CIVIL WAR FRONT PAGES

The Seventh Regiment marching down Broadway to leave for the war, May 1861

CIVIL WAR FRONT PAGES

A COLLECTION OF 157 FRONT PAGES FROM THE NORTH AND SOUTH

EDITED BY JOHN WAGMAN

THE FAIRFAX PRESS

AMERICAN LIGATURE PRESS
New York

The editor would like to thank the following newpapers for their kind permission to reproduce their front pages: the New York *Times*, the Philadelphia *Inquirer*, the New Orleans *Times-Picayune*, the Charleston *Courier*, the Washington *Post* © *the Washington Star* and the Richmond *Times-Dispatch*.

A special acknowledgment must also go to Ruth Webb for her expert typography and to Rita Rosenkranz for her faith.

First published in 1989 by Fairfax Press, distributed by Crown Publishers, Inc. 225 Park Avenue South, New York, New York 10003, by arrangement with American Ligature Press, Inc.

Book design by John Wagman

Manufactured in the United States of America

Library of Congress Cataloging-in-Publication Data

Civil War Front Pages: A collection of 157 front pages from the North and South/edited by John Wagman

ISBN 0-517-66572-7

1. United States—History—Civil War, 1861-1865—Sources.
I. Wagman, John

E464.C484 1989
973.7—dc19

88-31840
CIP

h g f e d c b a

To Ellen, Lauren and Molly B.

Abraham Lincoln in the White House with son Tad, 1864

"THE IMPULSE TO DISUNION
WAS COMING TO A LAND THAT,
MORE OR LESS
IN SPITE OF ITSELF
WAS IN THE VERY ACT OF
MAKING UNION PERMANENT."

—Bruce Catton
This Hallowed Ground

The Battle of Chancellorsville, May 1863

C O N T E N T S

The Philadelphia *Inquirer,* July 4
Field of General McClellan's terrific engagements
The Washington *Evening Star,* July 5
General McClellan's army safe
The Charleston *Mercury,* September 2
Defeat of the combined forces of McClellan and Pope
The Richmond *Daily Dispatch,* September 2
Battle of Second Manassas (Bull Run)
The Charleston *Mercury,* September 18
'Stonewall' Jackson captures Harpers Ferry, Virginia
The New York *Times,* September 20
The Battle of Antietam Creek
The Philadelphia *Inquirer,* September 20
Particulars of the bloody battle in Maryland
The New Orleans *Daily Picayune,* September 30
The battles in Maryland
The New Orleans *Daily Picayune,* October 21
Great battle in Kentucky
The Richmond *Daily Dispatch,* December 15
The Battle of Fredericksburg, Virginia
The New York *Times,* December 17
Evacuation of Fredericksburg by our forces
The Charleston *Daily Courier,* December 24
Reconstruction of Lincoln's cabinet demanded

1863

The Charleston *Daily Courier,* January 3
Great battle near Murfreesboro, Tennessee
The Philadelphia *Inquirer,* January 3
The great battle in Tennessee
The New York *Times,* January 6
Murfreesboro and its surroundings
The Philadelphia *Inquirer,* January 8
Sherman's assault on Vicksburg, Mississippi
The Charleston *Mercury,* January 13
The resignation of General Burnside
The New Orleans *Daily Picayune,* January 14
The capture of Galveston, Texas
The Philadelphia *Inquirer,* January 27
General Hooker succeeds to the command of the army
The Philadelphia *Inquirer,* February 11
Charleston and its defences
The New York *Herald,* March 26
The new Yazoo expedition
The Richmond *Daily Dispatch,* April 16
The Yankee account of the Charleston fight
The Philadelphia *Inquirer,* April 20
The advance from the Rappahannock
The New York *Times,* May 5
The Battle of Chancellorsville, Virginia
The Charleston *Mercury,* May 11
The death of 'Stonewall' Jackson
The Richmond *Daily Dispatch,* May 12
Funeral ceremonies for 'Stonewall' Jackson
The New Orleans *Daily Picayune,* May 16
The fight at Fredericksburg, Virginia
The New York *Times,* June 16
Rebel forces in Maryland and Pennsylvania
The New York *Herald,* June 18
Retreat of the rebels from Chambersburg, Pennsylvania
The Philadelphia *Inquirer,* June 29
The invasion of Pennsylvania
The Richmond *Daily Dispatch,* July 6
Great battle at Gettysburg
The Washington *Evening Star,* July 6
The greatest battle of the century
The Philadelphia *Inquirer,* July 6
The desperate battles near Gettysburg
The Charleston *Daily Courier,* July 8
Confederates victorious in Pennsylvania
The Philadelphia *Inquirer,* July 8
The fall of Vicksburg, Mississippi
The New York *Times,* July 8
The retreat of Lee
The New York *Herald,* July 23
The capture of Jackson, Mississippi
The New York *Times,* September 21
A great battle fought near Chattanooga, Tennessee
The Richmond *Daily Dispatch,* September 28
The Battle of Chickamauga
The New Orleans *Daily Picayune,* October 13
The situation at Chattanooga
The New York *Times,* November 26
General Sherman carries Missionary Ridge
The Richmond *Daily Dispatch,* November 27
The battle at Lookout Mountain, Tennessee
The Philadelphia *Inquirer,* December 7
The siege of Knoxville, Tennessee

1864

The Philadelphia *Inquirer,* March 5
The great cavalry raids
The New York *Times,* March 18
General Grant in command of the Union armies
The New York *Herald,* April 10
The Red River expedition
The Philadelphia *Inquirer,* May 7
The grand advance on Richmond
The New York *Times,* May 8
Lee confronts Grant with his whole army
The Charleston *Mercury,* May 9
The battles on the Rapidan
The New York *Times,* May 10
Lee's defeat and retreat fully confirmed
The Richmond *Daily Dispatch,* May 13
The death of J. E. B. Stuart
The New York *Times,* May 13
The gigantic struggle on the Rapidan and the Po

The Battle of Gettysburg, July 1863

FOREWORD

John Wagman was brimming with excitement when he first told me about a book project he was researching. A graphic designer by profession and an enthusiastic Civil War buff, he had become fascinated with newspapers from the period. Now he had compiled what seemed to be a simple collection of front pages of Civil War newspapers. But upon closer inspection, these pages tell a compelling story, of a nation hungry for news and of the men sent to the front to help satisfy that hunger.

It was "the look" of the pages that first attracted him. In the design and layout of the various papers he saw innovation. He noted similarities in some and vast differences among many others. This would be the first war in which correspondents sent their stories singing from the front across telegraph wires to their respective home offices. Competition to break a story was fierce, and new devices were employed on front pages to draw readers. The Civil War's front pages were among the first to be accented with bold type in headlines and illustrations.

Never before had a society had such an appetite for news. During the 1860s alone, America saw more than five thousand journals begin publication. In the two decades between 1850 and 1870, newspaper circulation rose 250 percent. The invention of the kerosene lamp in 1830 extended the day for reading printed material. By 1860 publishers were printing the news on rolls of paper, instead of single-stamped sheets. Without stopping, they could run off four thousand copies from rolls 3½ miles long. The process of bringing the word to the people had evolved into a science.

These front pages represent more than mere technology, however. In the days before film and television, the newspaper was the only information medium, aside from letters mailed back and forth among relatives and friends. The newspaper *was* the media. And its power in forming public opinion was unquestioned.

Today, historians—both serious scholars and casual buffs—know more about the events and personalities of the Civil War than any of the millions of people who actually lived through it. History books have culled for us the inaccurate, sensational, and censored reporting that influenced the civilian point of view during the war, and we now have a better understanding of what actually happened during the Civil War than we've ever had. But those books are unable to relay to us the war as it was happening. *Civil War Front Pages* offers the closest thing to a feeling of "you are there" than any history book can provide. Stepping back in time 125 years or so, it is not difficult to imagine how Americans reacted to the momentous events of the Civil War, as reported by the scores of journalists in the field. As imperfect a science as journalism was, and still is, there was no substitute for the firsthand account.

Aside from capturing the events on the battlefield for the reading public, Civil War newspapers unintentionally evoked something much more intriguing for the latter-day historian. The very style and manner of the reporting captured the essence of the Civil War society. Stories from the battle lines invariably affected lifestyles on the homefront. As Mr. Wagman started to read between the lines, stories began to emerge.

One such story unfolded quite early in the war. Imagine the reaction to reports in the September 5, 1861 edition of the New York *Herald*. That day readers in the North were greeted with startling news from the South. "Death of Jefferson Davis," it proclaimed. "Strong confirmatory evidence of the truth of the report—the Rebel flags at half-mast and the Confederate officers in mourning." The day before, a report had come from a correspondent at Manassas Junction, Virginia, the site of the First Battle of Manassas that took place only less than two months before: "Personal confirmation of the death of Jefferson Davis." The reporter not only confirmed that the Confederacy's President had indeed died, but "adds that all the officers wear crepe on their arms."

Of course, Jefferson Davis did not die in 1861, but rather presided over the government of the Confederacy in Richmond for the duration of the war. It is interesting to weigh the implications that his early demise might have had. A different Confederate president undoubtedly would have had a different impact on the outcome of the war.

Were people dancing in the streets of Northern cities over this news? Probably not, for newspapers were already known to advance what would be called "misinformation" today, a false report for the benefit of the people. Positive news about "our boys" and negative reports about "the enemy" in both Northern and Southern newspapers kept homefront morale high early in the war.

"Glorious News From Europe!!!" announced the December 18, 1861 edition of the *Daily Courier* from "Charleston, S.C. (Confederate States of America)." Even before the war started, the Confederacy had been seeking support of European countries, namely France and England. "Great Excitement in Great Britain," the headline went on. Then, continuing its optimism, the *Courier* proclaimed "Recognition of the Southern Confederacy by France and England." Of course, we now know that neither France nor England offered substantial support of the Confederacy. But in 1861, Southerners were comforted by news that the Northern blockade of Southern ports would be broken, that there would be a "probable blockade of the Northern ports." Equally startling this day was the news that Napoleon would serve as mediator. Even though the famous "Trent Affair" that November of 1861 would bring the Union frightfully close to war with Great Britain, the conflict never materialized and England never lent its full suport to the Confederacy, although Southerners waited for and counted upon that support throughout the war.

In the wake of the great Seven Days' Battles for Richmond in the end of June and the beginning of July, 1862, Union commander Major General George B. McClellan was making headlines across the country, in both Northern and Southern newspapers. But in Charleston, the *Mercury* ended his military career altogether. "The Great Battle of Richmond" it stated, brought on "desperate fighting on Monday afternoon on our right wing." According to a report it claimed to have received from the Richmond *Enquirer*, McClellan had been mortally wounded in the fighting. "A Federal officer brought in yesterday reports McClellan mortally wounded and the Yankee army completely demoralized." As we now know, "Little Mac" was never "mortally wounded." However, he was relieved of his command only a month after the *Mercury* item appeared. President Lincoln eventutally reinstated McClellan to command of the Army of the Potomac after the Union defeat at the Battle of Second Manassas, but it was another short-lived appointment. After the indecisive Battle of Antietam in September 1862 Lincoln relieved McClellan of command for good. Was the *Mercury*'s report of his mortal wound an omen?

Three months after the Battle of Antietam, the Charleston *Daily Courier* reported "The Latest News" about the Battle of Fredericksburg "By Telegraph." Because the telegraph was still in its infancy, and newspapers had begun to use this relatively expensive medium for reports from the field, "By Telegraph" appeared on many front pages. It was used to give more credence to the report transmitted in this manner, much the same way "Via Satellite" is used in news gathering today. According to the *Courier*'s report on the aftermath of the Fredericksburg battle, "Wm. H. Seward, Secretary of State, and his son, F. W. Seward, Assistant Secretary, have both resigned, and a reconstruction of the entire Cabinet is possible. The reason given for this step is the failure of Burnside's Army at Fredericksburg."

Reporters in camp with Meade's army, July 1863

As it turns out, the *Courier* report was only partially wrong. Secretary Seward threatened resignation in response to widespread charges that he was responsible for the long string of recent Union military defeats. But he did hold his Cabinet post through the end of the war dissuading European intervention into Confederate matters. And he was Secretary of State long enough to be wounded by one of the Lincoln assassination conspirators on April 14, 1865, the night the President was shot in Ford's Theater. Most of the rest of the Lincoln cabinet would not dissolve until 1864.

Who won the Battle of Gettysburg? We would never know by reading the early news reports. The July 6, 1863 edition of the Philadelphia *Inquirer* proclaimed "VICTORY!! WATERLOO ECLIPSED!! The Desperate Battles Near Gettysburg!! Repulse of the Rebels at All Points!!" A special correspondent had reported from the field that Confederate Lieutenant General James Longstreet had been killed in the battle.

Two days later, down in Charleston, the *Daily Courier* announced "Thrilling and Glorious News." From Richmond, their correspondent reported from a dispatch he had received from Martinsburg, West Virginia, that the Confederates had won a "Bloody Battle in Pennsylvania," that it was a "grand strategic movement." Claiming that the Confederates had taken 40,000 prisoners, the correspondent also wrote that, "Before the army under Meade had recovered from their defeat General Lee fell upon them with whole force, drove them three miles, inflicting on the enemy the severest defeat he had sustained in any previous battle."

The hundreds of books that have since been written on nearly every aspect of the battle at Gettysburg, of course, tell a much different story. General Longstreet contributed to that literature long after the war, most often defending his actions during the Gettysburg Campaign. and residents of the South did not learn that the Union Army's "severest defeat" was in truth its greatest victory until months later.

Reliability of Civil War news reporting did not improve much, even during the final years of the conflict. On May 14, 1864, the Philadelphia *Inquirer* ran a front page story on the late battle at Spotsylvania Court House in Virginia. While announcing a complete rout of the Confederates at the hands of the Union Army, the *Inquirer* also reported that Confederate General Robert E. Lee had been badly wounded in the fighting. The truth is, Lee was never wounded at all in the four years of the war, but nonetheless, the *Inquirer* reports had been "officially confirmed."

By the beginning of 1865 Union Major General William T. Sherman had completed his celebrated "March to the Sea" in North Carolina, while Major General Philip Sheridan had led successful raids through Virginia's Shenandoah Valley. On March 6, the New York *Herald* ran the bold banner headline: "Capture of the Rebel General Early." Lieutenant General Jubal A. Early was never captured, however. After his bout with Sheridan, he was relieved of command, and after the Confederate surrender at Appomattox, he fled to Cuba.

So how did all this "misinformation" find its way onto the Civil War front pages? Much of it came from lack of communication between commanders and reporters. Journalists at the time were both patronized and scorned by the commanders on both sides. The press—or the specials, as their respective papers called them—were for the most part a wild bunch, known more for their raucous behavior than for their writing. They fashioned a name for themselves that indicates their collective personality. They were the "Bohemian Brigade." Commanders generally detested the fact that these mere writers were forming public opinion, but they coddled the writers, nonetheless, just to get "good press."

The heat of the moment no doubt contributed to inaccurate reporting as well. Trying to collect the facts in the midst of flying bullets, battle smoke, mangled bodies, and the screams of agony from the wounded must have been a formidable challenge. And even after a reporter collected the information, the only means of transportation to the nearest telegraph office was by horseback. To be sure, much of the news, such as it was, never even found its way into a newspaper. Correspondents also had to contend with censorship imposed by some commanders, especially when sensitive troop-strength information was involved.

A Confederate raiding party cutting telegraph wires, June 1864

All this brings into question whether the journalists and their newspapers did either side any good. In the South, such personalities as Major General J. E. B. Stuart, the flamboyant cavalier, and other colorful commanders would not be nearly as well known today, had it not been for the "specials" who wrote about them from the field. Did the creation of these heroes have any redeeming value? Probably not, but it did make for good reading.

The most outspoken opponent of the Northern press was Major General William T. Sherman. He would refer to journalists as "dirty newspaper scribblers, who have the impudence of Satan . . . spies and defamers . . . infamous lying dogs."

Sherman, announced to be insane in the December 11, 1861 Cincinnati *Commercial*, questioned the propriety of Northern newspapers printing detailed descriptions of an attacking army. He contended that such reports were costing Union lives. He may have had a point here, because General Lee is said to have preferred reading battle accounts from the Philadelphia *Inquirer* rather than from any Southern newspaper.

Major General George G. Meade was certainly no supporter of the press, either. Early successes in the war catapulted him into command of the Union Army of the Potomac just days before the Battle of Gettysburg. A decisive victory there started political wheels turning, and Meade began contemplating a run for the Presidency. But Meade, like Sherman, had little tolerance for members of the press, and made the biggest mistake of his public career before it even started. He expelled Philadelphia *Inquirer* reporter Edward Crapsey from covering the Army of the Potomac. Craspsey, in turn, gained support from other reporters who agreed to omit Meade's name from any future stories. All positive news would be attributed to Ulysses S. Grant. Newsmen then, as they do today, had the power to make or to break.

The value of the press in the Civil War will continue to be a subject of debate among historians. The love-hate relationships between commanders and journalists, and inaccuracies of such as those highlighted here, have served to tarnish the true worth of Civil War journalism.

But for the most part, Civil War writers reported only what they thought was true. When we place these stories in context and consider the meager sources the newspapermen had at their disposal, it is evident that these "Bohemians" did a remarkable and valuable job. The majority of battle reports were grippingly accurate. Most of the time, the inaccuracies in contemporary reporting were, at worst, inadvertent. As a veteran newspaperman myself, I like to think that all journalists do some good. No matter what the news was in the Civil War, or is today, the people always have the right to know.

FRED L. SCHULTZ

Gettysburg, Pennsylvania
March, 1988

Fighting in the Wilderness, May 1864

INTRODUCTION

As a graphic designer and Civil War enthusiast, I originally became interested in the front pages of mid-nineteenth century newspapers for their artistic value. The typography, maps, charts, and woodcuts have a timeless beauty in this age of computer graphics and laser reproduction.

But it soon became apparent that these front pages tell a far richer story. Here is the beginning not only of contemporary newspaper journalism, but the forerunner of war coverage by the electronic media as well.

The correspondents who followed Civil War armies into battle are the direct descendants of the pioneering radio correspondents who broadcast their reports from inside Nazi Germany before the United States entered World War II, and of television reporters who plunged into the jungles of Vietnam to bring us the Vietnam War in living color on the six o'clock news.

The Civil War helped to hone the journalistic skills of many correspondents and led to the effectiveness in which future wars would be covered by the media. J. Cutler Andrews states in his definitive volume *The North Reports the Civil War:*

> Viewed through the eyes of the reporters who pictured the great drama of those years, the Civil War takes on a deeper, a more personal meaning.

No single event in our nation's history has been written about, covered, analyzed, or studied more than the Civil War. This violent confrontation between the North and South changed the face of the United States forever. Not a single aspect of American life was left untouched or unchanged as battle after battle raged on for four long years. Nowhere were these changes more evident than in the way the American public received their news of the war.

When Abraham Lincoln was elected President of the United States in 1860, most people received all of their news from local newspapers, mostly a week or two late, as much a reflection of the slow pace of life in nineteenth century America as of the relatively primitive state of communications. The telegraph, not yet perfected, was in its early stages of development. The majority of newspapers could ill afford this costly and unreliable service regardless of the demand.

The events at Charleston Harbor in South Carolina in mid-April of 1861 changed all that practically overnight.

With the firing on Fort Sumter and the coming of civil war, the demand for more accurate, up-to-date news virtually exploded and the rapid expansion of the newspaper industry was a direct result. Soon, in order to be first with a story, newspapers began to compete wildly for telegraph time, despite the cost. Correspondents often tied up telegraph lines by having operators transmit entire passages from the Bible or anything else that was handy, until *their* stories were written, to keep rival newspapers from sending in their stories first. The major papers allocated substantial portions of their operating budgets for telegraph time and put their ever growing resources squarely behind their war efforts.

The huge increases in circulation required newspapers to develop new printing methods. The web perfecting press, which enabled both sides of the paper to be printed simultaneously, greatly increased press speeds and enhanced reproduction. It was first put into use by the Philadelphia *Inquirer* in 1863.

More sophisticated typographic equipment made possible the use of display headlines, a design innovation which appeared for the first time during this period. Newspapers, particularly in the industrial North with its larger population, began to take on a look that more closely resembled the newspapers of today.

The competition between newspapers was every bit as fierce during the Civil War as today. Correspondents often risked their lives to get near the scenes of battles, sometimes sleeping in the saddle or staying up all night to write their dispatches after hitching a ride on a passing steamer or catching the last train out. Even after arriving at a telegraph station, many found the lines down, cut by a marauding party from one army or another.

In some cases reporters such as Henry Wing of the New York *Tribune*, were summoned to the White House to report directly to President Lincoln himself about the details of a battle. Once, Wing brought with him a message entrusted to him by General Grant for the President's ears *only*. In early May of 1864, with the Army of the Potomac locked in a death struggle with the Army of Northern Virginia commanded by General Robert E. Lee in the Wilderness of Virginia, General Grant wanted President Lincoln to know that "there would be no turning back."

Correspondents such as Henry Wing, Charles Webb of the New York *Times*, Whitelaw Reid of the Cincinnati *Gazette*, and many, many others were the unsung heroes of the Civil War. These nineteenth century 'Ernie Pyles' broke new ground in their efforts to report the news to an anxiously awaiting nation.

The New York *Times* stated in an editorial on September 25, 1901, on the occasion of its fiftieth anniversary:

> It was during the Civil War that the New York newspapers gained their first realizing sense of two fundamental principles that have made them what they are to-day—first, the surpassing value of individual, competitive, triumphant enterprise in getting early and exclusively news, and second, the possibility of building up large circulations by striving unceasingly to meet a popular demand for prompt and adequate reports of the day-to-day doings of mankind the world over.

The front pages I've selected for this collection reflect not *only* the battles, politics, and news of the day. Beneath the yellowing and faded surfaces lie far bigger stories, the passing of our country from one era into another, and no less than the coming of age of journalism, whose freedoms are zealously guarded by the First Amendment, so crucial to a free society.

JOHN WAGMAN

New York City
1989

The firing on Fort Sumter, April 1861

1861

Jefferson Davis

January 2, South Carolina's decision to secede from the Union prompts President Buchanan to order the reinforcing of the garrison at Fort Sumter in Charleston Harbor. **January 7,** Florida troops seize the Federal arsenal at Apalachicola. **January 29,** Kansas receives congressional approval to enter the Union as the 34th state, with a constitution banning slavery, aggravating tension between north and south. **February 4,** A peace convention convenes in Washington, D.C. headed by former President John Tyler in a last ditch effort at compromise, but none of the southern states send representatives. **February 9,** Jefferson Davis of Mississippi is elected provisional President of the Confederate States of America. **February 12,** State troops take possession of Federal munitions in Napolean, Arkansas. **February 22,** President-elect Abraham Lincoln declares, "there is no need of bloodshed and war", as it becomes increasingly clear that the reinforcement of Fort Sumter is impracticable. **March 4,** Abraham Lincoln is sworn in as the 16th President of the United States. Vowing to uphold the Union, he states, in his inaugural address, "in your hands, my dissatisfied fellow countrymen, and not in mine, is the momentous issue of civil war". **April 11,** Major Anderson, in command of the Fort Sumter garrison, is informed of the Confederate government's demand for his surrender.

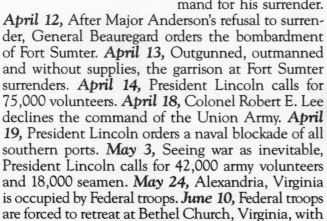

James Buchanan

April 12, After Major Anderson's refusal to surrender, General Beauregard orders the bombardment of Fort Sumter. **April 13,** Outgunned, outmanned and without supplies, the garrison at Fort Sumter surrenders. **April 14,** President Lincoln calls for 75,000 volunteers. **April 18,** Colonel Robert E. Lee declines the command of the Union Army. **April 19,** President Lincoln orders a naval blockade of all southern ports. **May 3,** Seeing war as inevitable, President Lincoln calls for 42,000 army volunteers and 18,000 seamen. **May 24,** Alexandria, Virginia is occupied by Federal troops. **June 10,** Federal troops are forced to retreat at Bethel Church, Virginia, with heavy casualties. **July 4,** President Lincoln, in reaffirming his position on the integrity of the union, calls for 400,000 men. **July 14,** Union General McDowell advances on Fairfax Courthouse, Virginia with 40,000 troops, while Confederate General Beauregard requests reinforcements to check the Union advance. **July 21,** the Army of the Potomac is routed at the Battle of Bull Run (First Manassas), as the notion of a quick war comes to a bloody end. **July 25,** The Crittendon Resolution, stating that the war is to be fought for the preservation of the Union, not the elimination of slavery, passes in Congress. **July 27,** General George McClellan assumes command of the Federal Division of the Army of the Potomac. **August 10,** In the western theater, Union General Nathaniel Lyon is killed at the battle of Wilson's Creek in Missouri. **October 4,** The cabinet approves a contract to have John Ericsson build ironclad warships for the Union Navy. **October 14,** President Lincoln orders the suspension of the writ of habeas corpus from Maine to Washington, D.C. **October 21,** The Union Army sustains severe casualties at Balls Bluff, Virginia. **November 1,** General-in-Chief Winfield Scott, hero of the War of 1812, resigns and is replaced by General McClellan. **November 6,** Jefferson Davis is elected President of the Confederacy. **November 7,** A Union naval squadron sails into Port Royal and successfully establishes a beachhead in this strategically important area between Charleston and Savannah.

Winfield Scott

November 8, Confederate commissioners James Mason and John Slidell, bound for England aboard the British ship *Trent,* are seized by the USS *San Jacinto,* provoking the possibility of armed conflict between the United States and Great Britain. **November 20,** General McClellan reviews 60,000 troops in Washington, D.C. **November 21,** Judah Benjamin becomes the Confederate Secretary of War. **December 1,** President Lincoln questions General McClellan about the movement of the Army of the Potomac. **December 4,** In his State of the Union address, President Lincoln declares, "the Union must be preserved." **December 11,** Charleston, South Carolina is ravaged by a fire that destroys nearly half the city. **December 19,** British Minister Lord Lyons gives Secretary of State Seward seven days to respond to the British demand for the release of Mason and Slidell. **December 26,** The United States agrees to release Mason and Slidell to Great Britain, ending the *Trent* affair. As the year comes to an end, President Lincoln harbors a deep concern about the lack of direction and focus of the Union armies, as the scene is set for a long, costly war.

James Mason

The New-York Times.

VOL. X.—NO. 2898. NEW-YORK, FRIDAY, JANUARY 4, 1861. PRICE TWO CENTS.

THE NATIONAL TROUBLES.

HIGHLY IMPORTANT FROM WASHINGTON.

The South Carolina Commissioners Sent Home.

Refusal of the President to Hold Further Communication with Them.

The Plot to Prevent the Inauguration of Lincoln.

GEN. SCOTT ON THE ALERT.

BELLIGERENT REPORTS FROM THE SOUTH.

Preparations for Operations Against Major Anderson.

More Seizures of Fortifications Reported.

Indications of Sentiment North and South.

The Views of Senator Douglas on the Position of South Carolina.

OUR WASHINGTON DISPATCHES.

WASHINGTON, Thursday, Jan. 3.

The President has returned the last communication of the South Carolina Commissioners unopened; and he has declined to receive anything more from them. They left in the morning boat for Charleston.

The Savannah forts were seized by citizens of Georgia, at suggestions telegraphed from this city by the Georgia Delegation in Congress.

The Augusta arsenal has been some days in their possession.

Prominent citizens of North Carolina, on hearing the report that troops were ordered South, called on Gov. ELLIS, and demanded the seizure of the forts at Wilmington. The demand being refused, they determined to act on their individual responsibility, when a dispatch received from Hon. L. O'B BRANCH contradicted the report, and stopped the movement.

North Carolina considers her forts and arsenal within her grasp whenever policy dictates the seizure.

The reports that armed bands were organizing to take possession of the Capital before the votes for President and Vice-President are counted, meet with credence everywhere. Gen. SCOTT is actively engaged in the preparations for putting down this jacobin mob. Capt. N. STONE, recently appointed Inspector-General of the Militia of the District of Columbia, issued his orders to-day for each volunteer Company to meet at the respective armories this evening for drill, and to carry home their guns with them in order that the seizure of the armories may be averted.

Republican members of the Senate and House have been apprised of a contemplated assassins' attack upon them, but are generally prepared.

The Committee of Thirty-three met this morning and discussed NELSON's proposition without coming to any definite conclusion. Slavery in the District was the subject under consideration.

The War Department is in receipt of official dispatches confirming the report of the massacre on Fort Walla Walla emigrant route. The tribe of Western Snakes is believed to be guilty. Capt. DENT promises a detailed statement, showing that the most horrible outrages have been committed.

The Indian Office has information of serious disturbances in the Creek Nation. Several parties that are suspected of tampering with slaves have been ordered to leave the country.

It is understood among Democratic Senators that the nomination of MCINTYRE as Collector at Charleston shall not be confirmed, as a Western Senator declares that, if necessary, he will consume every Executive session in debate in order to defeat it.

Mr. DOUGLAS, in his speech to-day, contended that the laws could only be enforced by civil process, or by a force headed by a civil officer, and that when rebellion becomes revolution, and a *de facto* Government is formed, then, and not till then, could war be declared. He would not contemplate war, as war would be disunion final and irrevocable.

DISPATCH TO THE ASSOCIATED PRESS.

WASHINGTON, Thursday, Jan. 3.

Intelligence was received last night that Fort Sumter is now besieged; that all Major ANDERSON's communications are cut off; that Fort Moultrie has been completely repaired and the guns remounted, and that everything is in readiness to open a fire on Major ANDERSON. New batteries are being erected around him by the Secessionists, and every day his danger and the difficulties of reinforcing him are increased. His frequent applications for reinforcements, and even the tears and prayers of his wife having failed to move the President, he has determined never again to renew his request, but will perish, if he must, in the fort. His men have bound themselves by an oath to stand and perish with him.

It is beyond a doubt that a combination is forming to take forcible possession of the Government at Washington on or before the 4th of March, but the precise time is not yet determined.

The above is from sources which leave no doubt of its reliability.

Gentlemen censure the apparent inactivity of the President, contending that by availing himself of the councils and services of Lieut.-Gen. SCOTT, all possibility of danger could be averted.

Mr. BINGHAM's bill, reported by him from the House Judiciary Committee to-day, provides whenever by reason of unlawful obstructions, combinations, or assemblages of persons, it shall become impracticable in the judgment of the President, to execute the revenue laws and collect the duties on imports in the ordinary way, it shall be lawful for him to direct the Custom-house for such district to be established and kept in any secure place within some port or harbor of said district, either on land or on board any vessel, and in that case it shall be the duty of the Collector to reside at such place, and there detain all vessels and cargoes arriving within the district, until the duties imposed on the cargoes by law shall be paid in cash, anything in the laws of the United States to the contrary, notwithstanding, and in such cases it shall be unlawful to take the vessel or cargo from the custody of the proper officer of the Customs, unless by a process from some Court of the United States, and in case any attempt shall be made to take such vessel or cargo by any force or combination, or assemblages of persons too great to be overcome by the officers of the Customs, it shall and may be lawful for the President or such person or persons as he shall have empowered for the purpose, to employ such part of the land or naval forces or militia of the United States, as may be deemed necessary for the purpose of preventing the removal of such vessel or cargo, and protecting the officers of the Customs in retaining the custody thereof.

It is believed, from what is known here, that in the course of a few days the forts at Pensacola and Key West, Fort Morgan, Alabama, the fort at Ship Island, near the mouth of Lake Borgne, together with the Arsenal at Baton Rouge, and Fort Johnson, on the Cape Fear River, will be seized and garrisoned by the troops of the respective States in which they lie.

Senator TOOMBS received a dispatch to-day, saying that the forts in Georgia were seized by order of Gov. BROWN. Private information says that if any attempt be made either to reinforce the Arsenal at Augusta, or remove the arms, it will at once be seized.

The South Carolina Commissioners considered the abrupt termination, by the President, of their business with him, as grossly insulting to themselves and the State. They treat it as a declaration of war, and in this spirit they left this city this morning for South Carolina. It is said the President yesterday returned their note without comment.

It is not true, as reported, that Senator BIGLER has sent dispatches to New-York, saying the national difficulties would be settled by the 10th of this month, nor has he sent any dispatches on the subject. These pretended dispatches were circulated in financial quarters. The use of his name was altogether without authority.

No motion was made to-day in the Senate to go into Executive Session on the nomination of Mr. MCINTYRE, for Collector of the Customs in the neighborhood of Charleston harbor. He is a resident of York County, Penn.

The following resolutions were adopted to-day as expressive of the views and feelings of the Committee of Thirty-three. The resolutions were offered by Mr. BRISTOW, of Kentucky:

Resolved, That we recognize Slavery as now existing in fifteen of the United States by the usages and laws of those States, and we recognize no authority, legally or otherwise, outside of a State where it so exists, to interfere with slaves or Slavery in such States, in disregard of the rights of their owners or the peace of society.

Resolved, That we recognize the justice and propriety of a faithful execution of the Constitution and "all" laws made in pursuance thereof, including those on the subject of fugitive slaves, or fugitives from service or labor, and discountenance all mobs or hindrances to the execution of such laws, and that the citizens of each State shall be entitled to all the privileges and immunities of the citizens of the several States.

Resolved, That we recognize no such conflicting elements in its composition, or sufficient cause from any source for a dissolution of this Government; that we were not sent here to destroy, but to sustain and harmonize the institutions of the country, and to see that equal justice is done to all parts of the same, and finally to perpetuate its existence on terms of equality and justice to all the States.

Representative PUGH, of Alabama, left for home to-day.

Private dispatches to Georgians say the indications are that the straight-out Secessionists have succeeded, and that Senator TOOMBS is elected a delegate to the State Convention.

OUR WASHINGTON CORRESPONDENCE.

THE REVOLUTIONARY DESIGNS UPON THE CAPITAL —PREPARATIONS TO MEET THE DANGER—MR. LINCOLN'S INAUGURATION—THE PRESIDENT'S CABINET.

WASHINGTON, Wednesday, Jan. 2, 1861.

For a week or ten days past, serious fears have been entertained that an effort will be made by the Secessionists to seize the Capital, and hold it as the permanent seat of Government of the much-talked-of Southern Confederacy. The date assigned for this *coup d'etat* was, first, the 4th of March next; but the rapid succession of revolutionary demonstrations in the South has caused the more sensitive and susceptible to fix, in their imaginations, upon an earlier day for the grand catastrophe. It is now said that on the 15th day of February, when the Presidential vote, in the ordinary course of events, would be counted, is to be made the occasion of the outbreak. Washington is to be filled by that time with the young bloods of the South; the galleries and lobbies of the House are to be occupied, and the issue is to be made upon the question of counting the electoral votes of certain Northern States which have Personal Liberty laws on their statute books. There is already a considerable number of Southern men here. Many of them, but almost invariably such as appear to be under age, wear the blue cockade, which is the fashionable badge of treason. Their number and power was attested by the uproarious applause which greeted the treasonable speech of BENJAMIN on Monday last. Men of this stamp, many of whom still hold office, have no hesitation in threatening the overthrow of the Government; and majors and colonels, who owe their titles to the courtesy of friends or, possibly, in a few exceptional cases, to the command of the corn-stalk militia, would put Hannibal to the blush by their fluent discourse upon the art of war.

But let me not underrate the importance of these threats. It is said that revolutions are always precipitated by the daring of a few leaders, backed by a minority of the people; and the history of the world proves that a hundred men, armed and organized for war, are more than a match for thousands of brave citizens who are peaceably going about their business. Weak as are the Secessionists, therefore, in point of numbers when compared with the great mass of law-abiding people, of all parties, it would be a fatal mistake to rest in quiet security, without an effort to counteract their machinations. They are not wanting in courage and audacity, and there are men among them who are not unfamiliar with military science. But their besetting sin is a passion for bluster and gasconade. Their addiction to boasting is irrepressible; and this folly, while it would have frustrated a far more skillfully conceived plot than their leaders are capable of making, may, at the same time, have saved them from the fatal consequences of a temporary success.

But the city and the country have been warned in time against a possible danger, and already we begin to see developed a spirit of patriotism which will sweep away the first symptoms of such a conspiracy against the Government as we have heard whispered about the national capital. Among the evidences of the soundness of public sentiment at this point, a fact already briefly alluded to by the Press, furnishes a striking illustration. It was announced yesterday in the journals of this city, that a strong police force was called out the night previous to prevent a very unmelodious serenade of the South Carolina Commissioners with tin trumpets, tin pans and similar instruments of discord. I learn that this movement originated not with the Republicans, who now number some two thousand or more, but among the Union men of other parties. All over the city the stars and stripes may be seen flying; and badges of Union are worn as off-set to the cockades of the Secessionists. The military companies are all, with an insignificent exception, for the Union.

But the great reaction, or more properly the great movement, of the Northern mind against the impudent outrages of the South Carolinians is, after all, the cause of the increasing confidence in this city, that whatever else may happen, nothing can prevent the inauguration of Mr. LINCOLN on the Fourth of March, on the east portico of the Capitol. There is talk of his inauguration at Springfield or elsewhere; but the American people will listen to no such cowardly suggestions. They will demand, as a point of honor, that he be inaugurated as usual, in the usual place, just as if no traitor had ever dared to raise his parricidal hand against his country. Members of Congress from the North are receiving a flood of letters from their constituents, assuring them of the firm and almost unanimous sentiment in favor of preserving the Union, at every cost, as the result of South Carolina's insults to the National flag. The influence of this sentiment is visible in the marked change which has taken place in the President's policy. Strong hopes are now entertained that he will not betray his country, and all parties seem disposed to forgive the past—to regard as the result of timidity, rather than treachery, his omission to reinforce the forts at Charleston—if from henceforth he will discard the counsels of traitors, and act upon the advice of patriots.

Mr. STANTON, the new Attorney-General, is regarded as the back-bone of the Administration. His old Whig and Republican opponents from Ohio say that he is as remarkable for strength of will as for legal talents. He is believed to be at the bottom of the new Administrative policy of enforcing the laws, which is driving out the Secessionists. Mr. HOLT, also, is highly praised for his firm and patriotic course. It is believed that he will act in full sympathy with Gen. SCOTT, in maintaining the national honor. As a Kentuckian he cannot fail to be proud of the gallant ANDERSON, who has so nobly taken the responsibility of preserving the national honor, at the risk of incurring the censure of the War Department.

If it shall turn out to be true, as I learned this evening, that the President, to-day, sent in the nomination of a new Collector for Charleston—a Philadelphian—the patriotic reaction in the counsels of the Administration has reached a point of which the country may well be proud. But "there's many a slip 'twixt the cup and the lip," and I greatly fear that the Old Public Functionary will be bullied into a withdrawal of the nomination. So deep-rooted is the superstitious reverence of Mr. BUCHANAN for Southern bluster, that I fear the dissolution of the Union itself could not cure his nervous susceptibility when assailed by the imperious command of DAVIS, and the sepulchral howl of TOOMBS. Still I shall be glad to find myself mistaken, and to know that his cure has been complete.

Republican Senators are in receipt of letters from the South threatening their lives, unless they immediately leave Washington. Senators SUMNER and WADE received missives of this character a day or two since, which would never have been honored with mention in the Press, but for the fact that the wretch who menaced the latter actually made his appearance yesterday, punctual to his appointment. He first called on the Senator's brother, Mr. EDWARD WADE, of the House; but after a conversation, in which he ascertained that he had mistaken the man, the would be assassin left, and repaired to the lodgings of the Senator WADE. He was invited into the parlor by the servant, and was observed by a member, who testifies to his suspicious appearance and to his singular conduct. He may be a deranged man; but is more probably a brutal fellow, whose heart fails him in the attempt to execute his bloody threats. OBSERVER.

CONGRESSIONAL PROCEEDINGS.

SENATE.

The galleries and lobbies were again crowded.

A message from the House, informing the Senate of the passage of the Indian Appropriation bill, was received.

Mr. BIGLER, of Pennsylvania, (Dem.,) presented memorials numerously signed by citizens of Philadelphia, asking the Senate to pass the Crittenden resolutions; also, the proceedings of the people at Harrisburgh. He said meetings had been held in several places in that State, all breathing the spirit of loyal devotion to the whole country, and all expressing a desire to have the Crittenden resolutions passed. If Congress would only give the people an opportunity, they would embrace it, and their friends at the South would discover that the people were prepared to meet their complaints in a spirit of conciliation and kindness.

Mr. CRITTENDEN, of Kentucky, (Am.,) offered the following resolutions:

Whereas, The Union is in danger, and it is difficult, if not impossible, for Congress to concur by the requisite majority, so as to enable it to take such measures to recommend to the States such amendments to the Constitution as are necessary to avoid the danger;

Whereas, In so great an emergency, the opinion and judgment of the people ought to be heard. Therefore,

Resolved, That provision be made by law without delay, for taking the sense of the people, and submitting to them the following resolution:

Whereas, Alarming dissensions have arisen between the Northern and Southern States as to the rights of the common territory of the United States, and it is eminently desirous and proper that the discussions be settled by constitutional provisions which give equal justice to all sections, and thereby restore peace, therefore.

Resolved, That by the Senate and House of Representatives the following article be proposed and submitted as an amendment to the Constitution, which shall be valid as part of the Constitution, when ratified by the Conventions of three-fourths of the people of the States.

First—In all the Territories now or hereafter acquired North of latitude 36° 30', Slavery, or involuntary servitude, except for the punishment of crime, is prohibited, while in all the Territory South of that latitude Slavery is hereby recognized as existing, and shall not be interfered with by Congress, but shall be protected as property by all departments of the Territorial Government during its continuance. All the territory North or South of said line, within such boundaries as Congress may prescribe when it contains a population necessary for a member of Congress, with a republican form of government, shall be admitted into the Union on an equality with the original States, with or without Slavery, as the Constitution of the State shall prescribe.

Second—Congress shall have no power to abolish Slavery in the States permitting Slavery.

Third—Congress shall have no power to abolish Slavery in the District of Columbia while it exists in Virginia and Maryland, or either; nor shall Congress at any time prohibit the officers of the Government or members of Congress whose duties require them to live in the District of Columbia, bringing slaves there and holding them as such.

Fourth—Congress shall have no power to hinder the transportation of slaves from one State to another, whether by land, navigable rivers or sea.

Fifth—Congress shall have power by law to pay an owner who shall apply the full value for a fugitive slave in all cases when the Marshal is prevented from discharging his duty by force or rescue made after arrest. In all such cases the owner shall have power to sue the county in which such violence or rescue was made; and the county shall have the right to sue the individuals who committed the wrong in the same manner as the owner could sue.

Sixth—No further amendment or amendments shall affect the preceding articles, and Congress shall never have power to interfere with Slavery in the States where it is now permitted.

Mr. CRITTENDEN said something must be done. It would be an open shame to the Government if ruin be allowed to come on the country. The sacrifice to be made was comparatively worthless. The peace and comfort of a great country were never purchased so cheaply. He would appeal with confidence to the people. They have the greatest interest in the Government. He had confidence that the people would give good advice.

The resolutions were read over, and unfinished business of yesterday taken up.

Mr. BAKER, of Oregon, (Rep.,) resumed his remarks. He said he was of the opinion that discussion on all points of difference was useful. He was willing to meet all just cause of complaint in a fair and honorable way. He contended that the attack on the men of the North for action in regard to the Territories was unjust, for men of all classes in the North believed Slavery the creature of local law. He quoted from Gen. CASS's speech at Detroit in 1854, against the so-called doctrine of equality; also from the speech of Senator HUNTER before the Breckinridge Club at Charlottesville, admitting that the opinion of the South in regard to Slavery has changed, and that her opinion was against the repeal of the Missouri Compromise, and for the extension of the system.

Mr. HUNTER, of Virginia, (Dem.,) said he never admitted that the South thought Congress had the right to restrict Slavery in the Territories.

Mr. BAKER said he understood that gentlemen on the other side, some time in their lives, were in favor of establishing a line between Freedom and Slavery.

Mr. BENJAMIN, of Louisiana, (Dem.,) never admitted that Congress had any power to exclude Slavery from any Territory. The South had been in favor of extending the Missouri line as a matter of compact merely.

Mr. BAKER thought we could do nothing as a matter of compact, which would violate the Constitution. He thought if the Senator from Louisiana believed in conscience that Congress had no right to exclude Slavery he must have violated his oath when he voted for such exclusion.

Mr. BENJAMIN said Congress had no such power under the Constitution.

Mr. BAKER said an act of Congress was sacred. The law was made under oath, and if he voted to prohibit Slavery by a certain law, when he actually believed Congress had no right under the Constitution to pass such a law, did he not violate his oath when he rendered such a vote? He said the Senator from Louisiana, in a dreary catalogue, complained that the Government interfered with Slavery in the South.

Mr. BENJAMIN said he did not complain of the Congress, but of the States.

Mr. BAKER was glad to hear the champion of Slavery admit that Congress had not interfered, but that his complaints were of the States. How could Illinois, for instance, interfere with Slavery in Virginia.

Mr. BENJAMIN said she could not by bill, but armed men might go to the State of Virginia and seize United States arms, and murder peaceful men, and try to excite slaves to revolt. A man in Massachusetts was found to say it was right, and Massachusetts elected him Governor, and thus indorsed murder. Massachusetts had sent Senators here to abuse and vilify the South.

Mr. BAKER said that was not a better scope of debate. He admitted that individuals might steal in Slave States. There were bad men everywhere. But this is no cause of separation and war.

Mr. BENJAMIN said that the Republican Party intend to surround the Slave States with Free States, so as to force emancipation.

Mr. BAKER argued that if even that were so it was no cause for dissolution.

Mr. BENJAMIN—I say, decidedly, yes.

Mr. BAKER said no, and proceeded to argue that it was a necessity that Slavery must be surrounded by free States. If Slavery is extended, it must be against the sentiment of the world. He claimed that the North were only allies of the South, and that they were bound to return slaves. France, England or Russia would not do that. If the slaves should revolt, the North would be bound to assist the South and would do it. He argued that the right of free speech could not be controlled in a free country, or a free Press, which was a greater safeguard to a free country. He would not restrict these to avert civil war, or maintain Slavery. The great principle of free government would not be surrendered. Come weal, come woe, Slavery shall never be extended by the powers of the Government of the United States. He would not yield one inch to secession, but there were things which he would yield; among them, the repeal of the Personal Liberty bills, should the Supreme Court pronounce them unconstitutional. Mr. CLAY had said, and he would say, yield not one inch or word to secession. He would agree to make all the Territories States now, and let the people decide on Slavery; but he would never agree to protect Slavery in the name of Freedom. Referring to power, he said, didn't it look a little as though, because they had lost the offices, the South had got up this rebellion? He said, after all, he had great confidence in the loyalty of the people of the South. He heard loyal sentiments everywhere, and could see the clouds breaking, and he was not without the hope that with time to allow the feverish heat to subside, the Union would yet remain safe if trusted to the hands of the people. The Senator from Louisiana had said that a State actually had seceded, and we must acknowledge its independence or make war. He said he would not acknowledge its independence, and said he thought it no very strange thing if a great Government had sometimes to enforce law. He quoted the ordinance of Gen. JACKSON in regard to collecting the revenue, when South Carolina once before revolted, as an answer to the Senator from Louisiana, when he asked how we would collect the revenue—"and, above all, let the laws be maintained and the Union preserved." He closed with the words of WEBSTER's speech in reply to HAYNE.

Mr. DOUGLAS, of Illinois, (Dem.,) asked that the report of the Committee of Thirteen be taken up. Mr. DOUGLAS proceeded to address the Senate. He said no act of his public life ever gave him so much pain as to vote for the resolution. The Committee could not agree. In order to see the real cause of the troubles, we must go back of the late election. We should assume that whenever Congress undertook to act on the question of Slavery, discord and agitation was sure to follow. When Congress let the question alone there was peace. He referred to the excitement at the time the Missouri Compromise was enacted. The fearful agitation of 1820 was settled by the establishment of the Compromise line. So long as that adjustment was carried out there was peace and quiet. Texas was admitted quietly under this rule, though there was a great contrariety of opinion. But no one objected, because it extended that line. Again, California and New-Mexico were acquired, and the extension of the line to the Pacific Ocean was demanded. The records show that he reported, as Chairman of the Committee on Territories, a resolution to extend the line to the Pacific. This was adopted in the Senate, but when it was sent to the House it was rejected by Northern votes. That opened the flood gates of the agitation of 1848, which only was settled by the Compromise of 1850. When we settle this question in the Territories, then we shall settle it entirely. The Abolitionists could never have brought the Union to the verge of dissolution, but for the question in the Territories. It was a rejection of the extension of that line in 1848 that reopened the agitation. The arguments of 1819 and 1820 were repeated. The positions of the North and the South were the same. The purest patriots in the land were alarmed, and Mr. CLAY came back to the Senate to see if he could not bring back peace. He found no trouble with the Southern members, but he could find no support of this line from the North. The Missouri line was abandoned, because its friends said they could not carry it out in good faith. Then they turned to see what was next best. There was a desire to take the question out of Congress, and secure the peace of the country. At last it was decided to leave the question to the people of the Territories themselves. The records show that he supported both compromises, and for the same reasons. Peace followed all over the country. But in 1853-4 it became necessary to organize the territory of Kansas and Nebraska. The Committee, in forming the bill, determined to carry out the compromise measures of 1850, though they had all been in favor of the Missouri Compromise as long as it could be carried out. A hue-and-cry was immediately raised that the Committee were violating a sacred compromise. But the bill did not mention the Missouri compromise, but did give the people the power of settling the question for themselves. The history of the Government might be divided into three parts. Before 1820 the Government admitted many Territories, but all was peace. After the agitation of 1820 was settled, all was peace again till 1850. Since then we have had a continual controversy, and the result of the late election has convinced the South that it is the fixed policy of the dominant party of the North to invade their constitutional rights. We come now to the consideration of that party which has plunged the country into this state of discord. It is folly for any man not to see facts which do exist. The result of the recent election, in connection with all the circumstances with which it is surrounded, have led the people of the South to form the conviction that it is a fixed policy of the dominant party of the North to invade and destroy their constitutional rights, and they are ready to rush, rashly I think, into all the horrors of revolution and disunion, rather than to submit to what they think the impending blow which hangs over them. The Senator from Ohio (Mr. WADE,) acknowledged the existence of this conviction in the minds of Southern people, and said he did not so much blame them as he did the Northern Democracy, who had misrepresented and falsified the purposes and policy of the Republican Party; yet he advocates a policy which will not relieve these apprehensions, but threatens them with war and coercion, rather than to give them security. It matters not whether the dangers were real or imaginary, if the Southern people are prepared to take a position which will plunge us into disunion and discord forever. I regret that any one on this floor should have introduced party politics, and endeavored to make party capital out of any question affecting the peace and safety of this country. But, since the Senator has attempted to make the Northern Democracy responsible for the revolution, I am forced to inquire whether the charge be true. There is no man living who would be better pleased to learn that he had misrepresented or misunderstood the policy of that party. I would like to know whether that Senator will now say it is not the policy of that party to confine Slavery within its present limits, by the action of the Federal Government? Whether it is not the policy of that party to exclude Slavery from the Territories we now possess, or any we may hereafter acquire? Whether or not that party are in favor of returning fugitives to their masters from whom they escape? In short, I will give him the opportunity of saying now, whether it is not the policy of that party to exert all the powers of the Federal Government, under the Constitution, according to their interpretation of that instrument, to restrain and cripple the institution of Slavery, with a view to its ultimate extinction in the States, old as well as new, North as well as South?

Mr. WADE, of Ohio, (Rep.)—All those questions are most pertinently answered in the speech to which he is now professing to make answer. I have nothing to add to it.

Mr. DOUGLAS.—I did not expect an unequivocal answer. I know too well that Senator will not deny that each of these interrogatories does express his individual policy, and the policy of the Republican Party, as he understands it. The harshest thing I have said of the Republican Party was that they intended to use the power of the Government with a view to the ultimate extinction of Slavery not only in the Territories but in the States of the Union. I have said and have believed it, and I would rejoice now to be corrected, that it is the policy of this party to prohibit Slavery in all the Territories of the United States now owned or hereafter acquired, with a view to surrounding the Slave States with a cordon of Abolition States, and thus keep Slavery confined till the number increases beyond the capacity of the soil to feed them, and thus force them to die of starvation, as a means of getting rid of the evil of Slavery in the name of humanity and Christianity. I have said that in Illinois, in the Abolition portions of the State, but never said it in a Slave State. I have always been exceedingly mild in speaking of that party in the Slaveholding States. But inasmuch as I did not get a direct answer from the Senator who makes the charge against the Northern Democracy, I will refer to the sentiments of the President elect, and see what he says on that subject. The Republicans have taken pains to publish reports of the debates between Mr. LINCOLN and myself and I may say they are unfair to me, as Mr. LINCOLN had an opportunity to correct his speeches, and the printer struck out many portions of my replies. [Mr. DOUGLAS then read from Mr. LINCOLN's speech, where he speaks of the House being divided against itself, and that the crisis must come, and the States must all become one thing or the other, &c., and proceeded.] When the Republican Committee publish an edition of Mr. LINCOLN's speeches containing sentiments like these, is it surprising that the people of the South think he was in earnest, and intended to carry out the policy which he then announced? I should not revive such revolutionary sentiments, but for the attempt to cast the responsibility upon the Northern Democracy, clearly intimating that Mr. PUGH and myself were the chief authors of these misrepresentations. I would like to find any one man, on that side of the Chamber, in the confidence of the President elect, who would deny that it is policy to carry out the very things to which I have referred. I feel bound, however, and take pleasure in saying, that I don't believe the Southern States are in any danger, or ought to have any apprehension, that Mr. LINCOLN or his party can do any harm, or render insecure their rights to persons or property anywhere in this country. I have some faith, that Mr. LINCOLN, after having emerged from the surroundings of a small country village, and assumed the high responsibilities of administering the law, and protecting the rights of a great nation, will sink the partisan in the patriot, and abandon the extreme doctrines, and step forward and avow his willingness to save the country by repudiating the extreme doctrines of a party. But be that as it may, neither he

[*Continued on Eighth Page.*]

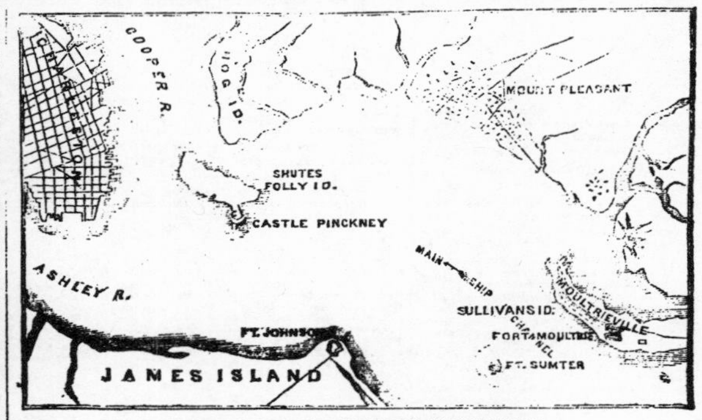

THE HARBOR AND FORTS OF CHARLESTON.

The Map given above presents an accurate view of the Harbor of Charleston, with the relative position of the several forts which were built by the General Government for its protection. It is reduced from the Chart of the Coast Survey. Persons familiar with New-York Bay will have no difficulty in tracing upon the map certain striking resemblances between the two harbors. Approaching Charleston from the ocean, it may be seen lying a few miles distant between the rivers Ashley and Cooper—the latter corresponding to the East, and the former to the North River. The low grounds on the right of the entrance will answer very fairly to Long Island; those on the left to Staten Island—the difference being best expressed by the supposition that the heights of our Northern islands had been flattened down, and as it were ironed out, almost to uniformity with the sea level. Upon these desolate flats plant here and there a few bare, straggling, stunted trees, stretching at rare intervals like sentinels along the shore; and an adequate idea may be had of the framework in which this tropical picture is inclosed. Proceeding inward, and keeping the map of our finer harbor in view, with due corrections for distances, and the substitution of Moultrie for Hamilton, Sumter for Tompkins, and Castle Pinckney for Castle William, and the similitude will be found sufficiently exact for all practical purposes. Fort Moultrie, on the right, is distant from Sumter at the left, a fraction over a mile; while Castle Pinckney, lying close to the city, is some 3¾ miles from both.

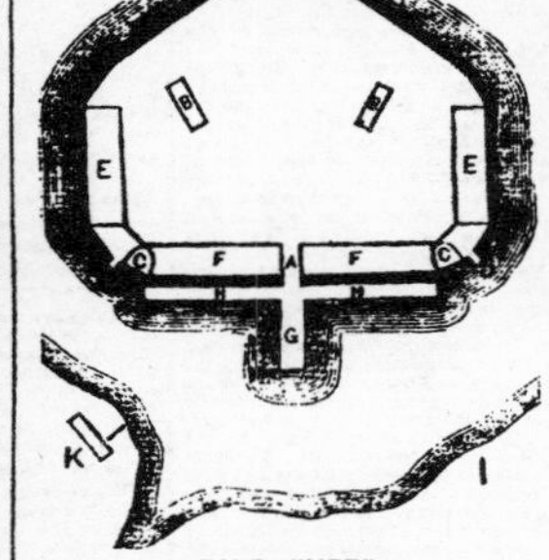

FORT SUMTER.

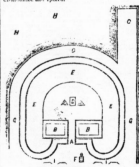

Fort Sumter, which just now attracts universal attention, is built upon an artificial island at the gate of the harbor, three and a half miles southeast of Charleston. It has been for ten years in course of construction; and only recently was so nearly completed as to admit the introduction of its armament. The fort rests upon a deposit of granite rocks, brought from New-Hampshire and placed there at great expense for the purpose, no point on the mainland adjoining on the South being sufficiently near or firm for the erection of a defence so necessary to aid Fort Moultrie in securing the approaches to the city. The cost of the work has been over $500,000. The fortress is in the form of a demi-octagon; the truncated side being at the South, and the exterior faces presented toward all points of the main ship channel, and overlooking Charleston and Fort Moultrie. The walls are of solid brick masonry, ten feet in thickness, and in height sixty feet from the water-line to the parapet. They are pierced for three tier of guns, numbering in all a hundred and forty pieces, of all sizes. The upper tier, which is designed for mortars and twenty-four pounders, is unsheltered, but at such a height as to be beyond the reach of danger from the balls of a naval attack. The others are beneath bomb-proof casemates, the lowest tier consisting of heavy Paixhans, carrying forty-two-pound shot, and the intermediate of ten inch Columbiads. It is stated in the Charleston papers that of seventy-five heavy guns now in the fort, only eleven of the Paixhans are fully mounted, nine of them being directed towards Fort Moultrie, and one toward Castle Pinckney. None of the Columbiads are in position. Four of the twenty-four-pounders on the summit of the wall are mounted upon pivots so as to sweep the horizon. They are at present on the side adjacent to Morris' Island. In addition to these weightier preparations for defence, the walls are pierced everywhere for muskets, of which there are endless numbers ready and loaded. The magazine is enormously stocked with grape, canister and shell. It contains seven hundred barrels of gunpowder. In his removal from Moultrie, Major ANDERSON carried with him all his stores and small arms. The place is, therefore, amply provisioned for a siege of six months. Water is furnished by four large cisterns; the only articles of which there appears to be a deficiency are men and fuel. With regard to the offensive abilities of the fort, its guns will sweep every point of the compass. Their range averages three miles; of course, commanding absolutely every approach to Charleston, and rendering the feebler defences of Fort Moultrie, or of any fortified places upon the mainland, wholly untenable. In a defensive point of view, the place is regarded as impregnable. From the mainland the nearest point of attack is 900 yards distant, but on ground so low as to be entirely at the mercy of the guns of the fortress; and besides there is no artillery in the possession of South Carolina which, even if undisturbed, could make anything like a breach in its massive walls. The garrison consists at this moment of sixty-four rank and file, fifteen musicians, and one hundred and seventy laborers. The utmost vigilance is maintained by all parties, sharing as they do to a man the determination to perish in defence of the place. The laborers are busily engaged in mounting the guns, so that each day adds to the number in position for effective service.

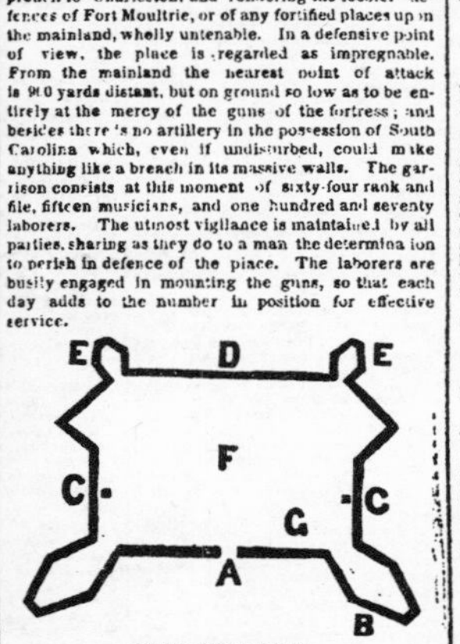

FORT MOULTRIE,

So named from the gallant defender of the city against the fleet of Sir PETER PARKER in earlier revolutionary times, is four miles distant from Charleston. It is nominally upon Sullivan's Island; but is actually separated from the land by a stretch of shallow water, which, at low tide, reveals the muddy bottom. Neglected through the long period of peace, the sand had drifted up against the south wall, so as to render the parapet easily accessible; and, but for the recent labors directed by Major ANDERSON and Capt. FOSTER it would have been quite feasible for a party of militia two hundred strong to have stormed and carried the place against its remnant of garrison. The greatest length of the fort from east to west is 300 feet; its breadth, 240 feet. The configuration is generally rectangular; but at each corner it is strengthened with strong bastionettes, and the sides have salient and reentering angles. It is well fitted, therefore, at any point to withstand assault or siege. The wall is composed of parallel erections of brick, fifteen feet apart capped with stone, the interval being filled with earth. From the bottom of the ditch to the coping, the wall is twenty feet in height. The ditch is about fifteen feet deep and as many wide. Among the works in progress at the time when Major ANDERSON found it necessary to abandon the post, was a heavy planking, destined to project over the edge of the wall as a defence against a scaling party; a deeper and more perfect excavation of the fosse; and a completion of one of the small bastions. The glacis and counterscarp, designed to reach attacking parties otherwise sheltered from fire by the walls, had been finished; new embrasures, with the same purpose, had been cut in the walls; and also in the citadel, where every arrangement had been made, in case of a successful attack upon the fort, for the garrison to shut itself up and explode the mines which were laid under the remainder of the fortification. The armament, after the departure of the troops, was found by the Charlestonians to consist of 8 or 10 Columbiads, the largest artillery used in the army, with a sufficient number of other heavy guns for the defence of the place, all, however, dismounted and spiked.

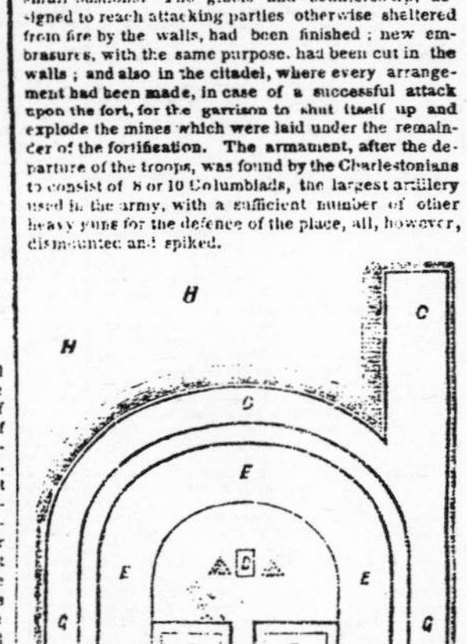

CASTLE PINCKNEY

has always been regarded by military authorities as an exemplification of all that is bad in engineering. It is, as we have said, situated relatively to Charleston as Castle William is to New-York. Shute's Folly Island, on which it stands, having the disadvantage, however, of being a mere marsh, rather than a beautiful elevation like Governor's Island. The fort is a half-moon, as the technical phrase is, the cresent being presented toward Fort Sumter. The lower batteries are pronounced worthless; the only available point for defensive operations is the exposed rampart, where there are ten twenty-four pounders mounted. In a lower tier are some fifteen smaller pieces, some of them said to be case-mated. The place is well supplied with munitions and provisions. Previous to recent events, there had been no garrison in the place, charge being left to a brace of watchmen. The day following the removal of Major ANDERSON to Fort Sumter, Castle Pinckney was occupied by a body of militia, two hundred strong, commanded by Colonel PETTIGREW and Major CAPERS, who now do garrison duty and strut in all the dignity and glory of active military service. It may be added that Castle Pinckney is quite beyond the reach of Major ANDERSON's guns, and that in case it should become necessary to land national troops at Charleston, its capture, which would be an indispensable preliminary, might give serious trouble. Perhaps, however, a broadside from one of our new frigates of weighty armament might suffice for the business.

MAJOR ANDERSON'S GRAND COUP.

EXTRACTS OF LETTERS FROM THE MAJOR.

The Boston *Journal* publishes the following extract from a private letter received in that city from Maj. ANDERSON: DECEMBER 24.

When I inform you that my garrison consists of only sixty effective men, that we are in a very indifferent work, the walls of which are only about fourteen feet high, and that we have, within 160 yards of our walls, sand hills which command our work, and which afford admirable sites for our batteries, and the finest covers for sharp-shooters, and that, besides this, there are numerous houses, some of them within pistol-shot, you will at once see that if attacked in force, headed by any one but a simpleton, there is scarce a possibility of our being able to hold out long enough to enable our friends to come to our succor.

Trusting that God will not desert us in our hour of trial, I am, very sincerely, yours,

ROBERT ANDERSON,
Major First Artillery, &c.

The following note of later date is given to the public by the Baltimore *Exchange*:

FORT MOULTRIE, S. C., Tuesday, Dec. 25, 1860.

——— ———, Esq., Baltimore:

DEAR SIR: I thank you for the trouble you were kind enough to take in correcting some of the rumors about me. You are right in the opinion that I could not and would not say anything contradictory of them. My plan always has been to try to do my duty honestly and fully, and to trust that in the good sense of justice of the people, they would give me credit for good intentions—even if my judgment should turn out to have not been good.

I must confess that I regret that the papers are making so much of my position here. I do not deserve the least credit for what I am doing—nothing more than any one else would do in my position—and, perhaps, not done half so well as many others would do. I receive, nearly by every mail, letters of sympathy, and many of them from strangers.

I hope that it will not be long before something will occur to give me a chance of being relieved from my present position.

Thanking you for your kind remembrance of me, I am, yours truly, ROBERT ANDERSON.

MAJOR ANDERSON AND THE STATE AUTHORITIES.

The Wilmington (N. C.) *Herald* says: "After Major ANDERSON removed to Fort Sumter, Gov. PICKENS sent Col. PETTIGREW and Major CAPERS down to him with a dispatch. The *Courier* says his reply had not transpired, but we learn that a gentleman who arrived here yesterday from Charleston says that Major ANDERSON received the above-named gentlemen courteously, and stated to them that he had acted upon his own responsibility, and for security; that he deprecated the necessity for it, and hoped no attack would be made upon him; that he should hate to turn his guns upon his countrymen, but, unless commanded by the Government of the United States, he would never surrender the post while he lived; and that if an attack was made upon him, he hoped the first shot fired at the fort would pierce *his* heart. It is said he has one year's provisions in the fort, and over 200 men."

Richmond Dispatch.

BY COWARDIN & HAMMERSLEY.

THE DAILY DISPATCH is served to subscribers at SIX AND A QUARTER CENTS PER WEEK, payable to the Carrier weekly. Price for mailing, $4 a year, or $2.50 for six months, in advance.

THE SEMI-WEEKLY DISPATCH is issued every Tuesday and Friday at $2, in advance.

THE WEEKLY DISPATCH is issued every Friday, and mailed to subscribers at $1 per annum.

DAILY DISPATCH.

VOL. XIX.—NO. 11 RICHMOND, VA., SATURDAY, JANUARY 12, 1861 PRICE ONE CENT.

SATURDAY MORNING......JAN. 12 1861.

THE NATIONAL CRISIS.

THE "ENGAGEMENT" AT CHARLESTON.

Full Particulars of the Firing into the Star of the West—The Capture of the Alabama Forts—From Charleston—Secession and Postage—Life at the Forts—Commercial Preparations for War, &c., &c.

The Charleston Courier, of Thursday, furnishes the particulars of the firing on the steamer Star of the West by the South Carolina troops. The troops had been notified fourteen hours in advance of the expected arrival of the steamer, and arrangements had been made to signal her. The account says:

SCENE IN THE CITY.

Early in the morning, between the hours of six and seven, the city was intensely excited at the expected reports of heavy ordnance in the harbor. "The Star of the West," was the exclamation of all. "One," "two," "three," "four" guns—the contest is begun. In a few minutes people from all parts of the city came from their houses, and were seen rushing out to the water's edge. The streets were soon thronged with eager men, hurrying towards the Battery and the wharves to ascertain all that could be learned of the noise made by the guns in the offing. The cannon, as long as they were discharged, went off in regular, deliberate succession, clearly evincing that in serving them the utmost military precision had been attained, and reflected great credit upon those managing them.

With the naked eye nothing of what was going on in the harbor could be discovered, and consequently the most intense excitement prevailed to find out what had caused the cessation of reports after seventeen or eighteen had been discharged.

It was not until half an hour or so that the populace, by this time fully aroused to the importance of the movement evidently made by our troops, was put in possession of the facts of the affair. In the meantime, crowds of people had gathered in the most convenient localities, for procuring information. The bulletin boards of the newspaper offices, the wharves and street corners, were filled with people, and every scrap of intelligence was greedily devoured.

NARRATION OF FACTS.

About six and a half o'clock, or thereabouts, the steamer General Clinch, Capt. Relyea, having discovered the approach of the Star of the West, signalled the fact to the occupants of the battery lately thrown up on the beach at Morris' Island. This vessel, it is known, left her wharf sometime during the evening before, with a guard of eighty men from the ranks of the Palmetto Guards and the Irish Volunteers. The duty assigned them was to keep strict surveillance over the harbor, and to make such signals as had been agreed upon in the event of the approach of reinforcements to the fortress in possession of the United States troops, as well as to report the approach of any vessel that may appear in the offing.—In the early grey of the morning the guard-boat first described the steamer heading in from the sea, and with as much celerity as possible performed the remaining part of the task assigned her.

As soon as signalled, the entire camp on Morris' Island was astir. There was no need for the reveille beat to quarters. The men were already at their posts before the orders were given. For some minutes they remained in anxious suspense, ready for what every one believed sure to come, and that—a volley from the heavy guns of Sumter.

As soon as the Star of the West rounded the point, she took to what is termed "Ship Channell," inside the bar, and proceeded straight forward, until nearly opposite the work on Morris' Island, not more than three-quarters of a mile from the battery, and within excellent range of the guns. At this position of affairs the command was given to fire, and a ball was sent whizzing athwart the bows of the steamer. This significant hint to proceed no further was noticed in no other manner by the vessel than by displaying a large flag of the Federal Union. As soon as the Stars and Stripes were run up to the mast-head, the act of defiance was met with a succession of heavy shots from the fortification. The vessel continued on her way, with increased speed; but one or two shots taking effect, she concluded to advance no further, and this conclusion was hastened by the shots from Moultrie, which, though harmless and out of range of the steamer, still gave evidence that hotter work was on hand if further attempt was made to proceed.

The "Star of the West" was clearly made out as the name of the vessel, so that there was no mistake on this point. She was possessed of no armament. As soon as five or six shots had been fired upon her from Morris' Island, and as many more from Moultrie, it was evident that she would lower her colors to half-mast. She veered about so as to avoid any further messengers of this kind from the fortifications, which, with one or two more discharges, finally ceased.

THE DAMAGE DONE

The steamer was very trifling, only two of about seventeen shots—all that was fired—took effect upon her. One struck the vessel about the forward part of the bow, the other amidships, in the vicinity of the wheel-house. No idea of the extent of damage done could be ascertained, indeed it could not have been known whether she had been struck at all had it not been for the heavy, dull sound, and subsequent crash, always accompanying the ball that "makes its mark" in a naval engagement. At all events she could not have been badly injured or disabled, for even while the firing continued she rounded to and started off seaward. As soon as this intention was shown, all firing was instantly suspended.

FORT SUMTER.

While the engagement lasted, no demonstration whatever was made by the command in possession of the frowning fortress—Sumter—except the opening of the port-holes and running out of the guns which bear upon Morris' Island and Moultrie. Major Anderson, however, prudently forbore to fire, and no doubt experienced great relief when he saw the vessel s eaming out of the harbor.

THE FEELING AT CASTLE PINCKNEY.

At Castle Pinckney, under command of Col. Pettigrew, the ardor of the men knew no bounds. The greatest eagerness was shown by all to have a shot at the stranger, with the intention of bringing out the fire of Fort Sumter. The guns of the Castle were all manned simply upon the spontaneous movement of the men themselves. Each sprang to his post, without command of the officer in charge. It was with the greatest difficulty that he could restrain them from firing; and it was not until a peremptory order to that effect was given that they held themselves aloof from the batteries. The eagerness at Forts Moultrie and Johnson was equally great—though the garrison at the former were gratified in the privilege of a number of harmless shots. Better luck to them next time.

WHO FIRED THE FIRST SHOT?

Since the event of the crisis, much curiosity has been excited to learn the man who fired the first shot. After diligent inquiry, we believe it is settled that the honor belongs to the Washington Light Infantry. Though this corps is not stationed in the entrenchments on Morris' Island, from which the first gun was fired, still, a single representative of the corps, we are informed, was at one of the guns, and to him befel the duty. We believe the name of the gentleman is Lieut. J. L. Branch.

THE CITY.

After all the facts of the affair in the harbor had become generally known throughout the city, the excitement in nowise abated.—Several companies of troops, never before in actual service, were called out and sent to different localities, where their presence might be needed, and every precaution was taken by the energetic administration to secure all points that might be useful.

In the streets, military uniforms were numerous. Old and young assumed the "cloth of war," and took their places in the ranks.—War, actual war, seemed inevitable; but with the thousand and one rumors that flew about, nothing could be set down as certain.

THE FLAG OF TRUCE.

Towards eleven o'clock, a boat from Fort Sumter, bearing an officer in full uniform, with a white flag, was seen to approach the city. The officer was met at the wharf by one or two gentlemen, and was suffered in quietness to land. He gave his name as Lieut. Hall, U. S. A., bearer of dispatches from Maj. Anderson, commanding Fort Sumter, to the Governor of South Carolina, and inquired the way to the Governor's quarters. Under the guidance of several gentlemen the Lieutenant was taken to the City Hall, followed by an immense, though orderly and excited throng—attracted by curiosity to learn the object of his mission.

After arriving at the City Hall, it was found that the Governor did not occupy any portion of the building, and after a delay of several minutes to learn where the Executive could be found, the officer was joined by a gentleman in military habit, who undertook to give him conduct.

While waiting at this point, the crowd outside increased at a tremendous rate. The Court-room was filled; the stairs were filled, and even the street was densely thronged, though not the slightest indignity, either by word or deed, was inflicted upon the representative of the United States. In perfect security he was allowed to take his way to the Governor, with whom he afterwards remained for over two hours.

The object of the mission not being known, created great excitement among the people—so much so that many of them lingered in the vicinity of the Gubernatorial quarters until after 2 o'clock, at which time Mr. Hall ended his interview. He was then escorted to a carriage, and driven, in company with two Aids of the Governor, to the wharf, where he re-embarked for the fort.

The correspondence between Major Anderson and Gov. Pickens has been published by telegraph; but as a part of the history of the important event, we publish in full the letter of the last-named gentleman, of which only a sketch came over the wires:

THE GOVERNOR'S LETTER.

STATE OF SOUTH CAROLINA,
EXECUTIVE OFFICE HEADQUARTERS,
Charleston, 9th January, 1861.

SIR: Your letter has been received. In it you make certain statements which very plainly show that you have not been duly informed by your Government of the precise relations which now exist between it and the State of South Carolina. Official information has been communicated to the Government of the United States that the political connection heretofore existing between the State of South Carolina and the States which were known as the United States had ceased; and that the State of South Carolina had resumed all the powers it had delegated to the United States under the compact known as the Constitution of the United States. The right which the State of South Carolina possessed to change the political relations which she had held with the other States, under the Constitution of the United States, has been solemnly asserted by the people of this State in Convention, and now does not admit of discussion.

In anticipation of the Ordinance of Secession, of which the President of the United States had official notification, it was understood by him that sending any reinforcements of troops of the United States in the harbor of Charleston would be regarded by the constituted authorities of the State of South Carolina as an act of hostility, and at the same time it was understood by him that any change in the occupation of the forts in the harbor of Charleston, would, in like manner, be regarded as an act of hostility. Either or both of these events occurring during the period in which the State of South Carolina constituted a part of the United States, was then distinctly notified to the President of the United States as an act or acts of hostility, because either or both would be regarded, and could only be intended to dispute the right of the State of South Carolina to that political independence which she has always asserted and will always retain.

Whatever would have been, during the continuance of this State while a member of the United States, an act of hostility, became much more so when the State of South Carolina had dissolved all connection with the Government of the United States. After the secession of the State of South Carolina, Fort Sumter continued in the possession of the troops of the United States. How that fort is at this time in the possession of the troops of the United States, it is not now necessary to discuss. It will suffice to say that the occupancy of that fort has been regarded by the State of South Carolina as the first act of positive hostility committed by the troops of the United States within the limits of this State, and was in this light regarded as so unequivocal that it occasioned the termination of the negotiation then pending at Washington between the Commissioners of the State of South Carolina and the President of the United States.

The attempt to reinforce the troops now in Fort Sumter, or to re-take and resume possession of the forts within the waters of this State, which you abandoned, after spiking the guns placed there, and doing otherwise much damage, cannot be regarded by the authorities of the State as indicative of any other purpose than the coercion of the State by the armed forces of your Government. To repel such an attempt, is too plainly a duty to allow it to be discussed; and while defending its waters, the authorities of the State have been careful to conduct the affairs of the State so that no act, however necessary for its defence, should lead to a useless waste of life. Special agents, therefore, have been off the Bar, to warn all approaching vessels, if armed or unarmed, and having troops to reinforce the fort on board, not to enter the harbor of Charleston, and special orders have been given to the commanders of all the forts and batteries not to fire at such vessels until a shot was fired across their bow, which would warn them of the prohibition of the State.—Under these circumstances, the Star of the West, it is understood, this morning attempted to enter this harbor with troops on board, and having been notified that she could not enter, was fired into. The act is perfectly justified by me. In regard to your threat in regard to vessels in the harbor, it is only necessary to say that you must judge of your responsibility. Your position in this harbor has been tolerated by the authorities of the State, and while the act of which you complain is in perfect consistency with the rights and duties of the State, it is not perceived how far the conduct which you propose to adopt can find a parallel in the history of any country, or be reconciled with any other purpose of your Government than that of imposing upon this State the condition of a conquered province.

Signed, F. W. PICKENS.

ENDORSEMENT OF THE ACT BY THE LEGISLATURE.

The following resolutions were adopted by the South Carolina House of Delegates on receiving the correspondence from the Governor:

Resolved, That this General Assembly looks upon any attempt to reinforce the troops now in possession of Fort Sumter, as an act of open and undisguised hostility on the part of the Government of the United States.

Resolved, further, That this General Assembly learns, with pride and pleasure, of the successful resistance this day, by the troops of this State, acting under orders of the Governor, to an attempt to reinforce Fort Sumter.

Resolved, further, That this General Assembly entirely approves and endorses the communication of the Governor this day made to Major Anderson.

Resolved, further, That this General Assembly pledges itself to an earnest, vigorous, and unhesitating support of the Governor in every measure adopted by him in defence of the honor and safety of the State.

ARREST FOR TREASON.

The Charleston Mercury, of Thursday, says:

J. N. Merriman, Collector of the port of Georgetown, S. C., was on Monday last arrested by the people of Georgetown on a charge of treason against the State. A letter was found written by him and addressed to Mr. Buchanan, stating that he (Merriman) had just cleared vessels in the name of the United States, and that he would continue to do so. The letter calls upon the President to send a boat and men to collect the Federal revenue, and informs him of the progress made in the construction of the works near Georgetown, and promises to keep him posted from time to time in relation to the same. The letter is signed by his initials, J. N. M. When arrested, he acknowledged having written it. Lopez, his deputy, was also arrested. He said he had been in the habit of writing out Merriman's letters, but had not done so in this case, as he considered it treason. Both have been committed for trial.

THE CAPTURE OF THE ALABAMA FORTS.

The Mobile News, of Saturday last, gives the following account of the capture, by Alabama troops, of the Federal forts within her limits:

The movement of the Mobile companies on Mount Vernon Arsenal up the river and Fort Morgan down the Bay, kept the city in a ferment of excited interest yesterday, and it was not until late in the day that intelligence arrived that both those points of Federal occupation and defence were in the hands of the soldiery of the State of Alabama. The sudden stroke of policy in Alabama, the *coup d'etat* and *coup de guerre*, was quietly and effectively carried out in this wise: Acting under the Governor's orders, at eleven o'clock on Thursday night, the following companies detailed for that service embarked on a steamer for Fort Morgan: the "Cadets," Capt. Sands; the "Fusiliers," Lieutenant Emrick commanding; the "Independent Rifles," Capt. Stikes, and the "Artillery," Capt. Ketchum. Steaming down the bay they arrived at the Fort about 3 o'clock and quietly occupied it, its only garrison being an Ordnance Sergeant and his family, and a laborer or so. The Fort is now held by the greater portion of the force which took possession, about two hundred men being under arms. The works are being put in more defensible condition.

The detachment detailed for the seizure of the Mt. Vernon U. S. Arsenal, located forty-five miles up the river, consisted of the "Mobile Rifles," Capt. Woodruff; the "Washington Light Infantry," Capt. Gracie, and the "Gardes Lafayette," Capt. Belloc. They embarked about the same time as the detachment for Fort Morgan. They arrived at the Arsenal about daybreak, and being provided with ladders for the purpose escaladed the walls of the premises at three different points simultaneously, and formed around the armory in the center. The garrison, consisting of a squad of about thirteen soldiers and as many Government employees, of course made no resistance, being captured before they knew of the presence of an enemy. Had they not been taken by surprise, however, and had they been so disposed, they might have given some trouble and shed some blood, as the arsenal is defensible against musketry, and their number was more than a third of that of their assailants. The arsenal contains 20,000 stand of arms, 1,500 barrels (*not kegs*) of powder, 300,000 rounds of cartridge and other munitions. It is now held by thirty men of the "Washington Light Infantry," who are having pleasant pic-nic duty, we suspect.

LIFE IN THE FORTS.

The Savannah Republican, of Tuesday, publishes the following letter:

FORT PULASKI, Tuesday, Jan. 8.

The work of the fort goes on rapidly; the guns are being overhauled, and will soon be in a condition to do effectual service.

The Chatham Artillery have had an offer from a lady in Savannah, whose husband is a member of the corps, to come down and act as nurse if her services are needed. Her letter was read in the quarters last night, and was received with three hearty cheers, and a letter of acceptance moved to be written her to that effect. Another lady sent us a splendid fruit cake, iced over, and the word "Secession" wrought in with sugar; still another, whose name is unknown, sent us a package of lint. There may be similar instances of kindness towards the other corps, but as I have no opportunity of finding it out, I do not mention them.

It is impossible to imagine a gayer and more animated scene than the fort is during the day; the men rapidly passing to and fro doing the various duties assigned them; the labor is severe, and one would suppose that by night nature would claim her rest, but up to tatoo, which is beaten at 9 o'clock at night every quarter resounds with gay sounds and shouts that come from many hearts. The "Marseillaise," "Dixie's Land," "Mickey, are you drunk," "Rap Rap," and other songs with like euphonious names, ring out upon the night. But after tatoo all is still and silent as death.

A schooner arrived last night, having on board a very large quantity of powder, and it is being put in the magazine to-day.

On Thursday there will be a relief sent down, and such soldiers as are compelled to go home will return. There are twenty from the Chatham Artillery who will return, and their places will be filled from town.

If anything of importance occurs, I will try and advise you. Very truly, BARRAKE.

P. S.—I learn by letters from town to-day that some consternation has been produced by the construction of Commandant Bartow's order in regard to any one found asleep on his post. The order simply stated that the exigencies of the times required that strict military discipline should be observed, and the penalty of being caught asleep was death, by the articles of war; but none of us anticipate the execution of such an order; in fact, the men are so alert at every duty that it will never be deserved. B.

THE FORTS AT KEY WEST.

The Charleston Mercury is appealing to the people of Florida to seize the forts and other Government property at Key West and Pensacola. It says:

"These forts can command the whole Gulf trade; and should Mr. Buchanan carry out what appears to be his present plan, he certainly must desire to hold possession of these forts. He may thus, with the assistance of war steamers, block up the whole Gulf; but let Florida hold these forts and the entire aspect of affairs is changed. Such vessels in time of war will have no port of entry and must be supplied in every way from a very long distance, and that at sea; while the commerce of the North in the Gulf will fall an easy prey to our bold privateers, and California gold will pay all such little expenses on our part. We leave the matter for the reflection and decision of the people of Florida."

THE STEAMER JOSEPH WHITNEY WITH TROOPS FOR THE SOUTH.

The Boston Traveller, of Wednesday, thus notices the announcement we had by telegraph of the steamer Joseph Whitney having been chartered to carry troops from Boston to the South:

It is announced that the detachment of United States troops now stationed at Fort Winthrop, in this harbor, have received orders to be in readiness to go South. They number seventy men. An agent of the General Government was in town yesterday, and chartered the steamer Joseph Whitney, of the Baltimore line, as a transport for the troops.

The Herald says:

"We understand proposals were previously made to engage the propellers forming the line between Boston and Charleston, but owing to the peculiary interest held in these propellers by Charleston capitalists, it was deemed not *advisable*."

It is stated that the Joseph Whitney will take on board seven hundred and fifty barrels of provisions and three hundred and fifty tons of coal. Her agents state that they are not at liberty to reveal her destination.

It is said that the company at Fort Winthrop are light artillery men.

The Boston Transcript says that the Whitney cleared for Norfolk, though her destination is understood to be the Coast of Florida.

FROM CHARLESTON.

The following weather item is from the Charleston Courier:

The mild weather of the past few days has produced its effect upon vegetation. Green buds have made their appearance on the trees, and fig trees, always most forward to welcome the warm breath of spring, are covered with tender sprouts.

The Columbia (S. C.) Guardian furnishes the following:

The news announcing the action of Florida, although expected, produced a great excitement on Monday night. On yesterday morning the ringing of the city bell "Secession," and the firing of cannon, by direction of the city authorities, announced the glad tidings to our citizens.

The Hamburg company of "Minute Men," and "Cherokee-pond Company," of Edgefield, both left Hamburg this morning, on the down eight o'clock train, for Charleston. Both companies numbered about 200 men.

DISPATCH FROM CHARLESTON.

CHARLESTON, Jan. 10, P. M.—The dispatches received here that the United States sloop-of-war Brooklyn is coming here with an armed force, has created an intense excitement.

Great preparations are making in the harbor for active warfare. A large steamer, called the Marion, of the Charleston and New York line, has been purchased by South Carolina, and ordered to be razeed for a man-of-war, her upper cabins to be taken off, and armament supplied. The buoys in the harbor have been removed.

The Brooklyn will no doubt be fired into when she makes her appearance, and it is expected that Fort Sumter will open on the South Carolina fortifications, when the fight will become general.

The people are preparing for it and for the worst. It is evident from the present determined hostile attitude of the people, that the Brooklyn cannot come in without a great fight. Major Anderson will doubtless protect her with the guns of Fort Sumter. He only pledged himself not to prevent communication between the authorities of South Carolina and the forts now in possession of the State till Lieut. Talbott came back.

A steam tug called the "Aid," Lieutenant Hamilton, formerly of the Federal Navy, commanding, left the wharf to-night for a reconnoitre. She mounted one gun.

There is much talk of sending to Savannah for steam tugs to be used as gun boats.

COMMERCIAL PREPARATIONS FOR CIVIL WAR.

Several of the Marine Insurance Companies of New York city, says the Commercial, have already adopted the "War Clause" in their policies, viz:

"*Warranted free from seizure or detention arising from the acts of any seceding or revolting State.*"

The subject will come before the Board of Underwriters to-morrow, when they will probably agree upon this clause; if so, all the companies will unite in the same restriction. We learn also that the companies have generally advanced their rates one hundred per cent. on risks from this port to Charleston—To ports in the Gulf of Mexico, the same advance will probably be demanded.

FLORIDA.

Before the secession ordinance was adopted in Florida, Mr. Edmund Ruffin, of Virginia, addressed the Convention.

Bishop Rutledge, of the Diocese of Florida, has handed to the Treasurer of the State of Florida an obligation to pay $500 to assist in defraying the expenses of the State, so soon as the Convention passes the Ordinance of Secession.

MEETING IN BALTIMORE.

A very large Union meeting was held at Baltimore on Thursday evening. Among the most distinguished speakers was Hon. Reverdy Johnson. He made a legal argument of great length against the right of secession—He also thought it necessary that time should be had to afford an opportunity to the Northern States to make the concessions which will guarantee to all the States their rights. The North was the aggressor and to blame, and the South was not blameless. But the time would come when all the difficulties could be healed, and peace and prosperity be restored. Mr. Johnson spoke at length, and his remarks were so protracted that but a faint idea of them can be given, so late was the hour when he concluded. Throughout he was frequently interrupted by applause, and once or twice by confusion on the floor.

At the conclusion of his remarks three cheers were given for Gov. Hicks, three for Major Anderson, three groans for President Buchanan and three groans for South Carolina.

Resolutions were adopted expressive of a desire for a compromise for the settlement of existing difficulties on a constitutional basis, and that such of the Northern States as have passed Personal Liberty bills shall repeal the same.

VIRGINIA.

The Norfolk Day Book says that a gentleman of that city has just received a letter from his son at the University of Virginia, asking if he shall pay his board for the next six months; that the young men at the University were rapidly enlisting in the various military organizations of the State, and making every preparation to leave in case the State needed their services.

The United States Marines still maintain their position at Fort Washington, without further reinforcements. Maj. Terrett has been relieved from the command of the fortress by Capt. Taylor, of the Marine Corps. Capt. Taylor is a native of Alexandria, Va.

There was a mass meeting at Nottoway Court-House, Va., on Tuesday. Although the mud was deep and the weather inclement, the attendance was very large. The Rev Edward Martin, of the Presbyterian Church, and Dr. Campbell, both made eloquent speeches in favor of arming the county, and $5,000 was subsequently raised in the form of county bonds. The Nottoway troop, numbering fifty-two, were on parade. A rifle company is to be organized at Blacks and Whites Saturday.

GENERAL ASSEMBLY OF VIRGINIA.
[EXTRA SESSION.]

SENATE.

FRIDAY, Jan. 11th.

The Senate was called to order at 12 o'clock by the President.

Prayer by Rev. Dr. J. L. BURROWS, of the Baptist Church.

The National Crisis.—A communication from the House of Delegates was read, informing the Senate of the passage of the following resolutions:

1. *Resolved by the General Assembly of Virginia.* That in view of the imminent danger of civil war, this Assembly, in behalf of the Commonwealth of Virginia, ask respectfully, on the one hand, of the President of the United States, and, on the other of the authorities of each of the Southern States, to the end that, if possible, peace may yet be preserved, that they will reciprocally communicate assurances in response hereto to the General Assembly of Virginia, now in session, and that the *status quo* of all movements tending to occasion collision, and concerning the forts and arsenals of the nation, shall, on either hand, be strictly maintained for the present, except to repel any actual aggressive attempts.

2. That the Governor of the Commonwealth be requested to communicate these resolutions, by telegraph immediately, to the President of the United States, and to each of the Governors of the Southern States.

Mr. PAXTON moved to commit the resolutions to the Committee on Federal Relations.

Mr. JOHNSON hoped that the resolutions would be acted upon speedily and promptly. He called for the yeas and nays on Mr. PAXTON'S motion.

Mr. STUART briefly advocated prompt action. The proposed reference would be equivalent to a vote of rejection. The nature of the case demands that there should not be an hour's delay.

Mr. PAXTON presented his objections to the resolutions. He understood them to signify that the seceding States should allow the forts and arsenals within their limits to remain in the possession of the Federal Government.

Mr. DICKINSON, of Prince Edward, said he would give the resolutions his cordial support. They do not compromit the interest or honor of Virginia. Surely, in an hour like this, it becomes every patriot and every Christian, before he commits his country to the horrors of civil war, to exhaust all honorable means for preventing it. There was everything to gain and nothing to lose by the adoption of the resolutions. As brave and magnanimous men—for brave men are always magnanimous—let us endeavor to avoid strife, by all honorable means. His constituents, though ready for war, desired peace. Mr. D. appealed to the Senate to adopt the resolutions unanimously.

Mr. PAXTON reiterated his objections to the resolutions.

Mr. COGHILL said that no possible good could result from the adoption of the resolutions. The Southern States may be lulled into a false security. Let us take time for reflection and deliberation.

Mr. WICKHAM remarked, that it seemed as if certain Senators were only willing for delay when propositions were introduced for peace. He argued in favor of prompt action. Called attention to the fact that Lt. Talbot had proceeded to Washington for orders, and that if this Senate desired that these orders should be of a pacific character, it is important that Virginia should step forward, and request the President to stay his hand.

Mr. COGHILL again addressed the Senate in opposition to the resolutions.

Mr. CLAIBORNE read a substitute, which he proposed to offer at the proper time, following the language of the pending resolutions, except the appeal by Virginia to her sister States of the South. They had committed no act of aggression, nor could commit any. South Carolina, though sinned against in the extreme, has acted with forbearance. Mr. C. avowed himself in favor of preserving the peace, and the Union, if possible.

Mr. AUGUST declared that no man desired more earnestly than himself to preserve the peace and to see the national banner wave in unimpaired brilliancy and equality; but he desired neither peace nor a continuance of the Union, if done at the expense of the honor of Virginia. This Legislature has already, by the resolutions adopted on Tuesday, sent a request to the Federal Government to stay its hand. Could any message be more productive of peace than that?

Mr. AUGUST commented on the clause, "for the present," as indefinite, and indicated other objections to the adoption of the resolutions, until, at least, they were considered by a committee.

Mr. NASH expressed the belief that the pending resolutions were not only inconsistent with, but antagonistic to those adopted on Tuesday, against coercion. It was, therefore, unbecoming the prestige and dignity of Virginia to adopt them. If he could understand them as a proposition for peace, he would be recreant to his constituents in failing to vote for them; but, believing that their adoption would embolden the Federal Government, he felt bound to vote for the motion to commit.

The debate was further continued by Messrs. THOMAS of H., and RIVES, in favor of the resolutions, and Mr. ISBELL against them.

The vote was then taken with the following result:

YEAS.—Messrs August, Brannon Bruce, Carson, Claiborne, Coghill, Day, Douglass, Early, Finney, Gatewood, Isbell, Layne, Logan, Lynch, Nash, Paxton, Pennybacker, Richmond, Thompson—20.

NAYS.—Messrs. Armstrong, Caldwell, Carraway, Jr., Carter, Critcher, Dickinson of Pr. Edward, French, Greever, Hubbard, Johnson, Marshall, Massie, McKenney, Neal, Neeson, Newlon, Newman, Pate, Rives, Stuart, Thomas of Fairfax, Thomas of Henry, Townes, Urquhart, and Wickham—25.

Mr. CLAIBORNE then offered his substitute, as follows:

1st. That the General Assembly of Virginia ask of the President of the United States, in view of the imminent danger of civil war, an assurance of the absolute preservation of the *status quo* for 60 days, except to repel hostile aggressions on all questions of difference between the General Government and the seceding States.

2d. That the Governor be requested to telegraph, immediately, this resolution to the President of the United States.

The substitute was adopted by the following vote:

YEAS.—Messrs. August, Brannon, Bruce, Carson, Claiborne, Coghill, Day, Douglass, Early, Finney, Gatewood, Greever, Isbell, Layne, Logan, Lynch, Nash, Neeson, Newman, Pate, Paxton, Pennybacker, Richmond and Thompson—24.

NAYS.—Messrs Armstrong, Caldwell, Carraway, Carter, Critcher, French, Hubbard, Johnson, Marshall, Massie, McKenney, Neal, Newlon, Rives, Stuart, Thomas of F., Thomas of H., Townes, Urquhart and Wickham—20.

Mr. THOMAS asked what is to become of us after the sixty days have expired. He infinitely preferred that no resolution should be adopted but that of Mr CLAIBORNE.

The subject was finally referred to a select committee, consisting of Messrs. Armstrong, Brannon, Newman, Paxton, Thomas of F., Thompson and Lynch.

Bills Reported.—Mr. COGHILL reported a bill changing the times for holding the Circuit Courts of the city of Williamsburg and county of Henrico.

Mr. AUGUST reported a bill to authorize the County Courts to arm the militia of their respective counties and provide means therefor.

Mr. THOMAS, of Henry, presented a substitute for the Convention bill reported yesterday by a special committee.

On motion of Mr. DICKINSON, of Prince Edward, the bill providing for the call of a Convention was made the order of the day for to-morrow, (12th inst.,) at half-past 12 o'clock.

Galt's Jefferson.—A communication from Mr. Galt, inviting the members of the Legislature to attend an exhibition of his Statue of Jefferson, was read, and the invitation accepted.

Resolutions of Inquiry.—The appropriate committees were instructed to inquire into the expediency of sending propositions, viz: By Mr. Coghill, of providing for the deposit of the revenue in some one of the Banks in the different divisions of the State; by the same, of repealing the law requiring the branch Banks to redeem their notes at the parent Banks, etc.; by Mr. Isbell, of authorizing the Governor to deposit muskets and ammunition at certain places, and under certain restrictions, etc., (designated in the resolutions;) by Mr. French, of a general stay law; by Mr. Neeson, of reporting bill 428 of last session; by Mr. Marshall, of providing for the voluntary enslavement of Clara and her children, in the county of Rappahannock; by Mr. Lynch, of erecting a magazine or arsenal at or near Lynchburg; by Mr. August, of extending the boundaries of the city of Richmond.—Several resolutions to inquire into the expediency of refunding taxes were adopted, memorials, etc., presented, after which,

On motion of Mr. THOMAS, the Senate adjourned.

HOUSE OF DELEGATES.

FRIDAY, Jan. 11, 1861.

The House was called to order at 12 o'clock M., by Speaker CRUTCHFIELD, and opened with prayer by Rev. J. A. DUNCAN, of the M. E. Church.

Bills Reported.—Bills were reported from committees as follows: By Mr Magruder, a bill releasing the Commonwealth's claim to a certain island in Chesapeake Bay to Edward I. Poulson; a bill for the relief of Edward McCabe, of Harper's Ferry; a bill to amend an act passed March 30, 1860, entitled "an act making regulations concerning licenses;" a bill to amend an act passed April 6th, 1858, entitled "an act to amend and re enact an act entitled an act for regulating foreign life insurance companies within this Commonwealth, passed March 6th, 1856;" by Mr. Chapman, a bill to incorporate the Arnoldsburg and Sandy Turnpike Company; a bill to extend the improvement of the Little Kanawha River to the falls thereof, in the county of Braxton; and a bill to incorporate the Lynchburg and North Carolina Railroad Company.

Petitions, &c.—The following petitions, &c., were presented and referred: By Mr. Christian, the petition of B. M. Smith, of Prince Edward, for relief from the payment of a fine inadvertently incurred; by Mr Kaufman, the petition of Col. E. E. Shryock and others, asking that compensation be paid the drummer and fifer for services rendered to the 51st Regiment of Virginia Militia; by the same, the petition of Capt. James Long and others, asking that leave be given to Henry Guard to peddle same articles without license; by Mr. Orgain, the application of Paul A. Farley, for the refunding of a pedlar's license.

Application Refused.—The Committee on Military Affairs asked to be discharged from the further consideration of the petition of Capt. James Kinney, of the Rockingham Rifles, the same having been considered and rejected.

The Convention Bill.—Mr. KEEN, of Pittsylvania, offered the following amendment to the first section of the bill providing for a call of a State Convention; all pending amendments being withdrawn to enable him to do so:

At the same time, the said Commissioners shall open a separate poll to take the sense of the qualified voters as to whether any action of said convention dissolving our connection with the Federal Union or changing the organic law of the State shall be submitted to the people for ratification or rejection; and in order to ascertain the sense of the voters upon the question aforesaid the said officers shall cause to be kept a poll, to be headed "Upon the question of referring such action to the people for their decision," which said poll book shall have two columns, one headed "For referring to the people," and the other "Against referring to the people," and the names of those who vote for the former shall be written under the former heading, and those who vote for the latter under the latter heading. When the said officers meet as aforesaid, they shall ascertain and make return of the number of persons voting for each of the propositions, and shall forthwith send to the Clerk of their respective counties or corporations a copy thereof, whose duty it shall be to transmit immediately a copy thereof to the President of the Convention, at Richmond, and also to the Governor of the Commonwealth.

Messrs. KEEN and BALL supported the amendment, advocating the policy which it proposed as essential to a strict adherance to the principle of republicanism and popular rights, which is its essence.

Mr. DUCKWALL offered the following as an amendment to the amendment offered by Mr. KEEN:

Provided, however, That the vote so taken in each county or election district, respectively, shall be considered only as declaratory of the popular voice of the electors of such county or election district, and as a popular instruction by the electors of such county or election district to their own delegate or delegates to the convention.

Mr. NEWTON, of Hanover, advocated prompt action in the matter, and deprecated in a very eloquent manner the hampering of the Convention with any such restrictions as the proposed amendments would impose, if adopted. It would be competent for the Convention itself to do what is here proposed, if they saw fit—and they would be the best judges of the expediency of such a policy, acting in full view of the events which shall present themselves at that time. He regarded it as decidedly impolitic at this early stage to prescribe any principle of action for that body, when the developments of every succeeding hour may suggest—nay, make necessary, a total change of policy from that which now seems best.

Mr. COWAN vindicated the fidelity of the Northwest to the institutions of the South, and maintained that the people of that section were as ready to stand forth in defence of Southern rights as the East.

Mr. ANDERSON advocated immediate action, and urged the passage of the bill as reported by the committee.

Mr. KEEN rose to a point of order; but the Speaker decided that Mr. ANDERSON had the right to proceed, the pending question opening the whole subject to debate.

Mr. ANDERSON resumed and concluded his remarks in advocacy of the bill.

Mr. CAPERTON, of Monroe, obtained the floor, but gave way to Mr. KEEN, who desired to make a personal explanation.

Mr. KEEN concluded his personal explanation, by some remarks in opposition to the amendment to his amendment, offered by Mr. DUCKWALL, and gave way to Mr. CAPERTON.

Mr. CAPERTON said, the friends of the amendment argued as if the people were dependent on the Legislature for the privilege of expressing their will. The Legislature had no power to control the action of a sovereign body. All it can do is to furnish a mode, a convenient mode, for making known their wishes. If this was the only mode by which their will could be communicated, it would be important to confer. But they could make known their will in a variety of modes. The people could communicate their wishes to their Delegates. The difference is only as to the convenience of the mode proposed and the other modes suggested. The mode contemplated in the amendment is most convenient, but are the advantages sufficient to compensate for the injurious effects which such a provision would have? He appeals to those who will unite with him in an honest and persevering effort to save the Union, to say whether the effect may not be far better than proposed, which ought to be to impress upon the Northern mind that, in the contingency of a refusal to accord such guarantees as we think important to our safety Virginia intended, and has prepared to sever her connection from them. The inference from this amendment, should it be adopted, would be, that Virginia was not prepared to say even that in any contingency would she dissolve the Union.

Mr. RIVES said the discussion had taken a very wide range, embracing the Constitution, Union, and other miscellaneous topics. He had heard a great deal of the "Union;" but had heard but little of the Constitution, and our rights under it, in connection therewith. He offered, in the way of argument, a proposition that when the people came to vote on the question of a Convention, they should indicate whether they were willing or not to stay in the Union under Lincoln.

Mr. EVANS, of Middlesex, said enough time had been consumed already in discussion, and he would, therefore, call the previous question.

The call being sustained, the SPEAKER stated the main question, which was on the adoption of Mr DUCKWALL's amendment to the amendment of Mr. KEEN. It was defeated. The question recurring on the adoption of Mr. KEEN's amendment, he called the yeas and nays, which were ordered, with the following result:

YEAS.—Messrs. Alderson, Arnold Ball, Bentley, Bisbie, Booker, Boreman, Brown, Cassin, Christian, Coleman, Collier, Cowan, Crane, Crump, Davis, Dickenson, Edgington, Ferguson, Ferrill, Fleming, D. Gibson, C. H. Gilmer, Goode, Gordon's, Hanly, Harrison, Haymond, Hackley, Hoffman, Holdway, Hopkins, Hunt, Jett, Johnson, Keen, Knotts, Kyle, Leftwich, Locke, Lockridge, Magruder, J. G. Martin, Jos. Martin, Wm. Martin, Massie, Matthews, McGruder, M Kinney, McKenzie, D. Miller, Morris, Myers, Patterson, Phelps, Porter, Preston, Pretlow, Randolph, Reid, Richardson, Riddick, Wyndham Robertson, Rives, Saunders, Scott, Segar, Snerrard, Sibert, Jones, K. Smith, Isaac N. Smith, Staples, Walker, A. Watson, Watts, Welch, Wood and Yerby—77.

NAYS.—Messrs. Allen, Anderson, Bailey, Ballard, Barbour, Baskerville, Bass, Bassell, Bell, Boisseau, Burks, Caperton, Carpenter, Carter, Chapman, Childs, Claiborne, Duckwall, Edwards, Evans, Friend, Garrett, J. T. Gibson, J. Gilmer, Graham, Grattan, Hunter, James, C. H. Jones, Warner T. Jones, Kaufman, Kemper, Kincheloe, Lundy, Lynn, Mallory, McDowell, Mayhew, Medley, Miles, J. R. Miller, Mong, Montague, Montgomery, Morgan, Nelson, Newton, Orgain, R. K. Robinson, Rutherford, Seddon, Shannon, R. Smith, Thomas, Tomlin, Tyler, Ward, Wilson, Wingfield, Witten, Woolfolk and Mr. Speaker—64.

After being debated *pro* and *con*, it was withdrawn by the mover.

Mr. COLLIER offered and advocated a motion to recommit the whole bill to the committee, but withdrew the same prior to a vote.

Mr. HAYMOND moved to reconsider the vote adopting the amendment offered by Mr. KEEN. He did so with a view of again submitting Mr. COLLIER's amendment, heretofore defeated.

Mr. KEEN said he heard it asserted in the House that the newspapers, politicians and Delegates were far behind the sentiment of the people. It was very strange, if that was the fact. It looks still stranger that the members were so afraid to let the question be submitted to the people.

Mr. CARTER called the previous question.

The ayes and noes being demanded, it was sustained.

The Clerk then called the ayes and noes, and Mr. HAYMOND's proposition was defeated by a tie vote—ayes 68, noes 68.

Pending the further consideration of the bill, the House adjourned.

The barn of Dr. W. Dorsey, of Granville county, N. C., was burnt on the 8th inst., with 1,800 pounds of tobacco, the property of John Tippett.

TELEGRAPHIC NEWS.

[Reported for the Richmond Dispatch.]

ALABAMA GONE OUT!

ORDINANCE OF SECESSION PASSED.

Rejoicings at Montgomery.

MONTGOMERY, ALA., Jan. 11.—The Ordinance of Secession was passed at 2½ o'clock yesterday.

Cannons are firing, bells ringing, and the city is in a blaze of enthusiasm.

[SECOND DISPATCH.]

AUGUSTA, Jan. 11.—The "ordinance to dissolve the Union between the State of Alabama and the other States of the United States, united under the compact and style of The United States of America," reads as follows:

Whereas, the election of Abraham Lincoln and Hannibal Hamlin to the offices of President and Vice President of the United States of America, by a sectional party avowedly hostile to the domestic institutions and to the peace and security of the people of the State of Alabama, following upon the heels of many and dangerous infractions of the Constitution of the United States, by many of the States and people of the Northern section, is a political wrong of so insulting and menacing a character as to justify the people of Alabama in the adoption of prompt and decided measures for their future peace and security; and, therefore,

Be it declared and ordained by the people of the State of Alabama in Convention assembled, That the State of Alabama now withdraws, and is hereby withdrawn from the Union known as the United States of America, and henceforth ceases to be one of the United States, and is, and of right ought to be, a sovereign and independent State.

SECTION 2. And be it further declared and ordained by the people of the State of Alabama in Convention assembled, That all powers over the territories of said State, and over the people thereof, heretofore delegated to the Government of the United States of America, be and they are hereby withdrawn from said Government, and are hereby resumed and vested in the people of the State of Alabama.

And as it is the desire purpose of the people of Alabama to meet the slaveholding States of the South, who may approve such purpose, in order to frame a Provisional as permanent Government, upon the principles of the Government of the United States be it also resolved by the people of Alabama, in Convention assembled, that the people of the States of Delaware, Maryland, Virginia, North Carolina, South Carolina, Florida, Georgia, Mississippi, Louisiana, Texas, Arkansas, Tennessee, Kentucky, and Missouri, be, and are hereby invited to meet the people of the State of Alabama, by their delegates, in Convention on the 4th day of February next, at Montgomery, Ala., for the purpose of consultation with each other as to the most effectual mode of securing concerted and harmonious action in whatever measures may be deemed most desirable for their common peace and security.

Be it further Resolved, That the President of this Convention be, and is hereby, instructed to transmit forthwith a copy of the foregoing preamble, ordinance and resolutions to the Governors of the States named, and the Governor of the State of Alabama.

Done by the people of Alabama, in Convention assembled at Montgomery, on this 11th day of January, 1861.

The preamble, ordinance and resolutions were adopted, by ayes 61, nays 39.

After the adoption of the ordinance, the hall was opened to visitors, a splendid flag was presented by the ladies of Alabama, and conveyed to the President's stand and formally given to the Convention, through Hon. Wm. L. Yancey, in a handsome address.

Mr. Smith, from Tuscaloosa, followed with a feeling reference to the Stars and Stripes, and invoked a blessing on the new flag.

Alpheus Baker, of Eufaula, returned the thanks of the Convention to the ladies.

The ordinance will be ratified Monday, when it is believed many other delegates will sign it.

An immense meeting is now in session in front of the Capitol. Distinguished co-operation delegates are pledging their constituents as a unit to sustain secession.

The flag presented by the ladies is now waving over the Capitol, amid the ringing of bells, firing of cannon, and intense enthusiasm.

[THIRD DISPATCH.]

MONTGOMERY, ALA., Jan. 11.—An illumination is lighting the city from the Capitol to the river.

An immense crowd is gathered in front of Montgomery Hall. Hon. J. L. M. Curry, and Mr. Mathews, of Mississippi, spoke.

Congressional.

WASHINGTON, Jan. 11.—*Senate.*—Several memorials in favor of the Union were received and referred.

Mr. Hunter's resolutions offered read as follows:

Whereas, certain forts, magazines, arsenals dock yards and other needful buildings, have been placed under the exclusive jurisdiction of the U. States by cession of the States in which they are situated, and with their consent, for the purpose of being used for the defence of the States; and whereas, such cessions cannot be made good and continued if the States where they are located, be set dissolved, if by the desire of one or more of these States to resume the jurisdiction thus ceded: Therefore, be it

Resolved, That the President of the U States be authorized to [illegible] the application of the Legislature or regular Convention of the people of any State, to retrocede the jurisdiction thus ceded, and providing for the proper security for the return and return of all the property of the United States; [illegible] any State making the application.

Mr. Hunter said, in offering the resolutions, that he had the hope of preserving the Union. His only hope now was to be ready to form a new Union stronger than the present one.—Many difficulties were in the way of this project, but the love of empire in the American mind might accomplish the result. He reviewed the history of the agitation of the slavery question, which, he contended, had induced the Southern States to believe that their social system was not safe in the Union without additional constitutional guarantees for its protection. The loss of their social system was the loss of their moral status and the reduction of their States to anarchy. He stated in form the demands of the South, and declared that to there should be annexed the right of veto by the South on all measures affecting slavery. He favored a dual Executive, founded on a plan somewhat different from that of Calhoun, providing for a President chosen by the electors chosen by the States in the Union to which the candidates reside. He suggested other vital reforms in the Executive branch of the Government. He also favored the reconstruction of the Supreme Court upon the basis of an equal number of Judges from each section. He did not believe coercion was proper, even if possible, and not possible, even if proper. He argued this position ably and at length, and illustrated it by numerous examples, drawn from the nature of the Federal Government. He depicted eloquently the evils which would follow in the train of civil war, and urged that it should be, if possible, avoided, in order to secure the reconstruction of the Government. He thought the retrocession of the forts and arsenals to the seceding States would do much to promote this object. The Government did not intend to coerce a State, it did not need them; and if it did intend to coerce a State, the arsenals would be needed. He declared the Union gone, but favored the assembling of a National Convention of each State to reconstruct it. He declared that Virginia would not submit to the coercion of any seceding State.

In conclusion, he appealed most eloquently for peace, and closed with a cheerful picture of the reconstruction of the Union.

Mr. Barker, of Oregon, asked Mr. Hunter if, should the Convention assemble to remodel the Constitution, he would use his influence in Virginia to maintain the present Constitution and laws until the amendments were decided upon?

Mr. Hunter said he had voted for Crittenden's resolution, and could do no more.

Mr. Baker said he only desired to know if the Senator would use his influence.

Mr. Hunter said if he did not satisfied the Senator from Oregon, he despaired of his power to do so.

Mr. Harlan, of Ia., addressed the Senate, attacking certain provisions of the Fugitive Slave law. He declared the Republican position. He said the Republicans would not yield an inch, before Lincoln's inauguration. He did not believe the war of coercion would last long, though it might be terrible, and would cost less than the merchants of New York had already lost by Southern sectional agitation, which was extended secession.

House.—Mr. Lovejoy asked leave to offer the following resolution:

Resolved, That in the judgment of the House, in the present state of the country, it would be wise to offer to the President, pending the present difficulties, [illegible] Army, and that the Republic receive no detriment.

Messrs. Jones and others objected to this resolution.

Mr. Curtis said the President had no such right under the Constitution, to delegate his powers.

Mr. Branch, of N. C., hoped the ayes and noes would be taken on the resolution.

No further action was had on the subject.

Mr. Hickman asked to be, and was, excused from serving as a member of the select committee on the President's recent Message.

Several private bills were passed.

The House went into Committee of the Whole on the Civil and Miscellaneous Appropriation bill, and discussed the same.

The Navy Appropriation bill was read, and the House

Adjourned.

From North Carolina.

RALEIGH, N. C., Jan. 11.—Both Houses of the Legislature were engaged yesterday and to-day on the State Convention question, which has become complicated by mixing State constitutional reforms with Federal matters in the amendment, for an open and a restricted Convention has been offered. No vote has been taken.

MORE FORTS TAKEN.

AN ENGAGEMENT EXPECTED

CHARLESTON, Jan. [illegible]—[illegible] dispatch to the Courier, from Montgomery, Ala., says:

"Fort Pike has been taken by Louisiana.

"The Federal troops have concentrated all the forts in Pensacola harbor except Fort Pickens, where they have concentrated. Three hundred men have left Mobile to surprise Fort Pickens."

[SECOND DISPATCH.]

NEW ORLEANS, Jan. 11.—Forts Jackson and St. Phillipe, on the Mississippi, and Fort Pike, at the entrance of Lake Ponchartrain, have been seized by New Orleans troops. There was no resistance.

LATER FROM EUROPE.

ARRIVAL OF THE AMERICAN.

HALIFAX, Jan. 1.—The American, from Liverpool on the 28 th, brings £162,000 in specie. It is stated that the late preparations of France exceed those of 1859.

COMMERCIAL.

LIVERPOOL, Dec. 28.—[illegible].—The market is quiet at [illegible]. Breadstuffs reported [illegible] [illegible]. Sales to-day of Flour [illegible]; Wheat is [illegible]; Corn [illegible]. [illegible] Consols 92¾@93½.

From Washington.

WASHINGTON, Jan. 11.—In the Executive session, Gen. Dix, of New York, was nominated Secretary of the Treasury, and was confirmed.

Great anxiety is felt about Seward's speech to-morrow, as it is believed it will be a fair exponent of Lincoln's views regarding the present state of affairs, and foreshadow his own case as Secretary of State.

Mr. Browne, editor of the Constitution, has received official notification of the withdrawal of Government advertisements from that paper. The supposed cause is his recent article on Secretary Holt.

Lieut. Talbot is reported to have arrived and had an interview with the President.

It is authoritatively stated that Mr. Holt will be appointed permanent Secretary of War.

The Interior and Post-Office Departments are still vacant.

The Mississippi delegation will withdraw from Congress to-morrow.

From Charleston.

CHARLESTON, Jan. 11.—The excitement here has somewhat abated, in consequence of pacific news from Washington.

Enlisting soldiers still goes on, but all is quiet.

The Legislature did nothing to-day.

Death of a Member of the South Carolina Convention.

CHARLESTON, Jan. 11.—Henry T. Conner, member of the South Carolina Convention, died at 6 o'clock this morning. He was a banker.

From Texas

NEW ORLEANS, Jan 11.—Galveston (Texas) dates to the 8th say the sentiment favoring a Southern Confederacy were chosen in that city for the State Convention.

The Indian depredations continued.

Federal Buildings at St. Louis.

ST. LOUIS, Jan. 11.—By order of Gen. Scott, a detachment of troops took possession of the sub-treasury, post-office and custom house here to-day.

Salutes for Secession.

AUGUSTA, GA., Jan. 11.—A salute of 100 guns for Florida, and the same number for Alabama, were fired to-day.

The Secession of Florida.

TALLAHASSEE, FLA., Jan. 11.—Florida seceded yesterday, at 20 minutes past 12 o'clock, by a vote of 62 to 7.

Warlike Movement at Norfolk.

NORFOLK, Jan. 11.—This morning before light a steamer went to the United States magazine wharf, loaded with powder, and left.—Its destination is unknown here.

The Star of the West.

WASHINGTON, Jan. 11.—It is stated that the Star of the West will return to New York.—The frigate Brooklyn will take the troops from here and carry them to Norfolk.

Secession Convention.

NEW ORLEANS, Jan. 11.—Returns indicate that the secessionists have a majority in the State Convention.

Northern Markets.

NEW YORK, Jan 11.—[illegible] Flour firm at [illegible]. Stocks higher and firm. [illegible] Virginia sixes [illegible]. Missouri's 62¼.

COUNTERFEITS.—The Liberty (Bedford co., Va.) Democrat, alluding to the recent arrest for passing counterfeit coin in Richmond, says:

Some three weeks ago, a young man of genteel appearance arrived in this place, and registered at the Hewitt House as Albert L. Riddell, Louisville, Ky. He came amongst us for the purpose of collecting a sum of money due the legatees in the estate of Benj. [illegible] Estes, dec'd. While sojourning in our midst, he became very intimate with David Saunders Gilton, a young man of this town, and they always to be an irreproachable character. On Thursday evening last the two young men left Liberty for the purpose of making a Western tour. When the news of their arrest reached this place, a number of our merchants examined their money, and found that they had received some of the spurious coin. [illegible] D. S. Gilton passed $30 to Wm Graves & Co.; $20 to Evans & Co.; $20 to J. M. [illegible] & Co., and $20 to Frank Braxton, which were afterwards redeemed by Riddell. J. M. England also received $30 in Riddell. We learn that the mail man from Lynchburg was in Liberty on Tuesday last with $120 he had received.

UNITED STATES ARMY.—The official register for 1860 contains, according to Regimental [illegible], 98 Colonels, 91 Lt. Colonels, 60 Majors, 468 Captains, and 768 Lieutenants, independent of the Pay and Medical Departments. They are distributed as follows:

	G.	Col.	Lt. Col.	Maj.	Capt.	Lt.	Lt.	Total.
Virginia	[illegible]	[illegible]	[illegible]	[illegible]	[illegible]	[illegible]	[illegible]	[illegible]
Slave	[illegible]	[illegible]	[illegible]	[illegible]	[illegible]	[illegible]	[illegible]	[illegible]
Free	[illegible]	16	16	31	163	248	[illegible]	521
Europe	[illegible]	[illegible]	[illegible]	[illegible]	[illegible]	[illegible]	[illegible]	[illegible]

S. H. Titcomb, a respectable citizen, was shot and killed at Nashville, Tenn., on the night of the 7th inst., by Leonard Simms, who mistook him for a burglar.

James M. Washington, editor and proprietor of the Bermudian, died at Hamilton, Bermuda, on the 25th ult., aged 42.

George Osborn and Patrick Egan were executed in New Orleans on Friday last, both for the murder of their wives.

Hon. Mr. Jenkins, of Virginia, did not vote for the Congressional resolutions in honor of Major Anderson.

Senator Trumbull, of Illinois, was on Wednesday re-elected Senator by a vote of 54 to 46 on joint ballot.

J. C. Mid [illegible] has been elected Mayor of Lexington, Va.

Lieut. Thomas B. Huger, U. S. N., of South Carolina, has resigned his commission.

A schooner arrived at Savannah, Ga., on the 5th inst., with 279 barrels of powder.

The Charleston Daily Courier.

NO. 18,787. CHARLESTON S. C..............MONDAY, FEBRUARY 11, 1861. VOLUME LIX.

THE LATEST NEWS!

BY TELEGRAPH.

Important from Montgomery.

THE SOUTHERN CONFEDERACY INAUGURATED!

A CONSTITUTION ADOPTED!

Great Unanimity Prevails.

HON. JEFFERSON DAVIS,

(OF MISSISSIPPI)

Elected Provisional President.

HON. ALEX. H. STEPHENS,

(OF GEORGIA)

VICE-PRESIDENT!

SALUTE OF ONE HUNDRED GUNS FOR "THE CONFEDERATE STATES OF AMERICA."

IMPORTANT FEATURES OF THE PROVISIONAL CONSTITUTION.

Speech of Mr. Stephens.

The Slave Trade and Tariff.

Important Proceedings of the Congress, &c., &c., &c., &c.

MONTGOMERY, February 9.—The Congress last night unanimously agreed upon a Constitution for the Provisional Government. It will be at once a strong and vigorous Government, and will go immediately into operation. It will have full powers and ample funds. No propositions looking to compromise or reconstruction will be entertained. The Congress will remain in session to make all the necessary laws.

The Constitution of the Provisional Government has been printed and made public. The preamble says: "We, the Deputies of the Sovereign and Independent States of South Carolina, Georgia, Florida, Alabama, Mississippi, Louisiana, invoking the favor of Almighty God, do hereby, in behalf of these States, ordain and establish this Constitution for the Provisional Government of the same, to continue one year from the inauguration of the President, or until a Permanent Constitution or Confederation between the said States shall be put in operation, whichever shall first occur."

The 7th section, 1st article, is as follows: "The importation of African negros from any foreign country, other than the slaveholding States of the United States, is hereby forbidden, and Congress is required to pass such laws as shall effectually prevent the same."

The 2d section, of the same article, reads: "The Congress shall also have power to prohibit the introduction of slaves from any State not a member of this Confederacy."

The 3d clause of article 4th, section 2d, says: "A slave in one State escaping to another, shall be delivered up on claim of the party to whom the said slave may belong, by the Executive authority of the State in which such slave shall be found. And in case of any abduction or forcible rescue, full compensation, including the value of the slave and all costs and expenses, shall be made to the party by the State in which such abduction or rescue shall take place."

Article 6th, 2d clause, declares "the government hereby instituted, shall take immediate steps in the settlement of all matters between the States forming it, and their late Confederates of the United States in relation to public property and public debt at the time of their withdrawal from them; those States hereby declaring it to be their wish and earnest desire to adjust everything pertaining to common property, common liability and common obligations of that Union upon principles of right, justice, equity and good faith."

All other portions of the Provisional Constitution are almost identical with the Constitution of the United States.

A grand and grand demonstration is now going on here.

A complimentary serenade was given to Hon. A. H. STEPHENS, which called forth from the Vice-President elect, an eloquent though brief speech. Mr. STEPHENS spoke as follows:

Gentlemen and Fellow-Citizens:—For though we met as strangers from different Independent States, we are once more citizens of a common country. [Applause.] Allow me, briefly and sincerely, to return you my unfeigned thanks for this compliment. The state of my health and voice and the night air, apart from other considerations, prevent me from doing more. This is not the time nor place to discuss those great questions now pressing upon the public councils. We are in process of a new formation. It is sufficient to say, this day a new Republic has been born. The Confederate States of America have been ushered into existence to take a place among the nations of the earth, [cheers,] under temporary or Provisional Government, it is true, but soon to be followed by one of a permanent character, which, while it surrenders none of our ancient rights and liberties, will secure, more perfectly, we trust, that peace, security and domestic tranquility that should be the object of all governments. [Applause.]

What is to be the future of this new Government? The fate of this new Republic will depend upon ourselves. Six States only at present constitute it; but six stars as yet appear in our constellation. More, I trust, will soon be added, and by the time we adopt a Constitution for permanent Government, may we have the number greater than the original thirteen of the original Union, with more than three times the population, wealth and power. [Applause.] With such a beginning the prospect of the future presents strong hopes to patriots of a bright and prosperous career. But what the future shall be depends upon ourselves, and those to come after us. Our Republic, and all Republics to be permanent and prosperous, must be supported by the virtue, intelligence, integrity and patriotism of the people. These are the corner stones upon which the temple of popular liberty must be constructed to stand securely and permanently. Resting ours upon these, we need fear nothing from without or within.

With climate unsurpassed in any nation on earth; with staple productions which control the commerce of the world; with institutions, so far as regards our organic and social policy, and in strict conformity to nature and the laws of the Creator,—whether read in the book of inspiration or the great book of manifestations—around us, we have all the natural elements essential to the attainment of the highest degree of power, glory and renown. [Applause.] These institutions have been much assailed, but it is our mission to vindicate the great truth on which they rest, and with them exhibit the highest type of civilization which it is possible for human society to reach. In doing this, our policy should be marked by the desire to preserve and maintain peace with all States and people. If it cannot be done, let not the fault lie at our door.

While we should make aggressions on none, we should prepare to repel them when made by others, let them come from whatever quarter they may. [Applause.] We ask of others simply to be let alone and permitted to look after our safety, security and happiness in our own way, without molesting or giving offence to other people. Let, then, peace, fraternity and liberal commercial relations with all the world be our motto. [Cheers.] With these principles, without envy towards other States in the line of policy they mark out for themselves, we will invite them to generous rivalship in all that developes the highest qualities in every nation. [Applause.] With my best wishes for you, gentlemen, and the success of our common Government, this day announced, I bid you good night.

As the speaker retired, three hearty cheers were given for the Hon. A. H. STEPHENS, of Georgia, the first Vice-President of the Confederated States of America.

Messrs. CHESNUT and KEITT, of South Carolina, CONRAD, of Louisiana, and others, also addressed the assemblage in glowing and patriotic language.

The popular demonstration progressed until a late hour on Saturday night. One hundred guns were fired on Capitol Hill. The people are wild with delight. Every one is pleased with the result.

[DISPATCH FROM THE SECRETARY OF THE CONGRESS.]

MONTGOMERY, February 9, 3 A. M.—I have just got through with preparing the first copy (for the printer) of the Provisional Constitution. Its title is "Constitution for the Provisional Government of the Confederate States of America." It follows, in the main, the Constitution of the United States. The Tariff clause is as follows: "The Congress shall have power to lay and collect taxes, duties, imposts and excise for the revenue necessary to pay the debts, carry on the Government of the Confederacy; and all duties, imposts and excises shall be uniform throughout the Confederacy."

The slave trade clause reads as follows: "The introduction of African negros from any foreign country other than the slaveholding States of the United States is hereby forbidden. And Congress is required to pass such laws as shall effectually prevent the same. The Congress shall also have the power to prohibit the introduction of slaves from any State not a member of this Confederacy."

The Constitution was adopted unanimously last night at half-past 10 o'clock.

MONTGOMERY, February 9.—Unusual interest has been manifested by outsiders to-day. The Convention Hall and galleries have been crowded.

Mr. MEMMINGER, of South Carolina presented a beautiful model flag made by South Carolina ladies. The design is a blue cross on a red field with seven stars on the cross. It is highly admired.

Mr. MEMMINGER also presented another model by a gentleman of Charleston. The design is a cross, with fifteen stars on a field of stripes.

A Committee was appointed to report on a flag, seal of arms, and motto for the new Confederacy.

The President has been directed to appoint Committees on Foreign Affairs, Finance, Military and Naval Affairs, Judiciary, Postal Affairs, Commerce, Patents and Printing.

Hon. JEFFERSON DAVIS, of Mississippi, has been elected Provisional President of the Confederated States of North America, and Hon. ALEXANDER HAMILTON STEPHENS, of Georgia, has been elected Vice-President. The choice was unanimous in both cases.

A resolution was adopted appointing a Committee of Three of the Alabama Deputies, to inquire and report upon what terms suitable buildings in Montgomery can be procured for the use of the several Executive Departments of the Confederacy under the Provisional Government.

A bill has been passed, continuing in force until repealed or altered by Congress, all laws of the United States that are now in force, not inconsistent with the Constitution of the Provisional Government. It is understood that under this law a Tariff will be laid on all goods brought from the United States.

A resolution was adopted instructing the Finance Committee to report promptly a Tariff for raising revenue sufficient to support the Government.

Another resolution was adopted authorizing the appointment of a Committee to report a Constitution for the Permanent Government of the Confederacy.

The Congress was about two hours in secret session, and the balance in open session to-day.

[Special Dispatch to the Charleston Courier.]

Important from Washington.

WASHINGTON, February 9.—The President has returned Col. HAYNE's last letter, deeming it offensive. He has even refused to transmit to Congress.

There is great excitement at the Capitol on account of the news from Savannah. Gov. BROWN's seizure of Northern vessels has disturbed the equanimity of the Republicans.

The House has called for official information in reference to the Savannah seizures.

From New York—Restoration of the Muskets, &c.

NEW YORK, February 10.—The muskets seized by the New York State Police, have been restored unconditionally to Mr. LAMAR, the agent of Georgia, who telegraphed the fact to the Collector of Savannah. [We are semi-officially informed that Gov. BROWN, of Georgia, on learning that the arms were restored, ordered the release of the vessels seized at Savannah.]

Important from Arkansas.

MEMPHIS, February 10.—We have positive information that the Little Rock Arsenal, with 9000 stand of arms, a large amount of ammunition, and 40 cannon, including BRAGG's Battery, has surrendered to the State authorities of Arkansas. It is now garrisoned by Arkansas State volunteers.

The Cutter Lewis Cass.

[The following is a *verbatim* copy of a dispatch from the Associated Press:]

NEW YORK, February 10.—Lieutenants ROGERS and SHERMAN; cutter *Cass*, from Savannah. Commander re-appointed by Georgia.

From Washington.

WASHINGTON, February 9.—Hon. THOS. J. JUDGE, Commissioner from Alabama, was received by the President only as a distinguished citizen of his State. The President repudiates his officiality.

The Peace Congress is still in Secret Session. A Committee was appointed for the purpose of engaging in preparing and receiving propositions for a peaceable adjustment.

Influential gentlemen, of all parties, continue to arrive here, urging a settlement of the national troubles. Millions of wealth are represented by them.

It is believed that KELLOGG's speech in the House, favoring his resolution to amend the Constitution, reflects the embodiment of LINCOLN's sentiments. The Unionists are jubilant at this, and other signs, indicating a willingness on the part of the leading Republicans to sacrifice party and Platforms for the sake of Union.

The Committee appointed by the Peace Conference will probably report on Tuesday. Various plans are now before them. It is believed that the Border State resolutions meet with most favor.

Congressional.

WASHINGTON, February 8.—*Senate.*—The usual number of peace memorials were received.

A resolution to extend McCORMICK's Reaper patent was discussed and carried.

During the debate, sharp language passed between DOUGLAS and FESSENDEN.

The President sent a message enclosing the correspondence with Col. HAYNE relative to Fort Sumter.

MORRILL's Tariff Bill was taken up and read.

Adjourned.

House.—A communication was received announcing that the President had signed the bill authorising the extension of the Alexandria, Loudon and Hampshire Rail Road to Georgetown.

Private bills were acted on.

A message was received covering the correspondence of the President with HAYNE.

The House refused to consider the report of the Committee of Thirty-Three.

Mr. HATTON, of Tennessee, made a conciliatory speech.

Mr. KELLOGG made a speech in favor of his resolutions, amending the Constitution. He said he repudiated his party platform for the sake of the Union. He did not speak to the politicians, but to the people of all parties.

Mr. SMITH, of North Carolina, followed in a conciliatory strain. He said his State would not be a party to the destruction of the Union as long as there remained a hope of maintaining her rights within it. He advocated CRITTENDEN's resolutions.

The House took a recess until 7 o'clock.

Additional by the Canada.

NEW YORK, February 9.—The Sardinians had entered the Roman States and dispersed the Re-actionary bands and burnt a convent at Casmalia.

The Paris Bourse was firmer.

There was great activity in the French Arsenals and Dock Yards.

It was reported that the King of Naples had resolved to continue the defence of Gaeta to the last extremity.

From Pennsylvania.

HARRISBURG, February 9.—The Legislature passed a Bill guaranteeing $2,800,000 of the new Government loan.

Mobile Cotton Market.

MOBILE, February 9.—The sales to-day were 1000 bales, at 10½¢. The market is very dull.

New Orleans Cotton Market.

NEW ORLEANS, February 8.—The Cotton market is dull; sales of 6000 bales. Middling 10¾@11¢. Sales of the week 67,000 bales. Receipts 81,500 bales, against 89,000 bales last season. Decrease 184,500 bales. Decrease in receipts at all the ports 583,500 bales. Exports 59,000 bales. Total exports 1,173,500 bales. Stock on hand 347,500 bales. Sterling Exchange 2½@4 per cent. premium. Exchange on New York ½@¾ per cent. discount.

New York Markets.

NEW YORK, February 9.—The Cotton market is declining; sales of 1200 bales. Middling Upland quoted at 11⅞¢. Flour—Sales of 8000 bbls.; market heavy. Southern is quoted at $5.40@$5.70. Wheat is declining; sales of 12,000 bushels. White quoted at $1.50@$1.52½. Corn is firm; sales of 42,000 bushels. Mixed is quoted at 65@67¢; New at 63@64¢. Sugar is heavy; New Orleans quoted at 5@6¼¢. Coffee steady; sales of 4500 bags at 11@12½¢. Spirits of Turpentine is dull at 35½@36¢. Rosin is dull. Rice is quiet at 3¾@4¼¢. Freights are firm.

NEW YORK, February 8.—Cotton dull, with sales of 1000 bales. Middling Uplands 11⅞¢. Flour declining; Southern $5.40@$5.75. Wheat dull. Corn heavy; mixed 66@67¢; choice Southern white 75½¢. Spirits Turpentine dull at 35½@37¢ ₩ gallon. Rosin dull at $1.20@$1.25 ₩ barrel. Rice dull.

Governor JOSEPH E. BROWN, of Georgia, is the man for his place and for the times, as will be seen in the report of his recent action.

The Southern Field and Fireside—a literary, agricultural and horticultural journal—is published every Saturday, at Augusta, Ga. Terms, two dollars per annum, in advance.

A Paper for the South.—It should now become a matter of pride with our people (says the Savannah *News*) to sustain and cherish a press, firmly established at the South, for the promotion of Southern interests. Such an one *The Southern Field and Fireside* has proved to be. It is published every Saturday, at Augusta, Ga., by JAMES GARDNER, at the low price of TWO DOLLARS per annum. Its columns are devoted to Literature, Agriculture and Horticulture, each department under the supervision of editors of talent and experience. Mr. JAMES N. ELLS of the Literary, Dr. DANIEL LEE of the Agricultural and Mr. WM. N. WHITE of the Horticultural departments, present a most acceptable paper, which should find its way, regularly, into every family throughout the South.

It is a large paper, in quarto form, containing forty columns, printed on fine material, with clear type, and makes a beautiful book when bound.

The South Carolina Flag.—The Norfolk *Day Book* says:

The flag presents a beautiful appearance. The ground is a rich blue with a white palmetto tree in the centre, and a white crescent in the upper corner next the flag-staff. It is extremely tasteful, and agreeable to the eye, and we think it will compare favorably with any other national ensign.

CONTINUATION OF CORRESPONDENCE

In Reference to Fort Sumter.

BETWEEN

COL. I. W. HAYNE,

SPECIAL ENVOY FROM THE STATE OF SOUTH CAROLINA,

AND

SECRETARY HOLT,

ON BEHALF OF THE PRESIDENT OF THE UNITED STATES.

MR. HAYNE TO THE PRESIDENT OF THE UNITED STATES.

WASHINGTON, January 31, 1861.

To His Excellency James Buchanan, President:

SIR:—I had the honor to hold a short interview with you on 14th instant, informal and unofficial. Having previously been informed that you desired that whatever was official should be, on both sides, conducted by written communications, I did not at that time present my credentials, but verbally informed you that I bore a letter from the Governor of South Carolina in regard to the occupation of Fort Sumter, which I would deliver the next day under cover of a written communication from myself. The next day, before such communication could be made, I was waited upon by a Senator from Alabama, who stated that he came on the part of all the Senators then in Washington from the States which had already seceded from the United States, or would certainly have done so before the 1st day of February next. The Senator from Alabama urged that he and they were interested in the subject of my mission in almost an equal degree with the authorities of South Carolina. He said that, hostilities commenced between South Carolina and your Government, would necessarily involve the States represented by themselves in civil strife, and fearing that the action of South Carolina might complicate the relations of your Government to the seceded and seceding States, and, therefore, interfere with a peaceful solution of existing difficulties, these Senators requested that I would withhold my message to yourself until a consultation among themselves could be had. To this I agreed, and the result of the consultation was the letter of these Senators addressed to me, dated 15th January, a copy of which is in your possession. To this letter I replied on the 17th, and a copy of that reply is likewise in your possession. This correspondence, as I am informed, was made the subject of a communication from Senators Fitzpatrick, Mallory and Slidell, addressed to you, and your attention called to the contents. These gentlemen received on the — day of January a reply to their application, conveyed in a letter addressed to them, dated ——, signed by the Hon. J. Holt, Secretary of War *ad interim*. Of this letter you, of course, have a copy. This letter from Mr. Holt was communicated to me under cover of a letter from all the Senators of the seceded and seceding States, who still remained in Washington; and of this letter, too, I am informed you have been furnished with a copy. This reply of yours through the Secretary of War *ad interim* to the application made by the Senators was entirely unsatisfactory to me. It appeared to me to be not only a rejection, in advance of the main proposition made by these Senators, to wit: that "an arrangement should be agreed on between the authorities of South Carolina and your Government, at least until the 15th February next, by which time South Carolina and the States represented by the Senators might in Convention devise a wise, just and peaceable solution of existing difficulties. "In the meantime," they say, "we think [that is, these Senators,] that your State [South Carolina] should suffer Major Anderson to obtain necessary supplies of food, fuel or water, and enjoy free communication by post or special messenger with the President, upon the understanding that the President will not send him reinforcements during the same period;" but, besides this rejection of the main proposition, there was in Mr. Holt's letter a distinct refusal to make any stipulation on the subject of reinforcement, even for the short time that might be required to communicate with my Government. This reply to the Senators, as I have stated, altogether unsatisfactory to me, and I felt sure that it would be so to the authorities whom I represented. It was not, however, addressed to me, or to the authorities of South Carolina, and as South Carolina had addressed nothing to your Government, and had asked nothing at your hands, I looked not to Mr. Holt's letter, but to the note addressed to me by the Senators of the seceded and seceding States. I had consented to withhold my message *at their* instance, provided they could get assurances *satisfactory to them* that no reinforcements would be sent to Fort Sumter in the interval, and that the peace should not be disturbed by any act of hostility. The Senators expressed in their note to me of the 23d inst., their "entire confidence that no reinforcements will be sent to Fort Sumter, nor will the public peace be disturbed within the period requisite for full communication between you (myself) and your (my) Government," and renewed their request that I would withhold the communication with which I stood charged, and await further instructions. This I have done. The further instructions arrived on the 30th inst., and bear date the 26th. I now have the honor to make to you my first communication as Special Envoy from the Government of South Carolina. You will find enclosed the original communication to the President of the United States from the Governor of South Carolina, with which I was charged in Charleston on the 12th day of January, instant, the day on which it bears date. I am now instructed by the Governor of South Carolina to say, that "his opinion as to the propriety of the demand which is contained in this letter has not only been confirmed by the circumstances which your (my) mission has developed, but is now increased to a conviction of its necessity. The safety of the State requires that the position of the President should be distinctly understood. The safety of all seceding States requires it as much as the safety of South Carolina. If it be so, that Fort Sumter is held as *property*, then as property the rights, whatever they may be, of the United States, can be ascertained, and for the satisfaction of these rights the pledge of the State of South Carolina, you are (I am) authorized to give." "If Fort Sumter is not held as property, it is held," say my instructions, "as a military post, and such a post within the limits of South Carolina cannot be tolerated."

You will perceive that it is upon the presumption that it is solely as property that you continue to hold Fort Sumter that I have been selected for the performance of the duty upon which I have entered. I do not come as a military man, to demand the surrender of a fortress, but as the legal officer of the State, its Attorney-General, to claim for the State the exercise of its undoubted right of eminent domain, and to pledge the State to make good all injury to the rights of property which arise from the exercise of the claim.

South Carolina, as a separate, independent sovereignty, assumes the right to take into her possession everything within her limits essential to maintain her honor or her safety, irrespective of the question of property, subject only to the moral duty requiring that compensation should be made to the owner. This right she cannot permit to be drawn into discussion. As to compensation for any property, whether of an individual or a Government, which she may deem it necessary for her honor or safety to take into her possession, her past history gives ample guaranty that it will be made, upon a fair accounting, to the last dollar. The proposition now is, that the law officer should, under authority of the Governor and his Council, distinctly pledge the faith of South Carolina to make such compensation in regard to Fort Sumter, and its appurtenances and contents, to the full extent of the money value of the property of the United States, delivered over to the authorities of South Carolina, by your command.

I will not suppose that a pledge like this can be considered insufficient security. Is not the money value of the property of the United States in this fort, situated where it cannot be made available to the United States for any one purpose for which it was originally constructed, worth more to the United States than the property itself? Why, then, *as property*, insist on holding it by an armed garrison? Yet such has been the ground upon which you have invariably placed your occupancy of this fort by troops; beginning prospectively with your annual Message of the 4th December, again in your Special Message of the 9th January, and still more emphatically in your Message of the 28th January. The same position is set forth in your reply to the Senators, through the Secretary of War *ad interim*. It is there virtually conceded that Fort Sumter "is held merely as property of the United States, which you deem it your duty to protect and preserve."

Again it is submitted that the continuance of an armed possession actually jeopards the property you desire to protect. It is impossible but that such a possession, if continued long enough, must lead to collision. No people not completely abject and pusillanimous could submit indefinitely to the armed occupation of a fortress in the midst of the harbor of its principal city, and commanding the ingress and egress of every ship that enters the port, the daily Ferry Boats that ply upon the waters, moving but at the sufferance of aliens. An attack upon this fort would scarcely improve it as property, whatever the result, and if captured it would no longer be the subject of account.

To protect Fort Sumter, merely as property, it is submitted that an armed occupancy is not only unnecessary, but that it is manifestly the worst possible means which can be resorted to for such an object.

Your reply to the Senators, through Mr. Holt, declares it to be your sole object "to act strictly on the defensive, and to authorize no movement against South Carolina unless justified by a hostile movement on their part," yet, in reply to the proposition of the Senators that no reinforcements should be sent to Fort Sumter, provided South Carolina agrees that during the same period no attack should be made, you say "it is impossible for me (your Secretary) to give you (the Senators) any such assurance," that it would be a manifest violation of his (your) duty to place himself (yourself) under engagements that he (you) would not perform the duty either for an indefinite or a limited period.

In your Message of the 28th inst., in expressing yourself in regard to a similar proposition, you say: "However strong may be my desire to enter into such an agreement, I am convinced that I do not possess the power. Congress, and Congress alone, under the war-making power, can exercise the discretion of agreeing to abstain 'from any and all acts calculated to produce a collision of arms' between this and other governments. It would, therefore, be a usurpation for the Executive to attempt to restrain their hands by an agreement in regard to matters over which he has no Constitutional control. If he were thus to act, they might pass laws which he should be bound to obey, though in conflict with his agreement." The proposition, it is suggested, was addressed to you under the laws as they now are, and was not intended to refer to a new condition of things arising under new legislation.

It was addressed to the Executive discretion, acting under existing laws. If Congress should, under the war-making power, or in any other way, legislate in a manner to affect the peace of South Carolina, her interests or her rights, it would not be accomplished in secret. South Carolina would have timely notice, and she would, I trust, endeavor to meet the emergency. It is added in the letter of Mr. Holt, that "at the present moment it is not deemed necessary to reinforce Major Anderson, because he makes no such request, and feels quite secure in his position." But should his safety require it, every effort will be made to supply reinforcements." This would seem to ignore the other branch of the proposition made by the Senators, viz: that no attack was to be made on Fort Sumter during the period suggested, and that Major Anderson should enjoy the facilities of communication, &c., &c.

I advert to this point, however, for the purpose of saying that to send reinforcements to Fort Sumter could not serve as a means of *protecting* and *preserving property*, for, as must be known to your Government, it would inevitably lead to immediate hostilities, in which property on all sides would necessarily suffer. South Carolina has every disposition to preserve the public peace, and feels, I am sure, in full force, those high, "Christian and moral duties" referred to by your Secretary, and it is submitted that on her part there is scarcely any consideration of mere property, apart from honor and safety, which could induce her to do ought to jeopard that peace, still less to inaugurate a protracted and bloody civil war. She rests her position on something higher than mere property. It is a consideration of her own dignity as a Sovereign, and the safety of her people, which prompts her to demand that this property should not longer be used as a military post by a Government she no longer acknowledges. She feels this to be an imperative duty. It has, in fact, become an absolute necessity of her condition. Repudiating as you do the idea of coercion, avowing peaceful intentions, and expressing a patriot's horror for civil war and bloody strife among those who once were brethren, it is hoped that on further consideration you will not, on a mere question of property, refuse the reasonable demand of South Carolina, which honor and necessity alike compel her to vindicate. Should you disappoint this hope, the responsibility for the result surely does not rest with her. If the evils of war are to be encountered, especially the calamities of civil war, an elevated statesmanship would seem to require that it should be accepted as the unavoidable alternative of something still more disastrous, such as national dishonor or measures materially affecting the safety or permanent interests of a people, or that it should be a choice deliberately made and entered upon as war, and of set purpose. But that war should be the incident or accident attendant on a policy professedly peaceful, and not required to effect the object which is avowed as the only end intended, can only be excused when there has been no warning given as to the consequences.

I am further instructed to say that South Carolina cannot, by her silence, appear to acquiesce in the imputation that she was guilty of an act of unprovoked aggression in firing on the Star of the West. Though an unarmed vessel, she was filled with armed men entering her territory against her will, with the purpose of reinforcing a garrison held, within her limits, against her protest.—She forbears to recriminate by discussing the question of the propriety of attempting such a reinforcement at all, as well as of the disguised and secret manner in which it was intended to be effected. And on this occasion she will say nothing as to the manner in which Fort Sumter was taken into the possession of its present occupants. The interposition of the Senators, who have addressed you, was a circumstance unexpected by my Government, and unsolicited certainly by me. The Governor, while he appreciates the high and generous motives by which they were prompted, and while fully he approves the delay which, in deference to them, has taken place in the presentation of the demand, feels that it cannot longer be withheld.

I conclude with an extract from the instructions just received by me from the Government of South Carolina:

"The letter of the President, through Mr. Holt, may be received as the reply to the question you were instructed to ask, as to his assertion of his right to send reinforcements to Fort Sumter. You were instructed to say to him if he asserted that right, that the State of South Carolina regarded such a right when asserted, or with an attempt at its exercise, as a declaration of war.

"If the President intends it shall not be so understood, it is proper, to avoid any misconception hereafter, that he should be informed of the manner in which the Governor will feel bound to regard it.

"If the President, when you have stated the reasons which prompt the Governor in making the demand for the delivery of Fort Sumter, shall refuse to deliver the fort upon the pledge you have been authorized to make, you will communicate that refusal without delay to the Governor. If the President shall not be prepared to give you an immediate answer, you will communicate to him that his answer may be transmitted within a reasonable time to the Governor at this place. (Charleston, South Carolina.)

"The Governor does not consider it necessary that you (I) should remain longer in Washington than is necessary to execute this, the closing duty of your (my) mission, in the manner now indicated to you (me.) As soon as the Governor shall receive from you information that you have closed your mission, and the reply, whatever it may be, of the President, he will consider the conduct which will be necessary on his part."

Allow me to request that you would, as soon as possible, inform me whether, under these instructions, I need await your answer in Washington—and if not, I would be pleased to convey from you to my Government, information as to the time when an answer may be expected in Charleston.

With considerations of high respect, I am, very respectfully, (Signed) I. W. HAYNE, Special Envoy.

LETTER OF MR. HOLT TO MR. HAYNE.

WAR DEPARTMENT, February 6, 1861.

Sir:—The President of the United States has received your letter of the 31st ult., and has charged me with the duty of replying thereto.

In the communication addressed to the President by Governor Pickens, under date of the 12th of January, and which accompanies yours now before me, his Excellency says: "I have determined to send to you the Hon. I. W. Hayne, the Attorney-General of the State of South Carolina, and have instructed him to demand the surrender of Fort Sumter, in the harbor of Charleston, to the constituted authorities of the State of South Carolina. The demand I have made of Major Anderson, and which I now make of you, is suggested because of my earnest desire to avoid the bloodshed which a persistence in your attempt to retain the possession of that fort will cause, and which will be unavailing to secure to you that possession, but induce a calamity most deeply to be deplored." The character of the demand thus authorized to be made, appears under the influence, I presume, of the correspondence with the Senators to which you refer, to have been modified by subsequent instructions of his Excellency, dated the 26th, and received by yourself on the 30th of January, in which he says: "If it be so that Fort Sumter is held as property, then as property, the rights whatever they may be, of the United States, can be ascertained, and for the satisfaction of these rights, the pledge of the State of South Carolina, you are authorized to give." The full scope and precise purport of your instructions, as thus modified, you have expressed in the following words: "I do not come as a military man to demand the surrender of a fortress, but as the legal officer of the State—its Attorney-General—to claim for the State, the exercise of its undoubted right of eminent domain, and to pledge the State to make good all injury to the rights of property which arise from the exercise of the claim." And lest this explicit language should not sufficiently define your position, you add: "The proposition now is that her (South Carolina's) law officer, should, under authority of the Governor and his Council, distinctly pledge the faith of South Carolina, to make such compensation, in regard to Fort Sumter and its appurtenances and contents, to the full extent of the money value of the property of the United States, delivered over to the authorities of South Carolina by your command." You then adopt his Excellency's train of thought upon the subject, so far as to suggest that the possession of Fort Sumter by the United States, "if continued long enough must lead to collision," and that "an attack upon it would scarcely improve it as property, whatever the result, and if captured, it would no longer be the subject of account." The proposal then, now presented to the President, is simply an offer on the part of South Carolina to buy Fort Sumter and contents as property of the United States, sustained by a declaration, in effect, that, if she is not permitted to make the purchase, she will seize the fort by force of arms. As the initiation of a negotiation for the transfer of property between friendly governments, this proposal impresses the President as having assumed a most unusual form. He has, however, investigated the claim on which it professes to be based apart from the declaration that accompanies it. And it may be here remarked that much stress has been laid upon the employment of the words "property" and "public property" by the President in his several Messages. These are the most comprehensive terms which can be used in such a connection, and surely, when referring to a fort or any other public establishment, they embrace the entire and undivided interest of the Government therein. The title of the United States to Fort Sumter is complete and incontestable. Were its interest in this property purely proprietary, in the ordinary acceptation of the term, it might probably be subjected to the exercise of the right of eminent domain; but it has also political relations to it of a much higher and more imposing character than those of mere proprietorship. It has absolute jurisdiction over the fort and the soil on which it stands. This jurisdiction consists in the authority to "exercise exclusive legislation" over the property referred to, and is, therefore, clearly incompatible with the claim of "eminent domain" now insisted upon by South Carolina. This authority was not derived from any questionable revolutionary source, but from the peaceful cession of South Carolina herself, acting through her Legislature, under a provision of the Constitution of the United States. South Carolina can no more assert the right of eminent domain over Fort Sumter than Maryland can assert it over the District of Columbia. The political and proprietary rights of the United States in either case rest upon precisely the same ground.

The President, however, is relieved from the necessity of farther pursuing this inquiry by the fact that, whatever may be the claim of South Carolina to this fort, he has no Constitutional power to cede or surrender it. The property of the United States has been acquired by force of public law, and can only be disposed of under the same solemn sanctions. The President, as the head of the Executive branch of the Government only, can no more sell and transfer Fort Sumter to South Carolina than he can sell and convey the Capital of the United States to Maryland or to any other State or individual seeking to possess it. His Excellency the Governor is too familiar with the Constitution of the United States, and with the limitations upon the powers of the Chief Magistrate of the Government it has established, not to appreciate at once the soundness of this legal proposition.

The question of re-inforcing Fort Sumter is so fully disposed of in my letter to Senator Slidell and others, under date of the 22d of January—a copy of which accompanies this—that its discussion will not now be renewed. I then said: "At the present moment it is not deemed necessary to reinforce Major Anderson, because he makes no such request. Should his safety, however, require reinforcements, every effort will be made to supply them." I can add nothing to the explicitness of this language, which still applies to the existing status. The right to send forward reinforcements, when in the judgment of the President the safety of the garrison requires them, rests on the same unquestionable foundation as the right to occupy the fortress itself.

In the letter of Senator Davis and others to yourself, under date of the 15th ultimo, they say, "we, therefore, think it especially due from South Carolina to our States—to say nothing of other slaveholding States—that she should, as far as she can consistently with her honor, avoid initiating hostilities between her and the United States or any other power," and you now yourself give to the President the gratifying assurance that "South Carolina has every disposition to preserve the public peace," and since he is himself sincerely animated by the same desire, it would seem that this common and patriotic object must be of certain attainment. It is difficult, however, to reconcile with this assurance the declaration on your part, that "it is a consideration of her (South Carolina's) own dignity as a sovereign, and the safety of her people which prompts her to demand that this property should not longer be used as a military post by a Government she no longer acknowledges," and the thought you so constantly present, that this occupation must lead to a collision of arms, and the prevalence of civil war. Fort Sumter is in itself a military post and nothing else, and it would seem that not so much the fact as the purpose of its use, should give to it a hostile or friendly character. This fortress is now held by the Government of the United States for the same objects for which it has been held from the completion of its construction. These are national and defensive, and were a public enemy now to attempt the capture of Charleston, or the destruction of the commerce of its harbor, the whole force of the batteries of this fortress would be at once exerted for their protection. How the presence of a small garrison actuated by such a spirit as this, can compromise the dignity or honor of South Carolina, or become a source of irritation to her people, the President is at a loss to understand. The attitude of that garrison, as has been often declared, is neither menacing, nor defiant, nor unfriendly. It is acting under orders to stand strictly on the defensive, and the Government and people of South Carolina must well know that they can never receive aught but shelter from its guns, unless in the absence of all provocation, they should assault it and seek its destruction. The intent with which this fortress is held by the President is truthfully stated by Senator Davis and others, in their letter to yourself of the 15th January, in which they say, "it is not held with any hostile or unfriendly purpose towards your State, but merely as property of the United States, which the President deems it his duty to protect and preserve."

If the announcement, so repeatedly made, of the President's pacific purposes in continuing the occupation of Fort Sumter until the question shall have been settled by competent authority, has failed to impress the Government of South Carolina, the forbearing conduct of his Administration for the last few months, should be received as conclusive evidence of his sincerity. And if this forbearance, in view of the circumstances which have so severely tried it, be not accepted as a satisfactory pledge of the peaceful policy of this Administration towards South Carolina, then it may be safely affirmed, that neither language or conduct can possibly furnish one. It, with all the multiplied proofs, which exist, of the President's anxiety for peace, and of the earnestness with which he has pursued it, the authorities of that State shall assault Fort Sumter, and peril the lives of the handful of brave and loyal men shut up within its walls, and thus plunge our common country into the horrors of civil war, then upon them and those they represent, must rest the responsibility.

Very respectfully,

Your obedient servant,

(Signed) J. HOLT, Secretary of War.

The Hon. I. W. HAYNE, Attorney-General of State of South Carolina.

P. S.—The President has not, as you have been informed, received a copy of the letter to yourself from the Senators, communicating that of Mr. Holt of the 22d of January. J. H.

LETTER OF MR. HAYNE TO MR. HOLT.

WASHINGTON, February 7, 1861.

To his Excellency James Buchanan, President:

SIR:—Your reply, through your Secretary of the War Department, to my communication of the 31st of January, covering the demand of the Governor of South Carolina for the delivery of Fort Sumter, was received yesterday. Although the very distinct and emphatic refusal of that demand closes my mission, I feel constrained to correct some strange misapprehensions into which your Secretary has fallen. There has been no modification of the demand authorized to be made and no change whatever in its character, and of this you were distinctly informed in my communication of the 31st of January. You have the original demand as delivered to me by Governor Pickens on the 12th of January, and you have an extract from the further instructions received by me expressly stating that he, the Governor, was "*confirmed*" in the views he entertained on the 12th of January by that very correspondence which you assign as the cause of the alleged modification. You assume that the character of the demand has been modified, yet you have from me but one communication, and that asserts the contrary, and you have nothing from the Governor but the very demand itself, which you say has been modified. What purpose of peace or conciliation your Secretary could have had in view in the introduction of this point at all, it is difficult to perceive. You next attempt to ridicule the proposal presented "as simply an offer on the part of South Carolina to buy Fort Sumter and contents as property of the United States, sustained by a declaration in effect that if she is not permitted to make the purchase she will seize the fort by force of arms." It is difficult to consider this as any other than intentional misconstruction. You were told that South Carolina, as a separate, independent sovereignty, would not tolerate the occupation, by foreign troops, of a military post within her limits, but, that inasmuch as you, in repeated messages and in your correspondence, had "laid much stress" upon the character of your duties, arising from considering forts as property, South Carolina, so far as this matter of property, suggested by yourself, was concerned, would make compensation for all injury done the property, in the exercise of her sovereign right of eminent domain; and this your Secretary calls a proposal to purchase. The idea of purchase is entirely inconsistent with the assertion of paramount right in the purchaser. I had supposed that an "interest in property," as such, could be no other than "purely proprietary," and if I confined myself to this narrow view of your "relations" to Fort Sumter, you, at least, should not consider it the subject of criticism. Until your letter of yesterday, you chose so to consider your relations, in everything which you have written, or which has been written under your direction. It was precisely because you had yourself chosen to place your action upon the ground of "purely proprietary" right that the proposal of compensation was made, and you now admit that in this view "it (Fort Sumter) would probably be subjected to the exercise of the right of eminent domain."

In your letter of yesterday (through your Secretary) you shift your position. You claim that your Government bears to Fort Sumter "political relations of a much higher and more imposing character." It was no part of my mission to discuss the "political relations" of the United States Government to anything within the Territorial limits of South Carolina. South Carolina claims to have dissolved all political connexion with your Government, and to have destroyed all "political relations" of your Government with everything within her borders. She is unquestionably at this moment *de facto* a separate and independent Government, exercising complete sovereignty over every foot of her soil except Fort Sumter. Now that the intention is avowed to hold this place as a military post, with a claim of exclusive jurisdiction on the part of a Government foreign to South Carolina, it will be for the authorities to determine what is the course proper to be pursued. It is vain to ignore the fact that South Carolina is to yours a foreign Government, and how with this patent fact before you, you can consider the continued occupation of a fort in her harbor a pacific measure, and parcel of a peaceful policy, passes certainly my comprehension.

You say that the fort was garrisoned for our protection, and is held for the same purposes for which it has been ever held since its construction. Are you not aware, that to hold, in the territory of a foreign power, a fortress against her will, avowedly for the purpose of protecting her citizens is, perhaps, the highest insult which one government can offer to another? But Fort Sumter was never garrisoned at all until South Carolina had dissolved her connection with your Government. This garrison entered it in the night, with every circumstance of secrecy, after spiking the guns, and burning the gun carriages, and cutting down the flag staff of an adjacent fort, which was then abandoned.

South Carolina had not taken Fort Sumter into her own possession only, because of her misplaced confidence in a Government which deceived her. A fortress occupied under the circumstances above stated, is considered by you, not only as no cause of irritation, but you represent it as held for our protection!

Your Excellency's Secretary has indulged in irony on a very grave subject.

As to the responsibility for consequences, if, indeed, it does rest on us, I can assure your Excellency we are happily unconscious of the fact.

I return to Charleston to-morrow.

With considerations of high regard,

I am, very respectfully,

(Signed) I. W. HAYNE, Special Envoy.

Pamphlets.—We have received several pamphlets worthy of more attention than we are now able to give, and we accordingly must content ourselves for the present with inviting the examination of intelligent readers:

"The State of the Country," re-printed from the *Southern Presbyterian Review*. By James H. Thornwell, D. D. Printed at the *Guardian* office, Columbia, S. C.

This is worthy of wide circulation, and careful perusal, and we earnestly commend it to all citizens and associations engaged in the good work of political colportage for Southern rights and interests.

"A Review of the Crittenden and other Resolutions, addressed to the South and to every adherent of the Constitution." Dodge & Christian Printers, 56 Gold-street, New York.

Very good for grocers and retailers, and makers of paper-bags, although for nice packages the blank paper would be preferred.

"The True Position, Interests and Policy of the South, Union or Secession, which is best (in four numbers) and the Crisis, in eight numbers." By J. H. Froeligh, citizen of Tennessee. W. M. Hutton & Co., Printers, Memphis, Tenn.

The leading position advanced and advocated by the writer, is "The principles involved in the secession of the Southern States, are identical with those that separated the colonies from Great Britain."

"The Crisis," designed to expose the vagaries, falsehoods and crimes of abolitionism.

Terms for all the numbers, $1. Single copies 25 cents. Twenty-five copies of any number $5. Fifty copies, $8. One hundred copies $14. Five hundred copies, $65. One thousand copies $120.—William B. Smith & Co., Publishers, New York. The trade supplied by Dick & Fitzgerald, 18 Ann-street, New York.

We commend this to the examination of all who are seeking documents for circulation.

Governor Letcher, of Virginia, does not hesitate to express the opinion that the State of Virginia will accept of no compromise guaranteeing less than the Crittenden propositions.

He says, moreover, that the Virginia Convention will recommend secession as their ultimate action, unless these demands are complied with.

Mr. Lincoln pronounces the letter purport to be addressed by him to Mr. Spencer, of Wheeling, a forgery.

CITY INTELLIGENCE.

FALSE ALARM.—There was a false alarm of fire last evening about half-past 7 o'clock, calling out our firemen unnecessarily.

COURT OF EQUITY.—The Court of Equity for this District adjourned on Saturday. An extra Court has been ordered by the Chancellor, to commence on the first Monday of May next.

MERCANTILE IMPROVEMENTS.—Messrs. D. F. FLEMING & Co., wholesale dealers, have nearly completed the improvements of their magnificent Boot and Shoe Emporium, at the corner of Hayne and Church-streets. The work was given out in October last to the late Mr. G. W. BLACK, master mason, with permission to remodel the whole building according to his well known taste and abilities.

The proprietors have been exceedingly pleased with the manner in which the trust was performed. The front of the building is on Hayne-street, and has been finished off in handsome style, presenting a very neat and elegant appearance. The building is three stories high, and runs back to Pinckney-street, covering an entire depth of 150 feet. There are two entrances to the first floor—one on Hayne-street and the other on Church-street.

The interior arrangements are of the most convenient and substantial order. Each story has been fitted up with special reference to the accommodation of visitors and customers from the city and country. The first floor has been divided into three apartments, viz: a commodious and well lighted story for the exhibition of gaiters, slippers and ladies' shoes generally. To the back of this is the office with windows opening on both Church and Pinckney-streets. On the West side of the office, is a division for the reception of an iron vault, where will be deposited the books, &c., of the firm. The main stairway to the second story starts from here. The second floor is used for the display of men's boots and shoes, and runs back the entire depth of the lot. This story is well ventilated and lighted up by spacious windows opening on Hayne and Pinckney-streets. On the right are convenient wash rooms, closets, &c., intended more particularly for the accommodation of country visitors. The third story is used at present mostly for storage.

One great advantage will be, the facility which this building possesses for the extinguishment of fires. In the basement has been fitted up a reservoir and force-pump, from which water is carried over the whole establishment. Another advantage is, the ease with which goods can be got out of the building in case of necessity, there being three openings for the exit of the stock, namely: Hayne, Church and Pinckney-streets.

The whole building exhibits the hand of a master workman, and is worthy of the enterprizing proprietors for whom it has been finished. Notwithstanding the critical state of the times, the work has been rapidly pushed forward to completion, and our country friends will no doubt be highly gratified in paying this establishment a visit when in the city.

Charleston and its Fortifications.

The New York *Herald* contains a card, which will receive a prompt and proper reply from those who can prove the falsehood of the most important allegations of the malignant author. We publish the card for information and for explanation of the forthcoming reply, which we hope will be reprinted immediately in the *Herald*, and in all other papers that insert the following:

CHARLESTON AND ITS FORTIFICATIONS.

107 EAST ELEVENTH-STREET, February 4, 1861.

To the Editor of the Herald:—Having just arrived from Charleston, S. C., where I have been for the past eighteen months engaged by the State authorities, teaching navigation on board of the Marine School-Ship, being obliged to resign my commission or take up arms against the flag of my country, I chose the former.

Seeing an article in the Herald of the 2d, from the correspondence of the Baltimore American, dated Charleston, January 29, 1861, stating that there were about fifty large pieces of ordnance, together with several bombs and howitzers, mounted on the Citadel Green and on the Battery (promenade) of Charleston, has induced me to submit to you a few facts, and through you to the public, if you feel disposed to give these few lines a space in your valuable paper. Up to the 25th of January there were but four guns mounted on Charleston Battery, and three on Citadel Green, at which latter place there were two more ready to mount, all only twenty-four pounders; there were neither bombs nor howitzers.

The nearest place at which a land force can be of any service against Fort Sumter is Cummings' Point, being only six-tenths of a mile distant. On this point a shell battery has been erected, together with a few pieces of cannon, the same as above. Fort Moultrie is the second place that can be of any service in reducing Fort Sumter. This fort has ten eight-inch Columbiads mounted directly in range with Sumter, and is the only fort which has any Columbiads mounted.

Fort Johnson is one and a half miles distant from Sumter, and is mounted with a few cannon of 24-pound calibre. The batteries on Lighthouse Island are three and three-eighths miles distant, and mostly of small artillery, and consequently cannot reach Sumter.

Castle Pinckney is two and a half miles distant, and can bring but three 42-pounders and eleven 32 pounders against Sumter—these, with little or no effect. The Green and Charleston batteries are 3¾ miles from Sumter, and are only to be used in case vessels should get into the harbor. Fort Sumter has four 42-pounders, five 10-inch Columbiads, and seven 32-pounders to bear on Fort Moultrie, the former in bomb-proof casemates; also an equal number against Fort Johnson and Cummings' Point.

Major Anderson has now nearly all his guns mounted, having thirty guns mounted on the ramparts to sweep the horizon, most of them 32-pounders, and can be so elevated as to strike an object at the distance of a quarter of a mile from the walls. Every part of the fort has been strengthened so as to make it bomb-proof.

Since my arrival in New York I have heard a great many say Fort Sumter cannot be reinforced without opposition from the troops or authorities of Charleston, and a serious loss of life. This I believe to be altogether wrong. Fort Sumter can be reinforced, and that, too, without the loss of a man. This, however, can only be accomplished in one way. Should opportunity offer I would willingly offer my services, and am confident of success. I am also of the opinion that the Charlestonians cannot take Fort Sumter. Major Anderson can, even with the small force at his command, repulse them from whatever quarter the attack may come, as long as his provisions and ammunition hold out.

CAPT. J. C.

Racing Summary.—For the convenience of all interested, we give a summary of the racing events, on the Washington Course, for the annual meeting which closed on Saturday, the 9th instant, as elsewhere reported:

FOUR MILE HEATS.

Albine	1	1
Planet	2	2

Time—7:36¼—7:42½.

THREE MILE HEATS.

Exchequer	1	1
Leisure	3	2
Oysterman	2	3
Julia Cooper	4	4
Bill Deering	5	dis.

Time—5:47¼—5:40¾.

HANDICAP.

Planet, 109 lbs	1	1
Leisure, 98 lbs	2	2

Time—5:45—5:47.

THREE MILE DASH.

Exchequer	1
Julia Cooper	2

Time—5:50.

TWO MILE HEATS.

Fanny Washington	1	1
Oysterman	4	2
Corinne	2	3
John Linton	3	4

Time—3:40¾—3:48.

HUTCHINSON STAKES.

Eugene	2	1	1
Rosa Bonheur	1	2	2
Joe Lane	4	3	3
Red Regis	3	4	4
c. f. by *Albion*	5	dis.	

Time—3:47¾—3:47¼—3:49.

MILE HEATS—HUTCHINSON STAKES.

Rosa Bonheur	1	1
Joe Lane	4	2
Red Regis	2	3
Tom Puryear	3	4

Time—1:50¾—1:50¼.

SOUTH CAROLINA STAKES.

ch. c. by *Lexington*	2	1	1
Little Ella	1	2	2

Time—1:53—1:53¼—1:57.

The memorable event of the meeting is, of course, the four mile triumph of *Albine*, making the best first heat time, and equaling the best second heat time ever made over this Course, and renewing the honor of her sire *Jeff Davis*.

The Montgomery (Ala.) *Mail* proposes, without interference with any chartered rights, the establishment of a Southern Telegraph Line, "controlled entirely by men Southern in sentiment," and recommends for the superintendency Mr. HUBERT, now chief operator of the American Telegraph Line in New Orleans.

We make no objection, of course, to any telegraphic extensions or improvements legitimately demanded, but we may protest against the implication conveyed against the American Telegraph Company. It is now largely controlled, if we are correctly informed, by "men Southern in sentiment," and such is the character of all the officers connected with it, with whom we have had intercourse.

The New-York Times.

VOL. X.....NO. 2949. NEW-YORK, TUESDAY, MARCH 5, 1861. PRICE TWO CENTS.

THE NEW ADMINISTRATION.

Abraham Lincoln President of the United States.

THE INAUGURATION CEREMONIES.

A Tremendous Crowd and No Accidents.

THE INAUGURAL ADDRESS.

How it was Delivered and How it was Received.

AN IMPRESSIVE SCENE AT THE CAPITOL.

Mr. Lincoln's First Audience at the White House.

Visit of the New-York Delegation to Senator Seward.

MR. SEWARD MAKES A SPEECH.

What was Done at the Grand Inauguration Ball.

MISCELLANEOUS INCIDENTS OF THE OCCASION.

OUR WASHINGTON DISPATCHES.

WASHINGTON, Monday, March 4.

THE DAWNING OF THE DAY.

The day to which all have looked with so much anxiety and interest has come and passed. ABRAHAM LINCOLN has been inaugurated, and "all's well."

At daylight the clouds were dark and heavy with rain, threatening to dampen the enthusiasm of the occasion with unwelcome showers. A few drops fell occasionally before 8 o'clock, but not enough to lay the dust, which, under the impulse of a strong northwest wind, swept down upon the avenue from the cross streets quite unpleasantly. The weather was cool and bracing, and, on the whole, favorable to the ceremonies of the day.

MR. LINCOLN.

Mr. LINCOLN rose at 5 o'clock. After an early breakfast, the Inaugural was read aloud to him by his son ROBERT, and the completing touches were added, including the beautiful and impassioned closing paragraph. Mr. LINCOLN then retired from his family circle to his closet, where he prepared himself for the solemn and weighty responsibilities which he was about to assume.

Here he remained until it was time for an audience to Mr. SEWARD. Together these statesmen conversed concerning that paragraph of the Inaugural relating to the policy of forcing obnoxious non-resident officers upon disaffected citizens

When Mr. SEWARD departed, Mr. LINCOLN closed his door upon all visitors, until Mr. BUCHANAN called for him to escort him to the Capitol.

THE THRONG IN THE STREETS.

From early daylight the streets were thronged with people, some still carrying carpet-bags in hand, having found no quarters in which to stop.

THE NOTE OF PREPARATION.

The busy note of preparation for the parade was soon heard on every side. The New-York delegation, over two hundred strong, formed in procession on Pennsylvania-avenue at 9 o'clock, and proceeded in a body to Mr. SEWARD's residence to pay their respects. J. H. HOBART WARD met them at the door, and JAMES KELLEY introduced the party to Mr. SEWARD in a pertinent speech. Mr. SEWARD, from the doorstep, responded as follows:

SPEECH OF MR. SEWARD.

FRIENDS, FELLOW-CITIZENS AND NEIGHBORS: I am very deeply affected by this unexpected demonstration of affection on the part of the people of the State of New-York. So many familiar faces, seen at this distance from my home, and under the circumstances which surround me, awaken memories and sympathies that I should find it difficult to describe. It is just twelve years since I came, a stranger and alone, to this Capitol, to represent the great State from which you have come in the councils of the Union. This day closes that service of twelve years—a period which now in retrospect seems so short, and yet it has filled up the one-sixth part of the Constitutional duration of this great empire. At this hour I appear before you a voluntary citizen, but, God be thanked! a citizen now as always, of the State of New-York—one of yourselves—your equal—no longer bearing the responsibilities of a representative. [Here one of the Deputy-Marshals stepped forward, and pinned a badge of the New-York delegation to Mr. SEWARD's coat, amid great cheering.] My public acts throughout that long, and to me trying period, are all upon record in the journals and debates of Congress. It is almost fearful to think that they are imperishable. Looking backward upon them, I will say and maintain here, and now, that I claim for them all the merit of good motives and honest intentions. Here in this presence, before you, a fair delegation of the constituency I have served, and in the presence of the God who is to be our Common Judge, I declare that there is not one word of that record which I desire should be obliterated. Although a representative of one State only, I have been all the while conscious that I was also a legislator for all the States—for the whole Republic—and I am not ashamed to appeal to every citizen of New-York and ask him to say what I have neglected. I am not afraid to appeal to every section—to the East, to the West, to the North, and to the South, equally—and to every State in every section, and to every man, to every woman, to every human being, freeman or bondsman, to say whether, in any word or deed of mine, I have done him wrong. And in labors which enhanced abilities I could not claim, and trials which exacted some equanimity of temper, I have here in this capital neither received nor given personal offence. I have not one enemy in this section to forgive. I know of no one who will utter a personal complaint against me. I have done little good, indeed,—far less than I have wished,—but I have been sustained and supported by the people of New-York with a generosity that is unparalleled. I know why this is so. The people of New-York are habitually constant, and faithful to conscience, to truth to liberty, to their country, and to their God. They have thought that I endeavored to be likewise faithful. I know their character well, and I know that in the new emergency which our country is now entering upon, they will be equally faithful. I rely on their intelligence, and their patriotism, as I do on the intelligence and patriotism of the whole people of the United States. They will preserve the inestimable legacy of civil and religious liberty which they have received from their heroic fathers. The administration which you have come here to inaugurate comes into power under circumstances of embarrassment and peril, never before known in the history of the Republic; but I believe I know the character and purposes of the Chief Magistrate: I believe that, while he will be firm, he will be also just to every State, and every section, and every citizen: that he will defend and protect the rights and interests, the peace and the prosperity, of all the States equally and alike, while he will practice the moderation that springs from virtue, and the affection that arises from patriotism in Confederated States. Under his guidance, and with the blessing of God, I believe and trust, and confidently expect, that an Administration that is inaugurated amid some distrust and painful apprehension, will close upon a reunited, restored, prosperous, free and happy Republic. The State of New-York, the greatest and most powerful of the States, will lead all other States in the way of conciliation; and as the path of wisdom is always the path of peace, so I am sure that now we shall find that the way of conciliation is the way of wisdom."

Mr. SEWARD was greatly affected during the delivery of his speech, which was frequently applauded, and followed by three hearty cheers. A gentleman standing near, who was evidently captured by the Senator, exclaimed: "I am a Virginian, and a Southern man all over, but I'll trust that man anywhere. I've watched his course for a long time, and I know he's honest." Mr. SEWARD shook hands with the delegation and then retired.

THE INAUGURAL PROCESSION.

It was nearly noon when Mr. BUCHANAN started from the White House with the Inaugural procession, which halted before Willard's Hotel to receive the President elect. The order of march you will get from other sources, and I will only observe that the carriage containing Mr. BUCHANAN and Mr. LINCOLN, was a simple open brett, surrounded by the President's mounted guard, in close order, as a guard of honor.

The procession, as usual, was behind-hand a little, but its order was excellent. Nothing noteworthy occurred on the route. As it ascended the Capitol hill, towards the north gate, the company of United States Cavalry and the President's mounted guard took their positions each side of the carriage-way, and thus guarded the inclosed passage-way by which the President's party entered the north wing of the Capitol to go to the Senate Chamber.

The procession halted until the President and suite entered, and then filed through the troops aforesaid into the grounds.

On the east front, the military took their positions in the grounds in front of the platform, but the United States troops maintained their places outside until the line took up the President and party again after the ceremonies were over, to escort them back to the White House.

ARRANGEMENTS AT THE CAPITOL.

The arrangements at the Capitol were admirably designed, and executed so that everybody who was entitled to admission got in, and everybody who could not go in could see from without. The Senate Chamber was the great point of attraction, but only the favored few were admitted upon the floor, while the galleries were reserved for and occupied by a select number of ladies. The scene which transpired there was most memorable, producing a great and solemn impression upon all present. Mr. BRIGHT spent all the morning in talking against time on some Gas Company's bill, greatly to the amusement of Senators, and the ill-concealed annoyance of spectators, who expected to hear some good speaking.

A few moments before 12 o'clock, Mr. BRECKINRIDGE came in with Mr. HAMLIN upon his arm, and, together, they sat by the side of the President's desk until noon, when, assuming the Chair, Mr. BRECKINRIDGE said:

MR. BRECKINRIDGE'S ADIEU.

SENATORS: In taking final leave of this position, I shall ask a few moments in which to tender to you my grateful acknowledgments for the resolution declaring your approval of the manner in which I have discharged my duties, and to express my deep sense of the uniform courtesy which, as the presiding officer, I have received from the members of this body. If I have committed errors your generous forbearance refused to rebuke them, and during the whole period of my service I have never appealed in vain to your justice or charity. The memory of these acts will ever be cherished among the most grateful recollections of my life, and for my successor I can express no better wish than that he may enjoy the relations of mutual confidence which so happily have marked our intercourse. Now, gentlemen of the Senate and officers of the Senate, from whom I have received so many kind offices, accept my gratitude and cordial wishes for your prosperity and welfare.

The oath was then administered to Vice-President HAMLIN, who announced his readiness to take it in a full, firm tone. Mr BRECKINRIDGE took him by the hand, and led him to the chair, after which, crossing over to Mr. SEWARD, he shook hands and extended greetings with him, and took his seat as the newly elected Senator. The Vice-President rapped to order, and addressed the Senate as follows:

SPEECH OF VICE-PRESIDENT HAMLIN.

SENATORS: The experience of several years in this body has taught me something of the duties of the presiding officer, and with a stern, inflexible purpose to discharge these duties faithfully, relying upon the courtesy and coöperation of Senators, and invoking the aid of Divine Providence I am now ready to take the oath required by the Constitution, and to enter upon the discharge of the official duties assigned me by the confidence of a generous people.

The Senate now waited in silence for the President elect. Gradually those entitled to the floor entered. The Diplomatic Corps, in full court dress, came quite early. The Supreme Court followed, headed by the venerable Chief Justice TANEY, who looked as if he had come down from several generations, and finally the House of Representatives filed in. For at least an hour Mr. HAMLIN was acting President of the United States, but at length, a little after 1 o'clock, the doors opened, and the expected dignitaries were announced.

THE OUTGOING AND THE INCOMING.

Mr. BUCHANAN and Mr. LINCOLN entered, arm in arm, the former pale, sad, nervous; the latter's face slightly flushed, with compressed lips. For a few minutes, while the oath was administered to Senator PEARCE, they sat in front of the President's desk. Mr. BUCHANAN sighed audibly, and frequently, but whether from reflection upon the failure of his Administration, I can't say. Mr. LINCOLN was grave and impassive as an Indian martyr.

APPEARANCE AT THE EAST PORTICO.

When all was ready, the party formed, and proceeded to the platform erected in front of the eastern portico. The appearance of the President elect was greeted, as he entered from the door of the rotunda, with immense cheering by the many thousand citizens assembled in the grounds, filling the square and open space, and perching on every tree, fence or stone affording a convenient point from which to see or hear. In a few minutes the portico was also densely crowded with both sexes.

On the front of the steps was erected a small wooden canopy, under which were seated Mr. BUCHANAN, Chief-Justice TANEY, Senators CHASE and BAKER, and the President elect, while at the left of the small table on which was placed the Inaugural, stood Col. SELDEN, Marshal of the District, an exponent of the security which existed there for the man and the ceremonies of the hour. At the left of the canopy, sat the entire Diplomatic Corps, dressed in gorgeous attire, evidently deeply impressed with the solemnity of the occasion, and the importance of the simple ceremony about to be performed. Beyond them was the Marine band, which played several patriotic airs before and after the reading of the address. To the right of the diplomats sat in solemn dignity, in silk gowns and hats, the members of the Supreme Court. Then came Senators, members of the House, distinguished guests and fair ladies by the score, while the immediate right of the canopy was occupied by the son and Private Secretaries of Mr. LINCOLN. Perched up on one side, hanging on by the railing, surrounding the statue of COLUMBUS and an Indian girl, was Senator WIGFALL, witnessing the pageant.

MR. LINCOLN INTRODUCED.

Everything being in readiness, Senator BAKER came forward and said:

"FELLOW-CITIZENS: I introduce to you ABRAHAM LINCOLN, the President elect of the United States of America."

Whereupon, Mr. LINCOLN arose, walked deliberately and composedly to the table, and bent low in honor of the repeated and enthusiastic cheering of the countless host before him. Having put on his spectacles, he arranged his manuscript on the small table, keeping the paper thereon by the aid of his cane, and commenced in a clear, ringing voice, that was easily heard by those on the outer limits of the crowd, to read his first address to the people, as President of the United States.

RECEPTION OF THE INAUGURAL.

The opening sentence, "Fellow-citizens of the United States," was the signal for prolonged applause, the good Union sentiment thereof striking a tender chord in the popular breast. Again, when, after defining certain actions to be his duty, he said, "And I shall peform it," there was a spontaneous, and uproarious manifestation of approval, which continued for some moments. Every sentence which indicated firmness in the Presidential chair, and every statement of a conciliatory nature, was cheered to the echo; while his appeal to his "dissatisfied fellow-countrymen," desiring them to reflect calmly, and not hurry into false steps, was welcomed by one and all, most heartily and cordially. The closing sentence "upset the watering pot" of many of his hearers, and at this point alone did the melodious voice of the President elect falter.

Judge TANEY did not remove his eyes from Mr. LINCOLN during the entire delivery, while Mr. BUCHANAN, who was probably sleepy and tired, sat looking as straight as he could at the toe of his right boot. Mr. DOUGLAS, who stood by the right of the railing, was apparently satisfied, as he exclaimed, *sotto voce*, "Good," "That's so," "No coercion," and "Good again."

THE OATH OF OFFICE.

After the delivery of the address Judge TANEY stood up, and all removed their hats, while he administered the oath to Mr. LINCOLN. Speaking in a low tone the form of the oath, he signified to Mr. LINCOLN, that he should repeat the words, and in a firm but modest voice, the President took the oath as prescribed by the law, while the people, who waited until they saw the final bow, tossed their hats, wiped their eyes, cheered at the top of their voices, hurrahed themselves hoarse, and had the crowd not been so very dense, they would have demonstrated in more lively ways, their joy, satisfaction and delight.

SHAKING HANDS.

Judge TANEY was the first person who shook hands with Mr. LINCOLN, and was followed by Mr. BUCHANAN, CHASE, DOUGLAS, and a host of minor great men. A Southern gentleman, whose name I did not catch, seized him by the hand, and said, "God bless you, my dear Sir; you will save us." To which Mr. LINCOLN replied, "I am very glad that what I have said causes pleasure to Southerners, because I then know they are pleased with what is right."

On the steps were Gov. KING, and many influential New Yorkers; Govs. HOPPIN and SPRAGUE, of Rhode Island; BUCKINGHAM, of Connecticut, and the entire Cabinet of the outgoing Administration.

WHAT MR. BUCHANAN SAID.

In reply to questions, Mr. BUCHANAN said, with a wretched and suspicious leer, "I cannot say what he means until I read his Inaugural; I cannot understand the secret meaning of the document, which has been simply read in my hearing."

WHAT MR. DOUGLAS SAID.

Mr. DOUGLAS said, "He does not mean coercion; he says nothing about retaking the forts, or Federal property—he's all right."

Subsequently, to another querist, DOUGLAS said: "Well, I hardly know what he means. Every point in the address is susceptible of a double construction; but I think he does not mean coercion."

GOING TO THE WHITE HOUSE.

After delaying a little upon the platform, Mr. LINCOLN, and Mr. BUCHANAN, arm in arm, and followed by a few privileged persons, proceeded at a measured pace to the Senate Chamber, and thence to the President's Room, while the Band played "Hail Columbia" "Yankee Doodle" and the "Star Spangled Banner." In a short time the procession was reformed, and in state, the President and Ex-President were conducted to the White House.

THE AUDIENCE.

After a few moments' rest, Mr. LINCOLN granted an audience to the Diplomatic Corps, who, with great pomp and ceremony, were the first to pay their respects to, and congratulate the President at his new home. Then the doors were opened, and the people, like a flooding tide, rushed in upon him. The Marshals, forming a double line of guards, kept all rudeness at a distance, and everything went off with great success, and to the eminent satisfaction of all concerned.

The thirty-four little girls who personated the several States of the Union, and rode in a gaily decorated car in the procession, halted at the door while they sang "Hail Columbia;" after which they were received by the President, who gave to each and all of them a hearty and good-natured salute.

After Mr. LINCOLN had been well shaken, the doors were closed, and the Marshals of the day were personally introduced to him. He thanked them for the admirable arrangements of the day, and congratulated them upon the successful termination of their duties.

They then retired, and the President repaired to his private apartment, somewhat overcome by the fatigue and excitement of the day, but thankful that all things had been so very pleasant, and that literally nothing had occurred to mar the perfect harmony of the occasion.

WHAT IS SAID OF THE INAUGURAL.

While conservative people are in raptures over the Inaugural, it cannot be denied that many Southerners look upon it as a precursor of war. They probably will take a calmer view to-morrow. Mr. WEED is delighted with it, and even Mr. WIGFALL publicly declares it a most able paper, certainly. Its conciliatory tone, and frank, outspoken declaration of loyalty to the whole country, captured the hearts of many heretofore opposed to Mr. LINCOLN, and its firm enunciation of purpose to fulfil his oath to maintain the Constitution and laws, challenge universal respect.

THE POLICE AND MILITARY.

The arrangements for the preservation of the peace were admirable. A large special police, with conspicuous badges, were distributed all along the line of procession, and about the Capitol, but their mere presence was generally sufficient to insure order. In a few cases, where individual fights occured, they interposed so promptly as to prevent a collision becoming general. So, too, they immediately dispersed every gathering of people who manifested the least improper excitement, or attempted to vociferate sentiments intended to be offensive or incendiary.

The several companies of United States Artillery, all under arms, were on the street near their quarters, with horses hitched up, and riders standing by their side, ready to vault into the saddle at an instant's notice. Files of mounted troops were stationed at different points of the City to convey to Head-quarters prompt intelligence of any disturbance.

The turn-out of the District militia was quite imposing. The Washington Light Infantry looked remarkably well. They are a fine-looking set of young men. The National Rifles, the corps whose secession sympathies are well understood here, failed to participate in the parade, but I understand they were on duty at the Armory, ready to turn out if needed to aid in the preserving of the peace.

THE CAPITOL FLAG.

Early in the forenoon, when the flag was unfurled upon the Capitol, one of the halliards gave way, and, splitting in two, the flag flung out like a pennant. For a long while it could not be taken down, though finally an adventurous man climbed to the top of the staff, and, tearing away the ill-omened standard, replaced it with an entire flag of the Union.

WIDE-AWAKES ABOUT.

After the Inaugural procession dispersed, large numbers of strangers in town pulled out of their pockets, and mounted the peculiar cap-cover designating Wide-Awakes, thus demonstrating the fact that they are here in large force.

There is a good deal of excitement in town to-night, but nothing angry or threatening.

RUMORED CHANGE IN THE CABINET.

The substitution of JOHN SHERMAN for CHASE in the Cabinet is still agitated, and it is stated, apparently on good authority, that the Ohio delegation have presented SHERMAN to the President as satisfactory to them. SHERMAN, however, emphatically denies any knowledge of the probability of his selection. From another very high source, I know the opinion was expressed very positively to-night that the substitution of SHERMAN for CHASE will be made, in which event it is intimated, that CHASE may be sent to the London Court. The fact that the Cabinet nominations were not sent to the Senate to day confirms the rumors that changes in the programme are under discussion.

Another rumor has it that WELLES will take the Navy Department, and BLAIR the Post office.

THE PEACE CONFERENCE PROPOSITIONS.

The Southern men express much regret at the failure to act upon the Peace Conference propositions, but think the passage of joint resolutions by Congress, and the positions taken by Mr. LINCOLN, will prevent all further trouble. Messrs. Crittenden, Johnson, Douglas, Clingman, Powell and Breckinridge, all concur in this opinion, and also several Southern members of the House. The wisest among them say to-night that the action of the past few days, with the Inauguration to-day, means peace and a settlement of all the National difficulties. WIGFALL, however, says war is inevitable, and has telegraphed home to that effect. He has been very boisterous all the afternoon and evening.

WHAT VIRGINIA WILL DO.

Senator MASON says he is very agreeably disappointed, but thinks Virginia will not be satisfied, and will secede at once. He thought so four weeks ago. The disunion Congressmen from Virginia have sent home to advise secession immediately.

THE CONSTITUTIONAL AMENDMENT.

The passage of the joint resolutions, amending the Constitution, in the Senate, gives very great satisfaction to the outspoken Union men of the South. Mr. CRITTENDEN and ANDY JOHNSON say that in it they see great hope for the future of the country. The Republicans who voted against it all took the ground, as expressed by Mr WILSON, that they intended nothing wrong, and preferred to show it by their actions rather than by declarations, and were opposed to useless amendments of the Constitution.

There were no serious accidents to-day, of any kind There was some surprise expressed that no salute was fired, but I learn that it was deemed inexpedient, as creating unnecessary confusion, noise and interruption.

MR. LINCOLN AND MR. BUCHANAN.

Mr. LINCOLN has invited Mr. BUCHANAN to remain at the White House some days. He probably declined, as he is stopping at the house of ROBERT OULDS, the District-Attorney. The unexpected and free intercourse between Mr. LINCOLN and Mr. BUCHANAN adds to the general tone of good feeling which prevails to-day.

Hon GEORGE ASHMUN was sent for to consult with the President, but is at Quebec upon legal business for BARING BROS., of London, in the great case of settlement with the Grand Trunk Railroad. He replied by telegraph that he could not be present for some time.

NEW-YORKERS VISIT THE PRESIDENT.

The New-Yorkers, numbering at least five hundred, proceeded this afternoon to the White House to call upon the President. Tharlow Weed, Gen. Scroggs, Amor J. Williamson, Justice John Quackenbush, Guy R. Pelton, D. D. Conover, and other prominent gentlemen, were in the procession. Mr. LINCOLN was at dinner, but on being informed of their visit, came out. STEWART L. WADFORD introduced the party, and the President replied as follows:

FELLOW-CITIZENS: I thank you for this visit. I thank you that you call upon me, not in any sectional spirit, but that you come, without distinction of party, to pay your respects to the President of the United States. I am informed that you are mostly citizens of New-York. [Cries of "All, "all."] You all appear to be very happy. May I hope that the public expression which I have this day given to my sentiments, may have contributed in some degree to your happiness. [Emphatic exclamations of assent.] As far as I am concerned, the loyal citizens of every State, and of every section, shall have no cause to feel any other sentiment [Cries of "Good," "Good."] As towards the disaffected portion of our fellow-citizens, I will say, as every good man throughout the country must feel, that there will be more rejoicing over one sheep that is lost, and is found, than over the ninety-and-nine which have gone not astray. [Great cheering.] And now, my friends, as I have risen from the dinner-table to see you, you will excuse me for the brevity of my remarks, and permit me again to thank you heartily, and cordially, for this pleasant visit, as I rejoin those who await my return.

At the conclusion, he was greeted with a hearty round of cheering, after which several gentlemen shook hands with him, but he found it necessary to break away from the company.

THEY THEN VISIT MR. CAMERON, ANDY JOHNSON AND GEN. SCOTT.

The delegation then reformed, and marched to the residence of Hon. SIMON CAMERON, who appeared in answer to their calls, and addressed them briefly. Upon motion of Judge QUACKENBUSH, the company then proceeded to pay their respects to Hon. ANDY JOHNSON, of Tennessee, at the St. Charles Hotel. He came out and made an eloquent, earnest Union speech, indorsing the President's Inaugural without qualification. They also called on Gen. SCOTT.

PAUCITY OF INCIDENTS.

The day was barren of incidents, other than those noted above. During the Inaugural ceremonies, strangers were still moving about on the outskirts of the crowd, carpet-bags in hand, and a long train left soon after, diminishing somewhat the crowd, which rendered so many unable to find a place to lay their heads.

THE INAUGURATION BALL.

The ball is a decided success. The room is very tastefully decorated with shields and flags, and is brilliantly lighted with gas. Dancing commenced precisely at 10 o'clock, at which hour the President had not arrived. ROBERT LINCOLN came in with Miss CAMPBELL, of Galena, Ill, accompanied by Col. LAMON, Col. ELLSWORTH, LOT TODD, and Private Secretary HAYS. The room is pleasantly filled, and toilettes of ladies are noticeable, with but few exceptions, for elegance and good taste. Capt. COMSTOCK, Capt. WOODHULL, of the United States Navy; J. WATSON WEBB, ABRAHAM WAKEMAN, JAMES HUMPHREY, wife and daughter; Gen. SCROGGS and wife: and Mrs. Chancellor WALWORTH, are among the prominent New-Yorkers present. Mrs DRAKE MILLS is gorgeously attired in two thousand dollars' worth of laces and twenty thousand dollars' worth of diamonds

The army is well represented. Lord LYONS and other diplomats, in plain dress, are present. Senator HARRIS and lady, MARSHALL O. ROBERTS, EDWARD FISKE and CHARLES SEDGWICK, of New-York, are also here. Mrs. CASSON, of Iowa, presented Mr. SEWARD with an elegant, but chaste bouquet, which was the envy of the Senator's *confreres*.

Mr. SEWARD entered the room with his daughter-in-law. A queerly-dressed man, with a long shepherd's crook, is on the floor endeavoring to find Mr SEWARD. At 10½ o'clock the Presidential party came in. Senator ANTHONY and Vice-President HAMLIN supported the President. Senator DOUGLAS escorted Mrs. LINCOLN; Senator BAKER Mrs. HAMLIN; Gov. YATES Mrs. BAKER, and Dr. BALOCHE Miss EDWARDS. The Band struck up "Hail Columbia," and the party marched from one end of the hall to the other, amid inspiring strains of the national air, causing an era of tremendous good feeling. After a brief promenade, the President, with Mrs. HAMLIN, took stations at the upper end of the room, and a large number of persons availed themselves of the opportunity of being presented to Mr. LINCOLN, who shook hands with everybody. At 11½ o'clock, the President and suite went into the supper-room, in the same order as they entered the hall. At 12¼ o'clock the quadrille of the evening was danced—DOUGLAS and Mrs. LINCOLN, HAMLIN and Miss EDWARDS, Mayor BERRET and Mrs. BERGMAN, Mr. HARRARD and Mrs. BAKER composing the set Miss EDWARDS, niece of Mrs. LINCOLN, is acknowledged to be the belle of the evening. The ladies of the Presidential party are dressed exquisitely, and in perfect taste.

Half-past Twelve—The ball is progressing. Everybody is in fine spirits. The President has gone home, but the ladies and younger portion of the family remain, and are dancing merrily. The ball is in every way a great success.

THE HUSSEY REAPER.

The application for an extension of HUSSEY's reaper patent was argued on Thursday. The patent was extended by Acting-Commissioner SHUGERT. The country needs no better evidence of how great a monopoly it was saved from by the action of Congress, in taking the McCormick reaper case out of his hands. The new Secretary of the Interior, if he does his duty, will decapitate the Chief Clerk of the Patent-office forthwith.

THE SARDINIAN MISSION.

The most prominent applicant for the Sardinian Mission is CARL SHURZ, the eloquent German speaker of Wisconsin. As a political exile, Sardinia is the only place abroad to which he could go with acceptability. It is to be hoped, however, that the Administration will not select any but Americans to represent the country abroad.

TWIGGS' TREASON LONG MEDITATED.

A private letter from San Antonio, Texas, states that TWIGGS planned his treachery months ago, and placed arms in the hands of the Knights of the Golden Circle, that they might drill, organize and be ready for the recent treasonable proceeding.

RESIGNATIONS IN THE NAVY.

Through the kindness of the late Secretary of the Navy I have been furnished with the following list of resignations of officers of the Navy accepted by President BUCHANAN, and for some of which acceptances a Committee of the House reported a resolution of censure upon Mr. TOUCEY.

CAPTAINS.	
D. N. Ingraham	South Carolina.
Lawrence Rosseau	Louisiana.
Josiah Tatnall	Georgia.
Victor M. Randolph	Virginia.
COMMANDERS.	
Ebenezer Ferrand	New-York.
Thomas W. Brent	Florida.
Raphael Semmes	Maryland.
Henry J. Hartstene	South Carolina.
LIEUTENANTS.	
J. J. Walbach	South Carolina.
Jas. H. North	South Carolina.
F. B. Renshaw	Pennsylvania.
Thos. B. Huger	South Carolina.
John Rutledge	South Carolina.
C. M. Morris	South Carolina.
John Kell	Georgia.
Joseph Fry	Florida.
John R. Eggleston	Mississippi.
R. T. Chapman	Alabama.
Thos. P. Pelot	South Carolina.
John M. Stribling	South Carolina.
Philip Porcher	South Carolina.
Eneas Armstrong	Georgia.
John R. Hamilton	South Carolina.
Geo. E. Law	Indiana.
Wm. G. Dozier	South Carolina.
A. F. Warley	South Carolina.
Robert Selden	Virginia.
SURGEON.	
W. A. Spottswood	Virginia.
PASSED ASSISTANT SURGEONS.	
Arthur M. Lynah	South Carolina.
Thomas J. Charlton	Georgia.
ASSISTANT SURGEONS.	
Charles E. Lining	South Carolina.
PAYMASTERS.	
W. W. J. Kelly	Florida.
Henry Myers	Georgia.
CHAPLAIN.	
Charles W. Thomas	Georgia.
MASTERS.	
W. E. Evans	South Carolina.
Thomas B. Mills	Louisiana.
John Pearson	Florida.
MIDSHIPMEN.	
Charles W. Read	Mississippi.
S. B. Paddock	Ohio.
John Grinball	South Carolina.

MARINE CORPS.

First-Lieutenant—Ed. Jones.
Second-Lieutenant—W. W. Kirkland.
Second-Lieutenant—C. L. Saver.
Second-Lieutenant—Geo. K. Howard.

Five Acting Midshipmen and eight Third Assistant Engineers.

THE PAWNEE A FAILURE.

The *Pawnee* arrived at the Washington Navy-yard on Saturday. Her model is pronounced a failure. She was built by Mr. GRIFFITHS, Naval Constructor, in pursuance of a contract independent of the Chief of Bureau of Construction. She is 1,300 tons burden, the largest of the seven new sloops. She took Mr. MCLANE to the Gulf, and has seen no other service. There was a defect in her main crank shaft, and a new one has been substituted lately at great cost. This is her first time out.

THE INAUGURATION CEREMONIES.

DISPATCH TO THE ASSOCIATED PRESS.

WASHINGTON, Monday, March 4.

The day was ushered in by a most exciting session of the Senate, that body sitting for twelve hours, from 7 o'clock yesterday evening to 7 o'clock this morning.

As the dial of the clock pointed to 12 o'clock last night, and the Sabbath gave way to Monday, the 4th of March, the Senate Chamber presented a curious and animated appearance. The galleries were crowded to repletion, the ladies' gallery resembling, from the gay dresses of the fair ones there congregated, some gorgeous parterre of flowers, and the gentlemen's gallery seemed one dense black mass of surging, heaving masculines, pushing, struggling and almost clambering over each other's backs in order to get a good look at the proceedings.

Some most ludicrous scenes were the result of the intense desire of the outsiders to get a peep into the Senate chamber, and the pertinacity with which the applicant for admission to the overflowing galleries would urge that he had come all the way from "Indianny" or "Varmount," or some other place, afforded the seated ones intense amusement.

On the floor, Messrs. Crittenden, Trumbull, Wigfall, Wade, Douglas and others kept up a rolling fire of debate, while those not engaged in the discussion betook themselves to the sofas for a comfortable nap during the session which it was known would last all night.

As the morning advanced, the galleries and floor became gradually cleared out, when, in the grey morning light, the Senate took a recess till 10 o'clock to day. A few minutes after 7 o'clock but few remained.

The morning broke clear and beautiful, and though at one time a few drops of rain fell, the day proved just calm and cloudy enough to prevent the unusual heat of the past few days, and the whirlwind of dust that would otherwise rendered it excessively unpleasant.

The public buildings, schools, places of business, etc., were closed throughout the day.

The Stars and Stripes floated from the City Hall, Capitol, War Department, and other public buildings; while not a few of the citizens flung out flags from their houses or across the principal avenues.

From early dawn the drum and fife could be heard in every quarter of the city, and the streets were thronged with the volunteer soldiery, hastening to their respective rendezvous.

Three or four hours elapsed before there was the least chance of entering the Capitol Pennsylvania-avenue was thronged with people wending their way to the famous east front. For four hours the crowd poured on towards the Capitol in one continuous stream of old and young, male and female—staid old Quakers from Pennsylvania, going to see friend ABRAHAM—tall lengthy Suckers, Hoosiers and Wolverines, desirous of a peep at Mr. LINCOLN—Buckeyes and Yankee men from California and Oregon, from the Northeast, Northwest, and a few from the Border States. The large majority, however, were Northern men, and but few Southerners, judging from the lack of long-haired men in the crowd, attended the Inauguration. The order of arrangements, as settled by the Committee, were as follows:

To the left of the Vice-President were the Committee of Arrangements. Immediately behind them the heads of the various Departments of the Government, Senators, Members and Members

[Continued on Eighth Page.]

The Philadelphia Inquirer.

ESTABLISHED 1829. | PHILADELPHIA, WEDNESDAY, APRIL 10, 1861. | PRICE TWO CENTS.

THE CRISIS CULMINATING.

Highly Interesting News.

A CONFLICT IMMINENT.

FROM CHARLESTON.

WAR VESSELS Off Charleston Harbor.

FORT SUMTER DISPLAYS SIGNAL LIGHTS.

Large Numbers of Secessionists Concentrating.

TALBOT REFUSED ACCESS TO FORT SUMTER.

THE POLICY OF THE PRESIDENT.

Explanations of its Operation.

NEW TARIFF SCHEME.

WAR MOVEMENTS ABOUT WASHINGTON.

PHILADELPHIA MILITARY.

MORE WAR VESSELS TO BE FITTED OUT.

Waiting the Result.

WASHINGTON, April 9.—Every one here is on the *qui vive* to hear from Charleston, as it is considered probable that the Secessionists may fire on Fort Sumter or Fort Pickens, or on those conveying provisions to them, in which case the strength of this Government will be fully tested. Many expect to hear, at any moment, that the cannonading has commenced, while others are positive that no hostilities will take place, feeling certain that the Secessionists will shrink from the contest. They are evidently in a dilemma. Before them is the gulf of financial confusion, home discontent, a latent Union feeling, and inevitable fratricidal war—while necessity goads them implacably on. Meanwhile a nation—divided though it may be—waits the result.

New Tariff Scheme.

Judge DOUGLAS does not, evidently, believe that we are to have a warlike separation, for he has shown his confidence in the recognition of the Confederate States by preparing a Customs Union, which he thinks preferable to the present tariff. This bill proposes a virtual free trade between the two sections of the dissolved Union, including, if desirable, Canada and Mexico, with a tariff of duties on exports from abroad acceptable to all. Of course, any such change of the tariff will be regarded with jealousy by those who have secured the passage of a scale of duties which will furnish the requisite revenue, and also protect our home industry. An examination of the new tariff at the Treasury Department has satisfied Secretary CHASE that the outcries of the New Yorkers are unfounded, and that it will not prove the unmanageable, oppressive burden upon the commerce of the country that has been represented. Any change, just now, is to be deprecated.

The Coup d'Etat.

With news of the firing of the first gun at the South, some expect to hear the booming of cannon and the fusillade of small arms in this metropolis. All sorts of cock-and-bull stories are circulated about the presence of BEN McCULLOCH, and the organizations of Knights of the Golden Circle and National Volunteers. But it is believed that the city is in safe-keeping, and that the regulars here and in the neighboring fortifications can preserve the peace.

Philadelphia Military.

The Secretary of War has been notified, by two of the best military companies in Philadelphia, that if a requisition is made on Governor CURTIN for volunteers, they will respond at a day's notice, ready to take the field. This spirit, doubtless, animates other bodies of the present organized force, and if they are needed, it will take but a few hours to bring them here.

Peace of the City.

The guard-house reports show that the "inauguration month" of March, usually so riotous here, has this year been very quiet. Only two hundred and twenty-eight arrests were made by the auxiliary guard of Government and by the day and night police of the city. Of these there were:—White, 169; colored, 59; males, 194; females, 34; white males, 151; white females, 18; colored males, 43; colored females, 16. The amount of judgments and costs obtained for violations of the corporation laws is $1119·22; cash collected, $713·43.

A bill has been introduced into the Common Council, to dispense with the services of twenty-five police officers, which shows that the "secession" of a few score of fire-eaters has contributed to the peace of the metropolis.

Snake Story.

The Post Office clerks are endeavoring to deny the statement that two copper-head snakes, which were probably sent from Florida in a mail bag, were killed in the court yard of the Department. But the story seems to be true—not always the case with snake stories.

Wide-Awakes.

When it was ascertained that Mr. LINCOLN was elected President, there was a large addition to a patriotic band of Wide-Awakes here, and in due time every one of them wanted an office, just to show that their services were appreciated. But now it is pretty certain that the Marshal, Navy Agent and Commissioner of Public Buildings will be taken from distant States, these enthusiastic Wide-Awakes are denouncing "Old ABE," and threatening to enlist in the brave battalions of Governor WISE.

California Appointments.

The latest rumor is that Dr. RABE, of San Francisco, has "smashed the slate" of Senator BAKER, and is to be Postmaster, besides placing his friends in other offices.

Bay State Troubles.

Our Massachusetts friends are in a terrible trouble about their Boston offices, which the Representatives undertook to meet and parcel out. By the "slate" thus adopted, Dr. PHELPS, a disappointed applicant for the Postmastership, was to be Surveyor of the Port, ousting FLETCHER WEBSTER, the only surviving son of the great expounder of the Constitution. But GEORGE ASHMUN, who presided over the Chicago Convention, has gallantly come to the relief of the son of his old associate, and there is a famous contest. Some three or four applicants for the place of Navy Agent have also entered a ring, and are striving hard each to outwit his competitors. The subordinate appointments at the Charlestown Navy Yard were arranged to-day, and divided around among the Republicans of that city and the neighboring towns.

THE GIBRALTAR OF THE GULF OF MEXICO.

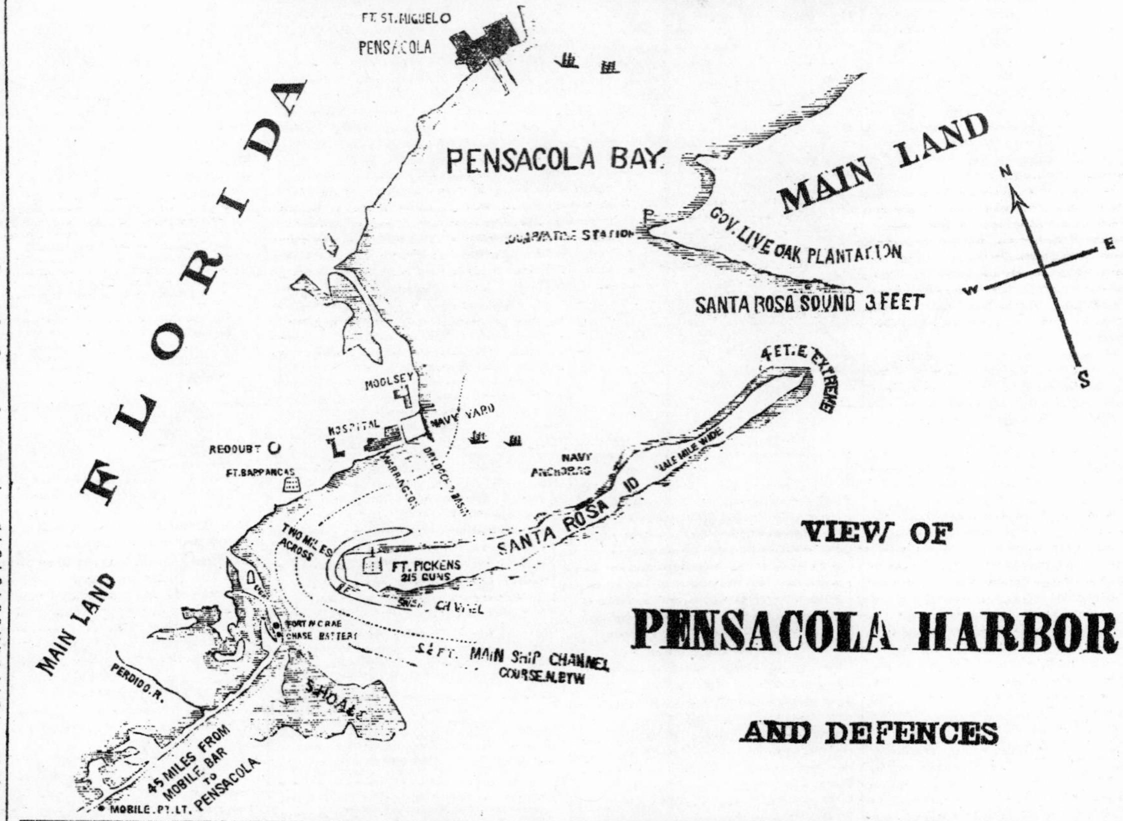

VIEW OF PENSACOLA HARBOR AND DEFENCES

The Latest from Charleston.

WASHINGTON, April 9.—The Government has received a telegram to-night from Charleston, which serves to show that the interest in the forts and Government property which President LINCOLN promised to possess and occupy is active and unabated, as well among the forces whose bayonets point toward the North, as among the anxious people in this section, who just now think war is a thing neither to be sought for or refused.

Talbot Refused Access to Sumter.

The official information is, that Lieut. TALBOT, on his return to Charleston, was not allowed to resume his connection with the little band at Fort Sumter, who alone in the entire State live and move under the shadow of their country's flag.

A Letter to Governor Pickens.

The President, a couple of days ago, despatched Mr. CHEW, a prudent and reliable clerk in the State Department, with a letter to Gov. PICKENS, notifying him that if it was attempted to cut off the supplies from Fort Sumter, recently obtained in Charleston, that the Government would undertake, at all hazards, to supply Major ANDERSON with fuel and provisions.

Anxiety of the Commissioners.

The three Commissioners from the C. S. A., who have been dodging about Washington, waiting for something to turn up, have become extremely anxious in regard to the exact position they occupy, and I expect to hear that they have suddenly packed up and left the Capital to avoid an arrest for that worst of all crimes, treason.

The Opinions of the Cabinet.

It is pretty well known that the Cabinet have become an entire unit in the present exigency of public affairs, but it is not so well known that Mr. SEWARD is now as determined and resolute for the honor of his country's flag as he was before desirous of obtaining a peaceful settlement by just and equitable compromises. His friends say that if war should unfortunately occur, he is in no degree to blame for it, because he exhausted every means of peaceful settlement.

War Movements About the Capital.

ROGER A. PRYOR has raised a company of soldiers in Virginia, and has tendered his services to JEFF. DAVIS. As an offset to this, Hon. JOHN B. POTTER is here, and may tender his services to President LINCOLN. After all it may be reduced to a single handed contest between these two distinguished warriors, at the head of their respective forces.

The North Aroused.

On every hand assurances continue to pour in from the Northern States, giving assurance that the people of the free States are ready to stand by the Government.

The Governor of Massachusetts has sent on a confidential agent, who gives assurance that she will furnish two thousand picked troops ready for service at any moment their services may be required.

Inspection of the Troops of the District.

Secretary CAMERON has issued orders to Colonel STONE, who has the direction of the volunteers at this point, to have them inspected without delay. A company of national volunteers, who have heretofore been accused of holding sentiments in sympathy with secession, will be inspected to-night.

Advices from Pickens.

Despatches have been received from Lieutenant SLEMMER, in command at Fort Pickens, in which he communicates the reasons why troops were not landed to reinforce that point according to the orders of the War Department.

War Vessels to be Fitted Out.

Special messengers left here to-day with instructions to have the *Savannah*, *Wabash* and *Vincennes*, at New York, and the *Jamestown* and *St. Lawrence*, at Philadelphia, fitted out for sea immediately. The preparations of the War and Navy Department are on the most extensive scale, and will embrace every means within reach of the Government. Confidential agents are in all of the Northern cities arranging for the charter and purchase of every merchant steamer whose frame is strong enough to enable her to carry a battery of even a single gun.

Fort Monroe.

It is rumored that the steamer *Pawnee*, instead of landing two hundred and fifty troops at Fort Monroe on Saturday last, actually received on board that number from the Fort.

Shaping the News.

It has been reliably ascertained that the agents of the Secessionists control much of the telegraph matter sent from here, and that it is ingeniously colored to advance the unholy cause in which they have embarked. They are well known and will be marked and watched.

The Defence of Washington.

Colonel CHARLES SMITH, a brave and experienced officer, in whom the President has the most unlimited confidence, and who has, until recently, been connected with the army in Utah, will be entrusted with the defence of Washington.

General SUMNER will take charge of the Pacific division of the army, superseding General JOHNSON.

Intense excitement prevails to-night, from the fact that the Battalion of Light Infantry have been ordered out for duty by nine o'clock to-morrow morning, by a messenger from head-quarters. No cause has been given for the order, and the residents of the Capital are anxious to know what prompts the unusual step.

An Officer Arrested.

It is rumored here that Capt. JOHNS has returned from New York under arrest, for refusing to go South with the troops ordered from New York harbor. Capt. JOHNS is a native of the District of Columbia.

The Policy of the Administration.

An Explanation of the Recent Movements.

WASHINGTON, April 9.—Extensive as are the recent military and naval preparations, it is persistently stated in Administration quarters that they mean defensive purposes only, and that nothing is intended not strictly justified by the laws which it is the duty of the President to enforce to the extent of his ability.

If resistance is made to his efforts in this particular, and bloodshed result, the responsibility must fall on those who provoke hostilities. And the assurance of the inaugural is repeated, that the Administration will not be the aggressor.

Various theories or reasons are given in the newspapers for the present military demonstrations; among them, that they were only recently stimulated by the result of certain State and municipal elections. But this is known to be an error; for, at the commencement of the Administration, the President and his Cabinet entertained the idea of reinforcing both Forts Sumter and Pickens; but, owing to the condition of the country at that time, and a non-acquaintance with the means at the command of the Government, the prosecution of the plans now progressing was impracticable. In other words, it was necessary first to ascertain the extent of the effects bequeathed to the present by the late Administration.

As to the secrecy of the objects of the military movements, this was deemed absolutely necessary, especially the sailing of vessels with sealed orders. Under the late Administration there were persons who clandestinely communicated its purposes from time to time to the Secessionists as frequently as they occurred, before they were reduced to an official form, and, according to a remark of an ex-Secretary, the Administration thus always found itself embarrassed at the threshold. The present Administration, however, with a full appreciation of such obstructions, has limited an actual knowledge of its purposes to the members of the Cabinet, and, perhaps, several trusty officers, and taken such precautionary measures as renders it next to impossible to improperly acquire the forbidden information.

The Administration, while constantly declaring its policy to be peace, claims that it can only be held to strict accountability by the people, and that however various and speculative may be the publications respecting its movements, it is under no obligation to announce, in advance, its purposes and plans—in other words, that the Administration should be judged by its acts.

That Fort Pickens has been, or will be reinforced, admits of no doubt. And, with regard to Fort Sumter, the Administration will do all in its power either to relieve Major ANDERSON or to secure his evacuation of the post, if needs be, without dishonor or committing the Government to the acknowledgment of any right claimed by the Confederate States, or in any way recognizing the doctrine of secession.

The proceedings in the Gulf, beyond the relief of Fort Pickens, will be governed by circumstances.

The above has been prepared *from reliable sources*, with a view to show, to some extent, the basis of the present military preparations.

THE FEDERAL STRONGHOLD IN THE SOUTH.

PENSACOLA HARBOR AND DEFENCES.

Description of the Fortifications.

THE PROBABLE SEAT OF WAR.

We present the readers of THE INQUIRER, this morning, with an accurate view of Pensacola harbor and its defences.

Fort Pickens.

Fort Pickens, the apparent stronghold of the Federal Government in the South, is built on a low, sandy spot on the westernmost end of Santa Rosa Island, and a little over one mile distant from Fort McRea, which forms another sentinel to the bay. Fort Pickens is a first class bastioned work, built of stone for foundation purposes, with walls of brick and bitumen. Its walls are forty feet in height, by twelve feet in thickness. It is embrasured for two tiers of guns in bombproof casemates, and one tier open or *en barbette*. The work has all the usual concomitants of a first class work, viz: covert ways, dry ditch *glacis* and outworks complete. The guns from this work radiate to all points of the horizon, with flank and enfilading fire in the ditches and every angle of approach. Its guns command Fort Barrancas, Fort McRea, the Navy Yard and the other works now in possession of the Confederate States troops. The work was commenced in 1828, and finished in 1853. It cost the Federal Government nearly one million of dollars. When on a war footing the garrison consists of 1200 soldiers. Its present armament consists of:—In bastion, 26 twenty four pound howitzers; casemate, 2 forty two pounders, 64 thirty-two pounders, 50 twenty-four pounders; in barbette, 24 eight inch howitzers, 6 eighteen pounders, 12 twelve pounders, 1 ten inch columbiad, mounted, and 4 ten inch mortars, in bad order.

The fort is only approachable by land on one side. Owing to the openness of the country, which is but a barren bed of sand, a party attacking from that quarter would be very much exposed. The Federal forces now in garrison at Fort Pickens consist of about two hundred and fifty men, under the command of Lt. SLEMMER.

Fort McRea.

Almost immediately opposite Pickens is Fort McRea, where the Secessionists have concentrated their forces. It is a powerful and castle like masonry structure, built on a low sand spit of the main land, and appears to rise out of the water. This fortification is situated on Foster's Bank and guards the west side of the mouth of Pensacola Bay. It is a bastioned fort, built of brick masonry, with walls twelve feet in thickness. The work is somewhat out of repair, and in view of this fact, General BRAGG recently ordered the removal of sixty heavy guns, and distributed them among the new sand batteries.

Fort McRae is embrasured for two tiers of guns under bombproof casemates, and has one tier *en barbette*. Its present armament consists of:—Lower tier, 22 forty-two pounders; second tier, 12 eight inch columbiads, 18 thirty-two pounders; in barbette, 62 twenty-four pounders, 3 ten inch columbiads, and in time of war requires a garrison of six hundred and fifty men. The work cost the Federal Government about $200,000. Its guns radiate at every point of the horizon. The full armament of the fort is not complete, but a sufficient number of guns are in battery to make a very good opposition to Fort Pickens. Below this fort is a water battery, which mounts some eight or ten guns. The interior of Fort McRae is provided with the necessary shot furnaces, officers' and soldiers' quarters, magazines, &c.

Fort Barrancas.

Fort Barrancas is on the north of Pensacola Bay, and directly facing the entrance to its mouth. The work is erected on the site of an old Spanish fort. It is a bastioned work, of heavy masonry, and mounts forty-nine guns, all of which are in battery and ready for action. It is at present garrisoned by three hundred troops of the regular army of the Confederate States. In the rear of the fort, and a short distance from it, is a redoubt from which Barrancas receives reinforcements in time of action. Some extensive repairs have recently been completed on this redoubt, and flanking howitzers of scarp and counterscarp mounted. In the flank defences of Fort Barrancas eight twenty-four pound howitzers have recently been mounted. Fort Barrancas contains 288 eight-inch shells, 993 twenty-four pound balls, 630 eighteen pound balls, and all the implements for working the cannon. Its present armament consists of eleven thirty-two pounders, three eight-inch paixhans, two eight-inch columbiads, eight twenty-four pounders, five eighteen pounders, two twelve pounders, eight twelve pound howitzers; flank defence, two eighteen-inch mortars.

The Chase Battery—Sand Fort A.

This is a new sand battery erected by the Confederate troops, and is so situated as to rake the front of Fort Pickens. The work has several columbiads in battery.

The Sand Batteries.

Along the bend from Warrington Navy Yard, to the extreme right of Fort McRea, there are efficient sand batteries erected at suitable intervals, with the guns bearing upon Fort Pickens. They are built at considerable distances apart, so as to scatter the fire of Fort Pickens, should an engagement take place with that work.

Fort Pickens, Junior.

This is a small outpost of defence or auxiliary of Fort Pickens, erected by Lieutenant SLEMMER's orders. It is situated about one mile and a quarter from Pickens, and commands the Warrington Navy Yard, in possession of the Confederate States troops. Fort Pickens, Jr., is now used as a station for picket guards, and it will answer the purpose of effectually preventing anything like a surprise of the main fort.

The Marine Hospital.

Gen. BRAGG has his head-quarters here; adjoining are the general barracks, a large three-story building, only a portion of the plan of which is completed, but even now having room for five or six hundred men. In the rear of these is the parade ground, with room for the manœuvres of a full regiment, and with convenient houses around for the quarters of officers, the whole encompassed with groves of live oak and other growth. From the barracks a railroad track furnishes means of conveyance for stores to and from the redoubt, about a thousand yards in the rear of Fort Barrancas.

Pensacola Bay.

Pensacola bay is twenty-seven miles in length, and in its broadest part twelve miles in width. It lies immediately at the mouth of the Escambia river. Running along the front of the bay for fourteen leagues, nearly east and west, is a long line of sandy shore, narrow, barren, and so low that in a severe gale the mad waves dash over it. Pensacola bay has rare properties as a harbor, and cannot be excelled on the Gulf, if by any in this country. It is accessible to frigates of large size, there being twenty-one feet of water on the bar; and when once inside, all the ships of our navy could ride in safety. The channel runs near this coast across the bar, which is short and easily passed. The harbor is completely landlocked, and the roadstead capacious. The upper arm of Pensacola bay receives the Yellowwater or Pea river, Middle river and Escambia river, eleven miles from the Gulf of Mexico.

Santa Rosa Island.

Santa Rosa Island is the great barrier that forms the main or sea enclosure of Pensacola Bay. The island is fourteen leagues in length, and, on an average, is not more than one-fourth of a mile wide, although in some places it exceeds this considerably. At high water there are many places where the waves run over the land. Upon the extreme western end of the island, and commanding the entrance to Pensacola bay, stands Fort Pickens. Near Pickens it is barren for a mile or thereabouts, and then commences a low growth of shrubbery, scraggy pines, live oak bushes, and small trees of different varieties. It is too sandy for cultivation, and is of no manner of use, except to protect Pensacola from the sea, and to form a reliable roadstead. The island is separated from the main land one and a quarter miles; there are two channels for the passage of vessels, one on the side of the main land, and the other on the island side. The outer shore of Santa Rosa Island is sometimes dangerous to incoming vessels. The island, however, affords the facility of making regular siege approaches by an attacking force.

From Harrisburg.

REPUBLICAN CAUCUS ON THE STATE OF THE COUNTRY.

HARRISBURG, April 9.—A caucus of the Republican members of both Houses of the Legislature is in session this evening, Senator Smith presiding.

Mr. PALMER desired an adjournment.

Mr. PENNEY made a speech, in which he declared that the party should at present take no other grounds than it had already taken.

Mr. McCLURE urged the adoption of the amendment to the Constitution, as recommended by the last Congress, declaring non-intervention with slavery in the States where it exists.

Mr. GORDON, of the House of Representatives, opposed the adoption of the amendment.

Mr. LANDON, of the Senate, declared that he would not vote for it.

Mr. McCLURE made a speech, in which he warmly defended this measure of compromise.

Mr. GORDON again spoke in opposition.

Mr. ARMSTRONG made a speech in favor of the amendment.

The caucus is still in session, but no vote will be taken to-night.

The Democratic members of the Legislature will hold a caucus on the military recommendation of Gov. CURTIN to-morrow morning.

Municipal Election at Trenton.

TRENTON, April 9.—The election in this city to-day resulted in the success of WM. R. McKEAN (Rep.) as Mayor, and SPAVIN (Dem.) as Marshal. A majority of Democrats on the City and Ward tickets were elected. There was very little excitement manifested.

FROM CHARLESTON.

A FLEET OF SEVEN WAR VESSELS REPORTED OFF THE HARBOR.

Signal Lights Displayed from Fort Sumter.

LIEUT. TALBOT DENIED ACCESS TO THE FORT.

His Departure for Washington.

THE CONFEDERATE FORCES UNDER ARMS.

NEW YORK, April 9.—The *Herald* has received a special despatch from Charleston, dated this morning, giving the following items of interest:—

A fleet of seven Government war vessels was reported off the Bar, and Major ANDERSON displayed signal lanterns from Fort Sumter during the night.

At midnight all the military in the city were ordered under arms.

Lieut. TALBOT, who had arrived at Charleston, with despatches for Major ANDERSON, was denied access to Fort Sumter, and has since started on his return to Washington.

Special despatch to the N. Y. Herald.

CHARLESTON, April 8, Midnight.—The authorities received a notification that supplies would be furnished to Major ANDERSON, by the United States Government, at any hazard. Immense preparations were immediately commenced to repel any such attempt, and orders were issued for the entire military reserve to proceed to their several stations. Four regiments, of a thousand men each, were telegraphed for from the country. Ambulances and other preparations for the wounded are being made.

At midnight seven guns from the citadel were fired as the signal for the assembling of the Reserves, and the city was thrown into the greatest excitement.

The Seventeenth Regiment, eight hundred strong, assembled in an hour, and left for the fortifications.

At three o'clock in the morning all the vessels in the harbor necessary for transportation of the troops, will be put in service.

A fleet of seven Government war vessels are reported off the bar, and Major ANDERSON has apparently been in communication with them by means of signal lanterns displayed from the walls of Fort Sumter.

It is believed that the fight will commence with the battery at Stony Island, twenty-five miles southward, and that the batteries along the coast being silenced in turn, after clearing Morris Island, the Government forces will cross to Fort Sumter while Major ANDERSON engages Fort Moultrie.

Lieut. TALBOT was denied admission to Fort Sumter by the authorities.

R. S. CHEW brought despatches from Washington to Governor PICKENS, announcing that Fort Sumter would be supplied with provisions, and in company with Lieut. TALBOT he left for Washington at 11 o'clock to-night.

CHARLESTON, April 9.—Affairs are culminating to a point.

About 800 men left this morning for different points.

It is estimated that nearly 5000 men are stationed at Sullivan's and Morris Islands, and along the coast.

Companies are arriving from the interior, and the posts will be further strengthened to morrow by nearly a thousand additional men.

All classes of our inhabitants are elated with the prospect, and the enthusiasm is general.

AUGUSTA, Ga., April 9.—A report has been received here that several war vessels are off Charleston, but it is not credited.

The Latest from Charleston.

CHARLESTON, April 9.—11 o'clock, P. M.—All is quiet on the surface, but there is a deep feeling, undercurrent.

Prodigious preparations are progressing.

WIGFALL is serving as a comon soldier.

Rifled cannon are arriving.

Mr. JAMISON delivered a farewell speech in the State Convention to-day, upon a complimentary resolution to the President, which was adopted.

The adjournment of the Convention is expected to take place to-morrow.

There are no war vessels outside so far as is known by your reporter.

NEW ORLEANS, April 9.—The news from Charleston is the all-absorbing topic. It creates a universal excitement.

WILMINGTON, N. C., April 9.—The Charleston news has produced an intense excitement here to-day.

From Baltimore—Union Feeling in the South.

BALTIMORE, April 9.—Private telegrams, which have been received from reliable sources in the South, confidently assert that Fort Sumter is to be reinforced, and that Government troops are to be sent to Texas to assist Governor HOUSTON. A gentleman who has just returned from New Orleans, *via* Montgomery and Charleston, informs me that the Union feeling is rapidly increasing throughout the whole South, with the exception of South Carolina, where the people are not permitted to express their true sentiments. Louisiana, it is said, is dissatisfied, and is fast verging to revolution. Many who voted in favor of Secession are now strong Union men. W.

The Federal Appointments.

WASHINGTON, April 9.—In addition to other California appointments, the following have been made:—

GEORGE H. WEBSTER, Register of the Land Office, and G. C. HAVENS, Receiver, at Stockton.

JOHN W. EDDY, Register, and WM. H. PRATT, Receiver, at Humboldt.

GEORGE B. TINGLEY, Register, and ROYALD G. WALL, Receiver, at San Francisco.

GEORGE M. HANSON, Superintending Agent for the Indians of the Northern, and MINOR FINK, Agent of the Southern Districts of California.

W. H. SHARP, United States Attorney, and Dr. WM. RABE, United States Marshal, for the Northern District of California.

Mr. DIMERCK, Attorney, and K. D. BORROWS, Marshal, for the Southern District.

GEORGE ROWLAND, Postmaster at Sacramento.

Postmasters.

The following appointments of Postmasters were also made to-day:—

SAMUEL RIDDLE, at Allegheny City, Pa.

ALEX. H. CONNER, at Indianapolis, Ind.

JOSHUA JONES, at Trenton, N. J.

JNO. T. JENKINS, at New Brunswick, N. J.

CHARLES B. GRIFFIN, at Newark, N. J.

WM. [illegible], at Springfield, Mass.

LEVI SMITH, at [illegible], N. Y.

J. S. VEDDER, at Schenectady, N. Y.

CHARLES H. ELDRIDGE, at Davenport, Ind.

Many appointments have been published as being made when the cases of the individuals named have not even received the consideration of the Executive. The only one for the District of Columbia thus far made, is that of Col. LAMON as Marshal.

Heavy Freshet on the Potomac River.

WASHINGTON, April 9.—The recent storm has raised the Potomac river to an almost unprecedented height, flooding the lower parts of Alexandria and Georgetown. Fears are entertained that considerable damage will be done to the merchandise in the stores along the wharves.

The New-York Times.

VOL. X.....NO. 2982. NEW-YORK, FRIDAY, APRIL 12, 1861. PRICE TWO CENTS.

THE WAR IMMINENT.

Formal Demand for the Surrender of Fort Sumpter.

THE REFUSAL OF MAJ. ANDERSON.

The Bombardment Probably to Commence Immediately.

THE WAR FLEET OFF THE HARBOR.

The Entire Government Forces Destined for Charleston.

WARLIKE PREPARATIONS AT SAVANNAH.

Departure of the Southern Commissioners from Washington.

OUR CHARLESTON DISPATCHES.

CHARLESTON, Wednesday, April 10.

The Floating Battery is now in position, commanding the barbette guns of Fort Sumpter.

It carries two thirty-four-pounders, two forty-two-pounders, and sixty-four men.

The Federal steamers are expected to-night. The city is filled with troops.

CHARLESTON, Thursday, April 11.

An officer has just arrived from Sullivan's Island, and informs me that three steamers were seen hovering off the coast yesterday for a considerable time.

Major ANDERSON fired a signal gun at 10 o'clock A. M.

An opening on Fort Sumpter by the batteries is expected every moment.

The Battery is crowded with people who wait in anxious expectancy.

The troops continue to pour into the city, and all business is suspended.

CHARLESTON, Thursday, April 11.

The Citadel Cadets are guarding the Battery with heavy cannon, and thousands are waiting there to see the attack commence.

One thousand mounted men and two thousand patrols, heavily armed, are guarding the city.

Absolute secrecy is still observed as to all future movements.

CHARLESTON, Thursday, April 11.

I am enabled to send you important information exclusively.

Ex-Senator CHESNUT, the Special Aid of the Governor, sent with Col. CHISHOLM and one of Gen. BEAUREGARD'S Staff, has just returned from Fort Sumpter with Major ANDERSON'S reply to the demand for an unconditional surrender.

The answer returned is at present denied to me at headquarters, but there is no doubt that it is a flat refusal.

Every man capable of bearing arms is called out.

CHARLESTON, Thursday, April 11.

WAR. JASPER.

DISPATCH TO THE ASSOCIATED PRESS.

CHARLESTON, Thursday, April 11

The excitement in the city has been intense, in consequence of rumors that a demand had been made for Fort Sumpter, and if refused, that an engagement would take place this evening at 8 o'clock.

The demand for the evacuation of Fort Sumpter was made at 2 o'clock this afternoon, and Messrs. CHESNUT, CHISHOLM and LEE were deputised to carry the message from Gen. BEAUREGARD.

Thousands of people assembled on the Battery this evening, in anticipation of the commencement of the fight at 8 o'clock.

Two hundred mounted guards patrol the city.

No fight, however, has occurred yet.

The *Harriet Lane* is reported to be off the bar, and signals are displayed by the guard-boats and answered by the batteries.

Immense crowds are now at the different newspaper offices, eagerly watching for news.

ROGER A. PRYOR, of Virginia, has received an appointment in Gen. BEAUREGARD'S Staff.

At this time the excitement has mostly subsided, and no conflict is looked for to-night.

One more regiment went down to Morris Island to-day.

CHARLESTON, Thursday, April 11—Midnight.

Gen. BEAUREGARD, at 2 o'clock this afternoon, demanded the surrender of Fort Sumpter, which Major ANDERSON declined to accede to, probably with a reservation.

A large portion of our people are collected on the wharves, and Battery, and every accessible point facing the harbor, anxiously awaiting the result.

The military in the city are under arms, but all is quiet.

Another regiment will arrive here to-morrow.

It is estimated that between 6,000 and 7,000 men are stationed on Morris and Sullivan's Islands, and points along the coast.

Gen. BEAUREGARD will leave at midnight for Morris Island.

It is reported that the *Harriet Lane* was seen off the bar this evening.

LATER.—It is currently reported that negotiations will be opened to-morrow between Gen. BEAUREGARD and Major ANDERSON about the surrender of Fort Sumpter.

Officers commanding different posts in the harbor and coast are on the alert, expecting an attempt will be made early in the morning to provision and reinforce Fort Sumpter.

OUR WASHINGTON DISPATCHES.

DESTINATION OF THE NAVAL FLEET—PROGRAMME AND PURPOSES OF THE GOVERNMENT.

WASHINGTON, Thursday, April 11.

The Administration is as yet without advices of the fleet of war-steamers, and steam transports, which sailed from your port. The telegraph south of this city is entirely in the hands of the seceding leaders, and they will let no information come over the wires that may be sure, in any way, to inform the Government, or gratify the curiosity of the people. You may depend that the port of Charleston is the destination of all the vessels, men, and munitions of war that have left Northern ports. The first call will be there, and the first service will be there required. If the objects of the Government are there attained, the surplus may then be forwarded to Pickens, and thence to Texas.

You will ask, "What are the objects of the Government?" Simply to assert its supremacy over the Government property. To do this, it has become necessary to feed its troops in the harbor of Charleston. This it will do. I think the Government expects to do it without the expenditure of blood. It will be disappointed, if the men and material now off the harbor are found necessary to accomplish its purpose; but if they are necessary, they will be unhesitatingly used. To the purpose of affording succor to the famishing men of Sumpter, the Government will unfalteringly devote all the resources of the country, believing the country will cheerfully respond to any demand which the Government may make.

SOUTHERN SUPPORT OF THE GOVERNMENT.

Mr. LINCOLN, and the great majority of the Cabinet who entertain the policy inaugurated, are receiving hourly assurances of the favor with which that policy is received. The North seems a unit, but it is not the North alone that sends the most hearty commendations. Strange as it may seem, the Border States are quite as earnest as the North. They seem to hail the positive position of the Administration as a prospective bulwark, protecting them from the desolation, anarchy, and taxation of secession. I shall be much mistaken, if the results do not prove that a firm maintenance of the rights of the General Government is the sole preventive of Border State secession.

Notwithstanding the denials of the *Herald*, I renew my assertion, given a week ago, that the great Powers cordially respond to the efforts making by Mr. LINCOLN to maintain the integrity of the Union. The assurances of sympathy and concurrence have been more positive and clear than the usual language of diplomacy. Though unofficially given, they are none the less reliable and satisfactory.

POWER OF GOVERNMENT TO CALL FOR AID.

The idea prevalent that the Government has no power to accept volunteers, or to call for aid from the States, or that it lacks authority to use all the reserved forces of the country, is an entire mistake. The Government has no doubt of its legal right to enforce the laws, and to collect revenue, in such manner as the exigencies of the case may demand—by blockade or otherwise. No Cabinet that has existed for years embraces more legal talent than that of Mr. LINCOLN, and on that point it is a unit.

GONE HOME DISAPPOINTED.

The Southern Commissioners left this morning for the South, having been disappointed in receiving anticipated advices from JEFF. DAVIS, directing their proceedings.

THE VIRGINIA COMMISSIONERS.

The Virginia Commissioners have not yet made their appearance. Their answer awaits them. It will be prompt and explicit. The Government has done treating secession with respect and consideration.

THE SOUTHERN LOAN A-BEGGING.

It is positively ascertained by the Government that the fifteen million loan, authorized by the Confederated States, cannot be taken. The offers are less than two millions, including the amount offered by the enthusiasts who happened to have a few dollars wherewith to gratify their passion for secession.

MEASURES FOR PROTECTING THE CAPITAL.

The militia of the District was mustered into service to-day. All the public buildings are guarded to-night, pickets being placed in such numbers as to prevent the possibility of surprise. Mustering these troops into service has made full developments of the strength of the secession feeling in this city. Strange as it may appear, the mass of those who refused to swear to support the Stars and Stripes are persons employed by the Government. Of the members of the National Rifles, the majority are clerks in the Departments, and of this corps I believe thirty-two declined the oath. Of another corps, sixteen refused to swear allegiance, and of this number twelve were employed in the Navy-yard, and one in the General Post-office. The duty of the heads of Departments would seem to be clear, at least so far as those gentlemen are concerned.

I do not discover that any fears are entertained of a sudden descent upon the Capital. The streets are hourly paraded by the military, but without interrupting the regular order of business.

BEN M'CULLOUCH AND HIS ENTERTAINERS.

I learn that during BEN MCCULLOUCH'S recent visit to this neighborhood, he was in the habit of stopping nights at the house of a prominent banker of this city, retiring to Virginia early in the morning; also that, while here, he was in consultation with the Commissioners, and with leading Secessionists of the District, and of Virginia and Maryland. The authorities have their eye on the man, who, by sheltering this traitor and his co-conspirators, has implicated him in their treason; and his money will not save him if he is not careful.

THE TRAITORS AT THE CAPITAL TO BE WATCHED

The lines are being closely drawn in Washington. Under the direction of CAMERON and Gen. SCOTT, well-known sympathisers and suspected men connected with the secession movement will now be closely watched. It is claimed that the calling out of the District Militia was not at all influenced by the reports of MCCULLOUCH'S movements. There are more dangerous and desperate men than he already detected in plots against the peace of the city. He is appreciated by the Government as a very clever and noisy humbug, and, thus far, his movements in Virginia have amounted to nothing, and probably will not. Many regard this call upon volunteers in this vicinity as an experiment to ascertain the state of public feeling here. The Government is gratified to find so healthy a tone here. Many of those who declined service have to-day gone back to their allegiance, prompted to do so by the general scorn and opprobrium which greeted them on all sides; but, aside from a desire to test the fidelity of the District Militia, there are strong reasons for vigorous preparations for the defence of the City. A decided Union Democrat, who has been spending some time at Richmond, says that the agents of secession openly advocate an attack upon Washington, and attempt to enlist and organize forces for that purpose. Mr. LINCOLN is in constant receipt of letters, some anonymous and some otherwise, warning him of personal danger.

The inspection of the District Militia was completed to-day, and not a single additional man refused the oath. Yesterday, over a hundred of the National Rifles refused the oath, leaving only about twenty of them sound. This is the company which has been notoriously suspicious all Winter. Being weeded of the traitors, over forty Union recruits joined it to-day.

It is designed to bring additional regular troops here within a few days.

FINANCIAL CONDITION AND PROSPECTS OF THE GOVERNMENT.

The bid for Treasury notes, opened to-day, thoroughly vindicates the wisdom of Secretary CHASE'S refusal to accept bids for the recent loan below ninety-four. Four millions more than the Department offered were bid for, and the awards were made at rates varying from par to twenty-seven one-hundredths premium. This, especially in view of the extraordinary efforts made to bear the market, and in view of the pending war panic, must be regarded as a brilliant success, and as a most satisfactory indication of the renewed confidence of capital in the Administration of the Treasury. Mr. CHASE'S operations in these last two weeks have saved the Government about $350,000 cash, to say nothing of the moral effect of this marked success of a man hitherto untried in financial affairs. There are about nine millions in the Treasury at present, and no unsigned warrants on hand. This is a far more favorable condition than the Treasury has enjoyed before for a long time.

Father WHITTLESEY resumes the First Comptrollership, on the 1st of May, which will further tend to restore public confidence.

MILITARY SPECULATIONS.

Among the speculations in military circles relative to the destination of the military forces and stores which recently left New-York, is one to the effect that the Government has determined to concentrate troops, &c., at Key West and the Tortugas,—as convenient points from which to strike a blow when required, either for Fort Pickens or Texas. This policy would make Pickens the Sebastopol, and Key West the Constantinople of the campaign.

A SOUTHERN CONTRIBUTION.

The President received a letter to-day from St Louis directed to "Old ABE or any other man." On one side was the Confederacy flag, on the other the seal and flag of the United States, with the words "played out." Inside was a five-dollar note on the Union Bank of South Carolina, "to help pay the expenses of reinforcing Fort Sumpter." This letter created much merriment at the White House.

LIEUT. HAMILTON AND THE NAVY.

I quote from a letter written by one of the officers of the United States sloop *Naragansett*, dated Callao, March 14, 1861.

"Lieut. HAMILTON, who resigned from the *Wyoming* at this station, has lost all his friends by his traitorous appeal to Southern officers to steal the ships they are attached to, if possible, and transfer them to the South. Some allowance should be made for him, as his father was one of the prime movers of nullification in 1832, and was snubbed by Gen. JACKSON. * * * All the officers feel it very mortifying to converse with foreigners concerning the present difficulties in our country, but I must do the French and English the justice to say that they are very sorry that anything has occurred to interrupt our progress and prosperity as a nation. They have no sympathy for the South and its traitors. * * * Peru, Equador and the other inter-tropical countries on the western slope of the Andes, with sufficient population, will, in five or ten years, outstrip the Cotton States in the production of cotton. The population is ready to be imported from the opposite coast of China, which you know is overflowing, and can easily be transplanted and adapted to this country. There are four kinds of cotton indigenous to the soil growing in Peru, all of which are superior to the American cotton, except the 'Sea Island.' Here there is no expense for re-planting, it being of the aborescent kind, and its trees lasting from thirty to forty years. It is now chiefly exported to France, where it brings the best prices, from the *silkiness of its fibres*. An American firm at Lima has introduced the American 'gin,' and shipped several lots for speculation, one cargo of which was sent to New-England."

THE NEW-YORK APPOINTMENTS.

The New-York appointments that were to have been made to-day, now go over to Monday. The coming crisis affords a plausible pretext for the delay. There is no perceptible difference in the status of the candidates, except that STETSON seems to be coming athwart the bows of Capt. SCHULTZ, and threatens to "cut him out" of the Marshalship, into which he was going "head on" last week, with a full crowd of sail and steam.

The "hope deferred" has driven most of the applicants for office "back again." The New-Yorkers have thinned out until hardly a corporal's guard mustered at Willard's this morning. What were on hand, however, were veterans. Mr. BARNEY came here this morning, probably to have some removals and appointments confirmed by the Secretary of the Treasury, who must *visé* all such documents. Postmaster TAYLOR is also here.

THE NEW-YORK POST-OFFICE SITE.

There is another hitch in the New-York Post-office site—this time in the Treasury Department. It is to be hoped that Secretary CHASE will think twice before he commences the expenditure of a half-million of dollars on a job that can well be deferred. The Government has a four-years' lease of the present premises, and therefore has no call to purchase.

THE BOSTON APPOINTMENTS.

The Boston Delegation had an interview with the President to-day, relative to appointments there, but effected no result, as they were not harmonious themselves.

EZRA LINCOLN has, to-day, been appointed Sub-Treasurer of Boston.

WM. STOWE, present Clerk of the Massachusetts House of Representatives, is reported appointed Postmaster at Springfield.

MINISTER TO GUATEMALA.

Mr. CROSBY, the new Minister to Guatemala, has left the city, on his way to his new post. I understand that he contemplates the introduction of the American cotton gin into Central America, with a view to stimulating the production of cotton, which grows there wild, and of excellent quality. Those who know Mr. CROSBY well cannot doubt that he will exert himself to the utmost to advance the commercial interests of the United States in Central America, and that in so doing he will encourage the development of the internal resources of the country to which he is accredited.

RECRUITING FOR THE C. S. A.

It is ascertained that there are recruiting officers in this city and in the surrounding Border States, attempting to gather recruits for the Southern Confederacy military service. Two were discovered in this city, to-day, and suddenly took themselves off

Please correct to-day's statement about Capt. SCHULTZ. The resolution against him in the Republican Committee was tabled and not adopted.

DISPATCH TO THE ASSOCIATED PRESS.

The general excitement occasioned, yesterday, by the calling out of the Volunteer Militia to be mustered into the Federal service has abated, and to-day four or five companies marched to the War Department and took the army oath, namely, "to bear true allegiance to the United States, and serve them honestly and faithfully against all their enemies and opposers whomsoever, and observe and obey the orders of the President of the United States, and the orders of the officers appointed over them, according to the rules of articles for the government of the armies of the United States."

Previous to taking the oath, the volunteers were informed that the obligation was for three months, unless they were sooner discharged; and an opportunity was given to such as might wish to retire. But as the men came there purposely to be mustered in, they assume the obligation accordingly. They now understand that they cannot be ordered beyond the limits of the District of Columbia, and will not be continuously on duty as guards to the armories, public buildings, etc. Not quite two hundred were accepted yesterday, but five hundred altogether will doubtless be mustered in during the day.

Army overcoats have been plentifully distributed among them.

When Col. ELLSWORTH, of Zouave fame, recently came to Washington, a company of Zouaves was organized, and this gentleman has been tendered the command. He has not, however, accepted it, but has been giving them the benefit of his proficiency in the drill.

The balance in the Treasury, last Monday, was $5,651,000. The receipts from Customs for the two weeks, ending April 9, 1861, were $1,471,211, and for the corresponding weeks, this year, were $1,500,667; increase, $29,416.

Owing to other engagements, the Secretary of the Treasury was unable to open the bids until after 7 o'clock, this evening. These exceeded the amount of the Treasury Notes offered, viz: $4 901,000, about 409,060 at rates ranging from par to 27-100 premium. The Treasury is now in good condition. No part of the proceeds of last week's loan has yet been used, nor will it be needed for some time. The receipts from Customs, for two or three weeks past, have nearly equaled all the demands upon the Treasury.

The following are the bids:

Name.	Place.	Amount.	Per Cent.
C. H. Baker	Philadelphia	$13 000	.26 prem.
Sam'l G. White	Philadelphia	2,000	par.
J. Cook & Co.	Philadelphia	200,000	.16 prem.
Sumner R. Stone	New-York	3,000	par.
Jno P. Elton	Waterbury, Conn.	15,000	.03 prem.
Jno. P. Elton	Waterbury, Conn.	10 000	.01 prem.
Bridgeport Savings Bk.	Conn.	10.000	par.
Bank of New-York		100 000	par.
Henry W. Z. Maisy & Co.		50,000	.01 prem.
H. Stowbridge & Sons	N. Hav.	5 000	.16 prem.
H. Stowbridge & Sons	N. Hav.	5 000	.11 prem.
C. Griswold	New York	2 000	.27 prem.
W. H. Macy on	New-York	10,000	.05 prem.
Colgate & Hoffman	New York	150,000	.05 prem.
James G. King Sons	New-York	100 000	par.
Reid, Drexel & Co.	New-York	185,000	par.
R. L. & A. Stewart	New York	110,000	par.
H. Howard, (sec'y)	Buffalo	100 000	par.
Institution for Savings	Roxbury, Mass	20,000	par.
Bank of Commerce	N. Y.	2,500,000	par.
S. Hooper, for self and others	Boston	1,100,000	par.
S. Hooper	Boston	350,000	par.
P. P. Rienlyn, by Assistant Secretary of Treasury, for benefit of Choctaw Indians		250,000	par.

The Secretary of the Treasury has prepared a circular of instructions to Collectors of Customs, by which, among other things, it appears that in all cases of the withdrawal and exportation of repaired or manufactured railroad iron, in order that the importation for such purposes may be exempt from duty, must be made at the same port where it was originally imported, and within six months from date of importation. The circular concludes as follows:

The control of the warehouses of the Government in the several States, South Carolina, Georgia, Alabama, Mississippi, Louisiana, Florida and Texas, having been usurped under the alleged authority of those States, and the Officers of Customs acting under the authority of the United States having been forcibly excluded from their functions in the custody of merchandise and the superintendence of the entries for warehousing and the withdrawal, it has become impracticable to continue the privilege of bonding for transportation to those ports. The Collectors of Customs are accordingly hereby instructed that no entries for transportation in bond to those ports can be permitted until otherwise directed by this Department. In the case of merchandise entered for transportation before the receipt by the Collectors of these instructions, transportation bonds to the ports of South Carolina, Georgia, Alabama, Mississippi Louisiana, Florida and Texas, will be canceled, on payment of the duties at the Collector's office at the port from which the goods were shipped, on the Collector being satisfied, by the affidavit of the party, to be filed with the bond, that the merchandise arrived at the port of destination after the United States officers at such port had ceased to issue the lawful canceling certificates.

It was heretofore stated that Secretary SEWARD, in reply to a note of the Confederate State Commissioners, refused to receive them in their diplomatic character. They responded, and were again answered on the part of the Government. Yesterday, the Commissioners sent to him their final communication. It is said to be written with ability, and reflects severely on the Administration, taking the ground that they have exhausted every resource for a peaceful solution of the existing difficulties, and that if civil war result, on the head of the Federal Government will rest the responsibility. They charge the Administration with gross perjury, insisting that under the shelter of the pretext and assertion that Fort Sumpter was to be evacuated, an immense armada has been dispatched to provision and reinforce that fort. They repeat they had almost daily indirect assurances from the Administration that Fort Sumpter was positively to be abandoned, and that all the Government's efforts were to be directed towards peace. The Commissioners allege that the Government at Montgomery was earnestly desirous of peace, and that in accordance with its instructions, as well as their own feelings, they left no means unexhausted to secure that much desired end; but all their efforts having failed, they were now forced to return to an outraged people with the object of their mission unaccomplished; and they express the firm conviction that war is inevitable. The Commissioners left Washington, to-day, for Montgomery.

EZRA LINCOLN, of Massachusetts, has been appointed Assistant United States Treasurer at Boston. WM. STONE has been appointed Postmaster at Springfield, Mass.

Col. LAMON, recently appointed Marshal for the District of Columbia, continues GEORGE W. PHILLIPS, who served under his two predecessors, as his deputy.

There is no truth in the rumors about Cabinet changes.

The New-York appointments have been postponed till Monday, and the Philadelphia till Tuesday.

D. C. JACKSON, of Madison, has been appointed Marshal, and J. B. COGGSWELL, of Milwaukee, District-Attorney of Wisconsin.

Hon. Mr. POTTER, of Wisconsin, has been forced by sickness to leave here for the sea shore.

The President has recognized PEMBRINCH RUDOLPH KEMHART as Consul of Hamburg; KARL AUGUST STOOTENFORT Consul of Lubeck, and GUIZEPPE AN FLORA DEI DUCHI DI LICIGNANO, Consul-General of Sardinia, all at New-York.

OUR WASHINGTON CORRESPONDENCE.

THE POSITION AND POLICY OF THE ADMINISTRATION—THE TREASON OF THE BUCHANAN CABINET—EFFECT OF THE SHORT CROP OF COTTON

WASHINGTON, Wednesday, April 10, 1861.

There can be no question that the policy of the Administration relative to the Seceded States should be either very vigorous or very lenient. The late Administration, by cowardice in its head, and treachery in its members, encouraged and emboldened the Secession traitors to push matters to the extreme of openly resisting, defying, and insulting the Federal authorities. If the Southern forts and arsenals had been strongly reinforced in the Autumn, immediately before or after the Presidential election, the Secession movement would never have assumed the formidable proportions to which it has attained; but now the question arises, how shall it be put down?

The natural and usual resort would be to armed intervention for the enforcement of the laws, to the extent, at least, of reinforcing the forts and collecting the revenue, or blockading the ports. A vigorous execution of this line of policy would destroy the great pecuniary resource of the rebels, which is the customs duties on imported goods,—and in this way the leaders of the movement would be compelled to resort to direct taxes as a means of carrying on their machinery of Government. This resort could not fail to be extremely odious, and its effect would be to awaken the deluded people to a consciousness of their folly, and strengthen the hands of those who never heartily entered into the movement, and who stand ready to re-unite themselves with the American Union.

But there is no disguising the fact that this vigorous policy would strengthen the disunion sentiment in the Border Slave States, and probably cause them to join the Confederates. Here lies the danger, and it should be looked in the face. It is possible that a resolute effort to maintain the laws may awaken the respect and confidence of the friends of Union in these States, and cause them to rally around the national standard; but it is to be feared that the hue and cry which will be raised by the secession demagogues will frighten the Unionists into acquiescence in their revolutionary schemes. A powerful exhibition of Federal force would prevent this result; but a merely passive policy, without additional military force, will be the signal for a general revolt of the Southern States, and a war of the sections.

The Administration must do one of two things in the present advanced stage of the rebellion: it must either appeal to the Southern friends of the Union and Constitution to stand firm, while giving them the assurance of unlimited support, or it must abandon the field and rely entirely upon the returning good sense of the people. In a word, they must act upon one of two theories, viz: that this is a Government, in the proper sense of the term, which can sustain itself by physical force, if necessary; or that it is, as some Utopians regard it, merely a Government of public opinion. The treachery and poltroonery of the Buchanan Cabinet have placed us in a position which renders it doubtful which of these two theories it is best to act upon.

Our Republican form of Government, in the hands of the late Administration, has exhibited to the world a new phase of crime—a new form of political depravity—which I will venture to say could not occur under any other system. I allude to the deliberate attempt to overthrow the Government under its charge, and the open sympathy which it manifested with the rebels against its authority. Dynasties have been overthrown through the agency of ministers employed by the sovereign: but in no instance, ancient or modern, until that furnished by FLOYD, COBB and THOMPSON, seconded by the cowardice, the political animosity and the faithfulness of BUCHANAN, did a party in power attempt to overthrow the Government. It was CRŒSUS, perhaps, or some equally luxurious monarch, who offered a premium to any one who should invent a new pleasure; but whether the ingenuity of that remote period was equal to the demand upon it, I am not informed. The idea was liberal, at any rate, and showed a practical spirit, not unworthy of the present age. It may be that the Prince of Darkness had put forth a similar temptation to the perpetration of a new crime, which has afforded FLOYD, COBB and THOMPSON the opportunity of achieving an immortality infamy.

The cotton crop has probably fallen off to the extent of a million bales, if we can form an opinion from the amount of receipts at New-Orleans during these political commotions. In ordinary times, a short crop is the signal for unwonted exertions the following year. The consequent rise in the price of the article causes thousands of slaveholders in the older States to remove South, and tens of thousands of slaves to be sent there for sale; and, in this way, the effect is oftener a benefit than a disadvantage to the planting States. But in the present perilous condition of affairs in these States it is not improbable that the short crop may only serve to stimulate the efforts of the Cotton Supply Associations of England to obtain the article from other countries, while in the South enterprise may be too relaxed to improve the opportunity. The defective supply from America, though really, as it regards the forthcoming crop, an ordinary casualty of the seasons, will be connected, in the minds of Europeans, with our political troubles, and will confirm the anticipated ill consequences of our domestic difficulties. The apprehension of a permanent deficiency will thus take root, and the efforts to provide against it by the application of all sorts of stimulants to the cotton-growers of other parts of the world, will be redoubled.

This has been an *excited* rather than an exciting day in Washington. The city has been filled with startling rumors from Charleston, all of which, however, turned out before night to be groundless. The talk of an attack upon this city has created very little sensation. A few nervous ladies have been rendered unhappy, but the people generally appear to regard the stories of invasion by BEN MCCULLOCH and WISE as entitled to very little attention. It is, however, well to be ready for them. If the rebels have their secret organizations, it would be folly not to guard against a surprise.

If the Secessionists have any common sense left,

[Continued on Eighth Page.]

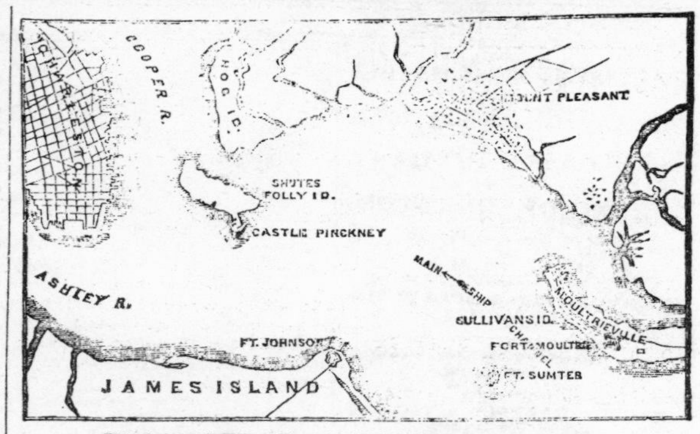

THE FORTS IN CHARLESTON HARBOR.

The above map represents the relative positions of the several forts in Charleston harbor. The one which we give below represents the means of approach to the harbor, and indicates the points from which the most formidable resistance may be expected:

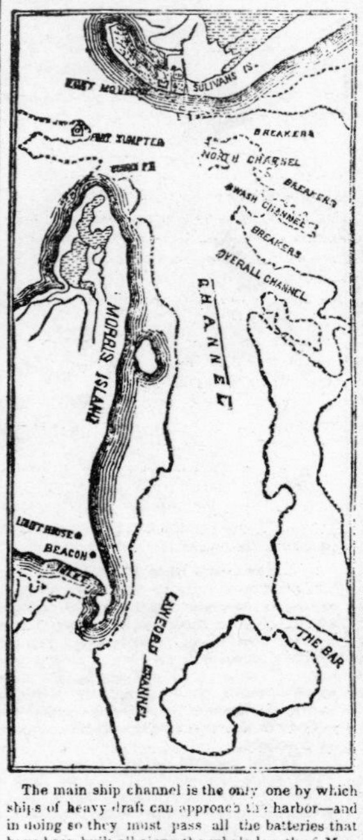

The main ship channel is the only one by which ships of heavy draft can approach the harbor—and in doing so they must pass all the batteries that have been built all along the whole length of Morris Island. This was the channel by which the *Star of the West* attempted to enter—though no serious impediment was offered to her progress until she was off *Cummings' Point*, as the batteries on Morris Island were not then completed.

But small boats, tugs, and steamers of light draft can enter the harbor through *North* Channel, *Swash* Channel, or *Overall* Channel, and thus escape the batteries on Morris Island altogether. The only fire they will encounter will be from the land batteries on Cummings' Point, and from Fort Moultrie.

There can now be no doubt that if the destination of the powerful fleet which has left this port within the last few days, is Charleston, a portion of it, at least, will be near Sumpter at the commencement of any attack that may be made upon it. This nearness of aid entirely alters the chances of a reinforcement, as the relieving party will be supported by the force of the powerful battery of the Fort, and the attack upon it will be directed by the necessity of guarding and defending a shore line of at least ten miles, with the numerous creeks and inlets, all of which are gateways to the harbor. Sumpter on the one side and the fleet off the North Channel on the other, will effectually cover any relieving expedition, whether of open boats, tugs, or small vessels, from any maritime attack, and confine all resisting operations to the land batteries. Experience has shown—as in the case of Gen. WILKINSON'S passage down the St. Lawrence during the last war, with five hundred boats, suffering but a trifling loss, in the face of strong shore batteries—that batteries cannot effectually prevent the mere passage of an armament. Still less can this be done when the batteries themselves will be exposed to such a terrific fire as Major ANDERSON can for some hours at least, pour with his whole force upon Moultrie and the battery near Cummings' Point, the only two places from which boats or light draft vessels can be fired upon to any purpose.

But ANDERSON'S fire will not be the only one to which Moultrie may be exposed, as the smaller vessels can take with impunity positions from which shell may be thrown with great effect. No matter how brave or skillful the Southern troops may be, they will be under a fire which will render the entire stoppage of relief to Fort Sumpter nearly impossible.

Two hundred fresh men once in Sumpter would render its provisioning a matter only of time, unless there are means of resistance of which at present we are ignorant.

It is almost impossible to form even a guess as to what may be the ulterior plan for the general and thorough relief of the Fort, as we are in complete ignorance of all the particulars upon which those plans must be based. The sword of the skillful General seeks the crevice of his antagonist's armor, and the distant spectator can rarely perceive it. So in this case we may be certain that the thrust will be made in the right place, and that we cannot now know where that place may be.

Why the Southern Commander, be he JEFFERSON DAVIS or Gen. BEAUREGARD, has delayed pouring on Sumpter his full force, and crushing it beneath an iron hail, if he could; why he has waited until, instead of concentrating his fire in security on one small point, he now has to defend a long, straggling line, from a powerful fleet, it is impossible to tell. The *reason* may have been political; it may have been that there was not the vaunted readiness; it may have been incompetency; and it is not impossible that when the yawning abyss opened before them with all its horror, they may have lacked the insane courage required for the final leap.

But be the motive what it may, there is little doubt that they have lost the golden opportunity, and that the Stars and Stripes will continue to wave over the old fort, unless puerile negotiations should again allow the Confederate force to prepare themselves for the new forces arrayed against them.

The Philadelphia Inquirer.

ESTABLISHED 1829. PHILADELPHIA, SATURDAY, APRIL 13, 1861. PRICE TWO CENTS.

WAR! WAR!! WAR!!!

HIGHLY IMPORTANT FROM CHARLESTON.

Correspondence between General Beauregard and the Confederate Secretary of War.

The Rebels Open Fire on Fort Sumter.

MAJOR ANDERSON REPLIES.

Two Guns Silenced in Sumter.

AN EMBRASURE MADE IN THE WALLS OF SUMTER.

Only Two Rebels Reported Wounded.

The Firing Ceased for the Night to Commence in the Morning

THREE STEAMERS OFF THE BAR.

Surveillance of the Telegraph Lines.

CHARLESTON, April 12.—The fight has commenced. This is all I can say at present.

SECOND DESPATCH.

CHARLESTON, April 12.—The ball has been opened at last, and war is inaugurated.

The batteries on Sullivan's Island, Morris Island, and other points, opened on Fort Sumter at 4 o'clock this morning.

Fort Sumter returned the fire, and a brisk cannonading has been kept up.

No information has been received from the seaward yet.

The militia are under arms, and the whole of our population are on the streets.

Every available space facing the harbor is filled with anxious spectators.

Correspondence between the Southern Authorities Preceding the Hostilities.

CHARLESTON, April 12.—The following is the telegraphic correspondence which took place between the War Department of the Confederate Government and Gen. BEAUREGARD, immediately preceding the commencement of the hostilities. The correspondence grew out of the formal notification of the United States Government, disclosed in Gen. BEAUREGARD's first despatch:—

[No. 1.]

CHARLESTON, April 8.—To Hon. L. P. WALKER, Secretary of War:—An authorized messenger from LINCOLN has just informed Gov. PICKENS and myself that provisions will be sent to Fort Sumter, peaceably if possible, otherwise by force.

(Signed) G. T. BEAUREGARD.

[No. 2.]

MONTGOMERY, April 10.—Gen. G. T. BEAUREGARD, Charleston:—If you have no doubt of the authorized character of the agent who communicated to you the intention of the Washington Government to supply Fort Sumter by force, you will at once demand its evacuation; if this is refused, proceed in such manner as you may determine, to reduce it. Answer.

(Signed,) L. P. WALKER, Secretary of War.

[No. 3.]

CHARLESTON, April 10.—To L. P. WALKER, Secretary of War:—The demand will be made to-morrow at 12 o'clock.

(Signed) G. T. BEAUREGARD.

[No. 4.]

MONTGOMERY, April 10.—Gen. BEAUREGARD—Charleston:—Unless there are especial reasons connected with your own condition, it is considered proper that you should make the demand at an earlier hour.

(Signed) L. P. WALKER, Secretary of War.

[No. 5.]

CHARLESTON, April 10.—To L. P. WALKER, Secretary of War, Montgomery:—The reasons are special for twelve o'clock.

(Signed) G. T. BEAUREGARD.

[No. 6.]

CHARLESTON, April 10.—To L. P. WALKER, Secretary of War:—The demand was sent at two o'clock. Allowed till six to answer.

(Signed) G. T. BEAUREGARD.

[No. 7.]

MONTGOMERY, April 11th.—Gen. BEAUREGARD, Charleston.—Telegraph the reply of ANDERSON.

(Signed) L. P. WALKER, Secretary of War.

[No. 8.]

Reply of Anderson.

CHARLESTON, April 11.—L. P. WALKER, Secretary of War.—Major ANDERSON replies as follows:—

"I have the honor to acknowledge the receipt of your communication demanding the evacuation of this fort, and to say in reply thereto, that it is a demand with which I regret that my sense of honor, and of my obligation to my Government, prevent my compliance."

He adds, verbally, "I will await the first shot, and if you do not batter us to pieces, we will be starved out in a few days." Answer.

(Signed) G. T. BEAUREGARD.

[No. 9.]

MONTGOMERY, April 11.—To Gen. BEAUREGARD, Charleston:—We do not desire needlessly to bombard Fort Sumter. If Major ANDERSON will state the time at which, as indicated by him, he will evacuate, and agree that, in the meantime, he will not use his guns against us unless ours should be employed against Sumter, you are authorized thus to avoid the effusion of blood. If this, or its equivalent, be refused, reduce the fort as your judgment decides to be most practicable.

(Signed,) L. P. WALKER, Sec. of War.

[No. 10.]

CHARLESTON, April 12.—To L. P. WALKER, Secretary of War:—He would not consent. I write to-day. G. T. BEAUREGARD.

The Plan of the United States Government Disclosed by Intercepted Despatches!

CHARLESTON, April 12.—Intercepted despatches disclose the fact that Mr. FOX, who had been allowed to visit Major ANDERSON, on the pledge that his purpose was pacific, employed his opportunity to devise a plan for supplying the fort by force, and that this plan had been adopted by the Government at Washington, and was in progress of execution.

[THIRD DESPATCH.]

Two of Fort Sumter's Guns Silenced.

REPORTED BREACH IN THE SOUTHEAST WALL.

Anderson to Surrender on the Exhaustion of his Supplies, if not Reinforced.

NO LOSS ON THE SOUTHERN SIDE.

The Pawnee, Harriet Lane, and Another Steamer Off the Bar.

CHARLESTON, April 12th.—(*Received in Philadelphia 9 30 P. M.*)—The firing has continued all day, without intermission.

Two of Fort Sumter's guns have been silenced.

It is reported that a breach has been made in the southeast wall of Fort Sumter.

The answer made by Major ANDERSON to Gen. BEAUREGARD's demand was, that he would surrender when his supplies were exhausted, if he was not reinforced.

Not a casualty has as yet happened to any of our men, (the Carolinians).

Of the nineteen batteries in position, only seven have opened on Fort Sumter. The remainder are held in reserve for the expected fleet.

Two thousand men reached the city this morning, and embarked for Morris Island and other points in that neighborhood.

FOURTH DESPATCH.

Three War Vessels Reported Outside.

CHARLESTON, April 12th.—(*Received in Philadelphia at 10 30 P. M.*)—The bombardment of Fort Sumter still continues.

The Floating battery and Stephens' battery are operating freely.

Fort Sumter continues to return the fire.

It is reported that three war vessels are outside the bar.

FIFTH DESPATCH.

CHARLESTON, April 12.—The firing has ceased for the night, to be renewed at daylight in the morning, unless an attempt be made in the meantime to reinforce Fort Sumter, to repel which ample arrangements have been made.

The Seceders worked their guns admirably well.

Only two were wounded during the day.

The *Pawnee*, *Harriet Lane*, and a third war steamer, are reported off the bar.

Fresh troops are arriving here by every train.

SIXTH DESPATCH.

CHARLESTON, April 12th—(*Received in Philadelphia April 13th. 2 o'clock, A. M.*)—The bombardment of Fort Sumter is still going on, every twenty minutes, from the mortars.

It is supposed that Major ANDERSON is resting his men for the night, as he has ceased to reply.

Three vessels of war are reported outside, but they cannot get in. The sea is rough.

Nobody on the Carolina side has been hurt by this day's engagement.

The floating battery works well.

Every inlet is well guarded.

There are lively times on the Palmetto coast.

THE LATEST.

SEVENTH DESPATCH.

CHARLESTON, April 13—12 30 A. M.—It will be utterly impossible to reinforce Fort Sumter to-night, as a storm is raging, and the sea is very rough.

The mortar batteries will be kept playing on Fort Sumter all night.

FURTHER FROM CHARLESTON.

CHANCES OF ANDERSON.

TWO GUNS OF SUMTER SILENCED.

SURVEILLANCE OF THE TELEGRAPH.

Special Despatch to the Inquirer.

BALTIMORE, April 12, P. M.—Private despatches from good authorities have been received here from Charleston.

It is positively asserted that fighting commenced about daylight.

The South Carolina batteries first opened fire from Cummings' Point, about three-fourths of a mile distant.

At last accounts an opening had been made in the weakest part of Fort Sumter. The walls had yielded to the heavy cannonading.

It has been impossible to obtain any information relative to the killed or wounded. Orders have been forwarded to Baltimore for large supplies of chloroform.

The firing during the day has evidently been very brisk from both sides.

Two of the guns of Fort Sumter have been silenced, but there is reason to believe that the garrison has escaped thus far with very little or no loss of life.

The telegraph line at Charleston is under the surveillance of the leaders of the Secession party, and it is therefore impossible to obtain accurate statement of the loss of the Rebels.

The excitement here is terrible. W.

Effect of the War News at Baltimore.

BALTIMORE, April 12.—Charleston news, which was not generally promulgated here until after night, has produced sensation.

Though there is a great diversity of news, the general expressions of the people, while regretting the prospect of bloodshed, are on the side of the Government.

Mrs. Anderson at New York.

NEW YORK, April 12, P. M.—Mrs. ANDERSON, the wife of the gallant commander of Fort Sumter, is now in this city, at the Brevoort House.—She is visited by numbers of persons, who desire to add their tribute of praise to the encomiums showered upon Major ANDERSON, and to testify their appreciation of the painful position in which Mrs. A. is now placed.

CHARLESTON HARBOR, ITS FORTIFICATIONS AND APPROACHES.

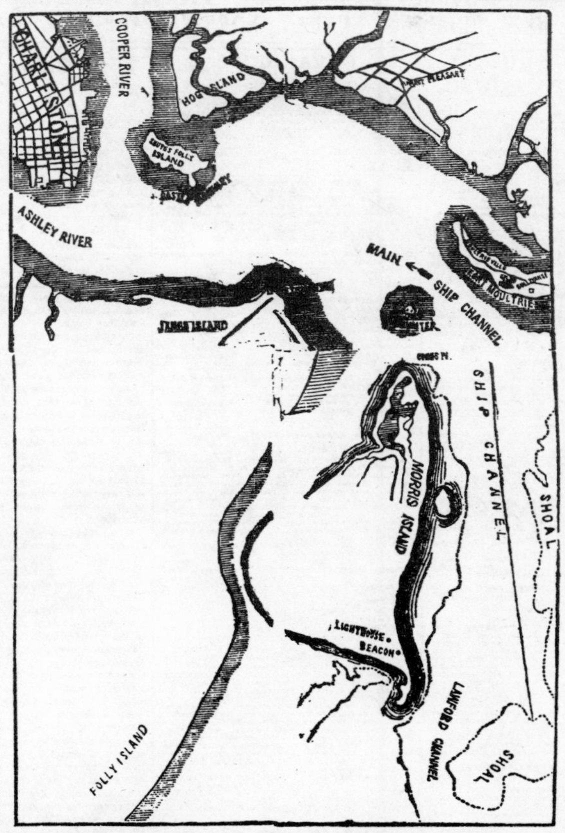

THE SEAT OF WAR.

POSITION OF THE FORTS.

THEIR CONSTRUCTION AND EQUIPMENT.

The Contending Forces.

As all eyes are now turned towards Charleston and the exciting scenes which are doubtless there transpiring, we present our readers, this morning, a map of the harbor, showing its defences and adjacent points of interest, coupled with a description of the various fortifications and military matters generally. The centre of attraction is

Fort Sumter,

Which is described as a modern truncated pentagonal (that is, of five sides), which is erected on an artificial island some 3 miles from the city. This island is composed of chips from Northern granite quarries, and of course is as firm as the rock itself. No better foundation could be formed. Its cost, and the fort as erected upon it, was a million of dollars. The walls are of solid brick and concrete masonry, built close to the edge of the water. They are sixty feet high, and from eight to twelve feet in thickness. It is pierced for three tiers of guns on the north, east and west exterior sides. Its weakest point is on the south side, of which the masonry is not only weaker than that of the other sides, but it is not protected by any flank fire, which would sweep the wharf. Once landed, an entrance may, at the present state of the construction, be easily made; for the blinds of the lower embrasures, though six inches in thickness, may yet be easily blown away, and even if this was impossible, scaling ladders can reach those of the second tier, which are not protected in this manner. The work is designed for an armament of one hundred and forty pieces of ordnance of all calibres. Two tiers of the guns are under bomb-proof casemates, and the third or upper tier open, or, in military parlance, *en barbette*: the lower tier for forty-two pounder paixhan guns; the second tier for eight and ten-inch columbiads, for throwing solid or hollow shot, and the upper tier for mortars and twenty-four pound guns. The full armament of the fort, however, had not arrived there when Major ANDERSON took possession; but since its occupancy by the present garrison no efforts have been spared to place the work in an efficient state of defence by mounting all the available guns and placing them in salient points.

Armament.

As we have remarked, the full armament of the fort is not in position, as only seventy-five of the one hundred and forty guns required for it are now mounted. Eleven paixhan guns are among that number, nine of them commanding Fort Moultrie, which is within easy range, and the other two pointing towards Castle Pinckney, which is well out of range. Some of the columbiads, the most effective weapon for siege or defensive operations, are not mounted. Four of the thirty-two pounder barbette guns are on pivot carriages, which gives them the entire range of the horizon, and others have a horizontal sweep of fire of 180 degrees. In addition to these weightier preparations for defence, the walls are pierced everywhere for muskets, of which there are endless numbers ready and loaded.

Ammunition.

The magazine contains seven hundred barrels of gunpowder and an ample supply of shot, powder and shells for one year's siege, and a large amount of miscellaneous artillery stores. The garrison is amply supplied with water from artificial wells, which are supplied by the frequent showers of rain. In a defensive strategical point of view, Fort Sumter radiates its fire through all the channels from the sea approach to Charleston, and has a full sweep of range in its rear or city side. The fort is sufficiently out of range from a land artillery attack, so that all apprehensions for breaching it from that source may be put at rest, unless by guns of superior calibre. The maximum range of the guns from Sumter is three miles; but for accurate firing, sufficient to hull a vessel, the distance would require to be reduced one half of that figure. The war garrison of the fort is six hundred men, but only seventy-nine of that number are within its walls, with the laborers—109 all told.

Having disposed of the only point occupied by the forces of the Federal Government, we now turn our attention to the various fortifications and batteries in the possession of the army of the Secessionists.

Castle Pinckney.

Castle Pinckney is a small work, situated on the southern extremity of "Shute's Folly Island," between Hog and Folly channels. Though in itself not a very considerable military work, yet, from its position, commanding as it does the whole line of the eastern wharves, it becomes of the utmost importance for it to be held by the State authorities. It is, in fact, the immediate outwork of the city, useful to annoy an invading fleet should it pass the outer forts, and to render their landing very difficult, if not impossible. In its plan it presents to the south a semicircular face; the eastern and western faces are formed by the line of ramparts following the direction of the tangent to the circular arc at the extremity, and for a distance of twenty yards; the northern side is plain; at both the northeastern and northwestern angles are semicircular bastions, the outer extremities of the arcs being tangent respectively to the eastern and western sides of the fort. There are two rows of guns—the lower being in casemates (bomb-proof), the embrasures for which are about seven feet above low water mark, and the upper being *en barbette*. The height of the rampart is twenty, and the width thirty-two feet. The width of the outer wall and of the parapet is six feet; the depth of the casemates is twenty feet, height ten; the diameter (east and west) of the castle is one hundred and seventy feet. The entrance is on the northern side, on either side of which are the officers' and privates' quarters, messroom, &c. The ascent to the barbette is made on the northeastern and northwestern corners of the *terre pereplein*. In the centre of the latter is the furnace for heating shot.—Around the foot of the scarp wall is a breakwater, about twelve feet in width, horizontally, which has its western side extended in a tangent direction to the south, to form the landing. The landing is protected by the fire of several guns sweeping its length. The armament of this castle consists of about twenty-five pieces, 24 and 32-pounders, a few sea-coast mortars and six columbiads—the latter not being mounted. In the magazine is a sufficiency of ammunition, including shot and loaded shell. This work has been of late put in as thorough repair as possible. Owing to the want of ventilation and the reverberation of the sound in an engagement, the lower tier of guns would soon become useless, and the occupants would be obliged to resort entirely to the barbette guns and mortars. In this case the exposure to the enemies' direct shot would not be great, for the perapet is higher than the hulks of most ships, and much higher than the adjoining shore.

Fort Johnson.

The present Fort Johnson is simply a huge sand battery erected on the site of old Fort Johnson, of Revolutionary memory. It is one and one-fourth miles from Fort Sumter, and at present is armed with four heavy guns, manned by two companies of regular artillery. The position of this old fort, which is of the utmost importance as a connecting point in the defence of the harbor, has been considered by the highest military authority as the key to all the defensive works in the harbor. Against the attack of forces by land, or a boat attack by the Stono river, it must be considered an essential element of defence.

Fort Moultrie.

Fort Moultrie is one of the sentinels that guard the principal entrance to Charleston harbor. It is opposite to and distant from Fort Sumter about one and a half miles. It is, more properly speaking, a huge water battery, without any guns under cover. Its armament consists of eleven guns of heavy calibre and several mortars. The outer and inner walls are of brick, capped with stone and filled with earth, making a solid wall fifteen or sixteen feet in thickness. This work has been much strengthened recently. It is now in command of Major RIPLEY, formerly of the United States Army, who has under his command several hundred experienced artillerists.

Stono Inlet.

Stono Point is a portion of Morris Island, facing the sea coast. Stono Inlet is about two leagues from the south channel of Charleston. Between them lie two islands, viz:—Morris Island, on which the lighthouse stands, and Coffin Island. In Stono Inlet there are nine or ten feet of water at low tide, but it was not much frequented until Charleston was blockaded in 1775, when it was visited by British vessels. In a strategical point of view, the landing of United States troops at Stono Point would appear to be for the purpose of getting in the rear of the Morris Island batteries, which now guard the sea approaches to Charleston. On Morris Island the Confederate States forces are pretty numerous, and if an attempt to land troops is made by the United States forces the conflict will be short and bloody. At our last accounts in regard to Stono Point, Gen. BEAUREGARD had ordered an immense battery to be erected at the very place where it is alleged the United States troops will attempt to land. A subsequent report stated that several large guns were in transitu from Castle Pinckney to that Point.

Cummings' Point Iron Battery.

The nearest land to Fort Sumter is Cummings' Point. On this point is erected the celebrated railroad iron battery. It consists of a heavy framework of yellow pine logs. The roof is of the same material, over which dovetailed bars of railroad iron of the T pattern are laid from top to bottom—all of which is riveted down in the most secure manner. On the front it presents an angle of about thirty degrees. There are three portholes, which open and close with iron shutters of the heaviest description. When open, the muzzles of the columbiads fill up the space completely. The recoil of the gun enables the shutters to be closed instantly. It is asserted on high military authority, that this inclined plane will effectually resist guns of the heaviest calibre—first, because no shot can strike it except at an obtuse angle, which would cause the ball to glance: second, because its power of resistance is sufficient to withstand the fall of the heaviest shells. The columbiad guns, with which this novel battery is equipped, bear on the south wall of Sumter, the line of fire being at an angle of about thirty-five degrees. This is not, of course, considered favorable for breaching; but owing to the fact that the wall is loop-holed for musketry throughout its entire length, which, of course, weakens it a great deal, the effect of shot upon it would, we think, even at the distance of 1150 yards, effect a breach within a reasonable time. The work is in charge of several companies of the regular army of the Confederate States. If employed to reduce Fort Sumter, this battery will prove quite formidable.

The Iron Floating Battery.

This is a novel war machine designed for harbor operations, and is at present anchored near Castle Pinckney. It is constructed of palmetto logs, sheathed with plate iron, and is supposed to be impregnable against shot. It is embrasured for and mounts four guns of heavy calibre. It requires sixty men to operate it. The first impression on seeing this machine is that of immense solidity. The outer or gun side is covered with six plates of iron—two of them of the T railroad pattern, placed horizontally, and the other four bolted one over the other, in the strongest manner, and running vertically. The wall of the gun side is full four feet thick, constructed of that peculiar palmetto wood so full of fibrous material that sixty-four pounders cannot pierce it. The main deck is wide and roomy. In nineteen open chambers, on the port side of the deck, we found a profusion of shot—thirty four pounders—while just beyond them is an immense pile of sand bags, which protect an overhanging roof, under which is to be placed the hospital. This also protects the magazines (three in number), under which is the hold proper. There are six entrances to the hold, which will contain, if necessary, over three hundred men. When moored it is kept in place by four heavy wedges, driven down by a species of ram, which will hold it fast, and prevent any swaying around by the tide.

Other Works.

There are other works at Hadrill's Point, Mount Pleasant, Stono, Morris Island, and fronting the entrance of Charleston harbor, which are constructed of palmetto logs and sand. They are all fully manned for action with large garrisons and guns of heavy calibre.

The Exact Distances of the Forts.

Fort Sumter is three and three-eighths miles from Charleston, one and one-eighth mile from Fort Moultrie, three fourths of a mile from Cummings' Point, one and three-eighths of a mile from Fort Johnson, and two and five-eighths miles from Castle Pinckney. The city of Charleston is entirely out of the range of the guns of Fort Sumter.

Approaches to the Harbor.

The main ship channel is the only one by which ships of heavy draft can approach the harbor—and in doing so they must pass all the batteries that have been built all along the whole length of Morris Island. This was the channel by which the *Star of the West* attempted to enter—though no serious impediment was offered to her progress until she was off *Cummings' Point*, as the batteries on Morris Island were not then completed. But small boats, tugs and steamers of light draft can enter the harbor through the *North* channel, *Swash* channel or *Overall* channel, and thus escape the batteries on Morris island altogether. The only fire they will encounter will be from the land batteries on Cummings' Point and from Fort Moultrie.

The Rebel Army

Is under the command of Brigadier-General BEAUREGARD, whose staff contains, among others, Colonels GIST, HATCH, PRYOR, WIGFALL, GIBBES, Major WHITNEY and Captain BOGGS.

The Artillery Regiment numbers 270 men, and is commanded by Col. LOCK.

The Infantry Regiment is a full one, under the command of Col. CUNNINGHAM, and is 825 strong.

The Riflemen amount to 787 men, divided into a regiment and a battalion, commanded respectively by Col. PETTIGREW and Major JOHNSON.

The dragoons number 360, divided into six companies; it does not appear that any commander has yet been designated.

There are also a number of other companies not attached to any regiment comprising artillery, infantry and riflemen—in all 1190 men, and a country regiment numbering 300 is not included in what has been named—making, in the aggregate, a force of nearly 1000 men, with which to assault and capture the stronghold of Sumter, defended by about 100, who have not yet "bowed the knee to Baal."

The Federal Expedition.

The expedition from New York, already described, was ordered to rendezvous off the Charleston bar. Commander PORTER, a son of Commodore PORTER, in command of the *Powhatan*, has full charge of the naval expedition, and has instructions from the President and General SCOTT as to the course he shall pursue. The military portion of the expedition, and the forces when landed, will be under the command of Lieutenant-Colonel HARVEY BROWN, who has been stationed for two years past at Old Point Comfort—a most gallant and discreet officer.

FROM WASHINGTON.

WASHINGTON, April 12.

Special Despatch to the Inquirer.

The Metropolis.

Plans for the seizure of Washington by the Secessionists have been received by the Administration, through the agency of adroit detectives, and Col. SMITH, who is in command of this military district, has taken every precaution to guard against the proposed *coup d'etat*. Dragoon picket guards have been posted on all the thoroughfares leading to the metropolis, and there is, at any moment, a good force of cavalry ready to spring into their saddles and to move off at a moment's warning. The volunteer companies are beginning to see the propriety of taking the oath, of which a copy was sent yesterday, and over eight hundred men have been "mustered-in" for three months. The idea of being "invincible in war, invisible in peace," does not meet with much favor, and those who hesitate about taking the oath of allegiance are endeavoring to get off by saying that they don't wish to leave the District. Yet some of the "National Rifles are talking about joining the Alexandria Companies!"

One—Two—Three—Zouave.

Mr. ELLSWORTH, who commanded the Chicago Zouaves, came here with the intention of establishing a "Bureau of Militia" in the War Department, and obtained a commission of second Lieutenant of Cavalry in order to give him military position. But Adjutant-General THOMAS did not, probably, appreciate the merits of the Zouave movements, or choose to be thus relieved of a portion of his duties, as the President recalled the request for establishing the proposed bureau. It will now be seen whether the Zouave will join his regiment on the frontier, and learn his duty as a soldier, or whether he will leave the service and promulgate, privately, his peculiar gymnastic drill.

Postal.

Postmaster JONES gives notice that on and after Monday next, the 15th instant, the morning train for Baltimore and the East will leave Washington at 4 30 A. M., instead of 6 20 A. M., and the afternoon train at 2 45 P. M., instead of 3 10 P. M. In view of this change, persons wishing to send letters by the afternoon train must deposit their letters in the office here not later than half-past one o'clock P. M., which is a very inconvenient hour for newspaper correspondents. Why the mail should be hurried away from here at this early hour is not stated.

By the morning train, leaving here at 4 30, a through connection is secured with the East, leaving Baltimore at 6 30 and Philadelphia at 11 A. M.) at New York, with the Sound steamers for Boston and New England generally. The arrival at New York will be at 3 30, some three hours in advance of the present time.

For the West, this train will connect (at Relay) with the early through fast train from Baltimore, reaching Columbus, Cincinnati, Dayton, Indianapolis, &c., fully twelve hours in advance of the present morning run, closely connecting for Chicago at Indianapolis.

City Post Office.

The quarterly returns of Postmaster JONES show that from January 1st to March 31st, no less than 633,118 free letters passed through the Washington City office. Stamps sold amounted to $9470 62; newspapers $755 70; unpaid letters $1495 02, and after paying salaries and all contingencies, the efficient officer pays over to the Government a balance of $2030.

City Republicans.

The Washington Wide-Awakes deny that their numbers have been increased since the election, which may be true, but the Republican Association received eighty-six new members in November, thirty-three in December, twenty in January, twenty-one in February, and sixteen in March, besides many others voted in, but who have not paid their initiation fees.

Intense Excitement.

Although it is a rainy night, yet crowds of persons are hovering around the hotels and telegraph offices. They are much excited, and all anxious to hear the news from Charleston.

The President to Gov. Pickens.

Friends of the Administration state that the President has notified Governor PICKENS that an unarmed vessel would be sent with supplies for the relief of Major ANDERSON and his command, and that this was a pretext for the commencement of hostilities.

Cabinet Meeting.

The Cabinet is in session, and vigorous measures are expected to be adopted.

Instructions to the Fleet.

It is reported that the war fleet, which recently sailed under sealed orders, has received instructions to throw shells into the city of Charleston, in case of hostilities.—[This is very doubtful.—ED.]

General Scott.

General SCOTT is holding a consultation with the officers now in the city.

For the Defence of the City.

The garrison of the city is now under arms; various parties of Dragoons are patrolling.

Council of Five.

A council of five officers have been appointed, whose duty it is to direct the movements of the military in the city.

National Volunteers.

The National Volunteers have been hastily called together this evening, and held a prolonged session. It is not known what action was taken.

The Boston Appointments Unsatisfactory.

The appointments which have been made for Boston are considered as not very satisfactory to the conservative portion of the Republican party, especially the removal of FLETCHER WEBSTER, Esq., as Surveyor of the Port, to make way for Doctor PHELPS.

Federal Appointments.

WASHINGTON, April 12.—The President has made the following Massachusetts appointments:

CHARLES A. PHELPS, Surveyor of the port of Boston, in place of FLETCHER WEBSTER, who was removed at the earnest request of the Massachusetts Congressional delegation.

EUGENE L. NORTON, Navy Agent at Boston.

RICHARD H. DANA, District Attorney, and JOHN S. KEIS, United States Marshal.

JOHN A. GOODWIN, Postmaster at Lowell.

C. C. P. BALDWIN has been appointed Marshal, and GEORGE HOWE District Attorney for Vermont.

JAMES C. AIKEN, Marshal, and EDWARD G. BRADFORD, Attorney for Delaware.

LANSING VANCE has been appointed Postmaster at Norristown, Pa.

HARMION BENNETT, Postmaster at Norwich, N. Y.

The Virginia Commissioners.

WASHINGTON, April 12.—Messrs. PRESTON, STUART and RANDOLPH, the Commissioners appointed by the Virginia State Convention to ascertain the purposes of the Administration, arrived here this morning.

During the afternoon they visited the President, but not in their official character, and were received by him directly after the Cabinet meeting adjourned.

Opening of the New York Canals.

SYRACUSE, April 12.—The Canal Commissioners have resolved to open all the canals in the State on the 1st of May.

The Daily Picayune.

VOLUME XXV. NEW ORLEANS, SUNDAY MORNING, APRIL 14, 1861. NUMBER 69.

The Daily Picayune.

THE DESIGN.

While rumors of the design of Lincoln's Administration to make a demonstration at Fort Sumter were most prevalent at the North, the journals most in his interest were ardently persuaded that the experiment would not be worth the cost. The fort was so fully beleagured that open attempts to relieve it would require immense armaments, and involve immense risks, for which its permanent occupation would not pay. They accordingly speculated upon the preparations in that quarter either as military feints intended to cover a more feasible attack at a more favorable point, or as a mere incident in a wide and comprehensive plan of hostility against the Southern States.

They suggested that Fort Sumter was to be threatened in order to keep the attention of the Montgomery Government fully occupied there, and its best forces and officers and a large part of its military means gathered for an anticipated conflict on that point, while the bulk of the Federal armaments were directed against less guarded places—to Fort Pickens, the mouth of the Mississippi, or the Rio Grande. The repeated rumors that a large fleet was concentrating upon Charleston, was regarded as part of the stratagem to deceive the Confederate Government as to the true point aimed at, which would be received and seized by surprise.

The suggestion gives credit, which is well merited by the Lincoln Cabinet, for meditating and preparing hostile expeditions in the face of its own professed desires and ostentatiously repeated pledges of peace. It would have redeemed them from the imputations of a wanton sacrifice of treasure and life without definite object, the throwing away of the peace of the country on a futile and isolated and desperate enterprise. But it substitutes for the charge of a more brutal and bloody caprice that of a perfidious scheme for a grand, organized enterprise for reconquering the States which have declared their independence.

As a serious attempt to reinforce Fort Sumter, the project was simply a piece of consummate weakness; as part of a general scheme of coercion, a subsidiary enterprise to cover more important expeditions, a feint or a snare, it rises to the higher crime of being the inauguration of a wanton war against a self governing community—a war which is treason against the fundamental truths of Civil Liberty, as expounded by American examples, and established by American blood, and which can effect nothing in the effort to overthrow or destroy them; but inflict calamity on both parties, and wrong, reproach and loss upon the common cause of civilization and humanity everywhere.

The Lincoln Cabinet mistakes if it supposes that a movement on Fort Sumter will help a movement on Fort Pickens, by lessening the vigilance and activity with which the latter will be watched, or the number of troops and quantity of munitions which the Confederate States can bring to bear there. There is no lack of soldiery anywhere on the Southern borders, nor of arms or ammunition for purposes of defence, and the spirit of the people runs high and ready for any emergency. It needs only the discipline and direction for which dependence must be had on the energy of those who have been called to the control of public affairs in this emergency; and it will be found ample for the maintenance of sovereign jurisdiction over every part of our territory, and the repulsion of invasion from whatsoever quarter it may approach. The hearts and the arms of the people are ready and sufficient to defend themselves and their country, their liberties and their territory.

☞ There has been a great point in the Northern Republican papers of the lack of confidence in the people shown by the Southern secessionists. They are just now exulting that Mr. Lincoln has got past the necessity of asking the people for their judgment on his war policy, and can go ahead for some time without them. The rejoicing is variously expressed to the effect that, "*the spring elections being over, and the loan effected,*" a decisive policy is to be adopted. The President has just got beyond the check of a popular election, and has raised the money, and he is not to care what the people or the money lenders may think, and *therefore* can go ahead in a decisive policy. He will soon be able to learn what will come of it.

The U. S. War Fleet.—The New York Journal of Commerce, of the 8th inst., says:

The alleged lists of officers of the home fleet, published by a morning paper yesterday, were cut from the Navy Register for 1861, which went to press last November. Of course they are filled with errors.

[illegible]	[illegible]	[illegible]	[illegible]
Flag ship, steam frigate Minnesota	400	[illegible]	[illegible]
Steam frigate Powhatan	500	[illegible]	2,415
Steam corvette Brooklyn	325	14	2,070
Sailing frigate Sabine	[illegible]	[illegible]	1,726
Sailing sloop St. Louis	300	20	700
Sailing sloop Cumberland	[illegible]	[illegible]	1,726
Steamer Water Witch	68	2	378
Steamer Crusader	110	10	549
Steamer Mohawk	110	6	464
Steamer Wyandotte	100	4	[illegible]
Steamer Pocahontas	95	4	[illegible]
Steam gunboat Pawnee	[illegible]	4	1,289

The Macedonian is not included, because she is in the Gulf of Mexico; the Falmouth and Supply, because they are mere transport storeships.

Annexed is the latest report from these ships:

Minnesota—Almost ready for commission at Boston.
Water Witch—Went in commission at Philadelphia Friday.
Powhatan—Sailed from New York harbor yesterday.
Brooklyn—Off Fort Pickens March 22.
Crusader—Sailed from New York March 18.
Cumberland—Flagship, Norfolk, March 25.
Falmouth—Moored at Aspinwall.
Mohawk—Sailed from New York March 16.
Macedonian—Vera Cruz, March 25.
Pawnee—At Washington, March 27.
Pocahontas—Norfolk, March 26.
Sabine—Off Pensacola March 23.
St. Louis—Off Fort Pickens March 23.
Supply—New York, for Gulf, March 2?.
Wyandotte—Off Fort Pickens March 2?.

Syria.—The Syrian correspondent of the London News writes that the proposed plan of the Porte for the future government of Syria has become very generally known there. To Fuad Pacha and all the advanced party of the Turks it is a death blow, but it has raised the hopes of the fanatical party, and has caused no small rejoicing among the Druses. The Christian population are preparing as one man to leave the country, and nearly all the European merchants say that if it is carried out, they will liquidate their affairs and abandon Syria. The writer intimates pretty broadly that Louis Napoleon is supporting the Sultan's proposed policy for the purpose of keeping the Syrian wound green.

Death of a Veteran Journalist.

The telegraph Friday brought us the painful announcement that Joseph Tinker Buckingham, the oldest American journalist of his day, died, the day before, at his residence, in Cambridge, Massachusetts. Few men have led a busier and more active life than this veteran of the press. His name has been connected with many literary and journalistic enterprises, one of which last, founded by him in 1824, and conducted by him until 1848—we mean the Boston Courier—remains a creditable monument to his enterprise and his usefulness.

The family name of the subject of our sketch was Tinker. His father, Nehemiah Tinker, of Windham, Ct., (says the New American Encyclopædia,) exhausted his whole property in contributing to the support of the American army, during the Revolutionary war, and died in 1783, leaving a family without any means of support. Joseph was apprenticed to a farmer, with whom he remained for several years. While in this family, he showed some desire for knowledge, and made himself acquainted with the rudiments of an English education. At the age of sixteen, he entered a printing office in Walpole, N. H., in which was printed the "Farmer's Museum." Here he became acquainted with the elements of the profession in which, in after years, he gained distinction. After remaining at Walpole a few months, he entered the office of the Greenfield (Mass) Gazette, where he staid until 1800, and then removed to Boston. In 1803, we find him officiating as prompter in a company of comedians, who played during the summer months, in Providence, R. I., and Salem, Mass. In 1806, having changed his father's name for his mother's, Buckingham commenced life for himself, by the publication of the Polyanthus, a monthly magazine, which, after a year's existence, was discontinued, and was not resumed until 1812. In 1809, Mr. Buckingham published, for six months, the Ordeal, a weekly magazine. He always had a great partiality for the drama, and in these two periodicals there was much good theatrical criticism, as there was in other journals published by him.

In the year 1817 Mr. Buckingham, assisted by Samuel L. Knapp, an eminent lawyer and facile writer of that day, commenced the publication of a paper in Boston, which will be remembered by many as one of the most witty, sparkling and clever weekly newspapers ever published in this country. This was the "New England Galaxy," which continued in his possession until 1828, when he sold it. It did not long survive his separation from its conduct. In 1831, in connection with his son, he commenced the publication of the "New England Magazine," which was continued, under his care, until 1834. Among the contributors to this monthly were writers who have since attained great literary eminence. In 1824, Mr. Buckingham, as we have already stated, founded the Boston Courier, which is yet in a flourishing and influential condition. It was the last publication with which Mr. B. was ever connected, though since his retirement from active life he has been a frequent contributor to the public press in the way of personal and local reminiscences of Boston and its history. He has given to the world two very readable autobiographical works, one called "Specimens of newspaper literature, with personal memoirs, anecdotes and reminiscences," in 2 vols., and the other, "Personal Memoirs and Recollections of Editorial Life," also in 2 vols.

Mr. Buckingham, in all the varied relations of life, alike public and private, was exemplary; and his society was ever eagerly sought for by the literary man, and those who were curious in historical research. He had a wonderful memory, was very observant, conversed well, was full of anecdote, possessed a fund of humor, not unmingled with playful satire, and was in all respects a remarkable person. His loss will be deeply felt throughout a circle much wider than that which embraces his numerous family connections.

Mr. Buckingham was several times a member of the House of Representatives, in the Legislature of Massachusetts, and for two terms sat in the Senate of that State.

A Fashionable Reform.—Willis, of the Home Journal, announces a reform in fashionable circles in the matter of dinner and other party invitations. Heretofore an invitation to the head of the family has been considered general, but it is now fashionable usage to ask any one of a family without the rest—even a wife without her husband.

Funeral of Mrs. Ellen R. Johnson.—The Nashville Patriot, of the 10th inst., says that the remains of the late Mrs. Wm. A. Johnson, having been brought from New Orleans to that place, for interment, the last sad obsequies were performed on the 9th. An unusually large number of citizens were in attendance, manifesting their esteem for the worthy dead, and their respect for the honored husband and relations. The death of Mrs. J. (says the Patriot) was indeed a mournful bereavement to those to whom she was nearest and dearest, and makes a void in society which cannot easily be filled. Rest thee, sweet saint! A purer spirit never ascended to the home of the blest.

The Zouaves off to Pensacola.—The Mobile Advertiser, announcing the departure of "our" Zouaves for Pensacola, Thursday morning, says:

As we came abreast of the boat, they were waltzing vigorously on the hurricane deck; as we stopped to copy the boat's manifest, they were employed, still more vigorously, in giving three cheers apiece for themselves, their country, the service, and a variety of other things; and by the time we got through, the Marseillaise was in full blast, from a hundred throats.

And thus our brave soldiers moved off, to almost certain combat, with that alacrity and cheerfulness which becomes the patriot, when the honor and liberty of his country are threatened.

Spain.—The spirit of religious freedom is showing itself in the Spanish Legislature. On the 8th ultimo a deputy, M. Olozoga, attacked the revolutionary policy of the old governments in Italy, and declared that, in his opinion, the temporal power of the Papacy is doomed to fall. He maintained that the Italians are right in seeking national unity, and argued that the Spanish government has no reasonable pretext for opposing them. The Minister for Foreign Affairs replied at considerable length; but it is interesting to notice that all the sympathy of that government goes only the length of words. Spain has no idea of undertaking a crusade on behalf of the Pope.

Telegraphed to the New Orleans Picayune.

LATEST FROM CHARLESTON.

PARTICULARS OF THE SURRENDER.

THE CONFEDERATE FLAG WAVING OVER FORT SUMTER.

Blockade of the Port of Charleston.

[By the American Line.]

CHARLESTON, April 13—2 P. M.—Major Anderson has hauled down the United States flag from Fort Sumter and run up the white flag.

The fort has been burning for several hours, from the effect of the bombshells. Two explosions have also been produced by the shells thrown from our batteries.

Maj. Anderson ceased his firing sometime since. The fire of all our batteries has been continued till the present time.

Upon the raising of the white flag the firing ceased, and two aids were sent by Gen. Beauregard to Fort Sumter.

[SECOND DISPATCH.]

CHARLESTON, April 13, 4 P. M.—The flag of the Confederate States of America now floats over Fort Sumter.

The port of Charleston has been blockaded by the U. S. ships of war which recently arrived in the offing of the harbor.

Rejoicing at Montgomery.

MONTGOMERY, April 13.—The above dispatches were addressed to the Secretary of War, by Gov. Pickens, of South Carolina. They were read by a clerk of the War Department in front of the executive building, and in the presence of President Davis and the Cabinet.

Seven guns were fired, and one for General Beauregard, and another for the Confederate States.

There is great rejoicing among our people.

Great Rejoicing in Mobile.

MOBILE, April 13.—The news of the surrender of Fort Sumter to the Confederate army was received with immense cheering. Crowds congregate about the streets to discuss the important intelligence.

The Confederate and Palmetto flags are unfurled to the breeze.

Cannon are firing, bells ringing, and the enthusiasm knows no bounds.

Important from Pensacola.

Fort Pickens Reinforced.

PENSACOLA, April 13.—Reinforcements were thrown into Fort Pickens last night.

Arrest of a Spy.

Secret Dispatches from Fort Pickens.

MONTGOMERY, April 13.—Lieut. Warden, [illegible], has been arrested in this city as a [illegible]. There were found on his person secret dispatches from Lieut. Slemmer, in command of Fort Pickens, to the Government at Washington.

It appears, also, that the prisoner violated his parole to Gen. Bragg, and carried in secret dispatches to Fort Pickens, while he showed to Gen. Bragg open dispatches.

He likewise failed to report himself to the General on his return from the fort.

The opinion of Mr. Benjamin, the Attorney General, has been asked on the points of law bearing on the case.

EXCITEMENT IN NEW YORK.

New Expedition Fitting Out.

Probable Suspension of Southern Mails.

(By the American Line.)

NEW YORK, April 13—A. M.—The bombardment of Fort Sumter creates intense excitement in this city and throughout the North, and business is everywhere suspended.

The friends of the South warmly commend the action of the Confederate Government, and lavish praises upon the troops at Charleston.

Further news from the scene of hostilities is impatiently awaited by all classes of people.

In the meantime the Lincoln Government is actively preparing to meet the issue with further reinforcements.

Commodore Stringham will command the new squadron.

The Southern mails will also probably be immediately suspended.

Virginia Troops for Charleston.

On the other hand it is rumored that several military companies have left Richmond for Charleston.

New Orleans Mails for Europe.

NEW YORK, April 13.—The steamship Kangaroo sailed from this port to-day for Liverpool, with New Orleans mails of the 5th, and telegraphic dispatches from New Orleans of yesterday.

The War News in Washington.

Troops Ordered to the Outskirts.

WASHINGTON, April 13.—The war news creates much regret, but no excitement here. The prospects of the future, however, cause a general depression.

The regular troops have been ordered to the outskirts of the city, and the volunteers to guard the armories and public buildings.

The President has dismissed from the army, Capt. W. B. John and Lieut. Abner Smith.

The War News in Massachusetts.

Profound Sensation Throughout the State.

BOSTON, April 13.—A profound sensation prevails throughout the city and State.

The general sentiment is that the Government is right and shall be sustained.

Offer of Troops from Rhode Island.

PROVIDENCE, R. I., April 13.—Governor Sprague, of this State, has tendered the services of the marine artillery, and a thousand of infantry to the Government, and will accompany them to whatever point [illegible] be ordered.

Naval Preparations [illegible]

NEWPORT, April 13.—The [illegible]

The Philadelphia Inquirer.

ESTABLISHED 1829. PHILADELPHIA, MONDAY, APRIL 15, 1861. PRICE TWO CENTS.

FORT SUMTER AFTER THE BOMBARDMENT.

Fort Sumter.

We present the readers of THE INQUIRER this morning with two views of Fort Sumter—one a ground plan, and the other a representation of the fort at the termination of the bombardment.

The Topographical Plan.

In the topographical plan the dangerous proximity of the soldiers' barracks to the powder magazines will be observed. The barracks, according to our report, were nearly or quite destroyed by fire, and to subdue the flames in this quarter appears to have been the principal object of Maj. ANDERSON during the morning of Saturday.

The Fort After the Engagement.

The representation of the Fort after the engagement tallies as near as possible with its actual state.

Throughout the whole exciting period during which Fort Sumter has been the theme of conversation, competent military men have doubted its ability to stand a protracted bombardment. Neither Sumter nor Pickens were constructed to sustain a siege, but rather to defend harbors against hostile fleets. For the latter purpose they are admirably adapted; no "wooden walls" could withstand the fire from their batteries, or do themselves harm; but a well-sustained fire from different points on the adjacent shores it has been shown has effectualty silenced Sumter, whatever might be the effect of a similar ordeal to Pickens.

The exterior of the Fort presents a sorry appearance. The portion which suffered most was that exposed to the iron battery at Cummings' Point. The walls, not constructed in a very durable manner (in despite of all heretofore said), were honeycombed, and several breaches were made. A portion of one of the corners was completely carried away. The heavy columbiads at Cummings' Point, capable of throwing balls of eight or ten inch calibre for a distance of two miles, did terrible execution.

It has been seen also that the forces of Major ANDERSON were entirely inadequate to effectually work the guns, and attend to the incidental requirements. It is not to be wondered at, under the circumstances, that Fort Sumter surrendered.

The men were on duty thirty-six hours, with balls or shells striking the casemates and guns of the fort constantly. Competent military men state that the intense vibration or shock produced on the brain and nervous system of those in the vicinity is terribly exhausting.

At the siege of Sevastopol the men who worked the guns were relieved every twenty minutes, and groomed with whisky and flannel to enable them to endure the concussion produced by the firing of their own guns and the shock of the enemy's balls and shells striking the fortification. The fearful hardships which Major ANDERSON's small band underwent, during the awful day and night of Friday last, may well have driven Capt. DOUBLEDAY insane, as our reporter telegraphs. The concussion attending the firing of a columbiad in the enclosed casemate of a fort, is said to be terrible.

Topographical Sketch of Sumter.

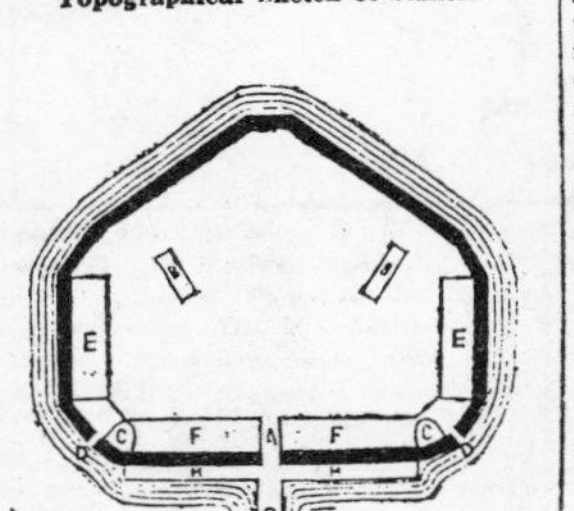

A Arched gateway in the southwest wall.
B Furnaces for heating shot.
C Powder magazines.
D Sally ports.
E Barracks for the soldiers.
F Officers quarters.
G Wharf—depth of water on east side sixteen to eighteen feet.
H Principal landing—extending along the entire soutwest wall.
I Morris Island beach.
K Fort Johnson, on James Island.

We would mention that the position of Morris and James Islands, owing to the small size of the ennraving, is not intended to be considered as more than indicating their proximity to Fort Sumter.

Cummings' Point Iron Battery.

Cummings' Point Iron Battery was three-fourths of a mile distant from Sumter, and brought three Columbiads to bear against the Federal stronghold. It consisted of a heavy framework of yellow pine logs. The roof was of the same material, over which dovetailed bars of railrod iron of the T pattern were laid from top to bottom—all of which was riveted down in the most secure manner. On the front it presented an angle of about thirty degrees. There were three port-holes, which opened and closed with iron shutters of the heaviest description. When open, the muzzles of the columbiads filled up the space completely. The recoil of the gun enabled the shutters to be closed instantly. It will thus be seen with what security the parties working the three heavy pieces of ordnance could operate upon Sumter. The shot of Major ANDERSON might fall like hail upon the inclined plane of railroad iron, and produce no impression beyond a slight indentation. Several companies of the Confederate troops worked this battery both day and night. The ship channel was commanded by this battery, although it does not appear that it devoted much of its attention to the war vessels—their distance probably being too great.

Fort Johnson Mortar Battery.

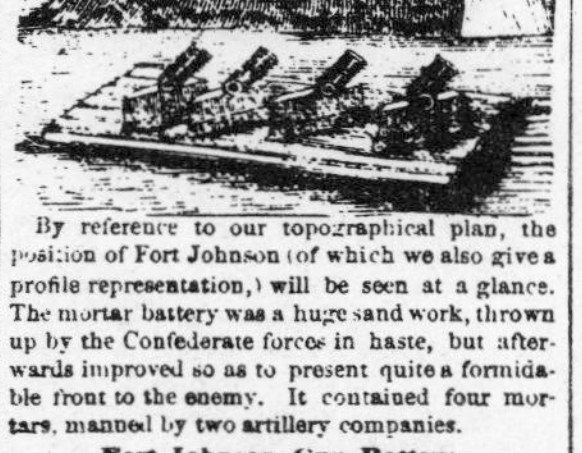

By reference to our topographical plan, the position of Fort Johnson (of which we also give a profile representation,) will be seen at a glance. The mortar battery was a huge sand work, thrown up by the Confederate forces in haste, but afterwards improved so as to present quite a formidable front to the enemy. It contained four mortars, manned by two artillery companies.

Fort Johnson Gun Battery.

The gun battery consists of sand bags, and is of more finished construction than its associate—the mortar battery alluded to. It was erected upon the site of an old fort. It contains seige guns and several mortars. The interior is represented in our view of the Gun Battery. The fort is in one of the best possible positions for the defence of the harbor.

GREAT NATIONAL TRAGEDY.

Details of the Bombardment of Fort Sumter.

THE FINAL SURRENDER.

Major Anderson on his Way to New York.

THE PRESIDENT'S PROCLAMATION ISSUED.

SEVENTY-FIVE THOUSAND MEN CALLED FOR.

A Special Session of Congress.

WAR MOVEMENTS ON FOOT.

ENROLLMENTS IN CITIES, TOWNS AND VILLAGES.

Strong Union Feeling in Baltimor

THE ACTION OF THE VIRGINIA STATE CONVENTION.

SECESSION DEMONSTRATION AT RICHMOND, VA.

CONTEMPLATED ATTACK ON WASHINGTON.

FORT DELAWARE TO BE SEIZED.

The Despatches from Charleston.

FIRST DESPATCH.

CHARLESTON, S. C., April 13.—At intervals of twenty minutes, the firing was kept up all night on Fort Sumter.

Major ANDERSON ceased to fire at 6 o'clock in the evening.

All night he was engaged in repairing the damages done to the fort, and protecting the guns in barbette on the parapet.

He commenced to return the fire this morning at 7 o'clock, but seemed to be greatly disabied.

The battery on Cummings' Point is doing Fort Sumter great damage.

At 9 o'clock this morning, a dense smoke poured out from the walls of Fort Sumter.

SECOND DESPATCH.

CHARLESTON, April 13.—*The Federal flag at Fort Sumter is at half-mast, signalling distress.*

The shells from Fort Moultrie and Morris Island fall into ANDERSON's stronghold thick and fast. They can be seen in their course from the Charleston battery.

The breach made in Fort Sumter is on the side opposite Cummings' Point. Two of its port-holes are knocked into one, and the wall from the top is crumbling.

Three vessels, one of them a very large-sized steamer, are over the bar, and seem to be preparing to participate in the conflict.

The fire of Morris Island and Fort Moultrie is divided between Fort Sumter and the ships-of-war. The ships have not as yet opened fire.

An explosion has occurred at Fort Sumter. A dense volume of smoke was seen suddenly to rise.

Major ANDERSON has ceased to fire for about an hour. It is thought that the officers' quarters in Fort Sumter are on fire.

THIRD DESPATCH.

CHARLESTON, April 13.—Two of Major ANDERSON's magazines have exploded. It was thought that they were only the smaller magazines.

Only occasional shots are now fired at Fort Sumter from Fort Moultrie.

The Morris Island battery is doing heavy work.

The greatest excitement prevails in the city.—The wharves, steeples, housetops, and every available place are packed with people. The ships in the offing have not yet aided ANDERSON.

It is now too late for them to come over the bar, as the tide is ebbing.

CHARLESTON, April 13—Noon.—The ships in the offing appear quietly at anchor, and have not fired a gun.

The entire roofs of ANDERSON's barracks are in a vast sheet of flame.

Shells from Cummings' Point and Fort Moultrie are bursting in and over Fort Sumter in quick succession. The Federal flag still waves over the fort. Major ANDERSON is only occupied in putting out the fire. Every shot appears to tell, and the spectators are anxiously expecting the striking of the flag.

FOURTH DESPATCH.

CHARLESTON, April 13.—Fort Sumter is undoubtedly on fire.

The flames are raging.

ANDERSON has thrown out a raft loaded with men, who are passing up buckets of water to extinguish the flames.

The fort is scarcely discernable for the smoke.

The men on the raft are now the objects of fire from Morris Island.

With good glasses the balls can be seen skipping the water and striking the unprotected raft.

Great havoc is created among the poor fellows.

It is surmised that ANDERSON is gradually blowing up the fort. He scarcely fires a gun.

The flames are bursting from all the port holes of Fort Sumter, and destruction is inevitable.

The few shots that ANDERSON fired this morning knocked the bricks off the chimneys on the officers' quarters at Fort Moultrie like a whirlwind.

It seems that ANDERSON's only hope is to hold out for aid from the ships.

CHARLESTON, April 13.—Two war ships are making in towards Morris Island, with the view to land troops to silence the batteries.

FIFTH DESPATCH.

CHARLESTON, April 13.—Four vessels, two of them being large war steamers, are in sight over the bar. The largest of the vessels appears to be engaging Morris Island.

The flames have nearly subsided in Fort Sumter, but ANDERSON does not fire any guns.

Gen. BEAUREGARD left the wharf, just now, in a boat, for Morris Island.

SIXTH DESPATCH.

CHARLESTON, S. C., April 13—P. M.—The bombardment has ceased. Major ANDERSON has drawn down the Stars and Stripes, and displayed a flag of truce. This has been answered from the city, and a boat is now on the way to Fort Sumter.

SEVENTH DESPATCH.

CHARLESTON, April 13.—The Federal flag was again hoisted at Fort Sumter, when PORCHER MILES, under cover of a flag of truce, went over to the fort.

In a few moments after his arrival there, the Federal flag was hauled down by ANDERSON, and a white one unfurled.

The Federal flag was shot away by the Palmetto Guards at Morris Island. In all, two thousand shots were fired. No South Carolinians were hurt. This news is reliable, and puts to rest all my previous reports about Fort Sumter. The bells are ringing a merry peal and our people are engaging in every demonstration of joy.

Our people generally sympathize with Major ANDERSON, but express abhorrence for those who were in the steamers off our bar and in sight of us, and did not even attempt to reinforce him.

Judge MAGRATH, who has just returned from Fort Sumter, reports that the wood-work of the fort and the officers' quarters were all burnt out.

The fort will be taken possession of to-night by the Confederate troops. Gen. BEAUREGARD, with two aids, have left for Fort Sumter. Three fire companies of Charleston were on their way to Fort Sumter to quell the fire before it reaches the magazine.

EIGHTH DESPATCH.

CHARLESTON, April 13—Evening.—A boat from one of the war vessels on the outside has communicated with General SIMMONS, in command of the forces on Morris Island, and made the request that one of the steamers be allowed to enter the port for the purpose of taking away ANDERSON and his command.

An arrangement has been agreed upon by the parties to stay further proceedings until nine o'clock to-morrow.

CHARLESTON, April 13.—Evening.—The Fairfield regiment, 1000 strong, have just passed the *Courier* office, on their way to Morris Island. There are now 10,000 men under arms in the harbor and on the coast.

NINTH DESPATCH.

CHARLESTON, April 13.—Evening.—Fort Sumter has unconditionally surrendered. The news has been received in a reliable shape.

Ex-Senator CHESNUT and ex-Governor MANNING, and W. PORCHER MILES have just landed, and marched to the Governor's house, followed by a dense crowd of people, who are wild with joy. They bring the particulars.

It was reported that ten of the garrison at Fort Sumter had been killed, but your reporter has just had an interview with W. PORCHER MILES, who has just returned from a visit to Fort Sumter, and is assured by him that no one was killed.

Major ANDERSON stated that he surrendered his sword to General BEAUREGARD as the representative of the Confederate Government. Gen. BEAUREGARD said he would not receive it from so brave a man. He says Major ANDERSON made a staunch fight, and elevated himself in the estimation of every true Carolinian.

During the fire, when Major ANDERSON's flag-staff was shot away, a boat put off from Morris Island, carrying another American flag for him to fight under.

The Conflict of Friday.

Major ANDERSON, during the greater part of Friday, directed his fire principally against Fort Moultrie, the Stevens and Floating Batteries—these and Fort Johnson being the only five operating against him. The remainder of the batteries were held in reserve.

Some fifteen or eighteen shots struck the iro Floating Battery, but made not the slightest impression upon its iron cased sides. The Stevens Battery was eminently successful, and did terrible execution on Fort Sumter.

The soldiers were perfectly reckless of their lives, and at every shot jumped upon the ramparts to observe the effect, and then jumped down cheering.

A party on the Stevens Battery are said to have played a game of cards during the hottest fire.

The excitement in the community was indescribable. With the very first boom of the gun thousands rushed from their beds to the harbor front, and all day every available place was thronged by ladies and gentlemen, viewing the solemn spectacle through their glasses. Most of these had relatives in the several fortifications, and many a tearful eye attested the anxious affection of the mother, wife and sister.

Business was entirely suspended. Only those stores were open which were necessary to supply articles required by the army.

Governor PICKENS remained all day in the residence of a gentleman commanding a view of the whole scene, a most interested observer. Gen. BEAUREGARD commanded in person the entire operations.

Troops were pouring into the town all day by hundreds, but were held in reserve for the present, the force already on the island having been considered ample. People also arrived every moment on horseback, and by every other conveyance.

The flag of Fort Sumter floated to the breeze all day. It was not struck by a single shot.

Quite a number of the contestants at the different Secession forts were struck by spent pieces of shell, but not seriously injured.

About six o'clock on Friday evening it became necessary to convey despatches from Sullivan's Island to Charleston. Capt. R. S. PARKER undertook the mission, and started in a small boat. He delivered the despatches to Gov. PICKENS, after having rowed through the warmest fire of Major ANDERSON, and escaped unhurt.

Senator WIGFALL in same manner bore despatches to Morris Island, through the fire from Fort Sumter.

Two rain storms occurred during the day, but did not interrupt the firing. Many of those engaged worked in their shirt sleeves. The excitement was intense.

The regularity of the replies of Major ANDERSON during the day led to the belief on the part of the assailants that by some means he had received reinforcements of men.

About eight o'clock in the evening the rain commenced to pour, and the uncovered batteries on the islands were obliged to cease firing regularly, and content themselves with occasional guns.

The interval is believed to have been made use of by Major ANDERSON to repair damages. He is said to have received twenty-nine full shots from the Stevens battery alone, making the bricks fly from the walls in all directions.

It is estimated that from twelve to eighteen hundred balls and shells were fired during the day. Over one hundred shells took effect inside the fort.

The shots from Sumter to Fort Moultrie generally went rather wide of the mark. They were from two of ANDERSON's barbette guns. The same was the case with the Floating Battery, to which he was very particular in his attentions.—A ball penetrated the Moultrie House, where a party of gentlemen were sitting in the parlor, watching the fight. It entered the second story, and traveled into the kitchen. The gentlemen scattered miscellaneously, and sought a better position.

Vessels were stationed at different points in the harbor. One of these, the schooner *Petrel*, Capt. S. F. COSTE, received four shots, but suffering no material damage.

It was known before evening that at least three, and perhaps four, Government vessels were outside the bar, and signals were believed to have been exchanged between them and Major ANDERSON.

The first shot was fired from Fort Johnson, on Morris Island, by Capt. JAMES, and the second by Lieutenant U. H. GIBBS. This was not answered until three o'clock this afternoon. The first shot from the Stevens Battery was fired by the venerable EDMUND RUFFIN, of Virginia.

It was anticipated by the Secessionists that the Government vessels would make an effort to reinforce Sumter during the night of Friday. To prevent this, extra forces were detailed to Morris and Sullivan's Islands, and guards were stationed both on the shores and in boats in the harbor, with orders to signal at once, if any reinforcement was attempted.

Orders were issued to send Major ANDERSON a bomb from all the batteries every twenty minutes during the night, to keep him wide awake, making about two a minute.

So passed the night of Friday.

The Conflict of Saturday.

Early on Saturday morning the regular cannonade was resumed with increased energy on the part of those in the shore batteries.

Lights were visible in motion on Fort Sumter all night, and Major ANDERSON was, doubtless, engaged in protecting his guns and making necessary repairs. He did not reply to any fire during the night.

Soon after the firing was commenced on Saturday morning, it was evident that some of the woodwork in the interior of Sumter had caught fire. Smoke and flames were seen issuing from the port holes.

The Secessionists were delighted. It was conjectured that the magazine of the Fort would explode. This was also feared by Major ANDERSON, for his guns remained silent and it is believed that efforts were made to subdue the flames.

The principal antagonist of Fort Sumter was the battery on Cummings' Point. The shells were thrown into and around the fort almost without intermission. From Moultrie and Morris Island there was no abatement.

Finally it appeared as though ANDERSON had yielded to the difficulties of his position. The flag of Sumter was put at half-mast—a signal of distress. It is believed that several of the smaller magazines exploded, as sudden clouds of smoke were seen to rise from Sumter. No aid was rendered by the Federal ships in the offing. It is not known whether they were able to cross the bar. The vessels were signalled, however, quite frequently by Major ANDERSON.

The wharves, steeples, housetops, and all available points within sight of the forts, were crowded with many women and children. Several of the Secession batteries opened upon the war vessels, but with what result is not known.

Finally the flag of truce was displayed on the ramparts of Sumter about half-past one o'clock.

The Fort surrendered.

Details of the Surrender.

VISIT OF OUR CORRESPONDENT TO THE FORT—EXPLANATION OF THE EXPLOSIONS—THE INTERIOR A MASS OF RUINS—THE WALLS HONEYCOMBED BY SHOT—DAMAGE TO FORT MOULTRIE—THE BARRACKS IN RUINS—DWELLINGS SHATTERED.

CHARLESTON, April 13—Evening.—Hostilities have for the present ceased, and the victory belongs to South Carolina.

With the display of the flag of truce on the ramparts of Fort Sumter at half-past one o'clock, the firing ceased, and an unconditional surrender was made. The Carolinians had no idea that the fight was at an end.

So soon after the flagstaff of Major ANDERSON was shot away, Colonel WIGFALL, the Aid of General BEAUREGARD, at his commander's request, went to Fort Sumter with a white flag, to offer assistance in extinguishing the flames. He approached the burning fortress from Morris Island, and while the firing was raging on all sides he effected a landing at Sumter. He approached a port-hole, and was met by Major ANDERSON, the commandant of the fort. The latter said that he had just displayed a white flag, but the firing was kept up nevertheless.

Col. WIGFALL replied that Major ANDERSON must haul down the American flag—that no parley would be granted—surrender or fight was the word.

Major ANDERSON then hauled down his flag and displayed only the flag of truce. All firing instantly ceased, and two officers of Gen. BEAUREGARD's staff, ex-Senator CHESNUT and ex-Governor MANNING, came over in a boat, and stipulated with Major ANDERSON that his surrender should be unconditional for the present, subject to the terms of Gen. BEAUREGARD.

Major ANDERSON was allowed to remain with his men in actual possession of the Fort, while Messrs. CHESNUT and MANNING came over to the city, accompanied by a member of the Palmetto Guards, bearing the orders of his company. These were met at the pier by hundreds of citizens, and as they marched up the street to the General's quarters, the crowd was swelled to thousands. Shouts rent the air, and the wildest joy was manifested on account of the welcome tidings.

After the surrender a boat with an officer and ten men was sent from one of the four ships in the offing to Gen. SIMMONS, commanding on Morris Island, with the request that a merchant ship, or one of the vessels of the United States, be allowed to enter and take off the commander and garrison of Fort Sumter.

Gen. SIMMONS replied that if no hostilities were attempted during the night, and no effort was made to reinforce or retake Fort Sumter, he would give an answer at 9 o'clock on Sunday morning. The officer signified that he was satisfied with this, and returned to his vessel.

Your correspondent accompanied the officers of Gen. BEAUREGARD's staff on a visit to Fort Sumter. None but the officers, however, were allowed to land. They went down on a steamer, and carried three fire engines for the purpose of putting out the flames.

The fire, however, had been previously extinguished by the exertions of Major ANDERSON and his men. The visitors reported that Major ANDERSON surrendered because his quarters and barracks were destroyed, and he had no hope of reinforcements, as the fleet lay idly by during thirty hours, and either would not or could not help him. Besides this, his men were prostrated from over exertions. There were but five of them hurt, four badly, and one, it is thought, mortally; but the rest were worn out and physically incapable of continuing the fight.

The explosions that were heard and seen from the city in the morning, were caused by the bursting of loaded shells ignited by the fire which could not be removed quick enough.

The fire in the barracks was caused by the quantities of hot shot poured in from Fort Moultrie.

Within Fort Sumter everything but the casemates is an utter ruin. The whole interior looks like a blackened mass of ruins. Many of the guns are dismounted. The side opposite the iron battery at Cummings' Point is the hardest dealt with. The rifled cannon from the battery played great havoc with Fort Sumter, and the walls look like a honeycomb. Near the top is a breach as large as a cart. The side opposite Fort Moultrie is also honeycombed extensively, as is that opposite the floating battery.

Fort Moultrie is badly damaged. The officers' quarters and barracks are torn to pieces. The frame houses on the Island are riddled with shot, and in many instances the whole sides of the houses are torn out.

The fire in Fort Sumter was put out, and recaught three times during the day.

Dr. CRAWFORD, Major ANDERON's Surgeon, is slightly wounded in the face.

It is positively asserted that none of the Carolina troops are injured.

Major ANDERSON and all his officers and men still remain in Fort Sumter. I approached near enough to the wall to see him bid his visitors adieu. In addition to this, conversations that were had with him were repeated to me.

A boat was sent from the Fort to-night, to officially notify the fleet that Major ANDERSON had surrendered.

It is not known when the Carolinians will occupy Fort Sumter, or what is to be done with the vanquished.

Every one is satisfied with the victory and happy that no blood was shed.

In the city, after the surrender, the bells were rung and salutes fired.

[The above is from a special correspondent of of the Associated Press, who reached Charleston early on Saturday, and may be relied on as entirely correct.—REPORTER.]

Departure of Anderson and His Men for New York.

THE FLEET STILL OUTSIDE.

CHARLESTON, April 14.—Major ANDERSON and his men will leave to-night, at eleven o'clock, in the steamer *Isabel*, for New York.

The war fleet is still outside.

The scene when ANDERSON and his men took formal leave of Fort Sumter was a thrilling and impressive one.

Beauregard's Report of the First Day's Engagement.

MONTGOMERY, April 13.—General BEAUREGARD telegraphed to the Secretary of War at a late hour last night, that heavy firing had been going on all day, and that four guns of Fort Sumter had been dismounted.

The Confederate batteries were all safe, and none of his men were hurt. Four steamers were in the offing, with a rough sea.

Nothing was received from Charleston, this morning, by the War Department.

Letter from Fort Moultrie.

CHARLESTON, April 13.—Your correspondent has just read a letter received from S. C. BOYLSTON, dated Fort Moultrie, 6 o'clock this morning.

He says not one man was killed or wounded during yesterday's engagement.

The iron battery has been damaged.

The rifled cannon of the battery did great execution on Fort Sumter. They were all aimed into Major ANDERSON's port holes.

Three of Fort Sumter's barbette guns were dismounted. One of them was a ten-inch Columbiad.

A corner of Fort Sumter, opposite Fort Moultrie, was knocked away.

The *Water Witch*, *Mohawk*, and *Pawnee*, it was thought were the three first vessels seen in the offing.

Reception of the News in the South.

AT MOBILE, ALA.

MOBILE, April 13.—The announcement of the surrender of Fort Sumter was received with immense cheering by the crowds who have been gathering in the vicinity of the newspaper offices all day. The Confederate and Palmetto flags are flying everywhere. Salutes are firing and bells ringing. The people are greatly rejoiced.

AT AUGUSTA.

AUGUSTA, April 13.—A hundred guns were fired here to-day in honor of the victory of the Confederate army.

AT MONTGOMERY.

MONTGOMERY, Ala., April 13.—Despatches from Governor PICKENS, to the Secretary of War, were read by the clerk of the War Department from the Executive buildings during the day in the presence of President DAVIS and his Cabinet. They gave rise to general rejoicing in all circles. Seven guns were fired in honor of the surrender of Fort Sumter.

War Spirit in New Orleans—Defence of the Mississippi.

NEW ORLEANS, April 13.—There was a grand muster of the city volunteer companies this morning. Preparations are being made to defend the Mississippi river in the best possible manner.

The War News at Boston.

BOSTON, April 13.—An intense excitement was created in this city this afternoon, by the receipt of the Charleston telegrams.

The announcement of the surrender of Fort Sumter is not believed by many. Others pronounce it a hoax. A more detailed account of this bloodless battle and surrender is anxiously awaited.

[This was received previous to the confirmatory despatches from Charleston.]

The War Spirit in Massachusetts.

BOSTON, April 13.—The Adjutant-General's office was crowded this forenoon with officers of the State military, tendering their commands to the Governor. An extreme war feeling has been aroused.

Governor ANDREW left for Washington this afternoon.

Arrest of a U. S. Naval Officer by the Confederate Government.

DESPATCHES OF LIEUT. SLEMMER INTERCEPTED.

MONTGOMERY, April 13—Major CHAMBERS, of the Alabama army, arrived from Pensacola to-day, bringing Lieut. REED WERDEN, of the United States navy, as prisoner of war. He was bearer of despatches to Fort Pickens and the United States fleet off Pensacola bay. He is held by the Secretary of War, who sent a detachment of troops to arrest him.

MONTGOMERY, April 13.—Lieut. WERDEN has been compelled to give up his despatches from Lieut. SLEMMER, of Fort Pickens, to the Government at Washington. The Attorney-General's opinion as to the law in his case has been requested.

It is charged against Lieut. WERDEN that he violated his promise to report to Gen. BRAGG, and carried in secret despatches to Fort Pickens, while he showed other despatches to Gen. BRAGG; and also, that he failed to report himself on his return.

From the Montgomery Government.

WAR TO BE DECLARED.

WASHINGTON, April 14—Official advices from Montgomery indicate that the Confederate Congress will, on re-assembling, at once declare war against the United States.

It is believed that in the act of declaration, a distinction will be made between alien friends and alien enemies, the former including the Border States and such citizens of the North as oppose the coercion policy of the Administration. All obligations to this class are as much to be respected as though in time of peace.

The War Feeling in Lancaster.

LANCASTER, April 13.—The war news has created an intense excitement here. The stars and stripes are displayed at different points in honor of ANDERSON. A call for a public meeting on Wednesday has already been issued to sustain the the Government. It is numerously signed. Volunteers are being enrolled.

Reinforcement of Fort Pickens.

MONTGOMERY, April 13.—Fort Pickens was reinforced last night. It is understood that Charleston is to be blockaded.

Excitement at Baltimore.

BALTIMORE, April 13.—The intelligence from Charleston has produced great excitement, and the anxiety to obtain further news is intense.

A man made his appearance in the streets with a large secession cockade on his hat. He was pursued by a mob, and was only protected from violence by the interference of the police.

Aid to Government from Rhode Island.

PROVIDENCE, April 13.—Governor SPRAGUE has tendered to the Government the service of the Marine Artillery and one thousand infantry, and offers to accompany them himself.

New York for the Union.

TWENTY-FIVE THOUSAND MEN TO BE CALLED OUT.

NEW YORK, April 14.—Advices from Albany state that Governor MORGAN will to-morrow issue a call for twenty-five thousand men for the assistance of the Federal Government.

A private letter from Governor CURTIN states that Pennsylvania can furnish one hundred thousand men and have them in Washington in forty-eight hours, if required.

DAVID DUDLEY FIELD has gone to Washington, on an invitation, for the purpose of consulting with the Administration.

The New York Regiments Volunteering for the Defence of Washington.

NEW YORK, April 14th.—The Seventh and Sixty-ninth Regiments have volunteered for the defence of Washington, but have not yet started.

The Twelfth Regiment will hold a meeting to-morrow.

Excitement in New York.

THE HERALD OFFICE THREATENED.

NEW YORK, April 15.—1½ o'clock A. M.—A body of policemen are on duty at the *Herald* office to guard against a rumored attack.

There will probably be no disturbance to-night

More Transport Steamers Chartered.

NEW YORK, April 13.—The Government has chartered the steamers *Philadelphia* and *Ericsson*. The former is rapidly filling with provisions, army stores, and munitions of war. The latter will be held in reserve for any emergency.

[The telegraph office closed at 1½ o'clock, the lines being down South.]

Continued on the Eighth Page.

The New-York Times.

VOL. X.....NO. 2984. NEW-YORK, MONDAY, APRIL 15, 1861. PRICE TWO CENTS.

FORT SUMPTER FALLEN.

PARTICULARS OF THE BOMBARDMENT.

The Fort on Fire and the Garrison Exhausted.

NO ATTEMPT AT REINFORCEMENT.

The Cessation of Firing and the Capitulation.

NO LIVES LOST ON EITHER SIDE.

Major Anderson and his Men Coming to New-York.

How the News was Received in Washington.

Call for Seventy-Five Thousand Militia.

AN EXTRA SESSION OF CONGRESS

War Feeling Throughout the Northern and Western States.

FORT PICKENS REINFORCED.

CHARLESTON, Saturday, April 13—Evening.

Major ANDERSON has surrendered, after hard fighting, commencing at 4½ o'clock yesterday morning, and continuing until five minutes to 1 to-day.

The American flag has given place to the Palmetto of South Carolina.

You have received my previous dispatches concerning the fire and the shooting away of the flag-staff. The latter event is due to Fort Moultrie, as well as the burning of the fort, which resulted from one of the hot shots fired in the morning.

During the conflagration, Gen BEAUREGARD sent a boat to Major ANDERSON, with offers of assistance, the bearers being Colonels W. P. MILES, and ROGER PRYOR, of Virginia, and LEE. But before it reached him, a flag of truce had been raised. Another boat then put off, containing Ex-Gov. MANNING, Major D. R. JONES and Col. CHARLES ALLSTON, to arrange the terms of surrender, which were the same as those offered on the 11th inst. These were official. They stated that all proper facilities would be afforded for the removal of Major ANDERSON and his command, together with the company arms and property, and all private property, to any post in the United States he might elect. The terms were not, therefore, unconditional.

Major ANDERSON stated that he surrendered his sword to Gen. BEAUREGARD as the representative of the Confederate Government. Gen BEAUREGARD said he would not receive it from so brave a man. He says Major ANDERSON made a staunch fight, and elevated himself in the estimation of every true Carolinian.

During the fire, when Major ANDERSON'S flag-staff was shot away, a boat put off from Morris Island, carrying another American flag for him to fight under—a noteworthy instance of the honor and chivalry of South Carolina Seceders, and their admiration for a brave man.

The scene in the city after the raising of the flag of truce and the surrender is indescribable; the people were perfectly wild. Men on horseback rode through the streets proclaiming the news, amid the greatest enthusiasm.

On the arrival of the officers from the fort they were marched through the streets, followed by an immense crowd, hurrahing, shouting, and yelling with excitement.

Several fire companies were immediately sent down to Fort Sumpter to put out the fire, and any amount of assistance was offered.

A regiment of eight hundred men has just arrived from the interior, and has been ordered to Morris Island, in view of an attack from the fleet which may be expected to-night.

Six vessels are reported off the bar, but the utmost indignation is expressed against them for not coming to the assistance of Major ANDERSON when he made signals of distress.

The soldiers on Morris Island jumped on the guns every shot they received from Fort Sumpter while thus disabled, and gave three cheers for Major ANDERSON and groans for the fleet.

Col. LUCAS, of the Governor's Staff, has just returned from Fort Sumpter, and says Major ANDERSON told him he had pleasanter recollections of Fort Moultrie than Fort Sumpter. Only five men were wounded, one seriously.

The flames have destroyed everything. Both officers and soldiers were obliged to lay on their faces in the casemates, to prevent suffocation.

The explosions heard in the city were from small piles of shell, which ignited from the heat.

The effect of the shot upon the fort was tremendous. The walls were battered in hundreds of places, but no breach was made.

Major ANDERSON expresses himself much pleased that no lives had been sacrificed, and says that to Providence alone is to be attributed the bloodless victory. He compliments the firing of the Carolinians, and the large number of exploded shells lying around attests their effectiveness.

The number of soldiers in the fort was about seventy, besides twenty-five workmen, who assisted at the guns. His stock of provisions was almost exhausted, however. He would have been starved out in two more days.

The entrance to the fort is mined, and the officers were told to be careful, even after the surrender, on account of the heat, lest it should explode.

A boat from the squadron, with a flag of truce, has arrived at Morris Island, bearing a request to be allowed to come and take Major Anderson and his forces. An answer will be given to-morrow at 9 o'clock.

The public feeling against the fleet is very strong, it being regarded as cowardly to make not even an attempt to aid a fellow officer.

Had the surrender not taken place Fort Sumpter would have been stormed to-night. The men are crazy for a fight.

The bells have been chiming all day, gun firing, ladies waving handkerchiefs, people cheering, and citizens making themselves generally demonstrative. It is regarded as the greatest day in the history of South Carolina.

FORT SUMPTER EVACUATED.

CHARLESTON, *via* AUGUSTA Saturday, April 13.

FORT SUMPTER HAS SURRENDERED.

The Confederate flag floats over its walls.

None of the garrison or Confederate troops are hurt.

Another correspondent says:

The bombarding has closed

Major Anderson has drawn down the stripes and stars, and displays a white flag, which has been answered from the city, and a boat is on the way to Sumpter.

CHARLESTON, Saturday, April 13—P. M.

The Federal flag was again hoisted over Fort Sumpter, when PORCHER MILES, with a flag of truce, went to the Fort.

In a few minutes the Federal flag was again hauled down by Major ANDERSON, and a white one unfurled.

CHARLESTON, Saturday, April 13.

Gen. BEAUREGARD, with two Aids, have left for Fort Sumpter.

Three fire companies from Charleston are now on their way to Sumpter to quell the fire before it reaches the magazine.

Fort Sumpter has unconditionally surrendered.

Ex-Senator CHESNUT, Ex-Governor MANNING and W. P. MILES have just landed and marched to Gov. PICKENS' residence, followed by a dense crowd wild with joy.

It is reported that the Federal flag was shot away by the Palmetto Guards at Morris Island.

In all two thousand shots have been fired. No Carolinians killed.

Major ANDERSON and his men, under guard, were conveyed to Morris Island.

The bells are ringing out a merry peal, and our people are engaged in every demonstration of joy.

It is estimated that there are nine thousand men under arms on the islands and in the neighborhood.

THE LATEST DISPATCHES.

CHARLESTON, Saturday, April 13.

I have seen W. PORCHER MILES, who has just returned from a visit to Fort Sumpter. He assured me that no one was killed at Fort Sumpter. This is reliable, and puts at rest all previous reports about Sumpter.

Maj. ANDERSON has reached the city, and is the guest of Gen. BEAUREGARD.

Our people sympathise with Maj. ANDERSON, but abhor those who were in the steamers off our bar and in sight of our people, and did not even attempt to reinforce him

The Fairfield regiment, one thousand strong, has just passed the *Courier* office, on their way to Morris Island.

There are now ten thousand men under arms in the harbor and on the coast.

Judge MAGRATH, who has just returned, reports that the wood-work and officers' quarters at Fort Sumpter are all burnt.

None of the officers were wounded.

The Fort will be taken possession of to night by the Confederate troops.

A boat from one of the vessels outside the harbor communicated with Gen. SIMONS, in command of the forces on Morris Island, and made a request that one of the steamers be allowed to enter the port for the purpose of taking away Major ANDERSON and his command. An arrangement was agreed upon by the parties to stay all proceedings until 9 o'clock to-morrow.

CHARLESTON, Saturday, April 13.

Hostilities have for the present ceased, and the victory belongs to South Carolina With the display of the flag of truce on the ramparts of Sumpter at 1½ o'clock, the firing ceased, and an unconditional surrender was made.

The Carolinians had no idea that the fight was at an end so soon.

After the flag-staff of ANDERSON was shot away, Col. WIGFALL, Aid to Gen. BEAUREGARD, at his Commander's request, went to Sumpter with a white flag, to offer assistance in extinguishing the flames. He approached the burning fortress from Morris Island, and while the firing was raging on all sides, effected a landing at Sumpter. He approached a port-hole, and was met by Maj. ANDERSON. The Commandant of Fort Sumpter said he had just displayed a white flag, but the firing from the Carolina batteries was kept up nevertheless.

Col. WIGFALL replied that Major ANDERSON must haul down the American flag; that no parley would be granted; surrender or fight was the word. Major ANDERSON then hauled down his flag, and displayed only that of truce.

All firing instantly ceased, and two other of Gen. BEAUREGARD'S staff—Ex Senator CHESTNUT and Ex-Governor MANNING—came over in a boat and stipulated with the Major that his surrender should be unconditional for the present, subject to the terms of Gen. BEAUREGARD.

Major ANDERSON was allowed to remain with his men in actual possession of the fort, while Messrs. CHESTNUT and MANNING came over to the city, accompanied with a member of the Palmetto Guards, bearing the colors of his Company. These were met at the pier by hundreds of citizens, and as they marched up the street to the General's quarters, the crowd was swelled to thousands. Shouts rent the air and the wildest joy was manifested on account of the welcome tidings.

After the surrender, a boat with an officer and ten men was sent from one of the four ships in the offing to Gen. SIMONS, commanding on Morris Island, with a request that a merchant ship or one of the vessels of the United States be allowed to enter and take off the commander and garrison of Fort Sumpter.

Gen SIMONS replied that if no hostilities were attempted during the night, and no effort was made to reinforce or retake Fort Sumpter, he would give an answer at 9 o'clock on Sunday morning.

The officer signified that he was satisfied with this, and returned. This correspondent accompanied the officers of Gen. BEAUREGARD'S staff on a visit to Fort Sumpter. None but the officers were allowed to land, however. They went down in a steamer and carried three fire engines for the purpose of putting out the flames. The fire, however, had been previously extinguished by the exertions of Major ANDERSON and his men.

The visitors reported that Major ANDERSON surrendered because his quarters and barracks were destroyed and he had no hope of reinforcements. The fleet lay idly by during the thirty hours of the bombardment and either could not or would not help him; besides, his men were prostrate from over-exertion.

There were but five of them hurt, four badly and one, it is thought, mortally, but the rest were worn out.

The explosions that were heard and seen from the city in the morning, were caused by the bursting of loaded shells. These were ignited by the fire, and could not be removed quick enough. The fire in the barracks was caused by the quantities of hot shot poured in from Fort Moultrie. Within Fort Sumpter everything but the casemates is in utter ruin. The whole thing looks like a blackened mass of ruins. Many of the guns are dismounted. The side opposite the iron battery of Cummings' Point is the hardest dealt with. The rifled cannon from this place made great havoc with Fort Sumpter. The wall looks like a honey-comb. Near the top is a breach as big as a cart. The side opposite Fort Moultrie is honey-combed extensively, as is that opposite the floating battery.

Fort Moultrie is badly damaged. The officers quarters and barracks are torn to pieces. The frame houses on the islands are riddled with shot in many instances, and whole sides of houses are torn out.

The fire in Fort Sumpter was put out, and recaught three times during the day.

Dr. CRAWFORD, Major ANDERSON'S surgeon, is slightly wounded in the face. None of the Carolinians are injured.

Major ANDERSON and all his officers and men are yet in Fort Sumpter. I approached near enough to the wall to see him bid adieu. In addition to this, conversations were had, which have been repeated to me.

A boat was sent from the Fort to night to officially notify the fleet at the bar that Major ANDERSON had surrendered. It is not known when the Carolinians will occupy Fort Sumpter, or what is to be done with the vanquished.

Everyone is satisfied with the victory, and happy that no blood was shed.

In the city, after the surrender, bells were rung and cannon fired.

CHARLESTON, Sunday, April 14.

Negotiations were completed last night. Major ANDERSON, with his command, will evacuate Fort Sumpter this morning, and will embark on board of the war vessels off our bar.

When Fort Sumpter was in flames, and ANDERSON could only fire his guns at long intervals, the men at our batteries cheered at every fire which the gallant Major made in his last struggles, but looked defiance at the vessels of war, whose men, like cowards, stood outside without firing a gun or attempting to divert the fire of a single battery from Sumpter.

Five of ANDERSON'S men are slightly wounded.

CHARLESTON, Sunday, April 14

The steamer *Isabel* is now steaming up, and will take Gen. BEAUREGARD to Sumpter, which will be turned over by Major ANDERSON to the Confederate States. ANDERSON and his command, it is reported, will proceed to New York in the *Isabel*.

CHARLESTON, Sunday, April 14.

Maj. ANDERSON and his men leave to-night in the steamer *Isabel* at 11 o'clock for New-York.

The fleet is still outside.

It was a thrilling scene when Maj. ANDERSON and his men took their formal leave of Fort Sumpter.

THE TIMES CORRESPONDENT IMPRISONED.

WILMINGTON, N. C., Sunday, April 14.

I saw the first gun fired at Fort Sumpter at 4 o'clock, A. M., April 12. I witnessed the battle for six hours. At noon I was arrested by order of Gen. BEAUREGARD as a Federal spy, and was imprisoned for twenty-four hours, and then sent out of the city by Gov. PICKENS, destitute of funds. In Wilmington I was aided by Mr. PRICE, of the *Daily Journal*, and will be with you in thirty-six hours.

There are conflicting reports as to the number killed. It is generally believed that nobody is hurt.

JASPER.

FORT PICKENS AND THE HARBOR OF PENSACOLA.

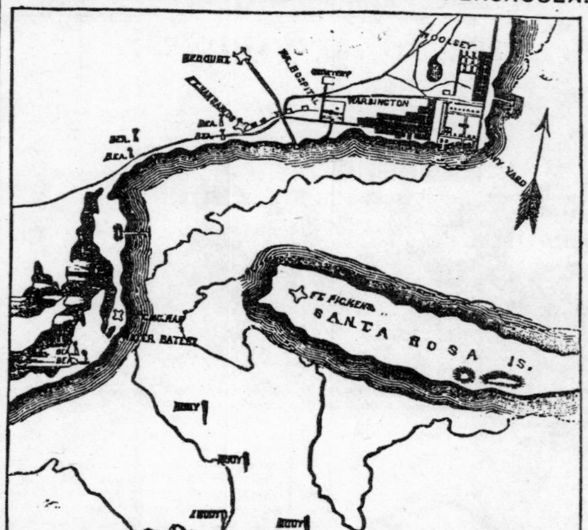

PROCLAMATION BY THE PRESIDENT.

SEVENTY-FIVE THOUSAND VOLUNTEERS AND AN EXTRA SESSION OF CONGRESS.

BY THE PRESIDENT OF THE UNITED STATES.

A PROCLAMATION.

Whereas, The laws of the United States have been for some time past, and now are opposed, and the execution thereof obstructed in the States of South Carolina, Georgia, Alabama Florida, Mississippi, Louisiana and Texas, by combinations too powerful to be suppressed by the ordinary course of Judicial proceedings, or by the powers vested in the Marshals by law,—now, therefore, I, ABRAHAM LINCOLN, President of the United States, in virtue of the power in me vested by the Constitution and the laws, have thought fit to call forth, and hereby do call forth, the militia of the several States of the Union to the aggregate number of seventy-five thousand, in order to suppress said combinations, and to cause the laws to be duly executed.

The details for this object will be immediately communicated to the State authorities through the War Department. I appeal to all loyal citizens to favor, facilitate and aid this effort to maintain the honor, the integrity and the existence of our national Union and the perpetuity of popular government, and to redress wrongs already long enough endured.

I deem it proper to say that the first service assigned to the forces hereby called forth will probably be to repossess the forts, places and property which have been seized from the Union, and in every event the utmost care will be observed, consistently with the objects aforesaid, to avoid any devastation, any destruction of, or interference with property or any disturbance of peaceful citizens in any part of the country, and I hereby command the persons composing the combinations aforesaid to disperse and retire peaceably to their respective abodes, within twenty days from this date.

Deeming that the present condition of public affairs presents an extraordinary occasion, I do hereby, in virtue of the power in me vested by the Constitution, convene both Houses of Congress. The Senators and Representatives are therefore summoned to assemble at their respective Chambers, at 12 o'clock noon, on Thursday, the fourth day of July next, then and there to consider and determine such measures as in their wisdom the public safety and interest may seem to demand.

In witness whereof, I have hereunto set my hand, and caused the seal of the United States to be affixed.

Done at the City of Washington, this fifteenth day of April, in the year of our Lord one thousand eight hundred and sixty-one, and of the Independence of the United States, the eighty-fifth.

By the President, ABRAHAM LINCOLN.

WILLIAM H. SEWARD, Secretary of State.

AID FOR THE GOVERNMENT.

Advices from Albany state that Gov. MORGAN will to-morrow issue a call for twenty-five thousand men, for the assistance of the Federal Government.

A private letter from Gov. CURTIN, of Pennsylvania, to a prominent citizen of New York, states that he can have one hundred thousand Pennsylvanians in Washington within forty eight hours, if required.

THE AVAILABLE MILITIA.

Should the Government require it, a military gentleman states that the following number of men can be forthcoming at short notice, and probably in a out the following contingents:

Maine	5,000	Michigan	10,000
New-Hampshire	5,000	Illinois	15,000
Vermont	5,000	Wisconsin	5,000
Massachusetts	15,000	Iowa	5,000
Rhode Island	2,500	Minnesota	5,000
Connecticut	5,000	Kansas	2,500
New-York	25,000	Indiana	5,000
New-Jersey	2,000		
Pennsylvania	30,000	Total	154,500
Ohio	12,500		

The estimate would give to an army of three divisions: 62,500 for the Eastern, 51,500 for the Central, and 37,500 for the Western Division. This would do to make a beginning.

THE NEWS IN WASHINGTON.

WASHINGTON, Sunday, April 14.

THE EXCITEMENT AT THE CAPITAL.

The excitement here throughout the day has been intense. People gather in groups on the streets and in the hotels, discussing affairs at Charleston and the probabilities of the future.

There is great diversity of opinion relative to the reliability of the news that Major ANDERSON has surrendered. The dispatches to the Associated Press are evidently full of blunders, which cast suspicion on the whole.

DISPATCHES TO THE PRESIDENT.

The President, nevertheless, has intelligence which satisfies him that the news is too true Private dispatches from Charleston, signed by trusty men, also confirm it; but as the telegraph is known to have been constantly tampered with by the secession authorities, it is feared that even private dispatches may have been mutilated for the purpose of cutting the Government off from all possible means of correct information.

THE CREDIBILITY OF THE TELEGRAMS.

The statement that the fleet had asked a cessation of hostilities until morning especially puzzles everybody, for if the Fort had surrendered the fleet could only have asked a cessation for its own sake, and we have thus far no information that it had been engaged. The vessels had only to steam out of range.

Still the opinion of men of high military authority here is that the news of the surrender is too true. They say no battery for the defence of the harbor could long withstand a skillful bombardment by heavy metal, where the garrison assailed is too weak to reply effectively and distract or annoy the assailants.

Besides, it is well-known here, and I have it from an authentic official source. Major ANDERSON'S provisions were all exhausted yesterday, leaving him without an ounce to refresh his men after their hard day's work There is apparently good reason here to believe the report that Major ANDERSON has embarked seaward.

Still many wagers were taken here to-day that the whole story of the surrender is false. The Union men absolutely refuse credence.

STREET FIGHTS IN WASHINGTON.

To-day's excitement has betrayed many secessionists who hold public office, and who could not conceal their joy at the reduction of Fort Sumpter. Several fights occurred, and decided knock-downs. Gen. NYE, among others, has knocked down a couple of secessionists within the last day or two. The fact is, Northern men have got tired of having treason crammed offensively down their throats, and are learning to resent it by force, the only argument the chivalry seem to appreciate.

JOHN M. BOTTS ON SECESSION.

Hon. JOHN M. BOTTS, who is here, is violent in his denunciations of secession. He has been all day the stoutest disbeliever in the story of Major ANDERSON'S surrender. He insists that the whole story is manufactured for the purpose of precipitating Virginia into the secession movement. He predicts that it will utterly fail.

THE COURSE OF VIRGINIA.

Everybody here sees that now war has commenced, the question which the Virginia Convention has to decide is simply whether Virginia will declare war against the United States or stand by the Government; whether she will invite the battle upon her soil, to her utter ruin, or aid in bringing the fratricidal strife to a speedy termination by sustaining the Government and Union.

THE NORTH A UNIT.

The news from the North of the unanimity of public sentiment in favor of the Government and the strongest policy for the suppression of rebellion gladdens every heart. It is fully believed that all partisan considerations henceforth will be suspended, and that every effort will be directed to saving the country.

THE PRESIDENT'S PROCLAMATION.

You have the President's proclamation, making a requisition for seventy-five thousand volunteers, called from all the adhering States except California and Oregon. That news will thrill like an electric shock throughout the land, and establish the fact that we have a Government at last.

UNANIMITY OF THE CABINET.

The Cabinet is a unit on these measures, and no man among them was more decided and active in their support than Mr. SEWARD, who urged conciliation and forbearance until the Disunionists were put clearly and thoroughly in the wrong.

THE QUOTA OF TROOPS FROM EACH STATE.

The War Department is engaged to-night in calculating the number of troops which each State is entitled to furnish. New York will be entitled probably to ten regiments. Pennsylvania and Massachusetts to a few less. The estimates are based upon the Federal representation of the States.

This proclamation is the fruit of a prolonged Cabinet meeting held last night.

THE BLOCKADE OF SOUTHERN PORTS.

No policy relative to closing the ports of the Seceding States is yet understood to be settled upon in detail. It is probable, however, that arrangements will be speedily made to cut off all communication with them by sea. There need be no doubt about the power of the Government to do this under its authority to prevent smuggling.

But, independent of that, the occasion justifies the Executive in assuming responsibility. He may well emulate Gen. JACKSON, who, when BOB LETCHER asked him under what law he could bring the Nullifier leaders of South Carolina to Washington for trial and execution, replied that if the Attorney-General could not find a law for it, he would get another Attorney-General who could. Self-preservation is the Government's first duty, and its masters, the people, will justify it in every wise measure addressed to that end.

ACTIVITY OF GEN. SCOTT.

Gen. SCOTT has been at work all day, with all the energy of the soldier in the prime of life, making calculations for the disposition of the forces to be raised.

PROBABLE ATTEMPT TO SEIZE WASHINGTON.

The Administration has satisfactory information that the Confederate States have proposed, immediately after reducing Fort Sumpter, to march on Washington with their army of twenty thousand men, for which they will have nothing else to do. Until recently, JEFFERSON DAVIS was disposed to postpone that step until the secession of Virginia and Maryland was effected, but as he despairs of that now, he believes that at the approach of his army those States will immediately unite their forces with his. Men who know those States well say he is in error.

PREPARATIONS FOR ITS DEFENCE.

There is one regiment of volunteers now in Baltimore ready to obey the call of the Government immediately, and they will be mustered into service. Virginia also is ready to furnish her quota The Government designs to bring a force of volunteers to this city not only strong enough to defend it against all comers, but to render an attack on it improbable. Several additional companies of regulars are also ordered here. It is not improbable that this point will be made a grand rendezvous from which troops can readily be sent wherever required.

THE SINEWS OF WAR.

Congress is called in extra session on the 4th of July,—a glorious day for a glorious work! This is essential in order to get the money that will be needed to enable the Government to sustain itself, and to pay as it goes. War is a costly experiment, as the Disunionists will find. It is no longer child's play, and will impoverish them utterly in a few months, if they persist in it, for they must themselves be the aggressors, and transport their troops and supplies long distances. The hopelessness of their unrighteous struggle must speedily force itself upon their minds when they learn how vigorous is the Government in its present hands, and how unanimous the people are in sustaining it.

MARTIAL LAW AT THE CAPITAL.

The President had not at nine o'clock to-night determined upon putting Washington under martial law. But there is little doubt that it will be done within a day or two. If so, it is hoped that possession will be taken of the telegraph office to prevent its employment by Disunionists for treasonable purposes.

CUTTING OFF THE MAILS.

The rumor that it has been decided to cut off all the mails from the seceded States is premature, to say the least. The Government does not recognize secession, and does not wish to punish the true men of the South together with the traitors. Wherever the mails are interfered with, they will be cut off, but probably not elsewhere. At least no determination otherwise has yet been arrived at by the President, notwithstanding his reference to the subject in the following letter to the Committee of the Virginia Convention, delivered by the President yesterday:

To Hon. Messrs. Preston, Stuart and Randolph:

GENTLEMEN: As a Committee of the Virginia Convention, now in session, you present me a preamble and resolution in these words:

Whereas, In the opinion of this Convention, the uncertainty which prevails in the public mind as to the policy which the federal Executive intends to pursue towards the seceded States, is extremely injurious to the industrial and commercial interests of the country, tends to keep up an excitement which is unfavorable to the adjustment of the pending difficulties and threatens a disturbance of the public peace; therefore,

Resolved, That a committee of three delegates be appointed to wait on the President of the United States, present to him this preamble, and respectfully ask him to communicate to this Convention the policy which the federal Executive intends to pursue in regard to the Confederate States.

In answer, I have to say that having, at the beginning of my official term, expressed my intended policy as plainly as I was able, it is with deep regret and mortification I now learn there is great and injurious uncertainty in the public mind as to what that policy is, and what course I intend to pursue. Not having as yet seen occasion to change, it is now my purpose to pursue the course marked out in the inaugural address. I commend a careful consideration of the whole document as the best expression I can give to my purposes. As I then and therein said, I now repeat, "The power confided in me will be used to hold, occupy and possess property and places belonging to the Government, and to collect the duties and imports; but beyond what is necessary for these objects, there will be no invasion, no using of force against or among the people anywhere." By the words "property and places belonging to the Government," I chiefly allude to the military posts and property which were in possession of the Government when it came into my hands. But if, as now appears to be true, in pursuit of a purpose to drive the United States authority from these places, an unprovoked assault has been made upon Fort Sumpter, I shall hold myself at liberty to repossess it, if I can, the places which had been seized before the Government was devolved upon me; and in any event I shall, to the best of my ability, repel force by force. In case it proves true that Fort Sumpter has been assaulted, as is reported, I shall, perhaps, cause the United States mails to be withdrawn from all the States which claim to have seceded, believing that the commencement of actual war against the Government justifies and possibly demands it. I scarcely need to say that I consider the military posts and property situated within the States which claim to have seceded, as yet belonging to the Government of the United States as much as they did before the supposed secession. Whatever else I may do for the purpose I shall not attempt to collect the duties and imposts by any armed invasion of any part of the country; not meaning by this, however, that I may not land a force deemed necessary to relieve a fort upon the border of the country. From the fact that I have quoted a part of the Inaugural Address, it must not be inferred that I repudiate any other part, the whole of which I reaffirm, except so far as what I now say of the mails may be regarded as a modification.

Postmaster-General BLAIR sent special agent BRYANT to Pensacola last week to reëstablish the Post-office there. BRYANT stopped at Montgomery on his way, where Confederate States Postmaster REAGAN forbade him to fulfill his mission, but failed to give any reason therefor.

RECRUITS FOR THE SECESSION ARMY.

Recruiting for the regular army of the Southern Confederacy has been going on sometime at Baltimore The men are sent South *via* Norfolk as rapidly as they are obtained. Recruiting was also going on for the same service in this city yesterday. No objection is made to it, as it is deemed desirable to be rid of such men. A reliable Union man as Collector at Baltimore now, would do much good in watching these enlistments and detecting anticipated efforts to obtain a navy for the Confederated States at that port.

FORT PICKENS.

The Government has no advices from Fort Pickens, but you may rely upon it that relief has been sent to it. Dispatches hence to Pensacola have positively announced the fact to Gen BRAGG, and it is very probable that fighting has begun there also by this time. No apprehension is entertained on its behalf, as it has abundant men and supplies, and, if needed, additional forces can be sent it from Fort Taylor and Tortugas.

While the Executive does not indicate his purpose in that respect, it is generally understood to-night that the contest will be waged at Charleston vigorously for the vindication of the flag at that point and the recovery of the public property there.

MISCELLANEOUS MILITARY MATTERS.

Five additional companies of the District militia were mustered into service to-day, making 2,500 men here now under arms.

The National Rifles, a Disunion corps, held a meeting last night to rejoice over the reduction of Fort Sumpter and reorganize their corps. Martial law would suppress this nest of traitors.

One POWELL, a clerk in the Sixth Auditor's office, and an officer in the District militia, who last week took the oath to support the Government, stated publicly on the street to-day, that if Maryland should secede he would go with her. He will probably lose both his office and commission to-morrow No mercy henceforth will be shown to Disunionists in the public employ.

Twenty men from the Second Cavalry were stationed all last night as a guard at the White House. Mounted troops are stationed to-night outside the city, with rations for their horses. They are guarding every approach to the city. They are stationed four at each point, and relieved every four hours. Signals have been arranged for more speedy communication. One hundred and fifty men are stationed in the Post-office Department; three hundred at the Treasury; two hundred at the Capitol, and two hundred near the White House. Gov. CURTIN, of Pennsylvania, who is in town, received dispatches to-day, assuring him that Pennsylvania volunteers to any

[*Continued on Eighth Page.*]

THE DAILY EVENING STAR
IS
PUBLISHED EVERY AFTERNOON,
(SUNDAYS EXCEPTED,)
AT THE STAR BUILDINGS,
Corner of Pennsylvania avenue and 11th st.,
BY
W. D. WALLACE.

Papers served in packages by carriers at $4 a year, or 37 cents per month. To mail subscribers the price is $3.50 a year, in advance; $2 for six months; $1 for three months; and for less than three months at the rate of 12 cents a week. Single copies, ONE CENT; in wrappers, TWO CENTS.

☞ ADVERTISEMENTS should be sent to the office before 12 o'clock m.; otherwise they may not appear until the next day.

Evening Star.

Vol. XVII. WASHINGTON, D. C., THURSDAY, APRIL 18, 1861. No. 2,547.

THE WEEKLY DOLLAR STAR.

This excellent Family and News Journal—containing a greater variety of interesting reading than can be found in any other—is published on Friday morning.

TERMS—Cash, invariably, in advance.

Single copy, per annum	$1 00
Five copies	4 75
Ten copies	8 00
Twenty-five copies	20 00

It invariably contains the "Washington News" that has made The Daily Evening Star circulate so generally throughout the country.

☞ Single copies (in wrappers) can be procured at the counter, immediately after the issue of the paper. Price—THREE CENTS.

BOMBARDMENT AT CHARLESTON.

The Evacuation of Fort Sumter—Embarkation of Major Anderson.

The Charleston papers of the 15th give the following further particulars:

An officer who visited the Fort soon after the terms of evacuation were made, states that the scene there presented is beyond conception. Without, the walls have the appearance, at a distance, of having been covered with an immense number of brick poultices spattered in every direction. This is the shattering effect of the shot. Within, the entire fort wore an aspect as if the hand of the destroying angel had swept ruthlessly by and left not a solitary object to relieve the general desolation. The blackened walls of the officers' and soldier's quarters were yet smoking, ashes and embers met the eye at every turn, while the shot and shell which had been rained upon the stronghold lay in great quantities upon all portions of the parade ground.

The appearance of both Major Anderson, his officers and the men, indicated the terrible nature of the ordeal from which they had just emerged. Deprived of sleep for many hours, fatigued with their labors at the guns, and prostrated by their battle with an element which waged beyond control, they looked worn, haggard and ready to drop with sheer exhaustion.

When the fire was at its greatest height Maj. Anderson stated that the only manner in which they could breathe was by laying flat upon the ground within the casemates, with their faces to the earth, while, added to the danger, was the occasional explosion of the piles of shells collected for service at different points within the fort.

It is to the fact that so few men were in the fortification, that is due the preservation of life. Major Anderson himself stated that had there been two hundred more, not less than one half of them must have been killed, owing to the absence of sufficient room, under the circumstances, for their protection.

As it was, their provisions would have given out in two days more, when an unconditional surrender would have necessarily resulted.

He also remarked that yesterday was one of the proudest days of his life, for while he had endeavored to do his duty as an officer, he had not taken the life of a fellow being.

The interview between Major Anderson and our informant was not a long one, and consequently many interesting incidents connected with Fort Sumter, which belong to the memorable occasion, must for the present remain unknown.

During the evening, a boat arrived at Morris Island from one of the northern vessels in the offing, bearing a lieutenant and a flag of truce, his object being to arrange for the evacuation of the soldiers with their property. He also assured the commanding officer at that point (Gen. Simons) that hostilities would not take place during the night. The matter was referred to Gen. Beauregard.

Meanwhile Major Anderson had himself addressed a letter to the latter officer, requesting that the steamship Catawba should be at the wharf of Fort Sumter at 9 o'clock this (Sunday) morning.

At half-past 12 o'clock his Excellency Gov. Pickens, with his aids, and Messrs. Jamison and Magrath, of his executive council, and Gen. Beauregard, with his aids, Messrs. Miles, Pryor, Manning, Chesnut and Jones, and many distinguished gentlemen, invited to be present, took their departure in a steamer from Southern wharf, and were borne in the direction of the fort. As we advanced it was apparent, however, that the evacuation was not completed. Though the steamer Isabel, at the request of Major Anderson, had been present from 9 o'clock, and the expectation had been occasioned that very soon thereafter his command would be under way, still causes of delay had intervened. To avoid the embarrassments of a premature arrival, the party was landed upon Sullivan's Island. Availing themselves of the opportunities thus afforded, they visited the floating battery, the Dahlgren battery, the enfilading battery, and were ascending the mortar battery, when the booming of the guns upon the parapets of Fort Sumter announced the lowering of the "stars and stripes." In the terms of capitulation it was allowed to Major Anderson to salute his flag, and it was perhaps expected that he would fire the usual compliment of twenty-one guns, but reaching that number, he still went on to fire, and the apprehension was that he might exhibit the discourtesy of numbering thirty-four. But he continued still to fire up to fifty, and then slowly lowering his flag, the shouts from assembled thousands upon the shores and the steamers, and every species of water craft, announced that the authority of the late United States upon the last foot of Carolina's soil was finally withdrawn.

It had been noticed, that the firing of the seventeenth gun, there was the sound as of two guns, and the impression was that two guns had been fired together; but, as the party, re-embarking, were on their way to Fort Sumter, they were met by a boat, which announced that one of the cannons had exploded, and made earnest request that the boat would return to Sullivan's Island for a fire engine, from the apprehension that the magazine might be in danger. This obtained, the party again started for the fort, and made their entrance.

It were vain to attempt a detailed description of the scene.

Shortly after the arrival, the garrison marched, and were received on board the Isabel; which, however, from the condition of the tide, was unable to move off, and it was a somewhat unpleasant circumstance that Maj. Anderson and his command should have been made unwilling spectators of the exultations inspired by their defeat.

Of those suffering from the casualty we have mentioned, one was killed upon the spot; two wounded, it is supposed mortally, and were left for medical treatment; and two others badly wounded, also, at their earnest solicitation, were carried off.

The occasion was not without the charm and interest afforded by the presence of the fair. The lady of his Excellency Gov. Pickens, and the wife and daughter of Attorney-General Hayne, witnessed the ceremony from the boat, and Mrs. Henry Bonnetheau has the distinction of being the first in the fort under the flag of the Confederacy. She was down to attend the sister of Lieut. Davis, her guest during the period of her brother's confinement to the fort, and with the eye and genius of an artist, it was doubtless with a feeling of especial pleasure that she was favored with the opportunities of this occasion.

Col. Ripley was put in command. The departments of the service necessary to bring the fort to order were distributed. The men were preparing such rude appliances for comfort as the place admitted of, and as, at twilight, we steamed for the city, of those standing upon the ledge around the base of the fort, the last to be seen was the venerable Edmund Ruffin, of Virginia, who, with canteen and blanket strapped upon his shoulder, seemed to be submitting with exemplary complacency to the experience of a volunteer.

The following incident connected with the surrender may be of interest:—Supposing that Sumter was about to surrender, and with a view of offering assistance in putting out the flames, several Aids of Gen. Beauregard were sent in a small boat from the city to the fort. When these gentlemen had nearly reached their destination, it was evident to them that Anderson was determined to continue the fight. They immediately turned back, and came half way to the city; but to the surprise of every one a white flag was directly seen to wave from Sumter. There was some difficulty in comprehending the meaning of this. Was it surrender? No. He had up the Federal flag, as well as a flag of truce.

Just then Col. Louis T. Wigfall, an Aid of Gen. Beauregard, left Cumming's Point in an open boat, with a handkerchief on the end of his sword, in lieu of a flag of truce. The batteries, it is true, partly ceased firing, [illegible] one wholly so; but Moultrie and the batteries on the left of the beleaguered fortress not being able to ascertain what was going on, continued to fire. Wigfall's position was therefore rather dangerous, but he kept on, notwithstanding the shot were falling thick around him. He made his way safely and unperceived to the ledge of rocks extending about five feet from the walls of the fortress. He landed, and walked quickly and alone up to a port hole, through which he poked his head. A soldier saw him, and asked: What do you want?

Wigfall—To see the commandant.

Anderson appeared at the moment, and said: Here I am.

Wigfall—I see, Major, that you have up a white flag. Do you surrender?

Anderson—Yes, I have up a flag of truce, but you still continue your fire.

Wigfall—And that they will continue to do so long as you keep up the United States flag.

Anderson—I decline a parley.

Wigfall—That is no use. We will help put out your fire, but there must be no delay; we will be content with nothing but unconditional surrender.

Anderson—Then I must surrender. I have no other resource. My men will shortly suffocate. We are all in flames.

The brave commander of Sumter then agreed that he would, unconditionally, surrender—subject to the terms of Gen. Beauregard, who, as was said by Col. Wigfall, "is a soldier and a gentleman, and knows how to treat a brave enemy."

MILITIA SERVICE.—The citizens of Baltimore may desire to know something of the militia laws which are applicable to them. We constitute two divisions under art. 4 of the public local code of the State. One division is called the third division of Maryland militia. The other is the first light division of Maryland volunteers. The third division consists of the third and fourteenth brigades. The third brigade is composed of the 6th, 27th and 53th regiments of infantry. The fourteenth brigade is composed of the 39th, 51st, 52d and 56th regiments of infantry. The third and fourteenth brigades are divided into regimental districts, which may be altered and arranged according to the judgment of the commanding officers of the brigade; and the regimental officers are authorized to divide their regimental districts into company districts.

All able-bodied white citizens between the ages of twenty-one and forty-five years, who are residents of the city of Baltimore, except members of Congress, judges and clerks of courts, members of the Legislature, school teachers, physicians, custom-house and post office clerks, pilots and mariners, and ministers of the gospel, are liable to militia duty.

If any private neglects or refuses to attend any of the parades provided for by law, or to answer to his name when called upon at such parade, he forfeits the sum of two dollars. We do not deem it necessary to refer to the case of the uniformed militia, for their rules are applicable to their own members only, and are sufficiently known to them.

The militia of which we have spoken is subject to be called out by the Governor "to repel invasion, to suppress insurrections and to enforce the execution of the laws," and it may also be called out by the President of the United States, whenever in his judgment "the laws of the United States shall be opposed, or the execution thereof resisted in any State, by combinations too powerful to be suppressed by the ordinary course of judicial proceedings." The power thus existing extends to the uniformed militia, as well as to the militia not in uniform, and the President of the United States may keep a militia force in service, if he deems it necessary, until the expiration of thirty days after the commencement of the then next session of Congress.

But of the militia, thus called out from time to time, no officer or private shall be compelled to serve more than three months after his arrival at the place of rendezvous, in any one year, nor more than in due rotation with every able-bodied man of the same rank in the battalion to which the militia officer or private belongs. If any militia officer or private fails or refuses to obey such call, he shall be fined a sum not less than one month's pay, nor more than one year's pay, which fine is to be imposed by a court-martial only, constituted either under laws of the United States or under the laws of the State of Maryland. These court-martial must be composed of militia officers only.—*Balt. Sun.*

PARTIES IN GEORGIA.—The Atlanta (Georgia) Intelligencer, in the course of an article upon the formation of political parties in the State, remarks:

The nucleus of a reconstruction party has already been formed in the State of Georgia, on the basis of the admission of free States into this Confederacy. At the head of this party stands Alexander H. Stephens, Robert Toombs and Ben. H. Hill. If we are mistaken in the information of which we are in possession, we stand open to correction. It is not our desire to do any man or set of men injustice. We will not do so if we know it. But upon the facts in our possession, we reiterate that a reconstruction party has been formed in the State of Georgia, with Stephens, Toombs, and Hill as the leaders. We will watch the future developments of this new move on the political chess-board with no small degree of interest.

The Augusta Chronicle and Sentinel of the 11th, commenting upon the views thus presented, says:

Whatever it be called, if there be such a party, and *with such leaders*, it will not require long for any man to become satisfied that it will sweep Georgia by 25,000 majority. With a party on such an issue, knowing the feelings of the people as we do, with the Cobbs, Jackson, Bartow and Crawford on one side, and Toombs, Stephens, Johnson, Hill, Warner, Wright, Judge Stephens, Nisbet, Kenan, &c., &c., on the other, we shall confidently expect to see the house of Cobb demolished forever—never to be reconstructed.

THE EXTRA SESSION OF CONGRESS.—We give below a list of the States which have yet to elect Representatives in the new Congress. In order to be represented in the extra session called by President Lincoln special elections will have to be held in six States:

Virginia, fourth Thursday in May, 13.
North Carolina, first Thursday in August, 8.
Tennessee, first Thursday in August, 10.
Kentucky, first Monday in August, 10.
California, Tuesday after first Monday in September, 2.
Maryland, first Wednesday in November, 6.

☞ The "Confessions of a Medium," says the London correspondent of the Evening Post, is the title of a singular publication, the writer of which professes to relate his experience as one of a spirit-rapping company. He has abandoned the art, but says it is not an imposture. He thinks the effects are pronounced "by some subtle agency whereby the human will operates upon inert matter." One day, however, when he was acting as a medium, the operator caused him to utter some grossly immoral advice; so he knocked the fellow down, cut the connection and now gives his "confessions" to the world as a warning.

A MOUSE SWALLOWED FOR A WAGER.—A gentleman on Ferry Point, some time back bet a twenty-five dollar overcoat that he could swallow a whole mouse. The bet was accepted, the mouse produced and down it went, in a style that would have shamed a Chinaman and done credit to a Chinese juggler. The loser then offered to bet $100 that the mouse-swallower could not swallow another, but the bet was declined. The swallowing of the mouse is as true as it is strange.—*Norfolk Day Book.*

DEFECTION OF THE UNITED STATES TROOPS IN TEXAS.—The Galveston News of the 9th inst. publishes the subjoined significant paragraph:

We understand that Captain Murray, of the steamship Fashion, which vessel was chartered to take the United States troops from Indianola to the steamships waiting for them outside the bay, has been informed by the United States officer having charge that his services would not be needed again until July next. What does this mean?

SOUTHERN CONGRESS TO MEET IN CHARLESTON.—The Charleston correspondent of the Richmond Dispatch, writing on Saturday last, says:

Our Southern Congress meets here on Friday next. Gen. Beauregard and about one hundred of the members of the late Convention, and his officers, are now in secret session. Great events hang upon them.

☞ "I sell peppermints on Sunday," remarked a good old lady who kept a candy shop, "because they carry them to church and eat 'em, and keeps them awake to hear the sermon; but I never sell pickled limes, you must come week-days. They're secular [illegible]."

[illegible]

MISCELLANEOUS.

PROPOSALS FOR POSTAGE STAMPS.

POST OFFICE DEPARTMENT, March 27, 1861.

PROPOSALS will be received until 12 o'clock m. of 26th April next for furnishing Postage Stamps of the general style and description of those now in use, on suitable paper of the best quality, for a term of six years, commencing first of July next.

Bidders will state the price per thousand stamps, deliverable in packages of ten thousand each at the Post Office Department in Washington.

Also, the price per thousand, in similar packages, deliverable to the Agent of the Department at the place of manufacture.

Also, the price per thousand, delivered in larger packages, as required, either at the Department or place of manufacture.

Also, the price per thousand, separated in such quantities as may be daily ordered for the use of Post Offices, never less than two hundred stamps, and securely packed in tin cases, suitable band ers' board boxes, with muslin or other equally strong covers, or lined envelopes, according to the quantity and distance to be conveyed, as may be required by the Department, stating the difference, if any, between the cost of delivery to an agent at the place of manufacture and at Washington, D. C. All such packages, before mailing, to be re-examined and the stamps recounted by an Agent of this Department.

Bidders will also give the additional cost for directing packages for the mails and preparing blank receipts, under the direction of an agent of the Department, either at the Department or manufactory.

Proposals must be made for the stamps in sheets, perfectly gummed, and perforated in such manner that each separate stamp can be readily detached and used.

The denominations of stamps now in use are one cent, three cents, five cents, ten cents, twelve cents, twenty-four cents, thirty cents, and ninety cents. The heads of Washington and Franklin are to be preserved as the leading designs; the former on all the stamps, except those of one cent and thirty cents, on which are to be the head of Franklin. On all of the stamps the denomination must be given distinctly, in figures as well as letters, and the whole work must be executed in the best style of line engraving on steel.

The whole number of postage stamps furnished to the Department during the year ending the 30th June, 1860, was 216 370 660.

From past experience it is supposed that the number of packages mailed will average above two hundred daily, varying in size from two sheets, or 200 stamps, up to 500 sheets, or 50,000 stamps; but by far the larger proportion of packages contain not more than 20 sheets or 2 000 stamps.

Each bid is to be accompanied with a specimen of the style of engraving and the quality of paper to be furnished, which will be submitted to a board of disinterested experts or artists for examination; and the accepted bidder, before the final consummation of a contract, will be required to prepare designs and furnish proof impressions of the engravings of the several denominations of stamps.

Specimens of board and tin boxes and lined envelopes must also be submitted with each bid. It is necessary to protect the boxes by muslin or other covers in the most effectual manner against wet and abrasion. The contract will require all dies and plates to be prepared and kept in repair, and that new dies and plates shall be made, either for the present denominations of stamps or others, without charge, at the pleasure of the Department; and all such dies and plates are to be the property of the United States for the service of the Post Office Department.

No bids will be considered except from parties who have been actually engaged in the business of copperplate and steel engraving and printing, and are thus engaged at the time of bidding, and who are occupying suitable fire-proof premises and provided with all the necessary facilities to execute the work promptly, and give the requisite protection to the stamps, dies, and plates in their possession.

Parties not known to the Department will furnish proof as to these points with their bids.

In awarding the contract the Postmaster General reserves the right of deciding which bid, in its practical results, may be most to the interest of the Department, having reference to the style of the work, security, mode of packing, &c.

Proposals should be carefully sealed, and marked "Proposals for Postage Stamps," and addressed to the "*Third Assistant Postmaster General.*"

M. BLAIR,
Postmaster General.
ma 28-law4w

FOR BALTIMORE AND THE POTOMAC RIVER LANDINGS.

The steamer ST. NICHOLAS, Captain JACOB KIRWAN, will leave Riley's Wharf, Washington, every SATURDAY MORNING, at 6 o'clock. Leave Commerce Street Wharf, Baltimore, every WEDNESDAY AFTERNOON at 4 o'clock, calling at her usual landings on the river for passengers and freight.

Since last season the steamer has been put in thorough order throughout every part of her.

For freight or passage apply to THOMAS W. RILEY, Agent, Riley's Wharf, foot of 11th st.
ma 19-Tu&Th2m

A STARTLING DISCLOSURE!
DECLARATION OF WAR!
GREAT OUTPOURING OF THE PEOPLE!
BEGINNING OF THE CONTEST BY
WINDSOR & BROTHER, 339 Seventh st., selling BOOTS, SHOES, HATS, CAPS, &c., at a great sacrifice on former rates. Good Men's Working Shoes at 75 cents; Misses' Sewed Morocco Boots 87½, well worth $1 25; and a general assortment of Gents', Ladies', Misses', and Children's Shoes, very cheap. We will sell as low as any one, and take off 5 per cent. discount for cash in current funds. ap 3-eolm

A CARD.

I WOULD Respectfully call the attention of the citizen and stranger to our new lot of Men's and Boys' CLOTHING, FURNISHING GOODS, HATS and CAPS. I can safely say that I am now prepared to sell goods on better terms than ever. Don't forget to call and look at our new goods.
J. H. SMITH, Clothier,
ap 5-1m No. 460 Seventh st., near F.

FIREMEN'S INSURANCE COMPANY
OF
WASHINGTON AND GEORGETOWN.
Capital............$200,000.

Office corner C street and Louisiana av., over Bank of Washington.

INSURE HOUSES AND OTHER PROPERTY AGAINST LOSS BY FIRE.

DIRECTORS.

Geo. Shoemaker,	Samuel Redfern,
Samuel Cropley,	William Wilson,
Richard Jones,	John D. Barclay,
Jacob Gideon,	Andrew Rothwell,
Thos. Parker,	Richard Barry,
B. B. French,	Charles W. Davis.

No charge for Policies.
JAMES ADAMS, President.
ABEL G. DAVIS, Secretary. oc 10-eo6m

N. B.—The undersigned begs to inform the public that he has on hand a large stock of MONUMENTS, TOMBS, HEADSTONES, &c., at Baltimore and Philadelphia prices. Also, a new style of Drawings can be seen at the yard, and a new style of Marble Mantels. Table Tops, &c., kept on hand. Brown Stone and Granite work promptly attended to. WM. BRADLEY,
ma 18-eo3m Pa. av., bet 18th and 19th sts.

Wood and Coal.

A No. 1 article of WOOD on hand, prepared to suit the wants of each customer. Wood sold cord length also, or in any way or any quantities desired.

☞ Coal kept in Coal-Houses, screened before delivering.

☞ 2,240 lbs. to the ton.

☞ Personal attention to every order.

T. J. & W. M. GALT.

Office 282 Pa. av., between 11th and 12th sts. Wood Mill and Wharf foot of Seventeenth street, below War Department. ma 23-tf

GREAT NUMBERS OF PIANO FORTES for sale or rent at all prices. Also, ten Melodeons of different makers for rent or sale. New Music received from all parts of the country weekly. JOHN F. ELLIS,
ma 30 306 Pa. av., bet. 9th and 10th sts.

SILK ROBES, MOUSLIN ROBES, LAWN ROBES, BERAGE ROBES.

We are selling at half their original price. All other goods of every description we are still selling at cost. Our stock is large and well assorted in every department.
fe 21 TAYLOR & HUTCHISON.

TAYLOR & HUTCHISON, No. 42 CENTER MARKET SPACE, Would call the attention of purchasers to our stock of SEASONABLE DRY GOODS, comprising some of the newest and most desirable imports, tions of the season. Our stock of Domestics, Linen and White Goods will be found very complete, and will be offered at prices that cannot fail to give satisfaction. We ask an examination. ap 3

JOHN F. ELLIS,
SOLE AGENT
FOR THE SALE AND RENT
OF
CHICKERING & SONS' PIANOS,
306 PENNA. AVENUE,
Between 9th and 10th Streets,
ma 2 North Side.

MAGNOLIA HAMS! MAGNOLIA HAMS!!

We are now receiving our first supply of Magnolia Hams for this season. They cannot be surpassed. KING & BURCHELL,
ap 4 corner 15th st. and Vermont av.

SOMETHING NEW "ON FREE EXHIBITION"—A very large lot of CLOTHING, FURNISHING GOODS, HATS and CAPS, at No. 460 Seventh st. N. B.—All of the above goods for sale at very low prices, at SMITH'S, No. 460 Seventh st., between E and F sts. ap 5-1m

THE PRINCE OF WALES HAS GONE, [illegible]

DENTISTRY.

DR. CHAS. S. BOTELER,
SURGEON DENTIST,

Having located himself permanently in Washington, offers his professional services to citizens and sojourners, in all the various branches of his profession, upon the most recently improved system of Dentistry.

Dr. B., having studied with one of the most eminent and experienced Dentists of Washington, and also with the Dental College of Baltimore, from whom he has received his diploma, feels confident that his operations will prove eminently satisfactory to those who will test his professional ability.

Office No. 336 Pa. avenue, between 9th and 10th sts., over Stevens's Lace Store; open from 9 a. m. to 4 p. m. ap 1-eo2m

DRS. LOCKWOOD & DARRELL ARE PREPARED to insert TEETH on VULCANITE BASE, a new and improved mode. When made on this plan they are comfortable to wear and much cheaper than any other. Also, Teeth inserted on Gold Plate, and all Dental Operations of any kind that may be desired. Office Room No. 5, in the Washington Building, corner Pa. av. and Seventh st. ja 10-4m*

TEETH.

M. LOOMIS, M. D., the inventor and patentee of the MINERAL PLATE TEETH, attends personally at his office in this city.

Many persons can wear these teeth who cannot wear others, and no person can wear others who cannot wear these.

Persons calling at my office can be accommodated with any style and price of Teeth they may desire; but to those who are particular and wish the purest, cleanest, strongest, and most perfect denture that art can produce, the MINERAL PLATE will be more fully warranted.

Rooms in this city—No. 338 Pa. avenue, between 9th and 10th sts. Also, 907 Arch street, Philadelphia. oc 15-tf

CLOTHING, &c.

460 SEVENTH STREET. 460

ALWAYS AHEAD.

I have just received a nice stock of SPRING CLOTHING, FURNISHING GOODS, TRUNKS, HATS and CAPS, to which I invite the attention of all in want of such articles. My motto is "A quick sixpence is better than a slow shilling." Those in want of Clothing we invite to come and look at our goods and prices; and if you want a nice Shirt and a pretty Tie, No. 460 Seventh street is the place to get them. I have a very large stock of SPRING HATS, which I am selling at 25 per cent. below their actual value. For those who want to travel, I have just received a large lot of TRUNKS, VALISES, and CARPET BAGS, varying in prices from $1 50 to $8. If you want a good Trunk, Clothing, Furnishing Goods, Hats, or Caps, there is no place where you can buy them as low as at the People's Clothing Store, No. 460 Seventh st., opposite Post Office.
J. H. SMITH, Clothier,
mar 14-1m No. 460 Seventh st., bet. E and F.

L. A. BEALL & CO.

TAKE Pleasure in informing their customers and strangers, that they have removed to No. 361 Seventh street, between I and K, just above R. B. Hall's. We have just received a new supply of CLOTHING, FURNISHING GOODS, TRUNKS, HATS and CAPS, which we offer to sell at very low prices. Call and see us before buying elsewhere, as we know that we can sell you goods at less than any other store in the city.
L. A. BEALL & CO., Clothiers,
mar 14-1m No. 361 Seventh st., bet. I and K.

JUST RECEIVED, a lot more of the celebrated TEN CENT TIES; also, a very large lot of SPRING CLOTHING, FURNISHING GOODS, TRUNKS, HATS and CAPS, at the People's Clothing Store, No. 460 Seventh st., opposite Post Office, between E and F sts. ap 5-1m

NEW ARRIVAL OF SPRING AND SUMMER CLOTHING, FURNISHING GOODS, HATS and CAPS, at the People's Clothing Store, No. 460 Seventh st., opposite Post Office, near F street. ap 5-1m

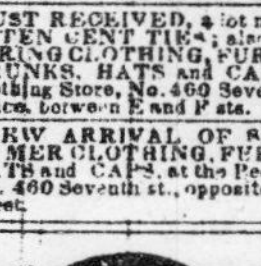

SCHWERIN'S
Annihilating
Powder

Is the only known and best article to exterminate Roaches, Bed Bugs, Ants, Moths, Flies, Fleas, Garden Worms, Vine Bugs, &c.

It contains no poison.

SCHWERIN'S PILLS are sure death to Rats and Mice. M. Schwerin has received certificates from the President of Girard College, Directors of House of Refuge, Pennsylvania Hospital, and other Prominent Institutions of Philadelphia; U. S. Jail, Washington, D. C.; and Charity Hospital, New Orleans, La.

The original certificates can be seen at the Wholesale and Retail Depot, 124 North Second street, Philadelphia, and for sale in this city by D. B. CLARK, corner Pa. avenue and 12 sts., and by all Druggists and Grocers.

BEWARE OF SPURIOUS IMITATIONS.

☞ Remember to ask for Schwerin's Annihilating Powder.

☞ None genuine unless signed M. SCHWERIN.
ma 13-6m

TOPHAM'S
PREMIUM TRUNK
MANUFACTORY,
499 SEVENTH STREET, WASHINGTON, D. C.

Silver Medal awarded by Maryland Institute of Baltimore, November 7, 1860.
Also, Medal by Metropolitan Mechanics' Institute, Washington, D. C., 1857.

I am constantly making, and always have on hand, of the best material, every description of Fine Sole Leather, Iron Frame, Ladies' Dress, Wood Box, and Packing Trunks, Pellisier, Carpet, and Canvas Traveling Bags, School Satchels, &c.,

At Low Prices.

Members of Congress and travelers will please examine my stock before purchasing elsewhere Trunks that are made in other cities.

Superior Leather and Dress Trunks made to order.

Trunks covered and repaired at short notice. Goods delivered free of charge to any part of the city, Georgetown, and Alexandria.
ja 23-1yeo JAMES S. TOPHAM.

THE EUROPEAN HOTEL; KEPT BY P. EMRICH, at the corner of Penn. avenue and Eleventh street, has been greatly improved recently and now offers greater inducements for the patronage of citizens and strangers than any other public house in the city, his prices being less than those of any other hotel on Penn. avenue, and his accommodations for permanent or transient boarders unexceptionable. The bar and restaurant arrangements of the European Hotel have already become very popular, being all that can be desired by the most fastidious. The proprietor pledges unremitted attention and continued liberal expenditures to give satisfaction to all, and thus renews his invitation to all to give the European Hotel a call. de 4-tf

TAKE NOTICE!

I WILL Take all kinds of Virginia money for my book debts and for Boots, Shoes, and Trunks. All persons indebted to me will please call and settle up, or I shall be compelled to give their accounts into the hands of a collector.
S. P. HOOVER, Iron Hall,
no 21 Pa. av., between 9th and 10th sts.

1861 DIARIES. 1861

Commence the Year with a Diary.

A valuable Pocket Companion for registering events past, present, and future; containing rates of postage, almanac, a blank space for memoranda for every day in the year, cash account for each month, annual summary of cash account, bills payable and receivable. Don't be without one of these useful little souvenirs. The most complete, elegant, and desirable assortment ever issued, comprising twelve sizes and upwards of fifty styles, at SHILLINGTON'S Bookstore,
Odeon Building, corner of 4½ street and
de 20 Penn. avenue.

PURE OLD RYE WHISKY.—On hand several brands of Pure Old Rye Whisky, Copper Distilled, made by the most reliable distillers in Pennsylvania, Maryland and Virginia, warranted pure. Also, Imported Brandies, Hennessy, Otard, Dupuy & Co., Jules Robins, &c. Also, Pelon and Apple Brandy, pure Holland Gin, old Jamaica and St. Croix Rum, and Wines of every variety, of all standard brands. A choice lot of Cigars and Tobacco. YOUNG & KEPHART, Agents,
ap 14-1y 289 Pa. av., between 9th and 10th sts.

LINCOLN AS HE IS.
STEEL ENGRAVED PORTRAIT.
The best Portrait yet published of
HON. ABRAHAM LINCOLN, (with whiskers,)
At FRENCH & RICHSTEIN'S,
No. 278 PENNA. AVENUE,
Washington, D. C.
Trade supplied at low prices. mar 7

HOME-MADE BOOTS AND SHOES,
FOR
LADIES', MISSES' AND CHILDREN'S WEAR,
At Exceedingly Low Prices.
At J. ROSENTHAL'S,
No. 15 Market Space,
ma 2-eo Pa. av., bet. 8th and 9th sts.

A VERY NICE PRINCE & CO. MELODEON which has been used a short time, for sale very low at METZEROTT'S Music Store. Also, several second-hand Pianos. ap 20

A SPECIAL BARGAIN IN TWO PIANOS, perfectly new. [illegible] for sale at [illegible]. Also, Melodeons for sale or rent very low.
JOHN F. ELLIS,
[illegible] 306 Pa. av., between 9th and 10th sts.

MEDICINES.

DR. JOHNSTON,
BALTIMORE
LOCK HOSPITAL,
Has discovered the most Certain, Speedy and only Effectual Remedy in the World,
FOR ALL DISEASES OF IMPRUDENCE.

LET NO FALSE DELICACY PREVENT.
APPLY IMMEDIATELY.

A CURE WARRANTED, OR NO CHARGE, IN FROM ONE TO TWO DAYS.

Weakness of the Back, Strictures, Affections of the Kidneys and Bladder, Involuntary Discharges, Impotency, General Debility, Nervousness, Dyspepsy, Languor, Confusion of Ideas, Low Spirits, Palpitation of the Heart, Timidity, Tremblings, Dimness of Sight or Giddiness, Disease of the Head, Throat, Nose or Skin, Affections of the Lungs, Stomach or Bowels—these Terrible Disorders arising from Solitary Habits of Youth—these Dreadful and Destructive Practices which render Marriage impossible, and destroy both Body and Mind.

YOUNG MEN

Especially who have become the victims of Solitary Vice, that dreadful and destructive habit which annually sweeps to an untimely grave thousands of Young Men of the most exalted talents and brilliant intellect, who might otherwise have entranced listening Senates with the thunders of eloquence or waked to ecstacy the living lyre, may call with full confidence.

MARRIAGE.

MARRIED PERSONS, or Young Men contemplating Marriage, being aware of physical weakness, organic debility, deformities, &c., speedily cured.

He who places himself under the care of Dr. J. may religiously confide in his honor as a gentleman and confidently rely upon his skill as a physician.

OFFICE No. 7 SOUTH FREDERICK ST.

left hand side going from Baltimore street, a few doors from the corner. Fail not to observe name and number. Letters must be paid and contain a stamp.

DR. JOHNSTON,

Member of the Royal College of Surgeons, London, graduate from one of the most eminent Colleges in the United States, and the greater part of whose life has been spent in the hospitals of London, Paris, Philadelphia and elsewhere, has effected some of the most astonishing cures that were ever known; many troubled with ringing in the head and ears when asleep; great nervousness, being alarmed at sudden sounds, bashfulness with frequent blushing, attended sometimes with derangement of mind, were cured immediately.

TAKE PARTICULAR NOTICE.

Young Men and others who have injured themselves by a certain practice indulged in when alone—a habit frequently learned from evil companions, or at school, the effects of which are nightly felt even when asleep, and if not cured, renders marriage impossible, and destroys both mind and body, should apply immediately.

These are some of the sad and melancholy effects produced by early habits of youth, viz: Weakness of the Back and Limbs, Pains in the Head, Dimness of Sight, Loss of Muscular Power, Palpitation of the Heart, Dyspepsy, Nervous Irritability, Derangement of the Digestive Functions, General Debility, Symptoms of Consumption, &c.

MENTALLY.—The fearful effects on the mind are much to be dreaded—Loss of Memory, Confusion of Ideas, Depression of Spirits, Evil Forebodings, Aversion of Society, Self-Distrust, Love of Solitude, Timidity, etc., are some of the evils produced.

NERVOUS DEBILITY.—Thousands can now judge what is the cause of their declining health, losing their vigor, becoming weak, pale, nervous and emaciated, having a singular appearance about the eyes, cough or symptoms of consumption.

DISEASES OF IMPRUDENCE.

When the misguided and imprudent votary of pleasure finds he has imbibed the seeds of this painful disease, it too often happens that an ill-timed sense of shame or dread of discovery deters him from applying to those who, from education and respectability, can alone befriend him. He falls into the hands of ignorant and designing pretenders, who, incapable of curing, filch his pecuniary substance, keep him trifling month after month, or as long as the smallest fee can be obtained, and in despair leave him with ruined health to sigh over his galling disappointment; or by the use of that deadly poison—Mercury—hasten the constitutional symptoms of this terrible disease, such as Affections of the Heart, Throat, Head, Skin, &c., progressing with frightful rapidity, till death puts a period to his dreadful sufferings by sending him to that undiscovered country from whose bourne no traveler returns.

DR. JOHNSON'S REMEDY FOR ORGANIC WEAKNESS AND IMPOTENCY.

By this great and important remedy weakness of the organs are speedily cured and full vigor restored. Thousands of the most nervous and debilitated, who had lost all hope, have been immediately relieved.

All impediments to Marriage, Physical or Mental Disqualifications, Loss of Procreative Power, Nervous Irritability, Trembling and Weakness or Exhaustion of the most fearful kind speedily cured.

ENDORSEMENT OF THE PRESS.

THE MANY THOUSANDS cured at this institution within the last seventeen years, and the numerous important Surgical operations performed by Dr. Johnston, witnessed by the reporters of the papers and many other persons, notices of which have appeared again and again before the public, besides his standing as a gentleman of character and responsibility, is a sufficient guarantee to the afflicted. mar 15-1y

DR. J. H. McLEAN'S
STRENGTHENING CORDIAL
AND BLOOD PURIFIER.
THE GREATEST REMEDY in the WORLD,
and the most
DELICIOUS AND
DELIGHTFUL
CORDIAL
EVER TAKEN.

Before taking.

It is strictly a scientific and Vegetable Compound, procured by the distillation of roots, herbs, and barks. Yellow Dock, Blood Root, Black Root, Sarsaparilla, Wild Cherry Bark, and Dandelion enters into its composition. The entire active remedial principle of each ingredient is thoroughly extracted by my new method of distilling, producing a delicious, exhilarating spirit, and the most infallible remedy for renovating the diseased system, and restoring the sick, suffering, and debilitated invalid to health and strength.

After taking.

McLEAN'S STRENGTHENING CORDIAL

Will effectually cure Liver Complaint, Dyspepsia, Jaundice, Chronic or Nervous Debility, Diseases of the Kidneys, and all diseases arising from a disordered Liver or Stomach, Dyspepsia, Heartburn, Inward Piles, Acidity or Sickness of the Stomach, Fullness of Blood to the Head, Dull Pain or Swimming in the Head, Palpitation of the Heart, Fullness or Weight in the Stomach, Sour Eructations, Choking or Suffocating Feeling when laying down, Dryness or Yellowness of the Skin and Eyes, Night Sweats, Inward Fevers, Pain in the Small of the Back, Chest, or Side, Sudden Flushes of Heat, Depression of Spirits, Frightful Dreams, Languor, Despondency or any nervous disease, Sores or Blotches on the Skin, and Fever and Ague (or Chills and Fever.)

OVER A MILLION BOTTLES

have been sold during the last six months, and in no instance has it failed in giving entire satisfaction. Who, then, will suffer from Weakness or Debility when McLEAN'S STRENGTHENING CORDIAL will cure you?

No language can convey an adequate idea of the immediate and almost miraculous change produced by taking this Cordial in the diseased, debilitated, and shattered nervous system, whether broken down by excess, weak by nature, or impaired by sickness, the relaxed and unstrung organization is restored to its pristine health and vigor.

MARRIED PERSONS,

or others, conscious of inability from whatever cause, will find McLEAN'S STRENGTHENING CORDIAL a thorough regenerator of the system; and all who may have injured themselves by improper indulgences will find in this Cordial a certain and speedy remedy.

TO THE LADIES.

McLEAN'S STRENGTHENING CORDIAL is a sovereign and speedy cure for Incipient Consumption, Whites, Obstructed or Difficult Menstruation, Incontinence of Urine or Involuntary Discharge thereof, Falling of the Womb, Giddiness, Fainting, and all diseases incident to Females.

THERE IS NO MISTAKE ABOUT IT.

Suffer no longer. Take it according to directions. It will stimulate, strengthen, and invigorate you and cause the bloom of health to mount your cheek again. Every bottle is warranted to give satisfaction.

FOR CHILDREN.

If your children are sickly, puny or afflicted, McLEAN'S CORDIAL will make them healthy, fat and robust. Delay not a moment; try it, and you will be convinced. It is delicious to take.

CAUTION.

Beware of druggists or dealers who may try to palm upon you some bitter or sarsaparilla trash, which they can buy cheap, by saying it is just as good. Avoid such men. Ask for McLEAN'S STRENGTHENING CORDIAL, and take nothing else. It is the only remedy that will purify the Blood thoroughly and at the same time strengthen the system.

One tablespoonful taken every morning fasting is a certain preventive for Cholera, Chills and Fever, Yellow Fever, or any prevalent disease. It is put up in large bottles. Price only $1 per bottle, or 6 bottles for $5. J. H. McLEAN, Sole proprietor of this Cordial; also, McLean's Volcanic Oil Liniment. Principal Depot on the corner of Third and Pine streets, St. Louis, Mo.

McLean's Volcanic Oil Liniment,
(THE BEST LINIMENT IN THE WORLD.)

The only safe and certain cure for Cancers, Piles, Tumors, Swellings and Bronchitis or Goitre, Paralysis, Neuralgia, Weakness of the Muscles, Chronic or Inflammatory Rheumatism, Stiffness of the Joints, Contracted Muscles or Ligaments, Earache or Toothache, Bruises, Sprains, Fresh Cuts, Wounds, Ulcers, Fever Sores, Caked Breast, Sore Nipples, Burns, Scalds, Sore Throat, or any inflammation or pain, no difference how severe or long the disease may have existed, McLEAN'S CELEBRATED LINIMENT is a certain remedy.

Thousands of human beings have been saved a life of decrepitude and misery by the use of this invaluable remedy.

McLEAN'S VOLCANIC OIL LINIMENT

Will relieve pain almost instantaneously, and it will cleanse, purify and heal the foulest sores in an incredible short time.

FOR HORSES AND OTHER ANIMALS.

McLEAN'S CELEBRATED LINIMENT is the only safe and reliable remedy for the cure of Spavin, Ringbone, Windgalls, Splints, Unnatural Lumps, Nodes or Swellings. It never failed to cure Big Head, Poll-evil, Fistula, Old Running Sores, or Sweeny, if properly applied. For Sprains, Bruises, Scratches, Cracked Heels, Chafes, Saddle or Collar Galls, Cuts, Sores, or Wounds, it is an infallible remedy. Apply it as directed and a cure is certain in every instance.

Then trifle no longer with the many worthless Liniments offered to you. Obtain a supply of DR. McLEAN'S CELEBRATED LINIMENT. [illegible]

J. H. McLEAN, Sole Proprietor,
Corner Third and Pine sts., St. Louis, Mo.
[illegible]

CARRIAGE FACTORIES.

WASHINGTON CARRIAGE FACTORY,
D Street, Between 9th and 10th Streets.

We have just finished a number of first class CARRIAGES, such as Light Family Wagons, Park Phaetons, Family Carriages, and Buggies, which we will sell at a very small profit.

Being practical mechanics in different branches of the business, we flatter ourselves that we know the styles and quality of work that will give satisfaction, combining lightness, comfort and durability.

Repairing promptly and carefully attended to at the shortest notice and most reasonable charges.
WALTER, KARMANN & HOPP,
Coachmakers, successors to Wm. T. Hook.
ap 27-d1y

CARRIAGES.

THE Subscriber having made additions to his factory, making it now one of the largest in the District, where his facilities for manufacturing CARRIAGES & LIGHT WAGONS of all kinds cannot be surpassed, and from his long experience in the business, he hopes to give general satisfaction.

All kinds of Carriages and Light Wagons kept on hand.

All REPAIRS neatly done, and all orders promptly attended to.

Second-hand Carriages taken in exchange for new ones. ANDREW J. JOYCE,
4 18-eo corner of 14th and D sts.

SOUTHERN MEDICAL HOUSE.

DR. SHUMAN has, after an experience of ten years, established the above refuge from quackery, self-labeled Indian or German doctors, and pretenders of witchcraft and impostors in general.

This is the only place where a sure and speedy cure can be obtained in the world for all improper and evil habits, gonorrhœ, gleet, seminal weakness, syphilis, primary, secondary, and tertiary, organic weakness, pains in the loins, strictures, general debility, prostration, nervousness, restless nights, palpitation of the heart, ringing in the ears, loss of memory, confusion, melancholy, affections of the head, throat, nose, and skin, and all those peculiar disorders arising from the indiscretion of youth, rendering them unfit for either business, study, society, or marriage.

Dr. S. has the greatest remedies in the known world for diseases of the blood, gonorrhœ, gleet, strictures, syphilis, seminal weakness, self abuse, &c. There is no case in which they fail to cure in from 3 to 6 days.

Victims of these horrible complaints, who would wish to be valuable men and ornaments to society, should embrace the earliest opportunity for relief.

Dr. Shuman has made the most complete arrangements for the comfort of his patients who come from a distance. They will be furnished with the most pleasant and agreeable quarters, necessary diet, and made as comfortable as they would be at a first class hotel at less than half the cost.

Do not forget the name and number. Dr. Shuman's office is on the corner of Sixth street and Pennsylvania avenue, Clarendon Hotel, opposite the National Hotel, Washington D. C.

Persons at a distance should enclose stamp for return postage. Office hours, 9 A. M. to 10 P. M.

Various parties have been detained from my institution by certain swindlers on back streets in this city, who will rue it till the day of their death. A word to the wise is sufficient. ap 9 1y

BROWN'S BRONCHIAL TROCHES

Cure Cough, Cold, Hoarseness, Influenza, any Irritation or Soreness of the Throat, Relieve the Hacking Cough in Consumption, Bronchitis, Asthma, & Catarrh, Clear and give strength to the voice of

PUBLIC SPEAKERS
AND SINGERS.

Few are aware of the importance of checking a Cough or "Common Cold" in its first stage; that which in the beginning would yield to a mild remedy, if neglected, soon attacks the Lungs. "Brown's Bronchial Troches," containing demulcent ingredients, allay Pulmonary and Bronchial Irritation.

BROWN'S TROCHES	"That trouble in my Throat, (for which the "Troches" are a specific) having made me often a mere whisperer." N. P. WILLIS.
BROWN'S TROCHES	"I recommend their use to PUBLIC SPEAKERS." REV. E. H. CHAPIN.
BROWN'S TROCHES	"Great service in subduing Hoarseness." REV. DANIEL WISE.
BROWN'S TROCHES	"Almost instant relief in the distressing labor of breathing peculiar to ASTHMA." REV. A. C. EGGLESTON.
BROWN'S TROCHES	"Contain no Opium or anything injurious." DR. A. A. HAYES, Chemist, Boston.
BROWN'S TROCHES	"A simple and pleasant combination for COUGHS, &c." DR. G. F. BIGELOW, Boston.
BROWN'S TROCHES	"Beneficial in BRONCHITIS." DR. J. F. W. LANE, Boston.
BROWN'S TROCHES	"I have proved them excellent for WHOOPING COUGH." REV. H. W. WARREN, Boston.
BROWN'S TROCHES	"Beneficial when compelled to speak, suffering from COLD." REV. S. J. P. ANDERSON, St. Louis.
BROWN'S TROCHES	"EFFECTUAL in removing Hoarseness and Irritation of the Throat, so common with SPEAKERS and SINGERS." Prof. M. STACY JOHNSON, La Grange, Ga. Teacher of Music, Southern Female College.
BROWN'S TROCHES	"Great benefit when taken before and after preaching, as they prevent Hoarseness. From their past effect, I think they will be of permanent advantage to me." REV. E. ROWLEY, A. M. President of Athens College, Tenn.
BROWN'S TROCHES	☞ Sold by all Druggists at TWENTY FIVE CENTS A BOX.

de 1-1y

THE ONLY PREPARATION
WORTHY OF
UNIVERSAL CONFIDENCE & PATRONAGE

FOR STATESMEN, JUDGES, CLERGYMEN, LADIES, and GENTLEMEN in all parts of the world testify to the efficacy of PROF. O. J. WOOD'S HAIR RESTORATIVE, and gentlemen of the Press are unanimous in its praise. A few testimonials only can be here given; see circular for more, and it will be impossible for you to doubt.

47 WALL STREET, NEW YORK, Dec. 20, 1858.

Gentlemen: Your note of the 15th instant, has been received, saying that you had heard that I had been benefited by the use of Wood's Hair Restorative, and requesting my certificate of the fact if I had no objection to give it.

I award it to you cheerfully, because I think it due. My age is about 50 years; the color of my hair auburn, and inclined to curl. Some five or six years since it began to turn gray, and the scalp on the crown of my head to lose its sensibility and dandruff to form upon it. Each of these disagreeabilities increased with time, and about 4 months since a fourth was added to them, by hair falling off the top of my head and threatening to make me bald.

In this unpleasant predicament I was induced to try Wood's Hair Restorative, mainly to arrest the falling off of my hair, for I had really no expectation that gray hair could ever be restored to its original color except from dyes. I was, however, greatly surprised to find, after the use of two bottles only, that not only was the falling off arrested, but the color was restored to the gray hairs and sensibility to the scalp, and dandruff ceased to form on my head, very much to the gratification of my wife, at whose solicitation I was induced to try it.

For this, among the many obligations I owe to her sex, I strongly recommend all husbands who value the admiration of their wives to profit by my example, and use it if growing gray or getting bald.

Very respectfully, BEN. A. LAVENDER.

To O. J. Wood & Co., 444 Broadway, N. Y.

My family are absent from the city, and I am no longer at No. 11 Carrol Place.

STANTON, ALA., July 20, 1859.

To PROF. O. J. WOOD: *Dear Sir*—Your "Hair Restorative" has done my hair so much good since I commenced the use of it, that I wish to make known to the public of its effects on the hair, which are great. A man or woman may be nearly deprived of hair, and by a resort to your "Hair Restorative" the hair will return more beautiful than ever; at least this is my experience. Believe it all!

Yours truly, WM. H. KENEDY.

P. S.—You can publish the above if you like. By publishing in our Southern papers you will get more patronage South. I see several of your certificates in the Mobile Mercury, a strong Southern paper. W. H. KENEDY.

WOOD'S HAIR RESTORATIVE.

PROF. O. J. WOOD: *Dear Sir*: Having had the misfortune to lose the best portion of my hair, from the effects of the yellow fever, in New Orleans in 1854, I was induced to make a trial of your preparation, and found it to answer as the very thing needed. My hair is now thick and glossy, and no words can express my obligations to you in giving to the afflicted such a treasure. FINLEY JOHNSON.

The Restorative is put up in bottles of three sizes, viz: large, medium and small; the small hold half a pint, and retails for one dollar per bottle; the medium holds at least 20 per cent. more in proportion than the small, retails for two dollars per bottle; the large holds a quart, 40 per cent. more in proportion, and retails for $3.

O. J. WOOD & CO., Proprietors, 444 Broadway, New York, and 114 Market street, St. Louis, Mo.

Sold in this city by C. STOTT, 370 Pa. avenue.
ap 27-eoly

3,000 LBS. CHOICE BUTTER;
[illegible] SUMMER BUTTER [illegible]
PENNSYLVANIA BUCKWHEAT.
CALVERT [illegible]
KING & BURCHELL,
[illegible] corner Vermont av. and Fifteenth st.

The New-York Times.

VOL. X....NO. 2987. NEW-YORK, THURSDAY, APRIL 18, 1861. PRICE TWO CENTS.

THE GREAT CONTEST.

Gathering of the Forces for the Struggle.

Wonderful Unanimity Throughout the North and West.

MOVEMENTS OF THE VOLUNTEERS.

The Seventh Regiment of New-York Going to Washington.

MOVEMENTS AT MONTGOMERY.

Letters of Marque and Reprisal to be Issued.

MORE VOLUNTEERS CALLED FOR.

The Virginia Convention Not yet Decided.

OUR WASHINGTON DISPATCHES.

WASHINGTON, Wednesday, April 17, 1861.

THE PRESIDENT AND GEN. SCOTT.

Nothing could be more untrue than all the statements that there has been any disagreement between the President and Gen. SCOTT, relative to the recent attempt to supply Fort Sumter with provisions. Gen. SCOTT, as is well known, advised that the Government had not at command regular forces sufficient to reinforce the Fort by force, because before that could be done, the battle must be fought ashore and won against all the secession batteries and troops. The President did not order an effort to reinforce it, and Gen. SCOTT was not called upon for, nor did he express, any opinion upon the political expediency of the attempt to "provision" the Fort, which the Administration considered it its imperative duty to make, whether it could succeed or not. That was a question with which the veteran soldier had nothing to do, and he is too scrupulous a disciplinarian, and understands his own duty too well to meddle with it.

THE FORT SUMTER EXPEDITION.

The presumption that the fleet was sent to Charleston as a feint, and to do nothing but divert Gen. BEAUREGARD from an attack on Washington, is equally erroneous. The purpose was to provision the fort in boats, and steam tugs provided to tow them in. The war vessels were not expected to engage the Morris Island batteries. That would have been madness, as one gun ashore is worth ten afloat, and the vessels would inevitably have been sunk or captured had they attempted the Quixotic exploit. They were designed simply to clear the way for the steam tugs, by dispersing and beating off armed boat parties from Charleston which might come down to oppose the landing of supplies. Why they did not make the attempt is not yet known here. It was expected by the officers in command of the war-steamers that Fort Sumter would coöperate with them by driving in or sinking the South Carolina boats in the harbor, within its range; and the fire of the fleet from outside the bar, in the same work, would lap the fire of Fort Sumter.

It is surmised that from a misunderstanding consequent upon Lieut. TALBOT's failure to reach the fort on his return from Washington, or from some other cause, Major ANDERSON failed to coöperate in this movement, and that for that reason the supply vessels were not sent in.

THE FIDELITY OF MAJOR ANDERSON.

I am able to state authoritatively that Maj. ANDERSON, in his defence of Fort Sumter, followed strictly the instructions of the Government. Nobody here doubts his honor and fidelity.

RUMORS FROM VIRGINIA.

The town has been rife with rumors to-day, especially from Virginia, towards which all eyes are turned, but as yet we have no information as to what she will do. A gentleman from Virginia, at the White House this morning, stated that she had passed the ordinance of secession in secret session, and that it was agreed upon to seize all United States strongholds and property within the grasp of the State. The President did not credit the report, although it gained general credence throughout the city, and created great excitement. The President said he was not yet prepared to believe that one of the founders of the Union, and the mother of so many of its rulers, was yet ready to break down her own work and blast her own glorious history by this act of treason.

THE FORCES AT THE CAPITAL.

There is a force of sixty additional men now stationed at the Capitol. The public buildings continue to be strongly guarded by increased forces. The avenues leading to the city are constantly regularly patrolled by mounted guards. To-night, in addition to the battery of two guns posted at the Long Bridge, fifty men of the Light Infantry Corps are stationed there.

The United States flag was displayed this morning at the Patent Office. The clerks at that Department have volunteered to do guard duty as often as required. A large force of volunteer troops passing the Patent Office to-day, halted in front of the flag and gave three cheers for "the Flag of the Union!" then for "the President!" and then for "Gen. SCOTT!"

PUBLIC SPIRIT IN WASHINGTON.

Hon. GREEN ADAMS, of Kentucky, was to-day commissioned as Sixth Auditor of the Treasury Department.

Many private citizens of Washington have raised the American flag over their residences. The National Hotel was the first to raise the colors permanently.

LIEUT. SLEMMER AND FORT PICKENS.

The statement that Lieut. SLEMMER has been superseded in command of Fort Pickens because his loyalty was suspected, is unjust. He is ordered to be superceded by an officer of higher grade and larger experience, but without the slightest intention to reflect on him. It seems to be well understood here now that Capt. MEIGS and his carpenters, with a corps of sappers and miners, has gone to the neighborhood of Pensacola, to aid in the relief and defence of Fort Pickens.

CAPT. HUGER'S RESIGNATION.

The resignation of Capt. HUGER, in command of Fort McHenry, who is a South Carolinian, and proves to be a Secessionist, created much surprise. He was supposed to be a strong Union man, and loyal to the flag and his oath. He has discarded all, and is execrated by many who hitherto esteemed him highly.

A company of Marylanders called upon the President to-day, to urge him to reinforce Fort McHenry at once with a garrison sufficient to hold it against all attacks. It will be done at once.

STRICKEN FROM THE ROLL.

Lieut. W. GWATHMEY, an Englishman appointed to the Navy from Virginia, having written an impudent and disrespectful letter to the President, his name was to-day stricken from the roll.

The following naval resignations have been received and accepted: Lieuts. WM. L. BRADFORD, of Alabama, and W. B. FITZGERALD, Virginia; SAMUEL V. TURNER, sail maker, from Virginia; GEO. D. LINING, South Carolina, Acting Midshipman, E. J. MCDERMOTT, Engineer, Texas.

WM. GWIN, son of the California Ex-Senator, appointed a cadet at large by Mr. BUCHANAN, has resigned to go South.

THE DEFENCE OF HARPER'S FERRY.

It was rumored, to-day, that several companies of troops had left here for the protection of Harper's Ferry Armory, but I can get no confirmation of the story. It is suggested that either two thousand men or a portrait of JOHN BROWN should be stationed there forthwith, as Gov. WISE threatens to march in that direction.

ENLISTMENTS IN BALTIMORE.

Advices from Baltimore indicate that thirty full Companies of Volunteers will be filled up in that city by Friday night. The President and Cabinet are in good spirits, and much gratified at the hearty response to the President's call for troops.

THE POSITION OF JOHN M. BOTTS.

The statement that JOHN M. BOTTS has turned Secessionist is laughed at by his friends, who say that when here, after the proclamation was issued, he fully indorsed the policy of the Government for its self-protection.

A TELEGRAPHIC ERROR.

In last night's dispatch I undertook to notice the promptness with which Capt. INNIS PALMER's company, of the Second Regiment of Cavalry, had been mounted. But a ludicrous error in the telegraphing conferred the honor upon JUNIUS PALMER, of the Indiana Cavalry. No such company as the latter is known to have arrived here.

DISPATCH TO THE ASSOCIATED PRESS.

WASHINGTON, Wednesday, April 17.

Gov. SPRAGUE has been telegraphed to come hither with Rhode Island's quota of troops without delay.

Additional volunteer companies were mustered in to-day by the War Department, and others are forming to offer their services to Government.

There is no intelligence here to warrant the belief that Harper's Ferry has been seized, as was currently reported to-day, together with other mere reports of an exciting character.

The Treasury Department has issued an order directing that the name of First Lieut. ROGERS be stricken from the roll of the Revenue service, for having, while in command of the Revenue cutter *Henry Dodge*, in violation of his official oath and of his duty to the Government, surrendered his vessel to Texas.

Col. CHARLES LEE JONES to-day resigned his commission as Adjutant-General of the District of Columbia Militia.

There is no ground for the report that JEFFERSON DAVIS is in Richmond.

IMPORTANT FROM MONTGOMERY.

PROPOSAL TO ISSUE LETTERS-OF-MARQUE AND REPRISAL.

MONTGOMERY, Wednesday, April 17.

Proclamation by the President of the Confederate States of America:

Whereas, ABRAHAM LINCOLN, President of the United States, has, by proclamation, announced intention of invading the Confederacy with an armed force, for the purpose of capturing its fortresses, and thereby subverting its independence, and subjecting the people thereof to the dominion of a foreign Power; and, whereas, it has thus become the duty of this Government to repel the threatened invasion, and defend the rights and liberties of the people by all the means which the laws of nations and usages of civilized warfare place at its disposal. Now, therefore, I, JEFFERSON DAVIS, President of the Confederate States of America, do issue this, my proclamation, inviting all those who may desire by service *in private armed vessels on the high seas*, to aid this Government in resisting so wanton and wicked an aggression, to make application for commissions or letters-of-marque and reprisal, to be issued under the seal of these Confederate States; and I do further notify all persons applying for letters-of-marque to make a statement in writing, giving the name and suitable description of the character, tonnage and force of the vessel; name of the place of residence of each owner concerned therein, and the intended number of crew, and to sign each statement, and deliver the same to the Secrethry of State or Collector of the port of entry of these Confederate States, to be by him transmitted to the Secretary of State, and I do further notify all applicants aforesaid before any commission or letter-of-marque is issued to any vessel, or the owner or owners thereof, and the commander for the time being, they will be required to give bond to the Confederate States, with at least two responsible sureties not interested in such vessel, in the penal sum of $5,000, or if such vessel be provided with more than one hundred and fifty men, then in the penal sum of ten thousand dollars, with the condition that the owners, officers and crew who shall be employed on board such commissioned vessel, shall observe the laws of these Confederate States, and the instructions given them for the regulation of their conduct, that shall satisfy all damages done contrary to the tenor thereof by such vessel during her commission, and deliver up the same when revoked by the President of the Confederate States. And I do further specially enjoin on all persons holding offices, civil and military, under the authority of the Confederate States, that they be vigilant and zealous in the discharge of the duties incident thereto; and I do moreover exhort the good people of these Confederate States, as they love their country, as they prize the blessing of free government, as they feel the wrongs of the past and those now threatened in an aggravated form, by those whose enmity is more implacable because unprovoked, they exert themselves in preserving order, in promoting concord, in maintaining the authority and efficacy of the laws, and in supporting, invigorating all the measures which may be adopted for a common defenbe, and by which, under the blessing of Divine Providence, we may hope for a speedy, just and honorable peace.

In witness whereof I have set my hand, and have caused the seal of the Confederate States of America to be attached, this 17th day of April, in the year of our Lord one thousand eight hundred and sixty one.

JEFFERSON DAVIS.

ROBERT TOOMBS, Secretary of State.

LATEST FROM THE CONFEDERATE CAPITAL.

MONTGOMERY, Ala., Tuesday, April 16.

One gentleman of this city has taken $125,000 of the Confederate loan at par, and paid the amount in gold.

There will be from 75,000 to 100,000 men in the field in less than thirty days.

The Government is likely to get large amounts of money from European ship builders.

MONTGOMERY, Wednesday, April 17—P. M.

The Cabinet had a long session to-day. A proclamation will be issued to-morrow, calling 150,000 more troops into the field.

Tenders have been made for letters-of-marque and reprisal.

Charleston has taken $2,000,000 of the loan at par $1,200,000 was paid in cash.

New-Orleans took $2,700,000 at par, and the people are not done subscribing at either place.

Mobile took $300,000, all taken by small bidders. Capitalists hold off till to-morrow.

FROM FORT PICKENS.

The following is an extract from a private letter received in this City yesterday:

MILTON, Florida, (20 miles from Pensacola,) Thursday, April 11, 1861.

I presume that before this reaches you, you will have news of an attack on Fort Pickens by Southern troops, which, for the past three or four weeks, have been pouring into Pensacola till they number 9,000 or 10,000 men. Mr. B went down yesterday morning and returned in the evening. *He reports it determined on by Southern officers to take Fort Pickens before to-morrow morning.*

I doubt if they can do it. I am satisfied that Fort Pickens has been reinforced, though the people at Pensacola doubt it. There are several United States vessels-of-war outside the harbor, and I know there will be hard fighting if an attack is made.

P. S.—6 P. M.—*Heavy cannonading for the past four hours at Pensacola.*

IMPORTANT FROM VIRGINIA.

Debate in Convention on the President's Proclamation.

SECESSION APPARENTLY INEVITABLE.

From Our Special Correspondent.

RICHMOND, Va., Monday morning, April 15, 1861.

The public mind of old Virginia is to-day boiling like one of the ocean's great whirlpools; or rather, I should say, rushing like the Gulf Stream's torrent; for it has ceased to meet in jarring conflict, resulting in a round of policy without progress, but is dashing onward to action—decided, open and irrevocable. What that action is, I need not repeat; I have already signified it clearly enough in the TIMES.

A man may live fifty years and see no such period of excitement as has prevailed in Virginia since the insurgent guns opened on Fort Sumter. When the news came that the "Stars and Stripes," that never fell before in the face of an enemy, had been lowered to the flag of the Confederate States, a delirium of joy seized the Disunionists of Richmond. They turned out by thousands, paraded the streets in companies, shouting the war cries of secession, were addressed at different points, as they passed through the city, by revolutionary orators, and finally proceeded to a State armory, and took without leave a number of field-pieces, with which they fired from Capitol Hill one hundred guns in honor of Sumter's surrender. Not satisfied with this, a passion seized them to exalt the secession flag over the State House, and a band instantly proceeded to execute the purpose. The State flag, renowned and honored in the old Commonwealth for its brave motto, "*Sic semper tyrannis*," was hauled down, and the banner of strange device—that of the seven Cotton States—dominated the haughty old State of Virginia! And many thousands of her sons and daughters shouted hosannas of *submission*!

Torchlight processions and illuminations at night succeeded the demonstrations of the day, and shouting, speech-making and revelry extended into the Sabbath morning. But "there are no Sundays in war," and repeating this declaration the streets were thronged from morning till night, and every available space near the newspaper offices occupied by hundreds and thousands of excited persons, waiting to read the dispatches that from hour to hour through the day were posted on the bulletin boards. Among the reports that came was one that President LINCOLN had issued his proclamation calling for 75,000 troops to quell insurrection in the Southern States. Of course it was intended to call on Virginia to furnish her quota. On this point it was awful to hear the savage comments and imprecations of the seceders.

But the crowning fardel on this raging flame of excitement was the telegraphic copy of Mr. LINCOLN's Proclamation, ordering the Southern insurgents to disperse, and calling for 75,000 men to restore the supremacy of the laws and retake the forts of the United States that had been captured. This was received by the Secessionists with a universal yell of defiance, and threats to march upon Washington City and drive the President from the White House! "Now, at last—now at last—will Virginia secede," was every seceders' consolation.

The Commissioners from the Virginia Convention to President LINCOLN, returned in the afternoon of Sunday, and this fact gave variety to the emotions of the hour. Mr. LINCOLN had replied to them in writing, and his reply was copied and published in this morning's papers. It jarred heavily on the popular heart, for its spirit was unmistakable.

With such excitement prevailing, you may well suppose that the Convention became to-day the centre of intense interest. At an early hour, Capitol Hill was dotted with gathering crowds, hoping to hear that the Convention, as soon as it should meet, would pass a secession ordinance. This hope was doomed to disappointment! Your correspondent was fortunate in obtaining his usual seat, though thousands of Virginians left disappointed. I will proceed to relate what ensued.

Immediately after the Convention was opened, Hon. WM. BALLARD PRESTON, Chairman of the Commissioners to Washington, presented a report of the result of their mission. The substance you have doubtless received by telegraph. The only point of interest in their interview with the President seems to have been this: That he had read of their appointment, and knew their business, and had prepared a written answer to them before they arrived. He so stated to them. I must be allowed to say that this was not dignified diplomacy. It is a dispatch, perhaps, only justified in war.

Mr. PRESTON submitted the report without the expression of any opinion as to what action should be taken in regard to it. Mr. HOLCOMBE, of Albemarle, Professor of Law in the University of Virginia, an influential member and a Secessionist, moved that the Convention go into secret session, suggesting that the public exigency was such as to make it politic to do so.

Hon. R. E. SCOTT opposed the motion. He was not aware of anything that made it proper to hide their counsels from the people. He thought there was but one sentiment now in Virginia. Mr. LINCOLN was in the exercise of a usurped power—his call for 75,000 men showed that his action was not to be limited to retaking the forts, but that he meant war—active, general, universal war. This Convention has deliberately declared how it will act in this emergency. We have declared it in terms explicit, and that cannot be misunderstood, that under no circumstances will Virginia be made a party to a war against the States of the South. The question now presented is—Will we make good this declaration? For one he was prepared to answer affirmatively.

If the proclamation which is reported to us to-day, as issued by the President, be authentic, we have no alternative. If it be responded to by the non-slaveholding States, we will have fierce, general war. In that view, it is our bounden duty and our public pledge to withdraw Virginia from the Federal Government. [Applause.] How this is to be done—in what manner—at what time—are grave questions for us to determine. By the law convening the Convention, we are required to submit to a vote of the people any measure that we may adopt changing the relations of this State to the Federal Government. We must keep that trust. *Secession, after all, is to be decreed by the people*; and, therefore, the Speaker saw no propriety in secret sessions of the Convention. The question now dividing the Convention was, whether secession should take place by separate State action, or on consultation with the Border States. The speaker approved the latter mode. He had heretofore approved it from motives of propriety and expediency. He approved it now for reasons of necessity. But the people of the State are divided, just as the members of the Convention are, on this question. It is proper, therefore, to submit the alternative propositions.

Mr. PRESTON interposed. He had not favored a secret session, because he held any secret opinions on the question involved. His mind was unalterably made up—he had nothing in thought or act to conceal. But he thought the whole question with the Convention now was, not whether the people of the State will accept their action. There was flagrant war commenced, and there were *prudential questions* in regard to meeting immediate emergencies, that they should consider.

Mr. CONRAD, of Frederic, (the Chairman of the main Committee of the Convention and leader of the Union men,) approved the motion for a secret session. He thought there were minor questions requiring action, besides the general course of policy to be pursued by the Convention.

Mr. MCFARLAND, of Richmond City, opposed the secret session. He thought it contrary to usage in Virginia, and that it was better to hold public sessions, that Representatives might act all the time under their responsibility to the public. The people had a right to know the opinions of members. If we hold a secret session exaggerated reports will go forth—the public anxiety will be increased—the excitement inflamed. Inasmuch as the Convention could do nothing that would not have to be announced, he thought there was no need of secrecy at all. It was contrary to Republican forms of government to deliberate upon public affairs in secret, where it was not feared an enemy would profit by a knowledge of your acts. Virginia has no enemy to fear. Only the Seceded States had set the example of legislating for a free people in secrecy. There was as much reason to have concealed their actions for weeks past as to conceal anything likely to be done or said now. Besides, their moral power would be lost, if they closed their doors upon the public. He wanted the moral power of their deliberations from day to day to be felt at Washington, as well as on the people of Virginia. And this could not be, if we sit in secret.

Mr. HOLCOMBE, (who had made the motion,) denied that the Secessionists cared for a secret session because they had aught to conceal. They were all openly and avowedly for secession, immediate and absolute. Himself had been for twelve months of the opinion that the election of a Black Republican President should be followed by the instant secession of the entire South. Not a day since the 6th of November last had found him unprepared for the act. And this very day, as the lightning was flashing LINCOLN's proclamation of four thousand words through the South, he (HOLCOMBE) would have seized the wires and sent ahead of that proclamation that declaration from Virginia that should have put every loyal son of the South "solid on his centre." He wished Virginia to go into the battle with the shout of a king. He left it for the Union men to direct the action of the Convention. They had confessed and accepted the full responsibility of their position as a majority of the body.

Mr. BRANCH, of Petersburgh, (elected Unionist, instructed now for secession,) wished to have the secret session. It could do no harm. If, when they had gone into secret session, they found that none of them had secrets to tell, they could come out and open their doors again. He was now for the conflict. His people were ready to march. If he could go with them, he would seek the front ranks.

Mr. SCOTT, of Powhatan, (elected Unionist, instructed for secession,) had thought there was no necessity for secession; the South had had Mr. LINCOLN's Administration in their power, but the Cotton States withdrew without cause, and lost the control of Congress. Mr. SCOTT had hoped to overcome that wrong step. He had loved the old Union and its flag too well to be willing to give them up without exhausting *every* expedient to save both. He thought this effort had been made, and the last hope was gone. He had, within the last moment, abandoned all hope, and now *he was for war*.

Mr. LINCOLN's inaugural had seemed to shut the door against hope, but Virginia had even after that thrown out her arms to save the Union. But there was no mistaking the signs. Why had the President called the Governors of non-slaveholding States to Washington? Why had he sent armed ships to the South? Even while we have been debating peace in this Convention, why has he thrown reinforcements into old Point Comfort? He had proclaimed that he intended merely to *provision* Fort Sumter. That was a *ruse de guerre*. If he meant but that, why were armed ships at hand?

Ex-Gov. WISE favored the secret session. The time for talking was past; the time for action was at hand. The entire purpose of secret sessions was misunderstood. It was not to tell or to hear secrets, but to debate subjects that in their nature required prudence and private handling. The United States Senate went into secret session on all the ordinary appointments of the Executive—not to tell secrets, but to discuss the qualifications of nominees, and to hear charges that may be made against their fitness. If such discussions were open, they would involve society in continual broils. There were secrets of peace and secrets of war. "Oh, the sweet secrets of peace! Oh, the infernal secrets of war!" Ex-Gov. WISE cared not whether the reported proclamation was authentic or not; the reply of the President to the Virginia Commissioners was enough. War was at their doors, and they must meet it.

Mr. DORMAN was in favor of immediate action. The gentleman from Montgomery (Mr. PRESTON) had suggested that there were facts to be made known, suitable only to secret session. That was enough for him. It had been said that much of their proceedings for a week past had as well been secret, as their present action. He assented to the proposition. It had been better that much of it had been secret, and kept so. Our differences are known to the world, and it were better that many sentiments expressed had been kept from the world.

One of the speakers had spoken of the policy of letting their deliberations be open, on account of their moral influence, not only in Virginia, but also at Washington. He (Mr. D.) was tired of trying "moral influence" on ABRAHAM LINCOLN.

Mr. J. EARLY opposed the motion to go into secret session. Suspicion had been cast upon the authenticity of the reported proclamation of the President. He doubted its genuineness. The Convention had been repeatedly assailed through sensation dispatches, and this might be one. He gave several reasons for the suspicions he entertained that the present dispatch was false. The Secretary of State (Mr. SEWARD) was a discreet and able statesman; and this proclamation would indicate an entire loss of common sense. He did not believe it a genuine proclamation, and did not mean to act in the dark.

Mr. BALDWIN (Union) had heard no reason assigned to justify the immediate action sought. He thought the people entitled to know all that themselves knew, and as fast as they knew it. The Convention should not cut themselves off from concurrent popular scrutiny and sympathy. He did not wish to be hurried. Efforts have been made to precipitate action. The crisis has been forced on Virginia. If we are "compelled to yield to it, let us sift every fact to the bottom, and have it clear as daylight to our minds. If a war of subjection is to be waged on the South, the Speaker's position was not doubtful. But before the Convention does an act to transfer war from the South to the soil of Virginia, let every man know to a certainty everything he ought to know, in deciding so momentous an issue.

Mr. GILLESPIE (Union) thought if any such proclamation had been issued as that published to-day, Gov. LETCHER, as Executive of Virginia, would be put in possession of it by the President, in making a call for troops. He thought, in such a grave matter, they might well wait for official papers. He therefore moved that the Convention adjourn till to-morrow (Tuesday) at 10 o'clock. This motion prevailed. And so Virginia did not secede, on the instant, as perhaps ten thousand Secessionists in all parts of the Union had predicted.

But secession is inevitable. Perhaps before this letter reaches you, the telegraph will tell that the deed is done.

MONTICELLO.

[BY TELEGRAPH.]

RICHMOND, Wednesday, April 17—5 P. M.

The Ordinance of Secession has not as yet passed. The Convention and they are still in secret session. Nothing certain is known of the proceedings transacted.

FALSE RUMOR ABOUT HARPER'S FERRY.

BALTIMORE, Wednesday, April 17.

It is not thought here that there is any truth in the rumor about Harper's Ferry. There is a company of regulars there.

LATEST REPORTS FROM CHARLESTON.

CHARLESTON, Wednesday, April 17.

Nothing of stirring importance has occurred to-day.

The prospect of the secession of Virginia gives great joy to the people of this section.

Two millions of the Confederate States' loan has been taken in Charleston alone. The paper is readily taken in the interior.

Not a word has to the present time been heard from Virginia, and great anxiety exists to hear from the Old Dominion.

CHARLESTON, Wednesday, April 17.

Two millions of the Confederate States loan has been taken in this city, and New-Orleans wants $5,000,000. The whole $15,000,000 will be issued immediately.

Gov. ELLIS, of North Carolina, has telegraphed to the Secretary of War that he has taken possession of the forts in North Carolina.

CHARLESTON, Wednesday, April 17.

Nothing of local interest has occurred here to-day.

Some excitement exists here about the secession of Virginia. If she secedes, it is supposed that troops will be sent from South Carolina to Virgina, but none will go before.

Private intelligence asserts that President DAVIS intends to assume command of the operations at Pensacola.

The iron battery on Cumming's Point is being taken down to-day, and the guns and rifled cannon are to be moved to posts commanding the channel.

The work of tearing down and clearing out continues at Sumter.

THE WAR EXCITEMENT.

MOVEMENTS OF THE METROPOLITAN MILITARY.

Rapid Organization of Regiments to Defend the Old Flag—Volunteers Flocking to the Recruiting Offices—The Zouaves Training for the Fight—The Seventh Regiment, &c., &c.

The ardor with which the City military have entered into the enrollment for the impending war is unparalleled. There is every probability of more volunteers from this City alone than required for the quota of the State. What with the enthusiasm of the Seventh, Seventy-first, Sixty-ninth, Seventy-ninth, Fifth, Eighth, and other favorite Regiments, quite a military *furore* prevails, which is in no way abated by the enlistments for Col. ALLEN's, Col. ELLSWORTH's and the Scott Life Guard Regiments.

THE SCOTT LIFE GUARD.

This veteran corps is being organized into a regiment, and a telegraphic dispatch was received yesterday from Senator MCLEOD MURPHY, who is a member of the corps, that the Governor has accepted their services. They have recruiting offices at No. 442 Broadway, at No. 37 Chatham-street, at Yorkville, opposite the Third avenue Railroad Dépôt, and will to-day have an office open in Brooklyn. They intend to include among their officers only efficient men who have seen active service, and they will be commanded by an experienced ex officer of the United States Army. For this reason their corps is a great favorite with those wishing to enlist, as additional guarantees will be given that the men will be taken care of by competent commanders.

The regiment will be uniformed in accordance with the lights of more modern military science. Their motto is that of Ex-Secretary JOHN A. DIX—

"The first man that attempts to haul down that flag, shoot him on the spot."

Already about four hundred men have been enlisted, and it is hoped that the ranks will be full by Saturday, ready for duty. The traitor *Express* upbraided them for not having a new flag, but their need was met yesterday by a timely presentation from two Broadway firms.

One of the volunteers was a member of the Kentucky regiment in Mexico.

COL. ELLSWORTH RECRUITING AMONG THE NEW-YORK FIREMEN.

The extreme danger to which the Federal Capital is now exposed, and the inadequacy of the available forces at command of the Government to afford it protection, have prompted an appeal to the New-York Firemen to organize into a Regiment of Zouaves, to assist in defending it from the threatened invasion. This idea of forming a regiment from the ranks of the New-York Firemen was originated by Col. E. E. ELLSWORTH, of Chicago Zouave fame, who arrived in this City yesterday, accredited with full power from the Administration to carry the matter to a successful issue. The emergency in question requires men inured to hardship—those already accustomed to a soldier's life—in fact, soldier's ready-made, which our firemen are known to be, and appreciating the compliment which is paid them, in soliciting their services for the important duty which has been designated, the greatest enthusiasm was created yesterday in the Department.

Col. ELLSWORTH only arrived in the City at 3 o'clock A. M., but before noon he had made his purpose known to the leading members of the Fire Department, who entered with spirit into the plan, and last evening offers had been made by five different men of Companies of one hundred each, one fire company—No. 14 Engine, it is said—volunteering *en masse*, while Brooklyn came forward and proffered 300 of her hardy sons.

Recruiting rooms have been opened by Col. ELLSWORTH at the Republican Committee Rooms, No. 618 Broadway, and it is believed that by this evening the full complement of picked men that he requires—800 rank and file—will have enlisted, and be ready to depart for Washington on Saturday.

The organization is to be precisely similar in character to the Zouaves of the French army, wearing a uniform like that of the famous Imperial Zouaves, provided at the expense of the Federal Government. The privates will receive board, medical attendance, all requisite clothing and $13 per month, while the pay of the non-commissioned officers will range from $17 to $22. Captains of companies will be elected by the members.

Col. ELLSWORTH's experience leads him to believe that, with the material which is thus at his command, he will not require a long time to drill the Regiment into the most efficient organization which the time demands. It is to be called the "First Regiment New-York Zouaves."

INDEPENDENT NATIONAL ZOUAVES.

This new element in military circles, through the indefatigability of Capt. MCCHESNEY, has achieved quite a success here, and are largely augmenting in numbers. Last evening they mustered at the Mercer House, and 84 men answered to their names. Without one dissenting voice, they resolved to tender their services to the Government. Patriotic speeches were made by Messrs. JACKSON and PEDDRICK, and their peculiar drill was witnessed by a large concourse of citizens. The Company meet again to-night.

THE SEVENTH REGIMENT DRILL.

The crowd assembled at the Armory of the Seventh Regiment last evening, to witness the left wing drill, was greater than ever before congregated in that building. No one was admitted to the drill room without a ticket, and hundreds who had tickets were obliged to await their turn for standing-room as the visitors passed in and out of the hall. There could not have been less than 3,000 persons visited the Armory last evening, at least half of whom were ladies. The rumor that the Seventh Regiment were likely to be called to Washington this week, drew hosts of their admirers to witness their splendid maneuvres before their departure.

It was extensively rumored about town yesterday that the Seventh Regiment had already been ordered to Washington, but, so far as we can learn, there is no truth in the report.

A member of the Regiment writes us as follows:

"During the day yesterday crowds of old members of the National Guard, who served their time out years ago, poured into Col. LEFFERTS' office, asking to be once more enrolled in the Regiment as active members, and hoping for active service in supporting the 'Stars and Stripes.' Among them was found *an enthusiastic German* in the person of NOLL, the old band leader, whose term of seven years expired about a year since. Mr. NOLL wanted the post of bugler, (whose duty is to sound the advance, charge, quick and double-quick movements, and, in fact, all such orders—*save the retreat*, which it is presumed there will be no call for.) He said, 'I have had offers of the post of band leader from other regiments, but I tell them the Seventh is my regiment. I served my time out there, and if I go back I could have command of a company, but I do not know how to be an officer. I *do* know the bugle, and I bugle for the Seventh Regiment, that business I know so well as any man.' He was promised the post, and departed happy.

At the armory in the evening the members were in full attendance; there was but one opinion, and that was in favor of volunteering.

The regiment is overwhelmed with applications for membership, but few, however, are admitted, as the companies are nearly all more than full."

During the evening Col. LEFFERTS received orders to proceed with his regiment to Washington to-morrow, (Friday,) at 3 P. M. The Captains were notified, and, later in the evening, the men, who responded with the greatest enthusiasm. Of one company alone of this reliable command, 125 men have volunteered to go, many more than the complement of a company in the regular service.

LAFAYETTE GUARD.

The Lafayette Guard met at the Arsenal, corner of White and Elm streets, last evening, and went through a regimental drill, the only peculiarity of which was the circumstance that it was an extra drill partially undertaken in view of the present condition of the country, and partly to pass away the time while awaiting the arrival of the Boston troop at midnight. The Lafayette Guard, as is well known, is entirely a French company, but the expressions of devotion to the Union last night might well cheer the heart of every native American. The "Lafayettes" are all sound.

MEETING OF THE DIVISION BOARD.

A special meeting of the officers of the First Division was called for last evening, in view of anxiety on the part of the Police Commissioners for the safety of the City Arsenals. In the absence of Gen. SANDFORD, Gen. HALL presided. After a general discussion it was decided to take no action at present, the usual police protection being deemed sufficient. The officers generally expressed the strongest determination to sustain the Union and the laws.

FIRST REGIMENT NATIONAL GUARD.

This regiment, which is being recruited by Col. WM. H. ALLEN, is not, as many suppose, composed of the Seventh Regiment solely. It is intended to make up the regiment mainly of volunteers from the First Division. Gen. SANDFORD is particularly interested in this regiment, and it will be composed mainly of his friends. The head-quarters for recruiting are at the Armory, corner of White and Elm streets. Other offices are open in Stanton-street, near Grand; at No. 83 Spring-street, near Broadway; and at No. 15 Centre-street—all of which are open from 10 A. M. to 10 P. M.

There have already been enrolled about 600 names, and it is expected that by Saturday there will be enough to fill the ranks of the companies—780 men—all enlisted for at least three months. They expect to be ordered to rendezvous at some point in the harbor on Monday, and be on the field to protect the National archives on Wednesday—at least such is the intention of Col. ALLEN.

It may be questioned by the uninitiated that so large a force could be uniformed in so short a time, but it must be recollected that the United States uniforms can be instantly put on the men, and fitted by the company tailors afterwards.

Besides the recruits at the stations already named, the regiment will receive additions of a company from Greene and Ulster Counties.

Sergeant CARPENTER, of the Union Volunteers, is raising a company for the regiment in the Thirteenth Ward.

A company is also organizing in the Ninth Ward, to be added to this regiment.

Col. ALLEN has already advertised for ten drummers and ten fifers, one for each company.

There were recruits offered and sworn in, yesterday, from the Third, Fifth, Seventh, Eighth, Eleventh, Sixty-ninth and Seventy-first Regiments. The services of the regiments have been proffered and accepted by the State.

THE SEVENTY-FIRST REGIMENT.

If any refutation was needed that the North was not true to itself and to the Union, it might have been learned last evening at the State Armory, on the corner of Thirty-fifth street and Seventh-avenue, where the Seventy-first Regiment, commanded by Col. VOSBURGH, have their drill-rooms. Last evening a battalion drill was had, Col. VOSBURGH commanding and directing the drill. There were over 300 members of the wing present, and more than twice that number of friends filled every possible location. Before the battalion was formed, the band played several martial and operatic airs, but the feature of the evening was the introduction of the "Star Spangled Banner," and on its appearance the immense audience, in which the troops must be included, arose and saluted it with so many cheers the reporter failed to count them. Having subsided into semi-quiescence, the band struck up the "Star Spangled Banner," which elicited more cheers and provoked more enthusiasm; but when they wound off with "Yankee Doodle," the enthusiasm reached its pitch, and was *encored* in as hearty cheers as were ever heard. After the regular drill, which was performed with an accuracy which promises to make the Seventy-first a formidable rival to the Seventh, Col. VOSBURGH formed his men into a hollow square, and addressed them briefly. He stated that, while he had, under present circumstances, no political or personal objects to advance, he was prepared to go with the regiment to any point to which it might be ordered, in defence of the flag under which he was born. He would gladly accompany the regiment to Mount Vernon, and lend all his power to protect the Government founded by the great and good man whose remains repose there. So far as he had been informed, there was as yet no official information that the services of the regiment would be required out of the City of New-York, but he felt assured that, if called upon, the Seventy-first would only ask "where to go and what to do."

The Colonel's speech, thus briefly and imperfectly sketched, was received with the most uproarious applause, and the hearty cheers given at its close for the Union was a sure test of the sentiments of the men he commands.

THE SEVENTY-NINTH REGIMENT, HIGHLAND GUARD.

Last evening our Scottish military, organized under the name of the Highland Volunteers, Seventy-ninth Regiment, met at the Mercer House, corner of Mercer and Broome streets, and after formally resolving to tender to the Federal Government the services of the Regiment, through the Governor of the State, they went into regular drill before a large company of visitors. During the evening the Regiment recruited 130 men, among them several well-known citizens. Gen. EWEN addressed the men, and expressed himself highly gratified with their performances. During the delivery of his remarks the General was called suddenly away by a dispatch from Gen. SANDFORD.

VOLUNTEERS FOR THE TWELFTH REGIMENT.

Great was the excitement yesterday evening at the drill room of Companies A and G, of the Twelfth Regiment, Independence Guard, Col. DANIEL BUTTERFIELD. Last Monday the whole of the regiment volunteered to go wherever and whenever the Commander-in-Chief pleases, for the purpose of upholding the honor of our National flag. At present the regiment consists of about 450 men; the meeting last evening was to receive the names of volunteers so as to get the full complement of a thousand men. The enthusiasm was intense, and Capt. GEORGE H. BARR was fully employed in enrolling the names of our patriotic citizens.

COL. WILSON'S REGIMENT.

The Head-quarters of Col. WILSON's regiment, at No. 618 Broadway, were crowded all day yesterday, and about 200 men were sworn in, swelling the numbers to 1,100, although the enrollments only commenced Monday. Drummers and fifers are wanted for this regiment.

Col. WILSON has issued an order directing all those in whose hands company rolls have been placed to to assemble their men to-night and go into an election of commissioned officers, and all the officers and men are directed to meet to-morrow night in the large hall in the second story of No. 618 Broadway, where, hereafter, all meetings of the command will take place.

A NEW VOLUNTEER COMPANY.

The martial spirit is hourly on the increase, and we hear of several volunteer corps about to be organized for the defence of the Federal Government. Hon. DANIEL E. SICKLES and Capt. WILLIAM L. WILEY are the officers of the latest of these bodies which has come to our notice, and the volunteers under their command will be all "picked men," Democratic, as they acknowledge, in politics, but Union to the very marrow of the back bone.

THE MEETING IN GRAND-STREET.

Company B, of the same regiment, also held a meeting for the same object at No. 552 Grand-st. These quarters are situated close to the Grand st. Ferry, and many gentlemen belonging to Williamsburgh and Brooklyn have entered their names as members, being determined to fight in such a cause by the side of their New-York brethren. Capt. HUSON, of this company, thought it would be a capital idea for the exempt men, who are over 45 years of age, and who are still in the vigor of manhood, to form a volunteer corps so as to protect the City in case it be necessary to call the whole of our regular militia away.

UNION VOLUNTEERS.

The Union Volunteers of the Ninth Ward, formerly the Young Artisans, are organizing an independent company, and are anxious for recruits. Their office is at No. 547 Hudson st., near Perry, and Capt. MCGRATH their commander. They want 100 men.

A POLISH REGIMENT TO BE FORMED.

The natives of Poland resident in this City and vicinity are preparing to organize a regiment or brigade for service under the President's Proclamation.

ARMY AND NAVY NEWS.

War business must be done whether it rains or shines. Accordingly Governor's Island, Fort Hamilton, Bedloe's Island and the Navy-yard yesterday reassumed the life-like aspect temporarily put off by bad weather.

The troops on the island were mustered at all the roll calls, as usual, and as the quarters may soon have additional occupants, no soldier is allowed two men's

[*Continued on Eighth Page.*]

THE NEW YORK HERALD.

WHOLE NO. 8989. MORNING EDITION—SATURDAY, APRIL 20, 1861. PRICE TWO CENTS.

THE WAR.

Highly Important News from Baltimore.

The Massachusetts Volunteers Opposed in Their Passage Through the City.

Bloody Fight Between the Soldiers and the Mob.

Two Soldiers and Seven Citizens Killed.

The Volunteers Succeed in Forcing their Way Through.

Total Destruction of the Arsenal at Harper's Ferry by the Federal Troops.

Seizure of Northern Vessels in Virginia.

Delaware Assumes the Position of Armed Neutrality.

IMPORTANT FROM WASHINGTON.

PROCLAMATION OF THE PRESIDENT.

BLOCKADE OF THE SOUTHERN PORTS.

Departure of the Rhode Island, Massachusetts and New York Troops for Washington.

The Seventh Regiment, Nearly One Thousand Strong, En Route for the Capital.

Immense Turnout of Ladies and Citizens to See Them Off.

Pathetic Leave Takings at the Railroad Depot.

Great Rush of Volunteers in the Metropolis.

Liberal Subscriptions in Aid of the Troops.

MOVEMENTS OF MAJOR ANDERSON.

Arrangements for the Monster Mass Meeting This Afternoon,

&c., &c., &c.

IMPORTANT FROM MARYLAND.

FIGHT IN BALTIMORE BETWEEN THE TROOPS AND THE MOB—TWO SOLDIERS AND SEVEN CITIZENS KILLED.

BALTIMORE, April 19, 1861.

A terrible scene is now going on in Pratt street. The track has been torn up. The troops attempted to march through, when they were attacked by a mob with stones and bricks, and then fired upon. The troops returned the fire. Two of the Seventh regiment of Massachusetts were killed. The fight is still going on.

There is intense excitement here. The soldiers are now forcing their way through. They fired on the mob, killing ten.

It is impossible to say what portion of the troops have been attacked. They bore a white flag as they marched up Pratt street, and were greeted with showers of paving stones. The Mayor of the city went ahead of them, with the police. An immense crowd blocked up the streets. The soldiers finally turned and fired on the mob. Several of the wounded have just gone up the street in carts.

At the Washington depot an immense crowd assembled. The rioters attacked the soldiers, who fired on the mob. Several were wounded, and some fatally. It is said that four of the military and four rioters are killed. The city is in great excitement. Martial law has been proclaimed. The military are rushing to the armories.

Civil war has commenced. The railroad track is said to be torn up outside of the city.

Parties threaten to destroy the Baltimore street bridge.

As the troops passed along Pratt street a perfect shower of paving stones rained on their heads.

The cars have left for Washington, and were stoned as they left.

It was the Seventh regiment of Massachusetts which broke through the mob. Three of the mob are known to be dead, and three soldiers. Many were wounded. Stores are closing, and the military rapidly forming. The Minute Men are turning out.

BALTIMORE, April 19—3:30 P. M.

Affairs are getting serious. Before all the cars got through great crowds assembled at various points and commenced obstructing the road.

Reports are now arriving that the mob are tearing up the track.

It is understood the principal portion of the troops have got through.

BALTIMORE, April 19—4 P. M.

A town meeting has been called for four o'clock.

It is said there have been twelve lives lost.

Several are mortally wounded.

Parties of men, half frantic, are roaming the streets, armed with guns, pistols and muskets.

The stores are closed, and business is suspended.

A general state of dread prevails.

Parties, a short time ago, rushed into the telegraph office, armed with hatchets, and cut the wires. Not much damage was done.

BALTIMORE, April 19—5 P. M.

R. W. Davis, of the firm of Pegram, Paynter & Davis, was shot dead during the riot near Camden station.

Four of the Massachusetts troops were killed and several wounded, but it is impossible to learn their names.

It is reported that the Philadelphians are now at the outer depot. The President of the road has ordered the train back at the urgent request of the Mayor and Governor. They are already off.

The citizens who were mortally wounded are John McCue, P. Griffin, G. Needham.

BALTIMORE, April 19—6 P. M.

As far as ascertained only two of the Massachusetts soldiers were killed, belonging to Company C. Their bodies are now at the police station. At the same station are the following wounded:—

Sergeant Ames, of the Lowell City Guard, wounded in the head slightly.

Private Colum, of the same place, shot in the head, not serious.

Private Michael Green, of Lawrence, Massachusetts, wounded in the head by stones.

H. W. Danforth, Company C, Sixth regiment, Massachusetts, slightly wounded.

So far as known at present seven citizens were killed, including Mr. Davis before mentioned and James Clark. Half a dozen or so are seriously wounded, though it is believed not fatally.

Comparative quiet now prevails. The military are under arms, and the police are out in full force. There is a large mass meeting here to-night, addressed by the Mayor. The Governor was present.

THE DEPARTURE OF THE SEVENTH REGIMENT.

The Scene at the New Jersey Railroad Depot.

BALTIMORE, April 19—10 P. M.

There was a town meeting at Monument square this afternoon. An immense crowd was present. The State flag was hoisted. Mayor Brown said he was opposed to the call of the President in spirit and object, but as Maryland was still in the Union he had exerted himself to his utmost ability to protect the troops in their passage through the city. He, however, felt that this should not be, and said that he had telegraphed the President, urging that no more troops be sent through.

Governor Hicks was sent for. He said he was opposed to secession, but the right of revolution could not be disputed. It was folly to attempt to subjugate the South, and he hoped the North and the administration would see the impracticability of doing so. He was still devoted to the Union, and hoped to see a reconstruction of it. (Shouts of "No, never.") The Governor replied that he should bow to the decision of the people of Maryland.

Several speeches were made by S. Teackle Wallis, W. P. Prestman, and others, justifying the determination of the people of Baltimore that no more Northern troops should invade her soil to subjugate and make war on her brethren of the South.

The speakers counselled peace and urged that the laws should be respected and obeyed.

The Mayor announced at the meeting that the President of the roads had promised that they would bring no more troops this way.

THE LATEST.

BALTIMORE, April 19—Midnight.

All is quiet to-night. The military and police are combined in guarding the city. The streets are comparatively deserted; here and there, however, small knots of people are discussing the events of the day.

THE KILLED AND WOUNDED.

The following is a correct list of the killed and wounded as far as known at this hour:—

The military wounded are:—

Sergeant Ames, of the Lowell City Guard, slightly.

Private Collum, of the same place, shot in the head, but not fatal.

Private Michael Green, of Lawrence, very slightly.

S. H. Needham, of Massachusetts, skull fractured, and now at the infirmary.

Another, whose name is unknown, is at the infirmary badly wounded.

Sergeant Ames and private Collum were to-night taken to a private house, and will receive the best attention.

H. W. Danforth and Ed. Cooper, of the same regiment, were shot in the thigh.

The names of the two Massachusetts men, dead and before mentioned, have not been ascertained.

The citizens killed are John McGhan, Sebastian Gies, Patrick Clark, P. Thomas Miles, Wm. C. Maloney, W. Reid and Mr. Davis—in all nine dead, including two soldiers.

Patrick Griffin was fatally wounded; others not known.

ATTACK ON THE PHILADELPHIA TROOPS.

The Philadelphians, who were unequipped and unarmed, remained in the last cars at the station, where they were assaulted with stones and other missiles. Some were slightly wounded. The train was taken back, but quite a number escaped to the city, and having no uniforms were not recognized.

The report of the difficulties on the road between here and Washington proves to be incorrect.

It is understood that all reached Washington safely except the Philadelphians, who were taken back.

PARTICULARS OF THE CONFLICT.

The following is the best account I can give you of the riot:—

At the President street depot of the Philadelphia Railroad a large crowd assembled in anticipation of the arrival of a large number of troops from New York and Massachusetts. Shortly after eleven o'clock the train from Philadelphia, comprising twenty-nine cars, arrived at the depot without disembarking the soldiers from the train. The several cars had horses attached, and about nine were drawn along Pratt street to Camden station, the first six without creating any marked sensation. For some reason the horses attached to the seventh car became restive, and were taken out from the car at the Pratt street bridge, and the car moved without them and he made a short distance of Gay street. Beyond Gay and Frederick streets a number of laborers were engaged in repairing the bed of the street, and just as the seventh car reached Gay street, were engaged in removing cobble stones from the principal portion of the street.

Some thirty or forty men assembled at this point, having followed the car from the depot, and with cheers for Davis and the Southern confederacy, hurled bitter taunts at Northern black republicans, as they termed them. This continued for several minutes, when, as the horses were again attached and the car moved off, it was proposed to stone it. Before the car had gone twenty yards almost every window therein was broken to pieces, and a portion of the crowd followed a considerable distance, hurling paving stones. Those persons not in uniform who were standing on the platform hastily jumped off to avoid the shower of stones.

The eighth car was treated in the same manner, but the ninth car, apparently being empty, or at least no person being visible, escaped with only one stone.

The crowd, exulted in their work, exclaiming that the black republicans should not pass through Maryland.

A lapse of five minutes succeeded. A number of respectable persons in the meanwhile urging the crowd to tear up the track.

After the first train had passed, one was observed on Pratt street bridge, when anchors were dragged on the track at the corner of Gay street and a part of the track was taken up.

Observing this, the cars were turned back to the President street depot, and the men disembarked and prepared to march through the city.

Mayor Brown, with a number of police, appeared at their head and led the way. They came along at a brisk pace, and when they reached centre market space an immense concourse of people closed in behind them and commenced stoning them. When they reached Gay street, where the track had been taken up, a large crowd of men armed with paving stones showered them on their heads with such force that several of them were knocked down in the ranks. After laying a few minutes they crowded into stores on Pratt street. At the corner of South and Pratt streets a man fired a pistol into the ranks of the militia, when those in the rear ranks immediately wheeled and fired upon their assailants and several were wounded. The guns of the soldiers that had fallen wounded were seized and fired upon the ranks with fatal effect in two or three instances. After they reached Calvert street they succeeded in checking their pursuers by a rapid fire, which brought down two or three, and were not much molested until they reached Howard street, where another large crowd was assembled. Some stones were thrown at them, but their guns were not loaded, and they passed on through the dense crowd down Howard street towards the depot.

The scene on Pratt street was of the most startling character. The wounded soldiers, three in number, were taken up carefully and carried to places of safety by the citizens along the street.

At Camden station, where the trains leave for Washington, was assembled a large detachment of police, under the direction of Marshal Kane.

It soon appeared that orders were given to clear the tracks near the main depot building. This was done, and soon after a large passenger car of the Philadelphia and Baltimore Railroad Company came up at a rapid rate, filled with the soldiers. The car was soon followed by about sixteen more, all of which were also occupied by the military. Upon inquiry it was ascertained that they consisted of a regiment of Massachusetts infantry, the Sixth, commanded by Colonel E. F. Jones and Lieutenant Colonel Shattuck, in all eleven companies, with an aggregate of 861 men.

As soon as the train arrived some of the troops were compelled to change cars, when they were hooted at by the crowd, but no overt act was committed. Several young men appeared at one of the cars and displayed revolvers, whereupon the captain of one of the companies drew his sword and declared he would protect his men.

Soon after the train was ready to start, under charge of Col. Shutt, assisted by Richard Armstrong. Many expected that the train would start immediately, but it did not move until about half past twelve, the delay being occasioned by the fact that President Garrett had received information that a large crowd of excited men had determined to tear up the track and blow up the bridges, and thereby prevent the passage of the train.

In a few minutes after the train left, a discharge of firearms attracted the attention of the crowd to the corner of Pratt and Howard streets, where a body of infantry from one of the Northern States, about 150 strong, was seen rapidly approaching the depot, and no doubt anxious to reach the cars. The excitement now was beyond description, and a man displaying the flag of the Confederate States, seemed to be the rallying point of the people. Some assailed the command with stones, when a number of the latter discharged their muskets. At least twenty shots were fired, but, as far as we could learn, no person was injured. There seemed to be but little discipline among the troops, especially as they rushed along pell-mell. When they were entering the cars a crowd of young men gave them several volleys of bricks and stones, some of which demolished the windows of the cars, whereupon three or four pointed their muskets through the car windows and fired. They aimed deliberately at the crowd, but no one was injured. While this body was passing near the corner of Pratt and Charles streets, they got into a collision with the crowd, and firing took place. One of the soldiers, named Robbins, of a company from Stonington, Conn., is supposed to be mortally wounded. He was wounded in the back part of the head, and fell to the ground.

The train with the second detachment left at a quarter past one.

There are rumors of an intended attack on Fort McHenry.

A crowd broke into the warehouse of Patterson & Walford, on Long Dock, this evening, and took therefrom some four hundred rifles and swords. Squads are parading the streets, fully armed, on the look out for the militia from the North who are expected to arrive to-night.

It can scarcely be true that any of the railroad bridges are to be blown up to prevent the passage of trains.

All sorts of reports are afloat, and it is impossible to discern the false from the true.

BALTIMORE, April 20—1 A. M.

I just hear that the Pennsylvania volunteers and the Seventh regiment of New York are coming. I fear there will be bloody work.

BALTIMORE, April 20—2 A. M.

It is reported the military are certainly coming.

All the city military have been ordered to meet in Monument square, and are now assembling.

AID WANTED BY THE UNIONISTS OF BALTIMORE.

A private despatch from Baltimore says:—"The position of our loyal citizens is becoming very critical. We hope that the North will stand by us; and in the forced passage of her troops to the capital will remember that there are many true men here. Our police force and many military companies are openly against the government."

PROCLAMATION OF THE GOVERNOR OF MARYLAND.

TO THE PEOPLE OF MARYLAND.

The unfortunate state of affairs now existing in the country has greatly excited the people of Maryland.

In consequence of our peculiar position, it is not to be expected that the people of the State can unanimously agree upon the best mode of preserving the honor and integrity of the State, and of maintaining within her limits that peace so earnestly desired by all good citizens.

The emergency is great. The consequences of a rash step will be fearful. It is the imperative duty of every true son of Maryland to do all that he can to arrest the threatened evil. I therefore counsel the people, in all earnestness, to withhold their hands from whatever may tend to precipitate us into the gulf of discord and ruin gaping to receive us.

I counsel the people to abstain from all heated controversy upon the subject, to avoid all things that tend to crimination and recrimination, to believe that the origin of our evil day may well be forgotten now by every patriot in the earnest desire to avert from us its fruit.

All powers vested in the Governor of the State will be strenuously exerted to preserve the peace and maintain inviolate honor and the integrity of Maryland.

I call upon the people to obey the laws, and to aid the constituted authorities in their endeavors to preserve the fair fame of our State untarnished.

I assure the people that no troops will be sent from Maryland, unless it may be for the defence of the national capital.

It is my intention in the future, as it has been my endeavor in the past, to preserve the people of Maryland from civil war; and I invoke the assistance of every true and loyal citizen to aid me to this end.

The people of this State will in a short time have the opportunity afforded them, in a special election for Members of the Congress of the United States, to express their devotion to the Union, or their desire to see it broken up.

TH. H. HICKS,
Governor of Maryland.

BALTIMORE, 18th April, 1861.

PROCLAMATION OF THE MAYOR OF BALTIMORE.

MAYOR'S OFFICE, April 18, 1861.

I heartily concur in the determination of the Governor to preserve the peace and maintain inviolate the honor and integrity of Maryland, as set forth in the above proclamation, and will earnestly co-operate with his efforts to maintain peace and order in the city of Baltimore.

And I cannot withhold my expression of satisfaction at his resolution that no troops shall be sent from Maryland to the soil of any other State. The great questions at issue must, in the last resort, be settled by the people of the city and State for themselves at the ballot box, and an opportunity for a free expression of their opinions will speedily be afforded at the approaching Congressional election.

If the counsels of the Governor shall be heeded we may rest secure in the confidence that the storm of civil war which now threatens the country will at least pass over our beloved State and leave it unharmed; but if they shall be disregarded, a fearful and fratricidal strife may at once burst forth in our midst.

Under such circumstances, can any good citizen doubt for a moment the course which duty and honor alike require him to pursue? GEO. WM. BROWN, Mayor.

IMPORTANT FROM DELAWARE.

ANTICIPATED RIOT AT WILMINGTON.

WILMINGTON, Del., April 19, 1861.

There is great excitement here, and a riot is hourly expected in the streets, to make people suspected show their colors. Great numbers are secretly armed.

A great Union meeting was held at Odd Fellows Hall to-night, Dr. H. F. Askew acted as President. The meeting was addressed by Mr. Patterson, L. E. Wales and others. Resolutions were passed unanimously for the immediate enrollment of volunteers for the protection of "home," and to sustain the Union by arms, if necessary, and that they don't belong to the North or South, but to the Union. Great enthusiasm prevailed. The enrollment has commenced.

THE TROOPS IN PHILADELPHIA.

PHILADELPHIA, April 20—3 A. M.

It is not known whether the troops have started for Washington—nothing having been seen of them since they arrived at the [illegible] street.

BLOCKADE OF THE SOUTHERN PORTS.

PROCLAMATION FROM PRESIDENT LINCOLN.

WASHINGTON, April 19, 1861.

The President has issued a proclamation stating that an insurrection against the government of the United States has broken out in the States of South Carolina, Georgia, Alabama, Florida, Mississippi, Louisiana, and Texas, and the law of the United States for the collection of the revenue cannot be effectually executed therein conformably to that provision of the constitution which requires duties to be uniform throughout the United States, and further that a combination of persons engaged in such insurrection have threatened to grant pretended letters of marque to authorize the bearers thereof to commit assaults on the lives, vessels and property of good citizens of the country lawfully engaged in commerce on the high seas and in the waters of the United States; and whereas, the President says an executive proclamation has already been issued requiring the persons engaged in these disorderly proceedings to desist, therefore calling out a militia force for the purpose of repressing the same and convening Congress in extraordinary session to deliberate and determine thereon. The President, with a view to the same purposes before mentioned, and to the protection of the public peace, and the lives and property of its orderly citizens pursuing their lawful occupations, until Congress shall have assembled and deliberated on the said unlawful proceedings, or until the same shall have ceased, has further deemed it advisable to set on foot a blockade of the ports within the states aforesaid in pursuance of the laws of the United States and the law of nations in such cases provided. For this purpose a competent force will be posted so as to prevent the entrance and exit of vessels from the ports aforesaid. If, therefore, with a view to violate the blockade, a vessel shall attempt to leave any of the said ports, she will be duly warned by the commander of one of the said blockading vessels, who will endorse on her register the fact and date of such warning, and if the same vessel still again attempt to enter or leave the blockaded she will be captured and sent to the nearest convenient port for such proceedings against her and her cargo as may be deemed advisable.

NO CLEARANCES TO BE GRANTED.

WASHINGTON, April 19, 1861.

To HIRAM BARNEY, Collector—

Grant no clearance for any south of Maryland till otherwise ordered.

S. P. CHASE, Secretary Treasury.

CLEARANCES TO THE REBEL STATES—FROM THE COLLECTOR.

CUSTOM HOUSE, NEW YORK,
COLLECTOR'S OFFICE, April 18th, 1861.

SIRS—In reply to your favor of this date, I have to say that owing to the very extraordinary exigencies under which the revenue and navigation laws of the United States are now compelled to be construed and executed, I am not at present prepared to grant any clearances to ports of the United States where the functions of the federal officers have been usurped by state authorities; and where the authority of the general government has been rebelled against, and repudiated—and more particularly since a belligerent proclamation from the quarter referred to indicates that the seizure or capture of your vessels would at once give aid and comfort to those now occupying a hostile attitude towards the government and people of the United States. I am, very respectfully, your obedient servant,

HIRAM BARNEY, Collector

Messrs. H. B. Cromwell & Co., New York.

PROCLAMATION OF THE MAYOR OF WASHINGTON.

MAYOR'S OFFICE, WASHINGTON, April 20, 1861

In the present unhappy condition of our national affairs, it is hoped, and believed, that the citizens at Washington will constantly feel and continuously respect the obligations of public order, which are in an especial manner incumbent on them. The presence of large bodies of troops, though it has given to the city an unaccustomed aspect, in no manner supersedes or interrupts the regular and orderly administration of the municipal government. It is not apprehended that any disturbance will occur, unless through heated and violent political discussions and harangues in public places upon topics, the agitation of which, at this time, and in this community, can be productive of nothing but unmitigated harm: therefore, I, James G. Berret, Mayor of Washington, do hereby earnestly exhort all good citizens and sojourners to be careful so to conduct themselves as neither by word or deed to give occasion for any breach of the peace.

Given under my hand, at the City Hall, this 20th day of April, A. D. 1861. JAMES G. BERRET, Mayor.

LIFE INSURANCE ON THOSE ENGAGED IN THE ARMY AND NAVY.

At a meeting of delegates from sixteen life companies doing business in this city and elsewhere, held this day, April 19, 1861, the following resolution was passed for the consideration and final decision of the Boards of Directors of the several companies:—

Resolved, That it is the opinion of this committee that the several life insurance companies should give their consent to those assured by them to enter into the military and naval service of the United States, for [illegible] [illegible] without any [illegible] [illegible].

OFF FOR THE WARS.

Departure of the Seventh Regiment for Washington—Scenes at the Armory—The Preparations for the Wars—March Down Broadway—The Embarkation at Jersey City,

&c., &c., &c.

Yesterday afternoon, in obedience to a requisition from the President and orders from Governor Morgan and Major General Sandford, the Seventh regiment, National Guard, left New York for Washington, via Philadelphia and Baltimore.

THE CROWD OUTSIDE THE ARMORY.

The orders issued from headquarters notified the men to be on duty at the armory, over Tompkins market, at three o'clock P. M., but long before noon the members of the regiment began to assemble in their rooms, and by one o'clock a crowd of over five thousand people gathered in the square upon which the market fronts, watching with intense interest everything connected with the departure for the wars of the celebrated and favorite regiment of New York. By two o'clock the crowd, both within and without the armory, became so great that policemen were stationed at the doors, and ingress refused to all persons not in the uniform of the regiment. By this means the crowd inside the building was restricted to manageable proportions, but that outside continued to increase until the streets were blocked up, and it was with the greatest difficulty that way was made for the passage of vehicles and for the Third and Fourth avenue cars. Orderly and easily managed as most American crowds are, the people occupied themselves with shouting and cheering for the Seventh, and with watching the arrival and reception of the officers' baggage, which was packed upon one of Adams Express Company's mammoth wagons. The wagon and the eight horses (of the size of small elephants), which were to draw it, were decorated with American flags, and the driver, like Longfellow's Youth, bore aloft—

"A banner with a strange device,"

which, after some difficulty, was understood to mean that "our glorious Seventh knew no North, no South, no East, no West, but only the whole Union." In looking at these objects, and in cheering until they were hoarse, the people outside kept themselves employed until, as the hour of rendezvous approached, carriages began to drive up conveying members of the regiment and their families. Then came the brief, half spoken adieus, the smiles which lightened only the face, the tears which welled up from the heart, the emotion which choked all utterance; and then the carriage drove off, leaving the cherished son or the beloved brother behind, perhaps forever. As every new arrival left his carriage he was cheered with the greatest enthusiasm, and these scenes, varied by occasional outbursts of the police, fully occupied the crowd outside until the regiment marched out of the building.

INSIDE THE ARMORY.

The crowd was almost as great as that outside. The company's rooms were filled with members of the regiment and their friends, and the large hall upon the lower floor of the armory resembled the vestibule of one of our most popular hotels. Gentlemen in uniform and out of uniform pushed and crowded each other about. The members of the regiment busied themselves in the last preparations for the journey. The officers journeyed from room to room, arranging details and obtaining instructions as to their movements. In the officers' room Major Stevens and other noted military men held a sort of informal reception. A few ladies, determined to be with their enlisted friends until the very last, moved about with the crowd, or whispered their farewell words to the loved ones, whose future dangers they, more than any one else, fully realized. Persons who belonged to the regiment, but were unable, for one cause or the other, to go with it, brought in their substitutes, and made and remade their half-ashamed apologies to their comrades. Outsiders, who felt an interest in each soldier only second to that of his more immediate friends, gathered to gratify their curiosity and give vent to their enthusiasm. Friends and pals of the boys swarmed about, shaking hands with every one, smoking furiously, and as full of ardor and fight as if they had been going to Washington also; members of the New York Zouave corps, in their loose blue uniforms, red shirts, fez and hairskin knapsacks, dotted the throng here and there, bidding the good byes, giving the God speeds and regretting that they, too, were not to be so soon en route; new recruits practising a little extra drill, or trying to fit themselves into uniforms too large or too small for them. Altogether a motley, varied assemblage, but all with one purpose and one sentiment: to express their sympathy with the National Guard and the cause it went to defend, and to show that sympathy by their presence, by their words and by their very faces.

PREPARING TO MOVE.

Presently, at about a quarter to three o'clock, a general hurry and movement throughout the rooms indicated that the time for muster was near at hand. The officers moved faster, and seemed more preoccupied. Col. Lefferts bluntly declined the offer of an escort from the Zouave corps, on the ground that it should have been made before, and that he had now no time to arrange for it. Recruits were told that it was too late to consider their cases now, and that they must report at some volunteer station. The members began to file off into their company rooms, from which outsiders were now excluded. Tardy arrivals were greeted enthusiastically, in the same spirit that the biblical shepherd rejoiced more over the one sheep he imagined lost than over the flock he had safely penned: "Why, here's Pete!" "I thought you wasn't coming." "Bully for you, old buffer," were the rough welcomes shouted to new comers. Yonder are a party of friends, some of whom are to go with the regiment while the others stay at home, and you may hear the request, "Kill one of the scoundrels for me, Billy;" the advice "take care of yourself, old fellow, and I'll see to things at home," the promise "I'll come back promoted, father, or I won't come at all;" and, then, in a woman's voice, "God bless you. I shall think of you and pray for you all the time. It's very hard to, but——" and then a few tears, low whisperings and a kiss. The most thoughtless began to grow serious now, and the most frivolous became earnest and anxious.

CIRCUMSTANCES OF THE START.

Then, as the soldiers began to engage more in conversation with each other, various interesting circumstances in connection with their departure began to be mentioned. Here were several Post Office clerks who had been granted leave of absence, with full pay, for the war; clerks in various mercantile houses had the same leave, with the same conditions. A Mr. Murphy had sent two sons and two employés with the Seventh, and armed them with fine revolvers. Other soldiers had been presented with revolvers also, and a general display of five and six shooters ensued. This man had been married only two days before, but his wife said "Go," and he came. Another was engaged to be married on Sunday, but the wedding was postponed three months, that he might serve his country. "I may die a batchelor, yet, you know," he lightly remarked, as he told of the circumstance. "I haven't had time to arrange my business, for I only received notice that we should move at ten o'clock to-day," remarked another, "but I'm here, my hearties." "I wonder will all the boys turn out," said a sergeant, "a day and a half is short work, eh?" "By George," laughed another, adjusting his sword belt, "I came up here to bid you good bye, but I couldn't stand it, so I jumped into these things, and will go along. Didn't have much time to bid the folks farewell, you bet." "What do you think the Governor said to me?" asked a young recruit, "why, he said 'remember Sumter,' and said he'd like to go too." "That's like Pa," shouted another, "she said she'd go if she were a man. Do you think I'd back out after that?" "How are you, my boy! You didn't back out, did you?" Then a long shake hands, and the response, "No! I didn't want to." "Here's a bouquet Mollie sent. Look at that. 'May peace soon bring you back to me.'" "Mother gave me this little flag. God bless her. I'll never disgrace it." "What do you think of that for a badge?" (displaying a beautifully worked rosette). "That goes over my heart." Breaking up these conversations there came, every once in a while, cheers upon cheers for the Seventh and for the Union, and snatches of national songs shouted with hearty, enthusiastic voices.

THE NEWS FROM BALTIMORE.

Then came the news from Baltimore, hurried up town by enthusiastic friends. It excited and saddened the soldiers vastly. The rumor spread that Colonel Lefferts had received a despatch instructing him to come through Baltimore at all hazards, and every one seemed to hope that it might be true. "Why should we go around to the Union?" remarked a sergeant; "if we can't railroad it, can't we march?" "Baltimore may serve as a little preliminary practice," said an officer, pulling a pair of white kids into his knapsack. "We have a character, and will sustain it, if it lays in our power," observed another. The members of the troop not being able to take their horses with them, and not expecting to get others at Washington, were ordered to act as artillerists, and lowered the two howitzers, which they were to take with them, down the stairs. "These are for Baltimore, if we want them," observed the captain, superintending the movement. Every one seemed inspired with a most patriotic spirit, recruits were obliged to be refused, and [illegible] [illegible] and a tiger made the building [illegible] [illegible] it was announced that every [illegible] [illegible]

Richmond Dispatch.
BY COWARDIN & HAMMERSLEY.

THE DAILY DISPATCH is served to subscribers at SIX AND A QUARTER CENTS per week, payable to the carrier weekly. Price for mailing, $4 a year; $2 for six months, in advance. THE SEMI-WEEKLY DISPATCH is issued every Tuesday and Friday at $3, in advance. THE WEEKLY DISPATCH is issued every Friday, and mailed to subscribers at $2 per annum.

DAILY DISPATCH.

VOL. XIX.--NO. 102. RICHMOND, VA., SATURDAY, MAY 4, 1861. PRICE ONE CENT.

SATURDAY MORNING......MAY 4, 1861.

MESSAGE OF PRESIDENT DAVIS, TO THE PROVISIONAL CONGRESS OF THE CONFEDERATE STATES.

Gentlemen of the Congress:

It is my pleasing duty to announce to you that the Constitution framed for the establishment of a permanent government for the Confederate States has been ratified by conventions in each of those States to which it was referred. To inaugurate the Government in its full proportions and upon its own substantial basis of the popular will, it only remains that elections should be held for the designation of the officers to administer it.

There is every reason to believe that at no distant day, other States identified in political principles and community of interests with those which you represent will join this Confederacy, giving to its typical constellation increased splendor—to its government of free, equal and sovereign States a wider sphere of usefulness—and to the friends of constitutional liberty a greater security for its harmonious and perpetual existence.

It was not, however, for the purpose of making this announcement that I have deemed it my duty to convoke you at an earlier day than that fixed by yourselves for your meeting. The declaration of war made against this Confederacy by Abraham Lincoln, the President of the United States, in his proclamation issued on the 15th day of the present month, rendered it necessary in my judgment that you should convene at the earliest practicable moment, to devise the measures necessary for the defence of the country.

The occasion is indeed an extraordinary one. It justifies me in a brief review of the relations heretofore existing between us and the States which now unite in warfare against us, and in a succinct statement of the events which have resulted in this warfare, to the end that mankind may pass intelligent and impartial judgment on its motives and objects.

During the war waged against Great Britain by her colonies on this continent, a common danger impelled them to a close alliance, and to the formation of a Confederation, by the terms of which the colonies, styling themselves States, entered "*severally* into a firm league of friendship with each other for their common defence, the security of their liberties, and their mutual and general welfare, binding themselves to assist each other against all force offered to, or attacks made upon them, or any of them, on account of religion, sovereignty, trade, or any other pretence whatever."

In order to guard against any misconstruction of their compact, the several States made explicit declaration in a distinct article—that "*each State retains its* sovereignty, freedom and independence, and every power, jurisdiction and right which is not by this Confederation *expressly delegated* to the United States in Congress assembled."

Under this contract of alliance, the war of the Revolution was successfully waged, and resulted in the treaty of peace with Great Britain in 1783, by the terms of which the several States were each *by name* recognized to be independent.

The articles of confederation contained a clause whereby all alterations were prohibited unless confirmed by the *Legislatures of every State*, after being agreed to by the Congress; and in obedience to this provision, under the resolution of Congress of the 21st February, 1787, the several States appointed delegates who attended a convention "*for the sole and express purpose of revising the articles of confederation*, and reporting to Congress and the several Legislatures such alterations and provisions therein as shall, when agreed to in Congress, and *confirmed by the States*, render the Federal Constitution adequate to the exigencies of government and the preservation of the Union."

It was by the delegates chosen by the *several States*, under the resolution just quoted, that the Constitution of the United States was framed in 1787, and submitted to the *several States* for ratification, as shown by the seventh article, which is in these words:

"The ratification of the *Conventions of nine States* shall be sufficient for the establishment of this Constitution *between the States* so ratifying the same."

I have italicised certain words in the quotations just made for the purpose of attracting attention to the singular and marked caution with which the States endeavored in every possible form to exclude the idea that the separate and independent sovereignty of each State was merged into one common government and nation; and the earnest desire they evinced to impress on the Constitution its true character—that of a *compact between independent States*.

The Constitution of 1787 having, however, omitted the clause already recited from the articles of confederation, which provided in explicit terms that each State retained its sovereignty and independence, some alarm was felt in the States when invited to ratify the Constitution, lest this omission should be construed into an abandonment of their cherished principle, and they refused to be satisfied until amendments were added to the Constitution, placing beyond any pretence of doubt the reservation by the States of all their sovereign rights and powers not expressly delegated to the United States by the Constitution.

Strange indeed must it appear to the impartial observer, but it is none the less true, that all these carefully worded clauses proved unavailing to prevent the rise and growth in the Northern States of a political school which has persistently claimed that the government thus formed was not a compact between States, but was in effect a national government, set up above and over the States. An organization created by the States to secure the blessings of liberty and independence against *foreign* aggression, has been gradually perverted into a machine for their control in their domestic affairs. The creature has been exalted above its creators; the principals have been made subordinate to the agent appointed by themselves.

The people of the Southern States, whose almost exclusive occupation was agriculture, early perceived a tendency in the Northern States to render the common government subservient to their own purposes by imposing burthens on commerce as a protection to their manufacturing and shipping interests. Long and angry controversies grew out of these attempts, often successful, to benefit one section of the country at the expense of the other. And the danger of disruption arising from this cause was enhanced by the fact that the Northern population was increasing, by immigration and other causes, in a greater ratio than the population of the South. By degrees, as the Northern States gained preponderance in the National Congress, self-interest taught their people to yield ready assent to any plausible advocacy of their right as a majority to govern the minority without control. They learned to listen with impatience to the suggestion of any constitutional impediment to the exercise of their will; and so utterly have the principles of the Constitution been corrupted in the Northern mind, that in the inaugural address delivered by President Lincoln in March last, he asserts as an axiom, which he plainly deems to be undeniable, that the theory of the Constitution requires that in all cases the majority shall govern; and in another memorable instance the same Chief Magistrate did not hesitate to liken the relations between a State and the United States to those which exist between a county and the State in which it is situated, and by which it was created. This is the lamentable and fundamental error on which rests the policy that has culminated in his declaration of war against these Confederate States.

In addition to the long continued and deep-seated resentment felt by the Southern States at the persistent abuse of the powers they had delegated to the Congress, for the purpose of enriching the manufacturing and shipping classes of the North at the expense of the South, there has existed for nearly half a century another subject of discord, involving interests of such transcendent magnitude as at all times to create the apprehension in the minds of many devoted lovers of the Union that its permanence was impossible.

When the several States delegated certain powers to the United States Congress, a large portion of the laboring population consisted of African slaves imported into the colonies by the mother country. In twelve out of the thirteen States negro slavery existed, and the right of property in slaves was protected by law. This property was recognized in the Constitution, and provision was made against its loss by the escape of the slave. The increase in the number of slaves by further importation from Africa was also secured by a clause forbidding Congress to prohibit the slave trade anterior to a certain date, and in no clause can there be found any delegation of power to the Congress authorizing it in any manner to legislate to the prejudice, detriment or discouragement of the owners of that species of property, or excluding it from the protection of the Government.

The climate and soil of the Northern States soon proved unpropitious to the continuance of slave labor, whilst the converse was the case at the South. Under the unrestricted free intercourse between the two sections, the Northern States consulted their own interests by selling their slaves to the South and prohibiting slavery within their limits. The South were willing purchasers of a property suitable to their wants, and paid the price of the acquisition without harboring a suspicion that their quiet possession was to be disturbed by those who were inhibited, not only by want of constitutional authority, but by good faith as vendors, from disquieting a title emanating from themselves.

As soon, however, as the Northern States that prohibited African slavery within their limits had reached a number sufficient to give their representation a controlling voice in the Congress, a persistent and organized system of hostile measures against the rights of the owners of slaves in the Southern States was inaugurated and gradually extended. A continuous series of measures was devised and prosecuted for the purpose of rendering insecure the tenure of property in slaves. Fanatical organizations, supplied with money by voluntary subscriptions, were assiduously engaged in exciting amongst the slaves a spirit of discontent and revolt; means were furnished for their escape from their owners, and agents secretly employed to entice them to abscond; the constitutional provision for their rendition to their owners was first evaded, then openly denounced as a violation of conscientious obligation and religious duty; men were taught that it was a merit to elude, disobey, and violently oppose the execution of the laws enacted to secure the performance of the promise contained in the constitutional compact; owners of slaves were mobbed and even murdered in open day, solely for applying to a magistrate for the arrest of a fugitive slave; the dogmas of these voluntary organizations soon obtained control of the Legislatures of many of the Northern States, and laws were passed providing for the punishment, by ruinous fines and long continued imprisonment in jails and penitentiaries, of citizens of the Southern States who should dare to ask aid of the officers of the law for the recovery of their property. Emboldened by success, the theatre of agitation and aggression against the clearly expressed constitutional rights of the Southern States was transferred to the Congress; Senators and Representatives were sent to the common councils of the nation, whose chief title to this distinction consisted in the display of a spirit of ultra fanaticism, and whose business was not "to promote the general welfare or ensure domestic tranquility," but to awaken the bitterest hatred against the citizens of sister States by violent denunciation of their institutions; the transaction of public affairs was impeded by repeated efforts to usurp powers not delegated by the Constitution, for the purpose of impairing the security of property in slaves, and reducing those States which held slaves to a condition of inferiority. Finally, a great party was organized for the purpose of obtaining the administration of the Government, with the avowed object of using its power for the total exclusion of the slave States from all participation in the benefits of the public domain acquired by all the States in common, whether by conquest or purchase; of surrounding them entirely by States in which slavery should be prohibited; of thus rendering the property in slaves so insecure as to be comparatively worthless, and thereby annihilating in effect property worth thousands of millions of dollars. This party, thus organized, succeeded in the month of November last in the election of its candidate for the Presidency of the United States.

In the meantime, under the mild and genial climate of the Southern States, and the increasing care and attention for the well-being and comfort of the laboring class, dictated alike by interest and humanity, the African slaves had augmented in number from about 600,000, at the date of the adoption of the constitutional compact, to upwards of 4,000,000. In moral and social condition they had been elevated from brutal savages into docile, intelligent, and civilized agricultural laborers, and supplied not only with bodily comforts, but with careful religious instruction. Under the supervision of a superior race, their labor had been so directed as not only to allow a gradual and marked amelioration of their own condition, but to convert hundreds of thousands of square miles of the wilderness into cultivated lands covered with a prosperous people; towns and cities had sprung into existence, and had rapidly increased in wealth and population under the social system of the South; the white population of the Southern slaveholding States had augmented from about 1,250,000 at the date of the adoption of the Constitution, to more than 8,500,000 in 1860; and the productions of the South in cotton, rice, sugar and tobacco, for the full development and continuance of which the labor of African slaves was and is indispensable, had swollen to an amount which formed nearly three-fourths of the exports of the whole United States, and had become absolutely necessary to the wants of civilized man.

With interests of such overwhelming magnitude imperilled, the people of the Southern States were driven by the conduct of the North to the adoption of some course of action to avert the danger with which they were openly menaced. With this view the Legislatures of the several States invited the people to select delegates to conventions to be held for the purpose of determining for themselves what measures were best adapted to meet so alarming a crisis in their history.

Here it may be proper to observe that from a period as early as 1798, there had existed in all of the States of the Union a party almost uninterruptedly in the majority, based upon the creed that each State was, in the last resort, the sole judge as well of its wrongs as of the mode and measure of redress. Indeed, it is obvious that under the law of nations this principle is an axiom, as applied to the relations of independent sovereign States, such as those which had united themselves under the constitutional compact. The Democratic party of the United States repeated, in its successful canvass in 1856, the declaration made in numerous previous political contests, that it would "faithfully abide by and uphold the principles laid down in the Kentucky and Virginia Legislatures of 1799, and in the report of Mr. Madison to the Virginia Legislature in 1799; and that it adopts those principles as constituting one of the main foundations of its political creed."

The principles thus emphatically announced embrace that to which I have already adverted—the right of each State to judge of and redress the wrongs of which it complains. These principles were maintained by overwhelming majorities of the people of all the States of the Union at different elections, especially in the elections of Mr. Jefferson in 1805, Mr. Madison in 1809, and Mr. Pierce in 1852.

In the exercise of a right so ancient, so well established, and so necessary for self-preservation, the people of the Confederate States, in their conventions, determined that the wrongs which they had suffered and the evils with which they were menaced, required that they should revoke the delegation of powers to the Federal Government which they had ratified in their several Conventions. They consequently passed ordinances resuming all their rights as sovereign and independent States, and dissolved their connection with the other States of the Union.

Having done this, they proceeded to form a new compact amongst themselves by new articles of confederation, which have been also ratified by the conventions of the several States with an approach to unanimity far exceeding that of the conventions which adopted the Constitution of 1787. They have organized their new government in all its departments; the functions of the Executive, Legislative and Judicial Magistrates are performed in accordance with the will of the people, as displayed not merely in a cheerful acquiescence, but in the enthusiastic support of the government thus established by themselves; and but for the interference of the Government of the United States in this legitimate exercise of the right of a people to self-government, peace, happiness and prosperity would now smile on our land. That peace is ardently desired by this government and people has been manifested in every possible form. Scarce had you assembled in February last, when, prior even to the inauguration of the Chief Magistrate you had elected, you passed a resolution expressive of your desire for the appointment of Commissioners to be sent to the Government of the United States "for the purpose of negotiating friendly relations between that Government and the Confederate States of America, and for the settlement of all questions of disagreement between the two Governments upon principles of right, justice, equity and good faith."

It was my pleasure as well as my duty to co-operate with you in this work of peace. Indeed, in my address to you on taking the oath of office, and before receiving from you the communication of this resolution, I had said, "as a necessity, not a choice, we have resorted to the remedy of separation, and henceforth our energies must be directed to the conduct of our own affairs, and the perpetuity of the Confederacy which we have formed. If a just perception of mutual interest shall permit us peaceably to pursue our separate political career, my most earnest desire will have been fulfilled."

It was in furtherance of these accordant views of the Congress and the Executive that I made choice of three discreet, able and distinguished citizens, who repaired to Washington. Aided by their cordial co-operation and that of the Secretary of State, every effort compatible with self-respect and the dignity of the Confederacy was exhausted before I allowed myself to yield to the conviction that the Government of the United States was determined to attempt the conquest of this people, and that our cherished hopes of peace were unattainable.

On the arrival of our Commissioners in Washington on the 5th of March, they postponed, at the suggestion of a friendly intermediary, doing more than giving informal notice of their arrival. This was done with a view to afford time to the President, who had just been inaugurated, for the discharge of other pressing official duties in the organization of his Administration, before engaging his attention in the object of their mission. It was not until the 12th of the month that they officially addressed the Secretary of State, informing him of the purposes of their arrival, and stating, in the language of their instructions, their wish "to make to the Government of the United States overtures for the opening of negotiations, assuring the Government of the United States that the President, Congress and people of the Confederate States earnestly desire a peaceful solution of these great questions; that it is neither their interest nor their wish to make any demand which is not founded on strictest justice, nor do any act to injure their late confederates."

To this communication no formal reply was received until the 8th April. During the interval the Commissioners had consented to waive all questions of form. With the firm resolve to avoid war, if possible, they went so far even as to hold, during that long period, unofficial intercourse through an intermediary, whose high position and character inspired the hope of success, and through whom constant assurances were received from the Government of the United States of peaceful intentions; of the determination to evacuate Fort Sumter; and further, that no measure changing the existing status prejudicially to the Confederate States, especially at Fort Pickens, was in contemplation, but that in the event of any change of intention on the subject, notice would be given to the Commissioners. The crooked paths of diplomacy can scarcely furnish an example so wanting in courtesy, in candor and directness, as was the course of the United States Government towards our Commissioners in Washington.—For proof of this I refer to the annexed documents, taken in connection with further facts, which I now proceed to relate:

Early in April the attention of the whole country, as well as that of our Commissioners, was attracted to extraordinary preparations for an extensive military and naval expedition in New York and other Northern ports. These preparations commenced in secrecy, for an expedition whose destination was concealed, only became known when nearly completed, and on the 5th, 6th and 7th of April, transports and vessels of war, with troops, munitions and military supplies, sailed from Northern ports bound Southwards.—Alarmed by so extraordinary a demonstration, the Commissioners requested the delivery of an answer to their official communication of the 12th of March, and thereupon received, on the 8th of April, a reply, dated on the 15th of the previous month, from which it appears that, during the whole interval, whilst the Commissioners were receiving assurances calculated to inspire hope of the success of their mission, the Secretary of State and the President of the United States had already determined to hold no intercourse with them whatever—to refuse even to listen to any proposals they had to make, and had profited by the delay created by their own assurances, in order to prepare secretly the means for effective hostile operations.

That these assurances were given has been virtually confessed by the Government of the United States by its sending a messenger to Charleston to give notice of its purpose to use force if opposed in its intention of supplying Fort Sumter. No more striking proof of the absence of good faith in the conduct of the Government of the United States towards this Confederacy can be required, than is contained in the circumstances which accompanied this notice. According to the usual course of navigation, the vessels composing the expedition designed for the relief of Fort Sumter, might be expected to reach Charleston harbor on the 9th of April. Yet, with our Commissioners actually in Washington, detained under assurances that notice should be given of any military movement, the notice was not addressed to them, but a messenger was sent to Charleston to give the notice to the Governor of South Carolina, and the notice was so given at a late hour on the 8th of April, the eve of the very day on which the fleet might be expected to arrive.

That this manœuvre failed in its purpose was not the fault of those who contrived it. A heavy tempest delayed the arrival of the expedition, and gave time to the commander of our forces at Charleston to ask and receive the instructions of this Government. Even then, under all the provocation incident to the contemptuous refusal to listen to our Commissioners, and the tortuous course of the Government of the United States, I was sincerely anxious to avoid the effusion of blood, and directed a proposal to be made to the commander of Fort Sumter, who had avowed himself to be nearly out of provisions, that we would abstain from directing our fire on Fort Sumter if he would promise not to open fire on our forces unless first attacked.—This proposal was refused, and the conclusion was reached that the design of the United States was to place the besieging force at Charleston between the simultaneous fire of the fleet and the fort. There remained, therefore, no alternative but to direct that the fort should at once be reduced. This order was executed by General Beauregard, with the skill and success which were naturally to be expected from the well known character of that gallant officer; and although the bombardment lasted but thirty-three hours, our flag did not wave over its battered walls until after the appearance of the hostile fleet off Charleston. Fortunately not a life was lost on our side, and we were gratified in being spared the necessity of a useless effusion of blood, by the prudent caution of the officers who commanded the fleet, in abstaining from the evidently futile effort to enter the harbor for the relief of Major Anderson. I refer to the report of the Secretary of War and the papers which accompany it, for further details of this brilliant affair.

In this connection I cannot refrain from a well-deserved tribute to the noble State, the eminent soldierly qualities of whose people were so conspicuously displayed in the port of Charleston. For months they had been irritated by the spectacle of a fortress held within their principal harbor, as a standing menace against their peace and independence. Built in part with their own money, its custody confided with their own consent to an agent who held no power over them other than such as they had themselves delegated for their own benefit, intended to be used by that agent for their own protection against foreign attack, they saw it held with persistent tenacity as a means of offence against them by the very Government which they had established for their protection. They had beleaguered it for months—felt entire confidence in their power to capture it—yet yielded to the requirements of discipline, curbed their impatience, submitted without complaint to the unaccustomed hardships, labors and privations of a protracted siege; and when at length their patience was rewarded by the signal for attack, and success had crowned their steady and gallant conduct—even in the very moment of triumph they evinced a chivalrous regard for the feelings of the brave but unfortunate officer who had been compelled to lower his flag. All manifestations of exultation were checked in his presence. Their commanding General, with their cordial approval and the consent of his Government, refrained from imposing any terms that could wound the sensibilities of the commander of the fort. He was permitted to retire with the honors of war—to salute his flag, to depart freely with all his command, and was escorted to the vessel in which he embarked with the highest marks of respect from those against whom his guns had been so recently directed. Not only does every event connected with the siege reflect the highest honor on South Carolina, but the forbearance of her people and of this government from making any harsh use of a victory obtained under circumstances of such peculiar provocation, attest to the fullest extent the absence of any purpose beyond securing their own tranquility, and the sincere desire to avoid the calamities of war.

Scarcely had the President of the United States received intelligence of the failure of the scheme which he had devised for the re-inforcement of Fort Sumter, when he issued the declaration of war against this Confederacy which has prompted me to convoke you. In this extraordinary production, that high functionary affects total ignorance of the existence of an independent Government, which, possessing the entire and enthusiastic devotion of its people, is exercising its functions without question over seven sovereign States, over more than five millions of people, and over a territory whose area exceeds half a million of square miles. He terms sovereign States "combinations, too powerful to be suppressed by the ordinary course of judicial proceedings, or by the powers vested in the Marshals by law." He calls for an army of seventy-five thousand men to act as a *posse comitatus* in aid of the process of the courts of justice in States where no courts exist whose mandates and decrees are not cheerfully obeyed and respected by a willing people. He avows that "*the first service* to be assigned to the forces called out," will be, not to execute the process of courts, but to capture forts and strongholds situated within the admitted limits of this Confederacy, and garrisoned by its troops; and declares that "this effort" is intended "to maintain the perpetuity of popular government." He concludes by commanding "the persons composing the combinations aforesaid"—to wit, the five millions of inhabitants of these States, "to retire peaceably to their respective abodes within twenty days."

Apparently contradictory as are the terms of this singular document, one point was unmistakably evident. The President of the United States called for an army of seventy-five thousand men, whose first service was to be to capture our forts. It was a plain declaration of war, which I was not at liberty to disregard, because of my knowledge that under the Constitution of the United States the President was usurping a power granted exclusively to the Congress. He is the sole organ of communication between that country and foreign powers. The law of nations did not permit me to question the authority of the Executive of a foreign nation to declare war against this Confederacy. Although I might have refrained from taking active measures for our defence, if the States of the Union had all imitated the action of Virginia, North Carolina, Arkansas, Kentucky, Tennessee and Missouri, by denouncing the call for troops as an unconstitutional usurpation of power to which they refused to respond, I was not at liberty to disregard the fact that many of the States seemed quite content to submit to the exercise of the power assumed by the President of the United States, and were actively engaged in levying troops to be used for the purpose indicated in the proclamation.

Deprived of the aid of Congress at the moment, I was under the necessity of confining my action to a call on the States for volunteers for the common defence, in accordance with the authority you had confided to me before your adjournment. I deemed it proper further to issue proclamation inviting application from persons disposed to aid our defence in private armed vessels on the high seas, to the end that preparations might be made for the immediate issue of letters of marque and reprisal, which you alone, under the Constitution, have power to grant. I entertain no doubt you will concur with me in the opinion that in the absence of a fleet of public vessels, it will be eminently expedient to supply their place by private armed vessels, so happily styled by the publicists of the United States, "the militia of the sea," and so often and justly relied on by them as an efficient and admirable instrument of defensive warfare.—I earnestly recommend the immediate passage of a law authorizing me to accept the numerous proposals already received.

I cannot close this review of the acts of the Government of the United States without referring to a proclamation issued by their President under date of the 19th April, in which, after declaring that an insurrection has broken out in this Confederacy against the Government of the United States, he announces a blockade of all the ports of these States, and threatens to punish as pirates all persons who shall molest any vessel of the United States under letters of marque issued by this Government. Notwithstanding the authenticity of this proclamation you will concur with me that it is hard to believe it could have emanated from a President of the United States. Its announcement of a mere paper blockade is so manifestly a violation of the law of nations that it would seem incredible that it could have been issued by authority; but conceding this to be the case so far as the Executive is concerned, it will be difficult to satisfy the people of these States that their late confederates will sanction its declarations, will determine to ignore the extermination on both sides, by treating as pirates open enemies acting under the authority of commissions issued by an organized Government. If such proclamation was issued, it could only have been published under the sudden influence of passion, and we may rest assured mankind will be spared the horrors of the conflict it seems to invite.

For the details of the administration of the different departments, I refer to the reports of the Secretaries which accompany this message.

The State Department has furnished the necessary instructions for three Commissioners who have been sent to England, France, Russia, and Belgium, since your adjournment, to ask our recognition as a member of the family of nations, and to make with each of those powers treaties of amity and commerce. Further steps will be taken to enter into like negotiations with the other European powers in pursuance of your resolutions passed at the last session. Sufficient time has not yet elapsed since the departure of these Commissioners for the receipt of any intelligence from them. As I deem it desirable that Commissioners or other diplomatic agents should also be sent at an early period to the independent American powers south of our Confederacy, with all of whom it is our interest and earnest wish to maintain the most cordial and friendly relations, I suggest the expediency of making the necessary appropriations for that purpose.

Having been officially notified by the public authorities of the State of Virginia that she had withdrawn from the Union, and desired to maintain the closest political relations with us which it was possible at this time to establish, I commissioned the Hon. Alexander H. Stephens, Vice-President of the Confederate States, to represent this government at Richmond. I am happy to inform you that he has concluded a convention with the State of Virginia, by which that honored Commonwealth, so long and justly distinguished among her sister States, and so dear to the hearts of thousands of her children in the Confederate States, has united her power and her fortunes with ours, and become one of us. This convention, together with the ordinance of Virginia, adopting the Provisional Constitution of the Confederacy, will be laid before you for your constitutional action. I have satisfactory assurances from other of our late confederates that they are on the point of adopting similar measures, and I cannot doubt that ere you shall have been many weeks in session, the whole of the slaveholding States of the late Union will respond to the call of honor and affection, and by uniting their fortunes with ours, promote our common interests and secure our common safety.

In the Treasury Department, regulations have been devised and put into execution for carrying out the policy indicated in your legislation on the subject of the navigation of the Mississippi river, as well as for the collection of revenue on the frontier. Free transit has been secured for vessels and merchandize passing through the Confederate States; and delay and inconvenience have been avoided as far as possible in organizing the revenue service for the various railways entering our territory. As fast as experience shall indicate the possibility of improvement in these regulations, no effort will be spared to free commerce from all unnecessary embarrassments and obstructions.

Under your act authorizing a loan, proposals were issued inviting subscriptions for five millions of dollars, and the call was answered by the prompt subscription of more than eight millions by our own citizens, and not a single bid was made under par. The rapid development of the purpose of the President of the United States to invade our soil, capture our forts, blockade our ports, and wage war against us, induced me to direct that the entire subscription should be accepted.—It will now become necessary to raise means to a much larger amount to defray the expenses of maintaining our independence and repelling invasion. I invite your special attention to this subject, and the financial condition of the Government, with the suggestion of ways and means for the supply of the Treasury, will be presented to you in a separate communication.

To the Department of Justice you have confided not only the organization and supervision of all matters connected with the courts of justice, but also those connected with patents and with the bureau of public printing.

Since your adjournment, all the courts, with the exception of those of Mississippi and Texas, have been organized by the appointment of Marshals and District Attorneys, and are now prepared for the exercise of their functions.

In the two States just named, the gentlemen confirmed as Judges declined to accept the appointment, and no nominations have yet been made to fill the vacancies. I refer you to the report of the Attorney General, and concur in his recommendation for immediate legislation, especially on the subject of patent rights. Early provision should be made to secure to the subjects of foreign nations the full enjoyment of their property in valuable inventions, and to extend to our own citizens protection, not only for their own inventions, but for such as may have been assigned to them, or may hereafter be assigned by persons not alien enemies.

The Patent Office business is much more extensive and important than had been anticipated. The applications for patents, although confined under the law exclusively to citizens of our Confederacy, already average seventy per month, showing the necessity for the prompt organization of a bureau of patents.

The Secretary of War, in his report and accompanying documents, conveys full information concerning the forces, regular, volunteer and provisional, raised and called for under the several acts of Congress, their organization and distribution. Also, an account of the expenditures already made, and the further estimates for the fiscal year ending on the 18th of February, 1862, rendered necessary by recent events. I refer to his report also for a full history of the occurrences in Charleston harbor, prior to and including the bombardment and reduction of Fort Sumter, and of the measures subsequently taken for the common defence, on receiving intelligence of the declaration of war against us made by the President of the United States. There are now in the field at Charleston, Pensacola, Forts Morgan, Jackson, St. Philip and Pulaski, 19,000 men, and 16,000 are now en route for Virginia. It is proposed to organize and hold in readiness for instant action, in view of the present exigencies of the country, an army of 100,000 men.—If further force should be needed, the wisdom and patriotism of Congress will be confidently appealed to for authority to call into the field additional numbers of our noble-spirited volunteers, who are constantly tendering service far in excess of our wants.

The operations of the Navy Department have been necessarily restricted by the fact that sufficient time has not yet elapsed for the purchase or construction of more than a limited number of vessels adapted to the public service. Two vessels purchased have been named the "Sumter" and "Macree," and are now being prepared for sea at New Orleans with all possible dispatch. Contracts have also been made at that city with two different establishments for the casting of ordnance, cannon, shot and shell, with the view to encourage the manufacture of these articles so indispensable for our defence, at as many points within our territory as possible.

I call your attention to the recommendation of the Secretary for the establishment of a magazine and laboratory for preparation of ordnance stores, and the necessary appropriation for that purpose. Hitherto such stores have usually been prepared at the navy-yards, and no appropriation was made at your last session for this object.

The Secretary also calls attention to the fact that no provision has been made for the payment of invalid pensions to our own citizens. Many of these persons are advanced in life, they have no means of support, and by the secession of these States have been deprived of their claims against the Government of the United States. I recommend the appropriation of the sum necessary to pay these pensioners, as well as those of the army, whose claims can scarcely exceed seventy thousand dollars per annum.

The Postmaster General has already succeeded in organizing his department to such an extent as to be in readiness to assume the direction of our postal affairs, on the occurrence of the contingency contemplated by the Act of 15th March, 1861, or even sooner, if desired by Congress. The various books and circulars have been prepared, and measures taken to secure supplies of blanks, postage stamps, stamped envelopes, mail bags, locks, keys, etc. He presents a detailed classification and arrangement of his clerical force, and asks for its increase. An auditor of the treasury for this department is necessary, and a plan is submitted for the organization of his bureau.—The great number and magnitude of the accounts of this department, require an increase of the clerical force in the accounting branch in the Treasury. The revenues of this department are collected and disbursed in modes peculiar to itself, and require a special bureau to secure a proper accountability in the administration of its finances.

I call your attention to the additional legislation required for this department to the recommendation for changes in the law fixing the rates of postage on newspapers, periodicals, and sealed packages of certain kinds, and specially to the recommendation of the Secretary, in which I concur, that you provide at once for the assumption by him of the control of our entire postal service.

In the military organization of the States, provision is made for Brigadier and Major-Generals, but in the Army of the Confederate States the highest grade is that of Brigadier-General. Hence it will no doubt sometimes occur that where troops of the Confederacy do duty with the militia, the General selected for the command, and possessed of the views and purposes of this government, will be superseded by an officer of the militia not having the same advantage. To avoid this contingency in the least objectional manner, I recommend that additional rank be given to the General of the Confederate Army, and concurring in the policy of having but one grade of Generals in the Army of the Confederacy, I recommend that the law of its organization be amended, so that the grade be that of General.

To secure a thorough military education, it is deemed essential that officers should enter upon the study of their profession at an early period of life, and have elementary instruction in a military school. Until such school shall be established, it is recommended that cadets be appointed and attached to companies until they shall have attained the age and acquired the knowledge to fit them for the duties of Lieutenants.

I shall call your attention to an omission in the law organizing the army, in relation to military chaplains, and recommend that provision be made for their appointment.

In conclusion, I congratulate you on the fact that in every portion of our country there has been exhibited the most patriotic devotion to our common cause. Transportation companies have freely tendered the use of their lines for troops and supplies. The Presidents of the railroads of the Confederacy, in company with others who control lines of communication with States that we hope soon to greet as sisters, assembled in Convention in this city, and not only reduced largely the rate heretofore demanded for mail service and conveyance of troops and munitions, but voluntarily proffered to receive their compensation at these reduced rates in the bonds of the Confederacy, for the purpose of leaving all the resources of the Government at its disposal for the common defence. Requisitions for troops have been met with such alacrity that the numbers tendering their services have, in every instance, greatly exceeded the demand. Men of the highest official and social position are serving as volunteers in the ranks. The gravity of age and the zeal of youth rival each other in the desire to be foremost for the public defence; and though at no other point than the one heretofore noticed have they been stimulated by the excitement incident to actual engagement, and the hope of distinction for individual achievement, they have borne what for new troops is the most severe ordeal, patient toil and constant vigil, and all the exposure and discomfort of active service, with a resolution and fortitude such as to command approbation and justify the highest expectation of their conduct when active valor shall be required in place of steady endurance.

A people thus united and resolved cannot shrink from any sacrifice which they may be called on to make, nor can there be a reasonable doubt of their final success, however long and severe may be the test of their determination to maintain their birth-right of freedom and equality, as a trust which it is their first duty to transmit undiminished to their posterity.

A bounteous Providence cheers us with the promise of abundant crops. The fields of grain which will within a few weeks be ready for the sickle, give assurance of the amplest supply of food for man; whilst the corn, cotton, and other staple productions of our soil, afford abundant proof that up to this period the season has been propitious.

We feel that our cause is just and holy; we protest solemnly in the face of mankind that we desire peace at any sacrifice, save that of honor and independence; we seek no conquest, no aggrandizement, no concessions of any kind from the States with which we were lately confederated; all we ask is to be let alone; that those who never held power over us shall not now attempt our subjugation by arms. This we will, this we must resist to the direst extremity. The moment that this pretension is abandoned, the sword will drop from our grasp, and we shall be ready to enter into treaties of amity and commerce that cannot but be mutually beneficial. So long as this pretension is maintained, with a firm reliance on the Divine Power which covers with its protection the just cause, we will continue to struggle for our inherent right to freedom, independence and self-government.

JEFFERSON DAVIS.

Montgomery, April 29, 1861.

GREAT BRITAIN AND THE SOUTHERN CONFEDERACY.—The question of the recognition of the Southern Confederacy by foreign powers is one of deep and absorbing interest, and we hesitate in giving currency to any information on the subject that is not well founded, especially since the Northern journals profess to have assurances that there is no probability of such a result. Still, it may not be amiss to publish any thing coming direct from the other side of the water, which shows the feeling among the commercial classes there. The following extract of a letter, dated April 6th, from a commission house in Birmingham, England, to a business firm in Columbus, Ga., possesses significance in this point of view:

"The feeling on this side about United States affairs is universally that it is not only *better* for both North and South to agree on amicable separation, but also that the North *must* cave in, (like it or not,) as neither England or France could recognize any partial blockade, which is the utmost the North can attempt. If it is the *will of the people* to separate, the thing is done, and will be recognized quick enough, especially with the Morrill tariff to spur all indifferent spirits."

A GALLANT EXAMPLE.—No instance of patriotic devotion to the South has come within our knowledge more entitled to honorable mention, than that of Gen. John W. A. Sanford, of our city, who will in a few days tender himself to the "Baldwin Blues," now in Virginia, as a *private* in their company.

Gen. Sanford, until his resignation a few months past, commanded a division of the militia of this State thirty years as Major General, with great efficiency, and with marked benefit to our citizen soldiers. His first connection with military life was in 1827, when he was the confidential Aid-de-Camp of Gov. Troup. He was subsequently elected a representative in Congress, but resigned before taking his seat, to accept a special agency tendered him by President Jackson as Commissioner of Indian Reserves in the Creek Nation. In the Cherokee District he also had a special military command under the administration of Gov. Gilmer, which he performed with credit to himself and with advantage to the public. More recently Gen. Sanford was appointed by the Georgia Convention as Commissioner to Texas, and through his able and zealous efforts the people of that State were fully aroused to the work of secession, which was soon nobly accomplished at the ballot box. Such a soldier, and such a gentleman of the most elevated character, seeking to serve his country as a private in her armies, is a sublime picture to contemplate!—*Milledgeville Recorder.*

A number of gentlemen of Washington, N. C., have borrowed $[illegible] of the banks, to buy provisions, to be sold to all who may need at cost.

FROM THE NORTH.

The New York Herald sharply lectures the Times, Tribune, and Courier and Enquirer, for their blood and thunder articles, but is itself not much behind them in its tone. In regard to these matters our people feel but little interest, and we therefore only copy the following from the Herald of Wednesday:

Baltimore is to be completely filled with troops, and Maryland is to be compelled to act like a State still in the Union. All the information which reached us up to a late hour last night plainly indicated that this is the policy of the Government at Washington. Let us state the points of the latest news in brief: The greatest activity prevails in Southern Pennsylvania, seventeen thousand troops being in the field there at the present time. At Camp Scott, York, Pa., there are 6,000 men; at Camp Sifler, near Chambersburg, 2,600; at Camp Curtin, near Harrisburg, 4,000; two regiments from Ohio are quartered near Lancaster, and 1,200 United States regulars at Carlisle. Scattered at different points between Philadelphia, Elkton and Perrysville there are 6,000 more.

Three thousand New Jersey troops are to march from Trenton to-day, which will constitute in all a force of over 20,000 men in that region, their destination being undoubtedly for Baltimore, to open the route to the Federal Capital. On the South side of Baltimore are stationed at Annapolis a force of between four and five thousand men, including the Providence Marine Artillery, which left Perryville yesterday. The Sixth and Thirteenth New York Regiments occupy a position directly opposite Annapolis, and the Sixty-ninth are at the Junction.

It will thus be seen that Baltimore is completely hemmed in on both sides with an effective force, which is to be immediately employed in opening a passage through that city for the Federal troops, and restoring free communication between the North and the capital of the Republic.

With this purpose Major General Keim, of Pennsylvania, was ordered to leave Philadelphia yesterday for the camp at York, with instructions to advance at once with an army of fifteen thousand men on Baltimore. If any resistance is offered, he will issue a proclamation announcing his intention to march his force through that city, and warning the loyal citizens, the women and children, to leave, and will then cut his way through at all hazards. It is probable, however, that the threat of visiting Baltimore with so severe a chastisement will bring the resistants to their senses, and thus save the effusion of blood.

The Philadelphia papers contain little of interest. They announce, however, the arrest of Charles A. Grinner, of Georgia, on the charge of treason. Mr. G. made the following statement:

My family are here; I came on to see them. The company I belonged to was nothing but a private company, that I belonged to for the last fifteen years. They enjoyed a good many privileges, and were exempt from jury duty. On the second day of January, there was a good deal of excitement in Georgia, and our Governor was apprehensive that Fort Pulaski might become occupied by an irresponsible party, and he requested our company to go there and take charge of it, which they did. I left there early in January and came up to the interior of Georgia, at my mother's place. I have been in Savannah very little. I am a Philadelphian by birth; went to school here; and believe I am as good a Union man as can be found anywhere. I was born under the American flag, and have a good many relatives residing in this city.

That was enough, and the officials, following the example of the petty despots of continental Europe, committed Mr. G. to prison.

A dispatch from Harrisburg, Pa., shows that the Hessians are beginning to count the cost:

Over 5,000 men are now in camp at Harrisburg. They consume daily 6,500 pounds of fresh beef, 6,500 pounds of bread, 808 pounds sugar, 300 pounds of coffee, 100 pounds of candles, 4 bushels of salt, and 18 bushels of beans. Not more than 15 barrels of mess pork have been used out of the 700 barrels sent here, the men refusing to eat it. It is estimated that the cost of subsistence alone is $1,200 per day.

The same telegram exposes an outrage committed by Pennsylvania soldiers:

Five soldiers attached to a Delaware county company were to-day sent out to arrest deserters. During their travel they abused several citizens, and subsequently entered a public house, got frenzied with liquor, charged bayonets in a crowded room, and wounded a citizen severely, though not dangerously. One of the soldiers was severely cut in the rencontre by a citizen. All five of the soldiers were arrested and lodged in jail.

The Toronto (Canada) Leader, Government organ, advocates an "armed neutrality" in respect to affairs in this country. A Toronto dispatch, April 30, says:

The Globe of to-day, in a long and able article on American affairs, says that the North, by their impatience with reference to President Lincoln's policy, ignore the stupendous and delicate task he has before him, and will drive the country to anarchy and chaos.

It advocates strengthening Mr. Lincoln's hands, and to abstain from perplexing his councils.

A committee on "Home Defence" at Pittsburg, have procured from the U. S. Arsenal, near that city, 2,380 muskets, 882 rifles, and accoutrements, besides over 100 cannon, to be used in the defence of that city. The Gazette says:

Captains McNutt and Brereton, and Lieut. Crispin, are now engaged in a reconnoisance of the heights and defiles surrounding the city, with a view to selecting the most available points for planting batteries. Scouting parties have also been sent out through Washington and Greene counties, to ascertain, if possible, if any hostile movements are on foot against this locality.

The following items possess some interest:

At a late hour on Saturday night information reached the United States Marshal of New Jersey, which induced him to invoke the assistance of Gen. Hatfield, of the New Jersey State Militia, who, with a force of men, proceeded with the Marshal to the Jersey flats, where they seized three schooners loaded with gunpowder, over which was spread a quantity of manure.

Col. Ellsworth's regiment of Zouaves, recruited entirely from New York firemen, made a magnificent parade on Sunday in New York, 1,100 strong, escorted by about 5,000 of their comrades of the Fire Department and 50,000 friends, of both sexes, who witnessed their embarkation on the Baltic for Washington.—The regiment are armed with Sharpe's rifles.

It is stated that James T. Brady, of New York, is about to join the army at Washington in a prominent position. Mr. Brady says that as the Breckinridge candidate for Governor of Massachusetts is in the field, he, as late candidate for the office of Governor of the State of New York, will not be behind-hand.

The New York Herald limits what it calls the "defensive attitude" of Lincoln's Administration, to the 5th of May—the "proclamation," which was dated on the 15th of April, requiring the "combinations" to "disperse and retire within twenty days."

DEATH OF BISHOP ONDERDONK.—Benjamin Treadwell Onderdonk, Episcopal Bishop of the Eastern Diocese of New York, died in New York on Tuesday, after a protracted illness, of dropsy, aged about 71 years. One of the papers of that city says:

About fourteen years after his consecration, in the year 1844, we believe, a circumstance occurred which cast a cloud over his character. A charge of indiscretion in conduct was preferred against him, which, not to be too prolix, resulted in his being indefinitely suspended from Episcopal functions by command of the House of Bishops. The scandal created an immense sensation at the time, having been published in almost every paper in the country. The suspension took place on the 3d of January, 1845, and has never been revoked since that time. Bishop Onderdonk never made what can be called a confession, and a strong feeling has ever been manifested in his favor by warm friends, who regarded him as a persecuted prelate.

SHIPMENTS OF PROVISIONS.—The following note was written by Secretary Memminger to the Collector at Savannah, in consequence of a vessel loaded with rice, for Boston, having been compelled to stop and discharge cargo:

The Government have entirely disapproved of any interference with private property before war is declared. Let us abide by the Law of Nations, and protect peaceful commerce which has trusted to our hospitality.—Tell your people to have patience; we gain more by respect for law than from the seizure of a few vessels.

ARREST OF AN ALLEGED SPY.—Dr. G. W. Ellis, of Miss., has been arrested in Cincinnati, on the charge of being a spy from the South. In his possession was found a large secession flag, copies of letters to Jefferson Davis, Robt. Toombs, H. V. Johnson and W. W. Berry; one handbill calling a meeting of secessionists; handbill advertising lectures on biology, &c. He has been committed to [illegible]

FROM WASHINGTON.

The Alexandria *Gazette*, of yesterday, furnishes the following:

WASHINGTON, May 2.—Washington to-day is quiet and orderly in the extreme; no facts or rumors of any importance, or even a sensational character, are discussed.

Arlington Heights, nor any other point on the Virginia side of the Potomac, have been occupied by the troops of the Administration.

The children of the lamented G. W. P. Custis still reside in their wonted ease and quietness at the family mansion on the Arlington estate.

More Northern troops are arriving, and a force of forty thousand well armed and equipped men will soon guard the city.

Government vessels come and go from the Navy-Yard and Arsenal, to all points on the Potomac and Chesapeake Bay without any interruption or inconvenience, whatever.

The rumor about the occupation of Alexandria by the Federal forces obtains no credence in any quarter whatever, though some of the Republicans say that it would be but a just retaliation for the seizure and firing into vessels bound to Washington, by persons on the wharves at Alexandria.

Major Henry B. Tyler, of the U. S. Marines, who has been in the service for over forty years, who has grown grey in serving his country, yesterday resigned and returned to his native State, Virginia.

Mr. James Tucker, master anchor-smith of the Navy-Yard, at Washington, has been removed, and a *shoemaker*, by the name of Brown, appointed in his place. Brown is a Republican.

The removal of Mr. Tucker, who is universally esteemed for his moral worth, created much excitement in the yard, and a general stampede, it is said, of the workmen was the consequence.

The women and children continue to fly the city. Martial law has not as yet been proclaimed.

The following is from another source:

WASHINGTON, May 1.—Contrary to the often repeated rumors, it is reliably ascertained that martial law will not be proclaimed here unless there shall be reason for it, which certainly does not now exist.

Among the unfounded reports to-day was one that the War Department had received a dispatch stating that the Confederate States troops were concentrating in Virginia for an immediate raid on Washington. Military men, however, have no fears on that subject.

The Government is sedulously and promptly providing for the equipment and comfort of such volunteers now here as hastily left their various employments for the defence of the Capital.

But few of the Government employees received their month's salaries to-day, the money for that purpose not having yet arrived from New York.

The intelligence of a marked improvement in affairs in Maryland in a peaceful aspect imparts general satisfaction.

Says the Washington Star, of Thursday:

John Conner, the Government messenger who recently tampered with confidential dispatches entrusted to him for conveyance between Washington and Philadelphia, is a Baltimorean. On the delivery of his dispatches in Philadelphia, Capt. Sanders discovered that they had all been opened and read somewhere on the road between Washington and that city. Conner is believed by the Government to have sold the information they contained at a round price. He is now in the custody of Col. Butler, at Annapolis, who, it is understood, will probably hang him.

There are now some 3,000 troops at Annapolis from New York and Pennsylvania.

The 71st (New York) Regiment are quartered inside the Navy-Yard.

The 12th (New York) Regiment are to be quartered in a few days in the public square, near Franklin Row.

W. O. Riddall, of Virginia, clerk in the State Department, has been removed. Geo. Rye, of Virginia, has been appointed to a $1,200 clerkship.

Under the head of "important commercial information," the National Intelligencer says:

We learn that on application made by some of the Diplomatic Corps at the State Department, the following points were ascertained:

1st. Vessels in blockaded ports when the blockade took effect, will be allowed a reasonable time to depart.

2d. Vessels bringing emigrants, though they had no notice of the blockade, will not be allowed to enter blockaded ports. That class of persons come to the United States chiefly to settle in the upper States of the Mississippi, it will be better for them to enter an open port, and thence make their way to their destination, rather than encounter the dangers and casualties incident to the insurrectionary condition of the Gulf States.

The Sun's Washington correspondent says:

Two persons were arrested by some of the Sixty-ninth New York Regiment, on criminal charges—one was detected in theft, but on the person of the other was found papers of a character suspicious, if not treasonable. His name is Granville. He was originally from Hoboken, N. Y., but has recently resided in Baltimore. He was sent down to Annapolis, and is now in the hands of the military under Gen. Butler.

HOUSE STRUCK BY LIGHTNING.—*Marvellous Escape of the Inmates.*—The first thunder storm of the season visited this region on Tuesday night. About midnight the lightning struck a dwelling-house at Forrestdale, near Slatersville, occupied by the families of Danforth Crossman and A. Butts, the members of which were all in bed. Nearly the entire north side of the house was torn off by the subtle element, while it played strange pranks within doors. The bed on which two persons lay *was moved across the room and its casters melted!* A bureau was smashed to pieces and a portion thrown upon the bed. Bed clothes and clothing were rent in twain, yet strange to say no person was seriously injured. A child was somewhat stunned. One of the ladies, in speaking of the event, said her first thought after the thunder clap was, "*Jeff. Davis has come.*—*Woonsocket (R. I.) Patriot.*

A NOBLE REPLY.—It is related to us, says the Portsmouth Transcript, that a native of Virginia, holding a pseudo office in the Lincoln Navy, and now on duty at New York, recently wrote to his children in this city—a son and daughter—to come on and join him, as he did not propose returning to the South. The young man, who has entered the army of Virginia, promptly answered by return mail, that he respected parental commands when they were either reasonable, lawful or biblical, but he could not, would not, desert the State of his nativity, and add another name to her list of ingrates. The sister united cordially in the sentiments and feelings of the brother, answering that though she might reap discomfort and even want by this separation from father and mother, her conscience bid her stay, and she would obey its mandates by contributing her labor in outfitting Southern soldiers.

AN ITEM FROM FORTRESS MONROE.—It is stated in a letter to the New York Herald that "Col. Dimick had a narrow escape, Sunday night from being himself a victim to the close watch of his sentinels. He had been in a boat to the light-ship, stationed between Capes Henry and Charles, and, upon his return, was challenged at the water battery. From some cause, he neglected to give the word, and a shot was fired, which narrowly missed him, and severely wounded in the shoulder a soldier standing behind him. In an instant twenty men were on the spot, and a volley would have killed every one on board, but for the promptitude of another man, who plunged into the water, and succeeded in acquainting those at the battery who their supposed enemies were."

WORTHY OF NOTICE.—The Montgomery Daily Advertiser says that a slave belonging to Mrs. Jobbert, of Marengo county, took $100 in the bonds of the Confederate States, and paid for it out of his own money; and another slave, belonging to Mr. Hatch, of the same county, took $500 worth of the same stock, and paid for it out of money which he had laid up from time to time.

A soldier named Marion Meacham, a member of Capt. May's company, fell from the cars in Calhoun, Ga., last Sunday, and was so badly injured that amputation of one of his legs became necessary.

A white woman named Strickney attempted to drown her three children a few days ago, at Washington, N. C., but was prevented, whereupon she stabbed herself three times, but not fatally.

A special dispatch to the New York Herald says "the schooner John Roach was seized on James River and converted into a war vessel by the secessionists."

In Barbour county, Ala., on the 27th ult., Mr. Lorenzo Faulk, an estimable citizen, accidentally shot himself, and died instantly.

Fifteen hundred free colored men in New Orleans have offered their services to fight for the South.

The residence of Col. B. Sims, in Waynesboro', Ga., was destroyed by fire on the 26th ult.

The Young Guards, from Covington, Ga., reached Portsmouth on Monday.

Samuel Hall accidentally shot and killed himself in Hyde county, N. C., on the 17th ult.

The Philadelphia Inquirer.

ESTABLISHED 1829. PHILADELPHIA, THURSDAY, MAY 9, 1861. PRICE TWO CENTS.

THE WAR

AND ITS DEVELOPMENTS.

THE LATEST FROM THE SEAT OF WAR.

PREPARATIONS FOR MARCHING THROUGH BALTIMORE.

THE PLAN OF THE CAMPAIGN.

MILITARY RECEPTION AT WASHINGTON.

Capture of a Privateer.

Protection to be Extended to all Union Men in the South.

SECESSION MESSAGE OF THE GOVERNOR OF KENTUCKY.

FLOATING BATTERIES FOR THE MISSISSIPPI.

The Departure of Colonel Patterson's Regiment of Infantry.

THE SCENES AT THE BALTIMORE DEPOT.

THE ARRIVAL OF TWO OHIO REGIMENTS IN PHILADELPHIA.

NEWS FROM WASHINGTON AND RICHMOND.

IMPORTANT INTELLIGENCE.

THE PENNSYLVANIA AND OHIO COMMISSIONERS—TREASONABLE CORRESPONDENCE INTERCEPTED—ALLEGED VOLUNTEERS FROM CANADA—CLERGYMEN FORMING COMPANIES—THE NEW JERSEY REGIMENTS—TROOPS FROM CONNECTICUT—30,000 SECESSIONISTS UNDER ARMS IN VIRGINIA—CONTEMPLATED REPUDIATION OF VIRGINIA BONDS—THE NEW CURRENCY—THE CONDITION OF ALEXANDRIA.

From our own Correspondent.

WASHINGTON, Tuesday, May 7th.

Judge JESSUP and MORTON McMICHAEL, Commissioners from Pennsylvania, with Judge SWAYNE and Colonel SNELL, of Ohio, arrived here this morning. They have been in close conference during the day with the President, Gen. SCOTT and Secretary CAMERON. They communicated the result of the conference of the Governors at Cleveland.

McCLELLAND is appointed to the command of the troops of Ohio, Illinois and Indiana.

A very important treasonable correspondence between certain high Southern officials has been intercepted. I am not at liberty to divulge particulars at this time.

A large number of volunteers from Canada have tendered their services to the Secretary of War, but for prudential reasons their generous offers have been declined. One, a distinguished Colonel, resigned his commission for the purpose of offering his services to this Government.

Large offers of volunteers from Maryland, Western Virginia and Kentucky have been made to-day. A number of clergymen of various denominations are getting up companies.

The New Jersey Regiments, numbering over three thousand men, are now parading on the avenue, exciting the greatest enthusiasm and admiration.

The Rhode Island Artillerists, with their famous batteries of rifled cannon, also showed themselves on the streets to-day, with their commander, Lieut. Governor ARNOLD and Governor SPRAGUE at their head.

Governor BUCKINGHAM, of Connecticut, left this morning, having been successful in inducing the acceptance of more troops from his State.

All express unbounded confidence in the Administration. Its ability and determination to carry on the war with vigor are conceded on all hands.

Arrangements on a scale hitherto unprecedented are rapidly being made. The rebels will soon quail before the advancing column of the grand army of Freemen, marching to battle and to victory.

News of a most exciting character may now be looked for daily.

WASHINGTON, Wednesday, 8th, A. M.—A gentleman who left Richmond this morning, after spending a couple of days there on business, gives me some information. He resides in New York, and, being an Englishman, traveled with a pass from Lord LYONS. He believes there are in Virginia upwards of 30,000 troops. Companies are constantly arriving, and a great determination is manifested to fight. The contemplated attack on Washington is given up, and the military officers declare they never did entertain anything more than a *defensive* warfare. This, however, is a canard manufactured out of whole cloth—a complete change of front since the determined stand taken by the Government.

There are about 8000 troops within three hours of Harper's Ferry, and a like number at Lynchburg, together with regiments at various other points.

The report of troops marching on Alexandria arose from the fact that several companies were obliged to return there, with a view of going on to Harper's Ferry by another route.

Virginia talks openly of repudiating her bonds and all Northern debts. My informant has with him some of the new shinplasters, which now take the place of other currency. It is not pretended they have any real value—being got up with special reference to present exigencies.

A company of Zouaves from New Orleans, and another, called the "Silver Greys," from Louisville, arrived in Richmond yesterday.

It is believed by all in the South that there are here upwards of fifty thousand troops. Alexandria is completely evacuated, and only sufficient food left to feed the few there who cannot get away.

Washington is kept full of Virginia spies, who buy up all the revolvers and everything else in the shape of arms to be had here from strangers and soldiers. Advantage is taken of the latter when they are intoxicated in the saloons. From henceforth a strict surveillance is to be kept upon all carriages going over to Alexandria.

The city is full of military excitement. The soldiers are all eager for active hostilities. X.

From Montgomery.

MONTGOMERY, May 8—The Postal Department is ready to take charge of the mails at any moment that Congress may direct. The official seal, books, blanks, routes, and clerical force are complete, and no detention of mails is feared in consequence of any policy of the United States Government.

DEPARTURE OF COL. PATTERSON'S REGIMENT OF INFANTRY.

Departure of Col. Patterson's Division.

The First Division of the Pennsylvania Volunteers is now on the *qui vive*, and will all be off just as fast as their equipment can be effected. The determination is to leave nothing wanting for their comfort in camp and their efficiency in the field. The fine old artillery regiment above named, now acting as infantry, and bound first of all for Perrysville, is nearly one thousand strong—officered and composed as follows:—Colonel, FRANCIS E. PATTERSON; Lieutenant-Colonel, ROBERT O. TYLER; Major, WM. A. LEECH; Adjutant, GIDEON K. CLARK; Surgeon, Dr. BACHE; Assistant Surgeon, Dr. SHIPPEN; Regimental Quartermaster, EUGENE D. DUNTON.

The companies, with their Captains, are as follows:—

Company A, Washington Greys, THOMAS P. PARRY.

Company B, Philadelphia Greys, DAVID F. FOLEY.

Company C, West Philadelphia Greys, JOHN H. GARDINER.

Company D, National Artillery, JOSEPH SINEX.

Company E, State Guard, ROBERT THOMPSON.

Company F, Second Company Washington Greys, ALEXANDER MURPHY.

Company G, Second Company Philadelphia Greys, WM. PRITNER.

Company H, Cadwalader Greys, ISAAC BASSETT.

Company D, Independent Greys, W. J. J. BRACELAND.

Company K, Second Company Cadwalader Greys, CHARLES TANNER.

The regiment, which has been organizing and fitting out for some time, was busied yesterday morning, from daybreak to 8 o'clock, in their final preparations. At 8½ A. M. they mustered on the west side of Washington square, and we were pleased to see that they seemed fully arrayed for comfortable marching and effective battle. Around the southwest corner of the square were congregated many vehicles, laden with baggage and provisions, including dry goods boxes, materials for tents, officers' valises, &c., &c.

A large and mixed assemblage surrounded the square, and in all the adjacent windows were many curious and interested lookers on. The standers and walkers below seemed more deeply absorbed in the scene around them than the outlookers above; for the first were mostly those who had business with the departing volunteers, or still oftener those who had come to take leave of acquaintances, friends, brothers, or sons; and of these leave-takers, whether the leaving or the left, the faces were as various as their characters, excepting that most of them, especially the soldiers, tried—and usually with success—to assume a cheerful look.

But a close observer could easily see that in most cases it was *merely* an assumption, and while the defenders of their country left their friends, and those friends gave them to the country with faces wreathed in smiles, the moistened eye and the close, hard wringing of the hand beneath showed that the face was a patriotic dissembler. Here a mother would part tearfully with her son, or a sister with her brother; for the grief of women usually *will* spring from the heart to the eyes. Here again brother shook farewell hands with brother, "while," in HOLMES' fine lines—

"—— the brave father stood with tearless eye
Smiling and choking with his last good bye."

Here a young fellow would accost his friend with something like this:—"Well, Charlie, old fellow, good bye. Sorry you're going; and glad too. Wish I were going with you. You'll *fight*, will you, fight in earnest?" "Well, I will, my boy. Good bye—God bless you!"

The same scenes, and between the same or different parties, were afterwards repeated at the depot. Some of these were truly affecting and and filled us with many and mingled emotions.—We ourselves, however, saw nothing as painful as two that we were told of by a lady. One venerable lady fainted on parting with her son, and his relatives took sorrowful leave of a young man, whose *own father* is serving in the Secession army! God grant that sire and son may not meet on the battle-field!

At a quarter past nine the regiment moved up Walnut street between a living wall of spectators: from door, window, balcony, a long line of waving handkerchiefs and banners, and a continuous roll of cheers and shouts, mingled with some tears shed, and kisses flung, and deeply-breathed "God bless you's."

Up and down all the streets near the depot, which they reached about ten o'clock, and along the track, and occupying all the fences, and swarming on every neighboring perch of car or building, was an immense gathering of citizens of both sexes, and all ages and ranks, to see the departure of their brave countrymen, and once more bid them "God speed" in their noble errand. There was much, but necessary, delay in the starting of the train, for it was no business of a minute to stow away properly such a mass of luggage. We need not say more of the final and general scene of parting, which was at half-past eleven. Perfect good order prevailed throughout the crowd, and a cheerfulness of look more general than one would expect.

The soldiers themselves mostly left singing, joking, laughing, and, apparently, but apparently only, as if they thought they were off for fun instead of very serious business, like that of so many determined men that have gone before, or will follow them. Honor, success and safety attend all their steps.

The first destination of these troops is Perryville; their subsequent movements, with those of the rest soon to follow, are not yet disclosed. But they are well provisioned and prepared for long service.

We accompany this account with a sketch of the scene at the depot, just as the soldiers were about entering the cars.

From Chambersburg—Flag Raising at Camp Slifer.

Special Despatch to the Inquirer.

CHAMBERSBURG, May 8—A new and splendid Flag was raised this afternoon at Camp Slifer, in front of the tent occupied by the Colonel of the Eighth Regiment. The men, under his command were drawn up in the form of a hollow square, to witness the ceremony. The flag was presented on behalf of the ladies of Chambersburg, by ex-Senator BREWER, who made an appropriate and pointed speech, and was received by Judge CONYNGHAM, of Wilkesbarre, whose remarks, though brief, elicited much applause. A detachment, comprising the best vocalists in the regiment, then sang a number of patriotic songs.

The ranks of WILSON REILLY's Rifle Company have just been filled, and they are now ready for active service. The troops are all in good health and anxious for the order to strike their tents and march. Probably this regiment will be moved Southward this week. The Seventh and Eighth Regiments received their uniforms last Sunday, and a portion of those for the Tenth reached here to-day.

Twenty-five hundred loaves of bread will be here to-day from Philadelphia, and the supply will be continued daily whilst the camp remains here.

The Unionists had kept their arms there, but had removed them before the fire broke out. From this circumstance some persons have suspected them of firing the building, while others contend that it was the work of secession incendiaries.

There has been no movement of our troops as yet, nor is any anticipated until their uniforms shall have arrived. J. R. D.

Secession Recruits from Baltimore.

Special Despatch to the Inquirer.

BALTIMORE, May 8.—A party of about eighty Baltimore Roughs, calling themselves the "Southern Rangers," took forcible possession to-day of a train on the Western Maryland Railroad, and went to Westminster. It is their intention to join the Southern army at Harper's Ferry. Efforts were made to arrest them, but with what success has not yet been learned.

The Maine Troops.

PORTLAND, May 8.—The First Regiment went into camp to-day, near the Marine Hospital. The Fifth Regiment will encamp on the Island Pond Race Course.

Fire at Memphis, Tenn.

MEMPHIS, Tenn., May 8.—The block of buildings at the corner of Front Row and Court street, were burned to-day. Loss $80,000.

THE LATEST FROM WASHINGTON.

Special Despatch to the Inquirer.

Plan of Campaign.

WASHINGTON, May 8—Many who profess to be posted up as to the plans of the Administration, expect to see an army of occupation march hence in a few days towards Richmond, while simultaneous movements are made on Norfolk and Harper's Ferry. Your correspondent does not find that these rumors have any authentic foundation. Harper's Ferry, if the rebels endeavor to occupy it, is a permanent fortified camp, and to obstruct the travel on the Baltimore and Ohio Railroad, will, doubtless, be retaken at no very distant day.

Alexandria will also doubtless be relieved from the presence of the Virginia troops, who left it on Sunday, but who returned to their old quarters yesterday. The citizens of the place continue to leave it daily, and in great numbers. It is said that the telegraphic order from Culpepper Court-House, intended to have been for the "*battery*" at Alexandria, was missent, so as to read "*battalion*," and that this was the cause of the temporary withdrawal of the Alexandria troops. But your correspondent has good reason to believe that no advance will be made upon Richmond, and that Lieutenant-General SCOTT has matured an elaborate plan of campaign, which will require at least six months to so prepare for as to render it effective and victorious beyond doubt. Meanwhile, the troops will be prepared for taking the field, and the necessary stores and munitions will be gathered.

Baltimore Open.

We hope to learn to-night that United States troops from Harrisburg and from Perryville, have passed through Baltimore, and joined the forces under General BUTLER at the Relay House.

Secretary CAMERON has endorsed an arrangement with the Post Office Department to have the mails between Washington and Baltimore and the East taken by the Norfolk steamers, running as a line between Baltimore and Perryville, opposite Havre de Grace. This arrangement at once restores to us a full and first-class communication with Philadelphia, and is of great importance to all our business and social relations, besides aiding the Government in its war operations.

In addition to the Government trains between here and Annapolis, Col. SCOTT has made an arrangement by which the passenger trains from Baltimore to Washington will start at 7.30 A. M., 3 P. M., and 7.30 P. M., and from Washington for Baltimore at 10.30 A. M., 2 P. M., and 10.30 P. M., occupying from two to two and a half hours in the trips. A regular freight train will also run daily, leaving Baltimore in the evening and returning early in the morning.

Military Reception.

By direction of President LINCOLN, the commissioned officers and their families, of the army, the marine corps, the navy, and the volunteer militia, now in this city, are invited to a reception at the Executive mansion, on Thursday evening, the 9th inst., at 8 o'clock.

Martial Concert.

The fine band of the Rhode Island Regiment performed this afternoon from five until seven.

The Colleges.

Columbian College is to be converted into a Military Hospital for the time being, as the few students remaining can pursue their studies in the building heretofore used for a preparatory school. At the Georgetown (Catholic) College, only about seventy students remain, and their studies are by no means interrupted by the quartering of the Sixty-ninth New York Regiment in a portion of the commodious buildings. On the contrary, the military services add interest and variety to the labors of the students, and afford them an insight into the routine of military life. Mass is celebrated every morning by Father MOONEY, chaplain of the Sixty-ninth.

Maine Volunteers.

The Maine Regiment, already started from that State, is under orders for Fortress Monroe, and Senator MORRILL, of that State, who is here, offers three more—*all to be enlisted for three years*, or during the war. It is proposed to form one of lumbermen and "loggers," those hardy raftsmen of the upper Penobscot and Arostook.

Debtors Easy.

It is stated in the *Intelligencer*, that upon the opening of the May term of the Circuit Court on Monday last, the members of the Bar held a meeting and conferred among themselves as to the best course to be pursued for protecting the interests of litigants before that Court, in view of the disturbed state of affairs. The result of their conference was an unanimous request that the Court would continue over all the cases upon the docket to the October term, and the postponement of all trials was in consequence of the unanimous request of those concerned in their disposition.

Major Anderson and Kentucky.

Major ANDERSON has been advised that twenty thousand Kentuckians hold themselves in readiness to fight with him in defence of the Union, whenever and wherever their services may be required.

Arrest of a Spy.

A spy, named SPENCER, alleged to have been one of the leaders of the Baltimore Riots, was arrested to-day at the Relay House. Papers of importance were found upon his person. He was sent to Annapolis, and will be tried at once.

Falling Back.

The Rebels, it is reported, are slowly falling back from Harper's Ferry, receiving meanwhile, continued accessions from the South.

Wigfall.

WIGFALL and Gen. BEAUREGARD are at Richmond, and BOULIGNY is in Washington.

Troops to Pass Through Baltimore.

A private letter which was sent by Secretary CAMERON to a prominent citizen of Baltimore, states that the troops from the camps on the Northern Central Railroad, and from Havre de Grace, will pass through the environs of Baltimore to-morrow (Thursday), at all hazards. They are en route for Washington.

An Infamous Rumor.

A rumor has been prevalent to-day, that many of the Massachusetts troops at the Relay House have been killed by eating poisoned cakes. The report is utterly unfounded.

New Jailor.

Marshal LAMON has appointed JOHN H. WISE, of this city, jailor at the Washington county jail, in place of PATRICK H. KING.

Our Markets.

The Secessionists having removed their "embargo," the farmers of Virginia and Maryland are beginning to come into the markets in greater numbers than for some time past, and, as a consequence, provisions are somewhat lower. The fish market continues to be supplied with shad from the Potomac fisheries, but there is a great scarcity of oysters, as the chivalric Virginians have seized several crafts.

Secret Correspondence.

A secret correspondence has been discovered between Governor MAGOFFIN, of Kentucky, and Governor BROWN, of Mississippi, in which it appears that MAGOFFIN has been trying to buy certain arms from BROWN that the latter stole from the Federal Government. MAGOFFIN, it is said, wished them to be used by the Secessionists in Kentucky.

Activity.

The greatest activity is going on in the War and Navy Departments, in the work of perfecting the details of encompassing and punishing the traitors who have thrown this country into its present condition.

Furlough to Anderson.

The Secretary of War has granted a furlough to Major ANDERSON, who will soon visit Kentucky, his native State, where many of his relatives still reside. The Secretary has the subject of the promotion of Major ANDERSON under consideration, and has not yet determined what rank above his present to assign him, but probably it will be nothing less than Brigadier-General.

Three Regiments from Baltimore.

There will be at least three regiments raised in Baltimore, of one thousand each, and accepted by the Government, notwithstanding the attempt of the rebel Legislature of Maryland to deprive Governor HICKS of his proper constitutional power. Troops will be concentrated in Washington to the number of forty thousand.

Floating Batteries.

The Government has under consideration the construction of six huge floating batteries for the Mississippi river.

Col. MANSFIELD has been promoted.

Shot.

SIMONTON, of the *Times*, has accidentally shot a sentinel this evening.

A member of the Metropolitan Rifles was shot by a secession policeman, in Brown's Hotel, at nine o'clock this evening.

The time which has been consumed in constructing the bridges on the Northern Central and Philadelphia, Wilmington and Baltimore Railroads, has delayed the movement of the Pennsylvania troops through Baltimore.

The Custom House in Alexandria.

It is rumored that the President has ordered the Rhode Island infantry and light artillery to take possession of the Custom House and Post Office at Alexandria.

President's Proclamation.

It is expected that the President will issue a proclamation, inviting the citizens to return to their homes, and promising protection to all who stand by the Union.

The New Regiments.

The new regiments are to consist of twelve companies each.

West Point Cadets.

The West Point Cadets arrived here to-day. They are to be detailed to instruct the volunteers in HARDEE's drill, including firing and target practice.

New York Regiment Reviewed.

President LINCOLN went to Georgetown this afternoon, where the New York Sixty-ninth Regiment is stationed, for the purpose of reviewing them.

Secretary CAMERON, together with several Philadelphians, visited the Meridian Hall to-day, and reviewed the New York Seventh.

A number of army officers were present at both reviews, and represent themselves highly gratified with the precision and celerity of movements which these troops have attained.

A Concert in Prospect.

The New York Light Guard are here. They have been enrolled in the Seventy-First Regiment. I am informed that they are to give a grand concert at the Navy Yard to-morrow, at which DODWORTH's Band and a number of amateur vocalists will assist.

The Pennsylvania Troops.

The Pennsylvania troops which have thus far arrived, are uniformed and are looking remarkably well.

The Troops Exasperated.

The troops are much exasperated against all Secessionists now on the police force, in consequence of a volunteer having been shot by one of them this evening.

The Massachusetts Sixth.

A lot of camp equipage was sent to the Massachusetts Sixth, who are stationed at the Relay House. They have felt the necessity of it keenly, but have uttered few complaints.

Provisions.

The Interior Department has information of large grain crops prepared at the West and South. One fourth of the cotton lands is put in corn. No more grain will be allowed to enter the Secession States from any quarter. Baltimore is allowed to send provisions to Washington, and twenty car loads came here yesterday.

Important from Perryville—Movement of Troops.

PERRYVILLE, Wednesday, May 8—6 P. M.—The train due from Philadelphia at 2 P. M. to-day, did not arrive here till 4 o'clock. It brought, however, the entire First Regiment of Pennsylvania Artillery, eight hundred strong; SHERMAN's celebrated battery of Artillery, with their brass field pieces, one hundred horses and one hundred and twenty men; and some companies of the Sixth Regiment Pennsylvania Volunteers. The entire arrivals of to-day number fifteen hundred men, which makes the force here two thousand strong.

The First Regiment of Artillery is commanded by Colonel PATTERSON. The men are armed with the new Minie muskets, and each man looks marches and acts like a soldier born and bred.—They are the men for fighting.

It is not likely that any of this reinforcement will remain here long. They will no doubt proceed to Annapolis, and thence to either Baltimore or Washington, at an early day. Part of them will probably proceed this evening on board the *Maryland* and *John A. Warner*.

LOYALTY OF HAVRE DE GRACE.

The people of Havre de Grace have been delighted with the recent advent of one of the companies of troops recently stationed here. There are now no less than seven beautiful American flags floating from houses in different parts of that pretty town.

IMPORTANT MOVEMENT OF TROOPS.

Five hundred men, in five companies, left here last evening, and crossed over to Havre de Grace. One hundred men remained *there*. The remainder proceeded to Bush river bridge, where they are now encamped.

Four new companies from Philadelphia, numbering four hundred men, arrived here last evening. Five other companies are expected in the next train. This will make the whole force here fourteen hundred or fifteen hundred men.

CAMP SUSQUEHANNA.

A cool southwest wind is the principal meteorological development here to-day, and the bay and river are both as rough as the most boisterous mariner could desire.

Yesterday evening, Col. DARE's Regiment Philadelphia City Guards, was sent over to Havre de Grace, and will be detailed down the Philadelphia and Baltimore Railroad below that point for its protection.

A portion of Col. NAGLE's Sixth Regiment, Schuylkill county, arrived here about 6 o'clock last evening. Several of the companies were left at Newark, Elkton, and other points on the road above here.

Col. PRATT's Twentieth New York Regiment and about fifty cadets from West Point, arrived at 11 o'clock last night, and were sent to Annapolis on the steamer *Georgiana*, while the passengers who came down by the same train, with the luggage of the regiment, went to the same destination by the *Ariel*.

The *John A. Warner* left this afternoon, taking a load of horses, and the *Maryland* is being fitted up to take SHERMAN's battery, now at Elkton, to Bush river.

The Schuylkill county troops are nearly all raw recruits, and need active and careful drilling, which they are very likely to get here.

The steamer *Hugh Jenkins* came up about noon to-day, with passengers from Baltimore, but was not allowed to land, and passed up to Port Deposit.

Society in camp to-day has been ornamented by the importation of two female nurses, and we feel ourselves happy in the belief that we shall have, of the most approved construction, "woman's smile to cheer the soldier."

The hospital is about the best arrangement, in point of construction and facilities for the relief of the men, that the camp can boast. It is under

Continued on Eighth Page.

The Philadelphia Inquirer.

ESTABLISHED 1829. | PHILADELPHIA. TUESDAY, MAY 14, 1861. | PRICE TWO CENTS.

OLD VIRGINIA!

WESTERN VIRGINIA TRUE TO THE UNION.

PROCEEDINGS OF THE WHEELING CONVENTION.

Twenty-five Counties Represented.

A NEW CAMP FORMED AT LANCASTER, PENNA.

THE COLLISION AT ST. LOUIS.

THE CAUSE OF IT.

THE PHILADELPHIANS IN CAMP AT WASHINGTON.

Opening of the Baltimore Railroad for Passenger Travel.

ADJOURNMENT OF THE SOUTHERN CONGRESS.

ITS NEXT PLACE OF MEETING UNCERTAIN.

Arrival of Fugitives from the South in Philadelphia.

ANNAPOLIS AND ITS DEFENCES.

The Philadelphia Regiments Under Marching Orders.

THE CITY ICE BOAT ON GUARD.

Attempt to Destroy Another Bridge by the Secessionists at Frederick.

MASSACHUSETTS AND NEW YORK REGIMENTS IN BALTIMORE.

THE TROOPS ENCAMPED ON FEDERAL HILL.

THE LATEST FROM WASHINGTON.

Special Despatch to the Inquirer.

Philadelphians in Camp.

WASHINGTON, May 13.—One of the finest military sights we have witnessed was the march of the First Pennsylvania Regiment, Col. PATTERSON, from their temporary quarters at the Capitol, to the camp ground assigned them at Kalorama. This magnificently beautiful and picturesque estate, the finest location in the environs of the metropolis, may be located on the map of Washington as situated without Boundary street, (which encircles the city,) and reaching down to Rock creek on the west. Massachusetts avenue, (which runs parallel with Pennsylvania avenue some eight blocks north,) leads to its gateway, where it is met by Twenty-second street, coming northward from the circle in which is the equestrian statue of GEORGE WASHINGTON. It is the commencement of the continuation of Georgetown Heights across Rock creek, and beyond it, in an easterly direction, is Meridian Hill, on which the New Jersey brigade is encamped. Next beyond comes Mount Pleasant, the location of the New York Seventh—next comes the Connecticut regiment, and next Rhode Island. So Pennsylvania has the right of this line of regimental camps.

Kalorama.

This estate was first fitted up by JOEL BARLOW, the American poet, who was Minister to France when NAPOLEON the First was Emperor. The house was fitted up in the Grecian style of those days, and the decorations of the parlors were superintended by his friend ROBERT FULTON, who experimented with models of steamboats in the mill-pond up Rock creek, which forms the southwestern boundary of the estate. Commodore DECATUR resided there after BARLOW's death, and went from there to fight a duel with Commodore BARRON, in 1820, in which both were supposed to be mortally wounded, and forgave each other as they lay bleeding. BARRON recovered, but DECATUR died on the field. Aside from these historical associations, it is a lovely spot, with fine shady groves, and a panoramic view of the whole metropolis, with the broad Potomac beyond, and Alexandria in the distance.

The First Pennsylvania.

Philadelphia has just reason to be proud of their fellow citizens, as the First Artillery marched up the avenue yesterday, with a large baggage train in the centre, laden with tents, chests, stores, &c.

Sunday Services.

The Fourth Pennsylvania had services on Sunday at their quarters, where Trinity Church, where Rev. S. W. McDANIEL, their worthy chaplain, preached.

The Seventh New York had services at Camp Cameron, their chaplain, Rev. Dr. WESTON, officiating.

The First New Jersey Regiment attended service in the afternoon, and listened to an able discourse from their chaplain, on the text, "God is our refuge and strength and very present help in time of trouble."

The Third New Jersey held appropriate services in the afternoon.

Rev. Dr. WOODBURY, chaplain of the Rhode Island Regiment, preached at the Unitarian Church in the evening, where many of his regiment attended.

The [illegible] Mounted Guard, Captain [illegible], attended Dr. [illegible] Church, in the morning.

The Constitutional Guards, Captain [illegible], attended the Thirteenth Street Baptist Church.

The [illegible] Massachusetts attended at the Church of the Epiphany, at two o'clock P. M., where the services were conducted by the Rev. Mr. [illegible], chaplain.

The [illegible] Massachusetts had services by their chaplain, Rev. [illegible].

Mr. [illegible] HALE SMITH, chaplain of the New York [illegible], preached at its encampment.

A Mail for Fort Pickens.

It is [illegible] that arrangements have been made by the Postmaster General for the regular transmission of mails to Fort Pickens, by means of the [illegible] mail steamers plying between New York and Havana, chartered by Government [illegible] Havana and Fort Pickens.

[illegible] for the first [illegible] to the New York post office for despatch thence [illegible] hereafter to be made up by that office for transmission by each of the United States mail steamers departing for Havana.

The Valiant Wigfall Heard From.

The great fire-eating WIGFALL has written a letter, fixing the 15th of June as the latest day to which he can be induced to postpone the capture of Washington. WIGFALL should be muzzled.

A Saving Determination.

It is rumored here that WINANS, of Baltimore, has fled, determined to save his neck from the halter, if he cannot save his great fortune from confiscation. It is also understood that McLANE, ex-Minister to Mexico, ex-Governor LOWE, of Frederick, and many others of the leading conspirators, are meditating flight. It will come to that, at last.

Not a Stampede.

It is not true that the greater portion of the female population has left the city in a state of alarm. A visitor to the President's grounds and other prominent places will find that there are thousands of women and children who evince no uneasiness whatever. No doubt some families have gone, but the churches on Sunday and the avenues on every day of the week show that there is full confidence in the means of defence already adopted.

Generosity.

I learn with pleasure that the members of the Rhode Island Regiment, who have already made themselves so popular with our citizens by their gentlemanly deportment and true soldierly qualities, on Saturday last, made up a purse of $1030 for the sisters of young HOWARD, who was murdered by the police on Wednesday night. This noble example will, doubtless, be followed by a number of other military regiments now in the city, as well as by our own District military.

That Wonderful Gun.

It now appears that the wonderful steam-gun which was captured by General BUTLER, is not, [illegible] after all. Mr. DICKINSON, the inventor, was not captured, as has been stated, but escaped with the most essential part of the machine—"the gun" itself—without which the machinery is of no more use than an old wagon. The machinery has all been taken to pieces and examined by the Massachusetts machinists, but they find that nothing can be made out of the wonderful gun. The [illegible] arrested was a Mr. BRADFORD, who, it is said, was interested in the sale of the gun to the Virginians.

Arrest.

A Potomac river pilot named DENNINGTON, who has passed some weeks latterly in the North, [illegible] returned to Alexandria, and has been arrested as a traitor to the South.

Accidents.

This morning, while the Providence Marine Artillery were firing one of their pieces, it was prematurely discharged by the carelessness of a man named [illegible]. He lost a hand, but was not dangerously wounded. Private ADAMS, of one of the New Jersey regiments, was badly wounded in the [illegible] by the accidental discharge of a revolver.

The Regiments in Washington.

The following is a correct list of the regiments that have reached this city, and reported to the Commander of the District since the President's proclamation:

From Massachusetts—The Sixth, Fifth and Eighth Regiments, and [illegible] Zouaves.

From New York—The Seventh, Seventy-first, Twelfth, Twenty-fifth, Sixty-ninth, Twenty-eighth and [illegible] Regiments, and Col. ELLSWORTH's Fire Brigade.

From Pennsylvania—The Fifth, Fourth and Sixth Regiments, and First Artillery.

From Rhode Island—One regiment and a Marine Artillery company.

From New Jersey—The First, Second, Third and Fourth Regiments.

Troops belonging to the United States service—[illegible] Battery, Second Artillery, Third Infantry, and [illegible] Cavalry.

The District militia are by no means undesirable aids, under command of Col. STONE. They have become proficient in drill, and are deservedly well spoken of.

The War to be Prosecuted with Vigor.

Every indication now goes to show that the existing war will be vigorously prosecuted by the Government. The troops now here are all fully uniformed and equipped, and are ready for the field at a moment's notice. They drill several hours daily, according to HARDEE's Artillery and Infantry practice, as published recently in THE INQUIRER.

A Volunteer Wounded.

While practising at target firing this morning, a member of the Rhode Island Artillery Company had his hand shot off by the premature discharge of the cannon he was serving.

Colonel Ellsworth's Zouaves.

With some other troops, it is rumored, will be stationed near the Relay House, under orders of General BUTLER.

The Route to Baltimore.

The Postmaster General has officially announced that the railroad route between Baltimore and Philadelphia is again open for the transportation of the mails and passengers.—From indications, however, it will probably be desirable to maintain an available force in the vicinity of the former city.

A Serenade.

LEWIS CLEPHANE, our new Postmaster, was serenaded to-night by his many personal friends, who engaged the Rhode Island Brass Band for the occasion.

A Re-Union at Seward's.

Secretary SEWARD entertains the officers of the New York Seventh and Seventy-first, the Massachusetts Fifth Regiments, with those from Rhode Island, to-morrow night.

Resigned.

Col. MUNROE, of the Massachusetts Eighth Regiment, resigned his commission to-day.

The Sloop-of-War Pawnee

Still maintains her position off Alexandria, with her guns shotted, ready to protect the fishing vessels, some of which have been shot on their way home.

Retrocession.

There is an earnest and growing desire here that Alexandria should be restored to her ancient place in the District of Columbia. The Union men say they will not dare to vote hereafter in Virginia.

A Dastardly Plot,

Having for its object the poisoning of the New York and other volunteers, has been discovered, and strict orders have been issued for the troops to purchase only at such stores whose occupants are known to the authorities.

Cairo Safe.

Captain POPE, who has just returned from mustering in the troops in Southern Illinois, reports Cairo to be perfectly secure against any force which the rebels can bring against it.

The Loan in Canada.

Messrs. IRA GOULD & Son, of Montreal, have offered, through JOSHUA R. GIDDINGS, to Secretary CHASE, to take one million of dollars in U. S. Treasury Stock, payable in drafts at three days' sight on Messrs. BARING, of London.

A Resignation Withdrawn.

President LINCOLN has requested Mr. CISCO, the Sub-Treasurer at New York, to withdraw his resignation, which was done to the great [illegible] office seekers.

THE ARMSTRONG GUN.

The efficiency of the rifle for the individual soldier having been demonstrated, the application of the same principle to cannon was a desideratum. As cast iron bullets are employed for large guns, of course they were inapplicable to rifled cannon. By coating such bullets with rings of lead, however, to prevent the stripping of the grooves, the success of rifled cannon was insured, and both the French and British military authorities have adopted them for their armies.

The Armstrong rifled cannon has obtained a great notoriety, and has gained for its inventor, Sir WILLIAM ARMSTRONG, a knighthood. The accompanying engravings illustrate it very fully—Fig. 1 being a longitudinal vertical section of the cannon, and Fig. 2 a view of an explosive ball which may be employed with it. When the pin F strikes an object, it explodes a charge of percussion powder inside, and the ball bursts to pieces with destructive violence. B B are the bands of lead around the cast iron shell. The carriage is of the usual form: the cannon is constructed with a steel core, which is bored out and rifled, and over this wrought-iron spiral bands are subjected to heat and shrunk, so as to combine great strength and tenacity. A conical bullet B is shown in the cannon, and it has a sabot in its rear chamber like that of a "Norton bullet." The breech entrance is a hollow screw, and the breech a screw-bolt, which is pushed back and forth on its slide C; then the screw is turned in its nut and the breech closed. B is an elevating platform, and E is a stop to support it. F is an elevating screw and a tightening nut. The elevating arrangement and the slide to the screw-breech are improvements recently made by W. GOSTLING, of London. This is the rifled cannon which our British cotemporaries state is to give them advantages in artillery warfare over every nation in the world. Sir WILLIAM ARMSTRONG states that at a distance of six hundred yards an object no larger than the crown of a man's hat can be struck with it at almost every shot, and at three thousand yards a target nine feet square (which appears like a mere speck at that distance) can be struck five times out of ten shots. It is four years since experiments were commenced with this gun, and a large factory has been erected for manufacturing them at Newcastle. The first cannons to be made are nine, twelve and eighteen pounders for the army, and after that large rifled guns will be supplied to the navy and the fortifications. It is, no doubt, a most deadly weapon of war, but those which are employed in the French army are stated to be equally as good; and there is nothing so very wonderful about it that cannot be copied and produced by our own armorers. It has been stated that this cannon is a breech loader on the principle of Sharpe's rifle; but this is not exactly correct, as Sharpe's rifle has a sliding bolt for a breech-closer, while the Armstrong cannon has a screw like the Prussian needle-gun. Some very interesting experiments have lately taken place at the Ames' Manufactory, Chicopee, Mass., with rifled bronze cannon, and from these we learn that any cannon may be rifled and made more efficient, also, that conical shot are more accurate, and have greater range with the same quantity of powder than round shot.

The London Gunmakers' Company lately entertained Sir W. ARMSTRONG at dinner, on the occasion of his receiving the honorary freedom of the company, which was conferred upon him by a unanimous resolution, "for the important service he has rendered to the nation by his great improvements in the science of gunnery." The visitors present consisted chiefly of officers and gentlemen in the Government Department officially connected with firearms. Sir WILLIAM ARMSTRONG made a speech in the course of the evening in which he said:—

I may state that all my experience leads me to the conviction that the principle of constructing cannon by the superposition of successive layers of iron coils welded into cylinders is the best, and to that principle I propose to adhere in the construction of guns of the largest dimensions. Layer after layer may be indefinitely applied, and I can scarcely see any limit to the size of gun which may by this process be constructed. The difficulties which had at first to be encountered in carrying this method into practice induced me to some extent to deviate from it. But now that those difficulties have been almost entirely surmounted I feel satisfied that it ought to be adopted in all its integrity. I can see no other mode of construction which affords so much strength, and, what is of still more importance, is so little liable to hidden and treacherous flaw. Publicity has lately been given in Parliament to the trials to which one of my twelve pounder guns had been subjected.

That gun sustained one hundred rounds fired with service charges of powder, and balls progressively increased in length until they projected beyond the muzzle. It afterwards went through a repetition of the same ordeal, not with a single but with a double charge of powder, and ultimately remained a serviceable gun. On the other hand, it has been announced that one of my 12 pounder guns had succumbed to what I must call very unmerciful usage. You have heard how it was fired at from a distance of only twenty yards, and broken with round shot. But you have not heard that the gun which was so treated was a defective one from the first, and one which the Ordnance Select Committee had been for weeks before vainly trying to burst. Although it had not been burst by those efforts, it had been cracked near the middle in a manner which greatly weakened it against an external blow. Now, one might have expected that after so gallant a resistance the poor thing might have been spared. Its wound was curable, and it might have lived to do good service to its country.

But no, the Committee ruthlessly sentenced it to be pounded to death by round shot. For this purpose a brass 9-pounder field gun, nearly twice as heavy as the poor victim, was used against it, and with a refinement of cruelty the Committee deliberately aimed at the wounded place, and succeeded in breaking the gun in two at the crack. I state all this in the presence of my friend Colonel LEFROY, who, I grieve to say, is deeply implicated in the murder. But a fate almost as bad awaited the brass gun, which in its turn was fired at from another brass gun at the same distance of twenty yards, and the very first stroke it received so crushed in the bore as to prevent the insertion of its shot. Each succeeding blow inflicted similar injury; and although the gun, from its greater weight and mass, was not broken in pieces, it was so crushed internally as well as bulged, as to be fit only for the melting-pot. It must be recollected that the carriage presents a far larger surface to the enemy than the gun, and little would be gained by making the gun invulnerable to round shot while the carriage must necessarily remain so much more liable to be disabled.

One of the 40-pounder guns has lately been tested in the same manner as the 12-pounder, and has endured 100 rounds, fired with projectiles progressively increasing in length until the entire bore was filled from the charge to the muzzle. The next step in advance was from 40-pounders to 100 pounders, a large number of which have now been proved without in any instance exhibiting any deficiency of strength. I have also very recently constructed a muzzle loading gun, designed to throw a projectile of 120 lbs. This gun is rifled upon a plan which I have called the [illegible] plan, and which enables the shot to go in easy and come out tight; for I need hardly tell you that there is nothing more essential to accuracy than to deliver the shot without vibration from the gun, while it is equally necessary, in the case of a muzzle loader, that facility of loading should be preserved. But it must not be supposed from the circumstance of my having made this gun a muzzle loader that I have in any degree given up the principle of breech-loading as applied to large guns. On the contrary, I am more than ever persuaded of the great advantages of breech-loading, more especially for the Navy, and I clearly see my way to the removal of every object on which can with any degree of reason be urged against it in heavy ordnance. At the same time, however, I believe that muzzle-loading guns, from their greater simplicity, will for some purposes be preferable to breech-loaders, and that both forms of guns will have to be provided.

Then as to the projectiles of the Armstrong gun.—It has become a common idea that one of the great difficulties incident to the lead covered form of projectile, is to give sufficient adhesion to the lead. I may therefore state that no such difficulty exists. Any amount of adhesion may be given; but there is a risk of giving too much, because if the lead were to stick too firmly to the iron, it would not separate from it and break into distinct pieces on the bursting of the shell. At present the premature separation of the lead is a matter of rare occurrence, and I do not think it would be expedient to guard more effectually against it at the risk of lessening the efficiency of the shell. With regard to the 100 pounder guns, the experiments with them and with the shells and fuses I have provided for them are proceeding satisfactorily. The destructive power of those large shells, which contain from eight to nine pounds of powder, is very great, and such as ought, I think, to settle the question of timber ships. I may mention that the copper ring, which in all the previous guns had been applied at the breech to resist the erosive action of the gas, was at first dispensed with in the 100-pounders, as I had reason to expect that, by using expanding cups to prevent the escape of the gas, the copper rings would not be required. I found, however, on trying one of these guns at Shoeburyness, that it would be necessary to resume the use of the copper for the preservation of the gun at the breech, and it was consequently returned to Woolwich to have the ring inserted. This has given rise to the foolish story that the gun was a complete failure."

Sir WILLIAM ARMSTRONG further stated that—"We have made about 780 guns during the year; and if we divide their cost (£195,000) by the number of guns, and take into account the value of the very large number of guns now in a state of progress and partially paid for, the result shows an average cost of about £320 per gun. This covers the expense of all experiments and alterations unavoidable in the commencement of a new and difficult species of manufacture."

Colonel LEFROY said he felt it right to justify the Ordnance Select Committee in the course they had adopted.—"They deemed it necessary to ascertain what would be the effect produced in the case of an Armstrong gun being struck by a round shot, as such an occurrence might be expected to happen even under the best regulated arrangements. For convenience, they had fired at a distance of only twenty yards; but, by way of compensation, they had used a reduced charge. The brass gun fired at was certainly quite shut up and therefore there was no disparagement to the Armstrong; but the result had shown that neither form of gun would bear the direct impact of a solid shot on its side without becoming disabled."

The Opening of the Baltimore Railroad—Arrival of Troops at Baltimore.

Special Despatch to the Inquirer.

THE FIRST TRAIN.

BALTIMORE, May 13.—The first train from Perryville arrived here this afternoon at four o'clock. It consisted of three passenger cars, which were well filled.

THE BRIDGES.

The bridges are all safe, and the people residing on the line of the road are "all right." The American flag was displayed at every station.

OUR CITIZENS PLEASED.

The streets of this city through which the train passed, were thronged with people, whose countenances were all indicative of the pleasure they felt.

ARRIVAL OF TWO REGIMENTS.

Two regiments have just arrived from the Relay House, and are lying on the grass on Federal Hill, unsheltered from the rain. They have no tents with them.

QUIETING DOWN.

There is now no trouble whatever experienced in passing through the streets. The American flag is flying everywhere.

HARPER'S FERRY.

The general impression prevails here that Harper's Ferry is absolutely impregnable against any force that the Government can send against it.

SENATOR DOUGLAS.

Senator DOUGLAS, I learn, is to be made a Major General in the Army.

Review at Camp Scott, York.

CAMP SCOTT, York, Pa., May 12, 1861.—Gov. CURTIN arrived in town by special train this morning, from Harrisburg. This afternoon the entire force of the Camp was drawn into lines, and the Governor, after being received with the proper honors, made a grand review. He was accompanied by Major-General KEIM and Aids, and Brigadier General WYNKOOP and Aids. The spectacle was of the most imposing and interesting character, and must have given ample evidence to the Governor of the patriotism of the volunteer soldiers of Pennsylvania. Not less than [illegible] spectators were present, and every available point affording a good view of the scene was occupied. Mrs. CURTIN was also present witnessing the review from General WYNKOOP's headquarters.

The troops are being rapidly equipped, and marching orders will no doubt be placed in the hands of the commanding officer in a few days. C.

Parade at Chambersburg.

Special Despatch to the Inquirer.

CHAMBERSBURG, PA., May 13.—The Tenth Regiment, Col. MEREDITH, made a street parade to-day. They looked remarkably well. It is not thought probable that the troops will move this week. Many of them are not yet equipped.

Non-Arrival of the Nova Scotia.

FATHER POINT, May 13—Evening.—There are no signs of the steamer *Nova Scotia*, now due at this point.

THE TROUBLE AT ST. LOUIS, MO.

General Harney Approves of the Course of Captain Lyon.

PROCEEDINGS OF THE MISSOURI LEGISLATURE.

STATE PENITENTIARY CONVERTED INTO AN ARMORY.

The Latest from St. Louis.

THE COLLISION BETWEEN THE SOLDIERS AND POPULACE—OFFICIAL STATEMENT.

ST. LOUIS, May 13.—The official statement of the recent collisions between the United States soldiers and the populace, published this morning, says that the first firing at Camp Jackson, on Friday evening, was some half dozen shots discharged near the head of the column of the First Regiment, occasioned by a volley of stones and pistol shot, from the crowd. No one was hurt at this point. The second firing occurred from the rear of the column guarding the prisoners.

The crowd here was large and very abusive, and one man discharged three barrels of a revolver at Lieut. SAXTON, of the regular service, many of the crowd cheering him and drawing revolvers and firing at the troops. The man who commenced the attack then laid his pistol across his arm and took deliberate aim at Lieut. SAXON, when he was thrust through with a bayonet and fired upon at the same time, and instantly killed.

The column then moved, having received orders to march, but the rear company being assaulted by the crowd, and several of them shot, they halted and fired, causing the deaths already reported.

The order was then given by Captain LYON to cease firing, which was promptly obeyed.

The principal arms taken from Camp Jackson were four large size howitzers, two ten-inch mortars, a large number of ten-inch shells, ready charged, and some four thousand stand of United States muskets, supposed to be a portion of those taken from the Baton Rouge Arsenal.

A thousand people left the city yesterday (Sunday) afternoon, in consequence of the reports of insubordination among the German troops, and threats to burn and sack the city; but the appearance of Gen. HARNEY's proclamation in a great measure restored confidence, and many of those who left will probably return to-day.

The city is now quiet, and the highest hopes are now entertained that no further disturbance will occur.

Twenty-two persons are known to have been killed during the collision at Camp Jackson, the following seventeen of whom have been identified, viz:—John Sweckerhardt, Casper H. Glencoe, J. Walters, Thos. A. Hand, Wm. Ireenhower, J. J. Jones, P. Doane, Eric Wright, Henry Jungle, James McDonald, Walter McDowell, Nicholas Krohlack, Francis Whedon, Job Carter, James Bodsen, Emma Somers, Wm. McAuliffe.

Three of these were soldiers belonging to the Southwest Expedition, and were among the prisoners captured at Camp Jackson.

ST. LOUIS, May 13.—The report which circulated in this city, on Saturday and yesterday, that General HARNEY disapproved of the action of Capt. LYON, with reference to the capture of Camp Jackson, is authoritatively denied this morning. He not only approves of the whole proceedings, but compliments that officer for the prompt and admirable manner in which he executed the orders of the Government.

Reliable information received from Jefferson City says that nearly all the objectionable features in the Harris Military bill, which had been debated during the secret session, had been materially amended, but when the news of the capture of Camp Jackson reached the capitol the amendments were immediately reconsidered, and the original bill passed both Houses by large majorities. Also, that no Secession ordinance had been brought before either House, nor was such an act contemplated.

The Legislature has passed, and the Governor signed, a bill providing for a military fund to arm the State. The fund will include the receipts from the assessments for the years of 1860 and 1861, after the regular expenses of the Government have been paid; a war loan from Banks and individuals; a special tax of fifteen cents on the hundred dollars, and $1,000,000 worth of bonds.

The bill also authorizes the Governor to establish an armory in the Penitentiary, for the manufacture of arms and munitions of war.

ST. LOUIS, May 13.—The city has been quiet and orderly to-day, and our citizens generally have been engaged in their usual vocations.

Capt. TOTTEN's battalion of regulars are still quartered in the city, and will be kept here as long as the Police Commissioners consider their presence necessary for the preservation of peace.

The troops at Camp Bissell, near Caseyville on the Ohio and Mississippi Railroad, are the Twelfth Regiment of Illinois Volunteers, under the command of Colonel McARTHUR, of Chicago. A telegraph office was opened to-day, putting the camp in direct communication with St. Louis and all Eastern points.

The *Evening Journal* publishes a statement signed by General FROST and his staff, explaining the reasons why Camp Jackson was surrendered. They say there were only five rounds of ammunition in the camp, and neither arms nor provisions enough to supply the force of eight hundred men under their command. To have attempted a resistance, surrounded as they were by six hundred or eight hundred troops, well armed and with every appliance of war, would have been suicide, and retreat was impossible, they being without means of transportation and without provisions and with no credit to procure either.

They censure the State authorities for not paying their just military debts, and affording proper supplies. They pronounce Captain LYON's demand as illegal, unconstitutional, and wanton, trampling under foot the laws of our common country.

It is estimated that over ten thousand persons left the city yesterday. A perfect panic is raging in some quarters, almost entire streets being deserted.

The Maryland Legislature.

BALTIMORE, May 13.—The Maryland Legislature did not adjourn to-day as was expected.

The House amended the resolution proposing to adjourn on Thursday next till the 4th of June. The Senate further amended it into a provision to appoint Commissioners to President LINCOLN and JEFF. DAVIS, and the Governors of Virginia and Pennsylvania, for a stay of hostilities till after the meeting of Congress; but the House refused to accede.

Mr. WALLIS reported a bill for calling a Sovereign Convention; but it was not acted on.

The Legislature adjourned till morning.

From Cairo.

CAIRO, Ill., May 13.—Several companies of Arkansas troops arrived at Memphis this morning.

An order has been issued that on and after to-day, all boats passing this point will be stopped. No provisions or munitions of war for the Southern States will be allowed to pass.

IMPORTANT NEWS.

Occupation of Baltimore by the Federal Troops.

SUDDEN MOVEMENT FROM THE RELAY HOUSE.

REJOICINGS OF THE PEOPLE.

MASSACHUSETTS AND NEW YORK VOLUNTEERS.

Every Hospitality Extended to them by the Baltimoreans.

THE TROOPS STATIONED AT FEDERAL HILL.

BALTIMORE, May 13, Midnight.—About eight o'clock this evening, a large train filled with troops arrived at the outer depot from the Relay House.

The train contained one thousand troops, comprising five companies from each of the regiments stationed at the Relay House—the Sixth of Massachusetts and the Eighth of New York, with a battery of artillery.

They marched through South Baltimore to Federal Hill, a high point of ground on the south side of the harbor, directly overlooking the city, and one mile west of Fort McHenry.

The sudden appearance of the troops from this direction took our citizens by surprise, but they were greeted with every demonstration of approbation.

Immense crowds quickly gathered, cheering at every step. The ladies waved their handkerchiefs, and many brought lamps and candles to the windows.

Prominent citizens accompanied the troops to the hill and assisted the officers in taking the best route thither, and procuring quarters for the troops until their tents could arrive.

The troops seemed to be highly pleased with their reception, and all expressed surprise and delight at the commanding position and fine prospect of the whole city and country spread out before them.

WESTERN VIRGINIA.

STATE CONVENTION AT WHEELING.

TWENTY-FIVE COUNTIES REPRESENTED.

FIRST DAY.

WHEELING, Va., May 13.—The city is wild with enthusiasm, and flags are flying from nearly all the buildings in honor of the meeting of the Union Convention of Western Virginia.

The Convention met at 11 o'clock A. M., and after appointing a Committee on Credentials, took a recess until 3 o'clock.

On re-assembling, the Committee reported favorable to the admission of delegates from twenty-five counties to seats.

A committee on permanent officers was appointed.

A resolution was adopted, appointing a Committee on State and Federal Relations.

Before its adoption, a discussion took place between Gen. J. J. JACKSON, of Wood county, and Mr. JOHN S. CARLISLE.

General JACKSON thought that the project for a division of the State was premature.

Mr. CARLISLE declared that we must have immediate and prompt action, and that this Convention must not satisfy itself with paper resolves.

The Convention then adjourned till morning.

The ceremonies attending the hoisting of the American flag over the Custom House, this afternoon, were very imposing. Thousands of people were on the ground. National airs were sung and speeches made by Mr. CARLISLE, and others.

Reported Secession Attempt to Destroy the Monocacy Bridge, near Frederick Md.

THE TELEGRAPH WIRES CUT.

BALTIMORE, May 13.—The *American* of this city has received the following special despatch from its correspondent at Frederick:—

FREDERICK, Md., May 13.—Some excitement was created here to-day by a report that late last night a party of twelve unknown men entered the telegraph office at Monocacy Junction, six miles east of Frederick, and cut the wires. They spent some time in examining the bridge at that point and left with the threat to return to-night and destroy the bridge.

A company of [illegible] to-night, to protect the bridge.

From Virginia, via Harrisburg.

CONDITION OF AFFAIRS AT HARPER'S FERRY—[illegible] OF PROVISIONS AND ARMS—NO BATTERY ON THE MARYLAND HEIGHTS.

HARRISBURG, May 13.—A person employed on special service, who visited Harper's Ferry last week, reached Harrisburg to-day, and reports that there were then [illegible] troops there altogether. About three-fourths of them were armed, and mostly with [illegible], but the balance were without arms. Only one Kentuckians were there and but one company of South Carolinians. The provisions of the troops there were very [illegible] under the existing circumstances. They had only one day's provisions on hand, their supplies [illegible] from Western Virginia being cut off by the stand taken by the people of that section of the State.

It was thought that the supplies, anywhere within reach in the surrounding country, must be exhausted within two weeks. It is positive that not more than [illegible] stand of arms were got out of the wreck of the arsenal buildings, and some of these were [illegible]. Not more than [illegible] are [illegible] per day in the shops in operation. There are only [illegible] men on the Maryland side of the Potomac; they have not erected any batteries on this side of the river, [illegible]. They must retreat or be [illegible]. This, however, does not [illegible] the probable advance of the main Confederate army on the southern Pennsylvania route, when JEFF. DAVIS discovers the impossibility of breaking the [illegible] around Washington.

Re-establishment of Railroad Travel.

THE FIRST TRAIN THROUGH BALTIMORE HAILED WITH DELIGHT.

BALTIMORE, May 13.—The train from Philadelphia came through this afternoon with the mails and passengers at 4 o'clock. It was hailed with evident satisfaction by the people along the route, and as it passed through the city, many expressions of welcome were given.

The national flag was displayed in various parts of the city to-day, the proscription against the colors having been removed by Councils.

Our citizens have been all day in expectation of the arrival of troops over the Northern Central, but up to this [illegible] o'clock P. M., none have arrived.

A Mexican War Steamer at New Orleans.

NEW ORLEANS, May 13.—The Mexican war steamer [illegible], from Havana, arrived at this port to-day.

THE NEW YORK HERALD.

WHOLE NO. 9019. MORNING EDITION—MONDAY, MAY 20, 1861. PRICE TWO CENTS.

THE WAR.

The Latest Intelligence from Washington.

Vigorous War Measures of the Federal Government.

Major General Butler Ordered to Fortress Monroe.

A Large Army to be Concentrated in Virginia.

The Formation of Two Large Cantonments Decided On.

President Lincoln Among the Rebels in Virginia.

The Capture of the Stolen Light Ship.

OUTRAGES BY THE REBELS IN VIRGINIA.

Masters of Vessels Robbed and Imprisoned.

Removal of the Seat of the Rebel Government from Montgomery to Richmond.

More Developements of the Policy of the British Government,

&c., &c., &c.

VIGOROUS MEASURES OF THE ADMINISTRATION.

WASHINGTON, May 19, 1861.

Major General Butler has been ordered to Old Point Comfort, with nine regiments, of about twelve hundred men each. This I know positively. Aggressive operations are at last actually to be commenced by the administration. General Butler left for Annapolis, on his way South, last evening.

The Fourteenth regiment, of Brooklyn, Colonel Wood, nine hundred and eighty men, have arrived this evening, via Baltimore. All well and in high spirits.

THE ADVANCE OF TROOPS INTO VIRGINIA.

WASHINGTON, May 19, 1861.

Brigadier Mansfield, of the army, it is understood, will take command of the *corp's d'armee* that will be advanced into Virginia from this point.

It will consist of twenty five thousand volunteers and five thousand regulars, nearly three thousand of whom are already concentrated here.

Colonel Henry L. Scott has been appointed Inspector General, in place of General Mansfield.

The forces that will be detailed to retake Harper's Ferry will probably be commanded by the newly appointed Brigadier General Reeder.

General Patterson and staff, including Senator Sherman of Ohio, are here to receive verbal instructions concerning the proposed movement of troops from southern Pennsylvania upon Virginia.

The Medical Committee, headed by Dr. Van Buren have been successful in their mission. The sanitary department of the army will be reorganized under the supervision of the Medical Board they represent.

Divine service was again held to-day in the open air in all the regimental encampments.

Commander Bartlett is here to urge the acceptance of his Naval Brigade.

PRESIDENT LINCOLN VISITS THE REBELS.

WASHINGTON, May 19, 1861.

The President has been absent from the White House nearly all day reconnoitering in the vicinity of Washington. Among other points of interest, he visited the Great Falls, sixteen miles above this city, on the Potomac. He crossed the chain bridge, and passed the secession pickets on the Virginia side, and returned the same way. The rebels might have caught a prize, but did not know so valuable a one was within their grasp.

A. D. Banks, the notorious secessionist, hailed a party of men on the Virginia side of the long bridge last night, and gave them a message for his personal friend from whom he had been in the habit of receiving his intelligence of the doings of the federal forces, and whom he supposed was in this city. Banks said he wished them to tell his friend to come over and see him this evening. This confederate of the notorious Banks left the city suddenly last night, and officers are in pursuit of him. I have reason to believe that a substitute of the friend of Banks, in the shape of a federal officer, went over the bridge to-night to see the latter, but he was missing.

For the benefit of the numerous callers at the White House upon Mrs. Lincoln, I am authorised to state that she will not return until Tuesday next, and will receive callers on Wednesday.

THE SEVENTH REGIMENT AND NEW YORK VOLUNTEERS.

WASHINGTON, May 19, 1861.

The rumors afloat respecting the Seventh regiment are not only unfounded, but most undeserved. They have no idea of breaking up their camp on the day when their period of service here expires. Their intention is to await the orders of the department. It is thought the Secretary will send them back to Staten Island, where their admirable drill will be useful in preparing the more raw material that will be collected there soon. The prompt manner in which the gallant Seventh rushed forward to the defence of Washington is appreciated by the government, and it ought to be a shield against the malicious reports of their returning to New York, with or without orders. They will never sully their colors by any act unworthy their high reputation. They will, probably, be ordered off soon for more important service, as just stated, near New York.

There is a good deal of strong comment here on the conduct of the Military Board at Albany. Whether the motives of these gentlemen spring from political manoeuvring or scheming for contracts, they are pronounced here both odious and disgraceful. The indignation of the country will crush any official body who at this crisis abuses its influence to obtain power or pelf. The Albany junta was denounced here in sharp terms by some members of the Union Committee of New York, and the government has conveyed its opinion of their proceedings by giving the organization of fourteen regiments solely to the Union Committee. It was the intrigues of these Albany hucksters that brought General Sickles to Washington this week, where his energetic remonstrances called the attention of the President to what was going on at Albany, and his decided action in accepting the Sickles brigade was the best rebuke he could pronounce on those who trade in their country's perils.

The War Department telegraphed yesterday to Governor [illegible] and the Union Committee that the Sickles brigade, consisting five regiments were to be included in the late [illegible] of fourteen regiments accorded to the Union Committee of New York. The chief [illegible] the government [illegible] [illegible] [illegible] former political opponent, and it is thought that the patriotic course of this gentleman in the last Congress in breaking off his long cherished political relations with the South deserved a marked compliment. General Sickles has his orders to remove his brigade at once into an encampment near New York, and to hold himself in readiness at a very early day for an important service to be confided to him. If it should turn out that he is incompetent for a delicate or dangerous task, his military career will close at the very outset. But his judgment and pluck are well thought of here by all parties. The General is eager for work, and desires the hardest job in the gift of the War Department. He is likely to get it, we hear, and very soon.

It is settled no more troops will be accepted by the government under the last requesition, either from New York or elsewhere. Already some two hundred and twenty thousand men are enlisted, and it will take time to muster them in and organize them for service.

A Cabinet officer was yesterday refused by the Secretary of War the acceptance of a single regiment, which he was most solicitous to have mustered in.

FORMATION OF CANTONMENTS.

WASHINGTON, May 19, 1861.

The War Department contemplates to establish shortly two large cantonments, one at Gettysburg, Pa., and another in the neighborhood of New York—probably at Staten Island. The object of these camps is to prepare two efficient *corps d'armee*, with which certain important operations can be promptly carried out. The force that will be collected in these camps is not yet settled upon, but will vary from fifteen thousand to twenty thousand men. They will be worked up by the best officers to the highest efficiency, and kept in constant readiness for active service. The force at Gettysburg will no doubt be employed at the right moment for an inland movement that it may not be proper at this time to disclose; whilst that at Staten Island is meant to be directed against various points of the seaboard bounding the rebel States.

Orders are issued to get ready at the earliest moment a fleet of steam transports that will rendezvous in the adjoining waters, so that in a few hours, when the signal is given, the whole of the force on the Atlantic coast can be embarked and proceed with all speed on the service designated. It has not transpired, of course, what points are selected for the exploits of this army of the Atlantic; but it is thought it is meant to assail in rapid succession various important positions along the rebel coast. All this is being carefully considered, and it is not to be doubted, from the quality of the troops that will be employed, and the energy of the officers that will be selected, that the operations of this corps will be the most important in its results of the whole war.

It does credit to the Secretary of War that, amid the multitudinous details of his office that harrass him night and day, he has had the time to devise these cantonments and suggest the mode of their organization. General Scott gives his hearty approval, it is understood, to these vigorous inspirations of the war office.

HEAVY REBEL BATTERY ON THE POTOMAC.

WASHINGTON, May 19, 1861.

A detachment of the Seventy-first regiment returned from a cruising expedition down the Potomac this evening. They report the erection of a heavy battery at Aquia creek. On the down trip the battery was masked with trees, but on their return, it was exposed to full view. As the government is determined to keep the navigation of the river open at all hazards, active measures will doubtlessly be instituted to secure its removal.

CAPTURE OF A STOLEN LIGHT SHIP.

WASHINGTON, May 10, 1861.

General Butler's forces have captured another light-ship, and smelt a little gunpowder in the undertaking. Captain R. S. Fay, one of the General's staff, was detailed on the 16th inst., with a detachment of fifty men from the Thirteenth New York regiment, under command of Lieutenant Underwood, and two guns and twenty men from the Eighth New York regiment, under Lieutenant Burns, the whole under command of Captain Fay, with orders from General Butler to find and capture one of the lightships that had been removed from their place in Chesapeake bay and concealed in a branch of the great Yeomico river. Besides the above force Gen. Butler ordered to the same duty Lieut. Hoezer, of the United States Navy, with the chartered steamer William Woodward, having on board thirty seamen from the Alleghany and the Forward, and a detachment from the force at Annapolis, named above.

According to a report made to the Secretary of the Navy, this service was faithfully performed on the 17th inst., and the lightship now lies in the harbor of Annapolis. It appears that a force of about thirty uniformed men in their shirt sleeves fired at the steamer from the Virginia shore. The rebels were covered in a dense thicket. Their shots went over the heads of the men on board the William Woodward. Captain Fay ordered the men under his command to fire upon the rebels. The report to the Secretary of the Navy says no casualties happened to the loyalists. Owing to the concealed position of the enemy it was impossible to say whether they incurred any loss or not.

General Butler compliments Captain Fay and his command for their gallantry. Some of the men under Captain Fay say they saw some of the rebels fall under the fire from the steamer. The rebels kept up their fire upon the steamer as long as she was within the range of their guns.

At Leesville, eight miles from Washington, there are [illegible] eight hundred men [illegible] [illegible] to watch the chain bridge that leads to Georgetown, and for the last few days this rebel picket has been annoying persons who have passed from Virginia to the District of Columbia.

Why don't the government disperse them and drive them from the Virginia side of the Long Bridge, and from that point to Alexandria, and beyond those who are daily annoying good citizens? It is time that this was done, and that the secession flag that has been flying for weeks within sight of the White House was taken down. Call for the boys to do the duty and thousands will volunteer.

The number of regular and volunteer troops accepted and soon to be mustered into the service of the United States, together with the old force, is over two hundred and thirty thousand. This is official. As many more could be called into the field in thirty days.

THE REBEL CAPITAL TO BE REMOVED TO RICHMOND.

WASHINGTON, May 19 1861.

The Montgomery *Advertiser* says that "Congress" has decided to remove the confederate capital to Richmond.

THE FOREIGN MAILS.

WASHINGTON, May 19, 1861.

Portland, Detroit and Chicago have been constituted new offices of exchange for the United States and Prussia closed mails, to be conveyed via England, by means of the Grand Trunk Railroad through Canada and the Canadian line of mail packets plying in summer between Quebec and Liverpool, and in winter between Portland and Liverpool. These offices will, in addition to the British and French mails already regularly despatched by them, commence to forward closed mails to Prussia, via Quebec and Liverpool, on the 1st of June next.

A private letter, dated on board the frigate Minnesota, Hampton Roads, Friday, says:—We arrived from Boston on the 13th, and have commenced our assaults on the enemy. We have seized about $300,000 worth of ships and tobacco. We are anticipating an attempt, on the part of the enemy, to fortify Sewall's Point. If they do, we shall attack them.

It is the intention of the government to render West Point Academy even more efficient than heretofore. A number of appointments have been recently made from civilians to occupy lieutenancies in the regular army.

The health of the volunteers in and around Washington continues unusually good. Twelve or fifteen of the regiments are already encamped in different localities. The troops manifest the most friendly feelings towards one another, while their general good conduct is remarkable.

OUTRAGES BY THE REBELS AT NORFOLK.

SINKING OF BARK D. C. PIERCE AT NORFOLK—WRECK OF BARK IDA, AND ROBBERY OF HER CARGO—IMPRISONMENT OF HER COMMANDER.

BOSTON, May 19, 1861.

The steam gunboat Pembroke, Captain Collin, from Fortress Monroe, 16th inst, arrived at this port this morning. She brings several passengers, including Captain Charles Gale, of the bark D. C. Pierce, of Cleveland, Ohio, and Captain Johnson, of bark Ida, of Boston.

Capt. Gale reports that his bark (the D C Pierce) was sunk by the rebels at Norfolk on the 5th inst. Besides losing his vessel, the cargo and $3,000 in specie, in all valued at $75,000, he was thrown into prison and kept there until released on bail through the intercession of a friend. Failing to obtain redress, and being closely watched, he made his escape, with nine others, in a long boat, and reached the frigate Minnesota in safety. Capt. Gale's daughter, who was with him, together with his crew, were in destitute circumstances in Norfolk, and were refused assistance on all hands, more especially by the English consul, one Myers, who, from his own acknowledgment, subsequently made in the presence of the officers of the Minnesota, had possession of the cargo of sugar and specie, valued jointly at $50,000, but refused to give Gale a receipt for it, as indemnity for his owners.

Captain Johnson reports that his bark (the Ida) was wrecked near Cape Henry: that he saved the cargo and rigging, and shipped it to Norfolk in a schooner, where he was robbed of nearly the whole property, and imprisoned for five days, when he made his escape with Captain Gale.

REPORTS FROM ANNAPOLIS.

ANNAPOLIS, May 19—9 P. M.

A despatch states that last night the wire was cut and the rails torn up at Mouscacy, on the Baltimore and Ohio Railroad, some twenty miles this side of Harper's Ferry. It was repaired to-day.

REPORTS FROM CHAMBERSBURG.

CHAMBERSBURG, Pa., May 19, 1861.

Judge Mason, arrested yesterday, was released to-day and sent over the Maryland line. He was known to entertain secession sympathies, but his character was too high to believe he would condescend to play the spy. There was no authority from the Secretary of War to retain him. His discharge meets with approval amongst the most judicious residents.

A deserter from Harper's Ferry, named Stanley, from Ohio originally, has arrived here, and reports that there were but twelve pieces of cannon, all told, there on Thursday night.

The Confederate troops on Friday visited a Maryland farmer three miles below the Ferry, killed seven hogs and drove off three head of cattle in open daylight. They have committed similar depredations on the Maryland side for ten miles above the Ferry. These are of daily occurrence.

The troops here are not fully equipped. Knapsacks will be here in a few days. The troops expect to receive marching orders [illegible] every day. They will certainly occupy Hagerstown in a few days.

[illegible] are arriving here daily. [illegible] stories are related by many.

A BIRD'S-EYE VIEW OF THE UNITED STATES.

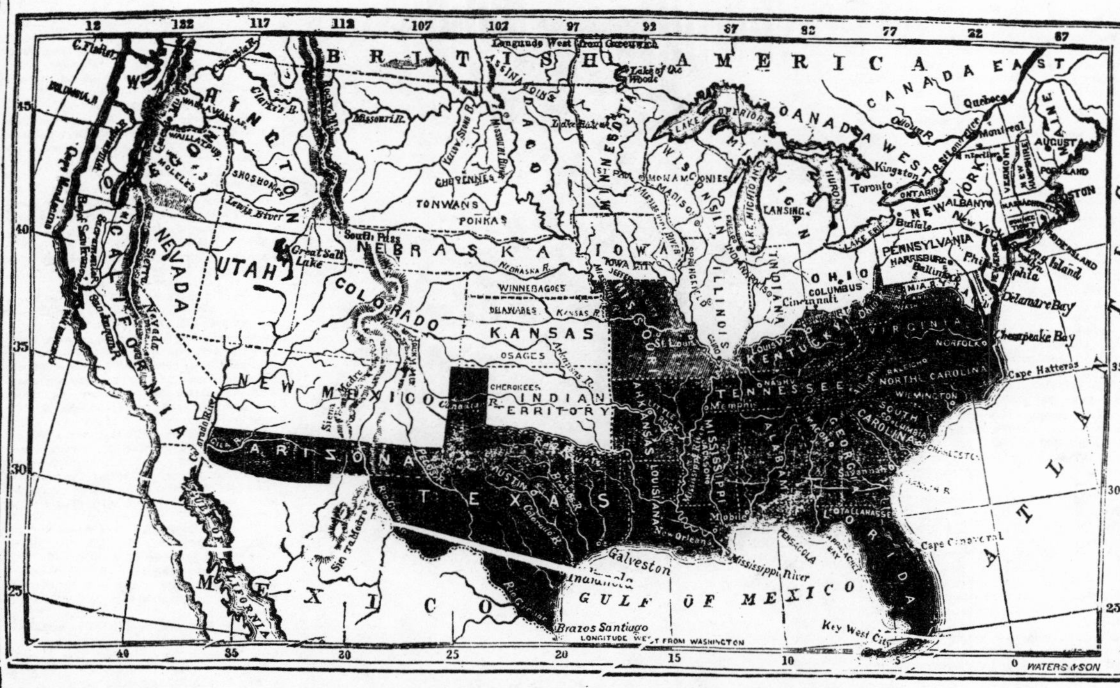

BIRD'S-EYE VIEW OF THE COUNTRY.

The above map gives a bird's-eye view of the United States, prepared in such a form as to show to the public at a glance the present status of each State in the Union. The seceded States are given in black, and the doubtful States, including the northwestern corner of Virginia, are given in shaded lines. The loyal members of the Union are in white. We add a sketch of each disloyal State.

In regard to the nominal fighting condition of the country, the census for 1860, just completed, shows the following number of males between the ages of eighteen and forty-five:—

THE CENSUS OF 1860.

FREE STATES.

State.	Aggregate Population.
California	384 770
Connecticut	460,670
Illinois	1,691,238
Indiana	1,350,802
Iowa	682,003
Maine	619,000
Massachusetts	1,231,494
Michigan	754,291
Minnesota	172,796
New York	3,851,563
New Hampshire	326,827
New Jersey	676,034
Ohio	2,377,917
Oregon	52,566
Pennsylvania	2,916,018
Rhode Island	174,621
Vermont	345,827
Wisconsin	763,445
Total	$18,602,124

SOUTHERN CONFEDERACY STATES.

States.	Free.	Slave.	Aggregate.
Alabama	520,444	435,473	955,917
Arkansas	331,710	109,065	440,775
Florida	81,885	63,809	145,000
Georgia	615,366	467,461	1,082,827
Louisiana	354,245	312,186	666,431
Mississippi	407,051	479,607	886,658
North Carolina	679,965	328,377	1,008,342
South Carolina	308,186	407,185	715,371
Tennessee	859,578	287,112	1,146,690
Texas	415,999	189,956	605,955
Virginia	1,097,373	495,826	1,593,199
Total	5,672,155	3,671,057	9,433,508

NEUTRAL SLAVE STATES.

States.	Free.	Slave.	Aggregate.
Delaware	110.548	1,805	112,353
Kentucky	920,077	225,490	1,145,567
Maryland	646,183	85,382	731,565
Missouri	1,085,595	115,619	1,201,214
Total	2,764,903	328,296	3,193,719

TERRITORIES.

Dacotah	4,839
District of Columbia	75,321
Kansas	143 645
Nebraska	28,892
New Mexico	93,024
Utah	49,000
Washington	11,624
Total	406,345

RECAPITULATION.

Free States	18,801,124
Seceding States	9,433,508
Neutral States	3,193,719
Territories	405,345
Total	31,835,696

According to our data, these numbers are somewhat exaggerated, because it is not to be expected that the whole population between those ages are always in a fighting condition.

THE PERIODS OF SECESSION OF THE CONFEDERATE STATES.

The disloyal States seceded in the following order:—

State.	Date of Secession.	Vote of Convention.
South Carolina	December 20 1860.	—
Mississippi	January 9, 1861	84 to 15.
Alabama	January 11, 1861	61 to 39.
Florida	January 11, 1861	62 to 7.
Georgia	January 19, 1861	208 to 89.
Louisiana	January 26, 1861	113 to 17.
Texas	February 1, 1861	166 to 7.
*Virginia	April 17, 1861.	
Arkansas	May 6, 1861	69 to 1.
North Carolina	Convention meets to-day.	—
†Tennessee	—	—

*To be ratified or rejected by a vote of the people, May 23, 1861—next Thursday.

†Adopted by the Legislature by a vote in the Senate, 20 to 4; House, 46 to 21, to be referred to the people for ratification.

THE DATE OF THE RATIFICATION OF THE CONFEDERATE STATES CONSTITUTION.

These States have ratified the constitution of the Confederate States by the following vote —

State.	Date of Ratification.	Vote of Convention.
Alabama	March 13, 1861	87 to 5.
Georgia	March 16, 1861	96 to 5.
Louisiana	March 21 1861	101 to 7.
Texas	March 25, 1861	68 to 2.
Mississippi	March 30 1861	78 to 7.
South Carolina	April 3 1861	149 to 20.
Florida	April 22, 1861	Unanimously.
Arkansas	May 6, 1861	Unanimously.
North Carolina	—	—
Tennessee	Not voted.	—
Virginia	Not voted.	—

SKETCHES OF THE SECEDED STATES.

We all know where the free States stand. The overwhelming uprising of Union sentiment, from the Atlantic to the Pacific, emphatically shows the position of the North. But what is the condition of the Southern States? This question is answered by the annexed brief sketches:—

VIRGINIA.

Virginia, the last of the seceding States, is 370 miles long, and 200 broad at its greatest breadth, containing 61,352 square miles of territory, with a population of 1,593,199, including slaves of the whites, [illegible] are liable to military duty. The State [illegible] Pennsylvania and the capital is now the theatre of war to put down rebellion. The aggregate number of troops within her border in the secession army cannot be far from 50,000 men, and opposed to them is an equal number of troops loyal to the American flag and the Union. The federal government occupy several important strategic military points within the border of the State, which, for the time being, give it a partial and not an unimportant degree of possession of the whole State. The ordinance of secession, which passed the State Convention on the 17th ult., will be submitted to the people for ratification or rejection on the 23d inst. The rebels have fortified themselves, and are in force at Norfolk, Harper's Ferry, Richmond and Lynchburg, Stanton, Yorktown, West Point and the advance from either side would be productive of a severe contest at arms.

WESTERN VIRGINIA.

The western part of Virginia, embracing twenty-five counties, with a population of over two hundred thousand (of which twenty thousand are liable to military duty), opposes the ordinance of secession of the State and claims its loyalty to the Stars and Stripes. The representatives of Western Virginia, with a patriotic determination, avow, in the event of the secession ordinance being adopted on the 23d, they will declare themselves an independent State, and claim the protection, if necessary, of the United States military forces. In this determination they have received the assurance of the Governor of Pennsylvania that they shall have all necessary succor from his State.

NORTH CAROLINA.

This State contains an area of 45,000 square miles. Although it has taken no steps to pass a secession ordinance, yet the action of its authorities has placed it in hostility to the Union. The Governor of the State has caused the seizure of Forts Caswell and Johnson, seized the Arsenal at Fayetteville and levied upon the public funds of the United States, and is now equipping a force to join the rebel army to oppose the defenders of law and order. The State has a population of 1,008.342, and of that number 132,000 males are liable to military duty.

SOUTH CAROLINA.

South Carolina, the pioneer of the States of the Southern confederacy, is two hundred miles long and one hundred and twenty-five broad, containing 28,000 square miles of territory, with a total population indifferently stated at 715,371, about one-half of whom are whites; of the latter 60,000 males are liable to military duty. This State seceded from the Union December 20, 1860. In the siege and bombardment of Fort Sumter this State rallied a force of between eight and ten thousand men. Since the evacuation of that fort by the United States troops five thousand of the former have been retained to hold the forts in Charleston harbor, and three thousand have been sent to Virginia to await further operations. The harbor of Charleston is effectually blockaded by the United States steam frigate Niagara, and all commerce will for the future be suspended. The blockade of Charleston is in effect equal to the occupancy of the city.

GEORGIA.

This State is three hundred miles long from north to to south, and two hundred and forty broad, and contains a population of 1,082,827, of which number 78,000 males are liable to military duty. Savannah, situated on the river of that name, about seventeen miles from its mouth, is the great seaport commercial mart of the State. The mouth of the Savannah river is defended by Fort Pulaski, on Cockspur Island. This fort is an immense work, built of brick, and mounts 150 guns, some of them of improved make and finish. The fort is garrisoned by six hundred men. To the south of this fort, on Tybee Island, the secession troops have erected an immense sand fort, in which has been placed a heavy battery of guns. This work has an extended sea range, and will prove a formidable customer to a blockading or attacking squadron. There are upwards of two thousand troops between the city of Savannah and the mouth of the river. Fort Jackson, a small fort two miles from Savannah, has a garrison of two hundred men and an armament of six or eight heavy guns. This State seceded from the Union January 19, 1861, by a vote of 208 to 89.

ALABAMA.

This State is bounded north by Tennessee, east by Georgia, south by Florida and west by Mississippi. It contains 50,672 square miles of territory, and has a population of 955,914, of which number 119,000 are liable to military duty. This State seceded from the Union, through its Convention, January 11, 1861, by a vote of 61 to 39. Mobile, the only seaport of any importance in this State, is situated at the head of Mobile Bay, forty miles from the sea coast. The bay is protected by Forts Morgan and Gaines, the first situated on a prominent sand spit, commanding all the sea approaches. The latter is situated on the opposite shore. These forts are now garrisoned by 1,500 troops of the Confederate States army, under Colonel Hardee. The forts are well equipped and ready for a good defence.

FLORIDA.

This State is [illegible] miles long and from 50 to 250 wide, containing 59,268 square miles. It has a population of 145,000, and of that number 6,000 are liable to military duty. The State, from its peninsulated position, embraces a large and extended sea coast, with few harbors, in which are included those of Key West and Pensacola, both of which are now in the military possession of the United States troops. The State, a hereditament to the Southern confederacy, [illegible] assistance in the present struggle, [illegible] except the few troops she may enlist. Financially [illegible] to sustain a State government, and is not prepared to raise money to any extent in the present civil war. Florida seceded from the Union January 11, 1861, by a vote of 62 to 7.

MISSISSIPPI.

The State of Mississippi seceded from the Union January 9, 1861, by a vote of 84 to 15. The State is 339 miles long from north to south, and 150 broad, containing 47,151 square miles. It has a population of 886,658 inhabitants; of that number 71,000 are liable to do military duty. The Mississippi river, with its various windings, forms the entire western boundary of the State, and its margin consists of undulated swamps. Like her neighbor State Arkansas, this State will have to afford her quota of protection from invasion from the north of the Mississippi river, and this force will have to be of such a magnitude as to detract considerably from her force to be furnished to the rebel Mobile force.

ARKANSAS.

This State is bounded north by Missouri, east by the Mississippi river, which separates it from Tennessee and Mississippi, south by Louisiana, and west by the Indian Territory. It is 240 miles long, and 228 wide, containing 54,000 square miles. It has a population of 440,775; of this number 65,000 are liable to military duty. This State having a large extent of border lying on the Mississippi, and within a short distance of the free States, it will require a large portion of her military force to guard against any movement of United States troops on the Mississippi river line—a measure not at all improbable. At present, and in view of the overwhelming force of troops being raised in the West, this State has called a large force into the field, and fortified important strategic points on the banks of the Mississippi. Arkansas seceded from the Union May 6, 1861, by a vote of 69 to 1.

LOUISIANA.

This State seceded from the Union January 26, 1861, by a vote of 113 to 17. In extent of territory Louisiana is 240 miles long from north to south, and 216 broad, containing 41,346 square miles. The population of the State is 666,431; of that number 75,000 are liable to military duty. The great Mississippi river outlet, and New Orleans, the great commercial mart of the extreme Southern States, being within the jurisdiction of the State, she will, in her present hostile attitude to the federal government, inflict severe injury on those within her borders. With the Mississippi closely blockaded, and her commerce with the West and Southwest cut off, it will be but a few months before her case will be pitiable. In regard to her mobile force for duty in the Southern rebel army, this State will be able to furnish a fair representation. A standing garrison will be required in New Orleans, and the same at the several forts commanding important points between the Belize and the Gulf to New Orleans.

TEXAS.

This State contains 325,000 square miles of territory, and a population of 605,955—84 000 of which are liable to military duty. The State, through its convention, seceded from the federal Union February 1, 1861, by a vote of 166 to 7, and joined her destinies with the Confederate States. At present there slumbers in the State a deep sentiment for the Union, which requires the whole moral force of the secessionists to keep from awakening to new vigor and increased life. The large extent of territory of Texas, with a sparsely settled population, and large inland frontier constantly menaced by hostile Indians and predatory bands of Mexican adventurers and robbers, renders the presence of a large military force within her borders necessary. Now that the United States military forces have been driven from the State, the Camanche Indians will make a desperate warfare upon its frontiers. The Camanches have many grievances against the Texans, and are brave and desperate. Their movements are very sudden, and in warfare merciless. Cortinas, the Mexican bandit, has recently reappeared in the south of the State, and will give the Texans much trouble. The anticipated presence of a United States blockading squadron near the mouth of the Mississippi river will have a tendency to isolate Texas in a great measure from the Southern confederacy, as her commerce with the neighboring States was by water—principally to New Orleans, land travel being next to impossible—and a blockade would cut off her sea transportation from New Orleans. It is thought that it will require the whole military force of Texas to keep the State intact from her Indian enemies, and that even were she ever so well disposed towards providing her quota of men in the military operations of the great body of Confederate State troops, her loss of sea communication would forbid the attempt.

KENTUCKY.

This State, which still continues faithful to the Union, we place in our pictorial illustration, in light shaded lines, with Missouri and Western Virginia, considering them at present as doubtful States. Kentucky in territorial extent is 400 miles long and 170 miles in breadth, containing 37,680 square miles. It has a population of 1,145,567, of which 186,000 are liable to military duty. This State, from its proximity to the free States, has among its citizens many thoroughly Union men. The secession leaders, under instructions from their master, Jeff Davis, are endeavoring to make the State adopt the suicidal course now being pursued by the confederated rebels. How far they will succeed, time will prove. At present Kentucky remains firm, and we shall not despair as long as she maintains her present course. The western part of this State occupies one bank of the Ohio river, and the trade between her and Ohio is so intimately blended that a separation would be very injurious to both, but especially to Kentucky.

TENNESSEE.

The territory embraced in this State in mean laugth is four hundred miles, and its mean breadth one hundred and fourteen miles, containing an area of terrriory of 44,000 square miles, and embracing a population of 1,146,690, of which 167,000 are liable to military duty. In regard to the present crisis, Tennessee has not directly severed the bonds which bind that State to the Union; but it has adopted a military league made between its Governor and three Commissioners of the Confederate States, in which it is agreed that all the force of the State shall be employed to assist the confederated rebels. The Legislature has also adopted a declaration of independence, and has permitted the people to vote upon it, which they will do on the 8th of June prox. The State is at present without effective military arms, and some inconveniences may arise before it can send an effective force into the field. At present a considerable force from this State, under the command of Major General Pillow, is assembled at Memphis and north twenty miles along the bank of the Mississippi. This force, it is reported, is co-operating with a force from Arkansas, whose ultimate design is to besiege Cairo, Illinois, now occupied by United States troops.

MISSOURI.

The State of Missouri contains 65,037 square miles of territory, and is two hundred and eighty seven miles long and two hundred and thirty broad. It contains a population of 1,204,214, out of the male population of which 221,000 are liable to military duty. The geographical position of Missouri, peninsulated as she is between Kansas, Iowa and Illinois, with her great river outlet near Cairo completely in the hands of the federal government, seems to render her alliance with the rebel confederacy of the South a hazardous experiment. The unloyal conduct of Governor Jackson, in refusing to comply with the proclamation of the President for troops to uphold the dignity of the laws, engendered a morbid desire among some of the citizens of the State to throw off their allegiance to the Union. For a time it seemed the seceders were gaining ground; but the Union men of the State made a grand rally and defence against the revolutionary spirit, and enrolled themselves as volunteers of the Union, despite of the perjured Governor. A State Convention will no doubt be held at an early day. The power of convening it is with a committee, whose chairman, though a Southerner, is utterly opposed to secession. This Convention will beyond doubt, in its first action depose Governor Jackson and the Legislature, a power clearly within their jurisdiction. Already four regiments of United States volunteer troops have declared their loyalty to the general government and been sworn into service. Other regiments are raising and will soon take the oath of allegiance to the Union.

ARIZONA.

The people of the embryo Territory of Arizona have, in an informal manner, declared their sympathies with the southern confederacy, and it is therefore viewed in the light of a seceded Territory. The population of the Territory is insignificant, and it is physically and pecuniarily unable to assist in the present movement. Its moral force will be insignificant. The people of Arizona are chiefly devoted to agricultural pursuits, and at present unable to afford means for their local protection, and for the past two years have been calling upon the federal government to send troops into the Territory to repel the constant incursions and forays of hostile Indians. Their secession ordinance was passed at a mass meeting of the people at Mesilla, March 16, 1861. The Territory cost the United States government $20,000,000.

For Additional War News see Fifth and Eighth Pages.

The Philadelphia Inquirer.

ESTABLISHED 1829. | PHILADELPHIA, SATURDAY, MAY 25, 1861 | PRICE TWO CENTS.

COLONEL ELLSWORTH.

It is sad to think that one of the first victims of the war was a man who, for spirit and energy, was as renowned as for bravery. Colonel E E ELLSWORTH, the subject of this sketch, was shot dead yesterday morning in Alexandria by a secessionist. His last act was to haul down the Rebel flag and to rear in its place the Stars and Stripes. The particulars of the event will be found elsewhere.

In the early part of the year 1860, the newspapers chronicled the appearance upon the public arena of Colonel ELLSWORTH, a young man of Chicago, who had organized a corps of Zouaves, and who by a thorough course of drill had brought them to such perfection as to extend a challenge to any company in the Union. The acceptance of the challenge and the trip made by the Zouaves to Detroit, Buffalo and the Eastern cities are matters of history, as well as the eminent abilities of the commander.

It was a feature of the corps, that irregularities of any kind were punished by expulsion. Doubtless an early New England training, as well as motives of policy, dictated this course to ELLSWORTH. The habits which he had acquired during a course of study at West Point were those most beneficial to a soldier. On his return home from the East, the young Colonel was of course much fêted by his fellow citizens, and new Zouave companies were formed on the model of his.

The engrossing scenes of the Presidential contest, which followed soon after, diverted public attention from the Zouaves and their captain. Among other persons who paid ELLSWORTH attention, however, was Mr. LINCOLN, then merely a candidate for the Presidency. After the election, Mr. LINCOLN signified his intention of attaching Colonel ELLSWORTH to his person; and when, in February last, he departed on his journey to Washington, ELLSWORTH was invited to form one of his escort. On the journey he won the esteem of all by his suavity and frankness. He was, the reporters tell us, one of the most useful of the party, ever watchful of Mr. LINCOLN's person, and always in good temper and ready for anything that could render the journey pleasant.

It was generally supposed that Col. ELLSWORTH would be placed in a prominent position in the War Department under Mr. LINCOLN. It is understood that his claims were urged by General SUMNER, and that some post—perhaps the Chief Clerkship—was mentioned in connection with his name. It is not likely, however, that he sought any such inglorious berth. On the outbreak of the war he sought active service. And having had an opportunity of judging what excellent material for soldiers was contained in the New York Fire Department, he bethought himself of forming out of them a Zouave Regiment.

The idea was a happy one. The firemen, brave as steel, would be restless under the stiff restraints of light infantry tactics, whereas the comparative freedom and dash of the Zouave drill suit them exactly. In the course of a couple of days over a thousand firemen volunteered. Some ten companies were accepted, the regiment was formed, and sent to Fort Hamilton for drill. They left for Washington, and since then have been almost daily under public notice. On Wednesday night last, one hundred of them, under ELLSWORTH, blockaded all the roads leading to the Alexandria Ferry.

Colonel ELLSWORTH was born in Massachusetts, and lost his parents while still very young. He lived sometime in New York, and in his early youth manifested strong military inclinations.—Some eight years since he removed to Chicago, arriving there penniless, and without a profession or certain means of support, but, by his industry, perseverance and energy, he soon acheived an honorable position in that city. The exciting exploits of the French Zouaves at Sevastopol first led him to investigate this description of drill.

At one time he studied law with Mr. LINCOLN.

It may not be amiss to mention at this time that Col. ELLSWORTH has been engaged for the last two years to Miss CARRIE SPAFFORD, a young lady of seventeen, the daughter of CHAS. F. SPAFFORD, a responsible resident of Rockford, Illinois. Miss SPAFFORD was recently a student in the Carroll Institute, Brooklyn. The marriage would probably have taken place ere this, but for the breaking out of the war.

THE GREAT REBELLION.

OLD VIRGINIA INVADED.

MIDNIGHT MARCH TO THE SOUTH.

Thirteen Thousand Federal Troops in the Old Dominion.

THE ATTACK OF THE NEW YORK ZOUAVES ON ALEXANDRIA.

THE ASSASSINATION OF COL. ELLSWORTH.

TERRIBLE SCENES.

RETREAT OF THE REBEL FORCES.

THREE REGIMENTS TENDERED FROM KANSAS.

A SENTINEL CAPTURED AT HARPER'S FERRY.

THE REBEL TROOPS IN MISSOURI DISBANDED.

LATER FROM EUROPE.

British Subjects Warned Against Engaging in the War.

ST. DOMINGO ACCEPTED BY SPAIN

Adjournment of the Kentucky Legislature.

OCCUPATION OF ALEXANDRIA AND ARLINGTON HEIGHTS.

WASHINGTON, May 24.—The Administration has struck a blow, at once decisive and important. The troops yesterday received orders to hold themselves in readiness to march at a moment's notice. Ammunition was furnished and every preparation made for a conflict. Nothing definite, however, was known as to their destination.

The order to march this morning was communicated to the officers of the different regiments at the evening parades, but it was kept from the men until shortly before midnight, when it was generally promulgated.

It was received by the various corps with true martial enthusiasm. The men having been kept in readiness since the night before last, the final packing up did not require much time.

About ten o'clock last night four companies of picked men moved over the Long Bridge as an advanced guard. They were sent to reconnoitre, and if assailed were ordered to signal, when they would have been reinforced by a corps of regular infantry and a battery. The Washington City National Rifles, Captain SMEAD, remained at the terminus until between one and two this morning, acting as an advance guard. Those were followed by other district volunteer companies, acting in a similar capacity.

At midnight the infantry regiment, artillery and cavalry corps began to muster and assume marching order. As fast as the several regiments were ready they proceeded to the Long Bridge, those in Washington being directed to take that route. The troops quartered at Georgetown, the Sixty-ninth, Fifth, Eighth and Twenty-eighth New York regiments, proceeded across the chain bridge under the command of General McDOWELL. The imposing scene was at the Bridge, where the main body of the troops crossed. Eight thousand infantry, two regular cavalry companies and two sections of SHERMAN's artillery battalion, consisting of two batteries, were in line on the Washington side of the Long Bridge at two o'clock.

The Twelfth New York was the first on the ground. The army crossed the bridge in the following order:—Twelfth Regiment, New York. Twenty-fifth Regiment, New York. First Regiment, Michigan. First, Second, Third and Fourth, New Jersey, in order named.

Two regular cavalry corps, of eighty men each, and SHERMAN's two batteries; next and last came the New York Seventh, with more men than any other regiment.

Following these was a long train of wagons filled with wheelbarrows, shovels, &c. Altogether there were at least thirteen thousand troops in the advancing army.

Major-General MANSFIELD commanded the movement of the troops until the last corps left the district. The first regiment of the main body that crossed the Long Bridge started at twenty minutes past two, and the last corps left the district at about a quarter to four o'clock.

The army could not have had a more beautiful night for their march. The atmosphere was balmy, and the moon never shone more clear. The only civilian allowed to cross the Long Bridge was Senator CHANDLER, of Michigan. So little noise did they cause that hardly any of the denizens of Washington were awakened from their peaceful slumbers.

The scene at the bridges was grand and impressive beyond description. The night was cool and clear, thousands of men were drawn up in line and defiling past, but hardly a whisper was heard from among them.

They all preserved a solemn silence as though sensible of the momentousness of the occasion, but the rumbling of artillery, the clatter of cavalry, the muskets and ordnance glittering in the moonlight, the suppressed commands of the officers imparted, nevertheless, a liveliness to the imposing spectacle.

Secretary SEWARD witnessed the crossing from the sidewalk near the foot of the bridge. He came very near being rudely treated by one of the pickets put out to keep the streets clear.

The troops took rations for only two days along, but large quantities of provisions will be sent across the river to-day. All the troops carried their knapsacks, blankets, canteens, etc., with the exception of the Seventh, which went without knapsacks.

At four o'clock, A. M., Major General SANFORD and staff left WILLARD's, and proceeded to Virginia, to take command of the advancing forces. He informed the reporter that he should establish his head-quarters on Arlington Heights, and should take possession of the Arlington Mansion.

Two thousand troops, the New York Zouaves and New York Twelfth, were to occupy Alexandria, the remainder were to occupy the heights by regiments from the chain bridge to Alexandria. Major-General MANSFIELD took the greatest care to instruct the troops just before entering upon the bridge to take the route step—that is, to avoid marching together, as the solid step might injure the bridge.

The main body of the troops were all across the bridges in two hours after they commenced entering upon them. Three or four companies marched over at a time. The few spectators that witnessed the crossing were momentarily expecting to hear reports of fire-arms from the other side, but they were sadly disappointed in their expectation, not a gun being fired.

It was soon known, however, that the Virginia pickets having been previously driven in by the advance guard, one of the regiments took the road leading to the Fairfax Court House, about twenty miles from Washington, while another one, the Jersey, stopped at the Forks, a mile from the Long Bridge, to await orders.

An advance into Virginia was also made from another point, namely, at the mouth of the Potomac Aqueduct at Georgetown. The Seventh New York Regiment was among the troops, and after several hours' march occupied a point between the bridge and Columbia Spring, on the line of the Washington and Alexandria Railroad.

The vanguard to Virginia was commanded by Inspector General STONE, under whom Captain SMEAD led the centre, Adjutant ABBOTT the left, and Captain STEWART; son of Hon. CHARLES STEWART, the right wing. They stopped within half a mile of the town, waiting for the main body; the coast was clear.

The excitement among the troops in Washington is most intense. All are anxious to join their comrades in the field, and every regiment hopes to be favored. The commanding officers are besieged with importunities for the privilege of being ordered out. Notwithstanding the departure of eleven thousand men last night, the force remaining in Washington is quite as large as it was a week since, and almost every train brings a regiment.

It is probable that the Ohio troops moved down from the West upon Harper's Ferry last night, and that they were supported by a column from Pennsylvania. It is also probable that a simultaneous movement was made against the rebels at Norfolk. Our communications do not extend to those points, so that I cannot say positively that these movements were executed, but it is likely that Virginia was invaded on all sides at the same time.

The Virginia troops now, having three railroad concentrations, from Richmond, Fredericksburg and Winchester, will probably advance and attack.

The Washington firemen were the first to show their respect for ELLSWORTH, by having their engine houses in mourning. This bloody murder is the only draw back to the success of the day.

There is a battery at each end of the Long and Chain Bridges, and one at Alexandria with the Zouaves. By peremptory orders from General SCOTT, no civilians are permitted to pass either way.

It is reported that as the Virginia troops retired from Alexandria, one of them was killed by a return shot from the Federal forces. There is a prospect of capturing the fugitives. Among the forces sent over to Virginia were two batteries and two companies of artillery. Numerous wagons with spades, picks, and other entrenching tools also passed into that State. The proceedings attending the movements of the troops were conducted with the best possible order.

MARCH OF THE ZOUAVES ON ALEXANDRIA.

ASSASINATION OF COL. ELLSWORTH

THE INCIDENTS OF HIS DEATH.

A SPEEDY RETRIBUTION,

WASHINGTON, May 24.—The Zouaves went on board the *Baltimore* and *Mount Vernon* before daylight, and at 5 A. M., reached Alexandria in good order. Just before reaching the wharf, the commander of the *Pawnee* sent a flag of truce to the rebel forces, giving them one hour in which to withdraw from the town. The Major commanding the Virginia troops refused the demand. The Captain then said the consequences would be terrible to the village and all its inhabitants, and prolonged the time till 8 o'clock. At 6 A. M., ELLSWORTH's Zouaves landed and took position on the dock.

The troops were accompanied by two guns from Sherman's Battery, and a company of U. S. cavalry. Sherman's Battery came like a whirlwind. As they marched into the street a whistle saluted them, and a train of cars steamed away, probably bearing the secession forces. One company of horse, numbering 45, were captured, with horses, accoutrements, and flag, mounted, mounting, and preparing to mount.

Simultaneously with the landing of the Zouaves the first Michigan regiment entered Alexandria via the Long Bridge, and proceeded to the railroad depot, of which they took possession, capturing a troop of the cavalry, numbering one hundred, with their horses and equipments.

The Zouaves landed in good order in double quick time, each company formed in company order on the street facing the river. Company E, Captain LEVERICH, first disembarked, and was at once detailed to destroy the railroad track leading to Richmond, which service they promptly performed.

After detailing Company E, Col. ELLSWORTH directed the Adjutant to form the regiment, and then with his Aid, Lieutenant WINSER, and a file of men, started for the telegraph office to cut the wires. Col. ELLSWORTH proceeded in double quick-time up the street. They had proceeded three blocks, when his attention was attracted by a large Secession flag flying from the Marshall House, kept by J. W. JACKSON. Col. ELLSWORTH entered the hotel, and meeting a man in the hall he asked, "Who put up that flag?" The man answered, "I don't know; I am a boarder here." Col. ELLSWORTH, Lieut. WINSER, the Chaplain of the regiment, Mr. HOUSE, a volunteer aid, and the four privates, went up to the roof, and Col. ELLSWORTH cut down the flag.

The party were returning down the stairs, preceded by private FRANCIS E. BROWNELL, of Company A. As they left the attic, the man who had said he was a boarder, but who proved to be the landlord, JACKSON, was met in the hall, having a double-barreled gun, which he leveled at BROWNELL. BROWNELL struck up the gun with his musket, when JACKSON pulled both triggers of the gun. The contents lodged in the body of Col. ELLSWORTH, entering between the third and fifth ribs. Col. ELLSWORTH was at the time rolling up the flag. He fell forward on the floor of the hall, and exclaimed "My God!"

He tore open his apparel, opened his wounded breast to all, then threw back his arms and expired almost instantly, before Surgeon GRAY, of the regiment, could arrive at the spot.

The instant that JACKSON fired, BROWNELL, quick as lightning, levelled his musket at JACKSON. The ball struck on the bridge of the nose, and crashed through his skull, killing him instantly. As he fell, BROWNELL followed his shot by a thrust of his bayonet, which went through JACKSON's body.

JACKSON's wife presently discovered the fatality, and approaching the body, uttered the most agonizing cries, and although treated with the utmost consideration that could be offered her in misery, she remained for a long time in the wildest state of frenzy. The house was in the utmost confusion. The lodgers darted from their rooms, but were held in control by the four or five Zouaves who accompanied the Colonel, and who at once established and maintained order.

Seven companies of ELLSWORTH's immediately posted themselves to command the halls of the hotel, and threatened to shoot the first man who showed his head outside of a door. In this way they stood for ten minutes. Their protracted absence alarmed Adjutant LEOSER, who ordered Company A, Capt. COYLE, to search for them. The Company found their commander dead, and their comrades in possession of the hotel.

His body was duly examined in the room where the event happened, and then sewed up in a red blanket and borne on a door through the streets to the boat, accompanied by as many of the Zouaves as could be spared from duty. An attack being every instant expected from Secession forces, said to be accumulated in the outskirts, the body was conveyed on board the *James Guy*, and carried to the Navy Yard, where it now reposes, kindly and affectionately protected by the Seventy first Regiment.

After fitting ceremonies, his remains will be taken to Mechanicsville, New York, for interment. His family reside at Mechanicsville. The persons around ELLSWORTH at the moment of his fall returned with him to Washington. The President, who was on terms of personal friendship with Col. ELLSWORTH, is greatly afflicted by his death.

Intelligence of Col. ELLSWORTH's murder was not communicated to the regiment until some time after the occurrence. I have never seen a more sorrowful and afflicted looking body than they. Revenge, the first passion that seized upon them at the announcement, was soon melted into most affecting and overwhelming grief. Though other officers in the service may be equally respected, none, I think, are more profoundly beloved. The affliction falls like a heavy pall upon Washington, and indignation and revenge are swelling the excitement to a fearful pitch.

The steamer *Mount Vernon*, it is said, narrowly escaped sinking before landing the Zouaves at Alexandria. Injuries were inflicted upon her hull, probably the work of some Secessionist at the Navy Yard.

To the Zouaves belong all the glory of taking Alexandria. They were assisted by no other regiment, and behaved themselves courageously.

Captain FOX made an official report of the circumstances attending the killing of Col. ELLSWORTH, as follows:—

TO THE PRESIDENT:—It appears that ELLSWORTH was marching up the street with a squad of men to take possession of the telegraph office, when, in passing along, he noticed a Secession flag flying from the top of a building. He immediately exclaimed—"That has to come down," and entering the building made his way up to the roof with one of his men, hauled down the rebel emblem, and wrapping it around his body, descended.

While on the second floor, a Secessionist came out of a door with a cocked double-barreled shotgun. He took aim at ELLSWORTH, when the latter attempted to strike the gun out of the way with his fist, as he struck it one of the barrels was discharged, lodging a whole load of buckshot in ELLSWORTH's body, killing him instantly. His companion instantly shot the murderer through the head with a revolver, making him a corpse a second or two after the fall of the noble ELLSWORTH. The house was immediately surrounded and all the inmates made prisoners.

The remains of the deceased were brought over to the Navy Yard this morning. The doleful peals of all the bells in the city are announcing the sad news to the citizens.

He was laid upon a bed in a room near at hand, with the rebel flag stained with his blood, and now a trophy to his glory, about his feet.

Lieutenant PRENDERGAST, of the Seventy-first Regiment of New York, was the first soldier who landed at Alexandria. He was in command of the steamer *Mount Vernon*, the vessel which conveyed the Fire Zouaves of New York from their camp to that point, and was in company with Colonel ELLSWORTH at the occupation of the city.

The news of the death of Colonel ELLSWORTH was not generally known throughout Washington until towards 10 o'clock to-day. The excitement was intense, especially among the military, who express the greatest desire to be sent over to Virginia. From a spy glass view of Alexandria, the Stars and Stripes are prominently flying from various quarters.

The President visited the navy yard and saw the remains of his friend Colonel ELLSWORTH.

ANOTHER DESPATCH—ALEXANDRIA QUIET.

Special Despatch to the Inquirer.

The Death of Col. Ellsworth.

WASHINGTON, May 24, P. M.—The most intense excitement prevailed throughout the city upon the receipt of the intelligence of Col. ELLSWORTH's assassination. Flags were all displayed at half-mast, and bells were tolled *in memoriam.*

Fate of the Assassin.

I learn that, as soon as Col. ELLSWORTH fell, JACKSON, his assassin, was completely riddled with balls. At least half-a-dozen Zouaves shot him in the head, spattering his brains all around, and then pinned him to the floor with their bayonets.

The Zouaves.

For two hours the fact was kept secret from his company. When, at length, they were made aware of it, they became nearly frantic, and it was with the greatest difficulty that they could be restrained from sacking the hotel.

The Remains.

The body was taken to the Washington Navy Yard, under a guard, and laid out with bouquets of flowers, etc. The scene was touching, and many of those present shed tears.

The Remains of Jackson.

The body of JACKSON, the assassin, was guarded several hours by the Zouaves, and then placed in the hands of his friends.

Rumored Arrest of Col. Lee.

I have just heard a rumor that Col. LEE, of the Southern army, has been arrested. Doubtful, however.

Alexandria Quiet.

At five o'clock P. M the Federal troops held quiet possession of Alexandria. The women and children have left. The Unionists, have, of course, no molestation to fear from the troops, at whose presence they express much satisfaction. The general belief is, that it will have a tendency to revive business, open further communications with Washington and the North, and afford greater security to the resident citizens. Some of them have expressed a wish that the entire State might be placed under Government protection. About 7000 of the Government troops are now in Alexandria. The New York Seventh Regiment are holding Arlington Heights. They are now desirous of continuing in the service, and it is believed they will do so, after their present enlistment expires.

No one Allowed to Visit Alexandria.

No one has been allowed to visit Alexandria to-day without a pass from the Government.

Arlington Heights well Fortified.

Arlington Heights is now well fortified, and the stars and stripes now float proudly from their summit.

The Remains of Col. Ellsworth.

The remains of Col. ELLSWORTH were embalmed to-day. The funeral will take place to-morrow at 11 A. M. The remains will be taken to New York, and thence to his home.

"Another Account."

Some of the Zouaves propose to open the polls in Alexandria on Monday next, and have a fair election.

The Sewall's Point Engagement.

Reliable intelligence has been received here, that in the Sewall's Point engagement, the United States steamer was not injured, nor were any of her crew. The Government, to-day, sent an immense quantity of tools and fortification implements to Arlington Heights, in special trains.

Ellsworth's Funeral.

All the engine companies in the city are making active preparations to attend the funeral of their late fellow-fireman, Colonel ELLSWORTH. The fire-bells have been tolling all the afternoon.

MISCELLANEOUS NEWS OF IMPORTANCE.

It is believed here that a simultaneous movement was made by the Government forces last night against Harper's Ferry and Norfolk.

The people of Alexandria are in great agitation and terror, as most of the able bodied men are away.

An advance of the Secession force at Culpepper Court House is anticipated. This outpost of the rebels is 62 miles from Alexandria, on the Orange Railroad. It has been reported that the force there is considerable.

Sherman's Light Artillery Battery and the District of Columbia militia command the Maryland shore above Georgetown, and will meet any attack that may be made by forces moving from Harper's Ferry.

The New York Sixty-ninth is throwing up breastworks at Arlington Heights, with the Seventh.

The telegraph at Alexandria was seized in time to prevent the transmission of messages South, announcing the movement of the Federal troops.

It seems to be true that a body of Federal troops has advanced to Fairfax Court House, to take possession of the junction of the Orange and Alexandria and Manassas Gap Railroad, with a view of intercepting the advance of Virginia troops toward Alexandria from Richmond and other points. Nearly three thousand troops arrived here yesterday, comprising some from New York and the two Ohio regiments. A third Connecticut regiment came in this morning.

The Sixty-ninth crossed the river below Georgetown, and took position on the Orange and Manassas Gap Railroad, which runs out of Alexandria. They took up some of the rails, and awaited in ambush the arrival of the train, which they supposed would leave Alexandria with the fugitives. When it came it was surrounded, and the train captured. About seven hundred persons were on board, including 300 men. The entire party were held as prisoners of war, and will be kept as hostages for the fair treatment of any loyal citizens that may fall into the hands of the rebels.

Among the prisoners captured by the troops this morning are several persons who have been ringleaders in the rebellion movements in Virginia. Dr. BOYLE is one. He will stand a good chance of treading air.

Capt. SHAFFER, a notorious traitor, from Washington, has also been caught at Alexandria.

A considerable number of regular troops are among the Government forces which now occupy Alexandria.

Several captures having been made in Hampton Roads before the expiration of the fifteen days from the notice of the blockade, restitution in such cases has been ordered.

Mount Vernon has been visited to-day, and the Virginia pickets were not seen. The tomb and all the grounds attached are reported undisturbed.

Mr. LYON, of New York, was told on Tuesday, at Alexandria, that if the North had any success in occupying that place, or even Arlington Heights, a committee would remove the treasure to Lexington, Va.

Col. ELLSWORTH was the only person killed.—Surgeon GRAY made an examination, and discovered that the slugs from the gun entered between the third and fifth rib, shattering the fourth rib, and pushed into the left auricle of the heart, destroying all the integuments with which it came in contact.

Postmaster General BLAIR prepared an order to-day discontinuing the transmission of the United States mails in Virginia, and other seceding States, and annulling all contracts for the same. Tennessee is excepted from the operation of the order, for the reason that State has not yet formally seceded. This course of the Postmaster-General is under the act in relation to the subject passed at the last session of Congress.—Contractors will be immediately notified of this decision. The mails for the South, from Washington, were stopped at the crossing place by the Federal troops, and were returned to the Post Office here.

Later from Alexandria.

CAPTURE OF SECESSION CAVALRY—RESPECT TO THE MEMORY OF COL ELLSWORTH.

WASHINGTON, May 24—Evening.—A company of cavalry, thirty five in number, were captured near Alexandria this morning, and have been brought to the Washington Navy Yard.

Passengers from Alexandria state that the Zouaves have been amusing themselves by riding about on the captured horses. Other secessionists are also in custody.

The United States troops are quartered in the Marshall House.

At two o'clock this afternoon the body of JACKSON, the proprietor of the Marshall House, still lay where he was killed.

The troops between this city and Alexandria have made good progress in throwing up entrenchments.

Col WILCOX, of the Michigan Regiment, is in command of Alexandria.

The ferry boats between Washington and Alexandria will resume their trips next week.

The flags all over the city are at half mast to-day, and the bells are tolling in respect to the memory of Col. ELLSWORTH. It is probable that his remains will be brought to the President's house, and conveyed thence to the cars to-morrow afternoon to be transferred to New York, of which State he is a native. He was about 24 years of age.

There are about twelve secessionists under charges in the common jail.

Many of the troops here are in readiness to march at a minute's warning.

In all there are twelve or fourteen regiments on the Virginia side. The New York Zouaves and the Michigan regiment are the only two as yet in Alexandria.

Last night, before the Michigan regiment started hence, it was desirable to procure an American flag. None suitable could be found except one belonging to the keeper of a restaurant, which was suspended across the street. The Hon. Mr. HOWARD, of Michigan, purchased it and gave it to the Regiment. It was, of course, carried by them, and now floats over that city.

Col. BUTLER, the brother of Gen. BUTLER, the Hon. Mr. DUNN of Indiana, Hon. J. N. ARNOLD of Chicago, and the Hon. M. ASHLEY, of Ohio, visit Fortress Monroe to-morrow, by way of Annapolis, to note the passing events in that quarter.

There is nothing known of any military movement being contemplated to-night.

Interesting from Chambersburg.

THE STRENGTH OF THE ENEMY—APPREHENDED ATTACK ON CUMBERLAND VALLEY.

CHAMBERSBURG, May 24.—There are now, beyond all possibility of doubt, 6000 troops between Point of Rocks and Williamsport, on the Potomac. Of these 2000 are Alabamians, Mississippians, North Carolinians and Georgians. The rest are Virginians.

There can be no doubt that there are 500 Cherokee Indians, armed as Indians are usually armed, with tomahawk, scalping knife and rifle, among this number. These Indians resided partly in North Carolina and Georgia.

The Virginia troops along the Potomac line are well armed but scarce of provisions—having only about three-fourths of the requisite army rations. Between Point of Rocks, which is eight miles below Harper's Ferry and Williamsport, twenty-three miles above, there are scattered at various points thirty-five pieces of cannon; twenty of these are brass field pieces.

Forward movements of the Virginia troops may be expected immediately.

Campbell's Flying Artillery of six pieces has positively been ordered back from York to Chambersburg. Two additional infantry regiments must be moved to this point, and a battalion of cavalry added, or devastation will overtake the whole valley. We want at least three batteries of six and twelve-pounders.

Important from Baltimore.

ANOTHER SEIZURE OF ARMS AND AMMUNITION—THE REBELS THWARTED BY THE PHILADELPHIA TROOPS.

Special Despatch to the Inquirer.

BALTIMORE, May 24.—A detachment of one hundred men from Col. WM. D. LEWIS' Regiment, under the command of Captain GOBLINS, accompanied by the United States Marshal, this afternoon seized a large number of loaded rifles, accoutrements, uniforms, and fatigue caps, in an old building near Barnum's Hotel. It is supposed that they were intended for the use of the rebels. They were conveyed to Col. LEWIS' encampment.

A gentleman, who left Richmond yesterday, says there are twelve thousand troops there, and more are arriving with every train.

Two North Carolina regiments arrived before his departure, and two from South Carolina left in the train in which he started; but turned to the left at Taylorsville, *en route* for Gordonsville.

The presence of General JOHNSON at Harper's Ferry, has been confirmed.

Arms from England.

OUR GOVERNMENT TO BE SUPPLIED.

WASHINGTON, May 24.—The Government has succeeded in securing all the products of all the arms manufactories and cannon manufactories in Great Britain, which are permitted to make arms for foreign States, for three months to come.

This decisive movement will at once strengthen the Government in its efforts to put down rebellion, and will also serve the farther purpose of convincing the British Government that there is to be no half-way work in the pending war.

Reported Attack on Harper's Ferry.

BALTIMORE, May 24.—A great variety of reports are in circulation this evening, relative to an attack on Harper's Ferry to-day. The coal trains were detained there this morning, and none have come down to-day. It is reported that a movement was certainly made to-day by the Federal forces in that direction.

[No despatches have been received from Wheeling or Chambersburg relative to any such attack.—REP.]

Disbanding of the Missouri State Troops.

ST. LOUIS, May 24.—The State troops at Jefferson City, numbering about 4000, were ordered to disband yesterday, by Gen. PRICE. At first they refused to obey, but it is believed that they will quietly disperse and return to their homes.

A ten inch howitzer, an eight and a half inch mortar, and three hundred rounds of cartridges, ball, shell and cannister, were shipped from the Arsenal yesterday. They are destined for Cairo.

Effect of the News at Baltimore.

MOVEMENTS OF COL MOREHEAD'S REGIMENT.

BALTIMORE, May 24.—The news from Washington this morning has produced a profound sensation here.

The Old Point Comfort boat, arrived this morning, reports that Gen BUTLER had thrown out a guard of three hundred men.

The United States Hotel was principally guarded, the splendid well water belonging to Colonel SEGAR being wanted for the use of the garrison.

A steamer arrived at Fort McHenry this morning, with a large supply of gun carriages and other military stores.

Col. MOREHEAD's regiment came across the river this morning and marched up Broadway, and proceeded to Patterson Park. They made a fine display.

From New Orleans.

NEW ORLEANS, May 24.—The news from Washington of the occupation of Alexandria, has considerably increased the military enthusiasm in this vicinity.

The *Delta* publishes a despatch from Montgomery, stating that the Government had received a letter from Mr YANCEY, in which he stated that he had no doubt of the success of his European mission.

The new tariff takes effect on the 31st of August.

The 13th proximo has been appointed by President DAVIS, in accordance with the recommendation of Congress, as a day of fasting and prayer throughout the Confederate States.

The Death of Col. Ellsworth.

NEW YORK, May 24.—The news of the death of Colonel ELLSWORTH has created the most intense excitement in this city. Regret of his loss is mingled with the universal feeling that it must be avenged.

PITTSBURG, May 24.—The intelligence of the death of Col ELLSWORTH was received here with profound regret. All the flags of the city are at half-mast.

The New-York Times.

VOL. X....NO. 3019. | NEW-YORK, SUNDAY, MAY 26, 1861. | PRICE THREE CENTS.

THE SECESSION REBELLION.

False Reports of Fighting at Alexandria.

All the Troops in Washington Ordered Under Arms.

Large Bodies of Them Thrown Into Virginia.

Astonishing Celerity of their Movements

ONLY A SKIRMISH BETWEEN PICKETS.

The Obsequies of Col. Ellsworth.

Highly Important from Fortress Monroe.

Reported Capture of the Sewell's Point Battery.

GEN. BUTLER RECONNOITERING.

SPECIAL DISPATCH FROM WASHINGTON

WASHINGTON, Saturday, May 25.

The false alarm of a fight in the neighborhood of Alexandria, which was raised about one o'clock to-day, had one great advantage—it tested the disposition of our troops, and made manifest their efficiency. As the signal went from camp to camp that the rebels were attacking the wing, there was a prompt and decisive response of "ready," and they were ready. I never realized until to-day the celerity of movement which drill and discipline insures.

SHERMAN'S battery of six-pounders made the distance from their quarters to Long Bridge at the rate of nine miles an hour. The Massachusetts Fifth were under arms, in line, and off to the Bridge before there appeared to be time for the orders to be ready.

N. P. BANKS is in town. It is understood to be settled that he will be made a Major General.

The Massachusetts Fifth were ordered to be ready with all their equipments, at 5 o'clock, but up to this time have not left the Treasury building. All the other Regiments ordered over the river to-day, when the false alarm was given, have gone back to their camps.

I have just seen a member of the New-York Seventh, who says he is from there this evening. He says everything is quiet. The work at Arlington Heights was going on lively. He says there was great excitement when the alarm was given on the other side; that a large body of men were advancing, some miles distant, upon their post.

The troops who went over the river confidently expected a fight but not a man flinching when the order was given, that I can learn.

Gen MANSFIELD regrets the false alarm, but is much gratified at the spirit manifested by the troops.

Col COOPER was at the Relay House to-day, with several companies reinforcements.

ANOTHER ZOUAVE SHOT.

JOHN BUTTERWORTH, of the Zouaves Sargant of the Guard, Company I., was shot about 3 o'clock this A. M, by the sentry. He was challenged three times, but failed to reply, thinking the sentry knew him. He died in five minutes. The sentry was justified, of course It is a good lesson.

Lieut. Col. FARNHAM will succeed ELLSWORTH in command by unanimous election.

JACKSON's body is in possession of his friends.

Lieut.-Col. NOBELSDORFF and Major KUNE, of Chicago, are here to urge the acceptance of a German Regiment, commanded by FRED. HECKER, Commander of Revolutionary forces in Baden in 1848. NOBELSDORFF was a distinguished officer in the Prussian army. KUNE was a member of Gen. BEM's staff in the Hungarian Revolution. Every member of the regiment has seen service. The Chicago Irish Regiment is accepted, which makes the Germans jealous.

If Col. MIX's Mounted Rifles are accepted, Col. PARKER, recently of BUTLER's staff, will probably join in the command.

ARLINGTON HEIGHTS.

The Sixty-ninth have been under arms all day, and are much exhausted, but full of spirit.

A body of the Seventy-first went across the river on the steamer *James Gay* to-night.

Dr BOYLE is not among the prisoners taken by the Federal troops. He barely escaped.

The Zouaves have the horses and arms of the captured cavalry. They have seized a case of Colt's revolving rifles, and one of double barrelled shot-guns.

The camps and equippage of the troops on the other side go over to-morrow.

I learn from Baltimore that JOHN MERRIMAN, one of the leading Secessionists, is now in confinement at Fort McHenry. He has been one of the most active and dangerous of the Maryland traitors, according to my informant. He is charged with being the leading spirit in the burning of the bridges.

The Secessionists are very active, holding secret meetings there every night. They are certainly plotting some new scheme of mischief. But the agents of the Government and Union men of Baltimore are on their tracks, and are sure to discover the movement.

They are becoming very restless under the lax order of the military rule now administered there. Scarcely a Union flag is to be seen in the streets while hundreds were to be seen when Gen. BUTLER was in command. Secession doctrines and abuse of the Administration are freely indulged in

These facts have been brought to the attention of the President and Gen. SCOTT.

SEWELL'S POINT BATTERY.

There are many doubts expressed by officers of the Government and military men of the truth of the report received last night at the War Department of the capture of Sewell's Point Battery by Gen. BUTLER. It is deemed impossible that in one day he could so dispose his forces as to assist the water force in such an undertaking. He reached the Post late Wednesday night, and it takes one day to get the news from there, so that he had necessarily but one day to do all this. I am positively assured by the chief clerk and operator at the War Department that they have no such positive news, but expect it will be done.

Last night Col. BUTLER, the General's brother, received from him a dispatch stating, "I shall take Sewell's Point as soon as possible." We expect, therefore, to hear of an attack there soon.

COL. ELLSWORTH'S FUNERAL.

The funeral of Col. ELLSWORTH to-day was an imposing spectacle. The ceremonies were held at the White House. The sermon, preached by Rev. Dr. PINE, was exceedingly appropriate to the occasion, the preacher giving a national character to the discourse by denouncing the killing of ELLSWORTH as murder. He stigmatized those engaged in this rebellion against the Government as assassins.

The purpose of the Government was to give to the funeral of Col. E. the solemnity and dignity of a national event. The President and the highest civil and military officers followed the body, and the military escort represented every branch of the service. The pall-bearers were J. G. NICOLAY, the private Secretary of President LINCOLN; AUGUSTUS HAIGHT, and ROBERT H. MORRIS, of the State Department, Col. STOVER, of New-York, and Hon. J. N. ARNOLD, M. C, from Illinois. Messrs. HAIGHT and STOVER accompanied the remains to New-York; and in addition, Messrs. L. D. BOOMER, E. C. LEARNER and STEPHEN GALE, of Chicago, Ill., accompanied the body by request, and as the representatives of the President.

The citizens of Illinois at present in Washington raised a sum of money for the purpose of purchasing a flag, to be presented to the Zouaves The regiment has already eleven flags, and so express a desire that the money shall be given to the parents of Col. ELLSWORTH.

SUBSCRIPTION FOR COL. ELLSWORTH'S FAMILY.

A meeting was held this evening of non-residents for the purpose of recommending a general subscription throughout the country. the subscriptions to be limited to one dollar each person Gov BANKS presided, and ABRAM WAKEMAN was Secretary. Messrs. JOHN COCHRANE, WALDO HUTCHINS and SIMON H MIX presented appropriate resolutions, and speeches were made by Gov. BANKS, CALEB LYON, ISAAC N. ARNOLD, M. C., of Chicago and JOHN COCHRANE.

Mrs. JOHN J. ASTOR was appointed General Treasurer, and REUBEN H. WALWORTH, EDWARD C. DELAVAN and JAMES M COOK, of Saratoga were appointed an advisory Committee.

MOVEMENT OF TROOPS.

LATER.—The Massachusetts Fifth will march to night to reinforce the troops in Virginia. They will be accompanied by two companies of Flying Artillery.

Speaking of Virginia, I looked to-day down ten feet into her sacred soil, the troops having penetrated to that depth in throwing up entrenchments They are making frightful scars upon the Old Dominion.

The Highland Regiment reached Washington to-night

Col. WESTBROOK has tendered to the War Department a regiment of thoroughly drilled troops, and they will probably be accepted. LEO.

FROM ANOTHER CORRESPONDENT.

FORT SEWARD, ARLINGTON HEIGHTS, VA., Saturday, May 25.

The troops along Arlington Heights have been under arms all day expecting an attack. Large bodies of U. S. troops crossed Alexandria bridge in consequence of firing in that direction.

The Sixty-ninth are rapidly completing formidable earthworks, and will work all night, an attack in force from Culpepper Court-house being expected to-morrow or the day after at furthest. As an acknowledgment to Gov. SEWARD for his kindness, since they have been here, their fort is called by his name.

The wildest reports have been in circulation all day, and the secession feeling showed itself strongly in Washington when it was believed that the Union forces had suffered a reverse. The men of the Fifth, Twenty-eighth and Sixty-ninth are well, and in high spirits. H.

DISPATCH TO THE ASSOCIATED PRESS.

WASHINGTON, Saturday, May 25

Western Virginia is an exception to the order of the Postmaster-General for the stoppage of the mails in the seceded States. Every facility will be afforded for postal accommodations in that section.

There is a great deal of coal on the way from Cumberland, Maryland, to tide-water, the principal or only difficulty in the way of which is the refusal of the rebel troops at Harper's Ferry to allow the boats to pass that point. From present indications, this obstruction will not probably long continue.

It cannot be ascertained that anything of especial moment took place at Alexandria last night. There is no doubt, however, the Government has sent out advance parties to take such measures regarding the railroads, bridges, etc., as to impede the advance of the Confederate troops.

The remains of Col. ELLSWORTH were this morning conveyed to the East room of the President's house where, for several hours, they lay in state. The coffin was draped with the American flag and adorned with choice flowers. The face was exposed to the public. Many persons, principally soldiers, visited the White House to take a farewell look at him.

WASHINGTON, Saturday, May 25—P. M.

Owing to the immense throng of anxious gazers on the remains of the deceased, the funeral *cortege* delayed moving from the Executive Mansion till near 1 o'clock. All along the line of Pennsylvania avenue flags were displayed at half-mast and draped in mourning. Every available point, including the windows, balconies and house-tops were thronged with anxious and sorrowful gazers. Various testimonials of respect were paid. All the bells of the City were tolled, and the heads of the soldiers and troops uncovered. Several companies of the City Corps, followed by the New-York Seventy first Regiment, Marines, and the local Cavalry Corps, formed the military escort, with their arms reversed and colors shrouded.

The hearse was followed by a detachment of Zouaves, one of whom, the avenger of Col. ELLSWORTH, carried the identical secession flag, torn down by the deceased.

Then followed the President, accompanied by Secretaries SEWARD and SMITH, and the rest of the procession was composed of carriages, containing the captains of the Zouave Regiment.

The head of the procession reached the depot at about 1:40, and the train, with the remains, will soon start.

THE FALSE ALARM.

WASHINGTON, Saturday, May 25—3 P. M.

At 2 o'clock this afternoon, the Massachusetts and other troops were hurrying to their quarters for a hasty advance towards Alexandria, where a fight is reported in progress, the extent of which is not known. Three guns have been fired, which is the signal for all the troops, here to get under arms Great excitement prevails throughout the city Soldiers and private citizens in crowds are hurrying in every direction. A full light battery, at a few moments notice thundered over the Long Bridge. Gen. MANSFIELD and Staff led the advance troops from Washington.

Intense anxiety prevails throughout the city.

WASHINGTON, Saturday, May 25—4 P. M.

The report of an engagement is incorrect, although believed at head-quarters and acted upon by signal guns.

There is no fight in progress.

WASHINGTON, Saturday, May 25—4½ P. M.

An account just received from Virginia, which seems to be truthful, says the cause of alarm was that the Federal picket guard at Little Falls Church near Arlington, were driven in by Secessionists The latter were soon put to flight. The Sixty-ninth New York Regiment left their work at the entrenchments and are now drawn up in line on the brow of the hill. The troops which hastily left the city this afternoon, are halting within a mile's [illegible] ce. The artillery and cavalry passed on in the direction of Alexandria.

WASHINGTON, Saturday, May 25—5 P. M.

Some of the troops who so hastily crossed the river this afternoon, have returned to this city, disappointed in their expectations of meeting the enemy. The proceedings, however, demonstrate the facility and expedition with which forces can be thrown into Virginia.

The President, while in the procession to-day, accompanying the remains of Col. ELLSWORTH to the cars, was informed by a courier of stirring hostilities on the Virginia side. Gen. MANSFIELD was similarly advised, and this was the foundation of the military movements here to-day. A dense smoke was meanwhile seen on the line of Arlington Heights, and cannon firing heard. The latter, however, were funeral minute guns, and the former probably from camp fires. The troops now here have been ordered to hold themselves in readiness to march at a moment's notice. The utmost watchfulness on the part of the military authorities to guard against the approach of the secession troops is everywhere manifest.

OUR WAR CORRESPONDENCE.

The March into Virginia—The Fifth, Twenty-eighth and Sixty-ninth New-York State Militia—First Night's Campaigning.

IN [illegible] ARLINGTON HEIGHTS, [illegible] Friday, May 24, 1861

Last night that event so threateningly denounced by Gov. LETCHER took place. The "sacred soil" of Virginia received the imprint of thirteen thousand feet on march in the vindication of the Union.

Visiting the Sixty-ninth Regiment in their quarters in the Catholic College, on Georgetown Heights, last evening, the scene was strange and impressive in the highest degree. The men had no idea they were about to start for Virginia, but knew that a move in some direction was contemplated, though few of them thought the line of march would be given until the beginning of next week.

Nevertheless, the main halls and corridors of the [illegible] presented a bustling and lively scene, the [illegible] Quartermaster and Adjutant superintending the distribution of vast quantities of clothing—red flannel shirts, woolen socks, heavy marching shoes [illegible] and general equipments.

Moving through the companies of men [illegible] up by their officers to receive these supplies, the dark robed figures of the Holy Fathers of the College presented a striking contrast. Calm, pale, clad in long black robes reaching to the ground, and wearing the peculiar black cap of their order, the ministers of religion formed a [illegible] background to the [illegible] of uniforms, the glitter of arms and the glare of light which made up the scene of entering.

Passing out into the moonlight, we could see, from the brow of the hill on which the College is built, the [illegible] Heights of Arlington across the river; the long aqueduct, which also serves as a bridge, at this end [illegible] by Uncle Sam's artillerymen; the city of Alexandria in the distance, [illegible] the water; and the beautiful tree-crowned islands lying between this point and that city. Before us, the calm of Nature seemed unbroken; not a breath of wind stirring, and the shadow of the smallest branch being reflected in the water.

Turning round, however, the two vast piles of red brick buildings which form the main portion of the College, were all alight with excitement—save in that wing of one of them still occupied by the fifty or [illegible] who remain, out of the three hundred [illegible] at this seat of learning. More than fifty of the older students, hailing from the South, are now, it is said, lieutenants in the Confederate Army. The peace of the Academy [illegible] given place to the clang of arms; and the Holy Fathers have only to fear that the regiment which succeeds the Sixty-ninth may not be so amenable to the mild discipline of religion and persuasion.

Let me say, at this point, that nothing can be kinder, more considerate or thoughtful than the Brotherhood of this institution have shown themselves. Father EARLY, in particular, might sit for the portrait of a model priest of the olden time—courtly, bland, acquiescent, polished, handsome and insinuating—a middle-aged, calm, resolute man, as much at home in the drawing-rooms of Washington or Paris as in his cloister; and yet never losing sight of "the Church" wherever he may be, or whatever his occupation. But to return:

By two o'clock last night everything was in readiness for the road, the men still believing that they were not to start until to-day, and expecting every moment to be dismissed and sent to their quarters. At half past two, however the orders were given to take up the line of march; and by three o'clock this morning the head of the Sixty-Ninth could be seen winding over the narrow pathway on one side of the aqueduct, while the rear guard were still defiling through the main gate of their quarters, and stretching in tortuous curves through all the intervening streets.

On this march were engaged the Fifth New-York Regiment, Col. CHRISTIAN SCHWARZWAELDER, almost entirely German; the Twenty-eighth, of Brooklyn, and a squadron of skirmishing cavalry known as the President's Body Guard. On the Georgetown side, the bridge is defended by a battery of flying artillery, completely enfilading its entire length; while on the Virginia side, two or three companies of District Militia have heretofore been stationed to prevent any attempt on the part of the Secessionists towards blowing up or otherwise destroying the aqueduct. As Washington so completely depends on this work—we might say for its very existence—this guard duty is one of the safest positions that could be assigned to the local soldiery of the Federal Capital.

Over the aqueduct marched the troops—their shadows, forty feet below, on the calm surface of the Potomac, advancing steadily along the water in fantastic procession. Suddenly, at the end of the bridge, the line wheeled upon the road for Alexandria—not a bugle sounding, not a drum beating; the deep silence of the trees on each side and overhead being utterly unbroken; every eye straining through the little patches of moonlight shimmering down through the leaves, to catch sight of any lurking foe; and every ear alert for the sharp ring that was to announce another officer picked off by some assassin marksman.

Then out into the broad moonlight, and over long patches of meadow land and grassy uplands—again plunging into the woods and again reappearing in open country. Here and there were beautiful mansions embosomed in trees, their white walls and green verandahs wearing none the less an air of comfort for the heavy dews that were falling; the weariness of the men under the novel weight of their full accoutrements and ammunition; the undulating character of the country, and the very doubtful prospect looming up in the immediate future of a nap or two hours on the wet grass, and then to work at entrenchments with the first daylight. Let the owners of those mansions sleep peacefully in their beds while they may! It is not forever that such acts as the murder of Col. ELLSWORTH, of which we have only this moment heard, can fail to draw down a frightful retribution alike on the just and the unjust.

Arriving at a distance of about four miles from Georgetown, the Fifth and Twenty-eighth were posted for camp duty, first breaking down the bridges in advance of them, to prevent a sudden attack by the Secessionists. These two regiments mustered in the march about 700 men each—the Twenty-eighth, perhaps, 800; but this latter body still need a good deal of drill and experience, being for the most part composed of men wholly new to military duties. The Fifth did very fairly and appeared in excellent spirits, the moonlight march, the silence, and the mystery of our destination having doubtless some attractions for the German mind.

As for the Sixty-ninth, they turned out more than twelve hundred muskets, leaving yet another hundred—the newly-arrived Zouaves—in their late headquarters at the College. This Regiment has grown into great favor in Washington—not a single one of its members ever having become amenable to the police authorities in any way; and its discipline and efficiency having frequently been made the subject of complimentary notice by Gens SCOTT and MANSFIELD. For very much of the good order and moral restraint existing in the ranks, it is doubtless indebted to the ceaseless and zealous exertions of Father THOMAS MOONEY, an admirable specimen-priest of the true Irish type, who, if he were not chaplain, would certainly be a candidate for Colonel—face and a sanguine temper giving him equal adaptation to the sword of the spirit and the "regulation sword"—a veritable son of the church militant. But this again is a digression.

The Fifth and Twenty-eighth being posted in a position which, to describe, must be seen by daylight, the Sixty-ninth then wheeled back, four of its companies being stationed on a hill about half way between the aqueduct and the advance, to keep open communication, three companies being detailed under orders of an engineer officer of the United States, to throw up fortifications and entrenchments for a camp, to be occupied by the regiment; and the balance having their post of duty assigned on a narrow strip of land, sloping down from the Aqueduct canal to the shore of that arm of the Potomac which runs up past Georgetown, where they are to keep open and protect a military ferry that has been established between the District of Columbia and Virginia—this ferry having its Virginian terminus exactly at the foot of the road to Alexandria. It is not difficult to conjecture what this means, and the less so as rafts laden with horses and boats carrying field pieces, are already passing over.

But your correspondent is very weary, as doubtless his readers may also be. In the first experience of campaigning, everything is so novel that one is apt to attach personal value to trifles which may prove of no general interest. This is a fault, however, of which time promises a speedy cure. Reluctant to complain of anything under the sudden and fearful pressure which has brought so many thousands into the field, he would only express a hope on behalf of the Regiment, that tents, artillery, a few waggons and a regular commissariat may be supplied as soon as possible by the War Department. Commissary RICHARD DOWNING has really been of invaluable service, and has the thanks of all the men. Quartermaster TULLY also labors energetically, and while the Regiment was in the College it had every reason to be satisfied. But there is reason to fear that the health of the men cannot long hold out, if kept working in the trenches all day under a broiling sun, and allowed to sleep at night without any other covering than their blankets and the sky for a counterpane.

Of Col CORCORAN, let me add that I have never seen a man so lavish of himself while so scrupulously careful of others. His health is very far from being robust, and yet he works without cessation, while paying the most minute attention to any symptoms of sickness or even weakness in the men under his command. Lieut.-Col. NUGENT is also an efficient and painstaking officer. I must now close, as this letter has to go by Engineer-Capt. JAMES B. KIRKER, who is sent back to New-York on business connected with the regiment. He is accompanied by Major TAYLOR, Inspector of the Fourth Brigade.

In a few days, if there be no immediate advance, I will endeavor to visit the other regiments, and report their movements and condition. Of the shooting of Col ELLSWORTH we know but little here, beyond the bare fact of its occurrence, and that the Fire Zouaves did not hang all the men in the house from which the shot proceeded. The indignation, however, is unspeakable; but there are matters not to be written about—not to be talked about. They are felt, remembered, and will bear their fruits. Lieut. GILES, who, with Lieut. MURPHY, captured DE GRANVALL, the spy, at Annapolis Junction, has been a little under the weather, but is now fully recovered. All the men of the regiment in good health. No signs of epidemic disease; nor will there be likely, as Arlington Heights are cool and pleasant, if they only give us tents and camp equipage. Capt. MEAGHER of the Zouaves, who came on with Major BAGLEY's command, is ill, and confined to bed in Washington. H.

IMPORTANT FROM FORT MONROE.

REPORTED CAPTURE OF SEWALL'S POINT BATTERY.

WASHINGTON, Saturday, May 25.

The *Yankee* arrived here to-day, from Fortress Monroe, and brings the report that General BUTLER yesterday captured Sewall's Point, with a loss of 84 killed and wounded; that the enemy lost between three and four hundred killed and wounded; that many prisoners were taken—perhaps 600, and that on Thursday evening the enemy's pickets near the Fort were surprised, and 300 prisoners brought to the Fort. The War Department has information to the same effect.

LANDING OF GEN. BUTLER AT HAMPTON.

BALTIMORE, Saturday, May 25.

The steamer *Adelaide* arrived from Fortress Monroe, early this morning. The correspondent of the Associated Press there sends the following:

FORTRESS MONROE, Friday, May 24.

Gen. BUTLER suddenly made his appearance yesterday in Hampton, at the head of the Vermont Regiment, on a reconnoissance. The rebels attempted to burn the Long Bridge, but were frustrated by the activity of the Advance Guard.

To-day (Friday,) he extends a reconnoissance several miles up the peninsula between James and York Rivers

The Troy and Vermont Regiments have encamped near Hampton, this being the occupation of Virginia soil by Federal troops.

The *James Adger*, after landing the Troy Regiment, sailed for New-York.

The *Harriet Lane* has gone to Charleston.

The blockading squadron off Fort Monroe consists of the *Minnesota*, *Cumberland*, *Yankee*, *Star*, (formerly *Monticello*,) *Quaker City*, and other small craft. The officers of the squadron, this morning, called on Gen. BUTLER.

There are several prizes in the harbor.

The arrival of the frigate *Mississippi* is expected, that active operations will be undertaken against Sewell's Point.

In the action of last Sunday, particulars of which you have, three of the four guns of the rebels were dismounted, and it is well understood here that at least half a dozen men were killed. The battery was to contain thirteen guns.

The Michigan Regiment is expected soon from Washington, also several regiments from New-York and Boston.

FURTHER FROM FORTRESS MONROE.

BALTIMORE, Saturday, May 25.

The morning steamer from Norfolk is in. Gen. BUTLER only took nine hundred men, and did not go as far as Lyndhaven, but to a point nearer Fortress Monroe, where he is encamped He will wait there until reinforcements arrive from New-York, when he will resume his march for Norfolk. He has expressed his determination to take the Navy Yard, or parish in the attempt.

The Virginians are busily engaged in strengthening their positions. A floating battery has been placed on the flats near Craney Island, and five new batteries are now completed between Lyndhaven and London Bridge. There are ten thousand men at Norfolk with outposts thrown out towards London Bridge, which is twelve miles east. There are five thousand men at Portsmouth and five thousand at Gosport. A gentleman from Richmond says that a millions of dollars have been expended in fortifying York River to defend Richmond, and that there are fifteen thousand troops there. He says the people of Richmond fully expect to be attacked but are confident of their ability to defend the city. The Petersburgh cavalry company is still there.

Later advices from Norfolk state that Gen. BUTLER has gone on a reconnoissance up the peninsula between James and York rivers.

The New-York and Vermont regiments are encamped near Hampton.

The officers of the steamers *Minnesota*, *Cumberland*, *Monticello*, *Quaker City* and *Yankee*, now blockading Chesapeake Bay, held a consultation this morning with Gen. BUTLER, when further details of the attack were agreed on.

Reinforcements of troops from New-York were hourly expected, when the attack on Sewell's Point would be made.

TRIP OF THE JAMES ADGER TO AND FROM FORTRESS MONROE

The *James Adger* left the dock at New-York on Wednesday afternoon at 5 P. M., and anchored off the Battery until Thursday at 12:30 A. M. at which time she got under weigh and proceeded to sea. We had on board the Second Regiment, New-York State Volunteers, of Troy, numbering 800 men.

During the voyage the men were in fine spirits, and with the exception of the indispensable accompaniment to the unaccustomed voyager, sea sickness, they enjoyed the best possible health.

On Friday, May 24, at 3 A. M, we arrived at the wharf at Fortress Monroe, and at 9 A. M all the troops were landed. Upon their arrival at the Fortress, they received orders from Gen BUTLER, who is now in command of the Federal troops at that For-

[Continued on Eighth Page.]

MAP OF THE SEAT OF WAR.

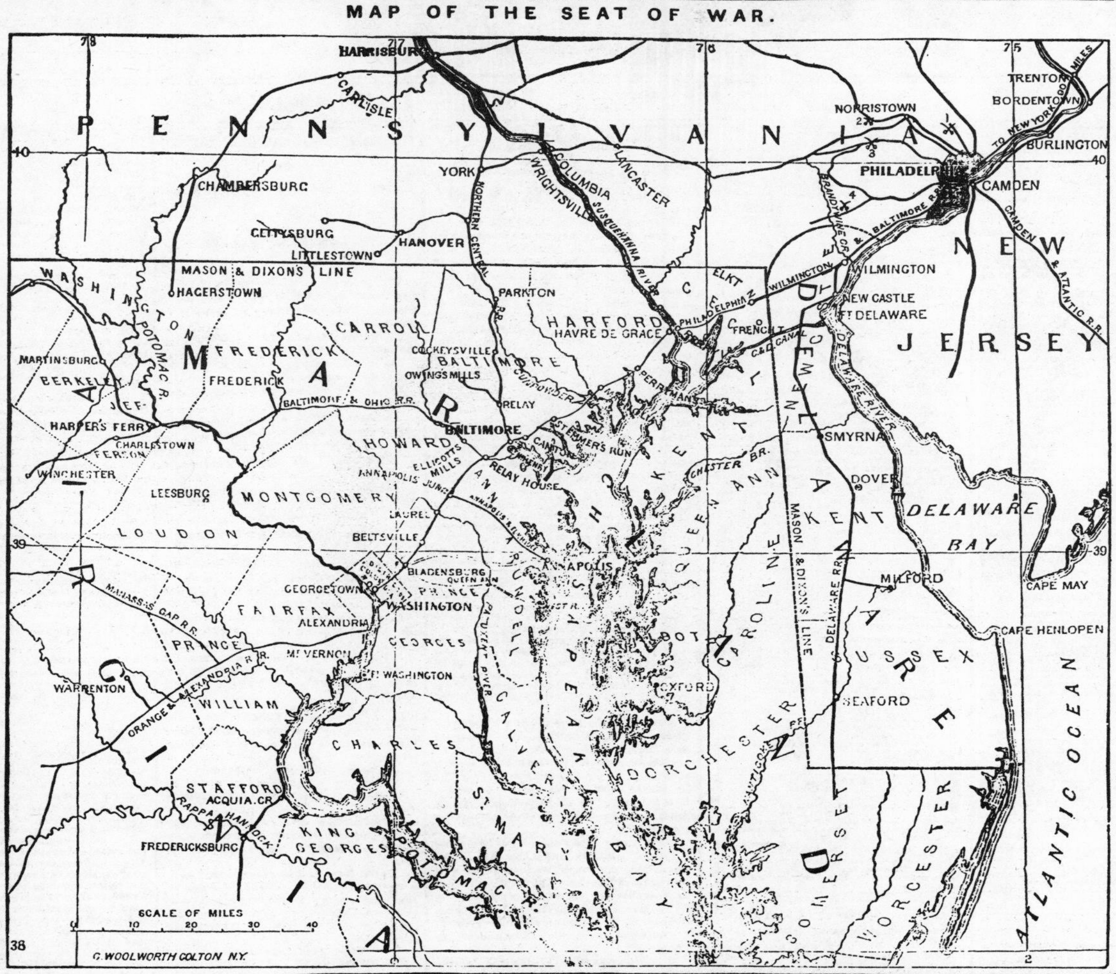

The Daily Picayune.

VOLUME XXV. NEW ORLEANS, TUESDAY MORNING, JUNE 4, 1861. NUMBER 119.

The Daily Picayune.

FROM OUR EVENING EDITION OF YESTERDAY

NORTHERN NEWSPAPER MENDACITY.

It is really pitiable, in looking over the journals of the North—journals conducted by men who assume to be gentlemen, and who would resent alike the imputation of knavery or imbecility—to see the recklessness with which the most apparent and patent falsehoods are inserted, without the expression of a question or a doubt of their accuracy, or even of their possibility, in their columns.

One example out of many falls under our eye, in turning over the exchanges that came to us to day. The Boston Transcript, of the 27th ult., says that "Dr. Charles McQuen, formerly a dentist in New Orleans," (who in this city ever heard of such a man?) "which city he was obliged to leave in consequence of his Union sentiments and sympathies, tells the Buffalo Express" "that on the day preceding his departure (Sunday) he witnessed a spectacle;" and that "spectacle" he thus describes:

A Mrs. Sarah Sanford, a native of New Haven, Ct., and a graduate of the South Hadley Female Seminary, has been for some time engaged as assistant teacher in a New Orleans grammar school. Some remarks, construed as abolitionistic, which she made a day or two before, in the hearing of her pupils, had been reported by them to their parents, and had got circulated abroad. On the Sunday mentioned, a mob was collected at her place of residence, she was seized, taken to Lafayette Square, *stripped naked, and tarred and feathered*, in the presence of an immense crowd of people, including many of her own sex, respectably appearing richly dressed women, who were heard by our informant to applaud and urge on the hellish atrocity. What eventually became of this brutally maltreated lady, he does not know.

Now we are curious to know if the editor of the Boston Transcript did not feel, in his own heart, that, in spreading before his readers this enormous lie, he was making himself responsible for what he knew was such? Did he believe it, or one word of it? If he did, he is to be pitied for his folly—if he did not, what words are competent to characterize his conduct?

It can hardly be necessary for us to say that no such "spectacle" as is described in the mendacious paragraph we have quoted ever took place in this city. The story is a wicked lie, manufactured out of the whole cloth—a lie in web, in warp and in woof—and, what is worse for those who copy and circulate it, a transparent lie, carrying on its face its own refutation.

A correspondent, in Washington, of the New York Times, under date of May 27th, tells about having, that afternoon, seen "a gentleman, direct from New Orleans, who gives a most interesting account of affairs in that city." The point of this account is the tremendous sensation caused in New Orleans, one day, by the reception and sale here of a batch of New York papers. This Mendez Pinto of informants is related to have told his credulous listener that "crowds of people gathered about the bulletins, where the newsvenders had posted the papers as signs, and so great became the tumult that the police authorities were compelled to interfere and order down the papers."

This reads amusingly enough in New Orleans circles, but the following, which winds up the letter, caps the climax:

The utter stagnation in business circles causes a deep gloom to pervade whole streets, and were it not for a continuance of public meetings, at which brass bands and fiery orations cheer their spirits, there would, without doubt, be some great popular demonstration of dissatisfaction.

☞ Mr. McKeever and the other gentlemen of the Adams Express, will accept our thanks for renewed attentions.

☞ We are indebted to the purser of the steamship Gen. Miramon for late Havana papers.

☞ We are indebted to our friend, Mr. W. P. Johnston, now in New York, for slips, by mail, from New York papers of the 28th ult., containing important news.

☞ We are indebted to Wilbur & Borge's Express for late Havana papers per steamship General Miramon.

☞ We have received from the publisher, Mr. D. Redmond, Augusta, Ga., a copy of the Southern Cultivator, for June.

☞ We have received from Chapel Hill, N. C., a copy of the Catalogue of the Trustees, Faculty and Students of the University of North Carolina.

☞ The New York Eclectic Magazine of Foreign Literature, W. H. Bidwell, for June. The frontispiece is composed of fine portraits, in mezzotint, of Webster, Clay and Jackson.

☞ The Mexican schooner Brilliante, Capt. Espinola, from Sisal and Campeachy, arrived at Pass-à-l'Outre on the 30th ult., and was ordered off by the U. S. war steamer Brooklyn. She left, stood for the entrance of the lake, ran in and arrived at the lake end of the New Canal on Saturday evening last.

More Louisiana Volunteers en Route. A telegraphic dispatch to our worthy fellow-citizen, Judge Edward Rawle, from his son, of the Louisiana Guards, and dated Atlanta (Ga.) June 2, says: "Just arrived, in good health and spirits. Bound for Richmond."

The Foreign Consuls and the Blockade. A deputation, consisting of British, French, Spanish and Bremen Consuls, residing in this city, with Mr. Baroche, agent of the French Empire, and also a deputation of the Towboat Company, left yesterday evening on board the towboat Ocean, Capt. Whitney, for the Balize, for the purpose of having an interview with the commander of the steam ship-of-war Brooklyn, in relation to the blockade of this port.

Time was given by the Lincolnite Government for all foreign vessels to leave this port, but it seems the captain of the Brooklyn has thought proper not to respect the nationality or rights of foreign vessels, by firing into them while in tow of tugs, which were taking them over the bar.

The Towboat Association have, in the meantime, laid up their vessels until they can have assurance that they will be protected in towing out vessels which have a perfect right to leave this port, and are protected by the laws of nations. If the interview shall not be satisfactory, the Governments of the Consuls will no doubt speak in another tone to the Abolition Government.

Telegraphed to the New Orleans Picayune!

THE WAR IN VIRGINIA.

Fairfax Courthouse Engagement.

Alexandria, June 3.—At the Fairfax Courthouse engagement, which occurred on Saturday, Capt. John Mann was the only Virginian killed.

Extra Billy Smith figured conspicuously in the fight.

The retreating horsemen were pursued, and two of their number captured.

A Federal colonel commanding cavalry was wounded.

It is raining here at present. There is no apprehension of another attack.

THE FIGHT AT AQUIA CREEK.

SOUTHERN TROOPS VICTORIOUS!!

Another Collision Anticipated.

Washington, June 3.—The Confederate forces at Aquia Creek, Va., have beaten off the Federal steamers Anacosta and Freeborn, killing a number of men.

These steamers are waiting the arrival of the Pawnee, which is in the offing, lying in wait for transports with Federal troops.

Provisions for Harper's Ferry.

Harrisburg, June 3.—Provisions continue to be forwarded from Maryland to Harper's Ferry.

The McDowell Case.

St. Louis, June 3.—Capt. or Col. Lyon will have legal proceedings instituted against him on account of his actions in the McDowell case.

The Removal of Gen. Harney.

Gen. Harney was removed because of his not using proper efforts to subdue the Missourians.

The Administration is evidently endeavoring to irritate Missouri beyond endurance, and wants an excuse for further coercive measures.

Negro Row in Chambersburg, Pa.

Chambersburg, Pa., June 3.—A fracas occurred last evening in the negro portion of this town, during which Frank Jones, a negro barber, shot two soldiers. He was afterwards killed.

From Fortress Monroe.

The Federalists at Fortress Monroe are motionless; 4000 Southerners at Yorktown hold them in check.

From Aquia Creek.

Gen. Washington is at Aquia Creek.

The Northern Light at New York.

Only $100,000 from California.

New York, June 3.—The steamer Northern Light has arrived from Aspinwall, bringing specie on freight to the amount of $100,000.

Our War of Independence.

The Uprising in North Carolina.

[Special Correspondence of the Picayune.]

Weldon, N. C., *May* 28, 1861.

Of all the States through which I have passed, from the banks of the Mississippi here, the good "old North State" seems best prepared for the great struggle before us. Never before have I seen so much military enthusiasm among any people; never, withal, a people who manifested a spirit so calm, so firm, and so determined. From the mountains to the seashore the whole State is in arms; every town through which I passed is bristling with bayonets; the railroads are filled with them, the depots, the highways; from every direction the people are rushing, apparently without thought of anything else, to the defence of their homes and their liberties. It is an uprising of the people *en masse*. Already 30,000 men have offered their services since the passage of the secession ordinance; in two weeks it is believed 50,000 men will be under arms. In case of invasion, indeed, the invader will meet an armed foe in every man, woman and child.

North Carolina is well provided with arms, in large quantity, of the latest improved. She has also recently received from Norfolk and Charleston an immense number of cannon, which have been planted into batteries all along the coast. Armed steamers, of light draught, have also been put on all the rivers and inlets conducting into the interior, so that now the State is believed to be safe against any sudden movement in that direction. "The only way now to reach us," says a companion at my side, "is to walk over the Virginians, and in doing that they will have to walk over us too."

And this is true. Apparently secure themselves, the North Carolinians are now rushing from every direction to the assistance of their neighbors. Two regiments left here but a few days ago for Norfolk, another leaves to-day, while others are prepared to leave any moment they are called upon.

The North Carolinians are not a moment behind any other people in the Confederacy. The secession ordinance was the last passed, it is true, but then "it could not be passed earlier." And why, I asked. "Because the 20th of May did not come round earlier. We contemplated a new declaration of independence, in open daylight, and the people would never have listened to its being made on any other day than the anniversary of our first one at Mecklenburg." And so it was. That day, honored above all others by every true son of the old North State, had no sooner come around, than it found the convention in session, and ready to act. There was but one thing to do. They had elected for that, and that alone. It was to declare the State out of the old and into the new Confederacy, and all in the same breath. So the two ordinances were combined in one, and before any other business was permitted to be done—before even the parliamentary rules of the convention had been adopted, the ordinance had passed.

There was no delay, no secrecy about it. The people would permit neither. Then, at Raleigh, on the 20th day of May, the eighty-fifth anniversary of the Mecklenburg declaration of independence, the people of North Carolina, in convention assembled, and openly, in face of the whole world, again asserted the sublime doctrines of self-government and State sovereignty, at the same time that they assumed new relations with their neighbors—destined to be more lasting, because more true and more in harmony with their true interests.

Those upon whom the defence of the State, however, depended, did not wait for this formal declaration. With the uncalculating patriotism of a people whose homes were in danger, the North Carolinians rushed to arms at the first note of alarm. Like ourselves, they seized every fort and stronghold on the coast, and prudently went to work to put every approach by sea in a perfect state of defence, so that now an invasion from that quarter is believed to be impossible. They seized also upon the well filled arsenal at Fayetteville, whereby they came in possession of 45,000 stands of the latest improved arms. Nor did they rest here. They hunted up the arms scattered through the State, and lost no time in putting them in the best possible condition for whatever emergency. Old Rip Van Winkle was wide awake all the time he seemed to be sleeping, and now the good old North State is able, not only to defend herself, but to hasten to the assistance of her neighbors.

H. P.

Letter from New York.

[Special Correspondence of the Picayune.]

New York, *May* 28, 1861.

You will see that Old Abe had a narrow shave with his nine million loan, and you will also see that it went at a lower figure than any of the recent loans, indeed lower than any loan since the foundation of the Government.

It was taken, too, as a purely business transaction; the bids did not top above the amount required, as was the case previously; but, on the contrary, they barely came up to the amount asked for. On a prior occasion the bids ran twenty million above the sum required, whereas now they barely reached the figure wanted! On a previous occasion, too, the offers ranged from 90 all the way up to par, whereas now 85 is the best that can be obtained. These are forcible and important changes—changes full of meaning—and they clearly prove two remarks made in previous letters; one of which was, that the eager patriotism of the North was dying out; and the other, that the loans, if taken at all, would be in a business way and at the market price. People are not such fools as to pay 100 for a bond that they can get at any moment for 86; and all the appeals to their patriotism, whether coercive or as mild as honey, will not induce them to commit so transparent a folly.

You will recollect in my last I alluded to the dictatorial appeals of a journal here for the people to come forward and take the loans at an exorbitant figure, by which they would show, in an unmistakable manner, their undying patriotism and the unbounded vigor with which they were anxious to push forward the glorious work. The result of these appeals is seen in the success of the loan awarded on Saturday. The coercive dose was too nauseating for our moneyed men, and many of them indignantly turned their backs upon the loan. Such is the fate of all unjust coercive measures; they are met with stern rebuke and withering defeat, and such a fate awaits the coercion that is now being undertaken on a grand scale at Washington.

The most refreshing incident in the loan just awarded is the fact that the domineering Abolition Secretary of the Treasury had to swallow all his pomposity and take just what the people chose to give him for his loan. At the award of the previous loan, when patriotism and speculation run neck and neck, and the offers were liberal, the high strung Secretary refused 94 for a large portion of the loan on the ground that he was determined the credit of the Government should be recovered and sustained. In other words, he would have par for his 6 per cent. stock, or the people should not have it. As no such proviso was to be found in the advertisement for the loan, the people who bid for the same were naturally very indignant at such proceedings, and gave copious vent to their feelings through the press and by letter to the "able" Secretary. Their turn, however, was to come; more money was wanted, and bids were invited. At the start it looked as though the loan would be a failure, and the time for receiving the bids was postponed for a week. The people also had the privilege of bidding for whichever they wanted—a twenty year loan or Treasury notes—and the people did just as they pleased, and took the loan at nine per cent. less than they offered for the previous one. So the very smart head of the Treasury Department has found the people more than a match for him; for what he indignantly and pompously refused 94 for, they (the public) have now obtained at 85.

The truth is, the Northern people are beginning to anticipate a vast amount of begging from the Treasury Department at Washington. The expenses for carrying on the diabolical crusade that has just been commenced are frightful, and they will increase rather than diminish. Besides, every additional loan but adds to the debt that is being saddled upon the people, and as they, after all, have to finally foot the bill, they are determined to make the load as easy as possible, and take the loans that may be offered on their own terms. This is only right, and the Government must consent to face the music.

Antelope.

The Gen. Miramon at Mobile.

Her Seizure and Release.

The Mobile Register, of yesterday, (June 2d,) has the following:

The British screw steamship Gen. Miramon, Capt. Golding, arrived last evening from Havana, which port she left on the evening of the 28th of May. From Mr. F. Ingate, one of the passengers, we learn the following particulars:

On the morning of the 31st, she arrived off the mouth of the Mississippi, and was chased and captured by the U. S. man-of-war Brooklyn. A prize crew was put on board, Lieut. Adams commanding, and the Miramon was ordered to be carried off Mobile Point to the officer of the Niagara, with a view of being sent North as a prize. In the evening the Miramon was chased by a steamer, supposed to be a privateer. The officers in command changed the course of the vessel, and on Saturday morning made Pensacola light.

The steamer Huntsville, provisionally armed with three guns, boarded, and after communicating, the Miramon was allowed to put about for Mobile Point. After sailing about ten miles, the U. S. steamer Mount Vernon hove in sight, and approaching the Miramon fired two shotted guns. The Niagara soon coming up, an investigation was had, and the Miramon was allowed to enter the bay of Mobile for supplies, the captain engaging to come out within a reasonable time. The Miramon brought over the following passengers:

Miss C. Puja, Major H. Harris, G. Malna, F. Ingate, R. Salas, Ed. Ewing, A. Panajo, O. Callahan, F. P. Ingan, Thos. Viadett, C. Hocha, J. Onetey, J. Simon, S. Redires, J. Miradjay, J. M. Lacoul, William Smith, Charles White, J. M. Campbell.

Later from Havana.

By the arrival of the steamship General Miramon at Mobile, we have files of Havana papers to the 28th ult., inclusive:

Business was excessively dull. Very little was doing in the sugar market, or in any departments. United States vessels were at a discount in the freight market; all vessels of other nations commanding a premium of 33 per cent., because of the protection from privateers assured by their flags.

The Habanese seem to be rejoicing in the idea that Havana must become the rendezvous of Gulf commerce during the war, and the papers put forth strong claims as to its merits for a general entrepot.

The arrivals of merchandise for the week were very large, though less than the previous week. The importations comprised large amounts of staple supplies of breadstuffs and provisions.

The editor of the Cuban Messenger, who, we regret to notice, leans strongly to the Lincolnite cause, visited the frigate Niagara, which is now blockading Mobile, and from his report we take the following statement of the armament of that vessel:

"She is 4,300 tons burthen, 320 feet long and 53 feet beam. She carries 500 men, and is armed with twelve bronzed Dahlgren guns, 11 inch bore, 15 feet long, weighing [illegible] pounds each, exclusive of the carriage, which weighs 5000 pounds more, making an aggregate of 20,822 pounds. The weight of the shell thrown by this gun is 149 pounds, and requires 15 pounds of powder at each charge, making an effective shot at 3½ miles. She also has four 24 pound howitzers, and 500 Minié rifles, with the accustomed supply of sabres, boarding pikes, revolvers, and all the horrible implements of warfare."

☞ We are much obliged to Mr. Davis, of the firm of Davis Bros., 93 Camp street, for a large budget of Northern and Western papers, of later dates than those yet received by mail. Such kind attentions as these are now, and are likely to be for some time, on the part of private friends, peculiarly valuable to us, our exchange list being now suspended, for the present.

THE CITY.

Accidents on our City Railroad.—Immense crowds besieged the city cars all day yesterday, and the rush for seats consequently was very great. A number of boys would follow the cars, and jump on behind for the novelty of the ride, and in this way a little negro boy, about eight years old, in attempting to jump on one of the cars, at the curve at the corner of Rampart and Canal, yesterday afternoon, fell under the wheels and was instantly killed. The driver, Owen Mead, was arrested, but no blame could possibly be attached to the driver.

A white boy sixteen years of age, named Laroque, had his left leg crushed in the same manner, on Esplanade, near Bayou Bridge. It is impossible for the driver to attend to the street crossing and in driving his "one mule" team act as conductor also. There should be a conductor on every car for to give attention and accommodation to passengers. In this respect we must confess the Lafayette city cars have a vast advantage over the new modern self conducting cars.

Uniform Time for the City.—Dr. Bonzano, the scientific and accomplished superintendent of the Mint in this city, Mr. Achille Hebert, the able superintendent of the Fire Alarm and Police Telegraph, and Mr. Fournier, the watchmaker of Royal street, whose devotion to the cause of science is so well known, have succeeded in jointly carrying out a scheme of their own to have uniform time for the city by the means of electric clocks. After several months of labor and considerable expense to themselves they now have each one of these splendid time recorders, which they put in permanent operation Saturday evening. They can be seen and inspected by the scientific and the curious at the Mint, City Telegraph office, and at Mr. Fournier's store. Dr. Bonzano regulates the main clock at the Mint by solar observations to the fraction of a second, and the working of that works the other clocks attached to it by a metallic circuit of wire. Instead of a pendulum or spring these clocks have a magnet and armature. At every half minute a current of electricity flashes over the wires, making the magnets attractive and springing to them the armature, which quickly rebounds by its spring. This motion of the armature at every half minute has the same action upon the works of a clock as does the ordinary pendulum, only that it moves the hands at half minute instead of second strides.

More Texans for the Field.—Two splendid companies of Texans arrived here this morning per steamer Texas, from Red River, the Marshall Guards, from Marshall, and the Star Rifles, from Bass county. They desire to express their thanks and gratitude to Capt. Stinde, and Mr. Orrin, of the Texas, for their great courtesy and hospitalities.

These two companies will be immediately mustered into service, and join the Texas battalion now in Virginia. The following is a list of the officers of the Marshall Guards:

Captain, F. S. Bass; 1st Lieut., Ed H. Bates; 2d Lieut., J. K. Taylor; 3d Lieut., A. D. Burns; Orderly Sergeant, T. P. Ochiltree; 2d Sergt., Tom H. Langley; 3d Sergt., W. B. Preston; 4th Sergt., G. W. [illegible]; 1st Corporal, Pratt Hughes; 2d Corporal, — Burnes; 3d Corporal, W. D. Prescott; 4th Corporal, [illegible] Willingham; Ensign, John Loyd.

Crescent Blues, Company B.—The Second company of the Crescent Blues organized on Saturday evening by electing their officers, as follows: Captain, M. G. Goodwyn; First Lieutenant, W. G. Crum; Second, J. H. Sanders; Junior Second, V. D. De Flaie; Orderly Sergeant, J. M. Goodman; Second, W. H. [illegible]; Third, A. M. Ashbridge; Fourth, George Williams; First Corporal, V. S. Goodin; Second, E. H. Guerague; Third, M. M. Stephens; Fourth, C. C. Hauge.

Sappers and Miners.—A company of sappers and miners, commanded by Major Smith, of the Confederate States Army, was mustered into service this morning by the gallant Capt. J. W. Phifer, C. S. A.

Polish Brigade.—The distinguished Major G. Tochman, whose military reputation is well known both in Europe and this country, arrived here this morning, having been authorized by the President to raise a Polish Legion.

The first regiment of this brigade is to be commanded by Col. V. Sulakowski, who has already two companies mustered in, commanded by Capts. Dolson and West, and four or five more are expected to be mustered in this week. Companies or individuals, wishing to be immediately mustered into the service of the Confederate States, should make immediate application at No. 37 St. Charles street, the headquarters of the first regiment.

THE NEW YORK HERALD.

WHOLE NO. 9034. MORNING EDITION—TUESDAY, JUNE 4, 1861. PRICE TWO CENTS.

THE INSURRECTION.

Important News from the Seat of War.

BATTLE AT PHILLIPPA, VA.

TWO THOUSAND REBELS ROUTED.

Colonel Kelly, of the Union Forces, Killed.

Concentration of Troops at Manassas Gap and Harper's Ferry.

Anticipated March of our Forces on Fairfax and Manassas Gap.

The Number of the Rebels near Harper's Ferry.

Twenty-five Thousand United States Troops on the March to Harper's Ferry.

THE NEW STEAM GUN BOATS.

Preparations to Receive the Privateers on the Pacific.

Reported Seizure of the Confederate Steamer Peerless at Montreal.

Departure of More New York Volunteers,

&c., &c., &c.

THE INTENDED MARCH UPON FAIRFAX AND MANASSAS.

WASHINGTON, June 3, 1861.

There is considerable flurry and excitement this evening among the various regiments on this side of the Potomac. It has been whispered about among the colonels of the regiments, by persons who are authority in such matters, that a fight is imminent, and preparations are accordingly being made. The Rhode Island regiment, with their beautiful battery, received an intimation this evening that marching orders might be expected between this and morning. Colonel Burnside promptly informed the commanding officer that his regiment was ready for action, and would move at a moment's warning.

There can be no doubt that a further advance of the federal forces into Virginia will be made in the course of the present week. It is not improbable that a forward movement will take place during the next forty-eight hours. The first move will be upon Fairfax Court House. Three regiments—probably the Fire Zouaves, the Michigan regiment and the Fifth Massachusetts—will form the advancing column, to be supported, in case of necessity, by the entire remaining force on the Virginia side, the numerical strength of which will be increased by several regiments on this side, that have received orders to hold themselves in readiness, and are expected to cross the river either to-night or to morrow.

Three hundred laborers marched to Alexandria this morning from this city, to follow in the wake of the column about moving on Fairfax Court House, and immediately put the railroad and telegraph between that point and Alexandria in working order.

General McDowell does not expect the rebels to make a stand at the Court House. He is said to have received positive intelligence to-day that the rebels at that point had received orders not to offer any resistance in case the federal troops should advance on the Court House, but to fall back on Manassas Junction.

Information derived by myself in Alexandria this morning, in a conversation with a heavy mail contractor, a strong secessionist, just arrived from Richmond, on his way to Washington, for the purpose of settling his accounts with the Post Office Department, confirms this. He stated positively that the firing of the secession pickets upon the federal cavalry on Friday night was against orders, and that they had instructions to retreat towards the junction as the federal troops advanced. My informant stated further, that the Confederate forces would not commence fighting until the invaders had reached the point to which General Lee has determined to allow them to advance, intimating, at the same time, that by a bold movement a strong secession column was to be thrown between the federal army and Maryland, so as to operate against the former from the rear.

It is certain that General Scott received an intimation some days since that such was the plan of the secession chief, and that he is preparing to frustrate any attempt to realize it. He cannot be caught in any trap the rebels are likely to set for him.

The Twelfth New York regiment have been ordered to sleep on their arms to-night, and reports are prevalent of additional troops to be dispatched to Virginia.

ALEXANDRIA, June 3, 1861.

Nothing definite has yet been received here of an authorized advance on Fairfax Court House, though such a movement from Arlington Heights is daily looked for. As soon as Fairfax Court House is occupied, the railroad from Alexandria to that point will be put in running order, and troops for the attack on Manassas Junction, which will speedily follow, will be transported from here. The arrangements for the immediate repair of the road are all completed, and the work can be done in two days.

The telegraph line will also be reconstructed, with similar or greater expedition.

Additional regiments are under orders to proceed from Washington to this place, some of which are expected here to-day.

INTERESTING FROM VIRGINIA.

The following interesting facts are supplied us by a gentleman who has just returned to the city from Richmond, Manassas Gap and Fairfax Court House:—

I left New York on Saturday night, the 25th ult., and reached Richmond, via Alexandria and Manassas Junction, on Tuesday afternoon. Mr. Davis, the President of the Southern confederacy, accompanied by Mr. Toombs, the Secretary of State, and Mr. Wigfall, arrived in Richmond on Wednesday morning, and met with a very enthusiastic reception. They were serenaded at the Spotswood House, where Mr. Davis made a short speech, in which he said that in less than a month every man in the Southern confederacy would be on Virginia soil, and that every cubic foot of the same would be disputed by an armed man.

On Thursday the President held a levee in the Governor's mansion, which was attended by a large number of the citizens of Richmond. Numerous offers of houses have been made to Mr. Davis, and it was understood that he had accepted that of Mr. Crenshaw, a miller at that place. On the same afternoon he drove out to the various camps, and made short but stirring addresses to the soldiers. General Lee left Richmond for Manassas on Tuesday morning, and returned Thursday night. From the best observation I was able to make, I do not think there were more than three or four thousand troops in Richmond up to Friday morning. Richmond was very quiet, and no business of any kind doing. A loan of fifteen millions for the Confederate States has been offered in that city. I arrived at Manassas on Friday afternoon, and left there about five o'clock the same evening. To the best of my judgment, there were not more than [illegible] there. There were, however, about eight thousand on the road between Manassas and eight miles from Fairfax Court House. I heard a report of the Virginia trooper who shot one of Ellsworth's Zouaves at Cloud's Mills, three miles from Alexandria. Tying his horse to a tree, he stealthily crept up and shot the Zouave through the head, and immediately returned to Fairfax Court House and exultingly boasted of his achievement. On Saturday morning I was awakened by the arrival of a company of United States cavalry, under Lieutenant Tompkins. The Virginia cavalry, about 200 in number, who were stationed in the place, had barely time to jump on their horses and escape before the federal troops arrived. The latter took up a station on a hill in the rear of the Court House, and there awaited the appearance of the enemy, who, taking a circuitous route, suddenly appeared in the rear of the federal cavalry, cutting off their retreat. After three volleys were fired the federal troops retreated on the road to Manassas. They, however, afterwards wheeled and charged the enemy, killing twenty-seven, with a loss of only two on their side. I arrived in New York this morning.

REBEL TROOPS AT MANASSAS GAP.

Recent arrivals from this most important strategic point of the rebels continue to give confirmation of the accounts before received, and certainly contradicts the statement said to have been made by General Scott, that only 2,600 troops were there congregated. The rebels know the value of this junction too well to leave it unguarded or merely defended by so small a body as above enumerated. They have at least 20 000 men under the leadership of General Lee, and the junction of the two railroads is as thoroughly fortified as possible. A glance at the plan will at once convince the doubtful of this fact. At present it does not seem to be the intention of this body of the rebel forces to make any attack, but to wait the action of our advancing columns, when, on their arrival at the Gap, they will receive them with a hot and raking fire.

ANTICIPATED ATTACK ON THE GOVERNMENT FORCES IN VIRGINIA.

WASHINGTON, June 3, 1861.

An opinion prevails in a high military quarter here that our troops in Virginia will be attacked to-night by the rebels. On the contrary, I have reason to believe that the rebels, instead of advancing upon our forces, are falling back for fear of being attacked themselves. The shock they received at Fairfax Court House will not leave them soon. I have good reason to believe that instead of twenty seven, there were twice that number killed in that skirmish.

There is no doubt that the advance movement alluded to in this correspondence some days since as soon to be made, for the purpose of cutting off communication between Richmond and Harper's Ferry, is about to be made, and you may now be prepared for it at any moment. It must be done soon in order to hem in the rebels at Harper's Ferry. General Patterson's arrival at Chambersburg is a part of the same programme.

MOVEMENTS OF TROOPS.

WASHINGTON, June 3, 1861.

The First Maine regiment and the New York Highlanders have arrived here this afternoon, *making fifty thousand troops now in and around the federal capital.* The number advancing towards Harper's Ferry from Ohio and Western Virginia is about fifteen thousand, and from Pennsylvania, in the same direction, about eight thousand. Another column is moving from the direction of Baltimore and the Relay House.

It will be only necessary to take and hold Manassas Junction, which will be done.

The First Maine regiment arrived at four o'clock this afternoon, being much fatigued, and they were glad to find quarters.

The Garibaldi Guard went into camp to-day on the eastern branch of the Potomac, near the Navy Yard.

THE NEW MAJOR GENERALS.

WASHINGTON, June 3, 1861.

The forward movements of General Butler in Virginia have been approved by Lieutenant General Scott, although they were made on General Butler's own responsibility, and without orders. This looks well for General Scott. General Butler will soon give a good account of himself if he is not held back in his glorious work by higher authority.

The report about the assignment to certain departments of Generals Fremont and Banks are premature, and will very likely prove erroneous. Nothing on the subject has yet been fully determined. Fremont has been appointed a Major General of the regular army of the United States. The government possesses no legal authority to do this, but has assumed it. Banks has been appointed a Major General of the three years' volunteers. Fremont, should he remain in the vicinity of Washington, being in the regular army, would rank Butler, who is a Major General of volunteers; whereas Banks would be ranked by Butler, who is his senior in service; therefore, it would seem to be preferable for Banks, and to afford him a more promising opportunity for distinction, to assign him to some department in the West.

Secretary Cameron is again pressing Governor Banks to accept the position of Quartermaster General, with the rank of Major General, and the subject is again reopened for consideration on both sides. Weighty reasons are presented which may induce Governor Banks to comply with the request of the Secretary of War. There are many complications already created in the Quartermaster's Bureau, that will require nice management on the part of Governor Banks or any other man to avoid being mixed up with. Hence the position is not one that any man would be over anxious to assume the duties and responsibilities of.

AFFAIRS AT ALEXANDRIA.

ALEXANDRIA, Va., June 3, 1861.

There was another alarm about twelve o'clock last night. It was caused by the accidental discharge of a gun in the hands of a sentinel, which was followed by the firing of other sentinels, who thought an attack had been made.

The government has taken possession of two cars at the depot of the Orange and Alexandria road, containing a quantity of musket stocks and two boxes of highly finished tools for the construction of implements of war. Each box is valued at $2,000.

Captain F. B. Medler has been appointed Provost Marshal, vice Whitteisey, relieved at his own request.

The Orange and Alexandria road, which is made a continuation of the military line, is rapidly being repaired by the federal forces. The work is under the charge of competent engineers. There are now at the depot here one good locomotive, two old castaways, one passenger car, fifteen baggage cars, one tender and five gondolas.

Another regiment is expected here to-day.

The Zouaves are picketed on the Fairfax road.

Captain Whittlesey, of the Michigan regiment, at his own request, has been relieved from the office of Provost Marshal, and Captain F. B. Medler, of the Pennsylvania Fifth, has been appointed to succeed him.

The women and children are gradually returning to town.

Important events are anticipated.

Everything is exceedingly quiet. A gentleman just from Arlington reports all quiet there up to two o'clock this afternoon. The New York Sixty-ninth, in encampment there, seemed quite contented and unalarmed.

The troops who have been quartered in the city are being moved to encampments outside, much to the gratification of the citizens.

Though the day has been exceedingly warm, there have been more people on the streets than any previous day since the troops occupied the town. Those now removing to the country are only those who are in the habit of doing so during the warm weather.

The Zouaves are amusing themselves in putting in order the fire engines of the city, and trying their capacity to "squirt."

ALEXANDRIA, June 3, 1861.

Active preparations are making here that indicate a change in the programme for the advance on the enemy. The repair of the Orange and Alexandria Railroad will require much less time than was anticipated. A requisition has been made on the Baltimore and Ohio road for for a large amount of rolling stock for this road, which will be shipped here at once from Washington. The road will be running in a day or two.

It is rumored that in the shooting at the depot last night one citizen and a soldier of the Michigan regiment were slightly wounded.

The general hospital at this post will soon be broken up and the sick transferred to Georgetown. Those permanently disabled will be sent home.

FROM BALTIMORE.

BALTIMORE, June 3, 1861.

Gov. Hicks this morning demanded and received the muskets of the Baltimore City Guard, numbering 160, and [illegible].

Several [illegible] Harper's Ferry were arrested this morning and taken to the fort.

THE SEAT OF WAR.

The Manassas Gap Junction and Surroundings—The Positions of the Rebel Troops, their Entrenchments, Batteries and Encampments.

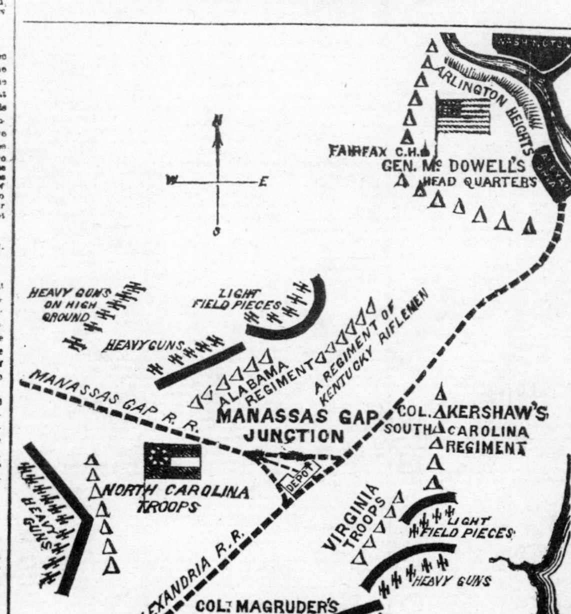

AFFAIRS IN AND AROUND WASHINGTON.

WASHINGTON, June 3, 1861.

At half past eleven A. M. to-day the President received telegraphic intelligence from Chicago that Judge Douglas died this morning.

There was no actual cause for an alarm on the other side of the Potomac last night; yet two lively scenes were enacted by the imagination of pickets. The New York Twenty-eighth pickets are on the extreme outposts. At half past twelve this morning two of them believed the enemy was approaching, and fired. The result was the alarm rang through the camps of the Twenty-eighth, Fifth and Sixty-ninth New York regiments, and my informant, who came into town about noon, states that the promptness of the men in preparing for the march was wonderful. With the greatest possible despatch the regiments were in battle array.

The second false alarm occurred about a quarter past three this morning, when they were again on the alert with the same despatch as before.

Efforts are making to avoid these unnecessary false alarms, which always occur with raw recruits, by placing regulars on guard.

The United States steamer Resolute, Captain William Budd, left this afternoon for a trip of exploration down the Potomac. The Resolute co-operated at Aquia Creek with the Freeborn, under Commander Ward. Captain Budd was the officer detailed to make the reconnoissance on shore at Mathias Point, which was a brave movement, inasmuch as he was entirely ignorant of the strength of the enemy, and might have been easily cut off had there been any considerable force to have opposed their landing. The Resolute goes down the river to-day prepared for warm work of some kind. She carries one rifled heavy twelve pound howitzer, one twenty-four pounder, smooth bore, besides a great supply of every kind of small arms and plenty of ammunition.

The steamer Page, heretofore used as a ferry boat, was seized not long since by the secessionists, the boat having got aground. She is now up in Aquia creek, about three thousand yards beyond the capacity of any of our light draft gun boats to go. She is the only boat in the possession of the rebels on the river or within the waters of Chesapeake Bay. If I am not very much mistaken, we shall hear soon of her capture.

General James, the proprietor of the celebrated rifled cannon, proposed two weeks since to take one or more of his one hundred pound shot and shell instruments, and go down the Potomac and silence all the batteries that could be discovered on the Potomac or Chesapeake Bay, but the proposition was refused. The proposal was made again to day, and the Secretary of the Navy accepted General James' proposition, and the General has left for New York to execute his pledges. The twelve pound rifled cannon is more properly for field service.

It is ascertained that the cannon used by the rebels at Aquia Creek was manufactured at Richmond, and is known as Parrott's gun. The projectile used in it is said to be an infringement of General James'.

Vice President Hamlin left for home yesterday.

Secretary Cameron has made several attempts to leave Washington and visit certain points of military importance just now; but the extraordinary pressure upon him of public business at the department has thus far prevented him executing his desires in this matter. For this reason he was obliged to abandon the idea of going down to Fortress Monroe on Saturday.

The HERALD's articles upon Lord Lyons are the principal topic in diplomatic circles. The ministers of the other leading powers of Europe are beginning to feel rather uneasy. In official circles these pungent articles are also read with interest, and they have excited much comment on account of their boldness. The administration will await advices from our ministers abroad before any action is taken. The next arrival from abroad is looked for with great interest.

The President and Secretary of State are again engaged upon foreign appointments. There will be a large number of consular appointments made during the week.

The Department of State to-day received the letter of Gen. Webb accepting the Brazilian mission.

While there is no doubt that three of the six Commissioners appointed by the Legislature of Maryland have waited on "President" Davis, no information can be obtained here to show that their associates, as instructed, have yet officially visited President Lincoln.

The plan of organization for the volunteer forces, designated in general orders, May 4, is so modified as to allow one surgeon and assistant to each regiment to be appointed by the Governors of the respective States, subject to the approval of the Secretary of War.

Lieutenants Chambliss and Horton having tendered their resignations to avoid being called upon for active service, their names have been stricken from the rolls of the army.

Captain Marr, who was killed at Fairfax Court House, was a member of the Virginia State Convention, and a member elect of the Legislature from Fauquier county.

It is understood that Colonel George [illegible] will be promoted to a Brigadier Generalship.

Reliable information has reached here that the secession troops at Fairfax Court House number 400, at Centreville 1,000; at Lee's, or Fairfax Station, 300, and Manassas Gap Junction from 4,000 to 5,000.

Thomas H. Nelson, of Indiana, has been appointed Minister to Chile.

The steam propeller Resolute left the Navy Yard at six o'clock this afternoon, for Aquia Creek, having on board a distinguished surveying officer. It is understood that that point is to be carefully surveyed, with a view to further operations.

Accounts from individuals residing in the vicinity of Fairfax Court House tend simply to confirm Gen. McDowell's official report of the number of killed and wounded in the recent skirmish there.

At the municipal election here to-day not much more than one-third the usual vote was polled, there being but little general interest in the result.

THE NEW STEAM SLOOPS.

WASHINGTON, June 3, 1861.

The seven steam sloops-of-war authorized by the last Congress are to be named as follows:—

Those to be built at Portsmouth, N. H., the Kearsage and Ossipee; the two at Boston, Housatonic and Wachusett; the one at New York, Adirondack; and those at Philadelphia, Juniata and Tuscarora.

The Naval Lyceum, at the Brooklyn Navy Yard, will take charge of all letters for the blockading squadron.

The Navy Department has increased its working hours.

There are now fifteen vessels of war in the Gulf of Mexico; twelve on the Atlantic coast, and ten in the Chesapeake and Potomac. Every exertion is being made to add to this list with the least possible delay.

The following document has at last appeared from Mr. John Lenthall, the loyal and scientific Englishman who is chief of the Bureau of Construction, Equipment and Repairs. It is sent to all who have expressed a desire to make proposals, a great number of whom have been detained in this city many days awaiting Mr. Lenthall's sage conclusions. Here they are:—

NAVY DEPARTMENT,
BUREAU OF CONSTRUCTION, EQUIPMENT AND REPAIRS,
WASHINGTON, May 30, 1861.

SIR:—You will herewith receive the specifications of the machinery of the screw gun boats, for the construction of which this Bureau invited proposals, by advertisement, dated May 22, 1861. You will find prefixed the conditions of the contract you will be required to execute in case your proposals are accepted. You will please make two distinct proposals, under the two following contingencies, namely: First, on the contingency that the hull of the vessel is constructed at the port where the machinery is built; second, on the contingency that the hull of the vessel is constructed at some other port, in which case the machinery must be carried to it, and these erected in the vessel. For each contingency your proposal will state First—The time from date of contract, in days of twenty-four hours each, in which you will contract to have the machinery, appurtenances, coal bunkers, instruments, tools, spare pieces, stoves, fuel, &c., complete in all respects, and ready for continuous sea service, on board the vessel, provided it be placed at your command within a certain number of days from the date of the contract, which number of days you will state in your proposal. Second—If the vessel should not be placed at your command within the number of days from date of contract stipulated in your proposal, then you will state the time, in days of twenty-four hours each, from the time you shall be notified that it is at your command, in which you will contract to have the machinery, entirely completed, on board, ready for continuous sea service with all appurtenances, coal bunkers, instruments, tools, spare pieces, stores, fuel, &c., delivered, and all the conditions of the contract fulfilled. The terms of payment will be as follows, namely:—First, when the machinery is complete, set up in the shop and fitted, ready for erection on board the vessel, you will be paid one half the total contract price. Second, at the expiration of the trial trip of ninety-six hours, as stipulated in the contract, provided the requirements of said contract up to that time be fulfilled, you will be paid one-fourth the total contract price, and if said requirements be not fulfilled, such deductions will be made as provided for in the contract. Third, at the expiration of the four months from the time the aforesaid trial trip of ninety-six hours shall terminate, or ought to terminate, you will be paid the third and final payment, which will be the remaining one-fourth of the total contract price, provided that all the stipulations and guarantees on the contract shall have been fulfilled, and in the event of their not being fulfilled such deductions will be made as are provided for in the contract. You will further state the number of gunboats for which you propose to contract the machinery, and in case of your proposing for more than one, the foregoing conditions will apply to each separately. A general drawing of engines and boilers, made to scale, and showing the form and arrangement of all the principal parts, can be examined at the Bureau. A copy of it will be furnished to those with whom a contract is made; but they will be required to make their own working drawings of the detailed parts, and to be responsible for the success thereof. No proposal will be received after the 15th of June.

Accompanying Mr. Lenthall's pronunciamento are specifications of the steam machinery, appurtenances and coal bunkers to be built and erected on board each gunboat; also general directions for building a screw steam gunboat. The length of each boat on the load lines, from the fore side of the rabbet of the stem to aft side of the forward stern post, is to be one hundred and fifty-eight feet. Extreme breadth, twenty-eight feet; hold, from inside of floor timbers to under side of deck plank, amidships, twelve feet. All the materials [illegible] of whatever kind, and in every department, are to be of the very best quality, [illegible] that the vessel shall be complete in every respect [illegible] which are not provided for in this contract, and any omissions there may be in these specifications will not relieve the party of the first part in this contract from furnishing the articles required or the labor to be performed, and no extra bills of any kind are to be presented.

The engine and boiler keelsons are to be placed as may be required for the steam machinery, and the necessary holes cut through the wood for pipes and valves. The contractors for the steam machinery are to be furnished with templets for the steam bracing, and for the composition knees to the steam posts, that they may be placed before the vessel is launched.

BATTLE AT PHILLIPPA, VA.

Rout of the Rebels—Colonel Kelly, of the First Virginia Regiment, Killed.

CINCINNATI, June 3, 1861.

Two columns of troops from General McClelland's command—one under command of Colonel Kelly, of the First Volunteers, and the other under command of Colonel Crittenden, composed of the Indiana Volunteers—left Grafton early last night, and after marching during the entire night about twenty miles through a drenching rain surprised a camp of rebels, 2,000 strong, at Phillippa, Va., and routed them, killing fifteen, and capturing a large amount of arms, horses, amunition, provisions, camp equipage, &c. The surprise was complete, and at the last advices, the federal troops were in hot pursuit of the rebels. It is probable that many prisoners will be taken.

Colonel Kelly was mortally wounded, and has since died. Several others of the federal troops were slightly wounded.

AFFAIRS AT HARPER'S FERRY.

THE NUMBER AND POSITION OF THE REBEL FORCES AT AND AROUND HARPER'S FERRY.

WASHINGTON, June 3, 1861.

A gentleman who was employed by government to visit Harper's Ferry, the Point of Rocks and the surrounding country, with a view of ascertaining as nearly as possible the number of troops, the strength and position of the fortifications, and the number of batteries at those points, has just returned and made his report to government, bringing with him also a map of the country. He was arrested immediately on arriving at the Point of Rocks, and was held as a prisoner for about thirty hours. He played the secession dodge upon them, and proved to the entire satisfaction of the commanding officer that he was an out and out secessionist, who had been driven out of Washington, and was on his way to his native State, Kentucky.

At the Point of Rocks three twelve pound batteries are erected on the Virginia side; on the Maryland side there were one hundred and fifty men stationed as a picket guard. They were just erecting batteries on the Maryland side. The guards took him from there to Harper's Ferry, where he was detained for sometime. Here he ascertained, through several of the soldiers who were in the guard house for various offences, the number and names of the regiments. There are fourteen full regiments at Harper's Ferry and the Point of Rocks.

After he was released he saw several companies arrive without arms. There seemed, he says, to be plenty of arms; for he saw them upon boxes and at once arm those that had just arrived.

At Harper's Ferry they had a large number of heavy batteries planted on all sides, and were busily engaged in constructing others at all the available points where they could be effectively used. He says they asked him a thousand questions as to the number of troops in and about Washington. They wanted to know how many colored regiments there were, and whether most of the soldiers were not Germans and Irish. He told them he saw quite a number of colored people in soldiers clothes, and as to the soldiers, he said he believed they were nearly all foreigners. At this announcement they shouted most vociferously.

My informant says they are perfectly certain of having possession of Washington in about two weeks.

OUR HARRISBURG CORRESPONDENCE.

OUR HARRISBURG CORRESPONDENCE.

HARRISBURG, June 3, 1861.

Guns for Fortress Monroe—Movements of Pennsylvania Troops—Flight of Maryland Rebels—Secession Troops South of the Potomac—Union Men Rallying to the Stars and Stripes—Desertions from the Rebel Camp, &c.

Three regiments of Pennsylvania volunteers passed through here to-day in the direction of Chambersburg. Major General Patterson and staff went by a special train to the same point last evening.

A movement of troops was to have been made to-day over the Franklin Railroad to occupy Hagerstown, Williamsport, Sharpsburg and several other towns surrounding Harper's Ferry. The Maryland rebels are hastening into Virginia, fearing arrest by the federal forces.

Colonel Allen's command, with the exception of a few companies, had moved towards Shepherdstown, Va., where, it is said, there are now two thousand troops. A portion of the party opposite Williamsport attempted to capture a ferry boat at that place, their object being to take it to Falling Waters. The Union men, however, rallied, armed and fired on the rebels, who returned the fire, though immediately retreating. Several were wounded.

On Saturday night, in the vicinity of Sharpsburg, a party of stragglers from Shepherdstown, on a marauding expedition, were attacked by a company of Union men, who had armed in defence of their State, and one man was killed and two wounded.

The Union men are rallying everywhere on the Maryland border, determined that they will repel the traitorous invaders. They are sadly in want of arms and ammunition. Our government should see that these men are supplied, although great discrimination should be made in their distribution to proper persons. There are still many disloyal Marylanders, but this Virginia invasion is lessening their numbers.

FROM HARPER'S FERRY.

I have seen to day gentlemen who left Harper's Ferry yesterday. There is no change in the condition of affairs there. There was no indication of any intention on the part of General Johnston to abandon his position. The defences on all points were completed, and the troops were being daily exercised at the guns and in various skirmishing manoeuvres. The drills in the bayonet exercise, which had been suspended for some days while the men were working at the roads and fortifications, had been resumed.

The traitors have perfect knowledge of the movements of the government forces, and all the men, except the picket guards, have been called in from all points. If the batteries on the Maryland heights are taken, the force on the opposite side of the river will make good their retreat. However, they will find that this will not be such an easy matter, as Major General Patterson will take good care to cut off all communication. The smallpox still claims its victims. Several cases of measles have also occurred. Over one thousand desertions from the rebel army have taken place since the commencement of hostilities. General Johnston says he does not know who to trust. He has lost confidence in his men, and fears that his troops will not stand the fire of the enemy. It is really believed there will not be much fighting at Harper's Ferry. The presence of the federal forces in the vicinity will prevent Maryland sympathizers furnishing food to them, and as they are at best but poorly provisioned, a few days' siege will compel them to evacuate.

General Philip Irwin, of this county, has been appointed a sutler in the United States Army.

A large shipment of heavy gun carriages has been made over the Pennsylvania and Northern Central Railroads for several days past. The carriages are of the most massive description, destined for mounting twenty-four and thirty two pounders. Yesterday two immense columbiads, from Pittsburg, went South, destined for Fortress Monroe. Norfolk must look out for a heavy bombardment.

Hundreds of fugitive slaves are daily escaping over the border into Pennsylvania. Our city is the rendezvous of many of them, but the great majority push on further north.

HARRISBURG, June 1, 1861.

The Attack on Harper's Ferry and Norfolk to be Simultaneous—General Beauregard Not Yet Arrived—A High Negro Insurrection—Nearly Ten Thousand Rebels Under Colonel Schnider—No Provisions—Governor Curtin's Appointments of Military Commissioners, &c.

By this time the rebels at Harper's Ferry are completely surrounded, with the exception of some thirty miles to the south. Unless they can have a chance to escape, troops have been accumulating in large numbers in Chambersburg, and from thence have been dispersed to hold the passes around to Harper's Ferry. [illegible] Norfolk [illegible] fallen back to Harper's Ferry. General Beauregard was expected there, but the redoubtable General will keep out of the dilemma of a capture, which will surely be the fate of the traitors there, and remain at Richmond.

The loyal people of the neighboring towns are awaiting the arrival of the federal forces with gladness, knowing thereby they will be relieved from the reign of terror which has cast such a terrible gloom over their respective communities.

A worthy Virginian informed me to-day that we have no idea of the dark pall that enshrouds every portion of Eastern Virginia. Planters are in constant fear of their lives, slaves are deserting, crops are poor, while only war, with its devastation and horror, stares them in the face.

A feeble attempt at insurrection was made in the vicinity of Winchester on last Sunday night, but the Southern army encamped there soon quieted the affair. Three negroes and a white man, from Massachusetts, it is said, were shot, and sixteen negroes lodged in the jail at that place.

Our informant, who passed through Harper's Ferry, was told by Colonel Johnston that he had 9,500 troops under his command, and expected more daily. Provisions, however, were not in sufficient quantity to maintain that body of men in case of a siege. He had been promised a large supply from the South, but it had not yet arrived. Desertions were numerous, and great trouble is experienced in keeping the disaffected ones there. He confirms my former despatch relative to sending such soldiers into the interior. The smallpox still claims its victims.

The Board of Medical Examiners having concluded their arduous labors, a report will be made in the course of a few days of the successful applicants.

Governor Curtin has appointed Jacob Fry, Jr., of Montgomery county, Benjamin Haywood, of Schuylkill, and Charles F. Abbott, of Philadelphia, commissioners to inquire into the well known frauds and peculations of military stores, clothing, &c. Governor Curtin is determined that this nefarious transaction shall be placed upon the right shoulders, and that he, at least, will be free from any attempt either to defraud the State or cheat those who, in the hour of our nation's peril, have mustered to its aid. The gentlemen named are men in whom the people of this Commonwealth have undoubted confidence, knowing they will present to them no "whitewashed" report of this iniquitous affair, which has been a burning shame upon the good name of the Old Keystone.

The government has taken possession of the Franklin Railroad from Chambersburg to Hagerstown, Md.

IMPORTANT FROM PHILADELPHIA.

OUR PHILADELPHIA CORRESPONDENCE.

PHILADELPHIA, June 1, 1861.

Movements of the Pennsylvania Troops—Their Present Locations—General Patterson and Staff, &c., &c.

For some days there has been great activity in this department. On last Monday Colonel Jarrett's regiment was moved from Lancaster to Perryville, Havre de Grace, and the line of the Philadelphia, Wilmington and Baltimore Railroad, to relieve Colonel Dare, who was ordered to move with his regiment to Chambersburg. Colonel Longnecker, of the Ninth Pennsylvania regiment, was ordered to Newcastle, where he remains, with instructions to be in readiness to move at a moment's notice. The Delaware regiment, under command of General Dupont, is ordered forward on the line of the railroad to relieve a portion of Colonel Dare's regiment. Colonels Owen, Grey and Ballier were ordered, and marched last Wednesday and Thursday from Suffolk Park to Chambersburg, to report to Major General Keim. The First City Troop, Philadelphia cavalry, marched on Thursday to Carlisle, to join Colonel Thomas, of the United States Army, in command of three companies regular cavalry at that place, where they duly arrived, and, with the three companies under Colonel Thomas, moved forward yesterday to Chambersburg and Hagerstown. The five regiments at York have all been pushed forward to Chambersburg, in the neighborhood of which there are now concentrated nine regiments, with two others within reach of co-operation.

To-day General Patterson broke up his headquarters in Philadelphia, and, together with his staff, proceeds to-morrow, at nine A. M., by the Pennsylvania Railroad, to Chambersburg, to assume command. His plan will be to threaten Harper's Ferry, and if possible turn their position. He will then operate on the valley of the Upper Potomac towards Cumberland, to aid in the movements of General McClelland.

The next week will develope the plan of operation, and may be illustrated with the first important battle in the campaign, of which you shall be kept promptly advised.

AFFAIRS IN RICHMOND.

WASHINGTON, June 3, 1861.

A very youthful duel was fought in Richmond a few days ago. Two boys, one aged ten and the other twelve, had a quarrel. A little negro, who had got through his thick skull some of the ideas of chivalry prevalent in that region, told them they had better fight a duel to settle it. To this the boys readily assented. The young darkey measured off the distance, and the boys took their positions. The elder, who was armed with a single barreled pistol, fired first, and missed. The younger had a five shooter. He took more deliberate aim, and hit his antagonist in the side, wounding him so that he died twelve hours afterward. The negro was severely whipped, and so ended the sad affair.

A gentleman just from Richmond reports provisions plenty, and fresh vegetables very cheap there.

CAPTURE OF SECESSION WAR MATERIEL.

ALEXANDRIA, June 3, 1861.

Last night, about one o'clock, suspicious persons were observed prowling about the depot of the Orange and Alexandria Railroad in this city, by the sentinels stationed at that point. The sentinels fired upon them, and they fled. An investigation this morning resulted in the discovery of a carload of gunstocks in the rough, and two cases of superior instruments for the manufacture of gunlocks, valued at several thousand dollars. These were loaded upon a freight train, which had evidently been made up to move South before the capture of the city. The property was seized by order of Col. Heintzelman.

It is supposed the prowlers who were fired upon were secession citizens, lurking about to ascertain the position of this property, and, if possible, secure it.

SECESSIONISM IN MARYLAND.

WASHINGTON, June 3, 1861.

Every day furnishes some new evidences of the existence of a secession undercurrent in the city of Baltimore and throughout Eastern Maryland. It is a well known fact that arms are secreted in large numbers in private houses throughout the State, and in many instances they are sewed up in bedding. The federal authorities should look well to it that nothing of the kind is allowed to pass into Virginia.

The people of Maryland, and especially of Baltimore, forget the fate of Pavia. The people of that city were loyal when Napoleon passed through it to Austria. Believing a false report that he was defeated at Austerlitz, the Pavians rose and destroyed Napoleon's garrison that he left. He returned a conqueror and destroyed the city as he passed. The law of nations recognizes the right of advancing armies to treat as traitors all those who rise in their rear. Let Baltimore take warning.

PREPARATIONS IN THE PACIFIC FOR RECEIVING THE SOUTHERN PRIVATEERS.

WASHINGTON, June 3, 1861.

The Navy Department has received despatches from Captain Ritchie, of the United States steamer Saranac, dated, "Bay of Panama, May 22," in which he says, after acknowledging the receipt of the President's proclamation in regard to pretended letters of marque, "having been notified by the Pacific Mail Steamship Company of the supposed presence of privateers in the Pacific, I had partly anticipated the orders of the department, by directing Commander Bissell, now at Ocapulco, to cruise with the Cayane between that port and Manzanilla, and have also despatched an order to Commander Porter, at San Francisco, to expedite the repairs on the St. Marys, and when in readiness to repair at once to Manzanilla and co-operate with Capt. Bissell in affording protection to the mail steamers along the most exposed line of the coast. By the English mail steamer sailing hence on the 24th inst. I will forward instructions to Capt. [illegible] immediately with the Narragansett to the relief of the Cyane, which (the latter vessel), after recruiting her stores at this port, will be despatched to Callao, and discharge the duties of the Narragansett at that place. Captain Ritchie's last communication states that he proposed to sail from San Francisco with the Wyoming for this port about the first of June. Should I hear, however, of the [illegible] detention of the vessel, I will direct Captain Mitchell to remain with the Wyoming at San Francisco, and afford protection to our interests at that place. In my orders to Commander Bissell I have directed special vigilance to be exercised on the arrival and departure of the mail steamers at the port of Acapulco, and will instruct Captain [illegible]."

THE IRON STEAMER PEERLESS.

[illegible], June 3, 1861.

The iron steamer Peerless, which is supposed to have been purchased [illegible], has been seized at Quebec, at the instance of the [illegible], Consul General.

Read Additional War News on Fifth and Eighth Pages.

The Charleston Daily Courier.

NO. 18,911. CHARLESTON, S. C. .... CONFEDERATE STATES OF AMERICA .... FRIDAY, JULY 19 1861. VOLUME LIX.

THE LATEST NEWS!

BY TELEGRAPH.

[Special Dispatch to the Charleston Courier.]

HIGHLY IMPORTANT FROM RICHMOND.

BATTLE OF BULL'S RUN!

Brilliant Victory of the Troops under General Bonham.

The Enemy Repulsed with Immense Slaughter, and in full Retreat to Alexandria.

Gen. McDowell Commanding the Federalists in person.

Deadly Effect of the Fire of the Washington Artillery.

Gen. Garnett's Opinion of the Georgians.

THE RICH MOUNTAIN BATTLE, ETC., ETC.

RICHMOND, July 18.—Dispatches have been received here, stating that General BONHAM to-day engaged the Federalists in large force—the fight lasting five hours, and repulsed them with great slaughter. The enemy were about ten thousand strong. Gen. MCDOWELL commanded in person. The enemy are retreating to Alexandria. If this is the result of the attack on the outposts simply, what will it be when it comes to the main body?

[SECOND DISPATCH.]

RICHMOND, July 18.—Further intelligence, states that the fight commenced at Bull's Run and continued several hours. The fight becoming general, our troops retired to their entrenchments, according to previous understanding, and repulsed the enemy at every point. The Washington Artillery, it is said, mowed the Federalists down like hail.

The battle covered an area of ten miles, extending from Centreville back.

[THIRD DISPATCH.]

RICHMOND, July 18.—The agent of the Associated Press will give you full particulars of the battle at Rich Mountain. The Georgians fought splendidly. Five hundred of them drove back 1500 of the Federalists at the point of the bayonet. Gen. GARNETT before being killed said it was a feat worthy of veterans.

[FOURTH DISPATCH.]

[FROM THE ASSOCIATED PRESS.]

RICHMOND, July 18.—We are compelled to depend upon passengers for the news. Those who are apparently reliable state that four hundred of Col. HECK's command surrendered, and also four companies of the Georgia Regiment.

The body of Capt. SKIPWITH, of the Powhattan Rifles, killed at Rich Mountain, was brought to the city to-night.

A gentleman from Gov. WISE's Legion states that the Companies were well and cheerful. They have had but few engagements, and always successful.

Gen. MCCLELLAN says that Gen. GARNETT's forces fought so hard and so determined that he felt no disposition to follow, but rather to leave them to their forces.

Apparently reliable advices from Fairfax say that the Federals advanced this morning with ten thousand men. After four hours' fighting, the Federalists were repulsed by seven thousand of the Confederate troops under Gen. BONHAM, with immense slaughter. The Federalists are retreating upon Alexandria.

W. E. STARK, Aid to Gen. GARNETT, who was with him when he fell, has arrived here. He says in the fight Gen. GARNETT lost twenty killed.—Four Georgia companies have two hundred men missing. It is believed they were surrounded and taken prisoners. He says the force retreated in good order and will reach Monterey to-morrow night. In the fight with Col. PEGRAM, forty Confederates were killed and [illegible] hundred taken prisoners. Among the prisoners was Col. PEGRAM.

From Washington.

IMPORTANT MOVEMENTS OF THE FEDERAL COLUMNS—FEDERAL CONGRESSIONAL PROCEEDINGS—THE $[illegible] BILL AUTHORIZING THE PURCHASE OF WAR VESSELS PASSED—WAR CONTRACTS TO BE INVESTIGATED—CONGRESS PETITIONED IN BEHALF OF THE BALTIMORE POLICE COMMISSIONERS.

WASHINGTON, July 17.—Gen. MCDOWELL will advance with his column to-night. Gen. SCOTT and Staff visited the troops on the Virginia side today.

In the House, the Bill to increase the efficiency of the volunteer force has passed.

In the Senate, the Navy Bill has passed.

The Baltimore Police Commissioners, confined in Fort McHenry, have petitioned Congress to interfere in their behalf. Referred to the Judiciary Committee.

The Bill authorizing Secretary WELLES to purchase vessels to suppress piracy, and to complete the blockade, and appropriating three million dollars, has passed.

Resolutions have been adopted, appointing a Committee to investigate all war and navy contracts. VAN WYCK, (Republican,) of New York, said for the past two months there had been a system of plunder going on, which, for audacity and wickedness, has never been surpassed. The resolutions were adopted—yeas 81, nays 32.

REPORTS OF SKIRMISHES IN WESTERN VIRGINIA—IMPORTANT NEWS FROM ARIZONA AND NEW MEXICO—CONFEDERATE AGENT IN MEXICO.

WASHINGTON, July 18.—Col. WOODRUFF attacked the Virginians between Madover and Barbourville, wounding several. One Federalist was killed.

The reserve force at Cumberland now occupy Piedmont and New Creek village. The Southerners attacked them at New Creek village, but were repulsed.

The Third and Fourth Massachusetts Regiments at Fortress Monroe, when their time has expired, will leave for home immediately.

At Grafton the Southerners escaped from Gen. HILL and passed within a mile and a half of his camp.

Reports from Arizona and New Mexico represent the Secession feeling very strong, making it necessary to reinforce Fort Bliss.

It is believed that J. F. PICKETT, late American Consul at Vera Cruz, is the Confederate agent in Mexico.

Later from Washington.

ADVANCE OF THE FEDERAL ARMY—MOVEMENTS OF GEN. McDOWELL AND STAFF—DIVERSION TOWARDS HUNTING CREEK—SUPPOSED OBJECT OF THE DIVERSION TO AVOID MANASSAS JUNCTION—SOUTHERNERS REPORTED FALLING BACK UPON MANASSAS.

WASHINGTON, July 18.—The army has advanced. Gen. MCDOWELL left at 3.30 P. M., to go somewhere. The advance guard is at Hunting Creek, ten miles from Washington.

In Washington it is believed that the design of the Federal Generals is to avoid Manassas. Their positive intention, however, is to allow no delay in pushing on to Richmond.

It is reported that the forces at Aquia Creek, Dumfries and several other points are falling back upon Manassas.

Still Later from Washington.

REPORTED ARRIVAL OF THE ADVANCE GUARD OF THE FEDERALISTS AT FAIRFAX—CONFEDERATES FALLING BACK ON CENTREVILLE.

WASHINGTON, July 18, 2 P. M.—The advance guard reached Fairfax at noon. The Confederate pickets had retired an hour before, falling back on Centreville, where they will probably make a stand.

From Richmond.

HEROIC CONDUCT OF THE GEORGIA REGIMENT UNDER GEN. GARNETT—THE DEATH OF GEN. GARNETT CONFIRMED—AND FOUR GEORGIA COMPANIES TAKEN PRISONERS.

RICHMOND, July 18.—An official communication has been received here, stating that the Georgia Regiment, under Gen. GARNETT, covered themselves with glory.

Another authority says that four Georgia Companies under Captains CRUMP, EVANS, WILLIAMS or WILKINS, and PINCKARD have surrendered, and that Gen. GARNETT has been killed.

From Germantown, Va.

MOVEMENTS OF THE FEDERALISTS—ARRIVAL OF GEN. McDOWELL AND STAFF—CONTEMPLATED ADVANCE ON MANASSAS JUNCTION.

GERMANTOWN, July 18.—TAYLOR's division moved early Wednesday morning, and the Southerners fell back towards Centreville.

At 1.30 P. M., MCDOWELL and Staff arrived.

Four divisions will move towards the Junction on Thursday.

[Germantown is a small village in Fauquier county, Virginia, 95 miles North by West of Richmond.—EDS. COURIER.]

LATER FROM EUROPE.

ARRIVAL OF THE ASIA.

NEW ORLEANS, July 18.—The steam ship *Asia* has arrived from Liverpool, with dates to the 7th inst. She brings $110,000 in specie.

The *Arabia* arrived out on the 7th inst.

LIVERPOOL COTTON MARKET.—The sales of Cotton on Saturday were 12,000 bales, speculators and exporters taking 3000. The market closed steady. Breadstuffs steady and Provisions quiet.

LONDON MONEY MARKET.—Consols 89½@89⅞.

HAVRE COTTON MARKET.—Havre Tres Ordinaire 115, Bas 109, the market buoyant. The sales of the week were 8,000 bales.

From St. Louis.

A TRAIN FIRED INTO—TEN FEDERALISTS WOUNDED—MOVEMENTS OF MAJOR HARRIS WITH THREE THOUSAND MEN—MOVEMENTS OF COL. McNEILL—J. W. TUCKER, THE PATRIOT EDITOR OF THE LATE STATE JOURNAL, ADDRESSING THE PEOPLE OF MISSOURI—REPORTED FIGHT OF FEDERALISTS AND MISSOURIANS AT A POINT THIRTY MILES ABOVE ST. CHARLES—FIGHT STILL PROGRESSING—ANOTHER FIGHT BETWEEN SEDALIA AND GEORGETOWN.

ST. LOUIS, July 17.—A military train was fired into about 12 miles above St. Charles, severely wounding ten Federals. The mail carrier reports that Major HARRIS with 3000 men is 12 miles beyond Fulton. Col. MCNEIL, Federal, was expected to reach Fulton to-night. All the houses along the road are deserted.

J. W. TUCKER is addressing the people throughout the State. Col. STRIFEL, at Alexandria, reports having discovered 200 kegs of powder and machinery for making cannon.

Steamers are prohibited passing Jefferson City unless displaying the American flag.

It is reported that 800 Federals have had an engagement with a few Missourians, number unknown, at a point 30 miles above St. Charles. The Federal loss was 3 killed and 7 wounded. The fight is still progressing.

A Missourian caught with a gun in his hand has been hung. Another attempting to escape was riddled with balls.

ST. LOUIS, July 18.—The Missourians under MAGOFFIN attacked a Federal force between Sedalia and Georgetown, killing 7 and losing 3. MAGOFFIN has 700 men.

BORNSTEIN announces that he will administer no more oaths of allegiance, but keep the suspected parties confined.

From Bunker Hill.

GEN. PATTERSON MOVING ON WINCHESTER WITH TWENTY-ONE THOUSAND MEN.

BUNKER HILL, July 15.—PATTERSON commenced moving on Winchester on Tuesday, and will reach there Tuesday night with a force of 21,000 men. It is supposed that JOHNSTON will skirmish heavily, but not fight a pitched battle.

From Louisville, Ky.

LOUISVILLE, July 15.—Strict search is being made here at the depot. Several trunks were seized last night.

Scarcity of Cotton in the Manufacturing Districts.—A letter from one of the largest manufacturers in the East, received at St. Louis, gives the stock of Cotton in New York, Philadelphia and Baltimore, all told, at about 9000 bales, with no stock of manufactured goods on hand, while the stock in Louisville, Cincinnati and Pittsburg is almost exhausted. The same letter states that the best informed Eastern merchants are of opinion that in sixty days Cotton will be worth twenty cents a pound.

All indications tend to approve the advice, "hold on to your Cotton." A correspondent of the Augusta *Constitutionalist* urges the importance of withholding the Cotton from the seaboard, pending the war:

I would press upon our planters the expediency of retaining their Cotton in the interior as much as possible. By crowding it into the large market towns and seaports, they will subject themselves to an expense and risk which would be unnecessary. Until the blockade of the ports has ceased, or there appears a prospect of its early cessation, there can be no market, or a very limited one. By placing his Cotton in the market towns, the planter will incur the storage and other expenses for a prolonged and indefinite time, or must sell at a sacrifice.

No greater inducement can be offered to the Lincoln Government for an attack upon any city or seaport, or for a continuance of the blockade, than the presence there of a large quantity of Cotton. Cities will be the chief objects of attack next winter, should the war continue; the country, they well know, is unassailable. Place one million bales of Cotton in New Orleans or any other port, and the Federal Government could cheaply afford to expend five millions of dollars and employ an army of one hundred thousand men for the capture of such a prize. If Lincoln's pirates and fillibusters were unable to effect its seizure, his secret incendiaries might effect its destruction. No better bait could be offered to the British and French to continue their non-intervention policy, than for Lincoln's Government to say to them "keep hands off in this quarrel, and when we have captured the ports the Cotton accumulated there shall go out to Liverpool or Havre, as it always has done." Better do this would Seward say, or even help the North, and permit trade to resume its former steady course, than by provoking a war with us, render your supplies precarious, uncertain and liable to capture on their passage across the Atlantic.

With crop stored in cities at a few assailable points, such would be the Northern argument to foreigners—scattered through the country, it would be beyond the reach of the enemy, and Cotton would still be King.

Is it not apparent that it is better that Cotton should be kept in interior towns, accessible to the chief markets in a few days, or, better still, be stored by the planter himself at home until there is a prospect of a revival of trade?

A PLANTER.

The Financial Convention.—The Macon (Ga.) *Journal & Messenger* says:

A correspondent of the Charleston Courier proposes a Mass Convention of the merchants, bankers, rail road presidents, and others of the Confederate States, to assemble at some central point within the Confederacy, (Macon or Atlanta, Ga.,) about the middle of August, for the purpose of devising some plan by which a system of credit may be established between the Confederate States and European countries, which may be used by all who desire it, on the most favorable terms, at the same time to make known to the world our wants and our resources, and materially aid our Government. The suggestion is a good one. It would be well for the business men of the country to meet and interchange views upon financial and commercial topics, and Macon will cordially welcome such a convocation.

Lincolnism Described.—The New York *News* gives a graphic and comprehensive sketch of Lincolnism:

The history of the world cannot furnish a greater accumulation of wrong and outrage, accomplished in so short a period, than has gathered during the brief rule of the present Administration, which promised the nation bread, and gave it a stone; promised a fish, and has bestowed a serpent. It was the cry of hostility to corruption, together with anti-slavery fanaticism, that carried this Administration into power. The change that has been accomplished in four short months has been a change from prosperity to ruin, from wealth to poverty, from Union to disunion, from comparative official honesty to the most flagrant corruption in high places, from peace to all the horrors of civil war, from the reign of law to the unlicensed despotism of the sword and the bayonet. These are a few of the radical changes effected in four months. Let an astonished country say what the Administration will accomplish in four years, if, indeed, the long suffering of an outraged people will tolerate it so long.

The Blockade in the North.—The N. Y. *News* of the 10th, remarks in the review of the markets in provisions:

A slight improvement in business is manifest this week—due, the dealers say, as a reaction to the inactivity immediately succeeding the 4th of July. But, after all, there is no encouragement to producers of staples of an enduring character, and until the present distracted state of national affairs has been succeeded by a period when reason and first principles will be regarded, we expect nothing more than a continuance of inactivity in every branch of domestic enterprize not immediately dependent upon a state of war.

The farmers, early in the season, excited by appearances, and anticipating a large demand for the army worm, planted extra breadths of ground for potatos. What is the consequence? The cause which shut off all other sources of supplying this market also destroyed the home demand, and with an overcrop on the eve of shipment hither, prices have already fallen within a week from $4 to $1.50 per bushel for new Long Island potatos, and with further decline. This rule holds good in other staple articles which are cultivated to an average full extent. The market, judging by the local demand, is amply supplied with everything in season; a short crop is no matter, in the fruit line, for the demand is much shorter, in proportion. The people have no money to spare, and producers must work for peace if they would save prosperity.

Tennessee Cut off from Mail Facilities.—The following notification has been issued:

POSTOFFICE DEPARTMENT, July 10, 1861.

By order of the Postmaster General the entire postal service, embracing the Postoffice routes and route agencies in Middle and West Tennessee, discontinue from and after this date. No mails will hereafter be made up for any office in these districts, until such service shall be restored and notice given, nor will prepaid postage thence be recognized. JOHN A. KASSON, Assistant Postmaster General.

It is the practice in the British army throughout the world for each soldier to frank his own letter, by merely putting on the corner of the envelope "Soldier's letter." This is respected by all the British Postoffices and mails throughout the world as a free frank.

Substitutes for Quinine.

Quinine is, after all, not as scarce as our friends of the North would have it in the South. From all the Southern States we hear of late supplies, and without extraordinary sickness both in camps and through the country, there will be found enough even for those who believe in drugging patients by the wholesale.

It is, nevertheless, interesting to learn the uses and value of any substitute or alterative, and we accordingly invite attention to the following communication from the Pee Dee *Times*:

Editor Pee Dee Times—Dear Sir:—As Quinine is becoming quite a scarce article, I propose the following as a substitute:

Thoroughworth (Eupatorium Perfoliatum) is known also by the following names—Thoroughstem, Cropsworth, Bonesett, and Indian Sage. The first of these names, Thoroughstem, has been imposed upon it from the peculiar structure of the leaves which are opposite, and appears as though the stem was thrust through them.

This plant flourishes in wet meadows, and other moist places. The stalk rises from two to four feet. The flowers are white, and appear in July and August. The leaves at each joint are horizontal, saw-edged and rough, from three to four inches long, and about one inch broad at the base, gradually lessening to a very acute point, of a dark green color.

This plant possesses very active powers, and during my practice I have used it with uncommon advantage in intermittent, remittents, and other diseases of debility. Its medical properties are, emetic, cathartic, diaphoretic and tonic. When used in the form of a warm decoction, a handful of the herb boiled in a quart of water, a wine glass full every two hours, has proved peculiarly beneficial in fevers, by exciting a copious perspiration. In doses oftener repeated, say every ten or fifteen minutes, it acts as an emetic.

The dried leaves in powder, in doses of twelve to twenty grains, operate gently on the bowels; by adding a little Epsom salts to the decoction, makes an excellent cathartic. The flowers, as a tonic bitter, are deemed equal to the bark of the Dogwood, and is a good substitute for Quinine in these scarce times. A wine glass of the juice of the green herb drank every hour, is celebrated as a certain cure for the bite of a rattle-snake. The bruised leaves should be applied to the part. S.

The plant above mentioned has long been known and esteemed in many portions of our State. The Dogwood (*Cornus Florida*) has also been substituted or preferred in some sections for autumnal and intermittent fevers. We believe with many observers that the *Materia Medica* of any well marked and defined region of country, has ample remedies for all the diseases of that region; and many believe that diseases would not be more frequent or fatal even under a diminished supply of medicines.

A Calm Appeal.

We will gratify many readers in giving in full the opening General Order of Major General POLK, the first prelate of the South who has accepted the position of a General. The clergy of all orders, and of all branches of the Church, are with us, and many are in the field; and the "best of all is, God is with us," as we humbly, yet confidently, believe.

The appeal of Gen. POLK is calm and worthy of the Christian Pastor and Prelate, as well as the General.

GENERAL ORDER NO. 1.

HEADQUARTERS DIVISION NO. 2, }
MEMPHIS, July 13, 1861. }

Having been assigned to the charge of the defence of that part of the valley of the Mississippi which is embraced within the boundaries of Division No. 2, I hereby assume command. All officers on duty within the limits will report accordingly.

In assuming this very grave responsibility, the General in command is constrained to declare his deep and long settled conviction that the war in which we are engaged is one not warranted by reason or any necessity, political or social, of our existing condition, but that it is indefensible and of unparalleled atrocity. We have protested, and do protest, that all we desire is to be let alone, to repose in quietness under our own vine and our own fig tree. We have sought, and only sought, the undisturbed enjoyment of the inherent and the indefeasible right of self-government—a right which freemen can never relinquish, and which none but tyrants could ever seek to wrest from us. Those with whom we have been lately associated in the bonds of a pretended fraternity have wished and endeavored to deprive us of this our great birth-right as American citizens. Nor is this all. They have sought to deprive us of this inestimable right by a merciless war, which can attain no other possible end than the ruin of fortunes and the destruction of lives; for the subjugation of christian freemen is out of the question. A war which has thus no motive except lust or hate, and no object except ruin and devastation, under the shallow pretence of a restoration of the Union, is surely a war against heaven, as well as a war against earth. Of all the absurdities ever enacted, of all the hypocricies ever practiced, an attempt to restore a union of minds, and hearts, and wills, like that which once existed in North America, by the ravages of fire and sword, are assuredly among the most prodigious.

As sure as there is a righteous ruler of the universe, such a war must end in disaster to those by whom it was inaugurated, and by whom it is now prosecuted with circumstances of barbarity which it was fondly believed would never more disgrace the annals of a civilized people. Numbers may be against us, but the battle is not always to the strong. Justice will triumph. And an earnest of this triumph we already behold in the mighty uprising of the whole Southern heart. Almost as one man this great section comes to the rescue, resolved to perish rather than yield to the oppressor, who, in the name of freedom, yet under the prime inspiration of an infidel horde, seeks to reduce eight millions of freemen to abject bondage and subjection. All ages and all conditions are united in the one grand and holy purpose of rolling back the desolating tides of invasion, and of restoring to the people of the South that peace, independence and right of self-government to which they are by nature and nature's God as justly entitled as those who seek thus ruthlessly to enslave them.

The General in command having the strongest confidence in the intelligence and firmness of purpose of those belonging to his department, enjoins upon them the maintenance of a calm, patient, persistent and undaunted determination to resist the invasion at all hazards and to the last extremity. It comes bringing with it a contempt for constitutional liberty, and the withering influence of the infidelity of New England and Germany combined. Its success would deprive us of a future.

The best men among our invaders opposed the course they are pursuing at the first, but they have been overborne and swept into the wake of the prevailing current, and now, under the promptings of their fears, or the delusion of some idolatrous reverence due to a favorite symbol, are as active as any in instigating this unnatural, unchristian and cruel war.

Our protests, which we here solemnly repeat in the face of the civilized world, have been hitherto unheeded. We are left alone under God to the resources of our own minds and our own hearts—to the resources of our manhood.

Upon his knowing as he does those whom he addresses, as well as those with whom you are co-operating throughout the South, the General in command feels we may rely with unwavering confidence. Let every man then throughout the land arm himself in the most effective manner, and hold himself in readiness to support the combined resistance. A cause which has for its object nothing less than the security of civil liberty and the preservation of the purity of religious truth, is the cause of heaven, and may well challenge the homage and service of the patriot and the Christian.

In God is our trust. LEONIDAS POLK, Major General P. A. C. S., Commanding.

Gen. Patterson.—The Wilmington (N. C.) *Journal* furnishes the annexed account of this hero of the Federal armies:

This rival of Napoleon is considerable on a dress parade, but his health is so seriously affected at the approach of a battle that he has always found himself unable to participate in such amusements. It must be said of him, however, that he has a keen eye to the commissariat. He is a good business man, and made much money in Mexico, as follows: During the Mexican war Gen. Patterson was for a good while placed in command of the department of the Rio Grande. A great many improper persons from the States were smuggling things into that department, selling them to the troops and probably also to the Mexicans. The General most virtuously prohibited all this—he would have nothing of that kind going on, so he issued an order prohibiting any traders bringing any more goods in. The point of the joke was that the house of which the General was a partner had already got in all the goods they wanted, and by the order prohibiting any more coming in, of course Patterson's house had a monopoly, charged their own prices, and made several hundred thousand dollars; some put the profit by this rather queer transaction at half a million.

Starvation Approaching.—The following call appears in the New York papers of the 11th inst.:

Public Meeting, Twenty-First Ward.—The undersigned respectfully invite their fellow citizens to meet at No. 466 Fourth Avenue, on Thursday evening, July 11, at 8 o'clock, to consider what action may be necessary to protect from starvation the families of our patriotic volunteers resident in the Twenty-first Ward.

Gardiner Spring, D. D., Pastor Brick Church.
J. P. Thompson, D. D., Pastor Broadway Tabernacle.
John Kelly, Sheriff City of New York.
Stephen T. Russell, Public Administrator.
A. V. Stout, President Shoe and Leather Bank.
John H. Sherwood.
Benjamin B. Atterbury.
W. H. Hoople.
Andre Froment, Alderman Twenty-first Ward.
Alexander Brandon, Councilman Seventh District.
Charles C. Pinckney, Councilman Seventh District.

Capt. Russell's Opinion.—W. S. writes from Washington to the N. Y. *Times*:

You were aware that Capt. Russel, of the French Navy, had been appointed by Napoleon to make a tour of the States North and South, with a view to reporting on the military *status* and resources of the two sections. He has just returned from a month's sojourn in the South. His comparative view of the two sides I have been able to learn is as follows: the Northern elements are greatly the superior both in quantity and quality, but the Southern forces are much our superior in military *organization* and in artillery! Capt. Russel, I may say, is no partisan of the insurgents, as he has been represented; on the contrary, he sympathizes wholly and heartily with the North. His conclusion accordingly is worth laying to heart—*we are deficient in a comprehensive scheme of military organization!* Throughout the whole North the confidence of the people in "the greatest captain of the age" is unbounded; but they will anxiously look to Gen. Scott that he immediately see to it that the cause, if it exists, of the reproach of the French officer be removed.

CITY INTELLIGENCE.

MEETING OF OFFICERS OF THE FOURTH BRIGADE.—At a meeting of the officers of the Fourth Brigade South Carolina Militia, held on Wednesday evening, two Committees were appointed—one to report a plan for the more thorough organization of the Brigade, and one to nominate a candidate for the office of Brigadier-General made vacant by the resignation of Gen. JAMES SIMONS.

PARADE OF THE PHŒNIX FIRE ENGINE COMPANY.—This fine and efficient Company passed our office on parade yesterday, numbering between fifty and sixty members. They made as usual a very handsome display. In the evening the members with their invited guests partook of an excellent supper.

A CAUTION.—Yesterday morning a gentleman had a severe fall, occasioned by treading on a piece of watermelon rind, which no doubt had been thrown carelessly on the side walk. There have been several cases of a similar character within the last week, and we have heard of complaints being made, but very little notice seems to have been taken of them. As there is a law against such practices, it should be rigidly enforced.

AT AN ELECTION held at Circular Church July 15th, for First and Second Lieutenants and Cornet, also Orderly Sergeant of the Charleston Light Dragoons, the following gentlemen were unanimously elected:

R. H. COLCOCK, First Lieutenant.
WM. DISHER, Second Lieutenant.
J. W. O'HEAR, Cornet.
C. C. NOWELL, Orderly Sergeant.

DR. REENSTJERNA, a great part of whose life has been spent in the most celebrated hospitals of Europe, offers his professional services in quality of Physician and Surgeon. See diploma and testimonials in his Office, 168 King-street.

N. B.—All secret diseases are cured certainly and with dispatch, according to a new method lately introduced in some Hospitals of France.

EDISTO RIFLES.—All letters and packages intended for the members of this company will be forwarded to Morris' Island, if left at the Office of the Quartermaster-General, or at Messrs. E. H. RODGERS & Co's.

TWO DAYS LATER FROM EUROPE.

ARRIVAL OF THE CANADA AT HALIFAX.

HALIFAX, Wednesday, July 17, 1861.

The R. M. Steam Ship Canada, from Liverpool at 10 A. M. of Saturday, the 29th ult., via Queenstown evening of the 30th, arrived here at 2.30 P. M. She has 36 passengers, and $516,000 specie for Boston.

The R. M. steam ship Australasian, from New York, arrived at Queenstown at 9 P. M. of the 28th.

Great Britain.—In the House of Lords, on the 27th, the new Lord Chancellor took his seat, under the title of Lord Westbury.

In the House of Commons the same evening, Mr. Berkely asked whether the Government recognized the right of New Granada or the Granadian Confederation to close or blockade certain ports. Lord John Russell replied that in the case of rebellion the Government had a right to close the ports, but if in case of civil war the ports were *de facto* occupied by the insurgents, they could not take that step according to international law. The British naval commander would not, therefore, recognize the right of closing of ports.

Lord C. Paget announced that the Admiralty survey of the Great Eastern was most satisfactory, and though it was not usual, the Government had no objection to publish the report.

The Times announces the following lay changes, in consequence of Sir Richard Bethel's appointment to the Chancellorship: Roundell Palmer, Attorney General; Sir William Atherton accepts the Judgeship; and the Solicitor Generalship will be conferred on one of the lawyers in the House of Commons.

Blondin was performing his tight rope wonders in Liverpool before immense crowds.

Advices from Jamaica mention that the Jamaica Cotton Company had commenced planting operations in the Eastern part of the Island.

France.—It was stated that Marshal Niel was about to proceed to Turin to notify officially the Italian Government of the recognition of the new Kingdom by France.

The Corps Legislatif was prorogued on the 27th. Count Morney, in his closing speech, congratulated the members on having appreciated the new privileges granted them in the Senate.

Two bills were passed, establishing postal services with India, China, and with the West Indies and the United States.

The annual subvention to the lines from France to New York, and West Indies and branches, is £372,000 sterling, but from it is to be deducted £37,000 sterling, to be paid by the Company yearly in discharge of the loan advanced by the State of £920,000 to start the Company. From 50° North to the Equator, from Newfoundland to the Amazon, there is not a port of commercial importance which the steamers will not communicate with. Branches to Mexico and New Orleans are to be optional. The Government reserves the right of extending the service beyond the Isthmus of Panama into the Pacific; the French port ultimately to be Brest.

The case of Patterson *vs.* Bonaparte was continued on the 28th. The Procurator-General concluded his speech in favor of the judgment pronounced by the first tribunal.

The legal proceedings against the Duke of Broglie for his work entitled "Views on the Government of France" had been stopped, and the copies seized were to be restored.

The Bourse was quiet; Rentes closing 67f. 75c.

Latest News by the Canada.—Halifax, Wednesday, July 10.—The steam ship Canada sailed at half-past six. She was detained off the harbor by fog for two hours.

The Berlin papers published a dispatch recently addressed by Baron Schlenitz to the Prussian Minister at Washington, in which the warmest sympathy with the welfare of the Union, and the deepest regret for the unfortunate discord is expressed.

Baron Geroet is instructed to discuss the important question of the treatment to neutral ships with the American Government in a friendly and open manner. The course which Prussia most desires to see adopted is a declaration of adversion to the Paris agreement of 1856. Should this be unattainable, Prussia would, for the present, content herself with a binding declaration that America would, for the duration of the present civil war, with respect to neutral shipping, adopt principles two and three of the Paris document, namely, that a neutral flag covers the enemy's property, with the exception of contraband of war, and that neutral property under a hostile flag with the same exception is inviolate.

Commercial Intelligence by the Canada.

LIVERPOOL BREADSTUFFS MARKET.—The weather has been favorable for the crops. Messrs. Richardson, Spence & Co., and Wakefield, Nash & Co. report Flour dull and freely offered at 24s. 6d.@28s. for American. Wheat steady: Red, 10s. 6d.@12s.; white, 12s.@14s. Corn dull; Mixed, 28s.@28s. 6d.; Yellow 28s. 6d.@28s. 9d.; White, 29s. 6d.@31s. 6d.

LIVERPOOL PRODUCE MARKET.—The same authorities report: Beef quiet. Pork difficult to sell. Lard dull at 50s.@51s. for choice.

The Brokers' Circular reports: Rosin dull at 4s. 4d.@6s. 5d for common. Spirits Turpentine dull at 43s. 6d. Sugar steady. Coffee firm and partially slightly advanced. Rice heavy.

LONDON MARKETS.—Baring's Circular reports Wheat dull and 1s.@2s. lower: White, 50s.@60s.; Red, 52s.@58s. Flour dull and 6d.@1s. lower; sales at 28s.@28s. 6d. Iron dull at £5 2s. 6d. for both rails and bars; Pig dull at 49s. Sugar dull, and quotations barely maintained. Tea dull at 11d.@11½d. for common Congou. Coffee steady. Rice quiet. Spirits Turpentine dull and offered at 43s.

LONDON MONEY MARKET.—Funds are dull and gloomy, but the fluctuations are unimportant. The demand for money had become extremely heavy, owing to the close of half the year. Six per cent. was liberally demanded. The West India mail steamer had arrived with £127,000 in specie.

Large instalments of the Chinese indemnity were paid into the Government Bank, at Canton, on the 23d of April.

LONDON MONEY MARKET.—Baring's Circular quotes Bar Silver nominal at 5s. 1½d.; Dollars 4s. 10⅝d.; Eagles nominal at 78s.

AMERICAN SECURITIES.—Baring Brothers report the market for American Securities unchanged. They quote United States Fives 70@72½ ex dividend; Illinois Central Shares 39@40 9¼ discount; Erie Shares 21@21½; New York Central Shares 68@70.

LIVERPOOL, JUNE 30.—Latest via Queenstown.—Cotton.—Sales Saturday 15,000 bales, including 8000 to speculators and exporters. The market closed with an advancing tendency at the full prices of Friday. Breadstuffs quiet. Provisions dull.

LONDON, JUNE 29.—Consols closed at [illegible]. Sales of Illinois Central Shares at [illegible] discount. Erie Shares 21@21¼.

HAVRE MARKET.—Cotton.—Sales of the week 9000 bales. The market opened dull, but closed active, with an advancing tendency. New Orleans Tres Ordinaire 111f; [illegible]. Stock 315,000 bales.

The Crops in Chicot County, Ark.—The Lake Village Press, of the 4th inst., says:

During the past week we have been blessed with copious rains. The corn crop is now a certain success; the yield being unprecedented in this county. Cotton looks promising and will be a good average crop. We are glad to state that those plantations on Lake Chicot which suffered so much from overflow, have been replanted in corn and cotton, and, if the weather is favorable, will give a satisfactory yield. The corn thus replanted has not suffered, so far as we learn, from the worm which overflows usually generate.

Crops in Louisiana.—The Homer (Claiborne Parish) Advocate of the 3d inst., says:

The generous showers which have blessed our Parish for the last few days, and in fact throughout the present season, have made our corn, oats, rye and wheat crops abundant beyond all precedent. Many of our planters tell us now that they will make corn enough this season to last them two years, and the oat crop is considered sufficient for feeding purposes for the next twelve months. We have any quantity of the finest fruit of every variety. Our Cotton crop was never more promising at this season of the year.

The Mount Lebanon (Bienville Parish) Baptist, of the 4th, says:

We have had bountiful rains during the last week and, the prospects for crops were never brighter.

Manufacture of Small Arms.—We have been informed that arrangements are being made to commence the manufacture of small arms in Athens, Ga. This is commendable, and should be imitated elsewhere. The machine shops of Augusta might engage in the work with profit.

Muskets and rifles are more needed than any other species of fire arms at present, and we have no doubt that the demand would equal the supply that could be furnished here. We hope that the subject will meet with the attention which it deserves, and that our machinists and gunsmiths will follow the example of those of Athens.—*Augusta Constitutionalist.*

Col. Blanton Duncan.—This gallant officer, finding no way of celebrating his birthday by a great fight with the enemy, determined that the day should not pass without in some way contributing to the great cause of Southern Independence. As a substantial evidence of his devotion to the cause, he sent a check of five hundred dollars to the Secretary of the Treasury.—*Richmond Whig.*

[FOR THE COURIER.]

War Finance.

NO. 1.

If success in war at the present day is based as much upon the skill of the financier as that of the strategist, in consideration of the interest involved in the present struggle, the matter of Southern finance rises to a magnitude truly colossal. It is, therefore, not surprising that the subject of the "Produce Loan" now before the country should be a matter of considerable discussion in the public prints. As far as we have information there are but three plans submitted to the people.

The first scheme is that proposed by the Government, a plan, according to the recent speech of Mr. STEPHENS, that succeeds only by the prompt sale of the incoming crop. The following objections to this plan are suggested: 1. Previous to the sale of the crop the possibility of Government succeeding in providing for its war expenditure rests upon a problematical and insecure basis. 2. The Government in its financial interests becomes too intimately identified with the prompt sale of Cotton. 3. It holds out to foreign Governments an invitation to play upon the necessities of the South in the management of their diplomacy. 4. The circulating medium by this scheme is not increased to proportions adequate to the present wants of the South, and thereby the industrial and mercantile pursuits will be checked in growth and efficiency. 5. The price of Cotton is endangered, inasmuch as for some time to come the importation of foreign goods is not likely to be equal to the purchase of the crop, and the exchange being thus against Europe should the importations fall off to a low figure, it is a question whether Europe could provide the requisite amount of gold without great damage to their financial operations at home. The consumption must necessarily be checked, and the supply exceeding the demand, the price of Cotton must go down.

The next scheme is, that the Banks should lend the Government a certain amount, according to their capital, and they (the Banks) pay said loan in their notes endorsed by Government. Against an unlimited issue of this paper, a wholesome check is provided, by the Banks not being able to issue more than the amount of their loan. The dangers connected with this scheme are patent. For the industrial and mercantile interests will need all the Bank circulation, which, although restricted, would be still in excess of the specie forming its basis—and the endorsed notes resting principally upon the credit of the Government, depreciation of the regular Bank issue would be highly probable.

The remaining scheme, (and we believe by far the most dangerous of the three,) is, that the Government should buy out and out from the planter the whole crop, and pay therefor in Treasury Notes—the object being principally, that the Government be possessed with the political power of the crop. When Governments are found to have souls, this plan might be ventured upon, but not until then. The objections to this scheme are on the surface.

1. The Government, instead of being an agent of the people for a *specific purpose*, and that purpose *alone*, would become the owner of property that should never be held by any but the producer, and pass into the hands of the consumer, through the media of regular trade, which are regulated by the healthful influences of unrestricted supply and demand.

2. The sale of the crops being placed in the hands of the Government, a dangerous patronage would certainly exist, or to say the least, suspicion and jealousy on the part of the mercantile community connected with the regular path of the crop, would be very probable, and the harmony of the South be thus jeopardized.

3. There is no certainty that the bulk of Treasury notes passed directly into the hands of the planter would find their way into general circulation, but that a large proportion would be locked up as a secure investment, and instead of safe and ample currency being provided for the South, at the simple option of the planter Treasury notes could be transmuted into the condition of bonds.

4. Large quantities of Treasury notes would be precipitated upon the community at once, and not issued according to the actual needs of the Government, and interest would be paid upon money not required by it.

5. The planter would cease to have a personal interest in the safety of the Cotton while in his charge, or in its safe and economical transmission to market when going forward; and further, the risk of loss by fire would be thrown upon the Government, and not where it legitimately belongs.

The leading object aimed at in this scheme can be easily attained by a way not so fraught with evils. If the Government for the time being desires to have the control of the crop for political purposes, a simple bill passed by Congress locks effectually every bale within the confines of the South, nor could a single pound pass the border without its direct sanction.

Let us now set forth the circumstances with which the South is surrounded.

The Confederate States need money for the successful prosecution of the war. Whatever safe scheme may be adopted during the war for the raising the necessary funds, it must result in the Government being in debt at the close of the struggle to the extent of the cost of maintaining it (we assume that the civil list will absorb resources from all other quarters). Direct taxation must be avoided, inasmuch as all monies withdrawn by this means must tend to cripple the industrial pursuits that are of vital importance to the cause of Southern independence. Nor can it be desired that this debt should be diminished by any appreciation in value of the produce loaned, for in proportion to the probability of this source of gain, so must be the likelihood of a possible depreciation and loss. The Government should not then entertain a scheme that contains the least element of speculation, but simply face a future debt in all its legitimate proportions.

If in the fall the Cotton crop should go *promptly* forward, (peace or independence having been attained,) the war expenditure could be easily provided for. But while this is exceedingly improbable, it must be confessed that not a few persons look with no little dread to the Government becoming too much identified in interest with the early movement of Cotton, or that Europe should presume to adopt a policy that would play upon Government's necessities, or that Southerners should fight their foes with British gold—the proceeds of shipments made, not in the regular course of trade between equals, but by the arrival of Cotton ships, entering Southern harbors by *permission* of the Northern despot. In order, then, to avoid the dangers in this direction, it behooves the South to at once provide for the war expenditure, while the Cotton crop *remains unsold*. Indeed, it is highly probable that the moral effect of the making known to the Governments of Europe that a system of finance had been adopted, rendering the Confederate States independent of the revenue derived by the sale of the incoming crop, the tortuous course of diplomacy would at once give way to a prompt recognition not only of the Confederacy as a nation, but of the Southern States as a power among the kingdoms of the earth, not to be trifled with or menaced.

The conclusion of this article is reserved for the issue of to morrow, in which a scheme will be submitted which, it is hoped, if it does not meet in great measure the exigency of the times, will at least prove suggestive, and thus assist in paving the way to Southern independence. J.

[FOR THE COURIER.]

Messrs. Editors:—In your paper of Thursday you ask to be informed as to what use can be made of the Sumah, so common in the Southern country! This question surprises me not a little, having taken it for granted that every man, woman and child, black and white, knew and has known ever since they knew any thing, that the Shumach berry is a regular article of commerce between South America and the United States, and is the only article except tar used in the manufactory of shoe maker's wax. It is prepared by boiling the berry to glue or wax, and then strain the berries out and mix the glue or wax with tar or pure rosin. Thirty years ago I could have given you all the minutiæ of making and preparing it for use, having often made it, both for sale and home use, as a country urchin of town. I have no doubt all our country people know all about it; if they do not it is high time they did. Its very name indicates its use.

[We asked for information concerning the "uses and varieties" of the Sumac. Our correspondent has mentioned one use, and given his account of the origin of the name. Others may report other uses.—EDS. COURIER.]

The Double-barrel Shot Gun with the Sword Bayonet.—Messrs. Haiman & Bro., of this city, have shown us a double barrel gun with the sword bayonet attached—the latter an invention and application of their own. The method of attachment is simple, strong and cheap, and, thus provided, we consider the ordinary shot gun the most effective weapon that can be carried to the field. [*Columbus (Ga.) Times.*

Patriotism of the Blacks.—Two of Mr. Bauknight's negro carpenters, who have been at work on our premises during the last two weeks, gave, without solicitation, half their rations for the support of the Volunteer Companies recently encamped at this place. They seemed to comprehend the fact that the war in which our Volunteers are to engage is one in which their interests are specially involved, and rightly regard our soldiers as their best friends.—*Ocala (Fla.) Companion.*

The Flags of Truce with Rebels—To the Editor of the Herald—New York, July 10, 1861.—What means this "flag of truce" business? If the Southern States are in rebellion, let them be treated as rebels. By giving them rights with a flag of truce we treat them as "belligerents," while we abuse European Powers for acting towards them in a manner we set the example of. If rebels and traitors, give them no such rights as belong to nations only at war with one another. S. D.

We have been assured by friends of Major Gen. Patterson that, in retreating back across the Potomac after he first entered Virginia, and in leaving the Baltimore and Ohio Rail Road for so long a time in the hands of the rebels, he simply obeyed orders from Washington. If this be so, he has been unjustly blamed; but we had previously supposed the facts to be otherwise. [*N. Y. Tribune, 11th inst.*

The Army Wagons.—It is doubtful whether Col. Meigs' thousand wagons will be finished by the 15th.

The Dinner Party at Gen. Scott's.—The denial in the New York Times of yesterday of the dinner party at Gen. Scott's was not merely a fabrication, but a declaration which might be characterised by a word of one syllable. Mr. Crittenden did dine there in the company stated by us to have been present.—*N. Y. Tribune, 11th instant.*

In Charlotte, Michigan, a woman, with a pipe in her mouth, went to answer a knock, when the door was pushed violently open, her pipe stem driven an inch into her throat, and [illegible]

IMPORTANT OPINION.

INTERCOURSE IN WAR.

THE DUTIES OF CITIZENS.

CHARLESTON, July 12, 1861.

Hon. I. W. Hayne, Attorney General:

DEAR SIR:—I would, as a citizen, ask your opinion on the following questions, viz.:

1st. Is it legal, according to the laws of our Confederacy, for houses in the Confederacy to be connected with individuals, or houses in the enemy's territory, those houses in the enemy's territory being composed of Southern men even?

2d. Is it lawful for houses in the Confederacy to sell any article to houses or individuals in the enemy's country?

3d. Is it lawful for houses in the Southern Confederacy to buy any articles of, or in any wise trade or traffic, with houses or individuals in the enemy's country? Very respectfully, S. WYATT.

OFFICE OF ATTORNEY-GENERAL, }
Charleston, S. C., July 16, 1861. }

To S. Wyatt, Esq.:

SIR:—You ask my opinion in reply to the three following queries, viz:

"1. Is it legal, according to the laws of our Confederacy, for houses in the Confederacy to be connected with individuals or houses in the enemy's territory, those houses in the enemy's territory being composed of Southern men even?

"2. Is it lawful for houses in the Confederacy to sell any article to houses or individuals in the enemy's country?

"3. Is it lawful for houses in the Southern Confederacy to buy any articles of, or in any wise trade or traffic, with houses or individuals in the enemy's country?"

The subject matter of enquiry has relation to a supposed violation of the laws of the Confederate States, and is not within the jurisdiction of the State Courts. I shall not, therefore, undertake to reply officially as Attorney-General, but as a lawyer I do not hesitate to answer all three questions in the negative. Any trading, any dealing, any intercourse, any correspondence whatever, kept up with any citizen of the enemy's country without the permission of our own Government, is illegal, and in violation of our duty as citizens of a belligerent power.

I refer you, however, for a full exposition of the law on this interesting subject to an opinion given by my partner C. Richardson Miles, Esq., who has been consulted as the acting District Attorney representing the Confederate States. I concur fully in the views presented by him in his letter of this date, addressed to Messrs. Aveilhé, Hopkins and Edgerton.

Very respectfully, your obedient servant, I. W. HAYNE, Attorney-General.

CHARLESTON, July 13, 1861.

C. Richardson Miles, Esq., Acting Confederate States Attorney for South Carolina:

DEAR SIR:—We, the undersigned, citizens of Charleston, desire to know whether the private transmission of mail matter between the citizens of the Confederate States and the United States is unlawful. And if so, what is the penalty, and what is the mode of procedure in such case to bring the offenders to punishment?

If not objectionable to you, we should like to publish your reply for the information and future guidance of our fellow citizens.

Your obedient servants,

(Signed) P. A. AVEILHÉ, JR., J. WARD HOPKINS, SAM. F. EDGERTON.

OFFICE C. S. DISTRICT ATTORNEY, }
Charleston, July 17, 1861. }

To Messrs. P. A. Aveilhé, Jr., J. Ward Hopkins and Saml. F. Edgerton:

GENTLEMEN:—I have received your communication asking my opinion, whether the private transportation of mail matter between the citizens of the Confederate States and of the United States, is unlawful; and if so, what is the penalty for the offence, and what is the mode to be pursued to bring the offenders to punishment.

As the questions submitted are novel ones to most of our citizens, and as the principles upon which they are to be decided involve many other cases which may arise, it is necessary for a satisfactory reply, that I should treat the matter at some length.

It is very difficult for those who have grown up in a state of peace, interrupted in this generation by only two short wars, with foreign nations, to realize the momentous and extensive consequences which follow from a state of war. And it is especially difficult, and seemingly almost impossible, for our people, hitherto bound to the citizens of the United States by such close social and business ties, to realize the absolute sundering of those ties, which necessarily follows a war between the two countries.

War, however, is not a matter between Governments in their political character merely; it affects every citizen of both countries. As soon as the Government, which is the acknowledged agent of the public will, has declared war, it is a war between all the individuals of the one and all the individuals of which the other nation is composed, irrespective of the ties of blood, and of social, political or business affinities.

It follows from this universal hostility, which is the necessary incident of war, not only, that the Government has a right to deal with the persons and property of the enemy which shall fall into its power, in such manner as it shall deem best for the interest of the whole, upon an enlarged view of policy and expediency—imprisoning their persons, and confiscating their property and debts, if it shall deem it expedient to do so—but also that all relations, other than those of hostility, between the subjects of the belligerent countries, must entirely cease.

This principle of international law has not only been laid down by every writer on the subject, but has been acknowledged and fully acted upon by every civilized nation of the world.

Accordingly, we find that the Courts of all countries have applied the rule to every variety of case which has arisen out of the complicated relations of commerce, with rigid inflexibility, and every endeavor to evade its requirements has been exposed and defeated.

It has been repeatedly decided that mercantile partnerships with residents of the enemy's country, are dissolved by the mere act of war; that every attempt to carry on trade with the enemy by the intervention of third persons, is unlawful; and no artifice has succeeded in legalizing the trade without the express license of the Government; that all contracts made with the enemy during the war are void, and the remittance of money to the citizens of the enemy, directly or indirectly, is a dangerous and illegal act. But further than this, it has been universally held by the Courts of England and the United States, that it is unlawful for the citizens of a belligerent country to withdraw their own money or property from the enemy's country, after the commencement of the war, except upon the express license of the Government. And this is on the ground that all intercourse and communication whatever between the citizens of the respective belligerent nations is unlawful, as tending to defeat the objects of the war.

It is obvious that it cannot be left to individuals to judge of the propriety of making exceptions to the general rule, upon the ground either of personal convenience or necessity, or of public policy. To allow this would at once give rise to the most dangerous consequences, and, in fact, would amount to an abolition of the rule. Nor can the citizen justly complain of the stringency of the rule, because, not only is he bound to sacrifice his individual interest to the public good, and his individual judgment to the public will, but, in cases which really constitute an exception, the Government which has declared war can relax its operation in the particular case, and can grant a special license to hold the communication which is desired, if compatible with the public good.

But as this is a question upon which the ablest jurists of England and America have written, it will be much more satisfactory, and will afford a much more certain guide for the conduct of our citizens, if I quote a few passages from their writings on this subject.

Chancellor Kent, in his Commentaries on the Law of Nations, says:

"One of the immediate and important consequences of the declaration of war, is the absolute interruption and interdiction of all commercial correspondence, intercourse, and dealing between the subjects of the two countries.

"Trading supposes the existence of civil contracts and relations and a reference to courts of justice, and it is therefore necessarily contradictory to a state of war. It affords aid to the enemy in an effectual manner, by enabling the merchants of the enemy's country to support their Government, and it facilitates the means of conveying intelligence and carrying on a traitorous correspondence with the enemy. These considerations apply with peculiar force to maritime States, where the principal object is to destroy the marine and commerce of the enemy, in order to force them to peace. It is a well settled doctrine in the English Courts, and with the English jurists, that there cannot exist at the same time a war for arms and a peace for commerce. The war puts an end at once to all dealing and all communication with each other, and places every individual of the respective Governments, as well as the Governments themselves, in a state of hostility. * * * *

"It follows as a necessary consequence of the doctrine of the illegality of all intercourse or traffic, without express permission, that all contracts with the enemy made during war are utterly void. The insurance of enemy's property is an illegal contract, because it is a species of trade and intercourse with the enemy. The drawing of a bill of exchange by an alien enemy, on a subject of the adverse country, is an illegal and void contract, because it is a communication and contract. The purchase of bills in the enemy's country, or the remission and deposit of funds there is a dangerous and illegal act, because it may be cherishing the resources and relieving the wants of the enemy. The remission of funds in money or bills to subjects of the enemy is unlawful. The inhibition reaches to every communication direct or circuitous.

"All endeavors at trade with the enemy, by the intervention of third persons, or by partnerships, have equally failed, and no artifice has succeeded to legalize the trade without the express permission of the Government. Every relaxation of the rule tends to corrupt the allegiance of the subject, and prevents the war from fulfilling its end." 1 Kent, 66.

Sir William Scott, whose decisions, equally distinguished for their learning, searching acumen, and for felicity of expression and eloquence of style, have been as much quoted and respected in America as in England, says:

"The sovereign alone who has the power of entirely removing the state of war, has the power of removing it in part, by permitting, where he sees proper, that commercial intercourse which is a partial suspension of the war. There may be occasions in which such intercourse may be highly expedient. But it is not for individuals to determine the expediency of such occasions on their own notions of commerce, and of commerce merely, and possibly on grounds of private advantage, not very reconcilable with the general interest of the State. It is for the State alone, on more enlarged views of policy, and of all circumstances which may be connected with such an intercourse, to determine when it shall be permitted, and under what regulations. No principle ought to be held more sacred than that this intercourse cannot subsist on any other footing than that of the direct permission of the State. Who can be insensible to the consequences that might follow, if every person in time of war had a right to carry on a commercial intercourse with the enemy, and, under color of that, had the means of carrying on any other species of intercourse he might think fit? The inconvenience to the public might be extreme; and where is the inconvenience on the other side, that the merchant should be compelled, in such a situation of the two countries, to carry on his trade (if necessary) under the eye and control of the Government, charged with the care of the public safety." *The Hoop*, 1 Rob.

But the case of the Rapid is still more interesting to us, not only as having been decided by the Supreme Court of the United States, at a time when its decisions commanded the highest respect, but also because the judgment was pronounced by a distinguished Judge of South Carolina—Judge William Johnson.

In that case, an American citizen having purchased goods in England long anterior to the war, and deposited them on the frontier of British America: after the declaration of war with Great Britain, sent a steamer to bring away his goods; she was captured by an American privateer, and vessel and cargo were condemned as prize of war, on the ground of trading with the enemy; and Judge Johnson thus defines the expression "trading with the enemy," and vindicates the justness and necessity of the rule:

"The object, policy and spirit of the rule which forbids trading with an enemy is to cut off all communication or actual locomotive intercourse between the individuals of the belligerent States. Negotiation or contract has, therefore, no necessary connection with the offence. *Intercourse, inconsistent with actual hostility*, is the offence against which the operation of the rule is directed, and by substituting this definition for that of *trading with an enemy*, an answer is given to this argument. * * * On the subject which affects this case, there has been no general relaxation. The universal sense of nations has acknowledged the demoralizing effects that would result from the admission of individual intercourse. The whole nation are embarked in one common bottom, and must be reconciled to submit to one common fate. Every individual of the one nation must acknowledge every individual of the other nation as his own enemy, because the enemy of his country." *The Rapid*, 7 Cranch.

The case submitted by you, of citizens of the Confederate States carrying letters to the United States is stronger than many which I have mentioned above. There can be no doubt of its illegality, not only upon the general principle that all intercourse and communication with the enemy's country without special license is unlawful, but also because it affords direct opportunity for carrying on a treasonable communication with the enemy by conveying intelligence which may afford him aid and comfort.

I have no doubt but that it is as unlawful for any citizen of the Confederate States to carry letters to the United States as it is for any citizens to write them.

The question of the remedy to be applied to prevent these acts is much more difficult, and one upon which I feel great hesitation in giving an opinion, in advance of any case made and prosecution commenced. I will only say, on this branch of the matter, that all the offences of which I have spoken seem to come within the designation of "offences against the law of nations," the power to define and punish which is, by the Constitution, expressly given to Congress.

Congress has, by virtue of the power vested in it by the Constitution, established certain Courts, and has, by the 35th section of the "Act to establish the Judicial Courts of the Confederate States of America," declared "that the said District Courts shall have exclusive cognizance of all crimes and offences cognizable under the authority of the Confederate States, except where the laws of the Confederate States shall otherwise provide."

I cannot decide in advance, whether the Courts of the Confederate States will take cognizance of this class of cases, by virtue of the jurisdiction conferred on them by the clause of the Constitution and the Act above quoted, and, having jurisdiction, will hold that their rules of action, as to the nature and extent of their authority and the mode in which it shall be exercised, where not prescribed by statute, are to be regulated by the rules of the Common Law; in accordance with the distinction that the Common Law is not a *source* of jurisdiction, but is to be considered merely as the *means* or *instrument* of exercising the jurisdiction conferred by the Constitution and the laws of the Confederacy; or whether they will accept as their rule on the subject, the construction which prevailed under the United States, that the Federal Courts could not take cognizance of any case where the offence was not created, and the punishment prescribed, by express statute.

I may add, that, even in the United States Courts the question of how far they could resort to the Common Law in the administration of their criminal jurisdiction, seems to have been determined rather upon precedent than reason; and that our change of government opens the question again, and it stands with us, as it did just after the adoption of the United States Constitution. Of the class of cases of which I have spoken, but one has been the subject of express legislation by the Confederate Congress, namely, the payment by citizens of the Confederate States of debts due to citizens of the United States, (except the States of Delaware, Maryland, Kentucky and Missouri, and the District of Columbia) which is expressly prohibited pending the existing war, by an Act approved on the 21st May, 1861. The Act prescribes no express penalty for a violation of its provisions, and a prosecution under it will raise one of the questions above indicated, as to the criminal jurisdiction to be exercised by the Confederate Courts.

It is to be hoped, however, that our citizens only require to be informed as to their duties and responsibilities arising from the state of war, in relation to these questions, to perform them fully; and that they will not be tempted by considerations of selfish interest, or peculiar conveniences of their private judgments, to run counter to the clear principles of right, simply because it may be difficult or impossible to punish them for its infractions. It is certainly the part of a good citizen to set the example of obedience to law, even if its sanctions are imperfect, rather than to violate its letter and spirit because he may do so with impunity.

Very respectfully,
Your obedient servant,
CH. RICHARDSON MILES,
C. S. District Attorney, *pro tem.*

Cotton Opening.—Our friend Major L. B. Vasser, has laid upon our table a Cotton boll which is fairly open. It was taken from his Dallas plantation on the 12th inst.—*Selma (Ala.) Register.*

Why is Gen. Scott like the Strait of Constantinople? Because he is the Boss-for-us.—*N. Y. Leader.*

PROCLAMATION.—STATE OF SOUTH CAROLINA, CITY OF CHARLESTON.—MAYOR'S OFFICE, MARCH 13th, 1861.—Know all men by these presents, that I, CHARLES MACBETH, Mayor of Charleston, do hereby issue this my Proclamation, notifying all concerned that the QUARANTINE RULES AND REGULATIONS, established by an Ordinance ratified in City Council on the 19th day of April, A. D., 1855, are of force, and will be continued without further notice; and I do hereby call upon and enjoin the Collector of the Port, the Port Physician, the Harbor Master and his Assistants, the Quarantine Master, the Pilots, and all other officers concerned, to perform their respective duties as prescribed by the following provisions of the aforesaid Ordinance, namely:

SECTION 1. *Be it ordained by the Mayor and Aldermen in City Council assembled*, That the following orders, rules and regulations, relating to the observance of Quarantine in the Harbor and Port of Charleston, be and the same are hereby established, to be in force at all times, until the same are altered and repealed by the Governor of the State.

1. The Quarantine Orders, Rules and Regulations, hereby ordained and established, shall be enforced by the City Council, when the Governor of the State may be absent from the City of Charleston, and shall be put in force by the proclamation of the Mayor, which proclamation, together with the said orders, rules and regulations, shall be published in two of the daily papers of the city, and the same shall continue in force from the day on which they shall be first established, as aforesaid, until they shall be suspended, altered or repealed, by order of the City Council, or by the Governor of the State.

2. The Quarantine Ground, or Anchorage Ground for vessels at Quarantine, shall be that part of the Harbor of Charleston, opposite Fort Johnson, lying and being between the Middle Ground and the said Fort Johnson, which shall be designated by buoys, to be anchored under the direction of the Port Physician.

Vessels arriving at the Port of Charleston shall be subject to Quarantine, as follows:

3. All vessels direct or indirect from any place in the West Indies, or from any place in America in the ordinary passage from which they pass South of Georgia, known to be liable to the prevalence of Yellow, malignant, or other pestilential or infectious Fever, or at which said Fever existed at the time of departure, or which shall have arrived at any such place, and proceeded from thence to Charleston, or on board of which, during the voyage, any case of such fever shall have occurred, arriving between the thirty-first day of May and the first day of October, shall remain at Quarantine for at least thirty days after their arrival, and at least twenty days after their cargo shall have been discharged, and shall perform such further Quarantine as the Port Physician shall prescribe.

4. All vessels embraced in the foregoing clause, arriving during the months of April, May and October—all vessels from a foreign port, on board of which, during the voyage or while at the port of departure, any person shall have been sick, and all vessels from any place (including islands) in Asia, Africa, or the Mediterranean, arriving between the first day of April and the first day of November, shall be subject to such Quarantine and other Rules and Regulations as the Port Physician shall prescribe.

5. During the period above specified, no vessel (except as hereinafter designated) shall pass the Quarantine ground without previous examination by the Port Physician, nor until permitted by him to come up to the city.

6. It shall be the duty of the Port Physician to board every vessel subject to Quarantine or visitation by him, immediately on her arrival, or as soon thereafter as may be practicable, to inquire as to the health of all persons on board, and the condition of the vessel and cargo, by the inspection of the bill of health, manifest, log-book or otherwise; to examine, on oath, as many and such persons on board of vessels suspected of coming from a sickly port, or having had sickness on board during the voyage, as he may judge expedient, and to report the facts and his conclusions to the Mayor, in writing.

SEC. 2. The Port Physician shall have power—

1. To remove and separate, on the Quarantine anchorage ground, such vessels as are infected, to a safe and reasonable distance from such as are only suspected to be so infected, and prohibit intercommunication.

2. To cause any vessel under Quarantine, when he shall judge it necessary for the purification of the vessel and her cargo, which judgment shall be imperative in cases of disease on board, actually occurring, or having occurred, during the voyage, to discharge her cargo at the Quarantine Ground.

3. To cause any such vessel, her cargo, bedding and clothing of persons on board, to be ventilated, cleansed and purified, in such manner, and during such time, as he shall direct, and, if he judge it necessary, to prevent infection or contagion, to destroy any portion of such cargo, bedding or clothing, which he may deem incapable of purification.

4. To prohibit all persons arriving in vessels subject to Quarantine from leaving Quarantine, until twelve days after the sailing of their vessel from her port of departure, and fifteen days after the last case of pestilential or infectious Fever shall have occurred on board, and eight days after her arrival at Quarantine, unless sooner discharged by him, by certificate of acclimation.

5. To permit the cargo of any vessel under Quarantine, or any portion thereof, when he shall judge the same free from infection or contagion, to be conveyed to the City of Charleston, or such place as may be designated by the Mayor, after having reported in writing to the Mayor of the city the condition of said cargo, and his intention to grant such permission; such permission, however, to be inoperative without the written approval of the Mayor.

6. To permit, with the knowledge and concurrence of the Mayor, if, in their opinion, it will not be dangerous to the public health, the cargo of any vessel under Quarantine, or any part thereof, to be shipped for exportation by sea, provided the vessel receiving the same shall not approach nearer than three hundred yards to the wharves of the city.

7. No lighters shall be employed to load or unload vessels at Quarantine, without permission of the Port Physician and Mayor, and subject to such restrictions as they shall impose.

8. Nothing in this Ordinance contained, shall prevent any vessel arriving at Quarantine from again going to sea before breaking bulk.

9. Whenever a vessel is boarded by a Pilot, it shall be the duty of the Pilot boarding such vessel to require a written statement, on oath, from the Captain of the said vessel, as to the condition of his vessel, officers, passengers and crew, in respect to health and the health of the place from which she last came and took in her cargo; and every Pilot omitting to require such certificate, shall forfeit fifty dollars, and be suspended from his branch for three months. And it shall be the duty of every Captain or Master of such vessel to render to the said Pilot such statement, under oath, immediately on being boarded; and every Captain or Master of such vessel giving a false bill of health to any Pilot, shall be liable to fine and imprisonment, provided by law for a violation of Quarantine regulations.

10. The officers, passengers and crew of any vessel brought to the Quarantine Ground, shall be detained and remain on board such vessel until they are examined by the Port Physician, and shall not leave or remove from such vessel until they are permitted to come up to the city by the Port Physician, excepting those who may be sent to the Lazaretto.

11. No vessel or boat shall pass through the range of vessels lying at Quarantine, nor shall any person be allowed to go on board of a vessel performing Quarantine, or hold any communication with her, except by the special permission of the Mayor or Port Physician.

12. At all times when the Quarantine orders and regulations shall have been put in force by the proclamation of the Mayor, as aforesaid, and so long as the same shall continue in force by virtue of the provisions of this Ordinance, it shall be the duty of every Pilot conducting over the bar of Charleston, any vessel liable to Quarantine, to bring such vessel to the Quarantine Ground hereby established, and to remain on board said vessel, or to go the Lazaretto, without coming up to the city, until the Port Physician shall permit him to do so; and during the time any Pilot remains on board, or stays at the Lazaretto, he shall be allowed four dollars for every day, and be found in provisions at the expense of the master, owner or consignee of such vessel; and every Pilot neglecting or refusing to bring any vessel to Quarantine, or coming up to the city without the permission from the Port Physician, shall forfeit and pay the sum of fifty dollars, and shall be deprived of his branch, and shall not obtain another.

13. In all cases where a Pilot brings a vessel to Quarantine for the inspection of the Port Physician, it shall be the duty of the Pilot, before crossing the bar, to have a flag hoisted at half-mast, which flag shall so continue to be hoisted at half-mast until the arrival at Quarantine and the visitation of the Port Physician; and any Pilot omitting this duty shall forfeit and pay fifty dollars; and it shall be the duty of the Captain or Master of a vessel performing Quarantine, to keep a flag hoisted at half-mast until the vessel is permitted to come up to the city. In cases of actual sickness on board, a yellow flag shall be hoisted at half-mast, which flag shall be furnished at the expense of the city.

14. Any Pilot bringing a vessel beyond the Quarantine Ground, without previous examination and permission of the Port Physician (except those hereafter excepted) shall, in addition to the penalties to which such Pilot is now subjected by the laws of this State, be deprived of his branch as a Pilot.

15. The officers, crew and passengers of vessels performing Quarantine, shall obey orders given by the Mayor or Port Physician, for the purpose of enforcing these regulations.

16. Persons ill of malignant or infectious maladies, on board of vessels performing Quarantine, shall be sent by the Port Physician, to the Lazaretto, where they shall be received and medically attended, from whence they shall not be permitted to come up to the city without the written permission of the Mayor or Port Physician.

17. All persons so sent or taken to the Lazaretto, shall be charged seventy-five cents per diem, during their continuance there, for attendance and other accommodations, and if incapable of paying, the captain, owner or consignee shall be responsible.

18. Whenever, in the opinion of the Port Physician or Mayor, or by virtue of any provision of this Ordinance, it is necessary or expedient that all infected, or presumed infected, cargo should be removed from the vessel in which it has arrived, all charges and expenses attending the same, with the charges and expenses attending the cleaning and purification of such vessels, shall be at the expense and charge of the owners, consignees or possessors of the same, and no charge shall be made beyond actual cost.

19. In any case in which the City Council may deem it necessary for the public safety, they may order an infected vessel to depart from the State, which order shall be given in writing; and in case any vessel so ordered to depart shall refuse to obey within the time prescribed, the commander of said vessel shall be liable to the fine and imprisonment provided by the aforesaid Act of Assembly of December, 1832, for the disobedience of Quarantine Regulations.

20. Any captain or master of a vessel violating any of these orders, rules and regulations, by passing the Quarantine Ground without permission, or by refusing to perform quarantine when ordered to do so, or by breaking Quarantine after being at Quarantine Ground, or by disobeying any order of the Mayor or Port Physician, relating to Quarantine, shall be indicted, and, on conviction, shall pay a fine not exceeding two thousand dollars, and suffer imprisonment not exceeding twelve months.

21. These regulations shall extend (so far as the same may apply,) to all vessels stranded or wrecked on any part of the seacoast or islands, within twenty miles of the City of Charleston, their cargoes, passengers and crews, and to all persons going on board or returning from vessels so stranded or wrecked.

22. Every vessel having had during the voyage, a case of small pox, cholera, or typhus or infectious or contagious disease, and every vessel from a foreign port, having passengers, and not hereinbefore declared subject to Quarantine, shall, at her arrival on Quarantine Ground, be subject to visitation by the Port Physician, but shall not be detained beyond the time requisite for due examination, unless she shall have had on board, during the voyage, some case of small pox, typhus or other infectious or contagious disease, in which case she shall be subject to such Quarantine as the Port Physician shall prescribe; and it shall be the duty of the Port Physician, whenever he thinks it necessary for the preservation of the public health, to cause the persons on board of any vessel to be vaccinated.

23. These regulations shall not apply to pilot or packet boats or coasters, or other vessels having no infectious or malignant malady on board, and arriving from Northern ports, at which no infectious malady prevailed at the time of their departure.

SEC. 3. 1. The Mayor or Port Physician, whenever in their judgment the public health may require it, may order any vessel at the wharves of the city, or in their vicinity, to the Quarantine Ground, or other place of safety, and may require all persons, articles or things, introduced in the city from such vessels, to be seized, returned on board, or removed to the Quarantine Ground or Lazaretto. In case the master, owner, or consignee of the vessel cannot be found, or shall refuse or neglect to obey the order of the removal, the Mayor or Port Physician shall have power to cause such removal at the expense of such master, owner or consignee, and such vessel or person shall not return to the city without a written permission of the Mayor or Port Physician.

2. If any person arriving in and belonging to any ship or vessel detained at the Quarantine Ground or in the Lazaretto by the Port Physician shall elope, or otherwise absent himself from the ship, vessel or Lazaretto, it shall be lawful for the Port Physician, or any constable or other person whom he shall call to his assistance—and they are hereby enjoined and required to lend such assistance—to pursue and apprehend the person so escaping and absenting himself or herself, and there again deliver him or her to be detained until he or she be duly discharged. If any master or captain shall knowingly receive or employ, or bring up to the city, on board of his ship or vessel, or if any housekeeper, or other inhabitant of Charleston, shall knowingly receive, harbor, or in any way entertain any person so eloping or absenting from the Quarantine Ground or Lazaretto, each and every master and captain, and each and every housekeeper or inhabitant of Charleston so respectively offending, shall, on being thereof legally convicted, forfeit and pay a sum of two hundred dollars; and the person so eloping and coming up to the City of Charleston, without first obtaining a discharge signed by the Port Physician, upon legal conviction of such offence, shall forfeit and pay the sum of two hundred dollars, besides being immediately remanded to the Lazaretto.

3. All persons arriving in, or going on board of vessels brought to Quarantine, shall be liable to be removed to such place as Council may appoint, and all expenses, of every kind, shall be paid by the person on whose account they may be incurred.

4. Nothing in this Ordinance contained shall prevent any ship or vessel, after she shall have been thoroughly cleansed and purified, if no malignant disease appear on board, to take in freight at the Quarantine Ground, by means of lighters, and proceed to sea, before the regular time for the performance of quarantine shall have expired: subject, however, to such restrictions as the Mayor or Port Physician shall impose.

5. It shall be the duty of the Port Physician, the Pilots, the Harbor Master, and all other officers connected with the enforcement of the Quarantine, to notify the Mayor of every infraction of these regulations which may come to his knowledge, that he may take measures for the prosecution and punishment of the offender.

6. The Mayor shall be authorized, whenever in his opinion it may be necessary, to have boats, or employ the City Guard, or other armed force, for the proper enforcement of Quarantine regulations.

7. In case of the sickness or absence of the Port Physician, he may appoint any other physician, to be approved of by the Mayor, to act in his behalf in the enforcement of Quarantine; which physician, so appointed, shall be invested, for the time being, with all the power and authority conferred on the Port Physician by this Ordinance, and his order shall be obeyed by all parties concerned, under the same sanction as if extended by the Port Physician in person.

8. The captain or master of every vessel released from Quarantine, and arriving at the City of Charleston, shall, within twenty-four hours after such arrival, deliver the permit of the Port Physician at the office of the Mayor, or to such person as he shall direct, (Harbor Master,) but such vessel shall not approach within three hundred yards of the city without the written permit of the Mayor.

9. Every person who shall knowingly or wilfully violate, offend against, or disobey any of these rules, orders or regulations, hereinabove named, established and ordained, shall, upon being convicted thereof in the Court of General Sessions, be imprisoned for a period not exceeding twelve months, and be fined in a sum not exceeding two thousand dollars for each and every offence; *Provided*, that such fines and penalties as are hereinbefore provided against pilots for violation of such of these rules and regulations as apply to the pilotage exclusively, shall be recovered as herein specified.

10. It shall be the duty of the Mayor and the Port Physician diligently to inquire into, and seek out such places, ports or cities, where there shall be reason to believe a pestilential or infectious fever actually existed, and to declare such place, port or city, to be infected, within the meaning of this Ordinance, and to direct that all vessels arriving in the port of Charleston, from such infected place, port or city, shall be subject to Quarantine, together with their officers, crews, passengers and cargoes, and to all the provisions, regulations and penalties of this Ordinance, in relation to vessels subject to a similar Quarantine.

SEC. 4. 1. To assist in the thorough execution of the provisions of this Ordinance, and to compensate for the occasional and necessary absence of the Port Physician, there shall be elected by the City Council an officer who shall be called the Quarantine Master, whose duty it shall be to reside at Castle Pinckney, or such other place as Council may direct, and immediately after the arrival of any ship or vessel liable to be detained at Quarantine, to direct and cause such ship or vessel to be properly moored, at such distance from other vessels as may prevent the communication of infectious disease; to prevent any personal intercourse between the persons on board different vessels at quarantine, and, for that purpose, to take possession of and secure the boats of such vessels, from sunset to sunrise of the succeeding day, until their respective terms of Quarantine shall be completed; to take charge of and superintend the unlading, transhipment, cleansing and purifying the cargo, bedding and clothing, or any part thereof, contained in such ship or vessel, under the direction of the Port Physician; and to preserve and enforce order and obedience to the Ordinance, and all such orders as the Mayor or Port Physician from time to time may issue. And in the absence of the Port Physician from the Quarantine Ground or Lazaretto, he shall be endowed with all the powers that this Ordinance confers upon the Port Physician, and he shall be required to execute the same, according to the provisions of this Ordinance, to the best of his ability and judgment; and it shall be obligatory upon the said Quarantine Master to provide, maintain and keep in repair, at his own cost, a good and substantial boat, and an efficient number of hands for the purpose of properly performing the duties assigned to him under this Ordinance, for which service he shall receive a salary after the rate of fifteen hundred dollars per annum, and shall not absent himself from his place of duty between the first day of June and the first day of October on any pretence whatever, for any time, without leave first obtained, in writing, from the Mayor, under the penalty of forfeiting his office and a fine not exceeding one hundred dollars. And immediately after the ratification of this Ordinance, an election shall be held for the said Quarantine Master, who shall hold until the next time for the election of city officers; and the said office shall be subject to the regulations now prescribed by Ordinance in relation to other officers. And the said Quarantine Master shall give bond to the City Council in the sum of one thousand dollars, with two or more sureties, to be approved by the City Council.

Given under my hand and the Seal of the Corporation of the City of Charleston, this 13th day of March, in the year of our Lord one thousand eight hundred and sixty-one. CHARLES MACBETH, Mayor.

By the Mayor.
JOHN R. HORSEY, Clerk of Council. March 13

BE IT ORDAINED BY THE MAYOR AND ALDERMEN OF CHARLESTON IN CITY COUNCIL ASSEMBLED, AND IT IS HEREBY ORDAINED BY THE AUTHORITY OF THE SAME—That from and after the first day of September next, there shall be laid down by the owner or occupant of each lot in the City, having an entrance for Carriage, Wagon, Cart or Dray, a PLATFORM OF WOOD OR STONE extending not more than four feet from the curb stone towards the centre of the street, and the owner or occupant of any such lot not having a platform as herein required to protect the pavement against the entrance of Carriages or other vehicles, shall forfeit and pay the sum of Five Dollars, and in the event that the said pavement becomes broken he shall pay, in addition to aforesaid penalty, the costs and charges of mending the same, and also the sum of Five Dollars for each day the same shall remain so broken.

Ratified in City Council this thirteenth day of August in the year 1851.

The above Ordinance will be rigidly enforced from and after this date. H. S. BAIL, Captain City Police.

THE BALTIMORE REPUBLICAN.

VOL. LXIX MONDAY EVENING, JULY 22, 1861 NO. 19 286

THE REPUBLICAN.

BALTIMORE, MONDAY, JULY 22.

Lincoln and Congress' Mode of Preserving the Union is Violating their Oaths, and Breaking the Constitution.

We again present to the people the oath taken by Abraham Lincoln when he was inaugurated President of the United States, not for the purpose of showing that he has complied with it, but for the reverse purpose of showing that he has violated it.

"I do solemnly swear (or affirm) that I will faithfully execute the office of President of the United States, and will, to the best of my ability, preserve, protect, and defend the Constitution of the United States."—Con., Art. 2 sec. 1.

"He shall (the President) take care that the laws be faithfully executed."—Con. Art. 1 Sect 3.

Among the powers delegated by the Constitution to Congress, exclusively, is the right of Congress to suspend the writ of habeas corpus. This can only be done by Congress when, "in case of rebellion or invasion, the public safety may require it."—Con. Art. Sec. IX.

Congress alone is authorized to suspend this writ, and only when and where "rebellion or invasion or the public safety requires it." Congress being but the agent to whom this power is delegated, it has no authority under the Constitution to delegate this or any other power confided to it by the Constitution, unless authorized by the Constitution; yet we find that Lincoln has usurped this and other powers vested exclusively in Congress, and that he has delegated these powers, which so belong to Congress, to others. Again, Lincoln has declared and levied war, augmented the army and navy, destroyed U. S. property, appropriated the public money, &c., all of which acts and powers belong exclusively to Congress, and cannot constitutionally be delegated by it.

Lincoln in his recent message admits that "the legality and propriety of what has been done [by him] are questioned," and he asks Congress to legalize and confirm what he admits he has unconstitutionally done. If Congress has no authority to delegate any of its powers confided to it, how can it legalize, or confirm, or make Constitutional, the illegal and unconstitutional acts of a usurper? The suspension of the writ of habeas corpus, the declaration of and levying war, the augmenting the Army and Navy, appropriating the public money, &c., are powers confided exclusively to Congress by the Constitution; all of these acts are to be performed by Congress; no other power, body, or person is authorized to perform any of these acts, therefore all acts of Congress sanctioning or confirming these acts of Lincoln are unconstitutional, illegal and void.

These are but a few of the unconstitutional acts of Lincoln, and they are admitted by him in his message to be so; yet the obligation of his oath to "preserve, protect and defend the Constitution," and to "take care that the laws be faithfully executed," and the oath which was taken by each member of Congress, who solemnly swore, or affirmed, that he would "support the Constitution of the United States," have been violated and totally disregarded both by Lincoln and a majority of the members of Congress.

Lincoln has declared and levied war, by means of certain Northern and Western States, against certain Southern States; he has blockaded the ports of the Southern States; he has destroyed their trade, commerce and mail facilities; he has captured vessels and cargoes and taken property belonging to the people of these States, when under the Constitution no such authority is vested in him or in Congress, because to use his own argument as the Constitution does not provide for the dismemberment or breaking up of this government, neither does it provide for waging war by a portion of the people comprising it against another portion of the people; he has by his unconstitutional blockade given a preference as to "commerce and revenue" to the ports of the Northern States over the ports of the Southern States in gross violation of the Constitution art. 1, sec. 9.

He and Congress, have abridged the freedom of speech and of the press; prevented and prohibited the organization of the militia in all of the Southern States, as well as the right of the people, there to keep and bear arms by his orders. Soldiers in time of peace in "loyal" States are quartered in houses, and in and upon other property of citizens without the consent of the owners; they have caused to be searched and seized the persons of men, women and children, as well as their houses, papers, letters and effects, without warrant or and process of law.

They have caused to be arrested, and imprisoned persons not in the land or naval forces or militia, &c., without warrant or process of law. whom they allege are charged with capital crimes, and whilst persons have been taken out of the State and district, in which the alleged crime or offence has been committed; They have appropriated private property to their use without the consent of the owners or by process or law.

All of which enumerated acts are in flagrant violation of Articles 1, 2, 3, 4, 5&c., of amendments to the Constitution.

It is now proposed by Congress to pass acts to abolish slavery in the Southern States when, at the last session of Congress, it was resolved by Congress that slavery should not be interfered with by Congress, in the States where it existed. The Supreme Court of the United States has also decided that Congress cannot create, prohibit or abolish slavery any where. Congress also proposes to pass export facto laws, and laws impairing the obligations of contracts, and as to rights of property so far as to apply to the Southern States, in violation to Art. 1, Sec. 16, &c., Constitution of the United States. The Supreme Court of the United States has, on various occasions, decided that "an act of Congress contrary to the Constitution of the United States is void." Cohen & Virginia, 6 Wheat, 264, 381; Hylton and [illegible] 3 Dalls, 171; Marbury and Madison [illegible], 137; U. S. and Smith, 5 Wheat, 158.

Notwithstanding all of these enumerated violations of the Constitution, which are admitted by Lincoln to be such, yet Lincoln and Congress did legalize and confirm them notwithstanding which their acts are yet, and will forever remain unconstitutional.

We confess that we are not surprised at any thing that this Congress has yet done, nor will we be, at anything it may yet do. In pointing out these glaring and flagrant violators of the Constitution, we do not do so under the expectation that the Congress or Lincoln desist from further violation of it. We look upon it as totally destroyed and trampled under foot by the despots who now wield the sword and the purse. We live no longer under the Constitution and laws, but under military despotism.

Our design simply is to point out to men in our own community as well as in others, (especially to those who rejoice to call themselves Christians and law abiding, and Union loving citizens.) The unconstitutional, illegal and despotic acts referred to, and to ask them, if by the President's and Congress' violation of the Constitution and laws, is the proper mode to "preserve, protect and defend the Constitution," and if that is taking care "that the laws be faithfully executed?" Are not these violations of the Constitution by the men who have sworn to "preserve, protect and defend" it more guilty and worse men than the rebels in the South, who have it not in their keeping, and who do not design to molest us, or deprive us, or rob us of our rights? Can it be supposed that if we were living under the "rebel" government we would be as we now are? If the "rebels" of the South have violated the Constitution, that is no reason why Lincoln and Congress should do so. "Let him that is without sin cast the first stone;" and, also, let him take the beam out of his own eye before he attempts to take the mote out of his brothers eye.

MESSAGE OF JEFF. DAVIS TO THE CONFEDERATE CONGRESS.

RICHMOND, (via New Orleans,) July 20.—Mr. Davis' inaugural message to the Confederate Congress commences by calling attention to the causes which formed the Confederacy. He says it is now only necessary to allude to such facts as have occurred during the recess and matters connected with the public defense. He congratulates Congress on the acquisition to the Confederacy of three sovereign States.

The accumulation of the enemy's forces on the Potomac sufficiently demonstrated that the efforts of the Lincoln government were to be directed against Virginia, and from no point could her defense and protection be so efficiently directed as from our own capital. The rapid progress of events during the last few months has stripped off the veil behind which the true policy and purposes of the Lincoln government had previously been concealed. They have now been, he says, revealed.

The message of President Lincoln and the action of the present Congress of the United States confess an intention of subjugating the seceded States by a war of folly equalled only by its wickedness—a war by which it is impossible to attain the proposed result, whilst its dire calamities will fall doubly severe on themselves. Commencing last March with an affectation of ignorance of secession, even of those States which had originated the Confederate Government. Persisting in April in the absurd assumption of the existence of a riot which was to be dispersed by the *posse comitatus*. Continuing for several successive months the false representation that these States intended offensive war, in spite of conclusive evidence to the contrary, the President of the United States and his advisers succeeded in deceiving the people of those States into the belief that the purposes of this government were not peace at home, but conquest abroad. Not defense of our liberties, but the subversion of the liberties of the people of the United States.

The series of manoeuvres by which this impression was created, and which were devised in perfidy, is already known, fortunately, for history. Lincoln's message minutely detailed the attempt to reinforce Fort Sumter in violation of an armistice, which he confesses to have been informed of only by rumors, too vague and uncertain to create any attention. The hostile expedition of the dispatch to supply Fort Sumter is admitted to have been undertaken with the knowledge that its success was impossible. He charged these States to be the Union. The world cannot misunderstand this unfounded pretence.

Mr. Davis then compares the present invasion with that of Great Britain, but which was conducted in a more civilized manner. Mankind will shudder at outrages now being committed on defenseless females by those pretending to be their fellow citizens. Who can depict the horrors which they regard with desperate malignity, and under a pretext of suppressing insurrection, make special war on sick women and children by withholding medicines necessary for their cure? The sacred claims of humanity, respected by alienations, even in the fury of battle, by a careful deviation from attack on hospitals is now outraged by a government which pretended to desire a continuance of fraternal connection.

THE WAR NEWS THIS MORNING.

The stirring intelligence received from the Seat of War during the last twenty-four hours creates intense excitement in the public mind. The accounts by telegraph, although copious and extended, do not satisfy the insatiable thirst for the details of blood and carnage. A fierce engagement seems to have taken place and the loss on both sides is doubtless severe. Upon which standard the prestige of victory has fallen, we are, in consequence of the notorious partiality of the telegraph, unable to decide. For the purpose of keeping our readers up with the progress of events, we condense below a summary of the most interesting news received by telegraph and otherwise since our edition of yesterday. We shall doubtlessly receive further details during the day, which will appear in our regular telegraphic column as well perhaps in an extra:

ANOTHER BATTLE AT BULL RUN.

WASHINGTON, July 21.—The following bulletins were received in official quarters to-day during progress of the battle, from the telegraph station, about four miles from Bull Run:—

FAIRFAX, July 21—11 A. M.—Rapid firing from heavy guns and frequent discharges of musketry.

11 40 A. M.—Firing very heavy, and apparently more on our left wing.

11 50 A. M.—There is evidently a battle towards our left, in the direction of Bull Run and a little north. The firing is very rapid and heavy.

1.45 P. M.—Heavy guns again, and apparently near; musketry heavy and near.

2 P. M.—The musketry is very heavy, and drawing much nearer. There is evidently a movement more to our left.

2.45 P. M.—Firing a little farther off, and apparently in the direction of [illegible] more light artillery, as near as I can judge.

3 P. M.—The firing ceased ten minutes since.

3.35 P. M.—The firing has almost entirely ceased, and can only be heard with difficulty.

LATEST FROM THE BATTLE FIELD.

HIGHLY INTERESTING DETAILS OF THE BATTLE

CENTREVILLE, July 21, P. M.—A most severe and general battle was fought to day at Bull Run bridge. The conflict was most desperate and bloody, lasting over nine hours!

The programme of the battle, as stated in my first dispatch, was carried out until the troops met a succession of masked batteries, which were attacked with great vigor and bravery, and successively stormed and taken, with severe loss of life.

Col. Key's brigade remained at Centreville as a reserve.

Information was received by Gen. Tyler's command of the existence of the enemy's battery commanding the road.

Our troops were then formed in battle array. The 2d New York and Ohio on the left, the 3d Ohio and 2d Wisconsin, and 79th, 13th, and 69th New York on the right. Colonel Miles' division formed in the rear. The first range gun was fired by Sherman's battery at ten minutes of 7 o'clock this morning.

The Confederates did not return his shot until an hour and a half afterwards, when Col. Hunter's division came up, and the battle became general.

Our troops advanced as follows: Colonel Richardson, who distinguished himself in the previous engagement with the batteries at Bull Run, proceeded on the left with four regiments of the 4th brigade, to hold the Federal battery stationed on the hill on the Warrenton road, in the vicinity in which the last battle (the Bull Run battle) was fought.

The flank movements were carried out as described in my first dispatch.

Colonel Schenck's and Colonel Sherman's brigades of General Tyler's division advanced by the Warrenton road, while Colonel Hentzelman's and Colonel Hunter's divisions took the fork of the Warrenton road, to move between Bull Run and Manassas Junction.

The most gallant charge of the day was made by the New York 69th, 79th and 13th regiments, who rushed upon one of the batteries, firing as they proceeded with perfect *elang*, attacking it with the bayonet point. Their yell of triumph seemed to carry all before them.

Our men were immediately ordered to lie down on either side of the road, in order to allow two pieces of artillery to pass through and attack the work. This battery then opened upon us and killed, on the third round, Lieut. Dempsey, of company G, New York 2d, and Wm. Maxwell, a drummer, and seriously wounded several others.

Our troops were kept in this position for fifteen or twenty minutes under a galling fire, not being able to exchange shots with the enemy, although within a stone's throw of their batteries. They succeeded in retiring in regular order with their battery.

They found that the Confederates had abandoned the battery as they approached, and had only succeeded in carrying off one gun. This success was acquired only after a severe loss of life, in which the 69th Regiment suffered most severely, and it is reported that the Lieutenant Colonel was among the first killed.

Among the Federal officers reported to be killed are Colonel Cameron, of the New York 79th regiment, and Colonel Slocum, of the 27th New York regiment of volunteers.

Colonel David Hunter, of the Third United States Cavalry, and acting Major General of the second division of Major General McDowell's army, is reported to have been mortally wounded.

The Confederates received reinforcements from Manassas Junction after the attack was opened. The battle consisted in a succession of fires from masked batteries, which were opened in every direction. When one was silenced its place was taken by two, and the daring charges of our infantry in unmasking them exhibited the most dauntless courage.

The 2d Ohio and the the 2d New Yor militia were marched by flank through the woods by a new made road, within a mile of the main road, when they came on a battery of eight guns, with four regiments flanked in the rear.

ANOTHER STATEMENT.

BULL RUN BATTERY CAPTURED AND RECAPTURED.

A prominent gentlemen of this city was in Washington yesterday and had a business interview with Secretary Cameron, and during the conversation the Secretary informed him that the Bull Run battery had been taken by the Federal forces at an early hour in the morning, but the Confederate forces rallied and retook the battery.

THE LATEST FROM OLD POINT, FORTRESS MONROE, &C.

The steamer Georgeana, Capt. Pearson, reached here this morning, at eight o'clock, on her return trip from old Point, but no news of interest could be learned from the passengers. Nearly the entire Sunday was devoted to a dress parade, and review, gotten up for the gratification of a party of officials, who passed through on Saturday, from Washington for the purpose of spending the Sabbath at Old Point. They consisted in part of Montgomery Blair, Postmaster General, Ex Gov. Morehead of Kentuck, Hon. Judge Hale, Senators Clark, Bingham and Wilkins, and Haskill; Roscoe and Conkling of House of Representatives. Col. Smith of the 13th Brooklyn regiment also arrived in the boat and will join his command forthwith.

No movements of the naval force had taken place, but as the Adelaide was coming up the bay, she saw the steam tug Young America having in tow a sloop, supposed to be a prize, as she was anchored near the stern of the Minnesota. The erection of different batteries near Sewell's Point was still going on, and the men could be easily seen hard at work. The only thing which indicated an aggressive policy at Fortress Monroe was that batteries of field artillery were being hastily prepared by the Ordnance department.

The Army Worm in New England.

Our country exchanges come to us to-day with the news that the army worm—that dreadful pest—has made its appearance in several parts of this State and Rhode Island. The Fall River News reports several grain fields in that vicinity completely ravaged and destroyed within a day or two. The News states that in several instances the farmers have built fires to arrest the progress of the worm towards their corn fields, but they are complete salamanders, the fire having only the effect of increasing their vigor. There are all sizes of the worm to be seen in the fields, from a half to two inches in length.

They have sixteen legs, the formost proplegs are shorter than the rest. They travel rapidly like the caterpiller, and go in droves across the streets and through stone walls. The worm is doubly striped with black on the back, and sprinkled with black spots. Their description answers to that of the army worm, which lasts from three to four weeks, though there is some doubt as to their identity with that species. In some other particulars they resemble the Brown wheat weevil, so destructive in New York and Northern Pennsylvania. The Providence, Taunton, and New Bedford papers speak of their appearance in the vicinity of those cities. Probably we shall hear of their simultaneous appearance in different sections of New England.—*Boston Herald.*

Punch asks the following "obstruse conundrum:" "What's the difference between the late Sultan Abdul Medjid, and his [illegible] Abdul [illegible] is Abdul at War, but the present Sultan is Abdul Aziz."

LATEST FROM THE SEAT OF WAR.

THE GREAT BATTNE AT BULL RUN.

Immense Loss of Life.

THE KILLED AND WOUNDED 12, 000.

Consternation and Retreat of the entire Federal Army.

DEATH OF CAPT. THOS. F. MEAGHER.

THE CONFEDERATE FORCES OVER 100,000.

The Washington Republican of this morning, in addition to the full details of the great battle at Bull Run, already received by telegraph, contains the following highly important announcement. It is a clear admission of the entire route and defeat of the Federal army in the direction of Washington:

All our military operations went swimingly on, and Colonel Alexander was about erecting a pontoon across Bull Run, the enemy were seemingly in retreat, and their batteries being unmasked one after another, when a terrific consternation broke out among the teamsters, who had incautiously advanced immediately after the body of the army, and lined the Warrenton road.

Their consternation was shared in by numerous civilians, who were upon the ground, and for some time it seemed as if our whole army was in retreat.

Many baggage wagons were emptied, and the horses gallopped across the open fields, all the fences of which were torn down, to allow them a more rapid retreat. For a time a perfect panic prevailed, which communicated itself to the vicinity of Centreville, and every available conveyance was seized upon by agitated civilans.

Wounded soldiers cried on the roadside for assistance, but the alarm was so great, that numbers were passed by. Several similar alarms occurred on previous occasions, when a change of batteries rendered necessary the retirement of the artillery on our part, and it is most probable that the alarm was owing to the same fact. The reserve force at Centreville was immediately brought up, and marched in double quick step, in the following order.

Col. Einstein's twenty-seventh Pennsylvania regiment, with two guns, the Garibaldi Guards, and Blenker's first rifle regiment, with its batteries, followed, at several miles distant, by the DeKalb regiment.

When our courier left, at half past four o'clock, it was in the midst of this excitement.

Two new masked batteries had been opened by the rebels on the left flank, and that portion of the division had had its lines broken, and demanded an immediate reinforcement.—The right flank was in good order. The battery erected on the hillside, directly opposite the main battery of the enemy, was doing good execution, and additional guns were being mounted.

On his arrival at Fairfax Court House, he was overtaked by Government messengers, who reported that our army was in full retreat towards Centreville.

They were followed by less agitated parties, who stated that the report of the retreat was owing to the fact that the alarm among the teamsters had communicated itself to the volunteers, and even, in some instances, to the regulars, and the lines were broken; and that a retirement of our forces across Bull Run was rendered necessary. Col. Hunter passed at the same time, in a vehicle, wounded. Ayer's battery was also reported as lost.

Crowds of carriages and baggage wagons came rushing down the road. The telegraph office was closed against all private busines, and in an hour the alarm had been communicated all along the road to Washington.—But this state of affairs is apparently without sufficient cause for agitating the public mind.

The movement was a grand one, and could only succeed by a desperate struggle.

The heavy loss of life, which is shared by the Confederates, only tends to show the brilliancy of the movement, and, with the immense reinforcements sent forward from Washington, will doubtless entirely succeed.

The unfounded alarm will probably prevent a continuance of visitors to the scene of conflict, as their conduct on this occasion tended greatly to inflame it among the teamsters.

STILL LATER PARTICULARS.

The struggle at Bull Run bridge was, in every respect, a severe one, and it is estimated that the number killed and wounded cannot be much less than 12,000. The conflict continued over nine hours. The foregoing programme was observed until the troops met a succession of masked batteries, which were attacked with great loss of life.

A Confederate prisoner reports the force under General Beauregard at and in the vicinity of Manassas Junction at over one hundred thousand men.

Among the killed is Capt. Thos. F. Meager and Colonels Heintzeman, Hunter, Barnside, Tyler and Schenck, badly wounded.

The above from the Republican, a government organ, told with circumspection, can only be understood as a general retreat of the federal forces. Private accounts from Washington state this fact was well known in that city last night and this morning.

The Federal loss is reported by some as high as fifteen thousand in killed and wounded. A reliable gentleman arrived this morning states that the War Department was in full possession of the above facts.—*Eds. Republican.*

THE VERY LATEST.

The head of the charger of Gov. Sprague which he rode during the engagement, was shot off from his body, while the horse of Gen. Burnside was shot from under him.

RETREAT OF GENERAL JOHNSTON TO MANASSAS JUNCTION—A BATTLE ANTICIPATED—MORE TROOPS SENT INTO VIRGINIA.

WASHINGTON, July 21.—It is not doubted in high military quarters that Gen. Johnston, was enabled to effect a junction with the Confederates at Manassas Gap some time during yesterday. Official despatches were sent to Gen. McDowell at two o'clock last evening.

The position of the enemy extended in three lines, forming a triangle, the apex fronting the centre of our column. The area seems to have been filled by masked batteries.

At 7 o'clock last evening, guns were still heard firing at short intervals.

COUNTERMANDED.—The order for General Banks to supercede General Patterson has been countermanded for the present, and the latter will remain in command of this Department.

BE MODERATE.

There is nothing that so much indicates true courage and a moral strength of character as calmness and moderation in the midst of the triumph of a just cause. This attribute, it has often been alleged, is not always a characteristic of our people. With regard to Baltimoreans, however true it may with others, we believe the imputation of deficiency in this respect is unjust. We, therefore, counsel our friends to let this day's record form no exception to this statement. We know the profound depth of feeling which animates the public heart on the receipt of this day's intelligence. We know that if free from the presence of foreign bayonets, and the no less unfortunate division of sentiment among our own citizens, that rejoicings, bon-fires, and illuminations, would manifest the spontaneous gladness of the people. Yet reason, prudence, and every incentive of correct judgment, counsel calmness, quietude, moderation.

John W Baughman, Esq.

We had a visit from this gentleman who was arrested at Sandy Hook by the Federal soldiery, and taken to Washington upon some idle pretence.

It has been stated that Mr. Baughman took an oath of allegiance to the Federal government. We are authorized to deny this statement most emphatically. Mr. Baughman refused most peremptorily to take any such oath. He wrote a form himself, simply a pledge to support the Constitution, and told the Justice before whom it was taken, that it not satisfactory to the Government, he would return and be subjected to such further treatment as might be deemed necessary.

But he, Mr. B., avowed that he would go to jail and stay there forever before he would take the oath to support the present Administration. Upon these conditions Mr. B. was released, and has not been sent for since, and it is presumed the Government intends no further interference with his liberty.

THE SHODDY CLOTHING CONTRACT—*Illgotten Gains Paid Back.*—The Buffalo Commercial Advertiser gives a solution of the willingness of Brooks & Co., to re clothe the troops viz:—that they made the officials whom they bribed refund the money:

Brooks Brothers exibit a late contrition by offering since the publication of this report, to furnish gratuitously 7000 first-class uniforms. The Argus shrewdly says upon this point, that "If they could have afforded to pay high for their contract."

We belive, though we do not charge, that they did pay high, for it, and that the righteous and patriotic clamor of the press of this State has so terrified those who connived at a fraud for the sake of gain, that they have paid back to Brooks Brothers the money which they received from them, so that the swindling tailors can well afford to spend the $60.000 which their present offer involves. That is our construction of the matter, and we submit that it is an exceedingly natural one."

SINGULAR VERIFICATION OF A PROPHECY.—A correspondent of the Petersburg (Va.) Express gives the following:

I have heard of a singular circumstance in connection with the affair at Vienna, in which a prophecy was literally fulfilled. A gentleman who is in our army, while on a visit last winter to his brother in-law in Ohio, urged him to leave that hot bed of Abolitionism and come to Virginia.

The latter replied that he would come, but it would be with a gun in his hand, to crush the rebels. "If you come on such an errand, I predict you will run away," replied the indignant Southerner. The prediction seems to have been speedily accomplished, for a blanket with the full name of the invader was found near the railroad track, where the enemy fled to the woods.

TERRIBLE SCENES IN WASHINGTON, GEORGETOWN AND ALEXANDRIA.

A gentleman of reliability, formerly an officer in the United States army, but now upon the retired list, arrived here on Saturday evening from Alexandria. He states that he beheld some most frightful spectacles at Alexandria, Georgetown and Washington.—Large trains of wagons were constantly arriving, loaded with killed and wounded, from the field at Bull Run, some of them most frightfully mangled, others with the loss of an arm or a leg. In the hospital at Georgetown he counted upon one floor *two hundred and thirty eight* wounded men, nearly all of whom were mortally wounded.

Decision in the Case of the Ship Genera Parkhill.

Judge Cadwalader rendered a decision on Friday last, in the District Court of the United States at Philadelphia, in the case of the ship General Parkhill.

This vessel was brought for adjudication into the above district, where a libel praying her condemnation as a prize has been filed by the United States, on the ground that she attempted to violate the blockade at Charleston, and is the property of insurgents, traitors and public enemies. Her proprietors exhibited a prayer for restitution, describing themselves to be of the city of Charleston, and citizens of the United States.

The issue thus raised presented a number of interesting and important questions which are reviewed by the Court. The claim for restitution by the proprietors was rejected.

So the ship will stand condemned as a prize.

A POTOMAC INCIDENT.

I have heard of a significant incident on the upper Potomac which goes to show that the hearts of the Union soldiers are far from being warm in the work of invasion. A party of the enemy's pickets, it is said, called across the river to a party of our pickets, and proposed that delegations of two from each side should meet in the middle of the river and take a drink together.

The proposition was accepted, and accordingly two of the "Yankees" stripped off their clothes to show their peaceful intent, and armed with nothing but their canteens, took a canoe and paddled out the stream, where they were met in like fashion by a couple of Confederate soldiers.

After a due interchange of drinks and compliments, the Confederate delegation jestingly remarked that they had a strong mind to take the Yankees prisoners. The latter replied that they would rather be prisoners than not. They were heartily sick of the war, they said, since it proved to be a war of invasion.

They were willing to fight for defence, but they could only be dragged by force of military discipline to go with an invading army into Southern territory. Their time of service would be out on the 10th of July, and with thousands of others they would go home with an unalterable determination not to take up arms again in the same cause.

Among the arrivals by the Asia is Lord Adolphus Vane Tempest, whose tempestuous character was recently commented upon by the journals of both hemispheres. If we mistake not he married a daughter of the Duke of of Newcastle, very much against the will of that nobleman.

A government dispatch has been received by the commanding officer at the Relay House, to the effect that the Federal forces are in full retreat on Washington, with a loss of all their baggage.

TELEGRAPHIC NEWS.

FOR THE REPUBLICAN.

DEFEAT OF THE FEDERAL ARMY

THE ARMY RETREATING TO WASHINGTON.

WASHINGTON, July 22.—After the latest information was received from Centreville at 7½ o'clock last night, a series of event took place in the intensest degree disastrous.

Many composed statements are prevalent, but enough is known to warrant the statement that we have suffered in a degree which has cast a gloom over the remnant of the army, and excited the deepest melancholy throughout Washington.

The carnage is tremendously heavy on both sides, and on ours represented as frightful.—We were advancing and taking their masked batteries gradually but surely, and were driving the enemy towards Manassas Junction, when the enemy seemed to have been reinforced by General Johnson, who it is understood took the command, and immediately commenced driving us back, when a panic among our troops suddenly occurred and a regular stampede took place.

It is thought that General McDowell undertook to make a stand at or about Centreville, but the panic was so fearful that the whole army became demoralized, and it was impossible to check them. either at Centreville or at Fairfax Court House, but our forces being in full retreat he could not accomplish the object.

Beyond Fairfax Court House, the retreat was kept up until the men reached their regular encampments, a portion of whom returned to them, but a still larger portion coming inside the intrenchments. A large number of the troops fell on the way side, from sheer exhaustion and scattered along the entire route, all the way from Fairfax Court House.

The road from Bull Run to Centreville is strewed with knapsacks, arms, &c. Some of the troops deliberately threw away their guns. the better to facilitate their travel. General McDowell was in the rear of the retreat exerting himself to rally his men, but with only partial effect.

The latter part of the army it is stated made their retreat in good order. He was completely exhausted, having slept but little for three nights.

His orders on the field did not at all times reach those for whom they were intended. It is supposed that the reserved force of the enemy sent against our troops consisted, according to a prisoner's statement, of about thirty thousand men, including large numbers of cavalry.

He further says that owing to the reinforcements from Richmond, Strausburg and other points, the enemy's effective force was 90,000 men. According to the statement of two of the Fire Zouaves, they have only about 200 men left from the slaughter, while the 69th and other regiments have frightfully suffered in killed and wounded. The number of the Federal loss cannot now be known.

Sherman's, Carlisle's and the West Point batteries were taken by the enemy, and the eight siege 32 pound rifled cannon, the latter being two cumberous to remove. They were two miles the other side of Centreville.

Such of the wounded as were brought to Centreville Hospital were left there, after having their wounds properly dressed by Sergeant Frank H. Hamilton.

The panic was so great that the attempt to rally the troops to make a stand at Centreville was entirely in vain. If a firm stand had been made there, our troops could soon have been reinforced, and much disaster prevented.

It is supposed that all the provision trains belonging to the Government are saved. Some regimental wagons were overturned by accident, or their wheels came off, and had therefore to be abandoned. Large armies of cattle were saved by driven back in the advance of the retreat.

It is supposed here to day that Gen. Mansfield will take command of the fortifications on the other side of the river, which are all it is said by military engineers, to be held against any force that may be brought against them. Large rifled cannon and mortars are being rapidly sent over and mounted.

THE LATEST FROM THE VIRGINIA SIDE OF THE POTOMAC.

An officer just from Virginia reached here at 10¾ o'clock, A. M., reports that the road from Centreville to the Potomac is strewn stragglers.

The troops are however resuming their occupation of the fortifications and entrenchments on the line of the Potomac.

Col. Marsten of the New Hampshire regiment reached here this morning. He was wounded.

Col. Hesntzleman was also wounded in the breast.

In addition to those reported yesterday, it is said that Colonel Wilcox, the gallant commander of the brigade, was killed. Also, Captain McCook, brother of Colonel McCook, of Ohio.

The city this morning is in the most intense excitement. Groups are every where gathered to inquire the latest news. Wagons are continually arriving, bringing in the dead and wounded. Soldiers are relating to anxious listeners the deplorable events of last night and early this morning.

Both telegraph and steamboat communication with Alexandria is suspended to day to the public.

The greatest alarm exists throughout the city, especially among the female portion of the population.

Southern Account of the First Battle at Bull Run.

LOUISVILLE, July 22.—A special dispatch from Manassas to the Nashville Union, dated July 18, says that in the fight at Bull Run General Beauregard commanded in person. The enemy was repulsed three times in great confusion and with heavy loss. The Washington Artillery of New Orleans, with seven guns, engaged Sherman's battery of fifteen guns, and after making a charge on their position fifteen times silenced them and forced them to retire from the field.

Large quantities of arms were taken. Our loss was trifling.

Major Harris and two parties were wounded. Federal officers of high rank were killed, and $700 in gold was taken from the body of one of the killed.

Attack on Cape Hatteras Battery.

LOUISVILLE, July 22.—The reported attack by the Federal steamer Wabash on the Confederate battery at Cape Hatteras is confirmed. It is stated that the attack was made on Oregon Inlet, and that the Confederates were dispersed by shells.

Governor of Tennessee.

LOUISVILLE, July 22.—The Knoxville Whig withdraws the name of Twigg, and hoists that of Polk, for Governor of Tennessee.

COL. GEO. P. KANE.—We regret to announce that Col. Geo. P. Kane, Marshal of Police, confined in Fort McHenry, is now lying dangerously ill in the Bastile, so much so, as to render it necessary to deny admission to all visitors, except his family. He is attended by Dr. Thomas Buckler of this city together with the surgeon stationed at the Fort.

The Philadelphia Inquirer.

ESTABLISHED 1829. | PHILADELPHIA, MONDAY, JULY 22, 1861 | PRICE TWO CENTS.

EXTRA

12 O'CLOCK, P.M.

otal Route of Our Army

URHEAVY GUNS LOST

he New Jersey First and Second Going to Our Rescue.

arribaldians, Einstein's Regiment and Blenker's Regiment trying to Cover Our Retreat.

IMMENSE LOSS.

WHOLE REGIMENTS CUT UP

JOHNSTON'S ARMY COME IN ON US FROM WINCHESTER.

Our Army Retreat in Confusion.

SOME ALL THE WAY TO WASHINGTON.

REBEL FORCE FROM 80,000 TO 100,000 MEN.

PART OF SLEMMER'S BATTERY, PART OF CARLISLE'S AND RICKET'S BATTERIES TAKEN BY THE ENEMY.

Davis, Beaureguard and Lee in the Field Cheering their Men On.

MASKED BATTERIES AT EVERY POINT

IMMENSE LOSS OF PROVISIONS, WAGONS, HORSES, STORES, GUNS, AND AMMUNITION.

Fiendish Action of Rebels towards our Wounded and Prisoners.

A FIRST COUSIN OF ROGER A. PRYOR'S TAKEN PRISONER BY A WISCONSIN AND CONNECTICUT REGIMENT.

Our own Special Reporter has just reached here from the battle field, having left at 6½ P. M., and a full account is now being prepared.

We witnessed the whole battle yesterday, having been upon the field from 11 o'clock A. M. until the rear of our army fled in infamous disorder.

At 10.45 General SCHENCK led his column, headed by the Eighteenth and Second Ohio and New York, right up within a few hundred feet of a masked battery of six guns.

They waited till our men got up close, and then opened on them, firing in rapid succession.

Ten men were killed and wounded belonging to the New York Second Regiment, and also four in the Second Ohio Regiment, by the premature discharge of our own muskets in their hands. A retreat was ordered, and our men fell back.

A battery in our rear upon a hill opened upon it, and they soon quit firing from that time.

SCHENCK failed to rally his column in any order. The Ohio and New York men scattered through the woods in pursuit of shelter and water. The sun was broiling hot, and almost suffocating, for the men were now out of water.

SECOND EDITION.

ONE O'CLOCK.

At six A. M. a heavy fire was opened upon the former battle field, and the Rebels did not answer, although it is known that they were there and our shell were making terrible havoc.

When the masked battery fired upon SCHENCK's column, Lieutenant DAMPSEY, Company C, New York Second Regiment, was killed at the first fire; WM. MAXWELL, drummer, who was at the time carrying water. Our troops were kept under this galling fire for fifteen or twenty minutes within a stone's throw of the battery, but brought off all the killed and wounded.

A few moments after our attack by SCHENCK, at Bull's Run, on the Warrentown Road, clouds of dust came from the direction of Manassas Junction and Brentsville, showing they were being reinforced. A white flag was run up at that point, to show that "we have been attacked by the territory of the army. Send help." General McDOWELL's large force had now got in the enemy's rear, and were driving them down towards the Junction.

POSITION OF THE UNION AND REBEL ARMIES

On the Morning of July 21st, before the Victory at Bull's Run, Recorded in our News Columns.

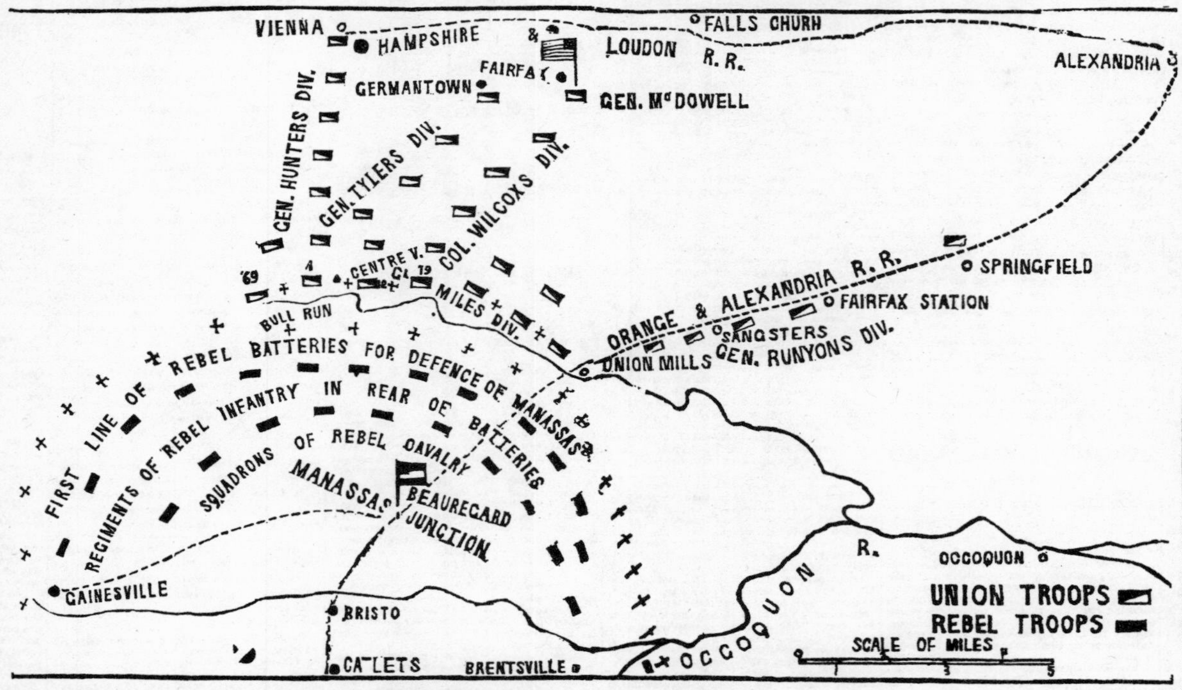

The most gallant charge of the day was made by the New York Sixty-ninth, and Nineteenth, and Thirteenth, who rushed upon one of the batteries, firing as they proceeded, and with great *eclat*, and attacking it with the bayonets' point.

The yell of triumph seemed to carry all before it. They found that the Rebels had abandoned the battery, and only taken one gun; but this success was acquired only after a severe loss of life, in which the Sixty-ninth most severely suffered, and that the Lieutenant-Colonel HAGERTY was among the first killed.

About noon the roar of artillery and peals of musketry was kept up incessantly for a mile or two along Bull's Run.

The fighting was so general and indistinct, it was impossible for us to learn reliably the exact position and result of the different brigades.

Wherever our men had a good chance in fair fight, they swept the field, up to about three, P M. Our army was victorious, but the men had a dread of the masked batteries that could not be overcome, they were placed all over the hill-tops and on sides of ravines, and would open fire upon us when least expected.

Col. RICHARDSON, who distinguished himself in the previous engagement, proceeded on the left with four Regiments of the Fourth Brigade, to hold the battery-hill on Warrenton road, in the vicinity of the place where the last battle was fought; the flank movements were described in the first despatch.

Information was received by TYLER's command of the existence of the enemy's battery commanding the road. Our troops were then formed in battle array. The Second New York and Second Ohio on the left, the Second Ohio and Second Wisconsin, and Seventy-ninth, Thirteenth and Sixty-ninth New York on the right. Col. MILES' division followed in the rear.

SCHENCK and SHERMAN's brigades, of TYLER's division, advanced by the Warrenton road, while HEINTZLEMAN's and HUNTER's divisions took the fork of the Warrenton road, to move between Bull's Run and Manassas Junction. KEYES' brigade remained at Centreville.

Up to the hour of three o'clock P. M., it was generally understood that we had hemmed in the enemy entirely, and that they were gradually retiring; that HUNTER had driven them back in the rear; that HEINTZLEMAN's command was meeting with every success, and that it required but the reserve of TYLER's division to push on Manassas Junction.

We were in the centre of TYLER's division, on the hill just east of Bull's Run on the Wemertown road. About 2 P. M. we saw clouds of dust rising to our left, as though they were trying to out flank us and come on us in the rear. We called several officer's attention to it, but there seemed to be no man who could have reinforcements sent for to cover our flank.

(Further particulars in Third Edition.)

Ordered to Charleston, Va.

Four New York Regiments have been ordered to Charleston to take the place of four Pennsylvania Regiments, whose term has expired.

More Contraband.

The Navy Department has received a despatch from Com STRINGHAM, stating that nine slaves were picked up near the mouth of the Rappahannock river, a few days since, by a Government vessel. They had made their escape in a row boat. According to their account, all the able-bodied male negroes in Essex and Middlesex counties, Va., were being armed. The only Union man in the latter county, who had dared to express his sentiments, was murdered a short time since. Com. STRINGHAM, in view of this new position in which the contraband has been placed by its owners, has written to the Department for instructions.

The Rebels Reinforced.

Well Ordered and Regular Retreat of the American Army to Washington.

OUR LOSS OVER TWO THOUSAND.

REPULSE OF GENRAL McDOWELL'S ARMY.

Official Despatch.

WASHINGTON, July 22.—Our troops after taking three batteries and gaining a great victory, were eventually repulsed and commenced a retreat on Washington.

The retreat is in good order, with the rear well covered by a good column.

Our loss is from 2500 to 3000.

The fortifications around Washington are strongly reinforced by fresh troops.

FROM OUR SPECIAL REPORTER.

WASHINGTON, Monday, July 22—Ten o'clock, A. M.—Our army, after taking three batteries, and really gaining a great victory, were repulsed by fresh troops, and commenced a retreat on Washington in good and regular order. The rear was well covered by good columns. The loss from 2500 to 3000 Our Forts at Washington have been strongly reinforced with fresh troops.

The news of the retreat and repulse is obtained by special reporters of THE INQUIRER from official sources, and it consequently can be relied on

The Battle at Bull's Run.

GREAT SLAUGHTER AND BRILLIANT VICTORY.

This has indeed been a glorious day for the Union. From morning till night the battle has been progressing, and on both sides have the troops shown their courage and fearless impetuosity. Hundreds on both sides have been slain and now sleep in death on the gory field of battle. The slaughter was indeed terrific, and the sight appalling to one unaccustomed to the horrors of war. General McDOWELL telegraphed at five o'clock this afternoon, that he had taken the batteries at Bull Run. A complete victory has been gained over the Rebels at this place, and they are now in full retreat towards Manassas, with our troops following them closely. The firing was so heavy that it has been heard in Washington for an hour past.

Still Later—The Rebels Driven to Manassas

Our troops have compelled the Rebels to retreat until they have reached Manassas, and our artillery are now triumphantly engaged in shelling the left of the enemy's entrenchments there. The bravery of our boys is the theme of praise, and it is believed by those competent to judge that more desperate valor was never seen; and it is plainly evident that it must have been so, considering the immense advantage of the Rebels in having everything fully prepared that time and labor would allow.

Another Vessel Recaptured from the Pirates.

NEW YORK, July 21—Arrived, the schooner *S J Waring*, captured by the privateer *Jeff Davis*, on the night of the 16th. When fifty miles south of Charleston, the colored steward, WILLIAM TILLMAN, killed three of the prize crew with a hatchet. The other two were captured, but set at liberty on promising to work the vessel. Their names were JAMES MILNOR and JAMES DAWBETT, of New Jersey. TILLMAN, with the aid of the rest of the crew, except one man, named DONALD McLEOD, who refused to assist in the recapture of the vessel, brought her to this port.

Later from the Battle-field at Manassas Junction.

THE ENEMY DRIVEN FROM BULL'S RUN

Union Reinforcements Thrown Forward.

WASHINGTON, July 21st—Received 9 P. M.—The orders to Gen McDOWELL to move forward at 6 o'clock yesterday, were suspended until early this morning. Our troops in the meantime were employed in cutting a road through the woods, in order to flank the enemy's batteries

The Secretary of War has received a despatch that the fighting was renewed at Bull's Run this morning. Our troops engaged the enemy with a large force, silenced their batteries, and drove the Secessionists to the Junction.

The city of Washington is wild with excitement and joy. The firing was distinctly heard here in the direction of Bull's Run, from eleven till about three P M, when a cessation took place till nearly five P M At seven this evening the reverberation was still audible

A gentleman who arrived here to night says that at three this afternoon the Second and Third New Jersey Regiments were ordered to march forward from Vienna, first sending back their baggage to Camp Trenton Other troops were hurrying forward to the scene of hostilities. There is great military bustle and excitement in the direction of all the camps

From the Head-quarters of the Army.

ARRIVAL OF JOHNSTON'S CORPS D'ARMEE AT THE JUNCTION.

Orders to Attack the Enemy's Stronghold

WASHINGTON, July 21—It is not doubted in high military quarters that the Rebel Gen JOHNSTON, recently at Winchester, was enabled to effect a junction, sometime yesterday, with Gen BEAUREGARD, at Manassas Junction.

Official despatches were sent at two o'clock this morning from head-quarters to General McDOWELL

General McDOWELL was to have moved upon the enemy at six o'clock last evening.

The Thirty-seventh New York passed over into Virginia this morning, the band playing "Dixie" amid the cheers of the soldiers and citizens.

Every possible arrangement has been made by the Associated Press agent to get the earliest reliable news of any result at Manassas Junction It is the impression in well informed circles here that the action is progressing there at this hour

FROM THE SEAT OF THE WAR.

ADVANCE OF THE GRAND ARMY

BEAUREGARD OUTFLANKED.

APPROACH OF GEN. McCLELLAN'S DIVISION.

A Decisive Battle Momentarily Expected.

RE-ENLISTMENT OF THE NEW YORK REGIMENTS.

CENTREVILLE, July 21—[By telegraph from Fairfax Court House]—We have successfully outflanked the enemy. At half-past two this morning the various regiments about Centreville were formed for the march, and at three they were in motion in the direction of Perryville, leaving Bull's Run to the left

At six o'clock the first shot was fired by one of the 32 pound rifled cannons, which was sent there to batter any masked batteries that might be encountered on the road. There was no reply from the enemy, and the advance guard moved on Gen McDOWELL's head-quarters were three miles beyond the town of Centreville.

The greater part of the army moved to the right to avoid a bridge some distance beyond, said to have been undermined. They will pass over the stream on pontoons prepared by Captain ALEXANDER, of the Engineers, who has previously reconnoitred the country minutely, and to whom in a great measure, the plan of the campaign is due.

A general battle is expected to-day or to-morrow, which will probably decide the fate of the whole campaign If General JOHNSTON has not yet effected a junction with General BEAUREGARD, he will be entirely cut off by this manœuvre [illegible] army utterly demoralized, and will probably fall into the hands of General McCLELLAN, who is now advancing beyond the Blue Ridge. If he has succeeded in reaching BEAUREGARD's camping ground, it offers a communication with General PATTERSON's division, and, thus reinforced, the Federal army can crush out the opposition. If we are driven back, the army can retreat upon Centreville, and keep an open communication with Washington

If Gen. BEAUREGARD remains where he is his communication with the rear is endangered, and Manassas being situated in the apex of a triangle formed by the rail roads, a movement in his rear would destroy his communication with Richmond.

The only danger our troops run by this flank march would be by the sudden advance by BEAUREGARD upon Centreville, thus interfering with our rearward communication, and cutting off supplies But this manœuvre would indicate a desperation on his part, as cutting himself off from supplies, and placing himself in an exhausted country between the Federal troops and the Potomac

The Sixty-ninth New York was assigned the post of honor in the advance movement. The members of this Regiment have unanimously agreed to remain in the service, although their time has expired All the New York regiments will follow their example

For five hours one steady column of troops has been passing through Centreville. The morale of the soldiers is excellent. All are anxious for a battle, and when informed of the purpose to advance, the enthusiasm was beyond description

It is supposed that BEAUREGARD's forces considerably outnumber our own

A battle is imminent at any moment, but it may not take place before to-morrow night

The telegraph wires are rapidly following the army, and offices were opened this morning at Fairfax Court House, with Messrs. BUELL and [illegible]TON as army operators.

[It is believed the foregoing was written about [illegible] o'clock this morning.—PHILA REPORTER]

[G]reat Battle at Manassas

[G]OVERNMENT BULLETINS.

[ST]ARS AND STRIPES VICTORIOUS!

WASHINGTON July 21—[Received at 11 P. M.]—[Th]e following bulletins were received in official [qu]arters to-day, during the progress of the battle, [fro]m the telegraph station, about four miles from [Bu]ll's Run

FAIRFAX, 11 A. M.—Rapid firing from heavy [gu]ns and frequent discharges of musketry.

11:40—Fighting very heavy and apparently on [ou]r left wing.

11 50.—There is evidently a battle towards our [lef]t, in the direction of Bull's Run, and a little [no]rth The firing is very rapid and heavy.

1 45—Heavy guns again, apparently nearer. Musketry heavy and nearer.

2 P. M.—The musketry very heavy, and drawing much nearer. There is evidently a movement nearer to our left.

2:45 P. M.—Firing a little further off, and apparently in the direction of the Junction. Less heavy guns and more light artillery, as near as I can judge.

3 P. M.—The firing ceased ten minutes since.

3 55 P. M.—The firing has almost entirely ceased, and can only be heard with difficulty. I shall telegraph no more, unless there should be a renewal of the battle which has been so gloriously fought for the old Stars and Stripes. From all indications here, our troops have at least stood their ground.

FAIRFAX C. H., 3:50—Our courier has not returned. Quartermaster BARTON, of the Second Michigan, has just passed, and says that the officers, men and citizens of Centreville say that a general engagement of the whole line has taken place three and a half miles this side of the Junction, and that our troops have driven and forced the Secession lines back to the Junction. We expect the courier now every moment.

CENTREVILLE, 4 P. M.—Gen. McDOWELL has ordered the reserves now here, under Col. MILES, to advance to the bridge over Bull's Run, on the Warrenton road, having driven the enemy before him. Col. MILES is now about three or four miles from here, directing the operations near Blackburn's Ford.

FAIRFAX, July 21, 4:45 P. M.—Two of our couriers have returned, but were unable to communicate in person with General McDOWELL. One of the couriers was on the field of battle. He says our troops have taken three masked batteries, and forced the Rebels to retire. He says the battle was general on Bull's Run for some distance. One of the batteries taken was in a wheat field, and the other some distance from it. The third battery was still further on

5 20 P. M.—Another despatch says that the Federals have won the day. The loss on both sides is very heavy, but the rout of the Rebels is complete. The batteries at Bull's Run are silenced, and two or three others taken.

5:40 P. M.—The firing has ceased. We shall send another courier there in a few minutes. The Colonel went at four o'clock and will be back soon.

STILL LATER.

A report, not official but from an apparently reliable source, says that the column under Col HEINTZELMAN has followed the Rebels to Manassas Junction, and has opened fire on their entrenched camp, and was then shelling them.

The cannonading can occasionally be heard in Washington and on Georgetown Heights.

The head-quarters of the army are inaccessible to night, the President and the Cabinet being privately with Gen. SCOTT and other distinguished gentlemen.

ANOTHER WASHINGTON DESPATCH

WASHINGTON, July 21, 12 o'clock, P. M.—The most intense excitement is everywhere existing to hear the news from the field of battle. Every returning spectator is immediately surrounded, and the demand for intelligence is insatiable. Many unauthorized rumors prevail, which serve to confuse the truth.

The smoke of the battle could be seen from the eminences in Washington. Numbers of Members of Congress, and even ladies, went to the neighborhood of Bull's Run to witness the battle. One of them reports that Col HUNTER, of the Third Cavalry but acting as Major General, was seriously, if not mortally wounded It is stated with confidence in all quarters that C. J. CAMERON, of the Seventy ninth New York, and brother to the Secretary of War, and Col SLOCUM, of the Second Rhode Island, were killed.

STILL LATER—DETAILS OF THE BATTLE.

WASHINGTON, July 21—Midnight —A most severe battle was fought to-day at Bull's Run bridge. The conflict was desperate, lasting over nine hours. The programme, as stated in the first despatch, was carried out until the troops met with a succession of masked batteries, which were attacked with vigor and success.

Our troops advanced as follows:—Col. RICHARDSON proceeded on the left with four regiments of the Fourth Brigade, to hold the Battery hill on the Warrenton road, in the vicinity of the ground where the last battle was fought. The flank movements have been previously described SCHENCK's and SHERMAN's Brigades, of TYLER's Division, advanced by the Warrenton road, while HEINTZELMAN's and HUNTER's Divisions took the fork of the Warrenton Road to move between Bull's Run and the Manassas Junction. Col KEY's Brigade remained at Centreville.

Information was received by Gen. TYLER's command of the existence of the enemy's battery commanding the road. Our troops were then formed in battle array. The Second New York and Second Ohio on the left, the — Ohio and Second Wisconsin, and Seventy-ninth, Thirteenth and Sixty-ninth New York on the right. Col. MILES' Division followed in the rear.

The first range gun was fired by SHERMAN's Battery at 10 minutes of 7 The Rebels did not return his shot until an hour and a half afterwards. When Colonel HUNTER's Division came up the battle became general The latter's movement to gain the enemy's rear was almost a success

The enemy's position was opened on by several of Captain CARLISLE's howitzers, followed by slight skirmishing. The Rebels rapidly received reinforcements from Manassas Junction after the attack was opened. The battle consisted in a succession of fires from the masked batteries, which opened in every direction; when one was silenced, its place was supplied by two, and in the daring charges of our infantry in unmasking them.

The Second Ohio and Second New York Militia were marched by flank through the woods, by a new made road, within a mile of the main road, when they came on a battery of eight guns, with four regiments flanked in the rear.

Our men were immediately ordered to lie down on either side of the road, in order to allow two pieces of artillery to pass through to attack the work, when this battery opened upon us, and killed, on the third round, Lieut. DEMPSEY, of Company G, New York Second, and WM MAXWALL, a drummer; also seriously wounding several others. Our troops were kept for fifteen or twenty minutes under a galling fire, not being able to exchange shots with the enemy, although within a stone's throw of their batteries. They succeeded in retiring in regular order, and with their batteries.

The most gallant charge of the day was made by the New York Sixty-ninth, Seventy-ninth and Thirteenth, who rushed upon one of the batteries, firing as they proceeded with perfect eclat, and attacking it at the bayonet's point

The yell of triumph seemed to carry all before it. They found that the Rebels had abandoned the battery, taking only one gun; but this success was acquired only after a severe loss of life, in which the 69th were the greatest sufferers, and it was reported that the Lieut Colonel was among the first killed. The Zouaves also distinguished themselves by their spirited assaults on the batteries at the point of the bayonet, but it is feared that their loss is immense.

Up to three o'clock, P. M., it was generally understood that we had hemmed in the enemy entirely, and that they were gradually retiring; that HUNTER had driven them back in the rear; that HEINTZELMAN's command was meeting with every success; and that it required but the reserve of TYLER's division to push on to Manassas Junction.

A Mississippi soldier was taken prisoner by HASBROUCK, of the Wisconsin Second. He turned out to be Brigade Quartermaster PAYOR, a cousin of ROGER A. PRYOR He was captured with his horses, he by accident riding into our lines He discovered himself by remarking to HASBROUCK, "We are getting badly cut to pieces." "What regiment do you belong to?" asked HASBROUCK. "The Nineteenth Mississippi," was the answer "Then you are my prisoner," said HASBROUCK.

Continued on Eighth Page.

The Daily Picayune.

VOLUME XXV. NEW ORLEANS, WEDNESDAY MORNING, JULY 24, 1861. NUMBER 154.

The Daily Picayune.

FROM OUR EVENING EDITION OF YESTERDAY

CONFISCATION.

Among the difficulties to the United States of the war they are so insolently waging against this Confederacy, the question of ways and means for carrying it on according to the programme presents one of the greatest and most insoluble. It is very easy for the Executive to demand of a supple Congress the appropriation of hundreds of millions of dollars. Mad Owen Glendower could "call spirits from the vasty deep," but did they come when he did call for them? We fancy that the chances of obtaining the necessary heavy loans required by that overweening Government will not have been greatly improved by the incidents of the 21st and 22d of July, on the western bank of the Potomac.

In casting about for alternative means of paying the expenses of the war, the sagacious advisers of the Lincoln administration have discovered a sure, safe and easy way "how to do it." Great as the task is of "suppressing the rebellion," and although it may cost any number of millions of dollars, the whole amount of the immense war debt must be paid out of the property and resources of the invaded and subjugated States! And the people of the North are encouragingly reminded that by the law and usage of nations, it is entirely legitimate to make the property of the citizens of the "rebel States" pay the whole debt incurred by the Lincoln government "in restoring the supremacy of the constitution and the laws. This they call the just penalty for treason, and urge its adoption as being perfectly consistent with the law and usage of nations. We will give a specimen of their reasoning, if so it can be called, on this point:

The debts incurred by the Confederate States for the support of their conspiracy and revolt are clearly without law and void, and will be so treated by all national courts. They will not, therefore, be a charge upon the property of the people of the seceded States when the Union is restored, or rather when the national jurisdiction over them is resumed. It will be within the ability, then, of the disloyal States to make up to the national Government the losses they have occasioned it; and the very revenues they have devised—the export duty on cotton, and the direct taxes they will lay—may be properly diverted by the national Congress from the support of treason to the extinguishment of the nation's war debt. The export duty on cotton will thus become a permanent regulation of American commerce, and as the English people, who are its chief purchasers, have no fault to find with the imposition of this duty by the rebels themselves, it is not to be supposed that they will complain if it is adopted and continued as a settled policy of the national Government.

That is one way. Another idea is that it would not be at all amiss for "the National," (i. e. the U. S.) Government, "in the exercise of its rightful power, to confiscate the property of rebels, to lay a special tax on that species of property in the seceded States that has, more than any other, been the cause of the present civil war."

These counsels bore fruit in the concoction of Mr. Secretary Chase's report on the state and the needs of the treasury at the opening of the extra session of Congress, in which, it may be remembered, he used this language:

The property of those engaged in insurrection, or in giving aid and comfort to the insurgents, may properly be made to contribute to the expenditure made necessary by their criminal misconduct. As a part of the punishment due to the guilt of involving the nation in the calamities of civil war, and thereby bringing distress upon so many innocent citizens, Congress may justly provide for the forfeiture of the whole or a part of the estates of offenders, and for the payment of the proceeds into the public treasury.

The New York Times, in concluding an elaborate article on this subject, expresses the hope that Congress would not hesitate to pass suitable laws embodying these principles. And here, again, the counsels of the Times and its coadjutors have fructified finely. As will be seen on referring to the telegraphic dispatches in this morning's Picayune, in the U. S. Senate, on the 22d inst., a bill, providing for the confiscation of the property of "rebels found in arms against the United States," was passed by a vote of 32 to 6, Messrs. Breckinridge and Powell, of Kentucky, Kennedy and Pearce, of Maryland, and Johnson and Polk, of Missouri, alone voting against it. The telegraphic dispatch adds that Trumbull, of Illinois, offered an amendment that "slaves employed to aid in this rebellion be forfeited by their masters." But it does not appear whether this proposition was adopted or not. Enough for our present purpose that the bill of confiscation was passed by the Senate, that it is sure to be passed by the House, and will with the utmost alacrity be approved by the President.

The spontaneous and voluntary enlistment of the entire fighting force of the Confederate States, the sagacity, experience and gallantry of their accomplished generals, the lukewarm indifference of thousands of the invading army, and the imbecility of the majority of its leaders, all combined, could hardly do more to assure the success of our glorious cause than will the adoption of that simple act of legislation by the Congress at Washington.

☞ It is said that arrangements are being made to commence the manufacture of small arms at Athens, Ga.

☞ The Second Florida Regiment arrived at Charleston on the 18th inst., *en route* for Virginia. They numbered 1003 men.

☞ Mr. Barr, at Louisville, has our thanks for valuable newspaper attentions.

☞ Mr. Sutterley, of Sutterley's news room, St. Charles Hotel, obliged us yesterday with a copy of the New York Daily News, of the 17th inst.

PERSONAL.—Among the passengers per Persia, from New York, on the 17th, were Messrs. John Gaudy and child, J. J. Browne, P. Massondet, Mrs. Froidevaux, and Mr. and Mrs. Tilton—all registered from New Orleans.

MAIL LINE TO MOBILE.—We would renewedly remind our readers that the California, as will be seen by the notice of the agent of the line, goes hence to Mobile on Wednesday (to-morrow) morning, on the arrival of the 6 o'clock, A. M., cars.

Telegraphed to the New Orleans Picayune

[SPECIAL TO THE PICAYUNE.]

BATTLE OF MANASSAS.

FURTHER PARTICULARS.

GLORIOUS VICTORY.

THE ENEMY 80,000 STRONG!

THEIR LOSS 10,000 TO 15,000.

GALLANT CONDUCT OF THE LOUISIANA BOYS.

MAJOR WHEAT'S BATTALION SUFFERED SEVERELY.

THE ENEMY COMPLETELY ROUTED.

CULPEPER COURTHOUSE, July 22.—There was a general engagement at Manassas yesterday, and a terrible fight all day.

The enemy was 80,000 strong, and was completely routed with immense loss, estimated at from 10,000 to 15,000.

Our loss was considerable.

Wheat's battalion suffered severely. Major Wheat and many of his men were wounded. The rest of the Louisianians suffered slightly.

The Washington Artillery and the Louisiana Infantry did splendid execution.

The victory was grand and decisive.

The enemy was pursued all night.

Centreville was occupied by our troops.

President Davis arrived here last night.

[SPECIAL TO THE PICAYUNE.]

BATTLE OF MANASSAS.

STILL FURTHER PARTICULARS.

Glorious Charge by Louisianians, Virginians and Mississippians under Beauregard.

Slaughter of the Enemy Dreadful.

MANY PRISONERS CAPTURED!

HEAVY LOSS OF THE ENEMY IN CANNON, RIFLES, BAGGAGE, &c.

OUR DEAD TO BE SENT HOME.

THE WOUNDED WELL CARED FOR.

CULPEPER C. H., July 22.—Our victory yesterday over the grand army of invasion at Manassas was glorious and complete.

Early in the morning the enemy, having obtained our badges and countersign, had got forward in front.

The enemy fought obstinately. The battle began at nine in the morning and lasted till five in the evening. At eleven o'clock the enemy suffered a repulse, but being reinforced, made a renewed effort for the mastery. At two they were again repulsed. Again renewing the struggle, they were finally outfought by our gallant men and were routed at five, fleeing in all directions, and pursued by our cavalry, and by President Davis, at the head of a body of fresh troops, which had been held in reserve, to Centreville.

Our army captured very many cannon, a large number of rifles, an immense number of prisoners, and a vast quantity of baggage.

All Sherman's Battery was taken and came in this morning. Gen. Beauregard charged in person upon Sherman's Battery at the head of a body of brave Louisianians, Virginians and Mississippians.

Our whole army covered itself with glory.

Our dead will be sent home. Our wounded are well cared for.

The slaughter of the enemy was dreadful. The battlefield was strewn with dead and wounded as far as the pursuit continued.

A large number of officers and New York politicians were taken prisoners.

THE BATTLE OF MANASSAS.

DISPATCH FROM PRESIDENT DAVIS TO THE SECRETARY OF WAR.

RICHMOND, July 22.—President Davis sends an official dispatch to the Secretary of War, announcing a complete and decisive victory near Manassas yesterday. The enemy, after ten hours fighting, fled precipitately in the direction of Leesburg and Centreville, pursued by our cavalry and light infantry, till night put an end to the pursuit.

The enemy left on the field large stores of munitions and arms.

Vast piles of slain are everywhere in the direction of the flight. The neighboring farm houses on the road are crowded with the wounded enemy.

The Confederate force immediately engaged was 15,000, and the Federalists are estimated at 35,000. This refers to the left wing, where the battle was principally waged, and don't include the right and centre, which was but partially engaged.

The entire Confederate force amounted to about 40,000 and the Federalists nearly 80,000.

The enemy lost several field batteries and one regimental stand of colors.

No particulars have been received up to one o'clock this afternoon of the dead and wounded on either side.

The Confederate Congress.

Reception of a Dispatch announcing the Victory.

RICHMOND, July 22.—Congress met at noon, opening with prayer.

The following dispatch to Gen. S. Cooper, Adjutant General, was read by the Clerk:

"MANASSAS, Sunday Night.—Night has closed upon a hard bought field. Our forces have won a glorious victory. The enemy was routed and fled precipitately, abandoning a very large amount of arms, munitions, knapsacks and baggage. The ground was strewn for miles with those killed, and the farm houses and grounds around are filled with his wounded. The pursuit was continued on several routes towards Leesburg and Centreville, until darkness covered the fugitives. We have captured several field batteries and a regimental stand of colors, and one United States flag. Many prisoners have been taken. Too much praise cannot be bestowed, whether for the skill of the principal officers, or for the gallantry of the troops. The battle was mainly fought on our left, several miles from our field works. Our forces engaged did not exceed 15,000. That of the enemy is estimated at 35,000.

"[Signed,] JEFFERSON DAVIS."

The following resolutions were offered by Mr. Memminger, and unanimously adopted:

"*Resolved*, That we recognize the hand of the most High God, the King of Kings and Lord of Lords, in the glorious victory with which He hath crowned our arms at Manassas, and that the people of the Confederate States are invited, by appropriate services on the ensuing Sabbath, to offer up their united thanksgiving and praise for this mighty deliverance.

"*Resolved*, That deeply deploring the necessity which has washed the soil of our country with the blood of so many of her noblest sons, we offer to their respective families and friends our warmest and most cordial sympathy, assuring them that the sacrifice made will be consecrated in the hearts of our people, and that they will there enshrine the names of the gallant dead as the champions of constitutional liberty.

"*Resolved*, That we approve of the prompt and patriotic efforts of the people of Richmond to make provision for the wounded, and that a committee of one member from each State be appointed to coöperate in the plan.

"*Resolved*, That Congress do now adjourn."

Richmond Full of Rumors.

The city is full of rumors about the number of killed and wounded on both sides, and of movements being made, but all are utterly unreliable.

Brig. Gen. Bartow.

The body of Brig. Gen. Francis S. Bartow, of Georgia, and perhaps others are expected on the train to-night.

Provision for the Sick and Wounded.

Large Meeting in Richmond.

A large public meeting was held this afternoon, and a committee appointed to go to Manassas and receive all the wounded able to be transported to Richmond. Other committees, also, to ascertain the number of families in Richmond who will receive and attend the wounded, and to solicit subscriptions and obtain comforts for the sufferings of the sick and wounded.

It has been raining all day, and the train due from Manassas at 3 o'clock this afternoon is not expected to arrive before midnight.

The telegraph to Manassas has been out of working order several hours, but is now working, with an immense business on hand and offering.

The Dead and Wounded.

It is impossible to obtain details of the dead and wounded yet.

The battle ground extended over a space of ten miles.

Receipt of the News of the Victory in Wilmington.

WILMINGTON, N. C., July 22.—The news of the battle of Manassas was received with great rejoicing.

A salute was fired in honor of the great event.

Proceedings of the U. S. Congress.

WASHINGTON, July 22.—In the Senate, the bill to increase the military establishment was returned to the House, the Senate refusing to concur in the amendments.

A message having been received from the President, the Senate went into executive session.

In the House, Mr. Wright offered a resolution that the reverses at Bull Run no way impair the ultimate success, &c., of the Federalists, which was tabled.

Army News from Washington.

Gen. McClellan has been ordered to the command of the forces on the Potomac, and is succeeded in Western Virginia by Gen. Rosencrantz.

The Federal army will be immediately reorganized and increased.

Gen. McDowell is at headquarters at Arlington. His division will resume its former position.

A large amount of arms, provisions, &c., were captured by the Confederates, who pursued and occupied the positions abandoned by us, as far as Fairfax Courthouse.

The cavalry of the Confederates was the terror of our volunteers, who kept the woods to avoid their charges.

Reports from Baltimore.

BALTIMORE, July 13.—The 13th New York Militia have re-enlisted for three years.

Banks joins Patterson, who is at Harper's Ferry awaiting him.

State of Affairs in Baltimore.

There is great excitement here. The Southerners are overjoyed, and the efforts of their friends to quiet their delirium is of no avail. It is said that a considerable military force will be required to keep them down.

Likenesses of Beauregard are selling through the streets.

The heavy rain prevents the people from congregating. Thirty arrests have been made for attempts to incite revolts.

Gen. Patterson under a Cloud.

The defeat at Manassas is attributed to the inactivity of Patterson, who had received a dozen official orders to engage Johnston at any odds.

What the New York Herald Says of the Great Battle.

NEW YORK, July 23.—The Herald's special correspondent says the retreat was nothing more or less than a stampede. The defeat is attributed in a great measure to Patterson's tardiness.

Gov. Sprague's bravery brought some degree of order out of the chaos.

McDowell displayed great bravery, but his efforts to arrest the panic were unavailing.

The New York 71st, 14th and 27th, and Maine regiments were mowed down like grass.

The list of killed and wounded embraces a large number of officers.

Col. Hawkins is thought to be dead.

Missouri Convention in Session.

JEFFERSON CITY, July 23.—The convention has organized; 61 members are present. Gen. Wilson has been elected *President*.

LATER FROM EUROPE.

ARRIVAL OF THE NORTH AMERICAN.

Liverpool Cotton Market Firm.

Breadstuffs and Provisions Steady.

FATHER POINT, July 23.—The Canadian mail steamship North American, from Liverpool on the 11th and Londonderry on the 12th, has passed this point bound for Quebec.

The steamships Jura and City of Baltimore, from New York, had both arrived out at Liverpool previous to the departure of the North American.

Liverpool Cotton Market.

LIVERPOOL, July 11.—The sales of cotton the past three days in Liverpool consisted of 37,000 bales, of which speculators and exporters took 12,000. The market closed firm at last week's rates, which were fully maintained.

Liverpool Breadstuffs Market.

Breadstuffs quiet and steady. Provisions steady.

London Money Market.

LONDON, July 11.—Consols closed at 89⅝ a ⅞ for money and 90⅛ a ¼ for the account.

General News.

The political news by the North American contains nothing of importance.

☞ We are indebted to Mr. McKeever, of the Adams Express, and his courteous coadjutors, for forwarding us our New York package of papers, of late dates.

Death of the first living Poetess.—By the latest arrival from England, we learn that Mrs. Elizabeth Barrett Browning died on the 29th of June, at Florence, Italy, in the fifty-second year of her age. Her life had been that of a literary woman. Born in England in 1809, she early displayed unusual ability, and her education received unusual care. That care was not thrown away. She made her debut on the stage of letters when only seventeen; her effusion was practical, and yet indicated the philosophical turn of her intellect, for it was styled "An Essay on Mind." Since then various publications have emanated from her busy brain. "Prometheus Bound," "The Drama of Exile," "The Seraphim," "Casa Guidi Windows," and "Aurora Leigh," have in turn engaged the attention of the literary world, and provoked the most various criticisms, some pronouncing them works of extraordinary genius, others, and perhaps the majority, finding them full of affectations, improprieties, and worse than all—dull.

In 1844 Miss Barrett published a collected edition of her poems which contained a graceful allusion to Mr. Browning, with whom the authoress was then unacquainted; the poet called on the poetess to express his thanks, and by mistake was ushered into the presence of Miss Barrett, then an invalid. The acquaintance thus singularly and almost fortunately begun ripened into friendship, the friendship into love, and love eventuated in marriage—a marriage said to have been remarkable for the completeness of accord between those whom it united, and for the perfection of the domestic felicity which it secured. In 1849 the only child of this union was born, a boy.

Mrs. Browning was undoubtedly one of the most gifted women of her time, perhaps overrated by the peculiar circle whose political and religious notions chimed entirely with her own, but undoubtedly a person of remarkable intellectual endowments. Some of her mental traits were masculine, and her taste was by no means correct or severe, and she always attempted in literature much more than she accomplished; but it is impossible for any one alive to the fascinations of splendid imagery, passionate language, earnest thought and profound feeling, to be insensible to the indications of these that abound in her works.

Mrs. Browning possessed rare attractions for her friends; attractions that were by no means confined to intellectual peculiarities. Whatever occasional manifestations of an unwomanly nature were visible in her writings, a very genuine and feminine sensibility is also displayed, while the universal agreement of those who knew her intimately, is, that this sensibility was conspicuous in all the actions of her life. She leaves no rival poet among living women.

THE CITY.

NEW ORLEANS JUBILANT.—*The Glorious Twenty-first of July.*—Throughout Sunday last, speculations ran high in our city, and predictions were freely made that a general fight and terrific battle was taking place in Virginia between our troops and the Northern hordes of the tyrant and usurper. An instinctive feeling seemed to possess many of our people to this effect, and the presentiment seemed to gain ground on the declaration that Sunday had ever been the grand battle day of nations. The day in New Orleans was unusually close and sultry, and the sun went down leaving a most remarkable blood-red sky, whose intense crimsoned hues attracted general attention, and were considered the omen of carnage and slaughter.

At 11 o'clock at night the prediction was fulfilled by the reception of a telegraphic dispatch from Richmond, stating that there had been a bloody battle—fourteen hours' fighting—and the enemy in retreat. The news spread in all directions, and the most intense excitement prevailed until after midnight. People were aroused from their slumbers, and the tale of glory and victory was repeated to the startled sleepers.

The confirmatory news the next morning sent a thrill of joy through the hearts of our people, like the upheaving of the mountain waves. Our office was besieged by multitude after multitude, anxious for the particulars; extra after extra was issued, and the most intense excitement reigned throughout the city until long after midnight. There were no wild [illegible] of inebriates, as in political victories—no firing of cannon—but an inward welling up of gladness and thanksgiving, an offering of the heart's deepest gratitude to God for the success of our [illegible] and the holy triumph of our arms, while [illegible] sisters, as they sank to slumber, [illegible] the safety of their kindred, and [illegible] of our country's cause.

THE NEW YORK HERALD

WHOLE NO. 9102. | NEW YORK, MONDAY, AUGUST 12, 1861. | PRICE TWO CENTS.

THE REBELLION.

The Latest News from Washington.

Important Letter of Secretary Cameron to Gen. Butler.

Fugitive Slaves to be Employed in the Service of the Government.

A Record of Them to be Kept for Future Adjudication.

THE VISIT OF MRS. LINCOLN TO THE NORTH.

THE BLOCKADE

Visit of the Assistant Secretary of the Navy to the New York Shipping.

THE REBEL PRIVATEER YORK BURNED.

Recapture of the Schooner George G. Baker.

The Schooner Wm. S. Tisdale, from Fort Pickens, Fired Into by a Pirate.

English Vessels Run Ashore to Dispose of Their Cargoes to the Rebels.

IMPORTANT FROM FORTRESS MONROE.

List of the Union Soldiers at Richmond.

THE SEAT OF WAR IN THE WEST.

Graphic Description of the Fight at Dug Spring,

&c., &c., &c.

OUR SPECIAL WASHINGTON DESPATCHES.

WASHINGTON, August 11, 1861.

IMPORTANT LETTER FROM SECRETARY CAMERON TO GENERAL BUTLER.

The following letter has just been despatched to Gen. Butler by the Secretary of War:—

WASHINGTON, August —, 1861.

GENERAL—The important question of the proper disposition to be made of fugitives from service in the States in insurrection against the federal government, to which you have again directed my attention in your letter of July 20, has received my most attentive consideration. It is the desire of the President that all existing rights in all the States be fully respected and maintained. The war now prosecuted on the part of the federal government is a war for the Union, for the preservation of all constitutional rights of States, and the citizens of the States in the Union. Hence no question can arise as to fugitives from service within the States and Territories in which the authority of the Union is fully acknowledged. The ordinary form of judicial proceedings must be respected by military and civil authorities alike for the enforcement of legal forms. But in the States wholly or in part under insurrectionary control, where the laws of the United States are so far opposed and resisted that they cannot be effectually enforced, it is obvious that the rights dependent upon the execution of those laws must temporarily fail, and it is equally obvious that the rights dependent on the laws of the State within which military operations are conducted must be necessarily subordinate to the military exigences created by the insurrection if not wholly forfeited by the treasonable conduct of parties claiming them. To this the general rule of right to services forms an exception. The act of Congress, approved August 6, 1861, declares that if persons held to service shall be employed in hostility to the United States, the right to their services shall be forfeited, and such persons shall be discharged therefrom. It follows, of necessity, that no claim can be recognized by the military authority of the Union for the services of such persons, when fugitives.

A more difficult question is presented in respect to persons escaping from the service of loyal masters. It is quite apparent that the laws of the State under which only the service of such fugitives can be claimed, must needs be wholly, or almost wholly, suspended. As to the remedies by the insurrection and the military measures necessitated by it, it is equally apparent that the substitution of military for judicial measures for the enforcement of such claims must be attended by great inconveniences, embarrassments and inquiries. Under these circumstances it seems quite clear that the substantial rights of local masters are still best protected by receiving such fugitives, as well as fugitives from disloyal masters, into the service of the United States, and employing them under such organizations and such occupations as circumstances may suggest or require. Of course a record should be kept showing a name and description of the fugitives; the name and the character, as loyal or disloyal, of the master, and such facts as may be necessary to a correct understanding of the circumstances of each case, after tranquillity shall have been restored. Upon the return of peace Congress will, doubtless, properly provide for all the persons it has received into the service of the Union, and for a just compensation to loyal masters. In this way only, it would seem, can the duty and safety of the government and the just rights of all be fully reconciled and harmonized.

You will, therefore, consider yourself instructed to govern your future action in respect to fugitives from service by the premises herein stated, and will report from time to time, and at least twice in each month, your action in the premises to this department. You will, however, neither authorize nor permit any interference by the troops under your command with the servants of peaceful citizens in a house or field, nor will you in any way encourage such servants to leave the lawful service of their masters; nor will you, except in cases where the public good may seem to require it, prevent the voluntary return of any fugitives to the service from which he may have escaped. I am, very respectfully, your obedient servant,

SIMON CAMERON, Secretary of War.

To Major General BUTLER, commanding Department of Virginia, Fortress Monroe.

THE VISIT OF MRS. LINCOLN TO LONG BRANCH.

The visit of Mrs. Lincoln to the North is postponed until Wednesday. The beau monde at Long Branch will have to restrain a while longer their impatience to shine in the atmosphere of the republican court.

DEPARTURE OF PRINCE NAPOLEON.

Prince Napoleon took leave of the President yesterday, and returned direct to New York.

THE IMPRISONMENT OF MESSRS. M'GRAW AND HARRIS AT RICHMOND.

When the train was about to leave Harper's Ferry for Baltimore yesterday, a letter addressed to the wife of Mr. McGraw, who is a prisoner at Richmond, was thrown into one of the cars by an unknown person. It proved to be an open letter from him assuring her that he was well cared for, but was not allowed to go out of the place of his confinement, except when attended by a sentinel, and that he had no expectation of being released until the termination of the war. There have been various surmises as to the cause of the detention of Messrs. McGraw and Harris under the circumstances, as their sympathy with the rebels was notorious. It is supposed by some that the imprisonment of Mr. Harris is in punishment for his failure to fulfill a contract he is said to have made to furnish a lot of arms to the rebels, and for having accepted an interest in a fat beef contract with the federal government, when compelled by circumstances to abandon the one for supplying arms to the rebels. The punishment should have fallen upon those who, in the name of the federal government, made a contract with notorious sympathizers with rebellion and men who had already a contract to furnish arms to the traitors.

THE SEAT OF WAR IN THE WEST.

Map of the Scene of Operations in Southeastern Missouri, Illinois and Tennessee, with the Positions of the Rebel Troops and Portions of the Federal Forces, and the Defences at Cairo and Bird's Point.

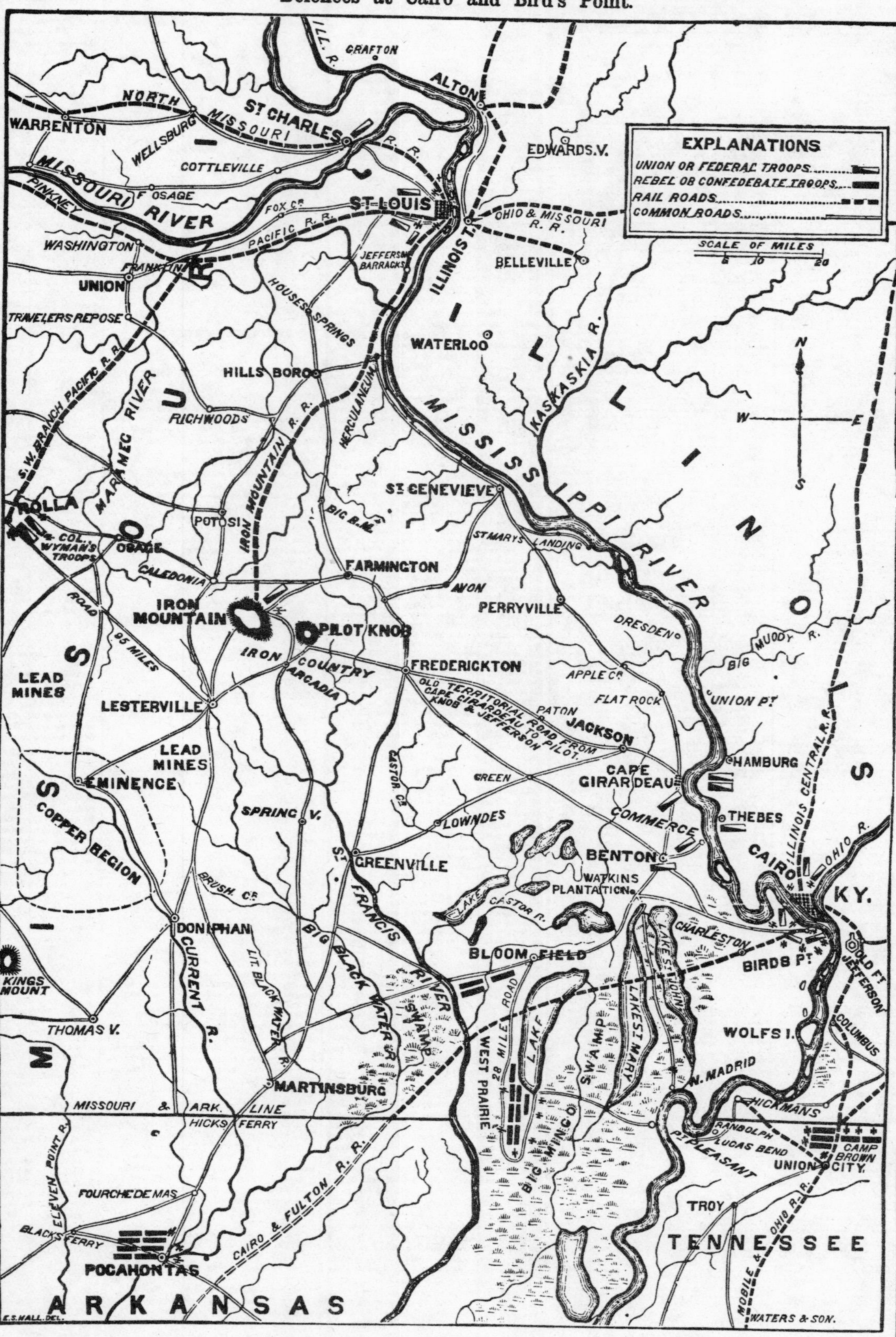

THE VESSELS CAPTURED BY REBEL PRIVATEERS AND SENT TO CUBA.

The Spanish Minister announced to the Secretary of State yesterday that the seven American vessels captured by the rebel privateer Sumter, and carried into the port of Cienfuegos as prizes, have been discharged by orders from his government.

WEST POINT GRADUATES IN CLERICAL POSITIONS.

It is well known that the study of southern statesmen, since the organization of the government, has been to crowd our military and naval schools with Southern students. This is not only so, but Southern politicians have always been most active to obtain for their graduates at these schools the earliest and most rapid promotion to places of trust and power. It is for this reason that so many army and navy officers have lately resigned and joined the rebellion. On account of the treasonable conduct of these officers the United States Army has been nearly thinned out, and it is not to be denied that we have been and are now deficient in men educated to the arts of war. In view of this fact is it not surprising that from forty to fifty of the assistants in the Commissary and Quartermaster General's departments are said to be the best artillery and infantry officers in the army. They were all, or nearly all, educated at West Point. The places they are now filling could be easily occupied by any good practical business man. They are exactly the duties that belong to the civilian, who, with a little practice, would be much better fitted for them than the man educated to the stern realities of the field. It does not look well to see the soldier sitting at a desk with a pen, in times of war, doing clerical work, when he has been fitted for other duties at the expense of the government, and for the skilful performance of which the government is suffering to an extent altogether too great to be mentioned. Soldiers in peace and civilians in war is a bad rule.

THE FOURTEENTH MASSACHUSETTS REGIMENT IN A THUNDER STORM.

The city was favored late this afternoon with a tremendous rain storm, which afforded great relief to all who had been suffering from the heat during the hottest day experienced here for eighteen years. In the midst of the storm, when the rain was pouring down in torrents, the Fourteenth Massachusetts regiment, Colonel Devens, marched up the avenue, *en route* for their camping ground. They had been quartered since last night at the Government Military Reception House, at the depot, but were required to move to make room for new arrivals. Their splendid horses and wagons had preceded them, and the men marched steadily through the driving storm, sometimes for squares through water two feet deep. Their songs, cheers and shouts mingled with the roll of the thunder, and the vivid flashes of lightning gleamed along their line of muskets and revealed their forms in the gloom of the night. It was a spirit stirring scene. The steadiness of the regiment under the circumstances shows both good discipline and good grit, in the material of which it is composed. Their songs, which the whole regiment seemed to participate in, heard above the loud thunder and terrible rush of waters, startled the people from their houses, who, as soon as they learned the cause of the demonstration, inspired by the patriotism of the gallant Massachusetts boys, rushed into the street and greeted the troops with loud cheers.

THE CONTRACT INVESTIGATING COMMITTEE.

Mr Van Wyck's Contract Investigating Committee had little opportunity to prosecute its labors during the session, as nearly all the members of it were also members of regular committees, to which they were required to give their chief attention. They will now apply themselves seriously and without intermission to the business of this special committe, which has been authorized to sit during the recess. Everything in the shape of contracts in the Army and Navy Departments will be thoroughly examined, wheresoever they may have been executed, and any wilful concealment of frauds by any officer of the government will be treated as complicity in the fraud itself. It is probable that the investigations of the committee may require some of its sessions to be held in New York and Philadelphia. But gentlemen who are interested in the contracts to be examined into need not expect to influence the decisions of the committee by brilliant *fetes* and grand dinners, for it is not intended to allow its sessions to degenerate into simple summer exercises; and besides, the Chairman is proof against such seductions, as he is a tetotaller.

THE POTTER COMMITTEE.

The Potter Committee have also been very active of late. A number of the old clerks in various departments, whose loyalty is undoubted, have been regularly summoned to testify before it, and a determination has been manifested to weed out disloyalty from every branch of the government service. The investigations of this committee have occasioned the use of the guillotine in several instances, and probably had more to do with recent resignations in the civil departments of the government than the law of the rebels defining treason and expatriating all who continued to hold office under the government of the United States after July 31, 1861.

DEPARTURE OF SENATORS.

Senator Wilmot has gone to Atlantic City, and Senator Hale to Rockaway, each to inhale sea air.

APPOINTMENTS.

Minian W. Edwards, brother-in-law of President Lincoln, has been appointed on the staff of General McClellan with the rank of Captain, to act as Commissary to the brigade.

THE PHILADELPHIA NAVY YARD.

PHILADELPHIA, August 11, 1861.

The Navy Yard presents a busy and bustling scene. About 1,700 hands are employed therein, and about 150 fresh hands will be taken in to-morrow.

The steamer Tuscarora is drawing towards completion. She is a second class steamer, will mount six guns, and will be launched in a week or ten days.

The steam frigate Susquehanna is receiving a new shaft. She mounts fifteen guns, and will be ready in a week.

The gunboats Albatross and Flag are being overhauled and will depart for the South in less than two weeks.

IMPORTANT FROM FORTRESS MONROE.

Another Pirate Burned—Recapture of Prize Schooner Geo. G. Baker—English Vessel Wrecked in Order to Sell the Cargo to Rebels.

FORTRESS MONROE, August 10,
Via BALTIMORE, August 11, 1861.

The Quaker City this morning brought up the prize schooner Geo. G. Baker, of Galveston, and her rebel crew of four men in irons. The schooner was captured by one of the United States blockading fleet off Galveston, and sent to New York with a United States crew on board. She was captured yesterday off Cape Hatteras by the rebel privateer York, who put four of her own men on board. Meanwhile the York was seen by the United States gunboat Union, who gave chase and burned the privateer, but not until the crew had beached her and escaped. The Union then recaptured the prize. The Baker made prisoners of her crew, and transferred them to-day to the Quaker City. The United States prize crew are still in the hands of the rebels; names unknown.

Lieut. Crosby's expedition to the Eastern Shore of Virginia, now absent four days, has not been heard from. He sailed with an effective force and three days provisions. No apprehensions are yet felt as to his safety.

A flag of truce came down this morning from Norfolk to make inquiries concerning several rebel officers, whom they supposed to be imprisoned here, among others Col. Pegram.

The few houses remaining in Hampton on Thursday morning have not yet been destroyed by the rebels, who are now near Big Bethel. One white woman, an invalid, was burned to death in the great conflagration.

It is reported that one of General Magruder's Captains penetrated within our line of pickets at Newport News, and declared the place too strong to be attacked.

One hundred rations are now issued to the contrabands at Old Point. Their services are invaluable to the Quartermaster, who provides for their various wants. They work with alacrity.

The captain and mates of the wrecked bark Glory, from Rio Janeiro to Baltimore, with a large cargo of coffee, came from Norfolk with the flag of truce. They sympathize strongly with the rebels. It is more than probable that the Glory was purposely lost, as the cargo was saved and sold at twice the ordinary price. As an encouragement for this manner of avoiding the blockade, the rebels paid promptly, and treated the captain with consideration.

NEWS FROM GENERAL BANKS' ARMY.

SANDY HOOK, Md., Aug. 10, 1861.

Captain Charles H. F. Collins, of the Zouaves d'Abrique, of Philadelphia, is here with a tender of his company, composed entirely, it is said, of soldiers who served in the Crimean war. He states that his proposition was well received by General Banks, who promised him a letter to the Secretary of War, requesting his acceptance as an independent corps.

Mr. Coggeshall, agent of the State of Pennsylvania, arrived here with supplies of overcoats, shoes, &c., for Colonel Mann's Pennsylvania Reserve regiment.

Captain Robert Williams, Assistant Adjutant General, has returned from Washington and resumed his position on the staff.

Captain Geary, of the Twenty-eighth Pennsylvania regiment, has been notified that one or more companies have been sworn in as additions to his regiment, already numbering 1,040 men; but it is to be increased to 1,550 men. This regiment, with its experience and able commander, promises to be one of the most efficient of this column.

The Lieutenant Colonel is Gabriel De Korponay, the greater part of whose active life has been spent in camp and on the battle fields of Europe and America, and commander of the British Foreign brigade in the Crimean war.

Col. Murphy's Twenty-ninth Pennsylvania regiment was inspected this morning by General Fitz John Porter Inspector General of Banks' division.

General Porter has not yet been assigned to any separate command.

HON. JOSEPH HOLT, EX-SECRETARY OF WAR, IN OSWEGO.

OSWEGO, N. Y., August 10, 1861.

Hon. Joseph Holt, of Kentucky, arrived in this city on the steamer Cataract, at eleven this evening, on his tour down the lake and river St. Lawrence. Although brief notice of his coming was given, more than five thousand persons, including the entire military of the city, assembled upon the wharf to welcome him, while the streets were illuminated with fireworks. On making his appearance he was welcomed to the city by Hon. Wm. Duer.

Mr. Holt, admid deafening cheers, replied:—

FELLOW CITIZENS:—

I beg you to be assured I am quite overwhelmed by the kindness and brilliancy of this unexpected welcome to the Empire State—a welcome for which every pulsation of my heart is grateful. I know, indeed, that this welcome is not to myself personally, but is rather given because you consider me a loyal man from a loyal State, devoted to the Union and this great and beneficent government. (Cheers.) But I am not going to make any thing like a political speech. The fires of patriotism are now burning all over this great State with such a glow that they need neither fuel nor kindling at my hands. But I may ask you have you heard the news from the great Commonwealth of Kentucky? (Cries of "We have," and "Three cheers for Kentucky.") That news has been flashed over the wires from one end of the country to the other, speaking a determination which nothing can shake to preserve all that Southern traitors would destroy—all that Northern patriots would save. It is a determination of the people of that old State to stand unalterably and forever for the Stars and Stripes. (Vociferous cheering.) Kentucky is determined, and by the recent election she tells New York that hereafter she will stand with her side by side. But I cannot detain you longer. Cries of "go on." I will only say that Kentucky never faltered, although her politicians did; but in the depth of her soul she has been determined to stand by the Union. Fellow citizen, I thank you again for this generous welcome so unexpected and so undeserved. The concluding portion of Mr. Holt's remarks were rendered inaudible by steam escaping from the engine. He retired amid a perfect shower of fireworks. The demonstration was entirely impromptu, but was such a welcome as Oswego has ever given "any other man."

NEWS FROM THE SOUTH.

LOUISVILLE, Ky., August 11, 1861.

On the 8th the steamer Massachusetts was about eight miles off Ship Island.

A special despatch to the Nashville *Union*, dated 10th, says that General Butler had burned Hampton.

The Richmond papers learn that the captured Southerners were to be handcuffed and made breastworks of!

GENERAL BEAUREGARD CLAIMED BY THE CANADIANS.

The *Courrier du Canada* of a late date contains the following paragraph relative to the commander of the rebel army:—The grandfather of General Beauregard, commander of the Southern army, was a Canadian. His name was Pierre Touton, and he emigrated to New Orleans from Batiscan, in the district of Three Rivers. At New Orleans he made a fortune and rapidly acquired considerable influence among the French population of Louisiana. As a reward for his political services, he obtained for his son an admission as a cadet into the Military Academy at West Point. The son figures in the books under the name of Pierre G. Touton. In the meantime he purchased an estate near New Orleans, which he called Beauregard. When his son obtained his commission as an officer in the army he cast aside the humble name of Touton, and adopted the more aristocratic one of de Beauregard, and thenceforth subscribed himself "Pierre Touton de Beauregard."

PROCLAMATION OF THE GOVERNOR OF TEXAS.

Mr. Edward Clarke, who signs himself Governor of Texas, has issued a proclamation, declaring that it will be regarded as treason for any citizen of Texas to hold any commercial intercourse with the inhabitants of any of the loyal States or Territories without special permission. It will also be treasonable for any citizen of Texas to pay any debts now owing to any citizen or citizens of said States or Territories during the war. The statute of limitations will cease to run, and interest will not accrue during that period. The Acting Governor then suggests that Texans owing debts to citizens of the United States deposit the amount of these in the Treasurer's office, to be retained until the United States shall pay to Texas the large amount now due her. In return for these, the parties will receive a certificate of deposit from the Treasurer. The people are also warned against purchasing property in Texas now held by residents of the States at war with her, as the Legislature may provide for the confiscation of all such property. "No act of treason, whether it may consist of aid and comfort to the enemy, or in language written, printed or spoken, which is intended to comfort or encourage them, will be knowingly permitted." Citizens of the loyal States will no longer be permitted to visit Texas, or if any such are now within her limits, they are warned to depart within twenty-four hours.

SAFETY OF OUR SOLDIERS' LETTERS.

TO THE EDITOR OF THE HERALD.

It is a notorious fact that many letters containing money, forwarded by mail to the soldiers in the army by their friends at home, never reach their destination. There are numerous cases where friends have sent money which has never been received.

A. VICTIM.

THE BALTIMORE REPUBLICAN.

VOL. LXIX. | WEDNESDAY EVENING, AUGUST 14, 1861 | NO. 1930

THE REPUBLICAN.

BALTIMORE, WEDNESDAY, AUGUST 14.

ANOTHER DEFEAT OF THE TYRANTS.

Our paper to-day will bear abroad the tidings of another defeat of the Federal forces and the death of the commanding General. It is to be hoped that a few more battles of a similar character may teach the infatuated despots at Washington the madness of their attempt to enslave the freemen of the South. The Government of Massachusetts, during the war of 1812, "resolved that it was unbecoming in a *moral* and *religious* people to rejoice in the *victories* of their countrymen." Perhaps the Puritanical Abolitionists may be able to rejoice in the defeat of the would be tyrants. Wheth er *they* do so or not, there are tens of thousands of moral and religious people who will rejoice and give God thanks for his interposition in behalf of those who are struggling for their rights against the most heartless despotism that can be found in the civilized world. We would only remind our readers that the present account is from *Federal* authority, and therefore will be satisfactory so far as the acknowledgment of another total defeat and rout is concerned. No doubt the real facts are much more disastrous to the Federal arms than is reported. It is more than probable too that the *"report"* of the death of McCullough is like that of the "wounding," "killing" and "capturing" of Wise, which has so often been circulated by Federal authority. We need not spend time in analyzing the account. Enough is known to show that defeat and rout is again the portion of the tyrants. There is one thing which should also be remembered—that these routed Hessians, true to their native instincts, *broke open and robbed the Bank* in their dastard flight. This is their own story, which will doubtless be *corrected* by the Administration and the robbery hereafter charged upon the Confederates.

THE WASHINGTON STAR.

This paper, which has been built up by the patronage of Southern men, is now among the most obsequious toadies of the Black Republican tyrants. It is not satisfied with the usurpations and outrages which Lincoln and his party have already committed, but is constantly inciting them to further and more daring acts of tyranny. We have noticed upon various occasions the efforts of this Swiss mercenary to induce the Administration to suppress the independent press of this city. Because the *Star* has submitted to the *gag* we suppose it is desirous that the freedom of speaking the truth should be denied to all others. Says this print—"our real wonder is that *up to this time* the government has *not* resorted to more summary measures for the preservation of its existence than it has essayed." Does the Star want the Guillotine erected, and suspected parties brought up and beheaded by the Provost Marshal? Is this the "summary process" which it wonders has not been adopted by its Black Republican masters?—How soon *this* may follow the existing list of outrages no one can tell. Citizens are now seized and imprisoned without law; how long it will before their executions may follow, depends more on the spirit of the people than upon the humanity or regard for law of their rulers. It would be well for the advocates of this "summary process" to remember that *their necks* may fall under the avenging knife as soon as those they are plotting against.

LINCOLN'S PROCLAMATION.

After having deliberately and with malice aforethought plunged the country into a most unnatural and destructive war, Lincoln and his hypocritical advisers come out now with a recommendation for prayer and humiliation upon the part of the people. It would be far more appropriate if Lincoln and his Cabinet advisers should *humble* themselves, and pray to be forgiven for the cruel wrongs inflicted upon the country by their instrumentality. We can only pray like David that "the tyrants may be confounded and put to shame and confusion before the people whom they have so foully wronged." We think the prayers of the hypocrites will avail about as much as their fighting. The Lord cannot heed the petitions of those who cherish the sin of murder and hatred in their hearts.

WENDELL PHILLIPS RIGHT.—It is a common saying that the most erratic old time piece will get right some time. So it appears that madness, be it ever so mad, will occasionally give utterance to a truth that "reason and sanity cannot so prosperously be delivered of." This is exemplified by Wendell Phillips in his late speech, in which he so ably argues that the idea of conquering the South is preposterous. Phillips needs attention at the hands of the Republicans. Is not his declaration a misprison of treason?

A RAILROAD INDICTED AS A COMMON NUISANCE.—The Grand Jury of the Superior Court at Boston, have been investigating a complaint against the Boston and New York Central Railroad, and have found it to be a "common nuisance." The cause for the indictment is the condition of the Company's track at South Boston, the embankments being in an unfinished condition, and stagnant water standing upon the track in several places. The people living in the vicinity of the track have for a long time been dissatisfied with its condition.

☞ Rhode Island has expended $207,164 for military purposes since the war commenced. Of this amount $140,665 has been allowed by the General Government, and will be paid at some indefinite time. The State has paid $97,267 for bounty, which, taken in connection with the $13,908 paid for a steamship, makes the sum of $111 175 for which the State has no claim upon the General Government.

☞ In the late extensive fire which occurred in London the loss of the insurance offices was estimated at £1,000,000. The premiums received by all the London and country offices for risks was only £350,000 a year, so that one fire has swept the whole amount—two and a half years' premium.

☞ A country Republican paper says:

"It is said that there are thirty thousand persons out of employment in the city of New York alone. This need not be the case; there are five hundred thousand men wanted for the war."

To which the Day Book replies:

"Oh, yes, that is good Republican doctrine —rob the people of all means of support, and then let them take their choice between starving at home with their families, or go away from home to be killed."

RUSSELL OF THE LONDON TIMES.

This gentleman has been in America now some four or five months, acting in the capacity of a special correspondent of the London Times, having been sent here by that great and influential organ of British opinion, as the faithful and impartial chronicler of the interesting events now transpiring on this side of the Atlantic.

His first letters—many of which we published—with all their vagueness and ambiguity evinced a decided leaning to the side of the South. To such an extent was this the case, that the imprecations of Abolition wrath were poured upon his devoted head without regard to the feelings of the unfortunate victim.—Every emanation from his pen which he supposed would be published in sufficient time to return to America, and to be read in the South before his advent among us, presented the war question very much after the manner of one whose intention it was to mete out sheer justice to the character of the cause in which we are struggling.

But no sooner had Mr. Russell reached Pensacola and New Orleans than he commenced to show the cloven foot of sympathy with the enemy, doubtless by way of palliating the indignation of the North so as to secure for himself a cordial reception among them on his return. His letter from Cairo (already laid before our readers) giving a description of his trip up the Mississippi Valley, with its sly flings and its slurring falsifications, was evidently manufactured for circulation in the latitude of Yankeedom. Its author shows himself to be little beyond a dishonest knave and a pensioned spy. He was received in our midst as a distinguished stranger and gentleman, and had accorded to him, by those in and out of authority, all of those kind amenities of social life for which the generous hearted Southron is so justly celebrated.

Yet we find him, in a communication which he knew full well would soon be displayed in the columns of Northern journals with a flourish of trumpets, not only insidiously libelling many of our prominent men, underrating the power and resources of our section, and falsifying historical facts, but betraying the confidence reposed in him by giving a full and ample description of our river defences and city fortifications, with suggestions as to the best means of assaulting and capturing them.

We risk nothing in saying that, under no circumstances would Mr. Russell have been allowed by our authorities to visit the forts around Memphis, had they known that he designed entering so far into the details of describing them as he did for the benefit of the enemy. Certainly his London readers found but little in that part of his letter either to instruct or interest them.

The conduct of this man has been such as to furnish our people with a salutary lesson for the future, especially in relation to the danger of being taken in by roving adventurers. The South fortunately escaped the humiliation of toadyism to the Prince of Wales, whose tour through the North last summer created so wild and disgraceful a furore; but the signs of the times forcibly indicate that we have been badly sold by the hypocritical Russell.—*Memphis Appeal.*

THE PERSONNEL OF THE CONFEDERATE CONGRESS.

The *personnel* of the Congress is both striking and remarkable. The delegates are mostly new men, that is, at least so far as 'Congressional' dignities are concerned; and the *tout ensemble* is that of plain, farmer-looking, serious men, invested with a sort of unaffected Revolutionary simplicity. There are recognizable, however, in the body, several of the old members of the Washington Congress, whom the South has honored by summoning them to her own independent national councils, worthily rewarding their former devotion to the cause of her rights by new trusts of dignity.

The President, the Hon. Howell Cobb, looks as familiar as he ever did in the political marbles of Washington, although his cheerful face is furzed with a new whisker, and one not of raven tints. As a chairman, he has the admirable qualities of ease, readiness, and dignity.

There was Toombs, too, another notability of Washington, looking dreadfully jaded, and speaking (as he did a few words to a motion on Saturday) in those careless and slovenly tones in which, in all his speeches, he precedes the sudden rise and swift and majestic flow of his eloquence. Then there was Mr. Reagan of Texas, with his open, practical face, no doubt as powerful a debater as ever; Mr. Benjamin, of Louisiana, classic and smiling as of yore; Mr. Keitt, of South Carolina, as incandescent and as unkempt as ever; and Mr. Curry, of Alabama, who, beneath an extreme youthfulness of appearance, and that simplicity of manner peculiar to the true gentleman, has given evidence of a mind of the rarest education, and depth, which has already placed him in the front rank of the former defenders of Southern rights in Washington, and had given a rare example there of the union of youth and modesty, with broad and solid faculties of statesmanship. Our recognition of Washington notabilities was of course partial. Neither Messrs. Hunter, Bocock, Pryor, Porcher Miles, "Aleck" Stevens, or Wigfall, of "Federal city" memory, were in their seats.—*Richmond Examiner.*

FLAGS OF TRUCE.

The following correspondence has taken place between Mr. Harris and Gen. Beauregard, in relation to the application to look for the body of Col. Cameron:

JULY 2, 1861.

To Gen. Beauregard, or Commanding Officer of Confederate Army:

SIR. I send this by a friend and trusty servant, who is well known to many officers in our Army. He is sent for the purpose of obtaining from you a permit for Mr. H. S. Mc Graw and myself to pass your lines to obtain the body of Col. Cameron, who fell in the action of yesterday. My solicitude in this matter is an impulse of private character. The rigid rules established in Washington with reference to flags of truce prevent me from carrying out my wishes without proceeding as I am now doing.

I believe General Beauregard will recollect me while a resident of New Orleans; but if President Davis, General Lee, General Johnston, General Wigfall, Colonels Miles, Keitt or Withers, are present, they will not hesitate to vouch for me, General Bonham, and, in fact, nearly all your officers know me. In addition to the gratification of performing a sacred duty, I would be highly delighted to meet in your camp many of my most valued friends. It is proper for me to add that I have not been in any manner connected with the action of the government here, and that I am neutral.

Very respectfully, yours, &c.,
ARNOLD HARRIS.

Please make the passport for A. Harris, P. S. McGraw, and two servants. I have not named my friend or servant for prudential reasons, but either of the gentlemen above named can vouch for them.

HEAD-QUARTERS ARMY OF THE POTOMAC,
Manassas Junction, July 22, 1861.

Sir: I am instructed by Gen. Beauregard, commanding the First Corps, Army of the Potomac, to say that he has received your note of the 22d, and to reply thereto.

The General declines giving an informal permit to any one residing beyond his advanced lines for any purpose which may be accomplished by those formal proceedings known to, and practiced by, civilized belligerent nations. By no act of his will he lower the dignity of the Confederates States as a nation by permitting that to be done indirectly which the usages of civilized warfare accomplish directly.

The arbitrary and unusual course adopted in such cases as you prefer to by the United States Government will be the guide of the General's conduct in return. Any one, therefore, coming within his lines without the proper flag, will be under an escort to the Confederate Government for examination.

The General deems proper for me to add that humanity should teach an enemy to care for its wounded, and Christianity to bury its dead.

I am, Sir, your obedient servant,
JOHN L. MANNING, Aide-de-Camp.
To ARNOLD HARRIS.

ANOTHER BATTLE IN MISSOURI.

OFFICIAL ACCOUNT OF THE BATTLE.

GEN. LYON KILLED AT THE HEAD OF HIS COLUMN.

THE FEDERAL TROOPS RETREATING TOWARDS ROLLA.

EIGHT HUNDRED FEDERAL TROOPS KILLED AND WOUNDED.

&c., &c., &c., &c.

WASHINGTON, August 13.—The following official report was received here to-night by Lieutenant General Scott:

HEADQUARTERS WESTERN DEPARTMENT,
ST. LOUIS, August 13, 1861.

Col. E D. Townsend:

General Lyon, in three columns under himself, Siegel and Sturgess, attacked the enemy at half past 6 o'clock on the morning of the 10th instant, nine miles east of Springfield. The engagement was severe. Our loss is about 800 killed and wounded.

General Lyon was killed in a charge at the head of his column.

Our force was eight thousand, including two thousand Home Guards. The muster roll *reported* to have been taken from the enemy gives their force at twenty-three thousand, including regiments from Louisiana, Tennessee and Mississippi, with Texan Rangers and Cherokee half breeds. This statement is corroborated by prisoners.

The enemy's loss *is reported* to have been heavy, including Generals McCullough and Price. Their tents and wagons were all destroyed in the action.

General Seigel left one gun on the field and retreated to Springfield, whence, at three o'clock on the morning of the 11th, he continued his retreat upon Rolla—the terminus of the southwest branch of the Pacific and Missouri Railroad—bringing off his baggage trains and two hundred and fifty thousand dollars in specie from a Springfield bank.

(Signed) J. C. FREMONT,
Major General Com'g.

THE LOUISIANA CROPS.

The Clinton Patriot of the 29th says:

Providence has smiled upon our land, and blessed the labors of the husbandman in rich returns from his orchards and fields. We are satisfied that East Feliciana has never been so generally successful in the abundance and quality of its products as is now being realized.

The Tensas Gazette of Thursday says:

E. Tullis, Esq., who last year shipped one of the first bales of cotton, had picked on his plantation on Tuesday, the 30th of July, over five thousand pounds of clean cotton. In about another week, picking throughout the parish will be general. The corn crop is now secured, and very abundant it is, and the cotton crop with hardly an exception gives general satisfaction. We have not heard of a single planter, however, who will ship his cotton before the entire removal of the blockade.

A COMPREHENSIVE PLAN.

A correspondent of the Memphis *Argus* writes, under date of Aug. 6:

"I am informed to-day by a friend from Manassas, who remained in the city but a few hours, that every thing is in readiness for an advance upon Washington. If we reach that city, drive the enemy from the Relay House and Baltimore, capture Fort McHenry, and be in readiness to march to Philadelphia, should it be necessary to do so, we may consider the war as virtually over. The Northwest, however, is just *now* in a critical position. Gen. Wise has retired to Lewisburg, and will probably await there the arrival of Gen. Lee, unless Gen. Cox should pursue him from Charlestown. In that event he will lead his 4,000 to some impregnable pass in the mountains, and if the worst comes, this spot he will consecrate as a second Thermopylæ."

HARD ON THE PET LAMBS.

It is said that not a single one of Billy Wilson's Zouaves have now the clothes they came to Fort Pickens in, having stolen each other's all around, and that old Harvey Brown has but one suit of clothes left, (the one he wears,) and has to sleep with a body guard over him to save them; and we are further informed that Wilson had to put his commission in the powder magazine to keep them from stealing it.—*Pensacola Observer.*

THE BOSTON BANKS AND THE U. S. GOVERNMENT.

A COMMITTEE TO CONFER WITH NEW YORK.

BOSTON, August 13.—Wm. Gray, Frank Hanen, J. Amory Davis, have been chosen a committee by the Boston Directors to confer with the committees of the New York and Philadelphia Banks. The meeting adopted the following instructions to the committee.

"That the committee be authorized to say to the gentlemen of the committees from the New York and Philadelphia Banks, that in the judgment of the gentlemen here assembled, the banks and bankers of Boston and of the State of Massachusetts, and its people, are prepared, ready, and willing, and determined, to do all in their power in view of their duty to themselves their trusts and their country, to aid in suppressing the present rebellion, by furnishing men and money to the utmost extent of their ability, now, henceforth and forever.

RESIGNATIONS.—The Richmond *Enquirer* says: "Capt. Robert R. Garland, U. S. Infatry, and Capt. Addisen Garland, U. S. Marines, both of Amhirst County, Va., have resigned their present positions to serve their native State in the present war. Lieut. Westwood McCreery, of this city, who resigned his post in the United States Army, reached here from Fort Pickens a few days ago, and has already taken service in the Confederate Army."

☞ During a thunder storm at Chicago, on Friday, the lightning struck the flagstaff of the Great Wigwam, shivering it to atoms, the fluid passing down one of the supporters of the building, and on its way entirely destroying the *bust of Lincoln.*

☞ The annoyance of the Princess Clothilde it seems continues in New York. It is affirmed that while going to her devotions, her carriage has been waylaid, the sidewalks blocked, and the church completely filled by a crowd of impertinent men and women—especially the latter—who would thrust themselves before her, behind her, and at her side, violating all the commonest dictates of decency, in order to obtain a glimpse of her veiled and indignant face.

HIGHLY IMPORTANT.

OPERATIONS OF THE PRIVATEER SUMTER.

She Sails into Curacoa, Takes in Coal, and Stays there Eight Days.

Protest from the U. S. Consul--The Protest Not Heeded.

Captain Boreham, of the brig Sea Foam, arrived yesterday at New York, and says that the steam privateer Sumter arrived off Curacoa on the night of the 17th of July, and fired a gun for the fort; but the people of the fort, not knowing her national flag, would not permit her to come in until the Governor had been consulted.

The Sumter then sent an officer with an armed crew ashore to talk with that official as to coming into port to coal up and refit, which the Governor allowed, against the protest of the U. S. Consul.

She lay at Curacoa for eight days. During the time, the crew had their libety ashore, and, as Capt. B. says, raised the devil generally.

The captain of the Sumter said he was very sorry he had not arrived 3 days sooner as he wanted ice badly—which article captain B. had a cargo of, and had only arrived the day previous.

Captain B. was detained four days waiting the departure of the Sumter which took place on the 24th. Saw no privateer or suspicious vessel on the passage home.

Later from Europe.

FRANCE AND ENGLAND ON THE AMERICAN QUESTION.

THE AMERICAN LOAN IN LONDON

FARTHER POINT, August 12.—The Canadian Company's screw steamship Nova Scotian, from Liverpool afternoon of the 1st instant, via Londonberry 2d; passed this point, en route to Quebec, at 2 30 this afternoon. She has 189 passengers and $140,000 in specie.

The steamship Anglo-Saxon, from Quebec Saturday morning, was passed off the west coast of Anticosta by the steamship Nova Scotia.

The steamship Etna sailed from Liverpool for New York on the 31st ult., with about £20,000 in specie.

GREAT BRITAIN.

The London Times, in the city article, asserts that it will be dangerous for England to have anything to do with the American loan.

The proceedings of Parliament on the 31st ult. were unimportant.

The House of Commons finally passed the bankrupt bill, as amended by the House of Lords.

The Ministerial whitebait dinner, in anticipation of the close of the session, took place at Greenwich on the 31st.

A Paris correspondent of the London Post states that the British Government is in correspondence with the French Government, in order that united action may be observed towards America by sea and land. As a real conflict is now to be expected, a perfect understanding is likely to be arrived.

Rumors of a probable compromise in America are again gaining strength in England.

Some of the London journals were speculating on the rate of the American loan in London.

Lord Palmerston stated in Parliament that the Government had not yet resolved upon the course relative to the postal service via Galway.

Mr. Gregory asked if the Government had received information of goods contraband of war being taken to America by the Kangaroo and that a loan for the Federal Government had been opened in London.

Lord Palmerston had no information on either point.

The Duke of Buckingham is dead.

FRANCE.

The Cherbourg Journal states that it is contemplated to establish a strategic railway along the French coast.

The Bourse was inactive but firm; Rentes closing 60f. 78c.

The King of Sweden is expected in Paris.

It is also reported that the King of Prussia will visit Paris.

The Bourse was firm. Three per cent. rentes 67f. 85c.

ITALY.

Italian politics are unimportant. The national loan was proving successful. It was more than bid for by the bankers, but some was reserved for the public.

It is reported that Napoleon had assured the Pope that he would defend Rome and the Papacy at any cost.

The other continental news is entirely unimportant.

BELGIUM.

The Moniteur Belge states that a new treaty of commerce between England and Belgium was about to be negotiated.

PORTUGAL.

There was some disturbance in some Portugal provinces. Reinforcements of military had been sent.

BRAZIL.

RIO JANEIRO, July 9.—Coffee, good firts, 5||400a5||500. All shipments since the last mail were to Europe.

INDIA AND CHINA.

The Calcutta mail has arrived with dates of June 23, and Hong Kong of June 12.

THE LATEST.

LONDON, Aug 2.—A telegram from Havre states that a vessel, name not given, has sunk at the mouth of the harbor, temporarily blockading the entrance for large ships. The Arago, from New York, will most probably come to Southampton instead of Havre. and the passengers and mails be sent on. The Arago passed Hurst Castle at 9½ A. M.

Mr Julius Dunier has been appointed to succeed the late Sir J. Mellville as Government Director on Indian Railways.

The suspended monthly China mail will be resumed on the 20th.

The reduction of the Bank rate has not had an immediate effect in Mincing lane.

The Board of Directors of the new Mercantile Fire Insurance Company comprise 14 names of unquestionable standing in the mercantile world.

A letter from China gives a most favorable account of the commercial advantages arising out of the opening of the Yang-tse. The writer says there is room for as many steamers as can come out.

London Markets—Breadstuffs steady, with a slight improvement in American. Wheat has advanced 1s. Sugar quiet and steady. Coffee has an advancing tendency. Tea flat. Rice firm. Tallow steady. Linseed oil firm at 32s.

London Money Market, August 1.—Consols closed at 90a90½ for money.

American Stocks—Illinois Central shares, 36 dis.; Erie 26½a27.

LATEST MARKETS.

(By Telegraph to Londonderry.)

LIVERPOOL, August 2—Cotton—The sales of the week reached 69,000 bales, the market closing firm but unchanged and quiet. The sales to speculators were 12,000 bales, and to exporters 9,500 bales. Sales on Friday 6,000 bales, the market closing steady.

COMMERCIAL.

Liverpool Produce Market.—Rosin is steady; common 7s. Spirits Turpentine dull at 47s. Sugar is quiet and unaltered. Coffee inactive. Rosin firmer. Ashes have an upward tendency: Pots 30s., Pearls 33s. Linseed Oil quiet at 31s 6d.

Trade Report.—Manchester advices are favorable, and quotations have an upward tendency.

Breadstuffs quiet and steady. Wheat has advanced 2d per cental, mostly on lower qualities.

Provisions inactive.

London Money Market.—Consols closed on Friday at 90a90¼ for money. The return of the Bank of England shows an increase in bullion of $476,000. American Stocks—The latest sales were: Erie shares, 26¾a27; Illinois Central shares, 35¾a36 discount.

"WHEN THE DEVIL GOT SICK, THE DEVIL A MONK WOULD BE."

By the President of the United States of America

A PROCLAMATION.

Whereas, A joint Committee of both Houses of Congress has waited on the President of the United States, and requested him to "recommend a day of public humiliation, prayer and fasting, to be observed by the people of the United States with religious solemnites, and the offering of fervent supplications to Almighty God for the safety and welfare of these States; his blessing on their arms and a speedy restoration of peace."

And whereas, it is fit and becoming in all people, at all times, to acknowledge and revere the Supreme Government of God; to bow in humble submission to his chastisements; to confess and deplore their sins and transgressions, in the full conviction that the fear of the Lord is the beginning of wisdom, and to pray with all fervency and contrition for the pardon of their past offences, and for a blessing upon their present and prospective action—

And whereas, When our own beloved country, once, by the blessing of God, united, prosperous, and happy, is now afflicted with faction and civil war, it is peculiarly fit for us to recognize the hand of God in this terrible visitation, and in sorrowful remembrance of our own faults and crimes as a nation, and as individuals, to humble ourselves before him, and to pray for his mercy—to pray that we may be spared further punishment, though most justly deserved; that our arms may be blessed and made effectual for the re-establishment of law, order and peace throughout the wide extent of our country; and that the inestimable boon of civil and religious liberty, earned under his guidance and blessings by the labors and sufferings of our fathers may be restored in all its original excellence:

Therefore, I, Abraham Lincoln, President of the United States, do appoint the last Thursday in September next as a day of humiliation prayer, and fasting, for all the people of the nation. And I do earnestly recommend that all the people, and especially to all ministers and teachers of religion, of all denominations, and to all heads of families, to observe and keep that day, according to their several creeds and modes of worship, in all humanity, and with all religious solemnity, to the end that the united prayer of the nation may ascend to the throne of Grace, and bring down plentiful blessings upon our country.

In testimony whereof I have hereunto set my hand and seal and caused the seal of the United States to be affixed, this 12th day of August, A. D. 1861, and of the Independence of the United States of America the sixty eighth.

{ L. S. }

ABRAHAM LINCOLN.

By the President:
WILLIAM H. SEWARD,
Secretary of State.

ADVENT AND ADVENTURES OF A STRANGE MUSIC TEACHER AT RED CREEK.

[Cor. Lyons (Wayne Co. N. Y.) Republican.]

RED CREEK, Aug. 5.

Within the past two weeks our quiet village has been thrown into a fever of excitement by the disclosure of circumstances which seem almost too shocking to relate.

Some eighteen months since there came into our village an ill looking individual, emanating from Syracuse, and professing to be highly skilled in the musical art. With a superabundance of brass, he succeeded in ingratiating himself in public favor to such extent that he obtained a class, and mingling his profession with that of a horse jockey, he succeeded in obtaining a support and paving the way to accomplish his designs the more successfully. Some months since he was promoted to the position of chorister in the M. E. Church.

By a course of conduct the most outrageous Parker had succeeded in seducing a young lady of about nineteen years, the idolized daughter of a respectable farmer living a short distance from the village. Suspicions having rested on him, young men of undoubted veracity became secretly eye witnesses of his most shameful performances, and they immediately disclosed the facts. The proof was so positive that both parties confessed the crime, and a hasty flight saved the villain from what we are sorry our "boys" were too slow in preparing for him.

Parker is a married man His wife is spoken highly of by all who knew her, and was living with him during the whole of this transaction, which it appears has been going on for months.

There are the strongest evidences that another young lady has been ruined by him since he has been here, and that this is but a repetition of his conduct in other places.

THE LATEST FROM OLD POINT, FORTRESS MONROE, &C.

The steamer Louisiana, Capt. Jas. Cannon, did not reach here this morning until nine o'clock, in consequence of the violent gale which prevailed in the Chesapeake. The bay was unusually rough, and the steamer brought up a rather small number of passengers. No news of interest could be obtained, and no active movements in the military line was going on.

General Butler and staff were very busy in packing up their luggage preparatory to their removal, in order to make way for General Wool, the new commandant. At the change universal satisfaction prevailed.

A FRENCH ZOUAVE HAS HIS EYES OPENED.—We have before us a letter written from Manassas by Capt. Aug. Carose, of the Bienville Rifles, to a gentleman of this city, from which we are permitted to make the following extract:

"One of the prisoners, a Frenchman, who served in the Crimean war, compares the Louisianians (Tiger Zouaves of New Orleans) and the South Carolinians, who took the celebrated Sherman battery, to real devils. They crawled on their bellies and knees nearly a mile through the bushes, and rising suddenly to their feet fired, and charging with the bayonet, killed nearly everybody, including horses. He says he never saw anything like it. He is slightly wounded, and declares that he was pressed into the service while intoxicated, and will join my company when sufficiently recovered. He is a stout, brave looking fellow, and expresses his astonishment at hearing so many of the Southerners speak French."—*N. O. Crescent.*

☞ Among the numberless stories told of the new arrangements of the Palace of the Sultan, is one relating to the Kislar Agha, or Chief of the Eunuchs—a man of immense height, and very corpulent. He was evidently chosen on account of his size; and his salary, 300,000 piasters a month, was of proportionate dimensions. On the accession of Abdul Aziz, this man was asked by the new Sultan if he would like to serve him in the same capacity at one tenth part of the salary. Upon some demur being made by the black, the Sultan quietly observed, "Why, you only cost 3000 piasters originally, and I thought I was very liberal in offering to purchase you over again every month."

LOCAL INTELLIGENCE.

CITY RETAIL MARKET.—The attendance at the old Centre market this morning was very fair, and the display of produce and provisions very extensive. There has been but slight change in the prices of meats, &c., since our last quotations, but fruit and vegetables can be purchased almost for a song. The following were the ruling rates:

Beef.		Lettuce......	3a 5 pr hd
Beef.........	12a14 per lb	Cauliflower...	8a12 "
Choice Cuts..	15a18 "	*Miscellaneous.*	
Rounds......	a10 "	Apples........	18a31 p pck
Chucks......	8 a10 "	Peaches.......	20a25 "
Corned Beef.	10a12 "	Butter, print..	18a30 pr lb
Pork.		" roll...	15a25 "
Sirloin & ribs.	10a12 "	Eggs..........	12a16 pr dz
Salt Should's.	a10 "	Roasting ears.	5a12 "
" Middling.	a10 "	Tomatoes.....	12a25 "
Ham, whole..	a12 "	Cucumbers ..	10a16 "
" sliced..	a15 "	Smearcase....	a12 pr qt
Shoulders....	a12 "	Gooseberries..	8a12 "
Middlings....	10a12 "	Blackberries..	4a 6 "
Sm'd Sausage	a12 "	Cherries ...	8a12 "
Fresh " ...	a12 "	Raspberries...	10a15 "
Lard.........	10a12 "	Apricots.....	18a25 "
Mutton.		Currants.....	8a10 "
Choice Chops.	a12 "	Dried peach's	12a25 "
Fore quarters.	8 a10 "	" apples...	6a12 "
Hind " ..	a10 "	Beans........	a 8 "
Shoul'rs&b'st	8 a10 "	Saur Krout...	6 a 8 "
Spr'g Lamb.	$1a150 pr q'r	Shll'd L Bean	a18 "
Veal.		Watermellons.	10a25 pr p
Choice Cutlet.	8 a10 per lb	Live Chick's..	25a50 pr pr
Shoulders....	a 6 "	" Pigeons...	18a25 "
Breasts......	a 8 "	" Geese....	100a150 "
Hind quart'rs.	a 7 "	Dress'd Tur's.	$1a125 single
Fore " ..	a 6 "	" Geese..	a100 "
Vegetables.		" Chick'n..	37a75 pr p'r
Potatoes, mer.	20a30 p pck	*Fish.*	
Spinnach.....	a18 "	Large Rock..	25a75 single
Parsnips......	15a20 "	White Shad..	50a75 pr pr
Kale Sprouts.	a16 "	Small Rock..	12a50 pr bh
Brocoli " ..	a16 "	Pike........	12a31 "
Beets........	a 4 pr bh	White perch.	6a25 "
Carrots......	a 6 "	Yellow " ..	6a18 "
Cabbage......	2a 5 single	W'te Catfish..	12a25 "
Radishes.....	3a10 pr bh	Codfish	a 6 pr lb
Asparagus....	10a12 "	Hard Crabs...	25a37 pr dz
Celery	6a12 "		

MILITARY MATTERS.—Yesterday afternoon a train arrived over the Washington branch railroad, having on board a body of about 350 men, the remainder of the organization of Ellsworth Zouaves, who gained such notoriety by their rascality in Alexandria, but since the battle of Bull Run have become so demoralized as to render them literally a "nuisance." The remainder of the regiment, with the exception of the lost at Bull Run, have already made tracks for home, having deserted and scattered in every direction. The party marched through various streets to the President street depot.

EXCITEMENT LAST NIGHT.—About nine o'clk last night considerable excitement was occasioned throughout the city, by the reception of the particulars of the heavy battle in Missouri. The news, as a matter of course, originated at the newspaper offices, but for some time, although it *was credited* to the Associated Press, it *was not* generally credited by the people, and the anxious inquiry upon every tongue was, "Is it true?" The confirmation of the news this morning by the press has set at rest all doubts.

A DULL SEASON.—The past week has been decidedly a dull season for Reporters, as there has an been unusual dearth of city news of any kind. The police records are comparatively blank, which may be accounted for by the absence of nearly the whole rough element, who have gone to the wars. Fortunately, through the efforts of General Dix, the Northern troops, who converted the city into a perfect pandemonium for some time, are kept at their various camps, to a great extent, at least, and the people are enabled to draw breath once more without fear.

PAINFUL ACCIDENT.—A most painful accident occurred about six o'clock last evening at the house of F. H. Roberts, residing on McElderry street. A small son, about eleven years of age, was amusing himself with a kite, upon a back building in the rear of the house, when by a misstep he was precipitated to the ground, a distance of about ten feet, striking in his descent upon the edge of a wash tub, and injuring himself, it is feared, quite seriously, three of his ribs being broken. He was attended by Dr. Collins, who gave partial relief to the little sufferer.

THE BOSTON STEAMERS.—The steamer Joseph Whitney, of the Merchants' and Miners' Transportation Company, Captain Loveland, reached her wharf this morning about six o'clock. Captain Loveland reports leaving Boston last Thursday for Old Point, which he made on Sunday, and had considerable difficulty in the Roads in consequence of the gale which prevailed, and the landing of eleven large boats, four of which were manufactured expressly for Captain Forbes' coast service, and the rest for the flag ship Minnesota. Some of these boats weighed over five tons each, and being on deck, were lashed to heavy timbers placed across the ship.

The Whitney had about two dozen passengers, some of whom were landers at Old Point. She is now the property of the Government and will probably leave to-night or to-morrow morning for New York. She has two brass six pounders on her deck as a means of defence, but these belong to Fort McHenry, and will be sent there. The other boats of the line, the S. R. Spaulding and the Ben Deford, at the the last advices were at Boston. The Spaulding, however, is expected here some time to-morrow. The freight of the Whitney consists in part of boots and shoes and dry-goods.—Soon as she reaches New York she is to be fitted out as a gun boat, for the purpose of strengthening the blockade of the Southern ports.

THE PEABODY INSTITUTE.—This splendid evidence of the ability and genius of our artizans is now rapidly approaching completion, and it is hoped but a short time will elapse before it will be thrown open for public inspection.—Notwithstanding the vast amount of money already spent upon it, and its location in one of the most commanding positions in Baltimore, it seems to have attracted but little attention on the part of the community, who seem to think that the Board of Managers manage their operations a little too secretly, or, in other words, that the Board should have by this time given to the community some account at least of their stewardship.

There are those in the community who greatly fear that the whole affair will prove another Smithonian Institute on a small scale, with its sphere of usefulness greatly contracted by the exclusive spirit of its managers. It is hope however that the intelligent and honorable gentlemen who have most influence in the Board will develope the generosity and extensive liberality of its founder, to the end that all [illegible] objects in its erection will be faithfully carried out for the benefit of all. We have already com[illegible]mended the Board for their wisdom in the electio[illegible] of the Rev. Dr. Morris as Librarian. He is one [illegible] of the most profound and erudite men in the State, [illegible] and the library which he will purchase, both in [illegible] Europe and this country, will be the most valuab[illegible] in Maryland.

ANOTHER UNPROVOKED ASSAULT.—A number of unprovoked assaults committed by soldiers, upon citizens have been recorded within the past week, and "still the work goes bravely on," as hardly a night passes that there is not a repetition of the offence, about 11 o'clock last night as Mr. W. H. Sherman, a merchant residing on West Lexington street; was passing near the corner of Lexington and St. Paul on his way home, he was approached by two men one of whom was a soldier who cheered for the Union and immediately set upon him knocking him down and beating him quite severely. Mr. S. happens to have been a staunch Union man heretofore but he is hartily disgusted with his affiliation

The New-York Times.

VOL. X....NO. 3106. NEW-YORK, THURSDAY, SEPTEMBER 5, 1861. PRICE TWO CENTS.

THE GREAT REBELLION.

Important News from the National Capital.

REPORTED DEATH OF JEFF. DAVIS.

Treasury Notes to be Used in Paying the Soldiers.

FACTS AND RUMORS FROM THE SOUTH.

Effect of the Victory at Hatteras Inlet.

THE REBELS PANIC STRICKEN.

Full Rebel Accounts of the Engagement.

Col. Corcoran Put in Irons for Refusing to Answer to Roll-call.

SPECIAL DISPATCH FROM WASHINGTON.

WASHINGTON, Wednesday, Sept. 4.

The proclamation of Gen. FREMONT is still the subject of much comment. The Government had not given instructions for any such declaration, nor was it known here that such was to be made. But, nevertheless, there is not one member of the Cabinet who does not approve and sustain the principles declared by Gen. FREMONT.

MARTIAL LAW IN MISSOURI.

Gov. GAMBLE, of Missouri, is here to remonstrate against the extension of Martial Law over the entire State, and to speak for the restoration of the Provisional Government, of which he is the Chief Executive, but he will be unable to induce any change. The President is determined to induce energy and firmness in commanders by sustaining them in such measures as they may deem necessary to insure success, and he will take no step backward.

THE REPORTED DEATH OF JEFF. DAVIS.

The report of the death of JEFF. DAVIS is received again to-day, and generally credited—not so much because of positive information, as because those here who are acquainted with him have for a long time entertained expectations of his breaking down under the excitement and responsibilities he has been called to endure, since he became the chief traitor of the rebellious States.

THE REBELS USING BALLOONS.

The rebels have availed themselves of the supposed advantages to be derived from balloon observations. Their balloons can be seen in the rear of their advanced works every calm day.

CLASHING OF AUTHORITY.

THURLOW WEED arrived at Washington, to-day, accompanied by Gov. MORGAN. There is more trouble, or clashing between the State and General Governments, about the volunteers. The men generally prefer to enter directly the service of the United States, in preference to going through the State mill, subjected to the treatment of Militia Quartermasters, and the circumlocution of the State routine. Gov. MORGAN is here, I understand, to induce the Government to bring volunteers into the State routine.

LORD TEMPEST IN WASHINGTON.

Lord ADOLPHUS V. TEMPEST is among the distinguished visitors in Washington. He comes to study our science of war, for which the present rebellion affords him abundant opportunity.

PAY OF BANDS.

Under the late law of Congress, ample provision is made for the pay of regimental bands, the compensation of a leader being equal to that of a Lieutenant, and the pay of privates the same as members of the Engineer corps. It has, therefore, been determined to organize full bands for all the regiments, and persons have been detailed for that duty from each of the New-York regiments.

THE NEW-YORK NINETEENTH.

From Maj. LEDLIE, of the Nineteenth Regiment New-York Volunteers, I learn that nearly all the members of that regiment have returned to duty, satisfied that they had really enlisted for two years, and were bound to serve the Government for that period.

RESIGNED HIS COMMISSION.

Maj. MINTURN, of the Second Irish Thirty-seventh Regiment, has resigned his commission, and his resignation has been accepted.

PRECEDENCE IN PROMOTION.

The precedence in the order of promotion of the newly-appointed Lieutenants of Marine and acting Paymasters is to be determined by lot. This measure will stop all efforts to determine the matter by political influence.

THE PRISONERS AT FORT LAFAYETTE.

Applications are daily received by the Government for permission to visit the prisoners at Fort Lafayette. They are all refused, the determination being to allow no communication with prisoners there.

EX-MINISTER FAULKNER.

Mr. FAULKNER still remains in custody. He is allowed no personal communication with his friends.

THE OFFICERS OF THE R. B. FORBES ARRESTED.

The steamer *R. B. Forbes*, purchased for a gunboat by the Government, arrived at the Navy-yard this afternoon from Fortress Monroe. The captain, first and second mates, boatswain and carpenter were immediately arrested by order of the Navy Department, and put in double irons. The charge against them has not transpired, but it is believed their arrest has grown out of their reckless conduct from the time of the boat leaving Boston.

SKIRMISHING ACROSS THE POTOMAC.

Considerable skirmishing transpired, this morning, near Bailey's Cross Roads. An hour before daylight the rebels, in considerable force from Munson's Hill, drove in our pickets from the Cross Roads, and took possession of the point. Four companies of the New-York Thirty-seventh, commanded by Capt. LEONARD, drove the rebels back, and again held the position. Our forces sustained a loss of two killed, and wounded nearly twenty of the rebels and took five prisoners. They state that no intelligence had been received of the death of JEFF. DAVIS. At 5 o'clock, this afternoon, our forces were in possession of the Cross Roads.

BALLOON RECONNOISSANCE.

This afternoon Prof. LOWE made another ascension from near Fort Corcoran. He was accompanied by Gen. MCDOWELL, Gen. FITZ JOHN PORTER and Dr. MAGRUDER. They ascended to an altitude of eight hundred feet, and had a fine view of the rebel camps in the vicinity.

SHOOTING PICKETS.

Yesterday afternoon a picket of the Fourth Michigan, stationed at Hall's House, beyond Ball's Cross Roads, walked a distance of twenty rods west of the House, when he was shot by a rebel picket. He died in an hour. Most of our pickets who have been shot are those who have ventured beyond our outposts.

ESCAPED CONTRABANDS.

Last night three contrabands escaped from the South Carolina Brigade, at Flint Hill, a short distance from Vienna, and reached our lines. They were slaves, one of B. B. FOSTER, of Spartenburgh District; one of Dr. HUNTER, of Laurens District, and one of Mr. COATS, of Newberry District. FOSTER is Lieutenant-Colonel of WILLIAMS' regiment. MIDDLETON, who belonged to FOSTER, is a negro of rare intelligence for a field-hand, and he gives a clear statement of the condition of the brigade. It is commanded by Gen. BONHAM, and the four regiments are commanded by Cols. WILLIAMS, CASH, BARTON and JENKINS. The measles and typhoid fever prevail extensively in their camps, and the sick are daily being sent to other places in Virginia. The regiments are reduced to below five hundred men each, and yesterday one of them, which left home with nine hundred men, only mustered a hundred and twenty-five at dress parade—the remainder being out on picket or in the hospital, dead or discharged. They have three or four brass field pieces, commanded by a man named KEMPER, of Alexandria. Until last week the men had been suffering much for the want of shoes and clothing, but a supply having arrived from South Carolina, they are now well shod and clothed. They have no want of provisions. Meats are plentiful, but vegetables, beans and rice are scarce. Meal or flour is given out to the men, which they have to bake for themselves. The breadstuffs and fresh meats are brought mostly from Loudon County, where wagons go almost daily to get supplies. Their means of transportation are limited. Nothing had been heard by MIDDLETON in camp of the death of JEFF. DAVIS, nor had their flags been at half-mast. One of the others states, however, that it was spoken of in his regiment, and that the officers were wearing crape. They had heard of the victory at Hatteras Inlet, but were waiting confirmation of the news by the Southern newspapers, which they receive by express from Fairfax Court-house. They have no intrenchments at Flint Hill. They estimate their own forces in Virginia at one hundred thousand men, and ours at two hundred thousand about Washington. MIDDLETON states that there are no colored regiments at Manassas; that the slaves, except in rare instances, are not allowed to have arms. Large numbers of free negroes in Virginia had been impressed into the service, and had been employed on the intrenchments at Manassas and as servants. He states that when he left South Carolina the greatest vigilance was exercised with regard to the slaves. In many instances they were not allowed to go to church, and being seen together in groups of three or four, except at work, they were severely punished. The slaves believed that the war promised good to them, and they were confidently expecting to be made free. With very rare exceptions they would run away, had they the opportunity.

DISPATCH TO THE ASSOCIATED PRESS.

WASHINGTON, Wednesday, Sept. 4.

The following order has just been issued by Lieut.-Gen. SCOTT:

HEAD-QUARTERS OF THE ARMY, WASHINGTON, Sept. 3, 1861.

The General-in-Chief is happy to announce that the Treasury Department, to meet future payments to the troops, is about to supply beside coin, as heretofore, Treasury notes in fives, tens and twenties, as good as gold, at all Banks and Government offices throughout the United States, and most convenient for transmission by mail from officers and men to their families at home. Good husbands, fathers, sons and brothers serving under the Stars and Stripes, will thus soon have the ready and safe means of relieving an immense amount of suffering, which could not be reached with coin. In making up such packages, every officer may be relied upon, no doubt, for such assistance as may be needed by his men. By command of

Lieut.-Gen. SCOTT.
(Signed.) E. D. TOWNSEND,
Assistant Adjutant-General.

The Executive Department has no information confirmatory of the reported death of JEFF. DAVIS. Intelligence received in Army circles renders such an event as merely probably true.

Commodore STRINGHAM has made his official report respecting the operations of the fleet at Hatteras Inlet. It contains no facts additional to those already published. He concludes his circumstantial narrative by saying:

"I have naught but praise to accord to the officers, seaman and marines, of the Navy, and officers and soldiers, of the Army, who were present, for their gallantry and cheerful devotion to duty and to their Government, the United States of America,—which they all cheerfully and heartily serve."

The Naval Board for retiring infirm and disabled officers, have been ordered to meet at the Brooklyn Navy-yard on the 16th inst.

The President has appointed Col. SEATON, of the *National Intelligencer*, a member of the Metropolitan Police Board to fill a vacancy; but although the appointment is popular it is probable he will decline the office.

The Board has elected Z. C. ROBBINS their President, and WM. B. WEBB, of this city, Superintendent of Police.

The Treasury Department has issued proposals for the construction of five steam screw revenue vessels.

Gov. GAMBLE, of Missouri, had an interview with the President to-day.

Capt. LYLES' National Guard Regiment, of Philadelphia, which was among the first of the three months' Volunteers accepted, was yesterday accepted for three years by the War Department.

At the Provost-Marshal's office, to-day, a pass to cross the Potomac was refused to a newspaper reporter, about whose loyalty there is no doubt. In Gen. PORTER'S absence a deputy attends to this business. It is presumed from the circumstance above related that the refusal to the Press is uniform.

MASSACHUSETTS MILITARY AFFAIRS.

BOSTON, Wednesday, Sept. 4.

Senator WILSON meets with great encouragement in raising his regiment. Over 30 companies have already tendered their services, of which 28 have been accepted, including 16 from the returned three months' regiments. The companies are accepted, with the understanding that their ranks will be recruited to the standard within a week. The recruiting officers are required to make daily returns.

FOLLETT'S new battery of light artillery is full.

Senator WILSON'S movement has given great impetus to the military spirit, and it is believed a brigade can be raised within a fortnight. The new cavalry regiment is rapidly organizing.

Orders have been received from the Navy Department to charter a steamer and send immediately 400 seamen from the recruiting ship *Ohio*. Their destination is unknown.

Col. JONES is recruiting the famous Sixth Regiment, and a large proportion of the men are reëntering the service for the war.

IMPORTANT FROM FORT MONROE.

HOW THE NATIONAL PRISONERS AT RICHMOND ARE TREATED.

FORTRESS MONROE, Tuesday, Sept. 3,
Via BALTIMORE, Wednesday, Sept. 4.

The gun-boat *R. B. Forbes* got off Cape Charles the night before last, with three feet of water in her hold, and proceeded to Washington this morning for repairs. She would have gone to pieces had not the weather been unusually mild.

The Confederate slaves at Old Point now number eighteen hundred, including women and children.

A flag of truce has just come in from Norfolk, with the crews of the barks *Rowena* and *Glen*, schooner *Mary Alice*, and brig *Joseph*, all captured by the privateer *Dixie*, with the exception of the *Joseph*, which was taken by the privateer *Savannah*. The Captain and mates of the *Glen* were retained as prisoners at Richmond. The Captain of the *Mary Alice* is almost direct from Charleston. He reports that the force there does not exceed four thousand men, and that they apprehended an attack from the recent naval expedition.

Congressman ELY is still at Richmond, and has to take his turn in cooking and carrying water for the prisoners.

Col. CORCORAN was lately put in irons several hours for refusing to answer his name at the roll call.

Butter at Richmond is worth 50 cents; ham 30 cents, and coffee 45 cents per pound.

Capt. DAVIS made a reconnoissance yesterday in the direction of Back River, and captured two of the mounted Worth Guards.

IMPORTANT ITEMS OF SOUTHERN NEWS.

BALTIMORE, Wednesday, Sept. 4.

A copy of the Richmond *Dispatch*, of Tuesday, received by a flag of truce at Old Point, contains the following items of news:

A dispatch from Charleston, dated Sunday night, says a brig, laden with coffee, run the blockade on Sunday morning; also, a vessel with fruit.

The ship *Gaudar*, from Liverpool, arrived at Beaufort last week.

The ship *Alliance*, which arrived at Beaufort last week, is spoken of by the *Examiner* as laden with arms, ammunition, thread, quicksilver, &c.

The *Dispatch* says, we may, in a few days, expect BEAUREGARD and JOHNSTON'S report of the battle of Manassas.

No mention is made in the *Dispatch* of the illness of JEFFERSON DAVIS, but it contains a proclamation of the "President" calling Congress together again on the 3d inst., on account of its failure to deliver to the President for his signature the bill containing the military appointments.

FROM GEN. FREMONT'S COLUMN.

CAIRO, Ill., Wednesday, Sept. 4.

The gun-boats *Taylor* and *Lexington* had an engagement off Hickman, Ky., with the rebel gun-boat *Yankee* this afternoon. Two batteries on the shore, supported by about 15,000 rebels, also fired upon our boats. None of the shots took effect. The *Taylor* and *Lexington* fired about twenty shots, with what effect is not yet known. They returned to Cairo this evening, and on the way were fired on with small arms at Columbus and Chalk Bluffs, Ky.

Col. HICKS, of the Fortieth Illinois Regiment, who was sent to exchange prisoners, returned last night from Charleston. The rebels had but three National prisoners.

It is reported that the rebels are falling back from Sykestown to New Madrid. Gen. GRANT took command of this post to-day.

IMPORTANT FROM MISSOURI.

HANNIBAL, Wednesday, Sept. 4.

Corporal DIX, of the Third Iowa Regiment, while out on a scout with five men, near Kirksville, last week, was surrounded in a farm-house, when at dinner, by twenty-five rebels, who demanded the surrender of his party. This was refused, and the Secessionists made an attack on them.

The fight was severe, but the National troops maintained the position in the house, driving the assailants from the ground, with a loss of 7 killed and 5 wounded.

Corporal DIX, on the National side, was killed, but none of the others were hurt.

JEFFERSON CITY, Tuesday, Sept. 3.

The latest information from Lexington confirms the safety of that place, and the withdrawal of the rebels. There is much disaffection in MCCULLOCH'S Army. He is in Arkansas. This is reliable.

An expedition crossed into Callaway County last night, destined for Columbia.

CAPE GIRARDEAU, Tuesday, Sept. 3.

Gen. PRENTISS' little Army, which left Ironton some days since, arrived at Jackson, some two miles west of here, yesterday morning. Gen. PRENTISS and Staff are now here. No enemy was met during the march. The report that Gen. PRENTISS took 180 prisoners is, therefore, false.

A scout arrived from HARDEE'S Camp last night, and reported that the rebels knew the exact time Gen. PRENTISS left Ironton, and immediately commenced retreating. HARDEE was rapidly moving toward Arkansas with 6,000 men. The enemy are reported to be strongly fortified at Sykestown.

ARRIVAL OF THE TWENTIETH REGIMENT OF MASSACHUSETTS.

GOV. ANDREWS TO DINE WITH THE MEN.

The Twentieth Regiment of Massachusetts, Col. LEE, will arrive in this City this morning. A deputation of the Sons of Massachusetts will receive the men on landing, and escort them to the Park Barracks, where they will partake of breakfast. Gov. ANDREWS, who is in this City, has been invited, and will partake of soldier's fare with them. It is expected the Governor will address them. The following gentlemen have had invitations sent them, and will no doubt be present: Gov. Morgan and staff, Wm. M. Evarts, Gen. Arthur, Com. Stringham, Col. Tompkins, Hiram Barney, David Dudley Field, W. Curtis Noyes, James Humphrey, Joseph Choate, F. Law Olmsted, George Godwin, Capt. Marshall, Judge Bonney, J. G. Brady, William Allen Butler, Rev. Dr. Bellows, Rev. Dr. Tyng, Rev. Dr. Adams.

ARRIVAL OF A COMPANY FROM MASSACHUSETTS.

A company of 161 men, under command of Capt. JOHN SAUNDERS, of Salem, arrived yesterday from Massachusetts. Upon landing in this City, the men were marched to the Park Barracks, where they are now quartered. To-day they will leave this City for the seat of war to join Col. SAUNDERS' regiment, which is already there. Accompanying Capt. SAUNDERS' command is a baggage wagon, two ambulances and eight horses.

ARRIVAL OF A NEW-HAMPSHIRE REGIMENT.

The Third Regiment of New Hampshire, Col. FELLOWS, arrived at Hunter's Point, L. I., yesterday by the steamship *Connecticut*. From there the men were marched to the camp of instruction at Hempstead, where they will be instructed in the art of war, and form part of a division, and taught to act in concert without regiments. The men are armed with the Enfield rifle, and are a fine set of athletic young fellows, all of whom are perfectly uniformed and equipped. The regiment numbers 1,010, exclusive of officers.

THE SEA-COAST OF VIRGINIA AND NORTH CAROLINA.

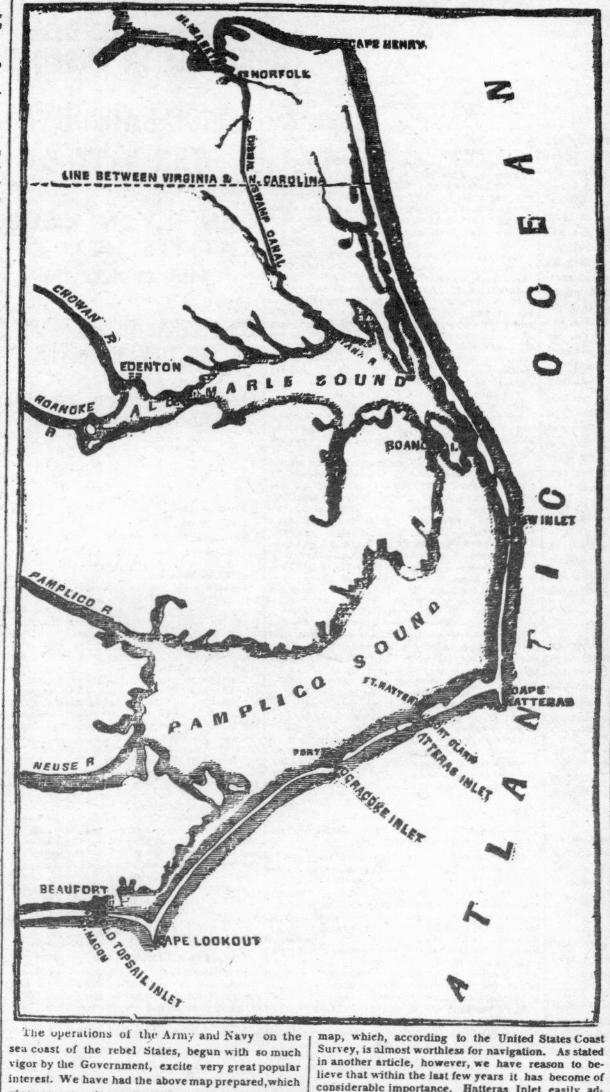

The operations of the Army and Navy on the sea coast of the rebel States, begun with so much vigor by the Government, excite very great popular interest. We have had the above map prepared, which gives an accurate representation of the theatre of the recent movements, and shows the immense advantages that the Government has gained.

The map commences with a margin of Hampton Roads, near Norfolk, and presents the entire Atlantic front of the States of Virginia and North Carolina for a distance of over 200 miles. It shows every inlet or harbor but one, on the North Carolina coast. It will be seen that Albemarle and Pamlico Sounds form large inland seas, with which Norfolk has connection by the Dismal Swamp Canal, and into which the Chowan, Roanoke and Neuse, the important rivers of North Carolina, flow. The point of land north of Norfolk, and near the end of the map, is the far-famed Sewall's Point, and just opposite to it, but not shown on the map, is Fortress Monroe. It is clear, therefore, that Richmond, Petersburgh and Norfolk, the three commercial towns of Virginia, and all communicating, could never be blockaded effectually by Fortress Monroe. Their vessels found comparatively easy outlet through the canal and the Sounds.

But it will be seen, on examining the maps, that the external commerce of the Sounds is dependent on three inlets—Hatteras, Ocracoke, and Old Topsail Inlet. Of these, Hatteras was the chief and almost only one used by all Virginia vessels. There is another inlet called New or Oregon Inlet, indicated on the map, which, according to the United States Coast Survey, is almost worthless for navigation. As stated in another article, however, we have reason to believe that within the last few years it has become of considerable importance. Hatteras Inlet easily admits vessels drawing fifteen feet of water. Ocracoke, in mean low water, admits over its bar vessels drawing 10 feet to 11½ feet. Its defences are believed to be insignificant even compared with those at Hatteras. Old Topsail Inlet, at Beaufort, is said to be the best on the North Carolina coast. It is defended by Fort Macon, and, the rebels say, in a very efficient manner. But so they thought of Hatteras. There is but one other harbor of importance on all the coast of North Carolina—that of Wilmington—the roads of the Cape Fear River, which empties into the Atlantic fifty to sixty miles down the coast from Beaufort. The navigation of the Sounds down to Beaufort is tortuous and tedious, and not at all reliable or safe. The closing of Hatteras Inlet therefore inflicts a heavy blow on all the contraband commerce and privateering enterprise in which Virginia and North Carolina have been indulging. Fort Hatteras is made a naval dépôt for our blockading fleet, and it is easy to see that a reasonable force within it, and a war-vessel near by to beat off landing parties, will make the position impregnable to the enemy.

We shall not wait long, we hope, to hear that Ocracoke Inlet and Fort Macon are under our control. The Richmond papers, which we quote freely from to-day, report that a "Yankee fleet," in great force, has already appeared off Beaufort. The rebels seem to be in great agitation and dismay by reason of our coastwise demonstrations.

THE HATTERAS PRISONERS IN QUARTERS.

Yesterday morning all the prisoners brought to this port on board the United States frigate *Minnesota*, were transferred to Fort Wood, on Bedloe's Island, and to Castle William, on Governor's Island. A large number of small boats, containing ladies and gentlemen, surrounded the steamboats *Saturn* and *S. A. Stevens*, which were employed to convey them to their quarters. They witnessed the disembarkation in silence; not a reproachful word was uttered, the spectators looking upon the prisoners more in sorrow than in anger.

At Bedloe's Island they were received by a few regulars, and a guard of Fire Zouaves drawn up in single file. The roll was called on the landing, and all being found correct, they were marched into the fort. The rebel officers were the last to leave the ship. Commodore BARRON was dressed in the uniform similar to that worn by the officers of the United States Navy. They all looked well, and appeared cheerful. The *Saturn* left the ship at 11 o'clock, and conveyed the officers with a part of the soldier-privates, to Castle William, where they were placed under guard.

FROM CINCINNATI.

CINCINNATI, Tuesday, Sept. 4.

Yesterday the United States Marshal seized the interest of citizens of the rebel States in merchandise now for sale on commission in this city, amounting to $50,000.

SEIZURE OF VESSELS IN PHILADELPHIA.

PHILADELPHIA, Wednesday, Sept. 4.

Bark *Benjamin Hallett* and schooners *G. W. Tyson*, *A. S. Shindler*, *Aribes* and *C. Barrows* were seized by the Marshal to-day, under the Confiscation act.

ARREST OF A SECESSIONIST.

BOSTON, Wednesday, Sept. 4.

JAMES LEGUIRE, hailing from Halifax, N. S., was arrested in this city to-day, on charges of conspiracy against the Government. He has been committed for trial at the next term of the United States District Court. Bail was refused. LEGUIRE was bound for Memphis, and a uniform was found in his trunk, and other suspicious circumstances led to his arrest.

FROM KENTUCKY.

CINCINNATI, Wednesday, Sept. 4.

The *Commercial* says that it is understood in Frankfort that Gov. MAGOFFIN refuses to play into the hands of the rabid Secessionists; that he has had a quarrel with Mr. BRECKINRIDGE; that he refuses to demand the breaking up of the United States camp in Garrard County, and that he declares that he will submit to the will of the majority of the people of Kentucky, as may be expressed through the Legislature.

THE KENTUCKY LEGISLATURE.

FRANKFORT, Tuesday, Sept. 3.

In the House, there was nothing of importance transacted to-day.

In the Senate, Judge ROBINSON, of Scott County, was elected President *pro tem*. Six or seven Senators more than the Constitution allows have been elected, and the permanent organization of the Senate is delayed on a question of contested seats.

ARRIVAL OF A PRIZE.

CAUGHT WHILE TRYING TO RUN THE BLOCKADE AT CHARLESTON.

The schooner *H. Middleton*, Capt. KEMPS, arrived at this port yesterday, a prize to the United States, having been captured on the 21st Aug., off Charleston, by the United States sloop-of-war *Vandalia*.

The *H. Middleton* was from Charleston, bound to Liverpool with a cargo of naval stores, and had attempted to run the blockade. During the chase she had thrown overboard the entire deck load. The Captain and crew were transferred to the United States frigate *Roanoke*.

The following note was found on board, showing that she had previously been intended for a privateer:

"In case of being boarded sink this package, as the letters were too late to take out privateer's papers for your schooner, and would criminate you.

(Signed,) F. J. PORCHER.

To Capt. BARKLEY."

The *H. Middleton* has gone to the Navy-yard.

ARREST OF A REBEL CAPTAIN.

SARATOGA, N. Y., Wednesday, Sept. 4.

JAMES CHAPIN, of Vicksburgh, reported to be a Captain in the rebel Army, was arrested at the residence of his father-in-law, in this village, to-day, by United States Marshal BURR, of Albany, by virtue of a warrant of the Secretary of State. He is to go to Fort Lafayette.

THE ARREST OF H. A. REEVE.

GREENPORT, L. I., Wednesday, Sept. 4.

The news of the arrest of H. A. REEVE, editor of the *Watchman*, published here, causes great rejoicing among our Union men.

ARREST OF TRAITORS IN MAINE.

PORTLAND, Me., Wednesday, Sept. 4.

CYRUS F. SARGENT and OCTAVIUS F. HILL, of Yarmouth, Me., who have been doing business at the South, were arrested to-day by the United States Marshal, by order of the Secretary of War. They are confined in jail, and will be conveyed to Fort Lafayette.

OPERATIONS OF THE FLEET.

RUMORED DEMONSTRATION AGAINST FORT MACON.

We have received a copy of the Petersburgh (Va.) *Express*, of Monday, the 2d inst., from which we glean considerable valuable information relative to the movements and operations of the National Fleet which recently left Fortress Monroe. The following is especially important:

"Our latest advices from North Carolina are up to 9 o'clock last night. At that hour it was known in Goldsborough that a formidable Yankee fleet was in sight of Fort Macon, and an attack this morning, even if deferred until daylight, will not surprise the garrison. We are pleased to hear that they are well prepared for an assault, and will resist with a determination and daring worthy of the glorious cause in which they are engaged. Fort Macon commands the entrance to Beaufort Harbor, and is said to be the most formidable fortification on the North Carolina coast.

It was reported in Goldsborough last night, that the Yankee pirates had burned the flourishing and spirited little town of Washington, in Beaufort County, but the report needed confirmation. We may add, that it was generally discredited.

Active preparations on the defensive still continue all over the State, and every man in it is prepared to die in defence of his native soil if necessary."

REBEL ACCOUNTS OF THE HATTERAS FIGHT.

From the Petersburgh Express, Sept. 2.

We find in such of our North Carolina exchanges as have reached us since Thursday, brief mention of the disaster to Confederate arms at Hatteras on Wednesday and Thursday last. They give but very few particulars that have not already appeared in the *Express*. The Newbern *Progress* of Friday has the following:

"Fort Hatteras was surrendered to the National authorities about 11 o'clock on yesterday, Thursday.

The steamer *Winslow*, which left there soon after the surrender on yesterday, arrived here about 10 o'clock last night.

She brought up five wounded men and one dead body. From Lieut. CITIZEN, of Capt. LAMB'S Company, who escaped and came up, we gathered the following particulars:

The National steamers, eleven in number, commenced the bombardment on Wednesday, and the Forts, Clark and Hatteras, returned the fire. It was kept up until dark, with but little loss on our side. On yesterday morning the conflict was renewed, and continued until about 11 o'clock, when, after a desperate resistance, our forces were compelled to surrender, and the whole garrison are now held as prisoners, save a few who escaped.

Commodore Barron, Col. Bradford, Col. Martin, Lieut.-Col. Johnson, Major Gilliam, Major W. S. G. Andrews, and all the Captains of the post are prisoners.

Our entire force at Hatteras on Wednesday night, another gentleman informed us, was 653. Some few escaped, perhaps 50 or more, and Lieut. CITIZEN thinks not more than 60 were killed and wounded. Probably 40 killed and about 20 wounded. He remained in the fort till half an hour previous to its surrender, and from the lucid manner in which his statements were made, we have great confidence in them.

The National fleet consisted of eleven steamers, four of which were large war-steamers. The bombardment is represented by our informers as most terrific.

Lieut. KNIGHT and Lieut. MURDOCK were brought up wounded—KNIGHT slightly in the arm, and MURDOCK with his arm badly injured. Probably amputation will be necessary. The dead body of a Mr. TINDELL, we believe, from Lenoir, was brought up.

The news is sad, and we can give no more this morning. We will give particulars hereafter as they reach us.

Lieut. CITIZEN says our men fought bravely, until they were compelled to surrender, and the defeat to our arms is only to be attributed to the superiority of the fleet over our batteries. The ammunition gave out at Fort Clark on Wednesday, and the guns were spiked and abandoned, but Fort Hatteras returned the fire of the Nationals till 11 o'clock and after, yesterday.

Men of Eastern Carolina, arouse! We have warned you heretofore, but many of you heeded not. Now your property, your homes and your families are in danger! Come to your arms, and drive the invaders from your soil. A little preparation might have saved this disaster, but now it is too late, and we must make the most of it.

Let the militia be called out to aid the regular forces, and if the Hessians dare advance, let us make them rue it. We can, we must. To arms! to arms!

The Goldsborough *Tribune* issues a small 'extra,' dated Friday, which we annex:

"We had not in our last issue sufficient reliable information to announce that the enemy have taken the forts and forces at Hatteras. The main fort, Fort Hatteras, is at a point commanding Hatteras Inlet. Fort Clark is a small battery two miles north of the former, and lies on the ship channel. The chief commander was Col. W. F. MARTIN, Colonel of the Seventh North Carolina Volunteers. The troops in both forts were under the command of Major W. S. G. ANDREWS, of Goldsborough.

The attack was made on Wednesday morning at 8 o'clock, and kept up till 11 o'clock A. M., on Thursday. Eleven of the enemy's vessels were engaged in the bombardment. Fort Clark was captured first, and Fort Hatteras at the time named above, as that of the close of the cannonade. From 600 to 800 prisoners were taken by the enemy. Among them is Col. MARTIN, Major ANDREWS and Commodore BARRON, son of the celebrated Commodore of that name. Some eight or ten escaped. Of the killed and wounded, we have no account at this time, but expect further details before we put this extra to press.

For this disastrous result somebody is to blame. Who that somebody is must remain a subject for future inquiry. In the mean time let us not hastily censure any of those engaged in the arrangement or execution of this affair. In ignorance of the truth, we may censure the bravest and the best.

We look for much good to come out of this present evil. We do not know the designs of the enemy. If they intend to demonstrate an invasion, let them *come*, if they can, we say—the Confederates will teach them how to go, as they have in every case of conflict, of any importance, since the first inroads of the ruffianly host. They have the advantage of us in the marine, that may skulk about the coast and annoy us—but let them come in contact whenever they dare, and we have no fears for the result. This event will perhaps give our boys something to do, who are ready and anxious to do something."

ACCOUNTS FROM RALEIGH.

The *Standard* of Saturday, says:

"On Tuesday last, Gov. CLARK received a dispatch from Gen. HUGER, at Norfolk, stating that two steam frigates, eight armed vessels, with other small craft, had left Old Point on Monday, and steered South. The impression was they designed an attack upon our coast. Gov. CLARK at once ordered the Seventh Regiment of State troops, commanded by Col. CAMPBELL, to Newbern. On Wednesday, a dispatch was received *via* Newbern, that the fleet had anchored off Fort Hattaras.

On Thursday afternoon an intense feeling was created here by the additional announcement that Fort Hatteras had been captured by the Nationals—that the guns of the fort were silenced at an early period of the day. From these rumors additional ones have been manufactured, and the most serious results are said to have occurred. At this writing, nothing is certainly known here as to the result. We had nineteen cannon mounted at that point, with about 500 troops. The force of the Nationals is variously estimated at from 4,000 to 6,000. We doubt if they had more than 4,000 if that, as more could not well have been spared from Old Point.

It is, however, quite certain that, according to our predictions and warnings for months, our coast is menaced, if not successfully invaded. If we are not prepared fully to meet the foe at the entrance of our inlets, it is not the fault of the *Standard*. We have labored earnestly to direct the attention of the Government to the absolute necessity of full preparation. If there be blame, let it fall where it ought.

But we must not give way to [illegible]. We must up and at them, and drive them from our coast. Gov. CLARK will do his utmost to [illegible] promptly, and we have no doubt President DAVIS will promptly meet the case. There is no time for delay. We hope and believe our friends in the Eastern Counties will rally promptly to resist the LINCOLN hirelings. Let them be cool, [illegible] and vigilant. Watch the enemy's [illegible] and be sure to provide against the [illegible] near approach. Remove [illegible] property of the enemy [illegible] beyond his reach at the first indication of his approach to the main land."

The *Standard* has also the following:

"We stop the press to announce the startling intelligence, that a dispatch has just been received in this city, that Fort Hatteras was taken by the Nationals at 11 o'clock on Thursday, and that our whole force, amounting to nearly 600 men, have been made prisoners. Arouse, North Carolinians, and drive them from your soil."

The *Register*, of Saturday, has the following:

"Raleigh was filled with rumors on yesterday and the day before, in relation to the bombardment and silencing of our battery at Cape Hatteras by the National fleet on Wednesday last. We have reason most reluctantly, to believe that these rumors are

[Continued on Eighth Page.]

THE NEW YORK HERALD.

WHOLE NO. 9126. NEW YORK, THURSDAY, SEPTEMBER 5, 1861. PRICE TWO CENTS.

THE REBELLION.

Confirmatory Reports of the Death of Jefferson Davis.

Unfounded Rumors of Conflicts in Virginia.

Eagerness of the Hostile Armies for Battle.

IMPORTANT NEWS FROM MISSOURI.

Particulars of the Attack and Repulse of the Rebels at Lexington.

Retreat of Ben McCulloch's Army Towards Arkansas.

Effect in the South of the Capture of Fort Hatteras.

Great Alarm of the Virginia and North Carolina Rebels.

Seizure of Rebel Property at Cincinnati and Philadelphia,

&c., &c., &c.

OUR SPECIAL WASHINGTON DESPATCHES.

WASHINGTON, Sept. 4, 1861.

ADDITIONAL CONFIRMATION OF THE DEATH OF JEFFERSON DAVIS.

Still further confirmation has been received here of the death of Jefferson Davis, on Monday instead of Saturday, at 7 o'clock A. M. A person arrived here to-day from Manassas Junction reiterates the statement already received, and adds that all the officers wear crape on their arms.

The Executive Department has no information confirmatory of the reported death of Jeff. Davis.

EXCITING RUMORS OF CONFLICTS WITH THE REBELS—AUDACITY OF THE ENEMY—BOTH ARMIES EAGER FOR BATTLE.

All day long the city has been filled with rumors of battles and captures of batteries. The rebel battery at Munson's Hill was said to have been taken early this morning, and details of the action were given. A furious battle was reported to be going on at the Chain Bridge, or Great Falls, or Seneca Falls, or somewhere up the river. Perhaps some of these rumors were telegraphed to New York. They were all utterly unfounded. There has been no engagement at any point of our lines during the day.

The rebels at Munson's Hill have been bold and tantalizing. They placed a band upon the parapet of their works, and entertained our outposts with "Away Down South in Dixie" and "Washington's March," alternately all day long. At one time they paraded about one hundred and fifty men before their works, as if it was their whole force, when we have accurate information that they have about 5,000 men there, under General Longstreet.

During the day parties and squads and companies of the rebels came down the road to within musket range of our pickets, and fired upon them upon several occasions; but the fire was not returned, as strict orders had been issued for our pickets not to fire. This order has probably been given by General McClellan to put a stop, if possible, to the firing between pickets, a practice that he condemns as murderous.

It is evident that the rebels are preparing for an immediate attack. They are swarming at all points along our lines. A large [illegible] approached last night to within a short distance of the Chain Bridge, but our troops are ready at a moment's warning, and, in fact, are anxious for the onset, so that they may have an opportunity to treat Monsieur Beauregard to a Bull run affair on the other track.

Mr. Ulrich Dahlgren, son of the distinguished commander of the Washington Navy Yard, is in command of one of our batteries in front of Munson's Hill.

CAPTURE OF REBELS AT HARPER'S FERRY.

Information has been received here that a detachment of a Massachusetts regiment captured twenty-two of the Charlestown Home Guard at Harper's Ferry, day before yesterday, and took them to General Banks' camp.

IMPORTANT ORDER FROM THE GENERAL-IN-CHIEF.

The following order has just been issued by Lieutenant General Scott:—

HEADQUARTERS OF THE ARMY, WASHINGTON, September 3, 1861.

The General-in-Chief is happy to announce that the Treasury Department, to meet future payments to the troops, is about to supply, besides coin, as heretofore, Treasury notes in fives, tens and twenties—as good as gold at all banks and government offices throughout the United States, and most convenient for transmission by mail from the officers and men to their families at home. Good husbands, fathers, sons and brothers, serving under the Stars and Stripes, will thus soon have the ready and safe means of relieving an immense amount of suffering, which could not be reached with coin. In making up such packages, every officer may be relied upon, no doubt, for such assistance as may be needed by his men.

By command of Lieutenant General SCOTT.
E. D. TOWNSEND, Assistant Adjutant General.

ARRIVAL OF THE STEAMER R. B. FORBES—ARREST OF HER OFFICERS.

The gunboat R. B. Forbes arrived at the Navy Yard to-night. Her officers were immediately placed under arrest.

THE PURSUIT OF THE PRIVATEER SUMTER.

The Navy Department to-day received official information from two points in the Gulf, dated the 13th ult., from which it is evident that three or four of our vessels of war have reliable information of the position of the privateer Sumter, and have probably by this time closed down on her, as they were then preparing to do from different points immediately.

REBEL REPORTS RESPECTING CAPTURED VESSELS—FLORIDA HARBORS BLOCKED UP.

It has been ascertained here that the Southern press have been in the habit of representing the prizes brought in by their privateers not only as prizes but also as vessels that have run the blockade. They thus make the most of a very little.

The prizes recaptured by our fleet on the Florida coast have been loaded with stone and sunk in the approaches to harbors along the coast, as has been done in the inlets of North Carolina, rendering the blockade entirely effectual, and enabling our blockading fleet to attend to more important points.

HASTY FLIGHT OF REBEL SYMPATHISERS.

Recent arrests of known aiders and abettors of treason have occasioned the sudden absence of several suspected persons, who probably feared being placed in durance. Many others of both sexes are under strict surveillance, and will be detained if circumstances require.

THE OFFICIAL REPORT OF THE CAPTURE OF FORT HATTERAS.

Commodore Stringham has made his official report respecting the operations of the fleet at Hatteras Inlet. It contains no facts additional to those already published. He concludes his circumstantial narrative by saying:—

I have [illegible] praise to accord to the officers, seamen [illegible] of the navy, and officers and soldiers of the army [illegible] were present for their gallantry and cheerful [illegible] to duty and to their government, the United States of America, which they all cheerfully and heartily served.

THE PROVOST MARSHAL AND THE PRESS.

At the Provost Marshal's office to-day a pass to cross the Potomac was refused to a newspaper reporter, about whose loyalty there is no doubt. In General Porter's absence a deputy attends to this business. It is presumed, from the circumstance above related, that the refusal to the press is uniform.

THE ARMY.

The following army appointments were made to-day:—Captains J. Nelson Smith, Pennsylvania; C. W. Golding, and Chas. D. Robinson, of Wisconsin, Assistant Quartermasters of Volunteers.

John A. L. Morrell, of Pennsylvania; Thomas B. Oakley, of New York, and M. Hoopes, of Pennsylvania, additional Paymasters.

Captains Alexander Morrison and John L. Hathaway, Commission of Subsistence.

Captains James Kelly and Patrick Kelly, late of the Sixty-ninth New York regiment, have been appointed Captains in the United States Army.

Captain Robert Nugent, of the Thirteenth United States infantry, late Lieutenant Colonel of the Sixty-ninth regiment New York State Militia, has been granted special leave of absence until further orders, to enable him to accept the Lieutenant Colonelcy of the new Sixty-ninth regiment New York Volunteers, and to aid in getting up the proposed Irish brigade. Captain Nugent goes to Philadelphia to-morrow to make arrangements for raising a regiment there to be attached to the brigade.

Captains Reid and Graham, late of the Second New York State Militia, are here, and have authority to raise a regiment for the Irish brigade.

Major Dennis E. Minton, of the Thirty-seventh New York regiment, has resigned, and his resignation is accepted.

Captain Lyle's National Guard regiment, of Philadelphia, which was among the first of the three months volunteers accepted, was yesterday accepted for three years by the War Department.

ORGANIZATION OF THE TENTH NEW YORK LEGION.

Hon. C. H. Van Wyck, Chairman of the Contract Investigating Committee, now in session at New York, arrived here to-day upon business connected with the organization of the New York Tenth Legion, to be made up in the counties of Orange, Sullivan and Ulster. The regiment is to have attached to it one cavalry and one artillery company. It is probable that Mr. Van Wyck will also while here endeavor to hurry up the statement required by the committee of the contracts made by the War and Navy Departments since March 4, which was asked for more than six weeks ago, but has not yet been furnished.

EXAMINATION OF CANDIDATES FOR ADMISSION TO THE MEDICAL CORPS.

A Board of Naval Surgeons is now in session at the Naval Hospital at New York for the examination of candidates for admission into the medical corps of the navy. It is understood that there are a number of vacancies. Gentlemen desirous to connect themselves permanently with the service would do well to avail themselves of this opportunity. Applications for permission to appear before the Board for examination must be addressed to the Secretary of the Navy, accompanied by testimonials of proper physical and moral qualifications. The candidates must be between the ages of twenty-one and twenty-five.

THE NAVAL RETIRING BOARD.

The Naval Board for retiring infirm and disabled officers have been ordered to meet at the Brooklyn Navy Yard, on the 16th instant.

THE PATRIOTIC LOAN.

A pamphlet, containing all the information necessary in reference to subscriptions to the national loan, is being prepared, and will soon be published under the auspices of the Treasury Department.

ARREST OF AN ALLEGED ROBBER.

John Gross, who was arrested about three weeks ago for robbing a jewelry store at Bethlehem, Pennsylvania, of a large amount, but made his escape from the officers while being conveyed to Philadelphia by jumping from the cars, was arrested to-day by Messrs. Lamon and Bartholomew, Philadelphia detectives, in one of the camps in this vicinity.

THE BARRON FAMILY.

There were two Barrons in the Revolution—Commodore James Barron and Captain Richard Barron—both in the Virginia navy. James had two sons, Samuel and James. The latter, late of the United States Navy, was the one who killed Decatur. It is his son, Samuel Barron, who was captured at Fort Hatteras.

LOYALTY OF THE EMPLOYES OF THE EXECUTIVE MANSION.

The recent intimations that some of the employes at the White House are secessionists are entirely unjust. Mr. Stackpole and all the other men there have been ready at any moment to take their guns in defence of the capital. They are faithful Union men, familiar with their duties, polite and attentive, and very much devoted to the President. It is small business, when the ranks of our army are flush with democrats, to ask the removal of these men on account of their former party politics, or—when we remember the gallant Sixty-ninth and Col. Corcoran—because some of them are Irishmen.

REMOVAL OF THE OFFICE OF THE SECRETARY OF THE TREASURY.

The office of the Secretary of the Treasury was to-day removed to a suit of rooms in the Treasury extension, which have been elegantly fitted up for that purpose. Rooms for Solicitor Jordan and First Auditor Smith will be prepared in close proximity to those of the Secretary, as frequent conferences are necessary between these officials. The rooms of Comptroller Whittlesey are already near by, but in the old building.

THE PROPRIETORS OF WILLARD'S KNOW HOW TO KEEP A HOTEL.

Willard's Hotel, under the management of Messrs. Sykes, Chadwick & Co., has already greatly improved. The table is better, and bills are actually made out now without any extra charges for articles which the guests have not had.

THE WASHINGTON POLICE BOARD.

The President has appointed Colonel Seaton, of the *National Intelligencer*, a member of the Metropolitan Police Board, to fill a vacancy. But although the appointment is popular, it is probable he will decline the office. The Board has elected Z. C. Robbins their President, and William B. Webb, of this city, Superintendent of Police.

CONTRACTS FOR STEAM NAVAL VESSELS.

The Treasury Department has issued proposals for the construction of five steam screw revenue vessels.

GOVERNOR GAMBLE AT WASHINGTON.

Governor Gamble, of Missouri, had an interview with the President to-day.

GEN. MITCHELL TO COMMAND AT CAMP DENNISON.

COLUMBUS, August 31, 1861.

Governor Dennison has been informed by telegraph from Washington, that, in compliance with his request, Brigadier General O. M. Mitchell will be immediately placed in command at Camp Dennison.

ARREST OF A REBEL AT BOSTON.

BOSTON, Sept. 4, 1861.

James Leguire, hailing from Halifax, N. S., was arrested in this city to-day, on charges of conspiring against the government. He has been committed for trial at the next term of the United States District Court. Bail was refused. Leguire was bound for Memphis, and a uniform was found in his trunk, and other suspicious circumstances led to his arrest.

ARREST OF A REPORTED REBEL CAPTAIN.

SARATOGA, N. Y., Sept. 4, 1861.

James Chapin, of Vicksburg, reported to be a captain in the rebel army, was arrested at the residence of his father-in-law in this village to-day by United States Marshal Burt, of Albany, by virtue of a warrant of the Secretary of State. He is to go to Fort Lafayette.

THE ARREST OF H. A. REEVE.

GREENPORT, L. I., Sept. 4, 1861.

The news of the arrest of H. A. Reeve, editor of the *Watchman*, published here, causes great rejoicing among our Union men.

ARREST OF TRAITORS IN MAINE.

PORTLAND, Me., Sept. 4, 1861.

Cyrus F. Sargent and Octavius F. Hill, of Yarmouth, Me., who have been doing business at the South, were arrested to-day by the United States Marshal, by order of the Secretary of War. They are confined in jail, and will be conveyed to Fort Lafayette.

ACQUITTAL OF AUGUST DOUGLASS.

PHILADELPHIA, Sept. 4, 1861.

The trial of August Douglass, of Baltimore, on high misdemeanor, on the charge of endeavoring to induce desertion, and enlistment for the rebels, resulted in his honorable acquittal, the jury finding him "not guilty."

COURT MARTIAL OF COLONEL DEHNA.

ST. LOUIS, Sept. 4, 1861.

Colonel Dehna, of the Indiana Legion, has been court martialed on a charge of conduct unbecoming an officer and a gentleman, and sentenced to be dismissed from the service of the United States. The court was presided over by General Pope, and the finding has been approved by General Fremont.

NEWS FROM FORTRESS MONROE.

Effect of the Capture of Fort Hatteras—Great Alarm in the South—The Blockade Violated—Release of Captured Seamen, &c., &c.

FORTRESS MONROE, Sept. 3, }
Via BALTIMORE, Sept. 4, 1861. }

The gunboat R. B. Forbes got off Cape Charles the night before last, with three feet of water in her hold, and proceeded to Washington this morning for repairs. She would have gone to pieces had not the weather been unusually mild.

The rebel slaves at Old Point now number eighteen hundred, including women and children.

A flag of truce has just come in from Norfolk, with the crews of the barks Rowena and Glen, schooner Mary Alice and brig Joseph, all captured by the privateer Dixie, with the exception of the Joseph, which was taken by the privateer Savannah. The captain and mates of the Glen were retained as prisoners at Richmond. The captain of the Mary Alice is almost direct from Charleston. He reports that the force there does not exceed four thousand men, and that they apprehended an attack from the recent naval expedition.

Congressman Ely is still at Richmond, and has to take his turn in cooking and carrying water for the prisoners.

Colonel Corcoran was lately put in irons several hours for refusing to answer to his name at the roll call.

Butter at Richmond is worth 50c., ham, 30c., and coffee 45c. per pound.

Captain Davis made a reconnoissance yesterday in the direction of Back river, and captured two of the Mounted Worth Guard.

BALTIMORE, Sept. 4, 1861.

A copy of the Richmond *Dispatch* of Tuesday, received by a flag of truce at Old Point, contains the following items of news:—

A despatch from Charleston, dated Sunday night, says a brig laden with coffee run the blockade on Sunday morning, also a vessel with fruit.

The ship Gondar, from Liverpool, arrived at Beaufort last week.

The ship Alliance, which arrived at Beaufort last week, is spoken of by the *Examiner* as laden with arms, ammunition, thread, quicksilver, &c.

The *Dispatch* says we may in a few days expect Beauregard and Johnston's report of the battle of Manassas.

The Petersburg *Express* of Monday gives an account of the taking of Fort Hatteras, and says a portion of the wounded escaped on a steamboat. It gives the number of killed and wounded at about eighty, and says that those who escaped from the fort contend that the magazine exploded, but the *Express* doubts this story, and adds:—

Our latest advices from North Carolina are up to eight o'clock last night. At that hour it was known in Goldsboro that a formidable Yankee fleet was in sight of Fort Mason, which commands the entrance to Beaufort harbor, and is spoken of as the most formidable fortification on the North Carolina coast. An attack was expected on Monday morning. The garrison is well prepared for the assault, and will resist with a determination and daring worthy of the glorious cause in which they are engaged."

The excitement throughout North Carolina and Eastern Virginia is intense.

It was rumored that Washington, N. C., had been destroyed by the Yankees.

No mention is made in the *Dispatch* of the illness of Jefferson Davis, but it contains a proclamation of the "President" calling Congress together again on the 3d inst., on account of its failure to deliver to the President for his signature the bill containing the military appointments.

OUR FORTRESS MONROE CORRESPONDENCE.

FORTRESS MONROE, Va., Sept. 2, 1861.

Affairs at the Fortress—Vigilance of Major General Wool—An Amusing Incident—Arrival of the R. B. Forbes in a Crippled Condition, &c., &c.

The even tenor of our way is still undisturbed. The business of every one in and about the fortress is attended to. Out of chaos and confusion all is now order and sunshine. General Wool personally inspects daily all the workings in his department, and with the happiest results. A very amusing incident occurred the other day, showing his vigilance and system of dealing with defaulters. He had heard that some of his men were in the habit of returning to their beds after reporting at reveille, which is beaten about the break of day. He decided to check it, and on the following morning presented himself at the bedside of one who was enjoying more than his share of sleep. The General nudged him, and was desired to let him alone. He repeated his efforts, and was told to go to the ——. The sleeper was then called upon to rise, and on hearing the voice of the old hero, was slightly "flabbergasted." The last word, though not often used in our language, nevertheless will convey an idea of the man's thoughts and situation. He, of course, apologised, and was told "improvement hereafter was absolutely necessary." I need scarcely say the General has endeared himself to all who have any love of order or pride, as soldiers.

The navy, or vessels attached to the same at this point, are all in excellent condition, with the exception of the R. B. Forbes, which came in last night about half-past eight in a most lamentable condition. On Saturday she ran ashore on Sand Shoal, about ten miles to the northward of Smith's Island. Our Harbor Master went to her relief with the Adriatic and Young America, and succeeded in getting her off, but in a damaged condition. On her arrival she had eight feet of water in her hold, and no [illegible] to keep her engine going. Her magazine was deluged and of course her ammunition spoiled. During the night her pumps were going continually—the only means to keep her afloat. Coal was sent to her from some of the vessels lying here. I could not ascertain the injury to her machinery. She is to remain here until the flag officer's return. It will be necessary to send her North for repairs, which, I think, will take considerable time and cost a large sum of money. This is the second time she has been ashore since she left Boston, only a week since. She is commanded by acting Master Gregory, of Boston; there were no regularly educated naval officers on board. The vessel was shamefully handled from the time she started, and all who have seen much coast service say that it could only have happened through gross neglect.

NEWS FROM THE REBEL STATES.

LOUISVILLE, Ky., Sept. 3, 1861.

A gentleman, just arrived in this city from Richmond, informs the *Journal* that he was captured at Mathias Point, while on his way to the North, and returned for trial to Richmond. He reports the number of troops in Virginia as greatly exaggerated in the North and Richmond, and that the actual numbers will not reach seventy thousand in the State, many of whom are down with sickness—in substance corroborating the statements of the Southern papers, that fully fifty per cent of the fighting force is in the hospital. He further says that on Saturday last Jeff. Davis was very ill, and little hopes were entertained of his recovery. The *Journal's* informant at the trial at Richmond proved himself an Englishman and was released.

A letter from Dublin, Groves county, Ky., says that two brothers named Bailey, with bowie knives, had killed Buck Smith and Bell Sherwood, in a quarrel, which arose from a political fuss. The Baileys are Union men.

LOUISVILLE, Ky., Sept. 4, 1861.

The Memphis *Appeal*, of the 3d, reports the receipt at that port of 130 bales of cotton and sales of 37.

A despatch from Columbus (Ky.) to the *Appeal*, says:—Three United States gunboats and one transport had arrived opposite Columbus with a large number of men, it is thought for the purpose to seize Columbus or attack General Pillow.

A meeting of native Kentuckians, at Memphis, on the 2d inst. resolved to pledge themselves to render their native State and her sons all the aid within their power whenever her freemen shall inaugurate a struggle for an assertion of her liberty against the tyranny of the federal power and despotism of abolitionists North.

A Richmond letter to the Memphis *Appeal* reports the arrival of two cavalry companies from Georgia, said to be the finest and most efficient troops, and with the finest horses ever seen.

The Charleston *Mercury* of Saturday announces the arrival at that port of the armed privateer Gordon from a six weeks' cruise. She had captured four prizes.

General A. Sidney Johnson had passed through Memphis on his way to Richmond.

THE THIRD IRISH REGIMENT GOING TO-DAY.

The Third Irish regiment are under orders to leave to-day, and the following has been issued by Colonel Enright:—

HEADQUARTERS THIRD IRISH REGIMENT, }
CAMP CARRIGAN, S. I., Sept. 4, 1861. }

GENERAL ORDERS NO. 4.

All officers and enlisted men of this command now on furlough, are hereby notified to report themselves to their headquarters on or before Thursday, the 5th inst., to alive [illegible] which this regiment is expected to leave for Washington, and absentees not reporting themselves [illegible] will be treated as deserters.

By order. RICHARD C. ENRIGHT, Colonel.

DEATH OF JEFFERSON DAVIS.

Strong Confirmatory Evidence of the Truth of the Report—The Rebel Flags at Half-mast and the Confederate Officers in Mourning—Biographical Sketch of the Rebel President, &c., &c., &c.

The continued rumors which are reaching us of the death of Jefferson Davis, would seem to indicate that there is some foundation for their truth. On Tuesday we published the following despatch from Washington:—

A despatch has been received here to-day from Richmond, via Louisville, announcing the death of Jeff. Davis. This accounts for the display of flags at half mast from the rebel ramparts to-day.

And yesterday the following:—

A negro, arrived here from Manassas to-night, reports that Jeff. Davis died at seven o'clock on Saturday morning. This report is believed by members of the family resident here. His physicians have long expected, from the condition of his health, that if at any time he should be subjected to protracted and extraordinary mental exertion, he would die suddenly. The report of his death is believed here.

The Washington *Star*, in an extra issued yesterday, says:—

At a late hour last night a branch of the government received a despatch from a reliable party in Louisville, notifying it that those in that city understood to be in the closest communication with Richmond, were satisfied of the correctness of the rumors of the death of Jefferson Davis that had reached Louisville from Nashville on the night before.

Our correspondent telegraphs, as will be seen elsewhere, that a gentleman from Manassas Junction, who arrived in Washington yesterday morning, states positively that Davis died on Monday (instead of Saturday) morning, at seven o'clock A. M., and that the rebel officers at the Junction were wearing crape on their arms.

Another gentleman, arrived in Washington yesterday from Richmond, reports the death of Davis as a certainty.

That such is really the case is borne out by many circumstance—among others the display of the rebel flag at half-mast on the intrenchments at Bailey's Cross Roads; an honor that would hardly be paid to the memory of so comparatively insignificant an officer as Colonel Stewart.

Another reason for concealment by the rebels of their chief's death is obvious, when it is considered what efforts are now being made by the secessionists of Kentucky to take that State out of the Union. The Legislature of Kentucky met on Monday last, and the rebels are resorting to every device of bribes and threats to compel that State to join her fate with that of the confederacy. The death of Davis, however, would dampen the ardor of the rebels there, and materially interfere with their cause. Hence the motive for concealment. It is significant, also, that we receive no reports of the affair through Louisville, which is the general source of news coming from the South.

We subjoin a brief sketch of the leading events in the life of the Confederate President:—

BIOGRAPHICAL SKETCH OF JEFFERSON DAVIS.

Jefferson Davis was born June 3, 1808, in what is now Todd county, Kentucky. While yet an infant, his father, Samuel Davis, a revolutionary soldier in Georgia, removed to Mississippi and settled in Wilkinson county. Jefferson Davis was sent, at the usual age, to Transylvania College, Kentucky, from which he was transferred in 1824 to the Military Academy at West Point, in 1828, which he left with the brevet appointment of Second Lieutenant. He was in the army about seven years, and distinguished himself in active service on the Western frontiers in the Black Hawk and other Indian wars. With the rank of First Lieutenant of dragoons, he resigned out of the army in 1835. He then returned to Mississippi and became a cotton planter in Warren county, where he lived in retirement until about 1844, when he first took an active part in politics as a democrat. We believe his first appearance as a public speaker was at a "barbecue" in Warren county, in answer to the celebrated S. S. Prentiss. From that moment he became the leader of the Mississippi democracy.

In 1844 Jefferson Davis was chosen one of the Presidential electors of Mississippi, in which capacity he voted for Polk and Dallas. In the succeeding year he was nominated by the democratic party of his State as a candidate for Congress, was elected, and took his seat in the body in December. His first opponent for Congress was Mark Valentine, then of Warren county, Miss., now of Carroll parish, La., who, though of the same party, thought Jefferson Davis not sound or pronounced enough on the repudiation question, and came out as an independent repudiation candidate against him. They came together in discussion at Vicksburg, where Davis succeeded in convincing his impulsive opponent either that there was no material difference between them on the repudiation hobby, or that, if there was such a difference, it did not make a material issue in the canvass for Congress. Mr. Valentine then withdrew, and left the field to Davis and the whig candidate, Mr. Tompkins, a lawyer of Vicksburg, a very popular man and a forcible and persuasive orator, who subsequently went to Congress. The election of Davis was the result.

While in Congress he was foremost among the members who assisted to organize the war against Mexico, and in July, 1846, when the First regiment of Mississippi Volunteers was enrolled for service in Mexico, he was elected its Colonel, when he left his seat in the House, and joining his regiment, led it to reinforce the army of General Taylor on the Rio Grande. His services in the army thenceforth are matter of history. It was just after the battle of Buena Vista that General Taylor, whose daughter Colonel Davis had married under circumstances displeasing to her father, consented to be reconciled to his long repudiated son-in-law. The present Mrs. Davis is his second wife, the former one having died some years ago.

On the return of his regiment, in July, 1847, Colonel Davis was tendered the appointment of Brigadier General of volunteers, which he declined, on the ground that the States, and not the federal government, had the right to appoint the officers of the militia. He was appointed by the Governor of Mississippi, in the same year, to fill a vacancy in the United States Senate, and was afterwards unanimously elected by the Mississippi Legislature for the remainder of the term, which expired March 4, 1851.

In September, 1851, Colonel Davis resigned his seat as Senator, on being nominated for Governor by the secession wing of the democratic party, in opposition to Henry S. Foote, the Union candidate, and was beaten by a majority of only 999 votes, although the Union party went into the field with a majority of 7,500 votes, as indicated by the Convention election a short time before.

Colonel Davis was in retirement, then, until 1855, when he rendered effective service on the stump for General Pierce, as democratic candidate for President. Appointed to the War Department by President Pierce, he continued in that position until the inauguration of Mr. Buchanan, in 1857. While in office he revised the army regulations; he introduced light infantry, or the rifle system of tactics; he caused the manufacture of rifled muskets and pistols, and the use of the Minie ball; he induced the addition of four regiments to the army, and organized a cavalry service peculiarly adapted to the wants of the country; he augmented the sea coast and frontier defences of the country; and had the western part of the continent explored for scientific, geographical and railroad purposes.

Colonel Davis was elected to the Senate by the Mississippi Legislature in 1856, before his retirement from the War Department. He again entered the Senate, therefore, in 1857, for the term ending the 4th of March, 1863. His State having seceded from the Union in January last, Colonel Davis, on being apprised of the fact, withdrew from that body and announced his withdrawal in a brief address.

On the 9th of February last he was elected Provisional President of the Southern confederacy, and in the event of his demise will be succeeded by Vice President Alexander H. Stephens.

REPORT FROM NASHVILLE.

LOUISVILLE, Sept. 4, 1861.

A Nashville despatch to-day says that there is no truth whatever in the reports of Jeff. Davis' death.

IMPORTANT FROM KENTUCKY.

CINCINNATI, Sept. 4, 1861.

The *Commercial* says that it is understood in Frankfort that Governor Magoffin refuses to play into the hands of the rabid secessionists; that he has had a quarrel with Mr. Breckinridge; that he refuses to demand the breaking up of the United States camp in Garrard county, and that he declares that he will submit to the will of the majority of the people of Kentucky, as may be expressed through the Legislature.

THE KENTUCKY LEGISLATURE.

FRANKFORT, Sept. 3, 1861.

There was nothing of importance transacted in the House to-day.

In the Senate, Judge Robinson, of Scott county, was elected President *pro tem.*

Six or seven Senators more than the constitution allows have been elected, and the permanent organization of the Senate is delayed on a question of contested seats.

FRANKFORT, Ky., Sept. 4, 1861.

Two Union members have been selected to fill the contested seats in the Senate. The temporary Speaker then resigned. The Senate will be regularly organized to-morrow.

CONTRADICTION.

LOUISVILLE, Sept. 4, 1861.

It is reported that the President has telegraphed the Union members who repudiated General Fremont's policy in regard to slaves.

NINTH REGIMENT, N. Y. S. M.

Recruits for this regiment are requested to report at headquarters, corner of Thirteenth street and University place, to-day, to receive uniforms and equipments.

THE NAVY.

ARRIVAL OF THE GUNBOAT WYANDOT FROM FORT PICKENS AND KEY WEST.

The United States gunboat Wyandot, Commander Baldwin, arrived yesterday morning from Fort Pickens August 28, via Key West 29th. Left at Fort Pickens United States ship Colorado, flag officer Marion. Left at Key West United States ships Santee, Capt. Eagle; Keystone State, Capt. Scott; Crusader, Capt. Corwin. All well.

Commander Baldwin reports the health of the troops at Fort Pickens good. The rebel troops had had a general stampede; large numbers of them had deserted and gone home.

The Wyandot brings a letter bag from Fort Pickens and a mail from the fleet at Key West.

Annexed is a list of the officers of the Wyandot:—

Commander—Augustus Baldwin.
Lieutenants—James Stillwell, Leroy Fitch.
Surgeon—R. Dean.
First Assistant Engineer—Wm. H. Cushman, acting Chief.
Assistant Engineers—W. K. Purse, E. J. Brooks and W. B. Clark.
Master's Mates—W. G. Wright, J. Paine.

The Wyandot has been cruising for the past two years. She was put in commission in September, 1859, shortly after which she left this port for the south coast of Cuba, where, after continuously cruising seven months, she captured the slave bark William, with five hundred and forty-six slaves on board. She continued cruising for slavers until November, 1860. In December she went up the coast of Florida in search of the then missing mail steamer Isabel, whose engines had been disabled, causing her return to Charleston. About the middle of December she proceeded to Pensacola Navy Yard, went into dry dock, had some slight repairs done, her bottom cleaned, and just got off in time to prevent the secessionists from capturing her with the Navy Yard, January 12, 1861. On the 10th of February she transported Lieutenant Slemmer and his command from Fort Barrancas to Fort Pickens. For nearly a month the Wyandot alone, by her constant activity day and night, along the inner shore of Santa Rosa Island, kept the rebels from crossing over, landing and attacking Pickens. During the day a portion of the crew assisted Lieutenant Slemmer's small command in mounting the heavy guns. At night the marines of the ship went ashore and did picket duty outside the fort to prevent surprise. Thus the Wyandot was by her presence and activity actually the protector of Fort Pickens, notwithstanding there was not a lieutenant aboard the ship, three having resigned, leaving Captain Berryman (peace to his ashes) and four engineers aboard, who performed all the various duties of the ship. After the Brooklyn and the rest of the fleet arrived outside the harbor, the Wyandot kept open the communication between them and the fort until the night of April 12, when she landed the reinforcements of marines and sailors of the squadron. She afterwards was actively engaged landing reinforcements, and for the last two months and a half she has been blockading the pass of the eastern end of Santa Rosa Island. On the 17th August she narrowly escaped shipwreck by being blown ashore during a hurricane, which caused her to drag both anchors, notwithstanding she was using all the steam power her worn out boiler and dilapidated condition would allow to assist in keeping the vessel off the lee shore. Had the gale continued fifteen minutes longer the faithful old Wyandot and all on board must have perished.

In consequence of her unseaworthy condition, the flag officer immediately ordered her to this port.

During the trying times off Pensacola the men suffered considerably from scurvy, living nearly five months without fresh provisions; and although three lieutenants and the assistant surgeon had resigned on account of their secession proclivities, the crew were to a man loyal.

The Wyandot has proceeded to the Navy Yard, Brooklyn.

THE BROOKLYN NAVY YARD.

There are quite a number of steamers and sailing vessels at present at the yard to be converted into cruisers. The workmen have already commenced on the barks Gem of the Sea and Brazileira. They will mount four thirty-two pounders of forty-two cwt.

Lieutenant Reed Worden has been ordered to command the steam gunboat Stars and Stripes; Lieutenant Hapobar Collins, the Unadilla; Lieutenant Parrot, the Augusta; Acting Master W. J. Hotchkiss, the General Putnam; Acting Master Gregory, the E. B. Hale, and Lieutenant Chaplin, the Valley City. The E. B. Hale will go into commission to-day and proceed to her station off the James river immediately. The old frigate Brandywine has been hauled into the dry dock, where she will be caulked and coppered. She is to be used as a hospital and receiving ship at Old Point Comfort. The steamer James Adger will soon be ready for sea. She will have eight thirty-two pounders, broadside guns, and a pivot. Commander Walke, we understand, has been ordered to her.

Last week the frame for a sidewheel steamer, two hundred feet long, and to draw only six feet of water, was set up. When completed she will mount a heavy battery. The steam sloop on the stocks will be ready for launching in a few weeks. There are 1,000 recruits at present on board the receiving ship North Carolina. The steamer Augusta came over to the yard yesterday afternoon to receive her guns.

OFFICERS OF THE STEAMER PAWNEE.

WASHINGTON, D. C., Sept. 3, 1861.

In your paper of yesterday I saw an incorrect list of the officers of the steamer Pawnee. Allow me, sir, to send you a correct one, viz.:—

Commander—S. C. Rowan.
Lieutenants—J. C. Maxwell, E. P. McCrea, T. H. Eastman, H. M. Blue.
Midshipmen—A. T. Snell, C. R. Daniels.
Surgeon—F. M. Gunnell.
Paymaster—C. Abbott.
Chief Engineer—W. H. Rutherford; Third Assistant Engineers—D. Hardee, J. Trilley, N. Champion, A. Adamson, H. Sellman.
Paymaster's Clerk—Wm. Robinson.
Captain's Clerk—C. Courtright.

OPERATIONS ON THE POTOMAC RIVER.

Under date of August 31 we learn that the United States steamer Resolute, under command of Amos P. Foster, formerly acting Master's Mate on the steamer Penguin, landed a crew and destroyed four boats capable of conveying three hundred men each, also the surrounding dwellings, at a place on the river called Ferry Landing. These boats were no doubt in readiness to transport troops across the river. The flames were seen at a distance of twenty miles. The Resolute, under command of Captain Budd, has been a terror to all rebels, and will continue to be, under command of Mr. Foster.

MISCELLANEOUS.

The BAINBRIDGE (brig) and FALMOUTH (storeship) were at Falmouth, August 26. All well. The Falmouth is stationed at Aspinwall as a storeship.

FOREIGN VESSELS HOMEWARD BOUND.—The corvette Saratoga, African station, and the Mystic and Sumter, Porto Grande, are on their way back under orders. The United States steamer Saginaw arrived at Swatow, June 17, with orders for the John Adams to proceed to Hong Kong on her way home.

Prudence Island, in Narragansett Bay, opposite East Greenwich, is about to be surveyed to ascertain its suitability for the new navy yard.

The Atlantic House, at Newport, has been hired by the government for the location of a branch of the Naval Academy there during the winter.

The gunboat Albatross is undergoing repairs at the Philadelphia Navy Yard.

The steamers Underwriter and Jacob Bell are at the Washington Navy Yard for repairs.

IS ALL SAFE AT HATTERAS INLET?

TO THE EDITOR OF THE HERALD.

Pamlico Sound is eighty miles long and from twenty to twenty-five wide, provided with steamboats and vessels intended for the privateering service in large numbers. From the western coast of the sound, and from Virginia on the north, an army might almost instantly be raised of several thousand for an attack upon the handful of men left in the captured forts by Messrs. Butler and Stringham. It is manifest, from the reports your enterprising journal has laid before the public, that there are on the inside, in the sound, plenty of vessels to transport these hostile troops from the mainland north, west and south of it, to the captured forts. If they have the spirit at the South which animated the people of Vermont when Plattsburg was invested by the British, before this time Pamlico Sound is swarming with volunteers going to the rescue, as was Lake Champlain with the Vermonters on the occasion alluded to. If they go, they carry with them the spirit of the bear robbed of her whelps in the field, and will not be sparing of their vengeance upon the handful of men left with only five days' provisions, and, for aught that appears, almost entirely destitute of ammunition. The cannon taken are many of them spiked. The ammunition shipped there by the federal force is not likely to be suitable for the thirty-two pounders which compose the armament. The Harriet Lane is there in a disabled state, without guns to fight with or coals to get away with: our men are left there in imminent danger of starvation, upon a narrow strip of sand hills, in forts that furnish them little or no protection from the overwhelming force that can easily be placed both north and south of them. I cannot myself see with what [illegible] and naval commanders can [illegible] stowed upon them for [illegible] important a position [illegible] who remain behind [illegible] a strip of land in [illegible] selves, to keep what [illegible] powerful and efficient as [illegible] they appear to have been [illegible] voluminously and promptly [illegible] of painful suspense in [illegible] I hope they may be able to show [illegible] perfectly safe. It would be mortifying [illegible] Russell to express, if we [illegible] advantage we have thus gained for want of [illegible] the troops and an abundant supply of [illegible] munitions of war.

INQUIRER.

IMPORTANT FROM MISSOURI.

A Brilliant Engagement in the Western Part of the State.

FIGHT AT LEXINGTON.

Four Hundred and Thirty Unionists Repulse Over Four Thousand Rebels.

SIXTY KILLED.

SEVERAL HOUSES DESTROYED,

&c., &c., &c.

[From the St. Louis Bulletin, Sept. 3.]

We learn from Mr. Wasson, a gentleman who left Richmond and arrived by the North Missouri Railroad Friday night, that a fight took place at Lexington, Lafayette county, on Thursday last, in the day time, between 4,500 rebels and 430 Home Guards and United States troops, in the intrenchments around Lexington. The attack was made by the rebels, who were repulsed with a loss of sixty killed in the battle, and three of their pickets. None of the Union force was killed.

During the engagement Arcana Hall, occupied by the Masons, and a private residence opposite to the Court House, owned by R. Aull, Esq., of this city, and occupied by T. Crittenden, Esq., temporarily absent in Kentucky, were shelled and burned. The impression was that the former contained powder designed for the use of the Confederates. Another attack was threatened and apprehended.

We learn further that ex-Governor King, of Ray county, who had been taken prisoner, had made his escape from the rebels, but that Judge Ryland and his son John were still prisoners.

Two regiments of infantry and a squadron of cavalry left Jefferson City yesterday morning, by land, for the relief of Lexington.

LATER FROM LEXINGTON.

A gentleman who arrived in the Pacific cars last evening from Warrensburg, Johnson county, gives some additional information in regard to affairs at Lexington. He had news direct from that city to Friday. At that time the troops in the intrenchments still held out against the rebels. He says that on Wednesday the rebel forces made a demand for the surrender of the troops in the intrenchments. This was indignantly refused.

On Thursday the Confederates attacked the Union troops, and were repulsed—the loss of the former being fifty or sixty killed. The Union men had none killed, but some were wounded inside of the intrenchments. Five or six Union men belonging to the Union troops, serving as scouts, had been killed in the neighborhood by the Confederates. The assailing party had no artillery. Their number was estimated at 2,500, but they claimed 4,000.

The commanding officer felt quite confident of being able to sustain himself against any further attacks until reinforcements could arrive. They were certain to be there on Saturday night, and consisted of a regiment of Illinois troops, under command of Colonel Marshall, part of the Johnson County Home Guards, and part of a regiment of Home Guards under command of Col. McClurg—numbering in all about twelve hundred men. This force would enable them to drive the Confederates from that section of the State, when aided, as they soon would be, by two or three regiments on the march from Jefferson City.

When near Georgetown the Illinois regiment was fired at by a person from a window, with a double barrelled shot gun, and one man killed and another wounded. The person firing was captured, and proved to be Colonel Magoffin, the leader of the secessionists in Pettis county. He is now a prisoner.

Captain Staples, who has been greatly instrumental in bringing on these troubles, was laying waste the country, seizing the wheat of Union men, and having it ground into flour for the use of the rebel forces. Their day will soon be over.

JEFFERSON CITY, Sept. 3, 1861.

The latest information from Lexington confirms the safety of that place and the withdrawal of the rebels. There is much disaffection in McCulloch's army. He is in Arkansas. This is reliable.

An expedition crossed into Calloway county last night, destined for Columbia.

CAPE GIRARDEAU, Sept. 3, 1861.

General Prentiss' little army, which left Ironton some days since, arrived at Jackson, some ten miles west of here, yesterday morning. General Prentiss and staff are now here. No enemy was met during the march. The report that General Prentiss took one hundred and eighty prisoners is, therefore, false.

A scout arrived from Hardee's camp last night and reported that the rebels knew the exact time General Prentiss left Ironton, and immediately commenced retreating. Hardee was rapidly moving towards Arkansas with six thousand men. The enemy is reported to be strongly fortified at Sykestown.

ROLLA, Mo., Sept. 3, 1861.

The correspondent of the St. Louis *Democrat* has furnished the following:—

A gentleman from Springfield on Friday evening reports that McCulloch, with five thousand Texas, Louisiana and Arkansas troops, was moving towards Arkansas. He was last heard from at the Chalybeate Springs, near Mount Vernon.

His wounded were also being moved from the Springfield hospital and taken southward. On Thursday, the 29th ult., Generals Price, Parsons, Slack and Churchill moved towards Bolivar, with a force of some 12,000 men. When last heard from they were marching towards Jefferson City, on the road between Bolivar and Warsaw.

Only a portion of General McBride's division remained in Springfield.

Thirty eight of the Dent County Home Guard were surprised Sunday morning early at Bennet's Mills by 350 rebels, and two of them killed and eight wounded, one mortally. The killed and wounded of the rebels filled a large wagon, but their number could not be ascertained. The Home Guard retreated. Eighteen rebel prisoners who were taken by the Guard the day before were confined in a house near by, and the rebels, mistaking them for Union men, fired on them, wounding several.

HANNIBAL, Sept. 4, 1861.

Corporal Dix, of the Third Iowa regiment, while out on a scout with five men near Kirksville, last week, was surrounded in a farm house while at dinner by twenty-five rebels, who demanded the surrender of his party. This was refused, and the rebels made an attack on them.

The fight was severe, but the Union troops maintained their position in the house, driving the assailants from the ground with a loss of seven killed and five wounded.

Corporal Dix, on the Union side, was killed, but none of the others were hurt.

CAIRO, Sept. 3, 1861.

Lieutenant Taft, who was sent with a flag of truce to General Pillow's camp at New Madrid, returned this night. Colonel Wallace's terms were [illegible] P., and an exchange of prisoners will take [illegible] row. 15,000 rebels are reported to be at New Madrid.

CAIRO, Ill., Sept. 4, 1861.

The gunboats Taylor and Lexington had an engagement off Hickman, Kentucky, with the rebel gunboat Yankee, this afternoon. Two batteries on the shore, supported by about fifteen hundred rebels, also fired upon our boats. None of the shots took effect. The Taylor and Lexington fired about twenty shots, with what effect is not yet known. They returned to Cairo this evening, and on the way were fired on with small arms at Columbus and Chalk Bluffs, Kentucky.

Colonel Hicks, of the Fortieth Illinois regiment, who was sent to exchange prisoners, returned last night from Charleston. The rebels had but three federal prisoners.

It is reported that the rebels are falling back from Sykestown to New Madrid. General Grant took command of this post to-day.

NINTH REGIMENT (HAWKINS' ZOUAVES).

Lieutenant Colonel Betts yesterday sent forward fifty more recruits, besides the band. This raises the regiment to the full complement of 1,046 men. The recruiting being finished, Lieutenant Colonel Betts starts this morning for Newport News, to take command of the portion of the regiment stationed there. The remainder of the regiment, under Colonel Hawkins, is at Fort Hatteras, having participated in the brilliant attack which led to the capture of that place.

FIRST REGIMENT WASHINGTON ZOUAVES.

This regiment is quartered at Camp Vanderbilt, Staten Island, and numbers 300 strong. They are under excellent discipline, and are [illegible] by companies, and expect to leave for the war on the 20th. Two companies will be accepted by making application at the tent in the Park, or at headquarters, 70 Varick street, to Colonel J. H. Romaine.

THE NEW YORK HERALD.

WHOLE NO. 9133. NEW YORK, THURSDAY, SEPTEMBER 12, 1861. PRICE TWO CENTS.

THE NATIONAL BATTLE GROUND.

The Armies of the Potomac---Encampments of Over Three Hundred Thousand Armed Men---Scene of the Coming Decisive Conflict.

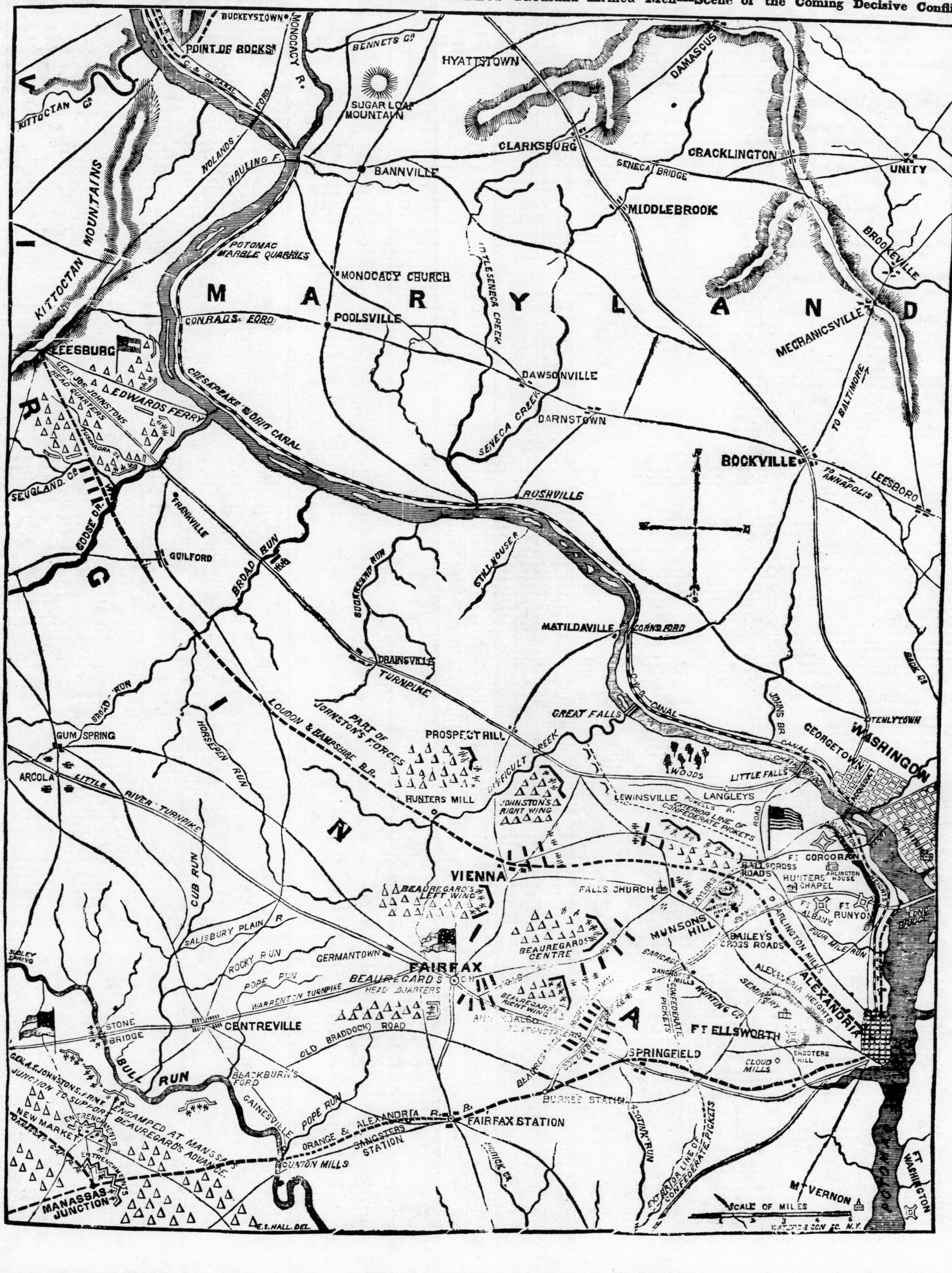

The New-York Times.

VOL. XI.....NO. 3154. NEW-YORK, THURSDAY, OCTOBER 31, 1861. PRICE TWO CENTS.

THE GREAT REBELLION.

Departure of the Naval Expedition from Fortress Monroe.

Affairs Unchanged Along the Lines of the Potomac.

The Rebel Batteries Down the River Shelling the Maryland Shore.

PROGRESS OF THE WAR IN THE WEST.

FIGHTING IN NEW-MEXICO.

Four Hundred Rebels Dispersed in Missouri.

IMPORTANT FROM HAVANA.

The Rebel Commissioners Slidell and Mason Received with Distinction.

The Steamer Theodora Gone to Charleston Again.

SPECIAL DISPATCH FROM WASHINGTON.

WASHINGTON, Wednesday, Oct. 30.

NOT GOING INTO WINTER QUARTERS.

I think I have sufficient authority for explicitly denying the statement that the army of the Potomac would go into Winter quarters within the lines of the present encampment or intrenchments. No such purpose is entertained by the Government, and no such suggestion has been made by Gen. McClellan. Indeed, within the past fornight the activity of preparation has been greater than within the same time for the last two months. Of course, an army is to remain in and around Washing to defend the Capitol, and doubtless we shall have a large camp of instruction. For the men and horses constituting this force, Winter barracks will be provided, and timely preparations are making for this; but beyond this there is nothing being done that looks like inaction during the Winter months.

NO NEW MOVEMENTS.

Since the rebels have ran away from Gen. McCall's division, there is nothing of interest to report. the movements and position of our own forces being contraband. Our scouts range the country round for ten to fifteen miles, but find nothing except the desolated tracks of the rebel hordes.

There is a report in circulation here that the rebels were firing on Banks' camp to-day, but there is no truth in it. All is quiet in his camp.

AFFAIRS ON THE LOWER POTOMAC.

The rebel batteries on the Potomac have been ineffectually playing upon our forces engaged in erecting counter batteries on the Maryland shore. The rebel steamer *Page* appears to be aground in Quantico Creek. She cannot escape without risking a few shots from our guns.

Two prisoners arrived at the Navy-Yard to-day, having been captured by our river force on suspicion of being spies. One was taken at Port Tobacco.

THE CONFLICT OF JURISDICTION.

Deputy-Marshal Phillips represented to the Circuit Court, to-day, that he did not serve the rule issued by that body on the 22d inst., to be served on Gen. Porter, Provost-Marshal for the District of Columbia, because he was ordered by the President of the United States not to serve the same, and to report to the Court that the privilege of the writ of *habeas corpus* has been suspended for the present, by order of the President, in regard to the soldiers of the army of the United States within this District. The Deputy-Marshal respectfully disclaims all intention to disobey or treat with disrespect the orders of the Court.

Chief-Justice Dunlop delivered an opinion to the Court, as follows:

Rule to show cause against Gen. Andrew Porter, Provost Marshal of the District of Columbia, why an attachment of contempt of court, issued against him for obstructing the process of this Court, and the administration of justice under it.

The return made by Deputy-Marshal Phillips, the 26th of October, we will order to be filed, though we do not doubt our power to regard it as insufficient in law, and to proceed against the officer who has made it. The existing condition of the country makes it plain that that officer is powerless against the vast military force of the Executive, subject to his will and order, as Commander-in-Chief of the army and navy of the United States.

Assuming the verity of the return, which has been made on oath, the case presented is without parallel in the judicial history of the United States, and involves the free action and efficiency of the Judges of this country. The President, charged by the Constitution to take care that the laws be executed, has seen fit to arrest the process of this Court, and to forbid the Deputy Marshal to execute it. It does not involve merely the question of the power of the Executive in civil war to suspend the great writ of freedom, the *habeas corpus*.

When this rule was ordered to give efficiency to that writ, no notice had been given by the President to the Courts or the country of such suspension here now first announced to us, and it will hardly be maintained that the suspension could be retrospective. The rule in the case, therefore, whatever may be the President's power over the writ of *habeas corpus*, was lawfully ordered, as well as the writ on which it was founded. The facts on which the rule was ordered by the Court are assumed to be true, as respects the President, because the President had them before him, and has not denied them, but forbade the Deputy Marshal to serve the rule on Gen. Andrew Porter. The President, we think, assumes the responsibilities of the acts of Gen. Porter, set forth in the rule, and sanctions them by his order to Deputy Marshal Phillips, not to serve the process on the Provost Marshal.

The issue ought to be and it is with the President, and we have no physical power to enforce the lawful process of this Court on his military subordinate. Against the President's prohibition we have exhausted every practicable remedy to uphold the lawful authority of this Court. It is, therefore, ordered this 30th day of October, that this opinion of the Court be filed by the Clerk and made part of the record, as explaining the grounds on which we now decide not to order any further proceedings in this case.

Associate Judge Marshall said: As a member of this Court and on its behalf I wish it understood that notwithstanding the blow leveled at this Court, I do distinctly assert the following principles:

First—That the law in this country knows no superior.

Second—That the supremacy of the civil authority over the military cannot be denied; that it has been established by the ablest jurists, and I believe recognized and respected by the great Father of the country during the Revolutionary war.

Third—That the Court ought to be respected by every one as the guardian of the personal liberty of the citizen in giving ready and effectual aid by that most valuable means, the writ of *habeas corpus*.

Fourth—I therefore respectfully protest against the right claimed to interrupt the proceedings in this case.

So the Judges of the Circuit Court here have decided that their edicts ought to be obeyed, and that if they had the power they would enforce them, but, "as the Court knows herself" that it cannot be done, the Judges content themselves with entering a protest against the military authorities, and Gen. Andrew Porter in partioular, and directs that all further proceedings in the case be stopped. The Court is discreet, certainly, and it is probahle that the sentinels will now be withdrawn from pacing up and down before the doors of the Judges.

THE GREAT EXPEDITION.

It is certain that no one outside of the naval expedition knows where the first blow will be struck. It is probable, however, that the earliest news concerning its operations will come through Southern channels.

THE STORY ABOUT CAPT. DUPONT'S CLERK.

The *Tribune's* story of the running away of Capt. Dupont's clerk grew out of what the boys call "a sell." Some wag innocently remarked that "the clerk had gone to parts unknown," with all the papers, orders, etc. Without stopping to think that he himself was ignorant of the destination of the fleet, the vigilant "special" at once informed the *Tribune* that the clerk had gone to secesh.

AFFAIRS IN ALEXANDRIA.

Gen. Montgomery, Military Governor of Alexandria, has issued an order forbidding the sale of liquor to soldiers in his District.

Provost-Marshal Griffith has been authorized by the Provost Court to seize a number of secession songs and pamplets, offered for sale by a bookseller of Alexander. Judge Freese says he will not permit the sale of any such documents, neither will he allow the utterance of secession sentiments in any shape.

I send you by mail a copy of the decision of Provost Judge Freese, of Alexandria, in the case of Bowen, Holmes & Co., of New-York, and Hallowell & Co., of Philadelphia, against Witmer & Co., of Alexandria. It is on this decision that an appeal is to be made to the President, and the opinion of Judge Freese is intended as a precedent to cover all civil cases of a similar nature. If the decision is sustained, it will equal in importance the *coup d'etat* of Gen. Butler as to the contrabands.

VALUE OF PROPERTY IN WASHINGTON.

I have before alluded to the enhanced rates of rents in Washington since the Army of Occupation came here. The effect has also been to raise the value of real estate. A gentleman showed me a piece of property to-day that last June would not have sold for twenty thousand dollars, that is now rated at fifty thousadd. Indeed, the owner will not not part with it at that price.

THE MILITARY EXAMINING BOARDS.

There are, at this time, in Heintzelman's and Franklin's divisions, two examining boards in full blast, and judging from the character and military reputation of their members, those gentlemen who have entered the service for pastime will discover, when too late, that they have mistaken their calling, or find their "occupation gone." The very names of the officers composing these Boards strike terror to aspiring military novices. In Heintzelman's Division they are Col. Pratt, Thirty-first New-York Volunteer Regiment; Col. Simpson, Second New-Jersey Regiment, U. S. A.; Col. Hawman, Thirty-seventh New-York Regiment, U. S. A. In Franklin's Division, Col. Ward, Thirty-eighth New-York Regiment; Col. Herbert, New-Jersey First Regiment; Col. Poe, Second Michigan Regiment, U. S. A. We sympathise with the victims who may come within their clutches.

A RARE PROMOTION.

Chas. A. Austin, of Massachusetts, has been promoted from an ordinary seaman to be master's mate. This is a most rare, if not the first occurrence of the kind, and will assure Jack that good conduct is sometimes rewarded with promotion.

A DEFAULTING OFFICER.

A Lieutenant-Colonel of a Massachusetts regiment has resigned his commission, and the resignatinn is accepted, when, unfortunately, he has borrowed several hundred dollars from the regimental fund.

UNIFORMS FOR THE ARMY CHAPLAINS.

The army Chaplains held a meeting this morning, at Trinity Church, in this city. The principal object appeared to be the concentration of their efforts so as to procure the passage of a law more clearly defining their position and rank, their relations to other officers, and the uniform they should wear. The law now prescribes that they shall have the pay of Captains of Cavalry, but does not designate their uniform. It was finally determined to present this matter to the President and the proper military authorities, through a Committee, and to agree upon what action it is necessary Congress shall take in order to remedy the evils complained of.

THE NUMBER OF THE SICK.

The weekly reports from the hospitals, show the following as the number of inmate for the week ending Oct. 25: On E-street, 80; Seminary, 120; Union, 163; Columbian, 231; Circle, 42; Alexandria, 134. Total, 820. This is a decrease since last week.

COL. EINSTEIN.

Col. Einstein has been mustered out of the service, and, indeed, mustered from Washington to Philadelphia.

NOTABILITIES.

Among the notabilities at Willard's to-day, I notice Gen. Butler, Wm. B. Thomas, Collector of Philadelphia, Hon. O. B. Matteson and Count Corwin.

SECRETARY SEWARD IN THE CAMPS.

Secretary Seward, and Assistant Secretary Seward, to-day visited the camps on the Virginia side.

SENATOR WILSON'S NEW POSITION.

Senator Wilson to-day entered the service, as a member of Gen. McClellan's Staff.

LEUTZE'S PICTURE IN THE ROTUNDA.

Leutze, the artist, has commenced painting the large picture for the vacant panel of the great rotunda. The subject is allegorical, typifying the advance of population Westward. The design was described last Spring, when it was first exhibited here. The sketch is very graphic and spirited.

SOLDIERS TO BE SHOT.

It is understood that Gen. McClellan has issued an order for the shooting of four soldiers found guilty of sleeping at their picket posts.

MISCELLANEOUS NEWS.

Some members of the Thirty-third New-York Regiment, owing to gross misconduct, to-day got into difficulty with citizens in the neighborhood of Lewinsville. Two of the former were severely injured. Gen. Hancock sent out a detachment and promptly placed the soldiers under arrest.

Col. Henry L. Scott, one of the Inspectors-General and son-in-law of Lieut.-Gen. Scott, has been retired by the Army Board, owing to his physical disability.

The Navy Department will take no notice of applications for places of masters or master's mates where the ages of the applicants are not stated, and references to the last employers given.

Capt. Henry B. Davidson, of the Tennessee First Cavalry, having left his regiment July 1st, on thirty days' leave, and having failed to report for duty, hes been dropped from the rolls.

IMPORTANT FROM HAVANA.

Arrival There of the Rebel Commissioners to Europe.

THEIR ENTHUSIASTIC RECEPTION.

Return of the Theodora to Charleston.

The steamship *Columbia*, Capt. Adams, from Havana at 5 P. M. on the 25th inst., arrived here yesterday morning.

The *Columbia* encountered strong northerly gales, with a heavy head sea, during most of her passage.

The *Columbia* brings intelligence that the Confederate steamer *Theodore*, formerly the *Gordon*, a vessel of 518 tons burden, Capt. Lockwood, left Havana on Wednesday afternoon, the 23d inst., for Charleston, having been in port a week. She sailed from Charleston for Cardenas, where she landed Messrs. Slidel and Mason, Confederate States Commissioners for Europe, and afterwards proceeded to Havana—Messrs. Slidel and Mason taking the land route to Havana. The Commissioners were received with the highest consideration, from the Captain-General down.

The *Theodora* is supposed to have taken with her a large quantity of arms and provisions, such as coffee, &c. She was presented while there with a silk flag by Southern ladies. She took out with her about twenty passengers, including Mr. Meade, late United States Minister to Brazil.

Consul-Gen. Shufeldt telegraphed to the Commander of the steam-frigate *San Jacinto*, at Trinidad, on the 24th, to proceed at once to Havana.

The British Consul called on the Confederate Commissioners, in full uniform, and presented them to the Captain-General.

From the *Diario de la Marina* we learn that the *Theodora* arrived at Cardenas on the morning of the 17th October, with a view to ascertain if the two Envoys were in time to take the Spanish mail steamer to Cadiz. The steamer in question had, however, left on the 16th.

The *Theodora* cleared at Havana for Nassau, N P., the British Consul giving the necessary papers.

The blockade seems to interfere very slightly with intercourse between Havana and the rebel ports. The British schooner *R. Burrows* reached Havana from Mobile on the 16th inst., with full files of Southern paper. The *Burrows* had of course run the blockade. A few days later the British brig *Maj. Barbour* performed the same feat at New-Orleans, reaching Havana in safety, bringing details of the Hollins victory.

The capture of the steamer *Salvor* by the *Keystone State* had caused much sensation at Havana.

Capt. Coxetter, late of the privateer *Jeff. Davis*, is in Havana. He came in the *Theodora*, and was left there for no good.

Things look quite warlike in Havana, a large vessel was in the harbor fitting out for Mexico.

From the Diario de la Marina, Oct. 18.

Yesterday, in the afternoon, the Confederate steamer *Teodora*, or *Theodore*, arrived at the port of Cardenas, having on board two distinguished persons from the South, sent by President Davis in the character of Ministers Plenipotentiary to the Governments of England and France.

The steamer in question sailed from the port of Charleston; but we are not aware why she has put into Cardenas. Certainly the mere fact that she brings two Ministers Plenipotentiary, *en route* to Europe, appears to indicate that some event has occurred of great importance in favor of the South. This is only conjecture on our part, but we do not believe it to be without foundation, and we would add that, in our opinion, these plenipotentiaries go to ask the recognition of the Confederation of the Southern States from the principal Powers of Europe. We expect shortly further advices in regard to this matter.

After the foregoing was written, we received the following dispatch from our Cardenas correspondent:

CARDENAS, Thursday, Oct. 17, 1861.

The steamer *Theodora*, from Charleston, brings the Envoys of the Confederate States near the Governments of England and France. The Envoys are Mr. Slidell, of New-Orleans, and Mr. Mason, of Virginia. They have touched at this port to learn if they can overtake the mail steamer for Cadiz.

From the Diario de la Marina, Oct. 19.

This morning, at 7 o'clock, the Confederate steamer *Theodora*, which arrived day before yesterday at Cardenas, entered our port. Mr. Slidell and Mr. Mason, the Commissioners from the South, have not arrived in her, but we understand will come by rail to this capital the day after to-morrow.

THE GREAT NAVAL EXPEDITION.

Its Departure on Tuesday Morning at Daylight.

THE FLEET SPOKEN OFF CAPE HENRY.

FORTRESS MONROE, Tuesday, Oct. 29, Via BALTIMORE, Wednesday, Oct. 30.

The great fleet sailed this morning—the *Wabash* taking the lead at daylight, when the gun was fired as a signal, and the *Cahawba* bringing up the rear. The vessels, about fifty in number, formed in line a few miles down the Roads, and went out between the Capes in splendid style. The *Baltic* had the *Ocean Express* in tow, the *Vanderbilt* the *Great Republic*, and the *Illinois* the *Golden Eagle*. The morning was the most beautiful of the season, and the scene the finest ever witnessed on this continent.

There is no news from Old Point.

REPORT BY THE TRANSPORT THOMAS SWANN.

The United States steam transport *Thomas Swann*, Capt. Hamilton, from Baltimore forty-eight hours, and Fortress Monroe twenty-four hours, arrived yesterday morning. The sailing vessels of the United States fleet were under way Monday, at 5 P. M., and the steamers were getting under way when the *Thomas Swann* left.

On Monday, the 28th, at midnight, off Hog Island, she passed four steamers bound south.

PROGRESS OF THE FLEET.

Capt. Hamilton, of the United States steam transport *Thomas Swann*, reports on the 29th inst., off Cape Henry, passed twenty vessels belonging to the Naval Expedition, all under convoys. Spoke them, and they all reported that they were bound South.

THAT STARTLING REPORT.

The following card appears in the Philadelphia *North American*:

TO THE PUBLIC.

My brother-in-law, Alexander McKinley, a native and citizen of Philadelphia, and a member of its bar, is the private and confidential secretary of Flag-Officer Dupont. To this post of honor and confidence he was invited by Capt. Dupont, and he is now discharging his responsible duty on board the flag-ship *Wabash*. Private letters have been received from him to-day dated Oct. 27. The New-York *Tribune* of to-day, under its editorial head, has circulated a report which has been copied into the *Evening Bulletin* of this city, under the caption of "Startling Report," that "the private secretary of Commodore Dupont had absconded, carrying with him the maps and charts, and even the sealed orders of the Commodore." The natural effect of this rumor is that Mr. McKinley's name has been most unkindly referred to. I pronounce the whole story to be a vile calumny, and have, by the advice of counsel, taken measures to trace it to its source, meaning to hold strictly responsible all who contribute to the defamation of an innocent and absent man.

J. W. FAIRES.
No. 245 South Thirteenth-street.

PHILADELPHIA, Oct. 29, 1861.

IMPORTANT FROM MISSOURI.

FOUR HUNDRED REBELS DISPERSED.

JEFFERSON CITY, Tuesday, Oct. 29.

A special dispatch to the St. Louis *Republican* says:

Gen. Prentiss, who left St. Louis on Monday last with a force of infantry to surprise and capture the rebels at Fulton, in Calloway County, has returned, and reports that before he reached Fulton, Gen. John R. Henderson, of the State Militia, had made a compromise with the rebels at Dyer's mills, near Concord, by which he agreed that the United States would not make any arrests if the rebels would lay down their arms and return to their homes.

Gen. Prentiss acquiesced in the compromise, but on the first violation of it will visit severe vengeance upon the offenders.

The rebels were 400 strong, and Gen. Henderson's force numbered 1,500. The proposition for compromise came from the rebels.

THE CONGRESSIONAL INVESTIGATING COMMITTEE.

ST. LOUIS, Wednesday, Oct. 30.

The Congressional Committee closed their labors last night. It is understood that they made a searching investigation into the alleged frauds and irregularities of the Government officers of this Military Department. The result of their examination will be made public in a few days.

IMPORTANT FROM MEXICO.

DEFEAT AND ROUT OF PARTIES OF REBELS.

KANSAS CITY, Tuesday, Oct. 19.

The Santa Fé mail furnishes the following interesting items:

"About the 4th inst. a party of New-Mexico volunteers, under Capt. Mink, was surprised at Alimosa, thirty-five miles bely Fort Craig, by 110 Texan rebels, and their horse stampeded. Capt. Mink proposed to surrender his company, but his men dissented, secured their horses and retreated to Fort Craig. Subsequently about one hundred United States troops, from Fort Craig, pursued the rebels, overtook them, killed their Captain and ten men, wounded about thirty, and killed thirty horses. The balance of the Texans escaped to Messella.

Another band of rebels who had been encamped on the Arkansas River were being pursued by a company of Confederate States dragoons, from Fort Wise, and a company of New-Mexicans.

THE TRIAL OF PIRATES AT PHILADELPHIA.

PHILADELPHIA, Wednesday, Oct. 30.

Eben Lane, the last of the *Jeff. Davis* pirates was acquitted on the ground that, being the navigator of the *Enchantress* after her capture, he must have delayed her progress, preventing her arrival at a rebel port; because, in sixteen days the vessel only made 250 miles. Lane alleges that he sailed the vessel North during the night and South during the day.

Thomas Quigley, David Mullens and Edward Rockford, were convicted of piracy last evening.

The schooner *Specie*, captured off Savannah, bound for Havana, has arrived at the Navy-yard.

DEPARTURE OF REBEL PRISONERS FOR BOSTON.

Yesterday evening, the rebel prisoners—numbering 900—who have been confined in Fort Lafayette, Fort Wood, and on Governor's Island, left on the steamer *State of Maine* for Boston, at which place they will be incarcerated in Fort Warren. A guard of 100 men, commanded by Capt. Updegraff, accompanied them, so as to make sure that none lose themselves on the way.

DIAGRAM OF THE BATTLE OF BALL'S BLUFF.

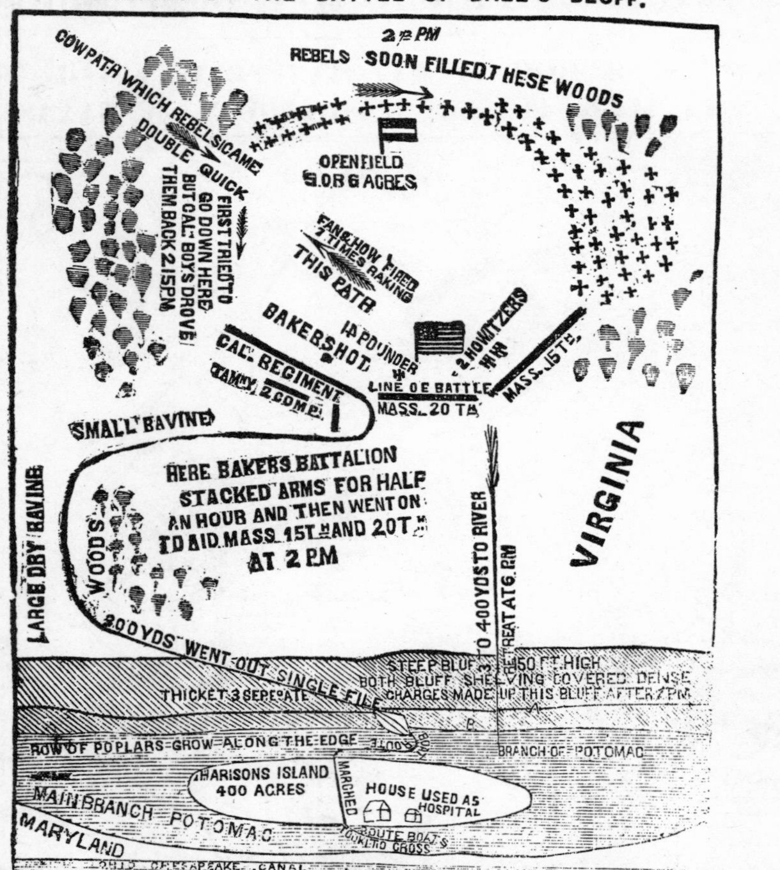

AFFAIRS ON THE UPPER POTOMAC.

THE LATE DISASTER.

A Full History of the Movement Across the Potomac, and the Disaster which Followed it—Where the Responsibility Belongs.

From Our Special Correspondent.

POOLESVILLE, Tuesday, Oct. 29, 1861.

It is now a week since the battle took place between the opposing forces which met this side of Leesburgh. During that time many versions of the affair have been given, all more or less incorrect, and the country has been balancing between the blame which certain correspondents insist should fall upon Gen. Stone and the unbounded praise which the same parties lavish upon the late Col. Baker. I have prepared, from official documents—the same from which Gen. Stone has made up his report—the following statement, which embraces every movement, every order and every result up to the time when Gen. Banks assumed the command and the general retreat was ordered. Before giving that statement, I will remark that the order said to have been found upon the person of Col. Baker, signed Stone, and ordering him to go on to Leesburgh, is a forgery. Gen. Stone is not Napoleon and does not sign his dispatches Stone, nor does he address Colonels as Generals, nor does he write ungrammatical orders. I have his word for it, that the document is a forgery.

It seems that on the 20th instant, Gen. Stone, having been advised of the movement of Gen. McCall to Darnestown, determined to make a demonstration to draw out the intentions of the enemy at Leesburgh. Consequently he proceeded, at 1 P. M., to Edwards' Ferry, from this point, with Gorman's Brigade, the Seventh Michigan Volunteers, two troops of the Van Alen Cavalry and the Putnam Rangers, sending at the same time to Harrison's Island and vicinity four companies of the Fifteenth Massachusetts Volunteers, under Col. Devens, (who had already one company on the island,) and Col. Lee, with a battalion of the Twentieth Massachusetts. And to Conrad's Ferry, a section of Vaughn's Rhode Island Battery and the Tammany Regiment, under Col. Coggswell. A section of Bunting's Y. Y. S. M. Battery, under Lieut. Bramhall, was at the time on duty at Conrad's Ferry, and Rickett's Battery, already posted at Edwards' Ferry, under Col. Woodruff.

The movement of Gen. McCall, on the day previous, seems to have attracted the attention of the enemy, as just previous to the arrival of Gen. Stone at Edwards' Ferry, a regiment of infantry had appeared from the direction of Leesburgh, and taken shelter behind a wooded hill near Goose Creek, 1½ miles from the position of the Union troops at the ferry. Gen. Stone ordered Gen. Gorman to display his forces in view of the enemy, which was done, without inducing any movement on their part, and then ordered three flat boats to be passed from the canal into the river, at the same time throwing shell and spherical shot into and beyond the wood where the enemy were concealed, and into all cover from which fire could be opened on boats crossing the river, to produce an impression that a crossing was to be made. Orders were also sent to Col. Devens, at Harrison's Island, some four miles up the river to detach Capt. Philbrick and twenty men to cross from the island and explore by a path through woods little used, in the direction of Leesburgh, to see if he could find anything concerning the enemy's position in that direction; but to retire and report on discovering any of the enemy. The launching of the boats and shelling at Edwards' Ferry caused a rapid retiring of the force which had been seen there, and Gen. Stone caused the embarkation of three boat-loads of thirty-five men each, from the First Minnesota, who, under cover of the shelling, crossed and recrossed the river, the boats consuming in crossing from three to seven minutes. The spirit displayed by officers and men at the thought of crossing the river was most cheering, and satisfied the General that they could be depended on for most gallant service, whenever more than demonstration might be required of them.

As darkness came on, Gen. Stone ordered Gorman's Brigade and the Seventh Michigan to fall back to their respective camps, but retained the Tammany Regiment, the companies of the Fifteenth Massachusetts and artillery near Conrad's Ferry, in their position, waiting the result of Capt. Philbrick's scout, he (Stone) remaining with his Staff at Edwards' Ferry. About 10 P. M., Lieut. Howe, Quartermaster of the Fifteenth Massachusetts, reported to Gen. Stone that Capt. Philbrick had returned to the island after proceeding unmolested to within a mile and a half of Leesburgh, and that he had there discovered, in the edge of a wood, an encampment of about thirty tents, which he approached to within twenty-five rods without being challenged, the camp having no pickets out any distance in the direction of the river. Gen. Stone at once sent orders to Col. Devens to cross four companies of his regiment to the Virginia shore, and march silently, under the cover of night, to the position of the camp referred to, to attack and destroy it at daybreak, pursue the enemy lodged there as far as would be prudent with the small force, and return rapidly to the island, his return to be covered by a company of the Massachusetts Twentieth, which was directed to be posted on a bluff directly over the landing place. Col. Devens was ordered to use this opportunity to observe the approaches to Leesburgh and the position and force of the enemy in the vicinity, and in case he found no enemy, or found him only weak and in a position where he could observe well and be secure until his party could be strengthened sufficiently to make a valuable reconnoissance, which should safely ascertain the position and force of the enemy, to hold on and report. Orders were dispatched to Col. Baker to send the First California Regiment to Conrad's Ferry, to arrive there at sunrise, and to have the remainder of his brigade in a state of readiness to move after an early breakfast. Also to Lieut.-Col. Ward, of the Fifteenth Massachusetts, to move with a batallion of a regiment to the river bank opposite Harrison's Island, to arrive there by daybreak. Col. Devens, in pursuance of his orders, crossed the river and proceeded to a point indicated by a scouting party, Col. Lee remaining on the bluff with 100 men to cover his return.

In order to distract attention from Col. Devens' movement, and at the same time to effect reconnoissance in the direction of Leesburgh from Edwards' Ferry, Gen. Stone ordered Gen. Gorman to throw across the river, at that point, two companies of First Minnesota, under cover of fire from Rickett's Battery, and sent a party of thirty-one Van Alen Cavalry, under command of Maj. Mix, accompanied by Capt. Chas. Stewart, Assistant Adjutant-General; Capt. Murphy, Lieuts. Pierce and Gouraud, with orders to advance along Leesburgh road until they should come to the vicinity of the battery, which was known to be on that road, and then turn to the left and examine the heights between that and Goose Creek, see if any of the enemy were posted in that vicinity, ascertain as nearly as possible their number and disposition, examine the country with reference to the passage of troops to the Leesburgh and Georgetown turnpike, and return rapidly to cover behind the skirmishers of the First Minnesota.

This reconnoissance was most gallantly made by all in the party, which proceeded along the Leesburgh road nearly three miles from the ferry, and when near the position of a hidden battery came suddenly on a Mississippi regiment about thirty-five yards distant, received its fire and returned it with their pistols. The fire of the enemy killed one horse, but Lieut. Gouraud, the gallant Adjutant of the Cavalry Battalion, seized the dismounted man, and drawing him on his horse behind him carried him safely from the field. One private of the Fourth Virginia Cavalry was brought off by the party, and as he was well mounted and armed his mount replaced the one lost by the fire of the enemy. Meantime Col. Devens on the right, having in pursuance of his orders arrived at the position indicated by the scouts as the site of the enemy's camp, found that the scouts had been deceived by the uncertain light, and had mistaken the openings in the trees for a row of tents. He found, however, wood in which he concealed his force from view and proceeded to examine the space between that and Leesburgh, sending back word to Gen. Stone that thus far he could see no enemy. Immediately on receipt of this intelligence, which was carried by Lieut. Howe Quartermaster of the Fifteenth Massachusetts, Gen. Stone ordered a non-commissioned officer and ten cavalry to join Col. Devens, for the purpose of scouring the country near him while he continued his reconnoissance, and to give him due notice of the approach of any enemy, and that Lieut.-Col. Ward, with his battalion of the Fifteenth Massachusetts, should move on to Smart's Mill, half a mile to the right of the crossing-place of Cols. Devens and Lee, where, in strong position, he could watch and protect the flank of Col. Devens on his return, and secure a second crossing-place more favorable than the first, and connected by a good road with Leesburgh. Capt. Candy, Assistant Adjutant-General in Gen. Lander's Staff, served on Gen. Stone's Staff during the day, and accompanied the cavalry.

For some reason never explained at headquarters, neither of those orders were carried out. The caval-

[Continued on Eighth Page.]

The New-York Times.

VOL. XI----NO. 3189. NEW-YORK, WEDNESDAY, DECEMBER 11, 1861. PRICE TWO CENTS.

TOPOGRAPHICAL MAP OF VIRGINIA.

From LEESBURGH to MATHIAS POINT and the RAPPAHANNOCK, including WASHINGTON and MANASSAS.

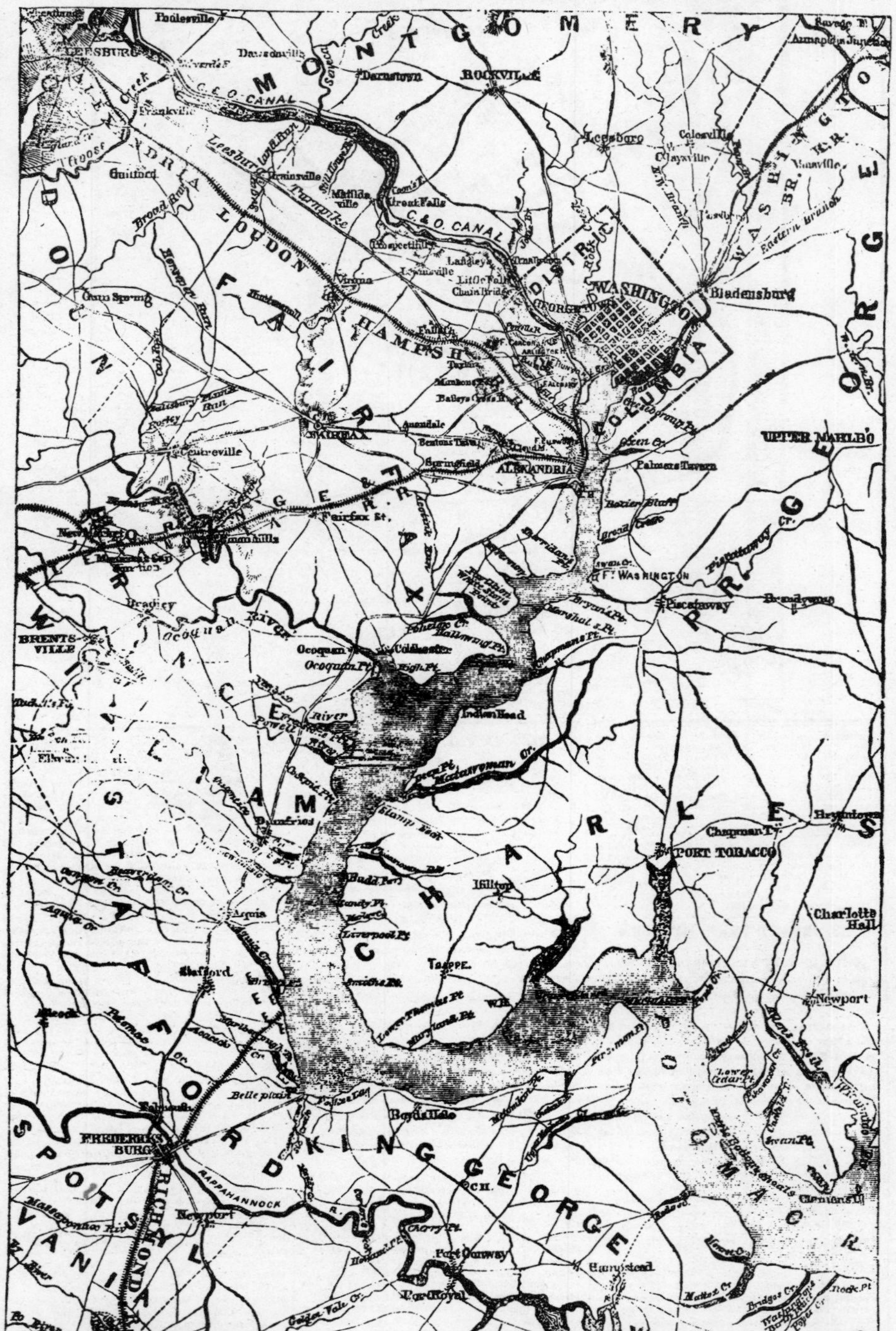

Brother Bennett (Profanely Styled "the Satanic,") Inflating his Well-Known First-Class, A No. 1 Wind-Bag, Herald.

From the Herald, Nov. 2.

Whether the *Tribune* or the TIMES has the larger circulation, we are unable to decide. According to recent accounts, they *both of them distribute somewhere between* TWENTY-FIVE AND THIRTY THOUSAND *daily.*

Of this we are not certain, but concerning the *Herald*, THERE CAN BE NO DOUBT. *Its daily sale of papers averages from* ONE HUNDRED AND FIVE *thousand to* ONE HUNDRED AND THIRTY-FIVE *thousand.*

From the Herald, Nov. 3

It remains doubtful whether the *Times* or *Tribune* will be discovered to be ahead, but in no case will it appear that *both of them together have* ONE-HALF *as many subscribers as the Herald, which sells from* ONE HUNDRED AND FIVE *thousand to* ONE HUNDRED AND THIRTY-FIVE *thousand of its daily issue.*

From the Herald, Thursday, Nov. 7.

We have attained a *daily issue as high as* ONE HUNDRED AND THIRTY-FIVE THOUSAND. Next to the *Herald* comes the *Tribune* and the *Times*, but far in the rear, for we presume that *neither the Times nor the Tribune can boast of an average beyond* TWENTY-FIVE THOUSAND *dailies.*

From the Herald, Saturday, Nov. 9.

In regard to our circulation we did not say that it was one hundred and thirty-five thousand every day, but that it *exceeded* ONE HUNDRED THOUSAND *every day.*

How the Aforesaid First-class Wind-bag was Punctured by the Following WAGERS OFFERED BY THE TIMES:

$2,500 that the *Herald's* daily issue is NOT	135,000
$2,500 that it is not	105,000
$2,500 that it is not	100,000
$2,500 that it is not	75,000
$2,500 that the TIMES' average daily issue is over	25.000
$2,500 that it is over	30,000
$2,500 that it is over	40,000
$2.500 that it is over	50,000
$2.000 that it is over	75,000

[The conditions of this wager were that one-half the whole amount should be forthwith deposited in bank, and that the whole sum should be handed over by the winner to the families of volunteer soldiers.]

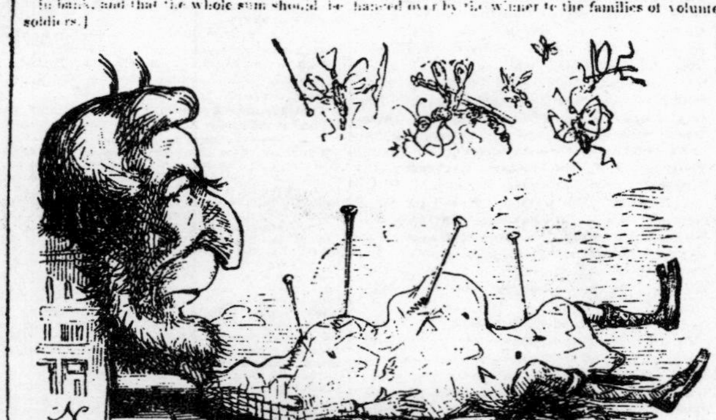

DISASTROUS RESULT!

Brother Bennett Resorts to the Consolations of Religion.

From the Herald, Dec. 5.

Betting, even when fair, is AGAINST OUR RELIGION, and we cannot consent to let him have the information he seeks in that way.

From the Herald, Dec. 7.

Mr. Mephistophiles GREELEY and that little villain RAYMOND are greatly moved upon the subject of the relative circulation of the *Herald* and their own petty papers, and are affected to tears about the matter. We are sorry for them,—but *their attempts to inveigle us into a silly bet are absolutely in vain.* THE PRACTICE OF BETTING IS IMMORAL. *We cannot approve of it.* It may suit GREELEY and RAYMOND, who have exhibited very little morality in the conduct of their journals, *but it will not do for us.*

DIPLOMACY OF THE WAR.

Secretary Seward's Letters to our Ministers Abroad.

Masterly Discussion of the Rebellion Movement for the English Government.

Interesting Letters to Ministers Adams, Dayton, Schurz, and others

MR. SEWARD TO MR. ADAMS.

DEPARTMENT OF STATE, WASHINGTON, April 10, 1861.

SIR: Although Great Britain and the United States possess adjacent dominions of large extent, and although they divide, not very unequally, a considerable portion of the commerce of the world, yet there are at present only two questions in debate between them. One of these concerns the line of boundary running through Puget's Sound, and involves the title to the island of San Juan. The other relates to a proposition for extinguishing the interest of the Hudson's Bay and Puget's Sound Agricultural Companies in the Territory of Washington. The discussion of these questions has hitherto been carried on here, and there is no necessity for removing it to London. It is expected to proceed amicably, and result in satisfactory conclusions. It would seem, therefore, on first thought, that you would find nothing more to do in England than to observe and report current events, and to cultivate friendly sentiments there towards the United States. Nevertheless, the peculiar condition of our country in the present juncture renders these duties a task of considerable delicacy.

You will readily understand me as alluding to the attempts which are being made by a misguided portion of our fellow-citizens to detach some of the States, and to combine them in a new organization under the name of the Confederate States of America. The agitators in this bad enterprise, justly estimating the influence of the European Powers upon even American affairs, do not mistake in supposing that it would derive signal advantage from a recognition by any of those Powers, and especially Great Britain. Your task, therefore, apparently so simple and easy, involves the responsibility of preventing the commission of an act by the Government of that country which would be fraught with disaster, perhaps ruin, to our own.

It is by no means easy to give you instructions. They must be based on a survey of the condition of the country, and include a statement of the policy of the Government. The insurrectionary movement, though rapid in its progress, is slow in revealing its permanent character. Only outlines of a policy can be drawn, which must largely depend on uncertain events.

The Presidential election took place on the 6th of November last. The canvass had been conducted in all the Southern or Slave States in such a manner as to prevent a perfectly candid hearing there of the issue involved, and so all the parties existing there were surprised and disappointed in the marked result. That disappointment was quickly seized for desperate purposes by a class of persons until that time powerless, who had long cherished a design to dismember the Union, and build up a new Confederacy around the Gulf of Mexico. Ambitious leaders hurried the people forward in a factious course, observing conventional forms, but violating altogether the deliberative spirit of their Constitutions. When the new Federal Administration came in, on the 4th of March last, it found itself confronted by an insurrectionary combination of seven States, practicing an insidious strategy to seduce eight other States into its councils.

One needs to be as conversant with our federative system as perhaps only American publicists can be to understand how effectually, in the first instance, such a revolutionary movement must demoralize the General Government. We are not only a nation, but we are States also. All public officers, as well as all citizens, owe not only allegiance to the Union, but allegiance also to the States in which they reside. In the more discontented States, the local magistrates and other officers cast off at once their Federal allegiance, and Conventions were held which assumed to absolve their citizens from the same obligations. Even Federal Judges, Marshals, clerks, and revenue officers, resigned their trusts. Intimidation deterred loyal persons from accepting the offices thus rendered vacant. So the most important faculties of the Federal Government in those States abruptly ceased. The resigning Federal agents, if the expression may be used, *attorned* to the revolutionary authorities, and delivered up to them public funds and other property and possessions of large value. The Federal Government had, through a long series of years, been engaged in building strong fortifications, a navy-yard, arsenals, mints, treasuries, and other public edifices, not in any case for use against those States, but chiefly for their protection and convenience. These had been unsuspectingly left either altogether or imperfectly garrisoned or guarded, and they fell, with little resistance, into the hands of the revolutionary party. A general officer of the army gave up to them a large quantity of military stores and other property, disbanded the troops under his command, and sent them out of the territory of the disaffected States.

It may be stated, perhaps without giving just offence, that the most popular motive in these discontents was an apprehension of designs on the part of the incoming Federal Administration, hostile to the institution of domestic Slavery in the States where it is tolerated by the local Constitutions and laws. That institution and the class which especially cherishes it are not confined to the States which have seceded, but they exist in the eight other so-called Slave States; and these, for that reason, sympathize profoundly with the revolutionary movement. Sympathies and apprehensions of this kind have, for an indefinite period, entered into the bases of political parties throughout the whole country, and thus considerable masses of persons, whose ultimate loyalty could not be doubted, were found, even in the Free States, either justifying, excusing or palliating the movement towards disunion in the seceding States. The party which was dominant in the Federal Government during the period of the last Administration embraced, practically, and held in unreserved communion, all disunionists and sympathizers. It held the Executive Administration. The Secretaries of the Treasury, War and the Interior were disunionists. The same party held a large majority of the Senate, and nearly equally divided the House of Representatives. Disaffection lurked, if it did not openly avow itself, in every department and in every bureau, in every regiment and in every ship-of-war; in the Post-office and in the Custom-house, and in every Legation and Consulate from London to Calcutta. Of four thousand four hun-

THE MASON-SLIDELL AFFAIR.

Report of Capt. Wilkes to the Navy Department.

Capt. Wilkes' Orders to Lieut. Fairfax.

UNITED STATES STEAMER, SAN JACINTO, }
AT SEA, Nov. 16. }

SIR: In my dispatch by Commander TAYLOR, I confined myself to the reports of the movements of this ship and the facts connected with the capture of Messrs. MASON, SLIDELL, EUSTIS and MACFARLAND, as I intended to write you particularly relative to the reasons which induced my action in making these prisoners.

When I heard at Cienfuegos, on the south side of Cuba, of these Commissioners having landed on the Island of Cuba, and that they were at Havana, and would depart in the English steamer of the 7th of November, I determined to intercept them, and carefully examined all the authorities on international law to which I had access, viz.: KENT, WHEATON, VATTELL, besides various decisions of Sir WM. SCOTT, and other Judges of the Admiralty Court of Great Britain, which bore upon the rights of neutrals and their responsibilities.

The Governments of Great Britain, France and Spain, having issued proclamations that the Confederate States were viewed, considered, and treated as belligerents, and knowing that the ports of Great Britain, France, Spain and Holland, in the West Indies, were open to their vessels, and that they were admitted to all the courtesies and protection vessels of the United States received, every aid and protection being given them, proved clearly that they acted upon this view and decision, and brought them within the international law of search and under the responsibilities. I therefore felt no hesitation in boarding and searching all vessels of whatever nation I fell in with, and have done so.

The question arose in my mind whether I had the right to capture the *persons* of these Commissioners—whether *they* were amenable to capture. There was no doubt I had the right to capture vessels with *written* dispatches—they are expressly referred to in all authorities, subjecting the vessel to seizure and condemnation, if the Captain of the vessel had the knowledge of their being on board. But these gentlemen were not dispatches in the literal sense, and did not seem to come under that designation, and nowhere could I find a case in point.

That they were Commissioners, I had ample proof from their *own* avowal, and bent on mischievous and traitorous errands against our country—to overthrow its institutions and enter into treaties and alliances with foreign States, expressly forbidden by the Constitution.

They had been presented to the Captain-General of Cuba by Her Britannic Majesty's Consul-General, but the Captain-General told me he had not received them in that capacity, but as distinguished gentlemen and strangers.

I then considered them as the *embodiment* of dispatches, and as they had openly declared themselves as charged with all authority from the Confederate Government to form treaties and alliances tending to the establishment of their independence, I became satisfied that their mission was adverse and criminal to the Union, and it therefore became my duty to arrest their progress and capture them, if they had no passports or papers from the Federal Government, as provided for under the law of nations, viz.: "That foreign Ministers of a belligerent on board of neutral ships are required to possess papers from the other belligerent to permit them to pass free."

Report and assumption gave them the title of Ministers to France and England, but inasmuch as they had not been received by either of those Powers, I did not conceive they had immunity attached to their persons, and were but escaped conspirators, plotting and contriving to overthrow the Government of the United States, and they were therefore not to be considered as having any claim to the immunities attached to the character they thought fit to assume.

As respects the steamer in which they embarked, I ascertained in the Havana that she was a mere hired vessel plying between Vera Cruz, the Havana and St. Thomas, carrying the mail by contract.

The agent of the vessel, the son of the British Consul at Havana, was well aware of the character of these persons, that they engaged their passage and did embark in the vessel; his father had visited them, and introduced them as Ministers of the Confederate States, on their way to England and France.

They went in the steamer with the knowledge and consent of the Captain, who endeavored afterwards to conceal them by refusing to exhibit the passenger list and the papers of the vessel. There can be no doubt he knew they were carrying highly important dispatches, and were endowed with instructions inimical to the United States. This rendered his vessel (a neutral) a good prize; and I determined to take possession of her, and, as I mentioned in my report, send her to Key West for adjudication, where, I am well satisfied, she would have been condemned for carrying these persons, and for resisting to be searched; the cargo was also liable, as all the shippers were knowing to the embarkation of these *live* dispatches, and their traitorous motives and actions to the Union of the United States.

I forbore to seize her, however, in consequence of my being so reduced in officers and crew, and the derangement it would cause innocent persons, there being a large number of passengers, who would have been put to great loss and inconvenience as well as disappointment from the interruption it would have caused them in not being able to join the steamer from St. Thomas for Europe. I, therefore, concluded to sacrifice the interests of my officers and crew in the prize, and suffered the steamer to proceed after the necessary detention to effect the transfer of these commissioners, considering I had obtained the important end I had in view, and which affected the interests of our country, and interrupted the action of that of the Confederates.

I would add that the conduct of Her British Majesty's subjects, both official and others, showed but little regard or obedience to her proclamation, by aiding and abetting the views and endeavoring to conceal the [illegible] of the Commissioners.

I have pointed out sufficient reason to show you that my action in this case was derived from a firm conviction that it became my duty to make these parties prisoners, and to bring them to the United States.

Although in my giving up this valuable prize I have deprived the officers and crew of a well-earned reward, I am assured they are quite content to forego any advantages which might have accrued to them under the circumstances.

I may add that, having assumed the responsibility, I am willing to abide the result.

I am, very respectfully, your obedient servant,
CHARLES WILKES, Captain.

Hon. GIDEON WELLES, Secretary of the Navy.

THE ORDERS TO LIEUT. FAIRFAX FOR THE ARREST OF MASON AND SLIDELL.

U. S. STEAMER SAN JACINTO, AT SEA, }
Nov. 8, 1861. }

SIR: You will have the second and third cutters of this ship fully manned and armed, and be, in all respects, prepared to board the steamer *Trent*, now hove to under our guns.

On boarding her, you will demand the papers of the steamer, her clearance from Havana, with the list of passengers and crew.

Should Mr. MASON, Mr. SLIDELL, Mr. EUSTIS, and Mr. MACFARLAND be on board, you will make them prisoners, and send them on board this ship immediately, and take possession of her as a prize.

I do not deem it will be necessary to use force—that the prisoners will have the good sense to avoid any necessity for using it; but, if they should, they must be made to understand that it is their own fault. *They must be brought on board.*

All trunks, cases, packages and bags belonging to them, you will take possession of and send on board this ship. Any dispatches found on the persons of the prisoners, or in possession of those on board the steamer, will be taken possession of also, examined, and retained, if necessary.

I have understood that the families of these gentlemen may be with them; if so, I beg you will offer some of them, in my name, a passage in this ship to the United States; and that all the attention and comforts we can command are tendered them, and will be placed at their service.

In the event of their acceptance, should there be anything which the captain of the steamer can spare to increase the comforts in the way of necessaries or stores, of which a war-vessel is deficient, you will please to procure them; the amount will be paid for by the Paymaster.

Lieut. JAMES A. GREER will take charge of the third cutter, which accompanies you, and will assist you in these duties.

I trust that all those under your command, in executing this important and delicate duty, will conduct themselves with all the delicacy and kindness which become the character of our naval service.

I am, very respectfully, your obedient servant.
(Signed.) CHARLES WILKES, Captain.

Lieut. D. M. FAIRFAX, U. S. Navy, Executive Officer *San Jacinto.*

Miscellaneous Items.

The Nashville *Banner* of Nov. 20 is reliably informed that a few evenings ago the family of ANDREW JOHNSON felt so assured that he would make his appearance in Greenville at the head of a Lincoln force, that they made preparations for giving the distinguished traitor a splendid supper upon his arrival. What a delusion!

The Lexington *Advertiser* of the 15th says: "We learn that two negroes belonging to Mr. BOYD, near Benton, shot their master with his own gun on last Sunday night, and then made their escape. The negroes were pursued and finally captured. Mr. BOYD is seriously wounded."

Under the caption, "Coals to Newcastle," the Memphis *Appeal* says: "The steamboat *Louisville* last evening took out 1,075 sacks of salt and 500 sacks of coffee for New-Orleans. After this we expect the day to come when New-Orleans will ship cotton to Memphis."

The Memphis *Avalanche* of Nov. 29 says: "The Federal prisoners, ninety-nine in number, reached the city last Friday afternoon. They were confined for safe-keeping in the large building known as Mosby's cotton shed, near the corner of Second and Jackson streets. No one is permitted to visit them."

The Nashville-Louisville *Courier* states that S. P. SEWELL, a Yankee school teacher at Memphis, has been arrested by the Committee of Safety, as a person inimical to the South.

The Natchez *Courier* states that parties in that city are actually purchasing the necessaries of life and sending them to New-Orleans on speculation.

The residence of the late Dr. HARNEY, in Baton Rouge, now the property of Gen. HARNEY, of the Federal army, is to be immediately confiscated.

The Charleston Daily Courier.

No. 19,040 ....CHARLESTON, S. C., (CONFEDERATE STATES OF AMERICA) WEDNESDAY MORNING, DECEMBER 18, 1861........VOL. LIX.

BY TELEGRAPH.

THE LATEST NEWS.

FROM NORFOLK.

Glorious News from Europe!!!

GREAT EXCITEMENT IN GREAT BRITAIN.

ARRIVAL OF THE EUROPA WITH THE QUEEN'S MESSENGER.

EXPLICIT INSTRUCTIONS TO LORD LYONS.

Demand for the Persons of Mason and Slidell.

Recognition of the Southern Confederacy by France and England.

The Blockade to be Broken!

PROBABLE BLOCKADE OF THE NORTHERN PORTS.

NAPOLEON AS MEDIATOR.

NEWS OF THE CONFLAGRATION IN THE NORTH.

NORFOLK, December 17.—The Baltimore *Sun*, of the 17th inst., just received, and news published in an Extra of the Norfolk *Day Book*, says the steam ship *Europa* arrived on the 15th inst., at Halifax, bringing the Queen's Messenger with dispatches to Lord LYONS, instructing him to demand the immediate restoration of the persons of the Southern Envoys and an apology from the United States Government.

The instructions are explicit, and meet the unanimous concurrence of the Council.

The London *Times* predicts three things will immediately follow, namely, the destruction of the Southern blockade, a complete blockade of the Northern ports, and a recognition of the Southern Confederacy by France and England.

The Paris *Patrie* says France will side with England and will take a decided attitude.

NAPOLEON has tendered his services as Mediator.

Troops have been ordered to Canada, and great excitement prevails throughout Great Britain and on the Continent.

The news of the conflagration in Charleston had reached the North, and caused great rejoicing. The papers contain a report of servile insurrections and exaggerated accounts of the event.

A ship is now loading at Woolwich with Armstrong guns and eighty thousand Enfield rifles, for Canada.

From Richmond.

SYMPATHY FOR MARYLAND—ILLNESS OF VICE PRESIDENT STEPHENS.

RICHMOND, December 17.—The *Examiner* of this morning publishes resolutions adopted in secret session of Congress, offering the sympathy of the Confederate States to the State of Maryland, and expressing a desire for her relief and admission as one of the Confederate States.

Vice-President STEPHENS is quite ill. PLINY MILES is somewhat better.

Northern papers of the 12th have been received here, but they contain nothing of importance.

[SECOND DISPATCH.]

"IMPORTANT, IF TRUE."

RICHMOND, December 17.—A report is current here of the reception in official circles of a dispatch, announcing the publication in the Louisville *Journal*, of a dispatch which states that information of the arrest of MASON and SLIDELL had reached Liverpool, and that an immense mass meeting had been held, at which resolutions of the strongest and most emphatic character were passed, calling on the British Government to demand the most summary reparation for the insult offered the British flag by the forcible seizure of Messrs. MASON and SLIDELL, on board a British vessel, by Capt. WILKES, of the *San Jacinto*.

[THIRD DISPATCH.]

FURTHER EUROPEAN INTELLIGENCE—IMMENSE MEETING IN LIVERPOOL—INTENSE EXCITEMENT ON MASON AND SLIDELL'S ARREST.

RICHMOND, December 17.—The Norfolk *Day Book* to-day published an extra containing important foreign intelligence brought by the steam ship *Europa* to Halifax, and extracted from the Northern papers. It gives the synopsis of the proceedings of a meeting held at Liverpool on the arrival of the intelligence of the arrest of Messrs. MASON and SLIDELL.

The Northern papers say the meeting was composed of Cotton men. The Chairman of the meeting, after the adoption of the resolutions, said: "When the news of the outrage reached Liverpool, the feeling created was one of surprise, mingled with indignation. This feeling was shared by the community generally, and it was our duty to press on the Government the imperative necessity of vindicating the honor and dignity of the British name and flag." Loud and continued cheering followed the address. Some slight effort was made in opposition to the adoption of the resolutions, but was overwhelmingly crushed.

The Northern papers are down on England for such manifestations.

The London *Times*, from a partial allusion evidently regards the MASON and SLIDELL arrest as a great outrage to the British flag.

A dispatch dated Liverpool the 29th ult., says the excitement here over the stoppage of the *Trent* has been most intense, exceeding anything of the kind since the Crimean war.

The funds at London are quite flat since the reception of the *Trent's* news, and speculators are quite at a loss what course to pursue.

The bark *Helen*, from Charleston, had arrived at Liverpool—thus affording further evidence of the inefficiency of the blockade. Cotton men in Liverpool now firmly believe that England will promptly interfere in the war and a consequent liberation of the Cotton crop by the raising of the blockade.

Saltpetre has advanced in Liverpool from ten to twelve shillings.

A letter dated Staunton, Sunday night, says the Twelfth Georgia Regiment lost in killed and wounded about thirty, and the Virginia regiments about eighty. The loss of the enemy is not known, but thirty-two Yankees were buried by our troops.

There is considerable expectation of an attack on the Peninsula indulged in, as well as at Manassas, but quiet still reigns.

The Baltimore *American*, of the 14th inst., received here, publishes a dispatch from Cincinnati on the 14th, claiming a victory in the recent battle on the Alleghany mountains, and says that the Federal loss was about thirty, the Confederate loss two hundred, including a Major, many other officers, and thirty prisoners. The dispatch says the rebels set fire to their camp and retreated to Staunton, and that the Federals left the field in good order.

From Lynchburg.

MORE PARTICULARS OF THE FIGHT IN WESTERN VIRGINIA—GREAT SLAUGHTER OF THE ENEMY.

LYNCHBURG, December 17.—A letter to the Lynchburg *Republican* from an officer at Camp Alleghany, in Western Virginia, says our loss was two Captains, three Lieutenants and fifteen privates killed and ninety-seven wounded. The enemy's loss was fully five hundred. General MILLROY commanded the enemy and it is supposed was killed from the reports made by prisoners and the people of the neighborhood.

Colonel JOHNSON acted most gallantly and appeared in the field dressed like a wagoner with a musket in one hand and a club in the other.

From Indianapolis—Northern Dispatches—More Troops.

INDIANAPOLIS, December 9.—Several of our regiments moved Southward on the Louisville and Nashville Rail Road to make room for regiments constantly arriving. If preparations mean anything a forward movement will certainly take place at an early day.

From Frankfort, Ky.

FRANKFORT, December 9.—Col. GAIRARD writes from London Saturday afternoon that Gen. GEO. B. CRITTENDEN is at Cumberland Gap with a large force, and that 5000 now at Morristown are coming to join him. He says CRITTENDEN has thirty days' rations, and fears that he will invade Kentucky from that point.

The Tennessee brigade and Col. GARRARD's regiment having gone to Somerset. There are no troops to check CRITTENDEN's advance.

A dispatch to the Cincinnati papers says that Gov. MAGOFFIN, of Kentucky, is much exasperated at the attempt of the Confederates to set up a Provisional Government for Kentucky in the Southwestern portion of the State. It is believed he is now willing to co-operate more heartily with the Union Legislature.

From Nashville—Movements of the Enemy.

NASHVILLE, December 16.—The Bowling Green correspondent of the *Union and American*, says the enemy is making an advance, with a force of five or six thousand, on Green river. He has some artillery, but shows no disposition to cross the river. They are repairing bridges, &c.

Reliable advices represent General HUMPHREY MARSHALL steadily advancing [illegible], Ky., meeting with little or no opposition.

A gentleman who left Paducah on the 11th, says that the enemy have only about 6,000 troops at that point, and 10,000 at Cairo and Bird's Point, 7000 at Smithland, &c.

There are no indications at Cairo of a speedy movement down the Mississippi.

LINCOLN's Message, with CAMERON's Report, has produced a great change among the Union men of Smithland.

Gen. N. G. EVANS, the hero and victor of Leesburg, has arrived at the Charleston Hotel, and has received the congratulations of many friends.

A few Enfield Rifles, COLT's Rifles and Navy Revolvers, may be obtained on early application at 44 East Bay, South of and near the Postoffice.

Madame FAVIER, who suffered the loss of everything by the great fire, may be found at Madame THAUSS', corner of King-street and McBride's lane.

Fifty dollars were demanded for a dray load, in some cases during the fire, and not five dollars, as the figures appeared.

We consider it the duty of all good citizens to report, publish and punish all such cases.

The "Carolina Guerilleros" have made rapid progress and their list now shows names enough for a very good company. A few more are desired as will be seen in the advertisement.

Dr. W. A. CARSWELL is Captain and J B. N. HAMMETT, a Lieutenant.

Next to the cheering tokens of sympathy, and offerings from friends, nothing is more encouragingly significant than the resolution and firmness exhibited by the sufferers in this city. Many of our hardworking artisans, who have been deprived of tools, materials and means, as well as of house and shop, are busily preparing to resume work without abatement of heart or hope.

South Carolina College.—The exercises of this College will be resumed on the first Monday in January, 1862, when applicants will be received for examination.

The Planters' Bank of Savannah has appropriated $1000 in aid of the Charleston sufferers.

From Columbia.—We learn from Columbia that the generosity and public spirit manifested by the Banks of the city in their conduct towards the Confederacy and the State, has made a profound impression on our Legislature, which must inspire confidence and hope to those who are charged with the responsible duty of providing the means *for the defence* of our country and of our beloved State. A Bill has been introduced into the House, which we learn has passed that body, proposing to raise $1,800,000—including the $300,000 already advanced by the Banks—by loan at an interest of seven per cent., payable semi-annually, on the first of July and the first of January, and redeemable in instalments of $100,000 per annum, commencing on the first of July, 1867. The interest, and the annual instalments—when these shall commence—are to be provided for by taxation. The interest for the coming year it is proposed to include in the Appropriation Bill—one hundred and twenty-six thousand dollars. This additional charge upon the Treasury, it is thought, will be met without any augmentation of the taxes of last year.

We also learn that provision is made in the Tax Bill to exempt from taxation all lands and negros that may pass into the hands of the enemy before the returns of the taxes are made; and to take at the present value only the lots without the houses, where the latter have been destroyed by the late conflagration. The Committee of Ways and Means, we further learn, have decided to recommend a Bill of a similar character to the one that passed the Legislature in 1838, which we believe called for a loan of two million of dollars.

The interest on the loan taken by the Banks last year has, we are informed, been made payable semi-annually.

It is not possible to ascertain the loss which has been sustained by the hundreds whose homes were consumed by the flames on Wednesday night. The rapidity with which the fierce fire rushed from building to building, the number of those who were burnt out, and the confusion and excitement produced by the terrible visitation, rendered it impossible for many to procure the needful assistance in the removal of their goods and furniture. A large amount of the property destroyed fell a prey to the devouring element after it had been placed where it was believed the fire would not reach.

It is melancholy to contemplate the number of paintings, statuettes, choice works of art and rare old books which met with the fate of the handsome and venerable buildings which they adorned. Much that was destroyed on that fearful night can never be replaced. But there are other losses which have caused heart rending distress, and it is to the relief and alleviation of this class of sufferers that we should address ourselves with christian liberality and promptitude. Their destitution appeals eloquently to our sympathies. We rejoice that the admirable measures adopted instantly, and carried out with vigor and discretion, have prevented suffering, the thought of which makes us sick at heart. The homeless have found shelter and the hungry have been fed.

Much has already been accomplished toward the temporary and permanent relief of the penniless and houseless, but a great deal remains to be done. Hearts have been touched by the great distress and the charitable have devised liberal things. The amount thus far subscribed will not nearly cover the immense loss which has befallen hundreds who are powerless to alleviate and relieve their own distresses. Our hearts glow with gratitude for the large and munificent donations which have been poured upon us from open hands. But the good work is but begun. We are confident it will be carried on in the spirit that has embarked those who have already come to our assistance.

We had the unspeakable pleasure on Tuesday of handing over to the gentlemen of the Committee of Relief, the sum of eleven hundred and seventy-nine dollars. While on the way to transfer that amount, three checks, each for five hundred dollars, were placed in our hands by fellow-townsmen. And before the gas was lighted our subscription list contained donations, whose total rose to two thousand dollars.

Among the responses we received on Tuesday are the following:

NORFOLK, December 13, 1861.

Please hand on our account, to those who may have charge of the poor in your city, $100 to be applied to the wants of those who suffered by the late fire in your city. Yours truly,

P. HOUSEBY & CO.

CHARLOTTE, N. C., December 14, 1861.

Messrs. A. S. Willington & Co.:

DEAR SIRS:—I sympathize with your people for the loss that they have sustained at the late fire. Enclosed you will find $10. You will please to help the sufferers with it that were deprived of a home. Respectfully, J. G. WILKINSON.

Inclosed find fifteen dollars. Place on the subscription list for relief of sufferers by the late fire of Wednesday night and Thursday morning last.

A FRIEND TO THE NEEDY.

The Spirit of our People.

The times demand all our forbearance, fortitude and courage. We must look the gravest calamities in the face and familiarize ourselves with their color and magnitude. We must learn to contemplate the dangers that frown on every side with unshaken nerves and high resolve. The vast interests at stake, the malignant spirit and diabolical purpose of our active and crafty foe, admonish us that citizenship is no meaningless phrase, but that this honor involves momentous duties and fearful responsibilities, which can only be met and discharged by the vigorous use of all our resources and powers. He is a traitor and coward who fails under any pretext to come up to the full measure of his solemn obligations.

Our all is threatened—all that religion has made holy, that humanity has made dear, that right has pronounced inviolable, that honor has made more valuable than life itself. The foe will fail of his iniquitous purposes only for lack of ability to execute them. The cause is equally the cause of all, rich and poor, high and low. And it invites and commands every one to take part in its maintenance and accomplishment. The call has fallen on open ears, and the South has responded with hand, head and heart. Cheerfully, generously, earnestly, bravely, have the citizens of the young Confederacy met the high requirements of patriotism. All classes and conditions have shown an equal ardor and promptitude. All are animated by the same spirit and nerved by the same resolve.

So grand and holy is the cause we are engaged in that it invests everything done and suffered for its advancement with its own dignity. They partake of its glory who have given to it their husbands, sons and brothers, and who keep their courage high and their determination immovable by words of heroic counsel, pious admonition, and the potent breathing of ardent prayers. The sword, the pen, the needle, the axe, the spade, every implement and instrument employed in this glorious work becomes a holy and beautiful thing. This is the sentiment that inspires every man and woman who is doing and enduring to attain the priceless boon of freedom. Under the inspiration of this feeling societies have been organized; delicate hands, unused to fatiguing labor, have toiled upon coarse fabrics, till they were weak from weariness, and the brow of the worker has throbbed with pain. Sacrifices against which comfort and pride have protested have been made with cheerfulness, and inconveniences and privations have been borne with, that a patriotism less ardent would have condemned as unnecessary.

But the most striking and impressive exhibition of the spirit that animates and sustains our people is manifested by our noble volunteers. We at home have but an imperfect idea of the duties and sufferings our volunteers are required to perform and endure. The privates in our army work harder and fare worse than their own slaves. They do the most menial and arduous work. They are subject to the severe requirements of military discipline. Their obedience must be quick and unhesitating. The distinction between the common soldier and the commissioned officer is broad and sternly observed. The cross-bars raise the one high above the other. The men in the ranks may be the others superior in social position, in wealth, in breeding, in education, but these advantages do not reduce the distance between himself and the person with the insignia of military rank. When the title co-exists with conceitedness and an overbearing disposition, the better man in undistinguished garb is made to feel keenly the vast difference between himself and he who has the right to command his services.

While we believe that our officers are actuated by a patriotism as pure and noble, as what animates our private soldiers, still the devotion of the latter because unsustained by the same bright visions of glory, appears the more grand. If the General or Captain fall upon the field his name is shouted far and wide, and there are eloquent pens and tongues to praise his prowess and make his fame immortal. But the common soldier who pours out his heart's blood on the field of war, is mentioned among the undistinguished many, and his deeds of heroism go down with him into an unmarked grave. When, in connection with these considerations and many others which readily suggest themselves to our minds, we contemplate the nature of their duties, and the numerous privations and hardships they have to bear, we feel that we are safe in affirming that the noblest illustration of the spirit which nerves and sustains the South in this eventful struggle, is furnished by the patient endurance, the ready obedience, the gallant valor of our army of volunteers.

The rescue of the Gas Office, papers, &c, was under the immediate management of the President, J. SCHNIERLE, and owing to the persevering efforts of Messrs. BEN. JOHNSON and B. M. HERIOT, and officers PURSE and W. J. HERIOT.

Among the volunteers of the Richland Rifles, who promptly responded to the call of the Governor, in January, and rallied to the aid and defence of Charleston, none was more gallant, ready and devoted than Color-Sergeant JOHN A. KAY. An engineer and architect, of approved qualifications, and, for his years, of long experience, he soon after resigned a lucrative position as assistant architect of the New State House, and abandoned a large and growing practice in his profession to enter the service of the State.

His skill, qualifications and experience as architect and constructing engineer and draughtsman, would render valuable service in the Engineer Department of the Confederate Army.

Jones' Portable Soup.—We have received specimens of this valuable preparation, of which the proprietor says:

"Jones' Portable Soup for Army and Navy Use.—This Soup, put up in the form of small square cakes, will be found very useful in situations where the articles for making Soup in the ordinary way are difficult to obtain.

Directions.—Each cake will make a pint of good, rich Soup. Cut the cakes into thin slices and put into a kettle, with one pint of cold water for each cake used. Let it boil about fifteen minutes, or until the cakes are thoroughly dissolved, and the Soup is then ready for use.

N. B.—Should the cakes be frozen, slice them into the cold water and let them stand a few minutes to thaw before putting them on the fire.

Made by J. W. JONES, corner of Line and Meeting-streets, Charleston, S C."

HAMILTON & SMITH, Grocers, 54 Market-street, will receive orders, and exhibit specimens and give information.

The Raleigh Register of the 14th says that D. F. Ferebee, Esq., who has just returned from a mission to the Confederate Government, upon which he was sent by the Convention, reports, among other things, that Secretary Memminger expressed a decided opinion that the blockade would be raised in thirty days.

Of course we do not know upon what facts Secretary Memminger predicates his opinion, or what sources of information he may possess, which are not yet before the general public. We wish it to be as he thinks it will be; but it must be evident that, after all, this opinion, although that of an able and cautious statesman, occupying a high official position, is still *only* an opinion, for we know enough of the caution which marks, and, indeed, ought to mark diplomatic intercourse, to be sure that it cannot be based upon any diplomatic assurances from foreign powers, assurances which they have not deemed it proper to make public, and which therefore Mr. Memminger, as a member of the Confederate Cabinet, would not feel justified in making public even in the form of an opinion.—*Wilmington Journal.*

Important from Washington—An Early Advance Contemplated.—Important information direct from Washington reached the Government in this city on Saturday night, which will not be permitted to transpire. It was confidently asserted when the informant left Washington, last Wednesday, that an attack from the Potomac would be made within ten days, and appearances seem to indicate that such was the intention. All the troops destined for the enterprise were said to be already on this side of the river.—*Richmond Dispatch, 16th inst.*

South Carolina Money.—We understand that a report has gained credence in this city, to the effect that the Charleston banks have been ruined by the late fire in that city, and that their bills are in consequence, worthless. Some of our citizens have been making unnecessary purchases, in order to get rid of their South Carolina money. We pen this paragraph for the purpose of assuring them that there is no cause whatever for alarm. The South Carolina Banks, and the Augusta Banks, are as sound as they ever have been, and it is the height of folly for holders of their bills to become panic stricken, and throw away their money.

[*Augusta Constitutionalist.*

CITY INTELLIGENCE.

ATTENTION IS DIRECTED to the sale of Carriages, Parlor and Bed Room Furniture, Mirrors, Pictures, &c., which takes place this day, by WILBUR & SON, corner State and Chalmers-streets.

SOUTH CAROLINA RANGERS.—GEORGE H. SMITH will leave the city for Camp Kinloch Thursday morning, December 19th. Packages or letters for members of the Company left at his residence, 33 Calhoun-street, this day, will be delivered with pleasure. 1*

LADIES' CHRISTIAN ASSOCIATION.—An extra meeting of the Ladies' Christian Association will be held at the hall this morning, at 12 o'clock. The members and all interested will please be punctual in attendance.

MASONIC.—At the Annual Convocation of Union Chapter, No. 3, R. A. M., held at Masonic Hall on Tuesday evening, the 17th instant, the following Companions were elected officers of the Chapter:

Companion R. S. FIELDING, M. E. H. P.
Companion WM. T. MILLAR, K.
Companion H. W. SCHRODER, S.
Companion H. W. KINSMAN, C. H.
Companion R. S. PARKER, P. S.
Companion J. SYMONS, R. A. Captain.
Companion B. FELDMAN, G. M. 1 V.
Companion W. J. BURK, G. M. 2 V.
Companion S. S. HANCOCK, G. M. 3 V.
Companion E. THAYER, Treasurer.
Companion THOS. ALLASON, Secretary.
Companion W. B. THOMPSON, O. S.

DARING BURGLARY.—The wharf office on BROWN & Co.'s wharf, was entered on Monday night by some daring burglar or burglars, who gained admission through the shed over an adjoining bar room. The burglar opened all the desks, stole what money had been left there, amounting to some forty or fifty dollars, opened and searched all the books and papers, and then scattered them about the floor. The locks of the desks were not broken, and it is therefore supposed that it was some experienced operator who is furnished with a complete set of burglar's tools.

After searching the desks and papers in the offices of Messrs. GRIFFIN and [illegible] & HALE, and scattering the papers as in the first office visited, the scamp departed, leaving traces of candle grease on the floor wherever he went. The supposition is that he must have made his exit through a window opening on Vendue Range.

Cannot some of our active police detectives ferret out these midnight robbers and incendiaries?

THE LATE FIRE.—Among those who suffered severely by the destruction of their home and other property, were four sisters, the Misses HARVEY, residing in Queen-street. The disaster to their property will cause a pang in the hearts of the orphan, and many a poor family who were the constant recipients of their bounty. A handsome income of $2000 to $3000 derived from the rent of several fine residences, belonging to these young ladies, had been annually devoted by them to charitable purposes. The poor always found in them an active friend ready to help and relieve in the time of trouble and difficulty. And although independent in circumstances they were ever busy with the needle or in teaching the little ones in their primary school which they had established at their own home. Their loss may be stated as follows:

One three story brick house and out-buildings in Queen-street, adjoining Dr. Myddleton Michel's, valued at	$6000
One three story wooden dwelling next to the above, with improvements	4000
Two wooden houses on Queen-street, opposite Sisters of Mercy, valued at	4000
One large house in King-street, with three small residences in the rear	6000
Two wooden houses on State-street, valued at	4000
Loss of furniture	2000
Total	$26,000
Insurance	7000
Total loss	$19,000

We learn that some fiend in (no doubt stolen) uniform forced a negro driver with his dray sent for the removal of the Misses HARVEY's furniture to another portion of the city, to [illegible] property.

The conflagration was arrested on the West side Meeting-street, above the Theatre, at the large brick building better known as "COHEN's Medical Depot." The upper part was occupied by Mrs. JANE WHITE. The yard attached was the Marble Yard of her son, ROBERT D. WHITE, (President of the Palmetto Engine Company) who suffered considerably from the destruction of his marble and large, beautiful Italian tombstones. We are pleased to perceive that, with his usual energy, he is again at work, repairing the damage. Dr. COHEN's entire stock was removed, and we regret to learn that his loss has been severe from breakage and stealage. Cannot our authorities do something to prevent this wholesale pilfering at fires? Wretches in human forms, who take advantage of the sufferings of our citizens at such times, should be summarily and severely dealt with.

ROBERT MINNIS, Plumber, Meeting-street, next South of Apprentices' Library. House owned by Dr. RODRIGUES. Totally consumed. Mr. MINNIS lost all his stock, tools and furniture, valued at $3000. No insurance.

J. BLANK, 157 King-street, Jewelry and Watch-making establishment. Loss about $2000. No insurance.

DR. T. REENSTJERNA, who has spent many years in the most celebrated hospitals in Europe, offers his services in quality of Physician, Surgeon and Man Midwife. See diploma and testimonials in his office, 9 Clifford-street.

N. B.—Secret diseases cured with certainty and dispatch. ws2*

BISHOP LYNCH requests that persons having in their possession any articles, saved from the Cathedral, or the residence of the Clergy, during the late fire, will kindly deliver the same at Mr. THOS. RYAN's, Archdale-street, opposite the Lutheran Church, or give information so that they may be sent for. 3

NOTICE TO SEA BOARD PLANTERS.—Attention is called to the advertisement of lands by Mr. JAMES R. BUTTS. Persons desirous of communicating with Mr. BUTTS will find him at the office of Messrs. GARMANY & CHAMPION, Savannah, until the 18th instant; after that he may be found at Macon, Ga. w2*

DR. WM. PETTIGREW, whose residence in Queen-street was totally consumed, will be found for the present and until further notice, at 64 Broad-street, the office and residence of Col. J. L. BRANCH.

LETTERS FOR THE FIRST REGIMENT OF RIFLES left at Maj. LEE's Office will be forwarded.

Also any Packages left at the Store of H. E VINCENT, Esq 12*

RECEIVED BY EXPRESS, direct from New Orleans, and opening this morning, a fresh lot of Alexander's Kid Finished Silk Gloves. Also new Ribbons and Worsted Talmas for children. "Terms cash." At DRAKE's.

Charleston Wayside Hospital and Soldiers Depot.

Every train will bring large numbers of soldiers, hungry, fatigued, and many, perhaps, sick and faint. Refreshments are essential immediately upon their arrival. Our City Council has appointed the undersigned a Committee to attend to this matter. The new building erected as a Depot for the South Carolina Rail Road Company, has been kindly given up for the reception of the Soldiers, and ample accommodation prepared for the sick and disabled.

We want cooks, waiters, nurses, fuel, hospital stores, etc., etc. Our citizens, we are assured, will immediately come to our aid.

All communications should be addressed to Prof. F. S. HOLMES, who is the Superintendent in charge, at his residence, corner of Calhoun and St. Philip-streets, or at the Depot of the South Carolina Rail Road Company.

H. E. BANKS,
F. S. HOLMES,
J. S. RIGGS, } Committee.

We learn that the Captain of the Key Stone State, who absconded from Key West, with his prize—Captain McKay's propeller Salvor—carried her into Philadelphia. On board the Salvor were found, besides the arms and other things already mentioned, several large drafts on houses in New Orleans, Memphis, Charleston and Savannah.—*Tampa (Fla.) Peninsular.*

Public Meeting in Spartanburg.

SPARTANBURG C. H., December 14, 1861.

A meeting of the citizens of Spartanburg was held on this day, Dr. J. J. BOYD was called to the Chair, and J. M. ELFORD requested to act as Secretary. SIMPSON BOBO, Esq., made some remarks explaining the objects of the meeting and especially our duty in helping our Queen City, in this her time of great distress and affliction.

Professor WARREN DUPRE offered the following resolutions which were unanimously adopted:

Resolved, That the late conflagration in the City of Charleston excites our deepest sympathies for the sufferers, and that we are willing to extend to them all the aid within our power.

Resolved, That a Committee of —— be appointed to ascertain the number of houses that may be obtained in this town and the terms upon which they can be rented; also, what families may be willing to receive as boarders the distressed citizens of Charleston.

Resolved, That as soon as the Committee obtains the necessary information, a report of the same be made to the Intendant of the City of Charleston.

After which, the following resolution was added:

Resolved, That the blank in the second resolution be filled with the number 9, and that the Chairman appoint the same.

The following gentlemen were then appointed by the Chair to act as said Committee:—SIMPSON BOBO, Esq., Prof. J. H. CARLISLE, Prof. WARREN DU PRE, PETER S. SMITH, A. H. KIRBY, A. J. DANIEL, J. W. WEBBER, A. BETHUNE and J. W. HARDY.

Which Committee soon after reported that, they, upon inquiry, find that there can be obtained in our town, for such citizens of Charleston as may be in need of homes, about thirty houses or more, for their use and occupation, at very low rent, ranging from houses of three rooms at three dollars per month to houses of ten and twelve rooms at twelve dollars per month—being some fifty per cent. less than the usual rent for said houses—and that numbers can be boarded at our public houses at reasonable prices, and several of our citizens will receive the distressed families at reduced rates.

On motion, it was ordered that the Committee will make farther inquiries and report to the Intendant of the City of Charleston; and the proceedings of this meeting be published in the papers of our town, and the Secretary be requested to forward a copy of the same to Charleston, to be published, by request of this Meeting, in the Charleston *Courier* and *Mercury*.

JAS. J. BOYD, Chairman.

J. M. ELFORD, Secretary.

Correspondence of the Courier.

NEW ORLEANS, December 9, 1861.

I have rarely known so strong a sentiment of disapprobation as has been aroused in the people of New Orleans by the rumor, vague as it is, that General PRICE is to be superceded in the chief command of the Missouri army, by a gentleman whose merits seem to be unknown to the public except that he is a graduate of West Point, and was an officer of the old army. The mere intimation of such a purpose, unfounded as it may be in fact, has provoked invidious comparisons between the results accomplished by General PRICE, and the results accomplished by those who entered the service with the prestige of scientific military training. He marches from the Southern extremity of the State to the Missouri River, takes Lexington, with its garrison of four thousand, all their arms, their horses, wagons, artillery and cash; toles Fremont down to the Arkansas line, at an expense to the Federal Government of twelve or fifteen millions of dollars, follows HUNTER up, and by these movements secures the Mississippi Valley from invasion. His aggressive movements, in popular estimation, are doing quite as much to redeem Kentucky and save Tennessee as Generals POLK and JOHNSTON are doing at Columbus and Bowling Green. He marches and countermarches an army of twenty or thirty thousand men through a remote and desolated country a hundred and fifty miles in each direction, and no one hears a word of complaint from him as to the insufficiency of his subsistence or the inefficiency of his transportation. In fact I am told he can park a whole wagon train in a five acre field, astonishing as it may be to the disciples of WINFIELD SCOTT, and, like the Roman legions, feeds himself as he goes. His victories bring fruits palpable to the common sense of the people, and in view of the fertility of his resources, his self-reliance, his incomparable economy, his skill and valor, they would deprecate his loss or the reduction of his authority as the removal of one of the grand pillows of their hopes. Nor is the fact to be denied that his proclaimed policy of defending his State by carrying the war into the enemy's country and subsisting upon them as they have been subsisting upon his people, is in accord with the wishes of the whole South.

Let him cross the Mississippi into Illinois with a column of thirty or forty thousand men, and the redemption of Kentucky and the advance of our lines to the Ohio river, menacing every farm, town and city North of it, becomes a comparatively easy task. NAPOLEON's military judgment refused to re-establish Poland as an independent nationality, for the reason that it was one dead level, embracing no point of strategic defence, and liable at any moment to be overrun by a neighbor. Such is exactly the condition of the West, between the Alleghanies and the Mississippi, and the centaurs of Missouri are fully as competent to demonstrate the vulnerability of such a country as the Cossacks of the Don. The West has no Pyrenees, no Balkan Pass, no Cumberland Gap, no Manassas, and whenever the towns and cities of that vast expanse of indefensible soil have to exhaust their energies and their means in the effort to protect their own homes, you on the Atlantic coast and we in the Valley will have little cause of anxiety. And it is gratifying to learn that the policy of Gen. PRICE in this regard, is likely to meet the approval of the distinguished soldier and statesman at the head of the Government. I am not at liberty to mention the source of my information, but the fact comes from high authority that President DAVIS has determined that the period has arrived when aggressive warfare, upon every favorable opportunity, is our policy.

JOHN LAW's financial theories as to money finds several disciples in the Legislature of Louisiana. The unsophisticated regrets of ARISTOPHANES that the depraved tastes of the people should induce the circulation of mutilated coin when whole coin was to be had, nor the astonishment of English politicians, in the days of WILLIAM of Orange, at the seeming preference for clipped shillings and crowns, are not more refreshing than the invincible belief which so generally obtains among us that an act of the Legislature has the faculty of converting a piece of paper into money. One bill has been introduced to "mobilize," as it is termed, the State bonds—which means that they shall be made available as money. This is the scheme: A thousand dollar bond, or upwards, may be exchanged at the Treasury for an issue of one hundred dollar bonds, drawing less interest. Another project looks to the relief of the Cotton planters, by issuing sixteen millions of State paper, also to be used as money. It requires no remarkable powers of ratiocination to foreshadow the results of such schemes. The country flooded with these issues, all attempts to fix values become wild conjecture, and the credit of the Confederate Government, that we have to rely upon for our success, vanishes, as every fresh utterance of State notes makes its appearance.

One of the signs of the times is an advertisement which appears in our papers from Messrs. J. & C. DAVIDSON, sisters, gravely announcing that they will accommodate the public by exchanging at two and a half per cent. premium their shin plasters for Confederate notes. Your readers must not mistake the quarter on which the premium is placed; it is on the issues of the Messrs. DAVIDSON. There is a great deal of presumption in the advertisement, but there is likewise a lesson which may be read profitably by our enterprising JOHN LAWS.

CHALMETTE.

NEW ORLEANS, December 10, 1861.

The scandal mongers of New Orleans have been sated with a very large and very noisome dish. WILLIAM G. STEPHENS, a paving contractor, well to do in the world, a widower and the father of adult children, who has been esteemed a model of propriety in social behavior, made his exit rather suddenly from the city in company with a notorious courtezan known as Mrs. FANNY SMITH or as Mrs. FANNY SWEET, on a mysterious journey to Mexico, and, while traveling through Texas, near the Rio Grande, made his exit from this world, after a short illness, into the mysteries of the next. His sudden death, the fact that he possessed large means, and the antecedents of his companion, known and putative, gave rise to a suspicion that his death was caused by her. Whereupon fecund nine pens traced with disgusting minuteness the licentious career of the supposed murderess, interspersing the narrative with vials, daggers and pistols as recklessly and shockingly as CARLYLE punctuates. The heroine was as seductive as CLEOPATRA and as merciless and vindictive as the dramatic BORGIA. She has returned, however, and her presence in the city has reduced a sensational romance to the dimensions of a very common place police item. That she went off with STEPHENS, she admits; that she had any hand in his death, she denies. And the circumstances go to show her innocence. The deceased was in possession of all her means as well as his own, in sterling bills, negotiable only by him or his administrator. She was of her own volition returning to the city when she was arrested. She had been his companion for months here. At his instance she attired herself in male habiliments, and thus disguised became an inmate of his house and was introduced to his family and friends as his nephew. A strong reciprocal attachment, she says, existed between them, and both sold out their property, intending to spend the remainder of their days in some land where was unknown. As a Magdalene she affects respectability and piety, and deprecates the cruel literature that not only perpetuates the recollection of her sinfulness, but also attributes attrocities to her which she never heard of until now. As there seems to be hardly any question that STEPHENS died a natural death, she will doubtless soon be at large again and at liberty to choose her own path of life.

The enemy's gunboats have been busy during the last two weeks, in Mississippi sound, intercepting traders between this place and Mobile. Two or three old steam boats and a couple of schooners have been captured. Latterly our vessels go under convoy of gunboats. An occasional brush takes place, but always at long taw, and, so far as we know, without result. Whenever the marauders are invited to close quarters, they take to their heels, and seek the protection of the larger vessels outside in the Gulf. Commodore HOLLINS has returned from Columbus, and again assumes the command here, having been succeeded above by Commodore WHIPPLE.

Yesterday arrangements were perfected in behalf of the State with the banks for a loan of $4,500,000. Of this sum the State had already received $1,100,000, leaving $3,400,000 to its credit. $2,000,000 of the remainder will be absorbed in paying the Confederate State direct tax, and the balance will be abundant to meet all the liabilities of the State and construct such additional defences as our exigencies may require. I am not yet informed as to the terms of the loan, but understand the banks have behaved with becoming liberality. The Legislature is in recess and for the time being we are spared a continuance of the empirical projects, with which the session was opened, to relieve every man's necessities by a flood of paper.

The weather continues as mild and genial as April, and the fields are as verdant as in that delightful vernal month. Coal speculators are tortured with apprehensions, and every body else contemplates their painful grievances with unalloyed pleasure. It is estimated that the stock on hand, in the absence of demand for sea going steamers, is sufficient for two years, and with half the winter over, and every promise of an entire season of remarkable mildness, the prospects of forestallers in the article, are of a darker hue than indigo.

A masters mate named O. A. CHILD and seven seamen of the Yankee frigate Santee, blockading Galveston, arrived here this morning prisoners. They were sent in a tender to the mouth of the Mississippi to procure fresh water for the frigate and were wrecked near the Sabine Pass. This occured on the 17th ult. They made their way in a launch to Last Island, subsisting on oranges and a few crackers. At Last Island they were met by a small party of fishermen who gave them liquor until they were drunk, and while in that condition disarmed them and bilged the launch. Thus destitute of means of defence or escape they were easily secured.

The failure of the Legislature to elect Mr. BENJAMIN as one of our representatives in the Confederate Senate, must not be taken as an indication of the weakness of that gentleman in Louisiana. Among all her public men there is not one esteemed more highly, but as I wrote you previous to the election, there were grave doubts if he could not be more serviceable to our cause in his present position than in the Senate. With this feeling among his strongest admirers, very little effort was made to secure his election. The gentlemen elected, however, will make excellent representatives. They are both men of talent and experience in public life. General EDWARD SPARROW is a native of Ireland, who has resided in this State since his boyhood. He was a prominent member of the old Whig party until the advent of Know Nothingism, when he joined the Democracy, and in the last Presidential contest labored strenuously for the election of BRECKINRIDGE. Our other Senator elect, THOMAS J. SEMMES, is a native of the District of Columbia and a graduate of Georgetown College. He has been several times a representative of this city in the Legislature and is at present the Attorney General of the State. He has always been a Democrat of the Southern Rights school.

The fall meeting over the Metairie Course commenced yesterday. The race did not afford much sport.

The race to-day was interesting; subjoined is the summary:

First Race—Single Dash of two miles—Club Purse, $250.

T. J. Wells' b. c. *Uncle True*, by Lexington, out of Edith, three years old........1
W. J. Minor's ch. f. *Regret*, by Brown Dick, out of Temptation, three years old........2
D. F. Kenner's ch. f. by Imp. Albion, dame unknown, three years old........3
H. B. Foley's ch. c., by Lexington, out of Minnie Mitchell, three years old........4

Time:—First mile 1:47; second mile 1:51½—3:38½.

One of the best informed merchants in New Orleans made a bet of $500 to-day on each of two propositions: First, That the Cotton crop is the largest ever gathered. Second, That the sugar crop is the largest ever grown in this State.

CHALMETTE.

Later from Europe.

New York, December 8.—The steamer *Africa* arrived here to-day, with advices via Queenstown to the 24th ult.

The steamer *Europa* arrived at Liverpool on the 24th.

The steamer Anglo-Saxon arrived at Londonderry on the night of the 23d, with news of the loss of the steamer North Briton.

The news of the arrest of Messrs. Slidell and Mason had not reached England when the Africa sailed.

Judge Aron Goodrich, Secretary of the American Legation at Brussels, left London on the night of the 23d, and reached Queenstown in season to embark on the Africa, as bearer of special dispatches to Washington.

The Latest via Queenstown.—The United States mail ship Arago, from New York, arrived at Southampton on the 23d.

London, November 24.—The Observer, ministerial organ, in alluding to the permission demanded to the Nashville to arm and coal at Southampton says "it became necessary to issue a proclamation by the Government respecting vessels seeking an asylum in our ports. A stay unnecessarily protracted for purposes of aggression, cannot be encouraged."

The "Observer" hints that in case of any violation of laws of strict neutrality by the Nashville, while in British ports, our courts might be moved to action, on the representation of the American Minister, as was the case of the seizure of the Sicilian ships by the Government of Naples, in 1858, and more recently in respect, to the issue of Kossuth notes.

Capt. Pegram, of the Nashville, denies the statement that he holds no commission, and has published his so-called commission—as a Lieutenant in the rebel navy.

Ragusa, November 22.—An official dispatch states that Pasha, with eight battalions, defeated eight thousand insurgents near Rivis, after four hours' fight. Eight hundred of the insurgents were killed, while the Turkish loss was only one hundred killed and wounded.

Paris, November 24.—The "Moniteur" publishes a decree, abolishing the entrance fee to the Bourse.

Liverpool, November 23.—Cotton quiet and unchanged. Sale to-day of 5,000 bales.

Breadstuffs quiet and prices firm.

Provisions inactive.

Consols closed this evening at 94@94¼ for money.

RELIEF FOR THE SUFFERERS BY THE LATE CONFLAGRATION.

A PROCLAMATION.

The calamitous fire which has spread through our city, upon all who have been within its reach inflicts loss and suffering. But there are many, who, in its ravages, have lost so much that the aid of all who have been fortunate in escaping its effects, should be and will be generously offered for their relief. To secure the most useful application of whatever may be thus contributed for the relief of those who are suffering, the following Committee has been appointed. It will forthwith organize itself, make immediate application to our fellow-citizens for such aid as they can afford, and promptly relieve, as far as possible, with shelter, food and clothing, those whose misfortunes have deprived them of these necessities.

CHARLES MACBETH,

December 12, 1861. Mayor of Charleston.

Committee under the foregoing Proclamation.

JUDGE MAGRATH.	GEORGE BUIST.
RT. REV. BISHOP LYNCH.	E. P. MILLIKEN.
REV. MR. PORTER.	W. C. COURTNEY.
J. K. SASS.	C. R. MILES.
HENRY GOURDIN.	WM. LEBBY.
W. J. BENNETT.	THEO. D. WAGNER.
Z. B. OAKES.	JAMES M. WILSON.
JAMES S. GIBBES.	JOSEPH T. CALDWELL.

The following notices have been ordered by the Committee to be published in the daily papers of the City

SUPPLIES OF FOOD,

Will be furnished *daily*, between the hours of *nine o'clock, A. M. and eleven o'clock, A. M.* Application must be made for *Tickets at the Confederate Court House*, to the Committee at the time above mentioned. No supplies will be furnished but to such as produce tickets from the Committee.

CLOTHING,

Will be supplied to those who are destitute, upon application at the *Confederate Court House*, between the hours of *eleven o'clock, A. M. and twelve o'clock, M., daily.* The attention of all charitable persons, who can contribute to the relief of the great want of clothing, experienced by those who suffered in the late conflagration, is particularly invited to this source of suffering.

SHELTER.

The benevolence of several of our citizens has enabled the Committee to provide temporary accommodation for the houseless. Applications for accommodations may be made at the Confederate Court House between the hours of *eleven o'clock, A. M. and twelve M., daily.*

DONATIONS

Of money may be sent to the Bank of Charleston, addressed to J. K. SASS, Esq., Treasurer, or to JOHN CHEESBOROUGH, Esq., Assistant Treasurer.

Of Provisions, may be sent to Mr. COPES' Cotton Press, in Chalmers-street, between Church and State-streets, where they will be received and acknowledged by Z. B. OAKES, Esq.

Of Clothing of all kinds, may be sent to the Theological Library, in Chalmers-street, opposite the Confederate Court House, where several ladies have kindly volunteered to superintend this department, and will receive and acknowledge all contributions.

Committee of Relief under Proclamation of the Mayor.

Wanted, by this Committee, a person to take charge of a large Building, to be appropriated to the shelter of the houseless. Apply to the undersigned at the Committee Rooms, Chalmers-street.

J. K. SASS,
C. R. MILES,
W. C. COURTNEY,
W. J. BENNETT, } Committee,

The daily meeting of the Committee will be held at the Confederate Court House, at 12 o'clock, M.

JAMES M. WILSON, Secretary.

CIRCULAR.

TO THE CLERGY AND LAY MEMBERS OF THE EVANGELICAL LUTHERAN CHURCH, SOUTH:

Dear Brethren:—The publication of a paper, reflective of the sentiments and interests of the Lutheran Church, South, is no longer a matter for speculation, but a thing of primary importance. It is unnecessary to state the reasons which have brought us to this conclusion; they are so apparent, that any attempt at explanation on our part might with great propriety be regarded as a reflection upon your judgment. We all realize that the act of separation between our churches and those of the North has already been effected, and needs but the formal declaration of our respective Synods to render it final and complete. Henceforth, in the great work the Master has commissioned us to do (so far as human instrumentalities are concerned,) we must rely upon ourselves. Let us, therefore, nerve ourselves to the task, and seek to become workmen who need not be ashamed of their labor. Our earliest efforts should, in our judgment, be directed to the establishment of a paper, which might strictly be regarded as the organ of the whole Southern Church, to be ultimately under the management and control of a General Synod. But as some months will probably elapse before such a Synod will be formed, the question presents itself, what are we to do in the interval for a medium of communication between our respective charges and the Church general? To meet this want, and provided it meets with the approval of the brethren generally, the Synod of South Carolina has undertaken the publication of a paper until a General Synod shall have been organized. We now solicit your co-operation in this important work.

PLACE OF PUBLICATION.

The paper is published in Charleston, S. C., which city affords facilities not furnished by any of the other places we might select.

EDITOR.

It is edited by a Committee of Clergymen appointed by our Synod, and whose services are gratuitously bestowed.

SIZE.

In size type, &c., it is made to correspond as nearly as possible with the Lutheran Observer.

NAME AND TERMS.

Its distinctive title is THE SOUTHERN LUTHERAN, and the price of subscription Two Dollars, in advance the amount to be paid upon the receipt of the first number.

It remains for us now but to entreat you, brethren, to sustain us in this undertaking. Let it be the determination of all of us, to cary it forward with becoming energy and spirit, and we will soon have a paper worthy of our Southern Church.

The names of Subscribers, with their Postoffice address, and all remittances of money, will be forwarded to Mr. ROBERT G. CHISOLM, Charleston, S. C.

All other communications will be addressed to "The Southern Lutheran," Key-box No. 52.

Yours in Gospel bonds,

E. B. HORT, *President*,

J. HAWKINS, *Secretary of the Synod of South Carolina and adjacent States*

September 2

The Battle of White Oak Swamp, June 1862

1862

George Brinton McClellan

January 1, Confederate commissioners Mason and Slidell are released and sail for England. ***January 19,*** The Confederate weakness in Kentucky is exposed at the Battle of Mill Springs. ***February 6,*** After being threatened by land and water, Fort Henry, Tennessee surrenders to Union forces. ***February 8,*** Confederate Colonel H.M. Shaw surrenders to General Burnside's superior forces in the Battle of Roanoke Island. ***February 16,*** Confederate General Simon Buckner surrenders Fort Donelson, Tennessee 'unconditionally' to General Ulysses S. Grant, opening Tennessee and the western theater to further Federal successes. ***February 22,*** Jefferson Davis is inaugurated as President of the Confederate States of America. ***February 25,*** Federal troops led by General Don Carlos Buell occupy Nashville, a vital supply base for western operations. ***March 8,*** The Confederates under General Earl Van Dorn are beaten in the Battle of Pea Ridge, Arkansas, the largest battle west of the Mississippi River during the Civil War. ***March 9,*** In an historic naval battle, the Union ironclad *Monitor* fights the Confederate ironclad *Merrimack* (officially the *Virginia*) to a draw, beginning the modern era of naval warfare. ***March 11,*** President Lincoln officially relieves General McClellan as General-in-Chief of the Federal armies, retaining him as commander of the Army of the Potomac. ***April 5,*** In the first major action of McClellan's Peninsular campaign, the Union Army begins the siege of Yorktown, Virginia. ***April 7,*** Confederate General Albert Sidney Johnston is killed at the Battle of Shiloh as the Federals led by General Grant and the Confederates sustain over 23,000 casualties. ***April 25,*** The Federals begin their occupation of New Orleans. ***May 3,*** Yorktown is evacuated by the Confederates. ***May 9,*** Norfolk naval base is evacuated by the Confederates. ***May 11,*** The *Merrimack* is scuttled to prevent her from falling into Union hands. ***May 25,*** Confederate General Thomas 'Stonewall' Jackson defeats a Union army under General Nathaniel Banks at the Battle of Winchester, Virginia in the strategically important Shenandoah Valley. ***June 1,*** General Robert E. Lee takes command of the Confederate Army on the Peninsula. ***June 12,*** Confederate cavalry commander Jeb Stuart begins a four day reconnaissance around the entire Federal Army on the Peninsula. ***July 1,*** The seven days campaign on the Peninsula comes to an end at the Battle of Malvern Hill with McClellan's retreating army making a strong stand against repeated Confederate attacks. ***July 17,*** President Lincoln signs the Confiscation Act, making slaves who support the rebellion free when they come within Union control. ***August 29,*** In one of 'Stonewall' Jackson's finest hours, the Confederates again defeat the Federals at the Second Battle of Bull Run, Virginia. ***September 2,*** General McClellan is restored to full command in Virginia. ***September 4,*** The Army of Northern Virginia led by General Lee, begins an invasion of Maryland. ***September 15,*** The Confederates capture Harpers Ferry. ***September 17,*** The Army of the Potomac repulses the Confederates in the Battle of Antietam, the bloodiest single day of battle during the Civil War. ***October 24,*** Major General William Rosecrans replaces General Buell. ***November 7,*** President Lincoln relieves General McClellan from command, replacing him with General Ambrose E. Burnside. ***December 13,*** Federals attack the Confederates strong defensive positions on Marye's Heights at the Battle of Fredericksburg, Virginia as General Lee remarks, "I wish these people would go away and leave us alone." ***December 15,*** The beaten and demoralized Army of the Potomac withdraws back across the Rappahannock River in the wake of its costly defeat at Fredericksburg. ***December 26,*** Union General Sherman's expedition down the Yazoo River in Mississippi lands near Steel's Bayou in the campaign to take the Confederate stronghold of Vicksburg, Mississippi. As the second year of the war comes to an end, President Lincoln meets with his cabinet to make final adjustments to the Emancipation Proclamation.

Thomas J. 'Stonewall' Jackson

Jeb Stuart

Ambrose E. Burnside

THE NEW YORK HERALD.

WHOLE NO. 9252. NEW YORK, FRIDAY, JANUARY 10, 1862. PRICE TWO CENTS.

NEWS FROM WASHINGTON.

Speech of Mr. Sumner in the Senate on the Trent Affair.

The Position of England and the United States as Regards the Law of the Ocean.

Great Britain Pledged to the Maritime Code of America.

The Secretary of the Navy Roughly Handled in the Senate.

The Financial Operations of Morgan and Cummings Under Consideration.

IMPORTANT ARMY BILLS BEFORE CONGRESS.

Arrival of the Released Prisoners from Richmond,

&c., &c., &c.

WASHINGTON, Jan. 9, 1862.

MR. SUMNER'S SPEECH ON THE TRENT AFFAIR.

The speech of Mr. Sumner in the Senate to-day, on the Trent affair, was a masterly and conclusive exposition of the triumph of American principles as applied to international law. In all his arguments and illustrations he left our respected mother England "out in the cold." He demonstrated that by all other leading European Powers the American doctrine had been recognized and admitted for many years, and that England alone had opposed it. The inconsistency of the present position of England, with her policy in all the past, was admirably illustrated, and the conclusion, that Great Britain is now stopped from any future assertion of her doctrine in reference to the right of visitation and search, was brilliant and effective. The speech was impressively delivered. The galleries of the Senate were densely crowded. Notwithstanding the inclemency of the weather, the ladies' gallery was filled to overflowing. Mrs. Vice President Hamlin and a party of her friends occupied seats in the diplomatic gallery, which was also filled. Secretaries Chase and Cameron occupied seats on the floor of the chamber, where were also the French, Russian, Austrian, Prussian, Danish and Swedish Ministers. Lord Lyons was not present, as etiquette required that he should not be there on such an occasion. The speech was listened to with fixed attention by Senators Bright and Powell and ex-Senator Green. M. Mercier, the French Minister, occupied a seat next to Mr. Bright, and exchanged salutations with Mr. Sumner at the conclusion of the speech, as did also most of the other foreign dignitaries.

Mr. Sumner's speech has created a marked impression on the public in regard to himself. It has removed much prejudice that existed against him, and added greatly to his reputation as a profound statesman. The impression prevailed that, with all his learning, his extraordinary acquirements, and splendid talents, he could not avoid the introduction of his peculiar views in reference to slavery; and on account of the strong anti-slavery proclivities of England hitherto, and the sympathy heretofore from this cause existing between leading English politicians and our own anti-slavery men of Mr. Sumner's class, it was apprehended by many that he would be inclined to lean towards Great Britain in this controversy. His course to-day was, therefore, an agreeable surprise. The absence of any allusion in his speech to the negro question demonstrated his ability and willingness to rise superior to the one idea attributed to him, and the scathing exposition of British inconsistency in regard to the right of search, and the dignified rebuke he administered to England, exhibited his capacity to regard public affairs with the eye of a genuine statesman.

The applause accorded to this really great production is universal and unqualified.

GENERAL STONE AND THE RENDITION OF FUGITIVE SLAVES.

Some three weeks since, it was announced that General Stone, commanding a brigade in General Banks' column, was tickling the rebels by returning fugitive slaves, and that he compelled Massachusetts soldiers in his command to perform that service. This announcement not only aroused the indignation of Governor Andrew, of that State, but that of the Senators and most of the representatives from Massachusetts. Senator Sumner, a few days afterwards, in commenting in his place in the Senate upon the order of Gen. Halleck concerning the disposition of slaves that came within his lines, took occasion to allude to Gen. Stone's course in returning fugitives, the facts concerning which I understand Mr. Sumner fully satisfied himself about. The Senator's notice of Gen. Stone was brief, but pointed. A few days afterwards Senator Sumner received a letter from Gen. Stone, the contents of which are the subject of street comment, and do not reflect creditably upon General Stone, who, it is said, employed language towards the Massachusetts Senator which is characterized by those who have read the letter as being unbecoming a soldier, much less an officer of the distinction and position of General Stone. Mr. Sumner treats the letter with contempt. The whole subject is in the hands of General McClellan at present; but it is the determination of several Senators to bring the subject before the Senate.

DISAGREEMENT BETWEEN GENERAL MANSFIELD AND GENERAL WOOL.

General Mansfield, who is at present in command at Newport News Point, is pressing a demand for removal to some other position, on account of an unpleasant disagreement between himself and General Wool. It appears that on the recent occasion, when a body of the rebels crossed New Market Bridge, General Mansfield went out with a force to repulse them. There was a group of houses on each side of the creek. Those nearest to the federal fortification afforded shelter to our soldiers, and those on the other side were used for protection by the rebels. In the skirmishes that occurred at that point, the rebels in retiring burnt the houses that sheltered our troops, and General Mansfield, to deprive the rebels of the advantage they had, burned those on the other side. For this he was severely censured by Gen. Wool, who, in general orders, characterized the act as a piece of Vandalism. This public censure, for doing what he deemed a duty in exercising a precautionary care for the safety of his troops, has rendered Gen. Mansfield's position peculiarly disagreeable, but his request for a change has not yet been granted.

IMPORTANT ARREST.

Mr. W. T. Smithson, a prominent banker of this city, was arrested yesterday afternoon, upon the charge of treasonable correspondence with the enemy. He is a Virginian, and has never made any secret of his sympathy with the rebels. Many of the leaders of the rebellion were his most intimate associates. He was a prominent and influential member of the Methodist Episcopal church South, and his friends are unwilling to believe that he has been guilty of any improper conduct.

CONDITION OF GENERAL M'CLELLAN AND GENERAL MARCY.

Neither General McClellan nor General Marcy were out to-day, the inclemency of the weather rendering their exposure imprudent.

ALL QUIET ALONG THE LINES.

Everything has been quiet to-day along the lines of the army.

THE REPORTED BATTLE AT ROMNEY.

So far as any conflict or skirmishing with the enemy is concerned, nothing of official of the fight at Romney, announced to-day, has been received at headquarters.

ARRIVAL OF THE PRISONERS FROM RICHMOND.

The Richmond prisoners arrived this afternoon. They will receive their pay, and those enlisted for three years are ordered back to their regiments. They complain that no ration allowance is granted, alleging that they were obliged to expend money to keep themselves from starving.

The prisoners number one hundred and ninety, and were comfortably cared for at the Government Voluntary Receiving House, near the railroad station. Dr. A. Tripp, of Scranton, Penn., is among the arrivals. The remainder of the party either went home after arriving in Baltimore from Old Point, or are detained there at the government hospitals, owing to their wounds breaking out afresh.

THE CONDUCT OF THE WAR COMMITTEE.

The joint committee appointed on the 19th of December, to examine into the conduct of the war, have assiduously applied themselves to that duty. They have been in session nearly every day since, and have obtained much valuable information. Senator Wade, the chairman, is so industriously engaged that he is seldom seen in the Senate, and then only when important votes require his presence.

A BILL TO PUNISH FRAUD AND BRIBERY.

In the House to-day Mr. Harris introduced a bill to prevent fraud in the public service and punish bribery in certain cases. This bill makes it a high misdemeanor, and a subject for indictment in any United States court having criminal jurisdiction, for any one to promise, offer or give, directly or indirectly, anything to any officer or public agent, either before or after his election or appointment, to influence his vote, decision or action in any proceeding, or in the discharge of any duty, or to induce him to neglect or omit the performance of any duty, or to use his influence to procure any appointment or emolument, or allowance, or payment. The penalty fixed is a fine of not less than the value nor more than three times the value of the thing offered or given or accepted, and imprisonment in the penitentiary for not less than one nor more than ten years, and disqualification forever from holding any office under the United States. The same penalty attaches to the officer convicted of receiving any such bribe, and the terms "officer" and "public agent" are made to include all who are performing any service for the United States. The bill also provides that any disbursing officer or agent to make contracts or purchases for the government, who shall directly or indirectly accept a present or reward, shall forfeit his office, and be promptly removed.

AFFAIRS ON THE LOWER POTOMAC.

There is considerable ice in the Potomac, but the iron clad steamer King Philip keeps the communication open. The steamer Stepping Stones came from the lower flotilla, past the batteries, last night, to the flagship of the upper flotilla. Nothing new had occurred down the river. The rebels are thought to be reserving their strength to attack the Pensacola when she goes to sea.

THE ARMY.

Colonel Friedman, of the Cameron Dragoons, received a despatch to-day from Governor Dennison, of Ohio, tendering him the command of a regiment of cavalry, to be assigned to Kentucky.

Robert J. Dallestier was to-day appointed Second Lieutenant in Captain Mott's old battery. He was at Bull run, where he acquitted himself gallantly.

First Lieutenant Stewart, of Captain Mott's battery, who was severely injured some time since at drill, to-day reported himself for duty.

All of Captain Mott's officers have been promoted from the ranks. The Captain is determined to admit of no other appointments if he can help it, and the men under him, knowing this determination, work with a hopeful zeal and courage.

First Lieutenant W. G. Mitchell, of the Forty-ninth Pennsylvania regiment, has been appointed Aid-de-Camp on the staff of Brigadier General Hancock.

PAYMENT OF THE TROOPS.

All the muster rolls are nearly completed, and arrangements about perfected for paying our troops across the Potomac. Major Ritter to day paid off the Forty-third New York Volunteer regiment, Colonel Vinton.

ATTEMPT TO BLOW UP A HOSPITAL AT ALEXANDRIA.

An attempt was last night made to blow up the Mansion House in Alexandria. This was formerly occupied as a hotel, but now as a hospital. A barrel had been secreted in the cellar filled with powder and projectiles, and a fuse was found extending from there to the stable. In proximity to the combustibles lucifer matches and Chinese crackers had been plentifully distributed. The fuse end at the stable had actually ignited; but the act was fortunately discovered by the guard, and the progress of the slow fire extinguished. But for this watchfulness and prompt action, not only would several hundred lives probably have been lost, but other casualties resulted.

NOTICE TO APPLICANTS FOR APPOINTMENTS IN THE NAVY.

Applicants for situations as master's mates in the Navy Yard are required to accompany their papers with recommendations from their last employers, and must have seen three years sea service, and not be over thirty years of age. Acting masters are similarly appointed, with the exception that they must not be over forty years of age.

MONETARY AFFAIRS.

Treasury notes are four per cent discount. Exchange on New York ½ per cent.

THE NEW GRANADIAN MINISTER.

It is implied in a recent publication that General Herran consented to act as Minister of the legitimate government of New Granada when he was made aware that he would not be received as the representative of Mosquera. This is not correct. It well known here that immediately after General Herran's arrival at New York our government was informed that he would proceed to Washington to act on his former credentials, and before any opinion in that respect could have been expressed by our government.

SENATOR BRIGHT NOT TO BE EXPELLED.

The Senate Committee on the Judiciary have come to the conclusion, six to one, to report against the expulsion of Senator Jesse D. Bright, of Indiana, the question involving his loyalty having been referred to them.

THE PRESIDENT AT THE CAPITOL.

The President, accompanied by his private secretaries, was at the room of the Vice President in the Capitol to-day, attending to public business.

NOT A DESERTER.

The name of Mathias Spoo, of the Fifth Wisconsin regiment, appeared among the list of deserters published in the HERALD. General Hancock assures me that Spoo is not a deserter. He was subject to attacks of insanity, and while suffering from one of these attacks is supposed to have wandered outside of our lines and to have been captured by the enemy's pickets. Aside from Spoo and another crazy soldier, who is now in an insane asylum, there has not been a desertion from General Hancock's brigade.

THE UNITED STATES AGRICULTURAL SOCIETY.

The United States Agricultural Society to day re-elected President Hubbard, Secretary Poor, Treasurer French, and nearly all the old Vice Presidents. The Executive Committee was reorganized, and consists of Marshall P. Wilder, of Massachusetts; Fredk. Smyth, of New Hampshire; Isaac Newton, of Philadelphia; Chas. B. Calvert of Maryland; Legrand Byington, of Iowa; J. H. Sullivan, of Ohio, and M. Meyers, of California. President Lincoln's recommendation of the establishment of an agricultural and statistical department was warmly commended, and he was elected an honorary member. The suggestions of the President's address were debated and endorsed, and a large edition was ordered to be printed. The establishment of an agricultural department was discussed and recommended. There was a decided expression of opinion against national exhibitions, unless they can be held at Washington.

THIRTY-SEVENTH CONGRESS.

FIRST SESSION.

Senate.

WASHINGTON, Jan. 9, 1862.

THE DEAD LETTER OFFICE.

Mr. COLLAMER, (rep.) of Vt., from the Post Office Committee, reported back the bill to promote the efficiency of the Dead Letter Office.

The bill provides that all dead letters be returned to the writers instead of being destroyed.

After a long discussion the bill was postponed till to-morrow.

EXPULSION OF WALDO H. JOHNSON, OF MISSOURI.

Mr. TRUMBULL, (rep.) of Ill., reported from the Judiciary Committee in favor of the resolution to expel Waldo H. Johnson, of Missouri.

MILITARY AFFAIRS, ETC.

Mr. WILSON, (rep.) of Mass., reported a bill to provide for the Signal Department of the army.

Also a bill for the organization of the staff of the divisions of the army.

Also a bill to increase the clerical force of the office of the Adjutant General.

Mr. SHERMAN, (rep.) of Ohio, from the Select Committee on Compensation, &c., in the departments, reported a bill.

Also a bill to regulate the compensation of officers of the army.

Mr. COWAN, (rep.) of Pa., presented a petition from the homoeopathic surgeons and physicians employed in the army.

Also a bill in relation to the appointment of chaplains in the army, and to allow Jewish chaplains.

ALLEGED GREAT FRAUDS BY ARMY AND NAVY CONTRACTORS.

Mr. HALE, (rep.) of N. H., presented a petition from citizens of Pennsylvania, which states as follows:—

Whereas, great frauds have been perpetrated on the Treasury by the appointment of Mr. Cummings by Mr. Cameron, and the appointment of Mr. Morgan by Mr. Welles, we therefore ask that a statute be enacted to prevent the appointment of persons without the statute therefor.

PUNISHMENT OF FRAUDS ON THE TREASURY.

Mr. HALE also introduced a bill to punish fraud on the Treasury. The bill provides that any person obtaining money fraudulently be punished with a fine to the amount of money and imprisonment at hard labor for not more than ten years. If any officer of the government do it he be discharged and punished, and ever after held ineligible for any office. Referred.

REPORT OF THE SANITARY COMMISSION.

A communication was received from the War Department transmitting the report of the Sanitary Commission. Referred.

THE TARIFF ON SUGAR AND COFFEE.

The House resolution in regard to bonded coffee and sugar, laid over yesterday, was taken up and passed by yeas 28, nays 15.

SPEECH OF MR. SUMNER ON THE TRENT AFFAIR.

The communication from the Secretary of State in regard to the Trent affair was taken up.

Mr. SUMNER, (rep.) of Mass., said—Mr. President, every principle of international law, when justly and authoritatively settled, becomes a safeguard of peace and a landmark of civilization. It constitutes a part of that code which is the supreme law, above all municipal laws, binding the whole commonwealth of nations. Such a settlement may be by a general congress of nations, as at Munster, Vienna or Paris; or it may be through the general accord of treaties: or it may be by a precedent established under such conspicuous circumstances, with all nations as assenting witnesses, that it shall at once become in itself a commanding rule of international conduct. Especially is this the case, if disturbing pretensions long maintained to the detriment of civilization, are practically renounced by the Power which has maintained them. Without any congress or treaties such a precedent has been established. Such a precedent ought to be considered and understood in its true character. In undertaking to explain it, I shall speak for myself alone; but I shall speak frankly, according to the wise freedom of public debate, and the plain teachings of history on the question involved, trusting sincerely that what I say may contribute something to elevate the honest patriotism of the country, and perhaps secure that tranquil judgment which will render this precedent the herald, if not the guardian, of international harmony. Two old men and two younger associates, recently taken from the British mail packet Trent on the high seas, by order of Captain Wilkes, of the United States Navy, and afterwards detained in custody at Fort Warren, have been liberated, and placed at the disposition of the British government. This has been done at the instance of that government, courteously conveyed, and founded on the assumption that the original capture of these men was an act of violence which was an affront to the British flag and a violation of international law. This is a simple outline of the facts. But in order to appreciate the value of this precedent, there are other matters which must be brought into view. These two old men were citizens of the United States, and for many years Senators. One was the author of the Fugitive Slave bill, and the other was the chief author of the filibustering system, which has disgraced our national name and disturbed our national peace. Occupying places of trust and power in the service of their country, they conspired against it, and at last the secret traitors and conspirators became open rebels. The present rebellion, now surpassing in proportions and also in wickedness any rebellion in history, was from the beginning quickened and promoted by their inspiring energies. That country to which they owed love, honor and obedience, they betrayed and gave over to violence and outrage. Treason, conspiracy and rebellion, each in succession, have acted through them. The incalculable expenditures which now tax our national resources, the untold derangement of affairs, not only at home, but also abroad, the levy of armies almost without an example, the devastation of extended regions of territory, the plunder of peaceful ships on the ocean, and the slaughter of fellow citizens on the murderous battle field—such are some of the consequences proceeding directly from them. To carry forward still further the gigantic crime of which they were so large a part, these two old men, with their two younger associates, stole from Charleston on board a rebel steamer, and, under cover of darkness and storm, running the blockade, and avoiding the cruisers in that neighborhood, succeeded in reaching the neutral island of Cuba, where, with open display and the knowledge of the British Consul, they embarked on board the British mail packet, the Trent, bound for St. Thomas, whence they were to embark for England, in which kingdom one of them was to play the part of embassador of the rebellion, while the other was to play the same part in France. The original treason, conspiracy and rebellion of which they were so heinously guilty, were all continued on this voyage, which became a prolongation of the original crime, destined to still further excess, through their embassadorial pretensions, which, it was hoped, would array two great nations against the United States, and enlist them openly in behalf of an accursed slaveholding rebellion. While on their way the embassadors were arrested by Captain Wilkes, of the United States steamer San Jacinto, an accomplished officer, already well known by his scientific explorations, who, on this occasion, acted without instructions from his government. If, in this arrest, he forgot for a moment the fixed policy of the republic, which has been from the beginning like a frontlet between the eyes, and transcended the law of nations, as the United States have always declared it, his apology must be found in the patriotic impulse by which he was inspired, and the British examples which he could not forget. They were the enemies of his country, embodying in themselves the triple essence of worst enmity—treason, conspiracy and rebellion—and they wore a pretended embassadorial character, which, as he well knew, according to high British authority, rendered them liable to be stopped. If, in the ardor of an honest nature, Captain Wilkes erred, he might well say:—

> Who can be wise, amazed, temperate and furious,
> Loyal and neutral in a moment? No man.
> The expedition of my violent love
> Outran the pauser reason.
> Who could refrain
> That had a heart to love, and in that heart
> Courage to make his love known?

If this transaction be regarded exclusively in the light of British precedents; if we follow the seeming authority of the British Admiralty, speaking by its greatest voice; and especially if we accept the oft repeated example of British cruisers, upheld by the British government against the oft repeated protests of the United States, we shall not find it difficult to vindicate it. The act becomes questionable only when brought to the touchstone of those liberal principles, which, from the earliest times, the American government has openly avowed and sought to advance, and which other European nations have accepted with regard to the sea. Indeed, Great Britain cannot complain except by now adopting those identical principles; and should we undertake to vindicate the act, it can be done only by repudiating those identical principles. Our two cases will be reversed. In the struggle between Laertes and Hamlet, the two combatants exchanged rapiers; so that Hamlet was armed with the rapier of Laertes and Laertes was armed with the rapier of Hamlet. And now on this sensitive question a similar exchange has occurred. Great Britain is armed with American principles, while to us is left only those British principles which, throughout our history, have been constantly, deliberately, and solemnly rejected. Lord Russell, in his despatch to Lord Lyons, communicated to Mr. Seward, contents himself by saying that "it appears that certain individuals have been forcibly taken from on board a British vessel, the ship of a neutral Power, *while such vessel was pursuing a lawful and innocent voyage*—an act of violence which was an affront to the British flag, and a violation of international law." Here is a positive assertion that the ship, notoriously having on board the rebel emissaries, was pursuing a lawful and innocent voyage; but there is no specification of the precise ground on which the act in question is regarded as a violation of international law. Of course it is not an affront, for an accident can never be an affront to an individual or to a nation. But public report, authenticated by the concurring testimony of various authorities, English and Continental, forbids us to continue ignorant of the precise ground on which this act is presented as a violation of international law. It was admitted that a United States man-of-war, meeting a British mail steamer beyond the territorial limits of Great Britain, might subject her to visitation and search; also that the United States ship-of-war might put a prize crew on board the British steamer, and carry her off to a port of the United States for adjudication by a prize court there; but that she would have no right to remove the emissaries, who were not apparently officers in the military or naval service, and carry them off as prisoners, leaving the ship to pursue her voyage. Under the circumstances, in the exercise of a belligerent right, the British steamer, with all on board, might have been captured and carried off; but according to the British law officers, on whose professional opinion the British Cabinet has acted, the whole proceeding was vitiated by the failure to take the packet into port for condemnation. This failure has been the occasion of much unprofessional objurgation; and it has been emphatically repeated that it was impossible to consent that the custody of the individuals in question should be determined by a navy officer on his quarter deck, so as to supersede the adjudication of a prize court. This has been confidently stated by an English writer, assuming to put the case for his government, as follows:—

It is not to the right of search that we object, but to the [illegible] without process of law. What we deny is the right of a naval officer to stand in place of a prize [illegible] judicate, sword in hand, with a sic volo sic jubeo on the very deck which is a part of our territory.

Thus it appears that the present complaint of the British government is not founded on the assumption by the American war steamer of the belligerent right of search; nor on the ground that this right was exercised on board a neutral vessel between two neutral ports; nor that it was exercised on board a mail steamer, sustained by a subvention from the Crown, and officered in part from the royal navy; nor that it was exercised in a case where the penalties of contraband could not attach; but it is founded simply and precisely on the idea that persons other than apparent officers in the military or naval service, cannot be taken out of a neutral ship at the mere will of the officer who exercises the right of search, and without any form of trial. Therefore, the law of nations has been violated, and the conduct of Captain Wilkes must be disavowed, while men, who are traitors, conspirators, and rebels, all in one, are allowed to go free. Surely, that criminals, though dyed in guilt, should go free, is better than that the law of nations should be violated, especially in any rule by which war is restricted and the mood of peace is enlarged; for the law of nations cannot be violated without overturning the protection of the innocent as well as the guilty. On this general principle there can be no question. It is but an illustration of that important maxim, recorded in the Latin of Fortescue, "Better that many guilty should escape than one innocent man should suffer," with this difference, that in the present case a few guilty escape, while the innocent everywhere on the sea obtain new security. And this security becomes more valuable as a triumph of civilization, when it is considered that it was long refused, even at the cannon's mouth. I do not forget, sir, that the question involved in this controversy is *strictly a question of law*—precisely like a question of trespass between two neighbors. The British Cabinet began proceedings by taking the opinion of their law advisers, precisely as an individual begins proceedings in a suit at law by taking the opinion of his attorney. To make such a question *a case of war*, or to suggest that war is a proper mode of deciding it, is simply to revive, in colossal proportions, the exploded ordeal by battle, and to imitate those dark ages when such proceeding was openly declared to be the best and most honorable mode of deciding even an abstract point of law. "It was a matter of doubt and dispute," says an early historian, "whether the sons of a son ought to be reckoned among the children of the family, and succeed equally with their uncles, if their father happened to die while their grandfather was alive. An assembly was called to deliberate on this point, and it was the general opinion that it ought to be remitted to the examination and decision of judges. But the Emperor, following a better course, and desirous of dealing honorably with his people and nobles, appointed the matter to be decided by battle between two champions." In similar spirit has it been latterly proposed, amidst the amazement of the civilized world, to withdraw the point of law now raised by Great Britain, from peaceful adjudication and submit it to trial by combat. But the irrational anachronism of such a proposition becomes more flagrant from the inconsistency of the party which makes it; for it cannot be forgotten that in times past, *on this identical point of law*, Great Britain persistently held an opposite ground from that which she now takes. The British complaint seems to have been narrowed down to a single point; but it is not to be disguised that there are yet other points on which, had the ship been carried into port for adjudication, controversy must have arisen. Not to omit anything important, let me say that the three following points, among others, have been presented in the case:—

1. That the seizure of the rebel emissaries without taking the ship into port, was wrong, *inasmuch as a navy officer is not entitled to substitute himself for a judicial tribunal.*

2. That had the ship been carried into port, it would not have been liable on account of the rebel emissaries, inasmuch as neutral ships are free to carry all persons not apparently in the military or naval service of the enemy.

3. Are despatches contraband of war, so as to render the ship liable to seizure?

These matters I shall consider in their order, giving special attention to the first, which is the pivot of the British complaint. If in this discussion I shall expose grievances which it were better to forget, be assured it is from no willingness to awaken the slumbering animosities they once so justly aroused, but simply to exhibit the proud position on this question which the United States early and constantly maintained. A question of international law should not be presented on any more argumentum ad hominem. It would be of little value to show that Captain Wilkes was sustained by British authority and practice, if he were condemned by international law as interpreted by his own country. It belongs to us now—nay, let it be our pride, at any cost of individual prepossessions or transitory prejudices, to uphold that law in all its force, as it was often declared by the best men in our history, and illustrated by national acts; and let us seize the present occasion to consecrate its positive and unequivocal recognition. In exchange for the prisoners set free, we receive from Great Britain a practical assent, too long deferred, to a principle early propounded by our country, and standing forth on every page of our history. The same voice which asks for their liberation, renounces in the same breath an odious pretension, for whole generations the scourge of peaceful commerce. Great Britain throughout her municipal history has practically contributed to the establishment of freedom beyond all other nations. There are at least seven institutions or principles which she has given to civilization: first, the trial by jury; secondly, the writ of habeas corpus; thirdly, the freedom of the press; fourthly, bills of rights; fifthly, the representative system; sixthly, the rules and orders of debate, constituting parliamentary law; and seventhly, the principle that the air is too pure for a slave to breathe—long ago declared and first made a reality by British law. No other nation can show such peaceful triumphs. But while thus entitled to our gratitude for glorious contributions to municipal law, we turn with dissent and sorrow from much which she has sought to fasten upon international law. In municipal questions Great Britain drew inspiration from her own native common law, which was instinct with freedom; but especially in maritime questions arising under the law of nations this Power seems to have acted on that obnoxious principle of the Roman law, positively discarded in municipal questions, *Quod principi placuit legis vigorem habet*, and too often, under this inspiration, to have imposed upon weaker nations her own arbitrary will. The time has been when she pretended to sovereignty over the seas surrounding the British isles, as far as Cape Finisterre to the south and Vanstaten, in Norway, to the north. But, driven from this pretension, other pretensions, less local, but hardly less offensive, were avowed. The boast of "Rule, Britannia, rule the waves," was practically adopted by British courts of admiralty, and universal maritime rights were subjected to the special exigencies of British interests. In the consciousness of strength, and with a navy that could not be opposed, this Power has put claims upon the sea. The commerce of the United States, as it began to whiten the ocean, was cruelly decimated by these arbitrary pretensions. American ships and cargoes, while, in the language of Lord Russell, "pursuing a lawful and innocent voyage," suffered from the British admiralty courts more than from rock or tempest. Shipwreck was less frequent than confiscation; and when it came, it was easier to bear. But the loss of property, stung less than the outrage of impressment, by which foreigners, under the protection of the American flag, and also American citizens, without any form of trial, and at the mere mandate of a navy officer, who for the moment acted as a judicial tribunal, were dragged away from the deck which should have been to them a sacred altar. This outrage, which was feebly vindicated by the municipal claims of Great Britain to the services of her own subjects, was enforced arrogantly and perpetually on the high seas, where municipal law is silent and international law alone prevails. The belligerent right of search, derived from international law, was employed for this purpose, and the quarter-deck of every British cruiser was made a floating judgment seat. The practice began early and was continued constantly; nor did it discriminate among its victims. It is mentioned by Mr. Jefferson, and repeated by a British writer on international law, that two nephews of Washington, on their way home from Europe, were ravished from the protection of the American flag, without any judicial proceedings, and placed as common seamen under the ordinary discipline of British ships-of-war. The victims were counted by thousands. Lord Castlereagh himself admitted, on the floor of the House of Commons, that an inquiry instituted by the British government had discovered in the British fleet three thousand five hundred men claiming to be impressed Americans. At our Department of State six thousand cases were recorded, and it was estimated that at least as many more might have occurred, of which no information had been received. Thus, according to this official admission of the British Minister, there was reason to believe that the quarter-deck of a British man-of-war had been made a floating judgment seat three thousand five hundred times, while, according to the records of our own State Department, it had been made a floating judgment seat six thousand times and upwards, and each time an American citizen had been taken from the protection of his flag without any form of trial known to the law. If a pretension so intrinsically lawless could be sanctioned by precedent, Great Britain would have succeeded in incorporating it into the law of nations. Protest, argument, negotiation, correspondence, and war itself—unhappily the last reason of republics as of kings—were all employed in vain by the United States to procure a renunciation of this intolerable pretension. The ablest papers in our diplomatic history are devoted to this purpose, and the only serious war in which we have been engaged, until summoned to encounter this rebellion, was to overcome by arms this very pretension which would not yield to reason. Beginning in the last century, the correspondence is at last closed by the recent reply of Mr. Seward to Lord Lyons. The long-continued discussion of conflict is now happily removed, and the pretension disappears forever—to take its place among the curiosities of the past. But I do not content myself with asserting the persistent opposition of the American government. It belongs to the argument, that I should exhibit this opposition and the precise ground on which it was placed—being identical with that now adopted by Great Britain. And here the testimony is complete. If you will kindly follow me, you shall see it from the beginning in the public life of our country, and in the authentic records of our government. This British pretension [illegible] startled the administration of Washington, and [illegible] Mr. Jefferson, his Secretary of State, was enlisted against it. In a letter to Thomas Pinckney, our Minister at London, dated June 11, 1792, he said:—

The simplest rule will be that the vessel being American shall be evidence that the seamen on board her are such.

In another letter to the same Minister, dated October 12, 1792, he calls attention to a case of special outrage, as follows:—

I enclose you a copy of a letter from Messrs. Blow and Melhado, merchants of Virginia, complaining of the taking away of their sailors on the coast of Africa by the commander of a British armed vessel. So many instances of this kind have happened that it is quite necessary that their government should explain themselves on the subject, and be led to disavow and punish such conduct.—State Papers, vol. 1, p. 876.

The same British pretension was put forth under the administration of John Adams, and was again encountered. Mr. Pickering, at that time Secretary of State, in a letter to Rufus King, our Minister at London, dated June 8, 1796, after repeating the rule proposed by Mr. Jefferson, says:—

But it will be an important point gained, *if on the high seas our flag can protect those of whatever nation who shall sail under it.* And for this humanity, as well as interest, powerfully plead.—*State Papers, vol. 2, p. 874.*

And again, at a later day, during the same administration, Mr. Marshall, afterwards the venerated Chief Justice of the United States, and at the time Secretary of State, in his instructions to Rufus King, at London, dated September 20, 1800, says:—

The impressment of our seamen is an injury of very serious magnitude, which deeply affects the feelings and the honor of the nation. * * * * Alien seamen, not British subjects, engaged in our merchant service, ought to be equally exempt with citizens. Britain has no pretext of right to their persons or to their service. *To tear them from our possession is at the same time an insult and an injury.* It is an act of violence for which there exists no palliative.—*State Papers, vol. 2, p. 489.*

The same British pretension showed itself constantly under the administration of Mr. Jefferson. Throughout the eight years of his Presidency the repeated outrages of British cruisers never for a moment allowed it to be forgotten. Mr. Madison during this full period was Secretary of State, and none of the varied productions of his pen are more masterly than those in which he exposed the tyranny of this pretension. In the course of this discussion he showed the special hardship found in the fact that the sailors were taken from the ship at the mere will of an officer, without any form of judicial proceedings, and thus early presented against the pretension of Great Britain the precise objection which is now adopted by her. Here are his emphatic words, in his celebrated instructions to Mr. Monroe, at that time our Minister at London, dated January 5, 1804:—

Taking reason and justice for the tests of this practice, *it is peculiarly indefensible, because it deprives the dearest rights of persons of a regular trial*, to which the most inconsiderable article of property captured on the high seas is entitled, and *leaves the destiny* to the will of an officer, sometimes cruel often ignorant, and generally interested, by want of manners, in his own decisions. Whenever property found in a neutral vessel is supposed to be liable, on any ground, to capture and condemnation, the rule in all cases is, that the question shall not be decided by the captor, but be carried before a legal tribunal, where a regular trial may be had, and where the captor himself is liable to damages for an abuse of his power. Can it be reasonable, then, or just, that a belligerent commander who is thus restricted, and thus responsible in a case of mere property of trivial amount, should be permitted, *without recurring to any tribunal whatever, to examine the crew of a neutral vessel, to decide the important question of their respective allegiances*, and to carry that decision into execution by forcing every individual he may choose into a service abhorrent to his feelings, cutting him off from his most tender connections, exposing his mind and his person to the most humiliating discipline, and his life itself to the greatest danger? Reason, justice and humanity unite in protesting against so extravagant a proceeding.—*State Papers, vol. 3, p. 84.*

Negotiations, on this principle, thus distinctly declared, were intrusted at London to James Monroe, afterwards President of the United States, and to William Pinckney, the most accomplished master of prize law which our country has produced. But they were unsuccessful. Great Britain persisted. In a joint letter dated at London, September 11, 1806, the plenipotentiaries say:—

That it was impossible that we should acknowledge in favor of any foreign Power *the claim to such jurisdiction on board our vessels* found upon the main ocean, *as this sort of impressment implied*—a claim as plainly inadmissible in its principle, and derogating from the unquestionable rights of our sovereignty, as it was vexatious in its practical consequences.—*State Papers, vol. 3, p. 134.*

In another joint letter dated at London, November 11, 1806, the same plenipotentiaries say:—

The right was denied by the British commissioners, who *asserted that of their government to seize the subjects on board neutral merchant vessels on the high seas*, and who also urged that the relinquishment of it at this time would go far to the overthrow of their naval power, on which the safety of the State essentially depended.—*State Papers, vol. 3, p. 123.*

In still another letter, dated at London, April 22, 1807, Messrs. Monroe and Pinkney say of the British commissioners:—

They stated that the prejudice of the navy and of the country generally was so strongly *in favor of their pretension* that the ministry could not encounter it in a direct form; and that in truth the support of Parliament could not have been relied on in such a case.—*State Papers, vol. 3, p. 160.*

The British commissioners were two excellent persons—Lord Holland and Lord Auckland; but though friendly to the United States in their declarations, and liberals in politics, they were powerless. At home, in the United States, the question continued to be discussed by able writers. Among those whose opinions were of the highest authority, was the late President, John Adams, who, from his retirement at Quincy, sent forth a pamphlet dated January 9, 1809, in which the British pretension was touched to the quick; and again the precise objection was presented which is now urged by Great Britain. Depicting the scene when one of our ships is encountered by a British cruiser, he says:—

The lieutenant is to be the judge, the midshipman is to be clerk, and the boatswain sheriff or marshal. * * * * It is impossible to figure to ourselves, in imagination, this solemn tribunal and venerable judge without smiling, till the humiliation of our country comes into our thoughts and interrupts the sense of ridicule by the tears of grief or vengeance.—*John Adams' Works, vol. 9, p. 322.*

At last all redress through negotiation was found to be impossible; and this pretension, aggravated into multitudinous tyranny, was openly announced to be one of the principal reasons for the declaration of war against Great Britain in 1812. In his message to Congress, dated June 1, of that year, Mr. Madison, who was now President, thus exposed the offensive character of the pretension; and his words, directed against a persistent practice, are now echoed by Great Britain, in the single instance which has accidentally occurred:—

Could the seizure of British subjects in such cases be regarded as within the exercise of a belligerent right, the acknowledged laws of war, which forbid an article of captured property to be adjudged without a regular investigation before a competent tribunal, *would imperiously demand the fairest trial where the sacred rights of persons were at issue. In place of such a trial, these rights are subjected to the will of every petty commander.*—*Statesman's Manual, vol. 1, p. 294.*

While the war was waging the subject was still discussed. Mr. Grundy, in the House of Representatives, in a report from the Committee on Foreign Affairs, said:—

A sub-lieutenant or any other officer of the British Navy ought not to be arbiter in such a case. The liberties and lives of American citizens ought not to depend on the will of such a party.—*State Papers, vol. 3, p. 605.*

Such was the American ground. The British pretension was unhesitatingly proclaimed in the declaration of the Prince Regent, afterwards George IV., given at the palace of Westminster, January 9, 1813:—

The President of the United States has, it is true, since proposed to Great Britain an armistice; not, however, on the admission that the cause of war hitherto relied on was removed; but on condition that Great Britain, as a preliminary step, should do away a cause of war now brought forward as such for the first time—namely, that *she should abandon the exercise of her UNDOUBTED RIGHT of search to take from American merchant vessels British seamen, the natural born subjects of his Majesty.*

His royal Highness can never admit that, in the exercise of the *undoubted and hitherto undisputed right of searching neutral merchant vessels in time of war, the impressment of British seamen*, when found therein, *can be deemed any violation of a neutral flag.* Neither can he admit that the taking of such seamen from on board such vessels *can be considered by any neutral State as a hostile measure or a justifiable cause of war.*

The war was closed by the treaty at Ghent; but, perversely the British pretension was not renounced. Other negotiations in 1818, under President Monroe; in 1823, also under Monroe; and again in 1827, under John Quincy Adams, expressly to procure its renunciation, were all unavailing. At last, in 1842, at the treaty of Washington, Mr. Webster, calmly setting aside all idea of further negotiation on this pretension, and without even proposing any stipulation with regard to it, deliberately announced the principle irrevocably adopted by our government. It was the principle early announced at the beginning of the republic by Mr. Jefferson. This despatch is one of the most memorable in our history, and it bears directly on the existing controversy when, in exposing the British pretension, it says:—

But the lieutenant of a man-of-war, having necessity for men, *is apt to be a summary judge*, and his decisions will be quite as significant of his own wants and his own power as of the truth and justice of the case.—*Webster's Works, vol. 6, p. 323.*

At a later day still, on the very eve of recent events, we find General Cass, as Secretary of State, in his elaborate instructions to our Ministers in Europe, dated 27th June, 1859, declaring principles which may properly control the present question. He says:—

It is obvious, from the temper of the age, that the present is no safe time to assert and enforce pretensions on the part of belligerent Powers affecting the interests of nations at peace, *unless such pretensions are clearly justified by the law of nations.* * * * * * * * The stopping of neutral vessels upon the high seas, their forcible entrance, and the overhauling and examination of their cargoes, the seizure of their freight, *at the will of a foreign officer*, the frequent interruption of their voyages by compelling them to change their destination, in order to seek redress; and, *above all, the abuses which are so prone to accompany the exercise of unlimited power*, where responsibility is remote; these are, indeed, serious obstructions, little likely to be submitted to in the present state of the world without a formidable effort to prevent them.

Such is an authentic history of this British pretension, and of the manner in which it has been met by our government. And now the special argument formerly directed by us against this pretension is directed by Great Britain against the pretension of Captain Wilkes to take two rebel emissaries from a British packet ship. If Captain Wilkes is right in this pretension, then throughout all these international debates, extending over at least two generations, we have been wrong. But it has been sometimes said the steam packet having on board the rebel emissaries was on this account liable to capture, and therefore the error of Captain Wilkes in taking the emissaries was simply an error of form and not of substance. I do not stop to consider whether an exercise of summary power against which our government has so constantly protested can be under any circumstances an error merely of form; for the policy of our government, most positively declared in its diplomacy, and also attested in numerous treaties, leaves no room to doubt that a neutral ship with belligerent passengers—not in the military or naval service—is not liable to capture, and therefore the whole proceeding was wrong, not only because the passengers were taken from the ship, but also because the ship, however guilty morally, was not guilty legally in receiving such passengers on board. If this question were argued on English authorities it might be otherwise; but, according to American principles, the ship was legally innocent. Of course, I say nothing of the moral guilt forever indelible in that ship. In the middle of the last century, the Swiss professor, Vattel, declared that on the breaking out of war we *cease to be under any obligation of leaving the enemy to the free enjoyment of his rights*, and the principle he applied loosely to the transit of ambassadors. (Vattel, book 4, cap. 7, sec. 85.) Sir William Scott, quoting this authority, at the beginning of the present century, let fall these words:—

The belligerent may stop the ambassador of the enemy on his passage.—*The Atalanta, 6 Robinson R., p. 440.*

And this curt proposition, though in some respects indefinite, has been often repeated since by writers on the law of nations. On its face it leaves the question unsettled, whether the emissaries of an unrecognized government can be stopped. But there is another case in which the same British judge, who has done so much to illustrate international law, has used language which seems to embrace not only authentic embassadors, but also pretenders to this character, and all others who are public agents of the enemy. Says this eminent magistrate:—

It appears to me on *principle* to be but reasonable that whenever it is of sufficient importance to the enemy that *such persons should be sent out on the public service and at the public expense*, it should afford equal ground of forfeiture against the vessel that may be let out for a purpose so intimately connected with hostile operations.—*The Orozembo, 1. Robinson R., p. 434.*

Admit that the emissaries of an unrecognized government cannot be recognized as embassadors with the liabilities as well as immunities of this character, yet, in the face of these words it is difficult to see how a government bowing habitually to the authority of Sir William Scott, and regarding our rebels as "belligerents," can assert that a steam packet, conveying emissaries from these belligerents, "sent out on the public service and at the public expense," was, according to the language of Lord Russell, "pursuing a lawful and innocent voyage." At least, in this assertion, this government seems to turn its back again upon its own history; or it sets aside the facts so openly boasted with regard to the public character of these fugitives. On this question British policy may change with circumstances, and British precedents may be uncertain, but the original American policy is unchangeable, and the American precedents which illustrate it are solemn treaties. The words of Vattel, and the judgments of Sir William Scott, were well known to the statesmen of the United States; and yet, in the face of these authorities, which have entered so largely into this debate, the American government at an early day deliberately adopted a contrary policy, to which, for half a century, it has steadily adhered. It was plainly declared that *only soldiers or officers could be stopped*, thus positively excluding the idea of stopping embassadors, or emissaries of any kind, not in the military or naval service. Mr. Madison, who more than any other person shaped our national policy on maritime rights, has stated it on this question. In his remarkable despatch to Mr. Monroe, at London, dated January 5, 1804, he says:—

The article renounces the claim to take from the vessels of the neutral party, on the high seas, any person whatever *not in the military service of an enemy*, an exception which we admit to come within the law of nations, on the subject of contraband of war. *With this exception, we consider a neutral flag on the high seas as a safeguard to those sailing under it.*—*State Papers, vol. 3, p. 83.*

Then again, in the same despatch, Mr. Madison says:—

Great Britain, then, must produce an exception to the law of nations in favor of the right she contends for. In what written and received authority will she find it? In what usage except her own will it be found? * * * * But nowhere will she find an exception to this freedom of the seas and of neutral flags, which justifies the taking away of any person, *not an enemy in military service*, found on board a neutral vessel.—*Ibid., p. 84.*

And then, again, in the same despatch, he says:—

Whenever a belligerent claim against persons on board a neutral vessel is referred to in treaties, *enemies in military service* alone are excepted from the general immunity of persons in that situation; and *this exception confirms the immunity of those who are not included in it.*—*Ibid., p. 86.*

It was in pursuance of this principle, thus clearly announced and repeated, that Mr. Madison instructed Mr. Monroe to propose a convention between the United States and Great Britain, containing the following stipulation:—

No person whatever shall, upon the high seas and without the jurisdiction of either party, be demanded or taken out of any ship or vessel belonging to citizens or subjects of one of the parties, by the public or private armed ships belonging to or in the service of the other, *unless such person be at the time in the military service of an enemy of such other party.*—*Ibid., p. 82.*

Mr. Monroe pressed this stipulation most earnestly upon the British government; but though treated courteously, he could get no satisfaction with regard to it. Lord Harrowby, the Foreign Secretary, in one of his conversations, "expressed a concern to find the United States opposed to Great Britain on certain great neutral questions in favor of the doctrines of the modern law, which he termed *novelties*." (State Papers, vol. 3, p. 99.) And Lord Mulgrave, who succeeded this accomplished nobleman, persevered in the same dissent. Mr. Monroe writes, under date of 18th of October, 1805:—

On a review of the conduct of this government towards the United States I am inclined to think that the delay which has been so studiously sought is part of a system, and that it is intended, as circumstances favor, to subject our commerce at present and hereafter to every restraint in their power.—*State Papers, vol. 3, p. 107.*

Afterwards Mr. Monroe was joined by Mr. Pinkney in the mission to London, and the two united in presenting this same proposition again to the British government. (State Papers, vol. 3, p. 137.) It was rejected, although the ministry of Mr. Fox, who was then in power, seems to have afforded at one time the expectation of an agreement. While these distinguished plenipotentiaries were pressing this principle at London, Mr. Madison was maintaining it at home. In an unpublished communication to Mr. Merry, the British Minister at Washington, bearing date 9th April, 1806, which I extract from the files of the State Department, he declared:—

The United States cannot accede to the claim of any nation to take from their vessels on the high seas *any description of persons, except soldiers in the actual service of the enemy.*

In a reply, bearing date 12th April, 1805, this principle was positively repudiated by the British Minister—so that the two governments were ranged unequivocally on opposite sides. The treaties of the United States with foreign nations are in harmony with this principle so energetically proposed and upheld by Mr. Madison. In the treaty of commerce with France, in 1778, it is expressly provided that:—

Enemies to both or either party are not to be taken out of the said ships, *unless they are soldiers and in actual service of the enemies.*—*Statutes at Large, vol. 8, p. 26.*

In the treaty with the Netherlands, in 1782, the exception is confined to "military men actually in the service of an enemy." (Ibid., p. 38.) and this same exception will also be found in the treaty with Sweden, in 1783, (Ibid., p. 64,) with Prussia, in 1785, (Ibid., p. 90,) with Spain, in 1795, (Ibid., p. 146,) with France, in 1800, (Ibid., p. 184,) with Columbia, in 1824, (Ibid., p. 312,) with Central America, in 1825, (Ibid., p. 328,) with Brazil, in 1828, (Ibid., p. [illegible]) with Mexico, in 1831, (Ibid., p. 416,) with Chile, in 1832, (Ibid., p. 436,) with Venezuela, in 1836, (Ibid., p. [illegible]) with Peru Bolivia, in 1836, (Ibid., p. [illegible], with Ecuador, in 1839, (Ibid., p. 540,) with New Granada, in 1846, (Statutes vol. 9, p. 888,) with Guatemala, in 1849, (Statutes vol. 10, p. 880,) with San Salvador, in 1850, (Ibid., p. [illegible]) and in the treaty with Peru, in 1851, (Ibid., p. 936.) Such is the unbroken testimony, in the most solemn form, to the policy of our government. In some of the treaties the exception is simply [illegible] the stipulation [illegible] "officers or soldiers." It is true that among these treaties there is none with Great Britain [illegible], that this is simply because this [illegible] not its assent when this principle was [illegible] by our government as an undoubted part of international law which it desired to confirm by treaty. Clearly and beyond all question, according to American principles and practice, the ship was not liable to capture on account of the presence of enemies, "not soldiers or officers;" nor could such [illegible] be legally taken from the ship. But the completeness of this authority is increased by the concurring testimony of the Continent of Europe. Since the [illegible] in 1813, the policy of the continental States [illegible] to sanction the removal of enemies from a neutral ship, unless military men in active service, and now, since this debate has commenced, we are [illegible] positive testimony of the French government to the same principle, given with special reference to the present case. M. Thouvenel, the Minister of the Emperor for Foreign Affairs, in a recent letter to Mr. Seward, published with the papers now before the Senate, earnestly insists that the rebel emissaries, not being military persons actually in the service of the enemy, were not subject to seizure on board a neutral ship. I leave this part of the subject with the remark that it is Great Britain alone whose position on this question can be brought into doubt.

But still another question occurs. Beyond all question, there were despatches from the rebel belligerents on board the ship—such "despatches" as rebels can write. Public report the statement of persons on board the ship, and the boastful declaration of Jefferson Davis in a public document, that those emissaries were proceeding under an appointment from him—which appointment would be a "despatch" of the highest character—seem to place this fact beyond denial. Assuming this fact, the ship was liable to capture and to be carried off for adjudication, according to British authorities; unless the positive judgment of Sir William Scott in the case of the Atalanta (6 Robinson R., p. 440), and also the Queen's Proclamation at the commencement of this rebellion, where "despatches" are enumerated among contraband [illegible] are treated as nullities, or so far modified in their application as to be words, and nothing more. But however [illegible] and peremptory these authorities may be in Great Britain, they cannot be accepted to reverse the standing [illegible] of the United States, which here again leaves no [illegible] doubt. In order to give precision to the rights which [illegible] claimed and at the same time accorded on the ocean [illegible] government has sought to explain in treaties what it [illegible] contraband. As early as 1778, in the treaty with [illegible], after specifying contraband articles, without mentioning despatches, it is declared that:—

Free goods are all other merchandise and things which are not comprehended and particularly mentioned in the foregoing enumeration of contraband goods.—*Statutes at Large, vol. 8, p. 16.*

In other treaties, subsequent to the judgment of Sir William Scott, recognizing despatches as contraband, and therefore practically discarding it, after enumerating contraband articles, without specifying "despatches," the following provision is introduced:—

All other merchandise and things not comprehended in the articles of contraband explicitly enumerated and classified as above, shall be held and considered as free.—*Ibid., p. 313; Treaty with Columbia and later treaties passim.*

Thus we have not only positive words of enumeration, without mentioning "despatches," but also positive words of exclusion, so that despatches cannot be considered as contraband. These treaties constitute the conclusive record of our government on this question. And here let me remark that while decisions of British Admiralty Courts on all these matters are freely cited, no decisions of our Supreme Court are cited. Of course, if any existed, they would be of the highest value. But there are none, and the reason is obvious. These matters could not arise before our Supreme Court, because under our government they are so clearly settled by treaties and diplomacy as to be beyond question. Clearly, then, and beyond all question, according to American principles and practice, the ship was not liable to capture on account of despatches on board. And here again we have the concurring testimony of continental Europe, and especially of the French government, in the recent letter of M. Thouvenel.

[CONTINUED ON EIGHTH PAGE.]

DAILY DISPATCH.

VOL. XXI.—NO 14. RICHMOND, VIRGINIA, THURSDAY MORNING, JANUARY 16, 1862. PRICE TWO CENTS.

Richmond Dispatch.

BY COWARDIN & HAMMERSLEY.

THE DAILY DISPATCH is served to subscribers at TWELVE CENTS PER WEEK, payable to the Carrier weekly. Price for mailing, $5 a year, or $3 for six months in advance.

THE SEMI-WEEKLY DISPATCH is issued on TUESDAY and FRIDAY at $3, in advance.

THE WEEKLY DISPATCH is issued every FRIDAY, and mailed to subscribers at $2 per annum.

GROCERIES, LIQUORS, &c.

NEW CROP NEW ORLEANS SUGARS, TOBACCO, CIGARS, &c.

70 Hhds. strictly prime New Orleans and Clarified sugars.

500 boxes low-priced, medium, and strictly prime quality Tobaccos, of the most approved brands.

25,000 Havana and German Cigars. [illegible]

We invite the attention of our friends and the public generally, visiting this market.

[illegible] & DOUGLASS, 13th st., Bet. Main and Cary, Richmond.

FAMILY STORES. [illegible]

MINNIS & CO., 23 and Main sts.

SUNDRIES. [illegible]

SALT. [illegible] MINNIS & CO.

CONFEDERATE MILLS. [illegible]

JUST ARRIVED. [illegible] E. W. PIERCE & CO., Corner Cary and 13th sts.

115 BOXES TALLOW CANDLES. [illegible] TYLER & SON, 1st Cary street.

LIQUORS, GROCERIES, &c. [illegible] THOMAS JONES, No. 8 Main st., Richmond, Va.

2,200 PAIRS MEN'S SHOES. [illegible] GROUND ALUM SALT. For sale by CONRAD & CREW.

COFFEE. We have for sale, a few bags of prime RIO COFFEE. JOHNSON, YOUNGER & OTEY, 15 Pearl street.

CASTILE SOAP.—140 boxes pure CASTILE SOAP, of recent importation. Just received and in store. For sale by BACON & BASKERVILL.

ALE, PORTER, &c. [illegible] S. WOLFF, New Orleans, La.

J. S. ROBERTSON, Corner Governor and Franklin sts., Richmond, Va. [illegible] FAMILY GROCERIES, AND FINE LIQUORS, AND CIGARS. [illegible]

CRUSHED SUGARS. [illegible] KENT, PAINE & CO.

OYSTERS, &c.

JOHNSON & WHITE, OYSTER DEALERS. [illegible]

YORK RIVER OYSTER HOUSE. [illegible]

THIRTY HORSE POWER STEAM ENGINE AND OTHER MACHINERY. [illegible] WM. B. GREEN. [illegible] RICH'D V. GAINES.

[illegible] DAVIS & HUTCHESON, JNO. O. JOHNSON, J. K. RIX.

Richmond Dispatch.

THURSDAY MORNING.....JAN. 16, 1862.

List of the General Officers in the Armies of the Confederate States.

The following interesting statistics of the Confederate Army organization are due to one of the Richmond correspondents of the *Courier*. In the list of Brigadier-Generals in the Provisional Army, the regular order of appointment is perhaps not always observed, but we believe the list is otherwise correct. The dates of graduation from West Point are taken from Gardner's Dictionary of the United States Army:

GENERALS IN THE REGULAR ARMY.

1. Samuel Cooper, Virginia, Adjutant-General.
2. Albert S. Johnston, Texas, commanding in Kentucky.
3. Joseph E. Johnston, Virginia, commanding Northern Virginia.
4. Robert E. Lee, Virginia, commanding South Atlantic coast.
5. P. G. T. Beauregard, Louisiana, commanding Army of Potomac.

Major-Generals in the Provisional Army.

1. *David E. Twiggs, Georgia, resigned.
2. Leonidas Polk, Louisiana, Commanding at Memphis.
3. Braxton Bragg, Louisiana, Commanding at Pensacola.
4. Earl Van Dorn, Mississippi, Army of Potomac.
5. Gustavus W. Smith, Kentucky, Army of Potomac.
6. Theophilus H. Holmes, North Carolina, Army of Potomac.
7. William J. Hardee, Georgia, Missouri.
8. Benjamin Huger, South Carolina, Commanding at Norfolk.
9. James Longstreet, Alabama, Army of Potomac.
10. John B. Magruder, Virginia, Commanding at Yorktown.
11. Thomas J. Jackson, Virginia, Commanding Northwestern Virginia.
12. Mansfield Lovell, Virginia, Commanding Coast of Louisiana.
13. Edmund Kirby Smith, Florida Army of Potomac.
14. George B. Crittenden, Kentucky, Commanding East Tennessee.

Brigadier-Generals in the Provisional Army.

1. Milledge L. Bonham, South Carolina, Army of Potomac.
2. John B. Floyd, Virginia, Commanding Army Kanawha.
3. Henry A. Wise, Virginia, waiting orders.
4. Ben McCulloch, Texas, Missouri.
5. *Henry R. Jackson, Georgia, resigned.
6. *Robert S. Garnett, Virginia, killed in action.
7. *William H. T. Walker, Georgia, resigned.
8. *Barnard E. Bee, South Carolina, killed in action.
9. Alexander R. Lawton, Georgia, Commanding Coast of Georgia.
10. *Gideon J. Pillow, Tennessee, Kentucky.
11. Samuel R. Anderson, Tennessee, Kentucky.
12. Daniel S. Donelson, Tennessee, Coast of South Carolina.
13. David R. Jones, South Carolina, Army of Potomac.
14. Jones M. Withers, Alabama, Commanding Coast of Alabama.
15. John C. Pemberton, Virginia, Coast of South Carolina.
16. Richard S. Ewell, Virginia, Army of Potomac.
17. John H. Winder, Maryland, Richmond.
18. Jubal A. Early, Virginia, Army of Potomac.
19. Thomas B. Flournoy, Arkansas, died in Arkansas.
20. Samuel Jones, Virginia, Army of Potomac.
21. Arnold Elzey, Maryland, Army of Potomac.
22. Daniel H. Hill, North Carolina, Army of Potomac.
23. Henry H. Sibley, Louisiana, Texas Frontier.
24. William H. C. Whiting, Georgia, Army of Potomac.
25. William W. Loring, North Carolina, Western Virginia.
26. Richard H. Anderson, South Carolina, Pensacola.
27. Albert Pike, Arkansas, Indian Commissioner.
28. *Thomas T. Fauntleroy, Virginia, resigned.
29. Robert Toombs, Georgia, Army of Potomac.
30. Daniel Ruggles, Virginia, Louisiana.
31. Charles Clark, Mississippi, Army of Potomac.
32. Roswell S. Ripley, South Carolina, Coast of South Carolina.
33. Isaac R. Trimble, Maryland, Army of Potomac.
34. *John B. Grayson, Kentucky, died in Florida.
35. Paul O. Hebert, Louisiana, Coast of Texas.
36. Richard C. Gatlin, North Carolina, Commanding Coast of North Carolina.
37. Felix K. Zollicoffer, Tennessee, Eastern Kentucky.
38. Benjamin F. Cheatham, Tennessee, Kentucky.
39. Joseph R. Anderson, Virginia, Coast North Carolina.
40. Simon B. Buckner, Kentucky, Kentucky.
41. Leroy Pope Walker, Alabama, Alabama.
42. Albert G. Blanchard, Louisiana, Norfolk.
43. Gabriel J. Rains, North Carolina, Yorktown.
44. J. E. B. Stuart, Virginia, Army of Potomac.
45. Lafayette McLaws, Georgia, Yorktown.
46. Thos F. Drayton, South Carolina, Coast of South Carolina.
47. Thomas C. Hindman, Arkansas, Kentucky.
48. Adley H. Gladden, Louisiana, Pensacola.
49. John Porter McCown, Tennessee, Kentucky.
50. Lloyd Tilghman, Kentucky, Kentucky.
51. Nathan G. Evans, South Carolina, Coast of South Carolina.
52. Cadmus M. Wilcox, Tennessee, Army of Potomac.
53. *Philip St. Geo. Cocke, Virginia, died in Virginia.
54. R. E. Rodes, Alabama, Army of Potomac.
55. Richard Taylor, Louisiana, Army of Potomac.
56. Louis T. Wigfall, Texas, Army of Potomac.
57. James H. Trapier, South Carolina, Coast of Florida.
58. Samuel G. French, Mississippi, Army of Potomac.
59. William H. Carroll, Tennessee, East Tennessee.
60. Hugh W. Mercer, Georgia, ————.
61. Humphrey Marshall, Kentucky, Kentucky.
62. John C. Breckinridge, Kentucky, Kentucky.
63. Richard Griffith, Mississippi, Army of Potomac.
64. Alexander P. Stewart, Kentucky, Kentucky.
65. William Montgomery Gardner, Georgia, on furlough.
66. Richard B. Garnett, Virginia, Army of Potomac.
67. William Mahone, Virginia, Norfolk.
68. L. O'Brian Branch, North Carolina, Coast of North Carolina.
69. Maxey Gregg, South Carolina, Coast of South Carolina.

Those having a * affixed are dead, or have resigned since the commencement of the war.

THE WEST POINT GENERALS.

The following Confederate Generals are graduates of West Point—the date of their graduation being prefixed:

Class of 1815—Samuel Cooper.
Class of 1820—John H. Winder.
Class of 1822—Isaac R. Tremble.
Class of 1825—Daniel S. Donelson, Benjamin Huger.
Class of 1826—Albert S. Johnston, John B. Grayson.
Class of 1827—Leonidas Polk, Gabriel J. Rains.
Class of 1828—Thomas F. Drayton, Hugh W. Mercer.
Class of 1829—Joseph E. Johnston, Robt. E. Lee, Theophilis H. Holmes, Albert G. Blanchard.
Class of 1830—John B. Magruder.
Class of 1832—George B. Crittenden, P. St. George Cocke, Humphrey Marshall, Richard C. Gatlin.
Class of 1833—Daniel Ruggles.
Class of 1835—Jones M. Withers.
Class of 1836—Joseph R. Anderson, Lloyd Tilghman.
Class of 1837—Braxton Bragg, Wm. H. T. Walker, John C. Pemberton, Arnold Elzey, Henry H. Sibley, Jubal A. Early.
Class of 1838—Wm. J. Hardee, James H. Trapier.
Class of 1839—Alex. R. Lawton, John P. McCown.
Class of 1840—Richard S. Ewell, Paul O. Hebert, Richard B. Garnett.
Class of 1841—Robert S. Garnett, Samuel Jones.
Class of 1842—Earl Van Dorn, Gustavus W. Smith, Mansfield Lovell, James Longstreet, Daniel H. Hill, Richard H. Anderson, Lafayette McLaws, Alex. P. Stewart.
Class of 1843—Roswell S. Ripley, Samuel G. French.
Class of 1844—Simon B. Buckner.
Class of 1845—E Kirby Smith, Bernard E. Bee, Wm. H. C. Whiting.
Class of 1846—Thomas J. Jackson, Cadmus M. Wilcox, David R. Jones, Wm. M. Gardner.
Class of 1848—Nathan G. Evans.
Class of 1854—J. E. B. Stuart.

GENERALS WHO WERE NOT GRADUATES AT WEST-POINT.

The following Generals were appointed to the old United States Army, without passing through the West Point Academy: David E. Twiggs, appointed in 1812; Wm. W. Loring, in 1836, Thos. T. Fauntleroy, in 1836.

The following Generals first saw service in the Mexican war: M. L. Bonham, Henry R. Jackson, Gideon J. Pillow, Samuel R. Anderson, Chas. Clark, Thos. C. Hindman, John C. Breckinridge, Benj. F. Cheatham, Richard Griffith, Albert Pike, Adley H. Gladden, Maxcy Gregg.

The following Generals participated in the Texan wars and the wars with Mexico: Ben McCulloch, Louis T. Wigfall.

The following Generals saw no military service previous to the present war: John B. Floyd, Henry A. Wise, Robert Toombs, Richard Taylor, Thos B. Flournoy, L. Pope Walker, F. K. Zollicoffer, William Mahone, L. O'B Branch, William H. Carroll, R. E. Rodes. Some, however, received military educations at State institutions.

Virginia has 16 Generals in the Confederate armies, South Carolina 9, Louisiana 8, Georgia 7, Tennessee 8, North Carolina 6, Kentucky 7, Maryland 4, Alabama 4, Mississippi 4, Texas 3, Arkansas 2, Florida 1, Missouri none.

The following were born at the North, though previous to the present war they were citizens of Southern States: General Cooper, born in New York; Ripley, in Ohio; Pemberton, in Pennsylvania; Whiting, in Massachusetts; Pike, in Massachusetts; Ruggles, in Massachusetts; Blanchard, in Massachusetts; French, in New Jersey.

The following Confederate Generals are South Carolinians, viz: Huger, Bonham, Bee, (dead,) D. R. Jones, Ripley, R. H. Anderson, Drayton, Evans, Trapier, and Gregg, and the following are natives of South Carolina, though citizens of other States, viz: Longstreet, of Alabama; Lawton, of Georgia; Donelson, of Tennessee; Withers, of Alabama; Hill, of North Carolina; Gladden, of Louisiana; and Wigfall, of Texas.

"A Soldier's Gratitude."

The mother to whom the following affectionate letter was written enclosed it to a gentleman of Richmond, requesting him to ascertain, if he could, to whom she is indebted for the kindness of which her son so gratefully speaks; and with his permission we lay it before our readers, not only because it contains a handsome and well merited compliment to one of Virginia's most accomplished matrons, but also daguerreotypes an incident which, alike in its occurrence and results, reflects infinite honor upon human nature:

MONTEREY, Va., Aug. [illegible] 1861.

My Beloved Mother: Among other promises which I made you when upon the eve of our departure from home, you gave me your parting kiss and blessing, I well remember to have told you that I would, when our regiment reached its destination, sit down and sketch you a history of whatever incidents of interest might transpire upon our journey. Between home and Richmond, however, nothing occurred to break the general monotony of dullness which generally reigns along railroad routes. But when we were about leaving Richmond an incident did occur which must forever still linger, haunt the greenest spot on my memory's waste.

For several days previous to the receipt of marching orders by our regiment, I had been quite indisposed, and some of the boys in our mess attempted, even on the very morning we struck our tents, to dissuade me from accompanying them; but I rallied my feeble energies and resolved to face the music; but before I had marched a half mile towards the depot, I found I would be bound to fall in the ranks if I attempted to stay there; so I got leave to withdraw and proceed to the depot in a vehicle. Charley was allowed to attend me, and as we were proceeding slowly along the street in search of a conveyance, we passed by the gate of one of the most splendid residences I ever saw in my life, at the door of which a lady about your age, dear mother, was standing. She was dressed in mourning, and as soon as I caught the glance of her dark, lustrous and intelligent eye, I read in an instant the history of a great and noble heart in her beautiful face. Yes, mother, she is very beautiful, illustrating the truth recorded by the poet when he said, "The autumn of the beautiful is beautiful."

Bending upon me a look of generous and motherly sympathy, she exclaimed to Charley, on whose arm I was leaning, in accents soft and sweet as the tones of an angel's harp, "Why, young man, is not your friend sick? Surely, he is very sick; come, bring him into my house and let me do something for him, or send for a doctor." If an angel had come sailing down out of the skies and lit before us, and offered to fan my fevered brow with its golden wings it could not have struck Charley and me more literally all up in a heap than this beautiful woman did.—We, however, after making a stagger or two at something polite to say, finally shook off our embarrassment, and thanking her, told her we were compelled to hurry forward.—But do you think she was to be turned aside after any such a fashion as that? Not a bit of it. "Hurry forward indeed!" said she—"You are not able to go at all," and with a graceful and hospitable wave of her hand, and a smile that I have seen, my dear mother, a thousand and one times since, and mingled its light with the light of those fond memories brought from home to span with the rainbows of hope the dark clouds that lower over a soldier's tent, she bade us "come in," and so completely were we mesmerized, that we obeyed her as promptly as if it had been the Colonel giving an order, or St. Peter inviting us into Heaven.

Well, we were soon seated in her spacious dining room, gloriously refreshed with some of the most delicious wine I ever smacked a lip over. Oh, mother, I can taste it yet. She then made us sit up to her breakfast table, and I found myself suddenly decidedly convalescent. Our appetites were soon with us, and it was precious little like a sick man—I came down to my work then and there. To tell you the truth, mother, I was at a loss to decide with which I was most infatuated, the beautiful hostess, her delicious wine, or her superb breakfast.

It would be a reflection upon all the good taste and sense among the educated gentlemen of Virginia, to suppose that any such woman can be single. That is clear out of the question, or, if it is not, it amounts to an awful commentary upon the *real* claims of Virginia gentlemen for worthiness. But, let her be married or single, I want you, mother, to pray that over her path, through this vale of tears, happy stars may shine, and in it the fairest flowers may bloom, for she has been more than a good Samaritan to your poor sick boy. When we rose to leave she pressed Charley and me to remain a few days, until I should recover my health, and when we assured her that could not be, she loaded us down with wine and nicknacks, which were as great a god-send to us, on our weary march, as the manna which was rained on the children of Israel in the wilderness was to them. And now, mother, after all, I blush to tell you I do not know her name—Her house is covered with quaker colored stucco, and stands on the corner of Grace and Sixth or Seventh streets, and you must not be surprised, my dear mother, if I tell you that, in those dreams Heaven sends to bless the soldier's pallet of straw in which he flies

'To those fields traversed so oft
In life's morning march, when his bosom was young."

That on my way through dreamland, back "to the home of my fathers," I also revert to that palatial residence where I met such gentle kindness; for never, no, never, while I breathe Heaven's vital air, will I forget the incidents of that morning. With the diamond-pointed pen of gratitude, they have been recorded upon the tablets of my memory, and there they will glow and glisten until, with me, the "silver cord is loosened, and the golden bowl is broken."

Your affectionate ROBERT.

A DESERTED VILLAGE.—Such is our town of Edgefield at this time; and although, unlike Goldsmith's "D. V.," she looks forward to a day when her pleasant places shall be again brightened with life and animation, yet for the nonce, Heaven knows she is deserted enough. You may walk out upon her public square any morning, at 9 o'clock, and you shall scarcely find a half dozen mortals of all colors and ages in view, and sometimes not a single business door open, always excepting that of the *Advertiser* office, which is ever ajar to accommodate applicants. The condition of things is indeed cheerless, but we keep our spirits up as best we may. Our incorporation best retains less than the legal remnant of men between 18 and 45; there are now only eleven, and several of those disabled. Our whole white male population may now be classed as follows: Fathers of families, 37; bachelors, 7 or 8; and of boys not a few. The entire population of our town is, in ordinary times, from 700 to 800.—*Edgefield Advertiser.*

[For the Richmond Dispatch.]

Random Thoughts on the War From a Georgia Stand Point.

RE-ENLISTMENT.

The feeling in Georgia is universal in favor of our twelve months' volunteers re-enlisting. Fathers who, like the writer, have their every son in the army, will go in if the young ones come out. If the old men are killed, the ladies will take their places.

DUELLING IN THE ARMY.

This barbarous practice should be suppressed in the army by the high hand of authority. If civilians choose to shoot each other, let them do it. But men who go forth to resist an army of invasion, should not be permitted to throw away their lives.

RESIGNATION OF OFFICERS.

This is another serious evil that should not be tolerated, except for ill health and incompetency. Men are put in office, and valuable trusts confided to them, and it is trifling with the service and inflicting a wound upon it, if they capaciously resign. If an officer does well, he deserves well, and promotion should come, but not at the bidding of such officer, or his friends. Let him bide his time until the proper authorities say the word, and then go up. But never let resignations be accepted, tendered capriciously, or from disappointed expectation.

FEUDS BETWEEN OFFICERS.

Feuds between officers are of the essence of treason; they hurt our cause and give aid and comfort to the enemy. The higher the standing of an officer, the greater the crime; and punishment should fall swiftly and surely on the offender. It is to be feared that large political influence may screen offenders in this particular.

WHISKEY.

This has been the scourge of our army.—Ye men at Richmond, high in authority, we, fathers and mothers, beg you to save our sons from the awful curse. If they fall by sickness or the sword, we are resigned. But, oh! save them from being poisoned and brutalized. In this connection the furlough system is much abused. Returned soldiers on furlough, drunk and besotted, are seen too often in our cars. Far better keep them under the restraints of the camp.

EIGHTH OF JANUARY.

It would gratify the people if the Congress at Richmond would do away with this day as a holy day and for military reviews, and substitute 21st of July. England must and will be our ally. Let us rejoice over Manassas.

A GEORGIAN.

Address of Frederick the Great.

To the Generals and Higher Officers, December 4, 1757, Before the Battle near Leuthen.

Gentlemen: You are aware that while I was obliged to stop the progress of the French and Austrians, Prince Charles of Lothringen has succeeded in taking Schweidnitz, beating the Duke of Bavaria, and in making himself master of Breslau, the capital of my Silesia, and a part of the Province are thus lost, together with all the provisions and ammunition therein contained, and my troubles would be very great, if I placed not an unbounded confidence in your courage, firmness, and love of your country, which you have shown on so many occasions. I acknowledge these services rendered to our fatherland and to me, with the tenderest movements of my heart.

There is almost not one amongst you who has not distinguished himself by some great and honorable deed; therefore I flatter myself you will fall short in nothing which the State has a right to expect of your valor, if circumstances demand it. This epoch approaches: I should believe I had done nothing if I left the Austrians in possession of Silesia: mark, therefore, I shall attack the army of Prince Charles, although nearly three times stronger, wherever I find it, and in opposition to all the rules of the art of war.

At this juncture, the number of the enemy is not the question, nor the importance of his position; for all this I hope the strong hearts of my army and the exact obedience to my orders, will overcome. I must venture this blow, or everything is lost; we must annihilate the enemy, or his batteries will bury us! Thus I intend to act. Communicate my orders to all the officers of the army, and prepare the privates for the work which must soon follow, informing them that I consider myself entitled to unconditional discipline. However, if you remember that you are Prussians, you will certainly make yourself worthy of this preference; if there should be one amongst you who fears to divide with me all the danger, he can obtain his dismission to-day, and without receiving from me the least reproach. [We follow your Majesty unto death! Our all and our blood for our King! called out loud the officers, and the King proceeded.]

Before now I was convinced none of you would forsake me. I count, therefore, totally on your faithful assistance, and on the certain victory. Should I fall, and not be able to reward you, our fatherland must do it. Go now into the camp, and repeat to your battalions what I have said: "If any regiment of horse should not fall upon the enemy at once, as ordered, they shall, after the battle, dismount, and be put into the garrison; and that battalion of foot, which only hesitates one minute, shall lose its standards and sabres, and the decorations from its uniforms, be it wheresoever it may! Now, gentlemen, farewell. Shortly we shall have either beaten the enemy, or we shall never see each other again."

LOST MAN.—A gentleman named Mr. Forward Movement has been missing for several months past. He was thought to have been seen at Manassas Plains, but it proved not to be him; it was Mr. Trotter, of the firm of Street Walker & Legget. He was again supposed to have been seen at Leesburg, but it proved to be Mr. Diver, of the firm of Sinker, Swimmer & Traveler, who left without paying Mrs. Potomac her wash bill. He was again thought to have been seen in Missouri, but it turned out to be Mr. Extravagance, of the firm of Woolly Horse, Rocky Mountain, Frank Blair & Dad. He was a few days since thought to have been near on one or both sides of Green river, Ky., but his friends met with another sad disappointment; it was not him. It was Mr. Slip Back-over-the-river & Co., doing a forwarding business backward for Squire Linkin.

Mr. Forward Movement is about 28 years old, more or less, five feet ten or ten feet five high; black whiskers, dresses fine, wearing a heavy gold fob chain manufactured from the finest candlestick brass; he is a tall, thin, thick set man, with very large feet; some think he has gradually wilted down in his boots. He will deny being any relation to James Buchanan, the Last Rose of Northern Summer. He is a blood relation to Mr. On-to-Richmond; his mother is almost distracted on his account, fearing he may be burnt.

On account of his sluggish temperament, she avers he was, when a child, so lazy he would not break out with the measles, or whoop with the whooping cough. The old lady is grieving for her sprightly offspring, but is yet willing to surrender him to the country, coming to the conclusion, on account of his monstrous feet, that he must have died standing.

All papers friendly to the friends of Mr. Forward Movement, will confer a favor upon the surviving relatives by giving this one insertion.—*Cor. Nashville Gazette.*

THE TOWN OF ROMNEY.—As Romney is becoming a place of some notoriety as a strategic point, a short description of the town and its vicinity may prove interesting to many of our readers. The town itself is beautifully located, resting upon the South Branch of the Potomac, about eighteen miles from its junction with the North Branch.—It is surrounded on all sides with declivitous hills and mountains, and if well fortified would be almost impregnable to an advancing army. It has been in a measure fortified by nature, and only needs the hand of science to make it a powerful post for purposes of defence. It is forty two miles from Winchester on the Northwestern Turnpike, sixteen miles from the Baltimore and Ohio Railroad, and twenty-five miles south of Cumberland, Md. It is the shire town of Hampshire county, and contains about five hundred inhabitants. The town was founded by Lord Fairfax, and is one of the oldest in that section of Virginia.

☞ LETTER FROM GEN. LEE.

CHARLESTON, S. C., Dec 16, 1861.

Mr. G. B. STACY, *Richmond*—Dear Sir: I received your MATTRESS just as I was leaving Richmond, and have not yet had an opportunity of testing it in field, but from its convenient construction, economy of space, &c., I have no doubt but that it will be found a valuable article of camp equipage. Begging your acceptance of my thanks,

I am, resp'y, your obd't serv't, R. E. LEE

ja 11—1w*

☞ THE ARMY MEDICAL BOARD, at Manassas, Va., for the examination of Medical Officers, (now in service,) and of professional applicants, has been reorganized.

The Board consists of Surgeons R. L. Brodie, S. L. Gaillard, and R. J. Breckinridge.

ja 7—9w

☞ S. WYATT & CO., of Charleston, S. C., beg to inform their friends everywhere that the great fire which occurred in our city last night did them no immediate injury, either in their stock or private houses.

We feel this announcement due to our friends who have a large amount of property in our hands. Charleston, Dec. 12th, 1861. de 16—ts

LOST, STRAYED, &c.

$100 REWARD—For the apprehension of the person or persons who broke into my house on Monday, about 5 A. M., and set fire to it in the closet under the staircase, thereby endangering the lives of many.

I will also give a liberal reward for the detection of the same party who stole many articles of value, some of which I enumerate: 1 pair cut glass pitchers, 1 table cover, small and large knives, 1 woolen crumb cloth, 1 overcoat, 2 plaid shawls, 1 black centro stella shawl, (colored border) 1 pair kid gaiters, 1 pair bootees, 1 basket of sundries, 1 silver pie knife, (marked J. E. T.,) mantel ornaments, &c., &c.

JAMES M. TALBOTT, Corner 19th and Broad sts. jy 15—3t

STOLEN—$50 REWARD—From the stable of the subscriber, on the night of the 9th inst., one beautiful light dun MARE, white tail and mane, about 14½ to 15 hands high, about 6 years old; paces well. She is supposed to have been stolen by two men belonging to the New Orleans Tigers. I will give $25 for the recovery of the mare, and $25 for the apprehension and conviction of the thief. They also stole at the same time a bay Horse belonging to Capt. Sam'l C. Williams, who, I believe, will pay a liberal reward for his recovery.

FREDERICK SCHEFFER, National Hotel, Woodstock, Va. ja 15—1w*

$5 REWARD.—Strayed, from Camp of Instruction, (new Fair Grounds,) a small, dark bay MULE, with the brand "C S" on the shoulder. The above reward will be paid for his return.

JOHN C. MAYNARD, Capt. and As't Q. M. ja 15—3t*

$5 REWARD—Lost or stolen from my office, a small pocket case of SURGICAL INSTRUMENTS, with my name on the back. The case was lined with blue silk, one or two of the instruments wanting, and one of the loops broken. I will pay $5 reward for its return, and ask no questions.

DR. JOHN F. JACKSON, No. 17 Main street. ja 15—3t*

STOLEN—From the subscriber, on the night of the 6th inst., a bay HORSE, with white hairs sufficient to induce some to consider him a roan; five feet high; twelve years old; all his feet white to above the ankle; blaze face; small ears; rides and draws well. A liberal reward will be paid upon his delivery to the subscriber.

THO. H. FOX, Junction, Hanover county. ja 14—eod3t*

$20 REWARD.—On Friday night, the 10th, a thief broke into the stable on my farm and stole therefrom a very dark bay MULE, with a scar on his left thigh.

The above reward will be paid if the animal is returned to me, or information given so that I get him again.

MRS. MARY E. HOBBS, Manchester, Va. ja 14—1w*

ESTRAY.—Came to my farm, in Chesterfield county, near Manchester, about one month since, a young Red COW and CALF.

The owner will please call, prove property, pay charges, and take her away. Apply to

MRS. MARY E. HOBBS, Manchester, Va. ja 14—1w*

STOLEN—A Child's Two wheeled GIG. From the porch of the house corner of Main and Monroe streets.

The party in possession of it is requested to return it this week, and no questions asked; if not, they will be dealt with according to law. ja 14—3t*

STOLEN OR STRAYED—From Reid's stables, a COLT, four years old; dark bay, a little lame in right hind leg, with some fresh cuts on the same; fore top and long tail; a slight sore on the back. Whoever has the Horse will please return him, without delay.

ROBERT REID, 6th, near Clay street. ja 14—3t*

LOST, STRAYED, OR STOLEN—On the 7th inst., a SORREL MARE about 14½ hands high, with white hind legs and blazed face. She is a little crest-fallen, well bred, and 9 years old. Had a new black Cavalry rigging on, with valice and bear skin, fringed with red cloth. Ten dollars reward will be paid and no questions asked, when delivered to DAVIS & HUTCHESON'S Livery Stables, Franklin street, below the Exchange Hotel. ja 13—1w*

$10 REWARD.—Stolen, from my stable, at Half-Sink, in the county of Henrico, 9 miles from Richmond, on the 10th of January, a small GRAY HORSE, very compactly made; has a knot on his tail, about 6 inches from the root; also, a scar on both fore knees, caused by being hung in the stable.

The above reward will be paid if delivered at the stable of N. C. LIPSCOMB, and Second st., between Broad and Grace.

T. I. CARTER. ja 12—6t*

STRAYED MULES.—Taken up, on the Falls Plantation, Chesterfield county, on January 7th, TWO MULES—one black mare mule and one sorrel horse mule, both old.—The owners are requested to come forward, prove property, pay charges, and take them away.

DANIEL F. WARD. ja 11—6t*

LOST—$25 REWARD—Between the First Market and Brooke Avenue, a BLACK BAG, containing two Account Books and sundry papers. I will give the above reward for their delivery to me, at Nos. 17 and 19, First Market.

JOHN LINDSEY. de 21—ts

HOSPITALS.

HOSPITAL OF THE MEDICAL COLLEGE OF VIRGINIA.—This Hospital, erected by the liberality of the State, at a cost of more than $30,000, is now completed, and open for the reception of patients. It is admirably adapted by its plan for the accommodation of the sick, and is furnished with every convenience requisite for their comfort and successful treatment. Its situation on Marshall street, east of 12th, immediately adjacent to the Medical College, while retired and airy, is at the same time central, and convenient of access from all parts of the city.

The patients are under the immediate charge of the Professors of the College, (who make daily visits,) assisted by a competent Resident Physician.

All persons requiring Medical or Surgical treatment are admitted, except the INSANE, and those laboring under SMALL-POX AND OTHER INFECTIOUS DISORDERS.

Lying in women, both white and colored, receive special care and attention.

CHARGES,

Including Board, Medical Attendance, &c.:

White Patients..........$6 per week.
Slaves..........5 " "

And at the same rate for fractions of a week.

For less than one week, $1 per day, up to the charge for a full week.

Several neatly furnished Private Rooms have been provided for those desiring separate accommodations. The charge for these will vary from $7 to $15 per week.

For surgical operations a fee ranging from $5 to $30 will be required, in addition to the above weekly rates.

☞ All charges payable on the removal of the patient.

A limited number of beds placed at the disposal of Charitable Associations, at $150 per annum, payable semi-annually, or at a corresponding rate for six months.

Patients conveyed to or from the Hospital in a suitable vehicle, provided especially for the purpose.

Citizens and strangers are invited to visit the Hospital and inspect its arrangements.

President—Dr. L. S. JOYNES.
Attending Physicians—Drs. TUCKER, CONWAY and McCAW.
Attending Surgeons—Drs. GIBSON, PETICOLAS and WELLFORD.
Resident Physician—Dr. ISAIAH H. WHITE.
Steward—F. M. PARISH. ap 22—1y

FOURTH STREET HOSPITAL.—The ladies of the First Baptist Church have procured a house on Fourth street, beyond Leigh, and propose opening it as a hospital for sick and wounded soldiers, on Monday next. They will be grateful for any supplies either of provisions or clothing, from the city or country, that may be adapted to the wants of the patients. Contributions for this purpose may be left at the hospital, or at the store of Mr. WM G. DANDRIDGE, 106 Broad street. se 11—ts

BELLEVUE HOSPITAL, CHURCH HILL, RICHMOND, VA.

WHITE PATIENTS—In wards, $6 per week; in private rooms, $7 to $15 per week.

SLAVES—$5 per week. Less than a week, $1 per day; but not to exceed $5 per week. Fractions over the week, 71 cents per day.

No extra charges except for surgical operations, and then an additional fee ranging from $2 to $30 will be charged. ☞ Bills payable on the removal of the patient. No small-pox admitted.

A covered spring wagon will convey patients to and from the Hospital when desired. Orders may be left at the Hospital, or at the office of A. L. HOLLADAY, Thirteenth street, between Main and Cary.

The subscriber, who has been connected with the Institution since its foundation, having taken it under his exclusive charge, aided by competent assistants, solicits a continuance of the liberal patronage of his friends and of the public generally.

Attending Physician and Surgeon, JAMES BOLTON, M. D., Grace st., between 4th and 5th.

ASSISTANTS: C. W. P. BROCK, M. D., Church Hill, cor. 26th & Marshall sts. W. W. COGGIN, M. D., Resident Physician. ja 18—1y

CASH advances made on consignments of merchandise by I. & G. B. DAVENPORT. ja 10

WANTS.

WANTED—One or two JOURNALISTS, or REPORTERS, On a leading daily paper. They must be men of industry and skill. Address, with reference, "A. B.," Dispatch office. ja 15—3t*

WANTED—A REGIMENT OF MEN FOR MANNING THE BATTERIES.—The Governor has authorized Messrs. J. PANNILL and WILLIAM P. BURWELL to say that he will receive for twelve months, a number of companies to organize a regiment, for the special purpose of manning the Batteries in and around the city of Richmond.

Any companies forming for this special service in the city or counties in which the militia has been ordered to hold itself in readiness, will apply forthwith.

Any persons in the city or country desirous to enlist in Company "A," now forming in this city can apply, by letter or in person, at J. PANNILL's Counting-room, Shockoe Warehouse, or WM P. BURWELL'S Law office, Bank st. ja 15—1m*

WANTED—NEGRO LABOR—The James River and Kanawha Company wants to HIRE negro CARPENTERS and LABORERS, to work on the repairs of the canal during the present year. Liberal wages will be paid, and rations, clothing, and medicine and medical attendance furnished. For further information address the undersigned in this city, or see the Company's Agents along the line of the canal, who are authorized to hire.

E. L. CHEW, Sup't J. R. and K. Canal. ja 15—dts

WANTED—SUBSTITUTES. I wish to employ four SUBSTITUTES, immediately, for artillery and infantry service. A liberal bonus given for good men.

THOS. J. BAGBY, Agent for Hiring out Negroes and Renting out Houses, No. 8 Wall st., between Main and Franklin sts. ja 15—3t

WANTED—A FOUNDER For a Blast Furnace in Botetourt county. Good wages will be paid to a competent man. Apply to J. R. ANDERSON & CO., Tredegar Iron Works. ja 15—3t

WANTED—A HOUSE—Containing six or seven Rooms, or a part of a House with three or four rooms, for a gentleman and his wife and servant. Any person having either for rent the balance of this year will address me, stating terms, through the city post-office. H. JONES. ja 15—4t*

WANTED.—Mrs. N. H. THORNTON wishes to hire a very superior COOK, CHAMBERMAID, and DINING-ROOM SERVANT. Corner Franklin and Foushee streets. ja 15—2t*

WANTED—VOLUNTEERS for 12 months, To man the Batteries in and around the city of Richmond. Call from 10 to 2 o'clock. Apply to R. A. MILLS, At J. Tinsley Jonson's, Shockoe Slip. ja 15—6t*

WANTED—A SITUATION as salesman in a grocery or commission house, by a young man from King William county, Va., who could influence considerable trade to his employer. Good references given. Address "W. C.," Dispatch office. ja 15—6t*

WANTED—SITUATION—By a Virginia lady, of several years' experience, a situation as TEACHER in a private family. No objection to going South. Address MISS S. E. M., Post-Office Box No. 110, Richmond, Va. ja 15—3t*

WANTED—To RENT, A ROOM suitable for a Sculptor's Studio. Central location preferred. Address "F. V.," Dispatch office. ja 15—6t*

WANTED—TEN MEN to fill an artillery company, and will pay a high bonus to get them to-day. ROBERT HILL, Substitute Agent, 6 doors above City Water Works. ja 14—3t*

WANTED—Bonds of the Confederate States, of the PRODUCE LOAN, by BACON & BASKERVILL. ja 8—ts

SERVANTS FOR HIRE.

FOR HIRE—A young NEGRO MAN that can Drive a cart or wagon, act as Porter, or almost any ordinary employment.

ALSO—A small BOY, that can wait in the house, will be hired low to a good home. Apply to C. S. MAURICE, Office 73 Main st. ja 15—3t*

FOR SALE—HOUSE SERVANT. A mulatto BOY, about 16 years old, handsome, and well grown. Apply to GODDIN & APPERSON. ja 15—ts

FOR HIRE—A likely young WOMAN, with a child six months old. She is a good Seamstress and House Servant. To a good home she will be hired low. Apply to LAWRENCE LOTTIER, at Wm. Ira Smith's, 74 Main street. ja—3t*

FOR HIRE—Two young MEN, as Dining-Room Servants, with good characters, and can be well recommended by former employers; one CHAMBERMAID and several other Servants. Apply to me, at the Paymaster General's Office corner of 10th and Bank sts. THOMAS P. TAYLOR. ja 14—6t*

FOR HIRE—A very sprightly and trusty BOY, about 11 years old; Very suitable for House service, &c. I. H. WALKE, Main st. ja 14—ts

FOR SALE—COOK, WASHER, and IRONER. I have for sale a good Cook, Washer and Ironer 22 years of age with her child, between 2 and 3 years old. She is strong, active and healthy. THOS J. BAGBY, Agent for Hiring out Negroes, No. 8 Wall street. ja 14—2t

BOARDING.

BOARDING.—Two gentlemen and their wives can obtain rooms and board in a private family in one of the most desirable parts of the city—Grace street. Also, one FURNISHED ROOM suitable for two single gentlemen.

One handsome front BASEMENT ROOM, suitable for a Doctor's office, with board. Address "R. D.," Dispatch office. [jy 15 4t*]

NOTICE.—A Gentleman and his wife can be accommodated with board in a genteel family, in a pleasant part of the city, at moderate rates, by early application at the corner of 7th and Clay streets, (left hand in going from Marshall.) ja 16—3t*

BOARDING. Persons desiring BOARD can obtain ROOMS at Mrs. HOOPER'S, on Grace st., between 25th and 26th sts. Also—Several gentlemen can be accommodated with day board. ja 9—eod2w*

STOVE PIPE AND SHEET IRON PANS. Persons in want of STOVE PIPE and Sheet Iron Baking PANS, can be supplied at short notice by applying to PAUL BARGAMIN, Cor. of Main and 10th streets. ja 15 3t

EDW'D DORAN, CUPPER AND LEECHER, North side of Broad street, between Mayo st. and Central Depot.

Having just received a large supply of foreign Leeches, I am now fully prepared to apply them on reasonable terms.

Mrs DORAN, Practical Leecher, attends to female leeching.

N. B.—Particular attention to all orders, night or day. ja 14—1m*

I HAVE ESTABLISHED A BROOM MANUFACTORY, And solicit orders, at 29 Pearl street. G. W. ROBINSON. ja 15—1m*

LUMBER FOR SALE. The undersigned will sell upon reasonable terms a very excellent lot of good SHIP-BUILDING TIMBER, lying in the county of Chesterfield, near Port Walthall, within a mile and a half of a good wharf or landing. For further information apply to, or address through the mail at Chester P. O., Chesterfield county. STRACHAN & WHITE. ja 11—6t*

PRESERVED GINGER, PRUNES, &c. 200 cases of PRESERVED GINGER, 75 cases PRUNES, in jars, 20 bags soft-shell ALMONDS. For sale by A. F. COCHRAN & HALL, New Orleans.

Richmond Dispatch.

TERMS OF ADVERTISING.

1 square, 1 day...	$0.50	1 square 5 days..	$1.50
1.. do....2 days..	0.75	1.. do....6 days..	1.75
1.. do....3 days..	1.00	1.. do....12 days..	3.0
1.. do....4 days..	1.25	1.. do... 1 month..	5.0

Larger advertisements in exact proportion.

☞ Advertisements published till forbid will be charged 50 cts. per square of EIGHT LINES for the first insertion, and 25 cts. for each continuance.

WANTS.

WANTED—A colored NURSE, without incumbrance, who is neat, and kind to children, to go about one and a half miles from the city. A good Cook, Washer and Ironer, for a very small family. Also, a Gardner, white or colored. To be sober and industrious are indispensable requisites.—Apply at the office of Mr. A D. Williams, on 11th st., between the hours of 11 and 12 o'clock, Tuesday, Wednesday, and Thursday. JAS. T. SUTTON, Jr. ja 14—3t*

WANTED—To RENT, A moderate sized HOUSE, In a pleasant neighborhood, for which we will pay a good rent. Apply to, or address MARCUS HARRIS & BRO., Next to American Hotel. ja 14—3t*

WANTED—Immediately, Eight BOOT and SHOEMAKERS; Six to work on Gent'emen's Fine Calf Boots, and two to work on Ladies' Fine Shoes. The best price given. None but the best of workmen need apply. Address FAGAN & BROWN, Staunton Va. ja 14—7t*

WANTED—To hire, at the General Hospital, Ten good SERVANTS, As NURSES. Apply at the General Hospital, near the Poor House, every day at 2 o'clock. CHARLES BELL GIBSON, Surgeon in charge of the General Hospital. ja 14—1w*

WANTED.—A Virginia LADY, of several years' experience, desires a situation as TEACHER in a private family. She is qualified to teach the English and Ornamental Branches usually taught in high schools, with the rudiments of French and Music. The best recommendation can be given. For particulars, address "Box 11," Charlottesville, Albemarle, Va. ja 14—12t*

WANTED—Permanent BOARD, for a small family, in a Private Family or Boarding-House, where there are but few boarders. For such accommodation a liberal price will be paid, provided the house is not over one mile from the Capitol. References exchanged. Address "GEORGIA" (stating where an interview may be had,) at this office. ja 14—3t*

WANTED—Ten WAGON DRIVERS For the use of the 4th Regiment Virginia Cavalry, near Manassas. Wages $20 per month. Apply to T. W. SYDNOR, at P. H. STARKE'S, Near St. Charles Hotel, Richmond. ja 14—3t*

WANTED—A GOOD COOK, WASHER, and IRONER. Apply at cor. 29th and Main sts., Church Hill [ja 14—3t*] LUTHER LIBBY.

WANTED—A copy of "INSTRUCTION IN FIELD ARTILLERY," By French, Barry & Hunt published under direction of the War Department of the United States. A *very liberal* price will be paid for a copy if left at this office. ja 14—3t*

WANTED—A FIRST RATE COOK, Without incumbrance. For such an one a liberal hire will be paid. HORACE L. KENT. ja 14—3t

WANTED—A WOMAN to act as Chambermaid and Assistant Nurse. She must be experienced and of good character. JOHN O. STEGER, 3rd st. bet. Clay and Leigh. ja 14—ts

WANTED—At the Carbon Hill Mines in this county, 10 good COAL DIGGERS, a first rate CARPENTER and BLACKSMITH, two skilful ENGINE RUNNERS, and twenty LABORERS, for surface operations.

Also, six LABORERS at the coke yards.

Also for my family, a good COOK, WASHER and IRONER. JNO. J. WERTH, Agent. ja 1—ts

WANTED—Two good PATTERN MAKERS. To such as will suit the highest wages will be paid. They must find their own tools. Address, or apply at the store of MEREDITH, SPENCER & CO., Under Spotswood Hotel. ja 13—3t

WANTED—A SITUATION—As COPYIST, At any of the Civil or Military Departments here. Best of references given. Apply to WM. SATTLER & CO., Main street, No. 142. ja 13—w

WANTED—A WHITE WOMAN, With good references, To WASH and COOK, For a small family. Apply at the corner of 8th and Franklin streets, from 9 to 11 A. M. ja 12—1w*

WANTED—NEGROES.—Wanted to hire Negroes, (free or slaves) Laborers Mechanics and Teamsters, for service on the Peninsula, on the following terms and conditions:

If hired by the month (not less than six months) fifteen dollars per month will be paid for laborers; with rations, comfortable quarters and Medical attendance free.

If hired by the year one hundred dollars per annum, paid quarterly, with rations, comfortable quarters and Medical attendance free, and usual allowance of clothing.

For Teamsters and Mechanics twenty dollars will be paid, and rations, comfortable quarters and Medical attendance free.

The Government will be responsible for the value of these Negroes, if captured by the enemy or allowed to escape to them, or killed in action.

In all other respects the contract of hire will be subject to and conformable to the Laws of Virginia.

For further particulars apply at the office of HECTOR DAVIS Franklin street near Wall, from 10 o'clock, A. M. to 4 P. M., until the 18th inst.

B. BLOOMFIELD, Quartermaster General of the Peninsula. ja 10—8t*

WANTED—25 MEN to enlist in a corps of Artillery and Artificers, stationed at Yorktown. Terms:

Sergeants..........$24.
Corporals..........23.
Privates..........17.

With an additional pay of 40 cents a day for each day's extra service, and also the bounty of $50 offered by the Confederate States for enlistment for the war.

For further information apply to Lieut. Pairo, at L. Baker's Saloon, corner of Main and 9th sts., or to Peyton Johnson, J. H. Dunlop, care of Q. M. Gen. Bloomfield, Yorktown.

T. W. PAIRO, Recruiting Officer, Transportation Office. ja 11—10t

WANTED—At the Carbon Hill Mines, an industrious and steady LABORING MAN, to act as FOREMAN of a gang of wood cutters and timber-getters. He must be a single man. Also, a FOREMAN and CAPTAIN of the drivers of the mule trains on the railroad. Also, a No 1 negro CARPENTER. JOHN J. WERTH, Agent. de 4—ts

WANTED—TO BUY—A young WOMAN, with or without incumbrance, competent and qualified as a house servant. Apply at corner of 12th and Franklin streets, over Confederate Commissioner's Office. ja 7—ts

WANTED—A situation as MINING CAPTAIN, by a thoroughly practical Miner, from Cornwall, England. The subscriber has had the most thorough experience in gold, silver, copper, iron, and lead mines; five years in the gold mines of Virginia, and four in Cuba. Good reference given. Address "P. C.," Wilderness Post-office, Spotsylvania county, Va. ja 4—1m*

WANTED—A LADY To teach FRENCH, in the Fredericksburg High School, For girls. WM. S. JOHNSON, Principal. de 30—1m*

WANTED—A WOMAN Who is a good washer and ironer, and a capable house servant. Apply at my residence, on Franklin st., between 23d and 24th. O. P. BALDWIN. ja 3—ts

WANTED—IMMEDIATELY—Twenty HANDS To work on KNAPSACKS. Apply at No. 131 Main st., or 114 Main street under Wm Ira Smith's. [illegible]

WANTED—A situation as TEACHER. A YOUNG LADY, a graduate of Buckingham Female College, desires a situation as TEACHER in a private family, or good Seminary. Reference given and required. Address "H. O. B.," Nelson Station, Nelson county. ja 10—1m

WANTED—30,000 lbs. BROOM CORN. 5,000 lbs. HOG BRISTLES. For which cash and a high price will be paid on delivery. G. W. ROBINSON, 29 Pearl st. de 10—1m*

WANTED TO EMPLOY—one man familiar with the manufacture of LAMP BLACK. To take charge of a Lamp-Black House at Wilmington, North Carolina. Address J. E. BLOSSOM & CO., Wilmington, North Carolina. de 27—1m*

The New-York Times.

VOL. XI—NO. 3242. NEW-YORK, WEDNESDAY, FEBRUARY 12, 1862. PRICE TWO CENTS

THE CAPTURE OF FORT HENRY.

Full Details from Our Special Correspondent.

The Land and Naval Forces in the Expedition.

The Preliminary Gunboat Reconnoissance.

Desperate Nature of the Engagement.

IMPORTANCE OF THE VICTORY.

The Fort a Very Strong and Well-Built One.

List of Casualties Among the National Forces

FORT HENRY, Friday, Feb. 7, 1862.

For several days, at Paducah, outsiders suspected that something was on foot, from the fact that the utmost vigilance was exercised at the headquarters of the Provost-Marshal, in issuing passes, and on Sunday and Monday no person was allowed to pass in or out of the lines. Suspicion grew into almost certainty when, Sunday night, half a dozen gunboat steamed leisurely into port and brought their black forms to anchor opposite the levee, in the centre of the river.

Monday afternoon, steamers commenced coming up from Cairo, laden with troops and stores, and by night the whole landing in front of the town wa crowded with the arrivals. The fleet which came up brought Gen. GRANT and Staff, and the First Division, under command of Brig.-Gen. MCCLERNAND. The steamers were under command of Commodore G. W. GRAHAM, and consisted of the following boats: *City of Memphis, Iatan, D. A. January, Chancellor, Alp, "W. H. B.," New Uncle Sam, Rob Roy, Alex. Scott Minnehaha, Illinois, Keystone, Emerald* and *Fanny Bullett*.

The First Division, on these boats, was made up of the two brigades, composed as follows, and commanded by Gen. JOHN A. MCCLERNAND:

FIRST BRIGADE, COL. OGLESBY, COMMANDING.

Seventh Illinois, Col. COOK.
Eighth Illinois, Lieut.-Col. RHOADES.
Eighteenth Illinois, Lieut.-Col. LAWLER.
Twenty-ninth Illinois, Col. REARDON.
Thirtieth Illinois, Lieut.-Col. DENNIS.
Thirty-first Illinois, Col. JOHN A. LOGAN.
SWARTZ's and DRESSER's Batteries.
STEWART's, DOLLINS', O. HARNETT's and CARMICHAEL's Cavalry.

SECOND BRIGADE, COL. W. H. L. WALLACE, COMMANDING.

Eleventh Illinois, Lieut.-Col. HART.
Twentieth Illinois, Col. MARSH.
Forty-fifth Illinois, Col. SMITH.
Forty-eighth Illinois, Col. HARNEY.
TAYLOR's and MCALLISTER's Batteries—in the latter, four siege guns.
Fourth Illinois Cavalry, Col. KELLOGG.
Seventh Illinois Cavalry, Col. DICKEY.

While giving details, I may as well give the gunboats which accompanied the expedition:

Tyler, 9 guns, Commodore FOOTE.
St. Louis, 13 guns, Commander PAULDING.
Essex, 7 guns, Commander PORTER.
Lexington, 9 guns, Lieut. SHIRK.
Conestoga, 5 guns, Lieut. PHELPS.
Carondelet, 13 guns, Commander WALKE.
Cincinnati, 13 guns, Commander STIMBLE.

Soon after arriving, Gen. GRANT and Staff paid a visit to Gen. SMITH, and held a conference, one of the results of which was, that it was determined to forward the division of Gen. MCCLERNAND that night, and after landing them at some point below Fort Henry, and out of range of its guns, send the boats back after Gen. SMITH's division at Paducah.

It was nearly midnight before the boats took their departure, and prior to that hour everything seemed ominous of evil. The sky was hung with gloom like a hearse. Not a single kindly star witnessed our departure—not a single cheering omen was there, unless it was the satisfaction everywhere visible in men's looks and words at the thought that *this* time here could be no failure in securing a decisive fight. External indications were all against us—heavy volumes of thick black smoke rushed away like mourning streamers upon a strong South wind, which beat against us as if it would fain deter us from our mission; the machinery clanked dismally below; the steam soughed in harmonious misery from the escape-pipes, or rushed with a hollow roaring from the safety-valves.

Omens, however, availed but little to retard us, and by midnight the most of the transports were under way, breasting a strong wind, a heavy rain, and the swift waters of the Tennessee. Gen. GRANT and Staff embarked on the *W. H. B.*, a gallant little craft, which although the last to back out, in an hour had distanced all the balance, and was the first to run her nose against the landing on the Kentucky shore. The point made was on the east shore of the river, about 10 miles below Fort Henry, and was reached at daylight. Soon after four of the transports arrived, and the work of debarking the troops commenced.

In the meantime, the gunboats *St. Louis, Essex* and *Cincinnati*, having on board Gen. GRANT and staff, steamed on up the river to make a reconnoissance. About four miles this side of the fort is Panther Island, and on both sides of this the boats crept till within about two miles, when the fortifications of the rebels, their flag, and even the number of guns, were visible.

The gunboats immediately opened on them with shells, and were replied to by some 24-pound guns, which, however, fell short about three-fourths of a mile. Finally a 9-inch shell from the *Essex* exploded exactly over the works, and being almost instantly followed by another, which burst nearly at the same point, the rebels seemed to lose their temper and opened upon the *Essex* with a 24-pound rifled gun. The first two or three balls whizzed over, in neighborly proximity to the heads of the officers, whereat there was considerable "ducking;" another followed, which pitched plump into the *Essex* just back of the wheelhouse, went on through the Captain's cabin, and tearing out through the rear, buried itself in the river. Nobody happened to be in the way of the heavy ball, and consequently nobody was hurt.

After dropping in a few more—throwing in all some fifteen or twenty—shells, and, satisfying themselves of the range of their guns, the officers determined to drop back out of range, and await the coming up of the balance of the force. They slowly fell back till a mile or so below the island, and there anchored.

At this time it was determined to effect the landing of the troops opposite this point, on the Tennessee shore, and under the protection of the gunboats. Accordingly, those who had landed during the morning at the point five or six miles below, were ordered to reëmbark, which they did, and at about 2 o'clock in the afternoon they had all arrived, and commenced once more the operation of landing.

While this was going on, a little target practice took place on the part of the *Essex*. About a mile above where the fleet was anchored a road leads down through the timber to the banks of the river, at which point there is a ferryboat. About an hour after the return of the gunboats, a squad of a dozen rebels came down this road to the water's edge, and stood here watching our movements.

"A shell, I think, would do those rascals good, Capt. PORTER!" said Gen. GRANT to the gallant Commander of the *Essex*.

Capt. PORTER appeared to be of the same opinion, for, a few seconds after, a 9-inch rifled shell, with a terrific whiz, described a most graceful curve, and fell some six yards to the left of the party, bursting just as it reached the earth. A half-dozen forms, ere the report had ceased rolling back from the hills, were seen scattering through the woods, with all the haste and want of unity natural under such peculiar circumstances. A little later in the day another squad ventured down the road opposite that followed by the others, but scarcely had their muskets reflected once the gleam of the bright sunlight ere a 9-inch messenger informed them they were treading on dangerous ground, which information was instantly repeated by another messenger of the same sort. Their retreat was incontinent, although slightly disorderly.

The point at which the troops were landed is about four or five miles below Fort Henry, and is opposite a small town in Kentucky, called Buffalo. Immediately at the place of landing is a clearing of about one hundred acres, surrounded on three sides by high bluffs, densely timbered, and reaching down to the river. The troops, on landing, immediately took possession of these, planted batteries so as to command the country in every direction, and then the troops made the best disposition possible to make themselves comfortable until the arrival of the balance of the force under Gen. SMITH.

Tuesday afternoon, while the troops were being disembarked, OSBAND Cavalry, and CARSON's and CARPENTER's scouts thoroughly examined the country in every direction, even up to within two miles of Fort Henry. Two squads of rebel pickets were driven in by CARSON, several arrests made, and a number of horses confiscated. Not a single atom of Union sentiment was found anywhere—even the women were as bitter and unrelenting in their hatred of the Yankees as is the most unregenerate son of "chivalry."

"I shan't run ef my ole man did!"—screamed one muscular termagant, in a highly-pitched key, as the scouts rode up—"shoot ef you want to; I just as lieve die now as any time. You think you're goin to take the Fort, but you'll git fooled—thar's a right smart heap of men thar!"

Just then some of the scouts came in, lugging a butternut native, whom they fished out from the bushes, and who proved to be her "ole man."

"I tole you you ougtener done, gone and tuk to the bush! But don't you let down an inch—if they shoot you, don't let down an inch!" and screaming like an enraged hyena, she banged the door in their face, and was seen no more. She is about an average specimen of the sex as found in the vicinity of Fort Henry.

Tuesday night was of the most beautiful description, and as unlike its immediate predecessor as the Vale of Cashmere, is unlike a Siberian Winter. A thousand camp fires glittered from out the darkness that rested upon the amphitheatre of wooded hills—the sky was as warm and tender as one that bends over the flowers of May, and was highly silvered by a crescent moon that glittered in the western sky, while, adding a charm to everything, came out the music of a half dozen bands, which now roused the soul with patriotic strains of "Red, White and Blue," and anon soothed it with some dreamy waltz.

Wednesday, but little of importance took place. Parties were out reconnoitering near the enemy's works, and in one case a squad of cavalry, when within a mile or so of the fort, ran against some two hundred rebel horsemen. Both sides immediately fired at the other, and then the rebels ran, leaving one of their number dead, and carrying off three severely wounded. One man on our side was shot through the brains and killed instantly. He was the first man who gave up his life in the vicinity of Fort Henry.

It being noticed that a steamer belonging to the rebels was busily engaged in running from the fortifications to some point up or across the river, and believing that it was bringing in reinforcements, two of the gunboats—the *Taylor* and *Conestoga*, ran up to nearly the centre of the Island, and dropped a few shells in the direction of the fort and the steamer, with what effect it was not known. Being up there, they concluded to stay—sound the west channel, reconnoitre the woods on either side, and prevent the rebels from putting up new batteries, either on the island or Tennessee shore. They effected a thorough reconnoissance on both sides, and also discovered two ugly torpedoes sunk in the west channel, which they carefully hauled out and towed down to the shore below. Their firing only elicited one shot from the rebels, and that burst some four hundred yards short of the boats.

During the day and night the Division of Gen. SMITH, from Paducah, arrived, and was landed on the west shore of the river, with a view of operating against batteries supposed to be on that side, and also to counteract a large body of troops, which our scouts said were concentrating opposite the fort.

Wednesday night was of the most disagreeable description. About 8 o'clock a heavy storm set in, which speedily took the beauty out of the numerous camp fires that, until then, had looked like a new and brighter creation of a mundane Milky Way spread over a sky of inky black. It soon dissolved the inspiring strains of the brass bands, and sent everybody grumbling, wet and disconsolate, to the best shelter he could find. The only offset to the general drizzly dreariness, was the fact that all over the southern horizon, and in the direction of Fort Henry, a tremendous thunder-storm went roaring and reverberating among the hills, and the white-blue lightnings leaped downward as if Heaven itself had become war-mad, and had opened its sulphurous batteries upon Earth. Coming from the south, we could not tell whether it presaged to the rebels what National wrath had in store for them, or whether it indicated the thunder-storm of vengeance that is awaiting our coming. We could only hope that the former was the truth, and then lulled by the roar of the electric strife, we pulled our wet blankets over us, turned again in the yielding mud, and gave ourselves to such slumbers and such dreams as the weather and thoughts of the morrow would permit.

Thursday dawned cloudily, but toward 9 o'clock it cleared up and the sun came out warm and gloriously—nature nowhere seemed to anticipate the bloody event which gives the day prominence. A few more troops arrived, among whom were the Iowa Seventh Col. LAUMAN, and the Iowa Twelfth, Col. WOOD, both from Smithland, and which, together with the Seventh Illinois, Lieut.-Col. BABCOCK: Thirteenth Missouri Col. WRIGHT; the Fiftieth Illinois, Col. ——, and Co. D' First Missouri Artillery, made the Third Brigade, Col. JOHN COOK commanding, and assigned the right wing of the advance up the Tennessee shore.

About 10 o'clock the gunboats started slowly up the river, the four iron clad steamers leading abreast—the *Essex*, Capt. PORTER, on the right, and the *Cincinnati*, Commodore FOOTE, on the left. The three wooden boats also ranged themselves abreast and followed, a half mile or so to the rear of the others. Before parting, Flag-Officer FOOTE shook hands with all his officers, and with a few words of encouragement bade them farewell. No one who witnessed the departure of the fleet had a moment's fear of the result—we were confident that Fort Henry was doomed, and that the hour of reckoning for its treasonable defenders was close at hand.

And so it proved—in just one hour and one minute from the time the first jets of smoke and flame burst from the guns of the flag ship, the traitorous flag of Fort Henry was in the dust, and its defenders strewed in the works or fleeing for life amidst one of the most terrific storms of iron hail that ever fell upon rebel stronghold.

The four boats moved up slowly abreast, keeping up the west or high water channel. Almost immediately on passing the lower end of the Island, the boats and Fort were in each others' range, but on both sides an ominous silence was preserved—a silence that betokened deadly intent on the part of the belligerents. On swept the boats, coming in full view of the long line of breastwork that lined the East shore—in full view of the black muzzles of the heavy guns which seemed watching the approach of the gallant little fleet in ominous silence—in full view of the flag which flaunted defiantly from a high staff in the centre of the works, until one could almost see down the huge bores of the guns, the bright straps of the shells, which seemed like leashes to pre-

[Continued on Eighth Page.]

THE SCENE OF OPERATIONS ON THE NORTH CAROLINA COAST.

Map Showing the Point of Burnside's Attack, Roanoke Island, and its Relations to Norfolk, Weldon, the Internal Navigation of the State, the Railroads, and Other Important Situations.

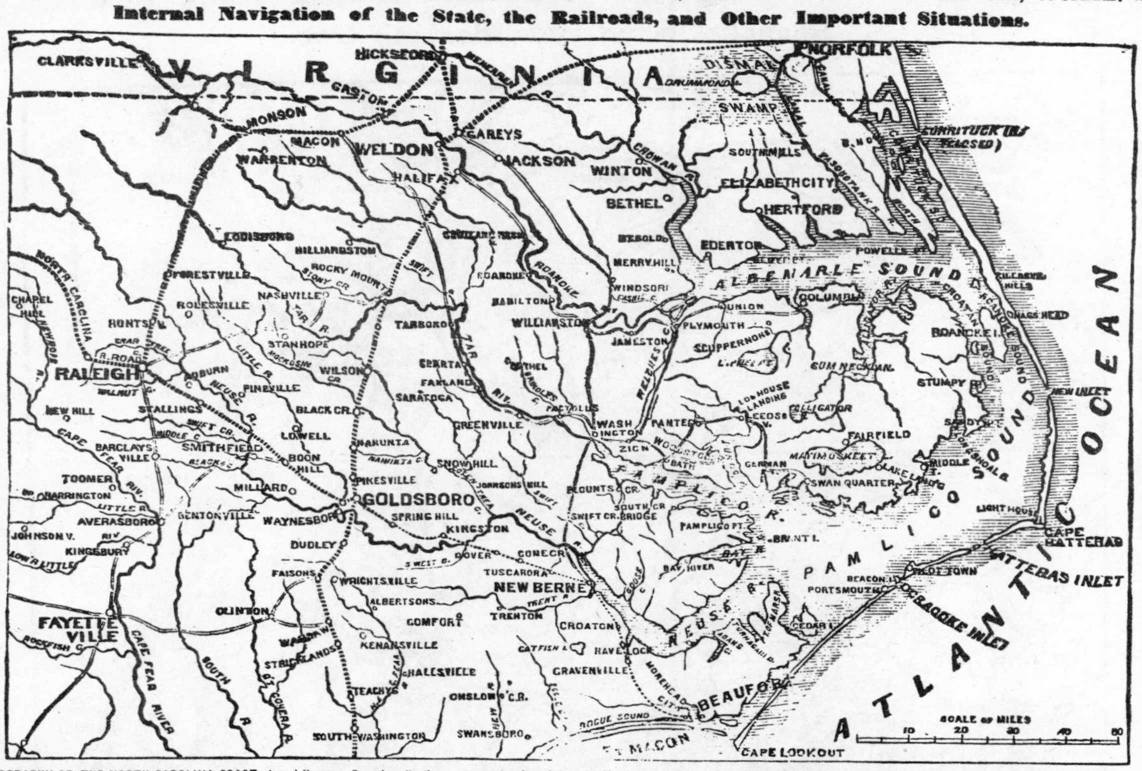

TOPOGRAPHY OF THE NORTH CAROLINA COAST.

North Carolina has no very populous towns. Raleigh, the capital of the State, has a population of 5,000; Newbern, formerly the capital, 5,000; Wilmington, (on the extreme southern point of the State, and its largest town,) 9,000; Fayetteville, 5,000; Beaufort, 2,000; Goldsboro', 1,000; Weldon, 1,000; and there are many other small towns scattered throughout the State, ranging from 1,000 to 3,000 inhabitants. By the last census, the population of the State was 661,586 freemen, and 331,081 slaves. These, free and slave, are nearly all native-born, only two or three thousand Europeans having taken up their residence there.

The topography of North Carolina is remarkable. The State has an extensive coast-line, which, commencing at Little River Inlet, on the borders of South Carolina, runs nearly northeast to Cape Lookout, thence in the same general direction to Cape Hatteras, and thence north to the Virginia line, a distance of nearly 400 miles. Along the whole length of the coast are sandy, barren, desert islands and bars, ranging from a half mile to two miles in width, traversed by numerous inlets, which, with few exceptions, are not navigable. From these islands shoals extend far into the sea, which render the navigation of this coast exceedingly dangerous. Cape Hatteras forms the headland of the dangerous triangular island-beach which separates Pamlico Sound from the ocean. The perilous navigation in the vicinity of Capes Fear and Lookout is sufficiently indicated by the names of those points. In the eastern part of the State, above Cape Lookout, are the two extensive Sounds, *Pamlico* and *Albemarle*, and one of lesser magnitude, Currituck, which are cut off from the ocean by the island or sand-bank before referred to. Pamlico Sound, which is the most southerly, extends from southwest to northwest 86 miles, and is from 10 to 20 miles in width, with a depth of 20 feet, and terminates westwardly in the wide bays of the Neuse and Pamlico Rivers. There are a number of shoals within this sound. On the north it connects with Albermarle and Currituck Sounds. Albermarle is sixty miles in length, and from four to fifteen broad; extends west into the mainland, and is not connected with the ocean except through Pamlico Sound. Its waters are nearly fresh, and not affected by the tides. It sends off a number of branches or little bays on either side, which extend from ten to fifteen miles inland. In the strait which connects Pamlico with Albermarle Sound is situated *Roanoke Island*, the scene of the present engagement. (See Map.) It is about forty miles north of Hatteras Inlet, and the waters on either side of it are designated as Roanoke and Croatem Sounds. On the narrow strip of sand to the East, between Roanoke Sound and the Atlantic Ocean, is a point called Nag's Head, where a force of rebels has for some time been stationed. Roanoke Sound is not navigable by vessels of large size, but Croatem Sound is about four miles broad, and navigable by the heaviest ships of the Burnside Expedition. Roanoke Island was strongly fortified by the rebels. It is the key to Albemarle Sound and its vicinity, and the main position for the defence of Norfolk against approaches from the rear, as well as for the defence of Weldon, and other important railroad points in North Carolina. The other Sound, Currituck, is from two to ten miles wide, and runs parallel with the coast, from which it is cut off by narrow sand islands. It connects with the ocean only through Pamlico Sound.

The seacoast of North Carolina, from fifty to eighty miles inland, including the turpentine region, is level, and abounds in swamps and marshes, the streams are sluggish and muddy, and the land sandy and barren, except along the banks of the streams, where it is very fertile, producing cotton, tobacco and maize, but the intervening country chiefly consists of pine barrens, valuable only for the turpentine yielded so abundantly by the pine forests. The Richmond *Dispatch*, in a late article, anticipating our operations in this region, said:

"It is quite certain, that if the Southern people had been allowed to choose the destination of this expedition for the enemy, they would have designated the very one which the enemy himself has selected. The coast of North Carolina, from Norfolk to Wilmington, with its sand-islands, shifting inlets and shallow sounds, its dismal swamps and everglades, its canebrakes and cypress-bogs, stretching out for miles to the right and left of river channels, constitute the most delightful Cretan labyrinth for the confusion and envelopment of an enemy to be found the world over.

By means of his vessels of shallow draft he may penetrate through the jungle and reach the firm and more elevated inland; but his safety in that case would be put in very great peril. If he masses his troops, we can mass ours likewise and fight him successfully inland, or confine him ingloriously in the narrow channels of the rivers. If he scatters his forces, he puts it in our power to attack and beat them in detail. If he cut our railroad connection with Charleston, that does not ruin us; for we shall soon have a better line under way far in the interior, beyond his reach. His scheme, it seems, is to get into the rear of Norfolk by shallow boats, through the Dismal Swamp Canal, and to destroy the railroad bridge at Weldon. *The natural defences of Norfolk from the Albemarle Sound are almost perfect, requiring but the slightest assistance of art; and as to Weldon, he will find it rather more difficult to reach it than to burn the bridge when there.*"

The Great Dismal Swamp extends north from Albemarle Sound into Virginia—area, 150,000 acres. From the Pasquatank River, through a great part of it, there has been a canal cut, which connects Norfolk with the North Carolina Sounds. Between Pamlico and Albemarle Sounds is Alligator, or Little Dismal Swamp, which is nearly as large as the other; and further south are other swamps, similar in character.

Advancing further into the interior of the State, however, the aspect of the country is quite changed. At a distance of sixty or seventy miles from the coast, the land begins to rise with small hills, stones appear on the surface, and the streams ripple in their course. A little further westward, there is all the variety of hills and dales which denote a fertile country fit for cultivation. West of the pitch-pine region, where we reach the falls of the streams, the soil improves, producing all the small grains in abundance. Still further west is an elevated region forming part of the great table-land of the United States, from one to two thousand feet above the level of the sea, and still beyond this region the Alleghany Mountains traverse the State from northeast to southwest, reaching here their greatest altitude. The people in this section are simple, peaceful and honest, and there is here a great deal of warm loyalty to the Union. They are very similar in character to the mountaineers of East Tennessee. There are but few slaves here, and there has even been an active Anti-Slavery element from time immemorial.

The people of the State are chiefly occupied in agriculture, raising tobacco, cotton, rice and the cereals. The most important branch of manufactures is that of spirits of turpentine, which is produced from the sap of a species of pine. There is an immense extent of territory in North Carolina covered by this sort of pine, extending from a point near the line of Virginia across the entire State, and varying in width from 30 to 80 miles. This belt is situated between the swampy country along the coast and the hilly region of the interior, and consists mainly of a level, sandy barren, called by the natives the "piny woods." The roads here are very poor, being the merest openings through the woods, and generally without bridges across the streams. A correspondent writing from that region thus describes the white and black residents:

"As you penetrate toward the interior, and reach the pine regions, you find the people of color, who are sparse on the coast, have increased in numbers. Here they are extensively employed in the manufacture of tar and turpentine, and in the agricultural pursuits of the country. Hence, when this rebellion was launched headlong on North Carolina by a few hot-headed, unprincipled and designing men, the colored labor of the State was considerably paralyzed. Many of the slaves were taken to the seaboard, and employed in the construction of coast defences. From bills found in Forts Hatteras and Clark, at Hatteras Inlet, we learned that nearly the whole of the work on those fortifications had been performed by the labor of slaves.

The poor whites, as a general thing, were all compelled to serve as soldiers. Out of the North Carolina Seventh Regiment, captured at Hatteras, numbering nearly one thousand officers and men, there were not more than thirty who could be called independent. The great bulk of the rank and file was composed of young men, who had been compelled to work for a living, and who were now compelled to serve as soldiers. They were, without exception, the most forsaken, unhappy, dejected body of men I ever saw. Generally thin in flesh, cadaverous in complexion, narrow across the chest, stooping in the shoulders, crooked in the legs, flatulent, pipe-puffing tobacco-squirting bipeds, in a kind of linsey-woolsey dingy gray, bedizened with yellow taffety binding, they presented a sorry pile of specimen bricks from the poor white foundations of the patriarchal institution of Slavery."

The annual turpentine product of North Carolina is 800,000 barrels, the value of which, to the makers, is about $2,000,000. There are 21,000,000 acres of farming lands in the State, of which only about one-fourth have been improved. Education is at a low ebb: less than half the white children of the State attend school, and a large proportion of poor white adults are unable to read. The census reports 1,790 churches in the State, all of which (except 6 Catholic) are of various Protestant denominations. One peculiar feature of the State Constitution provides that "no person who shall deny the being of a God, or the truth of the Christian religion, or the divine authority of the Old or New Testaments, or who shall hold religious principles incompatible with the freedom or safety of the State," shall hold any civil office. If it had also proscribed Secessionists, it would have been well for North Carolina. The railroads of the State are the North Carolina, extending from Goldsboro to Charlotte; the Raleigh and Gaston, from Raleigh to Weldon; the Wilmington and Weldon, between these points; the Wilmington and Manchester, from Wilmington to Kingsville, S. C.; the Roanoke Valley, from Ridgeway Junction to Clarksville, Va.; and the Atlantic and North Carolina, from Beaufort harbor to Goldsboro, and other uncompleted lines.

ROANOKE ISLAND.

The island is about seven miles long and three broad, and has good natural defences. On both the island itself, at Nag's Head and on the mainland, the rebels had thrown up strong fortifications and planted batteries. According to information furnished, there were five different fortifications and an intrenched camp in the centre. The garrison, some time ago, consisted of 5,000 troops, under command of Major-Gen. HILL, of North Carolina, with Gov. WISE acting as his Brigadier and general factotum; but the probability is, that heavy reinforcements were lately sent there from Manassas. On the mainland opposite, the works were extensive, provided with heavy ordnance, and well manned. Altogether, Roanoke Island was a pretty formidable position. If the attack was successful, as there is little doubt, and if it be, as none of our victories have been, followed up, it will prove one of the most important victories of the war.

THE BURNSIDE EXPEDITION

The First Blow Struck by the Combined Land and Naval Forces.

Capture of Roanoke Island After Three Days' Fighting.

Commodore Lynch's Mosquito Fleet Demolished.

Two of his Gunboats Captured and the Rest Sunk and Scattered.

The National Flag Flying Over the Confederate Batteries.

The People of Norfolk and Portsmouth Panic-Stricken.

FORTRESS MONROE, Monday, Feb. 10, via BALTIMORE, Feb. 11.

A flag of truce to-day brings the intelligence that our troops landed at Roanoke Island yesterday afternoon.

No particulars are given, but it was intimated that the island had been taken.

No papers had been received except the Norfolk *Day Book* of Saturday, the contents of which have already been made public.

REPORTS FROM BALTIMORE.

PHILADELPHIA, Tuesday, Feb. 11.

The Baltimore *Clipper* publishes an extra, stating that Roanoke Island was captured after three days' fighting. Two rebel gunboats were captured and the rest were sunk or scattered.

The people of Norfolk and Portsmouth are panic-stricken.

The news is confirmed by passengers by the Fortress Monroe boat.

INTERESTING PARTICULARS OF THE FIGHT.

Special Dispatch to the Philadelphia Inquirer.

FORTRESS MONROE, Sunday, Feb. 9—P. M.

By a flag of truce, to-day, I learn that the bombardment of the works on Roanoke Island continued during yesterday. About noon, Com. LYNCH got his Mosquito flotilla under way, and came down Currituck Sound to assist his rebel friend, Gen. WISE, on the Island.

The Federal gunboats then directed their fire upon the gunboats commanded by LYNCH, and at 5 o'clock yesterday afternoon three rebel gunboats had been sunk, two were captured, one of which had a Commodore's pennant flying during the action, and the rest dispersed in every direction.

The firing ceased at dark last night, but was recommenced with increased vigor and effect this morning, and kept up until about 8 o'clock, when, it is supposed, the rebel forces on the island surrendered.

A fireman on board the *Selden* said that the Federal troops had been landed in large numbers on Roanoke Island, and that the Stars and Stripes could be seen at Elizabeth City flying over the Confederate batteries. It was rumored in Norfolk, this morning, that three regiments had been recently sent to Roanoke Island, and that as there was no chance for escape, the probability was that they were all captured.

The rebels acknowledge that the only obstacles of importance to retard Gen. BURNSIDE's march inland and upon Norfolk, will be the natural ones of swamps, marshes, sickness, &c.

The rebels feel their recent defeats very sensibly, and are growing desperate in their fear.

THE EXPEDITION TO NORTH CAROLINA.

Details of the Military and Naval Forces Engaged.

FULL LIST OF REGIMENTS AND THEIR OFFICERS

The Gunboats—Their Armament, Officers, Size, &c.

Now that the Burnside Expedition has at last arrived at its point of destination and operation, at Roanoke Island, in the waters of North Carolina, we present our readers with full details of all the forces, military and naval, composing the Expedition, from which a clear and correct idea of its formidable nature may be obtained.

AMBROSE EVERETT BURNSIDE
Brigadier-General Commanding Expedition.

STAFF:

Capt. Lewis Richmond, Assistant-Adjutant Gen'l.
Capt. Herman Biggs, Division Quartermaster.
Capt. Wm. Cutting, Assistant Quartermaster.
Capt. E. R. Goodrich, Division Commissary.
Capt. Jas. F. DeWolf, Assist'nt Division Commis'ry.
Dr. W. H. Church, Medical Director.
Dr. J. H. Thompson, Medical Purveyor.
Lieut. D. W. Flagler, Ordnance Officer.
Lieut. Duncan C. Pell, } Aides-de-camp.
Lieut. George Fearing, }
Private Secretaries to Gen. Burnside—Daniel Larned and W. H. French.

FIRST BRIGADE.

BRIGADIER-GENERAL JOHN G. FOSTER.

STAFF.—Capt. C. S. Hoffman, Assistant Adjutant-General.
Capt. David Messinger, Quartermaster.
Capt. E. E. Potter, Commissary.
Capt. P. W. Hudson, Aid-de-Camp.
Dr. J. H. Thompson, Brigade Surgeon.
Lieut. E. N. Strong, }
Lieut. G. W. Pendleton } Volunteer Aids.
Lieut. J. B. Anderson, }

The following are the regiments and officers of this brigade:

MASSACHUSETTS TWENTY-THIRD REGIMENT

Colonel—John Kurtz.
Lieut.-Colonel—Henry Merritt.
Major—Andrew Elwell.
Captains—Brewster, Martin, Centre, Howland, Alexander, Whipple, Raymond, Sawyer, Hobbs, Hart.

MASSACHUSETTS TWENTY-FOURTH REGIMENT.

Colonel—Thomas G. Stevenson.
Lieut.-Colonel—F. A. Osborn.
Major—R. H. Stevenson.
Captains—Hooper, Redding, Richardson, Maker, Prince, Jr., Austin, Clarke, Stackpole, Deland, Pratt.

MASSACHUSETTS TWENTY-FIFTH REGIMENT.

Colonel—Edwin Upton.
Lieut.-Colonel—Aug. B. R. Sprague.
Major—Matthew J. McCafferty.
Captains—Pickett, Clark, Atwood, Foster, Neill, Foss, Wagley, Moulton, Parkhurst, Denny.

MASSACHUSETTS TWENTY-SEVENTH REGIMENT.

Colonel—Horace C. Lee.
Lieut.-Colonel—Luke Lyman.
Major—W. G. Bartholomew.
Captains—Vance, Caswell, Walker, Sloan, Fuller, Thayer, Swift, Sanford, Hubbard, Cooley.

[Continued on Second Page.]

THE NEW YORK HERALD.

WHOLE NO. 9286. NEW YORK, THURSDAY, FEBRUARY 13, 1862. PRICE TWO CENTS.

IMPORTANT NEWS.

The Capture of Roanoke Island Fully Confirmed by the Rebels.

TERRIBLE FIGHTING.

Three Hundred Rebels Killed and One Thousand Wounded.

THE ENTIRE REBEL FLEET DESTROYED

ELIZABETH CITY TAKEN.

The Place Burned by the Rebels.

Two Thousand Rebel Prisoners Taken.

Advance of the Union Troops on Edenton.

OPINIONS OF THE REBEL PRESS, &c., &c., &c.

We learn by the flag of truce which arrived at Fortress Monroe on Sunday of the complete success of the Burnside expedition at Roanoke Island.

The island was taken possession of and Commodore Lynch's fleet completely destroyed. Three hundred rebels were killed and wounded, and two thousand taken prisoners. Scarcely any escaped.

Elizabeth City was attacked on Sunday and evacuated by the inhabitants. The city was previously burned.

The first news of the defeat arrived at Norfolk on Sunday afternoon, and caused great excitement. The previous news was very satisfactory, stating that the Yankees had been allowed to advance for the purpose of driving them into a trap.

The rebel force on the island is supposed to have been only a little over three thousand efficient fighting men.

General Wise was ill at Nag's Head, and was not present during the engagement. When the situation became dangerous he was removed to Norfolk.

All the gunboats but one were taken, and that escaped up a creek, and was probably also destroyed.

One report says that only seventy and another that only twenty-five of the rebels escaped from the island.

General Huger telegraphed to Richmond that only fifty on the island escaped.

There appears to be no bright side of the story for the rebels.

THE REBEL DETAILS.

The following despatches on the subject are taken from the Richmond papers of Tuesday morning:—

NORFOLK, Feb. 10, 1862.

The latest news states that Captain O. Jennings Wise, son of Governor Wise, was shot through the hip and disabled, though his wound was not mortal. Major Lawson and Lieutenant Miller were mortally wounded. *About three hundred confederates were killed. Our wounded number over one thousand.* The number of Yankees wounded is about the same. Midshipman Camm has had an arm shot off. The other casualties are as yet unreported.

A late arrival this morning says that Elizabeth City had been shelled and burned by the Yankees, and that the enemy was pushing on to Edenton.

SECOND DESPATCH.

NORFOLK, Feb. 10, 1862.

A rumor has prevailed that Commodore Lynch's fleet of gunboats had been captured. It is not regarded as true, but *it is believed that all were burned by the confederates to prevent their capture*, with the exception of one, which was endeavoring to make its escape. The fleet went to Elizabeth City from Roanoke Island, and was probably burned at the former point.

THIRD DESPATCH.

NORFOLK, Feb. 10, 1862.

A courier arrived here this afternoon at four o'clock, and brought the intelligence that *Elizabeth City was burned this morning by its inhabitants.* During the conflagration the federals landed a large force. All our gunboats excepting one were captured by the enemy.

General Wise had not yet arrived at Norfolk.

THE VERY LATEST.

The following "very latest" we copy from the Norfolk *Day Book*:—

[From the Norfolk Day Book, Feb. 10.]

It is said that the enemy came up in their boats on the south side of the island, and by means of their boat howitzers *effected a landing in the rear of our batteries*, and that after landing about fifteen thousand on all parts of the island, they marched up and flanked the batteries. It is also reported that, notwithstanding our small force of twenty-one hundred men against about fifteen thousand, on some parts of the island the resistance was of the most desperate nature, and a hand-to-hand contest lasted for a considerable time, showing the most desperate courage. This is said to have been the case particularly with the Richmond Blues, under command of Captain O. Jennings Wise. Captain Wise, we learn, fell bravely urging his men on.

[From the Norfolk Day Book, Feb. 11.]

A courier arrived here yesterday afternoon about three o'clock, from whom we gather the following information:—

The enemy advanced in full force upon Elizabeth City yesterday about seven o'clock, and began an attack upon that place. *The citizens, finding resistance vain, evacuated the place, but before doing so set fire to the town, and when our informant left it was still in flames.*

We have also to record the capture by the enemy of all our little fleet, except the Fanny or Forrest—our informant is not certain which. This eluded the enemy and made up Pasquotank river. She was pursued, however, and fears are entertained that she was captured. It is said that before our boats surrendered they were abandoned, and that their crews succeeded in making their escape. If so, we are at a loss to conjecture why the boats were not fired before they were abandoned.

The disaster to our little fleet is attributed to the fact that, having exhausted their supply of coal and their ammunition, they proceeded to Elizabeth City for the purpose of obtaining a supply. Every effort was made to obtain coal, but without success, and the boats could not, therefore, return to the island and lend any assistance whatever to our forces.

All the details, as published, with reference to the capture of Roanoke Island, are confirmed by the courier, who represents our loss at three hundred killed and wounded, and that of the enemy not less than one thousand killed. Great havoc was made among the enemy while coming up the road leading to the fort. Our forces brought to bear upon them two thirty-two pounders, and at every fire their ranks were terribly thinned. The places of the fallen, however, were quickly filled.

The Pork Point battery was manned by the Richmond Blues, and most nobly did they defend it. During the fight they were attacked by a whole regiment of Zouaves, and though completely overpowered, they stood their ground. They did not yield a foot until all but seven of them had fallen bleeding to the ground.

There is good reason to believe that had Colonel Henningsen, with his artillery, been on the island, it would not have been forced to surrender. The lack of field pieces was sadly felt, and had they been at hand perhaps the enemy never would have been able to have landed their forces. Colonel Henningsen had orders, we understand, to report at Roanoke Island; but by some misunderstanding he mistook Elizabeth City for his place of destination.

Captain Taylor, of this city, is represented as having distinguishing himself for his coolness and bravery. He fought the enemy like a tiger, and not an inch of ground was yielded by him without its being well disputed.

In addition to the above there are many rumors we might give; but as they are nothing more than rumors we prefer withholding them. Among them, however, is one worthy of notice—that General Wise had been shot while on his way in an ambulance. The statement, so far as we have been able to learn, is untrue. We can only account for it by supposing that the name of the General was confounded with that of his son, who was reported among the killed.

BRILLIANT OPERATIONS AT ROANOKE ISLAND.

Scene of General Burnside and Commodore Goldsborough's Victories—Roanoke Island and Elizabeth City.

ADDITIONAL PARTICULARS.

[Special correspondence of the Richmond Dispatch.]

NORFOLK, Feb. 10, 1862.

With inexpressible sorrow *I announce the fall of Roanoke Island*, after a spirited and heroic resistance by our brave troops. This occurred between twelve and two o'clock on Saturday, and the news was received here with every indication of regret and indignation. We gather the following particulars from a young man from the Richmond Blues, who participated in the fight, escaped in a small boat and rowed to Nag's Head, where he was taken up by one of our gunboats and brought to this city. He is an intelligent lad, and I believe a son of your Postmaster. The enemy's ships, he says, opened fire on our batteries, at Roanoke Island, about seven o'clock in the morning, and kept up an incessant fire until seven o'clock in the evening, doing, however, but little injury to the island. About nine o'clock the next day (Saturday), the Hessians were allowed to land on a point to the east of Roanoke Island, where they marched upon that point. The booming of heavy cannon in the distance heralded the enemy's approach. Our brave troops prepared to meet them, supposing their numbers to be about 5,000. Gradually the sounds came nearer and nearer, and the shell came thick and fast over our intrenchments. Confident of their own strength, our troops moved rapidly forward, when, in a few minutes, the ball opened and the terrific contest ensued. Bravely did our boys stand up to the overwhelming forces of the enemy, and not till nearly every man was dead or wounded did they leave their stand. Nothing remained but retreat, which our men did, constantly turning and giving them a shot. Finding it useless to hold the island under such overwhelming numbers, the order to retreat from the island was given, and our remaining troops retired, leaving their stronghold in the hands of the enemy.

It will be a pleasure hereafter to record on the page of history the heroic fortitude of our gallant troops. Nobly and well did Captain O. Jennings Wise, of your city, stand up with his men to the fierce encounter, when, suddenly, he was shot through the side and instantly fell. One of his men asking him if he was much hurt—"Not much," said he, "but fight them yet." He was borne from the scene of action in a blanket. *About 300 of our brave boys fell, and nearly all the rest were either wounded or taken prisoners.* The enemy's loss is laid down at 1,000. *Four of their ships were sunk*, they doing but little damage to any of our boats. Commodore Lynch and other parts of our fleet did noble service, his ship being among the first to open fire on the enemy's shipping. At last accounts they were in pursuit of Commodore Lynch.

In the midst of this terrible struggle it will be regretted that General Wise was seriously indisposed at Nag's Head. Both he and his son are expected here to-day. I am sorry to say that but very few escaped from Captain Wise's company. Large quantities of ammunition were saved by our troops. The women, children and a number of negroes are reported now on their way to our city. The enemy will be successfully checked from getting possession of our railroad in that vicinity. Active preparations have been made here regarding this disaster, which it may be imprudent for me to mention. The news fell upon the ears of our citizens with fearful significance. Many would dare shut their eyes against the fact had not dread conviction come so direct. Every man was at his post, and our departments here were engaged in sending despatches to the various encampments. The alacrity with which every officer executed his orders is a theme of public praise; and especial praise is due to the Young Guard of our city for their services on the occasion. At a very late hour military movements were going on, and everything is in great excitement.

NORFOLK, Feb. 10, 1862.

The intelligence of the desperate and unequalled contest at Roanoke Island, and its result, have doubtless reached you by telegraph. Of course this is the principal subject of conversation here. Considering all the circumstances attending the fight, a more favorable termination of the affair could scarcely have been expected by those competent to judge. Our force on the island at the time of the attack was but small in comparison with the heavy and numerous force of the enemy. Of the bravery and gallant conduct of our troops too much can scarcely be said in commendation. That they were overpowered by greatly superior numbers, after fighting with a recklessness and desperation never surpassed, is a fact already established, and which will be placed upon the truthful pages of history.

I send you herewith such particulars of the battle as I have been able to gather. A true account cannot be given now. We know enough to cause a deep sigh of grief for the brave men slain, and the gallant sons of the South, who are now captives in this cruel war—of homes rendered desolate, of hearts wrung with anguish, and ties of love and friendship severed. But who believes, except the deluded and revengeful Yankees, that the South will ever yield to them?—that the great cause of Southern liberty, and honor, and humanity is not still onward?

True, the news comes that the hospitable town of Elizabeth City has been shelled and burned, and that the vandal hordes are desolating the pleasant places of the Sound coast. But they cannot go far into the interior, and the day is coming when these Northern minions shall be driven back in disgrace to their inhospitable and barren soil.

General Wise, though still sick, is, I learn, on his way to this city. Captain O. Jennings Wise was dangerously wounded. Major Lawson, Lieutenant Miller and Captain Coles, are reported among the killed. The enemy lost in killed and wounded one thousand, our loss three hundred, *besides more than two thousand prisoners.* We must be nerved for a vigorous resistance, and Providence will assist us as heretofore in this cause of honor, and truth, and human rights.

OPINIONS OF THE REBEL PRESS.

[From the Richmond Examiner, Feb. 11.]

The loss of an entire army on Roanoke Island is certainly the most painful event of the war. The intelligence of yesterday by telegraph is fully confirmed. Twenty-five hundred brave troops on an island in the sea were exposed to all the force of the Burnside fleet. They resisted with the most determined courage; but when fifteen thousand federal troops were landed against them, retreat being cut off by the surrounding element, they were forced to surrender. This is a repetition of the Hatteras affair on a large scale.

It is reported that one regiment from Massachusetts was badly cut up; but it is impossible to ascertain which of the five that were attached to the expedition it was.

All the Southern papers received to-day are unanimous in admitting a complete victory to our troops, and in saying that the loss of the island is a very serious one.

The prisoners captured, numbering at least two thousand, will arrive at Fortress Monroe in a few days.

[From the Richmond Dispatch, Feb. 11.]

THE DISASTER AT ROANOKE ISLAND.

The exciting occurrence at Roanoke Island, resulting in a reverse to our arms, was the theme of conversation yesterday in the city, to the exclusion of almost every other topic. The fact that some of our Richmond companies were engaged in the fight occasioned an intense and painful anxiety, particularly among those who had friends or relatives among them, which could not be well concealed. It is but a short period since the Wise Legion, after an arduous and toilsome campaign in Western Virginia, left here for the coast of North Carolina, and though now defeated in one of the most desperate conflicts of the war, it is at least consoling to know that the men fought with determined bravery, against overwhelming odds, and won for themselves the proud appellation of heroes, of which their present situation cannot deprive them. The Light Infantry Blues (Company A, of the Legion), date their organization as far back as the year 1793, and number among their honorary members many of our oldest and most venerated citizens. The history of the company is so well known that we need not repeat it here. Captain O. Jennings Wise was elected commander a short time before the war broke out, and the corps was one of the first to respond to the call of the country. Captain Wise is reported badly wounded, and Lieutenants Fred. Carter and Charles P. Bigger are taken prisoners, with, it is presumed, a majority of the men. The Jackson Guard and the Light Guard, both attached to the Legion, were enlisted here after the commencement of the war. Captain Hiram B. Dickinson, of the former, and Captain Geo. Wallace, of the latter, reported captured by the enemy, are well known citizens of Richmond. Lieutenant Miller, of the Jackson Guard, is said to be mortally wounded. Major Hugh W. Fry, who is among the prisoners, has many friends here, who regret his misfortune, but who are proud to believe that he sustained himself gallantly in the fight, and the same remark applies to Frank Johnston, of the Blues, as brave a young man as ever shouldered a musket.

The telegraph informs us that our killed and wounded amounts to 300, while that of the enemy reaches 1,000. The reader will find some further particulars of the affair in our Norfolk papers, from which it appears that the infamous scoundrels have shelled and burned the pleasant little town of Elizabeth City, and are threatening Edenton. Their operations in that quarter, however, will be limited; and instead of depressing the spirits of our people, such acts of vandalism will serve to make them more determined, and rouse them to thrice vigorous resistance.

Personally we regret the loss of our accomplished correspondent "Bohemian," whose letters from the Potomac and other points have for some time past adorned the columns of this paper. Dr. Shephordson is well known throughout the South, and in his captivity (which we trust will be brief) he has the sympathy of a vast number of friends.

THE CAMPAIGN IN CAROLINA.

[From the Richmond Dispatch, Feb. 11.]

Until within a day or two past, *the capture of Roanoke Island by Burnside was considered a foregone conclusion.* A fleet of nearly a hundred sail and an army of fifteen or twenty thousand men, with guns and equipments in profusion, were esteemed equal to the capture of any exposed piece of water bound land like the island in question. But the brave resistance offered for nearly two days by our troops, and the hopeful terms in which they spoke of their prospects, led our people to believe that the island might be held. It has, however been lost, and we are compelled to resign ourselves to the conclusion which a day or two of hope—we confess not strong in our own case—had unsettled.

Burnside has landed, after a hard fight, on a seaboard island, not as advantageously situated, nor encompassed by as rich surroundings of country as Beaufort. His object is supposed by some to be Norfolk; but if we are to believe the recent outgivings of Northern journals, his leading purpose is to make a demonstration against the Weldon and Wilmington Railroad, with a view to cutting our great line of Southern communication. *That thing seems, for the present, to be the especial aim of the enemy in every quarter.* His movements in Western Kentucky and Tennessee seem to have that single object for the present in view; and it has been repeatedly declared by Northern journals that Burnside's primary purpose is a demonstration upon our railroad. It remains to be seen whether such be his real design, and with what success he will prosecute it. The experience of Sherman in a similar undertaking may possibly be his own.

An assault upon Norfolk is the only object next after this railroad enterprise, commensurate in importance with the magnitude of the expedition. In such an undertaking the enemy's vessels could be of little direct use. The water approaches to that city from North Carolina are too narrow, tortuous and easily obstructed to admit the use of vessels; and if the enemy attempts a land attack the chances in our favor of repelling him are two or three to one. The reduction of Norfolk would be the work of months, and could only be effected by a large increase of Burnside's forces, an increase which the Yankee exchequer is not able to afford for an operation stretching through a protracted period. *Nothing at all can save their treasury, and nothing can keep the war on foot but rapid operations and decisive successes.* Yet we do not see wherein the Burnside expedition promises these results more unmistakably than Sherman's did, which landed in November, nearly three months ago.

Measured by its cost to the enemy, not even the capture of Norfolk, if it could be effected, would compensate him for his outlays, and this at last is the true standard by which his successes should be estimated. The South need not expect, and cannot rationally expect, that these huge expeditions, fitted out at immense expense, should fail to effect any achievement. Fifteen or twenty thousand men landed anywhere upon our seaboard must succeed in getting possession. It would be idle to expect otherwise, and imbecile to be discouraged by the fact. The true consideration is, whether such successes repay their cost.

Measured by this standard, the achievements of the Burnside expedition are not likely to be very important. *Its cost cannot have been less, in the first instance, than ten millions of dollars, and its charges every day are at least a quarter of a million.* It has been thirty-one days prosecuting its career to the point of capturing Roanoke Island, a feat which has cost the federal government several millions, independently of the first outlay in the enterprise, and the losses incurred by the storm. If the expedition should succeed in capturing the whole Carolina seaboard, and even a considerable slice of the country besides, together with Norfolk, still the fifteen or twenty millions of federal money laid out in the whole operation would not be reimbursed by half.

We are not of those who suffer discouragement from occasional successes of the enemy. They have far overtaxed the resources of the North in bringing their prodigious forces into the field. The effect may be to damage us considerably, but they are damaging themselves much more. The injury they inflict upon us is local and remediable; that which they bring upon themselves in debt and taxation, is general, universal and enduring. They have chosen a gigantic and expensive programme, which must break down, and which no successes, however great, can compensate the cost of.

THE REBEL ISLAND AND TOWNS.

ROANOKE ISLAND AND ITS ADVANTAGES.

A few days ago we gave a brief description of Roanoke Island, and pointed out the advantages to be derived from its capture and occupation. The news, however, which we lay before our readers this morning, of the brilliant victory of the Union arms under General Burnside and Commodore Goldsborough, is of so much importance that we think it not out of place to give a more detailed account of the island and of the advantages which have fallen into our hands by its capture.

Roanoke Island is twelve miles long and three miles wide, and is about fifty miles up Pamlico Sound. It was said to be fortified by the rebels on the southern, western and eastern shores, and defended with heavy ordnance, and on the 12th January, when the rebels learned of the arrival of Gen. Burnside at Hatteras Inlet, they instantly commenced the construction of a battery about midway of the island. In addition to this they had thrown up five forts, with an intrenched camp in the centre, and had their works garrisoned by some five thousand troops, in order to prevent the passage of our gunboats through the Croatan Sound—the only communication with Albemarle Sound. But the cheering news has now reached us of their being shelled out of their strongholds by the powerful Union expedition which was brought against them, consisting of seventeen gunboats most powerfully armed with rifled artillery, among which were a dozen nine-inch guns, two one hundred-pounder rifled guns, four eighty-pounders, and a large number of eight-inch shell and thirty-two-pounders.

The capture of Roanoke Island is of much importance, inasmuch as it commands all the water communication along the whole North Carolina coast, as well as a portion of Southeastern Virginia. Being in possession of it, we are enabled to cut off all supplies by water from Norfolk, so that hereafter the rebels will be compelled to get their supplies wherever they can, and entirely by land; for Norfolk can also be cut off here, as also from the course across Albemarle Sound northward to the point where the Pasquotank and North rivers empty. There are two routes from this last point to Norfolk—one by Pasquotank river, Dismal Swamp Canal and south branch of Elizabeth river, and the other by the North river of Albemarle and Pamlico Canal, Currituck Sound, the North river of Currituck, the upper cut of the Albemarle and Pamlico Canal, and the Elizabeth river. During the winter months the first is passable for vessels drawing about six feet of water. The Pasquotank river is three miles wide at its mouth, and gradually narrows until at Elizabeth City it is only about three hundred yards wide.

Currituck is about fifty miles long, ten miles wide, and is navigable for vessels drawing ten feet of water. Albe-

(CONTINUED ON EIGHTH PAGE.)

The Philadelphia Inquirer.

ESTABLISHED 1829. | PHILADELPHIA, SATURDAY, FEBRUARY 15, 1862. | PRICE TWO CENTS.

THE GREAT VICTORY!

STORY OF AN EYE-WITNESS.

Bombardment of the Rebel Forts.

AN ACTION OF EIGHT HOURS DURATION.

THE CHEVAUX DE FRISE!

LANDING OF THE TROOPS.

STANDING BY THE GUNS AT NIGHT.

A BATTLE IN A SWAMP.

Terrible Charge upon a Masked Battery

FORDING THE MOAT.

The Flags of New York and Massachusetts upon the Rebel Parapets.

FLIGHT OF THE ENEMY AND DEATH OF WISE.

THE FLAG OF TRUCE.

The Surrender of Thirteen Hundred of the Rebels.

THE DARING OF "DE MONTEIL."

Full List of Killed and Wounded.

TERRIBLE SCENES UPON THE BATTLE-FIELD.

Descriptions of Rebel Fortifications.

AFTER THE BATTLE.

THE OFFICIAL REPORTS.

From Our Special Reporter.

Departure of Burnside's Expedition from Hatteras Inlet for Roanoke Island.

SAILING ORDERS—GENERAL BURNSIDE'S ADDRESS TO HIS SOLDIERS.

At seven o'clock, Tuesday evening, February fourth, the steamer *Patuxent* went alongside the vessels comprising the fleet, and delivered orders to get ready for sailing from Hatteras Inlet the morning following. The news soon spread through the entire ship, and great was the joy manifested, from the colonel down to the cook. Games of whist, chess and backgammon were suddenly ended; captains shook hands with corporals, congratulating one another upon an early departure; even the "specials" who, it was believed, had become callous to everything that boded another period of interest, refilled their pipes, and looked at each other with deliberate astonishment. "O, no!" says one, "I've heard all that before. Hereafter, I shall believe a thing when I see it, and not before. Note that down." Incredulity seemed to hang from every projection like dusty cobwebs along the ancient walls of some gloomy monastery or gathering place of a few Platonic individuals who had become disgusted with the conventicles of social life, and secluded themselves from the gaze and knowledge of the world's people. "Look out for a movement to-morrow," was a sentence so familiar to the ear that it bordered upon the ridiculous, and a man who ventured to make the assertion, towards the last of our torpidity at Hatteras, was set upon as a fit subject for an asylum.

Sailing Orders.

To say that we retired early, however, and awoke at the call of "one bell" (half-past four) in the morning, denotes that a hope was left that another glimpse of blue sky above and blue water beneath might again be afforded us. Subjoined is a copy of our sailing orders:—

HEAD-QUARTERS SECOND BRIGADE,
Depart't of North Carolina, steamer *Patuxent*,
February 4, 1862.

GENERAL ORDERS, No. 8.—The following orders have been issued at the Head-quarters Department of North Carolina:—

SIGNALS.

For Starting.—The Union jack at the foremast, with the Brigade flag (blue letter A in the centre) underneath, with American flag at the stern, shall be the signal for the weighing of anchor and starting.

Anchoring.—The American flag at the foremast shall be the signal for coming to anchor, the vessels of each brigade close to each other.

Anchoring in a Fog.—Two whistles from the flag-ship, repeated at intervals of one minute. This signal will be repeated by the flag-ship of each brigade.

For Landing: Preparatory.—Union jack at the foremast.

Getting into Boats.—American flag underneath the Union jack.

Landing.—Brigade flag underneath the Union jack and American flag.

In case of Stranding or Distress.—The signal shall be the American flag, Union down. At this signal, the whole fleet will slacken speed, and look for the signal to anchor. All the tugs and light draught vessels will be sent at once to the assistance of the disabled vessels by the Commander of each brigade.

By order,

J. L. RENO, Brigadier-General.

E. M. NEILL, Assistant Adjutant-General.

GENERAL ORDERS, No. 9.—The following orders and directions as to disembarking will be strictly followed and obeyed by the commanding officer of this Brigade:—Let all the thole pins (of the small boats) be secured by lanyards underneath, so that when they are taken out they may not be lost. A large and strong pair of stairs, with man ropes, will be made to fit on each of the four gangways of the steamers, and one on each side forward, and one on each side aft of the propellers and sail vessels. One officer must be placed at each stair to disembark the men, receive their muskets and pass them to the men when in the boats.

Two sailors will be detailed for each boat, the rest of the crew to be supplied from the soldiers, and the crews will not be changed unless deemed necessary by the commanding officer. A steering oar, if there be no rudder to the boat, must be rigged, and a coxswain appointed to each boat.

At the signal of the Union jack at the foremast of the flag-ship of the brigade, (*Patuxent*,) the boats will be cleared away, lowered, and the rowers and coxswain placed in them at a signal of the American flag under the Union jack, at the foremast of the flag-ship of the brigade (with the letter A in the centre) under the Union jack and American flag. If the transports of the brigade cannot approach within easy rowing distance of the shore, all the boats of the different vessels of the brigade will, at the third signal, row to the *Patuxent* and attach themselves in two lines as they arrive in succession—the painter of each being attached to the stern of the preceding boat. The *Patuxent* will give one whistle in starting [illegible] the coxswain of each boat [illegible] the boat. At three whistles all the painters will be cast off, [illegible] boat the proper direction toward the shore, [illegible] will seize the oars and pull rapidly to land, when all the soldiers will jump out at once, holding up their cartridge boxes and muskets, and form rapidly in line by the colors of their regiment, without regard to companies. A field officer will accompany the first detachment. Having made one trip, the boat will return and land the rest of the regiment as rapidly as possible. In order that the officers and men may fully understand the movement, the commanding officers will drill the men in getting in the boats and out, when practicable, so that all in succession may be fully instructed.

It is absolutely necessary that the most silent, prompt obedience be rendered during the disembarkation, so that all confusion and consequent delay may be avoided, and the commanding officers are urged to give their personal attention to the preparing of all necessary detail, by designating boats, finding their capacity, and assigning the officers and men for each and every trip, &c.

Three days' cooked rations will be carried in the haversacks, and canteens will be filled with water; overcoats will be carried, but knapsacks left on board. The vessels will start in the following order, and retain their places in line:—*Northerner*, *George Peabody*, *Cossack*, *Lancer* and *Pioneer*. The *Patuxent* and tug-boat will not take places.

By order of J. L. RENO, Brigadier-General.

EDWARD M. NEILL, Assist.-Adjt.-Gen.

Each Brigadier-General commanding was supplied with a copy of the above, to which his signature was attached, previous to its being delivered to the Colonel of a regiment in his brigade; the orders, of course, designating different vessels and signed by the officer commanding each brigade.

Gen. Burnside's Address to his Soldiers.

HEAD-QUARTERS DEPARTMENT N. CAROLINA,
PAMLICO SOUND, Feb. 3, 1862.

GENERAL ORDERS, No. 5.—This Expedition being about to land on the soil of North Carolina, the General Commanding desires his soldiers to remember that they are here to support the Constitution and the laws, to put down rebellion and to protect the persons and property of the loyal and peaceable citizens of the State. On the march of the army, all unnecessary injury to houses, barns, fences and other property will be carefully avoided, and in all cases the laws of civilized warfare will be strictly observed.

Wounded soldiers will be treated with every care and attention, and neither they nor prisoners must be insulted by word or act.

With the fullest confidence in the character and valor of his troops, the Commanding General looks forward to a speedy and successful termination of the campaign.

By command of Brig.-General A. E. BURNSIDE,
LEWIS RICHMOND, Assistant Adjutant-General.

Across Pamlico Sound.

Wednesday morning came—not with a rosy east, nor balmy breeze, but a keen, raw atmosphere and leaden sky, that bespoke a rough passage whithersoever our way opined. Signals were watched, and every precaution taken to get under way as early as possible after orders were issued. Presently the boatswain's whistle, calling, "Away, away—heave anchor," denoted our departure for, to us, an unknown destination. It was nine o'clock before the wheels of our good vessel moved us forward, and the First Brigade had already got under headway, and were following, in the wake of the flag ship, towards the broad expanse of Pamlico Sound. Onward we rushed, each steamer towing from one to three schooners and brigs, laden with soldiers and munitions of war. Gay-colored streamers fluttered in the air, plaintive notes of the clarionet and trumpet, intermingled with the clanging of cymbals and drums, swelled out and sank away in delightful cadences; and just then, to increase the enthusiasm of the scene, the glorious sun burst forth in complete effulgence.

Within one hour from the time of our departure seventy-five vessels were under way and in sailing order, according to their classification in the three brigades—first, on the right; second, in the middle; and the third on the left.

Gradually the Forts Hatteras, Clark, and the spars at Hatteras sank down the southern horizon, and by one o'clock it was blue overhead, blue beneath and blue around. Save our own fleet no object appeared on any side, except it might be an occasional empty barrel or box thrown over from some of the war vessels.

Land Ho!—At Anchor.

About two o'clock in the afternoon we made out the North Carolina shore on the left, and then it was apparent to all that our destination was Roanoke Island. At length a six months' mystery was solved, and every doubter silenced. Nothing of unusual interest transpired during the balance of the day, and, at sundown, a gun, discharged from the *Picket*, announced the termination of our first day's voyage.—The rattling of chain cables on every side told the most inexperienced that the fleet was anchoring.—The low, dark shore of Carolina stretched along the western sky, while to the eastward nothing but the white-capped billows reared their heads to break the water line. The various sailing craft, which were attached by strong hawsers to the different steamers, retained their positions astern, and, as the sea became quiet and the moon shone brightly, they continued hanging on throughout the night. Early in the morning boats were lowered and filled with forty and fifty men, who went through the movements necessary to impart a limited knowledge of what would be necessary upon disembarking for a land attack.

We Enter upon Another Day—Fog and Rain—Cautious Movements.

About nine o'clock A.M., Thursday, the fleet again got under weigh, and in half an hour passed Stumpy Point, and made the dismantled Roanoke Marsh Light. The morning opened with a foggy and humid aspect, which finally culminated in a pouring rain, preventing any but a limited view, and finally compelling most of the fleet, with the exception of the gun-boats, to anchor, which they did within easy distance of the shore. Two or three apparently deserted buildings, and the light-house at the Marshes, were the only evidences of civilization yet evinced during a day's sail up Pamlico Sound.

Interminable forests of cypress, pitch pine, and other valuable timber, extend more than half the length of the North Carolina coast, approachable by light draught vessels at almost any place. There are also many valuable fisheries, where shad and herring are caught in such abundance that their cost is comparatively nominal.

The unfavorable weather continued with us throughout the day and night, but the morning brought indications of pleasant weather, which were soon verified by the breaking clouds.

The Attack on Fort Bartow, Roanoke Island.

STOUT RESISTANCE BY THE REBELS—A FEARFUL DISCHARGE OF SHOT AND SHELL FROM THE FEDERAL GUN-BOATS.

Satisfactory evidence having been gained the previous evening, by several of General BURNSIDE's staff—who were out on a reconnoitring cruise in four small tugs—that the enemy were disposed to make fight from four batteries commanding the main channel through Croatan Sound, preparations for an early advance were made, and by ten o'clock in the forenoon we were under way for the conflict. The gun-boats led off, running ahead of the transports two or three miles.

Having a position on board of the "relief boat" *Tempest*, which had been detailed to tow out any vessel that might happen to become disabled by the enemy's fire, or getting aground while passing before their battery, I had superior facilities for observing this contest. Sharp cannonading from both sides commenced a few minutes after ten o'clock, at which period such of our gun-boats as drew no more than seven or eight feet of water were actively engaged. About noon the action was hottest, and then it was that the barracks of the enemy took fire from our shells, and caused a dense smoke to rise for more than an hour, obscuring, at times, the fort and adjacent shore. At this juncture it was believed that the Rebels were getting the worst of it, for their fire soon became slower and extremely irregular.

The gun-boat [illegible], taking advantage of the temporary lull, ran close in to the fort, and opening her two heavy guns, plied them with such precision and quickness, that the Rebels again made a desperate effort to renew their [illegible] discharges. From that time until three P.M., the discharge of shot and shell from both sides was [illegible]ing; and although it was obvious that the Rebels could not withstand such a fire for many hour longer, they worked their guns faithfully, but without much effect—in fact, it may be said, none at all. The *Picket* received one hot shot, but two buckets of water effectually prevented any disastrous result. The *Hetzel* also had one gun dismounted, aft. With these trifling exceptions, no damage was done to our vessels. The gun-boat *Ranger* got aground twice about half-past four; but the *Tempest* went in, and placed her broadside to the fort, when she made four fine shots with her large Parrots.

The trim little sloop *Granite*, which had been anchored in the rear of the gun-boats, and apparently been forgotten in the midst of the excitement, suddenly hove up her anchor, about noon, and hauling close to the wind, sailed close up to the enemy's guns, and discharged her long 32-pounder, making the sand fly fifty feet in the air. She continued sailing up and down before the battery until darkness intervened, delivering her deadly messengers with unremitting energy. The vim of her commander was highly applauded, and she came off as perfect as when she went into action.

The *Stars and Stripes*, although not able to go as close in as several of the other gun-boats, made up the difference by the unceasing discharge of her seven long 32's, nearly every one of which told a tale of suffering and dismay wherever it fell.

GEN. BURNSIDE, COM'G MILITARY FORCES.

(See Second Page.)

COM. GOLDSBOROUGH, COM'G NAVAL EXPEDITION.

(See Third Page.)

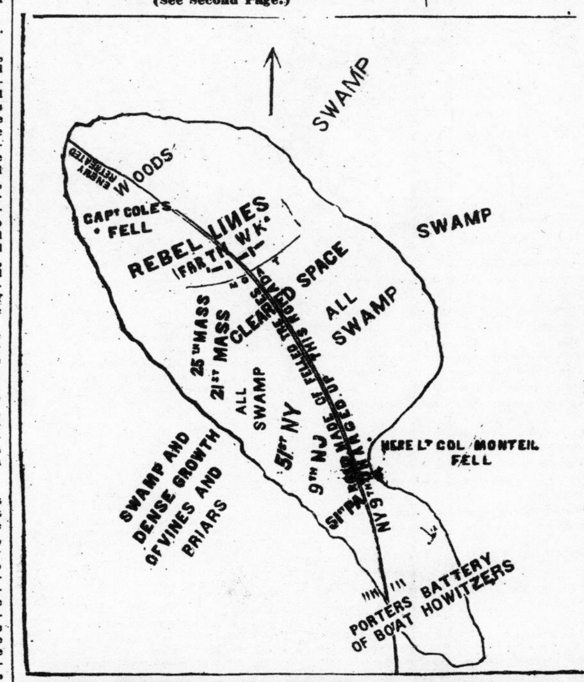

BATTLE GROUND IN THE CENTRE OF ROANOKE ISLAND.

We give above two exact views of the recent great battle grounds on Roanoke Island; one showing the position of the Rebel forts, and the manner in which the Federal gun-boats were stationed while bombarding them. And the other illustraring their inland battery, and depicting the location and movements of the Federa troops when preparing to drive the enemy from their trenchments during the conflict.

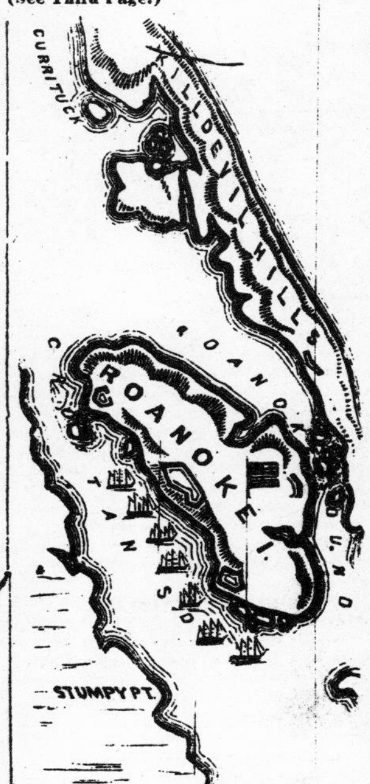

ROANOKE ISLAND.

The Channels and the Bombarding Fleet

THE NAVAL FORCE ENGAGED.

The naval force engaged under Commodore GOLDSBOROUGH were the following vessels:—

Southfield (flag-ship), carrying the flag of Flag Officer L. M. GOLDSBOROUGH; Commander, Acting Volunteer Lieut. BEHM, ably assisted by Lieut. TILLOTSON, of Union Coast Guard; armament, three 9-inch shells, 100-pound rifle. *Delaware*—Commodore STEPHEN C. ROWAN; Captain, S. P. QUACKENBUSH; armament, one 9-inch shell gun. *Stars and Stripes*—Lieut. Commanding REED WERDEN; armament, four 8-inch shell, one 20-pound rifle Parrot, and two rifled Dahlgren boat howitzers. *Louisiana*—Lieut. Commanding F. K. MURRAY; armament, two heavy 32-pounders, and two 8-inch guns. *Hetzel*—Lieut. Commanding H. K. DAVENPORT; armament, one 8-inch shell and one 80-pound rifle. *Commodore Perry*—Lieut. Commanding CHAS. N. FLUSSER; armament, two 9-inch shell guns. *Underwriter*—Lieut. Commanding WILLIAM N. JEFFERS; armament, one 8-inch gun and one 80-pound rifle. *Valley City*—Lieutenant Commanding, J. C. CHAPLAIN; armament, four 32-pounders and one rifled howitzer. *Commodore Barney*—Acting Lieutenant, R. RENSHAW; armament, two 9-inch shell guns. *Hunchback*—Acting Volunteer Lieutenant, CALHOUN; armament, two 9-inch shell and one 100-pound rifled gun. *Ceres*—Acting Master [illegible]; armament, one [illegible]-pound and one 30-pound Parrot gun. [illegible]—Acting Master, W. J. [illegible]; armament, one 30-pound rifle and one [illegible] 32-pounder. [illegible]—Acting Master, HAYES; armament, [illegible] gun. [illegible]—Acting Master, GRAVES; armament, one [illegible]-pound [illegible] gun and one [illegible]. [illegible]—Acting Master, WELLS; armament, two 30-pound rifle Parrots. Sloop *Granite*—Acting Master, BOWMAN; armament, one heavy thirty-two pounder. *Brinker*—Acting Master, GIDDINGS; armament, one 30-pound rifle gun. *Whitehead*—Acting Master, FRENCH; armament, one 9-inch shell gun. *Shawsheen*—Acting Master, HAYWOOD; armament, two 20-pound Parrot guns.

The army gun-boats engaged, under the direction of Commodore HAZZARD, of the navy, were the *Picket*, Acting Master J. PAYNTON IVES, carrying four guns, viz., one 30-pound Parrott, one Wiard 12-pounder, one boat howitzer, one 12-pound shell gun. *Hussar*, Acting Master ————, four guns, viz., two 30-pound Parrott and two Wiard 6-pounders.—*Vidette*, Acting Master ————, three guns, viz., one 30-pound Parrott, one boat howitzer, one shell gun. *Ranger*, Lieutenant Commanding NICHOLS; armament, four guns, viz., one 30-pound Parrott, one Wiard 12-pounder, one 12-pound boat howitzer and one mountain howitzer. *Chasseur*, Acting Master ————; armament, four guns, viz., two 30-pound Parrott and two Wiard 6-pounders.

Upon entering the Sound, above the marshes, the *Underwriter* went ahead taking soundings. The Rebel gun-boats were the first objects towards which our fire was directed.

A Rebel Trap.

Commodore GOLDSBOROUGH remained on board the *Philadelphia* until the fleet arrived at the Marshes, when he embarked on the *Southfield*.

The Rebels had contrived an ingenious sort of trap in the Sound, directly in range of the three forts on the island and the Robb's Fishing Battery on the main land opposite. Quite a number of sloops and schooners had been sunk in the deepest water toward the island, while farther across the Sound piles had been arranged in such a manner that our vessels would be led into an arrangement similar to fish-dams with a trap at the extremity, such as may be often seen in country streams. Had our vessels crowded onward, not stopping to engage the lower battery, they would suddenly have found themselves in a huddle and exposed to the fire of four forts and six Rebel gun-boats, which were stationed just above this *chevaux de frise*, apparently for the purpose of tempting us up that way. This shallow scheme utterly failed in its results, as our cautious commander did not intend to go any farther than was necessary to get an opportunity to chastise our pusillanimous foe.

As the *Southfield* cleared the marshes upon entering Croatan, she hoisted at her peak the following signal:—"This day our country expects every man to do his duty." Within five minutes it was understood through the entire fleet, and, as the flag-ship, the *Southfield* was thenceforward conspicuous in the engagement.

Landing of Troops—Night Closes the Scene.

At five P. M., troops were sent ashore, about two miles below the fort, the *Patuxent*, *Pilot Boy*, *Union* and *Phoenix* taking several loads, besides towing numerous surf and other boats full. At twilight the last gun from our gun-boats was fired at the fort, but no reply received from it. Camp fires began to illume the sky, and once more the shores of North Carolina were trodden by true Americans.

So far, everything had gone well. We had gained a footing on Roanoke Island, and it was evident that Fort Bartow could not withstand another day's bombardment. Why it was that the enemy failed to reply, except at long intervals towards night, we could not conjecture, as several of their guns were yet apparently in position, and the smoke from the burned barracks had subsided. Something was the matter; what was it? The morning would tell. Through the night our troops were being landed, as expeditiously and quietly as possible, for we anticipated an early attack from the Rebels, who were known to be in force, within a mile to the left, across a swamp, through which was a narrow road sufficiently wide to admit a wagon. This road was made passable by trunks of trees having been hauled in and settled down in the quagmire.

THE GREAT BATTLE ON ROANOKE ISLAND.

PLAN OF ATTACK—ARRANGEMENT OF THE FEDERAL FORCES—THEY STORM THE REBEL ENTRENCHMENTS, WADING KNEE DEEP IN MUD AND WATER—RETREAT OF THE ENEMY—CONSTERNATION AND DESPAIR—KILLED AND WOUNDED.

On Friday, P. M. about 5 o'clock, General RENO ordered the Twenty-first Massachusetts to move forward into the woods, to the main road, to occupy the place until morning. They proceeded as far as a ford; slight skirmishing commenced very soon, and they halted for a brief period, considering whether to advance or proceed. It was decided that the skirmishers should be called in, when it was found that two or three were missing of Company G. A cry of distress was soon heard, emanating from the woods on the left, and a corporal and two privates were sent out to institute a search for the absent ones. The party soon returned with one, but the other was not heard of. Picket duty was then performed by the whole regiment, aided by a five howitzer battery of the Union Coast Guard, which commanded the road. A reconnoissance being made soon after, the equipage of the missing soldier were found, and the camp-fires of the enemy discerned. At eleven o'clock in the evening it commenced raining, continuing all night. At 7½ A. M. General FOSTER passed up the road toward the suspected position of the enemy, having with him the Twenty-third, Twenty-fifth and Twenty-seventh Massachusetts, Tenth Connecticut and Fifth Rhode Island, of PARKES' Brigade.

Gen. RENO in the meantime brought out his brigade, of the Twenty-first Massachusetts, Fifty-first New York, Ninth New Jersey, and Fifty-first Pennsylvania. At 8½ o'clock firing was commenced by the Rhode Island skirmishers, in front of the battery, and a number of our men fell dead and several were taken to the rear in a wounded condition. Our skirmishers now rushed up, valiantly driving the enemy before them, until arriving at a clearing a battery was discerned ahead, masked, and surrounded by an apparently impassable swamp. Our troops then formed, supported by a four howitzer battery on the right, commanded by BENJAMIN H. PORTER. In this position they remained all night, standing by their guns and exposed to the storm, without shelter or proper food. The Twenty-fifth Massachusetts opened upon the enemy at an early hour, and after expending their forty rounds of cartridges fell back, moving both to the right and left up the curved road.

At this period the Second Brigade came up as follows:—Twenty-first Massachusetts, Fifty-first New York and Ninth New Jersey. The Twenty-first Massachusetts deployed to the left of the battery, and entered the swamp, followed closely by the Fifty-first New York. Both of these regiments endeavored to flank the Rebel entrenchment on the left. At this period the firing was terrific, volley upon volley succeeding so closely that it was difficult to distinguish the intervals. They fought there two hours, up to their waists in water. Lieut.-Col. MAGGI, on the extreme right of the battery, came up with flanking companies I and D, armed with Harper's Ferry rifles, and pushed around the right flank of the battery, to turn it. At this juncture, Capt. FOSTER, of Co. D, fell at the head of his column, pierced by two bullets. Our men were now contending against a murderous fire from the enemy's sharpshooters, stationed in the opposite woods at the rear and right of their battery, while 200 more were in the front of the battery itself. The other Companies of the Twenty-first Massachusetts were then brought up by Major CLARK, and formed in front of Companies A and D, who had sustained the fire for an hour and a-half, at this point. Three Companies of the Fifty-first New York came up behind the Twenty-first, and were led into the woods and formed on the left. They were followed by the remainder of the regiment, under command of Colonel POTTER. General RENO here came up to the front line with great gallantry, and asked if the Twenty-first would charge and take the battery—the men had to lay down in the water, and mud in order to load, rising up to fire—Major CLARK promptly responded "yes!" Lieutenant-Colonel MAGGI then gave the order to "charge upon the battery."

At this moment the enemy becoming aware of our intentions, instantly poured into our men an incessant volley of musketry, continuing, perhaps, for five or ten minutes, taking effect along the whole eight companies of the Twenty-first and the four of the Fifty-first New York. During this shower of bullets the men laid down on their faces in the water, General RENO only standing erect and firm on a hammock of of grass. The Union troops were soon upon their feet again, fired a deadly volley, and charged through the swamp up to their waists in the quagmire, towards the battery, the New York Ninth at the same instant coming up to the support of the line. They poured a heavy fire in while advancing, a portion of which unfortunately took effect upon a portion of the Fifty-first New York. Colonel FERRERO, finding that their fire was not properly directed, gave the bugle sound to cease firing.

The Rebels seeing the Union forces charging on them fled in terror and the utmost consternation, leaving their three guns unspiked, and throwing away every article that was likely to impede their progress—guns, pistols, bowie knives, knapsacks, clothing, food, etc. Our men struggled through the swamp, forded the moat, and climbed over parapets and through the embrasures, cheering wildly.

The first Union colors within the fort was the flag of the Twenty-first Massachusetts and that of the Fifty-first New York. Immediately the Ninth New York came up in the rear of the battery and the Ninth New Jersey advanced along the road, which was filled with Union soldiers.

The troops of the Second Brigade, under command of General RENO, now started in pursuit of the Rebels, who were half an hour ahead in full retreat. It would not be possible to describe the appearance of the road along which the enemy fled. The quantity and variety of articles were too extensive to describe. Numerous prisoners were taken along the route, the most of whom were wounded and exhausted, having fallen by the wayside. As we advanced on the road towards Nag's Head, several boat loads of Rebels were observed retreating across Roanoke Sound, towards the main land. A small sloop and surf-boat had just put off from shore, having thirty or forty persons on board, among whom were Captains SMITH and O. JENNINGS WISE, the latter mortally wounded. General RENO instantly ordered five companies of the Twenty-first Massachusetts to scour the beach to right and left, and also commanded the Rebel boats to return or be fired into. They immediately came ashore and surrendered to Major CLARK.

A contraband gave notice about this time that several Rebels were in a house near by, and a guard having been detailed, they were captured.

The afternoon had now half passed, so the brigade halted for some refreshment, after which they started on the route toward the Rebel Camp "Georgia," three miles distant. Company E, Twenty-first Massachusetts Regiment, were thrown out as an advance guard, and when three-quarters of the way through the forest, were fired on by the enemy, who were ambushed in the bushes and trees. Forty skirmishers were then deployed, all of whom returned safe, notwithstanding they killed three Rebels and wounded five others. Soon after this Lieutenant HOVEY observed a squad of Rebels approaching, bearing a flag of truce. Lieut.-Col. POOR, who was in command of the flag, asked to see the commanding General of the Union forces. Lieut. HOVEY received the messenger, and hastened with him to find Gen. RENO. This was near the junction of the road leading to the Rebel camp.

General FOSTER, with the Twenty-third and Twenty-fourth Massachusetts, had advanced a short distance beyond this road on his way to the north end of the island. Having learned that he was on the wrong route he was returning, when met by the Rebel Messenger and Lieutenant HOVEY. The Lieutenant-Colonel of the Rebel Regiment meeting General FOSTER, asked him what terms of capitulation would be granted? General FOSTER replied "None, except an immediate and unconditional surrender!" Lieutenant-Colonel POOR then acceded to the terms, and was escorted to the Rebel camp by our troops. Meantime General RENO advanced along the road with his brigade to the Rebel camp also, and took possession with the Twenty-first Regiment, who were drawn up in front of the barracks.

On this glorious occasion thirteen hundred Rebels laid down their arms and surrendered to General FOSTER and seven hundred to General RENO. Company I of the Twenty-first Massachusetts was detailed to take charge of the prisoners, and Company C to receive their arms, the greater portion of which consisted of flint lock Springfield muskets, Mississippi rifles and a few percussion lock muskets.

The men and officers were mostly without uniforms, being dressed in coarse regulation cloth and Kentucky jeans. A few of the officers had cloth cloaks and shoulder straps, and the French style of duelling swords.

The following is a list of officers of the Thirty-first and Eighth North Carolina Volunteers, who surrendered, unconditionally, to the United States troops, after the battle of Roanoke Island, February 8th. The Officers of the other regiments we have not yet obtained.

OFFICERS OF THE THIRTY-FIRST NORTH CAROLINA VOLUNTEERS.

Colonel—J. V. JORDAN.

Lieutenant-Colonel—D. G. Fowle.

Major—J. J. Yeates.

Captains—C. Goodwin, C. W. Knight, E. R. Liles, A. Betts, L. C. Manly, J. Miller, J. Picot, W. D. Jones, J. O. D. McKay, Jos. Whitty.

First Lieutenants—W. H. Hartman, S. J. Latham, W. W. Parker, Quintin Utley, H. R. Jordan, J. H. Hughes, J. Pipkin, F. H. Perry, C. H. Coffield, E. J. Bowen.

Second Lieutenants—R. Stingall, M. T. Lely, T. W. Massonett, S. H. Hyman, [illegible] Lindsey, [illegible], T. H. Wray, A. Betts, [illegible], J. [illegible], J. P. Collins, J. A. Haughton, A. S. [illegible], W. Debaume, Wm. Pulley, W. A. Prince, Wm. Pearson, J. H. Jenkins.

(Continued on the Eighth Page.)

The New-York Times.

VOL. XI—NO. 3246. NEW-YORK, MONDAY, FEBRUARY 17, 1862. PRICE TWO CENTS.

MAP SHOWING THE STRATEGIC POINTS CAPTURED IN THE RECENT VICTORIES IN KENTUCKY AND TENNESSEE.

Exhibiting Their Relations to These States and to the Contiguous Southern and Southwestern States; Giving the Location and Bearings of Bowling Green, Forts Henry and Donelson, Clarksville, Nashville, Columbus, Memphis, and also the Important Points in East Tennessee and Kentucky.

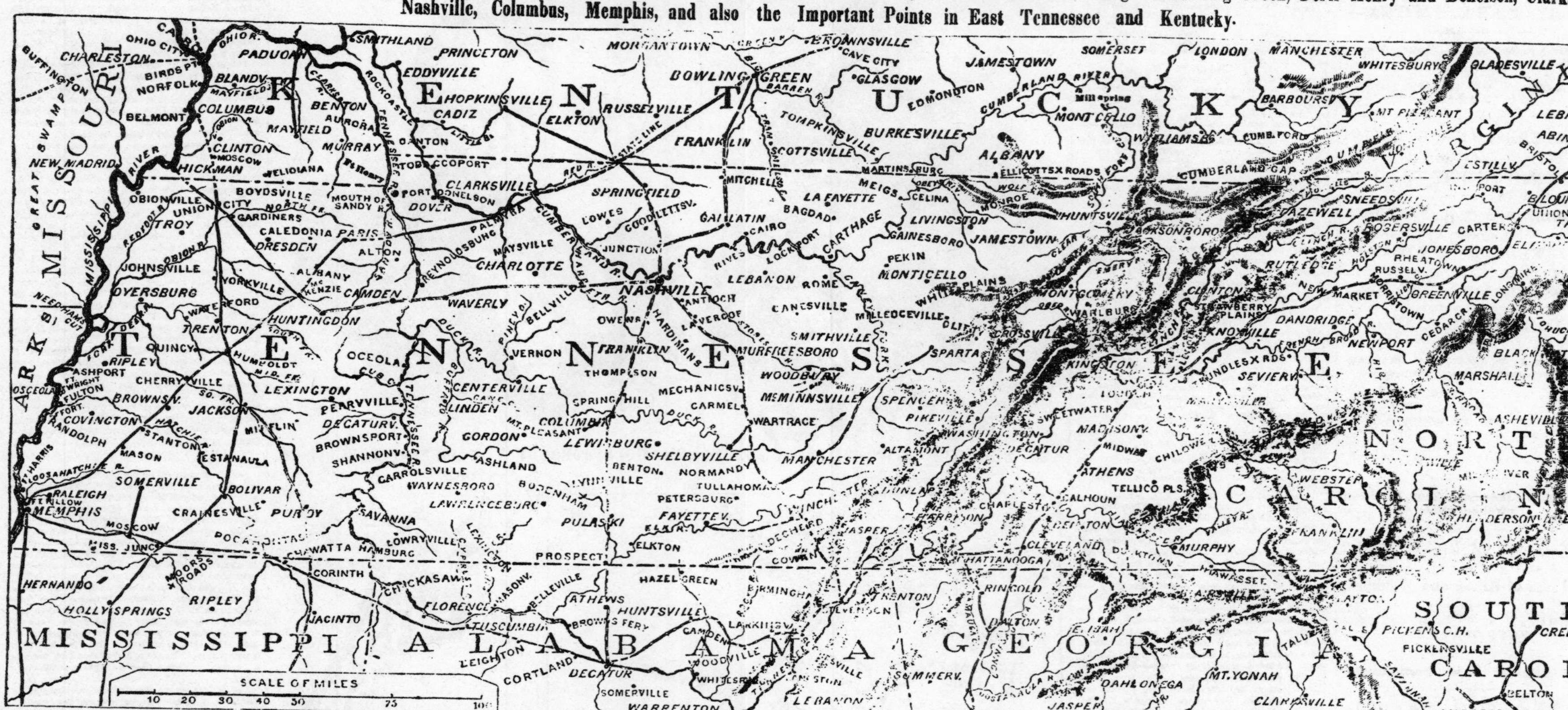

THE FORT DONELSON BATTLE.

Reports of Three Days' Desperate Fighting.

HEAVY LOSSES ON BOTH SIDES.

Two of our Colonels Killed and Two Wounded.

Capture of the Upper Fort Commanding Fort Donelson.

Six Gunboats in Action on Friday.

Several of them Disabled and Forced to Retire.

COMMODORE FOOTE WOUNDED.

Great Strength and Accurate Aim of the Rebel Batteries.

One of Gen. Grant's Batteries Captured and Retaken.

The Mortar Boats on the Way from Cairo.

The Rebels Flying the Black Flag.

REPORTS FROM ST. LOUIS.

ST. LOUIS, Sunday, Feb. 16.

This city is wild with excitement and rejoicing. *The news is just made public that the American flag waves over Fort Donelson.*

The loss is heavy on both sides.

One of Gen. GRANT's batteries was taken by the rebels, but was recaptured by our troops.

The gunboats are said to be badly damaged.

Further particulars expected to-night.

ST. LOUIS, Sunday, Feb. 16.

The following is a special to the *Missouri Democrat:*

CAIRO, Sunday, Feb. 16—P. M.

Commodore FOOTE reached here at 12 o'clock last night, on board the gunboat *Conestoga.* He stormed Fort Donelson Friday afternoon, with the gunboats *St. Louis, Louisville, Pittsburgh, Carondelet, Tyler* and *Conestoga,* and after fighting a little more than an hour, he withdrew. Fifty-four were killed and wounded on our gunboats. Pilots RILEY and HINTON, of the *St. Louis,* being among the latter. Com. FOOTE, while standing on the pilot-house of the *St. Louis,* his flag-ship, was slightly wounded. *The St. Louis was hit eighty-one times.* Two gunboats were disabled, the *Tyler* and the *Conestoga,* and remained out of range of the enemy's guns.

The line of battle was as follows: *St. Louis* on the right next the *Louisville,* then the *Pittsburgh* and the *Carondelet* on the left. *The enemy's firing was very accurate. They had three batteries, one near the water, one fifty feet above this, and a third fifty feet above the second.* The upper one mounted four 18-pounders. This one was held in reserve until our boats got within four hundred yards of the fort. Our fire was directed principally at the water battery. One of the enemy's guns burst, and a number were dismounted. The enemy could be seen carrying the dead out of the trenches.

All the gunboats were left up the Cumberland, except the *Conestoga.* She left there yesterday morning. A rifled gun on the *Carondelet* burst, killing six men. The rudder of the *Pittsburgh* was shot away.

The mortar-boats left here yesterday morning.

The above statements of the fight were received from gentlemen who were on board the *St. Louis* during the engagement.

LATER.—A gentleman who left Fort Donelson yesterday afternoon at 3 o'clock, and reached here this noon, says the fight had been going on all day yesterday (Saturday.) *The right wing of the enemy's fortifications were taken, and the Stars and Stripes were floating over them.* The forces were breast to breast, and the fight was to be renewed.

ST. LOUIS, Sunday, Feb. 16.

Dispatches received at headquarters say that all the gunboats are pretty effectually disabled, except one. Commodore FOOTE was wounded twice, but not fatally.

The upper redoubt was taken by our troops. This commands Fort Donelson, and Gen. Grant telegraphs that he would be able to capture that fort to-day, (Sunday.)

REPORTS FROM CAIRO.

CAIRO, Sunday, Feb. 16.

Steamer *Minnehaha* has arrived here from Fort Donelson, having left the fort at 5 o'clock last evening, bringing the military mail and dispatches, and 150 of the wounded to the hospital at Paducah. The fight commenced on Thursday, and *Friday's and Saturday's contest was desperate.* The Illinois Eighteenth suffered severely, and the Iowa Seventh sustained considerable loss. *Swartz's battery, which was taken by the enemy, was recaptured by our men.* Two Colonels were wounded and two killed. Loss heavy on both sides.

The upper fort was taken at 4 o'clock, and *the Union flag is now floating over it.* Our troops behaved with great gallantry.

The gunboats *St. Louis, Louisville* and *Pittsburgh* were disabled.

The *Minnehaha* met the mortar boats at Paducah, going up.

REPORTS FROM CHICAGO.

CHICAGO, Sunday, Feb. 16.

A special to the *Tribune,* dated Cumberland River, near Fort Donelson, 15th, says:

The firing commenced again at daybreak, and continued at intervals all day long. Up to four o'clock no movement or assault by the land forces had been made.

Night before last an attempt was made by the rebels to take TAYLOR's battery of light artillery, but they were repulsed by two regiments and driven back beyond their intrenchments. Our loss in wounded is considerable, but not more than three or four are dangerously wounded.

Six gunboats arrived yesterday, and commenced an attack on the fort at 2 in the afternoon. The firing was very rapid and severe, and lasted one hour and twenty minutes, when our gunboats fell back. The four iron-clad boats went within 300 yards of the fort. All the rebel river guns, except six, were either dismounted or silenced. The first shot fired from the gunboat *Louisville* dismounted the rebels 128-pounder. The *Louisville* received fifty-seven shots, two of which took effect, one striking the starboard side of her deck, and passing through the entire length of the boat, killing three men, and breaking her tiller-rope a short distance from the pilot-house. The rope was then managed by some of the hands, when a shell from the *Tyler,* which lay some distance astern, burst over the *Louisville,* scattering the men at the tiller-rope, and so much disabled her steering-tackle that the boat was compelled to drop astern.

A shot struck the *Pittsburgh* in the bows and stove an immense hole in her, which caused her to drop out of the action. The leak, however, has been stopped.

A shot struck the pilot-house of the *St. Louis,* passing through it between the pilot's legs without injuring him.

All the boats were more or less injured, but none but the *Louisville* seriously. There were five killed and two wounded on the *Louisville.* The gunboats will not be in a condition to renew the attack before to-morrow morning.

In consequence of the height of the bluffs on which the rebel fortifications are built, our shots cannot have as much effect on them as those at Fort Henry. It will therefore require a much longer time to reduce this fort.

The rebels have raised the black flag. It can be seen flying from the bank a short distance above here.

COMMODORE FOOTE'S OFFICIAL REPORT.

WASHINGTON, Sunday, Feb. 16.

The following dispatch was this morning received at the Navy Department from Flag-Officer FOOTE:

UNITED STATES FLAG-SHIP ST. LOUIS, NEAR FORT DONELSON, *via* PADUCAH, Saturday, Feb. 15.

To Hon. Gideon Welles, Secretary of the Navy:

I made an attack on Fort Donelson yesterday at 3 o'clock P. M., with four iron-clad gunboats and two wooden ones, and after one hour and a quarter's severe fighting the latter part of the day, within less than 100 yards from the fort, the wheel of this vessel and the tiller of the *Louisville* were shot away, rendering the two boats unmanageable. They then drifted down the river. The two remaining boats were also greatly damaged between wind and water. This vessel alone received fifty-nine shots, and the others about half that number each.

There were thirty-four killed and wounded, in the attack, which we have reason to suppose, would in fifteen minutes more, could the action have been continued, have resulted in the capture of the fort bearing upon us, as the enemy was running from his batteries, when the two gunboats drifted helplessly down the river from disabled steering apparatus, as the relieving-tackles could not steer the vessels in the strong current. When the fleeing enemy returned to the river battery guns, from which they had been driven, they again hotly poured fire upon us.

The enemy must have brought over twenty guns to bear upon our boats from the water battery and the main fort upon the hill, while we only could return the fire with twelve boat guns from the four boats.

One rifled gun aboard the *Carondelet* burst during the action.

The officers and men in this hotly-contested but unequal fight, behaved with the greatest gallantry and determination, all deploring the accident which rendered two of our gunboats suddenly helpless in the narrow river and swift current.

On consultation with Gen. GRANT and my own officers, as my services here, until we can repair damages by bringing up a competent force from Cairo to attack the fort, are much less required than they are at Cairo, I shall proceed to that place.

I have sent the *Tyler* to the Tennessee River to render the railroad bridge impassable.

(Signed,) A. H. FOOTE,
Flag-Officer Com'g Naval Force West'n Division.

THE GUNBOATS ENGAGED.

There had been, according to Commodore FOOTE, but six gunboats engaged in the bombardment up to latest advices. Four of these, the *St. Louis, Carondelet, Taylor* and *Conestoga,* took part in the reduction of Fort Henry; two, the *Louisville* and the *Pittsburgh,* were here brought into action for the first time; and three of those engaged at Fort Henry, the *Essex, Cincinnati* and *Lexington,* were not in this fight. We give a list of the officers of all the boats engaged in this gallant action, in the order mentioned by Commodore FOOTE:

GUNBOAT ST. LOUIS, COMMODORE FOOTE'S FLAG-SHIP.

Lieutenant-Commanding, LEONARD PAULDING, U. S. N.; First Master, Samuel Black; Second Master, James Y. Clemson; Third Master, Charles S. Kendrick; Fourth Master, Alexander Fraser; Acting Paymaster, Llewellyn Curry; Surgeon —— McDill; Master's Mates, S. H. McAdams, James P. Paulding; Pilots, Frank Riley, —— Hinton; Gunner, —— Hall; Chief-Engineer, W. Carswell; First Assistant, T. F. Ackeman; Second Assistant, James L. Smith; Third Assistant, John Wilcoxen; Carpenter, Robert H. M[illegible].

The *St. Louis* was Commodore FOOTE's flag-ship, and was rushed into the very jaws of the enemy's guns. It was within 100 yards of the fort. She was hit 61 times by the rebel guns. Commodore FOOTE and Pilots RILEY and HINTON were wounded.

GUNBOAT LOUISVILLE.

Commander, BENJAMIN M. DOVE, U. S. N.; First Master, Robert Getty; Second Master, R. A. Bausman; Third Master, Thomas M. Packer; Fourth Master, Samuel C. Harrison; Surgeon, A. L. Nail; Master's Mates, Robert Sherman, Charles L. Felton; Pilots, Samuel McBride, Samuel Williamson; Chief Engineer, James P. Fulton; First Assistant Engineer, A. W. Hardy; Second Assistant Engineer, John C. Patterson; Third Assistant Engineer, Deodatus Chapel; Carpenter, —— Boggs; Gunner, James G. Austin; Armorer, Charles Degleman.

GUNBOAT PITTSBURGH.

Lieutenant-Commanding—E. Thompson, U. S. N.; First Master—C. Bentley; Second Master—Andrew Watson; Third Master—W. Snyder; Fourth Master—L. P. Morgan; Paymaster—Cephas G. Gunn; Pilots—David E. Waite, Charles S. Tennson; Master's Mates—J. F. Nichols, Chas. H. Matthews; Chief Engineer—J. McDonald; First Assistant Engineer—George H. Atkinson; Second Assistant Engineer—George Sanford; Third Assistant Engineer—Charles W. Blessing; Gunner—vacant; Carpenter—George W. Rodgers; Armorer—Thomas Smith.

The rudder of this vessel was shot away in the engagement, and being thereby rendered unmanageable, she had to drop down the stream, but not before having rendered excellent service.

GUNBOAT CARONDELET.

Commander, HENRY WALKE, U. S. N.; First Master, Richard K. Wade; Second Master, John Dorety; Third Master, Charles C. Gray; Fourth Master, H. A. Walke; Pilots, William Henton, Daniel Weaver; Surgeon, James S. McNeely; Paymaster, George J. W. Nexsen; Master's Mates, Theodore L. Gillman, Edward E. Brennard; Chief Engineer, W. H. Faulkner; First Assistant Engineer, Charles H. Caven; Second Assistant Engineer, Samuel S. Brooks; Third Assistant Engineer, Augustus F. Crowell; Carpenter, O. Donaldson; Gunner, Richard Adams; Armorer, H. H. Rhodes.

A rifled gun on this gunboat bursted in the action, with what effect will be seen from the official report.

GUNBOAT TAYLOR.

Lieutenant Commanding, W. GWIN, U. S. N.; First Master, Edward Shaw; Second Master, Jason Goudy; Third Master, James Martin; Pilots, John Sebastian and David Hiner; Chief Engineer, Samuel Goble; First Assistant Engineer, D. Edward Weaver; Second Assistant Engineer, Edward W. Goble; Third Assistant Engineer, Oscar S. Davis; Armorer, Elihu Stevens; Acting Paymaster, W. B. Coleman; Assistant Surgeon, T. H. Kearney; Carpenter, Thomas Russell; Gunner, Herman Peters, U. S. N.; Master's Mates, Ferdinand T. Coleman and Edward D. Brainard.

GUNBOAT CONESTOGA.

Lieutenant Commanding, PHELPS, U. S. N.; First Master, John A. Duble; Second Master, Charles P. Noble; Third Master, Benjamin Sebastian; Assistant Surgeon, William H. Wilson; Acting Paymaster, Alfred Phelps; Chief Engineer, Thomas Cook; First Assistant Engineer, Alex. Magee; Third Assistant Engineer, Michael Norton; Master's Mates, James Kearney, Richard H. Cuttee; Gunner, Henry Hamilton; Carpenter, Andrew Woodlock; Armorer, Jas. O'Niel.

The two last-mentioned boats, the *Taylor* and *Conestoga,* are not of the same model of character as the others, being simply Mississippi River steamboats rebuilt with perpendicular bulwarks and pierced for guns. They were both disabled in the action.

The mortar-floats, which at latest advices were nearly ready to open on the parts of the fort still held by the rebels, are iron-clad, and of the strongest character.

ARMAMENT OF THE GUNBOATS.

	Guns.		Guns.
St. Louis	13	Carondelet	13
Louisville	13	Taylor	9
Pittsburgh	13	Conestoga	9
Total gunboat armament			72

These guns are all in battery, and none are less than 32-pounders—some are 42-pounders, some 64-pounders. In addition to these, each boat carries a Dahlgren rifled 12-pounder boat howitzer on the upper deck. Several of the larger guns on each boat are rifled, but most of them are smooth bore, those being most efficient in close action.

FORT DONELSON.

Its Position, Armament and Strategic Value.

The news of the capture of Fort Donelson—or at least its virtual capture by the taking of the redoubt commanding the rebel positions that still held out on Saturday—which is announced by telegraph this morning, and the still more important news of the rebel evacuation of Bowling Green, will attract undivided attention to the great military operations now being carried out in the Southwest. To render more clear to everybody the value of these victories, we give the above map, showing not only the important positions which have of late been the scenes of Union triumphs, such as Fort Henry on the Tennessee, Fort Donelson on the Cumberland, Bowling Green on the Big Barren, Mill Springs on the Eastern waters of the Cumberland, and other strategic localities, but showing also the bearing of these points on Columbus and Memphis, on Clarksville and Nashville, on Cumberland Gap and Knoxville, still in rebel hands; and exhibiting, too, the relation of the several places captured, and of those on which our army is now rapidly advancing, to the rebel States immediately south and east of Tennessee, to the Gulf States of Mississippi and Alabama, and to Georgia, North and South Carolina. If the reader will give a few minutes' study to this little reference-map, to its topography, railroads, rivers and mountains, he will gain a more accurate knowledge of our present military situation in the Southwest, and of the directions and places whence our banners will next be borne, than could possibly be given by verbal descriptions. As the scene of our main operations for some time to come is likely to be within the territory included in this map, those who wish to follow them up intelligently will find it convenient to clip out and preserve for reference.

Fort Donelson, as will be seen, is situated at Dover, Tennessee, on the west bank of the Cumberland River, a few miles south of the northern boundary of the State, and was built last Summer, about the same time as Fort Henry. It is located at a point where the river washes an obtuse angle in its northward course. It is twelve miles southeast of Fort Henry, which was captured just nine days before the present victory. The main object of the fort was to stand as a rear defence to Bowling Green, and also as a defence against our approach to Nashville by the Cumberland River. It was believed by the rebels that it would block up effectually our passage into Tennessee in this direction. Some seven or eight post roads here intersect each other, and the railroad from Bowling Green to Memphis passes but four miles south of it. This same railroad, it will be remembered, was cut a short distance west, at the Tennessee River, by our gunboats, immediately after the fall of Fort Henry, and is now again destroyed at the crossing of the Cumberland. Fort Donelson controls the river as far up as Clarksville, where the rebels may perhaps again make a stand as we advance onward to Nashville. At Clarksville they have fortifications and a pretty strong armament, and lately they had there also a considerable body of troops.

The enemy are supposed to have had three batteries at Fort Donelson—one near the river's edge, one fifty feet above this, on the high ground, and a third fifty feet above the second; this upper one mounted four 18-pounder guns. Our gunboats first attacked the water battery, but the rebels held back the fire of their upper and strongest work until Commodore FOOTE, with his usual daring, had brought his boats within 400 yards of the fort. He still advanced, however, until he got within 100 yards of it. At 4 o'clock on Saturday this upper redoubt, constituting the right wing of the enemy's fortification, and which commands the remainder of the rebel works, was taken by our troops, and from it the old flag was flung to the breeze. Of the exact armament of these various works we have not information, but, at the latest date to which our knowledge extends there were mounted some 20 heavy guns, 18, 32, and 64-pounders. It is not to be wondered, placed as these were, that they should have done considerable damage to even such strong boats as compose our iron-plated Western river fleet. And there is no doubt that large additions to the number were within a week made from Bowling Green—as Commodore FOOTE says, in his official dispatch, that in the upper and lower redoubts alone there were mounted 20 guns.

The number of rebels manning the fortifications was estimated, last Thursday, by our commanders on the field, in the dispatch published last Saturday, as high as 15,000. No further reinforcements could have been thrown in after that time, as our forces then had invested the fort. If Gen. HALLECK's statement was correct that FLOYD (the thief) was then inside the fort, it is likely that he had taken the division with which he left Bowling Green last Monday, along with him, instead of having taken it to East Tennessee to fight Gen. THOMAS, as was supposed. That division consists of three brigades, one of which was immediately commanded by FLOYD himself, another by HARDEE, and a third by SIMON BOLIVAR BUCKNER. The regiments were from Arkansas, Mississippi, Tennessee, Virginia and Kentucky, and were the flower of the rebel army in the Southwest. The four regiments also which fled from Fort Henry on its capture by Commodore FOOTE, had probably also taken refuge in Fort Donelson. The rebel troops at Clarksville too, could have been easily thrown forward after the fall of Fort Henry. There is no doubt that all the rebel forces that could possibly be spared were there. Up to the 20th of last month, the fort was occupied by only a few companies of Tennesseeans, and so strongly were the rebels there posted that they did not believe we would dare to assail even them. But give the rebels all the reinforcements and the largest number claimed, and there was still an immense preponderance of men on our side—the Union force investing the fort being stated by Gen. HALLECK to be fifty thousand strong. Considering the location of the fort, its defences, and the force manning it, and it will be seen that the rebels could make a severe fight. There are other things beside superior numbers to be taken into consideration in estimating the chances of a battle. The rebels succeeded, too, in disabling the most efficient of our gunboats. But as at the latest hour, the mortar boats were nearly ready to open fire on the positions the rebels still held, in connection with the guns from the commanding position we had captured, and as our brave troops were breast to breast with the rebels, we may at any hour anticipate news of the complete reduction of Fort Donelson.

THE WESTERN MANASSAS EVACUATED.

Flight of the Rebels from Bowling Green.

LOUISVILLE, Saturday, Feb. 15, 1862.

To Maj.-Gen. McClellan:

MITCHELL'S Division by a forced march reached the river at Bowling Green to-day, making a bridge to cross.

The enemy had burnt the bridge at 1 o'clock in the morning, and were evacuating the place when he arrived.

D. C. BUELL, Brig.-Gen. Com'g.

From the Washington Star, of Saturday.

Just as the *Star* goes to press to-day, the General-in-Chief has received a dispatch from Gen. BUELL, announcing that his advance, under Gen. MITCHELL, reached the river opposite Bowling Green yesterday by a forced march.

The enemy, fearing the passage of his force across the river by the remaining bridge there, burned that immediately, or sufficient of it to render it impassable.

Gen. MITCHELL at once set about constructing another, under the protection of his guns.

The enemy thereupon last night evacuated their Bowling Green stronghold, of which Gen. MITCHELL is now, doubtless, in possession, as no enemy was left to resist him in raising the Stars and Stripes over it, the river being but to cross.

Gen. BUELL had for some days past been concentrating a large force in the neighborhood, with which, doubtless, to march directly on to Nashville after having reduced Bowling Green.

It is the impression in military circles here, that on evacuating their Bowling Green stronghold last night, the main body, if not all the rebel army, fled directly toward Nashville; as to attempt to reinforce Fort Donelson instead, would be well-nigh a hopeless undertaking, and would inevitably be followed almost immediately by the fall of Nashville before the main body of BUELL's army, and the fall of Knoxville before the Division of Gen. THOMAS. Neither BUELL or THOMAS can meet with any resistance to speak of in marching directly on those most important strategic positions, if the army running away from Bowling Green has failed in its retreat to aim to cover Nashville, which, by-the-by, is the main object of the effort of the enemy to continue to hold Fort Donelson.

OUR TROOPS IN POSSESSION.

LOUISVILLE, Sunday, Feb. 16.

Gen. MITCHELL'S troops have crossed Barren River, and are in possession of Bowling Green.

BOWLING GREEN.

Our news from this point is as yet exceedingly meagre, consisting only of Gen. BUELL's very brief dispatch. That, however, is enough to show that the rebels have evacuated their Western Manassas, and that it is now in our hands. As will be seen by the map, there were only two feasible routes for the decamping rebels to take—one by railroad almost directly north to Nashville, and one in a western direction, toward Fort Donelson. They first began to evacuate the place about a week ago to-day, when FLOYD and his division marched out, apparently to the latter road. After these had gone, there was not a very great force remaining,—certainly not over ten thousand men. These, as it appears, on Saturday last fled in the direction of Nashville, where, at latest accounts, BEAUREGARD was working out his plans for the defence of the city. During the week they had removed nearly all their guns and property.

The rebel evacuation of Bowling Green was a "military necessity." The flank movements of Gens. THOMAS and CRITTENDEN, and the rear operations of Com. FOOTE and Gen. GRANT, rendered the place untenable. A few days more and the rebels would have been taken in their stronghold. It is unfortunate that they have been allowed to escape. But from Gen. BUELL's reticence, and his interdiction upon the telegraph, it looks as though he was carrying out some plan to prevent their rallying again at any other point, if not of overtaking them. This evacuation is certainly a very lame and impotent conclusion to the rebel boasts about the impregnability of their position at Bowling Green.

In all Kentucky, and we may say in all the Southwest, the rebels now hold [illegible] one position of importance, Columbus; and that [illegible] isolated and untenable. The rebels will soon fly from there, as they have fled from Bowling Green, if our Generals will only permit them to do

The Philadelphia Inquirer.

ESTABLISHED 1829. | PHILADELPHIA, MONDAY, MARCH 10, 1862. | PRICE TWO CENTS.

THE VESSELS AND SCENE OF CONFLICT IN HAMPTON ROADS.

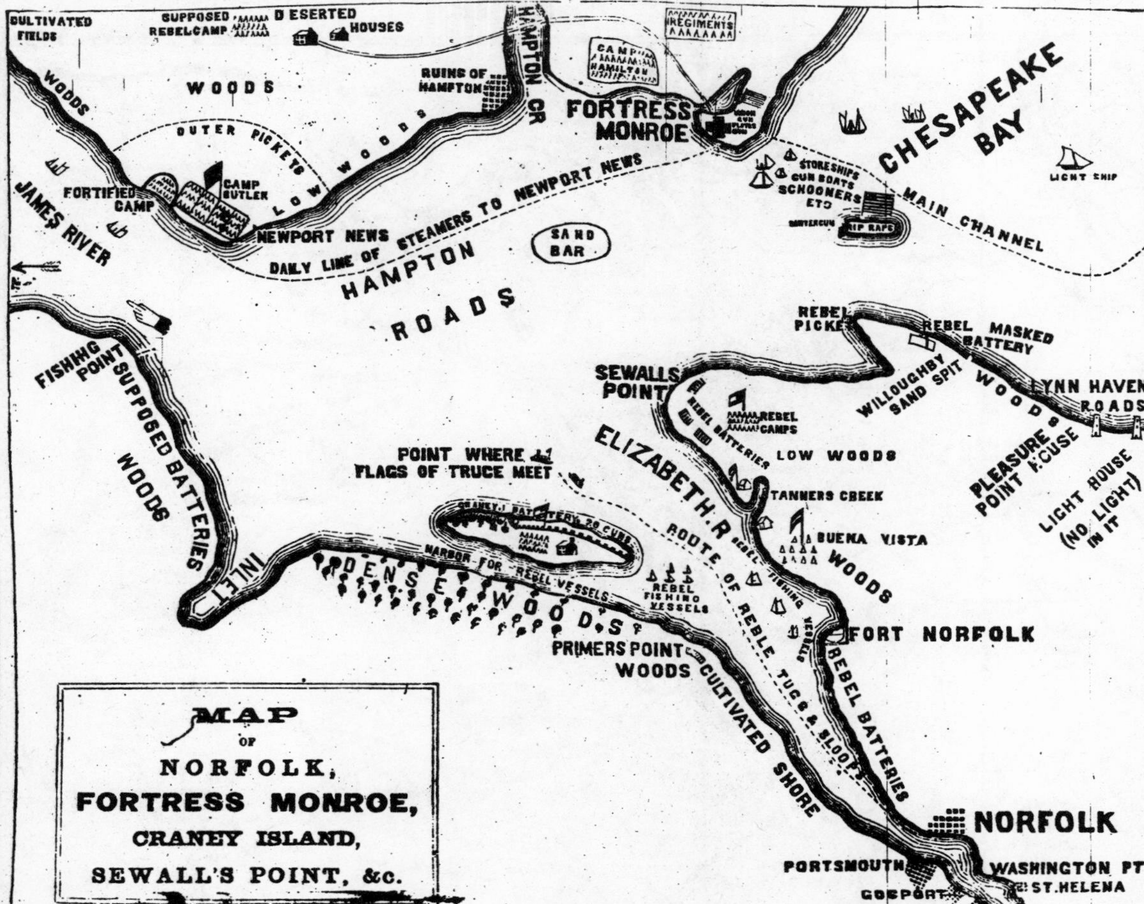

HIGHLY IMPORTANT NEWS!

OUR FLEET AT FORTRESS MONROE ATTACKED BY THE REBEL STEAMERS ! !

The U. S. Sloop Cumberland Sunk and Congress Burned!

Our Loss from One Hundred to Two Hundred and Fifty.

STILL LATER NEWS!

Iron-clad Steamer "Monitor" Attacked by the "Merrimac."

THE REBEL FLEET DRIVEN OFF.

THE MERRIMAC IN A SINKING CONDITION.

OPENING OF THE TELEGRAPH TO FORTRESS MONROE.

OFFICIAL DESPATCH.

Special Despatches to The Inquirer.

WASHINGTON, March 9, 1862.

The Union Fleet Attacked by Rebel Steamers Merrimac, Jamestown and Yorktown.

WASHINGTON, March 9—The Government has received information from Fortress Monroe, that, yesterday, the iron-clad steamer *Merrimac* and the gun-boats *Jamestown* and *Yorktown* attacked our fleet, and sunk the U. S. sloop-of-war *Cumberland*, and took the *Congress* The U. S. steamer *Minnesota* was aground when the Fortress Monroe boat left.

DETAILS OF THE DISASTER.

FORTRESS MONROE, March 8.—The dullness of Old Point was startled, at 10 o'clock to-day, by the announcement that a mysterious vessel, supposed to be the Rebel steamer *Merrimac*, and looking like a submerged house, with the roof only above water, was moving down from Norfolk by the channel in front of Sewall's Point. Signal guns were also fired by the United States sloop-of-war *Cumberland* and the frigate *Congress*, to notify the *Minnesota*, *St. Lawrence* and *Roanoke* of the approaching danger, and all was excitement in and about Fortress Monroe.

There was nothing protruding above the water but the flag-staff, flying the Rebel flag, and a short smoke-stack. She moved along slowly, and turning into the channel leading to Newport News, steamed direct for the *Cumberland* and *Congress*, which were lying at the mouth of the James River. As soon as the *Merrimac* came within range of the *Cumberland*, the latter opened on her with her heavy guns, but the balls struck and glanced off, having no more effect on her than peas from a pop-gun. Her ports were all closed, and she moved on in silence, but with a full head of steam.

In the meantime, as the *Merrimac* was approaching the two frigates on the one side, the iron-clad steamers *Yorktown* and *Jamestown* came down the James river and engaged our frigates on the other side.—The batteries at Newport News also opened on the *Jamestown* and *Yorktown* and did all in their power to assist the *Cumberland* and *Congress*, which, being sailing vessels, were at the mercy of the approaching steamers.

The *Merrimac* in the meantime kept steadily on her course, and slowly approached the *Cumberland*, when the latter, as well as the *Congress*, at the distance of one hundred yards, rained full broadsides on the iron-clad monster. The shots took no effect, glancing upwards and flying off, having only the effect of checking her progress for a moment.

After receiving the first broadsides of the two frigates she ran into the *Cumberland*, striking her about midships and literally laying open her side. She then drew off, fired a broadside into the disabled ship, and again dashed against her with her iron-clad prow, and knocking in her side left her to sink, while she engaged the *Congress*, which laid about a quarter of a mile distant.

The *Congress* had, in the meantime, kept up a sharp engagement with the *Yorktown* and *Jamestown*, and having no regular crew on borrd of her, and seeing the helplessness of resisting the iron-clad steamers, at once struck her colors. Her crew had been discharged several days since, and three Companies of the Naval Brigade had been put on board temporarily until she could be relieved by the *St. Lawrence*, which was to have gone up on Monday to take her position as one of the blockading vessels the James River.

On the *Congress* striking her colors the *Jamestown* approached and took from on board all the officers as prisoners, but allowed the crew to escape in the boats. The vessel being thus cleared it was fired by the Rebels, when the *Merrimac* and her two iron-clad companions opened with shell and shot on the Newport News batteries. The firing was briskly returned.

Various reports have been received, principally from frightened Sutler's clerks. Some of them represented that the garrison had been compelled to retreat from the batteries to the woods. Another report is, that the two smaller Rebel steamers had been compelled to retreat from the guns of the batteries.

In the meantime, the steam frigate *Minnesota* having partly got up steam, was being towed up to the relief of the two frigates, but did not get up until too late to assist them. She was also followed by the frigate *St. Lawrence*, which was taken in tow by several of the small harbor steamers. It is, however, rumored that neither of these vessels had pilots on board them, and after a short engagement, both seemed to be, in the opinion of the pilots, on the point, aground.

The *Minnesota*, either intentionally or from necessity, engaged the three Rebel steamers at about a mile distance, with only her two bow guns. The *St. Lawrence* also poured in shot from all her guns she could bring to bear, and it was the impression of the most experienced naval officers on the point that both had been considerably damaged.

These statements, it must be borne in mind, are all based on what could be seen by the glass at a distance of nearly eight miles, and by a few panic-stricken non-combatants, who fled at nearly the first gun from Newport News. In the meantime darkness approached, though the moon shone out brightly, and nothing but the occasional flashing of guns could be seen.

The *Merrimac* was also believed to be aground, as she remained stationary at the distance of about a mile from the *Minnesota*, making no attempt to attack or molest her. Previous to the departure of the steamer from Old Point for Baltimore, no guns had been fired for half an hour, the last one being fired from the *Minnesota*. Some persons declared that immediately after the last gun was fired, a dense volume of vapor was seen to rise from the *Merrimac*, indicating an explosion of her boilers. Whether this is so or not cannot be known, but it was the universal opinion that the Rebel monster was hard aground.

Fears were of course entertained for the safety of the *Minnesota* and *St. Lawrence* in such an unequal contest, but if the *Merrimac* was really ashore, she could do no further harm to them. It was the intention of the *Minnesota*, with her picked and gallant crew, to have run into close quarters with the *Merrimac*, avoid her iron prow, and board her.—This the *Merrimac* seemed not inclined to give her an opportunity to do, being afraid to approach her at close quarters when aground.

At eight o'clock, when the Baltimore boat left, a fleet of steam tugs were being sent up to the relief of the *Minnesota* and *St. Lawrence*, and an endeavor was to be made to draw them off from the bar on which they had grounded. The firing had been suspended, whether from mutual consent or necessity could not be ascertained.

The Rebel battery at Pig's Point was also enabled to join in the combined attack on the *Minnesota*, and several guns were fired at her from Sewall's Point, as she went up; none of them, however, struck her, but one or two passed over her.

Arrival of the Iron-Clad Ericsson Steamer Monitor.

BALTIMORE, March 9.—The Old Point boat left at eight o'clock last night. About half an hour after she left the wharf the iron-clad Ericsson steamer *Monitor* passed her, going in, towed by a large steamer. The *Monitor* reached Fortress Monroe by nine o'clock, and may have immediately gone into service. If not, she would be ready to take a hand early on Sunday morning.

The details furnished in the despatch from Fortress Monroe are all the facts, as far as can be ascertained, and are probably the worst possible version of the affair.

THE MERRIMAC.

The *Merrimac* was built at Charlestown, Mass., in 1855, was one of the finest steam frigates in the United States Navy, thirty-two hundred tons burden, and carrying forty large guns.

She was partially burned and sunk at the time of the destruction of the Gosport Navy Yard. The Rebels having succeeded in raising the vessel, cut down her hull to within three feet of her light water mark, and built a bomb-proof house of wrought iron plates, three inches thick, on her gun deck.

She is iron-plated, and her bow and stern steel-clad, with a projecting angle of iron for the purpose of piercing a vessel. She has no masts, and there is nothing to be seen over her gun deck, with the exception of her pilot-house and smoke-stack.

Her armament consists of four 11-inch navy guns on each side, and two 100-pounder Armstrong guns at the bow and stern.

THE JAMESTOWN.

The *Jamestown* is furnished with a heavy, clumsy and ridiculous looking iron prow in front, the *point* of which barely projects above the water.

To all appearance the ship is not razeed at all, iron plated or pierced for broadside guns. Her batteries seemed to consist of a 32-pounder rifled gun, fore and aft. They are similar to the Parrot gun. The question was once asked of the Rebel officer, "Are those Parrot guns?" to which a negative answer was given.

THE YORKTOWN.

The Rebel steamer *Yorktown* was formerly used on the New York and Virginia line of steamers. She is a side-wheel steamer of 1400 tons burden. was built in New York in 1859, and her size is as follows:—Length, 251 feet; breadth, 34 feet; depth, 18 feet. She has been completely fitted out at Norfolk, her sides having been plated with iron, and other means taken to strengthen her and to render her formidable.

THE MONITOR, OR, ERICSSON BATTERY.

This vessel is sharp at both ends, and consists of a lower and upper hull, the sides of the former inclining to an angle of fifty-one degrees, and coming to a point at each end at an angle of eighty degrees. The lower hull is iron-plated. The upper section is five feet high, with perpendicular sides and the same sharp ends, and is forty-one feet four inches wide, jutting over the lower hull three feet and seven inches on each side. The sides of this upper section are a little over three feet in thickness. First, there is an inner guard of six inch plate iron, and upon this a section of white-oak timber, thirty inches thick, and covered with an armor six inches thick, formed of six one-inch iron plates, lapped and firmly riveted together.

The deck or top of the battery is even with the top of the hull, and is covered with two thicknesses of inch plate-iron, fastened to eight-inch oak plank and ten-inch oak timber, but twenty-six inches apart. There is no railing or other obstruction on the top of the battery except a round tower or turret, twenty feet in diameter and nine feet high and eight inches thick, made of plate iron.

The turret has two port holes, each two feet in diameter, for two eleventh inch columbiads, and is also pierced for musketry. The turret is of immense weight, but made to revolve by machinery from below, so as to bring the guns in any desired range, and to remove the ports from the enemy's guns while loading.

To support, protect and give efficiency to this turret is the whole object of the battery, although its immense weight and power would sink any vessel with which it should come in contact.

The battery is steered from the front, the wheelhouse standing before the turret. The wheelhouse is strongly built of iron, and can be lowered into the hold like a bale of dry goods. When lowered, the top, which is bomb-proof, is level with and forms a part of the deck. The joints are water-tight. The house is pierced for sharpshooters.

The ends of the upper vessel project over the propellor, rudder and anchor. The propellor is, of course, at the stern, and the equipoise rudder behind that, and they are so protected by the upper vessel that they cannot be struck by a ball. The anchor is in front, and is short but very heavy. It is hoisted by a chain running into the hold, up into a place fitted for it, outside of the lower hull, but within the impregnable walls of the upper hull. The entrance to the hold is by small hatchways, which, when closed, form a part of the deck, and are equally secured.

The interior of the battery presents a novel and interesting study. In the bow are the cable and anchor chambers; next the cabin and quarters of the officers and men, and amidships the cook-room, and overhead the small engine which is to furnish ventilation and work the turret. Just abaft are the furnaces, and in the stern the engine working the propeller. The bunkers for wood coal and ammunition, and the water-tanks, occupy every conceivable vacancy. The cabin is neatly but substantially fitted up, and shows that it is meant for use more than pleasure. Taken altogether, it would be impossible to imagine more material, and that more substantial and serviceable, and at the same time more perfect, in a smaller space, than is embodied within this formidable engine of warfare.

Of the efficiency of the battery great hopes are expressed. It has no vulnerable part save the port-holes, which are exposed only for about half a minute in firing. Its shape and massive iron prow will enable it to sink any ordinary vessel with perfect ease. In case it is boarded, no harm is done. The only entrance is at the top of the turret, which cannot easily be scaled, and even then but one man at a time can descend. There are no places in the deck where an entrance can be forced, so that the boarding party may stand until the sea washes them off, or the sharp-shooters assist their departure. It is claimed that it can steam into any port, deliver its effective broadside, and retire in safety.

The battery is now about four feet above water, and weighs 1,400,000 pounds. With the addition of her armament, coal, water and provisions for a thirty day's cruise, she will be but eighteen inches above water and her entire weight will be nine hundred tons. Her two columbiads will carry round balls weighing each one hundred and eighty-three pounds, or conical balls of three hundred and fifty pounds.

THE FLAG-SHIP MINNESOTA.

The *Minnesota* is one of our largest screw steam frigates, 3200 tons burden, rates 40 guns, and was built in 1855 at Washington. She is what is termed an auxiliary propeller, and her engines are 450 horse power. She left Boston as the flag-ship of the blockading fleet, and has been in that service up to the time of the departure of this expedition from Fortress Monroe.

Her guns are very heavy and most effective, as has been proved in the last engagement; two of them are of eleven-inch calibre, capable of throwing balls of one hundred and sixty pounds weight She has made but one regular cruise previous to her present position; that was in the East Indies, from which place she returned in 1858.

THE CUMBERLAND.

The sloop-of-war *Cumberland* is 1726 tons burden, rated twenty-four guns, was built in 1842 at the Charlestown Navy Yard. She is a sailing vessel of good substantial build. She has been the flag-ship of the Home Squadron, sailing under the flag of Commodore PRENDERGAST.

THE CONGRESS.

The frigate *Congress* carries fifty guns. She was built at Kittery in 1841, and measures 1867 tons. She had recently arrived from the coast of Brazil.

THE ST. LAWRENCE.

The *St. Lawrence* also mounts fifty guns, and measures 1726 tons. She was built at the Gosport Navy Yard in 1847.

POSITION OF THE VESSELS WHEN ATTACKED.

The two vessels opposite Camp Butler represent the position of the *Cumberland* and *Congress*, stationed there to watch the James river. The *Minnesota* was aground on the point marked Sand Bar, midway between Sewall's Point and Hampton. The *Merrimac* pursued a course down Elizabeth river.

STILL LATER!

The Iron-Clad Steamer Monitor Attacked by the Three Rebel Steamers.

THE ASSAILANTS DRIVEN OFF.

The Merrimac in a Sinking Condition.

WASHINGTON, March 9—7 o'clock, P. M.—The telegraph line to Fortress Monroe has been completed, and the following despatch has been received direct from that point:—

"The Ericsson iron-clad steamer *Monitor*, arrived at Fortress Monroe last night, and early this morning she was attacked by the three Rebel steamers, the *Merrimac*, *Jamestown* and *Yorktown*. After a contest of five hours, they were driven off, the *Merrimac* in a sinking condition.

Official Despatches from Fortress Monroe.

WASHINGTON, March 9.—The following despatch was to-night received by Major-General MCCLELLAN from General WOOL:—

FORTRESS MONROE, March 9—6 o'clock, P. M.—Two hours after my telegraphic despatch to the Secretary of War, last evening, the steamer *Monitor* arrived. She immediately went to the assistance of the *Minnesota*, which was aground, and continued so until a few minutes since. Early this morning she was attacked by the *Merrimac*, *Jamestown* and *Yorktown*.

After a five hours contest, they were driven off, and the *Merrimac* in a sinking condition. She was towed by the *Jamestown*, *Yorktown*, and several smaller boats, towards Norfolk, no doubt for the purpose, if possible, to get her in the dry dock for repairs.

The *Minnesota* is afloat and being towed towards Fortress Monroe.

Despatch to the Secretary of the Navy.

FORTRESS MONROE, March 9—6.45 P. M.—To G. WELLES, Secretary of the Navy:—The steamer *Monitor* arrived at 10 o'clock last night, and went immediately to the protection of the *Minnesota*, lying aground just below Newport News. At seven o'clock A. M., the *Merrimac*, accompanied by two wooden steamers and several tugs, stood out towards the *Minnesota* and opened fire.

The *Monitor* met them at once, and opened her fire, when all the enemy's vessels retired excepting the *Merrimac*. These two iron-clad vessels fought part of the time touching each other, from eight o'clock A. M. till noon, when the *Merrimac* retired. Whether she is injured or not it is impossible to say. Lieutenant J. S. WORDEN, who commanded the *Monitor*, handled her with great skill, assisted by Chief Engineer STIMMERS. Lieutenant WORDEN was injured by the cement from the pilot-house beieg driven into his eyes, but I trust not seriously. The *Minnesota* kept up a continuous fire, and is herself somewhat injured. She was moved considerably to-day, and will probably be off to-night. The *Monitor* is uninjured, and ready at any moment to repel another attack.

(Signed) G. V. FOX,
Assistant Secretary of the Navy.

CREW OF THE CUMBERLAND.

REPORTS OF THE LOSS OF LIFE.

NEW YORK, March 9.—A special despatch from Fortress Monroe to the *Tribune* states that the *Cumberland* had a crew of five hundred men, nearly half of whom went down with her, but a negro states that some of the crew who swam ashore gave the number lost at one hundred. The guns of the *Congress* after her capture, were turned on our batteries at Newport News.

General WOOL sent two regiments of infantry, six companies of cavalry, and the Mounted Rifles, by land to Newport News to support General MANSFIELD, in case of an attack.

The Excitement at Washington.

WASHINGTON, March 9.—The excitement at the hotels, and elsewhere, all day, has been intense, consequent on the news from Fortress Monroe.

THE WAR IN VIRGINIA.

OPERATIONS OF GEN. BURNSIDE

Winton, North Carolina, Occupied in Force!

The Stars and Stripes Waving Over the Rebel Battery at Cockpit Point.

THE STEAMER "PAGE" BURNED.

The Rebel Batteries on the Potomac Evacuated.

THE POTOMAC ARMY TO BE DIVIDED INTO FIVE CORPS D'ARMEE.

Indians of Kansas and Nebraska.

FROM GEN. BANKS' COMMAND.

LEESBURG OCCUPIED BY COL. GEARY.

Forts Beauregard, Johnson and Evans in Possession of Geary.

THE REBELS RETREATING.

CHARLESTOWN, VA., March 8.—To day a Mr. CARTER, member of BAYLIE's Cavalry, together with three valuable horses, carriage and other articles, was captured and turned over to the custody of the Quartermaster. A considerable amount of Rebel scrip was also seized.

Private WHITNEY, of the Michigan Cavalry, who was accidentally wounded on Friday night, died to-day.

Colonel BRODHEAD, of the Michigan Cavalry, has been appointed Chief of the Cavalry for this Division.

During the visit to the residence of Col. LEWIS WASHINGTON, near Halliston, your correspondent was informed that subsequent to the departure of the proprietor in August last, the Rebels paid a visit to the establishment and appropriated a large collection of the portraits of Gen. WASHINGTON and his family, being probably the only collection of the kind extant.

It is to be regretted that previous to the order of General BANKS some wanton depredations were committed on private property in this vicinity, but it is probable that the perpetrators will be detected and severely punished.

LEESBURG, March 8.—Colonel GEARY has taken Leesburg and driven General HILL with his whole command, from the town and surrounding forts. The Stars and Stripes now wave over all the hills.

The Rebels fell back towards Middlebury, last night. Colonel GEARY left Lovettsville, with his command, and marched through Wheatland and Waterford, taking prisoners at both places, and putting the scattered forces of the enemy to flight.

Shortly after sunrise, this morning, he took possession of Fort Johnson, which was rechristened by the officers Fort Geary. He then entered the camp, with flags flying and bayonets fixed.

The Rebel troops, who had considered this as one of their greatest strongholds, could be discerned through a glass in full retreat.

The command took many prisoners and a quantity of army stores, and are in possession of the Bank, Post Office and public buildings.

Forts Beauregard and Evans are also in our possession.

This achievement, accomplished by a skillful manouvre, is of vast importance. The command is well and in good spirits.

A detachment of the First Michigan Cavalry did much service, under the direction of Col. GEARY, in this movement.

POOLESVILLE, March 8.—To Brigadier-General S. WILLIAMS:—

Leesburg was entirely evacuated yesterday morning. The reports are that Colonel GEARY's advance is there.

N. J. T. DANA, Brigadier-General.

THE OCCUPATION OF LEESBURG CONFIRMED.

CHARLESTOWN, Va., March 9.—The report of last night that the United States troops had occupied Leesburg, is officially confirmed. The Rebels evacuated the town on Friday morning, taking all their baggage and supplies to Middlesburg, but it is not known whether the troops retired thither or started toward Winchester. Colonel GEARY occupied the town unresisted yesterday morning, capturing considerable property belonging to the Rebel army.

All was quiet on our frontier last night.

A Scout within Four Miles of Winchester —Skirmishes with the Rebels.

CHARLESTOWN, Va., March 9.—Yesterday, for the first time since our arrival, the country carriages came into town, and the occupants held social intercourse with our officers and soldiers. Suits of secession grey are gradually giving way to other hues, and the ladies are beginning to frequent the streets on business and pleasure.

DR. WM. ALEXANDER, an eminent physician and unflinching Unionist, died at his residence, in this vicinity, last month. His son, yesterday, returned home from the Charlottesville College, deeply im-

The New-York Times.

VOL. XI—NO. 3264. NEW-YORK, MONDAY, MARCH 10, 1862. PRICE TWO CENTS.

HIGHLY IMPORTANT NEWS.

Desperate Naval Engagements in Hampton Roads.

Attack Upon our Blockading Vessels by the Rebel Steamers Merrimac, Jamestown and Yorktown.

The Frigate Cumberland Run Into by the Merrimac and Sunk.

Part of Her Crew Reported to be Drowned.

SURRENDER OF THE FRIGATE CONGRESS.

Engagement of the Rebel Steamers with the Newport's News Batteries.

The Minnesota and Other Vessels Aground.

CESSATION OF FIRING AT NIGHT.

Opportune Arrival of the Iron-Clad Ericsson Battery Monitor.

A Five Hours' Engagement Between Her and the Merrimac.

The Rebel Vessel Forced to Haul Off.

THE MONITOR UNINJURED.

FORTRESS MONROE, Saturday, March 8.

The dullness of Old Point was startled to-day by the announcement that a suspicious looking vessel, supposed to be the *Merrimac*, looking like a submerged house, with the roof only above water, was moving down from Norfolk by the channel in front of the Sewell's Point batteries. Signal guns were also fired by the *Cumberland* and *Congress*, to notify the *Minnesota*, *St. Lawrence* and *Roanoke* of the approaching danger, and all was excitement in and about Fortress Monroe.

There was nothing protruding above the water but a flagstaff flying the rebel flag, and a short smoke-stack. She moved along slowly, and turned into the channel leading to Newport's News, and steamed direct for the frigates *Cumberland* and *Congress*, which were lying at the mouth of James River.

As soon as she came within range of the *Cumberland*, the latter opened on her with her heavy guns, but the balls struck and glanced off, having no more effect than peas from a pop-gun. Her ports were all closed, and she moved on in silence, but with a full head of steam.

In the meantime, as the *Merrimac* was approaching the two frigates on one side, the rebel iron-clad steamers *Yorktown* and *Jamestown* came down James River, and engaged our frigates on the other side. The batteries at Newport's News also opened on the *Yorktown* and *Jamestown*, and did all in their power to assist the *Cumberland* and *Congress*, which, being sailing vessels, were at the mercy of the approaching steamers.

The *Merrimac*, in the meantime, kept steadily on her course, and slowly approached the *Cumberland*, when she and the *Congress*, at a distance of one hundred yards, rained full broadsides on the iron-clad monster, that took no effect, the balls glancing upwards, and flying off, having only the effect of checking her progress for a moment.

After receiving the first broadside of the two frigates, she ran on to the *Cumberland*, striking her about midships, and literally laying open her sides. She then drew off, and fired a broadside into the disabled ship, and again dashed against her with her iron-clad prow, and, knocking in her side, left her to sink, while she engaged the *Congress*, which laid about a quarter of a mile distant.

The *Congress* had, in the meantime, kept up a brisk engagement with the *Yorktown* and *Jamestown*, and having no regular crew on board of her, and seeing the hopelessness of resisting the iron-clad steamer, at once struck her colors. Her crew had been discharged several days since, and three companies of the Naval Brigade had been put on board temporarily, until she could be relieved by the *St. Lawrence*, which was to have gone up on Monday to take her position as one of the blockading vessels of the James River.

On the *Congress* striking her colors, the *Jamestown* approached and took from on board of her, all her officers as prisoners, but allowed the crew to escape in boats. The vessel being thus cleared, was fired by the rebels, when the *Merrimac* and her two iron-clad companions opened with shell and shot on the Newport's News batteries. The firing was briskly returned. Various reports have been received, principally from frightened sutler's clerks. Some of them represent that the garrison had been compelled to retreat from the batteries to the woods. Another was that the two smaller rebel steamers had been compelled to retreat from their guns.

In the meantime the steam frigate *Minnesota*, having partly got up steam, was being towed up to the relief of the two frigates, but did not get up until it was too late to assist them. She was also followed up by the frigate *St. Lawrence*, which was taken in tow by several of the small harbor steamers. It is rumored, however, that neither of these vessels had pilots on board them, and after a short engagement both of them seemed to be, in the opinion of the pilots on the Point, aground. The *Minnesota* either intentionally or from necessity, engaged the same steamers at about a mile distance, with only her two bow guns. The *St. Lawrence* also poured in shot from all the guns she could bring to bear, and it was the impression of the most experienced naval officers on the point that both had been considerably damaged. These statements, it must be borne in mind, are all based on what could be seen by a glass at a distance of nearly eight miles, and from a few panic-stricken non-combatants who fled at almost the first gun from Newport's News.

In the meantime darkness approached, though the moon shone out brightly, and nothing but the occasional flashing of guns could be seen. The *Merrimac* was also believed to be aground, as she remained stationary, at a distance of a mile from the *Minnesota*, making no attempt to attack or molest her.

Previous to the departure of the steamer for Baltimore, no guns had been fired for half an hour, the last one being fired from the *Minnesota*. Some persons declared that immediately after this last gun was fired, a dense volume of vapor was seen to rise from the *Merrimac*, indicating the explosion of her boiler. Whether this is so or not, cannot be known, but it was the universal opinion that the rebel monster was hard aground.

Fears were of course entertained for the safety of the *Minnesota* and *St. Lawrence* in such an unequal contest; but if the *Merrimac* was really ashore, she could do no more damage. It was the intention of the *Minnesota*, with her picked and gallant crew, to run into close quarters with the *Merrimac*, avoid her iron prow, and board her. This the *Merrimac* seemed not inclined to give her an opportunity to do.

At 8 o'clock, when the Baltimore boat left, a fleet of steam-tugs were being sent up to the relief of the *Minnesota* and the *St. Lawrence*, and an endeavor was to be made to draw them off the bar on which they had grounded. In the meantime the firing had suspended, whether from mutual consent or necessity, could not be ascertained.

The rebel battery at Pig Point was also enabled to join in the combined attack on the *Minnesota*, and several guns were fired at her from Sewall's Point as she went up. None of them struck her, but one or two of them passed over her.

The Baltimore boat left Old Point at 8 o'clock last night. In about half-an-hour after she left the wharf, the iron-clad Ericsson steamer *Monitor* passed her, going in, towed by a large steamer. The *Monitor* undoubtedly reached Fortress Monroe by 9 o'clock, and may have immediately gone into service; if not, she would be ready to take a hand early on Sunday morning.

The foregoing are all the facts so far as can be at present ascertained, and are, probably, the worst possible version of the affair.

THE LINE OF THE POTOMAC FROM HARPER'S FERRY TO CHETANK POINT.

Map Showing the Cockpit Point Batteries, Yesterday Evacuated by the Rebels, and Taken Possession of by Our Troops; Leesburgh, from Which the Rebels were Driven on Saturday Morning by Col. Geary, and All Other Important Points.

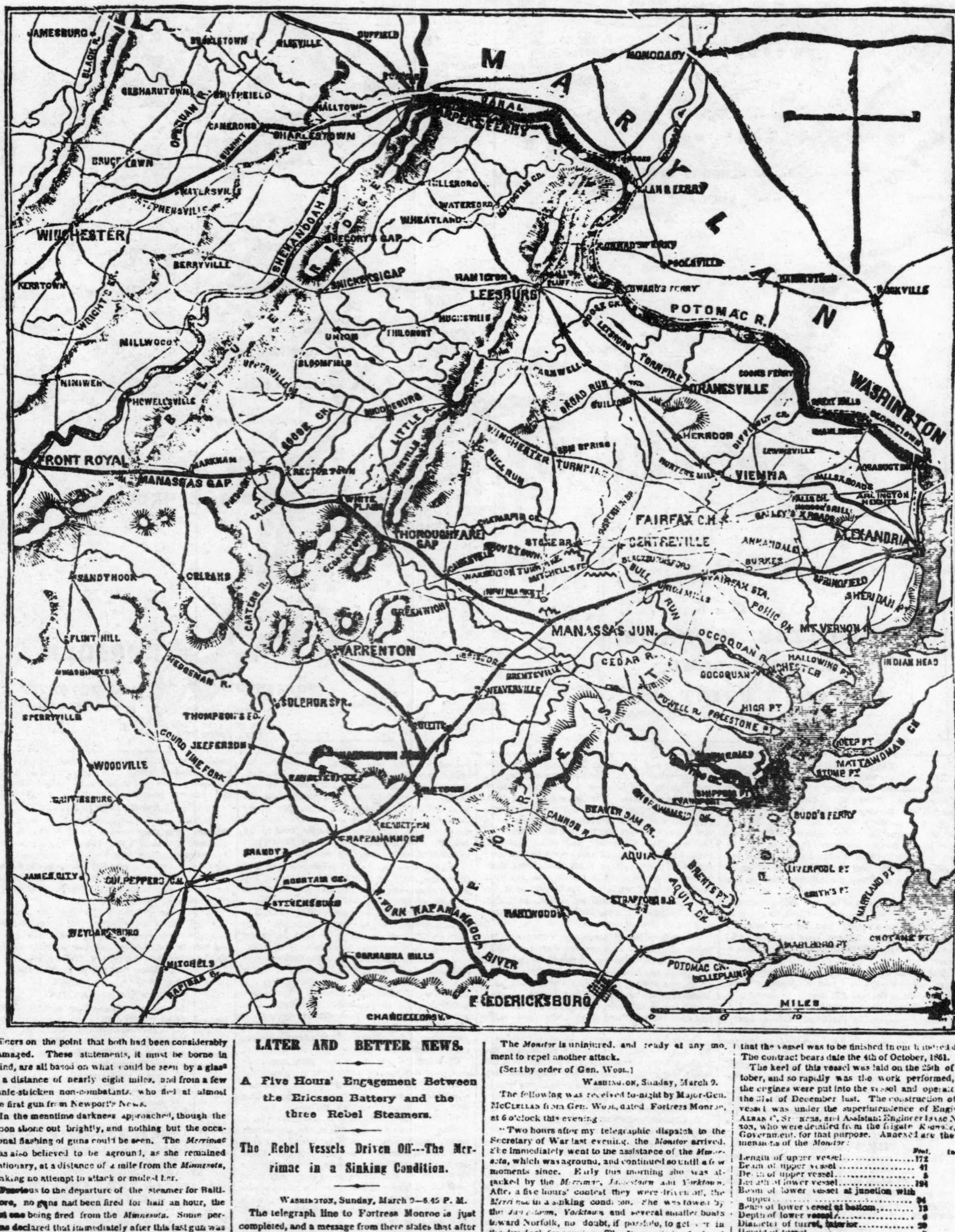

LATER AND BETTER NEWS.

A Five Hours' Engagement Between the Ericsson Battery and the three Rebel Steamers.

The Rebel Vessels Driven Off—The Merrimac in a Sinking Condition.

WASHINGTON, Sunday, March 9—6.45 P. M.

The telegraph line to Fortress Monroe is just completed, and a message from there states that after the arrival of the *Monitor*, last night, she was attacked by the *Merrimac*, *Jamestown*, and *Yorktown*. *After a five hours' fight they were driven off, and the Merrimac put back to Norfolk in a sinking condition.*

OFFICIAL.

[BY TELEGRAPH FROM FORTRESS MONROE.]

WASHINGTON, Sunday, March 9—7 P. M.

The *Monitor* arrived at Fortress Monroe last night.

Early this morning she was attacked by the three vessels—the *Merrimac*, the *Jamestown* and the *Yorktown*.

After five hours' contest they were driven off—the *Merrimac* in a sinking condition.

The above is official.

DISPATCH AUTHORIZED BY GEN. WOOL.

FORTRESS MONROE, Sunday, March 9.

The *Monitor* arrived at 10 P. M., last night, and went immediately to the protection of the *Minnesota*, lying aground just below Newport's News. At 7 A. M. to-day the *Merrimac*, accompanied by two wooden steamers, the *Yorktown* and *Jamestown*, and several tugs, stood out toward the *Minnesota*, and opened fire. The *Monitor* met them at once, and opened fire, when the enemy's vessels retired, excepting the *Merrimac*. *The two iron-clad vessels fought, part of the time touching each other, from 8 A. M. till noon, when the Merrimac retreated.* Whether she is injured, or not, it is impossible to say.

Lieut. J. L. WORDEN, who commanded the *Monitor*, handled her with great skill, assisted by Chief-Engineer STIMERS.

The *Minnesota* kept up a continuous fire, and is herself somewhat injured. She was moved considerably to-day, and will probably be off to-night.

The *Monitor* is uninjured, and ready at any moment to repel another attack.

[Signed by order of Gen. WOOL.]

WASHINGTON, Sunday, March 9.

The following was received to-night by Major-Gen. MCCLELLAN from Gen. WOOL, dated Fortress Monroe, at 6 o'clock this evening:

"Two hours after my telegraphic dispatch to the Secretary of War last evening, the *Monitor* arrived. She immediately went to the assistance of the *Minnesota*, which was aground, and continued so until a few moments since. Early this morning she was attacked by the *Merrimac*, *Jamestown* and *Yorktown*. After a five hours' contest they were driven off, the *Merrimac* in a sinking condition. She was towed by the *Jamestown*, *Yorktown* and several smaller boats toward Norfolk, no doubt, if possible, to get her in the dry-dock for repairs. The *Minnesota* is afloat and being towed toward Fortress Monroe."

THE VESSELS ENGAGED.

THE ERICSSON BATTERY MONITOR.

The new Ericsson battery, or, as she is now called, the *Monitor*, which left this port for Southern waters last Wednesday, has already had her first engagement with the enemy, and has come out victor. It appears that she arrived in Hampton Roads last Saturday night, just after the rebel battery *Merrimac* had been playing havoc with our blockaders. She came to the rescue precisely at the right moment. Yesterday morning she was set upon by the *Merrimac*, the *Jamestown* and the *Yorktown*. After a five hours' fight she drove them all off, the *Merrimac* putting back to Norfolk in a sinking condition. As the public will now be anxious to know something of the style and power of this iron-clad vessel, which has thus routed the famous rebel iron-clad destroying craft, we append a full account of her, furnished by our correspondent, who accompanied her on a recent trial trip from this harbor.

DESCRIPTION OF THE VESSEL.

The designer and builder of the *Monitor* was Capt. ERICSSON, famous in connection with the invention of a mode of propelling vessels and working engines by the motor-power of caloric or heated air. Capt. ERICSSON is a Swede by birth, but his remarkable and persevering scientific efforts have been carried on principally in this City for the last ten years.

By an act of Congress passed last Summer the Secretary of the Navy was authorized to advertise for proposals to build one or more iron-clad vessels, all proposers to furnish their own plans. An appropriation of $1,500,000 was made to build such vessels, providing that the plans met with the approval of three commanding officers of the navy. The Board appointed consisted of Commodores JOSEPH SMITH, HIRAM PAULDING, and Capt. CHAS. H. DAVIS. Capt. ERICSSON submitted a plan which was accepted, with the understanding that the vessel was to be finished in one hundred days. The contract bears the date the 4th of October, 1861.

The keel of this vessel was laid on the 25th of October, and so rapidly was the work performed, that the engines were put into the vessel and operated on the 31st of December last. The construction of the vessel was under the superintendence of Engineer ALBAN C. STIMERS, and Assistant Engineer ISAAC NEWTON, who were detailed from the frigate *Roanoke*, by Government for that purpose. Annexed are the dimensions of the *Monitor*:

	Feet.	Inches.
Length of upper vessel	172	—
Beam of upper vessel	41	—
Depth of upper vessel	5	—
Length of lower vessel	124	—
Beam of lower vessel at junction with upper	34	—
Beam of lower vessel at bottom	18	—
Depth of lower vessel	6	9
Diameter of turret, interior	20	—
Height of turret	9	—
Diameter of pilot-house	6	—
Height above deck	5	—
Draught forward	7	3
Draught aft	8	1
Draught with armament, coals and provisions on board	9	9
Height above the water line	—	21

THE ARMAMENT.

The armament consists of two 11-inch Dahlgren guns, which are the heaviest now used by the navy. The lower part of the gun-carriages upon which the upper part slides when the gun is run in or out, consists of solid, wrought iron beams, extending the whole diameter of the turret, with their ends secured to it in such a manner that they essentially form a part of it. These beams are planned perfectly true, are seven inches deep by four inches wide, and are placed perfectly parallel in the turret, both guns pointing in the same direction. This permits the officer working the guns to take his aim by sights fixed with the turret instead of with the guns, in the usual way, which requires personal exposure when taking the aim. The ports through the side of the turret are only sufficiently wide to permit of the passage through them of the muzzle of the guns, and with just enough addition, vertically, for the elevation required. Inside of these swing iron pendulums, which close them against the enemy as soon as the gun recoils. The whole is made to revolve by a pair of steam engines placed beneath the deck, the handle which governs them jutting up into the turret convenient to the hand of the officer who aims the gun.

HER AMMUNITION.

At the Novelty Iron Works a quantity of solid wrought iron shot was forged for the *Monitor*; each one weighing 187 pounds. These were intended for perforating and sinking iron-clad vessels of the enemy whose sides are the ordinary height above the water line. Besides these she carries a quantity of cast iron shot, weighing 175 pounds each, and one hundred rounds of shell, weighing 135 pounds each.

THE MACHINERY.

Mr. C. H. DELAMATER fitted this vessel with her machinery. It consists of two horizontal tubular boilers, containing 3,000 square feet of fire surface, and two horizontal condensing engines, of forty inches diameter of cylinder, by twenty-two inches stroke of pistons. The propeller is nine feet diameter, sixteen feet pitch, and has four blades. Her speed is about six and a half knots an hour. All her machinery is below water line.

THE MONITOR'S OFFICERS.

The following were the officers of the *Monitor* when she left this port, six days ago:

Lieutenant Commanding—JOHN S. WORDEN.
Lieutenant and Executive Officer—S. D. GREEN.
Acting Masters—L. N. STODDER and J. W. WEBBER.
Acting Assistant Paymaster—WM. F. KEELER.
Acting Assistant Surgeon—D. C. LOGUE.
Chief Engineer—A. C. STIMERS.
Engineers—First Assistant, ISAAC NEWTON, Second Assistant, ALBERT B. CAMPBELL; Third Assistants, R. W. SANDS and M. T. SUNSTROM.
Acting Master's Mate—GEORGE FREDERICKSON.

THE SCIENTIFIC PLAN OF THE MONITOR.

Capt. ERICSSON's idea in building the *Monitor* was to give the greatest buoyancy to the vessel, and as small a target as possible to the enemy, so as to enable him to completely protect every part, all its attachments and every person on board, when under the fire of an enemy. He conceived that to do this was to build a broad flat-bottomed vessel with vertical sides and pointed ends, so that it requires but a shallow depth to displace water sufficient to buoy itself up, though loaded with an impregnable armor upon its sides, and a bomb-proof deck upon which is placed a shot-proof revolving turret containing two of the heaviest Dahlgren guns. To insure such a vessel the power of locomotion, it was only necessary to append beneath it a vessel of ordinary strength, sufficiently narrow and sloping at the sides, that if, as actual experiment has proven possible, the enemy's missile should pass below the shot-proof upper vessel, these sides can only be hit at such an acute angle that little harm is likely to ensue, and in its length approaching the bow only so nearly that its raking stem may receive the shot fired from directly ahead in the same way, and at the stern giving sufficient space to permit the dipping shot coming from directly aft to pass under the shot-proof end, directly on its course, without hitting the rudder, which is placed abaft the propeller.

The sides of the upper vessel are first formed of plate-iron, half an inch thick, outside of which is attached solid white oak, twenty-six inches thick, which again receives the rolled iron armor of five inches thickness. The bomb-proof deck is supported by well-stanchioned and diagonally braced oak beams, ten inches square, placed with their faces twenty-six inches apart, upon which is laid planking seven inches thick, covered with rolled plate-iron one inch thick. As the bottoms of these beams are on a level with the water-line, the armor above water is supported by a backing of forty one feet in depth. The lower vessel is of iron, one-half inch thick, made in the usual manner, and contains, in its after part, the steam machinery and coal, and in the forward part—the poop being divided by a wrought iron bulkhead—the quarters for the officers and crew, and the ammunition and stores. In describing the upper and lower vessel, it must not be imagined that they are constructed separately: they form, together, one vessel; it is only as respects form that they can be regarded as two.

The Pilot-House and Anchor.

The pilot is protected by a shot-proof pilot-house which alone weighs 22,000 pounds. The house stands five feet above the level of the deck. The anchor is suspended from a circular well, open at the bottom, situated in the extreme bow of the upper vessel, and connected with the capstan in the bow of the lower one. An arrangement is also provided for taking soundings below the water line.

The Turret.

The turret spoken of above is for the protection of the men while working the guns; in fact, no one is exposed or seen by the enemy. The turret revolves, and consists, first, of a rolled plate iron skeleton, one inch thick, to which is riveted two thicknesses of one inch each, of rolled iron plates. Outside of these riveted plates are six thicknesses of one inch each, of rolled iron plates. Outside of these riveted plates are six thicknesses, of one inch each, of rolled plates bolted firmly to the first two thicknesses with screw bolts, having deep countersunk heads on the outside and nuts within, so that if in action the enemy's shot should loosen any of the plates they can easily be refastened. The seams are vertical, and these break joints with each other, consequently no shot can strike the seam of more than one thickness. The top is covered with a bomb-proof roof, placed six inches down within the turret, and perforated with holes. In addition to the above the gunners are protected by a shield, within the turret, of one and a half inch thickness.

FOR WHAT THE MONITOR WAS INTENDED.

The Ericsson Battery was not intended for an ordinary cruiser, but for the defence of our harbors and coast, and for operations such as those in which she has just achieved such a signal success. She is enabled to carry eight days' fuel, and thus can proceed easily from port to port along our seaboard. Provisions for three months can be stowed away in her, and a condensing apparatus for supplying fresh water to the officers and crew is fitted up on board.

THE LAST TRIAL TRIP OF THE MONITOR AND ITS RESULTS.

Last Monday the *Monitor* went on a trial trip down the Bay, about five miles beyond Fort Lafayette. Her steering qualities were found to be all that could be desired.

The guns were fired to test the question which had been mooted, of whether the concussion within the turret would not be so great as to injure seriously the ears of the men. First, a blank cartridge was fired, with the hatches in the roof open. Then a charge of canister, weighing 175 pounds, with 15 pounds of powder, with the hatches still open, and finally the same charge with the hatches closed, as they will be under the fire of the enemy. It was found that in every case the concussion in every part of the interior of the turret was considerably less than when standing near such a gun fired in the open air. The sailors stationed at the guns, and who expected to handle them shortly against the enemy, all expressed themselves delighted at the success of the trial. The speed of the vessel by the chip log was 6¾ knots, the engines making 65 revolutions.

The last heard of the *Monitor* previous to this news of her success, was by a bark which arrived here yesterday morning. The bark reported that, on the 7th inst., at 10 P. M., off Barnegat, she passed the *Monitor* in tow, bound for Fortress Monroe.

This magnificent success in her first trial, will settle all questions as to her efficiency.

LIEUT. WORDEN.

Lieut. J. L. WORDEN, it will be recollected, at the commencement of the rebellion was captured by the rebels, after having conveyed dispatches from the Government to the National fleet off Pensacola, and imprisoned several months at Montgomery. He was exchanged a short time ago, and was [illegible] assigned to the [illegible] from the [illegible] service.

THE MERRIMAC.

The *Merrimac*, the iron-clad rebel steamer which attacked the Ericsson Battery, was formerly the United States screw-frigate of the same name. She was built at the Navy-Yard at Charlestown, Mass., in 1855, and her last active service was in the Pacific Squadron. At the time of the rebel attack on the Norfolk Navy-Yard, she was lying there in ordinary, as a store and receiving ship. She was a ship of 3,200 tons burden, and was pierced for forty guns. When the Navy-yard was assailed, she was set fire to, scuttled and sunk, by the National officers, in preference to letting her fall into the hands of the rebels. A recent official report on the subject, made to the rebel authorities, stated that she was sunk and burned to her copper line and down through to her berth-deck, which, with her spacious gun-decks were also destroyed. As soon as the rebels had got possession of the Yard, they proceeded to raise the hull of the *Merrimac*, and to convert her into a vessel of war for their own purpose. Her hull was cut down to within three feet of her water line, and a bomb-proof house built on her gun-deck. She was then iron-plated, her bow and stern steel clad, with a projecting angle of iron for the purpose of piercing a vessel. She had no masts, and there was nothing to be seen over her hull, with the exception of the pilot-house and smoke-stack. The bomb-proof was three inches thick, and made of wrought iron. As a whole, she looked a most formidable war-ship. But when her armor was half on, it was tested and found to be insufficient. She was then additionally strengthened, until she was so heavy that she came near to being unmanageable, and every day she was in danger of sinking. In a description published some twelve days ago, her armament was stated to consist of four 11-inch navy guns on each side, and two 100-pounder Armstrong guns at the bow and stern, but many important changes have been made in her armament since that time. The *Norfolk Day Book* published an article describing the attempt to convert the *Merrimac* into an impregnable iron plated man-of-war as a failure. It began thus:

"We have scarcely patience enough left to contain in temperate language the reckless impropriety of two of our cotemporaries, who have seen fit in their [illegible] to [illegible] the public the fact that the *Merrimac* has proved an abortion."

It was further said, that:

"The calculation in displacement was erroneous. An error amounting to more than two hundred tons was discovered when the ship was floated off. The chief subject of regret is, that when she was shored up again the ship caught upon the blocks and received a considerable strain; consequently, some parts of the machinery have been taken up, and a quantity of dead-wood will have to be introduced to correct the

[Continued on Eighth Page.]

DAILY DISPATCH.

VOL. XXI.—NO. 61. RICHMOND, VIRGINIA, THURSDAY MORNING, MARCH 13, 1862. PRICE TWO CENTS.

Richmond Dispatch.

BY COWARDIN & HAMMERSLEY.

The DAILY DISPATCH is served to subscribers at TWELVE CENTS PER WEEK. Price for mailing $4 a year, or $2.50 for six months; two months $2, one month $1, in advance.

The SEMI-WEEKLY DISPATCH is issued Tuesday and Friday at $3, in advance.

The WEEKLY DISPATCH is issued every Friday and mailed to subscribers at $2 per an'm.

SPECIAL NOTICES.

OWING to the prohibition contained in the proclamation of the President, our store will be kept closed after this day, except for the purpose of settling accounts, and to supply orders previously received.

We request those who have any bills against the concern to present them at once for settlement, and those indebted to us will please call and settle without delay, as it is important to close up our affairs at an early day. All sales will be discontinued after 25th March.

YANCEY & HARRISON,
No. 219 Main st.

PERSONAL.

NOTICE.—The hospital in Richmond, or elsewhere, to which ALPHEUS [illegible], of Sumter District, S. C., a member of Col. Kershaw's 2d South Carolina [illegible], was assigned, will please report what has become of the said Grooms. Direct to
J. S. RICHARDSON,
[illegible] Sumter Volunteers, 2d Regiment S. C. Vols., Sumter, S. C. mh 13—6t*

LARGE AND WELL ARRANGED DWELLING ON FRANKLIN ST., BEYOND THE CORPORATION LINE, FOR RENT.—The large and excellent residence, located as above, now in the occupancy of Mr. Robert A. Lancaster. The house has five rooms, exclusive of the basement, with a large kitchen, stable, a well of good water, and a garden attached to the premises.

For terms, apply to Sam'l J. Rutherfoord, [illegible]
GODDIN & APPERSON.
mh [illegible]—6t

RUNAWAYS.

ONE HUNDRED AND TWENTY-FIVE DOLLARS REWARD.—The following Negroes absconded from the Carbon Hill [illegible] the 2d instant:

JOHN—Dark brown, stout, 5 feet 10 to 11 inches in height; heavy brows; round features; 24 to 26 years of age; purchased last year from King William county.

JIM—Light brown; very likely; intelligent countenance; oval face; 5 feet 8 to 5 feet 9 inches in height, 24 to 28 years of age; can read and write, purchased last year from Bedford county.

[illegible]—Brown; stout built; 5 feet 7 to 5 feet [illegible] inches in height; 22 to 24 years of age; round features and cheerful expression; purchased from Essex county.

PHILIP—Black; very likely; intelligent countenance; stout, well made, except being slightly round-shouldered; 5 feet 10 to 5 feet [illegible] in height; 22 to 24 years of age; purchased last year from Henrico county.

[illegible]—Black, rather [illegible], but clean [illegible]; 5 feet 8 to 5 feet 9 inches in height; 24 to 26 years of age.

[illegible] dollars reward and reasonable expenses of transportation, will be paid for [illegible] apprehension and delivery to me in Richmond [illegible] either one of them.

JNO. J. WERTH, Agt.

WANTS.

WANTED—RECRUITS. MAGRUDER LIGHT ARTILLERY. $50 BOUNTY.

Any cannoneers, mechanics, artisans, or others desirous of enlisting in the Magruder Light Artillery, will apply for information to STEPHEN D. YANCEY, at No. 7 Wall street, under St. Charles Hotel.

This company of Artillery, organized by authority of the Secretary of War, under the command of Lieut. T. J. Page, of Gen. Magruder's Staff, will for the present be stationed on the Peninsula, and a number of recruits are wanted to complete its organization, to whom extraordinary inducements are offered. The battery will be composed of rifled pieces and howitzers, with the best equipments on the Peninsula.

Apply also at the headquarters of the Army of the Peninsula, Yorktown. mh 8—6t

WANTED—FORTY RECRUITS—Being authorized by the Secretary of War to raise a Heavy Artillery Company. Usual bounty and clothing given.

Persons wishing to enlist for this service, which has many advantages over Light Artillery or Infantry, will apply at the Rendezvous, on 10th street, between Main and Bank sts.

JOHN T. ROGERS,
WM. P. ATKISSON,
SAMPSON JONES, Jr.
mh 8—1w*

WANTED—RECRUITS FOR MORRIS LIGHT ARTILLERY.—Twenty RECRUITS will be received into the above-named company, now comfortably quartered near Centreville. The company numbers eighty men, who have been in service since the 19th of August. It is provided with a field battery and a good lot of horses. Full uniform furnished free. Besides the regular pay, persons enlisting for the war will receive a bounty of $50. Apply to C. T. Wortham & Co., Richmond; Dr. Geo. Fleming, Wm. O. Winston, and Sergt. W. H. Toler, Villa Green, Hanover county, or address any of the subscribers, at Manassas Junction, care of Col. Wm. N. Pendleton, to whose corps the Morris Artillery belongs.

Capt. LEWIS M. COLEMAN,
1st Lieut. H. P. JONES,
2d Lieut. EDWARD W. MORRIS,
3d Lieut. WM. A. MASSIE.
fe 26—[illegible]

WANTED—RECRUITS, For a crack regiment—the 4th Alabama, and Law's Legion.

The undersigned, having been appointed recruiting officer for the 4th Alabama Regiment, has opened an office in this city, at 109 Main street, (up stairs) three doors above 14th, over Mr. W. S. Tupman's Furnishing Store.

This is an opportunity rarely offered to men desirous to enrol themselves under the banner of their country, in a regiment which has already won for itself a name for gallantry unsurpassed in history.

The $50 bounty allowed by Government will be paid upon enrollment in cash.

Clothing, rations, &c., furnished free.

I have given Lewis Warrington and John R. Plater authority to act as recruiting officers with me.

[illegible] B. TRAVIS,
Lieut. 4th Alabama Reg't,
Recruiting Officer.

N. B.—Those desiring substitutes for the war, and non-resident parties who desire to serve as substitutes, would do well to call at our recruiting office. mh 5—3w*

WANTED—100 RECRUITS. Major T. G. Peyton having permission to raise a regiment for the Confederate service, has kindly consented that the undersigned should raise a company to compose a part of said regiment. I can be seen at all hours day or night, at Battery No. 15.

JOHN F. TOMPKINS,
Lieut. Battery No. 15.

Any person calling on Lieut. Tompkins to enlist in the company which he proposes to raise, should he be absent on duty, will receive from me all attention in my power.

L. M. BURFOOT,
Captain Battery No. 15.
mh 5—6t*

WANTED—RECRUITS For THOMAS'S ARTILLERY. Lieut. E. J. Anderson, of this company, has been detailed as recruiting officer. Persons wishing to enlist in this company, will apply at the office of the Midlothian Coal Mining Co., on 12th street, between Main and Cary, or at Mr. E. A. Smith's office, on Main, between 20th and 21st streets, next door to the Georgia Dispensary. The bounty of $50 will be paid on enlistment. fe 17—1m*

WANTED! WANTED!! WANTED!!! One hundred able-bodied MEN, for the P. Army of the Confederate States, to whom will be given a bounty of $50, and $11 to $20 per month pay. The bounty will be paid immediately, and clothing and subsistence furnished at the same time. Recruits will be allowed to join any company and regiment they desire. Apply, immediately, at the General Recruiting office, corner Pearl and Main sts., up stairs.

C. W. BLAIR, 2d Lieut., and
Gen'l Recruiting Officer.
mh 6—2w*

WANTED—FIFTY RECRUITS. The undersigned are authorized to raise a VOLUNTEER COMPANY, for the service of the Confederate States. A bounty of $50, and uniform furnished. Also, comfortable lodgings and rations furnished to those desiring it. The company is to be commanded by a graduate of the Virginia Military Institute.

Recruiting Office at Bayly & Moncure's Shockoe Slip. Also, corner of 17th and Marshall sts.

THOS. J. MONCURE,
A. W. NOLTING, Jr.,
JULIAN VANNERSON.
mh 7—1w*

WANTED—To purchase a place containing 20 or 30 ACRES OF LAND, improved or unimproved, within from one to four miles of the city.

Address "Box 761," Post-Office, giving address and other particulars. mh 7—6t*

WANTED—Several SUBSTITUTES, Exempt from all military duty, for which a very high price will be paid. Apply to

SAM'L D. HICKS,
Commission Merchant, Shockoe Slip.
fe 26—2w*

WANTED—$50 BOUNTY—THIRTY MEN, to Dr. Courtney's Artillery Company, now at Manassas. Apply at Recruiting Office, in Franklin House, on 6th, between Broad and Marshall sts.

Lieut. R. H. VAUGHAN,
Recruiting Officer.
fe 27—12t*

WANTED—A SERVANT To Wash and do Housework, who can come well recommended. Apply to C. P. B. fe 28—ts

WANTED AN OVERSEER. Wanted, a steady, industrious MAN, To take charge of a small Farm in Powhatan county. Address "POWHATAN," through the Richmond Post-Office. [illegible]

WANTED—NATIVE GOLD! NATIVE GOLD! Wanted to purchase, native Gold, for the manufacture of an article of commerce much used in the Southern Confederacy. The highest market price will be paid for any quantity, either large or small. [illegible] GENNET, 140 Main street. mh 8—10t

WANTED—$120,000—$20,000 wanted for one year, secured by mortgage on valuable real estate in Mississippi.

$100,000 wanted for five years or more, secured by mortgage on valuable real estate in the State of Louisiana. For particulars apply to

R. H. MAURY & CO.
mh 6—ts

WANTED—RECRUITS—THOMAS ARTILLERY. Capt. P. H. STANARD will receive the names of all persons wishing to enlist in this Battery, at the office of the Midlothian Coal Mining Company, on 12th street, between Main and Cary, or at Mr. E. A. Smith's office, on Main, between 20th and 21st streets, next door to the Georgia Dispensary. The bounty of $50 given. fe 19—1m*

WANTED, RECRUITS FOR COMPANY F.—I have been detailed as recruiting officer for Company F, 21st regiment Virginia volunteers, from this city, and can be found at all hours during the day on Bank street, near 12th. The bounty of $50 will be paid when the recruits are mustered in. The Company is armed with Minnie rifled muskets.

R. H. CUNNINGHAM, Jr.,
Capt. Co. F, 21st Va. Vols.,
Recruiting Officer.
mh 12—10t*

WANTED—IMMEDIATELY—Five young LADIES, to work on Mantillas.

Apply at No. 87 Main street, to
Mrs. S. STRIDER.
mh 12—6t*

WANTED—A SITUATION, by a widow lady, who has been accustomed to keeping house and nursing the sick. Good references given. Address "P," at this office. mh 12—3t*

WANTED—A WHITE GIRL, to Wash and Iron, and do general housework. Apply at 221, corner of Main and 9th sts. mh 12—3t*

WANTED—BOARD by a gentleman and his wife in a private family in the country, not far from the city. Address "D. W.," Dispatch Office. mh 12—3t*

WANTED—By a steady man, of industrious habits, a situation on a Railroad, who has been in the business for several years—is a good Telegraph Operator, and acquainted with all the different branches pertaining to railroading. Best of references given. Address, "RAILROAD," care of Dispatch office. mh 12—3t*

WANTED—By an energetic and capable man, of considerable experience, a SITUATION in some active business. He is exempt from military duty. Apply, by letter or otherwise, "J. K. S.," at this office. Reference given, if necessary. mh 12—3t*

WANTED.—The undersigned, (exempt from military duty) solicits a position in some of the Departments, where dispatch, accuracy, and neatness of writing is required. He would take charge of Books, and close them with satisfaction. Best city reference given.

mh 12—3t* L. W. [illegible]

WANTED—Board for a gentleman, wife, and two children, in the vicinity of the Capitol and Post-Office. Address, "YELROSE," Dispatch Office. mh 11—3t*

WANTED—TWO YOUTHS, from twelve to seventeen years. One for service in the country, the other to attend in a store. Apply at No. 80 Main street. mh 12—3t*

WANTED—A MAN who understands farming, to take charge of a small place near town. One without much encumbrance preferred. Apply to PARKER, at No. 80 Main street. mh 12—3t*

WANTED—TO RENT—A DWELLING-HOUSE, in a good location, containing at least six rooms, or two good ROOMS, furnished or unfurnished. Address "C. C.," Dispatch office. mh 11—3t*

WANTED—TO PURCHASE—Fifteen or twenty head BARREN COWS.

JESSE WILLIAMS.
mh 11—3t*

WANTED—$4,000 for five years. Security on country property near the city. Address Box 749, Richmond Post-Office. mh 11—3t*

WANTED.—A gentleman wishes to engage a pleasant ROOM, in a genteel part of the city; a furnished room preferred. Address "G. L.," box 809. mh 11—3t*

WANTED—To Hire, A NURSE. One who can come well recommended. Inquire at the house of R. J. Higgins, 18th st., between Broad and Grace.

B. FULLER.
mh 11—3t*

WANTED.—ATTENTION, MARYLANDERS. Wanted a number of able-bodied MEN, to fill up Co. "C," 1st Maryland Regiment.

A bounty of $50 will be paid immediately on joining. Clothing and subsistence furnished. Apply immediately at the Maryland Recruiting office, corner of 9th and Main sts.

LT. ALEX'R CROSS,
Recruiting Officer.
fe 19—1m*

WANTED.—ATTENTION, MARYLANDERS. Wanted, a number of able-bodied MEN, to fill up Co. "E," 1st Maryland Regiment.

A bounty of $50 will be paid immediately on joining. Clothing and subsistence furnished.—Apply immediately at the Maryland Recruiting Office, corner 9th and Main streets.

LT. JOHN LUTTS,
Recruiting Officer.
fe 19—1m*

WANTED—Ten SUBSTITUTES For which the highest price will be paid. Apply, to-day, at the corner of 18th and Dock sts. mh 5—6t*

RECRUITS WANTED—40 Volunteers to fill up THE VIRGINIA LIFE GUARD. Being ordered on recruiting service I will receive new members for the above company at my office, near Shockoe Warehouse, between 10 o'clk A. M. and 2 P. M. This company was among the first in the field, and are re-enlisting for the war. Acquaintances of the present members of the company who prefer being in association with their friends to being drafted, will do well to volunteer at once in this company.

Substitutes will not be received.

Arms—Enfield Rifles.

The usual bounty, &c., given.

JNO. STEWART WALKER,
Captain Virginia Life Guard.
mh 10—9t*

WANTED—$50 Bounty—TWENTY-FIVE MEN, To fill up my company at Game-Point Battery, Aquia Creek. Come at once. Don't be drafted. Richmond to the rescue, as we want fighting men. Rendezvous on 10th street, next door to Crawford's Saloon.

WM. J. DABNEY,
Capt. Com'd'g.
mh 10—3t*

WANTED—SUBSTITUTES. We want eight Substitutes for friends in the country, and are willing to pay good prices for able bodied non-residents. Call at our office corner 13th and Cary sts., up stairs.

mh 10—6t [illegible]

WANTED—500 POUNDS SHEET BRASS, in large or small quantities, for which the highest market price will be paid. Call on or address [illegible]WIS & KAYTON, 13th street, between Main and Cary, Richmond, Va. mh 10—12t*

WANTED—BOARD For a small family, with a private family, where there are no other boarders, located from one to three miles West of Richmond. Address Box 1067, Richmond. mh 10—3t*

WANTED.—Two or three first-rate BOATMAKERS. SEERS, POINDEXTER & CO. mh 10—6t

TREDEGAR IRON WORKS, Richmond, March 10, 1862.

WANTED—We wish to purchase 100,000 feet best OAK AND HICKORY TIMBER. Apply at the works.

J. R. ANDERSON & CO.
mh 10—1w

WANTED.—MARYLANDERS, ATTENTION.—Wanted, a few able-bodied men for Company D, 1st Maryland regiment. $50 bounty paid. Apply at the Recruiting Office under Exchange Hotel.

JAS. R. HERBERT,
Capt. Co. D, 1st Md. Reg.
mh 8—2w*

WANTED—IMMEDIATELY—10,000 SILLS, Delivered on the line of the road between Richmond and Fredericksburg. Dimensions: 8 feet long, not less than 9 inches diameter at small end, barked and smoothly hewn to a thickness of 6 inches, clear of any defect calculated to impair strength.

No Sill will be received under size.

TERMS.

For white or post oak, 9 to 11 inches diameter, 45 cents, cash; 11 inches or more, 50 cents, cash.

For red or chestnut oak, 37 cents, each.

For further information, apply to Section Masters on line of road, or to

WM. N. BRAGG, Sup't Road.
Office R., F. & P. R. R. Co., Richmond, March 12, 1862. mh 12—ts

WANTED—A TEACHER. A Baltimore family wishes to engage an agreeable female Teacher for the present year. She must be a good musician and able to speak French. Address, immediately,

THOS. H. TRENT,
Appomattox C. H., Va.
mh 12—eod3t*

WANTED—A DRUG CLERK. One acquainted with the business and not subject to military duty, can hear of a good situation by calling on

R. W. POWERS, Druggist,
Corner Main and 15th sts.
mh 12—ts

WANTED! WANTED!! WANTED!!!—SEVENTY-FIVE RECRUITS, for the Governor's Mounted Guard, which company is now quartered at Manassas. $50 bounty. Clothing and subsistence will be furnished. Apply at the Recruiting Rendezvous, on Bank street, near the corner of 12th.

fe 25—1m Capt. F. W. CHAMBERLAYNE.

LOST, STRAYED, &c.

LOST—A SMALL TRUNK.—At the Central Depot, on Saturday evening last, a small hair TRUNK, much worn, with the name of the owner, (Mrs. R. T. Kern, Farmville, Va.,) written on leather, tacked on one end. It contains many family letters of value to the owner, but to no one else. The finder will be liberally rewarded by leaving the Trunk at the Capitol House, opposite Minnis's Gallery, Main st. mh 11—3t*

STRAY MULE.—Strayed, from Canal-Boat Thomas Jefferson, on the Basin, a small black MULE; tail and mane not trimmed; about four years old. A reward of Ten Dollars will be paid for his delivery to me.

JAS. F. GUNN,
Lumber Yard corner 19th and Cary sts.
mh 11—3t*

LOST—A POINTER DOG. I have lost my Pointer Dog, "Roscoe," 12 months old, liver-colored, with some white spots on him. A suitable reward will be given for his delivery at corner of Main and Foushee streets. CHAS. DAVENPORT. mh 10—3t*

STRAY HEIFER.—Came to my stables, near Dickinson & Hill's auction house, some three weeks since, a Red HEIFER, supposed to be some 14 or 15 months old. The owner can have her by proving property and paying charges. [mh 10—3t*] D. McDANIEL.

STRAYED—On 12th February from Adams's Store, six miles below Richmond, a HORSE or MARE, supposed to be a gray, and branded C. S. A suitable reward will be paid if returned to the undersigned. If found in possession of any person, they will be liable to criminal prosecution.

WESTON & WILLIAMS,
15 Pearl street.
mh 8—6t

ESTRAY.—Left the Government stable on the 16th February, a black MULE, lame and sweenyed. Five Dollars reward will be paid for his delivery to me.

WM. E. WARREN,
Capt. and Ass't Quartermaster,
Bank street.
mh 6—2w

$50 REWARD.—Lost, on the 18th inst., between R. Adam's Bakery, on Main street, and the stables of Davis & Hutcheson, on Franklin street, a Black Morocco POCKET-BOOK, containing about $400 in notes of the Confederate States, Farmers' Bank of Virginia, and Bank of Virginia, &c.; also, sundry important papers. The above reward will be paid to the finder if returned to the undersigned.

JOS. J. WHITE,
At the Capitol.
fe 20—ts

LOST—COUPONS.—Lost in transmission by mail to Charlottesville, Va., the following Coupons of the Orange and Alexandria Railroad Company:

No. 731 to 736 inclusive, $40 each	....	$240 00
" 64 to 66 " 20 "	....	60 00
		$300 00

Interest payable in May and November, at New York. All persons are cautioned not to buy or trade for them, as the same will not be paid.

ja 29—ts C. W. PURCELL & CO.

LOST—$20 REWARD—Between the First Market and Brooke Avenue, a BLACK BAG, Containing two Account Books and sundry papers. I will give the above reward for their delivery to me, at Nos. 17 and 19, First Market.

JOHN LINDSEY.

BOARDING.

BOARDING.—Board can be had at No. 115, on the South side of Broad street, between 8th and 9th. mh 11—3t*

BOARDING.—A gentleman and wife, and six or eight Day Boarders, can find comfortable accommodations by applying east side of 10th street, two doors south of Broad, to

MRS. JAMES H. LEWELLYN.
mh 7—6t*

BOARDING.—Ten or twelve gentlemen can obtain BOARD and LODGING in a private family, by the day, week, or month by applying at the corner of 29th and Marshall streets, on Church Hill, near the Chimborazo Hospital, and beyond the limits of the corporation, at the reduced prices of $1.50 per day, $7 per week, or $30 per month, washing and candles extra. fe 19—1m*

DISSOLUTION.—The copartnership of APPERSON & DUPUY was dissolved on the 1st January, 1862. All persons indebted are requested to make immediate payment; and those having claims against the firm are requested to present them for settlement.

R. W. APPERSON,
P. B. DUPUY.

The undersigned, having purchased the interest of R. W. Apperson in the late concern of Apperson & Dupuy, hopes, by personal attention and competent assistance to merit the former patronage of the house and the public generally.

POWHATAN B. DUPUY,
Graduate in Pharmacy.
mh 11—1m

SUNDRIES.—20 hhds. choice New Orleans Sugars. 15 bbls. white Clarified Sugars. 15 bbls. yellow Clarified Sugar. 50 boxes Tallow Candles. 20 boxes Soap. 20 bbls. Apples. 100 bags Beans and Peas. 20 gross Matches. For sale.

G. W. ROBINSON, Virginia st.,
Opp. Harvey, Armistead & Williams.
mh 11—3t*

VERY VALUABLE PRIVATE RESIDENCE FOR SALE PRIVATELY.—We are authorized to sell that really valuable residence situated at the southeast corner of Marshall and 12th streets and within three minutes' walk of the Capitol and business part of the city.

The buildings were erected in 1860 by the owner, using the best selected material throughout, and with all the modern conveniences.

The masonry work was done under the instructions of W. Gill, Esq., City Engineer.

Altogether, this is a No. 1 residence and most desirable property. For further information, apply to

JAS. M. TAYLOR & SON,
Auct'rs.
mh 11—6t

SPECIAL NOTICE.—JULIUS SYCLE having removed his entire stock of Dry Goods, Clothing, Boots, Shoes, Hats, Caps, &c., to the large store, No. 320 Broad street, directly opposite the old stand, wishes to inform his patrons and the public at large that, notwithstanding the blockade, he can show you as complete and well selected a stock of goods as can be found in any other store in the Confederacy, at wholesale and retail. Call at the new store, and examine for yourself.

JULIUS SYCLE,
320 Broad, bet. 2d and 3d sts.,
Richmond, Va.
mh 11—6t*

RAISINS, Baking Soda, Salts, Soda, and manufactured Tobacco, for sale by
I. & C. S. DAVENPORT.

Richmond Dispatch.

THURSDAY MORNING, MARCH 13, 1862.

Promotions for Merit.

History not only teaches the fallacy of the idea that military schools confer the high qualifications of generalship; but it also teaches that the country which has pursued the system of promoting for merit, and not by mere favoritism, has produced the greatest number of great generals. No country in the tide of time has produced a greater number of military heroes and distinguished captains than France since 1790; and it is astonishing to find how many of her great historical names have sprung from the ranks, and in almost every case from the bosom of the community, without the advantage of military education.

We have at considerable pains compiled a list of the most conspicuous French generals of modern times, with the dates of their promotions in rank. It is a remarkable fact that all of Napoleon's great marshals, with one or two exceptions, rose from the ranks, and that probably every one of them was without the advantage of a military education. There were indeed real generals before West Point undertook the manufacture of them.

Hoche—a celebrated General of the French Revolution—soldier 1784, General 1793, poisoned in 1797—one of the best Generals of that period.

Joubert—Soldier 1789, General 1795; very distinguished; killed at the battle of Novi.

Jourdan, Marechal de France—Soldier 1778, General 1793, Marechal 1804.

Junot, well known—Soldier in 1792, General 1797.

Kellermann—Soldier at 18 years old, 1750; General 1792.

Kellermann, (son of the above,)—Soldier 1793, General 1797; decided the victory of Marengo.

Kleber—Educated in a Bavarian military school, General in 1794, assassinated in Egypt.

Latour d'Auvergne—Alternately soldier and General; the latter when he was called upon to save the army, returning afterwards to the ranks as a simple grenadier; killed in the ranks as such 8th June, 1800. His heart was preserved and carried in a box for a long time by the oldest grenadier, who answered for him at roll-call even after Napoleon was Emperor. Honor to the patriotic soldier—a rare example of self-denial. No pay, no glitter of epaulettes, tempted him.

Lannes—Rose from the ranks to a Marshal's baton.

Lauriston—From schools.

Lefebvre, Marechal de France—Soldier 1773, Sergeant 1789, General 1793, Marshal 1804, died 1820.

Lefebvre-Desnouettes—soldier 1792, Colonel 1804, General 1806, refugee in America, drowned in the Albion.

Macdonald—Born in Sancerre, France, 1765, Lieutenant in an Irish regiment 1784, General 1796, Marshal at Wagram 1809.

Marceau—Born 1769, soldier 1784, Lieutenant Colonel 1792, was arrested by *representant* Bourbotte of the Convention, and, at the risk of his own life, saved that of the *representant* from the army; General 1793, killed in 1796. The Austrian army solicited an armistice to attend his funeral, so highly was he estimated by all.

Marmont, from the military school—Lieutenant 1774, General 1798, Marshal 1809.

Massena—Well known; surnamed "Enfant cheri de la victoire;" soldier 1790, General 1793, Marshal 1804, died 1817.

Moncey, Marechal de France—Soldier 1773, Lieutenant 1778, General 1794, Marshal 1804.

Moreau, a lawyer—Major 1792, General 1794, exiled conspirator 1804, killed 1813.

Mortier, Marechal de France—Captain 1791, General 1793, Marshal 1804.

Mouton-Duvernet—Soldier 1787, Captain 1794, Major 1806, General 1811.

Murat—Born 1768, sub-Lieutenant 1791, Major 1796, General 1797, Marshal 1804, shot 1815.

Nansouty—Born 1768, Lieutenant 1785, Captain 1788, Lieutenant Colonel 1792, General 1800, died 1815.

Napoleon, military school—Somewhat known as a General.

Narbonne (Count of)—Born 1756, Colonel 1789, General 1791, died 1831.

Ney—Born at Sarre-Louis, France, 10th January, 1769; enlisted very young as a hussar, and rose successively through the various grades, until he was made Captain in 1794, Major in 1796, General on the field of battle 1796, Marshal 1804, shot 7th December, 1815.

Oudinot—Born 1767, soldier 1784, Major 1792, General 1799, Marshal 1809.

Perignon (Marquis de)—Sub-Lieutenant about 1774, General 1791, Marshal 1805; not very remarkable.

Pichegru—Soldier 1782, officer 1789, General 1792, deserter and conspirator, died in prison 1804.

Reynier (Count)—Born 1771, Colonel 1792, General 1793, died in Paris 1815; nothing remarkable.

Salm-Salm (Prince de)—Major of cavalry in 1808, in Portugal, under Junot.

Sebastiani (Count)—Born 1775 in Corsica, Lieutenant, then Captain, Major, Colonel; General about 1796, went through all the campaigns until 1815, Ambassador to Turkey in 1806, and member of the Chamber of Deputies in 1819.

Segur (Count)—Born 1780, Soldier 1800, Major 1807, Colonel 1809, General 1812; occasionally Ambassador to Denmark and Spain.

Serrurier (Count,) Marechal de France—Born 1742, officer at first, General about 1796, died 1819.

Soult—Born 1769, soldier 1785, officer 1790, Major 1793, General 1794, Marshal 1804.

Suchet—Born at Lyons 1772, soldier 1792, then sub-Lieutenant, Lieutenant, Captain, Major in 1793, Colonel 1797, General 1798, Marshal 1811.

Tascher de la Pagerie, (Count,) a relation of Josephine, Captain before 1807, Major in 1807, General in 1816; the end.

Teste, (Count,) born 1776, Major at 17 (1793) Colonel 1800, General 1806; until Waterloo.

Valence, (Count of) born 1757, Lieutenant 1774, Captain 1778, Colonel 1784, General 1792; retired after Waterloo.

Vandamme, (Comte d'Unebourg) officer about 1790, General 1793, prisoner in 1813 in Bohemia, exiled in 1815.

Victor, Marechal de France, born 1766, soldier 1781, General 1793, Marshal 1807.

Vignolle (Count of) born 1763, officer 1793, Captain 1795, General 1796, retired in 1815.

The value of this catalogue is very great. It shows the importance of promotion for merit and service, and the exceeding hazard of promotion from mere caprice or favoritism. The experience of the present war has brought into conspicuous view and into great popular favor, four able generals, two of them happening to be thoroughly educated officers of the West Point school, and two of them men of great natural capacity and talent for command. The fact shows that West Point has little to do with making a general: it neither confers the talent for command nor takes it away.

The South Unconquerable.

We have never yet heard from the most despondent person the suggestion of any plan by which the South can be conquered, and made tributary to the North, provided the South prove true to herself, and determines never to surrender. What is the object of this war? It is simply Southern staples and Southern trade. Who supposes or pretends that if the South were unproductive to the North, instead of being its main dependence for commerce and revenue, that the North would spend five dollars to keep it in the Union? Suppose, then, that the Northern armies take every city in the South, how much nearer does that bring them to the object of the war, provided the South determines not to submit. It is not the cities which raise cotton, they are small affairs at the best, and made up in great part of Yankees. The country, the enormous cotton and tobacco-growing country, where white labor cannot be employed, and which is too vast for even the hosts of Xerxes to overrun, how is that to be made tributary to the North, if the planters do not choose to cultivate Southern staples for Northern benefit, and to raise wheat, corn, and vegetables? That is an impediment in the way of a Yankee triumph which does not seem to have entered into the calculations of the invaders.

The Battle of Hampton Roads.

[SPECIAL CORRESPONDENCE OF THE DISPATCH.]

NORFOLK, March 11, 1862.

The excitement occasioned by the great naval victory of Saturday, has nearly subsided. So decisive a triumph and so important results, naturally caused much joyous agitation of the public mind here and perhaps in many other places. A thrill of profound delight will, doubtless, be felt in every part of the South on account of the very satisfactory achievements of the Confederate iron steamer. The Yankees were, no doubt, taken by surprise; the officers and men on board the Federal frigates were almost bewildered with astonishment, and the terror occasioned by the death-dealing balls of the Virginia was intense. The whole affair was so sudden and violent that the consternation was beyond description.

As the Virginia neared the blockading frigates, it is said by prisoners who were on board, that the strange looking war steamer called forth many derisive remarks. They looked upon her with contempt, not dreaming that she could withstand the broadsides of the big Yankee frigates. The shots from her rifled guns, crashing through the timbers, and the storming jar and smash from her prow, sending the Cumberland quickly to the bottom, roused all hands up to a vivid and terrible evidence of the tremendous power of the great battering ram which they had derided and laughed at.

The bodies of the men slain and drowned in the battle will probably float ashore in a day or two. Occasionally a mattress floats ashore. One has been found apparently much stained with blood. Two suits of sailors' clothes have also floated ashore at Sewell's Point. In the pockets were found letters written by the friends of those who had worn the clothes. Other articles have gone ashore from the Cumberland, whose masts and spars now mark the location of the fierce engagement.

I regret to state that the Yankees succeeded in getting off the Minnesota, and towing her round to Fort Monroe. She is in a specially bad condition—her masts shivered; her hull riddled, and large timbers having been knocked from her upper and lower works. If she should be carried North for repairs, the work of months will be required to put her in a seaworthy condition.

The villainy and treachery of the officers and men on board the Congress, in firing upon our gunboats while approaching after she had raised the white flag, is denounced in strong terms. By this perfidious conduct valuable lives were lost, and among them that of Lieut. J. L. Taylor, of Virginia, who died yesterday, Midshipman Hutter, who was killed in the action. Captain Buchanan, and Lieut. Minor, were also shot under the white flag. I am glad to state that they are both improving.

It is probable that not more than two hundred and fifty to three hundred Yankees of the Cumberland were killed and drowned.—The statement that there were four hundred, is doubtless an over-estimate.

Those on board the Virginia state that when she fired at the iron battery Ericsson her tower revolved with great rapidity, and that when the ball struck, the sound was like the ringing of an immense gong. The Ericsson has a revolving circular tower, in which there are two powerful guns worked by an engine. The machinery, gun tables, and all the apparatus for working them, are said to be remarkable and complete. The guns being elevated, the balls probably struck the iron roof of the Virginia at nearly right angles, but the powerful timbers of our great marine battery resisted the well-directed and powerful blows of her antagonist.

It is reported that, in addition to the consternation and terror on board the Congress, there was mutiny among the crew, and that the scenes of violence, slaughter, blood, and death, are unparalleled in the history of naval warfare.

Another correspondent of the *Dispatch*, who witnessed the terrific engagement, sends a long and interesting account, a portion of which we append. After describing the successful attack upon the Cumberland and the Congress, the writer proceeds.

It was now about 3 o'clock P. M., when the Confederate steamer Patrick Henry, Capt. Tucker; the Jamestown, Lieut. Barney, and the Teaser, Lieut. Webb, which had been lying near the Rocks on James river, and were attracted by the cannonading, appeared on the scene, and were ordered at once by Commodore Buchanan to open upon the Congress and the perfidious shore batteries; and never was order more daringly executed, as these slight vessels dashed up to the enemy and literally vomited fire upon them. How they escaped destruction in this unequal conflict, it is impossible to explain, especially as at this hour the Minnesota, the heaviest steamer in the Federal navy, came up from Old Point, and opened upon our squadron, about a mile off. It soon appeared that she had grounded, but still her position and immense battery made her more than thrice a match in number and weight of metal for our whole fleet. But the Virginia took a position as near as she could approach her, and, aided by the other vessels, poured an incessant fire into her, et flaming her several times, and rendering her condition almost hopeless.—She returned our courtesies with much skill and power; and now, whilst the contest was hottest between the Minnesota, several gunboats, and the shore batteries, on their part, and the Virginia, Patrick Henry, and Jamestown, on our side, Buchanan, who had too daringly exposed his person on the elevated deck during the whole action, was wounded in the leg by a Minie ball, and was forced to go below, leaving the active command to Lieut. Catesby Jones, than whom none could be more worthy of the perilous office. Surely the Commodore must have borne a charmed life, for all this time shot of every description, from ship and shore, had passed and fallen like rain at his feet, whilst the [illegible] near which he stood, was pierced by at least two hundred balls. It was now between 5 and 6 o'clock P. M., when the Federal steamer Roanoke was seen approaching from Old Point, and following her the St. Lawrence and a large gunboat, and the hearts of the thousands who looked on from the surrounding shores of those magnificent roads trembled at the seemingly unequal war. But the Roanoke, the St. Lawrence and the gunboat, when about half way between the Rip Raps and Newport News changed their minds and their course, and returned to the guns of Fortress Monroe—why, we know not, but as they were fired upon by the great rifled battery at Sewell's Point, it may be that, in spite of the distance, they may have been damaged though it is more probable that they were appalled by the fate of the Cumberland and the Congress.

As the night spread over the Roads, the Virginia, with the other vessels, passed over and anchored near Sewell's Point, leaving the Minnesota aground, and the Congress in flames—up to midnight, the guns of the latter ship were heavily discharged as the fire approached them, and at about one o'clock A. M., her magazine exploded, illuminating the whole panorama, and causing the windows to rattle through the city.

Commodore Buchanan, and the brave Lt. Minor, who had been sharply wounded on board the Virginia, were landed at Sewell's Point, during Saturday night, and on Sunday morning the Virginia crossed and recommenced the firing upon the Minnesota, which was still ashore and greatly shattered. She was defended by her crew most pertinaciously and by the iron-cased steamer Monitor, and, after a conflict of several hours, the Monitor steamed off to Old Point, and the Virginia, from her draft, being unable to approach any nearer to the Minnesota, returned to Sewell's Point, and with the other steamers, arrived at 2 o'clock P. M., to Norfolk, welcomed by the grateful cheering of a whole population.

The damage to the Virginia is not material. Her killed is but two, and five or six wounded. The Patrick Henry lost five men killed, [illegible] by scalding, from the passage of a shot through one of her boilers. The Jamestown and Teaser lost none that I hear of, and were not damaged. The Patrick Henry, with the exception mentioned, and some eight or nine balls which passed through the upper works, is as sound as before the action.

Greater skill or greater courage was never exhibited by any body of men than the officers, pilots, and crews of our fleet. They have rendered eminent service to their country, and are panting to render more. They will be marked men in our history, and to have fought in this battle should be a passport for all time to the affections of their countrymen, for, let it be remembered, that until the demonstration of the 8th of March, the Virginia was an experiment.

I ought not to close this communication without a passing tribute of admiration and gratitude to the gallant Capt. Sevill, of the United Artillery of Norfolk, and a detachment of thirty of his most expert gunners, who gloriously shared the perils of the contest and the honors of these memorable days.

A SPECTATOR.

The editor of the Norfolk *Day Book* sums up the results of the fight thus:

As we looked up towards Newport News we saw the spars of the Cumberland above the river she had so long insolently barred, but of her consort there was not even a timber head visible to tell her story. But this was not all the Virginia had done. The Minnesota lay there riddled like a seive. What damage she sustained will never be known, but it must have been frightful. And within eight and forty hours the Virginia had successfully encountered, defied and beaten a force equal to 2,890 men and 230 guns, as will be seen by the following table:

	Men	Guns
Congress, (burnt)	480	50
Cumberland, (sunk)	300	26
Minnesota, (riddled)	550	50
Roanoke, (scared off)	550	50
St. Lawrence, (peppered)	480	50
Gunboats, (2 or 3 disabled)	120	6
Forts, (silenced)	300	20
Ericsson	150	2
	2,890	230

Here, perhaps in this short table, is a better picture of what she did and what she dared than any word painter, though he were a Vernet, could ever give.

Richmond Dispatch.

TERMS OF ADVERTISING.

1 square, 1 day...$0.50 | 1 square, 2 days...$0.75 | 1...do....3 days...1.00 | 1...do....4 days...1.25 | 1...do....6 days...1.50 | 1...do....12 days...2.50 | 1...do....1 month...4.00

Larger advertisements in exact proportion.

Advertisements published till forbid will be charged 50 cts. per square of EIGHT LINES for the first insertion, and 25 cts. for each continuance.

FROM SAVANNAH.

[SPECIAL CORRESPONDENCE OF THE DISPATCH.]

SAVANNAH, GA., March 7, 1862.

I gave an account in my last letter of the draft ordered by the Governor, to supply deficiencies in the requisition made by the Confederate Government for twelve regiments. The draft was duly effected, and it has caused universal indignation, especially among the unfortunate subjects of military or rather militia rigor. It has not apparently been administered with the impartiality which should accompany so grave a retrenchment of the ordinary civil rights of a citizen, and this has given just complaint to many. Savannah is not the only city which can lay claim to the pre-eminent honor of having stood a draft, and this unenviable distinction has originated solely from the numbers who feel so wrapped up in self, or involved in the intricacies of trade, or wedded to luxurious ease, so to shirk the performance of the duty which their country demands of them. Not a few in Savannah have remained idle spectators of the struggle now going on, in which they have more involved even than those noble ones who have stepped forward to battle for their country's cause. The city and the county of Chatham has, nevertheless, done its duty nobly; she has now in the field a full proportion of her population, and those who remain are the weak in spirit and in courage, the infirm, the wealthy, and those who have been employed in work as necessary to the prosecution of the war as the stout arm that wields the sword. Since the draft these establishments have been so severely crippled in their resources that the proprietors have seriously contemplated the arrest of any work towards the completion of Government contracts. In one establishment where the engines for the new gunboats are being built, and all other available means towards the defence of the city are put in requisition, where the calls for ordnance stores are constantly being supplied, the labor of the whole concern has been stopped since Saturday last; out of one hundred hands not ten men remain to-day to carry on the almost essential business of the Government. The gunboats are in the same predicament, not from mechanics now being employed on a work which General Lee a week since characterized as a very important and necessary means of defence. From this state of affairs apparently no redress can be obtained, the Confederate General commanding has no authority in the matter and General Jackson equally is incompetent to discharge from the service those drafted.

Since the departure of General Lee, the command has devolved upon General Pemberton, of whose energy and officer-like qualities I have already informed you. His stay in Savannah has been well received by the citizens generally, and wherever he has been known he is accepted as a worthy successor of Gen. Lee. Before leaving, the General completed, with his staff, the reconnoissance of the lines of defence which extend from the Savannah river north of the city towards the Louisville road, thus finishing the circuit of earthworks extending from river to river. It is well worth the notice of the student of history and the intelligent observer of our progress since the revolution, to trace the outlines of the British defences, and compare them with the present wide extent of the city limits and the new works of defence about it. It is only from history that these works and lines of defence can be traced, the march of progress has obliterated long since, all that the gentle finger of time had left, and twenty years has past since the green mound, the last evidence of a military work, has been completely erased. The left of the British lines rested upon the river, a[illegible] situated on a commanding bluff, now occupied by the gas company and adjacent houses, rendered the approach from that side over a small creek and extensive marsh impossible; that hill is now closely occupied, and extends back into pine woods, now sheltering the camps of Gen. Capers's brigade, the creek has been nearly filled, the marsh drained and planted, and the river front occupied by cotton presses, from which the fleecy product goes to support the poor of Europe, and to warm the dweller by the pole. The line continued in a semi-circle and traversed the ground now adorned by the beautiful square, which the city of Savannah has tastefully ornamented with a memorial of the gallant, but unfortunate Pulaski, who fell contending for the liberties which we now fight for. The right rested again upon the Savannah river, on the brow of a hill which led to the banks of a creek, beyond which the swamp extended, hemmed with moss. The swamp is still there—the hand of the adventurous pioneer has not yet effaced all the evidences of the rank growth of primeval nature, but the creek has become a canal, and from its course the city is supplied with the best of water, and which partakes of the color of James river water, but which always preserves its own temper, and is seldom ruffled to fire by violence. [illegible] works is now at least one mile within those of the present defences, but it is not unreasonable to say, see that Savannah then occupied a smaller proportion of the enclosed area than it does at present; the little germ which Oglethorpe planted has matured into a queenly city, and has become the centre of [illegible] for the commercial world of the [illegible], and famed for the intelligence and the refinement of its citizens. The siege of Savannah, conducted on the part of the Americans by Gen. Lincoln and Count D'Estaing, was a proof of how much energy and skill might effect. The British force, inferior in number, with a naturally weak position, especially in the centre, history tells us, rendered the works almost impregnable by assault. By diligent and unremitting labor, and compelled the American forces to retire from the siege.

Such was the position in 1779. The situation is not materially different now. The Georgians then were without a navy, as we are to-day, and D'Estaing's fleet were then lying in St. Augustine Creek, at Thunderbolt, nearly in the same place as that which the Yankees ventured to approach but one time since. We have, then, every reason to hope a defence of the result of the present attempt of the foe to [illegible] of Georgia, and despite the apparent invulnerability of their gunboats, we believe that they will not alter the final result, and will be forced to retire now as they did before.

One of our steamers (the Leesburg) ran aground between Skidaway and the main land, some days since, and has since remained in that position. The accident occurred from the breaking of a rudder iron. To-day the "[illegible] gentlemen" reported its cap ture by the Yankees, but it turns out to be untrue. We trust she will not remain long in her present position.

Fernandina has been occupied by the Yankees, not a gun being fired before our forces abandoned the post, leaving twenty-six guns in their possession.

The acquisition is one of little value, as to the guns captured, the country in the vicinity being poor, sparsely populated, and almost destitute of means of living, save the cattle ranging the country at large. They hold the terminus of the railroad, but whether the rolling stock was left for the enemy, or not, I have not been able to learn. Why we retreated from that post when we abandoned attempts, as if with the [illegible] of being defeated, why it was not defended, is a mystery to me. I suppose the effort to command has some good, [illegible] or reason for its abandonment.

THE NEW YORK HERALD.

WHOLE NO. 9325 — NEW YORK, SUNDAY, MARCH 23, 1862. — PRICE THREE CENTS.

THE PEA RIDGE BATTLE.

Additional Particulars of this Important Action.

The Killed and Wounded on Our Side.

INTERESTING INCIDENTS OF THE FIELD.

One of the Arkansas Regiments Disbanded.

Horrible Treatment of the Wounded by the Indians Under Albert Pike,

&c., &c., &c.

Our Arkansas Correspondence.

PEA RIDGE, BENTON COUNTY, Ark., March 11, 1862.

We have at length an opportunity to foot up our loss in the recent battle at this point. It is not as large as many had anticipated, and, considering the duration and severity of the engagement, does no particular credit to the skill of the enemy. The casualties in the various divisions are as follows:—

FIRST DIVISION—COLONEL OSTERHAUS.

TWENTY-FIFTH ILLINOIS REGIMENT.

Killed ... 3
Wounded ... 17
Missing ... 3

FORTY-FOURTH ILLINOIS REGIMENT.

Killed ... 1
Wounded ... 1

TWELFTH MISSOURI REGIMENT.

Killed ... 3
Wounded ... 28
Missing ... 3

SEVENTEENTH MISSOURI REGIMENT.

Wounded ... 1
Missing ... 8

THIRTY-SIXTH ILLINOIS REGIMENT.

Killed ... 4
Wounded ... 38
Missing ... 31

The principal loss of the Thirty-sixth Illinois regiment was in the skirmish of the 6th, near Bentonville.

WELFLEY'S BATTERY.

Killed ... 1
Wounded ... 6

HOFFMAN'S BATTERY.

Wounded ... 1
Missing ... 4

SECOND DIVISION—GENERAL ASBOTH.

SECOND MISSOURI.

Captain Francz Kohr, killed.
Lieutenant A. Jacquemen, wounded.

Killed ... 6
Wounded ... 34
Missing ... 11

SECOND OHIO BATTERY.

Lieut W. D. Chapman, wounded.

Killed ... 1
Wounded ... 3

FIFTEENTH MISSOURI REGIMENT.

Missing ... 11

FIRST FLYING BATTERY (ELBERT'S).

Killed ... 8
Wounded ... 8
Missing ... 8

BENTON HUSSARS.

Lieut. Ernst Kessenwelter, wounded.

Killed ... 3
Wounded ... 10
Missing ... 3

FREMONT HUSSARS.

Killed ... 4
Wounded ... 8
Missing ... 3

Brigadier General Asboth was slightly wounded in the arm on the evening of the 7th.

THIRD DIVISION—COL. DAVIS.

TWENTY SECOND INDIANA REGIMENT.

Col. J. A. Hendricks, killed.
Lieut. Perry Watts, killed.

Killed ... 9
Wounded ... 42

EIGHTH INDIANA REGIMENT.

Killed ... 5
Wounded ... 29

KLAUS' INDIANA BATTERY.

Wounded ... 6
Missing ... 2

THIRTY-SEVENTH ILLINOIS REGIMENT.

Killed ... 19
Wounded ... 80

FIFTY-NINTH ILLINOIS (LATE NINTH MISSOURI) REGIMENT.

Killed ... 14
Wounded ... 40

DAVIDSON'S ILLINOIS BATTERY.

Killed ... 1
Wounded ... 5

FOURTH DIVISION—COLONEL CARR.

Colonel E. A. Carr, commanding division, received three wounds in the first day's action. His horse was struck three times by musket and rifle balls.

Colonel G. M. Dodge, commanding Second brigade, wounded in the hand in the action of the 7th.

This division, unassisted, stood the brunt of the fight on the 7th, on the north of the camp, where the principal attack was made. Its loss was very heavy in proportion to the number engaged.

NINTH IOWA REGIMENT.

Lieut. Col. F. J. Herron, wounded and captured.
Major William H. Coyle, wounded.
Adjutant William Scott, wounded
Lieutenant F. M. Kelsey, wounded.
Captain A. W. Dripps, killed.
Captain A. Bevins, killed.
Lieutenant Nathan Rice, killed.
Lieutenant A. G. M. Neff, killed.

HAYDEN'S DUBUQUE BATTERY, ATTACHED TO NINTH IOWA.

Lieutenant W. H. McClure, wounded.
Lieutenant M. C. Wright, wounded.

The regiment entered action with 610 men, and lost—

Killed ... 33
Wounded ... 190
Missing ... 4

PHELPS' MISSOURI REGIMENT.

Colonel John S. Phelps, wounded.
Captain John W. Lisenby, wounded.
Captain John Adams, wounded.
Captain George B. McElhannon, wounded.
Lieutenant Robert P. Matthews, wounded.
Lieutenant C. C. Moss, wounded.
Lieutenant John A. Lee, wounded.
Captain Gideon T. Potter, killed.
Sergeant Major W. J. Chester, killed.

Entered action with 276 men.

Killed ... 12
Wounded ... 71
Missing ... 10

THIRD ILLINOIS CAVALRY.

Captain Charles P. Dunbaugh, wounded.
Lieutenant Samuel F. Dolloff, wounded.
Sergeant Major Wooster, killed.

Killed ... 9
Wounded ... 33
Missing ... 2

THIRTY-FIFTH ILLINOIS.

Colonel G. A. Smith, wounded.
Captain Thomas H. Dobbs, wounded.
Lieutenant Joseph Moore, wounded.
Lieutenant Colonel Wm. P. Chandler, missing.
Lieutenant J. C. Lapham, missing.
Lieutenant Moses C. Snooks, missing.
Captain James F. [illegible]nd, missing.
Lieutenant Dudley H. Maybry, missing.
Lieutenant Collins Jones, missing.

Entered action with 402 men.

Killed ... 15
Wounded ... 47
Missing ... 55

FOURTH IOWA.

Lieutenant Colonel John Galligan, wounded.
Lieutenant J. A. Williamson, A. A. G., wounded.
Captain George Burton, wounded.
Captain E. Y. Burgan, wounded.
Lieutenant James R. Chrisamilton, wounded.
Lieutenant Lyman Parcher, wounded.
Lieutenant Robert S. Jackson, killed.

Entered action with 368 men.

Killed ... 18
Wounded ... 136
Missing ... 2

FIRST IOWA BATTERY—CAPTAIN JONES.

Captain J. A. Jones, wounded.
Lieutenant O. W. Gamble, wounded.

Killed ... 8
Wounded ... 11

The following were not brigaded:—

Bowen's Cavalry battalion—no loss.
Stevens' Howitzer battery—no loss.

FIRST MISSOURI CAVALRY.

Loss not yet ascertained. About four killed and six or eight wounded.

THIRD IOWA CAVALRY.

Lieutenant Colonel H. C. Trimble, wounded.

Entered action, men ... 225
Killed ... 37
Wounded ... 8

Eight of the dead of this regiment were scalped by the Indians of Albert Pike's command. Their names are:—

Carl Foster,	R. H. Millard,
Hichs Hoss,	James P. Mercer,
David Carroll,	Spencer Minar,
Caspar Frush,	Henry Browne.

OPERATIONS ON THE COAST OF FLORIDA.

Occupation of Jacksonville and St. Augustine by Commodore Dupont.

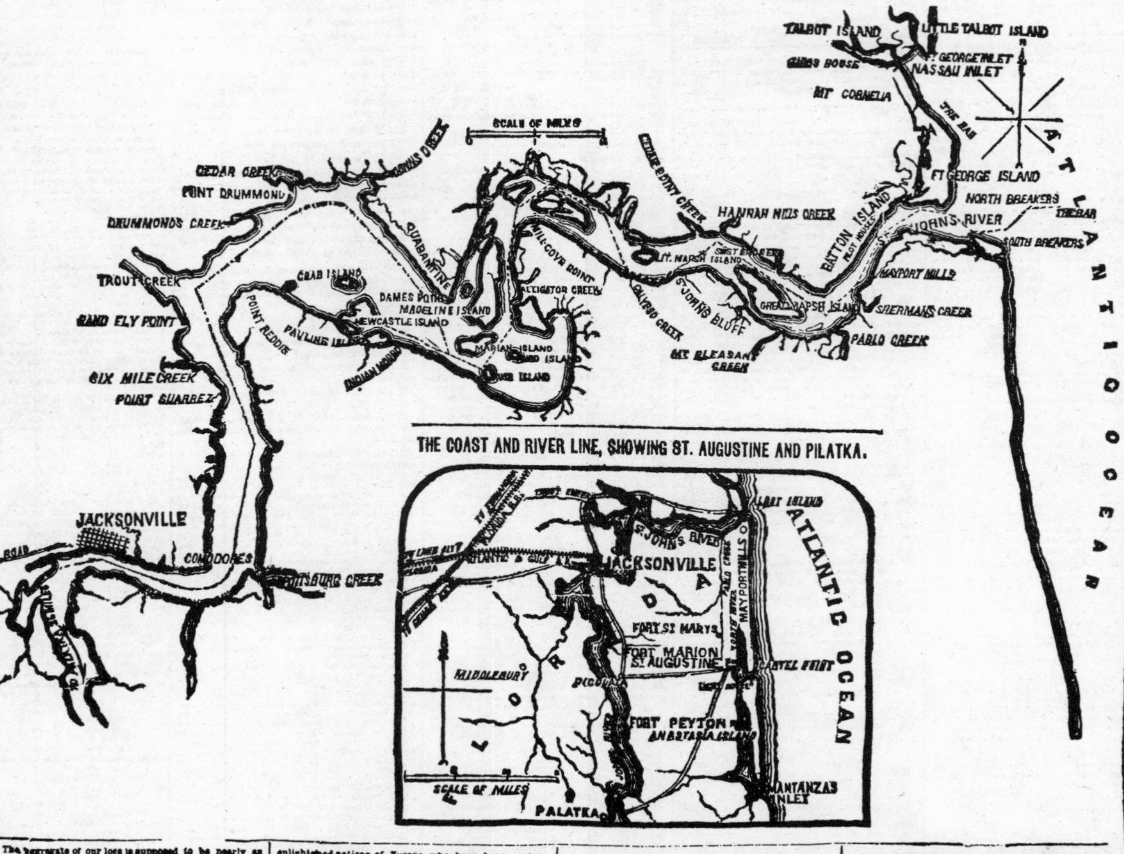

THE COAST AND RIVER LINE, SHOWING ST. AUGUSTINE AND PILATKA.

The aggregate of our loss is supposed to be nearly as follows:—

Killed ... 212
Wounded ... 926
Missing ... 174

Total ... 1,312

The casualties of the enemy are not yet known; but information received from the rebel army shows that it was from three to eight hundred greater than ours. The country for miles in all directions where the rebels retreated is full of their wounded, and the field after the engagement was covered with rebel dead double the number of the Union slain. Their loss in officers is considerable. All statements from prisoners, wounded, spies, &c., confirm the death of McIntosh and Colonel McCulloch, and most of them corroborate that of General McCulloch. General Slack and Colonel Clarkson are said to have fallen by Union missiles. Numerous colonels, captains and lieutenants are said to be among the officers that were. Some of the wounded officers now in our lines speak of their men as cowards of the worst description, and say that the loss of so many officers is owing to the cowardice of the men, necessitating the former constantly to expose themselves. The panic among the fleeing rebels was increased by the stories of Northern barbarity that have constantly been related by the officers to the rank and file. The roads were strewn with broken and disabled wagons, arms, provisions and various munitions of war. Several pieces of artillery were found a few days since with the woodwork of the carriages destroyed by fire and the guns carefully spiked. Two of them are bronze rifled twelve-pounders, of new and beautiful patterns. The whole will be remounted as speedily as possible.

Colonel F. A. Rector's regiment of Arkansas militia was disbanded by order of the commanding officer on the afternoon subsequent to the battle. Colonel Rector became disgusted and disheartened after the defeat, and, retreating about fourteen miles from the scene of action, ordered his men to stack their arms and disperse for their homes. Lieutenant Bradley, of Hayden's battery, yesterday went in search of these abandoned weapons, and, after a long and toilsome march, found them in a narrow ravine, stacked and without guard. Wagons sent out to-day to bring them in have just returned with upwards of 200 guns.

In the action of the 7th, a gun and a caisson belonging to the Iowa First battery became disabled, and were being abandoned by their gunners. Colonel Vandever ordered Captain Carpenter, of Company B, Ninth Iowa, to go forward with his company and remove them. Capt. Carpenter, under a heavy fire from the enemy's infantry, succeeded in the attempt, and safely removed both the gun and caisson. Reaching the rear, it was noticed that there were some burning gun wads among several loaded shell and case shot, with their cartridges, in one of the caisson chests, momently threatening an explosion. Captain Carpenter ordered the burning wads to be removed, and with his own hands aided in separating them from the deadly materials with which they were in close contact. By his promptness and coolness he saved all around from the consequences of a fearful explosion.

In nearly every instance where they fell into the hands of the enemy our dead and wounded were robbed of everything valuable about them. An artilleryman named Yost, in Hayden's battery, was wounded and left upon the field at the time the battery was withdrawn, on the afternoon of the 7th. Seeing the enemy approaching, he took out his wallet, and, removing fifty dollars in Treasury notes, and placing them in his mouth, he returned to his pocket the wallet containing a small amount in silver and two or three postage stamps. A few moments later his wallet was taken by the rebels, but his fifty dollars remained untouched and are still in his possession.

Lieut. Perry Watts, of the Twenty-second Indiana, was slain by a ten pound cannon shot that previously killed two men and then lodged in his breast. Col. Hendricks, of the same regiment, was instantly killed by a rifle ball in the breast at the time the advance was made upon the Indians posted in the thicket. Col. Hendricks was the only Union field officer killed in the battle.

The use of Indians by the rebels in the late battle has raised a cry of indignation among our men that will not soon be hushed. Seven of the Indians are now prisoners in our camp, and it was at first difficult to restrain our men from visiting summary punishment upon them. In addition to the eight of the Third Iowa cavalry that were scalped on the field, we have reports of several others scalped on other parts of the ground. It will be noticed that the report gives thirty-seven of that regiment killed, and only eight wounded. This disparity arises from the fact that *several who were left wounded on the ground were afterwards found pierced through and through with knives and bayonets and mutilated in the most horrid manner*. This statement I make, not upon hearsay, but from having been on the ground and seen with my own eyes what I have above written. What will the enlightened nations of Europe, who have been contemplating a recognition of the Confederacy, say to this mode of warfare?

By subsequent developments I find that the affair of the 7th, on our right of that day, though short, was particularly hot during the time it lasted. Colonel Julius White, of the Thirty-seventh Illinois, commanding the Second brigade of the Third division, claims to have opened fire on that morning and to have withstood the brunt of the fight. It is estimated that ten thousand of the enemy attacked us in that quarter, and that General McCulloch was killed in the encounter. The fact of his death is not yet fully established.

The enemy at last accounts was about forty miles from this point, in full flight for Van Buren or Fort Smith. There appears to be no probability of a battle before we move to attack the discomfited rebels.

Subjoined is General Price's report of his retreat from Springfield. His confidence of the future, as expressed in his last lines, appears to have been misplaced.

General Price's Official Report.

HEADQUARTERS, M. S. G., CAMP ON COVE CREEK, ARKANSAS, Feb. 25, 1862.

To His Excellency C. F. JACKSON, Governor of Missouri:—

SIR—I have the honor to lay before you an account of the circumstances surrounding my command within the last two weeks, compelling me to evacuate Springfield and retreat beyond the State line into the territory of Arkansas, the intelligence of which has no doubt reached you.

About the latter part of December I left my camp on Sac river, St. Clair county, fell back and took up my quarters at Springfield for the purpose of being within reach of supplies, protecting that portion of our State from both Home Guard depredations and federal invasion, as well as to secure a most valuable point for military movements. At Springfield I received from Grand Glaize considerable supplies of clothing, camp and garrison equipage, and, having built huts, our soldiers were as comfortable as circumstances would permit. I am pleased to say few complaints were either made or heard. Missouri having been admitted as an equal member of the Confederate States, and having my command much augmented by recruits, I was enabled to raise and equip about 4,000 men for the Confederate service. A brigade of these, consisting of two regiments of infantry, one regiment of cavalry and two light batteries of artillery, have been tendered the Confederate government.

About the latter part of January my scouts reported that the enemy were concentrating in force at Rolla, and shortly thereafter they occupied Lebanon. Believing that this movement could be for no other purpose than to attack me, and knowing that my command was inadequate for such successful resistance as the interests of my army and the cause demanded, I appealed to the commanders of the Confederate troops in Arkansas to come to my assistance. This, from correspondence, I was led confidently to expect, and, relying upon it, I held my position to the very last moment, and, as the sequel proved, almost too long, for on Wednesday, February 12, my pickets were driven in, and reported the enemy advancing upon me in force. No resource was now left me except retreat, without hazarding all with greatly unequal numbers upon the result of one engagement. This I deemed it unwise to do. I commenced retreating at once. I reached Cassville with loss unworthy of mention in any respect. Here the enemy in my rear commenced a series of attacks running through four days. Retreating and fighting all the way to the Cross Hollows in this State, I am rejoiced to say my command, under the most exhausting fatigue, all that time, with but little rest for either man or horse, and no sleep, sustained themselves, and came through, repulsing the enemy upon every occasion with great determination and gallantry. My loss does not exceed four to six killed, and some fifteen or eighteen wounded. That of the enemy we knew to be ten times as great.

Colonel Henry Little, commanding the First brigade, with Colonels B. A. Rives and J. Q. Burbridge, of the infantry, and Colonel E. Gates, of the cavalry, covered this retreat from beyond Cassville, and acted as the rear guard. The Colonel commanding deserves the highest praise for unceasing watchfulness, and the good management of his entire command. I heartily commend him to your attention. All these officers merit, and should receive, the thanks of both government and people. To all the officers and men of my army I am under obligations. No men or officers were ever more ready and prompt to meet and repel an enemy. Governor, we are confident of the future.

STERLING PRICE,
Major General Commanding M. S. G.

News from Port Royal.

The United States transport Star of the South, Captain Hobart, from Port Royal, March 18, arrived here yesterday morning. She has on board the crew of the prize schooner Alice, taken in the Gulf some time since. They are not prisoners. She reports all quiet at Port Royal, and the troops in the enjoyment of good health.

Safety of the Frigate Vermont.

BOSTON, March 22, 1862.

The steamer Saxon, from Philadelphia, in search of the frigate Vermont, put into Holmes' Hole to-day short of coal. She fell in with the Vermont on the 15th inst., in latitude 36 deg. 51 min., longitude 65 deg. 30 min., and left her on the 18th in latitude 37 deg. 50 min., longitude 68 deg. 45 min. She was in better condition than before reported. The rudder taken out by the Saxon was lost while attempting to hang it to the Vermont. The Saxon will return to tow her in.

Fire in Boston.

BOSTON, March 22, 1862.

The building on Devonshire street, occupied by the Union Print Works, used for sponging and finishing cloths, was nearly destroyed by fire at an early hour this morning, with most of its contents. The loss is estimated at $40,000.

THE FIGHT AT ISLAND NUMBER TEN.

The Bombardment Slowly Progressing—Reported Evacuation of the Island by the Rebels, &c.

CHICAGO, March 22, 1862.

A balloon was sent to the fleet of Commodore Foote yesterday, for the purpose of making a reconnoissance of the works of the enemy.

The despatch boat arrived this morning and represents that the condition of affairs at Island No. 10 is without change.

The mortars and gunboats indulge in occasional shots, but, so far, without further perceptible results.

A special despatch to the *Post*, of this city, says that only four shots were received from the rebel batteries at Island No. 10 yesterday, and that our fleet fired about thirty.

There are numerous reports that the rebels are evacuating the island and marching across the peninsula to Merriweather's landing. It is impossible to ascertain the truth of the reports, but existing circumstances favor them.

THE LATEST.

CAIRO, March 22, 1862.

The latest advices from Island No. 10, which are later than those brought by the despatch boat which arrived here at six o'clock this morning, state that the position of the Union gunboats and mortars has not changed.

Firing is kept up at intervals to prevent the enemy from strengthening or repairing their works.

THE NATIONAL FLAG FLOATING OVER NEW ORLEANS

WASHINGTON, March 22, 1862.

It is asserted as the generally prevalent opinion in naval and military circles that by this time the national banner floats over New Orleans, and it is believed that our mortar fleet attacked the rebel fort at the Rigolets within two days after the departure from Ship Island of the steamer bringing North the last intelligence from that point.

Personal Intelligence.

Major General Hunter, the newly appointed commandant at Port Royal, arrived in town yesterday, and is stopping at the Astor House. He will leave for the South during the early part of this week.

Major General Fremont arrived at his apartments in the Astor House by the late train from Washington last evening. He was announced to leave Washington on Friday, but failed to do so in consequence of his engagements with the Secretary of War. He visits the city just now to make some final arrangements in relation to his private affairs, and will leave here for his department in the course of three or four days. His staff has been completed, and though the names of the officers composing it have not publicly transpired, yet it is proper to say that it comprises several of those who were attached to his person while recently commanding in Missouri.

Colonel Percy and Major Danvill, of the British Army; S. Frothingham, Jr., and G. A. Gardner, of Boston; B. B. Smalley, of Vermont, and C. N. Emery, of Easton, Md., are stopping at the Brevoort House.

Rev. S. F. Vail, Warren Colburn and L. Rawson, of Ohio; D. B. Levy, of Caracas; J. J. Irwin, of Indiana and W. H. Jarvis, of Hartford, are stopping at the St. Nicholas Hotel.

Dr. Ten Broeck and J. Ocerson, of the United States Army; L. Fisher, of Boston; W. B. Chapin, of Rhode Island; S. J. Vail, of Hartford; E. L. Armstrong, of Illinois; C. D. Caldwell, of Dunkirk, and G. Gilman, of the Sandwich Islands, are stopping at the Metropolitan Hotel.

Lieut. Storrs of the Connecticut Volunteers; Major W. H. Cranston, of Newport, R. I.; J. S. Jay and Henry Doane, of Boston; S. S. Marshall and S. W. W. Sherwood, of New York, and Dr. L. W. Ogden, of San Francisco, are stopping at the Lafarge House.

Hon. J. C. Palfrey, of Boston; Captain Hunt, of the United States Engineers; W. S. Charnley, C. W. Bradley and H. B. Smith, of New Haven; G. R. Kelsey and J. Arnold, of Connecticut; J. A. Robinson, of New York; H. F. North, of New Britain, and D. Cope, of Lockport, are stopping at the Albemarle Hotel.

General H. Baxter, of Vermont; Baron Cadestrom, of Sweden, attache of General Fremont's staff; H. R. Stagg, of Buffalo; C. R. Sprague, of Baltimore; W. G. Weed, of Albany; G. and E. M. Winslow, of Boston; H. G. Stagg, of Buffalo; E. R. Sprague, of Baltimore; J. Butterfield and P. Cloagher, of Utica; G. Stetson and wife, of Bangor; F. W. Hemersley, of Philadelphia, and G. Mayo, of Maine, are stopping at the Astor House.

Major O. Holman, of the United States Army; Dr. E. G. Tucker, of Boston; ex-Governor Goodwin, of Maine; Judge Miller, of Rochester; Judge Aldis, of St. Albans; R. D. Hubbard and M. Jewell, of Hartford; S. A. Sawyer, of Oswego; A. G. D'Auby, of Ithica; W. A. Dana, of San Francisco; T. M. Hayes, of Maine; J. V. Buther, of Chicago, and John H. Wyman, of New York, are stopping at the Fifth Avenue Hotel.

THE TENNESSEE RIVER EXPEDITION.

Gen. Grant Reinstated in Command—His Arrival at Savannah—The Probable Force of the Enemy, &c., &c.

ST. LOUIS, March 23, 1862.

The Savannah, Tenn., correspondent of the St. Louis *Democrat*, under date of the 17th inst., says:—

No further move has yet been made. A second flood in the Tennessee river and its tributaries is prevailing.

Information in regard to the enemy is still quite meagre. His main force is supposed to be at Corinth, Miss., where it is probable he will be able to concentrate fifty thousand troops. Our force mostly remain on board transports.

Gen. Grant has been reinstalled in command of this expedition. He arrived here to-day.

It is not likely that operations will take place hereabouts for several days.

CHICAGO, March 22, 1862.

A special despatch from Cairo to the Chicago *Tribune*, says that the gunboat Lexington, from the Tennessee river, has arrived, and reports that our forces are concentrating into the country about Savannah, Tennessee, accomplishing nothing of importance besides the occasional capture of the scouts of the enemy, and bringing into our lines prominent rebels, charged with aiding the rebellion.

Our forces have entire possession of the Memphis and Charleston road, in the vicinity of Savannah, Tennessee.

The Ohio river is rapidly rising at this point (Cairo). In the last twenty-four hours it has risen a foot. The streets are covered to the depth of four feet in some places.

Steamers are continually arriving with troops from St. Louis and elsewhere.

A messenger just returned from Cape Girardeau reports that the rumored attack on that point by Jeff. Thompson is without foundation.

Skirmish Near Pittsburg Landing.

CAIRO, Ill., March 22, 1862.

A batallion of the Fourth Illinois regiment had a skirmish on Sunday last with a squadron of rebel cavalry, near Pittsburg landing, resulting in the defeat of the latter, with some loss. Four of the federals were wounded

THE CAPTURE OF YANCEY.

EASTON, Pa., March 22, 1862.

B. S. Kellogg, of Scranton, has received a letter from an officer of the Forty-ninth Pennsylvania regiment, dated Key West 10th instant, which says:—A prize arrived here last evening. She was captured in an attempt to run the blockade. Her sailors were taken to jail.

One of them, to whom attention was directed by the whiteness of his hands, was identified by several officers as the famous "Yancey." A newspaper correspondent also recognized him. He is confined in the calaboose here.

Our Harbor Defences and the Chamber of Commerce.

A meeting of the committee of the Chamber of Commerce who have on hand the subject of our harbor defences was held yesterday, at which were present quite a large number of the representatives of the capital and commerce of our city. The meeting was a strictly private one, no reporters being admitted, it being the desire of the Chamber that no proceedings of the committee should be published until more definite action is taken in the matter.

Action for Virginia Steamship Stock, Valued at Five Thousand Dollars.

SUPERIOR COURT—TRIAL TERM.

Before Hon. Judge Bosworth.

MARCH 19.—*Keay, Executor, vs. Vought.*—This was an action to recover stock of the New York and Virginia Steamship Company, valued at $5,000, and also a promissory note for $2,245, made by the deceased testator, which, it was alleged, was entrusted to the defendant by the deceased for the purpose of raising a loan upon it. The defendant asserted his right to detain it for an alleged debt. The case occupied two days, and the jury found a verdict for the plaintiff—value of stock $5,000, and the note to be given up to the plaintiff, value $2,245. Counsel for plaintiff, Messrs. Edwin James and Thomas Darphy. Counsel for the defendant, Messrs. McM[illegible] and Sherman. The Judge, on application, allowed $100 costs.

IMPORTANT FROM EUROPE.

The America at Halifax with Two Days Later News.

The Blockade in the English Parliament.

THE QUESTION SETTLED.

The Solicitor General Proclaims Its Efficiency.

SIGNAL FAILURE OF ITS ASSAILANTS.

RESIGNATION OF THE PRUSSIAN MINISTRY, &c., &c., &c.

HALIFAX, March 22, 1862.

The Cunard mail steamship America, from Liverpool on the 8th, via Queenstown on the 9th inst., arrived at this port at two o'clock this morning.

The advices by the America are two days later.

The Prussian Ministry has resigned.

The Sumter is still at Gibraltar, and the Tuscarora at Algesiras.

The steamer Annie Shields had arrived at Queenstown with a cargo of rosin, cotton and tobacco from Wilmington, N. C.

The steamship City of Baltimore, from New York on the 15th of February (reported by the Anglo-Saxon as missing), arrived off Holyhead on the 8th inst.

The steamship Edinburg, from New York 22d of February, arrived at Liverpool on the night of the 7th inst.

The steamship Jura, from Portland, arrived 22d of February at Liverpool on the night of the 7th inst.

The new Cunard steamship Scotia had arrived in Liverpool from the Clyde.

The ship Sarah Park was ashore near Southampton.

THE AMERICAN WAR QUESTION.

Debate on the Blockade in the British Parliament—The Cabinet Acknowledge the Measure as Effectual—The Rebel Statements of Mr. Mason Discredited, &c.

There had been an important debate on the question of the American blockade in the House of Commons.

Mr. Gregory denounced it, and expressed strong sympathy for the South.

Mr. W. E. Foster denied that the blockade was ineffectual, and stated that the list of upwards of three hundred vessels handed in by Mr. Mason as having broken the blockade, *had dwindled to nineteen*, and most of these escaped on dark and stormy nights.

Sir James Fergusson called on the government to interfere in the matter.

Mr. Milne could not believe in the final dissolution of the great American Union, and so long as it existed he deprecated any interference by England in the struggle.

The Solicitor General *strongly opposed any interference. The blockade had been as efficient as other blockades in former years.*

After further debate, Mr. Gregory's resolution for the correspondence on the subject was negatived without a division.

The Markets.

The sales of cotton in the Liverpool market on Saturday were 8,000 bales, the market closing buoyant.

Breadstuffs quiet.

Provisions quiet and dull.

Consols, 93¼ a 93⅜ for money.

Detention of the North American.

PORTLAND, Me., March 22, 1862.

The steamship North American will not sail from this port until to-morrow (Sunday) morning, the Canadian mails not having left until a late hour to-day.

Meeting of the Republican State Executive Committee.

ALBANY, March 22, 1862.

A meeting of the Executive Committee of the Republican State Committee was held at the Delavan House this morning, and the following resolutions were unanimously adopted:—

Resolved, That this Executive Committee have full confidence in the national administration, and in the patriotism, fidelity and ability of the republican President of the United States, and pledge to him their cordial and earnest support in carrying into effect the principles of public policy on which he was elected.

Resolved, That we hail with profound satisfaction the triumphs of our arms in the contest with rebellion, and believe the integrity of the Union will be restored, and the authority of the constitution re-established over all the States and Territories of the United States.

Resolved, That we hail with equal satisfaction the evidence that the political principles of the republican party have been firmly established in the conduct of the government, and are universally recognized as essential to its future administration; that slavery can hereafter never be extended into any Territory of the United States, nor can the political power which it wielded so long, and with such baneful effects over the national government, ever be restored.

Resolved, That the policy pursued by the Executive and other officers of this State in the management of the public finances and of the canals meets with the cordial approval of the republican party, accords with its principles and platform, and commends itself to the hearty approval of the people of this State. By this policy the surplus revenues have increased from $993,425 97, in 1858, to $2,695,842 16 in 1861. The requirements of the constitution have been more nearly complied with than at any period in the history of the State for many years. The canal debt has been reduced during the past three years nearly three millions of dollars. The canal enlargement has been nearly completed, and those great works have been rendered remunerative and prosperous.

Resolved, That the republican party recognise in the co-operation of the pure and patriotic men who have united with it in sharing the burdens and defending the principles of the administration of the national government, a disinterested love of country outweighing the trammels of party organization, and deserving the promised acknowledgement of our favored land.

Resolved, That deeming the action of the national administration wise and reliable, the Executive Committee earnestly request early action for the organization of the republican party for the protection of its principles, the efficiency of its labor, and its future success in maintaining the dearest principles that belong to an American citizen as well as lovers of freedom throughout the civilized nations of the world.

SIMEON DRAPER, Chairman.

JAMES TERWILLIGER, Secretary.
ALBANY, March 21, 1862.

NEWS FROM FORTRESS MONROE.

FORTRESS MONROE, March 21, 1862.

All is quiet here. There is no news.

A flag of truce was sent out this morning for the accommodation of an officer of the French navy desiring to go South. The rebel officers and crew were very uncommunicative, and we gathered no news from them.

No Southern newspapers were received.

Among the passengers who arrived here this morning from Baltimore were Prince de Joinville and Miss Dix.

Hopes are entertained that the telegraph cable will be repaired either to-day or to-morrow.

Letter Received by the Father of Lieutenant Frank Tryon, of the Fifty-first Regiment N. Y. State Volunteers, Who was Wounded at Newbern, N. C.

The following note from Captain Chase, of the New York Fifty-first regiment, was received here yesterday, written upon brown wrapping paper, bearing the manufacturer's stamp of a Goldsboro paper maker.

MARCH 15, 1862.

E. W. TRYON, Esq.:—

DEAR SIR—Yesterday we engaged the rebels at or near Newbern, N. C., and put them to flight, capturing many prisoners and arms.

But your son, who I am proud to say is my Lieutenant, while valiantly leading his men on to victory, was struck by a rifle ball in the thigh. Still I think it is not of a serious nature. All that can be done shall be done for him. He is quite easy and cheerful, and I hope ere long will be able to help to do what such men as your son alone can do, i. e., to restore our country to peace and tranquillity.

I miss him very much, and it pains me to be obliged to tell of such noble souls falling from the service they so much adorn. Yours, truly, STEPHEN W. CHASE,

Captain Co. B, Fifty-first New York Volunteers.

Southern Confederacy.

THE PUBLIC GOOD BEFORE PRIVATE ADVANTAGE.

BY ADAIR & SMITH. ATLANTA, GEORGIA, CONFEDERATE STATES OF AMERICA, APRIL 2, 1862. VOL. II—NO. 7.

WEDNESDAY, MARCH 26, 1862.

To His Excellency Joseph E. Brown, Governor of Georgia.

We hope you will not deem it impertinent in us to make a few suggestions in relation to our public defenses. It is a matter of the deepest moment to every citizen of Georgia.

In a very short time the services of the soldiers, whom you have called out and sent to the coast for State defense, will expire. So far they have had no opportunity to strike a blow at the invader, or in any wise repel his vandal tread, further than their presence at the right point has kept back his advance or held him in check.

The Legislature has appropriated a large amount of money to be used by you in defense of the State of Georgia; and as it appears to us that the large body of troops called out by you has been a partial failure—for which, however, we attach no blame to your Excellency—would it not be well to change our tactics and modes of defense? The recent engagement in Hampton Roads will doubtless materially change the programme of the invasion from our seaports. Already the Lincoln Congress has passed an appropriation for the construction of a number of iron-clad gunboats like the *Virginia*. With them they will easily pass all our fortifications and ascend our rivers. May we not devise some plan to meet and repel them? Would it not be well for you to bring your resources and energy to bear in the construction of invulnerable iron-clad gunboats to be placed in our rivers—the Savannah, Atlamaha, Chattahoochee, &c.—all that can be ascended by the enemy?

Give our coast army an honorable chance, in whatever way seems to you most fit, to enlist for the war in the Confederate service, that they may go when and where their valor is most needed—retaining only a sufficient number to man these invincible boats when placed in our rivers.

We make these suggestions with all due respect, and from the very best motives. It seems to us the cause will be better served in this way than by spending double the amount of the appropriations by the State in any other. Of course, of the practicability of our plan you will be the better judge; but if it be practicable in any way, let us have the rams in our rivers.

With great respect, we are, &c.,

THE EDITORS.

Glorying in their Shame and Perfidy.

The Fortress Monroe correspondent of the New York "Tribune" of the 12th, gives the following laudatory account of the atrocious violation by the enemy of their own flag of surrender at Newport News:

"* * * As the Merrimac approached she opened fire, which the Congress returned, but soon raised the signal to surrender. The Yorktown and Jamestown sent officers aboard *to receive the surrender and arrange for the transfer of the prisoners.* When some 25 of the crew of the Congress had been taken to the rebel boats, Capt. Howard, of the 4th Artillery, brought the guns of his light battery to bear on them, and fairly beat them off and compelled them to draw off and *give up the transfer of the prisoners.* One of his shells entered the steam chest of the Yorktown.—Therefore, all but the twenty-five, or so, that had been previously taken, the crew and officers of the Congress not killed, made their escape. Great praise is accorded on all hands to Capt. Howard, as well as to the Fire Zouaves and others, who lay down in the sand and picked off the rebels with small arms."

Such villainy was never before heard of. All the savage atrocities of cruel and relentless heathens are unequal to this. Many a tale of horror which chills the blood at its recital, is perpetuated in the history of the early wars with Indian savages in this country. That, however, we can readily account for, because they were savage and brutal in their nature and practice—having no pretensions to civilization or christianity, and no just conception of the obligations of humanity. But when people who make claim to being the most liberal and best educated on earth, and say they are most civilized and enlightened upon the face of the globe, will act with base perfidiousness to which a savage never made pretensions, and then proclaim it thro' the press to an astonished world with a self-complacency and self-approbation that is only tolerable at the conclusion of the most noble and worthy achievments, we may well stand back appalled at the low down depths of of meanness and rascality, which they have exhibited. Well may we thank God that we are cut loose from them—no matter what the cost may be; and pray that the last one of us may sink down in death rather than submit to a national affiliation with them again upon any terms whatever that mortals could suggest.

Iron-Clad Gunboats.

The Yankees, as we have heretofore predicted, have been taught a lesson by the exploits of the *Virginia*, and are making preparations to assail us with impregnable iron-clad vessels at all points. Unless we go energetically to work and are ready for them, with boats and ships superior in number and armament to theirs, and have them placed in every harbor, river and inlet on our coast, we will be outdone in this new naval engine of destruction which we have adopted. The naval Committee of the federal Senate introduced a bill on the 14th instant, with the following provisions:

"The bill introduced by Senator Hale, from the Committee on Naval Affairs, to-day, provides for the construction, under the direction of the Secretary of the Navy, of an iron-clad steam vessel, of not less than five or six thousand tons burthen, and of great speed and strength, to be used only as a ram, for which purpose $1,000,000 be appropriated; also, $13,000,000 for the construction of iron-clad gunboats, $783,000 for the completion of Stevens' battery, and $500,000 for extending the facilities of the Washington Navy Yard, so as to roll and forge plates for the armored ships.

The completion of the Stevens' battery, which has hung fire so long, is provided for in the bill."

Capt. Morgan.

The Knoxville *Register*, in alluding to Capt. Morgan's late exploit, says he "captured 40 prisoners, including 10 officers, besides one Yankee telegraph operator, the United States mail, and $60,000 in gold."

Battle of Pea Ridge.

St. Louis, March 11.—The following is the official report of General Curtis to General Halleck:

Headquarters Army of the South west,
Pea Ridge, Ark., March 9

General:—On Thursday the 6th inst., the enemy commenced an attack on my right wing, assailing and following the rear guard of a detachment under General Sigel to my main lines on Sugar Creek Hollow, but ceased firing when he met my reinforcements, about 4 p. m.

During the night I became convinced that he had moved on so as to attack my right or rear. Therefore, early on the 7th, I ordered a change of front to the right—my right, which then became my left, still resting on Sugar Creek Hollow.

This brought my line across Pea Ridge, with my new right resting on Head Cross Timber Hollow, which is the head of Big Sugar Creek. I also ordered an immediate advance of the cavalry and light artillery, under Colonel Osterhaus, with orders to attack and break what I supposed would be the reinforced line of the enemy. This movement was in progress when the enemy, at 11 a. m., commenced an attack on my right. The fight continued mainly at these points during the day, the enemy having gained the point held by the command of Col. Carr, at Cross Timber Hollow, but was entirely repulsed with the fall of the Commander, McCulloch, in the centre, by the forces under Col. Davis. The plan of attack on the centre was gallantly carried forward by Col. Osterhaus, who was immediately sustained and supported by Col. Davis' entire division, supported also by General Sigel's command, which had remained till near the close of the day on the left. Col. Carr's division held the right, under a galling, continuous fire, all day. In the evening, firing having entirely ceased in the centre, and the right being now on the left, I reinforced the right by a portion of the Second Division, under Gen. Asboth. Before the day closed, I was convinced that the enemy had concentrated his main force on the right, I commenced another change of front, forward, so as to face the enemy where he had deployed on my right flank in a strong position. The change had only been partially effected, but was in full progress, when, at sunrise on the 8th, my right and centre renewed the firing, which was immediately answered by the enemy with renewed energy along the whole extent of his line. My left, under Sigel, moved close to the hills occupied by the enemy, driving him from the heights, and advancing steadily towards the head of the Hollows. I immediately ordered the centre and right wing forward, the right turning the left of the enemy, and cross firing on his centre. This final position of the enemy was in the arc of a circle.

A charge of infantry extending throughout the whole line, completely routed the rebel force, which retired in great confusion, but rather safely through the deep, impassable defiles of Cross Timber. Our loss is heavy. The enemy's can never be ascertained, for their dead are scattered over a large field. Their wounded, too, may many of them be lost and perish. The force is scattered in all directions, but I think his main force has returned to Boston Mountains.

Gen. Sigel follows him toward Keittville, while my cavalry is pursuing him toward the mountains, scouring the country, bringing in prisoners and trying to find the rebel Major General Van Dorn, who had command of the entire force at this, the battle of Pea Ridge.

I have not as yet statements of the dead and wounded, so as to justify a report, but I will refer you to a dispatch which I will forward very soon.

Officers and soldiers have displayed such unusual gallantry that I hardly dare to make distinction. I must, however, name the commanders of divisions. Gen. Sigel gallantly commanded the right, and drove back the left wing of the enemy; Gen. Asboth, who is wounded in the arm, in his gallant effort to reinforce the right; Colonel and Acting Brig. Gen. Davis, who commanded the centre, where McCulloch fell on the 7th, and pressed forward the centre on the 8th; Colonel and Acting Brig. Gen. Carr, is also wounded in the arm, and was under the continuous fire of the enemy during the two hardest days of the struggle.

Illinois, Indiana, Iowa, Ohio, and Missouri proudly share the honor of victory, which their gallant heroes won over the combined forces of Van Dorn, Price and McCulloch at Pea Ridge, in the mountains of Arkansas.

I have the honor to be, General,
Your obedient servant,
SAMUEL CURTIS,
Brigadier General.

Perfidy of the North—Message from the President in Secret Session of Congress.

We learn that yesterday a message from the President was sent into Congress, in secret session, recommending that all our prisoners who had been put on parole by the Yankee Government be released from the obligation of their parole, so as to bear arms in the struggle for independence.

The recommendation was urged as a retaliation for the infamous and reckless breach of good faith on the part of the Northern Government with regard to the exchange of prisoners, and was accompanied by the exposure of this perfidy in a lengthy correspondence conducted by the War Department. We have been enabled to extract the points of this interesting correspondence.

It appears from this correspondence that, at the time permission was asked by the Northern Government for Messrs. Fish and Ames to visit their prisoners within the jurisdiction of the South, our government, while denying this permission, sought to improve the opportunity by concerting a settled plan for the exchange of prisoners. For the execution of this purpose Messrs. Conrad and Seddon were deputed by our government as commissioners to meet those of the Northern Government under a flag of truce at Norfolk.

Subsequently a letter from Gen. Wool was addressed to Gen. Huger, informing him that he, Gen. Wool, had *full authority* to settle any terms for the exchange of prisoners, and asking an interview on the subject. Gen. Howell Cobb was then appointed by the government to mediate with Gen. Wool, and to settle a permanent plan for the exchange of prisoners during the war. The adjustment was considered to have been satisfactorily made.

It was agreed that the prisoners of war in the hands of each government should be exchanged, man for man, the officers being assimilated as to rank, &c.; that our privateersmen should be exchanged on the footing of prisoners of war; that any surplus remaining on either side, after these exchanges, should be released, and that hereafter, during the whole continuance of the war, prisoners taken on either side should be paroled.

In carrying out this agreement, our government has released some three hundred prisoners above those exchanged by the North, the balance in the competing numbers of prisoners in the hands of the two governments being so much in our favor. At the time, however, of sending North the hostages we had retained for our privateersmen, General Cobb had reason to suspect the good faith of the Northern Government, and telegraphed in time to intercept the release of a portion of these hostages (among them Colonel Corcoran) who were *en route* from points further South than Richmond to go North under flag of truce at Norfolk. A number of these hostages, however, had already been discharged.

It now appears that, in contravention of the solemn agreement of the Northern Government, not one of our privateersmen have been released, and the Fort Donelson prisoners, instead of being paroled, have been taken into the interior, where they are still confined.

As a judgment upon this open and shameless perfidy of the North, it is proposed that our prisoners, who have been paroled by the Yankees, shall be released from their obligations. There is little doubt of the honor of such a proposition as there is of its justness and meetness as a retaliatory measure for an act of fragrant perfidy.—*Richmond Examiner, 21st inst.*

Doings in Yankeedom.

SLAVERY IN THE DISTRICT OF COLUMBIA.

WASHINGTON, March 11th.—The Committees on the District of Columbia of the two Houses have agreed upon a bill for the abolition of slavery in the District, which is substantially the same as that reported by Mr. Morrill, of Maine. The House Committee will report at the earliest opportunity, and Mr. Morrill will, to morrow (12th) amend it as agreed. The House Committee has been equally divided until this morning, when Mr. Fessenden, of Maine, appointed in place of Mr. Upton, of Virginia, after he was unseated turned the scale.

Visit of the Congressional Investigating Committee to Bull Run.

The Committee on the Conduct of the War have been to Bull Run and Manassas to investigate the cause of our defeat there last July. They gained some valuable information, and will clear up the mystery of this and all other doubtful things connected with the war in due time.

The United States frigate St. Lawrence, from Fortress Monroe, with a portion of the officers and crews of United States sloop of-War, Cumberland and United States frigate Congress, arrived off the Navy Yard at Philadelphia, yesterday afternoon March 14, where she is to repair damage sustained in the late battle from the rebel iron-clad steamer Merrimac.

Massachusetts Legislature.

BOSTON, March 14, 1862.—An order was unanimously adopted in the House to-day, authorizing the construction of one or two iron-clad steamers, on the plan of Ericsson's Monitor, for the protection of the harbor of Massachusetts.

General Fremont's Command.

General Fremont is expected to arrive here to day. Already a new German regiment is partially raised in New-York, it is said, to accompany him to East Tennessee and Georgia.

Enterprise of Speculators.

A number of itinerant speculators went to Fairfax Court House yesterday and took possession of the vacant stores to commence business. The Provost Marshal, however, ejected them promptly.

Burning Dwellings.

Yesterday evening a number of dwellings in the neighborhood of Centreville were wantonly burned by some of our soldiers.

Congress is determined to bring the war to a speedy close.

That Vile Trio in Nashville.

The Nashville "Times" of the 14th instant, contains the following:

Governor Andrew Johnson, Horace Maynard and Emerson Etheridge, arrived in the city on Wednesday night, from Washington, and are stopping at the St. Cloud.

Brig. Gen Johnson was serenaded last night by the military band, and in response he addressed them for about an hour. He stated that he returned to Tennessee for the purpose of restoring the Constitution and the laws as they formerly existed; that this was a war brought about by disappointed seekers after power. He argued that there could be no government unless the laws were enforced; that the time had come for treason to be crushed and for traitors to be punished. He called upon the Union men of Davidson Co. to come forth and fight for the Federal government, and predicted that it would not be long before they would buckle on their armor to assist the Unionists of East Tennessee.

Emerson Etheridge next addressed the band. He said nothing particular except that the meanest "secessionists" were the John Bell Whig secessionists, and that there were a great many silly ladies in Nashville.

Horace Maynard next spoke, but we did not hear him.

A general order issued by the Federal commander contains the following section:

"9. A board of officers to consist of Colonel Hambright, 79th Pennsylvania volunteers, Lieut. Col. Jones, 1st Wisconsin volunteers, and Capt. McNally, 78th Pennsylvania volunteers, will meet at Nashville, at 12 M., on the 14th instant, to examine into the rights of ownership in case of all stores and property in dispute in this city, between citizens on the one hand and officers and agents of the government on the other.

The "Times" also has the following:

OUR COTTON LANDS TO BE TAKEN.—In the Federal Senate on the 7th, the bill to provide for the occupation and cultivation of the cotton lands, (of "rebels" we presume,) was passed by the following vote:

Yeas—Anthony, Chandler, Clark, Collamer, Dixon, Fessenden, Foote, Foster, Grimes, Hale, Harlan, Howard, Howe, King, Love, Morrell, Pomeroy, Sherman, Simmons, Sumner, Ten Eyck Trumbull, Wade, Wiley, Wilmott, Wilson, of Mass—26.

Nays—Browning, Carlile, Cowan, Davis, Henderson, Kennedy, McDougall, Pearce, Powell, Rice, Saulsbury, Thompson, Wilson, of Missouri, Wright—14.

"Owing to circumstances" we have not seen this bill, or an abstract of its provisions, but from a brief report of some remarks of Mr. Carlile, of Virginia, previous to its passage, its character may be inferred. He said "he did not believe that the government held supreme control of all the lands in the country;" that "in place of the present masters and slaves," the bill "makes the government one great, lordly slaveholder, with a great brood of petty agents," and that "the provisions of the bill made humane treatment of the slaves impossible." Mr. Pearce of Maryland, declared that the bill was impracticable, and a most extraordinary political blunder," and that "the money that it would cost the government to provide for these indigent persons, would make the treasury more indigent than themselves even."

Tennessee Legislature.

This body, which recently assembled at Memphis, after having been driven out from Nashville by the Federals, closed up its business and adjourned on the 20th instant.

BY TELEGRAPH.

NORFOLK, March 24th.—Twenty transports and steamers entered the roads last evening—all except one painted white. They are crowded with troops, and apparently, came across the bay from the direction of the Eastern shore—supposed to reinforce Burnside or attack Magruder.

Between 90 and 100 steamers and sailing vessels were in the Roads yesterday. (Glorious time for the *Virginia*, if she was only in good plight.—Eds. Confederacy.)

RICHMOND, March 24.—*Congress.*—The House has passed a resolution, declaring that all army officers, whether holding State or Confederate commissions, ineligible to seats as Congressmen; and that all such, who are elected to Congress, must either resign their commissions or their seats in Congress.

The Yankees are landing wagons, baggage trains, &c., at Newbern, and decisive battles are expected at Kinston, (Lenoir county, N. C., between Newbern and Goldsboro',) and Suffolk, Va., in a few days.

The Yankees are said to be going back from near Strasburg, to Winchester, and General Jackson pursuing them.

Twenty-five Yankee steamers with troops on board, are in Hampton Roads, approaching from the Maryland side of the bay; and 100 sailing vessels and steamers are reported in the Roads, supposed to reinforce Burnside or attack Magruder.

NORFOLK, March 24.—Northern papers of the 22d, state, that Yancey had certainly been captured off Key West by the *Water Witch*; but a dispatch from Nashville announces his arrival at New Orleans.

It is rumored that the rebels at Island No. 10, had been seriously damaged by the fire from the mortars.

The tax bill in the Yankee Congress still drags its slow length along. Whisky insurrections kept the House occupied all day. It is supposed the bill will be finally crowded through the House in three weeks.

Fremont leaves for his new department, (Western Va. and Eastern Ky. and Tenn.,) to day.

The steamer *Roanoke* is to be iron clad.

Nothing official from the West. Senator Wade's friends are confident of his re-election from Ohio.

Information has been received of large quantities of cotton being taken through Texas into Mexico, and thence to Europe.

A dispatch to Chicago says Jeff. Thompson is marching on Cape Girardeau, pressing men and horses into the rebel service. He has had a skirmish—several were killed and wounded on both sides.

Fort Calhoun is to be changed to the name of Fort Wool.

General Wool has established a censorship over the press in his department.

A large number of troops landed at Fortress Monroe and Camp Hamilton yesterday, and to-day there is great activity at Old Point.

Yankee advices from Newbern state that 400 Confederates were killed, and 1,500 federals; and that the Yankees raised the white flag twice during the battle, and had ceased firing when the Confederates fell back. The Confederates were prevented from seeing the flag by the smoke. They say the Confederates had 13,000 in the field; that it was a hard fight; that the Yankees suffered severely, losing many of their best officers; that 500 Confederates were taken prisoners, and 50 pieces of cannon and a large quantity of arms and ammunition captured.

The Yankee troops at Newbern have good quarters. The rebels fired the town and railroad bridge. About 100 of the white population remains (old people.) Three stores are open.

There are no tidings of the frigate Vermont.

The Baltimore papers have positively asserted that Capt. Buchanan died on Sunday last.

The mortar boats cannonaded Island No. 10 all last Wednesday, doing much damage. The rebels are supposed to be evacuating the Island—though it is doubtful. A vigorous fire was returned from their batteries.

Position and Movements of the Enemy in Kentucky and Tennessee.

Some four or five regiments of Yankee troops are encamped in the vicinity of Louisville.

One regiment is stationed at Elizabethtown, another at Munfordsville and another at Bowling Green. Three regiments are marching between Bacon Creek and Bowling Green.

Only two or three regiments are stationed in the immediate vicinity of Nashville. The main body of Gen. Buell's army, some thirty or thirty five thousand, are marching southward, principally by the Franklin pike. Some six or eight thousand of them, were proceeding on the Murfreesboro' pike.

It was stated at Nashville that twenty thousand men were expected there, in transports to reinforce the army in East Tennessee.

Yankee Prisoners Taken.

It is reported that an entire regiment of Indiana troops, the advance of the Federal army, was taken prisoners on Tuesday last, about 30 miles from Nashville, on the Franklin pike, by a command made up of Texas Rangers, Col. Forrest's Cavalry and Colonel Scott's Cavalry, who surprised and surrounded them. We do not vouch for the truth of the report, but it was current and generally believed in Nashville on Wednesday last.

Left.

The Knoxville *Register* of the 22d instant says the Federals have left Jacksboro' quite hastily. They carried off 1,000 pairs of shoes and 800 pounds saltpetre—private property. The Register says that but for the presence of Gen. Kirby Smith and his prompt preparations to meet the vandals, it would have been any thing but a "bag," as the telegraph from Richmond a few days ago specified.

THURSDAY, MARCH 27, 1862.

From the Richmond Enquirer, March 8.

The Pretended Exposures by the Charleston Mercury and Richmond Whig.

The Richmond *Whig*, of the 6th inst., has attempted to sustain its assault of the day before on the President's administration, by the reproduction of an article from the Charleston *Mercury*, which professes to give "information from a good source" as to what "the President has done or failed to do" in relation to certain matters connected with the public defence.

We propose to show, from information which we have received from more reliable sources than any to which the *Mercury* has access, that all the allegations and their various specifications made by the *Mercury* are destitute of foundation in truth.

We do this not merely in order to refute the charges contained in this article, but also to show the public how utterly unreliable are the sources of the *Mercury's* information. To do this effectually, we propose to republish the various allegations, *seriatim*, in the *Mercury's* own language:

I. "The Provisional Congress, at its last session passed a bill granting bounties to the setting up and establishing of manufactures of arms, saltpetre and gunpowder. A certain advance of money was to be made to the manufacturer of these articles, when he had advanced a certain stage in putting up the factories, which was to be returned in the articles manufactured. The President vetoed the bill, and it failed."

The bill here referred to was so loosely drawn, and so completely put the Government in the power of speculators, that when the President gave his reasons for not approving it, the body which had passed it sustained the President's veto by an almost unanimous vote, and to this hour no injury or inconvenience has resulted from its rejection.

II. "The Harper's Ferry machinery, for the manufacture of arms, was turned over by Virginia to the Confederate States when Virginia seceded from the Union. It was sent, to be put into operation, to Fayetteville, North Carolina; a few months ago, and not a gun had yet been furnished to the army. It had not yet got into operation."

This charge is utterly untrue from beginning to end, as a simple statement of facts will show. The Harper's Ferry machinery consisted of two parts—that for the manufacture of muskets, and that for the manufacture of rifles. The musketry machinery was, after much negotiation, turned over to the Confederate States, in the month of July, in the boxes in which it was conveyed from Harper's Ferry to this city; was, as promptly as possible, set up and put in operation, and has been for several months furnishing as many muskets per month as the number of workmen which could be procured could make. The rifle machinery, to which the *Mercury* specially refers, has never been turned over to the Confederate States. It was lent to the State of North Carolina by Virginia, to be put up at Fayetteville, in the former State, and was transported thither in June last, every aid being given to the agent of North Carolina by the Confederate Government. When it was being put up in the Confederate States Arsenal at Fayetteville, it was found that the portion for making locks was missing, and immediate steps were taken to supply the defect by manufacturing the necessary machinery here. In the meantime locks were made here and sent to Fayetteville to be attached to the rifles, a number of which have been made monthly for several months.

III. "Three manufactories of arms were in Tennessee. Their proprietors sought to make contracts for the manufacture of arms with the Confederate Government. Not being able to succeed, one or more of them came to Richmond during the sitting of the late Congress, to interest the members of Congress from Tennessee in their behalf. The War Office declined to make contracts for the purchase of arms manufactured by these factories, on the ground that it had no money. On inquiry being made into the cause why there was no money, it turned out that the Treasury Department could not have Treasury notes signed fast enough. Five and ten dollar Treasury notes were at a premium of three and four per cent. at New Orleans, for currency. The contractors and creditors, of course, demanded these notes, instead of fifty or one hundred dollar notes, and the Treasury was most laboriously trying to meet their demands, altho' bound by no contract to do so. Hence the Government could not meet its engagements, or contract to buy these arms. The Treasury was twelve millions in arrears to the War Department."

To this count of the *Mercury's* indictment, we reply by the following narrative of the circumstances to which it has reference:

A field officer of a regiment of Tennessee volunteers, which had just been raised, accompanied by a Member of Congress from that State, applied to the Secretary of War for arms for his men. On being informed that the War Department could not then grant his request, he asked the Secretary why the ordnance officer in Tennessee did not contract with the three manufactories, referred to above, to furnish arms, alleging that they were ready to do so at $25 per piece. The Secretary replied that he authorized him to make a contract with them immediately, and to ensure speedy delivery, further authorized the payment of $30 per piece. These facts were stated by the above mentioned Member of the Provisional Congress, at a meeting of the Finance Committee. This gentleman's statement was subsequently distorted just as the *Mercury* has misconstrued it, and he reiterated his statement on the floor of the House, showing that the War Department had done everything in its power to secure the purchase of every arm that could be furnished. The other allegations of the *Mercury*, in relation to Treasury notes, &c., fall with the charge which they are designed to sustain.

IV. "When the *first* Congress of the Confederate States met at Montgomery, it was clear to every one that war was not an improbable event. Prudence required preparation. By the Constitution, Congress could make no appropriation of money but at the call of the Executive. It was urged on the Government to call for several millions of money, and to send it to Europe immediately to buy arms and munitions of war. The Government would call for only money enough to purchase some fifteen thousand small arms; and when the second Congress assembled, and war was declared, no agent had yet gone to Europe to purchase even these arms."

When the first Congress met in Montgomery there was much diversity of opinion as to the probability of war. Many believed that there would be a peaceable solution of our troubles, and that there would be no war with the United States. Among that number no one was more emphatic in the expression of his opinion than Mr. Rhett, of South Carolina upon whose authority these charges are now evidently made. The President, however, was not so sanguine of a peaceful solution of our difficulties, and immediately proceeded to take the necessary measures to prepare the country for war, and so far from the charges contained in the above paragraph being true, at the meeting of the second session of the Congress, 29th April, 1861, the Government had a *second* agent on his way to Europe charged with the purchase of arms and munitions of war, the first agent employed for that purpose having, after considerable delay, declined the service. Fortunately for the country and its defence, the President did not concur in the views and convictions of Mr. Rhett as to the improbability of war. A disclosure at this time of what the President has done in reference to the procuring of arms and war material, from the commencement of the Government to the present day, would show the utter falsity of the *Mercury's* charges; but every intelligent man will perceive that such a disclosure cannot be made without serious detriment to the public interest.

V. "Private enterprise has imported a considerable quantity of arms and munitions of war; but what has the Confederate Government done? The only effort, that we are aware of, to get arms *from Europe* is that of the Gladiator, which is now in Nassau. The arms lately brought by the Victoria in New Orleans are said to be a part of her cargo.—Even after war was certain, there was ample time to have imported a large quantity of arms, *before* the blockade was established, and since the blockade was established, the successful efforts of private citizens show that the Government might have imported large quantities of arms and munitions of war."

It would be highly improper to reveal what vessels have arrived, where they arrived, where from, what amount of arms they had brought, and what vessels are expected to arrive with a like freight. We shall not therefore make any such revelation, though we can assure our readers that it would conclusively dispel the belief which the *Mercury* desires to create by accusations which are evidently made with the assumed impunity derived from a knowledge that the Government ought not to contradict them by a specific exposition of the facts. It may be said, however, that the amount of arms imported by private enterprise does not amount to a fourth of that imported by the Government. The arms brought by the Victoria (about 150) were not a part of the Gladiator's cargo. So much for the *Mercury's* speculation and its facts.

VI. "So necessary was it for us to have an abundance of arms, that several of our naval officers proposed to the Naval Committee to put under their control one million of dollars, and that they would go to Europe with it—buy an iron-clad steamship, convert her into a war vessel, fill her with arms and munitions of war, and, if necessary, fight their way across the Atlantic into a Confederate port—Congress favored the gallant proposal, and passed the bill to carry it into effect. The President pocketed it, and it failed."

Upon inquiry, addressed to both the Executive and Legislative Departments of the Provisional Government, we cannot find any one who has any recollection of the proposition referred to; but if any such was made and failed to be acted on, it is attributable to the fact that every possible effort in this direction had already been made, the details of which, for reasons already given, it is improper to state. We can further add, that the President has never vetoed or "pocketed" any bill appropriating money for the public defence.

VII. "We will mention one other fact, amongst many others, going to show the military energy of the President. A new swift steamer lay at Wilmington, North Carolina. One half of it belonged to Northern citizens. Certain citizens of Wilmington desired to convert this steamer into a privateer; and, in order that good titles might be got for this purpose, they petitioned Congress to have the steamer sold, and the half of the proceeds of the sale belonging to the Yankees should be paid into the Confederate Treasury. Congress promptly passed a bill to accomplish this object. But the President pocketed it, and the bill failed."

At the close of a session of Congress a bill of the nature referred to was passed. As it undertook to decide questions of property which legitimately belonged to the courts of law, the bill was returned, and the President's reasons for so doing orally explained to Congress by the Attorney General. It was further discovered that the steamer to which allusion is made, was wholly unfit for the purposes for which it was proposed to be used.

We have thus met and refuted every charge and allegation made by the Mercury, by a plain and simple statement of facts which will so discredit any further assaults by that paper, as to render future notice of them wholly unnecessary.

We do not propose to discuss the motives which induced this attack. It will be for Mr. Rhett to justify before his own conscience and before the country, his violation of the injunction of secrecy which the Congress had placed upon its proceedings, and which he knows that body refused to remove for good and patriotic reasons.

No disappointed ambition, no private griefs can warrant any citizen in making an attack on the government, which, even if true, could only weaken the great cause for which the patriots of the South are struggling, and give "aid and comfort" to the enemy.

The Cost of the War to the North.

The North is beginning to feel the immense cost of this war, and her resources are becoming exhausted under its burden. The Milwaukie (Wis.) News, in calculating the expenses of the war, says:

The expenses of the government, according to the New York Tribune, are over $3,000,00 per day. This is at the rate of fifteen cents per day for every man, woman and child in the Northern States. At this rate, the war costs Wisconsin over $116,000 every day, and nearly $10,000 every hour, and over $150 every minute between sunrise and sunset.—The whole expense for one year would build a comfortable house for every family in the Northern States. It would pay the ordinary expenses of all the State Governments for twenty years. It would buy nearly one half of all the farms in the Northern States. It would take all the wheat produced in Wisconsin for three years to pay its proportion for twelve months. Such is the cost of war.

The Philadelphia Ledger, in its money article, says: For want of government revenues, and an adequate tax law, government credit is daily more and more at a discount. For the future, if the war ended to-morrow, we shall do well if we get on with an expenditure of two hundred millions annually. A large standing army will be required, the cost of which for each man, rank and file, is one thousand dollars per year. It is estimated in financial circles that on the 1st of July next we shall have an annual interest account of forty millions of dollars!

The Ericsson.

A correspondent of the N. Y. Tribune, writing from Fortress Monroe, gives the following account of the impression made on the Monitor by the Virginia:

I visited the Monitor to-day. Two shots of the enemy struck her on the edge, above the surface, and tore up a few inches of the deck plating, and penetrating about half the diameter of the ball, affording a complete illustration of her impregnability. As the worst the enemy, with the most powerful guns afloat could do, the fact, settles all question on that point. The shots referred to are as mere scratches on a pugilist after his antagonist has done his best for four hours to knock him down. On her tower, where the Merrimac's shots struck square and with full force, there are three or four indentions not exceeding three inches in depth. Her deck is blazed in several places where shots struck her and glanced off. The wheel-house has several similar indentations, though not as deep.—These are all the marks the Monitor bears as the results of the action.

EXTRAORDINARY GUN.—The immense 500 pounder Armstrong gun manufactured at the factory of Sir W. Armstrong, at Elswick, near Newcastle-on-Tyne, has been forwarded to the Woolwich Arsenal, to be subjected to a series of experiments at Shoeburyness, in the presence of the Ordnance select committee. This extraordinary weapon is constructed on the muzzle loading principle; it weighs 12 tons 8 cwt.; and should the experimental trials prove satisfactory, Sir W. Armstrong will have the merit of producing the most powerful agent of modern warfare.

BY TELEGRAPH.

MOBILE, March 25.—A dispatch from Bay St. Louis states that the *Oregon* and the *Pamlico* fought the *New London* for three hours and sunk her; and that a steamer is now coming to the aid of the *New London*.

SECOND DISPATCH.

A special dispatch to the N. O. *Picayune* from Memphis, says the enemy is moving cautiously towards Decatur, Ala. A column is moving Southward from Columbia, and another across Tennessee from the direction of Corinth. It is believed their purpose is to unite the two main columns at some point on the Memphis & Charleston Railroad near Decatur.

A special to the Mobile *Advertiser & Register* from Memphis, says the bombardment of Island No. 10 continues desperately day and night, the main attack is directed against Rucker's battery. The Confederates work knee deep in water, displaying great valor.—The loss on our side is slight. Two of the enemy's gunboats are certainly sunk.

The enemy is moving down on the west side of the river, through the swamps and back water, in "dug-outs." They have four saw-mills at work making lumber to build boats.

Island No. 10 is amply provisioned for a siege, and the Confederates are in good spirits.

MEMPHIS, March 25—Information from Island No. 10 was received last night that there was heavy cannonading on Sunday last. Two of the enemy's gunboats were destroyed. One sunk below Hickman, and the other in sight of the Island. The soldiers on the Island are in good spirits, and declare they can hold out against the world.

The enemy's land forces at New Madrid are estimated at 40,000. Sixty of them came down in small boats through the swamps to Gayoso, and captured seven citizens—formerly of Gen. Jeff. Thompson's army.

Yesterday the Confederate scouts at Corinth captured 100 artillery horses belonging to the Yankees. They were compelled to leave their guns, as the enemy was close at hand.

Bombardment of Island No. 10.

The Memphis "Appeal" of the 21st says:

"On Monday, (the 17th instant) the enemy brought down eight gunboats and six mortar boats, and commenced the fire again from a nearer point, say within two miles. Three of the gunboats were lashed together, and made a desperate attack upon Capt. Rucker's battery—the upper one on the shore line. The bombardment was terrific throughout the day, and considerable injury was sustained by [illegible] battery, which was, however, fully repaired during the night. Lieut. Clark, of this battery, a gallant soldier, was the only person killed on our side at any time during the four days' bombardment.

'One of the enemy's gunboats was disabled Monday afternoon, and had to be towed back by the tugs. She was not sunk as reported. Other boats were struck, but the extent of the damage done them could not be ascertained."

Removed.

The Raleigh "Register" of the 22d inst., announces that Gen. Gatlin, who was in command of all the Confederate forces in North Carolina, has been removed, since the Newbern affair. We sincerely hope this is true. If President Davis entrusted the management of military affairs in that State to him; and if he is to blame for the disaster at Newbern, he should be not only removed, but deprived of all command whatever.

We chronicle these evidences of the administration holding men to whom important trusts are confided, to a rigid accountability, with unfeigned gratification.

The Abolition Programme out in Motion.

Lately we published Lincoln's special message to Congress, proposing an abolition scheme as a means of prosecuting the war to a successful crushing of the South. The *House* of that body has responded to the recommendation by passing the following:

Resolved, That the United States ought to co-operate with any State which may adopt a plan for the gradual abolishment of slavery, giving to such State pecuniary aid to be used by such State in its discretion to compensate for the inconveniences, public and private produced by such change of system.

The resolution was adopted—yeas 88, nays 31.

Commodore Tatnall gone to take Command of the Virginia.

Commodore Tatnall received orders Saturday last to repair forthwith to Norfolk and take command of the battering ram Virginia. The whole country will be rejoiced to hear of it, and look with confidence to the future operations of the wonderful machine. We regret to lose his services at this post, but for his and the country's sake, we are pleased to see him in a position where he can be available to the latter, and sustain his well earned fame as a naval commander.

Commodore Tatnall leaves here this morning for the theatre of his future labors. He was accompanied by Capt. J. Pembroke Jones, late commander of the Resolute, who will act as his flag Lieutenant, and his son Paulding Tatnall, as Secretary.—*Savannah Republican, March 24th.*

DEATH OF WM. H. PRITCHARD, ESQ.—The Telegraph brings us the sad announcement of the death of Mr. Wm. H. Pritchard. He died at Richmond after a few days illness, on Monday night last at 12 o'clock. Mr. Pritchard was for several years connected with the editorial department of this journal, and was well and favorably known as the news agent of the Southern press. A good man has fallen.—*Constitutionalist, 25th inst.*

FROM POUND GAP.—We learn, from good authority, that on Sunday last, Major Thompson, who has command of the five companies from Scott and Lee, who volunteered for the protection of the Gap, had a brisk brush with 2,500 of the enemy, which lasted several hours. After driving the enemy back, Major Thompson learned that the enemy were attempting to flank him at a gap a few miles below the Pound. He immediately removed the most of his force to that point, where a fierce battle ensued, and the enemy repulsed. Our loss was none killed and wounded. The enemy's loss in killed, was supposed to be heavy. The Federals fell back to Pikeville, and Major Thompson to Gladesville.—*Abingdon Virginian.*

The New-York Times.

VOL. XI—NO. 3290. NEW-YORK, WEDNESDAY, APRIL 9, 1862. PRICE TWO CENTS

THE SEAT OF WAR IN THE SOUTHERN, EASTERN, AND MOUNTAIN PARTS OF VIRGINIA.

Indicating the positions now held by the Rebels, and some of the positions held by the Union Army; and showing, also, the Railroad Lines of Retreat for the Rebels.

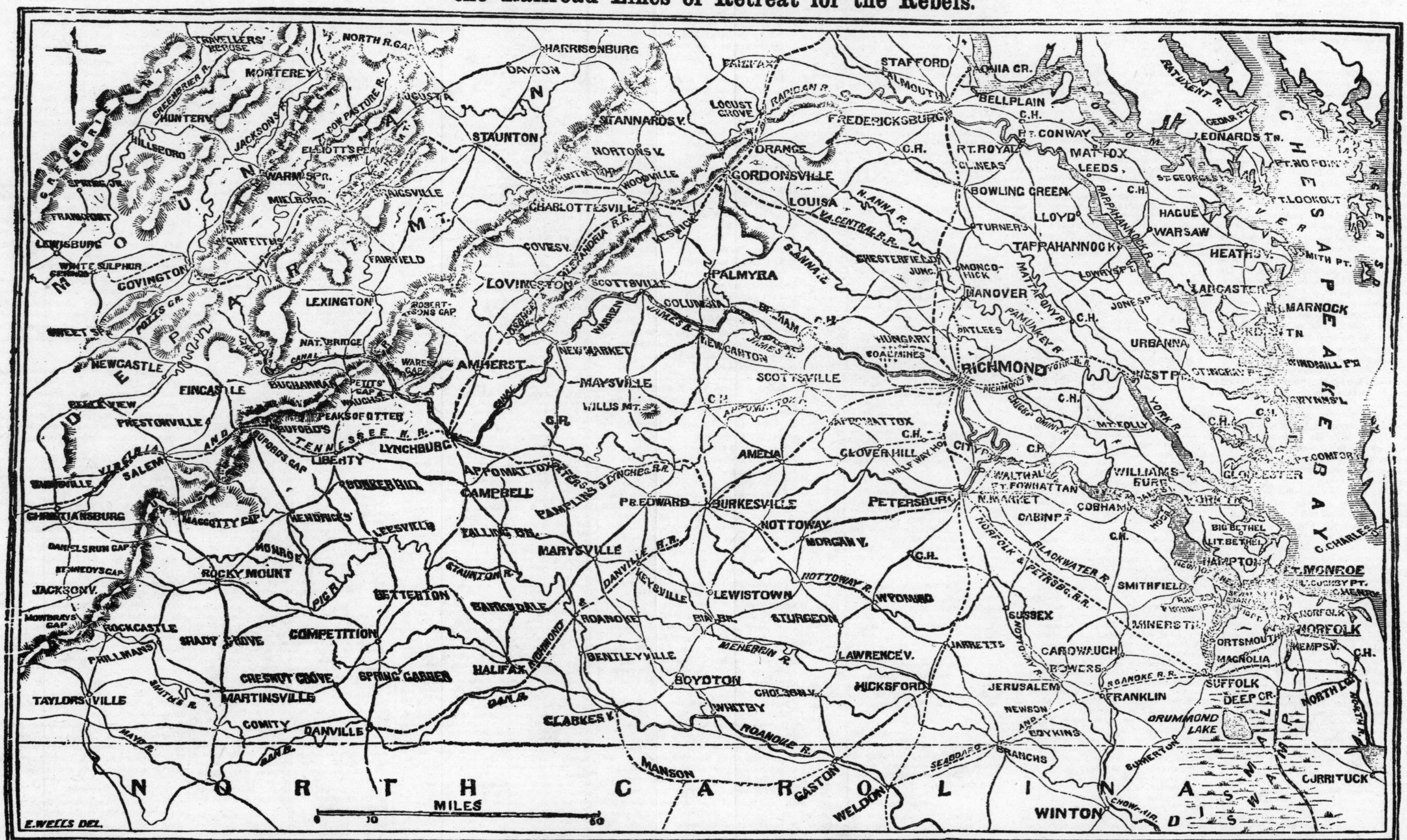

OUR ARMY CORRESPONDENCE.

GEN. PORTER'S DIVISION.

Departure from Alexandria—The Voyage down the Potomac—Arrival at Fortress Monroe—One Night Amid the Ruins of Hampton—Encampment Near New County Bridge—A Reconnoissance at Big Bethel.

From Our Special Correspondent.

NEAR NEW COUNTY BRIDGE, Va., Friday, March 28, 1862.

On the 21st of March, the Division under command of Gen. PORTER left its temporary quarters at Cloud's Mills, Va., and proceeded to Alexandria, where it embarked on a fleet of thirty-six steam and sailing vessels, and at 11 o'clock the following morning, commenced moving down the Potomac. The embarkation was conducted with the utmost order and precision, and without accident of any kind. A fall of rain the night previous made the roads somewhat yielding, but did not tend to dampen the ardor of the troops, who expressed their willingness to march a greater distance, along roads in worse condition, so delighted were they at the prospect of soon being brought face to face with the enemy.

The flight of the rockets from the *Daniel Webster*, Gen. PORTER's flagship, was the signal for the fleet to get under weigh, and shortly after the vessels with crowded decks and streaming pennants, amid the hearty shouts of the troops, glided slowly from their anchorage and piers on their way southward. The *Daniel Webster*, having on board the Fourth Michigan Regiment, took the lead, closely followed by the *Elm City*, *State of Maine* and *Knickerbocker*, bearing respective Gens. MARTINDALE, MORELL and BUTTERFIELD, with their Staffs. The other vessels of the fleet came in regular order. Your correspondent secured a passage on the flagship, thereby having facilities for becoming acquainted with any important event which might happen on board any of the vessels. Nothing of moment, however, occurred. Some uneasiness was caused on the afternoon of the 21st by a report to the effect that the *Knickerbocker* had sprung aleak, and the pilot deemed it unsafe to enter the Bay that night; but an investigation proved that the leak was not of a serious character.

A signal corps attached to the expedition rendered valuable service by their system of rapidly communicating from one vessel to another.

The soldiers, occupying every part of the boat, enjoyed themselves amazingly, and frequently engaged each other's attention by pointing out places and objects of interest on the banks of the river. Our point of destination was unknown to but few, consequently much speculation was had in reference to it, which continued to be indulged until the fleet had fairly arrived under the protecting guns of Fortress Monroe. At about 9 o'clock in the evening, it being considered imprudent to advance in the darkness, without the guide of lighthouses, the vessels came to anchor within ten miles of the mouth of the river, where they remained till 4 o'clock the next morning. They then proceeded on their course and arrived in good order at Fortress Monroe at about 4 o'clock in the afternoon. Some of the regiments disembarked that night and were marched to Hampton, which is three miles west of the fortress, where they were joined on the following day by the remaining troops of the division. HAMILTON's Division, which had sailed from Alexandria a few days in advance of PORTER's, was already encamped at Hampton. In referring to Hampton, it would be more proper to say the ruins of that place, for scarcely any thing remains of that once favorite rural district but lonely chimnies, heaps of mortar and brick, scathed trees, and despoiled gardens. The flaming torches of seven hundred rebel fiends, in a single night last Summer, was the cause, as is familiarly known, of this wholesale and wicked desolation. They did not even hesitate to wreak their insatiate vengeance on the sacred memories of the dead, as the defaced, dislocated, and shattered tombstones, plainly testify. Lest any desecration should be caused on the part of our troops, to the graveyard surrounding the ruins of a church, which was built over two centuries ago, a guard was stationed over it night and day. This precaution, however, was unnecessary, for not a Union soldier had the inclination to even speak but softly as he moved with cautious tread over that ancient and hallowed ground.

Gen. PORTER's Division left Hampton on Tuesday, the 25th, and proceeded up the peninsula to within about a mile and a half of New-County Bridge, and about two and a half miles from Hampton. At 3 o'clock on Thursday morning an order was issued to the Second and Third Brigades to prepare for a

RECONNOISSANCE AT BIG BETHEL.

At a few minutes past 7 the Third Brigade, Gen. BUTTERFIELD, accompanied by GRIFFIN's Battery, formed in line and led the way to Big Bethel, taking the direct road thither, and after proceeding some distance, met, unexpectedly, Gen. MORELL's Brigade, who intended to go by a different route. The two Brigades met upon the same ground where, on the 10th of June last, the unfortunate collision occurred between two Union regiments, but on this occasion every precaution had been taken to prevent a similar disaster. Here the brigades parted, the Second taking the road leading to the right, and the Third pushing forward as originally planned, preceded by a line of skirmishers, composed of a portion of Col. BERDAN's Sharpshooters, who were followed by Company H, Seventeenth Regiment, Capt. GROWER, supported by a line of skirmishers from the same regiment. Then came the other companies of that regiment, GRIFFIN's Battery, the Forty-fourth, Eighty third, Twelfth and STOCKTON's Michigan Regiments. The Brigade moved in the order indicated, and when arrived within a mile of Big Bethel, encountered an obstruction, consisting of a number of large trees felled across the road, which were soon thrown aside by the pioneers. Everything was then got in readiness for an attack in case the enemy should be found in position at the works of Big Bethel. A careful disposition was made of the force, and if the enemy had showed fight at that place he would bitterly have repented his rashness. A few rebels who were stationed behind the works fled precipitately at the approach of our skirmishers, and shortly after the American flag was planted thereon by Lieut. S. HOWLAND ROBBINS, one of Gen. BUTTERFIELD's aids. Gen. BUTTERFIELD, at the head of three regiments, then took a road leading to the left, and proceeded a distance of three miles, for the purpose of reconnoitering the country, and driving out the enemy, should he show himself at other works which were visible beyond. Upon arriving at these works, they were ascertained to be about a quarter of a mile beyond Heath's Corners, and to the right in front of a house owned by Mr. CARROL PRESSEY. At Heath's Corners five mounted rebel pickets were discovered, who sped away with the greatest possible dispatch. They were pursued by our skirmishers until the latter had come up to the works.

It was ascertained that these earthworks extended from Big Bethel to James River—a distance of ten miles—and were evidently designed to prevent a flank movement by our troops. This extensive range was the only formidable feature they presented. All the works were abandoned. In the rear of the works, at Heath's Corners, lives a man named CALLONY, who reported that a company of the Second Louisiana Regiment, Capt. CURTIS, had been there the preceding morning, also that the Tenth Louisiana Regiment was there about a fortnight ago, and staid one day. He further stated that the nearest works from that point were three miles distant, at WALL's farm, and were strongly built. On the right of the road leading to Heath's Corners, and across a morass, was another work, near the house of widow HEATH, which was unapproachable on account of the deep mire. On the return of the force they were followed by the rebels to Heath's Corners, near to the position where they were first seen.

The Second Brigade, under command of Gen. MORELL, with MARTIN's Massachusetts Battery and the Eighth Pennsylvania Cavalry, arrived at Big Bethel, and pursued a road leading to Rosetown, a distance of two miles. No earthworks or fortifications were observed on the route. They learned, however, from an inhabitant that two companies of rebel cavalry had left Rosetown fifteen minutes before their arrival. In one house an Irishman was discovered secreted under a bed. He had blackened his face, hoping by this means to pass himself off as a negro, but the imposture was detected, and the Irishman taken to headquarters.

A party of skirmishers advanced two miles beyond Rosetown to Smithville. A strong fortification was observed here, behind which were about 700 rebels. Our troops did not attack the fort, their purpose being only to reconnoitre. When turning a sharp corner three rebel cavalry officers were seen by the signal corps, who immediately gave chase. One of the rebels was shot, and his sword and belt were picked up.

The result of the reconnoissance was eminently satisfactory, and the whole force returned the same evening, in good order, to their quarters behind New-County Bridge.

WHIT.

GEN. SUMNER'S CORPS D'ARMEE.

The Advance Upon Manassas—Camp Life—A Letter from the Chaplain of the New-York Sixty-sixth.

HEADQUARTERS SIXTY-SIXTH REGIMENT, N. Y. S. V., (Col. PINCKNEY,) SANGSTER'S STATION, Va., Tuesday, March 11, 1862. Nine miles from Manassas.

I write on the ground by a camp-fire, under the strangest and most romantic circumstances. Nothing could surpass the grandeur of this extempore encampment, and words will fail, I am afraid, to give you much idea of it as it strikes the senses of those who are in the midst of it. Our exhilaration at leaving the dull monotony of the tented camp, where we have endured all manner of dull, wintry hardship, within sight of the Capital, and at last making the advance, of course adds zest to our feelings; and yet here is something truly grand. After two days' severe march, through deep woods, we at last emerged upon a wide expanse of open, hilly country, and Gen. SUMNER's Division now rests from its toils, full of the highest enthusiasm, in spite of the disappointment of having the enemy escape the anaconda, and give us yet a chase, perhaps to the Gulf.

Some twelve thousand troops are here resting on their arms for the night. A part rests on an immense open hill, a part in heavy woods on the left, on a steep hill, with woods intervening, while others occupy a hill in front.

I have just strolled through the whole command. Gen. SUMNER bivouacks on the right, on a little rise of land, and from this point the whole may be taken in at a glance.

Thousands of camp-fires glowing in every direction, showing a most variegated scene,—horses picketed by thousands,—artillery drawn up in grim array.

On the left of Gen. FRENCH's Brigade, the Sixty-sixth Regiment of New-York occupy the most prominent position. Bivouacking in a heavy piece of woods on a steep hill-side, their fires by hundreds light up the whole with wondrous splendor, the flames rising high among the lofty trees, and the smoke lit up with lurid light above, casting the forest in relief, as though the trees were interspersed with auroral columns. Here you may recall all that you ever read of romance in wild wood life, and multiply its multitudes and extent, and you can imagine something of what is not to us imagination or fiction, but *reality*.

The men are scattered around in booths, or under shelter-tents, made of India-rubber blankets, or by hundreds rolled up in blankets on the bare ground, like so many mummies. Others are discussing chickens, (rebels',) or even larger animals, making merry over their campaign cooking—so rich, compared with the ordinary camp rations. They have bid adieu to their tents with the utmost alacrity. Meanwhile the bands lend their inspiring strains, answering one another from hill to valley, and echoing through the woods with peculiar sweetness. Over the whole, serene, the same as from the beginning of creation, shine unclouded stars and moon.

The headquarters of the chiefs are, of course, object of peculiar interest. The veteran hero of Mexico, and Kansas, and Utah—a splendid man—Gen. SUMNER, now commanding a *corps d'armée* with as much composure as though it were a regiment, surrounded by a brilliant staff, and surveying the whole scene, with couriers coming and going; and not far away, the model of a Brigadier-General, pacing back and forth, with hands behind him, before his fire, every now and then stopping to receive a messenger or dictate an order—the heroic FRENCH—every inch a man of war, who defied Gen. TWIGGS in Texas, and brought off the only battery in the State, defying the rebels to take a gun, through a wild march of five hundred miles, from beneath his flag.

Or you may visit Col. PINCKNEY, of our Sixty-sixth, seated on a log before his booth, like a chieftain of the olden time, receiving his Captains and regulating the wild enthusiasm of his command.

I have tried to give you a picture most difficult to draw. But think of the money that it has cost to get up this little entertainment, the intelligence, science and experience here concentrated, and you may fill the details for yourself, drawing very deeply on imagination before you can come near what is real.

To-morrow we move on Manassas, but not through fire and blood, as we thought this morning. The anaconda, winding through so many woodland roads, with slow but determined advance from the Potomac toward the rebel strongholds, have frightened the foe, and he has slipped away from his hole, and we must have a long chase yet. * * * *

My desk has been the ground and the light precarious, so you must excuse all mistakes.

JAMES H. DWIGHT.

GEN. KEYES' CORPS D'ARMEE.

Sketch of the Commander—His Military Services.

HEADQUARTERS GEN. KEYES' CORPS D'ARMEE, WASHINGTON, Friday, March 21, 1862.

The Press, echoing the impulses of the great popular heart, developes the military spirit as fast as the people can follow it. At the outset of the rebellion we had a correspondent to each regiment; soon they became so numerous that a "Press Brigade" was formed, and now we make another leap and divide our brigades and divisions into *corps d'armées*. Your correspondent having been assigned to the above command, finds that he will have to describe, amplify and glorify the valorous deeds of some 400 Captains, 800 Lieutenants, some 40 Colonels, Adjutants, Majors, and Chaplains, and any quantity of Sergeants, Corporals and privates, making a grand total of over 40,000 men, selected from the volunteers of New-York, Pennsylvania, Maine, Massachusetts, Rhode Island, Vermont and Wisconsin—a tremendous responsibility for one pen, which, however, having shed considerable ink before, buckles to the good fight again, with a determination to lay before the public the truth.

Gen. ERASMUS D. KEYES, the commandant of the fourth *corps d'armée*, was born in Massachusetts. He was appointed a cadet at West Point in 1828, from Maine, graduating sixth in his class; in 1832 he was ordered to report to the Third Artillery as Brevet Second Lieutenant. Under Col. CUMMINGS, of the Second Infantry, he took an active part in the Black Hawk war. During the first whisperings of secession in South Carolina, in 1832, he was stationed at Charleston. Gen. SCOTT appreciating his services at that time, invited him to become one of his military family, and on his staff he remained nine years, being with him during the Patriot difficulties in Canada, the removal of the Cherokees, etc. In 1841 he was made Captain of the Third Artillery, and served in Florida. While passing through New-Orleans with a number of Seminoles, an insurrection broke out among the blacks, which was quelled by his promptness. In 1842 he was appointed head of the Department of Artillery and Cavalry at West Point; remained there four years, devoting himself to the study of military tactics. In February, 1849, he was ordered to the Pacific coast, and was stationed there eleven years. During this time he greatly distinguished himself in the Indian campaigns by his intrepidity, nerve and self-possession. Not forgetting the claims of civil life, he was assiduous in improving the tone of society, was a leading man in all matters appertaining to the improvement of San Francisco, and personally superintended the Harbor Improvements. In 1858, as a tribute to his daring courage in the Indian wars on the Pacific coast, as well as his civil services, he was made Major of the First Artillery, and in 1859 returned to New-York. Gen. SCOTT again recalled him to his Staff, making him Military Secretary, with the rank of Lieutenant-Colonel. Stationed at Washington during the stormy Winter of '60–'61, while YULEE and his traitor band were plotting treason in their Senatorial seats, Col. KEYES carefully watched the pulse of the tide which was so rapidly drifting the country into war, and, had his repeated warnings been heeded, measures would have been taken which might have rendered impossible the consummation of the designs of the arch conspirators.

In April, 1861, Col. KEYES received an order from the President to accompany Capt. MEIGS and Col. BROWN to New-York, and there superintend the expedition for the relief of Fort Pickens. When Washington was in such imminent danger, during the week subsequent to the bombardment of Fort Sumter, Col. KEYES took charge of the 5,000 volunteers that flocked to the National Capital.

At Bull Run Col. KEYES served under Gen. TYLER. After the rout commenced, instead of falling back on Washington, he retired to Fall's Church, where he remained two days, and saved and sent to Washington over two hundred wagon-loads of stores, ordnance, &c., which otherwise would have fallen into the hands of the enemy. He also recovered all the tents which were deserted by the panic-stricken soldiery. For this Col. KEYES received the thanks of the entire country, and the President was not slow in placing him at the pinnacle of his profession. After commanding a brigade for three months, under Gen. McDOWELL, he was ordered to the command of a division to relieve Gen. D. C. BUELL, and within a few days has been assigned to the Fourth Corps d'Armée. Can the country doubt that such a man will fail to lead his 40,000 to victory and imperishable renown?

JASPER.

GEN. HUNTER'S DEPARTMENT.

The Voyage From Hampton Roads—Arrival at Port Royal—Skirmish at Edisto—Loss of the Steamer Empire.

From Our Own Correspondent.

STEAMER ATLANTIC, PORT ROYAL HARBOR, Sunday, March 30, 1862.

The good steamer *Atlantic*, bearing Gens. HUNTER and BENHAM, with their Staffs, left Fortress Monroe on Friday afternoon at 4 o'clock, and reached this place this morning. The voyage was entirely devoid of incident.

The coast about Port Royal disappointed me. It is low and sandy; Hilton Head is but little above high tide. But the harbor is truly royal in extent, and the channel, though intricate, equal in depth to that of New-York. Government has replaced the buoys, and a light-ship lies each night near the bar. Over the site of the rebel Fort Walker, on the south side, the Stars and Stripes floated proudly in the evening breeze; and where was only an old plantation house a few months ago, now appeared a little village of barracks and government offices. A fine new wharf, T-shaped, has also been built out into the bay, on piles. Riding at anchor, in different parts of the harbor, were about fifty vessels of all sorts and sizes—mostly large. All the coasts in sight are covered with forests—mainly the emblematical palmetto; I could almost fancy that I saw the rattlesnake coiled around its stem. It was a satisfaction to see headless trunks of some which our shot have decapitated.

Of course, we had plenty of visitors, both from the shore and the ships in port. The mails have been sent in by the pilotboat; but numbers had old acquaintances to see or inquire after, and all were anxious for news by word of mouth. Fortunately, the passengers had no occasion to go ashore till they pleased, and so the evening was undisturbed by the bustle and care of departure.

My voyage ended, it is only proper that I pay my honest tribute to the admirable condition of the *Atlantic*, under the experienced charge of Capt. [illegible] and Purser FORDHAM. Everything makes for [illegible]

The Philadelphia Inquirer.

ESTABLISHED 1829. | PHILADELPHIA, FRIDAY, APRIL 11. 1862. | PRICE TWO CENTS.

LATEST WAR NEWS!

THE GREAT BATTLE NEAR CORINTH.

ANOTHER ACCOUNT OF THE TERRIBLE CONFLICT.

PROCLAMATION OF THE PRESIDENT.

THE VERY LATEST FROM FORTRESS MONROE.

THE REBELS GATHERING A LARGE FORCE AT YORKTOWN.

ANOTHER DESPERATE FIGHT PROBABLE.

THE TEXANS EVACUATING NEW MEXICO.

PROCEEDINGS OF CONGRESS.

DOINGS AT HARRISBURG, PA.

LATEST FROM WASHINGTON.

THE GREAT BATTLE NEAR CORINTH.

ANOTHER ACCOUNT.

HOW THE BATTLE COMMENCED.

CINCINNATI, April 10.—The correspondent of the Cincinnati *Times* gives the following account of the Pittsburg battle:—

"Our forces were stationed in the form of a semi-circle, the right resting on a point north of Crump's Landing, our centre being in front of the main road to Corinth, and our left extending to the river in the direction of Hamburg, four miles north of Pittsburg Landing.

At 2 o'clock on the morning of the 6th, 400 men from General PRENTISS' Division were attacked by the enemy, half a mile in advance of our lines. Our men fell back on the Twenty-fifth Missouri, swiftly pursued by the enemy.

The advance of the Rebels reached Colonel PEABODY's brigade just as the long roll was sounded and the men were falling into line. The resistance was but short and they retreated under a galling fire until they reached the Second Division.

At six o'clock the attack has become general along the entire front of our lines. The enemy, in large force, drove in the pickets of Gen. SHERMAN's division, and fell on the Forty-eighth, Seventieth and Seventy-second Ohio regiments. These troops had never before been in action, and being so unexpectedly attacked, made as able a resistance as possible, but were, in common with the forces of Gen. PRENTISS, compelled to seek support on the troops immediately in their rear.

At one o'clock the entire line of both sides was fully engaged. The roar of cannon and musketry was without intermission from the main centre to a point extending half way down the left wing.

The Rebels made a desperate charge on the Fourteenth Ohio Battery, and not being sufficiently sustained by infantry, it fell into their hands. Another severe fight occurred for the possession of the Fifth Ohio Battery, and three of its guns were taken by the enemy.

By eleven o'clock commanders of regiments had fallen, and in some cases not a single field officer remained; yet the fighting continued with an earnestness which showed that the contest on both sides was for "death or victory!" Foot by foot the ground was contested, and finding it impossible to drive back our centre, the enemy slackened their fire and made a vigorous effort on our left wing, endeavoring to outflank and drive it to the river bank. This wing was under General HURLBURT, and was composed of the Fourteenth, Thirty-second, Forty-fourth and Fifty-seventh Indiana, Eighth, Eighteenth and Twenty-first Illinois. Fronting its line, however, were the Fifty-fourth, Fifty-seventh and Seventy-seventh Ohio, and Fifth Ohio Cavalry, of SHERMAN's division.

For nearly two hours a sheet of fire blazed from both columns, the Rebels fighting with a valor that was only equalled by those contending with them. While the contest raged the hottest, the gun-boat *Tylor* passed up the river to a point opposite the enemy and poured in broadsides from her immense guns, greatly aiding in forcing the enemy back. Up to three o'clock, the battle raged with a fury that defies description. The Rebels had found their attempts to break our lines unavailing. They had striven to drive in our main column, and finding that impossible, had turned all their strength upon our left. Foiled in that quarter, they now made another attack on our centre, and made every effort to rout our forces before the reinforcements which had been sent for should come up.

At five o'clock there was a short cessation in the firing of the enemy, their lines falling back for nearly half a mile. They then suddenly wheeled, and again threw their entire force upon our left wing, determined to make a final struggle in that quarter; but the gun-boats *Tylor* and *Lexington* poured in their shot thick and fast with terrible effect.

In the meantime General LEW. WALLACE, who had taken a circuitous route for Crump's Landing, appeared suddenly on the enemy's right wing. In the face of this combination of circumstances, the Rebels felt that their enterprise that day was a failure, and as night was approaching, fell back until they reached an advantageous position somewhat in the rear of, yet occupying, the main road to Corinth.

The gun-boats continued to send their shell after them until they got out of range.

After a weary watch of several hours of intense anxiety, the advance regiment of General BUELL's army appeared on the opposite bank of the river, and the work of crossing the river began, the Thirty-sixth Indiana and Sixty-eighth Ohio being the first to cross, followed by the main portion of NELSON's and BRUCE's divisions.

Cheer after cheer greeted their arrival, and they were immediately sent to the advance where they rested on their arms.

All night long steamers were engaged in ferrying General BUELL's forces across. When daylight broke it was evident that the Rebels, too, had been heavily reinforced.

The Second Day's Fight.

The battle was opened by the Rebels at 7 o'clock, from the Corinth road, and in half an hour extended along the whole line.

At nine o'clock the sound of artillery and musketry fully equalled that of the previous day. The enemy was met by the reinforcements and the still unwearied soldiers of yesterday with an energy they certainly could not have expected. It became evident that they were avoiding the extreme of our left wing, and endeavoring with perseverance and determination to find some weak points by which to turn our forces. They left one point, but returned to it immediately, and then as suddenly, by some masterly stroke of Generalship, directed a most vigorous attack upon some division where they fancied they would not be expected; but the fire of our lines was as steady as clock work, and it soon became evident that the enemy considered the task he had undertaken a hopeless one.

Further reinforcements now began to arrive, and they were posted on the right of the main centre, under WALLACE. Gens. GRANT, BUELL, NELSON, SHERMAN and CRITTENDEN were everywhere present, directing the movements for a new stroke on the enemy. Suddenly both wings of our army were turned upon the enemy, with the intention of driving them into an extensive ravine. At the same time a powerful battery was stationed in the open field, and poured volley after volley of cannister into the Rebel ranks.

At 11½ o'clock the roar of the battle shook the earth. The Union guns were fired with all the energy that the prospect of the enemy's defeat inspired, while the Rebels' fire was not so vigorous, and they evinced a desire to withdraw. They finally fell slowly back, keeping up a fire from their artillery and musketry along their whole column, as they retreated. They moved in excellent order, battling at every advantageous point, and delivering their fire with considerable effect. But from all the divisions of our army they were closely pursued, a galling fire being kept upon their rear.

The enemy had now been driven beyond our former lines, and were in full retreat for Corinth, pursued by our cavalry.

The forces engaged on both sides, in this day's battle, are estimated at about seventy thousand each.

FURTHER DETAILS.

CAIRO, April 10.—An arrival from Pittsburg says the enemy, in making the first attack on Sunday morning, carried the Stars and Stripes and wore the Union uniforms. Gen. BRAGG is reported killed.

Provisional Governor JOHNSON, of Kentucky, is wounded and a prisoner.

It is stated that General PRENTISS escaped in the confusion of the enemy's retreat on the second day of the fight. Our total loss is about seven thousand. This is the estimate of military commanders who were in the engagement. Of these about two thousand were taken prisoners, and the balance killed and wounded in the usual proportions.

General WALLACE of Illinois, was reported dead, as it was thought impossible that he could live. He was, however, living on Wednesday, and improving. He was shot back of the ear, the bullet coming out at the nose.

General HALLECK passed Cairo to-day, *en route* for Pittsburg.

Five thousand prisoners are expected to-night from Island No. 10.

Every preparation is being made here for the reception of our wounded at Pittsburg.

CHICAGO, April 10.—We are beginning to get some reliable details from the great battle at Pittsburg from several gentlemen who were on the field after the fight. From their statements we gather the following:—

General PRENTISS' brigade, consisting of the Sixty-first Illinois, Seventeenth Wisconsin, Twenty-fourth Indiana and Seventy-first Ohio, were attacked while eating their breakfast, by what seemed to be the entire Rebel force. PRENTISS had no artillery. His Brigade was cut to pieces and forced to retire, and General PRENTISS and many of his troops were taken prisoners.

At 12 o'clock the entire line was fiercely engaged, but in full retreat. At 4 o'clock P. M. the enemy had taken SCHWARTZ's battery of six guns, DRESDEN's battery of four guns, WATERHOUSE's battery and also two Ohio batteries, the names of which are not given.

Thousands of our troops had taken refuge under the bank of the river, and utterly refused to fight: in fact, they could not, as the officers and men were mixed in inextricable confusion. The army at this time seemed utterly defeated.

At this juncture, the gun-boats *Lexington* and *Tylor* opened a tremendous fire of shot and shell upon the enemy, and kept it up every half hour.

THE HEROES OF THE RECENT GLORIOUS UNION VICTORY AT PITTSBURG LANDING.

MAJOR-GENERAL GRANT.

MAJOR-GENERAL BUELL.

MAJOR-GENERAL GRANT.

Major-General ULYSSES S. GRANT was born at Point Pleasant, Clairmont county, Ohio, April 27th, 1822, and entered West Point Military Academy, from Ohio, in 1839, where he graduated with honors in 1843, and was attached, as brevet second lieutenant, to the Fourth Infantry. He was promoted second lieutenant at Corpus Christi, in September, 1845, and served as such through Mexico, under General TAYLOR at Palo Alto, Resaca de la Palma and Monterey; and under General SCOTT from Vera Cruz to the city of Mexico, and was twice promoted for his bravery. He was regimental Quartermaster from April 1, 1847, and when he resigned the service on the 31st of July, 1854, he was a full captain in the Fourth Infantry of Regulars. After his resignation he settled in St. Louis county, Missouri, and moved from there to Galena, Illinois, in 1860.

Upon the breaking out of the present war he offered his services to Governor YATES, and was appointed Colonel of the Twenty-first Regiment of Illinois Volunteers, and served with his regiment until promoted a Brigadier-General, with commission and rank from the seventeenth of May, 1861. He was engaged as colonel and acting brigadier-general in several of the contests in Southeastern Missouri, and his course as commander of the Southeast district of Missouri has been thoroughly scrutinized; and among his most praiseworthy acts was the occupation of Paducah and stoppage of communication and supplies to the Rebels via the Tennessee and Cumberland rivers. The manner in which he conducted the battle of Belmont is still fresh in our readers' minds. The rest of his course, as commander there, is too well known to be repeated here, and certain it is that his action in every instance has been applauded both by his superior officers and the people. After the capture of Fort Henry a new district was created, under the denomination of the District of West Tennessee, and General GRANT was assigned by General HALLECK to the command of it.

He was in command of the Union forces at Fort Donelson, and his noted correspondence with General BUCKNER gained him the soubriquet of Unconditional-Surrender GRANT, answering to his initials of U. S. GRANT. For the success of that action he was created a Major-General; but, being unavoidably absent from the field during the early portion of the fight, it was reported that he was temporarily deprived of his command until the matter could be investigated. After a few days he was, however, again ordered into the field, and the manner in which he has conducted the present action will remove from him all the remains of his former discomfiture. General GRANT is a noble, brave and efficient soldier, as his actions have plainly proved throughout the present contest, and, in fact, throughout the whole of the Western war.

MAJOR-GENERAL BUELL.

General DON CARLOS BUELL, the commander of the District of Ohio troops in the field, is a native of Ohio, and is about forty years of age. He entered the Military Academy at West Point as a cadet in the year 1837, and was breveted second lieutenant of the Third Infantry July 1, 1841. In June, 1846, he was appointed first lieutenant, and was breveted captain September 23, 1846, for gallant and meritorious conduct during the several conflicts at Monterey, Mexico. During 1847 and 1848, he acted as adjutant of his regiment, and was particularly distinguished in the battle of Cerro Gordo. On the 20th of August, 1847, he was breveted major of the army for gallant and meritorious conduct in the battles of Contreras and Cherubusco, and was severely wounded in the latter. He was appointed in January, 1848, Assistant Adjutant-General, with the rank of captain, still holding his brevet rank of major. He relinquished his rank in the line during March, 1851.

At the commencement of the present troubles he was still holding the position of Assistant Adjutant-General. On the 11th of May, 1861, he was promoted to a Lieutenant-Colonelcy in the Adjutant-General's department, and by Congress he was created a Brigadier-General of volunteers, his commission bearing date May 17, 1861. With that rank he took charge of the Department of the Ohio, and under his direction the advance of the Union forces to Bowling Green and Nashville was conducted. At about the 20th of March, 1862, he was confirmed by Congress as Major-General of volunteers, and took command of the army in the field. The advance along the railroad from Nashville to Columbia, and from thence by turnpike roads to Savannah, has been performed with marked rapidity, and the junction with General GRANT's forces took place not a moment too soon.

THE REBEL FLOATING BATTERY AT ISLAND NO. 10.

This Battery, formerly the "Pelican Dock," at New Orleans, has no propelling power, but was towed up the river by four steamboats. The deck is about two feet above the surface of the river, but can be lowered or elevated by letting in or pumping out the water from the hollow space under its entire breadth. A steam engine which works the pump is inclosed in the circular iron-plated bomb-proof. The rectangular bomb-proofs, constructed of timber, are designed as quarters for the men. The guns are mounted *en barbette*, and none of them are smaller than 32-pounders.

JUST BEFORE THE BATTLE.

Special Correspondence of the Inquirer.

FIVE MILES INLAND FROM PITTSBURG LANDING, Tenn., on the Road to Corinth, Miss., Saturday, April 5, 1862.

Yesterday afternoon, about four o'clock, two regiments of the enemy made a reconnoissance on our right (General SHERMAN's Division), and succeeded in capturing five of our men—one major, one lieutenant and three privates—who were on picket duty. A brigade was immediately ordered out, as it was believed that the Rebels were in force, and, after moving one mile beyond our picket line, came up to a masked battery, but found it out in time to fall back to a safe position, in the meantime firing upon the Rebels, who endeavored to cut them off.

We obtained a position in the edge of a wood, and, in about two hours, drove them down the Corinth road, they taking their guns along. Subsequent observation showed twelve Rebels lying dead, and three wounded, the latter being captured. Night coming on, nothing has been done since, except a general distribution of cartridges, etc., and last night an order to sleep on our arms, which was done. We are anticipating a renewal of the scene this afternoon, and I have no doubt but that the ball is just now commencing in earnest.

Affairs here are of so entirely a military character that I cannot find an opportunity to lay hold of anything except it concerns the movements of troops, etc.; and aside from that, the system of espionage lately established prohibits me from saying what I feel it my duty to say with reference to many matters. I bide my time, hoping that a few days longer may produce results that will repay me for the risk and anxiety I experience here in these gloomy forests. Sickness in camp continues to increase, and it is to be hoped that some excitement will be afforded the men, for it would benefit them a thousand fold more than all the physic and tonics that could be administered in the form of drugs and medicines. We buried three from our regiment, Twenty-fifth Missouri, yesterday. H. B.

FROM NEAR YORKTOWN.

NEAR YORKTOWN, April 9th, 1·20 P. M.

To the Associated Press:—The weather still continues unfavorable for military operations. It has been raining for two days. The creeks are much swollen, and the low ground covered with water, making the road almost impassable for empty wagons.

Information received shows that the Rebels have a force of sixty thousand, which is rapidly being added to by troops from the neighborhood of Richmond, which is one day from Yorktown by railroad and river. They have four steamers and sixteen transports in use, and, by the time the roads are in condition for the Union army to move, the Rebels may be able to meet them with one hundred thousand men—the flower of their army, with their best arms. Besides, they are in a strongly entrenched position.

Previous to our troops occupying their present position, the military authorities had mo means of ascertaining the extent of the Rebel works. Information obtained through deserters, contrabands and other sources, show that the enemy have nearly five hundred guns, some of them of the largest calibre.

The Rebel General, JOHNSTON, with some of his forces, has arrived and taken command in person, showing that they intend making a desperate resistance to the advance of our troops at every point.

The entrenchments extend entirely across the peninsula from James to York river.

The cheering news from the Western Department arrived here to-day, and our troops are wild with enthusiasm over the result, and are anxious to be led to action, that they may perform similar deeds of valor.

LATE WASHINGTON NEWS.

A GIGANTIC RAILROAD SCHEME.

THE STEVENS' BATTERY.

Pennsylvania Reserves Out West.

A REBEL GENERAL.

SENTENCED TO BE HUNG.

Nominated a Brigadier-General.

Special Correspondence of the Inquirer.

WASHINGTON, April 10.

A Gigantic Speculation—Grand Railroad Scheme.

Mr. WRIGHT reported a bill into the House this morning, from the Committee on Military Affairs, entitled "An Act to facilitate the transportation of troops, munitions, stores and mails of the United States, between the cities of Washington, Baltimore, Philadelphia and New York." Its provisions will be found in the following brief synopsis:—

Section 1. The Secretary of the Treasury is authorized to guarantee the bonds of the Metropolitan Railroad Company to the amount of two millions of dollars, payable in thirty years at six per cent., to be issued when the said company shall execute a mortgage on their road, rolling stock and property, and also conditioned for two per cent. per annum for a sinking fund for the redemption of the bonds. The Company shall immediately construct a railroad to Gaithersburg, Md., and from there connect with the Philadelphia, Wilmington and Baltimore Railroad at such point, near Baltimore, as the Secretary of War may direct; also, to connect with the Northern Central or such other roads as now exist or may hereafter be finished or constructed running into Pennsylvania or New York, and to make extensions in any direction, and towards any point of the compass. In consideration of these inordinate and tremendous privileges, the said Company is to carry freight at four cents per ton per mile, and soldiers and sailors at two cents per mile.

Section 2 provides, that when the Company shall bring evidence of its owners or engineers that it has expended fifty thousand dollars, he shall deliver that amount of bonds.

Section 3. The Company is authorized to lay tracks through any of the streets of Washington and Georgetown.

Section 4 provides for the sale of the road in default of its interest, and its purchase by the United States.

Section 5. The Company is authorized to construct a double track upon the line of any railway, when the Secretary of War shall so direct, and authorizes the Secretary of the Treasury to issue bonds to an indefinite amount for such construction upon the demands of the owners of the road.

Section 6. The rate of fare to be two and a half cents per mile for through passengers, and three cents per mile for way passengers. *Provided*, That for better accommodations than are now afforded, the company shall have the right to charge an additional rate of one cent per mile.

Altogether, this bill designs to aid one of the most magnificent projects of the day, and confers upon a half dozen individuals privileges which are worth fifty millions of dollars. It completely tramples upon the clearest rights of five States, and aims to reduce to bankruptcy some of the most loyal corporations in the land. It is an instance of national ingratitude that ignores the services of the existing lines by whose labors the National Capital was saved exactly one year ago, merely to enable a handful of speculators to fasten a huge job upon Congress, while the shrieks of dying soldiers and sorrow-stricken families echo over the land.

It is evident that the Committee cannot have given the subject a thorough investigation, and there can be no doubt that it was hurried through in the immense press of business which has weighed so heavily upon the most laborious and hard working committee in the House. If this bill shall become a law it will establish a precedent for future bogus railroad grants and aid to flimsy corporations from a heavily taxed and depressed people, who, while willing to spend their last dollar for the public defence, will never consent to be taxed to enrich a hungry band of railroad jobbers and speculators.

Nominated to a Brigadier-Generalship.

The President yesterday sent to the Senate the nomination to a Brigadier-Generalship of Major SAMUEL W. CRAWFORD, of the Thirteenth Regular Infantry, Inspector-General of Gen. ROSENCRANS' division. Major CRAWFORD is a native of Philadelphia. He entered the army in 1851 as a Surgeon, at the head of his class. He was at once sent to the frontier, where he remained for several years. In 1857 he traveled throughout Mexico, and made a daring and successful ascent of the volcano Popocateptl. For his researches he was honored by the Geographical Society of Mexico with membership. He was subsequently made Bearer of Despatches to the State Department. In 1858 he was assigned again to duty on the frontier, with the late lamented General LYON, and he continued the warm friend and correspondent of that patriot until his death.

In 1860 Major CRAWFORD was ordered to Fort Sumter. During the long imprisonment of that brave band, and in the final bombardment, he bore a conspicuous part, and commanded for hours the battery exposed to the fire of Fort Moultrie and Sullivan's Island. After the fall of Sumter he was assigned to duty with General ROSECRANS' command, and took an active part in driving FLOYD from Western Virginia. So valuable have been his services in that section that the delegation from Virginia waited upon the President and requested his nomination to a General of Brigade. Philadelphia cannot but be gratified at the well-merited reward thus bestowed upon one of her sons.

The Stevens Battery.

The appropriation for the completion of this immense iron-clad frigate passed the House by the decisive vote of eighty-two to forty-one. The bill goes back to the Senate by reason of non-concurrence in some of the Senate amendments, but there is no doubt that it will be a law within the next week. The Secretary of the Navy, who has displayed commendable zeal and energy on the subject of constructing iron-clad ships, it is believed will cordially co-operate with Mr. STEVENS in making his renowned battery a credit to the nation.

Competent scientific and nautical men say that, when finished, she will surpass the *Warrior* or *La Gloire* as much as either of them excel an ordinary wooden ship. The Navy Department need desire no prouder monument of its efficiency than the completion of this single impregnable and destructive battle-ship.

Pennsylvania Reserves Out West.

It will be gratifying to Pennsylvanians to know that the Union gun-boat *Carondelet*, which recently made the gallant dash of running the blockade by the Rebel batteries at Island No. 10, on the Mississippi, getting safely into her desired position under a fire of forty shots, is manned entirely by volunteers from the Pennsylvania Reserve Corps, McCALL's Division. The quota of volunteers from the Division, for the gun-boat service, was sixty men, ten from each regiment, and they left General McCALL's Head-quarters here, after inspection of the detachment by the General himself, on Monday morning, the 17th of February. They are a fine body of men, and nobly are they sustaining the reputation of Pennsylvania. They left under charge of Sergeant H. S. FISHER, Fifth Regiment.

A Rebel General.

Considerable curiosity has been excited here to know something of a Rebel officer who figures in the reports.

General W. W. MAKALL, captured at Island No. 10, is a native of Virginia, and was formerly Assistant Adjutant-General in our army. No longer since than last June he came home from California at the expense of the Government, drew his pay, and resigned. For two or three weeks he hung around Elkton, Maryland, to the intense disgust of loyal men there, and suddenly disappearing, now turns up a "General." His whole family have lived on the Government all their lives.

List of Prisoners from the United States Ship "Congress."

The following has been received at the Navy Department:—

The subscriber, PETER J. HARGOUS, is, of course, included among the prisoners.

TOBACCO WAREHOUSE, RICHMOND, VA., April 3, 1862.

SIR:—The following is a correct list of the men taken prisoners from the United States ship *Congress*, on the 8th of March last, at Newport News, viz:—William Robinson, seaman; James A. Wicks, second master; Jeremiah O'Connor, captain of the hold; Arthur Clegg, do.; David Sherry, boatswain's mate; Amos Gitupe, carpenter's mate; Peter Barker, colored, cook; Charles Costello, seaman; Thomas C. Jones, do.; Samuel Kelly, do.; Michael Quinn, ordinary seaman; Jno. Tonson, do.; W. H. Williams, do.; Benjamin F. Wing, landsman; Math. Kenny, do.; Edward Morrissey, do.; Daniel Barton, colored, do.; James McCauley, do.; John Beard, ordinary seaman; John Williams, landsman; John O'Mailey, marine; Wm. Baldwin, coast guard, Ninety-ninth Regiment N. Y. S. V.; John Blackwood, do.; Richard Thomas, do.; Miller Delane, do.; Archibald McClain, do.; John Peterson, do.; Francis Kenny, do.; James Goodwin, do.

In the hospital at Portsmouth, Va., John Collins, quarter gunner, slightly wounded; Thomas Forward, landsman, badly burned; Flynn, do., left leg amputated.

I am, sir, very respectfully, your obedient servant,
PETER J. HARGOUS,
Master's Mate, United States Navy.

To Hon. GIDEON WELLES, Secretary of the Navy.

Sentenced to be Hung.

In the course of the past summer Mr. SAMUEL P. CARUSI, a native of this city, and son of our fellow citizen Mr. SAMUEL CARUSI, was arrested by the military authorities here on some charge implicating his loyalty. He was, however, promptly discharged on taking the oath of allegiance to the United States, and returned to his home in Westmoreland county, Virginia.

The Union prisoners last arrived in this city bring to his parents here the distressing intelligence that some time since he and two others were arrested by the Rebel authorities on a charge of being Union spies, and that he has been tried in Richmond, where he is now imprisoned under sentence of death. His father is endeavoring to enlist the influence of the Government here in his behalf; it is sincerely to be hoped with success.

The War in New Mexico.

WASHINGTON, April 10.—The following was received to-day by the Secretary of War:—

"KANSAS CITY, April 10.—The Santa Fe mail has arrived.

"The Texans, one hundred and fifty strong, had evacuated Santa Fe, and were marching along the river. It is reported that General CANBY had intercepted an express with orders commanding the Texan forces to evacuate the territory and return to Texas.

"Colonel SLOUGH had left for Union City with one thousand four hundred men, to make a junction with General CANBY.

"The Texans were exacting contributions and forced loans from the inhabitants, and clothing and provisions were being taken from the merchants without regard to their politics or circumstances."

FORT UNION, New Mexico, March 23.—[Correspondence of the Missouri *Republican*.]—Our column, under command of Colonel SLOUGH, is breaking up camp for a forward movement south towards the Rebel forces. The Texan army occupies a strong position in the vicinity of Albuquerque, 175 miles south of this depot, about midway between this fort and Fort Craig, where General CANBY was at last accounts.

The Texans have taken up this as the strategic point, doubtless intending to march upon either column as they leave their stronghold—Fort Union or Fort Craig—and by their superior force (which is estimated at 2400 strong and twenty-one pieces of artillery) whip one, face about and assault the other column before they can form a junction, and cut us up in detail.

It would seem that Col. SLOUGH and Gen. CANBY, the commanders of the two depots, are not acting in concert, and sound men of the army fear that this movement—one of the most difficult of military combinations—may prove successful, and render our depot at Fort Union—the only supply left us—comparatively defenceless. I sincerely believe Col. SLOUGH will march beyond supporting distance of the depot. The Texans are occupying Santa Fe, a hundred miles south of this, with from a hundred to two hundred troops.

From Fortress Monroe and the Peninsula.

BALTIMORE, April 10.—The Old Point boat has arrived. The news of the capture of Island No. 10 caused great enthusiasm and rejoicing. The storm still continued, but had somewhat abated last evening.

The accounts from the Peninsula report our troops meeting the storm with characteristic ingenuity in the way of improvised shelters. Their enthusiasm and confidence in General McCLELLAN is unabated.

Though the storm at this time is unfortunate, the time has not been lost, and the retreat of the Rebel MAGRUDER and his forces, or their defeat, is about as certain as any possible future event. The prospect of a clear-up in the weather is looked for with great anxiety at Old Point, from a belief that the sunshine and the *Merrimac* will come together. All seem confident that she will be captured or sunk if she comes out.

LATEST.

WASHINGTON, April 10.—The latest news received from Cherrystone reports everything quiet in the vicinity. A strong wind was blowing, and the sea was running very high.

The Baltimore and Ohio Railroad.

BALTIMORE, April 10.—The Directors of the Baltimore and Ohio Railroad have passed the following:—

Whereas, Publications have been made in some of the journals of the Northern and Western States, alleging disloyalty on the part of officers and employees of this Company, and assigning this as a reason why the Government of the United States have not, at an earlier period, assisted the Company in opening the road to its Western termini;

And whereas, The officers of this Company have the entire confidence of the Government, as is well known to this Board, and the delay by the Government in furnishing any assistance to enable the Company to open its road has not been owing to the cause alleged;

And whereas, This Board, in accordance with our views, are opposed to the employment of any persons by the Company who are known to be disloyal; therefore,

Resolved, That the employment, in any capacity whatever, of any person known to be disloyal to the Government, will meet with the unqualified disapprobation of the Board, and if any persons, now in the employ of the company, shall be discovered to be disloyal to the Government, the removal of such persons be imperatively demanded.

Resolved, That no person shall be appointed to any position, or employed in any capacity, by the officers of this company, except loyal citizens of the United States.

The Occupation of Corinth, Miss.

WASHINGTON, April 10.—Despatches have been received here to-day, confirming the report of the occupation of Corinth, Mississippi, by the troops under Gen. BUELL.

General Banks' Command.

EDENBURG, Va., April 10.—All is quiet in this Division.

The enemy's pickets have not been seen during the severe storm which has prevailed for the past two days.

Auction Sale of Wool at Boston.

BOSTON, April 10.—At the auction sale to-day 600,000 pounds of wool were sold at 43@48c., the bidding closing firm. Average price 45c.

Among the purchasers were [illegible] & Sons and ROBINSON & Co., of Philadelphia. The lots were all sold.

The New-York Times.

VOL. XI—NO. 3318. NEW-YORK, MONDAY, MAY 12, 1862. PRICE TWO CENTS.

THE CAPTURE OF NORFOLK AND THE ADVANCE UPON RICHMOND.

Map Showing Norfolk and the Various Places Referred to in the News of its Capture; Showing also the New Points of Interest in Gen. McClellan's March to Richmond.

GLORIOUS NEWS

Norfolk and Portsmouth Captured Without a Battle.

The Gosport Navy-yard Repossessed.

THE MERRIMAC BLOWN UP.

Five Thousand National Troops Landed at Willoughby Point.

THE ADVANCE ON NORFOLK.

Our Forces Met by a Delegation of Citizens.

THE CITY FORMALLY SURRENDERED.

No Property Destroyed by the Retreating Rebel Troops.

The Monitor and the Naugatuck Gone Up to the City.

DISPATCH FROM SECRETARY STANTON.

WASHINGTON, Sunday, May 11.

The following was received at the War Department this morning:

FORT MONROE, Saturday May 10—Midnight.

Norfolk is ours, and also Portsmouth and the Navy-yard.

Gen. WOOL, having completed the landing of his forces at Willoughby Point, about 9 o'clock, this morning, commenced his march on Norfolk, with 5,000 men.

Secretary CHASE accompanied the General.

About five miles from the landing-place a rebel battery was found on the opposite side of the bridge over Tanner's Creek, and after a few discharges upon two companies of infantry that were in the advance, the rebels burned the bridge.

This compelled our forces to march around five miles further.

At 5 o'clock in the afternoon our forces were within a short distance of Norfolk, and were met by a delegation of citizens.

The city was formally surrendered.

Our troops were marched in, and now have possession.

Gen. VIELE is in command, as Military Governor.

The city and Navy-yard were not burned. The fires which have been seen for some hours proved woods on fire.

Gen. WOOL, with Secretary CHASE, returned about 11 o'clock to-night.

Gen. HUGER withdrew his force without a battle.

The *Merrimac* is still off Sewall's Point.

Commander RODGERS' expedition was heard from this afternoon ascending the James River.

Reports from Gen. MCCLELLAN are favorable. EDWIN M. STANTON.

DESTRUCTION OF THE MERRIMAC.

DISPATCH TO THE NAVY DEPARTMENT.

FORTRESS MONROE, Sunday, May 11.

To Hon. J. H. Watson, Assistant Secretary of War:

The *Merrimac* was blown up by the rebels at two minutes before 5 o'clock this morning. She was set fire to about 3 o'clock. The explosion took place at the time stated. It is stated to have been a grand sight by those who saw it. The *Monitor, E. A. Stevens (Naugatuck)* and the gunboats have gone up toward Norfolk.

THE PREPARATORY MOVEMENTS.

SPECIAL DISPATCH FROM FORTRESS MONROE.

MOORE'S RANCHE, PLEASURE POINT, Saturday, 3 P. M., *via* WASHINGTON, May 11.

I have just arrived here, and meet intelligence from the army in advance. It seems that five regiments of infantry were sent forward this morning, and pushed forward as far as the bridge across Tanner's Creek, about seven miles from this place, on the road to Norfolk. They arrived just in time to see the secession troops *burn the bridge* in their faces, and plant four pieces of rifled cannon on the opposite bank to protect them in doing it. It was then discovered that our artillery, which had been ordered over, was still on board the transport, not a single piece having been landed. The result was, that we were absolutely helpless.

It was decided to take a roundabout road, which leads around the head of Tanner's Creek. Gen. MANSFIELD, who had been requested by Gen. WOOL to leave his command at Newport's News, overtook the advancing troops, MAX WEBER's Regiment taking the lead, just after the bridge had been fired, and was at once placed in command. He attended to everything in person, and has now gone back to attend to the landing and forwarding of the artillery, and to bringing up reinforcements. Five regiments are already in advance.

By the road which the destruction of the bridge has compelled them to take, our troops will be obliged to march some eight miles further—not far from twenty in all—to Norfolk, which they will scarcely be able to reach before morning. H. J. R.

DISPATCHES TO THE ASSOCIATED PRESS.

FORTRESS MONROE, Friday, April 9—Evening.

Old Point this evening presents a most stirring spectacle. About a dozen steam transports are loading troops. They will land on the shore opposite the Rip Raps and march direct on Norfolk. At the time I commence writing, (9 P. M.,) the moon shines so brightly that I am sitting in the open air, in an elevated position, writing by moonlight. The transports are gathering in the stream—they have on board artillery, cavalry and infantry, and will soon be prepared to start. The Rip Raps are pouring in shot and shell into Sewall's Point, and a bright light in the direction of Norfolk leads to the supposition that the work of destruction has commenced.

President LINCOLN, as Commander-in-Chief of the Army and Navy, is superintending the expedition himself. About 6 o'clock he went across to the place selected for the landing, which is about a mile below the Rip Raps. It is said he was the first to step on shore, and, after examining for himself the facilities for landing, returned to the Point, where he was received with enthusiastic cheering by the troops who were embarking.

The *Merrimac* still lies off Craney Island, and the *Monitor* has assumed her usual position. The fleet are floating quietly at their anchorage, ready at any moment for action.

It is evident that the *finale* of the rebellion, as far as Norfolk is concerned, is rapidly approaching. The general expectation is, that the troops now embarking will have possession of the city before to-morrow night.

10 P. M.—The expedition has not yet started, the delay being caused by the time required for stowing the horses and cannon on the *Adelaide*. The batteries at the Rip Raps have stopped throwing shells, and all is quiet. The scene in the Roads, of the transports steaming about, is most beautiful, presenting a panoramic view seldom witnessed.

11 P. M.—The vessels have not yet sailed.

The *Merrimac* exhibits a bright light.

It is said the *Seminole* will go up the James River in the course of the night.

BALTIMORE, Sunday, May 11.

The Old Point boat has arrived.

Our troops crossed to the Virginia shore during Friday night, whilst the Rip Raps shelled the rebel works at Sewall's Point.

A landing was effected at Willoughby's Point, at a spot selected the previous day by President LINCOLN, who was among the first who stepped ashore.

The rebels fled as our troops advanced.

At last advices Gen. MAX WEBER was within three miles of Norfolk.

The *Merrimac* remained stationary all day off Craney Island.

LATER.

WILLOUGHBY'S POINT, Saturday Morning, May 10.

The troops left during the night, and at daylight could be seen from the wharf landing at Willoughby's Point, a short distance from the Rip Raps. Through the influence of Secretary STANTON, I obtained this morning a permit to accompany Gen. WOOL and Gen. MANSFIELD and Staffs to Willoughby's Point, on the steamer *Kansas*, and here I am, on "sacred soil," within eight miles of Norfolk. The Point at which we have landed is known as Point Pleasant, one of the favorite drives from Norfolk.

The first regiment landed was the Twentieth New-York, known as MAX WEBER's regiment, which pushed on immediately, under command of Gen. WEBER, and were at 8 A. M. picketed within five miles of Norfolk. The First Delaware, Col. ANDREWS, was pushed forward at 9 o'clock, accompanied by Gens. MANSFIELD and VIELE and Staff. They were soon followed by the Sixteenth Massachusetts, Col. WYMAN. The balance of the expedition consists of the Tenth New-York, Col. BENDIX, the Forty-eighth Pennsylvania, Col. BAILEY, the Ninety-ninth New-York, (Coast Guards,) Major DODGES' Battalion of Mounted Rifles, and Capt. FOLLETT's Co. D of Fourth (regular) Artillery. Gen. WOOL and staff remained to superintend the landing of the balance of the force, all of whom were landed and off before noon.

The President, accompanied by Secretary STANTON, accompanied Gen. WOOL and Staff to the wharf, and then took a tug and proceeded to the *Minnesota*, where he was received with a National salute. It is generally admitted that the President and Secretary STANTON have infused new vigor into both the naval and military operations here, and that the country will have no cause for further complaint. As to the insulting course of the rebels in this quarter, the President has declared that *Norfolk must fall, that the Merrimac must succumb to the naval power of the Union, and that the Government property at Norfolk must be repossessed at whatever cost it may require.* What is more, he has determined to remain until it is accomplished.

The iron-clad gunboat *Galena*, accompanied by the *Port Royal* and *Aroostook*, went up the James River on Wednesday night, and although I have been unable to obtain any positive information from them since they all encountered the forts on the lower part of the river, it is understood that the President has received dispatches from Gen. MCCLELLAN to the effect that they have given him most valuable aid in driving the enemy to the wall. It is even stated to-day that the *Galena* not only captured the *Yorktown* and *Jamestown*, but has put crews on board and ran them up within shelling distance of the river defences of Richmond. Of the truth of this, however, I cannot vouch, as Old Point is becoming famous for fabulous rumors.

THE CITY OF NORFOLK.

Norfolk, by last census, had a population of 14,609, about 3,300 of whom were slaves. But on account of the fearful state of perturbation in which the city has been kept for the last year, and also on account of the rebel conscription, it is now probably reduced to a half of that number. It is situated on the right bank of the Elizabeth River, just below the confluence of the two branches, 8 miles from Hampton Roads, 32 miles from the Ocean, and 106 by land and 160 by water southeast from Richmond. The situation is low; the streets are irregular and mostly wide, with good brick and stone buildings.

The harbor is safe and spacious, admitting the largest vessels. The entrance to it is over a mile in width, and Fortress Monroe and Fort Calhoun, on the Rip Raps, were built for its defence.

Among the principal buildings, are the City Hall, having a granite front, and a cupola 110 feet high; the Norfolk Military Academy, Mechanics' Hall, and Ashland Hall. The city contains a court-house, jail, custom-house, three banks, and fourteen churches. There is a beautiful cemetery, handsomely laid out, and adorned with cypress trees. In the vicinity, at Gosport, is the celebrated United States Navy-yard, which was seized by the rebels last year, and at which they clad in iron the *Merrimac* and other vessels. The yard contains a dry dock, constructed of granite, at a cost of a million of dollars.

The foreign commerce of Norfolk exceeds that of any other place in Virginia; and there are only two towns in the State of greater population, Petersburgh and Richmond.

The Dismal Swamp Canal connects Chesapeake Bay and Albemarle Sound, and opens an extensive water communication from Norfolk to the South. The locks of this canal were recently partially destroyed by Gen. RENO, when the battle of Camden ensued; and the canal was subsequently obstructed by a detachment of Commodore ROWAN's naval force. There is a line of railroads running from Norfolk to Suffolk, in the adjoining county of Nansemond, which connects it with the whole Southern system of railroads.

Norfolk was the scene of important military events in the war of the Revolution. The British fleet, to which Lord DUNMORE, the Governor of Virginia, fled at the outbreak of hostilities, made Norfolk harbor its principal rendezvous. On the 1st of January, 1776, the town was bombarded by the British at the order of DUNMORE, and a party of troops were landed, who set fire to the houses. The fire raged three days, and the horrors of conflagration were heightened by the thunder of cannon from the ships; and many women and children lost their lives. The remaining edifices were afterward destroyed, and the mournful silence of gloomy depopulation reigned where once was the principal town of Virginia. But it rose again from its ashes, and has now, for the second time been taken, but by a more humane and civilized Government than the British.

THE TOWN OF PORTSMOUTH.

Portsmouth, directly opposite Norfolk, is a place of 9,500 inhabitants. It is built on level ground, has various institutions of learning, a military academy, five newspapers, and six churches. By the seaboard and Roanoke Railroad, and James River, it has extensive communications North and South. It, of course, falls with the fall of Norfolk. The Navy-yard is more properly said to be here than at Norfolk. It is half a mile from the central part of the town, or that part of it called Gosport.

THE NEWS IN WASHINGTON.

WASHINGTON, Sunday, May 11.

Washington has been in a state of tumult all day, growing out of the extraordinary war bulletins that have been posted at the hotels. People are bewildered, and their joy made grave and inexpressible by the unexpected immensity of the Union triumphs. Willard's Hotel has been crowded, the War Office besieged, and every place of public resort thronged by eager crowds pressing and breathless for news. Extra editions of the Sunday papers were issued, and sold at fabulous prices, until every man, woman and child of Washington knew the wonderful tidings. Shall I add it—need I add it—that the chorus of every congratulation between the people was the same—a pæan of enthusiastic praise of the noble General of the Union, who, in the unanimous declaration of Congress, has accomplished such great results with such small sacrifice of human life.

REJOICINGS OVER THE NEWS.

PHILADELPHIA, Sunday, May 11.

This city has been in a furore of excitement—flags are floating in every direction, and the chimes of St. Stephen's Church rang joyful peal this evening, on account of the news from Fortress Monroe.

BRIDGEPORT, Conn., Sunday, May 11.

A salute of one hundred guns was fired here to-day in honor of the recent victories.

THE MOUNTAIN DEPARTMENT.

The Defeat of Guerrillas by Gen. Kelley—Telegraphic Communication with General Schenck Cut Off.

Special Dispatch to the New-York Times.

PARKERSBURGH, Saturday, May 10, *via* BALTIMORE, Sunday, May 11.

The report of the capture of Arnoldsburgh by the rebels is contradicted. The rebels merely burned some stores at Running Creek. Their subsequent defeat is authoritatively reported by Gen. KELLEY.

The telegraph from here to Gen. SCHENCK's position has been cut, and useless all day. News has arrived, however, that our forces are at Franklin, safe. The army of FREMONT and SCHENCK has saved MILROY.

Southern Confederacy.

THE PUBLIC GOOD BEFORE PRIVATE ADVANTAGE.

BY ADAIR & SMITH. ATLANTA, GEORGIA, CONFEDERATE STATES OF AMERICA, JUNE 11, 1862. VOL. II—NO. 17.

WEDNESDAY, JUNE 4, 1862.

For the Southern Confederacy.

The Discovery of Salt Springs and Wells—Highly interesting account of some Experiments in Tennessee in 1825.

Messrs. Editors:

As the discovery of localities of Salt has become an object of paramount importance, I herewith send you a brief account of the experiments of Col. John Lyon, about the year 1825, in Tennessee.

His first attempt was by boring a well in the bed of the Calf Killer River, a tributary of the Cumberland, about four miles from Sparta. After boring to the depth of three hundred feet, they came to a vein of salt water two feet thick which yielded one bushel of salt to thirty gallons of water; (at the Salines, New York it takes thirty-five; at Abingdon, Virginia, twenty, and sea water of Georgia, three hundred and twenty gallons.) A furnace was erected, and from 30 to 40 bushels per day were made for several weeks, when the vast accumulation of carburetted hydrogen gas drove the tubing and pumps out through the roof, and continued to escape in immense quantities for several weeks, when it became exhausted, and the pumps were put to work, when lo! the salt water had disappeared.

The boring was again resumed, and at 360 feet another vein was found of greater quantity and better quality. To prevent a recurrence of so disastrous an accident, the colonel had the well enlarged from three inches to eight inches in diameter to the depth of 30 feet, and a cast iron cylinder inserted and fixed in with great strength; the pumps were rigged, and the work went on swimmingly for a month, when the accumulated gas forced the cylinder, pumps and house-roof out, and continued to rush out for a week, when the overseer applied a torch, as he said to burn it out. The ignition had well nigh burned him and two negroes to death before they could escape, and the undulating flame ascended to the height of over one hundred feet, and from side to side of the river—exhibiting one of the most sublime and magnificent spectacles in Nature. The light was so brilliant that the inhabitants of Sparta could read at night as readily as in day time—four miles off. This continued some ten days, when it exhausted, and upon trial the salt water was gone.

These repeated difficulties forced the parties to try lower down the river, where they found the salt water at the same depth, and with the same disastrous results. Being ignorant of science they abandoned the work altogether; whereas that troublesome element has since been converted into an active agent in boiling the water, instead of wood, at the great Kanawha salines, which are in the same formation, and consequently accompanied by this gas. As soon as the Yankees are driven from Tennessee, (which I pray may be early this summer,) the government ought to have these wells re-opened, or others sunk in the same neighborhood, and supply this great want of our people. We deem it to be the duty of all governments to relieve the pressing wants of the people, whic is not only natural, but without doing which there can be no government.

Samuel Turney, of White county, formerly Member of Congress, can give specific information relative to it.

I will now notice the saliferous region of Georgia, which is confined to the counties of Dade, Walker, Catoosa, Chattooga, Whitfield, Gordon and Floyd.

Though we may not find every member of the salt group in this district, there are certainly enough indications, both negative and positive, to justify the assertion that salt does exist, and may be found with but little expense.

"Salt licks" exist in Floyd county, west of the Oostanaulee River, and between John's Mountain and Taylor's Ridge.

Salt beds, like coal, are generally of limited extent. The coal fields of the Ohio Valley are on a magnificent scale; so are the beds of rock salt. The isolated bed found near Abingdon, Virginia, is not more than eight miles in extent; whereas the great western salt field has been opened at various places for five hundred miles, at all of which places the salt was found by "licks" or salt springs. This was the case in Abingdon, where Mr. King sunk a shaft at one of the "licks" to the depth of several hundred feet, without finding water, and after all his funds were exhausted, and his credit gone, and no hope left, the vein of salt water passing so near the shaft, gradually softened the wall, and finally burst into his abandoned work two hundred feet above the bottom, and filled the well with the strongest salt water on earth. His credit immediately arose. Money was advanced; furnaces were erected, and in a few years he was rich, and the surrounding millions provided with an indispensable blessing.

Cannot our patriotic Governor assist several practical as well as scientific citizens of Georgia to develope the salt beds of our State, and relieve her people from present want and suffering? That salt may be found in Floyd and Catoosa I have but little doubt. In most of the adjoining counties the strata are too highly inclined to hope for much.

Respectfully, yours.

M. F. STEPHENSON.

Large Families in the Army.

A few days ago, we mentioned the case of a Mr. Snead, living near Stone Mountain, who had six sons in the army.

Since then we have learned that Mr. Robert Thompson, of Henry county, formerly of Newton, has *eight* sons in the army, and has two more not quite old enough to do service, who are eager to be in ranks. The Confederacy can have the services of the old gentleman as soon as it needs him.

We are also informed that Mrs. Sarah Mangham, of Walton county, has *eight* sons now in service, who volunteered for the war. She has only one son at home, who has been a cripple from his infancy. The father of these brave sons lived to the age of 85 years, and was for forty years a resident of Walton county.

☞ See our New Terms.

ARMY CORRESPONDENCE

Of the Savannah Republican.

ARMY OF THE MISSISSIPPI,
Corinth, May 26, 1862.

This is the last letter I shall be able to send you from this point. Gen. Beauregard has issued an order, requiring all newspaper and other public correspondents to retire from the army. This step has been taken in consequence of the alleged indiscretion of one of the correspondents of the Memphis *Appeal*, who writes over the signature of "Sparta." No complaints have been made of anything I have written, or of the letters of other writers from the army. On the contrary, the letters of some of us have been referred to frequently, by persons high in authority, in terms of warm commendation, and information of interesting character has been voluntarily imparted to us that it might be laid before the public. And yet all of us alike, the innocent as well as the guilty, are made to suffer for the sins of one man.

It is believed by some that General Beauregard has been induced to issue this unjust and tyrannical order by Gen. Bragg, the most waspish officer in the army, or by some one of the swarm of gaudy butterflies who bask in the sunlight of his presence—many of whom are volunteer aids or officers whose merits have not been duly appreciated by the independent writers of the day. The truth is, the characters to whom I allude are the bane of the army. There is hardly a general officer in the service who is not surrounded by a multitude of volunteer aids, with *whip and spur*, (the latest style of riding,) who follow in the train of their chiefs like the tail of a comet, and who, though ornamental, are seldom useful. For the most part, they are young men who have wealthy parents, and who have not the patriotism to enter the ranks and perform the duties of a true man and a soldier. They are pert, insolent and impudent; they ride fine horses with gay trappings, use an immense amount of gold lace, swear like a trooper, and render themselves generally disagreeable and ridiculous. This is true not only of volunteer aids, but of many officers whose heads have been turned by their sudden elevation, and who think they are required to exercise their power every hour in the day, lest somebody forget what "mighty men of valor" they are. These characters are generally known, in the army, by the vulgar but expressive name of "squirts."

Gen. Beauregard, nevertheless, is responsible for the order to which I have alluded, and will so be held by the country and by the historian.

The freedom of the press, though guarantied by the fundamental law of the land, exists only in name. The military authorities have for some time claimed and exercised the right to inspect all telegraphic despatches, and to prohibit their transmission over the wires unless they were such as they saw fit to approve. Every telegram I have sent you since my return to this place, had first to be submitted to the Adjutant General, without whose approval the operators dare not send it. Not content with this imitation of the Lincoln government, they now issue a peremptory order, completely closing the door against all knowledge of the operations of the army, and in effect destroying the newspaper press of the country. Will the people submit to this unwarranted stretch of power? Ought they to submit to it?

A few short months ago Gens. Beauregard and Bragg were condemning the Northern despotism for the very thing they are now doing. The Federal Government was guilty of the outrage of searching the house of the citizen without due process of law, suspending the writ of *Habeas Corpus*, seizing private property, destroying the liberty of the citizen, and exercising a surveillance over the Press, which amounted to a virtual denial of all freedom of thought and speech. The military authorities of the Confederate States are following fast in the footsteps of the infamous tyranny that lords it over an enslaved people beyond the Potomac, and that now seeks to subjugate us to its ruinous rule. We had hoped it wouldd never be said of us, as it has been of our enemies, that freedom was incompatible with success, and that to achieve our liberties, we must first become slaves.

The complaint against the correspondent of the *Appeal* relates to a telegram which he sent to that paper. Before the telegram was sent, it was submitted to the acting Adjutant-General of the army, and by him approved. If blame attaches to any one, therefore, it is the Adjutant, whose duty it was to expunge all news of a contraband character.

I am glad to say the order of expulsion is universally condemned by the army. I have not met with a single individual, officer or soldier, outside of the "charmed circle" alluded to, who approves of the proceeding.—It is everywhere looked upon as a blunder, which, like Banquo's ghost, will return in life and in history to plague the authors of it.

When I came to Corinth, the first thing I did was to call upon the Adjutant-General of the army, who gave me permission to visit the camps and to pass in and out of our lines without let or hindrance. I expressed a desire to be placed upon a military footing, to be allowed access to such orders and despatches as it was proper to publish, and to be held responsible for my conduct like other men in the army. He courteously granted my request, and until his recent illness everything went on smoothly and pleasantly. But unfortunately, it became necessary some days ago for Gen. Jordan (the Adjutant-General) to go into the country on account of sickness. Had he been at his post, I have no idea that such an order, as that complained of, would ever have been issued. He is a soldier, a scholar and a gentleman, and his department is conducted with singular ability and courtesy.

When a correspondent or other person in the army transgresses any of the rules adopted for its government, it is proper that he should be punished; but there is no reason why the innocent should be made to suffer, and especially the people who have been lavish of their means and their blood in support of our cause. This war is the people's war. Their sons and brothers make up the army, and their means, and theirs alone, support and maintain it. And shall they not be allowed to know anything that is transpiring within that army? When their sons are maimed or slain in battle, shall they be denied the poor privilege of seeing a list of the killed and wounded? Is the army to be a sealed book to the country? Even in despotic France and monarchial England, literary men have been encouraged to accompany their armies, and to write freely of their movements; but it has been reserved for free (?) America alone to place a muzzle upon the Press.

Personally, I care nothing for the order. On the contrary, I am glad of an opportunity to return to my home in dear old Georgia. But I do regret its promulgation on account of the army, and the bleeding hearts at home, and General Beauregard himself, whom I have supported and defended for the last twelve month with whatsoever ability I possessed, and that, too, at times when I believed his course at least questionable.

Without the aid of the women, the Pulpit and the Press, the revolution in which we are engaged would long ere this have proved a lamentable failure. I, who have done least of all the writers from the army, can say this without presumption. This fact is patent to all the world, except the arrogant and silly officials in the civil and military service of the Government. And yet a "puff" as long as your finger would purchase from many of them permission to do and say almost what you please.

The truth is, a blunder was committed at Corinth on Thursday last, when the army marched out to attack the enemy, without having first made proper reconnoissances.—The movement was a failure, and it is now feared that the time has passed for *attacking* the enemy, whose position has been rendered next to impregnable. The obnoxious telegram in the Memphis Appeal did not reach here until after the enemy had been made aware of it. Any attempt, therefore, to saddle any part of the blame upon the correspondent in question is both unjust and disingenuous. A scape goat is wanted, however, and this writer has answered the occasion. Unfortunately, General Halleck does not look to the Confederate press for his information of our movements. Spies, dressed in the garb of citizens, enter and leave our lines without much difficulty, and desertions from the twelvemonths' regiments from the disaffected portions of Tennessee, are not unfrequent. In this way Halleck receives almost a daily report of our movements.

I have written thus plainly, not from any want of respect for Gen. Beauregard, whom I esteem as one of the most loyal and unselfish men of any country or age, but in vindication of the freedom of the Press, and of the rights and respectability of literary men everywhere.

There is but little to communicate in regard to the position of affairs here. The Federals are fast closing around us. It is reported, by an intelligent scout, that they have planted one of their heavy seige guns just across a swamp, and within one mile and a half of our work. Others will, doubtless, be got into position soon. Indeed, it is probable they will begin the work of shelling our camps before this week is out. They have also erected very strong defensive works, to guard against an attack by us.—*We must, therefore, go out and fight them in thier own strong positions, or submit be shelled in ours, or prepare to retire from Corinth.* No other alternative is left us.

P. W. A.

Northern News, Speculations, Gossip, and Lies.

Through the kindness of a friend near the Yankee lines, we are in possession of the Louisville *Journal* of the 24th May. It has a large amount of interesting matter in it, from which we take the following:

ANDY JOHNSON AND THE NASHVILLE BANKERS.

The several bankers and bank officers of Nashville were notified on Wednesday by Gov. Johnson, that they would be required to take the oath of allegiance. The *Dispatch* says it was stated, that, upon the notice being served upon Messrs. D. F. Carter and John Hartiford of the Bank of the Union, they peremptorily refused to take the oath, and were subsequently arrested. An officer of the Union Bank waited upon Gov. Johnson and informed him that the specie, and perhaps other assets belonging to that bank, were within the lines held by the Confederates, and that if they were required to take the oath, the stockholders being mainly Northern citizens, their specie would be confiscated by the Confederates. It is said that upon this representation Gov Johnson waived his requirement so far as it related to the officers of the Union Bank. The Planter's Bank is similarly situated with the Union Bank, and will, we presume, be treated by the Governor in the same manner. Mr. Porterfield, of the Traders' Bank, in an interview with the Governor, stated to him that the assets of his bank were almost wholly in the South, and that he could not take the oath. What the decision in his case was, the *Dispatch* did not learn. Neither did it learn what course the other banks and bankers intended pursuing. It heard that some of the banks, in anticipation probably that they would be closed up, had notified their depositors to draw out their deposits, which was being done.

REBEL THIEVES CAPTURED.—On Sunday last Major Brown, of Col. Williams' Ninth Regiment Pennsylvania Cavalry, with a squadron consisting of companies G and K, captured four men of Morgan's band near Allen's Springs. They had burned the house of a Union man and committed other depredations. They are now safely lodged in prison at Nashville. A portion of this fine Pennsylvania regiment has been for some time stationed at Gallatin, and has rendered very efficient service. Col. Williams, Lieut. Colonel James, Majors Jordan and Brown, are as fine officers as the Union has engaged in the holy cause of its preservation.

A TROPHY.—We have in our possession a fine specimen of the Porter repeating rifle, an eight-shooter, which was captured by the gallant Capt. Kurfis, of the Fourth Kentucky Cavalry, in the fight with Morgan's Cavalry at Lebanon, Tenn. The weapon belonged to Lieut. Shillman, one of Morgan's band

☞ It was rumored in Covington yesterday that the notorious secessionist, Judge Nutall, of Henry county, Kentucky, had been arrested at his home, near Springport, and conveyed to Louisville.

MORE TROOPS WANTED TO CRUSH THE REBELLION.—The Adjutant-General of Indiana issued an order on Thursday calling for an additional regiment of Infantry, in pursuance to a requisition from the President.

By Telegraph to the New York Times.

WASHINGTON, May 23d.—The War Department has called for no definite number of troops, but has re-opened the recruiting stations lately closed by order. Some new regiments will be raised for special service, as in Kentucky, for the Military Commandant appointed there. Beyond this, no formal call has been made on States for volunteers. The main object is to obtain a reserve to fill up existing regiments. The radicals exaggerate this matter.

The *Times'* Newbern correspondent states that attempts to raise a Union regiment in North Carolina progresses, but it is doubtful if more than one or two companies can be obtained.

SHOT.—We learn from the Richmond *Messenger*, that on Saturday night last, while Lieut. Sutton and a file of men, who were conveying six or seven prisoners of war from the Gap to Lexington, were stopping at Wm. Biggerstaff's, in Madison county, Benj. F. Richardson, (better known as Bud Richardson) a violent secessionist, rode up, and, it is said, created some disturbance, when he was shot by the guard. He died of his wounds the next day.

☞ P. W. Alexander, the army correspondent of the Savannah *Republican*, who writes over the initials P. W. A., says the Confederate loss at the battle of Shiloh on the 6th and 7th of April was fully 10,000 in killed, wounded, and missing.

☞ There has been an unusual demand for gold in this city for the past few days, with which to purchase cotton and other produce in Tennessee and North Carolina.

☞ In the late engagement with Morgan's Cavalry at Lebanon, Tenn., Jake Elderkin, a young man well known in this city, attached to Morgan's Cavalry, was shot and killed. A large sum in Confederate notes was found upon his person. Elderkin, it is stated, was killed by Henry Lamon, of this city, a member of Capt. Kurfis's Company of the Fourth Kentucky Cavalry

☞ All the Brigadier Generals, Colonels, Majors, and Captains of our armies profess the utmost anxiety to serve their country in the best way they can. Then let half of them resign immediately.

☞ The rebel Congress, after flying from Richmond, made a halt at Danville. We do not presume it will remain there, but, as its symptoms are so alarming, it will hurry home to Montgomery to die.

☞ The abolitionists are doing every thing in their power to make the Union's Southern friends its enemies.

☞ The rebels blew up the Merrimac when they saw that it was about to be captured. Isn't it about time for them to blow up their Confederacy?

THE INEFFICIENCY OF THE MORTAR FLEETS.—The mortar fleets on the Upper and Lower Mississippi cost a great deal of money and a great deal of time, and we think they have been very far from realizing general expectation. The general impression, before they were used in actual fight, was that a single bomb from one of them, exploding inside of a fort, would deal terrible destruction, and that half a dozen of the missiles would render any fort untenable, but the facts of the case turn out to be far different. The New York *World* says that 9,000 bombs were hurled at Forts Jackson and St. Philip, with scarcely any appreciable effect, as was proved by a subsequent examination of the forts by General Butler. Commodore Farragut could have passed the rebel defences with his sloops of war and gunboats as well on the first as on the sixth day of the bombardment; indeed, the only real damage the forts sustained was from his Parrott and Dahlgren guns. On the Upper Mississippi they have been equally ineffective, as witness Island No. 10 and Fort Wright. The official testimony of the engineers who planned the attack on Fort Pulaski was to the same effect; the rifled cannon alone were effective. This experience is that of all sieges in former times; bombs do very well to burn a large city, but are generally ineffective against earthworks and small forts, owing to the fact that they cannot be fired with a sufficient degree of accuracy, the slightest breeze baulking the most skilful aim. This war is repeating some old lessons in military operations as well as teaching us many valuable new ones.

CONFISCATION.

Our readers will recollect the confiscation bills before the Yankee Congress, full and intelligent abstracts of which we published a few days ago. They were discussed in the House of Representatives on the 23d inst. We extract the following:

The House resumed the consideration of the confiscation bills.

Mr. Sheffield argued that the first bill was, in effect, a bill of attainder, and it took property without due process of law. The second bill was for the emancipation of slaves This was in violation of the solemn pledge made in July last, not to interfere with the local institutions of the States. This breach of faith could not be justified on the ground of necessity, for the greatest necessities of the war were upon the country when we made that pledge. He (Sheffield) said the rebellion was to be put down by the army, not by legislation.

Mr. Sedgwick favored the employment of slaves to crush the rebellion, both of loyal and disloyal masters, compensating those of loyal masters, and giving freedom to those of rebel masters.

Mr. Mallery opposed confiscation, but favored the hanging of traitors, and offered a substitute to punish by fine and imprisonment all persons found guilty of aiding the enemy.

Mr. Blair favored confiscation, arguing that emancipation would accomplish nothing. He opposed an army of negroes, but favored colonizing them.

A Valuable Work.

The Charleston Courier, of the 2nd inst. says:

"We observe in the Atlanta *Confederacy*, in process of publication, a work entitled "a Handbook of Miscellaneous Information for Soldiers and Officers, by Major John M. Richardson."

Judging from the numbers already published, we safely pronounce it a work highly interesting and useful to all readers in or out of service. The work will be published in book form.

THURSDAY, JUNE 5, 1862.

The Battle of Chickahominy.

It would seem that the battle was between only a small portion of the respective forces. The battle of Sunday would seem to have between the commands of Gen. Longstreet on our side, and Gen. Keyes on the other—and that neither McClellan nor Johnston participated in the fight. It was only a skirmish, so to speak—a desperate set to between a portion of the hostiles forces, to test the spirit and fighting qualities of each, and is only a prelude to the mighty shock that is to come off when the two great armies come in collision. If we can get a fair fight we have no fears whatever.

The Boston Bankers and the Currency.

We extract the following from the Washington dispatches to the N. Y. "Herald" of the 21st May, now before us:

"The late resolution of the Boston Bankers, that the General Government is hereafter to furnish the currency of the country, is regarded at the Treasury Department as a pretty correct one. One hundred millions of dollars of demand notes are now out, and there is authority for issuing sixty millions more. Congress will doubtless authorise the issue of further amounts, as the public needs may require of them. It is desired that there shall be notes of a less denomination than five dollars. The necessities of trade may call for a currency circulating medium of three or four hundred million of Treasury paper, and for this form of government indebtedness there will be no demand for payment of either principal or interest. In this matter Gov. Chase has done a great service to the State.

Gen. Mitchell Issues an Order.

HEAD QUARTERS, THIRD DIVISION,
CAMP TAYLOR, HUNTSVILLE, ALA.,
May 2d, 1862.

To the Citizens of Alabama,
North of the Tennessee River:

Armed citizens have fired into my trains on the railway, have burned bridges, have attempted to throw my engines from the track, have attacked my guards, have cut the telegraph wires. All these acts will be punished with death, if the perpetrators can be found; and if they cannot, I will destroy the property of all who sympathise with the Southern rebellion in the neighborhood where these acts were committed.

Unorganized leaders have no right to make war. They are outlaws, robbers, plunderers and murderers, and will be treated as such.

O. M. MITCHELL,
Maj. Gen. Commanding 3d Division of the Army of the Ohio.

Corinth Evacuated.

We learn that Corinth is evacuated. Beauregard and all the army and stores have fallen back on the Mobile Railroad, to Rienzi, 12 miles. There was a considerable engagement on Wednesday last between the enemy and a portion of our troops, which was intended only to cover our retreat. All our stores and arms were successfully removed.

Before falling back, the enemy's cavalry came down upon our rear, to Booneville, the next station this side of Rienzi, and burnt up a train of thirty cars, two of which were laden with ammunition. The depot was also burnt.

A guard of 80 men were left to guard the place while the Yankee cavalry went out to commit further depredations. These 80 men were captured.

Our forces have good water and every advantage of position in a fight. Corinth was burned.

☞ We have before us the Mo. *Republican* of the 21st May. From it we see that Gen. Halleck has expelled all newspaper correspondents from his army, the same as Beauregard. It took place three days before Beaugard's order was promulgated.

Col. Morgan.

This gallant partisan chief arrived here last evening. He was greeted by an immense and enthusiastic throng at the depot. They called on him for a speech, but he thanked them for the compliment, and begged them to excuse him, as he was *not a politician.*

Army Telegraphs.

We see from the New York "Herald" of the 21st, now before us, that a telegraph line has been built from Fortress Monroe to Gen. McClellan's Head Quarters on the Chickahominy, so that he has direct communication with the War Department.

Whistling to Keep the Courage.

Prentice, in his Journal of May 24th tries to keep up the courage of the Northern people in reference to the expected fight at Corinth, on this wise:

Our whole country has confidence in Gen. Halleck. He is cool, brave, and scientific: There is no quality of a great chieftain that he lacks. Every great undertaking of his life has been successful, and genius, and his judgment. He now seems to be moving upon Beauregard in the same manner adopted by McClellan at Yorktown, and with the same certainty of success.

With respect to the efficiency of the national army, a correspondent of the St. Louis Democrat writes that nothing better could be wished. It is healthy, well armed, and disciplined, and supplied in the most ample and effective manner. When we add to this that Gen. Halleck has at the heads of his several corps, Pope, whose splendid strategy captured the entire rebel army at Island No. 10; Buell, whose magnificent fighting retrieved the fortunes of the day at Shiloh; Mitchell, whose brilliant campaign cleared out Northern Alabama like a lightning flash; and Thomas, the victor at Mill Spring, where the tide of victory was first effectively turned in favor of the Union arms; when these facts are considered, those who are apprehensive because movements are slow will be convinced that they are not slow without good purpose, and that we have both the army and the Generals at Corinth to make triumph certain

Special Correspondence of the Lynchburg Republican.

From Gen. Jackson's Command.

THE BATTLE OF FRONT ROYAL AND WINCHESTER.

Interesting Particulars by a Participant.

CAMP SIX MILES NORTH
OF WINCHESTER,
Sunday, May 25th, 1862.

Dear Republican:—We met the enemy at Front Royal, Warren county, Va., on Friday evening. He made but a short stand. The first Maryland Volunteers on the Yankee side, was charged by the first regiment of Maryland rebels who put their old acquaintances to flight in a short time, capturing a stand of colors, killing several and taking a number of prisoners, who were recognised by many old acquaintances.

We took the enemy by surprise and put them to flight before one-fourth of our forces had entered the town. The cavalry, among which were the Wise Troop and Jack Alexander's company, charged upon the Yankees in the retreat, killing many and capturing a large number of prisoners. Ashby's and Stuart's cavalry did good work by taking two railroad trains, which were loaded with provisions, and bringing in prisoners all day Friday.

The number of prisoners captured, as well as I could learn and see, amounted to about eleven hundred, most of whom are Marylanders.

We also captured a large amount of stores and arms. Among the latter are about 500 improved cavalry six-shooters, an article very much needed.

I am told that the stores captured amount to $300,000 to 400,000. We also took three pieces of artillery.

When we entered Front Royal, the women and children met us with shouts of the liveliest joy. As we passed through the place in double quick, we could not stop to partake of the hospitality so generously and profusely tendered on all hands.

On Saturday, at early dawn, we were again on the march to pay Gen. Banks a visit, who was encamped at Strasburg, twelve miles distant. After reconnoitering for several hours, Col. Ashby's cavalry marched down the road leading to Middletown, which is six miles in the rear of Strasburg, and General Ewell's command down the road to Newton, twelve miles in the rear of Strasburg. At 2 o'clock a courier reported that Banks was on the retreat, and had passed Middletown, but that two regiments of cavalry were still left behind at Strasburg and Middletown, as a baggage guard.

Gen. Ed Johnson's division, under the command of Brigadier General Elzey, was at once ordered down the road to Middletown, to pursue the enemy. On our march we met detachment after detachment of Ashby's men with prisoners and horses. Among one of the squads of prisoners, about twenty in number, was a woman, mounted. When we came to the Valley turnpike we found hosts of prisoners, and the road blockaded with dead and live horses, and wagons heavy laden with subsistence, &c., together with dead and wounded Yankees.

We pushed on our column for about eleven miles, when we halted for a few hours. We then learned that Banks had passed the road leading into the Valley pike near Newton, where Ewell's command had entered the road. Skirmishing was then kept up until a late hour of the night, and at about 8 o'clock in the morning we halted within three miles of Winchester.

We found along the road about 100 wagons loaded with baggage, together with a number of boats (not of the gunboat order) on wheels, which Banks had destroyed for fear of their falling into our hands.

At early dawn this (Sunday) morning, we advanced and attacked the mighty Banks in front of Winchester. After fighting about one hour, distributing shell and minnie balls profusely, our boys made a charge when the Yankees left at double quick, after setting fire to the town and burning their commissary stores.

The Lee Battery of Lynchburg, and two others were ordered to pursue in a gallop, and the command was obeyed, they shelling the enemy for five miles.

When the army passed through the town, men, women, and children were shouting, "thank God we are free—thank God we are free once more!" Confederate flags and white handkerchiefs were waved from every window, and the happy smiles of lovely women on all sides met the wearied soldier and cheered him as he hurriedly passed through the place in pursuit of the flying foe.

After pursuing the enemy for six miles we were brought to a halt, and left the finishing stroke to the cavalry, who have captured a large number of prisoners who have been sent in through the day. The final result of the achievements are yet unknown.

Prisoners tell me that Gen. Banks has said that he was afraid that he would have to surrender his whole command, and to be relieved of the painful necessity and to save his own bacon, left before day on an extra car.

The fire in the town was extinguished by our boys after the commissary stores were destroyed, but we succeeded in saving all of the medical stores and ammunition, both of which were very large. We also secured the depot and a train of cars, both of which were well filled with provisions.

The Yankees left behind all their knapsacks, a large quantity of arms which they threw away, and lots of trinkets, which the boys have been examining all day.

Having been on the march for 22 days, and all of the previous night, our General "Stonewall" allowed us to go into camp to rest, but I guess we will be off again in the morning in pursuit of the Yankees.

In neither of the engagements we have not had one-fourth, no, not one sixth of our forces engaged, and I cannot see why the enemy have fled in such confusion after so short a stand.

We recaptured a large number of stolen negroes. The Yankees had married a number of the women and were taking them home with them. I have seen some that refused to go, and others that had been forced off at other times that had returned.

At Front Royal we captured 1,470 prisoners, and eight or nine hundred at Winchester, and numbers from points north are being hourly brought in.

At Strasburg we took six pieces of artillery.

W. W. H.

TAYLOR'S HOTEL,
WINCHESTER, VA., May 28, '62.

This beautiful inland town has assumed quite a lively appearance since we drove the detested Yankees from its vicinity, and the people are once more breathing the air of freemen and not of slaves. To-day I heard a lady say that she was once more free, and the *niggers* were *niggers* again.

Up to this time we have captured, and have in this place, between 3,000 and 4,000 prisoners; and I am told that 1100 more of the Hessians have been captured near Harper's Ferry and Martinsburg.

We have now in this place 8,000 stand of arms, taken since we entered Front Royal, besides a number of pieces of artillery, together with the largest quantity of the best ammunition of all grades that I have ever beheld.

The medical stores captured are estimated by the druggists of this place to be worth at least $200,000. Among them are articles very scarce in the Confederacy and much needed by the government. We captured 500 pounds opium and 200 gallons castor oil, both of which are greatly needed, and have been shipped to the hospitals in Lynchburg.

To-day news was received that the Yankees had burnt the depot at Charlestown, together with all the stores.

A portion of the army moved this evening, and it is reported that the balance will follow in the morning. Their destination is unknown, but the impression prevails that they will not stop until the State of Maryland is free. God grant that it may be so.

During the sojourn of the Yankees in this place the people were not allowed to communicate with any one, either North or South, without the letters being first scrutinized by the Provost Marshal, and no Virginian who would not take the oath of allegiance was allowed to purchase goods from the North or elsewhere; but Yankee importers did all the business, and upon our approach on Sunday morning, left at double quick, leaving behind all the stocks of goods. Some few Jews were permitted to traffic who had the audacity to refuse our money for merchandize, but old Stonewall has had them all arrested, and their goods, like those of their Northern friends, have been confiscated, and their dens closed.

BY TELEGRAPH

(Private Dispatch.)

RICHMOND, June 3.

James Ormond, Esq.:

Corporal Stewart, and privates Ravel, Wooten and Haralson wounded slightly—none killed in Company "A," 19th Reg. Ga. Vols., in the action of Saturday.

J. M. JOHNSTON, Capt.

(Private Dispatch.)

RICHMOND, June 3.

Mr. E. R. Sasseen:

Inform Mrs. A. E. Black, of Carrollton, Ga., that Capt. Black, 19th Ga. Vols., was killed Saturday evening. His body is in possession of the enemy. If recovered, it will be forwarded. Also, Harry Bridges and Dock Boyle were killed. Barney Thompson, wounded in the leg. W. F. Garrison and James Holcombe, missing.

J. C. BENSON, Lieut.

RICHMOND, June 3.—All quiet along the lines to-day. The clouds threaten heavy rain to-night.

SECOND DISPATCH.

The only incident on the lines to-day was the advance of a regiment of Yankees reconnoitering, while our troops were engaged in strengthening their position. The 12th Va. moved forward, when the enemy receded in double-quick.

Gen. Lee issued an address to the army to-day, which had a fine effect. There will be no more retreating. The watch-word is, "*Victory or death.*"

(No *more* retreating! Private dispatches speak of some being killed, and in the *hands of the enemy*. The question arises, Were we defeated on Sunday? We ought to know, but are not allowed to.—Eds. Confed.

Infamous Letter from the Governor of Massachusetts—The Arming of Negroes Advocated.

COMMONWEALTH OF MASSACHUSETTS,
EXECUTIVE DEPRTMENT,
Boston, May 19, 1862.

Hon. Edwin M. Stanton, Secretary of War:

SIR—I have this moment received a telegram in these words, viz:

"The Secretary of War desires to know how soon you can raise and organise thee or four more infantry regiments and have them ready to be forwarded here to be armed and equipped? Please answer immediately, and state the number you can raise.

(Signed) L. THOMAS, Ad. Gen."

A call so sudden and unexpected finds me without materials for an intelligent reply. Our young men are all pre-occupied with other views; still, if a real call for three regiments is made, I believe we can raise them in forty days. The arms and equipments would need to be furnished here. Our people have never marched without them. They go into camp while forming into regiments, and are drilled, and practiced with arms, and march as soldiers. To attempt the other course would be to dampen enthusiasm, and make the men feel that they were not soldiers, but a mob.

Again, if our people feel that they are going into the South to help fight rebels, who will kill and destroy them by all means known to savages as well as civilized men, who will drive them by fraudulent flags of truce and lying pretences, as they did Massachusetts boys at Williamsburg; will use their negro slaves against them both as laborers and as well as fighting men, while they themselves must never fire at the enemy's magazine, I think they will feel the draft is heavy on their patriotism; but if the President will sustain Gen. Hunter, to cognize all men, *even black men*, as legally capable of loyalty, which the black are waiting to manifest—and let them fight with God and human nature on their side—the roads will swarm, if need be, with a multitude whom New England would pour out to obey your call.

Always ready to do my utmost, I remain most respectfully your obedient servant,

(Signed) JNO. A. ANDREW

Latest War News.

Since going to press, we have learned by telegraph of another splendid victory achieved by the invincible Stonewall Jackson—this time upon the soil of Maryland. Banks, reinforced by 10,000 troops from Washington, made a stand near Williamsport. Jackson attacked him and routed him, taking three thousand prisoners, and is now persuing the repeatedly vanquished Federal army towards Washington. The unfaltering career and unbroken success of this distinguished General are conspiring to make him the hero of this war.—*Knoxville Reg* 3d inst.

☞ See our new terms

The New-York Times.

VOL. XI—NO. 3346. NEW-YORK, FRIDAY, JUNE 13, 1862. PRICE TWO CENTS.

THE PURSUIT OF JACKSON.

Further Particulars of the Battle of Cross Keys.

Jackson Very Badly Defeated by Gen. Fremont.

The Dead and Wounded Left on the Field.

Flight of the Rebels on Sunday Night.

Advance of Gen. Fremont to Port Republic on Monday.

Communication with General Shields to be Opened.

The Casualties in the Battle of Sunday.

FREMONT'S HEADQUARTERS, PORT REPUBLIC, Va., June 9, 1862.

The army advanced early this morning in line of battle, but finding no enemy proceeded in column through the woods and over the country to Port Republic. Everywhere were evidences of the completeness of yesterday's success. The battle was fought at Cross Keys, and therefore takes that name. The rebel loss was greatly superior to ours. They left their dead and many wounded on the field. Not less than 500 dead were found and many wounded. Two of their guns were left behind, which we captured this morning.

Capt. DUNKKA, of Gen. FREMONT'S Staff, was killed Capt. GITTERMAN, of CLUSERET'S Staff, was severely wounded. No other staff officers were wounded. The rebel wounded were found in every house along the road. Ambulances, wagons, arms and clothing strewed the field. Forty of our wounded, taken prisoners, were left in a church, and were retaken. The Sixth Louisiana lost all but 30 men. The enemy retreated till midnight, and this morning their rear guard crossed the Shenandoah at this place and burnt the bridge.

REPORT OF GEN. FREMONT.

HEADQUARTERS, MOUNTAIN DEPARTMENT, PORT REPUBLIC, June 9,—12 M., via MARTINSBURGH, 12th.

To Hon. Edwin M. Stanton, Secretary of War:

There was no collision with the enemy after dark last night. This morning we renewed the march against him, entering the woods in battle order, his cavalry appearing on our flanks, Gen. BLENKER had the left, Gen. MILROY the right, and Gen. SCHENCK the centre, with a reserve of Gen. STAHL'S brigade and Gen. BAYARD'S. The enemy was found to be in full retreat on Port Republic, and our advance found his rear guard barely across the river, and the bridge in flames. Our advance came in so suddenly that some of his officers remaining on this side, escaped with the loss of their horses.

A cannonading during the forenoon apprised us of an engagement, and I am informed here that JACKSON attacked Gen. SHIELDS this morning, and, after a severe engagement, drove him down the river, and is now in pursuit. I have sent an officer, with a detachment of cavalry, to open communication with Gen. SHIELDS.

This morning detachments were occupied in searching the grounds covered by yesterday's action at Cross Keys, for our remaining dead and wounded. I am not yet fully informed, but think that 125 will cover our loss in killed, and 500 that in wounded.

The enemy's loss we cannot clearly ascertain. He was engaged during the night carrying off his dead and wounded in wagons. This morning on our march upwards of 200 of his dead were counted in one field, the greater part badly mutilated by cannon shot. Many of his dead were also scattered through the woods, and many had been already buried. A number of prisoners had been taken during the pursuit.

I regret to have lost many good officers. Gen. STAHL'S Brigade was in the hottest part of the field, which was the left wing. From the beginning of the fight the brigade lost in officers 5 killed and 17 wounded; and one of his regiments alone, the Eighth New-York, has buried 65. The Garibaldi Guard, next after, suffered most severely, and following this regiment, the Forty-fifth New-York, the Bucktail Rifles, of Gen. BAYARD'S Brigade, and Gen. MILROY'S Brigades.

One of the Bucktail Companies has lost all of its officers, commissioned and non-commissioned. The loss in Gen. SCHENCK'S Brigade was less, although he inflicted severe loss on the enemy, principally by artillery fire.

Of my Staff, I lost a good officer killed, Capt. NICHOLAS DUNKKA. Many horses were killed in our batteries, which the enemy repeatedly attempted to take, but were repulsed by canister fire generally.

I feel myself permitted to say that all our troops, by their endurance of this severe march, and their splendid conduct in the battle, are entitled to the President's commendations, and officers throughout behaved with great gallantry and efficiency, which requires that I should make particular mention of them, and which, I trust, will receive the particular notice of the President as soon as possible. I will send in a full report; but, in this respect, I am unable to make any more particular distinction than that pointed out in the description of the battle.

Respectfully, J. C. FREMONT, Major-General Commanding.

LIST OF KILLED AND WOUNDED

STAHL'S BRIGADE.

REPORT OF THE FORTY-FIFTH REGIMENT NEW-YORK VOLUNTEERS, OF KILLED, WOUNDED AND MISSING.

A. Kist, Co. B—slightly. J. Bender, Co. D—slightly. D. Lutjen, Co. K—killed. Sgt. F. Schader, Co. K—wounded. F. Kirk, Co. K—wounded. Carl John, Co. K—slightly. S. Schmidt, Co. K—slightly. A. Thomas, Co. K—slightly. Lieut. Czermely and Lieut. Durban—slightly. F. Stadler, Co. D—slightly. Lieut. Spangenberg, Co. F—killed. H. Dietz, Co. G—slightly. 1st Lt. Grassau, Co. K—seriously. B. Horming, Co. K—killed. M. Burkhard, Co. K—killed.

Nineteen privates are missing.

Total—35, killed, wounded and missing.

(Signed,) G. VON AMSBERG, Col. Forty-fifth Reg't N. Y. Vols.

LIST OF KILLED, WOUNDED AND MISSING OF THE TWENTY-SEVENTH REGIMENT PENNSYLVANIA VOLUNTEERS, COL. A. BURBECK, COMMANDING.

Killed.

Lieut. F. Leuders, Co. A. Sergt. Erans Faust, Co. A. Wm. Stroh, Co. A. Ludwig Oehns, Co. B. Corp. G. Grees, Co. B. Edward Roeth, Co. G. Fred. Pflugfelder, Co. G. Sergt. T. Kirhne, Co. H. Geo. Theiss, Co. H. Wm. Rauscher, Co. H. Abraham Hunter, Co. I. Fredk Withrock, Co. I. Hugh McGiverin, Co. K.

Wounded.

Leopold Gross, Co. A. Christian Wenzel, Co. A. Gustave Rechtep, Bach. Co. A. Phillip Lang, Bach. Co. Sgt. John A. Steens, Co. A. Corp. Henry Meyer, Co. A. Fred. Bodenstein, Co. B. Adam Wildner, Co. B. Joseph Hensel, Co. B. Geo. Biefreiter, Co. B. Paul Pranger, Co. C. Bernhd. Rossling, Co. C. Oscar Werter. Henry Springer, Co. D. Jos. Schepperle, Co. E. Jacob Schomaker. Jacob Stripler. Louis Milleck. Herrm. Miller. Corp. Abram Gotwals, Co. K. Wm. Mayall, Co. G. Emanuel Heist. George Collen. Capt. Dagebert Hujus, Co. G. Corp. Blumenthal, Co. H. Herrmann Schneider. Schoen Hunnzehuenn. E. Schoenemann, Co. C. Fred. Sellemair, Co. C. Sebastian Winter, Co. C. Sgt. Robt. Wagner, Co. C. John Bieswanger, Co. C. Abraham Dusch, Co. D. John Eiding. Chas. Kupke. Wm. Lindermann. John Markert. John Silberzahn. Frederick Stierle. Capt. Albert Heubel, Co. H—slightly. Otto Schmidt, Co. I. Leonhard Hoffmann. Jacob Briel. Jos. Schwindinger. Fredk. Hasher. Corp. Wm. H. Hughes, Co. I. Chas. Dougherty, Co. K. George W. Emery. George Eddes. Jesse Rinheuer. John Hillebrand. Chris. Schmidt, Co. K. Wm. Mitchell, Co. H.

Total, 13 killed, 56 wounded.

LIST OF OFFICERS AND MEN OF THE DE KALB REGIMENT—KILLED, WOUNDED AND MISSING.

Killed.

August Lea, Co. A.

Wounded.

Col. Leopold Von Gilsa. Or, Mr. August Rachel. August Konoguisky, Co. A. August Doerges, Co. A.

Missing.

Fred. Schmidt, Co. A. Henry Kohn, Co. A. Henry Meldt, Co. A. Frantz Mayer, Co. A. John Anderson, Co. A. Gottleib Haerle, Co. A.

(Signed,) DETLER VON KINSIDEL, Major-Com'g Regt., (De Kalb.)

WOUNDED AND MISSING IN THE GARIBALDI GUARD.

First Co.—Privates Valentin Szamjeszky, wounded; Chas. Stader, wounded; Chas. Back, missing.

Second Co.—First Lieut. Lescina, killed; Orderly Sergeant Chas. Meurel, wounded; Sergeant Lorentz, wounded; Privates Valentin Gibel wounded, Henvut wounded, Hintze wounded, Canon wounded, Breis missing, Budein missing, Hahn missing, Richter missing.

Third Co.—Capt. Venuti wounded, Giovanni Riggioni wounded, Jean Maria Olivri wounded.

Fourth Co.—Sergeant Jacob Cordet killed, Sergeant Matthias Monis wounded; Privates Heinrich Krabbe wounded, Albert Schwarzenberg wounded, Johan Hirsch wounded, Ferd. Leibnitz wounded, Heinrich Kempf wounded, Gottlieb Speck wounded, Heinrich Hochheimer missing, Jacob Matthias wounded.

Fifth Co.—First Lieut. Albert Jordan, wounded; Corp. Albert Mehl, killed; Sergt. Gustav Kauffmann, wounded; Corp. Chas. Sihling, wounded; Privates Heinrich Backer, wounded; Heinrich Scheiber, wounded; John Stefan, wounded; Joseph Weil, wounded; Wm. Ebeling, wounded; Gottlieb Kallenbach, wounded; Louis Lange, wounded.

Sixth Co.—Private Bernhard Weber, wounded.

Eighth Co.—Private Augustus Murton, wounded.

Ninth Co.—Private Antonie Fernander, wounded.

Tenth Co.—Second Lieut. Louis Riege, wounded; Private Louis Roth.

First Lieut. Keassau, of the Forty-fifth Regiment, wounded. Acted for a quarter of an hour in this Company. The horse of Acting Adjt. First Lieut. A. Shada was killed.

Killed, 3; wounded, 35; missing, 6. Total, 44.

PENNSYLVANIA BUCKTAILS, DETAILED TO GEN. STAHL'S COMMAND.

Killed. Corp. H. Hadley, Co. I.

Wounded. Capt. McDonald, commanding Battalion—face. Lieut. B. B. Rice, Co. I—arm. Chas. Millsen—shoulder. Frank West—shoulder. Sam. Beckwith—arm. Albert Leighly—arm. John Mucklehaney, Co. C—leg. Ed. G. Debeck, Co. G—leg.

COL. CLURIRET'S BRIGADE.

SIXTIETH OHIO, COL. TRIMBLE.

Killed. 1st Lt. Jas. M. Vance, Co. H. Jas. Gabriel, Co. K. Wm. Dodge, Co. C.

Wounded. Jos. Erwin, Co. A. H. B. Haughins, Co. B. Geo. Bowman, Co. K. Capt. Gittman, Staff—shoulder.

EIGHTH VIRGINIA—COL. LOESHER.

Killed. —— Rose, Co. I. J. Anderson, Co. F.

Wounded. H. F. Clark, Co. I—severely. Ch. Grass, Co. H—severely. C. Ballard, Co. I—severely. R. Bogast, Co. J. J. Cantly, Co. H—slightly. J. Ballard, Co. I—slightly. Wm. Turner, Co. I—slightly. —— Baldwin, Co. E—slightly.

MILROY'S BRIGADE.

SECOND VIRGINIA, COL. LATHAM.

Killed—Jonathan Benny, Co. H; Wm. Manil, Co. K.

Wounded—Second Lieut. Bellingsly, Co. I; Aaron Hollingshead, Co. K, seriously, thigh amputated; John Rhodes, Co. B; Saml. A. Sams, Co. K; Henry Heiser, Co. A.

THIRD VIRGINIA, COL. HUGHES.

Killed—Privates W. W. Cole, Co. A; John Frederick, Co. A; David Spangler, Co. B; Jas. Phillips, Co. [illegible].

Wounded—Privates T. Harrington, Co. A, severely; Jas. McGraw, Co. A, severely; F. Flanagan, Co. B, slightly; Jacob E. Irvin, Co. C, severely; Thos. McManan, Co. C, slight; Corporal M. B. Orr, Co. E, slight; Sergeant Chapman McCoy, Co. E, slight; Felix Bend, Co. E, slight; Elisha Martin, Co. E, slight; Wesley Moody, slight; Frances Reqrood, Co. E, slight; Jenny Hess, Co. E, slight; Sergeant R. G. Cather, Co. F, slight; Wm. Powell, Co. F, slight; A. C. Husted, Co. G, severe; B. Gehd, Co. I, severe.

EIGHTH REGIMENT NEW-YORK VOLUNTEERS.

Co. A.—Dead—Privates Breitbarth, Filer, Grothe, Greib, Henkel, Huf, Strauss. Wounded and Missing—Second Lieut. Bruck, Sergt. Baumann, Privates Behnck, Bohman, Grass, Geiger, Hartmann, Volt, Voitander. Wounded.—First Lieut. Gest. Corps. Fischer, Schoen, Lenzen, Bugler Heyer, Privates Amend, Becker, Bremer, Evert, Fischback, Briel, Graff, Hoffmann, Kaeppen, Sieberding, Rossler, Schwenk, Taechl, Tinnes, Wahrmuth.

Co. B.—Dead—Sergt. Luchinger, Corp. Gundelach Corp. Christ, Bugler Bretteraitz; Privates, Lewis Scheilhass, Pauli, Dautermann, Motz, Friedman. Wounded—Capt Pauli, Sergt. Wolff, Sergt. Muller, Corp. Barth; Privates Borchert, Seele, Baumann, Schnabel, Kosmina, Fred Hansen, Frank Fisher, Koss, Herboldt, Scheaffer, Lunt, Dutmann, Dutting, Heringen, Dahlmann, Rebteck, Futterer. Wounded and Missing—Second Lieut. Lehner, Corp. Dur or Dit; Privates Astheimer, Fusse, Kroecker, Fuchs, Brockman, Hagendorf, Newbauer, Paulsen, Nielsen.

Co. C.—Dead—Sergeant Lange, Corporal Ney, Corporal Nickel, Privates Schultz, Lambert, Kastritz. Missing and Wounded—Sergeant Meyer, Privates Faber, Weiss, Valentin, Satterer. Wounded—Corporal Koebler. Privates Mitchell, Pfeiffer, Knoz, Furst, Rudolph, Gross, Rohl, Scheuten, Philipsen, Fuhl, Weiss, Gruba, Grupe, Hand, Henning, Hartmann, Ettesberger.

Co. G.—Dead—Bugler Pfeller, Privates Schiner, Neuman, Oeikers, Schwerdt. Wounded—Second Lieut. Kinzel, Corporal Kliermann, Privates Obenningen, Huber, Loecher, Mohr, Schneider, Sauer, Hackenger, Gamerdinger. Missing—Privates Seitz, Schaum, Weaker.

Co. H.—Killed—Corp. Schurmann, private Wullenhorst. Wounded—Second Lieut. Wilhelm, Corp. Tack, Corp. Gimpel, Corp. Kron, privates Riesling, Lesser, Peters, Peeliffer, Schuliem, Sandhammer, Thurn. Missing—Sergt. Weilezahl, privates Ackermann, Berg, Schroeder.

Co. D.—Dead—Privates Kempff, Wolff, Franke. Wounded—Bugler Klotz, privates Schweinle, Bosse, Feibel, Grassman, Gries, Groeschel, Hahn, Energer, Kammerer, Knoll, Kranz, Lockle, Noerling, Rauscher, Schneider, Woerner, Kirschmeyer. Missing—Privates Ruhrold, Ulmann, Laser.

Co. E.—Killed—Corp. Schultz, Corp. Kraemer, Private Kaufman. Wounded—Orderly Sergt. Kahlbeyer, Sergt. David, Corp. Hupl, Corp. Lieltke, Corp. Lindner, Privates Sauter, Meyer Alek, Meyer Aug, Pfeiffer, Pfaff, Epple, Baake, Martens, Thier. Missing—Sergt. Schenk. Privates L. Kraus, Clark, Pielman, Schmidt.

Co. F.—Killed—Sergt. Thies, Corp. Behne, Corp. Ahrens, Corp. Heincke, Privates Dicht, Schwantz, Schonheim, Wauldhauer. Wounded—Sergt. Schneider, Corp. Grunder, Freunds, Corp. Olding, Baldauf, Dicht, Grimm, Juagmann, Lambert, Slemmihl, Weidmann, Brillmayer, Schunbrandt. Missing—Privates Meister, Ramas.

Co. K.—Killed—Corp. Heller, Private Bernhander. Wounded—Sergt. Bautsch, Privates Lutz, Matzel, Fickel, Zimer, Joseph, Branedschaus. Missing—Private Fallesen.

Co. I.—Wounded (no killed)—Privates Albert Schellhoun, Martin Schlemaer, Henry Weimer, Louis Otti.

TWENTY-FIFTH OHIO, COMMANDED BY LIEUT.-COL. RICHARDSON, (ONLY 250 MEN ENGAGED.)

Killed—Privates John J. Eastham, Co. B; T. S. H. Russell, Co. C; Jesse Little, Co. E; Geo. Wilson, Co. G; Corp. Friend P. Wilson, Co. I.

Wounded.

Capt. I. F. Charlesworth, Co. A, mortally; Sergeant [illegible] White, Co. A, slightly; Joseph Acres, Co. A, severely; Wm. Harrison, Co. A, slightly; Sergeant James D. [illegible], Co. B, slightly; private Samuel White, Co. B, severely; Sergeant Alonzo P. Henthorn, Co. C, severely; J. L. Hopper, mortally; Amida Province, Co. C, slightly; Fred Woodly, Co. C, severely; Joel Spoon, Co. E, severely; Charles Slaughterback, Co. E, slightly; J. H. Whitten, Co. F, severely; Patrick Burke, Co. F, severely; Michael Cantwell, Co. F, slightly; Sergeant A. A. Lambkin, Co. G, severely; Corporal H. H. Ogden, Co. G, severely; Corporal Samuel Baughman, Co. G, severely; Corporal W. J. Kyle, Co. G, slightly; Coonrod Smith, Co. G—severely; Ely T. Beard, Co. G—severely; Geo. Longstreet, Co. G—severely; L. W. Getta, Co. G—severely; M. O. Robinson, A. Myer, Co. G—slightly; J. N. Cline, Co. G—slightly; S. L. Kain, Co. G, Sg't J. Renny, Co. I—severely; W. H. Orton, Co. I, R. S. Gant, Co. C, D. McCulloch, Co. C, Seneca C. Rogers, Co. C—slightly; Samuel Cahand, Co. C, E. T. Lovet, Co. C, Coonrod Baum, Co. K—severely; C. A. Smith, Co. K—severely; C. M. Cass, Co. K—slightly; Michael Herbert, W. H. Coprer, R. Crawford, James Jones, Co. K—slightly.

Missing.

Wm. Mackey, Co. E; A. J. Collins, Co. I.

FIFTH VIRGINIA, COL. ZEIGLER.

Killed.

Thos. Stafford, Co. G; John Magraw, Co. H; John B. Craft, Co. I; Andy Lawrence, Color Bearer, Co. B; John Lenz, Co. H; Harris Flim, Co. H.

Wounded.

Capt. McFadden, Co. A, in thigh; Lieut. Kirkpatrick, Co. A, hand; A. C. Adams, Co. E, arm; S. Spann, Co. E, hand; L. Leffingwell, Co. E, face; Jacob Collins, Co. F, arm; T. T. Sparling, Co. A, arm; Thos. McKnight, Co. A, thigh; W. Daniels, Co. E, thigh; T. Duncan, Co. E, thigh; Robt. Flagg, Co. I, thigh; John Fudge, Co. E, shoulder; H. Thompson, Co. F, hip; Martin Freely, Co. F, foot; Jas. Defor, Co. H, both thighs; Jas. Dennison, Co. H, side and arm; T. O'Brien, Co. I, foot; Wm. Evex, Co. H, wrist.

PLAN OF THE BATTLE OF FAIR OAKS.

Sketch of the Battle-ground of "Fair Oaks," or the Seven Pines, on May 31, 1862, by Lieut. E. Walter West, A. D. C. to Brigadier-General Casey. Drawn Especially for the New-York Times.

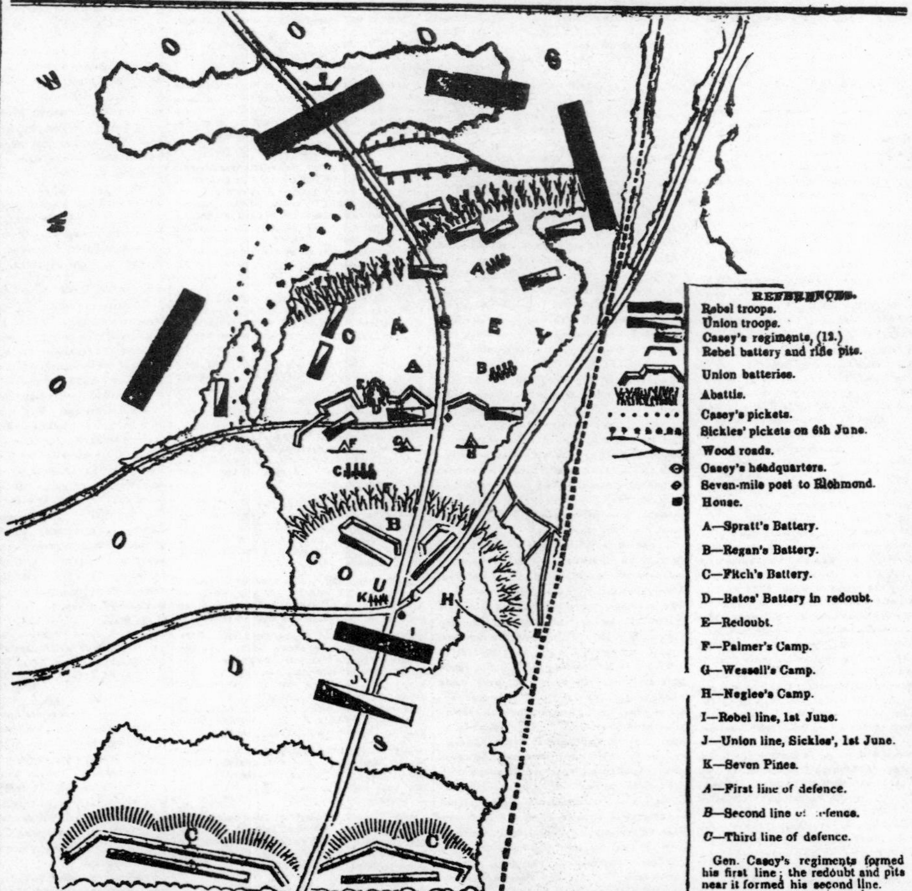

DEPARTMENT OF THE SHENANDOAH

The Floods—Gen. Banks' Headquarters at Winchester—Jackson's Force 60,000 Strong—Sigel Serenaded.

WINCHESTER, Saturday June 7.

The Potomac and Shenandoah Rivers are higher than for ten years previous, retarding the movements of the army corps under Gen. BANKS. The loss of the bridge at Harper's Ferry, and the impossibility of crossing with safety, cut off our supply trains, as well as a portion of the troops, and compelled Quartermasters to supply the troops by way of Cumberland. Yesterday, however, the supply trains of Gen. WILLIAMS' Division succeeded in getting over at Williamsport, and Gen. GREENE'S Brigade will cross to-day. There is no rail transportation between here and Harper's Ferry, the bridge over the Opequan having been destroyed, and the embankment at Shenandoah City washed away. The telegraph along the same route has been partially destroyed. Thus we are, just at present, cut off from any regular communication with the East.

Gen. FREMONT, at last accounts was at Mount Jackson pursuing the rebel force up the valley. Gen. SHIELDS after leaving Middletown, went up the Luray Valley as far as Elk Run, or Swift Run Gap, but failing to overtake or cut off the enemy, in consequence of the bridges having been destroyed, returned toward Front Royal. Beyond doubt JACKSON has escaped with but little loss. Returned prisoners say his force is reduced almost to the starving point for want of food, subsisting on two crackers per day.

A considerable number of paroled convalescent prisoners, left here by JACKSON on his retreat, go to Washington to-day, thence they will be sent home to await an exchange. Most of those remaining in the hospitals are doing well, and but very few deaths have occurred among them. Many ladies of this town are unremitting in attention to the sick and wounded, and Dr. ANTISELL, Medical Director, is indefatigable in his labors.

There are now in confinement here 60 rebel prisoners, under charge of Capt. COGSWELL, of the Second Massachusetts Regiment, and between 300 and 400 are now *en route* hither from Strasburgh. These will be sent to Baltimore to-morrow. In order to prevent any insult to the prisoners, as well as any demonstration on the part of secession sympathisers, a strong patrol will escort them through the town, who will promptly suppress and punish any attempt of the kind.

Gen. BANKS has his headquarters here at present. Capt. BERTRAM, (of the Third Wisconsin,) Deputy Provost-Marshal, maintains excellent order, and is quietly searching the houses of noted Secessionists for arms, articles contraband of war, and army and sutlers' supplies, which were appropriated to private use. The usual Provost-guard has been augmented by the Sixtieth New-York. The regulations concerning passes to citizens are much more stringent than ever before. Unless applications are indorsed by some of the best Union citizens they are refused, and a strict watch is kept on all the roads leading from the town.

It has recently come to light that on the Friday morning previous to the attack on Col. KENLY at Front Royal a large mail was received here from JACKSON'S army, conveying intelligence that he was approaching with an overpowering force. The female secession circles were jubilant as well as defiant. It is also known that other mails had been previously received from the same point; but all attempts to ferret out the parties engaged have thus far failed. A gentleman, well known to many of our officers, who was concealed several days in town, overheard conversations participated in by rebel officers. One, who appeared to be well informed in regard to rebel movements, said, if Richmond was evacuated, the whole force would be thrown into the valley, to maintain a guerrilla warfare to the last.

Gen. COOPER'S Brigade passed through town yesterday, in excellent health and spirits.

It surprises observers of the hostility exhibited toward our army on its retreat, to meet now with such numbers of "good Union men" here. The female Secessionists alone take pride in having their real sentiments known to us by words, gestures and deeds. Hereafter outward demonstrations of their secession proclivities will be promptly suppressed by the military authorities.

JACKSON did not hesitate to declare that the main object of his expedition had failed, and he attributed the failure to the non-arrival of his rear supports under LONGSTREET and SMITH. He said his whole force reached nearly 60,000 men.

Gen. SIGEL was serenaded last night at the Taylor House. He made a few remarks in response.

Capt. COTHRAN, of the First New-York Battery, has resumed his command here. The President reversed the finding of the Court-martial dismissing him from the service, and restored him to his battery. His return was gladly greeted by officers and men.

THE NINTH REGIMENT NEW-YORK STATE VOLUNTEERS.

The following private letter will be interesting to the friends of the Ninth Regiment New-York State Volunteers:

FRONT ROYAL, Thursday, June 5, 1862.

One week ago last Sunday, we were at Falmouth, opposite Fredericksburgh, as comfortable as could be. At 4 o'clock in the afternoon, we got orders to pack up and be ready to march at a minute's notice. We got off at 5 o'clock, and marched to Aquia Creek, a distance of 20 miles. We arrived there (after being on the road all night,) at 3 o'clock in the morning. There we slept until 9 o'clock, when we embarked. We took some old tugs which put us on board the steamship *C. Vanderbilt*, and started up the Potomac for Alexandria, but we only got about opposite Cockpit Point when we got aground. There we staid all day and night. It poured hard all the time, and I had to sleep on the deck all night and got soaked through.

About 9 o'clock the next morning the *John Brooks* and *North America* came alongside and took us all off. We arrived at Alexandria about 1 o'clock. We left for Manassas that night by railroad; were in the cars all that night. The next morning started on the march, and had a very long one of 17 miles to Thoroughfare Gap, where we pitched our shelter tents for the night.

At 3½ o'clock the next morning we were on the march again, and went 15 miles, to White Plains, where we encamped for the night. After we got all nicely fixed, a terrible thunder storm came up, and soaked us through. When I got up the next morning, at 3 o'clock, not a thing on me was dry. My knapsack was full of water, and my blanket was soaked through. We started to march at 3½ o'clock, went three miles, to Piedmont Station, where we left everything but our rubber blankets and haversacks. There we drew three days' rations of coffee, sugar and crackers. At 8 o'clock we started again, and that day we succeeded in reaching Front Royal—28 miles from the camp that we left—the longest march that we ever made. On Sunday we arrived at this place, and were up in line of battle all day, expecting that JACKSON would make his appearance, but we did not see anything of him. At 5 o'clock it began to rain hard, and we had to lay in the wet all night. The next morning the sun came out and dried us off. At 1 o'clock the long roll was beat, and in half an hour we were on the march again. We went up the railroad about four miles, toward Strasburgh, but had to halt for the night on account of the rain. At [illegible] o'clock the next morning we were ordered up, ready to march, but only marched four miles, when we halted and killed *six head of cattle*, the first meat of any kind that we had had since we left Falmouth. All that we had to live on was coffee and crackers, and that we had to cook ourselves. We left our camp near Strasburgh yesterday morning, in a most drenching rain, and arrived at Front Royal just in time to save ourselves from starving, as the bridge across the river was carried away by the flood just about one hour after we got across. We halted in the woods, stacked arms, and went down to the cars to get our knapsacks. We found them soaked through, and last night we spent most of our time in drying everything. We are out here to bag JACKSON, if we can, but I am afraid that he is too smart for us. We have seen very hard times for the past week. Just think of sleeping out in the rain with only a small rubber blanket for covering. I think it is a wonder that half of us are not sick; but we appear to stand it very well. We are on the same ground where Col. KENLEY'S First Maryland Regiment was cut up by the rebel cavalry. The graves of the dead soldiers are to be seen. In the town we have got 200 rebel prisoners. They are all from Georgia regiments, and a very hard-looking set they are.

IMPORTANT FROM THE GULF.

The City of Galveston Summoned to Surrender.

A BOMBARDMENT THREATENED.

The Houston (Texas) *Telegraph*, of May 23, has the following important news:

On Saturday morning the frigate *Santee* had a white flag up as a signal of a desire to communicate with the shore. During the day a messenger came ashore bearing the following demand:

UNITED STATES FRIGATE SANTEE, OFF GALVESTON, Texas, May 17, 1862.

To the Military Commandant Commanding Confederate Forces, Galveston, Texas:

SIR: In a few days the naval and land forces of the United States will appear off the town of Galveston, to enforce its surrender.

To prevent the effusion of blood and destruction of property, which would result from the bombardment of your town, I hereby demand the surrender of the place, with all its fortifications and batteries in its vicinity, with all arms and munitions of war. I trust you will comply with this demand.

I am, respectfully, etc., HENRY EAGLE, Captain Commanding the United States Naval Force off Galveston, Texas.

The bearer of the above message stated that an answer could be made any time within 24 hours.

Owing to the wires being down during the day, this message was not telegraphed up till in the evening.

This morning Gen. HEBERT has instructed Col. COOK to reply that when the land and naval forces make their appearance *the demand will be answered*. Meanwhile we can assure the people that the island will not be given up on a mere paper bombardment. Nothing will be left undone to provide for the enemy when he comes.

The General Commanding advises the people to keep cool—there is no danger. When the enemy lands and endeavors to penetrate into the interior, he will be fought on every inch of ground. In the meantime every man should stand by his arms, and be ready to take the field at a moment's warning.

The foreign Consuls have communicated with the captain of the *Santee*, with a view of fixing some point that might be respected in the bombardment, as a place of refuge for foreign subjects. The following is Capt. EAGLE'S reply to them:

UNITED STATES FRIGATE SANTEE, May 22, 1862.

GENTLEMEN: Let me assure you that no person can deplore more than myself the misery that would result from the bombardment of the town of Galveston and its fortifications, yet it is a duty that will become necessary to enforce its surrender.

It is not in my power to give you any assurance of security during the bombardment, for it is impossible to tell what direction the shot and shell will take.

HENRY EAGLE, Captain Commanding United States Naval Forces off Galveston.

To the Foreign Consuls, Galveston.

The Missouri State Convention.

JEFFERSON CITY, Wednesday, June 11.

The bill to postpone the election of State Officers, has been before the Convention nearly all day, and has elicited much discussion. Several substitutes and amendments were offered and rejected, and the bill was finally lost by a vote of 31 yeas to 35 nays. As the case now stands, an election for all State Officers, from Governor down, is authorized. An ordinance to enable citizens of the State in the military service of the United States, or State of Missouri to vote, was taken up, and, on motion, made the special order for to-morrow morning.

An ordinance to amend the Constitution, so that general elections shall be held on the 3d Monday in October, instead of August, as now, was referred to a Select Committee of Three.

Movements of War Vessels.

WASHINGTON, Thursday, June 12.

The gunboat *Paul Jones* has arrived from Baltimore for her armament.

BOSTON, Thursday, June 12.

The steam-frigate *Niagara*, from Key West, is below.

Headquarters of the Eleventh Militia.

HARPER'S FERRY, Thursday, June 12.

The headquarters of the Eleventh New-York Militia Regiment are now at Wadeville, Clarke County, Va. Everything for Col. MAIDHOF and the soldiers of his command, directed to that place, will reach them.

NEWS FROM THE MISSISSIPPI.

Favorable Condition of Affairs at Memphis.

Cotton Beginning to Come Forward.

Opening of Trade on the Mississippi.

Commodore Farragut's Fleet at Vicksburgh.

The Demand for the Surrender of the City.

MEMPHIS, Tuesday, June 10.

Quiet pervades the entire city. The ready submission of the inhabitants to the National rule, is not only surprising, but gratifying. The civil authorities continue to exercise their functions as heretofore. The Provost-Marshal's office is thronged with applicants for permits to proceed North. All persons are requested to take the oath of allegiance before the permission is granted.

JACKSON'S rebel cavalry, which have been hovering around the city ever since the National occupation of it, are said to have gone to Holly Springs. As most of them are largely interested in this city, it is improbable that they will make an attempt to burn it.

The City Recorder was yesterday arrested by the Provost-Marshal for causing the arrest of a citizen for conversing in the streets with a Union soldier.

Rebel cavalry are scouring the country around Grand Junction, destroying all the cotton that can be found.

Applications to ship 6,000 bales of cotton have already been made.

The Memphis *Argus* is still outspoken in its secession sympathy.

The *Avalanche* is much more guarded, and inclined to submit quietly.

Both advise peaceable submission to the National rule. Many stores have been opened and have resumed business. Some traders refuse Confederate money, but receive Tennessee bank notes.

The markets are rather sparsely supplied with meats and vegetables.

Two rebel steamers were captured yesterday above the city.

MEMPHIS, Monday, June 9.

Intelligence was received this morning that as soon as the news of the defeat of the rebel fleet here and the surrender of the city, reached St. Frances River, Arkansas, a steamer, acting under Gen. HINDMAN'S orders, went up and down that stream and destroyed several thousand bales of cotton. Some four hundred bales were burned at Madison, Arkansas, about 40 miles west of here.

Throughout yesterday and last night the city was as quiet as any Northern City. To-day some of the stores are open, and Confederate scrip is being pretty generally refused. There has been no movement either in the fleet or land forces since Friday. It is said as many as 30,000 bales of cotton have been burned here. Not much business is being done, and currency is left to regulate itself.

OUR MEMPHIS CORRESPONDENCE.

OCCUPATION OF MEMPHIS—FEELING OF THE PEOPLE—APPEARANCE OF THE CITY—DECREASE OF POPULATION—CONFEDERATE MONEY IN THE CITY—DESTRUCTION OF COTTON—THE FIRST THROUGH STEAMER.

GOYOSO HOUSE, MEMPHIS, Friday afternoon, June 6, 1862.

Memphis is taken—emphatically *taken*—not captured. The impregnable city, the valiant people, "who knew not how to surrender," have yielded without a struggle. Northern civilians, and officers in National uniform, walk its streets as quietly and as free from insult or molestation, as if they were in their own homes.

Transports at the levee, laden with Union troops, bear afloat the banner of the Union, and fifes and drums are making the air resonant with the strains of Hail Columbia, and the Star Spangled Banner, yet neither sign nor sound of indignation or displeasure can be seen or heard among the crowd on the levee.

A motley throng it is which has gathered to gape and stare and wonder at the invaders. Clergymen and courtesans, laborers and ladies of fashion, students and stevedores, clerks and contrabands, American, Irish, Dutch and Ethiopian, men, women and children, on horseback, in carriages and on foot, have come down to see the show. While there is little indignation displayed at our presence, there is as little show of a general welcome. The prominent feeling seems to be one of overwhelming surprise, almost of incredulity, at our being there. The totally unexpected abandonment of Fort Pillow, followed so immediately by the arrival here of our fleet, and the seemingly almost magical destruction of their own, appears to have dumbfoundered them, and they have scarcely begun to consider as yet whether they really ought to be the more glad or sorry; whether the restoration of their city to the Union is to be regarded as a calamity or an advantage.

The truth is, Memphis has suffered so severely under the Confederate rule, her business has been so crippled, her supplies cut off, her people burdened with taxation, her active, enterprising men, the class on which the prosperity of a city depends, cajoled or compelled into the army, her pleasant homes made desolate, that a majority of the people cannot help feeling, even while they do not acknowledge it openly, that they were sadly the losers by the change.

At the same time, the avowed public sentiment of the city has always been in favor of the rebellion. Their newspapers have been among the most bitter and malignant in the South in their vilification of the National Government and those who supported it. Their leading public men have assumed the same tone.

It is impossible for any one to remain for a length of time entirely unaffected by the current tone of popular sentiment around him, and it is perfectly natural, therefore, that a majority even of those who felt the disastrous effects of the rebellion most deeply, should come at last to feel a sort of National, or rather local pride, to be involved in the struggle, and feel somewhat hurt at being defeated, even though they knew their own condition would assuredly be bettered thereby. After the lapse of a few days, however, when this soreness shall have partly worn away, I am satisfied that a large majority of the peo-

[*Continued on Eighth Page.*]

The Charleston Mercury.

DAILY PAPER—TEN DOLLARS PER ANNUM, PAYABLE HALF-YEARLY IN ADVANCE.

SPONTE SUA SINE LEGE FIDES RECTUMQUE COLENTUR.—VINDICE NULLO

COUNTRY PAPER—THRICE A WEEK—FIVE DOLLARS PER ANNUM, IN ADVANCE.

VOLUME LXXXI. | CHARLESTON, S. C., WEDNESDAY, JULY 2, 1862. | NUMBER 11,490

NEWS BY TELEGRAPH.

THE GREAT BATTLE OF RICHMOND.

DESPERATE FIGHTING ON MONDAY AFTERNOON ON OUR RIGHT WING.

M'CLELLAN REPORTED MORTALLY WOUNDED.

THE ENEMY AGAIN DRIVEN FROM HIS ENTRENCHMENTS,

&c., &c., &c.

RICHMOND, July 1.—Yesterday afternoon the enemy was attacked by General HUGER's forces in the vicinity of White Oak Swamp. The divisions of Generals LONGSTREET and D. H. HILL were also engaged. The action soon became general, and lasted several hours, with heavy loss on our side. The enemy was driven back. About two miles farther down, Stonewall JACKSON's forces were engaged with a column of the enemy, and captured three batteries. The *Enquirer* states that a Federal officer brought in yesterday reports MCCLELLAN mortally wounded and the Yankee army completely demoralized.

(*Second Despatch.*)—*Afternoon.*—The fight yesterday took place on the Darbytown Road, about five miles northeast of Darbytown. It began about four o'clock in the afternoon. The forces engaged on our side were Gen. D. H. HILL's division and several brigades of LONGSTREET's division, embracing KEMPER's, PRYOR's, RICKETT's and FEATHERSTONE's. The Yankees made a desperate resistance, but were driven from their entrenched positions and pursued two miles. They were then heavily reinforced and had succeeded in checking the further advance of our men; but the arrival of MAGRUDER's division, about nine o'clock, again put them in motion; but darkness prevented our troops from following and routing the enemy. Our loss was very heavy, but that of the Yankees was immense. We captured six hundred prisoners, who have arrived in the city, and twenty pieces of cannon. Among the prisoners is Major-General MCCALL, who was captured by Lieut. ROLLINGS, of the 47th Virginia. Brigadier-General MEADE was also captured. This morning MAGRUDER went in pursuit of the Yankees, but had not yet overtaken them at eight o'clock, when our informant left. The engagement yesterday is represented to have been the most sanguinary of the series of conflicts which have taken place before this city. The valor displayed by our troops was beyond all praise.

We have received, through private despatches, the news of the following casualties:

Capt. BURNET RHETT, of the Brooks Artillery, attached to Gen. D. H. HILL's Division, was slightly wounded.

Capt. CHARLES BOAG, of the Richardson Guards, 1st Regiment S. C. V., killed.

1st Lieut. BRAILSFORD, of the same company, wounded.

2d Lieut. R. W. RHETT, of the same company (previously reported wounded), died near the battle field.

HOWELL TREZEVANT (son of Dr. D. H. TREZEVANT, of Columbia), killed.

Capt. EDWARD CHEVES (aid to Gen. LAWTON, and grand-son of the illustrious LANGDON CHEVES), killed.

Col. LANE, 28th N. C. Regiment, lost an arm.

Col. MCRAE and Major STONE, of the 16th N. C., killed.

Col. REUBEN CAMPBELL, of the 7th N. C., killed.

Capt. R. B. MCRAE, same regiment, wounded.

Lieut. Col. PARR, of WRIGHT's (Ga.) Legion, lost his left leg.

Capt. BUTLER, of the Oglethorpe Light Infantry, is shot through the lung.

Private COOMBS, very seriously wounded, and not expected to recover.

It is reported that Col. LAMAR, of the Eighth Georgia, has been recaptured from the enemy.

Lieut. Col. MAGRUDER, of the 8th Georgia, slightly wounded.

IMPORTANT FROM EAST TENNESSEE.

KNOXVILLE, June 30.—BUELL's entire army has left Corinth, and is now rapidly crossing the Tennessee river at Florence. They are concentrating at Bridgeport, thirty-four miles from Chattanooga. The enemy crossed a regiment of artillery over Battle Creek yesterday. Brig. Gen. HARRY HETH has been assigned to the command of Chattanooga.

IMPORTANT FROM THE WEST—BOMBARDMENT OF VICKSBURG—THE CITY TO BE HELD AT ALL HAZARDS, &c.

JACKSON, MISS., June 29.—Passengers from Vicksburg this morning report that on yesterday morning seven of the enemy's vessels succeeded in passing up by our batteries. A severe bombardment was immediately opened upon the city by the gunboats and the batteries which the Yankees had erected on the Louisiana shore of the river. This lasted about two hours. It is understood that several vessels, including the *Brooklyn*, were badly damaged, with heavy slaughter among their crews. The Confederate loss, so far, had been only nine (including one woman) killed. Our batteries were uninjured. The enemy's fire was directed chiefly against the city, and several houses had been shattered. It is supposed that the enemy will not renew the conflict for several days. A deserter reports the enemy's loss to be very heavy, and that they had expected an easy capture of the place.

Later.—We have just received later news from Vicksburg, that the enemy is to-day slowly bombarding the city from his mortar boats. The telegraph office is among the buildings which have been smashed.

On the 28th inst., General VAN DORN issued a general order to the forces under his command, declaring that "Vicksburg shall be defended unto death," and that "the Federal troops can never occupy Vicksburg."

The fleet appears to be too much crippled to engage our batteries with a prospect of success. The loss of property in Vicksburg has been heavy.

The Yazoo City correspondent of the Jackson *Mississippian*, writing under date of the 16th inst., says that two of the enemy's gunboats were reconnoitering in the Yazoo River, when Commodore PINCKNEY burned the Confederate gunboats *Van Dorn*, *Polk* and *Livingston*. "This action," adds the correspondent, "is considered to have been altogether unnecessary, and is much deplored here."

A gentleman just from New Orleans, says that BUTLER has issued orders levying a tax of two millions of dollars on the citizens.

CASUALTIES IN THE 2D REGIMENT OF RIFLES S. C. V., COL. JOHN MOORE.

We get the following lists from the Columbia *Guardian*:

Field and Staff—Killed—None.
Wounded—R. J. Bruns, slightly.

Capt. H. S. Kerr's Company—Killed—N. Knox, John W. Gelmer. Wounded none.

Capt. R. A. Thompson's Company—None killed or wounded.

Capt. Dene's' Company—Killed none. Wounded—Sergt. David Sanders.

Capt. D. L. Cox's Company—Killed none. Wounded none.

Capt. R. E. Bowen's Company—Wounded—B. C. Barret, Elias Hollingsworth, B. H. Farner.

Capt. D. L. Donald's Company—Killed none. Wounded—John Campbell, W. H. S. Brunt, Jesse Smith, O. T. Hewins, John McCarey.

Capt. Putnam's Company—Killed none.—Wounded: Lieutenant Larkin Hughes, Jackson Charles, Thos. Burnett, J. W. Crenshaw.

Capt. W. H. White's Company—Wounded; J. H Dunahoe.

Capt. E. M. Brown's Company—Killed: Dempster Cox, Elbert Hutchinson. Wounded: Lieut. E. J. Major, Corporal W. J. Hawkins, Jas. Davis.

The wounds were generally very slight.

W. S. SHARPE.

CASUALTIES IN COMPANY A, PALMETTO SHARP-SHOOTERS.

The following are the casualties in this company up to Saturday, at 4, p. m.:

Killed: Private B. P. Hopkins, G. W. Johnson.

Wounded: Lieutenant O. L. Beatty, slightly, in the breast; Corporal S. Y. Green, arm broke; Privates R. D. Dunlap, Geo. Peridge, J. W. Harris, in the arm.

G. W. GOSS, Captain.

CASUALTIES IN COMPANY D, ORR'S REGIMENT.

Killed—Sergt. W. R. Burrows, T. C. Burns, Birt Young, H. B. Grant, Thos. Brady.

Severely wounded—W. S. Simpson, S. S. McKee, L. C. G. Anderson, H. Yeaging, Warren Watkins, J. R. Hayne, J. Bates.

Slightly wounded—Capt. T. E. Harrison, Sergt. J. R. Jadler, S. J. Webb, J. F. Woolbridge, E. S. Hall, J. S. Strickland, R. P. Richardson, B. L. Mitchell, Jas. McConnell, Jos. McLees, G. W. Richardson, W. S. Cater.

T. E. HARRISON, Captain.

TOTAL LOSS IN ORR'S REGIMENT OF RIFLES.

Killed, 74. Wounded, 223.
This regiment carried into action 560.

J. T. PARKS, A. D. C.

CASUALTIES IN COMPANY E, 14TH REGIMENT S. C. V.

The following comprise the casualties in Company E, 14th Regiment, S. C. V.:

Killed—John Simpson. Wounded—Lieut. Dorrah, Sergeants Franks and Means; Privates Albert Boyce, J. F. Cox, Henry Daniels, Jno. Pearson, Ben Martin, Harrison Tumolin, S. H. Paul, Thos. Waddel, and also myself.

All are doing well, except the gallant Boyce, whose injuries may terminate fatally.

JOS. N. BROWN, Captain.

CASUALTIES IN THE NEWBERRY RIFLES.

The following are the casualties of the Newberry Rifles, 13th Regiment, S. C. V., at the battle of GOINS' Mill, June 27:

Killed—Privates W. H. Pitts and R. D. Suber.
Wounded—Private J. J. Ruff, severely; Capt. I. F. Hunt, slightly; Privates A. S. Conwell, Willie Caldwell, W. R. Lane, Job P. Senn.

J. H. HUNT, jr.

[The following despatch was received by Gov. PICKENS on Monday night.]

RICHMOND, June 29.—Yesterday was expended, not wasted, in establishing our forces. Our confidence has increased.

Later.—The enemy crossed their whole army over the Chickahominy. They are completely whipped, and are in full retreat for James river. We are pursuing them in three columns; have cut off a portion, and hope to do more. The victory is complete, but the enemy not quite annihilated.

THE MERCURY.

WEDNESDAY, JULY 2, 1862.

The Great Struggle in Virginia.

We know enough of the succession of battles which have been fought upon the Peninsula since Thursday evening last, to feel assured that the victory is certainly ours, and that no mischance at the eleventh hour is likely to turn the scale against us. But, at the date of our last accounts from the scene of action, the fighting was evidently not yet over. A large body of the enemy's troops had been hotly engaged with our right wing, and, after being at last forced back, were *reinforced* so heavily as to enable them, for a time, to make a second and successful stand.—And, when the approach of MAGRUDER's division compelled the Yankees again to give way, they fell back, it appears, under cover of the night, towards the James River and their gunboats. Yesterday morning MAGRUDER was in close pursuit, but had not yet come up with the retreating foe. Thus things stood then. The final blow, which is to end the "Grand Army," and, with it, the Yankee project of subjugating the South, was probably struck yesterday afternoon. We await the news of the result with the full confidence that the valor of our right wing will secure and complete the advantages which our left and centre have so nobly won.

Trade in Captured Southern Cities—the Duty of the Vanquished.

In his administration in New Orleans Butler, although he has outraged every law of civilization and the commonest instincts of decency, has managed to maintain and consolidate his rule by addressing the passion of avarice, and using the mean and mercenary influences which are found in the populations of great cities to corrupt the simplicity of the country Southern merchants have been permitted to go from the city to get rid of their Confederate money, and to persuade the country people to send cotton and supplies within the enemy's lines; proposing, under patriotic affectations, the most fatal measure which the cupidity and malice of New England could devise. The influences of the people living in cities have been always, in time of war, demoralizing to the country. It is the duty of the government to provide against these sources of corruption, to protect the simplicity of its rural population, and to erect the barrier, wherever it can, of commercial non-intercourse between cities occupied by the enemy and districts of country where its authority is still supreme.

The duties of subjugated cities are plain. They are not to make idle and cheap affectations of patriotism; they are to cultivate dignity of behaviour, and, while refusing to submit to social conversation with the enemy, to abstain with equal severity from holding commercial intercourse with him. We are satisfied that there is a large portion of the business community of New Orleans who have adopted this honorable rule of behaviour and policy; but in the heart of every man in that city whose avarice can be excited, or whose patriotic scruples can be conciliated, the leaven of corruption is at work. At least, the mischief and demoralization of commercial intercourse between New Orleans and the districts of the Mississippi must be stopped wherever the Confederate Government or the State authorities have the power to do so. The renewal of business relations with men in a city, where every measure of finance and commerce is aimed to destroy the currency and credit of our government, is to aid directly in the subversion of our government and the sacrifice of our cause.—*Richmond Examiner.*

One hundred and two Representatives and thirty-seven Senators have signed a paper, started by Wilson, of Iowa, asking Lincoln to make an arrangement for releasing, by exchange, all Federal prisoners in Confederate hands.

THE SPIRIT OF THE WAR.

WHAT M'CLELLAN INTENDED TO DO.

An editorial article in the New York *Times*, of the 24th ult., on the "Situation in Virginia," closes with the following grand programme, which, somehow, failed in the performance:

Though the evacuation of Richmond would not prove what the rebel leaders hope it would, it is useless to conceal that the successful flight from Virginia of the Confederate army, without a battle, would be a decided misfortune, and put back the *finale* of the war. General McClellan does not mean to allow this, if he can possibly prevent it. If he delays the attack an hour beyond the time when he is fully prepared, the country may be assured that it is for the purpose of arranging such subsidiary operations as will frustrate the hope the rebels have in flight. The Richmond journals have already told us that Gen. Mansfield occupies Suffolk, in the rear of the rebel capital, with a strong force. The visit of Burnside to McClellan, at headquarters, undoubtedly meant work in this direction. But more significant than all, there is yet encouragement that the gunboats in the James River are destined to play *their* prime part in the capture of Richmond and its rebellious defenders. The movements in this direction have been very properly shrouded in secresy; but there is every hope that our ironclads will be able to silence and pass the batteries that line the banks of the James River, near Fort Darling, and, this accomplished, to remove the obstructions that have been placed in the channel. It would be a heavy imputation on the courage of the navy should this enterprise not be *attempted*; and if attempted, it will in all probability be successful. The service they can render is incalculable. With a fleet of gunboats commanding the main line of retreat from Richmond, the last hope of the rebels, the hope of flight, is cut off. Is McClellan awaiting the echo of the guns of Fort Darling? If so, twenty millions wait with him, hushed in expectancy.

"THE IMPENDING CAPTURE OF RICHMOND AND FINAL ROUT OF THE REBELS."

The following choice bit of Yankee braggadocio, which we take from the editorial columns of the New York *Herald*, of the 15th instant, will be read with peculiar pleasure, now that the "Grand Army" of MCCLELLAN has "dissolved and disappeared:"

All quiet in front of Richmond. Hardly a musket shot from our advanced pickets has been reported for several days. In sullen silence the two hostile armies there confront each other. A dead calm prevails; but it is that ominous and awful calm which immediately precedes the outbreak and the swift, terrible, and irresistible march of a summer hurricane. Thus the army of General McClellan hangs, like a mass of heavy clouds still thickening, darkening, and extending around Richmond, and the moment approaches when its elements of destruction will break forth upon and sweep from that devoted city the last remaining organized vestiges of that great rebellious conspiracy, still feebly flaunting itself before the world as an independent Southern Confederation.

Let our patriotic readers patiently await the appointed hour. It cannot be much longer delayed. In the meantime, as every day's preparation serves to strengthen and consolidate the army of the Union, while it inevitably weakens and demoralizes the forces of the rebellion, we are steadily gaining ground. Thus the great victory which McClellan could win to-day, would be a greater victory if postponed till to-morrow; for we know that another of those so-called strategical retreats of the armies is utterly out of the question in reference to Richmond. That place is their chosen "Confederate" capital, their last remaining army of any moment is there concentrated to defend their capital, and Davis and his ruling associates are too well informed, by late events, not to know that if they are driven out of Richmond they cannot undertake to set up their tabernacle in any other city, town or hamlet in the South.

No fears need be entertained, therefore, that the rebel army of Richmond, one of these fine mornings, will be reported missing, like that of Beauregard at Corinth. If they abandon Richmond, they abandon Virginia; and with that obstruction out of the way, North Carolina instantly wheels back into the Union, and a hundred thousand fighting men of these two States will thus be lost to the rebel army, with the evacuation of Richmond. Accordingly, we may entertain no doubt of a desperate struggle by the rebels to hold their capital; and in this view, the more complete we make our preparations for a decisive victory, the more decisive it will be. We are assured, too, that the Government and Gen. McClellan are acting upon this idea, and that we may expect, when the final assault is made upon this last rebel stronghold, we shall not only carry the city, but capture the bulk of the enemy's forces, and perhaps, too, without any serious destruction of human life.

With the fall of Richmond, this rebellion will be virtually at an end. We shall have then nothing left to do but to settle with a few inconsiderable fragments of the two great routed and broken up rebel armies, and these demoralized fragments will dissolve and disappear at the approach of our superior forces.

SECRET HISTORY OF THE WAR—THE BROILS OF M'CLELLAN AND STANTON.

The Boston *Journal*, of a recent date, has a long and elaborate editorial defending STANTON, the Secretary of War of LINCOLN, from sundry accusations which had been brought against him by the friends of MCCLELLAN. In the course of this article much of the history of the Yankee campaign in the South, hitherto unknown to our readers, is developed, and the mysterious "anaconda" policy of the "Young NAPOLEON" comes in for a sharp criticism. We copy the more interesting portion of the *Journal's* editorial:

In what we have to say of General McClellan, we shall draw a clear line between his plans and acts as Commander-in-Chief, and his ability as a General at the head of an army in the field. We believe him to be fully competent where he is, and we shall not cease to believe in his eminent fitness and to hope for his triumphant success in his present campaign, *unless forced by events and by authoritative military criticism to another conclusion.*

It is clear that when the main direction of this war was left to a Commander-in-Chief, that more than purely military calculations must occupy his mind; that he must see the value of time in relation to national finances, to a democratic form of government, and to foreign intervention; in short, that he must have some of the qualities of a great statesman, as well as all of the qualities of a great general. When Mr. Stanton became Secretary of War, what was the posture of affairs under General McClellan's plan and direction? The country was under lasting obligations to his demonstrated faculty for organization. But it becomes necessary to state how little else had been done, why so little had been done, and to whom the country is indebted for what was done in February and March, and to its position before the world to-day.

Whether more could not have been accomplished in Kentucky, nearly all of whose strategic posts were occupied by the enemy, we are not competent to judge. But it is clear to military authorities and to the country that Eastern Tennessee, whose people are the most loyal and the most distressed of the border States, might have been relieved, Knoxville taken, and the great northern line of communication between Virginia and the great sources of her supplies broken, weeks or months before General McClellan ceased to be Commander-in-Chief. The country patiently waited, because we believed it bore wise relation to some great military plan.

The country saw the great Baltimore and Ohio Railroad not only abandoned to the enemy, but its rolling stock neither removed nor destroyed, but given up to him, to whom its value was immense. The responsibility for this loss we do not impute to General McClellan. The road remained in the enemy's possession.

Still patient, but in deep humiliation, the country saw a blockade of the Potomac quietly allowed, which cost this country millions of dollars, by reducing our immense transportation to one railroad, with a single track, and which placed our Government before the world as besieged in its own capital. We know whereof we affirm when we say that five months ago our navy department begged to be allowed to remove that blockade. They demonstrated its removal to be a simple certainty, and an eminent general was anxious to aid by landing troops, confident that he could capture the batteries and the men who manned them. Their repeated requests were peremptorily refused by the Commander-in-Chief.

The plan of the Hatteras expedition contemplated nothing more than the destruction of the forts and sinking obstructions in the channel, and the occupation of the forts was a wise transcending of instructions. In this Gen. McClellan may, perhaps, have had no responsibility. But the instructions for the Burnside expedition were substantially his, and by them Gen. Burnside was limited to perfecting the blockade, and prevented from striking at vital points and cutting important lines of railroad. Over all this the country wondered, believed, and waited.

We know that, beginning more than five months ago, Gen. Wool and the Navy Department joined in urgent and repeated applications to be allowed to take Norfolk, which they demonstrated to be a military and naval certainty. Besides its immense importance otherwise, the Merrimac would have been taken while building, the Cumberland and the Congress would have been saved, and the James as well as the York River would have been open for Gen. McClellan's march upon Richmond. Their request was peremptorily refused by the Commander-in-Chief.

We know that while Gen. McClellan was still Commander-in-Chief, Gen. Sherman reported that he was prepared and anxious to be allowed to take Savannah; that it was a military certainty, and that it could be done with very little loss of life. This, too, was forbidden by the Commander-in-Chief.

We have given these great selected facts, derived from central and authoritative sources, to indicate the whole circle which the people supposed bore relation to some sufficient and entirely justifying plan in the mind of the Commander-in-Chief. We will add, without assuming to pass judgment, that, while in great European wars, the spy system has often been such as to tap the very centre of military counsel, while there never was a war offering better opportunity for such a system than this, and while our enemy has notoriously been in possession of nearly all our plans as soon as made, we have lamentably failed in detecting his.

We will not stop to conjecture what Gen. McClellan's plan was, and we have no right to state such facts bearing upon it as are within our knowledge. Nobody questioned his loyalty and his faculty for organization, and we shall now show that it becomes entirely unnecessary to discuss his plan; for the plan itself becomes unimportant in the light of the facts we shall now state, some of which are already partially before the country.

Mr. Stanton came into power when foreign intervention seemed imminent, without one great military advantage yet followed up, and with capital distrusting the national finances, on which all depended. With the breadth and vision of a statesman, and with the terrible earnestness and force of will of a Cromwellian, he brought into the national councils, for the first time since the war began, comprehensiveness, decisiveness, and a thorough realization of the value of time to this nation. He found General McClellan virtually directing the whole war, responsible that no more had been done, and fixed in his determination that no advance should be made until April. In this determination General McClellan still further fortified himself by a vote of eight of his generals against four.

Mr. Stanton saw at once that no advance until April involved national despondency, a tax levied upon a people for an immense debt which had borne no fruit in victories, hot weather, and a fall campaign, distrust, and a great fall in national stocks, and a possible if not probable foreign intervention. *Then, through him, was issued the President's Order No. 1, over Gen. McClellan's head and against his protest, peremptorily commanding an advance at all points on the 23d of February.* Gen. McClellan was placed at the head of the Army of the Potomac, and ceased to be Commander-in-Chief. Mr. Stanton simply became a real Secretary of War, taking into his capable hands the reins which Mr. Cameron had either necessarily given to others or misused himself. The President had, at last, a great right arm to lean on, and each was strengthened and greater for the other.

The movements in the West under Commodore Foote, which sent joy and hope through the nation, were made without regard to General McClellan's plan, and sprang directly from Commodore Foote's communications and requests to the Navy Department and its orders to him; and without further enumeration, it is only necessary to say that the series of brilliant successes during February and March, which threw new life into the nation, which gave us Fort Henry, Bowling Green, Columbus, Donelson, Island No. 10, and Nashville, which brought national stocks to par, and which forced respect for us abroad, if it did not prevent intervention, was in direct contravention of the plan of the Commander-in-Chief, and against his protest. What that plan was, were it proper to discuss it, becomes of little consequence when we know that no advance was to be made under it until April, and when it was found that the Commander-in-Chief had communicated none to the other Major Generals.

While expressing, as we have, our faith in General McClellan as the commander of an army—all the more because, as civilians, we are entirely incompetent to form a judgment of his military acts since he was placed at the head of the Army of the Potomac—we are free to say, and we think all candid men will agree with us, that, in the light of the trustworthy acts we have given, it was the most fortunate event in the history of the war when Edwin M. Stanton became Secretary of War, and Gen. McClellan was placed where nothing more than purely military ability was wanting.

And now, what are the facts as to the charges of diversion of troops from Gen. McClellan which have taken contradictory and absurd shapes, which have had the support of some letters written by a few honest officers in the field, with only special and limited knowledge, as well as those of omniscient newspaper correspondents. In the first place, let it not be forgotten that the President and Cabinet have at their side a special military adviser, Gen Hitchcock, who has been called the Cæsar of our army, and whose skill as a strategist and whose powers of combination are consummate (on the highest military authority) with his general culture and comprehensiveness. And he is not the only general, eminent by nature, culture and experience, who is called into consultation. The idea that Mr. Stanton alone interferes with or changes military plans is simply absurd.

No agreement was ever made by the President or the War Department with General McClellan to send to the Peninsula the whole of McDowell's corps. For reasons no doubt sufficient to his mind, with reference to his position upon the Peninsula, he desired the whole, which would have left not a national soldier between the forts across the Potomac and Richmond, by way of Fredericksburg. A large part of McDowell's command was, however, sent to him, which was so much in excess of agreement, and when the correspondence of the War Department on that subject sees the light, it will be found that the President himself interfered to prevent the 23,000 men left to Gen. McDowell from going further sent in excess of original agreement. But for the President wisely insisting, that both for the safety of Washington and that General McClellan might be aided by a flank movement under General McDowell, these 23,000 men should make a part of a sufficient force, all of General McDowell's army would have gone to the Peninsula.

And yet Mr. Stanton has been charged with diverting troops from Gen. McClellan, in violation of original agreement, and with his having prevented this very flank movement upon Richmond, which was long delayed because more men had been sent to Gen. McClellan than he was entitled to by agreement. The simple truth is, that the reduction of Gen. McDowell's command, by sending so large a portion of it to Gen. McClellan, beyond agreement, if not in full compliance with his wishes, caused the very derangement of original plans which has been wickedly charged upon Mr. Stanton. Until Gen. McDowell's force was increased and the disposition of troops changed, these facts could not be publicly stated.

We have only to say further, that the major part of the facts stated in this article have been for weeks in our possession, and that their publication has been made proper and necessary by the lapse of time, and by the most ignorant, virulent and persistent attacks upon a Government whose lips have been closed against saying a word which might, even by implication, injure one of its own generals or the cause in which we are all engaged.

THE STORY OF ONE REGIMENT.

The following, which we copy from the New York *Post*, tells the story of one Yankee regiment which came to Virginia to plunder and destroy. Many others will meet a similar fate:

When the Maine Eleventh passed through Broadway last November, the "Hallelujah Chorus" was chanted by eight hundred and fifty sturdy fellows; few persons who saw them could have anticipated that those sturdy lumbermen would, within a twelve month, be almost decimated. Arriving in Washington, they built those famous barracks, which were visited by so many strangers; but in spite of the fine shelter, the typhoid was soon busy in their ranks, and when they went down with Casey's division, they were only 750 strong; one-eighth died of disease. While on the Peninsula they lived on hard biscuit and water for five weeks, owing to the inefficiency or rascality of some one, so that when they took up the double-quick for Williamsburg the men fell on the road and died from sheer exhaustion. At the battle of Fair Oaks they numbered, fit for duty, only 180 men. One-half of this number were in action, and were nearly all killed and wounded.

THE YANKEES IN THE DARK CONCERNING THE WHEREABOUTS OF BEAUREGARD'S ARMY.

All Yankeedom seems to be in sore tribulation in regard to the mysterious disappearance and present whereabouts of our Army of the West. The New York *Times*, in one of its late issues, asks:

Is or is not the great rebel army lately at Corinth still a coherent mass? Taking all the circumstances into account, there never was, in the military history of the world, an army of such magnitude, concerning whose movements and whereabouts the opposing commanders were so completely in the dark. Although such a host could not have been removed from Corinth in a day nor in a week, Gen Halleck knew not it had been evacuated until, by accident, Gen. Pope discovered that the rebel bird had flown, and that a few rebel pickets were keeping our mighty army at bay; and, though twenty days have elapsed since that event, we have yet nothing clearer than a lot of disjointed statements locating it here, there and everywhere. The 10,000 men said to have been captured by Pope is ascertained to have been a highly exaggerated statement of that dashing General's achievement, and though our cavalry were reported to be everywhere "in hot pursuit," and though Pope is now announced to be forty miles south of Corinth, it has not yet been ascertained where a single one of the rebel divisions has gone to. The possible lines of retreat for them were very few, and we know that they must have gone southward, and then probably east. But how far south, and to what point or points in the east? Information on this subject is awaited for by the public with the greatest anxiety. We have no doubt that if Halleck had not expelled all correspondents of the Press from his lines they would have informed us, and him too, long ago, of the location of every brigade of the rebel army.

There seems to be little doubt, however, that the divisions of Beauregard's army are not now coherent With great likelihood, detachments of it are reported to be at Richmond, Charleston, Mobile, and other places. Certain divisions are reported as being greatly broken up, though such statements, being without proof, must be received with caution. There have undoubtedly also been heavy rebel desertions; but eight or ten thousand, though it might be a large number of deserters, would be a small deduction from the rebel army which Gen. Halleck reported to be at Corinth. If the remainder of Beauregard's prodigious force—if Price, Polk, Bragg, Hardee, Breckinridge, Crittenden, and their respective commands, are still in Mississippi, or if they have left the State—we would be obliged to any one for some intelligent information on the subject.

AN ENGLISHMAN'S OPINION OF THE WAR.

A correspondent of the London *Times* (Mr. SPENCE) gives his opinion of the condition of affairs as follows:

In considering the aspect of the main Federal operations, it is necessary to keep in view that the real hardships of the war are yet unknown to them. They have travelled, so far, as cabin passengers, and have fought under the wings of gunboats; but before such a country is subdued, many a foot-sore march must be made to battle fields away from rivers. The commissariat and hospital services have not yet been spoken out.

The truth is, that during the past winter the Northern people, having no external hope, applied themselves to form an army with admirable energy and great success. The Southerners, on the other hand, were thoroughly convinced that the pressure of the blockade and its inefficiency, as reported by all the European Consuls to their respective Governments, would enforce an intervention of the Great Powers. The conviction lulled them into inaction, especially in the West, and the consequences were plain at the commencement of operations. The delusion passed away, the reality aroused them to action, and we see the result in the relative condition of the main armies. At the end of the summer their effective forces will probably be the more numerous of the two. That some positions have been badly held and some mistakes committed, cannot be surprising. We judge with a European standard, but the half-disciplined, whether of the North or South, cannot be expected to operate with the judgment or resist with the firmness of the professional soldier.

Here is a people shut out from the world; deprived of all the comforts of life; starting without tools, money, credit, ships or soldiers; disappointed in their political calculations; their commerce annihilated; the value of their property extinguished; overmatched in men and means of warfare; assailed with torrents of abuse, and depressed by a long course of adverse events. In the face of such difficulties as these, they have now 350,000 men under arms, and in the two great actions of the war they have taken home the prisoners and the guns. Is this the scheming of a few ambitious men, or is it the movement of a resolute people? And if such a people are to be subjugated, and such a country is to be held as a conquered province to gratify the ambition or swell the profits of others, for whom are liberty and self-government to be reserved?

But such an event may be regarded as an impossibility. The power of a resolute people against regular armies has often been proved on a small scale—La Vendee, Switzerland, the Tyrol, Holland, has exemplified; on a scale such as this, what army, American or European, could deal with it? New Orleans is taken only in name; its trade was gone and its people are unchanged. By a singular fatality its people had no chance to fight for it—a keen humiliation to a race whose courage amounts to recklessness of life. All of this will not make them loyal. In every community there will be found some few craven spirits to run up the flag of the conqueror or trade with his sutlers. But in every country the great majority have some respect for the land of their birth, and, whatever their original sentiments, they cannot welcome those who come to rule it as a conquered province. The people of New York are elated, naturally; but they forget the fact that their own city fell [illegible] hands in a manner not more glorious [illegible] York and the Hudson were quite as [illegible] the colonists as New Orleans and [illegible] are now; yet our possession of [illegible] effect in subduing the country; and [illegible] the "rebels" obtained their independence, may not the same result follow now?

BUTLER AS A JOKER.

[illegible] BUTLER is inclined to amuse himself [illegible] innocent alarms among his troops, [illegible] indulge himself in equally harmless [illegible]. The conduct of his soldiers he styles "admirable." What would the author of order No. "twenty-eight" consider "admirable" conduct in his soldiers? The last paragraph in the subjoined special order is decidedly cool:

HEADQUARTERS DEPART'T OF THE GULF,
New Orleans, La., June 14, 1862.

[*Special Order No. 99.*]

The Commanding General, desiring to test the vigilance, alertness, activity, and efficiency of his troops stationed in the city, unexpectedly caused the assembly to be beaten at half-past ten o'clock last evening.

The General was much gratified at the prompt manner in which all the troops performed their appropriate duty. In ten minutes every corps had either reported for orders, or was on its march to its station.

Soldiers, your behavior in New Orleans has been admirable! Withstanding the temptations of a great city, so as to present such discipline and efficiency, is the highest exhibition of soldiery qualities. You have done more than win a great battle; you have conquered yourselves.—You have convinced the people of New Orleans that you are worthy of the flag you bear in triumph. He is more of a coward who yields to his own weakness, than he who surrenders to an enemy.

Go on, as you have begun! True to your New England training and her religious influences, showing the men and women of the South that where your bayonets are, there are peace, quiet, liberty, safety and order under the law.

By command of

MAJOR GENERAL BUTLER,
Commanding Department.

R. S. DAVIS, A. A. A. G.

BUTLER'S SEIZURE OF GOLD IN NEW ORLEANS—SEWARD'S CORRESPONDENCE WITH THE DUTCH MINISTER.

A despatch from Washington, dated June 16th, says:

The diplomatic correspondence concerning the $800,000 forcibly seized by Gen. Butler from the hands of the Netherland Consul has been carried on with a great deal of urbanity, and in a fair spirit of conciliation by the Secretary of State and the Dutch Minister. It is hoped that the matter will soon be settled to the satisfaction of both parties. As the proceedings towards Mr. Couturie, the Dutch Consul, took place in the heat of battle and under martial law, and were not, consequently, in accordance with diplomatic usage and traditions, Mr. Seward sent his excuse for any infractions of the rule, but refused to comply with the request of the Dutch Minister referring to the removal of Gen. Butler. As regards the seizure of the money, against which the Dutch Minister objected, on the ground that it ought to be placed in third hands, Mr. Seward replied that the Federal Government was as responsible for the money as the third party, and that when the time shall come to return it, if it comes at all, the money will be found ready.

The question of form having been thus satisfactorily settled, the representative of Holland said that as to the question of property, he had in his hands evidences that the $800,000 were not the property of the Confederacy, but an amount deposited by the State of Louisiana for the payment of the interest of the Louisiana State Bonds, a large amount of which was in the hands of Dutch stockholders. To this Mr. Seward replied that he was not sure that this was the case, that he had evidences to the contrary, and that he could not decide upon the subject before Mr. Reverdy Johnson, who is going to-day to New Orleans for the purpose of studying the question, had made a report upon it. This, of course, ended the matter, which will not be resumed for some time to come.

THE FORT PULASKI PRISONERS AT THE NORTH.

Dr. MCFARLAND, the surgeon of the Fort Pulaski garrison, who has been released under the order for the discharge of all captured surgeons, furnishes the Savannah *Republican* with the following account of the movements of his late fellow prisoners

The garrison was placed on board the steamer Ben de Ford on the 13th April and taken to Hilton Head, where they remained under guard until the 18th, when they embarked on board the iron steamer Oriental, for New York There were sixteen negroes belonging to the garrison, who were allowed the privilege of accompanying their owners to New York, or remaining at Hilton Head, at their option. About eight decided to go, and they remained with the garrison about eight days after their arrival at Governor's Island, when they were taken away by order of the Secretary of War and set at liberty in the city.

Barren, Graves, Ayer and Westcott, citizens of Savannah, who were captured in the river, were at Hilton Head, and held as prisoners of war.

On landing at Governor's Island, the prisoners were supplied with comfortable quarters, the officers being separated from the men. The former were allowed the freedom of the island on their parole, but the men were confined to the fort, yet with ample privilege of exercise, etc.—The prisoners received every attention from citizens of the South now resident in New York, with offers of money without regard to the amount. Remittances from Savannah reached them, and all their wants were supplied. The prisoners feel under special obligations to Messrs Edward Padelford and Andrew Low, of Savannah, who placed any amount they might desire at their disposal. Other names it would be improper to mention. Their treatment from the officers of the fort was generally kind, though for some time after their arrival our officers were somewhat annoyed by comments on the criminality of the "rebellion," &c.

When Dr. McF. left the Island, the prisoners were in excellent health and good spirits. The officers were removed to Sandusky, Ohio, on the 20th June; the privates still remained at Fort Williams, on Governor's Island.

A "SNAG IN THE MISSISSIPPI."

The New York *Times* thus alludes to Vicksburg:

The only rebel snag interfering now with the free navigation of the Mississippi river is the town of Vicksburg. Our boats struck against it very unexpectedly, when they were dashing up the Father of Waters in the most triumphant style. The invincible fleet of Commodore Farragut, which had blown to pieces all the rebel gunboats, fireships and forts near the mouth of the stream, and captured all the towns on the river as far up as Vicksburg, was stopped short, and turned tail and went down the river again, after taking a look at this Mississippi town. The gun and mortar boats of Commodores Foote and Davis, which did such brave work at Island No. 10, at Fort Pillow, and above Memphis, and which, we are given to understand, after the capture of Memphis, were not to pause in their victorious course down the stream until they hailed the up-coming fleet from New Orleans—even they, it seems, have not thought it best to go to Vicksburg. And so, from the mouth of the Arkansas to Vicksburg, a distance of two hundred miles, the Mississippi River, which we all thought weeks ago was entirely ours, is still controlled by the rebels. We do not think, however, that Vicksburg will be a very difficult snag to root out or to break down, and we do not imagine that the country will need to wait very long now for its reduction, and the consequent opening of the river. Our New Orleans fleet only turned back from Vicksburg that it might return to it again in such force as to compel it to succumb without making any ado about the matter; and of our up-river fleet, we learn that Ellett's rams have passed down to see if there is any butting needed near Vicksburg. We suppose that some of Foote's old mortar boats have also gone down; and as part of Porter's mortar fleet, lately at Mobile, has gone up, we shall doubtless soon see warm work at Vicksburg, or else we shall behold, what the military commandant there said we never should behold, the surrender of another Mississippi town.

MISCELLANEOUS.

Birney, the Yankee general who was recently suspended for cowardice, has been tried, acquitted and restored to his command.

Rev. Dr. B. M. Palmer, the distinguished Presbyterian divine of New Orleans, is delivering war addresses at various towns in Mississippi. He is everywhere received with great enthusiasm.

Col. A. H. Colquitt has been promoted to a Brigadier General. His brigade consists of the 6th, 23d, 28th and 27th Georgia.

Lincoln has nominated to the Yankee Senate Col. John Cochrane and Gustavus Adolphus Scroggs, both from New York, to be Brigadier Generals of Volunteers.

The Naval Court Martial to try Commodore Tattnall for blowing up the Virginia, was ordered at the request of himself, and may be considered in the light of an appeal from the decision of the late Court of Enquiry.

Richmond Dispatch.

☞ The DISPATCH is published DAILY, Sundays excepted. Price for mailing $6 a year, or $3.50 for six months; three months $2; one month $1, in advance.
☞ The SEMI-WEEKLY DISPATCH is issued every TUESDAY and FRIDAY at $3, in advance.
☞ The WEEKLY DISPATCH is issued every FRIDAY, and mailed to subscribers at $2 per an'm.

DAILY DISPATCH.

VOL. XXIII. RICHMOND, VA., THURSDAY MORNING, JULY 3, 1862. NO. 3.

Richmond Dispatch.

TERMS OF ADVERTISING.

1 square, 1 day	$0.50	1 square, 8 days	$1.50
1 do. 2 days	0.75	1 do. 6 days	[illegible]
1 do. 3 days	1.00	1 do. 12 days	3.00
1 do. 4 days	1.25	1 do. 1 month	5.00

Larger Advertisements in exact proportion.
☞ Advertisements published till forbid will be charged 50 cents per square of EIGHT LINES for the first insertion, and 25 cents for each continuance.

THURSDAY MORNING.......... JULY 3, 1862.

THE GREAT BATTLE.

TERRIBLE FIGHTS OF MONDAY AND TUESDAY.

HEROISM OF OUR TROOPS—THEIR SPIRITS BUOYANT.

Critical Situation of the Yankee Forces.

&c., &c., &c.

Since the issue of our paper yesterday no information has reached us of the transactions of our own and the enemy's forces calculated to discourage the hope that the grand army of McClellan is completely discomfited. The determined stands made by the Federal forces on Monday and Tuesday were only the last desperate struggles against ignominious capture or utter annihilation. Their condition is one of desperation, and it is but natural that they should struggle with energy to avert the fate that awaits them.

MONDAY AFTERNOON'S FIGHT.

We have already laid before our readers such accounts of the desperate and determined fight of Monday evening as we were enabled to gather from the most authentic sources. An active participant in that memorable engagement has furnished a detailed account of the part borne by the division of Gen. A. P. Hill in this struggle. This division went into the fight about half past 5 o'clock P. M., and was actively engaged from that time until its close, after 9 o'clock at night.

The 40th Virginia Regiment, Fields' Brigade, Col. Brockenbrough commanding, was deployed as skirmishers, three hundred yards to the right, separating them from the balance of the brigade, which was ordered forward. The regiment was then withdrawn as skirmishers, and placed in the rear of the division, which was advancing rapidly to the field in regular line of battle. After advancing in this order for some distance, they were thrown out upon the left, through a heavy tract of woods—emerging from which they encountered a strong force of the enemy, who threw themselves upon the ground and awaited the approach of the regiment. When within one hundred and fifty yards of this body, which we learn, was partly composed of the 57th N. Y. regiment, a most murderous and destructive fire was opened upon them, and it is believed that not less than seventy-five of our men fell from the first volley. This, as might have been expected, produced some confusion in the regiment, and they fell back to the woods, hotly pursued by the exultant foe. Many of the regiment, it is believed, were captured in this woods, as at roll-call next morning but fifty were present to respond to their names—out of 450 that went into the fight.

On a hill, obliquely to the right of Gen. Hill's advance, was posted a battery of some twelve pieces, which had been twice captured during the afternoon by our forces under Gen. Longstreet, but recaptured by the enemy. This battery, the brigade of Gen. Fields—reduced in numbers and worn out with fatigue from their participation in every general engagement since Thursday—was ordered to charge. With spirit and alacrity they responded to the order, and with close rank and steady step they moved forward to its execution. In their approach to the battery, they fired three or four rounds, and then engaged the enemy with the bayonet. Here the struggle was bloody and determined, but after a most obstinate resistance, the enemy was driven from his pieces, and pressed back some two hundred yards in a hand-to-hand engagement. This charge was made by three regiments—the 47th, 55d and 60th Virginia.

The other brigades of the division coming up to the support of Fields, finding the enemy routed, commenced cheering vociferously. The Federal General McCall, hearing this cheering, and mistaking the source from whence it came, rode up and said, "Hurra, boys; I am glad you have held the battery. Hold on for a short time and reinforcements will be up to sustain you!" He was accompanied by Major Biddle, his Adjutant-General, Major Williams, another aid, and two couriers. Suspecting that he had, perhaps, made a mistake, he asked what regiment it was that held the battery. An officer present replied, the 47th Virginia. On obtaining this information, Majors Williams and Biddle and the two couriers wheeled about and endeavored to effect their escape. They were fired upon, and Major Biddle shot through the heart and killed instantly. The others, so far as is known, escaped without injury. Gen. McCall, being in advance of his party, was brought to a stand by a private in the 47th regiment, who drew his gun upon him and demanded his surrender. His sword was received by Major Mayo. The General was particularly solicitous that no indignity should be offered him, when he was emphatically assured by Major Mayo that he had not fallen into the hands of a soldiery unacquainted with the usages of civilized warfare. Under an escort, McCall was then sent to Gen. Hill.

About 9 o'clock the brigade of Gen. Anderson was advanced to the front and drawn up in line of battle. Several volleys were fired into the woods where the enemy had taken shelter, which had the effect to disperse them, and the fight closed for the evening. During the engagement Gen. Anderson was knocked from his horse by the fragment of a shell striking him on the side of the head. He was missed after the fight was ended, and it was feared that he had been captured; but on Tuesday morning he came in tolerably well, but considerably bruised about the head.

TUESDAY'S OPERATIONS.

During the forenoon of Tuesday there was no regular engagement, but much desultory firing along the whole extent of the retreating and advancing lines. In the afternoon, about 2½ o'clock, a brisk fight was commenced on the right of the left wing of our army, Jackson's corps, then situated convenient to Dr. Poindexter's farm, on the Williamsburg road, and directly opposite Turkey Island creek. The character of the country here is slightly undulating, the intervening ground between the belligerent parties consisting of open, cultivated fields, whilst the extremes are dense woods of heavy timber and thick undergrowth. From the situation occupied by our troops, the enemy was discovered in large force deploying their troops, and placing their artillery in position. Bodies of skirmishers were thrown out from our column with a view to test the disposition of the enemy. This required but a short time to accomplish, as a brisk fire was soon opened upon them. Our artillery then opened fire upon the batteries of the enemy which had the effect to produce another "artillery duel," lasting for one hour and a half, both parties serving their pieces with decided skill and alacrity.

Heavy bodies of infantry were advanced to the support of our artillery, and a general fight ensued, which resulted in the repulse and temporary withdrawal of the enemy; but, ultimately rallying and bringing to their aid a battery on their right, they opened a fierce oblique fire on the left flank of our forces then in action. This fire, which was excessively severe, was continued without intermission, and responded to with spirit by our own artillery until 6 o'clock P. M.

An intermission of some half hour then occurred, during which time, according to the representation of prisoners subsequently captured, the enemy at this point were heavily reinforced, when the fight was again renewed, our centre and right of line becoming engaged. For three successive hours there was kept up one unbroken roar of artillery and musketry, which, for its fierce intensity, exceeded anything that has occurred in the whole series of bloody battles around Richmond. The very earth trembled beneath the deafening and incessant peals. Notwithstanding the fatigue and well nigh exhausted condition of our men, from their almost superhuman labors of the previous six days, they entered this fight with an ardor and readiness, plainly indicating their unchangeable determination to conquer or die. About 9½ or 10 o'clock, our artillery ceased firing, having effectually silenced the batteries of the enemy. This, however, it is due to say, was the only perceptible advantage gained by this wing of the army in the afternoon's operations. The loss sustained by both contending parties was heavy. How many on either side it is impossible to state, or even give an approximate estimate.

Whilst these operations were going on on the left wing of our army, a scarcely less severe fight was progressing on the right, where the division of Gen. Huger was engaged. The brigades of Mahone and Armistead had been exerting themselves against a largely overwhelming force of the enemy, but being compelled to fall back in order to rest their men, Gen. Ranson's brigade was ordered forward. It consisted of five regiments, viz: 24th, Col. Clark; 25th, Col. Rutledge; 26th, Col. Vance; 35th, Col. Ransom, and 49th, Col. Ramseur, all North Carolina troops. They were ordered to charge two heavy batteries, that were supported by not less than five Federal brigades, and all the while they were marching up to make the charge were under three fires. They did not falter, however, but went forward into the very teeth of the enemy without so much as the slightest indication of hesitation. It was, beyond question, one of the hardest fights, and one of the most desperate charges, that has been made during the whole war. This one brigade engaged the main body of the enemy's army at this point, and when compelled to withdraw did so in the most perfect order, and with the most undaunted spirit. Gen. Ranson fearlessly and intrepidly led his brigade on horseback, and was, during the whole continuance of the fight, exposed to the leaden hail of the enemy.

Col. M. W. Ranson, of the 35th regiment, was wounded in the early part of the fight by a Minie ball in the arm, but remained at the head of his regiment, rallying and cheering his men, till struck by a piece of shell in the side and prostrated. Lieut. Col. Pettway then took command of the regiment but was almost immediately killed. Colonel Ramseur, of the 49th, was wounded, and the casualties are very large throughout the entire brigade. We held our ground, and Gen. Ranson and his men slept upon the field they had formerly occupied, and but for the pelting rain would have renewed the fight yesterday morning.

There were, doubtless, other divisions and brigades engaged at different points along the line, who acquitted themselves with the same heroic and determined courage as that of the gallant Ranson; but being unapprised of their particular participation in this grand struggle for the defence of liberty, we are not prepared to notice them specially.

YESTERDAY'S OPERATIONS.

Notwithstanding the heavy rains of yesterday, the two armies were not inactive, though we have no report of any severe fighting. The latest accounts we have inform us that the enemy, finding some difficulty in getting off the bulk of their forces by the way of Turkey Island, had moved to their left, in the direction of Deep Bottom, where there are good landings and deep water. But their retreat was cut off by our troops occupying the New Market road, while they were also being attacked along the lines of the Long Bridge and the Quaker roads. These three roads form a triangle of about one and a half or two miles area of low and heavily timbered land, with thick undergrowth and which, in wet weather, is almost impassable.

If this information is correct—and we cannot doubt it—the total surrender must be only a question of time; and, in the absence of supplies, cannot be postponed more than one or two days.

FEDERAL BARBARITY.

On Monday last, in the fight near Willis's Church, Winfield Byrd, of the 11th Alabama regiment, was taken prisoner by the Yankees uninjured. After his capture two Yankee officers assaulted him with their swords—one of them piercing him through the side, the other striking at his head. The blow was warded off by Byrd with his hand, and while his head was protected the blow was received on the arm and hand, inflicting a painful wound. The Yankees were subsequently driven back and Byrd recaptured. He is now at a house near the church. —— Woodward, of the same regiment, was wounded, and is at the same place.

YANKEE CAPTIVES.

There are over 4,000 Yankees registered at the different places appointed for their reception in this city. Yesterday nearly three hundred were sent in, including J. F. Guy, 2d Lieutenant, 7th Pennsylvania; R. Sherman, Sergeant Major, 42d Pennsylvania and F. W. Usher, 2d Lieutenant, company [illegible], 34th New York. As soon as some place can be fitted up for the accommodation of the many wounded left on our hands by the commander of the Yankee forces, they will be brought into the city and properly cared for. There are already several hundred of the enemy's wounded here.

CASUALTIES.

We learn that Major Baldwin, lately in charge of the Ordnance Department in this city, received a severe wound in the engagement of Tuesday evening. He entered active service in the field only a few days ago, and at the time he was shot was acting Colonel of an Alabama regiment. He is now with his friends in this city.

Colonel Thomas P. August, of the 15th Virginia regiment, was wounded in the leg and brought in yesterday morning. We are gratified to hear that his injuries are not considered dangerous.

Major John Stewart Walker, formerly Captain of the Virginia Life Guard, was killed on Tuesday.—He was a brave and gallant officer, and one of our best and most influential citizens. Elli. Munford, son of the Secretary of the Commonwealth, also fell mortally wounded in the same bloody engagement. R. T. Daniel, Jr., was wounded.

Captain Charles Bruce, of Halifax, and Captain Harrison, of the Charles City Troop, were numbered among the gallant dead of Tuesday's battle.

Captain Charles Pickett, A. A. General in Gen. Pickett's brigade, had his leg badly fractured in Sunday's fight, but it is believed that amputation will not be necessary. Captain P. is a resident of Richmond.

VIEW OF THE SITUATION FROM THE SOUTH SIDE OF THE RIVER—REINFORCEMENTS.

The Petersburg *Express* of yesterday has the following intelligence, which is of much interest:

We have reliable information that a portion of McClellan's army sought safety in flight as far back as Monday afternoon. This we knew Monday night, and so stated yesterday, but further confirmation of this retreat is furnished in the following communication which Col. Pannill, the Provost Marshal of this city, has kindly furnished us:

DREWRY'S BLUFF, July 1.

To Col. *Wm. Pannill*, Provost Marshal:

Capt. Upshur reports from Bermuda Hundreds on James river, at 11 o'clock last night, that the enemy (or a portion of them) was in full retreat; that their gunboats were near Shirley, on the Charles City shore, endeavoring to protect the retreat; that the Galena and two other gunboats had fired 200 shells into ranks, as they supposed, but that our forces had pressed the enemy hard, and he could hear fearfully rapid musketry firing until dark; that they were embarking their wounded above Shirley, and that many stragglers of all arms of the service were on the banks, without arms, also a large number of teams.

S. S. LEE, Capt. C. S. N.

All day yesterday, as we ascertained last evening from a gentleman who left Bermuda Hundreds at 4 P. M., gunboats, transports, and sailing vessels—the latter under the convoy of gunboats—were plying up and down the river with troops, which were embarked in the vicinity of Shirley. It is stated further that the banks of the river were lined with stragglers yesterday, and that they could be seen to rush eagerly to the transports as fast as they would reach the wharf. Four of the fugitives rushed into a small boat, and paddling out into the stream, were drifted to the Chesterfield shore. These were captured, and expected to reach Petersburg last evening.

Several hundred Federal army wagons were seen at Berkeley, Charles City county, yesterday morning early, by citizens of Prince George. They communicated with a small tug lying out in the stream, but none of them were embarked. The wagons were protected by Federal cavalry, and known to be empty from the rattling noise which they caused when they were driven up. A detachment of Stuart's cavalry could easily bag all this valuable game.

Parties from Drewry's Bluff, who arrived here last night, report heavy firing of cannon, and rapid discharges of musketry, all day yesterday across the river. The fight was evidently progressing on the north of the James, but no accounts of results had reached Richmond last night at ten o'clock.

We have positive information that the enemy were reinforced yesterday from below. We know not the extent of the reinforcements, but the *Vanderbilt*, a very large transport, was certainly in the lower James yesterday, crowded with troops. More reinforcements were probably carried up last night.—The immense train of wagons seen yesterday at Berkley are to be used, doubtless, for the purpose of carrying ammunition and provisions to the now much discomfited foe. It is gratifying to know that we are prepared to meet these reinforcements with fresh troops, man for man.

"I came off with flying colors," as the painter said when he fell from the ladder with [illegible] his thumb.

HIGHLY IMPORTANT FROM EUROPE.

FOREIGN INTERVENTION

Speeches in Parliament.

BUTLER'S PROCLAMATION.

THE BRITISH PRESS ON INTERVENTION.

&c., &c., &c., &c.

The New York papers to the 27th (one day later) contain the details of the foreign news by the Arabia from London, June 14th. They are very important, much more so than the telegraphic summary before published would have led us to believe. The following editorial in the *Herald* will show with what solicitude that paper regards the present attitude of foreign powers relative to intervention:

BRITISH INSOLENCE AND AMERICAN POWER.

[From the New York Herald, June 27.]

The details of the news by the Arabia are of a much more decided character than the telegraphic summary which we published on Wednesday seemed to indicate. Our Paris correspondence, too, throws great additional light upon the movements now going on in France and England. It appears that the programme is, that France will take the lead in the "mediation" or intervention scheme for the settlement of the civil war in America, while England secretly pledges her moral, and if necessary, her physical, support; that the basis of the intervention is to be, if not separation as a *sine qua non*, at least a decision of the question by the votes of the people of the Southern States, each State to determine for itself what is to be its future connection—whether with the Northern States or the Southern Confederacy—and that, to carry out this arrangement, an armistice should take place for six months—the proposition to be made at Richmond and Washington simultaneously in the middle of July—and in the event of the North refusing to accept the intervention, the European Powers will immediately acknowledge the independence of the revolutionary States, and will also consider what farther action it may be necessary and proper to take in the premises.

These views are confirmed by the tone of the French and English press, as well as by the full reports of the debates in the British Parliament. The London *Post*, the organ of Lord Palmerston and of Count Persigny, in an article dated June 14, has the following very suggestive observations:

"It is a matter of astonishment that long ere this some demand has not been made upon the Government to take some steps towards effecting a cessation of hostilities which have proved so disastrous in their consequences to this nation. The time may come, and that shortly, when it will become the paramount duty of neutral States to interpose; but now, as at the commencement of the war, they are undoubtedly bound to stand aloof."

The language of Lord Palmerston is in singular harmony with this. He says: "We have *at present* no intention of offering mediation between the two contending parties." And so Earl Russell in the other house: "Certainly there is no intention on the part of her Majesty's Government to mediate *at the present moment*." This implies that the time may soon come when England will "interpose."—Meanwhile, Napoleon is to go ahead, as the Manchester *Guardian* suggests. The Emperor would prefer to have England openly with him from the start, but she prefers that France shall bear the first shock resulting from the insolent proposition. Meantime, the English population are to be worked up to the fighting point by such unprecedented harangues against a friendly nation as those indulged in by the ministers of the Crown against the same people.

The London *Times* suggests the mediation at first of Napoleon and the Czar, while England holds back, and then goes on to say:—"If, as seems more than possible, the resolution of the Southerners avails to protract this war from month to month, then the time must come when the intervention of Europe will be demanded by the interests of humanity, and, perhaps, accepted willingly by the exhausted combatants." In another article the same journal, representing, as it does, the oligarchy of England, thus sounds the warning note upon another point:—"It cannot be doubted that we are approaching a time when a more important question even than that of an offer of mediation may have to be considered by England and France. The Southern Confederacy has constituted itself a nation nearly a year and a half. During that time the attachment of the people to the new Government has been indubitably shown. Immense armies have been raised, the greatest sacrifices have been endured, the persistence of the South in the war through a long series of battles—some victories, some defeats—has shown the 'force and consistency' which are looked upon as the tests of nationality." The writer proceeds to [illegible] recognition as an Independent Power, the precedents of the British and Spanish American colonies, of Belgium, and of Tuscany and Naples, forbid England "to question this right when asserted by the Confederate States;" and that "it is the duty of the British Government to anticipate this possible event."

For some time past British statesmen and their press have put a restraint upon their wonted hostility to the United States. They are beginning, perhaps, to forget the affair of the capture of their West India mail steamer, which so nearly involved them in a war with this country. They then blessed their stars that they escaped, as it were, out of the fire. At that time, too, they hoped that the insurrectionary States would succeed in their design. They are now disappointed. They see that the rebellion, fomented by British gold and influence, will soon be crushed, and they are becoming desperate. Their long cherished purpose to divide the country they know will prove a failure, and hence their rage and their insolence to the American Republic.

Lord Palmerston, for example, has the audacity to say that the English Government will consider what is the proper course for it to adopt with regard to the proclamation of Gen. Butler at New Orleans, just as if that were any business of Lord Palmerston or of the British Government. Earl Russell hopes that our Government, for its own sake, will repudiate the act of General Butler. This looks somewhat in the nature of a threat, as much as to say: "You had better of your own accord rebuke General Butler, or we will take you in hand as we did in the case of the Trent." Is England to become censor general of the manners of all nations in peace and war, and to punish them if they do not square with her ideas of propriety? Such impudence and presumption can find no precedent save in the folly of the British monarch who stood on the sea-shore and ordered the waves to recede; but they flowed on in their majesty, and poor Canute was soon compelled to escape from their power.

But let England rest assured, that by any European coalition she can form she will be as unsuccessful in her designs against the independence, the union and integrity of the American Republic, as were all her coalitions for the dismemberment and destruction of the Republic of France. At that time France had no naval force with which she could cope with her rival. Yet she held her own. But the navy of the Republic of the United States is more than a match for that of Britannia, which so long ruled the waves; and whereas France was surrounded in close contiguity by England and her allies, the field of operations in America would be separated from the foe by a vast ocean 3,000 miles wide. How much less, therefore, is her chance of success against a Republic mightier than France, and that has remained unconquered ever since she had an existence!

Let British statesmen, therefore, beware of what they do. The cup of their iniquity is nearly filled. They have come second best out of two wars with the United States; out of a third, perhaps, they would never come at all. The Southern fleet is completely used up. We have a powerful naval force left almost unemployed. With this reinforced, as it will be next fall, by a tremendous addition of iron-clad gunboats, we will be in a position to annihilate the navies of England and France, and of all the maritime Powers of Europe. Canada and the British West India islands would fall, like ripe pears, into the lap of the American Republic, and Great Britain would cease to own a foot of soil in the New World, while perhaps Ireland, taking advantage of her tyrant's difficulty, would at last work out a successful revolution, and leave "the sister" island alone in its glory.

GENERAL BUTLER'S PROCLAMATION BEFORE THE BRITISH PEOPLE.

In the House of Commons on the same night Sir J. Walsh rose to ask the Under Secretary of State for Foreign Affairs whether Her Majesty's Government had received official information authenticating a proclamation attributed to General Butler, the Military Governor of New Orleans, menacing the women of that city with the most degrading treatment as a punishment for any mark of disrespect offered to any officer or soldier of the United States army, and, if so, whether her Majesty's Government had deemed it right to communicate with the American Government against the issue of such an order. He said that when he placed the notice on this subject upon the paper, he hoped that the answer he should receive would be that the proclamation in question was only one of *those common fabrications* which had been so ingeniously circulated during the American war; for it appeared to him incredible that a military officer, bearing a high commission, and invested with responsible command in the service of a great Power, should have placed his name to a document which must entail so much obloquy. (Hear, hear.)

But he could not fail to observe from the journals of that morning, and from a letter written by the generally accurate New York correspondent of the London *Times*, that this matter had been long and angrily canvassed at New York, that it had excited great attention, and was there universally believed, and he regretted to add that there was no report or intimation of any formal contradiction or repudiation of the act on the part of the Government of the United States. (Hear, hear.) Under these circumstances the hope he had entertained was considerably weakened, but he still in-dulged the expectation that the Under Secretary for Foreign Affairs would by his reply be enabled to allay the deep, indignant feeling which pervaded all classes in this country at the announcement of so extraordinary a proclamation, utterly repugnant to the spirit of the nineteenth century and to the usages of civilized war. (Hear.)

In the few observations he was desirous of making he should refrain from entering into the merits of the great contest now going on the other side of the Atlantic. In that House they had hitherto maintained impartial and strict neutrality, and had exhibited a prudent and wise reserve, but it was necessary that he should make the observation that, in that unhappy civil war, it appeared, as all accounts agreed in stating, that wherever the Northern armies penetrated into the South they were uniformly received as invaders, and there was yet no evidence of the existence of any party, or fraction of a party, or of any individual scarcely, who entertained in the secessionist States other feelings than those of the most determined hostility to the Northern States of America. It would appear that such a feeling was universal, and that the Southern men, rightly or wrongly, identified their cause with the sacred cause of independence and liberty and with love of country. It was not wonderful, then, that throughout the Southern States of America the women should partake of the sentiments which their fathers, husbands, and sons entertained.

It might have been thought that the sentiments of honor which generally animated the members of a gallant profession would have made it impossible that anything like discourtesy or insult should have been offered to women by the officers of a Christian country in a civilized age. (Hear, hear.) The Northern States having established a military occupation at New Orleans found, as might have been anticipated, a bitter feeling of animosity awakened by the conquest of that city. That feeling ought to have excited their generosity and forbearance. Instead of that, however, General Butler had issued a proclamation stating, that "as the officers and soldiers of the United States had been subjected to repeated insults from women calling themselves the ladies of New Orleans, in return for the most scrupulous courtesy, it is ordered that, hereafter when any female shall, by word, gesture, or movement, insult or show contempt for any officer or soldier of the United States army, she shall be held liable to be treated as a woman of the town, plying her avocation."

Did that language mean that the ladies of New Orleans, because they might happen to make some gesture or movement which an officer or soldier might interpret as an insult, were to be dragged to the common jail and subjected to the most degrading association with the vilest of their sex? That, of itself, would be the most intolerable tyranny to which a civilized people in our day had been exposed. There was another construction which those words might bear, so horrible that it could hardly be intended by any mind but that of a demon, and he would not, therefore, further allude to it. But wherever this proclamation was spoken of in Europe it was sure to be visited with one burst of execration—(hear, hear)—and it would be seen, whether public opinion, which was said to be so influential in controlling despots, had any power over a rampant democracy. Some honorable gentlemen might think a remonstrance against this proceeding would be a departure from the line of non-intervention, and might lead us into difficulties and complications with the American Government. Let the House not listen to such mean and timid counsels. We had interfered, and interfered effectually, on former occasions.

Many years ago a civil war raged in the north of Spain, which was characterized by barbarous cruelty on both sides. The British Government endeavored by negotiation to stop those brutal practices, and, though the war went on, they succeeded in their object by means of the Elliott Convention. The noble viscount now at the head of the Government *had perpetually interfered* by way of remonstrance, and had tendered excellent advice to almost every Government in Europe. Not long ago, too, Earl Russell remonstrated with this very American Government for blocking up Charleston harbor with a stone fleet. But surely our interposition was now far more imperatively called for by an act which tended to degrade human nature itself—to throw back civilization, and revive the spirit of a Gheughis Khan or a Nadir Shah. (Hear, hear.) It would be most unjust, without more reliable information on the point, to accuse the American Government of any participation in this enormity.

If that Government at once signified its disapproval of this proclamation public opinion would applaud its conduct. On the other hand, if it showed any hesitation or delay in taking that course he earnestly hoped that her Majesty's Government would gravely point out to them the necessity of vindicating the national honor so foully stained.—(Hear, hear.) The honorable baronet concluded by moving for copies of any correspondence received from our Minister at Washington relating to Gen. Butler's proclamation.

Mr. Gregory was not surprised that such a motion should have been placed on the paper relative to the proclamation they were now considering.—The course which had been pursued in regard to it was neither improper nor unusual. The honorable baronet had quoted certain precedents; but he need not go further than the discussions which had taken place in that and the other House of Parliament to show that when a great act of inhumanity had been committed by a foreign nation they were perfectly justified in commenting on the proceeding. There had been a debate on the conduct of Russia towards Poland, and there had also been a discussion on the conduct of an Italian General in the south of Italy. Government had not failed to express their opinion in regard to both of these transactions.

He deprecated *any fussy or meddling interference* with foreign States. He entirely disapproved those homilies and lectures that were too often read by our ministers to foreign States, and which were infinitely more agreeable to the compilers than to the receivers. He also deprecated the conduct of those who ransacked the newspapers for the purpose of putting questions in that House which were of no possible use, and were received by foreign countries with great dissatisfaction. He entirely agreed with what was said in the vacation speech of the right honorable member for Huntingdon, (General Peel,) that such intermeddling tended to produce a general feeling of dissatisfaction towards this country on the continent, and led foreigners to say, in their hearts at least, with Orlando, "I do desire that we should be better strangers."

But when a proclamation repugnant to decency, civilization, and humanity, had been promulgated and put in force against a people endeared to us by every tie of family, language and religion, then he did think we had a right to protest against such an enormity—(hear, hear)—and appeal to the moral sense of the world against an outrage so wicked, so inexcusable, and so useless. (Hear, hear.) Taking the words of the proclamation as he read them, it could signify nothing less than that the ladies of New Orleans, if they showed by word, by gesture, or by movement, contempt for a Northern soldier, were to be subjected to the brutalities of the Northern armies, *and handed over to the tender mercies of the scum and the rowdery of New York.* (Hear, hear.) That was the interpretation which the words conveyed, and which they had a right to put on them. He had heard that very day that there was no punishment in New Orleans against unfortunate women of the town—they were not placed in the lock-up; there was hardly any instance in which that had occurred.

But let them put even the most merciful signification on the words—suppose these ladies were only to be locked up in the calaboose with drunken negroes and all the rascality of soldiery, and for what was this punishment to be inflicted on the ladies of New Orleans? If by word, movement, or gesture they offended the sensibilities of a Northern soldier. (Hear.) Suppose a case of gallantry on the part of such a soldier; if a lady replied to it with that feeling of loathing they felt towards the men, it might be construed into a mark of contempt. If a lady crossed the street to avoid an encounter with a Northern soldier, or made use of any unguarded expression which showed that, though subdued, the people were still unconquered in their determination for freedom, it might be construed into contempt, and for that the ladies of New Orleans might be locked up with the common women of the town. (Hear.) He spoke very strongly because he felt very strongly.

Not more than two years and a half ago he was at New Orleans himself, and *he should not readily forget the kindness, the geniality, the ever ready welcome with which he was received, or the charm, the grace and gentleness of these ladies.*—(Hear, hear.) A letter was put into his hand from a Southern young lady a few days ago, in which it was stated, "I am afraid when you see us again you will find us entirely changed—we have been so outraged that you will no longer find us the timid, retiring women we were." ("Hear," and a laugh.) He thought it too piteous to laugh at. It was sad enough for tears. He did not appeal to his honorable friend, the Under Secretary of State for Foreign Affairs, to reply to this question; but he did ask the Prime Minister of England if he was prepared to do that which he was convinced the ruler *of brave and chivalrous* France would do, if he had not already done it—(hear, hear)—namely, to protest against this, the greatest outrage which had been perpetrated against decency in the age in which we lived. (Hear, hear.)

Lord Palmerston rose amidst loud cheers and said—Mr. Speaker, appealed to as I have been by my honorable friend, I am quite prepared to say that I think no man could have read the proclamation to which our attention has been drawn without a feeling of the deepest indignation—(cheers from both sides of the House)—a proclamation to which I do not scruple to attach the epithet infamous. (Renewed cheering.) Sir, an Englishman must blush to think that such an act has been committed by one belonging to the Anglo-Saxon race. (Cheers.) If it had come from some semi-barbarous race that was not within the pale of civilization, one might have regretted it, but might not have been surprised; but that such an order should have been promulgated by a soldier—(cheers)—by one who had raised himself to the rank of General, is a subject undoubtedly of not less astonishment than pain. (Cheers.) Sir, I cannot bring myself to believe but that the Government of the United States, whenever they had notice of the order, would of their own accord have disowned it [illegible] their own [illegible]. (Hear, hear.)

We received yesterday a despatch from Lord Lyons, [illegible] and giving the text of, the proclamation to which reference has been made. There will be no objection to produce that paper. With regard to the course which her Majesty's Government may, upon consideration, take on the subject, the House, I trust, will allow me to say that will be a matter for reflection. (Cheers.) I am quite persuaded that there is no man in England who does not share those feelings which have been so well expressed by the honorable baronet and my honorable friend. (Loud cheers.)

The motion was then agreed to.

Newspaper Accounts.

THE ENGLISH IDEA OF INTERVENTION—THE LONDON TIMES THINKS THAT FRANCE SHOULD TAKE THE LEAD, &C.

[From the London Times, June 14.]

The task of intervening even in the most friendly way between the two hostile communities in America is one of so much delicacy that the country will gladly leave the matter in the hands of the Government, to choose such an opportunity and mode of action as it may think proper. The statements of Lord Palmerston and Lord Russell last night were to the effect that the British Government, at least, has no intention of offering mediation at present, and that no proposals on the subject have been made by the French Emperor. * * *

We should desire nothing better than that Napoleon or the Czar, who are the two most popular sovereigns across the Atlantic, should, either separately or conjointly, press on the Americans the counsels which would be indignantly rejected if offered by us. European mediation had better begin on the continent. All that we can now say has already been said by our politicians and by the press. The speeches of two or three Cabinet ministers and too well known opinions of almost every man of note in either house are equivalent to anything that the French Emperor can disclose to the Americans by a formal offer of mediation. The North knows well the opinions of this country, and, without further official communication, will feel assured that we give a tacit assent to any recommendations which other Powers may make in the interests of peace.

Without, therefore, pretending to divine the secrets of the French Emperor, or to say in what form and when his opinions will be expressed, we may admit that this country must allow him to take the lead. There exists so general a desire in Europe to bring this war to an end, and it is now so clear that the Union can only be restored in name, and by coercing a determined and unanimous people by military force, that every day will increase the number of continental politicians who think as we do. Lord Russell, who confines himself to deprecating mediation at the present time, and who alludes to the probability of some future action of the kind, will probably find the way to the re-establishment of peace, smoothed by the beneficent counsels of our neighbors. The time may come when this country will be able to offer its assistance to settle the dispute without certain misrepresentation or repulse.

In the country districts, at a distance from the points occupied by the Federal forces, there would be less expression, because there would be free scope for lawlessness and violence. The execution of the Federal laws, or the collection of taxes, would be impossible in places where a Federal official would be looked upon by the fierce and maddened Southerners as little less odious than a panther or a rattlesnake. A few thinking men at the North are looking forward to such a state of things, and are candid enough to admit that they know of no greater calamity for themselves than complete success; but if, as seems more than possible, the resolution of the Southerners avails to protract this war from month to month, then the time must come when the intervention of Europe will be demanded by the interests of humanity, and perhaps accepted willingly by the exhausted combatants. This country may, then, with prudence hold itself in readiness to support any proposition which may be urged by its more favored neighbors.

WHAT THE MANCHESTER COTTON MEN THINK OF MEDIATION.

[From the Manchester Guardian, June 13.]

* * * There are many objections to the scheme of the joint mediation which appears to be on the tapis. Our hands are not so free in this matter as those of the French Government, whose relations with America are not embarrassed either by ties of relationship or by recollections of recent rivalry.—But the Emperor Napoleon has gratified the taste of his subjects for foreign influence in many worse directions than that which he is now again represented to be thinking of; and he will have our active sympathy and approval in any steps he may take for the simple purpose of putting a stop to the most crying scandal which the 19th century has witnessed. For ourselves, we shall rejoice if the struggle can be any way ended without interference on our part.

THE LONDON TIMES ON THE "NATIONALITY" OF THE REBELS.

[From the London Times, June 12.]

It is plain that the time is approaching when Europe will have to think seriously of its relations to the two belligerents in the American war. A contest is raging of which we can predict nothing but that every week will add to the hatreds of the two communities, and will spread ruin wider and wider. The state of affairs disclosed to us by the last advices deserves anxious consideration. * *

It cannot be doubted that we are approaching a time when a more important question even than that of an offer of mediation may have to be considered by England and France. The Southern Confederacy has constituted itself a nation for nearly a year and a half. During that time the attachment of the people to the new Government has been indubitably shown; immense armies have been raised, the greatest sacrifices have been endured, the persistence of the South in the war, through a long series of battles—some victories, some defeats—has shown the "*force and consistency*" which are looked upon as the tests of nationality. Wherever the Government is unmolested, the laws are administered regularly as in time of peace, and wherever the Federals have penetrated they are received with an animosity which they resent, as at New Orleans, by a military rule of intolerable brutality. The vision of a Union party in the South has been dispelled, as the Northerners themselves are compelled, with bitterness and mortification, to admit.

All these circumstances point to but one conclusion: Either this war must be brought to an end, or the time will at last come when the South may claim its own recognition by foreign nations as an independent Power. The precedents of our American colonies, of the Spanish colonies, of Belgium, and of Tuscany and Naples the other day, forbid us to question this right when asserted by the Confederate States. It is our duty to anticipate this possible event, and it may be wise as well as generous for statesmen on this side of the ocean to approach the American Government in a friendly spirit with the offer of their good offices at this great crisis of its fortunes.

BRITISH WAR STEAMER IN CHARLESTON HARBOR.—On Saturday evening the British steam sloop-of-war Racer, Captain Lyons, crossed the Bar, and steamed past Fort Sumter into the Harbor of Charleston. She now lies at anchor off the Battery, a short distance from the city wharves. It was currently reported and believed that a French man-of-war is outside, and will, likewise, presently enter the harbor. The *Mercury* says:

While entering the port, a shot was thrown across the bows of the Racer from the Beauregard Battery. She displayed her colors, and was permitted to proceed, in accordance with orders issued, and without saluting our fortifications. We are informed that, by application of the British Consul accredited to the United States Government, the Confederate Government has assented to her ingress and egress, as may prove convenient, without the etiquette of recognizing our authority in our own waters.

It is of a piece with the position occupied on our soil by foreign consuls, acting officially under *exequaturs* of the United States, being parcel of the same policy, and doubtless a logical sequence. We conceive the policy to be weak and temporizing and injurious—a course derogatory to our claims to independence, and to our respectability as a people.—We so characterized it a year ago. The matter of the *Racer* appears to us unnecessary, while it opens an avenue of easy and possibly deleterious information with the enemy off our harbor.

The Confederate States have never been really so weak as to have to ask favors, cap in hand, of the Courts of Europe, as they have done. Our Commissioners should, we think, long since have been withdrawn, until it shall be signified that their official presence is desired, and then we should send Ministers Plenipotentiary. For our part, we recognize no proper ground, now or heretofore, for the Confederate States submitting to be put in an equivocal position by foreign nations. Strong facts will bring us foreign recognition and the lifting of the blockade. They will do it without our acquiescence in either snubbing in Europe, or slights here. Voluntary humiliation, upon whatever pretext of alleged convenience or supposed temporary benefit to ourselves, is, we judge, both unnecessary and unwise.

CONFEDERATE JOURNAL IN LONDON.—The Montgomery (Ala.) *Mail*, noticing a new journal in the interest of the Confederate States, published in London, says:

It is called the *Index*, and is edited by Henry Hotze, formerly of this city, and more recently connected with the editorial department of the Mobile *Register*. A volunteer private in the Confederate States Army, Mr. Hotze was, some months since, withdrawn from the ranks and sent to Europe upon important Government business, which he performed promptly and satisfactorily.

NOT GONE NORTH.—The report from the Charleston papers that the Oriviette, supposed Confederate gunboat, had been seized and was to be or had been sent to Halifax for some alleged violation of the neutrality laws appears to have been premature. The Petersburg *Express* has positive information that nothing of the kind had occurred as late as Saturday.

YANKEE PASTIMES.—Com. Goldsborough has a [illegible]

THE WAR.

A gentleman who visited New Kent on Tuesday has shown us two copies of Northern papers, in which there are maps of the "disputed territory." One shows the ground around Richmond with far greater accuracy than any of our county maps.—The locality of the tents of the "rebels," as seen from a balloon, are correctly given, and the different hills and fortifications properly drawn. Our informant says they have committed every sort of depredation on their line, even to stealing a sheep from a lady in Hanover. At another house, occupied by a widow lady, they dug up the brick floor and seized some money which they had heard from her negroes was buried there.

The Petersburg *Express* says:

The Federal gunboat John Bell, which was so severely peppered on Friday week last, while attempting to pass up James river, in the vicinity of Turkey Island, by a section of French's battery, under the direction of Col. Manning, of the 3d Arkansas regiment, has turned up at the North, and reports "severe injuries" sustained on the occasion above alluded to. Our boys fired 35 shots at her, (6-pounders, rifled,) at a distance of 250 yards, every one of which was seen to enter, and must have passed through and through. Her decks, which were crowded with sharpshooters, were cleared at the first shot from the Confederate battery, and as they all ran below the casualties must have been numerous. Even the pilots left the wheel, and the John Bell drifted slowly down the stream, with the flag flying at half-mast. This signal of distress Col. Manning did not respect, as he knew it was a miserable piece of deception to save the cowardly vandals who had deserted the deck and huddled below.

From a gentleman who has visited City Point within the last day or two, we learn that the malice of the commanders of the Federal fleet in James river was so far indulged in their recent beastly raid up our river as to impel them to the commission of many dastardly acts. Independent of their wanton destruction of private property and the great jeopardy in which they placed the lives of many peaceful citizens on the banks of the Appomattox, they applied the match to all the buildings under the hill at City Point, after shelling all on the hill, and afterwards fired the lumber houses and the wharf, all of which were entirely consumed. The wharf and the lumber houses could not be replaced under an expense of $30,000. What their object could have been in destroying these buildings, we cannot divine, unless it was pure malice.

A TRIP TO YANKEE LAND.

A Richmond correspondent of the Montgomery *Advertiser* furnishes that journal with an account of the experience of Dr. Bates, of the 10th Alabama regiment, who remained with Lieutenant-Colonel Henry Forney, who was wounded in the battle at Williamsburg. Dr. Bates staid at Williamsburg about ten days, was then sent to Washington city as a prisoner; but, in charge of some of our wounded, went first into a hospital, was then imprisoned awhile, then paroled for the District of Columbia—next paroled to come home, and finally discharged unconditionally. The letter says:

Dr. Bates decided to cast his lot with the Colonel, and as our troops departed and the Yankees were coming in, made himself assiduous in his attentions to the wounded. A squad of the enemy soon came hurrying in, and inquired who were there and what they were doing. They next asked the Doctor how to get on top of the building to hoist a flag. He told him he had not been up there and did not know anything about it, and applied himself more diligently in his attentions to the wounded. The Yankees were jubilant over the retreat of our army and many of them talked of going right "on to Richmond," but finally concluded *not to do it just then*. Several officers soon visited Col. Forney, and finally Gen. McClellan came in.—Some of them were old schoolmates of Gen. John H. Forney, and learning that the Colonel was his brother, inquired much about him, and treated the Colonel with a great deal of kindness. He assured him he should have every attention and any quarters in Williamsburg, and as much room as he pleased.

The Colonel's ebony boy Zenas was terribly frightened, and commenced crying from the fear of being carried off by the Yankees from "Mas. Henry;" but he was suffered to remain to take care of his wounded master, and up to the latest accounts was still with him. The citizens of Williamsburg, especially the ladies, ministered freely to the sufferings and wants of our wounded. The Federal Surgeons came in to look after the wounded, and visited Col. Forney, and tendered their services to him. The wounded were shortly after placed under the control of the Yankee Surgeons, after which Dr. Bates played a subordinate part, professionally, merely nursing, dressing and looking after the wants of the wounded. He boarded at a private house in Williamsburg, receiving every kindness from the Williamsburg people, whom he represents as staunch in their allegiance to the Confederacy, notwithstanding the presence of the enemy. A Major Dwight was wounded, captured by our troops during the fight, and sent into Williamsburg along with our wounded, and occupied a position near Col. Forney. Dr. Bates attended to his wants and sufferings, and they soon became acquainted on good terms. When our army left their wounded and the Yankees came in, the Major told Dr. Bates if he got into any trouble to let him know, and he would help him out of it. This turned out well, for subsequently in Washington, when the Doctor was sent to prison for refusing to do drudgery in the hospital at the bidding of some medical cadets, or unfledged "Doc's," Major Dwight at once interposed and had him paroled for the city.

The condition of things on board the transports to Washington is described as horrible, where the wounded Yankees and Southerners lay as close as they could be packed, with their now festering and offensive wounds. Our friend was sent into a hospital occupied partly by Yankees and partly by Southerners. The Doctor bears testimony to the uniform kindness of the enemy to our wounded. They were kindly cared for and well treated everywhere by their captors, and rarely received an unkind word, except from an occasional ignorant and vulgar fellow. He states that the respectable people never annoy our men with discussions of "secession;" that sometimes a big-mouth "politician," or some ignorant fellow, would endeavor to "deliver a lecture on the wickedness of secession and the enormity of fighting against the "Old Flag." Our men soon found plenty of friends in Washington. The Secession ladies were so open and profuse in their attentions and lavish in supplying the wants of the wounded prisoners, that the authorities interfered, and finally forbid their visits. He says it is true, as published in the Northern papers, that it was not uncommon to see wounded Southerners surrounded by groups of ladies in rustling silks, furnishing them all sorts of delicacies, books, papers, &c., while many poor Northern hirelings lay with such attendance as the hospital furnished.

After leaving the prison, he lived at Brown's Hotel, without being troubled with "your bill," and had his pocket full of money. The Doctor saw the great magician, Seward, who pulls the wires, and Old Abe and Mrs. Lincoln, several times. Old Abe he describes, as everybody else does, as a long, awkward, and kangaroo-looking person. Mrs. Lincoln was out in her carriage frequently, and is a genteel, quiet, amiable looking, middle-aged lady.—The Doctor thinks she has been misrepresented by newspaper correspondents. He did not hear a single Secession lady speak disrespectfully or unkindly of her.

The newspaper writers, politicians, and wire-pullers of the Lincoln dynasty are violent, abusive, and vindictive towards Southerners, and succeed in stirring up their followers and keeping up their power, while the [illegible] a large class of harpies, in the form of office-holders, manufacturers, contractors, and speculators, who are now fattening on the war. Many of the soberer and more intelligent people are heartily tired of the war, and despondent of final success. The most marvellous reports of great victories are often put into circulation, especially on the sailing of a European steamer. Great handbills are stuck about the streets, containing these announcements.

The Doctor managed by a little adroitness to avoid being paroled not to tell anything seen or heard, consequently is free in his communications, being untrammeled. While they were paroling the others, he engaged to be very busy talking to a Yankee lady, and was overlooked.

In Baltimore, Dr. Bates found plenty of friends. It is only necessary to be known that you belong to the Southern army.

They are compelled to keep "mum," as the sword of the Abolition Government hangs over them.—But in their private circles, clubs and little social parties, they enjoy their sentiments and discuss matters, and wait in hope for a "better day coming," singing "My Maryland," "The Bonnie Blue Flag," and other Southern war songs. One noble young captive officer, in the prison at Washington, seats himself in his prison window of an evening, and pours forth "My Maryland" to the passing crowd, in defiance of jailors and guards.

McClellan's army was about ninety thousand strong. It has been reduced more than twenty thousand by disease and battle. All the drilled troops are being removed from the fortifications and posts to make up his loss, and their places filled by recruits or militia. It is expected to reinforce the army by this means to its original strength.

DISCONTENT IN THE U. S. SENATE.

Mr. Saulsbury (Del.) said (in the U. S. Senate on the 26th) history would hand down to the future, with execration and condemnation, many acts of the present day. An arbitrary and despotic power now, not satisfied with trampling on every constitutional right of citizens, has dared profanely to enter the temple of justice and drag her ministers from the altar. Men who thus invade a court of justice prove himself a tyrant, capable of any assault on the liberties of the people. Under the pretence of suppressing a causeless rebellion, the Executive Department of this Government, in his judgment, was daily engaged in the greatest violations of the fundamental law.

The necessity who are thus [illegible] civil [illegible] [illegible] to the [illegible] of a civil war, and now evidence sincerity by shouting loyalty, while engaged in destroying the liberties of the people, and even go so far as to dare to impeach the loyalty of those men who stand by the Constitution. He said it was his deliberate and solemn conviction that either abolitionism or constitutional liberty must forever die—the two cannot exist together. Abolitionism has, for the time being, dissolved the Union, and while it lives it will remain dissolved. No free people either will or ought to submit to its sway. It has been the author of all our political woes.

Abolitionism always has been aggressive on the liberties of the Government, and had culminated in an attempt to invade a peaceful State. Then the Republican party, in the same aggressive spirit, nominated a man who declared that "a house divided against itself cannot stand." The war clouds immediately began to threaten. A Senator (Mr. Crittenden) offered a compromise, which would have averted the war, but the Abolitionists refused compromise, and deliberately chose war. Then arose the cry of "On to Richmond," when it was met with a bloody defeat at Manassas. Then Congress passed a resolution that the only object of the war was to suppress rebellion and nothing else, and the loyal people of the Border States took heart and courage. How has Congress kept this pledge?

They abolished slavery in the District of Columbia, and established a paradise for free negroes from Delaware and Maryland, where they were supported by taxing white men. They are paying negro teamsters thirty dollars per month, while our white soldiers are working at thirteen (13) dollars per month. They have legalized negro testimony and established diplomatic relations with Hayti and Liberia. The council chamber of the nation has been turned into a house of wailing for the wrongs of the negro. He contended that the present war was not merely an insurrection or a rebellion, but a great revolution.

He would take the admissions of the Senators from Vermont (Mr. Collamer) and Pennsylvania (Mr. Cowan) and assume that the present Confederate Government is a Government *de facto*, and contend that when the old Government was fully ousted and a new one firmly established, those who give allegiance to the latter cannot be punished for treason to the former. The right of revolution has been asserted in this country, and he thought it settled, that where a revolution is inaugurated under circumstances where success seems probable, it may become the duty of every citizen to yield allegiance to the new Government, and where there is only a reasonable probability of success, such support to a new Government is not a felony which would subject them to imprisonment and death, or confiscation.

It was not right to visit severe punishment on men for doing what they conscientiously believed to be right. A large mass of these men at the South believe that they have the right, and that they owe allegiance to the State as well as to the Government, and they had always given great weight to the former. Humanity, charity, and all the usages of the civilized world, cry out against a severe punishment to those who yield allegiance to Government *de facto*, where a Government *de jure* ceased to protect them or have any power.

He denied that there was any justification or cause for the present resolution. He admitted the right of the Government to prevent the secession of any State, but such right was not derived from any authority in the Constitution, but from the right of self-preservation. He thought that if there had been no slavery in the Southern States there never would have been any confiscation bills. The passage of this bill will only tend to prolong the war and make the separation complete.

THE ASSAULTS UPON GENERAL BLENKER.

It is said that the correspondence in the New York *Tribune* against Gen. Blenker emanates from Carl Schurz, who desires the command of the division. Since the battle of Cross Keys, Colonel Fremont has manifested less unfriendliness towards Gen. Blenker, because in that fight his military abilities and bravery were exhibited. It is contended by the friends of Gen. Blenker that the German division is not demoralized, as the *Tribune* asserts. The marauding attributed to this division is said to have been occasioned by the utter want of provisions, a consequence of the inefficiency of Gen. Fremont's commissariat, which compelled the soldiers to live on the resources of the country. It is remarkable that the *Tribune* should in this case evince so much sympathy with the rebels, while elsewhere, and through its followers in Congress, it has fiercely demanded that rebel property shall be appropriated for the use of our army, and has more than a hundred times assailed General McClellan on account of his alleged leniency towards the enemy. The whole attack upon Gen. Blenker smells very much of political intrigue to raise Carl Schurz to the command of this German division.

DEFENCE OF THE BALTIMORE AND OHIO RAILROAD.

It is understood that the military protection and defence of the Baltimore and Ohio Railroad, east of Cumberland to the city of Baltimore, and of the railroad between Harper's Ferry and Winchester, is especially assigned to the command of Major-General Wool. Officers on the line of that road will accordingly report to him. The operations of the Winchester and Potomac Railroad will remain under the direction of Major-General Banks, it being his line of supply.

ONE DAY LATER FROM THE NORTH.

Changes in the Federal Army.

We have received the New York *Herald*, of the 27th ult., one day later. It contains very little interesting war news. The following is its account of

THE SITUATION.

We have to announce to-day an important change in the military command in Western Virginia, proving that our predictions as to the object of the President's visit to West Point were perfectly accurate. General Pope has received the supreme command of affairs in the Shenandoah Valley, and will now be pitted against the rebel Stonewall Jackson. The forces under Major-Generals Fremont, Banks, and McDowell have been consolidated into one army, called "the Army of Virginia," and Major-General Pope has been especially assigned by the President to the chief command. The forces under General Fremont constitute the first army corps, to be commanded by General Fremont. The forces under General Banks constitute the second army corps, and are to be commanded by him. The forces under General McDowell constitute the third army corps, to be commanded by him.

General Pope enters upon his new command with the prestige of former successes in the Mississippi Valley and in Missouri surrounding his name, which no doubt will be a host in itself with the army of the Shenandoah, recently involved in a somewhat muddled condition of affairs, under the management of the political Generals. A soldier of great dash, combining a capacity for instant action with fine strategical power, as his conduct at Shawnee Mound, New Madrid and Island No. 11 evinced, General Pope is just the man for the position assigned to him.

We are in possession of some further particulars—which we publish—of the skirmish in front of Richmond, on Wednesday. The ground contended for was a swamp, scattered over with clumps of brushwood, with an open country in front. The main object of the advance appears to have been to obtain a dry and healthy location for that portion of our army then encamped in a swampy and sickly region. In this General McClellan *proved entirely successful, as but little more ground has to be gained in order to place our men beyond the effects of their previous unpleasant position.* The rebel camps in front of General Hooker's division are now occupied by our troops. Our total loss in killed and wounded in the action of Wednesday did not amount to over two hundred—the killed being exceedingly small—while that of the enemy was much greater. General McClellan conducted the affair in person, and his presence stimulated the valor of the men engaged.

A dispatch received at the War Department yesterday afternoon from Gen. McClellan, states that the affair of yesterday was perfectly successful; that we hold the new picket line undisturbed, and that all is very quiet on the banks of the Chickahominy.

The official lists of the rebel losses at the battle of Fair Oaks have been published. Eighty-five regiments and battalions in all were engaged, sustaining a loss of killed, wounded, and missing, of 5,897.

With the exception of some details of the recent expedition up the White river in Arkansas, and an engagement of our gunboats near Grand Gulf on the Mississippi river, between Natchez and Vicksburg, there is nothing important to report from the West to-day.

TELEGRAMS.

CITY POINT, VA., June 26, 1862.—Last evening one of our gunboats moved up and shelled the rebels on the Petersburg road, but without any casualties on the side of the rebels, according to their own account of the affair.

General Longstreet issued a flaming address to his troops on Monday, in view of the great conflict imminent, inciting them to new deeds of heroism, and advising them to aim low and make sure of the mark.

The official lists of the rebel losses at the battle of Fair Oaks have been published. Eighty five regiments and battalions in all were engaged, sustaining a loss of killed, wounded, and missing, of five thousand eight hundred and ninety-seven.

The rate of postage on letters in the "Southern Confederacy" has been raised from five to ten cents.

About ten o'clock this morning a conveyance arrived at City Point with Capt. Robertson and Lieut. Sykes, of the rebel army, who return under their parole of honor to Fort Warren, the rebel Government having decided not to make any individual exchanges until the United States Government shall agree upon terms for a general exchange of prisoners.

General Prentiss and fifty other Federal officers, taken at Shiloh, have been removed to [illegible].

A despatch from Chattanooga says the [illegible] have stampeded from that place, leaving their camp and everything behind.

CHARLESTON, June [illegible] [illegible] from Liverpool [illegible] P., ran the blockade [illegible] has on board Mr. [illegible] a valuable cargo of [illegible] a year from England.

The New-York Times.

VOL. XI—NO. 3364. NEW-YORK, FRIDAY, JULY 4, 1862. PRICE TWO CENTS.

FROM GEN. M'CLELLAN.

The Great Battle Continued Through Seven Days.

IMMENSE LOSSES ON BOTH SIDES.

Terrific Onslaught of the Rebels on Our New Position.

Final and Overwhelming Defeat of the Enemy.

Death of Stonewall Jackson and Gen. Barnwell Rhett.

Gen. Magruder Reported to be a Prisoner.

Gen. McClellan Safe and Confident in His New Position.

Arrival of Considerable Reinforcements.

OFFICIAL ADVICES FROM GEN. McCLELLAN.

WASHINGTON, Thursday, July 3—3:12 P. M.

A dispatch from Gen. McCLELLAN, just received at the War Department, dated "From Berkley, Harrison's Bar, July 2, 5:30 P. M," states that he has succeeded in getting his army to that place, on the banks of the James River, and *had lost but one gun*, which had to be abandoned last night, (Tuesday,) because it broke down: that an hour and half ago *the rear of the wagon train was within a mile of the camp, and only one wagon abandoned*; that we had a severe battle yesterday (Tuesday;) *that we beat the enemy to-day*, the men fighting even better than before; that all the men are in good spirits, and that *the reinforcements from Washington have arrived*.

ADVICES FROM FORTRESS MONROE.

FORTRESS MONROE, Tuesday, July 1.

A gunboat has just arrived here from the scene of action yesterday, ten miles above City Point.

That division of our army has been fighting four days, and has retreated about 17 miles.

The fight of yesterday was most terrific, the enemy having three to our one.

The battle commenced with our land forces, and after about four hours' fighting, our gunboats got in range, and poured into the rebels a heavy and incessant fire.

This fire the rebels stood about two hours and then retreated.

Our troops have captured, notwithstanding their disadvantages, a large number of artillery pieces and 2,000 prisoners.

Among the prisoners captured is the Rebel General MAGRUDER.

The place where this last action took place is near Turkey Creek.

The retreat of the rebels last evening was with great disorder, and their loss has been very heavy, much greater it is thought than ours.

There is nothing definite, however, in regard to losses.

In the retreat forced upon Gen. McCLELLAN by the superior numbers of the enemy, I learn that he had to spike his siege guns and leave them on the field, after burning the carriages. The nature of the ground rendered it impossible to move them.

[This, it will be seen, is denied by Gen. McCLELLAN himself.]

In the retreat many of our sick and wounded were necessarily left behind. There are, of course, innumerable reports and rumors here, but I send only what appears to be authentic.

FORTRESS MONROE, Tuesday, July 1.

The loss of the enemy in killed and wounded alone yesterday (Monday) is said not to have been less than four thousand, but we hear nothing definite of the loss on either side.

Gen. Shields' army arrived here this morning, and have proceeded up the James River. They came in vessels via Annapolis.

FORTRESS MONROE, Wednesday, July 2,—9 P. M.

The steamer *Daniel Webster* has just arrived here from City Point with upwards of 300 wounded on board.

A gentleman who came down in charge of them informs me that *yesterday was the sixth day that the battle has been going on, with the most terrific fighting the sun ever shone upon.* It has extended the whole length of our line.

We have lost a great many men in killed, wounded and missing, *probably fifteen to twenty thousand.*

He informs me that Gen. McCLELLAN's headquarters are at Hardin's Landing to-day and his lines extend five miles above toward Richmond. This move of the right wing of the army was predetermined upon and planned ten days ago, and would have been carried out sooner, but for certain reasons well known in the army, but which it would not be proper to state. The enemy's forces have greatly outnumbered ours in almost every action, *but notwithstanding this they have been repulsed oftener than we have and their loss far exceeds ours.*

Yesterday Gen. McCLELLAN is said to have *captured a whole rebel brigade, and took from them several rifle cannon, and other pieces.*

It is now said that we have lost very few of our siege guns, most of them having been recovered in safety.

There have been a great many wounded prisoners taken on both sides.

Our informant says that Gen. McCLELLAN and his Staff all agree that the present position of our army is *far more advantageous as a base of operations against Richmond than that hitherto occupied.*

The gunboats can now be brought to bear, and materially aid in carrying on the work.

Some of our regiments have suffered terribly, while others have but little. The New-York Fifth suffered terribly. They made a most heroic struggle, and made great havoc among the enemy. About one-half their number are killed, wounded, and taken prisoners. They were in the fight at Cold Harbor, and fought against desperate odds.

Our left wing was engaged yesterday, July 1, up to 2 o'clock, with the enemy, mostly with artillery.

The enemy's force, gathered from prisoners, who were members of Beauregard's Western army, was 185,000 men, whilst our effective force did not exceed 95,000.

The Richmond *Dispatch*, of Monday, announced the death of Gen. "Stonewall" JACKSON, and of Gen. BARNWELL RHETT, of South Carolina.

ADVICES RECEIVED IN THIS CITY.

A person arrived in this City last evening from the field of battle before Richmond, having left there on Tuesday evening, July 1, at 9 P. M.

At that time Gen. McCLELLAN's advance was three miles northwest of Hardin's Landing, and within fifteen miles of Richmond.

The enemy was terribly repulsed in the battle of Monday, which was sanguinary in the extreme. We were attacked at four different points, and summarily repulsed the enemy three, when they pressed HEINTZEMAN's left very hard, but SUMNER went to his relief, and they were finally repulsed with great slaughter. HEINTZELMAN captured eight guns and a whole brigade of rebels, 1,600, including their Colonels—PENDLETON, of Louisiana, ex-Congressman LAMAR, of Georgia, and McGEWAN, of South Carolina.

Our transportation was all safely removed but seventy-five wagons, which were burned in camp.

The enemy's attack, on Monday, was fierce in the extreme. Kearney, Hooker, Richardson, Sedgwick, Smith and McCall participated.

The reserve under McCALL suffered severely, and Gens. McCALL and REYNOLDS were probably taken prisoners, as they were missing Tuesday night. Gen MEADE is severely wounded, and Gens. BURNS and BROOKS slightly.

Stonewall JACKSON is undoubtedly killed. Gen McCLELLAN, after the fullest investigation, credits the report: all the prisoners corroborating it.

The rebel General J. R. ANDERSON was mortally wounded in the action at Savage's Station on Sunday.

On Monday night intrenchments were begun and prosecuted as rapidly as possible. The first boat of reinforcements arrived just as our correspondent left. Supplies were also coming in in abundance.

Our total loss in the whole six days' terrific fighting, from Wednesday up to Monday night, is about twelve thousand, seven thousand five hundred of which were lost in the battle of Friday on the right.

Col. McQUADE of New-York: Col. CASS, of Massachusetts: Maj. PATTERSON, of Pennsylvania, and all the field officers of the Duryea Zouaves heretofore reported killed or wounded and many others, are alive and well.

OUR FORTRESS MONROE CORRESPONDENCE.

CITY POINT, Wednesday, July 2, 1862.

I did not write you yesterday, because the reports were coming in so thick and contradictory, that, without having time to thoroughly sift them, you would be just as likely to receive wrong as right information. What little I am now permitted to tell you is, therefore, reliable; for I have taken pains to obtain it from trustworthy eye-witnesses, or from parties who ought to be thoroughly well posted.

Whatever may be the impression in New-York there is but one conclusion arrived at here by all intelligent people, in spite of all that the army pedlers and other skedaddling croakers have to say, and that is that the terrific battle which has been raging for the last four or five days has exhibited the most masterly strategy on the part of McCLELLAN, and bravery in himself, his officers and his men. So far from there being anything like defeat in his position, it is eminent success, and the enemy, without intending it, could not have better contrived to play into his hands.

I have just been on board the *George Washington*, which arrived this morning with 821 sick and wounded; among others, Gen. MEADE, and Brig.-Gen. W. A. GORMAN, of SEDGWICK's Division—the former wounded very severely by the fragment of a shell passing through his body, and the latter prostrate by sickness. I have had a long and interesting conversation with one of the patients—a Captain of the Twenty-third Pennsylvania, and a man of great intelligence—and I was glad to find, not only in the facts he advanced, but in the cheerful and confident view he took of the dreadful struggle now going on, a full corroboration of the opinion so earnestly sustained by the TIMES and its correspondents.

The whole affair is simply this: As soon as McCLELLAN discovered—by the bold raid of STUART near the White House, and other indications—that the enemy had an intent upon that point, he at once came to the conclusion to turn that to account; and, by luring them on to a spot that could be of no [illegible] to them, and too far removed from his own base of operations, concentrated his forces on the James River, where he could have the aid of our gunboats—the terror of the rebels. For this reason—and long before any descent was made upon PORTER's right wing—Gen. McCLELLAN had caused to be removed [illegible] all the army stores, provisions, &c., from the White House, and all the rest by transports down the York River, leaving but a small portion there (variously estimated at from $5,000 to $50,000, though probably nearer the first sum) to be destroyed, in the event of the enemy approaching sooner than they could remove it.

THE RECENT GREAT BATTLES.

Map Showing Richmond, Fort Darling, the Line of the James River, the Present Location of Gen. McClellan, and the Scene of the Recent Great Battles.

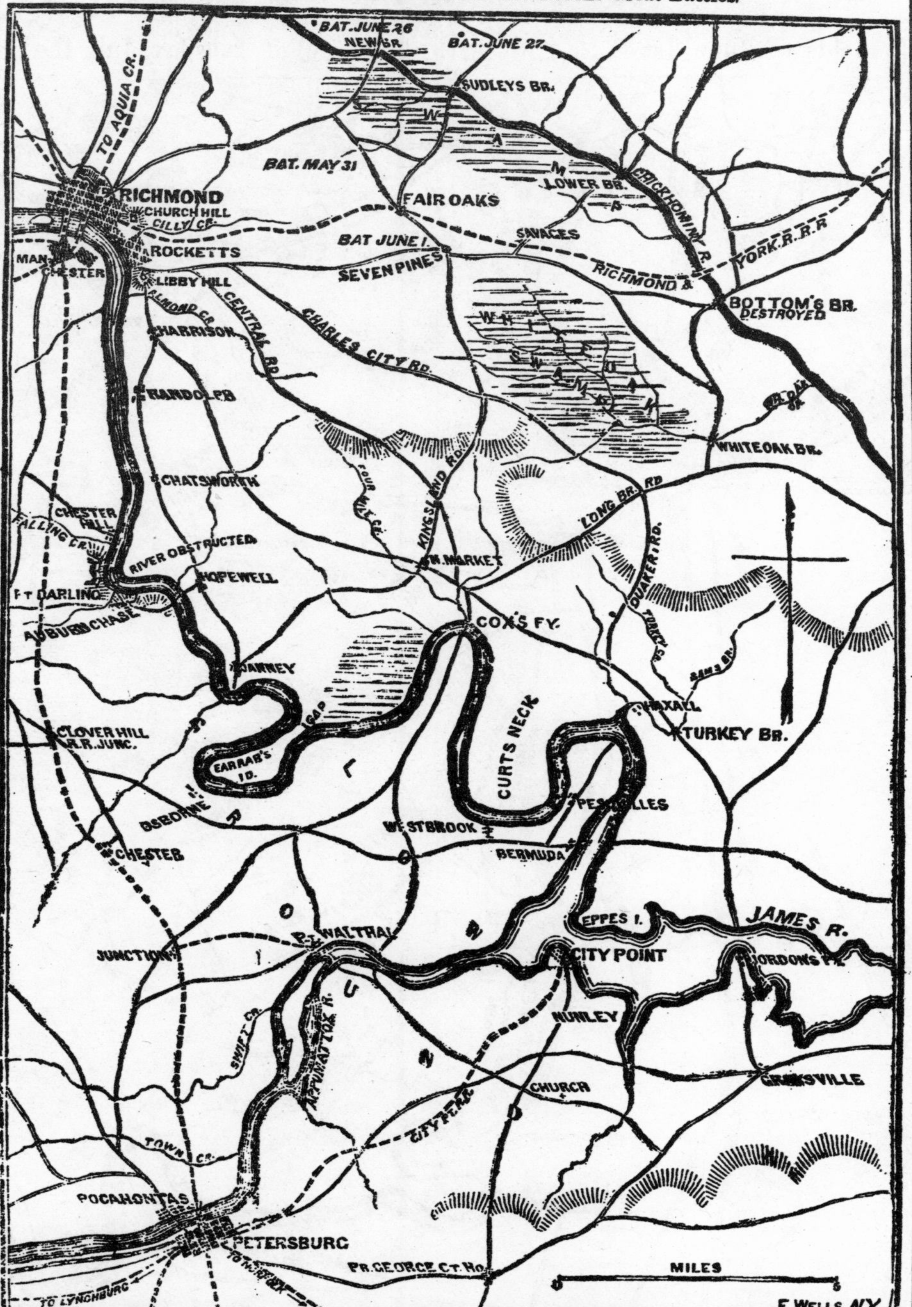

So certain is this, that many days elapsed before there was any demonstration at the White House, loaded vessels were seen coming down the York River and up the James, with what intent people did not *then* knew, though they do *now*. All this being arranged, orders were given for PORTER's wing to fall back, add *he was doing so when attacked by the rebels*. The result was that, after great slaughter on both sides, McCLELLAN has reached the very spot he intended on the Jame River, with all his equipments, and allowed the rebels to go into the very trap he had prepared for them. Does this look like defeat?

Much excitement prevailed here yesterday (Monday) when news came of the bloody work of the last two days, and the information that our army was on rations which must soon be exhausted. This fear is now, however, entirely removed. Boats, loaded with provisions, are rapidly going up the James River in abundance, and twelve vessels had already unloaded when my informant left, which was at 6 o'clock last evening. I was also informed that Gen. McCLELLAN is in a strong position, under cover from gunboats, and able to hold his own until reinforcements come. The latter we know are rapidly on the way to him—though whence and in what number I am not at liberty to say. Well sustained in the position he now holds, there can be no doubting his success.

Some people here are contemplating not only the possibility but the probability of the rebels venturing down the peninsula as far as Yorktown, and even further. It is almost to be hoped they will have the foolhardiness to do so. They might thereby gain the glory of shedding more human blood, but they will only be rushing on their own destruction. Shut up between the York and James rivers, without a plank afloat to confront our gunboats on them, it is difficult to see how they could either hold anything or sustain themselves there, while every man taken from their forces to go there is only increasing McCLELLAN's chances of entering Richmond.

It is the province of those of your correspondents who were on the battle-field to give the details of what passed under their own eyes. I am merely giving you impressions derived from those who actually took a part in the fights, and who betray not the remotest symptoms of despondence. They all assured me that never did a General live who commanded more thoroughly the love of his men, and one of them said, with deep emotion, that there was not a man in his army who would not die for him. Should calamity befall our noble young chieftain before Richmond, through lack of strength before overwhelming numbers—and under no other circumstances could he fail—God help the truckling politicians, who will have brought him and his country to such extremity! He has done all that man can do. He has the indorsement of men, both at home and from abroad, who stand high in the ranks of war: and if disaster attends him, the responsibility not only should, but *will* be placed upon other shoulders than his. To know how deeply the army feel upon this subject, one should mix with them, as we correspondents are compelled to do; and you may depend upon it, a long account is being scored up against some political marplots of the Press and Congress.

Among the reports here which I have heard, but know not whether to credit or not, is that Gen. McCALL was wounded in the neck on Sunday, and is now a prisoner in Richmond; also that "Stonewall JACKSON" is killed. Dr. STRONG, Chaplain of the Fourth Michigan, who is unceasing in his attentions to his men, begged me to correct the following mistakes in one of your cotemporaries:

Col. McQUADE, of the Fourteenth New-York, reported as killed on Friday last, was seen yesterday at the head of his regiment in good health.

Col. ROBERTS, First Michigan, also reported killed, is not dead, but only slightly wounded.

Capt. SPALDING, Fourth Michigan, also reported killed, was seen in perfect health yesterday.

Capt. R. G. DEPUY, Company K, Fourth Michigan, was instantly killed on Friday last; also Lieut. T. B. JONES, Company B, Fourth Michigan, in the same engagement.

We are awaiting, with intense excitement, the result of the next two or three days; but unless something worse arrives than we have yet heard, Richmond must and will be ours in a few days.

NEMO.

LIST OF KILLED AND WOUNDED.

The following list of killed and wounded is additional to that published yesterday:

NEW-YORK REGIMENTS.

FIRST NEW-YORK.

T. Ryan, Co. H—hand.	Sergt. S. W. Legoutz, Co. E—finger off.
Sergt. P. [illegible], Co. C—arm.	J. Stansbury, Co. A—arm.
James Higgins, Co. E—hand	

SECOND NEW-YORK.

W. E. Seaford, Co. K—wrist.	H. Wilson, Co. C—sick.
J. Penn, Co. [illegible]	D. Lamb, Co. I—arm.
M. Sheckle, Co. C—sick.	P. Costello, Co. F—sick.

FIFTH NEW-YORK.

Geo. Cartwright, Co. G—wrist.	James O. Reed, Co. H—mouth.
C. Albright, Co. C—head.	Sergt. J. W. Sharter, Co. D—arm.
E. Mormon, Co. H—leg.	Thomas Murphy, Co. C—shoulder.
G. F. Dorsan, Co. I—head.	Sergt. Geo. A. Mitchel, Co. F—head.
A. K. Wolomon, Co. [illegible]—leg.	[illegible] Co. C—rupture.
J. Fosley, Co. [illegible] leg.	[illegible] Shreffer, Co. K—arm. (amputated.)
J. W. Brown, Co. I—head.	F. C. Tucker, Co. H—foot.
Thos. Donovan, Co. C—arm.	
Andrew Williams, Co. B—thigh.	
John Bernan, Co. C—ship.	
C. Kilsman, Co. E—hand.	J. H. Stout, Co. F—woun'd
M. R. Powers, Co. H—hand.	Geo. W. Leavitt, Co. F—wounded.
Jas. Rupert, Co. C—arm.	Jas. Maloney, Co. F—wounded.
C. C. Miller, Co. H—hand.	J. W. Neal, Co. F—wounded.
F. Higgins, Co. H—thigh.	W. Sweeney, Co. F—woun'd.
C. Snyder, Co. G—hand.	T. Russell, Co. F—wounded.
J. A. Shore, Co. A—arm.	Capt. Partridge, Co. I—killed.
Wm. C. Ryan, Co. F—killed.	C. Allen, Co. F—killed.
S. Dealy, Co. F—killed.	A. Berrien, Co. D—killed.
H. Mandeville, Co. F—killed.	
C. O'Neill, Co. F—killed.	
Sergt. Phillips, Co. F—wounded and prisoner.	

TENTH NEW-YORK.

T. M'Connigal, Co. H—leg.	M. Bancroft, Co. I—thigh.
W. Collins, Co. F—foot.	H. Seymour, Co. D—hand.
Jos. Knees, Co. F—head.	

TWELFTH NEW-YORK.

Jas. Kelly, Co. E—breast.	Lt. Oliver, Co. E—wounded.
Philip Brady, Co. D.	S't. Richards, Co. E—wounded.
David A. Byre, Co. B—arm.	— Wetmore, Co. E—missing.
Sergeant S. A. Carpenter, Co. H—shoulder.	Corporal Garrison, Co. E—wounded and prisoner.
M. Dogg—arm.	

FOURTEENTH NEW-YORK.

R. Sprague, Co. H—side.	J. Beebe, Co. F—shoulder.
Corp. Sid. Day, Co. I—face.	N. Mathews, Co. E—hand.
Sergt. D. R. Butts, Co. I—hand.	P. Lishlen, Co. E—hand.
A. M. Gennacher, Co. I—head.	Lieut. Skillen—killed.
	Major Davis—missing.
	Capt. Harra—wounded.

SIXTEENTH NEW-YORK.

Col. Harlan—seriously.	I. Rodger, Co. I—hand.
C. H. Hollow, Co. F—hand.	J. A. Powers, Co. B—arm.
W. Wayne, Co. G—arm.	E. J. Sanford, Co. F—hand.
J. Rawson, Co. I—arm.	J. O'Connor, Co. C—hand.

EIGHTEENTH NEW-YORK.

S. S. Stevenson, Co. C—neck.	C. C. Starr, Co. H—arm.
P. Mullen, Co. F—head.	R. C. Selden, Co. B—shoulder.
A. King, Co. F—hand.	M. Carey, Co. I—neck.
J. G. Riley, Co. K—left arm.	S. L. Stevenson, Co. C—neck.
J. F. Shay, Co. F—forehead.	J. Flynn, Co. C—hand.
Sergt. R. Wiscoman, Co. G—arm.	Thos. Kerns, Co. F—head.

TWENTIETH NEW-YORK.

S. Solomon, Co. B—leg.	A. Hayes—neck.

TWENTY-FIFTH NEW-YORK.

A. Jack, Co. D—hand.	J. Goby, Co. A—killed.
Sgt. T. Toomey, Co. C—hand	

TWENTY-SEVENTH NEW-YORK.

W. Griffiths, Co. H—shoulder	H. Hammond, Co. G—breast.
G. Lady, Co. H—hand.	Sgt. E. B. Stilsord, Co. E—wounded.
F. Driscoll, Co. A—wrist and head.	J. K. Barboot, Co. E—w'nd'd.
J. Bonne, Co. E—elbow.	2d-Lt. J. Webster, Co. E—wounded.
R. M. Hibbard, Co. E—shoulder.	W. Crawford, Co. E—w'nd'd.
S. Bachman, Co. E—neck.	E. Butler, Co. E—w'nd'd

THIRTY-FIRST NEW-YORK.

Jas Kelly, Co. I—neck.

THIRTY-SECOND NEW-YORK.

S. Rosendale, Co. K—arm.	John Deal, Co. D—hand.
A. J. Formon, Co. C.	J. J. Peck, Co. I—head.
Wm. Simpson—arm.	

THIRTY-SEVENTH NEW-YORK.

Z. Roden—sick.	John Adams, Co. C—hand
L. Martin, Co. D—sick.	

THIRTY-EIGHTH NEW-YORK.

C. Grokert, Co. C—hand.	F. Hoffmaster Co. I—breast

FORTIETH NEW-YORK.

Sergt. J. A. Emory—hand.

FORTY-FOURTH NEW-YORK.

R. H. Burbaus, Co. C—hand	J. McGowan, Co. G—bruise

FIFTY-FIFTH NEW-YORK.

Fred. Coppa, Co. C—hand and side.	Ger. Chisholm, Co. B—leg.
	Felix Gallrans, Co. C—arm.

FIFTY-SIXTH NEW-YORK.

G. H. Avery.

SIXTY-SEVENTH NEW-YORK.

F. Hays, Co. B—hand.

SIXTY-NINTH NEW-YORK.

J. Quinn, Co. C—died in the hospital.

SEVENTIETH NEW-YORK.

G. Goodall, Co. C—elbow.

SEVENTY-SECOND NEW-YORK.

P. Donnelly, Co. F.

SEVENTY-THIRD NEW-YORK.

J. Wright, Co. H—hand and foot.	H. Hogan, Co. F—leg.
	A. J. Hickey, Co. F—arm.

SEVENTY-FOURTH NEW-YORK.

A. Doll, Co. B—finger off.	G. A. Caffon, Co. F—shoulder

SEVENTY-SEVENTH NEW-YORK.

D. S. Brown, Co. G—side.

EIGHTY-SEVENTH NEW-YORK.

S. E. Honington, Co. C—head.

ONE HUNDRED AND FIRST NEW-YORK.

I. Hall, Company B—hand.

PENNSYLVANIA REGIMENTS.

SECOND PENNSYLVANIA.

Daniel Conner, Co. A.	— Townsend, Co. C—wrist.
Corporal Jones, Co. A.	W. Goth, Co. C—arm.

THIRD PENNSYLVANIA.

H. Harbaugh, Co. A—arm.	J. Kocker, Co. A—back.
P. F. Holland, Co. A—shoulder.	

SEVENTH PENNSYLVANIA.

William H. Schively, Co. I—shoulder.	N. S. Horner, Co. A—left shoulder.
J. W. Davis, Co. K—shoulder.	J. Grimes, Co. B—shoulder.
Wm. M. Culp, Co. A—arm.	Wm. Portsine, Co. B—arm.
Solomon Saylor, Co. F—arm.	Joseph Winters, Co. B—arm.

EIGHTH PENNSYLVANIA.

A. Bane, Co. I—leg.	T. Britton, Co. H—leg.
R. Sayres, Co. I—wounded.	

EIGHTH PENNSYLVANIA.

S. M. Drum, Co. G—arm.	H. A. Steward, Co. B—arm.
Corporal Hugh Gattines, Co. K—thigh.	H. Larkee, Co. G—breast.
W. H. Miner, Co. I—breast.	E. H. Miner, Co. G—shoulder.
Job Franks, Co. I—arm.	Walter Grubbs, Co. B—leg.
Francis Groton, Co. E—nose.	John C. Gray, Co. B—breast.
J. H. Sweeney, Co. H—arm.	J. L. Francis, Co. G—thigh.

NINTH PENNSYLVANIA.

Robt. H. Rells, Co. I—leg.	C. Deits, Co. B—hand.
J. W. Donthile—hand.	

ELEVENTH PENNSYLVANIA.

Edward Hoffman, Co. C—face.

THIRTY-EIGHTH PENNSYLVANIA

D. W. Keever—hip.

FIFTY-SECOND PENNSYLVANIA.

F. Medlin, Co. K—hand.

SIXTY-SECOND PENNSYLVANIA.

Capt. T. B. Monks—wounded and prisoner.	Private Shenan, Co. F—k'ld
Capt. R. J. Crozier—wounded badly.	Private Mintzmer, Co. G—wounded.
Lieut. W. J. Patterson—w'nd	Corp. Randolph, Co. F—wounded.
Lieut. Bell—wounded.	George R. Gaily, Co. F—wounded.
Lieut. Cunningham—w'nd.	Robert Finnlrock, Co. F—wounded.
Lieut. Lowry, Acting Adjutant—wounded.	Capt. F. Brown—wounded and missing.
Lieut. Seitz, (accidentally burned) Co. B—wounded.	W. King, Co. K—dead.
Privates Coursin and Mack, Co. D—killed.	L. Eahamiah, Co. F—wn'd

SIXTY-SECOND PENNSYLVANIA.

R. Erwin, Co. G—wrist.	H. White, Co. F—leg.
S. Edwards, Co. G—finger.	W. Closson, Co. A—arm.
T. Ruth, Co. G—left leg.	Joel Martin, Co. K—face.
J. M. Stark, Co. H—shoul'r.	C. H. Miersch—leg.
S. Mersaick, Co. A—neck.	G. B. Gray, Co. F—hand.
J. K. Wilson, Co. F—face.	A. Fisher—hand

SEVENTY-SECOND PENNSYLVANIA—BAXTER'S ZOUAVES.

E. Allman, Co. H—finger off.	F. Hogg, Co. L—neck.
George Allen, Co. B—foot.	James Story, Co. I—foot.

EIGHTY-FIRST PENNSYLVANIA.

John Hughes, Co. E—hand.

EIGHTY-THIRD PENNSYLVANIA.

Thos. W. King, Co. C—foot.	O. L. Otis, Co. D—arm.
F. J. Tsook—chest.	J. A. Howe, Co. E—arm.
Sergt. J. E. Mozier, Co. H—breast.	Col. J. W. McLane—killed.
John Bovee, Co. B—hips.	Capts. Zeigler, Morris and Wood—wounded.
Maj. L. H. Nagle—wounded.	

NINETY-THIRD PENNSYLVANIA.

H. J. Penrose, Co. B—foot.	F. Kirtz, Co. A—face&hand.

NINETY-FIFTH PENNSYLVANIA.

Col. Gosline—sev'ly wond'd.	Corp. McAleer, Co. K—wounded.
Maj. Hobbs—sev'ly wond'd.	M. Pendergast, Co. K—wounded.
Lt. Donohue, Co. C—killed.	A. Stemm, Co. K—wound'd.
Lt. Robinson, Co. E—wounded.	J. Shannon, Co. K—wounded and prisoner.
Lt. Luginers, Co. F—wond'd.	E. L. Eddy, Co. K—wounded and prisoner.
D. McCarthy, Co. K—wounded and prisoner.	J. Barton, Co. K—wounded and prisoner.
E. Latham, Co. K—wounded and prisoner.	
G. McBride, Co. K—killed.	

NINETY-SIXTH PENNSYLVANIA.

P. Gosian, Co. I—arm.	J Divine, Co. I.
W. Strother, Co. G—left leg	D. Woodring, Co. E—head.
Milton Moyer, Co. D—finger.	

FIRST NEW-JERSEY.

Sergt C. G. Morton, Co. A—head.	J. Ellwood, Co. A—head.

SECOND NEW-JERSEY.

W. H. Warner, Co. A—sick.	W. Dougherty, Co. I—breast.
W. H. Beens, Co. K—face.	J. H. Worden, Co. K.

THIRD NEW-JERSEY.

Patrick Burn (or Brown), Co. B—nose, cheek and shoulder.	E. Trussill, Co. B—left arm.
Corp. S. Harris, Co. F—neck.	F. McRaund, Co. G—left wrist.
J. G. Lewallen, Co. B—arm.	R. B. McConan, Co. E—shoulder.
P. J. Fox, Co. B—arm.	C. Bennett, Co. H—breast.
J. Blair, Co. B—shoulder and neck.	Wm. Kelley, Co. I—left shoulder.
F. W. Coull, Co. B—right arm.	P. Shank, Co. B—mouth.
W. A Smith, Co. E—right arm.	R. C. Levick, Co. F—knee.
	J. Henry, Co. B—finger.
	J. Dillon, Co. G—shoulder.

FOURTH NEW-JERSEY.

Col. J. H. Simpson—missing and supposed to be killed.	A.—missing.
Lieut.-Col. Wm. H. Hatch—missing and supposed to be killed.	2d-Lt. H. Schroder, Co. A—missing.
Major Wm. Birney (brother of Brig.-Gen. Birney—missing and supposed to be killed.	1st-Lt. E. Wright, Co. D—missing.
Adjt. George H. Sturdiford—missing and supposed to be killed.	2d-Lt. George Bennet, Co. D—missing.
Capt. Wm. Mevis—killed.	Capt. B. Ridgway—missing.
Capt. Wm. Mulford—killed.	1st-Lt. T. C. Spear—missing.
Capt. A. Aaronson—killed	G. H. Stubbins, Co. C—wrist.
Capt. Wm. Fetter—killed.	G. S. Reen, Co. K—stomach.
Capt. H. M. Jewett—killed.	Sgt. J. E. Doughty, Co. G—head.
Capt. Wm. Nippins—killed	Sgt. H. Hopkins, Co. D—elbow.
First-Lieut. Wm. Myer, Co.	J. Lanx—shoulder.
	Jerome Shields, Co G—arm.
	W. Hubert, Co. I—groin.

According to the statement of an officer, this regiment went into the fight with 640 men and only 81 can now be found. The six Captains first mentioned above were all killed within an hour after the fight commenced.

FIRST MICHIGAN.

M. Cotter, Co. G—arm.

FOURTH MICHIGAN.

M. L. Parks, Co. H—w'nd'd.	T. Hogan, Co. I—dead.
J. M. Miller, Co. I—w'nd'd.	W. Ross, Co. E—wounded.
D. H. Cotterall, Co. F—wounded.	Lt. Smith, Co. E—wounded.
A. D. Clark, Co. I—w'nd'd.	A. J. Deal, Co. I—wounded.
Sgt. J. Plummer, Co. I—wounded.	W. R. Balcom, Co. F—w'nd'd.
R. McDonough, Co. I—w'nd'd	W. Robinson, Co. I—bayoneted.
W. Breen, Co. I—w'nd'd.	C. F. Carris, Co. G—w'nd'd.
M. T. Severance, Co. F—wounded.	C. A. Rouse, Co. F—w'nd'd.
G. H. Lee, Co. C—wounded.	Lts. Jones and [illegible], Co. D—mortally [illegible]
H. A. Clark, Co. I—wounded badly.	J. Fleming, Co. [illegible]—head.
Capt. Depuy, Co. I—killed.	L. Haviland, Co. K—arm.
Sgt. G. Maltz, Co. I—w'nd'd badly.	Corp. J. T[illegible], Co. K—two fingers off.
J. Clag, Co. I—dead.	A. B. Crane, Co. K—jaw.
	H. Peters, Co. H—shoulder.
	L. [illegible], Co. B—back.

Entire loss of this regiment is 152.

SIXTEENTH MICHIGAN.

J. Doubleman, Co. A—arm.	W. S. Conover, Co. G—right hand.
S. W. Hilton, Co. C—head.	H. Palmer, Co. I—arm.
A. Smith, Co. G—finger.	
Sgt. A. Cameron, Co. G—knee.	

SECOND MAINE.

J. Winslow, Co. K.

FIFTH MAINE.

F. C. Bradbury, Co. C—shoulder.	W. H. Everett, Co. C—head.
	W. Larraby, Co. C—arm.

SEVENTH MAINE.

E. Irvin, Co. H—head.

NINTH MASSACHUSETTS.

D. Sullivan, Co. G—arm and breast.	Corp. M. Burley, Co. H—right arm.
T. Slattery, Co. H—right arm.	P. Flynn, Co. H—hand and arm.

ELEVENTH MASSACHUSETTS.

James Browner, Co. C—side.	J. G. Helton, Co. I—contusion.

SIXTEENTH MASSACHUSETTS.

M. Gormley, Co. I—hand.	J. Sullivan, Co. I—foot.

[Continued on Eighth Page.]

The Philadelphia Inquirer.

CIRCULATION OVER 55,000. PHILADELPHIA, FRIDAY, JULY 4, 1862. PRICE TWO CENTS.

FIELD OF GENERAL M'CLELLAN'S TERRIFIC ENGAGEMENTS.

Showing the Battle Fields of June 1st, 25th, 26th, 27th, 30th, and of Tuesday, July the 1st, when the Rebels were terribly repulsed.

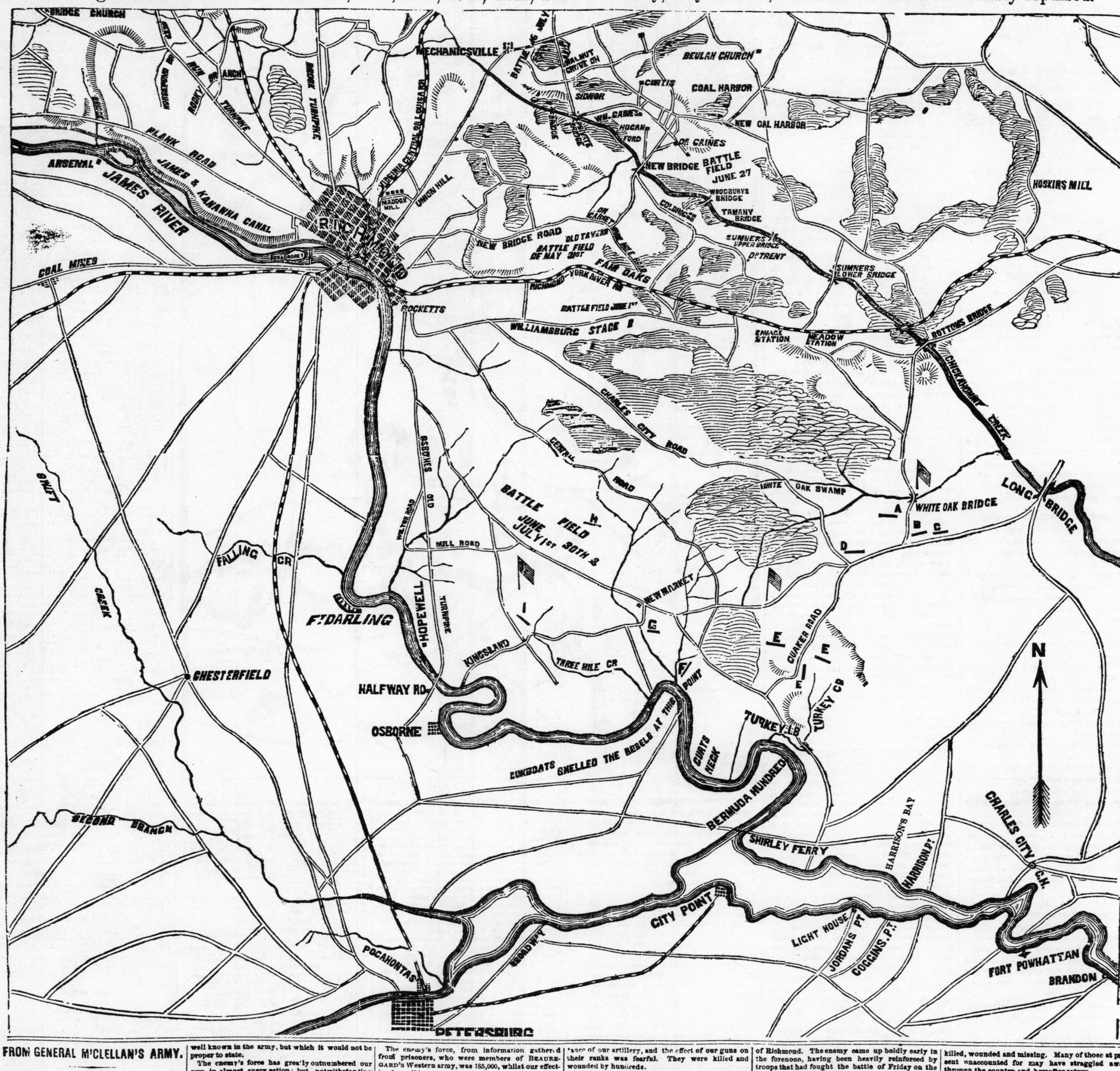

FROM GENERAL M'CLELLAN'S ARMY.

TERRIBLE BATTLES—FEARFUL SLAUGHTER.

Our Loss from 15,000 to 20,000 in Killed, Wounded and Missing.

MOST OF THE SIEGE GUNS SAVED.

FORTRESS MONROE, July 2—One o'clock, P. M.—The steamer *Daniel Webster* has just arrived here, from City Point, with upwards of three hundred wounded on board.

A gentleman who came down in charge of the wounded, informs me that yesterday was the sixth day that the battle has been going on, with the most terrific fighting the sun ever shone upon. It has extended the whole length of our lines. We have lost a great many men in killed, wounded, and missing—probably from *fifteen to twenty thousand.*

He informs me that General MCCLELLAN'S Head-quarters are at Handy's landing to-day, and that his lines extended five miles towards Richmond. The move of the right wing of the army was predetermined upon and planned ten days ago, and would have been carried out sooner but for certain reasons well known in the army, but which it would not be proper to state.

The enemy's force has greatly outnumbered our own in almost every action; but, notwithstanding this, they have been repulsed oftener than we have, and their loss far exceeds ours.

Yesterday, General MCCLELLAN is said to have captured a whole Rebel brigade, [very doubtful] and took from them several rifled cannon and other pieces.

It is now said that we have lost very few of our siege guns; most of them having been removed in safety.

There has been a great many wounded prisoners taken on both sides.

Our informant says that General MCCLELLAN and his staff all agree that the present position of our army is far more advantageous as a base of operations against Richmond than that hitherto occupied. The gun-boats can now be brought to bear and materially aid in carrying on the work.

Some of our regiments have suffered terribly, while others have lost but little. The New York Fifth Regiment has suffered terribly. They made a most heroic struggle, and caused great havoc among the enemy. About one-half of their number are killed, wounded and taken prisoners. They were in the fight at Coal Harbor, and fought against desperate odds.

Our left wing was engaged yesterday (July 1st) up to 2 o'clock, with the enemy, mostly with artillery.

The enemy's force, from information gathered from prisoners, who were members of BEAUREGARD'S Western army, was 185,000, whilst our effective force did not exceed 95,000.

THE BATTLES BEFORE RICHMOND.

DETAILS OF THE LAST THREE DAYS' FIGHTING.

HEAD-QUARTERS OF THE ARMY OF THE POTOMAC, TURKEY ISLAND, July 2d, 1862.—The following is an account of the battles fought in front of Richmond on Sunday, Monday, and Tuesday the 5th, 6th, and 7th days of the engagement:—

On Sunday morning, the corps of SUMNER and FRANKLIN were left in the works at Fair Oaks, with instructions to evacuate and protect the baggage and supply trains on their way to James river. They had hardly left their position, and were falling back on the railroad and Williamsburg turnpike, when the enemy discovered the movement, and immediately started in pursuit with their whole force.

So rapidly did they approach that our officers had barely time to place their men in position to receive them before they were upon them. The enemy advanced to an attack about two o'clock, which was promptly met by our men. The battle lasted until dark, during which the enemy suffered terribly. They advanced in a solid mass to within a short distance of our artillery, and the effect of our guns on their ranks was fearful. They were killed and wounded by hundreds.

At dark the enemy were repulsed and forced to abandon their position. This battle took place about 1½ miles above Savage's Station.

While the battle was in progress other important events were transpiring. The railroad bridge across the Chickahominy was burned and a train of cars under a full head of steam was run overboard. All the commissary and quarter master stores were committed to the flames together with a large amount of ordnance stores.

The large house at the station, and the adjoining grounds, which were filled with our sick and wounded, whom it was impossible to remove, were left under the care of our surgeons, with all the necessaries at hand for their comfort. They number about seven hundred, and are now in the enemy's hands.

The troops which had fought the battle of Sunday, retreated under the cover of night, to White Oak Swamp bridge, a distance of about twelve miles, there to await the approach of the enemy.

The disposition of the troops on Monday the 6th day, was as follows:—

Gen. SMITH'S Division, supported by General NAGLEE'S Brigade, occupied the right of the bridge, while SUMNER and FRANKLIN'S corps were on the left. HEINTZELMAN'S corps, with Gen. MCCALL'S Division, was posted on the Newmarket road to meet the enemy, who was approaching from the direction of Richmond. The enemy came up boldly early in the forenoon, having been heavily reinforced by troops that had fought the battle of Friday on the opposite side of the Chickahominy.

At about 2 o'clock it became evident that some portion of our lines must give way, as the enemy were evidently throwing fresh troops into action. Our troops in front of the bridge now fell back to within 3½ miles of Turkey Island Bridge, when the fight was shortly after renewed and continued with the greatest determination on both sides.

The loss on Monday was very heavy on both sides. During the day all the cattle and a greater part of the transportation had safely crossed Turkey Island Bridge. Some of the rear wagons were abandoned and fired on this day, in order to make room for the artillery.

The Battle on Tuesday.

The fight was renewed early on Tuesday morning by the enemy, who evidently expected to crush our army. It lasted about three hours, resulting in considerable loss to both parties.

The enemy then retired, leaving the field to our troops. They again advanced about three o'clock P. M. in considerable force, but retired after being shelled by the gun-boats and artillery for about two hours, without coming near enough for the use of musketry.

The loss of our army during these seven day engagements is not known, but 20,000 is considered as near an estimate as can at present be given in killed, wounded and missing. Many of those at present unaccounted for may have straggled away through the country and hereafter return.

The loss of the enemy in killed must have been very heavy, far exceeding that of our army.

We have taken about 700 prisoners, among whom are three Lieutenant-Colonels and one Major.

The reported capture of Gen. MAGRUDER is probably a mistake.

The loss in field artillery during the seven days amounted to about thirty guns.

General REYNOLDS and Captain KINGSBURY, of his staff, were taken prisoners, as was also Colonel STOCKTON, of Michigan.

General MEAD, of Pennsylvania, was severely wounded.

General BURNS was wounded in the face.

Generals SUMNER and HEINTZELMAN were both slightly wounded in the left arm, but they did not leave the field.

General MCCALL was seen to fall from his horse during the battle of Monday. He was taken prisoner. The extent of his injuries is not yet known

Col. GOSLINE, of the Fifty-fourth Pennsylvania Regiment, was killed; also, Capt. CAMBLOS, of the Fifth Regular Cavalry.

Capt. WHITING, of the Fifth Cavalry, was wounded and taken prisoner, and his son, a Lieutenant in the same regiment, lost his left arm.

Colonel PRATT, of the Thirty-first New York Regiment, was wounded in the face.

THE EVENING STAR
IS
PUBLISHED EVERY AFTERNOON,
(SUNDAY EXCEPTED,)
AT THE STAR BUILDINGS,
Corner of Pennsylvania ave. and Eleventh street,
BY
W. D. WALLACH.

Papers served in packages by carriers at $4 a year, or 37 cents per month. To mail subscribers the price is $3.50 a year, in advance; $2 for six months; $1 for three months; and for less than three months at the rate of 12 cents a week. Single copies, ONE CENT; in wrappers, TWO CENTS.

☞ ADVERTISEMENTS should be sent to the office before 12 o'clock M.; otherwise they may not appear until the next day.

Evening Star.

Vol. XX. WASHINGTON, D. C., SATURDAY, JULY 5, 1862. No. 2,923.

LATE FROM RICHMOND.

The Battle of Wednesday and Thursday—Rebel Accounts.

From the Richmond Whig, of June 27th, we obtain the following interesting items:

THE BATTLE OF THURSDAY.

Yesterday afternoon an engagement opened a few miles northeast of the city, which we have no reason to doubt is the beginning of the great conflict that is to decide the fate of this Capital, and perhaps of the Confederacy itself. The cannonading, till an hour or more after dark, was quick and heavy, exceeding in rapidity and volume that at Seven Pines. Not a word from the field has reached the city. The reason probably is, that the attack was made and the fight waged on the enemy's rear. The city is confident and calm.

LATER.

Information came to hand last night that the attack was made by General A. P. Hill's division on the enemy's position near the Meadow Bridge, about 3 o'clock. The enemy recoiled, leaving a battery, as it is reported, in the hands of our troops.

Retreating about two miles the enemy made a stand in their entrenchments at Mechanicsville and offered vigorous resistance for two or three [illegible]

THE WHITE RIVER EXPEDITION.

The Arkansas correspondent of the St. Louis Republican gives some interesting details of the expedition up the White river, from which we extract the following:

Of the rebel gunboats two more certainly yet remain—the Ponchartrain and Arkansas—both in the Arkansas. The former is commanded by J. W. Dunnington, formerly of the U. S. Navy. In the papers before me, the name of R. F. Pinkney, formerly of the U. S. Navy, frequently appears. These men, with Fry, Roby, and Comstock, of the Maurepas, were all educated by the United States, and are now arrayed against their alma mater with matricidal blood upon their hands.

I have before me the "log" of the Maurepas from the 23d of May to the time she was sunk. A few notes from it will not be uninteresting to the public.

At Clarendon the boat was greeted with "cheers from the ladies;" and at Des Arc large crowds visited her, "examining the wounds" that she "received at Tiptonville." May 24, she was lying inactive at Des Arc, "without much prospect of getting at the Yankees!" Sanguinary logographist! As the writer was "undecided what to do," he had his "clothes washed," which, from the fact of his underscoring the news, must have been a rare occurrence. The writer misses the "cheers from the ladies," so he went up into town, but had to report "ladies scarce." What a fate for a lady killer! He thus describes Des Arc:

"Des Arc is a very pretty little town, immediately upon the bank of the White river. The houses are all built in cottage style, mostly all frame, and painted white. Very pretty flower gardens about the houses. Nearly every other house is a store, or was before the present trouble [illegible]

TELEGRAPHIC NEWS.

FROM GEN. McCLELLAN'S ARMY.

Seven Days' Fighting—Fearful Slaughter—General McClellan's Army Safe—Death of "Stonewall" Jackson and Gen. Ewell.

BALTIMORE, July 3.—The Army Correspondent of the Associated Press has just arrived here, direct from General McClellan's headquarters. The following is briefly the state of affairs:

After seven days' incessant fighting, during which Gen. McClellan's army was compelled to fall back before vastly superior numbers, he reached a point on James river adjoining Turkey Island. Here he is in safe position, with the support of the gunboats.

His army are on high ground, out of the swamps with abundance of good water, and where he can be, and is now being, reinforced. The battle, or rather series of battles, has been one of the most destructive of human life that the world has seen, and has resulted in the killing and wounding, it is thought, of not less than 45,000 men both sides.

The enemy's loss has unquestionably been enormous—far greater than ours, which in killed and wounded will not exceed 15,000. We have lost many prisoners, but not more than 5,000.

All the bridges were blown up by Gen. McClellan as he retreated, and all the property, stores, etc., that he could not save were destroyed. The enemy got very little besides a portion of our siege guns and about forty pieces of light artillery.

We captured a number of the enemy's artillery, and also took many prisoners, but were compelled to release most of them rather than be encumbered with them.

The Richmond Dispatch of Monday announced the death of Gen. "Stonewall" Jackson and Gen. [illegible]

Hanging of Federal Scouts by Rebels.

LOUISVILLE, July 3.—A passenger just arrived from the South reports that Gen. Mitchell detailed fifty-five men from different regiments for scouting service. They were all captured by the rebels, carried to Atlanta, Ga., and there hung. One of them, Robert Buffum, formerly of Salem, Mass., (now of the 21 Ohio regiment, Col. Norton,) made a speech on the scaffold, saying "he considered it no ignominy to die for his country, even in that manner."

CONGRESSIONAL.

XXXVIIth CONGRESS—Second Session.

SENATE.—After our report closed Thursday—

The bill to establish provisional governments in certain cases, was postponed until Monday at 12 o'clock.

Mr. Wade called up the bill providing for a temporary government of Arizona; which, after some discussion, was postponed to the next session.

The bill for the relief of Alex. Ten Broeck was rejected.

Mr. Foster called up the bill relating to the judiciary.

Mr. Sumner moved to amend so that no testimony shall be excluded on account of color of the witness; rejected.

Yeas—Messrs. Chandler, Collamer, Foot, Grimes, Harlan, Harris, Howard, Howe, King, Kane of Kansas, Morrill, Pomeroy, Sumner, and Wade,—14.

Nays—Messrs. Anthony, Browning, Clark, Davis, Dixon, Fessenden, Foster, Hale, Henderson, Lane of Indiana, Nesmith, Powell, Saulsbury, Sherman, Simmons, Stark, Ten Eyck, [illegible]

AUCTION SALES.

By WALL & BARNARD, Auctioneers.

COMMISSIONERS' SALE OF THREE HOUSES AND LOTS ON THE ISLAND.—By virtue of an order and decree of the Circuit Court of the District of Columbia, bearing date on the 8th day of February, A. D. 1861, and passed in the case of John Adams and others, for a division of the estate of Alexander Adams, deceased, the undersigned Commissioners will offer for sale at Public Auction, on TUESDAY, the 8th day of July, A. D. 1862, at 5 o'clock p. m., on the premises, all the right, title, interest, and estate, both legal and equitable, of which the said Alexander Adams was seized and possessed at the time of his decease, of, in, and to the following valuable property, situated in the city of Washington, to wit: Lot numbered seventeen, (17) in square numbered three hundred and eighty-eight, (388) with the improvements thereon, consisting of a comfortable Frame Dwelling House, and Lot numbered thirteen, (13) and part of Lot numbered fourteen (14) in square numbered four hundred and sixty eight (468) beginning for the said part of lot fourteen, (14) at the southwest corner of said lot, and running thence north with the line of Seventh street west [illegible] feet, thence east one hundred and twenty-two (122) feet to an alley in the rear of said lot, thence south with the line of said alley five (5) feet, and thence west one hundred and twenty two (122) feet to the place of beginning, as described in the proceedings, with the improvements thereon, consisting of two neat and convenient Frame Dwelling Houses.

This property is eligibly located in the Seventh Ward—the first-mentioned piece fronting on E street south, between 9th and 10th streets west; and the last fronting on Seventh street west, between south G and H sts.

Terms of sale: One-third cash; the residue in 6, 12 and 18 months, the purchaser giving his bonds for the deferred payments, payable to the heirs respectively, and bearing interest from the day of sale. Title deeds to be retained until the whole of the purchase money is paid. [illegible]

THE WEEKLY STAR.

This excellent Family and News Journal—containing a greater variety of interesting reading than can be found in any other—is published on Friday morning.

TERMS—Cash, invariably, in advance.

Single copy, per annum	$1 50
Five copies	4 75
Ten copies	8 00
Twenty-five copies	20 00

It invariably contains the "Washington News" that has made the Daily Evening Star circulate so generally throughout the country.

☞ Single copies (in wrappers) can be procured at the counter, immediately after the issue of the paper. Price—THREE CENTS.

OFFICIAL.

DEPARTMENT OF STATE,
Washington, January 25, 1862.

The Secretary of State will hereafter receive Members of Congress on business on Saturdays, commencing with Saturday, the first of next month.

jan 27-tf WILLIAM H. SEWARD.

PASSENGER TRAINS TO MANASSAS. [illegible]

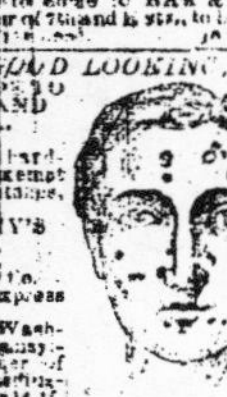

[illegible]

The Charleston Mercury.

DAILY PAPER—TEN DOLLARS PER ANNUM, PAYABLE HALF-YEARLY IN ADVANCE.

VINDICE NULLO
SPONTE SUA SINE LEGE FIDES RECTUMQUE COLENTUR.

COUNTRY PAPER—THRICE A WEEK—FIVE DOLLARS PER ANNUM, IN ADVANCE.

VOLUME LXXXI · CHARLESTON, S. C., TUESDAY, SEPTEMBER 2 1862 · NUMBER 11,542

NEWS BY TELEGRAPH

GREAT NEWS FROM MANASSAS!

ANOTHER GLORIOUS [illegible] VICTORY.

SIGNAL DEFEAT OF THE COMBINED FORCES OF McCLELLAN AND POPE.

OFFICIAL DESPATCH OF GENERAL LEE.

RICHMOND, Monday night, September 1.—The following despatch was received by the President this evening, about six o'clock:

HEADQ'RS. ARMY OF NORTHERN VIRGINIA,
GROVETON, August 30—10, p. m.,
Via Rapidan, September 1st.

To President Davis:

This army achieved to-day, (August 30), on the Plains of Manassas, a signal victory over the combined forces of Generals McCLELLAN and POPE.

On the 28th and 29th instants, each wing, under Generals LONGSTREET and JACKSON, repulsed with valor attacks made on them separately.

We mourn the loss of our gallant dead in every conflict, yet our gratitude to Almighty God for His mercies rises higher each day.

To Him, and to the valor of our troops, a nation's gratitude is due.

(Signed) R. E. LEE.

ENGAGEMENT AT STEVENSON—THE ENEMY EXPELLED, AND THE TOWN RECAPTURED BY OUR TROOPS.

BRIDGEPORT, ALA., August 31.—Gen. MAXEY's brigade, under command of Col. McKINSTRY, of the 32d Alabama regiment, attacked the enemy, 1200 strong, at Stevenson, at 11 o'clock to-day. The enemy's force consisted of infantry, artillery and cavalry. After four hour's shelling, the enemy evacuated their fortifications, leaving on the Nashville trains, by the common roads, and through the woods. A large amount of ammunition and stores was captured. Our command met with a most cordial reception from the citizens, the ladies urging them not to stop till they had killed or captured every Yankee foe. The joy of the citizens at once more beholding the "Stars and Bars" was unbounded. The regiments engaged on our side were the 32d Alabama, 41st Alabama and 25th Tennessee, with Major GUNTER's dismounted partizan rangers, Capt. RICE's cavalry, and FREEMAN and DURR's batteries. The whole number of men engaged was 900. Our loss was two wounded, none killed. The Yankee loss is unknown. The Yankee fortifications at Stevenson were very strong. Our troops displayed great gallantry in the action. FREEMAN's battery worked with great skill and signal effect. HARRY MAURY commanded the 32d Alabama with coolness and efficiency, exposing himself greatly to the Yankee fire. His conduct is highly eulogized.

IMPORTANT FROM TENNESSEE.

CHATTANOOGA, September 1.—The Yankees again occupied McMinnville in large force on Tuesday last. These are probably the forces from Pelham and the neighborhood, on their retreat to Nashville. They may be caught at any rate. Tennessee will soon be entirely in the possession of the Confederates. We have a rumor that Huntsville is evacuated.

THE CONVENTION AND THE EXECUTIVE COUNCIL.

NO. III.

To the Editor of the Mercury: The *abuse* of power charged upon the Convention, consists: First, in assuming to itself, or vesting in the Council, *legislative* power. Secondly, in encroaching upon the Executive, under the State Constitution. The first will be satisfactorily answered, by showing that the Convention being supreme, possesses all power in itself; the second by demonstrating the necessity which existed for the measure. I hold it to be indisputable, that, if the Convention represents the sovereign authority of the State, it was competent to do any sovereign act. The Constitution was intended to be the sole governing rule, *only when the Convention had ceased to exist.* If the latter could amend the former, it could exercise any of the powers conveyed in that instrument, in whole or in part. It saw fit to *amend* instead of *suspending* it, and while leaving the general power of legislating and appropriating money with the Legislature, it exercised some of those powers itself, and *with propriety.*

Not having the books for reference, I cannot say whether the Convention of 1832 exercised this power—probably not, as there was no occasion for it. It is likely that that Convention would have been the only one in the history of the State which was in circumstances to furnish a precedent. In default of such, we turn to the history of England, the country from which we derive our institutions, and to whose, ours are as closely assimilated as circumstances have permitted.

In Macaulay's History, vol. 4th, pp. 21 to 24, reign of William and Mary, we read that this very question came up in the Convention Parliament, and was decided in the affirmative, as the following quotations show, where the authority of the Convention which restored Charles the Second, and upon the force of reasoning which could not be resisted:

"As soon as the new Privy Councillors had been sworn in, it was necessary to submit to them a grave and pressing question. Could the Convention now assembled be turned into a Parliament? The Whigs were for the affirmative. The Tories were for the negative."

"It was plain that the Convention was the fountain head from which the authority of all future Parliaments must be derived, and that on the validity of the votes of the Convention must depend the validity of every *future* statute. And how could the *stream* rise higher than the *source*? Was it not absurd to say that the Convention was supreme in the State, and yet a nullity; a legislature for the highest purposes, and yet no legislature for the humblest purposes; competent *to declare the throne vacant, to change the succession, to fix the land marks of the Constitution*, and yet not competent to pass the most trivial act for the repairing of a pier, or the building of a parish church?"

"No royal writ had summoned the Convention which recalled Charles the Second. Yet that Convention had, after his restoration, continued to sit and *to legislate, had settled the revenues*, had passed an act of amnesty, had abolished the feudal tenures. These proceedings had been sanctioned by authority of which no party in the State could speak without reverence. Hale had borne a considerable share in them, and had always maintained that they were strictly legal."

"It is remarkable that the orator who took the most statesmanlike view of the subject, was old Maynard. In the civil conflicts of fifty eventful years, he had learned that questions affecting the highest interests of the Commonwealth were not to be decided by *verbal cavils*, and by *scraps* of *Law French* and *Law Latin.* And being, by universal acknowledgment, the most subtle and the most learned of English jurists, he could express what he felt without the risk of being accused of ignorance and presumption."

"We are," he said, "at this moment, *out* of the beaten path. If, therefore, we are determined to move *only in that path*, we cannot move at all. A man in a revolution, resolving to do nothing which is not strictly according to established form, resembles a man who has lost himself in the wilderness, and who stands crying: 'Where is the King's highway? I will walk nowhere but on the King's highway!' In a revolution we must have recourse to the highest law, *the safety of the State.*"

Our Convention could not become the Legislature, because it willed that the Legislature should still exist, but it did what the Convention Parliaments did. It legislated. The fact that the Convention had authorised the continued existence of the Legislature, could not deprive it of any right it possessed. If it could make an agent to do certain acts, it could do those acts itself. That agent was created to act when the Convention should cease to exist, or did not choose to act. It did choose to act itself, because we were, and are, in the midst of a revolution, and, in the words of old Maynard: "If we are determined to move only in the beaten path, we cannot move at all."

SOUTH CAROLINA.

THE MERCURY.

TUESDAY, SEPTEMBER 2, 1862.

A Great Battle—the last, we hope, that is to purple the soil of the Old Dominion—has been fought and won. The news is direct, official and satisfactory. General LEE is no braggart. He announces to the President that the valor of our troops has again prevailed upon the Plains of Manassas. On that memorable field McCLELLAN and POPE had marshalled their united hosts to meet our advancing columns. On Thursday, the 28th, and Friday, the 29th of August, the conflict was opened by the enemy. Our right and left wings, commanded respectively by Stonewall JACKSON and LONGSTREET, were successively assailed; but, in both instances, the attack was repulsed. On Saturday, the 30th of August, our whole army became engaged with the combined forces of the enemy, and achieved "a signal victory." This is the sum of our information. It is enough to indicate that the fight is likely to prove, in its fruits, the most important success, thus far, of the war.

The country will join with General LEE, in grateful acknowledgment to the Lord of Hosts, who has thus smiled once more upon our Cause. But vain indeed, and costly would be our triumph, if we should fail to grasp the advantages which it offers. We trust and believe that there will be no such failure.

The beaten and demoralized masses of the Yankee army can scarcely be rallied for another struggle south of the Potomac. The road lies open, to the gates of the Yankee Capital. Let our Generals but unleash their victorious legions, and Washington is ours. Maryland will arise and cast aside her fetters; and in thirty days the seat of war will be transferred "beyond the outer boundaries of the Confederacy."

We await with impatience the next tidings from the Potomac. For we believe that there can be no more delays upon the sod which covers the dead heros of Manassas.

The Convention.

Twenty members of the Convention, out of one hundred and eighty composing it, have at length signed a request to the President of the Convention to call that body together. The objects of the call on the part of those who have made it, we understand, are, to dissolve the Convention, and to abolish the Executive Council established by the Convention.

We do not understand that there is any practical evil alleged to exist from the continuance of the Convention. Its members, since its last adjournment, have been at their homes, or in Congress, or in the army, exercising no power whatever as members of the Convention, and receiving no pay. The evil of its continued existence, if any, must be theoretical—abstract. Accordingly, it is asserted that it is absolutely a despotism, and ought to be abolished.

One half of the false logic in the world is from an abuse of terms. What is a despotism? It is a *form of Government* in which the ruler wields absolute and unlimited power. Is the Convention a Government? It is no Government at all. To know what the Convention is, we have only to turn to the Ordinance of Secession, which every one of the twenty members who have requested the call of the Convention, voted for and signed. That Ordinance begins as follows: "*We, the People* of the State of South Carolina, in Convention assembled, do declare and ordain," &c. All the ordinances of the Convention begin in the same way. These gentlemen, therefore, being the authority, the Convention is the people of South Carolina, assembled in Convention. Now, can the people of South Carolina be a despotism against themselves?

The people, under our form of free Government, are the sovereignty of the State; and when they meet in Convention, undoubtedly they must possess all power; for the very definition of sovereignty is "the supreme ultimate authority in a State." The sovereignty of every State must be somewhere. In Russia it is in the Autocrat; in Great Britain it is in the King, Lords and Commons in Parliament; in our system of Government it is in the people. As the people cannot assemble personally to exercise their sovereignty, they elect delegates, who form a Convention, and there they are supreme. If sovereignty is despotism, then there can be no such thing as a free Government. But sovereignty is not despotism. It is the potential power by which all Governments exist, but it is not Government, and therefore cannot necessarily be a despotism. On the contrary, it is, under our system of Government, the grand source of all free Government vested in the people. To constitute a despotism, power must be thrown into the *form of a Government*, without limitation or responsibility. But whilst existing potentially in a sovereignty, it is nothing unless exercised. Exercised by the people to establish a free Government over themselves, or to throw off a dangerous despotism, such as lately existed in the Government of the United States, it is the terror of despotisms and the grand vindicator of liberty.

To elucidate our views, let us consider what the people, in the exercise of their sovereignty in Convention, have done in South Carolina. They set up the Government of South Carolina by a Constitution which Mr. CALHOUN declared to be the most perfect form of free Government which exists in the world. They placed the State under the Government of the United States, by adopting the Constitution of the United States. They have cast off the Government of the United States by seceding from the Union it constituted, and have placed the State in a Confederacy, by the adoption of the Constitution of the Confederate States. In doing all or any of these things, were the Conventions which performed them despotisms? or were they anything more than the people of South Carolina rightfully controlling, in their sovereign capacity, their own destiny? To assert the contrary, is merely an abuse of terms.

If these views are correct, the various objections urged against the Convention are very easily answered. It is asserted that the Convention is limited by the Act of the Legislature calling it. This, in the *first* place, is not true in fact. The Legislature merely designated in their Act calling the Convention the leading purpose for which they called it. This was proper as their justification to the people for their act; but the terms of the Act in no way attempt to limit the power of the Convention. Its terms are of the broadest kind, including the phraseology used by the Roman Senate when in the act of vesting all the powers of the State in the discretion of one man, for the preservation of the State in great emergencies. And if, in the second place, any attempt to limit the powers of the Convention had been made by the Legislature in the Act, it would simply have been nugatory. The Legislature is the creature of the Convention—the agent merely of the people. How can it limit the power of the people? If it could do so, the Legislature would be sovereign, and not the people; and if it was sovereign, why did it convoke the Convention? It convoked the Convention because it was *not*, and because the Convention was, sovereign; and even the power of convoking the Convention was by no inherent authority of its own, but the grant of a previous Convention.

It is further urged that the Convention has usurped powers. This is impossible, unless the people of South Carolina are not sovereign, and there is a power above them, whose attributes they may usurp. The particular matter in which it is alleged the Convention has practiced usurpation, is in establishing the existing Executive Council. Now the very presses and members of the Convention who make this charge, supported the Convention in the Ordinance of Secession, and the Ordinance placing South Carolina in the Confederacy of the Confederate States. If the Convention was competent to these high functions of sovereignty in changing the Government over the people of South Carolina, could it not give the Governor an Executive Council? These presses and members of the Convention have themselves answered this question in the affirmative, not only by their support of the above Ordinances, but by their support of the first Ordinance; for they supported the act of the Convention giving the Governor a Council. That was a very imposing Council. It established the highest dignitaries in the land. It consisted of a Secretary of State, a Secretary of War, and a Secretary of the Treasury—a striking and august miniature of the Government at Washington. No such Council is known in the Constitution of the State! Yet these gentlemen supported it. In what does it differ from the second Council, stamping the latter with usurpation? The Governor appointed the first Council, and the Convention itself appointed the second. "*Hinc illæ lachrimae.*" We will not do these gentlemen the injustice to suppose that they rest their charges of usurpation upon the kind of Council the Convention established. Admit the power, and the details of organization are clearly within the discretion of the Convention. But the power is denied, because it is not authorized by our State Constitution; and this denial is flatly refuted by their own repeated acts.

But it may be that the Convention, although exercising only its legitimate powers, may be tyrannical and oppressive, and, therefore, ought to be abolished.

The Acts of the Convention, it appear to us, have been governed by one single object—to save the liberties of the people and the existence of the State. These were threatened with destruction by the Government of the United States. They threw off that Government, and have succeeded in setting up another Confederate Government over the State of South Carolina. A savage war has arisen; and the Convention has passed various ordinances to enable the State to do her duty efficiently to herself and her confederates in carrying it on. Every act of the Convention has been honestly directed to this end. The only two measures that we have seen objected to, worthy of notice, are the establishment of the present Council, and the authority given to the Executive Council to call out and organize the slave labor of the State for the defence of the State. We do not know all the reasons for the Convention establishing the Executive Council, but we are satisfied that the authorities of the Confederate States at Richmond deemed it important if not necessary.

We are not aware that the good people of South Carolina have been disturbed in the enjoyment of their lives, liberties or property, by the acts of the Council, unless, indeed, the calling forth of the slaves to erect fortifications to defend the State against Yankee invasion can be called such. Here, we know, is a succession of labor for the defence of the State. To defend the State is a duty not only to the people of South Carolina, but to our confederates. It must be done by white or by black labor. Will any man hesitate, while our white laborers are in our armies, fighting for the liberties and independence of the Confederacy, to place our slaves in the trenches to build our fortifications? In the absence of adequate legislation, by our Legislature, the Convention would be faithless to its great mission of securing the liberties and independence of the State, if it did not pass efficient regulations to call forth the slave labor of the State to defend the State. The conquest of South Carolina by our enemies will be no trifling event to the slaveholder in South Carolina, or to the Confederacy. It will be full of miseries which the boldest may shrink to face. It will be full of horrors which the tongue may be ashamed to tell. Whether the Executive Council have abused the powers entrusted to them by the Convention, the Convention will judge. For ourselves, we have heard of no abuse actually practised, beyond the fact of their existence. As far as we can judge, they have done too little, rather than too much. They have failed in energy, rather than in aggressiveness. In the enrollment of troops they have done well. And in calling out slave labor they have at last done what ought to have been done.

If the Convention, as we believe, has been heretofore of inestimable service to the State, will the State be benefitted by its dissolution? It is a matter for the sound discretion of the Convention; but we doubt the policy of its dissolution. We are in the throes of a bloody revolution. Who will say, from the manner in which the war has been carried on, that South Carolina will not be overrun by our enemies? No Legislature might be able to meet or to call together the people again in Convention, if the existing Convention is abolished. Who knows whether a Governor will be elected; and if so, whether he will be equal to the duties of the crisis? To save the State, it might be necessary, as it was in the revolution of 1776, to place a Dictator over the State. The progress of this war is not determined. The character of the Confederate Government is not yet settled. The Constitution is already strained and warped from its integrity, by the assumed exigencies of the war. The tendency to centralization, with some of the worst features of the Government of the United States, is strongly developed. We hesitate not, to say, that if the broad ground of military necessity is used to set aside the Constitution, in the assembling of Congress, on six hours notice, given to a small remnant of the body, and in the building of railroads all over the country, and in establishing military law, &c., &c., the existence of the Convention may be important. Over the State of Texas, where there is no enemy, the President has declared martial law, and appointed a Provost Marshal in every county, thus superseding the civil authorities of that State by military power. Such is the statement of a Senator in Congress.

We are in the midst of a bloody and terrible struggle. We know not what will be the progress of events, and what will be the dangers of the fast coming future, either to our existence as a people, or to the integrity of our Government. In the very throes of this revolution, the attention of our people has been diverted from those with whom we battle, and from the conduct of those who direct for us the policy of this struggle and the powers of the Confederate Government. A petty issue has been got up between the Governor and the Executive Council of this State; and bitter attacks have been leveled against the Convention, a body not exercising any power, or costing the State any money, but merely holding in abeyance the authority with which it was invested for any emergency. Efforts have been made to excite the jealousy of the Legislature. We regard it as ill-timed and unfortunate. We think the Convention a body of men who will not abuse their powers. We think the assaults upon the Convention as uncalled for as they are injurious to the cause of the South and to the State.

PROGRESS OF THE WAR.

THE SPIRIT OF THE NORTH—WAR MEETINGS—A MILD LETTER FROM DANIEL E. DICKINSON.

War meetings continue to be held throughout the North. Preparations are being made to hold a great demonstration in Brooklyn. Among the speakers announced for the occasion are General SPINOLA, State Senator from New York; General SICKLES, Mayor KALBFLEISCH (Phœbes what a name?) Congressmen ODELL and HUMPHREYS, ex-Judge MORRIS, and others. Senator PUGH, of Ohio, had been invited to address a war meeting in Cincinnati, but he declined, alleging as his excuse that he thought "it was time for those who have not themselves enlisted to quit exhorting others on the subject." "Honorable DANIEL E. DICKINSON, of New York, is also out in a long letter, in reply to an invitation to address a war meeting in Pennsylvania.—To show the treachery of this man whom the South once regarded as her firm friend, and was anxious even to support for the last Presidential nomination—to expose the faith of our Northern friends—we quote some few passages from his letter. After expressing his regret at his inability to attend, he says:

"My views are, to-day, what they were when this hell-born rebellion assaulted the glorious flag of our country's pride and hope at Sumter—that it must be put down without regard to cost or treasure, put down upon the field of blood; and put down, too, by severing the head of the loathsome serpent from its body. It is not a mere rebellion or outbreak. It is the result of a dark and malign conspiracy, conceived and prosecuted by a worse combination of evil spirits than assembled at Milton's "Infernal Conference." It will never relax nor yield until it has overthrown the government or been crushed into the earth beyond hope or prospect of resurrection; and not only to its *overthrow*, but its *annihilation*, should we, as a people, address ourselves.

"The government should lay its hand with iron rigor upon every interest which will give it strength or weaken its adversary, and should strike hardest where it will be felt most; should condemn and confiscate to its use every species of property, of every name and kind, whether animate or inanimate, on two legs or on four.

"We have not now, nor have we ever had, over about one half men enough in the field to conquer and hold so vast an area of rebellion; and the occasion is now presented for us to crush the venom out of this pestilent curse.

"In raising such force, the President should understand that the people will not hesitate at any amount, for they mean that this rebellion shall be destroyed, cost what it will, or come what may.

"The people should understand that the popular demand of to-day is not only for the raising of three hundred thousand men already ordered, but for a further order for an equal number, with a recommendation that every able-bodied man, between the ages of eighteen and forty-five, should prepare to take the field in case of necessity. Let this be recommended, and so much of it as may be necessary carried into effect, even to the whole and conspiracy will find its reward, and rebellion go where it belongs. Let the people demand this, and our good President proclaim it, and little more will be wanted than an act of amnesty for the masses, and halters for the leaders.

"Let every one who has ability to shoulder a firelock come forward to do so, and help rescue this land our fathers loved from the hands of traitorous despoilers."

THE WAR IN ARKANSAS—IMPORTANT INTERCEPTED LETTERS FROM GEN. HINDMAN.

A correspondent of the New York *Tribune*, writing from Helena, Arkansas, under date of August 6, says:

Since the arrival of Gen. Curtis' army at this place, considerable bodies of troops have been kept at points within a circuit of twenty miles, and an expedition has been made up the St. Francis river. In two instances we have captured the rebel mail passing to and fro between Little Rock and the army of Gen. Bragg, east of the Mississippi. Several of the letters reveal important information, and will be read with interest. The two following are from Brigadier General T. C. Hindman, commanding the rebel army in Arkansas, to Major G. W. Brent, chief of staff, Headquarters, Western Department, Tupelo, Mississippi, dated July 19, 1862.

GEN. HINDMAN TO MAJOR BRENT.

HEADQUARTERS TRANS-MISSISSIPPI DIST.,
Little Rock, Ark., July 19.

MAJOR: I have now at my different camps of instruction in Arkansas, and on the march, thirty regiments of infantry, averaging very nearly, if not quite, 1,000 men to the regiment. Of these not 3,000 are armed.

In North Louisiana I have three regiments unarmed.

In Missouri six regiments are forming for which I have no arms.

In the Indian country there are four or five regiments whose arms are worthless.

I have gathered up by purchase and impressment, about all the arms in my district. It is perfectly certain that not one thousand more guns can be obtained. Of those that I have, only about eight hundred (800) are valuable, the balance being shot guns and common rifles.

In response to my previous appeal for arms, General Beauregard ordered turned over to my ordnance officer, Major Lockman, some four hundred and fifty (450) damaged guns and rifles, and sent me a worthless battery. These I have received.

Curtis is devastating Eastern Arkansas. A gunboat and transport fleet is at the mouth of the Arkansas River.

A Union force of between 2,000 and 5,000 is in the Cherokee Nation. Another Union column of the same strength is in Northwest Arkansas.

If arms and ammunition were furnished me, I could do something in the way of defence; without them I am nearly powerless.

There are old muskets and batteries in abundance east of the Mississippi. I apply for them. The requisitions I send do not cover the fourth of my wants. I have stated the facts. Begging and complaining cannot add to their strength.

Very respectfully,
T. C. HINDMAN,
Major General Commanding.

Major G. W. Brent, chief of staff, headquarters western department, Tupelo, Miss.

May I ask that a copy of this be forwarded to the Secretary of War immediately. T. C. H.

Of the same date of the above, the following letter is from Gen. Hindman to Gen. Bragg, and is marked "private."

HEADQUARTERS TRANS MISSISSIPPI DIST.,
Little Rock, Ark., July 10, 1862.

GENERAL: I hope not to be thought importunate, but if you only could realize the troubles that are upon me, I am sure you would send Cleburne and Marmaduke to me. I stand, except my staff, absolutely alone. There is no one to help me. For God's sake do you give me the relief I have asked. With these two officers, and the old muskets and batteries east of the river, I will be content, and will trouble you no more.

Respectfully and very truly,
T. C. HINDMAN,
Major General Commanding.

Gen. Braxton Bragg, commanding Western Department, Tupelo, Miss.

THE CONFEDERATE CONGRESS.

SENATE.

RICHMOND, Friday, August 29.

Mr. Sparrow, from the Committee on Military Affairs, reported back the memorials of the Theological Seminary of Louisiana, and of the Society of Friends of Guilford, North Carolina, requesting that the Committee be discharged from the further consideration of the subject. The Committee's request was acceded to.

Mr. Sparrow, from the same Committee, reported a bill to aid the completion of the Vicksburg and Shreveport Railroad, in the State of Louisiana, which was placed upon the calendar and ordered to be printed.

QUARTERMASTER AND PAYMASTER DEPARTMENTS.

Mr. Sparrow, from the same Committee, reported a bill to provide for the establishment of separate a bureau for the Paymaster's department.

Mr. Sparrow said that on account of the press of business in the Quartermaster's department, it was impossible to pay the troops regularly, and that many of them remained unpaid for months. He asked that it should be immediately put on its passage.

Mr. Burnett, of Kentucky, was opposed to the measure proposed by the bill. There were now a number of officers in the Quartermaster's department who were idle and inefficient. If the troops remained unpaid it was because the Quartermasters did not perform their duty. He should oppose establishing a Paymaster's department, unless a corresponding reduction of officers was made in the Quartermaster's department. He had never yet been able to find out what were the duties of Brigade Quartermaster. The bill was put upon the calendar.

SUBSTITUTES.

On motion of Mr. Semmes, of Louisiana, the bill "providing for substitutes, in certain cases, and detailing privates for police duty," was taken up.

Mr. Simms, of Kentucky, thought the consideration of the bill had better be postponed, but if it was to be taken up, he had a few remarks to make about substitutes. He had always been opposed to substitutes, but if they were to be taken into the army, he approved of the French system. The party wishing to supply the substitute should be obliged to pay the government whatever amount may be fixed, and let it procure the substitute. The practice of permitting individuals to furnish their own substitutes had led to enormous abuses. In this very city he had been informed that substitute agents had made as much as one hundred dollars, and that the same substitute had sold himself, in some cases, twenty times. He had also learned, from military men, that substitutes composed nine-tenths of the deserters. He hoped the consideration would be postponed, to allow him time to prepare an amendment. The bill was reported by sections.

Mr. Maxwell, of Florida, moved to amend so that the bill should read that in all cases where substitutes are received, the person furnishing the substitute shall guarantee his fidelity, and in case he deserts the principal shall be held to service, as if no substitute had been furnished by him.

Mr. Semmes, of Louisiana, had also personally been opposed to substitutes; he thought every man, high or low, rich or poor, should be forced to go into the army and do his part in the defence of the country; now the procurement of substitutes was confined to the rich; the poor or the moderately well off man could not afford to pay the enormous prices demanded; no substitutes should be allowed; all citizens should be put upon the same footing.

Mr. Barnwell, of South Carolina, opposed the amendment of the gentleman from Florida. The gentleman's sole object seemed to be to provide against the desertion of substitutes. He was opposed to substitutes. They were in all respects inferior to other troops, and, as we are told by all military men, more prone to desertion. He was for permitting only such persons to furnish substitutes as the good of the country required. Legislation should teach the people that the danger is not passed. If a rich man, he must be taught that he must fight. Men desire offices, but they are unwilling to go down into the ranks. Whenever a spurt of success takes place, our people are apt to take up the opinion that the danger is all over. Our enactments must convince the people of the error of this opinion. He was opposed to substitutes except whenever the Secretary of War should say a man would be more serviceable working at his trade than in the ranks. And as concerned the large slaveholder, he did not wish to favor him, but approved the section of the bill permitting him to supply a substitute, because it was more important to the prosperity of the country that he should remain on his plantation and keep his slaves in subjection. He favored the bill as it stood, and should vote for it.

Mr. Phelan, of Mississippi, thought either that no man should be allowed to furnish a substitute or that every man should be allowed the privilege. He was not prepared to vote for any middle policy. By the bill two classes of citizens only are entitled to obtain substitutes. The substitute of the gentleman from Florida puts every man on the same footing, and holds them responsible for the desertion of their substitutes. It had been said the rich should be allowed to remain at home to protect the poor man's family from the ravages of his slaves. Why not let the poor man stay at home and protect his own family against the slaves of the rich man? The poor man should be permitted to remain at home and attend to his pecuniar interests, if the rich man is permitted to do it. The poor man should be permitted to remain at home on account of his feelings of affection for his family, if the rich man is to be permitted to do it. In his own district, on one side of the river, were the prairie plantations of the rich, while on the other were the farms of the poor. The latter might ask him when he went home, why he had legislated to permit the rich to remain at home, while the poor were forced to go into the army? If I should tell them the rich were permitted to remain at home to guard the families of the poor, would they not at once reply, that they had much rather entrust the protection of their families to their own presence? The policy of the bill was class legislation; he was, therefore, opposed to it. He was opposed to it from the first to the last line. But if we are to have class legislation, let us legislate in favor of the poor. The rich will take care of themselves.

Mr. Clark, of Missouri, moved to strike out these words "or when such person is the only white male adult on a farm or plantation having thereon not less than fifty slaves." He thought the second section of the bill made ample provision for the keeping the slaves in subjection.

The substitute of Mr. Clark was adopted.

The question then recurred on the amendment of Mr. Maxwell, of Florida, viz: to strike out the entire section, saving the enacting clause, and the clause which makes the party furnishing the substitute responsible for his fidelity.

There being no further amendments to the first section, the Secretary reported, section the second, providing for the detail of privates for police duty.

On motion of Mr. Brown, of Mississippi, the words "with the approval of the Provost Marshal of such county or parish," were stricken out.

Mr Phelan, of Mississippi, moved to strike out the clause providing for the detail of one private, as a police, for the plantation of a *femme sole*, a minor, or a person in the military service of the Confederacy.

Mr. Phelan argued to show the indelicacy, the absurdity, and the impossibility of a *femme sole*, a minor, or an absentee to make a contract for the retention or maintenance on their respective plantations, of a whiskered grenadier. The amendment was lost.

Mr. Preston moved to strike out the entire section. He thought the slave should only be managed as the separate States might think proper. He did not desire to authorize brigadiers or any other generals, to meddle with domestic institutions. The conscript army should not be prostituted into a police guard for slaves.

After much more discussion the further consideration of the bill was postponed until Monday.

On motion of Mr. Sparrow, of Louisiana, the Senate went into executive session.

HOUSE OF REPRESENTATIVES.

The Speaker laid before the House the Joint Resolution relating to the Navy Department, sent back from the Senate, and reported as passed without amendment. It appeared, moreover, that an amendment had been made by filling the blank left by the House with the number of members on the part of the Senate. The resolution was, by unanimous consent, considered as without amendment. The Speaker subsequently announced the Committee on the part of the House, as follows: Messrs. Foote, of Tennessee; Barksdale, of Mississippi; Lyons, of Virginia; Dupre, of Louisiana, and Boyce, of South Carolina.

SOLDIERS UNDER EIGHTEEN YEARS OF AGE.

Mr. Chambliss, of Virginia, moved a suspension of the rules for the purpose of taking up for consideration the bill "authorizing the discharge of private soldiers under eighteen years of age." The motion was agreed to, and the bill was taken up. As reported from the Military Committee it reads as follows:

An Act authorising the discharge of private soldiers under eighteen years of age, and prohibiting the enlistment of such persons.

SEC. 1. The Congress of the Confederate States do enact, That any private soldier of the Provisional Army, who is under the age of eighteen years, shall be entitled to a discharge from all military service while he is under such age, on the application of himself, his parents, guardian or next of kin, to the Colonel of the regiment to which such private soldier belongs, sustained by proof satisfactory to said Colonel, of the age of said private soldier.

SEC. 2. *Be it further enacted.* That hereafter no person under the age of eighteen years shall be allowed to enlist in the military service of the Confederate States.

Mr. Chambliss addressed the House in favor of the immediate passage of the bill, which was also sustained by Mr. Goode, of Virginia.

Mr. Miles, of South Carolina, moved to amend the first section by striking out the word "colonel" and inserting the word "commander," and after the word "regiment" inserting "legion, battalion or independent company."

Mr. Foote, of Tennessee, approved the bill—thought it eminently proper—but could not vote for it, as he himself had sons in the army, and he could not aid in the passage of a law which forbid them to serve the country in their own way.

Mr. Ewing, of Kentucky, thought the bill had been introduced at an unfortunate moment.—While the country was calling upon Congress to furnish additional troops for the army, we pass a law taking from that army 20,000 of its best troops. He should vote against the whole bill.

The debate was continued by Messrs. Heiskell and Jones, of Tennessee; Singleton, of Mississippi; Lyons, of Virginia; Machen, of Kentucky; and Wright, of Georgia; after which the amendment of Mr. Miles was agreed to.

Mr. Singleton offered the following amendment as a proviso to the first section of the bill:

"Provided that the provisions of this act shall not apply to those persons who, though under eighteen years of age, have gone into the army as substitutes."

Mr. Chilton offered the following as a substitute for the amendment last proposed:

"But the provisions of this bill shall not extend to any minor who has gone into the army as a substitute by the consent of the parent or guardian of such minors; and in cases where substitutes may apply for a discharge by reason of the minority of such substitute, no discharge shall be granted until notice be given to the person whose substitute he is, if resident within the Confederate States, and time allowed such pary to controvert the grounds of discharge, and if it should appear that the substitution was made of a minor under the age of eighteen years, and that he still continues under that age at the time of making such application, and that his substitution was procured without the consent of the parent or guardian of such minor, then, in such cases, the party who procured the substitute shall be ordered to return to the service, and required to serve out the term of his enlistment."

After some debate, Mr. E. M. Bruce said that an objection to the passage of the bill might be found in the fact that in Kentucky the larger portion of the boys were Southern in feeling, and as they might be compelled to fly from their homes at any time, it would be a pity to exclude such fine material from our army. He thought the less legislation on the matter the better, and moved to lay the whole subject on the table.—The motion was not agreed to—ayes 31, nays 51.

Mr. Chilton's substitute was then rejected—ayes 33, noes 49.

The question then recurring on Mr. Singleton's amendment, it was adopted.

Mr. Heiskell, of Tennessee, moved to amend by inserting just before the proviso—"But no minor shall be so discharged except by his own free will and consent." The amendment was agreed to.

Mr. Crockett, of Kentucky, moved to amend by inserting immediately after Mr. Singleton's proviso—"And provided further, that nothing in this act shall prevent volunteers from the State of Kentucky between the ages of sixteen and eighteen from entering the service, if in the opinion of the proper authorities, they are capable of performing military service."

Mr. Crockett appealed to the House to exempt Kentucky from the operations of the bill, by the adoption of the amendment he had submitted. He hoped that our army would enter Kentucky at no distant day, and many of the chivalric youths of the State were impatiently waiting to enlist under the banner of the South.

Mr. Gartrell hoped the House would reflect before passing the bill now under consideration. There was danger that gentleman would be led away by sympathy into the adoption of a measure productive of vast injury to our cause. Let the boys remain in the army. If it can be made to appear that they entered the service without the consent of their parents their discharge could be obtained from the Secretary of War.

Mr. Lyons.—By what authority of law would the Secretary do this?

Mr. Gartrell.—Upon the ground that they were illegally held to service, and under the rules of the War Department. I now move to lay the whole subject on the table. The motion was lost.

Mr. Heiskell offered the following amendment in lieu of that offered by the gentleman from Kentucky.

"This shall not apply to any person who is a refugee, or the son of a disloyal person; the consent of no other person than himself shall be required." Lost.

Mr. E. M. Bruce moved to commit the bill and amendments to the Committee on Military Affairs. Lost.

Mr. Bonham moved the indefinite postponement of the bill, and the previous question was ordered thereon; the motion was decided in the negative—ayes 32, noes 46.

The question recurring upon the amendment of Mr. Crockett, of Kentucky, it was agreed to—ayes 48, noes not counted.

Mr. Clapp, of Mississippi, moved to amend the second section by adding—"Unless the parents of such persons are living and shall give their written assent to his enlistment before he is received." Agreed to. The bill was then ordered to its engrossment.

The bill was then read a third time and passed—ayes 48, noes 26.

The House adjourned.

Richmond Dispatch.

The DISPATCH is published DAILY, Sundays excepted. Price for mailing $6 a year, or $3.50 for six months, three months $2; one month $1, in advance.

The SEMI-WEEKLY DISPATCH is issued every TUESDAY and FRIDAY at $3, in advance.

The WEEKLY DISPATCH is issued every FRIDAY, and mailed to subscribers at $2 per annum.

TUESDAY MORNING.... SEPTEMBER 2, 1862.

DAILY DISPATCH.

VOL. XXIII. RICHMOND, VA., TUESDAY MORNING, SEPTEMBER 2, 1862 NO. 53.

BATTLE OF MANASSAS

TRIUMPH OF OUR FORCES OVER THE COMBINED ARMIES OF McCLELLAN AND POPE.

Our information is such as to give encouragement to the hope that the sacred soil of Virginia will soon be rescued from the hands, and divested of the polluting tread, of the Yankee invader. The great battle of Saturday last, fought on the memorable and classic ground of Manassas, resulted in the overthrow of the combined armies of the Federal Government, with a loss that is perhaps unequalled in the annals of the present war. We write without particulars; but the dispatches received by the President, and now given to the public warrants the belief that our triumph is complete and glorious, and that the Confederate army is probably to-day within hailing distance of the Federal capital.

The first dispatch received yesterday morning represented that the enemy had made several attempts to break through our lines, which intercepted their retreat towards Alexandria, but were repulsed each time with heavy loss. No mention of the casualties on our side was made, except that Gens. Ewell and Trimble were badly wounded, but not mortally, and Gen. Taliaferro slightly wounded.—A large number of prisoners were said to have been captured by our troops. This fight occurred in the vicinity of Manassas Plains. The indefinite character of this dispatch created some anxiety, and although it was stated that the enemy had been repulsed, still some uneasiness was felt, and some apprehensions entertained, for the safety of the gallant corps that, to the public, seemed to be between the two armies of the foe. These apprehensions were dispelled, however, by the later and more authentic intelligence of the day.

Late in the afternoon, a dispatch was received by the President from Gen. Lee, conveying information which left no grounds to question the glorious success of our arms. This dispatch stated that on Thursday Gen. Jackson's corps repulsed Gen. Pope; Gen. Longstreet repulsed McClellan on Friday, and that on Saturday Gen. Lee attacked the combined forces of McClellan and Pope, utterly routing them with immense loss. Our army, it was stated, was still pursuing them, but in what direction we did not learn. If it be true, as previously represented, that our forces had gained the rear of the enemy, and repulsed their attempts to recover their intercepted lines we do not understand by what route they are now endeavoring to effect their escape. Large supplies of valuable stores were captured, some of which were destroyed by our troops. Our loss is represented to be heavy in valuable officers, though no names are given.

FROM CUMBERLAND GAP.

If correct, the news from Cumberland Gap is scarcely less important than that from Manassas. Late last night it was asserted that news had been received in official quarters to the effect that the Yankee General Morgan had attempted to cut his way through our lines, and that he was repulsed with great slaughter, after which his entire command, amounting to some ten thousand men, with their arms and equipments, surrendered to our forces under General E. Kirby Smith. There is every reason to believe that this statement is correct, as it is well known that Morgan's position was decidedly precarious; but in view of the many similar reports received from the same quarter it should be taken with much caution.

FROM THE PENINSULA.

We learn from an intelligent gentleman, who has lately visited a portion of the Peninsula, that the Yankees, though keeping up a great show of strength in the counties of James City, New Kent, and Charles City, by means of foraging parties, which arrest every white man they find, are yet preparing to evacuate this portion of the State.—The 11th Pennsylvania regiment of dragoons occupy Williamsburg, and while they are engaged in removing everything of value to their vessels lying in James river, yet they have virtually given up possession of the town, having reinstated all the old officers in the lunatic asylum, including the former matron, for whom they sent to Norfolk; and to prevent an attack while thus engaged, the parties above named are sent out, and for lack of a few good men to meet them, they are practising outrages and indignities upon this actually desolated portion of our State. A great many of the negroes who were taken off by the Yankees have returned to their owners, and express themselves as heartily tired of their Yankee friends. The Union men, including Lemuel Bowden, who, it will be recollected, was a candidate for Judge at the last election, have gone to the North. But the worst feature in the intelligence which we have received is, that the rascals have appropriated to themselves a large portion of the provisions intended for the inmates of the asylum, and there is great danger of their suffering. From all that we can learn, a bold dash with a few hundred of Stuart's dragoons would accelerate their evacuation of Williamsburg, and restore much valuable property to its rightful owners. This gentleman also states that there are a large number of negroes at Yorktown, who are really suffering for the necessaries of life, the Yankees neglecting them in their care for their own safety and security.

THE WILL OF COM. URIAH P. LEVY.

The published will of Com. U. P. Levy, U. S. N., bequeaths Monticello, the residence of Thomas Jefferson, and all his property, with the exception of a few small legacies, "to the people of the United States"—the will making it incumbent on the United States Government to establish a school at Monticello. In case Congress fails to carry out the intention of the bequest, the property goes to "the people of Virginia;" and in case the Legislature declines to receive the trust, the property is to go to the Portuguese Hebrew congregation in Cherry street, Philadelphia, and the Portuguese Hebrew congregation of Richmond, Va., for the establishment of the said school at Monticello for the children of all denominations, Hebrew and Christian. Among the legacies is one of $100 to Benj. F Butler, (the Beast,) to purchase a mourning ring. The will directs the executors to erect a monument at Cypress Hills, to consist of a full length statue of Capt. Levy, in iron or bronze, in the full uniform of a captain of the U. S. Navy, and holding in his hand a scroll on which shall be inscribed: "Under this monument," or "In memory of Uriah P. Levy, Captain in the United States Navy, Father of the Law for the Abolition of the barbarous practice of Corporal Punishment in the Navy of the United States." The monument is to cost $6,000, and the body is to be buried under it.

ARREST OF A YOUNG LADY.

Miss Green, a loyal young lady in one of the northwestern counties in Virginia, was arrested and put in jail in Buckhannon, Upshur county, on a charge of cutting telegraph wires in the Yankee army. When interrogated, she confessed she had cut the wires, and said that she would do so again if set at liberty, at the same time refusing to take the oath of Yankee servitude. One end of the wire cut was found stuck in the ground several inches, and when asked why she did that, she replied that a great many Yankees had been killed, and as that wire pointed the way they had gone it would doubtless be used to know if there was room for any more.

PIG IRON.

This article is very scarce just now, and ready sale is found for all offered. Small lots of Scotch pig sell at $900, and Virginia iron at $100 @ $125 per ton. Good scrap cast iron is selling readily at three cents per pound.

MARRIAGE LICENSES.

The war does not affect the marriage market in any perceptible degree in Richmond, thirty licenses having been issued by the Clerk of the Hustings Court during the month of August. This is largely above the average number.

CONFEDERATE STATES CONGRESS.

[*ADJOURNED SESSION.*]

SENATE.

MONDAY, September 1st, 1862.

The Journal of Friday was read and approved.

Mr. MAXWELL, of Fla., presented a petition from twenty-three of the inmates of the Winder Hospital asking the passage of a bill "to send all the old and infirm men that are not able to double-quick in the army to their respective States." Referred.

Mr. SIMMS, of Ky., offered the following preamble and resolutions, which, on his motion, were laid upon the table for the present:

Whereas, our country must ever cherish with a grateful pride the heroic achievements of its brave and patriotic soldiery, who, in a noble struggle for independence of and resistance to the invaders and desolators of our homes, have won for themselves and our armies imperishable glory upon the field of battle; and whereas, these achievements, thus signalized by deeds of daring and personal valor worthy of any age, and rendered doubly dear to the hearts of our people by the precious blood that has been shed and the brave patriots who have fallen, must ever form one of brightest pages in our history, and through all time challenge the admiration and approval of the brave and generous of every nation. To the end, therefore, that the whole country may in the most honorable manner give some especial token of its appreciation of the noble services of its brave and heroic defenders:

Be it Resolved, That the President cause to be prepared medals, or badges, with suitable designs or inscriptions thereon, to be presented to such of our officers and soldiers as may have, or shall hereafter, distinguish themselves by deeds of personal gallantry upon the battle-field; which medal, or badge, when presented, shall be to such officer or private a lasting memorial of a nation's grateful tribute to its patriotic and heroic defenders.

Be it further Resolved, That in all cases where such officer or soldier shall be killed by the enemy upon the battle field, after having performed such deeds of personal bravery as would entitle him, if living, to such medal or badge, the President shall cause the same to be delivered to his widow, or children, if any; and if there be no widow or child, then to the father or mother, if any.

Be it further Resolved, That in order to execute faithfully the intention of Congress, as above expressed, the Secretary of War shall prescribe such regulations to determine the claims of each officer or private who by his conduct in battle may merit this especial honor at the hands of his country; and in cases of especial merit he is hereby authorized to confer upon brigades, regiments, and battalions, or other corps, such evidences of appreciation as will impress upon the mind of each soldier that he is in the service of a country proud to do honor to its patriotic sons.

Mr. HILL, from the Committee on Judiciary, reported a bill for the repression and punishment of counterfeiting C. S. Treasury notes. Ordered to be printed.

Mr. DAVIS, of N. C., from the Committee on Claims, reported back the memorial in behalf of Gen. Hardee, in connection with his work on Military Tactics, and requested to be discharged from the further consideration of the subject, the committee being unwilling, at this time, to inaugurate the policy of bestowing pecuniary rewards upon any person, however meritorious. The memorial was laid upon the table.

The calendar being taken up,

The bill creating a Paymaster's Department, separate and distinct from the Quartermaster's Department, was taken up.

The bill was postponed on the motion of Mr. HILL.

The bill concerning substitutes, which was postponed from Friday last, was taken up in its place.

After much debate the bill was passed in the following form:

SEC. 1. *The Congress of the Confederate States do enact*, That hereafter substitutes for persons liable to military duty shall not be allowed, except in cases where the person offering the substitute is skilled and actually employed in some mechanical pursuit, the prosecution of which, at the time, the Secretary of War may declare to be important to the public interest: *Provided*, That in all cases where substitutes are received, the person furnishing the substitute shall guarantee his fidelity, and in case he deserts the principal shall be held to service as if no substitute had been furnished by him.

SEC. 2. That the Secretary of War and commanders of brigades and divisions shall detail to any farm or plantation worked by slaves, when the owner thereof is a *femme sole*, a minor, or a person in the service of the Confederacy, one enrolled private for police duty thereon, and to act as overseer, under the direction and control of the owner thereof, or his legal representative: *Provided*, That said detail be made upon the application and designation of the owner, or the representative of the owner, of such farm or plantation, and that the person so detailed shall be withdrawn upon a like application of such owner or his representative: *And provided, further*, That said private shall not, whilst so detailed, receive any pay or allowance from the Government, but shall be paid by the owner of the farm or plantation an amount to be agreed upon between them; and when recalled said detailed private shall immediately proceed to brigade headquarters and report for duty, under the penalty of being punished as a deserter.

Mr. BROWN, of Miss., now called up the bill in relation to the organization of Partisan Rangers.

Mr. BURNETT, of Ky., in order to test the sense of the Senate, moved to postpone the bill until the first Monday in December next.

After some animated debate the bill was postponed, and the Senate adjourned.

HOUSE OF REPRESENTATIVES.

MONDAY, Sept. 1, 1862.

The House met at 12 o'clock.

Mr. DARGAN, of Ala., offered a joint resolution in reference to retaliation, which was referred to the Judiciary Committee. Also, an act entitled "An act further to protect the country, and to drive back the invaders"—referred to the Military Committee. Also, an act to regulate the mode by which sick soldiers shall be examined by the Medical Board of Examiners at Richmond—referred to Special Committee on Hospitals.

Mr. CLOPTON, of Ala., introduced an act to amend an act with reference to the exemption of certain persons from military duties—referred. Also, a joint resolution to prevent the escape of persons guilty of treason, and to provide for the removal of disloyal citizens—referred to the Committee on Military Affairs. Also, a resolution instructing the Committee on the Judiciary to inquire into the expediency of providing by legislation for the confiscation of property of persons guilty of treason, and appropriating the same to the benefit of persons despoiled of their property by the enemy. Adopted.

Mr. CURRY, of Ala., offered a joint resolution of thanks to Capt. Raphael Semmes, and the officers and crew of the steamer Sumter, for gallant and meritorious conduct in inflicting injury upon the commerce of the enemy. Adopted unanimously.

Mr. HANLEY, of Arkansas, introduced an act to provide for the payment of mail contractors for service performed by them after their States had seceded from the United States, and before the Confederate Government took control of the service. Referred to Committee on Post-Offices and Roads.

Mr. ROYSTON, of Arkansas, presented a memorial on the postal service, which was referred. Also, the following resolution:

Resolved, That the President be respectfully requested to communicate to the House of Representatives whether it be true that Maj.-Gen'l Hindman, the Commanding General of the Trans-Mississippi district, caused all cotton in said district to be seized, and the object for which such seizure was made; also, whether said Commanding General refused to have substitutes received as soldiers in the army of the Confederate States; also, whether said Commanding General has placed said military district under martial law; also, whether said Commanding General has caused to be organized into new companies and regiments the conscripts of said military district, and appointed officers to command the same; and if said acts, or any of them, have been done by said Commanding General, that the President be requested to communicate to this House the authority or instructions under which said Commanding General has taken this action. Agreed to.

Mr. WRIGHT, of Ga., presented two memorials, which were appropriately referred.

Mr. GARTRELL, of Ga., presented a resolution that the Committee on Military Affairs be instructed to inquire whether the officers and men of the Provisional Army have been regularly paid; and if not, what legislation is necessary to insure their prompt payment. Agreed to.

Mr. TRIPPE, of Ga., introduced a memorial in reference to the property of the infant children of Stephen A. Douglas. Referred, without reading, to the Committee on Claims.

Also, a resolution that the Committee on Claims be instructed to inquire into the expediency of increasing the salary of clerks in the different Departments. Agreed to.

Mr. MOORE, of Ky., introduced a resolution that it be referred to the Military Committee to inquire into the expediency of increasing the medical corps of the Provisional army of the Confederate States.

Mr. BRUCE, of Ky., offered a resolution to refer it to the Committee of Ways and Means to inquire into the expediency of employing a complete corps of competent reporters and printers to publish substantially the debates and proceedings of this House. Not agreed to.

Mr. PERKINS, of La., offered a resolution that the Secretary of War be requested to communicate to this House the result and finding of the court-martial convened in the case of Quartermaster Hesse, and whether he is still in the pay of the Confederate States; and if not, the date of his dismissal from the service. Agreed to.

Mr. DUPRE, of La., submitted a bill to amend the act with reference to the sequestration of the property of alien enemies. Referred to the Judiciary Committee.

Mr. CLAPP, of Miss., offered a resolution, that the Judiciary Committee be instructed to inquire what legislation, if any, is necessary in regard to persons residing within the limits of the Confederate States who have taken the oath of allegiance to the Government of the United States since the commencement of the pending war.

Mr. CHAMBERS, of Miss., presented a bill for the relief of subscribers of cotton to the produce loan in certain cases. Referred to the Committee on Commerce.

Mr. VEST, of Mo., introduced an act to provide for the payment of certain claims against the Confederate States in the State of Missouri. Referred to Military Committee.

Mr. LANDER, of N. C., introduced an act to amend the act to exempt certain persons from enrollment for service in the armies of the Confederate States. Referred to Military Committee.

Mr. [illegible], of North Carolina, offered the following, which was referred to the Military Committee:

Whereas, conflicting opinions exist as to the mode of filling vacancies in the offices of the regiments organized under the authority of the States and transferred to the Confederate Government, and still retaining their organization: Therefore,

Be it enacted by the Congress of the Confederate States, That where any such vacancies now exist, or may hereafter occur, the same shall be filled according to the laws of the respective States from which such regiments are received, applicable thereto.

Mr. BOYCE, of S. C., presented a memorial from the Faculty of the Theological Seminary at Columbia, S. C., for the exemption of theological students from conscription. Referred to the Military Committee.

Mr. AYER, of S. C., offered a resolution that it be referred to the Military Committee to inquire and report on the expediency of authorizing the Secretary of War to appoint an Adjutant for every independent battalion in the service of the Confederate Government. Agreed to. Also, a resolution requesting the President to communicate to the House, at as early a day as convenient, whether the work is being prosecuted by the Government, or in any other way, on the railroad for connecting the Richmond and Danville Railroad and the North Carolina Railroad, for which one million of dollars was appropriated by act approved February 10, 1862, and what has been accomplished, if anything, towards the completion of the same. Adopted.

Mr. FOOTE, from the Committee on Foreign Affairs, to whom was referred the resolution of Mr. Hartridge, of Ga., relating to the recall of our Commissioners from Europe, and of suspending the functions of European Consuls in the Confederate States, reported that the committee was without that information of our present relations with foreign nations, and of the number and character of our agents abroad, and of those of foreign nations residing in our midst, necessary to enable the committee to act intelligently on the subject, and they therefore ask the House to adopt the following resolution of inquiry:

Resolved, That the President be respectfully requested, if not incompatible with the public interest, to communicate to the House of Representatives the number and names of all persons engaged in the service of the Confederate States in foreign countries, either as diplomatic, consular or commercial agents, or in any other capacity, stating the places to which they have been sent, the date of their appointment, the salaries they receive, the duties they are expected to discharge, and how far they have been officially or otherwise recognized by any foreign Government; also, the number and character of foreign agents, whether consular, commercial, or other, known to our Government, representing in any capacity foreign Governments within the limits of the Confederate States, and whether in communicating with this Government they do so under exequatur from our own Government or that of the United States, and whether they are subordinate or subject to the control or direction in any way, and to what degree, of the Ministers of their respective countries, accredited to and residing in the United States.

The President is further respectfully requested to communicate such instructions as may have been given to our foreign agents, and such correspondence as may have been had with other Governments, either through the Secretary of State or our Commissioners abroad, as will aid Congress in its legislation regarding foreign nations and their citizens residing in our midst. The report was agreed to.

Mr. FOOTE also presented a report from the Committee on Foreign Affairs upon his resolutions concerning the future conduct of the war; which was laid on the table and ordered to be printed.

Mr. BALDWIN, of Va., presented a resolution that the Committee on Military Affairs be instructed to inquire into the expediency of exempting from military duty the cadets of the Virginia Military Institute. Referred. Also, a petition from citizens of Rockingham county, asking that Confederate notes be made a legal tender. Referred to the Judiciary Committee.

Mr. BOTELER, of Va., presented a memorial from a citizen of Hampshire county, asking pay for a horse lost in the public service. Referred to Committee on Claims, without reading.

Mr. CHAMBLISS introduced a bill to regulate the impressment of slaves by military commanders.—Referred to the Military Committee.

Mr. MILES, from the Committee on Military Affairs, reported a bill to provide for the filling up of existing companies, squadrons, battalions, and regiments, and to increase the Provisional army of the Confederate States. This bill provides for the extension of the Conscription act so as to embrace all persons between the ages of 35 and 45 years. He moved that it be laid on the table, printed, and made the special order of the day for Wednesday next at 1 o'clock. Agreed to.

The Chair laid before the House a communication from the President, submitting the report of the Secretary of the Navy, in response to a resolution of inquiry in reference to the construction of the iron-clad gunboats Arkansas and Louisiana—Laid on the table without action.

On motion of Mr. FOOTE, the House then adjourned.

From our Army on the Rappahannock—Interesting Diary—Executions on the Route.

As late news about the movements of our army is very properly "contraband," even if the press were able to get hold of it, we give some interesting extracts from the diary of "Personne," published in the Charleston *Courier*:

August 20.—Army crossed the Rapidan, the water thigh deep. Scene exciting and amusing. Nearly whole day thus occupied.

August 21.—The enemy in close proximity, and we have to move cautiously. Longstreet's corps is in the front. From a hill on the other side of the Rapidan we have a magnificent view for miles.—Three columns—long, black winding lines of men, their muskets gleaming in the sunshine like silver spears, are in sight, moving in the direction of Fredericksburg, or down the opposite bank of the river. More skirmishing in front. Good many stragglers by the wayside, but they are generally broken down soldiers, and trudge slowly along in the tracks of their comrades. An attractive part of the procession is the baggage trains, wending their way in the rear of the army. Thousands of wagons are in sight, and between the stalling of trains, the shouting of drivers, and the chaotic confusion which emanates from the motley mass, no man can complain of the *ennui* of a march.

Nothing can be more picturesquely beautiful than the bivouac at night. Thousands of troops line the woods on both sides of the road for miles.—Camp-fires are glimmering in the trees, muskets are stacked along the edge of the forest, and the men are disposed in every conceivable manner. Some are rolled up in their blankets, and already dreaming away the fatigues of the day; some are sitting around the camp-fires watching the roasting ears, and discussing the "coming events which cast their shadows before," and some are among the trees, moving to and fro in the gray film of smoke that has arisen from the myriad fires and rests upon the earth. Between the dusty figures of the soldiers, the various occupations in which they are engaged, the road filled with wagons and guns, the appearance of the illuminated trees and bushes, forming against the deep gloom of the night a fantastic background, and all the details combined with the almost unnatural beauty, the spectacle resembles one vast embroidered transparency that has been worked by goblin hands. Art, with her most opulent tents and fixtures, arrayed in her richest trappings, can never hope to equal those of the curious and careless efforts of nature. We live on what we can get—now and then an ear of corn, fried green apples, or a bit of ham broiled on a stick, but quite as frequently do without either from morning until night. We sleep on the ground without any other covering than a blanket, and consider ourselves fortunate if we are not frozen stiff before morning. The nights are both damp and cold.

August 22.—To-day, another busy scene. The army resumed its march at daylight, Longstreet's twelve brigades moving toward the Potomac on the right, and Jackson on the left. The latter has passed the Rapidan Station on the Virginia Central Railroad, and is pressing on northeast of Culpeper. Several small skirmishes have taken place on the front, and eighty or ninety prisoners went by on their way to the rear. Among the Yankees captured by Jackson were two men, who, as soon as they fell into our hands, commenced to ask after their old comrades in an artillery company. An inquiry being instituted, they confessed that eight months ago they were soldiers in our army, but that being tired of service they had deserted and joined the ranks of the enemy. Without further ado, the General ordered them to be hung to a tree, which was done in the presence of a large portion of his army.

In Longstreet's division there has also been active work. The enemy several times attempted to check our advance, but were signally repulsed.—Pickett's, Wilcox's, and Pryor's brigades were severally engaged at different periods of the day, and lost a few men killed and wounded. At Mountain Run, a small branch which joins the Rappahannock, a Federal battery of six pieces commenced this afternoon to throw shells by way of diversion, but were promptly engaged by the Donaldsonville battery, (Louisiana,) Capt. Mora, and soon after retired. In this affair Gen. Roger A. Pryor had a narrow escape. While sitting on a fence by the roadside, a shell burst immediately over his head, and the fragments dashed into the ground around him on every side, but fortunately without doing injury. As he wears a light felt hat, and was plainly in sight of the artillerists, the presumption is that he was made their mark. General Wilcox, likewise, received similar attentions. He was riding in advance of the army, attended by a single trooper, when the latter discovered one of the Yankee pickets peeping over the top of a boulder. "Shall I bring him down?" said the soldier. "No," replied the General, "better not waste your powder, the distance is too great." Hardly were the words out of his mouth, before "whiz"—a Minie ball flew within three inches of the [illegible]'s ear, and lodged in the bank behind him [illegible] quently he was wounded in the arm.

Among the incidents of the day which have kept the men in good humor, and [illegible] for a fight, was a charge by a regiment of [illegible] upon two companies of the 12th Mississippi regiment. Thinking they had the Confederates [illegible], the Yankee Colonel demanded a [illegible]. "Surrender be d—d," was the response, "[illegible] pians don't know how." In a moment more [illegible] cavalry were dashing forward at full speed. [illegible] allowed them to come up within short [illegible], and then opened. Thirty or forty saddles were emptied in less time than you can tell it, and without waiting for a repetition of the dose, the re[illegible] took to its heels, and, amid the cheers and je[illegible] of the boys, got out of sight in the most [illegible] manner possible.

To-day has been further [illegible] by the hanging of a spy—a man named [illegible] Mason, of Perrysville, Pennsylvania. [illegible] that as one of the couriers of Gen. Long[illegible] was carrying an order, he was met by this [illegible] inquired "whose division do you belong to?" "[illegible]ongstreet's." The courier then asked, "whose [illegible] do you belong to?" "Jackson's," was the [illegible]. A gray Confederate uniform favored this [illegible] a conversation ensued. As the two travele[illegible] the courier observed that there was a [illegible] on the part of his companion to drop b[illegible], and finally he was astonished by a pistol p[illegible] at his breast, and a demand for the deliv[illegible] of the papers he carried in his belt. Having [illegible] other resource, the latter surrendered the docum[illegible], when the spy deliberately shot him in the ba[illegible] ran. Soon afterwards the courier was [illegible] by some of his friends, and narrated the p[illegible] of the affair, describing the man so min[illegible] that when subsequently arrested, he was [illegible] beyond a peradventure. He had, [illegible] defective front teeth, was a pale faced, determined looking, and quick spoken person.

A search was at once instituted, but fortunately he fell into our hands by his own foolishness. It is stated (but I do not vouch for this) that this morning the spy rode up to Gen. Jones, who was at the head of his column, and said: "General, I am the chief courier of Gen. Jackson. He desires me to request you to order your column to be reversed at once." The order was of course given, and the pretended courier rode away. His next exploit was to ride up to the Colonel of one of our regiments, and give him the same command he had given to Jones. The Colonel was a shrewd officer, however, and remarked: "I am not in the habit of receiving my orders from Gen. Jackson." "Well, sir, those were my orders from him to you." "What cavalry are you from?" The courier hesitated a moment, and said, "from the Hampton Legion." "In whose division and brigade is that?" asked the Colonel.—This confused him still more, and he could only reply, "I don't know; I have forgotten." Being then taken into custody and examined, several papers were found upon his person written in short hand, and an abreviated long hand, embracing the information he had obtained. A pair of lieutenant's shoulder straps were also concealed in his pocket.—These discoveries being made, the man confessed that he was a Yankee, and belonged to the Union army, but in the capacity of an independent scout. He admitted further, that he had observed and reported the movements of our army, but denied having killed the courier. He claimed that it was done by a party of Texans with whom he was traveling.

These various facts being conclusive, the court-martial by which he was tried had little hesitation in finding him "guilty," and sentencing him to be hung. The execution took place this afternoon, under the direction of Gen. Evans, in the presence of his brigade and a large number of soldiers. The prisoner was mounted on a horse, his hands tied behind him, and he was driven beneath a tree. The rope, which was little larger than an ordinary bed-cord, then being adjusted, he was ordered to stand upon the saddle. As he did so, a soldier gave a sharp cut to the animal, and in a second more the spy was jerking convulsively from the limb above him. He met his fate with great stoicism, and appeared perfectly satisfied with what he had accomplished, but to the last denied all participation in the act of shooting Longstreet's courier. He said that he had an uncle and aunt living in Clarke county, Virginia, and that the latter had made him the Confederate uniform which he wore.

August 22, Friday.—At Stevensburg—once a fine old sober Virginia village, but now deserted, dilapidated, and as rough as if it had been evolved up from a lot of second-hand rubbish. The ancient burg has evidently been awakened from a long *coma*, and while I write is alive with a cosmopolitan humanity. Ascending the hill in the suburbs, we have one of the handsomest views in the country. Around the edge of the horizon is the Blue Ridge, hanging like a misty veil dropped from the clouds; the huge tops illuminated by the sunlight. Between here and there spreads out a broad plain, broken at intervals by hills and patches of woods. Four miles to the left of our line of travel is Culpeper Court-House. Four miles ahead is Brandy Station, on the Orange and Alexandria Railroad, and already there is filing away in that direction a train of a thousand wagons. In the meadows at your feet are camps of other wagon trains, containing ordnance, quartermaster and commissary stores, for the use of the various divisions of the army. Several brigades are also bivouacked here, while others are in motion, filing across the country. Roads in superb condition for marching, and weather bracing. The head of Longstreet's corps is now upon the banks of the Rappahannock—Jackson still to the left. Gen. R. H. Anderson's division has just come up from Richmond, and is hurrying forward to the front. It is soon after sunrise, and the camps are in a state of bustle—men cooking rations, eating breakfasts, and preparing to resume their march.

Near here is where a part of Col. Ashby's old command attacked the enemy's rear guard day before yesterday, and drove them back. Several killed and wounded on both sides. Some twenty Yankee prisoners, captured within the last two days, are confined in the town. They are generally a miserable, low-lived set of fellows, but evidently glad they are out of tribulation. Not one of them will acknowledge that he belongs to the army of Gen. Pope. They swear that they are Gen. Burnside's men. I asked one of them where the army appeared to be going. He replied, "Some to Warrenton Junction, and some towards Alexandria."—Citizens who live here report that they moved off evidently in great haste and confusion, and were terribly annoyed by our advanced cavalry. It is probably their intention to make a stand on the other side of the Rappahannock, and endeavor to prevent our crossing. Lee is pressing them with great pertinacity.

August 23, Saturday.—Twenty-eight miles from Manassas. Four miles from the Rappahannock.—It is now half-past six o'clock A. M., and heavy cannonading has commenced upon the front.—Jackson is reported to have sent word to Lee that he is in possession of Warrenton Springs, fifteen miles to the left of Longstreet. Ewell is also said to have crossed the river above the enemy. Two bridges across Cedar Run and the Rapidan having been burned by the enemy, we cannot use the railroad until they have been rebuilt. One of the prisoners states that the iron and materials for the purpose are always near them, and it is understood that the work of reconstruction is rapidly going forward. If this be true, the army can soon be subsisted more conveniently even than at Manassas.—There are no fortifications around Warrenton, but the position is naturally strong for either friend or foe.

LATER FROM EUROPE.

The Kangaroo, from Liverpool on the 14th ult., has arrived. The Federal gunboat Tuscarora had suddenly left Queenstown, owing to orders from the custom-house officials. There was nothing new from Garibaldi. The distress in the cotton manufacturing districts of England was increasing:

Agents are now in England making contracts in behalf of the U. S. Government for a supply of arms, &c. The contracts are proposed with a clause that they shall be null and void in case of a war with England.

It is asserted that the Confederate envoys have demanded a recognition of the Southern Confederacy, but that England refused to accede to their demands, while France did not give a reply.

It is believed that the Mexican expeditionary force from France is very large. The choicest officers and men of the Versailles artillery are under orders. A division of gunboats for Mexico were being armed.

The returns of the harvest in France were very favorable.

Another correspondence between United States Minister Adams and Earl Russell was published.—Mr. Adams wrote in May, while Earl Russell's letter is dated July 28. The *Times* characterizes his remarks as dry and caustic.

The *Times* editorially endorses Mr. Roebuck's late speech at Sheffield, as far as his lecture to the North is concerned, but totally dissents from his arguments in favor of mediation, which it considers would do more harm than good.

The *Daily News* bitterly reproaches Mr. Roebuck, and characterizes his course as the lowest depth of moral degradation. It says happily Mr. Roebuck's opinions have long ceased to have the smallest value or interest for anybody but himself. The article concludes by complimenting the American Government for its friendly and straightforward dealings with England, and says nothing is wanting but a little generous consideration towards the North to establish thoroughly cordial and friendly relations between the two countries.

The St. Petersburg *Journal* reiterates that the desire of the Russian Cabinet is to see the conflict ended by prudent and honorable compromise.—Russia's desire is not to divide, but bring together and reunite adversaries who ought to remain brothers.

Many of the cotton mills in Lancashire have stopped.

The *Times*, speculating on the probable demands of British subjects for protection from conscription in America, says it will be impossible to extend the British ægis to myriads who may want its momentary protection.

The Crown Princess of Prussia has been confined with a prince.

COMMERCIAL.

Cotton—The sales on Wednesday and Thursday were 16,000 bales. The market was buoyant and slightly higher, owing to the great advance and excitement in Bombay and Calcutta.

Breadstuffs were quiet and steady on Thursday. Provisions inactive.

Consols 93¾. Illinois Central shares 51@50 discount. Erie 28½@29¼.

LATER FROM THE NORTH.

New York papers of the 27th are received, but contain little of importance. Capt. Garnett, of the Confederate army, who was imprisoned in the old Capitol at Washington, has been released on parole in view of his ill-health. A riot had taken place in the Empire Brigade, at New York, because the troops did not receive the promised bounties.—Fresh troops are arriving at Fortress Monroe. The Hartford (Ct.) *Post* asserts, on "direct and reliable information," that McClellan is going to resign.—The New York *Times*, of the 27th, announces the death of Gen. Bohlen, of Philadelphia, who was killed on Saturday, the 23d, by a "rebel shell," near the Rappahannock. The same paper has the following "situation" article:

We gather from various sources a variety of interesting information from our armies in Virginia—all of it, we are glad to say, of an encouraging character. Passengers from Virginia, who reached Washington yesterday, report that there was an engagement at Warrenton on Monday, in which our forces were successful, having driven the enemy out of the town. We infer from this that the rebels have been making strenuous efforts to turn our right flank, as Warrenton is some distance this side of the Rappahannock. Our dispatch further states, however, that the rebel forces which have been engaged in the recent skirmishes are mainly cavalry, and it is probable that the force at Warrenton was of this character, and was not very formidable.—Heavy rain occurred on Friday afternoon and night, and continued through Saturday in the vicinity of the Upper Rappahannock. This swelled the river so as to make it unfordable below the mountains back of Warrenton, and of course put an end to all efforts of the rebel army to cross until the river shall again fall. There was artillery firing, nevertheless, at nearly all the fords throughout Saturday and Sunday, but with results which have not been deemed worthy of reporting. There is a rumor the rebels have been moving a heavy force in the direction of Luray, to operate in the Shenandoah Valley, but no doubt General Pope has taken measures to guard against any disaster in that direction.

The rebels have tried their hand at recapturing Fort Donelson; but have failed. The fort, garrisoned by four companies of the 71st Ohio regiment, under command of Major Nab, was attacked on Monday by the force of rebels under Col. Woodward—the same which captured Clarksville—but the Ohio boys repulsed the assailants, killing and wounding thirty of them. The rebel force consisted of 450 infantry, 335 cavalry, and two pieces of artillery.

News from Memphis, which we publish this morning, renders it probable that Breckinridge has thought better of his intention to make a second attack on Baton Rouge. It is stated that he is moving his entire army up to Stentobia, on the New Orleans, Jackson and Great Northern Railroad, about 42 miles below Memphis, and that his cavalry are scouring Northern Mississippi.

A letter to the Cincinnati *Commercial*, dated Cumberland Gap, Aug. 19th, says: "This place is completely surrounded by the enemy. His pickets are within four miles of the Gap, and extend entirely across the mountain. He is 20,000 strong in front, and reinforcements are still arriving from Knoxville. A heavy force has gone through Big Creek and Rogers's Gap. Capt. Martin's company of cavalry, sent out to watch those Gaps, was suddenly attacked by Ashby's cavalry, six hundred strong, and was cut to pieces or scattered to the winds.—Out of eighty men, but fifteen or twenty have come in. Col. Houck, of the 5th Tennessee, stationed at London, is probably cut off. The enemy expect to starve us out, but Morgan will neither evacuate nor surrender. Supplies are now entirely cut off, and sad disaster will come if the road to Lexington is not promptly cleared."

The latest intelligence from Cumberland Gap represents that Gen. Morgan is in no immediate danger. He had provisions and forage enough to last him thirty days. He had repulsed a large force of the rebels on the Tennessee side, and no doubt was entertained that he could hold the position until assistance arrived. This assistance was being rapidly hurried forward.

The rebel emissary who passed through Buffalo a day or two ago, supposed to be Wm. L. Yancey, turns out to be no more important a personage than Geo. N. Sanders. He sailed in the steamship Jura from Quebec on Saturday.

The citizens of Fairmont, Clarksburgh, Mannington, and other points in Western Virginia, have been greatly exercised of late, lest the guerrillas might make a dash upon them, Gen. Kelly having drawn off the troops stationed there, to meet Gen. Imboden, who was moving up from Pendleton with a rebel force.

It is believed that great numbers of the Maryland Secessionists have crossed the Potomac into Virginia, to join the rebel service, since the promulgation of the order for the draft. It is asserted that an entire company of cavalry left Montgomery county, on the Upper Potomac, last week, and that squads are constantly moving. It is, perhaps, easier to fight these men in Virginia than in Maryland.

DESPONDING VIEW OF AFFAIRS OUT WEST.

The correspondent of the Chicago *Times*, writing from Memphis, gives the following gloomy summary of Federal affairs in the West:

Arkansas is being overrun by strong guerrilla bands. Hindman has collected a force of twenty-five or thirty thousand, and there are almost as many more ranging the country for spoils. There have been a number of skirmishes, of which nobody seems to have the right accounts, and nothing is known except that strong Federal expeditions have been attacked and overpowered, and that a large number of prisoners and valuable stores have been taken from us. There will probably be some important movements in that locality before long.

A good deal has been said in connection with the Vicksburg affair, about sending troops there and reducing the place by a siege. This is all very well for those who know nothing of the climate and the country; but they who have been there are keenly alive to the perils of that campaign. None have ventured it and come off unscathed. Our flotilla is full of wan countenances, and death has been among its brave men to an alarming extent. Officers and men have both suffered. The former have been seriously ill, and the latter have died like rotten sheep. The soldier fared no better, and some of the regiments went back with almost decimated ranks. This is the true history of the siege of Vicksburg.

The Yazoo river was fitly named by the red-skinned hunters who traversed its tortuous channel in days gone by. Yazoo—Death river. What could be more significant? Their symbolical language never fails them, and in this instance it was well applied; for, if it be not a river of death, then none exist. Old settlers tell me that no man can drink its water in the hot season and live longer than a few months. It is impregnated with such rank vegetable matter, gathered from the tropical luxuriance which borders its banks and those of its tributaries, that its water is conveyed into slow poison, which is sure to destroy human life. If you would find a counterpart to its sombre shades and its stained, murky waters, you must go into the depth of swamps, which it drains, and look upon the green scum and crawling reptiles who shun the sunlight and breed pestilence and death alone.—The simple substance of it is, that an army of twenty-five thousand men would find their graves between now and the first of October without ever facing an enemy. The flotilla has already accomplished its destiny in that line, and, if an army is to be maintained anywhere in that locality it must be removed from the river and provided with pure water—and you might dig until you lost daylight in that red-hot soil, and not find enough to wet the palm of the hand.

I suppose by this time you have undergone various surmises in regard to the northern trip which Com. Davis and Gen. Curtis are making. The precise reasons for their pilgrimage to the seat of authority are not known, but the nature of their derelictions is public enough. Davis proved himself an infant in conception, and an imbecile in execution, from the moment he left Memphis to besiege Vicksburg until he came away with the indellible disgrace of having been whipped and bullied by the Arkansas into abject submission. The fear of losing a vessel was strong enough to overcome the hope of glory, and there was nothing but folding of hands and crossing of arms. The results of the expedition were these: Gained—nothing. Lost—the Carondolet shot to pieces, the Louisville disabled, the Benton riddled, the Tyler demolished, the Essex and Sumter thrown away, and the rams Lancaster and Queen sent into dry docks for weeks. The loss of the Essex alone to the river flotilla is irreparable. She has been under reconstruction for six months, and has cost a mint of money, and on her first trip she was cut off and compelled to go to New Orleans. The gunboat flotilla is actually ruined, and we shall know it to our sorrow before sixty days pass over our heads.

Gen. Curtis has made himself conspicuous in two or three ways. The unlicensed system which governed his movements in Arkansas has brought misery to thousands of unprotected families, and a corresponding degree of obloquy to the Union cause. He was of course compelled to subsist upon the country through which he passed, but that was no reason why houses should be despoiled and burned, innocent white women outraged, and black ones converted into the instruments of a promiscuous harlotage which it would be hard to find a parallel for. These performances were the work of stragglers and unknown persons, and should not be charged to the main army; but the cause will be made to father it all, and the commander must be held responsible. He should have prevented such discreditable occurrences.

SEIZURE OF REBEL NOTES.

INDIANAPOLIS, August 23.—John N. Garrett, formerly a resident of this city, was arrested last night, having in his possession three hundred and twenty-five dollars in Confederate notes. Garrett held a receipt from Adams's Express for three hundred and seventy-five dollars in money sent to him by E. D. Ramsey, of Philadelphia.

FROM THE SOUTH.

Morgan's last exploit is thus described by a letter from Lenoire, in East Tennessee, dated August 26th:

On last Wednesday morning an Indiana regiment was dispatched from Nashville by rail as far as the burnt bridge at Sandersville, from thence to proceed on foot to Gallatin, to recapture that place, and at the same time (if possible) to capture the redoubtable John Morgan. The Colonel of this regiment (Hefferen) entered Gallatin and arrested every male citizen, including many of the oldest in the county. He permitted his men to sack the stores and destroy the property of quiet, peaceable citizens, and also to enter the Masonic Lodge at Gallatin and scatter the furniture and paraphernalia of the order in every direction. They then proceeded with their captives down the road towards Nashville. In the meantime Gen. Morgan, with 1,200 men, returned to Gallatin from Hartsville, and hearing of the recent visit of the "Yanks," started with his command in pursuit.

He chased the Indianians to within ten miles of Nashville, killing some fifty or sixty, and capturing about fifty prisoners. At the junction of the Edgefield and Kentucky Railroad and the Louisville and Nashville Road the Yankees made a stand behind a triangular stockade work, and Gen. Morgan drew off his men, rather than sacrifice them in the attempt to capture the few Yankees that had taken refuge there, and returned to Gallatin. In the fight at the Junction two of his officers were killed—Lieut. J. A. Smith, of Company A, and Adjutant Niles. Only three of his men were wounded.

At Gallatin the next morning intelligence reached Morgan that Gen. Johnson, with a large Federal cavalry force, was rapidly advancing. Morgan rallied his men and moved out the Hartsville road to meet him. Both parties ran together at the first toll-gate on the Hartsville road, and the fight commenced, but ceased shortly at the appearance of a flag of truce from the Yankees. Johnson requested an armistice. He was taken by surprise and his men were not all together. Morgan sent word to him that he had been following him from point to point, and now he could get it. The fight was resumed, but shortly ended in a complete victory for Morgan—Gen. Johnson, with 600 of his men, having surrendered. About five hundred escaped by fording the Cumberland, swimming the river, and leaving their horses on the wrong side, and getting on the safe side of that stream in the speediest and most practicable way possible. As I came up to Lebanon about 4 o'clock on the evening of the fight, I saw Johnson's men "skedaddling" (to use a Yankee vulgarism) in the most disgraceful manner. Many of them were hatless and even bootless after their bootless effort to capture John Morgan. They tarried not in Lebanon, nor even till they landed safely in Nashville.

Many of them on foot were pressing horses and vehicles of every kind with which to get away from Morgan, and their guns and accoutrements were strewn from Lebanon to the toll-gate nearest to Nashville. They acknowledged themselves to be citizens of Lebanon, that they were badly whipped; in fact, "cut all to pieces." Morgan, I believe, is still at Hartsville, or perhaps at Gallatin, and Forrest must have joined him by this time. New recruits were flocking to Morgan from every direction in Kentucky and Tennessee, and the citizens are once again hopeful of deliverance from the Philistines. I was unable to ascertain Morgan's loss in the last fight. I have heard it estimated at 100 killed and wounded, but I do not believe it is half that.

The last raid of the gunboats on James river amounted to a little less than nothing. On Thursday last the flotilla off Harrison's Landing steamed up James river for the purpose, it was supposed, of "reducing" Drury's Bluff. A letter to the Petersburg *Express* gives the particulars of the reduction:

On arriving at the mouth of the Appomattox, a large 18-gunboat, which was in the advance, ran aground. This caused the balance, nine in number, to take positions along the Appomattox channel, while the iron-clads Galena and Monitor moved up the James, with the intention doubtless of going on; but finding the big sloop-of-war still aground, they slipped their anchors and formed in line of battle, extending from Bermuda Hundreds to Dr. McComer's late residence on the Appomattox.

The flotilla consisted of the two iron-clads already mentioned; one sloop-of-war, 18 guns; one of 16, and one of 10 guns; ten New York ferry-boats, carrying four 9-inch guns each; two steam tugs of two guns each, and two transports. They also brought with them many schooners loaded with coal, evidently intending to remain up the river for several days.

The vessels remained in the position above described until 6½ o'clock Friday morning, when all weighed anchor and moved down James river, seemingly in a great hurry, as one of the sloops slipped her cable instead of weighing it, leaving a small steam tug to grapple the anchor. While the tug was busily engaged in endeavoring to rescue the anchor, the Confederate picket stationed at City Point delivered a volley at the little tug, which seemed to surprise the bunkers very much. The tug immediately turned about and returned the fire from a small brass howitzer, but did no damage to our men. While thus engaged, the Monitor and two small gunboats came to the aid of the tug, and commenced shelling both sides of the Appomattox at City Point and Ray's farm. In the meantime, our pickets, nothing daunted, rushed down to the water's edge at City Point, and poured volley after volley at the exposed bunkers on the deck of the tug, evidently causing them to suffer severely.—The tug soon withdrew beyond the range of small arms at the Point, and brought their guns to bear on the signal station at Ray's farm, shelling the station for one hour and ten minutes, and cutting down trees and tearing up the ground in the yard where the station is situated. The signal men did not shrink from duty during this terrible shower of shell, but continued to wave their flags and pass messages along the line to Petersburg and Richmond.

At 2 o'clock the firing ceased, and the Monitor and consorts steamed down the river and joined the flotilla lying at anchor off Harrison's Landing.

Nothing more was heard from the fleet until Friday morning, August 29th, when, at 10 o'clock, the entire flotilla commenced the work of weighing anchor and making fast to their sail transports.—We at first thought this was preparatory to a move for Richmond, but to my great surprise they steamed down the river, taking with them all their schooners, lighters, and negroes. At 12 o'clock the last mast had disappeared from view at Berkley.

Thus ends the great work for the present, that Com. Wilkes, with his invincible fleet, was to have accomplished before the 15th of August.

LOCAL MATTERS.

Passing Counterfeit Money.—A detective connected with the Provost Marshal's office arrested, on Saturday night, a man named Robert Blossingham, for having in his possession a ten dollar and twenty dollar counterfeit C. S. Treasury notes, and a pass from Gen. McClellan. Blossingham yesterday had an examination before C. S. Commissioner Watson, when it appeared that he was a resident of Williamsburg, Va; had lived there a long time, and formerly kept the old Raleigh Tavern before it was burned; that being found there when the Yankees came into possession of the place, he had been forced to stay and accept their protection, such as it was. One of them passed on him as genuine the bogus money, and he received it not knowing its worthless character. A number of refugees from Williamsburg were examined *pro* and *con* in this case, which was finally sent before Gen. Winder to be determined by him.

Police Court.—Yesterday, as usual on a Monday morning, the court-room was crowded with spectators. There were not wanting a considerable number of criminals to give importance to the occasion. Surupa Guireaux was arraigned for feloniously stealing $120 from Julius E Bates. The larceny was not proved, but the fact that defendant sold liquor unlawfully was conclusively made out. For the latter offence he was fined $15.—Eliz'h Bass was fined $1 for permitting her son Henry to throw stones in the street, contrary to ordinance.—Elizabeth Lankford, who wore a meek and subdued aspect, was brought up on the complaint of William Lankford, her husband, who alleged that she had threatened to lick him and burn his house down. Being unable to disprove the allegation, $300 security for her good behavior was required.—Lavinia, slave of Mrs. A. Hill, underwent a partial examination on the charge of setting fire to her mistress's house. The case was continued.—Chastain, slave of Francis Fletcher, was arraigned for having in his possession seventy-four pairs of woolen socks, four shirts, five bags and $125, supposed to have been stolen. He was ordered thirty lashes, and the articles detained to await the call of their owner.—John R. Mayfield, a white man, brought from the Columbian Hotel for acting suspiciously, and trying to obtain a ticket for lodging without shelling out the rhino, was discharged, the Mayor thinking the imprisonment he had already undergone sufficient punishment for his offence.—Henry, slave of George D. Harwood, was committed as a runaway.—Lewis, slave of Samuel Hardgrove, was ordered fifteen lashes for getting drunk and straggling about the streets.—Jane Gorden, who said she was free, but could produce no papers to that effect, was discharged on promise to make tracks for home.—Elmira, slave of William Turbit, was committed as a runaway.

The City Post-Office Robbery Examination Concluded.—Several hours were consumed yesterday by the C. S. Commissioner, Wm. F. Watson, in an examination of the charge preferred against A. B. Martin, a member of the Washington Artillery battalion, arrested at the Spotswood Hotel on Thursday last, by detective Roache, at the instance of Wm. H. Truehart, a clerk in the Richmond Post-Office, on the charge of purloining letters from the Post-Office. The prisoner was remanded for trial before Judge Halyburton, of the C. S. District Court, and allowed to give bail for his appearance, if he could.

Shot.—On Saturday evening last, Robert Ratcliffe, a member of the Fayette Artillery, was shot while attempting to escape from an officer in Screamersville, who went to arrest him. The ball entered the left shoulder and came out on the left breast, near the region of the heart, inflicting what is supposed to be a mortal wound.

The Charleston Mercury.

DAILY PAPER—Ten Dollars per annum, payable half-yearly in advance.

—VINDICE NULLO
SPONTE SUA SINE LEGE FIDES RECTUMQUE COLENTUR.

COUNTRY PAPER—Thrice a Week—Five Dollars per annum, in advance.

VOLUME LXXXI — CHARLESTON, S. C., THURSDAY, SEPTEMBER 18 1862. — NUMBER 11,556

NEWS BY TELEGRAPH.

IMPORTANT FROM RICHMOND—SUCCESSES IN WESTERN VIRGINIA—STONEWALL JACKSON CAPTURES HAPER'S FERRY WITH EIGHT THOUSAND PRISONERS.

RICHMOND, September 17.—An official despatch from Gen. LORING, dated Charleston, Kanawha County, Va., says:—"After incessant skirmishing we took this place at 3 p. m., to-day. The enemy, six regiments strong, made a stout resistance, burning their stores and most of this town, in their retreat. Our loss was slight; that of the enemy heavy. He is now in full retreat, and Gen. A. G. JENKINS is in his rear."

The Secretary of War received despatches to-day from Major BROWN, commanding the post at Dublin, Va., stating that Gen. LORING's command entered the Kanawha salines last Saturday morning, and took possession of the Salt Works, closely pursuing the enemy, who was making his way towards Charleston. The Salt Works are not much injured. A very large quantity of salt was on hand when the works were taken. It is now selling at 35 cents per bushel. An order has been issued, urging the farmers to send forward their wagons, loaded with forage, &c., and return with salt.

An official despatch from Chattanooga, this morning, confirms the occupation of Iuka, Mississippi, by General PRICE's army. He captured there several hundred thousand dollars worth of army stores.

Private despatches from Staunton, to-day, say that the enemy's force at Harper's Ferry had capitulated to General Stonewall JACKSON on the 15th. Eight thousand Yankees and one thousand negros were captured.

IMPORTANT FROM CUMBERLAND GAP.

KNOXVILLE, September 17.—The enemy at Cumberland Gap had made arrangements to evacuate that position on the 14th instant—had sent all his sick to the rear, and had made preparations for blasting the overhanging rocks in order to block the road behind him. His advance had already reached London, when he received favorable news (which was false), and the order for evacuation was countermanded.

SCAN THE EVIL OMENS.—No. VI.

Obsta Principiis.

I shall now appeal to a source of information, that *approaches* the stringent force of *authority* upon the question of the true meaning of the phrase "to coin money." It *approaches* the force of authority, because I am not willing to attribute the force of absolute authority to the opinions of any man, not vested with competent express power to make an irreversible, binding exposition of any word in a Constitution, to which, by fair and express contract, directly or through my State, I am bound to yield obedience. I cite the observations of Mr. Madison, on the clause of the Constitution in question, expressed *before* its adoption, and in the face of that close and unsparing scrutiny with which its opponents would, and did, visit all his opinions and expositions in Conventions to be engaged in an examination of that instrument. I have, by no means, the same respect for the opinions of the same man, on the same subject, expressed *after* he became an administrator of the Constitution, or the expounder of it, being under the blandishments which spring from the possession and exercise of power, which, evermore, "grows on what it feeds on," or the disturbing influences of heated party bias, or that syren song, the unfailing lullaby of purpose to usurp and tyrannize—the plea of public necessity—the inexorable demands of the condition of war.

In the 42d No. Federalist, Mr. Madison says: "All that need be remarked on the power to coin money, regulate the value thereof and of foreign coin, is, that by providing for this last case" (*i. e.* as to foreign coin) "the Constitution has supplied a material omission in the Articles of Confederation. The authority of the existing Congress is restrained to the regulation of coin *struck* by their own authority or that of the respective States. It must be seen at once, that the proposed uniformity in the *value* of the current coin might be destroyed by subjecting that of foreign coin to the different regulations of the different States."

In the 43d No. of the same work, from the same pen, is the language following:—"The right of coining money, which is here taken from the States, was left in their hands by the Confederation, as a concurrent right with that of Congress, under an exception in favor of the exclusive right of Congress to regulate the *alloy* and value. In this instance, also, the new provision is an improvement on the old. Whilst the *alloy* and value depended on the general authority, a right of coinage in the particular States could have no other effect than to multiply expensive mints and diversify the forms and *weights* of the circulating *pieces*. The latter inconveniency defeats one purpose for which the power was originally submitted to the Federal head; and as far as the former" (*i. e.* State mints) "might prevent an inconvenient remittance of *gold* and *silver* to the central mint for re coinage, the end can be as well attained by local mints established under the general authority."

Now taking this exposition as our guide (and surely it is worthy of all acceptation), who will pretend to say, that "coin"—"to coin money"—in the sense of the Constitution, refers to anything, under the Heavens, but *metallic* currency? And, I add, of gold and silver only? For that alone could a State make a legal tender, when constituted current coin by the regulation or stamp of the federal head, and that alone could the federal head coin, or adopt, with a regulated value, as the constitutional currency; and the exclusive thing fit to be, and constitutionally pronounced to be, a legal tender in payment of debts.

Look at the words italicised—"alloy," "weights," "pieces," "gold and silver:" what doubt can there be, that a paper medium, or currency, or standard of value, no matter of what form or from what authority, is as effectually excluded from all idea concerning the act of coining, as the skin of a beast or a leaf of tobacco?

Yet, in the face of this reasoning and authority, in contempt of the voice of history that proclaims aloud the meaning of the language in question, and proclaims that gold and silver coin was the "money" which Congress was to provide, and that only, listen to the language of the writer for the Whig: Quoth he, "Who will deny that Congress may *stamp* the Treasury Notes, and thus make them money?" It is probable my readers will join me in asking a division of the question; and we shall unite in allowing that Congress may *stamp* Treasury Notes, but I surmise we shall equally join in utterly denying that Congress can thereby, or by any other means, make them *money*—*i. e.*, the money which the Constitution empowered Congress to coin. People may call a variety of devices money, and use them in lieu of money; and dictionaries may reflect this voluntary popular language and conduct; and they may, in special circumstances, and for certain periods, perform the office of money. But, is it a species of logic that can challenge our respect, which seeks to convert a substitute for a *specific thing* into that very thing—that calls the shadow the substance—the representative the constituent—a promise to pay, payment? Surely he reads in vain our annals, touching constitutional regulations of money—coining money, establishing a standard of value for commerce and contracts—who does not see that it was the special, identical, exclusive end of them all to extinguish and forever eradicate the pretension of a promise to pay money to become itself money; no matter by whom—Government or corporation or individual—the promise might be issued. The evidence of this truth is scattered broadcast over all the records of all discussions relating to the subject indulged by those who contrived, and those who adopted, the Constitution of 1787–'9.

CATO.

THE MERCURY.

THURSDAY, SEPTEMBER 18, 1862.

Thanksgiving.

To-day, the people of this broad Confederacy are called upon to unite in grateful homage to Almighty God, for the splendid triumphs, with which, under His providence, our arms have everywhere been crowned. Never, in the course of the long and unending struggle between Might and Right, has the Divine favor been more signally shown towards the cause of justice, than in the recent events of the contest between the North and the South. For months a selfish and unsympathising world has looked on, amazed at the obstinacy and success with which a brave people, thinly scattered over a vast extent of territory, ill supplied with most of the mechanical resources for war, and cut off from all intercourse with the rest of mankind, have resisted the overwhelming odds brought against them, for the subjugation and ruin of their country. And now, the scene is changing. The armies of the insolent invader, stricken with confusion and terror, are falling back at every point, hard pressed by the ragged and hungry soldiery whom they had so long striven in vain to crush; the tide of blood and desolation is fast surging over the border, and the people who were wont to exult over the destruction of our homes, begin, at last, to tremble for their own. Each day brings to us the tidings of some new success, and the shouts of victory which but yesterday rang through the Valley of the Mississippi, are echoed to-day from the banks of the Kanawha and the heights of Harper's Ferry.

Surely it is the Hand of God that has given strength to our gallant soldiers, thus to smite and smite again the ruthless foe, who thirsts for our destruction. And now that we have launched our hardy and victorious armies into the rich country of our enemies, and are about to strike once more, upon new fields, for Independence and Peace, it is right that our whole people should join to-day in hearty thanksgiving to the Lord of Hosts for past mercies, and implore for the future His blessing upon our cause.

Repudiation Foreshadowed.

At a recent "war meeting," held in Brooklyn, the Hon. H. B. STANTON, in order to stimulate the bellicose feelings of his auditors, said, amongst other things, that "if our Government went to pieces there would be no United States to pay the debt, and he would advise those who had anything invested in United States stocks to save all and spend half." This looks a good deal like preparing the public mind in Lincolndom for a repudiation of the enormous war debt which is running up there at the rate of some *six millions a day.*

THE NEWS FROM RICHMOND.

(CORRESPONDENCE OF THE MERCURY.)

RICHMOND, Monday, September 15.

From the Army—Picked Men in Maryland—Notable Yankee Items—Seymour—A Quandary—Young Soldiers—DeBow's View—Anti-Slavery Book—Caricatures, etc., etc.

Thursday's dates are the latest, either way, from our army in Maryland. The Yankees and ourselves are equally in the dark as to its position and future movements. LEE has sent for two millions in Confederate funds to pay for provisions; and that our army has certainly moved off from Frederick City, but whither, no one knows. The reins being again in MCCLELLAN's hands, we may be sure he will take his time about fighting, unless, indeed, the praise of the London Times and the sneers of his enemies act on him like the fire-coal on the turtle's back. But Lee means business, for, before crossing the Potomac, he purged the army of all men incapable of the hardest service. Hence the report about our ragged soldiers being turned back to Richmond, because Lee did not want them. It is said that 20,000 stragglers, convalescents and returned soldiers, have been turned loose at Rapidan Station, to find their way to the army as best they could.

The notable items in the late Northern papers are Seward's rumored resignation, the quietude in Baltimore, and the steadiness of gold and stocks. There must be a combination to keep stocks, etc., up, all parties struggling to delay the common downfall. Seymour, the joint nominee of the Democratic factions for Governor of New York, inaugurates his canvass by a speech against the radicals, and those who know him in this city, think he is opposed to the war. Probably—if that opposition will bring him into power. Northern Democrats have proved broken reeds to Southern leaners.

Saturday's proceedings in Congress are not spoken of. Legislation in this country will ever be a tedious farce until we adopt the English practice of coughing down the small potato gabblers and allowing the speaking to be done by the big guns—men of decided ability. With regard to the conscript extension, a high official is reported to have said that the taking of all men under 45 will bring all work in the country to a stand still, and the not taking them will leave the armies depleted and incompetent for the work in hand. This is a quandary, indeed. Must we then fall back upon the boys? They fight better than men, but wear out quickly under the fatigues of military life. In this connection let me insert a brief editorial from this morning's Dispatch. Here it is:

"We met on Saturday with two youths, who had been honorably discharged from the army, having seen more in a brief period than most men in a lifetime. One of the little fellows, Henry Woods, of Georgia, is just fifteen and a half years old; the other, Jesse Scott, of S. C., barely fifteen.—These two mere children, for such they are in appearance as in age, fought in all the battles round Richmond! What other country can produce such examples of infant heroism and patriotism? A happy journey home to them, and may every one who meets them on their way give them substantial Godspeed!"

DeBow, in the late number of his Review, shows that, notwithstanding the great disparity between the Confederate and United States, in point of population, our real fighting strength is more than one-half that of the North; in other words, statistics prove that they can bring into the field less than two to our one. Add the strength of our cause, our greater military aptitude and superiority in the use of arms and horses, and the view is most encouraging—if our legislators would do their duty and bring out the whole strength of the country.

The Yankees are rejoicing over an anti-slavery book recently published by a Mr. Cairnes, Professor of Jurisprudence and Political Economy in Queen's College, Galway. I give an extract to show the temper of this work, which the London Spectator thinks "will do much to arrest the extraordinary tide of sympaty with the South, which the clever misrepresentations of Southern advocates have managed to set running in this country"—*i. e.* Great Britain. Cairnes is caustic on us—says our cause is "intrinsically and wholly evil." "The Slave Confederation exhausts man and his energies, exhausts nature and her energies; and by the very law of its existence is aggressive and destructive to the life of neighboring States." Altogether, Cairnes considers the Confederacy a decidedly bad egg.

Some very funny caricatures, done by a young artist in this city, are exhibited privately among his friends. One shows the "Reliable Gentleman," in front of the War Office, pouring out his lies to a gaping crowd. Another represents Gen. Whiting (whose short stature and passion for high-topped boots is well known) immersed to his arm-pits in an enormous pair of cavalry boots, while his tall brother, six feet high, is bending over him, trying to draw him out of his boots by means of a mammoth corkscrew inserted in the top of his head. Still another, and the best of the lot, gives an inside view of the panic in Richmond during the gunboat fever. Two ladies are seen, in a state of the deepest distress, vainly endeavoring to compress a modern high-peaked bonnet into an old fashioned bonnet box, while out of the open window a couple hundred gunboats, mounted on human legs, are climbing furiously up the hills around Rockett's, with carpet bags in their hands.

Mr. Crocker, Superintendent of the Army Intelligence Office, puts down our losses in the late battles at only 500 killed; the wounded, most of them slightly, 1500 or 1600. He estimates the Yankee loss, in killed and wounded, at 12,000. Add 7000 prisoners, and we have 19,000 used up on their side, to 2000 on ours—nearly ten to one.

HERMES.

THE STATE CONVENTION.

COLUMBIA, Tuesday, September 16.

Mr. Allison introduced a resolution making the pay of the officers of the Convention equal to those of the Legislature, and making provision for paying the same.

Under the head of general orders, several reports of the Committee on Accounts were presented and passed.

Under the special orders, the majority and minority reports, with two amendments, were taken up, and discussed.

Mr. J. P. Richardson wished to explain his position. He had a claim on the indulgence of the Convention, as he had not spoken before. He considered himself instructed by his constituents to present their grievances and sufferings. When the Convention met last, the country was threatened with invasion, and much was done under the excitement of the moment which had better been left alone. They exceeded the bounds of law and the Constitution. He was opposed to clothing the Council with dictatorial powers. They had borrowed the idea from the classics, but it would not apply in this age. They had, however, reversed the ancient order, as we conferred the powers and then appointed the dictators. Ours was not, properly speaking, a dictatorship; it was an oligarchy, in spirit and in form; an oligarchy of five instead of ten. They held their councils in dark and murky chambers, where the light of day nor the prying eye could never penetrate. They claimed their victims and enforced their behests in secret. They carried the manacled subject across the Bridge of Sighs, from whence he would never return. He did not pretend to say that such a state of things existed now; far from it; but the powers, to some extent, are assumed under the right to arrest and detain persons, virtually suspending the *habeas corpus.* They had misconstrued the Ordinance; it conferred great powers indeed, but scarcely to that extent. With a little more age, a little more rust and dust on the record, and men could have been found bold enough so to construe it. He did not mean to accuse the Council of mean and sordid motives; far from it. Like Cæsar's wife, they were above suspicion. They were honorable, high minded men, and far above even a thought of over-reaching their powers or oppressing the country. If the Council were to be perpetuated, there are none he would prefer to those now composing that body. Let us clothe the Executive with the proper powers to meet the exigencies of the times, and let him act under the regularly constituted authorities. But let us have no Council, no oligarchy. The power, the dangerous and almost supreme power, with which the Council were clothed, or which, at least, they exercised, was what alarmed the people, and was the ground of the murmurings and complaints. They were placed too high on the dizzy pinnacle of power to stand with safety, either to themselves or the people. He doubted if Robespierre, Danton, or even Napoleon, ever exercised more supreme authority. He denied that the exigencies even of the present perilous condition of South Carolina called for the conferring of such power. It stripped the State of men, and took even the lame, the halt and blind. What are the urgent necessities of the State to justify that enormous stretch of power, the power to impress persons, labor and property? These things, be they right or wrong, has and will be done by the Confederacy, and all arrangements made to meet the contingencies of the state of war.

Where exists the necessity of this cumbrous machinery of government, the duties of which could all be performed by a judicial government? Is the State so rampant and unruly as to require the curb and bit to be put in her mouth and the reins held by five dictators? He could not believe that the necessities of the case justified such a state of things. But, even if she did, is this the best and surest mode of accomplishing the desired end? He thought not. If you were in the midst of the ocean in a storm, would you think it added to the safety of the ship to have five captains, mates and pilots, all clothed with equal power? Would you have two suns to rule and regulate the solar system? Instead of harmonizing, would they not be apt to cause confusion and disorder?

He owned that he voted for the Ordinance forming the Council. He did it in good faith, with the best lights he had before him. But now he would clothe himself in sack-cloth, and repent in dust and ashes. He would place his hand upon his mouth and his mouth in the dust and cry *peccavi! peccavi!* But he was not without excuse. It was asserted in Convention that the Governor could not execute the onerous duties of his office in time of war, without assistance. He, with others, believed it, perhaps, at the time, and were thus induced to lend the measure their aid. The Ordinance contained greater powers when it was first presented to the Convention than it did when it was adopted. It was modified to suit diversified opinions. The Governor and Council claimed, under it, the right to suspend the *habeas corpus*, arrest and detain persons, and suspend or repeal existing laws. The right even to do this in the cases of arson and murder, but this power was abstracted. But he never supposed it would be attempted to be enforced.

What positive good have they done? Or, in fact, what could they do? That they have faithfully and honestly tried to do good, no man can deny. Their efforts in the path of duty under the powers conferred are patent to all. But it is also pertinent to enquire what evil they have done? The dissensions and clamors of our oppressed people will tell the story. They have accustomed peaceful and law-abiding people to rebel, and rise up against their rulers, which is a lesson more easily learned than forgotten. Obedience to the constituted authority is the first lesson of the patriot.

The attempt has been made to override the civil by the military law. Powers potent for good, but omnipotent for evil. Angels could not have been equal to the accomplishment of the task imposed upon the Council. And in their desire to do good and accomplish the end of their organization, they have allowed their zeal to outstrip their prudence.

Mr. Barnwell said he did not, for a moment, doubt the powers of the Convention, or the existing necessity for them. This is the only mode in which the sovereignty of the people can speak. The State *en masse* could never speak its sovereign will. The power must be delegated, as it is in this instance.

This is the mode, and thus far we are the people of South Carolina, for all intents and purposes, under the sanction of our organization. There can be no want of power in the people; they are the legitimate source of all power. They have the power, through a convention, to secede from the Union and form new alliances. The power is necessarily supreme, otherwise there is no supremacy. We are the people, and they are supreme. How can the people abuse or transcend the power of the people? As his opinions in this matter differs from some others, he will here take occasion to express them. He thought the Council had done their duty and a vast amount of good. The objection to five, instead of one, was not a valid one. They had to act in concert; every act had to pass the concurrence of that that body. There was wisdom in consultation, and in the multitude of counsellers there is safety. This Convention did not act unwisely in delegating five instead of one.

He now proposed to proceed to the matter more directly in hand. He had listened to the arguments of gentlemen in favor of a compromise, but he had not yet come to such a conclusion. It proposes, to some extent, a yielding to what might have been mistaken for the popular clamor. The question for us now to settle is, have we mastered our business? Have we accomplished all that we undertook to do? And has the danger passed in which we were in duty bound to see that the State suffered no detriment? Are not Lincoln's iron-clad boats still expected in the harbor of Charleston? And may the enemy not penetrate the interior? Let us hold on till the danger is passed, and not shrink from our duty till it is fully and fairly performed. Till the danger is passed and the State safe, we are not at liberty to resign the trust committed to our hands.

There is but one reason why we should change, and that is the growing murmurs and disaffection of the people, which may in some degree confuse and distract our future proceedings. These things were before us on a former occasion; why not, then, prepare to dissolve? The question is not into whose hands we shall surrender the trust, but is the danger past that we had to meet? Is our work done that we proposed and it was our duty to do? Were the news to reach us to-day that a fleet of war steamers were menacing Charleston, the people would turn their eyes to this Convention to devise ways and means to furnish troops to defend it. Let us not quail before the popular clamor, but remain at our posts and do our duty to the country, regardless of the consequences; and when the issue comes we will meet it like men, conscious of having done all they could to see that the State suffer no detriment. When the injunction of secresy shall be removed from the proceedings of this Convention, and the journal shall be printed and circulated and read among the people, they will then look upon this matter in a different light. When we make out the case fairly and squarely and present it to the people, I have but little fear but that they will give a righteous judgment.

Mr. Hayne would make a few remarks by way of explanation of the amendment which he had offered to the amendment of the majority report of the Committee of Seven. He did not see that the necessities of the times demanded a dissolution of this body. But he saw a disposition among members to surrender their power to the Legislature; and as it seemed that something like that would have to be done, he wished to put the matter in its least objectionable form, which he had endeavored to embody in his amendment.

Mr. Reed opposed the amendment and the amendment to the amendment. He preferred the report of the minority of the Committee of Seven to either. He believed that the powers vested in the Convention and Council were not necessary to meet the present exigencies. If Lincoln's gunboats were riding in the harbor of Charleston, the demands of the State could all be met by the regular constituted authorities. There is no Executive Council in North Carolina, Georgia or Louisiana.

[Here Mr. Barnwell rose to remark that, though there were no Executive Councils in those States, yet the Governors had been clothed with extraordinary powers.]

Mr. Reed resumed. Did not know what extraordinary powers Governors had assumed, but he doubted not that they had exceeded the Constitution. This Convention has exercised no power which might not as well have been done by the regularly constituted authorities; and he had no doubt but that this sentiment was held by an overwhelming majority of the people of the State. He would go home and try to pour oil on the troubled waters, and unite and harmonize the people. South Carolina might yet be invaded, and we would have to meet the foe on our own soil.

He concluded by moving to lay the amendment and the amendment to the amendment on the table. The motion was not agreed to.

Mr. Hayne then withdrew his amendment.

Mr. Dunkin said he had not changed his opinion of the powers of the Convention. The people are sovereign, and must speak through their agents or representatives. The Legislature that called this Convention intended that it should in the first place dissolve the Union, and then see that the State suffer no detriment. A motion was made at a former meeting of this Convention to refer the matter to the Legislature, and it was not granted, for the reason that it would confer unlimited powers on that body, which would not be expedient. The right of not exercising the powers guaranteed to the Convention on the ground of expediency, is another thing.

Narrow-minded people are always jealous of powers which they do not possess themselves. But it is commendable to be jealous of unlimited power. He feared to confer it on others; he trembled to possess it himself. He voted for the Ordinance creating the Executive Council, and he had done no penance for it; he had nothing to reproach himself for. He is not prepared to dissolve the Council now unless he is satisfied that no danger shall accrue therefrom. But he is in favor of fixing a day to terminate its existence. Let the people know it, and let them elect their best men to assist in conducting the State through her present difficulties.

Mr. Brown was prepared to vote on the plain question, whether or not shall the Convention be dissolved. He would vote to stand as they are. The Legislature is yet to be elected; we do not know who they will be. The best part of the population are on the tented field. Every proposition made looks to the continued existence of the Council in some form or other. Upon this question, a compromise seems likely to be effected. He might be said to have come from the chair of despotism, and he came to sustain despots, if he could find them; but he found nothing in the Council to condemn except that they had not done enough; they had certainly not done too much.

FROM OUR ARMY IN MARYLAND.

Our latest news from the army, through private sources, is to Thursday last, which is derived from parties who left Frederick on that day. Up to that time our army was bivouacked around that city, but marching orders had been received. The direction contemplated was not understood by our informants, though it was conjectured that our forces would move on the Relay. Others state that on Thursday morning the army, or a large portion of it, moved in the direction of Hagerstown. These parties state that our soldiers were receiving every attention from the people of Frederick and the neighborhood, and articles were sold them at rates that seemed astonishingly low, compared with the high prices they have had to pay in Virginia. At Frederick hundreds of soldiers purchased shoes at $2.50 to $5, and other articles of clothing at proportionate rates. Coffee was bought by them in great abundance at 25 cents per pound.

A recruiting office was opened in Frederick immediately after our army took possession of the city, and the Stars and Bars were flung to the breeze. Up to the 10th inst. about fifteen hundred gallant Marylanders, from Frederick and Montgomery counties, had enrolled themselves in the service of the Confederate States. The condition of the army is said to be excellent, and the spirits of the men buoyant. The universal desire of the soldiers was to move on Pennsylvania. With regard to the movements of Stonewall JACKSON, we have no other information than that given in the following paragraph from the Richmond *Enquirer* of Tuesday:

We learn by a gentleman of high character, who arrived last evening, from Staunton, that a courier had arrived in that place, from the lower end of the Valley, with information that Gen. Jackson was at, or near Martinsburg, Va., in pursuit of the Yankees who were left in the Valley to protect the Railroad and Harper's Ferry. The force of the enemy is variously estimated at from 4000 to 18,000. When this force is disposed of, there will then be no enemy in our rear, and the line of communication by the Valley route will be open for our advancing army as they push Northward. It is supposed Jackson went from Frederick to Hagerstown, and then turned back on Martinsburg and Harper's Ferry.

FROM BALTIMORE.

A correspondent of the New York *Tribune*, writing from Baltimore on the 10th inst., says:

The present exceeding quiet in this city may be the indication of a loyalty that will manifest itself in a strong and determined stand for the Government, or it may be the result of a fear of the mortar boats and Fort McHenry, or it may be only the lull that precedes a storm. No doubt that, under present circumstances, there exists a check upon expressions of disloyalty that will prevent any open outbreak, unless the rebel army should knock at the gates, fresh from recent victories. The 6th Massachusetts regiment can now march through the streets, cheered instead of being fired upon, as they were in their famous march a year ago last Spring—it still remains an open question whether this quiescence is true or simulated patriotism.

There are 14,000 good men and true in this city, bound by solemn oath to sustain the Government and the laws. Their organization is of necessity a secret one so far as the oath, etc., is concerned, but the fact is so well known to the Secessionists, that no harm can be done in announcing it. Meanwhile, the Secessionists are secretly armed and awaiting their opportunity. But the league is well organized and ready to come forward to the assistance of the Government whenever their action shall be necessary. Meantime, the "Roughs" in the city, led by men whose Northern antipathies are the result of a life-long education, are equally ready to rise against it, and among these rebel leaders are some of the wealthiest citizens.

THE MOVEMENTS OF M'CLELLAN.

A correspondent of the *Tribune* writes as follows from Rockville, Maryland, on the 9th inst.:

Poolesville was again occupied by the National troops last evening. Gen. Fessenden, with his brigade of cavalry, entered the town about dusk, meeting but little resistance and losing but one man. By this evening our army corps will, without doubt, be encamped about it. The exact position of the main body of the rebel army seems to be difficult to ascertain. Sugar Loaf Mountain is occupied by them as a telescopic and signal station, and a more admirable one for that purpose could not have been found. It is a high peak, rising in the form of a sugar loaf, and upon any clear day can be seen distinctly from Washington.—From its summit the rebels can watch the movements of all the army corps as they leave by the different roads from Washington and Georgetown. The roads, too, are three inches deep with dust, and the cloud which floats over an army train can be seen a very great distance. Our Generals are unfortunate in having no high points from which to watch the movements of the rebel army. As in Virginia, they still have the advantage of us in obtaining accurate information of our movements.

The troops are again beginning to feel like fighting. Just at this moment they have no General to quarrel about.—Pope has been sent to the Indians, and McDowell has gone to see his wife. Their idol, General McClellan, is here among them, where they can see him almost daily; and if they will not fight under him, they would not fight under Gabriel, if he should blow his trump, descend from above, and offer to lead the Yankee host in their last extremity.

The Upper Potomac, like the Rappahannock, can be forded at almost any point. General Lee will meet with no difficulty in crossing his supply trains, if he has any with him.

The hotels all being full, I am stopping at the house of a prominent citizen of this village. In the morning, in addition to the songs of birds singing in the trees, I am entertained before rising with the choicest rebel songs, sung by the prettiest little rebels I have seen in my campaigns. The little imps—I just call them pretty—are now giving three cheers for Jeff. Davis, and talking in loud strains about that ugly old devil Lincoln. It is useless to disguise the fact, loyal Maryland is not half loyal. As in Baltimore, so in this portion of the State, the wealthy and aristocratic are with the South. While the army remains here they will be very civil and quiet, but as soon as it advances or falls back they will be, as before, blatant secessionists.

I believed when I left Washington that a campaign in Maryland was a part of the rebel plan. All evidence confirms it here. Whatever force is immediately in front of this army is the curtain behind which the rebel procession marches to Baltimore. Maryland, fair and false, half loyal in speech, wholly traitor at heart, welcomes with open hand an army that invades only to liberate her from Federal tyranny. Her soil shakes under the tread of armed feet, but the yoke is lifted from her neck.

Possibly, not Baltimore, but Harrisburg, is the point to be struck. Frederick is a base for either march. Whichever it be, the campaign begins in a country overflowing with supplies, and the army which advances through it needs to keep open no lines of communication. I suppose, if the enemy had crossed the Potomac in ships, he might have burned them on the hither shore.

NEW BRIGADIER GENERALS.—The following recent appointments of Brigadier Generals have been made: WILLIAM STEEL and J. F. FAGAN, of Arkansas; FRANCIS A. SHOUP, of Florida; Col. SKURRY and ALLISON NELSON, of Texas.

CLOTHING.—The Richmond *Whig* says: We have reason to believe, from information in our possession, that the prices for clothing will not be as high, during the winter, as many persons have anticipated. The probabilities are that shoes will also be lower. We will see.

THE COTTON FAMINE IN ENGLAND.

The London *Times* has been sending a special correspondent into the manufacturing districts to ascertain the truth in regard to the suffering and privation there, growing out of a stoppage of trade, consequent upon the American war, the loss of the cotton supply, &c. His first report appeared in the *Times* of the 26th ult. From him we learn that—

In Preston alone there are 23,000 persons receiving parochial and charitable relief. The population is only 83,000, so that more than one-fourth are steeped to the lips in misery. In addition to the 23,000, there are thousands endeavoring to subsist on half-wages, or less than one half. Half time does not imply half pay, for the use of Surat cotton renders it impossible for the hands to earn their customary wages. The amount lost to the operatives by the failure of employment is calculated at £13,000 a week. The slight compensation to the suffering amounts to little more than £1,000 a week; so that, in point of fact, £1 is made to do the duty of £12. In one court, says the reporter, I found a poor woman with three children, whose husband had three days' parish work and an extra relief of 3s., in all 6s. a week for all.

All their furniture was gone but a table and two chairs, and all five slept in one bed, which was placed in a dark hole with not a ray of light finding its way into it—such as we should hardly think too good to store coals in. All their clothes had been pawned, and most bitterly of all did the poor woman lament a good black suit of her husband which was "in" for 10s., and which they could never hope to "redeem." Another family of six people, in the same court, had to live on 8s. a week—that is, 1s. 2d. per week, or 2½d. a day for each. "In another house," he says, "I saw a sight which will be before my eyes for many a day to come."

It was a little low stone-floored room—its only furniture a table, a stool and a bed. On the bed was a stretched object—I could not tell whether it was a man or a woman—worn to the bone—a very skeleton, in fact—her body covered with putrid sores, with not a rag on her—literally naked, but for the coarse sheet which was spread over her. The bed on which she lay was a rough brown sacking stuffed with a handful of straw. She had lain there I don't know how long; her husband had lain there before her, and died on the same bed.

She was the mother of two girls, factory operatives, who earned, or were relieved, with a few shillings—I forget how many, for I own I was too much shocked at what I saw to listen to figures. Even among a somewhat better class, he continues, the suffering is hardly less extreme, and sad were the tales to which I had to listen of the gradual descent from comfort to utter destitution. In one little house, huddled all together, was a family of eleven, all of which had been twenty-eight weeks out of work, and for fifteen of these they had existed on something less than 1s. per head.

The Relief Committee had just raised their pittance to 16s. for the eleven. Before the bad times the family earnings had been about £3 15s., and they had had to part with nearly all their furniture. A man, his wife, three daughters and two sons, had only one bed among them, and only a dirty blanket and a dirty quilt, one to be under, and the other over them. Of course the children slept on the bare boards. The reporter illustrates the condition of a rather superior class as follows:

But perhaps the strongest illustrations of the distress actually chargeable on the present crisis are the cases of respectable men who have hitherto kept themselves in comfort and endeavored to provide for old age and infirmity.—There was no difficulty in finding plenty of these. At one house I visited a young couple, not long married, who, between them, had earned over £2 a week. They had both been out of work for some time, and when their savings were exhausted they had at last applied to the parish.—Their present income was exactly 5s. 6d. a week, out of which their rent was 2s. 7d., leaving them 8s. a week for subsistence. Another young couple had 2s. a week from the Relief Committee; but, living with their parents, they had no rent to pay. In the next house there were four grown-up people living, whose united incomes amounted to 9s., out of which they had to pay 2s. rent.

Little further on I came on an overseer with a family of five children. His salary had been 39s. a week, and though he had been out of work more than a twelvemonth, he had managed to struggle on until about a fortnight ago, when, all his resources being exhausted, he had been compelled to apply for relief, and was now receiving, from one source or another, about 9s. a week. An old woman and two daughters, both of them over twenty-one years of age—one employed half time, the other receiving relief—had among them 4s. 6d. a week.

A highly respectable reed-hook maker—whose wife cried bitterly as she told me her story—is earning, with the aid of one of her boys, 7s. a week, which has to keep four of them, by dredging stones from the bed of the river. They had pawned all their clothes and much of their furniture before applying to the Relief Committee.

The average amount derived from charity, the parish and half-time, when distributed amongst all the claimants, amounts only to 1s. 6d. a head per week. Many, of course, are living for less. The 1s. 6d. is not given in money, the Relief Committee distributing their bounty in bread, soup and coffee.

The cotton question is discussed by the London *Daily News* in a desponding spirit. It says:

The supply of American cotton is rapidly becoming extinguished, and these exports have consequently risen during the past week no less than 4d. to 5d. per pound. For the future American cotton, as being quite a "fancy" article, will command a "fancy" price,—indeed, just such a price as the limited number of holders may choose to demand for it. Accordingly an interesting revolution is taking place in the manufacture. American cotton passes out of of consumption, and the small quantity remaining will be husbanded and used only in those fine articles which are worn by the wealthier classes of society.

The cotton of Surat—the description now chiefly entering into consumption—cannot be worked into the finer sorts of yarns and goods; before it will become available for them its quality must be greatly improved. It is very suitable, however, to coarse fabrics, and with coarse fabrics we must be content until such time as America sends her produce here again, or the cotton of other countries improves in quality as well as increases in quantity. * * *

We have shown how small is the present stock of cotton, and, looking to the immediate future, the prospect is gloomy in the extreme.

Chief reliance is placed upon the supply of Surat sorts, but it is not by any means encouraging to find that the total quantity from this source now afloat, and on the way to England, is only 90,000 bales more than it was at this time last year, being 390,000 bales against 300,000 in 1861. From no other source can the deficiency now indicated be made up, save with time. Assuming that the American crop is not released, and allowing for the probable supplies from every other quarter, competent authorities estimate that during the next six months there will be only sufficient cotton to admit of the operatives having two days' work a week, and this is upon the supposition that not a single bale will remain in stock at the end of that period.

The latter anticipation, of course, will not be literally fulfilled, but there is too much reason to apprehend, as we have already hinted, that the pressure on the cotton manufacturing districts will become yet more intense. A well known Manchester firm have given public expression to an opinion that its severity will be the greatest during the autumn and winter months, from October to February next.

SNUBBED.—The "National War Committee" at New York resolved "that Gen. FREMONT and Gen. MITCHELL be and are requested, if the Government will consent, to organize in this State without delay a corps of 50,000 men, and that application for such consent be made to the General Government, and if it refuses, then to the State Government." This resolution was sent to General FREMONT (Gen. MITCHELL was not at the moment within reach), with the question whether, if Government would consent, he would undertake the organization of such a corps. Gen. FREMONT replied that he would cheerfully do so. Then the Committee asked the Secretary of War if the Government would give such consent, and Mr. STANTON said No—and there the matter ended.

THE CONFEDERATE CONGRESS.—In the Senate on Monday Mr. Hill, of Georgia, from the Committee on the Judiciary, reported a bill to declare certain persons alien enemies. The bill provides that the President shall issue his proclamation, requiring all persons within the Confederate States, who refuse to support this Government, to depart within forty days beyond the territorial jurisdiction of the Confederate States; provided, that if any of said persons shall, during the forty days, abandon the Government of the United States and renounce their oath of allegiance thereto, they shall be relieved of the penalties against alien enemies.

The Military Exemption bill was further considered, and the constitutional question involved, which has been discussed for several days past, was disposed of by the adoption of an amendment excepting from exemption such State officers as the several States may have declared by law to be liable to military duty. An amendment to exempt one editor of each newspaper was rejected—ayes, 8; nays, 14. A motion to strike out Ministers of the Gospel, was negatived—yeas, 5; nays, 27. The Senate then adjourned.

In the House, a resolution from the Senate fixing the 30th of September as the day for the adjournment of Congress, was agreed to. The Conscription bill was further discussed.

Advices received at New York from Key West, state that the Yellow Fever continued to rage there. One hundred and sixty deaths had occurred, including many officers of the Federal army and navy.

THE PAY AND APPOINTMENT OF PROVOST MARSHALS.

The following communication was last week presented to the Senate from the Secretary of War, in reply to a resolution requesting certain information from the President in relation to the pay and appointment of Provost Marshals:

His Excellency Jefferson Davis, President C. S. A.:

SIR: I have the honor to acknowledge the receipt of the enclosed resolution of the Senate, requesting you to give them information concerning the pay and appointment of Provost Marshals.

The army regulations provide for the employment, by a Commanding General or a General of Division, of Provost Marshals, who are charged with the custody of prisoners, and the performance of police duties. In garrisons non-commissioned officers are usually assigned to these duties, but, with armies of the field, deprived as they are of the assistance of the civil authorities, and often incumbered with large numbers of prisoners, the duties become more difficult and important, and commissioned officers are detailed for their discharge.

It will be observed that Provost Marshals are *employed, not appointed;* otherwise, officers of the army, already holding commissions, could not be assigned to such duty without holding two distinct appointments from the Government.

It having been found that large amounts of public property at our principal depots, and the peace and good order of many of our towns were endangered by the numerous stragglers from the army, and camp-followers hanging about them, and that desertion from the army was encouraged by the want of persons at those points authorized to make arrests, the Department employed Provost Marshals, and vested them with authority over all persons in the army found within their respective limits.

They have no authority whatever over persons not in the army, except where martial law is in force, in which localities their police powers are extended to citizens as well as soldiers.

Whether martial law exist or not, they are expressly prohibited by a general order from exercising civil jurisdiction, and the Department has checked them in all cases in which the exercise of such jurisdiction has been made the subject of complaint.

Many of the Provost Marshals of posts where martial law is not in force have fallen into the error of supposing themselves to be clothed with general police powers, but the Department has invariably informed them when such cases were brought to its attention, that they could derive the power to arrest citizens from the civil magistrates only.

Their compensation is usually fixed at that of a captain of infantry, but in some few cases they have been allowed the pay of field officers. The reference to the army grade is merely for the purpose of fixing their rate of compensation, and does not confer on them grade or commission.

The employment of Provost Marshals and provost guards is essential to the preservation of public property, to the peace and good order of our chief towns, and to the very existence of the army.

They are paid by the Quartermaster's Department, because the army regulations require that Department to pay the incidental expenses of the army, including, generally, all proper and authorized expenses for the movements and operations of the army, not expressly assigned to other Departments.

Provost Marshals being essential to the operations of the army and not being chargeable to any other department, seem properly to be assigned for their pay and allowances to the Quartermaster General's Department.

Very respectfully,
Your obedient servant,
GEORGE W. RANDOLPH,
Secretary of War.

The New-York Times.

VOL. XI—NO. 3430.

NEW-YORK, SATURDAY, SEPTEMBER 20, 1862.

PRICE TWO CENTS.

GREAT VICTORY

The Rebel Army in Full Flight Out of Maryland.

The Dead and Wounded Left Behind.

Our Cavalry Pushing Them Across the Potomac.

The Whole National Army in Good Condition.

Further Details of the Great Battle of Wednesday.

No Fighting of Consequence on Thursday.

Official Dispatches from Gen. McClellan.

HE ANNOUNCES A COMPLETE VICTORY.

DISPATCHES FROM GEN. McCLELLAN.

FIRST DISPATCH.

HEADQUARTERS ARMY OF POTOMAC, Sept. 19—8:30 A. M.

Maj.-Gen. H. W. Halleck, General-in-Chief:

But little occurred yesterday, except skirmishing.

Last night the enemy abandoned his position leaving his dead and wounded on the field.

We are again in pursuit.

I do not yet know whether he is falling back on an interior position, or crossing the river.

We may safely claim a victory.

GEORGE B. McCLELLAN, Major-General.

SECOND DISPATCH.

HEADQUARTERS ARMY OF POTOMAC, Friday, Sept. 19—10½ A. M.

Maj.-Gen. H. W. Halleck, General-in-Chief:

PLEASANTON is driving the enemy across the river.

Our victory was complete.

The enemy is driven back into Virginia. Maryland and Pennsylvania are now safe.

GEO. B. McCLELLAN, Major-General.

OUR LATEST WASHINGTON DISPATCHES

WASHINGTON, Friday, Sept. 19—11½ P. M.

A special dispatch from the TIMES' Baltimore correspondent says that Gen. McCLELLAN's bulletins have greatly discouraged the rebels there. They are inclined to believe that the Confederate combinations have failed, and that their cause is ruined.

WASHINGTON, Friday, Sept. 19—12 Midnight.

It is now clearly apparent that the rebel army is repelled from Maryland. Probably nearly or quite the whole has succeeded in crossing the Potomac, with slight additional loss of men, wagons and artillery. It is believed that the rebels can sufficiently defend the most important crossings to enable the bulk of their forces successfully to retreat to Winchester, which is probably their base, or to any other point they choose.

LATEST REPORTS FROM HEADQUARTERS

HEADQUARTERS OF THE ARMY OF THE POTOMAC, Friday Morning, Sept. 19, 1862.

Yesterday was occupied in burying the dead and caring for the wounded.

The rebels sent in a flag of truce in the morning, asking permission to bury their own dead, which was granted.

At first the orders were very stringent against holding intercourse with the rebels, but during the afternoon they were relaxed, and the troops of both sides freely intermingled.

The following is a list of some of the killed and wounded:

Brig.-Gen. Rodman, commanding a brigade in Major-Gen. Burnside's Division, was wounded.

Col. Stear, of the Fourth Rhode Island Regiment, was wounded in the hip.

Lieut.-Col. Appleman, of the Eighth Connecticut Regiment, was wounded.

Capt. Griswold, of the Eleventh Connecticut Regiment.

Lieut. Arenberg, of SEAMAN's Ohio Battery, lost a leg.

Major Giles, of the Eighty-eighth Pennsylvania Regiment, was severely wounded.

Col. Barlow, of the Sixty-first New-York Regiment, was wounded.

Col. Goodrich, of the Sixty-first New-York Regiment, was killed.

Col. Beall, of the Tenth Pennsylvania Regiment, was wounded.

Col. Crossdale, of the One Hundred and Twenty-eighth Pennsylvania Regiment, was killed.

Maj. Dwight, of the Second Massachusetts Regiment, was wounded.

At daylight, this morning, it was discovered that the enemy had changed their position. Whether their whole force has crossed the river, or taken a new position nearer the river, is not at present known.

Had the rebels remained, a general engagement between both armies would have taken place this morning.

OUR DISPATCHES FROM HARRISBURGH.

HARRISBURGH, Friday, Sept. 19—1 P. M.

A dispatch just in from Gov. CURTIN, on the battle-field, says that the battle is raging fearfully, and progressing favorably for our side.

McCLELLAN has been largely reinforced. The Pennsylvania militia were also advancing to the field, under Gen. REYNOLDS.

Surgeon-Gen. SMITH has telegraphed to prepare for the wounded to be brought here, and all the churches and other buildings are being got ready.

There is intense excitement, but every one is full of hope.

HARRISBURGH, Friday, Sept. 19—3 P. M.

By an official telegram just received, we learn that our victory is complete. The enemy is in full retreat, and our forces are driving them to the river.

No details at present.

FROM THE ASSOCIATED PRESS CORRESPONDENT.

HARRISBURGH, Friday, Sept. 19.

Information just received from the battle-field says our victory is complete, and that Gen. PLEASANTON is in hot pursuit of the enemy, and driving them across the Potomac. The whole Federal army is in good condition, and the enemy has been badly punished.

THE GREAT BATTLE OF WEDNESDAY.

BALTIMORE, Friday, Sept. 19.

A gentleman who left the battle-field at 9 o'clock on Wednesday night, confirms the statement of the reporter of the Associated Press at headquarters, in every particular.

He says that our forces occupied the position chosen by the enemy at the commencement of the battle, and that the rebels were driven back a mile and a half at all points, except upon our extreme right, which they still held at the close of the day.

Our informant was all day within a hundred yards of Gen. McCLELLAN, and says that the results of the day were regarded by him and his Staff as a glorious victory, though not a final one.

There was no faltering at any point of the line of our whole army.

Our soldiers were exultant at the results of the day's fight, and Gen. McCLELLAN was in the highest spirits.

The opinion of Gen. McCLELLAN and those around him was that the final result would depend on who got reinforcements first.

Our informant says that nothing had been heard on the field of the capture of Gen. LONGSTREET or the killing of Gen. HILL, and that there is no truth in either report.

Twenty thousand more reinforcements were expected to reach the field yesterday from Harrisburgh.

Our informant thinks the loss of the rebels fully equal to ours.

The gentleman who furnished us with the foregoing intelligence is one of our most respectable and intelligent citizens, and says that the battle of Wednesday was not a decisive one. It was a contest in which all the advantages were with Gen. McCLELLAN, who occupied the field of battle at the close of the day.

GEN. MANSFIELD.

Brig.-Gen. J. K. F. MANSFIELD, killed at the battle of Sharpsburgh on Wednesday, was a native of Connecticut, from which State he was appointed a cadet to the West Point Military Academy in Oct., 1817. He was at the time of his death about sixty years of age. He graduated on the 30th of June, 1822, standing No. 2 in a class of forty members, among whom are the names of Gens. HUNTER, McCALL, and others noted during the present war. On the 1st of July, 1822, he was brevetted a Second Lieutenant of a corps of Engineers, and received his full rank the same day. On the 5th of March, 1832, he was promoted to a First Lieutenancy, and on the 7th of July, 1838, became Captain. He served in the Texan and Mexican wars, and on the 9th of May, 1846, was brevetted Major for gallant and distinguished services in the defence of Fort Browne, in Texas. On the 23d of the following September, he was brevetted Lieutenant-Colonel for gallant and meritorious conduct in the several battles of Monterey, in Mexico, on the 21st, 22d and 23d of September, 1846.

On the first of those days he was severely wounded. He was breveted Colonel on the 23d of February 1847, for gallant and meritorious conduct at Buena Vista. During the campaigns of 1846 and 1847 of the war with Mexico he held the position of Chief Engineer of the army under Gen. TAYLOR. Previous to the war he had been appointed as member of the Board of Engineers, viz.: From Dec. 8, 1842, to Sept. 8, 1845, and after the war he resumed this same position, which he kept for some time. On the 28th of May, 1853, he was appointed an Inspector-General of the United States Army, with the rank of Colonel. This position he held at the breaking out of the rebellion. On the 6th of May, 1861, he was brevetted a Brigadier-General of the Regular United States Army, and on the 14th of May, 1861, was commissioned a full Brigadier-General. He was placed in command of the position at Newport's News, which he held until the advance upon Norfolk transferred his services to the other shore of the James River.

He was next placed in command at Suffolk, Va. When Gen. POPE met with his reverses in Virginia, and demanded a Court of Inquiry to examine into the conduct of certain of his officers, Gen. MANSFIELD was ordered to proceed to Washington to sit as one of the Court. The inquiry having been postponed, by order of the President, at the request of Gen. McCLELLAN, Gen. MANSFIELD was assigned a post of duty in the field. In the discharge of that duty he fell, at the post of honor.

COL. McNEIL.

Among the killed in this week's terrible battles in Maryland, is Col. McNEIL, the commander of the justly celebrated "Bucktail" Regiment, while leading a charge at the head of his men, near Antietam Creek. HUGH WATSON McNEIL was a son of Rev. A. McNEIL, a Cameronian clergyman, and was born in Seneca County, New-York, in 1830. He was educated at Yale College, and entered upon the study of the law in the office of CLARENCE W. SEWARD, at Auburn. In 1857 he commenced practice in this City, but was obliged to abandon his profession two years afterward, by reason of ill health. He removed to Pennsylvania, and engaged in business. Upon the breaking out of the rebellion he enlisted as a private in a company known as "Wild Cats," commanded by Capt. STONE, which was afterwards incorporated with the famous Bucktail Regiment. In a short time he was chosen First Lieutenant, and then Captain. In this capacity he led the regiment in a magnificent bayonet charge at Drainesville. The exploits of the regiment are familiar to all. While with McDOWELL on the Rappahannock; while in pursuit of Stonewall JACKSON up the Shenandoah Valley, under FREMONT, and particularly at the spirited battle of Cross Keys, the Bucktails gained the foremost name for valor and vigor. And since then they have not ceased for a day to harrass the enemy. They accompanied Gen. HOOKER in the recent expedition up the Potomac in quest of Stonewall JACKSON. On Tuesday they came up with the enemy under LEE, near Sharpsburgh. The National troops were disposed in order of battle. The Bucktails were at the front. The action commenced at dark and lasted two hours. Col. McNEIL had just charged upon the rebel forces, driving them back half a mile, when he received his death wound.

He was a daring and intrepid officer, a generous friend and kinsman, the idol of his family and regiment, and his loss cannot be replaced.

BATTLE OF ANTIETAM CREEK.

Full Particulars from Our Special Correspondent.

The Most Stupendous Struggle of Modern Times.

The Battle Won by Consummate Generalship.

The Rebel Losses Estimated as High as Thirty Thousand.

A GREAT NUMBER OF PRISONERS CAPTURED.

BATTLE-FIELD OF ANTIETAM CREEK, Thursday, Sept. 18, 1862.

Another great battle has been fought, and the cause of the Union has once more been vindicated upon one of the most bloody and well-contested fields known to ancient or modern times. Wednesday, Sept. 17, 1862, will, we predict, hereafter be looked upon as an epoch in the history of the rebellion, from which will date the inauguration of its downfall. On that day about one hundred and sixty thousand men met in deadly strife upon the field of Antietam—a name which will occupy a leading position in the history of the war—and there, marshaled by brave and able men, fought with a desperation and courage never before excelled, and rarely, if ever equaled, for twelve hours, leaving the Union army in possession of the contested ground. This victory was not gained, however, without the sacrifice of many valuable lives, and the maiming of thousands of individuals.

PRECEDING EVENTS.

Before attempting to present even a glance at this battle, let us first prepare the reader for a correct understanding of it by relating—in continuation of my last letter—the events immediately preceding the great contest. My last brought Gen. McCLELLAN's advance into Maryland up to midday on Tuesday, Sept. 16, at which time the army occupied a position in close proximity to the road leading from Boonesville to Sharpsburgh, and upon and near the left bank of the little creek known by the name of Antietam, which rises in Central Pennsylvania, and, after running in a southerly direction, its waters are mingled with the turgid waters of the Potomac, about five miles above Harper's Ferry.

The enemy occupied a position on the right bank of the Antietam, favorably located for both offensive and defensive operations, and in this respect had the advantage. To circumvent the enemy, and secure an equally favorable position, was the first object to be obtained. That this required the genius of a great leader, needed no military man to elucidate, for the whole position of affairs could be taken in at a glance. How well and successfully this object was accomplished, the success of our arms is abundant evidence. Of some of the details of the movement to this end we shall give in the proper place. Just across the creek, in plain view from the eastern bank, the enemy's skirmishers could be distinctly seen, and from elevated positions massed forces of infantry and cavalry could be discovered in every little valley and ravine for miles on either hand. Two hundred thousand men was what the enemy pretended to have within the scope of the eye, and from repeated personal inspection, aided by an excellent glass, while standing in a favorable position, I should judge the figure named not an exaggerated one.

PREPARATIONS FOR A MOVEMENT.

Between 12 and 2 o'clock P. M. all was silent along the lines. The German Battery of sixteen 20-pound Parrott guns, upon the eminence overlooking the river's bank were silent. Major ARNDT had fallen, and the infantry battalions were quietly resting upon the ground under the hill, upon the tops of which were planted our artillery. This quietness was like the quietness that precedes the storm. The Commanding General had arrived upon the ground at an early hour the day before, and had made himself familiar with the position, and at the time of which we write was busily engaged in giving the necessary instructions to the Commanders of Corps, so as to render our success in the impending conflict as much a matter of certainty as possible.

THE MOVEMENT.

Soon after 2 o'clock P. M. the Parrott guns, to which allusion has been made before, were opened upon the enemy and worked with great rapidity, and nearly every shell thrown, as I afterward ascertained, did fearful execution in the massed columns of the enemy. In a brief space after this terrible fire had been opened, there was a movement of the troops inexplicable to the uninitiated at the moment, but the object of which was soon revealed to the careful observer. The Antietam was to be crossed: Gen. HOOKER's Corps, by a flank movement, gained a point to the north of between two and three miles, and changing direction to the left reached the river at Kelly's Ford. A portion of the Pennsylvania Reserve, under command of Brig.-Gen. MEADE were thrown across the river and were deployed as skirmishers, and under their cover and the support of the German New-York Battery, Gen. HOOKER's column very speedily gained a foothold upon the opposite bank. Our skirmishers were met with a galling fire poured in by the skirmishers of the enemy, and before a battery of four or six pieces so located as to give a raking fire to the advancing column. Fortunately this battery was not well managed, and most of the missiles were thrown too high, hence our loss at this point was comparatively trifling. This battery was speedily silenced, and the rapid movements of Gen. HOOKER's column soon placed it in jeopardy; but the enemy, always on the alert, managed to get their pieces out of the way before a battery could be thrown across to sustain the infantry column in its local movements. The enemy's skirmishers were forced back step by step by the Reserves to their main body, by which time the whole of the advancing column was in position, and ready for more decisive offensive operations. The enemy rushed forward seemingly bent upon annihilating the comparatively small force sent against them, and several times there was some wavering under the terrible and impetuous resistance—but the troops quickly rallied, and, under the lead of their able commander, secured the much coveted and a necessary position to secure success. This movement across the river was one for which Gen HOOKER was peculiarly qualified, and he executed it in a manner highly creditable to his skill as a General. Here the battle of Antietam commenced in earnest. Until nightfall set in Gen. HOOKER pressed the enemy back, and every step was gained by hard fighting.

THE DEMONSTRATION TO THE LEFT

Tuesday afternoon Gen. BURNSIDE's column was brought up to the river and directed to make a demonstration on the enemy's right, by crossing the stream three or four miles below the point where Gen. HOOKER had crossed, with a view to secure a stone bridge—to facilitate the crossing of artillery and munitions—and also to threaten the enemy's right flank, to correspond with the demonstration of Gen. HOOKER on his (the enemy's) left, which was to be the real point of attack. This order was promptly obeyed, and carried out with alacrity. Gen. BURNSIDE, by dark, had arrived at the point of crossing, and on the following morning forced the enemy back from the bridge, and rendered important aid with his artillery.

TUESDAY NIGHT.

During the night of Tuesday, Gen. BANKS' Corps, then under the command of Gen. MANSFIELD, who was killed early the following day, Gen. FRANKLIN's Corps and two divisions of Gen. SUMNER's Corps—SEDGWICK's and FRENCH's—were thrown across the river at the ford to sustain Gen. HOOKER, when the line of battle was formed in the following order: Gen. HOOKER on the right; Gen. SUMNER—the line running nearly north and south—the left inclining toward the river and in a direction a little to the east of south. Gen. FRANKLIN's force was placed in a reserve on the right. On Wednesday morning early the balance of Gen. SUMNER's Corps—Gen. RICHARDSON's Division—was thrown across the creek and extended the line to the left; the commands of Gens. MORELL, FITZ-JOHN PORTER and COUCH were brought on to the field later in the day, but were not required, and were therefore held in reserve.

THE BATTLE OF ANTIETAM.

On Wednesday morning, Sept. 17, the sun rose in a cloudless sky, and all nature seemed to smile as if the world were filled with the elect of God. But its splendors were soon dimmed with the smoke rising from the battle-field.

To enable the reader to understand the events of this day, he should look at a map which has laid out the principal roads throughout the State of Maryland. With a pencil follow the road or "pike" from Boonsboro' direct to Sharpsburgh—which is nearly three miles west of the river, at the point where the road crosses it; the battle-field is on both sides of that road—between the river and Sharpsburgh—the bulk of it being north of the Boonsboro' road, and in the triangle formed by the roads connecting Bakersville and Middletown and Bakersville and Sharpsburgh. The surface is interspersed with hill and vale, and covered with cornfields and grass land, and skirting and stretching toward the centre from different points are thin belts of forest trees—all of which gives advantage to the enemy acting on the defensive, he having an opportunity to select his position for defensive operations, and when forced from one position he has only to fall back a short distance to find a position naturally as strong as the first. The engagement was opened early Wednesday morning by the advance of a strong line of our skirmishers. They were met by a similar movement on the part of the enemy. The latter were forced back until the right of our line (Gen. HOOKER's,) came into action with the enemy's left, commanded by Gen. HILL, who commands a portion of LONGSTREET's corps. BANKS' corps was, within a half an hour, at work, and was followed soon after by Gen. FRANKLIN's command. The first fire was at about 5 o'clock, and at 6 o'clock the infantry arm entered upon its work. The line thus formed,

THE ENEMY'S LEFT WAS FORCED BACK

for nearly three miles from the ford, where the bulk of our troops crossed the creek before 9 o'clock when they were relieved by Gen. SEDGWICK's coming to the front. Just previous to this, MORRIS' Brigade, of HOOKER's command, had advanced from a belt of timber across a plowed field into a piece of woods, where the enemy, massed in great force, were repulsed, and the troops fell back to the belt of timber in some disorder, but soon rallied again, and regained the field in front. It was at this time that Gen. MANSFIELD, in command of Gen. BANKS' corps, was mortally wounded, carried from the field and died soon afterward. Gen. WILLIAMS succeeded to the command of the corps, and Gen. CRAWFORD took command of WILLIAMS' Division until he was wounded and taken from the field. The repulse of MORRIS' Brigade was accomplished by an old and contemptible trick of the enemy. As the corps advanced to the woods across the plowed field, the rebels unfurled the Stars and Stripes, and waving them, cried out, "What the h—l are you doing? Don't fire upon your friends!" Our troops, deceived by this ruse, ceased firing, when the rebels opened upon them a murderous volley of musketry and cross fire, and creating a temporary panic. They rallied and drove the rebels back, but it was done at a great sacrifice of life.

These troops were relieved by

GEN. SEDGWICK'S COMMAND

coming up on their left. The enemy who had gained a point in the woods, extending some distance in front of our line, at the left of Gen. BANKS' corps, were driven out, and across a plowed field in front, to the timber beyond, with terrible slaughter—NEAD's battery covering them with grape and canister, strewing the ground with the dead. At one point, just on the brow of a little hill of the road I [illegible] the infantry, emerging suddenly upon the open field, supposed that it was a rebel force [illegible] for them, and the dead rebels got an extra volley. This corps came into action by brigades, between 8 and 9 o'clock—GORMAN's, DANA's and HOWARD's. While preparing for action, the enemy appeared from an unexpected quarter, and opened a terrific fire with a view of breaking the line by a sudden attack with musketry and artillery, he believing that it was composed of raw troops. But they soon discovered their mistake; these veterans, notwithstanding the sudden attack, though their lines were broken for a moment, were not disconcerted, but received it with cheers. While under this galling fire the Fifteenth Regiment Massachusetts Volunteers made a dash forward and seized the battle-flag of one of Gen. HILL's regiments, and now have it to show to their friends as a trophy of the day. In this connection it should be mentioned that Capt. HOWE and Lieut. WHITTIER, of Gen. SEDGWICK's Staff, distinguished themselves in the action by rallying the left of Gen. SEDGWICK's division, and on several occasions, by their example, they encouraged the men in discharging their duties faithfully. Gen. SEDGWICK's horse was killed, and he was wounded twice, but remained on the field until he was ordered to the rear with his command.

FRENCH'S DIVISION.

The division under Gen. FRENCH occupied a position to the left of SEDGWICK's, and was fairly engaged by 10½ o'clock. The fighting on the extreme right at this time was confined mostly to artillery, while the tide of infantry fighting swept along toward the left of our line. The left of this division gave way and fell back from the superior force they had to contend against—the rebel hordes making pell mell after them. The left fell back in pretty good order, and upon a walk, under as galling a fire of musketry as is often experienced. This movement was evidently no fault of the men. The rebels advanced, and as they ventured a little to the rear of our line at that point, Col. BURKE (acting Brigadier-General in Gen. RICHARDSON's Division,) changed his front, and poured in several volleys upon their flank, strewing the ground with dead. The balance, hastened somewhat by a cross fire from AYER's battery, fled in utter dismay. The left of FRENCH's Division advanced again, and fought like heroes until ordered to the rear.

RICHARDSON'S DIVISION.

Three Brigades of this Division, commanded by Gen. MEAGHER, Gen. CALDWELL and Col. BURKE' Tenth Pennsylvania, did not cross the creek until Wednesday morning, when Gen. RICHARDSON was ordered to form on the left of FRENCH's Division The Division crossed the river and moved up with alacrity near the line of battle, ready for action. Having filed about through the valleys to avoid letting the enemy know of the movement, the Division laid down under the brow of a hill, just in rear of the line of battle, until wanted. It was now about 9 o'clock.

THE IRISH BRIGADE.

In less than half an hour after taking this position Gen. MEAGHER was ordered to enter the line with the Irish Brigade. They marched up to the brow of the hill, cheering as they went, led by Gen. MEAGHER in person, and were welcomed with cheers by FRENCH's Brigade. The musketry fighting at this point was the severest and most deadly ever witnessed before—so acknowledged by veterans in the service. Men on both sides fell in large numbers every moment, and those who were eye-witnesses of the struggle did not suppose it possible for a single man to escape. The enemy here, at first, were concealed behind a knoll, so that only their heads were exposed. The brigade advanced up the slope with a cheer, when a most deadly fire was poured in by a second line of the enemy concealed in the Sharpsburgh road, which at this place is several feet lower than the surrounding surface, forming a complete rifle-pit, and also from a force partially concealed still further to the rear.

At this time the color-bearer in the right wing advanced several paces to the front, and defiantly waved his flag in the face of the enemy; as if by a miracle, he escaped without serious injury.

The line of the Brigade, in its advance up the hill was broken in the centre temporarily by an obstruction, the right wing having advanced to keep up with the colors and fell back a short distance, when Gen. MEAGHER directed that a rail fence which the enemy a few minutes before had been fighting behind should be torn down. His men, in face of a galling fire, obeyed the order when the whole brigade advanced to the brow the hill, cheering as they went and causing the enemy to fall back to their second line—the Strasburgh road, which is about three feet lower than the surrounding surface. In this road were massed a large force of infantry, and here was the most hotly contested point of the day. Each brigade of this Divison was in turn brought into action at this point and the struggle was truly terrific for more than four hours—the enemy finally, however, were forced from their position. In this work the New-York German Battery, stationed on the hill across the Creek, rendered efficient service by pouring in upon their massed forces a constant stream of 20-pound shells.

Gen. CALDWELL's Brigade was next ordered into action by Gen. RICHARDSON in person. They too advanced in good order, cheering, and were received with cheers by the Irish Brigade. It was at about this time that the left of FRENCH's Division, commanded by Col. BROOKS, of the Tenth Pennsylvania, was directed by Gen. RICHARDSON to wheel to the right, and a murderous flanking fire was poured into the flank of an advancing division of the enemy, causing him to recoil, and fall back in disorder.

This division was actively engaged for nearly five hours, and lost nearly half of the men taken into action.

The fight, which had opened by five o'clock in the morning, gradually swept down to the left of the main line, where it opened at about 9 o'clock. Soon after this time, Gen. BURNSIDE's guns were heard on the extreme left, on the flank of the enemy, he having obtained possession of the stone bridge across the creek on the Strasburgh road. This seemed to surprise the rebels, and a desperate effort was made to change their line of battle so as to meet the flanking movement on their right. To do this their line was extended, and large columns of infantry were thrown off to meet Gen. BURNSIDE, so that by 12 o'clock the rebel line of battle, having been forced back on the right, was crescent shape. Toward night our infantry got to work on the extreme left, the rebel ranks gave way at all points—but in good order, and the day's fighting was brought to a close by a heavy artillery fire—and

[Continued on Eighth Page.]

THE BATTLE OF WEDNESDAY.

Another Detailed Account of the Great Struggle

From the Tribune Extra.

BATTLE-FIELD OF SHARPSBURGH, Wednesday Evening, Sept. 17, 1862.

Fierce and desperate battle between 200,000 men has raged since daylight, yet night closes on an uncertain field. It is the greatest fight since Waterloo—all over the field contested with an obstinacy equal even to Waterloo. If not wholly a victory to-night, I believe it is the prelude to a victory to-morrow. But what can be foretold of the future of a fight in which from 5 in the morning till 7 at night the best troops of the continent have fought without decisive result?

I have no time for speculation—no time even to gather details of the battle—only time to state its broadest features—then mount and spur for New-York.

After the brilliant victory near Middletown, Gen. McCLELLAN pushed forward his army rapidly, and reached Keedysville with three corps on Monday night. That march has already been described. On the day following, the two armies faced each other idly, until night. Artillery was busy at intervals; once in the morning, opening with spirit, and continuing for half an hour with vigor, till the rebel battery, as usual, was silenced.

McCLELLAN was on the hill where BENJAMIN's battery was stationed, and found himself suddenly under a rather heavy fire. It was still uncertain whether the rebels were retreating or reinforcing—their batteries would remain in position in either case, and as they had withdrawn nearly all their troops from view, there was only the doubtful indication of columns of dust to the rear.

On the evening of Tuesday, HOOKER was ordered to cross the Antietam Creek with his corps, and, feeling the left of the enemy, be ready to attack next morning. During the day of apparent inactivity, McCLELLAN had been maturing his plan of battle, of which HOOKER's movement was one development.

The position on either side was peculiar. When RICHARDSON advanced on Monday he found the enemy deployed and displayed in force on a crescent-shaped ridge, the outline of which followed more or less exactly the course of Antietam Creek. Their lines were then forming, and the revelation of force in front of the ground which they really intended to hold, was probably meant to delay our attack until their arrangements to receive it were complete.

During the day they kept their troops exposed and did not move them, even to avoid the artillery fire, which must have been occasionally annoying. Next morning the lines and columns which had darkened cornfields and hill crests, had been withdrawn. Broken and wooded ground behind the sheltering hills concealed the rebel masses. What from our front looked like only a narrow summit fringed with woods, was a broad table-land of forest and ravine, cover for troops everywhere, nowhere easy access for an enemy The smoothly-sloping surface in front and the sweeping crescent of slowly mingling lines was all a delusion. It was all a rebel stronghold beyond.

Under the base of these hills runs the deep stream called Antietam Creek, fordable only at distant points. Three bridges cross it, one on the Hagerstown road, one on the Sharpsburgh pike, one to the left in a deep recess of sleepy falling hills. HOOKER passed the first to reach the ford by which he crossed, and it was held by PLEASANTON with a reserve of cavalry during the battle. The second was close under the rebel centre, and no way important to yesterday's fight. At the third BURNSIDE attacked and finally crossed. Between the first and third lay most of the battle lines. They stretched four miles from right to left.

Unaided, attack in front was impossible. McCLELLAN's forces lay behind low, disconnected ridges, in front of the rebel summits, all, or nearly all unwooded. They gave some cover for artillery, and guns were therefore massed on the centre. The enemy had the Shepherdstown road and the Hagerstown and Williamsport road both open to him in rear for retreat. Along one or the other, if beaten, he must fly. This, among other reasons, determined, perhaps, the plan of battle which McCLELLAN finally resolved on.

The plan was generally as follows: HOOKER was to cross on the right, establish himself on the enemy's left if possible, flanking his position, and to open the fight. SUMNER, FRANKLIN and MANSFIELD were to send their forces also to the right, coöperating with and sustaining HOOKER's attack while advancing also nearer the centre. The heavy work in the centre was left mostly to the batteries. PORTER massing his infantry support in the hollows. On the left BURNSIDE was to carry the bridge already referred to, advancing then by a road which enters the pike at Sharpsburgh, turning at once the rebel flank and destroying his line of retreat. PORTER and SYKES were held in reserve. It is obvious that the complete success of a plan contemplating widely divergent movements of separate corps, must largely depend on accurate timing, that the attack should be simultaneous and not successive.

HOOKER moved Tuesday afternoon at 4 o'clock, crossing the creek at a ford above the bridge and well to the right, without opposition. Fronting southwest his line advanced not quite on the rebel flank, but overlapping and threatening it. Turning off from the road after passing the stream, he sent forth cavalry skirmishers straight into the woods and over the fields beyond. Rebel pickets withdrew slowly before them, firing scattering and harmless shots. Turning again to the left, the cavalry went down on the rebel flank, coming suddenly close to a battery which met them with unexpected grape and canister. It being the motive of cavalry to retire before batteries, this company loyally followed the law of its being, and came swiftly back without pursuit.

Artillery was sent to the front, infantry was rapidly deployed, and skirmishers went out in in front on either flank. The corps moved forward compactly, HOOKER, as usual, reconnoitering in person. They came at last to an open grass-sown field, inclosed on two sides with woods, protected on the right by a hill, and entered through a corn-field in the rear. Skirmishers entering these woods were instantly met by rebel shots, but held their ground, and as soon as supported, advanced, and cleared the timber. Beyond, on the left and in front, volleys of musketry opened heavily, and a battle seemed to have begun a little sooner than it was expected.

Gen. HOOKER formed his lines with precision and without hesitation. RICKETT's Division went into the woods on the left in force. MEADE, with the Pennsylvania Reserves, formed in the centre. DOUBLEDAY was sent out on the right, planting his batteries on the hill and opening at once on a rebel battery that began to enfilade the central line. It was already dark, and the rebel position could only be discovered by the flashes of their guns. They pushed forward boldly on the right, after losing ground on the other flank, but made no attempt to regain their hold on the woods. The lights flashed, and glimmered, and faded, and finally went out in the dark.

HOOKER had found out what he wanted to

The Philadelphia Inquirer.

CIRCULATION OVER 60,000. PHILADELPHIA, SATURDAY, SEPTEMBER 20, 1862. PRICE TWO CENTS.

MAP SHOWING THE FIELDS OF OUR MARYLAND VICTORIES.

Middletown—South Mountain—Birkittsville—Fox Gap—Keedysville—Sharpsburg—and the Country South and West of these Historic Fields into which the beaten Rebels have Retreated.

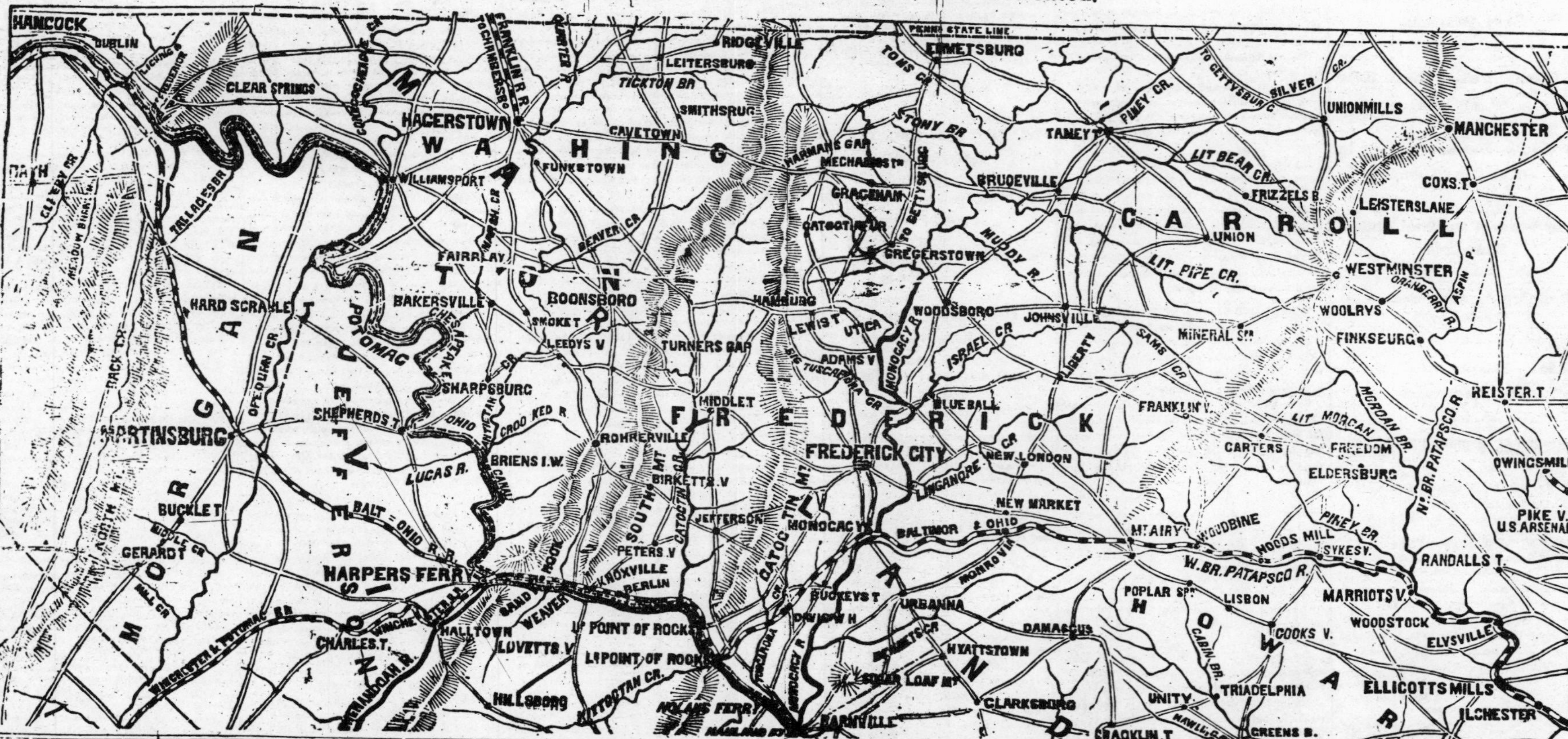

THE WAR FOR THE UNION!

GLORIOUS VICTORY!!

The Particulars of the Bloody and Fearful Battles in Maryland.

Gen. McClellan Clears the Rebels Out of "Maryland, My Maryland."

THE OFFICIAL DESPATCHES OF GENERAL McCLELLAN.

A Large Number of Rebels Still This Side of the Potomac.

RUMORED CAPTURE OF GENERAL LEE!!

An Immense Number of Dead and Wounded Rebels in Our Hands.

THE WAR IN KENTUCKY.

THE SURRENDER OF MUNFORDVILLE CONFIRMED.

LATEST FROM THE FEDERAL CAPITAL.

Daring Cavalry Reconnoissance.

LATER FROM EUROPE.

IMPORTANT AND GLORIOUS NEWS.

The Rebels Driven to Virginia—Maryland and Pennsylvania Safe.

More About the Battle of Wednesday.

BALTIMORE, Sept. 19.—I am satisfied now that all is right with the Army of the Potomac.

I have just had a conversation with a gentleman who left the battle-field at nine o'clock on Wednesday night. He confirms the statement of the correspondent of the Associated Press, published this morning, in every particular.

He says we occupy the position chosen by the enemy at the commencement of the battle, who were driven back a mile and a half at all points, except on the extreme right, which they still held at the close of the day.

My informant was all day within a hundred yards of Gen. McClellan, and says that the result of the day was regarded by him and his staff as a glorious victory, though not final. There was no faltering at any point of the line, and the whole army was exultant at the result of the day's fight.

General McClellan was in high spirits. His opinion, and that of those around him, was that the final result would depend on who got up reinforcements first. He says nothing was heard on the field of the capture of Longstreet or the killing of Hill, and there is no truth in either rumor.

Twenty thousand more reinforcements were expected to reach the field yesterday, from Harrisburg. He thinks the enemy's loss is fully equal to our own.

The gentleman from whom this information is derived (who is one of our most intelligent citizens) expresses the opinion that whilst the battle on Wednesday was not a decisive one, it was a contest in which all the advantages were with McClellan, who occupied the field of battle at the close of the day.

The Operations of Thursday.

HEAD-QUARTERS OF THE ARMY OF THE POTOMAC, Friday morning, Sept. 19.—Yesterday was occupied in burying the dead and caring for the wounded. The Rebels sent in a flag of truce in the morning asking permission to bury their own, which was granted. At first the orders were very stringent against holding intercourse with the Rebels, but during the afternoon they were relaxed, and the troops on both sides freely intermingled.

The following is an additional list of officers killed and wounded:—

General Rodman, commanding a brigade in Burnside's Corps, was wounded.

Colonel Strar, 4th Rhode Island, wounded in hip.
Lieut.-Colonel Appleman, 8th Connecticut, wounded.
Captain Griswold, 11th Connecticut, killed.
Lieut. Arenberg, of Shaken's Ohio Battery, lost a leg.
Major Gile, 88th Pennsylvania, severely wounded.
Col. Barlow, 61st New York, wounded.
Col. Goodrich, 60th New York, killed.
Col. Croasdale, 128th Pennsylvania, killed.
Col. Reall, 10th, wounded.
Major Dwight, 2d Massachusetts, wounded.

At daylight this morning it was found that the enemy had changed their position. Whether their whole force has crossed the river, or taken up a new position nearer the river, is not at present known. Had they remained, a general engagement would have been had this morning.

Reports from Harrisburg.

HARRISBURG, Sept. 19.—Evening.—Information which has just been received here from the battle-field, says that our victory is complete, and that General Pleasanton is in hot pursuit of the enemy, and driving them across the Potomac.

The whole Federal army is in good condition, and the enemy has been badly punished.

General Sigel is said to be in force on the opposite side of the Potomac, and no doubt will be able to annihilate the whole Rebel army.

Official Despatches from Gen. McClellan.

HEAD-QUARTERS ARMY OF THE POTOMAC, September 19, 1862, 8 o'clock A. M.—To Major-General Halleck, General-in-Chief.—But little occurred yesterday except skirmishing last night.

The enemy abandoned his position, leaving his dead and wounded on the field. We are again in pursuit.

I do not yet know whether he is falling back to an interior position, or crossing the river. We may safely claim a victory.

GEORGE B. McCLELLAN,
Major-General.

HEAD-QUARTERS ARMY OF THE POTOMAC, Sept. 19, 10 A. M.—To Henry W. Halleck, General-in-Chief.—Pleasanton is driving the enemy across the river.

Our victory is complete.
The enemy is driven back into Virginia.
Maryland and Pennsylvania are safe.

GEORGE B. McCLELLAN,
Major-General.

The Pennsylvania Militia Moving into Maryland.

HARRISBURG, Sept. 19.—A gentleman who arrived in this city from Chambersburg this evening, says that all the troops that were stationed there have been sent to Hagerstown and Boonsboro'. A company from Philadelphia refused to go over the line, whereupon General Reynolds told them they might go home and be ——, and disgrace forever would rest on their shoulders. After receiving this reprimand they finally went over.

Governor Curtin is still at Hagerstown.

A feeling of perfect security is now felt here, in official circles, regarding the defeat of Stonewall Jackson's plans for a raid into Pennsylvania.

Quite a number of wounded have arrived here and at other points on the Cumberland Valley Railroad.

The news of General McClellan's victory was received here with great rejoicing.

Many of the troops here are urgent to go forward, that they may yet assist in the rout of the enemy, and the great work of crushing the Rebellion.

The body of Captain George A. Brooks, of the Forty-sixth Pennsylvania Regiment, arrived here to-day. His funeral will take place this evening, at six o'clock.

The remains of Col. Samuel Croasdale and Captain W. H. Andrews, both of the One-hundred-and-twenty-eighth Pennsylvania Regiment, were also brought here to-day. The remains of Col. Croasdale will be sent to Doylestown, and those of Captain Andrews to Reading. The bodies are in charge of John W. Brown.

Travel to Chambersburg and Hagerstown was resumed to-day, and telegraphic communication is now open to Boonsboro'.

The Wounded in the Late Battles.

The following proclamation was issued yesterday, at Hagerstown, Md.:—

"PROCLAMATION.—The citizens are requested to suspend their ordinary business, and give aid in bringing in the wounded from the battle-field, and providing for them.

"Information as to what is wanted, and passes, will be furnished at this office.

"If this request be complied with, it may prevent the necessity of a peremptory order on the subject.

"E. SPENCER MILLER, Provost Marshal.
"WALTER McMICHAEL, Aid.

"Hagerstown, September 18, 1862."

LATEST FROM THE BATTLE-FIELD.

Skirmishing Yesterday—Fifty Thousand Rebels Still This Side of the Potomac—Rumored Capture of General Lee—Twenty Thousand Dead and Wounded Rebels Left in Our Hands.

Special Despatch to the Inquirer.

BALTIMORE, Sept. 19.—A large number of dead and wounded men arrived here to-night. There were two car loads of dead.

Lieutenant Duffy, who brings the body of his brother, Captain Duffy, Sixty-ninth New York, left the battle-field last night. He confirms all the previous statements of McClellan's brilliant success.

There was considerable skirmishing yesterday. The general impression is that fifty thousand Rebels are still on this side of the Potomac river, and must yet be captured. There is a rumor here to-night that the Rebel General Lee has been captured.

It is believed that at least twenty thousand dead and wounded Rebels have been left in our hands; many are still unburied. It is thought to be impossible for the Rebels to retreat through Virginia. The dead body of General Mansfield is here being embalmed; many others are coming in for the same purpose.

COMMENTS ON THE SHAMEFUL AFFAIR AT WILLIAMSBURG.

Correspondence of the Inquirer.

WILLIAMSBURG, Va., September 15, 1862.

The policy at present pursued by the Rebels of paroling all the prisoners they take holds out a strong inducement to our officers to give themselves up as prisoners of war at the first opportunity. This was clearly demonstrated on the 9th instant, at the time an attack was made on the Fifth Pennsylvania Cavalry at this place. If a previous arrangement was not made, it seemed very singular how it could have happened in the manner it did. Our pickets, which were at least four miles distant, were driven in, or taken, at three o'clock in the morning. This was known to certain of our officers; yet the camp was allowed to be taken by surprise, after six o'clock, without allowing the men the least chance for preparation. Then came a confused bustle, with conflicting orders. One officer, it is well known, ordered a retreat, for which he is now under arrest.

Some were inclined to fight, and did so to the number of perhaps one squadron; but the majority of the officers who were taken gave themselves up *without any resistance*; on the contrary, they had every chance either to make a stand or get away, if necessary. This can be proven by any number of witnesses. Some of the officers who at first ran, afterward threw down their arms, rode back and gave themselves up, swearing that they would go with the others to see Richmond. It would not be so bad if these same officers had not been heard to swear at the men, calling them *cowards*, when the appellation applied more properly to themselves. This will be better understood when it is known that after driving our men for some distance, while the confusion lasted, they were afterwards handsomely repulsed by the bravery of less than one company. I hope, in justice to the men of the regiment, that this will be inserted, that the blame may rest where it properly belongs, and also that other investigations may be made, which, I am persuaded, will show *something rotten in Denmark.*

IMPORTANT FROM KENTUCKY.

Surrender of Munfordsville—The Place Invested by Bragg with Thirty Thousand Men—Our Force Scarcely Five Thousand.

INDIANAPOLIS, Ind., Sept., 19.—Adjutant Stanton, of the Seventeenth Indiana Regiment, who escaped from Munfordsville immediately after the surrender of that place to the Rebels, has reached this city.

He reports that the garrison there, numbering from four to five thousand men, comprising the Seventeenth, the Fiftieth, the Sixtieth, the Sixty-seventh, the Sixty-eighth, and the Sixty-ninth Indiana Regiments, and one company of cavalry and ten pieces of artillery, have surrendered.

The surrender was made on Wednesday morning, our forces being completely surrounded by General Bragg's forces estimated at thirty thousand men.

Our loss in killed and wounded was fifty

The Rebels acknowledge a loss of seven hundred on Sunday.

LATE NEWS FROM WASHINGTON.

Daring Cavalry Reconnoissance—Eighty Miles in Twenty Hours.

THREE OF GENERAL EWELL'S STAFF CAPTURED.

Special Despatch to the Inquirer.

One of the most daring and successful reconnoissances of the present war was made yesterday by a force of cavalry from General Heintzelman's head-quarters. They went within three miles of Thoroughfare Gap, accomplishing the distance of eighty miles in twenty hours. Near the Gap they came upon a Rebel force acting as a body-guard to the Rebel General Ewell, who was wounded, and being conveyed toward Richmond in an ambulance. Three of his staff were captured, besides a number of prisoners of lesser note, wagons, &c. Our men returned safely, bringing along with them the prisoners.

George Francis Train.

George Francis Train made one of his characteristic speeches here to-night, in response to a crowd.

Miscellaneous News.

The Commissioner of Internal Revenue invariably returns orders and money sent to him for currency stamps, such stamps not being issued from his bureau. They are to be procured from the United States Treasurer, but no one need send to him at present, as he is now engaged in supplying the Government agents only.

Acting Master Edward Hooker has been promoted to Acting Volunteer Lieutenant, for gallant conduct during the attack on Washington, N. C., and has been ordered to to the command of the steamer *Victoria.*

George W. Marvin and James Pendger have been appointed Acting Assistant Surgeons.

The following officers have been ordered to the steam-sloop-of-war *Mohican*:—

Captain J. B. Marchand, Lieutenant R. K. Duer, Acting Master R. B. Ely; Boatswain, G. C. Abbott; Gunner, Wm Arnold.

Adjutant-General Thomas left Washington to-day, for Annapolis, on business connected with the large number of paroled prisoners now at that station. There is no doubt that he will at once take the initiative measures for their exchange as he is the Commissioner of the United States for that purpose, and has heretofore so satisfactorily performed similar service.

Brigadier-General Max Weber has been ordered to report for duty to Major-General Dix, at Fortress Monroe, and Brigadier-General Gilbert, now on duty with the Army of Kentucky, to General Wright, at Cincinnati.

Colonel A. M. Wood, of the Brooklyn Fourteenth Regiment, to-day received his commission as Collector of Inland Revenue for the Second District of New York.

When the President made Colonels Corcoran and Wilcox Brigadier-Generals a similar appointment was tendered to Colonel Wood, but it was declined on account of his impaired health.

The Collectorship has been awarded to him by the President as an equivalent. He has never fully recovered from the wound he received at Bull Run, and his physicians some time ago pronounced it unwise for him to again take the field.

Mr. George Francis Train will leave this city for Philadelphia to-morrow. He dined with Secretary Seward, yesterday, and had an interview with the President, Secretaries Stanton and Welles and Gen. Banks to-day.

FIRST NEW JERSEY BRIGADE.

Correspondence of the Inquirer.

BATTLE-FIELD, CRAMPTON'S GAP, Sept. 15, 1862.

We marched from our camp yesterday morning at five o'clock. It was a beautiful Sabbath morning, and little did we think when we started that, before the sun set, we should gain a glorious victory, and avenge our fallen comrades of Gaines' Mill and Manassas. As we passed through the little town of Jefferson, cannonading could be heard, and we formed in line of battle. Some troops were engaged at a mountain pass to our right. We, however, soon marched on some four miles further to the left, and, between four and five o'clock, formed in four lines—the Third and Fourth Regiments in the rear.

The first commenced the fight with the Rebels, who were posted in the mountain with artillery. Soon the second came up, and so on, until all were engaged, and we were ordered to charge. The line firing ceased, and at them we went with a will, over the fence, double quick. We drove them from their position behind a stone wall, at the foot of the mountain, and occupied it ourselves. Never did men take more deliberate aim. Every one seemed determined to kill his man. Now for another charge over into the woods, and after them we go, and again they run as we advance; but now we see a large body advancing beyond our lines to the right. We close in on their rear, catch them in their own trap, and cut them all to pieces.

We are now at the top of the mountain and the victory is ours. There have been two or three stands of colors captured. We took the mountain in about one hour and a half; the sun was just setting in the west as the fighting ceased. It was a glorious sight to see the Rebels run; and we all feel joyous to think how well we have paid them off for Manassas.

This morning, while writing this, a Rebel flag and quite a number of prisoners are passing. Their loss has been very severe. Our brigade, I think, has about fifty killed and one hundred wounded. Our officers did nobly. Col. Torbert, now in command of the brigade, acted bravely his part, and is richly deserving a commission of General. Col. Brown, of the Third, led us on as only a brave man could; ever at his post, none could falter where he was. Adjutant Fairly could be seen first at one end of the line and then at the other, giving his orders. He captured a color, and once or twice, as balls passed close before him, he rode on smiling as though it were a good joke.

Evening.—As I close the dead are nearly all buried, and the wounded cared for. The total loss in the brigade is one hundred and eighty-one.

The Publication of Army Movements Prohibited.

HEAD-QUARTERS OF THE ARMY, WASHINGTON, Sept. 19, 1862.—Major-General T. G. Foster, commanding the Department of North Carolina, has called attention to an article in the New York *Evening Post*, of September 6th, in which are published the numbers and positions of his troops. He remarks that New York papers always reach the enemy in a few days after publication, and that such information from our friends is more injurious than that gained by the Rebel spies. The newspaper press is earnestly requested to make no publication in regard to the numbers or movements of our troops. No information could be more desirable to the enemy than this. Such publications have done immense injury to our cause.

H. W. HALLECK, General-in-Chief.

From California.

SAN FRANCISCO, Sept. 10th.—Sailed, barque *Victoria*, for Liverpool, carrying 15,000 sacks of wheat. Business is still mostly confined to the jobbing trade. Butter has declined to 28c. ℔ lb.; candles are dull; crushed sugar quiet; anthracite coal $18, and Cumberland $21 ℔ ton.

J. L. Taggart & Co., prominent jobbing house of this city, failed to-day for about $80,000. The losses are pretty generally distributed among San Francisco merchants.

The news of the recent great Union victory produced the most unbounded joy here.

Subscriptions for the relief of our wounded soldiers has been opened. The subscription of our city alone amounts to about one hundred thousand dollars, and will probably reach a quarter of a million in a week.

A new line of stages has commenced running between San Barradino and the recently-discovered Colorado mines, to accommodate the increasing emigration in that direction.

Card of Cassius M. Clay.

WASHINGTON, Sept. 19.—Hon. Cassius M. Clay publishes a card to-day, denying that he has ever said a word to the President about Gov. Morton, or in favor of making him the commander of the Northwestern grand division of troops. He has never proposed any other way of carrying on the war than by the constituted authorities, nor desired the overthrow of the President, or the establishment of the dictatorship of Fremont, or any other man. He calls upon the country to trust the President as he himself does, and pronounces the assertions concerning him calumnious.

Funeral of the Late Col. Miles.

BALTIMORE, Sept. 19.—The body of Col. Miles, who was killed at Harper's Ferry, was conveyed this morning, with a military escort, to Sweet Air, Baltimore Co., his late residence, where the funeral services will take place.

THE CONTEST IN MARYLAND.

GREAT BATTLE OF WEDNESDAY.

Graphic and Interesting Particulars.

TERRIBLE ENCOUNTERS.

DESPERATION OF THE REBELS.

HEROIC DETERMINATION OF OUR TROOPS

Fighting Joe Hooker Glorious Again.

GALLANTRY OF OFFICERS AND MEN.

The Union Army Victorious in Each Day's Fight.

ACCOUNTS OF OUR LOSSES.

The *Tribune* has the following despatch, dated:—

BATTLE-FIELD OF SHARPSBURG, Wednesday evening Sept. 17, 1862.—Fierce and desperate battle between 200,000 men has raged since daylight, yet night closes on an uncertain field. It is the greatest fight since Waterloo; all over the field contested with an obstinacy equal even to Waterloo. If not wholly a victory to-night, I believe it is the prelude to a victory to-morrow. But what can be foretold of the future of a fight in which from five in the morning till seven at night the best troops of the continent have fought without decisive result?

I have no time for speculation; no time even to gather details of the battle, only time to state its broadest features, then mount and spur for New York.

After the brilliant victory near Middletown, General McClellan pushed forward his army rapidly, and reached Keedysville with three corps on Monday night. That march has already been described. On the day following the two armies faced each other idly, until night. Artillery was busy at intervals, once in the morning opening with spirit, and continuing for half an hour with vigor, till the Rebel battery, as usual, was silenced.

McClellan was on the hill where Benjamin's battery was stationed, and found himself suddenly under a rather heavy fire. It was still uncertain whether the Rebels were retreating or reinforcing; their batteries would remain in position in either case, and as they had withdrawn nearly all their troops from view there was only the doubtful indication of columns of dust to the rear.

On the evening of Tuesday Hooker was ordered to cross the Antietam creek with his corps, and, feeling the left of the enemy, to be ready to attack next morning. During the day of apparent inactivity McClellan had been maturing his plan of battle, of which Hooker's movement was one development.

The position on either side was peculiar. When Richardson advanced on Monday he found the enemy deployed and displayed in force on a crescent-shaped ridge, the outline of which followed, more or less exactly, the course of Antietam creek. Their lines were then forming, and the revelation of force in front of the ground which they really intended to hold was probably meant to delay our attack until their arrangements to receive it were complete.

During that day they kept their troops exposed, and did not move them to avoid the artillery fire, which must have been occasionally annoying. Next morning the lines and columns which had darkened cornfields and hill crests had been withdrawn. Broken and wooded ground behind the sheltering hills concealed the Rebel masses. What from our front looked like only a narrow summit fringed with woods, was a broad table-land of forest and ravine, cover for troops everywhere, nowhere easy access for an enemy. The smoothly-sloping surface in front and the sweeping crescent of slowly mingling lines was all a delusion. It was all a Rebel stronghold beyond.

Under the base of these hills runs the deep stream called Antietam Creek, fordable only at distant points. Three bridges cross it—one on the Hagerstown road, one on the Sharpsburg pike, and one to the left, in a deep recess of sleepy falling hills. Hooker passed the first to reach the ford by which he crossed, and it was held by Pleasanton with a reserve of cavalry during the battle. The second was close under the Rebel centre, and no way important to yesterday's fight. At the third, Burnside attacked and finally crossed. Between the first and third lay the battle lines. They stretched four miles from right to left.

Unaided attack in front was impossible. McClellan's forces lay behind low, disconnected ridges, in front of the Rebel summits, all or nearly all unwooded. They gave some cover for artillery, and guns were, therefore, massed on the centre. The enemy had the Shepherdstown road and the Hagerstown and Williamsport road both open

(Continued on the Second Page.)

The Daily Picayune.

VOLUME XXVI. NEW ORLEANS TUESDAY MORNING, SEPTEMBER 30, 1862. NUMBER 212.

The Daily Picayune.

FROM OUR EVENING EDITION OF YESTERDAY.

☞ Our thanks are tendered to Capt. Fletcher, of the steamship Potomac, for files of Northern papers to the 18th inst.

☞ Our New York correspondent, writing on the evening of the 18th, says: "Gold to-day is 16⅞ premium. The Roanoke is up for New Orleans on the 27th."

☞ By the arrival of the steamship Potomac we have Northern and Western papers containing a mass of interesting intelligence, which we will lay before our readers as early as possible. This evening we give the latest war news from Maryland, Virginia and Kentucky, also the latest news from Europe, &c., &c.

☞ We have received from the enterprising music publisher, L. Grunewald 26 Chartres street, the following: "Rosey Thorn, Reverie," written and composed by Theodore Von LaHache, and dedicated to M'me St. Leon Dupeire; "Danse Andalouse, caprice de concert," by J. Ascher.

ONE WEEK LATER FROM NEW YORK—*Arrival of the Potomac.*—The United States mail steamship Potomac, Capt. Fletcher, from New York on the 18th inst., arrived here yesterday, with mails, merchandise, dates to the day of sailing inclusive, and the following passengers:

Mrs. J. K. Hanly, Antoine Segur, Mrs. George T. Doughty, Mrs. Robert Scott, Miss Doyle, Mr. Charles Couteux, A. Thize, M'me Chauveau, L. A. Howes, Edward Nester, Allen Vening, Miss Smith, John Geddes, Mrs. J. Lewis, Miss Sallie Scott, John S. Gouche, T. Dromell, H. J. McDonald and wife, Miss Moret, John Burgess, John McAlery, M. J. McGovern, Julian Grassin, Mrs. J. Lewis, boy and infant, Miss Gouche, J. C. Denmar, T. L. McConkey, Sister Mary Margaret, Edward Schaffnit, D. D. Smith.

September 25, latitude 24 46 N., longitude 83 47 W., spoke bark Damon, sixteen days from Boston, bound for New Orleans—all well.

REPORTED INVESTMENT OF CHARLESTON—*Fort Sumter Seriously Damaged.*—The New York Express, of the evening of the 18th, says:

We have a report by way of Boston, that Charleston has been invested by our gunboats, and that "Fort Sumter has already received a preliminary dose of shot and shell, which resulted in serious damage." This information is contained in a letter written on board the United States steamer Bibb.

☞ Accounts from Labrador to the 12th inst. represent that the cod fishery was wretched on the whole coast, no herrings, and cod oil was scarce at £43 per ton.

THE CITY.

DANGEROUS TALK.—C. L. Marshall was arrested yesterday in the Fourth District on a charge of using seditious language against the United States, and of applying most opprobrious epithets to Gen. Butler.

THREAT TO KILL.—Rinehart Kinsley was yesterday arrested on Eighth street on a charge of disturbing the peace and threatening to kill a lady without rhyme or reason.

HURRAHING.—Geo. A. Heapal was arrested last night on Washington street, on a charge of hurrahing for Jeff. Davis.

PREPARING.—Sydney Armsby and James Whiteside were arrested last night at Gretna on a charge of having prepared, and indeed attempted to run the blockade.

SEDITION.—M. Myers was arrested yesterday on Canal street, on a charge of talking seditiously and resisting an officer in the discharge of his duty.

TRIED TO DROWN HERSELF.—Early yesterday morning a woman, apparently insane, was rescued from the river into which she had thrown herself, with a view to the termination of all her earthly sorrows. She said her name was Mary Durkey, but the story she told concerning herself was extremely confused and unsatisfactory. She was handed over to the police and conveyed to the First District lockup.

DRAWING A KNIFE.—Partalo Carrico was last evening arrested on a charge of having drawn a knife on J. McElroy, with intent to kill him.

DRAWING A PISTOL.—Bob Lyttle was arrested on Dryades street. He is charged with having entered the premises of Mary Armstrong, f. w. c., and drawn a pistol on her, with intent to shoot her.

TREASON.—Archy Coleman, a colored man, was last night arrested on Triton Walk for talking treason.

ACCESSORIES.—Mary Fitzpatrick and Margaret Fitzpatrick were arrested by Officer Foley, at the corner of Felicity and Camp streets, on a charge of being accessory to the crimes of forgery and embezzlement.

DRAWING WEAPONS.—Henry Gallagher, of the 30th Massachusetts Regiment, was arrested on a charge of entering an officer's residence and drawing a bayonet and a pistol on said officer and his wife.

STEALING A CHECK.—Thomas Sullivan is under arrest on a charge of having stolen a check for $111 30-100, which was found in his possession.

SWORD.—Officer Burkhard reports having found the sword of a sword cane at the corner of Felicity and St. Charles streets, and gives it as his opinion that said sword is the property of Ben. Harrison.

UNRULY.—James Boyle was arrested last night at the corner of Conti and Robinson street on a charge of disturbing the peace and threatening to kill James Mentha.

TAKEN TO THE HOSPITAL.—On Saturday night the First District police found Jas. Anderson, a sailor belonging to the bark Pathfinder, on Market street. He had fallen among thieves, and was terribly bruised and beaten. Furthermore, he was robbed, as he said, of $20. He was taken to the Charity Hospital. A man named Sam Caldwell was also sent to the Hospital in such a condition as to be wholly unable to give any account of himself.

STABBING.—A boy named Rudolph Steiffe was arrested in the Second District on a charge of having seriously stabbed another boy, younger than himself, named Anthony Powers. Young Powers was conveyed to the residence of his parents, on Laharpe street. It is said that Powers and another boy were fighting, when Steiffe went up behind Powers and stabbed him in his left side.

THRONGED.—The sidewalks are this morning thronged by people wending their way to the office of the Provost Marshal on business connected with Order No. 76. Some go to take the oath, some to take out their papers as aliens, and some merely to accompany their friends. Papers have also been handed to the police for distribution among householders in accordance with the proclamation of the Provost Marshal General.

DETAILS OF A WEEK LATER

NEWS FROM THE SEAT OF WAR

THE BATTLES IN MARYLAND.

THE LATEST.

The New York Evening Express, of the 18th inst., (Thursday,) says:

The latest news from the army (via Washington and Harrisburg) comes down to 5 o'clock Wednesday, P. M. The dispatches are meagre as regards detail, but state in general terms that the most terrific battle that ever was fought on this continent had been going on all day near Sharpsburg, the contests being entirely with artillery, and that the enemy has been driven back two miles. The slaughter had been prodigious. Longstreet is reported wounded and a prisoner. Hooker is wounded in the foot. Mansfield is reported killed. A bridge over a creek had been destroyed by our forces, so as to isolate one of the enemy's wings in an attack upon which our troops were massing. No official dispatch as yet confirms the report that Harper's Ferry had been reoccupied by our troops, or abandoned by the enemy, and it is doubtless untrue, notwithstanding paroled prisoners say they saw the enemy skedaddling much faster than they came in. If they did so, it was with the design of moving rapidly up to Shepardstown to reinforce the enemy at Sharpsburg, taking with them, doubtless, the 50 pieces of artillery which they are said to have captured.

At Washington, on Wednesday night, very little was probably known in regard to the battles in Maryland, except the fact that the contest is still going on. The Government has preserved silence in regard to whatever information it possesses, but we learn from some official sources that the tenor of the advices is favorable to the Union cause. Heavy firing had been heard in the direction of Dranesville, which leads to the belief that one of our columns may have encountered a foe in that neighborhood.

The same paper publishes the following telegraphic dispatches:

HARRISBURG, Pa., Sept. 17.—The battle fought yesterday between Sharpsburg and Middletown closed without a definite result.

No firing has been heard from Hagerstown since 4 o'clock yesterday (Tuesday.)

PHILADELPHIA, Sept. 17.—A dispatch from Harrisburg to Gov. Curtin states that the battle at Sharpsburg recommenced early this morning and raged with the greatest fury up to 4.45 A. M.

Our latest advices from Harrisburg say that the State troops are pushing forward to the border.

The New York Commercial Advertiser of the same date has the following:

WASHINGTON, Sept. 17.—It is the general impression here to-day that the enemy has succeeded in recrossing the Potomac, having met with success in the capture of Harper's Ferry, thus opening to them a route for retreat which it was believed would remain in our possession. The plan of the retreat was found to be carried out in strict accordance with the orders of Gen. Lee, which fell into our possession at Frederick.

The fall of Harper's Ferry was a grave error; for it was well understood that Gen. Miles was to have been reinforced last Saturday by a column from our left. Why this was not is not yet explained.

The capture of Harper's Ferry only deprives us for some time of six thousand men paroled for exchange, for the rebels have already evacuated the place. It is asserted that it was their intention to take and hold Harper's Ferry, and make it a base of supplies preparatory to an advance into Pennsylvania by way of Williamsport and the Cumberland valley; but the rapid advance of our army, as well as the known disposition of our forces, caused an immediate change of programme. It is therefore probable that there may be a rush of the enemy down the Virginia side of the fortifications in front of Washington, with a view, perhaps, if the way be clear, of making an attack on this city. The enemy will find it out before you will, and therefore there can be no harm in saying that the way is not clear.

But if the rebels do not take that step, the probabilities are that they will go to Winchester or to Manassas, for the purpose of establishing communications for supplies which they greatly need. Manassas they will not be able to hold, and Winchester will doubtless be their present headquarters, so they can use the valley of Virginia and its harvest crops. An opposite opinion prevails to some extent, and that is, that with the rebel army massed from Harper's Ferry to Martinsburg, the latter will yet be held, and an offensive movement made towards Pennsylvania, though the destitute condition of their army—now well known true—may prevent this. It is sincerely hoped that no ammunition was captured by the enemy at Harper's Ferry.

The campaign promises continued activity. With the executive abilities of Gens. Halleck and Banks here, and that of Gen. McClellan in the field, success upon success should follow rapidly. In addition to our large army of veterans more than a hundred thousand of the new volunteers are now in the field.

The Evening Express, of the same date, (18th,) has the following:

There is an enormous amount of rubbish news this morning, especially from Pennsylvania, and it is so buried up in the rubbish, that the reader will thank us for extracting the real kernel of fact. It appears then—

1. That on Wednesday Gen. McClellan drove back the enemy two miles, and that the reports of his progress and successes were very satisfactory.

2. That Harper's Ferry was ingloriously surrendered after a loss of but about 100 men killed—when McClellan was gloriously fighting for its rescue—and that the report is not reliable, that Gen. Burnside's corps had reoccupied it after the evacuation by the enemy. Harper's Ferry now would seem to be a pivot of the enemy's operations.

There are exaggerated reports of 10,000 of the enemy killed and wounded, and of 15,000 prisoners, but all these reports must be taken with "a great many grains of salt."

Gen. McClellan would seem to be going along successfully—but in the midst of blood and carnage, the details of which must be frightful, when they come along.

Our substantial news just now is no later than 5 P. M. Wednesday evening, when, it is probable, the battle was near closing for the day.

P. S.—The extras in the city to-day, announcing the retaking of Harper's Ferry give only Tuesday's news. Wednesday's news contradicts the report.

Capt. Fletcher, of the Potomac, which left New York on the evening of the 18th, says, in a private note:

In addition to the news contained in the papers accompanying this, the bulletins in New York, at 4 P. M., on the 18th, announced that Gen. Longstreet and his entire division, consisting of 15,000 men and 20 pieces artillery had been captured by the Union forces.

The Express, of the 18th, gives the following, under the head of "Reports via Hagerstown, Md., under date of the 17th:"

HAGERSTOWN, Sept. 17.—A battle has been raging furiously for the past two days on the Antietam Creek, a tortuous stream, having its source in the mountains and running down to the Potomac midway between Sohertsville and Sharpsburg.

The enemy, cut off from the iron bridge at Harper's Ferry by the advance of Gen. Franklin's corps, and fearing to cross the Potomac at any of the fords, with Gen. McClellan pushing down hard upon them, took this creek for a line of defence.

During yesterday the battle raged with great spirit, and the firing on either side was very heavy until towards sundown, when the enemy were flanked by Hooker and Porter, and were being severely punished. Their firing became desultory, and it was evident their ammunition was giving out.

This morning the battle was renewed by the rebels with redoubled vigor; they acted as if they had been reinforced and furnished with fresh ammunition.

The battle lasted until 4 o'clock this afternoon, when the enemy retreated, leaving Gen. Longstreet and the remnant of his division in our hands as prisoners of war.

Our victory is sure, but it has cost us many officers and men. Major Gen. Hooker was wounded in the foot by a Minié ball while leading a second brilliant bayonet charge today, and Gen. Mansfield is either killed or taken prisoner. He fought heroically during the entire affair to the time he was missed.

The loss of the enemy was much greater than ours. Longstreet's division of the ten brigades cannot muster seven thousand men.

The entire army will be captured or killed. There is no chance left for them to cross the Potomac, as the river is rising, and our troops pushing them continually, and sending prisoners to the rear by scores.

Stonewall Jackson is now in command in Maryland. Six batteries of artillery, belonging to Longstreet's division, were captured yesterday and to-day, and it is said we have taken nearly fifteen thousand prisoners since Sunday.

Jackson's army, with Lee and other distinguished wounded officers, will be forced to surrender in a day or two at the farthest.

Our immense army is all in motion, and our Generals are certain of ultimate and decisive success.

Stores for the army are coming by way of Harrisburg and Baltimore.

Three Days Battles.

The correspondent of the Philadelphia Inquirer, under date of the 17th, gives details of the battles of Sunday, 14th, Monday, 15th, and Tuesday, 16th, from which we select the most important particulars:

The battle of South Mountain, or, as it is called by some, the battle of Blue Ridge, commenced on Sunday morning, at 8 o'clock, in the valley at the foot of South Mountain, about four miles West of Middletown. The fight began by an artillery duel between one of our batteries and a few rebel guns planted on an eminence a short distance from the Mountain House.

Soon after the first firing another rebel battery commenced to shell our forces from an open field near the western turnpike, running from Middletown to Sharpsburg. At this point the contest became exceedingly warm, and Gen. Cox's brigade was ordered to advance. Immediately upon the approach of our men the rebel guns were withdrawn and planted a short distance up the mountain.

Here the fighting became general. Nearly the whole of Gen. Burnside's corps were ordered into line of battle, and the 11th, 15th, 23d, 38th, 30th and 31st Ohio regiments were sent forward to engage the rebels, covered by woods on South Mountain. Probably during the war no more desperate fighting has been done than in this locality, between the hours of nine and eleven.

Rebel prisoners informed me that they were positively assured by their officers that the Union forces could never ascend the mountain without being cut to pieces, and that it was their intention to hold the position until they were ordered elsewhere.

Shortly before 12 o'clock, the Ohio regiments succeeded in reaching the summit of the mountain, when they were fired upon by rebel batteries planted upon four prominent eminences, which completely covered a large cleared field, over which our troops must pass before they could again use their muskets on the enemy.

What made it still worse was the galling fire poured in upon them from three rebel regiments posted behind a stone wall, about three hundred yards distant, under cover of the woods. For a long time it seemed impossible for our men to advance without being exterminated.

Just at this juncture, the 45th and 100th Pennsylvania regiments came marching up the mountain, and were received by the Ohio men with cheers. The reinforcement by our gallant Pennsylvania troops turned the tide of battle, and before the afternoon had far advanced the rebels were in full retreat, leaving a large number of prisoners in our hands and their killed and wounded on the field.

Where several of the charges were made, the rebels fairly lay in heaps. I counted in one lane running up from Braddock's road, within a distance of ten rods, forty dead rebels, and this is but a fair sample of the desperation with which they fought.

In the fights to the left and right of the turnpike, about 700 rebel prisoners were taken.

But I have no time to comment further on the fight. Suffice it to say that night closed with our victorious army encamped on the field of battle.

I think I may safely estimate our losses at 200 killed and about 1000 wounded. Our dead were buried on the battle field, and our wounded were taken to Middletown and Frederick, where accommodations were found for them in the different churches.

Of the rebel losses nothing definite is known, but judging from the appearance of the battle-field their killed could not have numbered less than 1000, and their wounded probably 3000. I was informed by rebel officers that their loss in killed and wounded in this battle far exceeded any engagement in Virginia, except that at Malvern Hill.

Early on Monday morning our pursuit of the enemy was renewed. Several skirmishes occurred on that day, but no fighting of a serious character took place up to the time of reaching the heights, this side of Pleasant Valley, about four miles distant from Sharpsburg. As the rebels were apparently making a stand with a view to bring on a general engagement, most of the day, Tuesday, was occupied in forming our army in line of battle.

The following was the position of our forces at 3 o'clock in the afternoon, (Tuesday,) when the first firing commenced: To the right of Braddock's Road, and immediately west of Antietam Creek, was Sumner's corps, Gen. McClellan's headquarters, and a line of batteries.

To the left of the road, west of the creek, were Gen. Sykes's division of regulars, supported by batteries, and Gen. Burnside's corps. To the right of the road, and south of the creek, were Gen. Banks's corps and Max Weber's brigade.

Hence the left, where the first advance was made, consisted of Sykes's division of regulars, supported by Burnside, the centre Gen. McClellan supported by batteries, and the right Gen. Banks's corps supported by Max Weber's brigade.

I have mentioned the left of the army first, as it was on the left that all the fighting was done on Tuesday.

As I before mentioned, the first firing commenced at three o'clock in the afternoon. They opened upon us at that hour from a hill southwest of the main body of the army, and about one mile from the position occupied by Sykes's division.

Sykes's batteries at once replied, and after scarcely more than a duel of one hour's duration, the rebel batteries were silenced, and nothing further was done during the day, except the shelling of the woods in the direction of the rebels, about dark.

Our loss on this occasion was 4 killed and 7 wounded. For the second time during the war the rebels fired railroad iron at us. One of the pieces fell among a train of wagons, and killed three mules; but did no other damage.

Judging from the fact that the rebel batteries were so soon silenced, it is believed that our guns must have done considerable execution. Soon after the first firing had ceased the rebel army commenced retreating, and while it was yet daylight retired about two miles from their position occupied in the forenoon, to Sharpsburg.

Our army also advanced, and, this morning at 7 o'clock, our batteries opened upon them from the hill about half a mile South of Sharpsburg, the rebels being on an eminence about the same distance from that place, nearly opposite our army.

Up to 10 o'clock there had been no general engagement, but the fighting, carried on principally by the different batteries, was still going on. I was informed by old soldiers that they never witnessed a more severe artillery engagement than was progressing at that hour.

The loss on our side was small. To what extent the rebels were suffering could only be judged from circumstances, such as the carrying of men from the field, the appearance of ambulances, &c. From such circumstances, it would appear that fearful execution was being done in their ranks.

One fact during the fights since Sunday morning is worthy of mention. Every night large numbers of rebels took advantage of the confusion and the darkness, would secrete themselves in the woods, and as soon as our army advanced in the morning would give themselves up, declaring that they were sick of fighting and would rather throw down their arms than continue the contest.

Sharpsburg is on the direct road to Williamsport, and as the rebels have evacuated Hagerstown, which is only six miles from that place, it is thought that it is the design of Lee to retreat and cross the ferry at Williamsport with his whole army now in Maryland. We have reason to believe such a result is not possible.

The Washington Star, of last evening, says:

We have most interesting information concerning the progress of McClellan's army in pursuit of the main body of the rebel army under Lee, Longstreet and others.

At noon yesterday they were overtaken by our advance division, when they formed in line of battle on the crest of the hill skirting the west bank of Antietam creek, in the immediate vicinity of Sharpsburg.

Shortly afterwards more of our troops arrived on the ground, and at 4 P. M. both armies were in battle array, ours on the east side and and theirs on the west side of the creek, as explained above.

At half-past 5 our forces attacked them, and a heavy battle ensued, until 9 P. M. The rebel army was believed to have been almost surrounded and well nigh out of ammunition, as well as provisions. Our army rested for the night just where the last of yesterday's fighting left them, and expected to renew the engagement at daylight this morning.

This information we believe is reliable. It comes both by way of Harrisburg and Boonsboro'.

The Battle of Portersburg.

We find the following in the New York Evening Post of the 18th:

The Philadelphia Press of to-day has the following in relation to the great battle:

Early on Wednesday morning Gen. McClellan's army advanced from its bivouack on Tuesday night to attack the enemy's rear as he was crossing the Potomac. Gen. Longstreet's division was the rear guard.

About noon the advanced parties came up with the rebels, but halted until the main body came up. A large Federal force was soon concentrated in front of the enemy.

The rebels formed in line of battle on the west bank of Antietam Creek, between Rohrerville and Sharpsburg.

Just after 5 o'clock Gen. McClellan attacked them, and the battle lasted until 9 in the evening, when he had nearly surrounded the enemy.

Early next morning the contest was renewed, Jackson's troops having crossed the river to the aid of his almost defeated comrades on the other shore.

Jackson left Harper's Ferry Tuesday, ostensibly for Martinsburg, but diverted his march to join the forces in Maryland.

The battle continued all day Wednesday, but no official news has yet been received of its results.

The War Department, though unable to give any report of the day's proceedings, has nothing unfavorable.

There are numerous rumors of decided and brilliant successes, and the anxiety for news from the upper Potomac is most intense.

Further Particulars of the Great Battle.

BALTIMORE, Sept. 17, Midnight.—A special correspondent from the seat of war says:

The cannonading on Tuesday afternoon was very heavy, and continued, with some intermission, long after nightfall.

On this (Wednesday) morning it was renewed at day, with such violence and rapidity that the people of the vicinity, who had watched the progress of the first day's contest, say it was entirely unprecedented.

The position occupied by Gen. McClellan appears to be an advantageous one, his guns seeming to be stationed on a range of hills, from the apex of which the little clouds of white smoke rolled up in the distance, marking distinctly the line of conflict. The reports were so rapid as to be without intermission, and sometimes three or four reports struck the ear at the same moment.

The cannonading commenced at daylight, and was heard distinctly up to ten o'clock, causing the impression that the great battle of the campaign was in progress.

The wounded were being carried towards Hagerstown and Boonsboro', so that little could be heard direct from the field in the direction of Middletown.

The reports that were received from the scene of conflict were highly favorable, our forces having, at the time, the best position, and the battle being principally with artillery, in which we have a great superiority.

Tuesday's Battle—Desperate Conflict.

At a late hour to-night no official news had been received from the battle of yesterday.

The telegraphic communication between this place and Frederick is interrupted.

A messenger arrived from the army this evening, and reports that everything was progressing satisfactorily when he left the battle field, and that there could be no doubt of a successful result.

The fight has raged some twelve hours, and has been a most desperate one.

Recapture of Harper's Ferry.

The New York Commercial Advertiser, of the evening of the 18th, says:

Private dispatches to-day from points near Harper's Ferry, seem to confirm in all essential particulars the good news published this morning, and leave no reasonable doubt of the recapture of Harper's Ferry by Gen. Burnside, and the occupation by strong Union guards of all the river fords between Harper's Ferry and Williamsport.

The Rebels in a Desperate Condition.

Reported Capture of Hill and Jackson.

Under the above headings the New York Evening Post, of the 18th, has the following:

The Philadelphia Inquirer has the following dispatches:

WASHINGTON, Sept. 17.—Confirmatory reports have just been received that the rebels are doing the best they can to keep our forces from crossing the Antietam Creek to outflank them. They have destroyed the bridges and have thrown up earthworks to defend the fords. It is evident they are doing all they can to get across the river, but our men are forcing them hard, and it is believed they will not succeed in crossing the Potomac without great loss.

"HARRISBURG, Sept. 17.—Later accounts state that the rebel Gen. Hill had been captured. It is also rumored that Jackson is captured, although not confirmed in official quarters. The retreating enemy will, no doubt, fall into the hands of the Pennsylvania militia. The soldiers here are intensely enthusiastic and jubilant."

The War in the West.

The latest accounts of the war in the West are contained in the following dispatches to the New York papers of the evening of the 18th:

CINCINNATI, Sept. 17.—A considerable riot occurred about 7 o'clock this evening, between a portion of the 10th, 39th and 81st regiments Ohio volunteers, in which several of the parties were severely injured. No lives lost. It was finally quelled by the Provost Guard. A rumor is on the street that Gen. Wright is to be superseded in the command of this department; by whom it is not known, but it is thought to be Lew. Wallace.

CINCINNATI, Sept. 17.—The news from Mumfordsville is quite exciting. There is every prospect that Buell and Bragg will have a general engagement in that neighborhood. Each general has about forty thousand good troops.

Kirby Smith has gone to Lexington, where he is in command of the rebels in Kentucky. His force is still near here. All quiet on our front. Morgan's rebel cavalry, fifteen hundred strong, occupy Independence, Ky. News from Louisville is quite exciting. Rebel guerrillas are destroying property near the city.

Later.

A fight has been going on at Mumfordsville yesterday and to-day. We have no particulars.

[Mumfordsville, where the rebels are reported to be engaged by Buell, is the county town of Hart county, Kentucky. It lies on the north side of the Green river, and is a village of some three hundred inhabitants. It was a rebel stronghold last year, and has been fortified since by our troops. On the 13th, the advance of Bragg made an unsuccessful attack there on some Indiana regiments, who beat them off. Buell, who reached Bowling Green about the same time that Bragg reached Glasgow, probably struck at once for Mumfordsville, and here forced Bragg to a battle.]

CINCINNATI, Sept. 18.—The rebels commenced falling back yesterday, and at last accounts were between Demassville and Falmouth, burning the bridges on the Covington and Lexington Railroad.

A scouting party of fifty-three of the 10th Kentucky Cavalry engaged a hundred rebels near Florence last night, and killed five and wounded seven, and routed the remainder. Our loss was one killed and one wounded.

Gen. Wallace has been relieved of the command of the forces here, and directed to report for duty at Columbus, Ohio. The command of the troops here has been assigned to Gen. A. J. Smith. Gen. Nelson has recovered from his wounds, and will command the troops at Louisville.

The Indian War in the West.

A dispatch to the New York Evening Post, dated Washington, Sept. 18, says:

Gen. Pope telegraphs from the West that the Indian difficulties in Minnesota are more formidable than he had anticipated. He asks for authority to have two regiments of volunteers mounted, to pursue the Indian war parties.

The eleven thousand men surrendered at Harper's Ferry by Col. Miles and Gen. White are to be sent to the West to be used against the Indians. They can thus be at once made useful, and they could not serve against the rebels for some time to come.

NEWS FROM EUROPE.

BY THE ARABIA.

The New York papers have the following telegraphic summary of the news from Europe, brought by the steamship Arabia, which left Liverpool on the 6th inst., and Queenstown on the 7th, and arrived at Halifax on the night of the 15th, *en route* for Boston.

Great Britain.

The London Times, in an editorial on the message of Jefferson Davis says:

"We cannot deny him the credit of being as moderate in prosperity as he has shown himself bold, determined and unyielding in adversity."

The Times then adds:

"We read with much pleasure the measured and statesmanlike language in which the Southern President pays a well earned tribute to the gallantry and good conduct of his troops, deplores the desolating war, and expresses confidence of the final triumph of the desperate struggle against despotic usurpation."

After pointing to the horrors which may be expected from President Davis's threatened retaliatory measures, to the exigencies which require an extension of the conscription, and to the dangers which the South run if they fail to conciliate the Indians on their frontiers, the Times's article concludes as follows:

"Yet in such a situation they are able to speak and act with moderation and dignity. In the midst of reverses they can look forward with confidence to success. In the midst of success they can contemplate and look forward to the possibility of loss and failure. Such men would seem worthy of a better destiny than to be dragged at the chariot wheels of a conquering democracy, and live under a perpetual."

The London Daily News, in reviewing the message of Jefferson Davis, says that he has attempted to present a character of moderation and dignity, but the fierce and vindictive spirit that breaks through his habitual calmness and reserve, is significant proof of his exasperated temper, if not also of the desperate prospect of the Southern government. It denounces the savage policy which Davis inaugurates, and the atrocious measures which he recommends to Congress, and says that the treatment threatened to the officers of troops incongruously composed, causes not only every instinct of humanity and every sentiment of justice to revolt at it, but it is an outrage against civilization itself.

A later telegram from Gibraltar throws doubt on the reported chase of the steamer Massilla, in the Bay of Biscay.

France.

It was reported that at the last Council of Ministers on Italian affairs, it was decided that the *statu quo* should be maintained in Rome for some time to come.

It was reported that the Orleanists and Republicans had formed a coalition for the next elections, and that they expected to return forty Deputies.

The third division of the expedition to Mexico, consisting of three steamers, left Toulon on the 3d inst.

The Madrid (official) Gazette announces that in consequence of the explanations given by Gen. Concha to the Emperor Napoleon, all differences of opinion between France and Spain have ceased.

The Paris Bourse closed firm and steady on the 6th inst., at 69f.40c., for the rentes.

Italy.

The physicians attending Garibaldi had issued a bulletin, stating that his sufferings were not very acute, and that his symptoms generally were favorable.

The official *Gazette* says that a ball penetrated his ankle joint, and inflammation had set in, but that the symptoms were not alarming.

It was stated that a ministerial conference had been held, and that after a long discussion it was determined that the rebel Garibaldians, captured by the Royal troops, ought to be tried by a special military tribunal, but foreseeing the possibility of such a tribunal, declaring itself incompetent, the question was submitted to the Procureurs General.

The London Morning Post asserts that the Emperor Napoleon has determined to bring about a solution of the Roman question, and it believes that the French army in Rome will certainly be withdrawn before another year is over.

La France, in an article signed "La Gueroniere," argues against the total abandonment of Rome by France, and endeavors to demonstrate the possibility of Italy definitely constituting herself without Rome for her capital.

There was a rumor that Victor Emmanuel contemplated a personal visit to Garibaldi incognito, and it was anticipated that, as the marriage of Victor Emanuel's daughter with the King of Portugal was to take place on the 16th inst., that he would take that opportunity to exercise the prerogative of mercy and pardon Garibaldi.

Spain.

The Queen of Spain has signed a decree granting an amnesty to the persons imprisoned on account of the insurrection at Loga.

China and Australia.

By telegraph we have Suez dates of the 6th of September, and the following later news from China and Australia.

SHANGHAI, Friday, July 18.—The city is quiet. News has been received here from Jeddo of another attempt having been made to assassinate the British Minister at that place. Two marines were killed. The assassin committed suicide.

The attempt upon the life of the Minister is supposed to have been instigated by the leading Damios.

Japan was unsettled.

MELBOURNE, Saturday, July 26.—Three thousand pounds, the proceeds of a subscription in behalf of the needy Lancashire operatives, have been remitted to England by this mail.

New Zealand is still unsettled. The Maories will not accept the terms of peace offered to them.

Latest News via Queenstown.

LONDON, Sunday, Sept. 7.—The Herald's Paris correspondence says no doubt is is entertained there that, unless Rome is evacuated, there will be a terrible outbreak in Italy.

It is stated that Ratazzi will resort to a general state of siege.

Canton dates of July 5 are received. The loss of the ship Phantom is confirmed.

Twist advancing. Tea—higher prices demanded, but market inactive. Exchange 4s.

CALCUTTA.—Tea active. Silk active and advancing. Exchange 6s. 4½d. Freights for silk 130s.

Latest via Queenstown.

LIVERPOOL, Saturday Night.—*Cotton.*—The sales to-day were only 2500 bales, including 2000 bales to speculators and exporters. The market closed firm at unchanged quotations.

Breadstuffs.—The market closed quiet and unchanged.

Provisions dull.

LONDON, Saturday Evening.—Consols closed at 93½ a 93⅝, for money.

American Stocks.—The market is steady, no quotations.

Commercial per Arabia.

Havre Cotton Market.—The sales of the week have been 33,000 bales. Orleans tres ordinaire, 160f., bas 150f. The market opened excited with considerable advance, and closed quiet and easier. The stock in port is 40,000 bales.

Explosion at the Pittsburg Arsenal.

A dispatch dated Pittsburg, September 17, gives the following account of this terrible disaster:

A frightful explosion occurred at the U. S. Arsenal, this afternoon, at 2 o'clock, in a large frame building known as the laboratory. About 176 boys and girls were employed in the building at the time of the disaster, 75 or 80 of whom were killed.

The explosion was followed by another, until the entire building was destroyed. Those who could not escape in time were burned up. The scene was most appalling. Dead bodies were lying in heaps as they had fallen, and in some places, where the heat was intense, the whitened bones could be seen through the smoke and flame. In other places large masses of blackened flesh were visible.

Up to the present time sixty-three bodies have been taken from the ruins. The cause of the explosion is not known, but it is admitted by all to have been accidental.

New York Money Market.

WEDNESDAY EVENING, Sept. 17.—The market was much depressed for several days, but after the brilliant victory at South Mountain, there was a general revival of business, and a manifest improvement in the tone of public feeling. This was dampened yesterday by the capitulation at Harper's Ferry, but we hope to announce before we go to press a stirring offset to that disaster.

The demand for money has been less eager. Loans on call are easily made on prime security at 4 to 5 per cent. Selections of prime business paper are taken at the same range, while at 6 to 7 per cent. any good paper can be readily discounted.

Gold opened the week at 118⅛, advanced to 119⅛, then declined to 116⅛, recovering last evening to 117⅛, and closed to-day at 117⅛. Silver has sold as high as 115 to the brokers, and 116 for lots from the brokers, but 115 is now the outside rate. Old demand notes have gone up 111⅛.

Foreign Exchange has fluctuated widely; yesterday bankers' sterling was freely offered at 129, and commercial bills were picked up in some cases as low as 126⅛, but afterward the range was higher. The market closes to-day at our quotations.

We quote: Bills at 60 days on London 128⅛ for documentary; 128⅛@129 for commercial; 129@130 for bankers; do. at short sight, 130@131⅛; Paris at 60 days 4.40@4.30; do. at short sight, 4.32½@25⅛; Antwerp 4.37⅛@4.32⅛; Swiss 4.33⅛@4.31⅛; Hamburgh, 42⅛@43⅛; Amsterdam 48⅛@49⅛; Frankfort 49⅛@49⅛; Bremen 92⅛@93⅛; Prussian thalers 86@86⅛.—*N. Y. Journal Commerce.*

Steamer Explosion.—A dispatch from St. John's, N. F., says the steamer Blue Jacket blew up in Conception Bay on the 18th inst. Engineer and one passenger lost.

A Ride a Bear-Back.—Last week, three children of Mr. Hooker, farmer, of Centreville, Chatham, C. E., the eldest a boy of about twelve years of age, a younger brother about ten, and a little sister seven, having gone out to the edge of the woods in quest of wild cherries, the eldest boy in getting over the fence in advance of his brother and sister, fell on the back of a full grown bear that was lying under the cherry tree, regaling himself, doubtless, with the fruit within his reach. Alarmed at the unexpected occurrence, the bear immediately arose and made what haste he could for the woods. The boy clung to his back for a few yards, when he fell off, screaming "a bear, a bear," on which the other children ran home as fast as they could. The boy says that when he fell off, the bear turned round and showed his big white teeth, and then increased his speed towards the woods. The children had to run a distance of ten acres before reaching their home, which they did in a state of great excitement. [Missouri Republican, 9th.

The Daily Picayune.

UNION. JUSTICE. CONFIDENCE.

[illegible]UME XXVI. NEW ORLEANS TUESDAY MORNING, OCTOBER 21, 1862. NUMBER 230.

The Daily Picayune.

[FROM THE EXTRA PICAYUNE.]

☞ Purser A. B. Reid, of the U. S. mail steamship Marion, has our hearty thanks for very acceptable favors, promptly accorded on arrival.

☞ The steamship Parkersburg, from New Orleans, arrived at New York on the 11th.

☞ Mr. McDonald, library depot, under St. Charles Hotel, will please accept our thanks for a file of papers, the latest dates from New York.

☞ We are under many obligations to A. B. Reid, purser of the steamship Marion, for particular attentions.

ARRIVAL OF STEAMSHIP MARION.—The United States mail steamship Marion, Capt. Phillips, which left New York on Saturday, 11th inst., arrived early this morning, bringing the mails and the following passengers:

Mrs. Major Gen. Butler and servant, Mrs. J. M. G. Parker and two children, Mrs. Col. Warren and child, Mrs. C. J. MacLellan, Mrs. John Brooks, child and infant, Miss Emily Moore, Mrs. Emily Adams, Mrs. Hardee, Mrs. MacCullum, Mrs. E. Hempsteadt, Miss H. Mayor, Mrs. M. Morton, Miss S. B. Morton, Mrs. Geagan and child, Miss Lorinda Green, Mrs. R. Lloyd, Mrs. Haines, Mrs. Ulrich, child and sister, M'me Monile and infant, Miss M. Curtis and servant, Mrs. Capt. Melancthon Smith and servant, Major Chas. J. Hoyt, Capt. J. M. Magee, Capt. J. E. Cowan, Capt. H. Mackey, Lieut. H. Stark, J. F. Alden, S. Aaron, J. L. Appleby, A. H. Bement, H. R. Buckley, Wm. Brown, J. Benheim, R. A. Blair, Dr. C. P. Crane and boy, C. Cavaroc, C. Cavaroc, Jr., S. W. Clapp, J. L. Cooper, W. C. Corsan, Louisa Conroy, Thomas J. Durant, W. T. Dobson, Chas. Dennison, Geo. Falk, B. Finkle, lady and child, J. L. Florence, son and servant, W. Ferry, Dr. Fletschinger and two children, J. T. Farish, C. Garnett, G. Gath, T. F. Guion, Wm. E. Hoyt, M. Hochendell, Chas. Hughes, A. Harget and lady, A. Hess, Bradish Johnson, D. Jacques, Thos. Lawrence, Thos. P. May, M. McGrath, John C. Miller, S. Offner, Elliston Perot, Geo. R. Price, J. M. Prentiss, Mons. T. C. Payan and daughter, J. Read, J. R. Reed, W. Rohleeberger, C. Seaville, George A. Seaman, L. Sylvester, N. F. Safford, J. Tayes, J. J. Wilkie, Orin Tellson, Jacob Yondorf.

FOR NEW YORK, DIRECT—The splendid and fast sailing United States steamship Marion, Capt. Phillips, will leave here at 8 o'clock on Thursday morning for New York, direct. The Marion has splendid accommodations for passengers, and the polite and gentlemanly purser, A. B. Reid, Esq., will be found in his office, ready and willing to attend promptly to the wants of passengers. The agent of the Marion is Wm. J. Reid, 33 Magazine street.

From the New York Journal of Commerce, 11th inst.

New York Money Market.

MONEY MARKET, Friday Evening, Oct. 10.—The Philadelphia Ledger, whose brief editorials are remarkable for their practical good sense as well as their tone of independence, in some remarks upon the currency question, alludes to "the apprehension felt in New York financial circles that the issue of Treasury notes would operate unfavorably for the banks by driving in their circulation." There was such a fear expressed in some quarters, but no such apprehension was expressed here by the friends of a sound currency. We maintained that unless the Government issues were made totally irredeemable and thus become poorer than all other issues, they would encourage and stimulate rather than diminish the circulation of the banks. We urged this in a prominent editorial published Feb. 22d, and again on the 22d of April, wherein we stated that "the expansion of bank note paper must keep pace with the issue of Government bills."

There were writers in this city who alternately ridiculed and denounced those who believed that Congress could not repeal the laws of trade. These writers not only insisted that there could be no depreciation of paper money as compared with gold, but that every one who expressed a contrary opinion was essentially disloyal, and only anxious to embarrass the government. Within a few days our venerable contemporary, the Commercial Advertiser, gravely asserted that the premium on Silver, then 8 to 10 per cent., could not be maintained after the Postage Currency was issued, and that it wou[illegible] lower for remittance abroad. It is now 22 [illegible] and rising, and gold would not stay down, [illegible]standing the threats to "mark the men" who [illegible]. But the result is vindicating all which in[illegible] writers predicted, and their theories need no o[illegible]nce than a page or two of history.

A correspondent wishes to know why, if Government does not intend to repudiate the soiled postage stamps, it could not as well redeem them by permitting holders to affix them to letters in prepayment of postage, as by exchanging them in gross according to the plan now intimated at Washington. He is very green to ask such a question. He cannot have heard of *shoddy* and knows nothing of the word *job* except as spelt with a capital J, and standing for an Old Testament patriarch. If the stamps are redeemed and burnt, there will be an immense supply of new ones wanted, and somebody must have a fresh contract. Where has he spent the summer?

The bottom of things either fell out or was greatly loosened for a while this morning. The general plan of William street operations is to encourage outside speculation, and during a rising market to load everything possible upon those who have something to lose, but whose only idea is to go in and make a profit. When the latter are well burdened, then a favorable opportunity is watched, the knowing ones let go, and the poor fellows who are caught beneath the load come out stripped as gaunt as Pharaoh's lean kine. We have noticed within a few days the rising value of money, the disposition of certain sharp stockholders to sell, and the increasing difficulty in borrowing upon stocks, even with a liberal interest and a wide margin. To-day the scheme culminated. An east wind, with a disagreeable storm, a little stringency in the money market, and an apprehension of some reverse in Kentucky, magnified into a certainty by retailers of street gossip, all conspired to give a certain hue to the financial horizon, and everything that should be buoyant, is not only "depressed," but flat as a stale joke, or the sediment of yesterday's lager.

Gold went up to 129, afterwards fell back to 127⅞, with 128⅛ offered, and again advanced to 128 at 5½ o'clock. Silver advanced to 125, but this was an outside rate. Old demand notes sold at 121 in the street.

Foreign Exchange advanced to 142½ for bankers' sterling, but at the close was much unsettled and nominal.

We quote: Bills at 60 days on London 139 a 139½ for documentary; 139 a 140½ for commercial; 141 a 142 for bankers'; do. at short sight, 141½ a 142½; Paris at 60 days 4.05 a 3.95; do. at short sight, 3.97½ a 3.92½; Antwerp 4.05 a 3.97½; Swiss 4.00 a 3.95; Hamburgh 46 a 47½; Amsterdam 52½ a 53½; Frankfort 53½ a 54; Bremen 102 a 103½; Prussian thalers 91 a 95.

The Stock market, as above indicated, came down with a run. There was little done in Government, but fancies caught a tremendous fall. This, of course, was followed by a partial reaction in the afternoon.

Prompt Reply.—"Why did Adam bite the apple?" said a schoolmaster to a country lad. "Because he had no knife," said the urchin.

☞ "She struck me very much at first," said the witty daughter of a celebrated novelist, to a young lisping swell. "Did she, indeed?" said the dandy, "that was very rude in her!" "It was a rudeness of which you were not guilty," was the ready reply.

Famous Foragers no Doubt.—A correspondent of the Philadelphia Press, writing from Philadelphia on the 20th ult., says:

Col. Billy Wilson's famous regiment of New York Zouaves has been quartered here for the last fourteen months, during which time they have been [illegible] in the quiet enjoyment of every luxury that this part of the country could afford. The men of this regiment have grown famous in the "foraging" way. They have no scruples in appropriating to their own use every thing that they can lay their hands on, that has ever been, or is now, the property of secessionists. They spent a considerable time in Fort Pickens, forming a part of the garrison, and attaining the efficiency of the regular troops. They have been changed, in a most surprising manner, from New York fire boys into excellent soldiers.

TWO DAYS LATER FROM THE NORTH.

BY THE STEAMSHIP MARION.

PROGRESS OF THE WAR.

Great Battle in Kentucky.

PENNSYLVANIA INVADED.

Gen. Lee's Account of the Battle of Shepherdstown.

His Order to His Troops on the Late Battles in Maryland.

FIGHT AT SUFFOLK, VA.

The 290 off the Western Islands.

HER OPERATIONS, &c., &c.

By the arrival of the United States mail steamship Marion, at an early hour this morning, we have papers to the 11th inst., inclusive, giving us two days later intelligence than we had by the steamship Creole. The news is highly important. The following is a comprehensive summary:

The War in the West.

Great Battle in Kentucky.—Dispatches to the New York Herald furnish accounts of a great battle in Kentucky, &c., as follows:

LOUISVILLE, Oct. 8.—A general engagement is progressing between Buell and Bragg, at Perryville, but nothing definite has been received here as yet.

LOUISVILLE, Oct. 9—1:12 P. M.—The battle at Perryville commenced yesterday morning, the rebels attacking Buell's advance in great force. An artillery fight continued through most of the day, with no great results. Later in the day Buell's forces, having secured a good position, advanced and drove the rebels back. No definite particulars have yet been received.

It is reported at Gen. Boyle's headquarters that Gens. Rousseau and Jackson, commanding Union divisions, were killed, but the report is not credited.

Buell intended last night to advance and bring on a general engagement this morning. The result of this is not known. Gen Dumont's success over Morgan and Scott at Frankfort is fully confirmed. Morgan entered Frankfort yesterday morning at seven o'clock, with his own and Scott's cavalry, three thousand strong, meeting no opposition. This morning Dumont moved on them from Shelbyville and at noon had routed them. The rebels are said to be dispersed, wandering over the adjacent hills, endeavoring to avoid Dumont's pursuing forces. If not all captured, the command will be completely broken up. The rebels destroyed the turnpike bridge before they were attacked.

LOUISVILLE, Oct. 9, 1862.—The battle at Perryville commenced early in the morning by an artillery duel, which continued all day. Gen. McCook's corps was engaged alone. At two o'clock the rebels made an effort to turn our left flank, and desperate fighting ensued at close quarters. The rebels were twice driven back with heavy loss. The battle continued till dark, when both parties rested.

Gen. Terrell was mortally wounded; also Col. Webster, of the 98th Ohio. Gen. Jackson was killed. The report of the death of Gen. Rousseau is not confirmed. The Union loss is estimated at two thousand killed and wounded. The rebel loss is greater, if anything.

Gen. Crittenden and Gen. Gilbert have reinforced Gen. McCook, and the battle was resumed this morning.

CINCINNATI, Oct. 9.—Intelligence has been received here to-night of an attack on Gen. McCook's corps at Perryville, Ky., yesterday, by Bragg, who threw his entire force upon him.

Our loss was nearly two thousand in killed and wounded. Gen. Jackson was killed, and Gen. Terrell badly wounded. The enemy's loss is not ascertained, but is probably heavy.

There is a prospect of a general engagement being brought on by Gen. Buell to-day.

PERRYVILLE, Ky., Oct. 9, 1862.—Bragg's army attacked two divisions of Gen. McCook's corps d'armée near this place yesterday. The fighting was desperate. Gen. James S. Jackson, ex-Congressman of Kentucky, commanding a division, was killed. Gen. Terrell, of Virginia, commanding a brigade, formerly of Terrell's battery, was very seriously wounded.

On two occasions the fighting was hand to hand. The rebels were greatly superior to the Unionists in numbers. McCook was then heavily reinforced, and the battle was resumed to-day. The fighting was merely done by Rousseau's division, formerly Mitchel's.

Col. George Webster, of the 98th Ohio, acting brigadier of the 34th brigade, was severely wounded. Firing ceased about seven o'clock on the evening of the 8th. A doubtful rumor says that at the close of the engagement the rebels had possession of a part of the field.

Gen. Sheridan, of Illinois, is reported killed, but it is doubtful. Our loss is stated at two thousand killed and wounded. The rebel loss was unascertained. The enemy is noth of Perryville. A general attack is expected immediately by our troops.

CINCINNATI, Oct. 10.—Later intelligence from Buell's army is very encouraging.

Gen. Buell's forces drove Gen. Bragg's nearly ten miles on Thursday, with great slaughter. The rebels are retreating in disorder, and our forces are following closely in pursuit. Gen. Buell has his forces well in hand.

LOUISVILLE, Oct. 10.—Gen. Buell fought a great battle with Bragg's rebel army yesterday, at Perryville, gaining a signal and decisive victory. Bragg is used up.

LOUISVILLE, KY., Oct. 10.—There are various rumors circulating relative to the fight which took place yesterday (Thursday), which are said to be favorable to the Union side; but they can be traced to no authentic source, and headquarters, at 11 o'clock this (Friday) morning, have received no authentic advices from the battle field later than Wednesday evening.

Our force in that fight was about 15,000 infantry, assisted by eight batteries of artillery and 2500 cavalry; but this force was reinforced towards the close of the fight. The rebel force has not been estimated.

Among the casualties at Perryville, on Wednesday, are the following: Gen. Jackson killed; Gen. Terrill, killed; Acting Brig. Gen. Webster, killed; Acting Brig. Gen. Lytle, killed; Lt. Col. Jewett, killed; Major Campbell, of the 15th Kentucky Cavalry, killed; Colonel Pope, of the same regiment was wounded.

There is no confirmation of the death of Gen. Sheridan. Gen. Rousseau is reported slightly wounded. Col. Woolford, of the 1st Kentucky Cavalry, after making five charges, took two Kentucky batteries, and the enemy, after very hard fighting, were driven back some eight miles.

The foregoing relates to Wednesday's fight.

No accounts have yet been received of the losses on either side, but ours is supposed to be large, from the mortality among the field officers. A large ambulance train is now leaving Louisville to bring the wounded hither.

LOUISVILLE, Oct. 10, 1 P. M.—Early yesterday morning Gen. Buell attacked Bragg's forces at Chaplin creek, in the immediate vicinity of Perryville.

A short but terrific fight ensued, when the rebels broke and retreated rapidly over three diverging roads southward, our forces in close pursuit. It is hoped that the lot will be bagged.

At the last accounts Gen. Gilbert's forces were in the rear of the rebels and some distance below them. Military exigencies require the suppression of details. No further accounts of losses on either side have been received.

Louisville is in great excitement respecting the fate of our soldiers in the pending battle. Capt. Oldershaw, Jackson's Adjutant, is on the way hither from Bardstown with the remains of Gens. Jackson and Terrill, and Col. Webster of the 98th Ohio regiment.

The New York Evening Express, of the 11th, has the latest intelligence from Kentucky, in the following dispatch:

LOUISVILLE, KY., Oct. 10—12 o'clock, midnight.—A dispatch from Bardstown to Gov. Robinson says that Gen. Crittenden's force was not engaged in Wednesday's fight, and that Gen. Wood's force was but temporarily engaged, not having arrived in season.

At night the rebels retreated towards Harrodsburg, but were hemmed in.

Gen. Kirby Smith's detachment had departed from the other rebel detachments on Dick River.

On Sunday we occupied advantageous situations on all sides of the enemy.

Our troops are in high spirits and confident of victory.

Our loss in killed and wounded on Wednesday was 1500. The loss of the enemy is considered much larger.

The reports of a severe battle near Perryville on Thursday are incorrect. The report came from four persons who left Perryville at 7 o'clock on that morning, when skirmishing had commenced, with slight cannonading.

Others who left the battle-field at three o'clock on Thursday afternoon, say the firing ceased before 8 o'clock in the morning, and the remainder of the rebels were making their way towards Harrodsburg, pursued by the Federal army.

Col. Jacobs, of the 9th Kentucky Cavalry, was slightly wounded in a skirmish on Wednesday night, near Lawrenceburg, but he continued on duty on Thursday.

The 10th Ohio regiment lost 38[illegible] killed and wounded on Wednesday.

Company B, Capt. Forman, mostly from Louisville, of Col. Pope's regiment, lost in killed and wounded all except twelve.

Gen. Rousseau's and Col. Pope's wounds are very slight.

There are conflicting stories about the death of Gen. Lytle. Some report him wounded and a prisoner.

The remains of Gen. Jackson, Gen. Terrill and Gen. Webster have arrived here.

The Sanitary Committee have made every preparation for the relief of the wounded.

Gov. Morton, of Indiana, is en route hither with a large number of surgeons and nurses.

Skirmishing in Missouri—KANSAS CITY, Mo., Oct. 8.—About 3 P. M. yesterday, a skirmish ensued between a company of 80 men of the Missouri cavalry, under Capt. David, and a guerrilla band of 180 men, under Quantrell and Childs, near Sibley Landing, resulting in the defeat of the guerrillas.

Our loss is one killed and one dangerously wounded. The rebel loss is unknown. We captured the rebel Col. Childs, who is severely wounded. Capt. Davis is still in pursuit of the guerrillas.

KANSAS CITY, Oct. 8.—Last night a detachment of Gen. Jim Lane's negro brigade attempted to cross the river from Wyandotte, Kansas, it is thought to make a raid upon the citizens of Clay county, Mo., when they were met on the Missouri bank by a company of Missouri State militia and driven back. Several shots were fired, but little damage was done to either party.

Operations in Mississippi.—The World, of the 11th, says:

The report that Gen. Oglesby had died from wounds received at Corinth, is incorrect. The Federal troops have occupied Rienzi, not Grand Junction, as before stated. Gen. Price has been chased as far as Ripley, and the pursuit is said to be still kept up.

Pennsylvania Invaded.

The New York World, of the 11th, has the following dispatches:

HARRISBURG, Oct. 10—7:20 P. M.—Gov Curtin has just received the following dispatch from Col. McClure at Chambersburg:

"Mercersburg was occupied by Stuart's rebel cavalry to-day, and they are now advancing on Chambersburg. They took horses and all other property they wanted at Mercersburg, offering rebel scrip for it. They did no injury to individuals that I have heard of. The force is estimated at three thousand.

"The rebels are certainly advancing upon Chambersburg. They have cut the Bedford wire. They are reported as near St. Thomas, about seven miles from here. There is no doubt whatever of their being in Mercersburg. They will certainly give us a call to-night. We had the rumor at 4 o'clock, but it was not credited. We can make no resistance, as it would only exasperate, and cause the wanton destruction of property and life."

Latest.

CHAMBERSBURG, Oct. 10—8 P. M.—About fifteen men on horseback are in town, with carbines and a flag of truce. They want to see the principal men of the town. They have a large force about one mile from town, who will enter in an hour.

Col. McClure and Provost Marshal Kimmel have just gone two miles from the town to meet the rebel commander. Nothing can be done except surrender. We look for the whole force in half an hour. They crossed the Potomac at Hancock, and came over the country to the Pittsburg pike. The deposits of the Chambersburg bank have not been returned from New York since the last raid.

Latest.

HARRISBURG, 10 P. M., Oct. 10.—Gov. Curtin is now pushing troops up the valley.

Dispatches just received from Shippensburg confirm the news of the occupation of Chambersburg. The advance rebel force consists of 1,000 cavalry and six pieces of artillery.

The New York Evening Post, in giving the news from Pennsylvania, says:

Mercersburg is a flourishing town in Franklin county, sixty-two miles southwest from Harrisburg. It is next in population to Chambersburg, and is an active business town. Marshall College, under the direction of the German Reformed Church, is located at this place, a Theological department being connected with it. The population is about fifteen hundred. It is twelve miles from Hancock, Maryland.

Chambersburg is the capital of Franklin county, and is situated on the Conecocheague creek, at the junction of the Cumberland Valley Railroad with the Franklin Railroad, forty-five miles from Harrisburg (southwest) and one hundred and fifty miles from Philadelphia. It is connected with Philadelphia, Baltimore and Pittsburg by turnpike roads, and by railroad with Harrisburg, Philadelphia and Hagerstown. It has manufactories of cotton, wool, flour, paper and iron, and a population of five thousand.

Franklin county has a population of forty thousand.

St. Thomas, also referred to in the dispatch, is a post village in Franklin county, fifty-two miles southwest from Harrisburg, and ten miles from Chambersburg.

The N. Y. Evening Express, of the 11th inst., has the following:

HARRISBURG, October 11.—The rebel raid against Chambersburg is not deemed important here.

The disposition of the Federal troops at Cumberland, Chambersburg and other points, will force the rebels to a speedy return to Virginia by way of Hanover, or to make a detour above Cumberland.

In either case the movements of the rebels must be rapid to escape capture.

PHILADELPHIA, Oct. 11.—A dispatch from Governor Curtin to Mayor Henry states that no troops are needed from this point. The rebels are already reported as falling back.

The War in Virginia.

The Herald of the 10th, in its editorial summary, says:

There is nothing of importance from the army of the Potomac, with the exception of some successful reconnoissances towards Aidie.

It is confidently stated from Washington that, notwithstanding recent rumors, no change will take place at present either in the Cabinet or the army.

Gen. McClellan has issued the following congratulatory order to the army of the Potomac, thanking them for their valor in the battles of South Mountain and Antietam:

HEADQUARTERS ARMY OF THE POTOMAC, Camp near Sharpsburg, Md., Oct. 3.

The Commanding General extends his congratulations to the army under his command for the victories achieved by their bravery at the passes of the South Mountain and upon the Antietam creek.

The brilliant conduct of Reno's and Hooker's corps, under Burnside, at Turner's Gap, and of Franklin's corps at Crampton's Pass, in which, in the face of an enemy strong in position and resisting with obstinacy, they carried the mountain, and prepared the way for the advance of the army, won for them the admiration of their brethren in arms.

In the memorable battle of Antietam we defeated a numerous and powerful army of the enemy, in an action desperately fought and remarkable for its duration and for the destruction of life which attended it. The obstinate bravery of the troops of Hooker, Mansfield and Sumner, the dashing gallantry of those of Franklin on the right, the steady valor of those of Burnside on the left, and the vigorous support of Porter and Pleasanton, present a brilliant spectacle to our countrymen which will swell their hearts with pride and exultation.

Fourteen guns, thirty-nine colors, fifteen thousand five hundred stand of arms, and nearly six thousand prisoners, taken from the enemy, are evidences of the completeness of our triumph.

A grateful country will thank the noble army for achievements which have rescued the loyal States of the East from the ravages of the invader, and have driven him from their borders.

While rejoicing at the victories which, under God's blessing, have crowned our exertions, let us cherish the memory of our brave comrades who have laid down their lives upon the battlefield, martyrs in their country's cause. Their names will be enshrined in the hearts of the people.

By command of
MAJOR GEN. McCLELLAN.
S. WILLIAMS, A. A. G.

Important from Suffolk.—Under this heading, the Herald has a letter dated Suffolk, Va., Oct. 4, which says:

I have before advised you that the rebels had pushed their pickets some distance this side of the Blackwater, and had grown quite bold in their menaces of this post. On Thursday evening Maj. Gen. Peck ordered a reconnoissance in force, which was placed under command of Col. Spear, of the 11th Pennsylvania cavalry. Col. Spear started upon his mission about nine o'clock, and drove in the enemy's pickets upon the main body, which was commanded by Gen. G. W. Smith. A sharp skirmish ensued, in which the Colonel had one lieutenant and two sergeants wounded. He succeeded, however, in completely routing the foe, and pursued him as far as Franklin, on the other side of the Blackwater.

The object of the reconnoissance was fully accomplished, and much valuable information gained in regard to the strength and position of the rebel force in this quarter. There is not now a rebel soldier on this side of the Blackwater, and the probabilities are that they will not soon make another appearance in our vicinity. Col. Spear has won new laurels by the gallant manner in which he performed the mission entrusted to him. The loss of the enemy was not ascertained.

From the South.

Gen. Lee's Official Report of the Battle of Shepherdstown.

Richmond papers, of the 8th, received at New York, contain Gen. Lee's official account of the battle of Shepherdstown:

HEADQ'RS ARMY NORTHERN VIRGINIA, Camp on Washington's Run, October 2, 1862.

Gen. S. Cooper, Adjutant and Inspector General, C. S. A., Richmond, Va.

General—The enemy's cavalry, under Gen. Pleasanton, with six pieces of artillery, drove back our pickets yesterday, in front of Shepherdstown. The 9th Virginia Cavalry, which was on picket, repulsed the enemy several times, by vigorous charges, disputing the ground step by step, back to the main body. By the time his artillery reached him, Col. W. H. F. Lee, who was in command of the brigade, was obliged to place it on the west bank of the Opequon, on the flank of the enemy as he approached Martinsburg.

Gen. Hampton's brigade had retired through Martinsburg, on the Tuscarora road, when Gen. Stuart arrived and made dispositions to attack. Lee's brigade was advanced immediately, and Hampton's ordered forward. The enemy retired at the approach of Lee along the Shepherdstown road, and was driven across the Potomac with severe loss, and darkness alone prevented it from being a signal victory. His rear was overtaken and put to flight, our cavalry charging in gallant style under a severe fire of artillery, routing squadron after squadron, killing a number, wounding [illegible] and capturing several.

[illegible] was driven through Shepherdstown and crossed the river after dark, in no case standing a hand-to-hand conflict, but relying upon his artillery and carbines at long range for protection.

I regret to add that we lost one lieutenant and several privates.

I am, most respectfully,
Your obedient servant,
R. E. LEE, Gen. Com.
Official—Chas. Marshall, Major and A. D. C.

Also Gen. Lee's address to his troops, congratulating them on the valor they displayed in the recent battles in Maryland—as follows:

GEN. LEE'S ADDRESS TO HIS TROOPS.
HEADQ'RS ARMY NORTHERN VIRGINIA, October 2, 1862.
General Orders, No. 116.

In reviewing the achievements of the army during the present campaign, the Commanding General cannot withhold the expression of his admiration of the indomitable courage it has displayed in battle, and its cheerful endurance of privation and hardship on the march.

Since your great victories around Richmond, you have defeated the enemy at Cedar Mountain, expelled him from the Rappahannock, and, after a conflict of three days, utterly repulsed him on the plains of Manassas, and forced him to take shelter within the fortifications around his capital.

Without halting for repose, you crossed the Potomac, stormed the heights of Harper's Ferry, made prisoners of more than eleven thousand men, and captured upwards of seventy pieces of artillery, all their small arms, and other munitions of war.

While one corps of the army was thus engaged, the other insured its success by arresting at Boonsboro the combined armies of the enemy, advancing under their famous General to the relief of their beleagured comrades.

On the field of Sharpsburg, with less than one-third his numbers, you resisted from daylight until dark the whole army of the enemy, and repulsed every attack along his entire front of more than four miles in extent.

The whole of the following day you stood prepared to resume the conflict on the same ground, and retired next morning without molestation across the Potomac.

Two attempts subsequently made by the enemy to follow you across the river have resulted in his complete discomfiture and being driven back with loss.

Achievements such as these demanded much valor and patriotism. History records few examples of greater fortitude and endurance than this army has exhibited, and I am commissioned by the President to thank you in the name of the Confederate States for the undying fame you have won for their arms.

Much as you have done, much more remains to be accomplished. The enemy again threatens with invasion, and to your tried valor and patriotism the country looks with confidence for deliverance and safety; your past exploits give assurance that this confidence is not misplaced.

R. E. LEE,
General Commanding.

The No. 290.

Her Operations Off the Western Isles. Five American Whalers Burned.

The New York Herald, in giving the news by steamship Persia, from Liverpool, says:

We have important news of the operations of the rebel steamer Alabama, known as "No. 290." The Cairngorm, an English vessel, arrived at Gravesend, from Sydney, on the day the Persia left Liverpool. She reports that when at Flores, Western Islands, three whaleboats' crews from the Alabama came alongside and reported that their ship, the Ocmulgee, of Edgartown, Mass., had been burned by the Alabama, under command of Capt. Semmes, late of the Sumter. The Ocmulgee had two hundred and fifty barrels of oil, and her crew—thirty-four men—were made prisoners. The Alabama had already burned four whalers. She also captured an American schooner—name unknown—in sight of the Cairngorm.

LATER FROM EUROPE.

BY STEAMSHIP PERSIA.

The New York Herald, of the 10th, has the following editorial summary of the news brought by the Persia:

The Persia, from Queenstown on the 28th ult., arrived at this port yesterday afternoon. Her news is two days later than the advices of the Jura.

The Liverpool cotton market had an upward tendency on the 27th of September, and closed at a trifling advance on all descriptions of American. Breadstuffs were quiet, but steady. Provisions ruled heavy. Consols closed in London, on the 27th ult., at 93⅜ a 93½ for money.

The most important news from the continent of Europe is to be found in the Paris *Moniteur* of the 25th of September. The official journal publishes, for the first time, a letter from the Emperor Napoleon, dated in May last, addressed to Mr. Thouvenel, in which his Majesty defines his position on the Roman question, both towards Italy and the Pope. The State paper shows that on the 20th of May Napoleon ordered Mr. Thouvenel to propose an arrangement between the Papal and Italian Courts, upon the conditions that the Pope should "lower the barriers which separate the Pontifical territory from Italy," and that Italy should "give the necessary guarantees for the independence of the Pope."

On the 30th of May M. Thouvenel instructed the Marquis de Lavalette to urge Cardinal Antonelli to accept a compromise, Italy renouncing her pretensions to romove, and engaging to respect the Papal territory and assume the greater part of the Papal debt. On the 24th of June the Marquis de Lavalette informed M. Thouvenel that Cardinal Antonelli had decisively rejected all proposals for a "transaction" between Pius IX and Victor Emanuel. His Eminence replied just as he had replied to similar propositions previously, and just what it was well known he would reply to these—"*Non possumus.*" The Pope's conscience would not allow him to make any relinquishment of the territory he received.

The news of McClellan's victory over the rebels at South Mountain, Maryland, reached England on the 26th of September, and produced a very decided effect in favor of the Union cause. The rebel agents and sympathisers were very much depressed. The London Times itself praises the activity of Gen. McClellan in organizing and marching the Federal troops from Washington to meet the enemy. Virginia State stocks, which had been quoted at 5 per cent. premium, immediately declined in London.

Our Paris correspondence is dated on the 26th ult. The letters were written before the news of the rebel reverses had reached the French capital. One of our correspondents states that, if the war is not ended by the 1st of January next, Napoleon, with England, is likely to recognize the Southern Confederacy, and follow up the act by an armed intervention.

He adds, that the French Minister in Washington has been already instructed to repeat in reply to certain questions—forwarded to him by the previous mail—on the subject, his answers to change, in a great measure, the course of the Imperial interference. The writer says that the announcement of decisive Union victories in the meantime may tend to alter Napoleon's present plan of American policy, and in this view of the case it is important to recollect that his Majesty had not heard of the defeats of the rebels by Gen. McClellan.

The English military journals regard the invasion of Maryland as a mistake of the rebels in the first instance, and a [illegible] end.

A "Southern Club" was [illegible] in some of the towns of [illegible] had already [illegible] [illegible]

7

DAILY DISPATCH.

VOL. XXIII. RICHMOND, VA., MONDAY MORNING, DECEMBER 15, 1862. NO. 141

Richmond Dispatch.

☞ The DISPATCH is published DAILY, Sundays excepted. Price for mailing $6 a year, or $6 for six months; three months $3; one month $1, in advance.

☞ The SEMI-WEEKLY DISPATCH is issued every TUESDAY and FRIDAY at $6, in advance.

☞ The WEEKLY DISPATCH is issued every FRIDAY, and mailed to subscribers at $3 per annum.

MONDAY MORNING..............DEC. 15, 1862.

FROM FREDERICKSBURG.

GREAT FIGHT ON SATURDAY.

The Enemy Repulsed at all Points.

&c., &c., &c., &c.

Great anxiety prevailed in the community on Saturday, to hear further and more satisfactory reports from the seat of war, as previous rumors had induced the supposition that a general and decisive engagement was imminent; but no intelligence of a reliable character could be obtained until 9 o'clock P. M., at which hour the following dispatches were received at the War Department by General Cooper:

To General Cooper:

At 9 o'clock this morning the enemy attacked our right wing, and as the fog lifted the battle ran along the whole line from right to left until 6 P. M., the enemy being repulsed at all points. Thanks be to God!

As usual, we have to mourn the loss of many of our brave men.

I expect the battle will be renewed at daylight to-morrow morning.

R. E. LEE.

To General Cooper:

General Wade Hampton reports that he had entered Dumfries, and captured thirty wagons with stores and fifty prisoners, which he brought across the Rappahannock.

Gen. Sigel is expected to be at Dumfries to-morrow.

R. E. LEE.

The highly gratifying nature of these dispatches only increased the general desire to learn something further, and throughout the day the bulletin boards in front of the various newspaper offices were surrounded by eager crowds in search of later intelligence. The War office was also besieged by anxious inquirers, but nothing of an official character was disclosed.

A telegraphic dispatch was received at the office of the Provost Marshal at 7 o'clock last night, stating that five ambulance trains were then between Hanover Junction and Guinea Station on their route to Richmond. Up to the hour of 12 o'clock P. M. none of the trains had arrived, though a large number of ambulances and hacks were still awaiting them to convey the wounded to Seabrook's Hospital.

Passengers who left Guinea Station at one o'clock yesterday and arrived by the early train, report that heavy firing was heard all the morning in the direction of Fredericksburg, and the presumption was that a general engagement was then going on.—It was also stated by the same authorities that our army had advanced two miles nearer to the town. No official information whatever could be obtained by the press yesterday, and all that we can give concerning what took place since the dispatches of Gen. Lee, on Saturday night, is conjecture.

The battle of Saturday commenced at six o'clock in the morning and raged with great violence until after dark. Our loss is estimated to be 2,500 wounded and 500 killed. It is said that Jackson accomplished a flank movement, capturing 3,000 of the enemy, but this is not generally received with credit.

A soldier of A. P. Hill's division says the enemy charged our men in their rifle pits and entrenchments nine times, and were repulsed with terrible slaughter, until our ammunition gave out, when our men were again charged by overwhelming force and driven back. But having obtained more ammunition, our forces in their turn charged the enemy and drove them from the works in great disorder, taking a large number of prisoners.

Johnson's, Crenshaw's, Purcell's, and the 1st and 3d companies of Richmond Howitzers, were in the fight. Two guns of the latter battery having been struck by the shot of the enemy, were taken from the field in a disabled condition.

Johnson's Battery lost fourteen killed and wounded. Their names we did not ascertain.

The number of wounded brought down by the first train last night was 180.

Gen Cobb was killed. Gen. Hood is also reported killed, but the rumor lacks confirmation. Gen Gregg was mortally wounded.

ARRIVAL OF BODIES.

The 5 o'clock train yesterday afternoon brought down the bodies of several officers. Among them were those of Brig.-Gen. Thos. R. R. Cobb, of Ga., and Capt. D'Aquin, of the Louisiana Guard Artillery.

[FROM OUR OWN REPORTER.]

SUMMIT, Dec. 13, 1862.

Heavy firing was heard at the front for several hours yesterday afternoon, the result of skirmishing. Some parties state that our forces were shelling Fredericksburg, now in the hands of the enemy. Last night a brilliant light was observable in the direction of the town. The two armies, in line of battle, lay all night confronting each other, and it was expected that the battle would commence early this morning, but up to this time (7 o'clock) no firing has been heard.

In the fight of Thursday, a Mississippi regiment, of Featherstone's brigade, suffered severely. One shell is said to have killed and wounded twenty-eight men. Some ninety of the wounded arrived at this point last night, and were sent on to Richmond.

The committee for the wounded remained here during the night, but are preparing to move forward this morning. They have the facilities for doing good service, should anything occur to require the exercise of their labors.

The straggling, so much complained of on the eve of previous battles, seems to have been obviated in this instance, and very few men are to be seen absent from their posts. The condition of the army is such as to inspire confidence in the result.

Lieut James Ellett, of Crenshaw's battery, was killed this morning while placing a section of his battery in position. His body will be sent down this evening. Major Brockenbrough, Chief of Artillery of 1st Division, Jackson's corps, was severely wounded in the hand. Several others were wounded whose names have not been ascertained.

THE WOUNDED.

The following is a list of the wounded men brought to this city on Friday and Saturday evenings. As will be seen, nearly all of them are of Barksdale's Brigade, which is said to have sustained the brunt of the heavy skirmishing of Thursday and Friday:

Lt J J Accostar, co I, 8th Fla; J A Hoppy, co G, 24 N C, C C Cauthorn, co G, 18th Miss; G H Lebrane, do, do; W F Baily, co H, 13th Miss; Sgt J M Carswell, co A, 13th Miss; W Penn, co D, 18th Miss; S T Braten, co D, 17th Miss; J M Black, co B, 51st Va; J W Thompson, co H, 13th Miss; J D Dewolf, co D, 13th Miss; H J Hurley, co C, 17th Miss; J J Gordon, co K, 17th Miss; T Saunders, co C, 8th Fla; J Mandy, co K, 8th Fla; C Roberts, co I, 8th Fla; J W Alexander, co K, 13th Miss; G W Smith, co K, 8th Fla; J P Brackwell, co G, 8th Fla; Lt L Carnford, co A, 51st N C; Lt E G Jandon, co I, 8th Fla; F M Campbell, co C, 17th Miss; J T Hood, co E, 24th N C; M Collier, co E, 7th N C; S Lambert, co K, 7th N C, H W Barns, co G, 5th Ala; R S Moody, co D, 33d Va; B Johnson, co D, 33d N C, W A Grosen, co G, 16th Ga; G D Hilman, co D, 51st Ga, W D Boules, co E, 8th Fla; Lt J D Finley, co A, 18th Miss, Lt W Cashin, co K, 18th Miss; J H O'Kean, co G, 13th Miss; Sgt J V Prady, co D, 18th Miss; B Carroll, co C, 8th Fla; G Allen, co B, 18th Miss; R F Sellers, co B, 13th Miss; J H Eaves, co E, 13th Miss; N P Russell, co K, 21st Miss; J R Bounett, co K, 21st Miss; N Helm, co K, 21st Miss; J C Williams, co K, 21st Miss; Lt J W Price, co K, 17th Miss; Cpl C Gramer, co K, 17th Miss; J M Comer, co G, 18th Miss; J McCade, co G, 8th Fla; H Strong, co I, 21st Miss; J Schneckenburg, co B, 17th Miss; F M Carter, co G, 13th Miss; T J Tidwell, co C, 17th Miss; S S Lynch, co B, 17th Miss; J R Holt, co A, 21st Miss; Lt J B Clayton, co G, 17th Miss; J Brady, co A, 18th Miss; W F McDougal, co B, 17th Miss; S D Knapp, co D, 17th Miss; Sergt R J Begg, co C, 13th Miss; Sgt E D Sadler, co G, 21st Miss; Capt J F Sessions, co —, 18th Miss; R N Robertson, co I, 16th Ga; R J Hughes, co F, 17th Miss; J J Carn, co C, 13th Miss; P W Murphey, co I, 17th Miss; B F Hurst, co G, 21st Miss; G W Gannon, co F, 17th Miss; N Anthony, co G, 21st Miss; T J Hunt, co B, 13th Miss; Sgt W H Eason, co I, 17th Miss; J M Witherley, co I, 13th Miss; W J Lusk, co I, 17th Miss; Ass't Surg D Hooker, 8th Fla; W B Parker, co A, 15th S C; J J Barnard, co K, 13th Miss; J M O'Neil, co E, 13th Miss; J L Finley, co C, 18th Miss; D A Cole, co D, 13th Miss; J L Smith, co G, 17th Miss; J C Fields, co I, 21st Miss; W D Chapman, co C, 17th Ga; A G Williams, co E, 18th Miss; Thos Missel, co K, 8th Fla; R A Harrington, co H, 13th Miss; J M Fielding, co A, 8th Fla; T W Harper, co B, 8th Fla; Capt C Green, co L, 17th Miss; J W Hilburne, co D, 51st Ga.

The following are the names of those who have died since their removal to the hospital:

J Esser, co E, 21st Miss; James Maniden, co L, 21st Miss; W E Smith, co G, 17th Miss; J C Collier, co B, 21st Miss.

The following officers arrived yesterday afternoon:

Lieut J K Parker, co G, 8th S C, wounded in knee; Lt J K Wiggins, co B, 18th N C; Lt W H Holt, co D, 38th N C, throat and leg; Capt H C Fite, co H, 37th N C, left arm and breast.

LOSSES IN RICHMOND COMPANIES.

Losses of the Letcher Artillery, commanded by Capt. Greenlee Davidson, in the battle before Fredericksburg, on Saturday, the 13th inst.:

Lieut. Thos. A. Brander, of Richmond, slightly wounded in side.

Seriously wounded—Privates John Shea, of Richmond, both feet amputated; James Wilson, of Richmond, in leg; S. W. Coles, of Brunswick county, in arm, and F. Smith, of Richmond, in leg.

Slightly wounded—Corp'l Winston, of Manchester, in foot; and privates James Heinen[illegible]er, of Richmond, in hip; Opie Staite, of Richmond, in foot; Frank Bernard, of Richmond, in side; John A. Estes, of Madison county, in arm; Frank Delaney, of Richmond, in hand; Michael Eaumin, of Richmond, in head; M. Douglass, of Richmond, in leg, and Jno. Morrissey, of Richmond, in arm.

Sixteen of the horses attached to the battery were killed or disabled.

During the action Capt. Davidson had command of a battalion of seven rifle pieces and two light 12 pounders, composed of three of his own pieces, one of Capt. Braxton's, two of Capt. Brown's Chesapeake Artillery, and three of Capt. Latimer's—five of the pieces were under the immediate command of Capt. Latimer.

In Capt. Latimer's command, Lieut. Graysen, of the Chesapeake Artillery, was mortally wounded; four privates were killed, sixteen wounded, and eleven horses killed.

Lieut. Zeph. C. McGruder, of the Purcell battery, of Richmond, was killed.

Lieut. James Ellett, of the Crenshaw battery, was killed by a fragment of shell while standing in conversation with Major Pegram. His battery was not firing at the time. Lieut. E. was Clerk of the Circuit Court of Richmond. His body has been brought here.

In the 3d company Richmond Howitzers, Lieut. Jas. S. Utz and private W. T. Mathews were killed, and privates Geo. Nicholas, Geo. Smith, (lost an arm,) and Samuel A. Wakeham wounded.

In the 1st company Richmond Howitzers, private Murphy was wounded.

FIGHTING IN EASTERN NORTH CAROLINA—SUCCESSFUL ATTACK ON THE ENEMY—THEIR ADVANCE FROM NEWBERN.

A portion of the 17th regiment N. C. Troops (Col. Martin,) two squadrons of the 63d regiment N. C. Troops, (Col. P. G. Evans's Partisan Rangers,) commanded by Lieutenant Colonel S. B. Evans, and a section of artillery, commanded by Capt. Moore, the whole commanded by Lieut.-Col. John C. Lamb, 17th regiment, attacked the enemy near Plymouth, on Wednesday morning last, at 5 o'clock A. M., drove them into the town, and being fired upon from houses, the artillery battered them down. Our forces captured 25 Yankees and 75 negroes. Capt. John M. Galloway, of the 63d regiment, from Rockingham county, was severely wounded while leading a charge. Three privates of Moore's battery and three of the 17th regiment were wounded though not severely. We lost none in killed. One gunboat was seriously damaged by our artillery. Some two-thirds of the town was burned, and was still burning.

A letter from Kinston, N. C., dated the 12th inst., says the enemy were advancing from Newbern in that direction, by way of Trenton. It adds:

"A courier has just arrived from the picket lines. He brings a dispatch from Maj. Nethercutt, saying that he (Nethercutt) is pressed by the enemy, and is falling back towards Kinston. The Abolitionists are advancing in large force, number not known.

"A report on the streets says that the Abolitionists mentioned in Maj. Nethercutt's dispatch number 17,000. It is also reported that Maj. Nethercutt lost eight men on yesterday evening, killed and captured by the advance guard of the enemy.

"I have just seen Lieut. Whitford, of Capt. John N. Whitford's Partisan Rangers. He reports the enemy in large force at Newbern, numbering at least 20,000, if not more, and an advance is expected in this direction daily."

Still Later.

REPULSE OF FOSTER'S FORCES.

The following dispatch was received at the War Department yesterday:

KINSTON, N. C., Dec. 14th.

Gen. Foster attacked Kinston yesterday, with 12,000 men and nine gunboats. I fought him seven hours, and have driven him back to his gunboats. His army is still in my front.

N. G. EVANS, Gen. Com'g.

FIGHTING AT BLACKWATER.

A gentleman who came from the line of the Blackwater River on Friday evening, says that the entire Yankee army is supposed to have marched out from Suffolk Thursday afternoon, but the column observed by our scouts numbered only 1,500, consisting of about 1,000 infantry and 500 cavalry. This column moved off in the direction of Isle of Wight Court-House, but at dusk suddenly diverged and bore towards Zuni and Joyner's Ford, bivouacking for the night at the farm of Robert D. Marshall. Zuni and Joyner's Ford are near the sources of the Blackwater River, and but four miles distant from each other.

At day dawn Friday morning the enemy made a simultaneous attack upon our troops at Zuni and Joyner's Ford, there being one company of Col. Claiborne's Rangers at each place. The rangers were dismounted, and fought gallantly, repulsing the enemy at each place, and driving him from the opposite bank of the narrow stream.

About 8 o'clock, the enemy's cavalry having succeeded in fording or swimming the river, between Zuni and Joyner's Ford, suddenly made their appearance in the rear of Capt. Sykes's company at Joyner's Ford, charging upon them with a yell, which was distinctly heard at Ivor, three miles distant. Capt. Sykes and his 35 men were taken prisoners.

Capt. S. had dispatched three of his men to Gen. Pryor's headquarters for reinforcements, who were also instructed to remove all the horses and other valuables from the camp. This was accomplished, and the enemy got nothing but the men and their arms who were defending the ford.

About 9 o'clock reinforcements came up to Joyner's Ford, and the enemy's cavalry recrossed, but took their prisoners along with them.

When the cars left Ivor Friday afternoon, a fight was progressing at Zuni, but up to a late hour last night we were unable to obtain any of the particulars. And here we would mention a fact which shows that there are black hearted traitors in our midst. During Thursday night, the telegraph wires on the Norfolk line were cut at some point between Ivor and Petersburg, and no communication could be had yesterday with headquarters in this place. The Abolition army at Suffolk was supposed to number about 30,000 on Tuesday last.

OCCUPATION OF GLOUCESTER C. H. IN FORCE BY THE ENEMY.

A report reached this city yesterday that the Yankees occupied Gloucester Court-House on Friday with a force of several thousand, and were committing all sorts of depredations in the country surrounding.

DIRECT TRADE.

Hon. T. Butler King, who has visited Europe to secure the establishment of lines of steamers from European ports to the ports of Georgia, has made a report of the results of his mission to the Legislature of Georgia. His efforts were first directed to Belgium, in the hope of forming a contract with the "Belgian American Company." In this he failed. The Belgians are more a manufacturing than a commercial people, and the above company seemed averse to enter into any engagements as regards the management of steamships. Mr. King then directed his attention to France, in addressing a memorial to the French Minister of Commerce.—He succeeded in inducing the French Government to change the law granting a subsidy for a Northern line to New York, and substituting Savannah for New York, and extending a Southern line from Bordeaux to the West Indies, to the same port. This was accomplished after great labor by Mr. King. Mr. King's next step was to form a contract with Mr. Frederick Sabel, of Liverpool, for a line of steamers from that port to Savannah, on the payment of a subsidy of one hundred thousand dollars as soon after peace as possible, which he was authorized to do by the laws of Georgia.

MARTIAL LAW—A LEGAL DECISION IN PETERSBURG ABOUT IT.

In Petersburg on Friday, R. N. Wilkinson and Jacob T. Crowder, charged with selling liquor in the city, were carried before Judge Gholson and discharged from the custody of the military authorities. George N. Browder, who was also up on *habeas corpus* for selling liquor in the military camps around the place, was remanded into the hands of the military authorities. The counsel for the Government took an appeal from the decisions in the first two cases and they are to be carried before the Supreme Court of Virginia. The points made by Judge Gholson in the cases named are as follows:

1. That the objection to his jurisdiction was not a valid one.

2. That the President's proclamation of martial law was founded on the act of Congress of February 27, 1862, authorizing him to suspend the writ of *habeas corpus*, and that inasmuch as that act had expired martial law had ceased to exist:

3. That the order of Gen. French, prohibiting the sale of ardent spirits in Petersburg and for a space of ten miles around it, was not binding upon citizens, inasmuch as Petersburg is not a military camp, and a commanding officer has authority to establish such a regulation only over his camp.

4. That there was no distinction between the case of Crowder, who sold liquor in Petersburg to soldiers, and Wilkinson, who sold liquor in Petersburg to others than soldiers—both Crowder and Wilkinson being civilians, in no way connected with the army.

5. That Browder, who sold liquor to soldiers in the camp of Gen. Pettigrew was lawfully arrested, though he could not be tried by Court-Martial.

6. That Wilkinson and Crowder, having violated the law of the State, should enter into bonds to be of good behavior, and to answer indictments before the Hustings Court.

The Correspondence Between Gen. Wise and Gen. Keyes.

The following is a copy of a correspondence relative to the Williamsburg (Va.) Lunatic Asylum from General Henry A. Wise to General Keyes, to ascertain the truth of rumors that the United States forces occupied the Asylum for military purposes:

BRIGADE HDQ'RS, Chaffin's Farm,
Nov. 27, 1862.

To the Officer Commanding the U. States Forces at Williamsburg, Va.:

Sir—Relatives of the unfortunate inmates of the Lunatic Asylum in the city of Williamsburg have become greatly alarmed and distressed by seeing it stated in the newspapers of the day, and by reports and rumors seeming to confirm these statements:

1. That the United States authorities have removed, or intend to remove, either all or a portion of the inmates of the State Lunatic Asylum to some Northern locality or elsewhere unknown; and

2. That since the invasion of Williamsburg by the United States forces they have occupied a large portion of the building of the State Lunatic Asylum for military uses; and,

3. That they have so disturbed all discipline and regulations of police as to crowd the two sexes and the various classes of inmates in the Lunatic Asylum together in the same wards and apartments.

These complaints have been made by the families and friends of the patients to the President of the Confederate States. He has ordered proper inquiries to be made, and I am authorized to send a flag of truce to you at Williamsburg to ascertain the real state of facts in regard to these allegations. I trust I need not say that the Confederate authorities are not willing to believe these statements are true without being better vouched for than by rumor or newspapers, and without giving even an invading enemy the opportunity of vindicating his reputation before the civilized world against all doubt as to inhumanity like this. Therefore this flag of truce is sent to soothe and quiet apprehension, naturally and excusably excitable in mothers, fathers, brothers, sisters, husbands, wives, and friends, and to pay respect to the tenderest charities of life and the most awful afflictions of mankind—charities and afflictions so sacred that States and God only can deal with them with proper care, and such as are always kept safe from all intrusion. The Lunatic Asylum at Williamsburg is a State charitable institution, long established, and of that character of hospitals the most exempt of all from the least touch of war. When the buildings of the venerable William and Mary College were burned, her ancient volumes of learning and all the material monuments of her beneficence as Alma Mater of the sages and heroes of American Revolution and American history and Glory destroyed, the President of the Confederate States abided simply the verdict of all civilized men, and justly deemed that no protest was called for from him.—But, now that the State of Virginia's children of affliction are said to be inhumanly harmed, he appeals, in behalf of these "little ones," if they are or have been injured, to no lower authority than that of Heaven to Christianity. For Lieut.-Col. R. Harrison and Major Stark, of my command, I ask an interview with you in person, and that they may be permitted, under parole of honor, as officers and gentlemen, to make any and all proper inquiries and inspection necessary to enable them to report fully and accurately on that matter of this communication.

I am, sir, most respectfully, your ob't serv't,

HENRY A. WISE, Brig'r Gen'l.

On receipt of the above letter Gen. Keyes communicated with Major-General Dix, and sent the following letter in answer to Gen. Wise:

HEADQ'RS FOURTH ARMY CORPS,
Yorktown, Va., Dec. 3, 1862.

To Brig.-Gen. H. A. Wise, C. S. A., commanding, &c., Chaffin's Farm:

Sir—Your communication of the 27th ult., addressed to the officer commanding the forces at Williamsburg, and brought by Col. Harrison and Major Stark under a flag of truce, has been transmitted to me.

Major-General Dix, commanding the department, has decided that these officers cannot be allowed to come within our lines, but that Mr. Douglas, the Superintendent of the Lunatic Asylum, can see them and lay before them a statement of the exact condition of the institution and its inmates. It is not the intention of the United States Government, so far as I know or can learn, to remove any of the patients to the North, nor has there been any authority given to occupy the building of the asylum for military purposes, further than was necessary for protection. A surgeon of the United States forces has been directed to render his professional assistance to the lunatics, and full rations of provisions have been issued to them. Coal is now being sent up, and nothing in my power has been omitted to render the unfortunate inmates of the asylum as comfortable as circumstances will permit. Your communication, though based avowedly on rumor and newspaper reports, evinces a disposition to credit a charge of cruelty towards the insane, since you associate the rumors with the destruction of the venerable William and Mary College, assuming that to have been done by us. The college buildings were burned in the confusion of a raid made by your troops within our lines. I know not who burned them; but I must take this opportunity to assure you that I am opposed to all violence not sanctioned by the usages of civilized warfare. I fully agree with you, that the awful afflictions and the tender charities which they deserve to awake in our breasts, and which are the main subject of your communication, should be exempt from every touch of war. They shall be so far as I can prevent, and I would not, to spite you nor your cause, do acts deserving the condemnation of the civilized world, and in regard to the arbitrament of that higher tribunal to which you refer. Heaven shield us! Who knows which deserves the greater [illegible] the poor lunatic in the asylum at Williamsburg [illegible] the men who have made this war!

I have the honor [illegible] sir, respectfully, your most obedient servant,

E. D. KEYES,
Major-General Commanding Corps.

EUROPEAN NEWS.

Yankee Correspondence about Intervention—Extracts from Foreign Papers—The "290," &c., &c.

The Paris correspondent of the New York *Herald* writes, on the [illegible] ult., that there is a great deal of feeling there caused by England's refusal to second France, and the Emperor is much disgusted at her action. The writer says:

In conversation yesterday with a distinguished journalist, the leading editor of a paper which is on the Government side, he expressed the opinion that this refusal would go far toward widening a breach which really exists between France and England, and which, though bridged over at present by an unnatural alliance, must sooner or later divide the two nations.

The present act of the Emperor would, he thought, stand forever as an evidence of his friendship for the United States, of his desire to see brought to an end the fearful struggle which desolates our country, while he interpreted the refusal of England to unite with France as an evidence of the desire of the former country to see us ruined and destroyed; and this is the opinion, as you will see, expressed by the Government journalists, as far as they dare express it. It [illegible] here whether England has or has not formally rejected the proposal of France. The report received yesterday was to the effect that she had.—To-day this is modified into an adjournment of the question until the result of the elections shall be known, and until dispatches shall have been received from Lord Lyons.

In any event, the *Moniteur* does not seem to give up the idea of the proposition having an effect in the United States.

In its bulletin of this morning, in referring to the guarantee given by the masters of two vessels taken by the Alabama, to pay eighty-six thousand dollars to the Government of the South, "after the conclusion of peace," the official journal remarks: "If this statement is correct, this stipulation, imposed upon one side, accepted on the other, authorizes us to believe that in the United States itself a pacific solution is not considered as either impossible or far off. The question which the dispatch of the Emperor's Minister of Foreign Affairs has just put to Europe, will come, then, in good time on the other side of the Atlantic."

Although there has been no official statement to that effect, it is generally believed that Russia has also refused to join France in the proposition, and it is now an interesting question upon which public opinion is greatly divided, whether the Emperor will or will not make the proposition to our Government alone. The Southerners here say he will, and that in case of refusal on the part of the Federal Government to accept it, he will lend the physical aid of France to the South, raise the blockade, and recognise the Southern Confederacy. The blockade once raised, they say, England would be glad to avail herself of the advantages thus offered to commerce, and would, of course, in no manner interfere with France in the aid which the latter would render to the South.

Mr. Slidell was received by the Emperor at Compiegne, a few days ago, since the circular of the Minister of Foreign Affairs was written, and he is in constant communication with the Minister himself.

I am inclined to believe that the Emperor's future course upon this matter will be moulded entirely by what he considers his interest in Mexico, and it is very certain that he looks upon the prospective occupancy of Texas by a large body of Union troops with no very favorable eye.

In spite of the claimed "impartiality" of the document of the Minister of Foreign Affairs, it is evident where the sympathies of the French Government at present lie. The bare fact that through the whole of it the two "Governments" of Washington and Richmond are regarded as equally entitled to the consideration of France shows this: the French Government may be considered as committed to the Southern interest, and it behooves us to be on the alert and prepare ourselves for any future contingencies which may arise, we know not how soon.

A London letter in the Philadelphia *Inquirer* copies the following from a paper in that city:

"So great is the impunity which Capt. Semmes and the crew of the Alabama appear to enjoy, and the utter inability or unwillingness of the United States to capture, burn or sink the famous Confederate, that the commerce between Liverpool and the United States is almost completely paralyzed and the trade is likely, unless a stop is put to the doings of the Alabama, to fall entirely into the hands of British shipowners. Already it is difficult to effect insurances upon American owned vessels, and we are informed that a large American ship, with a valuable cargo on board, and in the Mersey outward bound for the United States, was suddenly sold as she lay, for ready cash, at nearly half her value. As soon as the necessary regulations were complied with, in order to give her a British registration, and sailed for her destination with a cargo on board valued at two and a half millions of dollars."

The London *Post*, of the 22d, says:

The steamer Nicolai I., which left Liverpool a few days ago, ostensibly for St. Thomas, but really to run the blockade, carried out an immense quantity of war material for the Confederates. The Nicolai I. cleared for St. Thomas, but she will make her way to Nassau, learn the latest news as to the position of the Federal cruisers, and act accordingly. Yesterday three vessels sailed from Liverpool for Nassau, laden with some things which are in great request by the blockade breakers at Nassau. The names of these vessels are the Thistle, Severn, and Monmouth.

The Paris correspondent of the London *Post* writes as follows on the 20th ult.:

Some French journals have declared that the relations between the Governments of England and France are by no means satisfactory, a coldness having arisen out of the refusal of her Majesty's Government to subscribe to the American dispatch of M. Drouyn de l'Huys. This is not true.—On the contrary, I have reason to suppose *that the French Government has rather modified its opinions as to the wisdom of precipitate intervention* between the North and South.

ARREST OF REV. J. R. GRAVES.—The arrest of Rev J. R. Graves, of North Carolina, and his imprisonment in Castle Thunder, has been noticed. The Raleigh (N. C.) *Standard* says that Gov. Vance, hearing by telegraph, late on Monday night, of this arrest, and being obliged to leave for Wilmington on Tuesday morning, addressed a letter to the Mayor of Raleigh, requesting him to attend at the depot on Tuesday morning, and arrest and detain the officer and his prisoner until his return. The Mayor attended, and went some ten miles with the train on the Gaston Road, thinking that the parties of whom he was in search might be on board the cars. But they had either gone on the night before or taken the Danville route.

The Raleigh *Register* says:

This Mr. Graves was the author of a letter which appeared sometime since in the Richmond *Enquirer*, and in which he gave an account of a visit to the North, and a glowing description of the great prosperity of that country, and its indomitable determination to subjugate the South. We thought at the time that it was a most extraordinary production, and so stated to several gentlemen. Mr. Graves is, we learn, a Canadian by birth and education, and has been but a short time a resident of this State. It is not true, as we learn, that he was imprisoned at the North. On the contrary, he was permitted to go to the North by Gen. Dix, where he remained a month. Since his return home he has, as we are informed, been boasting of the kind treatment he received from the Northern people, and using language well calculated to bring down upon him strong suspicion that he is anything but a man who should be permitted to go at large in the South.

THE YANKEE ROBBERIES.—A letter from Highland county, Va., gives some account of the Yankee robberies in the mountains West of the Valley. The writer says:

"The Yankees robbed our county of near one hundred horses, three hundred cattle, twenty negroes, a gold watch, $2,000 or $3,000 in money, a number of blankets, butter, honey, and other small articles, that could be carried with them. They carried off fifty-eight prisoners and burned two houses. They took a number of cattle and horses from Pocahontas county, and burned one barn.—James Lockridge, of Pocahontas, lost 40 head of fat cattle. So you see we have been again largely robbed. Our people are disposing of a portion of their remaining stock, and little will be left. Many persons here are concerned as to how they are to procure the necessaries of life, and there will be suffering beyond a doubt."

Upon entering Winchester, a few weeks since, a letter says:

So soon as they entered the Martinsburg road, every house and yard was infested with the brutes, stealing bread, meat, chickens, and everything they could lay their hands on. A lieutenant in the 5th Ohio grappled a chicken in the yard of a lady resident on the roadside; she collared and thumped him well, and obtained the chicken, while her daughter engaged another fellow, whose head she chucked under the hog-pen, while in the act of reaching for another chick. She, too, was conqueror. The night before they came in they stole about 3,000 lbs. of pork, ten or twelve horses, and robbed an old lady, 80 years of age, of everything they could carry off, even to her dress cap.

Gen. W. T. Sherman, who is the military commander at Memphis, recommends that, instead of shinplasters—which the Common Council of that city proposes to issue—five, ten, twenty-five, and fifty cent packages of raw cotton be done up and passed as currency—the cotton to be of the standard value of half a dollar a pound. An ordinary roll of what is termed cotton batting weighs about half a pound, and an armful of Gen. Sherman's proposed currency would not purchase a breakfast for an ordinary-sized family.

LOCAL MATTERS.

Arrested on Charge of Murder.—A man named James Gregor was brought to Richmond from Lynchburg on Saturday, having been arrested there as the party who killed Michael Horan alias Brockets Mick, in an affray at the house of Carter & Roache, in Henrico county, a few weeks since. He was lodged in the cage for examination before the Mayor. The city police on Saturday caged Daniel Summers for stealing a gold watch and chain, valued at $150, and $100 in C. S. notes from an unknown person. Also, Billy, a slave, for stealing lard molasses and salt from John O'Neal.

Prison Items.—The following parties were lodged in Castle Thunder on Saturday: James Broderick, an escaped prisoner; Nicholas Martin, for disloyalty; John Bradley, Rodger's cavalry, desertion and stealing a horse; Miles Murray, do, for desertion; Chas Johnson, Hampton artillery, Holbrook Taylor, Co G, 25th Va bat'n, and Jacob Kell, Richmond Sharpshooters, for desertion; Corry West, Andrew Hogg, Washington Hogg, and John Smith, for execution of sentence of Court Martial; Henry Mitchell, Alexandria artillery, for desertion; John Williams, sent from Drewry's Bluff by Col. Page, for punishment; James Pearson, of the steamer Jamestown, sent by the Hustings Court; Jas McMichael, 15th La., for desertion; eighteen men were received from Camp Holmes, N. C., to be returned to their regiments.

Richmond Thieves in Petersburg.—On Friday last three lads, purporting to hail from this city, and giving the names of Tazewell Lee, Edward Sullivan, Robert Lotsy, and Jerry Dunnavant, were arrested by the Petersburg police, near the Petersburg and Richmond Railroad Depot, charged with robbing two gentlemen of between two and three hundred dollars. The parties were suspected directly after the funds were missing, and being searched, the money was found on their persons.—The oldest of the prisoners appeared to be only fifteen years, though the appearance of all of them indicated that they were not unfamiliar with crime and scenes of debauchery. The parties, who were in jail at last accounts, will no doubt be recognized by the police as a part of the gang of juvenile thieves for which this city has long been noted.

Released.—Major Nordendorff, formerly on the staff of Gen. Banks, who was taken prisoner by our men at Warrenton, after he had resigned his position in the Federal army, and brought to Richmond, where he was held as a prisoner, was released from the Libby prison by order of the Secretary of War last Friday. This officer, by birth an Austrian, occupied a prominent position in the army of that Empire as a military engineer. Prior to his resignation of office under Banks he had behaved very kindly to the residents of Warrenton in preventing the pillage of their houses by the Yankees. It was probably the opportunity he thus acquired of seeing the superiority of our race over the other that induced him to throw up his commission in the U. S. army, and express the desire to make his home in the Confederacy.

The Grand Royal Arch Chapter.—The yearly convocation of the members of the Grand Royal Arch Chapter of Virginia, the highest order of Masonry, was held in this city, at the Masonic Hall, Franklin street, on Friday evening last. The following officers were elected at the meeting, which was fully attended by delegates from all sections of the State, viz: M E John W Potts, G H Priest; M E John R Purdy, G K; Wm H Harman, G Scribe; Thos U Dudley G T; John Dove, G S; Edward H Lane, C B; John P Little, P S; Robert E Withers, R A C; Geo W Dame, M, 3d; James A Scott, M, 2d; Wm L Lushbaugh, M, 1st; John C McCabe, C; Richard D Sanxay, Master; Emanuel Semon, Janitor.

Recruits for the Chain Gang.—On Saturday seven loafers who had, at various times, fallen in the hands of the police for petty infractions of the law were brought up from the jail and carried before the Mayor, who ordered that they should be set to work as members of the chain gang. Jacob Manning, John Thomas, Benj. Page, Dan Hickey, Thos. McDonald, and Charles Grace, were ordered to work for a period of sixty days, and Jerry Sullivan, an old customer at the jail, and an inveterate toper, was put in for ninety days.

Suspicious Character Arrested.—On Saturday officers Kelley and Griffin, of the day police, discovered in an alley in rear of the Exchange Hotel, a room kept by a man named Augustus Plume, used by him as a liquor and lottery or policy shop, much resorted to by that class of the colored population who may not inappropriately be called "fast." The officers carried off Plume and the implements of his trade, and some half dozen colored men, and locked up the whole party in the cage.

Death of a Lunatic.—Richard, a servant, owned by Mr. John Crew, died at the city jail on Saturday morning last. He was decidedly *non compos mentis*, though seldom dangerous. He had been in the prison since July last, having been committed to be sent to one of the Lunatic Asylums, which never was done, the enemy having in their possession the only one at which he could have been received. He finally died as stated on Saturday. The Coroner was summoned to hold an inquest, but on learning the circumstances declined to hold one, and ordered the body to be buried.

Accident.—Yesterday morning, about 9 o'clock, while some negroes were examining a pistol in the cellar of the building on the corner of Broad and 5th streets, known as "Schutte's Hall," an accidental explosion took place, which resulted in severely wounding in the leg Zachariah Copeland, a free negro. He was taken to the Medical College, where his wounds were properly attended to.

Death of a Public Officer.—James Ellett, Clerk of Richmond Circuit Court, was killed in action near Fredericksburg by the Abolitionists, on Saturday last, by a shell. On the formation of the Crenshaw battery, he was elected first lieutenant.

Lighted Up.—The street lamps were re-lighted on Saturday night, for the first time for several months past.

PROCEEDINGS OF THE COURTS.

Hustings Court, Saturday, Dec. 13—Recorder Jas. K. Caskie Presiding.—John M. Michie was tried for shooting at John J. Crawford, corner 13th and Main streets, a few months since, to the disturbance of the public peace. The jury found defendant guilty, and fined him $500, which he paid. The Court declined to add any imprisonment. It will be remembered that in the affray between these parties Crawford shot Michie through the face with a pistol bullet.

Dick Duff, a dangerous character, in jail on suspicion of committing a murder on 17th street, was tried for making his escape therefrom on the 14th of August last. The law makes an escape a penal offence when "force and violence" is used to effect the object. That both were used by Duff and his comrades, was proved to the satisfaction of the jury who tried the case. Defendant being found guilty, was sentenced to three months' imprisonment.

Mr. Beverley R. Wellford, Jr., addressed the Court at some length in support of an application submitted by him for a new trial in the case of the girl Margaret, tried on Monday, and sentenced to be hung on the 9th day of January next, for the murder of Frances Deane Tardy, infant child of Mr. Samuel C. Tardy, whose nurse she was. Mr. Wellford contended that the verdict of guilty against his client was not based on any actual evidence of her guilt, but on the opinions of the physicians summoned in the case, that death would ensue under a given state of things, and that these were apparent. The Court refused to grant a new hearing of the case.

The Court entered an order calling the attention of the City Council to the insecure condition of the jail; its total incapacity, with all the watching that can be brought to bear, to prevent the escape of determined and desperate felons, and the necessity for either rendering it secure or building a new one.

Mayor's Court, Saturday, Dec. 13th.—Joe, slave of Gen. Dimmock, was arraigned on the charge of stealing one turkey and three hens from the roost of Martha Alvis. The identity of Joe with the despoiler was sought to be established by a soldier's hat, found in the yard from whence the fowls had been abducted, and which hat the loser shrewdly surmised belonged to the prisoner, from its great resemblance to one which was oftentimes seen on his head. To offset this Joe produced his own hat and a note from his master, stating that at the time of the abduction of the fowls the accused was in a different part of the State. He was acquitted.

Mike Leary, who had been arrested by the police for being disorderly on 17th street, Friday night, while drunk, failing to give $200 security for his good behavior, was sent to the city jail.

James S. Mall, who had been arrested for disorderly conduct, at the military ball given at the Old Market Hall, Friday night, was committed in default of bail for $200 to keep the peace.

Case of Charles, slave of Wm. Redwood, charged with insolence to R. D. Mitchell, was continued on account of the absence of the witness.

Walter Stultz, a lad about ten years of age, was brought up for going into the grocery of Turner & Perry, corner of 6th and Broad streets, Friday evening, and taking $39.10 out of their till. The lad was apprehended in the act, but he being within the age which the law declares one incapable of crime from a want of knowledge, the Mayor returned him to his parents, with the request that they would adjudicate the matter at home.

United States Senator S. G. Arnold, of Rhode Island, having been classed by the radical journals as a Republican, has written a letter repudiating all sympathy with that party, and stating that he was elected in opposition to it. Arnold is a "Conservative."

The St. Louis *Democrat*, (radical Republican,) says a majority of the Democratic editors of the North are a pack of villainous traitors, manufacturing the grossest lies against the Government and its officers, for the purpose of dividing the people of the North.

The rumor that $500,000 worth of stores were destroyed by the Federals at Abbeville, Miss., is untrue. It is stated that $3,000 will cover the whole loss.

Dr. Wm. Steptoe, an old physician of Bedford county, Va., died on the 10th inst.

TELEGRAPHIC NEWS.

Cotton Burnt.

MOBILE, Dec. 13.—A special dispatch to the *Evening News*, dated Okalona, 12th, says Colonel Bartran's scouts burned 1,500 bales of cotton this week, belonging to the Yankee speculators near Corinth.

There is no movement of the enemy in this direction.

Richmond Dispatch.

TERMS OF ADVERTISING:

1 square 1 day	$0 75	1 square 5 days	$2 [illegible]
1 do. 2 days	1 25	1 do. 6 days	[illegible]
1 do. 3 days	1 75	1 do. 12 days	[illegible]
1 do. 4 days	2 25	1 do. 1 month	15 00

LARGER ADVERTISEMENTS IN EXACT PROPORTION.

☞ Advertisements published till forbid will be charged 75 cents per square of EIGHT LINES for the first insertion, and 50 cents for each continuance.

The New-York Times.

VOL. XII—NO. 3505. | NEW-YORK, WEDNESDAY, DECEMBER 17, 1862. | PRICE THREE CENTS.

FROM THE ARMY OF THE POTOMAC.

Evacuation of Fredericksburgh by Our Forces.

The Army Again on the Falmouth Side of the Rappahannock.

The Movement Executed with Success.

THE WOUNDED ALL SAFE.

Full Description of the Terrible Battle of Saturday.

Our Losses from Ten to Fifteen Thousand.

INCIDENTS OF THE DAY.

OUR DISPATCH FROM HEADQUARTERS.

HEADQUARTERS OF THE ARMY OF THE POTOMAC, FALMOUTH, Tuesday, Dec. 16—1¾ P. M.

During last night the Army of the Potomac evacuated their positions on the opposite side of the river.

The movement was a perilous one but it was conducted in safety.

The artillery was the first to cross over the river.

The last of the infantry brought up the rear shortly after daylight.

The enemy never discovered the movement until it was too late to do us any harm.

As soon as the last man had got safely across the river the pontoon bridges were removed, thus cutting off all communication between the two shores.

Our wounded are all safe and on this side of the river.

There was a heavy wind all last night, accompanied with considerable rain, which assisted us in our movement, as it prevented the rebels from learning our intentions.

SPECIAL DISPATCH FROM WASHINGTON.

WASHINGTON, Tuesday, Dec. 16.

Sabbath with the Army of the Potomac passed with comparative quiet, and there was only occasional firing between pickets, and desultory shots from the enemy's batteries. The movement of the army on its withdrawal from Fredericksburgh to the north bank of the Rappahannock began at dark on Monday night, and was successfully accomplished before daylight next morning. All the sick and wounded were removed during the day to hospital tents on this side, with the apparent purpose, on the part of Gen. BURNSIDE, of renewing the engagement in the afternoon of that day. Those most seriously wounded were conveyed on stretchers and in ambulances, while every one able to do so walked across. The middle pontoon bridge was chiefly used, that being more out of range of the enemy's batteries at the lower part of the town.

Gen. BURNSIDE inspected the position of the troops in the afternoon, in the town, and was greeted with cheers which must have been distinctly heard in the enemy's lines. Activity throughout every department indicated that a battle was imminent. The Irish Brigade assembled in and around the theatre, where the ceremony of presenting to it a set of beatiful colors, just sent from New-York City, was gone through with, Gen. MEAGHER making an address. The enemy's batteries kept a regular fire upon the upper crossing, in order to retard the passage of the troops. The Surgeons were ordered to be in readiness to receive and care for a large number of additional wounded, and red flags were displayed on the tops of many of the large houses in town which were to be used for temporary hospitals.

The withdrawal of our forces from Fredericksburgh had, however, been determined on at a council of all the Corps Commanders during the day. It was regarded as a perilous undertaking, but one that, if successful, would rescue the army from the necessity of risking another battle, with the prospect of accomplishing little except the destruction of valuable lives.

The troops had received no intimated of their having to retreat, and had laid down rest to upon their arms for the night. The order then for them to fall in. many supposed it was for a night assault upon the enemy's works, and were not undeceived until they found themselves upon the pontoon bridges actually returning across the stream.

A heavy gale of wind, which blew all sound away from the rebel lines, greatly facilitated the movement. Bridges were covered with earth, to deaden the sound of the moving artillery, and a dark night hid every object from view.

Gen. FRANKLIN'S Grand Division, occupying the extreme left, began to move as soon as it was dark, and the right and centre of Gen. SUMNER and HOOKER took up the line of march almost simultaneously, moving in good order, but silently away from under the very guns of the enemy.

All three of the crossings were used, making six bridges. No accident of consequence occurred. The troops obeyed with alacrity every order, and waited with patience their turn to cross. The artillery and infantry alternated in moving colums, very much in the order in which they went into battle.

Many officers and soldiers expressed great regret at being withdrawn from before the enemy, saying that they would have preferred dying in front of the rebel batteries. Nevertheless, every one acquiesced in the wisdom of the movement.

Few only of the wounded are believed to have been left on the field within reach of the enemy's rifle pits.

Two brigades, belonging to Gen. BUTTERFIELD'S corps, occupy the town as advanced pickets. Our artillery, placed on the hither bank of the river, will coöperate in keeping possession of the town.

The movement, from beginning to end, was a complete success, and the various commands returned to their former encampments to repose.

At sunrise on Tuesday morning our heavy guns were opened on the rebel batteries, but elicited little response.

THE SCENE OF SATURDAY'S ACTION.

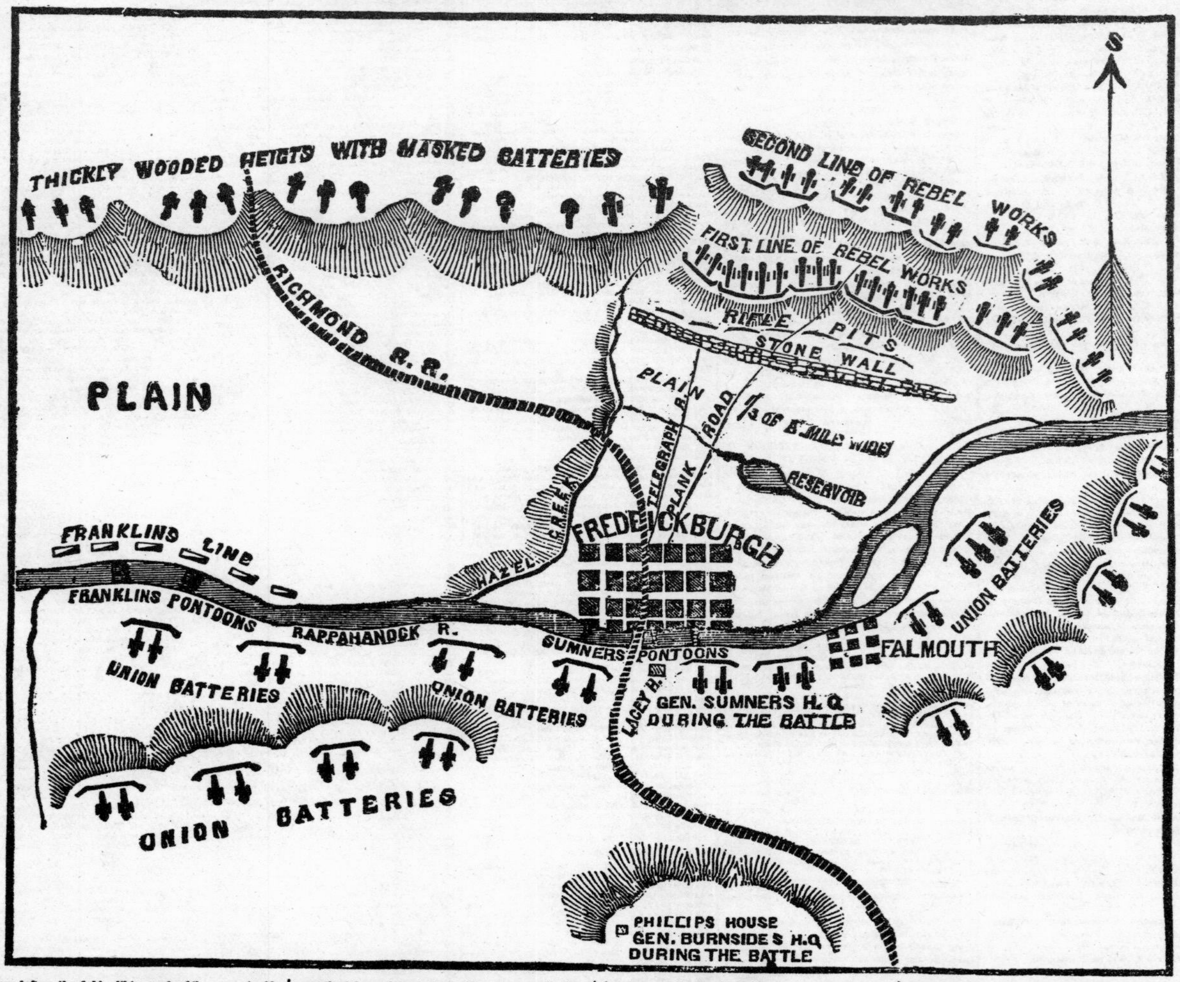

THE BATTLE OF FREDERICKSBURG.

Full and Reliable Details from Our Special Correspondent.

PHILLIPS HOUSE, HEADQUARTERS OF GEN. SUMNER, OPPOSITE FREDERICKSBURGH, VA., Saturday—Midnight, Dec. 13, 1862.

The battle of Fredericksburgh, which has been raging since 10 o'clock this morning, without a moment's pause, was closed by darkness to-night.

In its duration, its intensity, if not, also, in the losses it has occasioned, it caps the climax of the whole series of the battles of the campaign. The Nation will stand aghast at the terrible price which has been paid for its life when the realities of the battle-field of Fredericksburgh are spread before it.

Unhappily, like many of our engagements, though serving to illustrate the splendid valor of our troops, it has failed to accomplish the object sought. The sequel alone can tell whether the work of to-day is to be the prelude to a glorious victory or an ignominious defeat. But the result thus far leaves us with a loss of from ten to fifteen thousand men, and absolutely nothing gained. Along the whole line the rebels hold their own. Again and again we have hurled forward our masses on their position. At each time the hammer was broken on the anvil!

I have no heart, in the mood which the events of to-day have inspired, to write other than a bald record of facts. Whatever there was in the battle scene of picturesque or sublime—and viewed merely as a spectacle a great battle displays these qualities in a way that no manifestation of natural forces or of human energy ever can—must shrink and shrivel before the awful earnestness of the issue. Of course at this moment it is impossible to give more than the most general impressions;—the phenomena of a battle are too multifarious and complicated for the resources of any one observer; and the man does not live who can reproduce with life and truth the reality of even the smallest engagement.

The theatre of operations to-day extended from Fredericksburgh on the right and down the south side of the Rappahannock for two miles. The accompanying diagram, together with a brief description, may serve to make the account a little clearer.

Immediately behind the town of Fredericksburgh, the land forms a plateau, or smooth field, running back for about a third of a mile. It then rises for forty or fifty yards, forming a ridge of ground, which runs along to the left for about a quarter of a mile, where it abuts at Hazel Dell, a ravine formed by the Hazel River, which empties into the Rappahannock, west of the town. At the foot of the ridge runs the telegraph road, flanked by a stone wall. This eminence was studded with rebel batteries. To the right, along up the river, the ridge prolongs itself to opposite Falmouth, and beyond; and here, too, batteries were planted on every advantageous position. Back of the first ridge is another plateau, and then a second terrace of wooded hills, where a second line of fortifications were placed. Between the rear of the town and the first ridge, a canal runs right and left, and empties into the river some distance above Falmouth.

This plain, of a third of a mile deep, between the suburbs of Fredericksburgh and the first ridge of hills, was the theatre of operations of the Right Grand Division of the army, under Major-Gen. SUMNER. On this narrow theatre our brave troops surged and swept, forward and backward, in the tide of battle, for ten long hours.

A word now on the scene of operations of the Left Grand Division.

From the lower part of the town the ridge on which it is built slopes abruptly down to a comparatively level or undulating country, which stretches for some miles down the Rappahannock. About a couple of miles back of the river it rises into a wooded slope. At a point a mile and a half below Fredericksburgh, two pontoons had been thrown across on Thursday morning, and on Friday the whole of the Left Grand Division, under the command of Maj.-Gen. FRANKLIN, had marched over the river. Daylight of Saturday found the force drawn up in battle array on this broad plain skirting the Rappahannock.

The battle-ground, though very marshy in some places, presented a fine field for military evolutions. The turnpike leading to Fredericksburgh runs about one-half of a mile from and nearly parallel to the river. Beyond is the railroad, and still further beyond, the woody range of hills in which the enemy were strongly entrenched. About a mile and a half from Fredericksburgh, nearly on the river edge, is situated A. N. BARNORD's stone mansion, after the English style.

The line of battle as it appeared in the morning, was as follows: The Sixth Army Corps, under Gen. SMITH, (FRANKLIN'S old force,) on the right, composed of three divisions, namely: Gen. NEWTON, on extreme right and rear; Gen. BURNS, on the centre, and Gen. HOWE, on the left.

The First Army Corps, Gen. REYNOLDS', extending still further to the left, drawn up in the following order: Gen. GIBBONS' Division on the right, connecting with Gen. HOWE'S; Gen. MEADE'S, centre, and Gen. DOUBLEDAY, left, fronting to the southward and resting nearly on the river. This constituted the order in which our forces were drawn up, there being three distinct lines of battle.

Opposed to our right, under Gen. SUMNER, was the rebel left, under command of Gen. LONGSTREET. Opposed to our left, under Gen. FRANKLIN, was the rebel right, under Gen. JACKSON. Gen. LEE, Generalissimo of the Southern army, was in person in command of the Confederate forces during the whole day.

The plan of Gen. BURNSIDE, agreed upon in Council of War, was to endeavor to pierce the rebel centre. Early on the morning of Saturday the order was given that SUMNER'S left, composed of the Ninth Army Corps, under command of Gen. WILCOX, should be extended until it reached FRANKLIN'S right—thus forming a continuous line of battle along the river for two miles, the left resting on the river at the point where the lower pontoons cross, and the right on Fredericksburgh. The left wing, comprising the whole of FRANKLIN'S command, (fifty thousand men.) should then be swung round, as on a pivot formed by SUMNER'S extreme right, resting on Fredericksburgh. If successful in this manœuvre, FRANKLIN would divide the rebel line, take possession of the railroad, (the line of retreat,) and come in on the flank of the rebel works back of Fredericksburgh. While this movement was being developed, a division was to be sent up from Gen. SUMNER'S command, by the plank road, to storm the ridge. If there should be any failure in this, it was hoped the coöperation of FRANKLIN would presently make success certain. HOOKER'S corps was destined to act as a reserve.

The dawn of Saturday found the forces distributed as thus indicated. It was a fine Virginia morning—mild and balmy as a September day, though the mist and fog of a late Indian Summer hung over the field of battle. About 8 o'clock, the Phillips House (the headquarters of Gen. SUMNER, about a mile from the river on the north side, and where, by the kind hospitality of the large-hearted old soldier, I had been staying for some time during a spell of camp-fever) was the scene of a numerous assemblage of officers. Gen. BURNSIDE and Gen. HOOKER joined Gen. SUMNER here, and the balcony and grounds in front were presently filled with officers and Aides.

It was with alarm and pain I found a general want of confidence and gloomy forebodings among some men whose sound judgment I had learned to trust. The plan of attacking the rebel stronghold directly in front would, it was feared, prove a most hazardous enterprise, and one of which there is no successful example in military history. It was doubted that the coöperation of the right and left, according to the programme, would admit of practical executions, and things were generally at loose ends. "The chess-board," said NAPOLEON at Wagram, "is dreadfully confused; there is but I that see through it." We all felt that the first part of the remark was applicable to our own case. But did we all feel equally confident that there was in our case an "I" that "saw through it?"

About 11½ o'clock I crossed the Rappahannock on the upper pontoon bridge, and passed through the town of Fredericksburgh, along the main street. At this time brisk skirmishing was going on in the outskirts of the town, the rebel sharpshooters stubbornly contesting every inch of the ground as our skirmishers advanced. Caroline, or Main-street, was occupied by Gen. KIMBALL'S, Gen. FERRERO'S, and Acting Gen. ZOOK'S Brigade, with portions of HANCOCK'S Division; the latter, with his artillery, lined the bank of the river in the neighborhood of the middle crossing, which is just below the railroad bridge. Other troops from the corps of Gens. WILCOX and COUCH occupied the other streets of the town nearer the line of advance. Our batteries replied across the river, covering the advance of our forces.

In the meantime FRANKLIN had been for a couple of hours briskly engaged with the enemy on the left. The force in Fredericksburgh had driven the rebels out of the suburbs of the town and rested their column on the canal. The time had now come to attempt an advance on the rebel position.

The orders were to move rapidly; charge up the hill and take the batteries at the point of the bayonet. Orders easy to give, but, ah! how hard of execution!

Look at the position to be stormed.

There is a bare plateau of a third of a mile, which the storming party will have to cross. In doing so they will be exposed to the fire, first, of the enemy's sharpshooters, posted behind a stone wall running along the base of the ridge—of a double row of rifle-pits on the rise of the crest—of the heavy batteries behind strong field-works that stud the top of the hill—of a powerful infantry force now lying concealed behind these—of a plunging fire from the batteries on the lower range—of a double enfilading fire from "cannon to right of them, cannon to left of them." Sebastopol was not half as strong.

The line of battle was formed by COUCH'S Corps, (the Second,) composed of the Divisions of FRENCH, HANCOCK and HOWARD, the left of the line abutting on STURGIS' Division of WILCOX'S Corps, (the Ninth.) The first advanced was FRENCH'S, composed of the brigades of KIMBALL, MORRIS and WEBER, supported by HANCOCK'S Division, consisting of the Brigades of CALDWELL, ZOOK and MEAGHER.

Forming his men under cover of a small knoll in the rear of the town, skirmishers were deployed to the left toward Hazel Dell; STURGIS, supporting at the same time, moved up, and rested on a point on the railroad.

The moment they exposed themselves on the railroad, forth burst the deadly hail. From the rifle-pits came the murderously-aimed missiles; from the batteries, tier above tier, on the terraces, shot planes of fire; from the enfilading cannon, distributed on the arc of a circle two miles in extent, came cross showers of shot and shell.

Imagine, if you can, for my resources are unequal to the task of telling you, the situation of that gallant but doomed division.

Across the plain for a while they swept under this fatal fire. They were literally mowed down. The bursting shells make great gaps in their ranks; but these are presently filled by the "closing up" of the line. For fifteen immortal minutes at least they remain under this fiery surge. Onward they press, though their ranks grow fearfully thin. They have passed over a greater part of the interval and have almost reached the base of the hill, when brigade after brigade of rebels rise up on the crest and pour in fresh volleys of musketry at short range. To those who, through the glass, looked on, it was a parlous sight indeed. Flesh and blood could not endure it. They fell back shattered and broken, amid shouts and yells from the enemy.

Gen. FRENCH'S Division went into the fight six thousand strong; late at night he told me he could count but fifteen hundred!

The fire of the rebel batteries was not the only thing from which our men had to suffer. Thinking to silence the enemy's guns, our batteries planted on the bluff, on the north side of the river, embracing the 4½ siege guns, some batteries of 20-pounder Parrots and the artillery of the left and left centre opened fire. The intervening space is between twenty-seven hundred and three thousand yards: too great a distance to calculate on the projectiles carrying with accuracy—particularly contractors' ammunition. If shell should fall short, or take an oblique direction, and explode among our troops, it would be difficult to see how a panic could be prevented. Promptly seeing this danger, Gen. HUNT, Chief of Artillery, instantly dispatched orders to cease firing. It was well he did so, for immediately afterward an Aid came galloping from Gen. COUCH, from the other side of the river, begging that our batteries should cease, as they were actually firing into his command!

While the broken column retires to its original position in the outskirts of the town, to re-form for a new encounter, let us see what goes on on the left.

At daylight, the forces comprising the left Grand Division of the army appeared drawn up in battle array on the broad plain below Fredericksburgh and skirting the Rappahannock.

At early morn the Thirteenth Massachusetts, Pennsylvania Bucktails, and two or three other regiments, were deployed in front as skirmishers, between whom and the rebel skirmishers considerable firing took place. No sooner, however, had the heavy mist cleared away, than Capt. HALL'S Battery, (Second Maine,) planted at the right of GIBBONS' Division, opened fire upon the rebels. Artillery firing now became general along the whole line, which was returned by the rebels. Heavy siege guns in our rear, the First Maryland, First Massachusetts Batteries, and Battery D Fifth Artillery, on the right; Capt. RANSOM'S, and Capt. WALKER'S in front, and COWAN'S New-York, and Lieut. HARN'S Third New-York Independent on the left, and other batteries, kept up a terrific fire on the rebels. Orders now came to advance, and about 9 o'clock GIBBONS' and MEADE'S Divisions commenced moving slowly forward.

Gen. MEADE'S command, consisting of the Pennsylvania Reserves, arranged in the following order: First Brigade, embracing the First, Second, one Hundred and Twenty-first and Sixth Regiments at the left; Second Brigade—Third, Fourth, Seventh and Eighth, centre; and Third Brigade, (JACKSON'S,) Fifth, Tenth, Eleventh and Twelfth, at the right.

The advance resulted in almost straightening our lines, which were before somewhat of a crescent.

Considerable resistance was met with, yet the forces continued to move forward, until at mid-day the line of battle was three-quarters of a mile in advance of where it had been at the outset. But now came the reserve fire of the enemy with terrific force. Shot, shell and canister were poured into our men from various points, while the rebel infantry appearing, fired with rapidity. Still they continued to press on. Several batteries moved forward at the same time. As our troops saw the enemy giving way, cheer after cheer rent the air.

About 1 o'clock, Gen. MEADE ordered a charge, which was well executed—the men pressing on the edge of the very crest, and skilfully penetrating by a movement on the flank, an opening which happened to occur between the Division of A. P. HILL and EARLY'S Brigade, captured several hundred prisoners belonging to the Sixty-first Georgia and Thirty-first North Carolina.

While the fight was progressing at this point, the enemy sent four heavy columns down on our left, near the river. They were handsomely repulsed and driven back, however, by Gen. DOUBLEDAY'S Division—COWAN'S New-York and Lieut. HARNS' Fourth Artillery, and Third New-York Batteries aiding very materially in the discomfiture of the enemy. Owing to the lack of reinforcements, Gen. MEADE'S command was obliged to fall back a quarter of a mile, where they remained—three-quarters of a mile beyond the ground first occupied.

Very heavy musketry firing continued along the line, neither side gaining any material advantage. About 1½ o'clock the first line of battle in Gen. GIBBONS' Division was relieved by the second, when TOWER'S Brigade, now commanded by Col. ROOT, charged over an open field beyond the railroad, and down into the edge of the woods, occupying the breastworks which the enemy had constructed here, and capturing 200 prisoners, belonging to the Thirty-sixth North Carolina and a South Carolina regiment. Gen. GIBBONS was severely wounded in the right hand. They held their own for some time, but were eventually compelled to fall back. The Second Maine Battery advanced with GIBBONS' Division. When it fell back, three guns were left to bear upon the advancing enemy. An order came at that moment to cease firing, as the force coming from the woods were our own men. When it had advanced, however, to within fifty yards, the Commander of the battery became convinced that they were rebels, and moving on to capture this battery, five guns were opened upon them, but after five rounds had been fired, the battery was ordered to fall back. Having fallen back the Captain called for volunteers to return and bring off the battery. Sergeant BERRY, Sergeant STEVENS, Corporal R. GREELEY, and twelve men belonging to the 16th Maine Regiment, stepped forward. The undertaking though a hazardous one, proved successful, as the abandoned gun was brought off in safety. It was while the fight was progressing at this point that Gen. BAYARD was fatally wounded. He had just reached Gen. FRANKLIN'S headquarters in a small grove of the Bernard House, and taken a seat under one of the trees, when a ball, striking a few yards in front of him, glanced and then went through his thigh, inflicting a fearful wound. He was immediately conveyed to the Bernard House and placed in charge of Dr. PHILLIPS, Surgeon of the Brigade. As he was lying on the couch, the Chaplain of the HARRIS' Light Cavalry approached and inquired if he desired him to write anything for him. "By-and-by," he replied; then turning to Surgeon HOSKEY, he inquired if he should be able to live forty-eight hours. A negative answer being given, he further inquired if he should die easy. Several of the surgeons in attendance thought his life might be saved by amputating the wounded limb, but the chances were so small he preferred not to undergo the operation. He was perfectly sensible, and never for once lost that self-possession which has always characterized him on the field of battle.

About 2 o'clock Gen. BIRNEY'S Division, of Gen. HOOKER'S Grand Division, which had been delayed for some time in crossing by the enemy's shells,

Continued on Eighth Page.

Charleston Daily Courier.

NO. 19,349 CHARLESTON, S. C. CONFEDERATE STATES OF AMERICA. WEDNESDAY MORNING, DECEMBER 24, 1862. VOL. LX.

BY TELEGRAPH.

THE LATEST NEWS.

IMPORTANT FROM THE NORTH!

Effects of the Fredericksburg Battle!

RECONSTRUCTION OF LINCOLN'S ENTIRE CABINET DEMANDED!!

RESIGNATION OF WM. H. SEWARD AND HIS SON F. W. SEWARD.

REPORTED RESIGNATION OF BURNSIDE, ETC.

RICHMOND, December 22.—A special dispatch to the Richmond *Enquirer* brings Northern dates to the 20th instant.

WM H. SEWARD, Secretary of State, and his son F. W. SEWARD, Assistant Secretary, have both resigned, and a reconstruction of the entire Cabinet is probable.

The reason given for this step is the failure of BURNSIDE's army at Fredericksburg.

On the 18th instant a Committee of Republican Senators waited on LINCOLN, and asked a reconstruction of the Cabinet. SEWARD and his son immediately tendered their resignations. They had not been accepted, but the Philadelphia *Inquirer* says they will be. BLAIR, it is reported, will follow first, and HALLECK will be removed.

The Washington *Star* gives the history of the Republican caucus, showing that steps were taken there for a reconstruction of the Cabinet, and thinks all of SEWARD's colleagues will follow his example.

The Philadelphia *Inquirer* has a report that BURNSIDE has resigned. The Yankees admit a loss at Fredericksburg of fourteen hundred killed and eight thousand wounded.

The Richmond *Dispatch* has Northern dates of the 18th inst

BURNSIDE telegraphed HALLECK as follows in relation to the withdrawal of his army:

"The army was withdrawn to this side of the river because I felt the position in front could not be carried. It was a military necessity, either to retreat or attack A repulse would have been disastrous to us. The army was withdrawn at night, without the knowledge of the enemy, and without loss either of property or men.

(Signed) A. E. BURNSIDE."

Northern correspondents, however, acknowledge a complete failure at Fredericksburg.

The New York *World*, of the 19th inst., concedes the late battle at Fredericksburg to be the most terrible defeat of the war. It says "the loss will rather exceed than come under fifteen thousand five hundred, as previously estimated. MEAGHER's brigade went into the fight twelve hundred strong, and but two hundred and fifty could be found next morning. Other brigades suffered as much."

The *World* says editorially: "Heaven help us—there seems to be no help in man. The cause is perishing. Hope after hope has vanished, and now the only prospect is the very blackness of despair. Here we are, reeling back from the third campaign upon Richmond, fifteen thousand of the Grand Army sacrificed at one sweep, and the rest escaping only by a hair's breadth."

BURNSIDE telegraphs from Headquarters, December 17, that the whole army had re crossed the river without loss of men or property; that it was found impossible to carry the crest of hills, and re-crossing became a military necessity.

The New York *World* says the army will now go into winter quarters, because it cannot go anywhere else.

The Louisville *Journal*, of the 19th, speaking of the battle of Fredericksburg, says: "It is painful and absolutely sickening to read of the horrible slaughter of our troops at Fredericksburg. The carnage was truly frightful. The war cannot be carried on much longer as it has been."

The following dispatch occupies the telegraphic column of the *Journal*:

"NEW YORK, December 18.—Gen. FRENCH went into battle with seven thousand men, and two days after the battle only twelve hundred reported to him. The total loss in his Brigade alone was thirteen hundred and fifty five."

A writer in the Philadelphia *Inquirer* places the Federal loss at fifteen thousand.

Congress has appointed a Committee, who left Washington on Thursday, for the Rappahannock, to inquire into the facts of the late terrible disaster at Fredericksburg.

Gold in New York, on the 18th, closed at 132; on the 18th, at 132¼ to 132⅞ Foreign Exchange on the 18th was quoted at 145¼ to 146¼.

Several of BANKS' fleet had put into Hilton Head, short of coal, disabled, &c. The troops on board had suffered much.

Additional particulars of the battle of Prairie Cave, Arkansas, published in the Northern papers, show the Abolition loss in killed and wounded to be nine hundred and ninety-five, and the rebel loss twenty-seven hundred.

The "pirate" *Alabama* had been heard from. She was at Dominica, West Indies, on the 28th of November, in pursuit of a schooner which had taken refuge at Dominica. The U. S. steam ship *San Jacinto* had been at Point Petrie only a few days before, but had sailed for St. Thomas.

From Richmond.

PROCLAMATION FROM PRESIDENT DAVIS—BUTLER PRONOUNCED A FELON AND AN OUTLAW.

RICHMOND, December 22.—President DAVIS has issued a proclamation that the execution of MUMFORD, at New Orleans, was an act of deliberate murder; in view of which, and other atrocities, he pronounces BUTLER a felon who deserves capital punishment, and orders that he be treated not as a public enemy, but as an outlaw and an enemy to mankind, and when captured to be immediately executed by hanging.

No commissioned officer of the United States, captured, shall be released until BUTLER meets the punishment due to his crimes. All commissioned officers in BUTLER's command are to be considered robbers and criminals, deserving death, and when captured reserved for execution.

Rumors in circulation that the enemy are crossing the Rappahannock are not confirmed. HAMPTON's cavalry captured one hundred and seventy prisoners a day or two since near Dumfries.

[SECOND DISPATCH.]

SPLENDID DASH OF HAMPTON'S CAVALRY.

RICHMOND, December 23.—Gen. HAMPTON has made a circuit of the enemy's lines and found him in full force on Bull Run and Dumfries, moving slowly towards Washington.

In his dash upon the enemy's lines, General HAMPTON's Cavalry captured a number of sutlers' wagons loaded with Christmas supplies, some of which were marked for General BURNSIDE. A train of thirty-two new wagons with six fine mules to each was also captured and brought off.

The notorious Abolition spy, UNDERWOOD, was captured at his mother's house, in Prince William county.

Gen. HAMPTON has rendered important service with his brigade of cavalry since the winter campaign opened. About two hundred prisoners captured by his command will arrive here to-day.

The *Herald*, of the 18th, says the best appointed army the world ever saw has been whipped by ragamuffins.

[THIRD DISPATCH.]

ALL QUIET AT FREDERICKSBURG—ADDITIONAL FROM THE NORTH.

RICHMOND, December 23.—JOHN C. UNDERWOOD, the spy captured by HAMPTON's cavalry, was the first man to raise the Black Republican flag on Virginia soil.

Passengers by the evening train report that there is no change in the situation of affairs at Fredericksburg.

The Philadelphia *Inquirer*, received here, fully confirms the resignation of SEWARD and the other news forwarded yesterday.

A Washington correspondent says since the late disaster at Fredericksburg the feeling has grown almost universal that there must be a change in the Cabinet and the policy of the Administration before the war can be prosecuted further SEWARD and his son still remain at their desks awaiting the appointment of their successors.

The Richmond *Enquirer* has Northern dates of the 22d instant.

The *Herald* says SEWARD and CHASE have certainly resigned. SEWARD will not remain in office if HALLECK and STANTON are retained, and CHASE will not remain if SEWARD quits.

FREMONT is mentioned as the radical candidate for Commander-in-Chief, and McCLELLAN as the conservative candidate.

The *Herald* says: "Sunday was the gloomiest day at Washington known in history." It thinks if FREMONT is appointed, or STANTON retained, the newly elected Governors of six great States will withdraw their troops and demand a change of policy.

A dispatch from Washington, Sunday, at mid night, says: "The President has announced that he is the proper judge of the conduct of his armies, and will not be influenced by the dictation of Senators."

BURNSIDE was in Washington on Sunday. It was telegraphed from BURNSIDE's headquarters on the 21st inst. that his staff knew nothing of his resignation.

Gold rose one per cent. in New York when the news of SEWARD's resignation reached there.

Later from Europe.

ARRIVAL OF THE SCOTIA.

RICHMOND, December 23.—The steam ship *Scotia* has arrived at New York, bringing Liverpool dates to the 6th instant.

There is nothing new on American affairs.

The Paris *Moniteur*, in a quasi-official form alludes to the presence of the French squadron at New Orleans, which is represented to have greatly elated the dissatisfied population.

The Cotton famine distress in France is increasing in severity.

The London *Globe* thinks the situation of America promises striking results soon.

The Liverpool Cotton Market closed quiet. Uplands were quoted from 22 to 24 d.

JAMES SHERIDAN KNOWLES, the distinguished poet and dramatist, is dead.

From Chattanooga.

RAIL ROAD ACCIDENT—DEATH OF EX-GOVERNOR HOUSLY.

CHATTANOOGA, December 22.—Two soldiers, names unknown, were killed on Monday on the Northern and Central Rail Road by the turning over of a car. They belonged to a battery being transported South, and were with their guns when the accident occurred.

Ex-Governor WM. HOUSLY, of Kentucky, died on the 17th inst.

[SECOND DISPATCH.]

ANOTHER CONFEDERATE VICTORY—BRILLIANT SUCCESS OF GEN. FORREST.

CHATTANOOGA, December 23.—A special dispatch to the "Chattanooga *Rebel*" from Tuscumbia, December 22d, says: "A gentleman who arrived here to-day with his brother's corpse, killed in a fight at Lexington, Tennessee, says: "General FORREST attacked and routed the Federals there, on the 18th, capturing a battery, horses and all, and forty prisoners, besides five hundred carbines, two hundred horses, several hundred saddles and considerable commissary stores."

Citizens reported the enemy at Lexington five thousand strong, all new recruits. Our loss was very trifling. A man here says the Yankees had returned from Okolona.

From Mobile.

THE YANKEE ABOLITION CONGRESS—CONFEDERATE BONDS AND SOUTHERN PAPER IN NEW YORK.

MOBILE, December 23.—A special dispatch to the *Advertiser and Register*, from Murfreesboro', December 22, says: "Late Northern papers state that a bill has been introduced into the Yankee Congress authorizing the organization of one hundred regiments of contrabands, to serve seven years; also, to establish a line of steamers between New York and Liberia, and appropriates the proceeds of confiscated rebel property for these purposes.

The New York *Times* says parties in the North are eagerly purchasing Confederate bonds at fifty cents on the dollar, and that private paper of wealthy Southerners sells readily at par.

CANTON, Miss., December 22.—GRANT's army has fallen back beyond the Tallahatchie river. An important expedition, under General VAN DORN, which has been out several days, has not yet been heard from.

From Selma, Ala.

BRILLIANT EXPLOIT OF VAN DORN'S CAVALRY

SELMA, ALA., December 23.—The Selma (Ala.) *Reporter*, of this morning, says: "Passengers on last night's train from Meridian, report that five thousand cavalry, under Gen. VAN DORN, dashed into Corinth, Miss., on Sunday, dispersed the Yankees and took possession of the place."

Retaliation and Resignations.

The telegraphic column in this morning's issue of the *Courier* contains intelligence of tremendous importance. Since this sanguinary conflict began its course, there has never been borne over the electric wires news that has so shocked and stirred the heart, as that which appears in its proper place on this, the morning before the sacred festival of the Nativity. And it is worthy of remark that a portion of that intelligence, and by far the most important in its nature and consequences, is seemingly strangely out of keeping with the character of the day that will be ushered in by the sun of the morrow. But this Confederacy of independent sovereignties is before God innocent of offence and crime, in the adoption of those measures announced in the proclamation of President DAVIS. On behalf of the people of whom he is the ruler and representative, into whose hands the interests and destiny of a great people have been committed by the allotment of Providence, that high functionary now stands before the world as the avenger of atrocities that have horrified the universal heart of christendom, and placed LINCOLN side by side with those monsters of wickedness that have disgraced mankind in former days. Upon the Government which has maintained the mean and bloody wretch in the place of power he has occupied, and upon his own guilty head, rest the responsibility of the action of our President, and he stands acquitted of all blame in the judgment of God and man.

The proclamation of our Chief Magistrate pronounces BUTLER guilty of deliberate murder in hanging MUMFORD, and stigmatizes the infamous coward as an enemy to mankind, who, having forfeited his life to humanity and justice, deserves capital punishment in the most ignomious manner. That paper also characterizes all commissioned officers under BUTLER's command as robbers, as criminals who, when captured, shall be reserved for execution, and directs that no United States commissioned officer shall be released until the punishment due his crimes has been meted out to BUTLER.

That proclamation, while it does not enjoin a war to the knife, will undoubtedly intensify the bitterness of the animosity raging in the bosoms of the combatants, and make this strife the more fierce and sanguinary.

The demand for the person of the base fellow who is lording it with a heavy hand over the women and children and old men of New Orleans will, of course, meet with a stern and peremptory *refusal* from the kindred spirits at Washington. And all his antecedents assure us that the hero of the first Yankee expedition to Richmond will never adventure his precious self where brave men are bleeding and dying. He was at a safe distance from the battle field of Big Bethel, and entered New Orleans after it had surrendered to FARRAGUT's formidable fleet. And were he, under the pressure of extraordinary circumstances, to attempt the conduct of a battle he would fight his troops under a shelter where he would be secure from the swift winged messenger of death. No matter how long this contest lasts, we are certain that this miserable wretch who bears the guise of man will never be caught or killed in battle, and we are equally certain that his Government will never surrender the execrable creature to the demands of justice.

The sword which now hangs over the heads of his commissioned officers will remain suspended there, and those holding commissions in the Abolition army who fall into our hands will remain in captivity till the war comes to an end. But perchance, after waiting a reasonable time upon the Government waging war upon us, should that power persist in its refusal to accede to the just demands of our President, that sword may descend upon the partners of his guilt, and thus a war initiated that shall exceed all other wars in bloody rancor and savage ferocity.

The resignation of SEWARD and his son, the removal of HALLECK, BLAIR and BURNSIDE, and the reconstruction of LINCOLN's Cabinet, are items of news which, if true, give rise to many conjectures and surmises. But without indulging these conjectures, content meantime to await their effects upon the views and conduct of that conceited and changeful people, it is clear that confusion and dissatisfaction reign in the councils of our blatant foe, and we are fully justified in tracing that state of things to the disappointment and mortification consequent upon the severe repulse BURNSIDE's splendid army sustained at Fredericksburg; for that trial of arms was of such a character that even Yankee ingenuity and unscrupulousness cannot gloss the conflict so as to conceal or mitigate the fact of a complete and disastrous discomfiture. That vast army had crossed the Rappahannock for the purpose of marching on to Richmond, and, after joining battle with the forces under Gen. LEE, it was forced to retreat across the river under cover of night, and abandon altogether the accomplishment of the purpose it attempted to execute. These disagreeable facts, covered all over with the blood of their sons, husbands and fathers, stare the disheartened people in the face, and they are obliged to behold them.

We do not wonder that they are smitten with amazement and terror, and with grave evils among themselves, growing every day more serious, with France prepared at any moment to extend a helping hand to our Confederacy; with our Southern land ringing with the shouts of victory, and the whole people more confident and resolved; it does not surprise us that confusion prevails in their councils, and distrust and dissatisfaction are agitating the heart of the nation.

SEWARD discerns the approaching danger, and, true to the instincts of his sordid and selfish nature, will hide himself from the bursting storm. BURNSIDE of course has gone by the board, and some grave cause of difference with the President has forced HALLECK to retire from office. The Cabinet that will be formed will be composed of the most fanatical of the Republican party, and Generals identified with that party will be appointed to the places in the army made vacant by the resignation of BURNSIDE, HALLECK and BLAIR. We may well rub our hands in glee over these most pleasing events.

God, in whom we trust, is working mightily in our behalf. Let us acknowledge his goodness with adoring gratitude, and address ourselves with renewed energy and perseverance to the good work we have entered upon.

If most men could rise from the dead and read their epitaphs, some of them would think they had got in the wrong grave.

CITY INTELLIGENCE.

UNION PRAYER MEETING IN BEHALF OF OUR COUNTRY.—Thursday being Christmas Day, it is suggested that the meeting be postponed from Wednesday to Thursday afternoon, at half-past 3 o'clock. The clergy, and all praying people, are cordially invited to attend; especially to give thanks for the wonderful display of Divine power in our behalf in the victory at Fredericksburg. 2

INQUEST.—An Inquest was held, Tuesday, on the body of HENRY FISHER, a conductor's man, who was killed at the Seven Mile Pump. It appears that the deceased was walking on the top of the cars, and fell through. The morning was frosty, which is supposed to have caused him to slip. The wheels passed over the deceased. He lived about two hours. The verdict of the Jury was in accordance with the above facts.

MASONIC.—At the Annual Communication of Friendship Lodge, No. 9, A. F. M., held at Masonic Hall on Monday evening, December 22, 1862, the following brethren were duly elected officers for the next Masonic year:

Bro. H. S. JACOBS, W. M.
Bro. J. MENDEL, S. W.
Bro. S. HARRIS, J. W.
*Bro. L. COHEN, Treasurer.
Bro. S. VALENTINE, Secretary.
Bro. L. PISER, J. D.

*In place of Bro. A. Moroso, who declined a re-election.

Acknowledgments.

FOR GARMENT SOCIETY.

From Mrs. S. T. W. $10

FOR FREE MARKET.

From Col. Ben Allston $25
From Mrs. J. B. Lafitte 100

COMMUNICATIONS.

Candidates.

Editors Courier:—We hear of the following candidates for Sheriff in Horry District: Col. J. J. KIRTON, Capt. ——, G. R. CONGDON, W. J. GORE and W. H. JOHNSON. We are glad to learn the people of that District are resolved to elect one not able to bear arms. We need all men capable of bearing arms in the field. Let those who are not able to participate in the present struggle have such offices. *

Editors Courier:—Our camp was removed from Jacksonboro' to Pocotaligo on Thursday last. One of the Privates, PHILIP WATERS, being on furlough, did not hear of the removal until he got to the camp at Jacksonboro'. It was dark; no place to stay for the night—which was intensely cold; with no food for his horse, and a journey of some forty miles ahead of him. He was certainly in a dilemma; he thought for a little while and concluded to ask a night's lodging for himself and horse at the house of one Mr. R——, about three miles distance. On coming to the enclosure, he hailed and asked permission to stay all night, offering to pay for it; this was refused him He then asked for some corn to feed his horse, offering to pay for that, thinking he would camp out; this was also refused him, although Mr. R—— always keeps a house full of corn. Tired, hungry and sleepy, he had to stay all night at some negro houses, two or three miles further on. I did not think the boasted hospitality of South Carolinians would allow any man to turn a soldier, fatigued and worn, from his doors, and I only mention the fact at the solicitation of some of the members of the Colleton Rangers, and to let the citizens of St. Bartholomew's Parish know what an inhospitable man lives in their midst.

A MEMBER.

Soldiers' Relief Association.

The usual weekly meeting of this Association was held at the Depository, Chalmers-street, on Monday morning, December 22. Reports were read.

During the past week the following donations have been received:

From Miss Simpson, 3 homespun shirts, 3 pair drawers.

From a Charlestonian, now in Alabama, 2 worsted shirts, 2 pair worsted drawers, 2 pair socks.

From a Charleston lady, now in Columbia, 1 bundle lint

From Mrs. F. Fraser, 1 bag dried apples.

Through the Courier Office, 2 barrels of hospital stores.

From Dr. M., 2 blankets.

From Mrs. Charles Tennent, 6 pair socks, 2 scarfs, 1 cap.

From Sam, through Mrs. Wells, $3

From a lady, $6 18.

Through Dr. Backman, $500.

Through a member of the South Carolina Rangers, $5

Through Miss C. L. Bachman, $5.

Through Mrs. General B Huger, $20.

Through Mrs. J. S, $23.

From a Friend, $5.

From a Friend, through Mrs F. Fraser, for Virginia, $5.

From Ella and Yetta, proceeds of Infants' Shoes, $5.

Through Editors of the Mercury, for shoes in Virginia, $90.

From a lady friend, in Lower St. James, through Mrs. W. S., for soldiers in the West, $100

From J. Adger Smyth, Esq., $25.

The following donations have been made:

To Captain Frank Huger's company, Light Artillery, Northern Virginia, 20 pair drawers, 20 woolen shirts, 9 cotton shirts, 24 pair socks, 12 caps.

To Lieutenant Robert S. Millar, commanding Company A, Second Regiment South Carolina Volunteers 40 shirts, 40 pair drawers, 15 pair socks.

To Captain Thomas K. Legare, Company F, Second Regiment South Carolina Volunteers, 15 Shirts, 15 pair drawers, 10 pair socks.

To E. C. Metze, for the band of the Second Regiment, Lamar's Artillery, 9 shirts, 8 handkerchiefs, 9 pair socks.

To individual applications, 3 blankets, 5 pair socks, 17 cotton shirts, 22 pair drawers, 21 pair socks, 12 worsted shirts.

To Roper Hospital, grist, meal, peas.

To Ladies' Relief Hospital, peas, potatos.

To Marine Hospital, peas, potatos.

Dispatches are awaiting delivery at the Telegraph office for the following names:

Henry Hart, H. M. Owens, L. D Owens, J. J. Newman, H. S. Estes, John M. Livingston, Jacob Cohen, Fisher, Agnew & Co., Lieutenant R. E. Ames, Mary Alston, A. M. Guthrie, Mrs. Sarah Jane Williams, N. D. Birney, T J Kerr, Colonel Jas. Blanding, Geo. W. Logan, G. L. Campbell, (2) Colonel W. B. Wilson, M. Bollin, John Christopher.

The Yankee Congress.

The proceedings of this body are important. In the House of Representatives, on the 15th, Mr. FESSENDEN, of Maine, offered the following:

Resolved, That the Proclamation of the President of the date of September 22, 1862, is warranted by the Constitution.

Resolved, That the policy of emancipation as indicated in the said proclamation, is well adapted to hasten the restoration of peace, is well chosen as a war measure, and is an exercise of power with proper regard to the rights of citizens and the perpetuity of free Government.

Mr. HOLMAN moved to lay the above resolutions upon the table, but the motion was disagreed to—yeas 53, nays 80.

The resolutions were then adopted—yeas .. nays 51—the Democrats voting against them in a body.

Mr. CONWAY offered a series of resolutions declaring that a restoration of the Union as it existed before the war would be a greater calamity than the rebellion itself; that any person proposing to make or accept terms of peace on any basis which would restore the slave power to its former supremacy in the Government, or by any new compromise or amendment of the Constitution recognizing slavery as an element of political power, will be guilty of a high crime; that it is a matter of serious reflection whether another election for President must not supervene before the rightful authority of the nation can be established; and whether, in the meantime, it is not a flagrant waste of our energies to continue the war; that unless the army of the West shall have swept through the valley of the Mississippi to its mouth, and the army of the Potomac annihilate the legions of LEE and JACKSON, thus subverting the military power of the rebellion within a reasonable time, the best interests of the country and humanity will require a cessation of hostilities, &c, &c., &c. The resolutions were laid upon the table by a vote of 132 to 1—(Mr. CONWAY.)—

Mr. MAYNARD remarked that this was the first formal proposition asserting the dissolution of the Union and the recognition of the Southern Confederacy.

Messrs. Editors:—"Worrell" will no doubt be recognized by a good many of your readers here, and doubtless will prove of interest to some elsewhere; however, and in short, may not be objectionable to any, as he is not in the habit of offending or making "personal remarks," save in a complimentary way.

It is no use disguising the fact, that our town is in a state of great excitement, and, I may say, thrown into almost a panic. Thousand upon thousand of rumors are afloat; and, strange indeed, to each some degree of confidence is attached. Last night, and until a late hour this morning, Gen. BURNSIDE's head was left on the field, the entire Yankee army had been bagged, and there was no alternative but capitulation. Another now is, that fifteen hundred cavalry are dashing in the direction of a point near this place on the Wilmington and Weldon Rail Road, for the purpose of burning a valuable bridge and cutting off supplies. All such rumors are constantly in circulation, and let them be started by those whom we know are not authorized to report, or are not good authority, and there is still a class here of "the excitables" ready to credit them, and—springs the excitement.

Last week we were certainly going to be attacked. Last week has passed, and another, and still another, and the whole winter may pass leaving us undisturbed; but if the general appearance of things—the removal of all household ware, families, &c.—indicate anything, our days of grace are very short. Preparations of no ordinary kind are being made, and every available "machine" being put to play. We have some very formidable fortifications, which, manned as they are by brave soldiers, may prove successful in the resistance of an attack by water. But by land we must, as has already been said by our Commanders, have a large force, and to insure our town from falling into the hands of the enemy we must have that force quite sufficient to meet an attack by land.

Salt is still "boiling" in spite of the embargo, and selling at $20 in spite of the cry to put it down. New works are going up every day, and men eager to buy interests in them, notwithstanding the threatened attack of the place.

The town is nearly deserted of familiar faces. Every thing still keeps high. A man has only to ask and he gets any price for his goods. It is gratifying to know that we have some—though few there be—among us who "live and let others live." More anon. WORRELL.

Wilmington, December 22, 1862.

We are glad to know, says the Columbus *Sun*, that Gen. PEMBERTON is being heavily reinforced from East Tennessee, and that the enemy will be checked before he proceeds much further. From present appearances, there is reason to believe that there will be an entire change in the programme of the Western campaign, and that the great battle for the possession of the valley of the Mississippi will be fought in that State in a few weeks, at most. We are assured the Yankees will never reach Mobile by land from Mississippi, until they have reduced that city by an attack in front, and the time has gone by when that can be done

Death of Andrew Wallace.—The Columbia papers announce the death of ANDREW WALLACE, Esq, long an esteemed and useful citizen of Columbia, and we believe the oldest citizen. He was an exemplary and successful merchant, and was actively connected with the growth and progress of Columbia, which, during his career, grew from a village to a beautiful and thriving city. The *Carolinian* says:

"He had reached the term of four score years, without the usual labor and sorrow, and fell into the last sleep as the ripe and mellow fruit falleth to the ground. Identified with every interest connected with our city and State, we have known him for thirty-five years, enjoying the respect and esteem of the whole community. Our rail roads and banks, insurance companies and other corporations of interest have had the benefit of his large business experience, and he has reared up in our midst a numerous family, who, like him, are zealous of good works. Peace to his remains.

Greeley on Peace.—"Ora" writing to the Mobile *Register* from Murfreesboro', says:

A gentleman told me to-day that he saw a New York Tribune of the 2d, in which Horace Greeley re asserts his opinion that it will be best to let the Southern States separate from the North.

The Battle of Gettysburg, July 1863

1863

January 1, The Emancipation Proclamation goes into effect, opening the door to the eventual end of slavery. ***January 2,*** The Battle of Murfreesboro, Tennessee is fought with neither side gaining an advantage. ***January 11,*** In a rare ship-to-ship duel, the CSS *Alabama* sinks the USS *Hatteras* near Galveston, Texas. ***January 25,*** General Joseph Hooker replaces General Burnside as commander of the Army of the Potomac. ***February 2,*** The Union ram *Star of the West* runs past the Vicksburg, Mississippi batteries. ***February 8,*** The circulation of the Chicago *Times* is suspended due to allegedly disloyal statements. ***March 11,*** The Confederate's hastily built Fort Pemberton repels the Federal gunboat fleet on the Yalobusha River in Mississippi. ***April 7,*** Federal Flag Officer Samuel Du Pont leads an ironclad squadron into Charleston Harbor and attacks Fort Sumter. ***April 16,*** Union Rear Admiral David Porter's fleet successfully runs past the batteries at Vicksburg, Mississippi. ***April 28,*** The Army of the Potomac begins crossing the Rappahannock River in Virginia. ***May 1,*** Generals Lee and Jackson, defying the laws of military tactics, decide to divide their army in the face of the Army of the Potomac. ***May 2,*** Confederate Generals 'Stonewall' Jackson and Ambrose Powell Hill are wounded at the Battle of Chancellorsville, Virginia as the Confederates win one of the greatest battles of the war. ***May 10,*** General 'Stonewall' Jackson dies of wounds suffered at the Battle of Chancellorsville. ***May 16,*** Union forces under General Grant defeat the Confederates under General Pemberton at the Battle of Champion's Hill in Mississippi, opening the way to Vicksburg. ***May 18,*** The siege of Vicksburg begins, ending one of the great military campaigns in history. ***June 9,*** Union cavalry under Alfred Pleasonton defeat the Confederate cavalry in the Battle of Brandy Station, the greatest cavalry battle of the war. ***June 15,*** Federal forces under Major General R.H. Milroy are defeated at the Battle of Second Winchester, Virginia. ***June 27,*** General Hooker is replaced by General George Gordon Meade as commander of the Army of the Potomac. ***July 1,*** Major General John Reynolds is killed as the Battle of Gettysburg, Pennsylvania begins. ***July 2,*** After a day of bitter fighting at Gettysburg, both armies retain their positions. ***July 3,*** The climactic and disastrous charge by Confederate General Pickett's brigades at Gettysburg end the Confederate's hopes of victory. Both armies sustain over 43,000 casualties in the largest battle ever fought in North America. ***July 4,*** As General Lee retreats from Gettysburg, Vicksburg surrenders to General Grant. ***July 8,*** Port Hudson, Louisiana, the last Confederate stronghold along the Mississippi River, surrenders. ***July 26,*** Confederate cavalryman John Hunt Morgan is captured. ***August 8,*** Robert E. Lee offers to resign as commander of the Army of Northern Virginia. ***August 21,*** Confederate guerillas under William Quantrill sack Lawrence, Kansas. ***September 10,*** Confederates under Sterling Price withdraw as Little Rock, Arkansas falls. ***September 19,*** The Battle of Chickamauga, Georgia begins. ***September 20,*** The Battle of Chickamauga ends with the Confederates under General Braxton Bragg winning a costly tactical victory over the Federal Army of the Cumberland under General George H. Thomas. ***October 16,*** The Military Division of the Mississippi is created with General Ulysses S. Grant in command. ***November 19,*** President Lincoln delivers his Gettysburg Address at the dedication of the military cemetary near the battlefield. ***November 23,*** General Grant makes his first attempt to break the siege of Chattanooga, Tennessee. ***November 25.*** The Federals break the Confederate lines at the Battle of Missionary Ridge, Tennessee, forcing them back across Chickamauga Creek into Georgia. ***November 30,*** Confederate General Braxton Bragg resigns as commander of the Army of Tennessee. ***December 8,*** President Lincoln issues his Proclamation of Amnesty and Reconstruction pardoning those who participated in the rebellion upon the taking of an oath of loyalty to the Federal Government. As the year comes to an end, the prospects of the Confederacy appear to be fading and their heavy losses begin to exact its toll.

George Gordon Meade

Ambrose Powell Hill

Joseph Hooker

James Longstreet

Charleston Daily Courier.

NO. 19,356 CHARLESTON, S. C., CONFEDERATE STATES OF AMERICA, SATURDAY MORNING, JANUARY 3, 1863. VOL. LXI.

BY TELEGRAPH.

THE LATEST NEWS.

BRILLIANT VICTORY IN TENNESSEE.

GREAT BATTLE NEAR MURFREESBORO'.

A DISPATCH FROM GEN. BRAGG TO GEN. BEAUREGARD—CONFEDERATES ATTACK ROSECRANS' ARMY—TEN HOURS HARD FIGHTING—ABOLITIONISTS DRIVEN FROM THE FIELD—FOUR THOUSAND PRISONERS, TWO BRIGADIER GENERALS, THIRTY-ONE PIECES ARTILLERY, TWO HUNDRED WAGONS AND TEAMS CAPTURED—HEAVY LOSSES ON BOTH SIDES.

HEADQUARTERS MURFREESBORO', December 31st, 8.30 P. M.

To General Beauregard:—We assailed the enemy at seven o'clock this morning, and after ten hours hard fighting have driven him from every position except his extreme left, in which he has successfully resisted us. With the exception of this point we occupy the whole field. We captured four thousand prisoners, including two Brigadier-Generals, thirty-one pieces of artillery and some two hundred wagons and teams. Our loss is heavy. That of the enemy much greater.

(Signed) BRAXTON BRAGG, General Commanding.

SECOND DISPATCH FROM GEN. BRAGG TO GEN. BEAUREGARD—THE ENEMY FALLING BACK—OUR ARMY IN PURSUIT—GENERAL WHEELER'S CAVALRY STILL IN THIER REAR—BRILLIANT SUCCESS.

HEADQUARTERS, MURFREESBORO', Jan. 1, 1862

To General G. T. Beauregard:—The enemy has yielded his strong position, and is falling back. We occupy the whole field, and shall follow him.

General WHEELER, with his cavalry, made a complete circuit of their army on the 30th and 31st. He captured and destroyed three hundred wagons loaded with baggage and commissary stores, and paroled seven hundred prisoners. He is again behind them and has captured an ordnance train to-day. We secure several thousand stand of small arms. The body of Gen. HILL was left on the field, and three others are reported killed.

God has granted us a happy New Year.

(Signed) BRAXTON BRAGG, General Commanding.

ADDITIONAL FROM MURFREESBORO'.

THE ABOLITIONISTS DRIVEN SIX MILES—GENERALS SILL, McCOOK AND WOODRUFF, OF YANKEE ARMY, KILLED—ENEMY'S LOSS ESTIMATED FIVE TO OUR ONE—GENERAL RAINS, COLONELS McNAIR, AUTRY, AND LIEUTENANTS B. C. ENOS AND TRISTE, CONFEDERATES, KILLED—COLONELS BLACK AND FISK MORTALLY WOUNDED—CAPTURE OF PRISONERS, AND GREAT DESTRUCTION OF ENEMY'S STORES, WAGONS, &c.

CHATTANOOGA, December 31—A special dispatch to the *Daily Rebel*, dated Murfreesboro', December 31st, says: The bloodiest day of the war has closed. General McCown's division attacked the enemy's right, driving them back with great slaughter. By 3 o'clock in the afternoon the enemy had been driven six miles from our left and centre. General WILLICK, and a number of Abolition officers, have been taken prisoners. Generals SILL, McCOOK and WOODRUFF, of the Abolition army, were killed. Our loss is heavy; that of the enemy is estimated at five to our one.

General RAINS, Colonel McNAIR, Colonel AUTRY, of the 27th Mississippi regiment; Lieutenant B. C. ENOS and Lieutenant TRISTE, of the 1st Louisiana regiment, are among our killed. Col. BLACK, 5th Georgia regiment, and Colonel FISK, 25th Louisiana regiment, were mortally wounded.

WHARTON'S cavalry captured two thousand prisoners with a large supply wagon train, and four hundred beeves.

Yesterday WHEELER'S cavalry burnt two hundred and eighty wagons in the enemy's rear, and captured six hundred prisoners.

Our troops covered themselves with glory.—Generals BRAGG and POLK displayed great judgment and heroism.

The battle may be resumed to-morrow morning.

[SECOND DISPATCH.]

DISPATCH FROM GOVERNOR HARRIS.

CHATTANOOGA, January 1, 1863.—The *Daily Rebel* has just received the following from Governor HARRIS:

"MURFREESBORO', December 31.—We attacked the enemy in his position at 5 30 A. M. The battle raged till 5 P. M. Our left wing drove the enemy's right back upon Stone River. Our advance was steady, but the resistance of the enemy stubborn. We captured four batteries and about four thousand prisoners. Among them three Brigadier-Generals. The loss is heavy on both sides, but the relative loss is not known.

"General RAINS, of Nashville, was killed.

(Signed) I. G. HARRIS."

From Chattanooga, Tenn.

ARRIVAL OF PRISONERS—FIFTEEN THOUSAND CONFEDERATE CAVALRY IN THE ENEMY'S REAR.

CHATTANOOGA, December 31.—Eighty-eight Abolition prisoners, captured near Murfreesboro', were brought here last night. Seventy-three more, with eight negroes, have just arrived on this evening's train. The last party were captured yesterday by Gen. WHEELER'S cavalry, between ROSECRANS' army and Nashville.

Gen. MORGAN is returning from Kentucky, having accomplished his object, and is now in the rear of ROSECRANS. It is believed that BUFORD, FORREST and MORGAN have joined, making a force of fifteen thousand cavalry in the rear of the Abolition army.

Dispatches received here at 2 P. M. to-day announce the repulse of the enemy with the loss of one of their batteries up to that hour.

From Knoxville, Tenn.

REPORTS OF THE ENEMY'S MOVEMENTS IN EAST TENNESSEE.

KNOXVILLE, December 31.—A force of Abolition cavalry, said to be about four thousand strong, made an incursion through Pendleton Gap, led by General S. CARTER, a renegade East Tennes-

[illegible] hundred [illegible] burned the [illegible] Carolina Regiment, [illegible] Senator HAYNES [illegible] works at Saltville. [illegible] was countermanded by General [illegible] is thought we have force enough in [illegible] to repel the Abolitionists. [illegible] of two [illegible] Preparations have been made to repel them. The enemy's force do not number more than two thousand, and it is supposed they only designed destroying Saltville.

Later from Europe.

ARRIVAL OF THE ETNA.

RICHMOND, January 1.—The steam ship *Etna* has arrived at New York, with four days later intelligence.

The London *Times* says LINCOLN'S Message is a bid for peace. His emancipation plan it denominates a dream.

The London *News*, the organ of Exeter Hall, says it has no faith in LINCOLN'S emancipation scheme.

From Richmond.

CAPTURE OF MORE PRISONERS—DESTRUCTION OF BRIDGES IN EAST TENNESSEE BY THE ABOLITIONISTS CONFIRMED.

RICHMOND, January 2—Ninety-two Yankees captured at Dumfries arrived here to-day. Two hundred more will arrive to-morrow. They were captured at Occoquan.

The reported destruction of two bridges on the East Tennessee and Virginia Rail Roads, by a body of Yankee cavalry, is confirmed. The enemy advanced within six miles of Bristol. It will take several weeks to repair damages.

[SECOND DISPATCH.]

IMPORTANT FROM THE NORTH—CALIFORNIA STEAMER CAPTURED BY THE ALABAMA—CONFEDERATE STEAMER FLORIDA.

RICHMOND, January 2, 7:30, P. M.—The Richmond *Enquirer* has received Northern dates to the 31st ult.

The New York *Herald* reports that Port Hudson has been captured. The retreat of Gen. HATCH across the Tallahatchie, is confirmed.

The Underwriters in New York have doubled their risks on American vessels.

The Washington *Chronicle* notices important movements of General STUART'S cavalry and, supposes he is advancing on Frederick City, Maryland.

The supercedure of BUTLER by Gen. BANKS is confirmed. BANKS sent a force to Baton Rouge and re-captured the place.

The *Herald* says the Confederate Steamer *Florida*, Commander MAFFIT, succeeded in running out from Mobile unseen by the blockaders.

A Confederate vessel had arrived at Havana loaded with Cotton.

On the 7th December, the Confederate Steamer (290) captured the California Steamer *Ariel*, with a crew one hundred and forty strong. Her officers were paroled. Lieut. LAW, of the *Alabama*, boarded the *Ariel*, took possession of three thousand Treasury notes and fifteen hundred dollars in silver. Having destroyed all the sails of the Yankee steamer and removed one of her steam valves, she was bonded for $125,000 and the cargo for $135,000 more, to be paid to the Confederate authorities within thirty days after the establishment of the independence of the Confederate States.

The news of this capture produced a great sensation in New York and Washington.

GREELEY, of the *Tribune*, has been summoned to Washington.

The Paris correspondent of the New York *Herald* says it is rumored in diplomatic circles that PALMERSTON and RUSSELL will be ousted from the British Cabinet after the opening of Parliament.

[THIRD DISPATCH.]

ADDITIONAL FROM THE NORTH.

RICHMOND, January 2.—Two hundred Abolition prisoners arrived to-day from above.

Northern dates of 1st inst. have just been received by the *Enquirer*.

JAMES BROOKS made a speech in New York on Tuesday at a meeting, at which resolutions were unanimously adopted requesting New Jersey, on account of her revolutionary history and past assertions, to invite all the States to meet in Convention in Louisville in February. They also call upon New Jersey to ask permission from the President to allow her to send delegates to the States in rebellion and invite their representation in this Convention, and in the event the States in rebellion agree to be represented, they ask LINCOLN to proclaim an armistice by land and sea for six months.

BROOKS was applauded loudly.

There is no war news of importance.

Gallantry of the Georgians at the Battle of Fredericksburg.—[illegible] General EARLY awards great praise to the Georgia troops for their noble conduct in the battle of Fredericksburg. Much of the success of our army [illegible] contested [illegible] is due to the [illegible] The Lynchburg *Virginian*, [illegible] a high compliment. For some reason—otherwise probably without any good reason—the command has hitherto been under a cloud, and the present is a favorable opportunity for placing it in a position which it has a right to occupy. Troops that can win the approbation of General EARLY for coolness and courage on the field of battle, are entitled to it; for no officer we have possesses more of these qualities or despises more heartily the lack of them in others; and none are more honest to award praise where it is deserved. All honor to the gallant Georgians.

Death of Col. Fisk.—A private dispatch to his brother in this city, received yesterday, announces the sad news of the death of Col. FISK, of the Twenty fifth Louisiana Regiment.

Our telegraphic column states that he was mortally wounded in the battle near Murfreesboro' on the 31st ult.

The deceased had a large circle of friends in this community, by whom he was highly esteemed, and who will mourn his demise.

Thanks and Service.

[illegible] vouchsafes us, is a loud and emphatic call for gratitude and praise, to be [illegible] We do not fulfil the [illegible] of victories if we are [illegible] the honor and glory [illegible] and wisdom. We may [illegible] God as the author of [illegible] yet if we go no farther [illegible] the service He demands [illegible] and by far the [illegible] remain unperformed.

[illegible] increases our power and [illegible] honorable and glorious, calls upon us in earnest, not only to give God the glory, but also especially to cease from committing those [illegible] that make us odious in His sight, and provoke His wrath and indignation.

To return thanks for any blessing, especially if that boon be one we had set our hearts upon obtaining, and which we expect will yield much happiness, is at all times an obvious and pleasing duty. And it is withal so easily discharged, that the right-minded regard its neglect as a grave transgression. And indeed it is a huge offence.

But we must not fancy that Heaven is well pleased with us merely because we bless the name of God on receiving some good thing from the open hand of the universal Father. It is sweet and pleasant to listen to the singing of the birds in the early morning, and doubly grateful to our senses is the warbling of these creatures, the odor of flowers, and the soft sound of the breeze through the trees, when we associate these agreeable things with the intelligent praise of reasonable creatures, and regard them as expressions of gratitude to the beneficent Creator. But He who has endowed us with a mind, a heart and a soul, who hath made us in His own image, and redeemed us by an incalculable price, requires more of us than the rendering of thanks. As praise is only a part of prayer, so it is only one of the duties enjoined by Heaven. And praise becomes uncomely and unacceptable when not accompanied with penitence, humility and obedience.

In truth the performance of the duty of praise in a proper manner, involves the discharge of the other duties of repentance and obedience. For God is most honored and glorified by him who keeps his commandments, who walks before Him in righteousness and holiness. We praise Him most effectually, not with our lips, but with our hearts, not by singing songs to His name, but by living pure, humble, godly lives. What is the worded praise of that man worth who is habitually guilty of sin? Will the mere language of his lips, which costs him no act of self-denial, no conflict with the Evil One, be pleasing to Him whose laws he breaks wilfully and deliberately? "To obey is better than sacrifice," said the prophet and Judge to SAUL, "and to hearken than the fat of rams."

It is easy to ascribe the victories our troops win to the fact that the Lord of Hosts is on our side, and it is also peculiarly gratifying to our national pride to believe and declare that glorious fact. The assurance of that fact makes us the more brave, and the more hopeful, and endows us with a fortitude that is proof against any reverse or disaster. And indeed the marks of God's [illegible] manifest that we are conscious we would be guilty of a mean and damning crime did we not attribute our successes to the help vouchsafed us from Heaven.

But it becomes us as a people not only to be grateful, but humble, not only to return thanks to God for the victories that crown our arms, but to search our hearts, repent of our follies and crimes, and walk in the way of His commandments with all sincerity and earnestness.

We should give other and stronger proof of gratefulness to God for our glorious triumphs, than what is furnished by ascribing our successes to His outstretched arm. The recognition of His presence with us in this terrific struggle makes the obligation of repentance and faith and service the greater. For if He really be the power in whom we trust, whose wisdom will guide us successfully over the rough and dangerous road we are pursuing, whose strength will overthrow and humble our foes, and exalt us to a place of honor in the family of nations, surely we should endeavor to show ourselves in some sort worthy of His favor. If we are thus honored, should we not reverence and adore Him who gives us such potent assistance? If God has taken part with us, should we not show our gratitude by ceasing to do evil and learning to do well?

A Model Representative.—In our last issue we reported the election of one WARREN W. WING as Representative in the Yankee Congress for the Norfolk (Va.) District.

A well informed and trustworthy friend tells us that he knew WING, in 1844, as office clerk for Drs. TAYLOR & TUNSTALL, physicians of Norfolk. After a few years, these physicians abandoned the dispensary and prescription business, whereupon WING formed a partnership in the apothecaries line with one LUDLOW. Business promised and prospered very well, and WING exhibited his gratification by excessive drinking, and by a lucky hit in a lottery, LUDLOW, his partner, succeeded, after many disappointments and vexations, in buying out WING'S share, and getting rid of him.

WING, who was by this time an inveterate toper [illegible], took refuge at the farm of his mother-in-law, Mrs. [illegible], near Norfolk, and pretended to manage her business.

He became, however, from his drinking excesses, such an intolerable nuisance, that he was driven out and off by his wife and mother-in-law.

After some vicissitudes and shifts, he procured a small clerkship in the Norfolk Navy Yard, and, on a show of reform was re united to his wife and family.

He is a "model Representative" of and for the Yankees.

The Knoxville *Register* says: Dr. PRICE, who left Memphis Tuesday evening, reports VAN DORN as being in the vicinity, and having sent in a flag of truce demanding its surrender. The Abolitionists were removing everything to Fort Pickering. Only two Yankee Regiments were in the town.

We have received a specimen [illegible] made in this city by H. A. LATHAM & Co.

CITY INTELLIGENCE.

FIRE.—The alarm of fire Friday morning was caused by the burning chimney of a residence in Cannon-street.

ARRIVAL OF THE EUTAW REGIMENT.—The Eutaw (25th) Regiment, South Carolina Volunteers, Col. C. H. SIMONTON, returned from special service in the field on Thursday.

The regiment was reviewed while away by Gens. WHITING, SMITH and GIST, and highly complimented on the fine appearance of the men, their beautiful battalion drill and correct military movements.

The Eutaw Regiment is acknowledged to be one of the finest regiments in the service and an honor to their native city and State. We tender them a warm welcome to their homes, with the assurance that the Palmetto State will never cease to regard her sons with that pride and affection which their prompt obedience to her call and their services so cheerfully rendered in the hour of need so richly deserves.

MULLER'S favorite Charleston Band, attached to the Eutaws, was out last night and serenaded General BEAUREGARD. They afterwards visited the newspaper offices and paid both a handsome musical compliment. We tender them our warm acknowledgments.

SOCIETE FRANCAISE.—At the Anniversary Meeting of the Societe Francaise de Bienfaisance, held on the 1st January, 1863, the following gentlemen have been elected officers for the ensuing year:

Mr. A'LIS LEPRINCE, President.
Mr. P. J. BARBOT, Vice-President.
Mr. EUGENE ESDRA, Secretary.
Mr. H. V. FUGAS, Treasurer.

Committee on Charity.—Messrs P. B. Lalane, Edward Lacassagne, John Lege, B. Riols, C. P. Aimar.

Acknowledgments.

FOR GARMENT SOCIETY.

From George W. King $5.00

FOR FUEL SOCIETY.

From George W. King 5.00
From J. S. J. 10.00

Messrs. Editors:—Please acknowledge the receipt of one blanket, one pair of India rubber and five pairs of socks, for the South Carolina soldiers in Virginia, and oblige

Mrs. D. H. ELLIS.

Whippy Swamp, S. C., January 1st, 1863

P. S.—The package is sent by express from Pocotaligo.

"Gregg."

Editors Courier:—That Union District should be so called, in honor of our lamented hero, all Carolinians will heartily approve. May we not also suggest the popular name of BEAUREGARD in the place of Unionville, the County seat of Union District. UP COUNTRY.

Personal.—The Richmond *Examiner* says:—"MRS. CRITTENDEN, sister of Hon. J. J. CRITTENDEN, of the United States, came through the lines at Fredericksburg, and reached Richmond yesterday. The lady is on a visit South. She represents the feeling in New York since the battle of Fredericksburg to have grown into open expressions of a desire for peace."

Mrs. F. W. LANDER, formerly Miss JEAN DAVENPORT, the actress, and widow of the late General LANDER, has been appointed Lady Superintendent of Yankee hospitals in the Department of the South, and will soon proceed with her mother to Port Royal, South Carolina.

President DAVIS said in a speech in Mississippi, delivered near Grenada, that the prospects of our armies in the West were all that he desired—that if the people would do their duty the ruthless invader would soon be driven across the Ohio.

Progress of Free Navigation.—Another Gunboat Destroyed.—It is reported in our city that several gunboats, accompanied by a transport, came up the Yazoo river a day or two since, and while attempting to raise the guns from the wreck of a boat destroyed on the 12th instant, a torpedo exploded under the transport, shivering it into a thousand pieces. The Yazoo is a hard river for navigation, and it will be impossible for Yankee boats to effect insurance in Cincinnati hereafter.—*Mississippian.*

Obituary.

DIED, in Columbia, on Friday, January 2d, of Typoid Fever, Captain S. H. KINGMAN, Quartermaster 24th South Carolina Regiment.

His Friends and Acquaintances, and those of his Mother and Family, are invited to attend the Funeral Services, at the Methodist Protestant Church, Wentworth-street, *To-morrow*, 4th instant, at half-past Four o'clock, P. M. January 3

DIED, at Madison, Florida, on the 19th of November last, Mrs. MARY B. HUMPHREYS, aged sixty-eight years.

The deceased was a native of Charleston, S. C., and was warmly attached to her native city. She had been a resident of Jacksonville, East Florida, for several year past, where her Christian benevolence and usefulness, and her attachment to the church, of which she was a member, won for her the affection and respect of a large circle of friends and relatives.

Her extreme sufferings for the past fifteen months she patiently submitted to, trusting in her "Savior," who rewardeth those who "patiently wait his coming," and where her spirit is now at rest. A FRIEND.

Since the commencement of the present bloody and unholy war upon the rights and institutions of the South, not a day passes but witnesses the mournful spectacle of death, either in the Hospital or upon the field, of some one of our noble army of struggling freemen, whose character and deeds are worthy of note and entitled to remembrance. It is not our purpose to give even a biographic sketch of the deceased, E. FOSTER COACHMAN; we have not the material if we were competent to the task. Full of patriotic zeal early in the war he joined the Washington Light Infantry of Hampton's Legion. In the battle of "Seven Pines" he was wounded in his right arm and side, taken prisoner and conveyed to Fortress Monroe, where he suffered amputation of his arm, and from the effects of his wound he died August.

In his death his parents have lost an only son of whom they might justly have been proud; his State a gallant and uncompromising defender of her rights and honor, his comrades in arms an example of integrity in camp, of courage and endurance in the field. During his dreary confinement he at all times displayed a fortitude that commanded the admiration of friend and foe. Although an exile from his own sunny clime, a stranger in a strange land, doubtless often in his feverish dreams or midnight vigils, the tender memories of home and its sweet endearments would, birdlike, flutter around his heart. Yet so imperishable was his love of country, so deep his conviction of the justice and righteousness of his cause he was never heard to complain of his bitter repine at his sufferings. On one occasion a lady passing through the ward stopped at his bedside and asked him if he was not tired of the war. His eye kindled with smothered indignation, his pale face glowed with enthusiasm as pointing to his wound, he replied with startling emphasis, "No! I thank God I have yet one arm left with which to fight the battles of freedom." Noble sentiment and nobly expressed, worthy the patriot and hero, linking him in spirit with the martyrs of all ages who have so freely given their blood as a precious libation upon the altars of freedom. How sad that the life that could utter such sentiments should so soon be sealed in death, that a heart which throbbed with such heroic impulses should be forever stilled. Sorely as is felt his loss among his comrades, yet more keenly still does it fall on those who knew him best and loved him most. The army of the dead will not be forgotten by the hosts of the living, and their memories will be forever embalmed in the hearts of a virtuous and grateful people.

LIST OF LETTERS

Remaining in the Postoffice at Charleston, S. C., January 3, 1863.

Persons wishing advertised Letters are requested to state the date of the List.

A

Allison, Miss Mary L.
Albers, J. H.
Alderson, J. F.
Alexander, J. W.
Allen, W. S.
Autson, Catherine
Anderson, Miss S.
Arnold, Maj. J. W. 2
Arrington, Albert
Anderson, J. W.
Augustine, Mrs. U.

B

"B," Mrs. Eliza
Baker, Charles B.
Baker, Geo.
Baker, James A.
Bailey, E. B.
Bayly, W. H. C.
Balk, Theodore
Ballis, Meyer
Baldwin, J.
Barry, J.
Baumann, J.
Black, Geo. C.
Blakely, R. F.
Bradford, W. J.
Branford, Miss J. A.
Bedell, Columbus
Berrit, J.
Bedon, J.
Beattie, J. J.
Bettison, P.
Bitten, Mrs. M. E.
Briston, Lt. A. E.
Britton, Mrs. J.
Brickweider, P. M.
Bringlow, Sam'l 2
Bolger, H. E.
Boswell, J. A.
Boyce, Mrs. M.
Brown, A. G.
Brodie, Miss C. B.
Brown, Miss G.
Brown, John
Brown, John (James' Island)
Browdie, Wm.
Brooks, W. J.
Brother & Co. H.
Burnett, A.
Butler, Mrs. E.
Burns, G. F.
Burgess, Lt. J. C.
Bruce, T. W.

C

Clay, Dr. D. M.
Craig, C. T.
Chatters, Geo. W.
Chambers, James
Calvo, J. P. M.
Casson, J. P.
Cannady, J.
Clary, Capt. J. E.
Cades, John H.
Cammer, Mrs. M. J.
Chavird, E. J.
Coy, Miss Marg't
Causey, Z. J.
Carrier, Wm.
Casey, Wm. M.
Camp, Wm. C.
Calaway, Mrs. S. A.
Chapin, Mrs. S. A.
Chapin, Master
Campbell, Edward
Cherry, T. R.
China, W. A.
Collcock, B. H.
Crowford, C.
Cromwell, Miss E. O.
Choat, T. V.
Crovat, H. H.
Cohenelly, W. G.
Crosby, J. J.
Chovis, John
Crose, J. C.
Cooper, Jno. A. (Goundin's)
Coffee, Mrs. Mary
Cross, M. W.
Cohen, S. A.
Collins, Wm. H.
Curtis, Mrs. Ann
Cunningham, Mrs. J. B.
Curry, Serg't N. D.

D

Darby, Dr. A. T.
Davis, Erwin
Davis, H. L.
Davis, J. P.
Darnold, Evans
Dawkins, Gideon 2
Darcy, Miss Kate D.
Davidson, Miss S. C.
Davy, Robt.
Dreanen, Capt.
Deloatet, G. W.
Dixson, Mrs. S. 2
Dill, Miss S. H.
Dobosey, C.
Doyle, D. S.
Dozier, Dr. Frank
Drose, Miss S. C.
Dolen, Serg't Patrick
Dorough, Dr. Wm.
Duff, Miss A.
Dunning, Miss Miss F.
Dunny, Emma
Due, Mrs. T. E.
Dubose, H. J.

E

Eccleston, Mrs.
Edwards, C.
Ekliff, Thomas

F

Faulkner, L.
Farrel, Mrs. M.
Farris, Mrs. M. A. 2
Fraira, J. T.
Fraser, C. J.
Frazer, Miss Mary
Felder, J. S.
Fleming, G. B.
Freeman, Dr. H. G.
Frese, F.
Fischer, Mrs. D. 2
Fipp, J. W.
Finley, Miss Mary
Fitzpatrick, F.
Fishbeck, Wm.
Foster, H. F.
Fox, Wm.
Fullmore, J. H.
Flynn, Capt. J. J.

G

Garralde, P.
Gamer, J.
Gari, Mrs. M.
Gladden, Miss M. J.
Grant, J. A.
Gray, W. M.
Gralton, D.
George, A.
Gehrels, Miss M.
Green, Mrs. E.
Green, Wm. H.
Gibbe, Lander
Gibbs, Susan
Griffin, J. W.
Goodwin, John
Gower, Thos. C.
Glover, Mary
Gully, W.
Gruber, John

H

Hair, J. L.
Halke, John C.
Happoldt, Miss S. E. 2
Harrison, Mrs. Robt
Hall, T. H.
Heath, Mrs. L.
Heller, P.
Heren, P. O.
Heargroves, Thos
Hill, E.
Hilton, N.
Holmes, A.
Howard Association.
Howell, Capt.
Hotard, A. E.
Hodge, J.
Hodges, Mrs. L. E.
Horrace, John
Hunscombe, Mr. (for Emma)
Hudson, Miss C.
Huts, Miss E. C.
Hudgeons, James
Hutto, John
Hudgson, Mrs. M.
Hunt, Wm.

J

Jackson, C.
Jackson, Miss Ann
Jaudon, S. W. A.
James, Mr.
Johnson, W. S.
Johnson, S. M.
Johnson, J. C.
Johnston, J. Z.
Jordan, G. S.

K

Knauff, T. J.
Keadle, J.
Keane, Mrs.
Kebbmann, F.
Kennedy, J. E. 2
Kennedy, J. D.
Kimbrill, Wm.
Kiser, Geo.
Kruse, Mrs. C.
Kyall, Mrs. M. A. E.
Kyall, Thos.

L

Law, Aug. E. 2
Labatat, H. C.
Lacost, W.
Legare, Miss Eliza
Leitner, John W. 3
Leland, Maj. A. 3
Lemar, Miss M. A
Lee, Mrs. Mary
Lee, H. D. 2
Lee, Miss Emma
Lee, Dr. Thos.
Lindsey, John
Little, James 2
Little, William
Lirage, Theodore M.
Long, John H.
Lyons, Miss Mano

M

Maschel, F.
Marvin, J. A.
Martin, Mrs. M. M. (Rantowle's) 3
Mason, E. P. 2
Maull, Mrs. S. A.
Mazgik, T.
Mazgik, J.
Means, Mrs. J. P.
Meyers, Miss J.
Meier, Mrs. M.
Meldeau, Mrs. R. L.
Mitchell, J.
Mitchell, Mrs. Jane
Mitchell, Mrs. R.
Miller, Miss S. C.
Miller, H.
Milliner, Mrs. (Commercial House)
Mack, P.
Moran, Miss K.
Mourees, Lt. J.
Moses, J. L.
Monday, J. J.
Morgan, L.
Moore, P. F.
Malloy, P.
Mosely, E.
Morris, S.
Muller, Mr.
Mushington, Mrs. A.
Murray, Mrs. E.
Muller, Wm.
Myer, J.

Mc

McCarthy, D. L. 2
McCartney, Mrs. H.
McClure, A. R.
McClinton, J.
McClaux, Miss S. A.
McComb, Wm.
McCoy, W. P.
McKenzie, L. C.
McKenzie, Mrs. M. A. S.
McLendon, R.
McSweeney, (Butcher)

N

Newton, Peter
Night, Mrs. P.
Noster, W. J.
Nolan, John J.

O

Ortsend, S.
Orr, B. W.
O'Neill, Mrs. Rebecca
Owner, R. W.
O'Heven, P.
O'Herran, Miss Bridget
O'Meara, C.

P

Painter, Wm D.
Page, Menth
Parr, S. D.
Pardue, T. S.
Pattat, Miss Josh
Parker, Ben
Petit, W. O.
Peters, Nat
Peters, Mrs. H. C.
Presley, C. W.
Pearson, A. S.
Pearson, Moses
Prince, Mrs. Mary E.
Pinckney, Thirsa
Pipkin, Jos. R.
Phillips, F. D.
Phie, Mrs. Arthur
Pinner, B. W.
Prector, B. W.
Powe, Peter
Pohle, G. B.
Purcell, Jacob

R

Racker, Robt.
Rast, Jas.
Randall, Edw'd
Ritter, Mrs. Eliz'h
Rennett, Mrs. Wm.
Ripps, Wm.
Rodgers, Mrs. S.
Roy, Capt. John
Rowan, Henry A.
Russell, Mr.
Robinson, Peter
Russell, Jno. J.
Russell, Lt. J. E. 2
Russell, Capt. John
Ryan, Mrs. W. O.

S

Sams, Rev. J. J.
Skiark, Lewis
Sasportas, Jos.
Sparks, Jesse
Savage, D. C.
Staut, C.
Stacy, Miss Ann
Salt Works, (Venning's Wharf)
Sampson, Jos.
Schwartz, Isidor
Small, Thos.
Sanger, Mrs. S.
Strain, Miss Margie
Salvo, V.
Salvo, Madame
Sweeney, John
Sherfesee, Mrs. C.
Stewart, Bridget
Sledge, W. A.
Sedgwick, W. W.
Sherrett, Mrs. Mary
Stiles, Wilcby
Shingler, Col. W. J.
Stiles, Mrs. Susan B.
Symmons, Mrs. Martin
Sigwald, Mrs. M. N.
Smith, Jno. T.
Smith, H. D.
Smith, F. L. N.
Smith, T. H.
Shokes, Miss Julia
Sloan, J.
Shokes, Geo.
Shokes, Mrs. T. G.
Stone, S. J.
Shoett, Stuart J.
Sullivan, D. A. J.
Schultz, W.
Sully, Maj. T. O.
Shryock, Lt. Geo

T

Teal, David
Tea, John H.
Therritt, Jas.
Trescott, Paul
Thigpen, Jackson
Tilton, Henry A.
Toughill, Den'l
Thompson, D. L. Jr.
Thorn, Philip
Toomer, Miss Mary E.
Thomas, W.
Thruman, Geo.
Trunthral, Mrs. Anna
Turner, W. M.

U

Usedom, Theodore

V

Vaughan, T. R.
Venning, H. M.

W

Walker, Arch'd
Waulle, Miss E. A. 2
Wagner, Miss Ellen
Walles, Ernest
Warley, Wm.
Way, Mrs. S. B.
Walsh, Mrs. P.
Walker, Miss Maria
Ward, Mrs. M. C.
Wall, Lazarus
Walker, Mrs. Jane
Welsh, Miss A.
Weil, Henry
Westmoreland, S. R.
Webb, S.
Weston, S.
Wispeh, F.
Wideman, Dr. A. T.
White, E. A.
Withers, Wm.
Wingate, Wm.
Williamson, R. M.
Winger, Silas
Wickliffe, Robt.
Wightman, Mrs. Jas.
Wilson, Joshua
Wilson, Mrs. S. F. S.
Wilson, T.
Wilson, S. C.
Williams, Serg't J. G. H. 2
Williams, Mrs.
Williams, Mr. (for Daphne)
Womble, Enock
Wolfe, H. L.
Wotton, Mrs. H. C.
Woodward, H. A.
Wolf, Z. M.

Z

Zeigler, W.
Zeigler, J. D.

January 3. [335] ALFRED HUGER, P. M.

SHIRRA'S DISPENSARY.—THE TRUSTEES OF SHIRRA'S DISPENSARY will, at their first meeting in *January next*, elect TWO PHYSICIANS, one for the EASTERN and the other for the WESTERN DIVISIONS of the City, to attend the poor at an annual salary of Six Hundred and Fifty Dollars each. Also, a Secretary and Treasurer, with an annual salary of One Hundred Dollars, who will be required to give a bond for two Thousand Dollars, with two Sureties.

Letters of application to be left at the Mayor's Office, on or before December 31st, addressed to "Trustees Shirra's Dispensary."

H. H. DeLEON, Secretary and Treasurer.

December 22 9

The Philadelphia Inquirer.

CIRCULATION OVER 60,000. PHILADELPHIA, SATURDAY, JANUARY 3, 1863. PRICE TWO CENTS.

A BLOODY BATTLE!

A Great and Decided Victory!

A DESPERATE BATTLE NEAR MURFREESBORO', TENN.

The Regulars and the Anderson Troop Lose Heavily.

CAPTURE OF THE REBEL ENTRENCHMENTS.

The Fifteenth Wisconsin has Lost Seven Captains.

REBEL GENERALS CHEATHAM AND RAINS KILLED.

GENS. STANLEY, ROSSEAU AND PALMER WOUNDED.

Majors Rosengarten and Ward of Anderson Troop Killed.

THE REBEL MORGAN ROUTED.

He Loses Many Men, His Caissons and Ammunition Wagons.

ROUT OF REBELS IN WESTERN KENTUCKY AND TENNESSEE.

The Advance of Gen. Rosecrans' Army Upon Murfreesboro'—Rebels Driven Back at All Points—The Rebels in Force at Steward's Creek—The Armies in Line of Battle Facing Each Other.

LAVERGNE, Tenn., Dec. 28, via LOUISVILLE, Dec. 31.—Orders to advance on the enemy were given Christmas Eve, but were countermanded before morning. On the morning of the 26th our entire force was in motion, sweeping down the Wilson, Nolinsville and Murfreesboro' Pikes.

During the day, Colonel CARLIN'S Brigade, of General JEFF. C. DAVIS' Division, McCOOK'S Corps, had some lively skirmishing, and the One-hundred-and-first Ohio gallantly charged and captured one gun and a caisson from a Georgia Battery. We lost only two killed and three or four wounded.

The enemy were driven back at all points, and at dark we occupied Nolinsville and Lavergne, and THOMAS' Corps moved down the Franklin and Wilson Pikes, and all intermediate points; McCOOK'S Corps down the Nolinsville Pike, and CRITTENDEN'S down the Murfreesboro' Pike, two brigades marching to the left on the Jefferson Pike.

General ROSECRANS moved from Nashville, down the Murfreesboro' Pike, at half-past eleven o'clock, A. M., and passed to McCOOK'S front, his head-quarters being established on the Murfreesboro' Pike, twelve miles from Nashville.

General McCOOK was directed to press HARDEE'S two divisions at Triune on Saturday, and orders were issued to move up along the whole road. The enemy's pickets were soon met at various points, and there was sharp skirmishing all day long. HARDEE fell back rapidly before McCOOK'S eager advance, the Anderson Cavalry distinguishing themselves in skirmishing, and NEGLEY'S and ROSSEAU'S divisions moving up to the centre on the left.

CRITTENDEN drove the Rebels all day, carrying the bridges on the Jefferson and Murfreesboro' pikes in handsome style. Our loss in the left wing was two killed and twenty-seven wounded, most of the latter of the Twenty-sixth Ohio.

At a late hour General McCOOK forwarded despatches that HARDEE had retreated upon the Murfreesboro' Pike. It seems that his true line of retreat, if BRAGG did not intend to engage us, was down the Shelbyville road; therefore it was concluded that the enemy would resist, in force, from Stewart's Creek to Murfreesboro'.

Subsequent information confirmed the impression, and every preparation which had not been made was perfected. In consequence of the heaviness of the roads it required the whole of to-day to concentrate and rest our troops; and, with the exception of picket skirmishing, there was no fighting on the entire front.

The two armies now face each other, on opposite sides of Steward's Creek, twenty miles from Nashville. The main force of the enemy is six miles from the creek, and we are encamped upon it in line of battle. The General and Staff went to the extreme front on the Murfreesboro' pike this afternoon. The enemy's pickets were visible to the naked eye, and a considerable body of them, with a battery, were drawn up on the road, within distinct view, not more than a mile from us, keeping up a lively fire, with little effect.

We anticipated a shelling, but for some reason the enemy, though deeply interested in our movements, declined to expend their ammunition.

The enemy have the advantage of position—high, rolling territory, very much broken, with a deep creek intervening. Our troops are full of ardor, and the General appears confident of winning a great victory.

We estimate the Rebel effective force at thirty-five thousand men. They recently sent ten thousand from KIRBY SMITH'S Corps to Mississippi. This is certain.

The cutting off of our communication between Louisville and Nashville is not a good thing for us, but a great victory will relieve us of all embarrassments. REYNOLDS' and FRY'S Divisions are after MORGAN sharply.

Scouts inform us that BRAGG asserts that we shall lose ten thousand men before he leaves Middle Tennessee.

The Armies Confronting Each Other on Stone Creek.

CAMP TEN MILES FROM MURFREESBORO', Dec. 29—6 P. M.—General CRITTENDEN reports the enemy drawn up in line of battle on the east side of Stone river, menacing General ROSECRANS. He is ordered to form in line of battle, with two divisions in front, and one in reserve, covering his flanks. Generals NEGLEY and ROSSEAU are to close up.

General McCOOK also reports his command on Williamson's Creek, seven miles from Murfreesboro', with the enemy in line of battle on Stone river, from Murfreesboro' to Franklin pike. A similar disposition of his force is ordered as in Gen. CRITTENDEN'S line.

Later.

NEAR MURFREESBORO', Dec. 31.—The whole line has suffered terribly, this morning, in the battle with the Rebels.

Four regiments of regulars lost half their men, and all their commanding officers.

The Anderson Troop of Philadelphia also suffered severely.

Majors ROSENGARTEN and WARD were killed.

Generals STANLEY, ROSSEAU and PALMER were wounded.

Two O'CLOCK, P. M.—General THOMAS breaks the Rebel centre and drives the enemy a mile. We advance the whole line.

General ROSECRANS personally superintends the movements. One shot killed two of his staff.

The Fifteenth Wisconsin loses seven Captains.

General NEGLEY'S artillery is still mowing down the Rebels in the centre.

General CRITTENDEN'S left wing has taken the Rebel entrenchments at Murfreesboro'.

The Rebel Generals CHEATHAM and RAINS are killed.

The Secretary of War, to-day, was advised as follows:—

CLEVELAND, Jan. 2, 1863.—The following has just been received by telegraph from Cincinnati, dated Murfreesboro', Jan. 1st, 1863:—

"A terrible battle was fought yesterday. The latest from the field is up to noon. The Rebel centre had been broken and things looked favorable.

"The losses reported are enormous. STANLEY, ROSSEAU and PALMER were wounded, and the Rebels CHEATHAM and RAINES killed.

The Very Latest.

NASHVILLE, Jan. 2.—A terrible battle has been fought at Murfreesboro', involving the severest carnage of the war.

The United States forces encountered the Rebels on the 30th ult., near Stewart's Creek. After heavy skirmishing on both sides, the Rebels were driven back. We captured a hundred prisoners, and killed and wounded a large number. Our loss on this occasion was seventy killed and wounded.

At daybreak on the 31st, the fight was renewed with great fury. Gen. McCOOK'S Corps being opposed to HARDEE.

After desperate fighting, with heavy loss on both sides, Gen. McCOOK retreated two miles. He soon rallied his men, but was again driven back, and at night was four miles this side of the ground occupied in the morning.

The fight continued until ten o'clock at night, at which time we had maintained our position.

The Federal loss was very heavy. Among our killed are:—

Brigadier-General SILL.
Lieutenant-Colonel GARESCHE, Chief of General ROSECRANS' staff.
Brigadier-General WILLICH, of Indiana.
Colonel KELL, of the Second Ohio Regiment.
Colonel SHAFFER, Acting Brigadier-General.
Colonel FARMER, of the Fifteenth Kentucky Regiment.
Colonel JONES, of the Twenty-fourth Ohio.
Lieutenant-Colonel COTTON, of the Sixth Kentucky.
Lieutenant-Colonel JONES, Thirty-ninth Indiana.
Major CARPENTER, of the Nineteenth Regulars.
Major ROSENGARTEN, of Philadelphia (Anderson Troop).
Captain GARRETT, of the Nineteenth Illinois.
Colonel CARPENTER, of the Eighteenth Wisconsin Battery.
Lieutenant-Colonel McKEE, of the Fifteenth Wisconsin.

Wounded.

Brigadier-General E. N. KIRK, of Illinois.
Brigadier-General WOOD, of Indiana.
Brigadier-General VAN CLEVE, of Minnesota.
Colonel CASSALE, of Ohio.
Major-General ROSSEAU, of Kentucky.
Lieutenant-Colonel BERRY, Fifth Kentucky.
Major SLEMMER, Sixteenth Regulars.
Major KING, Fifteenth Regulars, and many others.

The Twenty-first, Twenty-fifth and Thirty-fifth Illinois Regiments lost two-thirds of their numbers, and the Fifteenth and Thirty-eighth Illinois one-half.

[illegible]

The Thirty-eighth Indiana lost about the same number.

The total number of killed and wounded is estimated at [illegible].

The Rebel loss exceeds ours.

General [illegible] E. RAINS was killed.

General CHEATHAM was wounded and taken prisoner.

We have captured five hundred prisoners.

The fight was renewed at three o'clock on the morning of January 1st.

Cannonading was heard at Nashville at ten o'clock, A. M.

WOOD'S and VAN CLEVE'S Divisions were in Murfreesboro' driving the enemy, who were in full retreat.

The following Rebel commissioned officers have been captured:—Major J. J. FRANKLIN, Thirtieth Arkansas; Captain W. E. JOHNSON, Second Arkansas; Captain J. R. EAGLE, Second Arkansas; Captain S. C. STONE, First Tennessee Cavalry.

Many buildings have been taken in this city for hospital purposes.

Great numbers of the wounded are now being brought in.

The river is falling and there are nearly eighteen inches on the shoals.

WASHINGTON, Jan. 3, 1 A. M.—No intelligence has been received during the night by the Government relative to the battle at Murfreesboro'.

A Victory over Morgan.

LOUISVILLE, Jan. 2.—Colonel HOSKINS, of the Twelfth Kentucky Regiment, commanding the forces at Lebanon, Ky, attacked the Rebels under JOHN MORGAN, eight miles south of the Columbia road, yesterday, killing and wounding several, and capturing sixty of the Rebels, together with their caissons, ammunition wagons and provisions. Colonel HOLLISSEY, Sixth Kentucky Cavalry, was killed.

Lieutenant-Colonel BOYLE, commanding the Ninth Kentucky Cavalry, with the Sixth Kentucky, are in pursuit of MORGAN—the infantry, under Colonel HOSKINS, following. MORGAN is retreating rapidly in the direction of Columbia.

WASHINGTON, Jan. 2.—The following official despatch has been received:—

LOUISVILLE, Ky., Jan. 1, 1863.—The Rebel General MORGAN crossed Cumberland river, cut off Nashville at Gainesboro', and appeared in front of Munfordsville on the 25th of December.

Colonel HOBSON, of the Thirteenth Kentucky, drove part of his force, killing nine and capturing sixteen.

MORGAN crossed Green river above Munfordsville and moved in the direction of Elizabethtown, burning the bridge at Bacon creek and Nolin. He destroyed the trestle-work at Muldrough's Hill, and moved for Rolling Fork. Colonel HARLAN, of the Tenth Kentucky, commanding a brigade, overtook him at Rolling Fork and attacked him, killing and wounding a number, and capturing a Captain and some privates.

Colonel DULL (Rebel) died of his wounds, and one of our Lieutenants of artillery. Colonel HARLAN crossed, pursued and attacked him at Rolling Fork and Salt River Bridge. This is the first instance, I believe, of infantry waiting and attacking cavalry.

MORGAN fled before HARLAN to Bardstown, and from there attempted to escape between Lebanon and Camp Boleville. Colonel HARKINS, One-hundred-and-twenty-eighth Kentucky, commanding there, attacked him this morning, killing a number and capturing ninety men, his caissons and ammunition wagons. MORGAN is flying precipitately. General REYNOLDS marched from Glasgow yesterday for Greensburg, and may intercept him. Colonel HOLLISEY, Sixth Kentucky Cavalry, killed. Our casualties are not yet reported. MORGAN has paid dearly for what he has done.

General ROSECRANS occupies Murfreesboro'.
(Signed) G. T. BOYLE Brig.-Gen.

Gallant Federal Victories Over the Western Guerrillas of Kentucky and Tennessee.

WASHINGTON, Jan. 2.—The following despatches were received at the Head-quarters of the Army this afternoon:—

HEAD-QUARTERS, CINCINNATI, January 2, 1863.—Major-General HALLECK, General-in-Chief:—Major-General GRANGER reports that he has received a despatch from Major FOLLEY, commanding an expedition sent by him to Elk Fork, Campbell county, Tennessee, composed of two hundred and fifty-one of the Sixth and Tenth Kentucky Cavalry, stating that, on Sunday morning last, he surprised a camp of the Rebels, 350 strong, at that place, killing thirty, wounding seventeen, and capturing fifty-one of them, without the loss of a man. All of their camp equipage was burned. Eighty horses and a large amount of arms were captured.

(Signed,) H. G. WRIGHT,
Major-General Commanding.

The Great Battle in Tennessee.

Map Showing the Position of Murfreesboro', Tennessee, the Scene of General ROSECRANS' Brilliant Victory.

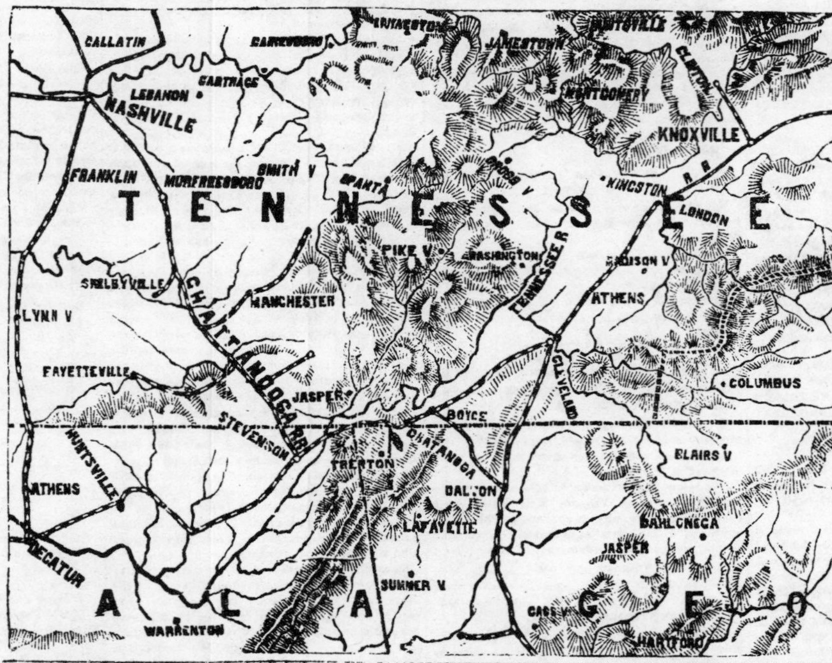

Another Victory Over Guerrillas.

HEAD-QUARTERS, CINCINNATI, Jan. 2.—Major-General HALLECK, General in Chief:—I have just learned from Major-General GRANGER that Major STEVENS, Fourteenth Kentucky Cavalry, with one hundred and fifty men, who were ordered by him upon a scout, to ascertain the whereabouts of a large body of guerrillas in the eastern part of Powell county, Ky., on the 26th ultimo, after traveling all night, over obscured and dangerous bridle-paths, came upon their camps as they were preparing to move, and dashed upon them, capturing their leader, a noted guerrilla, and eleven men.

The rest, though outnumbering Major STEVENS' force, were utterly routed, and escaped into the dense wood, brush and mountain gorges.

Twenty-five horses and a large amount of clothing, blankets, guns, pistols, &c., which were being transported to HUMPHREY MARSHALL'S camp, were also captured. (Signed.)

H. G. WRIGHT, Major-Gen. Commanding.

Still Another Victory.

LOUISVILLE, Jan. 2.—Major FOLEY, commanding one hundred and seventy-five men of the Tenth Kentucky Cavalry, surprised a body of three hundred and fifty Rebels, at their camp, at Elk Fork, Campbell county, killing and wounding seventeen, capturing fifty-seven, and burning all their camp equipage; also, capturing eighty horses and a large amount of arms.

FROM NEW ORLEANS—GEN. BANKS' EXPEDITION.

NEW YORK, Jan. 2.—The steamer *George Washington* arrived to-night, from New Orleans on the 28th.

The following vessels of General BANKS' Expedition were in port:—

The *North Star, Illinois, Arago, Empire City, Continental, United States, Matanzas, City of Bath, Honduras, J. A. Green, Saxon* and *M. A. Boardman.*

Also the following vessels of war:—

Hartford, Pensacola, Potomac, Mississippi, Winona, Sciota, Cayuga, Itaska, Katahdin and *Pampero.*

General BANKS had removed the restrictions upon the holding of Church services, giving notice, however, therewith, that clergymen are subject to restrictions imposed on all other men.

Quite a number of political prisoners have been ordered to be released on giving their parole to commit no acts of hostility to the United States.

The steamer *Creole*, from New York, arrived on the 24th.

GENERAL SHERMAN'S MISSISSIPPI EXPEDITION.

Severe Cannonading on the Yazoo River.

CAIRO, Jan. 2.—A steamer which has arrived here from below reports that the gun-boats accompanying General SHERMAN'S expedition had gone up the Yazoo River. At Drummgall's Bluff, twenty miles above the mouth, a Rebel battery was discovered and severe cannonading followed, during which the gunboat *Benton* was struck sixteen times, the shots penetrating her sides.

General SHERMAN'S force will debark up the Yazoo and march to the rear of Vicksburg.

A train with supplies was to leave Memphis, yesterday, for Holly Springs.

When Island No. 10 was evacuated, lately, sixty-nine pieces of cannon were spiked and ten thousand rounds of ammunition thrown into the river.

From the Army of the Potomac.

HEAD-QUARTERS OF THE ARMY OF THE POTOMAC, Jan. 2.—General BURNSIDE returned from Washington this morning, and has been visited by his grand division commanders.

Several contrabands came into camp to-day, and were received in accordance with the proclamation of the President.

From Danville.

DANVILLE, Jan. 2.—The report that fifteen thousand Rebels crossed the Cumberland, last Monday, and are moving towards Danville, is discredited at head-quarters.

Two Soldiers Burned to Death.

MILWAUKIE, Wis., Jan. 2.—The barracks at Camp Sigel, which were occupied by the Twenty-seventh Wisconsin Regiment, were burned last night. Two privates perished in the flames. The regiment has been removed to Camp Washburn.

FROM GEN. HOOKER'S GRAND DIVISION.

Muster Day—Uncle Sam's Boys Needing Money—The Rebel Raids—The Army in Good Spirits—New Commands—Philadelphia Brigadier-Generals—Colonel Collis and his Zouaves.

Special Correspondence of the Inquirer.

HOOKER'S GRAND DIVISION, OPPOSITE FREDERICKSBURG, Va., Dec. 31, 1862.

To-day is "muster day" throughout the whole army, which takes place every two months, preparatory to paying the troops. Many of the regiments have not been paid for four and five months; but, nevertheless, the ceremonies of "muster day" are gone through with the same regularity as if the troops received their pay punctually every two months. It is to be hoped that our respected Uncle Samuel will be more considerate to his "boys" than heretofore, and re-establish his credit and character by paying his troops more promptly than has been done for some time past.

Important Movements Impending.

From indications observable on all sides there is little doubt that important movements will take place before long, but where the army will go is a subject open to conjecture, and you are probably as able to guess as I am to indicate it to you, were I entrusted with the secrets of head-quarters, which I am not. You may rest assured that the army will not go into winter quarters here, notwithstanding the many predictions which have been made that it will.

The sick and wounded are being removed to Washington as rapidly as possible, and nearly every man who cannot perform a day's march has been sent away. The army is in good condition and in buoyant hopes that the next time they meet the Rebels they will do it on a fair field, where they can achieve success and revive the drooping hopes of the country. The mass of the men strongly desire to be home again with their families and friends, but they feel also that they have a duty to perform, and that they cannot return home honorably until that duty is done.

Rumored Rebel Raids.

The camps are filled with rumors of Rebel raids between this point and Alexandria, but they cannot be traced to any reliable source. The news of a Rebel raid upon Dumfries reached here via Washington, which was the first intimation we had of such an occurrence. As a matter of precaution, however, measures have been taken which will be likely to get the "raiders" in a bad fix, and probably "bag" a lot of them, "a consummation most devoutly to be wished," you will say.

To-day a report was current that two of our regiment of infantry had been captured and paroled, yesterday, not far from Alexandria, by a large body of STUART'S cavalry. This story is believed to be a "canard" of the first water, for it can scarcely be conceived that so large a body of infantry would allow themselves to be captured in such a hilly, rolling country as this part of Virginia—full of deep ravines and gulleys, almost inaccessible to cavalry, yet affording excellent cover for infantry.

It is said that the Rebel camps in our front, on the other side of the river, have been considerably thinned out within the past week, and conjecture is busy to determine the point where the Rebel troops have gone—if they have gone at all, for they still keep up a respectable picket appearance in our front. This state of uncertainty as to the whereabouts of our active and wary enemy, and the expectation that orders may be issued to move at any moment, keeps us in a healthy state of excitement.

Indeed, so far as health is concerned, the army never was in better condition, having been "weeded out" by the discharge of officers and men of feeble constitutions unable to endure the fatigue and privations of a winter campaign. Those who are left are hardy and rugged, and compare, in fine physical development, with any troops in the world. Their reverses have not dispirited them, but, on the contrary, nerved them to greater exertion.

The Spirit of the Troops.

As an evidence of the good spirits of the men, I need only mention that yesterday I saw a brigade ordered out on a reconnoissance, or "recon-*nonsense*," as one of the men facetiously called it, for three days. The day was cold, raw, and chilly, and the men waited in line nearly an hour on the bleak hill, side for the order to march.

When it came they started off gaily, some whistling and others singing patriotic airs. They had gone only a short distance when the rain came down heavily, but nothing daunted, they kept on as lively as ever. As they passed out of my sight night came on, and the rain came down in torrents. The poor fellows were to be out three days, without tents or shelter of any kind.

Care of the Wounded on the Battle-field.

It will be gratifying to the friends at home of the soldiers to know that the most perfect arrangements possible under the circumstances have been made for the proper treatment of those wounded on the battle-field. At Antietam and other battles regimental surgeons and those not attached to the army, such as volunteer physicians, fell to work, and in many instances cut and slashed away and amputated the legs and arms of many a poor fellow which might have been saved. It is a serious thing thus to maim a human being for life, unless the terrible remedy cannot be possibly avoided.

This evil has engaged the attention of the Surgeon-General, and measures have been taken to prevent a repetition of the cruelty. According to recent orders, the Medical Director of each division of the Army of the Potomac appointed one medical officer as operating surgeon for each brigade, without reference to rank, and gives him three assistant operators, and no other surgeon is permitted to operate except those thus specially detailed. Whenever doubt occurs as to the propriety of an amputation, these three surgeons consult and decide the matter.

One surgeon to each regiment is sent into the field of battle, and the remaining entire force of surgeons are collected at a reserve depot in the rear, where the wounded are brought by the ambulance corps. The result is, expedition in dressing the wounded, and giving proper attention to the care of the sick, many of which cases are brought in suffering from exhaustion in the heat of battle. This is what is professionally termed "conservative" surgery, in contradistinction to the "cut and slashing" system.

To further provide for the comfort of the wounded and sick, one surgeon has entire charge of the cooking arrangements at the reserve depot, and every possible preparation for the wants of the disabled soldier are made in this way. The Medical Corps press into their service all stragglers coming to the rear, many of whom are glad to have any excuse for their absence from the front, and the surgeons are thus well supplied with plenty of assistance in their humane labors.

Assigned to a New Command.

Brig.-Gen. JOHN C. ROBINSON, recently commanding the first brigade, BIRNEY'S Division, STONEMAN'S Corps, HOOKER'S Centre Grand Division, to-day assumed command of the division recently commanded by GIBBON, in REYNOLD'S Corps, FRANKLIN'S Left Grand Division. General GIBBON will return to the command of his brigade. Colonel S. B. HAYMAN, Thirty-seventh New York Regiment, has been appointed a Brigadier-General, and assigned to the command of the brigade vacated by Brig-Gen. ROBINSON.

Philadelphia Brigadier-Generals.

It is said that Colonel JOSHUA T. OWEN and Colonel TURNER G. MOREHEAD, of Philadelphia, both now in command of brigades, have been nominated for Brigadier-Generals, with a fair prospect of confirmation.

Colonel Collis' Regiment.

The behavior of Colonel COLLIS' Zouave Regiment in the battle of Fredericksburg has been highly commended. They made a gallant charge which, it is conceded, saved RANDOLPH'S and LIVINGSTON'S Batteries from capture by the enemy. They also took Colonel CHARLES LAMAR, four captains, one surgeon and one Assistant Adjutant-General of the Rebel army, and sixty-five men of the Sixty-first Georgia Regiment, prisoners from the rifle pits which they stormed.

They also manned the batteries of RANDOLPH and LIVINGTON, which had been decimated by the terrible fire of the enemy. General BIRNEY sent Colonel COLLIS a highly complimentary letter, congratulating his regiment upon its good conduct. The band of music attached to Colonel COLLIS' regiment, I learn, were taken prisoners, after the return of the army to this side of the river.

They had taken shelter in a farm-house a short distance outside of Fredericksburg, and not being notified that our army was about to withdraw, they were left behind, to find themselves next morning prisoners in the hands of "Secesh." They had their instruments with them, which, of course, were made a prize of by the Confederates. The loss in Colonel COLLIS' Regiment was eight killed and twenty-one wounded.

Gen. Meade and the Reserve Corps.

Major-General GEORGE G. MEADE, recently in command of the Pennsylvania Reserve Corps, before leaving that corps made a request to the Governor of Pennsylvania and Secretary of War that the old Reserves be sent back to Pennsylvania, for the purpose of recruiting their broken and shattered ranks with new men. This effort was made once before, after the battle of Antietam, but it did not succeed.

It is to be hoped that this application will prove more successful, for no corps in the army deserve such an indulgence more than they do. Their entire fighting strength in the battle at Fredericksburg, with the two new regiments recently added to them—the One-hundred-and-twenty-first and One-hundred-and-forty-second Pennsylvania Volunteers—was only about 4500 men, and out of this number they lost in killed, wounded and missing, 1800 men, or forty per cent. of the whole number engaged.

Why General Cadwalader Does Not Get a Command?

It has caused some surprise that Major-General GEORGE CADWALADER, of Philadelphia, has not been assigned a command in the field, as it is known that he possesses military talents of a high order, having sprung from a good fighting stock. I will give the reason, as mentioned hereabouts. It will be remembered that General CADWALADER served in the Mexican war as a Brigadier-General, with such distinction that after the close of the war, in 1848 or 1849, he was honored by Congress with the rank of Brevet Major-General as a reward for his services. It is understood that he claims priority by virtue of his brevet rank, dating back some fourteen years, which would give him precedence over all the other Major-Generals now in the field, and would entitle him to command the Army of the Potomac, if he were assigned to it for duty.

The Administration, probably desiring to avoid raising delicate questions of rank, which might occur if the General were ordered to take the field, have detailed him on Courts-martial and other special duties, and have lately appointed him one of a commission to codify the army regulations and report new articles of war, suitable to the changed condition of our military affairs. This will be an undertaking of no small magnitude, and will doubtless occupy the attention of the commission for a year or more to come.

Important Army Changes.

It is reported in army circles that an important change will be made in the Army of the Potomac, which, it is said, will be divided, and SUMNER'S Grand Division taken to Washington, and the other Grand Divisions—HOOKER'S and FRANKLIN'S—taken other points.

INTERESTING WASHINGTON NEWS.

Successful Experiments with Ordnance—Rebel Impudence—The Porter Court-Martial—Gen. McClellan's Evidence—The West Virginia State Bill Signed—The Loan of 1842 to be Paid in Coin.

Special Despatches to the Inquirer.

WASHINGTON, January 2, 1863.

A Trial of Projectiles, with Extraordinary Results.

To-day, another trial of STAFFORD'S projectiles was made at the Navy Yard in this city, with his rifled sub-calibre shot. The most astonishing results were attained, even surpassing former experiments. Three sizes or weights were used, for the purpose of ascertaining the one best adapted to the largest penetration with the same gun. A target construction of eight one-inch plates and twenty one-inch of oak, seven plates in front and one in the rear, was pierced and demolished, the timber being all rended into splinters and the bolts all broken. A penetration of six inches of iron was made with a shot of thirty-two pounds weight, with ten pounds of powder, from a fifty pounder Dahlgren rifled gun. Whitworth and Armstrong are distanced with one-sixth of the charge which they used. It has never yet been equaled. In these results Captain DAHLGREN is prepared to bid the Rebel iron-clads "a happy New Year," if they come within hailing distance.

The Loan of 1842 to be Paid in Coin.

The Secretary of the Treasury has decided to pay in coin the loan of 1842, amounting to two millions eight hundred thousand dollars, falling due yesterday. All bonds to be redeemed must be transmitted to the Secretary of the Treasury, endorsed by the legal holder to the United States, on the reception of which at the Department they will be referred to the First Auditor and promptly settled. Drafts for principal and interest upon the Assistant Treasurer nearest the residence of the owner, will be transmitted to the legal holder in the usual manner.

Rebel Impudence.

In his recent raid, the Rebel STUART caused his telegraph operator to intercept Union messages at Burke's Station, thus learning more or less concerning the efforts being made to intercept him, and the readiness of the forces at Fairfax Station and Fairfax Court House, to give him a warm reception should he venture to visit those points. He also sent various messages over the telegraph wires; one to Fairfax Station, purporting to order (from here) the instant destruction of the considerable quantity of army stores accumulated there. It, however, failed of its object. Among the messages found in the office at Burke's Station, having been sent over the wires by his order, is the following:—

BURKE'S STATION, Dec. 28, 2:30 P. M.—Q. M. General MEIGS, Washington:—In future you will please furnish better mules. Those you have furnished recently are very inferior. J. E. B. STUART,
Major-General C. S. A.

The Bill Admitting Western Virginia Signed.

All speculations as to the President's action upon the bill for the admission of Western Virginia into the Union are now ended, the facts having been ascertained on inquiry that he approved and signed it on Wednesday night; therefore it is a law.

Change of Military Storekeeper.

Captain DANIEL G. THOMAS, the efficient and courteous Storekeeper in this city, is shortly to be ordered to St. Paul, Minnesota, to take charge of the military depot at that post.

General Butler at Washington.

Major-General BUTLER has arrived at Washington.

Miscellaneous News.

The Commissioner of Internal Revenue has decided that naphtha and benzine are subject to a duty of three per centum, on account of manufactures not otherwise provided for.

H. G. FANT has been appointed United States agent for paying pensions for the District of Columbia.

The Coston night signals, adopted by our Government in the naval and military service, have been approved by the English and French Admiralties, and Mrs. COSTON, the widow of the inventor, goes out as passenger in the steamer *Great Eastern* to close the contracts with these Governments.

The Porter Court-Martial.

The following are the proceedings of the PORTER Court-martial, which resumed its sessions to-day.

The Court having called on General PORTER to bring forward his witnesses, he said that the first one whose evidence he most needed was Col. MARSHALL, who then lay ill at a neighboring hotel.

A question was raised as to the propriety of adjourning to the invalid's room, which was decided affirmatively by the Judge Advocate.

The members then proceeded to the hotel, where the Court-martial was reopened in the chamber of Colonel MARSHALL.

He was sworn and testified that he was Colonel of the Thirteenth New York Volunteers, attached to General MORELL'S Division, and a captain in the regular service; and also, that on the afternoon of August 29th, he had been detailed by General PORTER to deploy skirmishers and feel the position of the enemy near the line of the Manassas Railway. He stated all he knew of the enemy's force on that day; they seemed to come from the direction of Thoroughfare Gap. He supposed them to have been twice as strong as General PORTER'S force.

He thought it was impossible for General PORTER to have attacked the right wing of JACKSON, who, with another portion of the Rebel army, was at the same time fighting General POPE, since the direct road thereto was blocked up by the enemy in front, and the other roads were impassable by reason of the dense woods and the rugged nature of the country. The only path that PORTER could have taken would have been a backward one, which was of course impracticable under the circumstances, though he had achieved his retreat by this route on the following day.

Testimony of General McClellan.

He commanded the Army of the Potomac from immediately after the battle of Bull Run, in 1861, up to about the end of August, 1862.

Question.—Did General PORTER command a corps in that army? If so, at what time?

Answer.—He served in that army for some time in the month of September, 1861, first as commander of a division, and then as commander of a corps, from about the end of April to the beginning of May, 1862.

Question.—When did the Army of the Potomac reach Aquia Creek?

Answer.—It reached, by detachments, during the latter part of August.

Question.—Have you knowledge of any efforts made by General PORTER for the purpose of moving with his own command, in order to get to Aquia Creek to join General POPE?

Answer.—I have.

Question.—Please state them!

Answer.—Immediately after the commencement of the movement for evacuating Harrison Bar General PORTER was instructed to move his corps to the vicinity of Williamsburg, holding a position in front of it, so as to be able to support either wing of the army if attacked. While there he received information from contrabands and intercepted letters showing that the Rebel troops in the vicinity of Richmond were moving upon General POPE, and immediately, without waiting for further instructions from me, moved his command with the utmost rapidity to Newport News to embark. While at Newport News he used every effort to facilitate the embarkation of his command for Aquia Creek.

Question.—Did he know that the object of the movement upon his part was to go as quick as possible to the assistance of General POPE?

Answer.—He did.

Question.—At what time did he get off from Newport News?

Answer.—I think he embarked in person on the 20th of August; I could not tell certainly without reference to papers and despatches.

A despatch was handed to the witness and the question asked if that document refreshed his recollection. The following is the despatch alluded to:—

"FORTRESS MONROE, Va., Aug. 20, 1862.—Please push off your troops without one moment's delay. The necessity is very pressing—a matter of life and death. What progress is being made and when will you be through? See me before you sail.

(Signed) GEO. B. McCLELLAN, Maj.-Gen.
To Major-General FITZ-JOHN PORTER."

After reading the paper and acknowledging its authorship, General McCLELLAN said:—To the best of my knowledge and belief, General PORTER sailed on the evening of the 20th of August.

Question.—That order, as we understand it, was executed by him to your satisfaction?

Answer.—Entirely so.

Question.—You have stated that the first movement which he made for the purpose of getting to Newport

Continued on our Last Page

The New-York Times.

VOL. XII---NO. 3521. | NEW-YORK, TUESDAY, JANUARY 6, 1863. | PRICE THREE CENTS.

MURFREESBORO

VICTORY!

The Official Dispatches of Gen. Rosecrans.

The Enemy in Full and Disorderly Retreat Toward Tullahoma.

THEIR DEFEAT A COMPLETE ONE.

Reported Capture of Their Wagon Trains.

Our Losses 1,000 Killed and 5,500 Wounded.

THE REBEL LOSSES MUCH HEAVIER.

DISPATCHES FROM GEN. ROSECRANS.

HEADQUARTERS FOURTEENTH ARMY CORPS, DEPARTMENT OF THE CUMBERLAND, IN FRONT OF MURFREESBORO, Jan. 3, VIA NASHVILLE, Jan. 4.

To H. W. Halleck, General-in-Chief, Washington:

On the 26th of December we marched from Nashville, in three columns. Gen. McCOOK by Nolinsville Pike; Gen. THOMAS from his encampment on Franklin's Pike, *via* Wilson Pike, and Gen. CRITTENDEN on the main Murfreesboro Pike.

Our left and centre met with a strong resistance, such as the nature of the country permits, the rolling or hilly routes, skirted by cedar thickets and farms, and intersected by small streams, with rocky bluff banks, forming serious obstacles.

Gen. McCOOK drove Gen. HARDEE'S corps a mile and a half from Nolinsville, and occupied the place.

Gen. CRITTENDEN reached within a mile and a half of Lavergne.

Gen. THOMAS reached the Wilson Pike, meeting with no serious opposition.

On the 27th, Gen. McCOOK drove Gen. HARDEE from Nolinsville, and pushed a reconnoitering division within six miles of Shelbyville, who found that Gen. HARDEE had retreated toward Murfreesboro.

Gen. CRITTENDEN fought and drove the enemy before him, occupying the line of Stewart's Creek and capturing some prisoners, with slight loss.

Gen. THOMAS occupied the vicinity of Nolinsville, when he was partially surprised, thrown into confusion, and driven back. Gen. SHERIDAN'S Division had repulsed the enemy four times and protected the flank of the centre, which not only held its own but advanced until this untoward event, which compelled me to retain the left wing to support the right, until it should be rallied and assume a new position.

On the 1st inst., the rebels opened by an attack on us and were again repulsed.

On the 2d inst., there was skirmishing along the line, with threats of an attack until about 3 o'clock in the afternoon, when the enemy advanced, throwing a small division across Stone River to occupy the commanding ground there.

While reconnoitering the ground occupied by this division, which had no artillery, I saw a heavy force emerging from the woods, and advanced in line of battle three lines deep. They drove our little division before them after a sharp contest, in which we lost 70 or 80 killed and 375 wounded, but they were finally repulsed by Gen. NEGLEY'S Division, and the remaining troops of the left wing of Gen. MORTON'S Pioneer Brigade, and fled far over the field and beyond their intrenchments, their officers rallying them with great difficulty. They lost heavily. We occupied the ground with the left wing last night. The lines were completed at 4 o'clock in the morning.

The 3d was spent in bringing up and distributing provisions and ammunition. It has been raining all day. The ground is very heavy.

CAMP NEAR MURFREESBORO, Jan. 4, 1863.

To Major-Gen. H. W. Halleck, General-in-Chief:

Following my dispatch of last evening, I have to announce the enemy are in full retreat. They left last night.

The rain having raised the river and the bridge across it, between the left wing and the centre, being incomplete, I deemed it prudent to withdraw that wing during the night. This occupied my time until 4 o'clock and fatigued the troops.

The announcement of the retreat was known to me at 7 o'clock this A. M.

Our ammunition train arrived during the night.

To-day was occupied in distributing ammunition, burying the dead and collecting arms from the field of battle.

The pursuit was commenced by the centre, the two leading brigades arriving at the west side of Stone River this evening. [See diagram.] The railroad bridge was saved, but in what condition is not known.

We shall occupy the town and push the pursuit to-morrow.

Our Medical Director estimates the wounded in hospital at 5,500, and our dead at 1,000.

We have to deplore the loss of Lieut.-Col. GARESCHE, whose capacity and gentlemanly deportment had already endeared him to all the officers of this command, and whose gallantry on the field of battle excited their admiration. W. S. ROSECRANS,

Major-General Commanding.

SPECIAL DISPATCH FROM NASHVILLE.

NASHVILLE, Monday, Jan. 5.

From persons arriving from the battle-field, I learn that on Saturday night, during the storm, the rebels attacked our men in their rifle-pits along the

MURFREESBORO AND ITS SURROUNDINGS.

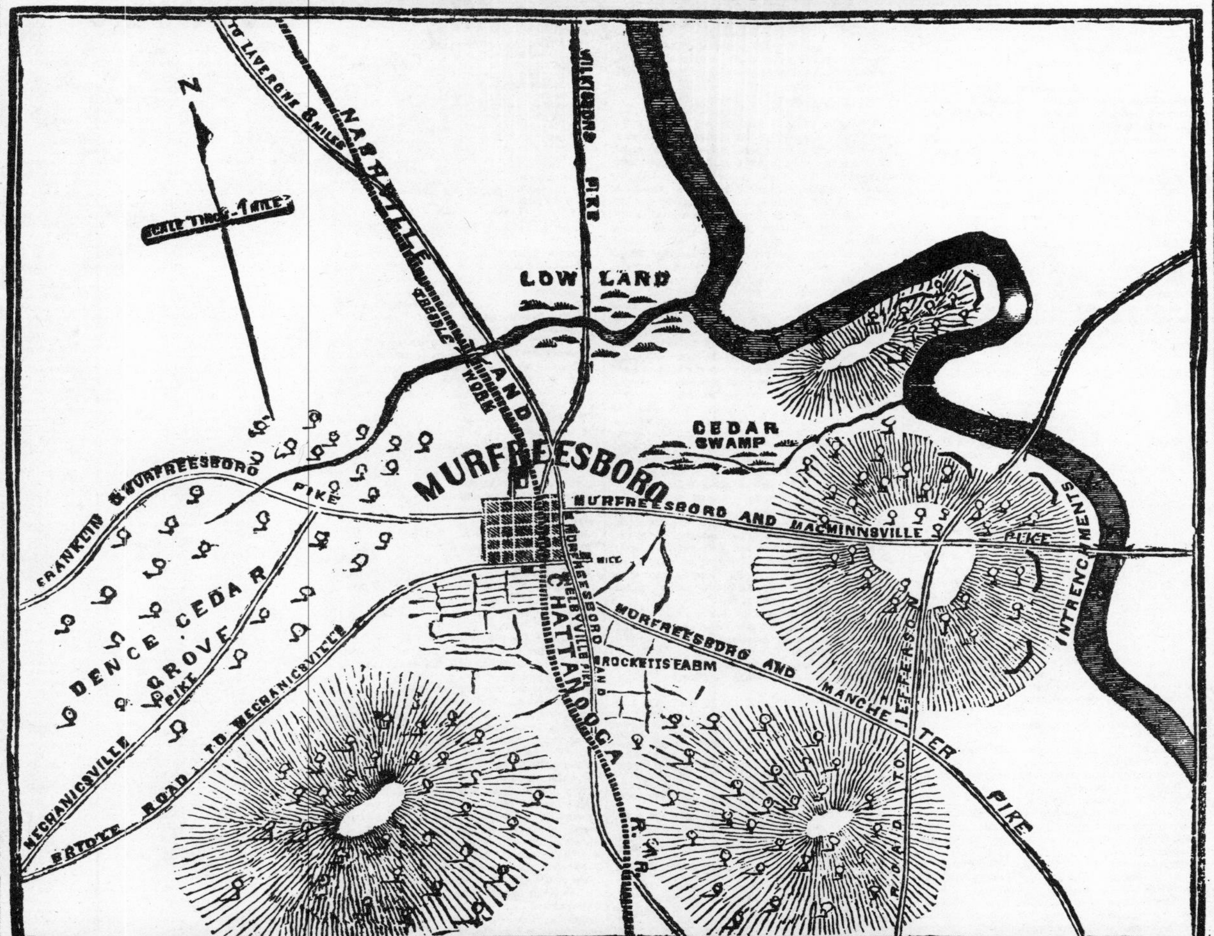

whole line. There was heavy fighting in the centre. We drove the enemy across Stone River. The Seventy-seventh Pennsylvania first carried the point.

On Sunday morning STANLEY'S Brigade entered Murfreesboro. The town is much injured by shells. Gen. SILL'S body was at the Court-house.

The rebels buried their own dead and our officers. There has been great loss of Confederate life.

We lose about 9,000 killed and wounded, and 5,000 prisoners.

The enemy retreated to Tullahoma.

Our forces are terribly scattered. Out of 136 Colonels engaged, we lost 19 killed.

PREVIOUS DISPATCH FROM GEN. MITCHELL.

HEADQUARTERS, NASHVILLE, Tenn., Jan. 4—1 P. M.

To Hon. E. M. Stanton, Secretary of War:

Skirmishing commenced on the evening of the 29th, our forces following the enemy closely, and driving them to the evening of the 30th. On the morning of the 31st, the enemy attacked our forces at daylight. Ever since that time the fight has been progressing. This is the fifth day in the same locality. If the whole Richmond army does not get here our success is certain. The fighting has been terrible. Our army has the advantage, and will hold it, God willing. I cannot give particulars. Our officers have suffered terribly. I have heard nothing of importance since 10 o'clock last evening. At that hour everything was favorable for us.

(Signed,) ROBERT R. MITCHELL,
Brigadier-General Commanding.

THE NATIONAL VICTORY COMPLETE.

The Enemy in Full Retreat.

LOUISVILLE, Monday, Jan. 5.

Murfreesboro advices represent the National victory as complete. The entire rebel army is fleeing toward Tullahoma in great disorder.

THE PARTICULARS.

LOUISVILLE, Sunday, Jan. 4.

There are three feet of water on the Cumberland Shoals, and the river is rising.

Everything is going on well in front.

Gen. ROSECRANS is in Murfreesboro. *He has captured the rebel trains and is driving the enemy.* Gen. ROSECRANS is unhurt. His Assistant, and Adjut.-Gen. McDOWELL is wounded in the arm.

The *Journal's* dispatches say that a fourth bloody fight occurred last night during the storm. The rebels charged us and were repulsed. Our troops hold Murfreesboro. Our advantages are decided. Gen. BRECKINRIDGE'S Division was cut to pieces, and routed Saturday. Our skirmishers decoyed a large number of rebels among our batteries. We routed them with great slaughter.

Capt. McCULLOCK, of the Second Kentucky Cavalry, (Union,) says the rebel General, WITHERS, was driven almost to madness by the slaughter of his men. Eye-witnesses say that the slaughter exceeds that of Shiloh. Gen. ROSECRANS and his soldiers are in the highest spirits.

On Saturday Col. McDOWELL McCOOK engaged WHEELER'S Cavalry six miles from Nashville, routing him completely. All is highly cheering.

Prisoners say that Gen. KIRBY SMITH is in the fight.

Rebel canteens were filled with whisky and gunpowder

The Murfreesboro *Rebel* of the 3d says the Federals fought gallantly, and admits a loss of 5,000.

The National prisoners were sent to Murfreesboro as fast as taken.

Capt. JOHN DESHA, of Kentucky, was wounded by a shell in the head. Adjutant CARR, of the same regiment, was shot by a cannon ball.

The following is from the Associated Press correspondent at Nashville:

It is reported that Gen. ROSECRANS shelled Murfreesboro this morning. There was no reply. Our forces would occupy it at noon. The rebels undoubtedly left. Our forces, it is reported, are pursuing.

McCOOK attacked WHEELER'S Cavalry near the asylum, six miles from Nashville, killing eight, who were left on the field, and many wounded. Seven Nationals were wounded.

Capt. PINNEY, of the Fifth Wisconsin, Lieut. HASTINGS, of the Twenty-fifth Illinois, and all the Commissioned Officers and Sergeants of Companies G, I, and K, are killed or disabled.

Col. SCOTT, of the Nineteenth Illinois, is seriously wounded.

Capt. AUSTIN, of Gen. WOODRUFF'S Staff, is taken prisoner.

Private dispatches say, that the rebels in their retreat are burning the cotton wherever they can get hold of it.

It is reported that FRANK WARD, of ANDERSON'S Troop, is killed.

All the reports of Gen. ROSECRANS having retreated to Nashville, are false.

The fight to-day is supposed to be in the vicinity of Christiana.

The interruptions of the rebel cavalry between Nashville and Christiana makes it difficult to get news, but everything thus far is favorable to the ultimate success of the National arms.

DISPATCHES FROM THE BATTLE-FIELD.

BATTLE-FIELD, STONE RIVER, Saturday, Jan. 3.

It rained hard all this day, and both armies suspended hostilities, save skirmishing. This evening we battered down a rebel house which concealed sharpshooters, and after short fighting drove the enemy out of a cover from which they had damaged us. Unless the enemy attacks, Sunday will perhaps be quiet.

Up to date, our killed and wounded, including skirmishing, amounts to nearly five thousand. An unusual proportion of the wounds are severe. The number of killed is about one-fifth that of the wounded.

The Murfreesboro Rebel *Banner*, of yesterday, admits a rebel loss of 5,000 in Wednesday's battle. They have lost at least 2,000 since. Prisoners state that Gens. HARDEE and HANSON were killed.

The following are additional names of Union officers killed and wounded:

KILLED.

Col. Fred. C. Jones, Twenty-fourth Ohio, gallantly leading his regiment into action.
Lieut. Taliafero, of Hickox Battery.
Adjt. Boynton, Sixty-ninth Ohio.

WOUNDED.

Col. Nick Anderson, Sixth Ohio.

Col. Charles Anderson, Ninety-third Ohio. Both of these officers were wounded quite severely, but after their wounds were dressed, they returned to the field.

Col. J. F. Miller, commanding 7th Brigade, returned to duty after his wound was dressed.
Lieut.-Col. Hall.
Lieut.-Col. Elias Neff, 40th Indiana—severely.
Capt. C. C. Webb, 18th Michigan—severely.
Lieut. A. G. Russell, 21st Michigan.
Lieut. Mark Walker, 15th Indiana—severely.
Lieut. Enoch Weiry, 21st Ohio—severely.
Lieut. Frank Pealer, 65th Ohio—severely,
Col. Leonard.
Col. C. C. Hines.
Maj. and Adjt. ELLIOTT.

These last are all of the Fifty-seventh Indiana, and are severely wounded.

Col. J. W. Tyler, Ninety-fourth Ohio, severely, but not dangerously.
Maj. HICKOX, Sixty-ninth Ohio.
Capt. McDONNELL, Adjutant-General of ROSECRANS' Staff.
Lieut. JAMES McCONNELL, Eighteenth Regulars.
Capt. C. W. BURKETT, slightly.
Lieut. S. T. SMITH, slightly.
Lieut. J. B. FERGUSON, Sixty-fourth Ohio, severely.
Lieut. JAMES C. HOWLAND, Sixteenth Regulars.
Adjt. MASSEY, Fifty-fifth Ohio, severely.
Col. Alex. Cassell, 65th Ohio—not dangerously.
Lieut. Grinsted, 3d Kentucky.
Lieut. McClana, 18th Ohio—seriously.
Capt. Brook and Lieut. Peter, 74th Ohio.
Maj. Marvine, 1st Wisconsin.

The Lieutenant-Colonel of the Sixty-ninth Indiana was saved by a breast-plate. A shot struck his breast and knocked him out of his saddle.

Lieut. WM. PORTER, of Gen. ROSECRANS' Staff, riding directly behind the General, received a piece of shell between his pants and haversack, cutting his breeches.

Since the above was written the skirmish developed into a bitter fight. Gen. ROSECRANS, worried by some rebels behind breastworks, sent Col. BEATTY, of the Third Ohio, with his regiment and the Eighty-eighth Indiana, and they carried the works at the point of the bayonet, capturing many prisoners and holding the works. All is quiet now, but the enemy is reported evacuating.

BATTLE-FIELD STONE RIVER, Monday, Jan. 5.

On Saturday it rained, and all was quiet until night, when the Third Ohio and Eighty-eighth Indiana charged and carried a rebel breastwork, capturing 50 prisoners and killing many rebels, with slight loss.

During the night the enemy evacuated, and are supposed to be retreating to Fayetteville.

Our loss in killed and wounded is about 6,000. The enemy claim that they captured 4,000 prisoners. Their loss is fully as great. Our loss of field-officers—valuable ones—is distressing. The rivers are all rising rapidly. Gen. WILLICH is a prisoner.

THE LOSS OF THE MONITOR.

Thrilling Particulars of the Disaster.

BALTIMORE, Monday, Jan. 5.

The *American's* special Fortress Monroe letter, dated Jan. 4, says:

"In conversation with several of the officers and crew of the *Monitor*, I gather the following narrative of the facts attending the loss of that noble little vessel and so many of her crew:

We left Fortress Monroe on Monday, the 29th of December, in tow of the steamer *Rhode Island*, with the *Passaic* in tow of the steamer *State of Georgia*. We passed Cape Henry Monday afternoon, at 5 o'clock, with a smooth sea and light wind. The *Passaic* was a little way ahead. The weather continued fine until 5 o'clock Tuesday evening, when it commenced to blow from the southwest, with a heavy sea running and making a clean sweep over all.

At 9½ Cape Hatteras bore N. N. W., distant 20 miles. The gale still increased. The vessel labored very heavily, the upper hull coming down upon every sea with fearful violence. Up to this time the Worthington pumps and bilge injectors were entirely competent to keep the vessel free.

At 10 o'clock several heavy seas struck the vessel in succession, when word was sent from the engine-rooms that the water was gaining on the pumps. Orders were then given to start ADAMS' centrifugal pump, capable of throwing three thousand gallons of water per minute. For a while the water appeared to be kept under.

In a short time, however, word was passed from the engine room that the water was again gaining on the pumps, and was at that time up to the ashpits, in a great measure stopping the draft. The water at this time was standing two feet deep on the ward-room floor.

All hands were then set to work with every bucket at hand to bail. Water, however, kept gaining upon the pumps until within a foot of the fires in the furnaces.

A "Coston" signal was then flashed to call the attention of the *Rhode Island* to our condition. After much delay consequent upon the heavy sea running, a boat was lowered from the *Rhode Island* and sent to our assistance. After several trials she succeeded in getting alongside of us.

The *Rhode Island* at the same time, in going astern, caught her launch between her own side and our vessel, crushing the boat badly and bringing her own counter down upon our side. For a time she could not move her engine, getting on a centre. She finally started ahead, and the launch, smashed as she was, succeeded in conveying to the steamer thirty of the crew of the *Monitor*.

After the departure of the launch, those remaining on board worked at the buckets with a will. The gale at this time was raging furiously, the seas making a clean sweep over the top of the turret. The water at this juncture had succeeded in rising up to the grate-bars of the furnaces, and was gradually extinguishing the fires. The steam in the boilers consequently ran down and the pumps could not be worked for want of sufficient steam.

At this time three boats were discovered coming toward the vessel. Word was passed that boats were at hand sufficient to take all from the vessel. The *Monitor* was now sinking. Every pump was stopped and her deck was under water. Several in coming off the turret were swept by the waves to the leeward, and must have perished, as no assistance could be rendered them.

The boats then shoved off from the sinking vessel. Although entreated to come down and get into the boats, several remained standing upon the turret afraid of being swept from the deck, stupefied with fear. The boats succeeded in reaching the *Rhode Island* in safety, and all in them got on board.

A picked crew with the gallant officer of the *Rhode Island*, Mr. BROWN, then shoved off in the launch to return to the *Monitor*. The moon, which up to this time had been throwing some light upon the waves, was shut in by dense masses of black clouds.

At 1, in the morning the *Monitor's* light disappeared beneath the waves. The *Rhode Island* then started for the spot where the *Monitor* was seen to go down. Coston signals were constantly kept burning. A strict lookout was kept up on all parts of the vessel to catch a glimpse, if possible, of the missing boat.

At daylight nothing was seen on the waves, and with heavy hearts we ran around the spot, as nearly as could be judged, where the *Monitor* had disappeared until late in the afternoon. Several steamers and other vessels were spoken, to learn, if possible, the fate of the missing boat, but nothing could be heard.

The survivors reached Fortress Monroe last evening in the *Rhode Island*. Nothing whatever was saved except the apparel the officers and crew stood in. The conduct of both the officers and men of the *Monitor* on that night was beyond reproach. No sign of panic was visible. Each stood to his post, confident in his commander, and it was hard to prevail upon the men to get into the boats, each wishing to remain by until the last.

The names of those officers who were saved are as follows: J. P. BANKHEAD, Commander; S. D. GREEN, Lieutenant; LOUIS N. STODDARD, Sailing Master; WM. F. KEELER, Acting Assistant-Paymaster; G. M. WEEKS, Acting Assistant-Surgeon; JAMES WATERS, First Engineer; MARK SUNSTRUM, Third Assistant-Engineer.

The names of the missing officers are as follows: NORMAN K. ATWATER, Acting Ensign, of New-Haven, Conn.; GEORGE FREDERICKSON, Acting Ensign, of Philadelphia; S. A. LEWIS, Third Assistant Engineer, of Baltimore; ROBINSON W. HANDS, Third Assistant Engineer, of Baltimore.

The first cutter of the *Rhode Island*, the boat referred to above, contained WILLIAM BROWN, master's mate, and seven of the crew, whose names I have not been able to ascertain. They have not been heard of up to this time. There is a possibility that they may have succeeded in reaching the *Monitor*, and taking off some more of the crew, and been afterward picked up by some coasting vessel, numbers of which were passing by the next morning.

Testimonial to Gen. Butler.

A meeting was held last evening at the Fifth-avenue Hotel, for the purpose of deciding upon some proper testimonial to be made to Major-Gen. B. F. BUTLER. Capt. MARSHALL was called to the Chair, and Mr. CHARLES GOULD appointed Secretary.

On motion of Gen. WETMORE, it was

Resolved, That, as the sense of the meeting, the loyal patriotism, indomitable energy and great administrative ability shown by Major-Gen. BUTLER in the various commands held by him in the service of the country, and especially in his military and civil adjustment of the duties pertaining to his command of the Department of the Gulf, unanimously entitle him to an expression of approbation on the part of the citizens of New-York. It was also

Resolved, That the hospitalities of the City be presented him in a public reception at the Governor's Room in the City Hall, and that a public dinner be also tendered him in behalf of the citizens of this City.

The meeting was then adjourned to meet this day, at 2½ o'clock, in the Chamber of Commerce.

VICKSBURGH.

VICTORY!

Continuous Fighting for Five Days.

Three Lines of the Rebel Works Captured by Gen. Sherman.

Probable Surrender of the Fourth and Last One.

The Fall of the City Admitted by the Rebels.

The Railroad Communication Cut Off.

The National Army Forty Thousand Strong.

CAIRO, Sunday, Jan. 4.

The Memphis *Bulletin*, just received, says the steamer *Rattler* has arrived direct from the fleet at Vicksburgh, which place she left on Monday evening.

Fighting had been going on for five days, commencing on Wednesday. Up to Monday morning Gen. SHERMAN had captured three lines of the enemy's works. The firing on the fourth and last line of defences, on the Jackson and Vicksburg Road, had ceased, and *the indications were that it had surrendered.* This line was just two miles from Vicksburgh. *There was nothing between Gen. Sherman and Vicksburgh but a trestle work of the railroad.*

Before taking the fortifications, Gen. SHERMAN sent a brigade to cut off communication with the city by the Shreveport Railroad, a work which was successfully accomplished.

Gen. SHERMAN was reinforced Sunday night by 9,000 men from Gen. GRANT'S army, by way of the river. The whole Federal force at Vicksburgh is now 40,000 men.

At the latest accounts, we had captured ten guns and 700 prisoners.

Nothing has yet been heard from the forces below.

The steamer *Judge Torrance* was twice fired on while passing Millikenville. In retaliation, the *Rattler* burned the town.

A DISPATCH FROM GEN. GRANT.

HOLLY SPRINGS, Miss., Sunday, Jan. 4.

Maj.-Gen. Halleck, Commander-in-Chief:

Dispatches from Gen. SHERMAN and the Naval Commander were received at Helena on the 31st. The gunboats were engaging the enemy's batteries. SHERMAN was inland, three miles from Vicksburgh, hotly engaged. From rebel sources I learn that the Grenada *Appeal* of the 31st says the Yankees have got possession of Vicksburgh.

Since the late raids this Department, except the troops on the river, have subsisted off the country. There will be but little in Northern Mississippi to support guerrillas in a few weeks more.

U. S. GRANT,
Major-General Commanding.

A REBEL REPORT.

FORTRESS MONROE, Sunday, Jan. 4.

The Richmond *Dispatch*, of the 28th of December, says that 26,000 Federal troops landed below Vicksburgh on the 21st, and made a land attack simultaneously with an attack of the gunboats on Vicksburgh. Several gunboats are said to be disabled, and and many prisoners taken.

THE VICTORY OVER FORREST.

A Severe Engagement Lasting All Day.

The Rebel Losses 1,400 Killed and Wounded, 400 Taken Prisoners, and 6 Guns, 1,000 Stand of Arms, and 350 Horses Captured.

CAIRO, Monday, Jan. 5.

Gen. SULLIVAN, with a force of 6,000 men, attacked Gen. FORREST on Thursday morning at Hunt's Cross Roads, twelve miles from Lexington, Tenn. It was a severe engagement, lasting all day. A gunboat patrolled the river, which prevented the rebels from crossing. They fought desperately, but were finally routed and scattered, with a loss of 1,400 killed and wounded, and 400 captured. We also took 350 horses, nearly 1,000 stand of arms, and a battery of six guns. Union loss, 600 killed and wounded. These losses may be exaggerated. It is certain, however, that they were very heavy.

Post-Office Notice.

POST-OFFICE, NEW-YORK, Monday, Jan. 5, 1862.

To the Editor of the New-York Times:

In consequence of the numerous cases of breakage which have occurred, and the injury resulting thereby to letters and packages, it is considered necessary to prohibit the forwarding of bottles containing medicines or liquids of any description through the mails.

In future, therefore, all such articles found in the letter boxes will be detained at the General Office in Nassau-street, instead of being sent, as heretofore, to their destination.

By order of the Postmaster-General.
ABRAM WAKEMAN, Postmaster.

The Monitor Nahant.

BOSTON, Monday, Jan. 5.

The Monitor *Nahant*, which left here Saturday evening, passed Cape Cod at 8 A. M. to-day; all well; sea smooth.

The Philadelphia Inquirer.

CIRCULATION OVER 60,000. PHILADELPHIA, THURSDAY, JANUARY 8, 1863. PRICE TWO CENTS.

THE WAR NEWS!

Sherman's Assault on Vicksburg

A DESPERATE BATTLE.

General Sherman Within Two Miles of the City.

He is Driven Back to His First Line of Defence.

Price, Van Dorn and Jos. E. Johnston Commanding the Rebels.

A FURTHER ACCOUNT OF THE MURFREESBORO' BATTLE.

Rebel Army Completely Demoralized

The Rebel Loss now Estimated at 12,000 to 15,000

GEN. ROSECRANS' OFFICIAL DESPATCH

Col. Carter's Raid into East Tennessee

AFFAIRS AT PORT ROYAL AND CHARLESTON.

THE ARMY OF THE POTOMAC.

Speech of Jeff. Davis at Richmond.

GOV. CURTIN'S MESSAGE.

The French Consul at New Orleans Dismissed.

THE BATTLE AT VICKSBURG.

NEW YORK, Jan. 6.—The following special despatch has been received by the *Tribune*:—

HELENA, Jan. 2, via CAIRO, Jan. 7.—The battle is still raging at Vicksburg with no decisive results.

Our forces took the main battery and rifle-pits of the enemy on Monday; but were afterwards repulsed.

Five cannon were taken and spiked; but they were afterwards lost.

General MORGAN and Colonel J. B. WYMAN were killed. Colonel MORGAN L. SMITH and Captain GRIM were wounded; but not mortally.

Both armies rested on Monday night, after a hard fought day. Our troops are still confident of victory. Generals PRICE and VAN DORN command the Rebels.

It is rumored that General SHERMAN was being largely reinforced by the arrival of General GRANT'S cavalry.

The gun-boats were not doing much.

Our army is well posted and protected in the flank and rear, and will not yield the contest till victory is in their possession.

Our loss in killed and wounded so far is estimated at three thousand.

THE LATEST.

A Desperate Battle—The Rebels Reinforced—General Sherman Driven Back.

CAIRO, Ill., Jan. 7.—We have one day's later intelligence from Vicksburg, of a highly interesting and exciting character.

The Rebels have concentrated al their forces from Jackson and Grenada and along the line of road, amounting to 65,000 men, at Vicksburg.

This overwhelming force attacked Gen. SHERMAN on Monday, causing him to fall back to his first line of defence.

The Rebel entrenchments and fortifications extend back from the city six miles.

Gen. SHERMAN'S force had fought itself to within two miles of the city, when he was attacked by the superior force of the Rebels.

The fighting on Monday is represented as having been desperate in the extreme. Batteries and fortifications were taken and retaken.

Whole regiments, and even brigades, fought hand to hand over their guns for the possession of the defences.

The Fourth Iowa Regiment lost six hundred men, killed, wounded and missing.

General HOVEY, with fifteen hundred men, was sent to execute a special order, but since then had not been heard from. Fears are entertained for his safety.

Nothing has yet been heard from the Federal forces below, nor can we learn that our gun-boats have taken any part in the action.

It is reported that Rebel steamers are crossing from the Tennessee shore to Vicksburg, and are supposed to be carrying reinforcements to the Rebels.

The last accounts stated that the Rebel General HOLMES was marching in the direction of Vicksburg, and it was not improbable that he had already arrived there.

General M. L. SMITH, of the United States Army, has been wounded in the breast.

There was some fighting on Tuesday morning, after SHERMAN had fallen back, but it was thought that he could maintain his position.

The report that SHERMAN was reinforced by GRANT is incorrect.

It is reported that General GORMAN is evacuating Helena, Arkansas, with the intention of occupying Napoleon.

General SHERMAN'S loss is estimated at from 4000 to 5000.

Trains are running on the Memphis Railroad to Lagrange.

General JOSEPH JOHNSTON commands the Rebel forces at Vicksburg.

THE ARMY OF THE POTOMAC.

Rebel Accounts of the Murfreesboro' Battle—Speech of Jeff. Davis at Richmond—The Enemy Withdrawing his Lines from Fredericksburg.

HEAD-QUARTERS OF THE ARMY OF THE POTOMAC, Jan. 7.—News from the Rebel side relative to the fight at Murfreesboro' is, in effect, that they have taken four thousand prisoners and twenty-six guns.

JEFF. DAVIS has returned to Richmond, where he delivered a bitter and violent speech against the Federal Government and its officers, denouncing them as guilty of the most enormous crimes.

Although the Rebel force on our front has been greatly reduced, and the army at Port Royal entirely withdrawn from view, it is not believed that any of the enemy's troops have been sent to reinforce General BRAGG from this point, but that they have merely fallen back upon the line of railroad for greater facility in procuring supplies.

The atmosphere is much colder to-day, indicating the approach of severe weather. No movement of any importance has taken place for several days.

All is quiet to-night.

THE BATTLE OF MURFREESBORO'.

The Demoralization of the Rebel Army—Breckinridge's Wounds—The Rebel Loss 12,000.

CINCINNATI, Jan. 7.—A special despatch to the *Commercial*, from Murfreesboro', dated the 6th inst., gives an additional confirmation of the demoralization of the Rebel army.

BRECKINRIDGE'S Division was terribly punished on Friday. BRECKINRIDGE was wounded in the ear, and his Adjutant-General was killed.

Wounded Rebel officers estimate their loss at from 12,000 to 15,000. There was great slaughter among the leading officers. Col. MULLIGAN, of Tennessee, was mortally wounded, and is in the hospital at Murfreesboro'.

The body of General HANSON was sent South to-day.

General RAINS' body has been sent to Nashville.

The enemy's rear guard was encountered at ten o'clock on Sunday night, by STANLEY'S cavalry. They retreated, with a loss of thirty men.

A negro from BRAGG'S head-quarters, who left the Rebel army within five miles of Manchester, heard General BRAGG say that he would go to Chattanooga.

GENERAL ROSECRANS' OFFICIAL DESPATCHES.

A Corrected Copy of His Despatch of the 3d Instant.

WASHINGTON, Jan. 7.—Nearly one-half of General ROSECRANS' despatch of the 3d instant, communicating the operations of his army up to that time, was omitted in its publication in the papers of yesterday. The following is a complete copy of the despatch, which includes a record of the most critical period of the struggle—the fight on the 31st:—

HEAD-QUARTERS FOURTEENTH ARMY CORPS, DEPARTMENT OF THE CUMBERLAND, IN FRONT OF MURFREESBORO', Jan. 3, via NASHVILLE, Jan. 4, 1863.—To H. W. HALLECK, General-in-Chief, Washington:—On the 26th of December we marched from Nashville in three columns—General McCOOK by Nolinsville pike, General THOMAS from his encampment on Franklin's pike, via Wilson pike, and General CRITTENDEN on the main Murfreesboro' pike.

Our left and centre met with a strong resistance, such as the nature of the country permits, the rolling or hilly routes, skirted by cedar thickets and farms, and intersected by small streams, with rocky bluff banks, forming serious obstacles.

General McCOOK drove General HARDEE'S corps a mile and a half from Nolinsville, and occupied the place.

General CRITTENDEN reached within a mile and a half of Lavergne.

General THOMAS reached the Wilson pike, meeting with no severe opposition.

On the 27th General McCOOK drove Gen. HARDEE from Nolinsville, and pushed forward a reconnoitring division six miles towards Shelbyville, and found that General HARDEE had retreated towards Murfreesboro'.

Gen. CRITTENDEN fought and drove the enemy before him, occupying the line of Stewart's creek, and capturing some prisoners with slight loss.

General THOMAS occupied the vicinity of Nolinsville. On the 28th General McCOOK completed his reconnoisance of HARDEE'S movements. CRITTENDEN remained, awaiting the result, and bringing up trains. THOMAS moved on to Stewart's creek, and on the 29th General McCOOK moved into Wilkinson's Cross Roads, seven miles from Murfreesboro', the end of a short pike road, rough, through a rolling country, skirted by bluffs, and covered with dense cedar thickets, tops and open timber. CRITTENDEN pushed the enemy rapidly, saved the bridges, and reached a point within three miles of Murfreesboro'. He advanced, driving all the outposts to within sight of the town. THOMAS' two divisions closed up with CRITTENDEN'S and took a position on his right.

On the 30th McCOOK advanced on the Wilkinson pike, having to make his way through dense woods, meeting with determined resistance, and got into position three miles from Murfreesboro', occupying the extreme right of our line. The left stood fast. The centre advanced slightly, and were engaged in cutting through an almost impenetrable growth of cedar, which separated them from our right, rendering communication with them exceedingly difficult. The combat and the roughness of the country had brought forward McCOOK'S right division so as to face strongly to the southeast, instead of being refaced to face to the south with the several divisions between the centre and right, and sufficiently far in the rear to support, and, if necessary, to extend it—the grave consequences of which were developed the next day.

On the 31st, found our left crossing Murfreesboro' pike and railroad—one division front, one forming a crotchet on Stone's river, and one in reserve in the centre—NEGLEY being between the left and right, and ROUSSEAU in reserve. The plan of battle was to open on the right, engage the enemy sufficiently to hold him firmly, to cross the river with our left, consisting of three divisions (to oppose which they had but two divisions), the country being favorable to an attack from that side of the town. But the enemy attacked the whole front of our right flank, which was partially surprised and thrown into confusion and driven back.

General SHERIDAN'S Division had repulsed the enemy four times, and protected the flank of the centre, which not only held its own, but advanced until this untoward event, which compelled me to retain the left wing to support the right until it should be rallied and assume a new position.

On the 1st instant the Rebels opened by an attack on us, and were agian repulsed.

On the 2d instant there was skirmishing along the front with threats of attack until about three o'clock in the afternoon, when the enemy advanced, throwing a small division across Stone's river to occupy the commanding ground there.

While reconnoitring the ground occupied by this Division, which had no artillery, I saw a heavy force emerging from the woods, and advancing in line of battle three lines deep. They drove our little division before them after a sharp contest, in which we lost seventy or eighty killed and three hundred and seventy-five wounded; but they were finally repulsed by General NEGLEY'S Division and the remaining troops of the left wing of General MORTON'S Pioneer Brigade, and fled far over the field and beyond their intrenchments, their officers rallying them with great difficulty. He lost heavily. We occupied the ground with the left wing last night. The lines were completed at four o'clock in the morning.

The 3d was spent in bringing up and distributing provisions and ammunition. It has been raining all day. The ground is very heavy.

W. S. ROSECRANS,
Major-General Commanding.

THE RAID INTO EAST TENNESSEE.

Return of the Expedition.

CINCINNATI, Jan. 7.—Colonel CARTER'S expedition reached Manchester, Ky., yesterday, on their return from East Tennessee. It left London, Ky., on the 21st ult., and comprised a thousand cavalry.

The results of the expedition are as follows:—

Two important bridges were destroyed; five hundred and fifty Rebels were killed, wounded or taken prisoners, and seven hundred stand of arms and a large amount of flour, salt and other Rebel stores were captured. A locomotive and two cars were also destroyed.

A brisk skirmish took place at Wautauga bridge, and another at Jonesboro'.

This raid was one of the most hazardous of the war, and attended with great hardships and privations, notwithstanding which we lost but ten men.

The Maine Legislature.

AUGUSTA, Me., Jan. 7.—The Legislature organized to-day, and the Governor will be inaugurated to-morrow. The Republican caucus to-night re-nominated the present Secretary of State, Adjutant-General and Attorney-General.

SPECIAL NAVAL CORRESPONDENCE.

A Flag of Truce—The Rebel Ram "Georgia"—The "Fingal" a Failure—New Rebel Batteries—Running the Blockade—United States Iron-Clads Wanted.

Special Correspondence of the Inquirer.

FORT PULASKI, Dec. 30, 1862.

On Saturday a flag of truce was sent up from this place to take a Reverend Mr. LOGAN, of Indiana, to visit his wife's sister, who resides in Savannah, and who is said to be so sick that if she is not immediately removed to the North she will die. Mr. LOGAN had influence enough to procure a passage to Port Royal in the United States supply steamer *Circassian*, and for several days after his arrival at that place he visited all the points of interest in that neighborhood, and also at Beaufort. He had excellent opportunities for visiting and making himself thoroughly acquainted with all our points of defence.

He may be a good and a loyal man, but it was wrong to allow even him to circulate about so much just at a time when he could give the Rebels much valuable information. His stay at Fort Pulaski has enabled him to see our defences here, and, if he chooses, he can make the most of his information. The steamer *Mattano* went up the river until within a mile of the obstructions, when she anchored and was boarded by a boat from the Rebel ram *Georgia*, commanded by Lieutenant PEMBROKE JONES, formerly of the United States Navy. While the *Mattano* was waiting, a Rebel flag of truce, under Captain STUART, Confederate States army, came down. Mr. LOGAN was transferred to await the disposition of the Rebel General, and, as he has not returned up to the time I write, it is fair to presume that his cause has found favor in the sight of the Rebels.

The Rebel ram *Georgia* is useless as a moving vessel, her engines being in so crippled condition that, with the appliances they have, she cannot be repaired. From present appearances she is hard and fast aground, as she does not swing with the tide. Her armament consists of five guns on each broadside, and one at each end. The Rebels acknowledge that she can be used only as a floating battery, auxiliary to Fort Jackson, and not as a ram.

The *Fingal* was not seen on the trip, and it is probable that she is up to the city. She is a failure, and, like the *Georgia*, is turned about when they desire to shift her position. The *Georgia* now lies off St. Augustine Creek, having a full crew on board, who, like "Micawber," are "waiting for something to turn up.

Our officers noticed that the "Rebs" have been strengthening their batteries of late, and, from appearances, one or two masked batteries have been built. The Rebel officer pointed out a schooner which they triumphantly asserted had lately run the blockade, bringing them a cargo of much needed supplies. As the vessel had not been seen before by our people, it is fair to suppose they tell the truth in relation to her. She has probably come in by the way of some of the numerous creeks which lead to the river above Fort Pulaski.

COSTON'S and the marine batteries have been lately strengthened in their build and armament, so that, in all probability, they together now mount in the neighborhood of say thirty guns, which render them very formidable.

Affairs here go on in the even tenor of their way. Our gunning parties are doing finely, and ducks, curlew, snipe, &c., come in without stint. We are having lovely weather, and the boys are enjoying themselves finely, but wait with anxious hearts the time when the Government will send a few iron-clads to clear out the rivers and give us an opportunity to occupy the city of Savannah. We trust it will not be long before our hopes are realized.

Lieutenant-Colonel O. T. BEARD, of the Forty-eighth New York Volunteers, stationed at this post, has resigned and gone home, prefering to do so rather than to stand the revelations of a court-martial in his case. He was arrested, a few days since, at Hilton Head, charged with many practices which rendered his name a discredit to the regiment as well as to himself. He was originally the Major of the regiment, but the death of Colonel PERRY advanced Lieutenant-Colonel BARTON and Major BEARD to the post of Lieutenant-Colonel. Of late he has been the Provost Marshal-General of this Department, and also in command of the celebrated negro regiment known as the First South Carolina Volunteers.

BEARD is a man of many talents, but he has used them unwisely, and is now reaping the reward of his sinful conduct.

We are anxiously awaiting news from the North in relation to the crisis in the Cabinet. When will our troubles end.

Arrival of the "Conemaugh" Stern First—An Effectual Blockade—Rumors of an Intended Attack upon Charleston—Movements of Naval Vessels, Etc., Etc.

Special Correspondence of the Inquirer.

PORT ROYAL HARBOR, S. C., Dec. 29, 1862.

At the present time we have here the flag-ship *Wabash*; *Vermont*, 74; *Vandalia*, 16; *Memphis*, 6; *Conemaugh*, 6; *South Carolina*, 6; *Daffodil* and *Dandelion*, steam tenders. The *Vandalia* returned from a practice cruise a few days since, and will leave for the North in a short time. The barque *Kingfisher* sailed on Saturday for the blockade.

The *Conemaugh* arrived on Saturday afternoon *stern first*. It is a remarkable and a disgraceful fact that none of the double bowed boats will steer well. Some of them go sideways about as well as any other way. They cannot be relied upon at any time. The *Conemaugh* will steer pretty well stern first, but how awkward that looks. Only imagine a man-of-war built from the plans of the Chief Naval Constructor of a country like this going crab-fashion. It is true that she by this means carries the flag ahead, but to see the gaffs of a schooner-rigged vessel pointing over the forward part of the boat, and the masts and smoke-stack raking forwards is disgusting to the eye of the sailor.

The blockade of Charleston now seems to be kept up with much vigor. Occasionally our vessels run in and give the "Rebs" a few shell so as to keep them accustomed to the sound thereof; but the day is not far off when they will hear a rushing sound like unto the moving of fierce winds and the roaring of mighty waters. Then let the Philistines flee, for the hand of vengeance is upon them. It is rumored here, for the fortieth time, that Charleston is soon to be attacked; but we must wait until we see more potent signs before we believe; and then, if such should be the case, it would not do for us to let the cat out of the bag.

The machinery is being taken out of the gun-boat *Mercury*, which has so long rendered such good service in this harbor. She was present and took a prominent part in the capture of Port Royal, and after much hard service the worms gnawed her bottom out, and she sank while in the performance of her duty.

The *John Adams*, Captain CLIFTON, has been turned over to the War Department, and is being put in shape for a very formidable gun-boat, being very heavily armed. She will, no doubt, do much valuable service in shoal water.

The *George Washington*, another army gun-boat, is to have one more gun of larger calibre to replace the one burst a few days since.

I have just returned from a cruise along the coast, but have no news to communicate. Our blockaders are all keeping a weather eye open for Anglo-Rebel vessels and prize money. On Christmas Admiral DUPONT visited Beaufort, where Generals BAMAN, SAXTON, TERRY and SEYMOUR spent the day. Gen. SEYMOUR, it will be remembered, was one of the Fort Sumter heroes, and some think that he has come down here to have a hand in operations connected with the recovery of his old home, which he assisted so nobly in defending. The boys on board of the *Wabash* had a good time on Christmas—no work, plenty of play, but no grog. Jack did not like that pretty much, and more than one of them will bet that the framers of the grog bill carries the sign of a gin mill on the end of his cutwater. A little grog is good, and there are but few men in the navy but what will say so. The abolition of liquor in the navy has done more to cause the practice of smuggling than any revenue act ever adopted.

The United States surveying steamer *Bibb* is now doing the duty of naval pilot boat at this port, and every one in naval circles is aware how well Captain BOUTELLE does his duty. He was the first to cross the bar at the time the fleet entered here, and sounded out the channel and placed temporary buoys, until others could be sent here, and then he set the buoys which now safely guide all vessels into this port.

The Adams Express Company have purchased two new and fast steamships which will soon commence their weekly trips to this place, carrying the mails, passengers and express freight. The Navy Department cannot bring down in their supply steamers half the express matter for the officers and men of the squadron, and the Adams Express Company will hereafter do their own work, which will, of course, be well done. They will be armed, so that if the "290" meets them they can make a defence worthy of Americans and expressmen.

The news has reached us of the seizure of the *Ariel* by the "290," and her bonding for the snug sum of one hundred and sixty thousand dollars. Additional vessels have been despatched from this station in pursuit of the pirate.

THE LATEST NEWS FROM WASHINGTON.

General Butler at Washington—Pennsylvanians for Brigadiers and Major-Generals—Vote of Thanks to Gen. Rosecrans—Judge Usher Secretary of the Interior—Dismissal of the French Consul at New Orleans—Gen. Butler Sustained.

Special Despatches to the Inquirer.

WASHINGTON, January 7, 1863.

General BUTLER, while here, asked for the reasons of his being removed from his command at New Orleans. None were given him. The President stated to him that it was not on account of any charge brought by foreign Powers.

We learn to-night, from a high source, he will probably be reinstated in a very short time at New Orleans. The President feels that BUTLER'S course has been sustained by the masses of the loyal people in the North. The only difficulty now being in the way is, what to do with BANKS. On the list of Generals to be sent to the Senate as soon as power is given to appoint more, we learn are the following from Pennsylvania:—

Brigadier-Generals—Col. STRONG VINCENT, Col. TYNDALE, of Philadelphia, Col. CHARLES CAMPBELL, Col. FISHER, Col. ROWLY, Col. H. L. CAKE, Col. HENDERSON, Col. SCHIMMELPFENNIG, Col. E. BREWER, Col. STONE, of Warren county, Col. HAMBRIGHT, of Lancaster, Col. D. LEASURE.

Major-Generals—Gens. REYNOLDS, MEADE, BIRNEY, and NEGLEY, of Pittsburg.

The House Committee of Ways and Means will recommend the issue of three hundred millions legal tender notes, three hundred millions currency bonds for three years, interest at five per cent., and four or five hundred millions bonds for twenty years, at six per cent. Senator WILSON, from the Senate Military Committee, will to-morrow introduce a resolution tendering a vote of thanks to General ROSECRANS, for his signal victory and the heroism displayed on the field of battle.

The Senate Military Committee, at their meeting to-day, authorized the Chairman to report a resolution: *Resolved*, That three presentation swords seized by Major-General BUTLER after the capture of New Orleans, as the property of DAVID D. TWIGGS, late brevet Major-General in the army of the United States, and abandoned by him in his flight from that city on the 25th of April, 1862, be disposed of by the President in the following manner:

The sword voted by Congress on the 2d of March, 1847, to Major-General BUTLER, as a reward for his distinguished military success during the present Rebellion; the sword presented by the State of Georgia, to be deposited in the library of the Military Academy at West Point, and the sword given by Augusta, his native city, to be preserved in the Patent Office, at Washington, as a trophy of the present Rebellion.

The Senate Committee reported favorably to the confirmation of Judge USHER as Secretary of the Interior. Under the rules it goes over until to-morrow, when he will be confirmed.

Colonel J. H. BELL, of the Thirteenth Illinois Cavalry, has been restored to service by the President.

Senator HOWARD is very low to-day, having been taken with hemorrhage last night.

A despatch to-night from W. P. SMITH, master of transportation on the Baltimore and Ohio Railroad, says:—

A train will reach Baltimore about 6 P. M., with passengers direct from Cumberland, and all parts of the West. The train that left Baltimore and Washington this morning for the West, is now near Cumberland, having passed through the newly built parts of the line all right. Tremendous trains of coal, produce and live stock are being moved through.

M. MERCIER, the French Minister, upon examining the records of the French Consul at New Orleans, became satisfied of his complicity with the Rebels against the Government of the United States, and yesterday dismissed him, and appointed another in his place.

It will be remembered that this Consul was suspected by General BUTLER as an agent for the Rebels, and BUTLER ordered the seizure of a large sum of money which was returned after the examination by REVERDY JOHNSON. The decision of the French Minister justifies this act of General BUTLER and shows that the return of the money was a mistake.

[BY THE ASSOCIATED PRESS.]

Miscellaneous News.

The Senate, to-day, confirmed the nomination of JAMES MONROE, of Ohio, to be Consul at Rio de Janeiro, in place of RICHARD C. PARSONS, resigned.

The President has nominated Commissioner PECK to be Captain in the navy, on the reserved list.

Representative HOOPER, to-day, introduced in the House a bill to provide a national currency, secured by a pledge of United States stock, and to provide for the circulation and redemption thereof. It designs to establish in the Treasury Department a separate bureau, with a Comptroller of the Currency, and to regulate associations or companies which may be formed in connection with this business. The bill is in accordance with the recommendation of the Secretary of the Treasury, is approved by him, and is similar in its leading features to that introduced at the former session of Congress.

The steamer *New York* left here this afternoon, with about four hundred and fifty women and children, for Richmond and other parts of the South. They are taken down by permission and at the expense of the Government. Nearly six hundred applications had been made and allowed, but only the above number availed themselves of the privilege to-day.

Eight officers were engaged last night in examining the baggage. In many of the trunks were found dress goods of various kinds and textures, pins, needles, shoes, thread, etc. When it was evident that the goods were intended for speculation, they were pronounced contraband. A number of sympathizing friends were at the wharf to bid farewell.

The Surgeon-General has approved, and the Senate Military Committee have before them, a measure designed to promote greater efficiency among, and a more careful selection of, female nurses in the army; also to encourage ladies to enter upon such duty as an honorable profession.

Major WM. McMICHAEL, Assistant Adjutant-General, has been relieved from service on the Staff of Major-General HALLECK, and ordered to report himself for duty to Major-General ROSECRANS.

This morning Senator HARRIS introduced into the Senate, and Hon. FREDERICK A. CONKLING to the House, a memorial from the Chamber of Commerce of New York, prepared by SAMUEL B. RUGGLES, showing not only the military importance but the resources and great advantages to the commerce of the country to be derived from the enlargement of the locks of the Erie and Oswego, and also the Illinois Canals. It was referred to the appropriate committee of each House.

The McDowell Court of Inquiry.

To-day the decision upon the written statement of Major-General McDOWELL was rendered, declining to receive it as testimony; but its retention by the Recorder of the Court was ordered.

General SIGEL was then re-examined to verify copies of numerous orders, messages and despatches between himself, General McDOWELL and other officers.

Message of the Governor of California.

SAN FRANCISCO, Jan. 7.—The ship *Gleaner* sailed to-day for Boston.

The message of the Governor of California, which has just been presented to the Legislature, estimates the floating debt of the State at $450,000.

He argues against the national taxation of the mines, believing that it would be a mere tax on labor, discouraging the development of the mines, diminishing their produce and injuring the whole community. The true policy, he thinks, is "to let well enough alone.

The markets are very dull. Sales of 1600 boxes of Candles at 18c. The stock of Coal Oil approximates 300,000 gallons.

The Washington Territorial Legislature has memorialized Congress in relation to fortifying the Columbia river and Puget's Sound, asking for the establishment of a branch mail route from Salt Lake to Walla Walla, urging the establishment of an ocean mail from San Francisco to China, and asking for a change of the port of entry from Port Angelo to Port Townsend.

MESSAGE OF GOV. SEYMOUR, OF NEW YORK.

ALBANY, Jan. 7.—Governor SEYMOUR sent in his message to the Legislature to-day. On the subject of national affairs, he says:—

"Not only is the national life at stake, but every personal, every family, every sacred interest involved. The truths of our financial and military situation must not be kept back. There must be no attempt to put down the free expression of public opinion. Affrighted at the ruin they have wrought, the authors of our calamities at the North and South insist that this war has been caused by the unavoidable contest about slavery. This has been the subject, and not the cause of the controversy. We are to look for the causes of the war in the pervading disregard of the obligations of the laws and constitutions, disrespect for the constituted authorities, and, above all, in the local prejudices which have grown up in two parties of the Atlantic States—the two extremes of our country. There is no honest statement of our difficulties which does not teach that our people must reform themselves as well as the conduct of the Government and the policy of our rulers.

"It is not too late to save our country if we will enter upon the sacred duty in the right way. Where it is the right of our Government to decide upon measures and policy, it is our duty to obey and give a ready support to their decisions. This is the vital maxim of liberty. This war should have been averted; but its flood-gates were opened. The Administration could not grasp its dimensions nor control its sweep. The Government was borne along with the current, and struggled, as best it could, with the resistless tide. Few seemed able to comprehend its military or financial problems. Hence we are not to sit in harsh judgment upon errors in conduct or policy. But while we concede all these excuses for mistakes, we are not to adopt errors nor sanction violations of principle. The same causes which extenuate their faults in judgment must make us more vigilant to guard against their influences."

The Governor urges that economy and integrity in the administration of affairs are vital in periods of war. He says meddling and intrigues have thwarted and paralyzed the valor of our soldiers and skill of our Generals within the influence of the capital, while our armies have gained victories in fields remote therefrom.

State Rights.

Not only must the National Constitution be held inviolate, but the rights of States must be respected as not less sacred. There are differences of opinion as to the dividing line between State and National jurisdiction, but there can be none as to the existence of such separate jurisdiction, each covering subjects of legislation and jurisprudence essential to the public security and welfare. A consolidated Government in this vast country would destroy the essential home rights and liberties of the people. The sovereignties of the States, except as they are limited by the Constitution, can never be given up. Without them our Government cannot stand. It was made, and it can be changed by State agency. This is shown by the following provisions of the instrument itself:—

"The ratification of the conventions of nine States shall be sufficient to the establishment of this Constitution between the States so ratifying the same."

Again, three-fourths of the States can add to or take away from the powers of the General Government, by demanding a Convention in which amendments can be proposed, which, if ratified by three-fourths of the States, become parts of the Constitution.

While they can thus take away or add to its power, the General Government can in no way touch one right of the States or invade their jurisdiction.

The obligations which rest upon the States to respect the Constitution, laws and authorities of the General Government, also demand that the General Government shall show equal respect for the rights and constituted authorities of States.

To State legislation and authorities we look for the good order of society, the security of life and property, the protection of our homes and all that is nearest and dearest to us in the relations, duties and actions of life. It is dangerous and demoralizing to show contempt for State authorities and laws. It undermines alike the foundations of State and National Government, by breaking up the social system. If home laws are not respected, the more general authority will not be regarded.

Arbitrary Arrests.

Our people have [illegible] with alarm practices and pretensions on the part of officials, which violate every principle of good order, of civil liberty and of constitutional law. It is claimed that in time of war the President has powers as commander-in-chief of our armies, which authorize him to declare martial law, not only within the sphere of hostile movements, where other law cannot be enforced, but also over our whole land. That at his pleasure he can disregard not only the statutes of Congress, but the decisions of the National Judiciary. That in loyal States the least intelligent class of officials may be clothed with power not only to act as spies and informers, but also, without due process of law, to seize and imprison our citizens, and carry them beyond the limits of the State, to hold them in prisons without a hearing or a knowledge of the offences with which they are charged.

Not only the passions and prejudices of these inferior agents lead them to acts of tyranny, but their interests are advanced and their positions secured by promoting discontent and discord. Even to ask the aid of counsel has been held to be an offence. It has been well said that "to be arrested for one knows no what; to be confined, no one entitled to ask where; to be tried, no one can say when, by a law nowhere known or established; or to linger out life in a cell [illegible] presents a body of tyranny which cannot be enlarged."

[illegible] of journals and the imprisonment of persons have been glaringly partisan, allowing to some the utmost licentiousness of criticism, and punishing others for the fair exercise of the right of discussion. Conscious of these gross abuses, an attempt has been made to shield the violators of law, and suppress inquiry into their motives and conduct. This attempt will fail. Unconstitutional acts cannot be shielded by unconstitutional laws. Such attempts will not save the guilty, while they will bring a just condemnation upon those who try to pervert the powers of legislation to the purposes of oppression. To justify such action by precedents drawn from the practice of governments where there is no restraint upon legislative power, will be of no avail under our system, which restrains the Government and protects the citizens by written constitutions.

I shall not inquire what rights States in Rebellion have forfeited, but I deny that this Rebellion can suspend a single right of the citizens of loyal States. I denounce the doctrine that civil war in the South takes away from the loyal North the benefits of the principle of civil liberty.

It is a high crime to abduct a citizen of this State. It is made my duty by the Constitution to see that the laws are enforced. I shall investigate every alleged violation of our statutes, and see that offenders are brought to justice. Sheriffs and District Attorneys are admonished that it is their duty to take care that no persons within their respective counties are imprisoned or carried by force beyond their limits without due process of legal authority. The removal to England of persons charged with offence, away from their friends, their witnesses and means of defence, was one of the acts of tyranny for which we asserted our independence. The abduction of citizens from this State for offences charged to have been done here, and carrying them many hundreds of miles to distant prisons in other States or Territories, is an outrage of the same character upon every principle of right and justice.

The General Government has ample powers to establish courts, to appoint officers to arrest, and commissioners to hear complaints, and to imprison upon reasonable grounds of suspicion. It has a judicial system in full and undisturbed operation. Its own courts, held at convenient points in this and other loyal States, are open for the hearing of all complaints. If its laws are not ample for the punishment of offences, it is due to the neglect of those in power.

Government is not strengthened by the exercise of doubtful powers, but by a wise and energetic exertion of those which are incontestible. The former course never fails to produce discord, suspicion and distrust, while the latter inspires respect and confidence.

This loyal State, whose laws, whose courts and whose officers have thus been treated with marked and public contempt, and whose social order and sacred rights have been violated, was at that very time sending forth great armies to protect the National Capital, and to save the National officials from flight or capture. It was while the arms of New York thus sheltered them against Rebellion that, without consultation with its chief magistrate, a subordinate Department at Washington insulted our people and invaded our rights. Against these wrongs and outrages the people of the State of New York, at its late election, solemnly protested.

The submission of our people to these abuses, for a time only, was mistaken at home and abroad for an indifference to their liberties. But it was only in a spirit of respect for our institutions that they waited until they could express their will in the manner pointed out by our laws. At the late election they vindicated at once their regard for law and their love of liberty. Amidst all the confusion of civil war, they calmly sat in judgment upon the Administration, voting against its candidates. Nor was this the only striking proof of respect for the Constitution. The minority, of nearly equal numbers, yielded to this decision without resistance, although the canvass was animated by strong partisan excitements. This calm assertion of rights, and this honorable submission to the verdict of the ballot-box, vindicated at once the character of our people and the stability of our institutions. Had the Secessionists of the South thus yielded to constitutional decisions, they would have saved themselves and our country from the horrors of this war, and they would have found the same remedy for every wrong and danger.

Martial Law.

The claim of power under martial law is not only destructive of the right of States, but it overthrows the legislative and judicial departments of the General Government. It asserts for the President more power as the head of the army, than as a representative ruler of the people. This claim has brought discredit upon us in the eyes of the world. It has strengthened the hopes of Rebellion. It has weakened the confidence of loyal States. It tends to destroy the value of our Government in the minds of our people. It leads to discord and discontent at the North, while it has united and invigorated the South.

If there is a necessity which justifies that policy, let us openly and honestly say there is a necessity which justifies a revolution. But this pretension is not put forth as a necessity which overleaps for a time all restraints, and which is justified by a great exigency; it is a theory which exalts the military power of the President above his civil and constitutional rights. It asserts that he may in his discretion declare war, and then extinguish the State and National Constitutions, by drawing the pall of martial law over our vast country.

* * * There is little to fear in periods of peace and prosperity. If we are not protected when there are popular excitements and convulsions, our Government is a failure. If Presidential proclamations are above the decisions of the courts and the restraints of the Constitution, then that Constitution is a mockery. If it has not the authority to keep the Executive within its restraints then it cannot retain States within the Union. Those who hold that there is no sanctity in the Constitution, must equally hold that there is no guilt in the Rebellion.

We cannot be silent and allow these practices to become precedents. They are as much in violation of our Constitution as the Rebellion itself, and more dangerous to our liberties. They hold out to the Executive every temptation of ambition to make and prolong war. They offer despotic power as a price for preventing peace. They are inducements to each Administration to produce discord and incite armed resistance to law, by declaring that the condition of war removes all constitutional restraints. They call about the national capitol hordes of unprincipled men, who find in the wreck of their country the opportunity to gratify avarice or ambition, or personal or political resentments. This theory makes the passion and ambition of an Administration antagonistic to the interest and happiness of the people. It makes the restoration of peace the abdication of more than regal authority in the hands of those to whom is confided the Government of the country.

He declares that the President's Emancipation Proclamation is impolitic, unjust and unconstitutional, calculated to create many barriers to the restoration of the Union, and to be misconstrued by the world as an abandonment of the hope of restoring it, a result to which New York is unalterably opposed and which will be effectively resisted. The Union, he says, will be restored by the Central and Western States, both free and slave, who are exempt from the violent passions which control at the extremes.

Those of the Central Slave States, which rejected the ordinance of Secession, which sought to remain in the Union, and which were driven off by a contemptuous, uncompromising policy, must be brought back. The restoration of the whole Union will be only the work of time, with such an exertion of power as can be put forth without needlessly sacrificing the life and treasure of the North in a bloody and calamitous contest. We must not wear out the lives of our soldiers, nor exhaust the earnings of labor by war for uncertain ends or to carry out vague theories of extermination—means not only destructive of lives and property in the South, but also a waste of the blood and treasure of the North. The exertion of the armed power must be accompanied by a firm and conciliatory policy, to restore the Union with the least possible injury to both sections.

The Governor concludes:—"At this moment the fortunes of our country are influenced by the results of battles. Our army in the field must be supported. All constitutional demands of our General Government must be promptly responded to. Under no circumstances can a division of the Union be conceded. We will put forth every exertion of power. We will use every policy of conciliation. We will hold out every inducement to the people of the South to return to their allegiance consistent with honor. We will guarantee them every right, every consideration demanded by the Constitution, and by that fraternal regard which must prevail in a common country. But we can never voluntarily consent to the breaking up of the Union of these States or the destruction of the Constitution."

OUR NEW YORK LETTER

Special Correspondence of the Inquirer.

NEW YORK, January 7, 1863.

The news from Vicksburg this afternoon created a feeling of disappointment, the public having been disposed to credit the lying statement of the (Rebel) Grenada *Appeal*, that the Yankees had entered the place on the 21st. It is now suspected that that story must have been a ruse only, intended, perhaps, to keep back Union reinforcements, by creating an impression that there was no necessity for them.

The anxiously looked for message of Governor SEYMOUR was laid before the public, this morning, and during the day it has been the subject of not a little criticism and remark. Not to put too fine a point upon it, the Governor—if he does not give "aid and comfort" to the enemy—takes good care to give as little aid and comfort to the Federal Government as possible.

However, don't be alarmed. The Governor is not yet the supreme power in this State. He is held in check, in the first place, by a Republican Senate; and in the second place by an Assembly in which the Democratic radicals are about equally balanced by Republicans and War Democrats. The salutary influences which thus surround him had the effect to restrain summary action in the matter of the Metropolitan Police Commissioners; and, should his Excellency ever be tempted to swerve from the path of patriotism and duty, rely upon it those influences will not be permitted to remain long passive.

An explosion occurred in the percussion cap manufactory of a Mr. GOFF, in Sixty-second street, near the Eleventh avenue, this morning, which entirely destroyed the building (a frame one), and killed one man. The force of the explosion was so great as to break all the panes of glass in the houses for several blocks around. Damage about $2000. The cause of the explosion is not yet ascertained. The name of the man killed is B. WHIPPLE.

The percussion cap manufactory of B. ROBERTS, in Seventy-sixth street, was also badly injured, last night, by an explosion of the ingredients used in the manufacture of caps. Damage to the building about $75. Fortunately, no one was injured.

The Money market is easy and unchanged. Call loans 5@6 ₩ cent., with a supply in excess of the demand. Foreign exchange rules quiet, at 146@148 for merchants' and 148@148½ for bankers' sterling. On Paris, 3f. 80@3f. 77½. American gold is firmer, opening at 34¼@34½, and closing firm at 35 ₩ cent. premium. Government stocks are dull. United States 6's, 1881, coupons, 98@98½; 7-30 Treasury notes, 102½@102¾. Stocks irregular. Michigan Southern Guarantied has advanced ½; New York Central, ⅜, and Reading, 2¼. Cleveland and Toledo has declined ¼; Erie and Michigan Southern, ⅜; Illinois Central and Harlem, ½.

SECOND BOARD.

$6,000 U. S. 6s, '67, reg. 98	600 sh Harlem RR........ 57¾
$10,000 U.S. 6s, '81. cpn. 98	200 sh Read. RR.......... 81
$2,000 U.S 5's,'71, reg. 90	200 do..........b30 81
$4,000 U.S 5's, '74,cpn. 80¾	800 sh Hud. Riv. RR. s30 86¾
$70,000 U.S. 1 year Cer. 96¾	200 do.............. 86¾
$5,000 U. S. D. Nts.....130¾	50 do..........s10 86¾
$15,000 Tenn. St.6s, '90. 61¾	50 do.............. 86¾
$50,000 Missouri 6s....... 65	50 do..........s60 86¾
$500 Cal. St. 7s.......116¾	250 sh M.S.& N.I.R.... 46¾
$13,000 Erie 6th mt. bs. 101¾	100 do.............. 46¾
$8,000 Ch.&N.W. A. bs.67	500 do.............. 46½
$5,000 Ch. &N.W.2 mt. 38¾	500 sh Ill. Cen. RR. Sc. 86¾
$1,000 P.F.W.&Ch. 1st 110	1500 sh Cl. & Pitts. RR.. 60
$5,000 P. Ft. W. & C. 2d 97	100 do.........s30 60
$5,000 Mich. S. Sk. Fd.107¾	1000 do.............. 60⅜
$6,000 Tol. & Wa. 2 mt. 87¾	1100 do.............. 61
$5,000 Cle.&Tol. Sk.F. 106¾	200 sh Cl. & Tol. RR.... 78
$7,000 Buff.N.Y.&E.1m100	1200 do.............. 79
$5,000 Han.&St.Jo. bs. 65	100 do..........s60 78½
$10,000 Tol. & W. 1 m. 105	355 sh Ch. & R.I. RR... 84
$10,000 A.&T.H.2 m. pr. 86	200 do.............. 84¾
$11,000 do........... 86¾	200 do.............. 84¾
$40,000 Amer. Gold.....134⅞	10 sh Ch. Bu. & Q. RR. 96¼
$6,000 do.......b30.135	50 do.............. 99¾
$20,000 do..........135	50 do..........b30 99¾
$25,000 do.......b3.135	100 do.............. 99
6 sh Bank of Com.... 94	200 sh A. & T. H. Pr.... 55
200 sh Cumb. Coal Pf.. 16¾	200 do..........b30 55¾
400 do............ 17	100 sh A. & T. H. RR..... 31¼
100 sh Pac. M. S. S b60.137¾	500 sh P. F. W. & C. RR. 59
100 do...............138¾	200 do..........b30 60
50 do.........s30..136¾	107 sh Del. La. & W. RR. 130
150 do...............137¾	49 sh To. Wab. & W. RR. 41
50 do.........s10. 137	1200 sh M. & P. du C. RR. 47
10 sh N. Y. Cen. R. 108¾	50 do.............. 47¾
500 do...............108¾	400 do..........s30 46
850 sh Erie Railway.... 67¾	200 do.............. 46¾
900 do............... 67	100 do..........b10 47
300 sh Erie RR. Pf...b30 98¾	100 do..........s30 45¾
100 do............... 98¾	30 sh M. & P. du C. 2 pf. 87
200 do..........s30 98	300 sh Mich. Cen. R.... 93
200 sh Harlem RR...... 28¾	15 do.............. 92¾
50 do............... 28¾	250 do.............. 92¾
200 do..........b30 28¾	275 sh Gal. & Ch. RR... 84
400 do............... 28¾	100 do.............. 84¾

CLOSING PRICES—*Reported by H. Toland & Son, Exchange Place*:—Erie, 67¼@67½; Reading, 81½@82; New York Central, 108½@109; Michigan Southern, 46¼@46½; Michigan Southern Guarantied, 87¾@88; Illinois Central, 86¼@86½; Canton, —@—; Harlem, 28¾@29; Harlem Preferred 57¼@57¾; Hudson, 87¼@87¾; Chicago and Toledo, 78¾@79.—Market firm.

OFFICE OF THE ASSISTANT TREASURER, NEW YORK, JANUARY 7, 1863.

Total Receipts	$6,290,100·41
Total Payments	1,817,502·68
Total Balance	12,8[illegible],[illegible]5·06
For Customs	110,000·00

The Charleston Mercury.

...Y PAPER—Ten Dollars per Annum, payable half-yearly in advance.

——VINDICE NULLO
SPONTE SUA SINE LEGE FIDES RECTUMQUE COLENTUR.

COUNTRY PAPER—Three a Week—Five Dollars per Annum, in advance.

VOLUME LXXXII. | CHARLESTON, S. C., TUESDAY, JANUARY 13, 1863. | NUMBER 11,653

TELEGRAPHIC NEWS.

LATEST FROM THE NORTH.

RESIGNATION OF GENERAL BURNSIDE.

THE MOVEMENTS OF ROSECRANS.

RAPID RISE OF GOLD.

THE TALK OF EUROPEAN INTERVENTION, &c., &c., &c.

RICHMOND, January 12.—Northern dates of the 9th and 10th instants have been received here.

A despatch from Washington to the New York *World* states that General BURNSIDE has resigned, and that General HOOKER has been appointed to succeed him.

Despatches from St. Louis admit that the Confederates had captured Springfield, Mo., with a very large amount of army stores, arms and ammunition.

The latest accounts from ROSECRANS state that his headquarters were fixed ten miles beyond Murfreesboro'. ROSECRANS has issued an "order that all captured rebel officers be confined and subsist on rations, until the recent proclamation of JEFF. DAVIS shall be revoked."

The New York *World* admits that the Yankees have met with a severe defeat at Vicksburg, with the loss of 5000 men, and several valuable officers.

Gold had suddenly risen at the North. In New York on the 8th it was quoted at 136. On the 9th it reached 138. Great excitement prevailed in the stock market.

THADDEUS STEVENS had delivered a speech in the House of Representatives, declaring that the States in rebellion were not only out of the Union, but had no constitutional obligations to respect, and that all relations between them and the Federal Government arose solely out of war measures on its part and their position as belligerents.

The London correspondent of the New York *World* writes that he has excellent reasons to believe that the Governments of England and Russia have reconsidered their action upon the proposition of the Emperor NAPOLEON for mediation. He says that "the prospect of success by the North has grown so much darker of late to eyes on that side of the Atlantic, that public opinion in Great Britain inclines more decidedly to the original advances of the French Government, and that an intervention, in the interests of peace and humanity, may become the positive duty of the European powers." He adds that no one there would be surprised to learn that the English Cabinet has at last made up its mind to act in that direction, and that a simultaneous communication to that effect was made that week from London and St. Petersburg to the Court of the Tuilleries.

The Washington *Republican* has an article which is reported to have caused much comment at the Federal capital. It says "it is evident that we [the North] are on the eve of some developments respecting foreign mediation;" that "it is utter folly to resist the inexorable logic of events;" and endorses an article in the New York *Tribune*, concluding as follows: "Only secure a capable and candid tribunal, and we shall be willing to submit without force to its arbitration."

In an editorial published a day later, the *Republican* says, it is proposed that Switzerland shall mediate between the two sections, and it thinks that there is reason in the proposition, as Switzerland is an independent republic, and admits that mediation will take place sooner or later. The *Republican* would rather see Switzerland lead in the movement than perfidious France or damnable England.

THE CONFEDERATE CONGRESS.

RICHMOND, January 12.—Congress re-assembled to-day. There were 9 Senators and 53 Representatives present. There being no quorum in either branch, both adjourned until to-morrow.

MOVEMENTS NEAR SUFFOLK.

PETERSBURG, January 12.—General PRYOR, yesterday, with two companies of cavalry, encountered DODGE's Mounted Riflemen, five miles from Suffolk, and routed them, inflicting considerable loss. Learning that there were 35,000 Yankees at Carrsville, PRYOR pushed across to intercept the fugitives, but they succeeded in making good their escape to the main body.

LATER NEWS FROM EUROPE.

FREDERICKSBURG, January 12.—The *Africa* has arrived at Cape Race, with Liverpool dates to December 29.

The news of the battle of Fredericksburg created great interest in England. The defeat was considered at Liverpool to be an event unfavorable to the hopes of an early peace.

The working men at Manchester had adopted a congratulatory address to President LINCOLN on account of his Emancipation Proclamation.

English revenue accounts show an increase during the year of £2,392,000. The London *Times* thinks that this shows that cotton is not King, and that it would be better for England to keep all her cotton operatives on a public pension until absorbed in other trades, than to vary one point from her national policy.

FROM THE WEST.

TULLAHOMA, Jan. 12.—Our pickets are now within six miles of Murfreesboro. The official reports of the several commands are being rapidly made up, and develope a more sanguinary conflict than at first supposed. Gen. HARDEE and his corps won imperishable renown. The loss in BRECKINRIDGE's division was two thousand and fifty. Every member of his staff was wounded or had his horse shot under him. Col. O'HARA, Chief of Staff, Major JAS. WILSON, Capt. A. J. MASTERS, had their clothes riddled with balls and their horses shot. Lieut. CABELL BRECKINRIDGE, son of the General, scarcely 18 years of age, was slightly wounded. The total loss in CLAIBORNE's division was two thousand and sixty two.

The Nashville *Union* of the 7th, mentions the arrival of nineteen rebel officers, including B. F. EDDING and J. D. LELAND of the 41st Alabama, together with six hundred and ten prisoners.

We learn from the Hinds county (Miss.) Gazette that President Jefferson Davis and his brother, Jo. E. Davis, have recently purchased plantations in that county, and removed their slaves to them. Colonel Jo. E. Davis has purchased the plantation owned and occupied for many years past by Dr. Thomas J. Catchings. President Davis has secured a place adjoining his brother's, being the same owned and occupied for some twelve years past by James P. Smith. These plantations are nearly between Vicksburg and Jackson. As both gentlemen own very superior plantations on the river below Vicksburg, we presume the lands just purchased are designed merely as places of refuge for negro property until the close of the war.

THE MERCURY.

TUESDAY, JANUARY 13, 1863.

Governor Seymour's State Rights Doctrines.

We yesterday noticed the concluding portion of Governor SEYMOUR's message, in which he argues that neither in a Northern nor in a Southern Union can the conflict of interests of agriculture, commerce and manufactures be adjusted; hence that the Union is indissoluble, and that "factions North and South must be put down." We endeavored, briefly, to point out that the whole difficulty of adjusting the relative interests of the two peoples, was the difficulty of obtaining justice for Southern interests, notwithstanding the barriers of constitutional law created for their protection. The overthrow of the fundamental compact, on the limited basis of which the fabric of the General Government was erected, and the attempt of the Northern majority to absorb all the powers of government within its control, and to employ them for the aggrandisement and gratification of the North, to the ruin of this section, rendered the dissolution of the Union and the independence of the South measures essential to the safety of the Confederate States.

Governor SEYMOUR's conclusion is a clear *non-sequitur* to his just and proper strictures upon the unconstitutional tyranny of the General Government of the United States. He admits that the cause of the war was "the pervading disregard of the Laws and the Constitution," and that it is necessary to "reform the people and the policy of the Government. The rights of the States must be respected. The consolidation of the Government of this vast country would destroy the essential rights and liberties of the people. The sovereignty of the States cannot be given up."

The political history of the United States for thirty years previous to the dissolution of the Union, was a long but unavailing effort, on the part of the State Rights men of the South, to "reform the people and the policy of the Government." South Carolina was once deeply attached to a Union, for the establishment of which she probably sacrificed more and suffered more, in proportion, during the revolutionary war, than any other of the old Thirteen. Her statesmen for thirty years have argued, and entreated, and warned the North against the destruction of the Constitution. Over and over they predicted the inevitable destruction of the Union as the consequence. They were called theorists, abstractionists, revolutionists. In their conservative efforts to preserve the Constitution and the Union, and to prevent the issue brought upon the country in 1860, with the evils under which we now suffer in a war for independence, they sacrificed their personal ambition and all hopes of office on the altar of their country's safety. As long as possible, they strove manfully. They waged a hopeless battle under a banner whose symbol was equivalent to proscription. Failing to save the Constitution and Union, they have engaged in a struggle for the salvation of the South. In this they have confidence of success.

The people and the policy of the United States could not be reformed. It is too late to save the Union or to reconstruct it. The immedicable wrongs suffered by the people of the Confederate States, at the hands of their *quondam* allies, constitute a wall of separation which cannot be broken down. Their sentiments as men, and the very instincts of our human nature, revolt at the proposition of re-union with these whose hands are dyed with the blood of our fathers and brothers and sons. The utter want of character, as manifested by the unvarying and almost universal falsification of facts at the North, as a matter of self-respect and self-preservation, independent of considerations of interest and security and honor forbid national association with such a people.

But for the sake of the United States themselves, and in the interest of mankind, we should be pleased to see the State Rights reform of Governor SEYMOUR carried into practice. It is the only alternative to anarchy and a military despotism in the end. A lawless majority must be a vulgar tyranny!

R. B. R. Jr.

BUTLER TO COMMAND THE ATTACK ON CHARLESTON.—A correspondent of the New York *Post* writes:

The Secessionists of Washington boast that the Government has already quailed before the threats of the rebel Jeff. Davis. They claim that the supersedure of Butler was caused partially by the demands of the rebel Government, which have been continually urged upon Mr. Lincoln since last summer. Butler, they say, has been occupied to oppose Jeff. Davis, and they point to the fact that Gen. Banks at once stopped proceedings under the Confiscation Act as soon as he arrived in New Orleans, these proceedings being counted by the rebels as the most offensive of any under Butler's administration. Of course, these boasts of the Secessionists are ridiculous. It is much more probable that the change in the command of the Government troops in Louisiana was made because of a vexatious diplomatic quarrel with the French Government.

The complaints of Louis Napoleon have been contentious, and indeed of such an insolent character, that more than one member of the Cabinet is in favor of taking a bold stand upon our rights, refusing any further attempts to pacify a man who seems bent on a quarrel with us. It is rumored here that Gen. Butler will soon have command of an expedition to Charleston, and this is not improbable, for the Government will hardly lay aside so successful a General as he has been. The President is known to be well affected towards the General, and that would hardly be the case if he were to be removed to private life.

The Charleston expedition was alluded to in this correspondence long ago, as if it were about to sail from New York. Such was at that time the intention of the Government, but for sufficient reasons it was postponed. There is little doubt that an attempt will be made to take Charleston within a few weeks, and Gen. Butler will make an excellent commander of the land forces engaged in the expedition, especially as he has the prestige of success in such undertakings. Baltimore and New Orleans are already inscribed on his flag, and if he can add the name of Charleston, it will be enough honor for one man to win in this war.

THE HARRIET LANE.—The *Harriet Lane*, a vessel of six hundred tons burden, was originally built for the Revenue service, but at the beginning of the war with the South she was turned over to the Navy, and at once underwent such alterations as were thought necessary to adapt her to her new service. At the time of her capture she mounted eight guns of heavy calibre, her bow gun being a fifteen inch rifle.

YANKEE FORCE AT NEWBERN.—The Raleigh *State Journal* learns from a perfectly reliable source that there were in the waters of Newbern, on Wednesday last, no fewer than *fifty five* Yankee transports. The forces there include the commands of three Major Generals, usually in the Yankee army 15,000 each, which gives the full force there at some 45,000 to 50,000 at least.

THE STATUTES AT LARGE of the Confederate States of America, passed at the second session of the First Congress, have just been published in handsome style at Richmond.

LETTER FROM RICHMOND.

(CORRESPONDENCE OF THE MERCURY.)

RICHMOND, Friday, January 9.

Capture of the Harriet Lane—Chance for Naval Men at Charleston—Letters from Englishmen—Rosecrans' Falsehoods—Lamar Fontaine—High Price for Ice, etc., etc.

We have just been cheered by the news of the capture of the *Harriet Lane*. It has been a long time since our naval arm has made itself felt, except in the sturdy blows of SEMMES. It is to be hoped that other surprises may follow that at Galveston. Very soon, if telegrams are to be trusted, there will be a chance for our naval officers at Charleston and Wilmington to show the "mettle of their pasture." The Examiner of this morning, commenting on the lack of enterprise in the Navy Department, derives consolation from the fact that the Yankees have defeated themselves by the rigidity of their blockade, thereby making us self-dependent and self-reliant, and making our paper money available for all the purposes of war, while Europe suffers.

The Whig gives up its first editorial column to a letter from an English gentleman of high position, who pays the highest compliment to the spirit displayed by the Confederacy, and assures us of the warm sympathy of the *people* of England, as distinguished from the Palmerston-Russell administration. He confesses, too, that the English are beginning to take more rational views of slavery. There is a letter copied into the Enquirer from the London Illustrated News, written by its correspondent, Mr. Vizitelly, who, as you are aware, follows Lee's army wherever it goes. This letter breathes the same cordial admiration of the virtues of the Southern people as that in the Whig. Such evidences of British good feeling can hardly fail to awaken a response in the warm-hearted people of the sunny South.

Rosecrans tries to produce the impression that the fighting at Murfreesboro' lasted continuously from Tuesday until Friday. He thus lends himself to a deliberate falsehood. The last fight was on Friday evening, and was not a general engagement, but an assault of the enemy's position by Breckinridge's division. I notice, however, that it is the cue of the Yankee papers, now more than ever—for recognition is imminent—to represent the rebels as defeated at every point. Could you see a copy of the Herald, you would find that not only Bragg but Morgan, Forrest and Wheeler have all been literally cut to pieces; not enough of them left to make a respectable grease spot. Rosecrans' Medical Director says there are 1000 killed outright and 5500 wounded in hospitals. Now a great many wounded never go into hospitals, and it is more than probable that many of Rosecrans' badly wounded can't get hospital accomodations. His loss was at first "truly enormous" and "heart-rending;" now it is 500 less than Bragg's.

I am glad to have been the means of bringing to light the name of Lamar Fontaine, the gallant dragoon from Texas, who can't walk, and carries his crutches with him on horseback. He is, by odds, the most wonderful man the war has produced, according to the letter published in the Mobile Register.

Ice is coming into town freely, and has been for weeks past. The Government buys it at eight cents a pound or $4 a bushel. HERMES.

GENERAL NEWS SUMMARY.

Gen. Floyd, Judge Allen, Charles W. Russell and W. C. Rives are mentioned in connection with the vacant Virginia Senatorship.

In the Virginia House of Delegates a resolution was passed urging Congress to pass a law to pay for slaves impressed into the Confederate service.

Sixty of the enemy's cavalry visited Strasburg, Va., on Saturday and levied upon the citizens of that place for corn, provisions and money. The citizens were compelled to submit, not only to the levy, but to every species of insult.

From Grenada, Miss., we hear that Gen. Price had been quite sick for some days, but was up again. The work of erecting defences is going forward rapidly, and it is intended to make the place impregnable.

Hon. John Bell, who has been driven from his home and estates in Tennessee, is now living with his family in a modest little village near Rome, Ga. Mr. Bell is quite advanced in years, and yet looks ruddy and hale. He has two sons in the army.

The Washington Republican, of the 29th says: "Rumor is again busy with the partial reconstruction of the Cabinet. It is now said that General Butler is to be made Secretary of War, and General Fremont is to command the armies."

Mr. Alexander George, of Atlanta, has invented an artificial leg, which is made of steel, so interwoven with springs, as to move as naturally as bone and muscle. Mr. George is an ingenious mechanic, at the head of the Georgia railroad wordshops in Atlanta.

A Washington despatch says that Burnside returned to his army on the condition that he would be allowed to do as he pleased, and that there would be no interference with him from Washington. The despatch adds that this was granted promptly, and that an offensive movement is immediately expected.

A large number of women and children, refugees who came by the flag of truce boat, have arrived in Richmond. The wife and children of John Ross, the Indian Chief, were among those who came by the flag of truce. The refugees seem impressed with the idea that peace will be declared in a short time.

A body of Col. Imboden's cavalry, numbering thirty-seven men, recently made a dash upon Milroy's ordnance and baggage train near Moorfield, and captured thirty-five prisoners and fifty-five horses. This feat was accomplished in full view of the whole Yankee force. The enemy shelled our men as they made off with their prisoners and booty, but without doing any damage.

Gen. Banks, the new commander at New Orleans, has removed the restrictions imposed upon the holding of church service, giving notice, however, that clergymen were subjected to the restrictions imposed upon all other men. He has also released a large number of political prisoners on their giving parole to commit no act of hostility against the United States.

The Chattanooga Rebel says it is rumored among army circles that General Bragg has asked to be transferred from the command of the army of Middle Tennessee to some other department, and more than intimates that this movement on Gen. Bragg's part is induced by the clamor and prejudice that has been excited against him by newspaper critics on his Western campaigns.

The Richmond correspondent of the Columbus Sun says that the Richmond, *alias* the Merrimac No. 2, has been completed some time, and it may not be improper to say she is already on the move to a point where she will "turn up" to the discomfiture of the iron-clads. She is truly formidable, and is commanded by the gallant Captain Pegram.

A Washington despatch says that General Butler has had a long consultation with the President and Cabinet, and has already been assigned to an important command in the Department of the South. Butler was serenaded in Washington, but made no speech, satisfying himself with simply returning his thanks, with the excuse that "this was no time for making speeches." The crowd was greatly disappointed.

SINGULAR LUSUS NATURÆ.—On Monday last there was an exhibition in our town of a two-headed colored girl. She forms one of the greatest curiosities of the age, and has excited the wonder of the medical world, both in Europe and America. The Siamese Twins have been regarded as a most wonderful production of nature, but in no respect are they comparable to this dual and yet single existence of this black girl. She has two distinct heads and a marked individuality above the waist and in the lower extremities. Instead of a lateral connection, as in the case of the Siamese Twins, there is a positive spinal junction, in part, by which one body is formed, the other parts being free and unrestrained. She seems to be a very intelligent girl, and has rather a fine musical talent. While talking or singing, you have before you two distinct persons, and yet there stands in inexplicable reality but one corporeal existence.—*Spartanburg Spartan.*

FROM BRAGG'S ARMY.

The condition of affairs in Middle Tennessee is gradually settling down into their new status. It seems to be quite certain that Duck River and Normandy Hills will be made our line of defence. The correspondent of the Chattanooga *Rebel*, writing from Winchester, Tennessee, on the 7th inst., says:

Don't be surprised if you hear of our victorious army advancing to a point nearer Nashville than the recent field of battle. Our forces, it is true, are in the neighborhood of Shelbyville, to which place General Bragg led them that they might freshen up their wasted energies and rest. It was a wise and judicious, not to say necessary, movement. General Bragg will certainly hold Middle Tennessee, and, with God's blessing, we shall yet get possession of Nashville. The troops are in the best of spirits, and, after a few days, will be as ready as ever to meet the foe. I am unable to give you other than "reliable" rumors from the front. Our cavalry under Wharton and Wheeler are close upon the enemy's line. General Morgan has just returned from his travels in Kentucky. He has destroyed the Louisville and Nashville Railroad for fifteen or twenty miles from above the Green River. At Mumfordsville there was an Abolition force of ten thousand posted to protect Green River Bridge. Leaving that structure, he burned a number of other bridges—miles of trestle work, a large amount of army stores, and paroled 2000 prisoners. General Morgan is with his charming wife, at the residence of our excellent friend, Frank McGhee, Esq.

The Rev. Dr. Pise, Rector of St. Peter's Church, Columbia, has left his home to devote himself to the care of our sick and wounded. He reached Winchester this morning, and will take some position of usefulness. A number of our wounded are to be brought to this place. One hundred and fifty will arrive to-night—all of Cheatham's division.

I have just learned that the pickets of the enemy are eight miles this side of Murfreesboro'.

From North Alabama we have a letter from an officer of rank, stationed at Huntsville, which throws some light upon the "situation" in that quarter. We make a brief extract:

There is no sign of an approach of the enemy in this direction, from Tuscumbia or Florence. We have daily communication with Roddy, at Tuscumbia, and he reports all quiet in that direction. Nothing heard from the enemy in the direction of Pulaski, where we have daily telegraphic communication. Duck and Elk rivers are both high and the enemy cannot cross them without difficulty.

FOREIGN MISCELLANY.

It is rumored in Paris that as soon as the French obtain any decided success in Mexico, the Emperor will order home the troops.

The notorious Yelverton marriage case had been brought to a conclusion in Edinburgh, the decision being in favor of Mrs. Yelverton. Lords Churchill and Deas were of opinion that the marriage was established according to the law of Scotland.

A commercial circular from Japan, dated October 25th, says a revolution has taken place in that Government, but of what character the published report did not make clear. The assumed power of the Tycoon is greatly restricted, and the policy adopted is adverse to foreign interests.

It is stated that Mr. J. Watson Webb, the American Minister at Rome, recently sent a challenge to the English Minister at that place, in consequence of some hard words that passed between them at a private party. The English Minister, as soon as he received the challenge, went on board the British storeship for protection, and there remained at last accounts.

Victor Hugo, encouraged by the wonderful success of his last novel, is said to be working harder than ever. He has a romance on the stocks entitled, "'93," and it is said that if any impediment is thrown in the way of the circulation in France of the cheap edition of the "Miserables," he has ready, *in terrorem*, the second volume of the "Chatiments," and the "History of the 2d December." which were begun ten years ago.

The mausoleum erected by Queen Victoria at Frogmore, having been solemnly consecrated, the remains of the late Prince Albert were removed to the tomb prepared for them in the mausoleum. The Queen had taken an active part in the proceeding, and the Court Circular adds that Her Majesty, though much overwhelmed with grief, had borne the touching event without any additional injury to her health.

A correspondent of the London Times states that the word "skedaddle" is not a Yankee invention. It is commonly used, he says, in Dumfries. "To skedaddle means to spill, in small quantities, any liquids. The same word applies to coals, potatoes or apples, and other substances falling from a cart in travelling from one place to another. But skedaddle does not apply to bodies of men scattered."

One of the interesting remains of old London—Crosby Hall, in Bishopgate street—has recently been converted into a wine merchant's store. The old India House, in Leadenhall street, which had historical and literary interest, has almost wholly disappeared. The rooms wherein an empire was built up, and the affairs of a score of kingdoms carried on, have been demolished. The sculptured pediment, at one time considered a fine work of art, and worthy of mention in the histories of London, was, after great difficulty in finding a purchaser, sold for ten pounds.

The increase of crime in Great Britain, so often spoken of, seems to be real. In 1861, committals for burglary increased forty-one per cent; for house breaking, fifty-six per cent.; for robbery, with violence, eighteen per cent. The total number of convictions for indictable offences increased by fifteen per cent.—a fact as grave as the cotton famine, and due almost entirely to the break down of the English system of ticket-of-leave, which turns the unreformed ruffian loose, with no hope but successful crime. In Ireland, the increase in convictions was only ten per cent, though the period was one marked by a revival of agrarian crime.

The Manchester Guardian learns, on good authority, that a wonderful discovery has recently been made in electricity, as applicable to the purposes of the electric telegraph. Incredible as it may seem to many of our readers, it is said that experiments established the fact that intelligible signals can be enchanged between distant stations without the intervention of any artificial conductor whatsoever, and that with equal success, whether the intervening space be wholly or partially land or water. The promoters of the new system believe it to be a reasonable expectation that this discovery may render unnecessary any future attempt to lay an Atlantic cable. We remember that, many years ago, this achievement was regarded by some scientific men as a speculative possibility.

At a meeting of the council of the Liverpool Chamber of Commerce, on the 1st of December, the following official notice was received from Earl Russell, in relation to British cargos destroyed by the Alabama:

SIR: I am directed by Earl Russell to reply to your letters of the 6th instant, respecting the destruction by the Confederate steamer Alabama of British property, embarked in American vessels and burned by that steamer. Earl Russell desires me to state to you that British property on board a vessel belonging to one of the belligerents must be subject to all the risks and contingencies of war, so far as the capture of the vessel is concerned. The owners of any British property, not being contraband of war, on board a Federal vessel captured and destroyed by a Confederate vessel of war, may claim in a Confederate prize court compensation for destruction of such property.

A writer in the Manchester Guardian says: "In consequence of the manufacturers having worked down their stock in every process to zero, it is impossible that the production of cloth can regain the rate of 1860 for many months to come, under the most favorable condition of the American struggle. Suppose the war terminated by the next mail; how soon can the cotton be got to England, and the various stocks in the preparations of blowing, carding, drawing, slubbing, roving, spinning, winding, warping, and, lastly, weaving, be placed in their regular working order? It is to those acquainted with the cotton business a matter of certainty that under no circumstances can the present small production be largely increased for at least five or six months, and the same facts apply to almost every large manufacturing town. Whether the Union is maintained or not, one thing is certain, that a tax will be levied on American cotton; and it is reasonable to ask whether, with taxed cotton, bare markets, and a diminished production, we can have a lower range of prices for cloth than 2s. per lb. now ruling for shirtings."

THE BATTLE AT VICKSBURG.

The Vicksburg *Whig* gives some interesting details of the battle of Chickasaw Bayou. We copy the following:

Some of the Abolition prisoners state that the 28th Louisiana Regiment, in the engagement of Sunday, the 28th ult., with Blair's brigade, killed and wounded upwards of four hundred of the enemy. On Monday, Colonel Thomas was placed by General Lee in charge of a brigade on his left, opposite the point where the enemy attempted to throw across a pontoon bridge. Four companies of the 42d Georgia, and two of the 28th Louisiana, posted on a mound commanding the position, served to turn the enemy at this point; the remainder of the 42d Georgia and 28th Louisiana were advanced to the right to meet a force sent to turn General Lee's flank. The enemy, advancing in solid column for this purpose, were repulsed with considerable slaughter, thus contributing greatly to securing a complete victory. We were in error when we stated that the 42d Georgia lost most men—the 28th lost most men, as they were most frequently engaged. The list we published was for Sunday, the 28th ult., only. On that day they lost forty killed, wounded and missing. Colonel Thomas and the regiment were complimented on the field by General Lee, for gallant conduct.

Companies A and B, of Major Ward's Artillery Battalion, took part in the fights, and are deserving of notice. They arrived here on Friday, and were ordered to the battle field immediately. On Sunday afternoon Company A, under the command of Major Ward, took position at the foot of the hill, in front of General Barton's brigade, and opened upon a battery of the enemy. They were under fire for some two hours, and behaved well. No one was hurt but Major Ward, who received a slight wound on the side of the head. They were assisted in silencing the battery by Lieut. Stowers, of Company B, in charge of three siege guns, on the crest of the hill. At night one section of Company A, in charge of Lieut. Tarleton, went up the lines of General Lee, and were all day Monday in the hottest of the fight. A shell exploded one of their caissons, killing Captain Hamilton, of General Lee's staff, a most excellent officer. He had just rode up to deliver an order to Lieutenant Tarleton. They shot away all their ammunition twice during the day.

Gen. S. D. Lee, who was in command, proved himself capable to lead and worthy of our trust in every way. The soldiers had perfect confidence in him, and felt sanguine that under him victory would be theirs. He was always among them, and wherever the iron hail was falling thickest, there was Lee, noting the progress of the contest, and encouraging his men. We thank President Davis for sending him to Vicksburg. Although we have not seen much of him, we are satisfied he will prove himself in every way worthy of the President's flattering eulogium.

WOMAN AND THE WAR.

What a beautiful tribute to the women of the South was that paid by Bishop ELLIOTT, in his recent sermon at Savannah. Said he:

"The attitude of woman is sublime. Bearing all the sacrifices of which I have just spoken, she is moreover called upon to suffer in her affections, to be wounded and smitten where she feels deepest and more enduringly. Man goes to the battle-field, but woman sends him there, even though her heart-strings tremble while she gives the farewell kiss and the farewell blessing. Man is supported by the necessity of movement, by the excitement of action, by the hope of honor, by the glory of conquest. Woman remains at home to suffer, to bear the cruel torture of suspense, to tremble when the battle has been fought and the news of the slaughter is flashing over the electric wire, to know that defeat will cover her with dishonor and her little ones with ruin, to learn that the husband she doated upon, the son whom she cherished in her bosom, and upon whom she never let the wind blow too rudely, the brother with whom she sported through all her happy days of childhood, the lover to whom her early vows were plighted, has died upon some distant battlefield, and lies there a mangled corpse, unknown and uncared for, never to be seen again, even in death! Oh! those fearful lists of the wounded and the dead! How carelessly we pass them over, unless our own loved ones happen to be linked with them in military association, and yet each name in that roll of slaughter, carries a fatal pang to some woman's heart—some noble, devoted woman's heart. But she bears it all, and bows submissively to the stroke. He died for the cause. He perished for his country. I would not have it otherwise, but I should like to have given the dying boy my blessing, the expiring husband my last kiss of affection, the bleeding lover the comfort of knowing that I kneeled beside him."

SAVE YOUR RAGS.

This would perhaps, in ordinary times, be quite an unnecessary piece of advice, but at this moment it is of vital importance. As our readers know, the price of paper has advanced enormously, and as a consequence, publishers have been compelled to make a corresponding advance on their prices. One great reason of this increased tariff on paper is the scarcity of rags with which to manufacture it. The manufacturers inform us that rags are exceedingly difficult to obtain, even when, as is the case, the rates paid are higher, by at least 800 per cent. than formerly.

We write this article solely with the view of calling public attention to the scarcity, that it may, as far as possible, be remedied, and that speedily. The press is one of the most potent auxiliaries of this Government in carrying forward its objects, and subserving its interests. As a medium of communication, in times like these, when every day adds some memorable event to our history, the newspaper is as indispensable as our daily food. And it is essential to our individual intelligence, and as a record of current events. And as we sit down to read the pages of the favorite book or journal, let us not fail to remember that the materials for its manufacture must be obtained, or we shall have no book or newspaper. Until the blockade is removed—a desideratum altogether among the uncertainties—we must rely upon our own resources. Let then every family carefully save up all the rags—all the shreds—all the scraps—either linen, cotton, or woollen, and furnish them to the Paper Mills, and the proprietors of those mills will pay them handsomely therefor. Husbands, tell your wives to see to this—and not only the wives, but let every member of the family, white and black, commence the saving of rags to make paper. The possible contingency of a country like ours deprived of newspapers is shocking to contemplate. And we will not believe but what, as we have thus sounded the note of alarm, every one interested (and who is not?) will do all in his or her power to keep the mills supplied with rags, that the press may thereby continue to dispense intelligence to the people.

Augusta Chronicle.

To the Editor of the Mercury:—To prevent any misunderstanding upon the subject, I will restate my proposition published recently in the *Courier*, to wit: "I, therefore, propose that a committee of gentlemen, competent to judge, be chosen by 'Dalton' and myself, and that this committee make a joint report, or separate reports, and offer it or them to different societies of science in America and Europe for final decision." And in my communication in Thursday's MERCURY, January 8, 1863, I stated the following: "And I will offer no objection to those mentioned by *Dalton Secundus*, should *Dalton Primus* feel disposed to select them for himself, according to my proposition in the *Courier* of the 25th inst." Intending, should "Dalton" accept my proposition, to select an equal number with himself, and leave the subject for the committee to prosecute to the end, desiring and expecting that the subject be discussed calmly, dispassionately and scientifically.

I select W. B. CARLISLE, JOHN VANDERHORST and P. F. STEVENS, Esquires. I do not know what views these gentlemen may have taken upon the subject, and I am acquainted with only one of them personally, but I am confident that the cause of Truth and Science will receive no detriment at their hands. I am, &c.,

LAWRENCE S. BENSON.

The Daily Picayune.

VOLUME XXVI. NEW ORLEANS, WEDNESDAY MORNING, JANUARY 14, 1863. NUMBER 301.

The Daily Picayune.

FROM OUR EVENING EDITION OF YESTERDAY.

ADDITIONAL THROUGH SOUTHERN SOURCES.

THE BATTLE AT MURFREESBORO.

Gen. Bragg's Dispatch to Gen. Beauregard

THE WASHINGTON ARTILLERY

Operations in North Carolina, Vicksburg, Arkansas and Kentucky.

STUART'S LAST RAID.

WRECK OF IRONCLADS.

THE EMANCIPATION PROCLAMATION.

BATTLE OF PRAIRIE GROVE.

We continue our gleanings from Southern papers. The annexed dispatches are from the Appeal of January 5th and 6th, and though not so late as those already given in our columns, they contain much that is new and throw additional light upon previously reported matters:

The Battle of Murfreesboro'.

MURFREESBORO', Jan. 3.—All is quiet along the lines to-day, and a rain has been falling with slight intermissions, which bears heavily upon our men, who have been now six days in line of battle. The enemy, in strong force, continues in position about three miles northwest of town, on each side of Stone river.

Nashville has been reinforced.

Brigadier General Hanson was severely wounded in the leg.

Gen. Bragg to Gen. Beauregard.

On the 1st Gen. Bragg sent the following telegram (from Murfreesboro) to Gen. Beauregard:

The enemy has yielded his strong position and is falling back. We occupy the whole field, and shall follow him. Gen. Wheeler, with his cavalry, made a complete circuit of their army on the 30th and 31st. He captured and destroyed three hundred wagons loaded with baggage and commissary stores, and took seven hundred prisoners. He is again behind them and has captured an ordnance train to-day. We secured several stand of small arms. The body of Gen. Sill was left on the field, and three other generals are reported killed. God has granted us a happy New Year.

BRAXTON BRAGG, Gen. Comd'g.

The Washington Artillery.—The Appeal says:

The following private dispatch has been handed us for publication for the benefit of the friends of the 5th Company of the Washington (New Orleans) Light Artillery:

To F. Walker, Canton, Miss.

MURFREESBORO, Jan. 1.—We have beaten the enemy. None of us killed.

From Vicksburg.—RICHMOND, Jan. 3, 2 P. M.—A dispatch to the Secretary of War, dated Vicksburg, January 2, says:

The enemy finding all his efforts unavailing to make any inroads upon our position, has re-embarked, leaving a considerable quantity of intrenching tools and other property, and apparently has relinquished his designs upon Vicksburg.

J. C. PEMBERTON, Lieut. Gen. Commanding.

Operations in North Carolina.—A Richmond dispatch, of the 3d, says:

Several thousand Federals recently left Suffolk for some point in North Carolina. Cochran's brigade now occupies Suffolk.

Two hundred prisoners arrived to-day from above.

President Davis—CHARLESTON, Jan. 4.—President Davis arrived at Raleigh on Saturday. He was enthusiastically received and addressed the citizens. He said unpleasant rumors caused his late visit West, but he was pleased to find the army in good condition and ready to meet the foe at all points. He was satisfied that success would crown our arms as heretofore on almost every battle field.

The Raid in East Tennessee—The Federals at Winchester.—RICHMOND, Jan. 4.—Advices from Bristol to the 1st state that the damage done to the bridges is not so serious as at first supposed. Gen. Marshall is said to be in pursuit of the enemy, and it was thought would overtake them in the vicinity of Moccasin Gap. The forces of the Federals at Winchester is estimated at two thousand. Their pickets extend to Middleton.

The President and suite arrived from their southwestern tour to-night.

The Virginia State Legislature meets in Richmond on Wednesday.

Members of Congress are beginning to arrive.

From Arkansas.—RICHMOND, Jan. 3.—The Herald, of the 1st, states that nine steamers, with cargoes of grain and provisions, have been burnt by Confederates at Van Buren, Ark.; that the Federals burned the arsenal and ferryboat at Fort Smith, to prevent them from falling into our hands. The Federals say they have a cavalry raid on hand which is to wipe out Stuart's.

Gen. Stuart's Last Raid.—A Richmond dispatch, of the 2d, says:

Gen. Stuart returned from a recent raid on New Year's eve. In his rounds he visited Dumfries, and proceeded up the Potomac. At Selectman's ford, on the Occoquan, he encountered a large force of the enemy's cavalry, when he charged through the stream. They fled in confusion, leaving the road strewn with overcoats, caps, blankets, arms, &c. He burned the railroad bridge over the Acatink creek, ten miles from Alexandria, and destroyed the railroad bridge at Anondale, seven miles from Alexandria. He dashed into the enemy's camps, destroying stores and capturing prisoners. Here he telegraphed Lincoln's quartermaster that he had not furnished sufficient transportation for the supplies he had taken between Fairfax and Vienna. He also encountered a large force of the enemy, who used artillery against him, when he retired.

At Aldie he routed the enemy's cavalry, taking a number of prisoners, and proceeded thence to Warrenton. On his return he was accompanied by Gen. Fitzhugh Lee, commanding cavalry brigade. Gen. Stuart was entirely successful, and captured and destroyed immense stores, wagon trains, camp equipage, &c., besides capturing about three hundred prisoners. His troops have supplied themselves with clothing, stores, arms, &c.

A dispatch from New York, dated 29th ult. says the Tribune's Washington special says Stuart's cavalry has made the entire circuit of Burnside's army, capturing 2500 prisoners. The 17th Pennsylvania cavalry was nearly demolished. He captured a battery of six guns, large train of wagons and Government property of every description.

The Emancipation Proclamation—New Orleans Exempted.—A Richmond dispatch, of Jan. 2, giving news from Northern papers, says:

The emancipation proclamation of Abraham Lincoln, which was to be issued on the 1st inst., would not include that portion of Virginia presumed to be loyal, nor the city of New Orleans, in its operation.

Operations of Morgan and Forrest.—RICHMOND, Jan. 3.—A dispatch to Gen. Cooper from Gen. Bragg, received last night at 11 o'clock, states that the expedition under Forrest had fully accomplished its object. The railroads in West Tennessee were broken in many places, and a large amount of stores captured and seven hundred prisoners paroled.

Morgan has done his work, but the full effect is not known.

The enemy in Tennessee and Mississippi are without railroad and telegraph communication with their rear.

Loss of Ironclads at Sea.—PETERSBURG, Jan. 5.—A reliable gentleman arrived by a flag of truce boat at City Point to-day, reports that the celebrated ironclad gunboat Monitor foundered off Cape Hatteras a few days since. All on board perished. The Galena also came near sharing a similar fate. She had to throw overboard her armament and everything. Their destination was supposed to have been Wilmington. Late Federal prisoners who came up on the boat confirm the above report, and say the information was received at Fortress Monroe yesterday morning.

Richmond dispatches of January 2d and 3d give the following news gleaned from Northern papers received there:

Mr. Brooks's Plan of Pacification.—Jas. Brooks made a speech in New York on Wednesday, Dec. 31, at a meeting at which resolutions were unanimously adopted requesting New Jersey, on account of her Revolutionary history and past association, to invite all the States to meet in convention in Louisville, in February. They also call upon New Jersey to ask permission of the President to allow her to send delegates to the States in rebellion, and invite their representation in this convention, and in the event the States in rebellion agree to be represented, they ask Lincoln to proclaim an armistice, by land and sea, for six months. Brooks was enthusiastically applauded.

Confederate Bonds in Europe.—The London News understands that agents of the Confederate Government are endeavoring to issue in England bonds bearing interest at the rate of eight per cent.

Kentucky to be the Battle Ground.—The Cincinnati Commercial says there is no longer any doubt that Kentucky is to be the great battlefield.

A Cincinnati dispatch says that Morgan was within thirty miles of Louisville. Marshall, Floyd and other generals are advancing from Cumberland Gap and other points into the heart of Kentucky, with thirty-five thousand troops.

Miscellaneous.—The Missouri Republican estimates the number of slaves lost in Missouri since the war at seven thousand one hundred and ninety.

The iron-clads at Fortress Monroe are said to be on the move. The Passaic, Monitor and Galena left there Tuesday for points not stated.

Northern papers say the "290" has been seen since the capture of the Ariel, cruising again in the track of the California steamers. There were three steamers of the line out, and it is feared that Capt. Semmes is cruising around in wait for them. There was great excitement in commercial circles of the North.

Theodorus Bailey, acting rear admiral, has assumed command of the Eastern Gulf squadron.

Propositions have been made in the Federal Congress to issue letters of marque to destroy Confederate privateers.

A Washington correspondent says information was received by last steamer that *Le Pays* says that Napoleon has postponed indefinitely the plan for interference.

The Minnesota is being fitted with 11-inch guns of immensely heavy calibre.

Later from the Rio Grande.—The Houston Telegraph, of December 17, contains the following:

The town of Brownsville is filled with strangers, who are buying goods or going abroad.

A steamboat load of goods arrived there about the 23d ult.

A cargo of superior bale rope and baggage has also arrived there for the rebels in Texas. It is said that two United States Consuls are engaged in supplying these things for the rebels generally.

There has been a rapid decline in the price of cotton. The Flag says:

We, in common with our readers, have erred in the supposition that the price of cotton here would be governed by its value in foreign ports. It is now discerned that our great staple is influenced by local circumstances. The extreme difficulty and danger of shipping cotton at this season of the year, over a bar that continues almost impassable to navigation for weeks together, necessarily depreciates its value in this market. Out of the eighteen thousand bales imported here from the interior, almost one-third remains unshipped in the hands of the buyers. It is estimated that five thousand bales are in this vicinity awaiting a favorable transportation to the shipping in the gulf.

Parties purchasing cotton to-day cannot reasonably expect to place it on shipboard before the beginning of another spring. Another reason assigned for the depressed state of the market is that the expenditure of two millions of dollars for cotton has depleted the long purses of our capitalists. For this cause the buyers have become diminished in number, and thus control the market. The reduced price of cotton is also attributed to the fact that one continued stream is pouring into our city, with the owners unable to hold and too anxious to sell. We quote cotton to-day 25½ to 26 cents.

From Mexico.—The Flag has also the following Mexican news:

Martial law has been proclaimed at the capital, and Gen. Comonfort appointed commander-in-chief of the Mexican army. This has done away with the Congress, and consequently all legislation for the moment.

The election for Governor of this State (New Leon) will take place next Sunday. There is no doubt but that Vidaurri will again be reëlected by an overwhelming majority. The election for members of Congress of this place took place last Sunday, and the candidates of the Vidaurri tickets were elected by large majorities.

A large conducta is now awaiting transportation if proper arrangement can be made with the customhouse.

King Cotton still wields the sceptre, and demands 32c. per pound. Owing to the failure of the crops, and on account of the drouth we suffer. The different corporations of the State have petitioned Gov. Vidaurri to prohibit the exportation of all kinds of breadstuffs, which measure has been adopted. This not only embraces Texas, but the adjoining State of Tamaulipas. The scarcity is such that the Government has procured a loan by subscription from the different merchants of the city of Monterey, of $20,000, to make importations of grain from the interior.

Battle of Prairie Grove.—We have conversed with Dr. Joel D. Conway, who has visited the army of the Northwest since the battle of the 7th. He reports that, upon burying the dead, under the flag of truce, and upon communication with the surgeons of the two armies, it was ascertained that the loss of the enemy far exceeds that reported by Gen. Hindman. He was credibly informed that it amounted to 3000 or 4000. The Fort Smith Bulletin says: "The Federals who conversed with our men, acknowledged their loss was much heavier than ours; some put it down three to one." Another paragraph of the same paper says:

"In the Prairie Grove battle, which came off on Sunday, the 7th, the Federal loss is set down at four or five thousand, killed, wounded and missing. Our loss is estimated at about a hundred killed, and fifteen hundred wounded and missing."

We take the following from the Gazette, of the 7th. We are glad to hear such good things of Hawthorn:

In a note accompanying the report Major Woodruff says that the official report of the losses in Gen Shoup's division was 721 killed, wounded and missing. Fagan's brigade suffered the most. The killed on the field only 81; wounded, about 400; remainder missing. Dr. Keller told him that the hospital subjects numbered about 250 of the wounded; residue being slightly injured. In McRae's brigade the killed numbered only about twenty-six.

Col. Pleasants had one of his legs broken—was doing well. Col. Polk, of Hawthorn's regiment, was wounded mortally, and since died. Col. Young, of Jackson county, was killed.

Three of Capt. Blocker's guns were temporarily captured by the enemy, but were soon recaptured by a most gallant charge of Hawthorn's regiment, who, at the same time, took a stand of colors. We learn from another source that, in this charge, no less than one hundred and fifty-seven of the enemy were left dead on the field.

Gen. Hindman retired after the battle to the Arkansas river, in the vicinity of Fort Smith. No army could subsist where he was. The Federal forces under Blount and Herron were, when last heard of, in the vicinity of Fayetteville.—*Washington (Ark.) Telegraph.*

LATER FROM MEXICO.

Progress of the War, &c.

By the arrival of the Bio Bio we have Havana papers of the 7th inst., from which we derive the following intelligence from Mexico:

We copy from the *Diario de la Marina* the following:

By the R. M. steamship Conway we have received files from Vera Cruz up to the 30th ult.

The *Opinion*, of Jalapa, announces the arrival at that place of Gen. Leonardo Marquez with 2000 men.

The *Boletin Oficial*, of Puebla, is confident that the troops stationed between that city and Mexico will not be withdrawn. The National Guard was reviewed on the Paseo Nuevo of Mexico on the 23d.

Don Domingo Martinez is temporarily in charge of the government of the State of Nuevo Leon. General Bazaine, commanding the 2d expeditionary corps, took possession of Jalapa on the 26th. There was a great military display on the occasion. The Mexican troops joined the Imperial army in the triumphal march through the city. Generals Marquez and Bertinier accompanied General Bazaine.

VERA CRUZ, Dec. 26.

The ship of the line Fourville has left Martinique, conveying 22 guerrillas, who are to be immured in Fort France until the end of the war.

On the 23d ult., a small detachment of the 81st Regiment of Infantry garrisoning Medellin surrounded a neigboring plantation known by the name of Novillero, where a party of guerrillas who have been devastating this section of country for some time make their rendezvous. The surprise was complete; all the band were captured but twenty-five, who lost their lives in resisting the assault. The French had two men slightly wounded. It is reported by a person of veracity, that a fight occurred on the 14th, at San Andres de Chalchicomula, between forty-nine Chasseurs d'Afrique and a company of 99th Regiment of Regulars, with some of Carbajal's forces. The latter were completely routed, after having suffered severe loss and leaving eighteen prisoners in the hands of the French. A horse ridden by an officer belonging to the 99th Regiment run away with his rider into the enemy's line; he was killed instantly. The French lost four men beside in the engagement.

On the 18th, 300 cavalry belonging to Marquez's corps made an attack on the forces commanded by Aureliano, Rodriguez and Quesada, numbering 1000 horsemen, encamped at Cerro Leon. The fight was severe for a short time, when the Mexicans fled in confusion, leaving their dead and wounded on the field. Marquez's forces captured 50 prisoners, several horses and accoutrements.

VERA CRUZ, Dec. 30.

The French Court, presided over by Lieut. Col. Magin, after two public sessions, pronounced the following sentences against some parties guilty of having poisoned some French soldiers:

Manuel Gonzales, Bartolo Banderas and Justo Pasos, death.
José Carmona, ten years hard labor.
Ramon Zamudio, five years hard labor.
Antonia Zamudio, hard labor for life.
Dolores Barafas, ten years hard labor.

The orders of the Commanding General are looked for before carrying the sentences into execution.

We read in the *Opinion*, of Jalapa, that on the morning of the 23d all the Mexican and French troops left that city *en route* to Perote. The first numbered 10,500 men. It was said that other troops belonging to Gen. Bazaine's corps were expected there daily.

At last dates the city of Mexico was in a deplorable condition. Great scarcity of money prevailed. Commerce was completely paralyzed on account of the innumerable taxes imposed on the people. Letters from that city say that a new tax has been imposed on merchants, to be paid in monthly quotas, varying from 100 to 7000 dollars. Great anxiety prevailed.

A decree has been issued in Puebla imposing on the citizens a contribution of $152,400, in quotas from $7000 to $50,000.

Gen. Negrete, Quartermaster General at Puebla, had been superseded by Gen. Mendoza. Gen. Doblado, having been appointed Constitutional Governor of Jalisco, left Guanajuato to defend Jalisco, which city was menaced by Fovar at the head of 3500 men. He arrived and took command, but having issued a decree demanding money from the people, which was disregarded, he evacuated the city with all the forces, leaving it to the mercy of the beleager.

At last accounts Gen. Mejia was very near San Luis Potosi. Through some letters from Orizaba, we have some interesting news up to the 12th.

Gen. Truyeque and Col. Layson have sided with the Imperialists, surrendering at Chalchicomula with 200 cavalry. On the 19th 100 more Mexicans came over.

It is said also that Aureliano, at the head of 800 cavalry, had tendered his services to Gen. Bazaine.

There is great confusion in the capital.

Large forces were gathering at Palmar, San Andres and Tehuacan. All these towns side with the Imperialists.

[FROM THE EXTRA PICAYUNE.]

LATEST NEWS THROUGH SOUTHERN SOURCES.

THE CAPTURE OF GALVESTON

GEN. MAGRUDER'S REPORT.

THE RESULTS AT MURFREESBORO'.

The First Day's Fight.

MOVEMENTS IN VIRGINIA.

LATE FROM THE NORTH

Mediation Rumors and Speculations.

MISCELLANEOUS NEWS.

We have received the Memphis (Jackson) Appeal, of Jan. 9, issued at 1 o'clock, A. M., from which we take the following interesting and important intelligence:

Capture of Galveston.

The Enemy's Fleet Destroyed.

NATCHEZ, Jan. 8, 1863.—The following dispatch (official) is taken from the Natchez Courier of this date:

HEADQUARTERS, GALVESTON, Texas, Jan. 1, 1863.

S. Cooper, Adjutant General, C. S. A.:

This morning, at 3 o'clock, I attacked the enemy's fleet and garrison at this place, and captured the latter, the steamer Harriet Lane, two barks and a schooner of the former.

The rest, some four or five in number, escaped, ignominiously, under cover of a flag of truce.

I have about six hundred prisoners, and a large quantity of stores, arms, &c.

The Harriet Lane is very little injured. She was carried by boarding from two high-pressure cotton steamers, manned by Texas cavalry and artillery.

The line troops were gallantly commanded by Col. Thos. Green, of Sibley's Brigade, and the ships and artillery by Major Leon Smith, to whose indomitable energy and heroic daring the country is indebted for the successful execution of a plan which I had conceived for the destruction of the enemy's fleet. Col. Bagby, of Sibley's Brigade, also commanded the volunteers from his regiment for the naval expedition, in which every officer and man won for himself imperishable renown.

I am, sir, very respectfully, your obedient servant, J. BANKHEAD MAGRUDER, Major Gen'l Com'g Dep't of Texas.

Result of the Battle of Murfreesboro.

MOBILE, Jan. 8.—A special to the Advertiser and Register says Gen. Bragg made a speech at Dechard on Monday to the citizens of Dechard and Winchester, assuring them he did not mean to desert them, but would make a stand between Alonza and Tullahoma.

He said he fell back because our troops needed repose, being perfectly exhausted.

He also said our loss was 7,000, while the enemy's loss was between 15,000 and 20,000.

The enemy has advanced his lines six miles this side of Murfreesboro'.

We find in the Knoxville Register the following additional particulars of the first day's engagement at Murfreesboro':

MURFREESBORO', January 1.—We are victorious. The enemy to-day yielded his strong points, and fell back. We now occupy the whole field of yesterday, and shall follow him to-morrow. There was little fighting to-day.

The enemy left an immense number of killed and wounded on the field. His loss must be near fifteen thousand—ours is five thousand. We have secured several thousand stand of small arms.

Gen. Wheeler, with cavalry, made the entire circuit, by Jefferson and Lavergne, of Rosecrans's army on Thursday night.

Yesterday they destroyed three hundred wagons loaded with baggage and commissary stores, capturing and paroling seven hundred prisoners.

He is again behind them and captured an ordnance train to-day. He got all of McCook's baggage and his body servant yesterday. Our wounded are receiving every attention from the patriotic ladies of Murfreesboro', though many necessaries for comfort are much needed yet. We have the wounded of both armies on our hands, but enough Federal surgeons have been captured to attend their wounded. The number of slight wounds is very great in our army. Those able to be moved are sent to Chattanooga as rapidly as possible.

Gen. Adams, of Louisiana, slightly wounded; also Col. Harry Maury, of Alabama, was shot, with regimental colors in his hand, while leading a charge.

Gen Cheatham's Tennessee division did desperate fighting. Indeed, all the troops fought with greater valor and determination than ever.

No Federal officers are paroled. They are sent immediately to Chattanooga under guard.

The Federal Gen. Sill's remains have been brought in. The top of his head was blown off.

The three generals previously reported are still believed killed.

The Day Before the Battle.

The Murfreesboro correspondent of the Mobile Register, writing on the 29th ult., gives us a very fair understanding of the strength and position of the two armies on the evening of that day. He says:

It was our confident expectation that the enemy would have commenced the battle this morning, but it seems he had not got his forces into position, having been carefully feeling his way. An advance of the enemy at this time was not looked for, it being the opinion of many that Rosecrans would not attempt to leave Nashville until the rivers got up, so that he might be aided by the gunboats. It is supposed, however, that the impression had reached him that we did not intend to hold Murfreesboro', and that we had been sending off our troops, leaving but a weak force here, and that under this belief he has advanced.

Besides this, there are other cogent reasons at this time to compel him to risk a little. The limited space of country around Nashville is too limited for foraging to supply his army, and he must now also know that his supplies are cut off by the destruction of the Nashville and Louisville road. In order to prepare for his falling back, in case of reverse, his heavy siege guns were crossed to the other side of the Cumberland, and two pontoon bridges erected over the river. This movement led to the report of the supposed preparations for evacuating Nashville. But the intention of the enemy is now clear.

I rode out to-day in front of our lines, on the Nashville pike to Stone river, where our line of battle is formed. The river is very shallow, being not over ankle deep at the ford, and is but a mile and a half from town. Polk's corps is on the opposite, or northwest side of the river. The character of the surrounding country is open and very slightly rolling, being mostly level. On this side of the river are numerous little brick chimneys, which were built in front of our tents, now struck, and which mark our former camp grounds. The enemy advanced this evening and took up their line of battle about a mile from ours. About four hundred yards in front of our line, on the left side of the Nashville road, stood a fine brick dwelling, which was set fire to this evening, with all the barns and out houses, in order to prevent the enemy from approaching us under shelter. Their signal corps, while the building was burning, approached near the house to reconnoiter, and were plainly seen.

On this side of the river there are small patches of thin woods, but as I have said, the ground is mostly open, and it must consequently be a fair field fight. The forces of the enemy are now estimated at from 55,000 to 60,000. Our full force is about 33,000, thus we have a far superior number against us, and must depend solely on the fighting qualities of our troops. That the battle will be a most bloody one there can be no doubt. Rosecrans has the advice and aid, it is supposed, of Buell, but I do not suppose the latter is on the field. The fight will most certainly come off to-morrow, the attack being expected at daylight.

In the skirmish this afternoon, on the Franklin road, some of our infantry fired upon the Texas Rangers through mistake, and wounded two or three. The Texans had a sharp brush with Woolford's cavalry this afternoon, killing several and driving them back.

By this time to-morrow night the fate of Middle Tennessee will be decided. God grant us a happy deliverance from our enemies. The following "memorandum for general and staff officers" was issued yesterday, Sunday morning, which anticipated the commencement of the battle to-day:

1. The "line of battle" will be in front of Murfreesboro'—half of the army, left wing, in front of Stone river; right wing in rear of the river.

2. Polk's corps will form the left wing; Hardee's corps the right wing.

3. Withers's division will form the first line in Polk's corps; Cheatham's the second line. Breckinridge's division forms first line in Hardee's corps; Cleburn's division the second line.

4. McCown's division to form reserve opposite centre, on high ground, in rear of Cheatham's present quarters.

5. Jackson's brigade in reserve to the right flank to report to Lieut. Gen. Hardee.

6. The two lines to be from 800 to 1000 yards apart, according to the ground.

7. Chiefs of artillery to pay special attention to the posting of batteries, seeing that they do not carelessly waste ammunition.

8. Cavalry to fall back gradually before enemy, reporting by courier every hour. When near our line, Wheeler will move to the right, and Wharton to the left, to cover and protect our flanks, and report movements of enemy. Pegram to fall to the rear and report to commanding general as a reserve.

9. To-night, if the enemy has gained his position in front ready for action, Wheeler and Wharton, with their whole commands, will make a night march to the right and left, turn the enemy's flank, gain his rear, and vigorously assail his trains and rear guard, blocking the roads and impeding his movements in every way, holding themselves ready to assail his retreating forces.

10. All quarter masters, commissaries, and ordnance officers will remain at their proper posts discharging their appropriate duties. Supplies and baggage should be ready packed for a forward or backward move as the result of the day may require, and the trains should be in position out of danger, teamsters all present and quartermasters in charge.

11. Should we be compelled to retire, Polk's corps will move on Shelbyville, and Hardee's on the Manchester pike, trains in front, cavalry in rear.

(Signed) BRAXTON BRAGG, General Command'g.
GEO. G. GARNER, A. A. General.

Federal Movements in Virginia.

RICHMOND, Jan. 7.—The Lynchburg Republican says the Federals are rapidly reconstructing the Baltimore and Ohio Railroad, and trains are running regularly west of Martinsburg. The Federals still occupy Winchester and continue depredations in the Valley.

We have nothing of interest from the lines.

Later from the North.

Petersburg dispatches of Jan. 7, give the following, derived from Northern papers of the 4th inst.:

Another Privateer at Work.—The Captain of the bark Trent reports the destruction of his vessel by a new rebel privateer on the 5th of December, and himself and crew set adrift.

Mediation Rumors and Speculations.—Advices by the Asia state that the distress in the manufacturing districts of France is deepening daily, and threatens to become serious. The Paris correspondent of the London Star says there is very little doubt that this fact inclines the Emperor to listen more attentively than he otherwise would have done to Mr. Slidell.

The New York Herald says Napoleon will address another circular to England and Russia upon the necessity of immediate intervention or mediation. The French Minister at Washington, it is said, openly states that during this month his Government will mediate in favor of the South. The Herald says this assertion, if true, puts all doubt upon that question at an end, and considers the present a moment of great peril to the country.

The Paris correspondent of the New York Commercial, under date of December 15, says there is no doubt of a secret league between Slidell and the French Government. Slidell being naturally interested in affairs in New Orleans, where his property has been confiscated, and as the French Government looks upon Louisiana as almost French property, the arrival of a French fleet at New Orleans was received with great joy by Southerners, and the official journals announced the fact in terms which would have been offensive to any Government but that of the United States.

He says that although indications for the moment are that while a better feeling is growing up towards us in England, the contrary is true of France.

Items.

Rumor says that Lincoln was shot at and his coachman wounded, while riding in the street.

The New Year's eve grand reception, given by the President, was largely attended by Congressmen and foreign ministers.

The Enquirer says the whole movement of the armies of the rebels show that they made a desperate exertion to cut Grant's army off, and that the movements were planned by Davis himself, but had signally failed.

Gold in Richmond.

RICHMOND, Jan. 8.—The premium for gold has declined here to two dollars. Previous quotations 220 to 225, selling rate.

The Battle of Chickasaw Bayou—Further Particulars.

The Vicksburg Whig furnishes the following additional particulars of the battle fought above Vicksburg, December 28:

In the engagement on our right on Monday last, the 3d and 30th Tennessee Regiments, the 28th Louisiana and 42d Georgia, as well as the 26th and the 31st Louisiana, deported themselves with great gallantry. The enemy first appeared at daylight, in force, in the woods in the bend of the river, beyond a ravine which was a few hundred yards in our front. Our skirmishers drove him back the first onset, with the assistance of the artillery

The Philadelphia Inquirer.

CIRCULATION OVER 60,000. | PHILADELPHIA, TUESDAY, JANUARY 27, 1863. | PRICE TWO CENTS

IMPORTANT WAR NEWS.

FROM THE RAPPAHANNOCK

Gen. Burnside Resigns.

General Hooker Succeeds to the Command of the Army.

GENS. SUMNER AND FRANKLIN RELIEVED.

General Burnside's Farewell Address to the Troops.

NATIONAL GUARD OF 250,000 MEN.

The Pirate "Alabama" Sinks the U.S. Transport "Hatteras."

LATER NEWS FROM THE SOUTH.

Bombardment and Capture of Acapulco by the French.

LATER FROM GENERAL ROSECRANS' ARMY.

IMPORTANT FROM GALVESTON.

The Pirate "Alabama" Sinks the United States Transport "Hatteras."

NEW YORK, Jan. 26.—The steamer *Mary A. Boardman* arrived to-night, from New Orleans on the 18th, and Key West on the 20th. She furnishes Galveston advices of the 17th, which were brought to Key West by the steamer *Northern Light*, from New Orleans.

On the 17th, the United States sloop-of-war *Brooklyn*, in company with six other United States steamers, were off Galveston. They saw a steamer in the offing. The steamer *Hatteras* immediately got under way to speak to her, and, when within hailing distance, asked who she was.

The answer was—"Her Majesty's ship of war *Spitfire*."

The commander of the *Hatteras* then told them to wait and he would send a boat to her, and had just lowered the boat with an officer and crew in her, when the steamer opened her broadside and fired it into the *Hatteras*.

The *Brooklyn* immediately got under weigh, and started in pursuit of the stranger, but night coming on, lost sight of her, and was compelled to give up the chase.

On returning she found the steamer *Hatteras* sunk in nine fathoms of war. The officers of the steamer *Mary Boardman* are unable to give further particulars. The steamer that fired was no doubt the pirate *Alabama*.

The steamer *Hatteras* was merely a transport, but carried four guns of light calibre, similar to those on the transport *McClellan*.

FROM THE ARMY OF THE POTOMAC

General Burnside Resigns the Command—General Hooker to Succeed Him—General Burnside's Farewell Address—Generals Sumner and Franklin Relieved.

HEAD-QUARTERS, ARMY OF THE POTOMAC, Jan. 26.—This forenoon General BURNSIDE turned over the command of the Army of the Potomac to General HOOKER, who came to the Head-quarters Camp for that purpose.

As soon as the change became known a considerable number of superior officers called on General BURNSIDE and took their parting leave with many regrets.

The following is General BURNSIDE's address to the army:—

HEAD-QUARTERS ARMY OF THE POTOMAC, CAMP NEAR FALMOUTH, Jan. 26.—General Orders No. 9.—By direction of the President of the United States, the Commanding General this day transfers the command of this army to Major-General JOSEPH HOOKER. The short time that he has directed your movements has not been fruitful of victory or any considerable advancement of our lines, but it has again demonstrated an amount of courage, patience and endurance that, under more favorable circumstances, would have accomplished great results.

Continue to exercise these virtues; be true in your devotion to your country and the principles you have sworn to maintain; give to the brave and skillful General who has long been identified with your organization, and who is now to command you, your full and cordial support, and you will deserve success.

In taking an affectionate leave of the entire army, from which he separates with so much regret, he may be pardoned if he bids an especial farewell to his long-tried associates of the Ninth Corps.

His prayers are that God may be with you, and grant you continued success until the Rebellion is crushed.

By command of Major-General BURNSIDE.

LEWIS RICHMOND, A. A. G.

It is understood that Generals SUMNER and FRANKLIN have also been relieved from their command of the right and left Grand Divisions, but the names of their successors have not been divulged, if appointed.

General BURNSIDE, with most of his late Staff, have been allowed thirty days' leave of absence. They will go to New York.

The weather is warm and pleasant, and the mud is fast drying up.

THE WAR IN MEXICO.

Bombardment of Acapulco by the French—Capture of the Fort.

SAN FRANCISCO, Jan. 26.—The steamer *Sonora*, which arrived here to-day from Panama, reports that four French war vessels bombarded the town of Acapulco, Mexico, for three days, commencing on the 16th. The fire was returned from the fort, doing some damage to the vessels.

The people abandoned the town. After killing thirteen of the Mexican garrison, the fort was finally silenced, when a hundred sailors landed and spiked the guns. The fleet then left.

The War in North Carolina—A Body of Rebels Driven from Pollocksville.

BOSTON, Jan. 26.—Private advices from Newbern, N. C., to Tuesday, the 20th, have been received. No mail had then left for the North for two weeks, but one was about leaving for New York.

The main expedition, of which so much has been said, had not yet started, but a land force was sent forward on the 17th, towards the railroad, which encountered a force of 1300 Rebels at Pollocksville. Our troops drove them from the town and took possession of it. Some of the New York cavalry were wounded. The general health of the troops was excellent.

FROM WASHINGTON.

Special Despatch to The Inquirer.

WASHINGTON, January 26, 1863.

The Assistant Secretaryships of War.

The law originally provided for but one Assistant Secretary of War. Mr. T. A. SCOTT was appointed to this office, under Secretary CAMERON. When Mr. STANTON was appointed Secretary of War he requested authority from Congress to appoint two more Assistant Secretaries for one year. This authority was granted by Congress, and Mr. WATSON and Mr. TUCKER were appointed. When Mr. SCOTT resigned, Mr. WOLCOTT was appointed to the permanent Assistant Secretaryship thus vacated. The term of office of Mr. WATSON and of Mr. TUCKER expired, by limitation, on Wednesday last. The Assistant Secretary, Mr. WOLCOTT, who is in very bad health, has since resigned, and Mr. WATSON has been appointed in his place; so that Mr. WATSON is now the permanent and only Assistant Secretary.

The fact that Mr. WATSON will remain in the War Department will be received with great satisfaction by all the friends of an earnest and honest Administration of the Department. His ability, untiring industry and integrity have won for him the respect of every one who has had intercourse with the War Department, and it is understood that he remained in the Department against his own wishes, but at the earnest request of the President and Secretary of War.

It is proposed to reorganize the Department still further, by creating the post of Solicitor to the War Department, to which Mr. WHITING will be appointed, and that of Special Commissioner, to which ROBERT DALE OWEN will be appointed.

The Selection of Gen. Hooker to the Command of the Army of the Potomac.

The appointment of General HOOKER to the command of the army of the Potomac has given the most sincere gratification to the army, and even here, where opinions are so diversified, a contrary sentiment is rarely expressed. It is true, the sympathizers with treason, of whom we have many still remaining in our midst, and, I regret to say, a few of the friends of other past and present commanders, have demurred somewhat at the present selection, but the masses, the majority of whom have long looked forward to and earnestly hoped for the promotion of General HOOKER, express unqualified delight and approval. Other changes in the army of the Potomac are rumored, and if the rumors are correct the changes have evidently been based upon a desire of the Administration to secure in the future the most perfect harmony among the commanding officers of the army—a desire which cannot fail to be gratified to the fullest extent under the new arrangement. The objects to be attained can admit of no interference by impolitic personal bickerings and misunderstandings, and with complete accordance on the part of the commanders with the views of Gen. HOOKER, the brave men of the respective corps can anticipate again being led on to victory.

Arrival of General Burnside.

A large number of army officers arrived in the city to-day, among whom are Major-Generals BURNSIDE, SUMNER and PARK, with a host of lesser lights. FRANKLIN is expected to-morrow.

WENDELL PHILLIPS was upon the floor of the House to-day, and was introduced by Mr. CONWAY, of Kansas. He received the attentions of many of the members.

A bill has been introduced, providing for the appointment of an Assistant Collector, to be located at Jersey City.

All Quiet on the Rappahannock.

Apparently all is quiet along the lines.

Miscellaneous Items.

A rumor is current to-day that FITZ-JOHN PORTER has been placed under arrest for improper conduct, but it is incorrect, he having been seen this evening on the avenue, in citizen's dress.

The large majority with which the Ways and Means Committee bill passed astonished even its own friends. There is but little doubt that it will pass the Senate, or should it not at first, the large majority now committed to it in the House will insure its final passage.

National Guard of 250,000 Men.

Senator WILSON, chairman of the Military Committee, introduced a bill to provide for the organization of two hundred and fifty thousand men, to be raised *pro rata* in the several States, from the militia; to be two hundred regiments, of twelve companies each, and one hundred men to each company—the men to be between the ages of twenty-one and thirty-five. This force is to be called the National Guard, and to be subject to all orders from the President.

Deaths of Soldiers.

Deaths of Pennsylvania soldiers in the hospitals in and about Washington, to-day:—GEORGE MAUK, Company E, One-hundred-and-twenty-fifth; ALFRED McCLAY, Company K, One-hundred-and-fourteenth; WILLIAM KENNEDY, Company K, Sixty-ninth; ABRAM HANNA, Company I, One-hundred-and-fiftieth; D. E. BLAKER, Company D, One-hundred-and-thirty-second; ABRAHAM BAGSLEY, Company G, One-hundred-and-thirty-first.

Officers Without Commands.

A list of "Major and Brigadier-Generals who are not assigned to any actual command, and the length of time since engaged in actual service:"—

Major-General GEORGE B. McCLELLAN. Relieved by General Order No. 182, November 5, 1862.

Major-General JOHN C. FREMONT. Not since August 12, 1862.

Major-General IRVIN McDOWELL. Not since September 6, 1862.

Major-General D. C. BUELL. Not since October 30, 1862. Before military commission.

Major-General FITZ-JOHN PORTER. Not since November 10, 1862. Undergoing trial. Since cashiered.

Major-General C. M. CLAY. Not since June 17, 1862, when appointed. Assigned to General BUTLER, but did not report.

Brigadier-General ANDREW PORTER. Not since May —, 1862. Now on duty, commanding camp at Harrisburg.

Brigadier-General WM. S. HARNEY. Not since May 16, 1861.

Brigadier-General ROBERT ANDERSON. Not since October 8, 1861.

Brigadier-General C. P. STONE. Not since February 8, 1862.

Brigadier-General GEO. A. McCALL. Not since July —, 1862. Now on court-martial.

Brigadier-General LOUIS BLENKER. Not since July 21, 1862.

Brigadier-General JAS. SHIELDS. Not since June 24, 1862.

Brigadier-General R. B. MARCY. Has been Chief of Staff with General McCLELLAN since appointment, September 18th, 1862. Now with General McCLELLAN.

Brigadier-General T. T. CRITTENDEN. Not since July 13th, 1862. Exchanged.

Brigadier-General J. B. TURCHIN. Not since appointed as Brigadier-General, July 17th, 1862.

Brigadier-General S. W. CRAWFORD. Wounded at Antietam, and in New York since September 17th, 1862.

Brigadier-General L. P. GRAHAM. Relieved as instructor Cavalry Camp Institute, Annapolis, August 18th, 1862. Sick.

Brigadier-General Z. B. TOWER. Wounded at Antietam September 17, 1862. Sick in Washington.

Brigadier-General R. J. OGLESBY. Wounded at Corinth, October 4, 1862.

Brigadier-General W. B. CAMPBELL. Not since appointed, June 30, 1862.

Brigadier-General F. C. BARLOW. Wounded at Antietam September 17, 1862. Not since on duty.

Brigadier-General J. H. H. WARD. Relieved November 1, 1862.

Brigadier-General H. S. BRIGGS. Not since September 22, 1862. Sick.

The Confiscation of Rebel Property.

In reply to the resolution of inquiry relative to property heretofore seized by the Military Governor of the District of Columbia as the property of Rebels, the Secretary of War encloses a communication from General MARTINDALE detailing the circumstances of the conflict of military and civil authorities with regard to the property of Judge CAMPBELL, which, after its seizure by the military authorities, was subsequently turned over to the Marshal of the District, upon a writ of replevin.

General MARTINDALE suggests further legislation by Congress, to embrace two points:—first, to authorize the seizure of Rebel property by military authority, as though martial law existed, but to be transferred to the civil authorities for condemnation and sale in those districts where the civil courts are in operation, and to courts-martial where Rebellion has interrupted civil courts; secondly, continued absence and general reputation of disloyalty to authorize condemnation and sale, unless the owner of the property seized shall appear and prove loyalty.

MAJOR-GENERAL HOOKER.

MAJOR-GEN. JOSEPH HOOKER,

The New Commanding General of the Army of the Potomac.

Major-General JOSEPH HOOKER, whose selection to the chief command of the Army of the Potomac has given such unbounded satisfaction to the army and the people of the country, is a native of Massachusetts, from which State he was appointed a cadet to West Point Military Academy in 1833. He graduated on the 30th of June, 1837, standing No. 28 in a class of fifty members, among whom were Generals BENHAM, ARNOLD, FRENCH, SEDGWICK and others of the Union army; BRAXTON BRAGG, W. W. MACKALL, J. A. EARLY and other noted Rebel officers. On the 1st of July, 1837, he was promoted to the second lieutenantcy of the First United States Artillery, and on the 1st of November, 1838, was further promoted to a First Lieutenantcy in the same regiment. From July 1st to October 3d, 1841, he was the Adjutant of the Military Academy at West Point, and from 1841 to 1846 was the Adjutant of his regiment. He served with distinction in Mexico, and was Aid-de-camp to Brigadier-General HAMER. He was, in May, 1847, brevetted Captain for gallant conduct in the several conflicts at Monterey, his brevet bearing the date of September 23d, 1846.

He was appointed on the staff as Assistant Adjutant-General, with the brevet rank of Captain, on the 3d of March, 1847, and in March, 1849, was further brevetted Major for gallant and meritorious conduct in the affair at the National Bridge, Mexico, his brevet dating from June 11, 1847. In the same month he received another brevet—viz: Lieutenant-Colonel—for gallant and meritorious conduct in the battle of Chapultepec. This brevet bore date September 13, 1847. On the 29th of October, 1848, he was appointed a Captain of the First Artillery, and on the same day vacated his regimental commission, retaining his position in the Adjutant-General's Department, with brevet of Lieutenant-Colonel. On the 21st of February, 1853, he resigned from the army and went to California, where he retired into private life.

At the breaking out of the Rebellion he considered that the education he had received at the expense of the Government was a sacred trust, and immediately offered his valuable services, which were accepted, and on the 17th of May, 1861, he was commissioned as Brigadier-General of Volunteers, his appointment being accredited to the State of California. He at first acted under instructions from General DIX, but afterwards was appointed to a separate command, under General McCLELLAN. He then proceeded to reorganize the two disturbed counties of Maryland—Prince George and Charles—and succeeded admirably, entirely re-occupying those counties and disarming the Rebel sympathizers, without loss of life. His division at this time took military possession of the northern and eastern shores, or left bank of the Potomac river, and several spirited excursions were made by portions of his command in the neighborhood of Budd's Ferry, Port Tobacco, &c., to the opposite Virginia shore. A portion of these troops afterwards crossed the Potomac, and took possession of the batteries which had blockaded the river for some time previous, and, having effectually removed these obstructions, and advanced a short distance into the interior, were finally withdrawn, and transferred to the immediate command of General McCLELLAN on the Peninsula.

In the contest at Williamsburg his division bravely stood the brunt of the battle. At Fair Oaks the General again displayed his splendid military talents and fighting qualities. In the seven days' battles and in the minor contests he never failed to attract the admiration of his men by his gallantry and courage, and the same noble traits distinguished him when, subsequently, he participated in the battles before Washington, under General POPE. On July 4th, 1862, he was promoted to a Major-Generalship of Volunteers, to date from May 5th, 1862. At South Mountain and Antietam we again find him battling zealously for the cause of his country, and from the battle-field was carried to the rear with a severe wound in the foot.

On the 20th of September, 1862, he was made a Brigadier-General of the Regular army, vice Gen. MANSFIELD, killed in battle. When he had recovered from his wound sufficiently to take the field on a litter, he did so, and was made commander of the Fifth Army Corps. On the 14th of November, 1862, he was placed in command of the centre grand division of the Army of the Potomac, and in the record of the battle of Fredericksburg we again find his name prominently mentioned.

No man in the service is more popular with the army, and none have attained a more exalted character with the public as a military leader.

Brave, talented and determined, and with but one object in view, the speedy crushing of the Rebellion, he has on every battle-field where his services have been engaged displayed those qualifications which always characterize the able military leader. His past acts of valor are but precursors of those to follow, and from the Army of the Potomac, in the future, may be expected such active, rapid movements as will add lustre to our arms, and insure the glorious termination of this protracted war.

The Proposed National Guard.

Senator WILSON's Volunteer Militia Bill provides for a force to be called the National Guard of the United States, comprising two hundred regiments of twelve companies each, every regiment to be divided into three battalions, commanded by Colonel, Lieutenant-Colonel, three Majors and twelve Captains, to be appointed by the Governors of the States, among which the force is to be distributed *pro rata*. Any portion of the militia may be called by the President of the United States into service during a war of invasion or a rebellion.

The McDowell Court of Inquiry

Sat with closed doors to-day. It is understood that they were awaiting the arrival of General MILROY and Lieutenant-Colonel LOCKE, formerly of General PORTER's Staff, who are the only witnesses yet to be examined.

Free Labor System in South Carolina.

The United States Tax Commissioners for South Carolina have made a preliminary report, in which they say it must be obvious that the system of free labor has not had a fair trial in the part of that State which is under United States control; indeed, scarcely any system has been put to a practical test. Owing to casualties, and the shifting circumstances of military events, no permanent labor policy can be inaugurated.

The great impediment in its progress is the uncertainty which overhangs the future of the colored people. It is a great mistake to suppose them to be unmindful of the uncertainty of their condition. Nevertheless, they are but tenants at will on the grace of the Government, subject to military caprice and necessity, with a strong desire to obtain permanent and free homes where they were born and reared. This class of people, the Commissioners say, are daily thronging their doors, anxiously inquiring about their destiny.

When the lands shall be sold for taxes they feel the necessity of some guiding minds to direct them in a new state of existence the immense magnitude of which they appreciate, but the details of which they are unable to comprehend. The males especially are anxious to return to their former labor, provided they and their families can be assured of their freedom, moderate compensation, good homes and permanent employment.

Nominations and Confirmations.

JAMES McBRIDE, of Oregon, was to-day nominated by the President as Minister Resident to the Hawaian Islands.

The Senate to-day confirmed the following nominations:—

FREDERICK ECKFELDT, of Pennsylvania, to be Melter and Refiner of the Branch Mint at Denver, Colorado.

Captains CHARLES STEWART and WILLIAM B. SHUBRICK, to be Rear-Admirals in the Navy. Captains GEO. S. BLAKE, CADWALLADER RINGGOLD, HENRY W. MORRIS, JAMES L. LARDNER, HENRY K. HOFF, CHARLES HENRY DAVIS, HENRY H. BELL, WILLIAM SMITH, JOHN W. LIVINGSTON, HENRY K. THATCHER, WM. D. PORTER, JOHN S. NICHOLSON and ROBERT B. HITCHCOCK, to be Commanders in the Navy on the active list, and Captain JOSEPH LANGMAN to be a Commander in the Navy on the retired list.

The Post Office Department.

In the bill passed by the House to-day, twelve millions were appropriated for the Post Office Department for the year ending with the 30th of June, 1864. For the first time during many years no appropriation from the Treasury for a postal deficit was required, there being enough of last year's appropriation unexpended to cover the small deficit of the coming year.

General Burnside.

General BURNSIDE has made arrangements to be in New York early this week. On Saturday morning he, at his own request, was relieved from the command of the Army of the Potomac, when the President immediately conferred the chief command on Major-General HOOKER.

The Navy Yard at League Island.

The Secretary of the Navy has sent a communication to Congress asking an appropriation of two hundred thousand dollars for establishing a Navy Yard at League Island.

PENNSYLVANIA LEGISLATIVE PROCEEDINGS.

HARRISBURG, Jan. 26, 1863.

SENATE.

The Senate was called to order at 3½ o'clock, P. M., by the SPEAKER.

Mr. NICHOLS, from the Committee on Railroads, reported, with an affirmative recommendation, an act relative to the bridges over the Wissahickon Creek, on the Philadelphia, Germantown and Norristown Railroad, (allowing the company to fill in certain of the spans with earth.)

Bills Introduced.

Mr. CONNELL read a bill relative to the culverts of Philadelphia.

Mr. REILLY, an act extending the charter of the Miners' Bank of Pottsville.

Mr. NICHOLS, a supplement to the act for the arrest of professional thieves in Philadelphia.

Mr. LOWRY, joint resolutions protesting against the enlargement of the canals of New York at the expense of the General Government.

Mr. BOUGHTER, an act extending the charter of the Harrisburg Bank. Also,

An act extending the charter of the Bank of Lebanon.

Exempts from the Draft.

Resolutions were adopted, calling upon the Adjutant-General to furnish the Senate with the number of persons who were exempted from the draft in each county on account of conscientious scruples.

League Island.

A resolution was also adopted authorizing a committee to be appointed, by the Speaker, to proceed to Washington, and urge upon the Government the acceptance of League Island as a Naval Depot.

Mr. CONNELL read a bill making the offices of member of the Legislature and of City Council incompatible. This bill was passed.

The Senate then adjourned.

HOUSE OF REPRESENTATIVES.

The House was called to order at 7½ P. M., by Speaker CESSNA.

Bills Introduced.

Mr. BROWN (Northumberland), an act requiring administrators, trustees and others to file with the County Prothonotary a copy of their respective accounts.

Mr. KERNS, a supplement to the act incorporating the city of Philadelphia.

Mr. BROWN (Mercer), an act relative to the payment of the State Militia.

Committee of the Whole.

The House then went into Committee of the Whole on Senate resolutions providing for the appointment of a committee of three from the Senate and five from the House, to proceed to Washington, accompanied by the Governor, to urge the acceptance of League Island as a proper place for the establishment of a naval depot. The committee reported the resolutions, which was then passed by the House substantially as above.

The House then adjourned.

FROM GEN. ROSECRANS' ARMY.

MURFREESBORO', TENNESSEE, January 26.—Gen. ROSECRANS hopes that the newspapers of Cincinnati, Louisville, and other cities will desist from the practice of publishing reports of the shipment of supplies to the department of the Cumberland, such publications being substantially a notification to the Rebels to prepare their forces for the capture of the supplies. It is understood, however, that the newspapers would not make such announcements if the quartermasters and commissaries did not furnish the items.

WHEELER's Rebel Cavalry made a dash at a train of cars, on Sunday, on the railroad between Nashville and Franklin, and succeeded in destroying two cars, but they were frightened away before destroying the balance of the train.

A convalescent Rebel soldier, who was riding in one of the cars, was killed, and a Sergeant of the United States troops was badly wounded.

Brigadier-General D. S. STANLEY followed the Rebels sharply, but they had too much a start of him. He rode a distance of fifty-two miles in twenty hours.

The Rebel cavalry, in considerable bodies, are constantly hovering on our flanks, watching our communication. The Government ought to reinforce our cavalry arm of this department, and supply horses to mount the infantry regiments in order that they may be able to pursue the Rebels.

The Rebel General WHEELER has been made a Major-General, and placed in command of the Rebel cavalry in Tennessee.

Captain ELMORE OTIS, of the Fourth United States Cavalry, who distinguished himself conspicuously in the successful charges on the enemy in the battle of Stone's river, and who now commands a brigade of cavalry, has been recommended by General ROSECRANS for a Brigadier-Generalship; also, Colonel STANLEY, and all the officers of his brigade, for promotion.

Brig.-General GARFIELD, who whipped HUMPHREY MARSHALL in Eastern Kentucky, and afterwards distinguished himself in command of a brigade at Shiloh, has reported to General ROSECRANS for duty. He will, probably, be assigned to command a division of the army of the Cumberland.

Brigadier-General R. W. JOHNSON, during the absence of General McCOOK, commands the right wing, and Brigadier-General GRANGER commands General ROSECRANS' old division.

It is reported that the enemy are being reinforced.

An intercepted letter from a member of General BRAGG's staff indicates that the feeling against BRAGG is so strong that he will be superseded. The writer admits that, notwithstanding the Rebels captured most of the guns, and several thousand prisoners from us, they were badly whipped. He says the slaughter of their officers was awful; and although the fighting of the Rebel army was splendid, they were beaten by superior Generalship and the obstinacy of the Yankees.

The weather continues stormy, and the rivers are swelling.

Dr. E. SWIFT, United States Army, Medical Director of this Department, whose services are almost invaluable, will be strongly recommended for promotion to rank as Lieutenant-Colonel.

Late Charleston News.

From files of Charleston papers from January 1st to 12th, received at THE INQUIRER office, we extract the following items:—

BRITISH DEMAND FOR ADMIRAL WILKES.—We learn by a private letter from Nassau that it is stated there upon the best authority that the British Government has formally demanded of the United States the recall of Admiral WILKES from his present station. Our readers will already have noticed that the English fleet in that quarter has lately been much increased. There can be no doubt that the Yankee Government will back out in this as meanly as it did in the case of the *Trent*.

THE REWARD FOR GENERAL BUTLER'S HEAD.—TEN THOUSAND DOLLARS REWARD! $10,000!—President DAVIS having proclaimed BENJAMIN F. BUTLER, of Massachusetts, to be a FELON, deserving of capital punishment, for the deliberate murder of WILLIAM B. MUMFORD, a citizen of the Confederate States, at New Orleans, and having ordered that the said BENJAMIN F. BUTLER be considered or treated as an OUTLAW and COMMON ENEMY OF MANKIND, and that, in the event of his capture, *the officer in command of the capturing force do cause him* TO BE IMMEDIATELY EXECUTED BY HANGING, the undersigned hereby offers A REWARD OF TEN THOUSAND ($10,000) DOLLARS for the capture and delivery of the said BENJAMIN F. BUTLER, DEAD OR ALIVE, to any proper CONFEDERATE AUTHORITY.

Charleston, S. C., Jan. 1. RICHARD YEADON.

SOUTHERN ESTIMATION OF THE STARS AND STRIPES.—Friday, 9th instant, was the second anniversary of that memorable event, the arrival of the *Star of the West*, Captain McGOWAN, off Charleston harbor, and the firing of the opening ball of the war, by the gallant cadets of the Citadel Academy. This was the first overt act of cowardly duplicity and artifice on the part of the Yankees, cunningly devised and designed under cover of peace to provoke and force the South to an act which would give the North a pretext for a howl about "the flag." The old rag for which Yankeedom is so indignantly exercised that the off scourings of the cesspools of European turbulence are engaged for its defence, was never dishonored while it was in the keeping of the South.—*Courier, Jan. 12.*

UNKNOWN ENEMIES ABOUT.—We learn, that as the train from Savannah to this city was on its way yesterday, a large log was discovered thrown across the track, near Coosawatchie, with the evident intention of throwing the cars off and periling the lives of those on board. No clue of the villainous perpetrator of this outrage has been arrived at, but a sharp lookout will be kept, and if the guilty wretch is discovered, it may lead to summary punishment.—*Courier, Jan. 6.*

Interesting from North Carolina.

NEWBERN, N. C., Jan. 17, via FORTRESS MONROE, Jan. 24.—The President of the Free Labor Association of Craven, Carteret, Hyde and Beaufort counties, has received letters from prominent Northern statesmen, irrespective of party, expressing the warmest commendation of their object and principles. They are also assured of the hearty sympathy of the President of the United States. Notwithstanding Governor STANLEY's persistent opposition to the movement, it is rapidly gaining strength. It already includes the entire First North Carolina Regiment. Hon. C. H. FOSTER, Free Labor champion of North Carolina, was serenaded last night by the band of the Fifth Massachusetts Regiment.

A movement is on foot to ask authority of Congress for the formation of ten loyal regiments in North Carolina, the material for which is abundant. The following resolutions were adopted by the First North Carolina Union Volunteers:—

"*Resolved*, That one JENNINGS PIGOTT, now claiming a seat as Representative from this District, who came down to Newbern a few weeks ago from Washington, D. C., where he has been 'Claim Agent' for fifteen years, for the purpose of getting elected to Congress, through Governor STANLEY's aid, and by promises to Secessionists to return their slaves and indemnify them for their losses, and by sympathizing with them generally, and denouncing free labor as Abolitionism, while he himself, at his home, in the District of Columbia, professes to be an Abolitionist, has earned the contempt of all decent men, and richly merits a coat of tar and feathers and a free ride on a rail, should he ever revisit North Carolina.

"*Resolved*, That as native citizens of North Carolina, and loyal men who have taken up arms for the Union, we claim the right to have something to say, as to who shall represent this District. And, inasmuch as the majority of our regiment were disfranchised through the trickery of Governor STANLEY and his confederates, and, with the exception of some fifty or sixty of our members, no opportunity given us to vote, we protest against the recognition of the election."

NEWBERN, N. C., 15th inst. via FORTRESS MONROE, Sunday January 25.—The following is among the resolutions adopted to-day by the Carteret County Free Labor Association:—

Resolved, That EDWARD STANLEY's attempted suppression of the freedom of the press by menaces of summary punishments of correspondents, and by threats to arrest and imprison any and all persons whatsoever who shall dare to speak or write in censure of his course, is in derogation of public liberty, and hostile to the fundamental principles of republican government.

Dr. JOHN M. DAVIES, Assistant Surgeon, Ninth New Jersey Volunteers, has been appointed Post Surgeon here.

New York Legislature.

MR. CALLICOTT ELECTED SPEAKER.

ALBANY, Jan. 26.—The Assembly has at length succeeded in effecting its organization. According to the agreement made before the adjournment on Saturday evening, the Assembly this morning proceeded to a ballot for Speaker, and Mr. CALLICOTT (Union Democrat), of Brooklyn, the Republican candidate, was selected.

All the Republican nominees for officers of the Assembly were elected.

A resolution was introduced charging Mr. CALLICOTT with bribery, corruption, &c.

After a long debate, the Assembly adjourned without action.

Honors to General Fitz John Porter.

NEW YORK, Jan. 26.—The Common Council of this city to-day adopted a resolution, requesting the counsel of General FITZ JOHN PORTER to furnish them with the full evidence in the late trial by court-martial, and tendering General PORTER the hospitalities of the city, and a reception in the Governor's room.

LETTER FROM CAIRO, ILLINOIS.

Special Correspondence of the Inquirer.

CAIRO, Jan. 23, 1863.

Dismissed the Service.

The late calamitous and almost unpardonable exploit of Colonel R. C. MURPHY, in surrendering Holly Springs to the Rebels, along with a large supply of stores and other valuable United States property, has been very properly and promptly punished by General GRANT, by the dismissal of the delinquent officer from the Government service. This righteous recompense of imbecility and unworthiness should not end here. Men like MURPHY and General DAVIES, who, upon the least pretext, are guilty of most heinous offences against the country, and who cast disgrace upon our noble volunteer soldiery, cannot too quickly be purged from the pay rolls. By the way, I learn that General ASBOTH, one of General FREMONT's foreign appointees, has already taken the seat of the latter General, DAVIES, who could not recover from the fright which caused him to spike guns and destroy ammunition when there was not the least use of it—and that DAVIES is under arrest by the Washington authorities. A few more such dismissals and arrests would not hurt the standing of our army in the West—nor in the East, either, for that matter.

The Arkansas Post Prisoners.

The prisoners taken on the occasion of General McCLERNAND's successful movement on Arkansas Post, to the number of four thousand seven hundred and twenty, arrived here yesterday, laden in rather compact masses upon three river steamers, the *Nebraska*, *John J. Roe* and *Sam. Gaty*. They were not as bad a looking set of men as were captured at Fort Donelson last year, and not quite as dirty in their dress and habits. But they were far from being what my fancy had painted the "Southern chivalry" to be. Uncouth, long, lean, lantern-jawed, tobacco-chewing, whisky-soaking fellows, as a general thing, they seemed to have but very little of the traits of manhood left about them. There were exceptions, however. Among these were General CHURCHILL and some of his staff, who were crowded upon the *John J. Roe*, the ladies' cabin of which appeared as though nobody would hereafter venture within its shabby bulkheads.

General CHURCHILL is somewhat of a gentleman, rather tall and thin, but possessing some of the habits and appearances, in his *personnel*, of a person of education and refinement. He was born in Louisville, Kentucky; at an early age became a resident of St. Louis, Missouri, and there remained until the breaking out of the Rebellion, when he quickly identified himself with the Secession element of the State. He raised some troops, entered the service, and fought at Wilson's Creek, and various other points in Missouri; and, latest, at Springfield, where he was Acting Brigadier-General, and where his command was almost entirely cut up. Since that affair, he has been made a Brigadier-General in fact, and placed in charge of Arkansas Post. He defended that place as well as he could against the assailants, and is now going back to St. Louis, his old home, a prisoner of war. He thinks that had the Union assault been delayed one day longer, he would have had a force within the fort which would have defied all our efforts towards its reduction. But, for once, our army moved swiftly, and conquered by moving swiftly. Gen. CHURCHILL says that he does not place his loss, killed and wounded, at less than two hundred. He had nine regiments. We captured 4720. Thus it would seem their regiments had been greatly reduced by death, desertion and capture.

The prisoners appeared to be in fine spirits, and conversed with Union soldiers and officers, standing upon the levee, quite freely. They were semi-comfortably, but shabbily clad, and appeared to have been poorly fed for some months past.

General G. B. McPherson.

Among the Generals at Memphis, the *Bulletin* of the 20th mentions General McPHERSON in the following flattering terms:—

"We understand that Major-General McPHERSON and staff arrived in the city last evening, and are quartered at the Gayoso House.

"General McPHERSON is one of the most distinguished officers in this Department. At Fort Henry and Fort Donelson and Shiloh he was Chief Engineer on the staff of Major-General GRANT, and earned distinction in each engagement. He is a young man, not over thirty-two years of age, and is now assigned to the command of one of the army corps in General GRANT's Department."

Gen. McArthur's Division

Moved from Memphis southward, by river, on the 19th, and four or five other divisions, including Generals QUIMBY and McPHERSON's, are preparing to move, the steamers having been congregated there for the purpose. It is not generally known where this movement is to be directed, but it is generally believed that it will join in the advance of the old expedition upon Vicksburg, which it will reinforce. Gen. GRANT has been down the river, held a conference with other Generals, and returned to Memphis. He is now very busy preparing to come and take the command of the expedition, at least so rumor has it, although we have had no official information of the fact that he proposes superseding Gen. McCLERNAND. Gen. McCLERNAND was appointed to the command of the former expedition, but failed to reach the point in time to become responsible for that failure. He may continue in charge of the movement now in progress, though, unless some one be especially sent on for the purpose, one would naturally suppose that General GRANT would supersede, as he does outrank him.

Cotton in Memphis.

The last news from Memphis reported cotton coming in quite freely from the newly opened Memphis and Charleston Railroad, and the portion of the Memphis and Tennessee road so recently explored by Colonel LEE's cavalry force. The price, on the 20th, was going up somewhat, and had, indeed, reached the figure above fifty when my informant left. A case was mentioned to me, a day or two since, where a man named STEWART had purchased a lot of three hundred bales, for which he paid an average of *sixty cents* per pound. This may, perhaps, be set down as the highest price yet paid for cotton this season.

General GRANT has just issued an order which is to be put in force in his entire district, which, while it will cause some speculators to grumble terribly, will be the means of adding to the comfort of our sick soldiers, and leave quite a surplus to be devoted to the secret service fund, a fund which our General will undoubtedly wield with proper judgment. The order provides that every person engaged in cotton buying in the district shall first take out a permit, for which the sum of one hundred dollars will be charged by the Provost Marshal granting the same. All other rules in regard to permits are rescinded. Traders in auction goods, where the civil authorities do not prescribe the license, and have control over the matter, are also to be charged the same sum for permits. Several persons had already taken out these permits on the 20th, and more seemed willing to do so. Those who were found grumbling, and who refused to take out the permit—especially those engaged in so profitable a business as purchasing cotton—may safely be set down as disloyal persons, to whom no courtesies should be extended. In fact, the order prescribes such, and makes their arrest incumbent upon the officers of the district in which they may be found.

The Election.

I believe that in former letters mention has been made of the Congressional election having been postponed to the 20th of the present month. Governor JOHNSON has recently been petitioned by loyal citizens of Tennessee to further postpone the election until August next, when a provision of the State statute makes it incumbent upon the people to elect a Governor and other State officials. But some tricksters in Memphis, who thought they had all the plans arranged for their full success, prevailed upon General VEACH, the new commandant there, to allow the election to proceed, even pending an expected answer from Governor JOHNSON to General GRANT's telegram. And hence there was a sham of an election on the 20th, but its results, whatever they may be, cannot be called an expression of the loyal citizens of the congressional district and the member elected, whoever he may be, should not—and probably will not—be admitted to a seat at Washington. There is no doubt of his possessing brass enough to make a trial to that end, should any one be elected. For any man who had not sense enough to see that an election, to be an election, should be held by consent of the voters, as well as by order of a General commanding, would certainly not be wanting in impudence enough to carry him to Washington, even though he had no hope of admittance, and merely expected to be sent back for his pains, but with *his mileage!*

One of the candidates for Congressional honors, B. D. NABERS, came out in a manly manner, in a card, refusing to let his name go before the people under such a state of affairs. Another, Mr. TOMENY, published a card, in which he avowed his determination to "run" at all hazards, and setting forth his patriotism and Union principles, which no one doubted before, in as strong a light as possible. A third, a Chicago ex-publisher, and since lumber dealer, says nothing, keeps quiet, pulls the wires, and probably will be the brassy man who will, ere long, be found hanging at the doors of Congress.

The Philadelphia Inquirer.

CIRCULATION OVER 60,000. | PHILADELPHIA, WEDNESDAY, FEBRUARY 11, 1863. | PRICE TWO CENTS.

THE VERY LATEST WAR NEWS

From the Army of the Potomac.

LEBANON (TENN.) OCCUPIED BY UNION TROOPS.

Capture of Six Hundred Rebels.

THE WAR ON THE MISSISSIPPI.

Exploit of the Steamer "Queen of the West."

A Supposed Pirate off the Balize.

AN EXCITEMENT AT WINCHESTER.

Capture of a Stage and Passengers by the Rebels.

THE VOICE OF ILLINOIS SOLDIERS.

The Fifth Pennsylvania Cavalry in a Skirmish.

MARRIAGE OF THE DWARFS TOM THUMB AND LAVINIA WARREN.

FROM WASHINGTON.

Special Despatches to the Inquirer.

WASHINGTON, Feb. 10.

General Burnside and the Army of the Potomac.

Since General BURNSIDE has been here, he again tendered his services to the War Department, and stated to the Secretary that he would not retain his commission unless he was assigned to a command. He said he had confidence in General HOOKER's ability and intention to take Richmond, and offered to take command of his old corps under General HOOKER, if the Department thought it best for the interests of the country.

He considers the forces of the Rebels much weakened by desertion, sickness and their reinforcing other points; and that the forces under HOOKER are ample for the purpose, and he entertains no doubts of his success, if he can only secure the confidence of his officers, and is allowed the privilege of weeding out the weak, cowardly and treacherous officers, and by rigid discipline, reforming the entire *morale* of the army. The Department have, however, concluded to give him the command of a most important department South, and as soon as the proper steps are taken we will announce his destination.

A Diplomatic Rumor.

It is stated in diplomatic circles that correspondence has been going on for some time between Secretary SEWARD and the French Government, looking to mediation or arbitration. With a view of ascertaining this fact, Senator FOSTER, to-day, after conference with a number of Senators, introduced the following:—

Resolved, That the President be requested, if not incompatible with the public interests, to lay before the Senate any correspondence which has taken place between this Government and France, on the subject of mediation, arbitration, or other measures looking to a termination of the existing civil war.

The Sherman Bank Bill.

Senator SHERMAN succeeded in having all amendments hostile to his bank bill voted down to-day. He made one of the ablest speeches yet delivered upon financial matters, and as he is known to be the representative of Secretary CHASE, his arguments were attentively listened to. It is thought the bill will pass to-morrow. The House bill, as amended by the Senate, will then come up; but as it will occasion considerable discussion, it will hardly pass this week.

Bill Increasing Major and Brigadier-Generals.

The Senate Military Committee to-day authorized the Chairman to report a bill for the appointment of thirty Major and seventy Brigadier-Generals. It is understood that selections will be made from fifty Major and one hundred and fifty Brigadier-Generals, now before the Committee for confirmation.

The New Orleans Telegraph.

The Senate Military Committee will consider, to-morrow morning, the House bill for a telegraph cable coastwise to New Orleans. The committee will hardly act upon it this session, owing to other important measures occupying all their time, and the project being deemed impracticable. There is no reliability in the foreign cable, and we have no factory in this country capable of making it in time.

Nominations.

The President, to-day, sent the following nominations to the Senate:—Paymasters, with rank of Major—JAMES R. TOFFLAND, of Delaware; HIRAM S. SLOOPER, Kansas; DAVID M. ADAMS, Kansas; T. H. STANTON, Iowa. Subsistence Department, with rank of Captain—JOSEPH P. LOUGHEAD, Pennsylvania. Quartermasters, with rank of Captain—First Lieutenant GEORGE W. MEADE, New York.

Secretary Seward and Le Minister Mercier.

Secretary SEWARD will send in to-morrow to the Senate an answer to the resolution calling for information as to his conversation, &c., with Count MERCIER prior to his visit to Richmond.

"Big Snakes," alias Big Swindles.

The air-line swindle, the big canal, little canal, ship canal and numerous other schemes for the depletion of the Treasury, are now considered defunct, but we have no doubt that vigorous efforts will be made to pass them all; but the friends of separate schemes have lost all confidence in one another, and personal wrangles are of daily occurrence.

The New Orleans Members of Congress.

The New Orleans Members, Messrs. FLANDERS and HAHN, will probably be admitted by a very small majority.

The Post Office Bill.

Senator COLLAMER succeeded to-day in passing his Post Office bill, but it is feared the lateness of the session will prevent its passage through the House.

Pacific Railroad.

Senator MCDOUGALL introduced his Pacific Railroad Bill to-day, amended as telegraphed you a few days ago. It will come up for action on the disposition of finance measures.

Additional Volunteer Generals.

The Senate Military Committee, in the bill reported for that purpose, recommend thirty Major-Generals and seventy Brigadiers, in addition to the present number in the army.

The Agricultural Department.

The House Committee on Agriculture have prepared a bill more particularly to define the duties and grade of officers of the Agricultural Department. It authorizes the appointment, in addition to the chief clerk, a botanist, chemist and entomologist, at $2000 salary each; a disbursing clerk and chief of statistics, at $1800 each; a translator and draughtsman, at $1400 each, and six clerks at $1200 each.

Naval Order.

Lieutenant-Commander FRANCIS H. BAKER has been ordered to temporary duty on board the receiving ship *Princeton*.

CHARLESTON AND ITS DEFENCES.

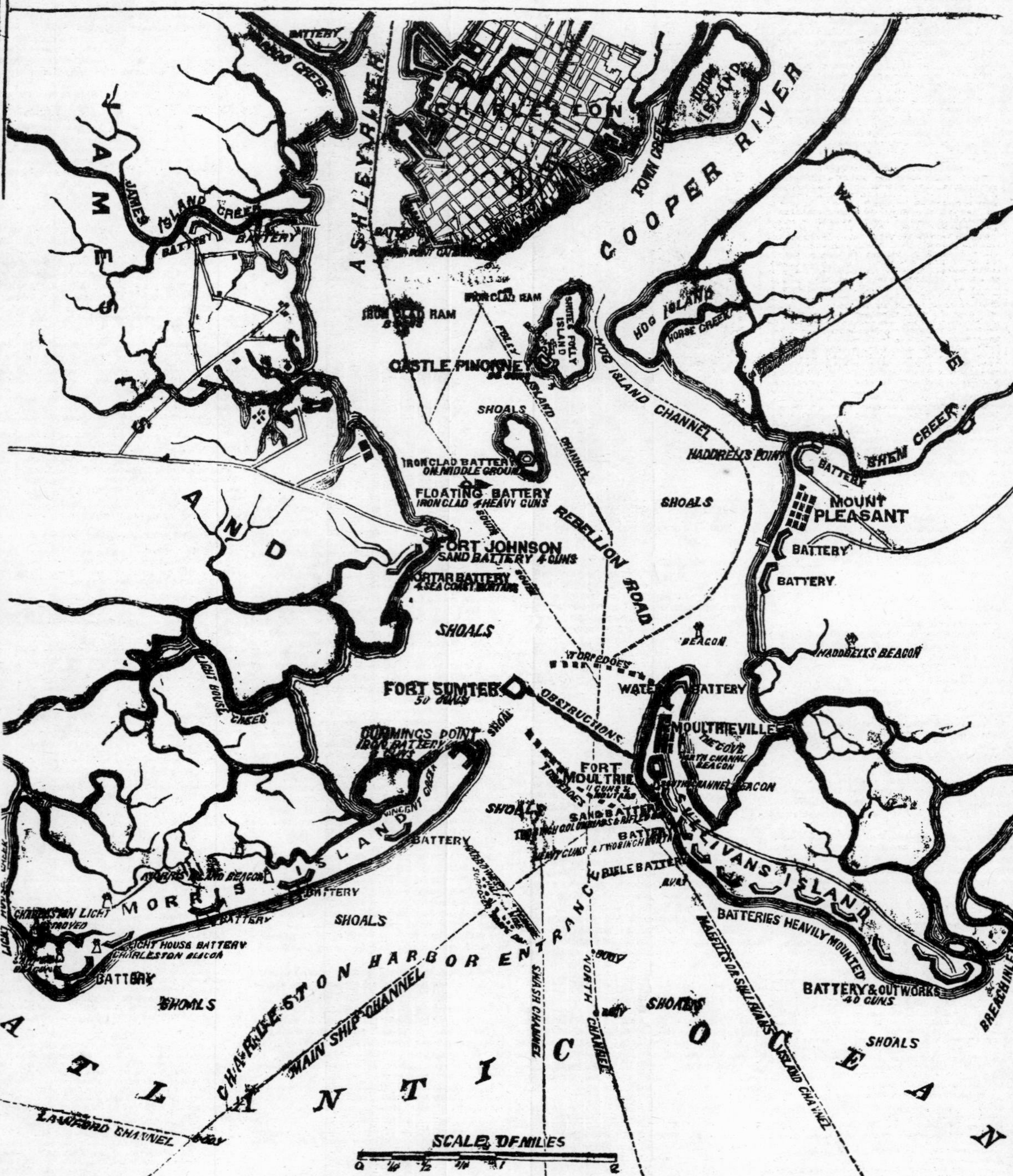

Capture of Contraband Goods.

A portion of Col. BAKER's detective corps last night seized 168 cases of boots and shoes, *in transitu* across the Potomac, from Leonardstown, Md., destined for the South. The goods and smugglers were sent to Washington under guard. The Secesh contraband trade is still carried on, there is no doubt, notwithstanding the frequent arrests of parties engaged in it.

The Attack on Fort McAllister.

From what is said here in well-informed circles, Captain WORDEN's object in proceeding to Fort McAllister with the *Montauk*, was not to reduce that work, but merely to test the effect of shot upon the turret of his vessel, upon which the Rebel steel-pointed projectiles had no injurious effect whatever. His proceeding in that quarter in nearly demolishing the Rebel parapet, &c., was not specified in the original programme.

The Sale of Condemned Vessels.

The Secretary of the Treasury has, in response to inquiry, transmitted a statement from the Collector of New York of the sales of vessels condemned under the act of July 18th, 1862. They are:—The schooners *Geneva, Mary C. Hopkins, W. H. Raritan, Claremont, Sunny South, Mobile* and *Virginia*; the barque *Bounding Billow*; brigs *Mary McRau, Gen. Bailey* and *Fanny*; and ships *John Cattle, Liberty* and *Sebastian Cabot*. The amount of sales was $7410, of which the United States received $1754.

Military Depot at Washington.

The Secretary of War has addressed a letter to the Senate Military Committee urging immediate action on the bill before them for the purchase of a site for an army and military depot at Washington.

A Senator from California Elected.

SAN FRANCISCO, Feb. 9.—On the first ballot for United States Senator to-night, by the Legislature at Sacramento, the vote stood—CONNESS, 59; SARGENT, 32; PHELPS, 1, and BROWN, 6. Mr. CONNESS was then declared unanimously elected.

SAN FRANCISCO, Feb. 10.—JOHN CONNESS was finally elected Senator, receiving 98 out of the 114 votes. He was formerly a Douglas Democrat, and latterly a member of the Union party.

The unrelenting feud between the friends of Congressman PHELPS and Mr. SARGENT prevented the election of a Senator of Republican antecedents, in accordance with the political bias of a large majority of the Legislature.

A fire occurred in Virginia city, Washoe county, to-day. Loss $30,000.

The money market is easy. Atlantic currency and exchange, 45 ⅌ cent. discount; gold, 5 to 6 premium; sterling exchange, 47@47¼ premium; legal tender, 64@65 discount.

The general market is slightly better with an increased demand for candles, coffee, butter and sugar.

The ship *Golden Fleece* has been chartered for a cargo of wheat for Liverpool.

EXCITEMENT AT WINCHESTER.

Capture of a Stage and Passengers by the Guerrillas—One of their Number Killed and Two Captured.

Correspondence of the Inquirer.

WINCHESTER, VA., Feb. 7th, 1863.
THIRTEENTH PENNSYLVANIA CAVALRY.

The town of Winchester, this evening, was thrown into great consternation. Lieutenant BURKHARDT, of General CROSELEY's Staff, passed down Main street, on horseback, in great haste, nearly breathless, and announced—"the stage and passengers are captured by the bushwhackers; I have barely escaped; I was a passenger in the stage," and passed directly on to the head-quarters of General MILROY.

Preparations were immediately made for a recapture, and in an hour's time five companies (Companies D, F and H of the Thirteenth Pennsylvania Cavalry; Company K, First Virginia Cavalry, and one company of New York Cavalry) were in the saddle and distributed upon the different roads.

About 1 o'clock this morning the stage was brought in without horses, and a trunk without its contents; since which the horses have been recaptured, Captain DIETRICH retaken, with Mr. KEYSER (the driver) and all the passengers, among whom were two ladies. A portion of the harness was found in the fields near Berryaville.

The banditti consisted of seven bushwhackers, under the charge of Sergeant-Major TIMBERLAKE. Two of his men have been taken prisoners and one killed.

JOHN C. ZELLER, the agent of the line, has made preparation to continue running the line, without a day's interruption.

It is generally conceded that the bushwhackers were on the look out for the Paymaster, as it was rumored he was coming from Martinsburg on that day.

Murder Trial at Trenton.

TRENTON, Feb. 10.—The trial of CHARLES LEWIS, for the murder of JAMES ROWAND, of Princeton, is progressing. The prisoner is ably defended by EDWARD JAMES and THOMAS DAUPHY, of New York, and Mr. BANGHARDT, of Jersey City. The defence relies principally on the cross-examination, which is conducted with great adroitness. The case is one of the most difficult character, the evidence being entirely circumstantial, and pointing strongly to the prisoner. Much reliance is placed on the ability of counsel to save him. Eight witnesses have been examined.

General Pope's Department.

MILWAUKIE, Feb. 10.—General POPE's Head-quarters for the Department of the Northwest, has been removed to this city.

Ogdensburg Municipal Election.

OGDENSBURG, N. Y., Feb. 10.—The whole Democratic ticket was elected to-day by an average majority of 75.

IMPORTANT FROM YORKTOWN.

The Fifth Pennsylvania Cavalry Drawn into an Ambuscade—Death of Capt. Faith.

FORTRESS MONROE, Feb. 9.—Mr. G. B. DAVIDS, for a long time Manager of the Government Machine Shop at Old Point, has been appointed Inspector of iron-clad gun-boats, and left for New York city last evening.

YORKTOWN, Feb. 9, 1863.—During last week a number of Rebels have been taken prisoners, and others have deserted and come within our lines at this place. Last Saturday five Rebel deserters came in, and reported sixteen others awaiting an opportunity to come in. Major KLINZ ordered out Captain FAITH, Company M Fifth Pennsylvania Cavalry, and Captain HAGEMASTER, Company L, ——. Lieutenant WILLIAMS and Lieutenant GEORGE SMITH volunteered and accompanied the squadron. They reached the six-mile ordinary without opposition or discovering the sixteen Rebels desirous of joining them.

The enemy's pickets stationed there retired before them, and Captain FAITH, without orders, pushed forward after them. Just this side of the nine mile ordinary, he, with his command, was drawn into an ambuscade and fired upon. He was brought off supposed mortally wounded. Capt. HAGERMASTER, upon whom the command devolved, fought like a hero. He charged upon and broke through the enemy's line, but got separated from his men and taken prisoner. Lieutenants WILLIAMS, SMITH and LITTLE were taken prisoners, and Lieutenant RHINEMILLER was seen to fall from his horse, supposed killed. Our entire loss was thirty killed, wounded and missing. The enemy's loss is unknown. The enemy is reported in some force at Burnt Ordinary, twelve miles from Williamsburg.

LATEST FROM KEY WEST.

Threatened Raid by Rebel Gun-boats—The "Alabama" Repairing Her Damages.

KEY WEST, Feb. 4th, 1863.—The steamer *Matanzas*, from Hilton Head, arrived in the harbor yesterday, with the Ninetieth Regiment N. Y. Volunteers, Col. JOSEPH S. MORGAN. The troops are sent to relieve the Forty-seventh Pennsylvania, Colonel GOOD. The latter, to the number of six hundred (six companies), return to Hilton Head, while four companies, in command of Lieutenant-Colonel ALEXANDER, remain at Fort Jefferson, to garrison that important point.

The United States steamer *Huntsville*, Lieutenant ROGERS, has arrived from Apalachicola.

It was believed on board our gun-boats blockading the Bay of Apalachiola that a formidable expedition was organizing on the Chattahoochee river, having for its object their destruction. It was generally believed that an iron-clad steamer was to take part in the expedition.

We have no further news from the *Florida*.

The *Alabama* was, at last accounts, repairing the damages she sustained in her conflict with the *Hatteras*. She was badly disabled, and lost her rudder. Six balls were put through her.

The steamer *Octorara*, Captain COLLINS, is in port, making some repairs to her machinery.

The schooner *Two Sisters* has just arrived with a prize captured off the Marquesas.

Admiral BAILEY's squadron are nearly all at sea and supposed to be in search of the *Florida* and *Alabama*.

The materials saved from the ship *Sparkling Sea* have been sold by the Marshal and amount to the sum of $7,442. The Admiralty Court have decreed salvage to the amount of fifty per cent. The hull of the ship has been sold to J. F. PACKER, Esq., for $75.

The schooner *Sarah Jane*, of this port, has been sold to parties in Havana for the sum of $4,600. She is to be employed in transporting stores for the French Army in Mexico from Havana to Tobasco.

THE WAR IN TENNESSEE.

Federal Occupation of Lebanon, Tennessee—Six Hundred Rebels Captured.

NASHVILLE, Feb. 10.—Our forces entered Lebanon, Tennessee, on the 8th. They captured some 600 Rebels, most of them being men of MORGAN's command. Many field officers were taken. Among the prisoners is PAUL ANDERSON, a violent member of the State Legislature of 1860 and 1862. He was an original Secessionist and one of the earliest advocates of the Southern Confederacy.

Over one hundred wounded reached here by the cars from Murfreesboro' to-night.

A number of Paymasters left for the front this morning.

The first train for Murfreesboro' will leave here to-morrow.

The river is six feet on the shoals and falling. The rain is now falling heavily.

A Supposed Pirate off the Balize.

NEW ORLEANS, Jan. 30.—On the evening of the 23d, a steamer, rigged as a barque, with a rakish appearance, came in sight of the Southwest Pass. She had nothing above the topmasts, and moved slowly by the Pass, apparently watching for signals, or expecting some. A number of the Pass pilots are now under arrest for communicating with a strange vessel some days since, and it is supposed further attempts will be made, preparatory to a raid on the river.

The schooner captured off the Sabine Pass by the Rebels was the transport *Velocity*. At the time of the capture a dead calm prevailed.

FROM THE ARMY OF THE POTOMAC

Special Correspondence of the Inquirer.

What Are We Going To Do?

STAFFORD COURT HOUSE, Va., Feb. 9, 1863.

In the absence of anything very absorbing, the attention reverts to what may be done in the future. An impression has firmly planted itself in the minds of many here, that the Army of the Potomac will be virtually dissolved, and transferred to some other locality where a more effective blow can be struck. Many have grown strong in this belief, from the fact that the Ninth, BURNSIDE's old corps, embarked from Aquia Creek Station, on transports, for some point southward during the past two days. Whether their opinion be correct, time alone can determine; but it is hardly likely that it is, as there is but little probability that those high in authority, who hold the military reins, will slacken them enough to allow the withdrawal of any considerable number of our troops from this locality as long as so many armed Rebels remain in Virginia.

There is much to confirm the statements that the Rebels have withdrawn some of their forces from the vicinity of Fredericksburg. But notwithstanding this, the Rebels are still strong and well fortified in our front. They evince a determination to remain as long as our army continues to be opposite to them.

Why we should abandon the field to the enemy at this point, no plausible reason can be given. Some urge that at other points he can be more easily attacked and weakened. This is undoubtedly so, but would anything justify the weakening of our army here to strengthen it at some other point?

Some opine that SIGEL will be sent to the West. Sometime since the General submitted a plan for the taking of Vicksburg, and from this many infer that he may be sent to co-operate with the forces in that locality.

The Changes.

In accordance with General Orders, No. 6, issued by General HOOKER, General SIGEL has resumed the command of the Eleventh Corps.

Brigadier-General STAHL, who commanded the corps during the period in which the Grand Reserve Division existed, resumes command of the First Division of the Eleventh Corps.

Generals SCHURZ and STEINWEHR retain their former positions.

General SIGEL has tendered his thanks to General SLOCUM, of the Twelfth Corps, for assistance and co-operation whilst serving under his command.

General SLOCUM now reports direct to General HOOKER.

The Late Rebel Raids.

Considerable talk has been occasioned consequent upon the late Rebel raids. The audacity of the Rebel cavalry is only equalled by their foolhardiness. If one or two raids by far superior numbers upon small parties of our men and pickets succeed, all may not!

The Secesh may themselves meet with a greater surprise than they have visited us with. Though they condescend to perform many base actions, of which we would not be guilty, an unexpected and humiliating capturing of them by us will take place when they least look for it. On several occasions they have missed their mark, and were made to share the fate of those whom they thought would be their captives.

War is a deep game, but by their cavalry it is played upon a paltry scale.

Though they may feel elated and speak of their achievements in glowing words, what honorable man will admit the capturing of a relief picket post, at the dead hours of night, and the wounding of the men patroling, are achievements. This is the manner in which the Rebels expect to gain prestige, but there is little honor in attacking pickets.

Whilst speaking of the late sad affair which occurred to the Seventeenth Pennsylvania Cavalry, it reflects but little credit upon those who have the posting of cavalry pickets and patrols. A reserve ought always to be near, in case of an emergency.

It is hardly five miles from here where the raid was made. To say nothing of the capture of seventeen horses and twelve men, the wounding and killing of unsuspecting pickets calls for a change of some kind, which will prevent a repetition of the sad affair.

The attack upon the foraging party of ours that started from the "Spotted Tavern," was less cowardly, though shabby enough. The bushwhackers that emerged from the woods so slyly were repulsed by a number far inferior to their own. They were compelled to retreat and seek shelter from the vengeance of those whom they assaulted. Both parties sustained some injury, but, undoubtedly, the Rebels were worsted, though they little expected it.

It is somewhat singular that the forests are still left open to the roving banditti to commit depredations upon both citizens and soldiers. It is time that the whole country should be thoroughly scoured for many miles around, and summary punishment be visited upon all that are caught acting with these dastardly rascals, who are too cowardly to enter an army and face the enemy upon a clear field.

Another Sutler's Establishment Captured.

During the early part of last week the establishment of the sutler of the Eighth New York was captured at Occoquan. The Rebels not only took his goods, but appropriated to their use his horses and wagon.

IN CAMP, NEAR FREDERICKSBURG, Feb. 8.

The cavalry in the late expedition, comprising about two hundred from the Third Pennsylvania, Colonel MCINTOSH; two hundred from the Fifth Regulars, Capt. HARRISON, and from the First Rhode Island, Lieutenant-Colonel THOMPSON, First Massachusetts, Colonel SARGEANT, and Fourth Pennsylvania, Colonel KERR, pushed through the town of Morgansburg to Bealeton, and from thence followed the line of the railroad to the Rappahannock river. Here they at once set "to work" to destroy the road bridge which spans the river near what is known as the Rappahannock Station.

Soon after emerging from the woods bordering the stream, they came in full view of the Rebel guards. Sixty men were first detailed and taken equally from each regiment of our cavalry as axemen, and after being provided with the proper implements, were marched to the centre of the bridge, and at once commenced chopping.

Up to this time not a gun had been fired by either side. As soon, however, as the "sound of the axe" was heard, the Rebels doing guard duty opened fire from their side of the stream upon us, directing their aim at those upon the bridge. But two or three of their missiles, however, fell among our men, the balance going over their heads.

The enemy thus "opening the ball," the main body of our troops dismounted and promptly returned their fire, and for nearly six hours kept up a continuous discharge of small arms, while, during all this time, the "Axemen" were busy with their chopping. The bridge in question was once before destroyed by our troops, when General POPE with his command were in occupation of that part of Virginia. It was some three hundred feet long, and from twenty-five to thirty feet high, and had been rebuilt in an unusually substantial manner. When the destroying party had so far weakened it as to permit it almost to fall by its own weight, turpentine was scattered about the entire woodwork and in the centre "set on fire, the flames spreading towards each end. So nicely had those who had been busy with the axes calculated how far to go with their chopping that the bridge, in less than five minutes after the fire was started, broke in the centre, and, with a terrific crash, sank to the bottom of the stream, each end still resting upon the abutments upon either bank. The entire structure, being soon in flames, was wholly consumed by the time our troops left the ground.

While engaged with the enemy, the Fifth Regulars, Capt. HARRISON, lost one killed and seven wounded.

While the fighting was going on some portions of this cavalry force were scouting up and down and back from the river, picking up much information of considerable value, and succeeded in capturing some thirty civilians, all of whom were known to be engaged in aiding and comforting the Rebels, by furnishing them subsistence, and giving them information respecting our strength and doings.

The object in destroying the above-named property was simply that, for the last two months, the Rebels have been using the railroad as a prominent means of supply, running sometimes as far as up to and beyond Warrenton Junction; and it has also been of service to the enemy in aiding such of their cavalry force as has been operating in our rear, in the neighborhood of Catlett's Station, Dumfries and Quantico. Should there be any of their forces in that neighborhood at the present time, they will doubtless hastily retrace their steps to a more southern clime, now that their means of sustenance is "cut off."

In addition to the small force stationed to guard the bridge now destroyed, back from the river and hid by the woods the Rebels had some five thousand troops, made up of a proportionate share of artillery, infantry and cavalry, and pretty strongly intrenched. One earthwork, mounting some six or eight guns was plainly seen from our side of the river.

Some of the scouting parties who were out with

Continued on our Last Page.

THE NEW YORK HERALD.

WHOLE NO. 9689. NEW YORK, THURSDAY, MARCH 26, 1863. PRICE THREE CENTS

THE ROYAL MARRIAGE IN ENGLAND.

The Arrival of the Princess Alexandra at Gravesend.

The Union of the Rose of England with the Flower of Denmark.

THE PROCESSION THROUGH LONDON.

The Bridal Dresses, Bridal Gifts, Bridal Cake, The Royal Carriages, &c., &c., &c.

All England was stirred, from its centre to the remotest border bounds, at the date of the sailing of the Europa, which left Liverpool on the 7th instant, in anticipation of the marriage of the Prince of Wales and the Princess Alexandra, which was to have been celebrated with regal pomp on the 10th. On the day previous to the steamer's sailing the royal squadron, convoying the Victoria Albert, royal yacht, having the Princess on board, arrived in the channel. On Saturday the Princess and royal suite arrived at Gravesend, where she was received by the Prince of Wales, amid the salvos of artillery and the most exuberant manifestations of loyalty from her future subjects.

The event is one of such universal interest that we lay before our readers full details of the reception of the Princess, the preparations for the marriage, the procession through London and the decorations along the route, with descriptions of the bridal dresses, bridal gifts, bridal cake, the royal carriages, &c.

ARRIVAL OF THE PRINCESS IN ENGLAND.

The royal yacht, having on board the Princess Alexandra with the Prince and Princess Christian, of Denmark, and other members of the royal family, arrived at Ramsgate about eleven o'clock on the night of Thursday, the 5th of March. The whole channel squadron lay off the town, and the following morning was heralded in with the booming of cannon giving a noisy welcome to the young Princess whose name is now a household word in every English home.

THE WELCOME AT RAMSGATE.

The usual formal welcome, enhanced, however, by the deep sincerity which in this case marked the ceremony, to the shores of England of its future Queen, was extended to the Princess by the Mayor and Council of Ramsgate, she having "graciously" granted them a "presence." After this ceremony was gone through the Princess walked on the deck of the royal yacht and conversed with members of the deputation. Her affability, sweetness of countenance and gracefulness of manner made a most favorable impression on the visitors from the loyal borough of Ramsgate. At three o'clock P. M. (Friday, 5th) the squadron weighed anchor and proceeded up the river.

ARRIVAL AT THE NORE.

The Victoria & Albert, royal yacht, arrived at the Gordler Deeps, at the Great Nore, at five P. M. on the same day, being accompanied by the Warrior, 40, and came immediately afterwards to anchor, the squadron following suit. A salute of twenty-one guns from the battery at Sheeburyness was then fired, followed by salutes in succession from the Formidable, 84, flagship; the Cumberland, 70, and the Leander, 51. The crews of each vessel manned yards on the royal yacht coming to anchor. A royal salute was also fired from the batteries at the Nore, by the royal artillery, and the Danish colors were hoisted. The beach at Sheerness was brilliantly illuminated, the word "Welcome" being displayed in gigantic letters formed with blue lights, which could be distinctly seen from the royal yacht. There were, besides, several large bonfires alighted along the shore.

ARRIVAL AT GRAVESEND.

The squadron sailed from its anchorage at the Nore at eight o'clock, on Saturday morning, arriving at Gravesend punctually at the appointed time. The royal yacht was immediately boarded by Admiral Johnstone, who was presented to her Royal Highness the Princess Alexandra. Soon after the Duke of Somerset and the Board of Admiralty arrived from Woolwich, and paid their respects to the Princess, who received them with easy dignity. A field battery from the Depot brigade, Royal Artillery, posted on the heights of Bristol Hill, fired a salute of twenty-one guns, followed by a salute from the saluting battery fronting the artillery barracks, which again was echoed by the broadside guns of the Fisgard on the river. Scarcely had the echoes of this last salute died away, when a field battery, drawn up at the back of the Charlton Railway station, announced by a royal salute

THE ARRIVAL OF THE PRINCE OF WALES AT GRAVESEND.

The royal train dashed into Gravesend with an impatience which was but characteristic, no doubt, of the ardor of the Prince's feelings in hurrying to meet his youthful fiance. Again the batteries and forts on shore, and the men-of-war on the river, thundered out their welcomes, and the whole fleet manned their yards on the appearance of the Prince on the deck of the royal yacht, from whence he soon after led his young bride, followed by the two royal personal suits and surrounded by a brilliant cortege. The usual civic ceremonies of welcome having been gone through, the royal party proceeded in carriages to the depot, where a special train was in waiting to convey them to London. The welcome of the people at Gravesend was as enthusiastic and exuberant as even a prince escorting his bride to her future royal home could desire. Away sped the train to London, past one continuous crowd of exultant people, halting not till it arrived at the Bricklayers' Arms station.

THE ARRIVAL IN LONDON.

The royal travellers arrived at the Bricklayers' Arms station at a quarter to two o'clock, where they were met by the Lord Mayor, the Sheriffs, the High Bailiff of Southwark, and the directors of the railway company. The Princess Alexandra, the Prince of Wales and Prince Christian, were ushered to an open carriage and four.

THE EXCITEMENT IN THE CITY.

The scene which the metropolis presented will not readily be forgotten. It may be truly said that by daybreak this morning all London was on the stir, and masses were moving in all directions to the line of route. Indeed, so great was the excitement and anxiety to see England's future Queen that thousands took up a position in the course of the night. At the early hour of six o'clock the line of route was traversed by vehicles of all descriptions, occupied by loyal subjects, who, despairing of witnessing the actual ovation, had thus contented themselves with their anticipatory glance of the reality which was to follow. As the morning advanced groups of elegantly dressed ladies were conveyed to the places arranged for them to witness the spectacle. Rifle volunteers, clad in their various uniforms of gray, green and red, were to be seen rushing in breathless haste to their different headquarters. The whole city seemed to have surrendered itself to a perfect abandonment of its commercial operations, which this day were destined to give way to the manifestation of exuberant loyalty; in a word, the metropolis and its vast population exhibited a total abnegation of its usual calling in order to give due honor to this memorable and, it is to be hoped, happy union.

As soon as the hour drew near for the arrival of the royal cortege the excitement in the metropolis became the most intense. Probably a greater multitude was never seen in the streets, and in the neighborhood of Temple Bar and London Bridge the pressure was something terrific. The line from Bricklayers' Arms station to Temple Bar was kept by the Royal Artillery, the fine band of the regiment being stationed on the south side of the bridge. The Royal Horse Guard kept the road from Temple Bar to Hyde Park.

THE PROCESSION.

From the railway station the royal party set forth in the following order:—

The Princess Alexandra, the Prince of Wales and Prince Christian, father of the royal bride, in the first carriage, drawn by four horses, escorted by a squadron of Horse Guards. The other members of the Danish royal family and their suite occupied five other royal carriages, and in this order the cortege proceeded on its route. The civic procession was the most magnificent ever witnessed in London.

THE DECORATIONS ALONG THE ROUTE.

The decorations along the line of route were far more imposing than any pageant within the memory of man. All that was of the lightness and airiness of foreign decorations, the flag and tinsel of the Boulevards, was supplied by a quality far more gratifying, the presence of myriads of the population, all anxious to give a loyal and generous welcome to a young Princess upon her arrival in the land of her adoption. The Bricklayers' Arms Station was fitted up in a very elegant and exceedingly tasteful style. Galleries, covered with crimson cloth, and festooned with garlands and flags, were erected inside the building and outside in the station yard, and were occupied by some hundreds of elegantly dressed ladies. A triumphal arch was thrown over the roadway near the entrance.

The decorations of London bridge surpassed anything that has ever been seen in this country, and the general effect was truly magnificent. Approaching the city from the Surrey side of the silent highway, the vista presented to the wondering gaze of the spectator was exceedingly grand. The parapets right and left were ornamented by the Danish national standards, supporting medallion portraits of the various monarchs who have filled the throne of that nation from the earliest period down to the reign of his present Majesty Frederick VII. The arch was of a mixed character of architecture, but each style was so blended as to produce an indescribable effect. Immediately over the carriage way are displayed the united armorial bearings of Great Britain and Denmark and right and left, over the footpaths, are medallion portraits of the Prince and Princess. Below the pediment were displayed, in silver letters, the subjoined lines, adapted from England's immortal bard:—

> Honor, riches, marriage, blessing,
> Long continuance and increasing;
> Hourly joys be still upon you,
> England showers her blessings on you.

The Fishmongers' Hall next demanded attention. The entire of its ample front has been devoted to the erection of a most spacious and elegantly constructed balcony, which to-day was graced by a galaxy of feminine beauty, whose presence, and the energy with which they waved their handkerchiefs, could not fail to gratify the fair object now the "observed of all observers."

The scene along Grace Church street and King William street was of a most exciting character. The *coup d'œil* formed by the decorations of the Mansion House was truly splendid, and the balconies, filled by most elegant company, commanded universal admiration. The scene in St. Paul's churchyard was one of a truly gorgeous character. The long line of galleries which were erected round the cathedral were most beautifully decorated with wreaths, garlands and flags, and medallions of the Prince of Wales and his youthful bride. Along Ludgate Hill and Fleet street flags and streamers waved from all points.

And so on along the whole route, the people everywhere exhibiting the most exuberant enthusiasm.

COST OF STANDS ALONG THE ROUTE.

The prices realized for sittings and windows are immense. A man in Piccadilly let first floor for £280. The same man got £450 for the whole upper part of his house. Messrs. Dakin, in St. Paul's churchyard—one of the very best situations—have let their whole window accommodation for £980.

THE ROYAL WEDDING CAKE.

This *chef-d'œuvre* stands five feet and a half high, and at the base two and a half broad, and one hundred pounds in weight. It has an ornamental elevation, which reminds us of one of our old English crosses of the time of the Edwards, such as we still see standing at Waltham in remembrance of Queen Eleanor. The design is divided into four parts or stories. The basement is octagonal, and within its arches two niches contain the arms of England and Denmark, with alternate arches occupied by figures of the Muses. Between the basement and the next tier of arches cornucopias hang over the parapet, and medallions of the prince and princess are hung from the bases of the pillars above. The shafts of these pillars are again hung with heraldic devices, the plumes of the prince and other such significant badges; while within, and occupying the centre, are figures emblematic of Hymen, surrounded by cupids and other mythological attendants upon the nuptial ceremony. On reaching the next story the shape contracts into an hexagonal form, within the arches of which the god of love sports, surrounded by a variety of complimentary emblems. Above this, the next story, quadrilateral, rises, which, being more contracted in size and approaching the apex, is dealt with as a sort of base for a slender vase surmounting the whole structure, out of which orange flowers depend. It is unnecessary to say that festoons of orange flower wreathes hang from column to column, and sufficiently designate the purpose for which this elaborate piece of confectionery is designed. Simple-minded folk will be ready to ask, "How is the bride to cut the cake?" We are happy to be able to answer the question, and to explain how this apparently Gordian problem is to be solved. The niches of the pediment, which contain the arms of England and Denmark, have been constructed as doors—and they open! When opened her Royal Highness the Princess of Wales will be enabled to draw the knife across the cake.

THE ROYAL PRESENTS.

The establishment of Messrs. Garrard, the Crown jewellers, has been eagerly sought by fashionable visitors anxious to see the costly presents manufactured for the Prince of Wales, as gifts to his bride.

Conspicuous among the beautiful objects is a complete *parure* of diamonds and pearls, comprising a necklace, a brooch and earrings. The necklace is composed of eight clusters, with large pendants, the centre cluster consisting of three and pear shaped pearl drops, and the whole being connected with festoons of diamonds. The brooch is composed of splendid pearls, surrounded by diamonds, with other pearls as drops. These jewels are all of the first quality, and were manufactured after the design and under the superintendence of the Prince.

Glittering on each side of the *parure* are two brooches, entirely of diamonds, formed so as to represent the Prince of Wales' feathers. These are of different sizes, but both very large.

The wedding ring, which, of course, is of plain gold, is remarkably massive, and its accompanying keeper is set with six precious stones, selected and arranged so that the initial letters of their names shall form the word "Bertie," an affectionate variation of "Albert." The stones of which this happy combination is effected are a beryl, an emerald, a ruby, a turquoise, a jacynth and another emerald. A plain gold ring has likewise been made to be worn by the Prince himself.

As presents for the bridesmaids eight lockets have been made. These are of coral and diamond, to signify the red and white which are the colors of Denmark. In the centre of each is a cypher in crystal, forming the letters A. E. A., after a drawing by the Princess Alice.

The eight bridesmaids themselves present to her Royal Highness a splendid diamond and enamel bracelet. This is made in eight compartments, in each of which is the miniature portrait of one of the young ladies, with her initials beneath in diamonds—one from her Majesty consisting of a most costly suit of opals and diamonds, as valuable and rare as those which the Prince of Wales presented to the Princess Royal, and similar in form to the suit designed for the Princess Alice by the Prince Consort. The second is another present from the Prince of Wales, and consists of a brilliant tiara. A magnificent, costly dressing case is to be presented by the principal members of her Majesty's household.

The city of Copenhagen is preparing to present the young Princess with a reproduction of the celebrated statue of Hebe, by Thorwaldsen. The execution of two pictures representing views of the capital of Denmark have been confided to two Danish painters, and will be also presented to her Royal Highness. Among other rich gifts from various sources may be enumerated a porcelain stand with rich figures from Flora Danica, a costly fan, old northern golden ornaments, an English Bible one hundred years old, busts of her Royal Highness' parents, a splendid pair of gold embroidered shoes, a large painting by Schott, representing a group of the Princess Alexandra's brothers and sisters; golden ornaments, diadem, clasp, bracelets, rings, &c., in the old northern style, executed by the Court jeweller, Michelsen; a marble group, two children kissing each other, one of the finest works ever executed by Bissen, the great Danish sculptor, and in the purest Carrara marble. The mould is destroyed, and the piece is little known, but all who have seen it unite in praising its elegance and expression.

A prayer book, containing the twelve chief prayers of the English church, painted in the style of the middle ages on vellum with a ground of gold and silver, splendidly bound in the old style by Michelsen.

A marble group, "Adam and Eve," executed by Jerichau.

A marble statue, "Hebe," executed by Bissen.

An album, with views in Denmark by the best Danish artists.

Two portrait medallions in porcelain, the Princess' grandfather and grandmother.

From the marine painter Sorensen a picture representing a part of Copenhagen and Long Line, as seen from the roads.

By the Corporation of the city of London a superb necklace of thirty-two fine and large brilliants, and a pair of top and drop earrings to correspond. The necklace is of the value of £10,000.

THE BRIDAL DRESS.

Finer specimens of needlework will not easily be found. The stitches are so fine and the work so delicate that they have excited universal admiration. No machine has been employed. On each piece has been embroidered her Royal Highness' initials, below the English crown, and this alone has given six hundred such embroideries. The time allowed being so short, several hundred persons have been employed, but the greatest accuracy and uniformity have been obtained.

The handkerchiefs have been ordered in Paris, and are masterpieces in their kind, the embroidery being remarkably tasteful and beautiful. The English crown, from its peculiar shape, has offered various difficulties, but they have been triumphantly overcome.

Only a few of the robes were exhibited, some being too delicate to bear any handling. Articles of this kind more glaring and costly might easily be obtained, but certainly nothing more quietly and fittingly appropriate as perfect specimens of what the needle can accomplish.

CARRIAGES OF THE PRINCE AND PRINCESS.

The carriages built for the Prince of Wales and the Princess Alexandra are four in number—a state carriage, for use on public occasions; a light and handsome waggonette, for country excursions, &c.; a barouche, for the personal use of the Princess, and a small brougham, designed for private use. The state carriage is a superb vehicle, the prevailing colors being chocolate and vermilion, the wheels being richly gilt. The corners of the roof are adorned with rich gilt crowns, and on the door panels the arms of the Prince of Wales and those of the Princess are emblazoned.

Magnificently gilt carriage lamps complete the appointments of this truly regal carriage. The barouche or landau, being intended for the use of the Princess, is a model of taste and quiet elegance. The prevailing colors are chocolate and vermillion, and the interior is tastefully lined with blue silk. The wagonette is a light vehicle intended for shooting or other excursions in the country. It is provided with Hadcock's patent contrivance for showing the distance travelled, which registers on a dial every yard of ground that is gone over up to thirty miles, when it can be wound up and set going again. The brougham is a neat and unostentatious vehicle, adapted for private use. It is small, but comfortably and tastefully fitted up.

THE PRINCE HAPPY IN HIS INTENDED MARRIAGE.

The Prince, replying to some congratulations, lately wrote:—"I beg to return my most sincere thanks to Lady Caithness and yourself for your good wishes; and I feel now what it is to be really happy. If I can make the future life and home of the Princess a happy one I shall be content. I feel doubly happy in the thought that my approaching marriage is one which has the approval of the nation, and I only trust that I may not disappoint the expectations that have been formed of me."

THE DANISH NATIONAL SONG.

> King Christian stood by the lofty mast
> In mist and smoke;
> His sword was hammering so fast,
> Through Gothic Helm and brain it past;
> Then sank each hostile hulk and mast,
> In mist and smoke.
> "Fly!" shouted they, "fly, be who can!
> Who braves of Denmark's Christian
> The stroke?"
>
> Niels Juel gave heed to the tempest's roar,
> Now is the hour!
> He hoisted his blood red flag once more,
> And smote upon the foe full sore,
> And shouted loud through the tempest roar,
> "Now is the hour!"
> "Fly!" shouted they, "for shelter fly!
> Of Denmark's Juel who can defy
> The power?"

THE NEW YAZOO EXPEDITION.

The Course of the Gunboat Diligent to the Rear of the Enemy's Works at Haines' Bluff.

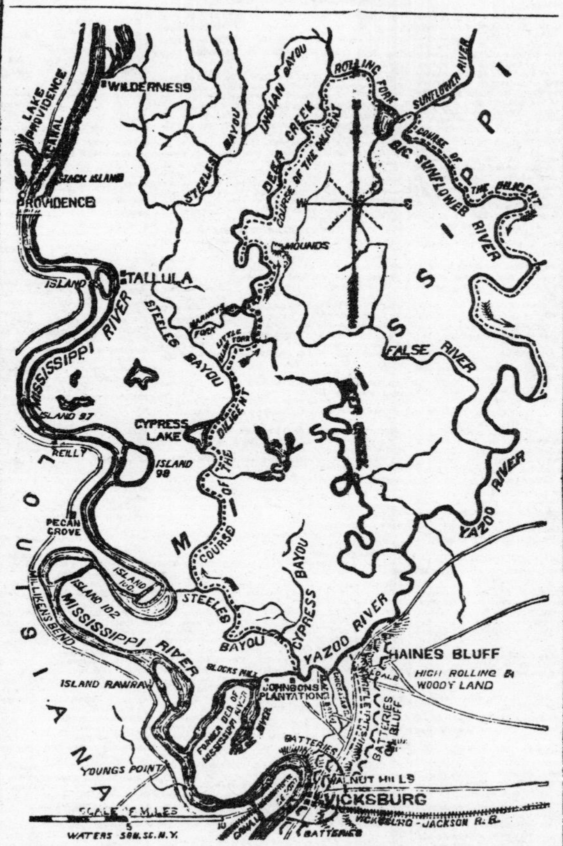

AN EPITHALAMIUM.

> God save the royal bride!
> That loved one by his side,
> Loving again!
> Denmark's fair daughter, she;
> England's proud scion, he;
> In them still united be
> Briton and Dane.
>
> Oh, on their nuptial day,
> Cause, gracious Lord, we pray,
> Thy face to shine!
> Hear Thou their solemn vows:
> Crown Thou with joy their brows;
> To Thyself their hearts espouse,
> And make them Thine.

The Reported Destruction of the Rebel Pirate Georgiana.

Rebel despatches from Charleston, S. C., of the 22d inst., state that "The enemy have been shelling the wreck of the Georgiana, off Long Island beach. Otherwise all is quiet." This brief telegram is one which probably gives us the first information respecting the destruction of a rebel pirate ship which was to have been dreaded more than even the far famed Alabama, as she was fully as fast and far heavier armed. We hope we are correct in our impression.

The Georgiana was built by Messrs. Laird, at Birkenhead, for the "Emperor of China." She is an iron vessel, brig rigged, and left England with an assorted cargo. She arrived at Nassau on the evening of the 27th of February, and, at our latest advices, the 16th inst., she still was lying there awaiting an opportunity to cross over and run into Charleston.

Our latest dates from Port Royal are to the 19th; and, as no mention is made of her capture, it is fair to presume that she attempted to run the blockade about the 20th, and was chased ashore by our blockaders.

The Georgiana no doubt desired to land her cargo at Charleston, probably having on board articles of great importance to the rebels; and, having completed that part of her mission, she would put her heavy battery in order and run out, or, if prevented, then she could be of good service in repelling any attack made upon that city.

By the attention and vigilance of the blockaders off Charleston this formidable piratical cruiser has, we hope, been entirely destroyed.

To the rebels her destruction is of course a great loss, while to us, under any circumstances, it is a great gain. They have already too many cruisers afloat, and our merchants naturally feel timid about risking their property on the seas while such merciless pirates are prowling about, with but slight chances of being captured.

It does not seem possible that the Englishmen who build these vessels will much longer submit themselves to the inconvenience of having their ships thus captured and destroyed; for it is fair to presume that the value of the Georgiana and her cargo will not fall short of nearly a million dollars.

As a steamer is now due from Port Royal, it will not be long before we shall hear the particulars of this affair.

Archbishop Hughes' Silver Plate.

TO THE EDITOR OF THE HERALD.

The Archbishop of New York respectfully requests the editor of the New York Herald to correct the following statement, found in the New York *Evening Express* of yesterday, to which the Archbishop's attention has been called:—

> Archbishop Hughes, of New York, when called on by the assessor for his return of silver plate liable to tax under the United States Revenue law, rendered twelve thousand and forty ounces, with the remark, "You need not exempt me forty ounces, the country requires all the tax."

This statement is entirely incorrect. The amount of silver plate belonging to the Archbishop was found to be nine hundred and seventy ounces, as reported and certified to by the official agent of Ball, Black & Co. Much of this consisted of personal and complimentary donations to the Archbishop. But to have it reported that his silver plate amounted to twelve thousand and forty ounces is no less a surprise than the Senatorial asseveration of Mr. Erastus Brooks some years ago, stating that the Archbishop owned on Manhattan Island alone five millions worth of real estate. Now, the forty ounces allowed by the law were not taxed by the assessor, nor did the Archbishop request that they should be taxed. The only thing that could give a coloring to this unfounded exaggeration is, that in the office of the assessor, having been complimented by the latter for promptness, the Archbishop remarked that, since the unfortunate circumstances of our country rendered it necessary that the government should be supported, he thought it wisest that each citizen should pay his share of taxation with as much promptitude and cheerfulness as patriotism could inspire. The Archbishop would respectfully request that the papers which may have copied the above paragraph, as found in the *Express*, will be kind enough to publish this correction of its misstatements.

NEW YORK, March 25, 1863.

Affairs in Cincinnati.

HONORS TO GENERAL BURNSIDE—DEATH OF AN EMINENT MERCHANT, ETC.

CINCINNATI, March 25, 1863.

Gen. Burnside was serenaded at the Burnett House last night. He takes command of this department.

Wm. J. Whiteman, of the late firm of Springer & Whiteman, of this city, died at St. Paul, Minnesota, yesterday.

Obsequies of Ex-Comptroller Haws.

The funeral of ex-Comptroller Haws yesterday afternoon was one of the largest and most respectable that has occurred in this city for a long period. The flags on nearly all the public buildings were suspended at halfmast, and most of the public offices were closed at noon, out of respect for the memory of the deceased gentleman.

A large number of people crowded the late residence of the ex-Comptroller, 95 Allen street, and the feeling among all was that of the most sincere and heartfelt regret at the loss of a man whose worth and ability were so generally recognized by all classes of the community. Mayor Opdyke, General Draper, Thurlow Weed, Wm. M. Evarts, James B. Nicholson, several of our city and county judges, and a host of officials of more or less distinction, were among those who mingled with the crowd of mourners.

The remains were laid in a neat mahogany coffin, on the lid of which were placed crosses, formed of camelias, and other floral decorations. The plate of the coffin contained the following inscription:—

> ROBERT T. HAWS.
> BORN FEB. 28, 1810.
> DIED
> MARCH 22, 1863.

About half-past three o'clock the funeral procession formed on the sidewalk, extending the distance of an entire block. The following gentlemen were among the pall bearers:—Thurlow Weed, Denning Duer, Moses H. Grinnell, William M. Evarts, Elijah F. Purdy, Andrew V. Stout, Joseph Hoxie and James Kelly.

The coffin was carried to St. Stephen's church, which was crowded in every part with ladies and gentlemen. Dr. Joseph Price, the respected pastor of the church, performed the solemn services over the dead, according to the forms of the Episcopal church, and also delivered a most touching discourse on the mystery of death, alluding to the many virtues of the deceased, as well as expatiating on the dreadful uncertainty of man's existence here on earth.

REPUBLICAN CENTRAL COMMITTEE OF THE CITY AND COUNTY OF NEW YORK.

At a special meeting, held on Tuesday evening, March 24, 1863, the President, Mr. Darling, announced the death of the Hon. Robert T. Haws, whereupon the following preamble and resolutions, presented by E. Delafield Smith, were unanimously adopted:—

Whereas, at the call of our President, we have assembled, as the representatives of the republicans of the city of New York, to offer a tribute of respect and affection to the memory of Robert T. Haws; therefore,

Resolved, That not in the terms of a cold formality, but in the sorrowing language of the heart, we desire to testify our sense of the purity and nobility which characterized him whose untimely death has just been announced. We would not mourn him as partisans; or his fidelity to principle was so softened by the amenities of his nature as to make the entire community mourners at his bier. Yet, as loyal Americans, we cannot but grieve that a citizen so useful and a patriot so true could not have been spared in this day of national gloom. When such men are taken the dependence of our country upon the God of our fathers is brought upon us with new emphasis.

Resolved, That to all his relations, both public and private, as a man and a public officer, Robert T. Haws had few peers and no superior. As a member of the Board of Health, during the ravages of the cholera of 1849 and '55, he developed a tenderness and fidelity, a courage and humanity, which must ever endear his name to the sick and the suffering; while the commanding ability and the unswerving integrity demonstrated by him during a long term as Comptroller of our city [illegible] placed him in the front rank of our public men. And, while we grieve over his death as that of a friend and associate, we sorrow over the loss sustained by the country in the death of one so eminently qualified for exalted public station.

Resolved, That as a testimonial of the sentiments with which this committee have received the sad tidings of the death of Mr. Haws, the members will attend his funeral, and will cherish with undying fidelity, and as a priceless heritage, his noble example of manliness and truth.

> Tears fell when he was dying
> From eyes unused to weep,
> And long where he is lying
> Shall tears the cold turf steep.

Resolved, That a copy of these resolutions, properly authenticated, be transmitted to the family of the deceased, and be published in the public newspapers.

WILLIAM A. DARLING, President.

A. M. PALMER, JOHN J. SHAW, Secretaries.

Sporting Intelligence.

THE M'COOL BENEFIT EXCITEMENT AMONG THE SPORTS—A LIVELY SET-TO, ETC.

Mozart Hall was filled to repletion last evening by a company of nearly one thousand persons, it being the occasion of the benefit of Mike McCool, the Western champion. The hall was so densely packed that the parties who had been pledged to spar could not get through, and only two exhibitions took place previous to the wind up. These were between two light weights—Walker and Hauly—and two middle weights—Cornell, a well known boxer of this city, and Conoran, the Colorado champion. These trials displayed a good deal of skill, and led the contestants into some warm work, which earned the applause of the house. The wind up between McCool, the beneficiary, and Australian Kelly was then announced. Sam. Davis, who acted as master of ceremonies, introduced McCool in a brief speech, returning his thanks to the audience for their attendance and the many courtesies shown him since his arrival in New York. McCool is a square built, powerfully made up man, weighing two hundred and three pounds, and standing six feet in his stockings. He has a long reach and stands well on his "pins," but is not yet quite up to the mark in the "science." His set to with Kelly was one in which he displayed his immense strength to some advantage; but the coolness and experience of the latter were more than a match for the advantage possessed by McCool in size and height. Kelly also is one of the best men with the gloves to be found in the metropolis, and is a hard hitter. He said that McCool's blows were perfect "auctioneers," however, and that the grip in the wrestle was like the hug of a bear. The excitement at the close of the contest was so great to see the champion that McCool with difficulty found egress from the hall. He goes back to the West [illegible]

VICKSBURG.

The Three Grand Expeditions to Open the Mississippi.

All of Admiral Farragut's Squadron Above Port Hudson.

THE RED RIVER BLOCKADED.

The Admiral's Flagship and the Albatross at the Cut Off.

The Tallahatchie Expedition Temporarily Checked.

Opening of a New Route to the Rear of Vicksburg.

Admiral Porter's Splendid Movement Through the Bayous.

The Iron-Clad Lafayette Above Haines' Bluff, &c., &c., &c.

The Port Hudson Expedition.

OFFICIAL DESPATCH.

CAIRO, March 24, 1863.

Hon. GIDEON WELLES, Secretary of the Navy, Washington:—

I have just received the following communication from Lieutenant Commander K. R. Breese, dated Black Hawk, March 20:—

The Hartford is below Warrenton. Admiral Farragut's secretary came on board this morning, *en route* to Admiral Porter. It will take him a week at least to communicate and get back.

He says that the Hartford passed the fort, but that the others were repulsed, and one was seen in flames. It is believed that the Mississippi was the ship destroyed.

A. M. PENNOCK,
Fleet Captain, Commanding Squadron at Cairo.

ADMIRAL FARRAGUT'S WHOLE FLEET ABOVE PORT HUDSON.

CAIRO, March 25—P. M.

Later news from Vicksburg confirms the arrival of the sloop-of-war Hartford and gunboat Albatross at the mouth of the canal on the 20th.

An officer from on board had arrived at Gen. Grant's headquarters, bringing despatches.

Seven of Admiral Farragut's steamers ran the blockade of Port Hudson. After coming up the river some distance, all but two returned, and have probably gone to the mouth of the Red river.

General Banks had not come up to make the land attack when the fleet ran the blockade.

Boats will pass into Lake Providence as soon as the current in that direction permits.

ADMIRAL FARRAGUT'S SQUADRON.

As far as known at present Admiral Farragut's fleet consisted of the following vessels:—

Hartford, flagship, Captain Palmer	25 guns.
Richmond, Captain J. Alden	26 "
Monongahela, Captain J. P. McKinstry	4 "
Genesee, Captain McComb	4 "
Kineo, Commander G. M. Ransom	4 "
Itaska, Commander R. F. R. Lewis	4 "
Essex, iron clad, Commander C. H. Caldwell	7 "
Sportsman, storeship.	

The following is a list of officers of the Hartford, Admiral Farragut's flagship:—

Rear Admiral—David G. Farragut.
Captain—James S. Palmer.
Fleet Surgeon—Jonathan M. Foltz.
Lieutenant Commanding—L. A. Kimberly.
Captain of Marines—John L. Broome.
Surgeon—Wm. M. King.
Paymaster—Wm. T. Meredith.
Lieutenant—John C. Watson, H. B. Tyson.
First Lieutenant of Marines—John H. Higbee.
Assistant Surgeon—Jos. Hugg.
Rear Admiral's Secretary—E. C. Gabaudan.
Acting Masters—T. L. Peterson, E. S. Goodwin.
Engineer-in Chief—Jas. B. Kimball.
Ensign—E. C. Hazeltine.
Second Assistant Engineers—E. B. Latch, Fletcher A. Wilson.
Third Assistant Engineers—C. M. Burchard, A. K. Fulton, Isaac Degraf, H. L. Pilkington, Jas. E. Speight.
Midshipmen—John H. Reed, H. J. Blake, C. D. Jones.
Rear Admiral's Clerk—Loyale Farragut.
Sailmaker—John A. Holbrook.
Boatswain—Jas. Walker.
Carpenter—C. S. Stimson.
Gunner—John L. Staples.
Master's Mates—J. B. Trott, H. B. Judson, H. Weston, Jr.

The Tallahatchie Expedition.

CINCINNATI, March 25, 1863.

The Tallahatchie expedition has come to a stand still.

The Chillicothe, in the last engagement, was temporarily disabled by shot battering the sides to her portholes so that they could not be moved.

Battery Wilson has been dismantled and the guns returned to the gunboat DeKalb.

Our troops are now acting on the defensive.

Gen. Quimby's division was on the Coldwater river on the 20th instant, and with good water would reach the scene of operations in two days.

The guerillas trouble the boats in that river and the Tallahatchie, and have killed three or four soldiers.

CAIRO, March 25—P. M.

Reports from Greenwood, Miss., to Wednesday afternoon state that the fight had not been renewed. Both parties were making active demonstrations. The rebels were mounting new guns and otherwise strengthening their position.

The New Yazoo Expedition.

OFFICIAL DESPATCH.

CAIRO, March 24—7 50 P. M.

Hon. GIDEON WELLES, Secretary of the Navy, Washington:—

I have just received a communication from Lieutenant Commander Breese, dated Black Hawk, March 19.

Admiral Porter has got through Steele's and Black bayous with five iron clads and the Price, and is into Deer creek, making all haste for the Yazoo. Doubtless he is there now.

General Sherman and the troops are following up.

A. M. PENNOCK,
Fleet Captain and Commanding Squadron at Cairo.

NEWSPAPER DESPATCH.

CINCINNATI, March 25, 1863.

The Monitor gunboat Lafayette is reported up the Yazoo, above Haines' Bluff. Other gunboats have gone up.

Stirring news is expected from that quarter.

The reported evacuation of Haines' Bluff by the rebels is not credited.

SKETCH OF THE NEW ROUTE.

The opening up by Admiral Porter of another route to the rear of the rebel works on Haines' Bluff is a matter of deep interest in a geographical as well as a naval point of view. It develops another of those curious systems of water courses which prevail in that part of our country, and points out a route of navigation almost, if not quite, unknown at the East until brought to light by this event.

By referring to our map it will be seen that the Diligent passed up the Yazoo river until nearly opposite Johnson's plantation. She next proceeded along Cypress bayou to Steele's bayou, along that water course and through Cypress lake to Little Black Fork, through which she reached Deer creek. Following that last stream for some distance, she branched off along Rolling Fork into Big Sunflower river, down which she proceeded until she reached its mouth, which opens into the Yazoo above Haines' Bluff.

[illegible] was very circuitous, [illegible] doubtless gained in obtaining an unobstructed channel to the Upper Yazoo. This series of water courses mainly pass through and along the borders of Issaquena county, Mississippi. This county contains about one thousand and thirty square miles, or nearly six hundred and sixty thousand acres. The Mississippi river forms its western boundary, the Yazoo its southern, and the Sunflower intersects it. The creeks, bayous and streams that fall into these principal waters are very numerous, and run in almost every direction. The surface of the country is subject to inundation, but the soil is very fertile. The population of the county, according to the last returns (1860), was 587 whites and 7,244 slaves. Half of these slaves are females. Deer creek, Cypress and Steele's bayous have heretofore been unimportant streams; but the Sunflower river has been often navigated by the planters as a means of transportation of their produce, via the Yazoo to the Mississippi. The Yazoo, at the point of junction with the Sunflower, is a very deep, sluggish stream, vessels of almost any draft being able to navigate it. The fleet of gunboats having safely passed through the Sunflower, there is barely a chance of their ever grounding while attacking the position at Haines' Bluff.

IMPORTANT FROM KENTUCKY.

The Rebel General Longstreet's Advance.

UNION TROOPS ARRIVING.

A Very Active Campaign Expected, &c., &c., &c.

CINCINNATI, March 25, 1863.

The rebel force which has occupied Danville, Ky., is believed to be the advance of General Longstreet's division. Their coming is not unexpected.

They will be promptly met. Several thousands of Union troops will arrive here to-day, and more are coming.

Look out for a very active campaign in Kentucky.

Enforcement of the Rebel Conscription Act in Kentucky.

LOUISVILLE, Ky., March 25, 1863.

We have had the usual quantity of exciting rumors respecting rebel movements to-day, but none of them are traceable to any authentic source, and headquarters are advised of no change in the rebel status since last night.

The *Democrat* says the rebels, in large force, under Breckinridge, are at Harrodsburg, and that the federal forces under General Carter are falling back on Frankfort.

Breckinridge is reported to have issued a proclamation declaring his intention of enforcing the Southern Conscription act, and rumor says that the act is being rigidly enforced in those portions of Kentucky now occupied by the rebel forces.

IMPORTANT FROM TENNESSEE

Fight With Rebel Cavalry at Brentwood—Surrender of a Detachment of Union Troops—Gallant Attack on the Enemy—The Rebels Within Four Miles of Nashville, &c.

NASHVILLE, Tenn., March 25, 1863.

A rebel cavalry force under Generals Forrest, Wheeler and Wharton, crossed Harpeth river this morning, six miles above Franklin. Part of the rebel force attacked our force at Brentwood, nine miles from Nashville, on the Franklin road.

Our troops, under command of Lieutenant Colonel Woodgood, consisted of parts of the Thirty-third Indiana, Twenty-second and Nineteenth Wisconsin, in all 300 men. After feeble resistance, with only one man killed and four wounded, our force surrendered to the enemy. All the government property was captured.

General Green Clay Smith sent to Franklin, came up with a force, and pursued them six miles west of Brentwood, when he met the entire rebel force, numbering five thousand, with only five hundred men. He succeeded in retaking all the wagons and ammunition, but, being attacked by superior numbers, he was compelled to destroy them. He then fell back. When reinforcements reached him the rebels had decamped.

We lost one officer and about fifteen men in killed, wounded and missing. The rebels lost some ten killed and wounded. Over fifty rebel prisoners have been brought in.

The rebel cavalry have been within four miles of the city on the Harding and Charlotte pike to-day.

CAVALRY SKIRMISH AT CHANTILLY, VA.

WASHINGTON, March 25, 1863.

A letter has been received from Fairfax Court House stating that on Monday, at five P. M., our pickets in front of Chantilly were attacked. The videttes were on the alert and gave the alarm. The reserve, of about ninety men, were immediately under arms, and charged the enemy, who fled for two miles along the Little river turnpike.

Between Sanders' toll gate and Cub run there is a strip of woods about half a mile wide, through which the road runs. Within the wood and about a quarter of a mile apart are two barricades of fallen trees. Our troops pursued the enemy between these barricades. Behind the latter some of the enemy were concealed. The head of the column was here received by a fire of carbines and pistols, and also by a fire upon the flank from the wood. The column broke, and was pursued by the enemy a mile and a half. It was then rallied by the exertions of Majors Bacon and White. Captains McGuire and Haberack, when they heard the alarm, proceeded on a gallop from Frying Pan, and, joining Major White's command, pursued the enemy for eight miles. Night coming on, and the enemy being more numerous than we were, and our horses being exhausted, the column halted and returned to Chantilly.

The line of pickets is now re-established.

Our loss was:—Killed, —— Gilles, Company H, Fifth New York cavalry; wounded mortally, John J. Harris, Company I, Fifth New York cavalry; wounded, Sergeant Layhey, Company C, Fifth New York cavalry; prisoner, Lieutenant Merritt.

NEWS FROM FORTRESS MONROE.

FORTRESS MONROE, March 24, 1863.

Twelve schooners from New York are now taking in cargoes of oysters near the mouth of Elizabeth river.

The new gunboat South Briggs, Captain Lee, of the Ninety-ninth New York commanding, received her guns at Fortress Monroe yesterday, and commences her services at once.

The steamboat Thomas Collyer, from New York, has arrived and will proceed to Newbern, N. C., as soon as she takes in coal.

The steamboat Hero sailed from Baltimore this afternoon with a schooner in tow, loaded with horses.

There are four schooners at Yorktown, loading with oysters for the Northern market.

The Yorktown *Cavalier* has the following:—

The storm that commenced on Thursday and continued till Saturday was the most severe of the season. The snow fell to one foot in depth. The soldiers enjoyed snowballing extensively.

The Hotel de Mallicotte, which for some time back has been the headquarters of rebel sympathizers and officers in United States uniforms, who would declare that Jeff. Davis is a better man than Abraham Lincoln, and that in less than four months he would occupy the White House, has been closed, and the building appropriated to better uses.

Another Prize Captured.

BALTIMORE, March 25, 1863.

The gunboat Reliance, of the Chesapeake squadron, captured yesterday the schooner Flying Cloud, loaded with percussion caps, pistols, shot, tools, arms, shoes, boots, &c., on the way to Dixie.

The warlike portion of her cargo was directed to the care of Major E. Griswold, the Yankee Provost Marshal of Richmond. Several persons on board were made prisoners. The vessel was brought here to-day.

Discharge of Mary Hartung.

ALBANY, March 25, 1863.

The Court of Appeals passed an order to-day discharging Mary Hartung, convicted of poisoning her husband, [illegible]

DAILY DISPATCH.

VOL. XXIV. RICHMOND VA., THURSDAY MORNING, APRIL 16 1863 NO. 91

Richmond Dispatch.

The DISPATCH is published DAILY, (Sundays excepted.) Price for mailing $12 a year; or $6 for six months; three months $5; one month $2—in advance.

The SEMI-WEEKLY DISPATCH is issued every TUESDAY and FRIDAY, at $6—in advance.

The WEEKLY DISPATCH is issued every FRIDAY, and mailed to subscribers at $4 per annum.

THURSDAY MORNING. APRIL 16, 1863

CONGRESSIONAL SUMMARY.

In the *Senate*, on Wednesday, Mr. Yancey submitted a joint resolution of thanks to Gen. G. T. Beauregard, and the officers and soldiers under his command in the battle in Charleston harbor on the 7th inst. Referred to the Committee of Military Affairs.

The House bill explanatory of the act authorizing the President to accept and place in the service regiments and battalions heretofore raised composed of persons liable to conscription was passed.

Also, the Senate bill authorizing the Secretary of the Navy to lease a site, with or without buildings, near the city for a laboratory, etc.

A report from the committee of conference on the Exemption bill was postponed until to-day, at 12 M.

The report of the committee of conference on the copyright question was agreed to.

In the *House*, Senate bills to abolish supernumerary offices in the Quartermaster and Commissary Departments, and to abolish all ports of delivery in the Confederate States, were appropriately referred.

The bill to refund to the State of Alabama the sum paid for the gunboat Florida was passed.

Several other reports from the Committee of Claims were made.

The Exemption bill, as reported from the Committee of Conference, was then taken up. After some discussion, the bill was postponed until Friday next, and ordered to be printed.

AFFAIRS ON THE BLACKWATER.

There is nothing from the Blackwater which can be relied on, except the fact that heavy firing was heard by citizens of Southampton county about daybreak Tuesday—some say they heard musketry as well as cannon. No intelligence had been received at the War Department last night of any movement or engagement near Suffolk.

THE WILLIAMSBURG AFFAIR.

From a letter written by an officer of General Wise's command to a gentleman in this city, under date of the 13th, we have some information with reference to affairs at Williamsburg. The letter states that the enemy had surrendered the possession of the town to our forces, and that we have troops there. The citizens of the place were moving out rapidly, perhaps in anticipation of further fighting, and were receiving the protection of our forces. The officers of the Insane Asylum have appealed to Gen. Wise for protection, which was accorded. A considerable number of conscripts and contrabands were captured by our men. The loyal people of that section have saved a large amount of forage, which was being hauled away as rapidly as the means of transportation would allow. There was, also, some bacon and salt secured.

Our forces were greeted by the people of the ancient town with marked manifestations of delight.

THE SIEGE OF WASHINGTON, N. C.

Much interest is felt in the progressing siege of Washington, N. C., by the Confederates under Gen. Hill, which is increased from the fact that a force of about 10,000 Yankees marched from Newbern, thirty miles, to the relief of the place, was met at Blount creek, seventeen miles from Washington, and defeated by Gen. Pettigrew. The Yankees were attempting to gain Gen. Hill's rear, but after their defeat fled precipitately, cutting down the forest for miles in their own rear to impede the progress of our pursuing troops. As the garrison at Washington can no longer receive reinforcements or provisions by the river they will be forced to surrender. A good deal of shelling between our batteries and the gunboats and town batteries has been going on. We have lost only two killed—Jas. McKinnie and —— Kelly, both of Wyatt's Virginia artillery. A letter to the Fayetteville (N. C.) *Observer* gives some account of the progress of the "siege." It says:

On Tuesday morning the firing commenced and was continued for some hours. The Yankees replied from two gunboats and their shore batteries. One of their gunboats—the Eagle—was severely damaged—the Whitworth, under Lt. Fuller, gaining much reputation for accuracy and rapidity.—The block house was struck several times and a 2nd battery of the enemy silenced. On Wednesday the Whitworths were moved to the former site of Fort Hill, and, with other guns, placed in position to affect a blockade of the river. During that day they were shelled by the enemy's gunboats.—On Thursday all was quiet. Thursday night a 12-pound Howitzer, from Wyatt's Va. Battery, was placed in position within 400 yards of the town, also in direct line to the steamer Louisiana. Soon after daylight it opened fire, and almost immediately the Louisiana dropped down out of range. The Howitzer had fired but a few rounds before it was the target for a hail of shot and shell. The embankment around it was completely leveled, yet the gun was not struck, and but two men hurt. It was brought out of the swamp on Friday night.—The behavior of the men was much praised.

From a position near our picket lines I could see the bridge, the steamer Louisiana, and a part of the town, and the Yankee pickets but a few hundred yards distant. On Saturday morning a gunboat ran by the Rodman's Point Battery, owing to the carelessness of the officer in command from Wyatt's Va. Battery. The men showed courage, and are not to be blamed. She was a small affair, though. Saturday afternoon the Yankee batteries shelled the Rodman's Point guns severely. No one hurt.

Sunday the gunboats below Fort Hill threw a number of shells at intervals. Our batteries did not reply. Sunday afternoon below Fort Hill there were ten steam gunboats and five sailing vessels all armed with cannon. The town batteries did not fire all day. Saturday and Sunday night the 5th, Col. Owens, and 6th Col Kenan's regiments were engaged in throwing up heavy earthworks on Rodman's Point. Behind these will be mounted to-night three heavy guns.

No firing anywhere this morning.

On the north side of the river the troops under command of Gen Garnett have been gradually drawing in their fold, and I was told on Sunday that Capt. Starr had his two Howitzers in 800 yards of the town. Whenever the signal for general attack is made, Gen. Garnett's brigade, with the North Carolina regiments he has, will advance and storm the town. When that will be, it is impossible to tell. To-morrow all the heavy guns necessary will be here and in place. Riley's battery is on the way, and may be waited for—but "delays are dangerous."

There was some skirmishing on the north side of the river on Saturday morning. I was informed that it was an attempt upon the part of some buffaloes and negroes to leave the town, but they were driven back.

THE BLOCKADE RUNNING FROM NASSAU.

Some developments made by the Nassau correspondent of the Charleston *Courier* about blockade running between the two cities demand the attention of the Confederate authorities. The mail carried by the steamers is nothing less than free and unrestricted postal communication between the Confederate and United States. At the office of the consignee in Nassau a bag is hung up, into which any person may drop a sealed letter, which is forwarded uninspected to Charleston, and thence by mail to its destination. At this end of the line no more caution is used than at the other. The mails are large enough to warrant their examination by an authorized Confederate officer at Charleston, where the letters from and for Nassau should be received unsealed. Another glaring piece of carelessness is the fact that there are no effective regulations to prevent improper persons coming into our ports on these blockade steamers. After getting to Charleston they are seen in all parts of the Confederacy, where the mere fact that they "ran the blockade" gulls silly people into regarding them as patriots who have gone through great danger for "the cause." The correspondent gives an example:

I know of one instance where a foreigner, who has just come back from Charleston, has talked loudly, and within ear shot of a score of Yankees, of the defences of our city and coast. He boasted that he had been shown over the fortifications, and related what Confederate officers had told him of the strong and weak points of the defences. While I write there are half a dozen persons here—who arrived from New York by the late steamers—who are striving to procure passages to Charleston.—They may possibly have the best intentions in view, but, if no discrimination is made, what is to prevent black sheep from slipping through? Our authorities should refuse to permit any persons to enter the harbor who cannot show passports from the official representatives of the Confederate States at either Nassau, Bermuda, or Havana.

With the crews of the vessels there would be more difficulty in excluding doubtful characters, as it is very difficult sometimes to man a vessel for a Confederate port, and a plausible Yankee can

might easily get an engagement. This, however, could be remedied when the ship arrives in Charleston, if measures were taken to prevent any stranger arriving there from going beyond the wharves of the city without a special permit from the local authorities. This may lead to embarrassment; but as long as the country is beleaguered by land and sea, extraordinary measures should be adopted to keep all its secrets inviolate.

DEATH OF A CONGRESSMAN.

Hon. Wm. M. Cook, of Missouri, representative of the St. Louis district in the Confederate Congress, died in Petersburg, Va., on Tuesday last, at the residence of Mr. D'Arcy Paul. He was one of the Commissioners who came from Missouri to Virginia, before the war, for conference with the authorities here. He was afterwards aid to Governor Jackson, and during the war was on the staff of Gen. Sterling Price, and went through several engagements in the West under that commander.—Judge Cook was about forty years of age. He was a native of Norfolk, Va., and a graduate of the University of Virginia. He leaves a widow and seven children in St. Louis. His remains will be interred in Petersburg to-day.

FROM FREDERICKSBURG.

[FROM OUR OWN REPORTER.]

FREDERICKSBURG April 15, 1863.

Last night and night before the Yankees had vivid lights and cars running all night. There appeared to be two large fires last night in the direction of Aquia Creek. What all this indicates I cannot say. It looks like a Yankee movement somewhere.

Firing was heard across and up the river yesterday morning. Perhaps Stuart is after them.

A heavy rain is falling, which began last night.

LATEST FROM THE NORTH.

THE YANKEE ACCOUNT OF THE CHARLESTON FIGHT!

A Successful Reconnoissance and Very Little Damage Done—Only One Iron-Clad Sunk—Thorough Examination of Charleston Harbor—Debate in the British Parliament on the Alabama, &c., &c.

[FROM OUR OWN REPORTER.]

FREDERICKSBURG, April 15.—I have received the Washington *Chronicle*, of the 13th instant. Among the news it contains is a dispatch giving the disastrous news from Charleston. It is as follows:

The Latest News from Charleston—A Detailed Account of the Attack—The Line of Battle—The Conflict Terrific—Heroic Conduct of the Officers of the Keokuk—Tremendous Fire Poured Upon Fort Sumter—The Gunboat Keokuk Sunk—Our Iron-Clads but Slightly Damaged.

Baltimore, April 12.—The gunboat Flambeau arrived at Old Point on Saturday afternoon, bringing the officers of the iron-clad Keokuk, which was disabled at the engagement at Charleston and sunk next day.

From participants in the engagement we gather the following interesting particulars:

The fleet after leaving Hilton Head rendezvoused in the mouth of the Edisto. Several days were here occupied in gathering vessels and making the final arrangements, issuing orders, and otherwise arranging for the great combat. All being completed, the fleet left in detachments and assembled off Charleston on Sunday, the 5th inst. The iron-clad fleet crossed the bar and entered Charleston harbor on Monday.

The Keokuk, drawing less water than any of the others, was sent in front to find the channel and replace the buoys. Proceeding up the main ship channel the Keokuk found an easy and unobstructed entrance, with full eighteen feet of water in the shallowest place, more than has ever been before found on Charleston bar. The buoys were replaced without difficulty, the rebels offering no opposition.

The Keokuk returned to the fleet, and on the morning of the 7th the order was given to the iron-clads to enter the harbor. The order was to proceed in single file, or in line ahead. The Weehawken was the leading vessel, having in front of her a scow, and then between the scow and herself the Ericsson torpedo exploder, or "Devil," as it has been called.

The Ironsides, with Admiral Dupont on board, was the fifth in the line, and the Keokuk was the last. In this order the bar was passed with safety and without detention. The orders given to the commanders of the various vessels was to keep on straight up the harbor until they came within a thousand yards of the forts, and then to attack, directing their efforts principally against Fort Sumter.

In this order the fleet moved on steadily and gallantly up towards Forts Sumter and Moultrie, the rebels withholding their fire until they got well up into the harbor. The Ironsides stopped off Fort Moultrie, and let go her anchor, it being dangerous to take her up further on account of her drawing over fifteen feet of water. At this moment there seemed to be a temporary misunderstanding, and from a fort erected on the middle ground the fire of from four to five hundred guns was concentrated in a terrible hail upon the devoted vessel. Such a fire has never, perhaps, been equalled in the history of the world. It was met by the officers of the Keokuk with heroic fortitude. Whilst the balls were striking her at the rate of one every second her guns were worked with vigor and precision, and their weight and force were already making their mark upon the walls of Sumter.

It soon, however, became apparent that the Keokuk had none of the impregnability of Ericsson's Monitors; that in fact, as an iron-clad, she was a failure. The rebel balls seemed to penetrate her as easily as though a wooden vessel.

The port holes or shutters of her turrets became jammed and her guns perfectly unmanageable.—During the thirty minutes she remained under the concentrated fire one hundred shots struck her, ninety of which were water line shots, or such as would cause her to sink in a sea way. In fact, she was perfectly riddled.

Her flag was shot into tatters, and the whole of her sides badly bruised or pierced. Perceiving the severe injuries she had received the Admiral signaled her to retire out of action and anchor beyond range.

This was safely accomplished. The Monitors Nahant and Catskill had moved on to the support of the Keokuk, and engaged Fort Sumter.

The Ironsides and other vessels, and at longer distance, were dividing their attention between Forts Moultrie and Sumter. Into and on the latter fort a heavy fire was thus poured, and it is believed not without effect.

The engagement was kept up from one until four o'clock, when, in obedience to the Admiral's signal, the fleet retired slowly, receiving and returning the rebel fire until they anchored out of range, within the bar.

The Weehawken was assigned the important duty, which was faithfully performed in the midst of the fight, to examine, and if possible to fire, the obstructions which the rebels have extended across the harbor from Forts Sumter and Moultrie.—Protected by the scow and the "Devil" in front of her, she pushed straight up towards the obstructions.

They were found to consist of a net-work of chains and cables stretched across the harbor, over which it was impossible for the Weehawken to run without fouling her propeller, and which she found it impossible to force. To this net-work the rebels are supposed to have suspended torpedoes and other submarine explosives.

Having completed the examination, and tested the impossibility of working up the harbor until means are devised for the removal of these obstructions, the Weehawken returned and reported to the Admiral, who then ordered a discontinuance of the conflict.

It is believed that the damage done to Fort Sumter by our fire was serious. So far as it showed externally, it consisted in two embrasures being knocked into one, and numerous indentations in the wall which it is believed a few hours' more pounding would convert into a serious breach.

What damage and loss of life was sustained in the interior of the fort is not, of course, known; but it is believed to have been considerable. Fort Moultrie was also well hammered, and at least one gun was dismounted.

Beyond the sinking of the Keokuk, the damage to the iron clads was very slight, not more than would require twenty-four hours to repair. They all came out of the contest in fighting trim, and able to have continued the conflict, had it been desirable. The Ironsides was hit frequently, but beside having one port shutter damaged was uninjured. Our informant heard of no serious casualties on board of any of the vessels except the Keokuk. This vessel sunk next morning about one thousand yards from Morris's Island beach. She had thirteen wounded, two of whom, including Acting Ensign McIntosh, will die.

The "Devil" was not lost, as stated by the rebel dispatches. When the Weehawken returned from the reconnoissance of the obstructions the scow she had in tow broke loose and grounded off Morris's Island. The rebels thinking it a dangerous affair peppered away at it, thinking it was the "Devil," or something worse, but our informant assures us the "Devil" is safe, and will yet be made use of against the rebels.

The affair may be summed up thus: We have entered Charleston harbor; made a successful reconnoissance; engaged the rebel forts for three hours, damaged Sumter pretty seriously; lost one vessel, and have had a crowning proof of the invulnerability of the Monitor fleet.

The foregoing is made up from an interesting account furnished to the Baltimore *American* by an eye witness who was in the fight.

LATER FROM CHARLESTON.—Geo. Leman telegraphs via Fortress Monroe, April 12, that arrangements are being made to blow up the Keokuk. Further action would be suspended. No torpedoes have been exploded. The Monitor Nahant had five holes in her chimney, and had 500 shots fired at her. Some rivets had been started from her turret.

DEBATE IN THE BRITISH PARLIAMENT ON THE ALABAMA—THE SHIPMENT OF ARMS TO THE NORTH—INTERVENTION UNFRIENDLY.

In a debate in Parliament on the 27th, in relation to the Alabama, the Solicitor-General made an offensive speech. The London *Chronicle* says: "Remonstrances were made by Mr. Baring and Mr. Bright. Mr. Laird said that the whole transaction with regard to the Alabama was most open and legitimate. Rifles were as deadly as vessels without guns, and he had seen manifests at the Custom-House of rifles shipped to the Northern States by the celebrated firms of the Barings and Brown & Co., of Liverpool. [Loud cheers.] He found, also, that (41,000 rifles, 16,500 gun flints, and 49,000,000 of caps, had been shipped to the Northern States, besides a fourth more as hardware. He had also been asked to build ships complete with guns for the Federal Government itself, and he read letters to prove this, amidst loud cheers.—He was therefore astonished at the outcry in America, and complained of the espionage of the Federal Government and its agents here, and said he would rather be handed down to posterity as the builder of a dozen Alabamas, than as a man who set class against class, and cried up the institutions of another country, which were to be found of no value when tested, and has reduced liberty itself to a mockery. [Cheers.]"

Lord John Russell, on the 21st of March, said:—"*It would be a failure of friendship on our part if at this moment we were to interpose and recognize the Southern States.*"

Lord Palmerston's observations on the 27th, though characteristically unfriendly in temper, yet bore the same general testimony to the necessity of avoiding all interference in American affairs.

MISCELLANEOUS.

The rebels in New Orleans had a report that Bragg had been defeated by Rosecrans.

The British steamer Dolphin and the Clara, both prizes, arrived at Key West on the 1st.

A special dispatch to the Chicago *Times* from Helena, Arkansas, the 8th, says the entire Tallahatchie fleet, consisting of the divisions of Ross and Quimby, and numerous gun and mortar boats, arrived the night previous. The expedition left Fort Greenwood Sunday, having been absent 43 days. The divisions under Quimby and Hovey have been ordered to Vicksburg.

The iron-clads Louisville, Mound City, Carondelet, Benton, Lafayette, and two others, are all prepared to run the blockade at Vicksburg, which it was thought would be attempted Friday or Saturday night last. It was also said transports had been prepared with logs and cotton bulkheads to run the batteries.

The reported arrival of Gen Osterhaus, with a heavy force at Carthage, ten miles below Warrenton, on the Louisiana side, is confirmed.

A special dispatch to the N. Y. *Herald* mentions a rumor that McClellan has tendered his resignation, and says the War Department has decided to muster out the two years' regiments, to date from the time of their muster into the service of the United States.

The conversion of legal tenders into five twenties for six days in Philadelphia, including Saturday night was $1,760,800. Total to the 12th, a little over $4,000,000.

The whaling vessel Ellen Risben was chased 12 hours by the pirate Retribution.

The prize schooner Rising Dawn, captured off Wilmington with a cargo of salt, on the 5th, has arrived at New York.

American silver is at a discount of 10 per cent. in St. Johns, N. B.

A bounty of $50, and a furlough of 30 days, are to be given to every soldier who enlists for a year after the expiration of his term of service.

An immense Union meeting has just been held in Chicago. Resolutions expressing the strongest and most decided Union sentiments and pledging a united support to the Government in prosecuting the war, were adopted. Trumbull and others made speeches.

The *Chronicle* alluding to the late arrests of certain ringleaders of an oath bound society in Berks county, Pa., says "there is one feature of their widely extended conspiracy against the Government which emphatically proves it dangerous and desperate character;" that is, "to rescue from the officers of the law those who may be arrested in attempting to resist the draft, or in carrying into effect any of the other known designs of the conspirators. The alacrity with which nearly three hundred men rallied to do what they conceived to be their sworn duty—that is, to rescue a traitor—shows that a number of ignorant and thoughtless men have been taught and are ready to discharge all the obligations imposed by their leaders."

Van Dorn is reported repulsed by Granger.—Van Dorn attacked him at Franklin with 15,000 men. The battle lasted most all day. Van Dorn was repulsed, with a loss of 300. Yankee loss, 100. Stanley's cavalry, led by himself, charged and captured a battery and 200 prisoners; but, being unsupported, was compelled to relinquish the battery and all but 10 prisoners. The enemy was pursued until dark.

Seven Yankee iron clads are expected to run the blockade at Vicksburg on Friday or Saturday night.

Gen. Osterhaus has arrived at Carthage, 10 miles below Warrenton, on the Louisiana side, with a heavy force.

The *Chronicle* editorially says: The Charleston "enterprise" may be abandoned for a time, but efforts to suppress the rebellion will go forward.

The horse artillery which President Lincoln recently reviewed "was bestrode by thirteen thousand men."

[Lincoln's visits to the army have generally been the precursors to defeat.]

The Position of Affairs—Ballooning—Diminution of Hooker's Army—The Elections.

[CORRESPONDENCE OF THE RICHMOND DISPATCH.]

OUT POST, NEAR PORT ROYAL, VA., April 13th, 1863.

This is a memorable day in the annals of the Southern Confederacy—the second anniversary of the fall of Fort Sumter—a propitious harbinger of the many brilliant triumphs of our arms subsequently.

While we are still in the midst of a struggle that has shaken the American Continent from centre to circumference, and excited the admiration of the whole of Europe for unprecedented prowess, we have reasons for feeling sanguine that, in the sequel, the Bonnie Blue Flag will float proudly over the land that has been drenched with the blood of her chivalrous sons. While we sorrow over the dead that are scattered profusely over countless battle fields, and feel the weight of the great sacrifices we have made, we are unwilling to sheathe the trenchant blade until we shall have avenged their lives and achieved a glorious independence.

A partial abatement of the spring tides, together with the amelioration of the roads, may induce "Fighting Joe" to move at any moment. Still there are no visible indications of an advance; he still lingers on the heights of Stafford, looking wistfully at the Confederate camps. The Confederates, in return, look back to the hills of Stafford, which are literally clad with tents, with a degree of indifference.

Professor Lowe makes daily aerial voyages, to ascertain if any new fortifications have been constructed, or if there has been any material "change of base" on the part of the Confederates. Notwithstanding he ascends to a great height, the information he gleans and imparts to "Fighting Joe" we presume is composed chiefly, if not entirely, of the same material that he inflates his balloon with, (gas.) Ballooning an enemy's camp or bivouac for information, in America, we have long since pronounced a complete humbug. A good scout is worth fifty balloons.

Hooker's army is not as powerful as many persons presume it is. From the most reliable information we have gleaned, he has lost forty thousand or more men by transfers and desertions since the battle of the 13th of December last. He has received very few, if any, reinforcements. His effective force will not exceed seventy thousand men.

The health of our army is good. The soldiers are elastic and bouyant, and march nimbly in the drills to the sound of the drum, and fife, and bugle. The profound silence in the field of Mars cannot continue long on the Rappahannock. Your readers may not be surprised to hear of the clash of arms at any moment.

We hear but few in camp speak of the approaching election in Virginia. But little interest is manifested for civil affairs. Soldiers are more absorbed about war, mothers, wives, and sweethearts, than political tricksters. Young men have left the old ones at home to attend to these matters, and we trust they will elect good and efficient men.

The most delectable season of the year, bringing countless rare and fragrant flowers, is upon us. The whole face of the earth begins to smile with beauty, and the prospects of rich harvests. The farmers on the Rappahannock are assiduously engaged in ploughing and putting in seed. DYKE

AN AFFAIR AT PASCAGOULA—*Yankees Landed and Repulsed.*—A party of the enemy 400 in number, and mostly "contraband" troops, landed at Pascagoula, Fla., on the 9th, under cover of two gunboats. They were attacked by Capt. John Marshall's company of mounted men, and repulsed with a loss of fifteen killed. Lieut. Hill and one private of the Confederates were slightly wounded. One gunboat, the "General Banks," put back to Ship Island with the wounded, and the others were still some three quarters of a mile from the shore.

A Retrospect of the Fight at Charleston—Report of a Captured Yankee.

The Yankee armada has left Charleston. On Sunday morning a steamer arrived in the fleet with dispatches, and soon after it was evident some important intelligence had been received. The day being the anniversary of the first battle of Fort Sumter the belief had obtained that the enemy would make their grandest efforts to reduce our fortifications and recapture the city. But when the afternoon arrived it was discovered that instead of advancing to another attack the Yankees were slowly picking up their anchors and moving away. The war correspondent of the Charleston *Courier* gives some intelligence of affairs transpiring since the fight, which is interesting. He says:

Notwithstanding the sinking of the Keokuk and evident damage to various members of the fleet, few among the officers in command were of the opinion the enemy would not give us a second trial, and when the several vessels got under weigh few thought the cowardly foe was about to take his departure. Yet it was even so, and at sundown the majority of the fleet were fading from view on the distant horizon. Of the iron clads, one alone remains—the frigate New Ironsides—which is anchored off the bar. The others took a Southerly direction, as did also the wooden vessels of the squadron, and by the time these notes are read will probably be safely anchored at Port Royal. The Ironsides was towed to her present anchorage, and one of the Monitors was in the same manner conveyed from her moorings. Whether this argues an inability to move of their own accord, is a matter of doubt. Twenty-four transports, supposed to be loaded with troops, have left the Stono, and the enemy are reported to be evacuating Folly Island. The latter rumor should be received with caution.

With reference to the injury inflicted on the Monitors during the late battle, (excepting, of course the sunken Keokuk,) there is no definite information, save what has been obtained from a prisoner captured on Little Folly Island Friday night, by Lieut.-Col. Dargan, of the 21st South Carolina regiment, and a squad of men. The name of the prisoner is John McDonald, and his regiment the 100th New York.

Although an intelligent man, he tells some of the biggest lies that ever issued from the lips of mortal man, and a careful examination only served to involve him in a tissue of fabrications and exaggerations which spoiled his entire story. The statement he made is that none of the iron-clads were seriously damaged, and that the attack was designed simply to test the strength of the fort—a sort of *reconnoissance in force*—and was regarded by naval men as eminently satisfactory. They now feel assured of their ability to reduce Fort Sumter in ten hours with two iron-clads, and intend to do it. McDonald adds that they have altogether a fleet of twelve Monitors, seventeen or eighteen vessels which are iron clad, and a large flotilla in the Edisto, on which are mounted the heaviest mortars.

With reference to the Keokuk, he states that her turret was not materially injured, and that she sunk, not from the effect of our fire, but from the concussion of her own guns, which "broke her back." Such is the Munchausen account of the prisoner. The only valuable part of it is that which refers to the concussion of the enemy's heavy guns. Taking the recent confession of a Northern correspondent, who was on the Montauk during the bombardment of Fort McAllister, in connection with the above, the inference is almost conclusive that the Monitors cannot safely withstand the shock of their own guns sufficiently long for a protracted bombardment. The effect on the systems of the men is not less than the effect on the vessels themselves, so that were it probable that the latter may hereafter be constructed in such a manner as to remove one part of the difficulty, ventilation and personal compassion are two obstacles that are inseparable to boats of that character. Four or five hours in battle, and firing at intervals of twenty minutes, is the most they can endure.

The destruction of the Keokuk is by no means a satisfactory test of the strength of the other Monitors as the latter are constructed upon an entirely different principle. The Keokuk was an experiment, which failed. Had we sunk one of the single-turreted monsters we should then have known something of the invulnerability of the others of her class. As it is, we are as much in the dark as ever.

On Saturday the city was filled with conflicting rumors as to the sinking of the Ironsides. Several gentlemen, with good glasses, observing the ship from the cupola of the Custom House, averred that she was surely settling by the stern, while a dummy engine was seen briskly pumping out water, or lowering her guns to the boat which lay alongside. No subsequent revelation has verified the correctness of these observations, however, and the probability is that the frigate is still comparatively sound. If not, why is she outside the bar?

The firing on Saturday evening about sundown is said to have been an effort by the enemy to shell Morris's Island.

The future movements of the fleet are enveloped in mystery. It is barely supposable that after two years of preparation the Abolitionists will be satisfied with the result of a two hours' bombardment. But they encountered what they did not fully anticipate, lost faith in their boasted prowess, and may have simply retired to gain strength and time, and organize another base of operations.—Perhaps they will now give Savannah or Wilmington a trial, hoping, if successful, to wipe out the disgrace of their present defeat, but that they will return to Charleston eventually.

"The Democracy for the War."

[From the Franklin (N. Y.) Gazette.]

This is the exultant shout of the New York *Tribune*, the vile oracle of Abolitionism, and it bases the foul slander upon the fact that James T. Brady, the Breckinridge candidate for Governor in 1860, and always an uncertain, unreliable politician, who never possessed the sympathy or confidence of his party, and John Van Buren, the erratic Prince of the house of Kinderhook, whose irregular, free-and-easy habits of life and political inconsistencies have rendered him a burden and source of anxiety to any party, attended and took an active part in an Abolition war meeting held in the city of New York a few evenings since. The Democracy in favor of this Abolition war! A blacker falsehood was never uttered, even by Greeley himself, and in behalf of the men who are bravely breasting the storm of fanaticism which is driving the country to destruction, and of the glorious old party of the Constitution, whose traditions give the lie to the *Tribune's* assertion, we hurl back the foul slander into the teeth of its author.

Whatever such shifting weathercocks as John Van Buren may say or do, the great Democratic heart beats true to the principles of constitutional liberty as taught by the fathers, which include the sovereignty of the States, the freedom of speech and of the press, the subordination of the military to the civil authority, the protection of the citizen from arrest and imprisonment except upon due process of law, and a speedy trial by jury. It is against all these sacred rights that the present war is waged by the Lincoln Government; and he who lends it his support or countenance, or does not oppose it by all lawful and constitutional methods, ought to blush to call himself a Democrat.

"In favor of the war, are we!" says the Rome *Sentinel* to a "war for the Union" neighbor—"Then how is it that we nominated Thomas H. Seymour in Connecticut—that we elected James W. Wall to the United States Senate from New Jersey—that in every State where we have had the Legislature, resolutions in favor of peace have been passed? How is it that our party in Congress vote solid against every one of Mr. Lincoln's war measures? But we are in favor of "the war for the Constitution and the Union," you mean. Then we ought to be able to state where that war is being carried on. Certainly not in Maryland, where congregations are directed by the Provost Marshal to conspicuously display the United States flag in their churches, or forbidden to worship; not in Western Virginia, where Milroy suppresses Democratic papers, and where Hooker fights to establish Pierpont as the lawful Governor of the part of the State which never voted for him; nor anywhere in the South, where slaves are all freed by proclamation, and every white man's estate confiscated without jury trial, by Congressional enactment. Not certainly in South Carolina, where San Domingo servile insurrection, with all its horrors, is being inaugurated by Hunter. Not in Missouri, where every property-holder is called a bush-whacker, and liable to be shot and his family and property placed at the brutal will of Kansas jayhawkers. Not in Kentucky, where a Democratic State Convention is dispersed by armed force before it has passed a single resolution or exhibited one sign of "disloyalty." Where shall we find this "war for the Constitution and the Union" of which we are in favor?

"We support the war in our Conventions, do we? Great war meetings those are. To them flocks every man who believes with Douglas that 'war is disunion.' In them every word against the war is cheered. Look at Gov. Seymour's message—nineteen-twentieths of it for the Constitution—hardly a bare reference to the war, and that only to recognize it as a fact, and to proclaim that war alone cannot restore the Union. If the Democratic party is in favor of the war and the Constitution it has the two feelings in very different proportions." [Better speak right out brother *Sentinel* and say that just in the proportion that it is in favor of the one, it is and must be opposed to the other. It is nonsense to talk about being in favor of both the war and the Constitution, when they are irreconcilably antagonistic to each other—the war being directed against the Constitution, against the liberties of the North, against the interests, prosperity, and happiness of the American people.]

MORE IRON CLADS.—The New York *Tribune*, of Wednesday last, states that all the contracts for iron clads (twelve in all) have been awarded. The prices for these will range from $330,000 to $400,000. They are to be finished and added to the Yankee Navy in about six months.

Dr. Andrews, of Charlotte, N. C., who went to Europe on important business, was arrested and is now in Fort Warren.

TELEGRAPHIC NEWS.

More Captures Near Nashville—The 'Horse Marines' at Work.

CHATTANOOGA, April 14.—Major Dick McCann has captured another train on the Nashville and Chattanooga Railroad. He has also destroyed a long wagon train.

Two more gunboats and three transports on the Cumberland river have been destroyed by Wheeler's command.

Van Dorn's Recent Fight.

CHATTANOOGA, April 14.—The rumors in regard to Van Dorn's fight at Franklin, Tenn., prove to have been exaggerated. The loss was only fifty on each side. Freeman's battery, which was captured by the enemy, was immediately retaken. All quiet along the line to-day.

From Charleston.

CHARLESTON, April 14.—All quiet to-night. The enemy occupies Cole's, Kiawah and Seabrook's Islands, in considerable force, protected by a few gunboats. All his transports have left this vicinity.

Destruction of Grain.

CHATTANOOGA, April 14.—The malt house attached to Snider's distillery, at this place, was destroyed by fire at noon to-day with a quantity of grain. Loss $7,000—insurance $2,000.

LOCAL MATTERS.

Escaped from Prison.—The following soldiers, charged with desertion and confined in the military prison, escaped on the 14th inst., by a "hole in the wall," which they made themselves, viz: Robert Burch, John Wrenn, M J Lannan, John Brismo, J O Gaynes, and Wm Clarke. On Tuesday night, Tim O'Brien, charged with forging checks to defraud the Government Treasury, and a Captain Buttrick or Butterworth, charged with forging soldiers' pay claims, who were confined in the jail of Henrico county, escaped by making an incision in the walls of that edifice. A guard was stationed around the building at the time, but it appears did not make any discovery till after the prisoners had gotten out.

Charge of Exhibiting Faro.—Messrs. Davis, Pleasants and others of the City Police, yesterday effected the arrest of Henry Hungerford on the charge of keeping and exhibiting, at the tenement No 149 Main street, the game of faro. James Bennett, E L Israel, John Abbot, O. H. Wilson, and J. A. Williams were also arrested at the same time, charged with being in the bank with Hungerford. After being carried to the cage, all of the parties gave bail to appear before the Mayor this morning, save Williams. The police seized during the raid a few chips and a table, said to have been used when the "tiger" was being exhibited.

Mayor's Court.—A number of cases were disposed of by the Mayor yesterday. A summary of which we subjoin:

Jack O'Donnell was brought up for assaulting and beating an old woman named Catherine Riley. The latter testified to a slap which she said O'Donnell gave her. *Per contra*, witnesses on behalf of O'Donnell proved that he had given Mrs Riley (who is a refugee from Baltimore) a house to live in, and that, proving quarrelsome and disagreeable, he had tried to get rid of her by persuasion. None of them had seen O'D. strike Mrs. R. The charge against O'D. was dismissed.

Richard Jordan was charged with stealing from Charles Mittledorfer a pipe worth $20 and Thos. Tunpin, a somewhat notorious youth, was charged with having the same in his possession. The evidence against the defendants was of such a character as to warrant the Mayor in requiring bail of each to the amount of $300 for their good behavior. On failing to give bail they were sent to the chain gang for 90 days.

Beverly Morris free, was charged with trespassing on Eliza Fagan's premises, and Patrick Murther with assaulting and beating him therefor. The Mayor sent Morris (who is an old jail bird) to prison, and required Murther to give security for his good behavior.

James McGee was charged with assaulting Alonzo Travers with an iron poker. It was in proof that the defendant and Wm. H. Travers were joint proprietors of the Alabama House, opposite the Spotswood Hotel, on Main street, and that they had had some difficulty relative to the proportion of profits to which each was entitled.—McGee thought Travers had set his son to watch his movements, and when Travers, the elder, had temporarily disappeared he commenced abusing the young man, and finally assaulted him with a poker. The opportune arrival of the father with a drawn pistol prevented further violence to the son. The Mayor remarked to McGee that difficulties might be settled with pokers in Baltimore, but such was not the case in Richmond. He held McGee to bail for his appearance to answer an indictment by the Grand Jury, and also required him to give security to keep the peace. It having leaked out that liquor had been sold in the house without a license, the Mayor fined Travers $5.

M. Jacobs gave bail to appear before Judge Meredith for trial for being engaged in the recent "riot."

The case against Melinda Emory and Jannet Williams, for the same offence, was continued, defendants giving bail for their appearance.

Hustings Court, April 15th.—Recorder Caskie and others presiding.—Mary Jackson, the alleged getter-up of the recent riot, was examined and sent on before Judge Lyons to be tried for felony.

Thomas Samani, who participated in the same affair, was also sent on for trial before the same Court.

Benjamin Kemper, charged with breaking into the storehouse of James Knotts and stealing a lot of boots and shoes, was committed for trial before Judge Lyons.

William H. Ross, a free negro, was tried for stealing $1,000 in C. S. Treasury notes, from Jos. Stickenburg, and was acquitted.

Malvina, a slave, was ordered 15 lashes for stealing $ 50 from E. S. L. Tighe, her employer.

Charged with Disloyalty.—William Wilson, a citizen residing within the lines of the army at Fredericksburg, was arrested on Tuesday, April 14th, by order of General Lee, for disloyalty, and sent to Richmond for trial. Wilson was sent to the military prison of the Eastern district, where he now is.

Libby Prison.—Twelve abolition prisoners were received into this prison yesterday. Two belonged to the 11th Pa Cavalry, six to the 1st New York Rifles, and four to the 7th N Y Artillery. They were captured near Suffolk, where the enemy is reported to have a large force of cavalry posted. Some 100 Abolitionists are now here awaiting transportation to the United States.

Fast and Slow People.—Oliver P. Baldwin, Esq., of this city, lectures before the Young Men's Christian Association to-night, at the Second Baptist Church, Main st., on the subject of "Fast and Slow People." A rich treat is promised the lovers of intellectual amusement.

Court of Appeals.—The Judges of this Court resumed their sittings on the 7th inst. They have since that time announced no decisions on cases pending before them. Arguments in pending cases were being heard yesterday.

THE OATH OF ALLEGIANCE TO THE UNITED STATES.—Mr. Robert Ould, Agent of Exchange of Prisoners for the Confederacy, has written the following in reply to an inquiry as to whether certain citizens of North Carolina were bound by the oath of allegiance to the United States, taken by them:

RICHMOND, April 1st, 1863.

All citizens heretofore arrested by Federal authority, and released upon parole, whether that parole was to return to Federal lines, or to procure the release of any other person, or for any other purpose, or with any sort of obligation, have been declared by the express agreement of the Federal Agent of Exchange released from said parole or any obligation named therein. RO. OULD, Agent of Exchange.

TAR DROPS FOR THE YANKEE GOVERNMENT.—The most laughable instance of the pitiable state of despotism under which Baltimore labors, is that related by the Baltimore *Gazette*, in a local paragraph:

M. Aukers was yesterday arrested by order of Col. Fish, Provost Marshal, for circulating a poetical advertisement of his tar drops, entitled "Uncle Sam Consumped; What Will Cure Him?" in which was recited, to the tune of "Yankee Doodle," some of the difficulties of the Government; the last verse intimating that the Government was in a deplorable condition, and that the only hope for it was in the use of the tar drops. He was released upon assuring Colonel Fish that he would not hereafter circulate or publish the objectionable doggerel.

HEAVIEST OF THE WAR.—An artillery officer writing from Port Hudson, says the cannonading there was the heaviest of the war, about three hundred large guns and mortars were belching forth their terrible thunders at the same time.

The South Carolina Legislature adjourned on Friday night.

The Philadelphia Inquirer.

CIRCULATION OVER 60,000. PHILADELPHIA, MONDAY, APRIL 20, 1863. PRICE TWO CENTS.

IMPORTANT ARMY NEWS.

THE ADVANCE FROM THE RAPPAHANNOCK.

Movements of Stoneman's Cavalry.

EXPEDITION to WARRENTON, SULPHUR SPRINGS, LIBERTY and BEALETON.

Kelly's Ford in Our Possession.

REBEL PARTISANS ROUTED.

Rush's Lancers in Active Service.

Success of the Expeditions.

Special Correspondence of the Inquirer.

NEAR FREEMAN'S FORD, BEYOND BEALETON, April 16, 1863.

Were it not for the violent storm of wind and rain that yesterday visited us, we should have had the pleasure of chronicling one of the most successful military movements that has had an existence during the continuance of this unholy war.

Up to the time it commenced raining, on Tuesday night last, our movement had been accomplished with unusual celerity, everything was working smoothly, all the plans of our leaders had been successfully carried out, and all were jubilant at the brilliant and glorious prospect before us. Yet, notwithstanding the elements are against us, the expedition is by no means abandoned, but will yet be fully carried out to a glorious and successful termination.

While it is still in being, and nothing of a permanent nature has been positively accomplished, we do not feel warranted in stating the force accompanying it, who are its leaders, what is its destination, or what advantages are to be gained by it. Still, in order to show your many thousand loyal readers that something really grand is in progress, we will make a *résumé* of what has been accomplished up to the present time.

On Monday morning early, the expedition, under command of that accomplished officer, Maj.-General STONEMAN, consisting of cavalry, infantry and artillery, left our old encampment opposite Fredericksburg; one portion, cavalry alone, proceeded to Bristerburg and there encamped for the night; another, likewise cavalry, bivouacked the same night at Elk Run; another portion, cavalry with a battery, encamped at Morrisville, and a fourth, accompanied by a brigade of infantry and two batteries of artillery, remained for the night at Grove Church, STONEMAN's head-quarters being at the Spotted Tavern, thereby making a complete semi-circle, and guarding and covering every road and by-path to our rear.

Before daylight the next morning, that portion encamped at Bristerburg sent out two squadrons, the Eighth Illinois and Ninth New York, under Capt. FARNSWORTH, with instructions to proceed to Warrenton, thence to Sulphur Springs, and there await orders. The remainder of this force were ordered to proceed to Liberty. In order that the movements may be more readily understood by the general reader, we propose to record the doings of each division or detachment, in the order as above mentioned.

The squadron sent towards Warrenton and Sulphur Springs fully obeyed their instructions in their [illegible]. They came upon several detached bodies of that celebrated partisan cavalry who rendezvous in this locality, to each of which they gave chase, and succeeded in capturing some and wounding others. Upon reaching the Springs they forded the river, and continued down on the opposite bank as far as Freeman's Landing, when, owing to the inclemency of the weather, the roads becoming impassable, they were obliged to return to the point at which they crossed. The gallant exploits of this squadron upon the other side of the stream we propose to elucidate at some future time, for the reason that, if told now, it might indicate to the enemy our future destination. The balance of the division to which these two squadrons are attached are at present encamped at Liberty.

The Division which remained at Elk Run left there before daylight the same morning, and proceeded to Bealeton, and upon their arrival there, they observed scattered about upon the hills and in the woods, parties of two, three, and up to a dozen, of the same partisan cavalry before spoken of, to whom they gave chase, but were unsuccessful in their capture. This Division is now lying in the woods near this point.

The Division remaining during the night near Morrisville moved down to Kelly's Ford. Here was discovered the first organized body of the enemy. Preparations were at once made to dislodge them, and after throwing a shell or two, the Rebels deemed it prudent to retire, which they did at a rapid rate, thus leaving the Ford in our possession.

A portion of this force then was sent on up the river to the Rappahannock Bridge, with instructions to hold it and prevent its spoliation. All has been done agreeable to directions given. They now hold one side of Kelly's Ford, and are strong enough in position at the bridge to hold it and prevent its destruction.

The remaining division on leaving their encampment, at Grove Church, traveled on to the junction of Eastham's and Hedgeman's Creek, and from there to Liberty, where they now are. These two met with trifling opposition, and have sent in some ten or twelve prisoners.

Thus were we moving quietly along; the roads were in a splendid condition, the streams almost dry, and unbounded success had been the result of our every movement, when the violent storm came, turning the soil into a thick, pasty concrete, rendering the hauling of artillery an utter impossibility, and it was with a great deal of difficulty that our lead horses could move along; all the time a perfect deluge of rain was falling, and at so rapid a rate as to cause the many streams emptying into the Rappahannock to swell to an enormous height. Streams which we crossed in the morning only an inch or two deep, were by noon rapidly flowing in absolute torrents, and so deep as to necessitate the swimming of horses in their crossing. The First Maryland Cavalry, in crossing one of these streams lost three horses by drowning.

At noon yesterday, our transportation wagons were concentrated at Bealeton, unloaded and sent back via Morrisville, and such supplies as were to be taken along were packed on the mules.

During the afternoon of yesterday frequent alarms were in progress, because of the doings of the beforementioned partisan cavalry, and at one time some dozen of them made a dash upon Bealeton Station, and succeeded in taking a trifling amount of property and capturing one man.

Orderlies, in their travels, are frequently chased, but so far as we are in possession of intelligence, none have been captured.

Towards night RUSH's Lancers were set scouring the country, in order to clear it of these strolling bands. They have succeeded admirably in so doing, and are almost hourly sending in some of them as prisoners, together with quite a number of civilians.

Towards noon yesterday, General STONEMAN, being fully convinced of the utter impracticability of proceeding further, called a consultation of his Generals, when it was determined to remain in possession of the position we then held, in order that he might, without delay, continue his tour when the weather and roads will permit.

We are in possession of data sufficient to make a narrative of considerable length and immense interest. We have the names of the parties commanding and the troops accompanying us, and we have, too, memoranda of many little incidents where courage, daring and splendid behavior have been apparent, but for prudential reasons refrain from mentioning them now. Suffice it to say we are splendidly officered and completely equipped, and the men brimming full of ardor, determination, and anxious to go on. So far it has been one continued success, and all are sanguine that so it will continue until the end; and when that end is accomplished we will be at liberty to write more explicitly than at present.

The Rebels appear in considerable force, but we doubt much if they will be able to greatly retard us should our able leader determine here to cross.

THE ADVANCE FROM THE RAPPAHANNOCK.

Map showing the position of Gordonsville, the junction of the Orange and Alexandria, and Virginia Central Railroads, and the Key to Richmond, Lynchburg, and Southern Virginia.

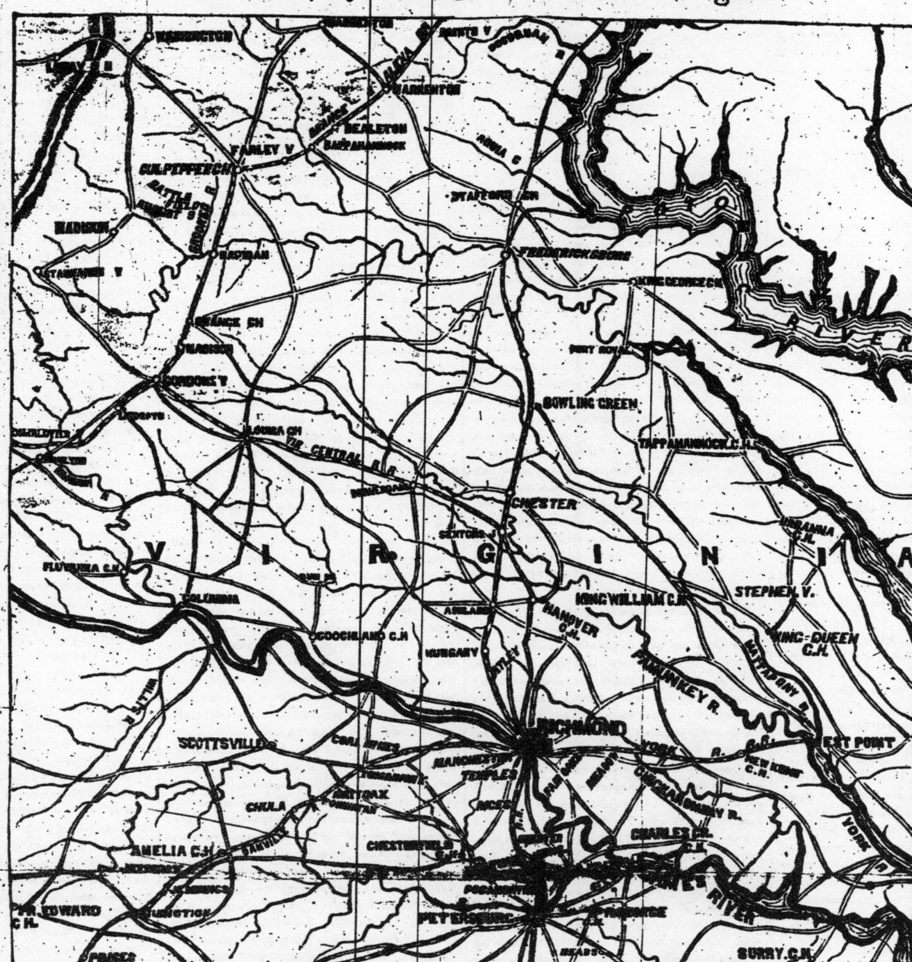

FROM WASHINGTON.

Special Despatches to the Inquirer.

WASHINGTON, April 19, 1863.

The Fight on the Nansemond River.

The steamer *Baltimore* arrived at the Navy Yard this morning from Fortress Monroe, bringing further particulars of the affair on the Nansemond.

The steamer *Mount Washington* was towed to Newport News on Saturday, where she will be repaired. She received two shots in her boiler and several struck her engines, damaging them considerably. Her woodwork is pierced through and through.

One of the seamen of the *Minnesota*, who was temporarily on the *Mount Washington*, was killed, but none of the men belonging to her were injured so as to keep them from duty, although many were struck by flying splinters and slightly hurt.

The pilot of the *Stepping Stones* lost one of his legs.

The gun-boats on the Nansemond have received a reinforcement of the following gun-boats from the Potomac flotilla:—*Yankee*, Captain IVES, *Cœur de Lion* and *Primrose*, Captain STREET; and the flotilla there, with these auxiliaries, will undoubtedly be able to keep the Nansemond clear of Rebel batteries.

Contradiction of the Gordonsville Rumor.

Rumors have been circulating here during the last twenty-four hours, that our forces have driven the enemy from and occupy Gordonsville. But it is ascertained, after inquiry in the proper quarters, that there is nothing authentic to sustain such reports. All is quiet on the front to-day. MOSBY's forces were in the neighborhood of Drainesville yesterday.

Officers Dismissed.

By order of General HOOKER, the following officers have been dismissed the service:—

Captain CHRISTIAN KUHN, Company A, Eleventh Pennsylvania Volunteers.

Lieutenant ORVILLE HARRIS, Company B, Fifth New York Artillery.

Lieutenant WILLIAM H. DAVIS, Company H, Twenty-fifth Ohio Volunteers.

Lieutenant FELIX HILFERTY, Company F, First Maryland Cavalry.

By order of the War Department, Lieutenant HARVEY COLTON, Sixth Virginia Volunteers, has been dismissed from the service, for drunkenness while on duty.

Deserters Sentenced.

The following soldiers, belonging to the One-hundred-and-Twelfth Pennsylvania Regiment, having been convicted by court-martial on the charge of desertion, are sentenced to confinement at hard labor in the Government works at the "Rip Raps," and to forfeit all pay during the same period:—

Private JAMES E. VERDIER, for one year.
Private HARRISON MOST, for one year.
Private JOHN COLLIGHAN, for one year.
Private WASHINGTON NOGLE, for one year.
Private JOHN NELSON, for one year.
Private THOMAS HARVEY, to confinement at Tortugas during the remainder of his term of enlistment.
Private FREDERICK T. SPRING, for one year.
Private JOHN REDMENT, for one year.
Private JAMES ABRAHAM, for selling, losing, or otherwise disposing of his uniform, six months at the "Rip Raps."

Agricultural Colleges.

The following States have accepted grants under the act of Congress of July 2d, 1862, donating public lands to the several States and Territories which may provide colleges for the benefit of agriculture and the mechanic arts:—New York, Pennsylvania, Illinois, Rhode Island, Minnesota, Vermont, Kansas, Kentucky, Missouri and Iowa. The General Land Office has in course of preparation the proper instructions which will serve as a guide to the officers charged with executing the act.

Contract Awarded.

The General Land Office has entered into a contract with DANIEL G. MAJOR, to establish, by a series of astronomical observations, the forty-sixth parallel of north latitude between the Columbia and Snake Rivers, constituting a part of the State boundary line between Oregon and Washington Territory.

Miscellaneous News.

HARVEY SHERMAN, one of Colonel BAKER's Detective Officers, has been captured near Drainesville by MOSBY's Rebel Cavalry Guerrillas, and report says that he was hung.

Colonel AMBROSE THOMPSON, of New York, Inspector of the Army of the Potomac, at head-quarters, has been relieved from duty with General HOOKER, and placed in command of the important post of Aquia, Virginia.

All the civilians lately released from Southern prisons and sent North, on their parole, have been exchanged.

It is understood that the case of the steamer *Peterhoff* is to be left to the jurisdiction of the Court now having it in charge, without interference from Washington.

It may not be generally known that Gen. SIMMONS was several weeks ago ordered to report to General WRIGHT, for service in the Department of the Pacific.

Governor JOHNSON having nearly completed the official business which brought him hither, will soon return to Tennessee.

The Hon. ROBERT J. WALKER has gone to Europe, partly in behalf of the Quicksilver Mining Company, to assist its claim in a suit against BARON FORBES, who represents the Company now in possession of the mines. He also will act for the Government for the purpose of effecting an arrangement to secure uniform weights and measures of coin, so as to be equal in weight and fineness, both in the United States and Great Britain, thus equalize the exchange for the convenience of commerce, as recommended in the annual report of the Secretary of the Treasury. His business is not, as stated, on the subject of loans.

Mr. ASPINWALL's business in Europe, it is understood, is connected with the Navy Department.

The Indian War in Minnesota.

ST. PAUL, Minn., April 18.—A party of Indians attacked an outpost of eighteen soldiers, on the 16th inst., at Medalia, thirty miles from Mankato, Minnesota. One soldier was killed and two wounded. The Indians also killed a boy and wounded two men (settlers.) A party of cavalry have been sent in pursuit of the Indians.

THE LATEST SOUTHERN WAR NEWS.

FORTRESS MONROE, April 17.—The flag of truce boat *State of Maine* arrived here from City Point at a late hour last night, in charge of Captain J. G. MULFORD, of the Third New York, bringing no passengers or news.

The Richmond *Inquirer* of the 16th contains the following despatch:—

CHATTANOOGA, Tenn., April 11.—Major DICK McCANN has captured another train on the Nashville and Chattanooga Railroad.

Two gun-boats and three transports on the Cumberland River have been destroyed by WHEELER's command. VAN DORN's fight at Franklin, Tenn., proved to have been exaggerated. The loss on each side was only fifty, and FREEMAN's battery, which was captured, was retaken.

A Committee of Congress is now engaged in investigating the conduct of Assistant Provost Marshal, GEORGE W. ALEXANDER, for charges of gross cruelty to the prisoners in his charge at Castle Thunder. The alleged cruelties bear several unpleasant charges, such as tying men up by the thumbs, kicking, beating, &c.

FORTRESS MONROE, April 18.—The Richmond papers of yesterday have been received here. They contain the following despatches:—

The War on the Mississippi.

"JACKSON, April 16.—The enemy's troops at Lake Providence have moved to Vicksburg and Grenada. The movement of the boats in going up to Vicksburg was a *ruse*.

"A heavy movement commenced on Thursday. A large fire was observed last night, right above Vicksburg, which is supposed to have been occasioned by the burning of transports. The Yankee forces are in possession of New Carthage.

North Carolina.

"WILMINGTON, N. C., April 16.—The steamers *Flora* and *Bell* arrived here this morning, from Nassau, with cargoes of coffee, saltpetre, &c.

"The Government warehouses at Branchville, were destroyed by fire on the 12th, with 50,000 rations of bacon and a large quantity of flour and sugar."

Tennessee.

"General WHEELER, on the 13th, captured two trains between Nashville and Murfreesboro', together with $30,000 in money. A number of prisoners were also taken, including three Majors, two Captains, and three of General ROSECRANS' Staff."

The Latest from Suffolk.

The following news has been received here from Norfolk:—

Yesterday afternoon the enemy drove back our skirmishers on the Somerton road, which is General CORCORAN's front, and opened on Fort Union with two pieces of artillery.

Our forts at once replied to them and drove them back. Our skirmishers on the South Quay road drove the enemy back some miles from our lines.

Deserters say that the enemy intend to make an attack this week.

A number of guerrillas were prowling about our flanks yesterday, cutting the telegraph wires, which were soon repaired. One man was killed.

Both railroads between Suffolk and Norfolk are in running order, and amply guarded by cavalry patrols.

No letters are now allowed to be sent forward by flag of truce, except to prisoners of war.

The *Herald's* Norfolk letter expresses the opinion that there will be no great battle at Suffolk. We outnumber the enemy there, and have the advantage of strong entrenchments, unless General PECK takes the initiative and advances on the enemy. We are confident there will be no battle.

The United States Gun-boat "Connecticut."

NEW YORK, April 18.—The barque *J. W. Andrews* reports, April 6th, in the Bahama Channel, was boarded by the British gun-boat *Signet*, who reported that on the 4th inst., she was fired into by the United States gun-boat *Connecticut*, who took the *Signet* to be the pirate *Alabama*. The captain of the *Signet* went on board the *Connecticut*, when the affair was amicably adjusted.

LATEST NEWS FROM CHARLESTON.

OPERATIONS SUSPENDED.

The Iron-Clads at Port Royal.

JOHN'S AND FOLLY ISLANDS HELD BY OUR TROOPS.

FURTHER DETAILS OF ATTACK ON CHARLESTON.

OUR IRON-CLADS INVINCIBLE.

Troops Sent to North Carolina.

The Future Operations.

REASONS FOR THE SUSPENSION, &c., &c., &c.

Special Correspondence of the Inquirer.

PORT ROYAL, S. C., April 15, 1863.

A Suspension of Hostilities.

The operations against Charleston have been suspended for the present, but not abandoned. This sentence I wish your readers would commit to memory, as it furnishes the key to the present movements in this department. Knowing that every one will wish to know why operations have been suspended, I have informed myself on this point from official sources. A portion of General FOSTER's troops had been surrounded by the enemy in North Carolina, and General HUNTER has despatched a part of the forces of this department to his relief. This, of course, weakens General HUNTER's command, which has never been as large as its exigencies would demand. Operations, therefore, by General HUNTER, are suspended for the present. Why Admiral DUPONT has not resumed operations with the iron-clads is something which I cannot at present state. You may rest assured, however, that *it is not because of any want of preparation or desire to attack, that the iron-clads have left Charleston*. This information, although it may be mystical and unsatisfactory, is perfectly reliable and semi-official.

A portion of General HUNTER's command still hold Folly Island, which they occupied before the naval attack upon Charleston. This island is immediately below Morris Island and about ten miles from Charleston. It commands Stono Inlet, which is serviceable to us, both as a naval rendezvous and safe anchorage for transports and supply vessels. You can see how important it is for the success of our future operations that we should keep possession of this island. If the Rebels should once gain a foothold on it they would fortify it, and thus deprive us for a time and perhaps altogether, of an important and necessary harbor. The same remarks apply in regard to John's Island, which commands North Edisto, another valuable harbor and convenient "back door" to Charleston. It is now held by General HUNTER, and he will not relinquish either of these positions, but will hold them as important auxiliaries to his future campaign. Part of the Expeditionary corps have returned to this place, and Port Royal has been made a busy spot by the unloading of troops, supplies and ammunition. The soldiers, while they do not know the reason for their return and debarkation, are nevertheless full of spirit, and have every confidence in the judgment and plans of their Commanding General

It seems to me that the force in this department should be greatly augmented for offensive operations. [illegible] of this State would gladden the hearts of the people more than any other achievement of the war. I have wished more than once, and not alone, I assure you, that General HUNTER had an army of a hundred thousand men or more, so that he could march from Pocotaligo directly upon Charleston and rout the Rebel hordes surrounding it. The army will take the decisive part in the next attack upon Charleston, and it should be so increased that not a shadow of defeat would attend its movements. General HUNTER is a man of undoubted bravery and talent, and deserves an army commensurate with his abilities. Such an army he would lead to victory and lasting renown.

The sooner such an army is sent to the Department of the South, the better it will be for the immediate success of our arms in this locality. *A land attack by a large and well organized army must resume successful operations against Charleston.*

One cannot remain here long without noticing the method and system with which the business in this department is transacted. Everybody knows his business and performs it. Lieutenant-Colonel HALPIN, Adjutant-General of the Department of the South, is particularly noted for his executive ability, and the ease and facility with which he conducts the varied affairs under his control. He is, moreover, a perfect gentleman, and while pressed by the cares of business, can find time and inclination to extend to strangers more than the bare civilities of life. General HUNTER has been fortunate in securing the services of so valuable and efficient an officer. While the Northern people have been gratified by receiving early intelligence concerning the late naval attack, their gratitude must be extended to General HUNTER, who had such an appreciation of the people's desires, that he placed a boat at the special disposal of the correspondents, in order that accurate and early intelligence of the affair might be published in the leading journals of the country. A General of such foresight and accommodation deserves the special commendation of the press and the people.

Aid for General Foster.

General HECKMAN's Brigade has been sent from this Department, by General HUNTER, to the assistance of General FOSTER in North Carolina. It is one of the most efficient brigades in the General's command, and will render material aid in foiling the plans of the enemy. The following is the special order issued on the subject:—

HEAD-QUARTERS, DEPARTMENT OF THE SOUTH, HILTON HEAD, PORT ROYAL, S. C., April 12, 1863.—Special Orders, No. 126.—It having been officially represented to the Major-General Commanding, by Brigadier-General HECKMAN, Major SOLOMON GILES, Third New York Artillery, and Captain WM. V. HUTCHINS, of the Staff of Brigadier-General STEVENSON, that Major-General FOSTER, Commanding Department of North Carolina, is besieged, and in danger of being captured by the enemy at Washington, N. C., Brigadier-General HECKMAN, United States Volunteers, is hereby ordered to proceed with his brigade, consisting of the following regiments, viz.: Ninth New Jersey, Twenty-third Massachusetts, Eighty-first New York and Ninety-eighth New York, to Newbern, N. C., where he will report to Brigadier-General PALMER, or whoever may be the General in command, for service in the relieving of Major-General FOSTER. This duty executed, or it being found that Major-General FOSTER has been already relieved, Brigadier-General HECKMAN will forthwith return with his command to this Department.

By command of Major-General D. HUNTER.
(Signed) ED. W. SMITH, Assistant Adjutant-General.
ISRAEL SEALLY, First Lieutenant, Forty-seventh New York Volunteers, A. A. A. General

Further Details of the Late Attack.

Now that the excitement is less intense than when we were at the scene of action, a better opportunity is afforded for arriving at truthful details of the late naval attack upon Charleston. The rumors and wonderful stories which filled the mouths and ears of officers and civilians in this department have contracted their huge dimensions, and the truth is gradually coming to light. It now appears that the iron-clads suffered more severely than was at first supposed or reported, and that, although they accomplished much, it was not in their power to overcome impossibilities. It is well known to the North for how long

Concluded on the Eighth Page.

The New-York Times.

VOL. XII—NO. 3623. | NEW-YORK, TUESDAY, MAY 5, 1863. | PRICE THREE CENTS.

FROM THE ARMY OF THE POTOMAC

Details of the Important Operations to Sunday Night.

Letters from Our Special Correspondents.

Terrible Battles Fought on Saturday and Sunday at Chancellorsville.

Unsuccessful Attempt of Stonewall Jackson to Turn General Hooker's Right.

A Terrific and Successful Night Attack upon the Enemy.

A Fierce Battle of Six Hours' Duration on Sunday.

A FAIR STAND-UP FIGHT.

The Results in Our Favor, but Undecisive.

THE OPERATIONS AT FREDERICKSBURGH.

The Two Ridges Behind the City in Our Possession.

OUR FORCES ADVANCED FOUR MILES

About Four Thousand Prisoners Captured

TERRIBLE LOSSES OF THE ENEMY.

CHANCELLORSVILLE, VA., TEN MILES WEST BY SOUTH OF FREDERICKSBURGH, Saturday, Midnight, May 2, 1863.

I.

The military operations which have been in progress on the line of the Rappahannock for a week past, have to-day culminated in what, if not precisely a great battle, only escapes that designation because we all feel that greater, by far, remains behind.

Gen. HOOKER, by a series of brilliantly audacious manœuvres and movements, of a celerity wholly unmatched in this war, has succeeded in crossing the Rappahannock River, and gaining for his army a position ten miles west by south, and in the rear of Fredericksburgh.

Gen. LEE, at first completely surprised by this move, and utterly puzzled as to his antagonist's intentions, has, however, had time to recover himself, and with a hand almost equally bold in the grand game of strategy—abandoning his position in Fredericksburgh, and the line of twenty miles down the Rappahannock which he has held for months—has changed his front, and stands opposite us in the horrid gage of battle.

We have secured a strong position, *completely turning the line of rebel defensive heights in the rear of Fredericksburgh*, against which our army on the 13th of last December madly dashed itself. This, as Gen. HOOKER expresses it in his inspiriting order of Thursday, gives us the advantage of compelling the enemy to fight us on ground of our own choosing.

Figure to yourself a huge triangle or redan, one leg of three miles long, resting on the south side of the Rappahannock, above Fredericksburgh, and between Banks and United States Ford, and the other on Hunting Creek, an affluent of the Rappahannock, with the apex at Chancellorsville, and you have, in epitome, the situation as it now stands. This position, naturally strong, has been rendered doubly stronger by breastworks and abattis thrown up in front to cover the troops.

Imagine, now, the enemy massed in front of this position—front to front, and flank to flank—and you have the rebel situation. Take into account, also, that the enemy have strengthened themselves by the same appliances adopted by us.

These relative positions were assumed three days ago, and the history of that period is that of skirmishing along the advance line, developed in front of both armies—we feeling the enemy at various points, the enemy feeling us at various points.

This afternoon and evening, however, the enemy was emboldened to depart from these minor operations, and make a bold *coup*, by attacking our right flank in force, and attempting to double us up. About 6 o'clock this evening, JACKSON—you will recognize as I go on the operations and all its circumstances as one quite in his style, and the affair will recall to you Cedar Mountain and other memories—with his whole corps of forty thousand men, threw himself impetuously on our extreme right, formed by the Eleventh Army corps, under command of Major-Gen. HOWARD. The assault was one marked by all the dash and audacity that characterize his mind, and as it was made precisely at our weakest point, and on a corps which JACKSON has already several times beaten, it was well calculated to succeed.

That he only *partially* succeeded in turning our flank was not owing to the conduct of the Eleventh Army Corps, which was disgraceful, but to the superb generalship of HOOKER, who promptly threw reinforcements on our right to stop the enemy's advance. Such changes in our position as circumstances dictated are to-night being made—I must not at present mention what they are—and there is little prospect that the enemy will succeed in his purpose of either breaking our line or cutting our communications, while a vigorous offensive will probably in a few hours be assumed. The rebels will do one of two things: either abandon their position here and seek to make good their retreat to Gordonsville—the only line now left them, as Fredericksburgh has been abandoned, and their line of communication with Richmond *is in all probability by this time cut*—or they will remain here and give us battle.

It is, of course, impossible for me to predict which alternative Gen. LEE will adopt; but a few hours will develop; and if the hopes of our leaders and our own do not prove deceptive, you may expect soon to hear of the greatest victory of the war.

To make the battle of to-day intelligible in all its relations, it is absolutely necessary that I should take a brief retrospect of the operations of the entire week. You have already received from your correspondents current accounts of events as they have transpired; but as it was inevitable that these should be written without a full appreciation of the meaning and relations of the movements and manœuvres, it will be necessary to go back and trace the development of the situation from the start. Let me add that owing to the accumulation of material, I must abandon all hope of entering into a *descriptive* account, as my note-book would fill several pages of the TIMES, and must, to the sacrifice of artistic effect, treat it purely in its military relations.

II.

It is Monday morning, (April 27,) and the army is all in motion. The vast area it covers of miles and miles in extent is an animated scene of bustle and stir. The camps are "broken," and the comfortable log huts and Winter-quarters, in which the men have been lodged for months, are abandoned. Columns of troops are moving on this road and that, and on a dozen different roads—carefully concealing themselves from the enemy's view by marching through the woods and behind the knolls and ridges of the broken ground along the Rappahannock. Long trains of artillery, pack mules and ambulances add their own features of the imposing and the picturesque to the scene.

The movement would many days ago have been inaugurated but for these fickle April skies, which have left but brief intermissions of fine weather, and during the rest of the time have been deluging the country with rain, and ruining these treacherous Virginia roads. At length, however, operations are actually begun, and a new life and vivacity stir the men.

The army, in all its aspects, material and moral, is in splendid condition.

The army is larger than it was ever before materially. The health of the troops is better than it ever was before. From the first day Gen. HOOKER took command, it was felt that a directing brain animated the mass. *Mens agitat molem.* Great mobility has been secured by prodigiously cutting down the amount of transportation, and by employing pack mules, which go anywhere in all weathers, instead of our heavy wagons, which are always stuck in the mud. But two wagons are allowed to a regiment. The army is no longer encumbered with that ponderous impediment which used to be the marvel of all who beheld it. In fact, we now approximate the French standard, which enables an army to carry fourteen days' provisions without a wheel behind it.

The moral transformation is not less complete. It may be in the recollection of some of your readers that I had occasion two months ago to give a minute dissection of the condition of the Army of the Potomac as it was at the time of the last bungling campaign on the Rappahannock. I was accordingly much interested, after an absence of a couple of months, to make a comparative study of the internal change that had come over it in the interval under the new military *régime*. The metamorphosis could hardly have been more complete, and I have often had difficulty in convincing myself that that army, where general croaking, jealousies, disaffection, desertion and universal demoralization prevailed, is the same with this in which a new vitality animates the men, system, harmony and organization are seen, and a true military spirit pervades the troops.

Nothing in this line of phenomena struck me more than the admirable secresy that existed in regard to the proposed plan and movements of the opening campaign. It was a new and somewhat tantalizing sensation; for any one who has followed the movements of the army in the field will bear me out when I say, that hitherto projected operations have always been known and discussed by nearly everybody—even the negro servants in the camps—for days and weeks before they took place. In this case absolute ignorance prevailed. Not even the corps commanders knew what was intended, and had only their specific individual order for the day.

Accordingly, early in the week every one was rubbing his eyes, and asking where is the army? No one could tell. Here was a column moving up, another moving down, and the column that was up yesterday proves to be down to-day. I confess I was heartily glad of the general bewilderment, though it was rather puzzling for a correspondent to observe movements along a line twenty-five or thirty miles in length. In this case, it was the spectators of the great game of chess that were blindfolded. The master player alone had his eyes open.

In the great game of war, time and space are the elements with which the General has to deal. Celerity (and for that purpose the greatest possible *mobility*) with secresy are the indispensable conditions of all military combinations. The mind of Gen. HOOKER is one that will put forth all the resources of these elements.

By Tuesday morning, however, an acute eye might begin to take in a rough outline of a plan from the dispositions then made of the troops. Three of the seven *corps d'armée* composing the Army of the Potomac—namely, the First Corps, (Maj.-Gen. REYNOLDS,) the Third Corps, (Maj.-Gen. SICKLES,) and the Sixth Corps, (Maj.-Gen. SEDGWICK,) had been moved from their camps the night before and had taken up their positions at the same point of the Rappahannock where Gen. FRANKLIN had his crossing at the time of the battle of Fredericksburgh—namely, two miles below that city—and covered from the enemy's view by the curtain of hills that fringe the Rappahannock. While these movements are going on, other columns, consisting of the corps of Gen. MEADE, (the Fifth,) and Gen. SLOCUM, (the Twelfth,) are moving on different roads, and have taken up positions up the Rappahannock, in the neighborhood of Banks' and United States fords, which are respectively eight and eleven miles above Fredericksburgh, and are, it will be remembered, the places selected by Gen. BURNSIDE for his crossing on the occasion of the mud campaign.

These circumstances made it probable that operations would be inaugurated at both points, though it still left one entirely doubtful as to *where* the main attack would be, whether below or above, and the more so, as—albeit the general disposition of the troops was as indicated—Gen. HOOKER still held the balance of power in his hand, ready to throw large reinforcements either up or down. It was fair to suppose, however, that the operations at one point would be merely of the nature of a demonstration, while the real attack would be made at the other. The points being fifteen miles apart, and out of supporting distance, it was not to be presumed that he would thus divide his army, and give the rebel commander (who held the centre position on the *chord*, while we occupied the *arc*,) this opportunity of falling upon and beating us in detail.

Before dawn of Tuesday the pontoon boats had been taken from the wagons, a couple of miles below Fredericksburgh, and under cover of a very heavy fog, were carried noiselessly down on men's shoulders to the river's brink and deposited in the water. They were immediately manned by the troops of RUSSELL's brigade, (BROOKES' division, Sixth Army corps,) and rapidly pushed over, in the manner taught us by Gen. HUNT at the time of the crossing in December. The rebels here, as at every ford for forty miles up and down the river, were posted along the river's margin in double lines of rifle pits, containing, perhaps, a couple of hundred men each. At the lower crossings, however, they made but a feeble resistance, and in a few moments our men were in possession of both lines of rifle pits, with the loss of half a dozen men. Indeed, a rebel Lieutenant captured here, a disingenuous young man, told us that they had been expressly instructed not to offer very serious resistance. This being accomplished, the whole of BROOKES' division was passed over the three pontoon bridges which were immediately constructed under charge of Chief-Engineer BENHAM, to hold the position and the bridge-head.

A mile and a half below the position of Gen. SEDGWICK's bridges, at an estate called Southfield, REYNOLDS' command was also instructed to effect a crossing. In doing this, however, they were not quite so lucky as those above them. Daylight had come while the engineers were still endeavoring to get the pontoon boats down to the water, but the fire from the rebel sharpshooters, who were placed in rifle-pits which had been thrown up opposite them, also succeeded in delaying operations so much, that it was 10 o'clock in the forenoon before they could be got into the water. To silence the fire of the sharpshooters, Col. WARNER, commanding artillery on the extreme left, under the able Chief of Artillery, Gen. HUNT, brought forty guns to bear upon them. This completely "corraled" them, for they were afraid of leaving their pits and exposing themselves to the murderous fire of the artillery. This detained them until a force was able to push over in boats, when, charging up the hill, they captured all the men in the first row of rifle-pits, numbering about one hundred and fifty. Immediately after the crossing of this force, a couple of pontoon bridges were built, and Gen. WADSWORTH's division of REYNOLDS' corps was thrown over. Gen. WADSWORTH himself, however, did not wait for the completion of the bridges, but while his men were crossing in the open boats, plunged in on horseback and swam his horse over to the other side.

Thus far, it is to be noticed that but *one* division of each of the two army corps had been sent across the river—the remaining *four* divisions stayed on the other side. But they were not idle. They were put in motion on the hill-slope on one side of the river, and in plain view of the enemy were marched along the crest of the ridge and down, as though to the crossing. But, instead of crossing, they were quietly drawn up *back* through a gully, round the rear of the ridge, and round again on its top. They made the appearance of an army of at least a hundred thousand men, and must have presented the appearance of a *massing* on our side, preparatory to a passage of the river under cover of the night. The same "circusing" was performed by the artillery, the same by the wagon trains.

Was this a *ruse de guerre!* It could hardly be anything else—and yet to any one but a careful observer, even on *our* side, the deception could not have been detected.

The effect on the rebels was prompt. Two hours afterward their columns began moving up the Bowling-green road from down the river. Here a considerable force, including the whole of JACKSON's corps—first, TRIMBLE's brigade, down opposite Port Royal, then coming up successively, A. P. HILL's brigade, D. H. HILL's division, and EALY's brigade—had been posted as a corps of observation. The Bowling-green road is at this point a sunken road; but we soon began to detect at various points the rebel column moving up—we were removed say a couple of miles—the bayonets glistening in the sun.

Were the same plains that witnessed the savage fight last December to see a renewal of it to-day? There was certainly every appearance of it. Our main force was massed here; a hundred and fifty guns were in position on the heights on our side, and the two divisions across the river were busily engaged strengthening the rebel rifle pits now occupied by them.

In the afternoon I passed over to the old battle-ground. It was now covered with a beautiful carpet of green; while the brilliant peach and hawthorn blossoms scented the air and delighted the eye. It is a superb plain for a review—several miles in length and one and a half in width—where *both* armies of the Potomac might march and countermarch; but a horrid place for a battle. At the rear of the plain the ridges rise, forming a perfect amphitheatre of hills around, thickly studded with rebel batteries, affording a hideous converging and enfilading fire on any troops attempting to pass across it. In the mind's eye one might see that battle raging and its fierce antagonisms painted on a cartoon of air.

History, it is said, repeats itself; but I knew too well Gen. HOOKER's ideas on throwing troops against fortifications, when the resources of strategy enable one to circumvent them, to think for a moment that he would repeat that horrid episode. Maugre all the array, therefore, I firmly held to the impression that this was, after all, but a demonstration, and that the hot work would be elsewhere.

Passing up the river we have fresh confirmation of this. During Sunday and Monday, HOWARD's corps, (the Eleventh,) SLOCUM's corps, (the Twelfth,) and Gen. MEADE's, (the Fifth,) had been moving to the upper fords of the Rappahannock. On the night of Tuesday, between 10 P. M. and 2 A. M., HOWARD's entire corps crossed the Rappahannock on the pontoon bridge at Kelly's Ford, twenty-seven miles above Falmouth. At day-light Gen. SLOCUM's corps followed, and during the forenoon Gen. MEADE's corps was thrown across.

This movable column then struck direct for Germania Ford on the Rapidan River, distant twelve miles, one of the main affluents of the Rappahannock, into which it empties at United States Ford. Gen. MEADE, however, instead of taking this direction on passing the river, struck a road diverging eastward, and made Ely's Ford on the Rapidan, eight miles nearer than Germania Ford, to the *embouchure* of that stream into the Rappahannock. At Germania Ford, a force of about a hundred and fifty rebel pioneers was discovered building a bridge. These, by a well executed manœuvre, were all captured.

Celerity of movement being the chief desideratum, it was resolved immediately to put the troops over by wading—an affair not very easy of execution, for the waters of the Rapidan, even at the ford, come up to a man's shoulder, and the current is very rapid. The men, however, plunged in, many of them stripping and carrying their clothes and cartridge boxes on their bayonets—and waded over, up to their armpits, amid Homeric scenes of laughter and gayety—a cavalry picket being placed below to catch those that were carried away by the current. In the meantime a foot bridge had been constructed on the abutments already placed there by the rebels, and during the night the whole remaining force was passed over, the piers being lighted up with huge bonfires. While this was going on at Germania Ford, MEADE's troops were crossing at Ely's Ford. Both columns now moved as ordered, for Chancellorsville, at the junction of the Gordonville turnpike with the Culpepper and Orange Court-house plank road—communication being kept up between the two movable columns by a squadron of PLEASANTON's cavalry, while another part of the same horsemen moved on the right flank of the outer column to protect it from rebel cavalry attacks. This manœuvre having uncovered United States Ford (which lies between Kelly's Ford and Falmouth—twelve miles from the latter,) COUCH's corps, which had, for three days, been lying at that point, was passed over the Rappahannock by a pontoon bridge on Thursday, without any opposition or indeed any demonstration more formidable than a brass band playing Hail Columbia. This force also converged toward Chancellorsville and on Thursday night four army corps—namely, HOWARD's, STEVEN's, MEAD's and COUCH's were massed at this point. That same night Gen. HOOKER and staff reached Gordonsville and established his Headquarters in the only house here.

III.

I think you will readily agree with me that there are few examples in history of a military movement of such proportions, executed with such celerity and success. To have marched a column of seventy-five thousand men, laden with sixty pounds of baggage, together with artillery and trains, thirty-six miles in two days, to have bridged and crossed two streams along a line which a vigilant enemy undertakes to observe and defend, with a loss of perhaps half a dozen men, one wagon and two mules, is an achieve which assuredly has had few parallels.

Remember how enormously difficult the task of crossing the Rappahanock proved last December, how two days were spent in the attempt after we had our force massed on the river's edge, and with what loss it was finally accomplished, and you will have the means of duly appreciating it.

There is no miracle about this result. It is simply the work of a planning and directing brain, with the most utter secrecy and the greatest possible celerity. But these qualities produce results which, in their *ensemble*, appear almost miraculous.

I remember, in my military reading, but one operation of precisely the same kind. It is the operation of Prince EUGENE against the French, who held the line of the Adige. EUGENE, by a series of skillful manœuvres, induced the French commander to scatter his troops along the line of the river; then, by dexterous feints, he entirely deceived his adversary as to the direction of his march, and the latter was suddenly surprised with the news that the line of the Adige was forced, and a detachment of his forces wholly routed at Carpi.

LEE's surprise could not have been greater when he heard that the Union army was across the river and had turned his flank. And, indeed, we have not merely material proof of this—such as that, when we were across the Rapidan the enemy was yet picketing the Rappahannock—but we have documentary evidence of it in a letter from Gen. LEE himself, which was found in the house at Chancellorsville.

This letter, signed by Gen. TAYLOR, LEE's Chief of Staff, was written to the rebel officer commanding the post at Chancellorsville, and was dated from LEE's headquarters at 4:29 o'clock P. M., of the day we arrived. It stated, in substance that "*the General had at that moment heard that the Federal force was across Ely's Ford*" (we had been across eighteen hours)—"*that Gen.* ANDERSON" (who commanded at United States Ford with a couple of brigades) "*knew nothing of our arrival*"—and asked him "*to come down immediately and consult with the Commanding General!*"

The order which the commanding General issued on Thursday, after the achievement of this position, is the key to the situation, and to the expectations of the commander. I repeat it here for its relations with the recital:

> HEADQUARTERS ARMY OF THE POTOMAC, NEAR FALMOUTH, VA., April 30, 1863.
>
> It is with heartfelt satisfaction that the General Commanding announces to the army that the operations of the last three days have determined that our enemy must ingloriously fly, or *come out from behind their defences, and give us battle on our own ground*, where certain destruction awaits him.
>
> The operations of the Fifth, Eleventh and Twelfth Corps have been a series of splendid successes.
>
> By command of Maj.-Gen. HOOKER.
>
> S. WILLIAMS, Adjutant-General.

The significance of the emphasized words will be seen from a glance at the map of the country. It will be seen that the position gained at Chancellorsville, which is ten miles west by south of Fredericksburgh, *completely turns the line of rebel defences on the series of ridges in the rear of Fredericksburgh*, and in fact there was now but one alternative: the enemy *must* either retreat along the line of the railroad toward Richmond, while that line was yet uncut, (for there was no other line of retreat, the communication with Gordonsville being threatened by our hold on that line,) or else come out and "give us battle on our own ground." LEE had been completely outgeneraled, and in a strategic point of view had suffered a defeat before we had fired a single shot. It was in this sense, and not in the meaning that they were actually destroyed, albeit he anticipated nothing less than that, that Gen. HOOKER on the night of our arrival at Chancellorsville proudly exclaimed, "The rebel army is now the legitimate property of the Army of the Potomac."

Gen. LEE seems to have felt himself strong enough to pursue the latter alternative, and he took prompt measures to carry his plan into execution. There is very little doubt that he had been heavily reinforced with troops from the South. We are at the present moment fighting Charleston. For, like the attack on Fort Donelson, that movement had been made too soon. A month had passed since that attack, and its result had emboldened LEE to call up the great portion of the force in South Carolina. The troops for the defences of Charleston numbered fifty-five thousand men, and he could afford to feel able to draw on forty thousand of that number. In addition, LONGSTREET's force had been recalled from North Carolina. Furthermore, it is the universal testimony of all the prisoners, (numbering several hundred taken during the past week) that their army has been heavily reinforced. What that force is, it is, of course, impossible to say. I think it would be unsafe to estimate it at less than *eighty thousand*, and there are those having good means of knowing who carry it to a *hundred thousand*.

Occupying, too, the interior line, LEE's facilities for a change of front were, of course, very great; and our army had hardly gained its position when a rebel column was marching up to confront it.

On Saturday, two prisoners were brought in from the Twenty-third North Carolina, belonging to HILL's division, of JACKSON's corps. Their testimony (I heard them keenly questioned by the able chief of the secret service, who knows the position of every rebel regiment) showed that that division started from below Hamilton's crossing, in the *rear* of Fredericksburgh, at 3 A. M., of Friday, and that they were portions of the same column which we saw moving up the Bowling Green road, *below* Fredericksburgh, two days before. I mention this circumstance as a slight clue to the great game which was now being played between the two able leaders of the respective armies.

On Thursday night we were massed in the vicinity of Chancellorsville, simply covering the approaches.

On Friday morning, Gen. HOOKER began the strategic disposition of his force. As the enemy has since been engaged with us all along this line, and as the disposition has, since then, been altered, there can be no objection to state that it formed a line of battle of a triangular or redan shape, resting with its wings respectively on the Rappahannock between Banks and United States fords and Hart's Creek, and having its apex at Chancellorsville.

The day was occupied with operations along the skirmish line, and reconnoissances for the purpose of feeling the enemy.

The night previously, Col. MCVICAR, of the Sixth New-York cavalry, had pushed out on the Spotsylvania road; but having, in the ardor that characterized him, got far beyond the point intended by the General, FITZ-HUGH LEE, with two brigades of cavalry and a battery of horse artillery, got on a cross road between him and us. He had two hundred men, and there was but one course for him—to pierce through the enemy's line, leading the assault, sabre in hand, and he fell at the first charge. I knew him well. He was a Scotchman and gallant soldier, and he died as he would have wished—cutting his way through the enemy. The intrepid band left fifty of its number behind.

At noon of Friday SYKES' division of MEAD's corps, occupying the extreme left, was sent out on a reconnoissance on the Banks' Ford road. They pushed the enemy steadily for an hour, gaining a mile of ground, which was in itself important as giving us possession of two successive heights, from which the enemy would annoy us with artillery. This accomplished, the order was given to fall back. There were those who were disposed to be captious at this, but the mind that took in the totality of operations knew well what he did. In itself the position was valuable; but it could not, without weakening us, have been made available in the general line.

In like manner a portion of SLOCUM's command was thrown out about three miles on the Fredericksburgh plank road, and other advances of the same kind were made on the right.

These "feelers" had the obvious purpose of causing the enemy to develop his force; but they had also another purpose, not so obvious, namely: that of a topographical survey, as existing maps are enormously defective. Gen. HOOKER, with the chiefs of the Topographical Department, busied himself all day in making himself thoroughly acquainted with the ground.

It will not be out of place for us here briefly to do the same. The situation of Chancellorsville is in the middle of a clearing in the woods, which takes the form of an irregular elipse, about a mile in length and half a mile in width. The solitary house that makes up Chancellorsville stands almost in the middle of this opening.

The ground in the region between here and Fredericksburgh is broken and wooded, there being occasional clearings in the forests. It rises as it nears Fredericksburgh, when it develops into bold heights. Its strategic importance, as already indicated, is derived from the fact that it covers the Fredericksburgh turnpike and the Culpepper and Orange Court-house plank road, and threatens the line of Gordonsville.

IV.

The military situation on Saturday morning, therefore, stands as follows: Our main force holds the position at Chancellorsville, confronting the main rebel army now massed opposite us. HOWARD's corps has the extreme right—then a division of SICKLES' corps—then SLOCUM—then COUCH—then MEADE on the left, HUMPHREY's division of MEADE's corps holding the extreme of the left. Working parties have been employed during the whole night in throwing up breastworks, and the woods have resounded with the strokes of a thousand ax-men felling trees for the purpose of constructing abattis. We hear the rebels, not half a mile distant, at work with the same view, and in the morning both armies are well entrenched. It will now be who will come out and give battle. HOOKER is determined to put forth all the resources of the craft of which he is a consummate master to tempt them out.

So much for the Right. Another, though minor force, is working on the left, independently, yet with its definite strategic bearings on the main operation. This subordinate operation is at Fredericksburgh. Balloon reconnoissances show clearly that the enemy have taken their main force from the heights of Fredericksburgh and the line down the Rappahannock, and massed it against us at Chancellorsville. They have also removed the greater bulk of their artillery with the same end; and Gen. SEDGWICK, who commands the left, thinks himself strong enough to carry the heights. The Commanding General assents, if there be good prospect of success; for it is of the utmost importance not to *anticipate* the golden moment to strike.

Still another coöperative *rôle* is assigned the powerful cavalry expedition under Gen. STONEMAN. This is nothing less than to cut the railroad bridges that cross the two affluents of the Pamunkey—namely, the North and South Anna—less than twenty miles from Richmond. The bridge over the North Anna is a hundred and fifty feet long and eighty feet high, and cannot possibly be reconstructed in less than a fortnight. You can see how tremendously this will embarrass the rebels.

Whether STONEMAN has by this time actually performed his task, is not yet reported. I have followed him only as far as Rappahannock Station, south of Culpepper, through which he dashed on Thursday night.

This rapid survey will indicate how colossal is the plan of campaign which Gen. HOOKER has marked out for the army. It contemplates nothing less than the destruction of the entire rebel force in Virginia. It is stupendously daring; but HOOKER is a man who thoroughly understands that, in war, to greatly gain one must greatly dare.

V.

The active operations of Saturday comprise a series of attempts in force on the part of the rebels to break our line at various points, which were in one case partially successful, in another completely successful, and in all the others completely *unsuccessful*.

In the morning, as we stood on the balcony of CHANCELLOR's house, the attention was aroused by a sharp rattle of musketry coming from a column of rebels coming up by the main Fredericksburgh plank road, directly in front of us. KNAPP's battery, however, which was planted directly in front of the position, opened upon them, and after a few rounds caused them to retire.

Immediately afterwards a battery opened from the height which I have mentioned as having been gained by SYKES, yesterday, and then abandoned by us. The position was rather upwards of a mile distant from the cleared space, and its object was to damage our ammunition train which was visible to the rebels from the tops of trees on the height. One of our batteries was, however, immediately opened in reply. The third shot blew up one of the caissons and a subsequent shot blew up another, and this settled their account.

Subsequently a reconnoissance was sent, on our part, consisting of the Twenty-sixth Pennsylvania Volunteers, (CARR's brigade, BERRY's division, SICKLES' corps,) on the same road by which the rebels had approached in the morning, for the purpose of feeling their strength. They went out on the plank road, deployed on both sides in the form of a letter V, chaced the rebel skirmishers a couple of miles, till they came to a heavy double line of battle, with artillery in position, when they retired, bringing us *that* piece of intelligence.

Another reconnoissance was next sent out on our right, consisting of BERMAN's sharpshooters. They met the enemy's pickets, drove them handsomely, and at 4 o'clock returned with fifty prisoners of the Twenty-third Georgia.

At 4 the rebels are moving down in force on the plank road, where we had a little before made the reconnoissance. GEARY's division of SLOCUM's corps is sent in on the double quick into the woods—their bayonets flashing in the sunlight. A sharp contest ensues, and in a few minutes they come back in disorder. A portion of KANE's brigade, composed of raw troops, had broken, and thrown the column into confusion.

An Aid from SLOCUM comes to ask Gen. HOOKER if he can have reinforcements. "No! he *must* hold his own. HOWARD will, of course, support him from the right. Let GEARY's division, however, be thrown to the right of the road, so that the artillery may be able to sweep the enemy on the left." This treatment presently repaired the damage, and checked the hope of the rebels being able to pierce our centre.

Foiled in this, they now prepared to make a still

Continued on Eighth Page.

The Charleston Mercury.

DAILY PAPER—TEN DOLLARS PER ANNUM, PAYABLE HALF-YEARLY IN ADVANCE.

VINDICE NULLO
SPONTE SUA SINE LEGE FIDES RECTUMQUE COLENTUR.

COUNTRY PAPER—THREE A WEEK—FIVE DOLLARS PER ANNUM, IN ADVANCE.

VOLUME LXXXII. | CHARLESTON, S. C., MONDAY, MAY 11, 1863. | NUMBER 11,751

TELEGRAPHIC NEWS.

IMPORTANT FROM VIRGINIA—MOVEMENTS ON THE RAPPAHANNOCK—DEATH OF GEN. (STONEWALL) JACKSON.

RICHMOND, May 8.—Passengers report all quiet at Fredericksburg. Several ambulance trains arrived this evening, and more are on the way hither. Crowds of ladies are at the depot dispensing refreshments to the wounded.

Gen. LEE has issued the following address to his troops:

HEADQUARTERS ARMY OF NORTHERN VIRGINIA, May 7, 1863.

[*General Orders No. 59.*]

With heartfelt gratification the General Commanding expresses to the army his sense of the heroic conduct displayed, both by officers and men, during the arduous operations in which they have just been engaged. Under the trying vicissitudes of heat and storm, you attacked the enemy strongly entrenched in the depths of the tangled Wilderness, and again on the hills of Fredericksburg, fifteen miles distant, and, by your valor, triumphed on every field, forcing him once more to seek safety beyond the Rappahannock.

While this glorious victory entitles you to the praise and gratitude of the nation, we are specially called upon to return our grateful thanks to the only Giver of Victory for the signal deliverance He has wrought. It is, therefore, earnestly recommended that the troops unite on Sunday next, in ascribing to the Lord of Hosts the glory due His name.

Let us not forget, in our rejoicing, the brave soldiers who have fallen in defence of their country, and while we mourn their loss, let us resolve to emulate their noble example. The army and country alike lament the absence, for a time, of one to whose bravery and skill they are so much indebted for success.

The following letter from the President of the Confederate States is communicated to the army, as an expression of his approbation of its services:

"I have read your despatch, and reverently unite with you in giving praise to God for the success with which He has crowned our arms. In the name of the people, I offer cordial thanks to yourself and to the troops under your command for this addition to the unprecedented series of great victories your army has achieved. The universal rejoicing produced by this happy result will be mingled with general regret for the good and brave who are numbered among the killed and wounded."

(Signed) R. E. LEE, General Commanding.

RICHMOND, May 9.—STONEMAN's cavalry broke camp on Thursday and started for the Upper Rappahannock, after capturing all the horses they could find. They cut the throats of 200 of their worn-out horses.

IMBODEN's cavalry has destroyed the great Cheat River Bridge, on the Baltimore and Ohio Railroad, built at an enormous cost, and regarded as one of the greatest triumphs of science.

Two thousand prisoners arrived here this evening, and the same number will come in to-night. The mail train from Fredericksburg arrived at 8 p. m. Passengers report that FRANK P. BLAIR, Jr., is amongst the Yankees captured.

Brigadier-General BARRY, HOOKER's Chief of Artillery, was killed on Wednesday. Major-General HOWARD and two other Yankee Generals were wounded. The Medical Director of BIRNEY's (Yankee) corps was killed.

[*The Latest.*]

RICHMOND, May 10.—Governor Letcher received a despatch this afternoon announcing the death of General THOMAS J. JACKSON, at Guinea's Station, at three o'clock this afternoon. He died from the combined effects of his wounds and an attack of pneumonia. His body will be brought to this city to morrow by special train.

IMPORTANT FROM THE WEST.

JACKSON, MISS., May 8.—Governor PETTUS has official information that our troops have driven the Yankees from Tupelo, and now hold that town.

We have news from New-Orleans that BANKS has published an order requiring that all registered enemies must take the oath before the 1st instant, or prepare to leave the Yankee lines before the 15th of May. The new oath will be far more binding than any hitherto offered, and will subject those taking it to the conscription.

VICKSBURG, May 9.—We have nothing new from the front. The enemy is landing troops below Young's Point, supposed to be destined to reinforce GRANT. The Vicksburg *Whig* office was destroyed by fire this evening.

A Yankee despatch, dated Cairo, May 6, says that advices had been received that the Union gunboats had been repulsed at Haynes Bluff, and the iron clad *Choctaw* badly damaged. Her turret was penetrated by a 64 pounder. The Yankee loss was 60.

INTERESTING FROM THE NORTH.

RICHMOND May 10.—We have received late Northern papers.

The Washington *Chronicle*, of May 4, publishes an order of Gen. HOOKER, dated April 30, and expressing to the Yankee army his heartfelt gratification that the operations of the last three days had determined "that the enemy must ingloriously fly, or come out from behind his defences to give us battle on our own ground, where certain destruction awaits him."

The *Chronicle* contains not a word of the defeat of the Yankee army at Chancellorsville. It says, however, that President LINCOLN has issued a draft for 500,000 men.—"This call of the nation, in its great agony, should reach every heart."

New York dates of the 5th represent the results of the great battles on the Rappahannock as still undecided.—Dates of the 7th, however, give advices from United States Ford, dated May 6th, 8 a. m., as follows:

"All our trains have been ordered back, and there is now nothing on the other side of the river except our infantry and artillery. The heavy rains are deluging the roads, tearing up the corduroy roads, sweeping away bridges and threatening the pontoons. The river has risen, and the upper pontoons have been taken to lengthen the lower ones. After several hours hard work they were passable, being covered with boughs to prevent the rebels hearing the crossing. At midnight the troops commenced the retreat; and it is understood they will be over by noon. It is hoped high water will not prevent the crossing. Great numbers of our wounded are in the enemy's hands. In Sunday's battle the dead were unburied and the wounded unattended. After consultation, a hasty return to our camps was decided upon. It is raining heavily and the river is rising rapidly.

FALMOUTH, May 6—10 a. m.—Three bridges destroyed between here and Acquia Creek. The river has risen ten feet. It is rumored that the enemy's cavalry crossed above and is advancing cautiously.

NEW YORK, May 7.—Nothing concerning war matters has been telegraphed from Washington. The *World* says we learn by a special messenger that a great battle was fought on Tuesday, and that HOOKER with the remains of his army was driven back across the Rappahannock. LEE is being heavily reinforced. The last battle exceeds in slaughter those of the previous days. Nothing heard of STONEMAN. It is impossible to doubt his force will be captured.

VALLANDIGHAM, according to the Washington *Chronicle* of the 6th, has been arrested. An attempt was made to resist the arrest, but it failed.

The *Alabama* has destroyed the ship *Punjaub*.

The accounts of the Yankee correspondents relative to the great battle on the Rappahannock are published with such sensation headings as: "The Rebels Shattered at Chancellorsville"—"Our Position Impregnable"—"SEDGWICK laurelled with Success," &c. The correspondents speak of HOOKER's great generalship and other Napoleonic qualities. Their entrenchments at Chancellorsville, they say, were the best they ever had. The Eleventh Army Corps are denounced as poltroons, for throwing down their arms and running from RHODES' brigade. The Baltimore *American* says: "The night attack of the rebels was the most brilliant thing of the war." The fight on Sunday was a desperate one, the rebels throwing themselves on the very muzzles of our guns. Our ammunition gave out, and, for one hour, the position was held with the bayonet. Our forces then fell back, in good order, from Chancellorsville.

The Northern papers report that a rebel raiding party on the Baltimore and Ohio Railroad, being reinforced by 4000 troops, had overwhelmed Colonel MULLIGAN's Yankee forces at Fairmount, Va. The statement of the Yankee loss is withheld from the public.

The Yankees report six divisions of BRAGG's army had moved to Shelbyville, and that BRECKINRIDGE's forces were close at hand.

(*The Latest.*)

We have Northern papers of the 9th. President LINCOLN has issued a proclamation calling out the militia to suppress the rebellion. All able-bodied male citizens between the ages of twenty and forty-five, and also all foreigners who may have declared their intention to become citizens are to constitute the "national forces."

An *official* despatch from Washington says that the President and General-in-Chief (HALLECK) had just returned from a visit to the army of the Potomac. No serious disaster had occurred to its organization or to the efficiency of the army. Not more than one third of HOOKER's force was engaged. STONEMAN's operations are declared to have been a brilliant success. A part of his cavalry had advanced within two miles of Richmond. HOOKER's army would soon resume offensive operations.

The trial of VALLANDIGHAM by court martial was concluded on the 7th, but the decision in his case was unknown.

The correspondent of the New York *Herald* is grandiloquent in his account of the battle, disguising the defeat, as far as possible, by the multiplication of words. HOOKER is said to have been stunned and thrown down by a shell, which shattered a pillar post against which he was leaning in Chancellorsville.

PETERSBURG, May 10.—The New York *World* of May 10 says that its worst anticipations of the result of HOOKER's advance had been more than confirmed. He has been out-generaled and out-fought. The *World* also says that HEINTZELMAN is on his way to HOOKER with 30,000 fresh troops, and that 18,000 are coming from another quarter [Suffolk?]

The following is a partial list of the Yankee killed and wounded: *Killed*—Brig. Gen. MOTT, Maj. Gen. BARRY and Brig. Gen. SCHUENHENFING of the 14th Corps, 17 Colonels, Lieut. Colonels and majors, with 28 Captains and Lieutenants. *Wounded*—Brig. Gen. WHIPPLE and Gen. DEVINE severely; 31 Colonels, Lieutenant Colonels and Majors, and 52 Captains and Lieutenants—many mortally.

VALLANDIGHAM is at the Burnett House, Cincinnati, under a strong guard. HALLECK had ordered all the stores and valuables from Acquia Creek. Over 4000 rebel prisoners, captured in the recent battle, had reached Washington up to Wednesday night. Ten guns of the famous New Orleans Washington Artillery were captured.

IMPORTANT FROM EUROPE.

PETERSBURG, May 10.—The *Australian*, with Liverpool dates to the 26th, has arrived at New York. A spirited debate had taken place in both Houses of Parliament in regard to the seizure of British vessels by Yankee cruisers. Mr. ROEBUCK made a strong war speech, asking Lord PALMERSTON whether the Government had come to any determination in the matter, and if it had, whether he could tell Parliament what that determination was. He (ROEBUCK) knew the consequences of the action PALMERSTON might take, he knew that it might lead to war; and, speaking for the English people, he would say they were prepared for war. [Loud cheers.] Justice must be done to the honor, the dignity of England, and the commerce of the country must no longer be subject to the sneering insolence of an upstart race. [Cheers.]

LETTER FROM RICHMOND.

(CORRESPONDENCE OF THE MERCURY.)

RICHMOND, Tuesday, May 7.

Not a Crushing Defeat—Hays' Explanation—Hooker Fortifying—His Desperation—He will "Peg Away"—General Jackson's Wounds—Charleston to be Again Attacked—Weather, etc., etc.

"It was a victory, but not a crushing defeat." So said a staff officer, just from Guineas, in my hearing yesterday. This he accounted for by the disparity of forces and the nature of the country. The Wilderness is well named—the land being thickly covered with scrubby trees and tangled vines, making evolutions extremely difficult. Moreover, the enemy was fortified with earth works and abattis in both of the positions from which he was driven. Hence our heavy loss.

In the first day's battle the enemy's infantry fought badly. Hays, the captured Yankee Brigadier, explained why Hooker's left rested on the Rapidan, and when the attack began he moved his forces near the river, supposing Lee's object to be against that point, with the view of cutting off his retreat. His best troops were there, while the nine months' men, whose term expires to-day, were on the extreme right. These, when attacked in rear by Jackson, ran at once, intending not to be killed two days before their time was up. This is Hays' explanation, which does not account for the reported stampede of Sedgwick's men on Monday.

Hooker was not routed. He retreated in disorder over the Rapidan to the Rappahannock, and partly across that, but was enabled, by Sedgwick's advance in our rear, to stay his flight. A despatch from Gen. Lee, received yesterday morning, stated that he (Hooker) was at the United States Ford, briskly fortifying himself on the south side. Later in the day, an Aide of the President said that he had recrossed the river to Stafford. Perhaps the heavy rain of the past two days alarmed him.

But he may still be on this side the stream. It is a matter of official life and death with him to do better than Burnside. He will hold on with desperation, and if he maintains his position on the south bank, will claim great things. Being an Abolitionist, his claim will be readily allowed.

As I feared and predicted in a letter last week, the battle was not decisive. Fifteen or twenty thousand *hors du combat* is a small matter to Hooker, with his 159,000. His losses have probably been more than repaired by the reinforcements which left Washington previous to his crossing the river. But a blow much like that at Murfreesboro' has been administered. Hooker, less cautious and wily than Rosecrans, may "peg away" without delay. Passengers yesterday reported another crossing at Deep Run and more fighting.

Gen. Jackson was certainly shot by his own men. A friend of mine heard him say so. The amputated arm will be well in six weeks, but Dr. Maguire fears the wounded hand will be troublesome.

Longstreet moves slowly. He is marching, and was said yesterday to be so near the city that his advance would reach here at nightfall. His operations at Suffolk are unknown, his officers being forbidden, on pain of dismissal, from communicating anything to the newspapers.

The Yankees say they are going to try Charleston again. No doubt you are ready for them. Cloudy and cold.

HERMES.

THE MERCURY.

MONDAY, MAY 11, 1863.

The Drift of the War.

The successive triumphs of the Southern arms have, thus far, served but to show the deliberate and settled purpose of the Northern Government to exterminate the people of this Confederacy, if need be, in order to grasp and retain those unfailing sources of wealth and prosperity, which nature has bestowed upon the South. It is time that our leaders should have done with the sickly sentimentality which has heretofore governed them, in their dealings with enemies, as treacherous in war as they are faithless in peace. We must prepare to meet, with their own spirit, the ruthless vandals who are spreading death and desolation in every quarter of our fair land. The inevitable tendency of a monstrous war like this, is at last beginning to develop itself. We give a significant extract from a leter from Gen. LEE's army. The writer is a gentleman perfectly trustworthy:

F—— has just come in. He brings this trustworthy account from C——, an inhabitant of Fredericksburg. On Sunday the enemy sent a flag of truce to ask leave to bury their dead. They took advantage of that to ascertain our force there, and finding it small, they came over very shortly after, fifteen thousand strong. They assailed Marye's Hill furiously. Our men fought desperately, killing great numbers, until the crest was reached, when they slayed us, and took the Washington Artillery in a hand to hand fight. The force was Barksdale's brigade and one or two Louisiana regiments. Next morning these Mississippians and Louisianians met Early, and told him they would follow him anywhere in the world on one condition: He must take no prisoners. "Them's my sentiments," says Jubal—and they went at it. They drove the Yankees off the hill, took three batteries, turned them on the enemy, and cut their position. No quarter was given, though the wretches begged for it like dogs. Then they got on the bridge; but still the slaughter continued, our men bayoneting, braining with the butts of their guns and bowie knifing. Finding they could not get over the bridge, the Yankees [illegible] the river roads in despair, our men following [illegible] when they were met by Lee, with McLaws and Anderson. F—— learns that nearly the whole were killed—not a prisoner taken—and [illegible], by Lee's command, and the whole town is one mass of bodies and brains. Good! Good!! Oh! Good!!! Jubal is said to have been radiant. Stuart, they say, brings in about 600 prisoners daily; and we have a young Yankee army at Guinea's Depot.

THE BATTLES ON THE RAPPAHANNOCK.

A week has passed since the defeat of HOOKER, and, as yet, no full or consecutive account of it has been obtained. The main facts, however, are now known. The Richmond *Examiner* thus briefly sketches the movements of the two armies:

Hooker's first object in crossing the Rappahannock above the town was to get in the rear of Fredericksburg. His second aim was to prevent a flank attack on the left by the Confederates, who, he supposed, would march up the bank of the river to cut his army at the fords. Hence, he determined to cross the Rappahannock above the confluence with the Rapidan, to march through a portion of Culpeper, and passing the latter river at Germanna and Ely's, to keep his communication behind him, the Rappahannock on his left flank, and the Confederate army and Fredericksburg always in front of him. On Tuesday week his troops were drawn up in full array on the hills of Stafford, in view of the town, pontoons were thrown over, and a strong detachment sent across at Deep Run. This first step was a mere feint to distract the attention. Next day his army disappeared, and the detachment was withdrawn, while the main body passed the fords above in the order stated. Still believing that Lee's onset would be made close to the river, and on his left flank, he rapidly strengthened that part of his line with field works, and then swung the rest forward to Chancellorsville.

It appears, however, from the despatches of the Confederate General, that his ways were not as the ways of Hooker, nor was his attack made in the manner which Hooker had decided he should make it. The Confederate operations were aimed at the right wing—that reaching to Spotsylvania Court House—of the Federals. General Jackson did flank them, after all, but it was the *right* flank—that nearest Richmond—not the left flank, which Hooker had carefully guarded with a river and field works. General Jackson appears to have turned the Yankee line somewhere beyond the Court House, and penetrating to the Wilderness, a creek between Culpeper and Spotsylvania, got partly in their rear. Attacked by the rest of the Confederates in front, while Jackson's corps came down from the Wilderness, the finest army on the planet, commanded, though it was, by General Judas Hooker, was shortly defeated with great slaughter, dislodged from all the positions around Chancellorsville, doubled up on itself, and pressed down in confusion to the banks of the Rappahannock. In this condition their rout and annihilation were nearly certain, could the attack have been continued as commenced.

But the Confederate victory appears to have been marred by the news from Fredericksburg. A part of the army, supposed to have been sufficient, had been put to guard the old heights back of the town. Hooker had left a large force—said to have been two full corps—on the opposite hill, under an old regular officer, General Sedgwick. His important part in the play was to pass the river and "carry the crest," if possible, while Lee had his hands full of Hooker, and then rush upon his rear. After a long delay, he crossed the river, and did actually get possession of Marye's Hill. Sedgwick was now in Lee's rear, and the event might have been fatal to that General if Hooker had held his own in front. But Hooker was already beaten, and at that time helpless. Lee, therefore, could turn on Sedgwick with safety. He did so, whipped him at once, sent him back to Stafford, and re occupied Fredericksburg. It is reported that he then went to finish Hooker.

It was too late! The Yankee General had gotten his beaten army in a very defensible position, supported by the Rapidan and Rappahannock, and had erected strong works in front. The Confederate General might well pause before he attacked him there without necessity.

Those who know the character of those rivers need not be told that there is no necessity to attack an army which depends on their fords for every particle of supply. It is possible to defend such a position as that which Hooker is said to have assumed; but impossible to remain in it. This is the season of heavy showers. One of these converts those streams in an hour from insignificant creeks into terrible torrents, which would sweep off Pharoah's host. No pontoon could live a minute on its flood. Hooker had the choice, to come out and fight forward, or get back to the northern bank as soon as possible. As his army is a beaten army, we were not surprised to hear that he has chosen the latter alternative, and retreated while still able.

DETAILS OF THE BATTLE.

The correspondent of the Richmond *Enquirer* writes from Fredericksburg, May 6th, as follows:

The battle seems to be over, and from all I can gather a glorious victory has crowned the Confederate arms. I propose to give you a history of the whole fight, beginning with the crossing below town on Wednesday morning last and bringing it down to the brilliant charge of Monday evening, when the enemy were driven in confusion across the river, their midnight cry being "*retreat to Banks' Ford.*"

The first movement of the enemy, *i. e.* the crossing below town, can hardly be said to have been a feint. It would be perhaps more proper to speak of it as a movement designed to co-operate with the main attack at Chancellorsville, or it is possible that this force was left in front of Fredericksburg to prevent a rear movement on our part, which, if successful, and the river once crossed by our troops, at a point near town, their egress to the railway could have been cut off and their base of supplies rendered useless to them. To guard his rear and protect his base, the force, which afterwards operated offensively, was at first intended to act defensively, in all probability.

How it afterwards acted on the offensive, and succeeded in carrying by storm "Marye's Heights," can probably be explained by the fact that Hooker had been hard pressed and whipped in the fight of Saturday and Sunday morning at Chancellorsville, and made this in order to create a diversion, and enable him to cover his retreat.

Chancellorsville having been the real point of battle it will be most fitting to treat of it first. On Thursday evening Gen Anderson, who was holding a position in front of the United States Mine Ford, twelve miles above Fredericksburg, ascertained that the Yankees, numbering five army corps, with at least eighty thousand men, crossed the Rapid Ann at Kelley's and Germanna Fords, having previously crossed the North Fork of the Rappahannock at Easley's Ford, in Culpeper county, and were advancing down the plank road. General Anderson at once fell back to Chancellorsville, and took up a line of battle in front of the plank road, and extending to the river, and reaching over towards the old Catherine Furnace. General Anderson, however, having too small a force to hold the enemy at this point, fell back to a position some four miles below Chancellorsville, and fronting the old mine road On Friday morning General Anderson was reinforced on the right by General McLaws, and on the left by General A. P. Hill. At this period General Jackson took command, and ordered an advance, himself leading it, and succeeded during the day in driving the enemy back, they making but slight resistance. On Friday night our forces rested fully two miles beyond the ground occupied by the Yankee forces on the previous evening. The forces principally engaged thus far in this quarter, belonged to Semmes' brigade of McLaws' division, and Mahone's brigade, of Anderson's division.

Saturday morning wore away without important results. There was some artillery firing and a little skirmishing, but the engagement did not become general until about five o'clock in the afternoon, from which hour the fight raged furiously until about eight o'clock. Jackson, at this time, had thrown a force on their upper flank, and was driving them fiercely down upon our lower line, which, in turn, was hurling them back, and rendering futile all their efforts to break through one lower lines, and making it necessary for them to give back towards the river.

There was an intermission in the firing from eight o'clock until about nine. But from nine until long past midnight the sound of artillery and small arms was well nigh deafening. The explanation was ready. Jackson was pressing them with a night fight. Our boys drove the Yankees, who stoutly held their ground, until near day; and at early dawn on Sunday the fight began on both ends of the line, and by eleven o'clock the firing had ceased. On the upper end of the line, near Chancellorsville, the Yankees were badly whipped, and were in full retreat towards the river. On the lower line, near Fredericksburg, however, they had succeeded in carrying Marye's Heights, and were rioting in the wild excess of joy. They had stormed, they said, the Gibraltar of America, and their route to Richmond was plain and easy, little remembering that they had hurled a column of fully ten thousand upon one regiment in front, and thus gaining the rear of the rest of Barksdale's brigade.

But "the best laid schemes of men and mice gang aft agree," and whilst the Yankees were felicitating themselves on their splendid successes, and in imagining themselves to be in the rear of our army, General Lee was so manœuvering as to meet the enemy, who were now throwing themselves forward from the town on the Plank Road. About four o'clock on Sunday evening McLaws' division, including Wilcox's brigade of Anderson's division, met the advance column of the Yankees, under General Sedgwick, at Salem Church, four miles beyond Fredericksburg, on the Plank Road, and our line of battle was formed at right angles with the Plank Road. The battle here raged for about two hours, but the Yankees were repulsed with considerable loss, including some five or six hundred prisoners. Our line on the telegraph road meantime had been formed at Smook's, about three and a half miles out from town. Early on Monday morning Lawton's old brigade, now General Gordon's, supported by General Smith and General Hayes, all of Early's Division, advanced towards Marye's Heights, and charged them without the firing of a gun, driving the enemy from a position from which less than twenty-four hours before he had dislodged Barksdale's gallant Mississippians, after a most heroic resistance, in which the enemy's loss was quite considerable. In this condition matters remained until about five o'clock in the evening, when a general advance was ordered. At the firing of a signal gun, General Early moved upon the enemy from the right, and Generals Anderson and McLaws from the left. The enemy, who held a position on the Plank road, extending up and down, were quickly dislodged and driven with great loss from the field. Their resistance was slight. The charge was grand. Early's men, and especially the Louisianians, under Hayes, walked over the enemy as giants over pigmies, while from above, the men of Anderson and McLaws, who had been constantly marching and fighting for five days, showed no signs of exhaustion, but marched boldly and fearlessly up to their appointed work. The result was the enemy was driven in confusion towards Banks' Ford, across which he succeeded in making his way during the night—not, however, without serious loss in killed, wounded and prisoners. General Hoke, of the North Carolina brigade, in Early's division, was wounded in this charge. Whilst this was going on, Barksdale's men were holding the stone wall, Marye's Hill and the heights commanding the Plank Road, so as to prevent a movement on our rear out from Fredericksburg. But this was hardly necessary. Yankee desire for a general advance had been satisfied, and by nightfall the remnant had begun to prepare for the third and last time to evacuate Fredericksburg—and by day-break our pickets were in the town, which is once again in the hands of Barksdale's men.

Though the enemy at Chancellorsville did not recross the river at the United States Ford until to-day, there has been no general engagement since Sunday—only some occasional skirmishing and feints of attack to cover up their retreat across the river. Hooker, though having the choice of position, did not act offensively after crossing, but fortified and threw himself on the defensive, thus forcing our men to contend against him in this fight against vastly superior numbers, aided by breastworks, fortifications and obstructions of all sorts. But they were of little avail. Jackson turned their flank and fell upon their rear. And Jackson's boys did their work with all their might and main. They charged faster over the battle field than they marched to it, and their cheering as they drove the enemy before them, broke upon the air with fine, inspiring effect, and told too plainly that our men were terribly in earnest.

The battle field, which reaches from Fredericksburg to a point above Wilderness, some twelve miles up from town, and out to the river, with the exception of about two miles between Salem and Zoar churches, attests the skillful aiming and deadly destruction of our artillery. The Yankee dead and wounded are strewn over the entire country Yet had it not have been one of the most thickly wooded sections of land in Virginia the Yankee loss would have been far greater. Over this same field of battle are scattered, in immense quantities, blankets, overcoats, canteens, knapsacks, haversacks, cartridge boxes, and any quantity of rifles, muskets, and various other equipments of the soldier. Our boys, however, found but little to eat. The Yankees had well nigh devoured the commissariat, still a good quantity of hard tack, with some good cooked meats and coffee, were found in the Yankee haversacks. We also captured some freshly slaughtered meats, and some corn and oats; all of which are quite valuable, and just the articles we needed.

Fredericksburg, on this occasion, did not suffer severely as she did before, though the Yankees managed to steal a good deal. Private houses, I believe, were in no instance entered, where the families were present, and the town was not shelled, nor were any citizens arrested or carried off in the town. A few were arrested outside, but in every instance I believe they were rescued by our own soldiery.

Hooker commanded in person at the Chancellorsville fight, and occupied a position near that place during the fight. Hooker has made a good fight. He has manœuvred well, and done better than any other Yankee General; but Hooker is not the equal of Lee. He has so manœuvred and combined as to surround the Yankees twice, and drive them back to the river, when they supposed, on both occasions, that they had gotten into his rear; and were about to surprise him; whilst General Jackson has outdone himself, and exhibited the highest characteristics of a strategist and skillful General, fully confirming all his past renown, and adding new laurels to the many already won in the service of his country.

Our losses are fully 5000, whilst those of the Yankees are confessed to be fully 25,000, and about thirty pieces of artillery. We have captured very near 8000 prisoners, and have lost, I suppose, about 1000 prisoners. These results of the fight point most conclusively to a most brilliant Confederate victory.

THE CASUALTIES.

Gen. T. J. Jackson, wounded; Gen. Paxton, killed; Gen. McLaws, struck, but not much hurt; Gen. A. P. Hill, contusion, has resumed his command; Gen. McGowan, slightly, but painfully, wounded; Brig. Gen. Heth, not much hurt, still in command; Col. J. Q. A. Nadenbousch, 2nd Regiment Infantry, slightly wounded; Capt Fulton, of the 4th Virginia Volunteers, lost a leg; in the 5th Virginia Volunteers Lieut. Bell was killed, and about 150 killed and wounded; Col. Edmundson, of the 27th Virginia Volunteers, lost an arm; in the 10th Virginia Volunteers (from Rockingham), Col. Warren, commanding the brigade, was shot through the right shoulder (not serious); Lieut. Col. S. W. Walker, killed; Maj. Stover, shot three times and killed. Nine out of eleven commandants of companies were killed, wounded and prisoners; Col T. S. Garnett, of the 48th Virginia Volunteers, commanding the brigade, was wounded, and is believed to be dead.

Maj. Rodgers (artillery) wounded; Col. F. M. Mallory, reported killed; this is doubted. Capt. Boswell, Chief of Engineers, on Jackson's staff, killed. Maj Price of Richmond, killed. Capt. Forbes, of A. P. Hill's staff, killed; all the staff of A. P. Hill either killed or wounded. Capt. Duncan McKim killed. Conway Howard of A. P. Hill's staff killed. In the 13th Virginia Volunteers, Capt. Field and Lieut. Morehead killed, and thirty killed, wounded and missing. In the 58th Virginia Volunteers, Lieut. Col. Casey prisoner; seventy killed, wounded and missing Col. Stafford, 14th Louisiana, wounded; Gen. Hope, of North Carolina, lost 120 men. Lieut. Bell, 5th Virginia Volunteers, was killed. This makes nine out of twelve in this family killed in that regiment. Lieuts. Calhoun and Ryan lost each a leg. Capt. Van Borsch, of Gen. Stuart's staff, a gallant Prusian officer, killed.

Rhode's brigade suffered severely, it is reported, in officers—one-third of whom were either killed or wounded—the proportion being ten wounded men to one killed.—In the 1st Washington Artillery, Captain Squires, Lieutenant Galbraith and Lieutenant Owens were taken prisoners. Lieutenant DeRussey, P. H. Von Cotton, Otto Frank, Barton Kirk and —— Vallentine were wounded. Sergeant Wm. West, Corporal Lewis and Robt. Many were killed. In the 51st Georgia Regiment, Col. Slaughter and Lieutenant Colonel Patten were killed; Colonel Mallory, of the 55th Virginia, Major Miles Selden, aid to Gen. Heth, Capt. Greenlee Davidson, Letcher Battery, Captain Edward Branch, of Richmond Grays, Capt Banks, of the Petersburg Grays, and Major Channing Price, of General Stuart's staff, were killed; also, Col. Purdy, of 18th North Carolina, and Capt. Paine, of Gen. Lane's staff.

FROM THE UNITED STATES.

Our dates from the North are as late as the 2d instant. We glean from the papers of that date the following intelligence:

SECOND ATTACK ON CHARLESTON—THREE GREAT CONTESTS CLOSE AT HAND—GENERAL GRANT AND ADMIRAL PORTER.

The Washington correspondent of the Baltimore *American* says:

The second attack upon Charleston is at hand, and Admiral Dupont will command it. Three great contests with the rebels will soon begin—at Vicksburg, Charleston, and somewhere between the Rappahannock and Richmond.

General Grant may be said to be upon his good behavior just at present. There has been a good deal of dissatisfaction with him at headquarters, as well as with Admiral Porter, and they will have to do something very soon or give way to men who will.

MARINE "DEVILS" ON THE WAY TO THE SOUTH.

The New York *Post* of Friday evening last contains the following:

The steamer Ericsson leaves this port to-day for the South with a heavy cargo of war material for our fleet. She takes in tow two of Capt. Ericsson's "Devils," designed to be attached to the bows of the iron-clads, for the destruction of torpedos and the removal of piles and other obstructions. On her last trip the Ericsson took one of these machines to Admiral Dupont and left it safely in Port Royal harbor. Thus the Monitor fleet has been for nearly three weeks in possession of a new "Devil," instead of the old one, which fell into the hands of the rebels in Charleston harbor. The general form of the machine is like that of a raft, and bars extending from it reach two or four feet below the keel of the vessel to which it is attached These will, of course, strike any torpedos or obstructions on which the vessel would otherwise pass. The arrangements for the removal of piles include immense torpedos, with ample means of explosion. The heavy, open frame work of iron will not, it is believed, be materially injured by the concussion or explosion of rebel infernal machines, or of the torpedos that are carried by the Devils, with which they perform their work. The length of the machine is about fifty feet.

HOOKER'S SENTIMENTS—BEFORE THE BATTLE.

The Baltimore *American* says:

A gentleman who witnessed the crossing assures us that the troops were in excellent condition and spirits, and that General Hooker remained behind to superintend the cutting loose of the bridges, declaring that there must be no coming back by that route. We learn that a despatch was received from him last night at Washington, stating that he had flanked the whole rebel army at Fredericksburg, and then had sixty thousand men between Lee and Richmond. The purpose of General Hooker is to attack and fight the rebel army away from Richmond, leaving the question of taking Richmond as an after consideration. If defeated, it must therefore be a terrible reverse, and if successful a glorious victory.

THE CONFEDERATE RAID INTO NORTHWEST VIRGINIA—DESTRUCTION OF RAILROAD BRIDGES, ETC.

Our telegrams notice the "gobbling up" of the Yankees under MULLIGAN by General JENKINS' force of rebel rovers in Northwest Virginia. The Northern papers of May 2 bring us the following details in regard to the previous movements of our forces in that quarter:

The intelligence from the line of the Baltimore and Ohio Railroad, received up to last evening, was that Gen. Mulligan had so disposed of his troops that it was thought the whole road might now be considered as amply protected, though much damage had been done at various points. The rebel cavalry, which made three attacks on Sunday and Monday last on Rowlesburg, retired, after their repulse, to Morgantown, in the direction of the Pennsylvania line. They reached there on Tuesday morning, and spent that day and part of Wednesday in plundering the people of both horses and goods. Those who sympathised with them were exempt from plunder, and in some cases horses taken were returned to disloyal persons. The object of the visit to Morgantown was to cross over the Cheat River and make a raid on Uniontown, Pennsylvania. There was, however, a flood in the Cheat River, rendering its fording an impossibility, and consequently they were compelled to abandon that part of the expedition.

On Wednesday they retired from Morgantown, striking across the country to Fairmont, on the Baltimore and Ohio Railroad, where they are reported to have committed extensive depredations. The Union troops there did not exceed three hundred infantry, and the rebels being about one thousand strong, mounted, with artillery, no defence was made. They entered and took possession of Fairmont, which is quite a large town, on Wednesday night, and immediately commenced their depredations on the property of loyal citizens, most of whom had fled on learning of their approach. A large number of horses, cattle and goods were appropriated. At Fairmont and the vicinity extensive damage was done to the property of the Baltimore and Ohio Railroad. The great Monongahela bridge, one of the finest structures on the road, is reported to have been destroyed, together with five other small bridges in the vicinity. The piers are, however, all standing, and trestle works will be immediately thrown over them, so that the business of the road may be renewed.

The enemy hearing of the approach of troops from the direction of Wheeling, are supposed to have left Fairmont on Thursday. Yesterday morning a rebel cavalry force from the direction of Fairmont were advancing on Clarksburg, on the Parkersburg road, doubtless with the intention of destroying the bridges of that company and plundering the inhabitants. A rebel infantry force was also reported as moving on Clarksburg from the opposite direction. The whole rebel force, cavalry and infantry, is said to be about 8000, and they have with them most experienced guides. General Mulligan has been joined by General Kenley, and is moving on the enemy in considerable force.

The latest intelligence from beyond Grafton, received last evening was that one of the railroad agents had gone up to Fairmont and found that the guerillas had left in the morning with their plunder. He found the structure of the Monongahela bridge entirely broken down, and in the water, though the piers were all standing.

From Grafton, where General Mulligan has his headquarters, intelligence was received that the rebel force, which had spent the day on Thursday at Fairmont, were approaching Bridgeport, on the Parkersburg road, which is sixteen miles from Grafton.

Despatches from Wheeling, received last evening, represented great excitement there. It was reported that a rebel force of ten thousand men were at Mannington, about sixty miles this side of Wheeling, and moving on that city. They were calling on Pittsburg and Ohio for aid, and making themselves very miserable, it was thought, without any cause At Grafton there was confidence felt that no rebels were beyond Fairmont, and those that had been there were moving as rapidly as possible from the line of the road. Their presence at Bridgeport was certainly known, and General Kenley was in pursuit of them.

The rebels first entered Morgantown, Virginia, at 2 o'clock on Monday, and were met by the Mayor with a flag of truce, who surrendered the place. The rebels remained four hours, and then returned to Ryan's farm, six miles south, where they encamped. Persons who saw the enemy's encampments say there were one hundred fires and twenty men around each, making two thousand men, all cavalry, no artillery or infantry. On Monday evening they returned to Morgantown and shot Lieut. Gensino, of the 1st Virginia loyal regiment, who was visiting his home on a furlough. They also stole fifty horses and all the available property. No women or children were molested. The rebels were under the command of the guerilla Jenkins. At 10 o'clock, Thursday evening, they moved to Bloomfield, nine miles south of Morgantown, and encamped—Various foraging and stealing parties were sent out; among others, one to Kingwood, Preston county, Va. Hundreds of horses were stolen. On Tuesday night the rebels attempted to cross Cheat River, but were unable to do so, owing to the high water, and to the fact that all the boats were on the Union side of the river.

THE CONFEDERATE FLEET IN ENGLAND—THE JAPAN, OR VIRGINIA.

[*Plymouth (April 12th) Correspondence of the London Shipping Gazette.*]

The screw steamship Alar, Bash, that put in here yesterday, brought decisive and important information in reference to the large iron steamship that left Greenock on April 2d, under the name of Japan, and was said to be proceeding on a voyage to the China Seas. Rumor then attributed her proclaimed voyage to be only a blind, and her real intention to fly the Confederate flag. The Alar's news confirms this rumor.

The Japan is an iron-built ship, laid down to very fine lines for speed, about six hundred tons, and having engines of from about two hundred to two hundred and fifty horse power. She has all the fitments for carrying heavy guns, shot and shell, and left Greenock with over one hundred men, who were all shipped at very high wages, and in perfect cognizance of the real intention of their voyage. They were shipped for two years for a voyage to Shanghae, Hong Kong, and any intermediate ports.—After they had proceeded to sea, another set of articles were produced by the captain, in which it was stipulated that they should fly the Confederate flag, and assist in capturing and destroying all Federal vessels with whom they might fall in. Thirteen only of the crew excepted to signing the new articles, and their alleged reason was that they thought they were to have higher wages. This was considered on board to be no excuse, as it was well known among them what were the wages offered. The captain, however, stated that he had no wish to take any man with him against his will, and landed these hands here by the Alar.

From Greenock the Japan proceeded to a creek on the coast of France, east of the Channel Islands. The Alar, that has been for several years a regular trader between Newhaven and St. Malo and the Channel Islands, took on board at Newhaven nearly one hundred tons of goods, in cases, and cleared for St. Malo. These goods consisted of twelve Whitworth guns, ten 40 pounders and two 10-pounders, with a large quantity of powder, shot and shell, and some provisions. She proceeded to the coast of France, and was there joined by the Japan and a French pilot. The two vessels ran in and anchored in the creek, where the transhipment of the goods between the two vessels took place during two nights. The Japan then left, and afterwards the Alar, the latter vessel being watched off the coast by a French frigate. The Alar laid two days in the channel before she made for this port. In addition to the thirteen disaffected seamen, she also landed two of the Japan's stokers, who were severely scalded by the burning of one of one of her condensers. The Japan is now sailing under another name, said to be the Virginia. The customs authorities here inquired into the circumstances attending the Alar's voyage, but not deeming themselves justified in detaining her, she was yesterday afternoon allowed to proceed, and she left for the eastward. The men report that on board the Japan everything is done to make the crew comfortable. Provisions of a high class and every accommodation are freely supplied.

The crew are all picked men, and in addition to being good seamen, the majority of them are old hands at the gun drill. The names of the officers are unknown, their present cognomens being considered mere pseudonyms.

THE CASE OF THE ALEXANDRA.

The Solicitor of the Treasury was engaged in a private inquiry into the merits of the case affecting the alleged Confederate gunboat Alexandra, and it was expected that the matter would soon be ripe for investigation in a court of law.

[*From the London Times, April 13.*]

Up to a late hour on Saturday no change had taken place in respect to the circumstances under which the screw steamer Alexandra had been seized at Liverpool, on the allegation that she was intended as a Confederate gunboat She still remained in charge of two officers of the customs, and no work is permitted on board of her, nor is anything allowed to be removed from the vessel. In regard to the Alexandra, it is understood that affidavits setting forth the grounds on which the vessel has been attached will be, or already have been, prepared and forwarded to the Court of Exchequer, and on the nature of those affidavits further ulterior proceedings will be taken or the vessel will be released.

In the House of Commons on 16th April, Lord R. Montague asked the Under Secretary of State for Foreign Affairs whether Her Majesty's Government would lay upon the table of the House copies of the papers or documents which justified them in seizing the Alexandra at Liverpool.

Mr. Layard—As the case of the Alexandra is still under consideration and discussion, I am unable to lay the papers upon the table of the House.

HEADQUARTERS 1ST MILITARY DISTRICT, DEPARTMENT OF SOUTH CAROLINA, GEORGIA AND FLA., Charleston, May 5, 1863.

[EXTRACT.]

[*SPECIAL ORDERS No. 163.*]

V. ALL BOATS OR VESSELS ANCHORING IN THE vicinity of Forts Sumter or Moultrie, will cast anchor at least 300 yards to the east or west of Fort Sumter. They will not be permitted on any account to anchor to the north of the Fort.

* * * * * * *

By command of Brigadier General RIPLEY.

WILLIAM F. NANCE, A. A. General.

May 6 6

DAILY DISPATCH.

VOL. XXIV. RICHMOND, VA., [illegible] MORNING, MAY 12, 1863. NO. 113.

The Daily Dispatch.

The DISPATCH is published DAILY (Sundays excepted.) Price for mailing $[illegible] a year; [illegible] for six months; [illegible] months $3; one month $[illegible] in advance.

The SEMI-WEEKLY DISPATCH is issued every TUESDAY and FRIDAY, $[illegible] in advance.

The WEEKLY DISPATCH is issued every FRIDAY, and mailed to subscribers at $[illegible] per annum.

TUESDAY MORNING.....MAY 12, 1863.

Gen Jackson.

Words have no power to express the emotion which the death of Jackson has aroused in the public mind. The heart of our whole people bleeds over the fallen hero, whom they loved so well because he so loved their cause, and vindicated it, not only with vast energy and courage, but with the most complete self-abnegation, simplicity, and single-mindedness. There was such an entire absence of pretension, vanity, ambition, and self in every shape about Gen. Jackson, that he had become a popular idol. The affections of every household in the nation were twined about this great and unselfish warrior, who, two years ago, was an unknown man! He has fallen, and a nation weeps, but not as those without hope. No grave more glorious can a soldier ask than the lap of victory; no future brighter than that which awaits one who united with the soldier the saint!

Nor is the loss to his country, great as it is, irreparable. No doubt the [illegible] will be encouraged to believe that, now that Jackson is dead, the subjugation of the South is certain. Let them cross the Rappahannock again, and the delusion will be dispelled. The veterans of Jackson's corps, the men whom he led and loved, will show at the first opportunity whether or not they are capable of avenging his death. True it is that amongst the galaxy of Confederate stars one has disappeared, but others are left equal in magnitude and brilliancy, and, as the darkness deepens, still others will be revealed, of which we now know as little as we did two years ago of the one we have lost. At the head of our armies is still the great Commander-in-Chief, whose masterly combinations Jackson assisted to execute with unsurpassed vigor and success. Around him are clustered a group of such men as Longstreet, Stuart, Hill, and others, and, no doubt, not a few in the ranks, (for this war has been the best kind of military school,) who will yet achieve a renown fully equal to that of the departed hero. Most of Napoleon's great Marshals were unknown men, and arose from the ranks, and why should not the Southern army, whose privates are in such large measure men of education as well as spirit, equal and even surpass in these respects the armies of France. Only let us cease to idolize man, and put our trust in that Providence which Jackson so constantly and reverently acknowledged as the hope and sheet anchor of our cause.

Vallandigham's Arrest.

The arrest of that brave and able defender of constitutional rights at the North—C. L. Vallandigham—is an event which ought to lead to some great consequences. Whether it will or not remains to be seen. It may be that the small riots, so soon suppressed, the arrest of a number of Vallandigham's friends, together with the extinction of the newspaper at Dayton called the *Empire*, of which Mr. V. was the editor, is to end the matter. If it stops at there, then indeed the Northern people are under the control of a despotism unsurpassed for its efficiency. Mr. Vallandigham was a candidate for the office of Governor of Ohio, and was receiving evidences from popular demonstrations which justified the hope of his election. It may be inferred that the step taken by the Government was prompted by the fact. For a long time it has discontinued the arrests of citizens of the North on suspicion of disloyalty, or for words uttered. Vallandigham never has ceased to declare his horror of the Lincoln despotism, and to denounce its usurpations of power. But even when Lincoln was arresting thousands, and filling his prisons, he would not put his hands on the fearless Congressman from Ohio. Therefore his arrest at this time betrays a sense of exigency not before entertained.

Whether or no the people agreeing with Vallandigham will tamely contemplate his imprisonment—will uncomplainingly and inactively acquiesce in the arrest of their great leader and hundreds of others of their fellow citizens—time must disclose. Certainly he is not the leader of a small party—certainly the wave agitated by his powerful intellect was no small one—and it would indeed be strange if the scenes depicted by the last arrival from the North should be the last of them all. The great reverses of the Federalists at the Wilderness and Fredericksburg may give some encouragement to the opposition and elicit some further evidence of its vitality. All we can say is, that if, after the demonstrations we have heard of at the North, there be a universal submission there to the atrocious despotism at Washington, then the Northern people are not fit for free institutions, and should not be allowed to enjoy them.

In Articulo Mortis

The Washington *Chronicle* says "the call of the nation, in her great agony, (for five hundred thousand men,) should reach every heart."

We have no doubt it will; but the sensations produced will be anything but agreeable. The nation (meaning thereby Lincoln & Co.) may call with all its lungs; but when the details of the ghastly carnage at the Wilderness come to be known, the call will awaken "an agony" of horror in every heart which it reaches. The natural response will be, "Why don't you go yourself? Old Abe, W. H. Seward, Washington *Chronicle*, and other bellicose throats of the nation, all nearer the scene of conflict than those you call upon, why don't you gird on your swords and hurry to the bloody banquet you are so fond of inviting other people to?"

But all these remonstrances will be of no avail. The five hundred thousand may as well make up their minds to follow the five hundred thousand who have gone before them.—And if they have not the courage to resist Lincoln's standing army, what may they expect when they come to confront the warriors who have so often cut the minions of Lincolnism to pieces? There is a dismal prospect before them. Their only encouragement is the confession which the late battle has scourged from the Washington *Chronicle*, that the nation is in "her great agony." We don't question it. She will be in a greater agony yet before she finds relief. The possibility that the rebels may get to Washington, which has always haunted "the nation," is now looming up to a fearful probability. Only suppose "the nation" should fall into the hands of Jeff Davis! It is too fearful to contemplate. Unfortunate nation! It is near its last gasp. With thundering words upon its lips, it is fighting against destiny, and slowly but certainly struggling to its dying grasp.—We know not what future effort it will make, nor how furious may be the flurry of the dying whale, but our confidence is calm and strong that the Power which has hitherto manifestly vindicated our cause will continue to confound the devices of our enemies and make us equal to every occasion that may arise.

The Richmond correspondent of the Charleston *Mercury* says that the Virginia salt works can now turn out 2,500,000 bushels annually.

THE DEATH OF GENERAL JACKSON.

THE FUNERAL CEREMONIES.

Last evening Gen. Jackson's remains were received in this city at 4 o'clock, from Guinea's Depot, in Caroline co. The announcement that they would arrive at 12 o'clock caused an entire suspension of all business in the city, and a turn out at the depot of nearly all the inhabitants of the city, who were anxious to pay the last tribute of respect to the departed chieftain. When it was known that the body would not reach the city before 4 o'clock, the immense crowd slowly dispersed, but assembled again at the last hour indicated in even greater force than before. The tolling of the different bells gave the signal that the cars were slowly wending their way down Broad street, when preparations were made for the reception of the body by an appropriate disposition of the military.

The train was stopped at the corner of 4th and Broad streets, and after a short delay the coffin containing the body was removed to the hearse in attendance. It was enveloped in the flag of the Confederacy. On the flag was placed wreaths of evergreen and rare flowers. A few minutes before 5 o'clock Gen. Elzey gave the command, and the procession started, marching in the following order:

Gen. Elzey and Staff, mounted; the Public Guard, Lieut. Gay, commanding; the 44th N. C. regiment, Pettigrew's brigade, Col. Singletary commanding; the Armory Band, playing a funeral dirge; Col. Frank Skinner, 1st Va. regiment, and some of the Governor's Aids; the hearse containing the body, surmounted by raven plumes, and drawn by two white horses; the Staff of Gen. Jackson, including Major Pendleton, Adjutant General; Maj. W. I. Hawks, Chief Commissary of the Corps; Major D. B. Bridgford, Chief Provost; Capt. Douglas, Lieut. Smith, Aide-de-Camp; Dr. McGuire, Surgeon, and others; the members of the City Council, two abreast, and lastly, an immense host of citizens and strangers.

The procession thus formed, (the military with reversed arms,) marched slowly to the corner of 9th street, and turned towards Main, entering the Capitol Square by the gate on Grace street. The military having formed a line extending across the Square past Washington's monument, the body was slowly conveyed down the line to the Governor's mansion, and carried into the large reception room. The bells were tolled till sundown, till which time hundreds of people remained on the Square. We have never before seen such an exhibition of heartfelt and general sorrow in reference to any other event whatever as has been evinced by all since the announcement of the death of Stonewall Jackson.

The body was embalmed, and to day the remains will lie in state in the Capitol.

HIS LAST MOMENTS

About 11 o'clock on Sunday it became known to his attending physician that there was no hope for Gen. Jackson's life. The General was informed of the fact, and was offered stimulants to prolong his existence.—These he refused to take, and a short time after his mind commenced to wander. Among his last words was a reference to his men. He said, speaking of his Commissary: "Tell Maj. Hawkes to send forward provisions to the men."

About 1 o'clock his wife entered the room, and took the last farewell which he bid on this earth, and at 15 minutes past 3 o'clock his spirit ascended to its Giver.

GEN LEE'S ORDER AFTER GEN. JACKSON'S DEATH.

The following is Gen. Lee's order to the army after the intelligence of Gen. Jackson's death:

Headq'rs Army Northern Va.,
May 11, 1863.

General Orders, No. 61.

With deep grief the commanding General announces to the army the death of Lieut. General T. J. Jackson, who expired on the 10th inst., at 3¼ P. M. The daring, skill, and energy of this great and good soldier, by the decree of an all-wise Providence, are now lost to us. But while we mourn his death, we feel that his spirit still lives, and will inspire the whole army with his indomitable courage and unshaken confidence in God as our hope and our strength. Let his name be a watchword to his corps, who have followed him to victory on so many fields. Let officers and soldiers emulate his invincible determination to do everything in the defence of our beloved country.

R. E. Lee, General.

THE LETTER OF GEN. LEE TO GEN. JACKSON.

The letter written by Gen. Lee to General Jackson before the death of the latter, is as follows:

Chancellorsville, May 4th.

General—I have just received your note informing me that you were wounded. I cannot express my regret at the occurrence. Could I have dictated events, I should have chosen for the good of the country to have been disabled in your stead.

I congratulate you upon the victory which is due to your skill and energy.

Most truly yours, R. E. Lee.

To Gen'l T. J. Jackson.

THE FUNERAL PAGEANT TO-DAY.

There will be a procession formed this morning at 10 o'clock precisely from the mansion of the Governor, to proceed down Governor st. to Main, thence up Main to Second, thence along Second to Grace, thence by the west gate of the Capitol Square to the Capitol, where the body will be deposited in State, in the Hall of Congress.

The procession will be under the charge of Gen. George W. Randolph, as Chief Marshal, with such number of assistants as he may select.

The order of procession will be as follows:

Military escort, composed of such force of the Confederate Government as may be detailed for the purpose;

The Public Guard,

The Hearse,

Pall Bearers, composed of six Major or Brigadier Generals, who are requested to attend and officiate as such;

The family and personal friends of the deceased;

Any portion of the old "Stonewall Brigade," wounded or other, who may be able to attend;

Officers of the Army and Navy not in command at present;

The President and Vice-President of the Confederacy;

The Heads of Departments of the Confederate Government and their Clerks.—Each Department will be organized by its head, or such officer as he may select for the purpose;

The Judiciary and District-Attorney, and attachees of the Judiciary Department;

The Governor and his Aids;

The Secretary of the Commonwealth, Attorney General, Auditor of Public Accounts, Treasurer, Second Auditor, Register of the Land Office, and their Clerks;

The Court of Appeals and Judges of Circuit Courts;

The Board of Public Works and its Clerk;

The Adjutant General and his Clerks; Inspector General, Quartermaster-General, Paymaster-General, and Ordnance Departments of the State Government and their Clerks;

The Mayor of the City;

Members of the City Council and its Officers;

Court of Hustings, Sergeant, Sheriff, and their Officers;

All Benevolent Societies who may wish to join the procession;

Citizens and strangers.

The Governor requests that the arrangement above indicated will be preserved, and that the procession be promptly formed.

By order of the Governor.

George W. Munford,
Secretary of the Commonwealth.

THE ENEMY ADVANCING UP THE VALLEY.

The latest advices we have from the Valley represent that the enemy had advanced his forces as high up as Hankinsville, nine miles below New Market, in Shenandoah county. Two regiments of infantry, one of cavalry, and a battery of artillery camped at that point on the night of the 6th. Our forces in the Valley had fallen back to Harrisonburg. Another report states that the Yankees have occupied Harrisonburg, but we think this doubtful.

FROM THE NORTH.

FURTHER ACCOUNTS OF THE FREDERICKSBURG BATTLE.

The New York *World* and *Herald*, of the 7th, from which we yesterday published some extracts, contained further news of interest. The *World* describes the operations of Sedgwick [illegible] as follows:

The capture of Fredericksburg by General Sedgwick was the last principal item of news from that quarter. After obtaining possession of the rebel batteries he marched four miles on the plankroad to Chancellorsville, where he met a large force of the enemy, doubtless a part of Longstreet's division, sent to meet him, from Suffolk. It appears that a portion of the rebel army got between Gen. Sedgwick and the force menacing Gibbons, who held possession of Fredericksburg. Thus Lee was between Sedgwick and Hooker, and Sedgwick in turn between two parts of Lee's army—Gen Sedgwick had been reinforced by some troops that had before been employed in holding the heights east of Fredericksburg, and the enemy took possession of a part of those deserted works. On Monday morning Gen. Sedgwick was attacked near Backford by a large force of the enemy, superior in numbers to his own. Pressed in front and flank, his men fought bravely, but were finally compelled to retire. As this movement was commencing the Vermont brigade charged furiously, and succeeded in driving the rebels from the ground. It was a bloody day for both sides, and the Federal command had done nobly in maintaining their ground against such numbers. A retirement across the river was determined on, with a view to recross at United States Ford and endeavor to join Hooker's main army. Accordingly, at a little past midnight he ordered the movement, and as silently as possible the troops took up the line of march over the bridge. The enemy soon discovered this movement, and opened a heavy fire on the bridge with artillery, killing and wounding a large number of our men. They did not succeed, however, in cutting off any portion by destroying the bridge, which was their principal object.

It may be, that instead of attempting to join Gen Hooker, Sedgwick will return to the relief of Gibbons, as the rebels were discovered on Monday morning only two miles below United States Ford, and at daybreak commenced shelling our trains on this side the Rappahannock. How large a force have thus got in the rear of Hooker's army it is yet impossible to decide:

The *World* gives the following account of Jackson's recapture of Fredericksburg:

The morning and evening attacks on Monday, by the rebels, under Jackson, and Gen. Gibbon's force at Fredericksburg, have resulted in their gaining possession again of the greater part of the place. It must not, however, be regarded as anything like a disaster. Fredericksburg now is not one-tenth as important as Fredericksburg before Gen. Hooker's first movement. Our armies are on its flank and rear, and our heavy pieces across the river on its front. About evening they rushed on our right, and for a long time the battle was hotly contested, each party alternately gaining the advantage. Finally our force was obliged to retire, and during the night held a defensive position. Next morning Col. Hall crossed his brigade over the river on the Falmouth side, and both bridges were taken up. It is suspected that the enemy have pontoons sufficient to cross the river, and a lively watch is kept up to prevent raids on their part.

Although it is believed that General Hooker is *master of his position* and able to combat successfully, yet, to make possibility *sure*, Gen Heintzelman, with 30,000 men, has been dispatched from Washington to his aid.

The trophies of Sunday's fight are just developing. It is found that a large number of rebel guns and flags were captured, and 6,000 or 8,000 prisoners. Ten guns of the famous Washington battery from New Orleans are among the trophies. Confederate prisoners are almost continually arriving in this city and turned over to the Provost Marshal. 850 Mississippians and Alabamians came yesterday.

The Philadelphia *Inquirer*, of the 6th, has the following account:

The news from General Hooker's army by the steamer Hero is of a very meagre and conflicting character.

Instructions have been given to those in the Government service not to impart information to any one regarding the progress of operations in and around Fredericksburg upon their arrival here.

Accounts pretty generally agree that the rebels have re-occupied Fredericksburg, and they held the town at the time of the Hero's departure.

The heights below are jointly occupied by the Union and rebel troops.

The position of the heights occupied by our forces on Sunday morning were retaken, after a desperate resistance, by fresh reinforcements from Gen. Longstreet's corps, and an enfilading fire was commenced by the rebels on portions of other redoubts occupied by our troops.

The fighting Monday was not as general or very terrific in its character as was generally anticipated.

It was thought that the shock of arms to-day (Tuesday) would be fraught with highly important, if not final results.

The general impression among the passengers from Aquia Creek appears to be that Gen. Hooker will hold his own; but still the news is indefinite from the front, and but little is known at the Aquia Creek station—almost within eye-sight of the scene of the mighty events *that now create the greatest solicitude and most intense anxiety*.

Passengers by the Hero state that everything is in immediate readiness for a removal of our stores, etc., from Aquia Creek if by any possible chance the fortune of war should turn against us, and an advance be made by the rebels in that direction.

Up to the present moment, Tuesday, May 5th, 3 o'clock P. M., nothing is known of a definite character beyond the fact that many thousands on both sides have been killed and wounded, and that the fight has been in progress since Wednesday last.

A dispatch from Washington, May 6, says since Saturday nearly 3,000 rebel prisoners have been brought to this city. Seven hundred and eighty arrived here at 2 o'clock to-day, and were, like their predecessors, marched to the Provost Marshal's office, under a strong guard. Thence they were conveyed to safe quarters. The number is already too large for convenient accommodation. Additional prisoners are to be sent up from the Rappahannock, making in all 4,000 and over certainly in our hands.

The prisoners present a shabby appearance. The much larger part are dressed in dirty gray, the remainder in brown, and generally in slouched hats. Many of them have good substantial boots, while others are nearly barefoot. Not a few, instead of having blankets, show that they have made an extensive levy on carpets. The prisoners are nearly all young men. Their appearance in the streets excited much curiosity, but no rude or offensive remarks were made by the spectators.

Ambulances were busy both last night and to-day conveying the wounded from the Army of the Potomac to the several hospitals.

SOME OF THE KILLED AND WOUNDED.

The following are among the casualties in the Yankee army:

Killed.—Brig-Gen Mott, of Sickles's corps; Maj-Gen Berry, of Maine; Brig Gen Schimmelfennig, 11th corps; Col Lee, 6th N J; Lt Col Walter, 19th Conn; Maj Watson, 36th N Y; Col McKnight, 105th Pa; Col Lancaster, 125th Pa; Col Stratford, 109th Pa; Col Stevens, 4th Excelsior Brigade; Lt Col Scott 3d Wisconsin; Lt-Col Chaplin, 86th N Y; Maj Keenan, 8th Pa cav; Maj Strouse, 46th Pa; Capt Ellsworth, 80th N Y; Col Kugar, [illegible] Maj John Haverin, [illegible] Maj Faison, 36th N Y; Maj Baske[illegible]

Wounded.—Gen [illegible] Mass, severely; Brig Gen Whipple, [illegible]man, 37th N Y; Col Sewell, 6th [illegible] Burling, 5th N J; Lieut-Col Norton, [illegible] badly; Capt Fry, aid to Sickles, in [illegible] Ross 21st Conn; Col Potter; Maj H[illegible] 36th N Y; Col Hecker, 82d Ill; Col [illegible] 20th Conn; Col Fontvegrauch, 20th N [illegible] Jones, 7th Mass, severely; Col Brown, [illegible] Y, knee shattered; Col Riley, 75th [illegible] a prisoner; Col Richardson, 25th [illegible] severely; Col Van Giesen, commanding [illegible] Adjutant Stevens, 115th Penn; Col [illegible] 1st N Y; Lieut-Col Cogswell, 2d Mass; [illegible] Col Cook 149th N Y; Col Miles, 61st [illegible] fatally; Col E M Gregory, 91st Penn[illegible]; Maj Auzelle, 5th N J; Lt Col Lowe[illegible] 5th Excelsior, severely; Maj Willoughby, [illegible] N Y; Maj Higgins, 86th N Y; Col [illegible] N Y; Col Hurlin, 6th N J; Col Willetts, 7th N J; Col Potter, 12th N H; Maj [illegible] Chasseur, mortally; Col W H Noble, [illegible] Conn; Adj't Thomas, 20th Ind, badly; Col [illegible], 8th N J; and 28 Captains and [illegible] killed; and 52 Captains and Lieutenants wounded, many of [illegible]. This is but a partial [illegible] officers.

Rebel Casualties.—The following rebel Generals are known to be wounded: Lieut Gen Jackson, slightly, and still in the saddle; Major-Gen D H Hill, severely; Major-Gen A P Hill, slightly; Brig Gen Mahone, severely; Brig Gen Nichols, slightly; Major-Gen Ransom.

THE SITUATION.

The *World* says, editorially:

The news from General Hooker's army is interpreted in official quarters as being favorable, but with the map before us we cannot so regard it.

It is idle to say that Fredericksburg was of no strategical importance. If that was the case, why was a loss of nearly a thousand brave fellows incurred endeavoring to capture it? The fact is, it was of supreme importance to hold the heights of Fredericksburg. By their possession Lee's rear was constantly menaced, and the railroad toward Richmond rendered unavailable for his army.

The mystery in connection with these rebel movements on Monday was the silence of Gen Hooker. The enemy must have detached over 30,000 men from his main body to overwhelm Sedgwick and Gibbons, yet Gen Hooker does not seem to have been able to take advantage of or prevent it. Sedgwick could not have been more than six miles distant from Hooker's left when attacked by the enemy, yet the Union commander was unable to aid him. This can be accounted for only on two theories—either Gen. Hooker's army was so crippled that it dare not engage the enemy, or it was retreating to the north bank of the Rappahannock.

In the absence of positive information to the contrary, and in the light of the facts before us, we are compelled to believe that Hooker has been out generaled—our army out-fought. We hear that 30,000 men, under Heintzelman, are on the road to reinforce Hooker, and that a large number of troops are also under way to the same destination from another quarter; all of which goes to show that the Union army on the Rappahannock is *in a bad box*. The reinforcements would not be needed if Lee was about to retreat.

It is difficult now to resist the conclusion that the Confederates deliberately allowed the Union army to cross without impediment, confident that it would be crushed under Hooker's leadership when once on the other side. Since last Saturday they have been doing pretty much as they pleased. Either Lee's army largely out-numbers Hooker's, or else the latter is unable to properly handle "the finest army on the planet."

Let us hope that the news to-day may be more reassuring. Some happy accident may yet interfere in our favor and give us an unexpected and glorious victory.

ARREST OF THE HON. C. L. VALLANDIGHAM.

Great excitement existed at Dayton, Ohio, on the 5th, in regard to the arrest of Hon. Clement Vallandigham, by order of General Burnside. A despatch from Cincinnati says:

At dark a crowd of from 500 to 600 proceeded to the *Journal* office, took possession of it, completely gutted the building, set it on fire, and burnt it to the ground. The fire communicated to the adjoining building, and all the property from the south end of the Phillips House to the middle of the square was destroyed. All the telegraph lines in the city were cut down and destroyed. The bridge on the Xenia road is reported to be destroyed.

At 10 o'clock at night Federal troops from Cincinnati and Columbus succeeded in putting down the rioters, and at half past 11 o'clock quiet was again restored.

Cincinnati, May 6—P. M.—Dayton has been comparatively quiet to-day. About thirty ringleaders in last night's riot have been arrested without resistance and placed in jail.

The *Empire* newspaper has been suppressed. Its editor has been arrested and brought here. The soldiers have removed a swivel from the *Empire* office, and also taken possession of two wagon loads of muskets, stored in the Light Guards' armory.

Mr. Vallandigham was brought before the Court-Martial to-day for trial. He refused to plead to the charges which were read to him. The Court proceeded with the evidence, the publication of which is not allowed. The charges were based on his Mount Vernon speech. Mr. Vallandigham is at the Burnett House to-night, under a strong guard. Dayton and Montgomery county are placed under martial law.

The total loss by the conflagration at Dayton was $39,000.

IMPORTANT FROM ENGLAND—EXCITING DEBATE

The Australasian, with Queenstown dates to the 26th, reached New York Wednesday.

A spirited debate had occurred in both Houses of Parliament in regard to the seizure of British vessels by Federal cruisers. Mr. Roebuck was among the speakers in the House of Commons, and during his remarks used the following language: Another outrage has taken place, and by the same men who perpetrated the insult offered to our flag in the case of the Trent. A vessel leaves the English shore—the Hon. member for London, Mr. Crawford, says he has seen her papers, and they are perfectly harmless. She was bound to a neutral port. [Cheers.] She was seized by an American man-of-war, taken into an American port, and the expectations of the English merchant in his honorable trade have been utterly destroyed by the conduct of the American Government. I say that conduct of the American Government you ought to resent. [Cheers.] But not only was this done. There were persons calling themselves English merchants, who applied to the American Minister for a permit to allow their ships to proceed in safety to its destination. That permit is granted, and why? *Because that ship carried out arms to the Mexicans to be used against our ally, France*—[Cheers.] Since then, other men calling themselves English merchants have applied to the same authority for the same permit. They have been refused because they are Englishmen, and because they are not carrying out arms to aid the Mexicans in the war, though they were trading to the same port. The permit I repeat, was refused, and now I must say that Mr. Adams, the American Minister, is the Minister for commerce in England. [Loud cheers.] Sir, I would put it to the noble Lord—the man who has hitherto shown himself alive to the honor and dignity of England—I would ask him whether the Government of which he is the head has come to any determination in this matter, and if they have, whether he is able to tell Parliament what that determination is? Sir, I know the consequences of the action he may take. *It may lead to war, and I, speaking for the English people, am prepared for war!* [Loud cheers, and "Oh! oh!"] I know that language will strike the hearts of the peace party in this country, but it will also strike the hearts of the insolent people who govern America, and we shall have justice done to the honor and dignity of England, and the commerce of this country will no longer be subject to the sneering insolence of an upstart race. [Cheers.] The question I have to ask the noble Lord is, whether the Government of which he is the head have formed any determination with regard to the conduct of Admiral Wilkes; whether they have addressed any remonstrance to the American Government, and whether he is prepared now to state the course the Government have determined to pursue? [Hear, hear.]

Lord Palmerston said the House would at once understand, from what had fallen from his honorable friend, that the matter to which his question referred was of the utmost possible importance. All he could say was, that it was receiving due consideration from Government; but he was not prepared at present to state at what result Her Majesty's Government might arrive.

THE RAID IN VIRGINIA.

The Washington *Chronicle*, of Saturday, May 9th, publishes the following:

The following official dispatch was received at the headquarters of the army last evening:

Yorktown, Va., May 7.

Major-General Halleck:

Col. Kilpatrick, with his regiment, the Harris Light Cavalry, and the rest of the Illinois 12th, have just arrived at Gloucester Point, opposite this post. They burned the bridges over the Chickahominy, destroyed three large trains of provisions in the rear of Lee's army; drove in the rebel pickets to within two (2) miles of Richmond, and have lost only one (1) Lieutenant and thirty men, having captured and paroled upwards of three hundred prisoners. Among the prisoners was an aid of Gen. Winder, who was captured with his escort within the entrenchments outside of Richmond. This cavalry have marched nearly two hundred (200) miles since the 3d of May; were inside of the fortifications of Richmond on the 4th; burnt all the stores at Aylett's Station, on the Mattapony; on the 5th destroyed all the ferries over the Pamunkey and Mattapony, and a large depot of commissary stores near and above the Rappahannock, and came in here in good condition. They deserve great credit for what they have done. It is one of the finest feats of the war.

Rufus King,
Brigadier General Comd'g Post.

The New York *Herald*, of the 7th, does not seem very hopeful about the results of the Fredericksburg fight. It says:

The public has been so often misled, duped, deceived, disappointed, and trifled with by the authorities at Washington that, in spite of the splendid fighting on the Rappahannock, it has at length relapsed into comparative indifference, and settled into the conviction that this Administration is totally incompetent to conduct the war, and that there is no longer any hope of the very speedy suppression of the rebellion.

THE LATEST,

We have received a copy of the Washington *Chronicle*, of Sunday, the 10th instant, and copies of other Northern papers. The New York *Herald* announces the battle as a "crushing defeat" to Hooker. Another Yankee paper says that the Federal army now numbers 70,000, and is strong enough to repel any attack.

Com. Porter gives an account of the attack on Grand Gulf, and says that he accomplished all he wanted *except* silencing the batteries, which, he says, "were fought with a desperation I never before witnessed."

A dispatch from Port Gibson, from General Grant, says he completely routed the rebels there on the 30th, capturing 500 prisoners besides the wounded.

An arrival at New York from Wilmington bar, on the 4th, says that the iron-clads are again off Charleston, and that an attack on the place is imminent.

Rosecrans has issued an order prohibiting women or non-combatants from entering his lines after May 8th—a sign of business.

The news of Van Dorn's death, and the cause, are published in the Yankee papers.

The decision of the Court-Martial in the case of Vallandigham has been submitted to Gen. Burnside, but no decision rendered as yet.

Lincoln has issued a proclamation, dated the 8th, declaring all foreigners subject to enrollment who shall have "declared their intention," and giving them 65 days to leave the United States.

The *Chronicle* has an editorial on the battle. It says the Federals "set their mark too high," and failed, but nevertheless gained something. The reason they did not gain all was the heavy reinforcement of Lee by Longstreet. The "something" gained, it seems, was frightening the people in Richmond, at the slight cost of about 12,000 men and officers killed and wounded, as published in the lists returned from Fredericksburg, of which the 2d division alone of Sickles's corps lost 1,985.

There was not a soldier left in Richmond or in Petersburg. Home guards, armed with shot-guns, did picket duty in front of Richmond, and department clerks, armed with horse pistols, guarded the prisoners in Libby prison. Nearly the whole of Longstreet's corps came to the army at Fredericksburg. Against these odds—much greater than we had any reason to expect—Gen. Hooker could not accomplish the magnificent task he had proposed to himself. It is a truth that will stand the test of all history, that he only failed in the *entire* accomplishment of what he had too confidently promised.

But we have gained much. General Lee is said to have reported that he has taken five thousand prisoners, though it is stated on good authority that this report was disbelieved in Richmond, where it was got up by Jeff Davis for effect. But even if it is true we have probably taken more than five thousand of their men, many of whom are ready to take the oath of allegiance to the Union, if for nothing else, for the sake of escaping from the Confederacy for which they have been unwillingly fighting. Two hundred took the oath in Baltimore yesterday. Authentic dispatches from General Lee and other officers in the rebel army captured by us, place their loss in killed and wounded at from eighteen to twenty thousand. Our whole loss can hardly exceed half that number.

The army was never—so we judge from all the accounts we hear—in better condition or better spirits. They have more confidence than ever, both in their commander and themselves, and in the next forward movement will again cover themselves with glory, and add new laurels to the army of the Potomac.

The *Chronicle* has the following two paragraphs:

The correspondent of the New York *Herald* who was captured on the Rappahannock a week or two ago and carried to Richmond, and was one of the party recently exchanged, says that all the prisoners were paroled when Stoneman was within a short distance of that city, or they would have overpowered the guard and probably captured the town. He says that our cavalry forces captured over a thousand rebels.

It is said that among the forces captured by Stoneman in the vicinity of the rebel capital was a battalion of the Richmond City Guard, an aristocratic organization for home duty.—They had been on a reconnoissance.

NOMINATIONS IN WESTERN VIRGINIA.

The Convention which met at Parkersburg, on the 5th inst., to nominate officers for the new State of Western Virginia, has adjourned, having nominated for Governor A. J. Boreman, of Parkersburg; Secretary of State, J. E. Boyer, of Middletown; Secretary of the Treasury, Campbell Tarr, of Brooke county; State Auditors, Samuel Brane of Wheeling, Judge B. O. Berckshire, of Morgantown; Wm. A. Harrison, of Clarksburg, and James H Brown, of Kanawha; Attorney General, A. B. Caldwell, of Wheeling.

A BRIEF ACCOUNT OF THE BATTLE.

Falmouth, Va., May 5.—Yesterday two terrible battles were fought by the 6th corps, Gen. Sedgwick, resulting in fearful carnage on both sides. Monday morning the rebels suddenly made their appearance on the hills to the left of Fredericksburg, and coming down rapidly, occupied the city, thus getting in the rear of the corps. Most of the supply trains, ambulances, mules, and soldiers in the vicinity were taken. A fleet horse saved me from capture. A serious blunder was perpetrated in pushing our forces on so rapidly without ascertaining whether or not there were any rebels on the woody heights to the left of the city. One whole corps came down, and forming in line of battle immediately marched after the corps.

The only way of retreat lay by Brooks's Ford, five miles above the city. Gen. Sedgwick was signaled from this side of the river of the condition of affairs and immediately [illegible] about formed a line of battle facing [illegible] way, holding the rebels in check, and working down toward the ford. The lines of battle remained in this condition until about the middle of the day, when the rebels attacked us, and were gallantly repulsed Howe's division capturing three hundred prisoners.—The rebel reinforcements had fought none, while our troops had been fighting more or less since the previous Tuesday night. For a time it was feared that the corps could not make communication at Banks's Ford, and that the whole of it must be captured. But by noon a connection was made, and Gen. Sedgwick sent for supplies. Meantime the wounded in Fredericksburg were being taken across the pontoon to this side, all of them being got away on the sudden appearance of the enemy on the outskirts above. The doctors supposing, of course, that the enemy would come down and take them, made all the arrangements for being taken prisoners; but for some reason, either through fear of our forces above or siege guns on this side of the river, the enemy did not advance into the town. The positions of the respective armies were then as follows: Our main force on the north, then the main force of the enemy, the 6th corps below, corps of rebels still lower, and our heavy guns on this side—a most extraordinary sandwiching of opposing forces together.

Skirmishing occurred along the whole line until 5½ o'clock in the evening, when the rebels attacked us from two ways. The Union forces were at the time arrayed in an arc, both wings resting on the river, the right at Banks's Ford.

We were arranged in two lines of battle.—The enemy attacking, the 2d division of the 2d corps and Howe's at first approaching them diagonally from Fredericksburg and the country directly beyond Gen Mills's brigade, consisting of the 33d, 77th, 20th and 49th New York together with the Vermont brigade and 7th Maine, bore the brunt of the charge, repulsing the enemy handsomely. The Vermont brigade were on the left of Gen'l Mills. Mills's brigade and other troops made a counter charge, but reinforcements coming up to the enemy, we were not able to drive them. The 77th acted nobly, but the 20th New York behaved very disgracefully, as it did at White Oak Swamp, and falling back brought a cross fire on the 33d. Their Colonel, however, conducted himself most bravely. The other lines of battle were now attacked by overwhelming numbers and obliged to fall back to the river.

STONEMAN'S RAID

A correspondent of the Washington *Chronicle*, who accompanied General Stoneman's cavalry raid, writing to that paper from Kelley's Ford, under date of May 8 gives a detailed account of the operations of the expedition.

He speaks of it as one of the most successful military enterprises of the kind ever undertaken in this or any other country. But we let the extravagant correspondent tell his own story, from which it will be seen that his own imagination accomplished more than Stoneman's raid. He says:

General Stoneman moved the main body of his command across Fleshman's river, and encamped for the night in an open field during a heavy rain storm. At this point the enemy made a dash upon our pickets, but did not alarm the camp. Thursday morning, early, General Buford crossed the Rapidan two miles below the Raccoon Ford, (Morton's Ford,) and advancing up the opposite bank caused a force of sixteen hundred rebel infantry, with one piece of artillery, to leave in great haste from Raccoon Ford, where soon after General Gregg crossed with his division. Here a Lieutenant and thirteen privates of a rebel artillery company were captured. Near this point an army beef contractor was overhauled and $28,000 in Confederate bonds taken from him.

A rebel engineer with a wagon load of material was also captured on the road. Friday morning heard cannonading on the right, which proved to be Gen. Averill's command having a little fight with the enemy at Rapidan Station, on the Orange and Alexandria railroad. Next day got close upon the heels of a large rebel force at Orange Springs, who, to escape, abandoned wagons, provisions, etc; captured a lieutenant of Jackson's staff returning from leave of absence. At night camped at Greenwood, just outside of Louisa Court-House. The town was surrounded and Col Kilpatrick took possession of the place at 6 o'clock A. M. May 2d, without opposition, capturing a few rebel soldiers.

The tracks of the Virginia Central Railroad, connecting Gordonsville and Richmond was destroyed at different points for ten miles, two trains of cars burnt, telegraph wires cut and destroyed, and some commissary stores were also appropriated. During the night a detachment of the 1st Maine cavalry, doing picket duty five miles up the Gordonsville road, was attacked, and had two men killed. The enemy disappeared the moment a brigade advanced, after firing a few shots. On the afternoon of the 2d the command moved on through Yanceyville to Thompson's Four Corners. From this point detachments were sent out in different directions. One party destroyed a portion of the railroad between Gordonsville and Charlottesville, another, consisting of four hundred men, under Col. Wyndham, proceeded to Columbia, on the James river, where the Lynchburg and Richmond canal crosses the river. An unsuccessful attempt was made to destroy the aqueduct.

Five locks were destroyed, the banks of the canal cut away at different points, three canal boats, loaded with materials for the rebel army, and five bridges were burned. A large quantity of commissary stores, medicines, &c., were also destroyed, and several hundred horses were captured. A party under Capt. Drummond, of the 5th cavalry, reached the river between Columbia and Richmond and destroyed locks, levels, and set fire to a bridge across James river. Gen. Gregg proceeded to the Fredericksburg and Richmond railroad, and destroyed at Ashland the depot buildings, railroad track, a train of cars, provisions, and telegraph. He sent a detachment to burn the railroad bridge over the South Anna, but it was strongly guarded by infantry, and the party sent out fell back. Gen. Gregg returned to Thompson's Four Corners, sent a portion of his command, under Col. Kilpatrick, moved eastward to the Central road, destroyed the bridge on that road over the South Anna, captured and destroyed a train of cars, culverts, and the railroad track for miles, and then passed down to the Peninsula.

Another portion of General Gregg's command, under Colonel Davis, Twelfth Illinois, crossed both roads nearer Richmond, destroying railroads, telegraph, bridge over Brook river, and railway trains. A detachment of Gen. Gregg's command also burned all the upper bridges over the South Anna, to prevent the enemy making a flank movement and catching Gen. Stoneman in a trap. Monday morning, the 4th, Hampton and D. H. Hill, with two brigades, attacked about sixty of the Fifth cavalry, on picket duty near Shannon Hill. A charge of the rebels was met by a counter charge; the rebel advance was temporarily repulsed, but rallying captured seventeen of the Fifth cavalry. Our force captured thirteen of the enemy. Gen. Buford advanced upon the enemy with his command, but they fled.

The night of the 4th Gen. Gregg moved to near Yanceyville, and was followed to that point next day by Gen'l Stoneman with Gen'l Buford's command. Here a man a native of North Carolina, came into camp, who had been concealed for a year to avoid serving Jeff Davis. Near Yanceyville seventeen C. S. A. wagons, with mules, were overtaken and captured. On the 5th the retrograde movement commenced, and crossing Raccoon ford the whole command arrived at Kelly's ford Friday morning, the 8th.

Confessing Their Own Vandalism.—Once and awhile even a Federal editor becomes disgusted with the vandalism of the Federal troops, and confesses that they commit acts that would disgrace even savages. The New York *Christian Inquirer*, in remarking upon these things, says:

In several libraries of New England clergymen we have seen choice volumes of great cost, bearing the names of Southern ministers, to whom they still belong, although they had been sent North by Yankee soldiers who had appropriated them. Some Massachusetts parlors are said to be carpeted with spoils of another kind. At Beaufort, South Carolina, tombs were violated. At Holly Springs, Mississippi, a communion table was used in behalf of "euchre" and "old sledge." Such tales of wrong have infuriated many who were disposed to be friends of the Union, and their righteous indignation has had something to do with reverses that have overtaken our arms.

The Daily Dispatch.

TELEGRAPHIC NEWS.

Reported Victory in Louisiana.

Jackson, May 11—The Natchez *Courier* has information from a person at Port Hud on that Gen. Kirby Smith, with ten thousand raw troops, whipped Banks—whipped him badly—driving him to Washington, La. The Confederate force consisted of men from the other side of the river.

From Vicksburg

Vicksburg, May 9.—Nothing new from the front. The enemy have been landing troops to day below Young's Point. It is supposed they are destined to reinforce Grant.

The *Whig* office was destroyed by fire this afternoon. The origin of the fire is unknown.

LOCAL MATTERS.

Meeting of the City Council—Resolutions Regarding the Death of Gen Jackson.—A called meeting of the Council was held at 11 o'clock yesterday in the City Hall. Present: D. J. Saunders, Richard F. Walker, David J. Burr, Samuel D. Denoon, Richard O. Haskins, Larkin W. Glazebrook, E. A. J. Clopton, Geo. K. Crutchfield, Wm. Holt Richardson, George W. Randolph, Nath. B. Hill, Fendall Griffin, Allen Y. Stokes, James A. Scott, and Thomas C. Epps.

The President announced the melancholy tidings of the death of the lamented Lieut.-Gen. Thomas J. Jackson, spoke briefly of the invaluable services rendered to the Confederacy by the departed hero, and the duty of the Council, in view of the sad event which caused his death, to pass suitable resolutions of respect to his memory.

Gen. Randolph said it was usual, on similar occasions, to appoint a committee to draft suitable resolutions, and he would move that one be appointed, to consist of three or five members, as might seem best.

The President adopting the suggestion for the larger number, appointed as said committee Messrs. Randolph, Hill, Scott, Haskins, and Glazebrook. The committee, after a brief retirement, returned, and through their chairman offered the following resolutions, which were unanimously adopted:

Resolved, by the Council of the city of Richmond, That profoundly impressed with the great calamity sustained by the country in the death of Lieutenant-General Thomas J. Jackson and desirous of expressing their sense of his virtues and his services in the most emphatic manner, they think that justice to his memory requires them to refrain from an attempt at eulogy which no language can adequately express. They leave, therefore, to others further removed from the times in which he lived, and when his public career shall have borne its full fruits, to portray character and conduct rarely equalled in the world's history.

Resolved, That they tender to his afflicted widow their most heartfelt condolence, and beg leave, as citizens of the Republic, to share in her grief for a loss alike irreparable to her and to the country.

Resolved, That the corporate authorities and the citizens of Richmond, and all strangers now in the city, be invited to join in the civil portion of the procession from the cars to the Capitol, and from the Capitol to such other point as may be hereafter indicated; that business be suspended, and the bells of the city be tolled while the procession is passing through the city, and that the Mayor be requested to adopt proper measures for the preservation of order in the civil procession, and publish a programme thereof.

Resolved, That the foregoing resolutions be entered upon the journals of the Council and that the Chamberlain be instructed to enclose a copy of the same, to the widow of General Jackson.

On motion, the Council adjourned.

Burglars About.—The neighborhood west of Brook avenue has been much infested with robbers lately; so much so, indeed, that the people residing in that section of the city are resorting to the expedient of hiring watchmen to guard their houses and property. On Saturday night, near the corner of Clay and Henry streets, two men went into the kitchen of Mr. T. C. Lipscomb, and assaulted a negro woman, and stole nine dresses, besides other articles, and escaped; and on Sunday night thieves made an attempt to break into Mr. Holdman's house, corner of Clay and Monroe streets, but were frightened off before they could effect anything. They left behind a lot of burglars implements, consisting of a saw, chisel, and jimmey.

Miscellaneous.—Seventeen Yankee prisoners were received at the Libby on yesterday—ten belonging to Stoneman's cavalry, were captured on the Rapidan. Eight hundred from Atlanta, Ga., were expected last night from Lynchburg. Several thousand will probably arrive to day from Guinea Station. A C Garey, of Harrison co, sent to Castle Thunder as a hostage, was discharged by order of General Winder yesterday. Ransom Washington and Roderick Wilson, free negroes, have been lodged in the Military prison on the charge of guiding the Yankees during their recent raid around Richmond. Robt S Parker, for assisting soldiers to desert, and Frank Livingston for being a spy, have been lodged in Castle Thunder for trial. John Orrell, a burglar, who recently escaped from the city jail, has been re-arrested and conducted to his old quarters.

Reprehensible Conduct.—It is stated on the best authority that the conduct of the armed guard stationed around the Fredericksburg cars, on their arrival in this city, is most disgraceful to them and insulting to gentlemen who have to put up with their impertinences, in the shape of rude hustlings from the cars, and threats of arrest if the party complains. Ever since the battle at Chancellorsville our citizens, and citizens of other States, have attended on the arrival of the cars for the purpose of succoring the wounded by refreshments, and lending assistance in getting them to the hospitals; but they cannot be expected to do so if they are rudely repulsed from the cars by the bayonets of the soldiers. In this matter we speak more in behalf of those citizens of other States who go to the cars to meet their wounded relatives, and are rudely denied the privilege, than our own, who have by experience learned to stand anything.

Hustings Court.—The regular monthly term of the Hustings Court commenced yesterday. Present: Recorder Caskie, and Aldermen Sanxay, Bray, Timberlake and Garey. Soon after the Court was opened it adjourned until this morning, in testimony of respect for the memory of Gen. Jackson. The Grand Jury which assembled yesterday also adjourned until to-day at 11 o'clock.

Denied.—It was stated yesterday that Patrick Curtis, who died from the effects of licks given him by a man named Lamb Schell, was "a substitute agent." This, we are informed by a friend of deceased, was not the case. Curtis had only been in Richmond four weeks when he received the wounds which resulted in his death, and during those four weeks had been engaged as an agent of the Government in buying leather. He was a shoe-maker by trade and came from North Carolina.

Not Dead.—The report published in some of the papers of the death of Conway Howard, of this city, a member of Gen. A. P. Hill's staff, and Capt. E. W. Branch, of the Richmond Grays, turns out to have no foundation in fact—Captain Howard being captured by the Yankees at the battle of Chancellorsville, and Captain Branch escaping a hurt.

Continued.—All the cases before the Mayor and Judge Meredith yesterday were continued until to-day, no business being transacted in either Court.

A Female Soldier Boy.—A young woman, apparently about 17 years of age, attired in military apparel, was arrested in this city Tuesday, and lodged in jail until a more satisfactory information in regard to her can be obtained. She says that she is a married woman, that she is from Mississippi, and was with a company stationed near Charleston; and that, having lost her dresses, she was unable to procure any other clothing than that in which she was attired.—*Augusta Constitutionalist, May 7th.*

A Chaplain's Badge.—The Chaplains of the army in Tennessee have adopted as a badge the Maltese Cross, yellow, about an inch in diameter, worn as a Major's star on the collar, on each side. They use also the staff buttons, and gray cloth with black facings and trimmings, like Surgeons.

The Daily Picayune.

VOLUME XXVII. NEW ORLEANS, SATURDAY MORNING, MAY 16, 1863. NUMBER 96

The Daily Picayune.

FROM OUR EVENING EDITION OF YESTERDAY.

☞ Capt. Couch, of the Creole, has, with his ever thoughtful courtesy, placed the Picayune under renewed obligations for new favors.

☞ Purser Cook, of the Creole, will please accept our sincere thanks for his very acceptable favors, made doubly acceptable from the prompt and courteous manner of the giver.

ARRIVAL OF THE CREOLE.—The U. S. mail steamship Creole, Geo. W. Couch, commander, arrived at her wharf early this morning. She left New York May 7th, at 4.25 P. M., and made the run in 6 days 23 hours to the bar. May 12th, at 6 P. M., off Tortugas, exchanged signals with steamship George Washington, hence for New York. The Creole brings the following passengers:

Capt S D Chadsey, B Abrams, R C Mildron, Lieut H C Hudson, John Bolg and son, Lewis Morgan, L Bowman, E B Walcott, John Hahn, A Moran, Miss F C Taylor, F Gilard, J N Peterson, M Gonzales, F M Tilton and lady, Bernard M Rice, R McKenzie, Miss Carrie Patterson, John Malony, F E Clement, F Brules, John Moran and lady, J C Seymour, Madame A Tujaque, W Washburn, and 7 in steerage.

SPLENDID TRIP.—Our readers will not fail to have noticed the remarkably short trip of the Creole, six days and twenty-three hours from New York to the bar. This, we are informed, is the best time ever made between the two ports.

Again we congratulate Capt. Couch. He has a noble craft, and she is most skillfully commanded.

FROM ALEXANDRIA.—We have seen the officer who came down, via Red River and the Atchafalaya, from Alexandria, the 12th inst., in charge of the United States transport Union, which arrived at Brashear City yesterday. This officer, and a bearer of dispatches, came on a special train from Brashear City, arriving here at 12 o'clock last night.

There is nothing of importance to communicate from Alexandria. Gen. Banks was there when the Union left, and all was quiet. We learn some interesting particulars with regard to the evacuation and occupation of that place. As has already been stated there was no opposition to the occupation of Alexandria. The few Confederate troops there had already abandoned the position when Admiral Porter's gunboats came up.

The following details with regard to the DeRussy affair are additional to what has already been published. On the 4th inst. the United States gunboats Albatross, Arizona and Estrella went up Red River as far as DeRussy, which is half-way between the mouth of the river and Alexandria. There were three earth works on the right bank of the river, which had mounted one gun each, and further back was Fort DeRussy, which commanded the bend of the river. The trees on the opposite side of the turn of the river had been cut down so as to give the guns the sweep of the river, and a raft had been stretched across below the works. But before Admiral Porter's arrival, and as soon as the news of Gen. Banks's advance reached Brig. Gen. Mouton, who was in command at DeRussy, he ordered the works to be dismantled, and we are informed that the guns were thrown into the river, and the place was abandoned.

There were, however, two Confederate cotton-clads above the raft which attempted to dispute the passage of the river. As has already been published, one of them, the Mary T., was soon disabled, and our informant tells us that the other, the Grand Duke, towed her up the river—that they went by Alexandria, and are supposed to have gone up to Shreveport. The raft was destroyed, and, as is known, the U. S. gunboats found no farther obstructions in their progress to Alexandria. Before leaving DeRussy, Gordon's house and another house on the river bank, in front of the evacuated works, were burned.

We learn that, before the arrival of the gunboats and of Gen. Banks's column, Lieut. Gen. Kirby Smith was at Alexandria with a small force of 4,000 or 5,000 men. The Grand Duke, in retreating up the river, carried the news of the advance of the United States gunboats. There were several steamboats then lying at Alexandria, and Gen. Smith, with his men and munitions, embarked on these boats and went up the river.

CITY NOTES.—Lieut. Miller has succeeded in recovering $2,500 of the unsigned city notes which were lost on board of the steamer Marion, and brought to this city by unauthorized parties.

☞ Attention is called to the advertisement in another colum of flour and pork, for sale by Messrs. S. H. Kennedy & Co., No. 36 Poydras street.

STEAMERS TO ARRIVE.—The steamship Quincy, Capt. Geo. W. Clapp, was advertised to sail on the 6th inst., and is now due.

The new steamship Merrimac, advertised to sail from Boston the 2d inst., cleared the 6th inst., and, as she is a fast steamer, is also due at this port.

The George Cromwell, Capt. John A. Post, is advertised to leave New York, for New Orleans direct, on the 9th inst.

The Morning Star, Capt. A. D. Perkins, was to leave New York, for this port via Havana, on the 13th inst.

The Columbia, Capt. D. D. Barton, is advertised to sail for this port direct on the 16th inst.

The Creole brought no mail. The mail to the 6th inst. is probably on board the Quincy.

FURTHER BY THE CREOLE.

ADDITIONAL WAR NEWS

The New York Tribune, of the 3d, says:

Private advices reached this city yesterday, to Friday afternoon, from Western Virginia, to the effect that the National forces, under Gen. Mulligan, had been repulsed near Fairmount, and that the Baltimore and Ohio Railroad bridge at that point had been entirely destroyed by the rebels, who also occupied Morgantown in large force.

The Herald, of the 4th, says:

Our army at Suffolk continues to be actively occupied. Yesterday morning at 9 o'clock Gen. Peck sent a force of infantry, cavalry and artillery across the Nansemond river on a reconnoissance. When two miles out they charged and took the enemy's rifle pits and some prisoners. Our loss was small, and the enemy's much greater. Skirmishing had been kept up all day.

The Herald, of the 6th, says:

We have some important news from Port Royal, by the arrival of the United States steamer New England, last evening, from Hilton Head. The captain reports that the Ironsides was to cross the bar at Charleston, on the 2d inst., and the monitors on the 4th. This, if true, would indicate the commencement of a second attack on the forts in Charleston harbor.

In its issue of the 7th, the same paper says:

Dispatches from Cairo yesterday bring one day's later news from Vicksburg. The attack of the gunboats on Haines's Bluff was repulsed, and they were returning to Young's Point. It is said that the Choctaw was much damaged, her turrets being penetrated with a 64-pound shot. Our loss was eighty killed and wounded. The Era was struck seventeen times by guerrillia batteries on her way up the river, but got through. The Duke of Argyle, with her 12 pound gun, however, drove the guerillas from their lurking place.

The Times says:

It is said that the rebels, in their last raid along the line of the Baltimore and Ohio Railroad, captured and took with them 3000 horses and 5000 head of cattle.

Arrest of Mr. Vallandigham.

Arraigned before a Court Martial—Rioting—Property Destroyed, &c.

Cincinnati telegrams, of May 6, give the following intelligence:

Great excitement existed at Dayton, Ohio, yesterday in regard to the arrest of Hon. Clement L. Vallandigham by order of the military authorities. At dark a crowd of from five to six hundred proceeded to the Journal office, took possession of it, completely gutted the building, set it on fire and burned it to the ground.

The fire communicated to the adjoining buildings, and all the property from the south end of the Phillips House to the middle of the square was destroyed. All the telegraph lines in the city were cut down and destroyed. The bridge on the Xenia road is reported to be destroyed.

At 10 o'clock at night Federal troops from Cincinnati and Columbus succeeded in putting down the rioters, and at half-past 11 o'clock quiet was again restored.

CINCINNATI, May 6, P. M.—Telegraphic communication being interrupted, we have no advices as to the condition of affairs at Dayton, Ohio, this morning.

All is quiet. There is no sign of any disturbance whatever.

Dayton has been comparatively quiet to-day. About thirty ringleaders in last night's riot have been arrested without resistance and placed in jail.

The Empire newspaper has been suppressed. Its editor has been arrested and brought here. The soldiers removed a swivel from the Empire office, and also took possession of two wagon loads of muskets stored in the Light Guards' armory. Every precaution has been taken to prevent a renewal of the outbreak. The liquor shops have been closed, and the telegraphs have been repaired, so that communication with the East is re-established.

CINCINNATI, May 6.—Mr. Vallandigham was brought before the court-martial to-day for trial. He refused to plead to the charges which were read to him, and the court proceeded with the evidence, the publication of which is not allowed. The charges were based on his Mount Vernon speech. Mr. Vallandigham is at the Burnet House to-night, under a strong guard. Dayton and Montgomery counties are placed under martial law.

The total loss by the conflagration at Dayton was $30,000. The damage otherwise by the riot was small.

General News.

The Herald, of the 5th, has the following:

The rebel steamer Cornubia arrived at Bermuda on the 20th ult. from Wilmington, N. C. This is the fifth voyage of the Cornubia to and from the rebel States. The Gen. Lee was nearly ready to sail for Charleston.

Reported Capture of the Retribution.—The course of one of the rebel privateers is at an end, which, though not as formidable as the Alabama, has accomplished much mischief in her short career. The brig Leonidas, from St. Domingo March 28, has just arrived at New Bedford, and reports that she was chased into St. Domingo by the rebel pirate Retribution. The captain states positively that the United States steamer Alabama came down and captured the Retribution, and when last seen had her safe in port at St. Domingo.

The Conscription to be Enforced.—The same paper says:

It would appear that the government intend to commence the enforcement of the conscription act at once, from the fact that they publish to-day—as will be seen in another column—the full list of provost marshals, as far as at present appointed, for the different districts.

Later from Central and South America.—New York papers, of the 7th, give the annexed:

The steamer Northern Light, from Aspinwall on the 27th ult., arrived at this port yesterday, bringing $205,057 in treasure, and later news from the Isthmus of Panama and Central and South America. It was believed that the Convention of the United States of Colombia would vote to remove the capital from Bogota to Panama, the "project" for that purpose having passed a second reading by an almost unanimous vote.

Among the items of news from South America is the announcement of the death of President San Roman, of Peru. Some excitement existed in Chili in consequence of a report that the British representative in Valparaiso had been instructed to take vigorous measures to enforce the payment of a claim considered by the Chilians as unjust. From Guatemala we have a report that President Carrera was making preparations for another invasion of Salvador.

Sent Across the Lines.—Nearly one hundred of the principal secessionists of St. Louis were arrested May 6 and will be sent South. Still further arrests will be made. A number of spies have been convicted, and are awaiting sentence. Several disloyal citizens were sent South from Nashville yesterday; among them was Neil S. Brown, formerly Governor of Tennessee.

[FROM THE EXTRA PICAYUNE.]

SEVEN DAYS LATER

FROM THE NORTH.

ARRIVAL OF STEAMSHIP CREOLE.

THE FOUR DAYS' FIGHT AT FREDERICKSBURG.

Rain Storm and Rapid Rise of the Rivers.

Gen. Hooker's Army Retreating Across the Rappahannock.

SEVERE LOSSES ON BOTH SIDES.

CONDITION OF THE ARMIES.

Highly Important from Europe.

THE UNITED STATES AND ENGLAND.

NEW COMPLICATIONS.

WAR VESSELS ORDERED TO SEA.

More Captures by the Alabama.

A EUROPEAN WAR IMMINENT.

The steamship Creole, whose arrival at Southwest Pass was announced in our morning edition, reached her wharf at 6½ A. M. She brings dates of the 7th inst., embracing a full account of the Fredericksburg fight to noon of the 6th inst.

The following is the Tribune's account, in its second extra published at 10½ o'clock on the morning of the 7th instant:

ARMY OF THE POTOMAC, Wednesday, May 6, 1863.

The army of the Potomac has recrossed the Rappahannock at United States and Banks's fords, and is marching back to the old camps along the Acquia railroad.

On Monday morning at daylight the enemy shelled from the heights below Scott's Dam the trains of Hooker's army at U. S. Ford. This circumstance increased the fears of the commanding general, and the longer he delayed to push forward the less was he able to advance.

After fighting the severe battle of Sunday morning, May 3, Gen. Hooker continued to strengthen his lines, throwing up double lines of rifle pits, and constructing abattis along the entire line of his camp. The enemy continued to make demonstrations along the works, driving in the pickets and delivering volleys of musketry at men most exposed.

His sharpshooters picked off the artillery horses and fired on any mounted officer seen behind the rifle pits. Troops could be seen marching and countermarching along the roads southeast from Chancellorsville. In all advantageous positions batteries were run out and vigorously used against Hooker's camp. As soon as counter guns were brought to bear on their flying batteries, they would disappear to show themselves in some new position.

The effect of a movement strategically offensive, made technically defensive, soon produced a damaging effect on the entire army. The question again was, the safety of the Army of the Potomac. Consultations were had with corps commanders; the question of the possibility of retreat was discussed. This once broached, and the campaign was a failure.

It was decided that the enemy was too powerful to be resisted, and that Sedgwick's corps must be rejoined to the army in order to make an offensive movement practicable.

Sedgwick's Repulse.

Sedgwick was overwhelmed by numbers, and pressed hard on both front and rear, and was barely able to make good his escape near Banks's Ford. Fredericksburg and the heights beyond have been reoccupied by the enemy, and the situation is substantially as it was previous to the advance.

Sedgwick has lost, in killed and wounded, about 5000 men. His artillery and trains were safely brought over on Monday night.

The artillery was placed on the heights below United States Ford, in a position to command the crossing.

At daylight a spirited cannonading was heard for half an hour at Banks's Ford, which was an unsuccessful attempt to shell Sedgwick's line. At United States Ford the crossing was effected without loss.

Sedgwick having failed to join Hooker, via the Fredericksburg and Gordonsville plank road, and being hard pressed he crossed the Rappahannock and saved his corps from annihilation. The experiment cost him some 6000 men. He inflicted, doubtless, a much greater injury on the enemy.

Retreat across the Rappahannock.

On Tuesday the order was given to retreat. New roads were cut. The trains and reserve artillery were sent back and the evacuation was at once commenced.

Sedgwick's repulse, added to the weak counsels of certain of his corps commanders, shook Hooker's confidence, and, forgetting that he was the aggressor, and that less than half his command had withstood the attack of the full force of the enemy, he, in a fatal moment, gave the order to evacuate the strong position and his fortified cam, and to retreat across the Rappahannock at U. S. ford.

The order for retreat was a surprise, as it was believed to be the determination to march out and attack the enemy in the front.

The crossing was commenced at 10 o'clock on Tuesday night. At 3 o'clock on Wednesday morning wagon and mule trains and the artillery had all passed, and the infantry was crossing on two bridges at U. S. Ford. Couch's corps was in the advance. The retreat was covered by the Fifth, Meade's corps.

On Tuesday, the Sixth Corps of Hooker's Army recently engaged at Chancellorsville, also recrossed the river at U. S. Ford, and are marching back to Falmouth.

The retreat of Hooker's Army produced a great panic at Acquia, and everything movable was placed on board the boats at the landing.

A defeat could have been little worse. The army is not panic-stricken, but it is certainly greatly demoralized by the inglorious retreat.

There was no time from Friday morning till Monday night that Hooker could not have attacked and defeated Lee's army. There only lacked the ability to give the order.

"The army is safe," with 10,000 fewer men in its ranks, and a much larger number unfit for duty. The heavy rain of Tuesday night and Wednesday, and the chilling atmosphere has severely impaired the health of the men, who were wholly without means of shelter. The tents were left behind, and many lost their knapsacks in battle.

[From the Washington Star, May 6.]

The Battle of Sunday.—The rebel dispatch says that on Saturday, Lee drove Hooker out of the Little Wilderness back to Chancellorsville, and on Sunday drove him from Chancellorsville to a position in that immediate vicinity. The falling back was on the part of Sigel's late (now Howard's) corps, only saved from annihilation by the gallantry of Hooker's original division under Berry, which checked the enemy's pursuit, and drove him back in turn with great loss.

Monday's Engagement.—On Monday afternoon the rebels attacked our left—Howard's corps—and after a desperate engagement, were completely repulsed with great loss. Yesterday forenoon they again advanced against us at the same point, but were able to stand the contest but for fifteen minutes, when they again fell back, repulsed with heavy loss.

Stoneman's expedition proved a great success, indeed. The Richmond papers of the 5th say that his forces played sad havoc with their railroad at Hanover junction and other points, destroying locomotives and a large amount of other valuable property, and all the railroad bridges to within five miles of Richmond.

Rebel Generals Killed and Wounded.—In the Richmond papers, mentioned above, is a dispatch from Gen. Lee to Jeff. Davis, saying that the (rebel) Gen. Paxton is killed, Stonewall Jackson severely wounded, and Gens. Heth and A. P. Hill also badly wounded.

The Philadelphia Press, of May 7, has the following, dated Falmouth, May 6, A. M.: A heavy column of rebels, under Gen. Early, attacked the 2d and 6th corps under Gen. Sedgwick, near Fredericksburg, on Monday, and after an engagement of several hours' duration, drove our forces back, and reoccupied the works, which had been partially destroyed by our troops.

Appreciating the position in which he was placed, Gen. Sedgwick at once determined to recross the Rappahannock by the pontoon bridges below Fredericksburg.

Yesterday morning, after all of our troops had arrived safely on this side, the rebels got several guns in position, and commenced shelling the pontoon bridges, but did little damage. The pontoons were taken up, and the rebels opened with some twenty-six field pieces from Fredericksburg, and reoccupied the city in considerable force.

Gen. Hooker was promptly apprised of this movement, and approved of it. He ordered the left wing of his army to advance, and after a spirited contest carried the field batteries of the rebels on the left, said to contain twenty six guns. The cannon and most of the cannoneers were captured.

A telegram from headquarters announces the fact that the entire rebel cavalry force, under Gen. Stuart, is concentrated on our right, and it is evidently the design of Gen. Lee to turn that flank of our army and operate on the upper portion of the Rappahannock.

It is also reported that General Stoneman has opened communication with General Keyes, or spoken a gunboat on the Pamunkey river, but of all this we know nothing positively. The fact that the rebel cavalry is concentrated on our right would indicate the entire success and safety of General Stoneman's expedition.

Rebel divisions under Generals Ewell, Early, Jackson, Longstreet and Anderson, and the two Hills, are said to be in front of us, with the cavalry of Gen. Stuart on our right. It is believed that the enemy is bringing up reinforcements overland, and he keeps up a splendid front.

The rebels are well supplied with ammunition and food, reports to the contrary notwithstanding. The region now occupied by our army is all ploughed, and most of it planted with wheat.

The New York Herald Extra, of the 7th inst., contains the following dispatches:

UNITED STATES FORD, May 6, 8 A. M.—Yesterday morning the trains were all ordered back to camp, and by dark the wagons, extra caissons, pack mules, &c., were at Falmouth. The wounded were hastily removed from the hospitals and sent to Washington, leaving nothing on the other side except our infantry and artillery.

About 5 o'clock it commenced raining. The water fell in torrents for over an hour, deluging the roads, tearing up the corduroys, sweeping away bridges and threatening the destruction of the pontoons. The river rose with great rapidity, and soon overflowed the ends of the pontoons, rendering crossing impracticable. The upper pontoon was taken up and used in lengthening out the others, and after several hours of very hard labor the bridges were once more ready.

Pine boughs were spread upon the pontoons to prevent the noise of crossing, and about midnight the troops commenced falling back. The First corps was the first to cross, and is now nearly all over. The Third corps remains in the intrenchments to cover the retreat. It is hoped that the army will reach this side before the enemy discovers the retreat; but cannonading has commenced quite fiercely at the front, and a desperate battle is not an improbable event.

We can doubtless retire across the river without serious loss; but, if discovered in our attempt, the struggle will be fierce. Unmolested the troops can get over by noon.

The roads are in a terrible condition—almost as bad as when Gen. Burnside foundered here last winter. Our sick are lying in the roads, but ambulances are coming up to remove them.

There was no fighting yesterday of any consequence. The sharpshooters were quite active, and the artillery opened occasionally, but results were unimportant. The enemy has evidently massed his army on our right, with a view, it is believed, of crossing above and attacking us on the flank and rear. The high water, however, will frustrate that movement.

Three pontoon trains are down near Hamilton's Crossing, and some fears have been entertained that the rebels would make a demonstration across the river below Fredericksburg.

A great number of our wounded have fallen into the hands of the enemy.

Our dead on the battle field of Sunday are still unburied, and the wounded are undoubtedly dying in great numbers for want of attention. Dr. Johnson, Medical Inspector of the Army, has volunteered to go over with a corps of surgeons and take charge of our wounded. He will probably be sent across as soon as practicable.

Gen. Hooker is very much depressed. Last night he held a consultation with his commanding Generals, in which it was urged that a longer stay in its present position would prove unsafe for the army. A hasty return to our camps is imperative.

The rain is falling heavily, and the river rising with great rapidity.

FALMOUTH, May 6, 10 A. M.—Three bridges were swept away on the railroad from Aquia last night. Building parties were at work all night, and the trains are again running.

It is rumored that the enemy's cavalry has crossed over upon the Northern Neck, and is advancing cautiously towards this place. A force has been sent down to oppose them.

Everything is quiet on the other side. The river has risen over ten feet and is still rapidly rising.

Heavy cannonading is heard in the direction of the United States ford.

The Latest.

The evening edition of the Commercial Advertiser, May 7th, contains the following:

A messenger from Washington to a large banking house in this city, brings highly important intelligence, in which they have all faith.

No battle has been fought since Monday. The movement of Hooker across the river was one dictated by prudence, in consequence of the rise in the rivers endangering his lines of communication.

He retired to the north bank of the Rappahannock to meet forty thousand men, which had not yet been engaged, and will now be reinforced by thirty thousand under Heintzelman.

No force of the enemy drove him on his retirement.

The messenger is in possession of a Richmond paper of Tuesday, which confesses that the communication of the rebel army with that city has been severed, and that the line of supplies to Gen. Lee is entirely cut off.

New York Money Market.

The Journal of Commerce, of the 7th, says:

WEDNESDAY EVENING, May 6.

The unfavorable news this morning, not being altogether unexpected, did not exert as much depressing influence as might have been looked for, and the market has borne up bravely, considering the weight of the burden.

The Evening Post of the same date contains the following:

Wall street this morning has been again disturbed by reports from the army. The prevailing opinion early in the day seemed to be that the news was disastrous.

Gold early this morning opened at 154, rising subsequently to 157. As we go to press the price is 155¾.

Exchange is dull to-day, as the changing price of gold paralyzes business.

LATE AND IMPORTANT FROM EUROPE

By the arrival of the Etna at New York on the 4th inst. we have news from Europe to the 23d of April—four days later. The advices are of considerable importance, and are thus given in the New York press:

Much uneasiness prevailed in London and Paris with respect to the near advent of war; but the affairs of Russia proper, Poland, Mexico and the United States were so mixed up, as constituting the alleged exciting causes of the struggle, that it was difficult to conjecture on which side of the Atlantic hostilities were likely to commence.

The notes forwarded by England, France and Austria to the Court of St. Petersburg, on the subject of the Polish revolution, had been presented to the Czar, and caused a "sensation" in the Russian Cabinet, as it was not anticipated that the three Powers would display such a uniformity of sentiment and language in the case. The Czar had not yet published his reply. In the meantime the Swedish Government was making considerable armaments.

Iron-clad ships had been ordered, and engineers were actively engaged in fortifying the port of Carlscrona, the chief dockyard of the Swedish navy, which is to be rendered capable of refitting, not only the Swedish men-of-war, but also "the squadrons of those Powers whose interest it might be to station a naval force in those waters."

Prussia adhered to her leaning towards Russia. The Russian amnesty was published at Warsaw, and found less comprehensive than it had been represented, as the leaders of the insurrection are excluded from its benefits. It had not induced a single insurgent to lay down his arms, and engagements continued between the Russians and the Poles with varying fortunes. Lord Palmerston had uttered some caustic remarks in the House of Commons with reference to the rule of Russia in Poland.

It was reported in Paris that Napoleon had ordered all the iron-clads of France to assemble at Cherbourg, and the iron war vessels now on the stocks to be completed without delay. His Majesty is described as being engaged hourly in studying maps of Russia and the surrounding countries.

The difficulties arising from the want of a supply of cotton in the manufacturing districts of France were becoming very serious. Napoleon expected that his troops would have taken Puebla by the 1st of May, and some correspondents in Paris thought that "after settling with Juarez" he would direct his attention to the blockade of the Southern ports of America.

The British journals were still incensed against Admiral Wilkes, and some of their writers affected to dread that the Cabinet at Washington were inclined to make a sudden war on their country.

Mr. Adams's letter to Messrs. Howell and Zirman, which was given to cover a cargo of munitions of war for the Mexicans, excited great "indignation" in France. Considerable agitation still prevailed in England on the subject, as well as the future regulation of neutral trade to the Mexican coast.

In the House of Commons Mr. Layard stated that the government had under their consideration the "ticket of leave" given by Mr. Adams. The British Government had declined to send out a mail agent on board the ship Sea Queen, lying at Falmouth awaiting orders to proceed to Matamoros, and the mails which had been put on board the vessel were to be sent ashore again.

The alleged rebel gunboat Alexandra had been "exchequered" at Liverpool, and it was stated that the Government contemplated legal proceedings against the builders. It was affirmed, on the other hand, that the authorities were conscious of the existence of a serious flaw in their case.

It was said that the English Government would inquire into the system of shipping able bodied men from Ireland to the United States, and put a stop to it unless it was shown to be a bona fide emigration movement.

The Confederate loan remained firm at ¼ a 1¼ premium. It was stated, however, that persons who had effected speculative sales in the loan were offering unusually high rates for the scrip, in order to enable them to fulfill their contracts. American securities were firmer.

Consols closed in London, on the 23d of April, at 93 a 93⅛ for money. The Liverpool cotton market was quiet on the 23d ult., with prices firm, but no actual advance. Breadstuffs were quiet and steady. Provisions were dull and inactive.

Later.

The steamship Australasian, from Queenstown on the 26th of April, arrived at New York early on the 6th. The news is three days later than the advices of the Etna, and is of a very exciting and important character. The Herald gives the following summary:

Animated debates had taken place in both

[CONTINUED ON FOURTH PAGE.]

The New-York Times.

VOL. XII—NO. 3659. NEW-YORK, TUESDAY, JUNE 16, 1863. PRICE THREE CENTS.

INVASION!

Rebel Forces in Maryland and Pennsylvania.

Their Advance to Hagerstown, Md., and Greencastle and Chambersburg, Penn.

HARRISBURG IN IMMINENT DANGER

A PROCLAMATION BY THE PRESIDENT.

One Hundred Thousand Militia Called Out.

Pennsylvania to Furnish 50,000, Ohio 30,000, and Maryland and West Virginia 10,000 Each.

A Subsequent Call for Twenty Thousand from New-York.

NEW-YORK TROOPS HURRYING TO ARMS.

The Advance of the Rebels Up the Shenandoah Valley.

A Desperate Battle at Winchester on Saturday and Sunday.

Gen. Milroy Surrounded by Jackson's Old Corps.

He Cuts His Way Out, and Falls Back to Harper's Ferry.

TWO OTHER BATTLES IN THE VALLEY.

WASHINGTON, Monday, June 15.

By the President of the United States of America:

A PROCLAMATION.

Whereas, the armed insurrectionary combinations now existing in several of the States are threatening to make inroads into the States of Maryland, Western Virginia, Pennsylvania and Ohio, requiring immediately an additional military force for the service of the United States,

Now, therefore, I, ABRAHAM LINCOLN, President of the United States and Commander-in-Chief of the Army and Navy thereof, and of the militia of the several States when called into actual service, do hereby call into the service of the United States one hundred thousand militia from the States following namely:

From the State of Maryland 10,000.

From the State of Pennsylvania 50,000.

From the State of Ohio 30,000.

From the State of West Virginia 10,000.

To be mustered into the service of the United States forthwith, and to serve for the period of six months, from the date of such muster into said service, unless sooner discharged, to be mustered in as infantry, artillery and cavalry, in proportions which will be made known through the War Department, which Department will also designate the several places of rendezvous.

These militia are to be organized according to the rules and regulations of the volunteer service, and such orders as may hereafter be issued.

The States aforesaid will be respectively credited under the Enrollment act for the militia service rendered under this Proclamation.

In testimony whereof, I have hereunto set my hand and caused the seal of the United States to be affixed.

Done at the City of Washington, this 15th day of June, in the year of our Lord 1863, and of the independence of the United States the 87th.

(Signed,) ABRAHAM LINCOLN.

By the President,

WM. H. SEWARD, Secretary of State.

A CALL UPON NEW-YORK.

ALBANY, Monday, June 15.

The Governor received, to-day, a telegram from Washington calling for 20,000 militia men immediately.

He has summoned the several Major-Generals of the State Militia to Albany for consultation, and taken steps for the rapid organization of the militia.

Gen. SANFORD telegraphs that he can bring out 5,000 men without delay, and the General commanding the Eighth division promises 2,000 more.

A draft will be made under the State law to fill up to their maximum number all the militia regiments in the State, and from these the 20,000 will be supplied.

They are called upon to serve six months, and will be credited to the State as three years' men under the impending National draft. They are to serve without State or National bounties.

CALL FOR THE FIRST BRIGADE.

HEADQUARTERS FIRST BRIGADE, N. Y. S. N. G., New-York, June 15, 1863.

SPECIAL ORDERS.—By order of the Commander-in-Chief of the State of New-York, the several regiments of this brigade will hold themselves in readiness to depart for Philadelphia at once—short service.

By order of

Brig.-Gen. C. B. SPICER.

R. H. HOADLEY, Brigade Major and Inspector.

WM. D. DIMOCK, A. D. C.

CALL FOR THE THIRD BRIGADE.

HEADQUARTERS THIRD BRIGADE, No. 543 BROADWAY, NEW-YORK, June 15, 1863.

ORDER. Commandants of regiments are hereby directed to report to Gen. WM. HALL, at his quarters, at 11 o'clock A. M. Tuesday morning. By order of the Commander-in-Chief, HORATIO SEYMOUR.

The brigade drill for the 17th inst., is hereby countermanded. By order of Gen. WM. HALL.

J. R. SMITH, Quartermaster.

THE THIRTY-SEVENTH REGIMENT.

HEADQUARTERS, THIRTY-SEVENTH REGIMENT, N. G., No. 506 BROADWAY, June 16, 1863.

GENERAL ORDER: In compliance with the orders of the Commander-in-Chief, and of Brig.-Gen. HALL, this regiment is directed to hold itself in readiness to march to Philadelphia on short service at one hour's notice.

Commandants of Companies will report to the Colonel at the Regimental Armory, No. 506 Broadway, at 10 o'clock this morning.

The parade order for the 17th inst. is hereby countermanded. By order of CHARLES ROOME, Col. Commanding.

A. G. MONTGOMERY, Adjutant.

THE BROOKLYN THIRTEENTH.

HEADQUARTERS, THIRTEENTH REGIMENT, N. G. S. N. Y. ARMORY, CORNER HENRY AND CRANBERRY STS., BROOKLYN, June 16, 1863.

GENERAL ORDERS: This regiment will assemble at the City Armory, corner of Henry and Cranberry streets, this Tuesday morning, at 9 o'clock, in full fatigue, knapsack, overcoat and canteen; having received orders from the Commander-in-Chief "to proceed to Philadelphia for short service."

By order, Col. JNO. B. WOODWARD.

WM. AUGUSTUS MCKEE, Adjutant.

THE NEW-YORK SEVENTH.

PHILADELPHIA, Monday, June 15.

The New-York Seventh have offered their services to aid in resisting the invasion of Pennsylvania, and are expected to leave for Harrisburgh to-morrow.

PROCLAMATION OF GOV. CURTIN.

HARRISBURGH, Monday, June 15.

The following Proclamation has just been issued by the Governor of Pennsylvania:

In the name and by the authority of the Commonwealth of Pennsylvania and ANDREW G. CURTIN, Governor of the said Commonwealth:

A PROCLAMATION.

The State of Pennsylvania is again threatened with invasion, and an army of rebels is approaching our borders. The President of the United States has issued his Proclamation calling upon the State for fifty thousand men. I now appeal to all the citizens of Pennsylvania who love Liberty and are mindful of the history and traditions of their Revolutionary fathers, and who feel that it is a sacred duty to guard and maintain the free institutions of our country, who hate treason and its abettors, and who are willing to defend their homes and firesides, and do invoke them to rise in their might and rush to the rescue in this hour of imminent peril. The issue is one of preservation or destruction. It involves considerations paramount to all matters of mere expediency and all questions of local interest. All ties, social and political, all ties of a personal and partizan character, sink by comparison into insignificance. It is now to be determined by deeds, and not by words alone, who are for us and who are against us. That it is the purpose of the enemy to invade our borders with all the strength he can command is now apparent. Our only defence rests upon the determined action of the citizens of our free Commonwealth.

I therefore call upon the people of Pennsylvania, capable of bearing arms, to enroll themselves in military organizations and to encourage all other to give aid and assistance to the efforts which will be put forth for the protection of the State and the salvation of our common country.

A DISPATCH FROM GOV. CURTIN.

PHILADELPHIA, Monday, June 15.

The following dispatch has been received by Collector THOMAS from Gov. CURTIN:

HARRISBURGH, June 15.

Mr. G. Thomas, Philadelphia:

The President calls for a hundred thousand men, for a term not exceeding six months. All men so raised are to be credited to the draft.

Gen. LEE's army is approaching in force.

We must have men immediately to check him.

Can you not raise a force at once?

The men are to be equipped and paid by the United States. A. G. CURTIN.

THE NEW REBEL MOVEMENT NORTHWARD.

Map Showing Winchester, Martinsburgh, Harper's Ferry, and the Line of the Potomac—Also, Chambersburgh, Penn., and its Relation to Harrisburgh and Baltimore.

PROCLAMATION BY GOV. TOD.

CINCINNATI, Monday, June 15.

Gov. TOD has issued a proclamation calling out 30,000 volunteers for the defence of the Border.

TROOPS FROM MASSACHUSETTS.

Gov. ANDREW, who is in New-York, has tendered to the Government the services of all the available Massachusetts militia, including the recently returned Forty-fourth, Third and Sixth regiments.

It is understood that all the New-York City militia regiments have been ordered to the seat of war.

THE LATEST BALTIMORE TELEGRAM.

BALTIMORE, Monday, June 15.

Gen. MILROY was surrounded at Winchester by 18,000 rebels; but, after a desperate fight, he cut his way through, and united with our forces at Harper's Ferry.

Our force at Martinsburgh has also fallen back on Harper's Ferry.

BALTIMORE, Monday, June 15.

The *American's* special report from Harper's Ferry, says that Gen. MILROY succeeded in cutting his way through the rebel lines, and reached there this forenoon, after evacuating Winchester.

The fighting was very desperate and we repulsed the rebels repeatedly with heavy loss, but finally they were largely reinforced and Gen. MILROY made his arrangements Sunday to abandon Winchester, finding that the rebels were endeavoring to closely invest the place.

He lost considerably—some 2,000 men in killed, wounded and prisoners.

Military movements are in progress to check the rebel movement in this direction, which it would not be proper to particularize.

THE LATEST CHAMBERSBURGH TELEGRAMS.

CHAMBERSBURGH, Monday June 15.

Lieut. PALMER, just returned from Greencastle, had to fight his way out two miles this side of that place. He reports that the enemy are advancing in three columns. One toward Waynesboro and Gettysburgh, one direct to Chambersburgh and one toward Mercersburgh and Cool Mountains. It is not known whether they will proceed in short columns or concentrate.

A large force is seen in the direction of Greencastle now. PALMER reports the column at Greencastle about 5,000 strong, principally cavalry, supported by infantry and artillery.

THE LATEST HARRISBURGH TELEGRAMS.

HARRISBURGH, Sunday, June 14.

Dispatches received to-day from the operators at Chambersburgh and Hagerstown give the information of negroes who have arrived there, to the effect that the rebel cavalry arrived at Perrysville and Martinsburgh about noon, and at the latter place there had been considerable hard fighting.

Gen. MILROY was contesting the advance of the rebels.

Telegraph communication is destroyed between Winchester and Martinsburgh. The lines having been broken by the rebels about 11 o'clock this morning.

Gen. REYNOLDS has been driven by a large force of the rebels from Perrysville to Bunker Hill.

The enemy are also at Winchester.

All Gen. LEE's army is moving.

The tidings from Muddy Branch and Nolan's Ferry indicate that warm work has been going on there.

The Capital and principal cities and towns of Pennsylvania, are in absolute danger.

The Governor will issue another call to-morrow.

The people of this State must respond if they do not want to experience all the ravages and horrors of war.

As there is some objection to the present plan of operations, by the instructions of the Governor, Col. SCOTT started for Washington on a special train this evening, to urge upon the National authorities such a modification of the plan as will suit the views of the people.

To this proposition no reply can be obtained as yet. The Government will no doubt accede to it.

The indications are that the capitalists will advance the money to pay the military, trusting to the General Government for reimbursement.

A meeting of the moneyed corporations of the State will be held to-morrow morning, to take into consideration the present startling aspect of affairs.

Gov. CURTIN will telegraph to Mayor HENRY, of Philadelphia, full news up to that hour.

The convalescent soldiers here and in the interior of the State, are being organized, armed and sent here.

Of the measures of defence I am not permitted to speak.

Every arrangement for the quick transportation of troops to this point has been completed under the direction of Gen. COUCH.

Special Dispatch to the New-York Times.

HARRISBURGH, Pa., Monday, June 15.

Communication with Chambersburgh is just broken. The Governor would be glad to have aid from New-York.

Danger is imminent.

HARRISBURGH, Monday, June 15.

The rebels entered Chambersburgh at 9 o'clock to-night.

THE LATEST PHILADELPHIA TELEGRAMS.

PHILADELPHIA, Monday, June 15.

A dispatch from Greencastle, Pennsylvania, dated at 10½ o'clock this morning, reports as follows:

"Our troops are now passing here in retreat from Hagerstown to Chambersburgh.

Hagerstown has been evacuated.

All the rolling stock of the railroad and all the stores have been removed.

Rumor fixes the rebel force at 10,000, but this is probably an exaggeration."

PHILADELPHIA, Monday, June 15.

The *Evening Bulletin* publishes the following news from dispatches received at the Pennsylvania Railroad Company's office:

"A dispatch received to-day from Bolton Station, on the Northern Central Railroad, says that Gen. TYLER had retreated from Martinsburgh at 8 o'clock last evening; that our force at Winchester had probably been captured yesterday, as the enemy are in force, probably 10,000 strong, at Hagerstown.

The dispatch adds that the danger is great, as the enemy is advancing in heavy force.

A private dispatch from a trustworthy source states that the rebels appeared near Chambersburgh this morning, and that it is probable that the place has already been occupied by them.

THE EXCITEMENT IN PHILADELPHIA.

PHILADELPHIA, Monday, June 15.

The movements of the rebels on the borders of the State caused much excitement at the Corn Exchange this morning, and trade was partially suspended.

PHILADELPHIA, Monday, June 15.

The principal citizens of this city have telegraphed to Gen. GEORGE CADWALLADER, now at Washington, asking him to obtain authority to repair immediately to Philadelphia, and organize the troops, his petitioners regarding him as a man fit for the crisis.

IMPORTANT NEWSPAPER REPORTS.

Advance of Ewell's Corps, of Lee's Army, Up the Shenandoah Valley.

A Desperate Battle at Winchester on Saturday.

The Rebels Repulsed with Great Slaughter by Gen. Milroy.

THE BATTLE RENEWED ON SUNDAY.

Advance of the Rebels Against Other Points.

From the Baltimore Sun of Yesterday.

For several days past, various rumors have been in circulation in relation to alleged movements of the Confederate army in Virginia. By information received from the military authorities of this Department, we are enabled to give the following highly important particulars:

On Friday, it was ascertained that a large body of Confederates were moving up the Shenandoah Valley, on the Strasburgh Pike-road, and from other directions. Every preparation was made by Maj.-Gen. SCHENCK to meet them. Gen. MILROY's pickets, a few miles from Winchester, encountered them on Saturday morning, and later in the day a general engagement took place between Gen. MILROY's forces at and near Winchester and the Confederates. The latter were repulsed in this engagement, losing a number of prisoners. Their loss in killed and wounded was said to be severe.

From the prisoners taken it was ascertained that the force attacking Gen. MILROY was Lieutenant-General EWELL's corps, variously estimated at from ten to eighteen thousand men.

The battle was renewed on Saturday afternoon, and again yesterday, and was in progress at last advices. Gen. MILROY's command is estimated at about 10,000. He has telegraphed Major-Gen. SCHENCK that he can hold out until reinforcements can reach him.

On Saturday afternoon Col. MCREYNOLD's, with a force of 3,000 men, stationed at Berryville, (between Harper's Ferry and Winchester, about eight miles south of the Winchester road,) was also attacked by a body of Confederates. The fight was said to be a very severe one.

Subsequently Col. MCREYNOLDS renewed the engagement, and at a late hour yesterday evening it was thought by the military authorities that he had succeeded in cutting his way through to reinforce Gen. MILROY, who was still fighting near Winchester.

About 4 o'clock yesterday afternoon a body of Confederates, said to number from three to five thousand, appeared in the vicinity of Martinsburgh, and demanded the surrender of that place. This force, it was thought, was a portion of the Confederates who had attacked Gen. MILROY's command.

Brig.-Gen. DANIEL TYLER, in command of the Federal forces at Martinsburgh, declined to surrender, and at 7 o'clock last evening a severe engagement was progressing.

The Thirteenth Pennsylvania cavalry, and Eighty-seventh Pennsylvania infantry, with one section of artillery, had a skirmish with some four hundred Confederate cavalry on Friday afternoon, near Middletown, Va. The Thirteenth skirmished with the rebels a short time, and drew them into an ambuscade of the Eighty-seventh and the artillery. Eight of the Confederates were killed, a number wounded, and thirty-seven, including a Captain and two Lieutenants, taken prisoners.

The Baltimore and Ohio Railroad was, at last accounts, uninjured. The freight and passenger trains, both West and East, passed safely through on Saturday. A large number of freight trains arrived at Mount Clare depot, yesterday, from Mount Airy. They contained a large quantity of freight from the Ohio country, which had been detained by the late raids on the western end of the roads.

The freight and passenger trains on the main stem, between here and Cumberland, will be suspended until the military troubles on or near the road are over. The Harper's Ferry and Frederick trains will still continue.

Major General SCHENCK, assisted by Col. DON PIATT and Col. CHESEBOROUGH, and the other members of his staff, have been, since Friday evening, assiduous in their labors, being at their posts almost incessantly day and night.

LATEST.

Up to the hour of going to press, nothing later was received from Gen. MILROY's or Col. MCREYNOLD's commands. The telegraph wires between Harper's Ferry and Martinsburgh having been cut about 7 o'clock last evening, nothing later was received as to the state of affairs at that point.

A dispatch received about 10½ o'clock last night from Harper's Ferry, reports that Col. COLE's Federal cavalry had fallen back from Kearneysville to Duffield's depot, the latter place being a few miles from Harper's Ferry, on the line of the Baltimore and Ohio Railroad. They do not report anything new from Martinsburgh, except that heavy firing was heard in that direction.

The Baltimore and Ohio Railroad Company have succeeded in saving all their engines and cars, and also in getting many of them on this end of the road.

At 11 o'clock last night a special car and engine arrived here from Philadelphia, via the Philadelphia and Wilmington Road, in which was a bearer of important dispatches for the Government. Mr. SMITH, master of transportation of the Baltimore and Ohio Railroad, supplied the important personage with a special car and engine, and at 11½ o'clock he was on his way to Washington. It was stated that his dispatches were of the most important character, but their nature or the name of the bearer did not transpire.

From the Baltimore American of yesterday.

Our city, yesterday, was filled with flying rumors in reference to the movements of the rebels in the Shenandoah Valley, and the most extravagant reports were circulated as to the presence of Gen. LEE there, with his entire army, *en route* for Maryland and Pennsylvania. The most reliable information we have been able to obtain is to the following effect:

An attack was made on Saturday morning on a small force of our men at Berryville under Gen. MCREYNOLDS, of which the First Maryland battery formed a part. They fell back before superior numbers, and joined Gen. MILROY at Winchester, after a sharp engagement, of which the results are at present unknown. At the same time Winchester was attacked in front (from the south,) by a force reported to be under command of Gen. EWELL, the successor of Stonewall JACKSON. The troops that made the attack at Berryville are reported to be under command of Gen. TRIMBLE.

A third force, after this encounter, are said to have captured a detachment of our men at Bunker Hill, and then moved on Martinsburgh. At 4 P. M., yesterday, they demanded the surrender of Martinsburgh, giving forty-five minutes for the women and children to leave town. Gen. TYLER, who commands at Martinsburgh, refused to surrender, and an artillery fight ensued. At 7¼ o'clock last night the wires were broken between Harper's Ferry and Martinsburgh, and what occurred after that is not known.

A battle was also in progress at Winchester yesterday, the result of which is unknown. Gen. MILROY repulsed EWELL on Saturday, and said he could hold out until reinforcements reached him. If unable to sustain his position, he would have to fall back on the line to Romney, as the Harper's Ferry and Martinsburgh roads are held by the enemy. The estimates of the rebel force in the Valley are so wide apart that they form no reliable data for any conclusion.

No danger was done to the Baltimore and Ohio Railroad as far as known. No cars or locomotives on the line are exposed to capture. Orders were sent to exposed points yesterday, and no less than 70 locomotives and some 1,200 cars were brought to Baltimore in safety. As a precautionary measure, no trains will be run beyond Harper's Ferry for the present.

From the Baltimore Gazette.

From the military authorities of this Department, we have received such information as enables us to lay before our readers the following facts, in regard to the movements of the Confederates in the Shenandoah valley, the battles fought there within the last three days, and of the engagements still in progress:

The Confederates made their appearance, in strong force, in the neighborhood of Winchester on Friday evening, but no engagement took place until Saturday. A most sanguinary battle is said to have taken place on that day, in which the Confederates were repulsed. Gen. MILROY succeeded in capturing quite a number of prisoners. The Confederates are also said to have lost heavily in killed and wounded.

The battle was renewed on Saturday night, and was still in progress at last accounts yesterday morning, but with what result was not stated. Gen. MILROY telegraphed that he could hold out until reinforcements could reach him.

From the prisoners captured he had ascertained that the Confederates attacking him were commanded by Lieut.-Gen. EWELL. Their numbers were variously estimated at from ten to eighteen thousand. The command under Gen. MILROY numbers about ten thousand.

On Saturday evening, Col. MCREYNOLDS, with 3,000 Federal troops, had a severe fight at Berryville with a much larger body of Confederates. The results were not known. At the last accounts, the authorities had reason to believe that Col. MCREYNOLDS had succeeded in cutting his way through to Winchester to reinforce Gen. MILROY.

A body of Confederates, supposed to be about 5,000 strong, had also passed around Winchester, and yesterday made their appearance at Martinsburgh. They demanded the surrender of the place. Brig.-Gen. DANIEL TYLER, in command, refused to comply, and an engagement at once took place, which was still going on at 6½ o'clock last evening.

The Baltimore and Ohio Railroad Company have succeeded in saving all their cars and engines. The freight and passenger business between here and the West will be temporarily suspended. The trains between here, Harper's Ferry and Frederick will run as usual.

LATEST.

The telegraph wires between Martinsburgh and Harper's Ferry having been cut by the Confederates at an early hour last evening, up to the hour of going to press nothing later had been received as to the result of the fight there.

A dispatch received at 10½ o'clock last night, from Harper's Ferry, reports that Col. COLE's Federal cavalry had fallen back from Kearneysville to Duffield, (both places on the line of the road, between the Ferry and Martinsburgh.) They report nothing from Martinsburgh. Nothing later was received, either from Gen. MILROY or Col. MCREYNOLDS, or the results of the battles fought by them.

THE NEWS IN WASHINGTON.

WASHINGTON, Monday, June 15.

The interest in Stuart's cavalry operations up the Shenandoah Valley has been absorbing here to-day. Nothing else has been talked of—but little else thought of. The heat has been awful, and Washington has sought its aliment of news literally in a furnace.

An exchanged officer of the *Indianola*, arrived to-night from Richmond, says that the window of his room in the Libby Prison commanded a view of the James River Bridges, and that in the last two weeks the trains which crossed them have carried daily from 2,000 to 3,000 troops to reinforce LEE. He also gives the number of STUART's cavalry and a large force of mounted infantry. He has organized 30,000 in all.

All the sick, wounded and disabled soldiers at Falmouth and vicinity, numbering about 8,000, have been removed to the Washington Hospitals.

Sale of Cotton.

CINCINNATI, Monday, June 15.

Two hundred and seventy-three bales of confiscated Cotton were sold at auction to-day. The prices ranged from 30½c.@45½c. [illegible] The quality was generally inferior.

THE NEW YORK HERALD.

WHOLE NO. 9773. NEW YORK, THURSDAY, JUNE 18, 1863. PRICE THREE CENTS

THE REBEL INVASION.

Retreat of the Rebels from Chambersburg.

Reported Evacuation of Harper's Ferry by Our Troops.

Maryland Heights Still Held and Strongly Fortified.

The Rebels in Strong Force at Williamsport and Cumberland.

South Mountain Occupied by the Enemy.

Operations of the Rebel Forces in Pennsylvania.

Reported Capture of Five Hundred Union Cavalry at Greencastle.

Energetic Preparations to Repel the Invaders,

&c., &c., &c.

Retreat of the Rebels from Chambersburg.

HARRISBURG, June 18, 1863.

No doubt whatever exists as to the presence of the enemy at Chambersburg up to about three o'clock this afternoon, when they retreated, it is supposed, towards Hagerstown. The operator is now at Chambersburg, and telegraphic communication has been reestablished.

Reported Evacuation of Harper's Ferry.

BALTIMORE, June 17—Noon.

I learn from an undoubted source that our forces have evacuated Harper's Ferry, and that we hold Maryland Heights, which are strongly fortified and capable of standing a siege against a vastly superior number.

The Harrisburg Telegrams.

HARRISBURG, June 16—Midnight.

Two of our reporters have just returned from in front of the rebel pickets, who are picketed forty-seven miles from Harrisburg, at Scotland Bridge, which they burned this morning.

A party of fifteen set fire to the structure.

The rebels are encamped at three points around Chambersburg, and are thirty-five hundred strong, under General Jenkins.

The rebels say that a brigade under General Rhodes is coming, and that they have seized two hundred horses to mount their infantry.

The rebels have fifteen pieces of artillery.

This morning a skirmish took place in the town between some rebels and some men from Carlisle Barracks. No lives were lost.

General Jenkins has ordered all the stores to be opened.

The rebels made prisoners of seven citizens, but injured no private property.

At Scotland Bridge the rebels spared a warehouse and two cars merely on the statement that they were owned by individuals.

They seized the flour mills near Chambersburg, and have placed a guard over them.

To-day the rebels were three times drawn up in line of battle, expecting an attack from our forces at Harrisburg.

At Greencastle matches were arranged so as to set fire to the government property at a moment's notice; but no property had been burned up to noon to-day.

Citizens were allowed to leave Chambersburg at first; but permission was afterwards refused.

At this late hour it is only possible to state that every appearance indicates that this raid of the rebels is only one of a usual character, and does not design any attack upon our cities, their object being to obtain horses and forage.

Additional artillery is on the way here for our fortifications.

The rebel force in Chambersburg have sent a special messenger to their forces in Greencastle, asking for reinforcements, as the Union forces have fortified and are supported in great force.

The rebels have, therefore, formed in line of battle to receive us.

Over five hundred government wagons, with government stores valued at $20,000, accompanied by contrabands and refugees, arrived here from Martinsburg to-day.

They left Martinsburg at four o'clock on Sunday evening, travelling very fast. The horses are very much jaded.

The refugees represent that the rebel attack at Martinsburg was by a force of four thousand mounted riflemen—a detachment from the main body of the rebel cavalry, which numbers from twelve to fifteen thousand.

General Milroy held this force at bay with but five hundred men until the government stores and wagons, which were the main object of the attack, could be got off heavily loaded. They succeeded in escaping all pursuit, and are safe in camp here. The drivers are nearly jaded out.

HARRISBURG, June 17, 1863.

The aspect of affairs, so far as can be judged by the reports from the border seems to be this:—

The rebel force occupy Hagerstown and such other points as leave them free to operate either against Harrisburg or Baltimore.

Apprehensions are entertained by the people of Altoona and other points on the line of the Pennsylvania Railroad that the rebels will strike for the West, and then go back to their own soil by way of Pittsburg and Wheeling.

The fortifications constructed on the hills opposite Harrisburg are considered sufficient protection for the city, and an offensive movement on our part is not unlikely.

The panic is over here, and the people are disposed to underrate the danger of the line of the Shenandoah becoming the seat of war, though there is high authority for stating that such an attempt may be made by General Lee.

Despatch from Governor Curtin—The Rebels Show no Disposition to Retire.

PHILADELPHIA, June 17, 1863.

The following despatch is just received from Governor Curtin relative to the Baltimore despatch, giving the opinion of military officials in Baltimore:—

HARRISBURG, June 17, 1863.

I regret to say your agent at Baltimore is mistaken. The rebels occupy Chambersburg and other points in Franklin county.

They burned the bridge at Scotland, five miles this side, and as yet show no disposition to retire.

I will get Major Beee to answer you fully.

A. G. CURTIN.

The Carlisle Telegrams.

CARLISLE, Pa., June 17, 1863.

The excitement here has much abated.

Almost all the good horses between here and Chambersburg have been taken out of rebel reach.

A train is now going to Newville, perhaps further, towards Chambersburg.

The Philadelphia Telegrams.

PHILADELPHIA, June 17, 1863.

A despatch from Harrisburg says that there are twenty-five hundred rebels at South Mountain, Md., and that there are thirty five hundred at and near Chambersburg. The latter have made no show of advancing to-day.

Business is mostly suspended in this city, and the merchants are devoting their time to the enlistment of troops for the defence of the State.

The Baltimore Telegrams.

BALTIMORE, June 17, 1863.

Reliable information relative to the invasion is that a small force of rebels, not exceeding 2,500, crossed the Potomac at Williamsport on Sunday, evidently in pursuit of General Kelly's baggage train, which arrived at Harrisburg last evening. This force passed through Hagerstown and entered Cumberland on Monday night. They did not proceed further than Scotland, five miles beyond Chambersburg, where they burned a bridge.

The military authorities here doubt that any rebels have entered Pennsylvania. They say that it was our forces retreating that caused the panic.

Hagerstown despatches are very unreliable. Trains arrived this evening from Westminster, bringing also passengers from Emmetsburg, who report no rebels in that section of the country. The excitement along the line towards Harrisburg was abating. Passengers said that the rebels were still at Chambersburg, and told the people they intended to stay there.

Passengers from Frederick represent that there are only a few rebel pickets at Hagerstown, though rumors were prevalent that an infantry force was coming across from the direction of Shepperdstown.

The Washington Telegrams.

WASHINGTON, June 17, 1863.

An official telegram from General Tyler at Harper's Ferry says the enemy has an infantry and artillery force of 7,000 or 8,000 at Williamsport, while the cavalry is running into Pennsylvania.

General Kelly telegraphs from New Creek, Va., that the rebel General Imboden is before Cumberland, Md., with two regiments of cavalry and a battery.

A letter from a reliable man, formerly an officer in the service, dated Harrisburg, June 16, P. M., was received here to-day. It states as follows:—

The trains of General Tyler, from Martinsburg, are just coming in. They report having left that place on Sunday afternoon, when the enemy's cavalry were within two miles of the town. They left unmolested, and have seen nothing of the enemy along their whole route since. One of the most intelligent men among them said they left Chambersburg on Monday night late, and up to that time the enemy had not made his appearance at that place.

This Pennsylvania raid puzzles the wisest among us. It has been definitely ascertained from various sources that the force advancing into Pennsylvania as far as Chambersburg could not have numbered more than twenty-five hundred to three thousand men. We have here positive information that General Jenkins, the junior brigadier general of cavalry in the rebel service, who has been detached for guerilla duty, with about twenty-five hundred men, composed of cavalry and mounted infantry, made the attack upon Martinsburg, and then crossed into Maryland and proceeded to Chambersburg.

The impression is hourly gaining strength that a portion of General Milroy's forces, escaping from Winchester and Martinsburg, have been mistaken by the timid farmers upon the Pennsylvania border for rebel invaders, and have been allowed to proceed on their way to Harrisburg before the mistake was corrected. One good effect, however, has been produced—the clamor of the copperheads for peace conventions has been momentarily silenced, and a thorough Union of the people of the North has been for a time effected.

There is now no doubt that General Lee has a large army. About one-third of it is occupying the country in the vicinity of Winchester and Martinsburg.

Senator Ramsay, of Minnesota is here. He says that when he started from St. Pauls the mercury was above ninety, and at La Crosse it was over a hundred. Considerable drought exists all along the route. In Ohio people were organizing and drilling. At Pittsburg places of business were closed, and archives and valuable property were in process of removal. Horses and cattle were being driven into the interior from the border. At Altoona valuable property had been sent forward towards Philadelphia.

The loss of Winchester laid open the Cumberland valley in Pennsylvania to invasion, and justifies the promptest measures to increase our army so as to make the free States impregnable from assault.

Our Harrisburg Correspondence.

HARRISBURG, June 16, 1863.

GOVERNOR CURTIN AND HIS PRESENT ACTION.

I called upon the Governor this morning at seven o'clock, and found him at the Executive chamber looking wearied and disappointed. He is resigned to the fate that awaits the capital of the glorious old Commonwealth of which he is the Executive. He has done everything that lay in his power to avert the dreaded blow. He has importuned and pleaded with the War Department to no avail. He has repeatedly warned the Cabinet of what might be expected, and his advice has never been hearkened unto. It is well to state, though, that, now that the raiders are in such close proximity, he bears up courageously and manfully, and will not desert his post until the last hope has been extinguished. Never had the people greater confidence in his wisdom, devotion and courage, and even political enemies, now present at the capital, in attendance upon the proposed Democratic Convention, testify to his eminent fitness, and sympathize with him in this to him dire calamity.

GENERAL DEPRESSION AND PANIC IN THE CITY.

Most of the stores in the city are closed, the markets deserted and private residences abandoned. The streets present much the same appearance that they do upon Sunday or fast day. The people are standing in knots, conversing upon the probable fate in store for them. Much speculation exists but very little excitement. Those who can are leaving, and already many have taken advantage of public and private conveyances to leave the city. The large hotels look as if stricken with a plague, the regular boarders having vamosed. The Jones House, the finest hotel here, was offered by its proprietor this morning for sale. He was willing to accept the moderate sum of $16,000, but could find no purchaser even at that price. The hotel and furniture cost nearly one hundred thousand dollars, yet no one appears willing to take the risk upon such apparently advantageous terms.

PACKING UP THE STATE DOCUMENTS.

I found a large force of assistants this morning in the various offices of the Capitol, busily employed packing up archives, reports, State library and other valuable papers. The original charter of the State and other prized papers, together with the portraits of the different Governors, have already been forwarded. Wein Forney, Esq., State Librarian, left at one o'clock P.M., with the valuable contribution of books belonging to the State. There is haste, but everything is being done orderly. The calm coolness of the Governor does much to keep down undue excitement, and his example is felt by the people.

NEW YORK'S OFFERING.

A despatch was received here to-day from Governor Seymour, offering the services of twenty regiments for the defence of Pennsylvania from the State of New York. This sympathy on the part of Governor Seymour is highly appreciated by the citizens. Troops are expected to arrive here to-day from Elmira.

THE OBJECT OF THE RAIDERS

is thought to be the tapping of the Pennsylvania Central road between this city and Lancaster. The Pennsylvania Central has another branch between the Columbia road between the two cities. This would not destroy the communication between Philadelphia and the capital, as the Reading road, by means of their branch, the Lebanon Valley, connect the two cities. The raiders, then, if that be their object, will have to proceed some distance up the Lebanon valley to do any great damage to that road. If they do destroy the Lebanon Valley road it will put a stop to any further travel between this and New York.

THE CALL FOR M'CLELLAN TO TAKE COMMAND OF THE FORCES.

Gen. McClellan is everywhere talked of as the only man capable to thwart the rebels in their late movements. Gen. Cameron, late Secretary of War, made a speech last evening eulogizing that officer in no measured terms. He was terribly severe in his strictures upon the War Department. He was of the opinion that if General McClellan was to head the militia the people would flock as one man to his support. *General McClellan's name was loudly cheered at every mention, and his popularity among the people was never so great as at present.* His open enemies now admit his ability and his capacity to drive the rebel horde from out the borders of his native State. Everywhere I hear the exclamation, "Oh, give us McClellan and we will whip the rebels." "He will come to the rescue of Pennsylvania" is a hope loudly expressed. If the government could but witness the enthusiastic hope his name creates he would be ordered here immediately.

WHAT THE REBELS ARE DOING.

This raid, in its conception and execution, surpasses anything yet attempted or performed by them. They are penetrating through a rich valley, helping themselves to whatever they please, and behave with unusual forbearance to the inhabitants, not disturbing them or injuring their private property.

The match is ready to put Carlisle barracks and other government property in flames.

The rebels were reported to be at Shippensburg, in Cumberland county, this morning.

TELEGRAPHIC COMMUNICATION STILL OPEN WITH GETTYSBURG.

The following despatch was received this morning,—

About one o'clock A. M. I asked operator at Hanover Junction if he was in communication with Hanover, and he replied he was in communication with both Hanover and Gettysburg. I asked if he had any news, and he replied he had not, as the scout went out from Gettysburg and had not returned. I think our line is down between York and Hanover Junction now. I will send men out to examine.

THE STARS AND STRIPES STILL AFLOAT.

The American flag is flying from the flagstaff upon the Capitol this morning. Its folds gracefully flutter in the pleasant breeze that is stirring. Many are looking upon it with feelings akin to worship. It may be that this will be the last day it will ever float from the present Capitol, and the feelings of the community can be better imagined than described.

THE REV. J. WALKER JACKSON,

a distinguished Methodist minister, and severely denounced by the Richmond *Whig* for his stirring addresses in favor of the Union, has been advised by Governor Curtin and other prominent gentlemen to leave. This Mr. Jackson firmly declines to do. He has sent his family to a place of safety, but says that he will abide the issue, and awaits his fate with as much nonchalance as it is capable in one man to express.

"DON'T BE SCARED."

The following I send you as I find it, issued in the form of a circular this morning. It is being attentively read and commented upon by large numbers of the citizens:—

DON'T BE SCARED.

We are ashamed of the cowardice exhibited by the "loyal" people of Harrisburg. We looked to them for an example of courage and coolness, and have been disappointed. We now appeal to the citizens to keep cool and make at least a show of courage. There are enough of us to drive off any rebel army likely to make its appearance—and besides, we have just been assured by Gen. Cameron that there will be ten thousand troops here in the course of the day. New York has tendered a whole division. Be brave! Keep cool, and all will be well.

GENERAL CAMERON

is at present immensely popular, and his speech in favor of McClellan and Franklin will do much towards securing the latter's nomination for the governorship by the democratic hosts to-morrow. I said the *proposed* meeting of the convention to-morrow; permit me to explain. The convention will, in case the rebs arrive to-night, have no place wherein to hold their meeting, as the court house, State Capitol and other buildings suitable, will, in all probability, have been destroyed. The members as yet express no intention of meeting elsewhere, but it may yet prove a necessity. William H. Witte, the more prominent of the candidates, is here. He expresses great confidence as to his being the nominee of the party, but Franklin's chances are decidedly favorable from the causes named.

PREPARATIONS TO MEET THE REBELS—WHO COMMANDS THEM.

There are many people who profess to despise and doubt the credence of the reports concerning this raid. They are of opinion that it is a ruse of the government to induce enlistments. If they were here their doubts would soon be removed by witnessing the stern preparations being made, and the realities of war, as it is variously exhibited through fear and other ways. Col. George H. Davidson, of Greencastle, Franklin county, Pennsylvania, near the scene of the raid, estimates the rebel force to be between five and seven thousand cavalry, supported by two batteries of artillery under command of Generals Imboden and Jones. A strong light was seen on Sunday night beyond Greencastle, which gave rise to the report of that place being in flames, but is now attributed to the rebel camp fires.

THE HON. THOMAS A. SCOTT,

late Assistant Secretary of War, who left Philadelphia in a special train for Washington, arrived here Monday. He has placed the resources of the Pennsylvania road at the command of General Couch. Colonel Scott's vast experience is of great service to the State at this moment. He is being seconded in his endeavors by the energetic assistant upon the Philadelphia end, G. C. Franciscus, Esq., and upon these gentlemen will devolve the necessity of providing transportation for troops.

CARLISLE BARRACKS TO BE BLOWN UP.

The following despatch was received from Carlisle:—

CARLISLE, June 16, 1863.

If we cannot defend the approaches to the town we will blow up the arsenal and barracks, and retire fighting.

ROUTE OF THE REBELS—A SKIRMISH.

Another despatch received, dated Shippensburg, says:—

The enemy is near here. He is avoiding the towns and passing north and east by the roads and through the fields. Cavalry is only believed to be near us. It is reported that the First Michigan cavalry met the rebels yesterday and gave them battle, dividing them, one part of the rebels leading off towards Broad Top, in Huntingdon county.

THE REBEL GUIDES—GEN. MILROY'S TRAIN.

The opinion is unanimous here that the raiders have experienced guides, well posted in the topography of the country, and their movements indicate that some of the natives of the country are with them in this raid. General Milroy's wagon train arrived this morning with two companies of his late command. Their march has been a very severe one, and their hardships of an almost unendurable character.

A train arrived here at half-past eleven o'clock in the morning, bringing what troops were stationed there, four pieces of artillery and a considerable baggage train.

The Post Office is closed; but a notice states that it will be opened again at one o'clock in the afternoon.

Both of the express companies decline to receive any more freight or receipt for any more packages. The excitement is greatly on the increase, and the populace much more alarmed, and hundreds of families are leaving.

HARRISBURG, June 17, 1863.

NO REBELS AT SHIPPENSBURG.

A train left here yesterday, on the Cumberland Valley road, and proceeded south as far as Shippensburg. They saw no rebels, and none had been there, notwithstanding reports to the contrary. The raiders advanced in a small body, upon foot, to the little town of Scotland, five miles distant from Chambersburg.

THE REBEL DOINGS AT CHAMBERSBURG—CAPTURE OF A BEARER OF DESPATCHES.

They purchased what goods they needed in Chambersburg, and paid for them in Confederate money; the officers informing the storekeepers they could either do that or take nothing. A bearer of despatches was captured yesterday by the rebels.

PURNELL'S CAVALRY FLANKED—ONLY TWENTY ESCAPE.

One of Purnell's cavalry arrived this morning at three o'clock, and states that about five hundred of their men were flanked at Greencastle by the rebels in force, and but twenty escaped. The rebels have burned the bridge at Chambersburg. They avoid the turnpike in their raids of this kind.

Correspondence of Mr. F. G. Chapman.

FREDERICK, Md., June 16, 1863.

The Advance of the Rebels to Hagerstown—Exaggerated Reports of Their Movements—Rebels Borrowing Horses from the Citizens—General Jenkins' New Mode of Paroling Deserters—Ewell Threatening Harper's Ferry, &c., &c.

After a hard ride of sixty miles I arrived here to day, and found the most excited set of people that could possibly be conceived of inhabiting the town. I had been led to expect that the town was occupied by the Confederate troops, (you see I must speak of the gentlemen composing General Lee's army respectfully under the circumstances) for all along the road from Baltimore I heard well authenticated stories of their presence here; nevertheless, I was determined not to turn back until I had obtained a view of their pickets at least, and the result was I came into the city as quietly and unharmed as if I had been the presiding elder entering a camp meeting. There were no troops here of any kind, save a few sick and wounded Unionists in the hospitals whom General Briggs had left in his movement back to the Relay House, below Baltimore. The most exaggerated reports were rife as to the movements of the enemy, many averring that the whole country between here and Harper's Ferry was lousy with graybacks, and others asserting that Lee's whole rebel (Confederate, I mean), army was crossing the Potomac at Point of Rocks, and that before night Frederick would be full of Southern troops. And it must be confessed that the female portion of the town seemed highly pleased with the prospect, while the sterner class, of all politics, looked upon the advent as anything but desirable. I found all communication with Harper's Ferry cut off, except by telegraph, though I do not see why the cars do not run through, as it is said the railroad is unharmed east of the Ferry. The cars now run as far as Monocacy Junction.

Shortly after my arrival here I made the acquaintance of a gentleman from Washington (whose name he does not wish mentioned), who left Hagerstown at eight o'clock this morning, and was in that place on business during the entire time that it was occupied by the raiders. From him I get some facts which have never before reached the public. The rebel force was composed of two regiments of cavalry and three regiments of mounted infantry, with four small cavalry howitzers, under command of General Jenkins—the same who commanded at the destruction of the iron bridge at Fairmont, in West Virginia, in April last. The advance guard arrived in the town about three o'clock in the morning, but the main body did not come up until about nine o'clock.

The troops were hailed by the citizens with manifest joy, and the best the town afforded was set before them for their breakfasts. General Jenkins issued an order before coming into Maryland forbidding pillaging, and promising any who might be caught in such vandalism in the State a speedy and severe punishment. Hence the troops were orderly and well behaved, bought freely of boots, shoes, clothing, hams, bacon and eatables for immediate use, for which they paid in greenbacks. They seemed to be well supplied with the last named article, and one captain jocularly remarked to a lady, in the presence of my informant, that their paymaster made the last payment all in greenbacks. Mr. ——— avers that he counted the troops as they rode in fours out of town, and he is confident that in the column there were not over twenty five hundred men, although he learned of one of much larger dimensions passing northward to the right some miles to the westward, and still another on the Mercersburg road. General Jenkins borrowed a few horses of the citizens to mount some of his men whose animals had become unfit for service, for which he gave receipts with a religious promise to return them as soon as he got over the line into Pennsylvania. The only damage sustained by the town was by the cutting of two telegraph poles on either side of the place. The rebels had with them quite a number of Union officers whom they had captured near Martinsburg, among whom was a paymaster; perhaps the one referred to by the rebel captain as having paid them off in "greenbacks."

While General Jenkins was in Hagerstown he exhibited many traits which it is to be hoped are characteristic of the man. An incident will illustrate. About noon yesterday, a lieutenant and five men, wearing the uniform of Union soldiers, crept out of some of the houses of the town where they had been hidden, and delivered themselves up. When they made their appearance before General Jenkins the following conversation occured:—

JENKINS—Hallo! who are you, and where did you come from?

LIEUTENANT—We belong to the Union army, or did belong to it, but we don't wish to fight any longer against our Southern brethren; so when our forces left here, we stayed behind, and to day we came out to be paroled.

JENKINS—What did you say about "Southern brethren?" By God, if I thought I had a twenty-fifth cousin who was as white livered as you are I would kill him and set him up in my barnyard to make sheep own their lambs. I'll show you how I parole such pukes as you are. You are too damned miserable to be paroled in military style.

So saying he ordered a detail of six men and a sergeant—"good lusty fellows, with thick boots"—who paroled the recreant federals to the west border of the town, where the paroling process ceased, and the detail and crowd came back highly pleased with Jenkins' mode of paroling cowards.

The whole rebel force left Hagerstown early last evening, and about ten o'clock a tremendous fire was discerned in the direction of Greencastle. Farmers from Pennsylvania who came into Hagerstown early this morning state that as soon as the rebels got into the State of Pennsylvania they took every horse, killed every other animal, and burned every house and barn and hayrick on their route.

Early this morning two cavalrymen came over from the Virginia side at the Point of Rocks, but soon returned. Our own forces had vacated the place the night before. There has been no fighting at Harper's Ferry yet, though it is said that General Ewell is menacing the place on the Virginia side. I think the cars will be running through to the Ferry to morrow.

Proceedings of the Common Council of Philadelphia.

THE M'CLELLAN RESOLUTIONS—SPICY DEBATE—$500,000 APPROPRIATED—THE MEMBERS TO VOLUNTEER TO GO TO HARRISBURG IN A BODY FOR THE DEFENCE OF THE STATE.

The city legislature of Philadelphia assembled on Tuesday afternoon at the call of the Mayor. The business was as follows:—

SELECT BRANCH.

Mr. LYND was in the chair, and a full quorum present.

Mr. BRIGHTLY read a written speech, in which he stated that it is the duty of every citizen, under circumstances like these, to support the constituted authorities. This calamity, however, he could not but see, was brought upon us by the miserable inefficiency of the War Department. He would vote any amount of money for the suppression of this rebellion, but would like to see it expended under a more efficient administration. Our patriotic Governor had gone long since to Washington to lay this subject before the War Department, but had been told to mind his own business. Mr. BRIGHTLY declared that in the dismissal of General George B. McClellan the government committed a fatal error; that the re-employment of that General would call to the army of the Potomac a great body of tried soldiers, whose term of service has expired. Mr. BRIGHTLY now offered a resolution that the President be requested to recall to the head of the army General George B. McClellan.

Mr. DAVIS desired to postpone this, at least for the present. It is a movement purely political in its character. Business of a graver character is on hand.

The motion to postpone was agreed to by a vote of 13 to 8.

The following message from the Mayor was then read:—

OFFICE OF THE MAYOR OF THE CITY OF PHILADELPHIA, June 15, 1863.

To the President and members of the Select Council of the city of Philadelphia:—

GENTLEMEN—The invasion of Pennsylvania by armed forces of rebels, which took place yesterday, and their rapid advance towards the interior of the State, have made it necessary to assemble councils, that they may take into consideration the measures essential to the defence of the city.

Official notice has been given by Governor Curtin that Colonel Ruff, United States Army, has been appointed by General Couch to superintend the organization of military in this city. A proclamation has been issued from this office, requesting all citizens to close their places of business, and to connect themselves, without delay, with existing military organizations. The Governor has authorized a publication of notice that all citizens will be received for the present emergency, without requiring an enlistment for six months.

The committee of citizens entrusted with the funds subscribed during the past year for bounties to volunteers have resolved to pay ten dollars to every private and non-commissioned officer, and twenty dollars for the expenses of each company enlisted for immediate service. In view of these circumstances, it will be desirable to make provision for any expenditures that may be incurred for the immediate organization of citizens, and you are requested to determine the amount and mode of disbursement.

Respectfully, ALEXANDER HENRY.

Mr. WETHERILL said the Committee on Defence and Protection had sat on the previous afternoon, feeling the importance of the task before them. They had nine months before sent a finely equipped force to the border for the same purpose, yet, while this force did what it could, it did not answer the purpose. To this day none of these men have been paid, though all of them went at a loss to themselves. The committee recommended that councils should guarantee this payment if the United States failed to pay it. When other arrangements are made we shall be able to drive every rebel from the soil of Pennsylvania. We cannot believe that the design is to hold Philadelphia, but like an army of locusts to devastate the State, which in the valley of the Cumberland they are probably now doing.

Mr. WETHERILL now offered the report of the committee. Mr. E. Spencer Miller is its chairman, and he is now about to start with his battery for Harrisburg. To the bravery, competency and patriotism of Captain Miller Mr. Wetherill paid a most handsome compliment.

To the report was annexed the following ordinance:—

The Councils of the city do ordain that the sum of $250,000 be and is hereby appropriated to provide for the enlistment, equipment and pay of all able-bodied citizens who may volunteer for the defence of the State or city, not exceeding three months, the said sum to be reimbursed to the city treasury out of the proceeds of a loan to be hereafter created.

The Mayor of the city, with the advice of the Committee on Defence and Protection, is hereby fully authorized to expend the said sum, and to carry out the provisions of this ordinance.

Mr. NICHOLSON desired to amend by inserting $500,000.

A further amendment was made to make the sum $1,000,000.

Mr. KING hoped that no such sum would be appropriated. The sum reported by the committee was ample for the purpose required.

Mr. WETHERILL said that the Bounty Fund Committee have appropriated $470,000. They ignored both Home Guards and Gray Reserves, which exist only in name. They call only for citizens. If ten thousand men are to be raised, $250,000 will scarcely be enough. It cannot yet be said how many men can be raised. Numbers of good men will doubtless come forward from the old organizations, but until we do see the citizens flocking in to the armories the $250,000 will be enough. It is to be hoped, however, that it will not.

Mr. BRIGHTLY said it was our duty to do whatever can be done to support the administration of the State. He saw nothing political in this, though his resolution recommending a leader was voted down by a strict party vote. But another quarter million, or more, can be added to the appropriation at a day's notice.

Dr. UHLER said that though a political opponent of General McClellan he was his personal friend. He knew him to be pure, just and honest, but the moment we adopt this resolution we place ourselves in opposition to the President of the United States. Though it killed his friend he was bound to submit to the judgment of the administration. The trouble here is the parsimony of the Finance Committee, who would "lose the sheep to save a pen'n'orth of tar." Dr. Uhler declared that if necessary he would vote for two millions. There is no need to waste the money. If it is not needed it is not spent.

Mr. CATHERWOOD believed that for the present $250,000 is enough. More can be appropriated at any time.

Mr. DAVIS also expressed his intention to vote for the sum named by the committee.

Mr. GREBLE said he would vote for whatever sum was needed. He believed that in an emergency like this no limit should be thought of.

The amendment making the figure $1,000,000 was lost.

The sum was fixed at $500,000 by a vote of 17 to 3, as moved by Mr. Nicholson.

Mr. CATHERWOOD now offered a resolution as follows:—

Resolved, That whereas the soil of this commonwealth has been ruthlessly invaded by a rebel foe, and not only the capital, but the metropolis of the State is in immediate peril, that the Mayor of the city be and he is hereby requested to desire his Excellency the Governor of the State to forthwith proclaim martial law throughout the State, enforce the same at all hazards, and require every able-bodied man between the ages of twenty one and forty five years of age to at once proceed to Harrisburg for the defence of the soil and property of the citizens of the State, for such time as a necessity for their services may exist.

Mr. BRIGHTLY said that the Governor had no power to enforce mit ers, and therefore the limit must be between the ages of twenty one and forty five.

Mr. KING moved to refer the whole matter to the Committee on Safety and Defence. He considered the resolution very ridiculous. He did not object to voting for it, but nothing could come from it. A similar resolution last year was so disposed of.

Mr. CATHERWOOD said he offered the resolution in good faith. He had not looked for opposition. With martial law fifteen hundred men could have been had in Independence square this very afternoon. The volunteer system is pretty nearly worn out. It is about time for coercion, as it is practised in the South. Let us close our stores and set to work. What consequence is our business now? No man who opposes this can be a friend to his country.

Mr. KING fired up, and said that the entertainers were now performing that very duty. Will the gentleman be the last to go or the first to go himself?

Mr. CATHERWOOD—I have given as much money to the cause as the gentleman (Mr. King) has.

Mr. KING—That isn't the thing. Will the gentleman go himself? Will he carry out his own resolution?

Mr. CATHERWOOD—The gentleman is a great deal richer than I am. I will guarantee that I have given as much as he has, will give as much as he will give, and will put down my name to go to night with Spencer Miller's battery if he will put his down under it, and I will serve as long as he will serve.

This was greeted with an involuntary and prolonged burst of applause from the galleries.

Mr. BRIGHTLY said he couldn't see the use of passing this resolution. It would be a dead letter.

Mr. CATHERWOOD said he had seen martial law enforced in Philadelphia, and with very decisive results. He was sorry to see men of his own (democratic) party differing from him in this respect. The present exigencies were greater than the claims of any party, and he would see his party disrupted and sunk rather than its dictates should rule to effect the ruin of the country.

Dr. UHLER said that there was a recent precedent for martial law, and whatever force we might raise here we could find in this very city a force of men who would be willing to rise against them. Martial law is what we need.

The motion to postpone was lost, and the resolution was unanimously agreed to.

Mr. ARMSTRONG offered a resolution that this Chamber hereby pledge themselves to proceed to Harrisburg and tender their services to the Governor at Harrisburg.

An amendment was offered that they attach themselves to the Third regiment of the Gray Reserves, in which Mr. Nicholson holds a high command.

Mr. NICHOLSON stated that the Third regiment Gray Reserves now has six hundred men, and will number a thousand in twenty-four hours.

Mr. ARMSTRONG said, in reply to some previous remarks from Dr. Uhler, that he would enlist this afternoon in Dr. Spencer Miller's battery, if he (Dr. Uhler) would go.

Dr. UHLER said I'll sign it a minute after you do.

Mr. ARMSTRONG now said that in consulting with some of his fellow members he found it to meet with so many objections that he would withdraw it.

Mr. KING insisted upon putting the resolution.

The motion to postpone was lost by this vote:—

Yeas—Messrs. Baird, Brightly, Nicholson, Riche, Spering, Uhler and Wetherill.

Nays—Messrs. Armstrong, Catherwood, Davis, Ginnodo, Greble, King, Manuel, Marcus, McElroy, Paullin, Weaver, Zane, Lynd, the President.

Mr. DAVIS moved an amendment, that the Chamber in a body report itself to Colonel Ruff for immediate service.

Mr. GREBLE said he belonged to an organized body, with which he should go. The amendment was lost.

A vote on the original resolution resulted thus:—Yeas 11, nays 9. It was therefore agreed to.

Mr. NICHOLSON asked to be excused. Mr. Greble ditto, as both belonged to other organizations. The former was already under arms.

Mr. BRIGHTLY said he must also ask to be excused, as no mustering officer, on account of his infirmities, would receive him.

Mr. WETHERILL offered a resolution that the heads of departments be requested to notify their employes that if they desire to enter service, their pay will be continued during their absence, and their places kept open till their return.

Mr. BRIGHTLY now moved that his resolution, recommending the President to recall Gen. McClellan to the head of the army, be taken up.

The Chamber refused to suspend the rules, by a vote of 12 to 8.

The Chamber now adjourned.

COMMON BRANCH.

President Wilson Kerr in the chair.

The call for the meeting and the Mayor's message were read and laid on the table.

A recess of fifteen minutes was then taken.

On reassembling, the ordinance from Select Council, appropriating $500,000 to equip and send out a force for the immediate defence of the State, was taken up and passed without discussion by a unanimous vote.

Mr. PAINTER introduced a resolution requesting the Governor to use his influence to have Gen. McClellan placed in command of the Pennsylvania troops.

Mr. LEIGH moved to lay on the table. Yeas 14, nays 19. Lost.

Mr. LEIGH expressed his regret that such a resolution had been introduced at this time. The intention of the resolution was to embarrass the Governor and Generals Couch and Brooks.

Mr. PAINTER denied that the intention of his resolution was harmful. If McClellan should be placed at the head of the Pennsylvania army, he would create great enthusiasm in the democratic ranks. If you give us this general you will have to-morrow fifty thousand men to fight for your constitution and your Union.

Mr. HARPER thought it was folly to pass the resolution.

A motion to postpone the consideration of the resolution was lost. Yeas 17, nays 19.

A motion to postpone till next Thursday was carried, and a motion to adjourn was lost.

The patriotic resolutions passed by Select Council in regard to martial law, &c., were taken up, and no quorum voting, a call of the house was made.

Mr. BARGER moved to adjourn, having stood just outside of the railing while the above call was being made, and not having answered to his name.

Mr. LEIGH raised the point of order that a member had no right to make a motion when he was not on the floor of the Chamber.

The Chair maintained the point of order.

Adjourned.

HOOKER'S ARMY.

The Union Forces Near the Old Bull Run Battle Field.

Thoroughfare Gap Completely Blocked Up with Regular Troops.

Capture of Rebel Prisoners and Contrabands.

A Rebel's Account of the Object of the Raid.

Pittsburg to be Invaded, Sacked and Burned.

Portions of Pennsylvania and Maryland to be Pillaged and Plundered,

&c., &c., &c.

BULL RUN, Va., June 15, 1863.

The grand Army of the Potomac is now on and near the old Bull run battle field.

The Third army corps arrived at Manassas Junction on Monday morning.

The First and Eleventh corps are at Centreville.

The balance of the Army of the Potomac—the Second Fifth, Sixth and Twelfth corps—will probably reach here to-night.

Major General Hooker and the retinue attached to the general headquarters are on their way to this point, and by to-morrow noon or night the army will be together again.

Our cavalry commands have during the whole time been on our flanks. They have done invaluable service as scouts, gaining information of the enemy's movements and making reconnoissances which impeded the enemy's progress.

General Gregg and his division are and have been operating in the neighborhood of Warrenton and White Sulphur Springs.

General Duffie's division, late General Averill's, are at the base of the Blue Ridge, near Ashby's Gap.

General Buford, with the regulars, has completely blocked up Thoroughfare Gap, thereby preventing the approach of the rebels to this neighborhood through that channel.

Colonel Taylor, of the First Pennsylvania cavalry, now temporarily in command of General Wyndham's brigade, has had the Orange and Alexandria Railroad under his special care.

General Pleasanton, now in command of the cavalry corps, has his headquarters in the neighborhood of Warrenton Junction.

Our cavalry have captured many prisoners and brought away numberless contrabands, from whom invaluable information has been obtained.

Among the prisoners captured is Captain Hutchins, of Stuart's cavalry. He was with General Twiggs in Texas when Twiggs surrendered his command and the government property.

Among the most important seizures made by our cavalry has been that of a bag containing mail matter—letters written by the rebel soldiers and addressed to their friends in the South.

Not only were the bag and its contents captured, but also the parties who had it in charge, thus breaking up a mail route that has doubtless been in constant operation for a considerable length of time.

Among the letters captured was one written by an aid to General Longstreet, to his wife living in Alabama. After talking of family matters, the writer goes on [illegible] [illegible] their movement North [illegible] they will ultimately send a cavalry force into Pittsburg, and sack and burn the town, while their infantry are to pillage and plunder sundry parts of Maryland and Pennsylvania.

Reorganization of the Artillery of the Army of the Potomac.

We learn that the artillery division of the army has been broken up and organized into a reserve for the whole army, except five batteries selected from each corps, which have been organized into artillery brigades, one to each corps.

The Situation in Front.

[From the Washington Star, June 16.]

Secesh in Washington last night discovered that Hooker's headquarters were at Fairfax Station, and argued disastrous things therefrom. It may quiet their nerves to know that wherever his headquarters were yesterday, or may be to-morrow, the Army of the Potomac is intact, in good spirits, well concentrated to deal rapid and telling blows upon the enemy, and is, on the whole, in better condition every way for effective service than it has been for a month or two past.

The indications are now that Lee's whole army is moving up to the valley in the same general direction with the advance of Ewell and Longstreet. Hooker, having the shorter line to travel, can doubtless keep pace with him, despite his advantages in starting time. And should Lee make a short turn, as some apprehend, with the idea of trying another fight on the old battle ground of Manassas, Hooker, by the same advantage of inside lines, will again be able to accommodate him.

In short, by Lee's new plan of campaign we are able to avail ourselves of the same advantage of moving across the chord instead of on the arc of a circle which the Confederates have heretofore enjoyed.

THE REBEL LEE'S ARMY.

The Main Body of the Enemy in the Shenandoah Valley.

The Whole Body of Rebels to be Thrown Into Maryland and Pennsylvania.

SKIRMISHING WITH THE REBEL REAR GUARD,

&c., &c., &c.

PHILADELPHIA, June 17, 1863.

A special despatch from Washington, dated last night, contains the following intelligence:—

The latest advices from the army show that General Lee has pushed a very large force up the Shenandoah valley.

General Ewell's corps is in the advance, accompanied by General Stuart's cavalry.

General Hill's corps is close behind, and General Longstreet is bringing up the rear.

There no longer seems to be any doubt that General Lee is throwing the whole of his forces up towards Maryland and Pennsylvania.

Our cavalry have been skirmishing with Lee's rear guard for two days, and all information now tends to show that the rebels are not moving to give us battle on the old field of Bull run, or in that vicinity.

Our forces evacuated Frederick, Maryland, and that vicinity, and fell back to the Relay House this morning. No enemy pursuing them, they returned to Frederick this morning with strong reinforcements.

Soon after the train passed the Point of Rocks some of General Hill's corps came in on a tour of observation.

It is said by some who watch military matters closely that the next battle will be fought in Maryland, and, perhaps, on the old field of Antietam again.

Some rebels appeared at Poolesville last evening, but withdrew without doing any damage.

An extra train went to Harper's Ferry last night and returned this morning.

General Lee is moving on a longer line than General Hooker; but he has not succeeded in outmarching him very far.

General Hooker was at Fairfax Court House this morning; but it cannot be said where he will be to-night.

It is not believed that the rebels have got into Pennsylvania in any great numbers. What they may do in twenty-four hours more is hard to tell.

It is believed that Harper's Ferry can be held against any force the rebels may bring against it.

Fredericksburg Abandoned by the Rebels.

WASHINGTON, June 17, 1863.

By an arrival from Aquia Creek to-day, information is received that three deserters report the remaining rebel force left the vicinity of Fredericksburg at sundown yesterday with their battery. Five rebel scouts were seen in the afternoon eight miles from the creek.

Fires in New York.

FIRE IN EAST TWELFTH STREET.

About one o'clock yesterday morning a fire broke out in the brick stables 2[illegible] East Twelfth street, owned by Joseph David and occupied by several parties. Three horses were burned to death—two owned by E. Riley and one owned by P. Brennan—valued at about $200. No insurance. Damage to stable about $300.

FIRE IN EAST THIRTEENTH STREET.

Shortly before three o'clock yesterday morning a fire originated in the stable No. 252 East Thirteenth street, owned and occupied by Cornell & Hayward. Two horses, valued at $350, were burned to death. Loss on stable about $300. Insured in the Broadway Insurance Company. The fire is supposed to have been caused by an incendiary.

FIRE IN CANAL STREET—LOSS ABOUT TEN THOUSAND DOLLARS.

About one o'clock yesterday morning a fire was discovered in the concert saloon Nos. 170 and 172 Canal street, kept by William Hitchcock. The flames spread rapidly and soon communicated to Nos. 174 and 168, damaging them considerably, and also to buildings Nos. 23, 25 and 27 Elizabeth street. Mr Hitchcock estimates his loss at about $5,000. Insured in the Bowery Insurance Company for $2,000.

Building No. 174 is owned by John B Cortier, is damaged about $400, and insured for $2,500 in the City Insurance Company. The upper part and basement of the building are occupied by Mrs. Florentine as a dwelling. Damage about $150, insured for $800 in the Bowery Insurance Company. The first floor is occupied by John [illegible], as a real estate office; damage about $50, no insurance.

No. 168, store, occupied by Jacob Davidson, boots and shoes; damage about $300. Insured for $2,000 in the Astor and Continental Insurance companies. The upper part of the building is occupied as a dwelling by J. H. Wetgen; loss $300; insured in the New Amsterdam Insurance Company for $600. Also by Robert Calahan, loss $300, insured for $400 in Stuyvesant Insurance Company. Also by H. F. Bush, loss $100, insured for $400 in New Amsterdam Insurance Company. Also by G. W. Davis, loss $100, no insurance.

No. 23 Elizabeth street—occupied by Jacob Horlath as a boarding house; loss $2,000, insured for $1,500 in the Stuyvesant Insurance Company.

No. 25—Occupied by Thomas Frith, Mrs. Stotts and W Chambers as a dwelling, loss $500, no insurance.

The buildings Nos. 23 and 25 are owned by J. J. Post; damage about $1,200; insured for $1,000 in the [illegible] Insurance Company.

No. 27—Occupied by P New as a dwelling and shoe shop, loss $100, no insurance.

Buildings Nos. 27 and 29 Elizabeth street, and stores as No. 168 Canal street, are owned by the Wetgen estate. They are damaged about $500, and fully insured in the New Amsterdam Insurance Company. The origin of the fire is unknown at present, but it is under investigation by the Fire Marshal.

Subscriptions for the Pacific Railroad.

SAN FRANCISCO, June 16, 1863.

Santa Clara county has voted to subscribe one hundred thousand dollars to the Pacific Railroad stock.

All the counties along the route have now subscribed their proportion, making two millions of dollars [illegible] subscribed by the State.

Temperance Convention at Halifax, N. S.

HALIFAX, N. S., June 16, 1863.

The Temperance Convention adjourned this evening, after a very pleasant session of five days.

A committee was appointed to arrange for the celebration of the twenty first anniversary of the foundation of the Order on the 29th of September.

The proposition to admit ladies to full membership was rejected.

No important constitutional changes were effected.

The members of the Convention have met with a continual ovation during their stay here, which kindness they have returned by drinking the health and happiness of our citizens in pure cold water.

Military Execution at Boston.

BOSTON, June 17, 1863.

William Lynch, a private in the Second Massachusetts cavalry, was shot at Fort Independence yesterday for mutiny, according to the sentence of the court martial. Lynch was one of the ringleaders of the revolt, when the chief one was shot dead by the consul at the time.

The Court of Appeals.

ALBANY, June 17, 1863.

The following is the calendar of the Court of Appeals for June 18:—Nos. 6, 6, 7, 10, 11, 12, 13, 14, 15 and 16.

The Philadelphia Inquirer.

CIRCULATION OVER 60,000. | PHILADELPHIA, MONDAY, JUNE 29, 1863. | PRICE TWO CENTS.

TO ARMS!

CITIZENS OF PENNSYLVANIA!!

The Rebels Are Upon Us!

YORK, GETTYSBURG, CARLISLE, HANOVER AND OTHER POINTS OCCUPIED BY THE REBELS.

SKIRMISH NEAR HARRISBURG.

The Northern Central Railroad Cut at York Haven.

A Skirmish Near Wrightsville.

COLUMBIA BRIDGE BURNED BY OUR RETREATING TROOPS.

Organization of the State Militia.

PHILADELPHIA TO FURNISH 7718 MEN.

The Army of the Potomac in Motion.

THE REBELS AT YORK.

The Burgess of York Offers to Surrender—General Gordon Expects the Citizens to Furnish Rations to Eight Thousand Rebels—He Will Burn all Government Property—Citizens of York Indignant at the Burgess.

Special Despatch to the Inquirer.

COLUMBIA, Pa., June 28.—Two officials connected with the military hospital at York, accompanied by the Assistant Postmaster, have just arrived here, bringing advices from York up to nine o'clock this morning. The statement that the town was surrendered at five o'clock yesterday is erroneous. At eight o'clock on Saturday evening, the Burgess, DAVID STRONG, accompanied by the Safety Committee, went nine miles beyond York, on the turnpike, to the head-quarters of General GORDON, commanding the Rebels, with a flag of truce.

They offered to surrender the place and asked GORDON whether he would respect private property? He said yes, but that he would destroy all Government buildings, including the hospital and barracks, unless the fire would endanger neighboring property. GORDON gave the Committee to understand that the town would be occupied to-day, and that he would expect citizens to furnish rations to his troops, about eight thousand strong. These troops are from Georgia and Louisiana, and GORDON himself is from Mississippi, having formerly been a Confederate Colonel.

The action of the Burgess and the Safety Committee was without the sanction or knowledge of the military authorities holding the lower end of the town, who would have fired on the Rebels had they advanced. At nine o'clock this morning the American flag was still flying from the public square in York. The Rebel pickets were then three miles distant. It is believed, but not positively known, that the original demand for the surrender of York was made yesterday afternoon by a paroled prisoner, whom GORDON sent to the Burgess.

This morning the action of the Burgess was commented upon freely by the people, some denouncing it bitterly, and others favoring the surrender.

YORK OCCUPIED BY THE REBELS.

Special Despatch to the Inquirer.

COLUMBIA, June 28.—I have been shown a letter, just received from Captain STRICKLER, on the outposts, to ROBERT CRANE, Esq., Superintendent of the Reading and Columbia Railroad, which says:—"The Rebels occupy York in force, with cavalry and infantry. They are General RHODES' Division of EWELL's Corps.

"All the Union cavalry and infantry from York, have passed this outpost for Columbia. I judge from the Rebel train of wagons that their force is very heavy." Another letter from the outposts just received, says:—The Rebels have driven us in on the front, and flanked us on the left. I have lost four men who are certainly captured, unless they can escape by the lower river route. One of them is Lieutenant SOUDERS.

FROM COLUMBIA.

An Attack Expected Hourly—The Bridge at Columbia to be Defended.

Special Despatch to the Inquirer.

COLUMBIA, Pa., June 28, 1863.—All the scouts have come in. The bridge at this point will never be permitted to be used by the enemy, who are at this hour understood to be but four miles from the river. Should they advance, a battle will take place before night within sight of this town. We are expecting the attack momentarily.

A body of eighteen Rebels have passed along the line of the Northern Central Railroad, and destroyed the bridges. One of these was opposite Bainbridge, about seven miles above this place.

The last of Colonel THOMAS' regiment escaped from the Rebels by crossing the Susquehanna, this afternoon, on a raft, near Bainbridge. They were fired on by the enemy before the crossing was effected, but not hurt.

THE REBELS AT WRIGHTSVILLE.

Our Troops are Compelled to Fall Back on Columbia—A Spirited Skirmish—Our Men Fire the Long Bridge Connecting Columbia and Wrightsville and it Burns Down without Damaging the Town—Excellent Behavior of the Militia—The City Troop Engaged.

Special Correspondence of the Inquirer.

COLUMBIA, Pa., June 28, 1863, 8·30 P. M.

The conflict on the opposite side of the river has terminated. The whole force of Colonel FRICK has retreated to Columbia, and just after they passed the long bridge over the river was set on fire. It is now burning. The sparks threatening to destroy Columbia, and the engagement lasting forty-five minutes. Our men were in trenches which had been thrown up during the preceding few hours, and fought valiantly.

The principal work was thrown across the turnpike, about two miles from Columbia, and on a hill. The Rebel force advanced not only on the turnpike, but on the right and left, completely flanking our forces, and obliging them either to retreat to the bridge and across the river, or be surrounded. They preferred the latter. The retreat was effected in the face of the foe, who harrassed our rear with cavalry and infantry. The first attack was by their skirmishers, who advanced, hiding themselves in the long grain; their artillery was then planted on a hill near our position, also, on the turnpike, and the shells fell not only in our trenches but into the town of Wrightsville and into the river. The smoke was visible from Columbia as well as the falling shells. In spite of the rattle of musketry and roar of cannon, it is not believed that our loss was over twenty, among whom was AARON TICE, of Company H, Twenty-seventh Regiment, and some members of Company H.

The artillery of the enemy numbered eight pieces, planted in various positions. To reply to this we had nothing but infantry. Their cavalry dismounted after the conflict had commenced, hiding in the grain and woods. The bridge was fired near the Wrightsville end, and at the time this was written the flames were gradually creeping towards Columbia. By the great light it is barely possible to discern some pieces of artillery planted on the opposite bank. There is reason to fear that the flames will extend to the hotel on this side. The first attempt to destroy the bridge was by filling holes with gunpowder. This would not succeed; the torch was then applied. The Pennsylvania Railroad despatches at this point had previously sent all the rolling stock to safe points. Two engines and a train of passenger cars are retained to meet any emergency. It is possible that the Rebel artillery may shell Columbia as soon as the flames of the bridge reach this side of the river so as to reveal objects distinctly. Some of the houses in Wrightsville were, no doubt, injured by the shells, but this could not be positively ascertained, as the haste with which our troops retired would not admit of an examination. Nearly all the women and children remained in Wrightsville. It is more than likely that they were injured. Two companies of colored troops remained in the entrenchments until ordered to retreat. They were volunteers, and behaved well, except in the retreat, which was accomplished rather hastily. Colonel FRICK and Major KNOX, with a guard, were the last to leave the bridge. They preserved order in the retreat, and kept the men together, so as to avoid a panic. The proceedings throughout were facilitated and aided by Major HALLER, Aid-de-Camp of General COUCH, who has been in the whole campaign. To the other Colonels and officers credit is certainly due for the manner in which they carried out the plans of the Acting Brigadier-General, Colonel FRICK. The bridge was fired by Messrs. CRANE and SMITH.

10 o'clock, P. M.—The bridge is still burning. An attack upon the town, either by fording the river, which may be possible, or by shelling Columbia, is apprehended to-night. It would be improper to give the present position of our forces.

10 P. M.—The City Troop took part in the conflict. All are well and at this place. The bridge was burned down, and no damage to Columbia from the sparks as yet.

Mass Meeting in Reading.

Special Despatch to the Inquirer.

READING, June 28.—A town meeting is being held in the public square. The County Commissioners will give extra pay to volunteers, and will raise a large force.

THE INVASION OF PENNSYLVANIA.

Map Showing Lee's Route from Fredericksburg, via Culpeper, Strasburg, Winchester, &c., into Maryland and Pennsylvania, together with the Towns Occupied by Ewell.

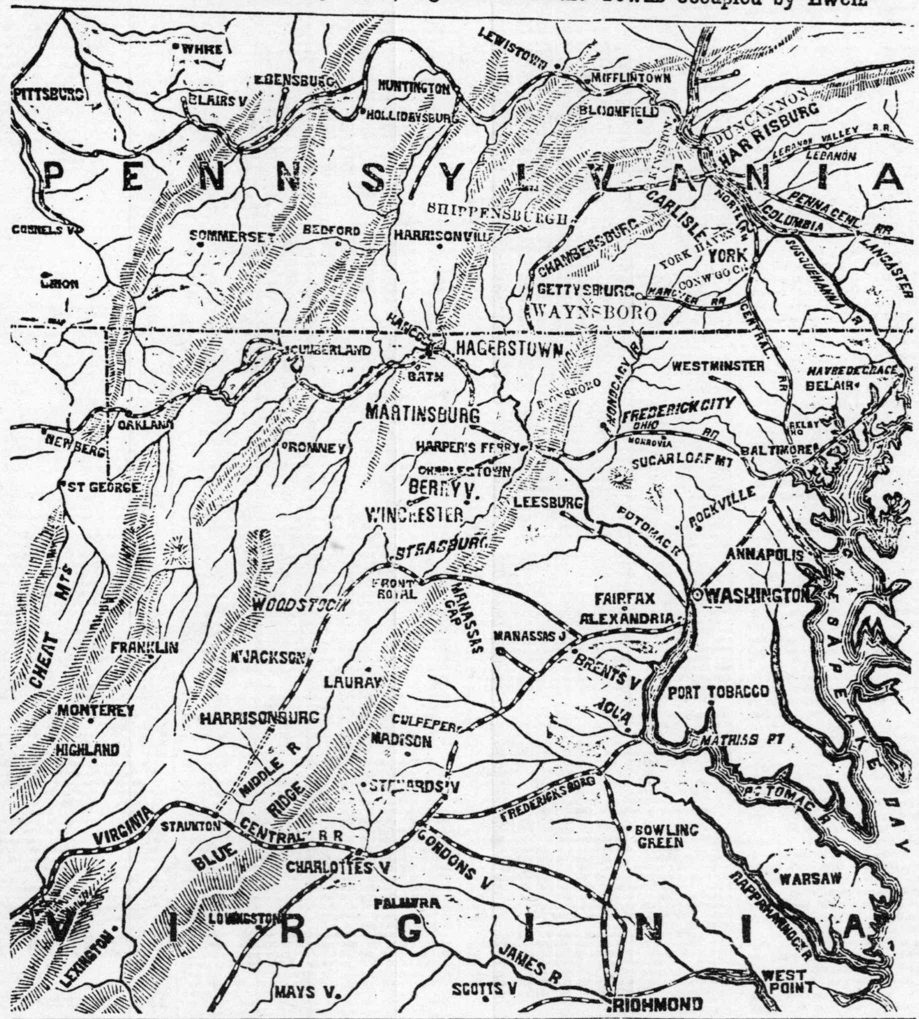

IMPORTANT FROM HARRISBURG!!!

The Rebels Within Four Miles of Our Works.

THE TROOPS IN POSITION, AWAITING THE ASSAULT.

A Battle Impending.

SKIRMISHING IN PROGRESS.

HARRISBURG, June 28, P. M.—The capital of the State is in danger. The enemy is within four miles of our works, and advancing. The cannonading has been distinctly heard for three hours. Our troops are in position, awaiting the attack. The authorities feel confident of their ability to repulse their assailants. A battle will probably take place before night.

The Pennsylvania Railroad is so far safe.

The Rebels Moving on Havre de Grace.

HARRISBURG, June 27, 10 P. M.—[*Special to the New York Herald.*]—Our pickets at Sterrett's Gap were driven in and a number captured.

It is reported that the Northern Central Railroad has been destroyed at York Haven. There have been no trains to-day to Baltimore.

It is rumored that the Rebels are moving on Havre de Grace, and also that General HOOKER has opened the ball.

All the citizens of Harrisburg are armed, and will cross the river to-morrow.

In a skirmish at Walnut Bottom, this morning, eleven men were wounded.

The Rebel cavalry scouts are seven miles this side of Carlisle, and a battle is expected here on Sunday.

A Kingston despatch, dated Saturday, 6 P. M., says, the enemy being on our flank our forces evacuated the position, and the Rebels are advancing.

At 9 o'clock the Rebel-advance halted.

Another despatch, dated in the field, four and a half miles east of Carlisle, 2·30 P. M., says, we are in line of battle, our forces in position on a hill supporting the artillery; Captain BOYD is in our front, with the enemy in sight. It was intended to blow up the earthworks on evacuating Carlisle, but the Regulars would not allow it. Several thousand dollars' worth of Quartermaster's stores fell into the hands of the Rebels.

About six hundred Rebel cavalry are in Carlisle.

A Mechanicsburg despatch, dated 10 P. M., Saturday, says, there is no prospect of the Rebels being there before Sunday morning.

LATER FROM HARRISBURG.

Skirmish at Oyster Point—Spencer Miller's Battery Engaged—Destruction of Columbia Bridge.

Special Despatch to the Inquirer.

HARRISBURG, June 28.—This morning, about 11 o'clock, a skirmish with the enemy took place at Oyster Point, about four miles from Harrisburg. Our advance, consisting of the Seventy-first New York and E. SPENCER MILLER's Philadelphia Battery, engaged the enemy's advance. Several shots were fired but without loss on our side. They advanced their forces and our troops then fell back towards our outer intrenchments, everything indicating an early struggle in the immediate vicinity of the city. York has been occupied and the enemy have advanced to Wrightsville, opposite Columbia, where a fight took place to-day. Colonel THOMAS' regiment, of Philadelphia, is there.

The Rebels are reported to have burned two bridges over Conawago creek. The Greys are sworn in and marched to the front. This morning the Rebels captured and brought in say that five thousand men are this side of Carlisle, and intend to take Harrisburg when the main body comes up. Crowds of people are on the banks of the river on this side, anxiously awaiting the opening of the ball. There is not much general excitement in the city. The people have kept up their spirits well, and numbers of the citizens have armed and formed into companies. We are expecting any moment to hear the booming of artillery. The Columbia bridge was burned by the Rebels, our forces getting safely over. An attack is expected on the town at any moment. The light of the burning bridge was seen here to-night. I have just arrived from the front, and know that a desperate resistance will be made.

THE LATEST FROM HARRISBURG.

A Fight at Wrightsville—Retreat of Our Troops—Burning of the Bridge—A Rebel Pontoon Train.

HARRISBURG, June 28.—The city to-day has been comparatively quiet, considering the near approach of the enemy. The banks of the river have been lined with men, women and children, hourly expecting the arrival of the enemy.

The trains departing from here to-day have been crowded with persons fleeing from the city.

York has been occupied, and a portion of the bridges on the Northern Central Railroad, this side of that place, have been burned.

When our troops fell back from Carlisle they left in the barracks equipments for one company of cavalry, one regiment of infantry and 20,000 rations, which have fallen into the hands of the enemy. There is a report that the barracks have been burned, but this needs confirmation.

The Governor has information that the Rebels are at Bainbridge, twelve miles above Columbia, with a pontoon train sufficiently large to construct a bridge.

The Rebels that drove our men from Sterrett's Gap yesterday, and then moved towards Duncannon, have returned to the Gap. No demonstration has been made on the Pennsylvania Railroad in that direction to-day, so far as known.

Major WYNKOOP has been appointed by General COUCH Chief of Cavalry in this Department, Captain BRISBIN having been ordered to his regiment.

Troops under the new call are rapidly arriving.

Two companies of colored troops, composed of citizens of this city, were armed to-day and sent across the river.

Colonel JENNINGS' regiment, which had the skirmish at Gettysburg, arrived here to-day. He lost about 200 men in prisoners and stragglers. The officers were sent to Richmond, and the men paroled. Some of the men have arrived here.

HARRISBURG, June 28.—[Special to N. Y. *Herald.*]—At nine o'clock this morning the Rebels demanded the surrender of Mechanicsburg, which was complied with, and our cavalry retreated in good order. The enemy pulled down the United States flag and raised the Rebel colors. The town was very quiet, most of the people having left. The enemy captured several thousand dollars' worth of property contracted for by the Government—salt, flour, &c.—at Kingston.

The enemy's cavalry was abreast of Shiremanstown by noon. The Rebels are said to be on several roads, and threaten to attack Harrisburg above and below.

The Rebel General JOHNSON's division entered Chambersburg on Wednesday, and on Friday moved towards Shippensburg. His force numbered from 8000 to 10,000.

The *Herald's* Lancaster despatch says that the Rebels have possession of York and have thrown out pickets towards Lancaster. There will be a battle at Harrisburg to-morrow.

MILROY's train from Harrisburg is passing through.

Placards are posted calling on the people to rally for defense. A mass meeting was held and six companies organized on the spot. The Rebels were supposed to be advancing.

Many of the store-keepers are forwarding their goods to Philadelphia, and some of the citizens are leaving.

The rolling stock of the Pennsylvania Central is passing east for security. One of the daily papers has suspended until the crisis is over, all the employees having entered the ranks.

FURTHER FROM HARRISBURG.

HARRISBURG, June 28.—(Special to New York *Herald.*)—General CAMERON has information that the Rebels, twenty thousand strong, are at Carlisle, with forty-eight pieces of artillery.

THE LATEST FROM HARRISBURG.

HARRISBURG, June 28.—Midnight.—The artillery firing heard to-day was a skirmish between the enemy's advance and our own outposts. No damage is known to have been done on either side. It occurred about five miles out. Our troops then fell back, and up to the present time the Rebel advance is four miles from here. The authorities expect an attack to-morrow.

The Governor has received notice of 25,000 men who have enlisted under the last call.

HARRISBURG, June 28.—The Grey Reserves, of Philadelphia, have been sworn in.

A gentleman who left York this morning says, that LONGSTREET's pickets were within a mile. Everything of value that could be had been removed.

Five Rebel companies of cavalry attacked four companies of the Twentieth Pennsylvania Cavalry last night, below York, and were driven off badly whipped.

There has been no fighting at Harrisburg yet.

The rolling stock of the Northern Central and Hanover Branch roads has all passed down.

A skirmish occurred at Wrightsville to-day. Col. FRICK's command fought the enemy in rifle-pits gallantly till they were surrounded and overpowered. Over 100 were captured and the rest retreated across the bridge, which was then burned.

HARRISBURG, June 28.—(Special to New York *Times.*)—Our troops slowly retired, and are now in and around the fortifications of Harrisburg.

The enemy is advancing slowly, and in all probability will soon commence an attack.

General SMITH has made the proper disposition of his troops. Throughout the day men have been coming to the defense of the city in responce to the Governor's proclamation. Among the number is a great many contrabands. They have all been furnished with guns and ammunition and sent across the river.

Captain BRISBANE, Chief of Cavalry, who was on a reconnoissance across the river, this afternoon, reports the Rebel scouts within three miles of our pickets.

LATER.—The enemy fired several shots from a position west of Oyster Point, this morning.

FURTHER FROM LANCASTER.

LANCASTER, June 28.—Great excitement here. The tap of the drum mingles with the chime of bells. Refugees from Harrisburg are flocking here, and horses are coming in droves.

Two spies came over the river at Marietta. They tried to escape, but one was killed and the other captured.

Our forces guard the river from Marietta to Columbia.

Bounties of twenty dollars are offered, at Columbia and other places, to encourage volunteering.

Four hundred cavalry attempted to ford the Susquehanna, but were baffled by the current.

The enemy has burned all the bridges on the Northern Central between Harrisburg and York.

The whole column moving towards Columbia is reported at 5000.

The enemy have shelled the village of Wrightsville, opposite Columbia.

Important Order—Organization of the Pennsylvania Militia.

HEAD-QUARTERS PENNSYLVANIA MILITIA, HARRISBURG, June 26.—General Order No. 44.—In organizing the troops responding to the Proclamation of the Governor, this day issued, calling for 60,000 men for the defense of the State, to be mustered into the service of the State for the period of ninety days, unless sooner discharged.

It is ordered, 1st. Camps of rendezvous will be established by the United States Government for districts, comprising the adjacent counties at such points as may be indicated by the Commandants of the Department of the Susquehanna and the Department of the Monongahela. In charge of which camps commanders and skillful surgeons will be appointed.

2d. Squads or companies will be received at the camps, and as rapidly as possible organized into companies of not less than sixty-four (64) men, and into regiments of ten (10) companies each, and mustered into the service of the State by officers appointed by the Adjutant-General for this purpose.

3d. Officers will be elected. Company officers by the men, and field officers by the company or line officers.

4th. Transportation to the camp of rendezvous nearest their location will be furnished by the United States Government, on application to any one actually having charge of a squad or company, to the agent at the nearest railroad station.

5th. Troops responding to this call of the Governor will be clothed, subsisted, equipped and supplied by the General Government, after arriving at the rendezvous.

6th. Annexed is the quota required from each county, in the present call, after crediting those counties which had already responded under the recent Order, with the number of troops furnished and actually mustered into service:—

Adams	469	Juniata	22[illegible]
Allegheny	3800	Lancaster	215[illegible]
Armstrong	820	Lawrence	46[illegible]
Beaver	600	Lebanon	51[illegible]
Bedford	584	Lehigh	90[illegible]
Berks	1730	Luzerne	144[illegible]
Blair	555	Lycoming	62[illegible]
Bradford	857	Mercer	74[illegible]
Bucks	1140	McKean	12[illegible]
Butler	648	Mifflin	82[illegible]
Cambria	680	Monroe	84[illegible]
Cameron	70	Montgomery	126[illegible]
Carbon	426	Montour	17[illegible]
Chester	881	Northampton	91[illegible]
Centre	540	Northumberland	47[illegible]
Clarion	520	Perry	46[illegible]
Clinton	286	Philadelphia	771[illegible]
Clearfield	365	Pike	15[illegible]
Columbia	821	Potter	24[illegible]
Crawford	980	Schuylkill	131[illegible]
Cumberland	587	Snyder	23[illegible]
Dauphin	744	Somerset	54[illegible]
Delaware	255	Sullivan	8[illegible]
Erie	1000	Susquehanna	65[illegible]
Elk	115	Tioga	55[illegible]
Fayette	800	Union	9[illegible]
Franklin	840	Venango	50[illegible]
Fulton	180	Warren	38[illegible]
Forrest	120	Washington	96[illegible]
Greene	480	Wayne	64[illegible]
Huntingdon	502	Westmoreland	108[illegible]
Indiana	675	Wyoming	18[illegible]
Jefferson	360	York	118[illegible]

By order A. G. CURTIN,
Governor and Commander-in-Chief.

A. L. RUSSELL, Adjutant-General of Penna.

[NOTE.—The Governor desires the Associated Press to request all the country newspapers to issue an extra for free distribution in the country, on their receiving a copy of the above order of the Adjutant-General.]

The Northern Central Railroad.

BALTIMORE, June 28.—The telegraph is working by Glen Rock, on the Northern Central, six miles this side of Hanover Junction.

From Port Royal.

NEW YORK, June 28.—The steamer *Fulton* has arrived from Port Royal, but brings no news. General TERRY is among the passengers.

DAILY DISPATCH.

VOL. XXV. RICHMOND, VA., MONDAY MORNING, JULY 6, 1863. NO. 5.

The Daily Dispatch.

The DISPATCH is published DAILY, (Sundays excepted.) Price for mailing $10 a year; or $5 for six months; [illegible] one month $1—in advance.

The SEMI-WEEKLY DISPATCH is issued every TUESDAY and FRIDAY, at $6—in advance.

The WEEKLY DISPATCH is issued every FRIDAY, and mailed to subscribers at $4 per annum.

The Daily Dispatch.

TERMS OF ADVERTISING.

[illegible]

MONDAY MORNING......JULY 6, 1863.

The Battle of Gettysburg

It is difficult to say, from the accounts which we publish to-day, (all Yankee, of course,) what portion, or whether all of our army was engaged. We presume, however, that it was only a portion, as the main body is supposed not to be in the immediate neighborhood of Gettysburg.

It is evident to us, at any rate, that our troops have gained a great victory. The *Philadelphia Inquirer* cannot conceal the fact, although it lies with an ardor and an earnestness that deserved better success. We are told, in the first place, that "our troops"—to wit, the Yankee troops—maintained their position in Gettysburg, in spite of the most obstinate attempts on the part of the rebels to capture it. A paragraph or two lower, we are told that at the "end of the battle" the rebel cavalry made a dash through the town, capturing all the sick and wounded, stores, &c. Now, dashing through a town, which the enemy has held during a severe battle, to ordinary comprehensions, certainly means that the town was carried and left in the rear by the victorious party in their pursuit of a flying enemy. Again, we are told that the "rebels" were triumphantly beaten back. But a little farther on we discover that towards the close of the action these same "rebels" made an attack upon one of the enemy's flanks, and that he fell back a mile, fighting valiantly, of course, as Yankees always do—*on paper*.—Lastly, the Yankees say the affair is "indecisive," which is proof enough that they have been badly beaten. Had it *really* been indecisive, they would have claimed a decided victory. It is only necessary to remember what McClellan did at Sharpsburg to be convinced of this. That affair was anything *but* indecisive. McClellan was beaten with immense slaughter. He retreated in the night, and the next day Gen. Lee could hear nothing of him, although he shelled all the woods in the neighborhood to start him from his covert. Had Gen. Lee followed him, beyond a question he would have continued his retreat. But the force of that General was too feeble, in comparison with the enormous Yankee army, to justify the risk. After holding the battle-field twenty four hours he withdrew, and McClellan, learning the fact by his scouts, sneaked up, occupied it, and wrote: "I think I may now say that we really have gained a victory." He was so crippled, in the meantime, that he would not follow, and was removed for not doing what was impossible. Can any one doubt, after this, that when the Yankees say an affair is indecisive, they are in fact badly whipped?

But if they are not whipped, why do they clamor so vociferously for reinforcements?

The Baltimore *American* tells us that up to Thursday they had captured 6,000 prisoners, but it accounts for only 800, although General Schenck announces that 1,500 more were to come on. On Thursday there was no general battle, but heavy skirmishing, in which 5,000 prisoners, making 11,000 in all, were captured. The gallant Dutchmen who distinguished themselves by running so at Chancellorsville, it seems, demolished Longstreet's corps and captured a thousand prisoners. These lies are too gross even for Yankee credulity.

The fact seems to be that a *division* of the army has kept the whole Yankee force at bay two days, and that Gen. Lee is rapidly concentrating in the neighborhood of Gettysburg. In a few days we expect to hear that Meade's army has been defeated, and probably annihilated.

Exit Hooker.

"Fighting Joe" has disappeared at last. He has gone the way of all Yankee Generals.—He brings up the rear of that illustrious procession,—Scott, McDowell, McClellan, Pope, Burnside,—last and least, Hooker. The grim shades of the departed rise to welcome him to the infernal pit,—the Young Napoleon, probably in the advance, greeting Hooker with an iron grip of salutation, and a significant smile, suggestive of Congress committees, and bubble reputations built up by bluster and blowing, and burst at the cannon's mouth.

Poor, dead Commanders-in-Chief of Doodledum—there they lie all in a row,—six green graves, and greener occupants, festering in the winding sheet of their dead reputations. Tread lightly on their ashes, Major-General Meade, successor of Hooker, and, instead of imitating their vain glorious and boastful ways, bend thine ear with humility amongst the long grass that covers their carcases, and—

> "Hark from the tombs a doleful sound,
> Thine ears attend the cry;
> Thou living man, come view the ground
> Where thou must shortly lie."

What is to become of Maj. Gen. Hooker alias "Fighting Joe," and Commander-in-Chief, "with the reins well in hand," of "the finest army on the planet," it is impossible to predict. Whether, like Pope, he is to be sent to hunting Indians, or, like Burnside, to console himself for his inability to cope with armed men by persecuting and hanging the defenceless and non-combatant, remains to be seen. As for the luckless McClellan, there seems no prospect of resurrection. No emergency, however pressing, can induce the Gorilla to entrust "the reins" of the army to the retreating hero of the Chickahominy. In the meantime Lee, who has swallowed one Grand Army after another, is standing with open mouth at the gates of the enemy, asking for more. The unappeasable appetite of this man is frightful to all beholders. One Grand Army after another, with innumerable cannon, small arms, and other munitions of war, has gone down his insatiable throat and he is still unappeased, endeavoring to stay his stomach with fat valleys and Pennsylvania militia, until, in the choice vernacular of the Yankees, he can "gobble down" another Grand Army. We are fearful that Meade will not organize his larder in time for the visitation of this ravenous Virginian, and that he may find it necessary, in order to allay the pangs of hunger, to bolt Washington whole, and all its horrid contents.

On to Richmond by the Political General

Dix is the only Politician General, save Butler, who has attempted that terrible Jordan of "On to Richmond." He is one of the most prominent of the foresworn public men of the North. He was one of the most ultra of State-rights men there, and carried his sympathies with the South to an extreme that threw almost into the shade the most zealous supporters of the same doctrines in the South. When the war broke out he promptly swallowed everything he ever said about the Constitution and Southern rights, and offered his services to the Government that had crushed the Constitution and was bending all its energies to destroy the South. He sought a place in the army, and being a man of influence in New York, it was given him as a matter of policy no doubt. He has distinguished himself by his bitterness and the malignity of his measures in the department assigned to him. He has been the rival of Daniel S. Dickinson, another man of New York utterly treacherous to his former principles and declarations. They were rivals for the public honors of their State, and are now rivals in their zeal in support of the Lincoln tyranny. They belong to the same political school with Butler, who is their equal in ability and somewhat ahead of them in infamy.

What put it into the head of the great General Dix that he could take Richmond after the failure of so many educated military men, it is hard to tell. Now, if Richmond had been in New York, and there was a chance to get into it by "bargain, intrigue, and corruption," this New York politician would be a first rate tactician to guide a charge upon it. But as this is not the case, and nothing short of strategic skill and bravery, superior to any yet employed against it, can succeed, why the expedition of the great Dix is an absurdity.—We begin to suspect that Dickinson suggested it to Lincoln and caused it to be determined upon, in order to wind up his old rival. He could not adopt a better plan to settle his hash, and a New York politician could hardly forego so good an opportunity to use up an enemy!

Vicksburg Fallen—A Trick.

The Yankees, desirous of infusing a little extra spirit into their soldiers, hit upon the expedient of reviving the old story that Vicksburg had fallen! How to do it was the question. There was some reluctance among the liars to venture forth with that stale falsehood. In this strait the story was ingeniously palmed off upon "a Captain of Marines!" They knew the marines would swallow it, and by reprinting the story it might help on a little the excitement in the army. In starting the report they profited by the old adage—"tell it to the *marines*, the *sailors* know better." The following is the dispatch:

REPORTED CAPTURE OF VICKSBURG.

PHILADELPHIA, July 3.—The *Inquirer* has the following posted on their bulletin board:

"A dispatch from Washington has just been received at the Navy-Yard, and read to the workmen, that Vicksburg has surrendered.

[*Second Dispatch*]

PHILADELPHIA, July 3.—At noon to-day a Captain of the marines, at the Navy-Yard, read a dispatch to the men announcing the capture of Vicksburg.

Health of the President.

Much concern has been felt for several days relative to the health of President Davis.—He has recently had a severe attack, and his health being indifferent at best, and he having been heavily taxed by the cares and duties of his office, it was reasonable that great anxiety should be entertained for his situation. We are gratified to be able to state that he is now convalescent, and not only able to leave his bed, but to walk about his house. He is recovering rapidly, and will, in a day or two, it is hoped, enjoy his usual strength.

The Southwest

The capture of Brashear City by General Taylor is one of the most important blows that has been struck in the Southwest since the war commenced. It is but ten miles above the city of New Orleans, and if it be held, as it can be, it will be impossible to feed the city by means of the Mississippi. Everywhere in Louisiana our forces seem to be clearing the scoundrels out. We hope to see the Confederate flag waving over New Orleans before the summer is over.

Auditor of West Virginia

The *Sentinel* of Saturday published a letter written in July of last year by Samuel Crane, the Auditor of the fraudulent Government of West Virginia. He is a very fit person for such a Government. He was Auditor under Pierpoint, who claimed to be Governor of Virginia from the Ohio to the sea, and was a suitable companion for Pierpont. He was elected to the same office under the new Government just established, with Boreman, of Taylor county, at its head. The letter was captured by one of our men in a recent expedition to Northwestern Virginia. It is addressed to William Bennett, Clerk of Randolph county. After some business matters, he says:

"The delinquent sales of 1860 you need not copy. I may need it, or may find it at Richmond, as soon as McClellan opens the door, which I know he will in a few days."

Crane, deeming the door as good as opened, proceeded in a most authoritative manner to indoctrinate Bennett with the proper feelings and policy towards guerillas and unsound persons—i. e., those who were loyal to Virginia. He says:

> I labored hard to return troops to Randolph, and I hope now you will all aid in capturing Bill Harper and other guerilla parties. You all have no other trouble in Randolph but guerillas. Let none be made prisoners, nor any that aid them.
>
> Petition no more for the return of prisoners unless it be in a more justifiable case. Let those who have not been sound remain in prison. It is far better that they and their friends should suffer than guerilla parties should receive aid or sympathy from any.—The Union men did not bring on the war, and let those who did suffer. They would gladly have put in prison, or to death, if they could only have carried their point.
>
> My best regards to my Union friends. The *Secesh* I do not care a *curse* for.
>
> Your friend, SAMUEL CRANE.

This is a very pretty record to treasure up against the immaculate and virtuous Auditor. "Let none be made prisoners," quoth he. He will assuredly stick to this injunction himself, as his flight to Ohio some day not far off will prove. Those same guerillas may audit their account with him before our own army reaches Wheeling.

Personal

Vice President Stephens, it is said, has gone to Fortress Monroe by the flag of truce boat. One story is that his business is to see about the exchange of prisoners, and another that it is to inform the Federal Government that if private property is not respected in the Confederate States, and the rules of civilized warfare strictly complied with, our forces in the North will receive instructions to retaliate in kind.

EUROPEAN NEWS

The steamship Hecla, from Queenstown, 17th ult., arrived at New York on the 29th.—The following summary is of the news from the *Herald*

Lord Palmerston, during a speech at Guildhall, London, stated that France and England were on accord in all questions "of peace or war on the East or on the West."

Earl Russel stated in the House of Lords that the blockade maintained by the American fleet was sufficiently efficient to entitle it to be observed. He believed also that there was every desire on the part of the American Government to prevent injustice from being done to neutrals.

The London *Times* anticipates that the Emperor of France "delivered from the Mexican war," will make his "powerful voice" heard in America in favor of peace.

The official report of the fall of Puebla caused much joy to Napoleon. He forwarded a letter of thanks to Gen. Forey, in which he disclaims the idea of a permanent rule by conquest. The order for reinforcements for the army was countermanded.

The Polish patriots had gained other victories over the Russians in the field. It is said that Napoleon's intentions on the subject of the revolution are pacific towards Europe, but the situation was still very serious.

THE MOVEMENT ON RICHMOND.

RAID ON ASHLAND.

The Yankees continue their movement on Richmond. They did not, however, attack the South Anna bridge, on the R. F. & Potomac R. R., Friday night, as was reported.—They came up through King William county, on the other side of the Pamunkey, as far as Littlepage, which is three miles from the bridge above named, but did not cross the river. The "heavy firing" heard in the direction of Hanover Junction by citizens here Friday night, turns out to have been a thunder storm which visited that place.

The force at the White House, or a great part of it, has gone to Barhamsville, about two and a half miles from New Kent C. H. This is a movement to the rear. On Saturday night they sent forward a small force and drive our pickets in at the Cross-Roads. Barhamsville is about 28 miles from Richmond, on the stage road. Two or three gunboats are still at the White House.

To ascertain anything reliable with reference to the operations of the enemy in the vicinity of Hanover, is exceedingly difficult. All we know is that they were in King William and Hanover counties, in heavy force, on Saturday and yesterday, and that they were unsparingly destroying the recently harvested crops in those counties, appropriating what stock was left from their former raids, and running off the negroes.

On Saturday night, about 12 o'clock, a small body of their cavalry, not over one hundred in number, made a raid upon Ashland, where they burned the station-house, wood-house and water tank, and tore up a small portion of the railroad track. This feat was accomplished without meeting any resistance, our military authorities not regarding that point of sufficient consequence to be provided with a guard. The raiders remained till nearly daylight yesterday morning, when they left, perhaps making their way back to their main body without meeting with a Confederate soldier.

The whole demonstration of the enemy is now beginning to develope itself as a reckless raid, to destroy what they can, and inflict all the mischief possible on our lines of communication.

Later.

A gentleman who left this city as an independent scout, on Saturday afternoon, and who left Hanover Court-House at half past 12 o'clock yesterday, has furnished us the following: About 7 o'clock on Saturday afternoon, he arrived at Hawes's shop, in Hanover, about 7 miles distant from the Court House. Upon inquiry, he could hear of no Yankees being in the county, save two who had crossed the river at Hanover Town Ferry, and who returned to the King William side without venturing very far. From Hawes's shop our informant went to within 2½ miles of the Court-House, where he received information from a reliable source that the enemy were in some force at the Court-House during the afternoon—their force consisting of infantry, artillery and cavalry. He also learned that they had taken the road leading to Ashland, leaving a picket force at the Court-House, and stationing a heavy picket about a mile distant, in the direction of Hawes's shop.

Finding it impossible to get to the Court-House, and being advised in the neighborhood not to stay at any house, our scout and one or two associates bivouacked for the night in a woods, about half a mile distant from the first line of the enemy's pickets. Between 9 and 10 o'clock they heard heavy firing in the direction of South Anna Bridge, which continued at intervals until after 2 o'clock yesterday morning. He could not distinguish anything but artillery firing, though he thinks there may have been infantry engaged.

On Sunday morning, ascertaining that the pickets had been withdrawn, with his party he cautiously proceeded in the direction of the Court-House; upon reaching which he found the enemy had left; and, also, that the force that had taken the Ashland road the evening previous had returned and recrossed the river at Littlepage's bridge. On their return they were heard to remark that they had not found the capture of Hanover Junction as easy a matter as they had anticipated. Along the road they asked for milk for their wounded, from which it is inferred they sustained injury by the firing the night before.

Leaving the Court-House, our informant went down to Littlepage's bridge, which he reached in time to see it enveloped in flames, the enemy destroying it after them. From a prominent position he could see, on the King William side of the river, a train of wagons, extending, he thinks, over a mile in length.—This train, he was informed by citizens, had been there a day or two.

At Hanover Court-House he was informed by a reliable citizen that the force of the enemy that passed that point on Saturday afternoon consisted of eight regiments of infantry, four companies of cavalry, and two pieces of artillery. He is confident that at 1 o'clock yesterday there was not a Yankee in Hanover county, unless as a prisoner.

Information received in the city from other sources, states that the enemy attacked South Anna bridge at 8 o'clock on Saturday evening, killing two of our men, wounding several, and taking eleven prisoners. They were repulsed, but with reinforcements renewed the attack at 1 o'clock yesterday morning, when they were again repulsed and driven off, with what loss is not known.

THE COTTON TRADE TO NASSAU.

The following is a statement of the receipts of cotton at Nassau by steamers from Charleston, Wilmington, Savannah, and other Confederate ports, from January 1st to June 24th, 1863:

Total by steamers from Charleston, Wilmington and Savannah	28 704
Received by sailing vessels from Atlantic ports	667
Received from Matamoras	2 704
Grand Total	32,075

The following is a statement of the exports of cotton from January 1st to June 24th, 1863:

Exported to European ports	23,817 bales.
Exported to ports in the United States	2 695 bales
Total exports	26,412 bales.
On hand	5 663 bales.

It will be seen from the statement of receipts of cotton in Nassau that 2,704 bales came from Matamoras, in Mexico. This cotton is all transhipped to New York by the firms who are engaged in the Matamoras trade. Since Jan. 1st, 2,381 bales of this Matamoras cotton has been shipped to the North, and 313 bales, a late arrival, remain on hand. By subtracting the exports of Matamoras cotton from the general cotton exports, we shall arrive at the following:

Exported to European ports	23,817 bales.
Exported to ports in U. States	264 bales.

It is presumed that none of the cotton sent to Bermuda finds its way to the United States, unless it is transhipped from England, which is not likely now, as it commands a better price in Liverpool than in New York.

The only steamers laden with cotton captured by the Yankees this year were the Douro and Cherokee. The sailing vessels captured have been much more numerous.

LATER FROM THE NORTH.

We are under obligations to the Signal Corps for Northern papers of the 29th and 30th ult. The most important news it contains is the removal of Fighting Joe Hooker from the command of the Army of the Potomac at his own request. The following is Gen. Hooker's farewell address to the Army of the Potomac:

HEAD'QRS ARMY OF THE POTOMAC,
Frederick, Md., June 28, 1863.

General Orders, No 65.

In conformity with the orders of the War Department, dated June 27, 1863, I relinquish the command of the Army of the Potomac. It is transferred to Major-General George G. Meade, a brave and accomplished officer, who has nobly earned the confidence and esteem of the army on many a well-fought field. Impressed with the belief that my usefulness as the commander of the Army of the Potomac is impaired, I part from it, yet not without the deepest emotion. The sorrow of parting with the comrades of so many battles is relieved by the conviction that the courage and devotion of this army will never cease nor fail; that it will yield to my successor, as it has to me, a willing and hearty support. With the earnest prayer that the triumph of its arms may bring successes worthy of it and the nation, I bid it farewell.

JOSEPH HOOKER, Major-General.

The *Herald*, in a double-leaded editorial announces the retirement of Gen. Hooker and the appointment of Gen. Meade "with no ordinary feelings of gratification." It eulogizes Gen. Meade's military qualifications and forbears to "deal harshly" with Gen. Hooker, who has displayed his patriotism by requesting to be relieved of the command of the Army of the Potomac.

A telegram from headquarters says that "nothing could have exceeded the surprise occasioned by this announcement"—the change of commanders. "Gen. Hooker was deeply grieved," etc.

A dispatch from Washington to the *Herald*, dated the 29th, says the main reason for the removal of Hooker, was a radical difference of opinion between him and Gen. Halleck as to the value of Maryland Heights as a military position during the present active operations.

Hooker was the sixth commander of the Army of the Potomac.

The following is the situation article from the *Herald*, of the 29th:

The enemy is pressing closely upon Harrisburg. Gen. Lee's whole army is undoubtedly in Pennsylvania. His own headquarters are at Hagerstown, Md., from which he is directing the movements. Gen. Longstreet's corps crossed near Williamsport on Saturday. A great battle is impending at Harrisburg today. Last night the rebels were within three miles of the city, and heavy firing was going on all day. This was probably the outposts, skirmishing as the enemy advanced.

Mechanicsburg was surrendered by our troops yesterday morning, and immediately occupied by the rebels. They also took possession of York, our troops clearing out before them. They have done serious damage to the Northern Central Railroad, both at York and Hanover Junction. They have burnt two bridges at York Haven. The splendid bridge across the Susquehanna at Columbia, a mile and a quarter long, which cost a million of dollars, was burned by our troops under Col. Frick, yesterday.

The utmost consternation prevails throughout the State of Pennsylvania, and at last there appears to be a disposition on the part of the people to rally for their defence. Fugitives, however, keep pouring into Harrisburg, Lancaster, and other cities, in a state of complete terror, bringing their cattle, merchandise and household goods with them.

The rebel Gen. Ewell has issued an order to his troops at Chambersburg, urging the necessity of vigilance and discipline in the safety of the army, and prohibiting all straggling, marauding, or plundering, on pain of the severest penalties. He says that all the material aid the army requires will be taken under the military rules which govern civilized warfare, and absolutely prohibits all individual interference with private property.

A train of one hundred wagons, loaded with supplies, and nine hundred mules, were captured by the rebels near Rockville, Md., yesterday. Several officers, who were on their way to join their regiments, were also captured.

A rebel force, which is said to be 7,000 strong, and composed of three brigades of cavalry, is reported to be moving eastward towards the Washington branch of the Baltimore and Ohio Railroad. They are reported to be commanded by Fitzhugh Lee. It has been ascertained that they passed within 14 miles of Washington, on the north side, and it is presumed that they are striking for the trestle work upon the railroad between the capital and Annapolis Junction.

Refugees who arrived yesterday report that quite a panic exists in Richmond. Only a very small guard was left there, and many of the citizens were leaving and going to Staunton.

The clergymen in Philadelphia have offered their services to the Mayor to work on the fortifications.

From the White House, on the Pamunkey river, we learn the full details of Col. Spears's operation to the South Anna, the capture of the rebel General Fitzhugh Lee, a rebel Colonel, a blockade-running Captain, and over two hundred other prisoners. Lee was captured at the house of a friend while he was trying to recover from his wound received at Kelly's Ford. A skirmish occurred at Hanover C. H., where our troops came out conquerors. A rebel baggage train on the way to Richmond, and of great value, was captured and destroyed, and with over a thousand saddles.

The *Herald*, of the 30th, has the following:

The enemy had not advanced on Harrisburg at latest accounts. Skirmishing at various points on the south side of the Susquehanna was going on yesterday, at Oysterville and Maysville especially. All our forces were within the defences at sunset yesterday. The rebels had torn up the track at Marriottsville and Sykesville, thirty-one miles from Baltimore. The damage at the latter place is but slight.

General Early has levied on the authorities of York for $150,000 in greenbacks, 40,000 pounds of fresh beef, 200 barrels of flour, 30,000 bushels of corn, 1,000 pairs each of shoes, stockings, coats, and hats, 50 bags of coffee, and large quantities of sugar and groceries. Gen. Early says "we will occupy the place permanently."

The defenders in the entrenchments at Harrisburg are prepared for an attack to-day.

The enemy is reported crossing the river at Bainbridge on pontoons, with the intention of cutting the Pennsylvania Central Railroad.

The greatest alarm and activity prevail in Philadelphia. The Mayor and Gen. Dana have issued stirring proclamations, appealing to citizens to prepare to defend their homes. There was a great panic in stock yesterday. The coal dealers held a meeting, and resolved to close their collieries until the crisis has passed, to enable the miners to volunteer. The merchants resolved to raise one million dollars for home defence. The Board of Brokers raised $25,000, to be divided among five hundred men, who may enlist for the emergency. A line of entrenchments will be commenced around the city of Philadelphia to-morrow. The splendid bridge over the Susquehanna at Columbia, valued at $157,000, was burnt on the 28th, to keep the rebels out of the town.

The rebel cavalry are committing considerable depredations upon cattle and horses around Washington city, at Drainesville and Long Bridge. They have also made their appearance at numerous points in Montgomery county, Md., on Sunday and yesterday, seizing all of the finest horses to take the place of their jaded animals.

Some few of them showed themselves as near Washington as Silver Spring, five miles from the city. They stopped the stage which connects with the railroad at Laurel, and took the horses.

The army of Rosecrans continues to advance at different gaps of mountains. His forces have had severe skirmishing with the enemy, in every case with success. The rebel Gen. Cleburne is reported killed at Liberty Gap.

The latest news from Vicksburg is to the 22d of June. The cannonading on the 20th was terrific from the army and the gunboats. The siege was progressing favorably.

The movements of General Johnston continue wrapt in mystery. He has gone beyond the Big Black, and is reported to be moving South. All the rivers and streams are rising.

All the bonds given by captains of captured vessels to the commander of the privateer Tacony have been found on board the schooner Archer, and are now in possession of the authorities.

Gold is quoted in New York at $1 47½; middling cotton 71.

THE LATEST.

GREAT BATTLE AT GETTYSBURG.

The Yankees Claim Not to be Defeated and to have Captured Six Thousand Prisoners—The Confederates Hold the Field—Yankee Generals Reynolds and Paul Killed—Heavy Loss of the Federals—The Grand Battle Expected Friday, &c., &c.

We are indebted to the courtesy of Dr. W. W. MACLURE for a Baltimore *American* of Friday evening last, the 3d inst. It gives the particulars of an important battle fought on Wednesday and Thursday last, between our troops under Generals Longstreet and Hill, and the enemy under Gen. Reynolds, who was killed. We give a summary of the news:

THE FIRST DAY'S BATTLE.

The Baltimore *American* has the following account of the first day's battle:

It appears that at 9 o'clock on Wednesday morning, (the 1st inst.,) the 1st and 11th corps of the Army of the Potomac reached Gettysburg, entering from the East side of the town, and marching directly through to the west side, the cavalry force of the enemy falling back as we advanced. On passing out of the West end of the town, the enemy was observed advancing rapidly from the Chambersburg pike, in line of battle, toward the town, evidently endeavoring to hold an advantageous position commanding the town. The first corps, under Gen. Reynolds, was in the advance, and pushed forward at double quick to secure the advantageous position. The enemy, under Longstreet and Hill, advanced steadily, and in a few minutes a heavy fire, both of artillery and musketry, was opened along the whole Federal and Rebel lines. The 11th army corps, under Gen. Howard, was also soon in position, and for a time a heavy battle raged. Several charges were made by the enemy to dislodge our forces, all of which were unsuccessful.

At 3 o'clock the enemy massed his entire forces and endeavored to turn our right wing. Gen. Reynolds advanced to meet them and a heavy infantry fight ensued, in which both parties suffered severely, volley after volley of musketry being poured into the opposing columns with deadly effect. In the charge Maj. Gen. Reynolds fell, mortally wounded, and died soon after being conveyed to Gettysburg. He was, as usual, leading his corps, and in the thickest of the fight. Gen. Paul, commanding the 3d brigade of the 1st army corps, was also killed on the field, and Cols. Wistar and Stone fell, severely wounded, and were taken prisoners by the enemy. The field between the contending armies was strewn with the dead and wounded, and it is said that the enemy suffered fully as heavily as we did, though it is not known what was their loss in officers.

The effort to flank our right wing entirely failed, and we held the prominent and commanding position for which the struggle was made at the close of the fight, which ceased for the day about 4 o'clock in the afternoon.—At this time two more corps of Gen. Meade's army reached the field, and during the night the main body of our army was in position to meet any demonstrations that the enemy might make in the morning, or to advance on him, as the Commanding General might decide.—The 1st army corps nobly maintained its position against the effort to flank its right, and scarcely faltered for a moment, when its gallant General fell, before the onslaught of the enemy. A great and decisive battle was considered imminent, and, notwithstanding our severe loss in officers, the advantages of the day were regarded as decidedly with our forces.

The army was in fine condition, full of enthusiasm for the coming battle, and confident of success. General Meade had also, it was thought, concentrated his forces to a greater extent than the enemy, a large portion of whose army was still scattered up through the Cumberland Valley.

Col. Wistar commanded the Pennsylvania "Bucktails," and Col. Stone also commanded a Pennsylvania regiment, and both were in the 2d brigade of the 1st army corps. Col. S., at the time of receiving his wound, was acting as Brigadier-General of the brigade. General Newton took command of the 1st army corps on the fall of Gen. Reynolds.

Gen. Paul commanded the 3d brigade of the same corps, and was a most efficient officer.

Some gentlemen connected with the press who arrived here last (Thursday) evening, from Gettysburg, having left before daylight in the morning, represent the condition of affairs at the close of the fight on Wednesday evening to have been still more favorable and promising of a successful issue than the previous information we had received. They state that the rebels had held Gettysburg for some time previous to the approach of our army, and had not only occupied but had commenced fortifying the hills west of the town, where they proposed to check our advance towards Chambersburg and the mouth of the Cumberland Valley.

The movement of Gen. Reynolds and the rapidity with which he advanced after entering the East end of the town took them somewhat by surprise, and he soon obtained the prominent position which the rebels were fortifying. The fighting through the balance of the day was in a futile attempt on their part to regain this important position, from which they were frequently repulsed.

Early in the afternoon both Longstreet and Hill combined their forces for a grand effort to turn our right flank, when Gen. Howard's 11th corps, (the Dutch corps,) which broke and ran at Chancellorsville, dashed in to regain their lost laurels, and most nobly did they repulse these two veteran corps of the rebel army. The repulse was so complete that no further attempt was made by the enemy during the balance of the day, and night closed in with our holding the position chosen by the enemy to give us battle from. The 3d and 12th army corps also came on the field after the last repulse of the enemy, but owing to the fall of Gen. Reynolds, and the lateness of the hour, as well as the exhaustion of the men, and the desire to take care of the wounded, it was *determined not to push the enemy for a renewal of the conflict.*

When our informant left the field yesterday (Thursday) morning, Gen. Meade had arrived, and the main body of our army was in position, ready to push the enemy so soon as day should dawn.

Gettysburg is just 25 miles east of Chambersburg, over a fine rolling country most of the way, which will doubtless be the scene of the great battle of the rebel invasion.

From one of the officers who came down in charge of prisoners, who arrived last night, who left Gettysburg Wednesday afternoon, we have accounts *not so favorable as those given by other parties*. He describes the fight on that day *as rather unfavorable to our arms, and states that the enemy held the field at the close of the day, our forces having fallen back after the fall of Gen. Reynolds*; that the attack of the enemy was so sudden and unexpected that both the corps of Hill and Longstreet were for a time engaged with Gen. Reynolds's corps, and that the 11th corps took but little part in the battle.

THE SECOND DAY'S FIGHTING.

The *American* learns from parties that left Gettysburg at noon Thursday, that up to that time everything was progressing favorably for the Federal arms. It says:

Up to that time they assert that over *six thousand prisoners had been captured*, and sent to Union Bridge for transportation to Baltimore. At nine o'clock last night a train with 800 prisoners, the first instalment of those captured, arrived at the Baltimore depot, and shortly after Gen. Schenck announced from his headquarters that those then in Baltimore and at the Relay House, which would soon be in his possession, amounted to 2,300. We learn that nearly 1,000 of these prisoners were captured on Wednesday evening by the 11th army corps in their gallant charge on Longstreet's corps. They are said to have at first slightly faltered, but their officers cried to them to "remember Chancellorsville," when they rushed into the fight with a fury that was irresistible, and the whole line of the enemy gave way before them.

During the early part of Thursday, up to noon, at which hour our informant left, there had been no general battle, though heavy skirmishing had been going on all the morning, resulting in heavy loss to the enemy and the capture of nearly 5,000 prisoners. In all these skirmishes, which were conducted under the direction of Gen. Meade, our arms were entirely successful; but the enemy studiously avoided a general engagement, and it was thought there would be none before to-day, when it was said to be the intention of Gen. Meade to press the enemy along the whole line.

The prudence and skill displayed by Gen. Meade in the management of his army and the strategy evinced by him in coping with Lee, had already won the confidence of his troops, and his presence along the lines drew forth the strongest demonstrations of attachment. The army evinced a determination to win at all hazards, and had been strongly impressed by their officers with the dreadful consequences that would ensue to them and the country if a disaster should occur to our arms in the coming conflict.

The *enemy was rapidly concentrating his troops yesterday from the Cumberland Valley towards Chambersburg, and General Meade's whole army had reached the field of battle.*—If Gen. Couch presses on the enemy down the Valley with his troops from Harrisburg, which is confidently expected, we may look for a glorious result.

THE FIGHTING ON WEDNESDAY—FURTHER PARTICULARS.

A correspondent of the Philadelphia *Inquirer*, writing under date of Wednesday, July 1, 8 o'clock A. M., says:

This morning, early, the First and Eleventh army corps, which had been during the night encamped near Emmettsburg, advanced—the 1st corps marching in the following order: 1st division, under Gen. Wadsworth; 3d division, Gen Doubleday; these followed by five full batteries under Col. Wainwright: bringing up the rear was the really splendid division of Gen. Robinson—this corps having been in the advance during the whole time of our march from Falmouth, were the first force of infantry to reach Gettysburg, and to come up with and fight the enemy.

During the day this corps had been under the direction of Gen. Doubleday, Gen Reynolds being in command of the right wing, comprising the 1st, 3d, 11th and 12th corps.

When some three miles from town, and while quietly marching along, the sound of heavy and rapid cannon firing was heard coming from the direction beyond Gettysburg. Almost at the same instant Capt Mitchell, a gallant aid upon Gen. Reynolds's staff, came dashing down the road with orders to the various division commanders to push forward their divisions as rapidly as possible. The order was given to *double quick*, which was instantly obeyed, and kept up until the intervening space where our batteries were engaged was passed over. These batteries, two in number, were a part of the artillery belonging to General Buford's division, and were stationed some half a mile to the South of the Gettysburg Theological Seminary, while the opposing force were stationed and strongly entrenched upon the East side of Marsh Creek, and about the same distance from the Seminary as were our own forces.—The latter was the first to open fire, and were for a time compelling our batteries to retire from their position. This they were quietly doing, and in good order, when the division of Gen Wadsworth came to their support, the two sole regiments, the 2d Wisconsin and 24th Michigan, rushing up and driving from in front of them the infantry force who were making desperate efforts to capture the pieces. When these supports arrived the batteries again took up a commanding position, which they were enabled to hold during the day.

In rear of the position so taken up, and to the right, the division of Gen. Wadsworth was drawn up in line of battle, with the division of General Robinson holding the second [illegible] their partial success in driving from position the batteries, attempted another charge, with the object of seizing the pieces, when the brigades of the 2d division, with fixed bayonets, made a charge upon them, and such as were not killed were taken prisoners. Two entire regiments—a Tennessee and Mississippi regiment—were then bagged.

Immediately after the arrival and going into position of the first corps, the eleventh, under the amiable and brave Gen. Howard, who had been in the rear and marching on the same road as the first made their appearance, marched directly through the town and at once formed a line of battle on the right of the Chambersburg road and some half a mile west of the college, which is located at the extreme end of the town. After some three hours of artillery duelling the rebels commenced to retire. There were massed two infantry corps, and in this formation a pursuit of their retreating column was commenced. After driving them back towards the mountain, something over a mile, soon after four o'clock it was discovered that with an extensive force of infantry and cavalry, they were endeavoring to turn our left flank, with a view probably to get between us and our supply trains. Before this being noticed, and it being evident that our reinforcements, the 3d and 12th corps, who had been anxiously inquired after during the entire day, were not yet up, no other alternative was offered us than to retire to the East of the town, and take up a better position upon the top of a hill and along the line of road leading to Emmettsburg. This was done, but in admirable order, no unusual haste being apparent, while at the same time all ammunition and supply wagons as were up to the front were sent to the rear.

A little after 4 o'clock the 3d corps, under command of General Sickles, came upon the field, and went into position upon the left of that held early in the morning by the 1st corps. The Twelfth, under General Slocumb, as well, arrived about the same time, and were stationed upon the right of the 11th corps. After those two corps, as well as those who had borne the heat and burthen of the day, were formed in battle array, they made an advance, and with but little resistance succeeded in driving the rebels from the town, and back into the position they first occupied early in the morning. In this manner, and in these locations, both armies are resting for the night.

The Second, Fifth, and Sixth Corps are moving this way, and by morning will be up and ready to do battle with us.

While the later mentioned movement was being made, the enemy kept up a continual rain of shot and shell upon the town, and when ceasing their cavalry dashed through the town, capturing all stray parties there congregated, together with the wounded, who were occupants of, and the surgeons and nurses who were in attendance in, the many hastily organized hospitals there located.—While the firing was in progress some few buildings were set on fire, but the town not being compactly built only such buildings as were struck by the shells were consumed.

A REBEL BRIGADE CAPTURED.

They also made an effort to capture a wagon train on the left and rear, and in attempting this movement nearly a whole brigade of rebels were captured, among them Brigadier General Archer, of the Rebel Army, formerly of the United States Army.

So rapidly were the rebels reinforced with fresh troops in their attempt to turn the left of the first corps that it obliged the order to be given to fall back a distance of perhaps a mile, fighting the whole time.

GEN. REYNOLDS KILLED.

While personally gallantly leading the first bayonet charge made by Gen. Wadsworth's division, the noble, popular and gallant Major-General John F. Reynolds received a wound which, in less than hour's time, resulted in death. The missile which robbed us of one of the brightest ornaments of our army, as well as one of its bravest and most useful members, was the sharp-pointed Minie rifle ball, it having entered the back of the neck, coming out at the temple.

Among other prominent officers killed is found the name of Gen. Paul. Gen. Wadsworth is severely wounded. Gen. Robinson, for the third time, had a horse shot under him. While among the names of officers of less rank who are more or less wounded, are found those of Col. Bates, of the 12th Massachusetts; Col. Leonard, of the 13th Massachusetts; Col. Fairchild, of the 2d Wisconsin; Col. Root, of the 94th New York; Capt. Robt. Williams, of the 12th Massachusetts; Lt. Thomas, Acting Aid to Gen. Baxter; Capt. Cane. Hovey, of the 12th Mass., Aid to Gen. Robinson, and Adjt. Weaver, 9th Penn.

Among those captured are the names of Dr. Nordquist, Medical Director of Robinson's division, and Capt. Fred. Gerker, of Philadelphia, of the same division. In the confusion occasioned by the charge of cavalry, and our approach to many hospitals being cut off, it is impossible to obtain a correct list of casualties. Our losses, though, are enormously heavy, especially among field and line officers. Neither are we warranted in guessing how seriously the rebels have suffered.

Of the rebels nothing definite as to their numerical strength is here positively known; at least, if known, is not stated, some placing their entire strength in Pennsylvania at 80,000, others at 125,000.

Our scouts report that to-night Hill is reinforcing the enemy, and that they are moving down the mountain by three different roads.—Their position to-day was one of unusual excellence, and selected with the same eye to natural defence and strength which has ever characterized them—upon the side of a broad running stream, and with a high mountain back of them; their artillery upon the hill side in a position one above the other, like seats in the parquette of a theatre.

THE FEDERAL GEN. REYNOLDS.

The Federal General, John Fulton Reynolds, who was killed in the battle at Gettysburg on Wednesday last, was born in Lancaster, Pa., and at the age of 17 entered the Military Academy at West Point, where he graduated in 1841, just 21 years of age, and received a commission as brevet 2d Lieutenant in the Third Artillery. In the Mexican war he was brevetted Captain and Major for gallant conduct in the battles of Monterey and Buena Vista. Subsequently he was an Aid-de-Camp to Gen. Wool. In 1855 he was promoted to a full Captaincy in his regiment, and served with some distinction in the severe battles with the Oregon Indians in 1856.

In August, 1861, he was appointed to the rank of Brigadier-General of Volunteers, and took command of one of the three brigades of the Pennsylvania Reserves, under Gen. McCall, the other two being under command of Gen. Meade, now in command of the Yankee Army of the Potomac, and Gen. Ord, who recently succeeded Gen. McClernand at Vicksburg. With this division Gen. Reynolds took part in nearly all the great battles in Virginia. Having been sent down to the Peninsula and marched to the front around Richmond, he was posted with his brigade on the extreme right of the Federal line, and, with McCall and Meade, sustained the first onslaught on McClellan's army at Mechanicsville. He was in all of the seven days' fight around this city, except the engagement at Malvern Hill, having the day previous been taken prisoner with General McCall and brought to this city.

After his release he took command of the division of Pennsylvania reserves and led them in Pope's disastrous campaign. Soon after the close of that campaign he was summoned by the Governor of Pennsylvania to the command of the militia raised for the defence of that State in September, 1862. When Gen. Lee recrossed the Potomac Reynolds rejoined his command in the Federal army and marched with it to Fredericksburg, where he was subsequently advanced to the command of the first army corps, having meanwhile been made Major-General by Lincoln. He commanded that corps in the fights at Fredericksburg and Chancellorsville. He is represented by the Northern press to have been a thorough, accomplished, and brave soldier.

THE CONFEDERATE EVACUATION OF CHAMBERSBURG—A PORTION OF THE PLACE BURNT.

The Confederates evacuated Carlisle, Pa., on the morning of the 1st inst., leaving on the Baltimore pike. During their stay they levied on the place for 25,000 lbs bacon, 100 sacks salt, 1,500 bbls flour, 5,000 lbs. each of coffee and sugar, 25,000 lbs dried fruit, 25 bbls molasses, 300 ounces quinine, 90 lbs. chloroform, 50 lbs. opium, &c., besides which they "generally took what they wanted." They destroyed the railroad bridge at the place, and among other outrages, Gen. Jenkins had the Manor Hotel searched, and seized a cold turkey for his dinner. [illegible] had a regular mail communication with Richmond while they occupied the town, and two mails were distributed. After they left in the morning, Gen. Smith (Federal) occupied the place in the evening, but a force of the rebels returned, and by shelling the place burnt the U. S barracks and the gas house.

THE VERY LATEST

The *American*, in its evening edition of the 3d inst., gives the following dispatches:

A special dispatch to the New York *Herald*, dated Hamburg, 2d, says: "The battle at Gettysburg to-day was fierce and bloody, and from all I can gather the rebel army has received its mortal wound. Cannon, small arms, and the field, are among the trophies. A column of rebels, 25,000 strong, passed through Dillsbury yesterday in the direction of Gettysburg.

ALBANY, July 2.—A dispatch from Gov. Curtin to Gov. Seymour was received to-day stating that *the battle at Gettysburg had not been decisive, and asking him to send all the troops he could raise without delay, as the need for them was pressing.*

PHILADELPHIA, July 3.—Parties arriving here from Gettysburg say that on Wednesday 10,000 of our troops were engaged with 30,000 of the enemy. During Wednesday night 75,000 men of Gen. Meade's troops came up and took favorable positions, while 25,000 other Union troops were near at hand. The rebels had mainly concentrated near Gettysburg on Wednesday night, and there is little doubt but the great battle of yesterday would involve every available man in both armies.

STATE OF AFFAIRS IN BALTIMORE—AMERICAN FLAGS TO BE DISPLAYED—THE MARYLAND CLUB DISPERSED.

Gen Schenck had issued an order that every "loyal" citizen of Baltimore should, on the 4th of July, display upon his house an U. S. flag from 10 A. M until 6 P. M. He issued an order the day before, seizing all the arms of any sort in the possession of the citizens.

Gen. Schenck also, on Thursday, closed the "Maryland Club House." The *American* says it was the rendezvous of the elite of secession in Baltimore, and was so exclusive that in six years only 352 visitors had been admitted there. Among them were Vallandigham, Voorhies, John C. Breckinridge, Marquis of Harlington, Bright of Indiana, and R. T. Merrick of Chicago. Among the members of the Club were Wm. Key Howard, S. Teackle Wallis, H. B. Latrobe, and others. A military guard was placed by the Yankees over the building. Several bundles of Vallandigham's speeches were found in the building.

DISPATCH FROM ROSECRANS ANNOUNCING THE OCCUPATION OF TULLAHOMA

The Washington papers publish the following telegram from Gen. Rosecrans:

HEADQUARTERS, TULLAHOMA, TENN., July 1.—I telegraphed you on Monday the occupation of Shelbyville and Manchester. On Monday it rained hard all day, rendering the roads impassable. It was found impossible to move our artillery or get our troops into position until this morning, when a general advance was ordered at daylight.

Gen. Thomas yesterday made a reconnoissance on two roads, and Gen. McCook on one road, reporting the enemy in force at this place, with the addition of Buckner's division, which arrived Monday evening.

On advancing this morning it was found that the enemy had fled in haste last night, much demoralized. Their strong fortifications, a small quantity of stores, and three siege guns in our possession.

They took the direction of Winchester.—Gen. Thomas should be on their right flank to-night. Gens. Sheridan and Brannan marched into town to-day at 11½ o'clock, taking a few prisoners.

W. S. ROSECRANS,
Major-General.

[A telegram from Atlanta, Ga., in another column of the *Dispatch*, dated the 3d instant, says that Rosecrans is falling back and Bragg re-occupying Tullahoma in heavy force.]

LATEST FROM VICKSBURG—EXPLOSION OF A MINE.

The Vicksburg correspondent of the St. Louis *Democrat* says that on the 25th ult. a mine was exploded, which was followed by a charge of the 45th Illinois, who rushed into the breach and planted their flag. Lieut. Col. Smith and Major Fish were killed in the

Evening Star.

Vol. XXII. WASHINGTON, D. C., MONDAY, JULY 6, 1863. No. 3,231.

THE EVENING STAR
IS PUBLISHED EVERY AFTERNOON.
(SUNDAY EXCEPTED,)
AT THE STAR BUILDINGS,
Corner Penn'a Avenue and 11th Street,
BY
W. D. WALLACH.

Papers served without wrappers by carriers 1 cent per copy, or 25 cents per month. In packages by carriers at $4 a year, or 37 cents per month. To mail subscribers the price is $4.50 a year, in advance; $2.50 for six months; $1.25 for three months; and for less than three months at the rate of 12 cents a week. Single copies, with or without wrappers, TWO CENTS.

☞ Advertisements should be sent to the office before 11 o'clock m.; otherwise they may not appear until the next day.

PROPOSALS.

PROPOSALS FOR WOOD AND COAL.

Post Office Department,
Washington, June 24, 1863.

Sealed proposals will be received by the undersigned until 12 o'clock M., on Wednesday, the 8th day of July, for furnishing for the use of this Department—
400 tons (2,240 lbs. to the ton) of the best White Ash Coal, furnace size.
50 tons Red Ash, same size, and
250 cords best seasoned Oak Wood.
Parties will be at liberty to bid for the Wood and Coal together, or for either one separately, and their bids will be considered accordingly.
Satisfactory arrangements must be made to secure to the Government full weight and measure.
The Wood is to be corded and measured upon the premises, and one half is to be sawed into three pieces and the other half into two, and all to be piled away in the cellar.
The Coal is to be placed away in the vaults, which are very accessible.
No bids will be entertained unless satisfactory evidence can be furnished of the reliability and loyalty of the parties.
Samples of Coal, such as is desired, can be seen by calling upon the Superintendent.
Payments will be promptly made after the delivery of the fuel.
Proposals should be addressed to the undersigned, and endorsed "Proposals for Wood and Coal." JAS. S. HALLOWELL,
je 24-d Disbursing Clerk, Post Office Department.

SEALED PROPOSALS are invited till the 18th day of July, 1863, at 12 o'clock m., for furnishing the Subsistence Department with 10,000 barrels of FLOUR.
Bids will be received for what is known as No. 1, No. 2, and No. 3, and for any portion less than the 10,000 barrels. Separate bids will be received for Flour put in good second-hand barrels of the same grade as above. Bids for different grades, and for second hand barrels, should be upon separate sheets of paper.
The delivery of the Flour to be commenced on or about the 20th July, or as soon thereafter as the Government may direct, at the rate of 300 barrels daily, delivered either at the Government Warehouse in Georgetown, at the Wharves, or at the Railroad Depot, Washington, D. C.
The barrels to be strong and head lined.
Payment will be made in certificates of indebtedness or such other funds the government may have for distribution.
The usual government inspection will be made just before the flour is received.
An oath of allegiance must accompany each bid.
No bid will be entertained from parties who have previously failed to comply with their bids, or from bidders not present to respond.
Bids to be directed to Col. A. BECKWITH, A. D. C. & C. S. U. S. A., Washington, D. C., and endorsed "Proposals for Flour." jy 1-td

PROPOSALS FOR HATS, CAPS, SHOES, DRY GOODS, &c.

Headquarters Department of Washington,
Office of Chief Quartermaster, July 1, 1863.
Written proposals are invited for furnishing for this Department, to be delivered in this city, the following articles, suitable for clothing contraband men, women, and children:
Russett Brogans, and other serviceable Shoes, for men, women, and children's wear.
Chip, felt, and woolen Hats, and cloth Caps.
Ready-made hickory and check Shirts, and Denham Over alls.
Kerseys, linseys, ginghams, blankets, and other Woolen and Cotton Goods.
Samples should be sent with each bid, at the expense of the party forwarding the same.
No bids will be entertained unless satisfactory evidence can be furnished of the reliability and loyalty of the bidder.
Proposals will be opened from time to time, and contracts awarded as the interests of the service may require.
Good security will be required for the faithful fulfillment of any contract made under this advertisement.
Proposals should be addressed to the undersigned, and indorsed "Proposals for furnishing Dry Goods, &c." ELIAS M. GREENE,
Lieutenant Colonel, Chief Quartermaster,
jy 2 1m Department of Washington.

MAYOR'S OFFICE, July 2, 1863.
PROPOSALS will be received at this office until 12 o'clock on Saturday, the 12th instant, for grading and gravelling Eleventh (11) street, from Maryland avenue to Virginia avenue, the gravel to be of a quality to be approved by the Commissioner and Assistant Commissioners, the gravel to be nine inches in the centre, tapering down to four inches at the gutter line, to be well raked of stone of improper size, and to be rolled with a heavy roller.
Bidders will state the price per cubic yard for grading, and per square yard for gravelling. No part of the appropriation will be paid the contractor except upon the certificate of the Commissioner of the ward and Assistant Commissioners that the work has been properly executed.
JAS. H. BIRCH,
Commissioner Seventh Ward.
CHARLES B CHURCH,
WILLIAM FENWICK,
jy 3 Assistant Commissioners.

PROPOSALS FOR CASES.

Department of the Interior,
Washington, June 22d, 1863.
Sealed proposals will be received at this Office, until 12 o'clock M. on Saturday, the first day of August next, for furnishing and Constructing the Cases for Models in the north saloon of the Patent Office building, including all materials and workmanship, except the iron pilasters of the lower tier of cases, the stairways and the railings. These will be furnished by the Government, but it will devolve upon the contractor to put them up.
These Cases will be similar in form and construction to those of the saloon of the west wing, but the lumber must be of the best quality, well seasoned, and free from knots and shakes, and the work must be done in the best and most workmanlike manner.
The contractor will be required to furnish the brass hinges and to fit them in; also to furnish locks like those of the present cases.
The whole work to be finished throughout with four coats of paint, composed of the best pure lead ground in oil. The glass must be equal in every respect to that of the cases in the West Saloon, and must be well bedded and bradded and left clean and whole on the completion of the contract.
The plans may be seen at the office of the Architect of the U. S. Capitol Extension, on the east Capitol Square every day, Sundays excepted, from 9 a. m. to 4 p. m.
The Commissioner reserves the right to reject any or all of the bids if he considers it to the interest of the Government to do so.
All bids must be addressed to the "Commissioner of Patents," and endorsed "Proposals for Cases for the U. S. Patent Office."
The said bids will be opened at 12 o'clock m. on the aforesaid first day of August, in the presence of such of the bidders as may see proper to attend.
jy 1-wtAu3 D. P. HOLLOWAY, Commis'r.

PROPOSALS FOR HAY, STRAW, AND GRAIN.

Assistant Quartermaster's Office,
Forage Department, Cor. G and 22d streets,
Washington, D. C., April 15, 1863.
Written Proposals are invited for furnishing HAY, STRAW, OATS, and CORN, for the use of this Depot, to be delivered at the Railroad Depot, or at any of the Government wharves in this city.
The proposals to be addressed to the undersigned, and they should state the quantity of each article offered, also the price and the date of delivery.
Proposals will be received for five thousand (5,000) bushels of Corn or Oats, and fifty (50) tons of Hay or Straw, and upwards, unless it should be for the interest of the Government to contract for a less amount.
All grain to be put up in good sacks, of about two (2) bushels each, which are to be furnished at the cost of the contractor.
The Hay and Straw to be securely baled.
All Grain and Hay offered to be subject to a rigid inspection by the Government Inspector.
Contracts will be awarded from time to time to the lowest responsible bidders, as the interests of the service may require. Good security will be required for the faithful fulfillment of any contract made under this advertisement.
Payment to be made at the completion of the contract.
S. L. BROWN,
ap 17-3m Captain and A. Q. M. U. S. A.

QUARTERMASTER GENERAL'S OFFICE,
Washington City, March 19, 1863.
Owners of steam vessels are invited to send to the Quartermaster General's Office tenders for their charter or sale.
Tenders should contain descriptions of the vessels, their dimensions, enrolled or registered tonnage, actual carrying capacity, material, whether coppered, whether side wheel or propellers, whether iron or copper fastened, size and power of engines and boilers, and should state the price at which they are offered for long or short charter, with the estimated value of the vessel in case of loss, or in case the Government should prefer to purchase instead of chartering.
Owners of steam vessels already in the service of the Quartermaster's Department are requested to make known to the Department any reduction in their present rates which they may be willing to grant, and also the price at which they will be willing to sell them.
All such tenders should be addressed to the Quartermaster General of the United States, at Washington, and should be endorsed "Proposals for charter or sale of steamers."
When received, they will be considered, and the Department will endeavor to reduce the heavy expense attending army transportation upon the ocean and the waters, by substituting, whenever it can do so, cheaper vessels of equal capacity, for those now employed.
M. C. MEIGS,
mar 19-3m Quartermaster General.

AMUSEMENTS.

THIS IS TO GIVE NOTICE, That the subscriber has obtained from the Orphans' Court of Washington county, in the District of Columbia, letters testamentary on the personal estate of Patrick Gibbons, late of Washington city, D. C., deceased. All persons having claims against the said deceased are hereby warned to exhibit the same, with the vouchers thereof, to the subscriber, on or before the 23d day of June next; they may otherwise by law be excluded from all benefit of the said estate.
Given under my hand this 23d day of June, 1863.
je 24-law3w* EDWARD BRENNAN, Executor.

THIS IS TO GIVE NOTICE, That the subscriber has obtained from the Orphans' Court of Washington county, in the District of Columbia, letters of administration on the personal estate of Thomas [illegible], late of Washington city, D. C., deceased. All persons having claims against the said deceased are hereby warned to exhibit the same, with the vouchers thereof, to the subscriber, on or before the 16th day of June next; they may otherwise by law be excluded from all benefit of the said estate. Given under my hand this 16th day of June, A. D. 1863. JNO. M. SEMMES,
je 17-law3w* Administrator.

FROM SATURDAY'S "EXTRA STAR."

Congratulatory Address of President Lincoln Upon the Brilliant Successes of the Army of the Potomac.

The President has just issued the following congratulatory order:

Washington, July 4th—10 a. m., 1863.

The President announces to the country that news from the Army of the Potomac up to 10 p. m. of the 3d, is such as to cover that army with the highest honor, to promise a great success to the cause of the Union, and to claim the condolence of all for the many gallant fallen, and that for this he especially desires that on this day He whose will, not ours, should ever be done, be everywhere remembered and reverenced with profoundest gratitude. (Signed,) Abraham Lincoln.

GREAT AND GLORIOUS NEWS!

THE UNION ARMS VICTORIOUS IN THE GREATEST BATTLE OF THE CENTURY!

After the last edition of yesterday's Star went to press official despatches reached Washington announcing that one of the most desperate battles of the war occurred on Thursday afternoon from 4.30 until 8.30 p. m., in which our General Zook and the rebel General Barksdale were killed. Prisoners invariably assert that Longstreet was also killed.

We take the following account of this great engagement from a special despatch to the New York *Times*, published in that journal's issue of yesterday afternoon:

At about 4½ p. m. the enemy sent his first compliments by a salvo of artillery, his first shell falling uncomfortably near Gen. Meade's headquarters. From this hour forth to 8½ o'clock occurred by all odds, the most sanguinary and bloody engagement yet chronicled in the annals of the war, considering its short duration.

The artillery attack which was made by the enemy chiefly on the left and centre, was rapidly followed by the advance of his infantry. The Third Corps received the attack with great coolness. The Rebels at once made an attempt to get on our flank, and kept moving heavy columns in that direction. This necessitated support which was quickly given by the Fifth Corps, the division of Gen. Barnes' being sent to the right and that of Gen. Ayres (regulars) to the left, with Gen. Crawford in reserve.

The battle now became terribly fearful. The armies engaged each other at a very short range, and for three long hours the roar of musketry was incessant. I have heard more noises, louder crashes in other battles, but I never saw or heard of such desperate, tenacious fighting as took place on this flank. The enemy would often bring up suddenly a heavy column of men and force our line back, only to be in turn forced back by our own line of glittering steel.

Our gallant columns covered themselves with glory over and over again. They fought a superior force in numbers; the dispositions of the enemy were very rapid, for look where you would on that field, a body of rebels would be advancing. Our dispositions were equally rapid, and the enemy found more than their equal in such gallant veterans as Sickles, and Birney and Humphrey's. At 6½ General Sickles was struck in the right leg by a piece of shell and borne from the field. The injury was so great that amputation became necessary, and it was performed successfully, the limb being taken off below the knee.

The struggle grew hotter and hotter, and many of our regiments, small enough before melted away into almost nothing. The Second Corps was called on for aid, and though its own position was strongly threatened, yet the First Division, formerly General Hancock's, flung themselves into the fight with desperation, and after a long and obstinate conflict, the enemy slowly and sullenly gave way. In this last charge the brigade of General Caldwell, Second Corps, and that of Col. Sweitzer, from the Fifth Corps, won great honors.

The charges made by our men deserve mention, but want of time forbids. The rebels made frequent attempts to capture our artillery; and at one time had Watson's battery in their possession, but it was retaken in a furious charge by Birney's division.

The battle lasted till fully half-past 8 o'clock, when the enemy fell back to his old position, and left our veterans the ensanguined victors of that field. Our pickets were thrown out, and our lines covered the most of the field, including great numbers of the enemy's dead and wounded. I visited some portions of the line by moonlight, and can bear personal witness to the terrible ferocity of the battle.

A great and magnificent feature of this fight is the splendid and extensive use of artillery. Though our line was only a mile and a half long, yet almost every battery belonging to the Army of the Potomac was more or less engaged. Every one of the Reserve batteries was brought into action, the positions for use being numerous.

The enemy also used artillery largely, but not to near so great an extent as we did. From this they suffered immensely, especially on the left, where canister was largely used. I believe we lost no artillery, unless it was two or three disabled pieces, though it was very wonderful we did not, considering how the enemy's forces were piled on to them. Some of their skirmishers were literally blown away from the muzzles of our guns.

Our losses at this hour cannot be computed. For the two days' fighting they must reach 10,000. We mourn the loss of many valuable officers, but they have been amply revenged in the hecatombs of rebel dead who lie piled along our lines.

The enemy withdrew his force from the city of Gettysburg yesterday, and occupies it now only with skirmishers. Our skirmishers advanced into it a short distance last night, and now hold considerably more than they did.

Capt. Dahlgren, volunteer aid to Gen. Pleasanton, made a daring scout into Hagerstown yesterday with twenty picked men, and captured more prisoners than he had men in his party. He also captured a dispatch bearer from Jeff Davis to Lee, with despatches of the greatest importance, the nature of which cannot to-day be properly disclosed. They have an important bearing on coming events."
L. L. Crounse.

On withdrawing from the field Lee left his dead and wounded in our possession.

The night was passed by our glorious veterans in confident preparations for the deadly conflict that seemed likely to be renewed at daybreak yesterday.

At four a. m., as was expected, our artillery opened fire along the whole line, and a hot engagement began, which continued until half past one p. m., with, as far as is now known here, invariable success on our side, though the rebels fought with terrible desperation and obstinacy, assuming the offensive early in the action, and expending themselves in many fruitless assaults of greater or less magnitude until prepared for their last grand and most fruitless effort of the day, which General Meade narrates in his dispatch of 8.30 p. m., which is as follows:

Official Dispatch of General Meade.

Headquarters Army of the Potomac, July 3d, 8.30 p. m., near Gettysburg.—*Major General Halleck, General-in-Chief.* The enemy opened at 1 p. m. from about 150 guns, concentrated upon my left centre, continuing without intermission for about three hours, at the expiration of which time he assaulted my left centre twice, being upon both occasions handsomely repulsed with severe loss to him, leaving in our hands nearly 3,000 prisoners.

Among the prisoners is Brig. Gen. Armistead and many colonels and officers of lower rank. The enemy left many dead upon the field and a large number of wounded in our hands.

The loss upon our side has been considerable. Major General Hancock and Brigadier General Gibbon are wounded.

After the repelling of the assault, indications leading to the belief that the enemy might be withdrawing, an armed reconnoissance was pushed forward from the left, and the enemy found to be in force.

At the present hour all is quiet.

My cavalry have been engaged all day on both flanks of the enemy, harrassing and vigorously attacking him with great success, notwithstanding they encountered superior numbers, both of cavalry and infantry.

The army is in fine spirits.

George G. Meade,
Major General Commanding.

We have to add that unofficial, though reliable, information to the same hour—8.30 p. m.—has also been received here. These various accounts speak of yesterday's battle as having been decisive, rendering Lee's retreat apparently absolutely certain unless willing to risk the annihilation of the remnant of his army. Without being able to pronounce upon the justice of this belief, which was general last evening in our army, we have to say that all accounts so far received here, official as well as unofficial, strengthen the hope of its correctness.

Though our loss has been heavy, especially in officers, that of the enemy has been terrific, evidently largely exceeding ours.

From the information before us we are not prepared to believe that Lee will venture to renew a general engagement on this glorious 4th of July, 1863, if he did not get into a full retreat for the Potomac some time last night, with what is left of his army; the recollections of the day, as well as of their great successes of the two previous days, being such as while they must doubly arm our gallant troops for another day's terrific fighting, if Lee remains competent to venture it, they must at the same time operate to the signal disadvantage of the rebels' possibility of success.

We need hardly add that, taken as a whole, the terrific battles of yesterday and the day before are victories for the glorious cause of the Union worthy of the history and memory of this sacred day on which they thus become known here.

The following are among the casualties reported:

Generals Zook, Weed and Paul killed. Generals Sickles, Barlow, Graham and Warren wounded.

Generals Ward and Barnes slightly wounded.

Col. Edward E. Cross, 5th N. H., very severely wounded.

Col. Revere, 20th Mass., badly wounded.

Col. Ward, 15th Mass., wounded in both legs.

Col. Thomas, 59th N. Y., breast, severely.

The Colonel of the 26th Ind. and the Colonel of the 124th N. Y. were both killed.

Col. Willard, 125th N. Y., was killed while gallantly rallying his command.

Col. Vincent, 83d Pa., commanding brigade Fifth Corps, severely in thigh.

Col. Prescott, 32d Mass., and Lt. Col. Stevenson, same regiment, both wounded.

Col. Sewell, 5th N. J., severely wounded.

Major Laurie, 53d Pa., killed.

Major Baird, of Gen. Gibbon's staff, has lost a foot.

Lieut. Brown, Battery B, R. I. artillery, wounded; Lieut. Col. Houston, 86d N. Y., do.; Major Lee, 3d Me., arm off; Lieuts. Cawgill and Patton, 20th Mass., both wounded—latter slightly; Lieut. Mallon, 42d N. Y., wounded severely; Col. Baxter, 72d Pa., wounded; Capt. Whitehouse, 16th Me., killed; Capt. Sell, 93d Pa., lost a leg; Lieut. Hazlitt, Battery D, 5th regular artillery, reported killed; Lieut. Watson, Battery I, 5th artillery, wounded; Capt. Duffy, 69th Pa., killed; Major Randolph, Chief of Artillery Third Corps, wounded shoulder; Capt. D. R. Ransom, 3d regular artillery, wounded; Lieut. Aiken, 1st regular artillery, seriously wounded. Capt. Freedly, 10th infantry, severely wounded.

This is only a small portion of the casualties among the officers.

THE FIGHT ON THURSDAY.

THE ENEMY REPULSED AT ALL POINTS.

HEAVY LOSSES ON BOTH SIDES.

Brigadier Gen'ls Paul and Zook Killed—Generals Sickles, Barlow, Graham and Warren Wounded—Gen. Barksdale, of Mississippi, Killed—The Rebel General Longstreet Reported Killed—Gen. Lee Concentrating His Whole Force.

Official Dispatches from General Meade.

An official dispatch was received here yesterday afternoon from Major General Meade, dated:

Headquarters Army of the Potomac, July 2, 11 o'clock p. m.—The enemy attacked me about four o'clock this afternoon, and after one of the severest contests of the war was repulsed at all points.

We have suffered considerably in killed and wounded.

Among the killed are Brig. Gen. Paul and Zook, and among the wounded Gens. Sickles, Barlow, Graham and Warren, slightly.

We have taken a large number of prisoners.

[SECOND DISPATCH.]

A later dispatch has been received from Maj. Gen. Meade, dated at 8 o'clock yesterday morning, which says:

"The action commenced again at early daylight upon various parts of the field. The enemy thus far have made no impression upon my position.

All accounts agree in placing the entire Rebel army in position in our front. The prisoners we have taken report that Longstreet's and A. P. Hill's forces were much injured yesterday, and many General officers killed. The dead body of Gen. Barksdale, of Mississippi, is within our lines.

"We have thus far about sixteen hundred prisoners, and a small number are yet to be started."

[This number of prisoners, sixteen hundred, is as stated in General Meade's official dispatch. He may possibly mean that they were captured in the fight of Thursday night and Friday morning, or the previous statements of correspondents may have been exaggerated.]

IMPORTANT FROM HAGERSTOWN.

REINFORCEMENTS FOR LEE MOVING FROM WILLIAMSPORT VIA THE OLD GREENCASTLE TURNPIKE.

We have information from Hagerstown as late as yesterday morning, to the effect that reinforcements for Lee were being hurried up from Williamsport, via the old Greencastle turnpike.

There is a report at headquarters that a considerable force of Confederate cavalry were at Gum Springs, in London county, yesterday, but the fact that Mosby's cavalry were at Hagerstown on Thursday—of which we have certain information—throws doubt on the story of the presence of rebel cavalry in London county.

ROSECRANS' IMPORTANT SUCCESS.

The capture of the enemy's strong position, of Tullahoma, Tenn., and its full occupation by our army under Rosecrans, official news of which last event has reached here, is an event of signal importance—worthy, indeed, of announcement on this glorious day.

It is the key to the possession of East Tennessee, and the point in front of Chattanooga for which the two great armies in that region have so long contended.

It necessitates that Bragg's army shall quickly retreat to the fastnesses of Chattanooga, releasing the large arms bearing Union population of East Tennessee to co-operate hereafter most effectively, we trust, with our gallant troops under Rosecrans.

LATE AND MOST IMPORTANT FROM RICHMOND.

We have news from Richmond up to the day before yesterday morning, when 950 Union prisoners (taken from Milroy in the Valley) left there on a flag of truce boat, to be exchanged. At that time there were no rebel troops there except the few manning the works. The citizens were being assembled every afternoon at three o'clock for drill. The fear of Dix's rumored approach was universal there. Our informant, an intelligent and experienced member of our quartermaster's department, estimates that, as now defended, the city will easily fall, if vigorously assailed.

VICKSBURG.

Information received here of late justifies us in the strong hope that Gen. Grant will dine to-day in Vicksburg.

OFFICIAL.

WAR DEPARTMENT,
Adjutant General's Office,
Washington, June 29, 1863.
General Orders, No. 195.
The Adjutant General will provide an appropriate medal of honor for the troops who, after the expiration of their term, have offered their services to the Government in the present emergency, and also for the volunteer troops from other States that have volunteered their service in the States of Pennsylvania and Maryland.
By order of the Secretary of War.
E. D. TOWNSEND,
je 30 Assistant Adjutant General.

HEADQUARTERS DEPARTMENT OF WASHINGTON.
Office Chief Quartermaster, May 23, 1863.
Dealers in Agricultural Implements, Garden Seeds, &c., are requested to furnish this office price lists of the various articles of their trade.
The same should be directed to Lieutenant Colonel Elias M. Greene, Chief Quartermaster, Department of Washington. my 25-tf

PROVOST MARSHAL GENERAL'S OFFICE,
Washington, May 22, 1863.
Notice.—The attention of all officers who have been honorably discharged on account of wounds or disability, and who desire to re-enter the service in the Invalid Corps, is called to the provisions of General Orders, No. 105, of 1863, from the War Department, published in the papers throughout the country. Such officers are requested to comply promptly with the provisions of that order, and to send their written applications, as therein provided, for positions in the Invalid Corps, (stating the character of their disability,) with as little delay as possible, to the Acting Assistant Provost Marshal General of the State in which they may be. Such Acting Assistant Provost Marshal General will at once forward the applications, with his endorsement, to the Provost Marshal General at Washington.
Officers for the Invalid Corps will be appointed immediately upon furnishing the papers required by General Orders No. 105, of 1863, from War Department. Their pay and emoluments will commence from date of acceptance of such appointments, and not from date of organization of the respective commands to which they may be assigned.
JAMES B. FRY,
my 23 Provost Marshal General.

WAR DEPARTMENT,
Washington, January 22, 1863.
In consequence of the pressure of business at the War Department, passes for citizens to visit the Army of the Potomac will be given at the office of Lieut. Col. Conrad, 182 Pennsylvania avenue [illegible]

The Philadelphia Inquirer.

CIRCULATION OVER 60,000. | PHILADELPHIA, MONDAY, JULY 6, 1863. | PRICE TWO CENTS.

VICTORY!!

Behold, now glories gild our flag!
New stars gleam from its azure sky,
While greener laurels round it twine
In this proud hour of victory!

WATERLOO ECLIPSED!!

The Desperate Battles Near Gettysburg!

REPULSE OF THE REBELS AT ALL POINTS!!

Gen. Lee Reported in Full Retreat, Pursued by Gen. Meade's Forces.

MANY THOUSANDS OF REBELS CAPTURED.

A Large Number of Cannon, and Immense Quantities of Small Arms, Ammunition, Etc., Etc., Part of the Trophies.

THE REBEL LOSS TRULY FRIGHTFUL.

Over Twenty Thousand Killed and Wounded.

LOSS OF MANY BRAVE DEFENDERS OF THE UNION.

Generals Hancock and Gibbons Among the Wounded.

REPORTED DEATHS OF HILL AND LONGSTREET.

Official Despatches from Gen. Meade.

Lee Ordered to Return to Richmond.

A REBEL PONTOON BRIDGE DESTROYED AT WILLIAMSPORT.

Lee's Army Retreating Down the Boonsboro' Road in a Disorganized Condition.

President Lincoln Congratulates the Union Army.

FROM THE BATTLE-FIELD.

Thursday's Terrific Battle—The Fighting on Friday up to 2 A. M.—The Heaviest Battle of the War—Major-General Sickles Loses His Right Leg—The Rebel Longstreet Reported Killed—A Rebel Mail Captured at Greencastle—Jeff. Davis Has No More Militia—Desperation of the Rebel Army—They Are Determined to Fight it out in Pennsylvania—The Traitors Finally Driven Back—Rebel Loss Estimated at 20,000—2400 Rebels Sent to the Rear—Battle Still Raging and Indecisive.

From Our Special Correspondent.

ON BATTLE-FIELD, NEAR GETTYSBURG, July 3, 1863.

When closing our letter telling of the doings of Wednesday, we left our commands, the Twelfth, Eleventh, First and Third Corps, drawn up in line of battle on the Emmettsburg road, and in the order as above stated, with the Twelfth on the extreme right. Yesterday and this morning our forces were splendidly managed, each corps within supporting distance of each other, all having nobly done their duty, and the result is that a glorious and complete success is ours.

Our Position on Thursday Morning.

During the night the three last fell back to the line of the Tarrytown road, where, after hastily throwing up slight fortifications in front of the batteries, they rested for the night, the Twelfth Corps holding a splendid position on the hill near the Cemetery, which is located at the eastern end of the town; to the left of this were the Eleventh, next the First, and then the Third Corps.

The Battle Commenced by Rebels.

At early dawn the following morning, the pickets of the Twelfth Corps discovered in motion, upon the road running alongside the Hanover Branch Railroad, what appeared to be a large body of the enemy, and moving rapidly towards York. This being made known to the officer of the guard, he, making a closer and more careful inspection, pronounced them Rebel cavalry, the guns then in position upon the hill opened at once upon the moving mass, and with such an effect as to break the column, and force the parties to make a retrograde movement back to where their main body was stationed, near the college, at the western end of the town.

While this was being done, the Third Corps had been pushed forward, up to and a mile beyond the Emmettsburg road, in order to intercept a similar movement to outflank us on the left, the latter being but a repetition of a similar movement the night before.

Longstreet's Corps on our Left.

This corps, after crossing a ravine, and when emerging from a thick wood located beyond, came in full view of, and at less than two hundred yards distance, the whole of LONGSTREET'S Division, all drawn up in line of battle. On the instant a terrific torrent of shot and shell was rained upon this gallant band, they promptly replying.

This rapid firing was kept up for nearly two hours, the Rebels continually moving, changing positions and trying in every way to out-manoeuvre those opposed to them.

Sickles' Corps Another "Stonewall."

Thanks to the skill, efficiency and military experience of the gallant SICKLES, every movement of theirs tending to their advantage was promptly met and defeated, while, notwithstanding their *real* superiority of force and position, the undaunted Third stood their ground nobly, and thus did they continue to hold their own.

A. P Hill Sends Reinforcements

General ANDERSON, with fresh troops from General HILL'S command, came up to reinforce LONGSTREET. Against such fearful odds, and knowing that our supply of ammunition was being rapidly depleted, they determined to retire, which they did in good order, fighting the whole distance. Soon after gaining the opposite edge of the woods in front of which they had been fighting,

The Second Corps and Artillery Reserve

Took up a truly splendid position upon the crest of the hill, to the east of the ravine which was crossed by the Third when advancing to the attack.

The line so taken up was of a peculiar character and worthy of imitation. First, six pieces of artillery; to their left a division of infantry; again, six pieces of artillery, then another division of infantry, and on the extreme left another full battery of artillery; while in the rear of all these and supporting them was another division of infantry, the third, going still further to the rear for rest and for the purpose of replenishing their ammudition.

Vigorous Assault of the Enemy.

While these changes were being made the enemy came out of the woods and renewed the attack, being met this time by the Second Corps.

The Fifth and Sixth Go In.

About three o'clock in the afternoon the Fifth came up and relieved the Second, while soon after six o'clock the Sixth Corps, who had been marching nearly thirty miles during the day, came to the assistance of and relieved the Fifth. All the whole day, and scarcely without intermission, the artillery and infantry of both sides were actively employed, the Rebels, however, constantly making changes in their lines, and bringing in what appeared to be fresh troops. It would take reams of paper and more time than we have at present writing, to tell of the gallant deeds done by detached bodies and individuals.

Let it suffice to say that all did well and nobly, and fought with the desperation of tigers. Never were troops so well handled—neither have they ever gained for themselves so much glory and renown. All this against a force twice their number, and although the loss on our side, and especially among the Third Corps, has been exceedingly heavy, yet, as we for once had a good position, the loss to the Rebels has been *four-fold that of ours.*

I must not forget to mention that during the day a brigade from Gen. SLOCUM'S Twelfth Corps was sent on to the left, and did admirable service. When night fell and a partial cessation of hostilities was apparent, it was deemed prudent that the Corps who had been so actively engaged during the day should retire to the rear of the fortifications erected the night before, and there comfortably rest. This movement was made and without molestation.

Operations of other Corps.

It must not be supposed, however, that while al this was in operation, the Twelfth, First and Eleventh Corps were inactive. They, too, were busily engaged, though not being so sorely pressed, were, with the single exception of losing a part of the line they were appointed to hold, able to maintain their position, which they are still in possession of.

Ewell Charges up the Hill.

After the batteries of the Twelfth Corps had set running their moving force of cavalry, EWELL, who had been during the night encamped near the College, formed his troops in battle order, and with the balance of LEE'S forces, came boldly marching up the hill, in front of our batteries and infantry there stationed, only to be sent back again, and with a fearful loss. This operation was repeated some four distinct times during the day, and each time with the same result.

A Review of the Fight.

The position of the contending parties, and the doings of this part of our line, remind us much of the first battle of Fredericksburg, and of that part of the then attack led by the brave and lamented SUMNER—with this exception, however, we held the hill and fortifications, while the Rebels came up to the attack.

There was but one single drawback to a complete success in the operations of the day with the forces holding the right, which was that, late in the evening, the enemy managed to charge upon and drive from a part of our line of defense a brigade of the Twelfth Corps. This advantage gained they were permitted to hold during the night, they being, however, closely watched, to prevent them from molesting us.

From early morn until late at night, the whole entire line has been engaged. Bayonet charges have been ordered and successfully carried out; skirmishes have been arranged, and the object to be gained fully attained, while, comparatively speaking, our loss has been trifling, compared to that of the Rebels.

Friday's Operations.

This morning, and up to 10 o'clock A. M., but little fighting has been in progress. No general engagement had been brought on. GREENE'S Brigade, of the Twelfth, *"cleared the ranche"* of the body of Rebels who had driven them out the previous night. Some few skirmishing parties have been sent out, while during the morning the Rebels were shelling that part of the line held by the Third, Fifth, Second and Sixth Corps, but doing no serious damage.

The Result.

We have been attacked by a force at least one-third larger than ours—a force elated with the idea that they have been able to transfer the seat of war to a loyal State, and a force that have, by reason of their eminent thieving qualifications, been able to gratify their palates with some of the substantials as well as the delicacies of Yankee land, and with all this have we been able to punish them severely. Our loss is comparatively light; theirs immensely heavy.

Our Captures.

We have captured six pieces of artillery, eight stands of colors, over four thousand prisoners and over two thousand stand of arms. Beyond the fact that many of our good and brave soldiers are numbered among the dead or are suffering from wounds, we have no cause to complain of the result of the past two days, other than that the position of the contending parties are such that neither are able safely to bury their dead or bring in their wounded.

Major-General Daniel E. Sickles,

He who so gallantly managed the Third Corps at Chancellorville, when they were cut off from the main body of our army, succeeded in safely bringing them through the mass of the enemy, and with them effecting a junction; he, too, who has, when with his command, ever been foremost at the point of danger, is now to be numbered among the wounded, having had his leg so badly shattered by a piece of shell, as to necessitate amputation. Rumors are current that one of his Division Generals was killed, and another wounded, but of this we have no positive information.

A Raid on Greencastle, the Enemy's Rear.

A squadron of cavalry, under command of Captain DAHLGREN, yesterday went out on a reconnoissance west and south of Chambersburg, and paid a flying visit to the town of Greencastle, on the Cumberland Valley road.

Rebel Mail Captured.

Here they made an important capture of a Rebel mail carrier who had upon his person many letters of an interesting character, prominent among which was one from JEFFERSON DAVIS to LEE, and one from LEE to DAVIS.

The former (DAVIS) tells LEE that he has been endeavoring to raise a militia force, and have such concentrated at Winchester, and to co-operate with him (LEE). "He regrets to state, however, that after urging the matter for the last month, he is unable to muster more than 800 men, and that he fears that the attempt to so assist him will have to be abandoned."

LEE, to DAVIS, says, "That, so far, my prospects are not cheering. I can barely seize enough to sustain life, while the Yankees have so largely and rapidly concentrated, and are so harrassing me, that I am fearful I shall have to abandon the State, and as well this present movement." Other letters were captured, some deprecating this movement North, and state that they never expect to get back alive, and tell their friends that, in case they don't, what to do with their different descriptions of property while many assert that they mean to desert at the first favorable opportunity.

The Rebels

Know and feel that they are in an exceedingly tight corner, and how to get out is their present dilemma. To-day, when we left the front, the general impression was prevalent that they would attempt a movement towards Hanover Junction, and at the point of the South Mountain, near Carlisle, effect a junction with such of their forces as may be in the Cumberland Valley, and then rapidly move down on Baltimore. If such a direction they should take, it would not only compel our moving further eastward, but would place them in a position from which there would be no extrication but death or surrender.

Hospitals Shelled.

On several occasions the enemy have opened their batteries upon our hospitals, which were farm houses, barns or cabins. No respect is paid to a yellow flag, and our wounded can only crawl away, or, if unable to get out, be torn to pieces by shot and shell of the most malignant foe that ever espoused a wicked and unholy war.

Our Losses.

It is impossible for us at present to obtain anything like a correct list of the casualties, for the reason that on the first day all our dead and wounded were left in the hands of the Rebels, when they gained possession of the town in which the hospitals were located. Yesterday it was one continued source of excitement along the whole line, and which has not subsided at present writing. When matters are calmed down we shall endeavor to obtain an official list and forward it at an early date. We have noted down such as came under our observation.

ONE-HUNDRED-AND-TWENTY-FOURTH NEW YORK.—Colonel Ellis killed.

Major Cromwell, killed, bodies brought to Westminster.

Lieutenant-Colonel Cummings, wounded in hip. Just as the One-hundred-and-twenty-fourth were making a charge upon the enemy, a volley was fired into them, one ball pierced the Colonel's forehead, another the Major's heart, and both fell dead at the same moment; a few minutes later, and the Lieutenant-Colonel fell shot through the hip; the loss of the regiment was heavy, but we have not yet secured more names.

SIXTY-THIRD PENNSYLVANIA.

Capt. G. W. McCullough, rheumatism in shoulder; sent to rear.

ONE-HUNDRED-AND-TENTH PENNSYLVANIA.

Major D. M. Jones, of Tyrone, wounded.
Capt. Cassidy, wounded.
The regiment suffered heavily.

SEVENTH NEW JERSEY.

Col. Francine reported mortally wounded.
Lieut.-Col. Price wounded.
Adjutant Dougherty, of Philadelphia, wounded.
The Jersey Brigade suffered severely.

SECOND WISCONSIN.

Geo. W. Stocker, leg.
Edward Atkinson, leg.
Col. Fairchild, lost left arm.
Lieut.-Col. Stevens, killed.
Major Mansfield, leg and hip
Capt. Perry, left leg.
Lieut. Jamison, wounded
Lieut. Lee, hip.
Lieut. Humphrey, killed.
Lieut. Humphres, killed.
Lieut. Winegar, killed.
Capt. Baldwin and First Lieut., Co. E, wounded.
Lieut. Daily, wounded and left.
Capt. Hewes, wounded and left.
Adj. Wood, wounded, head.
Capt. Sperry, wounded.

THIRD MAINE.

Samuel E. Foster, arm.

FOURTEENTH REGULARS.

Wm. Dwyer, leg.

SECOND NEW HAMPSHIRE.

G. H. Maye, leg.

ONE-HUNDRED-AND-FORTY-NINTH PENNSYLVANIA.

Abram Courtright, finger.
Charles William Lewis, hand.
Aaron D. Tilitson, shoulder.
John T. Jones, hand.

SEVENTY-SIXTH NEW YORK.

S. Darbell, arm.

THIRD WISCONSIN.

Nathan Tuttle, arm.

THIRD MAINE.

George W. Davis, shoulder.

SIXTEENTH MAINE.

Sheldon H. Tibbets, burned by explosion of ammunition wagon.

EIGHTY-EIGHTH PENNSYLVANIA.

Garrett Lukens, shoulder.

ONE-HUNDRED-AND-FOURTEENTH PENNSYLVANIA.

James Yocum, Co. F, forefinger.
Jeremiah Bancker, Co. F, hand and head.

EXCELSIOR BRIGADE.

Captain George Le Fort, wounded.
Colonel John S. Austin, wounded.
Major J. P. Finklemier, wounded.
All three got away and are at Westminster.

NINETY-FOURTH NEW YORK.

Calvin Carey, leg.
General Graham, reported mortally wounded.

FIRST MASSACHUSETTS.

Lieutenant-Colonel Baldwin, wounded.
Adjutant Mudge, wounded.
Lieutenant Hinckley, wounded.
Lieutenant Hartley, killed.

SIXTEENTH MASSACHUSETTS.

Lieutenant-Colonel Merriam, wounded.

ONE-HUNDRED-AND-TWENTY-FIFTH NEW YORK.

Colonel Woodward, struck in face by shell and killed instantly. He was acting as Brigadier. His body was secured, and will be sent to Troy, N. Y.
Lieutenant Gillis, in foot, amputated.
Captain Shelden, hand.
Lieutenant Stevens, leg.
Major A. B. Myer, missing.

The Latest—Battle of Friday Afternoon.

Our line of battle on Friday afternoon was in shape of an arc; our left was after a sharp contest pushed out a considerable distance, and we regained considerable ground we had previously lost; the battle rages, however, with great fury as we start a courier with this.

Prisoners to the Rear.

Over twenty-four hundred prisoners have been sent to the rear, about one hundred of whom were officers; and we are informed that the Rebel General BARKSDALE is wounded and in our hands. The Rebels are now marched to Baltimore under cavalry guard, it not being safe to send them by rail.

GLORIOUS VICTORY.

From the Battle-field up to Sunday, A. M.—Death of the Rebel Longstreet—The Most Terrible Battle of the War—Battle of Friday—Fourth of July in the Army of the Potomac—The Rebels have Lost 40,000 Men—Lee Asks for a Cessation of Hostilities—We Reoccupy Gettysburg—Recapture Our Wounded—Lee Retreating Towards Cumberland Valley—Popularity of General Meade—Heroism of the Army of the Potomac—Waterloo Eclipsed.

Special Correspondence of the Inquirer.

ON FIELD OF BATTLE, NEAR GETTYSBURG, Saturday, July 4—10 P. M.

Our last report left off at Friday morning. The battle was then raging with such ferocity as has never been known in the annals of war. Our lines formed an arc, something the shape of a horseshoe, the arc being directly in front of Gettysburg, one line of artillery being in front of the cemetery, which is located upon a high hill directly in front of the town on the east side. Our right ran along the Baltimore pike, and our left on the Taneytown plank road.

The troops occupied the following order, commencing on the left:—

Sixth Corps General SEDGWICK; then
Fifth Corps, General SYKES.
Third Corps, General BIRNEY—parallel to the Taneytown road.
Second Corps, General HANCOCK.
First Corps, General NEWTON—in front of town.
Eleventh Corps, General HOWARD.
Twelfth Corps, General SLOCUM.

The earliest dawn of day was ushered in by the opening of such a roar of cannon as would lead one to believe that all the fiends of hell were hurling thunderbolts at each other.

Quick as lightning the gunners of two hundred and fifty pieces replied, and a hundred thousand men of the Army of the Potomac sprang to their feet, and clasped the trigger of as many trusty weapons; the Rebel lines formed around our horse-shoe; our army lay upon five hills, between each of which were ravines, some wooded, some open, and others covered with low bushes; beyond them all, and distant from half a mile to a mile and a quarter were other hills, on which the Rebel battle flag was flying.

The very earth seemed to tremble, but our lines wavered not. The musketry in woods and in front of the batteries vied with one another in the incessant rattle. Now and then the fire would slacken in some quarter, and then again it would start up in some fresh place, as though our lines were swaying to and fro. On our extreme right the Rebels had the previous evening secured a position which rather broke into our lines, and it was determined to dislodge them.

The Twelfth and a portion of the Sixth went in, and by eleven the Rebels were driven back and our lines formed to be held. About 1 P. M. the enemy could be seen massing his troops in three columns. EWELL in the streets of Gettysburg, HILL to the left of the town, and LONGSTREET upon the right about two and a half miles. LONGSTREET made an attack east of the cemetery, and HILL on the opposite side of the town. On they came, up to the very mouths of the cannon, up the hill sides, along which were stone fences in all directions.

Our riflemen lay behind them, and as the Rebels played upon us at Fredericksburg, so we poured a sheet of flame into their faces as they came within range, and hundreds were piled up as quickly as grain would fall before the reaper's iron hand. About three, the Rebels, under LONGSTREET, succeeded in reaching the top of the hill just in the rear of the Cemetery.

Their battle-flag was planted boldly upon the crest and a shout went up from the demons who seemed to court death and destruction, but our lines swayed but for a moment; back they went, the ground was regained, and our lines again intact. At other points they succeeded in gaining temporary advantages, but ere they could realize their importance they were torn to pieces and hurled back upon their column, and so the column swayed until they could no longer get the troops to make a charge.

Then EWELL, who had laid in town all day, ready to cut his way through when our centre was once pierced, began to fall back. The reinforcements he had sent to the other columns were in vain, our left was pushed out nearly a mile, and the sun set over one of the most fearful scenes of carnage there has been during the *whole war.*

Our loss was comparatively small. Generals HANCOCK and GIBBONS, both seriously wounded, are the most important losses to us. We lost two or three guns, but they were recaptured. Several were destroyed by the fire of the enemy, and in one charge one was spiked by them, but the batteries around the cemetery kept up their steady roar the whole day long.

Every corps was engaged, and the whole army covered itself with such immortal glory that we cannot at present individualize the daring acts of heroism or the unparalleled manner with which our army received the assaults and hurled back their mangled columns.

LONGSTREET died this morning. A. P. HILL is reported wounded, and all day long we have been feeling for the enemy, who does not manifest himself in any force anywhere along the lines.

The past two days he has been hauling his wounded out on the road to Chambersburg, and last night he withdrew his forces from the town, and keeping up a line of sharp-shooters, from the outskirts has sought to pick off any of our men who ventured too far into the town. There are still a large number of his wounded in different houses in town, and many of his dead unburied.

Our dead were all buried by detachments of our men who were taken prisoners, but there still remains many who fell between the points where our picket lines are now drawn. What they are doing to-day we have not yet learned satisfactorily. The general impression is that they are retreating to Williamsport. It is not known positively that they are, but nearly all indications point that way.

Our pickets on the left and around the edge of the town have kept up continuous firing all day; his sharp-shooters are engaged in picking off any one who may show his head within their range. This morning a large force of Rebels appeared about four miles south of Gettysburg, on the Emmettsburg road, and commenced throwing up defensive works. No threatening move had been made in that quarter, and it is surmised that it is being done to enable them to hold their present position, which is as strong as the one we hold, until they accomplish some particular purpose they may have in view.

Torn to pieces as they are, having lost 30,000 or 40,000 men in the last five days, they are not yet used up. They have all their artillery yet, and those who remain, we are informed by one of our wounded men who was left beyond the town, marched out in solid columns as though they had been on dress parade. Their endurance, their desperation, their utter disregard of life, is certainly worthy of a better cause.

While EWELL had his corps drawn up in line ready for battle in the streets, on Friday afternoon, he made a speech, and told them that they were on the march now for Baltimore, and that HILL and LONGSTREET'S corps would smash our lines, and drive us towards Baltimore; while his old and trusty corps would dash on to Baltimore, and Washington; but perhaps the disarrangement of the first part of the work will prevent him from pushing "on to Baltimore."

STUART'S Cavalry started early yesterday in the direction of Frederick; had LEE succeeded in driving us, STUART would have made direct to Washington; where he will go to now is uncertain, but he may be watched.

Scouts and reconnoissances were pushed out to their rear and will report the condition of his movements to-night. Our troops have been replenished with ammunition and rations. We have not seen a man who is not willing to follow it up and settle it with them wherever they can be found, and the sooner the better.

Three days more fighting for them, like the last, and they are about exterminated! Should they fall back down Cumberland Valley, and endeavor to recross into Virginia, we have the shorter line, and can outmarch them and meet them where they least desire it. We learn that they have left ten thousand men to guard the fords at Williamsport and that vicinity; intercepted correspondence shows that LEE can get no more help from DAVIS! What will he do next?

Those who know him know that he will not fail to carry his point, if in so doing he sacrifices his whole command.

A heavy thunder storm set in about 2 P. M. to-day, and lasted for two hours without intermission. Copious showers also fell during last night. Towards evening it cleared off for a short time, but it is now raining heavily. All the streams in this locality rise rapidly every rain, and twenty-four hours' rain may be the means of our crushing the balance of the Rebel foe.

Our wounded who were left in Gettysburg were paroled by them, and many have to-day been brought out and placed in our hospitals, or sent to the rear.

There is scarcely a house or barn left in the town which is not more or less pierced by balls. It is not known that any citizens were killed during the engagement, but it is reported that several were shot down during the first assault upon the place.

No buildings were burned until this afternoon about three P. M., when the Rebels fired three houses on the Emmettsburg road, and the last ones outside of the village; the heavy rain prevented the fire from spreading, and they soon burned up. Southeast of the town about half a mile, was a large brick mansion, which they burned last night, and now behind its charred walls they fire upon our pickets.

About noon to-day we rode along the lines in front and such a Fourth of July the men never spent before. The long marching they have gone through during the last three weeks has been very severe. For the last forty-eight hours the whole army has been in line of battle. In some portions of the lines water was very scarce. No time has been taken to wash hands or faces, and the smoke of battle and the fearful excitement which they were under has given their countenances a ghastly look that will not soon be forgotten by them.

Cattle were driven up to the pickets, a ball soon crashed through a bullock's head, the knife was soon plied, and in an incredibly short time the ox would be eaten in sight of the enemy's pickets, and nothing but hard tack and sometimes coffee to accompany it. This shows coolness, determination and enthusiasm in behalf of our cause that no army has ever shown before.

Everywhere was the same spirit manifested. One of the pickets said he was about the last of his company, but five others remained; a shell last night had killed three of his comrades who stood by his side talking to him. He was eager to go in. "Oh," said he, "if we can only put the finishing stroke to them, I am ready to go too!"

When the Rebels flanked us and took the town of Gettysburg, we made a large number of hospitals all over town. The Rebels came up with their fiendish yells and fired right and left. In front of one of the hospitals of the First Corps two men of the New York Ninth were on guard. Some one said to them—"Run in the house." "No," they replied, "we were placed here by Dr. NORDQWIST, and he must order us away." The next moment both fell dead, and in another second Rev. Mr. HOWELL, of the Ninetieth Pennsylvania, *fell, shot through the head.*

Our wounded left in Gettysburg are well cared for by the people and by some of our own men, who were detailed by the Rebels for that purpose.

The cemetery fence is destroyed. Cannon balls, tearing through iron rails and marble monuments, have strewn them in all directions. This may not have been the first time a battle has been fought in a graveyard, but never one of such ferocity and desolation. Some of the men have raised up tomb stones and crawled under them for protection.

When the enemy poured cross fires into our men at this point our wounded would crawl between newly made mounds to escape.

Broken caissons, guns, and all the accoutrements of war are scattered over acres of ground, mingled with the dead and dying, friend and foe. The rapid putrefaction of horses and men has already made a stench in some quarters almost unbearable.

We dined with General ROBINSON, of the Second Division, First Army Corps, his head-quarters being at the foot of a large tree in rear of the graveyard, about the middle of the afternoon. A piece of canvass, stretched over a couple of rails, was all the protection from the storm, and several inches of water upon the ground. In the rear was a half-dozen mangled horses, in the front Rebels and horses lying side by side, the tree overhead splintered by the iron hail of the previous day.

Ten feet in front of where the General sat was a hole that looked as though it might have been for a grave. "That," remarked the General, "is where a shell struck instead of coming in under here, and I am perfectly satisfied that it did so;" and well he might be, for his Staff were mostly by him at the time. All around the field 6 and 12-pound shot and shell were scattered as though an ammunition wagon had upset. A cup of coffee and a slice of bread and butter was the old hero's dinner, and was eaten with avidity.

What a contrast between the soldiers of the Army of the Potomac at their Fourth of July dinner and that of the thousands of stay-at-home patriots! Let the Fourth of July, 1863, be remembered in the future.

It is to be hoped that the people of the vicinity of Washington have not been annoyed by "MOSBY, the guerrilla," lately, for on Thursday he was in Gettysburg, all day, with his command. He has been with STUART since he crossed the Potomac.

Major EWELL, aid to and brother of Gen. EWELL, was killed by one of our sharp-shooters in the streets of Gettysburg. One of our rifled guns was got in range of the open square in Gettysburg so completely, that whenever a group of Rebels show themselves there, down goes a shell right in their midst.

Large numbers of women and children passed out yesterday, and went out towards Hanover, fearing to remain longer for fear of the town being shelled and burned.

From those who saw the whole affair while lying among them we learn that their discipline is much more rigid than ours. They have no straggling; men are shot down like dogs if they fall behind or show any disposition to shirk.

On Friday some of the *Louisiana Tigers* got into the town and sacked the stores and many private houses.

North Carolina troops have suffered severely, and they evinced willingness to be captured in nearly every instance.

A Rebel officer, badly wounded, says there are two Brigades of the Eleventh Corps who fought so well as to elicit commendation of even the Rebels, but he could not tell which two they were.

The First Ohio Battery lost one section of their battery, but it was afterwards recaptured; the

Continued on the Eighth Page.

Charleston Daily Courier.

NO. 19,518. CHARLESTON, S. C., CONFEDERATE STATES OF AMERICA, WEDNESDAY MORNING, JULY 8, 1863. VOL. LXI.

BY TELEGRAPH.

THRILLING AND GLORIOUS NEWS.

BLOODY BATTLE IN PENNSYLVANIA.

GRAND STRATEGIC MOVEMENT.

CONFEDERATES VICTORIOUS

FORTY THOUSAND YANKEE PRISONERS TAKEN—LOSSES HEAVY ON BOTH SIDES—THE PRISONERS EN ROUTE TO MARTINSBURG.

RICHMOND, July 7.—The latest dispatches from Martinsburg report the enemy routed and forty thousand Yankee prisoners taken last Sunday.

MARTINSBURG, July 5.—At 6 A. M., Saturday, General LEE had changed his front and occupied the ground from which the enemy were driven on the 1st and 2d instants. The whole army was in splendid spirits and masters of the situation. Generals PENDER and PICKETT were wounded, Colonel AVERY, of North Carolina, killed, and Colonels BENNETT and PARKER wounded.

MARTINSBURG, July 6, A. M.—A courier, who has just arrived, reports that the enemy were defeated yesterday (Sunday,) and driven back three miles. Vast numbers of prisoners are reported to have been taken by Gen. LEE. The prisoners refused to be paroled, and are on their way to Richmond. This conflict is regarded as the bloodiest battle of the war. Our loss was very great—that of the enemy immense.

LATEST.—MARTINSBURG, July 6—Saturday Night.—Our centre, in yesterday's battle, fell back, drawing the enemy on until we gained the heights. A general fight then ensued, resulting in the rout of the Yankees. According to all accounts, LEE captured forty thousand prisoners.

Fighting is reported going on at Williamsport between IMBODEN'S cavalry and several regiments of infantry with a division of Yankee cavalry under the command of PLEASANTON.

Another telegram, dated Martinsburg, July 6, says:—"The latest news, which seems to be reliable, is that the fight on Sunday was the bloodiest of the war. Gen. HILL fell back in the centre, drawing the enemy on, causing him to believe that HILL was retreating. As the enemy advanced, EWELL and LONGSTREET advanced their right and left wing, thus surrounding the enemy. We took the heights for which we have been contending, and captured forty thousand prisoners. The latter refused to be paroled. PICKETT'S division is now guarding the prisoners *en route* to Martinsburg."

FURTHER DETAILS BY NORTHERN PAPERS.

RICHMOND, July 7.—The Baltimore *Sun*, of the 1st inst., says:

"STUART captured twelve hundred mules and four hundred prisoners in Montgomery County, Md. At Westminster he captured the Delaware cavalry. The wildest alarm prevails. The streets of Baltimore have been barricaded, and the secessionists of that city are threating to — on the offensive.

Our city papers contain extracts this morning from the New York papers of the 3d and 4th inst. The latest dispatches refer to the fighting of Friday. A Washington telegram of the 3d, says: "The latest intelligence received here from the field is up to eleven o'clock to-day." The purport of the dispatch is not given.

Gen. DIX's troops are believed to be leaving the Peninsula and evacuating Virginia, *en route* to Maryland. Rail Road and telegraphic communition with the Valley of Virginia has been resumed.

Latest from the North.

RICHMOND, July 7th.—The New York *Tribune* of the 4th instant, contains many details of the battle of Wednesday. Brig. Gen. BARTON is mentioned as twice wounded and taken prisoner. Brig. Gen. SCHIMMELFOON was taken prisoner, and Gen. MANSFETA wounded.

A telegram from Hanover's, July 3d, says: "The fight was most terrific and the loss on both sides tremendous. We have LONGSTREET a prisoner, sure. If COUCH arrives to-night the victory is ours beyond a chance.

PHILADELPHIA, July 3, 11 P. M.—Stirring rumors are in town. A report is current that LONGSTREET is killed.

The siege of of Vicksburg is said to be progressing satisfactorily, but the rebels are regarded as very obstinate.

New Orleans dates of the 27th ult. state that there is nothing new from Port Hudson. The rebels have overrun the Teche country.

A drawing took place yesterday at the Libby Prison for two Federal Captains, to be executed in retaliation for the shooting of two Confederate officers, in Kentucky, by BURNSIDE. The two names drawn were HENRY W. SAWYER, First New Jersey Cavalry, and JOHN FLYNN, Fifty first Indiana. No day has yet been fixed for their execution.

The community of Richmond are disposed to await official confirmation of the news of Sunday's battle, and defer fully crediting the Martinsburg telegrams. It is generally believed, however, that a decisive victory has been achieved. The account from City Point is regarded as a partial confirmation of the news.

News by Flag of Truce.

PETERSBURG, July 7.—The flag of truce boat to City Point arrived this morning. No papers were allowed to come ashore. The Yankee officers on board wore a dejected appearance. Paroled prisoners state that they overheard one Federal officer at Fortress Monroe say that the loss of General MEADE's army could not be less than sixty thousand killed, wounded and missing. Captain MULFORD, of the flag of truce steamer, reports General SICKLES killed in the late battle.

From the Southwest.

YANKEE CAVALRY DRIVEN BACK—OSTERHAUS' YANKEE FORCES CROSSING THE BIG BLACK—WARM WORK EXPECTED.

BOLTON'S STATION, Miss., July 5.—Yesterday about 12 o'clock a force of Yankee cavalry crossed the Big Black at Birdsong's Ferry, and advanced into the interior, but were promptly met by Gen. WHITFIELD'S brigade and driven back across the river.

A courier just in from Edward's Depot says OSTERHAUS' entire command crossed the river near that place last night. If so we will have warm work to-day. GRANT is evidently very uneasy in regard to events transpiring in his rear. There was but little firing at Vicksburg yesterday.

Reported Fall of Vicksburg.

JACKSON, Miss., July 6.—The mail carrier has just arrived and states positively that Vicksburg has fallen. The same news has been received here this morning from different sources, but not by any one here officially.

[The above report is discredited in official circles both here and at Richmond. No intelligence of the fall had been received at the War Department.—EDS. COURIER.]

From Wilmington, N. C.—A Fight Progressing.

WILMINGTON, July 7.—A letter from a reliable source, dated Kinston, last night, says: "A courier just arrived reports an engagement now progressing between the retreating enemy and our forces near Freebridge. The enemy is supposed to be cut off."

North Carolina Legislature.

RALEIGH, July 6.—The House was engaged deliberating the Militia Bill all day. No final action was had.

The Senate passed a Bill to punish aiders and abettors in military desertions.

From North Carolina.

TRAVEL ON THE WILMINGTON WELDON RAIL ROAD.

AUGUSTA, July 7.—A special dispatch received here dated Wilmington, July 3, states that the damage done to the Wilmington and Weldon Rail Road by the enemy was trifling, and will be repaired to-night. The trains will resume their regular trips to-morrow. The Federals retreated to Newbern.

Merited Reward of a Notorious Abolitionist.—"P. W. A.," of the Savannah *Republican*, writing to that paper from Hagerstown, Md., says:

All honest men throughout the world will be rejoiced to hear that that malignant demagogue and Abolitionist, Thadeus Stevens, of Pennsylvania, has received some of the punishment due for his enormous crimes against the happiness of the human race. He owns large iron works and mills in Adams County on the border, which I am informed have been utterly destroyed. His machinery, aqueducts, buildings, and supplies for his operatives, including, it is said, twenty thousand pounds of bacon, have been swept away. Amen! will be the involuntary exclamation of every lover of justice and every foe of hypocrisy. An effort is made, in the work of impressment, to distinguish, as far as possible, between the friends of peace and the aiders and abettors of Mr. Lincoln. Thus the red hand of war is made to fall heaviest upon those who were first to lift it. Some of the troops complain, however, that they are not allowed to appropriate and destroy as they go. If permitted, they would avenge Mississippi, Tennessee, and the Carolinas and Virginia, and leave behind a track of desolation as barren and enduring as the desert of Sahara. They give Gen. Lee high praise as a fighter and strategist, but they say "he has not a good pillaging mind." Gen. Lee is right, however, as all will acknowledge after a while.

A correspondent from Grant's army says the "rebels" are afraid to risk another engagement at Milliken's Bend.

CHARLESTON.

WEDNESDAY MORNING, JULY 8, 1863.

General Lee's Victory.

The battle at Gettysburg disclosed the important fact that the whole of General LEE's army is in Pennsylvania. That event removed every doubt touching the nature of that movement. It was seen that it is not a raid, but a real campaign of vast proportions. The consummate General who, under God, holds in his hands the destinies of one hundred thousand men, comprising his command, had other and higher objects in view than the replenishment of his stores and the capture of fat cattle. He aimed to accomplish results which will be felt throughout the hostile land—results that will strike terror and dismay into the mean and boastful foe, and fill our own bosoms with gladness.

Though ignorant of the plans and purposes of the great Southern commander, and fully aware of the hazardous nature of the mighty undertaking, the country awaited with calmness and confidence the time when some grand deed worthy of the cause and the genius and reputation of the General-in-chief and his coadjutors, disclosed the plan and proclaimed the objects.

The country watched the progress of events beyond the Potomac with intense interest, altogether free from doubt and anxiety. No mind was clouded with apprehension or disquieted with solicitude. It was felt that to harbor such feelings would be unjust to the magnificent army and its unsurpassed chiefs, for that army had invariably come off victorious from every battle it had fought. And these conflicts in which it had triumphed had taxed to the utmost the abilities of our leaders and the valor of our troops. In every one of them we were opposed to a largely superior number of men, not inferior to our own soldiers in discipline and spirit, and enjoying important advantages in equipment and ordnance. And, furthermore, in several of them the enemy fought behind entrenchments upon which science and labor had been liberally expended. If at any time apprehension stole into our minds we recollected the battles on the Chickahominy and the grand bayonet charges at Chancellorsville, and dismissed the uneasiness with shame and mortification at having given place to it even for a moment.

The report of the first battle on hostile soil increased that confidence to assurance. The truth that was wrung from the false pen of the most vile and shameless of Yankee journalists warranted the conclusion that our arms had been crowned with a signal victory. For we were certain that that unprincipled miscreant would never have told the Yankee public in the columns of his dirty sheet that the Confederates remained in possession of the battle-ground while the Federal army was forced to fall back several miles, had there not been some worse intelligence for Yankee ears which must shortly cause them distress and dark forebodings.

That news, though so meagre and communicated through such a channel, sent a thrill of joy through our hearts, and we reckoned with perfect confidence on hearing that the battle at Gettysburg had resulted in a decisive victory for the heroes under Gen. LEE.

The exultation we indulged in over that conflict was not altogether caused by the victory we had no doubt had been won on the opening day of July. We regarded that engagement as a prelude to a great battle, which would decide the fate of our army and of Washington. Having found the foe and given him a taste of his mettle, we supposed Gen. LEE would make haste to dispose of the host that interfered with his well contrived plans. He had thus far out-generalled him, and so skillfully had he manœuvred, that he had forced the foe to fight on ground of his own choosing. The severe drubbing the portion of his army that had participated in the fight had received must have dispirited them, and the demoralising effect of the defeat was in no small measure enhanced by their uncommonly heavy loss in officers of high grade.

That victory caused us to count upon another and a greater, and God be praised, we have not been disappointed. Before the army under MEADE had recovered from their defeat, General LEE fell upon them with whole force, drove them three miles, capturing an almost incredible number of prisoners and inflicting on the enemy the severest defeat he has sustained in any previous battle.

The telegrams that inform us of that splendid victory may have made misstatements, but we are warranted in accepting the result of that battle as the most decisive and brilliant victory the Almighty has yet vouchsafed our arms.

We must receive further reports before we can venture to predict and conjecture the effect of that magnificent success upon the mind of the North. In the meantime it becomes us to acknowledge the good hand of God in that victory, and to laud and magnify His adorable name.

The *Army and Navy Messenger*, published by the Evangelical Society, Petersburg, Va., the representative of all denominations, is furnished to private soldiers and sailors *gratuitously*.

The *Messenger* has ready and equal access to soldiers of ALL denominations, and to soldiers of NO denominations, and meets with a universal welcome in every camp. It has been recommended by General LEE and by many other eminent officers, who have contributed to its support. It is pre-eminently the soldier's and sailor's paper, specially designed to interest and profit them.

To meet the increasing demand for it from our armies, East, West and South, a much larger edition than has been heretofore issued is required. But the expense is great. Donations solicited from all who are disposed to sustain this enterprise, and who have at heart the moral and religious welfare of our defenders.

Address Rev. A. W. MILLER, Corresponding Secretary Evangelical Tract Society, Petersburg, Va.

Capture of Gen. Neal Dow.—A special to the Mobile *Register*, dated Jackson, July 4, says: NEAL DOW has been captured by LOGAN's scouts at a farmer's house, where he was convalescing. He is expected here to-morrow.

Reports from below go to confirm the capture of Kenner's Station.

A special to the Mobile *Tribune* from Jackson, of the 4th, says: Gen. Dow has arived here."

A courier from the front reports slight skirmishing for several days, beyond the Big Black, with our cavalry. Results unimportant.

A few prisoners almost hourly arrive.

Take any view of the matter we may, and it cannot be denied, says the Augusta *Constitutionalist*, that the South has much greater ability to continue the war than the North. We can and do produce an abundance of meat and bread. We have also Cotton and wool from our own soil. And we may, if we but will do it, produce also plenty of leather, of iron and of salt, and if we but do these things we shall be fully able to carry on the war just as long as the North is reckless enough to wage it.

Liability of Aliens.—The Mobile *Tribune* says the decision of Judge JONES in the Confederate States Court, respecting the liability of aliens, is regarded as one of the most important decisions that have yet been given, and will have a wonderful effect in bringing about a change in matters generally. For there is any quantity of these people who have resided in this city, married here, and have been doing business for years, and since the war have sworn that they never intended to become citizens, and were granted exemptions on this oath—men who are now engaged in every branch of speculation, and doing more to depreciate our currency than any other class in the community. We are told that there are hundreds in the interior who travel from towns to farms buying up all the produce they can get hold of and shipping it to the cities on speculation, which is partly the excuse for the exorbitant prices we have been paying all winter. Now that the Judge has declared them liable to conscription, the country will probably be rid of them, so far as their "business" qualifications are concerned at least.

South Carolina College.—An occasional meeting of the Trustees of the South Carolina College is hereby summoned to be held at Columbia, in the Executive Office, on Monday evening, the 13th July, at seven o'clock. A full attendance is desirable.

The Meridian (Miss.) *Clarion*, of Thursday last, says: "An employe of the Southern Express Company abstracted about $43,000 from the office in that place on Saturday last, but was detected in the attempt to send it up the Mobile and Ohio Rail Road, and all the funds recovered. He was placed under arrest."

The Yankee.—PARK BENJAMIN once wrote the following epigram on the Yankee, which is true to the life:

He would kiss a queen till he raised a blister,
With his arm round her neck and his old felt hat on;
Would address a king by the title of "*Mister*,"
And ask him the *price* of the throne that he sat on.

Good, if True.—A gentleman from Chattanooga informs us that when he left that place a report was in circulation and credited, that Morgan had captured Murfreesboro', Tenn., after a fight with the garrison. As a part of the fruits of his success, the destruction of all the vast stores accumulated for Rosecrans, and the burning of two rail road trains, were items mentioned.—The information was said to have been brought to Chattanooga by a courier from General M. This if true, must seriously interfere with Rosecrans' future movements.—*Memphis Appeal, 6th inst.*

As was to be supposed, the Canadian papers are justly angry at the offensive rhodomontade of the New York Times, charging the people of the British provinces with a want of military spirit, and boasting that 75,000 Yankee troops would take possession of British America without any difficulty.

New Orleans Reported Captured.

Colonel CLAIBORNE, of the army, who passed through Atlanta on Monday evening, direct from Mobile, reports New Orleans as having been recaptured by General DICK TAYLOR, and that General MAGRUDER was pushing on to Fort Jackson, which was garrisoned by three hundred negroes, and which, it was supposed, would fall an easy conquest before our arms.

The Memphis (Atlanta) *Appeal* is inclined to give credence to this report, for the reason that, by the latest dispatches, Gen. TAYLOR is represented to have captured an important point, ten miles North of the city, on the New Orleans and Great Northern Rail Road, and heavy firing was afterward heard in the direction of and nearer to the city. If the news shall prove true, it will send a thrill of joy throughout the Confederacy, and effectually put a check upon the future operations of BANKS in Louisiana.

Since writing the above, we have received the Mobile *Register* of the 4th, which says:

A number of private dispatches were received last night from Jackson, stating that New Orleans had been captured by our forces under Generals Magruder and Taylor.

The news was brought to Jackson, it is said, by Lieut. Scott, C. S. A. One story is that our troops crossed the river at Gen. Taylor's plantation, above New Orleans, and, perhaps, used three large steamers he had previously captured at Plaquemine for that purpose.

The news is of the first importance, and is calculated to change the whole aspect of the Western campaign, provided it be true.

It is a little singular that neither the Agent of the Associated Press at Jackson, nor our own special reporter at that place have telegraphed a word about it. We hear that the news has been officially received here, but the hour is too late to verify the report.

The *Tribune* of the same date has a dispatch referring to the report given by Lieut. SCOTT, as follows:

Jackson, July 3.—Lieut. Scott, of the artillery, has arrived here. He left New Orleans on Tuesday, and confirms the previous report of the taking of Kenner.

He says that Gen. Taylor crossed the river at his own plantation.

Gen. Magruder had captured some 7000 negroes at Brashear City and sent them to Texas. He was on his way below to take one of the forts, which was occupied by only 300 negroes, and he would then act with Gen. Taylor against New Orleans.

Lieut. Scott, he says, has no doubt but that New Orleans is now in the hands of the Confederates, as there were only four or five hundred troops there.

He says he saw the Confederate flag flying at Kenner's and below.

Duties of Officers.—From the little tract "On the Principles and Maxims of War," lately issued under the approval of General BEAUREGARD, we take the following directions, which we commend to the special attention of all officers who wish to discharge their duties faithfully:

When an officer is on active service in the field, everything connected with the daily life of his men should be an object of constant attention; no detail is beneath him. He must not think the arms and ammunition his most important charge, and that if they be in fighting order he need not trouble himself much about the rest. The arms are the fighting weapons, but the soldier is the machine which wields them; and it is to him—to clothing his back, and feeding his belly, and looking after his health and comfort—that the great attention is due. The arms and ammunition must of course be always in perfect order, but they are only required when in contact with an enemy. The natural condition of a soldier on service is the line of march. He will have at least twenty days marching to one of fighting; and he has to be preserved in health and comfort during those twenty days, otherwise his musket and pouch would do small service on the twenty-first day.

An officer should go among his men and himself look after their comfort. No fear of their losing respect for him because he does so. At the end of a march, he should never feel at liberty to attend to his own wants until he has seen his men engaged in cooking their meals. The rapidity with which a regiment has its fires lighted after a march, and meals cooked, may be regarded as a test of the attention paid by the officers to the comfort of their men.

Similarly before a march, an officer should take care that none of his men leave their encampment or bivouac without as good a meal as circumstances permit.

As regards equipments for the field, an officer must have as few wants as possible; and he should carefully study the art of putting up the articles it is necessary he should possess in the smallest possible compass.—The line of march must be considered as the natural condition of a soldier, and everything regulated with that view.

An officer charged with the arrangement of any military movement or operation should on no account trust to the intelligence of subordinates who are to execute it. He should anticipate and provide against every misconception or stupidity it is possible to foresee, and give all the minute directions he would think necessary if he knew the officer charged with the execution of the operation to be the most stupid of mankind.

Our Fibrous Plants.—EDWARD G. SQUIER has lately published a volume (CHARLES SCRIBNER, New York; JAMES MADDEN, London) on "Tropical Fibres; their Production and Economic Extraction." Although referring chiefly to strictly tropical plants, Mr. SQUIER's volume, we doubt not, would furnish much instruction to all explorers of our own botanical resources, as our bounteous and abundant flora runs almost into the tropical flora in some plants, and presents cognates of many others. From a review of this work in a foreign journal we take the following remarks:

The real importance of the subject is indicated by Mr. Squier, in the introduction to his work, as follows: "These *endogenous* plants not only furnish staple articles of food, oil, and refreshing as well as intoxicating drinks, but also are the productive sources of valuable fibres, of every degree of fineness and strength, and fit for the most delicate tissues as well as for the strongest cables. He will find that the hammock in which he reclines is netted from fibre almost as fine and soft as silk, and will probably be surprised to learn that it is supplied from the leaves of the wild pine apple, which he sees everywhere forming the hedges of enclosures, and scattered thickly through the forests. He will find the native boats rigged with cordage of superior description, and will be told that it has been procured from the agaves or *hennequins*, of which he will observe a small perennial patch, with their green, fleshy leaves, growing by the side of almost every hut. Or, if in Mexico, he will receive his passport on paper of surprising toughness and durability, made from the leaves of the *magney*—the price of which, supplying here the place of beer, cider, and the more potent whiskey, is sold in the shops over the way, under the name of *pulque*. Or, if in the East Indies, he desires to send home some souvenir of his travels, he will select from the stock of an itinerant pedlar a handkerchief of gossamer-like texture, almost as fine and as delicate as that which the spider weaves, made from the fibres of the leaves of the pine apple plant, the fruit of which he ate for his dessert. If, in Manilla, he will find ships of all nations filling out their cargoes with bales of excellent fibres, which he will mistake for hemp or flax, but which he will ascertain, on inquiry, are extracted from the stalks of the plantain, the forests of which, with their broad leaves, shadow over every path and by road of the island." The author lays forcibly before his readers the value and importance of these fibres, and urges the necessity of their being utilised on a large scale, now that the increasing deficiency in the world's supply so urgently demands the employment of every resource.

Army Correspondence.—By a masterly strategical retrograde movement, General Bragg has out witted Rosecrans, forcing him to follow our army across the mountains and leaving his base of supplies over 75 miles in the rear, greatly exposed to our cavalry.

Our army has fallen back to Bridgeport, with a force at Stevenson, at the junction of the Memphis and Charleston Road, thus protecting Huntsville and preventing our army being flanked—a chain of hills being in our front, and the river at Bridgeport only eleven miles distant, in our rear.

Rosecrans has been joined by Burnside's forces and all the troops garrisoning the posts from Louisville to Nashville.

Our retreat for the last two days has been conducted with great skill, the enemy following us up, and skirmishing having been continuous. The enemy holds Decherd, which gives them Winchester and Fayetteville.

Every confidence is felt in Gen. Bragg, his present position giving him great advantages over the enemy.

Gen. Morgan is in Kentucky with a clear road before him, so that we may soon expect to hear of good news.—*Atlanta Intelligencer.*

From Tennessee.—We have but little additional from the seat of war in Middle Tennessee. Verbally we learn that the impression prevailed in many army circles on Saturday last, that Rosecrans was moving Eastward from McMinnville and Winchester, as if for the purpose of crossing the river into East Tennessee, at some point above Chattanooga, and so strongly was it believed that steps were being taken to dispute his passage of the river. Our army is, as generally reported, at present in position on the South side of the Tennessee.

[*Memphis Appeal, 6th inst.*

A strange work is being carried out for exhibition at the Permanent Industrial Exposition at Vienna. It is a wooden library—that is, a hundred octavo volumes, the covers of which are formed of wood. On the backs, which are formed from the bark, are inscribed the trees they are made from. Inside are specimens of the leaves, flowers, fruits, &c., of the trees.

Blockaders are following in the track of the Southern army, gathering up trinkets and other useless articles, and hurrying them South to sell at exorbitant prices. If blockade goods were entirely prohibited, especially such trash as is daily brought to this market, the enormous premium on gold would decline, our own people would rely more on home industry and home ingenuity to supply their wants, and Southern Confederacy money would steadily advance in value.—*Richmond Dispatch.*

A few days since a party of our guerillas went round in the rear of Murfreesboro' and blew up two locomotives and trains, with torpedoes, one on the Nashville and Chattanooga, and the other on the Franklin and Nashville road. The torpedoes were placed underneath the track, with a screw percussion cap, or friction primer attached, which was so placed on the iron rail that the wheel of the car passing over it caused the fulminating powder to explode and ignited the magazine.

The Illinois Legislature has adjourned till January. The Governor informed the Committee who announced the adjournment, that he did not recognise the legal existance of the Legislature, as he had dissolved it by proclamation.

Abbeville Cotton Market.—The Cotton market during the last days of June assumed a more active feature than had been manifested for a month previous. The highest price paid was 35 cents.

Gen. Tuttle, of Grant's army, is the choice of the Iowa Democracy for Governor.

Cotton Interests and Prospects.

The following extracts are from a Circular of a Charleston house, furnished for publication in the Liverpool *Journal of Commerce*:

CONFEDERATE STATES OF AMERICA, Charleston, 6th May, 1863.

SIR:—We have hitherto deemed it superfluous to address a circular to our foreign friends, while the present war is being waged by the United States against the independence of the Confederate States, yet the present and future prospects of this country have such a forcible bearing on the production of Cotton, that it cannot but be a subject of interest to all.

The probable amount of Cotton likely to be available for shipment after peace is as uncertain as the duration of the war, but it has been generally estimated that the supply realized from the crops of 1860-1861 and that of 1862 would amount to 4,000,000 bales. From this must be deducted the large amount stolen by the enemy, burnt and destroyed by our own people, and the enormously increased consumption of our own Cotton Factories, &c., which must in the aggregate be computed at 1,000,000 bales. The exports during the above period cannot be correctly arrived at, but, from the official records in the Custom House in Charleston, we find the clearances from 1st July, 1861, to 1st May, 1863, to be 45,000 bales. Assuming, therefore, that the balance will be in a merchantable state, there is now available for export less than 3,000,000 bales in the Cotton States.

The production of this year's crop will be curtailed in part by legislative enactment and public opinion; the probable supply from this source is not worthy of comment, and from the want of bagging cannot be made available during the continuance of the war.

The business of running out Cotton through this so-called blockade is now extensively carried on, and facts demonstrate that the detention of the crop of Cotton and other articles of export on this side is to be attributed to the difficulties of transportation to other ports, and the scarcity of procuring steamers of sufficiently large capacity and such moderate draft of water as to effect a clear passage over our bar.

We find from official records that there have entered and cleared from this port from July 1, 1861, to May 1, 1863, 216 vessels of all descriptions, conveying 45,000 bales of Cotton, valued at near 5,000,000 dollars, and returning with merchandise of about 10,000,000 dollars, which is exclusive of many million dollars of army supplies for the use of our Government.

The extent of land planted in Sea Islands is small, and it will be years after the peace ere a large crop will be made.

Fully three-fourths of the open land in the Confederate States has been planted in grain, and the yield likely to be so far beyond the wants of our people, that an early peace would give a large amount for export.

We have not hitherto discouraged our friends sending out orders for Cotton, to remain in the interior until after peace; but in view of increasing risk from fire, loss of weight, depreciation and bursting of bales, expense of storage, insurance, and final shipments, we now recommend them, in preference, to invest in the Government 7 per cent. bonds, which guarantees Cotton at 6d. per pound, at the option of the holder, the only risk the buyer encounters in these investments being the security or stability of our Government; and what impartial observer of its progress, from infancy to its present strength, can doubt its success? The war may last for years, but the result must be the same.

We call the attention of our friends also to the tax bills just passed. Eight per cent is taxed by our Government on the value of every bale of Cotton owned by any party on the 1st July, 1863. The State of Georgia imposed a State and County tax of $1.50 per bale on all Cottons within her limits; and other States are likely to pursue a similar course.

Howard's Grove Hospital.

A correspondent of a Columbia paper writes:

I have just visited Howard's Grove Hospital, one division of which has lately been assigned to South Carolina, and the other division to Florida. The hospital has been built up by the energy and perseverance of Dr. C. D. Rice, of Colleton District, S. C., the surgeon in charge. Although a young man, he has already gained an enviable reputation. It is well located, in a fine grove, East of Richmond, where they have an abundance of fine water, far superior to any that I have found in the city.

I was highly gratified with the complete arrangements, the neat appearance, and the great cleanliness observed throughout, and the attention and politeness of the attendants. Mrs. Benson, of Greenville, S. C., is one of the matrons. Everything under her charge, and in her department, seems to be in perfect order. She is entitled to much credit for her industry and perseverance in the good work in which she is engaged. Dr. Rice informed me that he consumed the whole hospital fund in supplies. The sick ration is now $1.25 per day. This enables him not only to have the necessaries of life, but frequently what we now regard as luxuries. They have milk, butter, eggs, poultry, vegetables, and lately they have purchased for the sick 25 quarts of strawberries. These are selling in the market from $1 to $3 per quart.

I am induced to believe that Dr. Dice and the Government are both doing their duty, and are equally entitled to the thanks of our people. I wish very much that Carolinians would see this establishment throughout. They would certainly be comforted and relieved. A minister is provided for the hospital, at the expense of the Government.

The hospital at Manchester, heretofore a South Carolina hospital, has been discontinued, and all patients who were in condition for removal have been transferred to Howard's Grove; as well, also, those from all other hospitals in the city. Dr. Middleton Michel, the other and efficient surgeon from our State, in charge of this hospital, will soon be assigned to some other position. I sincerely trust that we will still have the benefit of his valuable services for the troops of our State.

The following is a list of officers in charge of Howard's Grove:

Dr. C. D. Rice, South Carolina, in charge.
Dr. W. A. Bellinger, South Carolina, now of Florida, Wards B and H.
Dr. H. E. Bissell, South Carolina, Wards D and H.
Dr. C. B. Finney, Virginia, Wards G and H.
Dr. A. Wallace, South Carolina, Wards C and E.
Dr. N. H. B. Goodwin, Virginia, Wards K and J.
Dr. P. P. Perkins, Virginia, Wards Q and L.
Wards M, N, C, P and R vacant as yet. The capacity of the South Carolina division is for 544 patients. The number of patients now in the division is 327.

A Remarkable Prophecy.—Private prophecies are of little account till verified by their fulfillment. We heard of one lately, nevertheless, that we offer to the reflections of our readers. Its author was a man in very humble life, a pious, good Catholic, who troubled not himself with politics, and hardly ever, if ever, looked at a newspaper. He died in December, 1860—the month after Abraham Lincoln was saddled on some of the States as President. He was near his death, and friends, visiting him, were discussing the political troubles, and speculating whether South Carolina would really secede. The good man had said nothing while they were talking. After they ceased, he said: "You have been talking of what is to come. There *will* be a war—a bloody war between the North and South. It will last three years, and the South will then become a separate Government, but not without the help of a foreign nation. When the North and South are separated, then there will be awful troubles at the North. The troubles will last for twenty years, and a hundred years from now the country will feel the effects of them. There will be a terrible persecution of the Catholics here after the country is divided."

This good man died soon after. His pastor, residing not far from this city, is a man of great learning and talents. He says that, for a long time, he had known the deceased as a man of very holy and meditative life. He was not a man of intellectual cultivation but a man of prayer. Whether it were the vagaries of a dying man, or the visions of coming troubles given to a true and humble servant of God we know not. We can only say that a subtile intellect, with a large reading of history and a keen appreciation of all the elements that are at work, if forced to utter the gloomiest and most probable of its provisions, would have said about what this pious, humble and unlettered servant of God uttered on his death bed.—*New York Freeman's Journal.*

Iron Shipbuilding on the Mersey.—There are now in course of construction no less than twenty-three vessels of various sizes, not including gunboats for the Emperor of China, and the frigate for the English Government at Birkenhead. An improvement in the building of ships has lately been introduced, and the reports from the experimental vessels are very satisfactory indeed. We refer to the building of vessels of steel. It gives ships double the strength of iron with plates just one half the thickness, thus allowing them to carry a cargo on a considerably less draft of water; it is also stronger than iron, and being of such light substance the vessels can be built with finer lines. So satisfactory have the experiments been that a keel has been laid down to build a ship of 1000 tons for Messrs. C. S. Lemon & Co., to trade between this port and the East Indies. The steel fleet are the steamers Banshee and Phantom (the latter now loading at this port for Nassau,) and the schooner Domitila, now on her way to the Sandwich Islands. Mr. Laird has also on hand the two gunboats for the Emperor of China, but about whose ultimate destination so much has been said. They are in a very forward state, and their launch may soon be looked for. Some of the plates used are five inch ones, and are bent to the requisite angle by hydraulic power. The vessels are beautiful specimens of naval architecture and very strong, built in Mr. Laird's well known style, and will certainly add efficiently to a fleet in either the China or Confederate waters. From these it will be seen that the trade is at present unusually brisk, and will bear favorable comparison with any other part of the Kingdom.

[*Liverpool Journal of Commerce, June 3.*

Artillery and Ammunition.—An official report from the chief ordnance officer of artillery of General Lee's army states, in reference to the performance of the ammunition of that army at the battle near Fredericksburg:

"I had an opportunity, during the action of Monday evening, of comparing the relative accuracy in the explosion of the rifle projectiles of our side and those of the enemy, and am satisfied that the advantage was with us. Many of their's were of the Schenckle pattern, with percussion fuse."

A report from the Chief of Ordnance of Jackson's corps says;

"This Confederate 12-pounder Parrotts and 12 pounder Napoleons are reported to be as good as the captured guns of the same kind in every respect, and, indeed, preference is shown for the Confederate Napoleon from its jarring less when fired."

It is a matter of congratulation that under all difficulties encountered the products of our laboratories and our Government workshops should prove reliable in the hour of trial. Few of those not engaged in labor involving mechanical appliances can estimate the disadvantages in spite of which those results are obtained.

The report also says: "Mr. McEvoy's fuze igniters proved perfectly successful with brass fuze plugs. With wooden fuze plugs they exploded the shells in all cases prematurely."

Mr. McEvoy is a well known and ingenious citizen of Richmond.

Cotton in Europe.—A friend has handed us ROSSMAN & CALDER's Cotton Circular from Liverpool, June 6th, 1863, from which we collate the following facts:

The stock of Cotton on hand in Liverpool, at the above date, was 371,530 bales, against 323,240 at the same period last year. Of the first mentioned amount, 45,344 bales were American. Increase of imports this year compared with the same date last year—191,906. Increase of stock, 48,290. During the five months ending 31st May, 1863, there were imported into Liverpool, from Charleston, 6763 bales, and during the same period last year 1,861 bales.

CITY INTELLIGENCE.

T. A. WHITNEY begs to call particular attention to the sales of valuable and desirable Stores, Residences, Vacant Lots, Wharf Property and Stocks, to be sold by him this day, 8th instant, at the Exchange. 3

UNION PRAYER MEETING at Trinity Church, this afternoon, at five o'clock. The praying public are solemnly called upon to unite in supplication to the God of battles, that our arms, especially in the far West, may be crowned with victory, and that an honorable and lasting peace may soon smile again upon these lands. The community, and the Clergy especially, are invited to attend. w

SUPERIOR SALT.—Persons in want of a superior article of dry, hard and clear Salt, made by an entirely new process, are invited to call and examine specimens at the Salt Works, West end of Broad street.

ANNUAL ELECTION.—At the regular meeting of the Cincinati Society of South Carolina, the following officers were elected.

H. A. DESAUSSURE, President.
JAMES SIMONS, Vice-President.
GEORGE B. REID, Treasurer.
JAMES SIMONS, Jr., Secretary.
Stewards.—Thos. R. Bateston and S. Wragg Simons.
Standing Committee.—Harris Simons, Wm. Hall, W. P. Finley, W. G. DeSaussure, J. Harleston Read, Thos. F. Drayton and Evan Edwards.

MR. JOHN T. SNEAD, of No. 274 King, near Hasell street, has presented us a box of Blacking, manufactured by G. D. BERNHEIM, Esq., at Charlotte, No. Ca. This Blacking is represented as affording a beautiful polish, and as made of ingredients entirely calculated to preserve any leather. Mr. SNEAD is the agent for its sale in this city.

The Missionary of St. Stephen's Chapel respectfully and thankfully acknowledges the receipt of the following sums in behalf of the poor, since his last acknowledgement, viz: from

Feb'y	11—A Lady	$10
	14—Mount Pleasant	10
March	8—Mrs.	10
	8.—Mr. J. W.	5
April	2—Miss C. G. P.	5
	5.—Mrs. J. G.	5
	5.—Mr. J. W.	5
May	5.—Mr. J. W.	5
June	1.—Mr. J. W.	5
July	2.—J.	20
	8.—Mr. J. W.	5

The Lord deliver these in the time of *their* trouble.

Soldiers' Relief Association.

The usual weekly meeting of this Association was held at the Depository, Chalmers-street. The Reports were read.

During the past week the following donations have been received:

From Miss M., 6 pair socks; from Mrs. J. G.'s servant Annis, 1 pair socks; through R. B. Rhett, Jr., 12 pair socks; from a Friend, 1 barrel of ice; from a Friend, half barrel limes from Nassau; through Mrs. Geo. Robertson, proceeds of a Raffle, $30; from a Member of Charleston L. D, through Mrs. J. G., $5; from Mrs. H., $2; from a Member, $10; Donation, $5; from a Lady, $5; from a Member of P. G., $2; from a Member of P. G., $3; from Mr. Harry McCarthy, proceeds of Concert, $180.

The following donations have been made:

To various applications, 40 pair drawers, 45 cotton shirts, 2 flannel shirts, 4 coats, 18 pair pants, 22 pair socks, 1 blanket, 1 bed comfort; to Hospitals in Columbia, limes; to Orangeburg Association, for Hospitals, limes, ice; to S. R. Hospital, limes, ice, eggs; to Roper Hospital, limes, ice, eggs; to Marine Hospital, limes, eggs; to Wayside Hospital, limes; to Citadel Square Hospital, limes.

The Sheriffalty—To the Voters of Charleston District.

The friends of Mr. JOHN T. MILLIGAN present him as a citizen worthy in every way to fill the responsible office of Sheriff of Charleston District. Mr. MILLIGAN well deserves the support of the community. His well known integrity, strict attention to business, long experience and familiarity with the duties of the office, gives him a claim to the suffrages of his fellow-citizens at the polls on Monday next. We trust he will receive the hearty and cordial support of the community. His Brother Mechanics and Firemen we feel assured will remember him. MECHANIC.

From Mississippi.—The Selma (Ala.) *Dispatch*, of the 1st instant, says:

We have been favored with an interview from an able and skilful observer of men and things, who comes immediately from Jackson and Canton. He is thoroughly satisfied that Grant's operations will turn out a dismal and bloody failure. There is no longer a doubt that his supplies are wholly cut off, and thirst and starvation stare him in the face. Not only do our forces command the passage of the river at Milliken's Bend, but General Chalmers also commands it at a point thirty miles above Arkansas, whilst a heavy Confederate force obstruct it on the Western side, eighteen miles below. The passage is completely barred, and the impression even at Johnston's headquarters is that Grant will immediately raise the siege, and, if possible, escape with the remnant of his army.

We learn that the Charlotte Depot is overflowing with the corn, peas, &c., collected for the *needy* soldiers.—The rats, it is said, and hogs are faring sumptuously, while the scarcity created has raised the price of meal beyond the reach of soldier's families.—*Yorkville Enquirer.*

The destructive operations of the Confederate cruisers in Northern waters continue unabated. The New York Herald, of the 27th ult., contains accounts of the destruction of no less than four more vessels, within a day or two before its issue. According to the Herald's statement there is a perfect nest of pirates off the Bay of Fundy, and great mischief is being done among the Yankee fishing boats.

Negro Women and Children Returned.—The Yankees have sent word to all the planters on the Mississippi River, whose negroes they have stolen, to send or come after their negro women and children, stating that they can afford to feed them no longer. The men are retained. It is said the poor negroes are in a deplorable fix.

The British steamer Seaquor, for which the United States Minister, Adams, lately granted a permit, much to the disgust of British merchants, to go to Matamoras, as she carried war material for the Mexicans, was captured at sea by the French, and sent as a prize to France.

Coal in New York.—The price of coal advanced one dollar per ton in New York in consequence of the invasion of Pennsylvania, and it is feared the price will be much higher.

Philadelphia papers are down on the Pennsylvania militia. They say the New York militia saved Harrisburg.

The Chicago Times says Lee is after Baltimore or Washington.

Consignees per South Carolina Rail Road, July 7.

62 bbls. and 24 sacks Flour, 212 bushels Corn, 85 bales Fodder, 260 bushels Peas, 100 bushels Rice, 175 sacks Meal, 50 bundles Paper, 27 boxes Tobacco, 8 tons Coal, Mdze, Cattle, &c. To H. Lee, H. C. Guerin, Mr. Kent, J. Larkin, Mrs. O. Norris, C. R. Brewster, E. H. Rodgers & Co, W. C. Bee & Co, J. R. Pringle, H. Stone, T. W. Johnson, W. M. Porcher, A. H. Atkinson, Wm. Ravenel, T. F. Capers, Mrs. Beckman, A. H. Mayor, J. S. McDonnel, M. Johnson, O. N. Averill, B. O'Neill, H. T. Peake, Miss A. Gray, J. T. Tresevant, O. Reeder, and Order.

Obituary.

The Relatives, Friends and Acquaintances of Mr. and Mrs. JAS. POWER are respectfully invited to attend the Funeral Services of Mrs. JAS. POWER, at Three o'clock *This Afternoon*. July 8

EDWARD KIVLIN,

An honest and worthy man who had been faithful in all relations and duties of life has gone to rest. EDWARD KIVLIN, one of the Clerks of the Southern Express Office of this city, died on Monday, 6th inst., from Consumption.

He was a native of Leitrim County, Ireland, and in his forty-second year. He was connected with the Express business in this city at and from its introduction under the ADAMS' Express Company, and continued under the Southern Express Company.

For most of the time he was the confidential and money clerk of the Charleston Office, and was always and justly rewarded with the fullest confidence of the Agent and Superintendent and of all his employers, and all patrons of the Company.

His leading traits in business were strict and exact fidelity to his employers, and so far as this allowed ample accommodation to all dealing with those employers. Faithful, courteous, diligent and exact in business, he exhibited an example which may be commended to all who are entrusted with the interests and business of others, and will be long and tenderly cherished by his sorrowing friends.

The Southern Express Company and all its widespread community of customers mourn in his departure the loss of a tried and faithful and most efficient agent. A widow and three children mourn the loss of a husband and father with a sacredness of sorrow into which, in this record, we cannot penetrate. We leave them for the present to the tender care of the God who has claimed it as a special and distinctive prerogative to be the God of the widow and the orphan.

The Philadelphia Inquirer.

CIRCULATION OVER 60,000. PHILADELPHIA, WEDNESDAY, JULY 8, 1863. PRICE TWO CENTS.

MAP OF VICKSBURG AND VICINITY.

Showing the Rebel Defences and the Union Approaches just before the Surrender, July 4, 1863.

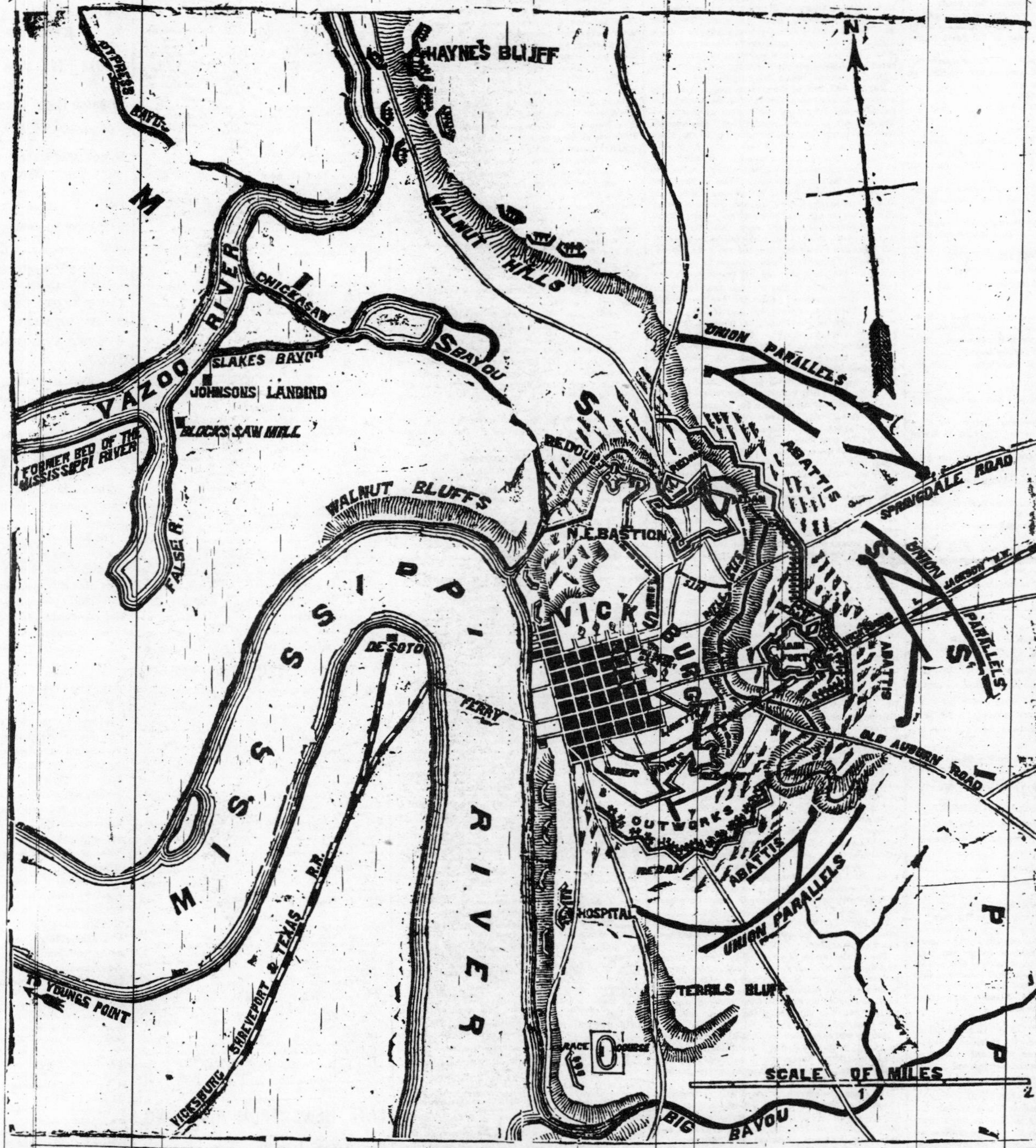

VICKSBURG IS OURS ! !

OFFICIAL REPORT.

WASHINGTON, July 7, 1 o'clock, P. M.—The following despatch has just been received:—

UNITED STATES MISSISSIPPI SQUADRON, FLAG-SHIP "BLACK HAWK," July 4.—Hon. GIDEON WELLES, Secretary of the Navy:—Sir: I have the honor to inform you that Vicksburg has surrendered to the United States forces on this Fourth of July.

Very respectfully, your ob't serv't,

D. D. PORTER, Acting Rear Admiral.

Conditions of the Surrender.

CAIRO, Ill., July 7.—The despatch boat has just arrived here from Vicksburg. She left at 10 o'clock on Sunday morning.

The passengers announce that General PEMBERTON sent a flag of truce on the morning of the 4th of July, and offered to surrender if his men were allowed to march out.

General GRANT is reported to have replied that no man should leave except as prisoners of war.

General PEMBERTON then, after consultation with his commanders, unconditionally surrendered.

This news is perfectly reliable.

THE REBEL RETREAT.

GETTYSBURG, July 6.—The report from the front is very cheering.

Our cavalry, supported by infantry, is close upon the heels of the enemy, and important results are likely to occur before night.

A despatch from General GREGG, of this morning, reports that the Rebels, instead of going to Chambersburg, are pushing to Greencastle. The roads are very heavy, and the Rebel trains are stuck in the mud, and the enemy are abandoning all their wounded in the retreat.

Every barn and house for fifteen miles is a hospital. They are leaving all their wounded, Generals and Colonels as well as privates. All their wounded will fall into our hands. We have taken, thus far, over 6000 prisoners, besides the wounded.

Another despatch states that the head of the Rebel retreating column passed through Greenwood, twelve miles northwest of Hagerstown, on Sunday forenoon.

On Sunday night, LONGSTREET'S head-quarters were at Jack's Mountain, ten miles from Gettysburg. EWELL'S at Fairfield, eight miles distant.

When the Rebels passed through Fairfield, they were moving rapidly, three columns abreast.

The slaughter among the Rebel General officers was very great. Major-General TRIMBLE is a prisoner in our lines, his left foot gone. Brigadier-General KEMPER is a prisoner in a dying condition. General ARMISTEAD, captured on Thursday, is dead. Major-General HOOD is wounded in the arm. Generals HETH, PENDER and PLUCKETT are also known to be wounded. Generals BARKSDALE and GARNETT were killed.

The enemy is reported to have a trestle bridge just built across the Potomac, above Williamsport. If so, their main force may escape.

A FIGHT NEAR BOONSBORO'.

FREDERICK, July 6.—General BUFORD, who set out with the intention of meeting STUART, had a fight with him to-day, somewhere in the vicinity of Boonsboro'. He whipped him badly. There is no further reliable information. STUART'S Cavalry, one thousand strong, commanded by himself, passed through Mechanicstown yesterday, with eight pieces of artillery. This is supposed to be the force that met BUFORD to-day.

Rebel deserters represent the army to be much dispirited, and out of ammunition. Yesterday General KILPATRICK, with his division of cavalry, attacked an ambulance train of Rebels under a strong guard, at Smithburg, eleven miles from Hagerstown. The train comprised one hundred and sixty ambulances and wagons, a great number of which he destroyed.

His artillery destroyed many wagons before the Rebels surrendered. He captured one hundred and sixty-seven prisoners, including wounded officers. He also captured two small pieces of artillery. Our loss was very slight, and that of the Rebels heavy, although they made but slight resistance.

THE REBEL ARMY NEAR THE POTOMAC.

Their Wagons Crossing on Flat-boats.

HARRISBURG, July 7—6 P. M.—Information from reliable sources proves, without doubt, the continued retreat of the Rebels towards Hagerstown and Williamsport. Their wagon trains are all in front, and are being ferried across slowly in two flat-boats. The Potomac is very high; in fact, bank full, and the troops cannot cross, their only pontoon bridges being destroyed. A large force of the enemy's infantry prevented the capture of Williamsport by General BUFORD with his cavalry. Our army is fast following them up, and a great battle will be fought before they succeed in getting away. This fight, it is hoped, will result in the capture or dispersement of the whole of LEE'S army.

There has been no intelligence received of any fight near Mercersburg. The report probably grew out of the cavalry fight of General GREGG, in which he captured 4000 prisoners.

THE REBEL ARMY ON THE POTOMAC.

A Battle at Williamsport.

HARRISBURG, July 7, 9 P. M.—A despatch received from Loudon says that a gentleman who had just arrived from Williamsport, brings the information that a big fight was going on when he left, and that there is no Rebels at Greencastle. The whole Rebel army appears to be on the bank of the river, and it is no doubt making a desperate fight.

FROM CARLISLE.

CARLISLE, July 7.—The railroad bridge here was finished to-day, and the road is now open to Scotland Creek bridge, six miles this side of Chambersburg. Between these two points about three miles of road is destroyed, and also about the same distance between Chambersburg and Hagerstown.

Eight dead Rebels were found yesterday in the wheat field which they occupied the night of the bombardment. This makes eighteen in all killed that night.

It is believed that none of the enemy now remain in this State. Hundreds of strangers arrived to-day in Harrisburg on their way to Gettysburg. Most of them go to seek their friends in the army.

Major BURT, Aid to General COUCH, commanding the troops here, sent yesterday to Harrisburg 188 Rebel prisoners, and this afternoon 34 more, including two captains. They are mostly deserters picked up by the militia.

There is no news of the late movements of General LEE.

MORE GOOD NEWS FROM NEW ORLEANS!

REBEL ATTACK ON DONALDSONVILLE.

A Disastrous Repulse.

THE REBEL LOSS SIX HUNDRED.

One Hundred and Twenty Prisoners Taken.

PANOLA, MISS., CAPTURED BY THE FEDERALS.

NEW YORK, July 7.—The steamer *Cahawba* has arrived with New Orleans dates to the 30th ult., via Fortress Monroe.

The New Orleans *New Era* states that a large Rebel force under Gen. GREENE approached Donaldsonville on the 27th, demanding a surrender. Of course, this was refused. The Rebels demanded the removal of the women and children, and at half-past one o'clock, on the morning of the 28th, the Rebels made a vigorous attack in force.

The battle lasted till daylight, three hours, when the Rebels were repulsed with heavy loss. Our loss was six killed and fourteen wounded, including among the latter, two officers. Our gun-boats participated in the action. Up to noon on Monday, our forces had buried sixty-four dead Rebels and were very busy burying more.

It is said that one hundred dead Rebels were left on the field and the entire Rebel loss is near six hundred. We took one hundred and twenty prisoners, including eleven commissioned officers, among whom are a colonel, two majors and a captain. A Rebel lieutenant-colonel, two majors and five contrabands were killed.

The Rebel newspapers received in New Orleans state that the Federals had captured Panola, Mississippi, destroying a large amount of Rebel property, and cutting off JOHNSTON'S communications and supplies.

VICKSBURG

HISTORY OF THE CAMPAIGN AGAINST VICKSBURG.

Farragut and Porter's Operations.

CAMPAIGN OF GENERAL SHERMAN

Brilliant and Successful Campaign of General Grant.

CAPTURE OF THE GIBRALTAR OF THE WEST

We give herewith a complete chronological sketch of all the operations against this formidably fortified place up to the period of its capture:—

Operations of the Fleet.

Flag Officer (since Admiral) FARRAGUT'S squadron arrived off Vicksburg, below the city, June 7th, 1862, and Commodore DAVIS, who had been successful in capturing Memphis, June 5th, descended the river with his squadron and took a position above the city, in the meantime communicating with FARRAGUT by land.

The Rebel iron-clad gun-boat *Arkansas* having escaped the blockade of the Yazoo, on the morning of July 15th, came down and succeeded in running the guantlet of the Union fleet, during which she fired seventy-three effective shots, and finally took refuge under the guns of Vicksburg. The same night Admiral FARRAGUT, with a portion of his squadron, undertook to sink her but failed.

We now pass over a period extending through five months, during which time little was done, owing to the low water, heat, and want of co-operation by the land forces, which were being concentrated under General SHERMAN.

General Sherman's Campaign.

Finally, on the 26th of December, an expedition under the command of General W. T. SHERMAN ascended the Yazoo about eighteen miles, where the troops were landed, and on the subsequent day attacked the advanced works of the city, six miles to the rear. In the meantime the gun-boats attacked the batteries on Haines' Bluff, and a portion of the expedition was also sent out to destroy the Vicksburg and Shreveport Railroad, in order to prevent the enemy from receiving reinforcements. On the 27th and 28th, after a stubborn contest, the Rebels were driven from their first and second lines of defense and the Union forces advanced to within two and a half miles of the city; but on the 29th the Rebels having been heavily reinforced from Grenada and along the railroad, attacked General SHERMAN with their whole force, and succeeded in forcing him back to his first line of defense.

General SHERMAN had counted upon the co-operation of General GRANT in this attack, but that general had been compelled to fall back from Holly Springs, which not only made it impossible for him to co-operate with SHERMAN, but had given the Rebels an opportunity of throwing in the reinforcements from Grenada. On the 1st of January, 1863, General SHERMAN was superseded by General McCLERNAND, and on the 2d the expedition withdrew from the vicinity of Vicksburg.

General McClernand's Campaign.

After assuming command of the "Army of the Mississippi," General McCLERNAND immediately began making preparations for a movement up the Arkansas River, for the purpose of capturing Arkansas Post, a strongly-fortified position, intended to defend the passage of the river, which is the great highway to Little Rock, the capital of the State of Arkansas.

This expedition was divided into two parts or army corps, one being under the command of General G. W. MORGAN, and the other under G. W. T. SHERMAN, but both under the supreme command of Major-General McCLERNAND, Commander-in-chief. Rear Admiral D. D. PORTER, commanding the Mississippi Squadron, effectively and brilliantly co-operated in the capture of this important place, which occurred on the 11th of January, 1863. From 7000 to 10,000 prisoners were captured, together with a vast amount of stores, animals and munitions of war.

About the last of January General McCLERNAND, with the United States forces, landed again five miles below the mouth of the Yazoo, on the Louisiana side of the river, and in full view of Vicksburg, and immediately commenced opening the canal across the Peninsula, which had been previously abandoned.

General Grant's Campaign.

General GRANT, with one Division, left Memphis January 27th, and arriving opposite Vicksburg at the close of the same month, took command. For several months subsequently he was never idle for a moment, being continually engaged in various projects to turn the Rebel flank and rear—such as the opening of the canal opposite Vicksburg itself; the attempt to get round into the Tensas River, by the Lake Providence Canal; the expedition down through the Yazoo Pass to Fort Pemberton, and the expedition by Steele's Bayou. None of these, however, were successful, and there is reason to believe they were only designed to divert the attention of the enemy from the great campaign to which we now come.

Admiral PORTER having succeeded in running by the batteries at Vicksburg, and several transports with supplies, having also gone down the river, General GRANT, about the close of April of this year, moved his troops through that part of Louisiana opposite Vicksburg, and, throwing them across the river, from New Carthage to Bruinsburg, commenced

The Great Campaign.

The following despatch from Major RAWLINS conveyed to the public the first intelligence of the brilliant successes of General GRANT in the opening of his great campaign:—

REAR OF VICKSBURG, WEDNESDAY, May 20, 1863. —The Army of the Tennessee landed at Bruinsburg on the 30th of April.

On the 1st of May we fought the battle of Port Gibson, and defeated the Rebels under Gen. BOWEN, whose loss in killed, wounded and prisoners was at least 1500, and loss in artillery five pieces.

On the 12th of May, at the battle of Raymond, the Rebels were defeated with a loss of 800.

On the 14th of May we defeated General JOSEPH E. JOHNSTON, and captured Jackson, with a loss to the enemy of 400, besides immense stores and manufactures, and seventeen pieces of artillery.

On the 16th of May we fought the bloody and decisive battle of Baker's Creek, in which the entire force of Vicksburg, under General PEMBERTON, was defeated, with the loss of twenty-nine pieces of artillery and 4000 men.

On the 17th of May we defeated the same force at the Big Black River Bridge, with the loss of 2600 men and seventeen pieces of artillery.

On the 18th of May we invested Vicksburg closely. To-day General STEELE carried the rifle-pits on the north of the city.

The right of the army rests on the Mississippi, above Vicksburg.

JOHN A. RAWLINS,
Assistant Adjutant-General.

The Capture of Port Gibson—Despatch from General Grant.

GRAND GULF, Miss., May 3, 1863.—Major-General HALLECK, General-in-Chief:—We landed at Bouilingsburg April 30, moved immediately on Port Gibson, met the enemy, eleven thousand strong, four miles north of Port Gibson, at two o'clock A. M. on

Continued on the Second Page.

The New-York Times.

VOL. XII—NO. 3678. NEW-YORK, WEDNESDAY, JULY 8, 1863. PRICE THREE CENTS.

THE RETREAT OF LEE.

The Whole Rebel Army Pushing for the Potomac.

The Route of Retreat Via Hagerstown and Williamsport.

The Army of the Potomac Pressing Closely Behind.

Desperate Efforts of the Rebels to Save Their Trains.

THE POTOMAC VERY HIGH.

Rumor of the Commencement of Another Battle Near Williamsport.

MOVEMENTS OF OUR CAVALRY.

Terrible Losses of the Enemy at Gettysburgh.

NEWS RECEIVED IN HARRISBURGH.

HARRISBURGH, Penn., Tuesday, July 7.

Gen. COUCH received information to-day, which is considered reliable, that Gen. LEE intends occupying and holding Maryland Heights until his army can recross the Potomac.

There is no news here to-day from the Army of the Potomac.

HARRISBURGH, Tuesday, July 7—6 P. M.

Information received here proves beyond a doubt the continued retreat of the rebels toward Hagerstown and Williamsport, with the intention of crossing the Potomac. Their wagon trains are all in front, and are being ferried across slowly in two flatboats.

The Potomac is very high—bank-full—and they cannot cross, their only pontoon bridge having been destroyed.

A large force of infantry prevented the capture of Williamsport by Gen. BUFORD, with his cavalry.

Our army is fast following them up, and a great battle will be fought before they succeed in getting away. This fight, it is hoped, will result in the capture or dispersion of the whole of LEE's army.

SECOND DISPATCH.

Later.—A dispatch from Loudon says a gentleman who arrived from Williamsport states, that a big fight was then going on, and that there were no rebels in the vicinity of Greencastle.

The whole rebel army appears to be on the bank of the river, and is no doubt making a desperate fight.

HARRISBURGH, Tuesday, July 7—Evening.

I have just received later and important intelligence from Williamsport.

The rebels were drawn up along the bank of the Potomac. The river was rolling and surging-brimful. The enemy had no pontoon bridges, and were ferrying their wagons across under great difficulty in two scows. The operation was so slow that it simply amounted to a stand-still.

Our army had already arrived at the scene, and *at 4 o'clock this afternoon a furious battle was progressing, in which the annihilation of the rebel army was almost reduced to a certainty.*

HARRISBURGH, Tuesday, July 7—10:20 P. M.

The latest report here is that the whole rebel army is routed in utter panic.

They are fleeing in all directions, throwing away arms, abandoning guns, trains and everything for life.

TELEGRAM FROM FREDERICK, MD.

WASHINGTON, Tuesday, July 7.

Mr. HENRY sends the following to this bureau from Frederick:

The rebels are known to be fortifying several gaps in the South Mountain, to cover their retreat across the Potomac. The main body of LEE's army will probably attempt to cross the Potomac at Hancock, for which point they are making in a disorganized, demoralized condition.

Our cavalry is operating vigorously on the rebel flanks and rear, capturing large numbers of prisoners. Several hundred wagons loaded with plunder, obtained in Pennsylvania, have been captured by our forces, and the prospect is that much of their ammunition and supply trains will be gobbled before they reach the Potomac.

Among the prisoners thus far captured are twenty-three Colonels, and a host of officers of inferior grades.

The rebels in the late battles lost thirteen General officers, killed, wounded or prisoners. A rebel Colonel, with whom I conversed, says that LEE's invading force did not exceed seventy-five thousand men. He had 180 pieces of artillery with him.

The rebel losses, as estimated by themselves, foot up thirty thousand. We have taken about twelve thousand prisoners, not including their wounded, who have all fallen into our hands.

Stirring news from PLEASANTON's cavalry may be expected within the next twenty-four hours. His forces are harassing the rebels in their retreat, playing havoc with their trains, &c.

Upward of fifty stand of colors were captured from the enemy.

NEWS RECEIVED IN PHILADELPHIA.

PHILADELPHIA, Tuesday, July 7.

The *Press*, of this city, has the following special dispatches:

GETTYSBURGH, Penn., Sunday, July 5—2 P. M.

A dispatch from Gen. HAUPT, who is in the advance, announces that the rebels are rapidly retreating.

We are now moving all our sick and wounded in this vicinity into town.

Four o'clock, P. M.—The Twelfth army corps is on the march, and is now moving in haste through Littletown, towards Williamsport, to cut off the retreat of the flying rebels.

Our left wing has just received marching orders.

Part of the artillery and cavalry belonging to Gen. PLEASANTON's command is in motion toward Frederick.

BLOODY RUN, Monday, July 6.

Gen. JENKINS has made off with his rebel cavalry.

A portion of the rebel cavalry, under Gen. LEE, is reconnoitering the Potomac for a ford.

HANOVER, Penn., Monday, July 6.

Our cavalry has not ceased to harass the rebel rear.

The rebels have abandoned their wounded, and they are now mostly in our hands.

We have buried large numbers of their dead.

Gen. FARNSWORTH's body was recovered to-day.

Our scouts report that Gen. LEE is straining every nerve to gain a strong position in the South Mountain Gap.

LEE is in the country roads, which are almost impassable, and his men and animals are reported to be exhausted with great fatigue.

Another battle is imminent.

FREDERICK, Md., Monday, July 6.

Gen. MCREYNOLDS sent forward a force to-day to discover the enemy toward Harper's Ferry.

The iron bridge at that place was so far destroyed as to be impracticable for the retreating rebels.

The rebels are retreating from Gettysburgh in all directions.

A wagon train conveying away wounded men was captured with its guard of 964 men to-day. They will be sent to Baltimore to-day.

Portions of the rebel army have passed through the South Mountain, but the Potomac is high and their pontoons are destroyed.

Gen. KILPATRICK is after the rebels sharply.

PHILADELPHIA, Tuesday, July 7.

The *Inquirer* has the following special dispatches:

CARLISLE, Penn., Monday, July 6—6 P. M.

Reliable accounts from the front state that the rebels are in full retreat toward Hagerstown. They were at Williamsport at 6 P. M. on Sunday.

Gen. SEDGWICK is close in their rear with 25,000 fresh men.

The rebel loss is estimated at 30,000.

The battle-field is strewn with dead and wounded for miles.

CHAMBERSBURGH, Monday, July 6—P. M.

Heavy firing is heard in the direction of Clear Spring and Williamsport.

It is supposed that MULLIGAN has come up from Hancock.

It was Gen. LONGWORTH, not LONGSTREET, that was killed.

The enemy appear to be retreating in all directions.

Gen. GREGG is in full pursuit.

Gen. BUFORD is reported at Hagerstown with the regular National cavalry.

Gens. FITZHUGH LEE, W. F. LEE, and WADE HAMPTON were at Marion on Sunday night with a wagon-train seven miles long and 2,000 cavalry.

The citizens are bringing in large numbers of prisoners.

All accounts agree that the Potomac is much swollen.

TELEGRAMS FROM CARLISLE.

Special Dispatch to the New-York Times.

CARLISLE, Tuesday, July 7.

Deserters are arriving hourly, picked up straggling on the mountains—glad to get out of the rebel army. It is probable there are no rebels in Pennsylvania to-day. The militia force is large, and daily increasing in effectiveness.

The railroad is repaired from here to Scotland. It will be all open in a few days.

Gov. CURTIN arrived here at midnight. WHIT.

PRISONERS ARRIVED IN BALTIMORE.

BALTIMORE, Monday, July 6.

The whole number of prisoners arrived here is 4,063, and more are on their way.

No intelligence has been received here of the capture of rebel prisoners by regiments or brigades.

IMMENSE STORES SAVED.

BALTIMORE, Tuesday, July 7.

Capt. E. P. FITCH, Depot Quartermaster at Martinsburgh, Va., arrived in this city to-day at about 1 o'clock, with his train of wagons, horses and Government stores, amounting in value to over a million and a half. It will be remembered that it was said that much of this property had been destroyed and captured by the rebels on Gen. MILROY's retreat from Martinsburgh last Sunday week.

MILITARY MOVEMENTS IN PHILADELPHIA.

PHILADELPHIA, Tuesday, July 7.

The first Union League regiment, with full ranks, is marching to the refreshment saloon, preparatory to starting for Harrisburgh.

MAJ.-GEN. BUTTERFIELD.

BALTIMORE, Tuesday, July 7.

Maj.-Gen. BUTTERFIELD passed through town to-day, for his home in New-York. His injuries are more severe than at first supposed. He suffers internally, and moves about with difficulty.

Gen. WARREN is now performing the duties of Chief of Staff.

OUR SPECIAL ARMY CORRESPONDENCE.

Further Details of the Great Battles of Friday.

GETTYSBURGH, Penn., Sunday, July 5.

As the details, the incidents and the general history of the great victory are brought to light, it is clearly defined as the most hotly contested and destructive engagement of the great rebellion. The peculiar feature of the battle is the ferocity and desperation with which it was fought by both armies, and the glorious issue places the lustre of the National arms, and the valor of the Army of the Potomac in the imperishable annals of brilliant history.

The battle occupied three days. Six hours fighting on Wednesday, four hours on Thursday, and including the artillery firing on Friday, thirteen hours that day, making a total of twenty-three hours, during which the battle raged with extreme fury.

The momentous and decisive part of the battle was that on Friday. It began really at daylight, and continued until 10 o'clock, the principal part of the musketry fighting being on the right, with SLOCUM's corps. A lull of three hours followed, during which the enemy massed his artillery on our centre, held by HANCOCK with the Second, and NEWTON with the First corps. At 1 o'clock one hundred and twenty guns opened on that position, and rained shot and shell in a perfect deluge for one hour and forty minutes. A graphic description of this awful period has already been furnished to the TIMES by an abler pen than mine, for that writer and one of the TIMES' messengers had the exciting felicity of enduring that storm of iron during the whole time. Mr. WILKESON is to-day engaged in the mournful duty of obtaining the remains and effects of his eldest son, the gallant young BAYARD, who was mortally wounded on Wednesday, left on the field, and dying finally, after ten hours' suffering, without a friend or a word to soothe the dying agonies of his soul. Lieut. WILKESON was but nineteen years old, yet had command of Battery G, Fourth regular artillery. His death adds another noble soul to the holocaust of this terrible war.

I rode this morning over the entire length of the battle-field, and it is not too much to say, for I have seen nearly every other battle-field in Maryland and Virginia, that the slaughter was perfectly unparalleled. Our details were busily engaged in collecting and burying the dead, and the ghastly, terrible sights were enough to shock a heart of adamant.

The vast number of dead lying in front of SLOCUM's line, on the right, and of HANCOCK's and NEWTON's on the centre, attracted much comment. They had been literally mown down by whole ranks at a single discharge. SLOCUM accomplished a bloody repulse of EWELL's corps on Friday morning, sustaining but small loss himself, his position being very formidable, against which the enemy insanely charged.

But the field, full of the greatest incidents and the scene of the most desperate fighting, was on the centre, in front of HANCOCK and NEWTON, against whom LONGSTREET's corps was precipitated. The enemy's front was that of one division in line of battle; there were two such lines, and a very heavy line of skirmishers, almost equal to another line of battle. Out of their concealment in the woods they came across the open fields and up the gentle crest, on the top of which was our line—a weak line of men behind a line of defences hastily thrown up and composed partly of stone walls, partly of rifle-pits, and partly of natural projections of soil and rock. The first charge was repulsed; the line broke and fell back before it had reached a point two-thirds the way over. A second line was formed; the officers came to the front, and with the onset of fierce and brutal hearts they rushed. Our men looked with astonishment, while fighting with great vigor; their line was dangerously weak; the defences were not formidable. A few men temporarily gave way; our advance, in some instances, slightly faltered. The artillery engaged was small in force, having been seriously weakened during the early part of the fight. The rebels came on so close that their expressions of fierce rage were plainly distinguished; some of them actually gained the inside of the first wall—but they never returned. Our immortal men, nerved to a degree of desperation never before equaled, poured forth such a devastating fire, and the artillery joining with its terrible canister, that the two long lines of the foe literally sank into the earth. Of the divisions of PICKETT and HETH, who made that charge, composed of eight brigades, positively not two brigades returned uninjured across the field. *The color-bearers of thirty-five rebel regiments*, who were in that charge, were shot down, the colors fell on the field, and were gathered by the victorious veterans of the Second corps. Being repulsed, large numbers of the enemy started back on the retreat, but our fire was so destructive that they fell flat on their faces, or again rushed about and implored mercy at our hands as prisoners of war. Seven Colonels of rebel regiments were buried on that field this morning; eight more were captured, beside those who were wounded and crawled or were taken off. Among the rebel officers killed and captured on that front were BARKSDALE on Thursday; Garnett killed, and Armistead wounded on Friday;—these general officers; Col. Magruder, brother of Gen. Magruder, killed; Col. Lee, of the Forty-eighth Virginia is a prisoner; Col. Allen, of the Forty-eighth Georgia is killed; Col. Miller, of the Forty-second Mississippi is a prisoner and wounded; Col. Frye, of the Thirteenth Alabama, and Col. Asborn, of Virginia are both prisoners. All these captured or destroyed by the brigade of Gen. Webb, a most intrepid officer, who won, with many others, the highest plaudits for his conduct.

A peculiar fact concerning our position is contained in the expression of surprise which the rebel officers uttered when they crossed our lines as prisoners of war. One of the Colonels said, as he looked at our thin line, "Where are the men who fought us?" "Here," said a Captain. "My God!" exclaimed the Colonel, "if we only had another line we could have whipped you;" and then, still gazing about him with astonishment, he continued, with great emphasis, "*By G—d, we could have whipped you as it was!*" This is a positive fact, and illustrates how the noble Army of the Potomac can yet fight, after all the imputations of demoralization and inefficiency which have been heaped upon it.

The Second division of the Second corps loses 42 officers killed and wounded, and 1,786 enlisted men killed and wounded.

The highest praise is awarded to Gens. HANCOCK and NEWTON, for their distinguished conduct on this portion of the field. HANCOCK was severely wounded in the thigh, but remained, laying on his back on the field, and giving the orders. Gen. NEWTON was especially active in supporting the line on the right with reinforcements.

History will never chronicle a tenth part of the gallant deeds performed during these bloody days; but the satisfaction of having nobly performed his duty shall be the sweet recompense of every patriot's heart.

The enemy, by a partially secret and ignominious retreat, has awarded to this gallant army the acknowledgment of victory. His forces are now on their way back to Virginia, beaten, weakened and demoralized by a terrible defeat; he is hotly pursued, a victorious army on his rear, a strong local force on his flank, and a swollen river in his front, are the obstacles to his successful retreat.

I regret to say that my esteemed friend, Capt. JAMES J. GRIFFITHS, of Gen. HOWARD's Staff, was severely wounded in the hip to-day while reconnoitering the enemy's rear line in company with the General. The wound is not dangerous.

L. L. CROUNSE.

DOINGS OF THE CAVALRY.

Gen. Kilpatrick's Attack upon the Enemy's Right Flank—Daring Movements—Loss of Gen. Farnsworth, &c.

ON THE BATTLEFIELD, Friday, July 3, 1863.

Gen. KILPATRICK this morning marched to attack the right flank of the enemy, with a view of forcing it in upon his parked train, and creating a panic in the enemy's ranks. Unfortunately, owing to a change of programme at a late hour, a misunderstanding occurred as to the point of concentration and one brigade, commanded by Gen. CASTER, went in a different direction from that intended, and the error was not discovered until the brigade was engaged, and could not then be well spared. This deficiency was in part supplied at a late hour by the arrival of Gen. MERRITT's brigade. Gen. KILPATRICK found the enemy—infantry, cavalry and artillery—occupying a strong position, and after skirmishing and driving in the enemy's line of skirmishers upon his support—in which the First and Fifth regulars took a prominent part, and notwithstanding his deficiency of force, determined to make an attempt to carry out his instructions. The First Vermont, Col PRESTON, and First Virginia, were ordered to charge. Led by Gen. FARNSWORTH, they moved forward rapidly, drove the enemy's infantry skirmishers from a stone-wall, leaped the wall and drove them pell-mell for more than a mile, under a galling fire of grape and canister in front, and rifles on our flank. Some of the men, indeed, went so far that, instead of returning with their command, they passed off a mile to the right, where they struck the left of our infantry line, and were thus enabled to regain their commands in safety. Gen. FARNSWORTH had one horse killed under him, and seizing another dashed on, and has not been seen since. It is supposed he was taken prisoner. ELDER's battery, as usual, was managed with consummate skill, and for the first time in this war, I believe, a battery was silenced, so situated that it could not be seen. This was done twice or three times. Some forty or fifty prisoners were captured, and a large number of the enemy's dead now cover the field. The position gained in this charge was an untenable one, and, therefore, at nightfall Gen. KILPATRICK withdrew his command to a position a little in advance of the one first taken in the morning. Although the special object of this flank movement was not accomplished, rebel prisoners admit that it prevented the enemy from massing their forces upon the right of our army, as they had intended to do.

At this hour I am unable to obtain a correct list of killed and wounded. The loss in killed is estimated at twenty, and wounded at about a hundred.

DANIEL HURLEY, of the Fifth New-York cavalry, was killed by a shell passing through his body. The same shell killed a horse, and afterward exploded and wounded several soldiers. JOHN BULKLEY, of the Fifth New-York, was wounded by this shell. The Fifth was at the time supporting ELDER's battery.

Albert Green, First Vermont—wounded.

—— Brounel, First Vermont—wounded.

Adjutant-General First Virginia cavalry—killed.

Lieut. Leisure, of this regiment, was also killed.

Capt. Phillips and Lieut. Wilson, of the Eighteenth Pennsylvania regiment, were wounded.

Lieut.-Col. W. P. Brinton, of the Eighteenth, had a horse killed under him—the second within a week.

The Chaplain, Capt. Harris, and another officer of the First Virginia, were killed.

Capt. Parsons, First Vermont—wounded in the shoulder.

Lieut. Cheney, First Vermont, was wounded in the hip.

Capt. Cushman, First Vermont—missing.

I shall forward a full list of the killed and wounded to-morrow.

Capt. DAHLGREN, of Gen. MEADE's Staff, yesterday captured one of JEFF. DAVIS' bearers of dispatches at Hagerstown. On his person was found a letter to LEE from JEFF. DAVIS, finding fault with the campaign in Pennsylvania, and urging him to return forthwith.

The heat during the day yesterday was very oppressive, and many men were prostrated in the ranks.

E. A. PAUL.

THE CASUALTIES.

List of Killed, Wounded and Missing in the Second Vermont Brigade, Third Division, First Army Corps, in the Battles of the 2d and 3d July instant.

We are indebted to Mr. GEORGE H. BIGELOW, proprietor of the Burlington *Daily Times*, and Acting Quartermaster of the Twelfth Vermont regiment, for the following list (nearly complete) of the casualties of the Vermont brigade.

Brig.-Gen. G. J. Stannard—leg.
Capt. A. G. Foster, Ins.-Gen. Staff—leg.

THIRTEENTH REGIMENT.

Lt.-Col. W. D. Munson—slightly.
Sergt.-Maj. H. H. Smith—killed.
1st Lieut. John T. Sennott, Co. A—mortally.
Sergt. Thos. Blake, Co. A—mortally.
John Shanaghan, Co. A—mortally.
John Cane, Co. A—missing.
J. Bruin, Co. A—missing.
J. Catlan, Co. A—missing.
Anthony Donnelly, Co. A—missing.
J. Herigan, Co. A—missing.
C. M. Nellis, Co. A—missing.
P. R. Ready, Co. A—missing.
W. Woodruff, Co. A—miss'g.
J. H. Wilson, Co. B—killed.
S. G. Dana, Co. B—severely.
D. Parker, Co. B—severely.
A. H. Chase, Co. B—severely.
J. Simmons, Co. C—sev'ly.
H. Martin, Co. C—sev'ly.
S. W. Benjamin, Co. C—sli.
J. S. Caswell, Co. C—slight.
A. Nye, Co. C—slightly.
W. C. Snow, Co. C—slight.
H. Wakefield, Co. C—slight.
C. Watson, Co. C—slightly.
H. Miles, Co. C—slightly.
G. Pierce, Co. C—missing.
V. Gemart, Co. C—missing.
O. Marseill, Co. D—killed.
W. Morch, Co. D—killed.
Sergt. J. F. Dinsmore, Co. D—wounded, severely.
Corp. J. M. Chapin, Co. E—severely.
Corp. D. Butler, Co. E—severely.
D. M. Dickenson, Co. E—severely.
W. Whitney, Co. E—severely.
John Hull, Co. E—severely.
Sergt. J. D. Catlin, Co. E—slightly.
J. Daniels, Co. E—slightly.
L. G. Seely, Co. E—slightly.
S. O. Wells, Co. E—slightly.
S. C. Sanborn, Co. E—slightly.
Corp. Henry Russell, Co. F—killed.
Corp. Geo. F. Baldwin, Co. F—wounded severely.
— Lawrence, Co. F—slightly.
— Kelly, Co. F—slightly.
— Mathews, Co. F—slightly.
— Byron, Co. F—slightly.
Capt. M. B. Williams, Co. G—dangerously.
Sergt. Albert Kingsley, Co. F—slightly.
Corp. J. W. Hitchcock, Co. G—severely.
Corp. John Combs, Co. G—slightly.
Horace Blaisdell, Co. G—severely.

D. Carey, Co. A—killed.
Michael McAnerny, Co. A—mortally.
M. Mulley, Co. A—mortally.
Corp. T. W. Sibley, Co. A—severely.
J. Hanlon, Co. A—severely.
A. Guinett, Co. A—severely.
J. Monaghan, Co. A—seve'ly.
J. Wallace, Co. A—severely.
Corp. J. Dolph, Co. B—slight.
D. L. Stoddard, Co. B—slight.
C. Carpenter, Co. B—slightly.
Z. Keyes, Co. B—slightly.
G. G. Mills, Co. B—slightly.
L. K. Dow, Co. B—slightly.
J. W. Richardson, Co. B—sli'y.
G. Stoddard, Co. B—missing.
S. A. Fiske, Co. B—missing.
Color Sergt. D. A. Marble, Co. C—severely.
J. E. Ballou, Co. C—severely.
S. S. Pratt, Co. C—severely.
Sergt. J. Harmon, Co. D—severely.
L. M. Bently, Co. D—sev.
M. P. Scullin, Co. D—sev.
Corp. R. G. Griffin, Co. D—slightly.
W. Crosby, Co. D—slightly.
John Johnson, Co. D—slight.
H. Tomlinson, Co. D—slight.
G. W. Lee, Co. D—slightly.
O. S. Kerr, Co. E—killed.
Lieut. F. Kenfield, Co. D—wounded, severely.
Corp. C. Wolcot, Co. E—wounded, severely.
Thos. Snell, Co. G—severely.
Corp. Geo. Cutting, Co. G—slight.
Jude Newcity, Co. G—slight.
John Tague, Co. G—severe.
Wm. Warner, Co. G—slight.
Henry Heath, Co. G—slight.
Corp. James L. Martin, Co. H—dangerous.
Andrew E. Osgood, Co. H—slight.
Wm. Roak, Co. H—slight.
Nelson Cattaract, Co. H—slight.
H. Wilson, Co. H—slight.
B. W. Wright, Co. I—dangerous.
C. E. Seaver, Co. I—dangerous.
Frank Jangraw, Co. I—slight.
W. L. Blanchard, Co. I—slight.
Martin French, Co. I—severely.
Corp. Church, Co. K—killed.
Serg't James Halloway, Co. K—slight.
John Elliott, Co. K—arm.
Oliver Parizo, Co K—slight.
C. H. Butterfield, Co. K—slight.
E. H. Richardson, Co. K—slight.

FOURTEENTH REGIMENT.

Sergt. Vaughn, Co. C—killed.
Thos. Burns, Co. C—killed.
— Sykes, Co. C—severely.
W. Sheldon, Co. C—slightly.
E. Stone, Co. C—slightly.
— Leonard, Co. C—slightly.
— Sheridan, Co. C—slightly.
Corp. J. H. Goodrich, Co. D—missing.
F. C. Howe, Co. D—slightly.
G. S. Lee, Co. D—slightly.
T. S. Hunt, Co. D—missing.
P. Carney, Co. D—missing.
Corp. W. C. Sturtevant, Co. E—killed.
John Brunell, Co. E—killed.
T. Dutton, Co. E—killed.
E. H. Fisk, Co. E—killed.
Sergt. D. G. Browne, Co. E—slightly.
Corp. C. Meade, Co. G—killed.
W. Green, Co. G—killed.
C. W. Ross, Co. G—killed.
Sergt. T. Bissonnette, Co. G—mortally.
M. Furlong, Co. G—severely.
Corp. H. Frazer, Co. G—slightly.
C. Delong, Co. G—missing.
C. E. Snow, Co. H—severely.
A. Noyes, Co. H—severely.
W. O. Doubleday, Co. H—severely.
Sergt. P. O. White, Co. H—slightly.
A. Bassett, Co. H—slightly.
L. L. Baird, Co. H—slightly.
P. Chenson, Co. H—slightly.
G. Hawley, Co. H—slightly.
L. E. Manley, Co. H—slightly.
C. Yettow—slightly.
G. N. Wright—slightly.
U. Jacobs—slightly.
E. Tatro—slightly.
H. B. Allen—slightly, mis'g.
T. Paane—missing.
W. Merrill—missing.
T. Barry—severely.
S. Carey—missing.
M. Ryan—missing.
J. Bower—slightly.

P. F. White Co. E—slightly.
J. B. Browlinan, Co. E—slightly.
H. R. Perry, Co. E—slightly.
W. H. Olmstead, Co. E—slightly.
N. S. Sherman, Co. E—slightly.
G. Merling, Co. F—killed.
Lieut. J. H. Bosworth, Co. F—severely.
S. B. Rice, Co. F—slightly.
F. W. Smith, Co. F—slightly.
A. Jones, Co. F—slightly.
L. Ward, Co. F—slightly.
A. Marnes, Co. F—slightly.
D. M. Ware, Co F—missing.
J. B. Perkins, Co. F—missing.
P. Humphrey, Co. F—missing.
M. Callaghan, Co. G—slightly.
C. Milleniff, Co. G—slightly.
H. H. Spooner, Co. G—slightly.
J. Levigne, Co. G—slightly.
E. Baldwin, Co. G—slightly.
L. Kent, Co. G—slightly.
H. Steiner, Co. G—slightly.
P. R. Rice, Co. H—missing.
Sergt. M. A. Clarke, Co. I—killed.
J. W. Dalliston, Co. I—killed.
Lieut. W. H. Hamilton—severely.
Sergt. L. Dickerman—mortally.
Corp S. M. Southard—mortally.
A. Dachne—mortally.
Sergt. E. F. Swett, Co. H—killed.
L. Allen—slightly.
J. Beaumont—slightly.
L. B. Gray—slightly.
H. Scradon—slightly.
J. Tifft—slightly.
J. O. Titus—slightly.
A. Wheeler—missing.
S. Geer—missing.

SIXTEENTH REGIMENT.

Chas. Morse, Co. A—killed.
Ira Emery—killed.
Capt. H. A. Eaton—sever'y.
Sergt. E. A. Eaton—sev'ly.
D. Abbott—slightly.
W. H. Gee—slightly.
P. Howard—slightly.
O. T. Larnerd—slightly.
A. A. Rice—slightly.
H. Ross—slightly.
G. Waldo—slightly.
M. A. Moody—slightly.
Lieut. J. Tarbell—slightly.
J. Fassett—slightly.
J. M. Joy—mortally.
J. J. Miller, Co. B—mortally.
H. B. Cobb, Co. B—slightly.
Sgt. P. Baldwin, Co. C—killed.
S. A. Winship, Co. C—killed.
Joseph Ashley, Co. C—killed.
Joel Spaulding, Co. C—killed.
Corp. H. Fletcher, Co. C—severely.
H. H. Carlisle, Co. C—sev.
Alfred Moore, Co. C—sev.
M. L. Bixbey, Co. C—sev.
Corp. V. N. Earle, Co. C—sev.
W. C. Lamb, Co. C—sli'y.
A. Rowell, Co. C—slightly.
J. W. Purse, Co. C—sli'y.
L. D. Miner, Co. C—slightly.
D. Johnston, Co. C—sli'y.
G. Kingston, Co. C—sli'y.
J. P. Johnston, Co. C—sli'y.
B. A. White, Co. E—slightly.
H. W. White, Co. E—slightly.
O. Rice, Co. E—slightly.
A. L. Thompson, Co. E—slightly.
W. S. Swift, Co. E—missing.
C. G. Tarbell, Co. E—missing.
Second Lt. C. B. Lawton, Co. F—severely.
A. Reed, Co. F—slightly.
E. Hascall, Co F—missing.
J. P. Cooper, Co. F—missing.
First Lieut. B. C. Dutton, Co. G—slightly.
H. E. King, Co. G—slightly.
J. E. Keith, Co. G—slightly.
C. F. Gardener, Co. G—slightly.
E. P. Davis, Co. H—killed.
C. P. Shepard, Co. H—killed.
Sergt. F. A. R. Packard, Co. H—severely.
Sergt. J. Carlisle, Co. H—severely.
Sergt. J. Mundey, Co. H—severely.
Sergt. A. J. Ellis, Co. H—mortally.
Sergt. B. J. Benjamin, Co. H—slightly.

W. Bennett—slightly.
W. Conant—slightly.
A. Leavitt, Jr.—slightly.
A. G. Barnes—slightly.
Sergt. L. S Emery—miss'g.
John Fowler—missing.
J. Goldthwaite—missing.
R. T. Hibbard—missing.
W. Waldo—missing.
Sergt. W. W. Ramsey—severely.
Sergt. J Mann—severely.
Corp. D. B. Stedman—severely.
G. A. Jacobs—mortally.
J. M. Martin, Co. D—killed.
M. L. Cooke, Co. D—killed.
John Dyer, Co. D—sev.
L. Cooke, Co. D—severely.
Corp. A. T. Wilder, Co. D—severely.
A. J. Stearns, Co. D—sli'y.
W. J. Howe, Co. D—sli'y.
R. W. Parks, Co. D—sli'y.
P. A. Chapman, Co. D—sli'y.
R. A. Hart, Co. D—slightly.
L. P. Daley, Co. D—sli'y.
P. D. Holbrook, Co. D—slightly.
J. C. Butler, Co. D—sli'y.
Corp. R. H. Tarbell, Co. E—killed.
Wm. Fenell, Co. E—killed.
Corp. H. C. White, Co. E—severely.
W. H. Rogers, Co. E—sev.
W. W. Walker, Co. E—sev.
Corp. A. J. Brannon, Co. E—severely.
A. Bugbe, Co. F—severely.
D. Chandler, Co. F—slightly.
C. C. Bemis, Co. F—severely.
C. Barker, Co. F—slightly.
A. Pike, Co. F—slightly.
T. Miner, Co. F—slightly.
E. Thompson, Co. F—severely.
Corp. D. S. Balls, Co. F—slightly.
W. H. Barrett, Co. F—slightly.
T. N. Marsh, Co. F—severely.
J. Hull, Co. H—missing.
Levi Blanchard, Co. H—missing.
W. Kelly, Co. K—slightly.
J. W. Haight, Co. K—slightly.
M. H. Graves, Co. K—slightly.
H. Hadley, Co. K—slightly.
E. H. Dudley, Co. K—severely.
C. Connell, Co. K—missing.
B. Lockwood, Co. K—missing.
J. Griswold, Co. K—missing.
D. Penkhouse, Co. K—missing.
Corp. H. S. Holden, Co. K missing.

SUMMARY.

355 killed, wounded and missing for the three regiments, as follows:

	Killed.	Wounded.	Missing.
Thirteenth	9	79	26
Fourteenth	17	69	26
Sixteenth	17	92	20

Casualties among Officers.

Col. Stone, commanding Bucktail brigade, wounded and taken prisoner.

Adjt.-Gen. John E. Parsons, missing.

Daniel Geish, Aid to Col. Stone, hit with spent ball.

ONE HUNDRED AND FORTY-THIRD PENNSYLVANIA VOLUNTEERS.

Capt. C. M. Cunningham Co. A—wounded.
Capt. G. N. Reichardt, Co. C—wounded.
Capt. Asher Gaylard, Co. D—killed.
Capt. Wm. A. Tubbs, Co. F—wounded.
Capt. C. K. Hughes, Co. E—wounded.
Lieut. C. C. Platz, Co. A—wounded.
Lieut. Wm. Lafrance, Co. E—wounded.
Lieut. H. M. Gordon, Co. F—wounded.
Lieut. Lyman Nicholson, Co. G—wounded.
Lieut. C. W. Betzenberger, Co. I—killed.
Lieut. O. E. Vaughn, Co. K—wounded.
Adjt. J. Jones—missing.

ONE HUNDRED AND FORTY-NINTH PENNSYLVANIA VOLUNTEERS.

Lieut.-Col. H. Dwight—wounded.
Capt. Alfred A. Scofield, Co. A—killed.
Capt. Brice H. Blair, Co. I—wounded.
Lieut. Lewis Bodine, Co. A—wounded.
Lieut. S. P. Seely, Co. F—wounded.
Lieut. Myron Fellows, Co. F—wounded.
Lieut. Alfred A. Thompson, Co. I—wounded.
Capt. J. H. Bassler, Co. C—wounded.
Lieut. John G. Botorf, Co. C—wounded.
Capt. Geo W. Soult, Co. H—wounded.
Capt. J. C. Johnson, Co. K—missing.
Lieut. H. F. Reynolds, Co. K—missing.
Lieut. C. F. Buckley, Co. K—missing.
Capt. F. C. Jones, Co. G—wounded.
Lieut. John F. Miller, Co. G—wounded.
Capt. John Irvin, Co. B—wounded.

ONE HUNDRED AND FIFTIETH PENNSYLVANIA VOLUNTEERS.

Col. Wister—wounded and prisoner.
Lieut.-Col. Huidekofer—arm amputated.
Maj. F. Chamberlin—w'n'd.
Adjt. R. L. Ashurst—w'n'd.
Capt. C. C. Widder, Co. A—wounded and missing.
Lieut. Chancellor, Co. B—wounded.
Lieut. Chetburn, Co. B—wounded.
Capt. Dougal, Co. D—w'n'd.
Lieut. G. B. Perkins, Co C—wounded.
Lieut. J. Q. Carpenter, Co. E—missing.
Capt. Gimbie, Co. F—miss'g.
Lieut. Sears, Co. F—wounded and missing.
Lieut. Keyser, Co. F—w'n'd and missing.
Capt. Sigler, Co. G—w'n'd.
Lieut. M. J. Rose, Co. G—wounded and missing.

TWENTY-SIXTH WISCONSIN VOLUNTEERS.

Lieut.-Col. Hanzborbel—wounded.
Maj. H'y Baletz—wounded.
Adj. Alb't Walter—missing.
Capt. Francis Lackner, Co. B—wounded.
Capt. Domschke, Co. H—missing.
Capt. Smith, Co. I—missing.
Lieut. Steinwheir, Co. B—wounded.
Lieut. Young, Co. C—killed.
Lieut. Lovak, Co. C—killed.
Lieut. Bartal, Co. D—wounded.
Lieut. Burkhardt, Co. D—wounded.
Lieut. Jwenger, Co. E—wounded.
Lieut. Troemel, Co. F—wounded.
Lieut. Fuerstenberg, Co. G—wounded.
Lieut. Marchauer, Co. H—wounded.
Lieut. Conrad Grode, Co. A—wounded.

MISCELLANEOUS.

Capt. John M. Stiffan, Co. H, 71st Penn. Vols.
Lieut. Granger, Co. D, 111th New-York Vols.
Lieut. Sutton Jones, Co. E, 72d Pennsylvania Vols.
Capt. A. McBride, Co. D, 72d Pennsylvania Vols.
Sergt. A. F. Strick, Co. D, 72d Pennsylvania Vols.
Capt. Wm. H. Dull, Co. B, 71st Pennsylvania Vols.
Lieut. F. Everetts, Co. D, 71st Pennsylvania Vols.—slightly.
Lieut. Stiles H. Bodin, Co. I, 71st Pennsylvania Vols.—missing.
Adj. S. D. Hutchinson, 71st Penn. Vols.—missing.
Lieut.-Col. Dickinson, Gen. Meade's Staff—arm.
Col. Colville, 1st Minnesota—wounded.
Lieut.-Col. Adams, 1st Minnesota—wounded.
Maj. Downey, 1st Minnesota—wounded.
Capt. Muller, Co. B, 1st Minnesota—killed.
Capt. Mesick, Co. H, 1st Minnesota—killed.
Lieut. Bruce, Co. I, 1st Minnesota—killed.
Lieut. May, Co. B, 1st Minnesota—slightly.
Lieut. Sinclair, Co. B, 1st Minnesota—slightly.
Lieut. Mason, Co D, 1st Minnesota—severely.
Capt. Farrell, Co. C, 1st Minnesota—severely.
Adjt. Teller—slight.

LATE NEWS FROM RICHMOND.

The Rebels in Profound Ignorance of the Whereabout of Lee.

Special Dispatch to the New-York Times.

WASHINGTON, Tuesday, July 7.

Officers arrived this evening from the flag of truce boat last sent to City Point, bring back rebel news, and files of Richmond papers to July 4. Profound ignorance was existing as to the whereabouts of LEE's forces, and the progress of the great battle. The rebel authorities had peremptorily ordered LEE's return. The belief was current that he was safe in the Shenandoah Valley.

The *Sentinel*, and *Enquirer*, of July 4, both contain accounts of the skirmish of the 2d inst., between the rebel forces under Maj.-Gen. D. H. HILL and our troops under Col. WEST, near Bottom's Bridge. They claim to have driven our forces four miles, to Tunstall's Station, and acknowledge a loss of only two men. On the same day, they say, two thousand Federal mounted infantry, with artillery, went into King William County and captured nearly all the Home Guard. They suppose DIX and KEYES to be making in a northwest direction, to cut off railroad connections.

The *Enquirer* of July 4 also publishes an arrival from Shippensburgh of a Georgian, reporting LEE's army anxious to get at the "Melish," but fear an opportunity will not be afforded them so long as the "St. Lawrence" is passable.

The *Sentinel* Extra of July 4, gives, under head of "Important from Louisiana," unofficial information by telegraph from Jackson, Miss. It states that an officer had just arrived, reporting that Gen. MAGRUDER and DICK TAYLOR crossed the Mississippi at Kenner, ten miles above New-Orleans, marching on that city, which is garrisoned only by fifteen hundred Federal troops.

VICKSBURG.

VICTORY!

Gen. Grant's Celebration of the Fourth of July.

Unconditional Surrender of the Rebel Stronghold.

THE NEWS OFFICIAL.

Dispatch from Admiral Porter to the Navy Department.

Great Rejoicing Throughout the Country.

WASHINGTON, Tuesday, July 7—1 P. M.

The following dispatch has just been received:

U. S. MISSISSIPPI SQUADRON,
FLAGSHIP BLACK HAWK, July 4, 1863.

Hon. Gideon Welles, Secretary of the Navy:

SIR: I HAVE THE HONOR TO INFORM YOU THAT VICKSBURGH SURRENDERED TO THE UNITED STATES FORCES ON THE 4TH OF JULY.

Very respectfully,

Your obedient servant,

D. D. PORTER,

Acting Rear-Admiral.

UNOFFICIAL REPORTS FROM CAIRO.

CAIRO, Ill., Tuesday, July 7.

The dispatch boat has just arrived here from Vicksburgh. She left at 10 o'clock on Sunday morning.

The passengers announce that Gen. PEMBERTON sent a flag of truce on the morning of the 4th of July, and offered to surrender if his men were allowed to march out.

Gen. GRANT is reported to have replied that no men should leave, except as prisoners of war.

Gen. PEMBERTON then, after consultation with his commanders, unconditionally surrendered.

This news is perfectly reliable

THE HERO OF THE MISSISSIPPI VALLEY.

Ever hopefully, but with feverish interest, the loyal people of the North have been watching more than seven weeks for the great news of the fall of Vicksburgh, that at last came yesterday as the crowning sheaf in the full harvest of Independence Day Victories. Now that the victory is assured, our readers will doubtless like to read somewhat of the history of the man who is the instrument of its achievement—Maj.-Gen. ULYSSES S. GRANT, in whom has centered so much of interest and of hope.

Gen. GRANT, whose brilliant exploits since the commencement of hostilities have fairly won for him the title of hero of the Mississippi Valley, was born at Point Pleasant, Clairmont County, Ohio, April 27, 1822, and entered West Point Military Academy, from his native State, in 1839, where he graduated with honors July 1, 1843, with the brevet rank of second lieutenant, receiving his appointment of Second Lieutenant of the Fourth Infantry Sept. 30, 1845. Though but 40 years old, he has been oftener under fire than any other man living on this continent, excepting that great chieftain now reposing on his laurels, Lieut.-Gen. SCOTT. He was in every battle in Mexico that was possible for any one man to be in. He followed the victorious standard of Gen. TAYLOR on the Rio Grande, and was in the battles of Palo Alto, Resaca de la Palma and Monterey. He was with Gen. SCOTT at Vera Cruz, and participated in every battle from the Gulf to the City of Mexico. He was breveted first lieutenant September 8, 1847, for gallant and meritorious conduct at the battle of Molino del Rey, and on the 13th of the same month he was breveted captain for gallant and meritorious conduct at the battle of Chepultepec. He has received the baptism of fire. No young officer came out of the Mexican war with more distinction than GRANT, and the records of the War Department bear official testimony of his gallant and noble deeds. He resigned the service on the 31st of July, 1854, being then full captain in the Fourth infantry, and in 1860, he settled at Galena, Illinois.

At the breaking out of the rebellion he was one of the first to offer his services to the Government, saying that, as he had been educated by the Government, that Government was entitled to his services in its time of perils. He was appointed Colonel of the Twenty-first regiment Illinois Volunteers, and went into actual service in Missouri, remaining with his regiment until promoted a Brigadier-General, with commission and rank from the 17th of May, 1861. His commands in Missouri were important, and he discharged every duty with great fidelity and advantage to the public service. With a military head and a military hand he everywhere evoked order from chaos. Military discipline, order and economy traveled in his path. In time, he was made a Brigadier-General, and intrusted with the important command of the district of Cairo, and how diligently, how faithfully, how satisfactorily he discharged all his duties, is well known to the country. While in that command, learning of a movement about being made by the rebels at Columbus to send out a large force to cut off Col. OGLESBY, who had gone into Missouri after that roaming bandit JEFF. THOMPSON, by a sudden and masterly stroke he fell upon Belmont, and after a brilliant and decisive action, in which he and his troops displayed great bravery, he broke up the rebel camp with great loss, and then returned to Cairo. The expedition was broken up, OGLESBY's command was saved, and everything was accomplished that was expected.

In time came the operations up the Cumberland and Tennessee, rivers and by a singular coincidence, on the 29th day of January, 1862, without any suggestion from any source, Gen. GRANT and Commodore FOOTE, always acting in entire harmony, applied for permission to move up those rivers, which was granted. The gunboats and land forces moved up to Fort Henry

[Continued on Eighth Page.]

THE NEW YORK HERALD.

WHOLE NO. 9807. | NEW YORK, THURSDAY, JULY 23, 1863. | PRICE THREE CENTS

CAPTURE OF JACKSON, MISS.

Another Brilliant Victory by Grant's Army.

General Sherman and His Gallant Forces in Possession of Jackson.

Joe Johnston's Rebels in Full Retreat Eastward.

Their Present Condition and Future Prospects.

The Rebel Paroled Prisoners Deserting En Masse.

Brilliant Success of the Union Arms at Various Points.

OFFICIAL DESPATCHES FROM GEN. GRANT.

Immense Captures of Prisoners, Cattle and Ammunition,

&c., &c., &c.

MEMPHIS, July 20, 1863.

By an arrival from below we have Natchez dates of the 20th, Jackson of the 13th and Vicksburg of the 18th instant.

General Sherman ordered a charge on General Johnston's forces on Friday; but they had so far escaped that capturing them was out of the question.

We only got a few stragglers, a few guns and some ammunition. A portion of General Sherman's army is now in Jackson, which is his headquarters, while the remainder are on the way back to Vicksburg.

Eight steamers left Vicksburg on the 6th instant for Natchez, having on board 1,200 soldiers, under the command of General Ransom. On arrival he captured five rebel officers, and, crossing the river, he captured a battery of nine guns, four of which were ten-pounder Parrotts.

He then marched back into the country nine miles, and captured 247 boxes of ammunition and nine more guns. The rebels fled in consternation. On returning to Natchez he found five thousand head of Texas cattle and four thousand hogsheads of sugar, all of which he took possession of in the name of the United States.

On the 8th instant two steamers arrived from New Orleans, via Port Hudson, bringing up 2,300 paroled rebel prisoners.

Two steamers left on the 8th instant for New Orleans, with large loads of cattle, and three more for Vicksburg with live stock.

The steamers Louisville and Elmira, captured up the Red river, arrived at Vicksburg on the 17th inst.

Official Despatches from General Grant.

WASHINGTON, July 24, 1863.

The following has been received here:—

VICKSBURG, Miss., July 12, 1863.

Major General HALLECK, General-in-Chief:—

General Sherman has Jackson invested from Pearl river on the north to the river on the south. This has cut off many hundred cars from the confederacy. Sherman says he has force enough, and feels no apprehension about the result.

Finding that Yazoo City was being fortified, I sent General Herron there with his division. He captured several hundred prisoners and one steamboat. Five pieces of heavy artillery and all the public stores fell into our hands. The enemy burned three steamboats on the approach of the gunboats.

The DeKalb was blown up and sunk in fifteen feet of water by the explosion of a torpedo.

Finding that the enemy were crossing cattle for the rebel army at Natchez, and were said to have several thousand there, I have sent steamboats and troops to collect them and destroy all boats and means for making more.

U. S. GRANT, Major General.

VICKSBURG, Miss., July 18, 1863.

Major General H. W. HALLECK, General-in-Chief:—

Joe Johnston evacuated Jackson on the night of the 16th instant. He is now in full retreat east. Sherman says most of Johnston's army must perish from heat, lack of water and general discouragement.

The army paroled here have, to a great extent, deserted, and are scattered over the country in every direction.

Learning that Yazoo City was being fortified I sent Gen. Herron there. Five guns were captured, many stores, and about three hundred prisoners.

Gen. Ransom was sent to Natchez to stop the crossing of cattle for the Eastern army. On arrival he found that large numbers had been driven out of the city to be pastured, also that munitions of war had recently been crossed over to wait for Kirby Smith. He mounted about two hundred of his men and sent them in both directions.

They captured a number of prisoners and five thousand head of Texas cattle, two thousand head of which were sent to General Banks. The balance have been or will be brought here.

In Louisiana they captured more prisoners, and a number of teams loaded with ammunition. Over two million rounds of ammunition were brought back to Natchez with the teams captured, and [illegible] rounds, besides artillery ammunition, were destroyed.

U. S. GRANT, Major General Commanding.

United States Gunboat Baron DeKalb.

We have news that the United States gunboat Baron DeKalb was destroyed by the explosion of two rebel torpedoes while proceeding up the Yazoo river.

She was built in the early part of the rebellion, and has done much excellent service.

The following were her dimensions:—Length, 200 feet; breadth on deck, 40 feet; depth of hold, 8½ feet. She was driven by two powerful side-wheels, each twenty-eight feet in diameter, with twelve feet buckets. Her hull was of immense strength, having walls of heavy gum timber of great thickness, sufficient to repel any ordinary cannon shot, and encased with heavy plate iron extending four feet below the water line. She was finished with a sharp prow, rising five feet above the water line, and having an immense solid wrought iron ram, weighing fifty-seven hundred pounds, so shaped that, in coming in contact with any opposing body, it should hit first directly at the water line, which is also the thickest portion of this ram. The ram set against solid timbers, crossed and bolted together into one compact mass, extending back thirty four feet. The force of a blow struck by such a huge mass of iron and timber can scarcely be estimated. With any reasonable degree of momentum, the blow would be irresistible. Running at a rate of ten miles an hour, it would penetrate and pulverize a solid rock. This powerful ram was further strengthened by three fore-and-aft bulkheads, extending the length of the vessel. These were again braced by cross bulkheads, water tight, by which her hull was divided into twenty-eight compartments. Thus, in addition to the strength imparted, her own side could be stove in by a ram, or she might be pierced or even "riddled" by a cannon shot, and still she would float. The filling of any two or three of these compartments would by no means cause her to sink.

Her main deck was open forty feet back from the front and thirty feet forward from the stern. From these points the casemates enclosing the gun deck commence. These casemates, like those on the old gunboats, rose at an angle of forty-five degrees with the deck and were eight feet high. They were of heavy gum timber, and plated entirely around with iron. She was pierced for thirteen guns.

The boilers were four in number, thirty-two feet each in length and forty-two inches in diameter. They were placed ten inches clear below the water line, and were entirely surrounded by coal bunkers, so that the possibility of a cannon ball reaching them did not exist. She had two high pressure engines, having twenty-six inch cylinders each and eight feet stroke. They stood on the main deck, but were so situated as to be secure from chance shots. She was also furnished with pumping engine and auxiliary steam apparatus for repelling boarders. Her pilot house was a six sided cone, its sides having an angle of forty-five degrees with the main deck. They were of heavy timber, and securely plated with iron. All her decks, wherever exposed, were covered with three-quarter inch iron, besides being strong in timber and planking themselves. The wheelhouses were covered with iron on the sides to a line even with the hurricane deck, and on the ends were protected from fore and aft shots by extra iron-clad casemates, having the same inclination as the sides of the vessel. The quarters for officers and men were on the main deck. Aft of the wheelhouses the enclosed portion of this deck was divided into rooms for the several officers' messes. The crew swung their hammocks on the gun deck, forward of the wheels. Two ranges of apartments were built on the hurricane deck, between the wheelhouses, one on either side of the boat, which were occupied for offices for the flag officer, paymaster and executive officer, and for kitchens, closets, pantries, &c.

She was a fast vessel, and had earned a name on the river of being an excellent one. The following is a list of her officers:—

Lieutenant Commander—John G. Walker.
Acting Volunteer Lieutenant—John V. Johnston.
Masters—C. S. Kindrick, R. H. Medill.
Ensigns—H. H. Gorringe, Chas. Hunter.
Acting Assistant Surgeon—John Wise.
Paymaster—Wm. A. Mann.
Engineers—Chief, Thos. Hebron; First Assistant, Jas. L. Smith; Second Assistant, Geo. L. Britton; Third Assistant, —— Willcoxsen.
Master's Mates—E. D. Bruce, F. C. Davis (dead), J. C. Meachunn.
Gunner—J. A. McDonald.

THE CAPTURE OF THE CAPITAL OF MISSISSIPPI.

The Defeat of the Rebel General Joe Johnston and His Evacuation of the City.

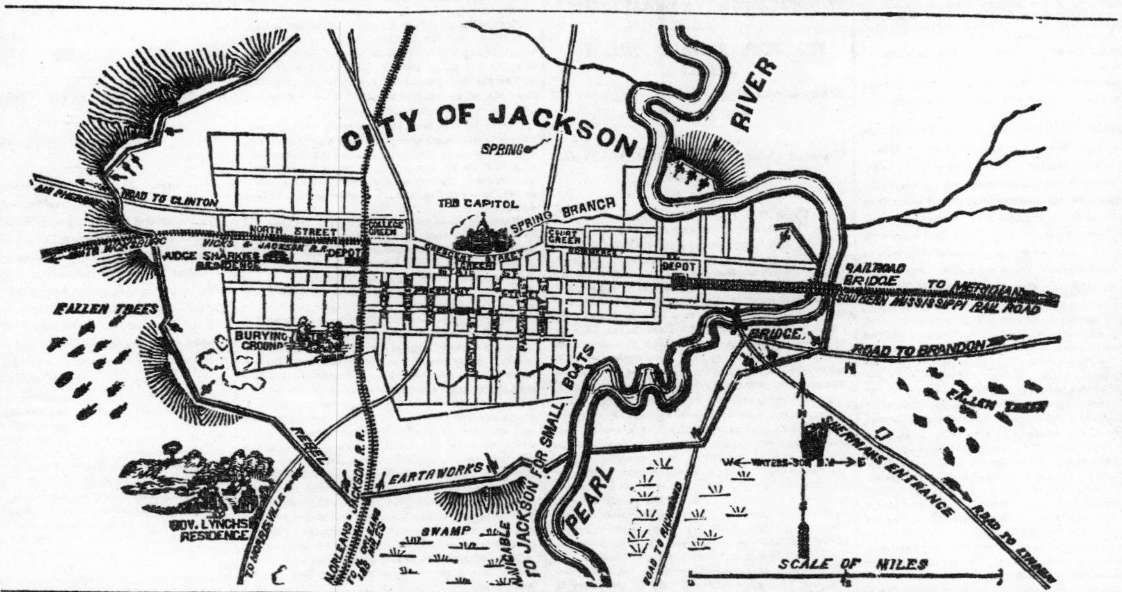

NEWS FROM NEW ORLEANS.

ARRIVAL OF THE STEAMSHIP CREOLE.

Effects of the Great Union Victories.

Changed Aspect of Affairs in the Department of the Gulf,

&c., &c., &c.

The United States steamship Creole, Captain Thompson, from New Orleans on the 16th inst., arrived at this port at about twelve o'clock last night. She brought the United States mails, passengers, and $300,000 in gold.

On the 19th inst., off Carysport reef, the Creole passed the bark Waltham, bound west. On the same day, off Cape Florida, passed the United States gunboat R. R. Cuyler, with a prize side-wheel steamer in tow, bound North.

We are indebted to Purser Cook, of the Creole, for the latest New Orleans despatches and papers.

Our New Orleans Correspondence.

NEW ORLEANS, July 15, 1863.

Change in the Aspect of Affairs in this Department—Particulars of the Surrender of Port Hudson—The Rebel Garrison and the Regiments Composing It—Artillery, Small Arms and Munitions of War Found Within the Works—The Strength of the Position—Arrival of Rebel Officers, Prisoners of War—Effect of Our Artillery Fire—Army Movements—Efforts to Recover Brashear City—The Result of Our Victories in this Department—What Will be Done With Port Hudson—Naval News, &c., &c.

As you may suppose, matters in this vicinity have assumed an entirely different aspect from what they were two weeks since. The rapid and overwhelming Union victories have thoroughly crushed the secessionists here; they are used up completely, and although some still doubt that Vicksburg has surrendered, the majority show by their extremely long faces the utter hopelessness of their cause. Two weeks since everything appeared gloomy enough, yet now the skies never looked so bright since the first gun was fired at Fort Sumter. This morning we have the news by the steamship Columbia of the great victory of General Meade over the favorite rebel General Lee. This is the "last feather that breaks the camels back," and we may consider the rebellion as being virtually crushed. There is a little work to be done in this vicinity yet; but it sinks into such perfect insignificance in comparison with affairs at the North that it is hardly worth mentioning.

We have received the particulars of the surrender of Port Hudson; but they are of very little moment. When the salutes were fired in honor of the surrender of Vicksburg the rebels very naturally desired to know what they were for. When the information was conveyed to General Gardner, the rebel commander, he addressed a note to General Banks and asked if he had any official information on the subject. General Banks replied by sending a copy of the despatch received from General Banks. Upon receiving this official information General Gardner at once asked that General Banks appoint a board of officers to arrange with three appointed by himself the terms of surrender. This was immediately done, and the terms of capitulation were agreed upon on the afternoon of the 7th. The formal surrender took place the next morning, our troops at that time occupying the famous stronghold. When it became known that the place had been surrendered the rebel soldiers flocked in crowds to the parapet of their line of works, and a most animated conversation was kept up for some time with our men, and after we marched in and had taken possession the utmost good feeling prevailed, from the generals commanding down to the drummer boys. No one would have supposed from the scene presented that only a few hours before these men were striving to shoot each other down, or that they had ever been anything else than the most dear and intimate friends. Such, however, is war. Although the surrender of Port Hudson was occasioned by the fall of Vicksburg, it could not have held out many days longer; for the garrison was reduced to a state of starvation. There was not a bushel of corn within the works, and officers and men were feeding on mule meat and rats, as I have before informed you.

The works at Port Hudson were found to be fully as strong as represented, but every part of them had been searched by our shot and shell. Large trees had been cut down and the earth torn up in every direction. Only one house was uninjured, and that is now occupied as a telegraph office. The nine-inch shot and shell from the naval battery had done the most damage: the effects of them could be seen on every side. It is very evident—at least officers say so who are capable of judging—that had Vicksburg not fallen, and a supply of provisions could have been obtained, we might have knocked in vain at the door of Port Hudson. Any assault we might have attempted would have been repulsed with great slaughter. The amount of artillery we have captured is smaller than I anticipated. It is represented to be as follows:—Two ten inch columbiads, one eight inch columbiad, two thirty-two pounders, rifled; one forty two pounder, rifled; one forty two pounder, smooth bore; one thirty two pounder, smooth bore, and four field batteries. Several other heavy guns were inside the works, but they had been disabled and rendered worthless by our fire. Six thousand stand of arms, with a large amount of ammunition, also form part of the spoils, and the number of prisoners will reach nearly six thousand, say fifty-five hundred at least. The troops that composed the garrison were the Tenth, Fourteenth, Fifteenth, Eighteenth and Twenty-third Arkansas, the First and Thirty ninth Mississippi, the First and Forty-ninth Alabama, Miles' Legion of Louisiana troops, and Wingfield's cavalry. The loss sustained by the enemy during the siege they report to be six hundred and ten, and but a small portion only was occasioned by the fire of artillery. Large caves had been dug in which the men slept, and covered themselves from the perfect hail storm of bullets and pieces of bursting shell. There does not appear to have been any females within the works, consequently the reports of two having been killed are without foundation. The sick and wounded of the enemy are being well cared by our own and the rebel surgeons. Yesterday the steamer Zephyr arrived from Springfield Landing, bringing a large number of rebel commissioned officers, who formed part of the garrison at Port Hudson; they are lodged in the Custom House, where they will remain until the pleasure of the Secretary of War is known. Those who have seen and conversed with them say they are a very pleasant, gentlemanly set of fellows, full of good humor, and not at all cast down at their misfortune. Their experience during the last six weeks has not been of a nature to increase their fondness for war and its honors. Generals Gardner and Beale have not yet arrived. They will come down, I suppose, with General Banks, the former having been his guest since the surrender.

It is not yet determined, I understand, what disposition will be made of the non-commissioned officers and privates. They will be paroled, however, I suppose, for it would be useless to bring them here to wait an exchange. They can be of no use to the enemy for a long time, if ever again; for the balance is now largely against them, and from present appearances will continue to be so.

Every effort will be made by General Banks to recover possession of Brashear City and the Opelousas Railroad. The division of General Grover, composed of Dudley's and Weitzel's brigades, are in advance from Donaldsonville, and the enemy have fallen back beyond Bayou La Fouche. We had an affair with them day before yesterday, in which we lost one hundred and fifty men and three pieces of artillery. This, however, amounts to nothing. It will not affect the ultimate result—viz: the reoccupation of all the Attakapas country. I have not the least doubt now, from the course that events are taking, that we will in a very short time be in quiet possession of not only Louisiana, but Mississippi also. The recent overwhelming victories North, South, East and West, must bring the South to its senses, and show the Southern people how entirely hopeless their cause is, and prove to them the determination of the North to compel the South to return to its allegiance or exterminate, if necessary, its people. Resistance now is worse than folly. Nothing can be gained by it: and the sooner Jeff. Davis acknowledges himself whipped, and leaves with his followers for a foreign clime, the better it will be for all concerned, and especially the Southern people.

The fall of Mobile, and with it Fort Morgan, must occur in a very few days. There is nothing to prevent General Grant from marching directly on Montgomery, Ala., and in that manner cutting off Mobile from all communication with the balance of the so-called confederacy. The rebel army will be driven into the Carolinas; Alabama will share the fate of Louisiana and Mississippi, and Georgia also. The movements of our armies have only to be made with rapidity, and the rebellion will be at an end by the first of October, if not sooner. It is most singular, the important change that has occurred between the 1st and 8th of July. Before that time everything looked dark and gloomy: now everything everywhere seems to say that we are to be successful. The fall of Vicksburg—the greatest blow yet struck against the rebellion—occurred on the Fourth of July. Could anything be more ominous? and the other great victories within a few days of that time. God now favors us. He is helping us in every way. Let us see that we help ourselves.

It is supposed Port Hudson will be strongly garrisoned, and in part by the Corps d'Afrique of Brigadier General Daniel Ullman. If this is the case: it will be a cause for congratulation; for it will remove General Ullman and staff from temptations of a large city like New Orleans, and enable them to learn something of their duties in the field and in heavy artillery practice, both of which the General and staff are sadly deficient in. Although Port Hudson has the reputation of being one of the most unhealthy portions of Louisiana, I am under the impression it only became so because the Yankee troops were investing it. It is high ground, with a fine rolling country in the rear, well wooded, and when there is a breeze it can always be found there; consequently I think it would not be a bad place for our invalid soldiers this summer. We might have large temporary hospitals erected that would be far preferable to keeping men confined in a small room, within the hot unwholesome atmosphere of a large city. It is worth the trial, at all events, even as late in the season as it now is.

A movement will be made by the squadron in a few days that will lead to important results. I am not at liberty to hint even as to the direction it will take. It is sufficient for the public to know that Admiral Farragut will command in person, and when that is the case fighting may be expected. We are in hopes that Admiral D. D. Porter will assume command of the entire Mississippi river. His fleet is adapted to the river service, while that of Admiral Farragut is not, and should only be employed on outside duty. We hear that the Hartford will leave for the north in a few days for repairs, and the other steam sloops—Pensacola, Richmond and Brooklyn—should go also, for they all stand more or less need of a few weeks at a navy yard. There is force enough in the squadron without them to accomplish the work before us.

I regret to state that night before last the United States steam gunboat Sciota was sunk by a collision with the steam gunboat Antonia, while coming up the river from the squadron off Galveston. Efforts are being made to raise her, but I consider the chances of saving more than her machinery and armament as very poor. I have not heard if any lives were lost, but think not, for she was run bows on to the mud before she went down. By the Sciota we learn that an expedition was fitted out from the squadron off Galveston to destroy some cotton loaded schooners lying at anchor within the bay. The party were successful, having destroyed three schooners with nearly three hundred bales of cotton on board. On their return, having to cross a neck of land, they were fired upon by parties in ambush, and Lieutenant Davenport, United States Navy, was severely wounded. He was shot in the right knee, slightly injuring the joint, in the right wrist, and had his left arm so badly shattered that it was amputated above the elbow. He returned on board the Sciota, and is now at the St. James' Hospital doing well.

The Spanish Consul and the commander of the Spanish steamer Pizarro have been notified by Governor Shepley that the steamer cannot come up to the city until after the first frost; and as that much wished for event is not likely to occur before the middle of November, the probabilities are that her commander will prefer going to sea rather than remain twelve weeks at least at the quarantine station, with only mosquitoes for his companions. The vessel, if not at once sent to sea, should have been ordered to Pass-a-l'Outre, out of the way of other shipping. She had her own medical officers, and would have been as well off in one place as another. The recent protest of Dr. Foltz, fleet surgeon, regarding the Quarantine, is having its effect, and may be the means of preventing yellow fever making its appearance here this summer. The city never was at any time more healthy than at present. The mortality report of to-day shows a great decrease in the number of deaths of the past week in comparison with the two former ones, and proper care will keep it on the decrease until the summer is over, and all danger of an epidemic is past and gone.

The result of our military operations since the 1st of July proves how utterly useless it is to speculate upon what is to be. No one supposed, on the 30th of June, that the hopes of the rebels would be so completely and entirely upset as they have been in less than two weeks time. We see this as plainly here as anywhere in the land. There was not a secessionist here that did not hold up her head on the first of this month and feel perfectly satisfied of their rapid and complete success, and not a few Northern people thought in the same manner. We could not see how or where the tide was to be turned. We felt confident that Hooker would be defeated whenever he met Lee, notwithstanding his powers of [illegible]. Johnston, we thought, might make a serious diversion in Pemberton's favor by attacking Grant in the rear, and it was feared that General [illegible] would not only be compelled to raise the siege of Port Hudson but would be cut off in his retreat from Springfield Landing or Baton Rouge. How completely every thing has been changed, for at every point where our armies were in front of the rebels have the latter been most thoroughly and overwhelmingly defeated, and in a manner to prevent their recovering from the utter demoralization of their armies. As a people, we have much, very much, to be thankful for. Let us see that we are in future, and let us profit in more ways than one by the experience of the past two years.

JULY 15—Evening.

Nothing of importance has "turned up" since three o'clock this afternoon. I had a short conversation to-day with a gentleman who has lately returned from Port Hudson. He was there when the place surrendered, and he confirms the report respecting the scarcity of provisions in the garrison. He declared to me there was no more corn in the place than Dr. Zacharie could have removed in a few moments without pain.

The United States steamer New London is here undergoing repairs. Her boilers and steam chest were much injured in passing up and down by the batteries below Donaldsonville. She is now commanded by Lieutenant Commander Potter, late of the United States steam sloop-of-war Lackawanna. The New London has been in twenty-three engagements since she arrived on this station, and although frequently struck has never had a man killed on board of her, and never was disabled until last week. She is truly a lucky vessel. Acting Volunteer Lieutenant Wiggin has been detached from the steamer Tennessee and ordered to command the United States steamer Estrella. We have no other naval news to communicate.

NEW ORLEANS, July 16—8 A. M.

The following is a copy of the last order issued by Gen. Gardner before he surrendered Port Hudson:—

GENERAL ORDERS—NO. 31.

HEADQUARTERS, PORT HUDSON, July 8, 1863.

I. Nobly have the troops performed their duty in the defence of this position, continued from the 21st of May to the present time. The cheerfulness, bravery and zeal displayed by the troops during the hardships and suffering of this long siege have never been surpassed, and every man can feel the proud satisfaction that he had done his part in the heroic defence of Port Hudson. The place is surrendered at the last moment it is proper to hold it, and after a most gallant defence in several severe attacks, in all of which the enemy have been signally repulsed. Let all continue during the duties that still remain to be performed, to show that cheerful obedience which has distinguished them as soldiers up to this time.

II. The troops will be paraded at six o'clock this morning for surrender, in line of battle, in the same order as they are now at the breastworks, with the heavy artillery on the right, on the edge of the praire in the rear of the railroad depot, the left extending towards the town of Port Hudson. All officers and men will be in their places under arms.

By order of Major General GARDNER.

Brigadier General J. W. Sherman, United States Army, will leave for the North on Sunday next in the steamer Columbia. He has entirely recovered, and has been moving about on crutches for ten days past. All he requires now is a "Palmer's patent" to render him fit for service.

General Payne is also nearly well. He has been sitting up and will be out in a few day. His chance of recovery has been very slim indeed.

OBITUARY.

Death of Mr. J. P. Dunn, Army Correspondent of the Herald.

[From the St. Louis Republican, July 20.]

Mr. J. P. Dunn, army correspondent of the NEW YORK HERALD at Vicksburg, died suddenly on board the steamer Minnehaha on the 13th inst. He was returning home, on account of ill health, and had complained during the day of not feeling well; but he sat up with friends until half-past nine o'clock in the evening, and expressed himself as feeling much better when he retired. He was found dead in his stateroom the next morning, having died apparently without a struggle. His effects are in charge of Mr. Raymond, another reporter for the HERALD.

From the above extract we learn of the decease of one of our army correspondents. We had been apprised of his illness, but his death was entirely unexpected.

Mr. John P. Dunn was the son of the late William Henry Dunn, Esq., counsellor-at-law, and nephew of the Rev. J. P. Dunn, parish priest near Philadelphia, after whom he was named. Previous to his having been attached to the HERALD he held the position of clerk in the New York Post Office, and while holding that situation he on one occasion nearly lost his life under the following peculiar circumstances:—He was a passenger on the Providence steamer which was run down in Long Island Sound by the steamer Commonwealth, and when the former vessel went under he sank with her, but, being a good swimmer, rose again to the surface. He struck out for the Commonwealth, which was then nearly stationary, and, grasping the wheel, was thus saved from a watery grave.

He became an attache of the HERALD about the year 1859, and since that date has been faithful and honest in the performance of his duties, giving entire satisfaction to his employer.

When the Burnside expedition was organized Mr. Dunn, in connection with Mr. Fitzpatrick, became attached to it as special army correspondent. He went with the forces to North Carolina, participated in the dangers of the storm off the Hatteras coast, took part in the battles of Roanoke Island, Newbern, &c., and gained great credit for his description of those contests. He remained in North Carolina until the Ninth army corps was added to General McClellan's command, when he also followed their fortunes. He took part in the movement to Fredericksburg in August, 1862, in the battles of South Mountain and Antietam, September 14 and 17, 1862, and was attached to the corps during the whole Maryland campaign. When General Burnside was appointed to the command of the Army of the Potomac Mr. Dunn still remained with the Ninth army corps, and participated in the terrific battle of Fredericksburg, December 13, 1862. Subsequent changes took place in the movements and commanders of the force, yet he remained with them and followed their fortunes into Kentucky, and subsequently down the Mississippi to Vicksburg. He took part in the siege of that formidable position, and, although sick, only left his post of duty after the place had fallen. He was on his way home, as stated above, when he died.

Mr. Dunn was the only son and support of an aged widowed mother, to whom his loss is irreparable. He was a young man of great promise, good education, and was possessed of an excellent and amiable disposition. He was admired and respected by all his associates and loved by his friends.

THE PRIVATEERS.

Operations of the Florida—A Prize Abandoned and Wrecked—The Natives Plunder the Wreck, &c., &c.

[From the Barbados (Bridgetown) Reporter, June 23.]

On Saturday a boat arrived here containing a lieutenant and nine seamen belonging to the Confederate man-of-war Florida. They form the prize crew of a Northern vessel snapped up by the Florida. Their intention was to take the vessel into some Southern port, if they could contrive to run the blockade. Being short of water, however, and in the neighborhood of Barbados, they thought it more advisable to set her on fire and take to the boat. Considering that part of her cargo was kerosene they do not seem to have accomplished the work of destruction with the facility of which abundant practice would have warranted the expectation. Before the fire had obtained full sway the vessel stranded on the St. Phillip's coast, and the breakers which washed over her soon obtained the mastery of their opposite element. Having fallen a victim to war she is now in her turn becoming the cause of strife. Her cargo of corn meal, flour, &c., is claimed by the laborers in the neighborhood to which she has drifted as a God send in these hard times. Of course this could not be allowed, and we hear that the yeomanry cavalry have been called into requisition in the interest of law and order, and that they have already been brought into unhappy collision with the mob.

NEWS FROM THE SOUTHWEST.

More Rebels Surprised and Captured.

CAIRO, Ill., July 22, 1863.

Information was received on Saturday afternoon that a force of rebels, three hundred or four hundred strong, would encamp that night at a point three miles from Rienzi, whose intentions were to attack Camp Davis, a strong stockade fort six miles south of Corinth, next morning, they being under the impression that the garrison was nearly all away upon a scout in Alabama. A detachment of the Sixth Illinois and the Third battalion of the Sixth Ohio cavalry were immediately sent forward, who completely surprised and captured the whole force.

Arrests at Barnum's Hotel, Baltimore,

BALTIMORE, July 22, 1863.

To-day Barnum's Hotel was visited by the provost guard, and two packages left there by C. H. St. Clair, of Tarrytown, Md.—arrested two days ago on the charge of being a spy—were found.

Four of the employes of the hotel were arrested on the charge of disloyalty. There is no charge whatever against the proprietor of the hotel, Zenus Barnum.

Sick Soldiers

BOSTON, July 22, 1863.

The steamer Kennebec arrived here this morning with invalid soldiers from Baltimore, via New York.

NEWS FROM WASHINGTON.

WASHINGTON, July 21, 1863.

THE ATTACK ON THE CHARLESTON FORTS.

The official advices received at the Navy Department from Admiral Dahlgren are to the morning of the 17th inst., on which day the attack on the harbor defences of Charleston was to be renewed. Everything was in readiness, and a favorable result was confidently anticipated. Unfavorable rumors were circulated to-day by speculators and rebel sympathizers in regard to the result of the attack; but they are without foundation.

GENERAL GRANT AND THE VACANT MAJOR GENERALSHIP IN THE REGULAR ARMY.

The recent action of the War Department, in placing General Wool and other officers upon the retired list leaves vacant one major generalship and one brigadier generalship in the regular army. It is said, upon good authority, that the major generalship will be conferred on General Grant, in recognition of his services in Tennessee and Mississippi.

TRADE WITH THE SOUTHERN PORTS.

The Treasury Department has issued notice to traders, shippers and carriers, or local rules and restrictions for the third special agency, which comprises so much of the State of North Carolina as is or may be within the lines of military occupation by the United States forces. It appears that commercial intercourse with localities beyond the lines of military occupation by our troops is strictly prohibited.

No permit will be granted for the transport of any articles to any blockaded port or place, except upon the request of the Department of War or of the Navy, either directly or through a duly authorized officer, accompanied by a certificate that the articles are needed for military or naval purposes. Authorized permits will be granted only by the Collector of Customs at Beaufort, or other officers specially despatched for that purpose, by or with the approval of the Secretary of the Treasury.

Until otherwise ordered, no permit will be granted to purchase, trade or barter in tar, turpentine or rosin, within the limits of this agency, or to transport the same therefrom, on private account. No vessel, boat or other craft, or vehicle used for transportation, shall put off any goods, wares or merchandise at any other place than that named in the permit or clearance as the place of destination. The supervising special agent for this agency (D. Heaton) will keep an office at Beaufort, N. C., till otherwise directed.

RECEPTION BY THE PRESIDENT OF THE DIPLOMATIC REPRESENTATIVES OF COLOMBIA.

Signors Murrillo and Parraga, the former the Envoy Extraordinary and Minister Plenipotentiary, and the latter Secretary of Legation and Fiscal Commissioner, were to-day received by the President. After a very interesting interview, and the presentation of their credentials, they were congratulated by him upon the cessation of all difficulties in the United States of Colombia (late New Granada). The diplomatic relations, interrupted by revolution, are now by this reception re-established between the United States of America and the United States of Colombia.

THE REPORTED EXPEDITION AGAINST DRURY'S BLUFF.

Some surprise was excited here by the report, via Fortress Monroe, that the attempt on Fort Darling, at Drury's Bluff, had been abandoned. No attempt to take Fort Darling has been made by Admiral Lee, as it has long since been established that it can only be reduced by a combined land and naval attack. Admiral Lee ascended the James river above City Point with two iron-clads, but not on the quixotic errand intimated.

THE COURT MARTIAL FOR THE TRIAL OF DISLOYAL CITIZENS.

The court martial organized for the trial of citizens charged with disloyalty concluded to-day the case of Hasel B. Cashel. The testimony sustained the charge of giving information to the enemy as to the situation of a herd of government cattle, the number of herdsmen, &c.

WAR MUNITIONS ORDERED TO NEW YORK.

Cannon and munitions of war have been sent from here to-day to New York, for the purpose of insuring the preservation of the peace hereafter.

THE INVALID CORPS.

The Invalid Corps is rapidly reaching its prescribed dimensions. Twenty companies of the First battalion have already been organized, and also seven companies of the Second battalion. Recruits are gathered at St. Louis, Washington, Michigan, Connecticut, South Carolina and Fortress Monroe, and will all soon be brought into the organization. At least two thousand five hundred men have already enlisted. Some of them are performing guard duty at the War Department and at other places. The men are delighted with the corps, which they regard as one of especial honor.

The statement is erroneous that the thirty invalid soldiers recently sent to the Provost Marshal's office in New York fired blank cartridges at those who assailed them. They each had sixty rounds of ammunition, and used them to the best advantage. Their friends think this correction is due to their character.

THE CONSCRIPTION ACT AND THE OHIO DEMOCRATIC LEADERS.

Leading democratic politicians of Ohio write here that compliance with the conscription will be urged by them; but that if it is carried out the democratic majority in the State will be immense.

THE GOVERNMENT AND THE BALTIMORE AND OHIO RAILROAD.

In view of the great service of the Baltimore and Ohio Railroad in military operations, the President has directed that payment for arrearages of its accounts against the government shall be promptly made.

THE INTERCEPTED DESPATCH FROM JEFF. DAVIS TO GENERAL LEE.

It is stated in high quarters that the intercepted despatch from Jeff. Davis to General Lee ordered the latter to retreat for the reason that troops could not be rallied in Virginia to defend Richmond.

THE NEW ASSAYER OF THE SAN FRANCISCO MINT.

Benjamin T. Larkin has been appointed Assayer of the Mint of San Francisco in place of Conrad Wiegand, resigned.

Base Ball.

ECKFORD, OF BROOKLYN, VS. MUTUAL, OF NEW YORK—THE CHAMPIONS MAINTAIN THEIR OWN.

Yesterday the above clubs met on the Mutual ground, Elysian Fields, Hoboken, and played the first game of a home and home match, which resulted in favor of the Eckfords by one run only. At least five thousand spectators were present, who witnessed the game with untiring interest, and the greatest order prevailed throughout. The arrangements for the accommodation of visitors and their lady friends—a large array of the latter being present—reflects great credit on the Mutual committee. A number of vehicles were also on the ground.

About half-past three the game commenced, the Mutuals going first to the bat; but the pitching of Sprague was very effective, and disposed of the Mutuals for small scores. The play on both sides at times was of the highest order and elicited general applause. In the fifth inning McMann made a splendid hit between centre and left field, for which he obtained the only home run made. But to particularize the play individually would occupy too much space, so the following score must suffice:—

MUTUAL.	O.	R.	ECKFORD.	O.	R.
Brown, 2d b	4	2	Wood, 2d b	[illegible]	1
Goldie, 1st b	3	1	Manolt, l. f	2	[illegible]
Kelly, c. f	3	0	Reach, 1st b	2	[illegible]
Mott, r. f	4	0	Beach, c	3	1
Beard, s. s	4	0	Sprague, p	1	2
Wansley, c	2	1	Duffy, 3d b	4	0
McKeever, p	3	1	Devyr, s. s	4	[illegible]
[illegible], 3d b	1	3	Swandell, r. f	5	0
Zeller, l. f	3	1	Snyder, c. f	3	2
Total		9	Total		10

RUNS.

	1st.	2d.	3d.	4th.	5th.	6th.	7th.	8th.	9th.	Total.
Mutual	1	1	0	0	1	0	3	2	[illegible]	9
Eckford	2	0	4	0	1	1	0	2	[illegible]	10

Umpire—Mr. Bigsby, Eagle Club.

Scorers—James [illegible], Mutual, Wm. [illegible], Eckford.

News from Albany.

ALBANY, July 22, 1863.

Mr. John E. Nafew gave bail to-day to [illegible] charge of having [illegible] county, two hundred and fifty dollars to [illegible] Broadway [illegible], and seven hundred [illegible] after [illegible].

The late rains have caused heavy damage [illegible]

News from San Francisco.

[illegible]

The New-York Times.

VOL. XIII—NO. 3742. NEW-YORK, MONDAY, SEPTEMBER 21, 1863. PRICE THREE CENTS.

HIGHLY IMPORTANT.

A Great Battle Fought Near Chattanooga.

The Engagement of a Desperate Character.

Fierce Dashes on Our Left and Centre.

THE ENEMY FINALLY REPULSED.

Our Lines Re-established as Before the Fight.

THE LOSS IN WOUNDED HEAVY.

Official Statement from General Rosecrans.

HEADQUARTERS OF THE ARMY OF THE CUMBERLAND, CRAWFISH SPRINGS, Ga., Sept. 19.

A desperate engagement commenced this morning at 11 o'clock.

The rebels made a heavy attack on the corps of Gen. THOMAS, forming the left wing of our army, and at the same time they attacked the right wing, which was thought to be a feint.

Gen. MCCOOK's and Gen. CRITTENDEN's troops were thrown into the engagement as convenience offered, the main portions of their forces being on the march at the time.

The fight on the left was of a very desperate character. The enemy were repulsed, but, on being reinforced, regained their position, from which they were subsequently driven, after a severe engagement of an hour and a half.

Gen. THOMAS' forces then charged the rebels for nearly a mile and a half, punishing them badly.

About two o'clock in the afternoon the rebels made a fierce dash on our centre, composed of the divisions of Gens. VAN CLEVE and REYNOLDS.

Gen. VAN CLEVE's forces were struck on the right flank, and being vigorously pushed by the rebels fell back, until Gen. CARTER's line was broken and the troops became much scattered.

Gen. THOMAS on the left, and Gen. DAVIS on the right, then pushed forward their forces vigorously toward the gap, and, after a hard fight, recovered the ground which had been lost on the extreme right.

The fight disclosed the intention of the rebels, which evidently was to get between us and Chattanooga.

The general engagement, which commenced at 11 A. M., ended about 6 P. M.

Gen. PALMER, who had gathered together our scattered forces, and Gen. NEGLEY, who had been sent from the right flank to feel the centre, pushed forward, and reëstablished our line as it had been before the battle began, along the Chicamauga Creek.

The country where the battle was fought is level, but thickly overgrown with small timber and brushwood, and is very unfavorable for the use of artillery, very little of which was used.

The casualties in wounded are heavy, but extremely light in killed for so heavy a musketry engagement.

The fight on the left was one continuous roll of musketry for an hour or more.

No general officers were injured.

Col. HEG and Col. BRADLEY, commanding brigades, were wounded.

Col. JONES, of the Thirty-sixth Ohio regiment, and Col. CARROLL and Maj. VANNETLA, of the Tenth Indiana regiment, were also wounded.

Lieut. JONES, of Company A, Tenth Indiana regiment, was killed.

Lieut.-Col. HUNT, of the Fortieth Kentucky regiment and Col. MAXWELL, of the Second Ohio regiment, were wounded.

Lieut. DEGRAW and Lieut. LUDLOW, Lieut. FESSENDEN of battery H, Fifth artillery, were wounded.

Lieut. FLOYD, of battery I, Fourth artillery, and Capt. BROWN, of the Thirty-first Illinois regiment, wounded.

Capt. SEARLES, Assistant Adjutant-General, of STARKWEATHER's brigade, was killed.

Battery H, of the Fifth artillery, was lost, and afterward recaptured by the Seventy-ninth Indiana regiment.

The battle is not yet over. It will probably be renewed to-morrow.

Rebel prisoners taken represent that the corps of Gens. HILL, POLK, JOHNSTON and LONGSTREET, were in the engagement.

Our men are in the best of spirits, and eager to begin anew.

Special Dispatch to the New-York Times.

WASHINGTON, Sunday, Sept. 20.

ROSECRANS, in a dispatch to HALLECK, says: "In the early part of the fight the rebels drove us some distance, capturing seven guns. Later in the action, however, we drove the enemy, reoccupying all our lost ground and capturing ten pieces of artillery. A number of prisoners, representing forty-five regiments, were captured by our forces." The battle was probably renewed yesterday morning.

FROM MEMPHIS.

Duel between Gens. Marmaduke and Walker—Changes in the Rebel Army.

A special dispatch to the Chicago *Times*, under date of Memphis, Sept. 15, *via* Cairo, states, upon the authority of a reliable gentleman just from Arkansas, that a duel was fought at Bayou Metaire, Sunday, the 6th instant, between the Confederate Generals, MARMADUKE and MARSH WALKER, in which the latter was mortally wounded. The circumstances are these: MARMADUKE, until lately, was the ranking officer of his, OWEN's and WALKER's divisions, stationed at Brownsville, but a commission of Major-General coming on for WALKER, he at once took command by virtue of his rank, and ordered his troops to fall back on Bayou Metaire, where PRICE was stationed. On falling back MARMADUKE accused WALKER of cowardice, whereupon WALKER challenged him, and they fought with pistols at eight paces. At the first fire Gen. WALKER was shot through the bowels. When our informant left, on the Tuesday following, he was not dead, but it was thought he could survive but a short time. The Arkansas troops, with whom he was a great favorite, are in a terrible state of excitement, and threaten to clean out MARMADUKE and his Missouri troops. The chagrin of MARMADUKE at being ranked by WALKER is said to be the sole cause of the difficulty. I have known Gen. WALKER for years, and know that a braver or more courteous man never lived.

I have just conversed with a gentleman direct from Atlanta, Ga., who states that Gen. JACKSON, formerly Chief of Cavalry on the Staff of Gen. BRAGG, and who succeeded Gen. VAN DORN in command of all the Confederate cavalry in BRAGG's Department, has, in turn, been superseded by Gen. S. D. LEE. The cause is said to be inefficiency and insubordination.

INTERESTING FROM KEY WEST.

No Symptoms of Yellow Fever—Few Vessels in Port—A Self-Sacrificing Surgeon.

Special Correspondence of the New-York Times.

KEY WEST, Monday, Sept. 14, 1863.

Our island has for the last two weeks undergone a period of unusual quietness and repose, resulting mainly from apprehension felt abroad concerning the health of the town, and more particularly as to yellow fever. Steamers pass by us both ways with no more of ceremony or notice than occasionally to stop at Sand Key and leave us a mail. And yet for all this apprehension there has not thus far this season been the slightest real cause, for our town never was more healthy at any season than it is now, and has been all Summer. In fact, we never have the fever here two successive years for palpable reasons. During the season of scourge, every person becomes sensitive on the matter, and the ensuing season every precaution is taken to ward it off. The police of the city is made thorough and complete. Quarantine regulations are rigidly enforced, and observed with willingness, and generally care is taken in all ways to do or avoid doing those things that are calculated to contribute to its introduction.

I noticed, in your number of the 19th ult., an account of the sadly destructive fever on the United States steamer *Alabama*, where it was stated that it was uncertain whether it was contracted at Havana or Key West. When we consider that there has been no case of fever in our harbor or on the island during this whole year thus far, we are undoubtedly safe in concluding that the seeds of disease were obtained at Havana, where the steamer stopped previous to her arrival here.

Our harbor is now quite bare of vessels, the only war vessels being the steamer *Tahoma* and ship *Dale*, with the small captured prize steamer *Neptune*, just arrived. The *San Jacinto* has gone on a cruise, the *De Soto* gone to the Mississippi, taking under convoy her prize, the steamer *Alice Vivian*, sent to New-Orleans for sale. She is a large river steamer about 450 tons burden, and appraised at $20,000, and the cargo which has been sent to New-York, consisting of 580 bales cotton, 36 barrels resin and turpentine, appraised at $177,103 50.

We have had very few prizes brought in here recently, probably owing to there being no Judge of the Court here at present, and that there is now a regular Prize Court at New-Orleans. It is hoped that the newly-appointed Judge for this place will present himself at an early day, as there is now very slight cause for any apprehension in regard to epidemic.

The naval coal depot, which has just been finished here at large expense to the Government, was last week partially filled up with 1,500 tons of coal, when the foundation commenced to settle and the centre column supporting the railroad and roof went down about ten inches, when they hurried the coal out again, and now the building must be appropriated for some other purpose. It is very well calculated for storage of provisions, clothing, materials, &c. The foundation is a sand bank, and the walls were sunk about ten feet below the surface by building coffer-dams, yet they are not equal to the immense weight.

Among the very many cases of self-sacrifice and devotion to country which this war has presented, there is none more deserving of notice than that of Dr. THOMAS MCHENRY, of Chester County, Penn., Acting Assistant Surgeon in our Navy, who died in this city last month. Dr. MCHENRY arrived here in August, 1862, in the height of the yellow fever season, when strong men were prostrated and carried to their final home in twenty-four hours. He was at once ordered to duty on the steamer *Huntsville*, where his first visit was greeted with the corpses of two young officers of that ship, Surgeon and Paymaster, who had died the previous day. Several of the crew were down with the fever; and amidst this did this young man devote himself to duty as only those do who have offered up their lives on the altar of their country. Much demand was made upon his time by the Fleet Surgeon, Dr. HORNER, on the flag-ship *St. Lawrence*, where a large number were sick and dying with the fever. His devotion amid these arduous and heavy duties was such that his fellow officers felt compelled to remonstrate with him and require that he should take more care of himself. Providence spared him through those scenes of death to periods of greater calm and restored healthfulness. He was subsequently attached to the schooner *Wanderer*, commanding and retaining the liveliest sympathies of his many friends. Of a retiring and modest disposition, he was the true hero, meeting difficulties and dangers with no motive but a discharge of duty. His death occurred at the Naval Hospital, whence his remains were attended to their resting-place by a numerous concourse of his brother officers and his friends.

F.

All Quiet at Knoxville—Severe Frost.

LOUISVILLE, Saturday, Sept. 19.

A dispatch from Gen. BURNSIDE reports all quiet at Knoxville and in that vicinity.

There was an extremely severe frost—the first of the season—last night. There are no reports of its ravages from any distance, but it is feared that all of the tobacco not gathered in is seriously injured, or entirely destroyed.

Government Loan.

PHILADELPHIA, Saturday, Sept. 19.

The sales of Five-twenties to-day amounted to $431,000. The advantage of the prompt delivery of bonds is shown by the increased orders. It is hoped that an arrangement will shortly be made by which the subscribers will receive their bonds at the time of subscription. Deliveries of bonds are made to Sept. 11.

Effects of the Storm.

WASHINGTON, Saturday, Sept. 19.

During the storm yesterday, among other damage done in the Lower Potomac, two schooners were capsized, the rain destroyed the crops, and the swollen stream carried away last night the Railroad bridge at Laurel. In consequence of the last, the trains to and from Baltimore were delayed.

Interruption of Canal Navigation.

ALBANY, Sunday, Sept. 20.

The storm of Friday and Saturday caused a freshet in the Mohawk and Hudson Rivers. At Hoffman's, on the canal, 150 feet of heavy embankment were washed out. It will take from five to seven days to repair the break.

The Canadian Parliament.

QUEBEC, Saturday, Sept. 19.

The debate on the motion of "No confidence in the Government," terminated this morning. The Government were sustained by two majority.

The Draft in Albany.

ALBANY, N. Y., Saturday, Sept. 19.

The draft in this District, which was to have commenced on Monday, has been postponed for a few days.

THE EXPEDITION TO TEXAS.

Naval Battle at Sabine Pass—Three Gunboats Engaged.

TREMENDOUS BOMBARDMENT.

TWO UNION GUNBOATS DISABLED.

Desperate Fight and Slaughter of the Enemy.

Gallant Conduct of Capts. Crocker and Johnson.

From Our Special Correspondent.

NEW-ORLEANS, Saturday, Sept. 12, 1863.

I told you in my recent letters that a military expedition, on an important scale, was on the *tapis*. As the movement has taken place, and results are now matters of public notoriety, I shall endeavor to give a clear account of all that transpired. Expecting to join the expedition at a later period with the Commanding-General of this Department, I did not go forward with the advance, and therefore, send you the account of another eye-witness, which is pronounced very accurate by all the officers with whom I have conversed.

DESTINATION OF THE EXPEDITION.

So carefully had matters been kept secret, that it was not until the transports had left, crowded with troops, and far toward their destination, that the truth began to leak out that the expedition was directed toward the mouth of the Sabine River; the dividing line between the States of Texas and Louisiana. We had plenty of force, the troops were in exuberant spirits, and everything promised success. But unfortunately we were not sufficiently informed of the *local* difficulties of the place we had to reduce. Like at Vicksburgh, Port Hudson, Sebastopol, and many other places to be attacked, we had to *feel our way*, and I am sorry to say it cost us something in valuable lives and property; but no more to affect us—as to the ultimate result—than a rain-drop affects the duck on which it falls.

On arriving at the spot on which our troops were destined to land, it was soon found to be impossible to attempt anything of the kind, owing to the marshy nature of the ground and the excessively shallow water. It soon, therefore, became evident that upon our gunboats would devolve the whole task of attacking; and gallantly did some of them go into an engagement, that is pronounced by all who saw it, one of the most desperately contested of the whole war.

THE NAVAL ACTION.

The attack was commenced about half-past 3 o'clock on the afternoon of the 8th, by the gunboat *Clifton*, Capt. CROCKER commanding, carrying nine heavy guns, two of which—one at the bow and the other at the stern—were 9-inch pivots.

Capt. CROCKER opened fire at a distance of about two miles from his bow pivot, and after an experimental shot or two, acquired the range, pouring in upon the enemy a continuous stream of fire, the bursting shells knocking huge holes in their works, and throwing the *débris* up in enormous quantities. The reports of the huge monster was absolutely deafening, and the ground fairly shook from the concussion.

The *Sachem*, Capt. JOHNSON commanding, in the meantime took up a position where she could pour a raking cross-fire, and also opened with her broadside of rifled pieces, which were served with equal precision and effect.

About the same time the powerful battery of the *Arizona*, Capt. TIBBETTS, from a position at the stern of the *Sachem*, also opened upon the enemy with screaming shell and hissing round shot,—every one of which could be plainly seen plowing up the interior of the fort and crashing through the breastworks.

This continued for some time before the enemy replied, the ships gradually nearing the fort and increasing the rapidity of their fire, until they were within point-blank range, and the *Sachem* had nearly passed by the works—on the right hand side of the oyster reefs fronting them,—when the enemy suddenly opened a terrific fire from his entire battery.

THE REBEL WORKS.

The fort is situated some distance below Sabine City—as shown by the map I send you. The first and main work consisted of a powerful earthwork of great length, mounted with six heavy guns, and garrisoned by a large number of men. To the left of this was a second work of similar character, mounting from three to five heavy guns, one or more of which was rifled. In addition to these two forts, the enemy had in sight, and rendering valuable assistance to the defence, three large cotton-clad river steamers, armed with one or more guns, and a schooner armed with one bow gun—probably of very large calibre, as she lay off at a distance of over two miles, and deliberately fired at the approaching fleet.

The firing now continued hot and fierce, the enemy's shot being generally aimed too high, passing over the tops of the vessels and striking in the water beyond them; while, on the other hand, nearly all the shots from the vessels were effective, searching every portion of the larger work, and, at times, with such effect that every man was driven from the guns.

AN ACCIDENT AND ITS RESULTS.

But just at this moment, when everything appeared most favorable, and the fortunes of war seemed about to assign the meed of victory to the gallant little vessels, the *Sachem* unfortunately grounded, broadside on, exposing her most vulnerable part to the concentrated fire of the enemy's largest work, the steamers and the sailing craft.

FURIOUS BATTLE OF THE GUNBOATS.

This was speedily taken advantage of by them, and a perfect storm of shot and shell fell upon, over, and around her, making the water hiss and foam like a boiling cauldron. Soon a heavy rifled shot struck her fair in the side, crushing in the iron-plating and wood-work, and, striking her machinery, exploded her steam chest, filling the vessel with the scalding vapor and leaving her a helpless wreck, with no hope of getting off the shore. Poor little *Sachem!*—a saucier craft never floated on the water nor a bolder man than her commander JOHNSON. We all remember the noble part she took in the affair at Galveston; one of the few bright spots in that otherwise dark and hideous piece of business.

The enemy now ceased their fire on the *Sachem* and turned their attention to the remaining two boats; the crews of which, realizing the position of their brave comrades, redoubled their exertions.

The *Arizona*, unfortunately, drew too much water to get to close quarters, and it devolved upon the *Clifton* alone to undertake the perilous task of silencing the works—a task that might have daunted the stoutest hearts.

But the *Clifton* was manned by brave men, and most nobly did the gallant CROCKER and his crew respond to the call upon them. Putting on a full head of steam, the devoted little craft ran down directly toward the largest fort, keeping up a hot fire all the time from her pivot guns, and as she neared the works, loading with double charges of grape, sweeping the parapet at every discharge.

The *Clifton* had now approached to within about 500 yards, and after giving the enemy a last discharge of grape from her pivot, attempted to throw her bow around, and take up a broadside position. But she had gone a few yards too near, and as she slightly swung around, her bow struck,—the velocity with which she was running driving her far upon the shore. She instantly commenced backing, keeping up a constant fire from her bow and port broadside guns, the former keeping the main parapet entirely clear of the enemy, while the latter played on the second battery.

This continued for some time, and faint hopes were entertained that the gallant Captain would succeed in extricating his boat from her terrible position. But this was not to be; for, at last, a shot from the battery at the left penetrated her boiler, in an instant reducing her to the same condition as the *Sachem*.

THE BATTLE ENDS.

The battle was now, to all intents and purposes, ended. Further resistance seemed utterly hopeless, but still the brave CROCKER could not endure the idea of giving up his vessel, and ordered his men to fight on. Without his knowledge, however, some party struck the white flag, and the enemy instantly ceased firing.

When informed of this, the Captain ordered the deck to be cleared, and, loading the after pivot-gun with a 9-inch solid shot, he fired it through the centre of the ship, from stem to stern, tearing the machinery in pieces, and rendering it utterly worthless to the enemy. After doing this, and spiking all the guns, the *Clifton* surrendered.

The remaining gunboat, the *Arizona*, quite unable to cope single-handed with the enemy, and drawing too much water to engage them in close quarters, reluctantly withdrew from the unequal contest, firing a farewell shot of defiance, as she steamed slowly down the bay, the enemy not replying to her challenge.

The *Clifton* had on board, beside her regular crew of one hundred and ten men, seventy-five sharpshooters; and the *Sachem* thirty sharpshooters—all of whom were captured, with the exception of seven men from the *Clifton*, who swam ashore, ran down the beach, and were taken off by a small boat.

The loss of the armament of the *Clifton* is unquestionably a serious one: her powerful battery of rifled guns being one of the most effective in the service. The boats, however, are so much damaged that the guns, to be of any service to the enemy, will have to be removed from them and remounted, and consequently it will be a long time before they can be made available.

The amount of killed and wounded I have not been able to ascertain, though they are not supposed to be heavy. I am happy to add that Capts. CROCKER and JOHNSON are neither thought to have been killed or wounded, but both prisoners.

A great deal will, no doubt, be attempted to be made out of this temporary check to our proceedings, but that will avail the enemy little. As we have shown them, upon many former occasions, all we require to know is *what* we actually have to contend with and then the difficulty is overcome. As the London *Daily News* very shrewdly remarks: We have now settled down into that passive, determined mood of warfare when we can neither be elated by petty successes, nor depressed by petty reverses. Our army and navy are safe and sound. They are composed of men of the right sort, and you may depend upon soon hearing of their paying back, with interest, this little affair of the *Clifton* and the *Sachem*.

NEMO.

ARMY OF THE POTOMAC.

The Late Cavalry Fight.

Correspondence of the New-York Times.

CULPEPPER COURT-HOUSE, Va., Tuesday, Sept. 15, 1863.

On the morning of the 13th the cavalry division of Gen. KILPATRICK crossed the Rappahannock at Kelly's Ford, and marched in the direction of Culpepper by Brandy Station. No rebels in force were encountered until reaching Brandy Station, where the advance, consisting of the Harris Light, or Second New-York, met them in some force. A brisk skirmish ensued, the rebels, however, immediately falling back toward Culpepper. At this place the division of KILPATRICK formed a junction with the divisions of BUFORD and GREGG, the whole under command of Gen. PLEASANTON. The whole corps advanced up the railroad toward Culpepper. Gen. KILPATRICK had the left, resting on the left of the railroad: Gen. BUFORD the centre, and Gen. GREGG the right—the skirmishing and cannonading becoming quite sharp as we advanced. As the cavalry moved across the plain in perfect order, some of the regiments in line, some in column, and a long line of skirmishers in front, with the batteries a little to the rear, the respective division and brigade commanders moving up with their Staffs, it presented one of the most brilliant spectacles of the war. The rebels did not make much resistance until we reached a point about one mile this side of Culpepper, where they opened three batteries upon KILPATRICK's division, but not checking the advance in the least. On approaching near the town, the rebels seemed disposed to dispute our further advance. A long line of dismounted infantry could be seen along a fence just across a deep creek, with two batteries in support. Gen. KILPATRICK ordered Gen. CUSTER to dislodge them, which he soon accomplished. The Sixth Michigan dismounted and engaged the rebel skirmishers, and soon routed them in good style. The Harris Light charged the battery on the edge of the town, capturing two guns. This brought the division of KILPATRICK to the edge of the town. BUFORD and GREGG were driving the enemy on the right, and Gen. KILPATRICK, with characteristic boldness, was about to charge the whole rebel force upon our left, and capture the train of cars that was moving off toward Orange, but was prevented by the unexpected discovery of a deep creek which was only passable at one place in his front. This enabled the train to escape, affording time to the rebel cavalry to take up a strong position, a little to the rear of the town, in the woods on the Cedar Mountain road. In the meantime, Gen. CUSTER at the head of the First battalion of the First Vermont, commanded by Major WELLS, dashed into town, driving the rebels out and capturing one piece of artillery to the right of the town. The rebels had two other pieces in the woods to the rear of the town, strongly supported by a strong force of cavalry. The Harris Light gallantly charged up into the woods where the rebels were posted, but were driven back by superior numbers. The First Vermont, consisting of two battalions, numbering about 150 men, under command of Major WELLS, now gallantly advanced to charge under a heavy fire from the enemy's battery. The Harris Light promptly rallied, and both regiments charged into the woods and drove the rebels further toward the Cedar Mountain road. Our loss here was the heaviest of any during the day. Gen. CUSTER, while leading the First Vermont, was wounded in the leg by the bursting of a shell, which also killed his horse, and the Harris Light sustained some loss, the extent of which I have been unable to learn. The rebels now formed just beyond the woods, where they had a battery in position. The Fifth New-York, and one battalion of the First Vermont charged upon the battery, but were repulsed, the rebels returning to the woods in great force, but were driven out the second time, whereupon they retreated for the Rapidan, closely pursued for four miles by Gen. BUFORD, when operations for the day ceased.

Our casualties on this day were three killed and forty wounded. On the 14th the cavalry advanced to the Rapidan, and found the enemy strongly posted at the respective fords on the other side of the river. In the fight the day previous the rebels were commanded by Gen. STUART—his force consisted of FITZHUGH LEE's and WADE HAMPTON's divisions of cavalry and five batteries.

TROOPER.

GEN. BLUNT'S CAMPAIGN.

The War in Western Arkansas and the Indian Country.

REVIEW OF OPERATIONS.

THE ENTIRE REGION RECLAIMED.

A LOYAL FEELING DOMINANT.

FACTS CONCERNING THE INDIANS.

From Our Own Correspondent.

LEAVENWORTH, Kan., Tuesday, Sept. 15, 1863.

By the arrival of messengers from Gen. BLUNT's headquarters at Fort Smith, Arkansas, we have confirmation most certain of the complete evacuation of the Indian Territory by the rebel forces. This gratifying result has been gained with but trifling loss on our part, and the complete disorder of the rebels.

Since the 5th of July last—a little over two months—when everything looked gloomy and disheartening in the Indian Territory, Gen. BLUNT has, with a force never exceeding 4,000 effective men, defeated and routed completely (both demoralizing and demobilizing) a rebel force doubling and trebling his own in strength. It may be that the comparative isolation of his field of operations, and the absorbing interest of the contest at other points, have engrossed the public attention, but certain it is that the movements of Gen. BLUNT have rarely received that notice they deserve. A brief *résumé* will show this.

When Gen. BLUNT assumed command of the District of the Frontier in the latter part of June, he had a force—whites, Indians and negroes included—of not more than 3,000 men. That force, by the addition of the Thirteenth Kansas and some cavalry, was raised to 4,000. At Fort Gibson on the Arkansas, 163 miles south from Fort Scott, Col. PHILLIPS, with three regiments of indifferent and partially disorganized Indians, a four-gun battery, and a few companies of nearly dismounted cavalry, had for four months been facing an enemy numbering not less than 7,000 men, who, if their leaders had had one tithe of the pluck of PHILLIPS, could at any time have "gobbled up" his entire force. There is not in the annals of this war a more striking example of tenacity and daring courage than that displayed by Col. PHILLIPS in so unflinchingly obeying the instructions of Gen. BLUNT and holding the Cherokee Territory, and thereby keeping Southern Kansas and Missouri from again being overrun.

Gen. BLUNT immediately pressed forward what troops he could gather, taking even the poorly armed and undrilled recruits just raised for the Fourteenth Kansas cavalry. Fortunately the Third Wisconsin cavalry, under Maj. CALKINS, was ordered to rendezvous at Fort Scott, with the intention of leaving the District. The emergency warranting it, Gen. BLUNT sent it to the field. Here commenced the rebel defeats. On the 1st and 2d of July, Col. WILLIAMS, of the First Kansas colored regiment, commanding escort, had severe engagements with the rebels under STAND WAITE, who with a superior force was strongly posted at Cabin Creek. The rebels were defeated and driven off in utter rout. BLUNT reached Fort Gibson on the 11th of July, and on the 15th, with 2,500 men, crossed the Arkansas, himself making a detour with cavalry, fifty miles, to outflank the enemy's advance, which he succeeded in doing, and on the morning of the 17th attacked the rebel COOPER, having a force of nearly 6,000, in a strong position. The rebels were badly beaten, losing 150 killed, 300 wounded, and 100 prisoners, with two guns, a flag, 500 stand of arms, and a lot of stores, etc.

On the 20th the rebels were largely reinforced, and numbering nearly 12,000, again advanced to Honey Springs, their pickets occupying the south bank of the Arkansas, and menaced Gen. BLUNT in rather formidable style. The latter, knowing that some reinforcements were on the way from Fort Scott, determined on their arrival to again attack the enemy.

Fortunately, while waiting for his own reinforcements, Col. CLOUD, Second Kansas, commanding a brigade, was moving to his assistance *via* Fayetteville, Ark. All having arrived, Gen. BLUNT, on the 22d of August, crossed the river, and moved upon the enemy. Though Gen. STEELE had at least 7,000 white troops, beside Indians, he had fallen back to Briar Town, North Fork, Canadian River, Creek Nation, fifty miles southeast of Fort Gibson. On hearing of BLUNT's movement he fled in haste to Perryville, south of the Canadian River, in the Choctaw Nation, not more than 50 miles from the Red River of Texas. Gen. BLUNT pressed on, in hot haste, with his cavalry, on the 25th ult., making, in one day, a march of 50 miles, surprising and capturing a strong rear-guard, and destroying all of STEELE's and COOPER's stores. The enemy had already broken in different bodies, and were fleeing in disorder. STEELE was fleeing with a portion of his army in the direction of Boggy Depot, 60 miles southwest of Perryville, about 18 miles from the Red River, and within a few miles of Fort McCullough, the only point left the Confederates in the entire Indian Territory.

The Creek regiments, (rebel,) under CHILI and UNI MCINTOSH, retreated by way of North Fork Town. Gen. BLUNT, understanding their desire to return to allegiance, sent Col. JUDSON and the First brigade to bring them. This was successfully accomplished, and the restoration of the Creek Nation to the National Government is now assured. The laying down of their arms on the part of the followers of the Creek Chief, CHILI and UNI MCINTOSH assures peace, because it heals a feud of thirty-five years' standing, which has more to do with the Indians espousing Slavery and the rebellion than a direct interest therein.

COOPER, TANDY WALKER (Choctaws,) and STAND WAITE (Cherokee,) fled directly south to the Red River, notifying the Indians that they must abandon their country, or be treated by the rebels as enemies. The result of this notification was to induce the Choctaws to report to Col. CLOUD in bodies, asking protection.

Gen. BLUNT returned to Briar Town with the Second and Third brigades. The Second brigade, under Col. BOWEN, Thirteenth Kansas, was sent to Webber's Falls, about half-way between Forts Smith and Gibson. With the Third brigade, Col. CLOUD, Gen. BLUNT pushed after CABELL, who was moving on to Fort Smith. CABELL was met with 3,000 or 4,000 men, twelve miles from the fort. It was night, and our troops camped two miles from him. CABELL left in the night. Col. CLOUD, with his own regiment, Capt. CRAWFORD commanding, the First Arkansas cavalry, and Rabb's battery, pushed after CABELL, who was traveling southward. CLOUD chased him fifteen or twenty miles, and had a brief engagement. The enemy fled in disorder, after a few rounds. Capt. ED. LINES, of the Second Kansas, was killed by an ambush, as was also SINCLAIR, one of Gen. BLUNT's scouts. Pushing on with the rest of the brigade, the General had in the meantime entered the fort and hoisted the flag, which Capt. STURGES (now General) removed when he evacuated that post in June, 1861.

This is a hasty *résumé* of the last campaign of Gen. BLUNT, one whose results for the peace and security of the Southwest, and in the territorial area of the region restored to the National Government, will be found to be of very great, though not of as paramount importance as other campaigns in the Mississippi Valley or the Western slopes of the Appalachian range, under GRANT, BANKS, ROSECRANS and BURNSIDE. It has been made against the opposition, not only of a Department Commander, but also that from a powerful politico-speculative combination interested in preventing the return of the 10,000 loyal Indians who were being fed as refugees in Kansas. With miserably meagre forces, a long line of communication, indifferently guarded, a foe largely outnumbering his own forces, Gen. BLUNT has within two months advanced the National lines southward two hundred miles to the border of Texas. He has restored Western Arkansas as well as the Indian Nations. A brief historical summary will best illustrate the value of the work done by his gallant army.

Fort Smith is in Sebastian County, Arkansas, on the Arkansas, at the mouth of the Portean River, one hundred and sixty-five miles west by north of Little Rock. It is a place of great importance to the rebels. Gen. BLUNT found here an extensive cartridge factory, as also other works. The post buildings are fine, and cost the United States Government $300,000. The centre of the plateau on which they are built is inclosed by a heavy stone wall, ditched and strengthened by earthwork. Fort Smith is the head of navigation on the Arkansas. Gibson is 66 miles west by land and 160 by water. The trade of Fort Smith is large, and as a military position and depot it was and is the controlling point on the Southwest Border. It was here that BEN MCCULLOCH assembled the army which coöperated with PRICE in the campaign that culminated at Springfield, Mo.

It is a well known fact that the people of Western Arkansas were at first strongly opposed to secession. A meeting held at Van Buren on the 15th of January, 1861, opposed it and declared that the election of LINCOLN was not sufficient cause for separation. The vote upon calling a convention to consider the question of secession stood 27,412 for, and 15,826 against. Nine-tenths of the latter votes were cast west of Little Rock. The vote on delegates stood; Union, 23,621; Secession, 17,927. While the convention was in session a test vote resulted, 39 against secession and 30 for. Salutes were fired both at Fort Smith and Van Buren in honor of the thirty-nine Union votes. Under the excitement of Sumter the ordinance of secession was passed. The Union feeling has always remained strong. Gen. BLUNT and Col. PHILLIPS raised three regiments in the northwestern counties, and in Scott County there has been a Union guerrilla force of 200 for some months past. The presence of Gen. BLUNT's army, and the movements of DAVIDSON and STEELE will insure success. Western Arkansas certainly, and probably the entire State, will soon be applying, with loyal officers, for restoration to its old rank in the Federal Union.

The extent of the Indian Territory may be readily seen when it is known that it extends east and west from the Arkansas west line to the east line of New-Mexico, a distance of 500 miles; and from Kansas to Texas, north and south, about 250 miles. It is watered by the Arkansas, Canadian and Red Rivers, and by a number of important minor streams, such as the Illinois, Neosho and Verdigris. It is in the same latitude as Southern Tennessee and Northern Mississippi and Alabama, a region admirably for cereal grains, fruits, cotton, tobacco, and other Southern staples. It was, previous to the war, one of the great grazing regions of the West.

There is a present population (Indian) of 65,650; whites, 1,[illegible]; slaves, 7,369, according to census of 1860, but according to present state of affairs, not more than half of that number.) These slaves were divided: Cherokees, 2,504; Creeks, 1,651; Chickasaws, 917; Choctaws, 2,294. The Seminoles owned no slaves, and but eight whites were resident in the nation. As a consequence, they were all loyal, except about 55 bribed by PIKE. Of the 75,000 living in the Indian Territory, at least 65,000 are more civilized than their neighbors of Arkansas, Missouri and Texas. The Choctaws were large cotton planters, some raising their 600 to 800 bales of cotton annually.

That the restoration of this Territory is complete, a glance at some facts in the history of the Indian nations will show. I mentioned the return to allegiance of the Creeks under CHILI and UNI MCINTOSH. These are the sons of the Agent, MCINTOSH, who was engaged in the Creek war with JACKSON in 1813, and who, in 1825, was murdered by the tribe for alleged treachery in ceding their lands by treaty to the United States. They had lived in Georgia, and in 1832 were finally removed to their present location. Out of the fraudulent treaty of MCINTOSH grew factions which have had more to do with the divisions of rebel and loyal than those sentiments themselves. It is curious to see how Slavery has tied itself to one side and embittered the quarrel. The MCINTOSHES lead, or led the half-breed, Slavery propaganda as well as pro-treaty party. OPOTHELEYHOLO, a large slaveholder, led the anti-treaty party. This party are now in favor of abolishing Slavery.

A similar quarrel, even more bitter, has existed among the Cherokee Creeks. Agent MCINTOSH seems to have been a useful tool of the Southern party. We early find him trying to bribe JOHN ROSS, in 1817–18. ROSS, or KOOWESKOOWE, is the son of a Scotch trader and half-breed woman. He, like all the leaders of these nations, has received a fine education, and is a man of considerable ability. He was opposed to ceeding the lands of his people, which were then part of the State of Georgia. In 1829, he, as agent of his nation, appealed from the State Legislature to the Supreme Court of the United States. In this he was successful. A series of aggressions was continued by the Georgians till 1835, when the Cherokee agent, J. F. S[illegible], with Major RIDGE, JOHN RIDGE and B[illegible], with 500 other Indians, entered into a treaty for the cession of their lands. JOHN ROSS and 15,000 protested against this fraud, known as the treaty of New-Echota. The Government, however, insisted on its provisions, and Gen. SCOTT was sent with a force to enforce the same. The Cherokees removed West. The RIDGES and BOUDINOT were put to death by the nation. This treaty was the cause of the bitterest feud existing among the nations. STAND WAITE is the leader of the Ridge party. His defeat and flight will heal the divisions among the Cherokees, and cement them all as a loyal people. Their Legislature not only abolished Slavery, but made the negroes citizens.

It is a curious speculation to know what will be the future of these nations. It cannot be possible to retain them in tutelage much longer. Wealthy, well educated, with large tribal, territorial and monetary possessions, and a population that, with the proposed removal of Kansas Indians to that Territory, will reach an 100,000, why is it not possible to organize a Territorial Government and let them be represented in Congress? It is certainly necessary for the security of this region that a form of Government under the direct control of the National authorities should be adopted, in place of the present loose tribal systems. This country is now in a condition to be administered into order and security. Well organized, with officers from among those who have led and are trusted by them, such a Territory would strengthen us greatly in the Southwest, and pave the way for a new Free State. We certainly can no more object to an Indian than a Mexican State, such as New-Mexico will make when it shall enter the Union. ALBERT PIKE, acting as Confederate Commissioner, held out, as one of the inducements for these Nations to go with the South, that they should have a delegate in the Confederate Congress to represent their interests. Certain it is that a Territorial Government would be the best method of educating them out of their present abnormal condition into that normal one of cit[illegible]

[illegible]

DAILY DISPATCH.

VOL. XXV. RICHMOND, VA., MONDAY MORNING, SEPTEMBER 28, 1863. NO. [illegible]

Richmond Dispatch.

The DISPATCH is published DAILY, (Sundays excepted.) [illegible]

The SEMI-WEEKLY DISPATCH is issued [illegible]

The WEEKLY DISPATCH is issued every [illegible]

Richmond Dispatch.

MONDAY MORNING..........SEPTEMBER 28, 1863.

THE BATTLE OF CHICKAMAUGA.

Further Particulars of the Fight—Scenes on the Battle Field—The Losses—Reinforcements, &c., &c.

The Atlanta papers contain some additional particulars of the battle of Chickamauga. The accounts include some meagre description of the fight of Sunday. We give a letter from the *Intelligencer*, written on the 22d inst.:

The preliminary fight commenced, it may be said, on Friday, the 18th inst., at Alexander's bridge, eight miles west of Ringgold. Walthall's brigade was principally engaged and suffered most, one regiment losing 73 killed and wounded. Gen. Bushrod Johnson's brigade moved up at the time from Ringgold, crossing the Chickamauga above at Reed's bridge, the enemy falling back before us and marshalling their forces in line of battle. Their advance on Georgia soil had been so successful and easy that they seemed surprised at the idea of being checked, contemplating a triumphant entrance into Atlanta.

On Saturday, the 19th, the two contending armies confronted each other in battle array. Our line extended from Reed's bridge to Lee & Gordon's mills, a distance of between seven and ten miles, over a rugged, barren country of hill and dale. Between 8 and 9 o'clock A. M. the battle opened on our right. In the course of an hour the firing became heavy and rapid, the batteries of Forrest's and Walker's divisions, and the reserve, Capt. Lumsden's battery, in command of Major Palmer, Chief of Artillery, keeping up a perfect roar of fire, which was fully returned by the enemy. The lines of both armies moved to and fro like the advancing and receding waves of the sea. Cheatham's division soon became under fire, with its artillery under command of Major Melanthon Smith. The fight was kept up with varied success, when the gallant division of General Cleburne charged the enemy after dark, by moonlight, and drove them two miles from their first line of battle and in front of Alexander's bridge. It was here the brave Gen. Preston Smith fell. After this victorious and most brilliant achievement our army rested on their arms for the night. During the fight Capt. Carnes's battery was captured, all the horses being killed, and all the artillerists being either killed or wounded. This battery was afterwards retaken by General Smith's brigade, and also one or two other pieces which had been abandoned, the horses being killed. That day we took the enemy's celebrated Loomis battery of six guns, and four other pieces, and 1,200 prisoners.

The fight on Saturday commenced on this side of the Chickamauga river, extending from the right of Lee and Gordon's mills to what is known as the new bridge across that stream, a distance of about five miles, with a flanking force well out on either wing. In the evening the Yankees retreated across that stream, burning the new bridge behind them, the river dividing the two armies for the night.

That night the Yankees were hard at work digging entrenchments, and threw up three lines of works towards the Missionary Ridge.

Sunday morning, the 20th, before day, the banks were dug down on each side of the stream, just below the point where the bridge had been burned, and our forces forded the stream and drew up in line of battle about 8 o'clock.

Gen. Polk, who commanced the right, had a hot day's work before him, but he felt confident of success. The battle-field was an undulating or rolling open wood, so much so that artillery had room and range enough for full play. The attack was commenced by our forces shortly after nine o'clock A. M. Our line of battle was four miles west of Chickamauga, and half a mile east of the main road leading from Lafayette to Chattanooga. We pressed the enemy sorely from the start, who, though strongly contesting the ground inch by inch, gradually fell back before our braves. Charge after charge was made on the enemy, and one vociferating yell prevailed our ranks, we turning their left on their centre, and driving back his right at the same time. In the afternoon the enemy attempted to throw reinforcements from the left to the right across an open field and the Chattanooga road. Major Williams's battery was concentrated on this road, and cut off the enemy, the whole forest being completely mowed down with grape, canister, shrapnel, and shell; it was at this time we took several thousand prisoners. It was after dark that Gen. Polk carried the last line of the enemy's entrenchments, when a thrilling yell of triumph rang out on the air, which told of our glorious victory.

The enemy was completely routed, and in full retreat. Gen. Breckinridge's division, and Gen. Preston's of Buckner's corps, also bore a most gallant part in the charging of the enemy's entrenchments, who were driven three miles, back to Missionary Ridge, and from which the enemy were driven to within five miles of Chattanooga. Gen. Bragg was on the field with the troops, night and day, and in riding down the lines in front of Gen. Breckinridge's division, on the night of victory, he was most enthusiastically cheered by Breckinridge and his brave Kentucky, Louisiana, Alabama and Florida troops.

We have captured over 40 stand of colors, 45 pieces of artillery, and taken over 6,000 prisoners. Our loss is estimated from eight to ten thousand, killed and wounded; the enemy's cannot be less than from twenty to twenty five thousand.

The battle-field extended about ten miles, and the carnage was the most frightful yet witnessed, far exceeding Chancellorsville, Gettysburg, Murfreesboro', or Shiloh. The constant and terrific roar of artillery never was exceeded. The fighting of our men on Sunday evening in carrying the enemy's entrenchments was magnificent, grand, and terrible. They faced the whirlwind of lead and iron with the steadiness and composure of a summer's rain. Then came charge after charge, the frightful gaps in our lines being immediately closed up, and with the yell of demons our battle cry arose above the roar and crash of musketry and artillery, while the terror stricken foe fell back aghast as our braves mounted and carried their entrenchments, line after line, over the dead carcases of the Abolition foe, who fell in heaps in the pits they had but dug for themselves.

The battle-field that night by moonlight—the glittering beams shining on the ghastly faces of the dead, distorted in expression from the wounds of their torn and mangled bodies, with heaps of the wounded and dying, with scattered arms strewn everywhere, broken artillery carriages and caissons, dead horses, and all that makes up the *debris* of a bloody contested field—was terrible and appalling.

Gen. Polk fought his corps with great skill and ability, and with all the coolness that bravery can command. The noble divisions of the heroic Breckinridge and chivalrous Cheatham carried the last entrenchments and they slept upon the field with the wreath of victory crowning their brows.—McNair's brigade, attached to Bushrod Johnson's division was on the left of Gen. D. H. Hill's corps, and charged the entrenchments Sunday with its famed and distinguished gallantry, taking 14 pieces of artillery. Gen. McNair was wounded, and the noble Col. R. W. Harper, commanding a brigade, was killed. Col. Harper was a Marylander, but a citizen of Arkansas, and had previously distinguished himself at Oak Hills, Elk Horn, and Murfreesboro'. Gen. Buckner's and Hill's corps also won imperishable renown. Capt. James Stone of Buckner's escort, (who took Gen. Willich prisoner at Murfreesboro',) also added to his laurels.

On Monday, the 21st, Gen. Forrest pursued the enemy, capturing a squadron of Gen. Stanley's Yankee cavalry, and general skirmishing taking place, the enemy retreating on Chattanooga. Gen. Wheeler had also captured a large train of wagons, burning a large portion, and securing over 1,000 prisoners. To-night, (Tuesday,) as I close this letter, which I send by private express, a courier just in reports that the enemy are burning their stores at Chattanooga and crossing the river.

When it is taken into consideration that our army had to, [illegible] deep in dust, over a wild, barren, [illegible] country, without affording any [illegible] and our men on half rations, undergoing forced marches and terrible sufferings without a murmur, and then to contemplate their heroism on the field, which has won [illegible] and glorious a victory, it cannot be [illegible] but that the God of battles favored our arms. But for the want of rations *Gen. Bragg would have followed up his victory the next day; but our troops were unable to move until our supplies came up.* In this great battle Gen. Bragg has exhibited a military capacity far over-reaching Rosecrans, and by his masterly manœuvres has handled his army with a skill and judgment that only could have secured to us such a glorious victory.

CASUALTIES.

Brig.-Gen. B. H. Helm, who was killed, was leading his men on to victory, when he fell mortally wounded in the abdomen by a minie ball. He was taken back to the hospital six miles above Ringgold, where he expired during the night. He was a grandson of Ben Hardin, the celebrated Kentuckian.—He entered the Southern army without a commission, but from the rank of private he was soon made Colonel, and commanded the 1st Kentucky cavalry [illegible] service. When the battle of Shiloh was brewing, he closely watched the movements of Gen. Buell, and kept Gen. Johnston constantly advised of the enemy's whereabouts and movements. He was made Brigadier General in March, 1862, and took command of a Kentucky brigade at Vicksburg last summer. His wife is a half sister of Mrs. Lincoln, and a sister of Alex. Todd, who was killed at Baton Rouge. It will also be remembered that Lieut. Todd, who was killed at Shiloh, was his brother-in-law. His wife is now in the city, and shares the sympathy of hosts of Kentucky friends and the people of the South generally. Before Gen. Helm died, the chaplain conversed and prayed with him, and he expressed perfect resignation to his fate, which he met in the same cheerful spirit that he has so well served his country. Thus, without a murmur, passed away another of the numerous throng of brave defenders of truth, justice and liberty.

In Helm's 1st Kentucky brigade 1,763 men went into action—432 only came out of it. Among the killed of this brigade we learn the following: Major Rice Graves, Breckinridge's staff; Col. J. M. Hewitt, 2d Kentucky regiment; Capt. Harry Rogers, do.; Lieut. M. M. Carson, do.; Adj't W. Bell, do.; Capt. Daniels, 9th Kentucky; Lieut. Bell, 4th Ky.

Cheatham's division is reported to be in possession of Gen. Thomas's body.

Col. Bland and Major Hard, 7th S. C., and Col. Gold, of the 8th S. C.; Col. Hewett, 2d Ky; Lieut.-Col. Inge, 18th Ala.; Col. Wheaton, 3d Ala., were killed. Col. John M. Lillard, 20th Tenn., and Major Haskell, 19th Tenn., dangerously wounded.

Col. Richmond, Gen. Polk's Aid-de-Camp, was killed by a Yankee sharpshooter just after the fight was over. He was riding between the lines of the two armies and after he was shot and had fallen from his horse he wrote in his memorandum book the request that his body should be taken to his home for interment, for which service his legal representative would pay $500 in gold.

The Federals have a jolly way of throwing down their guns and rushing to the rear of our troops when they have enough of our musketry. While Gen. Lytle was not far from our line his men suddenly rushed forward, and when he was for a moment amazed at the brilliant charge made without orders, and then when he saw that their muskets had been thrown away, he sought himself to escape with his staff. He turned his horse to fly, but it was too late; he, and every man near him, was killed. He was shot through the head, the ball entering just above the neck and coming out above his nose.

Brig.-Gen. Preston Smith, who was killed, was a brave Tennesseean.

THE PRISONERS AND WOUNDED.

The train on Tuesday evening brought down the first installment of Yankee prisoners from Bragg's army. They were part of some 2,500 captured on Saturday, and were full of bombast. In conversation one of them informed us that he believed "Rosecrans would get whipped this time, but he had too many pontoon-bridges to cross the Tennessee and get away with." They are the most hang-dog looking scoundrels we have ever seen, their appearance not being one-half as fine as the men of Grant's army. They appeared not in the least surprised at the intelligence of Rosecrans's rout on Sunday and Monday, but assert that they have a plenty of troops to protect their retreat after they cross the Tennessee. The number that arrived yesterday is 1,634. Among them are one Colonel and several Lieutenant-Colonels and Majors, all the remaining officers being subalterns. They mostly belong to McCook's and Thomas's corps, composed of Kentucky, Ohio, Missouri, and Illinois troops.

Some of the officers among the prisoners who arrived last night asserted that Rosecrans had a reserve which was not engaged in the battles on Saturday and Sunday, consisting of McPherson's corps from Grant's army, and sixteen thousand under Burnside. The former they stated were resting on the north bank of the Tennessee, and the latter were in the vicinity of Chattanooga. We doubt the correctness of these representations, but are glad to know that Gen. Bragg will not be without a large additional strength in the next conflict.

Among the prisoners we have soldiers from Meade's army, and they tell us that Sherman's corps is on the march from Huntsville, Ala; that Burnside is coming down from East Tennessee, and that Grant is ascending the Cumberland river.

A RECONNOISSANCE TOWARDS CHATTANOOGA.

Mr. Rushton, agent of the East Tennessee and Georgia railroad, endeavored to reach Chattanooga with an engine, Wednesday, for the purpose of ascertaining the condition of the track, via Cleveland. The report made of this reconnoissance at Dalton was, that on reaching a point within five miles of Chattanooga they met Pegram's cavalry, about 1 o'clock, who ordered the party back to Dalton, and informed them the Federals were still in the town. Pegram had received orders to fall back to Chickamauga. When the engine passed Cleveland on its return Bird's brigade of Federal cavalry were reported within six miles of the town. Our forces stationed there being small in numbers were obliged to leave. It is evident we must have another struggle before Rosecrans is driven across the river.

Rosecrans has certainly been concentrating his forces since Sunday, and that he has been able to gather as much physical force as he lost, may be true. Burnside's disposable force may have joined him, and his garrisons left lower down and north of the river may have been hurried to his support. And it will be remembered that the letter of our correspondent, "Kingston," published yesterday, (who writes advisedly,) informs us that five brigades of infantry, one of cavalry, and several batteries of artillery, left Huntsville, Ala, on the 13th inst. If this force had not come up in time to participate in the late battle, they will have had time to make the march ere this. It is the impression of our officers they were engaged before, but the Federal officers captured say not. It may be so.

GEN. BRAGG'S DISPATCH TO GEN. BEAUREGARD.

CHICAMAUGA RIVER,
9 miles Northwest of Ringgold,
September 22, 1863.

Gen. Beauregard—After several ineffectual efforts we succeeded in bringing the enemy to action on the 18th inst., on the Chickamauga river, between Ringgold and Chattanooga, and after four days' fighting have driven him from the State of Georgia, and are now still pursuing him. We have encountered the most obstinate resistance and endurance that the valor of our troops, under great privations, has overcome, all under God's providence. Our loss is severe, but the result is commensurate.

(Signed,) BRAXTON BRAGG.

Charles Halleck, son of the editor of the New York *Journal of Commerce*, who arrived in Augusta, Ga., some months since, as a "refugee," and obtained a situation on a newspaper there, deserted to the enemy last week.

FROM THE NORTH.

Baltimore papers of Saturday have been received. They contain only meagre accounts of the battle of Chickamauga, the substance of which we subjoin:

CINCINNATI, Sept. 23.—Special dispatches from Chattanooga to-day fail to get through. Though the news is *far from encouraging*, people here have confidence that Rosecrans will maintain himself till reinforcements reach him, and that he will then turn the tables on Johnston.

WASHINGTON, Sept 24.—A dispatch from Gen. Rosecrans, dated at his headquarters last night, says:

"I cannot be dislodged from my present position."

NASHVILLE, Sept. 23.—Very little news of an official character is received here, we obtaining all our news from officers directly from the front. It is rumored that we have lost four Generals in killed and wounded and two as prisoners.

CINCINNATI, Sept. 24.—Mr. Shanks, correspondent of the New York *Herald*, has arrived here from the battle-field. He says that the official reports of the battle from Washington are in the main totally incorrect; that really the Army of the Cumberland has met a defeat which must put it on the defensive for some time to come.

Gen. Rosecrans was falling back on Chattanooga, where he was perfectly safe from all that Bragg could do. His lines of communication were perfectly secure, and he had plenty of ammunition and provisions in Chattanooga to stand a month's siege.

The result is virtually a defeat, as we have lost tremendously in material—not less than fifty pieces of artillery falling into the enemy's hands, whilst they lost twenty taken by us.

Gen. Rosecrans is in no danger, but at the time Mr. S. left Chattanooga the danger to Burnside was very imminent.

The Washington papers of Friday evening say that dispatches from Gen. Rosecrans to 3 P. M. on Thursday show that he is in an impregnable position, feels entirely safe, and has no doubt about holding out.

Rosecrans invites battle in his present position. From appearances Bragg's army is massed in Chattanooga Valley, before the city.

MISCELLANEOUS.

A Washington telegram, dated the 24th, says that Gen. Meade's army is undoubtedly advancing towards Gordonsville, and a battle is daily looked for. General Lee's force is estimated at forty thousand.

Lincoln has removed the blockade of the port of Alexandria, Va.

Another Russian frigate had arrived at New York. Five more were expected in the course of a few days. The Baltimore *Gazette* says, whether they come by accident or for some ulterior purpose are questions it cannot satisfactorily answer.

Official information has been received at Washington of the detention of the rams at Birkenhead, by order of the British Government.

An official paper at St. Petersburgh says that the Czar will adhere to his policy in regard to Poland.

Gold advanced on Thursday to 140, but the latest quotation was 138½.

LOCAL MATTERS.

Accident.—On Friday evening, about four o'clock, a wagon, driven by a son of Mr. John W. Camp, containing his wife, another lady, and two or three children of Mr. Camp's, while coming down Grace street, was upset near the corner of 6th, the wheels of the wagon going over the body of the driver, who at the time, said that he was unhurt. Most, if not all, of the occupants of the wagon, were injured. A little girl, Mr. Camp's daughter, very sprightly and intelligent, received a severe cut on the head, as well as some bruises on her limbs; Mrs. Camp was cut upon the face, being also badly bruised—in fact, all of them were more or less injured. Some time after the occurrence Mr. Camp's son, who had been driving the wagon, complained of being unwell, (he had made no complaint at the time of the accident,) and experienced some difficulty in walking. Dr. Harrison was called in and rendered the necessary medical attention.—At the time of the accident the children were carried into the house of Mr. T. J. Evans, and the ladies into that Mrs. Wm. Mitchell, where they were treated with all the kindness which their situation required.

Regulating the Prices—Commendable Move on the Part of the Butchers.—We mentioned some days since that a move was on foot in this city to bring down the prices, and fix some standard governing the sale of all articles of provisions. Since that time we have ascertained that such is the fact, and, as a preliminary step, a meeting of all the butchers took place one day last week, in compliance with a request from Major Wm. H. Smith, to arrange some plan for the purchase of cattle. At that meeting a committee was appointed to consider the matter, which committee met on Friday evening last and drew up the following propositions, which have been submitted to the Government authorities:

"Major W. H. Smith—Sir: We, the undersigned butchers, having met together at your request to fix a standard price for purchasing cattle to be slaughtered for the inhabitants of this city, so as not to conflict with purchasers for the Government, and also to reduce the price of beef from our stalls, respectfully submit the following propositions:

"1. That all cattle en route to this market for sale on arrival shall not be impressed or interfered with by the Government.

"2. That it is quite inconvenient at times for us to leave our stalls to lay in our supplies, or to get suitable agents to do the same satisfactorily, and that the owners of stock may be permitted to bring it here, by allowing a price above the Government price sufficient to cover all risk—driftage and expense.

"3. That our profit will be principally regulated by the value of the fifth quarter, and the quality of the cattle must regulate the price thereof; we, therefore, request that we may pay in this market from 20 to 35 cents gross for fair to extra cattle, and that we retail the same from our stalls from 50 to 75 cents net by retail, which will be a reduction of about one-half from present rates.

"4. From the above propositions it will be seen that the farmer and butcher have reduced the present prices one half, while their expenses in all articles necessary and indispensable are still at inflated prices, with an upward tendency; and if everything useful for the support of the needy were likewise reduced 50 per cent. the evil which is sought to be remedied would in a great measure be averted.

"5. We earnestly hope, should the above liberal propositions be accepted, that you use all proper means to have all other necessaries of life reduced in a like ratio. Should the above result be not enforced, the above obligations to be null and void after 1st of November next.

"6. The above resolutions to be put in force from and after the 10th of October next."

Richmond, Sept. 25, 1863.

Charged with Stealing Clothing.—Jennett Lapinsky was on Saturday arraigned before the Mayor charged with stealing from Mrs. Lavinia Whitlock, of Henrico county, one brown merino dress, one blue check dress, one flowered silk do., one silk berege do., one cotton and worsted do., one man's shawl and one green crape shawl, all valued (in good times) at $200. The evidence in this case proved that some of the articles enumerated were found upon the premises of Mrs Lapinsky, and the supposition was that, as a part were traced to her house, the whole of them went the same way. For the defence two witnesses testified to having seen the accused purchase said articles of wearing apparel from another woman whose name they did not remember. At the conclusion of the testimony the Mayor announced that he should send Mrs. Lapinsky on to the November term of the Hustings Court, on the charge of larceny, and would admit her to bail.

Departure of Yankees.—A large number of Yankees will be sent North this morning, via City Point, under a flag of truce.

Heavy Robbery.—On Saturday [illegible] between one and two o'clock, the jewelry store of Mr. C. C. Walter, near the corner of Broad and 6th streets, was forcibly entered and robbed of about forty gold and silver watches, several fine bracelets, and two or three gold chains, valued in all at about [illegible]. This daring act was committed while Mr. Walter had gone to dinner, the thieves making an entrance through the back door by forcing out the staple which fastened it in the inside. A number of the watches stolen belonged to individuals who had left them there to be repaired, and some of them were of the most superior quality. This is the second or third time attempts have been made to rob Mr. W's store, and only on Saturday week some thief stole from him a very valuable double-case gold watch. This misfortune falls heavily upon him, and it is sincerely hoped his property will be recovered and the scoundrel who perpetrated the theft brought to justice.

Burglary.—Wm. H. [illegible], a free negro, was arraigned Saturday before His Honor on the charge of burglariously entering the house of John Graves, and feloniously stealing three vests, of the value of $[illegible]; one overcoat, worth $150; five shirts, valued at $40; one counterpane and three [illegible], worth $[illegible]; two dress coats, valued at [illegible]; one gray double blanket, estimated [illegible], the property of said John Graves. On account of the absence of witnesses the prisoner's examination was deferred, and in the meantime he was committed to prison.

Robbery of a Church.—Robberies in this city are becoming very frequent, and the operators seem to be indifferent as to where they make their raids. On Friday night last the Monumental Church was forcibly entered and robbed of one superior black silk gown, nearly new; one black silk scarf, belonging to the surplice; two table cloths, six damask napkins, two small napkins, and four damask towels.

Discharged.—A white man, named Walter Lacy, made his appearance before the Mayor on Saturday to answer the charge of stealing from the pockets of Patrick Hagerty, on Tuesday night last, one hundred and fifteen dollars. The complainant in this case being at the time of the alleged robbery in a state of beastly intoxication, and there being no other evidence to prove the guilt on Lacy, he was discharged from custody.

A negro man named Mathew was up before His Honor on the charge of stealing one coat valued at $20, and aiding and abetting a slave named Catharine to leave Thos. Bradford, her owner. Upon a failure to make the charge good, Mathew was discharged.

C. S. District Court.—Judge Halyburton's Court was again in session Saturday.

The petition of J. C. Rittenhouse, asking to be discharged from Capt. Hayward's company, was granted, and the petitioner discharged from custody.

The argument in the case of the Roanoke Valley Railroad Company against Col. C. F. M. Garnett and Capt. George E. Walker, was partly heard and its further disposition postponed.

The Judge will announce his decision on the petition of Thomas E. Kinney, praying to be discharged from military service, on Monday.

Judge Lyon's Court.—The following cases were disposed of Saturday in this Court:

John Conway was sentenced to the Penitentiary for five years on the charge of stealing a watch from Capt. Jackson L. Warner.

The charge against James Hill, of robbing Jacob Holder, was dismissed, and the accused released from custody. Hill has been in jail for nearly twelve months, during which time the witnesses have not appeared against him.

The Grand Jury will meet again this morning.

Arrest of Vanderlip.—On Saturday night last, about half-past ten o'clock, Elias Vanderlip, the convict who escaped from the Penitentiary guard a few days since, while they were taking him to work, was recaptured at a house in Lumbard alley. The watchmen who arrested him were shot at by V., but fortunately were not struck. He was taken back to the Penitentiary yesterday morning.

Passing Spurious Money.—A negro man named John was yesterday arrested by Officer Morris for passing a Yankee patent medicine card on another negro named Ben for a $100 note. John had bought something of the value of $50 from Ben, and gave him this card in payment, receiving in change $500 in good money. The Mayor will dispose of the case this morning.

Sent Back to Hanover.—Three negro women and one man, bearing the names of Robert, Jane, Louisa, and Judy Hogg, were arrested in a notorious free negro den on Friday night last and brought before His Honor on Saturday. All of these negro women having Hanover papers, and being in the city contrary to law, were ordered to return to that county forthwith. The negro man Bob was sent to the batteries.

Failed to Give Bail.—A paroled Irish Yankee, named Patrick Connell, arrested some time since on the charge of stealing a pot of butter from some one in the Second Market, was again brought before the Mayor on Saturday last. The prisoner failing to give security in the sum of $200 for his good behavior, was sent to prison.

Whipped.—Thomas, slave of R. P. Archer, was ordered by the Mayor on Saturday to receive twenty lashes for being without a pass and having in his possession a piece of plank supposed to be stolen.

Martha Bradly, a free negro girl from Chesterfield, was whipped for leaving her bailiwick without proper papers.

Bound Over.—A free negro, named Bob Smith, arrested on the charge of assaulting and brutally beating his wife, was held to bail on Saturday by the Mayor in the sum of $200 to keep the peace and be of good behavior.

The Prisons.—At the Libby since our last publication 401 Yankee prisoners have been received.

The commitments at Castle Thunder were fourteen Yankee seamen, captured from some schooners near Warwick.

Sudden Death.—Mr. William Hardgrove, a tobacconist, died suddenly at his residence in this city yesterday morning. On Friday he was apparently well, and attending to his business. His age was about 33 years.

Fined.—Robert Cardwell, a detailed soldier, was fined one dollar by the Mayor on Saturday for being drunk and noisy on the premises of the Stonewall drinking saloon.

Whipped.—Edward, the property of R. P. Archer, was ordered a whipping yesterday by the Mayor, for trespassing upon the premises of Daniel Y. Bowen.

FROM TRANS-MISSISSIPPI.—The Mobile *Advertiser and Register* has received a special dispatch from Memphis, dated the 17th, which says that Kirby Smith was reported to have fallen back from Little Rock. The Federals, under Blunt, had occupied Fort Smith, driving out Cabell. General Marsh Walker was recently wounded in a duel with Marmaduke. Burnside claims that he captured 3,000 prisoners and fourteen pieces of artillery at Cumberland Gap.

FROM SUFFOLK.—Parties directly from the vicinity of Suffolk report that all the Yankees have again left that place. For a week or two past only four companies of Spear's cavalry have been there, and on *Friday* last all left for some point unknown, going in the direction of Portsmouth. There are now no Yankees above Bowers's Hill. During the stay of the Yankee vandals at Suffolk the last time several raids were made in the surrounding country and many depredations committed. The unoccupied houses about the town were badly abused.

THE ENEMY IN WESTERN NORTH CAROLINA.—The enemy are reported to be advancing in force towards Morgan, N. C. Colonel Avery's plantation has been destroyed and his stock driven off.

TELEGRAPHIC NEWS.

From Northern Georgia.

ATLANTA, Sept. 26.—The train last night from Ringgold ran off the track four miles above Marietta, and is not yet in. No lives lost.

Mr. Adair writes from Ringgold, yesterday, to the *Confederacy*, that General Wheeler, with his cavalry, is over the river, and Gen. Forrest is in the right place.

A Confederate officer has just arrived who was wounded and a prisoner Saturday, and detained in a Yankee hospital until Monday, when he was relieved by Forrest's cavalry. He saw Gen. Rosecrans on Sunday at 12 M., and did not perceive any marks of wounds.

On Sunday night rockets were seen towards Harrison, which, the Yankees said, were a signal of the approach of General Burnside, with forty thousand reinforcements.

A heavy Confederate force was before Chattanooga and Harrison.

[SECOND DISPATCH.]

ATLANTA, Sept. 26.—Our lines extend around Chattanooga within striking distance of the enemy.

Our forces are well up to the front.—Full supplies of commissary and hospital stores are close at hand.

On Wenesday night our cavalry occupied Cooper's Gap, on Lookout Mountain, twelve miles from Chattanooga.—That night Gen. Wheeler made a reconnoissance toward Lookout Mountain, found an infantry force of the enemy, and drove them away.

The mountain is now held by Gen. Longstreet. The enemy's operations are plainly visible from Lookout.

Rosecrans has two lines of defence on the road to Chattanooga, six hundred yards apart. He has one pontoon bridge across the river, which is crowded with wagons, and the impression is that he brings them over as they are needed.

Gen. Longstreet commands the river and railroad below Chattanooga.

Gen. Hood was doing well Thursday.

Our loss in killed and wounded will not exceed twelve thousand.

The Yankee loss in killed, wounded, and prisoners will reach twenty-eight thousand.

Five Yankee hospitals are in our hands full of wounded.

The enemy's haversacks contain *corn bread only.* Prisoners state that they were four days on short rations.

The bridge over the East Chickamauga river is repaired, and trains will go to our lines to-morrow.

[THIRD DISPATCH.]

ATLANTA, Sept. 26.—Officers from Gen. Hood's division train, just in, report that they left Lookout Mountain yesterday morning. That important position was then held by Hood's division, now commanded by Gen. Jenkins.

It is not supposed that an assault will be made, *as we command the situation*, and need not sacrifice the lives of our troops.

When the train left the burnt bridge station this morning heavy cannonading was heard.

On Thursday night the enemy made two attempts on our lines. They were driven back both times to their entrenchments.

Further news of a cheering character has been received, but it is not deemed prudent to communicate it.

The Defeat of Rosecrans's Army at the North.

MOBILE, Sept. 26.—The *Advertiser and Register* has a special dispatch from Senatobia, which says:

Northern papers are mournful over Rosecrans's defeat. They acknowledge a loss of thirty thousand.

The insurance companies will not insure the Mississippi river steamers.

All quiet in Arkansas.

From Texas and Louisiana.

ATLANTA, Sept. 26.—A special to the *Appeal*, from Canton, Miss., dated 24th, says:

The Memphis *Bulletin*, of the 23d, states that Magruder had whipped Franklin's Yankee corps, taking many prisoners, sinking two gunboats, and disabling several transports, at Sabine Pass.—Franklin returned to New Orleans.

[ANOTHER DISPATCH.]

MOBILE, Sept. 26.—The New Orleans *Era* says that a most disastrous reverse to the Federals in Louisiana has occurred. This concurs with the rumor that Gen. Weitzel had been defeated and killed by Gen. Dick Taylor, at Napoleon, La.—[The particulars of this Confederate victory were published from the Northern papers on Friday last.—Rep.

From Charleston.

CHARLESTON, Sept. 26.—The Yankees have worked very little at their batteries to-day. Our fire is keeping them close under cover. Our mortars on Sullivan's Island work admirably. The shells are thrown with accuracy and fall with accuracy in the middle of the enemy's batteries at nearly every fire.

There was again considerable motion in the fleet to-day. It is supposed that Admiral Farragut was visiting with vessel.

[SECOND DISPATCH.]

CHARLESTON, Sept. 27.—The enemy is evidently attempting to make himself impregnable on Morris Island. Besides enlarging and strengthening batteries Gregg and Wagner, he has erected palisades around his works, to guard against any effort on our part to take the Island by assault.

The enemy has teams of mules constantly transporting supplies, &c., from South Island to Cummings's Point, notwithstanding our fire.

Our James Island batteries were shelling the enemy briskly last night.

From the Rapidan.

GORDONSVILLE, Sept. 26.—No movements of the enemy have been reported to-day. A strong brigade of Yankees went to Germanna Ford yesterday. An immense wagon train was at Mitchell's Station yesterday. The main fortifications of the enemy are supposed to be at Cedar Run.

Gen. Hood's wife is with him at Red Sulphur spring, Tenn.

Chickamauga is the Indian name for "river of death."

Gen. Howell Cobb has been promoted to be Major-General.

There was a heavy frost at Charlotte, N. C., on the 23d inst.

The Daily Picayune.

UNION. JUSTICE. CONFIDENCE.

VOLUME XXVII. | NEW ORLEANS. TUESDAY MORNING, OCTOBER 13, 1863. | NUMBER 221.

The Daily Picayune.

[From our Evening Edition of Yesterday.]

STEAMERS TO ARRIVE.—The Creole, which was advertised to leave New York for New Orleans on the 2d inst., is announced in New York papers of the 3d as being up for Havana, to leave on the 6th. The George Washington was to leave on the 16th, and the Evening Star would leave on the 17th inst.

☞ The Parkersburg, Capt Spencer, from New York September 30, arrived up this morning.

☞ We are indebted to Capt. Spencer, of the steamship Parkersburg, for favors.

☞ The purser of the steamship Parkersburg will accept our thanks for prompt delivery of our files.

☞ Dealers in cotton should attend R. T. Montgomery's sale on Monday, October 12th, at 1 o'clock P. M., at salesroom 93 Camp street. There will be sold 66 bales or more.

☞ We are indebted to Messrs. Gomez, Sales & Co., of Havana, for a copy of the Havana Prices Current, of Sept. 19.

☞ The well known Francis J. Grund died suddenly in Philadelphia on the 29th ult.

☞ A Boston (Oct. 2) telegram says that a movement is on foot in Massachusetts "to procure an elegant sword for presentation to Gen. Banks as a special recognition of the taking of Port Hudson."

☞ A gentleman who has just returned from England, after a prolonged tour in that country, informs the Boston Traveller that the United States Consul at Liverpool felt confident of being able to accumulate sufficient testimony to justify the course of the English Government in detaining the rams just completed at that port. Arrangements were making before the order of detention was received to man the vessels with British sailors, preparatory to their departure for the coast of the United States.

CASUALTIES IN THE N. O. WASHINGTON ARTILLERY.—We have already published the list of killed and wounded in the N. O. Washington Artillery in the battle of Chickamauga, as reported in the Memphis (Atlanta) Appeal. We have since received the following particulars of the casualties in this company, which we subjoin as follows:

Wounded.—Martin Mathias, shot through the thigh; Felix Arroyo, bruised slightly; C. R. Percy, slightly in calf of leg; J. A. Walsh, by fragment of shell in the region of groin; D. Weingard, slightly bruised in back by shell; W. G. Crawford, slightly in the head, piece of shell; W. Asa Wood foot amputated; George Pugh, very slightly by fragment of shell; J. Weber, slightly bruised; J. Frazier, in arm; sergeant E. J. O'Arien, ball in the face; corporal J. Beggs, run over; C. Ferrand, ball in leg; P. Capou, piece of shell in leg; George Brown, slightly, shell on arm; W. R. Murphy, run over; R. Vinson, run over; John Murray, very slightly in breast; E. S. McIlhenny, cannon ball on arm.

Killed.—Lieut. T. M. Blair; privates J. R. Anderson, C. P. Baily, Martin Duggan, Emile Reichert, L. D. Daigle, Joseph Belson, Jr., Fred. Morrel, Ben. Stakeman, James Boyle, Brocard, volunteer, (originally Maury's secretary.)

General News.

A letter from the steamer Seminole, dated Rio del Norte, September 12, says: "The most valuable prize of the war has been captured by the Seminole, under command of Com'r Roland. She is of British build, and over 300 feet long, and showed British colors. She has evidently been fitted out in England for a rebel man-of-war."

Brig. Gen. Robert Anderson, in response to an inquiry from the War Department, has stated that the flag which he hauled down from Sumter on the occasion of its surrender is still in his possession.

By order of United States Marshal Keyes, cargo of the prize steamer Cronstadt, consisting of cotton, turpentine and tobacco, was sold at auction on the 1st inst. at Boston.

A Washington telegram to the New York Tribune says:

We are enabled upon the best authority to say that no draft for 600,000 men, as reported by the Evening Post, nor any further draft other than the one last ordered and now in progress is contemplated by Government.

The late heavy rains occasioned a great freshet in the rivers of Newfoundland, damaging the telegraph lines so that they could not be worked for eight days.

Many of the Confederate prisoners recently taken in Virginia are clothed in clean new jackets, especially the cavalry men. They have also been supplied with new boots, of foreign manufacture.

Minister Burlingame officially communicates that the imperial Government of China has responded to his request for an extension of the time in which to re-export native produce, from three to twelve months.

FEARFUL ACCIDENT—*Confederate Prisoners Killed and Injured.*—A Nashville telegram in the Cincinnati Commercial of 14th inst says:

About 300 Confederates, confined in an unfinished hotel, known as the Maxwell House, were precipitated from the fifth story through the gangway, which was fitted up with temporary stairs, to the second floor. The prisoners made a simultaneous rush to breakfast, and the stairs gave way under the unusual weight. Two men have been taken out of the ruins dead; two have since died from injuries received, and 96 others are injured. Some have both legs and arms broken, and others are more seriously injured.

Reinforcing Rosecrans.—A Washington telegram of 1st inst. says:

Arrangements for prompt communication between Chattanooga and Washington are now perfected. It is not supposed here in military circles that any serious impediment will interfere with the reinforcing of the army of the Cumberland.

FROM CHINA—*San Francisco, Sept. 29.*—Hong Kong dates to the 29th of August have been received.

Business in the Chinese ports was generally prostrate. The Taeping rebellion was becoming more formidable owing to the assistance of numerous fillibusters.

Burgoine, who succeeded Ward as the leader of the American fillibusters on the Imperialiste side, has gone over to Tae-Ping, taking many skilled riflemen with him. His first exploit was the capture of an Imperial steamer, and immediately afterward the City of Desoon.

Hong Kong papers attach great importance to his movements. They ask, who can tell how many thousand fillibusters will flock to Burgoine's standard, since every inducement is offered which tends to gratify fillibustering expeditions, such as animosity to England, the plunder of women, and the boundless dreams of conquest.

Letter from New York.

[Special Correspondence of the Picayune.]

NEW YORK, Oct. 3.

The Saxonia's news, received from Cape Race and published in the city papers this morning, will no doubt furnish subject matter for "thundering" editorials in the New York journals for a week at least, and Wall street will be lively to-day. The summary is short but significant, especially in the semi-official announcement in the *Memorial Diplomatique* that England, in conjunction with France, will acknowledge the present Mexican Government so soon as Maximilian accepts the throne; that both powers will accredit official representatives; that the two powers will pursue the policy on this continent, as well as elsewhere, Napoleon announced to Mr. Dayton many months ago; and that England, apart from the alliance, will "go" a loan, and will see that Mexico is placed in a position, pecuniarily, to fulfill her engagements with other nations; thus doing away with that excuse for "interference," which favored France with so fair a pretence for the inception of her schemes in Mexico.

Those who believe fully in the Monroe doctrine will consider this joint action of the two powers as scarcely less an enormity than would be the recognition of the rebellious States of the South. The news also tells us that Mr. Mason has withdrawn from London and gone to Paris "by order." Street talk to-day expresses two opinions with regard to the withdrawal—to wit: that the Confederates are disgusted at the "coldness" of Great Britain and that Mr. Mason no longer hopes to influence the British Government in favor of recognition—in short, that he gives up the game. The second expression of opinion, and which is quite as current, is that Mr. Mason has gone to Paris for the sake of aiding in schemes for which Paris affords a better diplomatic field just now than London. The advices that the French Government intends (perhaps) to recognize Poland as a belligerent power will be eminently satisfactory to those who have charged France with inconsistency in refusing to rebellious Poland what she has already granted to the rebellious States of America.

The event of the week in this city was the reception of the Russian naval officers belonging to the five Russian vessels of war now in this port. I do not remember to have ever seen a better managed public display in New York, and much enthusiasm was manifested. The mail and the journals will give you the details of the affair. It is certainly a novelty, even in this city of cosmopolites, to see crowds of Russian officers and sailors daily on Broadway. The officers present a fine appearance. They are generally very fair, with Saxon-like hair and eyes, and would pass for jolly Englishmen almost anywhere. The common sailors are dark, and queer-looking chickens, as *outré* in appearance and costume as so many Arabs. They draw a crowd of *gamins*, newsboys, and others who drive a lively trade in the purchase of Russian coins. A day or two since, one of them amused a large crowd by a shrewd financial operation. A small boy was very anxious to invest in Russian coins, but had nothing to offer in exchange but his empty porte-monnaie. This he tendered. The sailor examined it, and concluded to trade. He pulled from some mysterious depth in his pantaloons a large greasy bag, turned out a handful of coppers of all sorts, a general exposition of the industry of all nations, spread them out in the palm of his broad, black hand, turned them over, and finally picked out four nickel cents, United States currency, and solemnly offered them for the porte-monnaie. There was a shout, of course. The boy declined the trade, as he doubtless wanted the coins of Alexander, and not those of Nickel-as.

New York was never so lively as now. Every where else, at the Springs, at Niagara, and by the sea shore, the season is over, and the campaign of fashion, luxury, and extravagance in the city has commenced. There is a gorgeous display of new shoddy carriages in the streets. The theatres are thronged. The shops and stores vie with each other in the splendor of their displays of stocks, and in their heretofore unheard of prices. Every one is rich in greenbacks. Beyond the place and contract applicants, there are now no beggars at the North. The war has made every one rich in greenbacks—or rich in hopes—of greenbacks. This, at least, is the surface story; and whatever grief, or sorrow, or suffering, or desolation, or despair there may be in the back streets, or in "the rural districts," is not manifest in the Central Park; and Broadway is very beautiful now.

The Legal Tender Question Decided.—The Albany (N. Y.) Evening Journal, of the 29th ult., says:

The Court of Appeals, at the opening of the session this morning, announced its decision in the case involving the validity of the notes issued by the National Government as a "legal tender" in the redemption of the circulating notes of State banks, and in the payment of obligations arising on contracts.

In the case of the Metropolitan Bank and others, respondents, vs. H. H. Van Dyck, appellant, the judgment of the Supreme Court of this District (which was in favor of "legal tender") was affirmed, while that of the Supreme Court of New York, in the Roosevelt case was reversed.

In the former case, the question involved was, whether "legal tender notes" were equivalent to specie, under the constitution and laws of this State, in the redemption of bank notes by the institutions issuing the same. In the other case the question arose on the reception of "legal tender" in discharge of a mortgage executed before the enactment of the law of Congress authorizing the issue of such legal tender notes by the General Government.

The opinion of Judge Emmott states succinctly the principles upon which the Court based its decision. Judges Davies, Wright, Balcom and Marvin also delivered opinions in one or the other of the two cases, sustaining the validity of the legal tender clause, in which Judge Rosecrans concurred. Chief Judge Denio delivered a contrary opinion, and Judge Selden also dissented.

☞ Attention is called to the advertisement of Drs. A. & A. F. Follin, who treat diseases of the throat and lungs.

☞ A lot of clean tarpaulins is advertised for sale by Bostick & Seymour, 35 Front Levee street.

☞ Kloppenburg, 481 Old Levee street, gives notice that he is prepared to gin and bale seed cotton. Orders left at 8 Carondelet street attended to. See advertisement.

☞ Schneider & Zuberbier have removed from the corner of Fulton and Lafayette streets to 33 and 35 Tchoupitoulas street. See advertisement.

LATE AND IMPORTANT.

From Mobile Papers of 2d, 3d and 4th.

THE SITUATION AT CHATTANOOGA.

ROSECRANS REINFORCED.

THE SIEGE OF CHARLESTON.

Movements in Virginia and Mississippi

THE PENNSYLVANIA CAMPAIGN.

GEN. LEE'S OFFICIAL REPORT.

The Bee of this morning publishes the following from the Mobile Advertiser and Register of 2d, 3d and 4th instant:

The Siege of Charleston.

CHARLESTON, Oct. 1.—There has been heavier firing to-day than for several weeks past. The enemy has been already pounding away at the ruins of Sumter from his old batteries on Morris Island, beyond Wagner. The enemy's fire was chiefly at Sumter, but he also shelled Fort Johnson. Our batteries and Fort Moultrie replied with a brisk and steady fire. All quiet to-night.

CHARLESTON, Oct. 2.—The enemy's movements on Morris Island indicate rather a design of permanent occupation than of immediate operations. Two monitors are kept close in, doing picket duty.

There has been scarcely any firing to-day.

CHARLESTON, Oct. 3.—The enemy to-day continued slowly firing at Fort Sumter.

Movements in Virginia.

GORDONSVILLE, Oct. 1.—Nine Federal prisoners were sent through to Richmond to-day, who were captured at Manassas Plains.

Mosby's troops are busy in the enemy's rear.

A Federal conscript deserter, who came through yesterday, reports many conscripts coming to Meade. They have a guard in front, rear and all around, to prevent their escape.

RICHMOND, Sept. 2.—The flag of truce steamer New York arrived at City Point this morning with official dispatches for Commissioner Ould, four Confederate officers long since declared exchanged, seven privates, three citizens and Mrs. Wilder, wife of the Russian Consul at Savannah.

RICHMOND, Oct. 1.—There is scarcely a doubt that Meade has sent heavy reinforcements to Rosecrans, and will concentrate the remainder of his army near Culpeper Courthouse, at which point the Federals are throwing up additional works, also building large hospital houses, quartermaster's and commissary's stores, with the apparent design of making that place the base of future operations. The Federal cavalry have again occupied Madison Court-house in force. It is supposed they contemplate a raid in the rear of Lee's army, to destroy the railroad.

The firing at Germania Ford yesterday was doubtless a feint to divert attention from movements in Madison and keep up appearances of a purpose to attempt crossing the river at the lower fords.

The indications are that Meade will not bring on a general engagement, as he threatened to do several days ago.

From Mississippi.

OXFORD, Oct. 2.—Gen. Johnston reviewed Gen. Chalmers's cavalry brigade yesterday. He expresses himself highly pleased.

Gen Chalmers has been placed in command of all the cavalry in North Mississippi.

Stirring events may be looked for soon.

The Pennsylvania Campaign.

GEN. LEE'S OFFICIAL REPORT.

RICHMOND, Oct. 1.—Gen. Lee's official report of the Pennsylvania campaign indicates that his purpose was to advance upon Harrisburg, but on the night of the 29th of June he ascertained that the Federal army had crossed the Potomac, and the head of his column had reached South Mountain.

As communication with the Potomac was thus menaced, it was resolved to prevent the further progress of the army in that direction by concentrating the army on the east side of the mountains at Gettysburg. The Federal army interposed between Stuart's command and our main body prevented communication with him until his arrival at Carlisle. The march towards Gettysburg was conducted more slowly than it would have been had the movements of the Federal army been known.

After referring to the first day's fight, the report says it had not been intended to fight a general battle at such a distance from our base, unless attacked by the enemy, but finding ourselves unexpectedly confronted by the Federal army, it became a matter of difficulty to withdraw through the mountains with our large trains.

At the same time the country was unfavorable for collecting supplies while in the presence of the enemy's main body, as he was enabled to restrain our foraging parties by occupying the passes of the mountains, and a battle thus became in a measure unavoidable. Encouraged by the successful issue of the engagement on the first day, and in view of the valuable results that would issue from a defeat of the army under Meade, it was thought advisable to renew the attack.

The report then gives a general description of the battles of the 2d and 3d of July; commending the heroic valor of the troops; explains the cause of the withdrawal of our army from Gettysburg, etc. It has been furnished to the Richmond papers for publication.

The Situation Before Chattanooga.

MISSIONARY RIDGE, VIA CHICKAMAUGA, Oct. 3.—The sun rose high and clear after two heavy rains. Once more the hostile lines of the enemy are plainly visible from Gen. Bragg's quarters. The enemy are again busy strengthening their positions, the most formidable of which is a star fort on an eminence, in the rear of Chattanooga, partially constructed by our troops before the evacuation. The health and spirit of the troops are very fine, and they are anxious to be led against the enemy, though everything indicates perfect quiet for some time. Rosecrans's forces seem to be massed in and immediately around the town. Three pontoon bridges are laid across the river, and wagon trains are packed on the opposite bank.

ATLANTA, Oct. 3.—Gen. Polk has arrived here, having been relieved from his command by Gen. Bragg. Alleged delay to attack the enemy on the 20th ult. is assigned as the cause. Gens. Hindman and Armstrong are also reported under arrest.

The trains report all quiet before Chattanooga.

A special dispatch to the Intelligencer, of the 30th ult., says the wounded prisoners were exchanged to-day. We had 2500 Federals; they had 41 Confederates. Gen. Dan Adams has determined to remain in the Federal lines until he can be safely removed. Gov. Brown has reached camp, and was enthusiastically cheered by the troops.

The enemy still hold Knoxville.

Additional from Europe.

In yesterday's Picayune we gave a summary of news from arrivals (to 23d ult.) from Europe. Our files furnish the following additional intelligence:

GREAT BRITAIN.

The Royal Mail steamship Persia, from New York, arrived at Queenstown on the 19th.

The United States frigate Constellation arrived at Gibraltar on the 11th.

The steamship Great Eastern and Hibernia arrived at Liverpool on the 19th.

The Rev. W. N. Channing had been lecturing in Liverpool on the American question. He predicted an early peace through the triumph of the North.

Rev. Mr. Stewart, late a chaplain in the rebel army, has been lecturing before the Southern Club at Liverpool. He charged the New England clergy with instigating the war, and asserted that the war would soon end when President Lincoln loses clerical support. He declared that the South had the means of carrying on the war for years to come, but was nevertheless ready to lay down the sword, and leave the questions at issue to the ballot.

The Paris correspondent of the Morning Post says a new loan for the Confederates is contemplated.

The London Herald, adverting to the withdrawal of Mr. Mason from London, says it is in consequence of the systematic rudeness with which he has been treated by Russell. The Herald hints that it has been through the suggestions of Mr. Adams that Mr. Mason has been excluded from official intercourse with the British Government.

SHIP BUILDING FOR THE CONFEDERATES.

The following reply to the memorial forwarded to Earl Russell by the President of the Union and Emancipation Society has been received from the Foreign Office:

FOREIGN OFFICE, Sept. 14, 1863.

Sir—I am directed by Earl Russell to state to you, in reply to your memorial of the 1st inst., that Her Majesty's Government have long had their attention turned to the question of building and fitting vessels of war for the so called Confederate States, and the subject will continue to receive their anxious consideration. I am, sir, your most obedient, humble servant, E. HAMMOND.

T. B. Potter, Esq., 51 Piccadilly, Manchester.

CAPT. MAFFITT'S EXPLANATION.

[Paris (Sept. 15) Correspondence of the London Herald.]

The Ocean, of Brest, publishes a long letter from M. Pecquet du Bellay, showing that the captain of the French ship Bremontier, on board which Capt. Maffit, of the Florida, is charged with having transferred his prisoners in spite of the commander of that vessel, took them off spontaneously, in pursuance of an arrangement between himself and the prisoners, to which the captain of the Florida was no party.

LIVERPOOL AND NASSAU COTTON TRADE.

[From the Liverpool Courier, Sept. 18.]

The export of cotton from Nassau for Liverpool continues unabated, and, notwithstanding the existing blockade, the stock there is very large. Vessels continue to arrive to load, five being reported from this port by the mail, and with arrivals from London, Cardiff, etc., made a very creditable fleet lying there on the 22d ult. The following had sailed for this port with full cargoes of cotton: Presto, Capt. Wingarden; Ella, Capt. Carter; Economist, Capt. Thomas; Lady of the Lake, Capt. Powell; Knight Bruce, Capt. White; Nina, Capt. Squires, and Emulous, Capt. Brown. The Presto and Ella have already been reported in the Mersey, and the remainder may be expected in a few days. The steamers Spalding and Smoker, reported at Nassau by last mail, had both sailed for Confederate ports.

MORE BLOCKADE RUNNERS.

[From the Scotsman, of Edinburg, Sept. 15.]

On Friday last a handsome looking paddle-wheel steamer of about five hundred tons measurement was launched by Messrs Stevens, of Kelvinhaugh, a sister to the Fergus, built by the same firm, and now about to proceed to Nassau. On Saturday Messrs. Caird & Co Greenock, launched a beautiful modelled paddlewheel steamer of seven hundred and fifty tons, a sister to the City of Petersburg, launched by Messrs. Caird & Co. lately. They are each to be supplied with powerful engines of two hundred and fifty horse power. These two vessels were first of all contracted for as steamers for the Glasgow and Belfast mail service, but were sold while being built. They are on the same model as the famous Lord Clyde, now on her way to Nassau as a blockade runner, and are expected to be very fast sailers. The Nola was christened by the wife of Captain Rollins, a thorough American sailor, who is nominal owner, and who will take command of this vessel when finished.

SPAIN.

MADRID, Sept. 15.—The Ministry is quite determined to chastise the Riff insurgents if the Emperor of Morocco does not keep his promise.

The Washington Cabinet has demanded that the distance to which Spanish jurisdiction extends around the Island of Cuba shall be reduced to three miles. It is asserted that the Government is little disposed to make this concession.

Marshal O'Donnell and Sir Y. Crampton, the English Ambassador, have arrived here.

IRELAND.

[From the Gazette de France, Sept. 15.]

French Reports of a Coming Revolution.—A piece of news has just arrived from England, which does not surprise us, and which we should not be sorry to see confirmed. It is published by the International, a French journal appearing in London, and is to the effect that a vast conspiracy is now openly organizing in Ireland against the English domination of course. The conspirators, who call themselves "Fenians" (!) and "Sons of St. Patrick," are said to be eighty thousand in number, all armed, and only awaiting an opportunity to shake off the Saxon yoke, and proclaim the independence of Ireland. If the English Government were engaged in a war with France, which is not probable, or with the United States, which is less probable, they would at once raise the standard of their country, and would be aided by their countrymen who have emigrated to America. The Irish would like to have France on their side; but they have resolved to act without her. The people in all the counties long for the day of deliverance, and do not make any secret of their hopes. We indulge no illusions as to the importance of this news. Ireland has for centuries groaned under English tyranny, and it is not astonishing that she should always long for freedom; but that day is not so near, perhaps, as we could wish. When it comes we shall hail it with joy.

POLAND AS A BELLIGERENT.

CRACOW, Sept. 16.—A leading article of the *Czas* to-day demands the recognition of Poland as a belligerent Power, declaring it would otherwise appear that the Powers approved the present condition of the conflict and the barbarous measures that are being taken. "This recognition," says the *Czas*, "would only be the logical consequence of the armistice accepted by Poland, and rejected by Russia. It would not cost a man nor a shilling; it would put an end to all conspiracy, secure Poland and Europe from revolutionary designs, and preserve the dignity of the Great Powers, while it protected the interests of Poland."

THE MEXICAN QUESTION.

The Paris correspondent of the London Morning Post learns that it is not the intention of the Government at Washington to throw difficulty in the way of French schemes in Mexico, but is disposed quietly to watch events.

The *Independance Belge* says that the date of M. Montholon's departure for his office in Mexico is not yet precisely known. He was doubtless waiting to learn the decisive intentions of the Archduke Maximilian. It was not therefore likely that he would leave France before the month of November.

A letter from Rome in the *Journal de Bruxelles* makes a statement to the effect that Cardinal Antonelli will shortly leave Rome for Lon. whence he will proceed to Mexico to regulate the religious affairs of the new empire.

THE LOAN, RECOGNITION, RUMORS, ETC.

We translate from the last number of the *Memorial Diplomatique*, received by our European mails, the following passage:

We are enabled to announce that a Mexican personage of elevated rank, and versed in financial affairs, after having visited Miramar for the purpose of paying his respects to the Archduke Ferdinand Maximilian, has returned to Paris, where he has had interviews with several financial notabilities. He is now in London, where he is engaged in preparing the way for a loan to be contracted by the Mexican Government.

The basis of this loan have been settled. It will amount to $500,000,000, one portion to be devoted to the repayment of the expenses of the French expedition, and the other portion to the partial extinguishment of the arrearages due to English creditors, still another to be capitalized, and the remainder to supply the expenditures of the Mexican Government. It said there was some talk of giving up Lower California to France as a guarantee for her claims, but we believe that this project is connected with another combination proposed by American (Mexican) citizens, with a view to develop their national industry."

[Paris (Sept. 15) Correspondence of London Telegraph.]

The report of the Mexican Commissioners on the government best suited to their country, and the reasons that render it so, has been a good deal criticised here. It is thought that the record indulges in rather strong language concerning the evils arising from a republic; and it is argued that a people cannot be mentally very good which is reduced to the state of demoralization mentioned in the report. The publication of this same report in the *Moniteur* is supposed to indicate that the Archduke Maximilian is about to accept the crown.

We hear—and I for one believe—that one of the first acts of the new government will be the recognition of the South. This seems to be also the opinion in America; and, to quote the words of the *Journal des Debats*, "In New York, as in Paris, no doubt is felt that the new government of Mexico, as soon as it is established, will hasten to recognize the confederation of the South, on condition that Mexico, in her turn, is also recognized." Whether the Northern States will believe that France is entirely disconnected from this policy remains to be seen. In the meantime Mr. Slidell is still dancing at the Villa Eugenie.

It is rumored to night that there is a strong feeling of jealousy between the French bankers and those of England and Germany, who are about to contract for a Mexican loan of 900,000,000f. The French wish for the consent at least, if not the guarantee, of the Government, but M. Fould is decidedly opposed to the measure. M. Hidalgo, the head of the Mexican mission to the Archduke, is to be *chargé d'affaires* for Mexico here; he is already appointed by the Provisional Government.

Commercial per Europa.

LIVERPOOL, Saturday, Sept. 19.—*Cotton.*—The Brokers' Circular reports the sales of the week at 116,500 bales, including 50,000 to speculators and 11,650 to exporters. The market has been excited and prices have advanced 1d.@2d. The sales on Friday were 10,000 bales, including 5,000 to speculators and exporters, the market closing quiet at the quoted rates of Thursday, which are as follows:

Orleans, nominal	27d.
Mobiles, nominal	26½d.
Uplands, nominal	26½d.

The stock in port is estimated at 172,000 bales, of which 33,000 are American.

STATE OF TRADE.—The Manchester market is firm.

LONDON.—Funds on the 18th were rather firmer, but there was no variation. Full demand for discount; notes unchanged.

The Stock Exchange was closed to-day. The effect of the Persia's news was not, therefore, developed on securities.

Consols closed on Friday at 93⅛@93¼ for money.

The bullion in the Bank of England had increased £116,000.

HAVRE, Friday, Sept. 18.—*Cotton.*—Sales of the week, 38,000 bales; market active and excited, and prices considerably higher, closing less firm; New Orleans tres ordinaire 345f; New Orleans bas 327. Stock in port 34,000 bales.

LIVERPOOL, Saturday, Sept. 19—Evening.—Cotton firmer but unchanged; sales on the day of the steamer's departure, 15,000 bales, of which speculators and exporters took 7000 bales.

THE CITY.

ON THE LEVEE.—It is true that our once crowded levee has now a dreary and vacant look, sadly in contrast with its anteriorly wild bustle and activity, but nevertheless there is yet some of its former glory remaining. Just now the landing of some 3,500 bales of cotton recalls the memory of bygone days forcibly to the view, and as these are themselves relicts of the past, the products of the industry of former years, they are surveyed with affectionate interest by even the moneyless and unemployed.

The comparatively few barrels and bags of "Western produce" are also the objects of great solicitude to the many who gather together around a newly landed steamer. Not only have these acquired an increased value in the prices current, but the daily decreasing means of all classes of our citizens gives augmented attraction to the necessaries of life. As evening approaches, our older citizens draw near to the ferry houses, sit a while and chat over the present or sigh over the past until the shadows lengthen and deepen into night, and then wend their way back again to their homes. So broad is our levee that it would seem now that all the commerce of the continent might there have room for its bestowal, and the walk across it seems wearisomely long; but were the good old *Ante-bellum* visit [illegible] this year again it would be difficult, from one day to the other, to land and carry off its products were all the "transportation" of the armies on foot in this department employed in the labor.

Let us go to the levee and there meditate!

CARELESS DRIVING.—A [illegible] drove over a child on the Levee yesterday, breaking one of its legs. He was arrested and locked up in the Second District guard-house.

BURGLARIES IN ALGIERS.—Not to be behind the times, our thrifty little neighbor has been visited for several nights past by [illegible] [illegible] and plunderers. [illegible] houses were entered and small sums of money and valuables were taken. Among those visited were Messrs. Lackey, Randolph, Steel, Sagee, Hannon and Gerard and Mrs. Martin. They even robbed the chicken coop of the Algerine Chief of Police, Mr. Mapley, and coolly built a fire back of the church near by to cook them. After such audacity, they can hardly hope to avoid detection if they continue their foraging operations.

SUICIDE CAUSED BY PECUNIARY TROUBLE.—A controversy is at present going on in the Second District Court as to who shall be appointed administrator of the estate of the late José Gonzales, who committed suicide by

CONTINUED ON FOURTH PAGE.

The New-York Times.

VOL. XIII—NO. 3799. NEW-YORK, THURSDAY, NOVEMBER 26, 1863. PRICE THREE CENTS.

GLORIOUS VICTORY!

GEN. GRANT'S GREAT SUCCESS.

Bragg Routed and Driven from Every Point.

SUCCESSFUL BATTLE ON TUESDAY.

Gen. Hooker Assaults Lookout Mountain and Takes 2,000 Prisoners.

General Sherman Finally Carries Missionary Ridge.

Gen. Thomas Pierces the Enemy's Centre.

Forty Pieces of Artillery Taken.

Five Thousand to Ten Thousand Prisoners Captured.

Flight of the Rebels in Disorder and Confusion.

Probable Interception of the Rebels at Rossville.

SPECIAL DISPATCH TO THE N. Y. TIMES.

WASHINGTON, Wednesday, Nov. 25.

Dispatches giving details of recent operations before Chattanooga were received to-night from Gen. Grant. He is in happy spirits and confident of success.

Atlanta he declares to be a prize already within his grasp.

DISPATCHES TO THE ASSOCIATED PRESS.

CHATTANOOGA, Wednesday, Nov. 25.

We are completely victorious. The enemy is totally routed and driven from every position. Our loss is very small and the enemy's is heavy in prisoners. Finding Gen. Hooker so successful in his movements against Lookout Mountain, the enemy evacuated that position during the night.

Gen. Hooker took possession early this morning. The enemy moved south and got on Missionary Ridge on the battle-field somewhere near Chickamauga. He is expected to intercept the flying foe. Gen. Hooker is said to have captured 2,000 prisoners in his magnificent assault of Lookout Mountain.

Gen. Sherman being all prepared to begin an assault at 8 A. M. to-day, upon the strong position of the enemy at the north end of Missionary Ridge. He had the day before taken a hill near the position of the enemy, but commanded by their artillery. He had to descend into a valley, and he then made another ascent to the position held by the enemy. Two unsuccessful assaults were made by Gen. Sherman, but, with the coöperation of the centre, he ultimately gained the position, and completed the great victory.

The brigade of Gen. Carse, with a portion of Gen. Lightfews brigade, composed the storming party in the first assault. They were repulsed with quite a heavy loss after an attack persisted in for an hour; but being reinforced they, were enabled to hold a part of the hills. In this attack Gen. Carse was wounded quite severely in the thigh. The Thirty-seventh Ohio and Sixth Iowa and One Hundred and Third Illinois regiments were in the attack. A second assault was made at 3½ o'clock, in which Mathias', Loomis' and Kaul's brigades were engaged. The fo ce reached within twenty yards of the summit of the hill and the works of the enemy, when they were flanked and broke, retiring to their reserves.

In this assault Gen. Mathias was wounded and Col. Putnam, of the Ninety-third Ohio, killed, their persistent efforts compelled the enemy to mass heavily on his right in order to hold the position of so much importance to him. About 3 o'clock Gen. Grant started two columns against the weakened centre, and in an hour desperate fighting, succeeded in breaking the centre, and gaining pessession of the ridge in which the enemy was posted, the main force was driven northward toward Gen. Sherman, who opened on them, and they were forced to break, and seek safety in disordered flight down the western slope of the Ridge, and across the western ridge of the Chickamauga. We have taken not less than 5,000 prisoners and perhaps 10,000. Gen. Hooker will probably intercept the flying enemy in the vicinity of Rossville and the region east of it.

There are reports that we have taken a whole corps.

Among the casualties are Lieut.-Col. Espy, of the Fifty-eighth Indiana regiment; Major McCawley, of the Tenth Iowa, Col. Omars, of the Ninetieth Illinois. Lieut.-Col. Stuart, of the Ninetieth Illinois; Major Walker, of the Tenth Missouri; Major Weirn, of the Fifty-sixth Illinois; Major Inniss, of the Sixth Iowa, wounded; Major Irwin, of the Sixth Iowa, killed.

Full reports of the killed and wounded cannot be obtained, as most of the killed were in Gen. Sherman's corps, and remained at dark in the hands of the enemy. The list will be telegraphed to-morrow. The prisoners say that Bragg was on the Ridge just before they were taken.

The successful storming parties consisted of Wood's and Baird's divisions on the left centre and Johnston's and Sheridan's on the right centre. Some of our wounded were left in the hands of the enemy after Gen. Sherman's unsuccessful assault, but were ultimately recovered.

CHATTANOOGA, Wednesday, Nov. 25—10 P. M.

The captured artillery is reported at about forty pieces. Gen. Hooker captured five boxes of new muskets on Lookout Mountain.

We are in entire possession of the field. We have control over the railway and river to Bridgeport. Two boats came through this morning. Our loss will not amount to more than 300 killed and 250 wounded in the three days operations. The success has been most brilliant.

The enemy is reported to be bivouacking two miles beyond Missionary Ridge. Col. Phelps, of the Thirty-eighth Ohio, and Major Glass, of the Thirty-second Indiana, are killed. Gen. John E. Smith is reported wounded. Col. Avery, of the One Hundred and Second New-York, lost a leg, and Major Elliott is the same as dead.

REPORTS FROM WASHINGTON.

WASHINGTON, Wednesday, Nov. 25.

The following was received here this afternoon from a responsible source:

CHATTANOOGA, Wednesday, Nov. 25—11 A. M.

We have had a brisk engagement this morning, and have driven the enemy entirely off Lookout Mountain, a considerable portion of which they held up to this morning. We have also taken Missionary Ridge from him this morning, and the troublesome rifle-pits, in possession of which yesterday's engagement left them at the close.

All firing has ceased for a sufficient time to warrant the conclusion that Bragg has retreated certainly, leaving all the ground and strong points in our possession for which we have been fighting for the last three days.

It is too early yet to enable me to state the casualties on either sides, which are not yet known. Our army is in glorious exultation indeed, over their series of victories.

WASHINGTON, Wednesday, Nov. 24.

Information has been received to-night at the War Department from Gen. Grant of a great battle fought to-day, resulting in a complete victory over the rebels.

Our army has carried at the point of the bayonet Lookout Mountain Top, Missionary Ridge, and all the intrenchments and rifle-pits around Chattanooga. The bravery exhibited in this great contest by our troops has never been surpassed.

OFFICIAL REPORTS FROM GEN. THOMAS AND GEN. GRANT.

WASHINGTON, Wednesday, Nov. 25.

The following official dispatch from Maj.-Gen. Grant has been received at the headquarters of the army here:

CHATTANOOGA, Tenn., Tuesday, Nov. 24—12 M.

Major-Gen. H. W. Halleck, General-in-Chief:

Yesterday, at 12½ o'clock, Gen. Granger's and Gen. Palmer's corps, supported by Gen, Howard's, were advanced directly in front of our fortifications, drove in the enemy's pickets, and carried his first line of rifle-pits between Chattanooga and Citer's Creek.

We captured nine commissioned officers and about 100 enlisted men.

Our loss is about 111.

To-day Gen. Hooker, in command of Gen. Geary's division, Twelfth corps; Gen. Osterhaus division, Fifteenth corps, and two brigades, Fourteenth corps, carried the north slope of Lookout Mountain, with small loss on our side, and a loss to the enemy of 500 or 600 prisoners; killed and wounded not reported.

There has been continuous fighting from 12 o'clock until after night; but our troops gallantly repulsed every attempt to take the position.

Gen. Sherman crossed the Tennessee River before daylight this morning, at the mouth of the South Chickamauga, with three divisions of the Fifteenth corps and one division of the Fourteenth corps, and carried the northern extremity of Missionary ridge.

Our success so far has been complete and the behavior of the troops admirable.

GEORGE H. THOMAS, Major General.

SECOND DISPATCH.

CHATTANOOGA, Tuesday, Nov. 24—6 P. M.

Maj.-Gen. Halleck, General-in-Chief, Washington:

The fighting to-day progressed favorably.

Gen. Sherman carried the end of Missionary Ridge, and his right is now at the Tunnel, and his left at Chickamauga Creek.

The troops from Lookout Valley carried the point of the mountain, and now hold the eastern slope and point high up.

I cannot yet tell the amount of casualties, but our loss is not heavy.

Gen. Hooker reports 2,000 prisoners taken, besides which a small number have fallen into our hands from Missionary Ridge.

U. S. GRANT, Major-General.

REPORTS FROM REBEL SOURCES.

FORTRESS MONROE, Wednesday, Nov. 25.

The Richmond *Dispatch*, of Nov. 24, has the following:

MISSIONARY RIDGE, Monday, Nov. 23.

The enemy massed a heavy fire on our right this morning, and advanced at 2 o'clock, driving in our pickets. It is not certain yet whether they intend an attack in force, or to advance their lines.

There are various rumors of the occupation of Knoxville by our forces, but nothing official, however.

Two thousand Yankees passed Rogersville, and five regiments through Jacksborough, *en route* for Kentucky. Our forces are active in front.

President Davis arrived at Orange Court-house on Saturday. He is stopping with Gen. Lee.

MISSIONARY RIDGE, Nov. 23.

To Gen. Cooper:

We hold all the roads leading into Knoxville, except the one between Holsten and French Broad Rivers. Gen. Jones' cavalry might close that. The enemy's cavalry is most broken up. Wheeler cut off his train between Cumberland Gap and Knoxville.

(Signed,) BRAXTON BRAGG.

EXTENSIVE FIRE IN MULBERRY-STREET.—Between 11 and 12 o'clock last night a fire broke out on the third floor of the tenement house No. 35 Mulberry-street, occupied mostly by Italian organ-grinders. The flames soon extended to No. 37, same street, and before the fire could be extinguished these two buildings were nearly destroyed. The latter building was a large tenement house, and was occupied by many families. Building No. 35 is owned by the Valentine estate, and is damaged to the amount of about $1,500. The loss to the inmates could not be ascertained. Several of them barely escaped with their lives.

CAPT. MAURICE W. WALL A BRIGADIER-GENERAL.—A private dispatch from Washington states that Capt. Maurice W. Wall, late acting as Adjutant-General of the Irish brigade, has been appointed a Brigadier-General of Colored Volunteers, to report immediately to Maj.-Gen. Schofield, of St. Louis, Mo. Capt. Wall is a veteran, having been in every engagement from Bull run the first to Gettysburgh.

FROM KNOXVILLE.

GEN. BURNSIDE'S POSITION SATISFACTORY

The Investment of the North Side of the Town Close.

Details of Three Days' Operations Before Knoxville.

CINCINNATI, Wednesday, Nov. 25.

The situation of Gen. Burnside at Knoxville is perfectly satisfactory.

There was heavy firing west of the town on Saturday.

The investment of the north side of the town is close, but the south side is open.

Gen. Burnside is confident of final success.

KNOXVILLE, Sunday, Nov. 22, 1863.

Thursday morning revealed a line of rifle-pits which the enemy had thrown up during the night. A house near our works was occupied by their sharpshooters, to the annoyance of our men, until our batteries shelled them out. During the day the rebels opened with a battery beyond the railroad depot, and threw a few shells. It was silenced by our guns.

On Friday a desultory fire was kept up between the skirmishers. Toward dusk the enemy opened with a new battery of six pieces and again threw a few shells. On the right a brilliant and successful sortie was made to burn a house on the Loudon road, which interfered with our range. The rebels were driven from their rifle-pits and the house burned, when our men came back, shelling them as they did so.

On Saturday a rain-storm set in, lasting nearly all day. The operations of the day were confined to skirmishing.

To-day skirmishing has been constant along the whole line. A few shots have been exchanged between the batteries. The enemy have invested the city with batteries. Their rifle-pits are quite close to our works, and sharpshooters occasionally pick off a man.

NEWS FROM WASHINGTON.

OUR SPECIAL WASHINGTON DISPATCHES.

WASHINGTON, Wednesday, Nov. 25.

ARMY OF THE POTOMAC MUD-BOUND.

Intelligence from the front to-night, is that the rains have rendered the roads almost impassable, and that the army is as completely mud-bound as it was at any time last Winter or Spring. Well informed officers hint that active operations of magnitude are at an end for this season. The ardent and hopeful persuade themselves that the mud will soon dry up. The natives of the sacred soil say there will be no more marching weather till next May.

THE NEW-YORK CUSTOM-HOUSE.

There is already shadowed a searching investigation, by a Committee of the House, of the administration of the New-York Customs Department, and particularly into the business of seizures and forfeitures. It is predicted that one of its results will be the refusal by the District Court, in a large number of cases, of the certificate of probable cause so customarily granted to the Collectors.

ANOTHER RAILROAD WANTED.

The present price of coal, sixteen dollars a ton, is made the basis of a demand already active, that Congress shall give a charter to somebody to construct a new line of railroad northward from Washington till it meets cheap fuel, and, incidentally, cheap food.

PERSONAL.

Senator Nesmith, of Oregon, arrived here to-day from Chattanooga. He was present at the last battle of Chickamauga, and says, after careful examination of the topography of the region, that if the rebels risk a fight on the first battle ground, they will not only be whipped but annihilated. He represents Grant's army in splendid fighting condition.

FURLOUGH TO VETERANS.

The Twelfth Illinois cavalry, which has been in the Army of the Potomac for nearly two years, to-day left in a body for Chicago, on thirty days' furlough. The entire regiment has reënlisted for three years.

GEN. MEREDITH WILL NOT BE RELIEVED.

The report that Gen. Meredith has been relieved as Commissioner of Exchange, travels faster than the policy of the War Department. He will be retained so long as Ould is retained. The present determination of the Government is to make no more exchanges until the military *status* and rights of our colored troops are definitely settled.

A CURIOUS PROCEEDING.

For several days past, Capt. Schutz's Detectives have been on the track of a notorious rebel ordnance officer named Lenostay, who came from Richmond to Washington to collect money rents, perhaps for renegade "Washingtonians" now in Dixie. His mission was successful. He gathered $150,000 and was on his way South *via* Baltimore, where he was arrested by the Detectives. Col. Fish, Provost-Marshal of that city, sent him South *via* Harper's Ferry, with all the money on him. There is much desire to know here why a rebel army officer with so large a pile is sent to a destination he desires to reach at our Government's expense.

COMMISSARY-GENERAL HOFFMAN

has returned from his tour of inspection in the West. He visited Johnson's island, Camp Chase, Helena, Ark., and all other places in the West where rebel prisoners are confined. He reports that rebel prisoners are in excellent condition—well clothed, well fed, in good quarters, and enjoying every comfort that they could desire—contrasting strangely with the condition of our prisoners in Richmond.

At Helena, Ark., buildings are being erected for the accommodation of such of the Southern chivalry as may be captured in the Southwest. The buildings are designed to accommodate 10,000 men.

AT PAROLE CAMP.

There are now at the Parole camp at Annapolis and Camp Chase, Ohio, fourteen hundred paroled Union prisoners, enlisted men, paroled since the 1st of September last. The last declaration of exchange by our Government included only those prisoners paroled to that date. Why our Government does not declare these men exchanged is not known, as the rebels have declared all those captured by Grant to be exchanged. Official figures show that the rebels are greatly in arrear in these exchanges.

THE LAND OFFICE.

During the month of October the cash sales at the United States Land Office at Marquette, Mich., (in the upper peninsula,) amounted to upward of $24,000, which shows that cash land sales are reviving.

SILVER AT LAKE SUPERIOR.

The General Land Office has received information to-day of large discoveries of silver in the neighborhood of Marquette, on Lake Superior.

DISPATCHES TO THE ASSOCIATED PRESS.

WASHINGTON, Wednesday, Nov. 25.

SOME OF MOSBY'S MEN CAPTURED.

Thirteen of Mosby's guerrillas, captured by Col. Lowell in the skirmish on Monday, and several of White's battalion have arrived here, and were sent to the Old Capitol Prison, together with seven prisoners of State

FROM THE ARMY OF THE POTOMAC.

The only information from the Army of the Potomac, to-night, is that all is quiet and nothing of a public character worth communicating going on. The roads are still in a bad condition.

NAVAL ORDER.

Lieut.-Commander Wm. T. Truxton has been detached from the Navy-yard at Philadelphia, and ordered to the command of the *Tacony*.

WHOLESALE DISMISSION OF OFFICERS.

Maj.-Gen. Thomas has issued General Orders dishonorably dismissing one Colonel, two Majors, fifteen Captains, twenty-six Lieutenants and one Surgeon, for various offences, including drunkenness, feigning sickness, spreading false rumors, permitting men to plunder, misbehavior in face of the enemy, shameful cowardice, gross disloyalty, dishonest practices, and conduct unbecoming officers and gentlemen.

Course of the National and State Authorities Concerning Colored Volunteers.

LETTER FROM GOV. SEYMOUR.

The "New-York Association for Colored Volunteers," formed at a meeting called by Peter Cooper, Gen. Sickles, Wm. C. Bryant, Gen. John Cochrane, Henry J. Raymond, Wm. Curtis Noyes, Wm. E. Dodge, David Dowd, David Dudley Field, and many other citizens—of which meeting Gen. Wm. K. Strong, late of the army, was President—took prompt measures for ascertaining the views of the National and State Governments concerning the conditions on which colored troops might be enlisted under the President's Proclamation for more volunteers. Gen. Strong was requested to telegraph the War Department, and Mr. James Rodgers went to Albany to learn the views of Gov. Seymour on the subject.

The callers of the meeting said: "If we allow our citizens to be drawn away by superior inducements offered by other States, we lose them in making up our quota, and the draft will fall heavily upon those who are left; or, if we raise men by volunteering at the last hour, we shall have to pay large bounties and heavier taxes. Let us move in this matter without delay. Other States are fast taking our men to fill their quotas—especially our colored men. Several thousand of these may be added to the strength of our army, and also *saved to the quota of our State*, by a prompt and vigorous movement. Our country's interest and self-interest here unite."

The General Committee of the Association, in their letter to Secretary Stanton, dated Nov. 21, said: "This application to the National Government results from the refusal of certain State functionaries to recognize *colored* men in the call for *volunteers*, notwithstanding the fact that the President's Proclamation makes no discrimination in color, and the additional fact that that class of citizens are subject, like white men, to *a draft*."

And, in their representations at Albany it was added that "justice and patriotism alike require that all men who are subject to draft shall have equal privilege in volunteering under the President's Proclamation"—it being desirable, also, "that our white fellow-citizens shall be measurably relieved from drafting by allowing colored citizens to volunteer for the war—in the course of which war the colored troops have evinced discipline and bravery worthy of the noble cause of National self-defence."

Answers have been received from Washington and Albany. Under date of the 24th the Secretary of War says: "On application, by suitable persons, special authority will be granted to raise colored troops in New-York, according to the rules and regulations relative to organizing and raising colored troops. The troops so raised *will be credited to the State*. Until Congress shall authorize it no bounty can be paid, and the pay is limited by act of Congress to ten dollars a month. The department will recommend that, in this respect, the act be amended so as to make the pay the same as for other colored soldiers. They will be enrolled as *United States Volunteers*, and the officers be appointed and commissioned by the President." (Signed Edwin M. Stanton, Secretary of War.)

Gov. Seymour replies thus to the inquiry made through Mr. Rodgers:

STATE OF NEW-YORK, EXECUTIVE DEPARTMENT, ALBANY, Nov. 24, 1863.

SIR: In answer to your inquiries about the enlistment of blacks and the organization of regiments and companies, I have to say:

First—That, under the State laws, the bounty is paid to all, without distinction, who are mustered into the service of the United States, of whom credits are given to New-York, under the President's call for troops.

Second—As to new organizations, I have no power to authorize any, either for blacks or whites, which will be entitled to the benefit of the bounty given by the General Government. The object at Washington is to fill up the ranks of the regiments in the field. If any new organizations, for either white or black troops, are made, they *must be authorized by the War Department*, to entitle those who join them to the benefit of the money paid to volunteers.

Yours, &c., HORATIO SEYMOUR.

These answers are published for the information of the Association and all others interested, and the coöperation of all loyal citizens is earnestly invoked in furtherance of the objects above mentioned.

By order of the General Committee.

HENRY O'RIELLY, Secretary.

Rooms of the Association, No. 26 Pine-street, Nov. 25, 1863.

THE WAR IN SOUTH CAROLINA.

Dispatches via Richmond—Vigorous Shelling Continued.

FORTRESS MONROE, Wednesday, Nov. 25.

The Richmond *Dispatch*, of the 24th, contains the following from Charleston:

CHARLESTON, Monday, Nov. 23.

There was no shelling of the city last night, but a slow fire on Sumter.

The second dispatch says there has been a vigorous fire kept up between the enemy's batteries and ours all day. The enemy has not shelled the city to-day, but divided his attention between Sumter, Moultrie, Johnson and Simkins. They also threw a number of shells on James Island; 290 shots were thrown in Sumter last night.

The Northwestern Convention of War Democrats.

CHICAGO, Ill., Wednesday, Nov. 25.

The Northwestern Convention of War Democrats organized this morning.

The business was transacted with closed doors.

None but accredited delegates were admitted.

All the States named in the call were represented.

Gen. John A. McClernand was chosen President of the Convention.

A Committee of nine, of which Judge Loverin, of Indiana, was selected as the Chairman, has been appointed to frame a platform or a call.

The Draft in Baltimore—Three Newspaper Reporters Drawn.

BALTIMORE, Wednesday, Nov. 25.

The draft is progressing in a most orderly manner. Three newspaper reporters were so fortunate as to be drawn this morning—one from the *American*, one from the *Clipper* and one from the *Daily Gazette*.

Quota in New-Hampshire.

A dispatch from Concord states that New-Hampshire is rapidly filling up her full quota of men by volunteers.

Sailing of the Asia.

BOSTON, Mass., Wednesday, Nov. 25.

The steamer *Asia* sailed to-day at 10 o'clock, taking 37 passengers for Liverpool and 23 for Halifax; also, $55,042 in specie.

Sale of Five-Twenties.

PHILADELPHIA, Wednesday, Nov. 25.

The Subscription Agent reports the sale of five-twenties to-day at $911,800.

Items from Boston.

BOSTON, Wednesday, Nov. 25.

Commodore William S. Walker, U. S. N., died in this city yesterday at the advanced age of 70 years.

Five of Mosby's guerrillas that were lately captured in the vicinity of Washington have reached Fort Warren for safe keeping.

The steam frigate *Niagara* is shortly expected at Charlestown Navy-yard to have her armament changed. The 200-pound Parrotts on the spar deck are pronounced too heavy, and guns of less calibre will be substituted for them. The *Ticonderoga* is in the Dry Dock.

THREE DAYS LATER FROM EUROPE

ARRIVAL OF THE ARABIA AT HALIFAX.

Opposition to the Proposed Peace Congress.

The Matter Considered Impracticable.

AMERICAN TOPICS AGAIN DISCUSSED.

The French Government Unchanged Respecting Southern Recognition.

MISCELLANEOUS CONTINENTAL NEWS.

Serious Illness of the King of Denmark.

FINANCIAL AND COMMERCIAL INTELLIGENCE.

HALIFAX, Wednesday, Nov. 25.

The steamer *Arabia*, Capt. Cook, left Liverpool at 10:30 on the morning of the 14th inst., and Queenstown on the evening of the 15th, and arrived at this port on the 25th, at 7 P. M., *en route* for Boston. She had on board 16 Halifax and 32 Boston passengers. She brings three days later news.

The *Arabia* sailed for Boston at 2 o'clock A. M.

The steamer *Hammonia*, from New-York, arrived at Southampton on the 12th.

The steamship *Scotia*, from New-York, arrived at Liverpool on the 13th.

On the 14th she passed the ship *Far West*, bound in. Off Fastwell passed a Galway steamer, bound in; 10 A. M., latitude 48°, longitude 48°, *Adriatic*, bound east.

The steam frigate *Phantom*, on the North American station, has been ordered to Charleston.

The extraordinary treble murder in a London cab, and the subsequent suicide of the murderer resulted a verdict of *felo de se* on the body of the latter and he was burried at midnight without funeral rites.

The Official Board of trades enquiring into the accident to the steamer *Africa* resulted in the suspension of Capt. Stone's certificate for 6 months for neglecting either to slow his engines or use the lead. The examination of the *Africa* shows no material damage. It was merely confined to the dead wood forward.

The London *Times*, expatiating on the disaster to the *Anglia* at Galway, and the shortcomings of the Galway Line in general, says the affair is a dead failure, and the question cannot be evaded, and whether the experiment has not been tried long enough. A survey of the *Anglia* shows but little damage, but the vessel is so strained that she is ordered to Liverpool to be Dry-docked.

AMERICAN TOPICS.

ANOTHER REBEL WAR VESSEL.

THE GOVERNMENT LOOKING AFTER HER.

From the London News, Nov. 11.

The Glasgow Emancipation Society lately sent a memorial to Earl Russell, Secretary of State for Foreign Affairs, regarding an iron screw steamer at one time named the *Canton*, but now named the *Pampero*. The memorial stated that this vessel had lately been launched from the building-yard of Messrs. James & George Thomson here, and was being rapidly fitted out in Glasgow harbor: that she was currently, and the memorialists believed truly, reported to have been constructed for the Confederate Government; that she was of a similar construction to the *Alabama*, and, like her, intended to prey upon the merchant ships of the Northern States; that she was fitted up with gun-ports, ring-bolts for guns, &c., although the gun-ports had since been filled up and the fittings removed, and these things disguised as much as possible; and that the Society, therefore, requested his Lordship would cause a satisfactory investigation to be made into the character, ownership and destination of this vessel, with the view that, if found to be of the description and for the purpose they believed her to be, she might be prevented from leaving Britain. The following reply has been received from Earl Russell:

FOREIGN-OFFICE, Nov. 7, 1863.

GENTLEMEN: I am desired by Earl Russell to acknowledge the receipt of the memorial dated the 4th inst., and signed by you on behalf of the Glasgow Emancipation Society, requesting the interference of Her Majesty's Government to prevent the departure from that port of the steam-vessel *Canton* until an investigation has taken place as to her character, ownership and destination, and I am to acquaint you in reply that the attention of Her Majesty's Government has already been directed to this matter.

I am, gentlemen, your most obedient humble servant, E. HAMMOND.

W. Smeal, Esq., and And. Paton, Esq., Secretaries Glasgow Emancipation Society.

PROJECT FOR PEACE.

The London *Times* publishes a project for peace in America, by a Northern gentleman writer. He says if the war is to go on for a time, from mere momentum, perhaps, it must be let alone; but it should be turned as soon as possible from a war of attempted conquest to a war for limits and terms of settlement. He suggests that negotiations be opened at once with the Richmond Government for such settlements, and for making a more formal recognition. One of the matters for discussion—the Confederates of course to be recognized *de jure*—must be the navigation of the Ohio and Mississippi; and in the event of Maryland joining the South, the Susquehannah and Chesapeake are to be free, with a common tariff for the two Confederacies.

THE PROPOSED PEACE CONGRESS.

It is rumored that Drouyn de Lhuys is drawing up an explanatory document, comprising the different questions which the Emperor intends to submit to Congress; in the meantime the English journals appear to be generally taking a view adverse to Congress. The *Globe*, Ministerial, opposes it. The *Daily News* and *Morning Herald* also oppose it, and agree that if it is held unfavorable results will ensue. The *Times* inquires what England will have to do in the Congress, should it ever prove more than an ideal conception, and points out that there is no place for England in it, all the honors being monopolized by France. The English Cabinet held meetings to consider upon the subject. The result has not transpired and other meetings is fixed for the 16th.

The Madrid *Correspondencia* says the Spanish Government has resolved to send representatives to the Congress, but some Spanish journals look cooly on it.

It is asserted that Austria will give no answer till the resolution of England is known.

FRANCE.

The Bank of France, on the 12th, raised the rate of discount to 7 per cent. The monthly returns of that institution show a decrease of cash in hand of 67 millions of francs. Bourse pretty steady; Rentes 67c.@35c.

POLAND.

Affairs remain unchanged in Poland. The withdrawal of the Grand Duke Constantine from the Governorship is confirmed. An additional taxation is imposed on Poland by the Russian Government, and a forced loan by the National Government of Prussia.

PRUSSIA.

The Chamber of Deputies elected Herr Von Grabow President. In his speech he pointed out that the King's desire for a solution of pending differences would be fulfilled if the Constitution were interpreted and stated in its obvious spirit.

DENMARK.

The King is ill with erysipelas and a slight fever. The Danish Regsraad adopted the Government project for a Constitution for Denmark and Schleswig.

Commercial Intelligence per Arabia.

LIVERPOOL PROVISION MARKET.

The Provision market is quiet and steady. Bigland, Athya & Co., and Gordon, Bruce & Co. report Beef inactive, Pork quiet and steady, Bacon still declining.

LIVERPOOL PRODUCE MARKET.

The Produce market is quiet and steady. Butter firm. Lard quiet, at 39s.@40s. Tallow easier, at 42s.@43s. 6d. Sugar was buoyant at the opening, but closed quiet. Coffee very dull. Rice firm. Ashes steady. Linseed Oil dull. Cod Oil steady, at 51s. Resin inactive, at 30s. Spirits Turpentine quiet and steady. Petroleum flat and irregular; refined, 1s. 9d.@1s. 10d.; £15 9s. for Crude ℔ ton.

LONDON MARKETS.

LONDON, Saturday, Nov. 14.

Breadstuffs firm. Iron steady. Sugar firm, and advanced 6d.@1s. Coffee easier and irregular. Tea steady. Rice quiet. Linseed Cakes dull. Linseed Oil still declining. Spirits Turpentine steady, at 85s. Petroleum dull. Sperm Oil quiet. Tallow dull, at 43s. Provisions inactive. Butter still advancing. Spirits Turpentine firmer. Resin steady. American Securities steady; sales small. Consols for money 92¾@92⅞.

LIVERPOOL, Saturday, Nov. 14.

COTTON—Sales of the week, 33,000 bales. The market opened to-day at an advance of ¼d.@½d., but subsequently lost, closing irregular. The sales to speculators reached 8,000 bales, and exporters 6,000 bales. The sales to-day foot up 5,000 bales, the market closing quiet. Of the above, speculators and exporters took 2,000 bales. The following are the authorized quotations: Orleans Middling, 38½d.; Mobile, 38¼d.; Uplands, 38d.

The stock of Cotton in port is stated at 182,000 bales, of which 38,000 are American.

TRADE REPORT.

The advices from Manchester are unfavorable. Market flat and still declining.

The Breadstuffs market is steady.

Richardson, Spence & Co. Wakefield, Nash & Co., and others report: Flour steady at 19s.@23s. Wheat firm; Red Western, 7s.@8s. 5d; Red Southern, 8s. 6d.@8s. 9d. Corn steady at 28s. 3d.@28s. 6d.

The Bullion in the Bank of England has decreased £338,000.

LATEST VIA LIVERPOOL.

LIVERPOOL, Saturday, Nov. 14—Evening.

Cotton flat; sales 2,000 bales, of which speculators and exporters took 1,000.

Breadstuffs quiet and steady. Sugar buoyant.

Consols for Money 92⅜@92⅞.

Illinois Central Shares 19¼@18½ discount, Erie 65@67.

Latest by Telegraph to Queenstown.

The Bank discount is unchanged.

The English journals generally oppose Napoleon's Congress.

The Paris Bourse was flat. Rentes closed at 67f. 25c.

The French Government had informed Mr. Dayton that their views on the American question were unchanged. They had not recognized the South, and consequently had not signed the treaty for the acquisition of Texas and Louisiana as reported.

BERNE, Sunday, Nov. 15.

The Juarez Government had addressed a note to the Federal Council, protesting against the modification of the Republican Constitution by French invasion, hoping for the sympathy of Switzerland.

COPENHAGEN, Sunday, Nov. 15.

The King of Denmark is seriously ill, at Flucksburgh, with tupplas, attended by fever, delirium and want of sleep.

MADRID, Sunday, Nov. 15.

A marriage is spoken of between the Infanta Isabella and the Count of Paris.

The steamship *America*, which sailed from Londonderry on Friday last, put back to Moville this morning, disabled.

LIVERPOOL, Saturday, Nov. 14—Evening.

The leading journals to-day continue their arguments against the proposed Congress. The *Times* treats the subject as a very unreal proposition, and says it may possibly turn out that the proposal was something in the nature of a fire-escape—the expedient of a man determined to come down some door from an untenable position. The Emperor may have made the proposition without desiring the Congress itself, and England, by declining to join it, may be doing the Emperor the greatest possible service.

A Paris letter says a cold shoulder is all that is to be seen with regard to the Congress, and the matter is drifting into an abyss of impracticability.

Wm. Cornell Jewett publishes a long pamphlet in advocacy of mediation in America, in which he maintains that the American question is designed to come before the proposed Congress as the most important matter affecting the peace and prosperity of Europe, and urgently appeals to England to support Napoleon.

A movement has been inaugurated among the shipping men of Liverpool to appeal against the sentence of Capt. Stone, of the *Africa*. A meeting will be held to-day on the subject.

Money is rather easier.

PERNAMBUCO, Sunday, Nov. 1.

Exchange, 28. Sugar—Whites, 3‖000. Cotton, 18‖000@20‖000.

RIO JANEIRO, Saturday, Oct. 24.

Exchange on London 27⅞@37⅛. Coffee—Good firsts 6‖900@7‖100. Shipments—73,900 bags; stock, 13,000. Freights 35s. 6d.@40s.

BAHIA, Thursday, Oct. 29.

Exchange 27⅞@27⅞. Sugar—Whites, 2‖200@2‖560; Browns, 1‖600@1‖800. Cottons, 24‖000@26‖000.

Union Officers Imprisoned in the South.

To the Editor of the New-York Times:

Having many letters of inquiry as to officers confined with me in the jail at Columbia, S. C., I inclose for publication in your columns the names of all who were there on the 6th inst., when I left for Richmond and City Point.

Respectfully, yours,

H. CLAY TRUMBULL,

Chaplain Tenth Connecticut Volunteers.

HARTFORD, Conn., Nov. 24, 1863.

ARMY OFFICERS.

Lt.-Col. John Bedel, 3d N. H. V., captured July 18.
Maj. John H. Filler, 55th Penn. V., July 18.
Capt. D. B. Hogeland, 76th Penn. V., July 11.
Capt. V. B. Chamberlain, 7th Conn. V., July 11.
Capt. Jerome Tourtellotte, 7th Conn. V., July 11.
Capt. Louis S. Payne, 100th N. Y. V., Aug. 3.
1st Lieut. and Adjt. H. W. Camp, 10th Conn. V., July 19.
1st Lieut. W. E. Phillips, 7th Conn. V., July 11.
1st Lieut. D. J. West, 6th Conn. V., July 18.
1st Lieut. C. L. Bittinger, 76th Penn. V., July 11.
2d Lieut. E. C. Jordan, 7th Conn. V., July 11.
2d Lieut. Rudolph Kost, 6th Conn. V., July 18.
2d Lieut. John King, 6th Conn. V., July 18.
2d Lieut. Elton W. Ware, 9th Maine V., July 11.
2d Lieut. F. J. O'Sullivan, 67th Ohio V., July 18.
Chaplain J. H. Fowler, 1st S. C. V., (col'd,) Sept. 13.

NAVAL OFFICERS.

Lieut.-Com. E. P. Williams, *Wissahickon*, captured Sept. 9.
Flag-Lieut. S. W. Preston, *Wabash*, Sept. 9.
Lieut. E. T. Brower, *Housatonic*, Sept. 9.
Lieut. G. C. Remey, *Canandaigua*, Sept. 9.
Ensign B. H. Porter, *New Ironsides*, Sept. 9.
Acting Ensign E. G. Dayton, *Wissahickon*, Sept. 9.
Acting Ensign M. W. Tillson, *Thos. A. Ward*, Oct. 20.
Acting Master's Mate C. P. Hovey, *Powhatan*, Sept. 9.
Acting Master's Mate C. S. McCarty, *Canandaigua*, Sept. 9.
Third Asst. Engineer J. H. Harmany, *Housatonic*, Sept. 9.
1st Lieut. R. L. Meade, (U. S. Marines,) Sept. 9.

Assistant-Surgeon John T. Luck, of the *Ottawa*, taken July 19, and Acting Master E. L. Haines, of the *Powhatan*, taken Aug. 4, confined for a time at Columbia, were removed to the Libby Prison, Richmond. All the above-named officers were in good health at latest dates.

Distressing Accident in the North River—Seven Russian Sailors Drowned.

Last evening soon after 8 o'clock, a boat containing twelve men from one of the Russian war vessels in the harbor, was run down by the ferry-boat *Jersey City*, of the Cortlandt-street line, while she was nearing the slip. All the sailors were thrown into the water and seven of them are believed to have been drowned. The other five were rescued by the crew of the ferry-boat.

Richmond Dispatch.
The DISPATCH is published daily, (Sundays excepted.) Price for mailing $20 per year; or $10 for six months; three months $6; one month $2—in advance.
The SEMI-WEEKLY DISPATCH is issued every TUESDAY and FRIDAY, at $10—in advance.
The WEEKLY DISPATCH is issued every FRIDAY, and mailed to subscribers at $6 per annum.

DAILY DISPATCH.

VOL. XXV. . RICHMOND, VA., FRIDAY MORNING, NOVEMBER 27, 1863. NO. 124

FRIDAY MORNING......... NOVEMBER 27, 1863.

REPORTED FIGHTING ON THE RAPIDAN—THE ENEMY SAID TO BE CROSSING.

By passengers who came down on the Fredericksburg train yesterday afternoon we learn that heavy firing was heard at Hamilton's Crossing, in the direction of the upper fords of the Rappahannock.

Passengers by the Central train, which arrived at a late hour, state that a report reached Orange C. H. yesterday morning that the enemy had crossed the Rapidan at one or two fords during the night before, and that heavy skirmishing was going on all the morning. Whether the enemy had crossed in force, or whether they consisted of infantry or cavalry, or both, we could not learn.

From movements of our own troops, we think it more than likely that a general advance of the enemy is contemplated. It will be seen that the correspondent of the *Dispatch*, writing from the army, announces an advance of Meade's pickets.

THE REPORTED SURRENDER OF BURNSIDE.

The reports from East Tennessee are very cheering, "if true." They state that Gen. Longstreet attacked Burnside in his outer line of defences at Knoxville, on Sunday, and drove him to his inner works at the point of the bayonet, killing and wounding large numbers of his men, and on Monday morning the attack was about to be renewed, when Burnside, finding himself surrounded on all sides, proposed negotiations for a surrender; that the former were finally agreed upon, and the "hero of Fredericksburg," and five thousand of his men, laid down their arms. As nothing of this kind has reached the War Department, we are compelled to put little faith in the pretty picture that is drawn by reliable gentlemen.

The Lynchburg *Republican*, of yesterday, publishes a letter from a soldier in Longstreet's corps, written on Thursday last, giving a short account of the fight at Campbell's Station on the previous day. The enemy, he states, were badly beaten, losing largely in killed and wounded, besides 700 prisoners, 900 horses, 110 wagons, four pieces of artillery, 3,700 blankets, and considerable amounts of commissary and quartermaster's stores, small arms, and ammunition. They fell back towards Knoxville, hotly pursued by our troops, and it was in the retreat that they lost the prisoners and property enumerated above. Our own loss the writer estimates at 150 killed and wounded.

DEATHS AT JOHNSON'S ISLAND.

One of the returned Confederate surgeons has courteously handed us the following list of deaths of Confederate officers who have died in the Federal prison at Johnson's Island since July 20th:

Lt Col A P Hamilton, 1st Miss; Capts G W Fuller, (commander of gunboat,) S C; D C Webb, 1st Ala cavalry; J W Mullins, 1st Miss batt; C Gillespie, 65th N C; C M Tugle, 33d Ga; J M D King, 9th Ga; F M Ezell, 13th Tenn; A E Upchurch, 55th N C; J D Hardy, 18th Arkansas; S W Henry, 9th Tennessee cavalry; J C Peden, regiment unknown.—Lieutenants W J Hudson, 2d N C batt'n; W A Harvin, 51st Ga; Jno Hufsetter, 1st Ark batt'n; J M Musselman, 14th La; M Lyon, 46th N C; J M D Stevenson, 15th Ark; S R Graham, 3d Texas cav; W P Harden, 5th N C; L B Williams, 63d N C; J M Dodson, 10th Tenn; E A M Orr, 62d N C; J B Gash, do; J Barnett, 9th La; J Smith Ray, 38th N C.—Privates Andrew Worthington, of Marshall, Ky; G M Cummings, Va; R D Copass, 60th Tenn; D C Jackson, 12th Va; H D Talbert, Marshall, Ky; D D Kelley, 2d Tenn cav; Daniel Rockerham, 5th Ky; S H Everman, 7th Ky; Robert Holt, 10th Tenn; Hugh Goble, 5th Ky; A P Allen, 2d Ky; Jno Kenny, Va.

Captain King and Lieutenant Graham died of wounds, the others of disease. Lieut. Ray died of smallpox, which disease had broken out on the island.

J. Emmett Scruggs, of Warrenton, Va., and formerly editor of the Warrenton *Whig*, who was a citizen prisoner on the island, died on the 9th inst. of dysentery. He will be recollected as a prominent speaker on the Whig side in several of the Presidential campaigns of other days.

Financial and Commercial.

There seems to be a steady advance in specie, and as the article becomes scarce the higher the figure to which it reaches in the market. $16 is now given as the buying, and $17 as the selling price for gold. The brokers are buying silver at $12, and selling it at $13.

BANK NOTES.—Southern bank notes are bought by the brokers at $2.75 to 3, and sold for $3.25.

BONDS AND STOCKS.—At the sale of bonds and stocks by Messrs. Lancaster & Co., on Wednesday, the following figures were realized: Confederate 8 per cent coupon bonds, 1864 '68, 101 to 101½; 8 per cent registered bonds, 1864 '79, 100¾ to 113; convertibles, 112½; 15 m loan, 186, for small bonds; large bonds of the same issue are worth from 198 to 200; Virginia registered bonds from 250 to 257; Virginia coupons, 446 to 448; North Carolina new 6's, 9½; North Carolina new 8's, 261; Richmond city bonds, 1887, 271; Bedford county bonds, 1866, 157; R. & Y. R. R. bonds, 1st mortgage, 174; Manassas Gap R. R. bonds, 1st mortgage, 142; Orange and Alexandria R. R., 2d mortgage, 235; Bank of Commonwealth stock, 166; Traders' Bank, 176 to 180; Bank of Virginia, 122 to 123; Virginia Central R. R. stock, 156; Richmond Importing and Exporting Company, 925; Richmond and Petersburg Importing and Export ing Company, 625; Old Dominion Trading Co, 525; James River Packet Co, 121.

GRAIN.—There is little if any improvement in the supply of Wheat, not enough being in market to establish a price. Good Wheat would readily bring $15 per bushel. Corn is worth from $16 to $15 per bushel, and very scarce.

COUNTRY PRODUCE AND VEGETABLES.—Bacon, hog round, $2.60 to $2.75, and very scarce; Lard $2.55; Butter $3.75 to $4; Eggs $3 to $3.25; Irish Potatoes $10 to $12; Sweet do. $12 to $14; Tallow Candles $4; Salt 40 to 45c.

The supply of Beef for the past week has been much more abundant than for some time. At the commission houses we have heard of sales at 65 to [illegible] cents by the quarter.

In the city markets fresh meats are worth $1.25 to $1.50 for Beef and Mutton, and $2 for Pork; Chickens, $6 to $8 per pair; Ducks, $7 to $8 per pair; Butter, $4.50 to $5 per lb.; Sweet Potatoes, $[illegible] per half peck; Irish Potatoes, $3 per half peck.

GROCERIES.—Coffee, wholesale, $9 per lb.; retail, $10; Sugar, $3 to $3.25; Sorghum Molasses, $12 per gallon, and $14 to $15 at retail.

LIQUORS.—Whiskey, $55 to $65 per gallon; Apple Brandy, $45 to $50; high proof Rum, $50; French Brandy, $80 to $100.

LEATHER.—The supply of Leather in the market is somewhat improved. We quote Sole Leather at $6 to $7.50 per lb.; Upper do., $7.50 to $8; Harness do., $5.50 to $6; Hides are quoted at $2.50 to $2.75 for dry, and $1.50 for salted green; Tanners' Oil, $4 to $5 per gallon.

TOBACCO.—The demand for the different brands of Tobacco is improved, and prices tending upwards.

THEATRICAL SUIT.—A verdict of $4,[illegible] has been rendered in the New York Supreme Court against the executors of the Burton estate for a breach of contract on the part of the deceased manager with the Escott opera troupe.

Virginia Annual (M. E.) Conference.

[REPORTED FOR THE RICHMOND DISPATCH.]

THURSDAY, Nov. 26th, 1863.

Conference was called to order at 9 o'clock.—Bishop Pierce in the Chair.

Revs. J. E. Edwards, Dr. Lee, P. Whitehead, and J. D. Coulling, were elected the Finance Committee of the Book and Tract Society.

Rev. W. W. Bennett submitted the report of the Soldiers' Tract Association, which was adopted.—Revs. Dr. Doggett, Dr. Lee, M. Read, J. E. Edwards, and H. B. Cowles, expressed high gratification at the report, which exceeded their highest expectations.

Wm. Willis, Jr., and Rob't J. Christian, were elected to fill lay vacancies in the Publishing Committee of the Richmond *Christian Advocate*.

The Committee of Twelve, to whom was referred the record of the trial of Rev. P. W. Archer on a charge affecting his moral and ministerial character, (had during the month of October, 1863,) with instructions "to report at the earliest day whether there is any necessity for a further judicial investigation," beg leave to report that, after a full and patient investigation, the committee are unanimously of the opinion that the charge is not sustained by the evidence, and recommend that no further action should be had in the case of Rev. P. W. Archer. [Signed by all of the committee.]

The report was unanimously agreed to by the Conference, and his character passed.

The Committee on Memoirs reported through Dr. Doggett on the death of Rev. D. W. Christian, who died in Petersburg in February, 1863, in the 68th year of his age.

Dr. Smith, from the committee to whom was referred the memorial from the [illegible] Church, submitted a report, recommending no further action at present, owing to the peculiar state of the country, except a further interchange of fraternal feelings and messengers; and, on motion, Revs. J. A. Duncan and Dr. Rosser were appointed fraternal messengers to the next session of the Conference of the M. P. Church.

The report of the Treasurer of the Conference was read, and funds distributed to the widows and orphans of deceased preachers and to necessitous preachers.

Dr. J. R. Finley, from the Committee on Sunday Schools, submitted a report, which was adopted.

On motion of Rev. James A. Duncan, it was

Resolved, That the Conference cordially approve of the publication of the *Children's Guide*, by Rev. J. W. Burke, at Macon, Ga., and recommend it to the patronage of our people as an excellent Sunday-School paper.

The Committee on Education submitted a report embodying the following resolution, which was adopted:

Resolved, That the Board of Visitors of Randolph Macon College be requested to take into consideration the subject of the removal of that institution to some more accessible point.

Dr. Smith's position excluded any remarks that he might have desired to make.

Dr. Doggett gave reasons why this should be done. That, although hallowed associations cluster around Randolph Macon College, still its being so inaccessible was the great cause of its want of success in the past, and therefore it should be removed to a more convenient point.

Lynchburg was brought before the Conference as a suitable place for the College. Danville was also spoken of.

Rev. Dr. Lee, J. E. Edwards, and others, urged its removal for some very important reasons.

The Conference then adjourned.

FROM GENERAL LEE'S ARMY.

[FROM OUR OWN CORRESPONDENT.]

ARMY NORTHERN VIRGINIA,
Near Orange C. H., Va., Nov. 26.

Advices from the front represent that Meade is advancing his picket lines on our front to within sight of the Rapidan river, and also that he is moving a force on our left flank, in the direction of Madison C. H. It is now affirmed, the railroad and the bridge being completed, that the bulk of the Yankee army is being transferred from Fauquier to Culpeper, preparatory, perhaps, to the forward move which the New York *World* tells us that Meade has been ordered by Lincoln to make contrary to his own judgment.

His Excellency President Davis and staff returned to Richmond via the Tuesday morning Central train, after spending two whole days and parts of two other days with Gen. Lee. During his stay nearly all of the principal officers of the army called upon "Uncle Jeff," and "Marse Robert," to pay their respects. The President and Gen. Lee rode to Clark Mountain on Monday, and had an excellent view of the situation and of the Yankees that were visible. But for the inclement weather the President would have reviewed the whole army. On his return to Richmond the President was accompanied as far as Gordonsville by Major Gen'l J. E. B. Stuart.

On Monday night the band of the 11th Mississippi regiment (Joe Davis's brigade) serenaded the President at Gen. Lee's headquarters. The band was accompanied by a large collection of soldiers. In reply to this compliment the President briefly addressed those present, thanking them for their patience under trial, their heroism and patriotism, and expressing the hope of soon seeing them at their respective homes under more favorable auspices.

The country will hear with deep regret that Lieutenant-General Ewell, who, as I mentioned in my last, is on a visit to Charlottesville, will probably be disabled from service during the coming winter by reason of an ulcer on his amputated limb. In his absence his duties devolve upon Major-General Jubal A. Early. In the event of his permanent retirement the country will lose one of its bravest, purest, and ablest Generals—a man whose deeds will illustrate the brightest pages of his country's history. The loss of such men as Jackson and Ewell is indeed great. But let us fear not; for the God of these heroes will raise up others to take their places if our faith is only equal to our trials.

Everything hereabouts indicates that we are permanent—at least for a while. The depot buildings have been considerably enlarged, the post office has been extended, and a new office has been erected for the passport clerks, and everything gives evidence of a disposition to have comfortable quarters during the winter. The men, too, are busy constructing their little huts for protection against the bad weather. This may, or may not, mean going into winter quarters; for it is always customary to fix up in this way whenever the army calls a halt at this season.

The death of the lamented Gen. Posey, of which your readers have already been apprised, makes vacant the command of his brigade, and speculation is rife as to his successor. Among the names prominent in connection with it are Lieut.-Col. Harris, of the 12th Miss.; Col. Baker, of the 16th; Col. Jayne, of the 48th; Col. Harris, of the 19th, and Col. Taylor, of the 12th.

Any number of court-martials are now in session all over the army dispensing justice. Every corps has one of these courts, and in many cases there are courts for the divisions and brigades.

Mosby, the gallant guerilla, has again been in rear of the enemy's lines. On Saturday last he came up with some three or four wagons, and captured them, together with their valuable contents, twenty mules, and ten prisoners, near Bealeton, in Fauquier county.

Yesterday was a bright and clear day, and to-day is of like character, and the roads are fast drying. Last night we had the heaviest frost of the season. If the enemy mean to fight, now is their time. There has been considerable activity in the Yankee camp for the last forty-eight hours; but what it means cannot yet be told. X.

A WORTHY PROVOST.—S. H. De Vaughan, formerly Provost Marshal of Lynchburg, who ran off to the Yankees, is leading prayer meetings in Alexandria. The Lynchburg *Republican* says:

We have before us now a letter from Alexandria, dated the 2d inst., in which this intelligence is confirmed, with the additional information that this consummate scoundrel visited a Sabbath School in Alexandria and prayed, and after his prayer, in a public statement, declared that it "was the first time he had been allowed to pray since he left the city to cast his fortunes with the Southern Confederacy." What think the members of his congregation in this city of this unblushing liar? and what will every honest man think when we tell him that De Vaughan was one of the loudest prayers at the revival of his church here! The laborer is worthy of his hire; so also is the liar, and this worthy subject of Lincoln has been rewarded for his treason, we are told, with a place in the Alexandria Post-Office.

IMPRESSMENTS IN ALABAMA.—A bill has been introduced in the Alabama Legislature making it a felony for any person to falsely represent himself to be either a State or Confederate agent for the purpose of impressing property. The bill proposes as a punishment a fine of five hundred dollars and imprisonment in the penitentiary for not less than five nor more than ten years.

WHEAT BREAD.—The *Southern Cultivator* has an excellent article on wheat bread, showing that so far as health is concerned, unbolted wheat flour is far better than the flour in common use. This is also the testimony of all intelligent physicians.—And in addition to this, there is a saving of about 25 per cent. in the quantity, which in these times of scarcity and high prices is an item worth caring for.

The tutor of the new King of Greece is Professor Kepper, late of Franklin College, Pa. He has spent fifteen years of his life in the United States.

The Position of Affairs Before the Battle of Lookout Mountain.

Anything from Gen. Bragg's army is interesting just now. The army correspondent of the Charleston *Courier* gives a view of the position of affairs before the battle of Lookout Mountain which will enlighten our readers relative to the situation as it then stood. The writer is combatting the "despondent views" which looked upon the loss of Lookout Valley as a disaster:

Firstly. Lookout Valley has never been occupied by a larger force of our troops than one small brigade—that of General Law—the object of which was simply to picket the Tennessee, watch the movements of the enemy, and cover the retreat of our sharpshooters and skirmishers (whenever attacked) engaged in harassing the wagon trains running to and from Chattanooga in the rear.

Secondly. We could not extend our lines beyond Lookout Mountain to the left, because of the disintegration of our forces which would be necessarily involved in such a movement, and the consequent weakening of our lines elsewhere. The difficulty of transporting troops or supplies across the mountain, within point blank range of the guns of Moccasin Battery, was in itself a bar to the permanent occupation of the Valley. From this cause alone it was found almost impossible to furnish regular rations to even the single brigade of General Law, every pound having to be carried at night, in panniers, on the backs of mules.

Thirdly. The advance of the Federals from Bridgeport was known to General Bragg from the start, and progress was reported from hour to hour as the troops marched up the valley. (This fact I learn from one of the signal officers.) Consequently there was no surprise and no lack of time for adequate preparation to give them battle. Both Generals Bragg and Longstreet were on the summit of Lookout Mountain, observing the movements of the enemy above and below—the six thousand at Brown's Ferry, who had already crossed the Tennessee from Chattanooga, and the eleven thousand more, who had simultaneously started, and were advancing from the opposite direction. The object of the Federals was penetrated at once; and if these officers, fully possessed of all information bearing on the present and future, with plans of operation elsewhere already matured in their minds, adjudged it prudent to allow the enemy to pass unmolested, it was a concession with which no one here or elsewhere, who desires to maintain public confidence, and unite and inspire the popular heart, ought to find fault.

Fourthly. Had an attack been made on the columns of the enemy while in motion up the valley, beyond doubt it would have precipitated a general battle. Reinforcements would have poured out of Chattanooga across Brown's Ferry three times more expeditiously than we could have thrown troops across Lookout Mountain, (through a demoralizing fire,) and sweeping down on our rear, or even encountering our front in the valley, would have rendered the result of an engagement, to say the least, doubtful. Granting success, however, what would have been accomplished? The defeat of two corps of the enemy—the retention of a valley whose occupation would have weakened our line and been of no permanent or practical benefit—the loss of five or eight thousand men without commensurate advantages, at a time when every strong right arm was indispensable to the service, and the grand issue involved in the investment of Chattanooga would not have been directly effected in the slightest degree. It is true that without the valley the Federals would have been compelled to rely for the rations on wagon transportation over mountain roads, and that eventually they may have been forced to retire to some point near their base of supplies; but this, if not a problematical, is a negative result. If the Federals had determined to hold Chattanooga, they would have done so in spite of mountain roads and a blockaded railway to Bridgeport. We have not, therefore, been "outgeneralled by the enemy," and their movement was not "masterly in conception and fruitless in execution." It was by a simple concession on our part that they were allowed to pursue their purpose—reopen communication with Bridgeport and establish themselves for the winter; and future developments will prove the correctness of the judgment by which that concession was made.

It is an error, too, to suppose that the mere possession of Chattanooga is the stake for which this army is contending, and the fact that the Federals may remain undisturbed there during the winter adds and subtracts nothing from our prospects of success. In truth, there are many officers who believe that we are better off where we are, with a railroad at our back, than if we were forty miles on the other side of the Tennessee river and dependent for supplies on the rugged roads and faulty wagons, which would be our bane during the winter.

Finally. We have not "lost the advantages of our position." Lookout Mountain is still in our possession, and, to all intents and purposes, the lines of the army have not been changed. With this great and almost impassable wall on our left, effectually barring the advance of the enemy from that direction, and Missionary Ridge, with its steep sides, on our front, no General can ask a more desirable place of defence than that which is now held by this army.

If the enemy have succeeded in provisioning themselves for the winter, it is only what they would have done, under any other circumstances, somewhere else—perhaps not so favorably to us—and this fact will, in no wise, interfere with the general battle which is eventually to decide the strength of the two armies, and, probably, the issue of the war. It is a question of fighting, and not of eating, with which we have to contend, and a winter's idleness in one place or another has little to do with the solution of the problem while the two armies confront each other intact.

A correspondent of the Atlanta *Confederacy*, writing on the 20th, says:

I notice in the few papers that now and then reach this elevated region that some despondency is felt by those at a distance concerning the situation of the campaign which extends itself along this great river. Will you believe me sincere when I say that I never felt more hopeful? I believe we shall winter around Nashville. If Gen. Longstreet gobbles Burnside, as I think he will, Grant must retreat from Chattanooga. And as sure as we get him moved we will keep him moving. The prospect is very cheerful. A large army, an animated spirit, a programme well arranged, nothing but extraordinary bad luck will foil our plans. It is true that we need Forrest. It is true that we shall miss Polk. It is true that Gen. Lee would inspire a deeper confidence. But it is equally true that things are not so bad as they seem, and that General Hardee's presence, his energy, his great talent for discipline, and his fine mind, have corrected a multitude of errors.

The Yankees down in Chattanooga are a sorry looking set of fellows, certain. They burrow away in the ground and are as muddy as minks. The pickets are now on mighty friendly terms. They converse freely, joke each other, and sometimes treat. You can ride from one end of our line of sharpshooters to the other without receiving a shot. Papers are not permitted to be exchanged. Flags of truce ply daily. By these, letters are frequently sent, and sometimes travel is also permitted. Mrs. Gen. Helm passed through the other day.

A letter to the Atlanta *Register*, dated Missionary Ridge, Nov. 15, says:

The signal corps, under the supervision of Captain G. C. Bain, has proven itself to be a valuable organization. Lookout Mountain converses with Missionary Ridge with expedition. Messages are borne on the air for five and six miles with a celerity barely to be believed. The signal flag transmits messages and orders throughout the whole army. Some of the corps having been consolidated, and all placed under the command of the untiring and indefatigable Bain, its efficiency and discipline will be more perfect, and its services far more useful. The signal corps always on the *qui vive*, their flag reports every movement of the enemy by day, while their lurid torch is ever watchful by night.

The roads are in a fine condition, and the weather beautiful.

The army is losing no time in preparing shelters, every description of a hut imaginable is built, and chimneys in all shapes that will vie with any.

THE "MARINE BRIGADE" ON THE MISSISSIPPI.—The St. Louis *Bulletin* gives some account of the operations of a Yankee "Mississippi Marine brigade," under Col. Currie. It had managed to capture three Confederate mails destined for the Trans-Mississippi Department. One of them was from Richmond, (says that paper) "contained very important documents and letters. One of these is a letter from Jeff. Davis, in reply to certain parties asking his opinion as to the propriety and expediency of empowering bands to destroy steamboats. He replies that he sees no objection to the plan, and construes the act of the rebel Congress to empower the formation of bands for the purpose. There were other documents of equal interest." Col. Currie has also captured in all some $1,350,000 in Confederate money, and fifty prisoners during the past month. One of the latter was a man going from Macon, Ga., to Camden, Ark., with a machine for spinning cotton, which he said would have been worth a million dollars to him if he had only got it through.

MATTERS IN NASHVILLE.—The Nashville papers of the 7th announce the sale of fifty bales of cotton at 60 to 63 cents per pound. The *Press* says that, owing to an increased demand and but little offering for sale, the quotations for Tennessee money have materially advanced in the last few days. Especially has this been the case with the notes of the State Bank. Brokers are paying, freely, sixty cents for the State Bank, and sixty-eight, and, in some instances, seventy cents for the notes the of Union and Planters' Banks.—In the penitentiary at Nashville 139 political prisoners are confined. On the 7th thirty-four were arrested and fifteen discharged. Twenty deserters were arrested, one hundred and eighty-eight prisoners sent North, and eighty-five now remain on hand. The *Press* also says that Captain Wm. Strong was badly wounded on the John A. Fisher, on her last trip, by a party of guerillas firing into his boat.

RACING.—At the Petersburg races, Wednesday, the match race was for $5,000, two mile heats, between W. R. Johnson's Oakland and D. McDaniel's bay colt, by Revenue. Oakland won the first heat, and was distanced in the third. Time 4:0[illegible], 4:0[illegible], 4:05. The winning horse was christened "Gen. Pickett."

GOVERNOR VANCE'S MESSAGE.—The North Carolina Legislature assembled at Raleigh, N. C., on Tuesday last. We make some extracts from Governor Vance's message:

The very important subject of feeding the poor, whose supporters and protectors are in the army, again demands our attention. The results of the past year's operations are most encouraging, and should serve to give our people confidence in the resources of their State. Great anxiety was felt last fall, as you know, on the subject of food, and fears were entertained that suffering, if not actual starvation, would be witnessed in many quarters. Under the authority conferred upon me by your body I purchased and stored away about 50,000 bushels of corn, 250,000 pounds of bacon, a quantity of rice, &c., which I expected would go but little way in supplying the general wants. When the season closed and the new crop came in, however, to my surprise and gratification, I found that Major Hogg, Commissary of Subsistence, had only issued to the County Commissioners about one-third of the bacon; less than one-half of the corn, and but very little of the rice. He reports still on hand some 70,000 lbs. of bacon, having fed a number of negroes engaged on the public works and sold to the army 100,000 lbs., with 20,000 bushels of corn. I have reason to believe that from various causes the crops this year have not been as abundant as usual, and that the public will be called on to do more than last season. But still I see no cause for alarm, and my last year's experience has encouraged me to believe that all can be fed from our own resources by proper prudence and economy. I respectfully recommend a liberal appropriation among the several counties, according to population, for this purpose—at least double that of last year—and that I be allowed to buy and store away corn, flour, and bacon, as heretofore. * * *

Reports are submitted herewith of the operations of the Ordnance, Subsistence, and Quartermaster Departments, which I trust you will find satisfactory. The experiment of running the blockade and importing army supplies from abroad has proven a complete success. You will see from the report that large quantities of clothing, leather and shoes, lubricating oils, factory findings, sheet iron and tin, arms and ammunition, medicines, dye stuffs, blankets, cotton bagging and rope, spirits, coffee, &c., have been safely brought in, besides considerable freight for the Confederacy. Two thousand and ten bales of cotton have been sent to Liverpool, the proceeds of which are deposited to the credit of the State, less the amount of expenses of the vessel. With what we have imported, and the purchases in our home markets, I think I can safely say that the North Carolina troops will be comfortably clothed to January, 1865—should God in his providence so long see fit to afflict us with a continuance of the war—except as to shoes and blankets. Neither the Ordnance nor Quartermaster's Departments placed too much reliance on foreign importation, but every effort has been made to stimulate home production.—Both the quality and quantity of arms and munitions manufactured have been improved in the past twelve months. * * *

We know at last precisely what we would get by submission, and therein has our enemy done us good service—abolition of slavery, confiscation of property, and territorial vassalage! These are the terms to win us back. Now, when our brothers bleed and mothers and little ones cry for bread, we can point them back to the brick kilns of Egypt—thanks to Mr. Seward—plainly in view, and show them the beautiful clusters of Eschol which grow in the land of independence, whither we go to possess them. And we can remind them too, how the pillar of fire and the cloud, the vouchsafed guidon of Jehovah, went ever before the hungering multitude, leading away, with apparent cruelty, from the fullness of servitude. With such a prospect before them our people will, as heretofore, come firmly up to the full measure of their duty if their trusted servants do not fail them.—They will not crucify afresh their own sons, slain in their behalf, or put their gallant shades to open shame, by stopping short of full and complete national independence.

THE NEW SENATOR FROM MISSISSIPPI.—The Confederate Senator elect from Mississippi, Hon. J. W. C. Watson, is said to be one of the ablest men in that State. The Atlanta *Register* names the following facts about him:

He stood at the head of a body of jurisconsults famed for their attainments, who, many years ago, made Holly Springs, by the attractions they contributed to social life, the most delightful interior city of the South. Mr. Watson has been distinguished, not less than his more noisy compeers, for his firm devotion to the cause of Southern independence. He was appointed last year by the President Commissioner for Mississippi under the Appraisement Act, and has sedulously devoted himself to the duties of his position. He is tall, slender, with blue eyes, light hair, and with an expression of face, benignant manner, and musical voice, remarkably attractive in social intercourse. In his professional habits he was the most laborious of men, and his success at the bar was brilliant. Not many months ago Judge Watson was arrested by a band of marauding Federal cavalry and taken to Pocahontas, where a Yankee Provost Marshal administered a horrible oath to Mississippians and others of debilitated moral constitutions. "By twos" the captured citizens were marched in and sworn by the Yankee official. Mr. Watson was the last brought before the Federal magnate.—He was very plainly dressed, and the officer knew nothing of him except his name. When "the book" and oath were placed before him, he remarked to the officer in the blandest, mildest tone conceivable that he might very well perhaps take that oath, but that he had conscientious scruples on the subject, and must therefore positively but respectfully decline. He said "that with his fixed convictions, his allegiance was primarily due to his State; no oath that could be administered would change the direction of that allegiance or of his duties as a citizen. The proposed oath to obey and respect the Government and laws of a foreign power, the United States, would be a nullity in the form of conscience." The officer said, "You seem to be an honest old gentleman, and if you will swear that you will reveal nothing that you have heard or seen within our lines that would militate against our interest, you may go." Judge Watson assented to this reasonable proposition.—He lost his horse, however, and all his clothing except that on his person, and is said to have reached the centre of Mississippi, on foot, within a shorter time than one of Morgan's men could have made the same distance.

HORRIBLE MURDER.—Mr. Irvie, an old citizen of Carroll county, Ga., was assassinated by one of his servants last week. The weapon used was a billet of wood, with which the victim was knocked senseless, when his throat was cut from ear to ear. He was then dragged to a cabin until night, and under cover of the darkness conveyed to a well near by and thrown in. The negro confided his bloody secret to a colored woman, who exposed the crime and brought the culprit to apprehension. He says that his mistress offered him a thousand dollars and his freedom to make way with her husband.

FATAL ACCIDENT.—Capt. James Dude, who has made several daring raids upon the enemy's shipping in the Gulf, was run over by the cars on the Mobile and Ohio railroad, on the 19th, and killed. He had just returned from an expedition after the enemy's vessels, and captured a schooner called the Norma within a mile and a half of Fort McRea, near Pensacola. Being hotly pursued by one of the Federal gunboats, he beached and burnt the vessel, and brought the Captain and crew to Mobile. After remaining with his friends there a few days, he started home to see his family, when the lamentable accident occurred.

YANKEE ROBBERY IN WESTERN VIRGINIA.—On their recent return the forces of Gen. Averill passed through Pendleton county, Va., and stayed over night at Franklin, where they took all the horses, beef cattle, &c., they could lay their hands on, and destroyed such things as they could not carry off. They took all of Mrs. Gen. Boggs's negroes, (some 15 or 20,) some of her stock, and plundered her house of silver ware, &c. Wm. McCoy, Col. J. F. Johnston, and others, were also sufferers to some extent from the depredations and robberies of these brigands.

HEADS TO THE NORTH.—The Abingdon *Virginian* says that a young man writing from the battle ground of Chickamauga to his brother in that vicinity, among other incidents, relates that he saw two Yankees burying a dead comrade.—They had dug the grave north and south, and when they were about to consign the body to it a dispute arose as to which way the head should be laid. "Let's put it south," said one. "No," said the other, "let's put it north, for it's already been too far South for its own good."

LOUISIANA ELECTIONS.—The election for State and Congressional officers took place in Louisiana on the 2d inst. Brig. Gen. Henry W. Allen was elected Governor without opposition; B. W. Pearce, Lieutenant Governor; P. D. Hardy, Secretary of State; F. S. Goode, Attorney General; H. Peralta, Auditor of Public Accounts; B. L. Defreese, State Treasurer. By official act of the Legislature, the vote for members of Congress was taken by general ticket. Little doubt is entertained of the election of the old members—C. J. Villere, C. M. Conrad, D. F. Kenner, L. J. Dupre, Henry Marshall, John Perkins, Jr.

PROVISIONS IN SOUTHWEST GEORGIA.—Corn is selling in Southwestern Georgia at $1.50a2; pork, 75ca$1, and still rising. No potatoes for sale.—Syrup brings from $7a8, and farmers do not want to sell at that. None of the owners of provisions wish to sell anything they have on hand. All are holding up for "good prices," and will let the people in other sections suffer rather than allow their hoards of accumulated provisions go into the hungry mouths of less favored communities.

ONE OF THE COLLARDS.—The Macon *Telegraph* is indebted to Mr. R. Dossett, of that city, for a collard four inches short of nine feet high. It looks for all the world, says the *Telegraph*, like a young Palmetto tree, and is capable of affording friendly shelter to four tall men in a thunder storm, or when the sun is at meridian. This collard grew in Mr. Dossett's garden in Macon, and is a product from seed sown last spring.

LOCAL MATTERS.

Destructive Fire.—Between the hours of 11 and 12 o'clock yesterday, dense volumes of smoke were seen to proceed from the sweat-house of Messrs. Jones & Childrey's large store and tobacco factory, on the north side of Main street, a few doors west of 17th street, and it being evident to the employees of the building that some of the tobacco casings had taken fire from the furnace used for heating that room, messengers were dispatched to the engine house for assistance. In an incredibly short time, the firemen, with their apparatus, were at the scene, and forcing one of the doors, poured in their streams of water upon the burning mass, thus checking the spread of the flames to other portions of the establishment, and finally extinguishing them.

We learn from Mr. Childrey that the stock on hand, in the sweat room alone, and which was then being prepared for European markets, was worth to the firm at least $150,000, the greater portion of which will probably be seriously damaged by fire and smoke, and the vast volumes of water which had to be thrown upon it to check the flames and to prevent their spreading to other portions of the establishment. Upon this amount the firm had an insurance of only $20,000.

Almost a Duel.—On Wednesday last the day police arrested Dr. William H Robertson, of Petersburg, and Dr. W. O. McCorkle, of Tennessee, charged with being about to engage in a duel, in violation of the laws of this Commonwealth. Yesterday morning the parties were before the Mayor, and each held to bail to keep the peace in the sum of $1,500. The parties were prisoners at Fort McHenry, where a difficulty occurred between them, which they determined to settle as soon as they were liberated. Arriving here on the flag-of-truce boat on Tuesday morning, Dr. Robertson soon after sent a challenge, which was accepted by Dr. McCorkle, and the duel would have taken place on Wednesday morning but for the serious indisposition of Dr. McC.'s second. In the course of the day the acquaintances of the parties got wind of the pending hostilities, and, to prevent the effusion of blood, called in the officers of the law to their aid—"Blessed is the peace maker," saith the good book.

Judge Halyburton, of the C. S. Circuit Court, heard the conclusion of Judge Crump's argument yesterday, in the case of C. F. Robertson, who was suing to be released from conscription, he having furnished a substitute in 1862, and complied with all the requirements of the law. Mr. R's substitute, after being in service some time, was claimed and carried off by officers of another company, without furnishing the company from which he was taken any evidence that he was a deserter, or from what company he had deserted. This cause was argued for Government by Mr. Aylett, for the Conscription Bureau by Col. T. P. August. Messrs. Howard and Crump appeared for Robertson, and enforced his claims to a release with great ability. The Judge decided that Robertson had complied with all the requirements of the law of Congress, and with the regulations of the War Department, concerning substitutes, and therefore discharged him from service.

Receiving Stolen Cloth.—Daniel Ryan, the well known keeper of a clothing establishment in the eastern part of the city, was arraigned before the Mayor yesterday to answer the charge of receiving a bolt of yarn cloth, worth $300, stolen from John D. Harvey & Co., knowing the same to have been stolen. The cloth was found on Ryan's premises, and is supposed to have been carried there by the negro that stole it. Ryan denied his guilt; but failing to prove his innocence when the charge was being investigated, he was remanded to the Hustings Court for a further hearing. If innocent of the charge, he will have an opportunity to prove it before that tribunal.

Hustings Court, Judge Lyons presiding.—In Judge Lyons's Court yesterday James Egan and Barney McNamee, for robbing Josiah King, of South Carolina, of his pocket book containing $30 in money, were sent to the Penitentiary for three years each.

Augustus Synco, formerly of Norfolk, Va., late C. S. detective, was arraigned for shooting Ella Johnson, a prostitute, in Exchange Alley, some weeks since. Hon. Humphrey Marshall and Daniel Ratcliffe, Esq., appearing for the prisoner, and Littleton Tazewell, Esq., for the Commonwealth. The jury, after an absence of some hours, brought in a verdict of guilty, and his punishment was assessed at three years in the Penitentiary.

Shooting at a Watchman.—Wm. Henry and Frank Wilson were before the Mayor yesterday on serious charges—the first for being drunk and disorderly, firing a pistol at watchman John O. Hall, and drawing a pistol on F. W. E. Lohman; and the last, for drawing a knife on Lohman, and being drunk and disorderly. The prisoners attributed all their troubles to the use of small quantities of bad liquors, a few drinks of which would make a preacher kill his father, or a soldier desert his flag. After a partial hearing, the Mayor adjourned their examination to a future day.

Stealing Liquor.—The police yesterday arrested two or three negroes, charged with being engaged in stealing a barrel of whiskey from the Powhatan House, but their statements were so contradictory that the truth could not be gathered from them.—Ned, a slave, in the employ of Mr. Herbert, seems to be one of the gang of thieves that raised the liquor, and it is equally clear that he had assistants; but who they were the Court will have to determine.

Hog Stealing.—Constable Robinson, of Henrico county, and the city police, have succeeded in arresting a gang of negroes whose nightly depredations on suburban hog-pens have produced no little uneasiness among that class of persons who have been husbanding their swine for fall killing. The county Justices can only punish these rogues by ordering them the lash, and they should, therefore, make that remedy as effectual as possible.

No Alarm.—Notwithstanding the close proximity to the first station-house of Messrs. Jones & Childrey's store, which was partially burned yesterday, the alarm bell was not sounded to call together the firemen until after one or two companies had reached the scene of conflagration with their machines, and had put streams of water upon the fire. A fireman reports that he went to the station-house to have the bell rung, but finding the door locked and no one present to admit him, he procured a ladder, entered a window, and rang the bell.

At a meeting of the City Council some few weeks since Mr. Scott made an effort to secure the appointment of officers to attend the station-houses at all hours of the day, but was defeated. Surely the Council will now see the importance of having these officers, and will appoint them. The city has no place where a policeman can be found at all hours, however urgent the necessity; nor has it any guard at the station-houses to prevent prisoners from escaping from them during the day. It needs officers to be in place at all times, and the sooner they are appointed the better for the public.

Sent On.—The lad, Charles Rose, arraigned before the Mayor on charge of receiving flour stolen from Peter Tinsley, knowing the same to have been stolen, was again called up yesterday, and remanded for a further hearing at the next term of the Hustings Court. Rose owned the wagon in which the stolen flour was hauled, and is supposed to be cognizant of the stealing.

Wheat, in small lots, has been selling in the streets for several days past at $12 per bushel. As the millers readily give one barrel of flour for five bushels of wheat, we can see no reason for the exorbitant prices asked for flour. Choice wheat at $15 per bushel, would make the best family flour worth but $75 per barrel.

KILLED.—Major Gist, of the 15th regiment South Carolina volunteers, was killed in a fight with Burnside's troops, near Knoxville, on the 18th inst. He was the son of ex Governor W. H. Gist.

A shrewd old gentleman once said to his daughter, "Be sure, my dear, you never marry a poor man; but remember the poorest man in the world is one that has money and nothing else."

TELEGRAPHIC NEWS.

[REPORTS OF THE PRESS ASSOCIATION.]

Entered according to act of Congress in the year 1863, by J. S. THRASHER, in the Clerk's office of the District Court of the Confederate States for the Northern District of Georgia.

THE BATTLE AT LOOKOUT MOUNTAIN.

FURTHER PARTICULARS.

[FROM OUR OWN CORRESPONDENT.]

CHICKAMAUGA, Nov. 25.—General Bragg abandoned Lookout Mountain last night, as no longer tenable or important, and massed his army on Missionary Ridge.

Our right extended well up to the mouth of the Chickamauga, where the enemy had sent a heavy force.

Gen. Hardee commanded the right wing, and Gen. Breckinridge the left.

The battle commenced at ten, and became general by twelve o'clock.

On the right Hardee repulsed the enemy's assault with great slaughter, capturing seven flags and some prisoners, but the enemy gained a ridge near our centre and enfiladed our lines. The men supposing that the enemy were successful elsewhere gave way on our left, when the Federals occupied that part of the ridge.

Our whole army was withdrawn at night, and is now crossing the Chickamauga.

There were no rails (?) by which to bring off our artillery, and in some cases several guns were lost and some prisoners.

Our loss in killed and wounded is slight.

The enemy's forces were two to our one.

SALLUST.

[Press Dispatch.]

ATLANTA, Nov. 26.—Trains from the front come in full of Yankee prisoners. No wounded have yet come in. The Atlanta Relief Committee commenced sending supplies to the front to day. The city is full of rumors, but nothing authentic has been received since Gen. Bragg's dispatch of yesterday.

[SECOND DISPATCH.]

ATLANTA, Nov. 26.—The news from our army is conflicting. It is believed that our troops are still falling back. No train has arrived since this morning. Every preparation has been made in the hospitals here for our wounded, but none have yet arrived.

The *Intelligencer's* correspondent, who has returned from the front, furnishes the following: The enemy, after a desperate and bloody struggle, gained Craven's House, on the northern slope of Lookout Mountain. Walthall's brigade suffered severely, holding two divisions in check, and a large portion of it was captured. Stevenson's division occupied the crest of the mountain. The assault continued by moonlight until midnight, the enemy suffering severely, and our forces gradually retired at day light from Lookout to Mission Ridge.

Seven regiments of the enemy's cavalry ferried the Tennessee at the mouth of the Chickamauga on the evening of the 24th.

Sherman's corps being on this side attacked Wright's brigade, which withdrew after a sharp contest.

The enemy's cavalry raided within a few miles of Chickamauga on the night of the 24th, burning 22 wagons.

The third day of the battle commenced yesterday on our left and centre. After several assaults our lines gave way, and fell back in some confusion. On our right Sherman was repulsed four times with great slaughter, and driven across the river; we burning his pontoons. The fighting yesterday was terribly desperate, probably the heaviest during the war. The enemy's loss is unusually heavy in proportion to ours. Ours severe.

It is reported that 5,000 of the enemy's cavalry came through Gos Gap, 15½ miles from Dalton.

SKIRMISHING ON THE RAPIDAN—THE ENEMY REPORTED ADVANCING.

ORANGE C. H., Nov. 26.—A Confederate scouting party under Lt. Duncan, of the 1st Va. cavalry, engaged a Yankee scouting party at Griffinburg, Culpeper co., yesterday, and captured twelve, who have been brought here.

Nearly all of the enemy's force has been transferred from Fauquier to Culpeper co. There was firing for two hours at the lower fords of the Rapidan to-day. The enemy's cavalry and infantry demonstrations indicate an intention to cross. Our artillery have opened upon them. They are reported to have crossed in force at Ely's ford, but to have gone back. Some musketry skirmishing to day at Morton's ford. No casualties reported.

FROM CHARLESTON.

CHARLESTON, Nov. 26.—The enemy's fire on Sumter has almost entirely ceased. Only twenty-one shots were fired on Wednesday, of which six missed. No casualties.

[SECOND DISPATCH.]

CHARLESTON, Nov. 26.—The firing to-day was principally mortar shelling between the enemy's batteries and our own. Forts Moultrie, Johnson, and battery Simpkins were engaged on our side, and a mortar battery, with Gregg and Wagner, on the part of the enemy. The number of shots fired on Sumter on Wednesday night was 243, of which 86 missed. Very little firing on Sumter to-day. No casualties. No further firing on the city.

BURNING OF A FEDERAL TRANSPORT.

MOBILE, Nov. 26.—New Orleans papers say that the Federal transport Tecumseh, loaded with cotton, sugar, and molasses, was destroyed by fire at Baton Rouge on the 15th inst. The vessel and cargo were valued at $300,000.

FROM EAST TENNESSEE.

BRISTOL, Nov. 26.—Nothing reliable from Knoxville, but rumors are numerous and conflicting.

The Philadelphia Inquirer.

CIRCULATION OVER 60,000. | PHILADELPHIA, MONDAY, DECEMBER 7, 1863. | PRICE TWO CENTS.

NEWS OF THE DAY.

IMPORTANT FROM TENNESSEE.

Retreat of General Longstreet.

HIS PROBABLE ESCAPE.

Full Accounts from Knoxville.

THE END OF THE SIEGE.

No Successor for Bragg.

The Union Losses at Chattanooga.

GILLMORE SHELLING STILL.

Incendiary Missiles for Charleston.

WHAT ADMIRAL DAHLGREN IS DOING.

Another "Scare" on the Rapidan.

ORGANIZATION OF CONGRESS.

The Contest for Speaker.

Mr. SCHUYLER COLFAX NOMINATED

Tricks of the Opposition.

THE MURDERER OF McCOOK ON TRIAL.

More Frauds Exposed.

ARKANSAS A FREE STATE.

A Brilliant Cavalry Affair in Louisiana.

THE CAPTURE OF 860 REBELS.

Latest European News.

Etc., Etc., Etc., Etc., Etc.

SIEGE OF KNOXVILLE.

LONGSTREET's Lines of Advance and Retreat—Scene of the Assaults of Nov. 23 and Nov 30—Fort Saunders, &c.

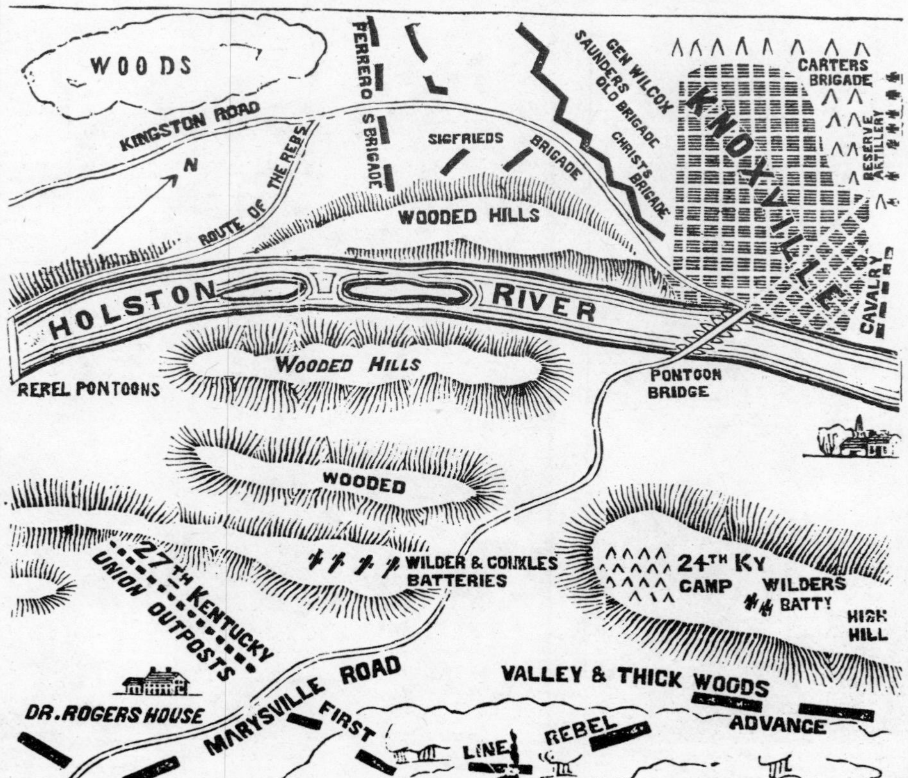

ARMY OF THE POTOMAC.

OUR SPECIAL REPORT.

Special Despatch to the Inquirer.

BRANDY STATION, Sunday, Dec. 6.—On Saturday evening, as the train was passing from Bealton to Warrenton Junction, a party of guerrillas fired at the locomotive, with the intention of shooting the Engineer. No one was hurt. Over a dozen balls struck the engine in various parts. The train kept on its way without stopping.

Two other trains were behind, and neither were molested.

The guerrillas disappeared in the woods soon after. All was quiet, yesterday, in the army.

An alarm was occasioned by the report that the Rebels were crossing the Rapidan to attack us, but it was without foundation. The report was brought in by two Rebel deserters who were, no doubt, sent in for that purpose; a trick they often play.

[DESPATCHES TO THE ASSOCIATED PRESS.]

Reconnoissance by the Rebels—Fight in Progress—Southern Accounts of Our Movements.

HEAD-QUARTERS ARMY OF THE POTOMAC, Dec. 4, P. M.—A light division of Rebel troops crossed the Rapidan this afternoon, at some point on Raccoon Ford, probably on a reconnoissance.

Since this information came to camp considerable cannonading has been heard in that direction, and it is supposed that their advance has been checked by our light batteries, which have been attached to the cavalry arm of the service, in pursuance of General MEADE's orders.

Rebel Reports.

The Richmond *Enquirer*, of December 2d and 3d, says:—

ORANGE COURT HOUSE, Dec. 1.—Our artillery opened on the enemy, yesterday, quite spiritedly. The enemy responded briskly. An artillery duel was kept up all day. The enemy has thrown up fortifications along their front.

Last night they built heavy fires in our front, and moved more to our right. One hundred and twenty-seven prisoners were sent to Richmond to-day. The Captain of the Lynchburg Artillery was killed.

ORANGE COURT HOUSE, Dec. 2.—There has been no fighting. The enemy still make a show in our front; but are believed to be falling back down the Rapidan, either to recross the river without fighting, or to go to Fredericksburg to winter.

ARMY OF THE CUMBERLAND.

All Quiet—Our Losses and Captures in the Late Battles.

CHATTANOOGA, Dec. 4.—All is quiet in this army. The expedition to relieve General BURNSIDE is under General SHERMAN, who has doubtless reached Knoxville.

The most important work now is to reopen the railroad from Bridgeport to Chattanooga, and the work is being pushed with great vigor.

Special despatches say that the rumor of the death of JOHN C. BRECKINRIDGE, from wounds received in the late battle is confirmed.

CINCINNATI, Dec. 5.—The *Gazette* has received a despatch from Chattanooga, dated yesterday, which says:—"Everything is quiet along the entire line.

"Our casualties in the late battle, both in killed and wounded, numbered 4580.

"We captured 6460 prisoners and 46 guns."

Rebel Raids in the Cherokee Nation.

WASHINGTON, Dec. 5.—Indian Superintendent Coffin has arrived in this city, bringing to the Indian Bureau an official report concerning a raid that was made several weeks ago into the Cherokee country, by, as is supposed, a party of QUANTRELL's guerrillas, who destroyed the public buildings at Tahlequah and the property of Union citizens, including that of JOHN ROSS. A son-in-law of the latter was murdered by the band.

INTERESTING FROM WASHINGTON.

[SPECIAL DESPATCHES TO THE INQUIRER.]

WASHINGTON, December 6.

The Canvass for Speaker.

We have had the exposé, within the last forty-eight hours, of what is deemed a conspiracy on the part of EMERSON ETHERIDGE, and of the Democratic leaders, to defraud the Union men out of an organization of the House, on a petty quibble as to the validity of their election certificates. Measures have been taken to have Mr. ETHERIDGE arrested should he insist upon carrying out his programme, which is as follows:—

At the last session of Congress a law was passed directing the Clerks to place such names, and only such, upon the roll of the House as produced certificates of their having been elected according to the laws of their respective States, or of the United States. ETHERIDGE construes this act to require that a certificate of election of a member must include either the phraseology of the act, or terms equivalent to it. He alleges that the usual certificate of a duly elected member does not meet the exigencies of the act, but he insists that the certificate must contain the express declaration either in the terms of the act or those equivalent to it.

The determination of this, he says, was arrived at some months ago, yet he made no announcement of it, and certificates he received some weeks ago were not returned until as late as Friday last. On some of the Missouri members offering their credentials, on Saturday, he refused to accept them, as they merely certified that they were "duly elected." Mr. ETHERIDGE announced that only Iowa, Delaware and Maine had brought proper certificates, but that others had "amended returns," and it was then found upon examination that every State that had a majority of Democratic members in their delegation had their returns "amended."

COX kindly procured those for Ohio, while HOLMAN took care of Indiana. New Jersey was amended, and a supplementary proclamation from Governor CURTIN made the Pennsylvania delegation all right. Telegraph despatches have brought in additional testimony, and up to noon to-day ETHERIDGE has only succeeded in throwing out Missouri, Oregon, Maryland, East and West Virginia, and Vermont. This still leaves the Republicans a small majority; although it is believed the list will be further tampered with, and a determined effort be made to secure the organization by the Democrats, unless prompt action is taken to meet such revolutionary proceedings.

The Kansas delegation arrived this morning, with certificates only of being duly elected. Mr. SMITHERS, of Delaware, brought a certificate of being elected, in pursuance of the laws of Delaware, which Mr. ETHERIDGE decides amounts to the same thing as the act calls for. A committee, appointed to wait on Mr. ETHERIDGE, will do so in the morning, and should he disfranchize enough Union men to defeat Mr. COLFAX for Speaker, no election will be allowed until the members who are thrown out shall have time to procure their amended returns. The President has been much annoyed at the matter, and this morning Mr. COLFAX called, by his request, to see him.

This afternoon Secretary SEWARD had a long interview at the hotel with Mr. COLFAX. A careful count, this afternoon, makes eighty-two Union men and seventy-seven Democrats as the House will stand to-morrow noon, if those now out are kept out; but the admission of the Louisiana delegation will give the Democrats a majority, should they act, as is claimed, with them. Mr. COLFAX is confident that ETHERIDGE will be forced to back down from his position, and that he will be chosen Speaker on the first ballot.

When the Union caucus met last night, at seven P. M., in one of the committee rooms at the Capitol, ninety-three answered to the call of the roll. FRANK BLAIR's name was omitted. MORRELL, of Vermont, was called to the chair. ROLLINS, of New Hampshire, and BOYD, of Missouri, were elected Secretaries. It was resolved to go into a ballot for Speaker, when SCHUYLER COLFAX was nominated for that office by ORTH, of Indiana; DAWES of Massachusetts, nominated WASHBURNE, of Illinois, and POMEROY, of New York, nominated FENTON, of New York.

After some little discussion FENTON and WASHBURNE withdrew their names, that entire unanimity might be procured, and COLFAX was then nominated by acclamation, on motion of HENRY WINTER DAVIS.

A committee of five was appointed to wait upon Mr. ETHERIDGE and learn his determination as to the seats of those men whom he has thrown out. The Committee consists of DAVIS, of Maryland; STEVENS, of Pennsylvania; GARFIELD, of Ohio; DAWES, of Massachusetts, and PIKE, of Maine.

The caucus to meet at the call of the Committee, and on motion further nominations were postponed and caucus adjourned.

The Democratic caucus was again in session last night, and after general discussion, and the candidate for Speaker narrowing down to Mr. COX, of Ohio, it was concluded to await further developments as to the complexion of the House, and they adjourned.

The Pennsylvania, New Jersey and Delaware members are now all here.

Border-State Men in the Union Caucus.

Three members from West Virginia, three from Maryland, three from Missouri, one from Delaware and two from Kentucky, were all the Border-State men who attended the caucus.

Enormous Army Frauds.

Enormous frauds have been committed in the Quartermaster's Department in Alexandria, amounting to several hundred thousand dollars. The facts that have come to light, in the last few months, since Colonel THOMAS assumed charge, vice General MEIGS, show that systematized frauds have been in operation for a long while, by which contractors and officers shared the spoils. The heaviest frauds were in the forage division, mostly in mixed grain. Capts. STODDARD and FERGUSON have been arrested, and sent to the Old Capitol Prison. Several of those defrauding contractors and others will, no doubt, follow suit, as the Secretary of War has determined to wage merciless war upon dishonesty and fraud, and investigations now in progress are making strange exposures.

President's Message and the Secretary's Reports.

The report of the Secretary of War was sent to the printer to-day. It will make about four columns in THE INQUIRER. The report of the Secretary of the Navy will make five or six columns, and the report of the Secretary of the Treasury about four and a half columns. It is not all in the hands of the printers yet. The President's Message is about four columns, and will be printed to-morrow.

Arrival of Wounded Officers and Men.

Dr. G. B. HOTCHKISS, Surgeon of the First Pennsylvania Cavalry, arrived late last night at Alexandria, in charge of seven wounded officers and eighty-six wounded men, all belonging to GREGG's Cavalry Division, and wounded during the late advance beyond the Rapidan.

The enlisted men were taken to Alexandria hospitals, and the officers were brought to Washington.

Rebels Reported Crossing the Rapidan.

It was currently reported yesterday that the Rebels were crossing the Rapidan above MEADE's army, and were about to attack him in force. Ample preparations were made to receive them; but, up to this morning, no attack had been made in force, though heavy skirmishing is reported.

Raise in Printers' Wages.

Last night the Printers' Society resolved to increase the wages for compositors and pressmen from sixteen to eighteen dollars per week. The rate will be paid at the Government printing offices.

Courtesy to the Russian Officers.

The Russian Minister, Mr. DE STOECKEL, this morning presented Admiral LESSOVSKY and the principal officers of the squadron to the Secretary of State, who expressed to them the President's regrets that his indisposition prevented him giving them an immediate audience. The distinguished visitors were then presented by the Secretary of State to the several heads of Departments, who received them with the kindest expressions of satisfaction.

At two o'clock this afternoon, attended by the Secretary of State, the Russian officers visited the Navy Yard, where they were received by the Secretary of the Navy with the naval honors due their rank.

Arrest of Rebel Spies.

Two supposed Rebel spies have been arrested here by the United States Detectives, and committed to the Old Capitol Prison. One of them is a Lieutenant of the Louisiana volunteer service, and the other a private in the Virginia Cavalry. The latter was on his way home to Lower Maryland, and says he came hither last night on the Underground railroad, by way of Baltimore. Eleven prisoners of violent Secession proclivities, were also committed to the Old Capitol to-day. One of them, a colored man, is charged with being disloyal and a dangerous character. They were sent to Washington from General CORCORAN's division in Maryland. Two other persons have been similarly domiciled on the charge of carrying despatches for MOSEBY and WHITE of the Rebel army.

The Washington Aqueduct.

Water from the Potomac river was let into the Washington Aqueduct to-day. Heretofore the city has been supplied, though insufficiently, from the neighboring creeks. The event was formally celebrated, the proceedings closing with a corporation dinner.

Members Arriving.

About two hundred members of Congress have already arrived, and there are accessions by every train. A number of ex-members are also here from various parts of the country.

THE MURDER OF GENERAL R. L. M'COOK.

Trial by Court-martial of the Murderer—The Prisoner Tells Two Stories—The Evidence Strong Against Him, Etc.

Special Despatch to the Inquirer.

NASHVILLE, Nov. 5.—FRANCIS GURLEY, charged with the murder of Brigadier-General ROBERT L. McCOOK, is now in prison here, and was tried yesterday before a Court-martial assembled by order of Major-General GEORGE H. THOMAS, and consisting of Colonel JOHN F. MILLER, President, Twenty-ninth Indiana; Captain JASPER PARTRIDGE, Forty-fourth Illinois; Captain THOMAS J. RHODES, Sixtieth Illinois; Captain A. V. P. DAY, Tenth Ohio Volunteer Cavalry; Captain ALBERT M. GREEN, Sixth Kentucky Cavalry; Lieutenant H. C. BLACKMAN, Eighth Kansas Cavalry, Judge Advocate.

Captain HUNTER BROOKS, Judge Advocate of the Department, who was with General McCOOK when he was murdered, was in attendance upon the Court as a witness, yesterday.

The Court granted a continuance of the case until the 18th, to enable GURLEY to procure a witness from among the prisoners at Camp Chase. GURLEY plead not guilty, but outside the Court admitted having shot General McCOOK while acting as a soldier in the Rebel service.

It will be difficult to convince the Court that GURLEY was acting as a soldier at the time, for the Rebel papers, detailing the murder, spoke of it as such, and spoke of him as a Partisan Ranger.

Prisoners are arriving by every train from Bridgeport. Six hundred and eighty arrived this evening, and among them the son of the Rebel General JOHN C. BRECKINRIDGE.

Supplies are going forward. The Rebel sympathizers here are making desperate efforts to prevent their property from being seized for Government use.

Our wounded have not commenced to arrive yet. No news from the front.

The Convicted Conspirators in Ohio.

CINCINNATI, Dec. 5.—The sentences of the Noble county conspirators were pronounced yesterday. McPHERSON and COGLE were fined $6500 and costs, each, and RACOON $1000, and to stand committed until the fines are paid.

Governor TOD has appointed the Hon. JOSHUA B. SWAN Supreme Judge, vice GHOLSON, resigned.

Fire in Baltimore—Destruction of Government Stores.

BALTIMORE, Dec. 6.—Five large warehouses on Fell's Point, which were used by the Commissary Department for storage of forage, &c., were destroyed by fire on Saturday evening. The loss will amount to some nine thousand dollars, about six of which is sustained by the Government.

Steamer "Saxonia."

NEW YORK, Dec. 6.—The steamer *Saxonia* will be up at one o'clock.

DEPARTMENT OF THE OHIO.

The Siege of Knoxville, Tenn.

A SKETCH OF ITS HISTORY.

The Retreat of General Longstreet.

SKIRMISHES IN TENNESSEE.

The Repulse of the Union Cavalry.

A FIGHT IN SOUTHWEST VIRGINIA.

Probable Escape of the Rebels.

AN ASSAULT ON FORT SAUNDERS.

The Rebels Repulsed With Heavy Loss

AN AFFAIR WEST OF THE HOLSTON.

Etc., Etc., Etc., Etc., Etc.

LATEST REPORTS BY TELEGRAPH.

Retreat of Longstreet.

CINCINNATI, Dec. 5.—A despatch to the *Commercial*, dated at Cumberland Gap on the 4th instant, says:—

"General FOSTER has driven the enemy from Clinch River, and is now in pursuit of him.

"The check which our cavalry received yesterday in attempting to cross the Clinch River, will doubtless secure the retreat of LONGSTREET's army."

Fighting Beyond Cumberland Gap.

CUMBERLAND GAP, Dec. 3, 7 P. M.—There was fighting yesterday and to-day at Walker's Ford, twenty miles from the Gap, between our forces under General FOSTER and the whole of LONGSTREET's cavalry. We attempted yesterday to cross the river Clinch, but were repulsed. Our loss at the close of yesterday's fight was fifty. We captured four pieces of artillery. The above I got from one of General WILCOX's staff, just in.

After the fight at Jonesville, Sunday, of which I telegraphed, the Third Battalion of the Sixteenth Illinois Cavalry left their two Surgeons back to care for the Rebel wounded. *They were yesterday found murdered!* One was Dr. HALSTED, formerly of Ohio. Major BEAM, with a portion of the Sixteenth, will leave here in the morning, on a mission of vengeance. They will take no prisoners. Much ill feeling exists against the prisoners we have here.

I expect to leave, to-morrow, for the scene of hostilities, on Clinch River, and telegraph authentic details.

Brilliant Affair in Virginia.

CUMBERLAND GAP, Dec. 2, 8 P. M.—On Saturday last, Col. LEMERT despatched a force consisting of two hundred and twenty-five men of the Sixth Illinois Cavalry, in command of Major BEARS, of that regiment, and under guidance of L. F. PAYNE, Esq., Provost Marshal [illegible] the Rebel force commanded by Col. PUTNAM, that has been roaming on a mission of plunder through the adjacent portion of Virginia. Thirty miles from the Gap, near Louisville, Lee county, they found the Rebels drawn up in line of battle, over three hundred strong. Major BEARS at once ordered a charge, but this proved too much for their pedal constancy, and their well-ordered line was at once dissolved into an aimless, fugitive mob.

We killed 21, wounded 16 and captured 21. The latter reached here this morning, under guard of their captors, who also brought in 50 Rebel horses and 100 guns. The latter were picked up on the line of retreat, in most instances charged, cocked and capped. We continued pursuit eleven miles; our loss nothing. Much praise is due Colonel LEMERT for the vigor displayed in demolishing the guerrilla hordes that have been prowling in this vicinity.

Further intelligence from BURNSIDE is vague and conflicting. Colonel LEMERT received intelligence that General FOSTER had engaged LONGSTREET this morning, near Maynardsville. Cannonading was heard for several hours to-day in that direction.

SOUTHERN ACCOUNTS.

BRISTOL, Tenn., Dec. 2.—The firing at Knoxville has ceased. The surrender of BURNSIDE is not officially confirmed.

Union advices from BURNSIDE, later than the above, show that LONGSTREET has been compelled to abandon the siege and retreat.

Fight at Kingston.

Last week WHEELER was ordered to Kingston; there is heavy firing at London.

[SECOND DESPATCH.]

A train came from Dalton, this morning, bringing wounded troops. Our forces are still falling back slowly, followed by the enemy. There was firing all day yesterday.

HISTORY OF THE KNOXVILLE SIEGE.

Advance of Longstreet.

On the third of November General BRAGG issued orders detaching the corps of General LONGSTREET, the division of General JOHNSON, and the cavalry corps of General WHEELER from the Army of the Tennessee, to operate against General BURNSIDE. This movement was a portion of the plan submitted by General LONGSTREET to crush BURNSIDE, compel a division of General GRANT's army about Chattanooga, and insure the overthrow of the Federal forces in Tennessee. Ten days were consumed in reaching London, near the Tennessee River, and on the 18th ult. an affair occurred, at Marysville, in which the Federal troops were repulsed with the loss of Gen. SANDERS wounded.

The Cavalry Skirmishes.

A Rebel correspondent with WHEELER's cavalry division writes as follows, under date of the 21st ultimo:—

Early on the morning of the 16th General MARTIN's splendid division of Alabamians and Georgians were moved forward to the front, Colonel MORRISON commanding the advance brigade, composed entirely of Georgians. At Rockford he met the enemy's pickets. These he drove without trouble for three miles, where he found the enemy in position with artillery. After a few minutes of sharpshooting General MARTIN dismounted his entire division, and moved them forward in line of battle to the attack. A few shots from some rifle and Parrott pieces caused the enemy to move their artillery, when the entire force followed. A line of skirmishers were thrown forward in advance of MARTIN's Division, led by General VAUGHN. The enemy stubbornly resisted his advance; but still he pressed on. For two miles he drove them, when they were again found in position, but, after throwing a few shell at our advance line of skirmishers, they fell back in the direction of Knoxville, not even giving our artillery boys an opportunity of throwing at them a single shot.

"The enemy retiring so soon, General WHEELER determined to press them before they took a new position, as they were not evidently more than ten regiments and two pieces of artillery strong. General MARTIN being dismounted, General ARMSTRONG moved forward his Division, distinguished for its fighting, DIBBRELL with his Tennesseeans, and charging HARRISON with his Texans and Arkansians; 'Texas brigade to the front,' shouted the dashing ARMSTRONG, the enemy's rear is in sight. The fearless VAUGHN has engaged them with some skirmishers, but they can't keep up with a fast retreating foe. The bugle sounds, the frontier yell is raised,

Continued on the Eighth Page.

The Army of the Potomac crossing the Rapidan River, May 1864

1 · 8 · 6 · 4

William Tecumseh Sherman

January 22, Union Major General William S. Rosecrans is made commander of the Federal Department of the Missouri. ***February 1,*** President Lincoln orders the drafting of 500,000 men in March. ***February 3,*** Union General Sherman's Meridian, Mississippi campaign begins. ***February 5,*** Sherman's army marches into Jackson, Mississippi. ***February 9,*** 109 Federal officers escape from Libby Prison in Richmond, the largest escape of the war. ***February 14,*** Sherman's Federals capture Meridian, Mississippi. ***February 17,*** An experimental Confederate submarine sinks the USS *Housatonic* off Charleston, South Carolina. ***February 22,*** Confederate cavalry under Nathan Bedford Forrest defeat a small Federal force at Okalona, Mississippi. ***March 1,*** A Union cavalry force under Judson Kilpatrick fails in an attempt to raid Richmond. ***March 9,*** Ulysses S. Grant officially receives his commission as Lieutenant General from President Lincoln. ***March 16,*** Federal troops occupy Alexandria, Louisiana on the Red River. ***March 24,*** Nathan Bedford Forrest's cavalry capture Union City, Tennessee. ***April 4,*** Major General Philip Sheridan becomes commander of the Army of the Potomac's cavalry. ***April 8,*** The Confederates under General Richard Taylor defeat the Federals at the Battle of Sabine Crossroads, Louisiana, forcing the retreat of General Banks' forces. ***April 12,*** Nathan Bedford Forrest's cavalry strikes at Fort Pillow, Tennessee, massacring soldiers after its surrender. ***April 21,*** General Banks' army withdraws back to Alexandria, Louisiana ending the unsuccessful Red River campaign. ***May 4,*** The Army of the Potomac crosses the Rapidan River as Confederate General Richard Ewell's division of the Army of Northern Virginia rushes up to meet the threat. ***May 6,*** Both armies sustain over 25,000 casualties in the Battle of the Wilderness in Virginia. ***May 7,*** General Sherman begins his march towards Atlanta and the entrenched Confederate Army of Tennessee under General Johnston. ***May 11,*** Confederate cavalryman Jeb Stuart is mortally wounded at the Battle of Yellow Tavern, Virginia. ***May 12,*** The Army of the Potomac sustains severe casualties at the Battle of Spotsylvania, Virginia, but attrition becomes a serious problem for the Army of Northern Virginia. ***May 23,*** General Lee misses an opportunity to attack the Army of the Potomac as it crosses the North Anna River. ***June 3,*** The Army of the Potomac launches an assault against a strongly fortified Army of Northern Virginia at Cold Harbor, Virginia, sustaining over 7,000 casualties before General Grant regretfully calls off the attack. ***June 8,*** Abraham Lincoln is nominated for a second term as President. ***June 14,*** The Army of the Potomac begins crossing the James River in Virginia. ***June 18,*** After deciding the city of Petersburg, Virginia could not be assaulted, General Grant orders a siege. ***June 19,*** The USS *Kearsage* sinks the highly successful Confederate raider *Alabama* off Cherbourg, France. ***June 17,*** Sherman's army is defeated at the Battle of Kennesaw Mountain, Georgia. ***July 11,*** Confederates under Jubal Early raid the suburbs of Washington, D.C. ***July 17,*** General John Bell Hood replaces General Johnston as commander of the Army of Tennessee. ***July 22,*** Union General James McPherson is killed at the Battle of Atlanta, which is put under siege. ***July 30,*** The Federals lose over 4,000 men after setting off an explosion and charging heavily fortified positions at Petersburg, Virginia. ***September 2,*** Sherman's army marches into Atlanta. ***September 4,*** Confederate raider John Hunt Morgan is killed in Greenville, Tennessee. ***September 19,*** The Federals under General Sheridan drive the Confederates back at the Battle of Winchester, Virginia. ***October 13,*** Maryland abolishes slavery. ***October 19,*** Confederates under Jubal Early defeat the Federals at the Battle of Cedar Creek, Virginia. ***November 8,*** Abraham Lincoln is re-elected. ***November 16,*** General Sherman leaves Atlanta on his march to the sea. ***November 30,*** Confederate General Pat Cleburne is killed at the Battle of Franklin, Tennessee. ***December 16,*** General Hood's Confederates are defeated at the Battle of Nashville, Tennessee. ***December 20,*** Confederates evacuate Savannah, Georgia. As the year ends, Federal Armies are poised for military victory and talk of peace is in the wind.

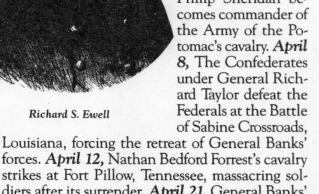

Richard S. Ewell

Nathan Bedford Forrest

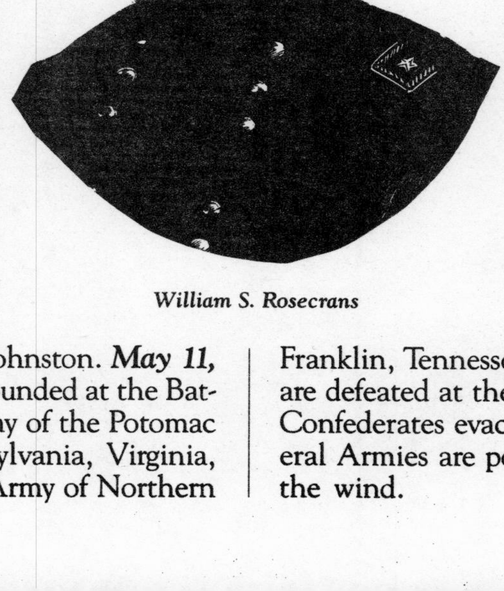

William S. Rosecrans

The Philadelphia Inquirer.

CIRCULATION OVER 60,000. PHILADELPHIA, SATURDAY, MARCH 5, 1864. PRICE TWO CENTS.

THE PHILADELPHIA INQUIRER

GENERAL KILPATRICK.

General BUTLER yesterday sent a telegraphic despatch to the President stating that General KILPATRICK had arrived the day before within the Union lines. He destroyed a large portion of the Virginia Central Railroad. This will prove a most damaging blow to the Rebel army on the Rapidan, as it is over this railroad they draw their supplies from Richmond. This road runs from Gordonsville to Richmond, crossing the Richmond and Fredericksburg Railroad at Hanover Junction. The Virginia Central Road is said to have been destroyed by General KILPATRICK from Beaver Dam to Hanover Junction, a distance of some ten miles. He also destroyed the Richmond and Fredericksburg Railroad from Mattapony Bridge to the Pamunkey River, a distance of some twenty miles. The destruction of these two railroads cuts off LEE's communication with Richmond on anything like a direct line, and cuts off Fredericksburg from Richmond entirely. The only way that LEE can now receive supplies from Richmond by rail is by the circuitous route southward on the Richmond, Danville and Petersburg Railroad, via Lynchburg; thence northward by the Orange and Alexandria road, through Charlottesville and Gordonsville. The distance by this latter route is some two hundred and six miles, while by the former route it was only seventy-six miles. The destruction of these railroads will probably cause LEE to shift his army to other quarters, for the greater convenience of receiving supplies; at all events, it will greatly embarrass and cripple his movements in his present position. General KILPATRICK had some pretty severe skirmishing on his way, it is supposed with WADE HAMPTON's Cavalry. He returned with a less of something less than one hundred and fifty men, which is, however, no trifle; and besides, three Colonels are reported missing—Colonels DAHLGREN, COOK and LITCHFIELD—who are supposed to be prisoners. The effect of General KILPATRICK's movement was to create another panic at Richmond, and rumors were current at Norfolk among Rebel sympathizers, that Richmond was about to be evacuated, but nothing definite, however, was known.

This has been a most brilliant and successful movement, and no doubt accomplished all that was originally intended. The destruction of the railroads will prove a most damaging blow to the Rebels at this juncture, and will place LEE in a comparatively isolated position, where he will have to depend more and more upon his own resources, and fight, in case of a further movement on our side, with the forces he has on hand now.

AFFAIRS IN THE SOUTHWEST.

News from Vicksburg and Nashville, via Cairo, gives us positive information that General SHERMAN occupied Selma. A despatch from Cairo yesterday says that on the 11th General SHERMAN was at a point twelve miles west of Meridian, and that he sent a portion of his force to Selma. This news is said to be official, and, if so, it settles the question as to General SHERMAN's whereabouts at that time, and also his occupation of Selma. The latest advices from the same source are that part of SHERMAN's forces are still at Selma, and that the rest were at Meridian.

Another despatch, yesterday, from Cincinnati, says that a gentleman arrived at Vicksburg, who had just escaped from Mobile, who states that when he left Mobile General SHERMAN was within forty miles of that place, and could easily have taken it if he wanted to. Then, again, a despatch comes from Washington, which says that intelligence has been received there that General SHERMAN had returned back from his extended reconnoissance and that he did not go near Selma, and never intended such a thing. These contradictions are rather perplexing, but we have the comfortable assurance that General SHERMAN is somewhere in the land of cotton, and that he is able to take care of himself.

No further news has been received from General THOMAS' army, or of movements in that quarter. At Chattanooga all is reported quiet in front. News from Knoxville confirms the previous statements that LONGSTREET had left, but for where is not known, but the impression is that he had bid a final adieu to East Tennessee. The Union people were returning to their homes, and preparing to put in their spring crops.

MOVEMENTS OF GENERAL SHERMAN.

CAIRO, March 3.—An officer arrived here to-day, from Vicksburg on the 28th ult., as a bearer of despatches from General SHERMAN, leaving his head-quarters when thirteen miles east of Meridian, on the 11th. He says the enemy numbered only seven or eight thousand men, and were much demoralized. No fighting had occurred after passing Jackson, Miss. General SHERMAN had sent a force to Meridian at that date.

CINCINNATI, March 4.—A despatch from Cairo states that when the steamer *Mississippi*, on her way up the Mississippi, arrived at Vicksburg, a gentleman, formerly the Captain of the steamboat *Scotland*, had just come in from Mobile, having escaped from the Rebels, into whose army he had been conscripted. He says that when he left Mobile, General SHERMAN was within forty miles of that place, and could easily take it if he wanted to. The Mobile papers of the 18th give no later news than has already been published.

WASHINGTON, March 4.—Intelligence has been received here that Gen. SHERMAN is back from his extended reconnoissance. He did not go near Selma, and never intended such a thing.

CAIRO, March 4.—The Fourth Iowa Regiment of Veteran Volunteers have arrived from Nashville, en route for home.

When General SHERMAN was at a point twelve miles west of Meridian, on the 11th, he sent a portion of his force to Selma, and not back to Meridian as reported. Last night's despatches, from which this information is derived, being official, settles the question as to SHERMAN's occupation of Selma. The railroad between Jackson and Meridian has been wholly destroyed. The latest advices are that part of SHERMAN's forces are still at Selma, and the remainder had fallen back to Meridian.

General Butler's Department.

FORTRESS MONROE, March 3.—Rebel General FITZHUGH LEE arrived, this morning, on the Baltimore boat from Fort Lafayette.

The steamer *Scotia*, recently captured while attempting to run the blockade off Wilmington, arrived this afternoon.

Steamer *S. R. Spaulding* arrived from Morehead City yesterday. She reports the following:—

NEWPORT BARRACKS, March 1.—The Quartermaster of Morehead reports heavy firing in front of Newbern. The citizens of Newbern are all arming themselves, and are ready for any emergency.

THE GREAT CAVALRY RAIDS.

Route taken by Kilpatrick in his Grand Dash on Richmond—Scene of Custer's Adroit Diversion in Kilpatrick's favor—Roads and Rivers between the Rapidan and Richmond

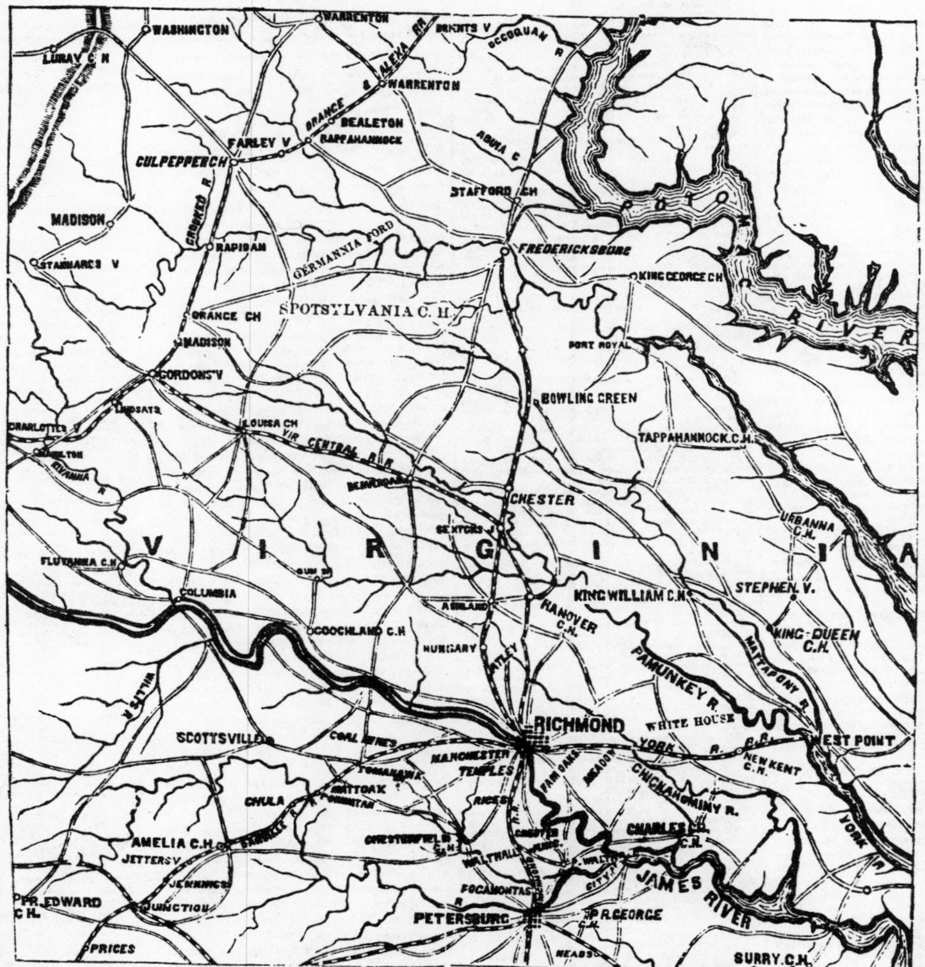

FROM GEN. GRANT'S ARMY.

The Late Movement on Tunnel Hill.

RECONNOISSANCE BY THE FOURTEENTH CORPS.

Heavy Skirmishing at Tunnel Hill.

THE ENEMY IN FORCE AT DALTON.

The Reconnoissance a Great Success.

FULL PARTICULARS OF THE AFFAIR.

Special Correspondence of the Inquirer.

NASHVILLE, Tenn., Feb. 27, 1864.

Our Occupation of Tunnel Hill—Our Assault on Dalton and Our Repulse.

On Saturday last I received a telegram from Mr. CONE, at Chattanooga, that General HOOKER's army was under marching orders, destination supposed to be Knoxville, and that General PALMER's Corps would start south with three days' rations.

I called at General GRANT's head-quarters and ascertained that the latter was true, but that the General would not leave, as the movement was only a heavy reconnoissance to divert the enemy in favor of SHERMAN, and to discover whether the enemy were in force at Dalton.

You will recollect that I had before informed you that the evacuation of Dalton was false, and in the same letter informed you what I had before telegraphed, that the Cumberland Gap road was cut off and abandoned. This latter I received from General FOSTER himself (and everybody knows it now), although the Washington *Republican* pompously denied it.

Well, the movement, as I learn it from Colonel BOWERS, at General GRANT's head-quarters, commenced on Monday morning, and was carried out as follows:—

It was known as early as Friday last that at least two divisions of HARDEE's corps had been sent to Meridian to reinforce Bishop POLK, who had at that place about sixteen thousand men, most of which, however, were raw troops. Prior to this, CHEATHAM's and WALTHAM's Divisions had been sent in the direction of Mobile. The divisions sent to Meridian were STEWART's and ANDERSON's, all four of which belonged to HARDEE's Corps. [There are only two *corps* in JOE JOHNSTON's army, each of which contains six divisions of infantry.]

The movement of the Fourteenth Corps was under the direction of General PALMER in the field, assisted by General WHIPPLE, General THOMAS' Chief of Staff.

The movement commenced early Monday morning General JEFF. DAVIS', General JOHNSTON's and General BAIRD's Divisions participating on the right and direct road to Dalton, and General STANLEY's Division, under the command of General CRUFTS, on the left. This latter division had been encamped in the vicinity of Cleveland for more than three weeks, which is distant from Chattanooga about twenty-four miles. It was to form a junction with the main force at a given place between Ringgold and Tunnel Hill, which was successfully accomplished.

The forces under CRUFTS were preceded by a brigade of cavalry under Colonel LONG, of the Fourth Ohio Cavalry, and the main body, upon the Dalton road, were preceded by a division of cavalry, respective parts of which were under the guidance of those distinguished horsemen and warriors, Colonel BOONE, of the Seventh Kentucky, Colonel HARRISON, formerly of the Thirty-ninth Indiana, and Colonel PALMER, of the Fifteenth Pennsylvania, the latter (the Anderson Cavalry) in advance. [You will recollect that a year or more ago, the men belonging to this gallant regiment, as an earnest of their courage, after their difficulties, stipulated that they should always have the advance].

The advance of the forces on the straight Dalton road passed to the left of the old Chickamauga battle-field, over a high lot of hills known as the Taylor Ridge, and through Ringgold Gap. Here our forces, as at the gaps generally in this country found some Rebel troops—the First Tennessee and First Alabama Cavalry Regiments—who fired a volley and precipitately retired. No one was hurt by this little exhibition of the chivalry, and after a rest the column moved on and occupied the town of Ringgold that night, distant from Chattanooga twenty-three miles.

On Tuesday morning the column moved at daylight, and during the forenoon our and the enemy's cavalry, under the command of General WHEELER, the ablest of the Rebel cavalry Generals, and the lesser scoundrel of the crowd in that department, skirmished continually, with but little loss of life to either party, however, as the Rebels fired but occasionally, but run all the time.

At about eleven o'clock a junction was made by General CRUFTS, although his infantry was nearly two miles to the rear. In a short time his whole force arrived, and the whole corps moved in line of battle, with cavalry in advance and on the flanks, until it reached the vicinity of Tunnel Hill.

On the ridge was a poorly-constructed fort and roughly-built earthworks, and a few men were to be seen therein.

The artillery came up within raking distance, and after the usual precautionary measures the column advanced, as it was evident no Rebel demonstrations would be made.

When, however, our forces were within a half mile of the base of the ridge, the enemy saluted, by a volley from a brigade of Rebel cavalry and shots from four guns. The musketry fire had some effect upon our cavalry, and they fell back, while all four of the first cannon shots, which were shells, burst in the vicinity of the brigade of regulars and Colonel HAMBRIGHT's brigade.

The Rebel battery was manœuvred capitally, and succeeded in killing and wounding several of our men.

In a few moments the Second Minnesota and Ninth Indiana Batteries were thundering away, and after a quarter of an hour's practice, succeeded in dislodging the enemy's guns. Our cavalry made great haste as soon as it was practicable, to endeavor to capture the battery, but when they gained the top of the ridge the battery was posted upon a neighboring crest. [This was General WHEELER's flying artillery, and more dreaded by our artillerists than any other battery in the Rebel service. During General ROSECRANS' advance upon Murfreesboro it brought up the Rebel retreat from Lavergne to the Stone River battle-field, and baffled all attempts at capture.]

The word "Forward!" was again given, and the infantry again advanced, and after a little exercise of climbing gained the top of the ridge. Here was a fine view of the town; time of day 4 P. M. The whole column again moved forward as before, except that the line was extended and the artillery not so much to the rear.

The cavalry, with everything open and clean before them, pursued a crowd of ragamuffins, who were making a precipitate rush for the town. All of a sudden our cavalry were "fetched up a standing," as six guns opened a cross-fire upon them from a gorge in what is known as Rocky Fall, and through which runs the railroad and the Dalton pike road.

The enemy moved up at a double-quick, and the cavalry moved back at the same rate. No working line of battle could be formed, and pluck alone had to be brought into requisition in the contest for the gorge. The enemy had managed to keep up a furious fire of musketry and cannon, and succeeded in holding their position, notwithstanding the brilliant dashes of the cavalry brigades of Gen. MORGAN and DAN MCCOOK.

It was now getting quite dark, which more than anything else, probably, contributed to the successful holding of the gorge by the Rebels. The further advance, therefore, was not attempted Tuesday night.

The next morning our forces, after considerable heavy fighting, marched into the town of Tunnel Hill and captured about a hundred and fifty prisoners.

The next movement was upon Dalton, which is seven miles from Tunnel Hill. The forces crossed the crest early Wednesday morning, and descended through the gaps into the Rocky Fall Valley. Gen. CRUFTS on the left, JOHNSTON on the right, BAIRD on left centre and DAVIS on the right centre.

The country here presents excellent advantages for defense, being diversified with valley and hills, bluffs and cover at all points. During the whole of the forenoon there was lively skirmishing, and as our forces advanced the enemy seemed to be more numerous.

About eleven and a half A. M. our forces were within three miles of Dalton, and considerable heavy fighting was going on. The cavalry especially conducted themselves with marked proofs of bravery and efficiency. General MORGAN's and Colonel DAN. MCCOOK's brigades having lost more men than the balance of the corps.

Our troops advanced cautiously to within two miles of Dalton, when it became evident that preparations were being made by the whole of JOE. JOHNSTON's Army to receive them. A large number of Rebel troops were seen in the distance; considerable activity was perceptible in the interior of the Rebel works; the cavalry began to hover about our flanks, and deserters and prisoners informed General WHIPPLE that all of CLEBURNE's and another division which had left Sunday morning had returned on Tuesday night, which was the object of the reconnoissance.

The diversion, as I said above, was made in favor of SHERMAN, and has resulted in bringing back to Dalton the division of PAT. CLEBURNE, and one other at least. This would still leave STEWART's and ANDERSON's divisions *en route* for Meridian.

The movement was also made to discover whether there was any truth in the evacuation of Dalton, which some green correspondents, from the fact that Colonel BURKE missed the Dalton road, and carried a flag of truce within sight of town, had reported, and stubbornly refused to contradict.

We have all known that divisions of troops left JOHNSTON's army as long ago as the first of the month, but there have been no signs of an evacuation of Dalton whatever, although I do not believe a regular battle will ever take place in that vicinity. When General GRANT gets ready to move I do not believe he will encounter much resistance at Dalton. But time must prove this. No military knowledge, just now, can determine what the Rebels will do in Northern Georgia. General PALMER's Corps is at present at Tunnel Hill, thirty-one miles from Chattanooga.

Our losses in the reconnoissance will not amount, I am informed, to more than three hundred and fifty killed and wounded. Probably the enemy's loss will reach the same number. We lost no prisoners; but took between four and five hundred.

General GRANT is still in this city.

Movements of General Hancock.

BOSTON, March 4.—General HANCOCK visited the State House to-day, and had an interview with the Governor. Subsequently he was informally introduced to the members of the Senate and House of Representatives.

GEN. KILPATRICK WITHIN OUR LINES.

He Did Not Enter Richmond.

RAILROADS AND MILLS DESTROYED.

A Great Panic in the Rebel Capital.

ITS REPORTED EVACUATION.

WASHINGTON, March 3.—The President has received a despatch from General BUTLER, stating that General KILPATRICK yesterday arrived within our lines, with a loss of something less than one hundred and fifty men, having had skirmishes on the way.

Among the missing are Colonels DAHLGREN, COOK and LITCHFIELD. DAHLGREN and COOK are supposed to be prisoners.

KILPATRICK destroyed a large portion of the Virginia Central Railroad, and several mills along the James River, as well as other valuable property. He penetrated to the suburbs or outer fortifications of Richmond.

Another Panic in Richmond.

BALTIMORE, March 4.—We learn from Norfolk that there was some excitement there yesterday among the Rebel sympathizers, who profess to have intelligence of a great scare at Richmond, owing to KILPATRICK's movements in the neighborhood of the city. It was generally understood that a force had been sent up by BUTLER to co-operate with KILPATRICK, but nothing has been heard from this force at the time the boat left last evening.

INTERERSTING FROM WASHINGTON.

[SPECIAL DESPATCHES TO THE INQUIRER.]

WASHINGTON, March 4, 1864.

Petition of the New Orleans Creoles.

A delegation of French Creoles from New Orleans, called on the President, to-day, and presented a petition signed by one thousand free colored citizens of New Orleans, asking that the rights of citizenship guaranteed to them by the French, when Louisiana was ceded to the United States, should be given to them in the new organization. Among the petitioners is MAXIMILIAN BRULEL, Lieutenant under NAPOLEON BONAPARTE, and three of his men, who also fought under General JACKSON. These petitioners have always been loyal and reliable, and now ask the President to give them the rights of which they have been deprived, some of them for sixty years. He promised to consider the subject.

General Meade's Movements.

General MEADE, with his personal staff, Captain MEADE and Captain BACHE, arrived this morning from the army, and has spent most of the day with the President and the Secretary of War. The result of his conference is not known positively, but appearances indicate that he will not be interfered with in his command.

The President and Kilpatrick.

The President remarked to-day that he finally gave his consent to KILPATRICK to make his raid; he was willing that he should try, although all the rest pronounced the scheme impracticable.

Destruction of a Bridge by Kilpatrick.

Information was brought in to-day by a Rebel deserter that KILPATRICK had burned the railroad bridge near Hanover Court House, over South Anna River.

Increase of Taxation.

Secretary CHASE urged upon the Committee of Ways and Means to take speedy action upon the tax bill, as time is rapidly passing away, and the revenue is far below what is absolutely necessary to meet our rapidly increasing expenses.

Crude and refined oils, tobacco in leaf and manufactured, spirits of all kinds, and other articles, must have a largely increased tax put upon them at once.

Seeking to be Reinstated.

GEORGE HARRINGTON, who left the Treasury Department last summer, at the invitation of Secretary CHASE, is in town, and rumor has it, is being pressed by his friends for some position in the same Department.

G. A. HENDERSON, who was arrested for having levied black mail upon persons having warrants to be passed, is also trying to get reinstated.

Resolution of Thanks to Generals Rosecrans and Thomas.

The House Military Committee to-day agreed to include the name of General ROSECRANS in the resolution of thanks to General THOMAS and the men of his command, for his conduct at Chickamauga.

Prize Steamer Sold.

The prize steamer *Ceres* was sold at auction at the Navy Yard to-day, by the United States Marshal, for seventeen thousand three hundred dollars. THOMAS CLYDE, of Philadelphia, was the purchaser.

The Sleeper-Rice Contested Case.

Owing to the contested election case of SLEEPER vs. RICE, coming up to-day, the House did not reach the gold bill, and as no business will be done to-morrow, it will not come up before Monday. If SLEEPER had any chance of getting a seat his own speech lost him that, and Mr. RICE was complimented by nearly a unanimous vote in his favor.

The Fighting near Norfolk.

Special Despatch to the Inquirer.

NORFOLK, Va., March 3.—The Rebels, in order to protect themselves in other localities, are endeavoring to divert our attention by making a demonstration on our front, which we, as well as they, know full well is nothing but a feint. Night before last a collision occurred between the Rebels, under General RAINS, and our troops, at Deep Creek. The Secesh, though in greatly superior numbers, retired after finding that they could not accomplish anything. Our brave soldiers are ever on the alert, and it takes more than the ingenuity possessed by General RAINS and his deluded followers to entrap them.

This morning the steamer *John Tucker* arrived here heavily laden with freed colored people from St. Mary's county, Md. Of those aboard one hundred and fifty were able-bodied men who have enlisted in our army. The remainder consisted of women, children and decrepid old men, to the number of four hundred, who will be properly provided for.

From Colorado and Kansas.

ST. LOUIS, March 4.—The Legislature of Colorado and many leading citizens of that Territory, have petitioned General CURTIS to retain Colonel CHAVINGTON in command, instead of General EWING, who has been assigned to that District. The Legislature of Kansas adjourned on the 1st inst.

Meetings continue to be held in all parts of the State, denouncing the late senatorial election.

From California.

SAN FRANCISCO, March 4.—Arrived, ship *William Chamberlain*, from New York. The dry weather has induced considerable speculation in breadstuffs. Offerings are made at $1.80@1.90 per hundred lbs. for wheat.

The sudden and unexpected death of the Rev. THOMAS STARR KING to-day at once surprised and saddened the whole community. Business was nearly suspended. The Courts adjourned and the public offices were closed, and flags placed at half-mast on every flag-staff, including those on every church.

It is universally conceded that no man ever did so much towards making California loyal; while his untiring zeal in forwarding every benevolent enterprise made him generally beloved.

The New-York Times.

VOL. XIII—NO. 3895. NEW-YORK, FRIDAY, MARCH 18, 1864. PRICE THREE CENTS.

GEN. GRANT IN COMMAND.

His Official Order Announcing the Fact.

Present Headquarters to be with the Army of the Potomac.

Departure of the General from Nashville for the East.

General Sherman Assumes Command at Nashville.

NASHVILLE, Thursday, March 17.

Gen. GRANT formally assumed the command of the armies of the United States to-day. The following is his order on the subject:

HEADQUARTERS OF THE ARMIES OF THE UNITED STATES, NASHVILLE, Tenn., March 17, 1864.

GENERAL ORDERS, No. 12.—In pursuance of the following order of the President:

EXECUTIVE MANSION, WASHINGTON, D. C., March 10, 1864.—Under the authority of the Act of Congress to appoint the grade of Lieutenant-General in the army, of February 29, 1864, Lieutenant-General ULYSSES S. GRANT, U. S. A., is appointed to the command of the armies of the United States.

(Signed) ABRAHAM LINCOLN.

—I assume command of the armies of the United States. Headquarters will be in the field, and, until further orders, will be with the Army of the Potomac. There will be an office headquarters in Washington, D. C., to which all official communications will be sent, except those from the army where the headquarters are at the date of their address.

(Signed,) U. S. GRANT, Lieutenant-General,

NASHVILLE, Thursday, March 17.

Gen. GRANT leaves for Washington on Saturday, and repairs immediately to the front.

His staff is composed of the officers formerly with him in the military division of the Mississippi. Among them are Brig.-Gen. RAWLINGS, Chief of Staff; Lieut.-Col. BOWERS, Capt. G. K. LEET, Capt. E. S. PARKER, Assistant Adjutant-General; Capt. H. W. JONES, Assistant Quartermaster-General, and Capt. BALLAN. Lieut.-Col. DUFF, late Chief of Artillery, goes as senior aide-de-camp.

Gen. SHERMAN is due here to-night, and will assume command of this military division.

Gen. DODGE is in the city.

NEWS FROM WASHINGTON.

SPECIAL DISPATCHES TO THE N. Y. TIMES

WASHINGTON, Thursday, March 17.

REPORTED RAID BY STUART.

There is some excitement in military circles, to-night, about the reported raid by STUART. He crossed at Fredericksburgh last night, with a force estimated at five thousand men. KILPATRICK and MERRITT are on his track.

THE SHELLING OF CHARLESTON AND THE FLORIDA EXPEDITION.

Gen. GILMORE's Chief of Staff arrived to-day with dispatches. He states that the City of Charleston is nearly all demolished. But one portion of it is occupied, and that only by troops. The Committee on the Conduct of the War, learning this officer was in the city, summoned him before them to testify in reference to the Florida affair. He gave a detailed account of the expedition, its objects and purposes. It was partly political, and partly for the purpose of destroying or capturing supplies of the enemy, in the shape of cattle and corn, which were on their way from Florida to the rebel army. The committee have not received the orders originating the expedition, and cannot tell whether they emanated from here or not. The officer examined to-day is not clear on that subject.

SHERMAN'S EXPEDITION.

A letter received to-day by a prominent citizen, from Gen. SHERMAN, gives some particulars of the late raid in Alabama. When the command returned, the Vicksburgh train was ten miles in length, and composed of negroes, horses and mules, and provisions in wagons, on horses and mules. In the section of country traversed everything of use to the enemy was destroyed. There was found to be no lack of supplies among the people, and in one day's foraging sufficient could be obtained for horses and men to last two days. Gen. SHERMAN could have taken Mobile had he known Commodore FARRAGUT was near the place to coöperate. The people, as well as rebel authorities, civil and military, were panic-stricken, and rendered unable to offer any formidable resistance. This raid, in every respect, was a complete success, and one from the effects of which the enemy cannot fully recover.

THE INTERNAL REVENUE.

It is understood that the Sub-Committee of Ways and Means have concluded their labors on the Internal Revenue Bill. The tax upon tobacco is not as heavy as was anticipated; no tax is put on leaf, and none on crude petroleum; twenty cents will be reported on refined. The additional tax on whisky has not yet been determined, but the recommendations of Secretary CHASE and Commissioner LEWIS of one dollar, from July, will probably be adopted. The tax on malt will be not less than thirty cents.

THE WILKES COURT-MARTIAL.

Commodore BALDWIN was cross-examined to-day before the Wilkes Court-Martial, and testified that the *Vanderbilt* being at anchor fifty days was caused by coaling and other necessary detentions. He did not mean to say she was idle. It was true that when the Admiral visited Laguayra, the American Minister had withdrawn his credentials, and the President had refused to hold interviews with him.

THE PRISONERS AT RICHMOND.

Capt. SAWYER, of the First New-Jersey Cavalry, who has just returned from Richmond, reports that he saw, on Monday last, Lieut.-Col. LITCHFIELD, Maj. COOK, Dr. KINSTON and three officers of a negro regiment, in one cell, chained to six negroes. The prisoners are fed upon corn bread and water, and have a limited supply even of that.

OCEAN NAVIGATION.

The House Commerce Committee to-day authorized Gen. WARD to prepare a bill looking to the establishment of a line of steamers between New-York and Southampton. The Committee is favorable to granting all aid necessary to place the new line on a permanent basis for promoting commerce.

THE HAVANA CONSULATE.

The Senate committee will report adversely on the nomination of HORATIO BALLARD, Consul at Havana; but his confirmation will probably be carried through the Senate.

THE WEST POINT BILL.

The Ways and Means Committee, accepting all the Senate's amendments to the West Point Bill, added a new one, providing one additional cadet from each Congressional District for the coming year.

AN UNFOUNDED REPORT.

The report that Senator POMEROY had made no account of the Colonization funds is unfounded. The whole amount was only $25,000; $14,000 was paid over on Mr. LINCOLN's order in favor of the Chiriqui land contract. More than $8,000 were paid over to the Treasury, leaving less than $3,000 to be expended by him in procuring outfit for colonists and incidental expenses.

COMMANDER OF DRAFTED MEN.

The Secretary of War has issued an order rescinding the authority to Governors to appoint Commandants for rendezvous for drafted men.

TRANSFER OF GEN. KILPATRICK.

There is a rumor to the effect that Gen. KILPATRICK will soon be transferred to another Department, and will have an important command.

DISPATCHES TO THE ASSOCIATED PRESS.

WASHINGTON, Thursday, March 17.

COLLISION ON THE POTOMAC.

The *Star* has the following: "The United States steamer *Harvest Moon*, Vol.-Lieut. WARREN, arrived at the Navy-yard this morning from Fortress Monroe, bringing up Admiral DAHLGREN, returning from an unsuccessful attempt to procure the body of his son. On the way up a collision occurred between the *Harvest Moon* and an unknown schooner twelve miles below Smith's Point, at four o'clock yesterday morning. When first discovered, the schooner was crossing the bows of the steamer. The latter's bow was stove in near the water line. The water immediately began to enter, and in about an hour the fire room floor was covered to the depth of several inches.

It being dark at the time, and a heavy sea running, the steamer could not stop to ascertain what damage was done to the schooner, which was soon lost sight of. The damage to the steamer rendered it necessary that every effort should be made to keep her afloat. All hands were promptly called out and got to work. During the first hour it is estimated that 16,000 gallons of water were thrown out by the pumps. Admiral DAHLGREN superintended the stoppage of the leak, and the pumps being kept constantly at work, the steamer was brought safely to the Navy-yard."

THE BLOCKADE IN THE GULF.

Rear Admiral FARRAGUT, commanding the West Gulf Blockading Squadron, reports to the Navy Department the following captures:

On the 20th of February, the United States schooner *Virginia* captured the schooner *Henry Colthwist*, near San Luis Pass. The *Colthwist* was from Kingston, Jamaica, with a cargo of 200 kegs of powder, 250,000 percussion caps, 500 ounces of quinine, and also some coffee, hardware, and dry goods.

On the 28th of February, the English schooner *Lilly*, when about eight miles from Velasco, Texas, was captured by the *Penobscot*. The *Lilly* was from Belize, Honduras, registered 43 tons, and had a cargo consisting in part of powder.

On the 29th of February, the schooners *Stingray* and *John Douglas*, when off Velasco, Texas, were captured by the *Penobscot*. The *Stingray* had a cargo of 60 bales of cotton and 52 half bales. The *John Douglass* had 100 bales.

The schooner *Camille* was captured, and a sloop was burned by the *Virginia*. Both vessels were cotton laden.

CHIEF JUSTICE TANEY'S EIGHTY-SEVENTH BIRTHDAY.

The Justices and Officers of the Supreme Court called on Chief Justice TANEY to-day and paid their respects, this being his eighty-seventh birthday.

OFFICERS VISITING WASHINGTON.

More care is hereafter to be observed in granting leaves of absence or permission for army officers to visit Washington. They are now required to address for the purpose Maj.-Gen. HALLECK, and must specify the business for which they desire the permission.

PROCEEDINGS OF CONGRESS.

SENATE.

WASHINGTON, Thursday, March 17.

BOUNTIES TO DISCHARGED SOLDIERS.

The Vice-President presented a petition of soldiers, praying for the allowance of the bounty under the Act of March, 1863, of $100 to soldiers discharged from the service on account of wounds or diseases contracted in the service. Referred to the Committee on Military Affairs.

EXPEDITION TO EASTERN ASIA.

Mr. FOSTER presented a memorial from the American Oriental Society in favor of Surgeon MAGOWAN's proposed expedition to countries in Eastern Asia. Referred to the Committee on Foreign Relations.

THE GOODYEAR PATENT.

Mr. WILSON, of Massachusetts, (Union,) presented the petition of 400 laboring men of New-York, remonstrating against the extension of the Goodyear patent.

PROPOSED ABOLISHMENT OF SECRET EXECUTIVE SESSIONS.

Mr. GRIMES, of Iowa, (Union,) submitted a draft of a proposed new rule of the Senate. "All executive nominations shall be submitted to and considered and decided by the Senate in open session."

THE MESSAGE AND DOCUMENTS.

Mr. TRUMBULL, of Illinois, (Union,) moved to print 5,000 copies additional of the Annual Message, with the accompanying documents. Referred to the Committee on Printing.

THE ECUADOR CLAIM CONVENTION.

Mr. SUMNER, of Massachusetts, (Union,) reported a bill to carry into effect the Convention with Ecuador for the mutual adjustment of claims.

By this bill, the Commissioner appointed to carry the Convention into effect, is allowed as compensation a salary of $3,000 and $10 per day for traveling expenses during the actual time of transit. If the President chooses to appoint him the Minister Resident, an increase of 50 per cent upon his salary.

SUMMARY TRIALS.

Mr. TRUMBULL, of Illinois, (Union,) called up the bill to provide for the summary trial of minor offences, which was passed without debate.

THE ANTHONY BURNS RESCUE.

Mr. DAVIS, of Kentucky, (Union,) called up the resolution of inquiry into the part taken by Col. HIGGINSON in the rescue of the fugitive ANTHONY BURNS, and read from the published history of the case extracts showing, as he thought, treason and murder on the part of said HIGGINSON.

On motion of Mr. TRUMBULL, the resolution was tabled, yeas 29, nays 20.

NAYS—Messrs. Buckalew, Carlile, Conness, Davis, Hendricks, Johnson, McDougal, Powell, Riddle and Saulsbury.

DISTRICT OF COLUMBIA MATTERS.

The bill to incorporate the Metropolitan Railroad Company of the District of Columbia came up in order, the pending amendment being that of Mr. SUMNER, providing that no person be excluded from the cars on account of color.

The amendment was opposed by Messrs. JOHNSON, SAULSBURY, CARLISLE and DOOLITTLE, and favored by Messrs. SUMNER and MORRILL.

The amendment was adopted—ayes, 19; nays, 17. The nays are as follows:

Messrs. Buckalew, Carlile, Davis, Doolittle, Harding, Harris, Hendricks, Johnson, Lane of Indiana, Powell, Riddle, Saulsbury, Sherman, Ten Eyck, Trumbull, Van Winkle, Willey.

The bill then passed.

KANSAS IMPROVEMENTS.

Mr. LANE, of Kansas, (Union,) introduced a bill providing for the erection of a court-house and post-office at Topeka. Referred to the Committee on Commerce.

THE PAY OF CHAPLAINS.

Mr. FOSTER, of Connecticut, (Union,) called up the House bill defining the pay and emoluments of Chaplains, which after an amendment, allowing them pay when absent on leave or on account of disability from service or in prison, was passed.

The Senate at 4:30 adjourned.

HOUSE OF REPRESENTATIVES.

WASHINGTON, Thursday, March 17.

THE PACIFIC RAILROAD.

Mr. BOYD, of Missouri, (Dem.,) introduced a bill to complete the Southwest Branch of the Pacific Railroad from Rolla to Springfield, Mo., asking the Government to refund the tariff on freight carried over said road since 1861 for Government purposes. Referred.

POSTPONEMENT OF THE GENERAL OFFICERS' BILL.

On motion of Mr. ASHLEY, of Ohio, (Union,) the House, by 20 majority, postponed for three weeks the joint resolution to drop from the rolls of the army unemployed general officers.

INCREASED RAILROAD FACILITIES.

The House proceeded to the consideration of the Bill declaring the railroad of the Camden and Atlantic Railroad Company, and the branches thereof built and to be built, and the railroad of the Raritan and Delaware Bay Railroad Company, and the branches thereof built and to be built, to be lawful structures and public highways of the United States, to be used as a continuous line between Philadelphia and New-York for postal and military purposes.

Mr. DEMING, of Connecticut, (Union,) explained the provisions of the bill, stating that the petitioners, viz.: the Raritan and Delaware Bay Company, that their roads and boats may be declared post and military roads. They state that, by means of these, there is a continuous through line between the Cities of New-York and Philadelphia. The Committee find that, after the battle of Antietam, (?) when a universal panic pervaded the country, and our interests were imperiled, this line carried from New-York to Philadelphia over 17,400 men, 649 horses, and more than 800,000 pounds of freight, under the orders of the Government. Both the Government and the public require constant and prompt means of communication, and anything which prevents this is a prohibition which ought not to be tolerated. He briefly argued the constitutional power to grant the relief prayed, and said the bill was the unanimous report of the Committee on Military Affairs.

Mr. DEMING moved the previous question.

Mr. RODGERS, of New-Jersey, (Dem.,) hoped that time would be afforded for discussion on the measure, so seriously affecting the interests of that State.

Mr. PRUYN, of New-York, (Dem.,) said that to pass such an important bill with only one hour's debate, would be an act of tyrannic power.

Mr. DEMING wanted to know whether that remark applied to him.

Mr. PRUYN replied that his remark was general, and not personal.

The morning hour here expired, and the further consideration of the subject goes over until Tuesday next.

THE ECUADOR CLAIM CONVENTION.

Mr. COX, of Ohio, (Dem.,) from the Committee on Foreign Affairs, reported a bill to carry into effect the convention between the United States and Ecuador for the mutual adjustment of claims.

It was passed, and provides for the appointment of a Commissioner, fixing his compensation at $3,500, together with the incidental expenses.

TERRITORIAL AFFAIRS.

The House then proceeded to the consideration of the special order, namely, business relating to the Territories.

The first bill was from the Senate, enabling the people of Nevada to form a Constitution and State Government, and providing for the admission of Nevada into the Union on an equal footing with the original States.

The bill was read and passed without debate.

The next Senate bill was taken up, enabling Colorado to form a Constitution and State Government preliminary to her admission into the Union on an equal footing with the original States.

Mr. PENDLETON, of Ohio, (Dem.) wanted the bill referred to the Committee of the Whole on the State of the Union for discussion.

Mr. ASHLEY, of Ohio, (Union) objected, saying that a similar bill had heretofore passed the House, and this one had passed the Senate.

Mr. COX remarked he had not had an opportunity to examine the bill, and would like to offer an amendment providing that the State be not admitted until Congress is satisfied that she has a population equal to that required for the election of a member of the House according to the Federal ratio under the last census.

Mr. ASHLEY replied that the population of Colorado was larger than that of Oregon to-day.

Mr. COX did not dispute that; but desired the insertion of a sound principle. He scarcely need ask whether by the provisions of this bill Slavery was excluded.

Mr. MALLORY, of Kentucky, (Dem.,) remarked that it had been said on the Republican side that Slavery was dead. If so, why prohibit its existence in Colorado and the other Territory?

Mr. STEVENS, of Pennsylvania, (Union,) in his seat—We want to bury it. [Laughter.]

Mr. ASHLEY said he never made the remark that Slavery was dead. If his colleague (Mr. COX) wanted an opportunity to offer an amendment establishing Slavery, he would have no objection to giving him that opportunity.

Mr. COX replied that his colleague knew that he had never proposed either to establish or prohibit Slavery, but to leave the decision of that question to the people themselves. The remark did not come with a good grace from that quarter, considering the antecedents of his colleague.

Mr. MALLORY moved to strike out that part of the bill prohibiting Slavery, so as to leave Congress uncommitted on the subject. He subsequently asked leave to withdraw the amendment, but the Speaker (COLFAX) decided that this could not be done, as the "previous question" had been seconded on the passage of the bill.

The House then voted on Mr. MALLORY's amendment, which was rejected by yeas 18, namely:

YEAS—Messrs. J. C. Allen, Ancona, Chanler, Cox, Dawson, Dennison, Eldridge, Hall, Harding, Knapp, Long, Mallory, Miller of Pennsylvania, Morrison, O'Neill of Ohio, Randall of Pennsylvania, Ross and Stiles.

The nays were 87.

The Colorado bill was then passed.

Mr. ASHLEY, from the Committee on Territories, reported the House bill enabling Nebraska to form a Constitution and State Government as preliminary to admission into the Union.

Mr. COX offered an amendment requiring Congress to be satisfied that Nebraska had sufficient population according to the Federal rates for the election of a member of the House.

The amendment was rejected—43 against 72.

The bill then passed.

The above enabling bills for Nevada, Colorado and Nebraska require each an election of delegates to a convention which shall submit a Constitution agreed upon to the people for their ratification or rejection, to be held on the second Tuesday of October. The Constitution shall be republican, and not repugnant to the Constitution of the United States and the principles of the Declaration of Independence. Slavery shall be prohibited therein by an ordinance forever irrevocable without consent of Congress. When the Constitution is ratified by the people, the President is to declare by proclamation the admission of these States on an equal footing with the original States, each of which is to be entitled to one member of the House until the next appointment, and two Senators in the Congress of the United States.

Mr. BEAMAN, of Michigan, (Union,) from the Committee on Territories, reported the bill organizing the Territorial Government of Montana. He explained that it proposed to divide Idaho, appropriating the southern portion of the new territory. Seventeen thousand of the inhabitants of Idaho have to travel seven hundred miles to reach the courts. The Committee proposed to make the dividing line the Rocky and Bitter Root Mountains, which could not be crossed for at least six months in the year. In reply to a question of Mr. SPAULDING, he said the Legislature of Idaho had asked for such division, and argued that it would be economical to create other territorial Governments, both for the protection of the citizens, which is the highest duty of the Government, and the quieting of Indian troubles.

Mr. COX suggested that the name of Montano be changed for an Indian name.

Mr. WASHBURNE, of Illinois, (Union,) suggested to the gentleman the name of Abyssinia. [Laughter.]

Mr. COX would propose the name of Douglas.

Mr. STEVENS, of Pennsylvania, (Union,) in his seat, suggested Fred. Douglass. [Laughter.]

Mr. COX thought the name of Douglass would suit both sides of the House, as the Republicans have a black DOUGLASS, and the other side a white DOUGLASS, whom they reverence.

The bill providing a temporary Government for Montano was then passed.

The House went into Committee of the Whole on the state of the Union on the bill appropriating $240,000 for public buildings in the several territories.

Mr. KENNEY, delegate from Utah, argued that territorial Governments, as now constituted, are not republican in character, and hence he insisted that the territories should be admitted as States as soon as practicable, to remove unconstitutional objections. He referred to the history and settlement of Utah, speaking of the patient spirit of the people under persecution, of their patriotism and of their wonderful achievements. He advocated the admission of Utah into the Union as a State, and asked for justice and equality.

Without further proceedings on the bill the committee rose, and the House at 5 o'clock adjourned.

ARMY OF THE POTOMAC.

Review of the Third Corps—Arrival of Escaped Prisoners—Winter Gayety still Prevalent—Injury to Gen. Custer.

HEADQUARTERS ARMY OF THE POTOMAC, Thursday, March 17.

The Third Corps was reviewed yesterday by Gen. FRENCH. It is the largest corps in the army. It presented a fine spectacle. Gens. SEDGWICK, CARR, ROBINSON and others were present, beside a large number of spectators from all departments, and ladies on horseback and in ambulances.

Some prisoners escaped from Richmond came into our lines yesterday. One of them was a scout of Gen. BUTLER's, who so adroitly managed to deceive the enemy as to obtain an opportunity to leave the rebel dominions.

A grand ball was given last night at the headquarters of Gen. BARTLETT's Division, of the Fifth Corps, near Rappahannock Station. A large number of ladies from Washington came down on special trains.

To-day the Irish Brigade celebrated St. Patrick's Day.

It is reported that Gen. CUSTER has been thrown from his horse and injured; to what extent is not yet known.

FRANCE AND THE UNITED STATES.

Rebel Vessels in French Ports—The Case of the Rappahannock.

The French Goverment to be Held Responsible for All the Damage She May Do—A Written Notification Served Upon the Emperor by Mr. Dayton.

From Our Own Correspondent.

PARIS, Tuesday, March 1.

The French Government, tired of the annoyances caused by the presence of Confederate ships in French ports, has announced, as its law of action, the same regulations as those published two or three months ago by the English Government. These new regulations are more stringent than the original neutrality proclamation, and tend to diminish and simplify the contestations between the two Governments. Among other things specified in these regulations, are two, to the effect that no vessel of either of the belligerents can remain in port more than twenty-four hours, unless by stress of weather or for necessary repairs, and that no vessel can return to a French port after leaving it, in a less time than three months. These rules the French Government hope will lessen the inducement for making of its ports a harbor of refuge on all occasions.

The *Rappahannock* has furnished a fruitful example of the nature of the annoyances these vessels are liable to provoke. In the first place, her Commander, Capt. CAMPBELL, declares that she broke some part of her machinery at sea, and drifted or was blown into Calais, which circumstance gives her the benefit of the stress of weather clause, and the contrary cannot be proved. But evidence has been obtained from England, that when the vessel escaped from Sheerness she was not in a fit condition to go to sea, as for example, among other things, that the masts were not stayed, and upon this very strong point it is urged that the French Government ought not to allow her to leave port as a Confederate vessel. Again, it was objected by the American Minister, that the packages sent to the vessel from England ought not to be permitted to go on board; but this objection was overruled by the French Government, on the ground that a part of the material in the packages was for the repair of the real or pretended accident to the machinery of the ship, and the rest insignificant and more or less superfluous articles for the furnishing of the cabin and kitchen. And again, a serious discussion has arisen in regard to the crew of the vessel, and into which the English Government has been drawn. Several crews, surreptitiously recruited in England by Confederate agents, have deserted, after arriving at Calais and learning the true situation of affairs, and Capt. CAMPBELL applied to the police authorities of the town to aid him in preventing these desertions. This circumstance brought Lord COWLEY, the English Ambassador at Paris, into the affair, so that the fight has now become a triangular one and bids fair also to become an interesting one. Calais, it will be understood, offers great advantages for desertion, since it is the port from which the English mail boats start twice a day to cross the channel, and a sailor once on board of one of these vessels is safe. For this reason, and to put a stop to a discussion which was annoying and irritating to all parties, the commander of the *Rappahannock* asked the privilege of transferring his vessel to Cherbourg or Brest, from which ports there is no ready way of escape to England; but as the matter of desertion was no business of the French Government, the request was very naturally refused. At present the number of sailors on board the vessel can hardly exceed half a dozen.

The American Minister at Paris has collected enough evidence in regard to the *Rappahannock*, to satisfy him that this vessel, if allowed to go to sea, ought, by every fair construction of international law, to stand in the same relation to the French Government as the *Alabama* and *Florida* do to the English Government, *and he has therefore given written notice to the French Government that it will be held responsible for all the damage she may do to American commerce.*

This official notice of the American Minister at once gave an increased gravity to the affair, and the Emperor, whose attention had been specially called to the subject, assured the American Minister, in a lengthy conversation, that the international law, whatever it should prove to be, should be stringently executed. His Majesty, in fact, could promise no less than this; for, since he sets himself up as an arbitrator in the world's affairs, he could not allow to go upon the record a precedent which would prove so prolific of trouble in the future as this one certainly would.

Thus, at the present moment the prospect is, that the *Rappahannock* will not be allowed to go to sea. But I have already made this statement, as also the contrary statement that she would be allowed to go out, and these opposite statements were true at the time of making them, for the chances have varied according to the evidences brought to light. At present, as I have said, the prospect is that the vessel will be retained, but international law is not construed in all countries alike, and the law counselors of the French Government may find some technicality we have not yet dreamed of across the Atlantic.

I believe I have not yet said that the *Rappahannock* is expected to meet at sea, if she gets out, a British vessel containing the armament necessary to complete her as a first-class privateer, and thus we will have another example of the new code set up by the rebels: that of imparting to vessels their nationality and distinctive character on the high sea instead of in port, as heretofore.

Messrs. ARMAN & VORUZ, the builders of the six Confederate vessels at Bordeaux and Nantes, have given their word to the French Government that these vessels shall not pass into the hands of the Confederates. One or more of the vessels are ready to launch.

The two supplementary elections for vacant districts at Paris are ordered by the Government for the 20th and 21st days of May. We will probably know this week who are to be the candidates. The democratic nominating committee consists of the Paris deputation in the Corps Legislatif and the three liberal editors who are not deputies.

At present there is little hope of arranging the dispute in the north of Europe. The German Powers declare that they cannot treat till Denmark abandons the part of the Duchy of Schleswig she still holds; and Denmark on her side declares that she cannot treat till the German troops evacuate the part of Schleswig they hold. And there they stand. The result is that there will be no conference, and that as soon as the weather permits the fighting will recommence.

The Emperor NAPOLEON, who has always declared that the civilization of Mexico was to be the "big thing" of his reign, appears yet to cling to this singular hallucination, as is shown by the decree just published, naming a scientific commission for the exploration of that country, and the accompanying report of the Minister of Public Instruction, M. DURUY. A commission of the same kind, says M. DURUY, was named under the first Empire to explore Egypt after its conquest by BONAPARTE, and rendered important services to commerce, science and literature, and a commission for conquered and benighted Mexico will probably have the same result. It is expected that M. MICHEL CHEVALLIER will be chairman and chief actor in this learned commission, and that the labor required will extend over several years. MALAKOFF.

FOREIGN NEWS.

Arrival of the Edinburgh—Miscellaneous English News—The Conference Rejected by Denmark.

The Inman steamer *Edinburgh*, from Liverpool March 2, via Queenstown March 3, arrived yesterday morning. Her dates are not so late by two days as those received, via Halifax, by the *Arabia*, but we have the following interesting items:

The Liverpool *Daily Post* strongly denounces the tenor of Mr. SALA's correspondence from America to the London *Daily Telegraph*, and charges him with prejudiced and unfounded assertions.

The first half-yearly drawing for the redemption of the rebel cotton loan at par took place on 1st March, and the numbers are published of 185 bonds, representing £71,300, being one-fortieth of £2,840,500, the amount of the loan unredeemed by cotton.

The English Board of Trade had presented to Capt. CUTTING, of the American ship *Adelaide*, a valuable binocular telescope, for having rescued the captain and crew of the ship *Polynesia*, of Liverpool, in December last.

The Berlingske *Tidende* semi-officially denies the Danish acceptance of the conference, and says should the basis of the conference be the political union of Schleswig-Holstein, the Danish Government will not accept the proposal.

The Galway *Gazette* says: "The directors of the Atlantic Mail Company have applied to the Post-office authorities for permission to discontinue the mail service via Galway until June next. They have also intimated their intention of entering into negotiations with another company for the use of steamers to commence the service at that time, as the ships of the company will not be in readiness to sail even then. The directors are reported to be of opinion that they can never carry out the contract with the ships at present in their possession; and will, in all probability, endeavor to effect a sale of their interest in the project, with a transfer of the mail subsidy to some existing company more capable of carrying out the project than they are. Two or three companies are said to be in negotiation with the Atlantic Company on the subject at present."

The *United Service Gazette* says:

"The Admiralty have sent persons to examine Mr. LAIRD's steam rams, and find out the thickness of the iron plates, what guns they will mount, etc. It is believed that this is with a view to buying them for the Government. The one that is all but finished is splendidly put together, and has two turrets on Capt. COLE's plan, to mount two guns each, and is plated with 4½-inch iron, with iron deck and iron masts. All the cabin fittings are up, coal on board, and she is in all respects ready for sea, except a little more work to the turrets and the guns putting in."

The *Railway News* has this paragraph:

"We understand that Government have granted the commission of a right of way through British Columbia for an electric telegraph, to connect the existing United States lines with those to be extended from Russia across Behring's Straits, a commission for the latter portion of this world-girdle telegraph having previously been given by the Russian Government to Mr. COLLINS, an American citizen. By the completion of these lines communication between this country and America will be established, without encountering the risks of a submarine cable across the Atlantic."

According to the *Memorial Diplomatique*, the Italian Government were very anxious to have a war between England and Germany. They offered, says the *Memorial*, to let the Cabinet of London have forty thousand men and all their fleet, if Great Britain would join with Sweden and Denmark in a war against Prussia and Austria. The *Memorial* "affirms" that this was the case; but the intelligence is, nevertheless, open to grave doubts.

EASTERN MARKETS.

CALCUTTA, Monday, Feb. 8.

Seven lbs. Shirtings, 10 rupees 40s.; mule twist, 12½ annas. Exchange on London 2s. 1⅜d.

BOMBAY, Monday, Feb. 8.

Cotton Dhollerah, 620 rs. Piece goods 7 lbs. 9r. 12a. Twist 23as. Exchange on London 2s.@⅞d.

CANTON, Friday, Feb. 26.

Grey Shirtings unchanged. Water twist quiet. Tea unchanged. Exchange on London 5⅛d. Freights unchanged.

SHANGHAI, Thursday, Jan. 21.

Shirtings declined. Tea unchanged. Exchange on London 7s. 2d. Freights improving.

THE WAR IN TENNESSEE.

A Freight Train Attacked by Guerrillas near Nashville—The Rebels Moving their Artillery from Dalton to Ringgold—The Rebels in Large Force.

LOUISVILLE, Ky., Thursday, March 17.

Special dispatches to the *Journal* say:

"Guerrillas attacked a freight train from Nashville, near Estelle Springs, on the night of the 16th inst., after displacing a rail by which the train was thrown of the track. The train was burned. Capt. BEARDSLEY, of the One Hundred and Twenty-third New-York, and seven men, arrived at Decherd, Tenn., on a hand car, having been paroled after being stripped of their clothing, money, watches and jewelry.

The rebels killed three of the negroes on the train. Two of the guerrillas were killed. There were no other losses.

The rebels are moving their artillery from Dalton toward Ringgold.

Taylor's Ridge Gap was picketed by rebel cavalry on the 15th inst.

We drive the rebels off one day, but they return the next.

The rebels have a large force of infantry, cavalry and artillery."

Movement for a Separate State Organization in Tennessee.

KNOXVILLE, Tenn., Wednesday, March 16.

The Executive Committee of the Knoxville "Grunville" Convention of 1861 met here to-day and adopted measures to reassemble the convention on the 12th of April.

The movement looks to a separate State organization for East Tennessee.

There has been some further but slight skirmishing at the front.

From Louisville, Ky.

LOUISVILLE, Ky., Thursday, March 17.

Maj.-Gens. SHERMAN and SHERIDAN have arrived in this city.

Col. BRUCE has been reinstated as Military Commander of Louisville.

Col. WOLFE has arrived here en route for Nashville, having been released from arrest and ordered to report in person to Maj.-Gen. GRANT.

The Chesapeake Case.

HALIFAX, Thursday, March 17.

The United States revenue cutter *Miami* arrived here this afternoon, and will leave to-morrow with the *Chesapeake*.

HORRORS OF THE REBELLION.

The Late Execution of North Carolina Unionists.

Twenty-four Loyal Southern Soldiers Hung at Kinston.

What it Costs a Southern Man to Fight for the Union.

Sufferings of Wives, Widows and Orphans.

Correspondence of the New-York Times.

BEAUFORT, N. C., Wednesday, March 9, 1864.

The unknown martyrs of this war are many. The madness of rebel leaders and the ferocity of the numerous guerrilla bands who hover about the advancing armies of Freedom, are not more noteworthy than the sublime but silent devotion with which hundreds of Southern men are continually yielding their lives, after passing through the ordeal of every form of torture the most devilish ingenuity can invent, as evidence to the existence, in the Southern States, of a widespread loyalty to the Constitution and the Union, which neither scourgings, starvation, bloodhounds nor the gallows can ever eradicate.

An illustration of this, recently furnished in North Carolina, upon a scale which in times less tragic than our own would have caused every heart on the continent to thrill with painful sympathy, but which, amidst the glare of great events, may be unnoted, or at best, only recorded in a brief paragraph.

When the attack was made on Newbern on the 2d of February last, Company F of the Second Regiment North Carolina Union Volunteers was stationed at Beech Grove, the extreme outpost from Newbern. When it became evident that the position could not be held against the overwhelming force of rebels, which was rapidly approaching, the men of this company, having the certainty of an ignominious death before them if they should be captured, proposed to the officer in command to pilot the force at the outpost in safety to Newbern, by paths through the woods known only to themselves. But unfortunately, they were temporarily in charge of officers, not belonging to their own regiment, who were either ignorant of the blood-thirsty character of the enemy, or too timid to fight to the death, if flight were deemed impracticable. Had these men been commanded by officers of their own regiment, they all would have escaped, or, as preferable to their inevitable doom if taken prisoners, would have found a more honorable death on the field. As it was, they were sternly forbidden to leave the ranks, and, without a shot being fired, or the stipulation secured that they should be treated as prisoners of war, they were surrendered; nineteen out of seventy only escaping. Of the fifty-one prisoners, twenty-four were immediately hung by order of the rebel Gen. PICKETT. On the scaffold, at Kinston, these twenty-four heroes met their fate with true courage. In the presence of the rebel forces, and surrounded by the people of their own State, they avowed their entire devotion to the Union. After receiving the consolations of religion, one of their number stepped forward, and, in a firm and clear voice, declared that he and his companions died, as they had lived, "Union men." One of the victims was a little drummer-boy, named JOEY NEAL, only fourteen years of age, a fair complexioned, blue-eyed child, an orphan, enlisted in Beaufort by the writer of these lines, out of pure compassion for his destitute state; another, a robust man, AMOS AMYETT, was tortured for fifteen minutes before the ill adjusted rope could strangle him to death.

Those twenty-four corpses swinging between heaven and earth, all that remains of as many brave and loyal North Carolinians, are not to be forgotten, nor the lessons they teach to be lightly passed over by the rich and prosperous people of the North. The rank and file of the Second Regiment North Carolina Union Volunteers, is composed of native North Carolinians, every one of whom is theatened with the fate of these twenty-four, if captured; and that that is no improbable contingency, may be gathered from the fact, that although the regiment has only been a few months in existence, and up to this time has not been fully organized, detachments from it have on several occasions, rendered services of sufficient importance to be recognized in General Orders. The men of the regiment fight with a halter around their necks, not merely because many of them are refugees from the rebel conscription, and Union men who have taken the first opportunity to leave the rebel army, but because every citizen of North Carolina taken in arms against the Confederacy, is declared by a statute of that State to be a traitor, and death is the decreed penalty of his offence. Hiding for months in swamps and thickets, and enduring perils and hardships that are almost incredible, these men, (or such of them as are not murdered by the guerrillas,) gaunt with hunger and clad in rags, at last reach our lines. Here they can find abundant and profitable employment as mechanics and laborers; but they are burning for the emancipation of their State and the rescue of their families from the horrors of the rebel despotism; and they enlist, without the lure of large bounties, in the service of the United States, which, on its part, guarantees them, or should do so, the same protection afforded to soldiers of the loyal States. Many of them have now been four months in the service, and have never received one cent of pay or bounty. This was the case with the twenty-four hung at Kinston; not a man of them had ever received a dollar from the United States.

But the saddest fact of all is that a much larger proportion of them than is usual in Northern regiments have large and helpless families dependent upon them, and these, when the father is killed in action, or murdered after being captured, are left to suffer. In North Carolina there is no "Freedman's Aid Society" to foster the destitute families of the "poor white man," who not only escapes from a worse than African bondage, but, despite the threat of the gallows, takes up arms for the Union.

Here there is no beneficent State Government, as in New-York and Massachusetts, to provide "State aid" for the families, and to furnish additional bounties for recruits. When the North Carolina refugee and his family arrive within the Union lines, without a crust of bread or a change of garments, the father enlists and receives the Government ration for himself and family. Belonging to one company of eighty men, there are thirty families; of these, two are still outside our lines, with small prospects of ever rejoining their kindred, and twenty families, comprising eighty-seven persons, forty-seven of them under the age of fourteen, are with the company in Beaufort.

Before the war these were, of their class, well-to-do people, owning a little land, a few cattle, and some household stuff, but now having scarcely anything beyond the Government ration. They are generally, almost universally, illiterate to a degree inconceivable to a Northern mind; on an average, not

Continued on the Eighth page.

THE NEW YORK HERALD.

WHOLE NO. 10,067. | NEW YORK, SUNDAY, APRIL 10, 1864. | PRICE FOUR CENTS.

THE RED RIVER EXPEDITION.

Full Details of the Military and Naval Operations.

Movements of the Main Column Under General Andrew Jackson Smith.

The Cavalry Operations Under General Albert W. Lee.

GENERAL MOWER'S BRILLIANT ACTION.

Success of the Expedition as Far as It Has Progressed.

Cotton, Corn and Contrabands Captured, &c., &c., &c.

Mr. Wm. Young's Despatch.

ALEXANDRIA, La., March 25, 1864.

OFFICIAL REPORT OF A CAVALRY SUCCESS.

Colonel T. J. Lucas, commanding the first brigade of General Lee's cavalry division, in compliance with orders, reported at five o'clock on the morning of the 21st inst., with the Sixteenth Indiana mounted infantry, the Sixth Missouri cavalry, the Second Louisiana mounted infantry and battery G, Fifth United States artillery, to Brigadier General A. J. Smith, then commanding Red river expedition, for orders, and was by him directed to report to Brigadier General Mower, who ordered him to place his command in the advance on the Bayou Rapides road.

Thirteen miles beyond Alexandria he met the enemy in small force and drove them seven miles to Henderson's Hill. The Second Louisiana rebel cavalry were holding the hill, occupying a strong position. Arriving in front of their position, he was ordered to report one regiment of cavalry and a section of artillery to the General, to make a detour, and to take the enemy in the rear, while with the remainder of his command he should occupy their attention and present a front, which, with the force thrown in the rear, would prevent their escape.

The Sixteenth Indiana mounted infantry, Lieutenant Colonel Redfield, and a section of Rawles' battery proceeded in accordance with directions, marching sixteen miles to the rear of the enemy, and reaching the pickets about half-past nine o'clock P. M. With the remainder of his command he occupied the enemy's attention until Colonel Redfield with his force had enclosed the rebel camp.

THE SURPRISE AND CAPTURES.

Colonel Redfield captured, when near the enemy's camp, a courier with despatches from General Taylor to Colonel Vincent. He successively captured, without firing a shot and without giving a general alarm, the pickets guarding the camp. A portion of the regiment advanced into the camp, while another detachment was thrown out in the direction of General Taylor's rebel troops, to guard against any attack upon the rear of the command from reinforcements. A body of the enemy then met, said by prisoners to be the advance of reinforcements, and driven back. A major, a captain on Taylor's staff, one lieutenant and thirty-six men were captured here, chiefly from the relieving force. This body of the enemy was as completely surprised as the other.

Captain Denny, with two companies of the Sixteenth Indiana, had the advance on entering the rebel camp; but infantry were soon deployed on his right, and the mounted and dismounted men advanced in line, capturing almost without resistance the astonished enemy. Four pieces of artillery were also captured.

The prisoners captured were immediately turned over to the infantry. Colonel Redfield's command captured the enemy's famous scout, Smith, and fifteen of his men.

At daylight next morning Colonel Lucas was directed to make a reconnoissance to Bowles' Ford, where he surprised and captured a picket post, consisting of a lieutenant and six men. Further on he captured two more men. His loss during the whole expedition was two men killed, one wounded and three missing.

RAPID MARCH AND GALLANT SURPRISE OF A REBEL CAMP BY OUR INFANTRY.

The Second brigade, First division, under command of Colonel L. H. Hubbard, of the Fifth Minnesota regiment; the Third brigade, of the same division, under command of Colonel S. G. Hill, of the Thirty fifth Iowa, and the Ninth Indiana battery, of the Third division of the Sixteenth army corps, from Gen. Sherman's command—the entire expedition being commanded by Brig. Gen. Joseph A. Mower—moved at six o'clock on the morning of the 21st inst. from Alexandria for Henderson's Hill, on Bayou Rapides. In their march they crossed the bayou over bridges three times, accomplishing a distance of twenty-one miles, and reaching a point within two miles of an encampment of the enemy. As it was the purpose of General Mower to take the rebels by surprise, he marched his forces by a circuitous route at least ten miles to get into their rear.

IMPORTANT CAPTURES.

He captured a courier, with despatches to General Taylor, from whom he learned that General Walker was within six miles and General Taylor within twelve miles, with their respective commands. He also learned the number of rebels in the command, the rear of which he was now approaching, the number of guns in their battery, and other valuable information. When within three miles of the enemy, at Henderson's Hill, he captured another courier on his way to Walker's command, conveying the information that they were short of ammunition.

After capturing their first picket General Mower secured the remainder of their pickets without creating an alarm. He then marched into their camp and surprised and captured two hundred and seventy officers and men, about two hundred horses and mules, Edgar's Texas four gun battery, comprising two brass field pieces and two brass howitzers, the caissons, horses and equipments. The horses were harnessed and attached to the pieces and caissons, and the battery was under marching orders when it was captured.

GENERAL MOWER IN THE ADVANCE—THE BRIDGES.

General Mower, with his staff, and the Thirty-fifth Iowa regiment, Lieutenant Colonel Keeler, led the advance into the rebel camp. Captain Sample, Assistant Adjutant General on General Mower's staff, headed a small detachment, which captured the first prisoners and the first section of the battery.

The bridge across the bayou nearest to the enemy's camp had been stripped of its covering by the rebels, who had thrown the planks into the bayou, and the next bridge below it had been burned by them. General Mower regarded it prudent to open speedy communication with his reserve, five miles distant, and immediately ordered the repair of the bridge which had been stripped, over which he marched his prisoners, his spoils and his own troops, and joined his reserve at one o'clock in the morning, performing a march of nearly thirty-five miles in nineteen hours, and surprising and capturing a force of the enemy nearly equalling that part of his own which was directly engaged in the capture. At eleven o'clock the following morning he marched to Trorone plantation, nine miles from Alexandria, where he remained until the next day, and then returned to Alexandria.

LIST OF OFFICERS CAPTURED.

The following is a complete list of the officers captured by the infantry and cavalry:—

Lieut. Col. James D. Blair, 2d Louisiana cavalry.
Major W. O. Brusseale, 2d Louisiana cavalry.
Adjutant Maj. W. [illegible], 2d Louisiana cavalry.
Capt. A. Purdhomme, 2d Louisiana cavalry.
Capt. A. C. Broussard, 2d Louisiana cavalry.
Second Lieut. Joseph [illegible], 2d Louisiana cavalry.
Second Lieut. D. C. Paul, 2d Louisiana cavalry.
Lieut. W. D. Calhoun, 2d Louisiana cavalry.
Lieut. E. A. Carmouche, 2d Louisiana cavalry.
Lieut. A. V. Carter, 2d Louisiana cavalry.
Lieut. J. Broussard, 2d Louisiana cavalry.
Lieut. C. F. Dresquis, 2d Louisiana cavalry.
Asst. Surgeon T. C. Thompson, 2d Louisiana cavalry.
Senior First Lieut. James M. Ransom, commanding Edgar's Texas battery.
Junior Second Lieut. J. C. Sibley, Edgar's Texas battery.
Lieut. J. D. Gambee, Edgar's Texas battery.
Lieut. [illegible], Edgar's Texas battery.
Lieut. [illegible], Ordnance Department.
Capt. [illegible], Taylor's staff.
Surgeon [illegible]
Lieut. J. J. [illegible]
Lieut. E. W. [illegible]

[illegible] CAVALRY MARCH.

General Lee's cavalry division reached Alexandria on Sunday evening, after marching from Franklin, across the Teche country, [illegible] by a hostile [illegible]. [illegible] to join the Red River expedition, [illegible] Banks' command, with portions of General Sherman's Sixteenth and Seventeenth army corps, under General Smith. The cavalry started from Franklin with three days rations, but the supply in the country through which they passed was so nearly sufficient that two days forage was brought into Alexandria by them. [illegible] thirty miles a day; [illegible] compensated for all the hardships which they were subjected to on the route.

NOW ALEXANDRIA APPEARS.

Alexandria is full of soldiers; but many of the citizens have departed, perhaps only temporarily, while many others welcome the arrival of the army and the gunboats as an indication that the Red river is to be opened and kept open to the head of navigation.

COTTON ON THE GUNBOATS.

Admiral Porter's gunboat fleet have secured, according to the estimates, from two to ten thousand bales of cotton, and it is probable that very much more will be obtained by the gunboats, the transports and the army. A considerable amount of cotton has been brought into Alexandria by the army, and more is to come.

CORN, CONTRABANDS, SHEEP AND SWINE.

General Mower's command captured only one or two loads of corn at Henderson Hill; but our foragers are constantly bringing in corn, sheep, swine and other supplies. Contrabands of all ages, sizes and every shade of color are coming into our lines.

The rebels are scattering through the country in every direction, burning cotton wherever they can find it. One planter, who is now in this town, had nearly three hundred bales of cotton burned by these rebels.

CONCENTRATION OF REBEL TROOPS.

It is rumored that the rebels are concentrating their forces to prevent our advance up the Red river to Shreveport, and that General Green's cavalry command, from the vicinity of Houston, Texas, has reinforced the enemy already.

APPROACH OF GEN. FRANKLIN.

Gen. Franklin's infantry command, which left Franklin and New Iberia last week, will reach Alexandria in two or three days, and perhaps before that time.

A SPEEDY ADVANCE

will probably be made, and there may be a series of severe battles before the Red river is entirely opened to navigation and commerce. Gen. Banks will undoubtedly succeed, though the unexpected capture by Gen. Smith of Fort de Russy, without a siege, perhaps prevented the combinations and concentrations from various points which had been arranged.

ALEXANDRIA, La., March 26, 1864.

REBELS CONCENTRATING—OUR CAVALRY ADVANCING.

Scouts report that Dick Taylor is concentrating a rebel force about fifty miles up Red river. Five brigades of infantry and four batteries of artillery are known to be up there as a nucleus of rebels.

This morning early our cavalry advanced in full force, Col. Dudley's Fourth brigade leading the advance. They may skirmish as they move, after they get beyond Henderson's Hill, the scene of the late successful dash upon the rebel camp.

SEIZURE OF COTTON—SPECULATORS.

The military authorities have seized eight or nine hundred bales of cotton on the plantation of General G. Graham, a disloyal citizen, who derives his rank from a commission he formerly held in the State militia. About six hundred bales of cotton have been seized on the plantation of Lucien Norman, near Fort de Russy, another disloyal citizen.

B. M. Poget, of New Orleans, a cotton speculator, who has been within the enemy's lines seven weeks, has been arrested by the Provost Marshal. G. L. Taylor, of New Orleans, claiming to be an agent for a house in that city, and a cotton speculator, has also been arrested by the same authority. Both of these men are held for going outside of our lines without a pass.

ARREST OF REBEL SYMPATHIZERS—THE TECHE COUNTRY.

James Busard, rebel Postmaster at Alexandria, and legal adviser of General Dick Taylor, has been arrested by the Provost Marshal's officers, and will be detained as an active associate or sympathizer with the rebels.

The Teche country was found by our forces which marched through there to be abundantly supplied with beef cattle, and there were several thousand bales of cotton and large quantities of sugar on the road, which could not be removed by our troops for want of transportation.

The route used by the rebels for driving cattle across the Mississippi has been at Morganzia bend, over which the flocks and herds of the rich and abundant Teche country have been transported to supply the rebel army. But that route, it is believed, is now closed.

COTTON AND CONTRABANDS—THE ADVANCE.

The Thirteenth and Nineteenth army corps and our cavalry columns have brought up small quantities of cotton and great numbers of contrabands, who flock into our lines wherever our troops march. General Lee's cavalry column, including contrabands and forage, was ten miles in length. [illegible] are bringing in cotton from short distances out in the country.

The guerillas yesterday fired two or three musketoes near here, which had been occupied by loyal men.

General Smith's column, from the army of General Sherman, which co-operates with General Banks, moved forward this morning from Alexandria.

VETERANS GOING HOME—FIFTY-SIXTH OHIO VOLUNTEERS.

The Fifty-sixth Ohio, veteran volunteers, which was among the first to respond to the call of July, 1861, has served a long time in Tennessee and Arkansas, went through the Mississippi campaign under General Grant and was engaged in the battles of Port Gibson, Fourteen Mile creek, Champion Hills, the siege of Vicksburg and capture of Jackson. This regiment lost over one-third of its number in these actions. It was subsequently ordered to the Department of the Gulf, where it has since been serving, and went through the campaign of last fall in the Teche country. The Fifty-sixth made a most successful charge with the brigade to which it was attached, at Grand Coteau, completely routing the enemy. The regiment has re-enlisted and has been promised a furlough to proceed to the North.

MOUNTED AND DISMOUNTED REGIMENTS.

All the Massachusetts infantry regiments in this department have been mounted, except the Thirty-eighth, now commanded by Colonel Richardson.

There are nearly as many regiments of New York troops in the Department of the Gulf as of all others combined, and they will do gallant service in the present campaign.

There is more music in this army than in the Army of the Potomac, and the bands and drum corps played their best marches as the Thirteenth and Nineteenth army corps came into Alexandria yesterday and General Smith's command moved out this morning.

GENERAL LEE'S STAFF.

Major John Tracey, Jr., of the Eighteenth New York cavalry, has been detailed for duty on the staff of Gen. A. L. Lee, commanding cavalry division. The entire staff of that officer is as follows:—

Major W. W. Howe, Aid-de-Camp.
Major J. E. Cowen, Acting Assistant Inspector General.
Major John Tracey, Jr., inspector of outposts and charge of pickets.
Capt. F. W. Emery, Assistant Adjutant General.
Capt. Cowie, Assistant Commissary of Subsistence.
Capt. H. Hoge, Assistant Quartermaster.
Capt. Brisban, Aid-de-Camp.
Capt. O. F. Nims, Chief of Artillery and Ordnance.

ADVANCE AND SKIRMISH.

General Smith's Sixteenth army corps will take transports on the Red river, some fifteen miles above here, immediately, and the whole army will probably advance within two days for Natchitoches, eighty miles from Alexandria, and situated on Old river, four miles from the Red river. It is not thought that the enemy will make any material or important fighting demonstrations before our troops reach that point.

A detachment of our cavalry skirmished with guerillas this morning a short distance from the river, nearly opposite Alexandria.

COLONEL GOODING'S STAFF.

The Second New York veteran cavalry and the Eighteenth New York cavalry regiments are in Colonel Gooding's brigade. Lieutenant Willard, of the Eighteenth New York, has been detached from his regiment, and is attached to the staff of Colonel Gooding as aid-de-camp.

The weather has been warm to-day and like summer, very much more pleasant than it has been previously.

PROVOST DUTY AT ALEXANDRIA.

The brigade commanded by Colonel Sharp, of the One Hundred and fifty-sixth New York regiment, is doing provost duty at Alexandria. Lieutenant Colonel Neafie, of that regiment, is Provost Marshal. The brigade consists in part of the One Hundred and Twenty-eighth New York, Colonel Smith; the One Hundred and fifty sixth New York, Lieutenant Colonel Neafie, and the Thirty-eighth Massachusetts, Lieutenant Colonel Richardson. In so conducting the military government of the town as to develope Union sentiment and protect the rights of Union citizens there are difficult and delicate duties to perform.

There have been two or three arrests on suspicion of contriving torpedoes and other infernal machines to obstruct the river. The falls above Alexandria are to be removed by the use of powder, to make the river navigable for larger draft steamers.

MR. ANDERSON'S PRISON HOME.

The jail where Mr. Anderson, of the HERALD, was confined as a prisoner of war is now vacant, and the Provost Marshal has the key. The jailor and his family have taken private apartments.

The band of the Twenty ninth Maine regiment serenaded General Banks at his headquarters this evening. The General made a brief speech, congratulating the troops on the prospects of entire success in the present campaign.

Before our troops came here there were two newspaper offices in town, one of which has been transferred to a gunboat and the other has been taken possession of by the Provost Marshal. A field is now open for ambitious printers to distinguish themselves and extinguish their greenbacks by publishing a paper for the army.

POST QUARTERMASTER AND COMMISSARY.

Captains Welsh and Delvecchio, Assistant Quartermasters, are doing the business here of Post Quartermasters, and Captain Irwin, Assistant Commissary of Subsistence, that of Post Commissary. One-half of the amount of the forage required for the army will be obtained in the country through which it passes; at least such is the Quartermaster's estimate.

Details of the Recent Military Operations Under General Andrew Jackson Smith.

MR. DE B. RANDOLPH KEIM'S DESPATCH.

CAIRO, Ill., April 3, 1864.

A Detailed Account of the Union Operations on Red River from the Fitting Out of the Expedition up to the Present—Quick Movements and Brilliant Fighting—Large Captures of Artillery, &c.—The Expedition Thus Far a Complete Success—Some Remarks Concerning the Country and the People—The Enemy Said to Intend Giving Up Louisiana and Falling Back Towards Texas—Impatience to Hear from General Steele's Column, &c.

Several gentlemen who have just arrived here from the lower Mississippi have furnished us with the most gratifying particulars of our operations on the Red river and some of its affluents.

It will be remembered, perhaps, that General Sherman, [illegible] through Southern Mississippi, left the main body of his army in the neighborhood of Canton, to carry out some further plans—which, however, did not require his personal superintendence—and with an escort of about three hundred cavalry reached Vicksburg on Sunday morning, February 28, the same evening he left, on board the United States Mississippi river marine steamer Diana, for New Orleans, and reached that city on the 2d of March. Immediately a consultation was held between General Sherman and General Banks upon the subject of an expedition into the Red river country. In the course of a few days, all preliminary arrangements being perfected and a complete understanding existing, General Sherman returned to Vicksburg, to complete the fitting out of the troops which were to start from that point.

As the troops were to move by water, all boats from above or below were detained at Vicksburg by military authority. After seizing about twice as many boats as were needed—the surplus being released after several days or a week's useless and expensive detention—the expedition was embarked.

I am not at liberty to give the numbers, but it may be said a considerable part of the Sixteenth corps, under General A. J. Smith, and a smaller force from the Seventeenth corps, under General T. Kilby Smith, constituted the land force from Vicksburg. The chief command was entrusted to General A. J. Smith. While these preparations were going on in Vicksburg some troops were also fitted out from the Department of the Gulf, the cavalry of that department, under Gen. A. L. Lee, being ordered to prepare for moving.

On the evening of March 10 the Vicksburg forces, under Gen. A. J. Smith, departed from Vicksburg on twenty transports, and on the day following were at the mouth of Red River. Here Admiral Porter had already rendezvoused a fleet of about twenty gunboats, of which the principal were the Benton, the Neosho, Eastport, Wachita, Osage, Conestoga, Lexington, Fort Hindman, Gen. Price and Cricket.

On the morning of March 12 the fleet weighed anchor, and being led by the Admiral's flagship, proceeded up the Old River, and thence passed into the Red. Some days prior to this movement Admiral Porter had sent an expedition, composed of six gunboats, up Black river, a tributary to the Red, and thence up the Wachita and Tensas rivers. This expedition was highly successful, succeeding in drawing the enemy out and capturing the towns and fort of Harrisonburg and Trinity, with little loss. This being effected, no enemy of importance was left in the rear, and the forces proceeded at once to demolish all barriers on the Red river.

By noon on March 12 the transports had reached the entrance to Atchafalaya river. It was arranged here that an escort of gunboats should accompany the transports, while the rest would push directly up the Red. The transports accordingly moved seven miles down the Atchafalaya river to the mouth of Bayou De Glaze, in the neighborhood of Simmsport. The gunboats having set out early in the morning, had arrived there in advance, and reported upon the coming up of the transports that the rebel cavalry was evacuating. On the morning of the 13th General Smith ordered a disembarkation, and marched with General Mower's division and General Kilby Smith's brigade on a reconnoissance towards a strong position the enemy had chosen on Yellow Bayou, about three miles distant, for the landing. Upon arriving an incomplete and evacuated fort was found, the enemy having decamped some time before. However, General Smith succeeded in capturing seven wagons loaded with camp equipage, thirty-four mules and fourteen prisoners. After accomplishing his purpose in that direction General Smith retraced his steps to the boats.

By this time the entire force, excepting a small guard for the boats, had landed and were ready to march. By ten o'clock on the same morning the entire column was in motion across the country towards another fort situated on Red river, and, as already known, called Fort de Russy. At two in the afternoon the expedition camped six miles out.

On March 14, at an early hour the command was again in motion; marched twenty-five miles, bridged a bayou, and at once attacked Fort de Russy, and in a short time stormed and took possession of the works, with little loss.

Our casualties will reach ten killed and forty wounded. Our forces captured two hundred and fifty privates, including one lieutenant colonel, six captains, and about fifteen lieutenants. Our forces also took eight siege guns and two field pieces. One of the heavy guns once formed part of the armament of the Harriet Lane, and another was from the Indianola. We also took a large quantity of ammunition and commissary stores. The troops of the enemy were all Texans. The fort is described as one of considerable strength, having a casemate with three embrasures and covered with railroad iron, double lined with four feet of solid oak. Mounted within the casemate was one nine-inch gun and one large rifled piece; the other gun [illegible] in position. The enemy [illegible] an immense amount of labor upon the fort, and if [illegible] and properly garrisoned [illegible] against a vastly superior force. [illegible] situated that it commanded the river for many miles. The enemy's troops are said to be of an excellent [illegible], but poorly officered. General Walker, who was at the fort a short time before, upon the approach of our troops decamped for Alexandria.

Let us now take a glance at the operations of the gunboats and transports. On the morning of the 14th Admiral Porter, with all the gunboats and transports, moved up the Red river. Upon arriving at a certain point some obstructions were discovered. The crew of the Eastport immediately set to work upon them, and in a short time had effected a passage. Thence the gunboats moved up to the fort and opened a bombardment from the river, meantime General Smith was successfully [illegible]. When all arrangements had been made [illegible], the gunboats ceased firing, and the fort [illegible] the enemy, under Walker, which [illegible] arrival of our forces, numbered, it is said, about five thousand.

From Fort de Russy General Smith moved upon Alexandria, and occupied the place on the 16th. General Taylor left beforehand for Shreveport.

Several days after, a junction was effected between General Smith and General Lee's cavalry, which had set out from New Orleans to co-operate.

On the 21st the combined forces attacked the enemy near Natchitoches, and captured two hundred prisoners and four pieces of artillery and caissons. The next place from which we may expect to hear will be Shreveport. This town is situated in almost the extreme northwestern corner of Louisiana, and is at the head of navigation on the Red river. The population of the place is small and considerably mixed. There seems to be an opinion that the enemy has accumulated a large amount of military stores at that point. This is no doubt a fact. It is the only place which seems adapted to the purpose, because of its security on account of its distance inland and the convenience of water communication with all parts of the State, in which their army has been operating during the past summer and winter.

For the holding of Shreveport the enemy is making great preparations. The rebel iron ram Webb, mounting some of the Indianola's guns, is in that neighborhood, and will get up, doubtless, quite a contest for the gunboats. The land forces of the enemy, both north and south of Red river, are concentrating there, and probably will aggregate twelve thousand. With all these means, and probably some fortifications and heavy artillery, the enemy will no doubt make an obstinate resistance. But not the least doubt, I understand, is entertained as to the ability of General Smith to cope successfully with his adversary.

The expedition thus far is pronounced a complete success, and will ultimately, there is no doubt, entirely annihilate the rebel military power in West and Northwest Louisiana.

The people are reported evincing the same implacable hostility for which they have always been famous. Certainly the impotent attacks of a powerless people very little affect the operations of our arms, and only bring down upon themselves the more terrible and deserved chastisement of the army.

The Red river country, like the larger portion of the Southwest, is thickly ramified by all sorts of water courses, from bayous—dry in summer—to quite respectable rivers. There is much swamp land in some sections, while in other parts fine prairies and a little table land and small hills are seen. This region is fertile and did abound in many large and well equipped plantations. The war has put an end to the cultivation of most of the estates, and what cultivation is done is for the raising of corn.

Rebel tactics have taken in many cases such singular and unaccountable twists that it is hard to determine, even in view of all their activity and concentration at Shreveport, whether or not they will make a stand for a last defence of Louisiana. Some rumors have reached here that they design falling back into Texas, where supplies are more plentiful, and, perhaps, for another reason, equally as influential, where Yankees are not so common.

Some impatience is felt in regard to the bearing of some particulars of Gen. Steele's movements. He left Little Rock and moved south about the time the other expedition left Vicksburg and New Orleans. Possibly the rebels will hear from him first knocking at their back door, into which, without a second knocking, he will certainly walk when he gets there.

THE RED RIVER EXPEDITION.

Location of Shreveport and of the Various Points on the Red River and Its Affluents Captured by Our Forces.

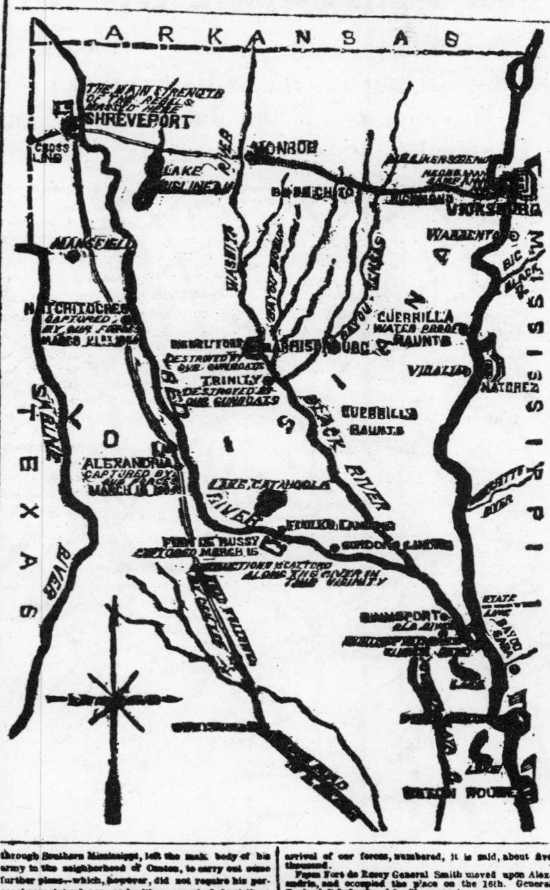

THE LATEST NEWS.

Reported Capture of Shreveport by Gen. Steele's Forces.

CAIRO, Ill., April 9, 1864.

The Red river correspondent of the New Orleans *Delta* notices an unconfirmed report that General Steele's forces captured Shreveport without firing a gun; that several of our gunboats had gone above the shoals of Red river to co-operate with our land forces, and that large numbers of cattle and ponies were being captured by our scouting parties as well as cotton.

Italian Opera.

IONE.

Petrella's grand opera, which has hitherto met with so much success, was given, without any deviation from its original splendor in *mise en scene*, at the Academy last night. The occasion was the benefit of Signor Mazzoleni. Glauco is perhaps one of Mazzoleni's finest parts. There is abundant opportunity for the display of the dramatic power which he possesses in an eminent degree, and in his performance last night he did not disappoint his many admirers. He sang well, looked well, and acted with a genuine passion which was sympathetic. The Romanza in the last act, a difficult and laborious effort, as those who are familiar with the opera know well, was very ably rendered, and called forth continuous applause. Medori, we need hardly say, was grand as Ione, and received a full measure of approbation, which was entirely deserved. To-morrow night we [illegible] again to greet the favorite Brignoli in Robert le [illegible], in which he always claims the fullest [illegible] of the public. On Wednesday [illegible] On Tuesday night the artists [illegible] worn out after a week's [illegible] rest.

MASQUERADE BALL OF [illegible].—The "Mo. Name" Carnival Junta, a [illegible], have obtained official permission to give a [illegible] ball at the Athenæum on [illegible] evening next [illegible] the 14th inst., the profits of which are to be given to [illegible] the charity fund of the Fourteenth Regiment Veteran [illegible] Society.

[illegible].—This organization will celebrate the [illegible] anniversary of the departure of the [illegible] regiment, for the seat of war, by a [illegible]. Our [illegible] are [illegible].

THE FAIR.

SIXTH DAY OF EXHIBITION.

Nearly Sixty Thousand Dollars Added to the Treasury.

THE ARMY AND NAVY SWORD RACE.

McClellan Four Hundred and Thirty-two Ahead.

Tremendous Excitement Among the Voters.

MORE TROUBLE ABOUT THE RAFFLE.

How a Lady Disposed of Her Eyeglass.

SCENES, INCIDENTS, ACCIDENTS, &c., &c., &c.

The weather yesterday was not so favorable for the Fair as during the other days of the week. The attendance was nevertheless very large, though there was a very appreciable falling off in the immense crowd, such as thronged every part of the Fair buildings the two days preceding. The decrease of numbers was no cause of faultfinding, for it enabled those who did go to enjoy themselves thoroughly, and to see everything worth seeing without incurring the risk of being mangled.

WHAT IT COSTS TO SEE THE ELEPHANT.

As some people do not yet know what it costs to visit the Fair and see all the sights, we supply the following table, which will afford the required information:—

Admission to Main Hall	$1 00
Admission to Art Gallery	25
Admission to Arms and Trophies	25
Admission to Indian Exhibition	25
Admission to Curiosity Shop	25
Admission to Cockloft House	10
Admission to Knickerbocker Kitchen	10
Charge for viewing a lady's hand	25
Charge for viewing a brick	10
Admission to Skating Pond	10
Total	$2 65

Some explanation is required respecting some of the departments stated in the above table.

THE VIEW OF A LADY'S HAND

is what it purports to be—an inspection of the soft, white hand of a beautiful female through a microscope. The exhibition proves quite a source of revenue and entertainment.

"THERE WAS AN OLD WOMAN WHO LIVED IN A SHOE."

At the Methodist stand a very pretty little bit of juvenile amusement has been provided. It consists in the representation of the "woman that lived in a shoe," by Miss Anna Belle Poole (four years of age). The little lady sits in a shoe of mammoth proportions, and vends dolls to all "who pass the way." The young folks are tickled to death by this, and the old folks doubtless recall the familiar words of early childhood, when they used to sing—

There was an old woman, who lived in a shoe,
She had so many children she didn't know what to do;
She gave them some broth, without any bread,
And whipped them, and beat them, and sent them to bed.

—All the young folks should visit the Methodist stand, where there is much besides the above to interest.

ANOTHER FORM OF RAFFLING,

and hence a growl has come up from parsondom against the "unrighteous practice." The Executive Committee have been somewhat exercised about the subject. Two meetings have been held, and another is to come off, to consider the albums, the subscription and the raffling. The committee, of course, intend to stand by their original anti-raffling resolution and the parsons. In justice to some members of the committee, it must be said that they have stuck out uniformly for the raffling; but, having been beaten, they intend to carry out the will of the majority, like true democrats. Mr. George Griswold Gray, chairman, was one of the stoutest opponents of the parsons; but he assured our reporter yesterday that he intended to enforce, to the full extent of his power, the anti-raffling resolution of his colleagues. In this resolve he is, perhaps, simply doing his duty, and should receive the entire support of the committee. In various parts of the Fair yesterday the following notice was tacked up:—

NOTICE.—RESOLUTIONS OF THE EXECUTIVE COMMITTEE.—Whereas, this committee has determined, upon the request of the Sanitary Commission, not to permit raffling at the Fair, and have made public announcement of such determination, therefore

Resolved, That it is due alike to the Commission and to the public that raffling shall not be allowed, directly or indirectly, in connection with and during the time of the Fair.

Resolved, That the heads of committees and all persons connected with the management of the Fair be requested to use their influence to check all attempts to dispose of articles by lot or chance in any form.

MARCH 19, 1864.

We understand that at the next meeting of the committee the album business will be ruled out of the pale of the church and the Fair unless the subscription dodge is abandoned.

AN EYEGLASS DISPOSED OF BY LOT.

Apropos of raffling, we were informed of a very pleasant little incident that occurred yesterday, and with which the name of Mrs. Demarest, one of the ladies of the Fair, has been coupled in an amusing manner. An impromptu dinner occurred yesterday afternoon on board the ocean steamer City of London. Among the party were Postmaster Wakeman, Captain Petrie, commander of the vessel, Mrs. Demarest, Mrs. Marsh and two daughters, Miss Demarest, and Messrs. Nicholson, Hallett and Coffin. During the meal the subject of the Fair came up, and Mrs. Demarest took advantage of the fact to make a "hit." She placed her eye-glass upon the table and solicited the company to take chances on it. The idea took; chances were subscribed to promptly, and in two minutes forty-four dollars were on the table for the benefit of the Fair. The next question was who should have the eyeglass. A number of lots were prepared and placed in a soup tureen, which was passed around the table, and each person drew as it came to his turn. Mr. Wakeman was the lucky winner of the prize. This forty-four dollars were added in an innocent manner to the great fund.

FIVE DOLLARS FOR A SEAT NEXT A LADY.

But this was not all. One of the gentlemen present (we omit his name) charmed at the whole affair, offered five dollars for the privilege of sitting for a few minutes beside the lady whose cleverness had exhibited itself so appropriately. The offer was accepted.

THOSE TWO SWORDS

continue to be the great feature of the Fair. The excitement respecting the voting is on the increase, and it is expected that thousands of dollars will be realized by this newest of "Yankee notions."

BETTING HIGH ON THE RESULT.

We are informed that a great deal of betting has been made on the result. There is one wager of six hundred dollars between a friend of Grant and a friend of McClellan. A number of smaller bets have have been made, and it is said by parties who have been about the place constantly, that thousands of dollars will change hands when the Fair is over in consequence of this sword contest.

WHEN THE LADIES VOTE.

Between the hour of opening and about six o'clock in the evening the ladies form the largest proportion of the voters. During that period the pressure of crinoline around the "keeper of the swords" is really appalling. The most fashionably dressed, the more plainly attired, and the unmistakably democratically decked females are all mixed up in a delightful heap, and keep up a highly exciting struggle in behalf of their army favorites for the sword. The lords of creation are in a glorious minority, and are almost swallowed up in the sea of silks, muslins and calicoes surging through the room. Occasionally a specimen of the *genus homo*, with more courage and perseverance than the ordinary run of his kind, shoves his way through the billowing throng of woman kind, and is rewarded by the honor of casting a vote, or several votes, suffering a corresponding depletion of his pocketbook.

THE LADIES WAX WARM

sometimes over this contest—at least so our reporter [illegible] by the [illegible], behind the [illegible] poll clerk, [illegible] of election, [illegible] of votes, &c. Once, since the commencement of the novel election, there was danger of a serious [illegible] among some of the female voters. One lady was rather loudly hostile to McClellan, and was snapped up quite sharply by another lady who went the "entire animal" for the "Young Nap. of America."

FIRST LADY—He's a traitor and a conceited coxcomb.

SECOND LADY—No such thing. No man was ever a truer patriot, and I'm sure everybody but contractors and fanatics acknowledge that he is an accomplished general.

FIRST LADY—I don't know what you mean by everybody. I know a good many ladies who believe very differently. He's a humbug.

SECOND LADY (very warmly)—He's no such thing.

FIRST LADY—I say he is.

The number of "he isn'ts" and "he is's" that followed it is unnecessary to state. The spirit of contradiction might have led to an open declaration of hostilities had not another lady came up to the rescue, just in time, by putting in a heavy vote in favor of one of the generals, thus creating a diversion and giving the disputants time to take breath and arrange their sweet little disordered tempers. It would never do, we fear, to extend the elective franchise to the women.

I'LL DO IT IF YOU DO.

There is a good deal of the bluff game about this voting. Yesterday, during the height of the excitement, a respectably dressed man passed the stand and was hailed by the keeper.

KEEPER—Don't you want to vote, sir?

GENTLEMAN—Vote? Vote for what? whom?

KEEPER—For one of the generals or naval officers.

GENTLEMAN—I'll tell you what I'll do, young man. If you get some one to fill up a page for one of the generals—I don't care which—I'll fill up another.

The bargain was struck immediately. The keeper without difficulty produced his man, and the challenger was obliged to lay down twenty-eight dollars, which represents in money the exact amount of voting it takes to fill a page.

Last night the excitement on the subject was more intense than at any time since the commencement of the Fair. The anxiety of everyone to learn how the vote stood was so great that occasional bulletins had to be issued and posted up in an elevated position so that they might be read with ease by all within four or five feet of the stand. At six o'clock the following bulletin appeared:—

TOTAL VOTE 3,561.

McClellan	2,006	Hooker	2
Grant	1,523	McCook	1
Rosecrans	8	Sherman	1
Fremont	6	Potter	1
Butler	5	Thomas	1
Fitz John Porter	4	Wadsworth	1
Burnside	2		
Total			3,561
McClellan over Grant			483

After six o'clock the friends of Grant poured in somewhat more numerously, and McClellan's majority continued to decrease thereafter. At half-past nine o'clock a new bulletin was issued as follows:—

McClellan	2,251	All others	33
Grant	1,816		
Total			4,100

During the evening the Gettysburg farmer, Burns, stepped up to the book and voted one for Grant. The act elicited loud applause. There were hundreds of interesting incidents which would fill a page of the HERALD to describe. One admirer of Grant paid for his vote in an old fashioned large silver dollar. A McClellanite marked the initial K, and paid up twenty-eight dollars. Q. T. C. emptied his purse of fifty dollars for an equal number of votes for McClellan. A Grantite filled three pages for his favorite, and was followed by two or three more enthusiastic Grant men, who rolled out the dollar bills in munificent style. At the closing of the polls, fifteen minutes past ten o'clock, the vote stood thus:—

McClellan	2,312	Scattering	33
Grant	1,880		
Total			4,225
McClellan's majority			432

There was a good deal of talk yesterday about

THAT JERSEYMAN'S PROPHESY,

to the effect that underhand means would be used to defeat McClellan. Much mysterious head shaking and dark hints were indulged in, and there were not wanting those who declared that they had seen those who had seen others who had heard others say that they had been told by others that the Union League Club had subscribed unnamed quantities of greenbacks to defeat McClellan.

THE NAVY SWORD

has not, as yet, emerged from the back ground into which it has been thrown by the struggle respecting the army sword. Few people stop at the navy side of the stand, unless it be to view the voting for Grant and McClellan. The total vote up to yesterday noon was thus:—

Farragut	119	Worden	2
Rowan	63	Ringgold	2
Dupont	20	Rogers	1
Porter	6	Loring	1
Lardner	4	Dekniffe	1
Boggs	4		
Total			225

SYSTEM NEEDED IN THE MONEY DEPARTMENT.

Though the Fair has been going on now for a full week, the financial arrangement does not seem yet to have got into perfect working order. As yet no report of the receipts obtained at all the branches of the Fair has been published, and apparently is not comeatable. The accounts which our reporter has published so far do not include the amounts received at the Union square building (except for the admissions), nor at the restaurant, nor at many other branches of the Palace Garden building. Why this is remained unexplained up to the closing of the Fair last evening. Some reform is needed here. The rule ought to be that all persons entrusted with receiving moneys should make a daily report, and hand over the cash to a common treasurer. The public have an interest in learning the daily receipts, and the Managing Committee should see that this hint is attended to.

The following were the receipts up to three o'clock in the afternoon for yesterday:—

Sales	$13,713
Admissions, Fourteenth street	12,538
Admissions, Union square	2,499
Donations	30,990
Total	$59,741

The Union Square Building.

There is no abatement in the rush at the Union square building. Yesterday there was a continual stream of visitors, and this building keeps pace with the Fourteenth street establishment in every particular. All the departments were freely patronized, and the sales were numerous. The ladies cannot receive too much praise for the energy and care with which they carry on the business allotted to them at this auxiliary building. To be gallant, it must here be remarked, without using flattery, that those ladies are all handsome, with some one or two exceptions. On an occasion of this description the fact of beautiful women being connected with the movements consequent upon their position is quite a large addition to the success attendant upon it. There are certainly many artificial embellishments to the building, but the natural beauties which everywhere meet the eye in passing through the various departments enhance tenfold the general splendor of the scene. The picturesque, though antiquated, dresses of the ladies in charge of the Knickerbocker Kitchen set off their forms to perfection. Hoops were dispensed with in those days, and of course the ladies of the kitchen do not don the present day encumbrances.

MUSICAL EXERCISES LAST EVENING.

Handel's grand oratorio of Judas Maccabeus was given last evening by the New York Harmonic Society, under the direction of Mr. L. F. Ritter. The solo parts were sustained by Miss Maria Brainard, Mrs. Motte, Mr. Gustavus Geary and Mr. J. R. Thomas. Mr. George F. Burton presided at the piano. The large room of the Children's Department was crowded to excess during the performance, and the artists as well as the Harmonic Society were greeted with frequent applause.

THIEVES ON EXHIBITION.

A male and female, who were detected in the act of stealing articles from one of the booths, were paraded around the rooms, with large placards attached to their front and rear, bearing the honorable cognomen "thief," printed in large letters. This degrading procession was received with much interest by the crowd of visitors. The unfortunate victims of their own indiscretion seemed to feel the degraded position which they occupied, particularly the woman, who cried bitterly on being brought into the police office. The example thus made of these thieves will no doubt have a wholesome influence upon others who may have a penchant for similar employment. The police department of this branch of the Fair is proving quite efficient in the detection of these thieves, as well as in the maintenance of order. Captain Speight is in command.

THE KNICKERBOCKER KITCHEN.

Visitors to the Knickerbocker Kitchen, if possible, seem to be on the increase. The strains of the violin, played by a colored gentleman, who sits contiguous to the spinning wheel, still reverberate throughout the kitchen and attract the curious as well as the musically inclined.

The portrait of the little Holland lady hanging next the entrance door of the Knickerbocker Kitchen is that of the grandmother of Mrs. Sharp, of Ulster county, who presides ably at the spinning wheel. This portrait was painted nearly one hundred and fifty years ago. The subject was the daughter of a Dutch physician who emigrated to Ulster county about that time.

Mrs. Sharp, who is the mother of Colonel Sharp, of Ulster county, is a fine specimen of a well preserved Dutch matron, and her ability on the spinning wheel is, at least in these days, unequalled. She declares it a much pleasanter machine to operate than the modern sewing machine.

The First Ward Public School Concert in Aid of the Sanitary Fair.

The concert given by the pupils of the public schools in the First ward on Friday evening at Niblo's Saloon was a complete success. It was a perfect jam, and hundreds, we understand, were compelled to go away, not being able to obtain even standing room. The performances would compare favorably with those of our best theatres. We have not space to notice all the excellent things given. The *finale* was the dialogue and tableau, "The Fairy Queen." The *tout ensemble* was perfect, the acting, scenery, and, in fact, every accompaniment, would do credit to any stage.

The choruses were finely executed. The music was given by Professor Nash, on one of Steinway & Sons' grand pianos.

Personal Intelligence.

Commodore W. D. Porter, United States Navy, has been lying very ill at the Whitney House. He was removed to the St. Luke's Hospital on Saturday in a sinking condition.

Hon. Benj. Wood has appointed, on the recommendation of the Board of Education, John Joseph Casey, of the sophomore class of the Free Academy, to the United States cadetship at West Point. Mr. Casey was born and has always resided in the Fourth Congressional district.

MR. AND MRS. BARNEY WILLIAMS resume their engagement at Niblo's on the 25th inst.

MISS LAURA KEENE, BROOKLYN.—Miss Keene, assisted by the choicest of her New York company, will commence a short season at the Academy of Music, Brooklyn, to-morrow evening, the performance being Rachel the Reaper, and the Soldier's Daughter.

The Philadelphia Inquirer.

CIRCULATION OVER 60,000. | PHILADELPHIA, SATURDAY, MAY 7, 1864. | PRICE TWO CENTS.

THE GRAND ADVANCE ON RICHMOND.

Scene of the Impending Battles between General GRANT and the Rebel Forces—Richmond and its Railroad Connections—The Flank Movements up the James River and the Peninsula—Petersburg and its Environs.

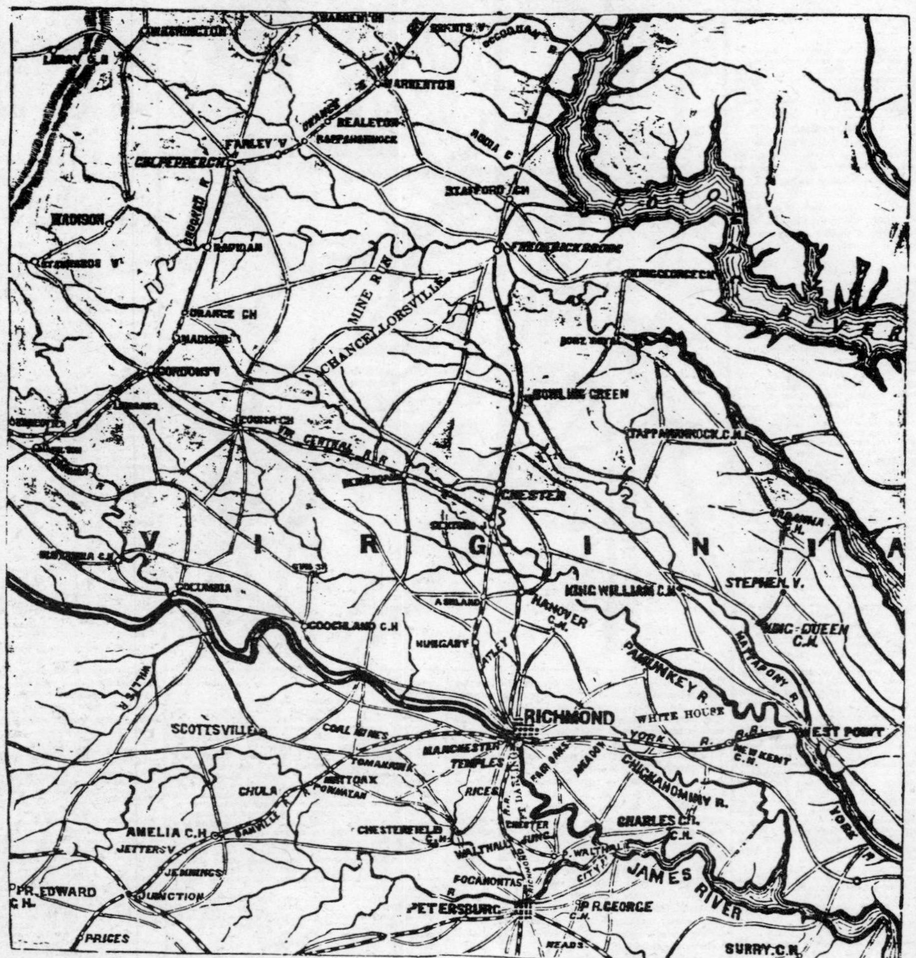

THE CAMPAIGN FOR THE UNION

Grant's Grand Advance on Lee.

THE REBELS REPORTED FALLING BACK

Burnside's Rumored Defeat, False.

NO COMMUNICATION WITH THE ARMY.

Gen. Butler Lands at City Point.

PETERSBURG THREATENED BY OUR TROOPS.

Rebel Communications Endangered.

REBELS ON THE LOWER POTOMAC

Beauregard at Petersburg

HIS FORCE 30,000 STRONG.

Grand Combination Movement of Our Armies.

OUR ARMY THROUGH THE WILDERNESS.

WASHINGTON, May 6.—Information has been received here that our army has passed safely through the Wilderness, but nothing further is known to-day of the onward movement. Rumors prevail of fighting, but they are founded on mere conjecture, as it is known that up to 7 o'clock on Wednesday no fight had occurred.

There are troops remaining on this side of the Rapidan, but it would be improper to state their exact location. Nearly all the colored soldiers are on this side of the river. Much of the rolling stock of the railroad has been sent back to Washington, as there is no further use for it below.

FURTHER FROM GENERAL GRANT.

WASHINGTON, May 6.—The impression in military circles here is that General LEE has gone to Richmond, by way of Gordonsville.

Nevertheless, the Government credits the theory entertained by the officers in the army.

Information received here to-day by the Government, via Fortress Monroe, states that General BEAUREGARD is at Petersburg, with a force of thirty thousand Rebels.

There is no information whatever, derived from any reliable source, that there has, up to this moment, been any fighting; while at the same time it is reasonable to suppose that two great armies occupying *the relative positions* of GRANT and LEE, must have come in collision before this time.

General GRANT has met with no opposition as yet in his onward movement. He has not found the enemy, who has retreated, it is supposed, to within the lines of his intrenchments at Richmond.

GENERAL MEADE BEYOND CHANCELLORVILLE.

WASHINGTON May 6.—The Army of the Potomac has passed the Wilderness, which includes the old Chancellorville battle-ground, east of LEE's army, until it reached an open plain east southeast of the Wilderness. He further states that General GRANT took that route in order to flank General LEE. Our informant states that the theory entertained by officers there was that General LEE was still in his works about Orange Court House. Many here believe that it will be found that General GRANT has flanked General LEE, and is between his army and the works of Richmond.

WASHINGTON, May 6—2.30 P. M.—There is no reliable information from the army front, because of the interruption of the means of communication. Rumors, therefore, take the place of known facts.

REPORTED DEFEAT OF GEN. BURNSIDE.

NEW YORK, May 5.—The *World* has issued an extra, containing a report that on Monday last Gen. BURNSIDE's advance was checked at Thoroughfare Gap by the Rebel forces under LONGSTREET. A battle is said to have occurred, resulting in our defeat, with the loss of 2000 to 4000 men. The negro troops are said to have become demoralized and threw down their arms, stampeding to the rear.

[This report is a base falsehood, as will be seen by referring to our Washington despatches. BURNSIDE has *not been* defeated by LONGSTREET, and the whole story is a lie of the first magnitude. He is in a position to defeat any attempt upon his lines whenever LEE can spare a force to attack him.]

BURNSIDE AT WARRENTON JUNCTION.

NEW YORK, May 6.—A special despatch reports that our army has passed through the Wilderness of Virginia, emerging into the open country.

A letter received from General BURNSIDE's headquarters at Warrenton Junction, on the 4th, locates the corps there, but it was expected to move on that day.

SKIRMISH AT THOROUGHFARE GAP.

Lee Calling in all his Cavalry Forces.

WASHINGTON, May 6.—Yesterday afternoon, at two o'clock, information was received by General BURNSIDE that a large force of Rebels was moving southward, by way of Thoroughfare Gap. This was communicated by signals, and General BURNSIDE at once started a large force of cavalry, who came up with the enemy as they were passing through the Gap. A volley from our men brought to the ground a Lieutenant, supposed from the mark on his shirt to be named MARCHAND.

He is believed to have been an aid to either LEE or STUART, as orders were found upon his person, signed by order of General LEE, directing IMBODEN and his cavalry, and all of the cavalry forces in Northern Virginia, to move at once and join General LEE. These orders were dated on the 4th inst., and it is supposed that the cavalry retreating south was not only that of IMBODEN, but all the Rebel cavalry in Northern Virginia, except, probably, a few guerrilla bands and marauders who could not in time receive the notice. This information shows that the statement telegraphed from New York of the defeat of BURNSIDE at Thoroughfare Gap was without foundation.

LANDING OF GENERAL BUTLER'S ARMY AT CITY POINT.

WASHINGTON, May 6.—Official despatches received to-day at the War Department, announce the advance of General BUTLER with his command, and their successful landing at City Point, Virginia.

Rebels on the Lower Potomac.

The *Primrose* of the Potomac flotilla, which arrived here to-day, reports that a few days since a party of Rebel cavalry were seen near Matthias Point, when the *Primrose* and *Teazer* opened on them with shell, causing them to take shelter behind the walls of an old building, whence they were driven by one of the shells of the former ship knocking down the wall.

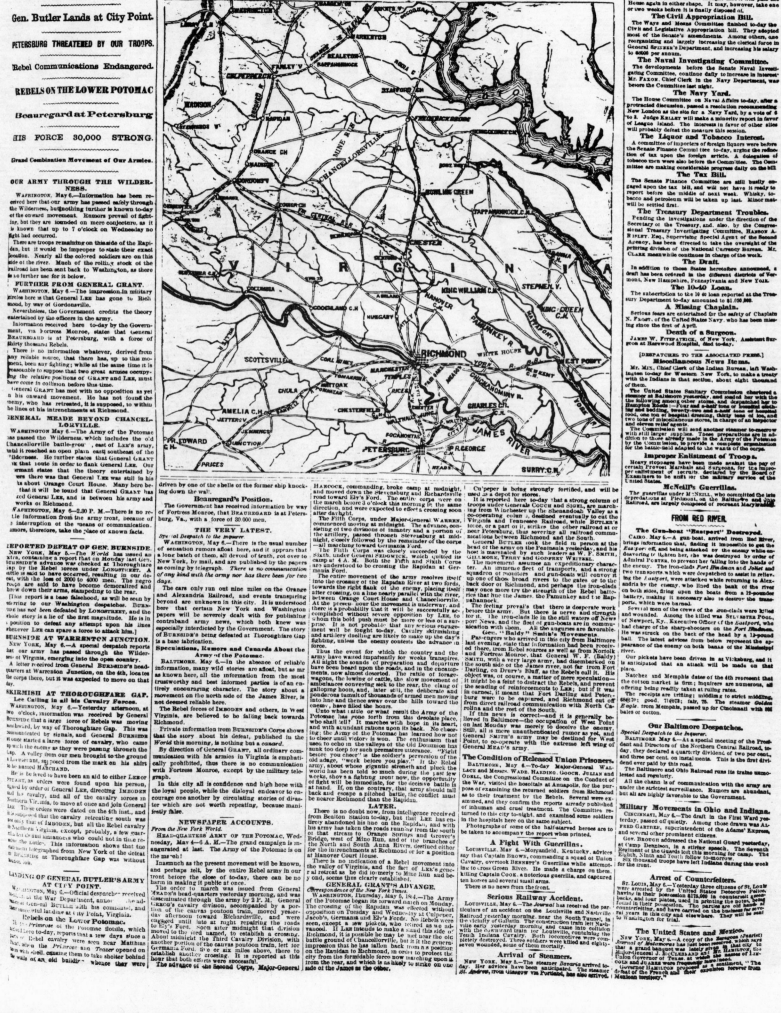

Beauregard's Position.

The Government has received information by way of Fortress Monroe, that BEAUREGARD is at Petersburg, Va., with a force of 30,000 men.

THE VERY LATEST.

Special Despatch to the Inquirer.

WASHINGTON, May 6.—There is the usual number of sensation rumors afloat here, and it appears that a long batch of them, all devoid of truth, got over to New York, by mail, and are published by the papers as coming by telegraph. *There is no communication of any kind with the army nor has there been for two days.*

The cars only run out nine miles on the Orange and Alexandria Railroad, and events transpiring beyond are unknown in this city. It is understood here that certain New York and Washington papers will be severely dealt with for publishing contraband army news, which both knew was especially interdicted by the Government. The story of BURNSIDE's being defeated at Thoroughfare Gap is a base fabrication.

Speculations, Rumors and Canards About the Army of the Potomac.

BALTIMORE, May 6.—In the absence of reliable information, many wild stories are afloat, but as far as known here, all the information from the most trustworthy and best informed parties is of an entirely encouraging character. The story about a movement on the north side of the James River, is not deemed reliable here.

The Rebel forces of IMBODEN and others, in West Virginia, are believed to be falling back towards Richmond.

Private information from BURNSIDE's Corps shows that the story about his defeat, published in the *World* this morning, is nothing but a *canard*.

By direction of General GRANT, all ordinary communication with his armies in Virginia is emphatically prohibited, thus there is no communication with Fortress Monroe, except by the military telegraph.

In this city all is confidence and high hope with the loyal people, while the disloyal endeavor to encourage one another by circulating stories of disaster which are not worth repeating, because manifestly false.

NEWSPAPER ACCOUNTS.

From the New York World.

HEAD-QUARTERS ARMY OF THE POTOMAC, Wednesday, May 4—6 A. M.—The grand campaign is inaugurated at last. The Army of the Potomac is on the march!

Inasmuch as the present movement will be known, and perhaps felt, by the entire Rebel army in our front before the close of to-day, there can be no harm in making it public at once.

The order to march was issued from General MEADE's head-quarters yesterday morning, and was disseminated through the army by 2 P. M. General GREGG's cavalry division, accompanied by a portion of the canvas pontoon train, moved yesterday afternoon toward Richardsville, and were engaged until late at night repairing the roads to Ely's Ford. Soon after midnight that division moved to the ford named, to establish a crossing. About midnight the Third Cavalry Division, with another portion of the canvas pontoon train, left for Germania Ford, five or six miles above, there to establish another crossing. It is reported at this hour that both efforts were successful.

The advance of the Second Corps, Major-General HANCOCK, commanding, broke camp at midnight, and moved down the Stevensburg and Richardsville road toward Ely's Ford. The entire corps were on the march before 3 o'clock this morning in the same direction, and were expected to effect a crossing soon after daylight.

The Fifth Corps, under Major-General WARREN, commenced moving at midnight. The advance, consisting of two divisions of infantry and a portion of the artillery, passed through Stevensburg at midnight, closely followed by the remainder of the corps—all marching toward Germania Ford.

The Fifth Corps was closely succeeded by the Sixth, under General SEDGWICK, which quitted its camp at 4 A. M. Both the Fifth and Sixth Corps are understood to be crossing the Rapidan at Germania Ford.

The entire movement of the army resolves itself into the crossing of the Rapidan River at two fords, towards the right flank of the enemy, placing itself after crossing, on a line nearly parallel with the river, between Orange Court House and Chancellorville. At the present hour the movement is underway, and there is a probability that it will be successfully accomplished without severe opposition by LEE, to whom this bold push must be more or less of a surprise. It is not probable that any serious engagement will be fought to-day. Cavalry skirmishing and artillery duelling are likely to make up the day's fighting, unless the enemy contests the advance in force.

Thus the event for which the country and the army have waited impatiently for weeks transpires. All night the sounds of preparation and departure have been heard upon the roads, and in the encampments, now almost deserted. The rattle of forage-wagons, the lowing of cattle, the slow movement of ambulances conveying sick to the rear, the clang of galloping hoofs, and, later still, the deliberate and ponderous tumult of thousands of armed men moving into line and thence away over the hills toward the enemy, have filled the hours.

Unto what battle or what result the Army of the Potomac has gone forth from this desolate place, who shall tell? It marches with hope in its heart, and with abundant rations upon its back. No cheering; the Army of the Potomac has learned how not to cheer until victory is won. The enthusiasm that used to echo in the valleys of the Old Dominion has sunk too deep for such premature utterance. "Fight before you cheer" is the soldier's perversion of the old adage, "work before you play." If the Rebel army, about whose gigantic strength and pluck the world has been told so much during the past few weeks, shows a fighting front now, the opportunity of fight will be immediate, for the decisive battle is at hand. If, on the contrary, that army should fall back and escape a pitched battle, the conflict must be nearer Richmond than the Rapidan.

LATER.

There is no doubt now, from intelligence received from Bealton Station to-day, but that LEE has entirely abandoned his line on the Rapidan, and with his army has taken the roads running from the south of that stream to Orange Springs and Grover's Bridge, west of Mine Run, and of the branches of the North and South Anna Rivers, destined either for the intrenchments at Richmond or for a position at Hanover Court House.

There is no indication of a Rebel movement into the valley of Virginia, and the fact of LEE's general retreat as he did formerly to Mine Run and beyond, seems thus clearly established.

GENERAL GRANT'S ADVANCE.

Correspondence of the New York Times.

WASHINGTON, Thursday, May 5, 1864.—The Army of the Potomac began its forward march on Monday. The crossing of the Rapidan was effected without opposition on Tuesday and Wednesday at Culpeper, Jacob's, Germania and Ely's Fords. No Rebels were seen, except a few pickets, who retired as we advanced. If LEE intends to make a stand this side of Richmond, it is possible he may be met near the old battle ground of Chancellorville, but it is the general impression that he has fallen back from his position on the Rapidan to Richmond, in order to protect the city from the formidable force now marching upon it from the rear, and which is as likely to strike on one side of the James as the other.

Culpeper is being strongly fortified, and will be used as a depot for stores.

It is reported here to-day that a strong column of troops under Generals COUCH and SIGEL, are marching from Winchester up the Shenandoah Valley as a co-operating column, destined eventually to cut the Virginia and Tennessee Railroad, while BUTLER's force, or a part of it, strikes the other railroad at or near Petersburg, thus severing all railroad communications between Richmond and the South.

General BUTLER took the field in person at the head of the army on the Peninsula yesterday, and his host is marshaled by such leaders as W. F. SMITH, GILLMORE, TERRY and GODFREY WEITZEL.

The movement assumes an expeditionary character. An immense fleet of transports, and a strong squadron of monitors and gun-boats will convoy it up one of those broad rivers to the gates or to the back door of Richmond, and perhaps the iron-clads may once more try the strength of the Rebel batteries that line the James, the Pamunkey and the Rappahannock.

The feeling prevails that there is desperate work before this army. But there is nerve and strength for it. The iron-clads lie in the still waters off News port News, and the fleet of gun-boats are in communication with them. All the auguries are favorable.

Gen. "Baldy" Smith's Movements.

Passengers who arrived in this city from Baltimore last evening, state that information had been received there, from Rebel sources as well as from Norfolk and Fortress Monroe, that General W. F. (Baldy) SMITH, with a very large army, had disembarked on the south side of the James river, not far from Fort Darling, on Drury's Bluff, as the Rebels call it. His object was, of course, a matter of mere speculation—it might be a feint to distract the Rebels, and prevent the sending of reinforcements to LEE; but if it was in earnest, it meant that Fort Darling and Petersburg were to be captured, and Richmond cut off from direct railroad communication with North Carolina and the rest of the South.

If this news is correct—and it is generally believed in Baltimore—the occupation of West Point on last Monday was merely to deceive the enemy. Still, all is mere unauthenticated rumor as yet, and General SMITH's army may be destined for West Point, to co-operate with the extreme left wing of General MEADE's army.

The Condition of Released Union Prisoners.

BALTIMORE, May 6.—To-day Major-General WALLACE and Messrs. WADE, HARDING, GOOCH, JULIAN and ODELL, the Congressional Committee on the Conduct of the War, visited the hospitals at Annapolis, for the purpose of examining the returned soldiers from Richmond as to their treatment by the Rebels. Several were examined, and they confirm the reports already published of inhuman and cruel treatment. The Committee returned to this city to-night, and examined some soldiers in the hospitals here on the same subject.

Photographs of some of the half-starved heroes are to be taken to accompany the report when printed.

A Fight With Guerrillas.

LOUISVILLE, May 6.—Morganfield, Kentucky, advices say that Captain BROWN, commanding a squad of Union Cavalry, overtook BENNETT's Guerrillas while attempting to cross Green River. He made a charge on them, killing Captain COOK, a notorious guerrilla, and captured ten horses and several small arms.

There is no news from the front.

Serious Railway Accident.

LOUISVILLE, May 6.—The *Journal* has received the particulars of an accident on the Louisville and Nashville Railroad yesterday morning, near the South Tunnel, in the vicinity of Gallatin. The construction train left Nashville early yesterday morning and came into collision with the downward train for Louisville, containing the Tenth Indiana Cavalry. Both locomotives were completely destroyed. Three soldiers were killed and eighty-seven wounded, some of them mortally.

Arrival of Steamers.

NEW YORK, May 5.—The steamer *Bavaria* arrived to-day. Her advices have been anticipated. The steamer *St. Andrew*, from Glasgow via Portland, has also arrived.

INTERESTING FROM WASHINGTON.

[SPECIAL DESPATCHES TO THE INQUIRER.]

WASHINGTON, May 6, 1864.

Payment of the Militia.

A paragraph sent from here by the Associated Press in reference to the bill for paying the Pennsylvania Militia, is incorrect. It was defeated at first, but when the motion was made to reconsider the motion to lay on the table, which would have settled the matter, LEONARD MYERS, to gain time, demanded the yeas and nays, and while they were being taken got enough members to change their votes to carry it, with an amendment appropriating fifteen millions to pay all similar claims from other States.

The bill is now before the Senate, and they will probably separate the Pennsylvania Militia pay from the other class of debts, and it is now thought that it will pass the House again in either shape. It may, however, take one or two weeks before it is finally disposed of.

The Civil Appropriation Bill.

The Ways and Means Committee finished to-day the Civil and Legislative Appropriation bill. They adopted most of the Senate's amendments. Among others, one reorganizing and largely increasing the clerical force in General SPINNER's Department, and increasing his salary to $6000 per annum.

The Naval Investigating Committee.

The developments before the Senate Naval Investigating Committee, continue daily to increase in interest. Mr. FAXON, Chief Clerk in the Navy Department, was before the Committee last night.

The Navy Yard.

The House Committee on Naval Affairs to-day, after a protracted discussion, passed a resolution recommending New London as the site for a Navy Yard, by a vote of 6 to 3. Judge KELLEY will make a minority report in favor of League Island. The interests in favor of other sites will probably defeat the measure this session.

The Liquor and Tobacco Interest.

A committee of importers of foreign liquors were before the Senate Finance Committee to-day, urging the reduction of tax upon the foreign article. A delegation of tobacco men were also before the Committee. The Committee are making considerable progress daily on the bill.

The Tax Bill.

The Senate Finance Committee are still busily engaged upon the tax bill, and will not have it ready to report before the middle of next week. Whisky, tobacco and petroleum will be taken up last. Minor matters will be settled first.

The Treasury Department Troubles.

Pending the investigations under the direction of the Secretary of the Treasury, and, also, by the Congressional Treasury Investigating Committee, HANSON A. RISLEY, Esq., Supervising Special Agent of the Second Agency, has been directed to take the oversight of the printing division of the National Currency Bureau. Mr. CLARK meanwhile continues in charge of the work.

The Draft.

In addition to those States heretofore announced, a draft has been ordered in the different districts of Vermont, New Hampshire, Pennsylvania and New York.

The 10-40 Loan.

The subscription to the 10 40 loan reported at the Treasury Department to-day amounted to $1,050,000.

A Missing Chaplain.

Serious fears are entertained for the safety of Chaplain N. FROST, of the United States Navy, who has been missing since the first of April.

Death of a Surgeon.

JAMES W. FITZPATRICK, of New York, Assistant Surgeon at Harewood Hospital, died to-day.

[DESPATCHES TO THE ASSOCIATED PRESS.]

Miscellaneous News Items.

Mr. MIX, Chief Clerk of the Indian Bureau, left Washington to-day for Western New York, to make a treaty with the Indians in that section, about eight thousand of them.

The United States Sanitary Commission chartered a steamer at Baltimore yesterday, and loaded her with the the following among other stores, and despatched her to Hampton Roads:—Four and a-half tons of hospital clothing and bedding, twenty-two and a-half tons of hospital food, one ton of hospital dressing, thirty tons of ice, and two tons of miscellaneous stores, in charge of an inspector and eleven relief agents.

The Commission will send another steamer to-morrow with still larger supplies. These preparations are in addition to those already made in the Army of the Potomac by the Commission, to provide a complete organization for the battle-field adapted to the wants of the corps.

Improper Enlistment of Troops.

Heavy stoppages have been made against the pay of certain Provost Marshals and Surgeons, for the improper enlistment of recruits, declared by the Board of Examiners to be unfit for the military service of the United States.

McNeill's Guerrillas.

The guerrillas under McNEILL, who committed the late depredations at Piedmont, on the Baltimore and Ohio Railroad, are largely composed of recreant Marylanders.

FROM RED RIVER.

The Gun-boat "Eastport" Destroyed.

CAIRO, May 6.—A gun-boat, arrived from Red River, brings information that, finding it impossible to get the *Eastport* off, and being attacked by the enemy while endeavoring to lighten her, she was destroyed by order of Admiral PORTER, to prevent her falling into the hands of the enemy. The iron-clads *Fort Hindman* and *Joliet* and two transports which were despatched to assist in relieving the *Eastport*, were attacked while returning to Alexandria by the enemy, who lined the bank of the river on both sides, firing upon the boats from a 12-pounder battery, making it necessary also to destroy the transports, which were burned.

Several men of the crews of the iron-clads were killed and wounded. Among the killed was SYLVESTER POOL, of Newport, Ky., Executive Officer of the *Eastport*, who had charge of the sharp-shooters on the *Fort Hindman*. He was struck on the back of the head by a 12-pound ball. The latest advices from below represent the appearance of the enemy on both banks of the Mississippi river.

Our pickets have been driven in at Vicksburg, and it is anticipated that an attack will be made on that place.

Natchez and Memphis dates of the 4th represent that the cotton market is firm; inquirers are numerous, all offering being readily taken at ruling rates.

The receipts are trifling; middling to strict middling, 68@70; good, 71@73; fair, 75. The steamer *Golden Eagle*, from Memphis, passed up for Cincinnati with 896 bales of cotton.

Our Baltimore Despatches.

Special Despatch to the Inquirer.

BALTIMORE, May 6.—At a special meeting of the President and Directors of the Northern Central Railroad, to-day, they declared a quarterly dividend of two per cent., and three per cent. on instalments. This is the first dividend ever paid by this road.

The Baltimore and Ohio Railroad runs its trains unmolested and regularly.

All the channels of communication with the army are under the strictest surveillance. Rumors are abundant, but all are highly favorable to the Government.

Military Movements in Ohio and Indiana.

CINCINNATI, May 6.—The draft in the First Ward yesterday, passed off quietly. Among those drawn was ALFRED GARTHER, superintendent of the Adams' Express, and several other prominent citizens.

Gov. BROUGH addressed the National Guard yesterday, at Camp Dennison, in a stiring speech. The Seventh Regiment of the Guards left this morning for camp. The Eighth, Ninth and Tenth follow to-morrow.

Six thousand troops have left Indiana during this week for the front.

Arrest of Counterfeiters.

ST. LOUIS, May 6.—Yesterday three citizens of St. Louis were arrested by the United States Detective Police, having in their possession $175,000 in counterfeit greenbacks, and four plates, used in printing the notes, being found in their possession. The parties are old hands at counterfeiting, and have carried on the business for several years in this city and elsewhere. They will be sent to Washington for trial.

The United States and Mexico.

NEW YORK, May 6.—A copy of the *Zaragoza* (*Juarist*) *Journal of Matamoras* has just been received, which says that a grand banquet was lately given in that city to Major-General J. McCLERNAND and Mr. HAMILTON, the Union Governor of Texas, at which the names of LINCOLN and JUAREZ were frequently introduced. Governor HAMILTON proposed as a sentiment, "The defeat of the French and their expulsion forever from Mexican territory."

The New-York Times.

VOL. XIII—NO. 3938. NEW-YORK, SUNDAY, MAY 8, 1864. PRICE FOUR CENTS.

THE BATTLE.

IMPORTANT NEWS FROM VIRGINIA.

A Great Battle Begun on Thursday.

Lee Confronts Grant with His Whole Army.

Severe Engagement Between Hancock and Longstreet.

HEAVY LOSS ON BOTH SIDES.

The Fifth Corps also Partly Engaged.

The Battle Renewed on Friday Morning.

Gen. Burnside's Corps on the Ground for Support.

STUART'S CAVALRY ROUTED BY SHERIDAN

The Troops Enthusiastic to a High Degree.

HIGHLY IMPORTANT FROM BUTLER'S ARMY

Very Successful Landing at City Point.

THE REBELS COMPLETELY SURPRISED.

Cavalry Expedition to Destroy the Richmond and Petersburgh Railroad.

Full Particulars from Our Special Correspondent.

WASHINGTON, Saturday, May 7.

The statements which were received here to-day, and which are entitled to belief, are that Gen. LEE made a tremendous and violent attack to pierce our centre, hoping thereby to divide our forces and to secure a victory; but Gen. HITCHCOCK's corps came to the relief, and, amid a murderous fire, formed in line of battle, and thwarted the designs of the rebels. The loss was heavy on both sides.

Gen. SHERIDAN was profitably engaged in another part of the field, and sent the Chief in command a message that he had routed STUART's cavalry.

The attack of LEE was on our advancing columns, who doubtless anticipated a victory by his onslaught, before the main body could advance to the field of battle.

The appearances on Thursday were that the hostilities would be renewed on Friday.

Battle Begun on Thursday—Grant Confronted by Lee's Whole Force—Severe Engagements Between Portions of Each Army—Hancock Engages Longstreet—The Battle-Ground near Chancellorsville.

From the Tribune.

UNION MILLS, Va., Friday, May 6—9 P. M.

The grand Army of the Potomac crossed the Rapidan on Wednesday. The Second Corps moved on Tuesday to the Mills, opposite Ely's Ford. On Wednesday morning, at 4 o'clock, the cavalry crossed and drove the rebel pickets from the opposite heights, meeting with no opposition.

A position was gained and the corps moved on at 7 o'clock, taking the road to Chancellorsville, at which place Gen. HANCOCK would establish his headquarters.

The Fifth and Sixth Corps crossed at Germanna Ford in the course of the day, taking the road to the Wilderness.

On Wednesday night Gen. WARREN's headquarters were at the Wilderness, Gen. SEDGWICK on his right, and the general headquarters at Germanna Ford.

On Thursday morning the rebels pressed our pickets, and appeared to be in strong force on our right. The Fifth New-York Cavalry, skirmishing on the Orange Court-house road, near Perkins' tavern, were driven in with a severe loss, leaving many wounded on the field. Gen. GRIFFITH's division was marched forward on our right about 11 o'clock to feel the enemy's position, and were met by the rebel Gen. A. P. HILL, supported by Gen. EWELL.

A severe action took place, in which we captured about 300 prisoners, though it is reported that we lost two guns. Meantime, Gen. HANCOCK marched his corps to the right to connect with WARREN, and had hardly got into position, his left resting on or near Chancellorsville, when he was attacked by LONGSTREET with his full corps, and a part of EWELL's.

Gen. HANCOCK, with the assistance of GETTY's division of the Sixth Corps, held his position under musketed fire of two and a half hours duration, in which his command suffered severely, inflicting much injury upon the rebels.

Other developments showed LEE to have his whole force in our front.

This knowledge of their position was, of course, highly important, and was thus obtained only by the greatest skill in the handling of our troops. It not being the purpose of Gen. MEADE to advance upon the enemy, he ordered the line of battle to be held till morning.

The position of our troops on Thursday night was parallel with and a little in advance of the road from Germanna Ford to Chancellorsville, the two flanks resting on those points, and general headquarters at the Wilderness.

Meanwhile, in the afternoon the advance of the 9th Corps crossed Germanna Ford, taking position on our right flank.

Gen. BURNSIDE's rear arrived this forenoon.

It was understood that a general attack was to be made this morning, and heavy firing had commenced on our right when I had left, at 5 o'clock.

Heavy cannonading was heard when I passed Kelly's Ford, about 9 o'clock this forenoon, which leads me to believe that we had driven them to their defences, as no heavy guns could be brought into action on the former position.

There ought to be no doubt that there has been a grand victory, as Gen. MEADE showed his strength yesterday by a stubborn and gallant defence withou using half the command that he has undoubtedly brought into the action to-day. The troops are in a high state of enthusiasm.

Reports from Washington—Doubtful Rumors—A Three Days' Battle Reported.

WASHINGTON, Saturday, May 7.

The *Republican* has the following:

"The Government has information this morning, whether from official sources or other we are unable to learn positively at the moment of going to press, that on Wednesday at daylight Gen. GRANT's whole army was entirely across the Rapidan. It marched to a plain a little beyond, and near the Chancellorsville battle-ground, when LEE was forced out of his works and offered battle, which was at once accepted. The fight became fierce, and lasted until dark, the enemy being forced back some distance, with great loss, leaving most of his killed and wounded in our hands.

The two armies lay on their arms all night Wednesday, and at daylight on Thursday the battle opened again, and raged with the greatest fury on both sides until dark, when it was found that the enemy had been forced back in the two days' fight about two miles and a half, leaving heaps of dying, killed and wounded on the field to be buried and taken care of by our troops. We have heard various estimates made of the number slaughtered, but at this moment it is useless to speculate on the subject. Everyone knows that it must have been terrible, and will speak to the senses when the facts are known.

On Friday morning, at 5 o'clock, the forces were marshaling for another conflict, Gen. GRANT moving on LEE's works.

Up to this time Gen. BURNSIDE's corps, numbering 30,000 men, had taken no part in the battle, but at half-past five was marching into position to engage in the bloody contest of the third day's battle.

Of the result of this day's battle we have no report up to the moment of going to press. The battle commenced at 6 o'clock in the morning. Unless LEE received reinforcements equal to BURNSIDE's corps, the battle of Friday must have proved terribly disastrous to him.

The fact that we have received no news of yesterday's fighting leads to the belief that LEE is endeavoring to get away to Richmond, and GRANT is in pursuit.

It is evident that the rebel forces about Richmond cannot be spared to reinforce LEE, as they have discovered ere this that they have enough to attend to there, probably from two attacks upon the city by Gen. BUTLER's force.

[The above dispatch is so extravagant in its statements, and corresponds so poorly with other and more reliable advices, that it is doubtless entitled to very little credit.—ED. TIMES.]

From Washington—Intense Excitement in the City—All Sorts of Reports, Rumors, &c.

WASHINGTON, Saturday, May 7.

The city has been intensely excited all day with the news from the Army of the Potomac, the early publications serving to excite the public curiosity concerning the military movements.

The bulletin boards of the newspapers attracted throngs of readers. Inquiries were repeatedly made of all who were supposed to have items of intelligence, while extra newspapers continued to be cried by the newsboys, and purchased in abundance.

Rumors of defeat and brilliant victories prevailed to a limited extent, but both classes of reports required authenticity to gain general belief.

The thoughtful, however, came to the conclusion that a single encounter would not determine the contest, and a series of battles may have to be fought before there can be any decisive result.

It was telegraphed hence by the Independent Telegraph Line, but refused by the other lines, doubtless for prudential reasons, that a great victory was achieved by Gen. GRANT on Wednesday and Thursday, he driving the rebels two and a half miles with immense loss, and that he was following up that victory on Friday morning by an assault on the rebel works.

The *Star*, in noticing a similar statement of an afternoon cotemporary, remarks:

"We should be very glad to be able to confirm this news, but have to say, after diligent inquiry, we are satisfied that the Government has received no such information, or any information of more decisive results than that furnished by the *Tribune* dispatch, elsewhere."

The fact that Gen. MEADE was able to stand the brunt of the Confederate onset with a portion of his command is considered a hopeful indication, and we hope soon to be able to announce a decisive victory; but we shall not trifle with our readers by manufacturing bogus victories for an hour's sensation."

The above contradiction of the *Star* is believed to be based on reliable information.

During the day many inquiries were made of officers of the Government, but without the satisfaction naturally desirable on the part of those who have imppatient desires for early and complete success, and who forget that the work must be necessarily stubborn, heavy and persistent on both sides, owing to the great importance to each of the result.

The fragmentary information received from time to time shows nothing decisive, but serves to contradict many rumors and speculations concerning the whereabouts and designs of the rebels which were so confidently asserted.

Further from Washington—No Later News Received by the Government up to 5 o'clock Last Evening.

WASHINGTON, Saturday, May 7.

Up to 5 o'clock this afternoon the Government had received no information of more decisive results than was furnished by dispatches published this morning. Therefore, the reports of a great victory achieved by Gen. GRANT on Wednesday and Thursday, and the pursuing of the enemy on Friday, etc., are, to say the least, not reliable.

WASHINGTON, Sunday, May 8—1 o'clock A.M.

It is said to-night that Gen. HAYS was killed in the fight on Thursday, and that several other generals were wounded.

Reported Casualties—Death of Brig.-Gen. Alexander Hays—Brig.-Gen. J. J. Bartlett and Col. Gurney Wounded.

PHILADELPHIA, Saturday, May 7.

A special dispatch to the *Evening Telegraph*, from Washington, says:

Gen. ALEXANDER HAYS was killed on Thursday, while deploying his troops as skirmishers.

Gen. BARTLETT and Col. GURNEY were severely wounded.

Gen. HAYS was a native of Pittsburgh.

The Forward Movement.

From the Washington Star, of Friday Evening.

We have information that up to 7 P. M. of Wednesday evening last no firing was heard in the direction taken by our Army of the Potomac the night before, and we have reason to believe that it was definitely known to Gen. GRANT that LEE had left his former positions before our advance took place. That up to this hour it is not known here by telegraph from Fortress Monroe, that LEE has attacked or confronted Maj.-Gen. "Baldy" SMITH's force, strikes us as embracing substantial proof that GRANT's pursuit commenced very shortly after LEE's movement—so soon after, as that, if he did move against our troops on the Peninsula, he could hardly open upon them before GRANT can attack his rear. But every succeeding hour of the absence of intelligence of a battle in that quarter strengthens the probability that LEE's movement was simply a retreat to get behind the Richmond fortifications; as by this time GRANT, if not seriously opposed, could have marched to within thirty or forty miles, at most, of the rebel capital, or to within supporting distance of where Gen. SMITH's army must be by this time, unless its advance has been delayed by the appearance of LEE in his front; in which case, GRANT's route to his support would be shorter than if his advance had been unopposed. Twenty-four hours at most must, however, solve all the so interesting questions as to what has happened in that quarter up to this time.

We have no fear of the success of any possible effort of LEE to attack and defeat Gen. SMITH's force before it can be amply sustained by the main army under GRANT, as we know many facts going to show that among Gen. GRANT's purposes is surely that of guarding against any disaster to SMITH's army that might otherwise result from LEE's movement.

THE COMBINED MOVEMENTS IN VIRGINIA.

Map Showing the Lines of Operation on the Rapidan, the North Anna and the James Rivers, where Grant and Butler, Lee and Beauregard are Manœuvering; and their Relations to Richmond.

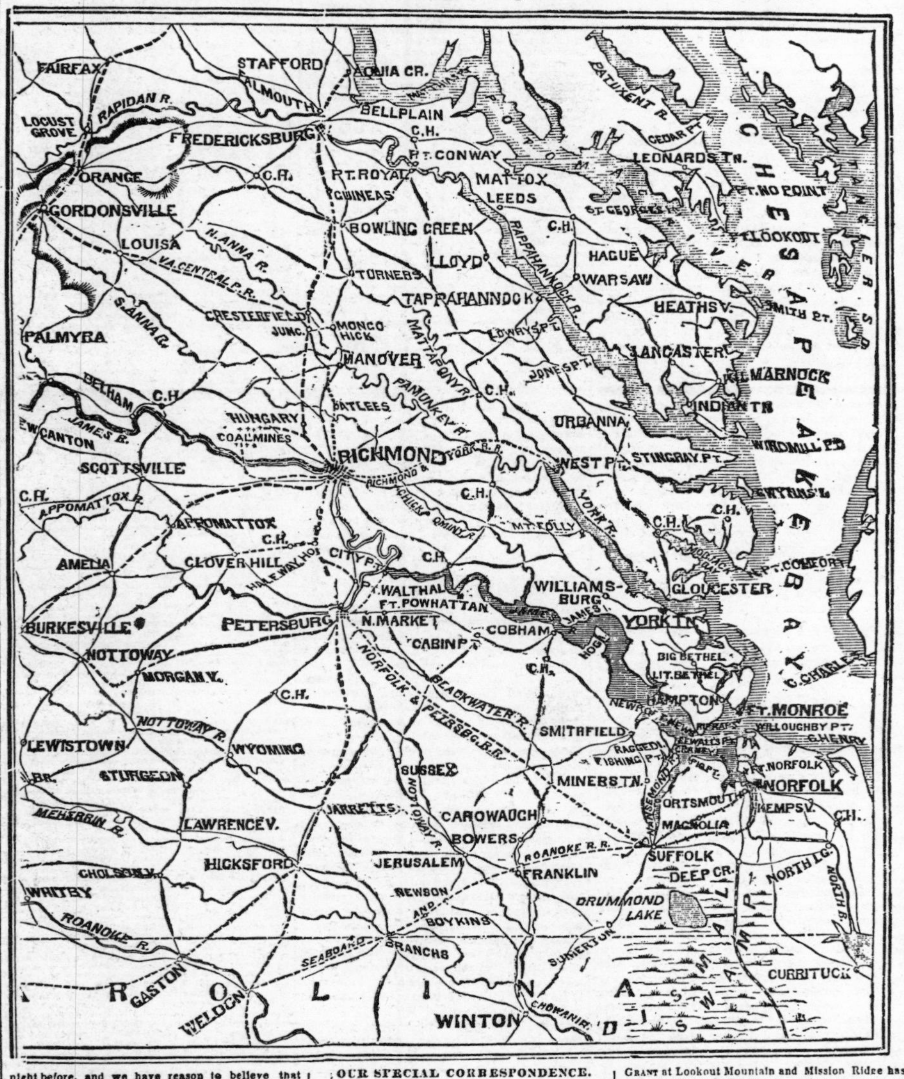

OUR SPECIAL CORRESPONDENCE.

GEN. BUTLER'S COLUMN.

Movements on the James River—A Complete Surprise—Our Forces Landed and Pushing Forward.

FORTRESS MONROE, Friday, May 6, via BALTIMORE, Saturday, May 7.

On Tuesday night, the 3d inst., about one-half of the large fleet of transports that have been lying in the Roads for some time were ordered to Yorktown, and commenced embarking troops on Wednesday.

The rest of the fleet went up and took the remainder of the troops on board and came back here.

The whole fleet then proceeded up the James River, passing here last night.

The movement was conducted with the greatest secrecy and with all possible quietness.

The fleet advanced up the James River, preceded by the army gunboats, under the command of Gen. GRAHAM.

During to-day and last night a very successful landing has been effected, and no resistance had been met with up to 4 o'clock this morning, at which time the steamboat *Thomas Powell* left with dispatches in charge of Capt. PFEIFFER.

No casualty had occurred beyond the killing of a colored soldier and the injury of two others by being caught between two boats.

Our movements were evidently a complete surprise.

At last advices, our forces were being rapidly landed and pushed forward.

We have landed at Wilson's wharf, Fort Powhattan, Landen, Bermuda Hundred, above the Appomattox River, etc.

Our monitors and gunboats are all over the bar at Harrison's Landing and above City Point.

The operations of the fleet have been characterized by great energy and success.

The Expedition up the James—The Start from Fortress Monroe—The Occupation of Fort Powhatan and Wilson's Wharf—The Successful Landing at City Point—Surprise of the Enemy—Important Cavalry Expedition from Suffolk.

STEAMER GRAYHOUND, OFF FORT POWHATAN, JAMES RIVER, Va., Thursday, May 5, 1864.

The movement of the Union army in this direction, which, for weeks past, has been vaguely expected, commenced this morning. The obligation to keep silence respecting the hostile preparations, which, for prudential reasons was imposed, is now removed; and here, under the shadow of the commanding fortification, erected by the rebels in 1862 for the purpose of interrupting MCCLELLAN's water communications after his reverses before the rebel Capital, known as Fort Powhatan, I commence the record of the campaign. Premising that up to this point every circumstance has been auspicious, and that not the slightest symptom of resistance on the part of the enemy to our advance in the direction of Richmond has been encountered, either from guerrillas, torpedoes or any other source, I shall go back a few weeks, and briefly trace from its conception the enterprise which, to the present point, in all its details, has been a wonderful success.

THE PLAN.

To Major-Gen. BUTLER, I am told, is exclusively due whatever credit shall result from the inception and execution of the plan. When, four weeks since, Lieut.-Gen. GRANT, the actual commander of the armies of the United States, visited Fortress Monroe, it was for the purpose of ascertaining the views of Gen. BUTLER respecting an advance upon the rebels by way of the Peninsula, to be carried out in co-operation with the Grand Army of the Potomac. Gen. GRANT had considered the various plans proposed with this object in view, but had committed himself to none, and was inclined, therefore, to listen attentively to what Gen. BUTLER might suggest. The sequel proves that the proposition of Gen. BUTLER fully commended itself to the judgment and acquiescence of the Commanding General, and measures were at once taken to put it in execution.

Briefly, the project was to advance upon Richmond by the James River; get a foothold as near the city as possible, on the south bank of the stream; seriously interrupt the communications of the rebel Capital southward, and eventually compel the evacuation by LEE's army of their strongly-fortified position on the Rapidan, thus forcing the rebels to give GRANT battle, or press rapidly rearward to the walls of their Capital. The plan will be generally admitted to be both bold and comprehensive, while the arrangement of its preliminaries has been marked by the rarest shrewdness and military sagacity.

THE ORGANIZATION.

The first step toward organization was made some weeks since, by the concentration at Yorktown, from the various posts in the Department of North Carolina and Virginia, the great bulk of the Eighteenth Army Corps. To the command of these troops was assigned Maj.-Gen. W. F. SMITH, whose glorious career under GRANT at Lookout Mountain and Mission Ridge has won for him the confidence of the army and the gratitude of the country. In addition to these war-worn heroes from the coast of North Carolina and the posts in Virginia, nearly all the brave and gallant fellows of the Tenth Army Corps, (under Maj.-Gen. GILLMORE,) fresh from the bloody field of Olustee and the more remote and scarce less bloody sands of Morris's Island, were sent to Gen. BUTLER to participate in the movement, forming their encampment at Gloucester Point, opposite Yorktown.

That Yorktown and Gloucester Point, both at the mouth of the York River, should have been selected for the rendezvous of these troops, naturally led to the supposition that the advance was intended to be made up the Peninsula by the route which proved so fearfully disastrous to MCCLELLAN. But this show of force was merely a stupendous *ruse de guerre*, and circumstances indicate that it succeeded admirably in deceiving the rebels. Their journals have constantly spoken of these troops as destined to follow the path of 1862, and that the assurance of their deception might be made doubly sure, a brigade of Union troops was dispatched by Gen. BUTLER even as late as yesterday to White House Landing, where, at sunset, when we last heard from them, they were sedulously engaged in felling timber and constructing a wharf, as if preparing to facilitate the landing of a large army. To aid in this scheme of mystification, all the light-draft steamers were kept until the last moment at Fortress Monroe, whence, early yesterday morning, they were dispatched to the York River, and the work of embarking the troops, whose arrangements for the purpose had been already made, was begun promptly. Soon after the shades of evening closed over the camping-ground, the last tent was struck and the troops were all on board.

Gen. BUTLER's order to his subordinate Generals, made it incumbent for them to repair to Hampton Roads, as quickly as possible after dark, where they were to anchor for the night. At day-break the order commanded an advance of the troops up the James River, convoyed by three army gunboats, under Brig.-Gen GRAHAM, and a naval force, consisting of five monitors and eleven gunboats, under Rear-Admiral LEE.

THE PLAN FOR THE CAVALRY.

The cavalry branch of the expedition is commanded by Brig.-Gen. A. V. KAUTZ, who has just received his stars, but who is pretty well known as the Colonel of an Ohio cavalry regiment, that last year, after a wearying chase, stopped the audacious career of the guerrilla General MORGAN, by a handsome charge upon the immensely larger force of the marauders, as they attempted to cross the Ohio River into Kentucky. KAUTZ, with a fine body of several thousand white troopers, left Suffolk, Va., also at daylight yesterday morning. The point at which he aims primarily to strike is Hickford, a town on the Petersburgh, Richmond and Weldon Railroad. A ride of about eighty miles, by the Surrey and Sussex roads, allowing him time to pay his compliments to the people as he passes along, would bring him to Hickford to-morrow evening. The railroad bridge there, which is a strong one, about three hundred feet long, will be destroyed, if possible; and then the dashing horsemen will do other damage to the enemy's means of supply as far as they can find opportunity. Gen. KAUTZ has received a roving commission, and if not too hardly pressed by the rebels he may penetrate as far South as Weldon, N. C., returning when it suits his convenience. We may not hear of him for a month, but meanwhile it is expected that he will make a good record.

Starting up the Peninsula from Williamsburgh, another cavalry force, somewhat smaller, commanded by Col. WEST, also set out at daybreak. Their object was to create a diversion in our favor by keeping the rebels excited and attacking guerrillas and the garrisons of the outposts. Col. WEST would try to cross the Chickahominy at Bottom's bridge and make his way to the main body on the James. Taking it for granted that the cavalry started at the proper time and are now having a good time and a glorious gallop, I must return to

THE ADVANCE OF THE MAIN FORCE.

As on every occasion when a large piece of machinery is put in operation, there is certain to be more or less friction of the parts, so this complex machine of a gallant and mighty army did not move smoothly according to the programme. The Eighteenth Corps (Gen. SMITH's,) having the advance, was promptly up to time, down finding all the steamers used in its transportation steaming by Newport's News into the mouth of the James River. But the steamers of the Tenth (Gen. GILLMORE's) Corps were still quietly at anchor off Fortress Monroe. Here was an unexpected source of detention. Gen. BUTLER had every reason to suppose that the sailing-orders were perfectly understood, and would be implicitly followed by his Corps Commanders. It was easy to perceive that he was both distressed and annoyed at the delay. He had hoped to reach his intended point of debarkation (City Point, fifteen miles below Richmond,) at three o'clock in the afternoon. This he expected to accomplish, even in case that the possession of two points on the way up the river, viz.: Wilson's Wharf and Fort Powhatan, should be contested by the enemy, as it was very likely would be done. There was nothing for it, then, but to learn the cause of this dilatoriness of the Tenth Corps, and to hasten the vessels forward. This was done.

The fleet new steamer *Grayhound*, the flagboat of the expedition, on board which Gen. BUTLER, with his staff, had come at midnight, went back from Newport's News to Fortress Monroe. Gen. GILLMORE was sent for, and made satisfactory explanations, I believe, to Gen. BUTLER. This accomplished, off we started at 8 o'clock up the river.

The scene in the hazy light of the beautiful Spring morning was picturesque and animated. Crowded steamboats labored heavily through the still water, pontoon trains and lumbering canal barges, to be used in disembarking, were in tow of the swifter transports. The long low lines and wedge-like shapes of those naval nondescripts, the monitors, with their high cylindrical turrets amidships, gave variety to the scene. The swift *Grayhound* flits among the slow-moving craft and slackens her speed an instant as she comes abreast each vessel, allowing Gen. BUTLER from the hurricane-deck to order them to advance with all the celerity possible. "Give her all the steam you can, Captain," shouts the General, with upraised cap, and as the crowds of blue-coats recognize him they burst out vociferously in cheers. The scene, as we pass up the river, is charming in the extreme. The high wooded banks of the stream present us every variety of delicate foliage with which the Spring delights to clothe the earth in vernal beauty. Occasionally a house is visible over the bluffs, and a man appears, beyond doubt very much amazed at the sudden appearance of so large a fleet of invading Yankees. The trip up the river is unbroken by any sign of war.

Taking the advance, Gen. BUTLER's boat reaches Wilson's Wharf, a point about 35 miles below Richmond. Here a regiment of Gen. WILDE's negro brigade have effected a landing, and are busily engaged in making preparations to hold the place. From this point up the river to Fort Powhatan is a clear straight reach of seven miles, which it would never do to leave in command of the enemy, who could fortify the bluffs and play the mischief with our water communications. So Gen. BUTLER takes possession of both these strong positions. The stalwart Africans gaily run up the bluffs, and are soon at work swinging axes with a will, and the giant trees fall with a mournful crash under their sturdy strokes. Soon a wide space of woods on the high banks are cleared away, and rebels approaching from toward Richmond must come within the sweep of our batteries. Bye-the-bye, there can be nothing mentioned, I think, which better shows the perfect surprise of this movement to the rebels, than the fact that, according to their own admission, they have a strong force at Charles City Court-house, six miles inland from Wilson's Wharf, engaged in collecting negroes together for work on the Richmond fortifications. It is strange if this force was aware of our approach that they did not come up and give us a few shots from a field battery. But no welcome of this left-handed sort greeted us. It is quite likely that our negroes may repair *vi et armis* to the Charles City rendezvous, and so reverse the kind of work their brethren have been assembled to perform on the strongholds of Richmond. The boat is just now leaving Powhatan, where a strong sable garrison has been landed, having little to do in the way of securing their position, but mount the ordnance in the works which the rebels two years ago so laboriously constructed.

The bell rings for the boat to move off for City Point. This place to us is of the first strategic importance, but the indications now are that we shall peacefully occupy it. I must, therefore, stop this hurried writing and go with the other passengers on deck to watch with anxiety the approach of our fleet to its proposed destination.

OCCUPATION OF CITY POINT.

There is a splendid chance for exultation here, and we are all devoutly thankful. City Point has become ours without a struggle. The Union forces are securely planted in a splendidly advantageous position within fifteen miles of the rebel capital. Our troops are landing as rapidly as possible. The negro soldiers, always in the advance, to-day are streaming up the steep bluffs like ants toward an ant-hill. It is now three o'clock, and before nightfall the greater part of this immense army will have disembarked. Our line will stretch across this narrow strip of land, the left resting upon the James River, and then passing over the little River Appomattox, the prolongation of the line will reach to the James again, holding that almost insular position called the township of Bermuda Hundred. Intrenched here, with both flanks of the army protected by gunboats, we can bid defiance to LEE's coherts, if GRANT's sharp pressing drive them down upon us. The position is considered admirable for seriously threatening Richmond. LEE's army is now between two fires, and should our cavalry raid seriously impair his communications south, starvation will be added to his other troubles. Before we left Fortress Monroe a dispatch from the War Department was received by Gen. BUTLER, announcing GRANT's safe passage of the Rapidan. We suppose that LEE ere this has given him battle or has hastened to the Richmond defences. In either case he must be at this time in a peculiarly unpleasant position. His army certainly was never in such an ugly place before. We are very thankful and joyous here at the perfect ease with which the entire plan of this expedition has been carried out.

THE SCENE AT CITY POINT.

The *Grayhound* having been delayed quite a while at Fort Powhatan, some of the transports went by and arrived at City Point just before her. I forgot to mention that three army gunboats, under command of Brig.-Gen. GRAHAM, led the advance the entire distance up the river, keeping a few miles ahead of the naval vessels. As we in the *Grayhound* came in view of the commanding bluffs of the Point, we

Continued on the Eighth page.

The Charleston Mercury.

DAILY PAPER—FIFTEEN DOLLARS, FOR SIX MONTHS—PAYABLE IN ADVANCE.

VINDICE NULLO
SPONTE SUA SINE LEGE FIDES RECTUMQUE COLLENTUR.

COUNTRY PAPER—THRICE A WEEK—EIGHT DOLLARS, FOR SIX MONTHS—PAYABLE IN ADVANCE.

VOLUME LXXXIV. | CHARLESTON, S. C., MONDAY, MAY 9, 1864. | NUMBER 12,056.

TELEGRAPHIC.

REPORTED FOR THE ASSOCIATED PRESS.

LATEST FROM THE SEAT OF WAR.

THE BATTLES ON THE RAPID ANN.

CONTINUED SUCCESS OF OUR ARMS.

OFFICIAL DESPATCHES FROM GEN. LEE.

GENERAL JENKINS KILLED, AND GENERALS LONGSTREET AND PEGRAM SEVERELY WOUNDED.

FIGHTING CONTINUED ALL DAY FRIDAY AND SATURDAY.

MOVEMENTS ON JAMES RIVER.

&c., &c., &c.

ORANGE C. H., May 6.—We have the following additional particulars of the fighting on Thursday:

HETH's and WILCOX's divisions were engaged. They checked and drove back three corps and two divisions of the enemy.

LANE's North Carolina brigade last night surprised and captured three hundred prisoners.

From 3 p. m. until nightfall there was very heavy musketry fighting. But little artillery was engaged. COOK's brigade fought well and suffered a heavy loss. THOMAS' and MCGOWAN's brigades (the latter consisting entirely of South Carolina troops) also suffered considerably.—ROSSER, with his single brigade, fought WILCOX's whole division of Yankee cavalry, driving them back at all points.

The fighting has been resumed this (Friday) morning. It is reported and believed that we are driving them. About 300 more prisoners have been received here, and more are on the way. Gen. BENNING was slightly wounded this morning, in the arm, and Gen. PEGRAM in the knee.

The battle field is about twenty-five miles below here. The Richmond ambulance committee have arrived here. The Press correspondent left for the battle field this morning.

LATER—THE BATTLE ON FRIDAY.

ORANGE C. H., May 6—9, p. m.—The attack of the enemy this morning was very violent, but it was repulsed in every instance. A strong effort was made to turn our right. We drove them on our left; but their line resisted stubbornly on the right. LONGSTREET, however, finally forced them to give way.

General LONGSTREET received a severe wound in the shoulder, and General JENKINS, of South Carolina, was mortally wounded. Col. BROWN, of Georgia, of the Virginia Artillery, was killed.

Amongst the other casualties reported are the following: Colonel JAMES D. NANCE, South Carolina regiment, killed; Colonel MILLER, 12th South Carolina regiment, killed; Lieutenant Colonel BOOKTER, 12th South Carolina regiment, mortally wounded; Lieutenant Colonel FRANKLIN GAILLARD, 2d South Carolina regiment, (and formerly editor of the Columbia *Carolinian*,) killed.

The fighting was principally with musketry, the ground being unsuitable for the use of artillery. The battle was fought near the "Wilderness," and the enemy has been pushed back nearly to Chancellorsville. Everything looks well. The Yankee General WADSWORTH, who was the Abolition candidate for Governor, against SEYMOUR, in the last New York election, was killed. Up to this time seventeen hundred prisoners have been received here.

GENERAL LEE'S OFFICIAL DESPATCH.

RICHMOND, May 6.—The following has just been received at the War Office:

HEADQUARTERS
ARMY NORTHERN VIRGINIA, May 6.

To the Secretary of War:

Early this morning, as the divisions of General HILL, engaged yesterday, were being relieved, the enemy advanced, creating some confusion; but the ground lost was recovered as soon as our fresh troops got into position, and the enemy was driven back to his original line. Afterwards, we turned the left of his fresh line and drove it from the field, leaving a large number of dead and wounded in our hands—amongst them General WADSWORTH.

A subsequent attack forced the enemy into his entrenched lines on the Brook Road, extending from the Wilderness Tavern, on the right, to Trigg's Mill. Every advance on his part, thanks to a merciful God, has been repulsed.

Our loss in killed is not large; but we have many wounded—most of them slightly, the artillery having been little used on either side. I grieve to announce that Lieutenant General LONGSTREET was severely wounded, and General JENKINS killed. General PEGRAM was badly wounded yesterday. General STAFFORD, it is hoped, will recover.

(Signed) R. E. LEE.

SATURDAY'S DESPATCHES.

RICHMOND, May 7.—The chief Monitor of the enemy's fleet in James River is the *Onondaga*, which has just been finished in New York. The Yankee gunboat destroyed by one of our torpedoes yesterday was blown into fragments. The official despatch says that hardly a piece as big as a row-boat was left. After the explosion, the rest of the fleet stopped.

Nothing has been heard of the situation of affairs on the Rappahannock this morning. GRANT's plan was to turn our right and get between LEE and Richmond. LONGSTREET turned the enemy's left and was pushing him back steadily when he received his severe wound. He was shot, owing to a mistake, by some of our own men, of MAHONE's brigade, and Gen. JENKINS was killed by the same brigade. Gen. KERSHAW commanded MCLAWS' division with distinguished honor. BATTLE's Alabama and GORDON's Georgia brigade suffered severely.

SATURDAY'S FIGHTING.

[An interruption of telegraphic communication with Richmond on Saturday afternoon, which was not restored until a late hour Sunday night, has prevented the receipt of the expected press despatches in regard to the operations of Saturday. Private telegrams, however, received on Saturday, before the interruption took place, render it certain that the conflict still continued on that day, with encouraging results.—*Ed. Mercury.*]

LATEST OFFICIAL DESPATCH FROM GEN. LEE.

RICHMOND, SUNDAY, May 8.—The following was received at the War Office this morning:

HEADQUARTERS,
ARMY NORTHERN VIRGINIA, May 8, 1864.

To the Secretary of War:

Gen. GORDON turned the enemy's extreme right yesterday evening, and drove him from his rifle pits.

Amongst the prisoners captured are Generals TRUMAN, SEYMOUR and SHALLOR. A number of arms were also taken.

The enemy has abandoned the Germania Ford Road, and removed his pontoon bridge towards the Ely's Ford Road.

There has been no attack to-day; only slight skirmishing along our line.

(Signed) R. E. LEE.

A despatch from Chaffin's Bluff says that one of the enemy's gunboats had been attacked and disabled, and afterwards boarded and burned on the 7th instant. Two iron clads bore down on our forces, but subsequently withdrew. We have no further particulars.

[*Note.*—In order that our readers may comprehend the state of affairs, we will explain the position of the roads and fords alluded to in General LEE's despatch. Germania and Ely's Crossings, on the Rapid Ann, are on the roads leading from Culpeper to Fredericksburg. Germania is the crossing for the plank road, and Ely's, which is lower down the river, for the old wagon road. These are the roads formerly used by the country people in passing from Culpeper to Fredericksburg. When the enemy crossed, he occupied both roads and both fords. But it seems that, on Saturday evening, our forces turned the right of his line, which was drawn up along the plank road, and at right angles to the course of the river. Being thus cut off from the south bank of the river at Germania Ford, the enemy appears to have withdrawn his line of battle to the old wagon road, lower down, at the same time removing his pontoons from Germania to Ely's Ford.—*Ed. Mercury.*]

Glorious News from the West.

VICTORIOUS ADVANCE OF GEN. PRICE.

Probable Surrender of Steele.

ANOTHER TRIUMPH ON RED RIVER.

RECAPTURE OF FORT D'RUSSEY,

&c. &c. &c.

JACKSON, MISS., May 5.—Officers, who left Gen. TAYLOR's camp, five miles from Alexandria, on the 29th ult., confirm the news of BANKS' retreat to Alexandria. The Yankee gunboat *Eastport* had been blown up and two transports had been captured. The rest of the enemy's fleet was above the Rapids, with no chance of escape. TAYLOR has certainly captured 4000 prisoners.

The success of Gen PRICE is complete. MARMADUKE had captured STEEL's wagon train; and STEELE being surrounded, Gen. PRICE demanded his surrender. STEELE consented, on condition that his negro troops should be treated as prisoners of war. PRICE refused to grant these terms, but referred the matter to Gen. KIRBY SMITH, who replied that the negroes must be sent back to their owners. STEELE refused to capitulate on these terms. What further action had taken place was unknown; but it was believed that the whole Yankee force would ultimately be compelled to surrender, as SMITH was reinforcing PRICE.

SUMMIT, MISS., May 7.—A gentleman who crossed the river below Bayou Sara on the 2d instant says that the Louisiana forces had pursued the enemy down Red River, recapturing Fort De Russey and Cheniville. On the 25th the enemy made a stand at Markham, where they were attacked and defeated with heavy loss, estimated at not less than 10,000 men.

Yankee transports going up Red River with reinforcements had been whipped back at Fort De Russey since we re-occupied the post. The Yankee wounded have been sent to Vicksburg.

General WALKER's division had crossed Red River in pursuit of the retreating enemy. The Yankees had burned four gunboats above the Falls.

NAVAL ENGAGEMENT IN NORTH CAROLINA.

THE "ALBEMARLE" AGAIN VICTORIOUS.

The following telegram from General BEAUREGARD was received at Department Headquarters last evening:

WELDON, N. C., May 8.

To General Samuel Jones:—General MARTIN reports, on the sixth instant, from Plymouth: "The iron clad *Albemarle*—with the enemy's raised gunboat, *Bombshell*—encountered yesterday, at four p. m., two monitors from the mouth of the Roanoke and nine of the enemy's gunboats, three of them being very large ones, from the blockading squadron. The fight lasted till night. We sunk the largest gunboat of the enemy and disabled at least two monitors, without serious injury to the *Albemarle*, but lost the tender. The result was encouraging."

(Signed) G. T. BEAUREGARD.

LATEST FROM JOHNSTON'S ARMY.

DALTON, May 7.—The enemy advanced in front of Tunnel Hill this morning and shelled our cavalry on the ridge this side of that place for two hours. They then fell back. They are reported as moving around to our left.

Our troops are in position.

LETTER FROM RICHMOND.

(CORRESPONDENCE OF THE MERCURY.)

RICHMOND, Monday, May 2.

President Davis' Bereavement—The Popular Heart Warmed—Organization of the House—Grant and Burnside—Fine Accounts from the Army—Ben Lane Posey and R. W. Cobb—What is Expected of Congress—Cartel Probably Knocked in the Head, etc., etc.

President DAVIS' sudden bereavement has excited very general and sincere sympathy. Whatever may have been the feeling towards him, this dispensation of Providence has softened all hearts. The burial of the beautiful little boy—for such he was, I am told—was somewhat hastened on account, doubtless, of the meeting of Congress to day.

The hearts of the people are warmed to the President for another reason. He has at length yielded to the popular wishes in regard to our Generals. Lee, Johnston, Beauregard and Price are all in the field, and just where the public would wish them to be. This gives great satisfaction.

The organization of the House will remain unchanged; Bocock, Speaker, Lamar, Clerk, and so on. A Sergeant-at Arms may be elected. If these officers give satisfaction, why continue the Yankee practice of changing them with every Congress? No good reason can be given.

It is thought Grant is going to use Burnside as he did Sherman, when the latter joined him at Chattanooga—that is, practice some ruse, by which a large force may be suddenly thrown upon one of our flanks. But the Rapidan is a better position than that at Lookout Mountain.

Gentlemen, who came down from Gordonsville Saturday, give fine accounts of Lee's army. There had been a review of Longstreet's corps by Gen. Lee, which passed off admirably. The army is strong in numbers and in the best spirits. I hear good reports also from our cavalry. The horses are fattening on the new grass, and the men well supplied with coffee, sugar, bacon and fish. Six fish to a man are served out nearly every day.

Captain Ben. Lane Posey comes out in a card in the Examiner against R. W. W. Cobb, an old Washington hunker, and newly elected member from Alabama. It seems Mr. Cobb has been very thick with the Yankees and very cold to Confederate prisoners.

We expect a death blow to the *habeas corpus* suspension as one of the first acts of Congress; prompt action in regard to the five dollar notes and officers' rations, and a short session, of not more than a month or six weeks.

A message sent by an officer on board the Yankee truce boat to a lady desirous of returning to Norfolk, induces the belief that there will be no more boats, and that all prospect of resuming the cartel has been abandoned—until we get more prisoners. HERMES.

THE MERCURY.

MONDAY, MAY 9 1864

The Signs of the Times.

The blasphemous saying imputed to President LINCOLN, that "he believed God Almighty was about to turn secessionist"—seems likely, in his sense, to be verified. Certainly no one can observe the late striking successes, of our army, and fail to perceive the finger of God in our behalf. Beginning with the defence of Charleston (the one great success to our arms, amidst the disasters which befel our cause, during the last summer and fall), to our late victories in Florida, North Carolina and Louisiana, the Giver of all victory seems to have rebuked our foes. In the Revolution of 1776, the victory of Fort Moultrie, in the Bay of Charleston, was the first signal rebound, amidst the deepest depression of our cause, which carried us on to successful independence. May we not hope, that history is about to repeat itself; and that again in this glorious Bay, the Gonfalon of victory lifted here, will pass on from battle field, to battle field, until it waves over us an acknowledged power amongst the nations of the world? *Here*, the grand movement for independence of Yankee domination began. *Here*, when this righteous cause was most depressed, rose up the courage and endurance which rebuked despair, and fired anew the grand spirit of a deathless resistance to our foes. *Here*, even amidst the ruins with which our foes have crowned our city—in silence and desolation sits enthroned the spirit of our new-born Confederacy,—suffering but patient,—calm but defiant,—grand and unconquerable. From the crumbling walls of Fort Sumter the voice of hope has gone out to the utmost limits of the Confederacy, and finds an echo in the triumphant shouts of victory which passes from State to State, as our Yankee foes go down beneath our arms. May we not humbly trust that the Omnipotent Disposer of the destinies of nations, is triumphantly carrying us, through the Red Sea of blood, with which it has pleased Him to baptize our cause; and that buffeting a few more waves, the happy shores of peace and independence will be ours. The blasphemous Buffoon, who began the war, seems fearful of the fate which awaits him. Now ordering the levy of conscripts, and then rescinding the order—now, forcing negroes into his ranks, and then leaving them behind—now threatening States with a levy for troops, and then begging them to send them—he presents the spectacle of an agitated and desperate combatant in a desperate cause.

MR. LINCOLN, AS PAINTED BY A FRIEND.—ORESTES BROWNSON "strenuously advocates the re election of Mr. LINCOLN," from the fear that by his defeat "the country would be condemned to worse rule." Who the worse man could be it seems difficult to imagine, from the following sketch which BROWNSON gives of his favorite.—Truly he must have a deplorable choice, if LINCOLN is his best. We copy from the Washington *Constitutional Union*:

His soul seems made of leather, and incapable of any grand or noble emotion. Compared with the mass of men, he is a line of flat prose in a beautiful and spirited lyric. He lowers, he never elevates you. You leave his presence with your enthusiasm dampened, your better feelings crushed, and your hopes cast to the winds. You ask not, can this man carry the nation through its terrible struggles, but can the nation carry this man through them, and not perish in the attempt? * * * * *

He never adopts a clear policy. When he hits upon a policy substantially good in itself, he contrives to belittle it, besmear it, or in some way to render it mean, contemptible and useless. Even wisdom from him seems but foolishness. We blame not, says the amiable Brownson, because he is mole eyed, and not eagle eyed, and that he has no suspicion of that higher region of thought and action in which lie the great interests and questions he is called upon to deal with as President of the United States. His only fault is in the misfortune of being unconscious of his own unfitness for his place.

* * * * *

Mr. Lincoln's is a renomination eminently unfit to be made. We have never been able to discern in him a single quality in any manner fitting him to be President of the United States at any time. We have found in him no quality not eminently unfitting him for this high office. As to his administration, its extravagance has been appalling, its expenditures enormous, and little to show for them. During four years it will have run up a national debt greater than that of Great Britain, and equal to one-third of the assessed values of the whole Union. And no small portion of the sum has been literally wasted.

LOUIS NAPOLEON'S PERSONAL APPEARANCE.—LOUIS NAPOLEON's present personal appearance is thus described in a late letter from Paris:

The personal appearance of Napoleon III. would puzzle the most accurate observer of physiognomy. The face of the man with the iron mask is not more devoid of expression than is his. One may study it for hours without deriving the slightest satisfaction as to the Emperor's mental characteristics. Those fishy, rayless eyes, the parchment like cheeks, the stiff, pointed moustache, all suggest a sort of artificial face prepared for the occasion, while the real man, like the priestess of Apollo, lies hidden, and delivers short, oracular responses behind it. He is short in stature, though his body is full the average size. Hence he appears to greater advantage in a posture. Of late years he has grown somewhat corpulent, like the first Napoleon and the other members of his family. His habits at the present day are said to be simple and regular, perhaps necessarily so, if the stories told of his early excesses be true. His appearance on horseback does great credit to his horsemanship, which is generally allowed to be the most skilful in Europe. He is very fond of horses, and has that thorough understanding of their nature which establishes a certain sympathy between the animal and his rider.

MEETING OF CONGRESS.

THE PRESIDENT'S MESSAGE.

RICHMOND, Tuesday, May 3.

The Senate met yesterday, at 12 o'clock, m.—Mr. HUNTER, of Virginia, in the Chair. The roll being called, sixteen Senators responded to their names:

The credentials of Messrs. Richard W. Walker, of Ala., John W. C. Watson, of Miss., and Wm. A. Graham, of N. C., newly elected Senators, were duly presented, and those gentlemen took the oath of office. The credentials of Messrs. R. W. Johnson, of Ark., and James M. Baker, of Fla., Senators re elected, being presented, also took the oath of office. Mr. Simms, of Ky., reappointed, also took the oath of office.

The Senate then proceeded to organize. Mr. R. M. T. Hunter, of Va., was re-elected President *pro tem*.—he receiving 15 votes, Mr. Brown 3, and Mr. Orr, 1. Mr. Jas. H Nash was re elected Secretary of the Senate, receiving 15 out of 22 votes cast.

On motion of Mr. Henry, of Tenn., the old incumbents of the offices of Sergeant-at-Arms and First and Second Doorkeepers, were declared re-elected.

On motion of Mr. Johnson, a Committee of three was appointed to wait on the President of the Confederate States and inform him that a quorum of the two Houses of Congress had assembled, and were ready to receive any message he might desire to communicate. In a few moments the following message was received and read:

To the Senate and House of Representatives
Of the Confederate States of America:

You are assembled under circumstances of deep interest to your country; and it is fortunate that, coming, as you do, newly elected by the people, and familiar with the condition of the various localities, you will be the better able to devise measures adapted to meet the wants of the public service, without imposing unnecessary burthens on the citizen. The brief period which has elapsed since the last adjournment of Congress has not afforded sufficient opportunity to test the efficacy of the most important laws then enacted, nor have the events occurring in the interval been such as materially to change the state of the country.

The unjust war commenced against us, in violation of the rights of the States, and in usurpation of power, not delegated to the Government of the United States, is still characterized by the barbarism with which it has heretofore been conducted by the enemy. Aged men, helpless women and children, appeal in vain to the humanity which should be inspired by their condition, for immunity from arrest, incarceration or banishment from their homes. Plunder and devastation of the property of non combatants, destruction of private dwellings and even of edifices devoted to the worship of God, expeditions organized for the sole purpose of sacking cities, consigning them to the flames, killing the unarmed inhabitants and inflicting horrible outrages on women and children, are some of the constantly recurring atrocities of the invader. It cannot reasonably be pretended that such acts conduce to any end which their authors dare avow before the civilized world, and sooner or later Christendom must mete out to them the condemnation which such brutality deserves.—The sufferings thus ruthlessly inflicted upon the people of the invaded districts has served but to illustrate their patriotism. Entire unanimity and zeal for their country's cause has been pre eminently conspicuous among those whose sacrifices have been greatest. So the army which has borne the trials and dangers of the war; which has been subjected to privations and disappointments (tests of manly fortitude far more severe than the brief fatigues and perils of actual combat), has been the centre of cheerfulness and hope. From the camp comes the voice of the soldier patriots invoking each who is at home, in the sphere he best may fill, to devote his whole energies to the support of a cause in the success of which their confidence has never faltered. They, the veterans of many a hard fought field, tender to their country, without limit of time, a service of priceless value to us, one which posterity will hold in grateful remembrance.

In considering the state of the country, the reflection is naturally suggested, that this is the third Congress of the Confederate States of America. The Provisional Government was formed, its Congress held four sessions, lived its appointed term, and passed away. The Permanent Government was then organized, its different Departments established, a Congress elected which also held four sessions, served its full constitutional term, and expired. You, the second Congress, under the Permanent Government, are now assembled at the time and place appointed by law for commencing your session. All these events have passed into history, notwithstanding the threat of our prompt subjugation, made three years ago, by a people that presume to assert a title to govern States whose separate and independent sovereignty was recognized by treaty with France and Great Britain in the last century, and remained unquestioned for nearly three generations. Yet these very governments, in disregard of duty and treaty obligations which bind them to recognise as independent, Virginia and other Confederate States, persist in countenancing, by moral influence, if not in aiding by unfair and partial action, the claim set up by the Executive of a foreign Government, to exercise despotic sway over the States thus recognized, and treat the invasion of them by their former limited and special agent as though it were the attempt of a sovereign to suppress a rebellion against lawful authority. Ungenerous advantage has been taken of our present condition, and our rights have been violated, our vessels of war detained in ports to which they had been invited by proclamations of neutrality, and in one instance our flag also insulted where the sacred right of asylum was supposed to be secure; while one of these governments has contented itself with simply deprecating, by deferential representations, the conduct of our enemy in the constantly recurring instances of his contemptuous disregard of neutral rights and flagrant violations of public law. It may be that foreign governments, like our enemies, have mistaken our desire for peace, unreservedly expressed, for evidence of exhaustion, and have thence inferred the probability of success in the effort to subjugate or exterminate the millions of human beings who, in these States, prefer any fate to submission to their savage assailants. I see no prospect of an early change in the course heretofore pursued by these governments; but when this delusion shall have been dispelled, and when our independence, by the valor and fortitude of our people, shall have been won against all the hostile influences combined against, and can no longer be ignored by open foes or professed neutrals, this war will have left with its proud memories a record of many wrongs, which it may not misbecome us to forgive—some for which we may not properly forbear from demanding redress. In the meantime, it is enough for us to know that every avenue of negotiation is closed against us, that our enemy is making renewed and strenuous efforts for our destruction, and that the sole resource for us, as a people secure in the justice of our cause, and holding our liberties to be more precious than all other earthly possessions, is to combine and apply every available element of power for their defence and preservation.

On the subject of the exchange of prisoners I greatly regret to be unable to give you satisfactory information. The Government of the United States, while persisting in failure to execute the terms of the cartel, make occasional delivery of prisoners, and then suspend action without apparent cause. I confess my inability to comprehend their policy or purpose. The prisoners held by us, in spite of humane care, are perishing from the inevitable effects of imprisonment and the home sickness produced by the hopelessness of release from confinement. The spectacle of their suffering augments our longing desire to relieve from similar trials our own brave men, who have spent so many weary months in a cruel and useless imprisonment, endured with heroic constancy. The delivery, after a suspension of some weeks, has just been resumed by the enemy; but as they give no assurance of intent to carry out the cartel, an interruption of the exchange may recur at any moment.

The reports of the Departments, herewith submitted, are referred to for full information in relation to the matters appertaining to each. There are two of them on which I deem it necessary to make special remark.

The report of the Secretary of the Treasury states facts justifying the conclusion that the law passed at the last session for the purpose of withdrawing from circulation the large excess of Treasury notes heretofore issued, has had the desired effect; and that by the 1st July the amount in circulation will have been reduced to a sum not exceeding $230,000,000. It is believed to be of primary importance that no further issue of notes should take place, and that the use of the credit of the Government should be restricted to the two other modes provided by Congress, viz: the sale of bonds and the issue of certificates bearing interest, for the price of supplies purchased within our limits. The law, as it now stands, authorises the issue by the Treasury of new notes to the extent of two-thirds of the amount received under its provisions. The estimate of the amount funded under the law, is shown to be $300,000,000, and if two thirds of this sum be re issued, we shall have an addition of $200,000,000 to our circulation, believed to be already ample for the business of the country. The addition of this large sum to the volume of the currency would be attended by disastrous effects, and would produce the speedy recurrence of the evils from which the funding law has rescued the country. If our arms are crowned with the success which we have so much reason to hope, we may well expect that this war cannot be prolonged beyond the current year, and nothing would so much retard the beneficent influence of peace on all the interests of our country, as the existence of a great mass of currency not redeemable in coin. With our vast resources, the circulation, if restricted to its present volume, would be easy manageable, and by gradual absorption in payment of public dues, would give place to the precious metals, the only basis of a currency adapted to commerce with foreign countries. In our present circumstances I know of no mode of providing for the public wants which would entail sacrifices so great as a fresh issue of Treasury notes, and I trust that you will concur in the propriety of absolutely forbidding any increase of those now in circulation.

Officers have been appointed and despatched to the Trans Mississippi States, and the necessary measures taken for the execution of the laws enacted to obviate delays in administering the Treasury and other Executive Departments in those States; but sufficient time has not elapsed to ascertain the results.

In relation to the most important of all subjects at the present time, the efficiency of our armies in the field, it is gratifying to assure you that the discipline and instruction of the troops have kept pace with the improvement in material and equipment. We have reason to congratulate ourselves on the results of the legislation on this subject, and on the increased administrative energy in the different bureaux of the War Department, and may not unreasonably indulge anticipations of commensurate success in the ensuing campaign.

The organization of reserves is in progress, and it is hoped they will be valuable in affording local protection without requiring details and detachments from active force.

Among the recommendations contained in the report of the Secretary of War, your attention is specially invited to those in which legislation is suggested on the following subjects, viz:

The tenure of office of the general officers in the provisional army; and a proper discrimination in compensation of the different grades;

The provision required in aid of invalid officers who have resigned in consequence of wounds or sickness contracted while in service;

The amendment of the law which deprives officers in the field of the privilege of purchasing rations and thus adds to their embarrassment, instead of conferring the benefit intended;

The organization of the general staff of the army, in relation to which a special message will shortly be addressed to you, containing the reasons which compelled me to withhold my approval of a bill passed by your predecessors at too late a period of the session to allow time for returning it for their reconsideration;

The necessity for an increase in the allowance now made for the transportation of officers traveling under orders;

The mode of providing officers for the execution of the conscript law;

The means of securing greater despatch and more regular administration of justice in examining and disposing of the records of cases reported from the courts martial and military courts in the army.

The recent events of the war are highly creditable to our troops, exhibiting energy and vigilance, combined with the habitual gallantry which they have taught us to expect on all occasions. We have been cheered by important and valuable successes in Florida, Northern Mississippi, Western Tennessee and Kentucky, Western Louisiana and Eastern North Carolina, reflecting the highest honor on the skill and conduct of our commanders, and on the incomparable soldiers whom it is their privilege to lead. A naval attack on Mobile was so successfully repulsed at the outer works that the attempt was abandoned, and the nine months, siege of Charleston has been practically suspended, leaving that noble city and its fortresses imperishable monuments to the skill and fortitude of its defenders. The armies in Northern Georgia and in Northern Virginia still oppose, with unshaken front, a formidable barrier to the progress of the invader; and our generals, armies and people, are animated by cheerful confidence.

Let us, then, while resolute in devoting all our energies to securing the realization of the bright auspices which encourage us, not forget that our humble and most grateful thanks are due to Him, without whose guidance, and protecting care, all human efforts are of no avail, and to whose interposition are due the manifold successes with which we have been cheered.

JEFFERSON DAVIS.

Richmond, May 2d, 1864.

On motion of Mr. Orr, the message and accompanying documents were laid on the table, and the former was ordered to be printed. Adjourned.

HOUSE OF REPRESENTATIVES.—The House was called to order at 12 o'clock. On the call of the roll sixty-four members answered to their names, more than a quorum. The first business in order was the election of a Speaker. Mr. Conrad, of La., nominated Hon. Thomas S. Bocock, of Va., and on motion of Mr. Welsh, of Miss., the election was made by acclamation. Messrs. Conrad, of La., and Farrow, of S. C., conducted the Speaker elect to the Chair, who returned his thanks to the body for the honor conferred upon him. He referred to the duties devolving upon the members of the House. The people were solemnly in earnest in the struggle, and their representatives must be in earnest; but they must also be careful to discriminate between the clamor of a faction and the voice of the people.

The oath of office was then administered to the members of the House.

Mr. A. R. Lamar, of Ga., was nominated for clerk of the House by Mr. Chambers, of Miss., and on resolution of Mr. Sexton, of Texas, the election was made by acclamation. Mr. Robert H. Wynne, of Ala., was nominated for doorkeeper by Mr. Russell, of Va., and elected without opposition.

On motion of Mr. Sexton, a committee was appointed to inform the Senate of the organization of the House. Also, a committee to wait upon the President, and inform him of the readiness of the House to receive any communication he might have to make.

The committee to wait upon the President reported through their chairman that they had discharged the duty assigned, and that the President would send a communication to the House forthwith. The clerk then read the message.

ADDITIONAL FROM THE NORTH.

NEWS SUMMARY.

The correspondent of the Richmond *Examiner* telegraphs from the Headquarters of General LEE's Army as follows:

From Northern papers of 30th, and other and higher authority, I learn the cause of the delay in the movement of the Army of the Potomac. It has transpired that when General Grant assumed command of the United States armies, he represented to the President that, in view of the magnitude of the trust confided to him, he felt it incumbent upon him to fortify himself by all the means in his power, and in particular he needed the moral support which the employment of Generals McClellan and Fremont, representing two great phases of public opinion, would give; he, therefore, desired permission to assign them to duty. This was refused on a trifling pretext, as respects Fremont, but peremptory as to General McClellan.

General Grant then proceeded to reorganize the armies on another basis. He thought it best to bring several Western Generals to his aid, and displace many who had served under McClellan. This has not worked satisfactorily, and General Grant is understood to have admitted, while satisfied with the number and material of his army, he is uneasy respecting the *morale*. He returned to Washington on Monday, therefore, with a peremptory demand for the services of General McClellan in the forthcoming campaign, and refuses to move the army until his demands are complied with. He is also very urgent that Gen. Fremont be assigned to duty. These facts are admitted by Lincoln's adherents.

The Pennsylvania Legislature has passed a joint resolution, urging Lincoln to discharge the Pennsylvania troops when their time is out.

The reserve troops from the Northwestern States are pouring forward to the reinforcement of the armies in Virginia.

My information shows clearly and unquestionably that neither the Potomac or Peninsula armies will move without further and larger accessions. It may, therefore, be safely concluded that battle is not immediately imminent. Grant was still in Washington on Saturday.

From Nashville we have it announced that the spring campaign in that quarter would probably open about the first of May. The camps were being cleared of all unnecessary incumbrances. Officers had been instructed to reduce their baggage, and all the detached garrisons that could possibly be spared have been ordered to Chattanooga.

The New York Tribune announces the abandonment of the siege of Charleston.

IMPORTANT ORDER OF GENERAL MEADE—ARRANGEMENT FOR HOLDING ON TO VOLUNTEERS WHOSE TIME HAS EXPIRED.

The Washington *Star*, of Friday week, has the following important announcement, showing that there is, and is to be, trouble in the Army of the Potomac with the expired enlistment men. It is because of this that BURNSIDE has gone to GRANT, instead of undertaking his independent expedition up the Peninsula. The *Star* says:

As the time is approaching when a number of the regiments belonging to the Army of the Potomac are to be discharged from the military service of the United States, by reason of the expiration of the term of service, for which they were mustered into said service, Maj. Gen. Meade has announced to such troops that the War Department has decided that the term of service of a regiment is to be computed from the date of muster into the service of the United States, without reference to the date of enrollment or any service rendered a State.

The Commanding General will, however, at all times, be glad to receive and forward, for the consideration of the proper authorities, any respectful communication touching the term of service of a regiment, when such term appears to be involved in doubt.

The Commanding General, in making this announcement, expresses the hope that regiments which may be discharged will cheerfully acquiesce in the decision of the Government with regard to their term of service, and that no organized bodies of individuals, after having borne an unsullied reputation during all the eventful scenes which have marked their connection with the Army of the Potomac, will suffer the honorable fame they have won by their gallantry and good conduct to be tarnished in the closing hours of their service by acts of insubordination, which, if ventured upon by any, will be promptly suppressed, and can only terminate in the speedy and certain punishment of the offending parties.

DISMISSAL OF ADMIRAL WILKES.

Admiral WILKES has been dismissed by court martial from the United States service. Among the queer things uncovered by the WILKES court martial is the successful endeavor of SANFORD, the Yankee Minister at Brussels, to have the war frigate *Vanderbilt* used to collect a claim of his against a South American State of $150,000. Com. WILKES says in his defence:

On the 15th of May I received a despatch from the American Minister at Brussels, saying he had been advised by the Secretary of the Navy in regard to a visit to Laguara by one of my squadron, and adding, "I hope that you or one of your squadron will be able, at an early day, to touch at Laguayra, or I fear that your intervention will come too late for any practical results."

In another place the Commodore says:

I proceeded to Caraccas, put myself in communication with the proper authorities, accomplished the object of my visit by securing the payment of $150 000 due to our citizens.

A CRY OF PATRIOTIC ANGUISH—THE PEOPLE MUST LEND MR. CHASE A DOLLAR OR TWO OR HE WILL BREAK.

The New York *Bank Note Reporter*, which is fully in the interests of LINCOLN, CHASE, and so fourth, says of CHASE and his efforts on the gold question:

He appeals afresh to the people in this the most trying military and financial period of the rebellion, to come forward with heart and money. He is reducing the volume of currency gradually, and will continue to do so. If the stock and gold gamblers shall again attempt the game they played last week, he will bring the whole power of the Government, and its whole means, both here and abroad, to checkmate them.

The Secretary of the Treasury relies upon the people for the ways and means, as the army for victories, and upon Congress for adequate taxation. The people will come to his help with every dollar that can be appropriated. This is their true interest; it is their true safety. The armies will now do their part—there is no alternative but victory. Congress will do its duty—it dare not falter.

To those capitalists who complain that Mr. Chase ought to pay a higher rate of interest, we say, pointedly, that a five per cent. negotiation against the American people is better than a loan at any higher rate of interest. For why? Your money righteously invested, free from taxation, generously invested for your country's cause, is, and will be through all time, valid. But grind your country—grind the American people in their time of distress and want—take Shylock's bond—and it will take more than the interest you get over five per cent. to defend you in coming against the political tribunals that will adjudge your bonds.

Well and wise would it be for you to come forward with the spirit that inspires the people, and for once, of this emergency, lay aside the spirit that governs the usurer. Your property, your money, your all is at stake. You are but a miserable minority at the ballot-box. Better either come to the standard of equity and right, or bag what gold you can and leave this continent [illegible].

EUROPEAN NEWS.

The House of Lords on the [illegible] delivered judgment in the *Alexandra* case. Six legal Lords were present. The Lord Chancellor [illegible] the judgement.

He argued that under the provisions of [illegible] known as the Queen's Remembrancer Act, there was no authority to [illegible] such an appeal [illegible] Barons of Exchequer [illegible]. He therefore moved that the appeal of the Crown be dismissed with costs. Lords St. Leonards, Chelmsford, and Kingsdown concurred, while Lords Cranworth and Wensleydale were in favor of the hearing of the appeal by the Exchequer Chamber. The appeal was therefore dismissed with costs.

The London *Times* remarks that this final decision has been pronounced on a technicality, [illegible] narrowness of law. For the present the victory remains with the defendants. But it is impossible to suppose that the Government will acquiesce in the law as laid down by the two Senior Judges of the Exchequer, or fail to bring any new offender to account, even if it should render necessary another struggle in the courts of law.

The London *Times* adds: If the the Foreign Enlistment Act be insufficient to repress enterprises endangering the peace of the country, surely it is better to apply to the Legislature than trust that, in some future case, a verdict or a bill of exceptions will carry the question to a tribunal which may reverse the judgment already given.

The Scotsman understands that the case of the Pampero [illegible] Crown and the nominal forfeiture of the vessel. They are, however, to retain possession of the vessel, to deal with her, make alterations on her, but not sell her for two years except with the consent of the Crown.

The Morning Post's City article says the Confederate loan is about to be placed on a new basis. A combined French and English undertaking, in which the Confederate Government has an active interest, is in active formation, having for its object to organize a regular system of blockade running from the various Confederate ports for the export of cotton.

The capital is £500,000 sterling. Shares are to be allotted only to the holders of Confederate bonds. The company's steamers are to take out cargoes to supply the wants of the Confederate Government. It is estimated that the whole of the bonds of the Confederate loan may be exchanged for cotton and produce exported from Southern ports within twelve months.

The promoters of the company are said to be gentlemen of capital, and long versed in blockade running. The fastest steamers are to be employed. But in order to reduce the risk a very large cargo will not be intrusted to any one vessel.

THE DANGER OF A CANNONADE.—The bloodlessness of a cannonade was shown on the North Carolina coast a few weeks since, when the blockade runner *Lucy* got aground. The authorities at the fort promptly sent down guns to protect her. A letter says:

Preparations were at once made by the crew and soldiers from the fort to bale and float the Lucy, which had been purposely filled with water to prevent the enemy from towing her off. In the course of the afternoon seven vessels advanced to attack the Lucy, feeling their way by the lead and forming in line of battle. From five o'clock until dark they continued to rain shot and shell at the unarmed and stranded little blockade runner. The greater proportion of the crew of the Lucy declined to leave her, thereby displaying sound discretion, as not a single shot struck her. For an hour and a half this farcical and harmless discharge of shot and shell continued, and was repeatedly replied to by the cool tars of the Lucy with round upon round of laughter. While the balls were whistling over head and tearing up the beach, the sailors on board the Lucy were comfortably enjoying their tea, and such of them as were on shore had much amusement in running after the spent shot on the beach.

The New-York Times.

VOL. XIII—NO. 3940. NEW-YORK, TUESDAY, MAY 10, 1864. PRICE THREE CENTS.

VICTORY!

"ON TO RICHMOND."

Lee's Defeat and Retreat Fully Confirmed.

OUR ARMY IN VIGOROUS PURSUIT.

Official Dispatches from Grant and Meade.

LEE'S REPORT OF THE BATTLES.

The Rebel Dead and Wounded Left on the Field.

ADVANCE OF HANCOCK.

He Passes Through Spottsylvania on Sunday.

Two Thousand Prisoners Captured.

FREDERICKSBURG AGAIN OCCUPIED

A Depot for the Wounded Established There.

IMPORTANT FROM GEN. BUTLER.

A Severe Battle Fought on Saturday.

The Railroad Destroyed Between Petersburgh and Richmond.

CAPTURE OF THE GUNBOAT SHOSHONE.

THE CASUALTIES OF THE BATTLES.

GEN. WADSWORTH KILLED

The Rebel Longstreet Mortally Wounded.

PROCLAMATION FROM THE PRESIDENT

EXECUTIVE RECOMMENDATION

For Prayer and Especial Gratitude to God, in View of the Great Victory.

EXECUTIVE MANSION, WASHINGTON, May 9, 1864.

To the Friends of Union and Liberty:

Enough is known of army operations within the last five days to claim our especial gratitude to God. While what remains undone demands our most sincere prayers to and reliance upon Him, (without whom all human effort is vain,) I recommend that all patriots at their homes, in their places of public worship, and wherever they may be, unite in common thanksgiving and prayer to Almighty God. ABRAHAM LINCOLN.

DISPATCHES FROM THE WAR-OFFICE.

FIRST DISPATCH.

The General Result a Success—The Fighting Desperate—The Cool, Determined Courage of the Army—The Death of Gen. Wadsworth—Gen. Sherman Heard From.

WASHINGTON, Monday, May 9—10:45 A. M.

Maj.-Gen. Dix:

We have intelligence this morning by scouts direct from the army, as late as Saturday evening, but no official reports.

The general results may be stated as a success to our arms.

The fighting on Friday was the most desperate known in modern times.

I deeply regret that the country will have to mourn the death of that accomplished soldier, Brig.-Gen. WADSWORTH, who was struck in the forehead by a ball, at the head of his command, while leading them against one of the enemy's strongest positions. His remains are in our hands, in charge of Col. SHARPE.

Gen. WEBB was wounded.

Gen. JONES, of the rebel army, was killed.

The condition of our army is represented to be most admirable. The cool, determined courage, in every instance, proved too much for the desperate fury of the rebels, who have been driven at all points. There has been no straggling.

At the last accounts HANCOCK was pushing forward rapidly by the left to Spottsylvania Court-house, and yesterday heavy cannonading was heard at Aquia Creek from that direction, until 3 o'clock.

We have lost some prisoners.

One regiment, the Seventh Pennsylvania Reserves, charged through an abattis of the enemy, but were unable to get back, and most of them were captured. We have also taken a large number of prisoners, supposed to be more than we lost.

The wounded had not yet arrived at the point whence the trains were to receive them. The Medical Director reports that a large proportion are slight wounds.

Artillery was not used on either side the first two days.

There is nothing later from Gen. BUTLER than the date of my last dispatch.

Gen. SHERMAN was heard from last night. He had been all day reconnoitering the enemy's position and would attack to-day. EDWIN M. STANTON.

SECOND DISPATCH.

Lee's Report of the Battle—Gen. Jenkins Killed—Longstreet, Pegram and Stafford Wounded.

[OFFICIAL.]

WASHINGTON, Monday, May 9.

To Maj.-Gen. Dix:

This Department has just received from Gen. BUTLER the official report of Gen. LEE of the operations of Friday. He says their loss in killed is not large, but they have many wounded. He grieves to announce that Gen. LONGSTREET was severely wounded, Gen. JENKINS killed, and Gen. PEGRAM badly wounded on Thursday, and that it is supposed that Gen. STAFFORD will recover. He thanks a merciful God that every advance on their (Gen. GRANT'S) part has been repulsed. He states that our forces attacked them, and caused some confusion. Gen. WADSWORTH'S body fell into their hands, but our reports this morning state that it is now in our possession under charge of Col. SHARPE, as stated in my first dispatch this morning.

The belief here is that Lieut.-Gen. GRANT is achieving a complete victory.

EDWIN M. STANTON.

THIRD DISPATCH.

Gen. Grant "On to Richmond"—Capture of Two Thousand Prisoners.

WASHINGTON, May 9—4 o'clock P. M.

Maj.-Gen. Dix:

Dispatches have just reached here direct from Gen. GRANT. They are not fully deciphered yet, but he is "On to Richmond."

We have taken two thousand prisoners.

EDWIN M. STANTON, Secretary of War.

FOURTH DISPATCH.

Lee Retreats Friday Night—Grant's Pursuit on Saturday—Hancock Passes Through Spottsylvania Court-House on Sunday Morning—Headquarters Twenty Miles from the Battle-field on Sunday—Occupation of Fredericksburgh—Depot for the Wounded Established There.

WASHINGTON, Monday, May 9—4 P. M.

A bearer of dispatches from Gen. MEADE'S headquarters has just reached here. He states that LEE'S army commenced falling back on the night of Friday. Our army commenced the pursuit on Saturday. The rebels were in full retreat for Richmond by the direct road. HANCOCK passed through Spottsylvania Court-house at daylight yesterday. Our headquarters at noon yesterday were twenty miles south of the battle field. We occupy Fredericksburgh. The Twenty-second New-York Cavalry occupied that place at 8 o'clock last night. The depot for our wounded is established at Fredericksburgh.

EDWIN M. STANTON, Secretary of War.

SPECIAL DISPATCHES TO THE N. Y. TIMES

The Defeat of the Enemy Complete—The Death of Gen. Wadsworth—Gen. Webb not Killed—The Wounded not yet Received at Rappahannock Station.

WASHINGTON, Monday, May 9.

Intelligence received this morning is of the most cheering character, modified only by individual cases of national bereavement. The rout of the enemy's forces is complete. They are flying in a demoralized condition toward the intrenchments at Richmond, leaving their killed and wounded in our hands. Victory is complete.

Our loss is very heavy. Among the brave men who are lost is Gen. WADSWORTH, of New-York. He was killed while charging at the head of his division by a ball through the brain. The rebel Gen. SAM. JONES was killed, and his body is in our hands.

Gen. WEBB is not killed, as reported.

The bridges on the railroad as far as Rappahannock Station have been guarded during all this movement by small detachments, and there has been uninterrupted telegraphic communication between Rappahannock and Alexandria until 9 o'clock last night.

The telegraph is in operation this A. M. Not a single wounded man had reached Rappahannock Station at last accounts. Six trains of empty cars went to the front yesterday morning, and more will follow as soon as they begin to load.

The Operations of Saturday—Heavy Skirmishing—Lee's Retreat—The Army in Vigorous Pursuit—Our Loss 1,800 Killed, 10,000 Wounded.

WASHINGTON, Monday—2 P. M.

Reliable information from the front up to 3 o'clock Sunday afternoon states that on Saturday morning Gen. GRANT opened the fight by a general advance of his pickets and skirmishers. During the whole day there was very heavy skirmishing, amounting sometimes to a severe musketry battle; and it was during one of these that the gallant WADSWORTH was killed at the head of his division. LEE retreated in the direction of Spottsylvania Court-House, and it was reported from the front on Sunday morning that Gen. HANCOCK was in occupation of that place. Gen. GRANT'S whole army was in vigorous pursuit. Our loss is reported at about 1,800 killed and 10,000 wounded. The order for sending the wounded to Washington has been rescinded, and other arrangements will be made.

WASHINGTON REPORTS.

Dispatches from Grant and Meade—The Pursuit of the Enemy—The Capture of Two Thousand Prisoners.

WASHINGTON, Monday, May 9.

Dispatches from Gen. MEADE and Lieut.-Gen. GRANT have just been received by the War Department.

Our army was in full pursuit of the enemy toward Richmond.

We have two thousand prisoners.

Our forces occupied Fredericksburgh at 8 o'clock last night.

The hospital for our wounded was established there.

The supplies, nurses, physicians and attendants have been ready for two days, and have gone forward.

The wounded are now estimated at about twelve thousand.

Reported Battle on Sunday—Lee's Report of the Battle of Thursday.

WASHINGTON, Monday, May 9.

The *Republican* Extra says: "There is reason to believe, from dispatches already received since our first extra to-day, that LEE was forced to fight at Spottsylvania on Sunday, and was again repulsed and compelled to retreat.

Another statement is that Gen. GRANT had flanked him and got between the rebel army and Richmond.

LEE'S report of the battle of Thursday last, published in the Richmond papers, has been telegraphed to this city by Gen. BUTLER. LEE says that Gen. GRANT attacked him, which contradicts the report received here that LEE made the attack upon our army. LEE employs this language, "*Thank God we have repulsed the attacks of the enemy.*" He states that LONGSTREET is badly wounded.

LEE says nothing in his report about the fight on Friday.

Dispatches state Gen. BUTLER is still holding the line of railroad between Petersburgh and Richmond, preventing BEAUREGARD from reinforcing LEE.

Richmond and Petersburgh Not Evacuated—Gen. Hancock in Vigorous Pursuit of Lee—The Casualties.

WASHINGTON, Monday, May 9.

The *Star* publishes an extra this evening, saying:

There is no foundation for the report that the rebels are evacuating Richmond, nor that Petersburgh is evacuated.

The following is a list of the casualties, so far as received at the present time:

Brig.-Gen. ALEXANDER HAYS, of Pennsylvania, killed.

Brig.-Gen. JAMES S. WADSWORTH, of New-York, killed.

Brig.-Gen. WEBB, of New-York, wounded,

Col. WILSON, of the Forty-third New-York, wounded.

Col. STONE, of the Second Vermont, wounded.

Col. LEWIS, of the Third Vermont, wounded.

Col. STONE, of the Pennsylvania Bucktails, injured by a fall from his horse.

Col. WEST, of the Ninth Maine, killed.

Lieut.-Col. TYLER, wounded.

Lieut.-Col. WEST, wounded.

Major DORLIN, of the Forty-ninth New-York, wounded.

Major DARLINGTON, of the Eighteenth Pennsylvania, wounded.

At the latest dates received by the War Department, Gen. HANCOCK was rapidly pushing by the left to Spottsylvania Court-house. Heavy cannonading was heard from that direction, yesterday, at Aquia Creek.

An official report of Gen. LEE to the rebel authorities at Richmond, transmitted by Gen. BUTLER to the War Department, states that the rebel loss in killed is not large, but that many are wounded.

Gen. LEE also states that he regrets to say that Gen. LONGSTREET is dangerously wounded; also, that Gen. PEGRAM and STAFFORD are wounded, and that Gen. JENKINS is killed.

Gen. JONES is also killed and his body is reported to be in our possession.

The Result of Friday's Fighting Very Advantageous—Lee Falling Back—He Leaves his Dead and Wounded in our Hands.

WASHINGTON, Monday, May 9.

The extra *Star* says:

"Reports from the front, not official, by parties that left there on Saturday, are to the effect that the result of the fighting on Friday was yet more advantageous to the Union cause than that of Thursday, resulting in LEE'S falling back, according to some reports, twelve miles, leaving his dead and wounded in our hands.

GRANT, according to the same report, has a field full of prisoners, and had advanced to Spottsylvania Court-house.

A verbal message received at Gen. HALLECK'S headquarters, by a messenger from the Army of the Potomac, is to the effect that the battle closed on Friday, the enemy having fallen back about twelve miles, leaving his dead and wounded on the field.

On Saturday, at 3 o'clock, LEE'S army was in full retreat through Spottsylvania, and when the messenger left, Gen. HANCOCK was entering the place in pursuit.

We have captured many prisoners, but the number is not known.

Gen. WADSWORTH is reported killed, and Gen. WEBB wounded.

Gen. BUTLER is reported to be within ten miles of Richmond. This information comes by a boat from Alexandria, passengers from there reporting the arrival of parties from GRANT'S army with news to that effect.

Parties in Alexandria County yesterday heard firing, as from heavy siege guns, in the direction of Spottsylvania Court-house, from 11 A. M. until 1 P. M. The distance is over sixty miles, but the day was quiet and the wind from the southwest, making it not improbable that the firing was from the battle going on yesterday between GRANT and LEE.

Owing to the fact of the Rappahannock bridge being out of repair, the order directing that the wounded be brought to Washington has been countermanded for the present.

LATER.

WASHINGTON, Monday, April 9—noon.

A messenger who left the front of the Army of the Potomac at 3 o'clock Saturday afternoon, reports that Gen. HANCOCK was then at Spottsylvania Court-house, pursuing the rebels, who were retreating in good order by two roads.

From the Field of Battle—The Fighting of Friday—The Desperate Character of the Battle-Ground.

OLD WILDERNESS TAVERN, Friday, May 6—9 P. M.
Via WASHINGTON, Sunday, May 8—Midnight.

Our correspondent with the Army of the Potomac sends us the following:

The most terrific battle yet fought closed to-day. LEE'S entire army has made repeated and furious assaults upon our right and left wings, commanded by HANCOCK and SEDGWICK, with temporary successes, but has been driven back with great slaughter.

An attack was made about 4 o'clock this afternoon, simultaneously, upon our whole line, which was gallantly repulsed.

Toward dark the enemy concentrated upon our extreme right and fell suddenly upon SEDGWICK, crushing in a portion of his line.

Gen. SEDGWICK succeeded in reforming his line and securing it against further disaster, and the enemy withdrew from his front under cover of the darkness.

Our losses have been heavy.

Our army to-day has certainly achieved a decided success. It has baffled all the offensive efforts of the enemy.

The almost impenetrable woods with which the battle-ground is covered saved the rebels from a crushing defeat, as it enabled them to conceal their movements almost perfectly until the very moment of their execution.

The number of our wounded is estimated at from 6,000 to 8,000.

They have been forwarded to Rappahannock Station, and thence to the Washington hospitals.

I will send a detailed account by the next train.

THE VERY LATEST.

Gen. INGALLS telegraphs from the Old Wilderness Tavern, at 11½ A. M. on Saturday, that "the enemy are said to be retiring."

Gen. BUTLER has sent a dispatch from Bermuda Hundreds, saying that he has made a demonstration against the railroad between Petersburgh and Richmond, and has succeeded, after some pretty severe fighting, in breaking the communication.

Gen. BEAUREGARD is in command of the rebel forces at Petersburgh and Richmond.

This authentic account disposes of the statement that the rebels have burned Petersburgh after evacuating it.

[The foregoing dispatch is a special one to the Boston *Advertiser*.]

PHILADELPHIA REPORTS.

The Advance on Saturday—Casualties—Longstreet Fatally Wounded.

PHILADELPHIA, Monday, May 9.

The following is bulletined here:

HEADQUARTERS ARMY OF THE POTOMAC, Saturday Evening.

At noon to-day our skirmishers advanced and formed, and found that LEE had retreated. Lieut.-Gen. GRANT pushed out strong picket forces on all the avenues leading westward, and resumed his original plan of campaign.

Gen. HANCOCK'S corps is now at Spottylvania Court-house.

The *Evening Telegraph* has the following list of killed and wounded:

Col. Woodward, son of Judge Woodward, of Pennsylvania, killed.

Col. Carroll, of the 95th Pennsylvania, killed.

Col. Gwynne, of the 118th Pennsylvania, wounded in the leg.

Maj. Darlington of the 18th Penn., killed.

Capt. Briggs, of the 11th Pennsylvania, wounded in the thigh.

Capt. Byrnes, of the 2d Penn., captured.

Gen. Longstreet was shot by a bullet in the neck and is stated to be mortally wounded.

The following is a special dispatch to the *Evening Telegraph:*

WASHINGTON, Monday, May 9.

The telegraph is working to Rappahannock Station. Up to 5 o'clock this morning none of our wounded had arrived there. This creates surprise, and many rumors are in circulation in consequence.

Communications have been opened with Gens. SMITH and GILLMORE, who are near Richmond, and have been fighting.

It may be that some of our wounded have been sent to the York River.

There was no fighting yesterday, and our army is believed to be advancing successfully.

Fredericksburgh has been occupied, and the railroad is being repaired.

Mrs. Gen. MEADE has received a dispatch from her husband, dated Saturday, stating that "*We are all well.*"

GEN. BUTLER'S ARMY.

THE BATTLE NEAR PETERSBURGH.

The Demonstration Against Petersburgh—A Severe Engagement on Saturday—Col. Barton's Brigade Destroys the Railroad—Beauregard in Command—Capture of the Gunboat Shoshone.

From Our Special Correspondent.

BERMUDA HUNDRED, Va., Saturday Evening, May 7, 1864.

I was in error in my last night's letter in saying that the Petersburgh and Richmond Railroad had been tapped by Gen. HECKMAN at its junction with the City Point branch. The information was brought to me, and I unfortunately used it without stopping to seek proof of its truth. Such a thing could not have been done without first visiting Petersburgh, as the City Point branch starts from that place. What the gallant HECKMAN really did was, to advance, by order of Gen. SMITH, with his brigade, (the First of WEITZEL'S division,) for the purpose of feeling the rebel position. He moved out on the Petersburgh road until he came to the enemy, whom he found posted upon the Port Walthall branch railroad. A lively skirmish followed, and it was apparent that the rebels were in strong force. They had no artillery, which fact gave us the advantage, and HECKMAN, after a lively musketry fire, succeeded in driving them off the railroad. The rebels brought two brigades of infantry into action, and at times the fighting was at such close quarters that they could be heard calling out to our men, "You are cowards to use artillery! Wait until to-morrow and we will pay you off." As Gen. HECKMAN had received orders not to bring on an engagement, he retired. The brilliant little affair lasted about an hour, and resulted in a loss to us of eight killed and sixty wounded.

Dr. SUCKLEY, Medical Director of the Eighteenth Corps, established a hospital at the house of a rebel named STRONG, which is delightfully situated on a bluff commanding a splendid view of the opposite side. Here the wounded were removed, and received excellent care. Following is a list of the names:

Edward Rahn, Co. G, 25th Mass., knee.
Leveret Clark, Co. H, 27th Massachusetts, arm.
Corp. Lorenzo R. Lovell, Co. H, 27th Mass., shoulder.
Michael Coughlan, Co. G, 25th Mass., knee.
William Ward, Co. G, 9th New-Jersey, abdomen.
William Lamb, Co. G, 25th Mass., finger.
James Rent, Co. E, 9th New-Jersey, leg.
Absalom Howe, Co. K, 9th New-Jersey, arm.
J. Q. Stearns, Co. K, 9th New-Jersey, arm.
John Jennings, Co. E, 9th New-Jersey, hand.
Francis Barnes, Co. I, 25th Mass., hand.
Frederick Weisser, Co. G, 25th Mass., hand.
Casth. Barman, Co. I, 25th Massachusetts, hand.
Charles L. Nye, Co. E, 27th Massachusetts, arm.
Newton Wallace, Co. I, 27th Massachusetts, face.
William Gillom, Co. E, 9th New-Jersey, thigh.
A. Gillmore, Co. F, 27th Massachusetts, leg.
Lafayette Smith, Co. A, 27th Mass., shoulder.
Nathan Nixon, Co. F, 25th Massachusetts, head.
J. B. Gaston, Co. K, 9th New-Jersey, thigh.
Corp. C. D. Gunn, Co. G, 25th Mass., head.
C. D. Toldy, Co. E, 9th New-Jersey, shoulder.
D. R. Bruce, Co. K, 27th Mass., abdomen.
George A. Draper, Co. D, 27th Mass., abdomen.
John Q. Irvin, Co. H, 27th Mass., scrotum.
Henry McCombs, Co. E, 27th Mass., both thighs legs and scrotum.
Frank Akar, Co. B, 9th New-Jersey, shoulder.
Wm. Mies, Co. E, 9th New-Jersey, leg amputated.
Ben. Yeager, Co. A, 9th New-Jersey, leg amputated.
Henry J. Pulsifer, Co. G, 27th Mass., thigh.
James S. Sickles, Co. E. 9th New-Jersey, thigh.
Henry Pittinger, Co. G, 25th Mass., abdomen; died in hospital.
John Munch, Co. E, 9th New-Jersey, head; died in hospital.
Thomas Sales, Co. D, 9th New-Jersey, neck; died in hospital.
Edwin Wilbur, Co. H, 25th Mass., hand, slight.
Frederick Brander, Co. G, 9th N. J., right arm.
David S. Giles, Co. K, 9th New-Jersey, leg.
John H. Loges, Co. B, 9th New-Jersey, arm.
John Edmonds, Co. H, 9th N. J., contusion right breast.

This morning the enemy paid us their compliments, both on the river and land. About ten o'clock, a battery of field artillery came down from Richmond on the north bank of the river, and popped away at the naval vessels, which were fishing for torpedoes near Turkey Bend. The small gunboat *Shoshonee*, a purchased vessel, technically known as a "pasteboard" boat, was some distance in advance of the others. The second shot from the rebel battery exploded the gunboat's boiler, and she surrendered. A few of the crew jumped overboard and swam to the opposite bank of the river, where they found shelter until the other boats came up and drove the impertinent rebels away. The men report that the explosion of the boiler injured no one on board, and that all the officers of the boat were taken prisoners. Admiral LEE kept up a vigorous shelling of the woods for some time after the rebels were driven away.

The fight on shore began about the same time as the affair on the James River. Anticipating the attack, a plan was formed by our side having the object of advancing upon the Petersburgh and Richmond Railroad to destroy it. Five brigades were organized, and marched in three columns to meet the enemy. HECKMAN'S brigade again went out on the left, and three brigades, under Gen. BROOKS, were assigned to the centre. These forces were designated to engage the enemy at the position which he held yesterday in the encounter with HECKMAN, and divert his attention while the column on the right advanced to the railroad near Chester Station. The day being excessively warm, it seemed to me almost impossible that any fighting could be done until the cool of the evening. But the rebels did not allow the heat to trouble them, and by 11 o'clock A. M., having received their artillery during the night, they opened fire briskly on our advancing columns, from about the point whence they had been driven last evening. Our men replied splendidly and in a short time the engagement on the left and centre became general. We could now and then hear the arrival of the trains both from Petersburgh and Richmond, which prisoners told us brought down reinforcements. They also said that Gen. BEAUREGARD had come up from Charleston with troops some days since, and was then commanding the forces in front. While the left and centre were engaged, for the most part in artillery practice, the right column, consisting of one brigade commanded by Col. BARTON, of the Forty-eighth New-York, hurried forward upon a road leading to the Petersburgh Railroad near Chester Station, where also is the junction of the Port Walthall road. Here they set a bridge on fire and destroyed the track for some distance, but being savagely pressed by the enemy, the order was given to retire. The damage to the road, I believe, is not thought to be very great. The fighting continued with unwavering vigor on both sides until 4 o'clock, when the rebels were reported to be falling back. After following them some distance an order was given for our troops to return to the line held in the morning.

The casualties of the day I have been unable to learn. Our loss is reported, however, not to have been very serious. Most of the wounds are from fragments of shells. Twelve or fifteen officers are reported to have been killed or wounded—among the latter Col. DANDY, of the 100th New-York, whose injuries are said to be slight. Gen. HECKMAN'S horse was killed, and a ball tore his glove, grazing his hand. I picked up the names of a few of the wounded:

Aaron A. Brown, Co. F, 9th New-Jersey—shoulder, by piece of shell.

John E. Kelley, Co. A, 9th New-Jersey—ankle.

Wm. Harmon, Co. F, 9th New-Jersey—arm and thigh, by shell.

Cornelius Van Ness, Co. G, 9th New-Jersey—head, mortally.

Corp. Woodhull, Co. F, 9th New-Jersey—side, by shell.

Lieut. Frederick K. Hobert, Co. G, 9th New-Jersey—thigh.

The following named soldiers were sun-struck: Edmund Boese, Co. C, 27th Mass.; Casper Heisler, Co. H, 27th Mass.; Frederick Williams, Co. A, 27th Mass.; Wm. Saxon, Co. C, 27th Mass.

The position of our forces here is considered impregnable. If we cannot get out of the Peninsula which contains us, it is certain that the rebels cannot get in. The natural defences of the place are perfect, leaving little to be done in the way of intrenching, and the gunboats are depended on to keep the river open to Hampton Roads. We are very anxious to hear from GRANT, but beyond the knowledge of a battle having commenced near Chancellorsville, have nothing definite. A negro refugee from Richmond came to us to-day, reporting that LEE and RICKETTS had both been seriously wounded.

We hear nothing from our cavalry expedition under KUNTZ. It is thought that he was too late to cut the railroad at Hicksford in time to prevent the mass of BEAUREGARD'S troops coming up. Col. WEST, with his negro cavalry on the Peninsula, returned to Williamsburgh, after frighting the rebels badly, and was sent out again. H. J. W.

The Landing at Bermuda Hundreds—The People Remaining in the District—A Lieutenant Promoted for Gallantry.

HEADQUARTERS OF GEN. BUTLER'S DEPARTMENT, BERMUDA HUNDREDS, Va., Friday, May 6, 1864.

The work of landing the troops, stores, horses and artillery, went on last night with uncommon dispatch, considering that the necessary wharves had first to be constructed. The shallow water near the banks of the James River at this point, does not admit of the very close approach of the transports, and pontoon bridges and other temporary landing-places had to be made. Everybody having anything at all to do with the debarcation, exhibited great energy and heartiness in the work, and this morning there were plenty of evidences that very few persons connected with the expedition had passed the night in sleep. On the river banks, and in the fields some distance inland, huge piles of ordnance, commissary and quartermaster stores—all the bulky and vast material needed for the effective working of a grand army—reared themselves as monuments to the industry of the chiefs of the Engineer and Quartermaster's Departments. Finding my way on shore early in the morning from the steamer Greyhound, where I am comfortably quartered, I threaded my way carefully through the labyrinth of field-batteries, artillery and cavalry horses, pyramids of stores, boxes of arms, and the incongruous and confused incidents and choking dust of the Summery weather, to a place where I could think and talk. From one of the Brigadier-Generals, whom I was lucky enough to encounter, I learned that during the night our pickets had been thrown out a couple of miles on the Petersburgh road, and that at dawn the Eighteenth Corps, under Maj.-Gen. W. F. SMITH, had taken up the march and pressed on, while Gen. GILLMORE'S corps (the Tenth) was preparing to follow. The military aspect being encouraging, I next visited a few of the straggling houses on the beach, still occupied by rebel families, to have a chat with those inclined to be communicative. The first house contained a Mrs. CRAWFORD, whom I could at once see was a good specimen of the "poor white trash" of Virginia. She was exceedingly non-committal, and very ignorant on every conceivable topic. She did not know whether our army was expected nor the distance from City Point to Richmond. Her husband was a conscript and had left his home as our boats appeared around the bend in the river. She and her three little children appeared to be very poor. The feet of the little girl were swathed in rags for want of shoes, and the little boys wore jackets made of ladder and worn-out ingrain carpets. Our good-natured soldiers, as they were called at the house of this poverty-stricken woman, offered her plenty of rations of salt pork and biscuit from their superabundant supply, and she seemed to appreciate the gift. I learned from her that the precise point where we had landed was a favorite fishing ground for shad, and that the rebel Government at Richmond for some time back had monopolized this business. Her husband, from his familiarity with the location, had been selected to superintend the Government nets. A free negro, living near this rebel woman, told me that he had been forbidden, upon penalty of severe punishment, supplying his wants from the river, and was dependent altogether for piscatorial supplies upon the Government fishermen. The Richmond monopoly verily surpassed the Camden and Amboy.

On a very large plantation, near here, at a delightfully located house on the river bank, I found an old Virginia gentleman named WATKINS. With stately courtesy he offered me the hospitalities of his house, but I could not conscientiously accept them, and preferred to talk with him beneath the stately oaks in his door yard. He acknowledged that the arrival of the Union army here, just at this time, was the largest kind of a surprise to everybody. They expected us here sometime, but as far as they had been able to learn of Gen. BUTLER'S intentions, this movement was destined to advance up the Peninsula. The old man's manner showed him to be a very coward, and miserable at the expected loss of his farm stock—negroes and cattle. He said that he was a "*neutral*," and hoped that Gen. BUTLER would protect him. He hoped that I would speak to the General and have a guard placed over his house to prevent intrusion upon him. His negroes he trusted would not be carried off. They loved him and he was sure would not leave him unless we compelled them to. I left the old man and his three shrewish looking daughters who had come out of the house to listen to the conversation, and went down to the quarters of his servants to hear if their story respecting the happiness and contentment of their lot coincided with the statement of their master. Not a bit of it. Old and young, they were busily packing up their homely traps to follow the army of liberation. They had prayed the good Lord for this day, they said, and seemed vaguely happy because it had come. Their old master, instead of being loved as before, was hated. They accused him of cruelty, in starving and overworking them. His daughters were worse than he. One old woman who had borne thirteen children, some of whom had been sold to other plantations beyond her power of seeing them, by this hoary old rebel, told me as she packed up her rags in a bundle, that all her life long she had slaved for her master, who still expected from her as much labor as when she was young and strong, and she would leave him if she had only a year to live in freedom. These negroes told me that the news of our coming up the river reached them early yesterday morning, and as soon as he heard it, old WATKINS gathered together the largest part of his slaves and carried them to Petersburgh. He then visited those whom he did not take away, and threatened all sorts of punishment if they did not express to the "Yankees" their satisfaction at being his chattels. He had endeavored to frighten them also, with horrible tales of the barbarity of the "Yankees" toward those who had gone to them. It is needless, however, to say that these stories were not believed. I am assured that Gen. BUTLER will put a spade into Mr. WATKINS' hands, and make him work in the intrenchments, if these charges of the negroes can be proved against him. He probably will be confronted with his accusers.

I learned this morning that as the army gunboats, under Gen. GRAHAM, advanced up the river yesterday, they drove the rebel signal officers from their stations along the banks, and, in some instances, in such a hurried manner that dispatches, proving beyond question that the movement here was a surprise, fell into our hands. Lieut. WM. H. BLEDENHEISER, commanding the gunboat *Brewster*, captured fourteen signal flags himself at Swan Point and Bermuda Hundred, landing at the latter place and driving the rebels a mile and a half. Upon Gen. GRAHAM'S recommendation, Lieut. BLEDENHEISER was promoted, by Gen. BUTLER, to a Captaincy in the First United States Volunteers, for his gallantry.

A sad accident happened a few hours since on board the transport *Curlew*. JOHN P. MAULL, the Second Engineer, was accidentally caught by the crank of the engine and horribly mangled. He died within an hour. He was a native of Boston, but his friends, it is supposed, are living in Maine.

I have hurriedly noted the results of my morning's work and must close. This afternoon I shall probably have some news. H. J. W.

A Ride along the Lines—The Gunboat Commodore Jones Destroyed by a Torpedo—Petersburgh only Defended by the Militia.

AT THE FRONT, Friday Night, May 6, 1864.

With Gen. BUTLER and his Staff, I was privileged this afternoon to ride along our lines. The army has advanced on the Petersburgh road, a distance of about eight miles, where it will remain for the night. Its left flank is protected by gunboats in the Appomattox, and its right by gunboats in the James. From Gen. SMITH'S headquarters, it is easy to see the spires of Petersburgh, and the general impression is that there will no great impediment to our advance upon that town.

A report, abundantly verified, has come to me, of a sad mishap on the James River. The gunboat *Commodore Jones*, Volunteer Lieut. WADE commanding, was entirely destroyed about 1 o'clock this afternoon, seven miles below Fort Darling, by a torpedo. About fifty lives were lost, and Lieut. WADE was seriously if not mortally wounded. My statement of the occurrence is from an eye-witness. He says that the *Jones*, with other gunboats, was fishing in the river for torpedoes, when one exploded beneath her, directly amidships, with a smothered sound. The boat was crushed like a piece of paper, and huge fragments of the wreck were lifted high in air. The executive officer of the *Jones* retained his foothold on a piece of the deck, and as a rare instance of coolness in such a sudden and trying event, it must be told that he drew a pistol and shot dead a rebel on the bank of the river, who had exploded the diabolic contrivance by means of a galvanic battery. This remarkable incident is vouched for. Subsequently the river bank was examined by

Continued on the Eighth page.

Richmond Dispatch.

BY J. A. COWARDIN & CO.

THE DISPATCH is published daily, (Sundays excepted.) Price for mailing, $30 per year, or $16 for six months; 3 mos., $7.50; 1 month, $2.50—in advance. All remittances by mail, are at the risk of those who make them. Checks and drafts must be made payable to order.

DAILY DISPATCH.

VOL. XXVI. RICHMOND, VA., FRIDAY MORNING, MAY 13, 1864. NO. 114

THE MOVEMENTS ON RICHMOND—THE FIGHTING AROUND RICHMOND.

Speculation was rife in Richmond yesterday as to the strength of the force now in the vicinity of the city and their designs. The prisoners who were brought in give very different accounts of the force, though all agree that there are "three divisions." What three divisions in the Yankee army number we are unable to say; but of this we may be certain, that if the force had been a very strong one it would never have allowed Stuart's cavalry to dog it all the way from Ashland, attacking it whenever it chose and gaining advantages, without having turned upon it and given battle. The design of the enemy, as at first planned, was doubtless to come to Richmond and make a demonstration upon it, which was to be answered by co-operation from the force on the south side of the river. The appearance of a very large army of Confederates on the southside has interfered with Butler's plans, and prevented the co-operation which was expected, and the heavy force of troops in the city was also a surprise to them. This cavalry raid has now been away from its base of operations for six days, and by this time the forage for their horses and provisions for their men must be nearly exhausted. Their departure from our front, when it does take place, must be made by way of the Meadow Bridge road, the bridges over which have been burnt by our forces.

THE FIGHTING WEDNESDAY EVENING.

During the fight on Wednesday afternoon three pieces of Stuart's Horse Artillery, under Major Breathed, were captured by the enemy at Half Sink, a point near Yellow Tavern.

Col. Randolph, of the 4th Va. regiment, (cavalry,) was killed in this fight.

MOVEMENTS DURING YESTERDAY.

Yesterday morning, about sunrise, the enemy, finding that the Meadow bridges, over the Chickahominy, were burnt, attempted to go down the Mechanicsville road. On this road they were met by a body of infantry (the name of which command need not be stated) and repulsed, after a brisk fight. They then fell back into a dense body of woods, on Mr. H. P. Taylor's farm, near Strawberry Hill. To the edge of this woods, which is distant from the city fortifications about a half mile, across a field, they advanced their artillery and some infantry skirmishers, and commenced a brisk fire.—Our infantry skirmishers advanced and drove them from the edge of the wood. During most of the day the fighting here was kept up without much effect on either side, very few of our men being killed or wounded.

Yesterday morning, about 9 o'clock, the [illegible] Virginia regiment, with three companies of the City Battalion, were ordered to attack the enemy on the right of the turnpike, near Brook Church. They went into the fight and with great gallantry attempted to dislodge the enemy from some breastworks of logs and rocks that he had thrown up, but found them too strongly posted. They then fell back across a field to a wood on this side within range of the enemy, and here a spirited firing was kept up until 12 o'clock, when the 19th Virginia, Col. Gant, was sent to relieve the battalion companies. They, however, declined being relieved, and remained until their ammunition was exhausted. At 4 o'clock the whole force was ordered back, and the firing ceased.

The following is a list of the killed and wounded in the battalion companies:

Company B.—Killed: J S Layne. Wounded: Jas Ashford, (in hands of the enemy;) Corp'l John Taylor, side; privates Geo W [illegible], thigh and shoulder; D W McCraw, thigh; C W Norris, breast; W R Patterson, [illegible]; Jas Tilman, neck; David Thomas, [illegible]; R L Wilkinson, hand.

Co C.—Killed: Serg't J H Thackston, private B C Morris. Wounded: Lieut Jno [illegible]dolph, thigh and hand; Sergt's Lewis S [illegible]es, breast, (in hands of the enemy;) R Spencer, leg and hand; privates E F Coleman, wrist; T B Harris, breast; Wm Hen[illegible], head; Rob't Alice, shoulder and neck; [illegible] Richardson, leg; W M McParr, shoulder. Missing: Corp'l A H Brown, private [illegible] Ralter.

Co D.—Wounded: Lt R Motley, private [illegible] Baker. Missing: W G Andrews.

COMMANDER AND NUMBER OF THE ENEMY'S FORCES AROUND RICHMOND.

The commander of the force which is now [illegible]ing around the fortifications of Richmond is Gen. Sheridan, who was formerly commander of the cavalry with the Federal army at Chattanooga, and was taken from there with Grant when he came to Virginia. His experience as a cavalry commander we know of nothing very dashing or successful, nor is his reputation that of a great General. The force under him is represented by others at the round figure of 20,000, all mounted infantry. That its strength is exaggerated is quite certain; that it consists of mounted infantry is equally certain, as in the fight at Brook Church yesterday the enemy's bayonets were plainly seen.

In the fight yesterday the enemy used two pieces of artillery, and seemed to have plenty of ammunition.

THE LATEST FROM SHERIDAN.

The latest report from the enemy around the fortifications was brought in last night by a courier, who reported that at seven o'clock they were in force on the Mechanicsville road, cooking their suppers. Some movement was expected to be made by them this morning.

OUR WOUNDED.

The following is a list of the officers wounded in the fight near the city yesterday up to nine o'clock last night were received at the officers' hospital: Leut. W. T. [illegible], G, 33d N. C; Leut. J. W. Tate, F, [illegible]; Capt W. J. Collins, G, do. do.; Leut. [illegible] Bedrick, G, Cobb's cav.; Lieut. R. F. [illegible], I, 38th Va.; Capt. W. G. Mitas, G, [illegible] Ala.; Lieut M. L. Barber, D, 43d Ala.; Lt E. G. Redwood, K, do. do.; Lieut. P. [illegible], C, 5th N. C. cav.; Lieut. T. W. [illegible]ding, G, 5th S. C. cav.

[illegible] Gen. Gordons, of N. C., is at the hospital, suffering with a musket-ball wound in the left arm, which it is feared will have to be amputated. He was holding his bridle-rein when struck. The ball entered the forearm, breaking the bone, passing through the muscle of the same above the shoulder.

Most of the other officers enumerated are slightly wounded.

The following is a partial list of the wounded in yesterday's fights about the city received at the Seabrooks Hospital up to [illegible] o'clock P M: R Hudgins, G, 53d Va; J [illegible]ings, F, 38th Va; C Everett, I, do; P [illegible]ed, G, 42d Va bat; J B Slaughter, D, [illegible]; S H Pollard, I, 32d do; J L Tosh, C, [illegible]; J C Destin, C, do do; C Childress, C, 9th do; W T Owens, G, 38th do; R R Sadler, K, 14th do; J Grommange, I, 38th do; W G Anderson, D, 25th Va bat; R M Robertson, F, 32d Va; T Wooten, F, do do; T S Hubert, I, do do; J W Clark, C, do do; W Watts, A, do do; J S Baker, D, 25th Va bat; J F Hall, F, 32d Va; W Wickson, F, do do; S Brooks, Thornton's art'y; R B Shelburne, 32d Va; J C Sadler, C, 19th do; J H Higginbotham, I, do do; G Hann, C, 14th do; F S Armorn, C, 33d N C; G Campbell, I, 54th do; J W Dry, F, 1st N C cav; D Johnson, K, do do; J Ray, A, do do; W A Mathews, A, 5th do; V E May, G, do do; Lt C Patru, C, 5th do; W J Watts, G, 1st Tex; E Newsome, G, do do; A Lawson, C, 5th do, Lt S J Woodward, B, 1st do.

DEATH OF GEN. J. E. B. STUART.

During the fight at Half Sink on Wednesday afternoon, Gen. Stuart was shot through the body, the ball entering one side of the abdomen and coming out through the back. He was brought to this city and carried to the residence of Dr. Burwell, where, we learn, he died last night.

THE ENEMY ON THE SOUTHSIDE—ANOTHER SKIRMISH NEAR CHESTER.

From the southside we learn that a small force of the enemy's cavalry and artillery made their appearance again on the turnpike between here and Petersburg.

About 11½ o'clock they attacked a force of our cavalry near Chester, and a skirmish ensued, in which they were driven off, and went back to the river. Our loss was three killed and six wounded.

They pulled down the telegraph wire and tore up the railroad track near the Junction for nearly a mile.

At Drewry's Bluff yesterday morning there was some skirmishing between our pickets and the enemy, with no result of importance.

THE HEAVY FIRING AT DREWRY'S BLUFF.

The firing heard in the city yesterday from siege guns was from some heavy pieces at Drewry's Bluff, shelling the woods. It is stated that in addition to this, the enemy's gunboats on the river were also shelling the woods along the banks.

EXPECTED RAID ON THE DANVILLE RAILROAD.

Yesterday afternoon Mr. Gill, the Superintendent of the Richmond and Petersburg Railroad, having gone towards Chester to ascertain the damage done to the road, discovered a large body of Yankee cavalry crossing the road and moving towards the Clover Hill Pits. The force was afterwards ascertained to be about 3,000, and it is believed that they have gone up to cut the Richmond and Danville Railroad, and perhaps to keep on to the canal.

THE SPEARS RAID UPON PETERSBURG—IT MARCHES TO CITY POINT.

We have some further particulars of Spears's raid on the rear of Petersburg. On Monday, after burning Maj. Belsches's mill and dwelling, and every out-house on his plantation, they proceeded to the premises of Mr. Niblett, not far distant, when they burnt that gentleman's mill, but did not molest his dwelling or out-houses. Late in the day they swung around towards James river, and burnt Baxter's and Temple's mills in Prince George county. On Thursday night they camped at Mt. Sinai Church, in Prince George county, where they cooked up their stolen sheep, hogs, cattle and poultry. A gentleman who saw their camp fires, says they extended for a distance of a mile or more, and presented quite a novel sight to the people in that section.

Tuesday morning, at seven o'clock, the column was moving by the old Baxter road to City Point, leaving Disputanta about a mile and a half to the right. Col. R. M. Harrison, of Prince George county, who saw them, states that their column was about three miles in length, numbering possibly between 1,500 and 2,000 men, and comprising an immense train of stolen buggies, carts, wagons, and pleasure carriages. But few negroes were observed. They had in one of their wagons a dead officer who had died of wounds received in the fight at Nottoway river or Jarratt's. He was evidently an officer of note, or his body would have been buried where he died. In this connection it may be interesting to state, that our troops heard at Jarratt's that Col. Spears himself was mortally wounded.

The enemy burnt the entire village at Jarratt's, except a small dilapidated building, occupied by an aged widow lady. In this case, the claims of humanity were for once regarded, even by Yankee hearts, and the building spared. Mr. Wm. Jarratt, we regret to hear, lost not only his elegant residence, but all his furniture, and much else of great value. Railroad and Government property of every description was of course consigned to the flames. This band of marauders, unlike many of their predecessors, arrested every man they caught who had any connection whatever with the State or Confederate Government. All clerks of Courts, magistrates, salt distributors, tax collectors, assessors of the revenue, constables and sheriffs, were secured.

THE FALLING BACK OF THE ENEMY ON THE SOUTHSIDE.

The retiring of the enemy from their advanced position towards Bermuda Hundreds was first known in Petersburg. A general engagement, it appears, was expected at that city on Tuesday. On every hand he seemed to be pressing his forces, and extending his lines—his extreme right reaching around to Brander's Bridge, north of the city. Contrary to this universal expectation, however, a general engagement did not come off, but there was little or no picket firing or skirmishing. At an early hour it was ascertained that the enemy had withdrawn his advanced lines, and retired several miles.

At a late hour Tuesday evening our scouts reported the enemy rapidly retiring on the road to Bermuda Hundreds. On the east bank of the Appomattox, in Prince George county, where the enemy advanced his negro regiments from City Point Monday, he was not to be found Tuesday, although a movement was made to ascertain his whereabouts, which pushed its search nearly to City Point.

The enemy left many valuable articles on the ground abandoned Tuesday in front of Swift Creek, such as Belgian rifles, canteens, haversacks, muskets, saddles, harness, etc. A gentleman saw the body of one negro soldier, stiff and stark. He had received a bullet through the breast, and his carcass was left unburied by his friends. There was every evidence of a hasty retreat. The retreat was as sudden as precipitate, for they had thrown up breastworks Monday, and made other preparations for a regular siege.

A GALLANT NIGHT ATTACK.

About half-past 11 o'clock on Monday night, the citizens of Petersburg were startled by several heavy discharges of musketry in Chesterfield county, the sound proceeding from a point due north of Petersburg.—Anxiety was on tip-toe to ascertain the cause but it was not ascertained until nearly four o'clock, just before the dawn of day. At that hour a guard came in with a Yankee who had come into our lines, and gave the particulars. On the enemy's extreme right, which had been pushed around Monday afternoon, to Brander's Bridge, he placed a heavy picket guard, consisting of a New Hampshire regiment, amounting to 800 men, picked troops. They were somewhat isolated from the main body of the Yankee forces, a fact which our Generals were not slow to perceive. Two companies of the 51st N. C. Regiment, General Clingman's Brigade, were selected to make a night assault on these sons of New Hampshire, and see if they could not be induced to "change their base."

The assault was sharp, sudden, and decisive. With a rush the brave Carolinians got within close proximity of the foe, and poured into him a deadly volley. Before he could recover from his surprise, another galling fire greeted him, and yet another a moment or two after, which proved rather warm for frigid New Hampshire, and the blue coats started off in wild confusion, shaping their course towards Bermuda Hundreds. It was a beautiful star-light night, and the dark moving mass could be distinctly seen, so the Carolinians had but to aim at the mass, and they were bound to hit. The race progressed until we had driven the New Hampshire Yankees back and across the turnpike and on over the railroad, a distance of some two miles or more. It was ascertained Tuesday that we killed and wounded a large number of the enemy in this night assault.

CONFEDERATE STATES CONGRESS.

The *Senate* met yesterday at 12 o'clock M. Prayer by the Rev. Mr. Duncan, of the Methodist Church.

The journal having been read,

On motion of Mr. Johnson, of Ark, the Senate resolved into secret session.

Mr. Caperton, of Va., presented the petition of J. Bassett French, asking that certain cotton and stocks contributed for the erection of an equestrian statue of Gen. Thos. J. Jackson, be released from taxation and export duties. Referred.

Mr. Barnwell, of S. C., from the Finance Committee, reported back, without amendment, House bill continuing till the first of January next the increased pay of Government clerks.

Mr Johnson, of Ark., offered an amendment that no one should be entitled to the benefit of the act unless they made affidavit that they had no other means of support. Rejected, and the bill was passed.

The resolution relative to the day of adjournment was, on motion of Mr Burnett, of Ky., laid on the table.

The Senate again resolved into secret session, and soon after adjourned.

The *House* met at 12 o'clock, and was opened with prayer by Rev. Dr. Moore, of the Presbyterian Church.

A Senate bill, to provide transportation for members of Congress living beyond the Mississippi river, was referred to the Military Committee.

Mr. Lyon, of Ala., from the Finance Committee, reported a bill to provide the prompt return of money paid into the Treasury Department by the Navy Department. Passed.

Mr. Russell, of Va., from the Judiciary Committee, reported back a bill concerning the malicious arrest of commissioned officers of the army, and asked that the same be referred to the Military Committee.

Mr. Russell, from the same, reported a bill to provide for the speedy settlement of claims for property impressed in the Trans-Mississippi Department. Passed.

Mr Russell, from the same, reported back a bill to repeal the act authorizing the suspension of the writ of *habeas corpus*.

The committee unanimously recommended that the bill do not pass, and that the same be laid upon the table. Laid on the table—yeas 58, nays 2.

Mr. Orr, of Miss., laid before the House resolutions of the State of Mississippi, requesting their Representatives and Senators in Congress to have the *habeas corpus* bill repealed. Ordered to be printed.

He also offered a resolution that the Judiciary Committee be instructed to report a bill repealing the act of the last Congress suspending the writ of *habeas corpus*. Laid on the table.

The vote having been taken, the resolution of Mr. Orr was laid on the table.

Mr Lyon, of Ala, reported a bill to authorize the Secretary of the Treasury to pay out of the Treasury the amount of money deposited there by the ladies of South Carolina for building a gunboat. Passed.

Mr E M Bruce introduced a bill that so much of the above recited act as authorizes the issue of two dollars in new currency for every three dollars of old currency which has been or may be funded, is hereby repealed.

Mr. Foote, of Tenn., introduced a resolution to repeal the *habeas corpus* act, which was, on motion of Mr. Miles, postponed till Thursday next, and made the order of the day for the morning hour.

On motion of Mr. Goode, of Va., the House adjourned.

City Battalion.

To the Editors of the Dispatch:

Gents: Please oblige the undersigned by inserting the following:

Learning that it is a current rumor in the city that in the recent engagement with the U. S. gunboat Shassheen, in the lower James river, my company was much cut to pieces, and desiring to correct such rumor as well as to relieve the anxiety of the relatives and friends of the members of the company, I will state that, though the only infantry used upon the occasion, none were hurt.

NOTE.—No dismounted cavalry, acting as sharpshooters, were used as stated in your issue of to-day, (May 9th, 1863.) Very resp'y,

LUCIEN L. BASS,
Capt Co G, 25th Va Battalion.

Fort Clifton.

CAMP, May 12th, 1864.

To the Editors of the Dispatch:

Gentlemen: For the benefit of the families of the parties concerned, please state that none of the members of Martin's Richmond battery, who are from Richmond, were hurt in the recent gunboat engagement at Clifton. The members of the battery are all well and in fine spirits.

Yours, &c, S TAYLOR MARTIN,
Capt Comd'g Art'y at Clifton.

Henley's Battalion.

To the Editors of the Dispatch:

Be kind enough to state in your paper that persons wishing to send provisions to Henley's battalion, can do so by leaving the same at the Post Office Department before 10 o'clock to-morrow (Friday) morning, marked with name and company.—The men are suffering for something to eat, having been in the rifle pits since yesterday morning.

May 12th.

RED RIVER COTTON.—The other day a Yankee dispatch read that Banks had captured forty thousand bales of cotton on the Red river. The truth about the amount captured is contained in the following extract from a letter written in New Orleans to the *New York World*:

"One of the most important civil officers of the Government residing here has recently received a letter from Alexandria, from a sufficiently high personage to be reliable, assuring him that all the cotton which may be expected from Red river has already been sent down, and as this is only one hundred and twenty bales the prospect is a poor one. As far as heard from, the torch has been put by the planters to every bale of cotton on the river above that point, which is chiefly attributed to the lawless conduct of the naval part of the expedition, which commenced the work by the indiscriminate destruction of all private property within its reach. The planters are finishing the work on their own account."

The thieving part of the expedition was as great a failure as anything else connected with it.

REV. DR. PLUMER.—By a [illegible] letter from the United States we learn that Dr. Plumer is engaged in preparing for the press a new work on the Commandments.

The Yankee Iron-Clad Navy—Admiral Dahlgren's Opinion of Monitors.

We have before us a copy of Rear Admiral Dahlgren's report to the Secretary of the Navy, of the services of the monitors before Charleston. The concluding portions of the report are of a general character as to the services and capabilities of the monitors, which we give in full. The accompanying report is from Commodore John Rodgers, who has had more experience with monitors in actual warfare than any other officer of the navy:

AFTER CONFLICTS.

The operations of the iron-clads against Morris Island were appropriately closed by a severe contest with Fort Moultrie, Batteries Bee, Beauregard, &c., to relieve the Weehawken, which had grounded under their fire, and was finally got off with some severe injuries, owing to the falling tide having exposed the hull under the overhang.

There were other occasions when severe conflicts occurred with the rebel works on Sullivan's Island. And besides the principal attacks in force there were few days from the first attack (July 10th) to its evacuation (September 7th) that some iron-clads or gunboats were not engaged in firing at the enemy's works, so as to facilitate the labor of our troops ashore, as will be perceived by the following sample from the record:

Date—1863	Object	Vess's Engaged.
July 18......	Assault on Wagner....	Montauk, Flag, Kaatskill, Nantucket, Weehauken, Patapsco; gunboats Paul Jones, Ottawa, Seneca, Chippewa, Wissahickin
July 22......	Wagner.......	Nantucket, Ottawa, (gunboat.)
July 24......	Wagner to cover advance	Weehauken, Flag, Ironsides, Kaatskill, Montauk, Patapsco, Nantucket.
July 25......	Wagner.......	G'bts Paul Jones, Seneca, Ottawa, Dai Ching.
July 28......	Wagner.......	Gunb'ts Ottawa, Dai Ching, Paul Jones
July 29......	Wagner.......	Weehauken, Kaatskill, Ottawa, (gbt.)
July 30......	Wagner.......	Ironsides, Patapsco,
July 31......	Rebel batteries on Morris Island......	Ironsides, Kaatskill, Patapsco, Ottawa, (gunboat.)
August 1....	Wagner.......	Ottawa, (gbt.)
August 2....	Wagner.......	Montauk, Kaatskill, Patapsco, Weehauken, Nahant, Passaic, Marblehead, (gunboat.)
August 4....	Wagner.......	Marblehead, Ottawa, (gunboats.)
August 6....	Wagner.......	Montauk, Marblehead, (gunboat.)
August 8....	Wagner.......	Marblehead, (gbt.)
August 11...	Wagner and vicinity.....	Ottawa, Marblehead, Mahaska, (gbts.)
August 13...	Rebel batteries on Morris Island......	Patapsco, Kaatskill
August 14...	Rebel batteries on Morris Island......	Gunb'ts Dai Ching, Ottawa, Mahaska, Wissahickin, Racer
August 15...	Wagner.......	Gunboats Wissahickin, Mahaska, Ottawa, Dai Ching, Racer, Dan Smith.
August 17...	Rebel bat'rs on Morris island to divert fire from our batteries, which opened on Sumter.....	Mortar boats Racer, Dan Smith.
August 18...	Wagner to prevent assault.	Weehauken, Ironsides, Montauk, Nahant, Passaic, Kaatskill, Patapsco; Gunboats Canandaigua, Mahaska, Ottawa, Cimerone, Wissahickin, Dai Ching, Ladona.
August 19...	Wagner.......	Ironsides, Passaic, Weehauken, gunboats Wissahickin, Mahaska, Dai Ching, Ladona, Ottawa.
August 20...	Rebel batteries on Morris Island......	Ironsides.
August 21...	Sumter and Wagner...	Ironsides, gunboats Mahaska, Ottawa, Ladona, Dai Ching.
August 22...	Wagner.......	Ironsides, Patapsco, gunboats Mahaska, Dai Ching
August 23...	Sumter.......	Weehauken, Ironsides, gbt Montauk
September 1.	Sumter.......	Weehauken, Passaic, Patapsco, Montauk, Nahant.
September 5.	Obstructions bet'n Sumter and Greg	Weehauken, Nahant, Patapsco, Montauk, Passaic, Lehigh.
September 6.	Wagner and Gregg......	Lehigh, Nahant.
September 7.	Batt'rs on Sullivan's Isl'd.	Ironsides, Weehauken, Montauk, Passaic, Patapsco, Nahant, Lehigh
September 8.	Batt'rs on Sullivan's Isl'd.	Ironsides, Patapsco, Lehigh, Nahant, Montauk, and Weehauken, (ashore.)

I shall now briefly comment on the various qualities of the monitors:

1. Capacity for resistance.
2. Power of ordnance.
3. Draft of water.
4. Speed.
5. Number of crew.

1. *Endurance.*—During the operations against Morris Island, the nine iron clads fired eight thousand projectiles, and received eight hundred and eighty-two hits. Including the service at Sumter in April, and the Ogechee, the total number was eleven hundred and ninety-four, distributed as follows:

SERVICE OF THE IRON-CLADS.

	Number of Shots Fired: 15 inch	Number of Shots Fired: 11-inch	Hits......	Hits April 7th, 1863	Hits at Ogechee	Total Hits......
Kaatskill.......	138	425	86	21	..	1 6
Montauk.......	301	478	154	14	46	214
Lehigh.........	41	28	36	..	..	36
Passaic.........	119	167	91	35	9	134
Nahant.........	170	276	69	36	..	165
Patapsco.......	178	239	96	47	1	144
Weehauken....	264	643	134	53	..	187
Nantucket.....	44	155	53	51	..	164
Ironsides.......	..	4439	164	[illegible]	..	164
	1255	6771	882	256	56	1194

	No. shots fired.		Weight projectiles fired in tons.	
By Ironsides........	4439			228½
11-inch by Monitors	2332	3587	151⅛	365
15-inch by Monitors	1255		213⅞	
		8026		653⅜

Of the eight monitors, one was always absent at Warsaw (Nahant or Nantucket) to blockade the rebel ram.

The Lehigh did not arrive until August 30th, therefore was only able to participate in the operations of the remaining seven days, but did good work.

For some time only five monitors were available for general attack, and then six, which was the greatest number disposable at any one time. The consequence of the protracted firing and hard usage to which the monitors were exposed during these two months of incessant service, were unavoidably very considerable in the aggregate; and the greater also that all repair which could possibly be dispensed with was postponed to the conclusion.

It was, therefore, necessarily extensive when entered upon. The battering received was without precedent. The Montauk had been struck two hundred and fourteen (214) the Weehawken one hundred and eighty-seven (187) times, and almost entirely by 10-inch shot.

What vessels have ever been subjected to such a test?

It is not surprising that they should need considerable repair after sustaining such a severe pounding for so long a time, but only that they could be restored at all to a serviceable condition. The force of a 10-inch shot must be experienced to be appreciated. Any one in contact with the part of the turret struck falls senseless, and I have been nearly shaken off my feet in the pilot-house when engaging Moultrie.

All the little defects of detail were marked by such a searching process. Decks were cut through; cannon were [illegible] out; side armor shaken; tops of pilot houses crushed, &c. But all these were reparable, and no vital principle was seriously touched. With such workshops and means as a Northern Navy Yard includes, the repair of all monitors would have been speedily effected; but when machinery, tools, labor and material have all to be obtained, as they were here, from a great distance, [illegible] of necessity considerable delays; and moreover, it was not admissible to withdraw but a portion of the Monitors at a time from the blockade.

The additions that were deemed advisable for strengthening the pilot-houses and turrets were also put on at this time, and the bottoms cleaned, for they had now become so foul with oysters and grass, that the speed was reduced to three or three and a half knots, and with the strong tide of this harbor, added considerably to the difficulties of working the vessels properly under fire.

One night I was caught by heavy weather from southeast, while close up to Sumter, when I had gone to attack it, and it was well that the darkness of the night prevented the slowness of our motion being perceived, while extricating the monitors from their position.

POWER OF ORDNANCE.

Each turret contains two guns, and from the peculiar facility which it has for giving direction to the heaviest ordnance, no doubt arises the desire to make these of the heaviest description. How far other considerations should control the character of the ordnance, is necessarily an unsettled question.

To strike an armored ship, it may be best to use a gun capable of the greatest power; but whether this shall be derived from a projectile of great weight, driven by low velocity, or of less weight and high velocity; whether it shall be a 15-inch gun, fired with thirty five or forty pounds, or a 13 inch, fired with fifty pounds of powder, is not here material; the weight of the gun for either purpose will not vary to any important degree. But in operations against earthworks, whose material cannot be damaged permanently, but only disturbed, and which are only to be dealt with by keeping down their fire, a much lighter projectile would be preferable, in order that the practice may be as rapid as possible. Hence a piece of 16,000 lbs for 10 inch or 11 inch shot and shell.

When a number of monitors are brought together, it would be better also to have guns of like kind in each turret, and bringing into action whichever might be preferable.

Each of the monitors of this squadron had a 15 inch and a smaller gun, 11 inch or 8 inch rifle, and hence the rapidity of fire which was most desirable was not attained. That this was due to the calibre of the gun, and not to its being located in a turret may be shown by one notable instance.

November 9, 1863, the Montauck, Capt Davis, was engaged in battering Sumter. In so doing, the 11-inch gun fired twenty five shells successively in one hour, of which twenty one hit the wall of the fort aimed at—distance sixteen hundred yards. This is at the rate of one shell in 2½ minutes, which is not only rapid, but also exceedingly accurate practice.

There is no reason why another 11 inch, if placed in the adjoining carriage, instead of the 15 inch, could not have been fired in the same time, at which rate that monitor would have delivered an 11-inch shell every 1.2 minutes.

The rates of fire reported for the Ironsides by Capt Rowan are:

	Time. Hours—Minutes.	No. Fired.	Time for each fire. Minutes.
Most rapid..	0.05	25	1.74
Continuous	2.55	490	2 86
Assumed...	1.00	360	1 33
Montauk....	1.00	25	2.40

It will be perceived that for a short space of time the frigate delivered a shell from each gun in 1.74 minutes for three hours in 2 86 minutes; and it is believed that a fire could be sustained at the rate of 7.33 minutes. The last rate is, therefore, possible; but I am sure it would be difficult to sustain it long with much regard to good aim and considerable distances; and I believe, on the whole, that for every practical purpose there would be all desirable rapidity of fire from the 11 inch turret.

Thus it is to be presumed that there will be equality of advance power in the same number of 11 inch guns as to the rapidity of fire whether in a turret or broadside.

DRAFT OF WATER.

The monitors of the Passaic class draw about 11⅛ feet of water when properly trimmed. On this coast 10 and 11 feet is the most convenient draft of water for penetrating all the principal sounds and rivers, and navigating them to any extent. A greater draft restricts a vessel in movement, and in many instances excludes her from several ports, except under very favorable circumstances.

SPEED.

The speed of the monitors is not great, (seven knots,) but it is quite respectable with a clear bottom, and is fully equal to that of the Ironsides.—Their steerage is peculiar, but, when fully understood and rightfully managed, not difficult of control. They pivot with celerity, and in less space than almost any other class of vessels.

NUMBER OF MEN.

The number of men required to work them and the guns is only eighty, which is very moderate.—In common with all iron clads, the scope of vision is much restricted, for the plain reason that in such vessels apertures of any size must be avoided.—There are some other defects, but they are not inherent, and, it is believed, are susceptible of being remedied wholly or in part. So much for the monitors.

THE IRONSIDES.

The Ironsides is a fine powerful ship. Her armor has stood heavy battering very well, and her broadside of seven 11-inch guns, and one 8-inch rifle has always told with signal effect when opened on the enemy. Draft of water about 15⅞ to 16 feet.—Speed 6 to 7 knots, and crew about four hundred and forty men.

The defects of the vessel are the unplated ends, which are consequently easily damaged by a raking fire, and involve the rudder and screw more or less, while she can return no fire in either direction. This was particularly and frequently inconvenient in attacking the works on Morris Island, for at certain stages of the tide vessels tail nearly across the channel, and present bow and stern to the beach of Morris Island. So that sometimes it was necessary to delay placing the vessels in position, and at others she would swing around very awkwardly when engaged.

The monitors, on the other hand, were almost equally well defended on all sides, and could fire in any direction. The Ironsides was also open to descending shot, and her scope of fire too much restricted by badly placed ports. The desire for comparison which rages just now can easily be satisfied by bringing the above data in juxtaposition. Just as they are, the Ironsides is capable of a more rapid and concentrated fire, which, under the circumstances, make her guns more effective than the 15 inch of the monitors.

On the other hand, she was restricted by draft to the mid-channel, was very vulnerable to the raking fire, and the direction of her own guns was very limited laterally. The monitors could operate in most of the channels, could direct their fire around the whole circle, and were almost equally well defended on all sides. The defects in both classes of vessels are susceptible of being remedied partially or entirely. The defence of the Ironsides could be made complete, and that of the monitors equally so. The armament of the monitors could be perfected so as to give all desirable rapidity of fire, but by no contrivance could the Ironsides be enabled to use much heavier guns than those mounted. Yet when such changes were made as experience suggested, there still would remain to the monitors the lighter draft, choice of guns from the heaviest to the lightest, defensibility, and direction of fire around the whole circle; consequently the ability to carry a heavier battery into the least depth of water, with equal power of offence and defence in any direction, and that with half the number of guns carried in broadside by another vessel.

COMPARISON OF IRON-CLADS.

The comparison now made is to be understood as having relation to existing circumstances, and not at all intended as conclusive in regard to the general merits of iron-clads.

It is in this sense that the action of the Navy Department is to be considered with reference to the selection of one class of vessels over another.

It is evident that it was not designed to adopt any one style exclusively, for of the three vessels first ordered, two were of the ordinary broadside class—the Ironsides and the Galena. The latter was quickly proved to be absolutely inefficient, and so must any armored steamer of that size. It is universally admitted that plates of less than four and a half (4½) inches cannot stand the shock of heavy projectiles, and vessels so armored must be of considerable tonnage. I presume the Department only intended to build such vessels as were best adapted to the service at the scene of war.

Keeping in view the peculiar exigencies of the case, which required light draft and great ordnance power, it appears that the selection of the Department could not have been more judicious in preferring a number of monitors to operate from a heavy frigate as a base; and if the intent of the Department could have been carried out in regard to numbers, we should now have been in entire possession of the coast from the Capes of Virginia to New Orleans, including Wilmington, Charleston, Mobile, &c.

Many defects of both classes are easily remediable, but some of those in the monitors could only be determined by the test of battle; before that, approximation only was possible.

What other style of vessel could the Department have chosen? Certainly none that has been built by English or French naval authorities. The Warrior and her class are exceedingly powerful, but could not get within gunshot here. On the other hand, there is very little navigable water on the coast which is not accessible to the monitors. They command supremely all that is near the shore, and cannot themselves be reached by vessels of heavier draft. So that when there was some reason to apprehend the appearance of certain rams in this quarter, I assured the Department that the iron clads could maintain position so long as coal and provisions lasted.

It may appear that I speak too positively on the subject, but some experience with them certainly gives a right to do so.

With a single exception, I have been on board a monitor in all the principal actions, and the recurrence of casualties to the Fleet Captains over me shows that I was in a situation to judge. I was once in the Ironsides in an attack on Moultrie and Sumter. I have also watched the behavior of the monitors at anchor through all the phases of winter weather in this exposed situation.

The completeness with which four little monitors, supported by an iron-clad frigate, have closed this port to their [illegible] is striking. Very soon after entering the Roads, I advanced one monitor well up towards the inner debouches of the Northern Channel, supported by another. On the night of the 19th of July, an English steamer attempted to run in, and having eluded the hot pursuit of the outside blockade, no doubt indulged in the belief that all danger was past. But the gallant Captain Rodgers was in advance that night with the Kaatskill, and a shell sent suddenly by him ahead of the culprit steamer signified no escape. In despair or alarm the latter grounded on a shoal, and her wreck has since served as a warning to like evil doers. Two or three steamers that were in, managed to get out immediately after, and one or two may have gotten in, for the crews of the monitors were often too fatigued then with a day's battle to keep watch at night; but there ended the business as such, and for several months not a vessel has passed in or out.

These four monitors, who thus keep watch and ward, muster eight (8) guns and three hundred and twenty (320) men, which is almost insignificant in contrast with the work done.

I have thus put on paper the general impressions now uppermost, but very hastily and under great pressure of business, which will, I hope, excuse such imperfections as may have inadvertently occurred. With more leisure I could do full justice to this interesting subject.

I have the honor to be, &c.

JOHN A. DAHLGREN, Rear Admiral,
Commanding S. A. B. S.
Hon. *Gideon Welles*, Secretary of the Navy.

The Trans-Mississippi.

The Atlanta *Appeal*, of the 3d inst., has the following encouraging view of affairs in the trans-Mississippi Department, written before the report of Steele's surrender to Price:

If our intelligence from the West be true, and we have no reason to doubt it, Kirby Smith and Price are doing their work up nobly on the west side of the Mississippi river. The campaign of Banks in Louisiana has proved a complete failure, and he is represented as having been driven on the north side of Red river, and is seeking refuge at Natchez, on this side of the Mississippi. This leaves all West Louisiana free from the enemy, and will play hob with those Yankees who have emigrated thither with the view of raising cotton and sugar. They will be compelled to give up their farms, of course, and re-emigrate to the North.

Gen Magruder seems to have no foe to contend with in Texas, and Gen Smith will remain idle during the spring and summer, as it will be impossible for Lincoln to supply Banks with a new force sufficiently strong to renew the campaign.

Gen Price, too, since he has been relieved of the incubus of Gen Holmes, is beginning to loom up, and will again signalize himself as the deliverer of Arkansas and Missouri. His victory over Steele seems to have been a complete one, and we doubt whether Steele will be permitted to remain long in Little Rock, even if he should get there.—Now that the work has commenced, and Gen Price has his face once more set towards the North, we may rest assured he will not remain idle. His army will gather strength as he moves through the country, and we predict that the summer months will find him once more within the borders of his own State, rallying the people to action.

These victories will inspire the hearts and nerve the arms of our people west of the river, who, we doubt not, will rally to the support of the army in such numbers as will insure that country from further invasion. Many of them, probably, will be enabled to cultivate the crops which the Yankees have planted and reap the proceeds before Lincoln will be able to send another effective force against them, even if he shall ever have the power of doing so, which we do not believe will be the case. He now has his hands too full on this side of the river to give much attention to the West, and Gen. Banks will call for reinforcements in vain. The greater probability is, that this individual will be called to Washington to give an account of his stewardship.

These victories and triumphs in the West will go far to teach the people of the North the utter folly of attempting further subjugation of the South.—They will teach them the impossibility of holding the country and turning it to advantage, even after they have once made a conquest of it. If there was any portion of our country which they considered to be firmly within their grasp, it was West Louisiana; yet this has been wrested from them, and we believe without the hope of recovery. So it will be with Arkansas, so with Missouri, so with Tennessee, and so with Kentucky. The return wave is now flowing back upon the North, and no earthly power can stay its progress. It will roll on and on, gathering strength and volume as it progresses, until the entire South is redeemed from the despotic tread of the Yankee invader.

Our dastard and unprincipled foe have had their most jovial revels on Southern soil. From this day forth they will be made to feel a more infuriating sting of Southern steel than they have hitherto felt. Our people, long oppressed, are now thoroughly aroused, and our soldiers may be said to be just beginning to fight. The Yankee will no longer find the South an asylum for him. He is now required to "take up his bed and walk," and "go home where he belongs." [illegible] battles thus far fought this spring have had a most powerful and persuasive effect upon him in this direction, but nowhere more so than in the West. The great Union slider, Banks, would now seem to be on a big slide himself, and no doubt thinks the ghost of Stonewall Jackson is after him. If he has not already discovered, he will find out before the summer closes, that Massachusetts is a more healthful place of residence for him than Louisiana.

Altogether, the Trans Mississippi Department is in a most promising condition. If Banks is driven on this side of the river, we know of no other Federal troops in Southwestern Louisiana. Magruder has little or nothing to contend with in Texas, and we may rest assured that Gen. Price will give Steele no rest until he gets him out of Arkansas. This leaves the Western department comparatively clear of the enemy, and, as remarked above, we do not think the people there need live in any fear of their return. Our opinion is they have started home, and will not stop until they get there. As the West is clear, let us now look to the East, give our best attention to Grant at Richmond and Dalton, and the war is over, at least so far as the South is concerned.

QUEEN VICTORIA AND THE PRINCE OF WALES.—The Queen is for Germany, not only in obedience to the proclivities of her dead husband and in friendship of his brother Prince Augustenburg, but because her niece, the Princess Leiningin, is Augustenburg's wife, and has always been high in favor with her Majesty, who appointed the lady's brother, the Prince of Leiningin—an officer in the British navy—to the command of the royal yacht. The Prince of Wales and his party hold with Denmark, and for war on its behalf and that of the papa of the pretty Princess. I believe it is a historical tradition that all reigning monarchs are at issue with their heirs apparent, and if Queen Victoria and her first born be not greatly belied by those who pretend to know, they are no exception to the rule. Not to put too fine a point upon it, it is said that they quarrel like cat and dog. Her Majesty likes to have her own way, as was very well known in Prince Albert's time, and the Prince needs none of the inevitable reminding that he is heir to the Empire on which the sun never sets, which must have attended him from his cradle—hence antagonism. They say, too—I think a newspaper correspondent is fully justified in using those two "dreadful words," denounced by Aaron Burr, who had good reason for detesting them—that the Queen cannot approve of her son's "goings on"—in the direction of George IV., of odorous memory, in illustration of which I might tell you more stories than are worth repeating. When the Prince got married and set up for himself at Marlboro' House, his mother desired him to put his servants into mourning for his dead father; this the young man flatly refused to do, and left Windsor in a huff, not returning for some time.—*London Correspondence of the New York Tribune.*

A VERY FRENCH INCIDENT.—A late French journal relates the following well invented story, which, it will be seen, is French all over:

While Mons. Godard was filling an immense balloon in the Champ de Mars, he amused the spectators by sending up the small figure of a man, the perfect semblance of M. Thiers without spectacles. The little man being filled with gas, rose majestically into the air, and was soon lost to view among the clouds. His adventures, which became known the next day, were curious. Thanks to a strong and favorable gale, which impelled him on his course, the little balloon man arrived the same afternoon in the sight of a fine country house in the neighborhood of Sevres. It was near the hour of dinner, and the lady of the mansion, who naturally thought herself perfectly safe, was occupied in the mysteries of her toilet.

It was a warm day, and she had opened one of the windows which looked out upon the park, and was safe from any prying eyes. While tranquilly engaged, by the assistance of corset lacing, in reducing her waist to a size and shape that would reflect credit on her husband's taste, she was suddenly startled by a blast of wind, followed by a strange noise; and immediately the casement was thrown open, and our little balloon man entered her chamber unannounced. The lady uttered a cry of terror and threw a shawl over her shoulders. The little man driven by the wind, threw himself upon the unhappy woman, who, screaming louder than ever, pushes him off, and he conceals himself under the bed.

Just as the wife, in a supplicating voice, says to this novel Don Juan, "Ah, Monsieur, go away, or you will ruin me!" the husband furiously rushed in, crying, "Ah, the wretch, I have him now!" and goes in search of his sword to run him through the body. The wife, more dead than alive, [illegible], in the midst of sobs, "Fly, fly, Monsieur! and save me the sight of a dreadful tragedy!"

The husband [illegible], armed to the teeth, followed by the whole household, who seek to satisfy his anger. While two of his [illegible] hold the husband, a third, stooping down, [illegible] the [illegible], who, for good reason, [illegible] not a word, and catching him by the leg [illegible] him forth from his concealment—[illegible]. Monsieur [illegible], no longer held down by the husband, raises himself erect, [illegible] out, and [illegible] to the ceiling, to the [illegible] of the spectators; while the poor jealous husband [illegible] away, sword and all, heartily ashamed of his [illegible] wrath.

LOCAL MATTERS.

Richmond Dispatch.

JOB PRINTING NEATLY EXECUTED

Advertisements will be inserted at the rate of one DOLLAR AND FIFTY CENTS per square, for each insertion—eight lines (or less) constitute a square. Larger advertisements in exact proportion. Advertisements published till forbid will be charged $1.50 per square for every insertion.

Hunting Yankees.—Three of the clerks of the Central Railroad Company being at leisure, owing to the temporary stoppage of business on their road, thought to amuse themselves yesterday by walking out and taking a shot at the enemy north of the city. Carefully loading their guns, they strolled out the Central road to our entrenchments. Here they found all quiet, and our men in the earthworks told them there was no danger in proceeding further, as our pickets were still some distance ahead of them. Assured by this information, they continued their walk across a wheat field in front of our line and in the direction of a heavy piece of woods on the left of the railroad. On getting within three hundred yards of this wood they perceived a line of troops drawn up in battle array, and the line looking particularly *blue*, they began to suspect they were venturing upon dangerous ground, and halted to confer and reconnoitre. But any doubts they may have had as to who were before them were speedily solved by a volley of a hundred muskets. The hostile bullets whistled about their ears most uncomfortably. The three hunters threw themselves on the ground without loss of time, and one of them is said to have dived into the soft mud up to his ears. Afraid to rise or look back in this their woful predicament, they bethought themselves of trying the efficiency of a flag of truce, and simultaneously pulled out their white pocket handkerchiefs and waved them in a frenzied manner. This, however, was far from having the desired effect, for the Yankees instantly opened on them again, and harrowed up the mud about them in a style which taught them the necessity of changing their base. Failing in their flags of truce, they sprang to their feet and ran for their lives. At every step the Yankee bullets hurried them. They had a quarter of a mile to run, and are said to have made it in the shortest time on record. Luckily none of them were hit, and breathless and spattered with mud to the crowns of their heads, they at last ran safely into our lines, where they were received with such yells and cheers as have seldom waked the echoes of the Chickahominy.

All three of the gentlemen express themselves as thoroughly satisfied for the present on the subject of Yankee hunting, and say the next time they go out it will be in rather stronger force.

Lightning and New Milk.—During the heavy thunder storm on Wednesday afternoon the residence of Secretary Mallory, on 10th street, was struck by lightning, the fluid tearing away a portion of the brick cornice, shattering a window frame and sash, and entering and setting fire to the small room in the northeast corner. Dense smoke instantly issued from it, and to all appearance the fire was beyond control, when a young son of Mr. Mallory rushed into the room and succeeded in extinguishing it. His demands upon the terror-stricken servants for water were answered by screams of murder, and by yelling that water would not put out God's fire, and that nothing but new milk would do any good; and but for his presence of mind and persistent energy the building would have been destroyed.

Struck by Lightning.—During the thunderstorm of yesterday morning the residence of Major Louis J. Bossieux, southwest corner of 19th and Franklin, was struck by lightning, but fortunately sustained no further damage than the knocking off of a quantity of slate from the roof. The building is high-roofed, with a pointed gable, and is unprotected by a lightning-rod. Several ladies in the house at the time were very much frightened, but no one was hurt, or received any shock.

Libby Items.—The clerks at the Libby prison yesterday were very busy receiving and disposing of prisoners. One hundred and eighty of the raiders captured about the city were brought in, among them three commissioned officers. Since the beginning of this raid ten Yankee officers have been captured and deposited in this prison, among a list of whom we noticed the name of Surgeon M. D. Ferguson, of the 8th Pennsylvania.

The prisoners are being fed on corn instead of flour bread, and are said to prefer it. We saw and tasted some of the bread last evening, and found it of most excellent quality.

Ragged Man.—The raggedest man this war has produced was paraded through our streets yesterday to the Provost-Marshal's office. His name was Tom Jones. He was brought down as a deserter from Powhatan county, where he has been skulking in the woods for five months. He had but one whole piece of cloth about his clothes, and that was a patch of black cloth twelve inches square in the seat of his faded grey homespun pants. He was committed to Castle Thunder. The Confederacy guarantees him a new suit when he emerges from this place of durance.

The Weather.—The weather continued cloudy during Wednesday night, and yesterday morning there was a heavy fall of rain, attended with considerable lightning and thunder. The rain lasted during most of the day.

THE WILL OF THE LATE JOHN C. RIVES.—John C. Rives, well known in the history of the United States as the printer of the *Congressional Globe*, died a few days since in Washington. His will is dated April 4, 1861, and bequeaths his estate to his six children, Wright Rives, Caroline R. Williams (wife of Samuel T. Williams,) Franklin Rives, Lucy Rives, Jefferson Rives and Blair Rives.

The *Globe* office, situated on Pennsylvania avenue, between Third and Four and a Half streets, is bequeathed to Franklin and Jefferson Rives, with the contents, excepting copies of the *Congressional Globe* and the stereotype plates of that work, which is devised to the other five children.

Franklin and Jefferson Rives are to have no benefit of the balance of the estate, which is to be divided between the other five children, together with $50,000 in Missouri State bonds.

The country residence in Prince George's county, with the ground, 51 acres, some of which lies in Washington county, is not to be sold out of the family; one of the heirs may sell their portion to the other, and he provides that the heirs may live on the place in common, contributing equally to its support.

When any of his blood relations cease to reside on the place, then the house and land is to revert to the Government then having dominion over them.

He wills that his slaves shall be free as follows: the day of emancipation being July 4: Gilbert Kay, 1866; James Brown, 18[illegible]; Jane, 18[illegible]; [illegible] Brown, 1878; Henry Brown, 1878, William Brown, 1851, Judson, 1867, Lucy, 187[illegible], Charles [illegible], 18[illegible]6; and Ben, an old man, whenever he sees proper to take his freedom.

He desires that the remains of his late wife shall be interred in the Congressional Burying Ground, and put in a coffin made of granite, the top to be placed on two granite [illegible], one inch in diameter, and one inch in height, so that they may be placed in a fire proof building to be erected in the southeast end of the garden, which is to hold the stereotype plates of the *Congressional Globe*. He directs that his body be disposed of in the same manner, as also all the children who might die before him.

George W Jones, of Fayetteville, Tenn., Samuel T Williams, of P G county, Md, and Wright Rives, are nominated as executors, the first of whom is not required to give any security, and the two latter required to bond in the sum of $[illegible] each. If either refuse or neglect to act as executor, the next oldest son to be appointed.

TERRIBLE DEATH.—Hon. Ezekiel Mowry, of [illegible], Wyoming county, Pa., met his death under the following circumstances:

He was engaged in the plaster mill, grinding corn, and while [illegible] about the cracker his coat caught by the [illegible] on a screw that held the coupling of the shaft together, just above the crusher, and before he was aware of his situation had wound up so closely that he could not extricate himself. In this position he remained until his [illegible] coat, a thick flannel and cotton shirt, and his vest, were torn into shreds, and he was only liberated when his body had been forced through a space of [illegible] inches between the [illegible] and a post. From this he fell into the [illegible] to the floor, where he lay about an hour [illegible] was discovered. He died in a few minutes. [illegible] deceased was an excellent man, and highly esteemed by all who knew him. He [illegible] Wyoming county in the Legislature in [illegible] 1850.

The New-York Times.

VOL. XIII—NO. 3943. NEW-YORK, FRIDAY, MAY 13, 1864. PRICE THREE CENTS.

THE GREAT CAMPAIGN.

The Gigantic Struggle on the Rapidan and the Po.

Comprehensive and Authentic Account.

The Strategy, Fighting, Gains and Losses.

Full Details from Our Special Correspondent.

THE BATTLE OF THURSDAY, MAY 5.

TODD'S TAVERN, Va., Sunday, May 8, 1864.

The details of the wonderful three days' battle of the Wilderness, which closed last night just as the blood-red sun went down behind the margin of the Rapidan, will have given you some idea of the labyrinth of action through which its course ran, and the maze of tactics out of which it was evolved; but the battle of the Wilderness must remain, for the present, undescribed, for the reason that it is really indescribable. I remember a pregnant observation of Gen. ROSECRANS, that with us war is only "bushwhacking on a large scale." Now, if this is true of the kind of ground on which many of our battles have been fought, the analogy holds still more forcibly in the wild, tangled pine woods in whose thickets and along whose margins the prodigious Indian fight of Thursday, Friday and Saturday raged.

No man can claim that he saw this battle, and although undoubtedly it had a line and formation of its own, it would puzzle even the Commanding General to lay it down on the map. There is something horrible and yet fascinating in the mystery shrouding this strangest of battles ever fought—a battle which no man could see—and whose progress could only be followed by the ear. It is, beyond a doubt, the first time in the history of war, that two great armies have met, each with at least two hundred and fifty pieces of artillery, and yet placed in such circumstances as to make this vast enginery totally useless. Not a score of pieces were called into play in the whole affair, and I may mention it as a fact strikingly illustrative of this battle, that out of the three thousand wounded in the hospitals of HANCOCK's command alone, not one of the wounds is a *shell* wound. In like manner our cavalry has been totally useless, *as* cavalry. In all their engagements the men have been compelled to dismount and fight on foot, and the horse, except for locomotion, has been a hindrance rather than a help. In such circumstances, in the utter impossibility of manœuvering or effecting any grand combination, the difficulty of generalship is enormously increased. It will also be inferred, from the circumstances in which the battle of the Wilderness was fought, that it was quite impossible for it to be decisive in its results. The combat lasted three days, but it might have been prolonged a fortnight longer and still have left the issue undecided. Now that it is ended by the withdrawal of the enemy, though we are hardly justified in calling the result a *victory* in the positive sense of the word, yet, if it be considered that the enemy was signally foiled in the purpose with which he sought battle in the Wilderness, that he was compelled to fall back, discomfited, and that we are in vigorous pursuit, under circumstances that give us the shorter line of advance on Richmond, even the most cautious and skeptical will admit the gross and scope of the action to be a most substantial advantage to our arms.

When GRANT, on Wednesday night and Thursday morning, threw his army across the Rapidan at Germanna and Ely's Fords, and the labor of a twelvemonth brought to nought. The chief consideration that the enemy's fortified position was turned, prompted the flanking movement on the enemy's right rather than on his left, was, doubtless, that a successful movement by the former direction would uncover for us water communications by Aquia Creek and Urbana—an advantage not to be overlooked, and, indeed, indispensable in any protracted march toward Richmond. The disadvantage is, that the line of march southward from the points of crossing leads through a region in which no General would seek to fight a battle. I mean, of course, the "Wilderness," a wild tract of barren country, overspread with a thick growth of stunted pine, extending from Chancellorsville up to Mine Run. By changing front by the right, LEE had it in his power, using the Orange and Chancellorsville turnpike and the Orange and Chancellorsville plank-road, to strike us at right angles. The only escape would be to make our passage of the Rapidan a surprise—a conception which was very happily carried out. The march to the river having been made during the night of Wednesday, Thursday morning found the whole army planted safely on the south side of the Rapidan, and well in hand. So complete indeed seems to have been the surprise, that even after the whole army had passed the river, our signal officers reported the rebels still busy on their works on the Rapidan.

But, of course, it was not long before LEE became fully aware of the situation, and he promptly changed front, and pushed out to strike us by the two roads already named, which, as you will observe, runs from west to east, and strike the road on which we must advance, (the Germanna and Chancellorsville plank-road,) precisely at right angles. This was a masterly movement, for it obliged GRANT to halt, form line of battle, and dispose his force in such a way as to cover the fords, by which all our teams were yet to pass, and which it was absolutely necessary to keep open in order to preserve our line of communication.

This, then, was how it came, strategically, that we were compelled to fight the battle of the Wilderness—an encounter which I am very sure both Gen. GRANT and Gen. MEADE would gladly have avoided, had it been possible to do so. This much credit at least is due to Gen. LEE, whose manœuvre was one of great boldness and rapidity. Whether Gen. LEE intended merely to delay our advance and gain time for the new combinations necessitated by our successful crossing of the Rapidan, or whether he chose this line as one on which to try the gage of a decisive battle, in the hope of defeating us in the same way as he did in the same region (Chancellorsville) at the same period of last year, is a question which I have no means of determining, although the desperate vigor of the three days' attack would give strong color to the probability of the latter design. And it must be confessed his advantages were great. He crowded us into a restricted triangle, densely wooded, with few roads, which we knew imperfectly, and with the whole of our vast trains yet to be brought over the river. On the other hand, the enemy knew the country; with fifty thousand men he could here do as much as we with a hundred thousand, and he had the strong line of Mine Run, six miles in his rear, to fall back upon in case of repulse. When I say that after three days' fight, in which he with desperate fury threw himself repeatedly against every point of our line—right, left and centre—in the hope of breaking through and rolling us up, he has been compelled to retire discomfited, the sum and substance of the story is told.

Thursday morning found WARREN's corps (the Fifth) at Old Wilderness tavern, on the Germanna and Chancellorsville plank-road, five miles south of the ford, and SEDGWICK in his rear, on the same road, and extending down to the river. HANCOCK's corps, on the same day, crossed the river at Ely's Ford, five or six miles further down the river, under orders to move to Shady Grove Church. BURNSIDE's corps was to remain behind for twenty-four hours at Culpepper, and then join the main column. The manœuvre of the enemy compelled Gen. MEADE to form line of battle north and south, and this was done about a mile west of the Germanna plank-road and parallel to it, SEDGWICK's corps forming the right and resting on the river at Germanna Ford, and WARREN joining his left. Finding the enemy was determined to make a stand here, the order to HANCOCK to move to Shady Grove Church was countermanded, and he was directed to diverge by what is called the "Brock road," swing round, come up and form the left of the line.

The disposition above given will have shown that there must be for a considerable time a great interval between our centre (WARREN) and our left (HANCOCK)—an interval which could only be filled by HANCOCK swinging round and connecting with WARREN. The attempts of the enemy were mainly directed to getting possession of the plank-road, and planting himself between the two halves of the army. In this he was completely foiled, for WARREN and SEDGWICK held the front firmly until HANCOCK in the afternoon arrived, and completed the line. This was not done without severe loss, especially on the part of WARREN, two of whose divisions, namely, those of WORDSWORTH and GRIFFIN, lost each a third of its numbers.

From Chancellorsville, where HANCOCK had bivouacked on Thursday night, he advanced to the intersection of Brock road and the Orange and Chancellorsville plank road, where he found GETTY's division of the Sixth Corps. Forming line of battle he attacked at 4 o'clock, and fought very severely until 8, engaging HILL's corps. The enemy held a strong position behind improvised breastworks and was already formed in line of battle, while HANCOCK had great difficulty in getting in as he was marching by the flank to mass, but he stoutly held his position at the cross-roads, from which all the efforts of the enemy could not drive him.

The engagements of Thursday were so far successful that they defeated the purpose of the enemy to advance up the Orange road and penetrate between HANCOCK and WARREN. It was, however, only by the utmost skill and vigor that this was effected, for had the rebels been able to penetrate a mile further they would have achieved their end.

THE BATTLE OF FRIDAY, MAY 6.

Unwilling to remain on the defensive, Gen. GRANT, on Thursday night, ordered a general attack along the whole line for 5 o'clock the next morning. BURNSIDE, who had been hitherto in reserve was ordered in, and HANCOCK, who, as was realized had a severe part to perform, was strengthened by four divisions taken from the Fifth and Sixth Corps, so that he now commanded nearly one-half the army.

Promptly at the hour the flame of battle burst forth all along the line, which, from SEDGWICK's right to HANCOCK's left, had an extent of about seven miles.

On the right SEDGWICK attacked, engaging EWELL, who, however, showed a strong front. The two divisions WARREN has left, namely, those of GRIFFIN and CRAWFORD, badly handled yesterday, content themselves with repulsing the rebel attack. WADSWORTH, connecting with HANCOCK's right, puts forth a desperate valor, leads in person several charges at the head of his division, has two horses shot under him, and is then himself shot in the head and left in the hands of the enemy, but whether dead or alive is not yet known. BURNSIDE, somewhat tardy, is only skirmishing as yet, and has had no serious business. HANCOCK, on the left, attacked promptly at 5 o'clock and gallantly drove the enemy about a mile and a half, taking the rebel line of rifle-pits and five colors. In their turn the rebels attack vigorously, and the ammunition of HANCOCK's men being exhausted, they are forced back to their original line at 11 o'clock. The enemy even turns the extreme left, formed by FRANK's brigade of BARLOW's division, which broke in considerable confusion down the road. This, however, was promptly repaired, and the enemy prevented from following up his advantage. After this all remained quiet with HANCOCK until 4 o'clock in the afternoon.

Hitherto HANCOCK had met only the corps of HILL, but at 4 in the afternoon, LONGSTREET's corps, which had marched twenty-five miles to get into the fight, came up, and LEE prepared to hurl the main weight of his force, with a view of doubling up our left flank, and rolling us back on the enemy. The rebel attack was made at precisely 4½, and was made in four lines, the left on the plank road. It was marked by the greatest vigor, and succeeded in breaking our lines. Part of our breastworks got afire, and a portion of the Third and Fourth Divisions broke. GIBBON's division was, however, promptly formed in rear of the break. The brigade of CARROLL (who conducted himself with distinguished gallantry, and though shot through the arm, would not leave the field,) forming by the left; the brigade of BROOKS by the right. This was effectual in checking the rebel advance, and after forty-five minutes of most desperate fighting, the crisis had passed. The heroism and skill of HANCOCK, and the valor of his command had saved our army. Failing on the left, the rebels repeated their usual tactics by a night assault on our right, and they succeeded in rolling up the brigade of Gen. T. SEYMOUR, who was himself captured, but the break did not extend to the other portions of the line, and though some confusion was inseparable from a night assault, the rebels had gained nothing after all.

The rebels expended their utmost strength in the battle of Friday, and failed to accomplish any decisive results. It was obvious that they were in very great strength, for they showed a full line along our whole front, extending beyond our right and overlapping our left.

SKIRMISHES OF SATURDAY, MAY 7.

It was, therefore, difficult on Friday night to say whether the enemy would resume the attack or retire. In case of the former alternative, a new and stronger line, considerably contracted, was selected on Friday evening. The attack, however, was not resumed in the morning, and reconnoissances and skirmishes made during the day along the whole line, though developing on the part of the enemy a strong skirmish line, left little doubt that the main portion of his army was retiring.

In this state of facts, Gen. GRANT formed the determination of throwing forward this army by a rapid night march toward Spottsylvania. Accordingly, a march of 15 miles was made during the night, and this morning finds the whole army massed at Todd's Tavern. We shall doubtless, to-day, feel forward toward Spottsylvania Court-house, where we shall probably find the enemy in position.

Although we have no reliable returns of our losses in the three days' fight, it is probable they will reach 15,000. The loss of the enemy cannot vary much from that figure, and we have taken 2,000 prisoners.

THE BATTLE OF SUNDAY, MAY 8.

NEAR SPOTTSYLVANIA COURT-HOUSE, Va., Monday, May 9—2 P. M.

I have this morning returned from our advanced line of battle, which lies within two and a half miles of Spottsylvania Court-house, the enemy confronting in force. Our army reached this position yesterday morning, WARREN's corps having the advance, and heavy fighting took place during the day. It was hoped that we could have reached Spottsylvania before the enemy would be able to make that point; but in the foot race which the two armies ran on Saturday night, from the battle ground of the Wilderness, the rebels beat us. LONGSTREET, it appears, started at 11 P. M. of Saturday; our advance left at 10 P. M. The two columns marched by parallel roads, but LONGSTREET's corps had time to arrive and form line of battle, and when our force was thrown out to feel the enemy this morning, he was found in position. Our first attack was made by BARTLETT's brigade of GRIFFIN's division, on the right of the road, with ROBINSON's division on his left. BARTLETT had been ordered by Gen. WARREN to attack in column, under the belief that only rebel cavalry would be found. Instead of this, however, he ran on the whole of LONGSTREET's corps, and his brigade, already reduced by the fearful losses of the three days' battle of the Wilderness, was frightfully cut up. One of his regiments, the First Michigan, went in a hundred strong and came out with but twenty-five, having lost three-fourths of its numbers in fifteen minutes. ROBINSON's division, which held the left, was also roughly handled, and broke in disorder. Seeing this, Gen. WARREN seized the division flag and rallied the men in person. Fresh troops were thrown in, and after fighting from 8 A. M. till 12 M., our troops had gained the object sought—an open space up to the woods in which the rebel line was formed. In this engagement Gen. ROBINSON was severely wounded in the leg, and will have to lose his limb.

At 6 P. M., two fresh divisions, namely, those of CRAWFORD, (Fifth Corps,) and GETTY, (Sixth Corps,) were thrown in, and after a severe engagement lasting for an hour and a half, CRAWFORD carried the rebel position, took their first line of breastworks and captured over a hundred prisoners. This ended the action of yesterday. For the numbers engaged, our losses were extremely severe, and will count up to 1,500.

This morning found our line established two and a half miles this side of Spottsylvania Court-house, and securely intrenched. LONGSTREET has also been strengthened by the arrival of EWELL's corps. The rebel line lies on a ridge a mile in front of the Court-house, and it will be a position somewhat difficult to carry, should it be decided to make a direct attack.

It will be observed on the map that our present position carries us many miles south and in the rear of Fredericksburgh, whose famous fortified heights are in our possession without the need of firing a shot. It will be used as a depot and for hospitals, and several thousand of our wounded were, yesterday, sent there. A small army of 2,500 greybacks have also just been marched by headquarters en route to the same point. They are generally hearty-looking fellows, and rather better clad and shod than I have before seen them.

Everything thus far has gone on satisfactorily, although it would doubtless have been better had we been able to find an opportunity of fighting a decisive battle.

The Army of the Potomac is in superb condition and spirits—in fact, was never before in any such condition. We are going on to Richmond, depend upon it; at least, some more formidable obstacle than has yet appeared will have to present itself to stop us. BUTLER, we see by the Richmond papers of yesterday, is between Petersburgh and Richmond; SIGEL and AVERILL are in the right place, and you will presently hear from the cavalry corps of this army, under the bold and energetic leadership of SHERIDAN, in a way that will throw all previous raids into the shade.

The headquarters of the Lieutenant-General and Gen. MEADE, are always established near each other, and in action the two Generals and their staffs are always together. Gen. MEADE retains the immediate command of this army, while Gen. GRANT exercises a general supervision over the movements over the whole field. In regard to the operations of this army, the two Generals are in constant consultation, and it would, I think, be hard to say how much his own practical share in the actual command is. Perhaps I may say that Gen. GRANT indicates the strategic moves and combinations, while Gen. MEADE takes charge of their technical execution.

The rebel papers acknowledge a loss of two general officers killed and two mortally wounded, while it is now positively ascertained that LONGSTREET also is wounded.

P. S.—We have this moment been shocked by the announcement that Gen. SEDGWICK, Commander of the Sixth Army Corps, has just been killed by a shot through the head. He was standing up with his staff in his advanced line of breastworks, and was picked off by a rebel sharpshooter, perched in a tree. The ball entered the face a little below the eye, and came out at the back of his neck. He lived for half an hour after being struck, and then expired. His body has just passed headquarters in an ambulance. It will be embalmed and sent North. The profoundest grief is felt at the death of the lion-hearted chieftain, and it is felt that we could better afford to lose a whole division of the army than one whose valor, illustrated on so many fields, we can ill spare at this time. He never fought so well as in the arduous three days' fight in the "Wilderness," and it was a matter of general remark how splendidly SEDGWICK had been doing. It is presumed that Gen. WRIGHT will take the vacant command of the Sixth Corps.

SKIRMISHES OF MONDAY, MAY 9.

[In order to make our account continuous from day to day, we insert again a part of a letter given yesterday.]

IN FRONT OF SPOTTSYLVANIA COURT-HOUSE, Va., Tuesday, May 10, 1864.

The military situation at this hour (Tuesday, 12 M.) finds the line of the army drawn around Spottsylvania Court-house in the arc of a circle, the concave toward us. The enemy is in force at that point, and seems determined to dispute the passage. I mentioned in my letter of yesterday that the two armies ran a race from the Wilderness for Spottsylvania, but unfortunately the enemy won the race. This should not be interpreted as conveying any censure on the Army of the Potomac, which has marched with new inspiration and a rapidity never before seen in its history. But the very necessities of our condition as the invading party, with our old base abandoned and a new one not yet opened, obliges us to take immense trains, which, of course, retard the general movement of the army; the rebels constantly falling back on their base, and favored by their very poverty, can readily beat us on an equal start. It would certainly have been a great point gained had we been able to make Spottsylvania Court-house in advance of the enemy. An inspection of the map will show you that it is an important strategic point, being the point of divergence of the roads leading southward, both to the right and left. The enemy's command of it enables him to cover the withdrawal of his trains and at the same time bars our further advance, unless on the condition of an assault—which, in the country in which we are now fighting, is very destructive of life—or of a turning movement. It is probable that to-day will decide the question; and if, as we hope, it gives us Spottsylvania Court-house, we shall then be out of the Wilderness, and have a clear road on to Richmond.

Yesterday was intended to be a day of quietude, during which the army, fatigued by five days incessant marching and fighting, would have an opportunity to recuperate and renew the supplies of rations. Little occurred to interfere with this programme, although the rebels made an attack on WILCOX's Division of BURNSIDE's Corps, early in the afternoon. They were, however, handsomely repulsed, and BURNSIDE has the extreme left of our line, within a mile and a half of the Court-house.

About 6 o'clock last evening, Gen. HANCOCK, holding the right of our line, crossed Po Creek and seized the Block House Road, the direct line from Parker's Store to Spottsylvania Court-house. Immediately afterward, WARREN, who now has centre, advanced his line of battle, drove the rebels for half a mile, and took up a strong position. Up to the present hour, the situation remains as here described.

The rebels have as yet shown no disposition to assume the offensive at this point. It was confidently expected on Sunday night that an attack would take place on HANCOCK's front, toward the Catharpen Road, and on a line with the Brock Road. The troops showed great diligence in throwing up breastworks, and a brigade was advanced out for a mile or more from the main front over some cleared land. About an hour before sunset this attack was made. Immediately upon the retirement of the advance brigade, the enemy charged toward our line, but never reached it. They put a few guns in position, and shelled the woods for a while, but did no harm. A small number of Gen. BIRNEY's troops, on whom the attack was principally made, were wounded by the enemy's musketry before they withdrew, having received more harm than they had done. Before this attack, our advance could see HILL's Corps marching south to join the main body, opposing our progress in front on the branch of the Po. As it was necessary to hold this position until it was certain the enemy were gone, Gen. HANCOCK did not stay the progress of the men engaged in forming breastworks, but added another line in the open ground around Todd's Tavern, a regiment of heavy artillery working all night to finish them. It was a very pretty sight. The lanterns of the workmen hung to the blossoming cherry-trees, and picturesque groups of soldiers digging and erecting the works, while batteries stood harnessed up, their cannoniers lying on the ground around the carriages, in wait for any emergency. At sunrise scouts advanced and found the enemy in small force; and about noonday Gen. HANCOCK left Gen. WARD's brigade to hold the position, and advanced with his corps toward the River Po, which by night he had, after considerable resistance, passed. Gen. BURNSIDE pushing out on the extreme left, advanced to a place in front of SEDGWICK's (now WRIGHT's) corps. A reconnoissance by two regiments was made. These advanced some distance without meeting much resistance. At the same time the cannonade along some portions of the front was quite brisk between ours and the rebel artillery.

The prisoners we have are in apparent good condition. One fellow, who was taken with much trouble, explained his determined efforts to avoid capture, on the ground that it was currently reported that we should massacre all our prisoners, in revenge for the slaughter of our negro soldiers.

We have fewer stragglers than usual, though not so few as might be. It is not easy to straggle in a country where there is no communication, and guerrillas loaf around the army to pick up any waif or estray sleeping in the woods. The Provost-guard has all it can do, to keep the lingerers up to their duty.

Gen. PATRICK had quite a brigade of them one day, and I believe had serious thoughts of making a charge with them.

The same intolerable heat which we have had ever since this movement commenced still continues, and numerous cases of *coup de soleil* happen every day. It is, however, one compensation for the heat that it keeps the roads in excellent traveling condition, saving and excepting the dust, which is here of a most malignant type.

Gen. WRIGHT, who formerly commanded a division of the Sixth, is now in command of that Corps so grievously deprived of its head by the death of the beloved SEDGWICK, the details of which I yesterday sent you. The grief at this sad event intensifies as it becomes known throughout the army. An effort was at first made to keep the sad fact from the knowledge of his men. Gen. WRIGHT is an excellent soldier, and will command the Sixth well.

The road which our troops faced runs from Orange Court-house to Fredericksburgh, and is forty-one miles long. It crosses no river. Proceeding from Orange Court-house, we come at a distance of ten miles to Verdiersville; ten miles further brings us to Parker's Store, six miles further to Wilderness; five miles further to Chancellorsville; ten miles more to Fredericksburgh.

Just as I close this letter a heavy cannonading has commenced in the front, for which I leave immediately.

THE BATTLE OF TUESDAY, MAY 10.

WASHINGTON, Thursday, May 12.

The following dispatch has just come to hand:

HEADQUARTERS ARMY OF THE POTOMAC,
NEAR SPOTTSYLVANIA C. H., Wednesday, May 11.

My dispatch dated 6 P. M. yesterday gave an outline sketch of the operations of that day down to the hour named, and included the announcement of the turning of our right flank [This dispatch has not yet come to hand.—ED. *Times.*] I would gladly have avoided leaving the situation suspended in this perilous condition, but the messenger by whom I had the opportunity to send my dispatch left just as the courier bearing the tidings arrived. I hasten to add that the menacing break was speedily repaired, and that the army holds at present a position not differing greatly from that we have held for the past two days, with the exception that our right is somewhat more strengthened.

Yesterday's operations now assumed the character of the most bitter and perhaps the most bloody of the series of battles which have been fought since we crossed the Rapidan. Knowing, as we do, that our cavalry force has been working havoc with LEE's communications, that his supplies are almost exhausted, that the lines of investment are being drawn around Richmond, and that echoes of disaster reach his ear from afar-off Tennessee, and presage the downfall of the fabric of the rebellion, we are left to infer that the attack of yesterday was a desperate, and, let us hope, final attempt to retrieve the rebel fortunes by dealing a crushing blow at this army. It is enough to say that it failed, and though he inflicted a severe loss of life upon us, he suffered not less himself, and we still hold a position against which the rebel fury may dash itself in vain. It would seem to have been the policy of LEE in the series of battles which he has delivered during the past week, to contest the advance to Richmond at every available point, to wear us away by degrees, and then, perhaps, to fall upon the Union forces under BUTLER, and endeavor to annihilate them. This plan he has carried into execution with a masterly skill, inspired by a fury perfectly diabolical.

We are steadily pressing the rebels southward. The enemy have been greatly favored by the nature of this country, in whose dense woods and tangled chapparal the lithe and wary are much more at home. Fortunately, if we once carry the position which they now hold in front of Spottsylvania Court-house, we shall be out of the "Wilderness" and reach open country.

The operations of yesterday were opened by a reconnoissance on the left by BURNSIDE's corps, which developed the fact that the enemy was in no force there—nothing but cavalry disputing the advance. This caused the division of MOTT to be withdrawn from its position on the extreme right and it was sent to the left to connect with BURNSIDE. The rebel position now very much resembled ours at Gettysburgh, a curved interior line, well protected by breastworks, with the additional defence of a marshy run in front: Holding us at bay in the centre, they discovered the weakness of the right, now held by BARLOW's division. This division of HANCOCK's command, as I yesterday mentioned, had made the passage of the Po, throwing out skirmishers on the east bank. This gave it a coigne of vantage, from which it not only enfiladed the entire rebel position, but commanded the road on which their trains were passing. At the same time, however, it isolated it from the rest of the army—a false position, of which the rebels could hardly have failed to take advantage, and of which they did take advantage, as we shall presently see.

Gen. WARREN's corps held the centre of the line. [illegible] it was resolved that a vigorous assault should be made there, while HANCOCK and BURNSIDE endeavored to assail and turn the two flanks of the enemy. With this view, two divisions of the Second Corps were thrown over to connect with the right of WARREN and support him. In execution of the projected design, WARREN's corps moved forward during the day, pressing the rebels through the woods to an open space behind, close to the enemy's breastworks. This was attended by very heavy shelling from the enemy, and it was three or four o'clock P. M. before the woods were cleared. After this, the corps advanced to assault the breastworks. In this, however, it did not succeed, although the attempt was gallantly made. CARROLL's brigade went in on the charge and lost eight hundred men.

Gen. MEADE realizing the critical position in which the extreme right of our line (BARLOW's division,) was placed, had ordered it to draw back. The rebels had, however, anticipated us, and making a detour came in on its rear, making it a matter of considerable difficulty to withdraw; supports coming up, however, it was successfully accomplished. A general attack was ordered along the line, to take place at 5 o'clock, but owing to the tardiness of some of the Commanders to get into line it was postponed, first to 6 o'clock, and then to half-past. A furious cannonade from our artillery preceded the charge. The worst of it was that the lateness of the hour prevented its being perfectly successful.

Gen. WRIGHT advanced the flower of the Sixth Corps. Nobly and well they sustained their reputation. UPTON's brigade leading, they advanced rapidly upon the enemy's breastworks without

Continued on the Eighth Page.

LOCALITIES OF THE LATE BATTLES ON THE RAPIDAN AND THE PO.

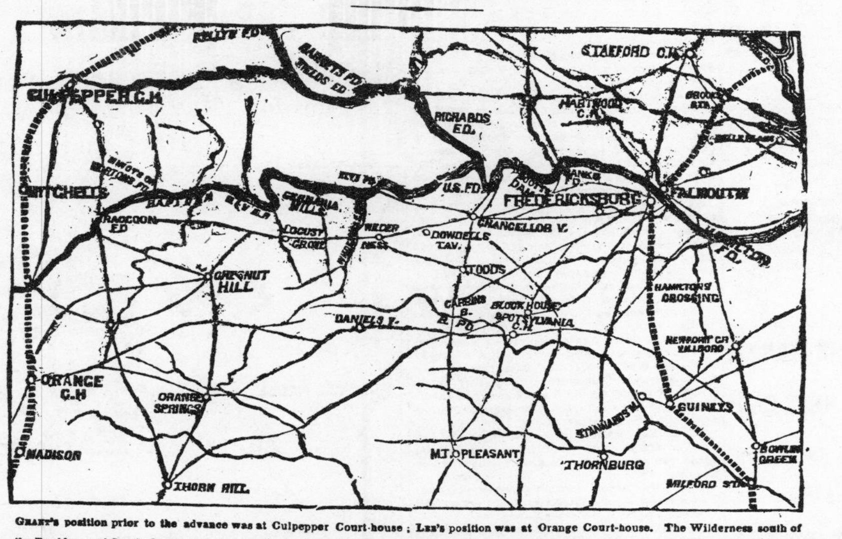

GRANT's position prior to the advance was at Culpepper Court-house; LEE's position was at Orange Court-house. The Wilderness south of the Rapidan, and Spottsylvania Court-house on the Po, will be seen above. Richmond is about fifty miles south of Spottsylvania Court-house.

The Philadelphia Inquirer.

CIRCULATION OVER 60,000. PHILADELPHIA, SATURDAY, MAY 14, 1864. PRICE TWO CENTS.

VICTORY!

LATEST FROM THE FRONT.

GEN. LEE IN FULL RETREAT.

Hancock and Warren in Pursuit.

Rear Guard of the Enemy Overtaken.

LEE REPORTED BADLY WOUNDED.

He Has Been Taken to Richmond.

Rebels to Make a Stand on the North Anna.

THURSDAY'S GREAT BATTLE.

SPLENDID UNION VICTORY.

The Reports of the "Inquirer" Officially Confirmed.

DESPATCHES FROM GEN. GRANT

War Bulletins of Sec'y Stanton.

DESPATCH FROM GEN. SHERIDAN

What He Has Done and Will Do.

THE SIEGE OF FORT DARLING.

Gen. Butler's Operations.

SHERMAN HAS A BATTLE.

Gen. Averill on a Grand Raid.

GEN. CROOKS MOVING TO STAUNTON.

LATEST FROM GENERAL GRANT'S ARMY.

Special Despatch to the Inquirer.

WASHINGTON, May 13, 2 A. M.

We have advices from the field of battle up to [illegible] A. M. to-day. Yesterday the battle raged with great fierceness all along the lines, and the Rebels held their positions with considerable tenacity.

General GRANT ordered a general advance with fixed bayonet all along the line at 5 P. M., but the troops were so worn out and fatigued that it was thought best to give them some rest, so at daylight to-day a charge was ordered, but it was found that the enemy had retreated during the night.

Pursuit was at once ordered, and HANCOCK and WARREN started upon two different roads. About eight A. M. their rear-guard was overtaken, and a brisk engagement was in progress when our informant left.

Their next stand will be on the banks of the North Anna River, which have been well fortified for some time.

We have well founded reports from Rebel prisoners that General LEE was badly wounded yesterday and sent on towards Richmond.

THE BATTLE OF THURSDAY.

Preparations for the Battle—Hancock Surprises Ewell—The Captures Made—Gen. Johnson at Head-quarters—Grant's Coolness in Action.

Special Correspondence of the Inquirer.

NEAR SPOTTSYLVANIA COURT HOUSE, VA., May 12th, 1864.

The annals of warfare can probably furnish no parallel to the fighting of the glorious Army of the Potomac for the past eight days. It seems almost incredible that human nature has either physique or spirit enough to accomplish the herculean feats of valor, fortitude and daring that have characterized that gallant body of men since the crossing of the Rapidan at Germania Ford was effected.

Each day's fighting since that time seems to have acted as an additional stimulus to our men, and we now fight as probably man never fought before. To-day death seems to have no effect on the fear of our soldiers, for they are pressing forward and charging line after line of the enemy's intrenchments with as little care or thought of the immediate consequence as though no enemy were in front of them.

It was evident from the general disposition of things last evening that active hostilities would be resumed this morning. Troops were marching, under cover of the night, to different positions. Gens. GRANT and MEADE were in close consultation in their respective tents. Staff officers and orderlies were dashing through the wooded roads in different directions, carrying despatches to the different Corps and Division Commanders, which contained directions as to the disposition of their different commands in the impending morning's battle.

By ten o'clock at night everything was hushed in repose. The preparations for the following day were completed, and the two vast armies lay on their arms facing each other, and eagerly waiting for the dawn of day to recommence the work of death.

While the Rebels lay in perhaps fancied security on their arms and behind their intrenchments, the "Yankees," true to their natural instincts, were working like beavers, taking time by the forelock and making disposition for a complete surprise of the enemy in the morning.

The sequel will show that these night preparations on our part were not without the reward that such labors should reap.

After a brief rest from the labor and fatigues of the previous day, General HANCOCK late at night, or rather early in the morning ordered a slow advance of his line of battle in the direction of the line of intrenchments held by EWELL'S Corps, who were in his front. Slowly and surely did his men creep forward and the dawn of day found them close upon the sleeping and unsuspecting Rebels.

At the proper moment the order was given to charge, when, with a yell the devoted band of heroes sprang forward, and ere the Rebels were aware of the proximity of their opponents and before they had time to finally recover from the surprise of the attack, HANCOCK'S men were leaping over their intrenchments and using the butt ends of their muskets in all directions, on the devoted heads of the Rebels.

The firing amounted to little or nothing; there was no time or necessity for such work. The shelter tents of the enemy, erected near their line of entrenchments, were entered by our troops before the Rebels had time to escape from them; they were surrounded, cornered, hemmed in and fairly dumbfoundered, and on the command being given to surrender they at once dropped their arms and became passive, resistless prisoners of war.

The artillery had not time to limber up and get away or fire a single volley before our dashing troops were among them. Even their General, whose quarters were somewhat in the rear, could not escape, and he, together with the greater portion of his command, became subservient to the orders and commands of the redoubtable HANCOCK.

The results of this morning's surprise are as follows:—Between thirty and forty pieces of artillery were taken, all of which were successfully brought within our lines. No time for spiking them was allowed, and they will most likely be turned upon their original possessors in the subsequent days' fighting, if LEE can, by any possibility, present a belligerent front for another day.

General E. JOHNSON, who commanded the surprised and captured Rebel division, was brought to General GRANT'S head-quarters about 7 o'clock A. M. He was treated with becoming courtesy and entered freely into conversation with Generals GRANT and MEADE and other officers. Information was imparted by him to some of our Generals regarding the condition of different Generals in the Rebel service, with whom some of our own were class-mates at West Point.

Shortly after his capture the general Head-quarters were removed about two miles, when a horse was furnished him and he rode with General GRANT'S escort. After spending a short time at the new head-quarters and being apparently a close observer of everything going on around him, he was furnished with transportation and sent North, accompanied by an escort.

At nine o'clock this morning the artillery firing on the right of HANCOCK'S Corps was tremendous. In addition to the brilliant night advance just mentioned which culminated so successfully, the whole line of HANCOCK'S Corps advanced during the morning, and although ground was gained inch by inch, the Rebels contesting every point with great determination, still we advanced, and in the face of such desperate resistance every foot of ground gained was a triumphant success.

Before noon the whole line was actively engaged in the fierce and bloody strife. All the morning it rained in torrents, and the terrible nature of the contest in the front, the uncertainty as to the issue, the tired condition of the troops after seven days' hard fighting, the drenching rain, the incessant volleys of musketry and roar of cannon, the anxiety depicted upon every countenance at head-quarters, all combined to make the time a trying one. But still every one possessed an innate feeling that everything was going right, and that GRANT would soon be issuing orders to his troops from his head-quarters in Richmond.

An incident occurred during the morning that illustrates the coolness and self-possession of the Commander-in-chief of the Armies of the United States. While the heaviest artillery firing in the morning was in progress Gen. GRANT was standing in company with Gen. MEADE, near a fire, talking and endeavoring to keep themselves dry, when a Rebel shell struck within a few feet of the twain. A disposition to move was manifested on the part of a number of officers standing around, when General GRANT, looking slowly around and fixing his eye on the spot where the shell struck, asked at once for a pocket compass, which, being furnished, he examined the course of the shell, found out the location of the battery, and it was not long before shells were thick among the men working said battery.

At three o'clock, this afternoon, heavy cannonading was heard on our extreme left, and a report is being spread that the Rebels are endeavoring to turn our left flank. BURNSIDE is said to be pressing forward to that point to check any such movement of the enemy, but owing to the distance and horrible state of the weather, it is impossible to arrive at a correct statement of facts regarding the condition of things at that point before I must forward this despatch.

The Rebel prisoners captured within the past four days are quartered in an open field, about five miles south of Fredericksburg. They are so numerous that at a distance they have the appearance of a division of soldiers, ready to be moved forward into action. A strong guard surrounds them, and so large a space of ground do they occupy, that it takes nearly a regiment of men to keep guard over them.

Each division of the different army corps have temporary hospitals erected about two miles in the rear of General Head-quarters. Numberless tents have been erected for the accommodation of the wounded, and the different roads leading to them are filled with ambulances, containing the sufferers by the fierce conflict of the morning. The number of wounded are so great that not enough ambulances are at hand to convey all from the battle-field to the hospitals, and consequently baggage wagons, ammunition wagons, and various other modes of conveyance are resorted to to bear off the wounded to the different quarters.

All who are able to walk are threading their way from the front to the rear and urgently inquiring the location of the hospitals of their respective divisions. Amputations of legs and arms are hourly occurrences, and the Surgeons are at present among the busiest men in the army. Thousands of the wounded are being transferred to Fredericksburg, where they are temporarily quartered in the stores and even private dwelling houses, previous to being sent North by way of Belle Plain, where transports are in readiness to convey them to Washington and other points North. Many of the slightly wounded are walking to Fredericksburg, thirteen miles distant from the battle-field, and they can be seen strung all along the road.

OFFICIAL WAR GAZETTE.

First Bulletin.

WASHINGTON, May 13, 5·30 A. M.—Major-General DIX:—Special despatches have just been received by this Department, dated yesterday at 8 o'clock A. M., at the battle-field, near Spottsylvania Court House. They state that during the night General HANCOCK marched from his previous position on our right, and occupied the ground between WRIGHT and BURNSIDE.

At daylight he attacked with his accustomed impetuosity, forcing the first, then the second line of the enemy's works, capturing the whole of EDWARD JOHNSON'S Division, and a part of EARLY'S, together with Major-General (EDWARD) JOHNSON, Brigadier-General JOHNSON, General STEWART, and from thirty to forty cannon.

The number of prisoners is not given, but it is to be counted by thousands. BURNSIDE, on the extreme left, opened at the same time with HANCOCK, and advanced with comparatively little opposition. His right formed a junction with HANCOCK, and his left is now actively engaged. WRIGHT'S troops attacked at 7·15, and are now at work. WARREN is demonstrating, to hold the enemy in front of his lines. The Rebel works at that point are exceedingly strong.

A despatch has been received from General BUTLER, dated in the field, near Chester Station, Va., May 12, 3·30 P. M. He is now pressing the enemy near Fort Darling, and has before him all the troops from North Carolina and South Carolina that have got up.

BEAUREGARD'S courier was captured this morning, going to General HOPE, in command of Drury's Bluff. He had a despatch stating that BEAUREGARD would join him as soon as the troops were up.

GILLMORE holds the intrenchments, while SMITH demonstrates upon Drury and the enemy's lines.

General KAUTZ, with his cavalry, has been sent to cut the Danville Railroad, near Appomattox Station, and can perhaps advance on the James River.

We have had no telegraphic communication with General SHERMAN since Wednesday.

EDWIN M. STANTON, Secretary of War.

Second Bulletin—General Grant Announces the Victory.

WASHINGTON, May 13, 2·30.—To Major-General DIX:—A despatch from General GRANT has been received, dated near Spottsylvania Court House, May 12, 6·30 P. M., which is as follows:—

The eighth day of battle closes, leaving between three and four thousand prisoners in our hands for the day's work, including two General officers and thirty pieces of artillery.

The enemy are obstinate, and seem to have found one last ditch. We have lost no organization, not even a company, whilst we have destroyed and captured one division (JOHNSON'S), one brigade (DOBBS'), and one regiment entire of the enemy.

(Signed) E. M. STANTON, Secretary of War.

Third Bulletin—Lee Abandons the Fight.

WASHINGTON, May 13.—To Major-General DIX:—The following despatch from Mr. DANA has just reached this Department. EDWIN M. STANTON, Secretary of War.

SPOTTSYLVANIA COURT HOUSE, VA., May 13, 8 A. M.—To Hon. E. M. STANTON, Secretary of War:—LEE abandoned his position during the night, whether to occupy a new one in the vicinity or to make a thorough retreat, is not known. One Division of WRIGHT'S and one of HANCOCK'S are engaged in settling this question, and at 7·30 A. M. had come upon his rear guard. Though our army is greatly fatigued from the enormous efforts of yesterday, the news of LEE'S departure inspired the men with fresh energy.

The whole force will soon be in motion, but the heavy rain of the last thirty-six hours renders the roads very difficult for wagons and artillery.

The proportion of severely wounded is greater than on any of either the previous days' fighting. This was owing to the great use made of the artillery.

CHARLES A. DANA.

Major-General DIX, New York:—The Acting Surgeon-General reports that of five hundred patients from the recent battle-fields admitted into the Harwood Hospital, not one of them will receive any surgical operation, and that, in his opinion, two-thirds of the whole number wounded will be fit for service in thirty days.

Reinforcements are going forward to the Army of the Potomac. EDWIN M. STANTON, Secretary of War.

Despatch from General Ingalls.

WASHINGTON, May 13.—The extra *Star* says the following despatch has been received from General RUFUS INGALLS, Chief Quartermaster of the Army of the Potomac. It brings positive information from as late as noon yesterday:—

"We have made a ten-strike to-day. HANCOCK went in at daylight. He has taken over four thousand prisoners and over twenty-five guns, and is still fighting. Everybody is fighting and have been for eight days.

"We shall have them this pop, though it may take a day or two more. They fight like devils.

"Our losses are heavy. Cannot say how many.

"HANCOCK captured General NED JOHNSON and two other Generals, besides lots of lower grades.

"The old Republic is firm. Bet your pile on it. GRANT is a giant and hero in war. But all our Generals are gallant; and our men, the world never had better. Yours, in haste, RUFUS INGALLS, "Brigadier and A. Q. M.-General."

THE GREAT VIRGINIA CAMPAIGN.

Map showing the Scene of the Great Battle of Tuesday, May 10th, between Generals Grant and Lee.

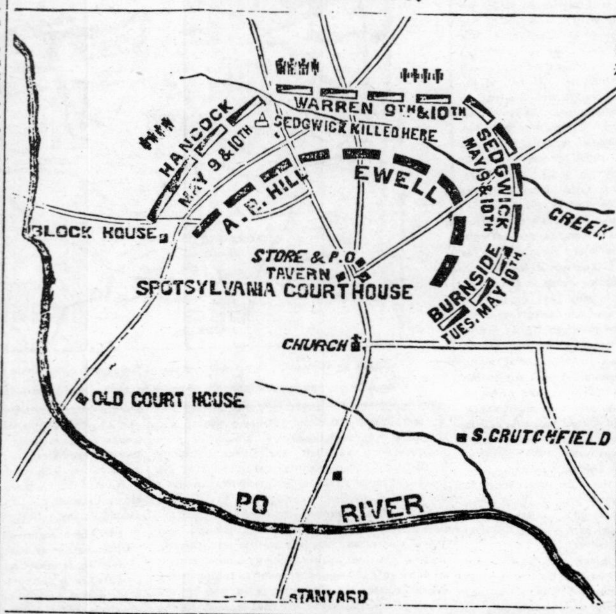

NEWSPAPER ACCOUNTS.

Terrible Defeat of the Enemy—General Lee Proposes to Capitulate.

WASHINGTON, May 13.—Despatches have been received from the battle-field up to last night.

Our victory continued to augment during the whole day, and the rout of the enemy's right and centre was complete.

We have taken nearly fifteen thousand prisoners since yesterday morning, and they are still being brought to the rear by hundreds.

The news this morning indicates a total rout of LEE'S entire army before the week is done.

Many of the Rebels taken say he cannot fight any more, as he is out of ammunition, and his army is utterly demoralized and broken up.

I am informed that Secretary STANTON has received a despatch from General GRANT to-day, stating that General LEE asked for a cessation of hostilities and a brief parley, offering to surrender with seventy thousand men. General GRANT promptly refused this unless Richmond and all its defending armies, works, munitions, stores, and inhabitants were to be surrendered at once.

General Crawford Captured—Colonel Jackson in Command of the Reserves.

WASHINGTON, May 13.—Colonel McCANDLESS reports that General CRAWFORD was captured on Tuesday, and the command of the Pennsylvania Reserves was given to Colonel S. W. JACKSON, of the Eleventh Regiment.

The corps has suffered very severely in killed, wounded and prisoners.

Accounts of Rebel Prisoners.

WASHINGTON, May 13.—Prisoners captured yesterday morning, in HANCOCK'S charge upon JOHNSON'S Division, report the Rebel army in a state of almost total insubordination on account of the want of food.

One hundred and fifty skedaddlers from General GRANT'S army, who were taken from the boat which arrived at Sixth street wharf at a late hour last night, were this morning sent to the Provost Marshal's office. Not one of these men is wounded in the least, but some represented themselves as having been sun-struck. It is the intention of Col. INGRAHAM to place these men in the various forts around the city, and compel them to do garrison duty.

THE GREAT CAVALRY RAID.

Despatch from General Sheridan.

HEAD-QUARTERS ARMY OF THE POTOMAC, May 12.—The following from General MEADE was issued last evening, and was read to the troops. Its effect can be imagined:—

HEAD-QUARTERS CAVALRY CORPS, May 10, 1864.—Major-General MEADE, Head-quarters Army of the Potomac—General:—I turned the enemy's right and got into their rear. Did not meet sufficient cavalry to stop me. Destroyed from eight to ten miles of Orange Railroad, two locomotives, three trains and a very large amount of supplies.

The enemy were making a depot of supplies at Beaver Dam. Since I got into their rear there has been great excitement among the inhabitants and with the army. The citizens report that LEE is beaten. Their cavalry has attempted to annoy my rear and flank, but have been run off. I expect to fight their cavalry south of South Anna River. Have recaptured five hundred of our men—two Colonels.

Very respectfully, your obedient servant,

P. H. SHERIDAN, Major-Gen. Commanding.

THE FIRST NEWS FROM SIGEL.

Destruction of the Railroad between Lynchburg and Charlottesville.

WASHINGTON, May 13.—The *Star*, extra, says an officer who arrived here to-day reports that at three o'clock yesterday afternoon a despatch was read at the front from General SIGEL'S command, dated at Butler's Mountain, between Charlottesville and Lynchburg, on Wednesday, at 10 A. M., announcing that our cavalry had torn up the railroad between Charlottesville and Lynchburg for a distance of twenty-six miles below the former place, and also that the track of the Gordonsville road, between Charlottesville and Keswick, has been destroyed. When returning our forces encountered a body of cavalry who came from the direction of Carter's Mountain, and a skirmish ensued which resulted in the repulse of the Rebels, who fled in the direction from which they had come. This was the only Rebel force met with during the raid.

FROM THE KANAWHA VALLEY.

CINCINNATI, May 13.—On the 4th Gen AVERILL'S expedition had reached Logan Court House, without opposition.

CROOK'S Infantry Column had reached Princeton, without opposition. All communication with the expedition had been abandoned.

The Good News Gone to Europe.

HALIFAX, May 13.—The royal mail steamship *Europa*, from Boston, arrived here this morning, and sailed for Liverpool. The latest war news was placed on board of her.

LETTER FROM AN OFFICER AT THE FRONT.

The following letter from Major O'NEILL, of the One-hundred-and-eighteenth Regiment Pennsylvania Volunteers, dated May 11, 1864, Battle-field, Virginia, has been kindly handed to us for publication:—

To-day is our seventh day of hard fighting, and thank God I am still unhurt, except a few scratches. Yesterday the fighting was fearful from 12 noon until night. All goes well and successfully, but we have had tremendous losses, and very heavy in officers. My regiment has been wonderfully spared, only one officer missing. Colonel GWYN is wounded. Our number this morning is two hundred and ninety-seven men and twenty officers. We have been fighting every day. Our brigade has made several charges on batteries and breastworks. In fact, the Fifth Corps has done much of the fighting. There is no way of sending letters from the front, and I do not know whether you will get this. Where I am writing the bullets are dropping all around me. We are very much fatigued, but strong in the hope of victory, which must soon end our present struggle.

THE GREAT BATTLES.

Partial List of Wounded in Pennsylvania and New Jersey Regiments.

Special Correspondence of the Inquirer.

NEAR SPOTTSYLVANIA COURT HOUSE, May 12, 1864.

The following is a partial list of the wounded in the Pennsylvania and New Jersey Regiments during the late engagements:—

Names of wounded at the battle of Spottsylvania Court House, May 10th and 11th:—

Fourth Division, Second Army Corps—Gen. Hancock.

FIFTH NEW JERSEY.

John Casady, B, head. Pat. Martin, A, arm.

SIXTH NEW JERSEY.

Sergt Wm. R. Marseillas, H, thigh. And. Holland, B, knee.

SEVENTH NEW JERSEY.

Lt. W. W. Barnes, K, hand. Aaron L. De Groot, H, hand.
L. W. Hoffman, I, arm. Captain D. Hart, General
Theo. Van Pelt, H, neck. Mott's staff, hip, slight.

Pennsylvania General List.

A. Garrison, C, 99, arm.	Lt. C. H. Dougherty, thigh.
Cpt. J. H. Lyons, A, 5[illegible], throat.	Peter M. Kane, K, hand.
G. Lawson, A, 1[illegible], hand.	B. F. Ogden, hand.
Lt. Stanley Gaines, A, leg.	Capt. S. J. Hopkins, hand.
Robt. B. Dyer, C, 115, leg.	Davis Skoss, H, 84, neck.
Alex. McCary, F, 118, leg.	Fred Fetcher, I, 115, side.
Wm. Hodges, F, 118, hand.	Aaron Safford, D, 83, thigh.
H. J. Turner, H, 83, hand.	R. Steward, E, 83, shoulder.
Stephen Cook, F, 8[illegible], wrist.	B. J. Stephens, F, 118, elbow.
G. H. Platt, F, 83, neck.	Chas. Murr, I, 83, hand.
Israel Gibbs, G, 83, arm.	G. Vance[illegible], [illegible], 83, arm.
John Jolly, G, 83, stomach.	[illegible], lung.
John. D. McIlenny, G, 83, thigh.	Jacob P. S[illegible]er, G, 84, hip.
	W. Huntle[illegible], K, 83, thigh.
L. Sheppards, B, 83, thigh.	H. McMurtree, H, 118, arm.
Steph. Leaney, A, 83, hand.	Michael Cole, K, 83, thigh.
E. J. Ross, A, 83, arm.	Russell Coburn, H, 8[illegible], arm.
Com. Reynolds, A, 83, arm.	Benj. F. Cox, B, 118, hip.
John Mullarkey, A, 83, head.	Anthony Rabel, I, 83, hip.
Phil. Smith, A, 83, stomach.	Amos Smith, F, 118, arm.
Jas. W. Osborn, I, 84, hand.	Jas. n Gillis, E, 83, thigh.
John Reynolds, A, 83, hand.	Hiram C. Nolan, K, 115, hip.
Eli Grant, I, 83, hand.	Theo. B. Frair, K, 118, hip.
Chas. Rich, I, 84, thigh.	Sylvester Martin, B, 118, leg.
Wm. Conners, K, 83, head.	John C. Cole, K, 118, side.
Jas. Mahoney, K, 83, hand.	Francis Long, K, 115, shldr.
J. D. Fish, H, 83, hand.	S. J. Hegerman, G, 118, hand.
Don H. Se[illegible]ar, H, 83, hand.	Robt. Kase, K, 118, hand.
W. Dickson, G, 83, thigh.	Eugene Cedar, A, 83, thigh.
C. H. Hable, I, 83, knee.	G. W. Maxfield, E, 83, neck.
Thad. May, D, 83, side.	Sgt. L. Burfield, G, 83, head.
John Jones, I, 84, thigh.	H. Sas[illegible], E, 83, leg.
Alex. McKee, K, 84, hand.	John Lawson, E, 83, leg.
T. W. Hyde, K, 83, arm.	G. Richardson, E, 83, leg.
H. L[illegible]dwin, F, 83, side.	Simon A. Amy, I, 83, leg.
Ed. A. Cole, D, 83, elbow.	Adam Snyder, B, 83, leg.
H. McGann, D, 83, leg.	D. L. Foote, K, 83, thigh.
J. D. San[illegible]ford, H, 84, thigh.	O. J. McAllister, K, 83.
Warren Bowen, C, 84, knee.	L. Eaton, G, 83, shoulder.
Robt. Hunter, I, 155, side.	Wm. [illegible]ke, E, 155, hand.
Jas. Faucett, D, 155, side.	W. H. Kuseman, K, 155, finger.
Pat. Lyons, B, 155, knee.	Jas. Webb, C, 155, thigh.
H. McLaughlin, H, 155, finger.	C. McManners, B, 155, back.
J. D. Gavenboner, A, 91.	Jas. Reighner, G, 155, leg.
Wm. H. Loftt, C, 91, finger.	Frank Martin, F, 155, hip.
Silas Chapman, I, P. R., arm.	Jas. O'Neal, E, 155, stomach.
Alpheus Conn, B, 62, Ear.	Wm. H. Justice, A, 155, foot.
Wm. C[illegible], M, 62, shoulder.	T. B. Mett, A, 155, side.
Frnklin Gilmore, A, 155.	Geo. Sharp, A, 155, head.
Rich'd Monroe, A, 155.	Jos. Stevan, E, 62, hand.
Jas. Flanegan, D, 155, hand.	M. Baidsberger, E, 62, leg.
J. Landsburger, F, 155, head.	Wm. Lindsay, M, 62, elbow.
E. McGowen, C, 155, thigh.	M. J. Murray, M, 62, leg.
James Bish, G, 155, arm.	Jas. A. Maratha, A, 62, side.
John Date, C, 155, head.	And. J. Wolf, C, 62, leg.
W. W. Wells, K, 155, thigh.	D. V. Dane, A, P. R., breast.
John Frisher, G, 62, hand.	E. Bumgardner, H, 149, thigh.
O. M. Christy, G, 62, hand.	H. Buchanan, E, 62, thigh.
Geo. Coarson, C, 62, leg.	J. W. Clark, F, 62, foot.
S. P. Smelter, D, 62, shoulder.	A. T. McCalmont, G, 83, thigh.
J. A. Beaver, A, 91, thigh.	Wm. Harvey, D, 91, foot.
R. Wilkinson, F, 91, bowels.	Wm. H. Care, D, 91, hand.
F. P. Donahue, E, 91, hip.	Wm. Aldridge, H, 91, hand.
Thos. O'Neill, C, 91, foot.	Jos. Green, E, 91, back.
Jere. B. Jacob, A, 91, hand.	W. Wurtzell, B, 155, hand.
Sgt. W. D. Chandler, D, 91, tgh.	Ferd. Deitch, B, 155, leg.
John F. Juster, A, 91, thigh.	S. Culbert, I, 155, side.
Wm. Tanney, D, 91, head.	Geo. K. West, A, 155, head.
W. F. Wankoll, D, 91, head.	Wm. S. Bell, H, 155, thigh.
J. P. Chester, H, 91, head.	S. Lebert, A, 155, finger.
S. H. Keen, D, 91, shoulder.	Jas. Niglan, K, 155, finger.
M. C. Johnson, C, 141, thorax.	J. Rosesteel, K, 1st Res, thigh.
Sgt. J. Gause, A, 110, leg.	P. Morton, I, 62, leg.
Sgt. C. P. Oust, A, 57, arm.	O. M. Jones, L, 62, finger.
J. Starliper, G, 146, shoulder.	J. L. Vanank[illegible]n, K, 56, thigh.
J. Morgan, H, 110, hand.	H. Anwester, H, 118, hand.
G. Yingland, D, 105, face.	P. H. Wilson, I, 118, hand.
J. McAttee, A, 63, hand.	Sgt. Wm. Holt, K, 83, thigh.
E. S. Bloom, K, 1st Pa. Rifles, thigh.	J. L. Black, G, 155, hand.
	J. Hutchins, E, 91, wrist.
G. A. Orne, D, 110, thorax.	E. E. Chemin, A, 91, thigh.
Sgt. T. R. Bently, E, 110, hand.	

FIRST NEW JERSEY.

P. C. Donnell. H. Creigden, jaw.
J. Stafford, C, hip. A. Hamilton, jaw.
L. Diehl, D, hip.

ONE-HUNDRED-AND-NINTH PENNSYLVANIA.

J. McElwee.

EIGHTY-FOURTH PENNSYLVANIA.

Lieut.-Colonel Milton Copp, shot through lungs.

ELEVENTH NEW JERSEY.

D. Schrader, H, arm. A. B. Serring, B, shoulder.
Joshua Barber, elbow.

TWENTY-SIXTH PENNSYLVANIA.

J. Hope, I, arm. Serg. R. Anderson, E, hand.
Pat. Stanton, C, hip. C. Monroe, arm.

ONE-HUNDRED-AND-FIFTEENTH PENNSYLVANIA.

M. Frankford, head. P. Sloan, A, side.
J. Ragar, D, foot. B. Ruff, hip.
Serg. J. Doyle, E, leg.

The Fate of General Wadsworth.

NEW YORK, May 13.—A letter from Captain SCHUYLER, of General PATRICK'S Staff, dated May 10th, states that a prisoner says he saw General WADSWORTH on Sunday morning or Saturday night lying on a couch in a hospital tent, with one of our officers attending him. He was shot in the head, and was breathing with some difficulty. From the fact that he was playing with the buttons of his coat it is thought that his mind was wandering, and that he was severely wounded.

Capture of a Valuable Prize.

BALTIMORE, May 13.—The *American* publishes a letter from on board the United States gunboat *Grand Gulf*, announcing the capture on the 7th, off Wilmington, of the blockade runner *Young Republic*, of Nassau, formerly the *Conqueror*, of New York, from which port she sailed about forty days since. Her cargo consists of six hundred tons of tobacco and one thousand three hundred and eight bales of cotton, all on Confederate account, and she was commanded by Rebel navy officers, Captain FRANK W. HARRIS acting as commander.

United States Christian Commission.

BOSTON, May 13.—The subscriptions at the Exchange, to-day, amounted to ten thousand dollars. Thirteen thousand dollars previously received at the same place. All to be appropriated to material supplies for the army in Virginia.

THE NEW YORK HERALD.

WHOLE NO. 10,120. NEW YORK, WEDNESDAY, JUNE 1, 1864. PRICE THREE CENTS.

ON TO RICHMOND!

Splendid Success of Grant, Meade, Warren and Hancock.

VICTORY ON THE TOLOPATOMOY

Warren Within Seven Miles of Richmond on Tuesday Morning and Intrenched.

Another Great Battle Probably Fought Yesterday.

TERRIBLE SLAUGHTER OF REBELS.

Interesting Reports from Richmond.

Consultation as to Whether the City Shall be Surrendered or Burned.

The Mayor is in Favor of Surrendering, and is Put in Castle Thunder, &c., &c., &c.

Secretary Stanton to General Dix.

WAR DEPARTMENT,
WASHINGTON, May 31—4 P. M.

Major General DIX:—

We have despatches from General Grant down to four o'clock yesterday afternoon.

There seemed, the despatch says, to be some prospect of Lee's making a stand north of the Chickahominy. His forces were on the Mechanicsville road, south of Tolopatomoy creek, and between that stream and Hawes' shop, his right resting on Shady Grove.

Dispositions for an attack were being made by General Grant.

Wilson's cavalry had been ordered to destroy the railroad bridges over the Little river and South Anna, and break up both roads from those rivers to two miles southwest of Hawes' shop, where the headquarters of our army were established.

There is as yet no telegraphic line of communication with Washington.

A despatch from General Sherman, dated yesterday, May 30, at eight A. M., reports no change in the position of the armies. Some slight skirmishing had occurred subsequent to the affair of Saturday.

No intelligence from any other quarter has been received by this department.

EDWIN M. STANTON,
Secretary of War.

THE SECOND DESPATCH.

WAR DEPARTMENT,
WASHINGTON, May 31—8 P. M.

Major General DIX:—

A despatch from General Grant, dated at six o'clock this morning, at Hawes' shop, has just been received. It is as follows:—

"The enemy came over on our left last evening, and attacked. They were easily repulsed, and with very considerable slaughter. To relieve General Warren, who was on the left, speedily, General Meade ordered an attack by the balance of our lines. General Hancock was the only one who received the order in time to make the attack before dark. He drove the enemy from his intrenched skirmish line, and still holds it. I have no report of our losses, but suppose them to be light."

Other official despatches, not from General Grant, were received at the same time, and gave more details. They are as follows, the first being dated yesterday, 30th of May, at eight o'clock P. M.:—

"In the course of the afternoon Warren has pushed down on our left, until his flank division, under Crawford, reached a point abreast of Shady Grove church. Crawford, having got detached from the rest of his corps, was attacked and crowded back a little. The enemy then threw a force, which appears to have consisted of Ewell's corps, upon Warren's left, attempting to turn it, but was repulsed. *The engagement was short, sharp and decisive. Warren holds his ground at a distance of seven miles from Richmond.* He reports that he has taken a considerable number of prisoners, and that there are many rebel dead on the field. Of his own losses he has not yet made report. His latest despatch says the enemy are moving troops to his left, apparently to cover the approach to Richmond in that direction."

"On our right an active conflict has been raging ever since dark, but has just closed. As soon as the enemy attacked the left of Warren, Wright and Hancock were ordered to pitch in, but do not seem to have got ready until after nightfall. No report has yet been received from them."

The other despatch above referred to is dated at six o'clock this morning, and states that, on Hancock's attack last night, Colonel Brooks drove the enemy out of a strongly intrenched skirmish line, *and holds it.* The losses are not reported. Burnside's whole corps got across the Tolopatomoy creek last evening, and is in full connection with Warren's. The left of Hancock's rests upon this side of the creek. The Sixth corps is upon Hancock's right, and threatens the left flank of the enemy.

Smith ought to arrive at Newcastle by noon, whence he can support Warren and Burnside, if necessary.

Sheridan, with Gregg's and Torbert's divisions of cavalry, is on our left flank.

Wilson is on the right and rear, for purposes reported in a former despatch.

The country thereabouts is thickly wooded with pines, with few good openings.

The indications this morning are that the enemy has fallen back south of the Chickahominy.

Nothing of later date has been received by this department.

EDWIN M. STANTON.
Secretary of War.

RICHMOND IN SIGHT!

The New Field of Operations----The Brilliant Affair on the Tolopatomoy----The Great Battle Field of the Rebellion.

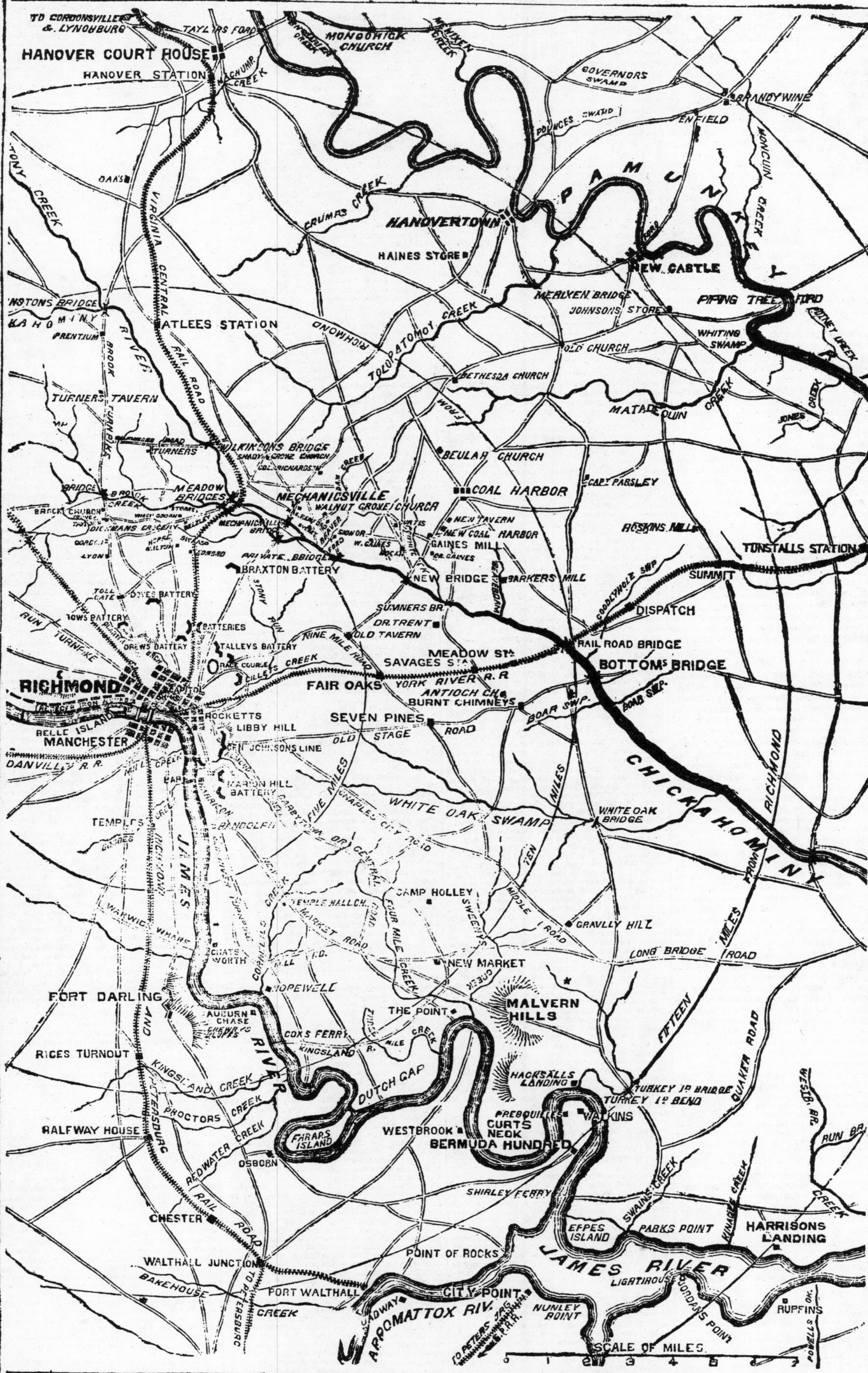

THE THIRD DESPATCH.

WAR DEPARTMENT,
WASHINGTON, May 31—11.25 P. M.

Major General DIX:—

The following despatch has been received from General Butler:—

"Yesterday all day heavy firing in the direction of Mechanicsville.

"Six refugees from Richmond report that Grant was on the Mechanicsville turnpike, fourteen miles from Richmond, yesterday; that they heard the firing, and that Grant was driving Lee.

"A woman reports that a meeting was held yesterday, while she was in Richmond, to see whether the city should be surrendered or burned. The Mayor advocated surrender, and was put into Castle Thunder.

"The enemy attacked my lines yesterday and were repulsed. To-day, all day, they have been demonstrating against my work on Spring Hill, on the easterly side of the Appomattox, but are repulsed."

Nothing further since my telegram of this evening from General Grant.

EDWIN M. STANTON,
Secretary of War.

Mr. J. C. Fitzpatrick's Despatch.

NINTH ARMY CORPS, BANKS OF THE NORTH ANNA,
May 2d—5 P. M.

THE RECONNOISSANCE OF LEDLIE'S BRIGADE

on Tuesday evening, however disastrous it was to the individual command, was of incalculable benefit to the whole army. From the vigor with which Gen. Ledlie made the attack at this point the rebels imagined it was the precursor of a grand assault upon the centre of their army to cut it in two, somewhat after the manner of Gen. Grant's strategy at Chattanooga. Acting upon this supposition, they contracted their lines elsewhere, withdrew their artillery, covering our advance at other points, and concentrated in the centre. In consequence Hancock was enabled to extend his lines upon the left, and obtain positions for his artillery which had been previously occupied by his skirmish lines. Similar advantages were gained by the corps of Wright and Warren.

A GRAND ATTACK

was to have been made this morning; but it was postponed on account of a heavy rain storm which commenced about seven o'clock. The weather cleared up this afternoon, with indications of its continuing fine. So to-morrow morning we expect another great battle, that is if the enemy are in force on our front—a matter about which there is considerable doubt. Prisoners taken represent the corps of Longstreet on our right, and Hill's in the centre—whether the main body or a rear guard, however, is not positively known.

LIEUTENANT COLONEL CHANDLER.

There is as yet some doubt about the fate of this gallant officer. It is known that he had an arm shot away; but as he subsequently fell into rebel hands it is uncertain whether he survived his wound.

CASUALTIES.

The following are some additional names of the wounded in the Ninth corps:—

W. C. Miner, Co. H, 100th Pa., right side.
James Mayhew, Co. D, 100th Pa., left side (died 20th).
J. L. Haven, Co. A, 100th Pa., forearm.
J. B. Ravi, Co. D, 100th Pa., head.
M. R. Garvan, Co. K, 100th Pa., right shoulder.
O. H. Kelly, Co. E, 100th Pa., leg.
Corporal J. H. Reed, Co. E, 24th N. Y. cavalry, mortally.
M. J. Hill, Co. B, 24th N. Y. cavalry, right hand.
J. J. Martin, Co. A, 6th N. H., left hand.
Thos. Lougherty, Co. D, 21st Mass., left leg.

The Washington Despatches.

WASHINGTON, May 31, 1864.

The Sanitary Commission's steamer John R. Thompson left Baltimore last evening with sixty tons of sanitary stores—her second load—bound for Bermuda Hundred, where she has been stationed during the past fortnight.

The propeller Elizabeth, one of the Baltimore and Philadelphia line, has also been chartered by the Sanitary Commission, and was last night loaded with some forty tons of ice and eighty tons of assorted sanitary stores, and despatched to the James river. The Thompson and Elizabeth each carried its corps of relief agents. Three other boats in the employ of the Sanitary Commission left the mouth of the Rappahannock at daylight yesterday morning for the new base of the Army of the Potomac.

The steamer Georgia, from Port Royal, Va., brought up to-day about one hundred sick men. She left Port Royal at eleven o'clock yesterday morning. All the government property at Port Royal had been placed on transports, which had been ordered to clear the river by nine A. M. to-day. No cannonading was heard there when she left, and if there had been any fighting it was with musketry.

Parties who came up on the Georgia report that Fredericksburg had been totally evacuated by our forces, and is now in possession of rebel scouting parties or guerillas.

The transports Wawassett and Swan, having become disabled, have been sent from Port Royal to Baltimore to be repaired.

BUTLER'S DEPARTMENT.

FORTRESS MONROE, May 30, 1864.

Generals Smith and Brooks, with their commands, arrived at Fortress Monroe last evening from Bermuda Hundred, and, after a short stop for coal, &c., left for the White House.

Generals Gillmore, Ames and Wild remain at Bermuda Hundred with General Butler.

The base of supplies for General Grant is now established at the White House, and fifteen vessels have gone there laden with supplies for General Grant's army.

The Italian brig Nova Granta, from Baltimore, in ballast, bound to New York, was run into at three o'clock yesterday morning, about one mile from Smith's Point light, in the Chesapeake Bay, by an unknown three-masted propeller. The entire rigging of the brig was carried away, and the captain, mate and pilot are missing. The crew were landed on Smith's Island.

The following persons died yesterday in the McClellan Hospital:—Daniel Parr, 9th New Jersey; A. A. Terry, 27th Massachusetts; J. C. Crommett, 23d Massachusetts; J. Griswold, 10th New York; J. H. Keller, 11th Pennsylvania cavalry; Wm. Cook, 24th Massachusetts; E. A. Moody, 24th Massachusetts.

Three hundred and fifty sick soldiers, from Bermuda Hundred, were admitted into the McClellan Hospital last evening.

Lieutenant Colonel John Cochrane, of the Sixty-seventh Ohio Volunteers, died yesterday in the Chesapeake Hospital of his wounds.

John Burrell, of the Thirty-ninth Illinois, was admitted yesterday, being wounded.

THE SHENANDOAH VALLEY.

Mr. T. C. Wilson's Despatch.

RECONNOISSANCE IN FORCE—STRENGTH OF THE ENEMY—SLIGHT SKIRMISHING, ETC.

EDINBURG, SHENANDOAH VALLEY, May 30—10 A. M.

The army has made a reconnoissance in force, and find the enemy four thousand strong in front of us.

We have had very little skirmishing up to this time.

SHERMAN.

General Sherman's Headquarters Established at Dallas, Ga.

LOUISVILLE, May 31, 1864.

Sunday's Chattanooga *Gazette* says that Sherman had reached Dallas, Ga., on Friday last, and made his headquarters there.

THE RED RIVER EXPEDITION

Despatch from Admiral Porter—Sharp Fight on the Atchafalaya—Two Cannon and One Hundred and Eighty Prisoners Captured, &c.

WASHINGTON, May 31, 1864.

The Navy Department has received an official despatch from Admiral Porter, dated Cairo, May 26, announcing his arrival there (before reported), and in which he states that he arrived at Cairo in four days from Red river.

On the 20th the army had all crossed the Atchafalaya, and General Smith's division embarked. The gunboats covered the army until all were over. General Smith, who brought up the rear, turned on the enemy with part of his command, under General Mower, killed and wounded a number and captured one hundred and eighty prisoners and two field pieces.

This makes eight or nine pieces captured by General Smith, besides the guns of Fort de Russy, in all of which captures Gen. Mower bore a conspicuous part.

The river is quiet between this place and Red river.

The rebels had a battery on the bank below Tunica Point; but the gunboats drove them off after a sharp engagement.

News from California and Mexico.

SAN FRANCISCO, May 30, 1864.

Arrived last night, steamship St. Louis, crowded with passengers.

The town of Forest Hill was destroyed by fire to day. Loss $60,000.

Dates to May 4 say that affairs in Northwestern Mexico are quiet.

Generals Negrete and Ortega have withdrawn their troops to Saltillo.

Juarez cannot place much reliance on his generals, who act very independently.

Much anxiety exists relative to the Congressional action on the taxing of mines.

The movement for a change of currency in Nevada Territory is not sustained by the capitalists.

Mr. Willet's Death.

TO THE EDITOR OF THE HERALD.

NEW YORK, May 30, 1864.

My attention has been called to an editorial this morning in your paper, under the heading of "City Improvements," in which, in your reference to the Washington Heights Commission, you say "one very respectable member of it, the late Mr. Willet, died from a complaint hastened by self reproach and mortification for ever having allowed himself to become identified with some of its absurd acts of usurpation and folly."

Mr. Willet's family and friends feel much aggrieved that a misstatement of the cause of his death should have been made in your paper. I think nearly all of my father's friends and acquaintances know the cause of his death; but, as some may not, I deem it my duty to correct your error and defend his unblemished character against calumny.

My father, the late James C. Willet, died after an illness of about three weeks, from the effects of a carbuncle on his neck, and from no other cause.

JAMES S. WILLET.

The Dollar Subscription Sword for McClellan.

TO THE EDITOR OF THE HERALD.

NEW YORK, May 30, 1864.

Please find enclosed the sum of one dollar, to pay for a vote in favor of Major General George B. McClellan, for the sword now on exhibition at the Metropolitan Fair in this city, which you will please deliver to the person in charge, and oblige, yours, respectfully,

JORDEN P. WIGGIN,
of State of Maine, and seaman brig Water Lily.

TO THE EDITOR OF THE HERALD.

WASHINGTON, D. C., May 30, 1864.

Please put these two dollars I send you with the good people's and brave soldiers' fund for a sword for General George B. McClellan, the brave and good man, our second Washington. Little Mac is like our brave New York firemen, always ready. The love, honor and friendship the brave officers and soldiers have for Little Mac [illegible] take from us. God bless Little Mac is a soldier's prayer.

A [illegible]

TO THE EDITOR OF THE HERALD.

[illegible] Kill, Rensselaer County, May 5, 1864.

Enclosed please find the sum of five dollars, which I cheerfully donate to be expended in purchasing a sword for the noble chief Little Mac, [illegible] in our midst.

[illegible]

DAILY PAPER—[illegible]—PAYABLE IN ADVANCE.

VOLUME LXXXIV.

The Charleston Mercury.

VINDICE NULLO
SPONTE SUA SINE LEGE FIDES RECTUMQUE COLUNTUR.

CHARLESTON, S. C., THURSDAY, JUNE 9, 1864.

COUNTRY PAPER—THRICE A WEEK—EIGHT DOLLARS, FOR SIX MONTHS—PAYABLE IN ADVANCE.

NUMBER 12,083.

TELEGRAPHIC.

REPORTED FOR THE ASSOCIATED PRESS.

THE CAMPAIGN AGAINST RICHMOND.

BATTLEFIELD, NEAR GAINES' MILL, June 7—5 p. m.—The press telegram sent last evening should have read "EARLY followed the enemy *two* miles," and not "*ten*." After pursuing two miles, and finding the enemy entrenched on Totopotomy Creek, with a swamp in their front, EARLY went no further.

The condition of affairs on our left is unchanged to-day. The enemy is still in front of HILL'S and ANDERSON'S corps, but is reported moving to the right.

Last evening GRANT sent another flag of truce asking permission to bury the dead. This was granted, and three hours (from 7 until 10, p. m.) fixed as the time. But it seems GRANT did not get General LEE'S answer in time; and the dead are still unburied. Another flag of truce has come in this morning.

Some artillery and picket firing is going on to-day.

SECOND DESPATCH.

RICHMOND, June 8.—GRANT sent Gen. LEE the flag of truce yesterday for the purpose of returning a detail of ours, improperly captured, while burying the dead last night, and apologized for taking them.

Nothing of interest has transpired to-day.

LATEST FROM THE UNITED STATES.

RICHMOND, June 7.—The Washington *Chronicle* of the 2d instant says that GRANT'S communications with the White House are complete. A railroad will be put into operation between West Point and the White House.

Brownsville, Texas, at last accounts, was threatened by 2000 rebels.

Gold in New York 89½.

We have European dates to May 20. Parliament had reassembled. PALMERSTON'S health was restored. There are alarming accounts of the health of the Pope. Some credit was attached, on the London Stock Exchange, to the report of GRANT'S victories over LEE. The Confederate loan declined 3 per cent., and the news caused unsettled feeling in commercial circles.

LATER.

RICHMOND, June 8.—United States papers of the 4th instant have been received. They quote gold at 192.

GRANT, in his despatches of May 2d, claims that the rebel works at Cold Harbor were carried on the afternoon previous. The rebels' repeated assaults, he says, were repulsed with loss in every instance. Several hundred prisoners, he adds, were taken.

Other despatches, equally false, from BUTLER and other sources, are published, probably with a view of influencing the action of the Republican Convention, which met in Baltimore yesterday.

CONSCRIPTION BEFORE THE FLOOD, WITH INCIDENTAL REFERENCE TO EATING AND DRINKING.

Methuselah lived to what would now be considered a good old age. Few people in these latter days can reasonably hope to attain their nine hundred and sixty-ninth year, though at the rate some have grown old under the operation of the conscription law, it has been slyly hinted that they will soon approximate the antediluvian standard.

But that is not the thing which we had in our mind when we wrote the caption of this brief article. The fact is, that something suggested to us yesterday the idea of a militia muster in those early days when people counted the stages of their lives by centuries. We seemed to see some of the cotemporaries of Tubal Cain, or some colonel or enrolling officer of the Land of Nod, calling upon the able-bodied men, between one hundred and eighty and four hundred and fifty, to be and appear, armed and equipped, as the law directs, at the usual muster ground near Tubal Cain's blacksmith shop. And then we could fancy the subsequent call for the reserves, including all the youths, between one hundred and fifty, one hundred and eighty, and all the men, between four hundred and fifty and five hundred. If they had substitutes over the conscription age, they probably came from the class between five and six hundred—hale, hearty men, a little over their prime, but still equal to good military service.

And the antediluvians were a pretty hard set—that much is evident—and it follows that although they may not have had Colt's revolvers or minnie muskets or rifled cannon, they were not without means for doing each other harm, nor wanting in the disposition to use them.—They also got drunk at militia gatherings, no doubt, for about the first thing Noah did after the flood subsided was to plant a vineyard, make wine and get overcome. He had learned that before he had seen so much water, and his long swim around in the ark does not seem to have made him a convert to the Maine liquor law.

We can fancy the light-headed boys from one hundred upwards, and sympathise with the fears of their discreet parients when they found these innocent and unsuspecting juveniles exposed to the temptations of the camp, and acquiring a taste for cider-royal and other potent beverages dealt out by the sutlers, for of course they had sutlers; and of course the sutlers had something to sell that would make drunk come, although distilled spirits for that purpose is a modern invention. That opens up a new field of reflection. Just to think of our superiority over the Greeks, Romans and Egyptians, antediluvians and other ancient peoples. Solomon in all his glory never had a mint julep. The grandest feasts of the Roman Emperors could not boast a Turkey—the most meditative philosopher never soothed himself with tobacco.—Fancy Plato walking through the groves of the Academy with a pipe in his mouth. Imagine Achilles, who was no philosopher, getting "high" on Puryear's best, while Thersites stole his cock tail, and railed at it for not being stronger. How that jolly "wandering minstrel," Homer, would have relished a good Irish whiskey punch after a day's wandering during a spell of that inclement weather from which "the Isles of Greece" are not exempt."

By the way, during the prevalence of this warm weather, such things must give place to thinner potations. We would, therefore, suggest the following as not hard to swallow:

Take a sufficient quantity of ice—clear, sparkling, and well broken—(if you can get it); put it in the bottom of a glass—the largest size of glass is preferable; fill the glass about three-fourths full of champagne (if you can get it), then let the balance be claret (if you can get it)—then—why then, try it, that's all. There are worse things, and the only serious objection consists in the difficulty of obtaining the materials.

But we have nearly consumed what the parliamentarians call "the morning hour," and have no more time for maundering.—*Wilmington Journal.*

FEDERAL PRISONERS SHOT.—We learn that two Federal prisoners—one an officer—were shot by the guard, while attempting to make their escape between Columbia and Augusta. Both were killed—one at Rowe's Pump, and the other at the 110 mile post, on the South Carolina Railroad.

HON. J. L. M. CURRY, of Alabama, has accepted an appointment as missionary in Gen. JOHNSTON'S army, under the auspices of the Virginia Sunday School and Publishing Board, and has entered regularly on his work.

THE MERCURY.

THURSDAY, JUNE 9, 1864.

The Campaign in North Georgia.

The Atlanta *Confederacy* has an interesting editorial review of the pending campaign in North Georgia. The "On to Atlanta," it says, was to be accomplished by a series of flank movements. The "On to Atlanta" has not been consummated, but as much of it as we have been permitted to see, has been conceived ingeniously, and executed not without some display of strategic brilliancy. If some enterprising Confederate sharpshooter had shot a bullet through McPHERSON'S head, and knocked out SHERMAN'S brains, the Yankee raid might have been handled with less skill, and with more damaging result to the enemy. As it was, it will not be denied, that SHERMAN has accomplished much more than some of us could have desired. The possession of Dalton was but the work of a few days rapid march by flank, which culminated in a spirited encounter at Resaca. Another flank movement and he possesses Rome and Kingston, crosses the Etowah, and is somewhat abruptly checked at New Hope and Dallas. Any further attempt to flank an enemy who shows his claws so pluckily and defiantly as did JOHNSTON in all of these little passages at arms, would be attended with imminent danger to an expedition "thus far into the bowels" of the enemy's territory. To make another right flank would be dangerous; to advance direct, with a veteran and disciplined enemy and a sagacious general confronting him, equally so; to retreat across the Etowah disastrous. SHERMAN immediately seizes the Altoona Hills, by a movement to the left, and he will there entrench himself, plant his pontoons behind him, reconstruct the Etowah bridge, and gather his strength for another hug. Except the acquisition of a great deal of valuable territory and several important villages, he has gained nothing but a closer proximity to Atlanta and a longer and more hazardous rear line of communication to his supply depots.

Looking upon the Southern side of the picture, while we have gained no material advantage over the enemy, we have lost nothing in regard to strategical advantage or position. SHERMAN advanced in the outset with upwards of one hundred thousand men. Rockyfaced Ridge, Resaca, and PAT CLEBURNE, have cost him dearly in the loss of many good fighting men, which, with a reasonable deduction for stragglers and deserters, have seriously diminished his stupendous raiding party. His men are more or less dispirited and demoralized, while ours were never in better trim or stomach for the fight. We do not believe he will attempt any further advance for sometime yet; and when he does, it will be a repetion of his original advance by flank. When that is attempted it will precipitate a battle, as is generally anticipated, between the Etowah and the Chattahoochee.—With the latter river, well bridged with pontoons, in his rear, and his trains and supplied on the Southern side of it, JOHNSTON will have his adversary at an advantage, whenever the prowess of the two armies may be brought to the test. His gallant and patient army, much inferior numerically to SHERMAN'S force in the beginning, has increased considerably in the retrograde, and is now more than a match for the enemy in "an open field and a fair fight." General JOHNSTON will hardly attack SHERMAN in his present position, and the latter will not be likely to continue the aggressive until his losses are made good and his raid is strengthened by reinforcements.

The Chicago Times and Old Abe.

A correspondent of the Chicago *Times*, at Washington says "Mr. LINCOLN has done much in three years to develop his real character. By the end of another year the development will be perfect. For a person in such a station to be a smutty joker, is bad enough. To be a hypocrite in the sphere that he occupies is still worse. He will sit down on the 4th of April and write a letter to gentlemen in Kentucky, in which, with shocking blasphemy, he attributes to God the crimes for which he and his abettors are responsible, and dares to attribute to the Almighty the great wrong that he has done to the black race in forcibly depriving them of their comfortable homes and kind masters; and then, rising from the task with one of his hideous smutty jokes, he sets to work with STANTON to plan his campaign in North Carolina. As he has penned it, so it has resulted. The successful defence of Plymouth would have enabled BURNSIDE'S corps to have landed there. The march of the united columns of BURNSIDE, PECK, WESSELS and BALDY SMITH towards Richmond would have enabled GRANT to move the Army of the Potomac also towards the rebel capital, and, between the two great armies, Richmond might have fallen. This must be prevented, and it has been prevented. Richmond must not yet be taken. The war must still go on, in the interest of God and humanity; but no great victory must be won, lest the renomination of honest old ABE be imperiled."

LIST OF CASUALTIES in 8th S. C. Regiment from the 5th May to the 3rd of June:

Company L—Killed: Private E Lane, May 24. Wounded: S E Spears, 8th May, and died on 18.

Company M—Killed: None. Wounded: Privates J H Privett, in foot, 6th May; M A McCown, in body, 8th May; John Privett, in arm, 1st June.

Company H—Killed: None. Wounded: Private C Rogers, in thigh, 8th May; Sergt W P Stone, in leg, 14th May.

Company F—Killed: None. Wounded: Lt W E James, in leg, 8th May; Private Erwin Rodgers, in arm, 1st June.

Company I—Killed: Private Joe Freeman, May 8. Wounded: Lieut G W Cussack, foot amputated, June 1; Private S A Owens, in thigh, June 3.

Company E—Killed: Sergt A J Ham, May 8. Wounded: Private W T Anderson, in body, May 30. Missing: Private J McKay, since May 8; Lieut J G Hallford and Corpl J R Phillips, since May 30.

Company K—Killed: None. Wounded: Corpl N T Alford, in shoulder, May 8.

Company G—Killed: None. Wounded: Private M A Roundtree, in leg, May 8.

Company C—Wounded: Private Allen Hays, shoulder, May 24.

Company D—Wounded: Lieut Hugh Blakeny, mortally, May 8; Private Louis Therrell, mortally, May 9. Missing: Privates T J Miller, R J Timmons and W H Lowell.

Company B—Killed: Private J Hancock. Wounded: Private S Sweat, 8th May. Missing: Sergt J B Douglass, since 8th May.

RECAPITULATION.

Killed	4
Wounded	16
Missing	7
Total	27

C. M. WEATHERLY,
Adjutant 8th So. Ca. Regiment.

Great Battle of May Twelfth at Spottsylvania Court House.

The Conflict, as Described by an English Correspondent.

MR. HEWSON, the correspondent of the London *Herald*, is writing a series of very interesting letters for that journal, descriptive of the operations of the spring campaign in Virginia. We regret that the pressure upon our columns will not allow us to publish these letters in full. We must content ourselves with reproducing the most interesting portion of his last, giving a minute and graphic account of the great conflict of the 12th of May:

RICHMOND, May 25, 1864.

* * * * *

On the 12th of May the battlefield lay, before dawn, enveloped in a heavy fog. At 4 o'clock in the morning of that day the hostile lines burst, as under the sudden bidding of an electric wire, into a fierce cannonade. An explosion in its suddenness, it raged from the first moment of its opening in the full depth of its fury. The metalic peal of the solid shot, the sharp clap and the flat crash of the shell rose from side to side with rapidity. They seemed to shake the very earth with their thunders. That terrific storm, while undiminished in depth, underwent immediately after its first outburst a change in character, for the sharper peals of shot and shell were succeeded in a moment by the duller thurls that hurling forward grape and canister, told of a struggle deepened into the sternness of close quarters.

The suddenness of the thunders with which the artillery rent the air was not greater than that with which the deafening storm burst from the infantry. The musketry that followed immediately after the very first gun, was so great in volume from its opening that it bespoke clearly the presence of large masses of men. Rising in a deep roll one and unbroken, its blended ringing clared that the hostile thousands from whom it swelled up must have met in conflict, hand to hand. The peals in quick succession of the artillery, did not drown its voice; but on it went distinctly, a flowing roar that rose to Heaven, like the constant outcry of a rushing river. Divination was not necessary with all those evidences to tell me, as I rose from my blanket in the rear, that, as in the case of our own conflict at Inkerman, an attack, prepared with deliberation, in close proximity to the Confederate lines, had moved suddenly from the cover of the morning fog.

The field works that protected Ewell's right on the morning of the 12th extended through a wood. They occupied the line of a low ridge; and, by what appears to me to be a grave error, lay somewhat down its reverse slope. An enemy approaching them could not be seen from some part of the works until he had appeared over the rise in their immediate front. Retreating from them, he received, once behind that swell of the ground, protection from the fire of part of those defences. The course of the breastworks followed that of the ridge; and accordingly formed, at one place, a salient with an angle so small as to be almost acute. They consisted of two lines which ran one parallel with the other; and containing between both, a space sufficiently wide for a line of battle, would be decribed by military engineers as a "double sap." Epaulments were placed in support of the whole at several points of the line; and at the salient, sufficient for so many as twenty guns. A general understanding of the position may be obtained from this description, after, it has been stated that the sides of the salient, subject, as they were, in the event of an attack, to enfilade from its apex, were protected for some distance down the line, with a series of short traverses.

General J. M. Jones' brigade occupied the salient. On the left of Jones' men were formed the Stonewall, under Walker; and next in order of the line of battle, the Louisianians under Hays. The right of Jones—who, be it recollected, held the salient—rested on the brigade of Stuart. Such was the distribution on the morning of the 12th, behind the breastworks of Ewell's right wing, of the men constituting the division of General Edward Johnston. On the right of this division was an unoccupied part of the works about two hundred yards in length, and further on that staunch brigade of Wilcox's division—Lane's, Jones' brigade had sent one of its best regiments, the 21st Virginia from the salient, to cover the gap between Stuart and Lane as skirmishers. Two others were also sent out of the works in the same capacity, with the view of protecting the angle of the position from sudden attack. But three regiments of the brigade remained to defend a weak point that had been held previously by six. Of twenty guns that had been planted in the salient, sixteen had, under an expectation entertained during the night of an attack upon the extreme right, been withdrawn. Such was the array and strength of Ewell's right on the morning of the 12th.

Johnston, informed at three o'clock a. m., that the enemy was massing in his front, sent off in hot haste for guns to replace those that had been removed from his works during the night.

In the meantime the signs in the front began rapidly to take the definite form of attack. His skirmishers came in short notice; and the forest behind them impressed the senses with the feeling that, wrapped as it was in fog, it was swarming with masses of human life. Page's battalion of artillery had, in response to the demand of General Johnston, come up to the salient in a trot; but a tremendous column of the enemy having at that moment emerged from the haze, it had arrived only to have its horses shot dead in their traces, and its men mowed down in the act of unlimbering. So terrible was the fire of the enemy that but one of the guns was brought into action. Captain W. Carter had, with great devotion, succeeded, unassisted, in making that ready for work; and, standing at it, heroically alone, continued, until his capture, to fire it, charged with grape and canister, into the Federal ranks.

General Johnston had no sooner become aware of the exact point of the attack than he rushed towards the salient. He was too late. The column that had burst from the fog upon that weak point, held it already in possession. The three regiments which had been left in line for its defence, had fled before the storming mass, without firing a shot, Johnston, caught in the rush of friend and foe, was made a prisoner; and was thus left, by the bad conduct of some of his own men, to waste his brave spirit ingloriously in prison. His bravery is of the antique. His conduct as a general officer was marked by constancy and address. A great favorite with Lieutenant General Ewell, he was known amongst the rank and file, in affectionate recognition of his courage and obstinacy, as "Old Blucher."

The salient carried, and one-half of Jones' men killed, wounded or captured, the enemy poured through the Confederate line in immense force. The Stonewall Brigade, on the immediate left of the gap thus opened in the Confederate ranks became exposed on the right flank. Gen. Walker, its chief, attempted immediately to swing that wing around; but, while in the act, was disabled by a very severe wound in the side. Pressed hotly by the Federal advance, that movement became then, after even the brief delay consequent on that accident, impossible. The pressure upon its flank having commenced, many of the men forced into disorder were killed, wounded or captured; but several of the regiments wheeling into position behind the short traverses running back from their breastworks, disputed every foot of the ground they held with a steadiness worthy of their traditions. Colonel Terry, while holding, with unflinching firmness, one of those short fronts, received a severe wound. The Stonewall Brigade, however, overborne by the movement upon its flank, was finally forced back; and what of it was neither captured, wounded nor killed, found protection behind the battle array of the brigade that had been in line on its left—Hays' Louisianians.

Stuart's brigade, on the right of the regiments that had occupied the salient, was taken by the surging masses of the Federalists in flank. Those of them who were neither captured, killed nor wounded, found shelter behind the brigade that had been in line [illegible] Lane's of Wilcox's division. Engaged in front with a heavy column of the enemy, Lane, on learning of the miscarriage at the salient, became alarmed for his left flank; and having immediately swung his line around almost squarely with its original position, encountered the enemy's triumphant advance. Charging in fine style, he drove it back after a contest that must have cost it dearly. His North Carolinians thus won the glory of being the first to stem the tide of Federal victory on the right.

While the Stonewall Brigade fought and fell back, the next on its left—Hays'—had time to swing round. Colonel Monaghan, its senior Colonel being in command, it confronted the rushing advance to the left. Standing behind a traverse that extended perpendicularly from the original position of the brigade, it presented a front as firm as a ledge of rock. The wave of the enemy's triumph surged up to that barrier; but, having broken upon it in mere spray, left the honor of the arrest of its overflow on that side of the field to those houseless, landless warriors of Louisiana.

Between Hays' men on the one side and Lane's on the other, the Federalists had driven all opposition from their path. For a width of a mile they had swept the works of their defenders; but though complete masters within that limit, were confronted by an impassable barrier on the one hand and on the other. Pouring through the gap they had made, their masses formed rapidly from the right and from the left, with the view of turning the line of Hays on that side, and of Lane on this, by pressure on those officers' exposed flanks.

Apprehension of attack during the night on the front of Hays, had led to the transfer to its support of the fine brigade of Pegram. The other brigades of the division under the command of Gordon—two—were, at the time of the assault upon the salient, half a mile to the left. Springing forward without orders, Gordon moved at "double quick" in the direction of the fire that had burst upon the dawn in sudden thunders. Rushing into the fog, he could see neither friend nor foe; but guided by the instincts of a soldier, still sped forward rapidly under the bidding of the battle's hoarsest roar. The thick haze into whose unknown depths he drove on, soon lit its murderous terrors, as he closed into the conflict, with lurid flashes; and, in the next moment, flung out a sheet of lightning that hurled about the ears of his advancing ranks a very tempest of bullets.

Gordon had come up in column. General R. D. Johnston's Brigade first upon the field, he threw rapidly into line; and launching it against the enemy through the fog, checked the advance. Having arrested, thus, at one point, the surging ranks of the foe, he sought to stop him as they swept around his right. The torrent streaming rapidly in that direction, he was about to be borne back by the flank, when, bringing up his own brigade, its firm line presented to the river-like rush an additional width of barrier. The living flood of Federal triumph dashing against it in vain, swept still farther around, again threatening the Confederate right with destruction under a rapid movement upon its flank. Gordon having by that time brought up his third brigade—Pegram's—formed it under the command of Colonel Huffman, somewhat detached from the others, across the new front of the enemy's advance.

The whole line then delivered a murderous volley into the dim masses of human life that stood before its shrouded—and very, very many of them winding-sheeted—in that morning fog. Instantly seizing the colors of the centre regiment of his own brigade, Gordon spurred forward under a storm of bullets, ordering a charge. His men rushed upon the misty ranks that they had just cut gashes through with their deadly fire. Their fury bore down all resistance. The charge had become a chase. Huddling the Federalists in headlong flight over the breastworks that had been held during the night by Stuart, that murderous race was continued for half a mile beyond. Opposition had disappeared before the pursuit; still, however, it held its way in unabated fury. Starting out suddenly from the fog upon a hostile force in line, Gordon's demand for surrender having, in the confusion of his sudden appearance, obtained no reply, the Federalists fell where they had but a moment before stood in lusty life, a battle array of dead and dying!

The enemy still held the ground he had won on Stuart's left. Gordon falling therefore back, occupied the works he had carried so gloriously. His charge had cost the Confederates the services for a time, of Brigadier General R. D Johnston. That gallant officer was disabled by a wound, that is, however, not very severe. Col. Jones, a soldier of high promise, lay upon the field mortally wounded. Lieutenant Colonel McArthur, and Colonel Garrett, both officers of ability, gave up upon that field their life blood in manly assertion of the liberties that have been handed down to them from our common ancestors of the days of Runneymede. Terribly, however, were the Confederate lives, lost in that movement, avenged. For a width of three hundred yards the Federal slain were scattered over a length of three-quarters of a mile; and, in all the open fields included in that space, lay in a sickening slaughter. Four guns that had been taken at the time of the enemy's advance were, during the charge, recaptured; and in the absence of horses, sent by manual labor for some distance to the rear.

The Federalists continued to hold their ground in the salient, and along the line of works to the left of that angle, within a short distance of the position of Monaghan's (Hays') Louisianians, Ramseur's North Carolinians, of Rodes' division, formed, covering Monaghan's right, and ordered to charge, were received by the enemy with a stubborn resistance. The desperate character of the struggle along that brigade front was told terribly in the horseness and rapidity of its musketry. So close was the fighting there for a time that the fire of friend and foe rose up rattling in one common roar. Ramseur's North Carolinians dropped from the ranks thick and fast, but still he continued with glorious constancy to gain ground foot by foot. Pressing under a fierce fire, resolutely on, on, on, the struggle was about to become one of hand to hand, when the Federalists shrunk from that bloody trial. Driven back, they were not defeated. The earthworks being at the moment in their immediate rear, they bounded to the opposite side, and having thus placed them in their front, renewed the conflict. A rush of an instant brought Ramseur's fellows to this side of the defences, and, though they crouched close to the slopes, under enfilade from the guns of the salient, their musketry rattled in deep and deadly fire on the enemy that stood in overwhelming numbers but a few yards from their front. Those brave North Carolinians had thus, in one of the very hottest conflicts of the day, succeeded in driving the enemy from the works that had been occupied during the previous night by a brigade which, until the 12th of May, had never yet yielded to a foe—the Stonewall.

The Confederate line had been re-established by Ramseur to the position held during the night by Gen. J. M. Jones' left, it had been restored by Gordon to the point occupied during the same time by Jones' right. The gap originally made remained however, still in the possession of the enemy, and with it all the guns—with the exception of the four retaken by Gordon—that had been captured at the time of the rush into the salient. Through that the Federal masses swept out between the flank of Gordon—of Pegram's brigade—on the one hand, and of Ramseur on the other, endeavoring, by movements to the right and to the left in conjunction with heavy attacks in front, to give the uncovered space greater width. They still protruded from the open interval between the flanks of those officers and continued to press still forward with the view of preventing their connection by an intervening array of battle. Moving out in tremendous force with the ultimate purpose of driving them still farther apart and of turning their lines, they were encountered by the stern front of Battle's Alabamians of Rhodes' Division.

Battle met the crushing weight of the advance unaided. He sought to insert his line between Gordon's left—Pegram's men—and the right of the brave fellows under Ramseur. Receiving the shock of the forward movement as a rock hurls back a wave of the sea, he pressed after the recoil, foot by foot. Closing in on it slowly, he succeeded, after a severe struggle, in pressing it back into the breastworks of the salient—for a part, be it recollected, a "double sap"—under a fire of [illegible] that exceeded anything I ever heard in its rapidity and volume. It roared unceasingly, a very river of death. Forcing his way on with heroic resolution; now straining forward; then standing in obstinate resistance; and next, for a moment, yielding stubbornly, as the mottled struggle swayed from side to side, Battle kept, with indomitable courage, laboring onward, inch by inch. Aided by the fire of Ramseur's men on the left flank of the Federalists, he succeeded, finally in driving them from a part of the works on that officer's right.

The gap in the Confederate array had been reduced to a small extent by Battle's left. The other part of his line continued to swing heavily backwards and forwards as the tide of battle rolled from side to side. Shattered terribly by the severity of the contest, he was reinforced by Harris' Mississippians, of Anderson's division, and McGowan's South Carolinians, of Wilcox's division. The heaviness of the fire at the point where these brigades went into action was terrible. Two young oaks, each upwards of twelve inches in diameter, pierced so often across their trunks, were thus actually cut down, to the serious injury of some of McGowan's men, by minie bullets.

Fresh troops being put in continually, in front of Harris and McGowan, the contest grew in fierceness. Reeling to and fro, for the width of a brigade front, it surged now to this side, then to that, over a bloody space of over two hundred and fifty yards. The guns that had been captured in the salient by the rush of the first attack, lay, during the fierce struggle in their original position—at one time within the onward roll of the Federal lines, and at another closed within the surging ranks of the Confederates. Major Cutshaw, a gallant officer of the battalion of artillery, whose pieces lay thus between the ebb and flow of battle, hung devotedly in their immediate rear, and watching the moment that saw them included in the advancing array of the Confederate infantry, sprang forward from his lair in the thicket to load them with canister and grape.—Bang! bang! bang! he plied them in hot haste; and thus tearing the ranks of the enemy at close quarters into shreds, he continued, with rare steadfastness, hurling his thunders until the line of his supports had begun once more to yield.—Retiring again and again as the tide of strife rolled back upon him, he continued, on each occasion, to watch his opportunity in patient resolution, and whenever the battle surged onward, bounded to his guns to work them with the same ardor and with the same havoc.

McGowan behaved, in the struggle for the works at the salient, gloriously. He fell, in its progress, painfully, but I hope not dangerously wounded. Several of his best officers yielded up their lives on that field of blood. General Harris set a brilliant example in the stern strife, to his brigade, but though he escaped accident in the tempest of bullets which swept on the wings of death around him, he lost heavily. His losses in officers includes some men of high promise. Colonel Baker and Lieutenant-Colonel Feltus, of the 16th Mississippians, and Colonel Hardin, of the 19th, are not amongst the least of the gallant soldiers who fell dead from the Confederate lines in that murderous salient. South Carolinians and Mississippians continued, however, to rival each other in their persistent striving to recover the captured works; and finally obtained firm possession of them still further in advance of the foothold that had been secured in them previously by Battle. Consolidating within the defences thus far recovered on the left of the salient, the strife was renewed in their front—and very often so close to the muzzles of their rifles as the opposite slopes of the breastworks behind which they crouched under enfilade from the apex of the salient.

Perrin's brigade of Anderson's division, sent up to reinforce Battle, formed behind some light works in the rear. Ordered to charge into the salient, its chief, as he rode at the head of its left wing, received a Minnie bullet in the thigh.—The femoral artery cut, he had hardly time to say "carry me back, boys," when the poor fellow had bled to death. Two of his regiments had been, at the time, rushing at the works on the right, under the direction of a gallant and promising young officer, now commanding the brigade, Colonel J. C. Saunders. They succeeded in making a lodgment in the defences on the left of Gordon. The other three regiments, bounding on to the left as Perrin fell, swept also without opposition into the breastworks on the right of the men of Harris and McGowan. The width held by the enemy at the salient had thus been reduced to about one hundred yards; but, included within it, at the appex, a battery of artillery, that, captured in the morning, swept both sides by enfilade.

Captain Wynne, the Adjutant General of Perrin's brigade, attempted to communicate with the Colonel commanding; but, venturing recklessly with that view across the immediate rear of the salient—where nothing human could apparently survive—returned to the left, after having run the gauntlet of the enemy's skirmishers, with a painful wound in his arm. Saunders, in the meantime, threw out some of his Alabamians as sharpshooters; and by the accuracy of their aim, succeeded in silencing the guns that had been hurling shell into his ranks in deadly enfilade. Opening again from time to time, they burst upon him repeatedly; but in a moment afterwards the hands by which they had been worked fell under his unerring rifles, stiff in death. The enemy's grasp upon the "double sap" at the angle of the salient, still undisturbed, Col. Saunders maintained his ground in this way on both sides of it, with admirable resolution.

From four o'clock in the morning until half-past one, the struggle within the salient had raged in terrible fierceness. At the expiration of that time it sank into a comparative lull. The roll of the heavy skirmish-shooting went on without intermission, however, around that angle of blood, and awaited, after a brief break in the main contest, into the furious roar of a renewed attack. The restored front on each side of the salient burst into thread like flashes; and from two o'clock, throughout the evening until nightfall, and from nightfall until midnight, and from midnight until the approach of dawn of the 13th, a close and rapid fusilade rushed up in commingled roar from the contending ranks. At one time bursting through the gap on Gordon's right, and endangering his flank; at others raging up to the face of the very works held by that officer, by Saunders, by McGowan, by Harris, by Battle, by Ramseur, the conflict raged furiously until the enemy repelled firmly at all points of his attack, it settled, long after midnight, into the sharp and venomous whizzings of the skirmishers.

The four guns that Gordon had recaptured still remained two hundred yards in his rear. They could not be removed under the terrible fire that swept over the ground they occupied. Fourteen guns remained in possession of the enemy, and, with those four, constituted substantially the only object of continuing the murderous struggle for the salient. The conditions of that contest had changed Lee's policy of defence for that of attack, and had thus made a further maintenance of it highly inexpedient. A material advantage, of some importance to the enemy, lay in the possession of the height on which the salient stood, but even this did not, in the opinion of the Commander-in Chief justify an avoidable waste of the lives of his men.

Before dawn, on the morning of the 13th, a line of works had been thrown up by the pioneers of the 2d corps, under Major Green, half a mile in rear of the point to which the contest of the day had been narrowed, and, connecting the original defences on the right with those on the left, by a route considerably shorter, presented a favorable position for return to the policy of defence. Covered by skirmishing, the gallant fellows who had fought their way so stubbornly over the bloody ground within the salient, into the works that had been captured by the enemy in his rush of the morning of the 12th, retired before day on the 13th to that new line.

In the battles of the Ny, no officer earned such glory as General Gordon. His admirable flank movement at the Wilderness, his repulse of the enemy's rush through the position of Dole, and his dash and skill in stemming the Federal torrent from the salient on the 12th, won the admiration of the army. General Lee acknowledged, on the field, publicly, the great services of that officer, and informing him at the time that he should ask for his promotion, has had him rewarded with the rank of Major General.

The battles, ending with the morning of the 13th, had closed. A more stubborn contest than that of the 12th has not been witnessed during the war. The losses of the Confederates, during these struggles, include between two and three thousand prisoners, eighteen guns, and from six to seven thousand killed and wounded. Those of the enemy in the conflicts of the 10th and of the 12th, including as they do the disaster at the hands of Early's flanking force, of the murderous repulses from the front of Field, and from that of Dole, and the terrible havoc of Gordon's charge on the right of the salient, cannot have been less, in killed and wounded, than from twenty to thirty thousand. The rotting dead found unburied on the ground the Federalists occupied during those contests presented a spectacle utterly horrible in the immensity of their number. During the campaign the losses in Ewell's corps, according to an official statement of the chief of its medical staff—Dr. Hunter Maguire—does not exceed in killed and wounded, after summing the losses of each of its brigades up to the 13th of this month, 3,500.

With this basis of approximate estimate, and the further fact that the number of wounded that had been sent to the rear up to the 19th, by those devoted men, the Richmond committee for the relief of the wounded, had not reached, including those disabled by *sickness*, ten thousand, there can be very little doubt of the conclusion that Lee's total losses, in killed and wounded, inclusive of the battle of the 12th, have not overrun, at most, eleven or twelve thousand. About three thousand five hundred prisoners added to that, the depletion of his forces by the battles of the campaign, up to this time, is fully represented, I should think, by fourteen or fifteen thousand men. Grant's army has shown, in the increasing feebleness of, and longer intervals between his attacks, in his change from offence to defence, from fighting to manœuvring, unmistakable evidence of the crippling unavoidable, under losses that, including about four thousand prisoners, must certainly amount to fifty, but that fall, in all probability, not much short of sixty thousand.

Defeated in forcing the roads covered by Lee at the battle of the Wilderness, and again at that of the Ny, Grant slid a second time upon our front. Moving off from his position before Spotsylvania Court House, at an angle forty degrees to the east of the line to Richmond, he marched fourteen miles to a place called Bowling Green. By way of Port Royal on the deep waters of the Rappahannock, he might have reached that village, if it had been in the route of his first intention, without firing even a shot. Once there, however, he has admitted that the original plan of his campaign has been abandoned, and that having ceased to contemplate the inland route, he has settled down on the adoption of that attempted in vain by McClellan.

Lee had maintained his original line of defence—that of the Mattapony—unbroken. The offensive having brought the contest within the limits of tide-water, the Confederate chief was, therefore obliged to adopt a policy in keeping with those new conditions; and for that purpose, crossing the North Anna, placed in his front the navigable depths of the Pamunkey. He thus covered Richmond and his own rear from any attempt at a *coup de main*. His front [illegible] itself to Grant's change of [illegible] around to the eastward. The Federal [illegible] der has crossed the Chick[illegible], and is now within a few miles of the White House. He has, therefore, reached a position [illegible] he might have occupied, by [illegible] to adopt McClellan's route, without any serious opposition, whereas, that by which [illegible] he has cost his army [illegible] even terribly in its [illegible]. Shorn of his strength, he yet may—if L[illegible] find it expedient to take the offensive [illegible] his position near Richmond, [illegible] upon the North. I think it very probable that he may not take the aggressive until after the meeting at Baltimore of the Black Republican Convention for nomination of a candidate for the Presidency.

The danger of the opening campaign in Northern Virginia is now virtually passed. If that in Georgia should not then [illegible] unfortunately in the face of all my reasonable [illegible], and thereby arouse the war spirit at the North, I think we have arrived at the beginning of the end. Last August, you will recollect, I ventured to condition the return of peace during this coming August, on the miscarriage of the heavy and quick blows that I [illegible], and now that these have taken a form which [illegible] the conclusion of their total failure. I find some justification in them, and even now, somewhat bold speculations touching peace, in the fact that regiments, whose term of service have expired, have already commenced to stream from the army of General Grant homeward.

THE BEAUTIFUL CITY.

MAY, 1864.

We stand upon the deck of a noble ocean steamer; behind us is a thronged and bustling wharf, piled with bales and alive with drays; before us spread the waters of an ample bay, upon the bosom of which, like another Venice, sleeps a historical city. In the middle distance a great ship swings idly upon her cable, "her pride, her majesty, her glory gone." The silent waters around are unvexed with the keels of busy commerce and ungraced with the sails of fluttering pleasure craft. In the morning the rippling waves flash back the golden sunbeams, and in the evening the purple flush steals dreamily over the polished surface as quietly now, as when more than a century ago, the Huguenots sang their hymns in the shades of the oak and palmetto. Occasionally the still air is startled with the thunder of cannon, and instantly a huge projectile hurtles through the air and crashes amid the architecture of the city. Anon, a cloud of smoke bursts from a building, the fire bells ring an alarm, a confused sound of rushing engines, of shouts and of trampling is heard. The smoke disappears, and quiet broods over the scene. Let us enter the city. At first, the streets exhibit life and activity. Bronzed soldiers in gray uniform hurry by, an officer canters up, dismounts, and enters a sentineled gateway, a few ladies in black are seen; a few merchants saunter listlessly by. As we advance the streets become more quiet, and soon we are surrounded by luxurious homes, now the scenes of no domestic joys; by stately warehouses, where no eager merchants congregate; by beautiful temples, where resound no more the organ's swell or the notes of praise. All is solemnly still. Occasionally the facade of a building has been shattered by artillery, the slate, bricks and glass being scattered on the pavement. Weeds spring up under our feet and mould gathers on the walls, while blackened ruins occasionally attest the presence of devastating fires. The destruction caused by bombardment is not great, but the air of desolation and abandonment is extreme. Nature, ever ready with her generous ministrations, seeks to compensate for man's violence, flowers are everywhere; the gardens are a mass of bloom. We are haunted with delicious odors as we tread the desolate streets. With no soft eye to gaze upon their loveliness, and no tender care to develop their beauties, these heaven-sent messengers hallow with their silent influences the sad desolate city. As we gaze around us the air trembles with the dull roar of artillery, and, with a devilish shriek, a shell buries itself in the frieze of a neighboring building. Should we meet, by chance, a former habitue of the place, we shall find that the present desolation and the probable ruin of this beautiful city, has not provoked in his breast anything of submission or suggestion of despair; no, rather destruction than the polluting tread and ruffianly domination of a Vandal enemy! Better Herculaneum than New Orleans! And so with sorrow and pride, we leave the noble old city, breathing a prayer that the All powerful will take it under his protection, and vouchsafe a speedy and complete deliverance.—*Macon Index.*

The Charleston Mercury.

DAILY PAPER—FIFTEEN DOLLARS, FOR SIX MONTHS—PAYABLE IN ADVANCE.

SPONTE SUA SINE LEGE FIDES RECTUMQUE COLENTUR.—VINDICE NULLO

COUNTRY PAPER—THRICE A WEEK—EIGHT DOLLARS, FOR SIX MONTHS—PAYABLE IN ADVANCE.

VOLUME LXXXIV. CHARLESTON, S. C., WEDNESDAY, JUNE 15, 1864. NUMBER 12,088

TELEGRAPHIC.

THE NEWS FROM THE ARMIES.

MOVEMENTS IN VIRGINIA.

Active Operations Resumed in North Georgia.

DEATH OF LIEUTENANT-GENERAL POLK.

Interesting Details of Forrest's Great Victory.

GOLD IN NEW YORK 199! &c., &c., &c.

FROM GEN. LEE'S ARMY.

RICHMOND, June 14.—The following was received at the War Office this morning:

HEADQUARTERS ARMY NORTHERN VA., June 13—10 p. m.

To the Hon. Secretary of War: A despatch just received from Gen. HAMPTON, states that he defeated the enemy's cavalry near Trevillians with heavy loss, capturing 500 prisoners besides their wounded. The enemy retreated in confusion, apparently by the same route he came, leaving his dead and wounded on the field.

At daylight this morning it was discovered that GRANT's army had left our front. Our skirmishers advanced two miles, failing to discover the enemy and were withdrawn.

A body of cavalry and some infantry from Long Bridge advanced to Riddle's Shop, and were driven back this evening nearly two miles, after sharp skirmishing.

(Signed) R. E. LEE, General.

FROM THE ENEMY IN THE VALLEY OF VIRGINIA.

LYNCHBURG, June 13.—Rumors of the movements of the enemy are plentiful, but nothing definite is known outside official circles. It is reported that the force which occupied Lexington is moving in the direction of Bufords, on the Virginia and Tennessee Railroad, 39 miles west of this place. The force in Amherst county is reported moving towards Buffalo Springs, 26 miles from here. This force is about 2000 strong under General STAHL. They are all cavalry, and have to subsist off the country, having no supplies with them. They have two pieces of artillery only. Eight of them visited the Orange Railroad, burnt the depot at Arrington, tore up 200 yards of the track, and removed several head of cattle. Our guards destroyed the telegraph. The damage can be repaired in three or four hours. The people here are calm and resolute, and will defend their city at all hazards.

FROM OUR LINES IN NORTH GEORGIA—FALL OF GENERAL POLK.

ATLANTA, June 14.—The enemy opened slowly with artillery on our position yesterday afternoon, after the storm had passed over, and continued up to nightfall. This morning his artillery again opened and the firing still continued when the trains left Marietta. Both armies are gradually moving towards our right. As the rains have ceased, it is supposed that active operations will again commence. Two trains have come in from the front to-day; but they bring very few wounded.

The following despatch from Major WEST, of General POLK's staff, was received at noon to-day:

"Lieutenant General Polk was struck by a cannon shot to-day, about 11 o'clock, and instantly killed. Generals JOHNSTON, HARDEE and JACKSON were with him when he fell."

FORREST'S LAST VICTORY.

MOBILE, June 13.—General FORREST, with BELL's, CROSSLAN's and LYON's rangers, of JOHNSTON's brigade, and RICE's and MORTON's batteries, whipped the enemy, 12,060 strong of all arms, with great slaughter, capturing all things promiscuously. It is reported that General FORREST lost from six to ten hundred, among them Colonel HALL, of BELL's brigade, and Adjutant POPE of 7th Tennessee, killed. RICE's battery, of the 7th Kentucky, was ambushed, and is reported badly cut up. The enemy scattered, and FORREST pursued them beyond Ripley. The heavy rains may retard the enemy's retreat. FORREST is said to be on all sides of him.

GUNTOWN, ALA., June 13.—General FORREST's victory was greater than at first supposed. Our loss was 150 killed and 440 wounded. The enemy's loss was 1000 killed and 3000 captured. The rest of the enemy's forces are scattered through the woods and are still being pursued, having traveled 58 miles in 31 hours. The enemy's army is, in fact, completely destroyed. "Fort Pillow" was the battle cry during the fight and hence the anxiety of the Yankees to escape. They are still being pursued and many more will be captured before reaching Memphis. We have captured about 3000 prisoners, 250 wagons, with supplies and ordnance stores, 3000 stand of small arms and about 20 pieces of splendid artillery. The fight was stubborn, the enemy in many instances standing their ground until knocked down with the butts of our muskets. We had about 3000 in the fight; the enemy 10,250.

LATEST FROM THE UNITED STATES.

RICHMOND, June 14—The New York *Herald* of the 10th instant says gold opened on the 9th 198¼, and closed at 197.

MORGAN is running riot in Kentucky. He occupies Williamston, thirty miles from Cynthiana.

The *Herald* is very severe on LINCOLN.

RICHMOND, June 14—The *Herald* of the 11th inst., has been received. On the 10th gold touched 99, and closed at 98 and a fraction. In consequence of the rise of gold resolutions have been introduced into the Yankee Congress prohibiting sales on time, and sales made elsewhere than at the place of business of the seller or the purchaser.

The New Orleans correspondent of the *Herald* says, that a fire in Alexandria, La., has destroyed buildings covering twenty-six squares.

The Mississippi River is blockaded by rebel batteries at Greenville, above Vicksburg.

CONGRESSIONAL.

RICHMOND, June 13.—In secret session on Friday night, Congress adopted a manifesto, declaring nothing more ardently desired by us than peace. The manifesto recites that the series of successes with which it has pleased the Almighty to bless our arms since the opening of the present campaign enables us to profess this desire we feel in the interests of civilization and humanity, without danger of having our motives misinterpreted The world must now see that we can never be conquered; and will not our adversaries begin to feel that humanity has bled long enough, and desist from longer perseveance in this wanton and hopeless contest. The war on our side has been strictly defensive. We do not wish to interfere with the peace and prosperity of the States arrayed against us. All we ask is the undisturbed enjoyment of the rights which our common ancestors declared the equal heritage of all parties in the social compact. If our adversaries are deaf to the voice of reason and justice, and shall determine upon a final prolongation of the contest, upon them be the responsibility of an illusion so injurious to the interests of mankind. We have no fear of the result.

The most important action in either house of Congress to-day was the passage of the bill amending the tax laws, which was reported from the Committee of Conference. Among the provisions of the bill as passed are the following: Land purchased and occupied by refugees to be assessed at the market value of 1860. Property assets of corporation associations to be taxed the same as the property assets of individuals; the tax to be paid by the company, provided no bank shall pay tax upon deposits. The stock of corporation associations and all property within the enemy's lines are exempted from taxation. Five per cent. of the tax on the amount of specie bills of exchange, &c., to be paid with specie or its equivalent in Treasury notes; an additional tax of thirty per cent. is to be levied upon the amount of profit of the sale of articles mentioned in the first two paragraphs of the fourth section of the tax act, from February 17th to July 1st. The old issue five dollar notes are to be taxed a hundred per cent. after the 1st of January next.

FROM THE UNITED STATES.

MORE MEN WANTED.

The United States army, and the people, too, feel the enormous losses inflicted upon it by Gen. LEE. The Philadelphia *Inquirer* has an article on the want of more men, in which it holds this language:

It is the fashion to account for the superior energy and desperation of the rebels by saying that they have everything at stake. It is almost time for us to recognize that we are in the same predicament. No people in history has submitted to sacrifices greater than those of the South—whether willingly or unwillingly, is immaterial as to practical result. With all our superiority of resources we must fail unless we are animated with a similar spirit. All that has value in the eyes of a free people hangs in the balance, and will inevitably be lost unless we can rise to the magnitude of the occasion.

Large as are the armies which we have put into the field, they are not in themselves sufficient.—Constant recruiting is necessary to preserve their effectiveness. The waste of war is fearful, and reserves are indispensable if we are to strike a final blow at the heart of the rebellion. Herein has been our error previously, and it is a cheering sign that General Grant intends not to allow himself to be crippled, as our other commanders have heretofore been, unable to follow up an advantage or to properly retrieve a disaster.

The order which we publish in another column from the Provost Marshal General shows that our policy henceforth is to keep the national forces up to the highest mark, and that when this is not accomplished by volunteering, the efficacy of the new enrolment law is to be vigorously and perseveringly tried. But little more than a month remains in which to furnish volunteers, and it is for our citizens to determine whether they will aid their Government now in the most effectual manner, or by inaction force the authorities to obtain men by drafting, after a delay which may have an unfortunate influence on the results of the campaign.

The rebels are now playing their last cards. They have not the material with which to repair inevitable losses. On the other hand our strength is virtually unimpaired. If successful at the outset, we thus have the means of rendering their defeat irretrievable. If we should be worsted we can, by exerting ourselves in time, convert misfortune into eventual triumph. Every motive, therefore, summons us to unrelaxing effort, and no time should be lost in raising reinforcements to keep in fighting trim the regiments of the gallant Army of the Potomac.

BUTLER'S ROBBERIES TO BE INVESTIGATED.

General BUTLER is at a large discount for his failure on the Southside. His "patriotism," however, is greatly praised for consenting so cheerfully for the larger part of his command, under BALDY SMITH, to leave him and go to GRANT. GARRETT DAVIS, however, has taken advantage of his present grief to attack him by resolution in the United States Senate, as follows:

Whereas, it has been frequently charged in the public prints and other modes, that when the leaders of the present rebellion were engaged in plotting and maturing it, Benjamin F. Butler was cognizant of and privy to their treasonable purpose, and gave them his countenance, sympathy and support, and that he, the said Butler, after some of the rebel States had published ordinances of secession, turned against the conspirators whom he had sustained, to get position and office under the Government of the United States, to enable him to consummate his own personal and corrupt objects; and that after he was appointed to, and while he was acting in the military service, he was, by himself and his accomplices A. J. Butler, and many others, guilty of many acts of fraud, peculation and embezzlement against the United States, and many acts of extortion, plunder, spoliation, oppression and cruelty against individuals: Therefore, be it

Resolved, That the present Senate appoint a committee of three to investigate all such charges against the said Butler; that the said committee have power to sit during the recess of the Senate, to send for persons and papers; and that it report all testimony and its proceedings to the next session of the Senate.

A PEACE LETTER.

The birthday of THOMAS JEFFERSON was celebrated in New York by the Anti-Abolition or State Rights Association, at which toasts of peace and recognition were drunk, and speeches made by EX-GOVERNOR SEYMOUR, of Connecticut, and others. Among the letters read was one from Hon. WM. B. REED, of Pennsylvania, which expresses in the following paragraph the spirit of the celebration. He says:

In all that you say about this wicked war I entirely concur. It ought at once to stop; and if recognition for the purposes of negotiation, or even ultimate recognition of Southern Independence, be necessary to arrest bloodshed then there should be recognition. Two years ago I thought I saw this necessity, and honestly said so. The dreary chapter of blood which has since been written has not weakened my faith. I cling to it resolutely, and am proud of the obliquy which, in certain quarters, such faith attracts. If peace does not come soon we may have anarchy, as we now have oppressive despotism.

CAPTURE OF PRIZES.

We find the following list of prizes recently captured by Yankee blockaders, in the *Inquirer:*

Sloop Fortunate, captured off Florida, with a small cargo. The Prussian schooner Frederick II, and the English schooner Agnes, captured off Brazos, after running the blockade.

THE MERCURY.

WEDNESDAY, JUNE 15, 1864.

A War Problem.

The South (says the Atlanta *Appeal*,) is engaged in solving a problem new in socialistic science. That problem is, how to combine military power with productive capacity in such degree as to put forth the whole martial power of the South, without impairing its industrial resources. Such a question could never have arisen in the ancient republics, because they did not subsist their armies from their internal resources, but by the plunder of their enemies. Nor could such a question have originated in any social condition in which slavery was not an element.

According to the theories of European writers, slavery is deemed a source of weakness in war, and a drawback on material prosperity in peace. It was not thought possible to withdraw a large proportion of productive laborers from the spheres of industry, without so curtailing the progress of wealth as to check its increase, and even to abridge the means of a bare subsistence. We have refuted this theory completely. We have not only laid by an annual surplus for three years, but placed in the field one-tenth of our population, a larger proportion than any State of equal numbers in modern times. The productive power of the Confederacy has not been impaired, while it has exhibited the maximum of military efficiency in a population of little more than five millions of souls.

By what agency has this been accomplished?—Simply by the superior efficiency of slave labor acting on a productive soil. When we speak of efficient labor, we mean its maintenance at a comparatively small cost. No modern State could maintain from three to four millions of laborers at so small a charge as we do, and no country possesses a soil that will yield so fruitfully at so small an expenditure of labor. It is for this reason that we can maintain so large a number of unproductive consumers as constitute our armies and their dependents.

We have, therefore, practically solved the problem, how most effectually to combine the utmost military strength with the largest productive power, in a State whose social condition embraces the two apparently discordant elements, in nearly equal proportions, of freedom and slavery. Without our slaves, a constituent of our wealth and material power, we could not have maintained our armies in the field, and without those armies we could not have preserved the sources of our subsistence.

The "Monroe Doctrine" as Asserted by the Yankees.

The New York *Herald* lately published an article, which purported to give the manner in which the French Government became "satisfied" regarding the resolution against the Emperor's policy in Mexico, recently adopted unanimously by the Yankee House of Representatives. The *Herald* made it appear that upon a mere assurance from LINCOLN that the resolution was but an expression of sentiment, and that the Government of the United States had no *present* intention of taking action in the premises, the French Government was perfectly satisfied. This, of course, is a very lame story.

The Paris correspondent of the Richmond *Enquirer* discusses the matter at length, and gives some further insight into the very singular affair. We take the following extract from his letter, in which he introduces the explanation made by the new Government organ, the *Moniteur du Soir*. In this connection he says:

The third paragraph of the first number of this paper, destined for circulation at the small charge of one *sous* in every part of the French Empire, is textually as follows:

"The Government of the Emperor has received from the Government of the United States satisfactory explanations on the meaning and bearing of the resolution passed by the Assembly of Representatives at Washington on the subject of Mexican affairs. It is, besides known that the Senate had adjourned indefinitely the consideration of this resolution, to which, in any case the Executive would not have accorded its sanction."

This is still further corroborated by the statement given the same day in one of what are called the Government papers, to the effect that Mr. Seward charged Mr. Dayton to impress upon the French Government that the vote had not been confirmed by the Senate, and *that the President is opposed to every manifestation of this kind.*

THE VALUE OF SOUTHERN COTTON, AS ESTIMATED BY A YANKEE.

A correspondent sends us the following, clipped from an old number of the Yankee pictorial known as *Harper's Weekly*, dated November 13, 1858 It is quite refreshing, nowadays, to hear this Yankee talk about "our" cotton:

WHAT COTTON IS DOING FOR US.

Many reliable estimates set down the cotton crop of the United States this year at the high figure of 3,500,000 bales. It is coming to market much earlier than usual. The receipts at Southern ports are 250,000 (in round numbers) in advance of the receipts of last and other average years of same date. So large have been the arrivals at Charleston, Savannah, Mobile and New Orleans, that specie has been shipped from New York to the South to buy bills on England more cheaply than they can be had here. The price is satisfactory. And, considering the condition of Europe; peace everywhere; prosperity in Germany, Ireland, Spain, and other countries which have often lately been in the deepest distress; a large accumulation of money at the financial centres; a fair prospect that new markets for European manufactures will be open in China, Japan, British Columbia and elsewhere; there is no reason to expect that the prices will decline.

In an article published some months back in this journal, we showed that in the most active commercial year the United States ever knew—1856—the cotton of the South was our chief stand by and set off against the enormous consumption of foreign goods in the great cities and throughout the country. But for the copious supply of cotton, and the high price it commanded, the United States would have incurred a debt to the foreign world which it would have taken years to discharge.

It seems now that the cotton crop is going to be the means of setting the trade of the country on its legs again. Our other great staple—breadstuffs—is in an unpromising condition. Excellent harvests have been the rule throughout Europe, and the prise of all kinds of breadstuffs rules so low that it is estimated that a loss of at least a million of dollars has been incurred by the parties who sent breadstuffs to New York this fall. At present rates—and they are likely to be unchanged for some months—flour and wheat cannot be sent abroad and sold so as to repay the producer in the West.

Our cotton, on the contrary, if the crop fulfills present expectations, will not only nobly reward the planter, but will go a long way toward liquidating the debt we are incurring to Europe for dry goods and foreign manufactures. More than this: the early receipts at the Southern ports, by suggesting shipments of specie from New York, have given trade the first wholesome impetus it has had since the revulsion. The four or five millions of specie we have sent to the South were worse than useless in our bank vaults here. In the South they will be eminently useful. They will generate and feed traffic throughout the Southern country. And coming back to us, as they will, by various channels through the South and West, they will, on their journey, serve usefully to restore credit and foster wholesome commercial enterprise. The revival of trade will hereafter be dated from the early fall receipts of cotton at the South, and the movement in specie which they occasioned.

BRITISH COTTON TRADE.

The following is the complete letter of Mr. MCHENRY on the Cotton Trade, Cotton Supply, &c., of which extracts have occasionally appeared. It will be found to present a very interesting and instructive exhibition of the growth and present extent of the demand for cotton, and the present and prospective supply. The large stocks on hand, both of the raw and the manufactured article, when the American war commenced, have made England comparatively independent of further supplies from us until the present time. A different state of things is henceforth to exist, and Cotton, if not King, is at least about to make itself felt as a power in the earth. We resign a large portion of our space to-day to this interesting paper:

DEAR SIR: The enclosed tables, compiled chiefly from the Board of Trade returns, show the course of the British cotton trade for the last six years. The period begins at the cessation of the commercial panic of 1857, when over production commenced, and ends with the close of last year, thus furnishing, at a glance, the history of the cotton imports, exports, manufactures and sales for home consumption, for the three seasons anterior, and the three seasons subsequent, to the secession of the Southern States from the Federal Union; and likewise exhibiting the increase in the stocks of cotton and cotton goods during the first division, and the decrease during the second division of the time.

The largest importations of raw cotton took place in 1860, when 1,390,938 752 pounds were imported at a cost of £35,756,889; and the smallest receipts were in 1862, when 523,973 296 pounds came to hand, valued at £31,093,045. The quantity in 1863 was 669,582,264 pounds, worth £56,277 953 The exportations of raw cotton in 1860 were 250,448 640 pounds; for 1861, 298,287 920 pounds; for 1862, 214,714 528 pounds, and for 1863, 241,570,992 pounds—the rate of increase in comparison with the importations being very great. The yarn producing properties, or nett weight of the cotton after spinning, that remained in the United Kingdom for manufacturing purposes was, in 1860, 969,433 595 pounds, and in 1863 only 285,221,154 pounds, proving the fact the extra loss in working inferior sorts, and accounting for the additional amount of cotton required to make a yard of goods in 1863, over what was needed in 1860.

Though the cost of the imports of raw cotton was so much greater in 1863 than in 1860, the value of the exports was likewise augmented, making the nett cost for that material in 1860, £30,368,699, and in 1863, £35,139,037. It has been estimated that the profits on the old stocks of cotton goods held over in foreign markets, belonging to English merchants, and disposed of in 1863, amounted to £16,000,000—thereby reducing the exchange to about £20,000,000, or £10,000,000 less than in 1860. As the old stocks are now exhausted, this means of payment will cease, and, of course, a greater amount of money will be required to settle for the cotton supplies of 1864, even should the importations be no larger than in 1863; and this, too, without allowing for the advance in price.

The freight on the raw cotton did not average in 1860, over ⅝ of a penny per pound; while in 1863 that charge was about doubled in consequence of the produce having been brought a longer distance in some cases, and in others of more expensive means (steam) of transportation. The rates from the Mediterranean were very high, and the expense of running the blockade was equal to the former entire cost of the cotton.

The largest exportations of cotton piece goods were in 1860, when 2,2776,218,427 yards were shipped, along with 197,343,655 pounds of twist and yarn—the value of clearances reaching, including hosiery and small wares, £52,012 380. Except for hosiery, etc., the figures for 1862 were smaller than in any other year—the total exports being £36,770,971. In 1863 1,706,572,858 yards of piece goods, and 74 643,146 pounds of twist and yarn were sent abroad, valued, with hosiery and small wares, at £47,448,964.

There has been a very slight reduction in the home consumption of cotton manufactures. The prices of cotton goods have not kept pace with the advance in cotton, cent for cent, in consequence of the cost of the raw material not being in ordinary times more than 30 per cent. of the value of the manufactured article. But now that cotton forms the chief cost of the fabric, and the stocks of goods made from cheaper cottons, are so much diminished, they are only one-fifth in extent when compared with those of 1860—a continuous rise may be expected to take place. The natural yearly increase in the consumption has merely been checked.

The rich purchase nearly as freely as ever; the poor, never, even in the most prosperous times, purchased more than sufficient for their wants. This is clearly demonstrated by the quantity of cotton goods imported; the receipts from abroad in 1863 were about the same as in 1860—the value, however, was augmented from £758,030 in 1860 to £1,039,904 in 1863.

The expense of cotton clothing to the inhabitants of Great Britain and Ireland was as follows:

In 1858	£23,000,000
In 1859	23,500,000
In 1860	25,000,000
In 1861	28,000,000
In 1862	33,000,000
In 1863	48,000,000

At present prices for cotton goods, the expense for 1864 will be about £60,000,000, or an increase over the figures of 1860 of £35,000,000 That amounts as equal to 33 per cent. more than the interest of the British national debt, and is about one-half the yearly outlay of the Government. But, unlike the annual expenditure of the nation, the whole of the sum will be sent to foreign countries, thereby causing an actual drain upon the resources of the people, to the extent of double the cost of all the food imported, and as a consequence, must, before long, bring about a financial panic. An increase in the cost of breadstuffs, after a bad harvest, if only a few millions of pounds sterling, creates a disturbance in the money market.

What a revulsion must then take place, when not only the £35,000,000 additional for the cost of home consumed goods, but the extra capital absorbed in conducting the commerce in cotton with other nations, will be added thereto? Nor will this anticipated panic lower the price of cotton. In the case of a bad harvest, the high rates for money do not affect the price of wheat, because wheat is then wanted. So it will be with cotton. This is the first time in the history of the world that there has been a "raiment" famine, and few persons, therefore, seem to comprehend the difficulty. The hiatus caused by the loss of three cotton crops in the Southern States, 1862, 1863 and 1864, must be felt; the quantity cultivated since the second year of the war has not more than half compensated for that which has been destroyed in order to prevent it falling into the hands of the enemy.

There was two years' supply of cotton and cotton goods of every shape in 1858; in 1860-61, three years' requirements in all parts of the globe. Now, including the quantity in the Southern States, there is not over a year's wants. High prices have not had the effect of stimulating production to any great degree in other countries, because their labor could not be diverted from their accustomed pursuits. Only a few months' extra consumption has been cultivated, under the influence of extravagant quotations. A careful calculation, made a short time since, shows that the increase in the cotton grown in all countries, other than the Southern States of America, in 1863 over 1860, was only equivalent to 367,906 bales of American cotton, which, with about 200 000 bales attracted from the interior of those countries, threw into the various markets an excess over former years of 567,906 bales, of the old average weight of yarn producing properties.

The excess in 1863 was about 200,000 bales; and the Southern States have, since the establishment of the blockade, parted with about 700,000 bales, making a grand total of about 1,500,000 bales received at the consuming points, besides the usual supplies from the small cotton growing countries. Formerly, the number of bales of American cotton manufactured in Great Britain formed 85 per cent. of the entire quantity taken by the mills; but the American bales were heavier, and the cotton produced more yarn to the pound than the growth of other countries. British cotton fabrics, therefore, contained 90 per cent. of American cotton. In order to work the inferior sorts, and to augment the weight of of the fabrics, a large admixture of mineral and other substances was and is being used.

This is regarded as a fraud, as most of the sales of goods have been negotiated with the understanding that they were composed of the usual proportion of American cotton. No description of merchandize is so long reaching the consumer, from the producer, as cotton goods; and but few complaints have, therefore, yet been heard of in reference to the inferiority of the texture of the articles. So soon, however, as the deception is generally discovered, British cotton fabrics must necessarily lose their reputation. East India and other inferior cottons, unless in very small proportions, are unfit for machine-made goods—they may look nearly as well when overloaded with "size," but they certainly will not wear so long.

Cotton is grown in about forty different countries; but the Confederate States present the only instance where it is cultivated as a leading crop. India has never produced in any one year as much as 2,000,000 bales, which, considering her enormous population, is a very small quantity. The delusion in regard to the yield of cotton in India—which is now being dispelled—arose from the fact of her "fine" cotton goods having been mentioned in the earliest history; also from the fact of her having at one time supplied the whole world with cotton goods. But then, it must be borne in mind that her production of fine cotton was very limited, and confined to one district, while her growth of coarser cottons, although larger was insignificant in comparison to the present ideas of cotton crops.

At the period when India supplied the world with cotton goods, the quantity of those goods purchased was very trifling—wool and flax then constituted the chief materials for human clothing. Mexico holds with respect to cotton almost an identical position to India; for, as far back as her history is known, she has been a cotton producing and cotton manufacturing country. Her cotton fabrics, as recorded by her discoverers, rivalled the long famed goods of India. Indeed, so valuable were they, that small pieces of exquisitely fine cotton cloth were used by the Mexicans for currency. Yet no one has ever attempted to claim for Mexico the position of a large grower of cotton.

The quantity of cotton and cotton goods in the hands of all classes in the United Kingdom, was greater on the 1st of January, 1862, than at any other time; and the stocks were less on the 1st of January, 1864, than on any previous occasion. The chief falling off was in yarns and goods—a diminution in clothing material that is seldom alluded to, and the importance of which has not been fully considered.

The following may be regarded as a fair estimate of the wants of the United Kingdom for 1864:

		POUNDS.
The home consumption will require in weight, of present inferior sorts of cotton		275,000,000
The exportation of cotton goods, if only the same as last year		600,000,000
The exportation of raw cotton, if only the same at last year		240,000,000
		1,115,000,000
The quantity of cotton of all kinds, in warehouses on the 1st of January was	128,000,000	
On spinners' hands, same time	20,000,000	
In yarns and goods, same time, in the hands of all classes, from the spinner to the retailer	100,000,000	
Importations at the rate of increase since the 1st January to 1st April over last year	810,000,000	
		1,058,000,000
Deficiency		57,000,000

with stocks of everything in the shape of cotton and cotton goods exhausted!

Included in the receipts of last year, as before remarked, were all the old stocks of cotton attracted from the interior of India, China, Egypt, etc., by reason of the high prices that prevailed in England in the latter part of 1862 It cannot be supposed that the increase in production this year will more than balance those old stocks, though in the preceding table an addition of 23 per cent. has been made in the importations of raw cotton in 1863 for the estimate of 1864. To be sure, the increase so far this year has been at that rate, but there is no likelihood of its being kept up when reference is made to the sources of supply through the whole twelve months. The importations into the United Kingdom for January, February and March, 1863 and 1864, are thus given:

	1863—POUNDS.	1864—POUNDS.
Confederate States	4 050,000	18 500,000
Brazil	9,000,000	9,900,000
West Indies, etc	1,500,000	150,000
East Indies, etc	95,200,000	105,600,000
Egypt, etc	89,000,000	48,000,000
	148,750,000	182,150,000

The increase, as already stated, was 22 per cent.; but nearly one-half of this increase was owing to the contributions from the Confederate States, having risen from 4,050,000 pounds to 18,500,000 pounds. That as well as the Chinese source of supply may soon cease, and there may be a very sudden termination to the supplies from India and the Mediterranean as the year advances. The people of those cotton growing regions have for some time past been making every effort to hurry forward their crops. So instead of "doling" them out as formerly they may long before the year closes rid themselves of all their cotton.

The consumption of cotton by the mills in January, February and March, 1864, was 50 per cent. greater than in the corresponding period of 1863. This, of course, has given additional employment to the operatives. Had it not been, however, for the augmented receipts from the Southern States it would have been impossible to have consumed so much cotton as even with the "size" fraudulently used, the goods require on the average about 20 per cent. of the good American staple. In other words, every bale of American facilitates the use of five or six bales of other sorts. This is evidenced by the weekly sales in the Liverpool market. In the work entitled "The Cotton Trade," it is stated that "before many months, unless the fortunes of war or the intervention of foreign Powers should cause a more ample portion of the staple to come to hand than has hitherto eluded the illegal blockade, for the first time in the history of commerce a cotton famine will be experienced." "A more ample portion" has eluded the blockade, and "the fortunes of war" have caused a considerable quantity—80,000 bales—to be received at New Orleans. 150,000 bales have reached the United Kingdom and the Continent of Europe since the 1st of September last, and about the same quantity has arrived at the ports of the Federal States. Much of the Southern cotton reexported from Mexico, Cuba, the Bahamas, Bermuda, etc., has been sent to those States in exchange for provisions, clothing, boots and shoes, cotton cards, and, in fact, many necessaries for the Confederate army shipped from New York to those intermediate places; the vast majority of Yankees having had their pockets, not their hearts, in the wicked crusade against the South.

Had it not been for this course of trade, the Federal cotton manufacturers would have been obliged to continue their importations of the raw material from Europe, and this have drawn largely on the already scanty stocks of cotton on this side of the Atlantic—enhancing the quotations here, and draining the Northern States of the precious metals, as the merchandise shipped to the Islands would not have found a market anywhere in Europe. It is a singular coincidence that no sooner did the large export trade in breadstuffs between the Northern States and Europe, which began after the last Presidential election, decline to its former limited amount, than these new outlets for Yankee produce were opened up. This, along with sales of clipper and other ships in Europe, driven from the seas by the activity of Southern cruisers, and captures of British property, furnishing supplies which otherwise would have had to have been bought in Europe, and paid for in England, have materially assisted Federal finances.

It is quite clear that if the Southern States had been in a position to have withheld their cotton from the "outer world," the Powers of Europe would by this time have been forced into recognizing their independence. People generally are not aware of the quantities of cotton that have been received from the South. The Board of Trade tables only credit the Confederate States with the cotton that comes direct from their ports while all that is imported indirectly is placed to the account of the country of intermediate export. And it is upon these Board of Trade returns that the statesmen and journalists of England have been basing their arguments—laboring under the vain delusion that "other countries" have greatly increased their growth of cotton—The Cotton Supply Association has not had the candor to acknowledge the facts of the case; on the contrary, its organs have reproduced, without explanation, the erroneous figures furnished by the Government; and the association itself has been publishing weekly the most visionary statements from its correspondents abroad; so ambiguously worded as to deceive the public mind upon the important question of cotton supplies.

What matters it if, in countries where only a few hundred weights of cotton have been grown, the cultivation should have, under the influence of high prices, been augmented one hundred or two hundred per cent? The whole additional quantity is but a drop in the bucket, in comparison to the void left by the loss of the Southern crop. Surely, if cotton was coming forward in sufficient quantities to run "five days" in the week, as has been alleged, the prices would tumble back to something like their normal condition, instead of being at four rates, because the currency in which they are quoted is in no way inflated; and there never were more than "six days" in the week—the mills, even in the most active times, rested on the seventh day. The deficiency of only one-sixth of a full supply would not make such an enormous difference in the value.

The truth is, strange as it may seem, the cotton manufacturers of the United Kingdom, although they have done a smaller business in quantity, since the breaking out of the war, have done a larger business in value, and their profits were never so large before in any period of three years. They have had the advantages of gradually hardening prices, and the other classes of the community have assisted them in the support of their idle operatives. Their sales, 1858 to 1860 inclusive, were £214 715 927; 1861 to 1863, inclusive, £240,067,424. Very respectfully,

(Signed) GEO. MCHENRY.

Quantity of raw cotton, cotton yarns, and goods in the world, civilized and uncivilized, at the following periods:

January 1,	1858	5,000,000,000
"	1859	6,000,000,000
"	1860	7,000,000,000
"	1861	7,500,000,000
"	1862	7,000,000,000
"	1863	5,500,000,000
"	1864	2,500,000,000

NOTICE.

ORPHAN HOUSE,

OFFICE CLERK OF COUNCIL, April 29, 1864.

PERSONS ENGAGED IN THE PURCHASE AND SALE of all second hand articles, JUNK, OLD METALS, and other like Commodities, in the City of Charleston, are hereby notified to call at this Office and make application for Licences to carry on the same, in compliance with the following Ordinance:

STATE OF SOUTH CAROLINA,

CITY OF CHARLESTON.

An Ordinance to license and regulate shops for the purchase and sale of all second-hand articles, Junk, old Metals, and other like commodities, in the City of Charleston.

SEC. 1. *Be it ordained by the Mayor and Aldermen in City Council assembled*, That, from and after the ratification of this Ordinance, the keeper or keepers of every shop within the limits of the City of Charleston, where any kind of second hand articles, junk, old metals, or other like commodities are purchased, sold, bartered or exchanged, shall obtain from the City Council a license to do so, and shall pay to the City Treasurer for said license the sum of fifty dollars; and such license (which shall continue for one year) shall not be transferred from one person to another without the consent of the City Council.

SEC. 2. Application for license shall be made to the City Council, and every application shall be accompanied by the recommendation of at least three respectable freeholders, who shall certify that the applicant is a fit and proper person to be entrusted with such license; the person so applying shall deposit with the City Treasurer the price of the said license, and upon the license being granted, shall execute a bond, in the penal sum of one thousand dollars, with two sureties, to be approved of by the City Council, conditioned for the faithful observance of the provisions of this Ordinance, and all other Ordinances hereafter passed in relation thereto.

SEC 3. Every person receiving such a license shall put up over the principal entrance to his or her shop, a sign designating that he or she is licensed, and containing his or her name, and shall keep a book in which shall be written, at the time of every purchase or barter, a description of the article or articles purchased or bartered for, the name and residence of the person or persons from whom received, and the day and hour when such purchase or exchange was made; and such book shall be at all times open to the inspection of the Mayor of the city, Chief of Police, or any person duly authorized by them, or either of them, to inspect the same.

SEC. 4. Such shops shall not be kept open for the purchase of any of the articles mentioned aforesaid; nor shall any purchase be made by the keeper or keepers of any such shop, or by any person or persons for them, except between sunrise and sunset; and said shops shall be open at all times to the inspection of the Mayor of the city, the Chief of Police, or any person duly authorized by them, or either of them.

SEC. 5. No keeper of any such shop shall himself, or through any other person, either directly or indirectly, purchase or receive by way of barter or exchange, any of the articles mentioned aforesaid from any minor or apprentice, nor from any slave or free person of color, without the written permission of the parent, guardian, master, or owner of any such minor, apprentice, slave or free person of color, which written permission shall be filed, and produced whenever required, by any one authorized to inspect such shops.

SEC. 6. Every person having obtained a license who shall violate any of the provisions of this Ordinance, shall forfeit the same, and upon conviction thereof, shall pay a fine of not less than ten dollars, nor more than fifty dollars; and every person keeping such a shop, and carrying on business therein, without having first obtained a license to do so, shall pay a fine of not less than fifty dollars, nor more than one hundred dollars, all of which said fines shall be recovered in the City Court, and shall be disposed of as follows, viz: one half to the use of the person who shall prosecute the offender to conviction, and the remainder to the use of the city.

By order, W. H. SMITH, Clerk of Council.

April 30

ORPHAN HOUSE—OFFICE CLERK OF COUNCIL, MAY 30, 1864.—The following persons have made application to the City Council to grant them Retail and Tavern Licenses, to take date from 1st April, 1864:

L F Koester, King and Radcliffe streets—sureties, C Amme and L J Moses.

Mrs A Morgan, 6 Chapel street—sureties, Jno Hargrave and F Wienholtz.

P J Coogan, 414 King street—sureties, C Amme and Henry H Bolger.

H Buck, Line street and Sires Alley—sureties, E W Passailaigue and N Hollings.

D Ratteman, 893 King street—sureties, H W Dowe and F Kressel

G H Linstedt, Calhoun and King streets—sureties, C Bart and C Amme.

R Meredith, 511 King street—sureties, C R Cassiday and N Hunt.

C H Korrigan, 554 King street—sureties, T Claffey and P J Coogan.

M Grattin, Warren and King streets—sureties, P Brady and Jas Melvin

John A Cook, No. 1 License, Mary and King street—sureties, Henry Stender and H Wittschen.

May 31 W. H. SMITH, Clerk of Council.

The New-York Times.

VOL. XIII—NO. 3974. NEW-YORK, SATURDAY, JUNE 18, 1864. PRICE THREE CENTS.

IMPORTANT.

PETERSBURG CAPTURED.

The Fortifications Stormed by General Smith.

BOTH LINES CARRIED.

Four Hurdred Prisoners and Sixteen Guns Taken.

Distinguished Gallantry of the Black Legion.

Gen. Smith Tenders His Thanks to Them.

PETERSBURGH UNDER OUR GUNS.

The Rebels on the West Side of the Appomattox.

The Army All Across the James.

HANCOCK IN JUNCTION WITH SMITH.

GRANT WELL AHEAD OF LEE.

SECRETARY STANTON TO GENERAL DIX.

[OFFICIAL.]

WASHINGTON, June 17, 1864.

To Major-Gen. Dix:

The following dispatches have been received by this Department:

CITY POINT, June 15, VIA JAMESTOWN ISLAND, 5:30 A. M., 16—1864.

SMITH, with 15,000 men, attacked Petersburgh this morning.

Gen. BUTLER reports, from his observatory near Bermuda Hund.ed, that there has been sharp fighting and that the troops and trains of the enemy were, as he writes, moving from the City across the Appomattox as if retreating.

HANCOCK is not near enough to render Gen. SMITH any aid.

The Richmond papers have nothing to indicate a suspicion of our crossing the James River. They expect to be attacked from the direction of Malvern Hill.

CITY POINT, Va., 5:30 P. M., June 15, 1864.

Our latest report from SMITH was at four P. M. He had carried a line of intrenchments at Beatty's House, the colored troops assaulting and carrying the rifle-pits with great gallantry, but he had not yet carried the main line. He describes the rebel artillery fire as very heavy.

He expected to assault this line just before dark. HANCOCK is within three miles of SMITH.

CITY POINT, Va., 7 A. M., June 16, VIA JAMESTOWN ISLAND, 11:45 A. M.

At 7:20 P. M. yesterday, SMITH assaulted and carried the principal line of the enemy before Petersburgh, taking thirteen cannon, several stands of colors, and between three and four hundred prisoners. This line is two miles from Petersburgh. HANCOCK got up and took position on SMITH's left at 3 A. M. to-day. There was heavy firing in that direction from 5 to 6 o'clock. No report has been received yet.

DON'T HARD LANDING, Va., June 16—1 P. M.

After sending my dispatch of this morning from the heights southeast of Petersburgh, I went over the conquered lines with Gen. GRANT and the engineer officers. The works are of the very strongest kind, more difficult to take than was Missionary Ridge, at Chattanooga. The hardest fighting was done by the black troops. The forts they stormed were the worst of all. After the affair was over, Gen. SMITH went to thank them, and tell them he was proud of their courage and dash. He says they cannot be exceeded as soldiers, and that hereafter he will send them in a difficult place as readily as the best white troops.

They captured six out of the sixteen cannon which he took.

The prisoners he took were from BEAUREGARD's command. Some of them said they had just crossed the James above Drewry's Bluff.

I do not think any of LEE's army had reached Petersburgh when SMITH stormed it. They seem to be there this morning, however, and to be making arrangements to hold the west side of the Appomattox.

The town they cannot think of holding, for it lies directly under our guns.

The weather continues splendid.

CITY POINT, Va., June 16, 1864—4:15 P. M.

Gen. BUTLER reports from Bermuda Hundred that the enemy have abandoned the works in front of that place. His troops are now engaged in tearing up the railroad between Petersburgh and Richmond.

The following dispatch does not designate the hour, but it is supposed to be later than the preceding ones:

JAMESTOWN, Va., Thursday, June 16.

I came down from the pontoon above Fort Powhatan with dispatches from Secretary STANTON. Just as I left Capt. PITKIN reported to me that Petersburgh was in our possession.

Nothing of recent date has been heard from Gen. SHERIDAN, but the Richmond *Whig* of the 15th, contains a dispatch from Gen. LEE, stating that SHERIDAN had been routed in an engagement with FITZ LEE and HAMPTON, losing 580 prisoners and leaving his dead and wounded on the field.

From Gen. SHERMAN, a dispatch dated last night at 9 o'clock, has been received. It only states the relative position of the forces. No serious engagement had yet occurred.

EDWIN M. STANTON,
Secretary of War.

CROSSING OF THE JAMES.

Valuable Services of Gen. Benham's Brigade—A Skirmish with the Rebel Cavalry on Wednesday Night—The Fighting on the Roads which Lead to Richmond.

Special Dispatch to the New-York Times.

CHARLES CITY COURT-HOUSE, Va., Wednesday, June 15.

The army is again in motion. Yesterday afternoon transports commenced taking the Second Corps from Wilcox's and Swynard's Wharves, two and a half miles from here, across the James River, to Windmill Point. By daylight this morning the whole corps had crossed. The Eighteenth Corps marched to the White House last Sunday, and took boats for the same vicinity, whence they moved yesterday noon. The Fifth Corps is crossing to-day near the Second. The Sixth and Ninth Corps commenced crossing last night on a pontoon bridge and in boats, from a point a little lower down the river, and nearly opposite Fort Powhatan. Gen. BENHAM, who has charge of the Engineer brigade, and the officers and men under his command, deserves special mention for the display of zeal and energy in preparing the way for the rapid and extensive marches of this numerous army. For weeks past this brigade has had no rest to speak of, but has been constantly on the move and constructing bridges and wharves and repairing roads. Up to this time the army has moved with but slight molestation from the enemy. Sunday night Col. CHAPMAN's brigade of Third Cavalry Division, Gen. WILSON, had a skirmish with the enemy's cavalry at Long Bridge, a skirmish line driving the enemy away so as to enable the engineers to lay a pontoon bridge. The whole brigade then crossed and drove the enemy to White Oak Bridge, where they were engaged until relieved by BATES' brigade, of Gen. CRAWFORD's division, Fifth Corps. The cavalry brigade then moved toward Richmond. Two miles up the road the enemy made a stand at a small creek, and held the position. Previous to reaching this point the rebels made several stands. At one time they succeeded in piercing the centre of our skirmish line, when the Third Indiana Cavalry on the left, and the Eighth New-York on the right, swept in upon them like a pair of shears, throwing them into disorder and forcing them back, killing and wounding a large number. The cavalry and part of CRAWFORD's division also had some fighting on Monday, within two miles of New-Market. In these several skirmishes the cavalry lost about one hundred and the infantry about fifty men in killed and wounded. The enemy's loss is estimated to be much larger. The several roads on which the fighting occurred all lead in the direction of Richmond, and the enemy were made to believe that the army intended to move in that direction, and had already commenced digging intrenchments. The First New-Hampshire Cavalry and Twenty-second New-York Cavalry were for the first time in a fight on Monday. They behaved in a very creditable manner. A portion of HILL's corps was engaged at White Oak Swamp Bridge. Some of the enemy's cavalry engaged were armed with Enfield rifles, with bayonet attached.

From Headquarters—Crossing of the Army—Hancock Advancing on Petersburgh.

HEADQUARTERS ARMY OF THE POTOMAC, Thursday, June 16—6 A. M.

Nothing of an exciting character occurred yesterday, our troops and trains being engaged in crossing all day.

Gen. HANCOCK's corps has advanced toward Petersburgh, which place he was expected to reach last night, but nothing official has been heard from him up to this hour.

Heavy cannonading has been going on in that direction, supposed to be either he or Gen. BUTLER engaging the enemy.

The entire army will be across the James River by to-night.

The Passage of the James River—Skirmishing with the Rebels—They are Driven to White Oak Swamp.

WASHINGTON, Friday, June 17.

A dispatch dated Headquarters Army of the Potomac, says:

The army is now crossing the James River at two places, one from Wilcox's Wharf to Windmill Point, and the other about two miles below.

The Second Corps crossed yesterday at the first-mentioned place.

The Fifth Corps start at ten o'clock this morning.

Some rebel infantry were found on the way, supporting rebel cavalry, but a part of the Fifth Corps came up and drove them from the position to White Oak Bridge.

At this place the rebels were found in a strong position, with their artillery posted, and HILL's corps supporting them.

Skirmishing commenced, and was continued until darkness set in.

Our forces withdrew toward Harrison's Landing.

Our loss was about one hundred killed and wounded, while that of the rebels was heavier.

Gen. GRANT returned from his visit to Gen. BUTLER this evening, having found everything satisfactory.

Premature Reports—The Crossing of the James by the Army of the Potomac.

FORTRESS MONROE, Thursday, June 16, via BALTIMORE, Friday, June 17.

Yesterday morning at 4 o'clock, the Eighteenth Army Corps, under the command of Gen. W. F. SMITH, left City Point and marched into Petersburgh.

Gen. KAUTZ's cavalry, comprising the Fifth and Eleventh Pennsylvania and District of Columbia Regiments, attacked the intrenchments of the rebels outside of Petersburgh, and at 11 A. M. yesterday succeeded in carrying them and entered the city.

They were supported by the advance guard of Gen. SMITH's forces.

The troops were, at last accounts, marching in the direction of Petersburgh as fast as they landed.

The crossing of the James River by the army is described by those who had the good fortune of viewing it, as one of the most brilliant scenes of the war.

An endless stream of transports, barges and schooners have been making their way up the James River to the new base of supplies all day to-day.

BALTIMORE, Friday, June 17.

The above appears to be based on the reports prevailing at Fort Monroe last evening, and may be premature. No official confirmation has yet been made.

Details of the Crossing of the Chickahominy.

CHARLES CITY COURT-HOUSE, Va., Wednesday, June 15, 1864.

The Chickahominy has been safely crossed. GRIFFIN's Division of the Fifth Corps, preceded by a brigade of cavalry, advanced from Providence Church to Long Bridge on Sunday night. After a brief skirmish our advance guard drove off the few rebel pickets guarding this place. The bridge had been destroyed by the rebels, but we laid pontoons across the river. A column moved up the south side of the river toward Bottom's Bridge, and drove every rebel out of sight.

On the margin of White Oak Swamp our cavalry ran against a considerable number of the enemy. For a few minutes there was a sharp skirmish, in which a number of cannon were freely used on both sides, and two regiments of infantry were deployed as skirmishers. About twenty men were killed and wounded in this short affair.

Some of the rebels were made prisoners. They report that LEE was massing his troops at Bottom's Bridge. But he was too slow. Our advance along the road to Bottom's Bridge kept the enemy back and gave the Second Corps ample opportunity to pass over the Chickahominy.

The Sixth and Second Corps crossed lower down at Jones' Bridge.

On Sunday the Eighteenth Corps embarked on transports at the White House, and have since moved past this place on the James River, going toward Bermuda Hundred.

The Second Corps is now being ferried to-day from Wilcox's Wharf to Windmill Point.

Our present position on the banks of the James is much healthier than that in the Chickahominy swamps, where many of our men commenced to suffer from fever and ague, and are now rapidly recovering.

The Wounded at Washington.

Special Dispatch to the New-York Times.

WASHINGTON, Friday, June 17.

LIST OF WOUNDED SOLDIERS SENT TO NEW-YORK IN HOSPITAL TRANSPORT ASHLAND, JUNE 16.

J. Y. CANTWELL, SURGEON-IN-CHARGE.

Sergt John Schmeot, C, 39th New-York.	L E Redfield, F, 2d N Y H A.
P Anthony Schbal, E, 120th New-York.	James Morgan, H, 7th N Y Heavy Artillery.
Corp H J Griffin, E, 156th New-York.	H Collins, H, 7th N Y H A.
Sherwood Ehle, F, 2d H A.	Geo Cotman, A, 2d N Y H A.
H H Frasier, A, 93d N Y.	1st Sergt John Davis, L, 2d N Y Heavy Artillery.
Sergt John Daball, F, 52d New-York.	Wilson Dodge, L, 2d N Y H Artillery.
Corp G C Chase, D, 8th N Y Heavy Artillery.	A J Shape, K, 120th N Y.
Sergt D C Buren, 39th N Y.	John Gropam, B, 43d N Y.
M Labone, A, 164th N Y.	John Couy, F, 62d N Y.
F Millet, F, 52d N Y.	C Elsmer, B, 32d Mass.
W Zoller, 2d Mass Light Art.	G Thompson, H, 22d Mass.
W Forbes, F, 3d Mass L Art.	R M Lack, F, 12th Mass.
W A Colmer, 9th Mass.	C Carter, D, 31st Me.
W Parson, B, 32d Mass.	I Hodgkins, H, 59th Mass.
D Waters, F, 6th N H.	A Butterfield, B, 1st M H A.
H M Tibbets, I, 31st Me.	J Lawler, A, 9th Mass.
J B Goodman, B, 32d Mass.	N J Wheeler, A, 12th Mass.
Sergt-Maj E P Light, 1st Mass Cavalry.	E Caff, 20th Me.
John Bigelow, B, 6th Vt.	B Rediker, A, 3d Me.
C Sylvester, H, 10th Vt.	Capt J Donley, C, 10th Vt.
A Hagar, D, 5th Vt.	G B Merritt, D, 6th Vt Cav.
Sergt J W Eldridge, H, 11th Vermont.	A F Ebon, H, 10th Vt Cav.
J Clark, K, 6th Vt.	W Murray, A, 10th Vt Cav.
Lewis Peo, B, 1st Vt Cav.	H Dillingham, E, 11th Vermont Cavalry.
C Fairbanks, E, 2d Vt Cav.	A S Whipple, 2d U S Sharpshooters.
I Piper, D, 2d Vt Cavalry.	F Miner, E, 17th Vt.
F H Delany, I, 10th Vt Cav.	Giles Fruster, A, 17th Vermont.
L W Griswell, H, 11th Vermont Cavalry.	D Clement, H, 10th Vt.
Anthony Rollin, K, 10th Vt.	J Blanchard, H, 3d Vt.
S Sharland, A, 1st Vt.	W Blowers, H, 10th Vt.
Sergt F Hoyt, C, 17th Vt.	David A Johnson, E, 43d N Y.
	Allen Bell, E, 2d Vt Vol.

FROM JUDICIARY HOSPITAL.

James Gould, D, 7th Me.	Joseph St. Johns, K, 5th Vermont.
O H Gerrish, D, 5th N. H.	M W Learned, A, 5th Vt.
C W Simpson, H, 18th Mass.	S A Wright, D, 6th Vt.
Michael Krins, H, 28th Mass.	C J Read, G, 10th Vt.
R C Gingell, E, 2d Conn.	Rollin M Carl, D, 6th Vt.
John Lawler, A, 2d Conn.	C J Eastbrook, I, 10th Vt.
E A Grow, D, 3d Vt.	H K Bickford, D, 10th Vt.
Joseph D Shaw, I, 3d Vt.	N O'Donnel, C, 11th Vt.
Chris Bredgman, L, 11th Vt.	
N W McCambra, C, 11th Vt.	

TO BRATTLEBOROUGH FROM ARMORY-SQUARE HOSPITAL.

John Mcgovern, C, 6th Vt.	E Reese, D, 1st Mass.
Lewis Mees, I, 5th Vermont.	R W Sibley, A, 1st Mass.
Jerome B Hatch, C, 1st Vt Cavalry.	D A Knowles, M, 1st Me.
John B Sturtevant, C, 5th Vermont.	G F Toplin, E, 12th N H.
P D Clark, B, 3d Vermont.	S O Blake, D, 7th Mass.
E R Brown, H, 15th Mass.	Joseph W Cutler, I, 1st Me. Art.
Edward R Harrington, H, 15th Mass.	Daniel Fletcher, H, 13th N Hampshire.
Thos A Briggs, D, 40th Mass.	E G Arlin, H, 13th N H.
Dan Gregory, A, 11th Conn.	C H Wheeler, F, 1st Me Art.
N W Lindall, A, 5th Me.	Or Gowne, F, 1st Me Art.
Almon G Lowell, E, 5th N H.	J P Hitchins, 1st Mass Art.
Jas Williams, H, 11th N H.	J H Poor, G, 10th Vt.
John S Ellis, A, 10th N H.	Sam S Oastroom, N, 2d Conn Art.
N D Filbrook, F, 1st Me.	W S Averell, I, 1st Me Art.
Tim Nickles, M, 1st Me Art.	F Columbian, Hospital.
Edward Duffy, B, 14th Con.	Robert Murray, A, 11th Vt.
J W Smith, F, 1st Me Art.	Henry Chonyou, H, 2d Vt.
Julius D Hill, H, 25th Mass.	Nelson J Lee, K, 10th Vt.
John Hegan, H, 6th Vt.	Thos Foster, K, 1st Vt Art.
Wentworth Harris, E, 5th Vt.	Thos G Mayne, L, 1st Vt Art.
James Horton, I, 3d Vt.	Homson Law, C, 10th Vt.
A G Fullerton, A, 1st Vt Art.	Phillip McKensie, F, 3d Vt.
Pattin Bober, G, 1st Vt Art.	David Wright, H, 3d Vt.
	Chas Wilder, K, 10th Vt.

FROM HAREWOOD.

Rollin A Phillips, K, 2d Vt.	W H Shepherd, E, 11th Vt.
Joseph Rooney, B, 5th Vt.	N N Vancar, G, 17th Vt.
Oral E Dudley, D, 5th Vt.	John W Farr, C, 17th Vt.
Moses Labelle, E, 11th Vt.	Wm Wells, D, 11th Vt.
C R Mansfield, E, 11th Vt.	Moses Whitehill, G, 17th Vt.

FROM CARVER HOSPITAL.

Chris C Wheeler, D, 6th Vt.	J W Windsor, K, 17th Vt.
Rufus Emerson, C, 2d Vt.	Sam Stewart, G, 17th Vt.
H E Baker, E, 2d Vt.	N W Chan, A, 6th Vt.

FROM CAMPBELL HOSPITAL.

T A Bradford, E, 17th Vt.	Martin Andrews, E, 17th Vt.
H O Magoon, G, 4th Vt.	E A Bowman, L, 1st Vt Cav.
Chas Eaton, F, 2d Vt.	C H Hochin, D, 4th Vt.
Henry McCole, H, 4th Vt.	Ed Kennedy, D, 14th Vt.

FROM EMERY HOSPITAL.

Henry Goodell, D, 2d Vt.	H Y Freeman, G, 10th Vt.
H Y Wood, B, 6th Vt.	C H Lackey, A, 10th Vt.
L Bessett, B, 3d Vermont.	B Y Whitny, K, 11th Vt.
A Wheelock, I, 17th Vt.	G Church, A, 17th Vt.
Charles Rich, I, 10th Vt.	John Dunn, C, 10th Vt.

FROM LINCOLN HOSPITAL.

A P Bodwell, E, 11th Vt.	E Berney, D, 3d Vt.
John Trask, H, 3d Vt.	H A Scoot, L, 1st Vt Art.
R Watson, D, 10th Vt.	H McCarter, H, 1st Vt Art.
W Chase, E, U S S S.	G H Wiggins, H, 1st Vt Art.
A H Smith, N, 11th Vt.	J Gillman, E, 10th Vt.
R Randall, F, 11th Vt.	G B Kedes, F, 1st Vt Art.

FROM ALEXANDRIA.

S D Lord, B, 17th Vt.	Rufus Lease, D, 4th Vt.
W E Bradford, I, 6th Vt.	Chas Poole, D, 10th Vt.
E Porter, G, 2d Vt.	S A Page, G, 10th Vt.
W S Stoddard, H, 6th Vt.	A Bellows, G, 10th Vt.
G O Gorman, H, 10th Vt.	H S Marshal, B, 10th Vt.
W P Brown, I, 10th Vt.	James Carroll, A, 1st Vt Cavalry.
Jos P Lyndis, I, 3d Vt.	W H Nelson, B, 10th Vt.
Michael Egan, C, 4th Vt.	

Dr. J. Y. CANTWELL goes on the *Ashland* in charge of the patients. The Doctor and his assistants are assiduous in their attentions to the men, some of whom are suffering severely.

THE BLOCKADE.

From the North Atlantic Squadron—Capture of Blockade Runners—Three Captured and One Run Ashore.

The United States supply steamer *Newbern*, Capt. HARRIS, from the North Atlantic Blockading Squadron, and 24 hours from Fortress Monroe, has on board 73 prisoners from the blockade-runners *Thistle*, *Georgiana*, *McColl* and *Syren*, recently captured.

On the 9th inst. the *Newbern* ran ashore the blockade-runner *Pevensey*, nine miles north of Beaufort. She was laden with arms, lead, bacon and shoes on Confederate account. Her engines and boilers were blown completely out of her a few moments after she struck. She was a fine iron sidewheel steamer of 543 tons register, and new, this being her second trip. The vessel and cargo were valued at $1,000,000.

The Central Sanitary Fair.

PHILADELPHIA, Friday, June 17.

The Fair continues to be crowded daily from 10 A. M. until 10 P. M., and will probably remain open until the 25th inst.

The vote for the sword now stands as follows: MEADE, 2,167; HANCOCK, 1,302; MCCLELLAN, 180; GRANT, 126; scattering, 65. Total, 3,870.

Death of an Editor.

BALTIMORE, Friday, June 17.

WILLIAM N. TUTTLE, Esq., one of the proprietors of the Baltimore *Clipper*, died to-day after a brief illness, aged 65.

GRANT'S LAST MOVEMENT.

Its Military Aspects and Objects—Its Probable Effect upon the Campaign.

From Our Special Correspondent.

WASHINGTON, Thursday, June 16, 1864.

The clear and succinct dispatches of the Secretary of War have made the country acquainted with the outline facts of the last great move of Gen. GRANT—the transfer of the Army of the Potomac from the Chickahominy to the James River. I can add no details of fact to the official statement, having been absent from the army since the battle of the Chickahominy on the 3d inst. There are, however, some suggestions of moment that may not be out of place.

Your readers will recollect that in my letter on the battle of the Chickahominy, in which I endeavored to recognize the true military character and bearings of that battle, I put on record the opinion that Gen. GRANT would make no further effort to pass the Chickahominy, and hinted that his eyes were even then "turned away to lines and combinations more bold than any yet essayed." Well, what could then only be thus obscurely foreshadowed, is to-day a realized fact. Indeed, I may now go further, and state that *from the very start, the transfer of the army to the south side of Richmond has formed an integral part of Gen. Grant's plan of campaign*; and while the battle of the Chickahominy was still in progress, the whole question of the pontooning of the James River was elaborately discussed. And now recognizing the relations which that action holds to the general plan of operations—noting that it now stands defined as the pivotal point of the whole campaign—would it be too much for me to ask those presses that abused me for having so recognized it a fortnight ago, to take back their abuse?

The battle of the Chickahominy was an experiment made for a specific purpose—to test the feasibility of an assault on Richmond from the northern side. It was an experiment perfectly proper to be made; and it was satisfactory. It convinced every reflecting mind that nothing was to be gained in that direction. This was obvious to every one; and every one waited to see what card GRANT would play next. But it was only those who knew something of the boldness of his military conception, that could have ventured to anticipate a repetition of the Vicksburgh strategy—the same strategy, the same audacity, only on a far grander scale!

This splendid stroke, comparable only to MOREAU's passage of the Rhine and flank march on Ulm, stands to-day an accomplished fact; the Army of the Potomac, taken up, as in the arms of a giant, is transported from the Chickahominy and planted south of the James River and south of Richmond. Now begins a new act in the grand war drama. We shall operate on new and unattempted lines, looking to new and hitherto unattainable results. I think there are few military men who do not now feel that *the present position of the Army of the Potomac gives us reason to indulge brighter hopes of ultimate success than has been possible any time since the war began.*

The south side is the true line of operation against Richmond looking to great ulterior results. Of the three cardinal maxims of strategy, the most important of all prescribes "to operate on the enemy's communications without endangering your own." Now, the operations of the Virginia campaign have been conducted under circumstances that made it impossible to apply this principle. Gen. GRANT has aimed assiduously to bring on a great decisive field fight with the hope of *crushing* the rebel army. But from the nature of the country, its prodigious facilities for defence, and the skill of the opposing General, this has been impossible. We gained victories; we steadily pushed the enemy back, and in an unparalleled campaign of twenty-nine days, forced LEE from the Rapidan to the front of Richmond. But no *decisive* results were accomplished. LEE's army is an army of veterans: it is an instrument sharpened to a perfect edge. You turn its flanks; well, its flanks are *made* to be turned; that effects little or nothing. All that we can reckon as gained, therefore, is the loss of life inflicted on the enemy, and of having reached a point thus near the objective; but no brilliant military results. In loss of life we were undoubtedly suffering more severely than the rebels; I think we may fairly say in the proportion of *five* to their *three*. Now it is obvious that we could not have long stood thus. Whatever preponderance of numbers we might have would soon disappear—would soon become an equality, and presently an inferiority. The rebel army might have been worn away by attrition; but we should ourselves have been exhausted in the process. The hammer would have been broken on the anvil.

By the present move a new order of operation begins. We not only threaten the communications of the enemy, we plant ourselves across his communications. The communications of the rebel army are the great lines of railroad by Petersburgh and Danville and their connections.

Richmond, as a city, Richmond, as a military centre, is strictly dependent on these lines for its supplies. Cut it off from these and you have a tourniquet around its throat. It may have a month's supplies, or three months', or six months'; but these exhausted and it must succumb. If LEE allows himself to be shut up within Richmond, therefore, the problem reduces itself to a repetition of Vicksburgh over again. Will he do so? That is a question.

But this is the pitiless alternative to which LEE is now reduced; to stay in Richmond and suffer the fatal lines of circumvallation to be drawn around him, or to come out of his works and give battle. Now a fair field-fight is precisely what the Army of the Potomac invites and welcomes; it will gladly give the rebels man for man, and engage to defeat them withal. If LEE is unwilling to run this risk, he retires within the defences of Richmond, *and we then hold precisely the relations held by the Allies to Napoleon defending Paris in 1814.* It was in vain then that that consummate master put forth a generalship that recalled the splendors of the first great Italian campaign; in vain he threw his masses on different points of the investing line. If LEE is not a better General than NAPOLEON, he can hardly hope for a much better fate.

With the army of the Potomac planted at or north of Petersburgh, we there tap the great railroad line connecting Richmond with the Atlantic seaboard and Gulf States. When there GRANT may be able to throw his left across the Danville Road, and in this case Richmond is isolated. If his plan does not contemplate so great a development of front, he will at least provide for the effectual *destruction* of the latter road; and this, as well as the destruction of the Western (Lynchburgh) Road and the James River Canal, will be an easy prey to our cavalry, which, under the hands of SHERIDAN, has almost put the rebel cavalry out of existence. The reduction of Fort Darling is an incidental piece of work, which will be gladly contended for by some of the able engineering heads of the Army of the Potomac. In the meantime, we have a perfectly secure and convenient base—the James River—to which all the transportation lately at White House has been forwarded.

There is another aspect of the move to the south side of the James, which from the point of view of its relations to the whole theatre of war, is not less important than its bearing on the problem immediately before us. *It is a division of the two great rebel armies, and gives us an interior position relative to the army of Lee in Virginia, and the army of Johnston in Georgia.* It has been reported that large detachments of JOHNSTON's army are already en route to reinforce LEE, and, if not actually under way, we may depend upon it that the able military heads that rule the war councils at Richmond, thoroughly imbued with the conception of *concentration*, and willing to risk everything to save Richmond, would willingly have sacrificed Southwestern territory to secure the great point in Virginia. But how does it stand now? JOHNSTON coming to reinforce LEE *would find his progress to Richmond barred by the same opponent who stopped his junction with Pemberton in Vicksburgh!* We secure this, therefore: first, that the enemy shall receive no addition to his strength, while our position effects a concentration of both the forces of BUTLER and HUNTER with the main operating force.

While, however, we have reason to look forward to great and important results as coming from the new position of the army, I am very far from looking on our success as a foregone conclusion. We have opposed to us an enemy of the highest skill, handling an army of sufficient strength still to attempt great things, and animated by a spirit of desperation. I fully expect some bold, audacious initiative on the part of LEE, and the greater the straits in which he finds himself, the more energetically he will attempt to retrieve himself, and the fortunes of the Confederacy bound up with him.

WILLIAM SWINTON.

SOUTHERN NEWS.

Rebel Extracts—The Cavalry Attack on Petersburgh—Orders from Gens. Colston and Wise.

From the Petersburgh Express, Monday, June 13.

THE REPULSE OF THE ENEMY AT PETERSBURGH—CONGRATULATORY ORDERS.

HEADQUARTERS FIRST MILITARY DISTRICT, Dept. N. C. and So. Va., June 12, 1864.

SPECIAL ORDERS No. 11.—VII. To the troops of my command for the defence of Petersburgh, on the south side of the Appomattox, on the 9th inst., I have, with the approval and under the instructions of the Commanding-General, to offer my grateful acknowledgments for their gallant conduct, and my congratulations upon their successful repulse of the enemy. Approaching with nine regiments of infantry and cavalry, and at least four pieces of artillery, they searched our lines from Battery No. 1 to Battery No. 29, a distance of nearly six miles. HOOD's and BATTE's battalions, the Forty-sixth Regiment Virginia Volunteers, and one company (Capt. WOOD's Company F,) of the Twenty-third South Carolina, with STURDIVANT's battery and a few guns in position, and TALLIAFERRO's cavalry, kept them at bay, and punished them severely until they reached the Jerusalem Plank road in front of Battery 29, defended by Maj. ARCHER's corps of reserves, and second-class militia, and by one piece of STURDIVANT's battery, a howitzer, under the temporary command of Brig.-Gen. COLSTON. Then, with overwhelming numbers, they were twice repulsed, and succeeded only at last in penetrating a gap in the line, and in flanking and gaining the rear of a mere handful of citizen soldiers, who stood firmly and fought bravely as veterans until ordered to fall back. Alas! some of the noblest of them fell "with their backs to the ground and their front to the foe," consecrating with their blood the soil of the homes they defended. Their immediate Commanders have reported the heroism of them all, the living and the dead, and now with pride and gratitude I announce that BEAUREGARD himself has thanked ARCHER and his comrades on the very spot of their devotion. If they lost killed, wounded and missing, 65 out of less than 150 men, they spent their blood dearly to the enemy; if STURDIVANT's battery lost one gun a better was captured, and another disabled, and if they lost a half a mile of ground, they gained about a half hour of time and saved their beloved city by holding on long enough for STURDIVANT's and GRAHAM's and YOUNG's batteries, DEARING's cavalry, and the Forty-sixth Virginia Infantry, with WOOD's South Carolina company, a company of convalescents, and a company of penitents, to drive back the insolent foe from approaches which their footsteps for the first time polluted. With the help of God it shall be the last time. With such troops as all have proved themselves, Commanders may well give assurance with confidence to the people of Petersburgh. A people who can thus fight for their altars must be aided, supported, guarded by every arm which can be outstretched for their defence. Comrades! their wives and daughters are daily and hourly nursing our sick and wounded, they wipe the hot brow, cool the fevered lips, and tenderly nourish and comfort the suffering soldiers in their hospitals. The angel nurses and the stricken patriots of this patriotic place shall not fall into the hands of ruffian invaders. Its very militia has set an example which inspires the confidence that Petersburgh is indomitable, and which consoles and compensates for every drop of blood which has been spilt at Nottaway, at Walthal Junction, and at Drewry's Bluff and Rowlett's Neck, for the defence of the old Cockade City. Let the reserves and second class militia of the surrounding counties now come in promptly, one and all, and emulate this bright and successful example—let it hotly hiss to blood-red shame the laggards and skulkers from the streets and alleys of the city to the lines; and let it proclaim aloud that Petersburgh is to be and shall be defended on her outer walls, on her inner lines, at her corporation bounds, in every street, and around every temple of God and altar of man in her very heart, until the blood of that heart is spilt. Roused by this spirit to this pitch of resolution, we will fight the enemy at every step, and Petersburgh is safe.

HENRY A. WISE, Brig.-Gen.

Official: J. V. PEARCE, A. A. G.

THE LATE RAID ON PETERSBURGH.

From the Petersburgh Express, Monday, June 13.

In the defeat of the Yankee raiders before Petersburgh last Thursday, the hand of Providence was plainly visible. A mere handful of untrained and undisciplined militia were nerved to the repulse and holding in check of 1,800 regulars, whose calling is war, and whose business is to fight. To these militia the city owes an incalculable weight of gratitude. For mainly to their bravery and heroism we owe it that our depots of supplies, our public buildings, our bridges, and probably much private property, are not now in ashes.

Gen. BEAUREGARD, who visited this city on Saturday, took occasion, we understand, to express to Major ARCHER, the gallant Commander of the militia, his high admiration of the distinguished bravery shown by him in the fight on Thursday, and his deep appreciation of the valuable services rendered by them. They fought, he said, like veterans. Such a compliment coming from such a source was no doubt doubly appreciated. We have already published the names of many of those taken prisoners, in which list occurred several errors. Thus far we have been unable to get a correct list, and only publish the names as they reach us. Since our last issue we have ascertained that Mr. THOMAS W. CLEMENTS, Mr. JOHN F. GLENN, Mr. GEORGE CAMERON and Mr. BRANCH T. ARCHER, all well-known citizens, were also made prisoners.

* * * * * * *

We understand from one of our wounded, who was carried by the Yankees to Mr. WM. A. GREGORY's residence during the conflict, that while there the notorious Col. SPEARS came in, cooly ordered his orderly to bring a basin of water, bathed his head, and casting himself upon a lounge, slept for an hour. Col. SPEARS is represented to have shown great kindness to our wounded, giving strict orders to his subordinates regarding their comfort, and supplying them with brandy and such other delicacies as he had.

* * * * * * *

It is now understood that the enemy's loss was much heavier than at first represented. They lost some thirty or forty killed, and a large number wounded. The roads near the battle-ground will testify to numerous burials of their dead.

[Communicated.]

THE ATTACK ON PETERSBURGH.

From the Petersburgh Express, June 13, 1864.

To the Editors of the Express:

Now that Petersburgh has been reinforced, we can speak freely of the past. Gen. WISE, commanding the First Military District of the Department of North Carolina and Southern Virginia, having gained information that the enemy were advancing on the City of Petersburgh, placed his troops in position to meet them. Major HOOD, Major BATTE, Capt. STURDIVANT, and the Forty-sixth Virginia Regiment, Col. HARRISON, were on the left, extending from the Appomattox River, covering the Broadway, City Point, Jordan's Point, and Prince George Court-house roads. Gen. COLSTON and Col. ARCHER, with the militia, were on the right, from the Baxter road, across the Jerusalem Plank Road. On the 9th instant, at an early hour, our pickets were driven in on the Broadway, City Point, Jordan's Point and Prince George Court-house roads, and the enemy soon appeared in force in front of the left of our line, and were soon engaged with Col. TALLIAFERRO's Seventh Confederate Cavalry. The boom of BATTE's and STURDIVANT's guns echoed far in the morning breeze, while the small arms of HOOD and the Forty-sixth Virginia, Col. HARRISON's, chimed in to tell mothers, wives, sisters, and *others as dear*, that this day brave hearts will defend the town which before the war was hospitable and kind to strangers, and which since the war has proven the soldier's friend.

Though it was the work of death, my heart throbbed with joy as I saw shell after shell fall and explode near our direful foe, who strove to force our works that he might sack the town. Gen. WISE sat on his horse and commented on the firing of our men; a smile played on his face as the enemy were driven back. Though repulsed with loss, the enemy's infantry remained in heavy force in front of our left, engaging us through the day, he sent his cavalry with some artillery from the left to feel our lines on the right. Here the eagle eye of Gen. WISE, our skillful, firm, bold Commander, as he rode from point to point, exposing his body to the Yankee lead, watched their work. When the cavalry, with several pieces of artillery, reached the Jerusalem plank road, he found the militia, with one piece of Capt. STURDIVANT's artillery, defending that point. Here, too, were brave men ready to die for their loved ones at home. Veterans never fought better.

Gen. COLSTON says this of them, and he knows what a soldier should be, for he is gallant, brave and true. Though many tears will be shed for the dead, Petersburgh will ever be proud of Col. ARCHER and his men. The militia—why 120 were flanked right and left by the enemy, still they stood under a cross fire until ordered to fall back. The enemy entered the line of fortifications, and rode up near the town. The ladies, who crowded housetops, expected now to be under Yankee rule, and to know all the horrors of Yankee wrongs. But the enemy, as if by the lurid lightning's flash, were brought to a stand. The reinforcements ordered to the right by Gen. WISE came in time; one of — guns, which had done good service in the morning, routed them again, and soon GRAHAM's battery from the Reservoir Hill opened on them again, and soon Col. TALLIAFERRO, who began the fight outside our lines at early dawn, together with a portion of Gen. DEARING's cavalry, YOUNG's Battery, the Forty-sixth Virginia infantry, with WOOD's South Carolina company, many of the sick and wounded, under the command of Capt. LOCKHART and Lieut. LINDSAY, who have been so kindly nursed by "angel hands," were ready to begin again for their country's cause, and even the Confederate prisoner's under command of the Provost-Marshal, Lieut. HAWES, who has already lost the use of one leg in defense of his country; all aided to repel the foe.

The Yankee force consisted of four regiments of infantry and five of cavalry. We had killed, 10; wounded, 33; missing, 28: total, 71. The enemy, as far as known, had 35 killed, 80 wounded, and 4 prisoners. We lost one piece of artillery and captured a better piece.

Gen. WISE has ever been for defending the City of Pittsburgh. His brigade has lost 400 men in the fights around the town. When placed in command here, he proclaimed he would hold the place or fall with it. His defence on the 9th proves him to be as good as his word. The hero of Charleston will stand by him. We'll trust in God and fight.

The One Hundred and Second New-York Volunteers.

LIST OF CASUALTIES—THE BATTLES IN WHICH THE REGIMENT HAS BEEN ENGAGED.

The friends of this regiment will be glad to learn that they have, as usual, nobly done their part in the grand movement of SHERMAN's army upon Atlanta. They participated in the battles of Rocky-faced Ridge, May 7; Resaca, May 15; and of Dallas, May 25. On the morning of May 15, the One Hundred and Second New-York and One Hundred and Eleventh Pennsylvania Regiments, forming a forlorn hope, were ordered to charge up a hill occupied by the enemy, and capture a battery that was interfering with the movements of our forces. The One Hundred and Second New-York, led by their gallant Colonel, JAMES C. LANE, marched up the hill in line of battle as steadily and in as straight a line as if on a dress parade, although all the way under a severe fire from the enemy. Immediately in front of the battery were rifle pits, occupied by a strong force; but after a severe fight, the enemy were driven out, and the battery, consisting of four guns, captured and sent into our lines. This brilliant operation was considered so hazardous, that officers high in rank who saw it commenced, expected both regiments would be annihilated. After its successful completion, Gen. HOOKER, the Corps Commander, personally complimented Col. LANE and his brave command for the splendid manner in which they had executed the work.

At the battle of Dallas this regiment was in the extreme front during the whole fight, and acquitted itself nobly. New-York may justly be proud of the record made in blood by this regiment. The following is a list of the casualties in the One Hundred and Second New-York up to June 2:

KILLED AND WOUNDED OF THE 102D REGIMENT N. Y. V. AT BATTLES OF ROCKY FACED RIDGE AND RESACA.

Killed.

Corp Thos Highland, B.	John Brophy, B.
Jos Bowden, B.	

Wounded.

1st Sergt Neils Christensen, B—hand and side.	Abram Lincoln, I—hand.
Ord Sergt Hermann Wesemuller, D—arm.	Sergt Thos S Mahan, G—arm amputated.
Thos Scantleberry, K—arm.	John W Albin, H—hand.
Robt Benjamin, B—hand.	Christopher Cruger, H—arm.
Corp Chas Steylesale, B—chin and breast.	Corp Strong Soper, K.
	Jas H Van Tassel, E—hand.

REPORT OF KILLED, WOUNDED AND MISSING OF THE 102D REGIMENT NEW-YORK VOLUNTEERS, SINCE MAY 25, 1864.

Killed.

Archibald Henderson, Co K.	Adam Y Stenes, Co B.
David L Crosby, Co B.	

Wounded.

D Cunningham, A—stomach.	1st Sgt D Shannon, I—head.
R M Heston, A—hand & arm.	Corp R Downs, I—hand.
George Golden, A—hand.	Enos Chapin, I—arm.
Sgt S D James, C—head.	John Hopkins, I—side.
Charles Reilly, C—arm.	Corp Edwd Lyons, I—hand.
Densil M Gould, D—leg.	1st Sgt J Richardson, K—arm.
Wm Moran, E—arm.	Corp Geo Harrison, K—leg.
Sgt M Whitbeck, G—head.	J Brown, K—leg amputated.

Missing.

1st Sgt W H Nevins, G—since May 25, '64.	John Colwell, A—since May 25, '64.
L Smith, B—since May 28, '64.	

Killed, 3; wounded, 16; missing, 3. Total, 22.

The Eleventh Massachusetts.

WASHINGTON, Friday, June 17.

A portion of the Eleventh Massachusetts Volunteers passed through the city to-day, on their way home, their time having expired. Those who remain in the army have been incorporated with the First Massachusetts Volunteers, and are commanded by Col. BLAISDELL, of the former corps.

The Berkshire Disaster.

POUGHKEEPSIE, Friday, June 17.

Two more bodies were found on the wreck of the *Berkshire* to-day. One of them is supposed to be that of Mr. VAN TASSELL, and the other has been identified as that of Mr. STEVENS.

The derrick for raising the steamer has arrived, and by Monday it is thought that the wreck will be brought to the surface, and the worst will be known.

The Charleston Mercury.

DAILY PAPER—Twenty Dollars for Six Months—Payable in Advance.

VINDICE NULLO
SPONTE SUA SINE LEGE FIDES RECTUMQUE COLLENTUR.

COUNTRY PAPER—Thrice a Week—Twelve Dollars for Six Months—Payable in Advance.

Volume LXXXV. CHARLESTON, S. C., MONDAY, JULY 11, 1864. Number 12,109.

TELEGRAPHIC.

ANOTHER CAMPAIGN IN PENNSYLVANIA.

Early and Breckinridge Over the Border.

ALARM AT THE NORTH!

The Alabama Sunk by the Yankee Gunboat Kearsage.

General War News, &c., &c., &c.

GLORIOUS NEWS FROM ARKANSAS—PRICE AGAIN VICTORIOUS.

CLINTON, LA, July 6.—A gentleman of this town, just from the other side of the river, reports the capture of Little Rock by PRICE, with all of STEELE's supplies, ammunition and transportation, and with all his army, excepting 4000 men.

Our army was marching on Fort Smith. The enemy has been driven entirely out of Arkansas, except around Helena, where his gunboats protect him.

News has been officially received at Alexandria that General KIRBY SMITH has ordered the impressment of half of the cotton in the Trans-Mississippi Department, for the purpose of buying military supplies.

THE ENEMY REPULSED IN MISSISSIPPI.

MOBILE, July 8.—The operator at Jackson, Miss., reports that the force which moved from Roddy simultaneously with that which marched from Vicksburg and which was commanded by Colonel ELLETT, of Maine, consisted of 500 white cavalry and 1500 negro infantry. This column was met at Coleman's Cross Roads, 10 miles south of Port Gibson, by Colonel WOOD, with his regiment, MORGAN's battalion, and a few State troops, all being a portion of ADAMS' brigade, and amounting to about 1000 men.

The enemy were driven back to Roddy after a sharp fight. The enemy's loss was 67 killed and a large number wounded. We captured many horses, small arms and equipments. Our loss was six killed. The number of our wounded is not known as yet.

MOVEMENTS IN VIRGINIA.

RICHMOND, July 8.—Nothing further from the Valley. It is reported that another large force of Yankees has been crossing to the north side of the James River to-day.

PETERSBURG, July 10.—About 5 o'clock on Friday evening our artillery, along the whole line, opened upon the enemy. At the time our men mounted the works and defied the enemy, who sought the cover of their entrenchments. They replied with artillery, and the firing lasted about thirty minutes. The enemy have made no assault upon our lines for a week past. The impression is that the enemy have drawn off the bulk of their forces from our front. For several nights past the rumbling of artillery wagons has been distinctly heard. The enemy, however, still keep up a show of force in our front. All quiet to-day.

HIGHLY IMPORTANT FROM THE UNITED STATES.

SENATOBIA, Miss., July 7.—Northern dates report EWELL's corps, in the vicinity of Harper's Ferry. HUNTER and SIGEL had evacuated Martinsburg.

The return of WILSON's raiders to GRANT's army is also announced. They claim to have destroyed sixty miles of railroads, burning the bridges to within twenty miles of Danville.

The N. Y. *Herald's* Bermuda Hundreds correspondent says that the armies are now taking their last repose before girding up for battle.

FESSENDEN has not yet accepted the post of Secretary of the Yankee Treasury Department.

SHERMAN's advance is bulletined by the Yankee papers as a great success.

The N. Y. *Herald's* Washington correspondent says that LINCOLN will call for 500,000 more men immediately after the adjournment of Congress.

Gen. WASHBURN has issued special orders taking 10 Confederate citizens as hostages for the safety of his railroad trains.

PETERSBURG, July 9.—The Washington *Chronicle* of the 6th has been received.

Great excitement prevails at the North in consequence of the rebel raid. Martinsburg had been captured with large quantities of supplies. The Baltimore and Ohio Railroad and Canal are badly injured. RANSOM is supposed to command the rebel cavalry and EARLY the infantry. The rebels are believed to have reached Hagerstown by the 6th, bound on an extensive raid in Pennsylvania. Gov. CURTIN had issued a proclamation saying "the enemy of the Government, in their desperation are threatening the State with an armed force in the hope that General GRANT may be withdrawn from before Richmond. The rebel force is not known.

SIGEL has again saved himself by a timely flight.

The latest foreign intelligence gives an account of a great naval engagement between the *Alabama* and the United States steamer *Kearsage*. The former was sunk in an engagement which lasted an hour and forty minutes. The fight took place ten miles from Cherbourg, on Sunday, June 19. The *Kearsage* was commanded by Captain JNO. A. WINSTON, who sent a challenge to the *Alabama*, which was accepted by Captain SEMMES. The *Alabama* was disabled by a shot through her boiler, while attempting to board the *Kearsage*. Captain SEMMES and a portion of the crew of the *Alabama* were saved by the English yacht *Greyhound*. SEMMES was slightly wounded in the hand. He reports his loss at nine killed and twenty-one wounded. The *Kearsage* was considerably damaged. Capt. SEMMES left all his chronometers, specie and ransom bonds at Cherbourg, previous to going out to fight. He was landed at Southhampton by the *Greyhound*, where he was offered a public dinner, but declined it, and proceeded to Paris to report to the Confederate Commissioner.

The Yankee Congress adjourned *sine die* on the 5th inst.

Ex-Gov. RHODES, of Kansas, is dead. Gold 248.

RICHMOND, July [illegible] [illegible] the *Alabama* [illegible] unseaworthy condition. [illegible] cial report says that the enemy fired at the *Alabama* five times after her colors were struck. Her rudder was disabled. During the action the crew displayed the utmost bravery. The shell that did the mischief struck the *Alabama* just above the water line, knocking her bunkers to pieces. The water almost immediately put out her fires. A steam tug was sent from Cherbourg by the *Prefet de Marine* to afford assistance to the *Alabama*, but arrived after all the survivors had been picked up.

LATER AND HIGHLY IMPORTANT.

RICHMOND, July 9.—The Baltimore *Gazette* of the 7th says that Martinsburg, Harper's Ferry and Point of Rocks have fallen into the hands of the Confederates. They obtained a very considerable amount of booty at those places. Governor CURTIN has issued a proclamation calling for 12,000 men for a hundred days. LINCOLN has made a requisition on New York for the same number. Hagerstown, Md., was occupied by the Confederates on Wednesday. The Federal troops retreated to Greencastle.

Gold in New York on the 6th, was 259.

LINCOLN has issued a proclamation declaring martial law and suspending the *habeas corpus* in Kentucky.

RICHMOND, July 9.—Citizens of Fredericksburg, carried off by GRANT's orders as hostages for the Yankees captured in the town after the battle of the Wilderness, have been exchanged. They left Washington on Wednesday, and arrived at Fredericksburg the same day.

Intense excitement prevailed at Washington from the announcement that 40,000 rebels were approaching the city. LINCOLN had called out the militia of the adjoining States. A telegram from Harrisburg states that the excitement there was intense, in view of the rumors that BRECKINRIDGE was moving in the direction of Chambersburg. One report says that BRECKINRIDGE has 20,000 men, and has whipped General SIGEL.

THE MERCURY.

MONDAY, JULY 11, 1864.

Early's Diversion.

Our people have heard, with great incredulity, the Yankee statement, that General EARLY has been detached, with some twelve thousand men, from the army near Richmond and sent up the Valley of Virginia to cross the Potomac and threaten Washington and its frowning fortifications. Diversions and the division of our forces have uniformly proved disastrous; and the time for invading the North or capturing Washington—the first year of the war—has long since past with its opportunities and advantages. Last year, when BRAGG defended Tennessee with forces inferior to the enemy, and when Vicksburg and the Valley of the Mississippi was endangered by GRANT, thirty thousand troops from the unoccupied army of Virginia might have enabled BRAGG to recapture Nashville and Memphis and save Vicksburg. But a grand diversion into Pennsylvania was projected. It ended in the disaster of Gettysburg, with the loss of half our army, and the doubling of the Yankee army by recruits; Vicksburg fell and Tennessee was lost. LONGSTREET with his corps had to be sent out in the fall to save Georgia at Chickamauga. Then another diversion and division of our forces was ordered in the attack on Knoxville LONGSTREET was unable to take Knoxville with his thirteen thousand men, fighting an equal number behind strong works; and BRAGG was so weakened by the detachment that we lost the battle of Missionary Ridge and Northern Georgia.

We allude to these facts of the last damaging campaign, as a commentary on what we cannot but fear may be a great blunder now.—EARLY will not take Washington, but may raise a large force for LINCOLN by his appearance.—The experience of larger and stronger expeditions has been unfortunate, and he is likely to come to grief in such an attempt. We hope he may weaken GRANT's army by compelling large detachments, but the means to such an end appears very unhopeful. We should much rather have trusted to prompt concentration and a vigorous attack upon GRANT on the south side before his heavy works were thrown up. And if troops can be spared from the army of Virginia JOHNSTON certainly has need of them.—We do not like EARLY's expedition, and these views can go for what they are worth.

The Bombardment of Fort Sumter.

The Richmond *Dispatch* has seen some interesting statistical tables descriptive of the different kinds of missiles thrown at Fort Sumter, and other matters connected with the protracted bombardment, a brief summary of which will doubtless prove acceptable to our readers. The missiles embrace almost every description of shells, shrapnell, bolt and shot, from 10 to 26 inches in length and from 3½ to 15 inches in diameter. The heaviest shot fired weighed 425 pounds. A classification of the shot fired by the enemy, from April, 1863, to February 21, 1864, shows the following results: From monitors, 1,443; land guns by day, 14,225; land guns by night, 4,402; mortars, 7,167; total 27,247; of which number 20,316 struck and 6,964 missed. Yet, shattered and crumbling under the hailstorm of iron hurled against it, the energy and skill of Southern engineers has raised a new fort like a Phoenix from the debris, whose resistive strength defies the utmost malice of the foe. The weight of metal fired by the enemy against the fort is estimated at 3,627,990 pounds, or 1,630 tons. The number of men killed was 41, of whom 13 were killed by the falling of the wall of the garrison barracks, and 11 by the explosion of the magazine, leaving 17 killed by the enemy's shot.

The writer gives an estimate showing the amount of metal thrown by the enemy to cause the loss to us of one man: 41 men killed by 3,627,990 pounds of metal, that is, 88,487½ pounds, or 39½ tons of iron to the man. Deducting the number killed by accidents, 24, it leaves 17 men killed by 3,627,990 pounds of metal, that is, 213,411 pounds, or 95½ tons of iron to the man. The following is an estimate showing the number of miles of railroad track the amount of metal wasted on Fort Sumter would have laid. A single rail weighs 50 pounds to the yard, which would require 80 tons to lay a track one mile; therefore, 1,630 tons, or the amount thereon, would have laid a track 20½ miles.

The writer proceeds to give an account of the several assaults upon the fort, and, in conclusion, says: "It will thus be seen that [illegible] attempts have been made by the enemy to reduce this noble fortress, [illegible] six or seven times [illegible] [illegible] against her from the [illegible] used in war, and still to-day she stands proudly defiant, and stronger in her defensive qualities than ever before. The kind providence of God has wonderfully shielded her and her garrison in their hours of trial, and to Him would we confidingly leave her future history, in the hope that, as in the past, she may ever dwell under the shadow of the Almighty."

ADDITIONAL FROM THE NORTH.

THE SINKING FINANCES OF THE NORTH—ENORMOUS ACCUMULATION OF DEBT.

The enormous accumulation of debt incurred by this war is beginning to arouse serious attention in the North. A writer in one of the New York papers makes an elaborate review of the finances of the Washington Government, in which, after proving it by figures, he says:

The annual rate of expenditure is now at least one billion dollars per annum. There are sagacious and well informed men who insist that it is not less that four millions a day. Of present reduction of expenditure there is no possible prospect. The taxation which Mr. Chase invokes as essential to insure success to the finances of the Government is not less than five hundred millions of dollars a year—that is, five hundred millions of fixed, permanent revenue are necessary, even if there be a military success. Otherwise "all measures will fail." It requires military success now to make five hundred millions of taxation sufficient to carry on the Government. That, too, be it noted, will be for a peace establishment. What would be needed for a continued war establishment, if success shall not come in time, and so completely as to close up the war and stop the expenditure. Mr. Chase does not profess to compute; for it is plainly in his thoughts that unless the war be thus finished the present year the Government is bankrupt.

The Chicago *Times* is equally frank, and says, in the course of an article on the same subject:

When the new tax and tariff bills take effect the people will realize the cost of the war.

Despite enormous taxes and duties, the expenses of the Government will continue to exceed the receipts by two millions per diem. The public credit cannot long endure such a strain without a prospect of relief. The financial situation, the enormous tax and depreciated currency, the awful magnitude of an accumulating debt, and the imminence of an explosion more destructive than any country has ever known, are bringing people to their senses.

The re-election of Lincoln decides the continuance of the war till national bankruptcy and exhaustion close it.

EFFECTS OF OPERATIONS IN GOLD.

A Philadelphia paper in some observations on the gold disturbance, says:

But these gambling combinations in gold stimulate and invite combinations in flour, and beef and pork, and other necessaries of life, and in this way the people are made victims all around. A successful "corner" in gold begets in some other operator a desire for a "corner" in beef, or butter, or mess pork, or coffee, or clover seed, or any available commodity. Thus beef was forced up to 40 cents a pound a few weeks ago, when there was an ample supply; and thus a combination of kindred character is trying to force up the price of mess pork in New York now. In this way the passion for that species of gambling spreads, and the people not only have to pay the increase of price in consequence of the rise in gold, but they suffer from the extortion of all other combinations for "corners" in the necessaries of life. The Government, by the late act of Congress struck a blow at the root of all these evils, by making false transactions in gold penal offences, and "that's what's the matter" over in Wall street.

OPERATIONS ON JAMES RIVER—THE FAILURE OF OF THE IRON-CLAD NAVY.

The New York *Herald* is greatly dissatisfied with the tardiness of Admiral LEE, and pours into that Yankee officer the following proper broadside:

It is announced in the news from the James River that Generals Grant and Butler visited Admiral Lee, on one of the gunboats, on Saturday last. What took place at this interview between the Lieutenant General and the commander of the James River flotilla, we of course do not know; but we know very well what ought to have taken place; and we can only hope that the presence and the words of the victorious commander of our armies may have stirred up Admiral Lee to a sense of his position, and inspired him to make some attempt, even though a lame one, to go on forward to the performance of his plain duty, in opening the James River, and taking his iron-clads to the wharves of Richmond.

There is no disguising the fact that, under their present commander, the James River gunboats are having a shamefully easy time of it. They are ignominiously compelled to look on in idleness, while the army loses eight or ten thousand men in glorious struggle that they should have rendered unnecessary. It is reported that even Commodore Goldsborough has growled at the inactivity of the gunboats on the James River. But, as if mere idleness were not enough, Admiral Lee has just performed an act that, we doubt not, has called an honorable blush to the cheek of every officer in his fleet. He has sunk boats in the river—obstructed the channel—to prevent the rebel rams from getting out at his ships. He has iron-clad vessels enough to blow every ram in the Confederacy to atoms; but he is afraid of the trial. If he fears to meet these vessels down the river where his own boats lie, when may we expect that he will go up the river and fight them where they are supported by batteries on shore?

If it be urged against his advance up the James that the obstructions are dangerous, and that the fire of the forts is too severe, it must then be admitted that iron-clad vessels are a failure, and that the immense sums spent in their construction have been thrown away.—Early in the war Admiral Dupont silenced shore batteries under a terrible fire with only wooden ships. Admiral Farragut went to New Orleans despite obstructions in the river, and running the fire of perfectly constructed forts, all with wooden ships. He ran the fire of the Port Hudson batteries with wooden ships, and Porter ran past the formidable and well served Vicksburg batteries with even the army transports. If so much more can be done by some commanders with wooden ships than can be by others with iron ones, we ought either to waste no more money in the construction of iron ships; or we ought to change commanders.

We do not object to Admiral Lee because he is a relation of Mr. Blair, nor yet because he is a Virginian, but we do object to him because he has no energy in the discharge of his most obvious duty, and because he is for that most simple reason palpably unfit for the important position which he now occupies.

THE CASE OF MR POLLARD AND THE GREYHOUND—CORRESPONDENCE WITH THE BRITISH MINISTRY.

It appears that Lord LYONS has applied to Secretary SEWARD for the release of the British steamer *Greyhound*, which was captured by a Yankee vessel, 125 miles out of Wilmington, on the high seas, and out of the jurisdiction claimed by the United States. The application also requests the release of Mr. EDWARD A. POLLARD, of Richmond. The correspondence on the subject, including three letters from Mr. P., and a protest from the Captain of the *Greyhound*, addressed to Lord LYONS, is published in the [illegible] [illegible] to England to fulfill an engagement for a literary work on the Confederate States, &c., with publishers in London, who had already printed two volumes I had composed of a similar nature; and also to discharge a private and domestic duty in visiting the relatives of my wife, who is a native of England and a subject of Her Britannic Majesty. I am not connected with the military service of the Confederate States, and am charged with no public office or trust on their behalf. These facts may be readily established by appropriate evidence; and in consideration of them, I submit to your Lordship that, if interposition be necessary, I may be protected in those very obvious rights, which I invoke in the character of an innocent passenger on the high seas, under the British flag.

And in another letter he shows how entirely unjustifiable was the capture of the steamer:

BOSTON, May 20, 1864.

Lord Lyons, Envoy Extraordinary, &c., for Her Britannic Majesty, near Washington, United States:

MY LORD: I have been detained here as a prisoner one week to-day, notwithstanding the notification, under date of 20th instant, with which your lordship obliged me, to the effect that you had applied to the Secretary of State of the United States for my release.

There are two points in my case, which I beg to bring to your attention again in a precise and brief recapitulation.

1. The Greyhound had passed out of the port of Wilmington without sight of a blockading vessel, and was taken by a cruiser about 150 miles out at sea. I desire to put the question to your lordship if the Government at Washington can so change its tactics of blockade as to omit an efficient guard of the coast, and take up vessels which have come out of Confederate ports by fast sailing cruisers on the ocean highway; for such I was informed by an officer of the United States steamer Connecticut was the recently adopted and easy plan of taking prizes, the fruits of which your lordship may have observed in the capture of four vessels as prizes in a single week, each taken far out on the high seas.*

2. The Greyhound was thoroughly a British vessel; the British flag she carried was not a decoy, and that flag covered me, after I had passed out of the territorial jurisdiction of the United States, and, even in case it did not protect vessel or cargo, (granting, for argument, these to be of an illicit character), protected me as an innocent passenger; else, having no other egress from the Confederate States, the passenger would be the victim of his necessity; and, else again, if a citizen of the Confederate States, not contraband, could be outlawed on the high seas under that flag, flying on a *bona fide* British vessel, why not a subject or citizen of any other Government? If the flag was a reality at all, it certainly should give protection on the ocean highway to a passenger who was pursuing objects of private convenience, and certainly was not amenable to any military penalties of the Government at Washington.

Begging that your lordship will acquit me of the charge of importunity in a matter, the importance of which is by no means altogether personal to myself,

I have the honor, &c.,
Your obedient servant,
EDWARD A. POLLARD.

P. S. I telegraphed your lordship on the 24th instant to obtain liberty for me to see you in Washington, in the interest of the Greyhound, but have received no reply, hence these lines.

*Another circumstance: It is true that if the blockade runner be seen in *flagrante delicto* passing the territorial lines, she may be pursued and taken on the high seas. But the Greyhound was not pursued, she was waylaid on the highway of the seas. Such a practice would convert the blockade into a system of roving commissions, and might as well be predicated on the coast of Bermuda as of that of the Confederate States.

CIRCULAR FROM MINISTER DE L'HUYS ON THE MONROE DOCTRINE.

The following is a circular from the French Minister of Foreign Affairs to the French Agents in foreign ports, (dated May 4,) upon the subject of the recent Monroe Doctrine resolution of the Yankee Congress:

Gentlemen—The recent vote of the House of Representatives at Washington, on the subject of Mexico, has given rise to certain interpretations which it will be as well to rectify. The idea has arisen that this vote might induce the United States to adopt towards us a new attitude, of such a nature as to effect the cordial feelings existing between the two countries, or, at any rate, to complicate the Mexican question by embarrassments arising from without. We need only, however, observe the circumstances under which the manifestation alluded to took place to understand that the vote is very far from possessing the importance imputed to it. It is doubtless the reflection of the feeling so carefully fostered by the American press in the United States, which leads that people to consider as an indirect attack upon their rights the most legitimate intervention of a European Power, on any point of the American continent. But we must consider that, in the United States, above all others, the legislative assembly may indulge in demonstrations of this character without pledging the government in any way or forcing it to regulate its conduct accordingly. The Imperial Government had, therefore, no reason to conceive any apprehension on that subject, even if the incident has elicited no explanation from the Federal Government; but the Cabinet at Washington has made it a duty spontaneously to anticipate and obviate any unfavorable impressions that we might have formed from it. Mr. Dayton called upon me to read a despatch addressed to him by the Secretary of State for the Union, repudiating all responsibility on the part of the Cabinet of Washington in this matter, and establishing the principle that a vote of the House of Representatives or of the Senate, or even of both Houses, while it would naturally be a subject for the serious attention of the cabinet, could not possibly oblige it to modify its policy or deprive it of its liberty of action. Mr. Seward sees no reason for adopting in the Mexican question any line of conduct other than that which he has followed up to the present time.

I answered Mr. Dayton that nothing, according to our ideas, could justify a change; that our confidence in the wisdom and prudence of the American Cabinet was too great for us to suspect it of any thoughts of compromising, by hasty acts, the true interests of the United States. In expressing to Mr. Dayton how much satisfaction the assurance he was commissioned to give me caused to the Government of the Emperor, I added that I thought, in fact, that, even seen from the point of view of the United States themselves, the choice could not be doubtful between the establishment of a stable and regular Government in Mexico and the perpetuation of an anarchy and its attendant evils, which they themselves had first felt the effects of and called attention to. The reorganization of a great country, which the return of order and security will enable to play an important economical part in the world, should be, for the United States especially, a real source of advantage, because it opens for them a new market, and one by which they more than any one, will profit, on account of their proximity. The prosperity of Mexico corresponds with their truest interests, and I could not believe that the Cabinet of Washington would recognize this truth. This answer to Mr. Dayton's communication, and the fact of this communication itself, must show you sufficiently in what light the incident on which I now write to you must be regarded.

DROUYN DE L'HUYS.

Editor Mercury: Permit me gratefully to acknowledge the receipt of thirty pounds of crush sugar and five pounds of green tea from the Importing and Exporting Company of S. C., through their Agents, Messrs. [illegible] & Richards and Street & West, for the sick and wounded South Carolinians at Hospital in Richmond.

T. A. LAFAR.

Richmond, June 20th, 1864.

The French people are wild with excitement at the [illegible] French horse [illegible] English [illegible] [illegible] the victory.

SOUTH CAROLINA CASUALTIES.

List of casualties in 8th S. C. Regiment, from 5th June to the 20th, 1864:

Company L—Corp R T Banfield, severe in neck, 5th June.

Company G—Private S J McInnis, severe in shoulder, 5th June.

Company B—Private H Funderburk, severe in body, 6th June.

Company A—Private H Carter, severe in body, 6th June.

Company K—Sergt Eli Willis, severe in leg, 8th June.

Company A—Private J J [illegible], killed, 11th June.

Company F—Private J H Privett, slight in head, 18th June.

Company A—Sergeant W H Reddick, killed, 18th June.

Company G—Private C F Webster, slight in head, 18th June.

Company L—Captain W D Carmichael, slight in head, 19th June.

Company I—Lieutenant D C Stafford, severe in head, 19th June.

Company D—Private Peter Holly, killed, 19th June.

Company B—Private Henry Therall, killed, 19th June.

C. M. WEATHERLY, Adjutant.

ELEVENTH REGIMENT.

Report of killed and wounded, 11th S. C. Regiment in the engagements around Petersburg, June 18th and 19th—Major J. J. GOODING commanding:

Company B, Lieutenant Jno Black, commanding—Killed: None.

Wounded: J W Ritts, thigh dangerously; M Doyle, left ankle slightly; J Hudson, hip slightly; J Barr, arm slightly.

Company C, Sergeant W Weatherford commanding—Killed: None.

Wounded: R Driggers, head severely.

Missing: T Powell, J Pelgler.

Company D, Lieutenant McD Gooding commanding—Killed: Privates Robert H Rivers, Charles Crews.

Wounded: A Stanley, little finger amputated; A Altmon, hand severely; Frank Rivers.

Missing: J Shipes, R N Mathews.

Company E, Captain J H Mickler command ing—Killed: Privates A Ginn and A Freeman.

Wounded: Privates F T Rivers, left lung dangerously; G Horton, left arm and side severely; W Bennet, left leg severely; W J Smith, right shoulder slightly.

Missing: J Angley, Sergeant A W Crosby, T H Smith, W S Shuman, L H Smith, B B Winn, J H Zehe, R C Wynn, Lieut T Hamilton, J J Dobson, C R Dobson, J T Daring, Cooper Cone.

Company F, Captain B F Wyman commanding—Killed: None.

Wounded: None.

Company G, Lieutenant Samuel Brownlee commanding—Killed: None.

Wounded: None.

Missing: Privates H Gosly, R R Dewitt, J L Darr, A B Larisey.

Company H, Captain T E Raysor commanding—Killed: Sergeant F E Howell, Private C T Canaday.

Wounded: Privates Z Lowe, head severely; J A Judy, left ankle severely.

Missing: Privates C T Heaton, H Murray, A D Murray, J G Murray, A H. Millard, W McElhany.

Company I, Lieutenant J Reilley commanding—Killed: None.

Wounded: None.

Missing: Privates Lawrence Hiott, J R Griffin, Joe Hiott, W Spell, W B Hagens.

Company K, L B Murdaugh commanding—Killed: Private A E Smoke.

Wounded: Privates G Johns, right knee and hip severely; J B Crosby, right leg severely; W A Copeland, right hand severely; J R Jones, fracture lower jaw severely.

Missing: R Fender, B Hudson, Wm Carter.

A. ENGLISH WILLIAMS,
Surgeon 11th S. C. Regiment.

COMPANY D, TWENTY-SEVENTH REGIMENT S C. V.

List of casualties in Company D, 27th S. C. V., HAGOOD's Brigade, HOKE's Division, from 7th May to 29th June, inclusive:

John Saxon, taken prisoner at Port Walthall Junction.

T Caissey, taken prisoner at Port Walthall Junction.

W E Bee, killed, May 9, at Swift Creek.

Lieut A St J Lance, killed, May 14, at Drewry's Bluff.

S V Martin, wounded near Drewry's Bluff, May 14; died in Hospital Camp, Jackson, 26th June.

Color bearer J Tupper, wounded through leg at the battle of Drewry's Bluff, May 16.

Jno Turner, wounded at Drewry's Bluff, May 16.

— Withers, wounded at Drewry's Bluff, May 16.

J F Fowler, wounded at Drewry's Bluff, May 16.

A Pool, wounded a Drewry's Bluff, May 16.

R Moore, wounded in lines near Bermuda Hundreds, May 21, right arm amputated at shoulder.

T W Atkinson, killed at Cold Harbor, June 1.

Sergeant H A Smith, wounded at Cold Harbor, June 3.

H T Susan, wounded at Cold Harbor, June 3.

W H Garland, wounded at Cold Harbor, June 5.

Jack Saxon, wounded at Cold Harbor, June 5.

C Arlington, wounded at Malvern Hill.

Captain J W Hopkins, killed in lines near Petersburg, June 16.

Orderly Sergeant W W Beckman, wounded in lines near Petersburg, June 16, leg amputated, died in Hospital, Petersburg June 25.

Corp J J Saylor, wounded in lines near Petersburg, June 16

C P Aldrich, killed in lines near Petersburg, June 16.

T J Bryson, killed in lines near Petersburg, June 16.

W A Gyles, wounded near Appomattox River, June 18.

R Beadle, killed near Appomattox River, June 18.

— Milford, wounded near Appomattox River, June 18.

J Fowler, mortally wounded near Appomattox River, June 22.

Corp Jno Birkedale, killed in assault, June 24.

James Cook, killed in assault, June 24.

Sam'l W Fisher, missing in assault, June 24.

Jas Pitts, missing in assault, June 24.

H. P. Foster, wounded in assault, June 24.

J A. Madden, slightly wounded, May 25.

B. M. Welles, arm broken, June 29.

H. Reddin, wounded near Petersburg.

Casualties among the officers in the 27th Regiment, S C V, from May 7th to June 29.

Company A—Capt B W Palmer, killed June 16. Lieut J W Axson, killed June 24.

Company B—Lieut Sinkler, wounded; Lieut. Masterman, killed, June 7.

Company C—Capt G Brown, killed; Lieut. Gelling, killed, June 16.

Company D—Capt J W Hopkins, killed, June 16; Lieut A St J Lance, killed, June 14; Lieut J T Wells, wounded, left ankel.

Company E—Lieut Proctor, wounded; Lieut Kemmerely, wounded, May 7; Lieut Crocker, wounded, May 16.

Company F—Capt J B Allston, wounded, May 16; Lieut J Huguenin, wounded; Lieut C Porcher, wounded, May 16.

Company G—Captain H Buist, wounded and prisoner; Lieut Hoffman, wounded; Lieut White, wounded and missing.

Company H—Capt Mulvaney, wounded and prisoner; Lieut A A Allemong, wounded, since dead.

Company I—Lieut J C [illegible], prisoner; Lieut W Trim, wounded [illegible]

Company K—Lieut [illegible], wounded, arm; Lieut E H Lang, [illegible] while on picket.

Editor Mercury:—In addition to the list of casualties sent you for publication, please insert the following:

Killed—[illegible] J Joy and [illegible] Lewis.

Wounded—Privates Charles B Prentiss, shoulder, besides body burned; Howell Cooper, hand and head, also burned considerably; J D Simpson, bruised.

* These casualties were occasioned by the explosion of a limber chest by the enemy's shell, on the 20th inst., near White House, Va.

L. C. STEPHENS,
Acting Assistant Surgeon Hart's Horse Artillery, Hampton's Cavalry Division.

Camp Hart's Battery, Hampton's Cavalry Division, near White House, Pamunkey River, June 21, 1864.

ACKNOWLEDGEMENTS.

* *Editor Mercury:* I beg leave to report the receipt of the following contributions for the Soldiers' Wayside Home for the three weeks, ending the 9th July. The Register Book show the Home has fed and sheltered 38,875 soldiers free of charge in ten months:

Friends of the Home, Columbia, S C	$500 00
A W T Simmons, Stono Scouts	10 00
Lieut R J Means, C S A	10 00
A Navy Officer	20 00
Bureau Clerk	40 00
J S Whaley, Stono Scouts, (old issue $10)	6.66⅔
Mrs J H Cooper, Mayesville, S C, (old issue $60)	40.00
Through Dr Bachman, from a Refugee of St Stephen's Depot	50 00
A Soldier	10 00
Through Mr H L Jeffers, from P D Klugh	10 00
Miss Mary McKeller	5.00
Total	$701.66

JAMES S GIBBES,
Treasurer Soldiers' Wayside Home.

Editor Mercury:—The following donations have been received at the Soldiers' Wayside Home during the past two weeks, ending the 9th July:

From Mr. Chas Heyward, city, 1 basket containing irish potatoes, squashes, onions and cabbages.

From Mrs Geo H Gruber, City, 1 dozen head cabbages.

From Mr Oliver Moore, Belvidere Farm, 1 bag irish potatoes and a lot of squashes and cucumbers.

From Mr O V Chamberlain, City, 1 large basket tomatoes.

Detachment from Fire Brigade, doing duty in City of Charleston, S. C., 1 ration each for 86 men.

From Maj. Chambliss, C. S. Arsenal, a lot of cabbages and cucumbers

From Mrs Wittpen, City, 1 basket tomatoes and 1 basket irish potatoes

From Mr J H Hilken, King street Road, 1 basket tomatoes, a fine lot of cabbages, 1 basket squashes, 1 basket irish potatoes and a lot of onions

Through T D Wagner, Esq, 1 box clothing and pamphlets, and 1 case wine from Edward Decker, Esq, Nassau, N. P.

Through Mr J W Davant, per J A Salters, Esq, Williamsburg, S C, through the following donors—Mr Thomas China, 2 bags corn; Dr Boyd, 2 bags corn, Mr W J J Lafrage, 2½ bushels corn and 1 piece bacon, Mr J A Salters, 2 bushels corn and 2 pieces bacon.

From a family in the country, 1 box containing 2 bushels corn and 1 side bacon, 1 shoat in a coop.

Mr O V Chamberlain, city, a fine lot of tomatoes and squashes.

From Captain George E Brown, of the steamer Fox, sugar, coffee and tea.

Through Dr L Dantzler, Vance's Ferry, S C, from the following donors—Mr David M Shuler, 2 bags grist Mr Jas A Felder, 2 bags grist; Mr R Evans, 1 bag grist, Mrs Maggie Evans, 1 bag grist; Mrs Julia Evans, 1 bushel grist; Mrs E M Shuler, 1 bushel grist; Mrs C Shuler, half bushel grist and half bushel rice; Dr L Dantzler, 3 bushels grist; Mrs Elizabeth Dantzler 1 bushel grist.

Mrs Wittpen, City, 1 barrel irish potatoes.

Mrs David Riker, 6 head cabbages and 1 basket tomatoes.

J H Colclough, Esq., Santee, S C, 5 bushels rough rice.

Mrs D B Heyward, 1 bag grist.

Mr O V Chamberlain, a fine lot of tomatoes.

Mrs Chas Heyward, 1 basket containing tomatoes, squashes, cucumbers, green corn, irish potatoes and cabbages.

Mr Oliver Moore, Belvidier Farm, a fine lot of tomatoes.

From Capt Wm F R Harden, City, 2 camp kettles, writing paper and ink.

W. H. HOUSTON.

Editor Mercury: Please allow me, through your columns, to acknowledge the receipt of donations to Florence Wayside Home:

Cash, through I. B Prince	$141 66
Cash, of Citizens of Anson County, N C	[illegible].32
Cash, of Ladies of Marion C H, S C	315.67
Cash, of Citizens of Cheraw, S C	150 00
Cash, of Ladies of Timmonsville, S C	1017.75
Cash, of Dr W Cropland, S C	100 00
Cash, of Ladies of Parnassus, Marlboro, S C	200 00
Cash, of Ladies of Salem (R B), Sumter, S C	329 00
Cash, of Ladies of Cheraw, S C	100 00
Cash, of Ladies of White Plains, S C	[illegible]
Cash, through W Godfrey, S C	156.85
Cash, through Z A Drake, Marlboro, S C	50 00
	$1876 55

Ladies Aid Society, Cheraw, lot of crockery, spoons, tubs, &c.

Ladies Salem (R B), Sumter, bacon, rice, molasses, peas.

Ladies Mount Zion, Sumter, bacon, rice, eggs, potatoes, meal, vinegar, candles.

Citizens of Marlboro, through Z A Drake, 335 lbs. bacon, 4 sacks peas.

Mrs McIver, Society Hill, ham, rice, butter, peas, vinegar.

Mrs Macfarlan, Cheraw, 2 baskets vegetables.

Mrs Benton and Mrs Ellerbe, Cheraw, 1 basket vegetables.

Marlboro Aid Society, 1 basket vegetables and bundle rags.

A W Dozier, Williamsburg, 2 bushels meal and 1 ham.

Mrs Moore, 2 baskets vegetables and 1 loaf bread.

Mrs E Lide, 1 bucket butter.

A Friend, half mutton and bag meal.

Ladies' Aid Society of Cheraw, 1 basket vegetables.

Ladies of Society Hill, 1 basket vegetables.

Respectfully,
J. H. McIVER, Treasurer.

Editor Mercury: Permit me to acknowledge the receipt of the following donations for the support of the Free Market of Charleston:

From a Lady of Williamsburg District	$10
From "Shiloh"	100
From two Refugees, through Dr. Bachman	25
Total	135

GEORGE W. WILLIAMS,
Treasurer Free Market.

CHANGE IN THE NAVY.—The following letter from the Secretary of the Navy to Commodore F. FORREST explains a recent change in the command of the James River Squadron:

RICHMOND, June 18, 1864.

Sir: Your letter of the 15th instant has been received. In response to your letter of the 9th instant, requesting a statement of the reasons which influenced the action of the Department "to relieve you from the command of the James River Squadron," it is deemed proper to say that, while the right of an officer to require of the head of a Department the reasons for relieving him from duty is not admitted, the expression of your apprehension that "the action of the Department may be regarded as based upon charges affecting your character as an officer and gentleman," and "upon the supposition that you had applied to be relieved to avoid an impending conflict with the enemy," induces me to say that nothing affecting your standing as an officer and a gentleman, or inconsistent with your acknowledged zeal and patriotism, has been heard of by the department.

Under the organization of the Provisional Navy an officer of that service was required to command afloat, and you have not been assigned to the Provisional Navy. I am, respectfully, your servant. (Signed) S. R. MALLORY.

To Capt F. Forrest, Richmond, Va.

The Philadelphia Inquirer.

CIRCULATION OVER 60,000. PHILADELPHIA, MONDAY, JULY 11, 1864. PRICE TWO CENTS.

INVASION!!!

Breckinridge Occupies Frederick.

BATTLE OF MONOCACY JUNCTION.

Repulse of the Union Forces.

GEN. WALLACE FALLS BACK.

Enemy at Towsontown.

HEAVY FIRING HEARD IN THE REBEL REAR.

Howe and Couch Probably on Hand.

Reinforcements Arriving for the Enemy.

HILL'S CORPS CROSSES THE POTOMAC

Rebel Force Estimated at 40,000 Men.

GEN. HUNTER'S ADVANCE AT MARTINSBURG.

IT CAPTURES 1000 REBELS.

Great Excitement in Baltimore.

THE CITIZENS RUSHING TO ARMS.

Rebels Moving Toward Washington.

Northern Central Railroad Destroyed

REBEL CAVALRY AT COCKEYSVILLE.

Bush and Gunpowder Bridges Threatened.

THE WESTERN MARYLAND RAILROAD TORN UP.

Proclamation by Gov. Curtin.

A STIRRING CALL TO ARMS.

OUR SPECIAL DESPATCHES.

REPORTS FROM BALTIMORE.

First Despatch.

Special Despatch to the Inquirer.

BALTIMORE, July 10.—Intense excitement prevails here to-day. A joint proclamation of Governor BRADFORD and Mayor CHAPMAN was issued late last night and posted throughout the city, calling upon the citizens generally and the Union Leagues to turn out for the defense of the city. This circular states that a strong force of Rebels is approaching Baltimore, and that General WALLACE has been obliged to fall back, after severe fighting, his numbers being too small to oppose the Rebels, who are believed to be twenty thousand strong.

At six o'clock this morning all the bells of the city rang the alarm for an hour, and subsequently after half an hour's intermission rang another hour. To this the Union men, City Guard and Union Leagues promptly responded, and now, ten o'clock A. M., large companies of citizens, Union Leagues, &c., numbering altogether probably ten thousand men, are marching through the streets, armed, and proceeding to the different fortifications and defenses. In all the past history of this war I have never witnessed such an excitement, and such a gallant determination to die, if necessary, to repel invasion.

Secessionists generally are very quiet and mute. They are mere lookers on, and take no part in our defense, and are seemingly more frightened than the Union people. They all think the Rebels do not design coming into Baltimore, but purpose demonstrating upon Washington. Our police are all armed and at their posts. Very many Southern sympathizers attempted to ride out of town with their horses, buggies, etc., but were pretty generally stopped and their horses impressed. Even the Secesh women are frightened and mute, fearing after consequences if they expose their feelings.

The churches are closed and every one is absorbed in the intense excitement. Rumor, of course, is thousand tongued and intensely wild. The report of General WALLACE being wounded is untrue. Gen. TYLER is a prisoner. Our forces have suffered a pretty severe loss, but still stand up confronting the enemy nobly. Some stragglers arrived here last night, but comparatively few in number. Several ambulances of wounded are on the way to our city.

A despatch, dated midnight, from Westminster, says the Rebels were at New Windsor, seven miles above, destroying the Western Maryland Railroad, the rolling stock of which is all safe in Baltimore. It is also reported to-day that the Rebels possess Westminster, and have sacked the town, and intend proceeding to cut the Northern Central Railway. It is also currently reported, and probably true, that small squads of Rebel cavalry are at several points, from fifteen to eighteen and twenty miles from Baltimore, in different directions.

This is not unlikely. Great activity is visible at military head-quarters, and hope is strong in our ability to defend the city and repel the invaders, if they come, but Secessionists assert they do not design marching on Baltimore. Terrible appliances exist to give them a fatal reception. Our banks and other institutions have taken the precaution to secure their valuables. Public property is also carefully attended to.

There are some apprehension of an attempt to cut the Philadelphia Railroad, but it is well guarded. Northern Central trains run cautiously. Washington trains run regularly. Our streets are crowded with a deeply anxious, and excited populace. Confidence is felt in our ability to repel the invaders if the North does her duty properly. Now is her time to act.

Second Despatch.

Special Despatch to the Inquirer.

BALTIMORE, July 10.—Military movements are contraband; therefore I cannot send them, but I merely say hopeful news prevails at head-quarters. It is now eleven o'clock A. M., and the excitement continues increasing, but all perfectly orderly. The Union Leagues and Union men are behaving nobly. Thousands of citizens are now under arms, stationed at various points of defence, and others are marching to the suburbs.

No doubt General WALLACE will retire upon the defenses of Baltimore. It is still believed that the Rebel leader's ostensible purpose is to attempt the capture of Washington, but they will, if they can, cut all communications this side.

Various seemingly well-founded reports leave no doubt that the Rebel cavalry, in small squads, are now in different parts of Baltimore and Carroll counties, and some of them probably not ten miles from Baltimore.

Colonel LAWRENCE and Colonel WOOLEY, of General WALLACE's staff, with all other officials here, are busily engaged. The entire Union populace seems resolutely determined to defend the city to the death. Secessionists, generally, keep close to their houses, and are very shy as well as frightened. They studiously refrain from invidious language or overt acts, apprehending serious ulterior retaliation.

The telegraph wires to Westminster are cut, and there is no doubt of the Rebels being in that county. Rumors are also circulating of some Rebel scouts being near Laurel.

The main column of the Rebels is somewhere on the Baltimore and Ohio Railroad, probably twenty miles distant; and also others on the Baltimore and Frederick Turnpike. Rumors of all kinds are innumerable, but, upon the whole, the aspect of affairs is alarming, and unprecedently exciting. Persons cannot go outside the city without passes.

Thousands of refugees are arriving in the city. Immense crowds of persons throng all the thoroughfares, and the excitement, if possible, is greater than on and after the 19th of April, 1861. But the Union people hold entire sway. The negro population is much frightened.

Later.

TWELVE O'CLOCK.—It is reported that a considerable force of Rebels is at Cockeysville, fourteen miles out on the Northern Central, and have cut the railroad there, but it is believed the main body is moving on to Washington.

All able-bodied negroes here are being impressed to work on the fortifications. The Custom House and Post Office Departments are acting with approved caution regarding the archives and valuables. Our banks are also assuming some caution.

General WALLACE is still safe. The North and the whole people must arouse without a moment's delay, and rally to the defense of the Capital.

Third Despatch.

Special Despatch to the Inquirer.

BALTIMORE, July 10, 1864.—The Rebels have undoubtedly cut the Northern Central Railroad at Cockeysville and also at Texas, three miles this side, and it is now confidently believed they are making for the Philadelphia, Wilmington and Baltimore Railroad to endeavor to cut it and destroy the bridges. This is merely a small cavalry raid, and the impression still prevails that the main body of Rebels have gone towards Annapolis Junction. Of course the Baltimore and Ohio Railroad is badly damaged. The Northern Central and Baltimore and Ohio Railroads have sent considerable portions of their rolling stock towards Philadelphia. The excitement still continues, but good order prevails. There are some encouraging features, though not prudent to publish.

Fourth Despatch—Excitement Abating—The Fight at Monocacy.

BALTIMORE, July 10, 5 o'clock P. M.—Since so many persons have left the streets and gone to the defenses of the city, the excitement has somewhat abated, but is still very great, and large numbers of people are gathered in the streets, anxious to hear the news.

The Rebels are not known to be nearer Baltimore than Texas, on the Northern Central Railroad, and those only a cavalry corps to cut the road and proceed to cut the Philadelphia road, but the force on that line is believed now amply strong to protect it from depredations.

The cars on it are still running, and the road is safe. The Union citizens of Baltimore, in large force, are still under arms at various points around the city. The feeling is confident, but not altogether sure. Secessionists continue to say that their friends will not enter the city, as it could not be held by them, and all sympathizers would be handled roughly afterward.

It is still believed that the main column of Rebels diverged towards Washington, and some believe for the purpose of retreating, but this is doubtful. All of the Government archieves here, money, and valuable property, have been prepared for instant removal, if necessary, and much of it is already on board of ships in the port.

Drays, carts, and every description of vehicle, have been busy throughout the day. Horses are still being pressed into service, and likewise negroes for labor. There is a guard all around the city, and no one is allowed to leave without a pass. There is a throng at the Baltimore and Ohio Railroad Depot, awaiting news and the arrival of troops.

Some wounded from the late battle on the Monocacy are arriving in the city. The casualties were considerable. The Eleventh Maryland (one hundred days' men) was badly cut up. ALEXANDER's Battery was saved with small loss. General WALLACE is uninjured.

The general aspect of affairs is less alarming. We now hope eventually to hem in and capture the invaders. Let the North send forth every man that can possibly be sent, and all will be well.

Baltimore Last Night.

BALTIMORE, July 10—7 P. M.—The mail and passenger train leaves for Philadelphia and New York to-night at the usual hour. It is strongly guarded. All is quiet, and we have no later news.

Armed citizens and soldiers appear in some parts of the city. Extreme vigilance is observed. Confidence is strengthening as well with the people as with the authorities. The Washington Railroad is uninterrupted.

Fifth Despatch—Fight Near Ellicott's Mills.

BALTIMORE, July 10—7 P. M.—The Independent Telegraph Line bulletins that a fight is now in progress at a point between Elysville and Ellicott's Mills. General WALLACE is holding his ground and driving the Rebels, with considerable loss to them.

Rebel Cavalry Near Baltimore.

BALTIMORE, July 10.—A small Rebel cavalry force is reported to be on the York road, this evening, at a point within five miles of Baltimore.

Sixth Despatch.

BALTIMORE, July 10, 6 P. M.—General SIGEL's wagon train arrived here to-day in charge of a large detachment of infantry and cavalry.

One of the officers who was in the fight says that in all his experience in this war he has never seen more desperate fighting, and he thinks we placed fully as many Rebels *hors du combat* as our own loss.

ALEXANDER's Battery is all safe. Our loss in prisoners is about a thousand, and we have yet no estimate of the number of killed and wounded.

Later.

7 P. M.—It is reported that the advance of a Rebel cavalry force is within seven miles of this city, on the York road. Later intelligence has reached here that a portion of General HUNTER's force, under General SULLIVAN, has recaptured Martinsburg and has taken about one thousand prisoners, also all the stores captured there, and much plunder collected by the Rebels at that point.

10 o'clock, P.M.—Late and reliable accounts represent a Rebel cavalry force at Towsontown, nine miles from Baltimore, this afternoon. Some accounts say they are in strong numbers. The excitement continues to-night, and thousands of Union Leaguers are under arms, guarding the different points. Many citizens were pressed into service to-day, to help load vessels with Government stores. It is now thought from the firing heard south of Ellicotts Mills, that HUNTER and HOWE are attacking the Rebels in their retreat.

Reported Arrival of Hill's Corps in Maryland.

HARRISBURG, July 10, 11 P. M.—Reliable despatches received here, estimate the strength of the enemy at forty thousand, most of which force is now in Maryland.

The advance of General HUNTER's force has arrived at and occupies Martinsburg. It is reported that General A. P. HILL is in command of the Rebel forces, and that his old corps crossed into Maryland at [illegible] Ferry.

To-day the Northern Central Railroad was cut by the enemy at Texas, between Parkton and Baltimore.

The late call for troops by the Governor is meeting with much success, and squads and companies are now arriving by every train.

THE REBEL INVASION.

Map Showing the Region Traversed by the Rebel Army of Invasion—Williamsport, Frederick, Cockeysville, &c.

BATTLE OF MONOCACY.

Stubborn Fighting of Our Forces—Gallantry of the One Hundred Days' Men—Our Little Army Flanked by the Rebels—It is Compelled to Fall Back—Our Loss One Thousand Killed, Wounded and Missing—Rebel Loss Equal to Ours—Breckinridge's Force 12,000 Veterans—Partial List of Casualties.

Special Correspondence of the Inquirer.

NEW MARKET, July 9, 9 P. M.,
VIA BALTIMORE, BY TELEGRAPH, July 10.

The situation in the last two days has changed entirely, and a preliminary glance is necessary to the full appreciation of events. On Friday afternoon last General WALLACE, with a small observing force, was at Frederick, watching the movements of BRADLEY JOHNSON, who was threatening the city from the west with about fifteen hundred infantry and cavalry, and a battery of artillery.

In the middle of the afternoon scouts brought General WALLACE information that BRECKINRIDGE was moving to the support of BRADLEY JOHNSON in such force as would render Frederick untenable, and General WALLACE immediately began preparations for falling back on Monocacy. At twelve o'clock on Friday night the evacuation of Frederick was completed, and our force gathered in hand on the east side of Monocacy."

At about eight o'clock on Saturday, A. M., we had formed a line of battle with our right resting on Gambles Mills, some six hundred yards south of the railroad, and stretching parallel with the river

At 5 in the morning of Saturday, two Rebels rode into Frederick from the Hagerstown Pike, and in a few minutes after, BRADLEY JOHNSON entered with his column, and took possession of the town.

Immediately they moved down the Washington Pike until they met our skirmish line, when brisk firing commenced. The One-hundred-and-tenth and One-hundred-and-twenty-sixth Ohio held their ground firmly, and only fell back when compelled by weight of superior numbers. Thus giving ample time for the completion of our preparation for battle.

General WALLACE, by nine o'clock, when the line of skirmishers were forced back across the river, had his line formed as stated, and was in complete readiness, having burned the turnpike bridge across the Monocacy. The Rebels soon appeared stretching across the fields to the left of the railroad, in strong force, with three batteries of artillery, and the action commenced, the firing being across the river.

At four P. M., however, the Rebels succeeded in getting six regiments and a battery across the river two miles below our position, and coming up across the fields, struck us heavily on our left flank. This movement, with a large force still hammering on our front, made the line of the Monocacy instantly untenable, and our troops were forced in some disorder from their position, and crowded back across the railroad.

Our line of retreat was straight across the country, towards the Baltimore pike, which we struck two miles east of New Market.

Our losses, to-day, are estimated at one thousand, mostly captured after we were flanked. The Rebel loss in killed and wounded is believed to be fully as large as our entire loss. It is rumored and believed that General TYLER is captured, but how it happened is not known.

The testimony is universal that our troops all behaved most admirably, and only yielded to the pressure of overwhelming numbers, which enabled the Rebels to display heavy forces in our front and still throw six regiments on our flank.

General WALLACE was on the field during the entire fight, in personal command, and made the most of his small force.

I hear that Colonel SEWARD, Ninth New York Heavy Artillery, is wounded.

The impression is general that the enemy's force to-day numbered at least ten thousand or twelve thousand veterans, and supposed to be under command of BRECKINRIDGE.

FROM THE SAME CORRESPONDENT.

Special Despatch to the Inquirer.

BALTIMORE, July 10.—I send the following partial list of casualties in the Eighty-seventh Pennsylvania Volunteers in the fight at Monocacy:—[illegible] Martin, mortally; Wm. Crabb, Co. E; Wm. Long, E; John W. Robert, C; George Bloutcher, E; Robert Dice, C; Thomas McLean, I; Lieut. Charles Holtke, K; Sergeant Elias Sheets, F; Lewis Rush, K; Lieut. Spangler, A; Sergeant H. Waltimore, C; Corporal James Henry, C; Jonas Snyder, C; Henry Bordner, C; Captain Lanaes, staff; John L. Ritter, H; Anthony Wolf, H; George Long, F, Sergeant W. F. Eckert, G; Sergeant Henry Stine, G; Corporal Jacob Schultz, G; John Wychtenberger, G.

Killed—Lieutenant D. P. Dietrich, Company H; Sergeant D. L. Welsh, Company G.

Casualties in the One-hundred-and-Thirty-eighth Pennsylvania Regiment

I have not yet obtained.

The Sixty-seventh Pennsylvania Regiment was not engaged.

Captain ADAM G. KING, Assistant Adjutant-General on the Staff of General RICKETTS, is mortally wounded.

Colonel SEWARD, of the Ninth New York Heavy Artillery, is reported wounded; but not a prisoner.

Lieutenant-Colonel TAFT, of the same regiment, is reported killed.

In the One-Hundred-and-Twenty-second Ohio, Captain THOMAS HUTCHINSON is wounded; One-Hundred-and-Tenth Ohio, Captains HASAWAY, SNODGRASS, BROWN and TRIMBLE, are killed. This regiment suffered heavily.

Heavy firing was heard this afternoon, in the direction of the Rebel rear, and the probabilities are that the enemy was being pressed by our forces in the rear.

The enemy is not pushing WALLACE at all, and has not at any time during the day. His whereabouts are exceedingly difficult to locate, and it is hardly worth while sending you any of the wild rumors to be heard on the streets. I do not think Baltimore is seriously threatened. The enemy is aiming for a different point, or else is endeavoring to escape, and it is hard to tell which now.

This city is being rapidly put in a state of complete defense, and is behaving admirably. I see no signs of the wild, aimless excitement usual in cities on occasions like this, but in its stead a vigor and systematic industry in preparation for meeting the enemy that augur well.

This morning all the various loyal organizations of the city assembled in obedience to the proclamation of Governor BRADFORD and Mayor CHAPMAN, and are being rapidly rendered into an effective army by General LOCKWOOD. The military situation at this moment is not considered critical, and all reports of heavy fighting at any point are unfounded. The enemy is reported to be nine miles out on the York road, but it is not believed.

General WALLACE, in a despatch of this morning's date, said the enemy was not pressing him. I can not now state definitely the force and the whereabouts of the enemy, nor can any one else.

The impression is general at Ellicott's Mills that HUNTER or HOWE is pressing the enemy in the rear, heavy firing being heard in that direction.

OUR LATEST SPECIAL.

Attack on the Rebel Rear.

BALTIMORE, July 10, 11·30 P. M.—The advance of the enemy is about seven miles beyond Ellicott's Mills. General WALLACE has had no fighting to-day.

It is confirmed that heavy firing has been heard near Monocacy, in the enemy's rear, and his actions there indicated that he feared danger from that quarter. The city is perfectly quiet at this hour, no [illegible] the streets or excitement of any kind.

Continued on the Eighth Page.

The Charleston Mercury.

DAILY PAPER—TWENTY DOLLARS FOR SIX MONTHS—PAYABLE IN ADVANCE.

VINDICE NULLO
SPONTE SUA SINE LEGE FIDES RECTUMQUE COLLENTUR.

COUNTRY PAPER—THRICE A WEEK—TWELVE DOLLARS FOR SIX MONTHS—PAYABLE IN ADVANCE.

Volume LXXXV | CHARLESTON, S. C., MONDAY, JULY 25, 1864. | Number 12,121.

TELEGRAPHIC.

Glorious News from Atlanta.

DEFEAT OF SHERMAN'S ARMY!

Capture of Two Thousand Prisoners, Twenty-Five Cannon and Seven Stand of Colors.

HARDEE AT WORK IN THE ENEMY'S REAR.

HEAVY LOSS OF GENERAL OFFICERS.

General Hood's Official Despatch.

How the News was Received in Richmond.

&c. &c. &c.

FROM THE FIELD OF BATTLE.

ATLANTA, July 22.—About 2 o'clock this afternoon, the enemy attacked our left under STEWART. They were received with a galling fire from both our artillery and infantry, which caused them to falter, when the order was given to our line to charge. Our troops sprang from their breastworks and charged with great gallantry, driving the enemy, with immense slaughter, from two lines of his entrenchments, and capturing twenty-two pieces of artillery and a large number of prisoners. Among the killed on the Yankee side, are Maj Gen. MCPHERSON, shot through the heart, and Brig. Gen. GILES A. SMITH and the Yankee Gen. HOOD. Gen. GRESHAM lost a leg.

General HARDEE, having passed round the enemy's flank, is now in his rear, doing great execution. The fighting still continues.

OFFICIAL DISPATCH FROM GEN. HOOD.

RICHMOND, July 23.—The following was received at the War Office at noon to-day:

HEADQUARTERS, Atlanta, July 22—10 p. m.

To the Secretary of War: The army shifted its position, fronting on Peach Tree Creek last night. STEWART'S and CHEATHAM'S corps formed our line of battle around the city, while HARDEE'S corps, having made a night march, attacked the enemy's extreme left to-day about 10 a. m. He drove him from his works, capturing sixteen pieces of artillery and five stand of colors.

CHEATHAM also attacked the enemy, capturing six pieces of artillery. During the engagement we captured about two thousand prisoners. WHEELER'S cavalry also attacked and routed the enemy in the neighborhood of Decatur, to-day, capturing his camp.

Our loss is not yet fully ascertained. Maj Gen. W. H. T. WALKER was killed, and Brig. Gens. SMITH, GIST and MERCER were wounded.

Our troops fought with great gallantry.

(Signed) J. B. HOOD, General.

RECEPTION OF THE NEWS IN RICHMOND.

RICHMOND, July 23.—The telegrams conveying the glorious tidings of the success near Atlanta, yesterday, was posted on the bulletin board at an early hour to-day, diffusing general joy throughout the community. Whilst the battle was deemed imminent, people here were somewhat taken by surprise by the announcement of the victory, and anxiously awaited the official confirmation of the news, which came to hand at noon. Everybody is applauding General HOOD and his noble army for the skill and gallantry displayed by them in this engagement.

THE LATEST.

ATLANTA, July 23.—General WHEELER last evening attacked the enemy's left, in the neighborhood of Decatur. He drove them back, capturing five hundred wagons, laden with supplies, and a large number of prisoners. He is still in pursuit.

There was very little fighting after dark yesterday. Two thousand prisoners, seventy-five commissioned officers, twenty five pieces of artillery and seven stand of colors have been brought in.

The losses on either side are not yet known. Ours was severe in officers.

Comparative quiet reigns this morning. There is some little skirmishing going on along our left.

[Despatch to the South Carolinian.]

ATLANTA, July 22.—The great struggle for Atlanta commenced to-day, immediately surrounding the city on the north side, in the form of a semi-circle, and opened with artillery, which continued until about 2 o'clock. HARDEE and WHEELER were detached the night before by Gen. HOOD, and by this time struck the enemy's left, making a flank movement, when HOOD's old corps, under CHEATHAM, advanced from their breastworks and drove the enemy's lines over their breastworks more than a mile, capturing a large number of guns, flags and prisoners. The battle is not yet concluded—HARDEE is still pressing on the Federal flank, having captured 16 guns and about 2500 prisoners. The total number of guns on hand from 23 to 24; prisoners, nearly 4000. The Federal General MCPHERSON is reported killed, also several brigadiers. Gen. W. H. WALKER and Col. MAURY were killed; Gens. GIST, GILES A. SMITH, COLQUITT and STAPLES wounded; Col. PRESSLY, of the 19th South Carolina, shot, though not dangerously; Lieut. JOLLY and C. HABERSHAM, of Savannah, killed.

There was much hand to hand fighting. The enemy is crippled both in *morale* and losses, while our troops are in splendid spirits, and expect to renew the battle every moment. The Georgia militia, under General GUSTAVUS W. SMITH, won golden opinions. They were as steady as veterans. WHEELER'S cavalry greatly distinguished themselves, carrying a line of formidable breastworks, and capturing the garrison, camp equipments and many prisoners.

SEVERE STORM ON THE COAST.

WILMINGTON, July 24.—A storm has been raging seaward, from the northeast, all day long. At this hour (8 p. m.) it is quite severe.

THE YANKEE PRISONERS.—We are informed that the Yankee officers at Camp Oglethorpe are very confident of an early release from confinement. They say that Sherman will have possession of Macon before many weeks are over, and then they will have no occasion to await an exchange. Perhaps Sherman will come here. There is no knowing what the chances of war are. He may be taken prisoner by some enterprising cavalry man, and brought to this city for safe keeping, but we do not believe that the Federal army is likely to reach Macon for some [illegible] Atlanta [illegible] doubt in our mind [illegible]

[*Macon Telegraph.*

THE MERCURY

MONDAY, JULY 25, 1864.

Sennacherib and our Yankee Foes.

History is repeating itself every day, because human nature is the same at all periods of the world and amongst all nations. The course of SENNACHERIB towards the Jews was strikingly like that of the Yankees towards the Confederate States.

1. Without just cause, the Assyrians had exacted tribute from the Jews. HEZEKIAH, the King of the Jews, refused to pay it, and SENNACHERIB "came up against all the fenced cities of Judah, and took them," and invested Jerusalem.

The Yankees exacted of us tribute, through their protective tariffs, &c., which we have refused to pay, and they have made war upon us—taken many of our cities, and assailed Richmond.

2. SENNACHERIB knew how to bully and boast; "and RABSHAKEH said unto them, speak ye now "to HEZEKIAH—thus will the great King, the "King of Assyria—what confidence is this where "in thou trustest.

"Thou sayest (but they are but vain words) I "have counsel and strength for the war: Now on "whom dost thou trust, that thou *rebellest* against "me.

"Hearken not unto HEZEKIAH when he persuadeth you, saying, the Lord will deliver us.

"Hath any of the Gods of the nations delivered at all his land out of the hands of the King "of Assyria?"

SENNACHERIB called the Jews *rebels* ("thou rebellest against *me*"), just as our Yankee foes do the people of the Confederate States; whilst against our saying, like that of HEZEKIAH—"the Lord will deliver us"—they set up their strength and power.

3. But SENNACHERIB, would be pious, as well as boastful. He affected to consider himself under the special guidance of God. He said: "Am "I now come up without the Lord against this "place to destroy it? The Lord said to me, go "up against this land and destroy it."

And thus it is with our Yankee foes. They affect to consider themselves as acting under the divine impulse and direction, in desolating our country and murdering our people. When they accomplish a huge slaughter, they offer up thanksgiving and praise to God; and they have lately appointed a day of humiliation and prayer to obtain his aid and blessing, in their efforts, by fire and sword—rapine and murder, to destroy our people and desolate our country.

4. SENNACHERIB was a politician as well as a warrior, and quite adroit in deceitful promises. He said to the Jews: "Hearken not unto HEZEKIAH; for thus saith the King of Assyria: "'Make *an agreement* with me, *by a present*, and "*come out* to me, and then eat ye every man of "his own vine, and every man of his own fig "tree, and drink ye, every one, the waters of "his cistern.'"

Is not this exactly the policy of our Yankee foes? Make "*an agreement* with them," "and come out to them"—that is, separate from the Confederate States, and go under their authority; and "make an agreement with them *by a present*"—that is, pay them tribute; and then the traitors are to have great prosperity—"then eat ye, every "man, of his own vine, and every man of his "own fig tree, and drink ye, every one, the "waters of his cistern." Unfortunately the state of things in some small portions of the Confederate States shows that such an appeal may still have its delusions.

5. But may we not hope, that as our Yankee foes, have imitated SENNACHERIB in his boastfulness—his blasphemy—and his lying, so they will be, like him, discomfited?

"Therefore thus with the Lord, concerning "the King of Assyria, he shall not come into "this city, nor shoot an arrow there, nor come "before it with shield, nor cast a brick against "it. By the way that he came, by the same shall "he return, and shall not come into this city, "with the Lord. For I will defend this city, to "save it, for my own sake, and for my servant "DAVID's sake. And it came to pass that night, "that the angel of the Lord went out and smote "in the camp of the Assyrian's a hundred four-"score and five thousand; and when they arose "early in the morning, behold! they were all "dead men. So SENNACHERIB King of Assyria "departed, and went and returned and dwelt in "Nineveh."

The Western Side of the Mississippi.

The New York *Herald*, in an editorial, speaks as follows:

Our private advices from the Lower Mississippi represent affairs there to be in a most unsatisfactory state. We may consider the whole Western bank of the river as gone—lapsed into rebel hands once more—lost to us by the inconceivable mismanagement of the administration. New Orleans is all that is left to us; and the reason is apparent enough. We have lost all that country just as an army is cut to pieces, when, having won a battle, it loses all organization, and gives itself up to a wild riot of plunder, while its enemy rallies and returns to the fight. No sooner was this Mississippi country in our possession than it was fairly deluged with plunderers under the designation of treasury agents, navy agents, army agents, and all other sorts of agents. Hordes of these men were everywhere, and they had no thought but to make money. Bribery was as common as the air, and a universal demoralization ruled and ruined us. Great disasters will yet come to us from this very quarter, if the President does not change his policy in relation to it. But to change his policy he must change his Cabinet.

The *Herald*, like all Yankee sources of information, does not disclose the whole truth. Its correspondent correctly discloses the condition of things on the Western bank of the Mississippi. It says, truly, that the whole country on the other side of the Mississippi "*is gone,—lapsed into rebel hands once more; and New Orleans alone is left to us*"—but it does not assign the true cause for this state of things. The Yankee [illegible] and corruption, no doubt, has been enormous, but this would not return that whole country to the possession and control of the Confederate States. It was accomplished by successful fighting on the part of the Confederate States, in which BANKS was whipped by KIRBY SMITH and TAYLOR, and driven down the [illegible] New Orleans. The fact, however, that we have undisputed possession of this country, is one of vast significance. What is our large army on the Western side of the Mississippi now doing? General TAYLOR, in a congratulatory address to his command, intimated that New Orleans was to be recaptured. It is clear that it is free to operate against the enemy in any other direction most advantageous to the Confederacy. Where is that direction? Can any man, having the least knowledge of the state of things in the West, doubt the proper field for its operations? The Army of Tennessee has been forced to retreat, by the greater numbers of the enemy, from Chattanooga to Atlanta. Northern Georgia, and Alabama are being overrun by the enemy, whilst Montgomery and Atlanta are in danger of falling into their hands. Why has not General KIRBY SMITH, with his army, been ordered a month ago across the Mississippi, and march to the relief of the Army of Tennessee? A union of these two armies would secure the defeat of General SHERMAN, carry the tide of war through Kentucky, and command peace.

The New Commander of the Army of Tennessee.

Gen. HOOD was born in Bath County, Kentucky, on the 29th of June, 1831, and is consequently only a little over 33 years of age. He graduated at West Point in the class of 1853, and was assigned to duty in the Fourth infantry, in California, where he served twenty-two months. In July, 1855, he was transferred to the 2d cavalry, commanded by the late General (then Colonel) ALBERT SIDNEY JOHNSTON, and of which General R. E. LEE was Lieutenant Colonel. In the winter of 1855—'56 he entered upon the frontier service in Western Texas, where, in the July following, he was wounded in a spirited engagement with the Indians. He continued in the service of the United States, and a short time previous to the beginning of the present war was ordered to report for duty at West Point as instructor of cavalry. At his own request, however, he was allowed to return to duty in Texas, being desirous of casting his destinies with that portion of the country to which he was most devotedly attached. On the 16th of April, 1861, he resigned his commission and tendered his services to the Confederacy. His name was entered upon the roll with the rank of First Lieutenant, and he was ordered to report to Gen. LEE in Virginia. He served with distinction on the Peninsula, and so rapid was his promotion that on the 30th of September he received the commission of Colonel of Infantry, and was placed in command of the Fourth Regiment of Texas Volunteers, then in camp near Richmond. Subsequently the Fourth and Fifth Texas Regiments were organized into a Brigade, and on the 31 of March, 1862, Colonel HOOD was appointed to the command. Thus within the brief space of ten months and seventeen days he rose from the rank of First Lieutenant to that of Brigadier. At the battle of Chickamauga, as in every other battle in which he was engaged, General HOOD bore a prominent part, and was so severely wounded in the right leg as to render amputation necessary. For signal courage displayed on that hard-fought field, he was made Lieutenant-General. As soon as he had sufficiently recovered, he resumed his active duties in the Army of Tennessee, of which he has now the command.

IMPORTANT FROM GEORGIA—SHERMAN'S RAIDERS AT WORK ON THE RAILROADS.

While the main armies of SHERMAN and HOOD are confronting each other around Atlanta, the Yankee raiding parties are very active in their depredations upon the railroads. The Augusta *Constitutionalist* of Saturday, in noticing the raid on the Georgia Road, says:

By passengers that arrived on the train this morning we learn that the Federals captured two trains, yesterday morning, at Conyers. One of the engineers escaped, and procuring a mule, made his way towards Covington. When he arrived there he saw a force of the enemy approaching the place, and continued on down to Rutledge. All the stock of the company, we learn, was moved from Rutledge to Union Point last night. Rumor also says the enemy have burned Yellow River and Alcova Bridges, and the depot at Covington. We give place to these reports in order to satisfy the anxiety of our people for intelligence of operations from Atlanta and vicinity, not that we give them full credit, but in order that they may not be deceived and unnecessarily excited by wild and unfounded rumors.

The same paper, in its issue of Sunday, tells us that—

A despatch from General Hood states that the Yankee raiding force now making havoc along the Georgia Railroad numbers three brigades of cavalry. A Confederate cavalry force had left Atlanta in pursuit. Ample preparations have been made to give the raiders a warm reception in case they progress much farther in this direction. A gentleman who came from Athens yesterday evening states that the enemy had not been seen this side of Alcova bridge. The rumor that the Yankees were in force at High Shoals nine miles from Athens, on Friday, needs confirmation.

The Columbus Ga. *Sun* Extra, of Thursday, says, that the citizens of that place were all agog and under arms to repel a raid expected from the direction of the Montgomery and West Point Railroad. The negro men had all been ordered to work on the fortifications. The *Sun* gives the following account of the doings of the raiders:

From the best information that our reporter could obtain—who returned last evening from the front—the raiders most thoroughly did their work of destruction of the superstructure of the Montgomery and West Point Railroad, from a point near Chehaw to another some two or three miles east of Opelika, and also of one and a half miles of the Columbus branch road. The stringers and ties were piled first, the iron rails on top, fire applied underneath, and as the rails became sufficiently heated other means were applied to aid in distorting them. The number of miles of road thus destroyed is probably between thirty and thirty-five. The raiders destroyed no private property, so far as now known, and committed no robberies excepting, perhaps, those of live stock and provisions. They destroyed Government property wherever found. They said that they came solely for the purposes of damaging the road and destroying Government property. They also said that they came with the expectation of being captured. This accounts for their having destroyed so much within the short space of two days. The raiders left the railroad Tuesday evening, and the last news from them is that they had passed through Lafayette, Chambers county, Alabama, that night. It is reported that Col. Lery, with a detachment of General Clanton's Alabama brigade, was in pursuit of them; and also that a detachment of General ——'s brigade, from West Point, is trying to intercept the raiders.

A CHARACTERISTIC YANKEE TRICK.—It appears from the annexed note that a quantity of forged Confederate bonds of £20 each, have been put in circulation in this country:

I have discovered that a large amount of counterfeit Confederate $100 bonds have been sent here from New York and sold. I know of one batch of $62,000 sold here to go to Holland. I have no doubt an enormous amount has been put in circulation. Of course, the trade will continue. It certainly is the duty of somebody to make this thing known, and to caution the public to avoid all bonds coming from doubtful sources. I have now before me five $100 coupon rights, purporting to be of July, 1872 per Act of Congress August 19, 1861, and dated 7th and 8th of May, 1862. The engraver of the genuine (B. Duncan) is here, and pronounces them counterfeits beyond question.

[*London Times* (*City Article*), *June 15.*

ADDITIONAL FROM THE NORTH.

We give below some additional intelligence from our latest Northern papers:

THE NEW SECRETARY OF THE YANKEE TREASURY

The Yankees are painting up their new Secretary of the Treasury. His name is PITT, which is considered a big thing in Yankeedom, though it is suggested that, if he expects to pay all the debts LINCOLN has contracted, he must be the "bottomless pit." A letter to the Washington *Republican*, describing him, says:

William Pitt Fessenden stands at this time, without a doubt, at the head of the American Senate. I suppose him to be nearly six feet in height, possibly two inches under that measurement, and he would not, in my judgment, weigh over one hundred and fifty or sixty pounds. His face long and rather severe in expression, heavy eyebrows, dark brown hair streaked with gray, were rather long and with a slight inclination to curl. I judge him to be about forty-five years of age. I should not think him a man of strong friendship, and yet he seems to be on familiar terms with all the Senators, occasionally enjoying a kind of dry laugh with those who come to him, or to whom he goes to chat. He pays little attention to style in dress, being behind the fashion, but there is nothing of the sloven in his appearance. His voice is clear, rather sharp in tone, and speaks naturally and with about the proper amount of gesture. He impresses any one that hears him that he is not talking for talk's sake, but simply filling his position as a statesman, by bringing the powers of his mind to the elucidation of the subject matter under discussion. There is nothing florid in the style of Mr. Fessenden, but, on the contrary, his oratory is solid, probing, and yet sufficiently graceful to secure the attention of his audience.

The correspondent of the Springfield, Massachusetts *Republican*, writes the following account of how he was appointed:

The President was very low spirited on Thursday—the day on which he sent in the nomination of Dave Todd. He seems to have been deserted of his usual good sense when he sent in this name to the Senate. The feeling was unanimous in Congress that for such a man to succeed Mr. Chase was ruinous to the finances. On Thursday night Governor Todd sent his declination, and Mr. Lincoln went to bed upon it, and, as he says, before morning he was satisfied that Pitt Fessenden was the man. Early Friday he ordered the nomination to be made out, and Major Hay took it down to the Senate. Five minutes after he had left Senator Fessenden entered the Presidential apartment and was soon discussing the "situation." Mr. Lincoln did not tell him what he had done, but discussed Mr. Chase's resignation for a short time, and then said, "Mr. Fessenden, I have made a new nomination this morning which I hope you will approve; I have sent your own name in." Mr. Fessenden was greatly surprised and amazed. He replied, "You must recall it; you can overtake Hay with a messenger now if you will. Please send for him at once, for I cannot possibly take it. My health will not permit me to think of it for a moment." But the President was firm. "You must take it," he said, and later in the day he sent word as follows: "Tell Fessenden to stick." Meantime telegrams from all parts of the country came pouring in upon him, congratulating him upon his admirable selection. At night Mr. Lincoln was in fine spirits, and he exclaimed to Mr. Seward who was present: "The Lord has never yet deserted me, and I did not believe he would this time!" It was Mr. Lincoln's intention to send in the name of Ex-Governor Boutwell if Mr. Fessenden had positively declined.

GOVERNOR SEYMOUR'S CONDUCT IN ORGANIZING THE NATIONAL GUARD.

The Washington correspondent of the Boston *Traveller* thinks Governor SEYMOUR, of New York is taking a rather mean advantage of LINCOLN in his distress. While the "rebels" are holding his head down, it looks to the correspondent very much like Governor SEYMOUR was quietly tying his legs. He says:

Governor Seymour is making the General Government trouble. He seems to think that the present moment is his opportunity, and he therefore orders his District Attorney to execute the laws of the State without reference to the orders of the President, and General Dix is in hot water. The President will probably give way, as he did in the case of Vallandigham, doubtless being satisfied that the seizure of the World and Journal of Commerce newspapers was a mistake. But the difficulty is to extricate General Dix from his dilemma. He is held by the State authorities, and if punished, it will be because he obeyed the President.

It will be extremely hard, and even cowardly, for the Government to desert him, and it cannot afford to do it. Yet Mr. Lincoln is greatly troubled upon the subject. Everybody knows that if Gen. Grant had succeeded in capturing Richmond, Gov. Seymour would not have taken such a defiant stand against the General Government. Like all cowards, he puts on airs when his opponent is in trouble. The rebels are threatening Pennsylvania, New York is called upon to furnish twelve thousand three months' men. Gen. Grant needs reinforcements. A draft is impending. And of course Gov. Seymour is courageous.

THE ESCAPE OF GEN. FRANKLIN.

Major General Franklin arrived in Baltimore during Wednesday night, and was Thursday at Barnum's Hotel, resting from his fatigue and exposure. The following is a brief account of his capture and escape:

He was seated in the car, at the time of his capture, alongside of a wounded Lieutenant Colonel, when a rebel officer came in the train and addressing himself to the wounded man, said: "Are you Major General Franklin?" He replied that he was not and gave him his name and rank.

General Franklin was in citizens dress, but the rebel also put the question to him, and frankly answered that such was his name and rank. There was no doubt in his mind, from the manner of the interrogator, that he had been pointed out by some of the passengers. The rebel said: "General, I am happy to see you." The General replied: "I cannot say that I am pleased to see you, under the circumstances."

About ten minutes afterwards Gilmer came into the car, and addressing himself to Major General Franklin, said: "General, you will consider yourself my prisoner." He was then put in a carriage, and with other prisoners driven through the country, stopping awhile at Towsontown, and then across to the Reisterstown road, where they arrived about 1 o'clock on Tuesday morning, and immediately bivouacked for the night.

The General was put in custody of Captains Owens and two guards, who were charged with his safe keeping. Expressing himself as sick and weary, he immediately laid down and feigned sleep. Soon after the captain and his guards laid down, and he listened anxiously for indications of sleep on their part. He had not to wait long before he heard the guard nearest to him commence to breathe heavily, momentarily increasing in volume and profundity, until it became sufficiently loud to wake an ordinary sleeper. The captain and his other guard had also in the meantime commenced to breathe rather heavy, and the General continued, with his ears open, also to feign sleep. He laid in this way for some time, until all three gave unmistakable signs of sleep. Fearing that they were playing possum, he got up and walked carelessly around them, moved over to the fence, and still watched them. He then coughed loudly and made considerable noise, thinking that they wanted an excuse to shoot at him, each man laying with the right hand grasping the muzzles of their rifles.

The indications of profound sleep being so unmistakable on the part of all three of them, he now thought that he would test the sincerity of their slumbers by jumping the fence. This he did, and on looking back could see no movement of the dusky forms of his guardians, and off he went across several fields, jumping fences, and keeping straight ahead in the direction he thought would take him towards the city. He ran for about three quarters of an hour, when he entered a thick woods, and in his weakly state, being really broken down by fatigue, he sought a place of concealment.

STARTLING DECLINE IN THE SHIPPING OF THE UNITED STATES.

The *Florida*, while sending to the bottom some Yankee vessels, has been the means of bringing to the top some statistics which show a startling decline in the shipping of that nation. From the first place in the maritime world the United States has descended to about the fifth. The New York *World* says:

In 1860 the total tonnage of the United States, exclusive of whaling and steam tonnage, was five million two hundred and nineteen thousand one hundred and eighty-one tons. In 1864 it is in the neighborhood of one million six hundred and seventy-four thousand five hundred and sixteen tons. That is, we have lost in four years three million five hundred and forty four thousand six hundred and sixty-five tons. We say nothing of the loss through the involuntary idleness of our vessels—nothing of the number of ships that lie rotting at our wharves and at foreign ports. We would simply ask, at the rate given above, how long a time must elapse before our commercial marine will be entirely wiped out, and the American flag unknown in any foreign port, or even on our own seas, save as seen upon ships-of-war? From being actually greater than that of any other nation on the face of the earth, our tonnage has dwindled below the standard of the third rate maritime powers.

More than nine hundred vessels that in 1860 were owned by citizens of the United States, and floated the Stars and Stripes, are now in the hands of foreign owners and sailing under foreign flags. On Thursday morning last we published a list of the names and owners of six hundred of these vessels—having an aggregate tonnage of three hundred and twenty eight thousand six hundred and sixty-five tons—sold during the single year 1863 to British owners, as compiled from British authority, and to which list the reader can easily turn. Foreigners will not ship goods in American bottoms, and so our vessels must either rot in port or become the property of people of other nationality. Not a single American steamer crosses the ocean at the present time—our steamships doing a pitiful duty as coasters, and even then with no sense of security. Foreign steamers carry our mails and freight, and transport such of our citizens whom business or pleasure calls upon a foreign soil.

THE REBELS AT HAGERSTOWN—HOW THEY BEHAVED—LEVY OF MONEY AND BACON—THEY GATHER A HARVEST.

The following interesting statement of the "outrageous doin's" of the rebels at Hagerstown is taken from the Chambersburg (Pa.) *Repository:*

On Tuesday afternoon the rebel advance drove our pickets into the town. On Wednesday afternoon General McCausland, the successor of General Jenkins, entered the town with about one thousand five hundred cavalry. He levied twenty thousand dollars upon the town, and seized Mr. Thomas A. Bolt, a silversmith, and we believe, a member of the Council, to be held as a hostage for the payment of the money. The money was raised and paid in Maryland funds—rebel currency being contemptuously refused. There were large Government stores in various places in town, and General McCausland didn't seem to have an appetite for applying the torch, so he placed Mr. Isaac Nesbit, Clerk of the Courts, under heavy bonds to have the stores destroyed.

The bond was given, and the stores burned after the rebels departed. An additional ransom of one thousand five hundred dollars was paid by Messrs. Nesbit, Hamilton, and a few others to save the warehouses of Messrs. Thurston & Eichelberger, as their destruction would have periled private property seriously. Zeller & Co having no Government stores in their warehouse, it was not disturbed, although taken possession of by the rebel officers. There was a large amount of private corn, oats, &c., in it; but, when they were satisfied that it was all owned by individuals, it was not moved or injured. The following receipt was given Mr. Zeller when his warehouse was seized:

QUARTERMASTER'S DEPARTMENT, FOURTEENTH VIRGINIA CAVALRY, July 6

"By order of General McCausland I have taken charge of all stores in Zeller & Co.'s private warehouse. The amount of goods I cannot estimate, but this will show the disposition of them.

H. R. CUSHAW, Acting Brigade Quar.

Considering that Mr. Zeller was one of the most earnest Union men in the place, he was treated rather fairly. The Government stores, however, more than supplied their wants, and any injury to Mr. Zeller would have been wanton destruction of private property. We do not learn that they so destroyed property of any description, violent as were their threats at times. About 2 a. m., on Thursday morning, McCausland's command left.

Scouting parties still hovered in and about the town, and about daylight of the same day Gen. Imboden came in with about one hundred and eighty men, to supply his command with certain articles not to be had conveniently in the dominions of Jeff Davis. The hat store of Messrs. Rouskulp and Updegraff, and the shoe store of Mr. Knoble, did a large trade with them—the trade being wholly on the side of the rebels, and Judge Small's shoe store narrowly escaped by the rebels being called off suddenly by the startling cry that "the Yanks are upon us!" Major Davis had the immediate command under Imboden. The only property burned was the railroad water tank and wood house.

A reporter who witnessed "the whole rebel movement in Hagerstown," and was present at several conversations between Gen. MCCAUSLAND and the citizens, says:

The spokesman of the Council and citizens was Col. Schley, aided by Mr. Seyster and several others who occupy a conservative position—so conservative, indeed, that they lean a little over perpendicular on the rebel side. When the demand was made for twenty thousand dollars, Messrs. Schley and Seyster called upon General McCausland and declared their inability to raise the money and clothing. The insurgent chief—a fierce, middle-sized man, with red, bushy whiskers—answered them in the following rather emphatic than poetical manner: "By ——, if you don't have the money and clothing by half-past eight o'clock this evening, I will burn every house in town, if it costs me my own life and that of all my command!" Schley was almost equally emphatic in returning compliments with the rebel chief. He intimated that he was a thief and a freebooter, but it did not disturb the guerilla's equanimity, nor lessen his taste for plunder. The demand was for fifteen hundred suits of clothing in addition to the twenty thousand dollars, but the clothing could not be found.

The rebel General was inexorable, and, whether the clothing was there or not, he must have it. Finally, all the clothing that could be found was gathered up—including children's shoes and many other articles entirely useless to the army—and when about everything was got that could be found "Southern brethren" of "My Maryland" were content. It was remarkable that they made no discrimination between rebel sympathisers and Union men. Mr. Bell, druggist, who has a brother in the rebel army, and who is said to lean that way himself, had his stock "confiscated" in the most approved freebooter's style; and when a rebel sympathiser expostulated with them for robbing their friends—one who had a brother in the "service—they politely answered that if Mr. Bell was their friend he should be with his brother in their army. The rebel sympathisers generally were very indignant at the indiscriminate propensities for stealing manifested by their constitutional friends, and curses loud and deep might have been heard on every corner from the disappointed and humiliated allies of treason.

A special committee of the right shade called on General McCausland to remonstrate about some order he had issued, and he dismissed them summarily by saying that as they could send these abolition delegates to Annapolis, they could certainly comply with any reasonable demand made by the rebels. Many of the fiercest rebel sympathizers openly declare that they hope General McCausland may receive the first Yankee bullet that is fired into his command. Altogether, secesh is by no means pleased with secession. It is rumored that they levied on Middletown for five thousand pounds of bacon, on Boonsboro' for one thousand, and on Frederick for two hundred thousand dollars.

On Saturday the rebels left the vicinity of Hagerstown, and moved towards Frederick, where they doubtless joined the main forces across the Potomac. On Saturday evening and during Sunday and Monday, there was a steady stream of horses and contrabands returning South, where we hope that they may gather their harvest in peace.

BLOCKADE ITEMS.—We get the following paragraphs from the latest Northern papers received:

The British prize steamer Boston, from Bermuda for Wilmington, North Carolina, which was captured on the 8th instant, off the latter port, by the United States steamer Fort Jackson, arrived at Boston last week. She is a double-decked, side wheel, wooden steamer, of about three hundred and fifty tons burden, and has a walking beam engine. She was purchased at Halifax about seven months ago for thirty five thousand dollars, and fitted up for running the blockade. On the first attempt at this business she was captured. Her cargo consisted of four hundred and fifty sacks salt, twenty-four bales of copperas, and one hundred boxes of soap.

The prize steamer Little Ada, from Nassau, N. P., arrived at Boston last week, having been captured on the 8th instant while attempting to run the blockade into Charleston by the United States steamer Gettysburg. She has a general cargo of merchandise, is an iron propeller of about one hundred and twenty tons, carries only one mast, and hails from Savannah.

The prize steamer Greyhound, captured about the 10th of May, while running out of Wilmington, was sold last week at Boston for forty thousand dollars. Her cargo of cotton, tobacco and spirits of turpentine was sold for over five hundred thousand dollars, and the total amount of money, realized by the capture will be upwards of six hundred thousand dollars. The Greyhound is a three masted, schooner rigged iron propeller. She is considered a very fast steamer, having several times run the blockade at Wilmington.

MRS. ABE LINCOLN "AT HOME"—A writer in the Mobile Register remarks that before the advent of Mrs Lincoln, the White House was the scene only of those simple, republican forms of reception observed in the stately yet plain style of Mrs. Madison, the agreeable soirees of Mrs. Tyler, the unostentatious levees of Mrs Polk, and the chaste elegance that adorned the little reunions of Miss Lane. But the present mistress proceeds on a different plan, and gorges her guests not so much with cultivated hospitality as with the grosser luxuries of the larder and wine cellar.

Mrs. Lincoln has learned something from her first lesson. Soon after she became the lady of the Executive Mansion, she went to Gautier and asked him if he could furnish a dinner for thirty persons, wine included, for three dollars a piece? The old Frenchman opened his eyes. "Pardon, madame," said he, "but seven dollar a plate, but cbust pay me for the leetle trouble I should do myself the honor to take for you"—Madame reasoned, and M. Gautier apologized, and the upshot was, that she retired in disgust and cooked her own dinner. But the story was too good to be lost. It first crept into gossip, then into the newspapers, until the good woman was so mortified that she has pursued the opposite extreme ever since, loading her tables in a manner to rival those of Caligula or Mark Anthony.

OFFICIAL NOTICES.

HEADQUARTERS
DEPARTMENT OF SOUTH CAROLINA, GEORGIA AND FLORIDA,
CHARLESTON, S. C., July 23, 1864.

[*GENERAL ORDERS NO. 68.*]

OFFICERS OF THE PERSONAL AND GENERAL STAFF of the Major General Commanding including the Chief of Artillery, Chief Engineer, Chief Quartermaster, Chief Ordinance Officer, Medical Directors and Inspector of the Field and General Hospitals of the Department, and the Chief Commissary and Chief Engineer of the State of South Carolina, will communicate with and receive instructions from these Headquarters direct. All other officers of the various Staff Departments, as well as of the line, will be under the control and supervision of the Commanders of the several Districts in which they are stationed, especially in all matters of military discipline and police.

This order will not be so construed as to interfere with the General Orders from the War Department on similar subjects.

By command of Major General JONES.

CHAS. S. STRINGFELLOW, A. A. G.

July 25 3

[EXTRACT.]

HEADQUARTERS
1ST MILITARY DISTRICT,
CHARLESTON, S. C., July 22, 1864.

[*SPECIAL ORDERS No. 83.*]

* * * * * * *

III. MEMBERS OF THE RESERVE TROOPS WHO have been furloughed or detailed from these Headquarters will consider themselves, during the existence of such furloughs or details, under the immediate command of Brigadier General Chesnut, commanding Reserves of the State of South Carolina.

* * * * * * *

By command of Brig. Gen. RIPLEY.

WM. F. NANCE, A. A. General.

July 25 mw8

DEPARTMENT OF SO. CA., GA. AND FLA.,
OFFICE CHIEF Q. M., 2D AND 6TH MILITARY DISTRICT,
ADAMS' RUN July 23, 1864

WANTED TO PURCHASE, BY CONTRACT OR otherwise, for the use of these Districts, FORTY THOUSAND (40,000) BUSHELS OF CORN, to be delivered at points convenient to these Districts, in such quantities, and at such times, as may be agreed upon. Cash payments will be made for every separate delivery of Corn, if so desired; and, in addition to the regular schedule price to be paid for the Corn, the hire of teamsters and transportation to such point of delivery will be paid, according to the prescribed schedule, from the points where it is now held by owners. Bags will be furnished by this Office, and every assistance will be rendered to facilitate its prompt delivery.

Address as above by mail E. POWELL,

July 23 12 c Major and Quartermaster.

HEADQUARTERS,
1ST MILITARY DISTRICT SOUTH CAROLINA,
CHARLESTON, S. C., July 15, 1864.

[*GENERAL ORDERS No. 4.*]

I. ATTENTION IS CALLED TO PARAGRAPH X., General Orders No. 84, current series, Adjutant and Inspector-General's Office, which is hereby republished for the benefit of all concerned:

X. "Soldiers retired from the service, as herein provided, will be furnished with descriptive lists which, in addition to the usual history given, will exhibit the fact that they have been placed on the retired list, and designate the post at which they will be entitled to receive pay and allowances. They will report to the commandant of such post—which will be nearest their places of residence, and deliver to him their descriptive lists."

To ensure a more prompt observance of this order the Medical Examining Board at this Post will notify these Headquarters, at the expiration of each week, of their action on each application under the above recited order.

II. Commanders of other posts within the limits of this Military District will acquaint themselves with and strictly observe this order.

III. Surgeons and Post Commanders will direct their attention to the requirements of Paragraph IV., G. O. No. 89, Series of 1863, from A. and I. General's Office, prescribing the necessary formality in cases of application for discharge, for physical disability, of men in hospitals; compliance with which is also enjoined.

By command of Brigadier General RIPLEY.

July 18 WM. F. NANCE, A. A. Gen.

TO THE PEOPLE OF SOUTH CAROLINA.

HEADQUARTERS,
DEPARTMENT SOUTH CAROLINA, GEORGIA AND FLORIDA,
CHARLESTON, S. C., July 19, 1864

TWENTY-FIVE HUNDRED ABLE BODIED NEGROES are immediately needed to work on the fortifications around Charleston, and, under the pressure of this necessity, impressments have been ordered. I feel confident, however, that the people of this State need only be informed of the wants of the military authorities to ensure a prompt response to this appeal; and I, therefore, call upon them to furnish, without delay, their respective quotas as established by the law of the State.

Full credit will be given upon the next call for labor for all such negroes as may be voluntarily sent forward, and the Government assumes all responsibilities that attach in the case of negroes impressed, and will take the same care of them.

If the Planters in different neighborhoods will have their negroes collected at particular Depots, and will notify Major W. H. ECHOLS, Chief Engineer, of the time and place selected, Agents will be sent to receive them. The same officer will, upon notification, have agents at the different Depots in this city, to receive and provide subsistence, medical attention, &c., for all negroes sent to him.

SAM. JONES,
Major-General Commanding.

July 20 10

The Daily Picayune.

VOLUME XXVIII. NEW ORLEANS, SUNDAY MORNING, AUGUST 28, 1864. NUMBER 148.

NOTICE OF ELECTION.

Pursuant to a Writ of Election, bearing date August ..th, 1864, to me directed by His Excellency J. Madison Wells, Lieutenant and Acting Governor of the State of Louisiana, the qualified voters of the Parish of Orleans are hereby notified that an election will be held on MONDAY, the Fifth day of September, 1864 for the ratification or rejection of the Constitution adopted by the Convention lately assembled in the city of New Orleans, for the Revision and Amendment of the State Constitution, and for Members of Congress, to fill vacancies in the representation of the State of Louisiana in the Thirty-eighth Congress of the United States, to wit:

One Representative from the First Congressional District of the State of Louisiana, comprising that portion of the Parish of Orleans lying on the right bank of the Mississippi river, and the Ninth, Eighth, Seventh, Sixth, and Fifth Representative Districts, and that portion of the Fourth Representative District of the Parish of Orleans, in the city of New Orleans, which is bounded by St. Louis, Rampart and Canal streets and the rear line of said Representative District.

One Representative from the Second Congressional District of the State of Louisiana, comprising that portion of the Parish of Orleans, in the city of New Orleans, which comprises the Third, Second and First Representative Districts of the Parish of Orleans, and that portion of the Fourth Representative District which is bounded by St. Louis, Rampart and Canal streets and the Mississippi river, and also that portion of the Tenth Representative District of the Parish of Orleans which is known and designated by existing statutes as the Tenth Ward of the city of New Orleans.

One Representative from the Third Congressional District of the State of Louisiana, which comprises that portion of the Tenth Representative District of the Parish of Orleans which is known and designated as the Eleventh Ward of the city of New Orleans.

And, whereas, It is further ordered that there shall be chosen on the same day Senators and Representatives to the General Assembly of the State of Louisiana, as follows:

SENATORS.

The First and Fourth Municipal Districts of the city of New Orleans shall elect Five Senators.

The Second and Third Municipal Districts of the city of New Orleans shall elect Four Senators

And all that portion of the Parish of Orleans lying on the right bank of the Mississippi river shall be entitled to vote for One Senator.

REPRESENTATIVES.

The First Representative District of the Parish of Orleans shall elect Three Representatives.

The Second Representative District shall elect Five Representatives.

The Third Representative District shall elect Seven Representatives.

The Fourth Representative District shall elect Three Representatives.

The Fifth Representative District shall elect Four Representatives.

The Sixth Representative District shall elect Two Representatives.

The Seventh Representative District shall elect Three Representatives.

The Eighth Representative District shall elect Three Representatives.

The Ninth Representative District shall elect Four Representatives.

The Tenth Representative District shall elect Eight Representatives.

And that portion of the Parish of Orleans lying on the right bank of the Mississippi river shall elect Two Representatives.

The Polls will be open in each Election Precinct from the hour of eight o'clock a. m. ... on the day above mentioned—to wit, the FIFTH DAY OF SEPTEMBER, 1864—for the purpose of receiving the votes of the qualified voters of the Parish of Orleans, under the superintendence of the Commissioners and Clerks to be appointed by the authorities designated by law. The Election to be conducted and triplicate returns made to the designated returning officer, according to law.

Sheriff's Office, Parish of Orleans, New Orleans, August ..th, 1864.

ALFRED SHAW, Sheriff.

OFFICIAL,

HEADQUARTERS MILITARY DIVISION OF WEST MISSISSIPPI, New Orleans, La., August 20th, 1864.

General Orders, No. 39.

I.—The following order from the War Department is hereby republished for general information:

WAR DEPARTMENT, ADJUTANT GENERAL'S OFFICE, Washington, August ..th, 1864.

General Orders, No. 67.

By the 57th article of the act of Congress, entitled An Act for establishing Rules and Articles for the government of the Armies of the United States, approved April 10, 1806, "holding correspondence with, or giving intelligence to the enemy, either directly or indirectly," is made punishable by death or such other punishment as shall be ordered by the sentence of a court martial. Public safety requires strict enforcement of this article. It is therefore ordered that all correspondence and communication, verbally or by writing, printing, or telegraphing, respecting operations of the army, or military movements on land or water, or respecting the troops, camps, arsenals, intrenchments, or military affairs, within the several military districts, by which intelligence shall be, directly or indirectly, given to the enemy, without the authority and sanction of the General in command, be, and the same are, absolutely prohibited, and from and after the date of this order, persons violating the same, will be proceeded against under the 57th Article of War.

By order:

(Signed) L. THOMAS, Adjutant General.

II. T. H. Cook, correspondent of the "New York Herald," and J. B. Chadwick, correspondent of the "New York Tribune," who were permitted to accompany the troops operating in Mobile Bay, having abused the confidence reposed in them, by making public information of value to the enemy, and engaging in a controversy calculated to disturb the harmony of the troops, will be sent beyond the lines of this command.

The Provost Marshal General is charged with the execution of this order, and the Quartermaster's Department will furnish the necessary transportation.

By order of Major General E. R. S. CANBY.

C. T. CHRISTENSEN, Major and Assistant Adjutant General.

Official: R. H. W. CORBY, Acting Assistant Adjutant General.

BANKS OF LOUISIANA.

Headquarters Department of the Gulf, NEW ORLEANS, August 22, 1864

General Orders, No. 115.

The Banks of the State of Louisiana having so far failed to comply with important provisions of the laws of the State as to justify the forfeiture of their Charters, are hereby required, as a condition of the further transaction of the business of Banking, to receive the Treasury Notes of the United States in exchange, at par, for their own notes respectively. Any institution aggrieved by this order may demand investigation of its affairs and show that its credit is superior to that of the United States.

By command of MAJOR GEN. BANKS.

GEORGE B. DRAKE, Assistant Adjutant General.

The Daily Picayune.

DOUBLE SHEET

[For the Picayune.]

BY THE SEA.—By Ruth N. Cromwell.

All day, all day long, I walk by the solemn sea,
All night, all night long, he singeth a song for me—
A weird, wild song, solemn and grand—
While I lie by his side on the cold damp sand;
A strange, wild moan, a sad monotone,
While I lie by his side, alone—alone!

For a year or more he hath sung me to rest,
For a year or more she hath lain on his breast,
While the pitiless moon goes wandering by
'Mid the joyless stars in the cold gray sky—
The moon will not hear; but the winds so drear
Howl back their anthem, far and near.

All her life, all my life, we had loved so well—
The moon knows, and the stars, but they will not tell.
Oh! he was her sire—I was gentle and mild,
Tho' he laugh'd me to scorn when I asked for his child.
Ah! this heart which is cold was once ardent and bold;
Could its blood have been coined, I'd ne'er wanted for gold!

But they bore her away, far away to her fate;
They left me alone, with my love and my hate;
But her face grew pale—I saw in my dream—
Like the pale-faced lilies, that live by the stream;
Then I cursed them aloud, while every cloud
Gleamed in the heavens, like a white-fringed shroud.

But so wan and so silent they bore her along,
'Mid the splendor of beauty, 'mid sunlight and song—
Nor dreamed that they smiled on an image of clay,
That her beautiful soul, with its love was away—
'Mid dazzle and show, where the south winds blow,
Where the pomegranate blooms and the orange trees grow.

In vain—'twas in vain—the ship cut the foam!
In vain—'twas in vain—they hurried her home!
I had youth and my love, the sea is old and so rough;
But she sleeps on his breast, she hath glitter enough—
A right royal bed, down, down with the dead,
She hath gold at her feet and gold at her head!

All day they sit lone, in their fine old hall,
Alone with the face, that looks down from the wall;
They would give me their gold for the life that hath gone—
I flung back their pity, and laughed them to scorn!
O! I watch with the tide, on the lone sea-side,
And wait for the morn, that shall give me my bride!

New York, August, 1864.

LATE SOUTHERN NEWS.

THROUGH SOUTHERN SOURCES.

Atlanta, the Potomac, Mobile, Memphis, Florida, etc.

The Times of yesterday afternoon contained the following intelligence, obtained from the Woodville, Miss., Republican, of the 22d inst.

Atlanta.

Atlanta, Aug. 18.—Heavy skirmishing began at midnight on the left and centre, and continued until 2 o'clock without ... this morning, the artillery of Stewart's corps opened on the enemy; their batteries replied feebly. The firing was very heavy, and produced great consternation among the enemy.

Prisoners report that our cavalry captured a large number of beeves at Kingston a few days since. Numerous reports are in circulation in regard to their operations, but it is beyond a fact that they had cut the road at Ackworth, and were destroying the track between the Etowah and Oostenaula rivers. Thus far they had been entirely successful. Nothing official has been received. The enemy seems to be ignorant of the magnitude of the operations in their rear, and were preparing another raiding expedition under Kilpatrick, which had rendezvoused at Sweet Water, preparatory to starting, but which it is believed had been recalled yesterday—they going in pursuit of our cavalry.

Potomac.

Raleigh, Aug. 20.—The Confederate has news from Petersburg and Richmond to yesterday. The enemy reached the Weldon road on Thursday morning, the 19th inst., and drove in Dearing's cavalry, capturing a few prisoners. They occupied the railroad at Yellow Tavern, four miles from Petersburg, and burnt a mile and a half of it. Our infantry came up and charged them and drove them back, capturing 200 and killing and wounding 90. Several charges were made during the day; the enemy were repulsed always. They were expecting to renew the fight on Friday evening.

The enemy's loss in the battles of Tuesday, 17th, below Richmond, was 6000, ours 1000.

There are rumors of victory by Early, but they are not confirmed.

Memphis.

Mobile, Aug. 21.—A special to the Register from Senatobia, dated August 21st, says Forrest attacked Memphis at 7 o'clock this morning. Heavy firing was heard for three hours. It is supposed the city was captured. The Federal forces are reported to be small. The Federals occupied Oxford to-day.

Later—Forrest, with 2000 men, left the enemy's front on Friday to attack Memphis. He expected to reach that vicinity last night. Heavy firing was heard this morning. A man arrived to-night from near Memphis, who says the city and fort were captured, with 5000 prisoners, but there is nothing official from there.

The enemy occupied Oxford this evening. Chalmers is retreating slowly.

Senatobia, August 22.—Gen. Forrest surprised and captured Memphis at 4 o'clock yesterday morning, killing and wounding about 400 Federals, and capturing between two and three hundred—a large number being officers. One brigadier general was killed. Our loss was comparatively slight, the surprise being complete. Among our wounded is Lieut. Col. Robert McCulloch, of the 2d Missouri, shot through the breast. Forrest found the Federals outnumbered him four to one, and had to fight his way out, making a fortunate escape. Amongst the spoils are five hundred fine horses, new hats, clothes, etc. The prisoners are arriving. It was the most daring raid and complete surprise of the war.

Charleston, Aug. 20.—An official dispatch from Gen. J. K. Jackson, dated Lake City, Florida, Aug. 9th, to Gen. Jones, received late last night, says Capt. Dickerson with his command engaged the enemy's cavalry, 340 strong, at Gainesville yesterday, completely routing them. We captured 150 prisoners and one piece of artillery, besides we recaptured 100 stolen negroes. Among the prisoners are one captain, two lieutenants and one surgeon. The whole command would have been captured if Capt. Dickerson's horses had not been worn out. The enemy were scattered and pursued fourteen miles. The enemy's infantry consisted of four colored regiments. Col. McCormick is in pursuit with some additional force.

Kentucky.

Raleigh, Aug. 20.—It is reported that 2500 Confederates under Adam Johnson, in Union and the adjoining counties, are preparing to attack Mount Vernon.

Burbridge says Kentucky is disloyal.

☞ A lady, who was a strict observer of etiquette, being unable to go to church one Sunday, sent her card.

TELEGRAPHIC.

FURTHER FROM THE NORTH.

[BY THE RIVER.]

FORTRESS MONROE AND CITY POINT

AN ATTACK ON THE FEDERAL LINES REPULSED.

A Federal Attack on the James River Successful.

FIGHTING ON THE APPOMATTOX.

A FIGHT AT HURRICANE CREEK, MISS.

The Rebels Repulsed.

BATTLE NEAR FRONT ROYAL.

Gold on the 19th in New York 257 1-2.

Middling Cotton Same Day, 179 to 180.

[From our Extra of Yesterday Evening.]

By the military telegraph, from Port Hudson, we have the following dispatches, taken from the Missouri Democrat of the 20th inst., brought down by the steamer Minnehaha:

Fortress Monroe, Aug. 18, P. M.—The mail steamer Vanderbilt has just arrived from City Point. At one o'clock this morning the rebels made a furious attack on our lines, or rather upon that portion of them consisting of Burnside's Corps, on the left. The fighting was chiefly with artillery, and lasted two hours, when the rebels fell back without attempting an assault on our works. Our loss is small.

The Vanderbilt reports that there was a rumor at City Point that strong reinforcements, sent by Hancock, had arrived at Fair Oaks.

Indianapolis, Aug. 19.—Dispatch to Gen. Carrington from Gen. Hovey, commanding the forces sent in pursuit of Adam Johnson's guerrillas. He had reached Morgan's field and White Oak Springs, Ky.; had attacked the enemy, captured a few prisoners and scattered the balance of the guerrillas in all directions. Gen. Hovey levied an assessment on the disloyal citizens of Union county, Ky., to cover the damages sustained by Government.

Washington, Aug. 19.—A letter from the Army of the Potomac, Wednesday noon, says the Twenty-Second Corps having been unsuccessful in the attack on the enemy on the north side of the James River, on Sunday, fell back to a safe position, which it occupied till yesterday, when another assault was determined and carried out successfully. The enemy were driven from their works with heavy loss. The Second Corps also captured several hundred prisoners and some heavy guns. Our loss quite large. We still hold our position.

Our cavalry, under Gen. Gregg, had an engagement with the enemy and drove them from some works near the New Market road, but were finally forced to fall back. Col. Gregg was severely wounded. It is reported that Butler's troops had a slight engagement, without advantage to either side.

Thursday, Aug. 18, A. M.—The rebels opened a most vigorous fire, which extended along the whole line from the Appomattox to the Jerusalem plank road, and which lasted about two hours. It is thought to be a prelude to an attack. Heavy firing was also heard from Butler's direction. Nothing is known about it.

Memphis, Aug. 19, via Cairo, Aug. 18.—On the 13th inst. a detachment of Gen. Smith's command, consisting of one brigade of infantry and two of cavalry, attacked three brigades of Forrest's command, who held a partially fortified position on Hurricane Creek, Miss., and after a short but sharp fight the rebels were dislodged and obliged to retreat, leaving fifty of their dead on the field. Our loss was slight—not over forty killed and wounded.

Major Gen. Washburne has just issued an important order regulating the prices of provisions in Memphis. The most exorbitant prices were being demanded for everything. This order is intended to remedy the evil, and will no doubt have a wholesome effect upon speculators.

New York, Aug. 19.—The Times has the following special:

"Baltimore, Aug. 18.—Battle took place at or near Front Royal on Tuesday, the 16th, between a portion of our cavalry and a heavy force of rebels, of Longstreet's command. Portions of Wilson's and Custar's brigades were engaged. The fight was a severe one for the numbers operating, and a charge made by Custar at the head of his brigade was most brilliant, resulting in the capture of 358 prisoners and two stands of colors. The fight is considered an important one, as it reveals some of the enemy's positions."

New York, August 19—9 P. M.—Cotton 1@2c. better, at 179@180 for Middling Uplands.

New York, August 19.—Sterling Exchange dull at 108¾ for specie. Gold a shade firmer; opened at 257, advanced to 257⅞, declined to 257½, and closed quiet at 257.

FURTHER BY THE ARIEL.

ONE DAY LATER THAN BY HER DATES.

News to the 18th.

The Atlantic Mail Steamship Company's first class side-wheel steamship Ariel, which left New York at noon on the 17th, and the lower bay on the 18th inst., arrived here early last evening, with a large freight, a mail, and a goodly number of passengers.

We have already given, by telegraph from the Southwest Pass, some of the most important news brought by this steamer, in extras published yesterday afternoon, and which may be found in other columns of this morning's Picayune. We append some further and fuller interesting details to the 18th, which is one day later than the papers from which our telegraphic dispatches of yesterday were made up. To the courtesy of Gen. de Goicouria we are indebted for the opportunity of doing this:

ONE DAY LATER.

From the Valley of the Shenandoah.

MARTINSBURG AGAIN.

The New York Herald, of the 18th, under the heading "The Situation," says:

By dispatches from Martinsburg, last night, we have the important and somewhat significant information that the rebels have again advanced up the Shenandoah Valley, and that they have been considerably reinforced by a division of Longstreet's corps and two divisions of cavalry. Great activity prevails in Martinsburg, and the excitement throughout the valley is intense. Indeed, rumors—still unconfirmed—were circulated that Gen. Lee, with his whole army, was moving in that direction. An engagement was said to be going on at Front Royal yesterday. A variety of rumors would seem to verify the statement that the enemy are in the valley in large numbers.

Martinsburg, Va., Aug. 17.—There is much activity in Martinsburg to-night, in consequence of a reported readvance of the rebels. Skedaddlers have already commenced a Northern movement, and some down the valley, bringing various reports.

We have information of an engagement at Front Royal.

It is said that the enemy have been reinforced by one division of Longstreet's corps and two cavalry divisions.

Prisoners are reported to have stated that the whole rebel army is moving.

There is much excitement in the valley.

[We have the Tribune, Times and World of the 18th, but neither of those prints makes any mention of the above—*Ed. Pic.*]

MARTINSBURG SAFE.

Martinsburg, Aug. 14, P. M.—Again this town is lively and considered to be safe. As on many other Sunday nights, the houses are lit up, the windows open and the streets full of promenaders. And yet but a few hours ago it was, in every sense, "as still as a Sunday" here.

Perhaps it will not be amiss for the rebels to know that their "reported" great damage to the railroad has been almost repaired; that we have telegraphic communication from here to-night, and that passengers will be able to go through from Wheeling to Baltimore over the railroad line (by changing cars at this point) in a very few days. So much for the enterprise of the railroad and telegraph companies.

MOSBY.

We hear to-night that the indefatigable Mosby is again in the field, and looking towards this section of country with an eye to his usual style of mischief.

GEN. AVERILL

is again reported in the field, and may be expected to be heard from favorably before long.

It is reported that Gen. Kelley's command will be extended so as to take in the line of the railroad from Wheeling to the Monocacy. People along the line are pleased at this report.

GEN. R. E. LEE.

In the Field, Aug. 15—P. M.—A report has come in that, if the report is true, he is looking after the general military situation, and providing for the defence of Staunton and Lynchburg.

THE MAIL.

There are two thousand six hundred letters at Cumberland for the post at Martinsburg, besides another heavy mail for the same post at Williamsport.

GEN. EARLY AND EX-MINISTER FAULKNER.

When the rebels were in Martinsburg, ex-Minister Faulkner visited his wife, on which occasion there were some words between him and Gen. Early, in consequence of the latter locating a few tents on the former's grounds.

The rebels did not do much damage at Hancock. They burned some small bridges and a few buildings of railroad property.

EARLY'S PLANS.

Baltimore, Aug. 16.—It is evidently Early's plan to withdraw south of the Shenandoah River, making that stream, if possible, a cover until reinforcements arrive. The menacing attitude of his troops at Cedar Creek, we learn, was merely designed as a ruse to induce our forces to be more cautious, and thus slacken the pursuit.

THE REGION OF COUNTRY

in which the two armies are now operating is excellently adapted to defensive warfare. There are three parallel ranges of mountains, between which numbers are less effective than resolution and discipline. It is not expected that a severe battle will take place unless the enemy has, according to his own mind, the advantage of position and fresh troops.

EARLY INTENDS TO HOLD THE VALLEY.

It is not supposed here by persons advised that Early intends leaving the valley permanently, unless defeated, driven out and kept out. The sending to him of fresh troops is convincing proof to this effect. The rebels seem to have their very existence in Virginia upon their keeping up a force to threaten the Potomac line, and keep a large body of troops in that region. I hope the coming few weeks will enable us to cover all points with the large number of men taking the field, and crush the enemy everywhere.

THE BALTIMORE AND OHIO RAILROAD.

Officers of the Baltimore and Ohio Railroad state that the working parties between Hancock and Harper's Ferry are pushing the repairs of the road with the greatest speed, and it is thought ten days will suffice to find trains again running.

REBEL ATTACK UPON OUR SUPPLY TRAIN.

Harper's Ferry, Aug. 16.—The attack upon our cavalry supply train proves that our losses will amount to about fifty wagons, four hundred mules, two hundred head of cattle and from one hundred and fifty to one hundred and seventy men. The property belonged to the reserve brigade. The train was the rear of a large supply train for the whole army, which was guarded by a brigade of one hundred days' men, under the command of Gen. John R Kenley. The General was at the head of the train, and his command was distributed at the rate of fifty or sixty men to every twenty wagons, the cavalry cattle herd being in the rear of the train.

MOSBY THE ATTACKING PARTY.

It appears, that Mosby came from Snicker's Gap to Berryville, four miles, and cut off the reserve brigade and the 1st Cavalry Division just as it was pulling out of park in the morning.

CAVALRY PICKETS

at Snicker's Ferry and Island Ford, two miles below, should have given notice of Mosby's approach; but there were none, it appears, and the rebels came upon the rear guard and made a charge, accompanied with one of their peculiar yells. The guard were panic stricken and made little resistance, but dropped their guns and fled in all directions. Some of the wagons were fired, the teams unhitched, and, together with the cattle, driven off in great haste toward the ferry.

MAJOR SAWYER,

with a chest of greenbacks, was in an ambulance, and, with two or three others, made a good show of resistance. He escaped with his money.

Capt. E. P. McKinney, Commissary of Subsistence, in charge, was shot through the thigh.

PURSUIT.

The 1st Rhode Island Cavalry, on duty near Winchester, hearing of the attack, dashed down to the river at full gallop, in pursuit, but were too late to recapture the property. There is a rumor to-day that Gen. Wilson came upon Mosby near Snicker's Gap and recaptured some of the animals and prisoners.

Sheridan Fallen Back.

The Times, of the 18th, says:

It is reported that Gen. Sheridan has fallen back to Winchester, where he will fortify himself and act on the defensive. This movement indicates that the reports lately brought by rebel deserters, of the heavy reinforcement of Gen. Early, were well founded, and that he was too strong to be attacked by Sheridan.

Fitzhugh Lee's Cavalry.

Headquarters Second Cavalry Division, in the Field, Aug. 15.—We learn through scouts and citizens that Fitzhugh Lee's cavalry is in the valley, and that a portion of our forces had a skirmish or engagement with him at Millwood on Friday and Saturday. The report is that Fitzhugh Lee was driven back.

Gen. Lee Reported Wounded.

We also learn that Gen. Robert E Lee was slightly wounded on the occasion of the explosion of the rebel mine before Petersburg.

Harper's Ferry, Aug. 17.—The guerrillas continue very annoying in the vicinity of Charlestown. A corporal and three men coming down to-day were fired upon, and two of the men are missing.

Lieut. Philip Duryea, of the Fifth U. S. Cavalry, wounded yesterday, is reported to have died last night.

Captain Henry Page, Assistant Quartermaster, has been appointed Chief Quartermaster of the cavalry corps, with the rank of lieutenant colonel.

Major Russell, of the Adj't General's Department, reports for duty to Gen. Torbert, commanding the cavalry corps.

We have no news of interest from the front to-day.

FROM GEORGIA.

A Contest at Dalton.

Louisville, Ky., Aug. 17, 1864.—The rebel Gen. Wheeler, with seventeen hundred cavalrymen, demanded the surrender of Dalton, Ga., on the evening of the 14th inst., of Col. S. C. Bold, of the 2d Missouri, commanding at that post.

The force of Col. Lieboldt numbers eight hundred men.

A slight skirmish was going on when the last train left Dalton.

This train had Col. Collum and three other railroad men on board, returning from between Adairsville and Calhoun.

These men were obliged to repair the road, which had been destroyed by small detachments from Gen. Wheeler's force.

The rebels had also captured about seventeen Government wagons on their way to Atlanta and nearly all the officers in charge of them.

The railroad men escaped after the train had left Dalton.

Gen. Steedman, being telegraphically advised of the movements of the rebels, started with a large force from Chattanooga in pursuit of them.

The latest heard from Dalton was just at nightfall on the 14th, when cannonading was going on.

Rumor says that as the trains were leaving Resacca fourteen of our men were captured by the rebel force that captured the cattle.

This raid had been anticipated by Gen. Sherman, and he was prepared to meet the rebels at important points.

Louisville, Aug. 17, P. M.—Three hundred and fifty head of cattle, captured by Wheeler, have been recovered.

The damage to the railroad near Calhoun has been repaired. Four trains were at Dalton when last heard from.

On the refusal of Col. Seiboldt to surrender, Wheeler attacked Dalton and gained some buildings in the town, where they kept up a harassing fire, driving Sieboldt's men from their position to the station, where they checked the rebels. The enemy was on both sides of the railroad, trying to cut the road.

Steedman will probably reinforce Sieboldt in time. A down train is reported captured at Altona Pass.

Wheeler's force is probably divided and operating at different points. That portion at Dalton is aiming to destroy the tunnel at Tunnel Hill. Telegraphic communication with Dalton has ceased by the cutting of the wire.

THE ARMY OF THE POTOMAC.

Hancock's Fight.

New York, Aug. 18.—The Herald, of this morning, says:

Everything is quiet in Grant's army. The rebels remain still in position, and forces are in front of their works.

The court of inquiry appointed to investigate the facts and circumstances concerning the unsuccessful assault on Petersburg on the 30th of July has temporarily suspended its sittings in consequence of the absence of Gens. Hancock and Miles, two members of the court. (Gen. Hancock being President) who are north of the James River, engaged in important military operations.

This is what the World of the same date says:

It is represented that Gen. Hancock's lines have been advanced to a point within six miles of Richmond since the movement of Sunday, and that there was some fighting, in which our forces were successful in driving the enemy back. Butler is co-operating with the 18th Corps, and a portion of the 5th Corps has been thrown across to aid Gen. Hancock. The latest advices state that our troops hold the centre line of works, which are very strong. The canal which is being built by Butler is stated to be for the purpose of enabling our gunboats to pass up the James River without inviting the fire of the rebel gunboats and batteries on the shore in the bend. A new telegraphic cable will be laid from Fortress Monroe immediately, and when it is complete the public will not be dependent upon steamers to bring the news of operations of Gen. Grant's army.

[Special Dispatch to the World.]

Headquarters Army of the Potomac, Near Petersburg, Aug. 16.—Since Thursday there has been constant movements, and numerous wild rumors have prevailed both as to what had occurred and what was intended. In the midst of these it was impossible to discern the truth, and especially so when officers of high grade were unable to give opinions respecting the reports. On Sunday morning, however, the booming of cannon on the north side of the James River advised us that Gen. Hancock, with his gallant Second Corps, had only been engaged in a cleverer strategic movement, attempting to march upon the vigilant foe. He embarked his corps in the morning, and ran down the river to Light House Point, in full view of the rebels, but returned under cover of darkness during the following night and disembarked at Deep Bottom. Early next morning Gen Gregg's cavalry made an extended reconnoissance, driving the rebel pickets to within nine miles of Richmond, to prevent their discovering our movements and communicating to the enemy. In the meantime the main body moved forward. They had not proceeded far before finding the enemy, who, although taken by surprise, fought vigorously for several hours, retiring slowly from one position to another, until in one part of the line they were within six miles of Richmond. Here they received reinforcements, and renewing the contest with unusual vigor, succeeded in driving back a portion of our forces beyond the position they occupied in the morning. The result of the day's fighting on our side was the capture of six or seven hundred prisoners, six pieces of artillery, and ... killing and wounding a large number of the enemy. Our loss in killed and wounded is severe—reports say between seven and eight hundred. Of these, a small proportion only are killed or seriously wounded. The fighting was not resumed yesterday.

The Tallahassee.

Yarmouth, N. S., Aug. 16.—The schooner Sophia, from Turks' Island, arrived here today with the crews of the following vessels, sunk by the pirate Tallahassee:

Ship James Littlefield, of Bangor, from Cardiff to New York, was sunk on the 14th inst., in latitude 42, longitude 66.

Schooner Lamont Dupont, of Wilmington, Del., was sunk on the 13th, in latitude 40, longitude 68.

Schooner Mercy A. Howe, of Chatham, was sunk yesterday, in latitude 43, longitude 66.

After the crews of the above vessels were put on board of the Sophia, the Tallahassee sunk four other schooners, one of which was the J. H. Howen, of Gloucester.

Smoke from a steamer was seen this morning in the direction of Seal Island.

Thomaston, Me., Aug. 17.—The rebel steamer Tallahassee yesterday destroyed twenty-five vessels off Matinicus Rock. She was manned mostly by Nova Scotia men. After sending the crews and passengers of the vessels destroyed by her into Friendship by a small craft, she steered in an easterly direction.

Boston, Aug 17.—A dispatch from J. M. Merrill, United States Consular Agent at Yarmouth, N. S., to Carleton Goodrich, of Boston, states that six vessels were destroyed by the Tallahassee on Monday, six miles from Cape Sable. Thirty men of the crews of the vessels were landed at Yarmouth in a destitute condition. The pirate was in sight on Monday morning.

Capt James Watts, of the bark Glenalvon, of Thomaston, Me., arrived at Newport, R. I. on Sunday night last. He furnishes the following particulars of the destruction of his vessel by the Tallahassee:

On the 13th inst., about 7 o'clock A. M., forty miles from Nantucket, the Tallahassee ran alongside the bark. Capt. Watts asked what vessel she was, and her commander replied, "the Confederate war steamer Tallahassee." Capt. Wood, of the pirate, then ordered Capt. Watts on board his vessel, and after he had arrived there Wood examined his papers and ordered his boarding officer to return and scuttle the bark. She was loaded with pig iron, and sunk almost immediately. Capt. Watts, with his wife and crew, were then on board the Tallahassee, where the clothing of the men was confiscated by Wood. They remained on board seven hours, and were then transferred to the bark Atlantic, of St. Petersburg, bound from Bremen to Newport.

Capt. Watts describes the pirate as being a steam vessel of about one thousand tons burden, painted a dull white color. She has two masts; but the mainmast is broken off, and two smokestacks. She carries two pivot guns, one forward and one aft, and one hundred and forty men all told. They have burned the pilot boat which they captured and used for a decoy boat as long as they could. The officers of the Tallahassee stated that they left Wilmington about eight days before they captured the Glenalvon.

Portland, Aug. 17.—The schooners Carl and Magnolia were burned on the afternoon of the 16th inst. by the privateer Tallahassee. Both vessels belong to Friendship, Me.

The pilot boat Favorite No. 5 reports seeing in latitude 40:23, longitude 72:10, a lot of burnt wood and a lower-mast and topmast, supposed to be from the Adriatic. Yesterday, Sunne cock, bearing N. N. W., saw a vessel, bottom up, supposed to be a schooner, with a green bottom.

Saw a gunboat yesterday standing in N. N. W. Boarded the ship J. F. Wheeler, from Glasgow.

More Retaliation.

New York, Aug. 18.—Six hundred rebel prisoners have been sent to Morris Island to be placed under fire, in retaliation for the placing of a like number of Union prisoners under fire in Charleston. The last effort of our Government to retaliate in this manner resulted in an exchange of prisoners. It will be a happy conclusion to the act if similar results are attained in this instance.

Rebel Opinion of the Surrender of Fort Gaines.

[From the Richmond Dispatch, Aug. 1..]

Each fresh development in regard to the surrender of Fort Gaines goes to prove that it was an act of cowardice or treachery on the part of its commanding officer, Col. Anderson, of the 21st Alabama Regiment. The fort is a casemated work, mounting some 50 guns, was well manned and provisioned for six months; and we have the assurance of Gen. Maury that it was in good condition, and that the garrison had suffered but little. All this looks very dark for Col. Anderson, though there is a vague hope—very vague, we confess—that when the facts are developed they may justify the surrender and save his reputation.

New York Markets.

New York, Aug. 17.—The demand for the new 7 30 per cent. Treasury notes at the Department amounted to two and a quarter millions. Some of the new notes have already appeared, so that the delay to subscribers cannot be long. Interest is settled as on the 15th August. The other stocks of the United States were steady at the Stock Exchange. The railways are quiet. Gold 256½ per cent. Money easy at 7 per cent.

Flour and wheat were heavy and lower. Corn was in fair request and firmer. Less activity was discernible in provisions. Pork was cheaper. Whiskey was more sought after and was advancing. Freights were dull and drooping, with 563 vessels of all classes in port. The changes in other branches of trade were not important.

The Launch of the "Guiding Star."

On the afternoon of the 13th inst. the successful launch of the new mail steamship Guiding Star came off at the foot of Houston street, East River, New York, at the large ship-building yards of Messrs. Roosevelt, Joyce & Waterbury. Prior to the hour thousands had congregated at the yards to witness the auspicious event, among whom was James A Raynor, Esq., the President of the New York Mail Steamship Company, who appeared to take a lively interest in the whole affair. The Guiding Star is a noble vessel, and shows to what perfection shipbuilding has been brought in this country. The vessel is intended for the Havana and New Orleans mail route. The men commenced to unloose her from the stocks at half past 4 o'clock, at which time her upper decks were crowded. In ten minutes afterwards she glided into the watery elements amidst the cheers of the vast crowds around the yards and docks. Not the slightest accident occurred, and every matter was very successfully carried into effect.

All the mail ships of the company have been erected by these builders, and the Day Star is on the stocks in their yards and is in a very forward state. The Guiding Star will make her first trial trip in October. When the Day Star follows she will be commanded by Capt. Bell, now in charge of the Evening Star.

The following are the dimensions of the Guiding Star: Extreme length, 313 feet; breath of beam, 41 feet; depth of hold, 32 feet; measurement, 416 tons.

We congratulate our fellow-citizen, Capt. Courtenay, the courteous and efficient agent of the "Star" line here, upon this auspicious event, it being one he has a peculiar right especially to felicitate himself.

Later from Europe.

The Inman steamship City of Baltimore, Capt. Mirehouse, which left Liverpool at 11 ... on the morning of the 3d, and Queenstown the 4th of August, arrived at New York on the morning of the 17th.

The ... Capt. Van Santen, from South... the 3d of August, ...

The Cunard ... from Liverpool 6th and Queenstown ... reached Halifax the same day, on her way to Boston.

The United States Consul at Liverpool publishes an order from the State Department at Washington requiring that all persons embarking for America, with the exception of emigrants intending to settle in the country, shall be provided with passports.

The decision of the Emperor Napoleon with reference to the Suez Canal has been published. The total indemnity to be allowed to the company for surrendering the stipulations of July 20, 1856, and for relinquishing certain territories, is fixed at 54,000,000 francs.

The English Postmaster General had at length finally canceled the postal contract with the Galway Atlantic Mail Company. An official liquidator had been appointed to wind up the affairs of the company, and all creditors are required to send in their claims for the purpose of adjustment and payment.

The London Star says that Lord Clarendon's departure from Paris to Wiesbaden has caused immense disappointment. They would infer it that Lord Clarendon was going to Vichy on some highly important and confidential mission to the Emperor Napoleon.

The *Moniteur de la Flotte* announces as an important fact that an English mercantile house has ordered a ship of twelve hundred tons to be built at St. Nazaire. The *Moniteur* adds that French merchants formerly ordered ships to be built for them in England, but now the case is reversed.

Advices from Tunis had reached France to the effect that, in consequence of a reduction of taxation, an arrangement had been concluded between the Government and the insurgents. Fourteen of the principal tribes had already given in their submission, and the chief of the revolt had been permitted to leave the Regency.

According to advices from Manilla, of the 8th of June, eighty thousand quintals of tobacco were burned in the Government stores on the 6th.

The Persian Gulf cable is broken.

The United States war steamer Sacramento arrived at Falmouth, on the 2d inst., from Queenstown.

The United States steamer Iroquois anchored in Brest Roads, coming from New York.

The steamship Australasian, from New York, arrived at Cape Clear early on the morning of the 6th.

The United States steamers Wachusett and Onward were at Rio Janeiro July 9th.

THE WAR IN GEORGIA.

The reported capture of Atlanta by the Union forces under Gen. Sherman was received with much satisfaction by the friends of the North in England, and caused a depression of two and a half per cent in the rebel loan.

The London News editorially expatiates on the great importance of the fall of this place.

AMERICAN QUESTION.

[From the London Times, Aug. 2.]

Discount requirements are active, and an impression in some quarters that peace in America might be followed by a further great increase in the demand for money seemed to contribute to the flatness of prices on 'change, although, as America is bare of nearly all kinds of produce, it is difficult to see, after allowing for any stores of cotton that may be available, how she could draw capital on balance from Europe. Moreover, the reduction that would ensue in the price of cotton would at once check the transmission of specie to the East. At the same time it is to be remarked that the belief in any possibility of an early and permanent peace being negotiated is entertained by very few. A period of suspense between this date and the presidential election at the end of the year is the utmost that is hoped for.

THE ALABAMA—FRENCH REWARDS.

[Paris (Aug. 2) Correspondence of London Herald.]

The Minister of Marine has awarded a gold medal of the second class to the pilot Manger, and silver medals to the pilot Gosselin and the apprentice pilot Dounet, for their conduct in saving the lives of a part of the crew of the Alabama, after the naval combat off Cherbourg.

AMERICAN NAVAL AFFAIRS.

The steamer Niagara, after taking in coal and provisions, left Liverpool on the 5th. Her destination was unknown.

Rumors were current on the 5th of August that the late rebel cruiser Georgia had been seized by the order of the Government, as she was about leaving Liverpool. It turned out, however, that she was simply detained by her owner. It is alleged that the Georgia is now the *bona fide* property of Mr. Bates, by whom she has been put in thorough repair, and was about leaving Liverpool for Lisbon under a charter to the Portuguese Government, to carry troops to the west coast of Africa and the mails between Lisbon and the Azores. It was alleged that the Niagara waited outside the Mersey for the Georgia, but it was contradicted.

EX-PRESIDENT BUCHANAN.

[From the Birmingham (England) Journal, August 2.]

Mr. James Buchanan, the ex-President of the United States, and Mr. Mason, the Confederate Agent, are at present staying at the Regent Hotel, Leamington, England. (Guess not!)

The Latest News.

Liverpool, Aug. 6.—The Australasian's news to-day had no effect.

The friends of the North were much disappointed that the alleged capture of Atlanta was not confirmed, while the Southern sympathizers loudly rejoiced.

The London Post to-day has an editorial denouncing the kidnapping of British subjects for the Federal service. It refers especially to the case of seven Irishmen, who were subjected in June last to gross indignities after their release was obtained, and says if the facts are proved, the British Government should not be satisfied with anything less than the exemplary punishment of all concerned in the outrages.

The London Times has an editorial on the same subject, holding it up to Irishmen as a warning, not only against the Federal service, but against emigration to America.

The London News editorially refutes the representations against the labor market in America; shows that it is in a most healthy state, and offers irresistible attractions to emigrants.

WHAT SPAIN THINKS OF IT.

[From the Epoca of Madrid, Aug. 2.]

The adhesion of Dobiado and Uraga to the

[Continued on Fifth Page.]

The Charleston Mercury.

DAILY PAPER—Twenty Dollars for Six Months—Payable in Advance.

VINDICE NULLO.
SPONTE SUA SINE LEGE FIDES RECTUMQUE COLLENTUR.

COUNTRY PAPER—Thrice a Week—Twelve Dollars for Six Months—Payable in Advance.

Volume LXXXV. CHARLESTON, S. C., MONDAY, AUGUST 29, 1864. Number 12,151.

TELEGRAPHIC.

ANOTHER GLORIOUS VICTORY.

THE ENEMY DRIVEN FROM THE WELDON RAILROAD.

Captures of Guns, Colors and Prisoners.

The Gallantry of our Cavalry.

INTERESTING NORTHERN INTELLIGENCE.

IMPORTANT NEWS FROM ATLANTA,

SHERMAN RETREATING ACROSS THE CHATAHOOCHEE.

&c., &c., &c.,

RICHMOND, August 26.—The following official despatch was received at the war office last night:

HEADQUARTERS, ARMY NORTHERN VIRGINIA, August 26.

To the Hon. J. A. Seddon:

General A. P. HILL attacked the enemy in his entrenchments at Ream's Station yesterday evening, and, at the second assault, carried the entire line of works. MCRAE's North Carolina brigade, and WILCOX's division, under General CONNER, with PEGRAM's artillery, composed the assaulting column.

The line of the enemy's breastworks was carried with great gallantry, by our cavalry, under HAMPTON, who contributed largely to our success.

Seven stand of colors, nine pieces of artillery and two thousand prisoners are in our possession. The loss of the enemy is reported heavy; ours relatively small.

Our profound gratitude is due to the Giver of all victory, and our thanks to the brave men and officers engaged.

(Signed) R. E. LEE.

FURTHER PARTICULARS.

PETERSBURG, August 26.—The affair of Wednesday, on the Weldon Railroad, was a very gallant one, and most successful in its result.—While the enemy's cavalry, under SPEARS, were engaged in tearing up the track several miles beyond Reams' Station, General HAMPTON attacked and forced them back behind their infantry supports. HAMPTON then dismounted his men and fought them as infantry, gradually but steadily pushing them back, until they reached their strong works, one mile this side of Reams', and capturing about 800 prisoners.

At five o'clock in the afternoon General HILL attacked the enemy's works, and, after a short but sharp fight, took them, capturing a large number of prisoners and nine pieces of artillery. The enemy fled in great confusion. Colonel PEGRAM, of Richmond, turned the captured guns upon the enemy with terrible effect. The number of prisoners will probably reach 2500. Brigadier General CUTLER is amongst the captured. The prisoners belonged to HANCOCK's corps, and have been brought to town.

There has been considerable firing down the road this morning.

Our cavalry in the late engagement acted with conspicuous gallantry.

LATEST FROM ATLANTA.

ATLANTA, August 27.—The enemy disappeared from our entire front last night, except on our extreme left. It is supposed he is moving upon our left. Picket firing ceased at midnight, during the rain.

Rumors are current this morning that SHERMAN is crossing the Chattahoochee.

Louisville papers of the 20th state that Colonel WOODWARD, of Kentucky, was mortally wounded and taken prisoner on the 17th, while making an attack on Hopkinsville.

LATER.

The enemy is still in force on our left. Heavy cannonading in that direction this evening. Nashville papers of the 25th have been received. WHEELER destroyed the railroad for 15 miles on the east side of Athens, Tennessee. This force is said to consist of 6000 cavalry and 10 pieces of artillery. The Cincinnati correspondent of the Chicago *Times* states that all the Kentucky delegates to the Chicago Convention have been elected with instructions to vote for SEYMOUR, of Connecticut, for President. The Chattanooga correspondent of the Cincinnati *Gazette*, writing on the 24th, says neither General STEADMAN or STRAIGHT were injured.

THE EXCHANGE OF PRISONERS.

RICHMOND, August 26.—The Confederate authorities have offered to exchange officer for officer and man for man with the Federal authorities. Heretofore, the point of contention has been the delivery of the excess of prisoners, our government insisting upon the fulfilment of the terms of the cartel, which required the delivery of all prisoners on both sides, the excess on either side to be paroled.

The Confederate Government has now receded from this demand, and proposes that the excess, if any, shall remain in the hands of the enemy until we can make up for it by capture.

Though the offer was made early in the present month, it has not yet been accepted. The correspondence on the subject will shortly appear.

LATEST FROM THE UNITED STATES.

RICHMOND, August 26.—The Washington *Chronicle* of yesterday has been received here.

A despatch dated Memphis, August 21, says: "This city was attacked at 4 o'clock this morning by FORREST, with 3000 cavalry. They drove in our pickets and then dashed directly for the headquarters of Gen. WASHBURNE, who, however, succeeded in making good his escape. They then attacked the Irving Prison, but were repulsed by the guard. They next visited the Gayoso House, expecting to capture Gen. HURLBERT, but they did not succeed. The Federal troops then attacked the rebels and soon drove them from the city, killing thirty or more. Our loss was about the same as that of the rebels."

Another despatch from Memphis, dated August 22, says: "The rebel raid on the city yesterday was a complete failure. Our troops being without leaders, the rebels succeeded in carrying off some plunder, and captured quite a number of prisoners."

Telegrams from New York say: "Rumors are current here, and credited in the best financial circles, that the Government has decided to send five commissioners to Richmond to arrange the preliminaries of peace."

Gold closed in New York on the 24th at 254½.

The Governor of Ohio has issued a proclamation, warning all persons who may be preparing to resist the draft to desist from such purpose.

FERNANDO WOOD, in a speech delivered at Dayton, Ohio, on the 23d, asserted that a peace man, on a peace platform, would be nominated at Chicago. It is announced that Governor HORATIO SEYMOUR, of New York, will call the Convention to order, and that the proceedings will be opened with prayer by Bishop HOPKINS, of Vermont.

FORREST'S ACCOUNT OF THE CAPTURE OF MEMPHIS.

MOBILE, August 22.—The following despatch was received from General FORREST, dated Hernando, 21st: "I attacked Memphis at 4 o'clock this morning, driving the enemy to his fortifications. We killed and captured four hundred, capturing their entire camp, with about three hundred horses and mules. WASHBURNE escaped in the darkness of the morning, leaving his clothes behind. My loss is twenty killed and wounded.

(Signed) "N. B. FORREST, Maj. Genl."

D. B MAURY, Major General.

THE MERCURY.

MONDAY, AUGUST 29, 1864.

The New Secretary of the Treasury.

The recent measures and utterances of Secretary TRENHOLM, in regard to the reform so much needed in the financial affairs of the Confederacy, are the theme of much favorable comment. Since he has assumed the management of the operations of the Department, a better tone prevails throughout the community, confidence is being reinstated, and the country feels encouraged in the belief that the present incumbent of the Treasury office is "the right man in the right place." One fact must have already been observed. Mr. TRENHOLM recognizes the importance of communicating with the people, of laying before them the actual condition of affairs, and suggesting financial measures which ought to be adopted by those who represent the various interests of the community. The following article from the Richmond *Examiner* needs scarcely a comment:

Mr. Trenholm has lately written a remarkable un-official letter to South Carolina, extracts from which have been given in these columns. It assumes the singular position that the currency and credit of the Confederate Treasury depend almost altogether for their support upon the confidence of the people; and it actually contains the following sentence: "I regard the Treasury of the Confederate States as most peculiarly the treasury of the people, and there is nothing in the power of man that would so soon restore it to a condition of ease and prosperity as the universal and generous support of our people."

The strangeness of these declarations of Mr. Trenholm consists, not in their want of truth—for nothing could be more true than that the Treasury is the people's, and that the value of the currency depends exclusively upon the price which the people themselves put upon it—but it consists in the fact that the head of an Executive Department of the Confederate Government—a Government notorious for its defiance of public opinion, its indifference to the popular good will, its absolute segregation from all relations of cordiality or confidence with the people—should have the sense, the heart and the patriotism to conceive the opinion and utter the sentiment which Mr. Trenholm expresses in his letter. The idea that the people of this Confederacy have anything to do with any affair of their Government—much more, that they have everything to do with the success of a great public measure—is bran new with this administration; and Mr. Trenholm, its author, has, in consenting to address one of the people at all, and especially in promulgating the acknowledgment of his dependence upon them for the successful Administration of his Department, entitled himself, and doubtless secured to himself, a degree of popular confidence and support, which no member of any department of the Government has ever before deserved or received. The policy of this Government from the beginning has been to inculcate a wholly different idea from that announced by Mr. Trenholm, in the popular mind; to erect itself into a close corporation rigidly exclusive, repulsive and self-sufficient; to regard the people as no other than the materials and subjects of power; and to realize for its head the character ascribed by Phillips, in one of his florid orations to the first Napoleon: "Grand, gloomy and peculiar, he sat upon his throne, a sceptered hermit," &c.

We welcome this letter of the financial Secretary as the first dawn of coming reason in the Administration; and we participate fully in all his cheerful hopes of the re-establishment of the Confederate credit and currency; but we do so exclusively because he has conceived the true idea, that his success in the responsible and difficult duties before him depends entirely upon the people's confidence in his measures, and because he is disposed to act upon that most rational conviction.

Neither the Confederate credit nor the Confederate currency is beyond the reach of salvation in the hands of any right thinking or right feeling man of experience and capacity, like Mr. Trenholm. Nothing is more demonstratable than that the solvency of this Confederacy in regard to any debt which this war is likely to create. The value, therefore, of its currency and bonds depends exclusively upon the estimate which the people themselves shall attach to them; and no effort should be spared to inspire the people with that confidence in them which they are entitled to receive. The Secretary himself should employ all legitimate methods for establishing this popular confidence, and public opinion should be made a unit in frowning down every effort to depreciate them, or to reject them in public and private dealings.

THE KIRKE-JAQUES VISIT TO RICHMOND.

[From the New York Herald, 15th August.]

THE INTERVIEW WITH JEFFERSON DAVIS—HIS ULTIMATUM INDEPENDENCE OR SUBJUGATION.

The Atlantic Monthly, for September, contains an article entitled "Our Journey to Richmond," by J. R. Gilmore (better known under the *nom de plume* of Edmund Kirke), who, in company with Colonel Jaques, visited Richmond, and had an interview with the rebel President. The particulars of how they got to Richmond have already been published, and we therefore give only that portion of the article describing their meeting with Davis.

Upon arriving at the Spotswood Hotel Mr. Gilmore and the Colonel sent a note to the rebel Secretary Benjamin, requesting an interview with President Davis. The Secretary, in reply, sent them his compliments, and stated that he would be happy to see them at the State Department. At nine o'clock in the evening they called and met by appointment.

JEFFERSON DAVIS.

Mr. Benjamin occupied his previous seat at the table, and at his right sat a spare, thin featured man, with iron gray hair and beard and a clear gray eye, full of life and vigor. He had a broad massive forehead, and a mouth and chin denoting great energy and strength of will. His face was emaciated and much wrinkled, but his features were good, especially his eyes—though one of them bore a scar, apparently made by some sharp instrument. He wore a suit of greyish brown, evidently of foreign manufacture, and as he rose I saw that he was about five feet ten inches high, with a slight stoop in the shoulders. His manners were simple, easy and quite fascinating, and he threw an indescribable charm into his voice as he extended his hand, and said to us:

"I am glad to see you, gentlemen. You are very welcome to Richmond."

And this was the man who was President of the United States under Franklin Pierce, and who is now the heart, soul and brains of the Southern Confederacy.

His manner put me entirely at my ease (the Colonel would be at his if he stood before Cæsar), and I replied—

"We thank you, Mr. Davis. It is not often you meet men of our clothes and our principles in Richmond."

"Not often, not so often as I could wish; and I trust your coming may lead to a more frequent and a more friendly intercourse between the North and the South."

"We sincerely hope it may."

"Mr. Benjamin tells me you have asked to see me, to—"

And he paused, as if desiring we should finish the sentence. The Colonel replied:

"Yes sir. We have asked this interview in the hope that you may suggest some way by which this war can be stopped. Our people want peace; your people do, and your Congress has recently said that you do. We have come to ask how it can be brought about."

"In a very simple way. Withdraw your armies from our territory, and peace will come of itself. We do not seek to subjugate you. We are not waging an offensive war, except so far as it is offensive defensive, that is, so far as we are forced to invade you to prevent you invading us. Let us alone and peace will come at once."

"But we cannot let you alone so long as you repudiate the Union. That is the one thing the Northern people will not surrender."

"I know. You would deny to us what you exact for yourselves—the right of self-government."

"So, sir," I remarked, "We would deny you no natural right. But we think Union essential to peace, and, Mr. Davis, could two people, with the same language, separated by only an imaginary line, live at peace with each other? Would not disputes constantly arise, and cause almost constant war between them?"

"Undoubtedly—with this generation. You have sown such bitterness at the south, you have put such an ocean of blood between the two sections, that I despair of seeing any harmony in my time. Our children may forget this war, but we cannot."

"I think the bitterness you speak of, sir," said the Colonel, "does not really exist. We must talk here as friends; our soldiers meet and fraternize with each other; and I feel sure that if the Union were restored a more friendly feeling would arise between us than has ever existed. The war has made us know and respect each other better than before. This is the view of very many Southern men. I have had it from many of them—your leading citizens."

"They are mistaken," replied Mr. Davis. "They do not understand Southern sentiment. How can we feel anything but bitterness towards men who deny us our rights? If you enter my house and drive me out of it, am I not your natural enemy?"

"You put the case too strongly. But we cannot fight forever; the war must end at some time; we must finally agree upon something; can we not agree now and stop this frightful carnage? We are both Christian men, Mr. Davis. Can you, as a Christian man, leave untried any means that may lead to peace?"

"No, I cannot. I desire peace as much as you do. I deplore bloodshed as much as you do; but I feel that not one drop of the blood shed in this war is on my hands; I can look up to my God and say this. I tried all in my power to avert this war. I saw it coming, and for twelve years I worked night and day to prevent it, but I could not. The North was mad and blind; it would not let us govern ourselves; and so the war came, and now it must go on till the last man of this generation falls in his tracks, and his children seize his musket and fight his battles, unless you acknowledge our right to self-government. We are not fighting for slavery. We are fighting for independence—and that or extermination we will have."

"And there are at least, four and a half millions of us left; so you see you have work before you," said Mr. Benjamin, with a decided sneer."

"We have no wish to exterminate you, answered the Colonel. I believe what I have said, that there is no bitterness between the Northern and Southern people. The North, I know loves the South. When peace comes it will pour money and means into your hands to repair the waste caused by the war, and it would now welcome you back and forgive you all the loss and bloodshed you have caused. But we must crush your armies and exterminate your government. And is not that already nearly done? You are wholly without money and at the end of your resources. Grant has shut you up in Richmond. Sherman is before Atlanta. Had you not, then, better accept honorable terms while you can retain your prestige and save the pride of the Southern people?"

MR DAVIS ON THE CONFEDERATE PROSPECTS.

Mr. Davis smiled.

"I respect your earnestness, Colonel, but you do not seem to understand the situation. We are not exactly shut up in Richmond. If your papers tell the truth, it is your Captain that is in danger, not ours. Some weeks ago Grant crossed the Rapidan to whip Lee and take Richmond. Lee drove him in the first battle, and then Grant executed what your people call a 'brilliant flank movement,' and fought Lee again. Lee drove him a second time, and then Grant made another 'flank movement;' and so they kept on—Lee whipping and Grant flanking, until Grant got where he is now. And what is the net result? Grant has lost seventy five or eighty thousand men—more than Lee had at the outset—and is no nearer taking Richmond than at first; and Lee, whose front has never been broken, holds him completely in check, and has men enough to spare to invade Maryland and threaten Washington. Sherman, to be sure, is before Atlanta; but suppose he is, and suppose he takes it. You know the further he goes from his base of supplies the weaker he grows, and the more disastrous defeat will be to him, and defeat may come. So, in a military point of view, I should certainly say our position was better than yours.

"As to money, we are richer than you are. You smile. But admit that our paper is worth nothing, it answers as a circulating medium: and we hold it all ourselves. If every dollar of it were lost, we should, as we have no foreign debt, be none the poorer. But it is worth something: it has a solid basis of a large cotton crop, while yours rests on nothing, and you owe all the world. As to resources, we do not lack for arms or ammunition, and we have still a wide territory from which to gather supplies. So you see, we are not in extremities. But if we were—if we were without money, without food, without weapons—if our whole country were devastated, and our armies crushed and disbanded—could we, without giving up our manhood, give up our right to govern ourselves? Would you not rather die, and feel yourself a man, than live and be subject to a foreign power?"

"From your stand point there is force in what you say," replied the Colonel. "But we did not come here to argue with you, Mr. Davis. We came hoping to find some honorable way to peace, and I am grieved to hear you say what you do. When I have seen your young men dying on the battle field, and your old men, women and children starving in their homes, I have felt I could risk my life to save them. For that reason I am here, and I am grieved, grieved, that there is no hope."

"I know your motives, Colonel Jaques, and I honor you for them; but what can I do more than I am doing? I would give my poor life, gladly, if it would bring peace and good will to the two countries; but it would not. It is with your own people you should labor. It is they who desolate our homes, burn our wheat fields, break the wheels of wagons carrying away our women and children, and destroy supplies meant for our sick and wounded. At your door lies the misery and crime of this war, it is a fearful account."

"Not all of it, Mr. Davis. I admit a fearful account, but it is not all at our door. The passions of both sides are aroused. Unarmed men are hanged and prisoners are shot down in cold blood by yourselves. Elements of barbarism are entering the war on both sides that should make us—you and me, as Christian men—shudder to think of. In God's name, then, let us stop it. Let us do something, concede something, to bring about peace. You cannot expect, with only four and a half millions, as Mr. Benjamin says you have, to hold out forever against twenty millions."

Again Mr. Davis smiled.

"Do you suppose there are twenty millions at the North determined to crush us?"

"I do—to crush your Government. A small number of our people, a very small number, are your friends—secessionists. The rest differ about measures and candidates, but are united in the determination to sustain the Union. Whoever is elected in November he must be committed to a vigorous prosecution of the war."

Mr. Davis still looked incredulous. I remarked;

"It is so, sir. Whoever tells you otherwise deceives you. I think I know Northern sentiment, and I assure you it is so. You know we have a system of lyceum lecturing in our large towns. At the close of the lectures it is the custom of the people to come upon the platform and talk with the lecturer. This gives him an excellent opportunity of learning public sentiment. Last winter I lectured before nearly a hundred of such associations all over the North, from Dubuque to Bangor, and I took pains to ascertain the feeling of the people. I found a unanimous determination to crush the rebellion and save the Union at every sacrifice. The majority are in favor of Mr. Lincoln, and nearly all of those opposed to him are opposed to him because they think he does not fight you with enough vigor. The radical Republicans, who go for slave suffrage and thorough confiscation, are those who will defeat him, if he is to be defeated."

"But if he is defeated before the people the House will elect a worse man—I mean worse for you. It is more radical than he is—you can see that from Mr. Ashley's Reconstruction Bill—and the people are more radical than the House. Mr. Lincoln, I know, is about to call out five hundred thousand more men, and I can't see how you can resist much longer; but if you do you will only deepen the radical feeling of the Northern people. They will now give you fair, honorable, generous terms; but let them suffer much more, let there be a dead man in every house, as there now is in every village, they will give you no terms—they will insist on hanging every rebel South of ———. Pardon my terms. I mean no offence."

"You give no offence," he replied, smiling very pleasantly. "I wouldn't have you pick your words. This is a frank, free talk, and I like you the better for saying what you think. Go on."

"I was merely going to say that, let the Northern people once really feel the war—they do not feel it yet—and they will insist on hanging every one of your leaders."

"Well, admitting all you say, I can't see how it affects our position. There are some things worse than hanging or extermination. We reckon giving up the right of self-government one of those things."

"By self-government you mean disunion—Southern independence?"

"Yes!"

"And slavery, you say, is no longer an element in the contest."

"No, it is not. It never was an essential element. It was only a means of bringing other conflicting elements to an earlier culmination. It fired the musket which was already capped and loaded. There are essential differences between the North and the South that will, however this war may end, make them two nations."

"You ask me to say what I think. Will you allow me to say that I know the South pretty well, and never observed those differences?"

"Then you have not used your eyes. My sight is poorer than yours, but I have seen them for years."

The laugh was upon me, and Mr. Benjamin enjoyed it.

"Well, sir, be that as it may; if I understand you, the dispute between your Government and ours is narrowed down to this: Union or disunion."

"Yes; or, to put it in other words, independence or subjugation."

"Then the two Governments are irreconcilably apart. They have no alternative but to fight it out. But it is not so with the people. They are tired of fighting and want peace; and, as they bear all the burden and suffering of the war, is it not right they should have peace, and have it on such terms as they like?"

"I don't understand you. Be a little more explicit."

MR. DAVIS REFUSES AN ARMISTICE.

"Well, suppose the two Governments should agree to something like this: "To go to the people with two propositions, say peace with disunion and Southern independence as your proposition; and peace, with union, emancipation, no confiscation and universal amnesty, as ours. Let the citizens of all the United States (as they existed before the war) vote 'Yes' or 'No' on these two propositions at a special election within sixty days. If a majority votes disunion, our Government to be bound by it, and to let you go in peace. If a majority vote Union, yours to be bound by it, and to stay in peace. The two Governments can contract in this way, and the people, though constitutionally unable to decide on peace or war, can elect which of the two propositions shall govern their rulers. Let Lee and Grant meanwhile agree to an armistice. This would sheathe the sword; and if once sheathed it would never again be drawn by this generation."

"The plan is altogether impracticable. If the South were only one State it might work, but as it is, if one Southern State objected to emancipation it would nullify the whole thing; for you are aware the people of Virginia cannot vote Slavery out of South Carolina, nor the people of South Carolina vote it out of Virginia."

"But three-fourths of the States can amend the Constitution. Let it be done in that way, in any way, so that it be done by the people. I am not a statesman or a politician, and I do not know just how such a plan could be carried on; but you get the idea, that the people shall decide the question."

"That the majority shall decide it, you mean. We seceded to rid ourselves of the rule of the majority, and this would subject us to it again."

"But the majority must rule finally, either with bullets or ballots."

"I am not so sure of that. Neither current events nor history shows that the majority rules or ever did rule. The contrary, I think, is true. Why, sir, the man who should go before the Southern people with such a proposition, with any proposition which implies that the North was to have a voice in determining the domestic relations of the South, could not live here a day. He would be hanged to the first tree without judge or jury."

"Allow me to doubt that. I think it more likely he would be hanged if he let the Southern people know the majority cannot rule," I replied, smiling.

"I have no fears of that," replied Mr. Davis, also smiling most good humoredly. "I give you leave to proclaim it from every house top in the South."

"But, seriously, sir, you let the majority rule in a single State; why not let it rule in the whole country?"

"Because the States are independent and sovereign. The country is not. It is only a confederation of States, or rather it was; it is now two Confederacies."

"Then we are not a people; we are only a political partnership."

"That is all."

"Your very name, sir, 'United States,' implies that," said Mr. Benjamin. "But tell me, are the terms you have named—emancipation, no confiscation, and universal amnesty—the terms which Mr. Lincoln authorized you to offer us."

"No, sir; Mr. Lincoln did not authorize me to offer you any terms. But I think both he and the Northern people, for the sake of peace, would assent to some such conditions."

"They are very generous," replied Mr. Davis, for the first time during the interview showing some angry feeling. "But, amnesty, sir, applies to criminals. We have committed no crime. Confiscation is of no account unless you can enforce it. And emancipation! You have already emancipated nearly two millions of our slaves; and if you will take care of them you may emancipate the rest. I had a few when the war began. I was of some use to them; they never were of any to me. Against their will you 'emancipated' them, and you may 'emancipate' every negro in the Confederacy, but we will be free. We will govern ourselves. We will do it if we have to see every Southern plantation sacked and every Southern city in flames."

"I see, Mr Davis, it is useless to continue this conversation," I replied; "and you will pardon us if we have seemed to press our views with too much pertinacity. We love the old flag, and that must be our apology for intruding upon you at all."

"You have not intruded upon me," he replied, resuming his usual manner. "I am glad to have met you both. I once loved the old flag as well as you do; I would have died for it; but now it is to me only the emblem of oppression."

"I hope the day may never come, Mr. Davis, when I say that," said the Colonel.

CLOSE OF THE INTERVIEW.

A half hour's conversation on other topics, not of public interest, ensued; and then we rose to go. As we did so, the rebel President gave me his hand, and, bidding me a kindly goodby, expressed the hope of seeing me again in Richmond in happier times—when peace should have returned; but with the Colonel his parting was particularly cordial. Taking his hand in both of his, he said to him:

"Colonel, I respect your character and your motives, and I wish you well; I wish you every good I can wish you consistently with the interests of the Confederacy."

The quiet, straightforward bearing and magnificent moral courage of our "fighting parson" had evidently impressed Mr. Davis very favorably.

As we were leaving the room he added:

"Say to Mr. Lincoln from me that I shall at any time be pleased to receive proposals for peace on the basis of our independence. It will be useless to approach me with any other.'

When we went out Mr. Benjamin called Judge Ould, who had been waiting during the whole interview—two hours—at the other end of the hall, and we passed down the stairway together. As I put my arm within that of the Judge, he said to me—

"Well, what is the result?

"Nothing but war—war to the knife."

"Ephraim is joined to his idols—let him alone," added the Colonel, solemnly.

THE CASUALTIES IN HAGOOD'S BRIGADE.

Editor Mercury:—Enclosed please find list of casualties in HAGOOD's Brigade for the week ending August 21st, including fight of same date, which you will please publish and oblige

Yours, &c., SAM'L LOGAN, Surgeon S. A. C. S.

Company A, Lieut Ross commanding—Wounded, and in hands of the enemy, Lieut Ross, Private H G Proctor.

Wounded: Corp J H Dickinson, in head and fingers slight; Private W B Cowperthwait in leg slight; J L Honour, in thigh severe, finger amputated.

Missing: Privates Jno Klinck, C T Black, John W McCabe.

Company B, Sergeant McLeod commanding—Killed: None.

Wounded: Corpl F Oliver, calf leg severe; Privates L E Molloy, thigh severe; S Graham, wrist severe; Acting Adjutant H J Greer, ankle bruised slight.

Missing: Sergt R A McLeod, Corpl A W Force, Privates J B Gibbes, A Gray, J T Grady.

Company C, Lieut Montgomery commanding—Killed: None.

Wounded: Lieut Montgomery, in leg slight; Sergt McCleary, in leg severe; Privates J H Young, in leg slight; H D Shaw, arm severe.

Missing: Act Lt J E Scott, Corp McCleary, Privates J N Brown, J G McCants, J W Kelley, D W Logan, E Johnson.

Missing and wounded: Privates E J Kelley, J B Mitcham, J B Montgomery, T W Montgomery.

Company D, Capt McKerrell, commanding—Killed: Jno Nuse.

Wounded: Corporal W J Lovell.

Missing: Capt McKerrell, Lieut Bethea, Sergeant McIntyre, Sergeant D A Keever, Corporal Hewen, Privates W K Foxworth, E W Hays, N F Horlong, J W Redman, S A Owens, W J Whittington, James Wilkes.

Company E, Lieutenant V Duc commanding—Killed: none.

Wounded and missing: Lieutenant Duc, Corporal H T Milligan, Private L M Phillips.

Wounded: Michael Bsim, in arm and leg severe, John Brenan, back severe.

Missing: Henry Hutson, S Weatherlin, Jno Metz.

Company F, Capt Sellers commanding—Killed: None.

Wounded and missing: Capt Sellers.

Wounded: Lieut Harper, in leg severe; Privates D V Thompson, thigh contusion; D F Ott, wrist severe; H L Rucker, breast slight.

Company G, Lieut S Kennedy commanding—Killed: None.

Wounded and missing: Lieut S Kennedy.

Wounded: Acting Lieut B Jzler, in arm and side slight, Corporal Wm Paulding, face and neck slight; Privates J P Bruce, in arm severe; J Graves, in face severe; A J Smook, in thigh severe; H Bailey, concussion severe.

Missing: Sergt J S Ouller, Privates T J Fruse, J D Ott, W W Taylor, S B Crider.

Company H, Lieutenant Bartless commanding—Killed: None.

Wounded: Private J E Parker, in hand, severe.

Missing: Corporal P Kunan

Company I, Sergeant J W Cochran commanding—Killed: None.

Wounded: Sergt Cochran, contusion, left side; Privates H T White, in leg, severe; S W Barwick, slight.

Missing: Sergeant Fleming, Corporals Evans, A W Burgess, Privates H L B Fleming, W D Freeman, J A Timmons

Wounded and Missing: Private F M Stukes.

Company K, 1st Sergeant Davis commanding—Killed: None.

Wounded and Missing: Corpl W B Gordon, Private W C Lesesne.

Wounded. Corpl Terry, neck, slight.

WM. C RAVENEL, Surgeon 25th S. C. V.

27TH REGIMENT, S. C. V., NEAR PETERSBURG, AUGUST 21ST., 1864

1 Sergt J W Guy, Company I, flesh wound left ankle.

2 Sergt W C Wood, Company C, flesh, calf right leg, (severely.)

3 Sergt J M Jackson, Company K, right hand fracture head of metta-tarsal bone and right thigh. (severely.)

4 Sergt J R Davis, Company E, middle finger left hand, amputation.

5 Corp W Y Lovett, Company G, palm left hand, (severely.)

6 Private J W D Bowen, Company F, right foot, (severely.)

7 Private W C Page, Company B, left arm, (severely,) upper section.

8 Private J McNeal, Company C, flesh, right fore arm, (slightly.)

9 Private D G Bullington, Company I, right hip, (slightly.)

10 Private J P McAbee, Company C, right thigh, flesh, (severely.)

11 Private W J Seyle, Company I flesh wound of back, fracturing inferior angle of scofula, (severely.)

12 Private Henry Adricks, Company I, shell wound of right thigh, (dangerously) amputation of middle third.

13 Lieut C P Porcher, Company F, right foot, (slightly.)

14 Private D J McElrath, Company B, shell wound of right leg, (severely,) amputation below knee, August 20th.

JOSEPH L. PRESSLY, Surgeon 27th Regiment.

11TH REGIMENT S. C. V., LIEUT J F. MORRISON COMMANDING.

Field and Staff—Missing. Lieut Morrison.

Company B—Killed: Private G Newton.

Missing: Lieut H W G Bowman.

Company C—Killed: None.

Wounded: Private S Fryar, thigh severe.

Missing: Private A Paramour.

Company D—Killed: None.

Wounded: Privates J P Stripes, thigh and arm, severe; W B Barnes, slight; W H Lewis, slight; R Thomas, slight.

Missing: Corporal W T Mixson and W A Fennel.

Company E—Killed: Sergeant A C Mew.

Wounded: Sergeant D Woods, stunned by shell; Privates W F Deloach, arm severe; W F Dobson, arm slight; R O Reynolds, thigh severely.

Missing: Lieut T S Tuton, Privates H Garrin, H Rushing.

Company F—Killed: None.

Wounded and Missing: Privates J Phillips, M Padgett.

Company G—Killed: None.

Wounded and Missing: Private T Brownlee.

Company H—Killed: None.

Wounded: Lieut J P Minus, thigh severe, Sergeant C P Brothers, foot severe; Private W J Waters, leg severe; Corporal W B Murray, ear slight.

Missing: Corporal D R Bowman, Sergeant A W Appleby, Sergeant B A Easterling, Corporal J D West, Private W J Hussy.

Company I—Killed: Corporal M Schmidt.

Wounded: Sergeant J W Saunders, slight; Privates S G Tant, ear and shoulder, slight.

Missing: Corporal S Martin, Privates C C Davis and J W Willis.

Company K—Killed: None.

Wounded: Lt F J Cassady, slight; Privates G F Fralix, arm severe; W Nettles, foot severe; W D Bishop, leg severe; T W Cummings, head severe; A N Walker, in hand, leg and thigh severe.

Missing: Corp J Peters, Sergt G W Rentz, Sergt J C Folk, Privates J D Buchanan, J S Buchanan, W B Godley, J H Nettles, J E Walker, F Padget, D Padget, J Rentz, J B Black lost finger in charge.

The above list is very nearly full—lists of the following Regiments are not complete, only those that have reported to hospital being included.

7TH BATTALION S. C. V.

Company A—Sergt J W Burns, right knee fractured.

Company B—Wounded: Private D Abbot (since dead), Sergt H D Duke, left eye severe; Lieut S W Douglass, thigh severe; Privates Jno Neal leg severe; C Price, back severe; O B Young, foot amputated

Company C—Wounded: Lieut J Mankin, right side severe; Privates R Goins, hand severe.

Company D—Wounded: Private Hogin, both thighs severe.

Company E—Wounded: Privates L C McKenzie, scalp slight; H C Gerald, leg severe; H Morris, left leg severe.

Company F—Wounded: Captain Dave Segars, left side severe; Private L Haugh, face slight; Lieut G P King, groin slight; Privates J D Shaw, back severe; W C Hall, fracture arm severe.

Company G—Wounded: Private H Smith, cheek and shoulder severe; Lieut L L Clyburn, leg severe; Sergt W Murray, thigh severe; Privates S Motley, forehead slight; Thos Jeffers, forehead slight.

Company H—Wounded: Lieut Weston, thigh severe; Privates W Tison, leg severe; H M Addison, hip slight.

R B. HANAHAN, Surgeon P. A. C. S.

Casualties in 21st S. C. Regiment, in engagement on Petersburg and Weldon Railroad, August 21st, 1864:

Captain S H Wilds commanded the regiment in this engagement and received a slight flesh wound in the thigh

Company A, Lieut Thos Ford, commanding—Killed: Private James Haywood.

Wounded: Sergeant John Ford, leg fractured, severe; Privates Z J Exum, in leg severe; J Rodgers, leg amputated.

Missing: Lieut Thos Ford, Sergeant J R Avant, Corporal H Cribb, Corporal D C Cornble, Privates B Cornble, J Goude, Joseph Goude.

Company B, Sergeant Z P King commanding—Killed. None.

Wounded: None.

Missing: A E San, A M Heath, L N Hutchinson

Company D, Sergeant F Rivers commanding—Killed: Private J C Carrie.

Wounded: Sergeant J C Campbell, Corpl A Smothers, in leg severe.

Missing: J H Edwards, also wounded; J O Edwards and B F Edwards.

Company E, Sergeant F Rivers commanding—Killed. None.

Wounded: Private Jacob Ban, in foot severe.

Missing: Sergeant A M Wilkes, Privates Wm Purvis, Wm Jones, Jas Polk and J W Dixon.

Company F, Sergeant W F Adams commanding—Killed: None.

Wounded: Sergeant W F Adams, in arm and side, severe.

Missing: Lieut N A Easterling, Acting Lieut Colonel, Sergt A B Easterling, Corpl G V Easterling, Privates G W Heustis, A Munship, N C McCaskill.

Company G, Lieutenant F Bowles commanding—Killed. None.

Wounded: T F[illegible], in head, severe; E Tyner, in hand, slight.

Missing: Lieut P Bowles, Sergt Jno Boyle, Privates Jerry Vaner, J Johns, E Bowle, Samuel Skipper

Company H, Sergeant Joel Odam, commanding—Killed: None.

Wounded: N B Rest, in side dangerous; Private Wm Harris, finger amputated

Missing: Lieut P W Atkinson, Acting Adjutant, Sergeant Joel Odam, Private A E DuBose

Company I, Lieut H M Cannon, commanding—Killed None.

Wounded: Sergeant J W Brown, leg amputated, Private R H Williams, in hand severe.

Missing: D H Johnson, also wounded.

Company K, Corporal W H Young, commanding—Killed: None.

Wounded: None.

Missing: Corporal W H Young, Privates G W R[illegible], M Scaff, J Thompson.

Company L, —— commanding—Killed: None.

Wounded: Privates N B R Gasque in arm and shoulder severe; O E Gibson, in shoulder slight.

Missing: None.

GEORGE B SMITH, Assistant Surgeon 21st S C Regiment.

CAMP CULPEPER C. H., VA., August 10, 1864

Casualties in Company H, 15th Regiment S. C. V. (Lieut. FARR commanding), near Richmond, Va.:

May 6—Killed: Privates James Adis and John Smith.

Wounded: Lieut Farr, in leg, Sergt D Griffin, Corpl A W Spronse, Privates Richard Adis, R Burges, J George, A D Spears, N Farr, E C Vaughn, Joel Weeks.

May 8.—Killed: None.

Wounded: Corpl D V Morgan, J Garner, G Garner, J M Fowler, F Gregory, L Spronse

May 21—Killed. W E Conley.

May 26. Wounded W T Codd, Noah Nat[illegible], C W[illegible], Wm Howell, A D Spears (the second time), John Spronse

Missing: Jackson Palmer, D R Vaughn (supposed to be killed or prisoners).

Burges, Farr and Spears all lost a leg.

J. T. R. WITHERST

☞ Columbia papers please copy.

TWELFTH QUARTERLY REPORT OF THE SOLDIERS' RELIEF ASSOCIATION OF CHARLESTON.

ORPHAN HOUSE, July 20, 1864.

Three years ago a few friends met at the house of one of our citizens, and then and there formed the Soldiers' Relief Association of Charleston, elected their officers and unanimously pledged themselves to do all in their power for the relief of our brave defenders, who had left the comforts of home and all that man holds dear, to be a bulwark of defence to us from a ruthless foe. We have endeavored, dear reader, to fulfil that pledge, and to you who must be the judge, we submit our report, hoping that you will accord us after a careful perusal, and in consideration of the many disadvantages we have labored under, a hearty "well done." Our efforts to do good have not been confined to our own "Palmetto Boys," but a helping hand has been extended to all who needed it, whenever in our power to give it unrestricted by State lines, for should not all who are thus battling for our rights and liberties share alike.

We trust that our friends both in the city and country will continue their donations of money, provisions, hospital stores, material for clothing, &c., and thus enable us, by the blessing of God, to continue our good work and assist our soldiers and sailors suffering in hospitals on their sick and dying beds, or exposed to all the dangers and hardships of war in the camp and on the field

Contributions directed to the Soldiers' Relief Association, Orphan House, Charleston, will be thankfully received, judiciously disposed of and duly acknowledged.

MRS GEORGE ROBERTSON, President.
MISS F. M. BLAMYER, Secretary.

TREASURER'S REPORT.

By cash balance on hand from last quarter		$[illegible]
By 4 per cent. Confederate bonds		[illegible]
By donations during the last quarter		[illegible]
		$7,[illegible]
To cash paid for freights and cartages	$58 50	
To cash paid for stationery	24 75	
To cash paid for discount on uncurrent money	146 99	
To cash paid for sewing and washing	161 00	
To cash paid for yarn and cloth	2,012 26	
To cash paid for hospital stores	242 40	
To cash paid Ladies' Hospital Committee	58[illegible]	
To cash paid depository expenses	[illegible]	
		$3,827 90
Balance in cash and 4 per cent. bonds		$4 494 [illegible]

MISS F. M. BLAMYER, Treasurer.

Charleston July 20, 1864.

During the quarter the Association contributed to various companies and hospitals 54 flannel shirts, 210 cotton shirts, 26[illegible] pairs drawers, 162 pairs socks, besides distributing, through its Committee of ladies, a large amount of hospital stores. It has also supplied several of the outposts with cooked provisions and refreshments.

RECAPITULATION FOR THE THREE YEARS

By amount of cash received		$36,666 48
To amount of cash expended	$32,171.63	
To amount of 4 per cent. bonds	3600 00	35,771 63
Cash on hand		$894.85

AMOUNT OF CLOTHING, ETC., DISTRIBUTED.

11,302 flannel and cotton shirts 3961 pairs drawers, 6429 pairs socks, 812 pairs pantaloons, 206 coats, 452 pairs gloves, 812 caps, 828 pairs slippers and shoes, 1796 pocket handkerchiefs, 861 dressing gowns, 618 mattrasses, 519 pillows, 1532 bed and pillow sacks, 278 mosquito nets, 1162 sheets, 412 scarfs, 1842 blankets and carpets, 1808 towels.

A large quantity of rice, hospital stores, liquors, wines, meats, vegetables, fruit, ice, herbs, books, tracts and papers have been distributed.

The Association also made up a large quantity of work for the Quartermaster and various companies, besides refilling a large number of bed and pillow sacks for various hospitals.

☞ Columbia papers please copy.

CHARLESTON, August 29th, 1864.

Editor Mercury: Please acknowledge, through your columns, the receipt of seven barrels biscuits, a donation to the Free Market from Mr. S. C. Hambleton, through Mr. E. Chapman, for which the Committee return their thanks.

H R JACOBS, Clerk of Free Market.

Consignees Per South Carolina Railroad, August 27.

160 bales Fodder, 1512 bushels Grain, 400 sacks Meal, 827 sacks Flour, 56 barrels [illegible], Mdse, &c. To Major McClenaghan, Maj [illegible], W S Henerey, H Kirch, L F [illegible], C D Ahrens, N Wynne, N M Porter & Co, Maj Burke, A Von Dohlin, J M Bally, M Burns, C Sahlman, W H Easterby, E H Rodgers & Co, J F Readhimer, Supply Association, Maj Seabrook, F Richards, J A Duffus, A [illegible], J H Graves, D Werner, P Muikal, E W West, J L Ward, S H Cunningham, W Hockaday, Capt Crafts, F A Mitchell, S Mathewes, J Qualls, J Giemenerato, L B Cline, J C Cozman, W F Paddon, J P Flonen, J G Martin, A Langnick, W McComb, J B Togni, C Macbeth, R Spriggs, J Campson, and Order

Richmond Dispatch.

BY J. A. COWARDIN & CO.

THE DISPATCH is published daily, (Sundays excepted,) at FORTY DOLLARS for twelve months; TWENTY DOLLARS for six months; TEN DOLLARS for three months, or FOUR DOLLARS for one month, in advance. All remittances by mail are at the risk of those who make them.

DAILY DISPATCH.

VOL. XXVII. RICHMOND, VA., MONDAY, SEPTEMBER 5, 1864. NO 58.

EDUCATIONAL.

MISS A. E. PARKER WILL RESUME the duties of her SCHOOL for BOYS and GIRLS, on Twenty-seventh street, between Clay and Leigh, on the 15th of SEPTEMBER. As she has had six years' experience, she flatters herself she will be able to give satisfaction. Thankful for past favors, she hopes, by unwearied efforts, to merit a continuance of the same. Proper attention will be paid to the manners and morals of all who may be entrusted to her charge. se 2—6t*

EDGEWOOD MALE SEMINARY.—The next session of this SCHOOL will commence the first MONDAY in October next and end the 15th of February. For terms, apply to the subscriber, Amelia Courthouse, Virginia. [illegible]

LETTER LIST.

LIST OF LETTERS remaining in the RICHMOND POST-OFFICE on the 2d day of September, 1864.

☞ Persons calling for Letters in the List will please say they are ADVERTISED.

☞ The postage will be TWO CENTS on each letter advertised.

LADIES' LIST.

A.—Mrs A Acree, Mrs A Adams (2), Mrs L Adams, Mrs W A Anderson, Mrs Sarah Anderson, Mrs S A Anderson, Mrs Wm Allen, Mrs R C Allen, Mrs H B Anderson, Mrs Ella Anderson, Mrs L Adams, Mrs N Allen, Mrs L G Allen, Mrs R V Augyle, Mrs L Armstrong, Miss M Allen, Miss A Anthony, Miss Va Aldridge, Miss E Austin (3), Miss M A Ander- [illegible]

[illegible]

John Brantley, Joseph Binford, John Bennett (2), J H Bradley, Henry P Browning, Howard W Baker (2), Harris D Burruss, Geo R Birchett, G M Bates, Geo E Brown, Geo R Bell, Geo Bailey, George H Burch, G H Ball, Capt Geo W Bowton, G W Brown, Geo W Barker, C H Ballington, Bairy Braxton, Chas Brady, B W Berry, J F Beuan, B M Brown, I & L Belsoly, A J Benett, A S Bacon, A J Brown, I & A L Belisoly, Albert Balls, A M Burk, Dr A G Beale.

C.—Wm Cook, W J Crawford, Wm Carter, Wm C Childs, Capt Wm H Christian, Capt W L Campbell, W R Coleman, W Caspary, W Craddock, W D Caw, Thos Cauthorn, J J Corfew, S C Cain, Thos R Calviz, Lieut T J Cannon, Col G Crutchfield, Dr S P Christian, Capt S R Chisman, Samuel R Cocke, S Cohen (3), Robt Cooke, R H Carter, P Cole, O E Chamley, [illegible]

[illegible]

Richmond Dispatch.

The DAILY DISPATCH is [illegible] News Dealers at TWENTY CENTS per copy. City [illegible] are authorized to charge ONE DOLLAR [illegible] FIFTY CENTS per week to regular subscribers.

MONDAY MORNING.......SEPTEMBER 5, 1864.

THE EVACUATION OF ATLANTA.

INTERESTING ACCOUNTS FROM THERE—SHERMAN'S EVACUATION OF HIS POSITION ON OUR RIGHT—HISTORY OF HIS FLANK MOVEMENT, &c.

The news of the evacuation of Atlanta by our forces gives interest to any news from there bearing upon the military situation. The movement by which Sherman has gained this advantage was a bold one, though not conducted with such secrecy as to hide from our commanders there its progress. To enable our readers to comprehend the change of position made by Sherman, we take from the Charlottesville *Chronicle* the following about

SHERMAN'S CHANGE OF BASE.

Four lines of communication meet at Atlanta—the Chattanooga, Augusta, West Point and Macon railways. General Hood relies on the Macon road. General Sherman is dependent on a single line. The enemy's cavalry have temporarily destroyed the Augusta railway. We learn to-day that his army is concentrated along the West Point road "between East Point and Fairburn." This intelligence is significant of an active campaign around Atlanta.—The West Point road follows the course of the Chattahoochee from northeast to southwest. East Point is distant six miles from Atlanta. Fairburn is twelve miles farther south. It will be observed, Sherman's army is on the left flank of General Hood, facing east. His line stretches from Atlanta to (and probably beyond) East Point junction of the Macon and West Point roads, facing west. This manœuvre of General Sherman is a repetition of his movement around Dalton, with this important exception—at Dalton he operated on both flanks of General Johnston's army. To occupy the West Point road, and menace the Macon road (south of East Point) he has withdrawn his army from the east and north of Atlanta and thrown it southwest of Hood's. Nay, he has abandoned the line of the Chattanooga road from Atlanta to the Chattahoochee, and communicates with Marietta—his fortified base—by wagon route from Fairburn via Sandtown, on the river below the railroad bridge. Marietta is held by Major-General McArthur, and the "crossings of the Chattahoochee are strongly guarded." Communication between Chattanooga and Marietta is now uninterrupted—Wheeler being in Tennessee.

THE EVACUATION OF THE ENEMY'S POSITION ON OUR RIGHT.

A letter from Atlanta, dated the 27th ultimo, gives the following description of the evacuated works of the enemy in front of our right wing, three miles from Atlanta:

It is thought that Sherman is massing on our left to make a desperate attempt to cut our line of communication and hold the Macon and Western railroad, with the belief that it will compel our army to fall back, thereby giving up the much-coveted prize, Atlanta.

I visited the Yankee camps to the west of Atlanta to-day. I find their earthworks to be very substantial, but not as much so as I had anticipated from the reports of parties who had visited them the day previous. The camps are well arranged. From the appearance of everything, each man had a bunk made to sleep on. The bunks are made by driving four stakes in the ground about two feet one way and four and a half feet the other, two cross bars or boards laid across the stakes and fastened on, and then small poles, about six or seven feet long, are laid on the cross bars and fastened on with withes or ropes, and hemp sacks spread on a great many of them. I have several of the sacks now in my possession, which I picked up around these bunks. I could have procured at least a thousand. These bunks all have dirt thrown up in front of them, which makes them very secure from Minie balls.—The camps which the Yankees occupied around this city are about the best arranged ones I have ever seen. Nearly every camp has from one to two Dutch bake ovens, which are made of brick, and put up in the best style. In fact, everything is fixed up as though they intended to remain in them for years to come.

All the houses which the people vacated between here and the river have been torn to pieces, and the lumber used to make shelters of. The houses, where the families remained in them, are left standing, but they look rather worsted. Some of them are pretty well riddled. The Yankee camps are crowded daily with people who are out viewing them. Every one you meet has a bag of plunder, which they are bringing home as curiosities. There is some very fine furniture scattered over the camps. In a day or two there will be nothing left worth bringing off.

It is reported here this evening that two brigades of Yankees crossed the Atlanta and West Point railroad, and struck out for the Macon and Western railroad.

I give you below a note which I discovered written in a large bold hand with charcoal on the headboard of one of the Yankee bunks. The bunk is about three miles west of Atlanta. The note is as follows:

"Good-bye, Johnny. We are going to see you soon, and when we come to Georgia we will remember Kennesaw.

YANK."

A letter dated the 28th says:

Many persons think that the long agony is over—that the investment is raised, and that the city is safe. I am not so fast in my conclusions. Among the prisoners who are brought in every day, I do not perceive the slightest demoralization. They are all plucky, and have no idea of abandoning Atlanta.

I see in late Northern papers hints which squint at a movement on our left; that is, upon East Point, the junction of the Macon and Montgomery roads, six miles from town. Sherman thinks—and truly—that if he can seize and hold this seat in our rear he will force us out of our works for the purpose of attacking and driving him away, or for our evacuation and retreat. But, be it remembered, we are as strongly fortified at East Point, and thence along the line of the railroad to the city, as we are around Atlanta. Sherman will be compelled to attack our works if he gain East Point; and no fear is felt for the result. So that if the movement is an attempt at a flank, it is still considered highly favorable to us, and among other good things, relieves the city from bombardment.

HISTORY OF SHERMAN'S MOVEMENT.

We find two very interesting letters in the Augusta *Chronicle* giving a description of what was known of Sherman's movements, and how they were accomplished. We give extracts from them:

ATLANTA, Sunday, August 28, 1864.

Something of the position of the Federal army has been ascertained—enough, at least, to convince every one that the late movement from the trenches was not made with a view of retreating, and, perhaps, sufficient to warrant reasonable conclusions as to what are Sherman's purposes, and where he will next strike.

The observations of our scouts, and reports from citizens in the rear of the late Federal lines, inform us that for some days back the enemy has been preparing a line of works, commencing on this side of the Chattahoochee a short distance above the railroad bridge, on the State road, and running down the river about two miles to a ferry, where they have built a permanent bridge. From thence the works run to a point at the left of their extreme right wing.

Behind those works the forces withdrawn so quietly on Thursday night were thrown, and during Friday and Friday night the centre was moved to the rear of this line. The works are said to be formidable, particularly in front of the railroad bridge. This position leaves the Federal line at least one-third shorter than it was before, and of course they have men to operate with elsewhere. At the second ferry below the railroad bridge their pontoon has also been taken up and a permanent bridge erected. The pontoon will, it is expected, be moved to ferries lower down the river.

These preparations, and the position into which Sherman has thrown his army, indicate very clearly that all his late unexpected movements are the result of his having arrived at the conclusion that he could not capture Atlanta by attacking its defences, and a matured plan for another attempt to flank our army from the city by cutting its railroad communication to the rear. The raiding policy was a failure, but the purpose might be accomplished by throwing his main line across the West Point and Macon roads, and that this is the grand movement that will be attempted there can be no longer any doubt. The topography of the country on the north side of the river is said to be favorable for transportation by wagon, the roads numerous; and with the ferries bridged, as [illegible], supplies can be moved from Vining's station above the river with facility. This is the opinion of the old citizens who are acquainted with the country.

ATLANTA, August 29, 1864.

The movements now going on are big with importance, and promise a very early development of results. Sherman has so far progressed with his new plan that strategic movements to prevent its fulfillment can be safely made with a certainty that renders an error almost impossible; and the time is at hand when General Hood will be called upon to demonstrate all the soldierly qualities of a great commander it is acknowledged he possesses. Of the result, if his resources are sufficient, fears are entertained by but few.

My former letter mentioned the fact that a heavy force of Federal cavalry occupied the West Point road Sunday morning. In the vicinity of Red Oak a battery was at once planted, and of course all transit by rail at once effectually blockaded. We also had rumors that skirmishing was going on during the day.

The reports from our scouts, brought in this forenoon, were to the effect that at an early hour this morning a strong Federal column of infantry and artillery commenced crossing the West Point road four miles below East Point, and that they were entrenching as they advanced. They were, thought, moving for Rough and Ready. Counter movements are, of course, going on, but of their character I may not speak. Of the progress made by the enemy in this direction, nothing definite has been ascertained; in fact, the only information I have been able to obtain was from passengers by the Macon train just arrived, who bring reports current at Rough and Ready when the train passed, that the Yankees had reached a point four miles west of the station, and were busy digging. No firing was heard as the train passed up the road to-day.

The movement the Federal commander is now endeavoring to carry on is a hazardous one, unless the numerical strength of his army has been greatly increased. This is asserted by some, and it may be the case. There is, therefore, a probability that General Hood may need more men. At all events, the contingency should be provided for at once. Now is the time to hold up his arms. Every available resource should be at once drained, be it from the State forces, or the idling and useless Government officials, of whom there are so many hugging safe and nominal positions in the rear. If urging all to the front who owe duty in the field will not send them forward, let the scorn of the community attach to them forever. They are needed now, and urgently.

It will not do for General Hood to uncover Atlanta by withdrawing all his forces from the long line around the city they so long and patiently held. Some five or six miles must be watched, while the more active operations will probably take place on a line extending nearly, if not quite, to Jonesboro', on the west side of the Macon road. This simple statement will serve to show the magnitude of the work the Army of Tennessee will probably be called upon to perform; and will the situation induce the forwarding of every aid that can be controlled? I am no alarmist, but cannot forego these expressions, which are freely indulged in at the front, and among officials who cannot well be mistaken as to the situation.

ADDITIONAL FROM THE NORTH.

From our latest Northern files we gather some very interesting intelligence, which we give below:

PLOT TO LIBERATE CONFEDERATE OFFICERS.

The fact that six hundred Confederate officers were sent to Hilton Head on the Crescent City, to be placed under fire on Morris island, has been stated. A letter to the New York *Times* gives the following incident of the voyage:

Immediately on landing, Captain H. Prentiss, in command of the guard, reported to General Foster his suspicions of an attempt on the part of William Baxter, the second mate of the vessel, to run her ashore at Cape Roman, with a view of allowing the prisoners to escape. The Crescent left Fort Delaware last Saturday under convoy of the naval supply steamer Admiral, and, when off Cape Roman, it is alleged the Crescent forsook her regular course and made a direct line for the shore. The mate was in charge of the steamer at the time—the captain having gone to his berth.

When the Admiral saw the Crescent making inland she showed lights and sent up rockets, of which the mate took no notice, although he was informed that signals were being made. The Crescent ran aground at nearly low tide; consequently at high water she was enabled to get afloat. While the vessel was ashore, it is reported that one of the prisoners, Lieutenant-Colonel Woodford, jumped overboard, and escaped by swimming, although the captain of the guard suspects that he is concealed on board the vessel. Both the captain and mate were arrested, and the latter was put in irons by order of General Foster. It is thought that the rebel officers bribed the mate to run the steamer ashore; but as to that matter, as well as other matters attending the whole affair, we shall be better informed when the Board of Inquiry, about to be convened, shall have made this report. At present the subject is too delicate to warrant speculation, and I am unwilling that the parties under arrest should be made to bear the burden of an unfavorable opinion until the facts of the case are proven against them. As to the guard, they were ready to a man to do their duty to the fullest extent. A strict eye was kept on the mate, and preparations were made to shoot the first rebel who should attempt to escape. The guard was composed principally of the One Hundred and Fifty-seventh Ohio regiment—hundred day men, and volunteered their service on the occasion, their time of enlistment having expired on the 23d instant. The Admiral signalled to a gunboat in the vicinity, which gunboat ran up as near the Crescent as possible, in order to repel any attack that the rebels might make from the shore. Fortunately for the rebels no hostile demonstrations were made. One of the prisoners has since stated that if the vessel had remained aground an hour or two longer a considerable force of cavalry would come down to assist the prisoners in escaping. The prisoners are all officers, ranking from colonel downward.

YANKEE VIEW OF THE INTERIOR SUPPLY OF DIXIE.

A Yankee who has conversed with some of Stoneman's raiders who escaped thus writes their impressions of "Dixie," as he calls it:

All agree in representing the Confederacy to be agriculturally in a most flourishing condition. The whole land is fat with corn and plenteous pork of corn, while negroes are huddled in only less abundance than mules and horses. The region which they penetrated is level and exceedingly fertile; the women are described as no longer the gaunt, sallow, whining creatures whom we see in Northern Georgia, but bitterly defiant and hostile toward the Yankees; but the men are absolutely swept out of the country. The vast tracts, stretching mile after mile, unbroken by the roadside, formerly devoted to cotton, now flourish with corn—the Government allows only a quarter of an acre of cotton per hand. Georgia alone has enough corn in cultivation to subsist the whole rebel army for a year. They found considerable old corn, and plenty of pork, stored in cellars in bulk. At Madison they destroyed five hundred sacks of genuine Rio coffee, and large quantities of rebel shoes, made of stout cotton cloth.

In short, the rebels have of imported luxuries but little to spare; but of the substantials—the material for sturdy muscle and the basis of hard fighting—*they have an abundance.*

But, socially considered, the South is described as being as gloomy and as cheerless as it is otherwise prosperous. The absence of nearly every adult white man from the household, and the redoubled multitudes of negroes, give an air of dismal loneliness to the whole land, which is described as something appalling. We who are near to the army miss nothing, but they wandered for days as through a great desert. Every one between sixteen and sixty-five is put into the army; in one county, ——, they found a gray-haired patriarch, who told them there were but twelve white male persons old enough to be called men in the county.

The negroes swarmed about them in vast numbers, so that General Stoneman had finally to establish a guard and drive them off to enable his forces to proceed at all. Each one brought in, as the price of his deliverance, a fine horse or two, or several mules of prodigious size, and an order had to be issued to disencumber the army of them when they began to be hemmed in. Three thousand were turned away at one time.

THE UNITED STATES ELECTORAL VOTE OF 1864.

Under the present apointments the following is the electoral vote of the several States of the "Union" which will participate in the coming Presidential election:

California	6	Missouri	11
Connecticut	6	New Hampshire	5
Delaware	3	New Jersey	7
Illinois	16	New York	33
Indiana	13	Ohio	21
Iowa	8	Oregon	3
Kansas	3	Pennsylvania	26
Kentucky	11	Rhode Island	4
Maine	7	Vermont	5
Maryland	7	West Virginia	5
Massachusetts	12	Wisconsin	8
Michigan	8		
Minnesota	7		231

STATES PROBABLY VOTING.

Arkansas	5	Nevada	3
Colorado	3	Tennessee	10
Louisiana	7	Virginia (part)	5
Nebraska	3		36

The following States, now in rebellion, would have been entitled to fifty-four electoral votes:

Alabama	8	North Carolina	9
Florida	5	South Carolina	8
Georgia	9	Texas	6
Mississippi	7	Virginia (part)	6

In the event of a vote of all these States, the whole number of electoral votes would have been three hundred and twenty-one, making necessary to a choice for President and Vice-President, one hundred and sixty-one. If we omit the votes of the States and the districts in rebellion, and include those which will enter the Union, or will have returned to allegiance, the whole number of votes will be two hundred and sixty-seven, of which one hundred and thirty-four will be sufficient to elect.

THE DRAFT IN INDIANA—THE EXPECTED RESISTANCE.

To-day the draft takes place in Indiana. There will be bloodshed there, though not those "rivers of blood" which sanguine people in the Confederacy look for. There will be scrimmaging in odd corners, large cities, and at various villages, in which, it is to be hoped, citizens of sufficiently prominent position, and Federal officers of sufficiently high rank, may be killed, to furnish the blood for drawing a clear line between the State sovereignty of Indiana and the central power of Lincoln. As anything about the state of affairs in that Commonwealth is interesting just now, we copy from the Indianapolis *Daily Journal* the following additional information about the treason in Indiana:

On Saturday afternoon Governor Morton received a letter from an Eastern city, which was as follows, except some names, which we omit for prudential reasons:

——— ———, August 17, 1864.

Governor O. P. Morton:

Sir: The facts hereby stated have come to my knowledge in a manner and from a source such as to leave no doubt in my mind of their reliability.

The Copperheads of Indiana have ordered and paid for thirty thousand revolvers, with forty-two boxes fixed ammunition, to be distributed among the antagonists to our Government for the purpose of controlling the Presidential election.

August 5th, the steamer Granite [illegible] landed in New York forty-two boxes of revolvers and ammunition; August 6, the steamer City of Hartford landed twenty-two boxes ammunition, destined for Indianapolis. Thirty-two boxes of the above have been forwarded to J. J. Parsons, Indianapolis, via Merchants' Dispatch, and marked ———; the balance is stored at No. — ——— street, New York, awaiting the convenience of the Copperheads to pay for the same before shipping.

Immediately on the receipt of this letter, Governor Morton placed the information it contained in the hands of policeman John S. Russell, who was able in a short time to report progress to Colonel James G. Jones, Assistant Provost-Marshal, who, with Colonel Warner, of the Veteran Reserve corps, with a proper detail, made a descent on the printing and book-binding establishment of H. H. Dodd & Co., on Saturday night, where they found thirty-two boxes, such as were described in the letter.—After the boxes were opened, their contents were found to consist of four hundred large navy revolvers and one hundred and thirty-five thousand rounds of fixed ammunition for the same arm.—Among the captures made at the same place were the great seal of the "Order of the Sons of Liberty," the official list of the members of the Order at this place, and several hundred printed copies of the ritual; also, a large amount of correspondence of an important character, which may be given to the public at the proper time. The people will begin to understand now how much these unmitigated scoundrels desire peace. Thirty thousand navy revolvers, with ammunition [illegible] for an army, coupled with the negotiations of Mr. Voorhees for the purchase of twenty thousand Garibaldi rifles, would indicate that there is a good deal of the disposition of the tiger hid under their [illegible] garb of peace.

When we look at the large sum of money which the amount of arms and ammunition named in this letter must cost, the question presents itself of the ways and means. The pistols alone would cost close on to one million of dollars at manufacturers' prices, and the twenty thousand rifles, without the import duties, would cost two hundred and eighty thousand dollars. Of course no such sums are provided by the members of the Order in this State, but there have been some peace commissioners prowling along the Canada border for several weeks. John C. Walker, and other peace men of Indiana, have been visiting them. Some months since the Confederate Government borrowed fifteen million dollars in Europe, for which they issued cotton bonds, and every blockade-runner carries out cotton to repay the loan. The object of the loan was, primarily, to purchase a navy in European ports, including the celebrated rams. That speculation having failed by the refusal of the Governments of England and France to permit the rams to depart, and they having been sold to other persons, the peace commissioners are in funds, and they could not make an investment more to the advantage of their master than to purchase arms and ammunition for Northern traitors, and to pay Northern demagogues liberally for shrieking for peace, free speech and liberty. William H. Harrison, Secretary of the Order of which H. H. Dodd is "Grand Commander," was arrested, and is still in custody. Messrs. John J. Parson and Charles P. Hutchinson, partners of Dodd, were also arrested, but were discharged on their affidavits that they were not members of the Order and were not advised of the contents of the boxes.

We have given a brief account of this, the most startling event in the attempted drama of civil war. The event naturally created an intense excitement in our city, and it will be an admonition to the people of the State of the danger which surrounds them. Dodd is absent from the city, probably making arrangements for the distribution of the arms and cartridges on hand and expected, but which, to his surprise, will be devoted to other purposes than enforcing the peculiar peace notions of a gang of conspirators against the peace and safety of the State.

The *Journal* also publishes a number of the papers and letters seized in the office of Daniel W. Voorhees, member of Congress:

ONE HUNDRED THOUSAND MEN TO HELP THE SOUTH.

HARRISONBURG, February 27, 1861.

My Dear Nephew:

* * * * * * *

We want you to hold that one hundred thousand men in readiness, as we do not know how soon we may want them.

* * * * * * *

J. HARDESTY.

Addressed on envelope:

Hon. DANIEL W. VOORHEES,
Terre Haute, Indiana.

ARMS FOR VOORHEES'S ARMY OF ONE HUNDRED THOUSAND MEN.

LONG BRANCH, August 21, 1863.

My Dear Sir: I enclose you two letters from a man by the name of Carr in reference to arms. A letter directed to him simply Philadelphia will reach him. I can vouch for the excellent quality and great efficiency of the rifles. Yours in haste,

JAMES W. WALL.

Envelope endorsed:

[Free.] JAMES W. WALL, U. S. S.
Hon. Daniel Voorhees, Terre Haute, Indiana.

E. W. CARR TO HON. JAMES W. WALL.

PHILADELPHIA, August 14, 1863.

Hon. James W. Wall:

Dear Sir: Your letter, with one enclosed about rifles, has been received. If the parties wish to buy them the best way would be for them to have some one in New York appointed to purchase them and confer with you and me.

I am satisfied that it is the very article they want, and as you know all about them you can "speak by the card." You have seen the article tried, and no doubt are well satisfied that it will speak loudly in a good cause.

We will sell them in bond for fourteen dollars, and I have no doubt that if the proper course is pursued the duty can be remitted. The rifles are better and cheaper than anything ever offered in this country, or made here, and as good as any ever imported. We challenge a comparison with any rifle execution whatever.

There are about twenty thousand rifles, and we desire to sell them all at once. They are a great bargain, and are worth to-day more in Europe than we offer to sell for here.

The price of fire-arms will advance within a year at least thirty-three per cent., as arms are in demand all over Europe. As you know, there is no more effective arm in the world than this.

I am, with great respect, yours truly,

E. W. CARR.

J. J. BINGHAM TO DAN VOORHEES—HAVE THE SOUTH RESOURCES ENOUGH TO KEEP THE UNION FORCES AT BAY?

INDIANAPOLIS, July 11, 1861.

My Dear Voorhees: I should like your private opinion as to the prospect of affairs, so that I may have some basis to go upon. Do you think the South have resources enough to keep the Union forces at bay, and finally force a recognition of their independence, or will Lincoln's army crush them out? You must have sources of information which I have not to enable you to form some opinion upon these matters.

If the *Congressional Globe and Appendix* is published and bound, I should be obliged to you for a set, and any other public documents of general interest.

I think there is a re-action taking place in Indiana in reference to the war, and Mr. Lincoln's message and Chase's report will aid it. Let me hear from you at the earliest convenience. What is Merson doing in Washington? Yours truly,

J. J. BINGHAM.

THE SURRENDER OF FORT MORGAN.

The New Orleans papers of the 24th contain the following particulars of the surrender of Fort Morgan:

All of Sunday and Sunday night a regular artillery duel was kept up between the fort and General Granger's men, about one gun being fired by the enemy every fifteen minutes. No damage resulted to either side as far as known. On Monday morning at daylight a combined attack by the land and naval forces was begun, and shot and shell were fiercely rained upon the doomed place until between six and seven o'clock yesterday morning. At this time a white flag was hoisted over Morgan, and firing immediately ceased. General Page was given until 2 o'clock P. M. before the final capitulation took place, which was unconditional. At two o'clock Fort Morgan was taken possession of.

At 5 o'clock on Monday afternoon the inner works and quarters of the fort caught fire from our shells, but the flames were speedily extinguished. At 8 o'clock the same evening another fire broke out, which spread rapidly and burned with great fury until 2 o'clock A. M., when it exhausted itself. During the whole of this terrible time our fire was poured in upon the garrison from all sides, rendering the place as near a hell upon earth as the imagination can well conceive. So fierce and continuous was our fire that the enemy were unable to respond in a way that in the least interfered with our operations. But *one gun* was worked by the rebels during the whole engagement.

Our losses during the conflict are stated at one killed and three slightly wounded. The rebel loss is about twenty killed and wounded. Fort Morgan is badly shattered by our terrific fire, and is but the wreck of the stronghold over which proudly waved the rebel flag on Sunday last.

The following is an extract of a letter from Admiral Farragut:

FLAGSHIP HARTFORD, MOBILE BAY, August 23, 1864.

Dear Commodore: Fort Morgan makes an unconditional surrender at 2 P. M. to-day to the forces of the army and navy. Page did not make us wait as long as I expected. We will cheer our flag and salute it, when hoisted, with one hundred guns by the fleet.

Congratulate General Canby upon the great success of his first effort in this department. Nothing could have been more harmonious than our combined operations. We had no ambition to excel each other but in the destruction of the enemy's works, which was effectually done by both army and navy. Very truly, yours,

D. G. FARRAGUT.

To Commodore Palmer, commanding at New Orleans.

Six hundred prisoners captured, and now coming up the river on the Tennessee and Manhattan. General Page is on board the [illegible].

Richmond Dispatch.

JOB PRINTING NEATLY EXECUTED.

Advertisements will be inserted at the rate of ONE DOLLAR AND FIFTY CENTS per square for each insertion—eight lines (or less) constitute a square.

Larger advertisements in exact proportion.

Advertisements published till forbid will be charged $1.50 per square for every insertion.

It appears that Colonel Anderson surrendered Fort Gaines after being shelled by one gunboat.—The following is his letter, offering to surrender on the 7th, after being shelled by the Chickasaw on the afternoon of the day before:

HEADQUARTERS, FORT GAINES, August 7, 1864.

To Admiral Farragut, Commanding National Forces off Dauphin Island:

Feeling my inability to maintain my present position longer than you may see fit to open upon me with your fleet, and feeling also the uselessness of entailing upon ourselves further destruction of life, I have the honor to propose the surrender of Fort Gaines, its garrison, stores, &c. I trust to your magnanimity for obtaining honorable terms, which I respectfully request that you will transmit to me and allow me sufficient time to consider them and return an answer. This communication will be handed you by Major W. H. Browne.

I am, sir, very respectfully,
Your obedient servant,
C. D. ANDERSON, Colonel Commanding.

SPEECH OF LINCOLN TO OHIO SOLDIERS.

The time of the One Hundred and Sixty-sixth Ohio regiment, one hundred days' men, having expired, they paid their respects to Lincoln, who made them a speech in front of the Executive mansion.—He said:

I suppose you are going home to see your families and friends. For the service you have done in this great struggle in which we are engaged I present you sincere thanks for myself and the country. I almost always feel inclined, when I happen to say anything to soldiers, to impress upon them in a few brief remarks the importance of success in this contest. It is not merely for to-day, but for all time to [illegible] children this great and free government, which we have enjoyed all our lives. I beg you to remember this, not merely for my sake, but for yours. I happen temporarily to occupy this big White House. I am a living witness that any one of your children may look to come here as my father's child has. It is in order that each of you may have, through this free government which we have enjoyed, an open field and a fair chance for your industry, enterprise and intelligence; that you may all have equal privileges in the race of life, with all its desirable human aspirations. It is for this the struggle should be maintained, that we may not lose our birthright—not only for one, but for two or three years. The nation is worth fighting for to secure such an inestimable jewel.

Three cheers were then given for the President.

A REPUBLICAN VIEW OF THE PLATFORM.

[From the Washington Chronicle, September 1.]

The platform adopted by the so-called Democracy is an admirable attempt at "how not to do it." It contains not a single expression of opinion upon any question of public policy, except that in a mild and inoffensive manner it takes sides in favor of the Union. This is the purport of the first resolution. The second declares that after four years of failure to restore the Union by war, efforts should be made for a cessation of hostilities with a view to calling a convention of all the States. But suppose the rebels refuse to go into a convention, or, going in, suppose they refuse peace except on terms of final separation? What then? The platform is entirely silent on this point. It neither indicates the terms which should be offered the rebels nor informs the country whether the war should be resumed in the event of the refusal of the rebels to come back into the Union.

* * This forcible, feeble manifesto from Chicago is more remarkable for what it omits than for what it embraces. It contains not one sentiment of approbation or censure upon the financial policy of the Administration during the last three and a half years. It neither condemns nor approves the legislation of Congress upon the subjects of tariff duties, internal revenue laws, bank-note currency, and the national banking system. It is silent even upon emancipation, confiscation and conscription. What are we to infer from this silence? Must we not assume that the Convention approves these measures; that it regards them as settled, and no longer open questions? Of course we must; and if during the campaign any champion of the Chicago nominees shall arraign the party in power on any of these issues, it will be a sufficient answer to refer him to his platform for proof that they are no longer in controversy.

The platform is also remarkable for its entire freedom from all malice and uncharitableness towards traitors and rebels. Not a word of censure for secession in theory or rebellion in practice is permitted to find place in the platform; and all the indignation is directed at the efforts of the Administration to suppress the rebellion. In a word, the veriest rebel may read the platform without taking offence, while no truly loyal man can fail to be disgusted with its manifest truckling to the disloyal elements in the loyal States. Upon the whole, the platform is a pitiful affair, and will be expectorated upon by all sorts of people.

WHEELER'S OPERATIONS IN TENNESSEE.

The following is the latest Yankee dispatch about General Wheeler's movements:

LOUISVILLE, August 30.—Passengers by the Nashville train say that Wheeler, with his entire force, has appeared at the bend of the Cumberland river, three miles below Gallatin, where they captured a company of United States troops, and were attempting to cross the river this morning for an advance upon Gallatin. His force is variously estimated at from five to twelve thousand, (the former number is probably nearly correct.) A report has reached Cave City, Kentucky, that the colonel commanding the post at Gallatin ordered the depot there to be burned, as it was without the range of his guns.

THE ENEMY'S TORPEDOES AT CHARLESTON.—On Sunday night last the enemy attempted an attack on Fort Johnson, in Charleston harbor, with the aid of a torpedo. The *Courier* gives the following account of the failure:

"About nine o'clock Sunday night a terrific explosion, which shook the buildings in this city, took place. Many supposed it to be a two hundred-pounder Parrott time-fuse shell. It appears, however, that about nine o'clock some musketry firing was heard at Fort Sumter. Upon examination, Captain Huguenin discovered that the firing was about two hundred yards from the fort, in the direction of Fort Johnson. The firing continued a few seconds only, when three Yankee barges were seen coming in towards the west face. Captain Lewis, with a detachment of the Thirty-second Georgia, mounted the parapet and opened a fire of small arms upon the parties; but had not fired more than one or two rounds before a tremendous explosion occurred about thirty feet from the west face of the fort, near the wharf. After the explosion the enemy were seen in rapid retreat towards Morris island. Our men kept up the fire of small arms until the enemy had got entirely out of sight. The Yankees, it seems, had floated down a torpedo from the direction of Fort Johnson. The torpedo exploded near the wharf of the fort. No damage was done to the works. The shock was distinctly perceptible all over the fort, and some of the officers on the southwest angle were knocked down."

BRITISH COURTESY TO THE TALLAHASSEE.—The Wilmington (North Carolina) *Journal* is informed that neither the Confederate States nor the officers or men of the Confederate cruiser Tallahassee owe much to the courtesy of the British authorities at Halifax. The Halifax *Chronicle* of the 19th states that she was only permitted to remain in port twenty-four hours, nor was she, as we learn, allowed to take on board any other supplies than one hundred tons of coal—a mere trifle for a ship of her steam—nothing at all for a cruiser. The people of Halifax, and even the officials, appeared to be personally friendly to the Confederacy, and private hospitality was freely tendered to the people of the Tallahassee. But there seemed to be stringent orders from the home government compelling them to act officially in a very unfriendly manner. Since the failure of the opposition in the British Parliament to defeat the ministry by a vote of want of confidence, the unfriendly tone of Earl Russell and his minions has been more decided.

RENTS IN WILMINGTON.—Tuesday was a big renting day in Wilmington, North Carolina. The London tenements went off comparatively high. As an instance, the store about twenty by forty feet, on the southeast corner of Market and Front streets rented for twenty thousand dollars. The rooms in the same building in about the same proportion.—This piece of property brought over sixty thousand dollars rent for the next twelve months, commencing the first of October next.

BROWNLOW'S paper says that the late Federal jury sitting at Knoxville found six hundred and sixty bills of indictment for treason against rebels.

M. W. CLUSKEY, Adjutant-General to Vaughn's brigade, is elected to Congress over Sneed in the Eleventh Tennessee District.

"THE PACIFICATOR."—This is the title of a new Catholic weekly journal to be issued in Augusta, Georgia, on the first of October.

The Philadelphia Inquirer.

CIRCULATION OVER 60,000. — PHILADELPHIA, MONDAY, SEPTEMBER 5, 1864. — PRICE THREE CENTS.

ATLANTA CAPTURED!

SHERMAN'S GREAT VICTORY.

Confirmation of His Success.

SLOCUM'S CORPS IN THE CITY.

Hood Blows Up His Magazines.

81 CARS AND 7 LOCOMOTIVES DESTROYED

Capture of 14 Cannon.

HOWARD'S VICTORY AT JONESBORO'.

1750 Rebel Prisoners Captured.

Gen. J. C. Davis Carries the Enemy's Works

HE CAPTURES TEN GUNS.

Sherman's Official Despatch.

THE REPORTS AT RICHMOND

Rebels Have No "Official Advices."

GRANT'S OFFICIAL DESPATCH.

His Opinion of the Triumph.

BATTLE NEAR WINCHESTER.

Gen. Averill Whips the Rebels.

GEN. SHERIDAN IN PURSUIT OF EARLY.

Gen. Rousseau Defeats Wheeler.

REBEL GEN. KELLY CAPTURED.

Latest from Gen. Grant.

THE VICTORY AT ATLANTA.

OFFICIAL WAR GAZETTE.

First Bulletin — Confirmation of the Good News, Etc.

WAR DEPARTMENT, WASHINGTON, D. C., Sept. 3. Major-General DIX, New York:—No intelligence from Atlanta, later than my telegram last night, has been received.

The telegraphic lines between Nashville and Chattanooga were broken last night, and we have had nothing south of Nashville to-day. This accounts for the absence of later information from Atlanta.

No doubt is entertained here of the correctness of the reports received here last night, which came from two independent sources, besides the official despatch of General SLOCUM.

An official report this evening from Nashville states that the damage done by WHEELER to the railroad will be speedily repaired, and that WHEELER had retreated. General ROUSSEAU is in pursuit. Also, that in an engagement between ROUSSEAU and WHEELER'S forces, the Rebel General KELLY was mortally wounded, and is in our hands.

A telegram from General SHERIDAN states that EARLY has retreated up the Shenandoah Valley, and is pursued by SHERIDAN, with his whole army; that AVERILL had attacked VAUGHN'S Cavalry and captured twenty wagons, two battle-flags, a number of prisoners and a herd of cattle.

EDWIN M. STANTON, Secretary of War.

SECOND BULLETIN.

THE CAPTURE OF ATLANTA.

Great Battle at East Point—The Rebels Admit a Loss of 40,000.

WASHINGTON, Sept. 4, 1864.—Major-General DIX, New York—The following telegram from General GRANT has just been received:—

CITY POINT, Sept. 3.—Hon. E. M. STANTON:—I have Richmond papers of to-day. They contain rumors of a battle at Atlanta, but say that the War Department, having no official information, declines to form an opinion from the rumors.

I have no doubt, however, but that SHERMAN has gained a great success there.

Before the despatch of last night was received, announcing the occupation of Atlanta by our troops, the fact was known to our pickets, the Rebels having halloed over to our men that SHERMAN had whipped HOOD, that the latter had lost forty thousand men, and that our troops were in Atlanta.

All is quiet here.

U. S. GRANT, Lieutenant-General.

Our southwestern telegraph lines continue down, and this, with a heavy storm that commenced in the afternoon, and is still prevailing beyond Louisville, may damage the lines, so as to hinder the arrival of the details from Atlanta for a day or two.

EDWIN M. STANTON, Secretary of War.

SHERMAN'S GLORIOUS VICTORY!!

THE CITY OF ATLANTA—ITS LINE OF DEFENCES.

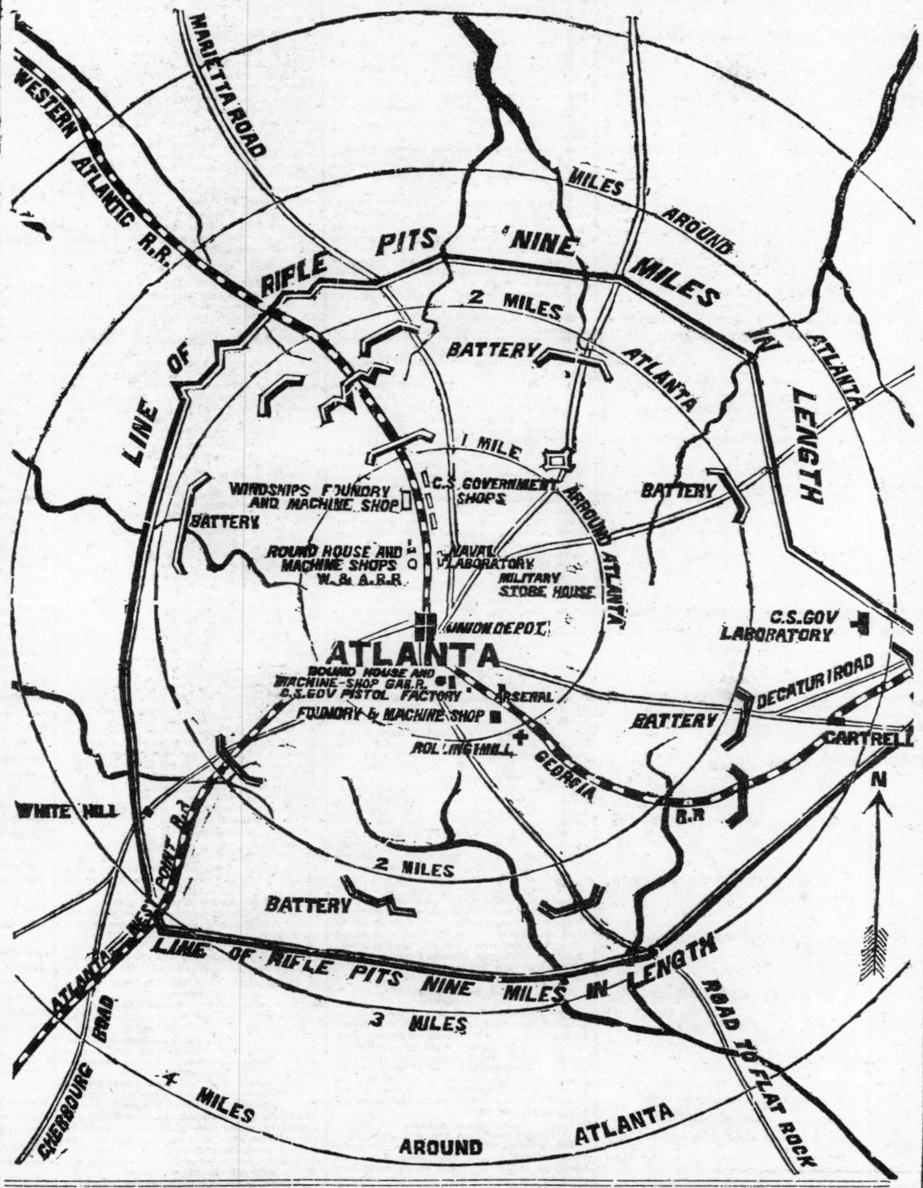

LATEST OFFICIAL DESPATCH.

THE CAPTURE OF ATLANTA FULLY CONFIRMED.

WASHINGTON, Sept. 4, 8 P. M.—To Major-General DIX, New York:—General SHERMAN'S official report of the capture of Atlanta has just been received by this department. It is dated twenty-six miles south of Atlanta, at 6 o'clock yesterday morning, but was detained by the breaking of the telegraph lines, mentioned in my despatch of last night.

"As already reported, the army drew from about Atlanta, and on the 30th had made a break of the West Point road, and reached a good position from which to strike the Macon road. The right (Gen. HOWARD) near Jonesboro, the left (Gen. SCHOFIELD) near Rough and Ready, and the centre (Gen. THOMAS) at Couch's. HOWARD found the enemy in force at Jonesboro, and intrenched his troops, the salient within half a mile of the railroad.

The enemy "attacked him at three P. M., and was easily repulsed, leaving his dead and wounded. Finding strong opposition on the road I advanced the centre and left rapidly to the railroad, made a good lodgment and broke it all the way from Rough and Ready down to HOWARD'S left, near Jonesboro, and by the same movement I interposed my whole army between Atlanta and the part of the enemy intrenched in and round Jonesboro.

"We made a general attack on the enemy at Jonesboro', on the 1st of September, the Fourteenth Corps, Gen. JEFF. C. DAVIS, carrying the works handsomely, with ten guns and about one thousand prisoners. In the night the enemy retreated south, and we have followed him to another of his hastily constructed lines near Lovejoy's Station.

"HOOD, at Atlanta, finding me on his road, the only one that could supply him, and between him and a considerable part of his army, blew up his magazines in Atlanta, and left in the night time, when the Twentieth Corps, General SLOCUM, took possession of the place, so Atlanta is ours and fairly won. Since the 5th of May we have been in one constant battle or skirmish and need rest.

"Our loss will not exceed twelve hundred, and we have possession of over three hundred Rebel dead, two hundred and fifty wounded, and over fifteen hundred well. (Signed) W. F. SHERMAN, "Major-General."

A later despatch from General SLOCUM, dated at Atlanta, last night, the 3d, 9 P. M., states that the enemy, on evacuating Atlanta, destroyed seven locomotives and eighty-one cars loaded with ammunition, small arms and stores; and left fourteen pieces of artillery, most of them uninjured, and large number of small arms. Deserters are constantly coming into our lines.

EDWIN M. STANTON, Secretary of War.

UNOFFICIAL DETAILS.

Sherman's Victory in Washington—His Masterly Strategic Movement.

WASHINGTON, Sept. 3.—There is great rejoicing in Washington this afternoon over the news that Atlanta is in the possession of the Union forces. It appears that while the Rebel cavalry was operating upon General SHERMAN'S rear, that officer was prosecuting his movements successfully, and at 11 o'clock this morning entered the city of Atlanta, and found that his combinations had compelled its evacuation by HOOD. Transmission of this intelligence over the wires, which have been cut for several days, proves that ROUSSEAU has been successful in his effort to dislodge the cavalry expedition of FORREST, WHEELER and MORGAN, and driven them from the road. The capture of Atlanta secures the possession of the whole State of Georgia, and renders the condition of the Rebel leaders more desperate than ever before.

It was by an apparent retreat, one of those masterly strategic movements for which this General has been so noted, that he has been enabled to achieve so brilliant a result. For some time past it has been apparent, not only to General SHERMAN, but to the majority of his officers, that the position could not be taken by direct assault. The works which JOHNSTON was enabled to build around Atlanta during the time he occupied SHERMAN'S attention by his slow retreats are represented to be of the most formidable character and strength.

On the other hand, a complete investment of the place was impossible from a want of men, General SHERMAN'S army being too small to establish the line around the city as strongly as would be necessary to prevent successful sallies by the enemy. It is now well known that HOOD has added materially to his strength by the conscription of numerous boys and old men, who, behind works, could render very good service. Outside of the works this very strength would prove a great weakness and a terrible cost of powder and provender.

The purpose of General SHERMAN, in the movement which began on the night of the 25th, was to deprive the Rebel commander, General HOOD, of this strength, and of his protection of the works at Atlanta. In other words, SHERMAN hoped, by flanking Atlanta and cutting off his supplies, to force HOOD out to fight, and then, with his largely preponderating force of veteran troops, to whip him in an open field. With this view SHERMAN moved on the night in question with twenty days' rations, and all his army, except the Twentieth Corps (SLOCUM'S), which was left ... in front of Atlanta, ... of observation, and to occupy Atlanta in the event of HOOD abandoning it. It was also employed to look after the communications and hurry forward the railroad and supplies to whatever new position SHERMAN might assume.

The army is reported to have moved in the following order:—The Twenty-third Corps (SCHOFIELD) in advance, followed by the Fourteenth (DAVIS), Fifteenth (LOGAN), Sixteenth (RANSOM), Seventeenth (BLAIR), and the Fourth (STANLEY), in the order named, all making the flank movement with strong skirmish lines on either flank and front and rear. East Point was left to the east, and at dawn HOOD found SHERMAN gone; at least the following from the Richmond papers of August 29 looks like it:—

"It was rumored yesterday that official intelligence had been received that SHERMAN was retreating from Atlanta, and that HOOD was pressing him heavily. We are much disposed to believe this report, though no information on the subject has been given the press. WHEELER and others have been playing such pranks in SHERMAN'S rear as must have rendered his position before Atlanta dangerous and extremely uncomfortable."

Rejoicings over the Victory at Atlanta.

OSWEGO, N. Y., Sept. 3.—A salute of a hundred guns was fired to-day by the 16th United States Infantry, stationed in Fort Ontario. The military subsequently paraded in commemoration of the victory at Atlanta.

TROY, N. Y., Sept. 3.—A salute of a hundred guns was fired in this city to-day in honor of General SHERMAN'S victory at Atlanta.

BOSTON, Sept. 3.—A salute of a hundred guns was fired at Boston Common to-day, as an expression of the public rejoicing at the capture of Atlanta.

There were salutes also at Lynn, Belfast and other places.

BUFFALO, N. Y., Sept. 3.—The fall of Atlanta was celebrated to-day by the display of flags, and this evening by the discharge of cannon.

NEW LONDON, Conn., Sept. 3.—A hundred guns were fired to-day in honor of SHERMAN'S brilliant victory and the fall of Atlanta.

SARATOGA, N. Y., Sept. 3.—The bells were rung and a salute of one hundred guns fired in honor of the fall of Atlanta.

READING, Sept. 3.—Quite an excitement prevails in Reading to-day. The bells are ringing, cannons are firing, and the people generally are rejoicing over the victory at Atlanta.

BURLINGTON, N. J., Sept. 4.—The Union League rooms were illuminated and a salute was fired here on Saturday evening, in honor of the victory at Atlanta.

Speeches were made by Messrs. WRIGHT, ROBERTS, RODGERS and the Rev. Mr. KELSO, a refugee from Western Missouri. The greatest enthusiasm prevailed.

[Despatches from Rochester, N. Y., New Haven, Conn., and other places, indicate the popular enthusiasm in General SHERMAN'S movements and the reported capture of Atlanta, Ga.]

From Harrisburg.

Special Despatch to the Philadelphia Inquirer.

HARRISBURG, Sept. 3.—Colonel H. D. ... will ... [illegible] ... to pay the expenses of ... Rebel raid of 1863.

ARMY OF THE POTOMAC.

Special Correspondence of the Inquirer.

A Quiet Day.

HEAD-QUARTERS ARMY OF THE POTOMAC, August 31, 1864.

This has been the quietest day we have had for some time. Hardly a gun has been heard anywhere along our front. At some points the pickets appear to be on terms not merely friendly, but sociable. I have heard of parties of our own men and Rebels playing cards and discussing politics with a degree of harmony and good feeling well worthy of imitation in bar-rooms, corner groceries and political assemblies generally. "Who're you going to vote for, Yank?" a Rebel shouts to one of our men. "Don't know; han't made up my mind about it yet." "Have they nominated any one at Chicago?" No, not yet." "Well, theirs'll be the man to vote for, Yank."

The Ream's Station Fight.

I am told that a Petersburg paper brought into our lines a few days ago, which, however, I have not been able to get sight of, has an article in which the attack at Reams' Station on the 25th inst., is deprecated as a useless sacrifice of men, the writer asserting that the enemy lost more men in killed and wounded than HANCOCK had there in all. Richmond papers have, I believe, stated the Rebel loss at one thousand, but there can be no doubt that this is very far below the truth. The writer in the Petersburg paper is probably nearer the mark. The latter thinks the capture of a few guns but a poor consolation for the great slaughter sustained in making the assault.

Suspended Publication.

The Petersburg *Express* has suspended publication for the want of paper to print on.

On Half Rations.

It is said that the Rebel army at Petersburg has been on half rations for some days past.

The War Correspondents' Order.

BYRON says, "'tis pleasant, sure, to see one's name in print." I am not so sure on that point, but pleased or not, your correspondent and all his confreres in the Army of the Potomac will henceforth be restricted to the alternative of having their names appended to their letters and despatches or leaving the army. Newspapers failing to publish the names of their correspondents will also be excluded from admission within the army lines. This order has, I believe, been in existence for some time, but appears to have been forgotten, or for some reason to have fallen into disuse. Indeed, I presume the majority of the correspondents now in the army were unaware of its existence. Our attention has again been called to it, however, and the order is now understood to be imperative. The object of the order is to enable the authorities to place the responsibility of newspaper publications on the writer.

L. T. PEYREE.

[DESPATCH TO ASSOCIATED PRESS.]

LATEST FROM THE ARMY OF THE POTOMAC.

HEAD-QUARTERS ARMY OF POTOMAC, Sept. 3, 6 A. M.—Private SELDEN C. CHANDLER, of Battery K, Fourth United States Artillery, suffered the extreme penalty of the law, for having deserted his command during active operations.

A detail from the provost guard of the Second Division, of the Second Corps, performed the sad duty.

The culprit addressed his fellow soldiers, admonishing them against the crime of desertion. He then sat down on his coffin, when the chaplain made a prayer, after which his eyes were bandaged. In a few moments he gave a sign that he was ready, and eight bullets entered his breast and head, killing him instantly.

He leaves a wife and two daughters to mourn his fate.

Another culprit named ALMEYER was to have suffered the same fate, but managed to effect his escape through the lines to the enemy a day or two since.

Dr. JOHN D. HERITAGE, of the Eleventh New York Volunteers, has been missing since the fight of the 25th ult. on the Weldon road. It is not known whether he was killed or captured.

The enemy's cavalry made their appearance on our left yesterday morning, near Ream's Station, and after some slight skirmishing with our pickets, fell back.

Deserters come in every night, claiming the benefit of General GRANT'S late order, giving them protection and employment, if they wish it, but not forcing them into the service. Twelve came in yesterday. All is quiet along the line to-day, scarcely a shot being heard.

W. W. McGREGOR.

ACCIDENT ON THE BALTIMORE RAILROAD

BALTIMORE, Sept. 3.—At an early hour this morning an accident occurred at Perrymansville, on the Philadelphia, Wilmington and Baltimore Railroad, by which eight or ten persons were more or less injured. The mail and passenger train, composed of eleven cars, from Philadelphia, due at President street depot at 8.45 in the morning, was about passing the station, when the switch at that point by some means became opened, causing the five rear cars to run off the track, three of them overturning and being broken badly.

The two last cars, the sleeping ones, fortunately were not overturned. There were about two hundred and seventy-five passengers in the entire train. Among those injured were DAVID W. SWEIGHER, Company A, Nineteenth Veteran Reserve Corps; HENRY A. FISHER, Sixth Connecticut Volunteers; HENRY A. WATTERS, One-hundred-and-fifty-second New York Regiment; HARRY T. CHATMAN, Third Assistant Engineer, United States Navy, late of steamer *Tallapoosa*, and WILSON MOTT, citizen, residing on Atlantic street, Brooklyn. These were brought to this city in the train which reached here at 8.30 o'clock. The soldiers were conveyed in an ambulance to West's Buildings Hospital, CHATMAN to the Lombard street Infirmary, and Mr. MOTT to the residence of a friend in this city.

A passenger states that, in addition to the above named, there were three other soldiers injured, one of them having both legs broken; another had one arm broken in three places, and the other received a serious cut on the right side of his neck, and his ear was partially cut off. A lady, name not learned, had a leg fractured, and another had her hand sprained. Another passenger had her collar-bone broken and arm dislocated. Two surgeons, one of the Army and the other of the Navy, were fortunately on the train, and gave their services to the injured passengers.

The accident was one of a kind which is unavoidable, as it is evident that the switch was locked, as the first part of the train passed over it safely.

DAMAGE BY THE STORM.

CINCINNATI, Sept. 4.—The heavy rains on Saturday night and Sunday morning caused an unprecedented rise in the Licking River. Kelly's and Kimbrough's bridges, on the Kentucky Central Railroad, near Cynthiana, were washed away. A large number of coal barges, lying near the mouth of the river, were carried off and one or two sunk. A log struck the steamer *Fitz Hugh*, sinking her, flooding the cabin and carrying it off into the Ohio. It is supposed that other damage has been done in this neighborhood.

Arrival of Union Prisoners at Annapolis.

ANNAPOLIS, Sept. 3.—Four hundred wounded men, with twenty-five officers and ten ..., have just arrived by boat from Richmond. They are in needy condition. The United States Christian Commission made arrangements for their immediate relief.

Burning of the Frigate ...

WASHINGTON, Sept. 4.—The Navy Department last evening received a despatch ... burning of the United States frigate ... at Norfolk, Va., with ... cause of the ... known, nor ... particulars.

The Daily Picayune.

UNION. JUSTICE. CONFIDENCE.

VOLUME XXVIII. NEW ORLEANS, THURSDAY MORNING, SEPTEMBER 8, 1864. NUMBER 157.

The Daily Picayune.

ADDITIONAL BY THE CONTINENTAL.

FURTHER NEWS DETAILS.

We gave, in yesterday morning's Picayune, exclusively, pretty full details of news received by the United States transport Continental, from New York on the 30th ult. We give below some additional intelligence derived from the New York journals of that date:

McClellan and Chicago in New York.

The Herald, of the 30th ult., thus describes the excitement in that city in favor of McClellan:

As the proceedings of the Chicago Convention are daily developed, the interest which concentrates on the name of Gen. McClellan as a candidate for the Presidency grows more intense at every hour. There is no news from any source of so much paramount interest in the city at present as the unfolding narrative of the great work of reform at this grand Democratic Convention. The friends of Gen. McClellan in New York city are legion, and therefore it is that so much anxiety is everywhere expressed for the success of the efforts of his friends to obtain him the Presidential nomination.

On 'Change there was a decided feeling in favor of his nomination, and gold fluctuated accordingly. Our reporter endeavored to glean as much information from this source as possible, and found the feeling to be almost unanimous in favor of Little Mac for the Presidency. A private dispatch was received in Wall street about 2 o'clock, to the effect that the Chicago Convention organized early yesterday morning with Gov. Seymour as President, and that McClellan was nominated on the first ballot. This had the effect of producing a decided sensation among the "bulls and bears," who seemed at a loss to know which way to turn. Gold, that indicator of popular opinion, seemed to suffer considerably under this intelligence, and fell at various intervals during the afternoon from 247 to 237½ at which quotation it stood at 5 o'clock in the evening.

The sudden fall in the precious metal seemed to exercise a good effect on the people generally, and many who had recently been strongly in favor of Mr Lincoln's reelection were loud in their protestations of fidelity to McClellan's cause.

> For Guelph or Ghibelline, or both of these,
> At certain seasons all the people please;
> 'Tis rank and pelf, and love of power,
> That truly rule the passing hour.

A visit to the various hotels and places of amusement in the evening, by our reporter, found the McClellan excitement still unabated, and bets were freely offered at ten to one in favor of McClellan. Wherever our reporter went throughout the city there was but one feeling and one opinion manifested. There were very few persons inclined to think otherwise than that Gen. McClellan will be nominated. Those who are most opposed to him, and it cannot be denied that there are some, have long since concluded that he will get the nomination; but they console themselves with the hope that it will not be so easy to elect him. Of Gen Grant very little is said, except that he is a great fighting general, and that he may become President after "Little Mac" has got through his term. Old Abe is left severely alone, nobody seeming to think that he has the slightest chance. Everybody in the city seemed to be carried away by the McClellan furor. Even the Copperheads and ultra peace men, now that they see Seymour's and Vallandigham's chances growing smaller by degrees, are gradually edging round to Gen. McClellan.

The Kearsarge.
OFF CHERBURG.

The *Phare de la Manche* states that the Federal corvette Kearsarge made her appearance off the port of Cherburg on Friday, Aug 12. Two of her boats were sent on shore—one to take on board three of her crew who had been wounded in her affair with the Alabama and sent to the naval hospital, and the other to procure provisions. On their return on board in the evening the corvette stood out to sea under full steam.

SAILS FOR NEW YORK.
[From the Dover (Eng.) Express, August 16.]

The Federal cruiser Kearsarge, which has been stationed in this neighborhood for some time past, quitted the roads on Thursday evening last for New York. The Kearsarge is relieved by the Iroquois, a war vessel of about the same tonnage, which arrived on Wednesday evening. On entering the bay she ran up the English ensign and saluted—a compliment which was returned by a salute of artillery from the Castle batteries. The commander of the Iroquois afterwards paid a complimentary visit to Gen. Ulice, the commandant of the garrison.

The Tallahassee Among the Fishermen.
[From the Cape Cod (Mass.) Republican, Aug. 25.]

Two fishing schooners of Harwich—the D. Ellis, Capt. Jehial Baser, and the Diadem, Capt. Joseph Robbins—arrived at the port (Harwich) on Saturday last, having been boarded off Sherburne a few days previous by the officers of the pirate Tallahassee. The crews of the fishermen state that, seeing a large schooner burned by the Tallahassee a short distance from them, and as they could see none of the crew taken off or leave the vessel, they naturally felt alarmed for their own safety, and as any attempt to escape with their own vessels would be useless, they at once trimmed their sails, secured the helms so that the schooners would make towards the shore, and after securing what they could, they took to their boats to go ashore, but were soon overhauled by a boat's crew of the pirates. There it was decided that as the two fishing vessels were within three miles of the British coast that they were in neutral waters, and were released, with they assurance that had they been outside of that their vessels would have shared the fate of the other numerous victims of their piracy. The crews then returned to their respective vessels, and arrived home as above-stated, with full fares of mackerel.

The crew of the fishing schooner Mercy A. Howes, of Chatham, sunk by the Tallahassee on the 15th inst., latitude 42°, longitude 66°, arrived home at Chatham on Monday evening last. One of the crew states that on being taken aboard the pirate he immediately recognized the sailing master as one Norris, formerly of Hyannis, and was, at the time of the building of Minot's Ledge Light-House, engaged with him on that work. It is also reported that there are other Cape Cod men on board the Tallahassee, who inquired particularly concerning various persons in this vicinity with whom they were acquainted.

It will certainly be remarkable if others of our fishermen escape from the hands of this pirate, as she is a fast sailer and determined to do all the mischief possible. But we trust the day of retribution is not far distant when the piratical crew of the Tallahassee will meet with their just deserts.

A Hartford Boy After the Tallahassee.
[From the Hartford Times, Aug. 26.]

We learn that Capt. Fred. T. King, of this city, sailed from New York yesterday, in command of the United States ship Horace Beals, to cruise for the famous Tallahassee. Capt. K.'s voyage is peculiar in one respect—his vessel goes out as a decoy. She has a strong armament, but it is all concealed under the guise of a merchantman, and if the rebel engages her he will cause her to show an unexpected row of teeth, that may leave him second best in the encounter. Having been attached to Admiral Farragut's squadron for three years, during which he participated in several trying encounters, Capt. King has had abundant opportunity of getting acquainted with rebel guns and gunnery, and at the same time to win for himself a marked distinction for his bravery and good conduct.

Muller, the Murderer's Arrest in New York.

Muller, the alleged murderer of Mr Briggs, a retired banker of London, was, on the 25th ult., brought before United States Marshal Murray, who has him in custody until such time as the London detectives can produce sufficient evidence to warrant his delivery under the extradition treaty. Ex-Judge Beebe volunteered to defend the prisoner, and to give him an opportunity to prepare his defence United States Commissioner Newton adjourned the hearing of the case till 11 o'clock on the 20th. There was great excitement on the occasion of the arrest, on the arrival of the victim at New York.

Foreign Items.

Mrs. Yelverton has brought an action in the Scotch courts against the Saturday Review for libel in the comments which that journal had made upon her. She lays her damages at £3000.

The London Court Journal says the day fixed for her Majesty's departure from Osborn for Windsor was Thursday, the 29th, being the day prior to the birthday of the late Prince Consort. The Queen would remain about four days at the castle, and then proceed to Scotland.

In the trial of Rae vs Cunard, at the Liverpool Assizes, involving a claim for damages against the auctioneer for not having knocked down the steamship Great Eastern to the plaintiff, instead of to the New Great Eastern Company, a verdict was entered for defendant, with leave for plaintiff to move.

Miss Kate Southey, the third daughter of the poet, died at Keswick, England, on the 15th of August.

The frigate Niagara had sailed from Lisbon. Her destination was unknown.

A Vessel Run Down by the Sacramento.

PLYMOUTH, Aug. 16.—The United States sloop of war Sacramento, ten, Capt Henry Walker, which left Falmouth this (Tuesday) morning for a cruise, put into Plymouth Sound in the evening. She had come in contact, at 4½ o'clock P. M., with the Norwegian brig Ceres, with salt from Cadiz for the Baltic. The brig sunk immediately, and her crew was saved by boats from the sloop. In a quarter of an hour the brig rose again, and she is now floating about in the channel. The collision occurred about nine miles S. S. W. of Plymouth.

The Privateers.

By the Brazil mail we learn that on the 28th of July news was received at Bahia that the rebel cruiser Florida, in company with the Electric Spark, had just captured the Federal merchantman Imlican. Nicholas Dalls, bound from California to New York, having $70,000 in specie on board and an extremely valuable cargo. The Florida took out the treasure and portions of her cargo and crew. The vessel and cargo, valued at £20,000, were then set fire to and destroyed.

The Florida was spoken on July 17, latitude 36.18 north, longitude 31.58 west, by a vessel which arrived at Liverpool.

The Florida Spoken.

The ship Preston Wakem, at Liverpool, sailed from Bombey April 2, reports: July 25 saw a very suspicious looking steamer to leeward, under sail. Shortly afterwards it fell calm, when she got up steam and came alongside, and very kindly offered to give us some late papers, containing the particulars of the destruction of the Alabama. She then wished us a good passage, and steamed away to the eastward. Saw her in latitude 36 18, longitude 36 18. She proved to be the Confederate steamer Florida—all well and jolly.

A Suspicious Looking Steamer in the Shannon.

CLOTHING FOR THE REBEL ARMY, ETC.
[From the Dublin Freeman's Journal, August 15.]

A magnificent and rapid sailing steamer, with three funnels, visited the Shanon on Saturday last. She proceeded to the Foynes Island, where she lay at anchor until evening, when she suddenly steamed westward towards Turbert. While at anchor near Foynes a warlike party landed and made inquiries at the railway station about a special train for Limerick, and they appeared exceedingly disappointed when they could not proceed by rail to Limerick. It is supposed that the vessel is a blockade runner, and it was rumored here that a lieutenant of the Alabama was one of the party who landed at Foynes.

It appears that the steamer has arrived to convey an immense supply of clothing to the Confederates.

Commercial Intelligence.

THE LONDON MONEY MARKET.

The English funds opened steadily on Monday morning, (Aug 5,) and in consequence of a further diminution of pressure in the discount market, and the fact that a good amount of gold having been taken to the bank, consols ultimately experienced an advance of an eighth, at which they closed with firmness, viz: 89¼ a ⅜.

The discount demand of the bank was again moderate.

The rebel loan, on the news of the defeat of Gen. Grant before Petersburg, experienced a rebound of 3 per cent., closing at 77 a 79.

£101,000 was taken to the bank on August 15.

AMERICAN STOCKS.

Atlantic and Great Western, New York section, second mortgage, improved 1, and Virginia 6 per cents, Erie paid up shares and Illinois Central paid up shares severally declined 1 each, and do. ordinary 1½.

The English funds were quiet on Tuesday, August 16, and consols remained at 89⅜ a ½.

Rebel loan, 77 a 79 on August 16.

LONDON, Aug. 16, Evening.—Consols closed at 89⅛ a 89¼ for money.

AMERICAN SECURITIES.

Illinois Central shares 46 a 44 discount. Erie shares 39 a 41.

LIVERPOOL COTTON MARKET.

A good amount of business (August 15 and 16) transacted, and sales for the two days amount to 20,000 bales, 8000 on speculation and for export. Prices steady at one quarter of a penny to a half of a penny per pound higher than Friday.

THE LATEST MARKETS.

LONDON, August 18.—Consols closed at 89⅛ a 89¼.
Illinois Central shares, 46 a 45 discount. Erie shares 40 a 42.
LIVERPOOL, August 18.—Cotton dull and quotations barely maintained; sales of two days 12,000, including 1500 on speculation and for export.
Breadstuffs dull and tending downward.
Provisions quiet and steady.
Petroleum firm.

The Chicago Nominees.

SEYMOUR, OF CONNECTICUT, FOR VICE PRESIDENT.

We received by the steamer Paragon, arrived here this morning, the following brief letter from our Cairo correspondent:

CAIRO, Ill., Aug. 31, 8 P. M.—The regular telegraphic reports to the Associated Press are not yet in, but the operator at Chicago has just telegraphed to the operator here that G. B. McClellan, of New York, and T. H. Seymour, of Connecticut, have been nominated for President and Vice President of the United States by the National Democratic Convention to day.

This news I derived at the telegraph office, a few moments since, from the operator there. I have no doubt but the gentleman states what has been communicated to him, and I believe the result is as stated. It is said there has been some disagreement on the adoption of the platform. In haste, R. K.

8½ o'clock, P. M.—The nominations are the talk of all here. The Democrats are enthusiastic and jubilant. "Wait for the wagon," boys.—*True Delta of last evening.*

☞ "It is with narrow-souled people," says Swift, "as with narrow-necked bottles: the less they have in them the more noise they make in pouring it out."

TELEGRAPHIC.

FROM ATLANTA.

Atlanta Evacuated by Hood on the 1st.

Sherman Entered Atlanta on the 2d.

FEDERAL AND REBEL ACCOUNTS.

Several Fights Preceding these Events.

[From our Extra of Yesterday.]

We have just received the following interesting and important dispatches:

MORGANZA, Sept. 7, 10 A. M.
To Major Gen. Canby:

Capt. Foster sends the following extra with his compliments. Atlanta is ours beyond doubt.
M. R. LAWLER, Brig. Gen.

From the Woodville extra Sept. 5th, Macon, Ga., Sept. 3d. Parties from the front report that our losses on Wednesday will probably exceed 600.

On Thursday the enemy made four assaults on our lines in heavy column, and each time was repulsed with great slaughter. They then concentrated on Govan's front, and breaking our lines, our retreat became necessary, which was effected on Thursday night.

Prisoners report that only four Federal corps were engaged. They are menacing, and guarding their communications. There is no reliable information regarding yesterday's operations, or the operations of Hood.

MACON, GA., Sept. 3.—During the last two days the city has been full of wild rumors relating to the operations on the line of the railroad. Communication with the press reporter is impracticable.

The result of the action on Thursday was that Hardee, opposed with overwhelming numbers, fell back to Lovejoy's Station, while Lee, by order of Hood, withdrew toward Atlanta, leaving the railroad in possession of the enemy. It is now ascertained that the 6th Corps of Sherman's troops were thrown on the railroad, only Hardee's and Lee's corps confronted them. The losses upon both sides were large, but as the Federals on Thursday attacked our entrenchments, it is supposed they suffered much more heavily than ours. No reliable details can be obtained. A collision occurred yesterday on the Macon road near Barnesville, which resulted in killing 2[illegible] persons and breaking up the trains seriously.

RICHMOND, Sept. 2.—An official dispatch states that the enemy has withdrawn from the Memphis and Charleston road to Memphis. The troops are supposed to be destined for Northern Virginia.

RICHMOND, Sept. 3.—The Baltimore Gazette says a dispatch from Nashville, dated Tuesday, states that 1500 of Wheeler's cavalry entered Lebanon that day. They captured Gen. Milligan and 30 privates. Wheeler's main force, 6000 or 8000 strong was near McMinnville advancing towards Murfreesboro. There is great excitement in Nashville under the apprehension that the city will be attacked.

RICHMOND, Sept. 4.—The following official dispatch was received from Hood, dated the 3d: "The enemy made a lodgment across the Flint River, near Jonesboro'. We attacked them there on the evening of the 31st, with two corps, but failed to dislodge them. This made it necessary to abandon Atlanta, which was done on the night of the 1st."

Our loss on the evening of the 31st., was small. On the evening of the 1st inst., Hardee's corps, in position at Jonesboro', was assaulted by superior numbers, and being outflanked, was compelled to withdraw during the night, with a loss of 800. The enemy's prisoners report their loss very severe.

MACON, GA., Sept. 4.—No doubt about the fall of Atlanta. It was evacuated on Thursday morning and occupied by the enemy at 11 o'clock on Friday morning. Gen. Hood destroyed his ordnance and burned his commissary stores, and drew off on the McDonough road, leaving Atlanta nothing but blood stained ruins. Yesterday our whole army was concentrated at Lovejoy's Station, on the Macon and Western Railroad.

The enemy are reported to be retreating from that point towards Atlanta. In the fight at Jonesboro', on Thursday, Gen. Govan, together with the 6th and part of the 2d Arkansas, were captured. We lost six pieces of artillery and captured six.

LOVEJOY, Sept. 4.—The army is in line of battle, confronting Sherman's advance on this point.

The trains were brought up safely. The Federals entered Atlanta in column by Peach Tree Road, on Friday morning at 9 o'clock. They left a garrison and post commandant, and passed through to join the main army. The city is very quiet and orderly, and citizens who remained were unmolested. The lines were comparatively quiet this morning.

☞ Water kept in a leaden vessel for only a day has been found to contract a sweetness of taste, and become poisonous for internal use. Consequently, water standing for some time in leaden pipes should be thoroughly drawn off before it is used for culinary purposes or for drinking.

☞ Establishments on the New York streets where the weaker sex can get their "bitters" in a quiet way when out shopping, are said by the veracious Herald to be indicated by a placard bearing the words "If you don't see what you want, ask for it!"

Letter from Franklin Pierce.

The following is the letter from ex-President Pierce, brought to the notice of the Chicago Convention, on the second day, as expressive of the wishes of that distinguished gentleman, by R. T. Spofford, a delegate from Massachusetts:

CONCORD, N. H., Aug. 17, 1864.

My Dear Spofford—I received your note on Saturday evening; but do not see how, consistently with your convenience or my own, we can meet again before you leave for Chicago. Nor, indeed, is there any special occasion for it. You know my views, and I rely upon your friendship. What I wish to have done will be no task. It will be easy to check any word that may by possibility be said about me in connection with the nomination. The New Hampshire delegation will take no steps from first to last which favor or give sanction to my being a candidate. I wish you, as early as you can, to see them together. At all events, you must understand from what I have more than once said to you, how painful it would be to me to have my wishes in this relation disregarded by my friends in any part of the country.

Whoever may be nominated will, I have no doubt, in obedience to what will be the voice of the Convention, declare in the name of the Democracy of the United States, that the approaching election shall be a *free* election—an election conducted in obedience to the laws of the land—with no military presence to overawe the unarmed citizen. And that if, in any sovereign State recognizing the authority of the Federal Government, military usurpation shall come to suppress the people in the exercise of their rights under the constitution and enacted laws, we will meet that military usurpation with all the power we can command.

But if your Convention will act cordially and in harmony, there need be no apprehension that bayonets will attempt to control the judgment of the voters.

No audacity in defiance of the constitution will dare to confront with arms the united democracy of the Southwestern, Middle, North-Western and Eastern States. No man, defying the constitution which he has sworn to uphold and obey, can bring the army to support open rebellion against a fair and free vote. They will hold that we are a free people yet,—let us be thankful for that,—a free people living under a written constitution, which binds the highest official not less firmly than the humblest citizen of the Republic. Of this, I think, you may be sure. The critical—the vital thing, will be united action on your part, and that such may be the result is my most earnest wish. Always your friend,

FRANKLIN PIERCE.

The Louisiana Application.

The following is the text of the application of the Louisiana delegation claiming a right to seats in the Chicago Convention:

The Chairman suggested that the communication addressed to the chair was still before the Convention, from gentlemen who claimed to represent the State of Louisiana, whereupon Mr. Vallandigham suspended his motion, to allow the communication to be read, as follows:

"Gentlemen, the undersigned delegates, selected by the Democracy of the State of Louisiana to represent that State in your Convention, under a call duly signed and published, respectfully represent that they have presented their credentials to the National Committee, which body, without a hearing, have refused tickets of admission as members of this Convention. Assuring the Convention that we have come in no spirit of disorganization, but to unite with the Democratic party of the entire Union in the glorious work of rescuing the country from this corrupt administration, and believing that the Democratic party of the North are ready to unite with us in such a work, we desire that as delegates from Louisiana we be allowed a hearing.

Respectfully, J. L. RIDDELL,
Chairman of the Delegation."

Referred to the Committee on Credentials.

From St. Paul.

A special dispatch to the Chicago Tribune, dated St. Paul, Monday, Aug. 29, 1864, says:

Dispatches have been received here by Gen. Sibley from Gen. Sully, announcing a glorious and decisive victory by his forces over 1,500 lodges of hostile Sioux, near Little Missouri River, July 30th. He destroyed immense quantities of their provisions and property. The dispatch was dated Heart River, Aug. 2d, indicating that the expedition is returning to Fort Rice.

A letter received from St. Cloud this morning by Mr. Mendleson, a merchant of this city, announces that a brother of his, a peddler, and another man named Dueland, were killed by Indians on last Monday, on Whiskey Creek, a few miles this side of Fort Abercrombie. A force of sixty cavalry had been dispatched from that post in pursuit of the murderers.

The quota of St. Paul is now filled, and every recruiting committee has ceased its labors. Of the one hundred and sixty men obtained, twenty-two were half breeds. They are tough and active, and prove serviceable soldiers.

Guerrilla Robbery and Murder near Rolla, Mo.

[From the St. Louis Democrat of the 31st ult.]

Mr. Myron Coloney, of Southwest Missouri, who is temporarily engaged in the news room of the Democrat, yesterday received telegraphic dispatches from Rolla, informing him that guerrillas had visited and robbed his premises, and had murdered the overseer.

Mr. Coloney is the proprietor of the extensive and well known "Union Farm," six miles south of Rolla. The tract is under active cultivation, and furnishes hay for Government use. Having been threatened by the guerrillas, Mr. C. some weeks ago left his place in charge of his father-in-law, Mr. Chauncey Tuttle, as lessee, and Mr. Andrew M. Darling as overseer. Their families and the family of Mr. Coloney also remained on the premises.

The dispatches simply say that at 3 o'clock Tuesday morning the place was visited by thirty bushwhackers, who killed Mr. Darling and carried off all the portable property.

Mr. C. is apprehensive that, his people fleeing to Rolla, the villains may have since fulfilled their threats to burn the buildings. Some thirty tons of Government hay would also tempt the guerrilla torch.

Mr. Darling is an old Minnesota pioneer, and lived on the Indiana frontier amid perils from the raiding savages, where he earned a reputation for personal courage and bravery. At Union farm he invariably slept with a rifle at hand, and probably was killed after using or attempting to use it.

Mr. Tuttle, lessee of the farm, happened to be transiently in St. Louis at the time.

Gen. McNeil has just taken charge of the Rolla district, and will soon make it a region to be avoided by bushwhackers.

P. S.—The leader of the gang who murdered Mr. Darling was one Bill Lenox, son of Hamilton Lenox, former owner of the Union farm. This man swore, in presence of the family, that no one should ever live on the premises outside of the Lenoxes. Mr. Darling's daughter heroically stood over and administered water to her dying father while the murderers were firing upon him.

☞ One of the fashionable colors in Paris at the present moment for ladies is called "Havana tobacco," perhaps out of a delicate compliment to the growing taste for the weed they indulge in.

THE NEW YORK HERALD.

WHOLE NO. 10,251. NEW YORK, WEDNESDAY, SEPTEMBER 21, 1864. PRICE FOUR CENTS.

VICTORY!

Secretary Stanton's Despatches.

Splendid Achievement of General Sheridan Over the Rebel Early in Shenandoah Valley.

Fifteen Battle Flags and Five Pieces of Artillery Taken.

Over Three Thousand Prisoners Captured.

The Gallant Union General Russell Killed and McIntosh, Upton and Chapman Wounded.

The Rebel Generals Rhodes, Wharton, Ramseur and Gordon Killed.

General Imboden Reported Killed.

Five Thousand Rebels Killed and Wounded.

Their Killed and Wounded in Our Hands.

PURSUIT OF THE FLYING REBELS.

General Sheridan Promoted by the President,

&c., &c., &c.

Stanton's First Despatch.

WAR DEPARTMENT WASHINGTON, Sept. 20—9:30 A. M.

Major General JOHN A DIX:—

Yesterday Major General Sheridan attacked Early, fought a great battle, and won a splendid victory.

Over two thousand five hundred prisoners were captured. Nine battle flags and five pieces of artillery were captured.

The rebel Generals Gordon and Rhodes were killed, and three other general officers were wounded.

All the enemy's killed and most of their wounded are in our hands.

The Department learns with deep regret that we lost General Russell, killed.

The details are stated in the following official telegrams, received by this Department:—

GENERAL STEVENSON TO SECRETARY STANTON.

FIRST DESPATCH.

HARPER'S FERRY, Va., Sept. 19—12 M.

Hon. EDWIN M. STANTON, Secretary of War:—

General Sheridan moved on the enemy this morning at daylight.

Soon after the movement commenced there was heavy and continued firing for two hours. It then ceased, apparently receding. It was resumed about nine o'clock, and has continued to this hour (twelve, noon), apparently in the vicinity of Bunker Hill.

JOHN D. STEVENSON, Brigadier General.

SECOND DESPATCH.

HARPER'S FERRY, Sept. 19—3 P. M.

Hon. E. M. STANTON, Secretary of War:—

Just received report from the signal officer as follows:—Continuous firing between Opequan and near Winchester. Very heavy since ten o'clock this morning. Think the engagement is general. Line about five miles long.

Averill is heavily engaged with the enemy near Darkesville. I have sent a party of scouts and couriers to the front, and shall report promptly all reliable news.

JOHN D. STEVENSON, Brigadier General.

THIRD DESPATCH.

HARPER'S FERRY, Sept. 19—4.30 P. M.

Hon. E. M. STANTON, Secretary of War:—

Fighting in the direction of Winchester much heavier. Our forces near Bunker Hill seem to be driving the enemy rapidly. JOHN D. STEVENSON, Brigadier General.

FOURTH DESPATCH.

HARPER'S FERRY, Sept. 19—7 P. M.

Hon. E. M. STANTON, Secretary of War:—

Just heard from the front. Our cavalry, under Averill and Merritt, engaged Breckinridge's corps at Darkesville at daylight, and up to one o'clock had driven him beyond Stevenson's depot, a distance of seven miles, killing and wounding quite a number and capturing two hundred prisoners from Gordon's division.

On the centre and left the enemy were driven about three miles beyond the Opequan into a line of earthworks, our infantry attacking them in position. Since then, as the officer left he could distinctly hear heavy musketry fire and continuous and heavy artillery firing as he came in. We have heard here heavy artillery firing, and still continuing to this hour. Every indication is most favorable to us.

JOHN D. STEVENSON, Brigadier General.

FIFTH DESPATCH.

HARPER'S FERRY, Sept. 20—7:40 A. M.

Hon. E. M. STANTON, Secretary of War:—

Just heard from the front that Sheridan has defeated the enemy, capturing two thousand five hundred prisoners, five pieces of artillery and five battle flags.

The rebel Generals Gordon and Rhodes were killed, and York wounded. Our loss was about two thousand. General Russell, of the Sixth corps, was killed. General McIntosh lost a leg.

The enemy escaped up the valley under cover of night. Sheridan is in Winchester.

Generals Upton, McIntosh and Chapman are wounded.

J. D. STEVENSON, Brigadier General.

General Sheridan [illegible] to General Grant the following official report, which has just been received by the Department:—

GENERAL SHERIDAN TO GENERAL GRANT.

WINCHESTER, Va., Sept. 19—7:30 P. M.

Lieutenant General U. S. GRANT:—

I have the honor to report that I attacked the forces of General Early over the Berryville pike at the crossing of Opequan creek, and after a most stubborn and sanguinary engagement, which lasted from early in the morning until five o'clock in the evening, completely defeated

THE VICTORY IN SHENANDOAH VALLEY.

Scene of Sheridan's Brilliant Achievement on Monday, September 19, 1864.

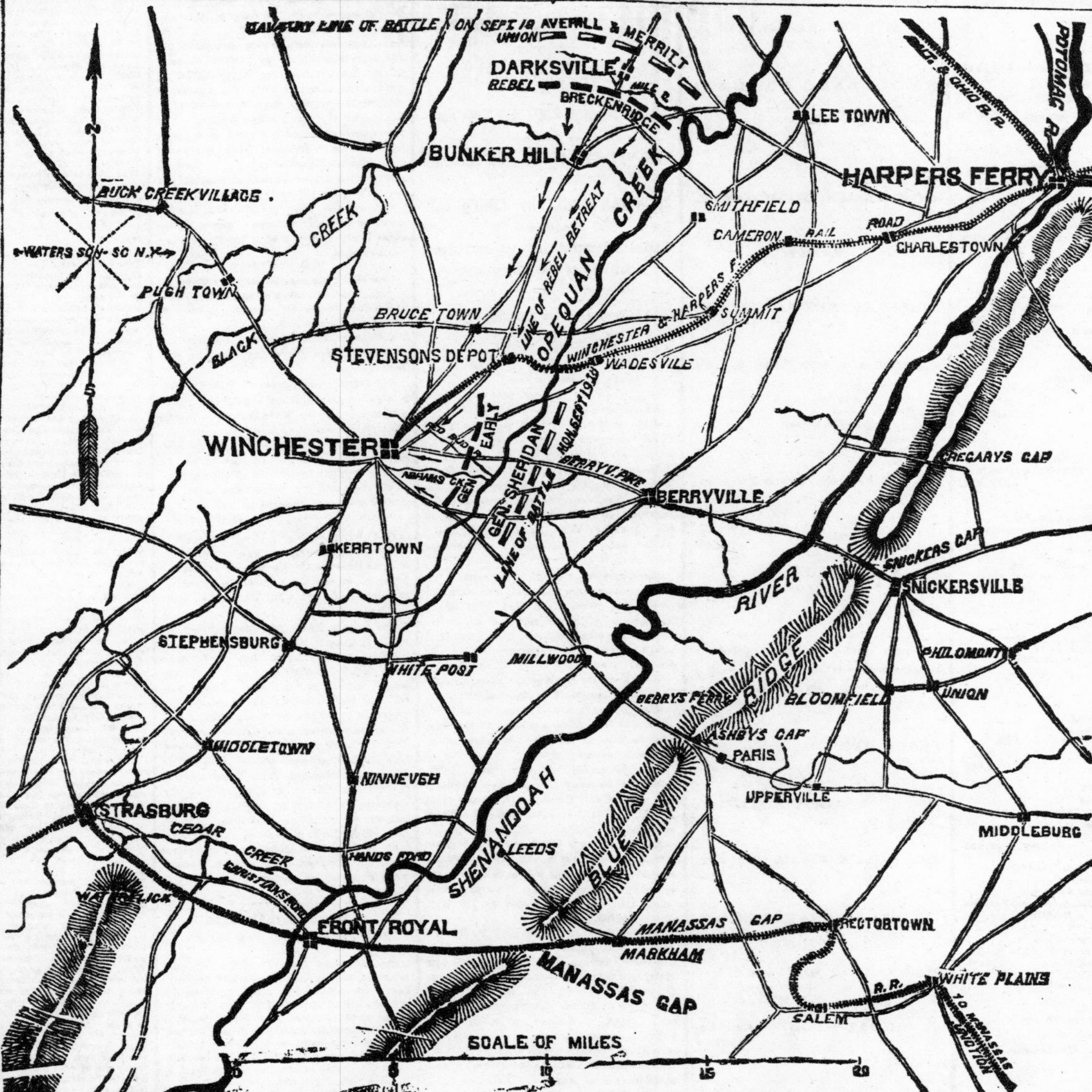

him, driving him through Winchester, capturing about twenty-five hundred prisoners, five pieces of artillery, nine army flags, and most of their wounded.

The rebel Generals Rhodes and Gordon were killed, and three other general officers were wounded. Most of the enemy's wounded and all their killed fell into our hands.

[The rebel General Rhodes is a native of Alabama, and has figured extensively in the operations in Virginia under General Lee. When he drove our forces out of Martinsburg, on the 29th ult., it is said that on subsequently retiring from the town he left his compliments for Gen. Averill, saying that he was sorry to trouble him, but that he had come down to get information of the nominations made by the Chicago Convention. It now appears, however, that his great desire for information has eventually cost the rebel general his life.—ED. HERALD.]

Our losses are severe. Among them is General A. D. Russell, commanding a division of the Sixth corps, who was killed by a cannon ball.

Generals Upton, McIntosh and Chapman were wounded. I cannot tell our losses.

The conduct of the officers and men was most superb. They charged and carried every position taken up by the rebels from Opequan creek to Winchester.

The rebels were very strong in numbers and very obstinate in their fighting.

I desire to mention to the Lieutenant General commanding the army the gallant conduct of Generals Wright, Crook, Emory, Torbert, and the officers and men under their command. To them the country is indebted for this handsome victory. A more detailed report will be forwarded.

P. H. SHERIDAN, Major General Commanding.

Full details of casualties will be given when received by the Department.

EDWIN M. STANTON, Secretary of War.

Stanton's Second Despatch.

WASHINGTON, Sept. 20—12 M.

Major General JOHN A. DIX:—

The following despatch has just been received, giving further particulars of Sheridan's great victory. A salute of one hundred guns has just been given:—

HARPER'S FERRY, Sept. 20—11:40 A. M.

Hon. E. M. STANTON:—

Just received following official from General Sheridan, dated one o'clock to-day:—

GENERAL—We fought Early from daylight till between six and seven o'clock P. M. We drove him from Opequan creek through Winchester, and beyond the town. We captured two thousand five hundred to three thousand prisoners, five pieces of artillery, nine battle flags and all the rebel wounded and dead.

Their wounded in Winchester amount to some three thousand. We lost in killed General David Russell, commanding a division of the Sixth army corps, and in wounded Generals Chapman, McIntosh and Upton.

The rebels lost in killed the following general officers:—General Rhodes, General Wharton, General Gordon and General Ramseur.

[The only rebel General Wharton we know of in the rebel service is the Wharton who was operating in the Southwest a few months ago. On the morning of the 19th of June he had command of a brigade, which crossed the railroad between Kingston and Dalton, capturing and burning five freight trains loaded with supplies.—ED. HERALD.]

We have just sent them whirling through Winchester, and we are after them to-morrow.

This army behaved splendidly.

P. H. SHERIDAN, Major General Commanding.

I am sending forward all the medical supplies, subsistence stores and ambulances.

JOHN D. STEVENSON, Brigadier General.

EDWIN M. STANTON, Secretary of War.

Stanton's Third Despatch.

WAR DEPARTMENT, WASHINGTON, Sept. 20—9 P. M.

To Major General DIX, New York:—

The following is the latest intelligence received from General Sheridan:—

HARPER'S FERRY, Va., Sept. 20—8 P. M.

Hon. EDWIN M. STANTON, Secretary of War:—

The body of General Russell has arrived. As soon as it is embalmed it will be forwarded to New York. Gen. McIntosh, with his leg amputated, has just come in, and is in good spirits.

Several officers from the front report the number of prisoners in excess of three thousand.

The number of battle flags captured was fifteen instead of nine.

All concur that it was a complete rout.

Our cavalry started in pursuit at daylight this morning. Sheridan, when last heard from, was at Kearnstown.

I sent forward this morning ample medical supplies. Full subsistence for the entire army goes forward. If you do not hear from me often it will be because of the distance we are from the scene of action, and because I only send you such information as I esteem reliable.

JOHN D. STEVENSON, Brigadier General.

The President has appointed General Sheridan a brigadier general in the regular army and assigned him to the prominent command of the Middle Military Division.

General Grant has ordered the army under his command to fire a salute of one hundred guns at seven o'clock to-morrow morning in honor of Sheridan's great victory.

EDWIN M. STANTON, Secretary of War.

PRELIMINARY MOVEMENTS TO THE BATTLE.

Mr. Charles H. Farrell's Despatches.

HARPER'S FERRY, Sept. 18, 1864.

The rebels occupy Berryville in force, and occupy a line of old earthworks, which have been improved to meet the exigencies of the hour. Our army is drawn up in line of battle, watching the enemy at all points. The Richmond papers seem to exult over what seems to be the fact, that General Early has twice and thrice offered battle to General Sheridan, which the latter has as many times declined. Perhaps the exultations of the rebel press may yet be transformed into regrets, as, from present appearances, hunger promises to effect with the rebel army what would cost General Sheridan many valuable lives to effect. It is not always considered good military policy to rush into battle when a commanding general sees the enemy. A battle is often half won by simple manœuvres before a gun is fired, and a campaign may be won by strategy alone. I do not pretend to fathom or divine General Sheridan's plans, nor is it necessary at this juncture. He stands before the country as a cool, careful, skilful commander, enjoying the full confidence of the President, General Grant and every officer and man in his command. He is evidently acting in concert with our other armies in Virginia, and in due time he will develop the work he is now doing. There is one thing very sure, and the facts have been obtained from rebel prisoners, that when General Early followed General Sheridan's army up the Peninsula his object was the invasion of Maryland and Pennsylvania, with an express understanding from the Richmond government that those portions of our territory through which their army should march should be devastated by fire and sword and the country made a chaos. Without going further into the subject, I must say that the rebel plans have simply failed.

Since they have been in this vicinity they have manœuvred for position, making a feint here and there, massing their columns on the right, left and centre, then falling back and anon demonstrating towards the fords of the Potomac; but in all these movements their designs were quickly interpreted by General Sheridan, through the medium of his cavalry officers—Generals Torbert, Merritt, Wilson, Custer and Averill. These officers for weeks have been constantly in the saddle day and night; they have moved from point to point of our position with a celerity that insures success to our cause, and whenever they have met the enemy they have inflicted damage upon his columns beyond that sustained by ourselves. An invasion of our territory by the enemy while Sheridan leads his army is simply an impossibility, or, if possible, it would be foolhardy on the part of the enemy, unless he was in overwhelming force. If the rebels cross the fords Gen. Sheridan would be on their rear and flank; if they retreat up the valley he is on their rear; if he stays in his present position starvation, or at least short rations, will effect the work of defeat.

Our army is in an excellent climate and position. They are daily recuperating. They have plenty of good, wholesome food, and plenty of clothing, and during the last week six paymasters have been dispensing greenbacks with cheerful hands. Our communications between the main army and this point, which were temporarily disturbed by Mosby's guerillas, were reopened yesterday. Lieutenant Colonel Page, of the commissary of General Torbert's cavalry corps, had the honor of effecting this. He came through the other day from General Sheridan's headquarters, escorted by a cavalry detachment. In the afternoon and during the night supply trains were sent to the front with supplies.

Rebel prisoners report that General Early has been reinforced instead of retreating to Richmond, and that it is the design of their government to keep a large force in the valley of the Shenandoah for the present.

HARPER'S FERRY, Va., Sept. 19, 1864.

The recent visit of Lieutenant General Grant to this department was to put in motion some active movement of the army. The visit was brief and significant.

On Friday morning last the enemy disappeared entirely from the left wing of our army, on the Winchester and Berryville pike, and only made a feint show on our right. This gave rise to the surmise that they had either taken up their line of retreat towards Strasburg, or had massed over to their left (our right) for a concentrated movement against us.

General Sheridan at once took measures to ascertain the facts in the case, and from the information obtained soon came to the conclusion that this attempted clever movement of General Early was only a feint to get troops on our left over to the west side of the Opequan creek. The trap was discovered and the rebel general thwarted in his designs. General Sheridan did not have any apprehension of any result but victory had he crossed when the rebels fell back; but he was not ready at the time.

The affair yesterday morning at Martinsburg, between the rebels, consisting of artillery and infantry, and our troops under General Averill, showed that the rebels were stoutly guarding the Baltimore and Ohio Railroad, with a view of preventing its reopening from here to Cumberland.

Shortly after daylight this morning the enemy were discovered in force on the west bank of the Opequan, when sharp skirmishing and a brisk cannonade took place between the armies. Major General Crook, with his noble veterans of the West Virginia army, occupied the right of our line, the Nineteenth corps the centre, and the Sixth corps the left.

The great battle for the possession of the Valley of the Shenandoah has commenced. It is said that the rebels have a large reserve concealed in the valley, between North Mountains and [illegible] Mountains, with headquarters at Jamesburg. The reports of rebel deserters and others in regard to the strength of this force are so conflicting that it is difficult to settle down upon any stated number as accurate. The fact of the enemy offering General Sheridan battle shows they have a good sized army and hope to meet with success.

Early's Last Order to Obtain Favor with the People of the Valley.

MR. THEODORE C. WILSON'S DESPATCH.

IN THE FIELD, NEAR LEETOWN, Va., Sept. 17—A. M.

On the 12th of this month General Early issued an unusually lengthy general order, of which the following is in part a copy:—

I. Commanding officers will be held responsible that the troops commit no depredations. When camps are formed the inspector, with the quartermaster of each command (and in the absence of these officers the commander shall detail an officer for this purpose) will make an inspection of the houses, fences, &c., near the camps, both on reaching and leaving them, and any property destroyed will be paid for by the quartermaster at the charge made by the owners, and the money will be stopped from the pay of officers of the troops camped nearest to where the property may have been destroyed. In each case of such stoppage the commanding officer will forward at once to these headquarters the names of the officers against whom these stoppages have been made.

II. Straggling, the greatest disgrace of any troops, for it produces every evil, will at once be stopped. Soldiers, and even officers, are prohibited from entering the houses of the citizens, except upon invitation. Neglect to enforce this regulation will cause any officer to be relieved of his command. Officers commanding, or on duty with troops in the field, will camp with their respective commands. The practice of officers taking houses of citizens or public edifices is prohibited. Officers and men falling out of ranks on account of sickness must do so with the written permission of the medical officer, otherwise they will be arrested and brought forward by the guard.

III. All commanding officers will hereafter use every exertion to procure leather with which to shoe the troops of their respective commands, and a detail will be made from each regiment of such as know how to make and repair shoes, to engage in this work whenever the army is lying idle, even if it be but for a day at a time.

IV. The general commanding relies upon the energy of the proper officers of this command to supply many of the deficiencies which it has been impossible for the departments at the capital to prevent.

V. Division commanders will order their commissaries to purchase wheat and have it ground at the mills in the neighborhood. Where wheat cannot be procured they will purchase corn for grinding.

VI. It has been proven to the commanding general that soldiers are in the habit of selling government property of all descriptions. This unwarrantable, demoralizing and vicious practice must and shall cease. Hereafter any soldier detected in such an act will be punished with the utmost severity. Any mounted soldier who shall sell his horse, or attempt to do so, shall, on the fact being established, be immediately transferred and sent to a post command at a distant and disagreeable position, and his horse turned over to the quartermaster for public use. Any officer becoming aware of any violation of this order, and not doing his utmost to bring the guilty party or parties to punishment, will be relieved from command and brought before a court martial for trial for neglect of duty. This order will be read at the head of each company in this command on at least three consecutive days.

VII. Quartermasters will hereafter be instructed to pay for the wood cut and burned on the encampments of the commands to which they are severally attached. Such payments will be made in accordance with the market price of wood, but not for larger quantities than are allowed by the regulations of the army.

VIII. No passes will now be granted to either officers or men to go more than six miles from their respective commands, unless it be to visit these headquarters.

IX. In future, cows will not be slaughtered unless it becomes absolutely necessary to do so in order to supply the pressing wants of this army. Commissaries should ration the commands with beef and pork as far as practicable.

X. Commanders of divisions and artillery battalions must do all they can to keep their men in as comfortable a condition as possible. They will direct their quartermasters to take charge of all the tanneries within reach, and cause all the hides and leather they can procure to be dressed and prepared for the use of the troops. Subsistence officers will cause to be collected as many supplies as possible; and they will use the men of the army and the government teams to have wheat ground where the farmers have not the means at hand to do so. The order relative to impressment must be strictly adhered to. Rigid economy is enjoined in the use of all supplies, and commanding officers will be held responsible for any destruction or unnecessary wastage.

XI. No more wheat shall be fed to stock.

XII. Quartermasters of this army are hereby authorized to exchange raw hides for leather. If it is found to be impossible to procure sufficient leather, shoes may be made out of the raw hides to supply the immediate wants of the men. Cold weather is approaching, and promptness in this matter is exacted.

XIII. Complaints have been made to the commanding general of this army, by farmers and defenceless women, of the bad conduct and depredations committed by some enlisted men unworthy to be called soldiers. Hereafter if any more complaints of the kind specified are made to these headquarters the commanding general will place one-half of the army on guard to keep the other half in camp.

XIV. In conclusion, the general commanding appeals to every officer and soldier now with him, by that love which we all bear for our government and the protection of families and their interests, to be ever ready to meet the foe, ever watchful to defeat his designs, and always on the alert to check his advances. Then, by the grace of a protective Providence, ever watchful, ever guiding us on to the great end of victory, our cause will succeed as sure as it is just and holy.

JUBAL EARLY, Lieutenant General Commanding.

THE BATTLE.

Mr. Theodore C. Wilson's Despatch.

IN THE FIELD, SOUTH OF WINCHESTER, Sept. 20—A. M.

Ere this reaches you the public will be apprised of another battle having taken place in this quarter. It was a hard contest, commencing at daylight on the 19th, and ending only temporarily with the cloud of night.

The whole movement was made up of a series of eminently successful combinations. Everything on the field was more or less engaged. The cavalry did some very hard and splendid fighting. Merritt and Averill joined and repeatedly charged. It was Averill who turned the enemy's left flank, taking one piece of artillery, on the Romney road.

General Rhodes' body is in Winchester, in a private house.

General Imboden is reported dead.

General Crook's corps did the hardest of the infantry fighting, and in all probability lost the heaviest.

Colonel Duval, commanding a brigade in Crook's corps, is slightly wounded and in a private house in town.

The battle was a decided success and our achievements were brilliant ones. No branch of the service more than the cavalry deserves credit for gallantry on the field.

Details of the Engagement.

HEADQUARTERS, MIDDLE MILITARY DIVISION, WINCHESTER, Va., Sept. 19—9 P. M.

General Sheridan's army has this day fought one of the most successful and decisive battles of the war. Victory again perched on our banners, and the rebel army which so recently threatened the invasion of the loyal North has been defeated and utterly routed, with the loss of at least three thousand killed and wounded, including five generals, namely:—Rhodes, Wharton, Bradley T. Johnson, Gordon, York and Godman, the two first of whom were killed and the others badly wounded; and we have captured two thousand five hundred prisoners, nine battle flags, representing nine different regimental organizations, five pieces of artillery, with caissons.

The recital of the victory ought to make every loyal heart at the North glow with admiration and gratitude to the brave men and gallant officers who have achieved so signal success.

In order to more thoroughly understand the nature of the battle, with all the surrounding influences, it will be necessary briefly to refer to the operations of Sunday.

On Sunday morning Early sent Gordon's division of rebel infantry from Bunker Hill, where it had been stationed for the past few days, to drive Averill out of Martinsburg and destroy the bridge on the Baltimore and Ohio Railroad across the Opequan, which they erroneously thought had been repaired. They occupied Martinsburg for a short time without doing any damage to the railroad, and were eventually driven by Averill as far as Darkesville.

General Sheridan, learning their movements, ordered the whole command to break camp and prepare to march. Accordingly at three o'clock on Sunday the tents were all struck and packed in wagons. The different divisions were all under arms and prepared to move at a moment's notice, and remained in this state for about an hour, when the order came to go into camp again for the night, and everything remained perfectly quiet. About nine o'clock orders were received from Sheridan for the Sixth and Nineteenth corps to be ready to start at three o'clock, and the Army of Western Virginia, under Crook, at five the following morning, the order of march to be as follows:—The Sixth corps to move out on the Winchester and Berryville pike, and move in two parallel columns on both sides of the road, with the artillery, ammunition and supply trains on the road; the Nineteenth corps to follow on the same road and in similar order; the Army of Western Virginia, under Crook, to move from its camping ground in the vicinity of Summit Point, and, striking across the country in a southwesterly direction, was ordered to form a junction at the crossing of the Opequan, on the Berryville and Winchester pike. And shortly after five o'clock Wilson's division of cavalry crossed the Opequan at the Berryville and Winchester pike, moving his command rapidly along the road. Driving in the enemy's skirmish line, he gallantly charged the enemy's field works with the First brigade, and carried them at the point of the sabre, capturing thirty prisoners. In this charge Colonel Brinton, Eighteenth Pennsylvania cavalry, was wounded within a few feet of the enemy's works, while gallantly leading his regiment.

These field works were constructed by the rebels to guard the ford at the Opequan, and prevent our passage at that point. It will be seen how signally they failed to accomplish the object for which they were constructed.

Our cavalry having secured a safe passage for the infantry, the Sixth corps was moved across the Opequan and along the pike towards Winchester, leaving its train in park on the opposite side of the stream, to a point about a mile and a half distant from the ford, where it formed in line of battle and threw out a strong skirmish line. At the same time the artillery opened on the woods, into which the enemy's infantry had retired, and kept up an incessant cannonade, the enemy replying briskly with parts of two batteries.

There was a delay of at least two hours, caused by the non-arrival of the Nineteenth corps, which, through misconception of orders, had failed to come up at the proper time. General Emery had moved his column to the rear of the baggage train of the Sixth corps, instead of keeping his command closed up in the rear of the advancing column of the Sixth corps.

General Sheridan having learned on Sunday that the main portion of Early's forces were encamped in the vicinity of Bunker Hill and Stephenson's depot, resolved to mass his forces on the Winchester and Berryville pike, and by a rapid movement hurl them on Early's rear. There is no doubt that the enemy were completely surprised and outmanœuvred by Sheridan.

While his different columns were being marched to the appointed place of rendezvous, a portion of our cavalry, under Generals Torbert and Averill, kept up a strong picket line along the Opequan, and by demonstrating in force at Burns' ford kept a large portion of the enemy at that part of the field, which was nearly twelve miles distant from the point where it was intended our infantry should operate and strike a blow which should result in the signal defeat of Early's army.

The delay in the arrival of the Nineteenth corps enabled Early to move Gordon's division at the double quick from Bunker Hill, distant about ten miles, and bring it up in time to form in line of battle with Breckinridge's, Ramseur's and Rhodes' commands, which had already arrived and were formed in a belt of woods skirting Berryville and Winchester.

As soon as the Nineteenth corps arrived it was formed in four lines of battle, about three hundred yards apart, on the right of the Sixth corps, and everything being in readiness the advance was sounded at about twelve o'clock, and the different lines moved forward.

The two corps advanced in splendid style, and just as composedly as though marching at a review or on parade, drums beating and colors flying, presenting such an imposing spectacle as has seldom been witnessed in the present war. In fact, some of the oldest and most experienced staff officers present declared they had never before witnessed so truly grand a spectacle.

The first line had not advanced more than two hundred yards before it became warmly engaged with the enemy, who were posted in line about six hundred yards distant. At the same time our artillery opened a furious cannonade, throwing shells and solid shot into the opposite woods, where the enemy could be distinctly seen moving up reinforcements.

Our different lines of battle continued to advance steadily until within nearly two hundred yards of the enemy's line, when the rebels opened a furious cannonade

CONTINUED ON FIFTH PAGE.

The Daily Picayune

UNION. JUSTICE. CONFIDENCE.

VOLUME XXVIII. — NEW ORLEANS, WEDNESDAY MORNING, SEPTEMBER 28, 1864. — NUMBER 174.

The Daily Picayune.

TELEGRAPHIC.

Northern Dates to the 20th inst.

WAR NEWS.

THE VALLEY OF THE SHENANDOAH.

SHERIDAN'S VICTORY CONFIRMED.

Official Dispatches to and from the War Department.

Gold in New York on the 20th, 223 7-8; Cotton, 172 to 173.

To the New Orleans Associated Press:

PORT HUDSON, Sept. 27, 1864.

NEW YORK, Sept. 20.—Cotton quiet at 172 and 173 for Middling. Gold heavy, unsettled and lower, opened at 226¾, declined to 223½, advanced to 224, closing at 223⅞.

WASHINGTON, Sept. 20.—*To Gov. Hall*: Yesterday morning, the 19th Army Corps, Major Gen Sheridan, attacked the rebels under Breckinridge and Early, near Bunker Hill, in the Shenandoah Valley, fought a hard battle all day, and a brilliant victory was won by our forces.

The enemy were driven over twelve miles 2500 prisoners were captured, nine stands of colors, five pieces of artillery were taken, and the rebel killed and wounded left in our hands. The rebel Generals, Rhodes and Gordon, were killed, and four other rebel generals were wounded. E. M. STANTON.

We have also received the same dispatch from Gen. Rosecrans's headquarters:

WAR DEPARTMENT, Washington, Sept. 20. *To Major Gen. Dix*: Yesterday Major Gen. Sheridan attacked Early, fought a great battle, and won a splendid victory.

Over 2500 prisoners were captured. Also, nine battle flags and five pieces of artillery. The rebel Gens. Gordon and Rhodes were killed, and three other general officers wounded.

All the enemy's killed and most of their wounded are in our hands. The details are stated in the following official telegrams received by this Department. The Department learns with deep regret that we lost Gen. Russell, killed.

HARPER'S FERRY, Sept. 19, 7 P. M.—*To Hon. E. M. Stanton*: Have just heard from the front. Our cavalry, under Averill and Merritt, engaged Breckinridge's corps at Dranesville at daylight, and up to 1 o'clock had driven him beyond Stevenson's Depot, a distance of seven miles, killing and wounding quite a number and capturing 200 prisoners from Gordon's division. On the centre and left the enemy were driven about three miles beyond the Ocoquan, into a line of earthworks. Our infantry attacking them in position. Since then, as the officer left, he could distinctly hear heavy cannonading, and it is still continuing to this hour.

Every indication is most favorable to us.

J. D. STEVENSON, Brig. Gen.

HARPER'S FERRY, Sept. 20, 7:40 A. M.—*To Hon. E. M. Stanton*: Have just heard from the front that Sheridan has defeated the enemy, capturing 2500 prisoners, 5 pieces of artillery, and 9 battle flags. Rebel Gens. Gordon and Rhodes were killed, and York wounded.

Our loss is about 2000. Gen. Russell, of the 6th Corps, was killed. Gen. McIntosh lost a leg. Enemy escaped up the Valley under cover of the night. Sheridan is in Winchester. J. D. STEVENSON, Brig. Gen.

Gens Upton, McIntosh and Chapman are wounded.

Gen. Sheridan transmits to Gen. Grant the following official report, which has just been received by the Department:

WINCHESTER, Sept. 19, 7:30 P. M.—*To Lieut. Gen. Grant*: I have the honor to report that I attacked the forces of Gen. Early on the Berryville Pike, at the crossing of Occoquan Creek, and after a most stubborn and sanguinary engagement, which lasted from early in the morning until 5 P. M., completely defeated him, driving him through Winchester, capturing 2500 prisoners, five pieces of artillery, nine battle flags, and most of their wounded.

The rebel Gens. Rhodes and Gordon were killed, and three other general officers wounded. Most of the enemy's wounded and all his killed fell into our hands. Our losses are severe. Among them Gen. D. A. Russell, commanding a division of the 6th Corps, who was killed by a cannon ball. Gens. Upton, McIntosh and Chapman were wounded. I cannot tell our loss.

The conduct of the officers and men was superb. They charged and carried every position taken up by the rebels, from Occoquan Creek to Winchester. The rebels were in strong force, and very obstinate in their fighting.

I desire to mention to the Lieutenant General Commanding the gallant conduct of Gens. Wright, Crook, Emory, Torbett, and other officers and men under their commands. To them the country is indebted for this handsome victory. A more detailed report will be forwarded. P. H. SHERIDAN.

Full details of casualties will be given when received by the Department.

E. M. STANTON.

WAR DEPARTMENT, Sept. 20, 6 P. M.—*To Major Gen. Dix*: The following is the latest intelligence received from Gen. Sheridan:

HARPER'S FERRY, Sept. 20, 8 P. M.—*To Hon. E. M. Stanton*: The body of Gen. Russell has arrived. As soon as it is embalmed it will be forwarded to New York. Gen. McIntosh, with one leg amputated, has just come in, and is in good spirits. Several officers from the front report the number of prisoners in excess of 3000. The number of battle-flags captured was 15, instead of 9. All agree that it was a complete route.

Our cavalry started in pursuit at daylight this morning. Sheridan, when last heard from, was at Reamstown. I sent forward this morning ample medical supplies and full subsistence, for the army goes forward. If you do not hear from me after this, it is because we are from the scene of action and because I only send you such information as I deem reliable.

J. B. STEVENSON, Brig. Gen.

Gen Grant has ordered the army under his command to fire a salute of one hundred guns at 7 o'clock, to-morrow morning, in honor of Sheridan's great victory.

A dispatch just received from Gen. Sherman at Atlanta, says everything continues well with us.

The President has appointed Gen. Sheridan a brigadier general in the regular army, and assigned him to the command of the Middle Military Division.

The reports of to-day allow that the draft is proceeding quietly in all the States. In most of the districts vigorous efforts continued to fill the quota by volunteers before the drafted men were mustered in.

E. M. STANTON.

NEW YORK, Sept. 20.—The Western Union Telegraph Company, in conjunction with the Russian Government, are actively engaged in fitting out an expedition under the immediate supervision of Capt. Chas. Buckley, U. S. A., for Oregon.

The post of Russia and the country beyond Behring's Straits to survey the route of the telegraph line, and make other needful arrangements to put the whole extent of the line under contract the ensuing winter, and understand the projectors of the enterprise are sanguine that the line will be in successful operation between New York and San Francisco and St. Petersburg and London by the middle of 1866. Hiram Sibley, of the Western Union Telegraph line the Russian Consul, in company with Mr. Cowling, the enterprising projector of the Russian and American Telegraph Line, left in the Scotia to-day for Liverpool and St. Petersburg. with a view to complete the arrangement already initiated with the Russian Government for expediting the early completion of the line.

A Southern Opinion

On Peace and Peace Propositions.

The Richmond Enquirer of the 8th, now before us, has the following, which seems to have been inspired by articles from the Republican pen of Col. Forney. The Enquirer affects to believe that even Mr. Greeley, as well as Messrs. Raymond and Forney, are prepared to compromise on "National Unity," as a basis of peace adjustment. This certainly is not the theory of Mr. Lincoln's dispatch to Niagara Falls. The Enquirer says:

Our enemy will not even dismiss the question of dividing the "National Unity," that the immense territorial empire once known as the United States of America shall be severed into two Confederacies. Notwithstanding the irreconcilable animosities and bitter, undying hatred which this war has mutually bred between the two sections, our enemy would still endeavor to unite in indissoluble bonds the people that thus mutually despise each other. This effort to make "brethren" of these who for four years have been cutting each other's throats cannot and ought not to succeed. The unnatural alliance is repugnant to every sentiment of sympathy and affection that exists between fellow-citizens or fellow-subjects. Its results are to be daily seen, and the bitter fruits periodically experienced, in the animosity of Ireland to England, of Poland to Russia, of Hungary to Austria. The wars with which such an alliance exacts the peace of Europe should warn our enemy against such an experiment on this continent. Could the children of those whose bones whiten the many battle-fields of this war ever look upon each other as brethren, as fellow-citizens? The very supposition is unnatural, and its accomplishment impossible.

Citizenship of a great empire is, indeed, to be desired, and it is what men of every great station pride themselves upon, but when purchased at the expense of internal peace and domestic harmony, it brings the nation into contempt, and robs that citizenship of all that made it enviable and desirable.

But the pride of "National Unity" seems to be swallowing up all other issues among our enemies. "The Federal Basis of the States" in the Chicago platform is but another expression for "National Unity." The Republican party seem to be about abandoning Mr. Lincoln's Abolition condition, and narrowing the questions in dispute to that of "National Unity." The phrase is sometimes varied into "National Dignity"—but both mean the same thing: territory—empire. The "Explanation from Forney," which is to be found in another column, appears to be given in elucidation of his article on "The Road to Lasting Peace," which appeared in the Washington Chronicle and Philadelphia *Press*, and which has been "assailed by suspicious and ignorant partisans." Forney retires behind the imposing authority of the "Hon. Henry J. Raymond, the Chairman of the National Union Committee," and, to silence all caviling, his readers are informed that the said Raymond "has been in consultation all day with the President, the different members of the Cabinet, and other friends of the Administration of the Federal Government," and that the said Raymond occupies a higher place and bolder platform than Forney has dared to assume.

The article from the Chronicle, on "The Road to Lasting Peace" never reached us, and we do not know through what regions of sacrifice that "road" would lead the people of these Confederate States. But Forney has seen proper to do us justice in the objects for which we are fighting. He says very correctly: "The blood poured out in this war for liberty mingles with the blood that is poured out, not for slavery, but for an ideal Southern independence," and he adds, "If we can change this latter sentiment into the belief that Southern independence can be better maintained in the old Union, why should not all issues, except that of national unity, be entrusted to a National Convention," which we understand to mean that the result of that "all day" consultation between Mr. Raymond and the President and his friends to be, that if the States of the Confederacy will waive or abandon the subject of territorial disruption, and meet the States of the Union in National Convention, that all questions will be remitted to the arbitrament of that body. In other words, the Administration, through its Washington City organ, professes a willingness to stop the fight and try the experiment of discussion. If Forney's "explanation" has any meaning, it can be nothing less than this. Why, then, does not Mr. Lincoln propose an armistice, and offer the National Convention? Whatever may have been determined by that consultation on the "[illegible]" the fall of Atlanta has altered it, and remitted the discussion from the proposed Convention to the ordeal of battle. The bloody work for "national dignity" is to be again tested on the battle-field, and the Convention postponed to a less favorable military situation.

After mentioning Mr. Calhoun's once proposed dual government, suggesting the applicability of it at the present time the Enquirer says:

The war has created the necessity for two Presidents, two Congresses, two judiciaries, in fact, for two nations. Each independent, but not necessarily indifferent to the welfare of the other. The domestic affairs of the two sections should be managed separately and exclusively by the authorities selected by the people. The necessities of each require a separate government; the good of both would be promoted by two governmental organisms, and the power and influence of all, undiminished by the separation, would always exist in unity as against an assailant of either. The American continent for American civilization is as much a Confederate as a Federal sentiment, and, notwithstanding the passions excited and aroused by this war, the people of the two sections must ever lean more on each other than on any other nation. Our conquest could only make us the ally of a foreign power against the United States. Subjugated, the people of the Confederate States would become the Ireland, the Poland, the Hungary of the American Continent, welcoming any and every enemy of the United States as their friend and deliverer, and ready at all times to reopen the contest. But as an independent nation the closest alliances that can unite the peoples should exist between them, and an insult to one would be an offence to the other.

At the beginning of the war, neither section expected it to assume the proportions it has since reached. Both were unprepared for it, and it grew to its present gigantic proportions imperceptibly to both parties, and now it has become almost unmanageable. Our enemy would make peace if national pride did not restrain them. "National Unity" is but another name for national pride. The power it implies would not be diminished by a separation, because the resources of each would always exist for the defence of both against any foreign power, and the development which separate governments would give to the resources of the respective sections would greatly increase their power.

No conflict of civilization, or institutions, or rights would arise between the two peoples; the desperate passions that now alike influence both nations would be left to the ameliorating and soothing hand of time, and the good offices which cautious intercourse might effect. By conquest, to make "brethren" of deadly enemies; by war, to "insure domestic tranquility;" by the outrage of confiscation, "to establish justice;" to "provide for the common defence" by the destruction and devastation of one section, are results incompatible with "the blessings of liberty," or the promotion of "the general welfare." The "national unity" of an empire or kingdom may be preserved by conquest, but force belongs not to constitutional governments. Compromise is the only principle by which popular governments can perpetuate their existence. When the appeal to arms was made, the peaceful remedy of compromise was impossible, and now four years of war has so widened and deepened the gulf that separates the two sections, that they can never be again united in peace. Intoxicated by sudden and partial success, Mr. Lincoln may imagine that our conquest is within his power and means. No words of ours can be more convincing than four years of war, but the in interest of humanity will the sober thought ever dispel the delusion that by conquest, by arms, by war, a "lasting peace" can be made between the parties to this disgraceful conflict! We regard this "explanation" by the editor of the Washington organ, referring as it does to the example of Mr. Raymond for its justification before the party, as a step towards a "lasting peace." It abandons the negro entirely, and points to Mr. Greeley as ready to forego philanthrophy and "freedom" for "National Unity." When partizan frenzy and fanaticism thus reduce their extravagant demands, the more reasonable and sensible mass of the people, who are bearing all the burdens, enduring all the sufferings and making all the sacrifices, will not long continue the war for the shadow of "National Unity." That people, as well as our own, will soon see the folly of attempting to live together after such a war. They will soon learn that in an offensive and defensive alliance of the two nations as against the world, with separate governments for domestic affairs lies their true and real interests, as well as the "road to lasting peace."

The Richmond Enquirer's Candidate.

It is often said that the Richmond Enquirer is the organ of Jefferson Davis. Others declare the Sentinel so to be. While this cannot properly be said of either, yet there is no doubt that these papers more often reflect the opinions which prevail in his administration than do the Examiner and the Whig, which are antagonistic to his management of public affairs. The Enquirer is the especial opponent of the views of the Virginia administration party, and thus must not only know, but impart the general sentiment in this council.

The Enquirer, of the 5th, thus pronounces its choice for President of the United States:

The Democratic nominees in the United States are McClellan for President and Pendleton for Vice President. What concern have the people of these Confederate States in the fate of these candidates at the approaching election? In our opinion, the interest and hope of peace is not greatly advanced by these nominations. From Gen. McClellan our people can have but little hope of peace, other than a reconstruction peace. * * * What hope do his antecedents hold out that should encourage our people to believe that he would yield our nationality any sooner than Mr. Lincoln? He is by far the more dangerous man for us; had his policy been persistently followed, and the war conducted on the principles of civilized warfare, he might have divided our people and, perhaps, conquered our liberties. With consummate abilities he clearly foresaw that emancipation might possibly free the negroes, but could not unite the sections; that confiscation might enrich his soldiers, but could not reconcile our people; hence, with an earnest and honest love for the Union, he avoided those fatal acts, and conducted the war for the restoration of the Union, rather than the destruction of the South. His policy was the olive branch in one hand and the sword in the other, to conquer by power and conciliate by kindness. It was a most dangerous policy for us; for if the ameliorating hand of Federal kindness had softened the rigors of war, our people would not have been subjected to those terrible fires of suffering by which Mr. Lincoln has hardened every heart and steeled every sentiment against our merciless foes. As a sincere secessionist, prefering war and nationality to peace and the Union, we looked upon the fact of a difference between Mr. Lincoln and Gen. McClellan as to the proper policy of conducting the war as peculiarly fortunate for our cause. We hailed the proclamations of emancipation and confiscation, and the policy of plunder and devastation as sure pledges of our ultimate triumph; they were terrible ordeals, but they most effectually eradicated every sentiment of Union, and arousing the pride as well as the interest of our people, inflamed the patriotism of the whole, until they would have accepted death as preferable to ultimate defeat.

Now, between McClellan and Lincoln there are many points of difference—the former is a man of talents, of information, of firmness and great military experience and ability—the latter is a supple, pliant, easy fool, a good but vulgar joker. While McClellan has the interest of the Union only at heart, Mr. Lincoln has the fanatical object of freeing negroes for his inspiration. Between "my plan," as Gen. Grant has conducted it, and one by Gen. McClellan, there could not have been the same success that has already attended our arms, for we lost more men fighting the science of McClellan on the Peninsula, than we have in repelling the furious but ill conducted assaults of Gen. Grant.

Thus, whether we look at this nomination in the light of peace or of war, we prefer Lincoln to McClellan. We can make better terms of peace with an anti-slavery fanatic than with an earnest Unionist. We can gain more military success in a war conducted on "my plan" than one of a real soldier like McClellan, and sooner destroy the resources and strength of our enemy where they are managed and manipulated by the light fingered gentry of Messrs. Chase and Fessenden, than when husbanded and skilfully controlled by such a man as Guthrie. Our best hope is from the honest fanatics of the United States, men who believe in their hearts that slavery is the "sum of all villanies," and who really and sincerely believe it to be their duty to separate their country from this "relic of barbarism." Such men, when they find that their people are tired of the war, will end it by a peace that sacrifices territory to freedom, and will let the South "go," provided she carries slavery with her. These men believe no less that the just powers of government are derived from the consent of the governed, than "that all men are created free and equal." The two postulates are of like importance to an abolitionist.

Both the Abolitionist and the Democrat is our enemy—the one because we have slaves, the other because we are disunionists. Nor does their enmity differ in degree; they both hate us most intensely. The Chicago platform is, that "peace may be restored on the basis of the Federal Union of the States"—that is, reconstruction of the Union as it was, with slavery protected by the nominal laws, but warred upon by a real sentiment, aggravated and embittered by the war. The reconstructed Union of the Chicago platform would be the certain destruction—first, of slavery, and next of slaveholders. With Lincoln and the Baltimore platform, we of the Confederate States know where we are—outside of the pale of mercy, devoted to ruin and destruction, with no hope save in the justice and protection of God, and the courage and manliness of our soldiers. With swords and muskets and cannon we fight Lincoln, and the past affords no reason of apprehension of the future. But in the reconstructed Union of the Chicago platform we would be deprived of our weapons without being reconciled to our foes.

There is no question that between the two men Gen. McClellan enjoys far more of the respect of the people of these States than Lincoln, and the Democratic party far more of our confidence than the Republican, and that if reconstruction were possible it would be more probable under Gen. McClellan and the Democracy than under Lincoln and the Republicans. The Northwest inspires one, and New England the other; but as long as New England imposes the dogmas of her civilization, and the tenets of her fanaticism upon the mind and people of the Northwest, there may be peace and separation, but there can never be Union and harmony. If the Northwest desires the restoration of the Union, let its people shake off the bondage of New England, and show to the world that a new era of toleration and fraternal kindness has arisen in the place of fanatical Puritanism and selfish ostracism.

Proclamation from the Rebel Governor Allen.

We find the following in a late New York journal:

To all persons residing within the Confederate lines in the State of Louisiana who have taken the oath of allegiance to the United States Government:

Having received many letters asking advice on this subject, I take this method of replying:

By the laws of Louisiana, whoever takes the oath of allegiance to the United States is disfranchised, and cannot enjoy any civil right. If you are true to such oaths you must be false to us, our country, and its cause. You should take your choice, either keep your oath and go with the enemy, or repudiate it and remain with us. As you did not depart with the enemy, I believe that most of you (and I hope all) did not design to forswear your fealty to your State and country. I will not discuss the right or wrong of what you did under stress of danger to yourselves, or whether that danger was small or great, real or imaginary, but I will simply advise you as your Governor, all the premises considered, and the hereafter we are to have, what you ought to do.

As an oath, imposed under any duress whatever, is not binding, finally, morally or religiously, my counsel is—to join the army at once, and wash out the stain on your names in the blood of your enemies. Let no occupation, nor age, nor infirmity, keep you at home another hour. If you can carry a musket, or march only a mile in a day, join the army, get face to face with the base foe who has robbed, and insulted, and tried by every means to dishonor you. In your case revenge is sweet, and right and holy in the sight of an all-wise and ever just God. All who are physically able should go immediately into active service. Those who are unable, by reason of age or infirmity, should join the reserve corps and be ready to do their duty whenever called upon.

I give you this advice in full view of all the circumstances. I would give it to my brother or my son. It is the counsel I would myself adopt. All persons pursuing the course laid down shall be recommended to the next General Assembly as good and patriotic citizens, worthy of being restored to all their former rights and privileges.

Violating the Oath.—Mr. A. B. Babbitt, citizen of Natchez, Miss., has been sentenced to confinement in the military prison at Alton, Illinois, for one year for violating oath of allegiance in attempting to smuggle goods through the lines. "The way of the transgressor is hard."

☞ Editor Greeley and District Attorney Oakey Hall are discussing and expounding scripture in the New York papers. Oakey is some, but Horace rather "gets him" in exegesis. *"Ne sutores ultra crepidam."*

☞ A few days ago the marshal of Newburg, Ia., shot two men, killing one and mortally wounding the other. Said to be in self-defence.

☞ The three tongues that were written upon the cross—Greek, Latin and Hebrew—to witness Christ to be the King of the Jews, do each of them, in their several idioms, avouch this singular axiom, that Christ is an all sufficient Saviour; and a threefold cord is not easily broken.

DAILY DISPATCH.

VOL. XXVII. RICHMOND, VA., SATURDAY, OCTOBER 8, 1864. NO. 86.

Richmond Dispatch.

BY J. A. COWARDIN & CO.

The DISPATCH is published daily, (Sundays excepted,) at FORTY DOLLARS for twelve months; TWENTY DOLLARS for six months; TEN DOLLARS for three months, or FOUR DOLLARS for one month, in advance. All remittances by mail are at the risk of those who make them.

Richmond Dispatch.

SATURDAY MORNING.......OCTOBER 8, 1864.

The DAILY DISPATCH is sold to News Dealers at TWENTY CENTS per copy. CITY CARRIERS are authorized to charge ONE DOLLAR AND FIFTY CENTS per week to regular subscribers.

THE WAR NEWS.

FROM BELOW RICHMOND.

At eight o'clock yesterday morning our forces advanced on the enemy's lines in front of Fort Harrison. After pushing forward some distance, the enemy sent out a heavy line to meet us, and the columns met about a mile from Fort Harrison. Our troops pressed their attack with great vigor, driving the opposing line in confusion back to their works, inflicting severe loss upon them. On arriving at their entrenchments they made a stand, and, being well supported, our troops were brought to a stand-still, but retained their ground at last accounts.

Battery Harrison is said to be a most uncomfortable position for the enemy.—They are subjected nightly to a gunboat shelling, and during the day the inmates are regaled with round shot and shell from land-batteries, while our sharpshooters besiege them so closely that no one dares to show his head above the parapets for fear of the deadly aim of our men.

As an instance of the fatality of the firing of our sharpshooters, we were informed by a gentleman, who was witness to the fact, that one of them killed eleven of the enemy in one day.

A rumor reached the city last night that we had, by a flank movement, isolated Fort Harrison, and that it was now completely in our power, all communication with the main army being cut off. This, however, is doubtful, and, at least, needs confirmation.

Simultaneous with the advance above mentioned, our troops, in the vicinity of the Darbytown road, were put in motion, and pressing on with their usual alacrity, compelled the whole line of the enemy to give way. Following up their advantage, our men continued to advance, the Federals retiring stubbornly at first, but finally breaking into a double-quick, they were soon in confusion, and abandoned in their flight nine field pieces, which our men took possession of.

After a brisk march of about two miles—the enemy all the while retreating before us—we came upon their first line of earthworks of any strength, having already passed two temporary lines, at which the enemy made but a short stand. Here, however, the entrenchments were held by fresh Yankees, and they poured into our ranks a terrible fire from cannon and small arms. Unfortunately, at this juncture, one of our brigades faltered, threw our line into confusion, and thus stopped our advance.

Here we lost most heavily. Charging the works with fury and dogged determination, we endeavored to regain our advantage, but in vain; and finally, falling back out of range of the enemy's guns, we established our lines two miles in advance of our position of the morning. The track of battle led to the right of the Darbytown, and in the direction of the Newmarket road, our extreme right finally resting in front of the line of entrenchments thrown out from Fort Harrison, and about a mile and a half north of it. Our loss was not very severe, as a whole, but some of our best officers fell. Brigadier-General Gregg, commanding the Texas brigade in Fields's division, was killed. His body arrived in the city last night. Brigadier General Gary was wounded; Brigadier-General Bratton, of S. C., seriously wounded; Colonel Haskell, Seventh South Carolina cavalry, painfully, but not seriously, wounded in the head; Major Haskell, South Carolina artillery, wounded. Some of the local troops, among them some of the War Department clerks, were slightly engaged, but we hear of no casualties.—We captured, besides the nine guns, about a hundred horses and some three hundred prisoners. Among them, Major A. S. Ashe, Kautz's adjutant-general, and a number of the staff of the notorious Spears, who, it is said, narrowly escaped capture.

The engagement was renewed last night about dark, but we could obtain no particulars.

PETERSBURG.

Some little skirmishing took place yesterday in the vicinity of Petersburg, with some heavy firing. A number of deserters came in yesterday morning.

GENERAL LEE'S OFFICIAL DISPATCH RELATIVE TO THE BATTLE OF YESTERDAY.

Last night an official dispatch was received from General Lee, stating that, yesterday morning, General Anderson attacked the enemy on the Charles City road and drove them from two lines of entrenchments, capturing ten pieces of cannon, with their caissons and horses, and a number of prisoners.

The enemy were then driven to the New Market road, when, being found strongly entrenched, they were not pressed.

Our loss is small; that of the enemy unknown.

The brave General Gregg died at the head of his brigade.

THE YANKEES BURN RAPID ANN BRIDGE.

An official dispatch from Gordonsville last night states that Yankee raiders burnt the railroad bridge over the Rapid Ann yesterday.

FROM THE VALLEY.

A dispatch from General Early to General Lee, dated the 8th instant, says: "Sheridan's whole force commenced falling back down the Valley last night along the pike."

Our cavalry were in pursuit.

Mr. Powhatan Weisiger, company E, Fourth Virginia cavalry, was severely wounded in the foot in an engagement at Waterbridge, near Staunton, on Sunday, 2d instant, but is now here, doing as well as could be hoped for.

FROM GEORGIA.

It was rumored last night that Hood had defeated Sherman in a general engagement and captured several thousand prisoners.

Specie Sent Abroad.

The Wilmington *Journal* states that the steamer Lynx, which left that port a few nights since for Bermuda, was attacked by the blockading squadron, and, being struck by their shot, was beached to save her from sinking. The *Journal* gives much credit to the captain, Gordon, for saving fifty thousand dollars of Government specie and a large amount of bonds, both on Government and private account, all of which he saved by his individual exertions, sacrificing his own interest to do so.

What may be the necessity of transmitting specie from this country to foreign ports by our Government, we do not know. But Mr. Memminger was much censured for shipping gold by the blockade-runners when sterling exchange was freely offered him. Three ships, having each twenty-five thousand dollars in gold, were captured by the enemy, and the sums with which they were freighted passed into his hands. The loss was considered heavy; and as it could have been easily avoided, the Secretary of the Treasury was thought to have acted most unwisely. The fifty thousand dollars on board the Lynx seems to have had a very narrow escape. We do not know, we repeat, what necessity may prompt the Government to ship coin, and can hardly suppose that Mr. Trenholm is so impractical as to send it out of the country if an equivalent is within his reach. Gold certainly ought not to be sent away if a substitute can be found to be remitted in its stead. It is quite scarce enough in the country, and will be greatly needed as the basis of our circulating medium when the war is over. It is, moreover, so unsafe in running the blockade that that is enough of itself to induce Government and individuals to send anything else in preference that will answer as a medium of exchange. When the enemy gets hold of the gold, it is gone from us forever. Not so the bills of exchange, which are payable to order.

Yankee Prisoners Entering Our Service.

The Augusta *Constitutionalist* says that some of the Yankee prisoners whose term of service has expired, and who are detained in captivity because Lincoln, having no further use for them, will not exchange them for our own men, have entered our service and are now doing duty on James island.

Captain Davis, son of the Rev. Mr. Davis, of Charlottesville, was killed in one of the late fights near Petersburg. Another son of Mr. Davis is now a prisoner in the enemy's hands.

Commander of Cavalry in the Valley.

Major-General Lunsford L. Lomax, who now commands the cavalry in the Valley, succeeds General Ransom. He is a young and very excellent officer, and is doing much to improve that part of his command which needs improvement. He was a second lieutenant of cavalry in the old United States army, and is a son of Major M. Page Lomax, deceased, also an old United States officer.

The Death of Mrs. Greenhow.

The death of a woman by drowning is an event that always excites the tender sympathies and pity of generous minds. It was the fate of Mrs. Rose A. Greenhow, formerly of Washington, to meet such a death at Wilmington, as already announced. Her life had been eventful. She was a native of Maryland, and quite distinguished in Washington society.—Her strong intellect and energy of character led her take a very great interest in politics. She possessed personal graces as well as mental, that added no little to the distinction she enjoyed. She was the widow of Dr. Robert Greenhow, son of Mr. Robert Greenhow, of this city, well known in other days. He was a gentleman of much learning, who filled the office of translator of several languages for the State Department of the old Government. Mrs. Greenhow had visited Europe to publish a book she had written on the war and her imprisonment by the Lincoln Government.—This she had accomplished, and was just returning to the Confederacy, when, on Saturday last, she met her death. The Wilmington *Journal* thus notices the event:

"As we write—at half past four o'clock on Saturday afternoon, October 1, 1864,—the corpse of Mrs. Rose A. Greenhow, a well known, and, we may add, a devoted Confederate lady, just returned from Europe, is laid out in the chapel of General Hospital No. 4. All the respect due to Mrs. Greenhow's position and character is, no doubt, paid to her remains by the ladies of the Soldiers' Aid Society, and, indeed, we may say, by the ladies generally.

"Up to the time of writing, we have obtained few particulars. We know that, on Friday night or Saturday morning, the steamship Condor, in endeavoring to come in over the New Inlet bar, got aground, and that a boat from her got swamped on the 'rip,' and that Mrs. Greenhow, being a passenger on board that boat, was drowned. We have not learned that any other of the passengers on the boat perished."

General Taylor and Provost Marshals.

The Montgomery *Advertiser* announces that General Dick Taylor has abolished all provost offices in the district of Alabama, Mississippi and East Louisiana. The *Advertiser* thus speaks of the measure:

"It has been a common remark that more men were engaged as provost guards on the streets and trains than had been secured by such means to the service, and the country will heartily thank General Taylor for the inauguration of a policy looking both to the restoration of law in this regard, and to the strengthening of our armies by the use of the abundant material hitherto withheld from their support and scattered broadcast over the land. The provost marshal system, as at present organized, is a nuisance, and ought to be dispensed with everywhere except in the immediate vicinity of our armies."

We learn from the Macon (Georgia) *Confederate* that the President has tendered Captain Desha, of Kentucky, command of the Confederate forces in Southwestern Kentucky, with the rank of brigadier-general, a change in the command there being necessitated by the unfortunate loss of sight to Colonel Adam R. Johnson, who had been but recently promoted to a brigadiership, and who, by this sad calamity, has been rendered unfit for further service.

Captain J. L. Griffith, of Kentucky, captured with General Morgan, died on the 14th of August, and Captain E. D. Warden, of Louisville, Kentucky, died on the 15th of August—both of typhoid fever, in Fort Delaware.

THE TACTICS OF JOHN PHŒNIX.—A correspondent of the Boston *Courier* writes the following:

A neighbor told him that he had seen a man only the day before, who was just from the "front," who assured him that Grant might have taken Richmond at any time within a month, and the only reason he had not done so was that he wished to hold Lee where he was to prevent his going to the relief of Atlanta.—I asked him if he had ever read the works of John Phœnix. "No," he replied; "who was he?" "A distinguished writer on tactics," said I, "who once described 'a military position' somewhat similar to your conception of Grant's. He was engaged in a street fight, and says: 'When we fell, I came undermost, and held my antagonist down by my nose, which I inserted between his teeth for that purpose.'"

SUGAR-CANE FLOUR.—While the papers are all giving very general and useful information with regard to the manufacture of syrup and sugar from the Chinese sugar cane, we do not recollect to have seen a reference to its advantages in the production of bread. An intelligent gentleman writes:

"As wheat crops were light in some parts of the Confederacy, and the staff of life likely to be scarce, it may be well for your readers to know that excellent biscuit and fair light-bread may be made from the flour of the seed of sugar cane. I have eaten of the bread myself, and found it to be very good. The gentleman at whose house the bread was prepared informed me that from one acre of the white sorghum cane he obtained four barrels of flour. I understand the crop is remarkably promising in all parts of the Confederacy, and as the time for harvesting it is approaching, much suffering may be saved by carefully saving the seed."

As this information comes from one who has seen the thing tested, it would be well to give it a trial.

LATEST FROM THE NORTH.

We have by flag of truce Northern dates of October 5.

In the engagement of September 30, near Squirrel Level, the Federals acknowledge a loss of two thousand in killed, wounded and prisoners, more than half of whom were prisoners.

On Sunday last a shell from a rebel battery grazed General Meade's boot leg, took a piece from the tail of General Humphrey's horse, and entered the ground between Generals Bartlett and Griffin. The shell did not explode.

The *Tribune* is silent as regards operations north of the James, but says Farragut arrived at Fortress Monroe on the 4th and proceeded up James river.

A dispatch to the *Tribune* from Louisville, dated October 4th, says that "a band of thirty-five guerrillas captured two upward-bound freight trains on the Nashville railroad at 10 o'clock last night, between Richland station and Fountainhead. They burned nineteen cars, but they contained no stores. To-day the trains will be slightly disarranged by the disaster."

Accounts from Missouri state that General Price is moving on Rolla in three columns, the right under Shelby and Marmaduke, the centre under himself, and the left under Cooper—the latter being composed mainly of half-breed Indians. About five hundred rebels entered Union, the county seat of Franklin county, on Saturday, and captured about one hundred of the county militia.—Washington had a garrison of six hundred men, under Colonel Gale, who evacuated the place on the approach of the rebels, and took his men and stores across the Missouri river. The depot at Jacksonville, on the North Missouri railroad, was burned by guerrillas on Monday morning.

General Schofield has received information that General Burbridge captured the salt works near Abingdon, Virginia, with little resistance.

[He received a bloody repulse.—DISPATCH.]

On Saturday last a portion of Forrest's command shelled Athens, Alabama.—Guerrilla bands are operating near that city, and last week two or three commissary trains were captured.

On Monday, Forrest appeared before Dalton, Georgia, and demanded its surrender.

On the 4th, gold opened at 192, fell to 189 1-2, and closed at 190 1-4.

Judge J. S. Baldwin, late chief justice of the California Supreme Court, died in San Francisco last Saturday. He was a native of Virginia.

LATE FROM NEW ORLEANS.

We have received a copy of the New Orleans *Era* of the 22d instant. It contains the proclamation of "Governor" Hahn announcing the adoption of the new constitution. The entire vote polled in the twenty parishes reported is only eight thousand four hundred and two, of which 6,836 were for, and 1,566 against, the precious budget. In St. Charles parish, all told, only 37 votes were polled; in St. James, 7; in St. John the Baptist, 9; in Iberville, 28; in East Feliciana, 165; and in St. Landry, 32. In Orleans the vote was 4,662 for, and 789 against, the constitution. What a farce! It must make even Hahn blush.

The steamer Gertrude, Captain Kerr, was capsized near Baton Rouge on the 20th instant. Two ladies, Madame Kendrick and Miss O'Meara, a little daughter of Mrs. Burton, of Bayou Sara, and four of the hands of the boat, were drowned.

On the 21st, a fire at Baton Rouge destroyed half a block of frame and brick buildings, including Piper & Badford's furniture warehouses. We copy the following from the *Era*:

A private letter from Pensacola, received in this city, gives the subjoined interesting particulars of the expedition in Florida, sent out by General Asboth in the latter part of last month:

"Captain Eugene F. Roberts, and his noble company A, (the regiment is the Eighty-second United States Colored Infantry,) was complimented in General Orders for a successful charge on the rebel earthworks known as Fort Hodson, at the Fifteen-Mile House, on the Pensacola railroad, where the colors of the Seventh Alabama (rebel) cavalry regiment were captured, besides a large number of horses, sabres, rifles, corn, cattle, ammunition, etc.; and some twenty-two rebel privates and three lieutenants were either killed, wounded or made prisoners. The rebel loss was as follows: Three privates killed, eight wounded and eleven captured; two officers wounded and one captured. The only loss on our side was one man mortally wounded and a horse killed.

"We destroyed by fire their new earth and log breastworks, besides all the buildings at the station. Before the charge was made, Captain Roberts skirmished three miles through the pine woods, the rebels steadily falling back before him, when he suddenly came upon the breastworks. It was at once perceived that the enemy was endeavoring to entrap our men, but, as the line of rebels rose above the works to fire, an order was given for the black troops to lie down, and the whole volley whistled harmlessly over their heads.

"In the dense smoke, Captain Roberts and his men crawled up to within fifty yards of the works, when the captain ordered a charge. With bayonets fixed, they started with a yell and cleared the works, and made the captures, as above stated."

LAKEPORT, Sept. 21—10:30 A. M.

To the New Orleans Associated Press:

The gunboat Selma just arrived from Mobile. She left day before yesterday. The rams Tuscaloosa and Nashville are reported to have gone [illegible] Montgomery, Alabama, but the report is not credited. It is believed they have gone up Spanish river to get a nearer position to the city.

[The Selma, our readers will remember, is one of the vessels captured from the rebels in Mobile bay.—*Editor Era.*]

A PRUDENT FORECAST.—If, after this war, there remain but two North American nations, there will still be a danger of their consenting to bury their animosities in the prosecution of ambitious purposes, which may be highly inconvenient to us, and may involve the whole world in the wars of the American continent. That this apprehension is not altogether chimerical has been shown by what has transpired, of certain negotiations, a few weeks since at Niagara. The self-constituted diplomatists, who would have arranged terms of peace and separation between the American nations, discussed a programme which was put forward, we trust, without authority from their respective Governments. A frontier line was to be drawn between North and South; but measures were to be at once taken with the view of swelling the territory of each section to dimensions equal to those of the old Union. The plan was simple. The armies of North and South being united, a million of men were to march northward and conquer Canada for the North. The victorious army would then move southward, and annex Mexico to the dominion of the cotton planters. The programme was unscrupulous and wicked; but who shall say that it was not feasible? If we have misrepresented the views of these precious negotiators, we shall be glad to be corrected. There is too much reason to believe that such propositions were seriously debated between Messrs. Clay and Greeley. As we are ill prepared to make head against a million of men on the American lakes; and as even the Emperor Napoleon will recoil from the thought of having to defend his newly-crowned brother against such a horde, the ventilation of his nefarious plot can have but one result in England and France. It makes us desire the utter ruin of the North. We rejoice to hear that Mr. Lincoln is becoming every day more unpopular; that a committee of Congress has denounced him; that governors of States and mayors of cities openly controvert his authority; that powerful secret societies are agitating against him; that discord is growing up between the States, New England being at variance with New York, New York with Pennsylvania, Pennsylvania with Illinois.—We trust that the principle of secession, having taken root, will bear seed and multiply. With a dozen jealous principalities on the English frontier, the loyal Canadians will have no cause to fear American aggression. Mexico will be safe, and Europe will not be dragged into war.—*Morning Herald, 17th ult.*

CUTTING A LION'S CLAWS.—The Brussels journals give an account of a curious surgical operation just performed on the great African lion belonging to the Zoological Society of that city. For some time past the animal has been suffering from disease in the feet, which necessitated the cutting of its claws. In order to do this without danger, a large box was prepared with a grated bottom, covered by a wooden floor, which could be withdrawn so as to allow the lion's feet to pass between the bars. The top of the box was also made to descend by means of screws, so as to press on the animal and prevent it from drawing in its foot. When the lion entered the box the latter was turned on its side and the sliding bottom withdrawn. The paws then slipped between the bars, and the screws above were tightened. M. Thiernasse, assisted by five pupils of the Veterinary school, then proceeded to cut away the claws. The patient bore the operation tolerably well, only uttering a short roar occasionally, and seemed relieved when the first paw had been cut and dressed. A keeper, to whom the lion is much attached, sat near its head and endeavored to calm it by talking, evidently not without effect. The operation was successfully performed, and there is every reason to believe the cure will be complete.

ABOLISHING PROVOST OFFICES.—General Dick Taylor has done one thing for which he ought to be thanked, if he never does another. He has abolished all the provost offices in the district of Alabama, Mississippi and East Louisiana, over which he presides. Captain Taylor, former provost-marshal at this place, has been ordered to report to Forrest, and the employees in his office to Major Jones, commandant of this post.—*Montgomery Advertiser.*

DIED,

On the 7th of October, WILLIAM JAMES, youngest son of Thomas Addison, aged five years and thirteen days.

Dear little WILLIE has gone to rest,
Without one sigh, among the blest;
Without one doubt, without one fear—
Too young to know that God was near.

His funeral will take place from the residence of his father, on Seventeenth street, THIS DAY, the 8th instant, at 3 o'clock P. M. The friends of the family are invited to attend.

On Tuesday, October 4th, at 12 o'clock, Mr. J. H. BECKTEL, of this city.

Mr. BECKTEL was on duty with the local forces, and, while viewing the battle-field at Fort Gilmer, was struck by a ball from a sharpshooter and instantly killed. He was an exemplary citizen and christian, and leaves a wife and seven children.

Yesterday evening, of diptheria, in the eleventh year of her age, SALLIE E., second daughter of E. C. and Janet C. Crump.

The friends of the family are invited to attend her funeral THIS AFTERNOON at 3 o'clock from the Leigh Street Baptist Church. The little scholars of the Sabbath School (of which she was so fond) are also invited.

FUNERAL NOTICE.—The funeral sermon of Mrs. ROBERTA A. LOGAN will be preached on SUNDAY MORNING NEXT at 11 o'clock at the Leigh Street Baptist Church.

Richmond Dispatch.

JOB PRINTING NEATLY EXECUTED.

Advertisements will be inserted at the rate of [illegible] DOLLARS per square for each insertion—eight lines (or less) constitute a square. Larger advertisements in exact proportion. Advertisements published till forbid will be charged $4 per square for every insertion.

LOCAL MATTERS.

EXECUTION OF A NEGRO.—At half past eleven o'clock yesterday morning, a negro named Henry, slave of the Virginia Central Railroad Company, was hung in the jail yard of Henrico County Court house. On the 28th of July last the unfortunate victim was guilty of setting fire to the hay and wheat stacks of William C. Day, of Hanover county, and was subsequently guilty of an attempt to assassinate Mr. Day by waylaying him on the public highway. For these offences he was tried by the County Court of Hanover on the 26th of August, and condemned to be hung; but on account of the insecurity of the jail and the proximity of the enemy the condemned man was transferred to the Henrico county jail and the execution ordered to take place in the jail yard of that county. The execution was witnessed by a very small concourse of persons, and his death was unaccompanied by any incident of interest. Rev. John E. Edwards visited the condemned man in the capacity of a spiritual adviser, but failed to elicit any satisfactory expression of spiritual repentance.

ACCIDENT.—Between 1 and 2 o'clock yesterday, as an ammunition wagon was coming up Seventh street from the Virginia Armory, a little boy, who was running before it, fell, and was severely injured in the right leg and arm by the wheels passing over him. He was taken to his father's residence, on Cary street, and properly attended to.

THE COURTS.—The business disposed of in the different courts yesterday was of such a character as to render it unnecessary to make an extended notice. A few cases were disposed of by the Mayor, the most of which were negroes without passes and soldiers taken up for imbibing too freely. The former were ordered to be whipped and the latter sent to their commands.

SENT TO SALISBURY.—Several hundred Yankee prisoners were sent to Salisbury yesterday morning. Within the past week, the large lot, amounting to thousands, who have been confined on Belle Isle and other prison camps, have been sent off, and now everything in the way of accommodations is again ready for the reception of the many Yankees which it is expected will be captured within the next few days.

ROBBERY.—On Thursday night Mr. Conway's storeroom, in the rear of his residence, on Marshall street, near the end of the corporation line, was broken into and robbed of groceries to the amount of several hundred dollars. The thieves were frightened off before stripping Mr. Conway of all the stock he had.

BOGUS WATCHMAN.—Philip [illegible] way was arrested on Wednesday for passing himself off as a watchman and capturing a negro on the street. At a special levee, held yesterday at the lower station-house, the Mayor dismissed him upon the payment of a small fine.

CHARGED WITH BEING A SPY.—An English woman, calling herself [illegible] wood, was arrested at Pole [illegible] Wednesday, on the charge of [illegible] and committed to Castle Thunder. She claims to have a husband [illegible] Washington for desertion from the Yankee army, and that she was on her way to General Grant to have him released when she was arrested.

SENT OFF.—Five hundred Yankee sick and wounded were sent North, via flag of truce, yesterday morning; among whom were [illegible] officers. A number of [illegible] marines will be sent off [illegible] flag of truce.

The New-York Times.

VOL. XIV.—NO. 4096. NEW-YORK, WEDNESDAY, NOVEMBER 9, 1864. PRICE FOUR CENTS

VICTORY!

GLORIOUS RESULT YESTERDAY.

Election of Lincoln and Johnson.

Terrible Defeat of McClellan.

THE UNION TRIUMPHANT.

New-England a Solid Phalanx.

New-York for Lincoln and Fenton

Defeat of Governor Seymour and His Friends.

Gain of Five Union Congressmen in the State.

Election of Raymond, Dodge, Darling, Conklin and Humphrey.

Pennsylvania Union on the Home Vote.

HEAVY UNION GAINS.

MARYLAND AND DELAWARE ALL RIGHT.

Heavy Union Gains in New-Jersey.

The Great Northwest Solid for Lincoln.

DETAILS OF THE RETURNS.

THE VOTE OF THE CITY.

PRESIDENT AND GOVERNOR.

Ward	District	Lincoln (President)	McClellan (President)	Fenton (Governor)	Seymour (Governor)
1st Ward	1	42	604	44	602
	2	63	491	61	493
	3	34	640	36	634
	4	40	116	26	97
	5	32	311	32	307
Total		213	2161	207	2138
2d Ward	1	127	144	128	140
	2	59	194	60	195
Total		186	338	188	335
3d Ward	1	77	223	73	224
	2	86	121	84	120
	3	53	112	53	112
	4	11	44	11	44
Total		227	500	221	500
4th Ward	1	163	259	165	266
	2	77	406	79	402
	3	34	349	34	351
	4	85	324	60	336
	5	17	255	17	256
	6	14	228	12	319
	7	45	843	29	303
Total		434	2379	397	2422
5th Ward	1	92	199	83	196
	2	92	159	86	163
	3	103	285	103	282
	4	277	239	273	238
	5	86	361	78	364
	6	137	269	146	266
	7	168	269	157	263
	8	78	278	89	274
Total		1022	2038	1012	2030
6th Ward	1	18	64	21	61
	2	32	347	31	347
	3	41	238	42	236
	4	55	383	60	377
	5	21	518	19	519
	6	61	666	63	658
	7	29	289	29	284
	8	45	286	86	281
	9	28	689	....	....
Total		329	3457	....	....
7th Ward	1	169	367	167	365
	2	58	569	51	563
	3	120	301	115	302
	4	70	289	65	288
	5	96	419	96	419
	6	275	405	—	—
	7	169	367	—	—
	8	119	342	118	335
	9	118	370	114	366
	10	59	476	59	472
	11	73	331	63	326
Total		1230	4090	—	—
8th Ward	1	132	266	127	265
	2	177	410	179	415
	3	110	266	106	283
	4	131	182	132	178
	5	76	156	63	196
	6	180	176	126	226
	7	271	380	216	288
	8	230	284	217	333
	9	159	264	169	269
	10	71	266	72	264
	11	207	255	94	297
	12	46	215	46	213
Total		1619	3202	1620	3274
9th Ward	1	266	476	314	476
	2	263	378	266	398
	3	613	463	608	468
	4	297	272	292	179
	5	311	201	316	201
	6	223	183	224	183
	7	364	242	381	240
	8	268	328	266	326
	9	208	291	219	268
	10	217	266	220	277
	11	288	408	283	407
	12	196	306	196	301
Total		3488	3744	3655	3714
10th Ward	1	292	331	277	333
	2	315	422	313	413
	3	278	457	264	464
	4	201	396	194	398
	5	316	402	296	407
	6	288	319	275	346
Total		1690	2347	1619	2361
11th Ward	1	119	383	114	386
	2	112	672	102	672
	3	144	398	142	399
	4	178	369	172	371
	5	162	317	149	318
	6	84	157	78	156
	7	75	410	71	409
	8	109	345	106	343
	9	140	190	144	185
	10	94	183	96	178
	11	140	203	136	203
	12	65	293	81	303
	13	78	406	78	403
	14	156	263	148	264
	15	60	186	61	181
	16	107	311	108	306
	17	48	254	51	252
	18	112	353	—	—
Total		1930	5532		
12th Ward	1	83	249	90	248
	2	298	440	292	444
	3	283	679	240	681
	4	421	389	417	388
	5	89	404	91	402
	6	181	337	183	331
Total		1,306	2,488	1,273	2,485
13th Ward	1	199	366	195	369
	2	173	414	172	419
	3	122	525	123	519
	4	117	409	117	411
	5	163	306	147	304
	6	139	267	133	265
	7	58	183	53	181
	8	142	297	137	301
Total		1,106	2,767	1,077	2,769
14th Ward	1	59	187	....	....
	2	29	670	20	678
	3	102	620	76	634
	4	41	609	37	38
	5	130	363	129	30
	6	139	356	136	369
	7	116	250	114	252
	8	80	319	80	362
	9	82	561	80	511
	10	82	285	78	267
Total		859	4229	....	....
15 Ward	1	289	260	275	262
	2	271	275	263	276
	3	137	294	131	299
	4	251	225	343	219
	5	161	86	162	85
	6	273	127	268	130
	7	159	85	162	82
	8	231	285	—	—
	9	209	160	—	—
	10	163	171	—	—
Total		2244	1970	—	—
16th Ward	1	307	278	302	280
	2	302	464	305	451
	3	303	351	360	470
	4	303	351	—	—
	4	183	393	294	378
	6	424	382	—	—
	7	211	463	211	456
	8	29	125	—	—
	9	387	275	390	276
	10	236	287	237	285
Total		2,685	3,959	—	—
17th Ward	1	251	248	238	255
	2	264	377	250	374
	3	252	352	243	354
	4	257	358	253	361
	5	319	409	319	408
	6	287	228	293	222
	7	403	327	400	324
	8	104	364	103	365
	9	61	489	47	502
	10	66	210	67	209
	11	108	412	108	411
	12	141	426	133	430
	13	165	290	151	293
	14	43	451	44	450
	15	98	404	89	402
	16	213	361	208	362
	17	99	435	99	433
	18	106	449	360	444
	19	211	441	208	448
Total		3425	7031	3613	7047
18th Ward	1	356	214	370	210
	2	452	371	—	—
	3	488	287	479	286
	4	178	124	177	122
	5	176	154	184	152
	6	266	365	265	353
	7	181	290	181	284
	8	87	200	90	197
	9	158	243	157	244
	10	68	306	67	368
	11	154	317	142	321
	12	46	346	46	342
	13	34	428	31	475
	14	38	318	33	320
	15	58	411	54	467
Total		2673	4424	—	—
19th Ward	1	203	507	208	502
	2	157	434	153	425
	3	247	392	251	389
	4	240	467	239	472
	5	163	298	163	295
	6	302	348	266	382
	7	191	467	188	472
	8	191	261	198	276
	9	247	369	252	362
Total		1941	3674	1918	3575
20th Ward	1	32	443	276	546
	2	189	303	192	303
	3	273	568	—	—
	4	173	360	—	—
	5	101	506	102	506
	6	328	245	326	246
	7	321	224	311	220
	8	161	419	162	416
	9	170	474	168	474
	10	169	367	169	366
	11	224	807	226	573
	12	186	336	184	337
	13	182	357	189	352
	14	311	427	318	431
Total		2874	5553	—	—
21st Ward	1	159	310	156	303
	2	127	426	132	419
	3	164	414	152	418
	4	141	446	140	441
	5	125	437	127	431
	6	84	278	82	277
	7	66	334	61	333
	8	158	145	190	145
	9	205	255	208	250
	10	238	309	241	303
	11	247	258	287	250
	12	290	264	298	201
	13	376	185	333	131
	14	320	176	321	275
Total		2,767	4,177	2,788	42,28
22d Ward	1	136	396	138	389
	2	248	420	247	419
	3	248	394	283	388
	4	281	280	275	284
	5	169	227	166	222
	6	137	165	131	167
	7	144	278	141	282
	8	200	218	198	229
	9	232	356	228	360
	10	163	314	173	310
	11	187	434	200	433
	12	60	306	66	307
	13	78	218	78	215
	14	70	138	74	138
Total		2360	4136	2348	4130

New-York City Recapitulated.

Ward.	Lincoln.	McClellan
First	213	2,162
Second	186	338
Third	207	500
Fourth	435	2,379
Fifth	1,022	2,038
Sixth	326	3,457
Seventh	1,230	4,090
Eighth	1,619	3,202
Ninth	3,488	3,745
Tenth	1,690	2,347
Eleventh	1,928	5,482
Twelfth	1,365	2,490
Thirteenth	1,106	2,767
Fourteenth	859	4,229
Fifteenth	2,244	1,970
Sixteenth	2,746	3,478
Seventeenth	3,425	7,031
Eighteenth	2,678	4,424
Nineteenth	1,941	3,674
Twentieth	2,874	5,553
Twenty-first	2,767	4,177
Twenty-second	2,366	4,127
Total	36,912	73,769

The Vote for Governor.

The vote for Governor by Ward Districts is incomplete. The following is the total in the several wards:

Ward.	Fenton.	Seymour.	Ward.	Fenton.	Seymour.
1	207	2,133	12	1,273	2,485
2	188	336	13	1,077	2,769
3	221	500	14	809	4-247
4	397	2,422	15	2,247	1,969
5	1,012	2,030	16	2,864	3,425
6	348	3,429	17	3,613	7,047
7	1,199	4,061	18	2,261	4,370
8	1,520	3,274	19	1,918	3,575
9	3,655	3,714	20	3,071	5,689
10	1,619	2,361	21	2,788	4,228
11	1,948	5,533	22	2,340	4,130
Totals				36,555	73,717
Seymour's majority					37,162

Lieutenant-Governor.

Ward.	Alvord.	Jones.	Wards.	Alvord.	Jones.
1	207	2133	12	1268	2483
2	188	334	13	1078	2770
3	221	498	14	810	4246
4	396	2422	15	2228	1968
5	1010	2030	16	2852	3421
6	346	3435	17	3355	7043
7	1196	4060	18	2247	4388
8	1518	3276	19	1913	3592
9	3496	3820	20	3055	5694
10	1621	2268	21	2767	4148
11	1950	5538	22	2342	4133
Total				36064	73790

Canal Commissioner.

The vote for Canal Commissioner in this city stands Alberger, Union, 36,081; Lord, Democrat, 73,757.

State Prison Inspector.

The vote for State Prison differs but little from that of Canal Commissioner—Forrest, Union, receiving 36,092, and McNeil, Democrat, 73,722.

Fourth Congressional District.

William Walsh, 5,099; Carolin O'Brien Bryant, 1,628; Morgan Jones, 8,445.

The First District of the First Ward, First, Second and Fourth District of the Sixth Ward are missing. Jones is elected.

Fifth Congressional District.

Nelson Taylor........9,144
Wm. B. McCay........4,174
E. E. Ellery........3,948

Sixth Congressional District.

Ninth and Fifteenth Wards complete, with Sixteenth Ward, except Third District:
Henry J. Raymond, 7,156.
Elijah Ward, 6,640.
E. P. Morton, 438.
R. C. Hawkins, 129.

Seventh Congressional District.

Chandler, 9,461.
Boardman, 4,711.
The First, Second, Third, Ninth, Eleventh and Eighteenth Districts of the Seventeenth Ward are Missing.
Chandler is elected.

Eighth Congressional District.

W. B. Dodge........6,573
James Brooks........6,329
T. J. Barr........3,302

1st and 2d District, 18th Ward; 1st, 9th, 11th and 14th, of the 20th Ward, and 1st, 5th, 11th and 14th, of the 21st Ward, are missing.

Ninth Congressional District.

Darling........5,201 Henrick........3,667
Wood........4,408 Smith........240

The Third District of the Twelfth Ward is missing. Darling is elected.

New-York Congressmen Elected.

Dis.		Dis.	
1	S. Taber, Dem.	17	C. T. Hulburd, Union.
2	T. G. Bergen, Dem.	18	
3	J. Humphrey, Union.	19	D. Hubbard, jr., Un.
4	M. Jones, Dem.	20	A. H. Laflin, Union.
5	N. Taylor, Dem.	21	R. Concklin, Union.
6	H. J. Raymond, Un.	22	S. T. Holmes, Union.
7	J. W. Chanler, Dem.	23	T. T. Davis, Union.
8	Wm. E. Dodge, U.	24	T. M. Pomeroy, Union.
9	Wm. A. Darling, U.	25	D. Morris, Union.
10	W. Radford, Dem.	26	G. W. Hotchkiss, Union
11	J. A. Ketcham Un.	27	H. Ward, Union.
12		28	R. Hart, Union.
13	E. N. Hubbell, Dem.	29	B. Van Horn, Union.
14	C. Goodyear, Dem.	30	
15	J. C. Griswold, Union.	31	H. Van Aernam, Union
16	O. Kellogg, Union.		

Assemblymen Probably Elected.

First District—Jacob L. Smith, Dem.
Second District—Bryan Gaughan, Dem.
Third District—Geo. Leutrell, Dem.
Fourth District—Joel Sammis, Union.
Fifth District—Chas. T. Polhemus, Union.
Sixth District—Wm. Higgins, Union.
Seventh District—Thomas E. Stewart, Union.
Eighth District—Jacob Geebacher, Dem.
Ninth District—Samuel C. Reed, Union.
Tenth District—Patrick McGrave, Dem.
Eleventh District—Robert Usher, Union.
Twelfth District—Joseph A. Lyons, Dem.
Thirteenth District—Joel W. Mason, Union.
Fourteenth District—Michael N. Salmon, Dem.
Fifteenth District—Col. J. B. Van Buren, Union.
Sixteenth District—Henry Arcularius, Dem.
Seventeenth District—S. P. Ingraham, Jr. Union.
Union, 8; Dem. 9. Union gain of 6 over last year.

County Ticket Election.

SHERIFF—John Kelly.
COUNTY CLERK—Wm. C. Conner, (probable.)
DISTRICT ATTORNEY—A. Oakey Hall.
CITY JUDGE—Abm. D. Russell.
SUPERVISOR—John Fox.
CORONERS—Dr. Schirmer, Robert Gamble, John Wildey, Wm. C. Gover.

THE TOTAL VOTE AND THE REGISTRY.

The following table shows the total vote in each of the wards of the city on President and its total registration. It will be readily seen that the wards, which polled such a heavy increase of the Democratic vote, are those in which the vote exceeds the registration—undoubtedly the work of fraud.

Wards.	Total vote.	No. registered.
1	2380	2122
2	524	603
3	727	993
4	2813	3162
5	3060	3457
6	3788	4142
7	5320	6138
8	4821	4992
9	7263	8067
10	4067	5010
11	7522	8731
12	3858	4228
13	3873	4629
14	5088	3829
15	4214	4670
16	6224	7099
17	10456	12756
18	7102	8288
19	5515	6779
20	7622	9409
21	6944	8306
22	6492	6877
Total	109,653	124,591

No returns have been received from two districts. The registration in six districts was not reported.

NEW-YORK STATE.

Kings County Election Returns.

Wards. Dis.	M'Clellan.	Lincoln.	Wards. Dis.	M'Clellan.	Lincoln.
I.—1	262	239	5	172	336
2	335	140	XII.—1	687	52
II.—1	400	96	2	736	126
2	653	257	XIII.—1	278	385
III.—1	208	311	2	376	465
2	209	398	3	307	466
3	207	478	4	278	490
IV.—1	287	375	XIV.—1	575	90
2	419	424	2	632	220
3	344	343	3	378	176
V.—1	545	84	4	247	218
2	487	227	XV.—1	—	—
V.—3	402	242	2	409	542
4	469	205	XVI.—1	—	—
VI.—1	774	304	2	368	416
2	254	295	3	—	—
3	573	369	4	548	241
VII.—1	317	232	XVII.—1	472	464
2	—	—	2	311	465
3	240	238	XVIII.—1	261	163
4	177	276	2	209	260
VIII.—1	367	255	XIX.—1	129	152
2	511	263	2	183	333
IX.—1	741	260	3	283	290
2	240	215	XX.—1	150	335
3	488	419	2	242	532
4	205	200	3	332	461
X.—1	238	343	4	167	240
2	568	270	New Lotts	—	—
3	302	343	Flatbush	—	—
XI.—1	351	351	Flatlands	—	—
2	538	213	New Utrecht	299	126
3	181	289	Gravesend	136	98
4	656	316		—	—
Total				23,515	18,191

Flatbush, Lincoln 191; McClellan, 214.
Flatlands, Lincoln 164; McClellan 119.

The election in Brooklyn passed off quietly. Nothing whatever occurred to warrant the interference of the police authorities. A large vote was polled resulting in the election of the following officers:

Congress—2d District—Tunis G. Bergen, Dem.
Congress—3d District—James Humphrey, Rep., by about 300 majority.
Register—Hugh McLaughlin, Dem.
County Clerk—John J. White, Dem.
Coroner—James Devaucene, Dem.
Superintendent of Poor—Joseph Attebram, Dem.
Justice of Sessions—Stephen I. Voorhis, Dem.
Police Justice—James H. Cornwell, Dem., prob'ly.
Justice of Peace, First District—Michael Walsh, Dem.
Justice of Peace, Second District—James Buckley, Dem.
Assembly, First District—Jarvis Whitman, Dem.
Assembly, Second District—William D. Veeder, Dem.
Assembly, Third District—Stephen Haynes, Dem., probably.
Assembly, Fourth District—Patrick Burns, Dem.
Assembly, Fifth District—John Perry, Rep.
Assembly, Sixth District—Henry C. Boswell, Dem.
Assembly, Seventh District—Jacob Worth, Rep., probably.

ALDERMEN.

Second Ward—Daniel McLaughlin, Dem.
Fourth Ward—Lewis F. Newman, Dem.
Sixth Ward—George P. Willey, Rep., probably.
Eighth Ward—Joseph Wilson, Democrat.
Tenth Ward—Francis Kelly, Democrat.
Twelfth Ward—Dennis O'Keefe, Democrat.
Fourteenth Ward—Edward Murphy, Democrat, probably.
Sixteenth Ward—John A. Saal, Democrat.
Eighteenth Ward—Fred. W. Kalbfleisch, Democrat.
Twentieth Ward—John K. Bulmer, Republican.

SUPERVISORS.

First Ward—Alex. Maggrothy, Rep., probably.
Third Ward—John J. Studwell, Republican.
Fifth Ward—William H. Furey.
Seventh Ward—E. W. Bloom, Dem., probably.
Ninth Ward—George G. Herman, Democrat.
Eleventh Ward—John Lawrence, Dem., probably.
Thirteenth Ward—Charles W. Cheshire, probably.
Fifteenth Ward—Charles C. Talbott, Republican.
Seventeenth Ward—Stephen Clark, Republican.
Nineteenth Ward—Fred. W. Sholes, Republican.

RICHMOND COUNTY.

Middletown, Second District, 473 majority for McClellan, and 487 for Seymour.

Sixth Districts gave McClellan 1,058 majority.

The returns from Richmond County indicate that the Democrats have carried it by from 1,500 to 1,600 Democratic majority.

WESTCHESTER COUNTY.

West Farms—McClellan, 58 majority; Seymour, 36; Radford, Dem., for Congress, 53 majority; Strong, Union, for Assembly, has 12 majority.

Yonkers gives McClellan, 233 majority; Seymour, 244 majority; Radford, Dem., for Congress, 194 majority.

Vote of New Rochelle complete. McClellan, 381; Lincoln, 239.

East Chester, First District, Lincoln, 269; McClellan 308. Fenton, 269; Seymour, 367. Radford, Democrat, for Congress has 97 majority. Second District, McClellan 92 majority.

Pelham 78 Union majority.
Tarrytown, 4 for Lincoln.
Beekmantown, McClellan 71 majority.
Manhattan, 314 Democratic majority.
Peekskill, 22 Democratic majority.
Mamaroneck, McClellan's majority, 25; Seymour's 24.
Portchester—Dem. majority, 111; Seymour's, 108; Radford for Congress, 114.
Sing Sing gives McClellan 134 majority.
Brandreth, (Union,) is probably elected to the Assembly.

CHAUTAUQUA COUNTY.

Sheridan, 79 Union majority; Fenton, 92 majority.
Fredonia, 173 Lincoln majority; Fenton, 168 majority.
Randolph, Lincoln, 116 majority.
Jamestown, Lincoln, 649 majority.
Westfield, Lincoln, 231 majority.
Chautauqua, Lincoln, 172 majority.
Ripley, Lincoln, 92 majority.
Portland, Lincoln, 87 majority.
Forrestville, 47 Union majority.
Perrysburgh, 130 Union majority.

DUTCHESS COUNTY.

Pawlings, Lincoln 278; McClellan, 154; Fenton, for Governor, 281; Seymour, 150; Ketcham, (Rep.,) for Congress, 283; Nelson, (Dem.,) 145; Howard, (Rep.,) for Assembly, 284; Hopkins, (Dem.,) 144.

Rhinebeck, 96 Union majority; Fenton, 96 majority; Ketcham, Union, for Congress, 87 majority.

Poughkeepsie City—Lincoln's majority, 249; Fenton's majority, 247; Ketchum, (Union,) for Congress, 305 majority.

Armenia—Lincoln, 311; McClellan, 221; Fenton, 312; Seymour, 211; Ketcham, for Congress, Republican, 333; Nelson, for Congress, Democrat, 195.

North Salem—Lincoln, 236; McClellan, 110; Fenton, 236; Seymour, 110; Brandeth, Republican, 129 majority.

Northeast—McClellan, 188; Lincoln, 136; Seymour, 187; Fenton, 136; Nelson, Democrat, for Congress, 183; Ketchan, Republican, 236.

ALLEGANY COUNTY.

Cuba, Lincoln, 116 majority.
Belvidere, Lincoln, 14 majority.
Harsdale, Lincoln, 33 majority.
Angelica, Lincoln, 180 majority.
Phillipsville, 154 Union majority.
Frenchville, 122 Union majority.
Scio, 26 Union majority.
Alfred, 24 Union majority.
Andover, 210 Union majority.
Alleghany, 78 Democratic majority.

CATTARAUGUS COUNTY.

Little Valley, Lincoln 74 majority.

STEUBEN COUNTY.

Cameron, Lincoln, 127 majority.
Addison, Lincoln, 10 majority.
Canisteo, Lincoln, 174 majority.
Adrian, 76 Union majority.
Hornellsville, 86 Democratic majority.
Rathboneville, 76 Union majority.
Bath, 278 Republican majority. Fenton, 288.
Campbell, Rep., majority 170.
Condorton, Rep., majority 71.
Wayland, Dem., majority 79; Seymour 81.

ORANGE COUNTY.

Newburgh, 150 Union majority.
Goshen, 196 Dem. majority.
Blooming Grove, 123 Union majority.
Southfield, 86 Union majority.
Mount Hope, 40 Union majority.
Deerpark, 102 Dem. majority; Seymour, 112 majority; Winfield, Dem., for Congress, 76 majority.

TOMPKINS COUNTY.

Trumansburgh, 54 Union majority.
Ithaca, 43 Union majority.
Danbury, 150 Union majority.

CORTLAND COUNTY.

Homer, 480 Union majority.
Homer, 480 Union majority.
Cortland, 488 Union majority.
Scott, 172 Union majority.
Marsipos, 125 Union majority.

ONONDAGA COUNTY.

Syracuse, 72 Union majority.

All three of the Union members of the Assembly are elected. Hon. I. T. Davis is reëlected to Congress. Returns from towns give Union majorities as follows: Dewitt, 79; Fabius, 253; Gedder, 34; Lafayette, 85; two districts of Manlius, 224; Lysander 236; one district of Clay, 146; Camellus, 10; Union gain, 16. First district of Onondaga, 137; first district of Pompey, 64; Van Buren, 71; Spofford, first district, Lincoln's majority, 70; Fenton, 74. The county has given over 2,700 Union majority.

CHEMUNG COUNTY.

ELMIRA, Tuesday, Nov. 8.

This city goes Lincoln—162 majority.
Afton Union majority 80.
Bainbridge Union majority 150.
Sixteen towns give a Union majority of 1,190. The remaining towns will make it 1,250.

WYOMING COUNTY.

Athica, 14 Union majority.
Warsaw, Democratic majority, 170.
Wyoming County gives Lincoln 1,579 majority.

MONROE COUNTY.

Rochester City, complete, 62 Democratic majority. Union gain over last year 137 and 290 over 1862. Hart, Union, is elected to Congress.

LIVINGSTON COUNTY.

Lima, 59 Union majority.
Springwater, 270 Union majority.
Livonia, 219 Republican majority.
Leroy, Republican majority, 71.
Alexander, Union majority, 164.

ORLEANS COUNTY.

Two-thirds of the county give a gain for the Union ticket thus far over last year, when the majority in the county was 1,164. This indicates a majority in the county of 1,300.

SULLIVAN COUNTY.

Mount Hope 4 Democrat majority. The following is the vote for Gov.—Seymour 193; Fenton, 193—a tie. Morvin for assembly has one majority.
Cochecton, Democratic, majority 295.

QUEENS COUNTY.

Newtown, Second District, Lincoln 218; McClellan, 353.

Flushing, McClellan, 365 majority; Seymour, 374 majority; Turner, (Democrat,) for Assembly, 331 majority; Faber, (Democrat,) for Congress, 300 majority; Hunter's Point, McClellan, 231 majority; Seymour, 231 majority.

Jamaica—McClellan's majority 234; Seymour's, 237. Hempstead—Lincoln's majority 338.
Newtown, Dem. majority, 576.
North Hempstead, Union majority, Fenton, 109.
Queens County complete will probably give 1,000 Dem. majority.

WAYNE COUNTY.

Palmyra, Union majority 40.
Arcadia, Second District, Union majority 78, Fenton 79.
Walworth, Union majority 179.
Marion, Union majority 326.
Savannah, Union majority, 122.
Fenton's majority, 119.
Rutler, Union majority, 194.
Lyons, Democratic majority, 94.
Arcadia, third district, McClellan majority, 15.
Williamson, Union majority, 195.
Macedon, Union majority, 108.

GENESEE COUNTY.

Batavia, Union majority 117, Fenton 121 majority.

MADISON COUNTY.

Lennox, Union majority 209.
Hamilton, Lincoln 291; McClellan 135. Fenton 293; Seymour 136.
Eaton, Union majority 138; Union gain 33.
Brookfield, Lincoln, 577; McClellan, 348. Fenton, 578; Seymour, 350.

ST. LAWRENCE COUNTY.

Potsdam, 786 Union majority.
Lawrence, 364 Union majority.
Oswegatchie, 275 Union majority.
Madrid, 267 Union majority.
These towns show a Union gain of 75 over last year.
Chateauguay, 20 Dem., majority; Union gain, 64.
Constable, 62 Lincoln majority; Union gain 83.

ERIE COUNTY.

Official returns from 16 out of 25 towns in this county give 1,096 Democratic majority against 685 Republican majority; nine towns yet to hear from. Democratic majority in the county will be from 500 to 600.

Tonawanda, McClellan, 353; Lincoln, 171.

The Democratic majority in Erie County will be about 400 or a trifle less. The towns of Clarence and Newstead give about 250 Republican gain, which uses up the Democratic gains in the strong towns.
Alden, Democratic majority, 114; Seymour, 109.
Perry, Union majority, 336.

COLOMBIA COUNTY.

Hudson City—216 Democratic majority.
The Town of Claversack—4 Democratic majority, a Union gain of 57.
Greenport—39 Democratic, a Union gain of 35.
Stockport—69 Union majority, a Union gain of 26.
Gallatin—51 Union majority.
Ghent—69 Union majority, a Union gain of 65.
Germantown—47 Union majority, a Union gain of 51.
Livingston—3 Union majority.
Laghkanic—148 Democratic majority.
Hillsdale—26 Democratic majority.
Copake—14 Democratic majority.
Ancram—53 Democratic majority.
New-Lebanon—Democratic majority, 31.
Town of Ghent—McClellan, 246; Lincoln, 333; Seymour, 267; Fenton, 331.
Town of Austerlitz—Lincoln, 214; McClellan, 140. Fenton, 212; Seymour, 143.

RENSSELAER COUNTY.

City of Troy—Democratic majority, 758.
Berlin—Union majority, 2.
Schaghticoke—Union majority, 13.
Poistenkill—Democratic majority, 55.
Brunswick—Union majority, 3.
Lansingburg—Union majority, 277.
Greenbush—Democratic majority, 261.
Schodack—Democratic majority, 116.
Sandlake, First District, Union majority, 69.
North Greenbush, Dem. majority, 59.
Grafton, Union majority, 73.
Troy city complete. McClellan over Lincoln, 788. Seymour over Fenton, 602. Van Alstyne, (Dem.,) for Congress, over Griswold, 713. Democratic Assembly, Bartlett by 650 majority.
McClellan's majority in this county is probably 300. A portion of the Republican county ticket is probably elected. Griswold is elected to Congress in the district of Rensselaer over Van Alstyne.

ONEIDA COUNTY.

Rome, 471 majority for McClellan, Seymour's 475, Kernan for Congress 469.

Utica City—Democratic majority, 259; Union gain over last year, 21.

Oneida County will give Lincoln from 1,300 to 1,500 majority, and Fenton 100 better. Roscoe Conkling (Union) has probably 800 majority for Congress, defeating Francis Kernan, the present member. For Assembly, A. B. Weaver and T. D. Penfield, Democratic, and Lorenzo Rowe and G. W. Cole, Union, are elected.

HERKIMER COUNTY.

German Flats, Union majority 6. Fenton 10.
Herkimer, Democratic majority 164.
Richfield, Union majority 126.
Warren, Democratic majority 40.
Columbia, Union majority 94.
Stark, Union majority 49.
Little Falls, Democratic majority 228.
Manheim, Democratic majority 60.

MONTGOMERY COUNTY.

St. Johnsville, Democratic majority 95.
Winden, Union majority 81.
Canajoharie, Democratic majority 11.
Root, Democratic majority 173.
Palestine, Democratic majority 156.
Mohawk, Democratic majority 53.
Amsterdam, Union majority 125.

OSWEGO COUNTY.

Oswego City and ten towns in the county, give a Union majority of 1,702. The remainder will probably increase this to 2,500. Three Union members of Assembly are elected.

FRANKLIN COUNTY.

Malone, 523 Union majority; gain over 1860 of 260.

OSWEGO COUNTY.

Volney, Union majority, 190.
Granby, Union majority, 102.
Palermo, Union majority, 264.
Schroppel, Union majority, 73

BROOME COUNTY.

Lisle, 270 Union majority.
Triangle, 160 Union majority.

SCHENECTADY COUNTY.

City of Schenectady, Democratic majority 229.

CHENANGO COUNTY.

Greene, Democratic majority 22.
Oxford, Union majority 34; Fenton's majority 37.
Norwich, Union majority 2; Fenton's majority 19.
Sherburne, Lincoln 457; McClellan 312.
Smyrna, Lincoln 318; McClellan 82.
Columbus, Lincoln 268; McClellan 60. Fenton 265; Seymour 62.

ALBANY COUNTY.

Albany City—The vote in this city is as follows: McClellan, 7,540; Lincoln, 5,066. Majority for McClellan, 2,476. Seymour, 7,541; Fenton, 5,078. Seymour's majority 2,463. The Democrats elect three of the four members of Assembly. Goodyear, (Dem.,) for Congress, has about the same majority as Seymour.

SCHOHARIE.

Wright, Democratic majority, 73; Seymour, 78.
Fulton, Democratic majority, 358.
Middleburgh, Democratic majority, 241.
Broome, Democratic majority, 18.

ULSTER COUNTY.

Kingston—Democratic majority, 828; majority Seymour, 511.

PUTNAM COUNTY.

Four towns give Lincoln 78 majority and Seymour 79. The Dem. majority in the county will be about 250.

Town of Patterson, Lincoln, 99 majority; Fenton, 100 majority; Larkin, for Congress, 99 majority; Penny, (Rep.,) for Assembly, 131 majority.
Town of Southeast: McClellan, 26 majority; Radford, 28 majority.

DELAWARE COUNTY.

Tompkins—Union majority, 115; Fenton's, 114. Gain of 46.
Sanford—Dem. majority, 3.

SUFFOLK COUNTY.

River Head, Union majority, 73.
Southold, Union majority, 164.
Southampton, Union majority, 262.
Easthampton, Union majority, 9.
Shelter Island, Union majority, 26.

SENECA COUNTY.

Seneca Falls, Democratic majority, 200.
Waterloo, Democratic majority, 171.

CAYUGA COUNTY.

Auburn City, Union majority, 380.

ULSTER COUNTY.

Saugerties, McClellan, 123 majority; Democratic gain, 89. Seymour, 89 majority. Bubbell, Democrat, for Congress, is elected. Bookstaver, Democrat, for Assembly, is elected.

SCHOHARIE COUNTY.

Experience gives 63 Republican majority.

SCHENECTADY COUNTY

Complete, gives McClellan 62 majority. The Republican county ticket is elected. Page, Democrat, for Congress, has 50 majority. Stanfield, Union, for Assembly, is probably elected.

DUTCHESS COUNTY.

Complete gives Lincoln 559 majority. Fenton, 725 majority. Ketchum, Union, for Congress 850 majority, electing him by over 1,000 in the district over Nelson, the present incumbent. Howard and Nilbur, both Union, all elected to the Legislature.

The State—Reported and Estimated.

	Lincoln.		McClellan.
Chatauqua	5,000	New-York	36,857
Allegany	3,500	Kings	4,300
Orleans	1,400	Albany	2,500
Monroe	1,050	Richmond	1,500
Columbia	200	Schoharie	1,500
Delaware	1,000	Ulster	800
Suffolk	300	Herkimer	1,200
Livingston	2,000	Rensselear	500
Cortland	2,200	Erie	550
Onondaga	2,800	Queens	1,500
Broome	2,100	Seneca	500
Wayne	2,000	Schenedtady	62
Madison	2,800	Sullivan	500
Montgomery	200	Westchester	2,100
Genesee	1,500	Rockland	1,000
Oswego	2,500	Putnam	400
Franklin	1,000	Green	800
St. Lawrence	7,000	Orange	200
Chenango	1,350		
			55,369
Oneida	1,400		
Wyoming	1,579		
Cayuga	3,200		
Steuben	2,000		
Washington	2,200		
Jefferson	2,800		
Cattaraugus	2,000		
Essex	1,000		
Lewis	500		
Ontario	1,300		
Saratoga	1,000		
Schuyler	500		
Tioga	800		
Tompkins	1,300		
Yates	1,000		
Otsego	600		
Warren	500		
Dutchess	550		
Niagara	500		
Clinton	200		
Chemung	200		
Fulton and H	200		
Total	66,129		

NEW-JERSEY.

MILBURN, N. J., Tuesday, Nov. 8.

Lincoln, 141; McClellan, 88.
Theodore Little, (Union,) for Congress, 141; Andrew J. Rogers, (Dem.,) 89.
Legislature—Rufus F. W. Harrison, (Union,) 142; Joel D. Mead, (Dem.,) 88.

SUMMIT, N. J., Tuesday, Nov. 8.

New-Providence township gives Lincoln 98; McClellan, 136.
For Congress—Charles Scranton, Union, 97; Charles Sitgreaves, Dem., 137.
For Assembly—Joseph T. Crowell, Union, 96; Scudder, Dem., 138.
Delaware Township, in Camden County, Union majority, 97; gain, 52.
Morris Township, McClellan 80 majority. Rogers, Dem., for Congress, 53 majority. Treadwell, Dem., for Assembly, 48 majority.
Mercer County, West Windsor Township, Dem. 166; Rep. 159.
Elizabeth City—Democratic majority, 366. Rahway City gives 113 majority to the Union ticket. Plainfield—Union majority, 162. Cape Island—One township gives 88 Union majority.
Chatham Township, McClellan 9 majority. Little, Union, for Congress, 2 majority. For Assembly, Democratic 19.
Mendham Township, in Morris County, Lincoln 10 majority; Little, 18 majority; Gage, Union, for Assembly, 36 majority.
Newark—Full returns from four wards give a Union majority of 108.
Newark—Later—Nine out of fourteen wards show Republican gain of 358. The Democrats carry the city by reduced majorities.
Morris, Union and Essex Counties—The returns show indecisive Republican gains.
Springfield—McClellan, 25 majority; Sitgreaves, Democrat, for Congress, 25 majority; Scudder, Democrat, for Assembly, 7 majority.
Returns from Pequannock, Morris County, are as follows:
Lincoln 359 majority.
Little, (Republican,) for Congress, 362 majority.

GLOUCESTER COUNTY.

Two townships give 158 Union majority.

CUMBERLAND COUNTY.

Melville, Union majority, 115. Stave, for Congress, 111.

NEWARK, Tuesday, Nov. 8.

Essex County has gone Union by over 150, making a Union gain of over 1,000 over last year. The Legislative delegation is six Union to three Democrats.
Camden County, 500 Union majority.
Trenton, 255 Democratic majority.
Bordentown, 148 Democratic majority.
Middlesex gives a Democratic majority of 775.
New-Brunswick gives McClellan 148 majority.

MERCER COUNTY.

McClellan's majority, 110; Middleton for Congress 91 majority.
Trenton—McClellan's majority, 255; Democratic Assemblyman, 117 majority. The whole Democratic County ticket is elected.

CAMDEN COUNTY.

Union majority, 300.

CUMBERLAND COUNTY.

Union majority, 400.

BURLINGTON, Wednesday, Nov. 9—4 A. M.

BURLINGTON COUNTY.—Wright, Union, is elected Senator. Stockton, Hailings, Quick and Lathrop, all Union, are elected to the Assembly. Union gain in the Senate, 1; in the Assembly, 2. The county gives 1,800 Union majority.

PENNSYLVANIA.

GLORIOUS PHILADELPHIA.

Special Dispatch to the National Union Committee.

PHILADELPHIA, Tuesday, Nov. 8.

Philadelphia gives LINCOLN 11,000 majority—4,000 gain on October. Lancaster 5,400 majority—1,400 gain on October. Pittsburgh large gains.

FROM HARRISBURGH.

Dispatch from Gen. Cameron.

HARRISBURGH, Tuesday, Nov. 8.

Hon. H. J. Raymond:

Returns indicate large Union gains in the State.
S. CAMERON.

CHESTER COUNTY.

Nine districts shows Union gain of 120.

(Continued on the Eighth Page.)

The Philadelphia Inquirer.

CIRCULATION OVER 60 000. PHILADELPHIA, WEDNESDAY, NOVEMBER 9, 1864. PRICE THREE CENTS.

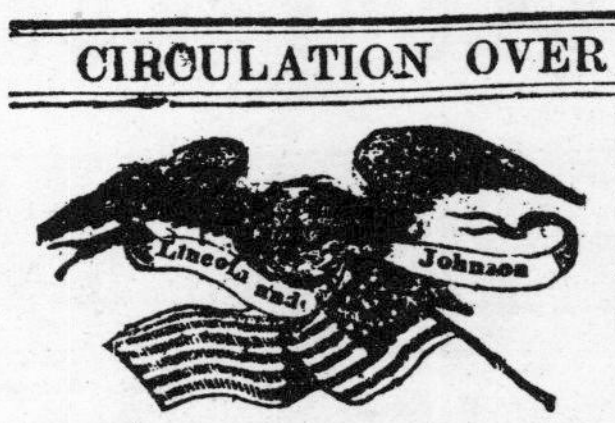

VICTORY!

THE UNION TRIUMPHANT!!

LINCOLN AND JOHNSON!!!

HONEST ABRAHAM RE-ELECTED

PEACE PARTY DEMORALIZED

Northern Rebels Sent Whirling

NO COMPROMISE WITH TRAITORS

THE UNION PYRAMID

IOWA.
OHIO.
MAINE.
KANSAS.
INDIANA.
ILLINOIS.
VERMONT.
MICHIGAN.
NEW YORK.
DELAWARE.
MARYLAND.
MINNESOTA.
MISSOURI.
WISCONSIN.
CONNECTICUT.
PENNSYLVANIA.
RHODE ISLAND.
WEST VIRGINIA.
MASSACHUSETTS.
NEW HAMPSHIRE.

ITS ELECTORAL VOTE 206.

THE RESULT IN THE CITY.

We present our readers this morning with a table of the full vote of the city of Philadelphia for President of the United States, and the different majorities at the October election. It will be seen that the Union vote has largely increased since the October election, and it may be assumed as a settled fact that ABRAHAM LINCOLN will occupy the Presidential Chair of the Republic for four years to come.

Wards.	October, 1864. Sheriff. Union.	Dem.	November, 1864. President. Lincoln.	McClellan.
First	1911	1068	1928	1028
Second	2278	2195	2498	2321
Third	1187	1451	1330	1566
Fourth	885	1503	927	2268
Fifth	1102	1397	1280	1415
Sixth	1060	1249	1160	1260
Seventh	2159	1352	2402	1502
Eighth	1581	1119	1767	1218
Ninth	1527	1303	1682	1425
Tenth	2343	1107	2680	1219
Eleventh	966	1474	898	1113
Twelfth	1863	1267	1429	1322
Thirteenth	2055	1325	2192	1366
Fourteenth	2284	1328	2539	1384
Fifteenth	2202	2174	3539	2395
Sixteenth	1619	1618	1698	1673
Seventeenth	1184	2056	1296	2310
Eighteenth	2312	1200	2503	1228
Nineteenth	2469	2320	2639	2489
Twentieth	3214	2480	3656	2361
Twenty-first	1617	1330	1670	1331
Twenty-second	2092	1123	2070	1150
Twenty-third	1773	1856	1589	1189
Twenty-fourth	2284	1772	2503	2215
Twenty-fifth	811	1211	847	1241
Twenty-sixth	1830	1189	2168	1401
Total	47,093	39,367	50,885	41,485
	39,367		42,485	

Howell's maj. 7,723 Lincoln's maj. 9,400

Majorities in October and November.

Wards.	Maj. Oct. 11. Union.	Democrat.	Maj. Nov. 8. Union.	Democrat.
1	843	..	900	..
2	78	..	172	..
3	..	264	..	236
4	..	1,018	..	1,341
5	..	295	..	135
6	..	189	..	100
7	807	..	900	..
8	462	..	554	..
9	224	..	257	..
10	1,236	..	1,461	..
11	..	518	..	215
12	96	..	107	..
13	730	..	826	..
14	956	..	1,155	..
15	1,028	..	1,144	..
16	..	25	1	..
17	..	872	..	1,014
18	1,112	..	1,275	..
19	139	..	150	..
20	734	..	995	..
21	287	..	339	..
22	969	..	920	..
23	417	..	400	..
24	512	..	488	..
25	..	400	..	804
26	641	..	767	..
Total	11,282	3,556	12,835	3,435
	3,556		3,435	
	7,726 Howell's maj. for Sheriff.		9,400 Lincoln's majority.	

PENNSYLVANIA.

Alleghany County.

HARRISBURG, Nov. 8.—Alleghany county gives a large gain for the Union ticket. Democratic reports estimate the Union majority at 7100, which would be a gain of 500. But Lincoln will no doubt have 8000 majority in that event.

PITTSBURG, Nov. 8.—Forty-five districts in Allegheny county, including Pittsburg and Allegheny City, give Lincoln an increase of 1500 over the October vote. Lincoln's majority in the entire county will be about 8500.

Lancaster County.

LANCASTER, Nov. 8.—This city gives 197 Democratic majority. Democratic gain, 54. Eight rural districts give over 200 Union gain. Large Union gains throughout the county.

Lancaster county gives LINCOLN 5500 majority, a clear gain of some 1500 for the Union party.

Lancaster county, with fifteen districts to hear from, gives 5050 Union majority. The districts to hear from will probably increase it to 5500.

Montgomery County.

Norristown borough gives 84 Union majority, a Union gain of 72.

Conshohocken borough gives a Union majority of 54, a Democratic gain of 11.

NORRISTOWN, Nov. 8.—Ten districts in Montgomery county show a Union gain of over 100.

Pottstown Borough gives 145 Democratic majority, Union gain of 15 over Congressional vote of October.

Chester County.

WEST CHESTER, Nov. 8.—Three districts of West Chester have been counted. Over the October vote on Broomall for Congress the Fourth District will probably run the gain of West Chester up to 60.

Twenty-seven townships give a Union gain of 175 over the October vote. There are thirty-five towns to hear from yet. The Union majority in Chester county will probably exceed 2500.

Charlestown Township—Union, 111; Dem., 86; Union gain, 5.

East Vincent—Union, 183; Dem., 222; Union gain, 4.

PHŒNIXVILLE, Nov. 8.—Schuylkill township, Union, 161; Democratic, 95. Union gain 22.

East Pikeland. Union gain 5.

Phœnixville, North Ward, Union, 42; Dem., 225. Dem. gain 32. South Ward, Union, 300; Dem., 199. Union gain, 15.

Seventeen townships show a Union gain in all but three, and the returns indicate a Union majority of 2500 in Chester county.

Chester county.—The Union majority is now reported at 2350.

Berks County, Pa.

READING, Nov. 8.—The Fourth Ward of this city gives Lincoln 117 majority; Union gain of 23.

Reading Ninth Ward—Democratic majority, 185; Union gain of 1.

Third Ward—Union majority, 28; Union gain of 16.

Seventh Ward—Union majority, 28; Democratic gain of 4.

Eighth Ward—Democratic majority, 68; Democratic gain of 24.

Union Township—Union majority, 42; Union gain of 15.

Alsace Township—Democratic majority, 152; Democratic gain of 12.

Sixth Ward—Union majority, 26; Union gain of 25.

First Ward—Union majority, 90; Union gain of 27.

Fifth Ward—Union majority, 71; Union gain of 20.

Cumeril Township gives a Democratic majority of 42; the same as the vote in October.

Reading City—Complete Union majority, 90; Union gain of 63.

Amity Township—Democratic majority, 144; Democratic gain of 36.

Spring Township—Democratic majority, 217; Democratic gain of 81.

Exeter Township—Democratic majority, 182; Union gain of 11.

Kaulstown Borough—Democratic majority, 60. Democratic gain, 4.

Maxatauney Township—Democratic majority, 248. Democratic gain, 26.

Richmond Township—Democratic majority, 404. Democratic gain, 40.

READING, Nov. 8.—Midnight.—Berks county give from 6400 to 6500 Democratic majority. The Invincibles and Young Men's Lincoln Club is now parading the streets with brass and calithumpian bands, banners and torches. The enthusiasm is intense. The Democratic head-quarters are closed, dark and silent.

Bedford County.

SAXTON'S JUNCTION, Nov. 8.—The Democratic majority in Saxton's is 35, a Union gain of 2 over the last election.

Northampton County.

Easton Borough, Bushkill Ward, Lincoln majority 99; Union gain, 66.

Lehigh Ward, Lincoln majority 48; Union gain, 8.

West Ward, Democratic majority 222; Democratic gain, 37.

Freemansburg Borough gives McClellan 10 majority, a Democratic gain of 7.

Forks Township, Democratic majority 185; Democratic gain 30.

Palmer Township, Democratic majority 87; Democratic gain 1.

South Easton Borough, Union majority 56; Democratic gain 4.

Bethlehem Borough, Democratic majority 86; Democratic gain 45.

Hanover Township, Democratic majority 78; Democratic gain 11.

Lehigh Township, Democratic majority 212; Democratic gain 82.

Lebanon County.

LEBANON, Nov. 8.—This county gives about 1000 Union majority.

Lebanon borough, East Ward, Union majority 48; Union gain, 25 West Ward, Union loss of 9.

Swatara township, Union majority 209; Union gain, 42.

South Cornwall township, McClellan 77 majority; Democratic gain, 7.

This county gives 960 Union majority. In October the Union majority was 716.

Lehigh County.

ALLENTOWN, Nov. 8.—Allentown borough, Fourth Ward, Lincoln, 49 majority; Union gain of 21. Fifth Ward, Democratic majority, 90; Democratic gain 9.

Catasauque borough, Union majority, 109; Union gain, 9.

Hoquendaqua district, Democratic majority, 20, Union gain, 6.

Wacingil township, Democratic majority, 209, Democratic gain, 2.

This county gives about the same vote as in October last.

Dauphin County, Pa.

HARRISBURG, Nov. 8.—The following is the official vote of the city:—

First Ward—McClellan, 196; Lincoln, 120. Democratic majority, 76. Union gain, 6.

Second Ward—Lincoln, 255; McClellan, 244. Republican majority, 11. Republican gain, 25.

Third Ward—McClellan, 13 majority. Union gain 33.

Fourth Ward—McClellan, 37 majority. Union gain, 24.

Fifth Ward—Lincoln, 24 majority. Union loss, 2.

Sixth Ward—McClellan, 52 majority. Union gain, 6.

The Union gain in this city amounts to 93 votes.

Middletown gives a majority for Lincoln of 59, a Union gain of 12.

The Union gain in Dauphin county will be 500. The returns from eight districts warrant this conclusion.

Millersburg gives 4 Union majority, a Union gain of 22.

Upper Paxton, Dauphin county—Democratic majority, 18.

Carbon County.

EASTON, Nov. 8.—Mauch Chunk borough, Carbon county, gives Lincoln 80 majority, a Democratic gain of 20.

Franklin township, Carbon county, gives a Union majority of 3; Union gain, 31.

Summit Hill borough, Union majority, 212; Union gain, 313.

East Mauch Chunk borough, Democratic majority, 8; Democratic gain of one.

Lower Towamensing Township, Democratic majority 215; Democratic gain, 6.

Huntingdon County.

HUNTINGDON, Nov. 8.—Forty-two Democrats this morning formed a procession and marched to the polls, where they voted for Lincoln and Johnson. All of them were solid men of the old Democratic party.

Sixteen Districts out of twenty-eight have been heard from. The county will give about 675 Union majority. A Union gain of 158.

Bucks County.

DOYLESTOWN, Nov. 8.—This borough gives a Democratic majority of 45. Union gain, 20.

Doylestown township, Democratic majority, 81; Union gain, 7.

Warwick Township—Union majority, 8. Democratic gain, 5. Plumstead, Union majority, 97. Union gain, 11.

Haycock Township—Democratic majority, 218. Democratic gain, 10. East Rockhill, Democratic majority, 149. Democratic gain, 11.

Buckingham Township—Union majority, 245, a Union gain of 6.

EASTON, Nov. 8.—Lower Makefield Township gives 142 Union majority, a Union gain of 2.

Falls Township gives 176 Union majority, a Union gain of 18.

Morrisville gives 41 Union majority, a Democratic gain of 5.

Warrington gives 50 Democratic majority, a Union gain of 3.

Warminster Township gives a tie vote, being a Union gain of 6.

Thirteen districts heard from show a Union gain of 50.

Lycoming County.

Williamsport 60 Union Majority.

Franklin County.

Chambersburg gives a Union majority of 163. About even, a Union gain of 50.

Bedford County.

About 650 for McClellan.

Schuylkill County.

POTTSVILLE, Nov. 8.—Eleven districts are in, and show a McClellan gain on the Congressional vote of 74.

Schuylkill county will give McClellan from 1950 to 2000 majority.

TAMAQUA, Nov. 8.—Democratic majority in this borough 88. Union gain 10.

Wayne Township—Democratic majority 76.

Union Township—Democratic majority 258. Democratic gain of 192.

Schuylkill Haven—Union majority 52. Union gain 20.

Pottsville Borough—Union majority 423. Democratic gain 47.

St. Clair—Union majority 159. Union gain 8.

Mount Carbon—Democratic majority 58. Democratic gain 13.

Pottsville Borough—Union majority 434. Union loss 367. Loss of one on Governor Curtin's vote.

Norwegian Township (Mining District)—Union loss 15.

St. Clair Borough—Union gain 8. Democratic majority in county about the same as on Governor's vote.

Adams County.

GETTYSBURG, Nov. 9.—Adams County will give about 500 majority for McClellan; a Democratic gain of 90.

Cumberland County.

CARLISLE, Nov. 8.—In Cumberland County thirteen townships and towns give a Democratic gain of 130. The estimated majority in this county for McClellan is 750.

The majority for McClellan in Carlisle District is 827; a Democratic gain on the Congressional vote of 114.

Blair County.

ALTOONA, Nov. 8.—Sixteen districts in Blair county give a Union gain of 143. The majority will be 425.

Mifflin County.

The Democratic majority is 99.

York County.

Hanover 110 Union majority.

Northumberland County.

Sunbury 133 Union majority.
Northumberland 23 Democratic majority.

Bradford County.

Bradford county gives 3500 Union majority

MASSACHUSETTS.

BOSTON, Nov. 8.—Union majority nearly 75 000. This city gives Lincoln about 5000 majority. Rice's majority in the Third District is 3326. Hooper, in the Fourth District, has nearly 5000 majority.

Returns from the State indicate that Lincoln's majority will be nearly 75,000 in the State. In 1860, it was about 43,000.

Messrs. Rice and Hooper have been re-elected to Congress in the Third and Fourth Districts. They will meet their constituents to receive their congratulations in Faneuil Hall, this evening.

The Republicans have carried all the Congressional districts.

BOSTON, Nov. 8, 10 o'clock.—Returns from 127 towns in Massachusetts foot up for LINCOLN, 75,273, for MCCLELLAA, 32,072. LINCOLN'S majority will reach over 80,000.

The Unionists have elected every member of Congress by a heavy majority; also, the entire State ticket, and probably every State Senator and nearly the entire House.

BOSTON, Nov. 8—11 30 P. M.—One hundred and seventy-six towns in Massachusetts foot up:—

For Lincoln....................90,000
For McClellan..................36,631

A grand Union jubilee was held in Faneuil Hall to-night. Among the speakers were EDWARD EVERETT, Senator WILSON, Representatives HOOPER and RICE, Dr. LORING, Rev. Dr. KIRK and others.

VERMONT.

MONTPELIER, Vt., Nov. 8.—A very heavy vote has been polled in this State to-day. Returns from thirty-four towns show an increase in the vote of 2907 over that in September. In these towns the vote stood 8355 for the Union, and 2919 for the Democrats. To-day it stands 10,986 Union, and 3240 Democratic, showing a net gain on the Union vote of 2260.

Fifty towns in Vermont give Lincoln a majority of 11,775.

MONTPELIER, Nov. 8.—Fifty towns give Lincoln 16,644; McClellan 4869. Union gain 8741. Vermont is good for 30,000.

NEW HAMPSHIRE.

One hundred towns give Lincoln 1700 majority,

One hundred and ten towns in New Hampshire give Lincoln 22,395, and McClellan 20,291. The above embrace nearly two-thirds of the whole vote of the State.

CONCORD, N. H. Nov. 8.—Sixty-one towns give Lincoln 15,326; McClellan, 13,772.

New Hampshire has gone for Lincoln by 2500 majority on the home vote.

CONCORD, 9 P. M.—One hundred towns gave Lincoln 20 785; McClellan, 18,596.

CONCORD, Nov. 8.—The vote of one hundred and ten towns and cities in this State stand as follows:—Lincoln, 22,995; McClellan, 20,291. Democratic gain, 2050.

The above embraces nearly two-thirds of the entire State.

CONNECTICUT.

HARTFORD, Nov. 8.—Lincoln, 2479. McClellan, 2890.

New Haven gives McClellan 895 majority.

Toland county gives Lincoln 2193; and McClellan 1840.

Middlesex county gives Lincoln 3083; McClellan 3207.

Thirty-one towns, including the cities of New Haven, Hartford, Bridgeport, Waterbury, Norwich and New London, give Lincoln 1169 majority.

DANBURY, Nov. 8.—The election passed off quietly in this part of the State.

Union Majorities.		Democratic Majorities.	
Danbury	182	New Fairfield	82
Bethel	98	Sherman	56
Ridgefield	79	Brookfield	56
Reading	41	Newtown	141
Wilton	82	New Milford	3

RHODE ISLAND.

PROVIDENCE, Nov. 8.—Returns from nearly the whole State show a majority for Lincoln of about 5000.

PROVIDENCE, Nov. 8.—This city gives 2200 majority for Lincoln.

Newport gives Lincoln 376 majority.

MAINE.

Twenty-eight towns give Lincoln 6000 majority.

PORTLAND, Nov. 8.—No returns yet from the eastern towns. 28 towns give Lincoln 13,264; McClellan, 7954. Union gain, 380. The full vote of Portland is Democratic, 1879; Union, 2856. Union loss of 6.

OHIO.

CLEVELAND, Nov. 8.—Scattering returns from Ohio and Indiana show Union gains over the October election, and indicate that LINCOLN has carried the two States by heavy majorities.

Sandusky, 629 Republican majority
Huron, 178 Republican majority.
Talmadge, 204 Republican majority.
Ravenna, 147 Republican majority.
Toledo, 624 Republican majority.
Cleveland, 964 Republican majority
Corry, 129 Republican majority.

Cleveland gives 3500 Union majority, on the home vote.

Ohio is conceded to LINCOLN by from 30,000 to 35,000 majority on the home vote.

WISCONSIN.

MADISON, Wis., Nov. 8.—Scattering returns show a Union loss on the vote of last fall, when the Union majority was 16,000. It is estimated by the Republicans that the State has given 10,000 Union majority on the home vote, which will be largely increased by the soldiers' vote.

NEW JERSEY.

ATLANTIC CITY, Nov. 8.—This city gives twenty-eight Union majority.

WOODBURY, Nov. 8.—Mantua township gives 46 Democratic majority. Union gain of 25.

CAMDEN, Nov. 8.—Delaware township, in Camden county, gives 97 Union majority, a Union gain of 52.

CAPE MAY, Nov. 3.—Cape Island, Lower Township—Union majority 88 on Electors, 87 on Congressmen, 64 on State Senate, and 76 on State Legislature.

MILLVILLE, Nov. 8.—Millville township, Cumberland county, Lincoln 114 majority; Starr 111 majority; Nixon 117 majority.

Trenton.—198 Democratic majority—one ward to hear from.

Gloucester County.

Woolwich Township.—Lincoln's majority, 48; Greenwich—Lincoln's majority, 110.

Burlington County.—Stockton, Union candidate in the Second District, for Assembly, is elected.

Wright, Union, is elected to the Senate from Burlington county.

CAMDEN, Nov. 8.—Camden county has gone Republican by about 800 majority.

Cumberland county about 400 Union majority.

Egg Harbor City—Lincoln 4 majority.

Mullica Township—Lincoln's majority 139.

Delaware Township—Union majority 69.

Newton Township—Union majority 88.

Centre Township—Democratic majority 8.

Middlesex county, New Jersey, gave 770 majority for McClellan.

New Brunswick, New Jersey, gives 148 majority for McClellan. Union Assemblymen elected by 64 majority.

WOODBURY, Nov. 8.—Lincoln, 1899; McClellan, 1495. Starr, Union, 1931; Dickerson, Dem., 1509.

NEWARK, N. J., Nov. 8.—Essex county has gone Union by 150 majority; being a Union gain of over 1000.

The Legislative delegation will consist of 6 Union and 3 Democrats.

Mercer county gives a Democratic majority of 119. In Trenton the whole Democratic ticket is elected.

NEWARK, Nov. 8.—Essex county has gone Union by 150 majority; Union gain of over 1000. The Legislative delegation stands 6 Union and 3 Democratic.

Full returns from four Wards give a Union majority of 198.

LATER.—Nine out of fourteen Wards show a Republican gain of 363. The Democrats carry the city by a reduced majority.

In Morris, Union and Essex counties the returns show Republican gains.

CAMDEN, Nov. 8.—Waterford Township—Democratic majority, 41.

The Union ticket will have a clear majority of 300 in the City of Camden, and at least 500 in the county.

Salem county gives a Union majority of 59.

The entire Union county ticket is elected by 80 majority.

MARYLAND.

BALTIMORE, Nov. 8.—Frederick City gives 452 majority for LINCOLN; a gain of 98 compared with October election.

EDWIN H. WEBSTER, the Union candidate for Congress in the Second District, has a majority of 5097 in seven of the lower Wards, and is undoubtedly elected by a large majority.

ELKTON, Nov. 8.—The Third District gives 48 Union majority, a Union loss of 7; the Fifth District, 175 Union majority, a loss of 2. No other districts heard from.

The Second District gives 80 Democratic majority.

The Fourth District polls were closed at two o'clock, caused by a row. The vote will not be counted.

Worcester county—Salisbury District—Democratic majority, 10.

Somerset county—Salisbury District— Democratic majority, 120.

BALTIMORE, Nov. 8.—Baltimore city gives a majority for LINCOLN in every Ward, as follows:—

Wards.	Union Maj.	Wards.	Union Maj.
First	779	Twelfth	397
Second	698	Thirteenth	59[illegible]
Third	1006	Fourteenth	[illegible]
Fourth	798	Fifteenth	90
Fifth	381	Sixteenth	711
Sixth	835	Seventeenth	357
Seventh	590	Eighteenth	not in.
Eighth	888	Nineteenth	705
Ninth	619	Twentieth	500
Tenth	35		
Eleventh	295	Total	9365

BALTIMORE, Nov. 9.—The city complete, except one precinct, gives 12,000 Union majority, a gain of 4300 over the October election. The State has undoubtedly gone for the Union ticket on the home vote by a considerable majority, and the election of SWAN, for Governor, and five majority for the Union Legislative ticket.

The Fifth Maryland Brigade is reported as giving 1100 majority for the Union ticket.

Colonel PHELPS is, of course elected, in the Third Congressional District.

KENTUCKY.

Lexington, Ky., gives 612 Union majority; Falmouth, 69 Union majority; Covington, 601 Union majority; Paris, 68 Democratic majority; Cynthia, 126 Democratic majority.

Lexington, 612 Union majority; Covington, 601 Union majority; Paris, 63 Democratic majority; Cynthia, 601 majority.

LOUISVILLE, Nov. 8.—Partial returns from 28 counties in Kentucky, excluding Jefferson, give Lincoln, 250 majority.

Louisville city—McClellan, 4873, Lincoln, 1849.

The returns are meagre, but indicate the success of the Democrats.

MISSOURI.

ST. LOUIS, Nov. 8.—The returns are meagre. The Republicans estimate Lincoln's majority in this county between 4000 and 5000 on the home vote, and the Democrats give him from 1500 to 2000.

John Hogden, Democrat, is elected to Congress the Twelfth District over Knox.

H. T. Blow is elected to Congress in the Second District.

Lincoln will undoubtedly carry the State, and the election of the Radical State ticket is regarded certain.

DELAWARE.

WILMINGTON, Nov. 8.—This city gives about 800 Union majority, a Union gain of 500 over the little election in October.

New Castle County.

WILMINGTON, Nov. 8.—Brandywine Hundred. Union majority 54; Red Lion Hundred 24; Mill Creek Hundred, 62; a Union gain.

Pencader Hundred, Democratic majority 19; New Castle Hundred, Democratic majority 101. Both these latter are Union gains.

ILLINOIS.

CHICAGO, Nov. 9.—Nine Wards in Chicago give 2565 Republican majority; six Wards to hear from.

CHICAGO, Nov. 9.—Cook county gives about 4000 Union majority. The wires are working badly, and the returns come in slowly. Those received so far show gains over LINCOLN's majority in 1860, leading the Republicans to claim a majority of 30.000.

CHICAGO, Nov. 8.—Eleven Wards of this city give LINCOLN 2577 majority. The other Wards reduce this majority to 1600.

CHICAGO, Nov. 8, midnight.—Communication with Iowa is interrupted by a storm, but the leading Republicans and Democrats admit that it has gone for Lincoln by 25,000 majority.

CHICAGO, Nov 8.—Complete returns from this city show 1746 majority for Lincoln.

A Republican Senator and Union members to the Assembly have been elected.

MICHIGAN.

DETROIT, Nov. 8, 10 P. M.—The Republicans claim to have carried the State by 15,000 majority. The returns are meagre.

Detroit city gives about 1000 Democratic majority.

Adrian, 65 Republican majority.

WEST VIRGINIA.

WHEELING, Va., Nov. 8.—Returns from nine counties show large Union gains. It is believed Lincoln will carry the State by large majorities in every county.

NEW YORK.

THE NEW YORK PRESS ON THE RESULT.

Kentucky the Only State for McClellan.

NEW YORK, Nov. 8.—Midnight.—Returns from Brooklyn show the following vote:—LINCOLN 18,191; MCCLELLAN 23,515.

Returns from sixty-five towns and two counties give LINCOLN 10 611 majority.

Ninety towns give MCCLELLAN 4734 majority. All these are outside of New York and Brooklyn.

The *World* claims New York, State for MCCLELLAN by 10,000 to 20,000 majority. The *Times* claims to have carried the State by a Republican majority of 10,000. It also says that the returns indicate that the Republicans have carried New Jersey; have certainly carried Maryland, Delaware, Pennsylvania, Maine, Indiana, Vermont, Massachusetts, and it is not probable MCCLELLAN has carried any State but Kentucky.

NEW YORK, Nov. 9.—The *Tribune* claims from 5000 to 10,000 Union majority in this State. It also says that New Jersey has probably given a small Democratic majority, and that Pennsylvania has given at least 10,000 for Lincoln on the home vote.

The *Tribune* gives LINCOLN 3000 majority in Connecticut and 5000 in Maryland.

NEW YORK, Nov. 8.—The total vote of the city shows the following:—

For LINCOLN....................36,442
For MCCLELLAN..................73,329

Democratic majority............36,887

One Ward, the Fifteenth, gave LINCOLN a majority of 274.

The total majority for MCCLELLAN in the city is 36 618.

NEW YORK, Nov. 9—2 A. M.—Morgan Jones (Democrat), is elected to Congress in the Fourth District; Nelson Taylor (Democrat), in the Eighth District; Henry J. Raymond (Union), in the Sixth District; John W. Chambers (Democrat), in the Seventh District; William E. Dodge (Union), probably in the Eighth District; and William A. Darling (Union), in the Ninth District.

The *Herald* reports that the indications are that New York has gone for Lincoln by from 10,000 to 15,000.

NEW YORK, Nov. 8.—It is reported that Humphrey, Republican, is elected to Congress from Brooklyn, and also that H. J. Raymond is elected to Congress, and that Fernando Wood has been defeated for Congress by Darling, Republican. Roscoe Conkling is elected to Congress over Kernan. This city gives Seymour, for Governor, 73,727, and Fenton 36.122. In eighty-three towns and cities, including Albany, Buffalo, Troy and Utica, and also three counties, McClellan has 16,094 majority.

In nineteen towns that have been heard from so far the aggregate majority for LINCOLN is 2403.

Eight additional towns give MCCLELLAN 1286 majority.

Fifty-five towns outside of New York city show a clear majority for LINCOLN of 5000.

Kings county, complete, McClellan 5424 majority.
Rochester City, 63 Dem. maj.
Riga 47 Union maj.
Brighton, 41 Union maj.
Henrietta (First District), 90 Union maj.
Wheatland, 109 Union maj.
Brooklyn (seven Wards) 3876 Dem. maj.
Brooklyn (two wards) 752 Union maj
Plattsburgh, 89 Dem. maj.
Malon, 523 Union maj.
Canton, 268 Union maj.
Bockman, 48 Union maj.
Dannemora, 28 Union maj.
Chateaugay, 76 Dem. maj.
Potsdam, 786 Union maj.
Laurence, 364 Union maj.
Oswegatchie, 275 Union majority.
Madrid, 267 Union maj. Union gain of 700.)
Constable, 62 Union maj.
Genesee county, complete, 1388 Republican maj.
Columbia county, Hudson City, 220 Dem. maj.
Orleans county, 1400 Repub. maj.
Greenport, 41 Repub. maj.
Stockport, 60 Repub. maj.
Utica, county, 1800 Repub. maj.
Utica city, 259 Repub. maj.
Poughkeepsie, 286 Repub. maj.
Buffalo, 500 Dem. maj.
Howelsville, 66 Dem. maj
Dunkirk, 61 Repub. maj.

INDIANA.

INDIANAPOLIS, Nov. 8.—Election returns from all parts heard from show large gains over the October election.

LINCOLN'S majority will be 30,000 to 35 000. The vote of the Ohio soldiers here is Union, 202, MCCLELLAN 18.

The Union majority is not less than 30,000.

SPECIAL DESPATCH TO THE INQUIRER.

The State Gives 30,000 Majority for Lincoln.

INDIANAPOLIS, Nov. 8.—The State returns indicate over thirty thousand Union majority for Lincoln and Johnson.

MINNESOTA.

ST. PAUL, Nov. 8.—This city gives 36 majority for McClellan. There is no telegraphic communication with the interior of the State, but leading Republicans claim a majority of 5000.

[SPECIAL TO THE INQUIRER.]

THE SOLDIERS' VOTE.

Vote of Pennsylvania Soldiers at Washington.

Executive Mansion (Bucktails)—Lincoln 67, McClellan 1; Finley—Lincoln 11, McClellan 1; East Capitol Barracks—Lincoln 37, McClellan 18; Armory Square—Lincoln 30, McClellan 5; Camp Fry—Lincoln 225, McClellan 25; Cavalry Bureau—Lincoln 81, McClellan 21; Harwood Hospital, Lincoln 54, McClellan 7; Lincoln Hospital — Lincoln 160, McClellan 44; Soldiers' Rest—Lincoln 19, McClellan, 7; Washington Street Tent—Lincoln, 230, McClellan, 109; Prince Street Barracks—Lincoln, 107 McClellan, 25; Sickels Barracks—Lincoln, 19 McClellan, 3; Carver Hospital—Lincoln, 67. McClellan, 30; Battery I, Fort Worth—Lincoln, 63, McClellan, 28; Camp Stoneman—Lincoln, 127, McClellan, 74; Battery H, (NEVINS)—Lincoln, 130, McClellan, 50; Battery C, Camp Barry—Lincoln, 74, McClellan, 71; Marine Barracks—Lincoln, 35, McClellan, 19; Fort Marcy—Lincoln, 65, McClellan, 30; Camp Distribution—Lincoln, 193, McClellan, 115. Ten (10) more polls to hear from.

Camp Curtin, at Harrisburg.

Soldiers' vote in Camp Curtin:—

For Abraham Lincoln, 93 votes; George B. McClellan, 20 votes.

[DESPATCHES TO THE ASSOCIATED PRESS.

The Soldiers' Vote.

WASHINGTON, Nov. 8.—The vote taken in Alexandria and Washington at the different barracks and city hospitals shows in part:—

	Union.	Dem.
Ohio	491	[illegible]
Iowa	74	[illegible]
Wisconsin	639	1[illegible]
Maine	406	78
Pennsylvania	1988	80[illegible]

A despatch from Alexandria states that the aggregate vote of all the soldiers there is as follows:—Union, 547; Democratic, 108.

The Soldiers' Vote.

BALTIMORE, Nov. 8.—The Pennsylvania soldiers in Jarvis' Hospital, in this city, voted to-day as follows:—Lincoln, 50; McClellan, 7.

CAMP CURTIN, HARRISBURG, Nov. 8.—The soldier's vote is Lincoln, 98, McClellan, 20. Union majority, 78.

Government Loans.

WASHINGTON, November 8, 1864.

The statement that a loan of sixty or one hundred millions of gold-bearing bonds is about to be offered is without foundation.

It is understood that a loan, receivable partly in certificates of a 7 3-10ths currency interest, is under consideration, which is the only loan thought of at present.

The Daily Picayune.

VOLUME XXVIII. NEW ORLEANS, FRIDAY MORNING, NOVEMBER 18, 1864. NUMBER 218.

The Daily Picayune.

THE CITY.

PROCEEDINGS OF THE LEGISLATURE.

Thursday, November 17, 1864.

THE SENATE.

The Senate met at 12 o'clock. C. W. Boyce in the chair. At roll call nineteen members present.

Prayer by the Rev. Mr. Gilbert.

Minutes of yesterday read and approved.

The Committee on Federal Relations reported a bill instructing the delegation to Congress to use their influence to have post offices established in all places within the Federal lines where it may be deemed prudent.

The Committee on Parochial Affairs reported an amendment to the bill prohibiting the city corporation from having public works done by contract, to the effect that said amendment shall not be enforced when the interests of the city would suffer. Said report accepted.

Father Murphy, of the Baronne street Church, was, according to Archbishop Odin's autograph letter, to open proceedings of the Senate with prayer on Fridays.

Mr. Hills offered a bill authorizing the laying of thirty inch pipes along the Levee in part of the First and Second Districts, for the purpose of providing water sufficient for the extinguishment of fires. The expense was estimated at $20,000, to be raised by taxing the property benefited.

Mr. Nicholas offered a bill to render valid marriages between aunt and nephew, and uncle and niece.

As some error had occurred in the election of R. K. Cutler, to the Senate, Mr. Montamat offered a joint resolution that the Governor be authorized to issue proper credentials to said persons elected.

The Senate agreed to pay Messrs. Hills and Delage their per diem from the commencement of the session.

Several bills previously referred to passed to their third reading. After which the Senate adjourned till to-morrow at 12 o'clock.

THE HOUSE.

The House was called to order at 12 o'clock M. Hon. S. Belden in the chair.

Prayer was delivered by Rev. Dr. Newman.

Sixty members present, and quorum for business. Minutes read, amended and adopted.

J. C. Michel, Chairman of the Committee on Claims, reported that the committee had dispensed with the committee clerk, having no occasion for his services. Report adopted.

Mr. Prescott, of the Committee on Public Education, reported that a bill will be submitted to the House providing for all demands claimed in the report of the Board of Directors of Public Schools for the education of colored children. Report adopted.

Mr. Christie, of the Committee on Banks and Banking, asks for certain books and papers. Report adopted, and the Sergeant-at-Arms instructed to furnish the necessary books and papers.

The following notices of bills were given by several members:

A joint resolution to instruct the Auditor of Public Accounts not to pay any bills on account of printing and publishing the works of the late convention until otherwise directed by the General Assembly. Passed its first reading, and was referred to the Committee on Printing.

An act from the Senate relative to the adoption of children was read and referred to the Judiciary Committee.

A bill relative to the organization of six district courts in the parish of Orleans passed its first reading and was referred to the Judiciary Committee.

An act relative to public lands was adopted on its first reading.

An act relative to harbor masters of the port of New Orleans was withdrawn for an amendment.

An act to abolish the office of Superintendent of Public Education was read the first time. Debate.

Mr. Hannon was permitted to withdraw the act for amendment.

The title of the "Lien Law Bill" was adopted; also the title of the bill relative to Justices of the Peace in the parish of Orleans.

An act from the Senate for the relief of the Deaf, Dumb and Blind Asylum in Baton Rouge, adopted on its first reading.

The Senate notifies its concurrence and amendment of an act relative to to Federal Relations (Mr. Meeks's) Accepted.

The joint resolution from the Senate, relative to the elected United States Senators, Chas. Smith and R. K. Cutler, asking the Governor to furnish the credentials to these Senators, after the suspension of the rules, passed its third reading and was adopted with the title.

An act to authorize the city corporation of New Orleans to build a bridge over the Carondelet Canal at the foot of Galvez street was read the second time. Debate.

Adopted this second reading and ordered to be engrossed.

A bill entitled "An act to authorize the city corporation of New Orleans to build a bridge across the New Basin Canal, on Liberty street." Adopted on its second reading and ordered to be engrossed.

An act for the relief of the parish of East Baton Rouge adopted with an amendment.

The House adjourned till to-morrow at 12 o'clock M.

FIRST DISTRICT COURT.—The case of Paul Decores and Charles Leomons having been set for trial, was proceeded with; though the principal witness relied on by the two young men, who were about 18 years old, had not appeared—not having been subpœnaed, according to the declaration of the prisoners; but according to the records of the court, at the place indicated, no such person could be found. They were arraigned on a charge of larceny, of $190, in current money of the United States, from Mr. Lee, on the 15th October last. In Recorder Vennard's court, before whom the case had been examined, the two prisoners confessed the charge and pleaded guilty. One of the prisoners had a confident air, and conducted his own case; the other, who was charged as the recipient of $30 of the sum, knowing it to be stolen, had a less serene countenance. The clothes which they had bought with a part of the money were in court. A part of the confession seemed to be that the money belonged to the sister of one of the prisoners. The verdict of the jury was "Guilty."

The case of the State against Jacob Smith, charged with the larceny, on the 22d day of September, 1864, of eight sacks of cotton, property of A. McDonald, who stated he was the owner of a barge on which the cotton was, and that he found his cotton on a Government barge lying near. The larceny was committed at 11 o'clock at night, while McDonald was asleep. Smith was near McDonald's barge that night, and had asked leave to go on board, and was afterwards found on the Government barge near the cotton. Each bag of cotton was worth about $30. Smith, by his own statement, was a special officer of the police. The officer in charge of the Government barge then stated that he assisted Smith in removing the cotton, and that Smith stated to him he was a special officer and had a right to remove it. Smith did not actually convey the cotton himself, but induced the officer in charge of the Government barge to do it. By the testimony of a lieutenant of police it appeared that Smith, on the night the cotton was stolen, had asked leave of absence, stating his family was sick. Verdict of jury, "Not guilty."

In the case of the State against colored Rose and Lizzie, both had pleaded not guilty, but by suggestion of counsel, colored Rose withdrew her plea of not guilty and pleaded guilty, the object appearing to be to make her a witness in favor of the other. They were charged with stealing a pair of sleeve buttons and one gold locket, property of Alexander Leon. The two girls were in the employ of Mr. Leon, and the articles were stolen about the 2d of October. They were employed as nurse and washerwoman. Rose testified that Lizzie did not take the things and knew nothing about the larceny. The jury decided that the parties were guilty of the larceny.

Robinson Rome, a man of color, was arraigned on the charge of assault and battery, committed on the 25th of January, 1864, on John Sullivan, a white man of advanced age, who at the time was engaged in driving a cart on Tchoupitoulas street. Both were going the same way and the street was blocked, so the accuser told Rowe to "hold on" for five minutes, but the colored man cracked his whip, drove on his team, the wheel of which struck the accuser, knocked him down, inflicting a severe wound on his head, of which he lay four months in the Charity Hospital, his life being most of the time in great danger. Verdict: "Guilty."

From the vigor and energy which our Recorders and Judges are now acting, it may be supposed the Workhouse and Parish Prison must soon teem with a large population. The number of cases of colored persons is very large in proportion to the population. It is probable the population of New Orleans is about 150,000 at the present time, of which number about 15,000 or one-tenth are blacks. Yet it is probable that more than one half of the violators of law and order adjudicated on by our Recorders originate among this species of human beings. It is hoped the efforts that are now being made to enlighten their intellects will have some effect also on their morals and manners.

PROVOST COURT.—In the Provost Court today Mr. Samuel Warner, who had been intrusted with the care of a dwelling-house and furniture, No. 63 Customhouse street, was charged with larceny of several articles, such as a table, chair, &c, belonging to said house, all of which was Government property. The sentence of the court was three months hard labor on Ship Island.

Jas. Whiteside, of the steamer James Battle, was arrested on the charge of having Government property, and also carelessly causing a fire to be made under the boilers of said boat. The case was continued till Saturday next.

The cases of Robert Clark, Wm. Roy and Joshua Ketchum, were also continued.

RECORDER WOOLFLEY'S COURT.—George Kroft, in the Vegetable Market, for disturbing the peace and resisting the officer, was fined $5.

Three colored women, Mary Williams, Elizabeth Steele, and Sarah, for disturbing the peace on Canal street, were fined $2 50 each.

Various other small cases—drinking, quarreling, disturbing the peace—were each fined $5, or dismissed, or continued.

RECORDER VENNARD'S COURT.—A negro named George went into a house on Franklin street, and insulted the wife of the owner of the same, whose name is Skillman. Skillman ordered him out of the house; instead of doing which the negro knocked him down. Another man named Kenner, a friend of Skillman, wounded the negro in the shoulder with a razor, inflicting a wound about eight inches long. The parties were sent to the First District Court to be tried.

A man named Andrew Robinson was found at 8 P. M. on Carondelet street, with a pan of fresh meat, of which he could not give a satisfactory account. On suspicion of larceny he was sent to the Workhouse for ten days.

E. Martin was exquisitely drunk, and in that condition entered a City Railroad car, making a disturbance there and refusing to leave. He was fined $5, which he paid, and departed perhaps a "sadder and wiser man."

Patrick Hoskins became considerably elated. He drove very fast up and down Canal street. A police officer requested him to drive slowly, which Pat was not in a hurry to obey. He was fined $10, which he paid.

Mrs. Roley was charged by John Kelley with railing too much at his wife. John's patience gave way, the treatment being too much for a moderate minded man to bear. $50 bonds to keep the peace and hold her tongue was what she got for her conduct.

Lewis Duval was charged with selling liquor after the proper hours, at the coffee-house corner of Gravier and St. Philip streets. The officer who arrested him could not prove that he received money for it, so the case was dismissed.

There were several drunken cases. Some were fined $5, others discharged.

☞ At 395 Liberty street, the body of Christopher Barkee, aged 43 years, a carpenter, a native of Mississippi, was found. The verdict of the jury of inquest was that the deceased came to his death by accidentally falling from the front gallery of his house to the banquette, thereby injuring his spine.

Victoire Gasang, 33 years of age, born in France, was found dead in his bed, corner of Chippewa and Louisiana streets. He was nearly blind. Verdict of inquest: "Death from disease of the heart."

☞ In Amherst, Massachusetts, they report a wild man of the woods, who amuses himself by setting fire to all the barns he can get at.

There have been several such men in the Shenandoah Valley lately.

LATE SOUTHERN NEWS

Mobile Dates to Tuesday Last.

ATLANTA.

SHERMAN DESTROYING RAILROADS

FEDERALS HUNG BY MOSBY.

FROM THE SHENANDHAH VALLEY

LATE FROM THE NORTH

THE PRESIDENTIAL ELECTION

Lincoln Receives 190 Electoral Votes.

M'CLELLAN RESIGNS HIS COMMISSION IN THE ARMY.

NAVAL ENGAGEMENT.

THE WACHUSETTS CHASED BY BRAZILIAN STEAMERS.

Gold in New York on the 9th, 260.

[From Our Extra of Yesterday.]

We are in possession of Mobile papers of the 10th, 13th and 15th, embracing the latest dates from the most important points in the South. We extract the following dispatches:

AUGUSTA, Nov. 14.—Gov. Brown publishes a letter in the Chronicle in which he states that Baylor, the traitor, was never clothed with any political or diplomatic functions. He had a commercial commission to Europe and was appointed in accordance with a resolution passed by the Legislature. The statement made that he was a member of his staff, the Governor says is false.

AUGUSTA, Nov. 14.—A call for a convention of the dentists of the Confederacy, to meet in this city on Monday, the 28th day of this month, has been issued.

AUGUSTA, Nov. 14.—Ex-Gov. Hammond, of South Carolina, died at his residence at Beach Island, S. C., Sunday, aged fifty-seven.

AUGUSTA, Nov. 14.—The large warehouse of Keningham & Co., Hamburg, C. S., was burned with contents this morning. Fifteen hundred bales of cotton were destroyed; loss over $1,500,000, partly insured. Fire accidental.

A letter to the Chronicle and Sentinel states that a fight occurred at Rough and Ready between the State troops and the Federals. The Federals were driven back.

There are about 9,000 Federals in Atlanta.

From all appearances the place is being evacuated.

The trains running from the city are loaded and return empty.

Five hundred mules were captured by our scouts a few days since.

The Federals have burned most of Canton and Cherokee counties in retaliation for some tories who were hung.

The latest rumors from Atlanta state that the city was evacuated Saturday.

RICHMOND, Nov. 14.—New York papers and the Baltimore American, evening edition of Saturday, are received.

A telegram from Chattanooga, 11th, says that on Wednesday morning the enemy made three attacks on Atlanta. Their shells went as far as the rolling mills.

The most desperate attack was made on the Rough and Ready road, the enemy's artillery being within 100 yards of our works, and their infantry and dismounted cavalry within 200 yards.

Our forces quietly manned the defences and drove the rebels off. We sustained no loss.

The enemy was a part of Young's command, and finally retired toward Macon.

A telegram from Louisville, 10th, says that news has been received from Sherman's army of an important and favorable character, but it is not published, being considered contraband.

Hood's exact whereabouts is unknown to the authorities.

The Federal movement will be developed at the proper time and will electrify the nation.

McClellan has resigned his commission in the army.

Lincoln's majority in Grant's army is reported at 80,000.

The portion of A. J. Smith's command has arrived at Paducah.

The Tribune says Fenton is elected Governor of New York by 9,000 majority.

Gold, 242.

RICHMOND, Nov. 14.—According to the Tribune, New York gives Lincoln 8500, the New England States 150,000, including the soldiers' vote, Pennsylvania 20,000 to 30,000, including soldiers' vote, Maryland 10,000, Ohio 5000, Iowa 50,000, Illinois 25,000, Wisconsin 10,000. No opposition to Lincoln in Western Virginia. Missouri voted for Lincoln.

McClellan's majority in New Jersey is 7000. He carried Delaware and Kentucky.

The Republicans gained largely in the congressional delegations.

In Nashville Lincoln received 2000 and McClellan 27.

Lord Lyons is very ill with typhoid fever at Washington.

RICHMOND, Nov. 14.—Seymour has been re-elected Governor of New York.

It is reported that Lincoln has called for a million of men.

Lincoln received about 190 electoral votes.

RICHMOND, Nov. 14.—An official telegram from the Valley says the army is entrenched between Newton and Kernstown.

Two divisions of cavalry attacked Rosser on the 10th, but were repulsed and driven several miles, losing 200 prisoners, but no horses.

Rosser's command behaved very handsomely, particularly Lomax's brigade, under Col. Hayne, and Wade Hampton's brigade, under Lieut. Col. Morgan.

About the same time another cavalry division attacked McCausland's brigade at Cedar Hill, on the Front Royal Road, and drove them across the river.

RICHMOND, Nov. 14.—The Senate has passed a bill which authorizes the exchange of four per cent. coupon bonds for seven thirty treasury notes.

The House was in secret session.

PETERSBURG, Nov. 13.—All quiet along the lines.

The enemy's pickets yesterday were unable to exchange papers. They said the papers of the 10th were taken from them by their officers after distribution. They thought it a strange proceeding, but could not tell the cause. The latest dates here embrace the 9th only.

Three of Hampton's scouts captured twenty-six Yankees two or three nights since near James river, and brought in twenty-three, three escaped.

PETERSBURG, Nov. 13.—The Herald of the 10th is just received.

Lincoln is certainly elected. The vote is close in New York and Pennsylvania, and McClellan carries New Jersey, Delaware, and Kentucky.

The captain of the Arago, from New Orleans, reports a naval engagement off the coast, on Tuesday, between three Federal war steamers and a rebel vessel, believed to be the Tallahassee. The rebel had long range guns, and was apparently cornered when the Arago left.

Reports from Sheridan's army say that Early is actively preparing for another offensive movement on New Market.

Mosby is still annoying the Federals between Winchester and Martinsburg. He had hung seven Federals in retaliation for a like number of Confederates executed by Custer.

It is reported that Sherman had destroyed the railroad between Chattanooga and Atlanta, burned the latter place, and at the head of four corps was marching on Charleston. The report is not credited in military circles at Washington.

Nothing from Forrest.

The Wachusett was pursued out of the port of Bahia by two Brazilian war steamers, but could not be overtaken.

Gold sold in New York on the 9th at 260, but closed at 257½.

All quiet around Petersburg.

SAVANNAH, Nov. 13.—About 2000 of our prisoners returned last night and to-day, and 1200 will come up to-morrow and next day. The men are looking well for the most part, and in the finest spirits. Many are ready for the front without furlough.

CLINTON, La., Nov. 12.—Two transports loaded with wounded have come down White River and gone to New Orleans. This indicates fighting somewhere in Northern Arkansas.

Eight transports loaded with troops and two Parrott batteries have left Morganza for White River.

The Federals landed at Bayou Sara, a few days ago, and commenced pulling down houses, carrying the material to Morganza to build winter quarters. While there they committed such outrages upon ladies that thirty of them were put in irons, and the officers who permitted it are to be cashiered.

RICHMOND, Nov. 12.—It was reported this morning, on good authority, that the authorities at Washington had issued a proclamation prohibiting the communication of any intelligence to the rebels regarding the election, either by railroad, telegraph, stage coach or otherwise.

The Mobile Tribune of the 15th has the following editorial article:

The news from Hood's army is actually nothing. What papers have struggled through since the mail was cut off have thrown no light on the subject—showing, we imagine, that there is a strict command that secrecy shall be observed, least otherwise, harm might come to the purpose of the movement. We implicitly assent to the wisdom of this. There have been gentlemen from the army as late as last Wednesday; but even they know little, although something, and even that, under what we understand to be the policy, we shall not make public. It is, however, we may observe, not very important.

The people here, as we suppose is the case elsewhere, are in great anxiety in respect of Hoods army; and more especially because, it is "rumored" that Sherman may take up his march in the direction of the Gulf, under the belief that the way would be easy; or that he may endeavor—supposing the path is open to him—to move towards Augusta and Savannah, and finally, accomplish the capture of all places in his route, and also Charleston. Either of these marches, if successful, would be of great detriment to the Confederacy; but we know that they cannot be easily made. We know also that, they were taken into consideration in laying out the campaign of Hood's army, and also that means have been provided to make the road of the Federal General, if he should choose either of these routes, through a devastated country, wherein not a blade of grass or an ounce of food for man or beast could be discovered. Sherman, we have no doubt, is the ablest general in the service of the enemy; and able as much by his prudence as his coolness and tenacity of purpose. He has won Yankee laurels both by his skill as an officer and his heartlessness and unscrupulousness as a man. He may, therefore, not hazard this gain by the risk, and more especially if he be, what we suppose he is, a prudent man.

It requires, however, some knowledge to judge of the business; and that we have not. We imagine that not a dozen men know what Hood's purpose is, and so we must wait for such developments as cannot be long kept in secrecy. We may observe, that we do believe that Sherman has not done what Hood anticipated as the necessary result of his movement, and thus new combinations for new purposes may have to be formed. In the meantime, while the *denouement* is not before us, let us be hopeful that we shall presently hear good news.

☞ Knowledge is treasure, but judgment is the treasury. Form is good, but not formality. Be cautious in giving advice, and consider before you adopt advice. A mule laden with salt, and an ass laden with wool, went over a brook together. By chance the mule's pack became wetted, the salt melted, and his burden became lighter. After they had passed the mule told his good fortune to the ass, who, thinking to speed as well, wetted his pack at the next water! but his load became the heavier, and he broke down under it. Pause, therefore, before you follow the example: that which helps one man may hinder another.

☞ A few weeks ago, Sarah Wise, aged about 23, left Portland, Me., for Lawrence, in search of employment. After remaining there a day, and not finding any, she wrote to her friends that she was going to Lowell, and would inform them of her success. Not hearing anything from her for about three weeks, and becoming alarmed for her safety, her brother went to Lowell in search of her. He obtained trace of a body of a woman, which was found in the waters of the Lawrence, with her throat cut from ear to ear, and identified it as that of his sister, but all trace of the murderer has been lost.

The Queen Consulting the Spirits.—A London letter says:

I hear from a reliable source that Queen Victoria has been to see the Davenport Brothers, and has appointed a trial of their spiritual, dark lantern jugglery game at Windsor Castle. She has gone quite daft with spiritualism, and these impostors have promised to bring back Prince Albert to this world for an hour, in the very room where he died. They have promised, moreover, I am told, to not only allow the Queen to have a conversation with him, but to actually touch him. As their performances are conducted in the dark, they will no doubt succeed in carrying out the delusion. Pray, what are the guardians of the poor Queen about to permit such a criminal imposture to be practised on one who is already far on the road to lunacy? Such an arrant imposture is a melancholy exhibition of human weakness and folly.

The New-York Times.

VOL. XIV.—NO. 4116. NEW-YORK, FRIDAY, DECEMBER 2, 1864. PRICE FOUR CENTS.

TENNESSEE.

A Severe Battle at Franklin, Tenn.

HOOD DEFEATED BY THOMAS.

The Rebels Desperately Assault Our Works.

They are Repulsed with Fearful Carnage.

Six Thousand Rebels Killed and Wounded.

TWELVE HUNDRED PRISONERS CAPTURED

Our Loss Less than One Thousand.

MAGNIFICENT BEHAVIOR OF OUR TROOPS

Full and Graphic Account from Our Special Correspondent.

OFFICIAL ANNOUNCEMENT.

WASHINGTON, Thursday, Dec. 1.

The following official dispatch concerning the report of the victory in Tennessee, has been received at headquarters:

FRANKLIN, Tenn., Wednesday, Nov. 30.
FRANKLIN, Tenn., Wednesday, Nov. 30.

Major-Gen. Thomas:

The enemy made a heavy and persistent attack with two corps, commencing at 4 P. M., and lasting till after dark. He was repulsed at all points, with heavy loss—probably of five or six thousand men. Our loss is probably not more than one-fourth of that number. We have captured about one thousand prisoners, including one Brigadier-General.

(Signed,) JOHN SCHOFIELD, Major-General.

OUR SPECIAL ACCOUNT.

Special Dispatch to the New-York Times.

FOUR MILES SOUTH OF NASHVILLE, Thursday, Dec. 1.

Gen. SCHOFIELD yesterday fought one of the *prettiest* fights of the war, resulting most disastrously to the rebels, with little loss to ourselves. After three days' skirmishing, the rebels crowded our first line of works yesterday afternoon, and at 4 P. M. made a most desperate attack on our right and centre, forcing our lines to our breastworks, which were thrown up from river to river in an open field on the Cumberland Pike, which ran through the centre of the field.

At least half the rebel force engaged endeavored to pierce our centre, and come down viciously on WAGNER's Division, which, after desperate fighting, fell back, and MANY's rebel division, of FRANK CHEATHAM's corps, got inside our works and captured two guns. Our centre was not broken, however, and, better still, Gen. WAGNER successfully rallied his troops, who charged on the enemy, recaptured the two guns, and *drove the division over the breastworks, capturing one entire brigade and its commander.*

At 4:30 o'clock the battle was waged with unabating vigor, the enemy having made during a half hour several attempts to break our centre.

The Federal position was a magnificent one, and the result of these four days' work were magnificently grand.

All this while the rebels had appeared in front of our right. The plan was to pierce our centre and crush our right wing before dark. A portion of our infantry were engaged three-quarters of an hour firing on the rebel columns who stood their ground like madmen. During every charge made on our right and centre, volleys of grape and canister were hurled into their lines, and only darkness prevented their sacrifice being more awful. It is said that no canister shot was used by the rebels during the day, but fired shot and shell.

After the first break of WAGNER's division and its recovery, our line never budged a step. All was quiet after 10 P. M. It was not only one of the *prettiest* but *cleanest* battles of the war. The excessive slaughter of the enemy was owing to our wholesale use of canister and grape, and our selection of the ground. The battle was fought in an open field, with no trees or undergrowth, or other interruption. The enemy's loss in killed and wounded approximates 7,000, and we have over 1,200 prisoners, and one general officer and several field officers. The Colonel of the Fifteenth Mississippi, a Northern man, of Illinois, was wounded and taken prisoner. Four-fifths of his regiment were killed, wounded and captured. Our loss does not reach a thousand, *hors du combat.* Gen. BRADLEY, of Illinois, while gallantly leading his troops, was severely wounded in the shoulder. Our loss in field officers is very small. Our troops behaved handsomely. SCHOFIELD commanded on the field, STANLEY on the right, and COX on the left. Gen. STANLEY was wounded slightly in the neck, but remained on the field and is all right to-day.

I have told you all along the programme of Gen. THOMAS would electrify you, and this is but the epilogue of the battle to come off.

After our dead, wounded and prisoners were cared for, our army fell back to this point, and are in line of battle while I write. Up to this time, 3 P. M., the enemy has not made his appearance. The Third Corps of Veterans are in readiness, and a battle is expected before daylight to-morrow. All Government work is suspended, and all are under arms, from Gen. DONALDSON down to the unscientific laborers.

The falling back of our troops was accomplished at 5 o'clock this morning, and bridges burned across Harpeth River to retard the transportation of rebel supplies. The cavalry was handled prettily by Gen. WILSON, between Spring Hill and Triune.

A. J. SMITH's corps is in line of battle, and the situation is particularly grand. Forts Negley, Morton, Cairo and Houston are alive, and the infantry movements perfectly satisfactory. Something must immediately transpire, as Gen. THOMAS is ready to strike no matter how the rebels move.

BENJ. C. TRUMAN.

ANOTHER ACCOUNT.

NASHVILLE, Tenn., Thursday, Dec. 1—9:30 P. M.

About noon on Wednesday our main army reached Franklin, when Gen. SCHOFIELD prepared to give the enemy battle. There was very little skirmishing, as HOOD's object was to attack us before we had time to throw up defensive works.

About 4 o'clock the enemy commenced advancing on our lines, when the ball was opened by our batteries shelling their advance, and soon after a regular cannonading opened along the whole line. The rebels, who had been protected by woods, now emerged from cover, and opened with a fierce volley of musketry along the lines and then charged. For a moment part of our line wavered, and fell back before the desperate charge of the enemy. Gens. RUGER and COX, however, rallied their men and charged the enemy, who had crossed over our abandoned line of works.

The rebels were now fighting with the desperation of demons, charging our lines furiously, some leaping our works and fighting hard.

Now was the critical moment, but our Generals, rallying their troops, swung on the rebel flank, doubling them in the centre, where our artillery and musketry mowed them down by hundreds.

The tide was now turned. Our men, inspired with success, gave a wild huzza and swept back on the rebel line like an avalanche, hurling the enemy back in the wildest disorder and confusion.

Night was now setting in, yet we followed up our advantage. What once threatened to be a disastrous defeat was thus turned into a glorious victory. The courage of our officers and the desperate bravery of our men was unexampled.

Our loss is about seven hundred killed and wounded. We captured over one thousand prisoners and eight battle-flags. Two rebel Brigadier-Generals are in our hands. A rebel Division-General was left on the field mortally wounded. The rebel loss in killed and wounded is estimated at three thousand.

The rebel Gens. CHEATHAM and LEE's corps were engaged. The brunt of the battle on our side fell on the Second Division of the Fourth Corps.

Capt. COUGHLIN, of Gen. COX's staff, was killed, and several regimental commanders and officers were killed and wounded, whose names have not been ascertained. Gen. STANLEY was slightly wounded in the neck, but did not leave the field.

Gen. COX states that one could walk fifty yards on dead rebels in his front.

The excitement is allayed here by the knowledge of the above facts.

Our troops have taken position in a line of works between Nashville and Franklin.

Further Details.

NASHVILLE, Tenn., Thursday, Dec. 1.

The Federal forces under Gen. THOMAS retired from Franklin last night, and have taken position and formed in line of battle south of Nashville about three miles. Skirmishing has been going on all day about five miles south of here. Heavy cannonading can be distinctly heard in the city. No want of confidence is felt by the citizens in ultimate success by the *Federals.* The employes of the Quarter-Master's Department are under arms and in the trenches.

One hundred and seven Confederate officers, including one Brigadier-General and one thousand prisoners, arrived in the city this morning. They were captured in the fight last night near Franklin. A great battle may momentarily be expected.

A Most Desperate Attack by the Rebels—The Rebels Charge Our Masked Batteries—Terrible Loss of the Enemy—Forrest Reported Killed—Reinforcements for Schofield.

NASHVILLE, Thursday, Dec. 1.

Parties who have arrived from the front, and who witnessed the battle of yesterday, describe the attack of the rebel forces as desperate. Four charges were made upon the Federal masked batteries in columns four lines deep. Each time the rebels were repulsed with fearful loss.

The fort is on the north bank of the river, opposite the town, extending up the river, and encircling the town was the line of masked batteries. Eye-witnesses say that this engagement, in desperation and furious fighting, was hardly equaled by the battle of Stone River.

FORREST in person was on the field rallying his men. A rumor is in circulation that he was killed, but it lacks confirmation.

About 7 o'clock last night heavy reinforcements reached SCHOFIELD, which caused a complete rout of the rebel forces.

The city to-day is full of fleeing residents of Williamson and other counties south. They state HOOD is gathering up all the horses, hogs and mules that he can find, and sending them south.

There is great panic among the negroes in the counties south of Nashville. Numbers are fleeing to the city for protection.

THE VERY LATEST.

NASHVILLE, Thursday, Dec. 1.

HOOD's Infantry force crossed the Harpeth River this morning, and he has not advanced that portion of his force since. His cavalry crossed Harpeth River on the fords above Franklin this morning at daybreak, closely following Gen. WILSON, who retired in this direction. Skirmishing with the advance has occurred all day. Gen. WILSON occupies a strong position a few miles south of Nashville, and is able to resist any force the rebels may bring against him.

The rebel General captured yesterday was Col. GORDON, of the Eleventh Tennessee, brevet Brigadier-General.

An officer who witnessed the fight yesterday, describes the battle as one of the most sanguinary of the war. The determined bravery of the rebels exceeded anything before seen. Although slaughtered by hundreds, they still advanced against our batteries. Within five hours, eleven distinct attacks were made against our works, each a failure.

The battle being ended our forces quietly withdrew from the town.

Among the casualties is Maj.-Gen. Stanley, wounded by a shot in the neck. The rebel Gen. Cheatham is reported wounded. Capt. Bissell, of the Twelfth Indiana, and Capt. Staley, One Hundred and Twenty-fourth Indiana, were killed; Capt. Hinton, One Hundred and Twenty-fourth Indiana, mortally wounded; Col. Lowrey, One Hundred and Seventh Illinois, killed; Capt. Coughlin, of Gen. Cox' Staff, was killed; Capt. Dowling, One Hundred and Eleventh Ohio, was wounded; Col. Walters, Third Brigade, First Division, was wounded in the shoulder; Col. Conrad, who commanded a brigade in the Second Division, was wounded.

The following are rebel casualties: Brig.-Gen. Adams, killed; Brig.-Gen. Scott, wounded. The enemy's total killed, wounded and prisoners are estimated at 4,000, 3,000 being either killed or wounded.

The Federal loss in killed and wounded was 700. The loss in prisoners is trifling.

Gen. BRADLEY is wounded and in the city.

COL. STOCKTON and Major JAMES, of the Seventy-second Illinois, are also wounded.

It is rumored this evening that HOOD is moving eastward, toward Murfreesboro'.

PRELIMINARY DETAILS.

Dispatches to the Associated Press.

NASHVILLE, Tenn., Wednesday, Nov. 30.

Army movements for the last few days have been simply for position.

The National forces have not retreated except to improve the location, and occupy Franklin to-day; but they will probably select for the battle-field a place much nearer Nashville.

Some skirmishing has occurred, with little or no advantage to either side.

The probabilities are that a great battle will be fought within the next forty-eight hours.

Our forces are in eager and anxious expectation for the fray, while our Generals are hopeful and confident of victory.

Large accessions of Federal troops have reached here, who have been sent to advantageous positions.

Small detachments of rebel cavalry are operating not far from Nashville, doing, however, no real damage to the rail communications, which still remain intact, trains running regularly.

There is much excitement among the citizens of Nashville on account of the near approach of HOOD's army.

Maj.-Gen. A. J. SMITH's corps reached here to-night.

Hood's Advance at Spring Hill, Tenn., Thirty-two Miles South of Nashville.

NASHVILLE, Wednesday, Nov. 30—Midnight. RECEIVED Dec. 1—9 A. M.

Heavy skirmishing for the past few days, and still going on between our troops and FORREST.

There was a sharp fight yesterday at Spring Hill, twelve miles south of Franklin. Our cavalry was driven back on our infantry lines which checked the enemy. A squad of rebel prisoners were in charge of these troops, when the rebel cavalry made a dash on them, releasing their men and capturing ours.

A train was attacked near Harpeth River. The engineer detached the locomotive, and both are supposed to be captured. The rest of the train was saved.

A squad of rebel cavalry dashed across the Chattanooga line yesterday, near Cheshire, tearing up the track.

The train was detained all night, but came in next morning.

Our troops have fallen back around Franklin.

The main part of HOOD's army is across Duck River.

Every indication of a heavy battle in a few days, but we are confident of the result.

Franklin.

Franklin, the scene of the great victory over HOOD on Thursday, is the capital of Williamson County, Tenn., and is situated on the south bank of Big Harpeth River, about 18 miles from Nashville, on the line of the Nashville and Decatur Railroad. Before the war it was a beautiful village, with a population of about 2,000 people. Franklin has changed hands several times during the war. After VAN DORN's success in capturing a Union brigade at Spring Hill, near Franklin, in March, 1863, that rebel Commander moved upon the latter place, which he attacked on the 10th of April. Major-Gen. GORDON GRANGER was in command of the village. His forces comprised two infantry divisions of 1,600 men, 2,000 cavalry under SMITH and STANLEY, and eighteen guns. The only artificial defence was an uncompleted fort, which mounted two siege guns and two three-inch rifled guns. VAN DORN's force was estimated at nine thousand infantry and two regiments of cavalry. The rebels were handsomely repulsed, losing three hundred, while GRANGER's total loss was only thirty-seven.

The town proper is built upon an open, level spot; but circling round to the west and south of it are the Harpeth Hills. Big Harpeth River has its source in Bedford County, and flows northwest through Williamson, past the town of Franklin, enters Davidson County, and falls into the Cumberland River thirty-five miles below this city, after a general comparative course of sixty miles.

Rebel Speculations.

From the Richmond Whig, Nov. 29.

The care which the Yankee newspapers take to represent the movement of HOOD as ineffectual and despicable; the ridicule which they cast upon his present position; their constant declaration that THOMAS is more than a match for him, and that he has entirely failed, prove beyond a doubt that he has not failed. He has succeeded in placing SHERMAN in a most embarrassing situation, from which he could only escape by a desperate plunge, which he has taken, and the effect of which we shall very shortly witness.

The *Whig* of the 29th says Gen. RIPLEY has been placed in command of South Carolina.

FROM NEW-ORLEANS.

An Important Success by Gen. Lee—A Raid Through Mississippi—Capture of Three Guns and a number of Prisoners.

The steamer *Matanzas*, from New-Orleans, Nov. 23 has arrived at this port. She brings the following news:

RAID IN MISSISSIPPI.

The *True Delta*, of Nov. 21, publishes the following:

SIX MILES EAST OF PORT HUDSON, Nov. 21.

Brig.-Gen. Burton:

I am en route home, and shall arrive to-night; have captured 200 prisoners, including 25 commissioned officers. We had a strong fight at Liberty, Miss., in which we whipped the enemy badly. We captured one piece of artillery, and two at Brookhaven, one of them is a siege gun formerly captured at Port Hudson. I have all of Gen. HODGES staff from 600 to 800 head of horses and mules, rode by negroes; and destroyed immense stores on the railroad.

(Signed) A. L. LEE, Brig.-Gen.

The above is a copy of a dispatch received by Brig.-Gen. BURTON.

Brig.-Gen. LEE with his whole command, prisoners and captures, as previously reported, has just arrived in Baton Rouge.

IMPORTANT CAPTURE.

LARGE HAUL OF MONEY, ETC.

From the Era, Nov. 20.

The steamer *Grey Eagle* arrived here this morning, having on board Capt. NED MONTGOMERY and twenty-six other rebel prisoners, captured at Choctaw Bend on Wednesday last. The party at the time of the capture were on their way to Texas, where Capt. MONTGOMERY is said to have purchased a rancho, on which he intended to reside for the balance of his days.

On MONTGOMERY was found $250,000 in foreign Exchange, and a quantity of money besides, and all the party were mounted on fine blooded horses.

Capt. MONTGOMERY is well-known here, having been in charge of the construction of the Confederate fleet at the time FARRAGUT passed the forts. He skedaddled at that time, and we believe has since been engaged in guerrilla business, which seems to be profitable, judging from what was found upon him. It is said that he has quit the rebel service, and had determined to become a peaceable citizen, but he may now have cause to change his purpose. "The best laid schemes of mice and men," etc.

THE REBELS DEFEATED AT THIBODAUX.

From the True Delta, Nov. 20.

The talk was current on the streets last evening that an expedition had recently started from Thibodaux, and was successful in defeating a large body of rebels, burning their boats, barracks and baggage. On inquiry, last night, of the proper authority, we found the report to be correct, and that the expedition was under command of Major MILLER. No further particulars had been received by us up to the hour of going to press.

ARRIVAL OF THE MANHATTAN.

From the Era, Nov. 23.

The ocean iron-clad steamer *Manhattan* arrived here on Sunday last from Mobile Bay. She is the first of the monitor class of boats that has made so long a voyage as from New-York to these waters. The *Manhattan* bore a conspicuous part in the great naval and land fight in Mobile Bay last Summer, and still bears the marks of that fearful contest. The following is the list of her officers:

Commander, J. W. A. Nicholson; Acting-Lieut. and Ex. Off., Robert B. Ely; Acting-Ensigns, George B. Mott, J. B. Trott, Chas. H. Sinclair and J. Lewis Harris; Assistant-Paymaster, H. G. Thayer; Surgeon, H. W. Mitchell; Chief-Engineer, Charles L. Carty; First Assistant-Engineer, W. H. Miller; Second Assistant-Engineers, James B. Farrand and Thos. Finney; Third Assistant-Engineer, William Stollery; Captain's Clerk, A. W. Maxwell.

TORNADO AT RIO JANEIRO.

Terrible Hail Storm—Great Damage to the City and Shipping—Serious Loss of Life.

By the arrival of the bark *Mirago*, Capt. MERRILL, we have advices from Rio Janeiro to Oct. 13th. The ship *Alexander*, Capt. J. BROWN, arrived the night previous from Cardiff, and while off the port Capt. BROWN was washed overboard by a sea and drowned.

A most violent tornado visited that place on the 10th inst., at 6 P. M., accompanied by tremendous large hail stones and torrents of rain. The city for about one quarter of a mile in width suffered severely, many houses being blown down and others completely riddled by the hail. The tornado lasted about 15 minutes.

The shipping has sustained a great deal of damage.

The bark *Leighton*, Capt. BLATCHFORD, was capsized, and his (the Captain's) son, a lad of 10 years, drowned; his wife was saved almost exhausted. The bark *Lapwing* was considerably damaged about the stern. The Brazilian brig *Manuel* was capsized, also several other foreign vessels capsized and a number of lives lost. A boat from the English line-of-battle ship *Bombay*, while going ashore during the tornado, was upset, and all the crew with several officers, lost.

FROM MEMPHIS.

Rebel Incendiaries Caught Firing Government Buildings.

CAIRO, Thursday, Dec. 1.

Memphis papers of yesterday give detailed accounts of a plot by rebel agents to burn the Memphis and Charleston Railroad Depot and Government stores, worth two millions.

The plot was discovered by the United States Detectives, to whom the matter was intrusted by Gen. WASHBURN, and the incendiaries were caught in the act of firing the buildings.

It is alleged that these emissaries were to receive from the rebel Government ten per cent. of the value of the property thus destroyed.

Dr. MCMILLAN, proprietor of the Charleston House of Memphis, is among those arrested. He is charged with being the agent of the rebel Government and concocting the plot.

The prisoners have been confined in Irving Block. They will be tried by a military commission, and probably hung.

Major-Gen. Banks.

HE IS TO RESUME HIS COMMAND IN NEW-ORLEANS.

WASHINGTON, Thursday, Dec. 1.

The *Daily Chronicle* of this morning, speaking of Major-Gen. BANKS' preparations to shortly leave here for New-Orleans, to resume his position as head of the Department of the Gulf, including Louisiana, Arkansas and Missouri, says:

"His civil policy has met the approval of the President of the United States, and he returns to his post at the request of the Executive, and it is no less pleasant to announce that the friendliest relations exist between Major-Gen. BANKS and Major-Gen. CANBY, in charge of the military operations in the Division of West Mississippi."

From Port Royal.

The steamer *Melville*, from Port Royal Nov. 27, brings the report that on the 26th inst. Gen FOSTER had issued orders for all citizens to be enrolled at that place, and report for duty on the 29th. These were to be formed in companies for home protection. The United States forces there were to move immediately, destination unknown. The *Melville* reports that after leaving port, at about 6 P. M., heard heavy and quick firing at Port Royal, but could not tell its meaning.

The Lake Erie Raid Case.

TORONTO, C. W., Thursday, Dec. 1.

The case of BURLEIGH, one of the Lake Erie raiders, came before the court to-day. Mr. RUSSELL, District Attorney of Detroit, conducted the case. Witnesses identified the prisoner, and testified to the part taken by him in the raid. The case was then adjourned to next week.

Seizure of Ammunition, &c.

COLLINGWOOD, C. W., Thursday, Dec. 1.

The customs authorities yesterday seized some boxes which, on examination, were found to contain a gun-carriage, with canister, grape, shot, etc., for 18-pounder guns. The *Georgian* is expected daily.

The City Railroads.

DRY DOCK, EAST BROADWAY AND BATTERY RAILROAD COMPANY, OFFICE No. 262 ELEVENTH-STREET, Dec. 1, 1864.

To the Editor of the New-York Times:

In reply to that portion of the article in your issue of this morning which refers to this road, I desire to state that the drivers in the employ of this company are instructed to drive on a *slow* trot the whole length of the City Hall Park, and to walk their horses around *all* curves, or when crossing the tracks of other roads. The conductor and driver who were on car No. 30 on Tuesday last have been suspended from duty until the charge made against them can be investigated. I have only to add, that every well founded complaint made to me against any employe of this company will receive immediate attention and prompt redress. Very respectfully, your obedient servant,

WM. RICHARDSON, Superintendent.

New-York Historical Society.

The first of a series of three lectures on Egypt and Egyptian Antiquities, was delivered before this society, last evening, by Prof. JOHN WILLIAM DRAPER, LL. D.

The Professor spoke of the position of Ancient *Egypt* in the family of nations, and what might be learned from their example. He spoke of their antiquities, pyramids, &c., and the peculiar opinions that led to their erection, and more particularly those that induced the people to embalm their dead. He then spoke of the causes which led to the permanence of the Egyptian system, showing that it lasted without material change for about forty centuries. He attributed this durability to the homogeneous character of the people, as arising from the unvariable climate in which they live. He then drew a contrast between that climate and the climate of the United States, showing how the latter produces great differences in the character of man, more especially in those who live in the North, as compared with those who live in the South. He then proposed the inquiry whether it is possible in any manner to compensate for these variations of climate, and to correct the disturbance that perpetually arises through emigration. He showed that, to a great extent, this can be done by public education and intercommunication, and that thus an approach can be made to the condition of things that gave such remarkable permanence to the Egyptian political system.

At the close of the lecture it was announced that Mr. PRIME would give the next lecture, on the Burial-places of Egypt, and that on the following Thursday Dr. ANDERSON would unroll the mummy he had given to the Society.

GEORGIA.

LATER FROM GEN. SHERMAN.

Savannah and Augusta Papers to November 26.

Sherman Still Reported on the Oconee.

A PROBABLE MOVEMENT ON SAVANNAH.

Rebel Troops Concentrating at Augusta.

Bragg Brings Reinforcements from Wilmington.

The Rebels Factories at Augusta Removed,

INTERESTING MISCELLANEOUS INTELLIGENCE.

From Our Special Correspondent.

SAVANNAH RIVER, Georgia, Sunday, Nov. 27, 1864.

We are scarcely less excited here on the question of Gen. SHERMAN's movement than the rebels themselves, and we know that they are stirred as they never have been before at the boldness of his advance. The Savannah journals are not brought to us now until after they are two days old, for fear that we shall be too highly elated at the strait in which the Confederacy finds itself. The last authentic information from the rebels tells us that SHERMAN is advancing in three columns, with a force estimated at 60,000 men, at least one half of whom are cavalry and mounted infantry. The public buildings of Milledgeville, the capital of Georgia, have been burnt, and the Legislature, being in session at the time of SHERMAN's advance force entering the town, adjourned in confusion, some of the members paying as high as *one thousand dollars for transportation a distance of eight miles.* You will be able to form an idea of the reign of terror that now obtains in Georgia and South Carolina, from the files of newspapers which I forward. A levy en masse has been ordered, and BEAUREGARD is in command of the troops. There seems to be most perturbation because SHERMAN has shrouded his objective point in mystery, by sending out immense bands of mounted men to ravage the country on the flanks of his main columns. On Monday last he was at Gordon, with artillery, about fifteen miles from Milledgeville, and had fortified the Georgia Central Railroad between Gordon and Griswoldville, cutting off 2,500 of our prisoners that were to have been brought up from Camp Sumter, at Andersonville. To impede his progress, the bridges over the Oconee River have been destroyed and the country devastated in his front, so that he shall be unable to subsist upon it. The roads have been to a great extent rendered impassable by felled trees and pitfalls, and the rebels claim that during the past three days the progress of the Union troops eastward has not exceeded six miles. They also claim that their cavalry are picking up large numbers of our stragglers, by dashing upon our rear and flanks. From all that I can learn, I believe SHERMAN's main body to be within 125 miles of Savannah, with nothing to oppose him save the militia and such other unorganized forces as the emergency has brought together, and that the chances of his reaching the seaboard are at present altogether in his favor. Should he be delayed, by artificial obstructions of the road, long enough for LEE to detach a part of his army to confront him, GRANT in that case would be able to drive the rebels out of Virginia, and SHERMAN would doubtless find a mode of retreat, from the heart of rebeldom, southwestwardly to Mobile. A tremendously bold game is in progress on the military chess-board, and it is easy to see that the enemy believe it to be in our hands.

H. J. W.

NEWS FROM REBEL SOURCES.

Our correspondent on the fleet in the Savannah River, Mr. H. J. WINSER, has supplied us with full files of Augusta and Savannah papers to the 26th ult., from which we glean the following intelligence about the campaign in Georgia:

SHERMAN'S PROGRESS.

OPERATIONS ON THE OCONEE.

From the Augusta Constitutionalist, Nov. 25.

The latest reliable intelligence from the direction of Macon comes from our scouts sent out from Sparta. These scouts, who came in last evening, *report that a body of from 600 to 1,000 Yankee cavalry had crossed the Oconee,* and were moving slowly and nervously toward Sparta. Beyond some burning and stealing, this small band of troopers has no special significance. We have reason to believe that they will be seriously bushwhacked, and, we trust, cut to pieces.

One of the most encouraging features of this "invasion" is the fact, which we have from the most undoubted testimony, *that hundreds of the enemy are straggling from their main bodies,* and searching for somebody to take them into custody. *They are sprawling all about the country, and those who are not willing to surrender can be beautifully bushwacked.* Let all the old and young folks turn out and give the rascals a taste of Georgia State sovereignty. *The demoralization of our enemy is most providential for us, and ought to stiffen the backbone of the most timid amongst us.*

Three hundred prisoners arrived last evening from up the Georgia Road, and four hundred more are to arrive to-day.

These prisoners report that a division of three thousand of our cavalry had followed them all the way, dashing upon them constantly, picking up stragglers and capturing wagons.

Hampton's invincible cavalry will be with us in a day or two, and hang upon their eastern flank.

Gen. Wayne has whipped Kilpatrick's cavalry division at the Oconee Bridge, driving them headlong and in confusion. He telegraphs that he is perfectly able to take care of himself.

Wheeler, with many thousand men, has intercepted the enemy at a point, at present unmentionable, and is giving them no rest, night or day.

The main body of the enemy is moving down the western side of the Oconee, and has shown no disposition, thus far, to attempt its passage.

The skies are brightening. Everything looks glorious, and ere long Mr. SHERMAN will get a lashing that he little dreamed of when he made his "On to the Gulf." The gulf of perdition be upon him!

From the Savannah News, Nov. 26.

We have no reliable information from the front to-day, of any movements that are going on. We learn that the opinion prevails to some extent in military circles, *that Sherman intends yet to fall upon Macon, and not press on toward the coast at present.*

Our own forces are gathering and going to the proper place. *We are informed that over three thousand rations were issued in this city this morning to newly arrived veteran troops,* and we are also officially informed *that four or five thousand more will pass through here in two or three days.*

LATEST FROM THE FRONT—THE ENEMY REPULSED AT OCONEE.

From the Savannah News, Nov. 24.

Yesterday an official dispatch was received here stating that the enemy, with a large force, *had flanked Gen. Wayne at Oconee Bridge, C. R. R., and compelled him to retire;* and furthermore, that the former had crossed his forces at Ball's Ferry, some four miles below the bridge. This was most unwelcome news, and produced many long faces.

At a late hour last night, however, we were favored with the following dispatch to Gen. HARDEE, who is now in the city, containing the cheering news that the enemy had been repulsed and driven across the river. All honor to our gallant young townsman:

AUGUSTA, Nov. 23—9 P. M.

Lieut.-Gen. Hardee, Savannah:

Major HARTRIDGE has driven the enemy back across the Oconee River. Gen. WAYNE has returned to the Bridge and opened the office there.

J. BRENNER, Supt.

ANOTHER VERSION OF THE ABOVE.

From the Augusta Constitutionalist, Nov. 23.

Gen. WAYNE, having been pressed back by a superior force from Gordon, retired to Oconee Station. At this point he was receiving reinforcements from the proper quarter. His position is an exceedingly strong one, being flanked on either side by impenetrable swamps, and only approachable by the narrow defile of the railroad. This pass is well protected by log forts and stockades, and will baffle the assault of heavy columns.

FROM THE GEORGIA ROAD.

From the Augusta Chronicle and Sentinel, Nov. 25.

Trains ran up as far as Greensboro yesterday. Passengers could impart no information concerning the whereabouts of the enemy.

One hundred and forty-six Yankee prisoners were brought down last night from Athens. They were "gobbled up" by GRAHAM's scouts, Texan Rangers, and squads of other commands.

There was a rumor in town last night *that the main body of Sherman was progressing towards the Altamaha River. Another rumor stated that a body of the Federals was within sixteen miles of Sparta.* We cannot vouch for the truth of either of these rumors. We merely give them as reported to us.

FROM THE CENTRAL RAILROAD

From the Augusta Chronicle and Sentinel, Nov. 25.

Gen. WHEELER with about ten thousand men has crossed the Oconee and effected a junction with Gen. WAYNE. *Gen. Wayne has successfully defended the bridge over the Oconee River.* On this road the cadets of the Georgia Military Institute, who fought under him, have acquitted themselves nobly.

The enemy have left Gen. WAYNE's front and are supposed to have joined the main body.

There are no Yankees this side of the Oconee River.

WAR RUMORS

From the Savannah News, Nov. 24.

It was reported in the city yesterday, on the authority of a private dispatch, that Milledgeville had not been visited by the Yankees, and the capitol and other public buildings were still safe.

The Augusta *Register* of the 23d says: "The depot at Madison is burned, also all other depots on the road. The column advancing on the Georgia road is composed of SLOCUM's corps. It is attended by cavalry, variously estimated at from two to five thousand."

Reports from up the Central Railroad indicate that the right wing of the enemy are still advancing, but the exact progress made is not clearly understood. There is a report that they have crossed the Oconee, four miles below the railroad bridge. WHEELER is close on their rear. Our dispatches give some Yankee news of SHERMAN's intentions.

The Augusta *Constitutionalist* of Wednesday, Nov. 23, has the following:

"It is reported that the enemy has crossed the Oconee in force, near Milledgeville. This rumor, however, is strenuously contradicted by other parties. Milledgeville is reported as burned."

The column operating on the Georgia Road kept the western side, and struck off in the direction of Macon, as though contemplating a junction with the force in that vicinity.

Prisoners captured from the enemy on the Georgia Road state that the intention of SHERMAN was to avoid Augusta, and strike Macon probably—Savannah certainly. Atlanta is now in our possession. A strong force of cavalry is following SHERMAN, and it is not impossible that the invincible FORREST—SHERMAN's evil genius—may, ere long, hang like a wolf on his rear and flanks.

From the Augusta Register, Nov. 22.

We conversed with an intelligent gentleman who arrived last night by the passenger train up the Georgia Railroad.

He informed us that on Monday the Federals left the line of the Georgia road, going directly to Eatonton.

The only Yankees who came to Greensboro' were a few stragglers, who were captured.

The trains ran up to Greensboro' and Athens yesterday.

A portion of Maj. GRAHAM's command reached this city last night. They report that they visited Atlanta several days since and found it completely evacuated and burned. They state that the Federals took all the cattle and forage in their route, but did not molest those who staid at home.

They captured two or three hundred Yankee stragglers, who will probably reach here to-day.

They also corroborate the statement of the Federals leaving the Georgia Railroad and going in the direction of Eatonton.

THE WHEREABOUTS OF THE YANKEES.

From the Augusta Chronicle & Sentinel Nov. 25.

The whereabouts of the main body of the Yankee army is involved in mystery, and there is not a military man in this city that can definitely locate them, in our opinion. We should not be like Micawber, waiting for "something to turn up," but should "turn up something" ourselves.

CHEERING.

From the Augusta Constitutionalist, Nov. 23.

We have intelligence of the most important character, which we deem contraband at present. Suffice it to say, that matters are beginning to assume a comfortable appearance, and Mr. SHERMAN had better keep his weather eye open, or mayhap he will get it closed.

PRISONERS.

Several Yankees, white and black, were captured on this side of the Oconee, and brought to this city.

PREPARATIONS FOR RESISTING SHERMAN.

REINFORCEMENTS FROM WILMINGTON UNDER BRAGG.

From the Augusta Chronicle and Sentinel, Nov. 24.

It will be seen from a dispatch in another column that Gen. Bragg has left Wilmington with reinforcements for this place. These, we are told, number about ten thousand. These, in addition to those who started for Augusta from another section on Saturday, will make quite a formidable array.

The following is the dispatch referred to:

WILMINGTON, Nov. 22.

Hon. R. H. May, Mayor of Augusta:

I leave here to-day with reinforcements for Augusta. Exhort your people to be confident and resolute.

BRAXTON BRAGG.

Reinforcements are constantly arriving in our city. The air resounds with the shriek of the engine whistle day and night. The soldiers appear to be in excellent spirits, and to enjoy the prospect of a fight ahead. The gloom which overspread our city a short time since has disappeared entirely. Everything wears a cheerful aspect.

From the Augusta Constitutionalist, Nov. 23.

Our citizens were gratified last evening by seeing, among the troops arriving in our city, *a portion of Hampton's splendid cavalry from Virginia.*

With the exception of the buzz created by the militia enrolling officers, all remains quiet. The "reliable gentleman" did not have so much to say as usual up to a late hour last night. No one believes that SHERMAN is half so crazy as to venture on a collision with the forces at this place. *The splendid fortifications that surround the city* would require the expenditure of more ammunition than he can afford to lose without any base of supplies.

He will not risk a battle, but avoid our forces wherever they appear in formidable proportions; destroy

(Continued on the Eighth Page.)

The New-York Times.

VOL. XIV—NO. 4130. NEW-YORK, MONDAY, DECEMBER 19, 1864. PRICE FOUR CENTS.

VICTORY!

Sherman at Savannah—Thomas in Tennessee.

GREAT NEWS FROM BOTH ARMIES

The First Official Dispatch from Gen. Sherman.

His Short Record of the Great Campaign.

SAVANNAH INVESTED.

Its Doomed Garrison of Fifteen Thousand Men and Hardee.

SHERMAN'S ARMY IN SPLENDID ORDER

The Quick Capture of Fort McAllister and Its Garrison.

GREAT RAILROAD DESTRUCTION

Sherman's Most Agreeable Trip in Georgia.

THE TENNESSEE NEWS

The Great Triumph of Gen. Thomas Near Nashville.

THREE DAYS' FIGHTING.

The Victory Over Hood's Army Still in Progress.

Over Ten Thousand Prisoners Captured in Three Days.

FORREST KILLED.

Fifteen Hundred of His Cavalry Captured.

[OFFICIAL.]

War Department, Washington, Dec. 18—9 P. M.

Maj.-Gen. Jno. A. Dix, New-York:

An official dispatch from Gen. Sherman was received to-day, dated near midnight, Dec. 13, on the gunboat *Dandelion*, Ossabaw Sound. It was written before Gen. Foster had reached him. He reports, besides some military details of future operations, (which are omitted,) the following interesting particulars of his operations:

On Board Dandelion, Ossabaw Sound, 11.50 P. M., Dec. 13.

To-day, at 5 P. M., Gen. Hazen's division of the Fifteenth Corps carried Fort McAllister by assault, capturing its entire garrison and stores. This opened to us the Ossabaw Sound, and I pushed down to this gunboat to communicate with the fleet. Before opening communication we had completely destroyed all the railroads leading into Savannah and invested the city. The left is on the Savannah River, three miles above the city, and the right on the Ogeechee, at King's Bridge. The army is in splendid order, and equal to anything. The weather has been fine, and supplies were abundant. Our march was most agreeable, and we were not at all molested by guerrillas.

We reached Savannah three days ago, but owing to Fort McAllister could not communicate; but now we have McAllister, we can go ahead.

We have already captured two boats on the Savannah River, and prevented their gunboats from coming down.

I estimate the population of Savannah at 25,000 and the garrison at 15,000. Gen. Hardee commands.

We have not lost a wagon on the trip, but have gathered in a large supply of negroes, mules, horses, &c., and our teams are in far better condition than when we started.

My first duty will be to clear the army of surplus negroes, mules and horses. We have utterly destroyed over two hundred miles of rails, and consumed stores and provisions that were essential to Lee's and Hood's armies. The quick work made with McAllister and the opening of communication with our fleet, and the consequent independence for supplies, dissipates all their boasted threats to head me off and starve the army.

I regard Savannah as already gained.

Yours, truly, W. T. Sherman, Major-Gen.

The following official reports were received this evening from Gen. Thomas, dated at his headquarters near Franklin:

Headquarters Department of the Cumberland, Near Franklin, Tenn., Dec. 17, 1864.

A report just received from Major-Gen. Wilson, states that at 6 P. M. to-day he attacked and dispersed Stevenson's division of rebel infantry and a brigade of cavalry, capturing three guns. The Fourth United States Cavalry and Hatch's division of cavalry, handsomely supported by Knipe's division of cavalry, did the work, making several beautiful charges, breaking the rebel infantry in all directions. Had it only been light, the rebel rear guard would have been entirely destroyed. As it is, it has been severely punished. The whole army will continue vigorous pursuit in the morning. This attack was made six miles beyond Franklin.

(Signed,) George H. Thomas, Major-General.

Headquarters Department of Cumberland, Near Franklin, Tenn., Dec. 17—8 P. M.

We have pressed the enemy to-day beyond Franklin, capturing his hospitals, containing over 1,500 wounded and about 150 of our wounded, in addition to the above. Gen. Knipe, commanding a division of cavalry, drove the enemy's rear guard through Franklin to-day, capturing about 250 prisoners and five battle-flags, with very little loss on our side. Citizens of Franklin represent Hood's army as completely demoralized. In addition to the captures of yesterday, reported in my dispatches of last night, I have the honor to report the capture of Gen. Rucker and about two hundred and fifty prisoners of the enemy's cavalry, in a fight that occurred about 8 o'clock last night between Gen. Rucker and Gen. Hatch, of our cavalry. The enemy has been pressed to-day both in front and on both flanks. Brig.-Gen. Johnson succeeded in striking him on the flank just beyond Franklin, capturing quite a number of prisoners—number not yet reported. My cavalry is pressing him closely through, and I am very much in hopes of getting many more prisoners to-morrow.

(Signed) Geo. H. Thomas, Maj.-Gen.

Other dispatches (unofficial) from Nashville, state that 1,000 prisoners were captured by Wilson, and that Gen. Rousseau, commanding at Murfreesboro, reports Forrest killed and 1,500 of his men captured.

The Superintendent at Nashville reports that the railroad from Nashville will be open to Franklin to-night, and will rapidly follow Thomas, thus furnishing him supplies, and enabling him to push on after Hood.

Edwin M. Stanton, Secretary of War.

OFFICIAL DISPATCHES.

The Armies in Tennessee and in Georgia—Further Details of the Fighting on the 16th at Nashville—The Enemy Pressed at all Points in His Line of Retreat—Immense Captures of Guns and Prisoners—Details of the Battle of the 15th—The News from Sherman—Savannah Closely Besieged—A Formal Demand for the Surrender of the City.

[The following important official dispatches (less important, however, than those in the preceding columns) were published in our edition of yesterday morning.]

War Department, Washington, Dec. 17—8:35 A. M.

Major-Gen. John A. Dix:

The following official report of the great victory achieved yesterday by Major-Gen. Thomas and his gallant army over the rebel forces under Gen. Hood in front of Nashville, was received this morning. One of the most surprising circumstances connected with the great achievement is the small loss suffered by our troops, evincing, among other things, the admirable skill and caution of Gen. Thomas in his disposition of the battle. In our rejoicings at the defeat of the enemy, thanks are due to the Almighty for his protection to our gallant officers and soldiers in the great conflict they have passed through.

The report of Gen. Thomas, and also an unofficial report containing interesting details are subjoined:

Headquarters Department of the Cumberland, Eight Miles from Nashville, 6 P. M. Friday, Dec. 16, 1864.

To the President of the United States, Hon. Edwin M. Stanton, and Lieut.-Gen. U. S. Grant:

This army thanks you for your approbation of its conduct yesterday, and to assure you that it is not misplaced, I have the honor to report that the enemy has been pressed at all points to-day, in his line of retreat to the Brentwood Hills.

Brig.-Gen. Hatch, of Wilson's corps of cavalry, on the right, turned the enemy's left, and captured a large number of prisoners, the number not yet reported.

Maj.-Gen. Schofield's corps, next on the left of cavalry, carried several hills, captured many prisoners and six pieces of artillery. Brevet Major-Gen. Smith, next on the left of Maj.-Gen. Schofield, carried the salient point of the enemy's line with McMillan's brigade of McArthur's division, capturing 16 pieces of artillery, two Brigadier-Generals and about 2,000 prisoners. Brig.-Gen. Garrard's division, of Smith's command, next on the left of McArthur's division, carried the enemy's intrenchments, capturing all the artillery and troops of the enemy on the line. Brig.-Gen. Wood's troops on Franklin pike took up the assault, capturing the enemy's intrenchments, in his retreat captured eight pieces of artillery, something over 600 prisoners, and drove the enemy within one mile of the Brentwood Hill Pass.

Maj.-Gen. Steedman, commanding detachments of the different armies of the Military Division of the Mississippi, most nobly supported Gen. Wood's left, and bore a most honorable part in the operations of the day. I have ordered the pursuit to be continued in the morning at daylight, although the troops are very much fatigued. The utmost enthusiasm prevails. I must not forget to report the operations of Brig.-Gen. Johnson in successfully driving the enemy, with the coöperation of the gunboats under Lieut.-Commander Fitch, from their established batteries on the Cumberland River, below the City of Nashville, and of the success of Brig.-Gen. Coxton's brigade in covering and re-turning our right and rear. In the operations of yesterday and to-day although I have no report of the number of prisoners captured by Johnson's and Croxton's command, I know they have made a large number. I am also glad to be able to state that the number of prisoners captured yesterday greatly exceeds the number reported by telegraph last evening. The woods, fields and intrenchments are strewn with the enemy's small arms abandoned in the retreat. In conclusion, I am happy to state that all this has been effected with but a very small loss to us. Our loss probably does not exceed three hundred and very few killed.

GEO. H. THOMAS, Maj. Gen. Commanding.

Nashville, Tenn., Friday, Dec. 16—9 P. M.

During last night, Hood withdrew his right from the river, and took a position covering Hillsboro, Grannywhite and Franklin pikes, which line had been carefully prepared for just this contingency. He was driven from the first line easily, but the second was very stubbornly defended, and at last heavily assaulted three times before succeeding. It was carried, however, and twenty pieces of artillery, two thousand men, including Gen. Jackson, with the remnant of his division, were taken. The enemy were forced back two miles, and his army broken into two parts, one on the White pike and the other on the Franklin, with range of Bluffy Hills between them. Steedman and Wood pressing down the latter, and A. J. Smith, Schofield and the cavalry down the former. Small arms lay as thick on the contested line as the rebels had stood there. Hood can't make another such day's fight, while Thomas is in good condition to press him. Caught more wagons. Can't say number. Everybody, white and black, did splendidly.

EDWIN M. STANTON, Secretary of War.

SECOND DISPATCH.

War Department, Washington, Dec. 17—10 P. M.

To Maj.-Gen. John A. Dix:

Nothing has been heard from Gen. Thomas to-day.

Unofficial dispatches state that the Provost-Marshal at Nashville reports 5,000 prisoners and 49 pieces of artillery as being already secured.

It is ascertained that in transmitting Gen. Thomas' report last night, a telegraphic mistake was made at Louisville or Nashville in the estimated number of our casualties.

The dispatch written by Gen. Thomas stated that his whole loss would not exceed 3,000, and that very few were killed.

A dispatch from Lexington, this evening, states that on the 13th inst., at Kingsport, Tenn., Gen. Burbridge had a fight with Basil Duke's brigade, formerly John Morgan's, and routed it, with a loss to the enemy of one hundred and fifty killed, wounded and prisoners, and their train. Dick Morgan, a brother of John, was captured.

Dispatches have been received to-day from Gen. Foster, who had a personal interview, on the morning of Wednesday, the 14th inst., with Gen. Sherman, at Fort McAllister, which had been taken by assault the preceding day.

Savannah was closely besieged, and its capture, with the rebel forces there, was confidently expected. It was to be summoned in two days, and if not surrendered, Sherman would open his batteries upon it.

Gen. Foster reports that Sherman's army is in splendid condition, having lived on its march on the turkies, chickens, sweet potatoes and other good things of the richest part of Georgia.

E. M. STANTON, Secretary of War.

REPORTS VIA FORTRESS MONROE.

Arrival of the Dispatch Steamer Eliza Hancock—Important from Sherman's Army.

Baltimore, Sunday, Dec. 18.

The Fortress Monroe correspondent of the Associated Press, under date of Dec. 17, has the following:

"The special dispatch steamer *Eliza Hancock* arrived this morning from Hilton Head, with Maj. Anderson Reaver, with important dispatches from Sherman and Foster.

The news brought by the *Hancock* is of the most encouraging character. The van-guard of Sherman's army succeeded in reaching with safety, on the 13th inst., and with very little loss to his main army, the outskirts of Savannah, and on the 14th Gen. Sherman completely invested the city, hemming in, and cutting off from all means of escape, Hardee's army of 15,000 men. Should the place not be immediately surrendered, a regular siege will be at once prosecuted with vigor. Secure lines of communication had been opened between the army of Gen. Shermon and that of Gen. Foster, and on the 14th inst. the two Generals dined together at Fort McAllister. No doubt was entertained at Hilton Head but that Savannah must soon fall; and when that takes place the attention of Sherman will be, in all probability, turned toward Charleston."

THE BATTLE OF FRIDAY.

Preparatory Manoeuvres—The Enemy Completely Deceived—Full Details of the Victory.

Nashville, Tenn., Thursday, Dec. 15.

The army commenced moving at daybreak to-day, with Gen. Steadman's corps on our left, the Fourth Corps next, and then A. J. Smith's corps. The cavalry force moved to the right, and the Twenty-first Corps were held in reserve.

Very little except reconnoitering was done until after meridian, but at 12:30 o'clock the order to advance was given, and the whole column moved onward.

The rebels evidently expected that Gen. Thomas would attempt to turn their left flank. All the indications would cause us to suppose this, and they offered numerous inducements for us to do so, and had carefully prepared their works to receive our forces if we should attack them in that quarter.

To keep up the delusion, Steadman's command was ordered to skirmish heavily on the rebel left flank, and he moved in the direction of the point which the rebels believed we were threatening.

While Steadman was manœuvring in this manner, the rebels were massing on their left, and we were concentrating the Sixteenth and Twenty-third Corps, and Gen. Wilson's cavalry on our right.

The result of this was that when the bugles sounded the advance, our right wing advanced rapidly between the left of the rebels and the Cumberland River, completely doubling upon a rebel division which the rebels had posted to blockade the river. A battery was taken here by our forces and sent to the rear.

The rebels had by this time perceived that our attack on the right was a feint, and Hood soon attempted to atone for his mistake, but he was too late, as our right had established a force on the main bank of the river, and were steadily advancing.

The whole Twenty-third Corps had taken a position on the extreme right, while Smith's Corps executed a half wheel, driving the columns of rebels before him easily and rapidly.

Soon the hill where the rebels were posted was taken with little loss and less difficulty.

In an hour or so the rebels had presented a strong front, and our progress for the moment was checked.

It was now visible that the contest was about to commence.

Another diversion on the left was made, to enable our men on the right to get into position and strengthen themselves so as to be ready for a charge.

In front of the Fourth Corps and about one mile beyond Acklin, the rebels had a strong line of works defended by a heavy line of skirmishers. Gen. Wood ordered a charge upon it, and the word "forwar" was shouted by the Division, Brigade and Regimental Commanders, and with prompiness and decision the men leaped over the breastworks and advanced.

In less than twenty minutes our forces had possession of the rebel works, and the banners of the Fourth Corps were planted on them.

Our men, flushed with victory, without orders, pushed forward and reached the second line of rebel works by the most strenuous exertions and captured some prisoners, which with those captured previously, amounted to over 1,000.

The second line of rebel intrenchments were now in sight, located on the verge of a hill, one mile from their skirmish line. These intrenchments were built with great skill, and some time elapsed ere our men were got in position to advance upon them.

Our cavalry had advanced meanwhile until its right rested on the hills six miles beyond Nashville. Moving from the river they could now manœuvre without difficulty. Instead of facing to the west, they now faced directly south. The Second Corps of Schofield and Smith's corps were in position directly parallel on the left. The skirmishers were advanced to the Hillsboro pike, sheltering themselves behind fences on the north side, while the Fourth Corps was formed at right angles, the front division lying directly across the Hillsboro pike, and the remainder being to the left of it.

While these movements were going on and our lines were forming and batteries being placed, the rebels could be distinctly seen moving to the left toward Hillsboro, with the view to prevent our turning their left flank.

As far as could be ascertained the entire rebel reserve was thus thrown in front of our right and centre.

In the meantime our Commanders sent reinforcements equally strong to our posts menaced by the rebels.

At 3:30 o'clock all was ready for the charge on the second line of the rebel works.

The position was a strong one, to reach which our forces had to ascend hills to an elevation of fifteen degrees, without any probation, but the lines were four columns deep, with ample reserves.

Our forces were massed against the rebel lines, and the veteran columns were hurled against the rebels with irresistible force, and at 4:50 P. M. the charge commenced.

The First and Second Divisions of the Fourth Corps moved west, and the Third Division, at right angles with it, moved south.

On the right of the Fourth Corps was the corps of A. J. Smith.

The First and Second Divisions of the Fourth Corps had the hardest part of the task to perform. They had to move, in an exposed position, to the rebel works in their front, and these works were more formidable and stronger than those elsewhere.

Under a heavy fire of grape, cannister and musketry our men moved steadily forward, but owing to the rebels firing too high, it mostly passed over them—otherwise the slaughter would have been terrible. Some of our men were killed, but the list of casualties was less than expected.

After advancing within one hundred and fifty yards of the rebel works, their fire became very severe. Our troops never wavered, but with a shout along the lines and ringing along the Hillsboro pike, they again advanced, and were almost immediately upon the intrenchments.

The distance yet to be passed did not exceed one hundred yards, and reinforcements were in sight coming, yet the rebels evinced no signs of retiring, and discharged volley after volley into our ranks at a distance of twenty-five yards. A few of our men had now reached the works and were using the bayonet, when some few of the rebels fled, followed by others, and soon all broke and fled in the wildest confusion.

Four twelve-pounder Napoleon guns their artillerists attempted to secure, but they only succeeded in getting one of them off the field. We secured three and two caissons, with a large lot of small arms. We also captured in this charge about 400 prisoners.

The prisoners report that Hood told them that they could hold their position against any Yankee force which could be brought against them.

Our losses in this charge did not exceed 100 killed and wounded.

Smith's and Schofield's corps had in the meantime advanced half a mile to the south of the Hillsboro pike, capturing there a whole battery of six guns.

This makes the total of artillery captured, five guns being taken on the extreme left by the Fifteenth Ohio, amount to eighteen guns.

Several battle-flags were also taken.

The rebel loss in killed and wounded is not less than 600, while ours is only about 300.

The rebels have taken up another line, and may defend it to-morrow, if they do not retreat to-night.

One of the most brilliant charges made to-day was by the Eleventh, Twelfth, Thirteenth, Fourteenth, Seventeenth and Eighteenth Colored Regiments. The charge was on Rail's Hill, near the Nolansville pike, and broke the rebel line.

The colored troops behaved splendidly and lost severely.

Col. Shaffer's colored regiment and the Seventeenth Colored Regiment lost nearly all their officers.

On the White Pike, in front of Acklin's residence, Gen. Beatty led the charge on the first rebel line, and at 12 o'clock to-day our forces carried it at the point of the bayonet, and planted our guns on the works abandoned by the rebels. Fifty prisoners were captured in this charge. Our losses were very slight, although we advanced in great confusion.

Lieut. J. Watson, of the Fifth Iowa, was shot through the breast while gallantly charging the enemy's batteries and mortally wounded.

The steamer *Pike*, in the Quartermaster's service, while proceeding up the river, when three miles from the city, was fired into by the rebels. One man named George Blakely was killed and four others wounded. She turned back.

The gunboat fleet were engaged down the river, about fourteen miles from the city, shelling the rebel left very vigorously.

The headquarters of Gen Chalmers were captured, with fifteen guns, and all his books, papers, valuables, etc. They are now at Capt. Goodwin's headquarters.

The Provost-Marshal-General says that about 550 have reached this city up to this hour (9 P. M.) The total amount of prisoners captured will not fall short of 1,200.

Capt. Grosvener, a brother of Col. Grosvener, commanding a brigade, was killed.

Adjt. Clayberne and Gen. Roberts were wounded.

One of our shells from Fort Negley fell short, killing four of our own wounded.

THE GREAT NAVAL EXPEDITION

The Fleet Seen Off New Inlet, North Carolina.

List of the Vessels Composing the Expedition.

Fortress Monroe via Baltimore, Sunday, Dec. 18.

The special dispatch steamer *Hancock*, from Hilton Head, passed off New Inlet, N. C., while on her way to Fortress Monroe the expeditionary fleet under command of Butler and Porter, which sailed from here some days since.

ADMIRAL PORTER'S FLEET.

Flagship, *Malvern*.

First Division.

Commodore H. K. Thatcher, commanding.

Colorado	10	Fort Donelson	5
Nyack	7	*Rhode Island	10
Aries	5	Maumee	7
Grand Gulf	9	James Adger	10
Howqua	6	Huron	5
Iasco	5	Mohican	7
Monticello	7	Cherokee	5
Agawam	9	Tallapoosa	9

Second Division.

Commodore Joseph Lanman, Commanding.

Minnesota	50	Eolus	5
Mackinaw	9	Yantic	5
Seneca	5	Massasoit	9
Kansas	5	Gettysburgh	5
Nereus	8	Juniata	9
*Fort Jackson	10	*Keystone State	9
Osceola	9	Calypso	5

Third Division.

Commodore James F. Schenck, commanding.

Powhattan	19	Lillian	5
Undilla	5	Shenandoah	10
Mount Vernon	5	Cambridge	7
Mattabesset	9	Brooklyn	26
Emma	5	*Alabama	—
Saco	5		

Fourth Division.

Commodore S. W. Godon, commanding.

Susquehanna	14	Tristam Shandy	5
*Quaker City	10	Gov. Buckingham	5
Victoria	5	Dumbarton	5
Montgomery	9	Britannia	5
R. R. Cuyler	9	Wabash	50
Vicksburgh	9	Peuqot	5
Maratanza	9	Pawtuxet	9
Tuscarora	10	*Santiago de Cuba	9

Division of Iron-Clads.

Commodore Wm. Radford, commanding.

New Ironsides	18	Dictator	2
Canonicus	2	Mahopac	2
Saugus	2	Monadnoc	4

* Vessels marked thus * are designated for hospital vessels.

NEWS FROM REBEL SOURCES.

Special Dispatch to the New-York Times.

Washington, Sunday, Dec. 18.

From Southern papers of Friday last received at the office of the Philadelphia *Inquirer*, we extract the following items of news, not contained in the official bulletin of yesterday.

IN FRONT OF RICHMOND.

From the Richmond Dispatch, Nov. 16.

Nothing worthy of notice has occurred on the military lines north of the James river. Four-fifths of Grant's army is now on the south side, the Sixth and Ninth corps at the front, the Second and Fifth in reserve. On the lines north of the Appomattox all intercourse between the pickets of the two armies has been stopped by peremptory orders from their respective Generals.

From the Richmond Examiner, Dec. 16.

The lines of Richmond and Petersburgh remain quiet. The whole force of the enemy from Fort Harrison to the river now consists of negroes, with the exception of two companies of white men, with cannon in Fort Harrison itself. Our men do not fire on them at present.

ADVANCE UPON KINSTON.

From the Goldsboro State Journal, Dec. 13.

The enemy, whom we announced on yesterday as advancing upon Kinston, were met on yesterday at daylight, and after a brisk engagement were driven back, our forces still pursuing. Still further reinforcements have been sent to Kinston, amply sufficient for any force the enemy can bring to bear at that point. Lieut.-Col. Starr's prompiness and courage has thus easily frustrated an attack upon Kinston, which, if successful, might have resulted in serious consequences.

COL. STARR'S REPORT.

Kinston, Dec. 12, 1864.

Having been reinforced, I left the breastworks at daylight to find the enemy. I discovered him in considerable force on the Neuse road, two miles from town. He showed two pieces of artillery and five or six hundred infantry. After a brisk engagement of thirty minutes, he was driven across the southwest bridge, destroying it behind him. Our cavalry and infantry are still pressing him.

J. R. STARR, Colonel Commanding.

LYNCHBURGH.

A telegram to the *Whig* from Lynchburgh, dated December 14, has the following additions about the Union raid on the Virginia and Tennessee Railroad:

No positive intelligence of the enemy's number is received, but it is supposed to be five or six thousand, a portion of whom, it is said, yet occupy Bristol. A body of the enemy, returning toward Beans' Station, encountered our forces at Zollicoffer Station, on the East Tennessee Road, nine miles west of Bristol, where a fight was said to be progressing at last accounts.

A PROCLAMATION BY GEN. BRECKINRIDGE.

From the Richmond Whig, Dec. 15.

On the 10th, Gen. Breckinridge issued the following proclamation:

Protection having been guaranteed to all citizens of East Tennessee, who, having entered the Federal service, shall in good faith return home and enter upon their pursuits as peaceable citizens, this privilege is hereby extended to all who, not having belonged to the Confederate army, have gone within the lines of the enemy, to avoid service, or for other reasons. Such as are above or below military age shall not be required to perform military duty, and all shall be free from punishment except such as have been guilty of murder and other high crimes. All citizens and soldiers are requested and enjoined to receive with kindness those who avail themselves of this order, and to cultivate such a spirit as will put an end to the internal strife and domestic warfare which has so long desolated this portion of the State.

JOHN C. BRECKENRIDGE, Maj.-Gen.

FROM MIDDLE TENNESSEE.

From the Richmond Whig, Dec. 15.

Capt. Reynolds, of the army, who has just reached Montgomery, informs the Montgomery *Advertiser*, that the day he left Cherokee information was received from Gen. Roddy, to the effect that all the Federal posts southeast of Tullahoma had been called in, including Chattanooga, Bridgeport and Stevenson. The Lagrange *Reporter* has information from a gentleman from Carrolton, whose brother's neighbor, living in Van Wert, was in Chattanooga on Wednesday of last week. He states that there was not a Yankee either in Chattanooga or Bridgeport, nor was it believed there were any this side of Nashville.

THE FALL OF FORT M'ALLISTER.

From the Richmond Examiner, Dec. 15.

An official dispatch from Gen. Beauregard, received yesterday, states that the enemy stormed and carried Fort McAllister on Wednesday. The same dispatch mentions the appearance of an increased number of enemy's vessels at mouth of Savannah River. The fall of Fort McAllister does not by any means involve the loss of Savannah, but will necessitate the reinforcement of the troops defending that city. There was some heavy artillery on the fort, and it will be remembered that an experimental attack of Yankee iron-clads on this position, about fifteen months ago, was successfully repulsed. Fort McAllister commanded the entrance to Ogeechee River, and has prevented the enemy heretofore from ascending the river. We believe there are other works further up the stream, which would render the navigation of the stream by the enemy extremely uncomfortable.

NEWS FROM WASHINGTON.

Special Dispatch to the New-York Times.

Washington, Sunday, Dec. 18.

DISUNIONISTS DOWNCAST.

Secessionists are extremely downcast over the unexpected reverses of the past week to their Southern friends. They attribute the loss of so many officers in the fight at Franklin, Tenn., to the fact that Hood's men were tired of the war, and would not fight. Their officers were compelled to lead them, and for this reason so many of them fell in the contest. They also prophecy that Hood's army will desert him, and never go back to Georgia. Besides thus giving up all success in the Southwest, these Secessionists acknowledge that Sherman's campaign has been a perfect success, because he was able not only to divide his army and march through Georgia, but even to leave the inferior portion of it to annihilate Hood. It is quite evident, from all conversations on the street to-day, that the Southern sympathisers have given up all hope of their friends' success.

FINANCIAL MATTERS.

A quorum of the Ways and Means Committee will remain here during the coming recess, for the purpose of maturing various financial schemes which have been submitted for their action. Secretary Fessenden is preparing a letter upon this subject, which will be transmitted to both the Senate and the House Financial Committees in a very few days.

THE RECONSTRUCTION BILL.

The Reconstruction Bill has been so amended as to meet the views of almost all the Administration Senators and Representatives. It will pass Congress at once, and receive the signature of the President. Louisiana will be admitted under its recent reorganization, and the delegation now here will be at once admitted to seats in Congress.

THE BILL RELATING TO UNEMPLOYED OFFICERS.

There is a strong pressure being brought to bear on the Senate Military Committee to defeat the House bill, dropping all unemployed general officers not on duty within the last three months. The Committee will take action on this subject to-morrow.

THE WHISKY AND TOBACCO TAX.

An attempt will be made by the Ways and Means Committee to get definite action upon the whisky and tobacco tax before the holidays. The Committee meet to-morrow morning to confer on this subject. Members of the House, however, are desirous that the whole subject shall be postponed until after the holidays.

DISTRIBUTION OF MEDALS OF HONOR.

Thursday last, at Maj.-Gen. Humphrey's headquarters, Gen. Meade presented to the following soldiers medals of honor, which had been awarded them by the War Department, for distinguished gallantry in battle:

NAMES, RANK, AND WHERE DISTINGUISHED.

Sergt.-Maj. W. B. Hincks, 14th Conn.—Gettysburgh.
E. W. Bacon, Co. F., 14th Conn.—Gettysburgh.
Corp. Christian Flynn, Co. K., 14th Conn.—Gettysburgh.
Sergt. W. Westerhold, Co. K., 52d N. Y.—Spottsylvania.
Sergt. G. H. Dare, Co. D., 126th N. Y.—Gettysburgh.
Jerry Wall, Co. B., 126th N. Y.—Gettysburgh.
John Mayberry, Co. F., 1st Del.—Gettysburgh.
Corp. J. De Castro, Co. I., 19th Mass.—Gettysburgh.
Sergt. Benj. Tellison, Co. C., 19th Mass.—Gettysburgh.
Corp. M. C. Henson, Co. F., 19th Me.—Bristow Station.
L. Bundy, Co. C., 4th Ohio—Spottsylvania.
L. Morgan, Co. C., 4th Ohio—Spottsylvania.
Oliver Rood, Co. F., 26th Ind.—Gettysburgh.
Sergt. W. P. Thomson, Co. G., 20th Ind.—Wilderness.
A. Freeman, Co. E., 124th N. Y.—Spottsylvania.
Philip Haughter, Co. F., 73d N. Y.—Spottsylvania.
F. A. Bishop, Co. C., 57th Penn.—Spottsylvania.
Corp. C. J. Russell, Co. H., 93d N. Y.—Spottsylvania.
Corp. J. M. Kendag, Co. A., 63d Penn.—Spottsylvania.
John U. Ossel, Co. G., 7th Ind.—Spottsylvania.

Medals were also due Sergt. T. Brigley, Seventh New-York Artillery; Privates George Harris, Co. B, One Hundred and Forty-eighth Pennsylvania; and J. H. Weeks, Co. H, One Hundred and Fifty-second New-York. The two former were sick in hospital, and unable to be present at the presentation. The latter died gallantly in the battle of Reams' Station.

THE BILL TO ENCOURAGE ENLISTMENTS.

To-morrow, Senator Wilson's "bill to encourage enlistments" will come up in the Senate. It proposes to free the wives and children of all the colored men who have and who may enlist in the Union army. It applies more particularly to enlistments in Delaware, Kentucky, West Virginia, Tennessee and Missouri. It is believed that by the operations of this bill more than one hundred thousand persons will be freed.

PERSONAL.

Hon. H. E. Chittenden, former Register of the United States Treasury, is here to testify in the case of Stewart Gwynn.

DEATH OF MISS MYRTLE MINER.

Miss Myrtle Miner, for a long time identified with the cause of educating colored children in this city, died here yesterday.

EXECUTIONS.

On Friday last, the following soldiers were hung for desertion: John Thompson, Fifth New-Hampshire; Christopher Luken, Co. E, Seventh New-York; and Charles Hammel, of the same company, all of the First Division, Second Corps. William Kane, *alias* W. Carter, Eighth Indiana Volunteers, belonging to Second Division, Fifth Corps, was also executed in the presence of his division.

PARDONED.

Private John McNulty, *alias* James Riley, Co. E, Sixth New-Hampshire Regiment, also sentenced to death for the same crime, was pardoned by Gen. Meade.

The Late Firemen's Fight—Prompt Action of the Fire Commissioners—Both Engine Companies Disbanded.

A special meeting of the Board of Commissioners of the New-York Fire Department was held at Firemen's Hall on Friday evening, 16th inst. Present, John J. Gorman, President, and Commissioners Bonfell, Lawrence and Flender.

The meeting was called to investigate the charges of Chief Engineer Decker and Assistant Engineer West, against Engine Companies Fifty-three and Forty. These were the companies engaged in the disgraceful fight which occurred on Tuesday morning last. A thorough investigation was had. The Commissioners remained in session from 8 o'clock in the evening until 2 o'clock the next morning, during which time they examined about one hundred witnesses; they then adjourned, to meet on Saturday afternoon at 4 o'clock P. M. At that hour they again met, when, after a short consultation, they, by a unanimous vote, disbanded both companies, expelled their foremen from the Fire Department, and directed the Chief Engineer to take charge of their houses and apparatus.

The difficulty occurred on the 13th inst.; the complaints were made on the 14th inst.; the trial took place on the 16th, and on the 17th the decision was rendered and names of the companies expunged from the rolls of the department. In this prompt action and decision, the Commissioners have done themselves great credit, and will receive the thanks and indorsement of all worthy firemen and citizens. The firemen of New-York have proved themselves in many an emergency to be a noble set of men, and worthy the great confidence the public have in them, and it is a shame that a few unworthy members should thus bring discredit upon so worthy an institution. The department is now governed by gentlemen of responsibility and position, who are determined to rid it of all "roughs" and "rowdies" and restore it to the position it originally held. In this endeavor they ask the assistance of the public, and every complaint brought before the Commissioners will receive their immediate attention.

THE NEW YORK HERALD.

WHOLE NO. 10,343. NEW YORK, THURSDAY, DECEMBER 22, 1864. PRICE FOUR CENTS.

SHERMAN.

The Gallop Through Georgia.

Forty-two Counties of the Rebel Empire State Laid Waste.

The State Capital Formally Surrendered to Ten Scouts, who Stampede Two Hundred Rebel Soldiers.

THE COUNTRY STRIPPED OF EVERYTHING

All the Railways Destroyed and Iron Burned.

THE BATTLE OF GRISWOLDVILLE.

Walcott Almost Annihilates Three Rebel Brigades with One and Captures the Rebel Commander.

Sherman Subsists on the Fat of the Land and Does Not Lose a Wagon or Gun.

The Spoils of the Campaign 4,000 Prisoners, 15,000 Horses, 10,000 Negroes, Thirty Pieces of Artillery, &c.

MILLIONS WORTH OF COTTON BURNED.

Sherman's Total Loss Only Fifteen Hundred.

STORMING OF FORT McALLISTER.

The Garrison and Twenty-four Guns Captured.

THE FLEET GOES UP TO THE NEW BASE.

The Siege of Savannah Opened.

MUTINY OF THE PEOPLE OF SAVANNAH!

They are Ready to Give Up—Warehouses Thrown Open and All Told to Help Themselves,

&c., &c., &c.

The United States steam transport Fulton, Capt. Wotton, from Port Royal on the 18th, via Fortress Monroe on the 20th inst., arrived at this port yesterday morning.

The Fulton touched at Fortress Monroe to land Lieutenant Colonel O. E. Babcock, bearer of despatches from Gen. Sherman to the War Department. Also Colonel A. H. Markland, General Sherman's mail agent.

Savannah was still in possession of the rebels. Its surrender had not been demanded by Gen. Sherman up to the time of the sailing of the Fulton.

Among the passengers per Fulton are Col. W. Gurney, One Hundred and Twenty-seventh New York Volunteers, nineteen other officers of lesser grade, who were wounded in the late battle at Pocotaligo, South Carolina, and our correspondents who accompanied General Sherman in his march through Georgia.

SHERMAN'S TRIUMPHANT MARCH.

Routes of the Army from Atlanta to the Atlantic----The Investment of Savannah.

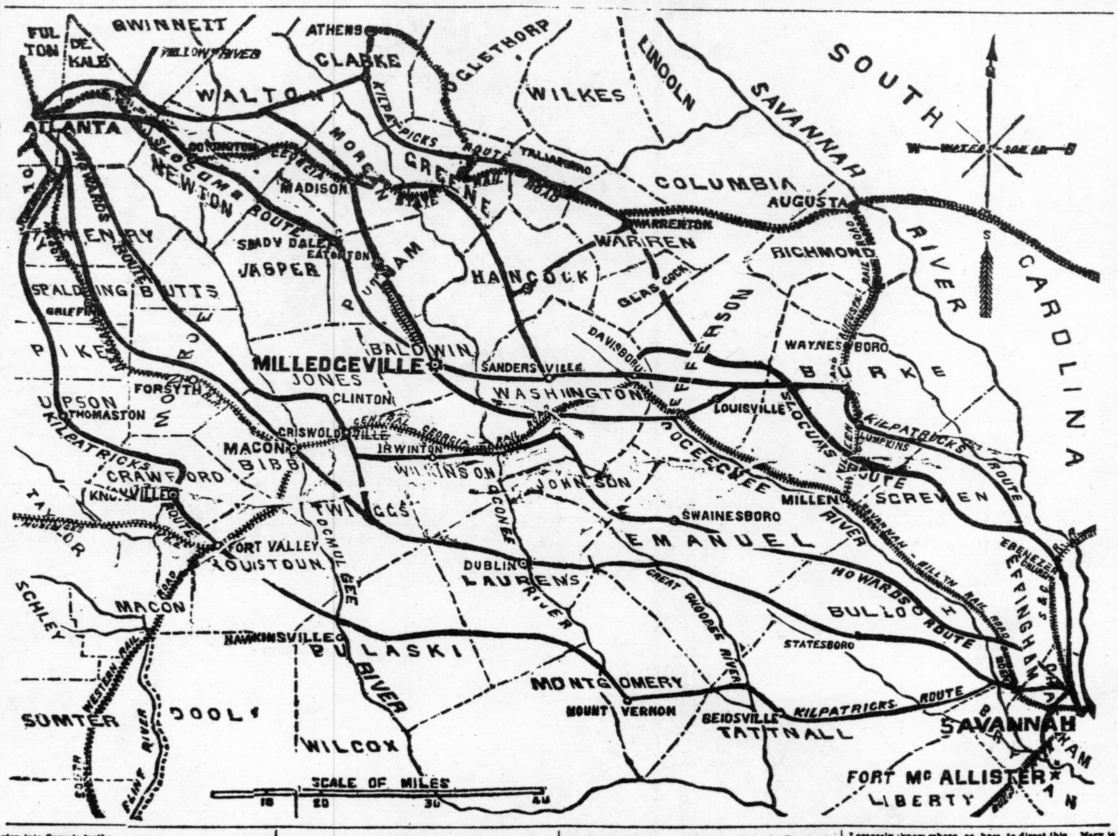

THE GRAND MARCH THROUGH GEORGIA.

Our Expeditionary Correspondence.

FORT McALLISTER, OGEECHEE RIVER, Dec. 1, 1864.

The winter campaign of Sherman, which for the past two weeks has caused so much anxiety in the minds of the loyal people of the nation, and spread terror and alarm throughout the confederacy, from Richmond to Arkansas, may now be considered ended for the present. To the casual observer its importance in a military point of view may not be at first apparent; but a careful study of the route traversed, and the situation previous to its inauguration, will exhibit the fact that Sherman's mouth of raiding in the confederacy has produced results even greater than that which followed the fall of Atlanta. I propose, briefly, to inform the reader of

THE GENERAL SITUATION.

Previous to the commencement of this bold and audacious movement through the enemy's country, going as far back as the commencement of the spring campaign, I will renew the situation and record what seems to me to have influenced the recent movements of Sherman.

On assuming command of the Military Division of the Mississippi, Sherman found Johnston in force at Dalton, and Longstreet wintering in East Tennessee, confronted by Schofield. Before the campaigning season arrived Longstreet withdrew, leaving but one large army (Johnston's) in the Southwest to be assailed. Military men all agree that the East Tennessee route to Virginia is the most feasible mode of investing Richmond, by the capture of Lynchburg, the key to the whole military position in the East and I believe that Sherman's keen sagacity pointed that way. But he had no alternative. With an army of only a hundred thousand he could not hold his long line of supplies from Louisville and protect Middle Tennessee from invasion while operating from Knoxville, consequently he was forced to follow Johnston into Georgia further and further from his base, until Atlanta fell into our hands, and Sherman found that Hood's army was still formidable for mischief. With Atlanta we severed the railway communications for a time, but the branch roads around Milledgeville and Macon still enabled the enemy to draw supplies from Florida, Southern Georgia, Alabama and Mississippi, for the subsistence of their armies, while it gave us one hundred and forty miles more of railway to guard against raids upon our flanks and guerilla depredations in the rear.

The further pursuit of Hood, consequently, seemed fraught with danger and perplexity, and Sherman seems to have studied well the problem how to shorten his line of supplies, and at the same time hold Chattanooga, the key to Tennessee. The campaign of the summer had ended, Hood's army being not less than thirty thousand, while the draft had very largely swelled Sherman's ranks. It was then that the great genius of the man solved the question; and this campaign was created and worked out upon the map. The moment he could draw Hood away from his front, beyond the reach of railway communication with the rebel base of supplies, Sherman saw that by dividing his large army he could with the one wing keep Hood employed and by bold and rapid movements strike the coast and open up a new line of supplies, via some of the large rivers, from which he could operate against the interior of Georgia, Alabama and the Carolinas.

I have the best authority for saying that the subsequent advance to the coast was of Sherman's own conception, submitted and explained by him to General Grant and the War Department, and by them heartily approved.

With the subsequent movement of Hood to Sherman's rear, the cutting of his communications, the apparent tardiness of Sherman in pursuit, and the escape of Hood into Northern Alabama, the reader is familiar, and at the time, no doubt, felt like censuring Sherman for not showing more determination and energy against inferior numbers. But they must now see that this was a part of Sherman's well matured plan.

While Hood was boldly pushing away from his base Sherman was gathering all his strength for a desperate blow that was destined to break the outer shell of the rebellion and expose its vitals.

PREPARATIONS FOR THE MARCH.

Sending the Fourth and Twenty-third corps to Thomas as a nucleus for a new command, a new army was organized under that well tried general, and then Sherman bade the North good bye, destroyed the railroad from Atlanta to Chattanooga, refitted his army at Atlanta and cut loose—destination, the coast; object, a new base.

Loading his wagons with sixteen days rations for a march of over three hundred miles through an enemy's country, he first divides his command into four columns, marches via the Augusta and Atlanta Railway, destroys it in his march as well as the road to Macon. While his right wing threatens Macon the left occupies the capital of the State and lays waste the railways, cotton mills, foundries and machine shops. In his march he subsists his armies upon the fat of the land, branches off, threatens Augusta, cuts the railway communication with Savannah; then rapidly turns south, crosses the Ogeechee river, and concentrating his command covers his flanks with the two streams and moves direct upon Savannah and the coast, completely destroying the railways of Georgia, leaving not enough subsistence behind him to winter a kid, invests Savannah, and in thirty days from the time he cut loose, opens up a new line of supplies with his base only ten miles from his army.

And all this marching of over three hundred and fifty miles through an enemy's country is performed without the loss of a wagon or mule, a gun or a pound of ammunition.

The intelligent reader will now see the importance of this campaign in a military point of view. With Georgia stripped of all its summer crops the railways all destroyed, Hood's army cannot subsist upon or occupy it until the return of another crop, and with Thomas confronting him he cannot hurry to the relief of Savannah and Charleston, which are now tottering to their downfall.

With a large army under Sherman and a grand navy under the gallant sea dog Dahlgren threatening them, their possession by us is only a question of a few weeks.

But it has had another important effect upon our common enemy. Heretofore Lee has drawn a large amount of subsistence from Florida, Georgia, Alabama, Mississippi and Texas. This raid of Sherman's has not only cut every line of communication with the Southwest, but blotted out the machine shops and iron works that furnished the material for repairing these railway arteries and veins. Hence for the future Lee must depend entirely upon the Carolinas and Virginia for subsistence for his army. He may endeavor to invade East Tennessee and obtain supplies from that quarter, but the withdrawal of any considerable force for that purpose would endanger Richmond and open the gates to Grant.

Taken as a whole, I am forced to the conclusion that this campaign of Sherman's own creation and execution is one of the most fruitful the war has produced. It is a blow from which Davis and his satellites will never recover; the effects of which will be felt from one end of the country to the other.

But there is still another effect it will have. It demonstrates to European Powers the weakness of the rebels and the power of the national government to cope with armed treason and rebellion.

But to the detailed narrative, which opens with

THE CONCENTRATION OF THE ARMY.

On the 11th the army was located as follows:—The Twentieth corps at Atlanta, the Fifteenth and Seventeenth corps at Powder Spring road, on the Chattahoochee river, and the Fourteenth corps at Kingston, Ga. Sherman's headquarters were at the latter place.

On the morning of the 12th the army commenced concentrating around Atlanta. The Fourteenth corps, Brevet Major General Davis commanding, remained at Kingston to cover the shipment north of the government property and rolling stock of the railway, and at noon of that day the Third brigade of the First division, Colonel H. A. Hambright, Seventy-ninth Pennsylvania, commanding, who, by the way, was the first commandant at Kingston, moved out, and the place was evacuated. Notwithstanding that the Colonel took every precaution to prevent a wanton destruction of the place, the negroes, who brought up the rear, fired several buildings, which were consumed. The corps reached Cartersville at night, and, after provisioning the troops, the public property was destroyed, and on the following day (the 13th) Big Shanty was reached, and the troops bivouacked for the night. Next day the corps, reached the Chattahoochee river, and on the 15th Atlanta.

CHATTANOOGA RAILWAY DESTROYED.

The railway was torn up from Chattanooga to Atlanta, and all the bridges laid in ashes, as well as every building that could be of benefit to the enemy. The straggling negroes and cavalry destroyed quite a number of uninhabited houses, and, I regret to say, three or four churches.

On the 14th and 15th, the Fifteenth and Seventeenth corps, under General Howard, marched to a camp one mile south of Atlanta, to which point Slocum, commanding the left wing, moved on the morning of the 15th, leaving the city entirely empty, except a few citizens, who remained scattered over the city, preferring to dwell in the city until the return to its ruins of their disloyal friends than to accept of free transportation to the land of "Yankee mudsills" and "Puritanical abolitionists." The afternoon was spent in emptying the storehouses of clothing, commissary supplies, &c., and their transfer to the persons of the troops of the Fourteenth corps.

During the entire day Atlanta presented a very busy appearance, every street of importance being blockaded by wagon trains and mounted officers and men. Quite a number of houses were fired during the day, and regular detailed parties from the Twentieth corps destroyed all the public buildings of value to the enemy.

GENERAL SHERMAN'S ORDERS TO HIS TROOPS.

After the men had bivouacked for the night the following orders, issued by General Sherman, were read to the troops, and were greeted with many manifestations of approbation by the veterans, who, in so many bloody battles, have followed the lead of Sherman:—

SHERMAN'S ORDERS.

Special Field Orders—No. 119.

HEADQUARTERS, MILITARY DIVISION OF MISSISSIPPI, IN THE FIELD, KINGSTON, GA., Nov. 8, 1864.

The General commanding deems it proper at this time to inform the officers and men of the Fourteenth, Fifteenth, Seventeenth and Twentieth corps, that he has organized them into an army for a special purpose, well known to the War Department and to General Grant. It is sufficient for you to know that it involves a departure from our present base, and a long and difficult march to a new one. All the chances of war have been considered and provided for as far as human sagacity can. All he asks of you is to maintain that discipline, patience and courage which have characterized you in the past, and he hopes, through you, to strike a blow at our enemy that will have a material effect in producing what we all so much desire—his complete overthrow. Of all things the most important is, that the men, during marches and in camp, keep their places and not scatter about as stragglers or foragers, to be picked up by hostile people in detail.

It is also of the utmost importance that our wagons should not be loaded with anything but provisions and ammunition. All surplus servants, non-combatants and refugees should now go to the rear, and none should be encouraged to encumber us on the march. At some future time we will be enabled to provide for the poor whites and blacks who seek to escape the bondage under which they are now suffering.

With these few simple cautions in your minds, he hopes to lead you to achievements equal in importance to those of the past. By order of

Major General W. T. SHERMAN.

L. M. DAYTON, Aid de camp.

MILITARY DIVISION, MISSISSIPPI, IN THE FIELD, KINGSTON, GA., Nov. 9, 1864.

Special Field Orders—No. 120.

I. For the purpose of military operations this army is divided into two wings, viz:—

The right wing, Major General O. O. Howard commanding—the Fifteenth and Seventeenth corps.

The left wing, Major General H. W. Slocum commanding—the Fourteenth and Twentieth corps.

II. The habitual order of march will be, whenever practicable, by four roads, as near parallel as possible, and converging at points hereafter to be indicated in orders. The cavalry, Brigadier General Kilpatrick commanding, will receive special orders from the Commander-in-Chief.

Paragraph III. relates to the position in the line of the ambulances and wagons.

IV. The army will forage liberally on the country during the march. To this end each brigade commander will organize a good and efficient foraging party, under command of one or more discreet officers, who will gather near the route travelled corn or forage of any kind, meat of any kind, vegetables, corn meal, or whatever is needed by the command: aiming at all times to keep in the wagons at least ten days' provisions for the command and three days' forage. Soldiers must not enter the dwellings of the inhabitants, or commit any trespass, but during a halt or in a camp they may be permitted to gather turnips, potatoes and other vegetables, and to drive in stock in sight of their camp. To regular foraging parties must be entrusted the gathering of provisions and forage at any distance from the road travelled.

V. To army corps commanders alone is entrusted the power to destroy mills, houses, cotton gins, &c., and for them this general principle is laid down:—In districts and neighborhoods where the army is unmolested no destruction of such property should be permitted: but should guerillas or bushwhackers molest our march, or should the inhabitants burn bridges, obstruct roads, or otherwise manifest local hostility, then army commanders should order and enforce a devastation more or less relentless, according to the measure of such hostility.

VI. As for horses, mules, wagons, &c., belonging to the inhabitants, the cavalry and artillery may appropriate freely and without limit, discriminating, however, between the rich, who are generally hostile, and the poor, or industrious, usually neutral or friendly. Foraging parties may also take mules or horses to replace the jaded animals of their trains, or to serve as pack mules for the regiments or brigades. In all foraging, of whatever kind, the parties will refrain from abusive or threatening language, and may, when the officers in command think proper, give certificates of the fact, but no receipts, and they will endeavor to leave each family a reasonable portion for their maintenance. * * * *

By order of Major General W. T. SHERMAN.

L. M. DAYTON, A. D. C.

ATLANTA ON FIRE.

"Now negress night came solemn down" upon the city, and as the flames spread from the public buildings and the depot that had been fired the whole heavens became illuminated by the lurid glare, while the unexploded shells in the dwellings and storehouses became heated, and as they exploded in rapid succession one almost imagined that the scenes of August last, when one hundred thousand heroes confronted the rebel stronghold, were being re-enacted.

Standing upon an eminence overlooking the doomed city, I had an excellent view of the conflagration, and never had I beheld so grand a sight. As night waned the gentle breezes carried the destroying element from house to house, and block to block, until one-half of the rebel city was in flames, the glare of which was so bright that the soldiers a mile distant read their last letters from home by the light. Next morning I rode over the city among the ruins, where nothing remained to tell the tale but tottering walls and blackened chimneys, that, like gravestones, stood there as monuments of departed glory.

ON THE WAR TRACK AGAIN.

On the morning of the 16th, at daylight, the whole army once more took up the line of march—the Seventeenth corps on the McDonough road, the Fourteenth on the Augusta road (running parallel with the railroad), with the Twentieth on the left and the Fifteenth on the right flanks. I accompanied the column of the Fourteenth corps, which passed out through Decatur, and the same evening encamped in Lithonia—a small town twenty miles southeast of Atlanta—without encountering any enemy.

On the 17th the march was resumed at daylight, through a country teeming in stock, vegetables and grain, that were found in abundance on all the large plantations that lined the route. This part of the State gives evidence of wealth and prosperity, and as we moved further into the interior the works of war's ravages became less frequent.

THE COUNTRY

is quite open, well watered, good roads and delightful climate. About half-past nine o'clock in the morning,

CONYERS,

a town of about five hundred inhabitants, was reached, but no halt was made, and the troops continued the march without interrupting the citizens, who flocked in large numbers to the doors and windows to see the long expected and much feared Yankees, and listen to the music of a score of bands that gave forth their martial strains. Only one man was seen in the town. All the others had "refugeed," as the ebony children classically expressed themselves. A rebel lieutenant, named Lewis A. Middleton, who acted as provost marshal at that place, left very hurriedly, forgetting to call at the post office for several letters, which were taken possession of by an aid de camp, and turned over to General Sherman for examination. The letters disclosed the fact that the Georgia militia accompanied Hood as far as Gadsden, Ala., when Governor Brown ordered them back to the State, where they arrived on the 6th, after a march of nearly five hundred miles.

One of the letters is worth producing here:—

A REBEL LETTER.

MONTGOMERY, August 13, 1864.

MY DEAR BROTHER—I have deferred writing to you for the past two weeks, daily hoping to get a few lines from you to tell us where you are and how you fared during and after the Yankee raid—but in vain; so I'll venture to write, even though my letter never reaches you. In fact, I scarcely know where or how to direct this. Mary is down at Greenville on a visit to Miss King, where she has been over two weeks. She went for her health, which had been very bad all the spring and summer. She writes me that she has improved and is enjoying herself very much; but no wonder, for she says she gets so well fed; that no one at Greenville seems to feel the war, but live in full and plenty, as they did before; though Margaret King always did live well; but she has plenty of money and nothing to do with it but support herself.

We had a terrible alarm the night the raiders were expected in Montgomery. This is the most excitable family the world ever produced, from the Judge down to the smallest negro child in the lot. Words of mine would fail to give you an idea of the time we had. Sufficient to say that the Judge snatched up his papers and money, flew down to the cars to take care of his own precious self, leaving orders that we all should follow at the first alarm bell, &c. Such a scene of confusion I never saw, and, without stopping to reflect, I jumped out of bed and commenced gathering together my clothes, for I was determined to try and save them, as I never expected to get any more, and where to get trunks or boxes to pack in I knew not. So I was up the whole night long, flying here and there, half dressed, and six o'clock came in the morning before I even sat down. Of course my servants were of no use whatever, and the Judge's, whom he thinks paragons, were in open rebellion. What influence they would have had on Polly when the time came to leave I cannot tell. Fortunately they were not tried, as the vandals did not get here; but when the excitement was over, and I had time to reflect, I thought how foolish it was in me to worry about running away any more, especially with Judge Jordan; for, in any great danger, he is a broken reed to lean upon—self is No. 1, and I have resolved hereafter to just stay where I am, and only regret that I was induced by the entreaties of the Judge to leave my all in Pensacola, not that I would have taken the Yankee oath. Selfish motives were at the bottom with the Judge. I hope I may do him injustice. The day after the alarm I was taken with a violent, nervous pain in my head, which seemed to get worse daily for about ten days, until I suppose the climax came, and then such excruciating pains run down the back of my head and neck that I was senseless for some time. A powerful remedy was administered—opiates and quiet—and in a few days I was myself again. In any great alarm, or excitement or rumor, I seem composed and do all that I can; but afterwards the reaction comes and prostrates me. But after this I think I shall have to stand my ground and take the Yanks as I find them. Now, I have reserved the *bonne bouche* for the last. On Monday, greatly to my surprise, a letter came from the post office, directed to Mary. It was so like your handwriting, though from Wilmington post office, that I was sure it was from you, and, while breaking the seal, wondered how you came to be there. Just think! it was a blockade letter from dear Peyton, written ever since the 20th of January—only seven months since. He had just arrived at Panama and found in the post office there two letters from Mary and one from you, dated, I think he said, 22d of July. It seems he has been in New York for the last two years. His health had been wretched, and after seeking and travelling about to various places in search of a climate to suit him, found that New York was the only place. His intention was to come into Dixie, but could not succeed; and after the fall of Vicksburg had to give up. Some of his good friends tried hard to get him in Fort Lafayette, but failed. His pecuniary matters are as usual; but it takes all he can raise to pay travelling expenses. He expected to meet his agent at Panama; but as he was not there he should go to Nicaragua, from thence to California, or perhaps accompany his agent to Europe; but would write and let us know; that we must write to him and direct our letters as we used to, to his agent in New York, and he would forward them to him, no matter in what part of the world he was. I have lost and forgotten his direction. I know it was a Mr. Sidell, Wall street; but what were the initials of the Christian name or the number of Mr. Sidell's store I have forgotten. Do you remember? If so, write and let me know, though if I write I don't see how we can get a letter to him; and as so much time has passed he may be dead. Write as soon as you can. The servants say, "Give their love to Massa Lewis." Goodby. May God bless and take care of you is ever the prayer of your affectionate sister.

I'll adopt Peyton's plan and not sign my name, in case it should fall into other hands. Love to Mary when you write.

The afternoon of the 17th was spent in destroying the Atlanta and Augusta Railway from Conyers to Yellow river, where Davis' column halted for the night, and Colonel Buell, of the Pioneer corps, threw down pontoons, upon which the army crossed on the following morning.

THE REBELS APPEAR IN OUR FRONT.

To day the First brigade, First division, Colonel Hobart commanding, had the advance, with Major Fox, of the Twenty-first Michigan, in command of the advance guard. While riding in advance of his command, he was suddenly confronted by a rebel cavalryman, who demanded his surrender. The Major was unarmed and on the point of surrendering when his regiment appeared in sight, and the rebel and his companions, who had come up, retreated without taking the Major.

AN ADVANCE BY THE LADIES.

On the 18th the army moved at half-past six, the First division in the advance, and the Seventy-ninth Pennsylvania, Lieutenant Colonel Miles, the advanced guard. The first place of importance encountered was the beautiful little town of

COVINGTON,

noted, as geographers say, for its water power and pretty women. As Hambright's brigade entered the town the Lancaster (Penn.) band struck up "Dixie's Land," when two hundred women rushed to the piazzas and doors to view the Yankee invaders of whom they had so often read. Every window and door swarmed with blooming war widows, stately matrons and shy virgins in homespun and coarse linen. But when the band had finished "Dixie" and broke off on "Yankee Doodle," oh, what a retreat. The piazzas were cleared of their beautiful inhabitants, windows came down with a slam and doors closed very abruptly, until not a fair face was visible. The troops as they moved at the right shoulder shift, the State and national colors floating in the silken Southern breeze, and the nicely paved streets resounding to the tread of the soldiers of the Union, presented an imposing appearance, not soon to be obliterated from the memories of the rebellious sympathizers with Davis and the Devil. The column encamped at eleven o'clock A. M. near Alcohovie river, distant ten miles north of Social Circle, and halted for the day.

FORAGING PARTIES

were sent out in the afternoon, and at night returned to camp with a large amount of fine stock, grain and vegetables.

THE RIGHT WING.

To-night (18th) Howard's (right) wing is encamped at Jackson, and has met no enemy. Slocum, on the left, is parallel with Howard, and has had no fighting.

SHERMAN'S HEADQUARTERS.

General Sherman makes his headquarters with Thomas' veteran corps, now commanded by Brigadier General Jeff. C. Davis.

SHERMAN TASTES SORGHUM.

Many little incidents occur daily that go to show a leader like Sherman can make himself familiar with his soldiers, and still retain their confidence and maintain thorough discipline. A colonel commanding a regiment, who witnessed it, informs me that to-day a number of soldiers who were filling their canteens from a molasses barrel, near Sherman's headquarters, were quarreling over the division of the syrup, when Sherman passing by cooly crowded in among them, and dipping his finger in it put it to his lips, remarking, "Don't crowd, boys, there is enough for all."

A PLANTATION SCENE.

About six miles south of Covington we struck the plantation of Judge Harris, who is a Massachusetts man and owns over two hundred negroes. The plantation is one of the most extensive in Central Georgia for the production of cotton and cerials of all descriptions. As the column moved past the Third brigade First division band struck up a quick step, when from the village of negro huts the dusky sons of Ham swarmed forth in large numbers and rushed to the fences. A rich scene followed. The negroes—men, women and children—struck off into a dance, swinging themselves round and twisting themselves into grotesque shapes that called forth peals of laughter from the soldiery, while shouts of "Glory be to de Lord, de Lincom's hab come!" "Won't we go long wid yous!" "Ize off to glory!" "Bress de Lord!" were heard on all sides. They followed the troops for half a mile, making the air resound with their exclamations of gladness, until driven back to the rear.

ANOTHER REBEL ATTACK.

On the 19th the column moved at daylight, Morgan's division leading, Baird next and Carlin covering the rear. The column took the Sandtown road, and when out about three miles, were fired upon by a few rebel scouts, who retreated.

WET WEATHER AND BAD ROADS.

Up to this time we had beautiful weather, but at daylight the roads were found almost impassable from the rain that had fallen in torrents during the night. Nevertheless, nine miles were made through a pouring rain, and we encamped at eight o'clock in the evening three miles south of Sandtown.

On the 20th the command moved at the usual hour, rain still falling, and the roads in a horrible condition. About noon we arrived at Shady Dale, the plantation of an old man named Matthew Whitfield, who owns nearly the whole of Putnam county, and an abundance of stock and crops. There we found

ANOTHER VILLAGE OF NEGROES,

who worked the large plantation upon which Mr. Whitfield resided, and where another scene similar to that enacted at Harris' greeted the men. About twenty-five women followed the column a mile, and were driven back by the staff officers. Nearly all the male negroes went with the army voluntarily. At night the command encamped near Eatonton, and on the morning of the 21st resumed their march, making

MURDER CREEK

before night closed in upon them and rendered marching over muddy roads and swollen rivers too dangerous to be attempted. The country through which we passed was the garden of Georgia, the plantations furnishing an abundance of everything necessary for the subsistence of man and beast, which was very generally appropriated by the foraging parties, who obtained so much potatoes and meat that the commissary wagons were not called upon to disgorge a portion of their hard tack and bacon.

THE ARMY TEAMS

had become thoroughly rejuvinated by the acquisition of hundreds of fine mules captured from the wealthy nabobs who had hidden them in the woods, where they were found by the aid of the negroes. Some of the finest horses I have seen in the South, were also impressed into the United States service.

HOWELL COBB'S "NAG" GOBBLED.

Among the blooded stock captured was General Howell Cobb's celebrated pacing mare, that cost $25,000. She was found in a swamp near Milledgeville, by private Walter Burns, Company E, Twenty-first Ohio, who, ten or twelve days after, was captured while riding her and murdered. He was acting as orderly, and when his companions dug open his grave they found that the enemy had cut his throat after shooting him through the head.

THE APPROACH TO MILLEDGEVILLE

The rain cleared off on the 20th, and the cold north winds came down like good spirits to aid the onward march of the victors by drying up the roads and relieving the faithful friend of the soldier—the mule. The bracing wind and warm sun were balm to the toiling veterans, whose clothes for four days had been drenched with Georgia rains and mud, and as they were near Milledgeville—the capital of the State—where was passed the ordinance of secession, increased speed was plainly discernable in the movement of the men.

At twelve o'clock noon, Davis' advance, composed of Baird's division, encamped in the city, and by dark the woods and shrubbery around the city were illuminated by the camp fires of Sherman's grand army of "invaders."

But let me here dwell a moment upon the

OPERATIONS OF THE TWENTIETH CORPS,

which formed the left, and moved from Atlanta on a road parallel with Davis' route, through Decatur, Madison, Eatonton, &c. General Williams, of Michigan, commanded the corps; Jackson, the First; Geary, of Pennsylvania, the Second; and Ward, of Kentucky, the Third divisions. The corps made excellent time from Atlanta to Milledgeville, encountering no enemy, nor even firing a shot, except at venturesome swine and cattle which strayed too near foraging parties.

NEW YORK PLANTS ITS COLORS ON THE CAPITAL.

Major General Slocum, the well tried commander of the left wing, accompanied the corps, which moved on a better road than that travelled by Davis, and reached the city one day in advance of him, planting upon the State House of Georgia the national colors of the One Hundred and Fourth New York regiment, which regiment, with the Third Wisconsin, who fought in the Valley of Virginia under Banks, were detailed as provost guard.

These, however, were not the first troops to enter the capital. The news that "Old Lightning" (which is now applied to Sherman) was coming spread like the wind, and on Saturday Governor Brown and the Legislature, which was in session, packed up their valises and vamosed the ranche, leaving about [illegible] rebel cavalry to cover their retreat to Augusta where they hoped to find rest for their wearied feet.

CITY CAPTURED BY [illegible]

The cavalry left the same night, and on Sunday, the 20th, Captain Duncan rushed into town on a three [illegible] cavalry charge, frightening the old granny who occupied the Mayor's chair into a surrender and stampeding all the male population, with a small squad of ten men. One rebel lady, whose husband is a high official in the State, and whose family is among the *bon ton*, described the surrender in the following words:—

"Early in the afternoon five Yankee scouts came dashing pell mell into the town, when the men—the mean, craven-hearted wretches, fully two hundred strong—skedaddled, leaving our baby Mayor to go out and surrender the place unconditionally to five greasy Yankees, ten miles in advance of their army. Oh, the men are mean, chicken-hearted wretches, and the Mayor a puffed up old fool. Had I been in town I'd collected all the women and driven the skunks out with mop handles and broom sticks."

This is the whole story in a nutshell. The craven-hearted bipeds of the masculine gender ran away and left their wives to the tender mercies of the Yankees, who, they have time and again asserted, come here to ravish, burn and plunder indiscriminately.

THE REBEL CAPITAL

is a very pretty little city, capable of accommodating

Sherman's veterans marching in Washington, D.C., May 1865

1865

Abraham Lincoln

John Wilkes Booth

Ulysses S. Grant

Robert E. Lee

January 6, Republican J.M. Ashley, brings up the proposed Thirteenth Amendment to abolish slavery in the House of Representatives. ***January 13,*** Confederate General John Bell Hood resigns as the commander of the Army of Tennessee. ***January 15,*** Fort Fisher, North Carolina is captured by the Federals. ***January 31,*** General Lee is named Commander-in-Chief of all Confederate armies. ***February 3,*** President Lincoln meets with Confederate representatives aboard the *River Queen* in Hampton Roads, Virginia and repeats his demand for unconditional restoration of the Union. ***February 6,*** John C. Breckinridge is named Confederate Secretary of War. ***February 17,*** General Sherman's army captures Columbia, South Carolina. ***February 22,*** The Federal Army enters Wilmington, North Carolina as Confederate General Braxton Bragg withdraws his troops. ***March 2,*** Jubal Early's cavalry is defeated by a Federal cavalry force at Waynesborough, Virginia. ***March 13,*** The Confederacy calls for enlisting negroes in the army. ***March 21,*** The Battle of Bentonville, North Carolina ends with the Confederates under General Joseph Johnston failing to stop the advance of Sherman's army. ***March 25,*** The Confederates attack Fort Steadman at Petersburg, Virginia, but are forced to withdraw with over 4,000 casualties. ***March 27,*** President Lincoln meets with Generals Grant and Sherman aboard the *River Queen* at City Point, Virginia to discuss plans for the final campaigns of the war. ***March 29,*** The Appomattox campaign gets under way as the Federal Armies of the Potomac and the James, totaling over 125,000 men, move against General Lee at Richmond and Petersburg. ***April 1,*** General Lee's right flank is broken at the Battle of Five Forks, Virginia, putting his entire retreat in jeapordy. ***April 2,*** The Confederate Government boards a train bound for Danville, Virginia as it begins its evacuation from Richmond. ***April 3,*** Union troops enter and occupy the Confederate capital of Richmond, raising the United States flag over the State House. ***April 4,*** President Lincoln enters Richmond and tours the city surrounded by cheering crowds of grateful negroes. ***April 6,*** The troops of Confederate General Richard Ewell are forced to surrender to the Federals at Sayler's Creek, Virginia in the last major engagement between the Army of Northern Virginia and the Union Army of the Potomac. ***April 7,*** General Grant writes to General Lee, stating "The result of the last week must convince you of the hopelessness of further resistance. . .". ***April 8,*** General Grant receives General Lee's response which states, ". . . before considering your proposition, ask the terms you will offer on condition of its (the Army of Northern Virginia) surrender." ***April 9,*** The Confederates attack near Appomattox Station, Virginia, hoping to break through the Federal force blocking their retreat and, when the attack fails, Lee formally surrenders to General Grant. ***April 12,*** Mobile, Alabama becomes the final major Confederate city to fall. ***April 14,*** President Lincoln is shot by Actor John Wilkes Booth in the presidential box at Ford's Theater in Washington, D.C. ***April 15,*** President Lincoln dies of his wounds in the Peterson House across the street from Ford's Theater at 7:22 A.M. At 11 A.M., Vice President Johnson is administered the oath by Chief Justice Salmon P. Chase and becomes the seventeenth President of the United States. ***April 18,*** General Sherman and Confederate General Joseph Johnston sign an agreement calling for an armistice by all armies still in the field, but go far beyond Grant's terms for Lee's surrender. ***April 19,*** The bells of Washington toll after brief funeral services for President Lincoln. Throngs of mourners come to view the body at the Capital rotunda. ***April 24,*** President Johnson disapproves of Sherman's surrender terms and orders him to renew hostilities unless Johnston surrenders under the same terms as General Grant. ***April 26,*** Confederate General Joseph Johnston surrenders his army near Durham Station, North Carolina, while in Virginia John Wilkes Booth is found and killed by Federal soldiers. ***May 4,*** Confederate General Richard Taylor surrenders the last Confederate forces at Citronelle, Alabama. ***May 10,*** Jefferson Davis is captured in Georgia and President Johnson declares armed resistance at an end. The agonizing years of reconstruction would now begin, but the four long years of civil war would forever have an impact on future generations of Americans.

The Philadelphia Inquirer.

DOUBLE SHEET. | PHILADELPHIA, WEDNESDAY, JANUARY 18, 1865. | PRICE TWO CENTS.

VICTORY!

Fall of Fort Fisher!

2000 REBELS CAPTURED!

72 Heavy Guns Taken!

SPLENDID BEHAVIOR OF THE ARMY!

Gallantry of the Marines and Sailors!

TERRIFIC ASSAULT OF OUR TROOPS!

Dreadful Hand-to-Hand Combat

FEARFUL CARNAGE DURING THE NIGHT

500 Dead Rebels in the Fort!

OUR LOSS 900 KILLED AND WOUNDED

The Rebel Pirates "Tallahassee" and "Chickamauga" Cornered.

EXPLOSION OF A MAGAZINE

Terrible Loss of Life!

200 MEN KILLED AND WOUNDED

Rebel News from Wilmington.

Lee Acknowledges the Fall of Fort Fisher

THE ARMY.

OFFICIAL WAR BULLETIN.

WASHINGTON, Jan. 17—10·40 A. M.—Major-General Dix, New York.—The following official despatches have just been received at this Department:—

General Terry's Despatch.

HEAD-QUARTERS UNITED STATES FORCES ON FEDERAL POINT, N. C., Jan. 15, 1865, via Fortress Monroe, Jan. 17.—Brigadier-General J. A. Rawlins.—General:—I have the honor to report that Fort Fisher was carried by assault this afternoon and evening, by General Ames' Division, and the Second Brigade of the First Division of the Twenty-fourth Army Corps, aided by a battalion of marines and seamen from the navy.

The assault was preceded by a heavy bombardment from the Federal fleet, and was made at 3·30 P. M., when the First Brigade (Gen. Curtis) of Ames' Division effected a lodgment upon the parapet, but full possession of the work was not obtained until 10 P. M.

The behavior of both officers and men was most admirable. All the works south of Fort Fisher are now occupied by our troops. We have not less than twelve hundred prisoners, including General Whiting and Colonel Lamb, the commandant of the fort.

I regret to say that our loss is severe, especially in officers. I am not yet able to form any estimate of the number of casualties.

(Signed) ALFRED H. TERRY,
Brevet Major-General,
Commanding the Expedition.

Report of Chief Engineer Comstock.

FORT FISHER, Jan. 16—2 A. M.—Hon. C. A. Dana, Assistant Secretary of War:—After a careful reconnoissance on the 14th it was decided to risk an assault on Fort Fisher. Paine's Division, with Colonel Abbott's Brigade, were to hold our line, already strong across the Peninsula and facing Wilmington, against Hoke, while Ames' Division should assault on the west end of the land front, and four hundred marines and sixteen hundred sailors on the east end.

After three hours of a heavy navy fire, the assault was made at 3 P. M. on the 15th. General Curtis' Brigade led, and as soon as it got on the west end of the land front, was followed by Pennypacker's, and later by Bell's.

After desperate fighting, gaining foot by foot, and severe loss, at five P. M. we had possession of about half the land front. Abbott's Brigade was then taken from our line facing Wilmington and put into Fort Fisher, and on pushing it forward at ten o'clock P. M., it took the rest of the work with little resistance, the garrison falling back to the extreme point of the Peninsula, where they were followed and captured, among others General Whiting and Colonel Lamb, both wounded.

I think we have quite one thousand prisoners. I hope our own loss may not exceed five hundred, but it is impossible to judge in the night.

Among the wounded are the commanders of the three leading brigades; General Curtis being wounded, not severely, but Colonels Pennypacker and Bell dangerously.

The land front was a formidable one, the parapet in places fifteen to twenty feet high, but the men went at it nobly and under a severe musketry fire.

The marines and sailors went up gallantly, but the musketry fire from the east end of the land front was so severe that they did not succeed in entering the work.

The navy fire on the work, judging from the holes, must have been terrific. Many of the guns were injured. How many there were on the point I cannot say—perhaps thirty or forty.

(Signed), C. B. COMSTOCK,
Lieutenant-Colonel, Aid-de-Camp and Chief Engineer.

Another Salute from General Grant.

Another despatch estimates the number of prisoners captured at 2500, and the number of guns at 72.

General Grant telegraphs that in honor of this great triumph, achieved by the united valor of the army and navy, he has ordered a salute of 100 guns to be fired by each of the armies operating against Richmond. C. A. DANA,
Assistant Secretary of War.

WILMINGTON!

Admiral Porter and General Terry. The Capture of Fort Fisher. The Approaches to Wilmington.

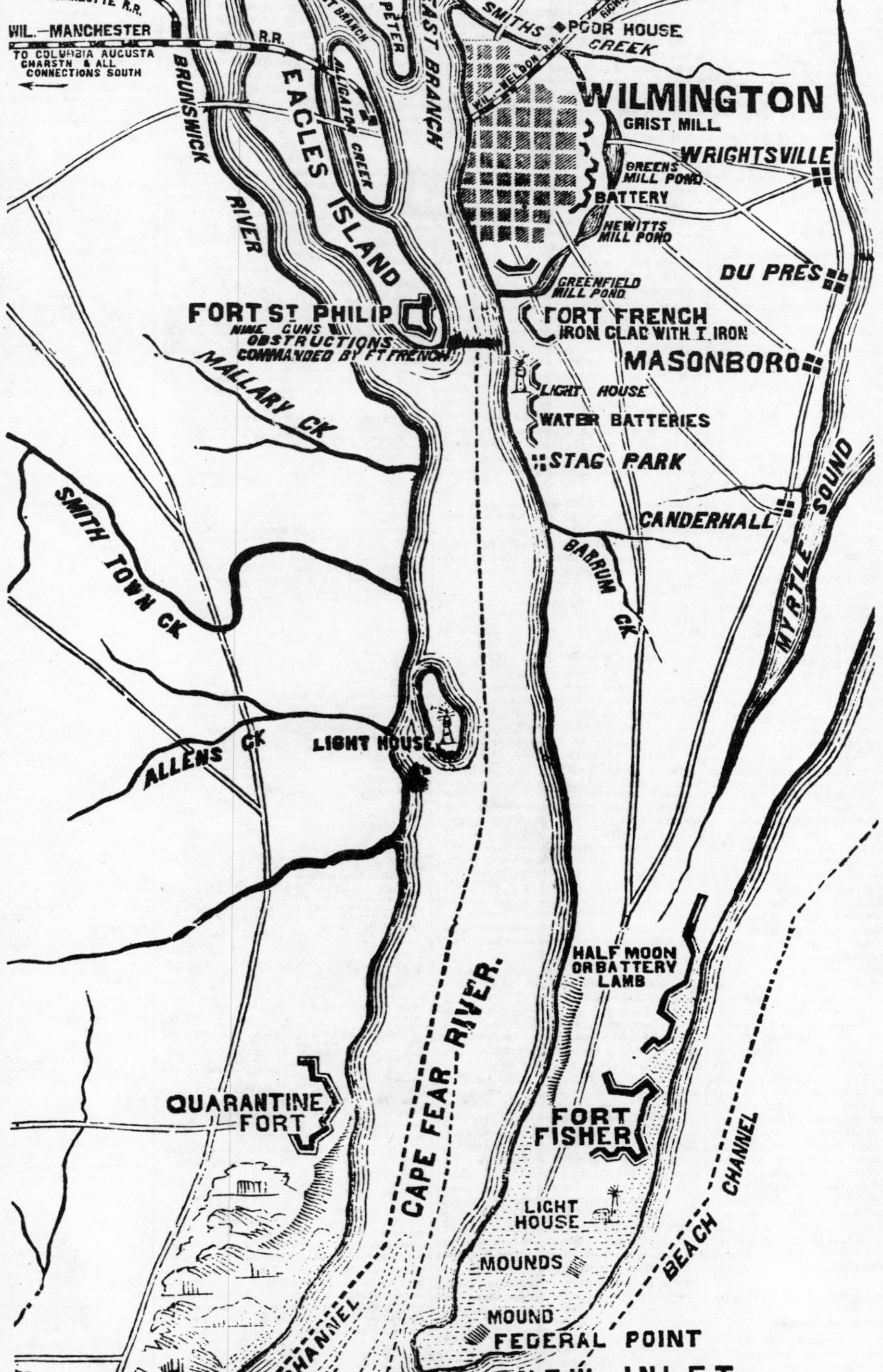

SECOND OFFICIAL DESPATCH.

Rebel Accounts of the Capture.

WASHINGTON, Jan. 17, 9 o'clock P. M.—Major-General Dix, New York.—The Richmond *Whig*, of this morning, contains the following account of the capture of Fort Fisher by the naval and land forces of the United States:—

Fall of Fort Fisher.

The unwelcome news of the fall of Fort Fisher, commanding the entrance to the Cape Fear River, was received this morning, and occasioned in the community a sensation of profound regret.

The capture of this fort is equivalent to the closing of the harbor of Wilmington by the enemy's fleet. It is situated about eighteen miles below the city, but is the main defense of the entrance to the river, and its fall, therefore, will prevent in future the arrival or departure of blockade runners. How far this source of revenue may prove injurious to our cause remains to be seen, but at present we regard it rather as an unfortunate than a disastrous event.

The following is the official report:—

HEAD-QUARTERS OF THE ARMY OF VIRGINIA, Jan. 16.—Hon. J. A. Seddon:—General Bragg reports that the enemy bombarded Fort Fisher furiously all day yesterday. At 4 o'clock P. M. their infantry advanced to the assault, a heavy demonstration at the same hour being made against their rear by our troops.

At half-past six o'clock General Whiting reported that their attack had failed and the garrison was being strengthened with fresh troops. About ten o'clock P. M. the fort was captured with most of its garrison. No further particulars are at this time known.

(Signed) R. E. LEE.

No despatches have been received from General Terry since that of Sunday night, announcing the result of the assault.

C. A. DANA, Assist. Sec. of War.

THE VERY LATEST.

A Bloody Struggle—Two Thousand Prisoners and Seventy-two Guns Captured—Our Loss Nine Hundred—The Pirates "Tallahassee" and "Chickamauga" Chased up the River—Explosion of the Magazine—Two Hundred of our Men Killed and Wounded.

FORTRESS MONROE, Jan. 17, 6·30 P. M.—After three days and nights bombardment Fort Fisher is ours, with all the contiguous works commanding New Inlet. The assault was made by the army and the naval brigade at three o'clock on Saturday afternoon. One corner of the fort was secured in half an hour, but there was a hand-to-hand fight with the garrison, which lasted until nine o'clock at night. There was a stubborn and bloody resistance, and the fort and its approaches were strewn with the dead.

The garrison had been heavily reinforced, and the number of prisoners taken is over two thousand. We captured seventy-two guns. All the forts, including the Mound and Zeke's Island batteries, surrendered. The Rebel loss in the assault was five hundred dead besides the wounded. Fleet Lieutenant Preston and Lieutenant Porter, commandant of the flag-ship, were both killed in the assault. General Whiting and Colonel Lamb are both prisoners and wounded.

The Rebel pirates *Tallahassee* and *Chickamauga* were in the fight, and were driven up the river. Our gun-boats went up the river on Monday morning.

Our prisoners will be immediately sent North. We had several days of delightful weather.

The magazine in the fort exploded by accident, on Monday morning, killing and wounding two hundred of our men.

The *Santiago de Cuba* brings the bodies of Lieutenants Preston and Porter, and the wounded of the navy.

THE NAVY.

Admiral Porter's Official Despatch.

WASHINGTON, Jan. 17.—The Navy Department has received the following:—

FROM OFF FORT FISHER, Jan 15.—Telegraphed from Fortress Monroe, Jan. 17.—Hon. Gideon Welles, Secretary of the Navy—Sir:—Fort Fisher is ours. I send a bearer of despatches with a brief account of the affair. General Terry is entitled to the highest praise and the gratitude of his country for the manner in which he has conducted his part of the operations. He is my beau ideal of a soldier and a General. Our co-operation has been most cordial. The result is victory, which will always be ours when the army and navy go hand in hand. The navy loss in the assault was heavy. The army loss is also heavy. D. D. PORTER, Rear-Admiral.

Congratulatory Order of the Secretary of the Navy.

WASHINGTON, Jan. 17.—Secretary Welles has addressed the following congratulatory telegram to Admiral Porter:—

NAVY DEPARTMENT, Jan. 17, 1865.—To Rear-Admiral D. D. Porter, Commanding North Atlantic Blockading Squadron, off Wilmington, care Commandant Navy Yard, Washington.—Sir:—The Department has just received your brief, but highly gratifying despatches announcing the fall, on the 15th instant, of Fort Fisher, under the combined assault of the navy and army, and hastens to congratulate you and General Terry, and the brave officers, sailors and soldiers of your respective commands on your glorious success. Accept my thanks for your good work. (Signed) GIDEON WELLES,
Secretary of the Navy.

Immediately upon the receipt of the news the following telegram was sent to the Commandants of each of the Navy Yards:—

NAVY DEPARTMENT, Jan. 17, 1865.—Fire a national salute in honor of the capture on the 15th instant of the Rebel works on Federal Point, near Wilmington, by a combined attack of the army and navy.

(Signed) GIDEON WELLES,
Secretary of the Navy.

OPERATIONS OF THE NAVY.

Preliminary Report of Admiral Porter.

WASHINGTON, Jan. 17.—The following has been received at the Navy Department from Admiral Porter:—

FLAG-SHIP MALVERN, OFF FORT FISHER, N. C., Jan. 14, 1864.—Sir:—I have the honor to inform you that operations have been resumed against the forts at the entrance of Cape Fear River. Since the first attack on that place, and the subsequent withdrawal of the troops, I have been employed in filling the ships with ammunition and coal. The difficulties we have had to encounter no one can conceive. All our work had to be done with the larger vessels anchored on the coast, exposed, you may almost say at sea, with the violent gales, that blow here almost incessantly. On these gales the enemy depended to break up our operations. We will see. We have gone through about the worst of it; have held on through gales heavy enough to drive anything to sea, and we have sustained no damage whatever. After the troops arrived the weather set in bad, and the gale was very heavy. As soon as it was over I got underway on the 12th instant, and forming the vessels in three lines, with the transports in company, I steamed for Fort Fisher.

On the morning of the 13th the fleet took its station in three lines, close to the beach, and the boats were sent at once to take off the troops. These were landed with about twelve days' provisions, at about 2 o'clock P. M. This time I pursued a different plan in attacking the Rebel works. I sent in the *New Ironsides*, Commodore Radford, leading the monitors *Saugus*, *Canonicus*, *Monadnock* and *Mahopac*. At 7·30 A. M., the forts opened on them as they approached, but they quietly took up their old positions, within one thousand yards of Fisher, and when ready they opened their batteries. In this way I tempted the enemy to engage the monitors, that we might see what guns they had, and seeing where they were, be able to dismount them by our fire. Quite a spirited engagement went on between the forts and the *Ironsides* and monitors.

It was soon apparent that the iron vessels had the best of it. Traverses began to disappear, and the southern angle of Fort Fisher commenced to look very dilapidated. The guns were silenced one after the other, and only one heavy gun in the southern angle kept up its fire. The fire of this gun was not at all accurate, as it inflicted no damage on the iron vessels. They were hit, though, several times. By way of letting the enemy know that we had some shell left on board the wooden ships, and did not intend to take any unfair advantage of him by using the iron vessels alone, I ordered line No. 1 on the plan, led by Captain Alden, of the *Brooklyn*, and line No. 2, led by Commodore Thatcher, of the *Colorado*, to go and attack the batteries. This was done in the handsomest manner. Not a mistake was committed except firing too rapidly, and making too much smoke. The heavy fire of the large vessels shut up the enemy's guns at once, and after firing till after dark the wooden vessels dropped out to their anchorage.

The *Ironsides* and monitors maintained their positions through the night, firing a shell now and then. They were lying within one thousand yards of the fort and one of the monitors within seven hundred yards, and the fort does not fire a gun at them, thinking, no doubt, that it is a waste of powder. The firing from the fleet will commence as soon as we get breakfast, and be kept up as long as the Ordnance Department provides us with shells and guns. There is a perfect understanding between General Terry and myself. I believe everything has been done to suit him. I have heard no complaints, and know that we have felt every disposition to help the army along.

A detailed report of our operations here will be sent in when we get through. I see no reason to doubt our success. The forts will be used up soon. We have a respectable force landed on a strip of land which our naval guns completely command, a place of defense which would enable us to hold on against a very large army. I will report to you by every opportunity.

I have the honor to be, very respectfully, your obedient servant,

DAVID D. PORTER, Rear Admiral.

To Hon. Gideon Welles, Secretary of the Navy, Washington, D. C.

Getting Ready.

BALTIMORE, Jan. 17.—The following are the details of the operations of the navy before Fort Fisher:—

Friday, Jan. 13, 1865.—At 8 bells (4 o'clock), this morning, we were aroused from slumber by a gun from the flag-ship, and the burning of Coston's preparatory signals, red and green, as an indication to the fleet that it is time to be up and stirring, preparing breakfast, getting through with the morning routine of duty, so as to be in readiness at dawn to commence the serious work of the day.

The moon is still shining brightly, with a coloriess sky and brilliant with stars. The throng of vessels sit calmly on the sea, the wind being too light to stir even a ripple. This, too, it should be remembered, just out of cannon range of the dreaded coast of North Carolina. Truly the elements promise to favor the great enterprise of Admiral Porter.

Under Way.

At 5 o'clock a second signal was given by the flag-ship, "Get under way," when the work of raising anchor commenced at half-past five. The signals of division commanders to move forward were given and responded to, causing a brilliant pyrotechnic display.

The gun-boat *Tacony* having been sent ahead last night, to anchor off the Flag Pond Battery and the day not having yet dawned, her lights can be seen as the steering point of the fleet, in shore about three miles ahead of us.

The three frigates, *Wabash*, *Minnesota* and *Colorado*, moved off first, led by Admiral Porter's flag-ship, followed by the *New Ironsides* and the monitor fleet. The army transports' signals also added to the scenic attractions.

At the first dawn of day the whole armada was in motion. The wind has changed due east during the night, and being off shore tends to make the landing of troops comparatively easy.

Line of Battle.

At a quarter of seven o'clock the Admiral signaled "form line of battle," when the *Brooklyn* with her line of vessels moved along close to the beach, in the following order:—

	Guns.		Guns.
Brooklyn	26	Kansas	8
Tacony	10	Huron	4
Unadilla	7	Patuxent	6
Maumee	5	Pontoosuc	10
Seneca	4	Yantic	7
Nyack	7		—
Mercus	11	Total	116
Mohican	7		

This division was ordered to prepare for action.

Continued on the Eighth Page.

The Charleston Mercury.

DAILY PAPER—TWENTY DOLLARS FOR THREE MONTHS—PAYABLE IN ADVANCE.

VINDICE NULLO — SPONTE SUA SINE LEGE FIDES RECTUMQUE COLENTUR.

COUNTRY PAPER—THREE A WEEK—FIFTEEN DOLLARS FOR THREE MONTHS—PAYABLE IN ADVANCE.

Volume LXXXVI. — CHARLESTON, S. C., TUESDAY, FEBRUARY 7, 1865. — Number 12,289

TELEGRAPHIC.

CONGRESSIONAL NEWS.

RICHMOND, February 3.—The House passed the Senate bill increasing the compensation and emoluments of the President, and increasing the salaries of officers and employees of the Government in Richmond, also adopted resolutions expressing the gratification of Congress for the additional evidence of patriotism of the different commands who have declared their purpose to maintain the war for independence.

FROM THE NORTHERN PAPERS.

THE GUNBOAT FIGHT IN JAMES RIVER—FARRAGUT GONE TO THE JAMES.

The most fanciful accounts of the naval excursion down James river, last week, are given in the New York papers. A correspondent of the New York *Tribune*, telegraphing from Washington on the 25th, says:

News reached here yesterday afternoon, from Grant's headquarters, that rebel rams and war steamers (we understand six in number) came down early in the morning from Richmond, and drove our armed vessels down the river, and swept them and the transports, and everything afloat, as far down as City Point. Details have not transpired here; but the emergency was deemed to be so great that Admiral Farragut was summoned to the James river, by telegraph, instantly.

Yesterday morning, at 3 o'clock, taking advantage of the high water in the Potomac, five rebel war vessels, including, we understand, two rams, ran past the obstructions we had placed in the river with the purpose of destroying our transports and warehouses at City Point. Our batteries on the shore opened fire at one of the rams, which had got aground, and was so hotly peppered that the rebels blew it up, setting a slow match to the magazine and escaping in their boats. Two others also got aground and were shelled warmly. It was doubtful whether they could escape. The fourth ram returned toward Richmond.

One is said to have got below our batteries. She caused a sensation, certainly, at least. If she did damage, and how much, if any, is not yet known. There will probably be a removal from command in the James River flotilla as a punishment for the negligence in this case.

The Washington *Star* says:

Despatches received here state that, yesterday morning at 3 o'clock, a rebel fleet of five vessels—the Richmond squadron, so long being prepared—came down the river to destroy our depots and works at City Point.

The high water caused by the freshet enabled them to pass the obstructions which our commander had placed above City Point for the better protection of the place.

A battle quickly ensued between the rebel fleet and our nearest battery or fort, in which one of the rebel vessels was blown up and instantly and entirely destroyed, while two others were so badly damaged by shot and shell as to compel them to seek safety by speedy flight back in the direction of Richmond, accompanied by the other two, which escaped damage to speak of.

Admiral Farragut left here yesterday evening for the scene of action, and it is understood that he will at once assume naval command there.

STOPPAGE OF THE WILMINGTON BLOCKADE RUNNING.

A telegram from Halifax, Nova Scotia, announces the arrival of a steamer there from St Thomas and Bermuda, and gives the following intelligence [illegible]:

The blockade runner Owl succeeded in reaching Fort Caswell the night it was evacuated, and immediately returned to Bermuda, arriving on the 21st with the news of the capture of Fort Fisher, and stopping the Maud, Campbell, Old Dominion, Florence, Deer, and Virginia, all ready to sail. The Charlotte and Stag sailed for Wilmington at the same time with the Owl, and the Rattlesnake, Chameleon and Snag between the 13th and 20th, and had not since been heard from.

The bark Sacramento, from New York for Rio Janeiro, put into Bermuda on the 16th instant, to land the captain and crew of the ship Ganges, which was fallen in with on the 7th instant, latitude 35, longitude 60, in a sinking condition.—The above is probably the brig Ganges, Captain Johnson, from Cadiz, November 4, for Boston.

The island of St. Thomas has been declared an infected port.

THE BURNING OF THE SMITHSONIAN INSTITUTE.

The losses by the burning of the Smithsonian Institute, at Washington, on Tuesday night, were quite heavy. A Washington letter says:

The fire in the Smithsonian Institute had probably been smouldering for days in the loft at the west end of the main building. The pipe of a stove had been placed in a flue in the south wall, and there was a joist running directly into this flue. But four or five pictures were saved in this gallery. "The Dying Gladiator" (a copy by John Gott) was utterly ruined, crushed to pieces and burned to lime. The books and records in the Regent's room, over the south door of the building, including the effects of the founder of the building, James Smithson, consisting of silver plate, the library of Bishop Johns, of Virginia, and the Beaufort, South Carolina, library, placed in the institution by the Governor for safe keeping, were totally destroyed. The sarcophagus brought from Syria by Commodore Elliot for President Jackson was damaged. The large collection presented to the Institute by Dr. Robert Hare, of Philadelphia, was mostly destroyed.—Some that was got out was broken, and many of the pieces are missing. In the offices over the north front entrance, with but little exception, all the correspondence of the institution and a large number of back reports were burned. The east wing was not in the least injured, although the staircase leading from the professors' apartments to the apparatus rooms was several times in flames. The lecture room is gutted completely. The towers on the north front appear to be cracked, and some of the walls are warped. The library in the east end was uninjured, and much of the apparatus, having been stored below, was also saved. There was no insurance on the building or effects.

HORACE GREELEY ON THE BLAIR MISSION.

[From the New York Tribune, January 30.]

There are men who talk as if the war were a normal condition, and who stare at the suggestion of peace as if some wrong was done the nation. But all wars must have an end, even those carried on as so few ever have been, for the highest good of the people, though all may not be attained which the victorious party, at the outset, promised itself. Ordinarily it is a struggle of endurance. It is a question of pluck and resources, and resources, as in all human affairs, are the ground work of courage. Which can hold out the longest? Which can hold out the longer? There comes always a time when the last is the vital question, and when it comes, peace is inevitable. We may or we may not have reached that point; but the signs are, at least significant, and wise men will give them due consideration. Unwise, or at least, thoughtless men, remember only that we have been at war but four years, while other nations have, with more or less patience, endured its calamities ten, twenty, thirty years; with far less at stake. They do not remember that one year of modern warfare, in the exhaustion attending it, in its enormous expenditure of blood and treasure, is equal to five years of war a century or half a century ago.

The desolation that followed the thirty years of war in Germany was not greater, probably not so great, as that which, in the last four years, has been visited upon the rebellious States of the South. Half of Virginia is a desert; Tennessee is a barren waste; the young men of the South are in their graves; the old men are reduced to poverty; the industrial system of all the slave States is destroyed; from Mason and Dixon's line to the Rio Grande, desolation covers the land.

In the natural course of things, then, peace is imminent. It may be the imminence of weeks or of months; certainly it cannot be delayed beyond the duration of one more campaign. The North wants peace, provided the terms and conditions shall suit it. There is unquestionably a party at the South that demands it, caring little what the terms are; ready to accede to anything that we demand. It is ready to grasp our utmost demand—lay down its arms and submit. Some facts are known to us which it is not safe now to make public. But they must be known ere long, and from that moment our public affairs will assume a new aspect.

Mr. Blair's first visit to Richmond was neither fruitless nor useless, or it would not have been repeated. Without pretending to know anything of its details, we, in common with every body else, arrive at this conclusion. Not less significant is the gradual but steady decline in the price of gold.

We are not more sanguine than our neighbors, nor are we more hopeful of or anxious for peace, neither do we pretend to more wisdom. But we hail the flush of those bright streaks of the coming day, and do not choose to shut our eyes to them because others, with closed eyelids, keep out the light. We do not prophesy immediate peace, because we do not mean to prophesy at all, but we believe the utter exhaustion of the rebels portend the result which exhaustion always brings to all wars.

THE MERCURY.

TUESDAY, FEBRUARY 6, 1865.

A Tandem Team!

The whole country was horrified yesterday to hear by the telegrams from Richmond, that "Commissary General NORTHROP has not resigned, as reported."

We are really so much astonished at this information that we are confounded. We don't know exactly how to begin to express ourselves on the subject. The fact is, the matter is beyond the reach of any words. It is a matter for *action*, not for words. It is a matter, if we comprehend it, for which somebody should be hurt.

Everybody knows that Mr. DAVIS' Cabinet are but his head-clerks of the several Departments, to record his wills and pleasures. Everybody knows that if Mr. NORTHROP stays where he is, after the expression of official opinion that has just taken place, it is because he is held there by Mr. DAVIS. It is a maxim in Kingly Governments that the King can do no wrong—(notwithstanding Mr. CHARLES STUART lost his head, because it was thought in England that he *did* wrong). Now, if Mr. DAVIS has already ascended to the title of JEFF. 1st, Autocrat of the Confederate States, in God's name let us hold somebody responsible, as was done in England with STRAFFORD. To what pass have we come, when the people of the Confederate States in Congress assembled, are to be treated with the defiance and the scorn with which Mr. JEFF. DAVIS undertakes to treat them now.—What are we all—white negroes, of serfs, or what? What is this little man JEFF. DAVIS? [illegible] authority has he? Where did he get it? Is this man one of the CÆSARS?—or is he one of the Medici?—or perhaps the last of Gothic Amahls?—or is he veritably "the last of the Bourbons?" Can it be so? Or is he indeed that little backwoodman from Mississippi that performed that wonderful and immortal military feat of the figure V,—made the worst and most meddlesome Secretary of War ever known under the old United States Government—and is now making the very worst Executive officer known in the modern world, since the time of his prototype, JAMES 2d, of England. Is this really the man who has the audacity thus to defy the authority of the People of the Confederate States, and to spurn their expressed wishes? Impossible! Surely, surely, the thing is utterly impossible! Has the monomania of this man's egotism utterly overthrown his whole reason, and reduced him to the condition of a mere lunatic? What does the man mean?

And what is Congress after? Have they forgotten the power of the people to impeach? Is there no high toned gentleman in the land, like General LEE, or General JOSEPH E. JOHNSTON who could be raised by Congress to the position now held by this incompetent man, tried now for four long years, and always found equally wanting in capacity and in patriotism? Can not this body, if composed of men too insignificant, individually, to have any respect for themselves, entertain and summon up some respect for the entire people in their official capacity?

Is the mellenium coming or the day of judgment? What is the matter?

HABEAS CORPUS.—The following is the vote of the Confederate House of Representatives on the suspension of the writ of *Habeas Corpus*:

Yeas—Messrs Anderson, Atkins, Ayer, Baldwin, Boyle, Branch, Clopton, Colyar, Cruikshank, Darden, Echols, Farrow, Foster, Gaither, Garland, Hanley, Herbert, Holden, Lampkin, Lester, Marshal, Menees, Miles, Simpson, J M Smith, W E Smith, Smith, of Ala; Smith, of N C; Wickham and Witherspoon—31.

Nays—Messrs Aiker, Barksdale, Batson, Blanford, E M Bruce, H W Bruce, Chilton, Chrisman, Clarke, Clusky, Conrad, Dickinson, Dupree, Elliot, Ewing, Funsten, Gholson, Goode, Hartridge, Hatcher, Holliday, Johnson, Keeble, Kenner, Lyon, Machen, Norton, Perkins, Pugh, Sexton, Shewmake, Snead, Swan, Triplett, Vest, Villere, Welsh, Wilkes and Mr. Speaker—41.

A SAMPLE OF SAVANNAH RULE.—We find in New York *Commercial* the following paragraph, which will show how delightful the Yankee rule in Savannah is becoming:

A Savannah belle stepped off the sidewalk the other day to avoid walking under the American flag, which hung in front of an officer's head-quarters. General Geary, military commandant of the city, immediately gave orders to have her promenade back and forth under the hateful symbol for an hour, as a warning for similar offenders."

LIEUT. GEN. PEMBERTON is in town, it is said, upon official duty of inspection. Our city is glad to welcome him back.

FIRE AT MIDWAY.—At four o'clock last Saturday morning, a fire broke out, at Midway, in the dwelling house of Dr. HOPSON PINCKNEY, which was rapidly consumed, with its entire contents, the family escaping with only a portion of their clothing. The flames quickly communicated to the Post and Telegraph offices, and the dwelling of the Postmaster, Mr. SHARR. Fortunately the contents of these buildings were saved. The fire originated in a defective chimney.

The Governor of the State

To the People of South Carolina.

The doubt has been dispelled. The truth is made manifest; and the startling conviction is now forced upon all. The invasion of the State has been commenced; our people driven from their homes; their property plundered and destroyed; the torch and the sword displayed as the fate to which they are destined. The threats of an insolent foe are to be carried into execution, unless that foe is checked and beaten back.

I call now upon the people of South Carolina to rise up and defend, at once, their own rights and the honor of their State. I call upon every man to lay aside selfish considerations, and prepare to do his duty to his State. Let the suggestions of ease and comfort become inglorious and unworthy; let those ends only be honorable which conduce to the defeat of the foe; let all who falter now, or hesitate, be henceforth marked. All who have lived under the protection of the State, who have flourished under its laws, and shared its prosperity, will gladly rise to protect it from subjection. If any seek to escape from duty and danger at this time, let them depart. The hour approaches when all who are true to the State will be found in the ranks of those who arm in its defence. There is no room in the State but for one class of men; they are the men who will fight in her cause.

I give now timely warning to all. The period is near when private business must be for a season suspended. While there is yet time let all prepare to set their houses in order. Let us hope that the interval may be short in which we will pass from doubt to hope; let us feel that as we grapple danger, we will pluck safety. In every district of the State the men will be organized. From a portion of these districts only will the militia be drawn. In others, more remote, it will be left for protection to persons and security to property. In such cases, the duty will be as imperative as in others, where the men are called from home.

In every quarter of the State, in every district, village and town, let the men stand with their arms in their hands. When required to move, let them do so with expedition and hope. Until required to move, let them be vigilant and prepared to repress disorder, and put down all violence.

It is the duty of every man to oppose all the resistance he can to the approach of the enemy. It is the command of the State that he shall do so. The foe now upon the soil of the State is here to kill; let him be killed. The foe now upon the soil of the State is here for rapine and lust; let him meet resistance unto death. That foe devotes us to a doom worse than death; let him receive the fate he designs for us.

If any one is so ignorant of the temper with which this war has been waged by the foe, as to suppose that resistance provokes punishment, which unarmed he would not incur, let him be quickly undeceived. He is only safe who is armed; he is only spared who defends himself. The stale, and not unsuccessful practice of the foe, is to promise pardon and threaten punishment. The threat is always executed when he dares; the promise never. Moreover, the State, your country, requires you to arm in its defence. It is not given to any man or any men within its territories to choose whether they will arm or not. When a merciless foe is abroad ravaging the fields, wasting the property, taking the lives of the people, insulting the sovereignty, and impeaching the independence of the State; where the State plants its banner, there will all true men gather. When the State calls, as it now does, to arms, all will echo that call; all must obey that summons.

Remove your property from the reach of the enemy; carry what you can to a place of safety; then quickly rally and return to the field. What you cannot carry, destroy. Whatever you leave that will be of use to your foe, what he will not need, that will be destroy. Indulge no sickly hope that you will be spared by submission; terror will but whet his revenge. Think not that your property will be respected, and afterward recovered. No such feeling prompts him. You leave it but to support and sustain him; you save it but to help him on his course. Destroy what you cannot remove. He will make your return to your homes over a charred and blackened road; prepare you the same way for him as he advances. Let him read everywhere and in everything, that in this State, from one portion of it to the other, there is but one purpose and fixed resolve—that purpose is to meet him at every point; fight him at every road; that resolve is to undergo all suffering, submit to every sacrifice, welcome any fate, sooner than subjection by his army, or submission to his terms.

You have led the way in those acts which united the people of your sister States in this confederation of States, and their secession from the Government of the United States. You first fired the gun at the flag of the United States, and caused that flag to be lowered at your command. As yet, you have suffered less than any other people. You have spoken words of defiance—let your acts be equally significant. In your sister States, with the people of those States, you have a common sympathy in the determination to be free, and in your hatred of the foe: you will not falter in that stronger sympathy which is derived from a common suffering.

You have defied a tyrant; do not apprehend his power. You have dared to do; fear not to die. No worse fate can befall him who has pride in the ancient honor of his State than to see it governed by those who hate it; and insult, with their vices, the virtues we have been taught to cherish.

Once more I say to you your State is invaded. Once more I call upon you to arm in its defence. All who unite with us are more than brothers; all who desert us are as false as the foe which assail us.

It is said there are some who think they are not bound to fight with us; who affect a desire not to forfeit what they call their allegiance to some foreign Power. It may be that there are some who hitherto have been misled. I will not believe that there lives in South Carolina now, any man who, having been under the protection of the State and treated as that State treats its own citizens, will, at this time, attempt to find in this affected zeal for an allegiance he has practically abjured, an excuse for the succor he is bound to render. If there are such, let them depart. They shall not remain here and be the cold witnesses of the sufferings which others endure, while they are secure from danger. If they remain, they will do so with the full knowledge that the State expects and intends that every man shall do his duty.

Be as resolute as your cause is just, and triumphant success awaits you. What right have they to expect success in the sight of God who pursue, with unrelenting hatred, you, who seek nothing more than the privilege of accomplishing the great ends for which your God has given you being? You have not invaded their soil, nor sacked their cities, nor wasted their fields; nor murdered their relatives, nor violated their wives and daughters. They pretend not to the plea of visiting upon you the terrible punishment of retaliation. They claim a right to reduce you to subjection—to hold you in bondage—to strip you of more than life, when they deprive you of the privileges dearer than existence. Rise, then, with the truth before you, that the cause in which you are to arm is the cause of Justice and of Right! Strike, with the belief strong in your hearts, that the cause of Justice and of Right is the cause which a Power superior to the hosts seeking to oppress you will not suffer to be overthrown. And even upon [illegible] the fate it deserves, [illegible] honor will be awarded those [illegible] great consummation, in [illegible].

By the Governor:
A. G. MAGRATH.
Official—HENRY BUIST, Lt. Col. and A. D. C.
February [illegible]

OFFICIAL NOTICES.

HEADQUARTERS, DEPARTMENT OF [illegible] AND FLA., CHARLESTON, S. C., February 5, 1865.

ATTENTION.

[illegible] TELEGRAPH OPERATORS JAMES B. SHAIN AND F. H. COHEN, will report at this Office immediately. By order [illegible] Gen. HARDEE. C. G. MEMMINGER, Jr., Chief Signal Officer. February 6 2

HEADQUARTERS, DEPARTMENT OF SO. CA., GA. AND FLORIDA, Charleston, S. C., February [illegible], 1865.

GENERAL ORDERS No 11.]

MAJOR H. D. BULKLEY, C. S., IS, UNDER THE orders of the War Department, announced as CHIEF COMMISSARY of the troops in the Department of South Carolina, Georgia and Florida. By command of Lieut. Gen. HARDEE. (Signed) T. B. ROY, A. A. Genl. Official: H. W FEILDEN, A. A. Genl. Augusta papers will copy three times and send bills to these headquarters. 3 February 4

[EXTRACT.] HEADQUARTERS, 2D AND 3D SUB DISTRICTS, S. C., DEPARTMENT OF SO. CA., GEORGIA AND FLORIDA, CHARLESTON, S. C., December 14, 1864.

[SPECIAL ORDERS No. 98.]

* * * * * *

I. ON NO ACCOUNT WILL NON-COMBATANTS be allowed to enter the City of Charleston except in passing through to more interior portions of the State after the promulgation of this order.

II. All Slaves whose owners are now living beyond the limits of the City of Charleston, except one Slave to take charge of Real Estate, which such owners have left unprotected will be at once removed from the city.

If in fifteen days after the issue of this order any such are still found in the city, they will be at once arrested and sent out of the city to seek their owners.

* * * * * *

By command of Major General RANSOM. WM. F. NANCE, Assistant Adjutant General. December 16

OFFICE PROVOST MARSHAL GENERAL, DEPARTMENT OF SOUTH CAROLINA, GEORGIA AND FLA., CHARLESTON, S. C., January 16, 1865.

[SPECIAL ORDERS NO. —]

ALL PAPERS EMANATING FROM THIS OFFICE, signed by Captain S. A. MOBLEY, Assistant, will be considered as official. WM. J. GAYER, A. A. G. and P. M. General. January 19

HEADQUARTERS, CITADEL, CHARLESTON, January 17, 1865.

[GENERAL ORDERS NO. 1.]

I. THE UNDERSIGNED, ON ENTERING UPON the responsible duties of Provost Marshal of the City of Charleston, respectfully invites the cordial co-operation of the Military [illegible] Civil Authorities, and of all [illegible] to secure to ALL the [illegible] consistent with [illegible]. The duties of a Provost [illegible] as this is, are [illegible] character, and should [illegible] to the general good.—[illegible] its inhabitants [illegible]. It is an important [illegible] hearty co-operation of those most immediately interested, the task will be of easy performance, and the good results seen and felt by all. My Sentinels, Guards and Patrol will be required to demean themselves as gentlemen, and to treat all persons with the utmost courtesy and respect, exacting reciprocal respect from all classes of persons. This rule will be strictly enforced, and all violators, whether citizen or soldier, will be held to strict accountability.

II. In order to avoid confusion or annoyance all Passports, Passes or Permits, except those granted for a few hours to my own command, must be presented at the Office of the Provost Marshal General, on King street, for approval by Captain WM. J. GAYER, A. A. G. and P. M. G.

III All persons knowing just cause of complaint against any officer or man of my command, will confer a favor by reporting the name of the party and facts in the case to these Headquarters. C. E. HANLEITER, Captain Commanding. January 18

HEADQUARTERS, 2D AND 3D SUB DISTRICT SOUTH CAROLINA, CHARLESTON, December 19, 1864.

GENERAL ORDERS NO. 96.]

* * * * * *

IV. NO RICE WILL BE SHIPPED FROM THIS city until otherwise ordered. The Agents of Railroad and Express Companies will see that this order is rigidly enforced.

* * * * * *

By command of Major General RANSOM. WM. F. NANCE, A. A. Gen'l. December 19

STATE OF SOUTH CAROLINA.

ADJ'T AND INSPECTOR GENERL'S OFFICE, [EXTRACT.] COLUMBIA, January 26, 1865.

[SPECIAL ORDERS No. 80.]

CAPT. WM. F. NANCE, A. A. GENERAL, P. A. C. S., having been assigned for temporary special service with these Headquarters, will be obeyed and respected accordingly until otherwise directed.

* * * * * *

By order of the Governor. (Signed) A. C. GARLINGTON, Adjutant and Inspector General S. C. Official—G. A. FOLLIN, A. A. General. January 30

STATE OF SOUTH CAROLINA.

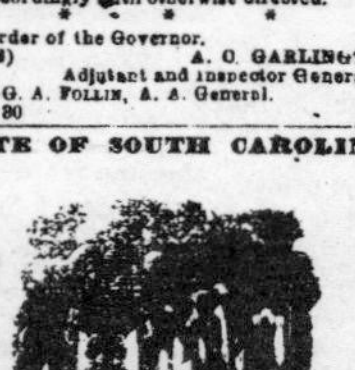

EXECUTIVE DEPARTMENT, January 21, 1865.

TO THE PEOPLE OF SOUTH CAROLINA:

GENERAL BUTLER, WITH HIS DIVISION, IS ON his way to the aid of our State. General HAMPTON is with him. He needs horses, and I have told him he shall have them. You will not hesitate to give up your horses when your friends and brothers require them to defend your State from invasion, your property from pillage, your wives and daughters from insult. Put aside your pleasure-carriages for the time; cease your ordinary pursuits for this occasion, and bring or send in your horses to Columbia!

Colonel CHRISTOPHER F. HAMPTON is charged by me with the duty of receiving, with thanks, all that will be sent; of taking all that are withheld. The horses will be paid for. No one shall suffer from his devotion to the State.

By the Governor: A. G. MAGRATH. Official: HENRY BUIST, Lieut. Col. and A. D. C. January 26

STATE OF SOUTH [illegible]

ADJUTANT AND INSPECTOR [illegible] COLUMBIA, [illegible]

[GENERAL ORDER NO. 5]

THE FOLLOWING APPOINT[MENTS BY HIS EX]CELLENCY the Governor [illegible] Chief, are announced for the in[formation of all con]cerned.

I. Board of Visitors State Milita[ry] [illegible] Hon. R. S. Davant, Chairman, [illegible] resigned.

Hon. J. W. Harrison, vice T. C. Perrin, Esq., re[signed].

Hon. A. P. Aldrich. vice Wm. Gilmore [illegible] signed.

Col. W. H. Evans, vice Isaac D. Wilson, resigned.

II. Col. John T. Sloan, Quartermaster General [illegible] Gen. James Jones, resigned.

William E. Elliott, Esq., Private Secretary [illegible] vice B. F. Arthur, Esq., resigned.

Nathan S. Hart, Esq., Assistant Private [illegible]

III. Lieutenant Colonel Henry [illegible] the Governor, is assigned to the [illegible] and Details. All correspondence on these [illegible] be addressed accordingly.

By command of the Governor. WM. F. NANCE, A. A. [illegible]. February 7

WAR TAX OFFICE, 30TH COLLECTION DISTRICT, KINGSTREE, February 6, 18[65].

I WILL ATTEND AT THE TIMES AND [places] named in the annexed Schedule to collect [the] Agricultural Tax, Soldiers' Tax and Tax on Sales:

Kingstree, on Thursday and Friday, the 9th [and 10th] instants.

Oades' Depot, on Saturday, the 11th inst.

Cross Roads, on Monday, the 13th inst.

School House, on Tuesday, the 14th inst.

Myersville, on Wednesday and Thursday, 15th [and 16th] insts.

Kaddy's, on Friday and Saturday, the 17th [and 18th] insts.

Indiantown, on Monday and Tuesday, the 20th [and 21st] insts.

Johnsonville, on Wednesday and Thursday, the [22d and] 23d inst.

Black Mingo Academy, on Friday and Saturday [24th] and 25th insts.

Potato Ferry Methodist Church, on Monday [illegible] insts.

Cedar Swamp, on Tuesday, the 28th inst.

Anderson, on Monday, the 6th of March next.

Oak Ridge, on Tuesday, the 7th March next.

Sutton's, on Wednesday, the 8th March next.

Gourdin's, on Thursday and Friday, the 9th [and 10th] March next.

Elon Church, on Saturday, the 11th March next.

Kingstree, on Monday, the 13th, and Saturday [illegible] days of March next.

The Assessor will be in attendance to make [assessment] of those whose returns are not yet made. JOHN F. BROCKI[NTON], T. C. 30th Collection Dist[rict]. February 6 c

WAR TAX OFFICE, 9TH COLLECTION DIST[RICT], CHARLESTON, February [illegible]

THIS OFFICE WILL BE OPEN FOR TW[ENTY days] from date for receipt of TAXES on Sales. Office open from 10 a. m. to 2 p. m. ALFRED H. DU[illegible], 9th District C[ollector]. February 7

WAR TAX OFFICE, 10TH COLLECTION DISTRICT, CHARLESTON, 6th February [illegible]

THIS OFFICE WILL BE OPEN FOR [illegible] days from date for receipt of Taxes on Sales. Office open from 10 a. m. to 2 p. m. T. L. HUTCHI[NSON], Collector. February 7 tuths

WAR TAX NOTICE.—36 COLL[ECTION] DISTRICT.

APPEALS WILL BE RECEIVED AND [HEAR]D relative to any erroneous or excess[ive assessments] by the Assessors, during the next fifteen [days; all] appeals must be made in writing and state the inequality complained of.

Collections will be made on non-agricultur[al] and quarterly sales, 4 per cent. bonds receiva[ble]; soldiers tax of (1-5th) one fifth of the amount to be paid in Treasury notes. At The Barr[illegible] 16th January; Eighteen Mile House, 17th; [illegible] Mile House), 18th; Strawberry Ferry 19th, Mo[nks Corner] Depot, 21st; Black Oak, 27th; Gala [illegible] Roads, WEDNESDAY, 1st February; [illegible] Wassamasaw Chapel, 8th; Summe[rville] [illegible] Field, TUESDAY, 14th. Collector 36th [illegible]

Mr. HARVEY, Assessor of Tax in [illegible] above appointments to receive retur[ns]. 1864. 6 mth4

SOUTH CAROLINA—COLL[ETON DIS]TRICT.—THOMAS S. CHAPLIN, [illegible] LIN, and others, vs. ROBERT L. BAKE[R, FRANCIS L.] ROUX, and others.—Bill for account and [relief.—It] appearing to my satisfaction that FRAN[CIS L. ROUX,] one of the defendants in the above case [resides] and without the limits of the State, on mo[tion of] DeTREVILLE, complainants Solicitor, it [is ordered that] said FRANCIS L. ROUX do plead, answe[r or demur to] the said bill within three months from [the publication] hereof, or an order *pro confesso* will be ta[ken against him]. C. [illegible] Commissioner in Equity, Col[leton District]. November 22 0

The New-York Times.

VOL. XIV......NO. 4192. NEW-YORK, THURSDAY, MARCH 2, 1865. PRICE FOUR CENTS.

THE SOUTH.

Great Excitement in the Rebel Capital.

THE ABANDONMENT OF RICHMOND

The Removal of Guns and Military Stores in Progress.

CONSTERNATION OF THE CITIZENS.

Unseemly Flight of Rebel Congressmen---Congress Reduced to a Mere Skeleton.

Extraordinary Article from the Richmond Examiner.

The Fall of Richmond the Fall of the Confederacy.

The Prospective Westward Flight of the Rebel Army.

VIRGINIA.

THE PROPOSED ABANDONMENT OF RICHMOND.

Special Dispatch to the New-York Times.

WASHINGTON, Wednesday, March 1.

Richmond papers of Monday contained very important admissions. The *Sentinel* admits that the removal of guns and stores from Richmond is going on, and endeavors to quiet the apprehensions of the people. The *Sentinel* says that the members of the rebel Congress have fled one by one until there is only a quorum left for business. Gen. LEE begs that Congress will not now adjourn, and leave his hands fettered and unprepared for further resistance.

From the Richmond Examiner, Feb. 27.

In the extraordinary message which Mr. DAVIS recently addressed to Congress he declared that "if the campaign against Richmond had resulted in success instead of failure; if we had been compelled to evacuate Richmond as well as Atlanta, the Confederacy would have remained as erect and defiant as ever. Nothing could have been changed in the purpose of its Government, in the indomitable valor of its troops, or in the unquenchable spirit of its people. The baffled and disappointed foe would in vain have scanned the reports of your proceedings at some new legislative seat for any indication that progress had been made in his gigantic task of conquering a free people. There are no vital points, on the preservation of which the continued existence of the Confederacy depends. There is no military success of the enemy which can accomplish its destruction. Not the fall of Richmond, nor Wilmington, nor Charleston, nor Savannah, nor Mobile, nor of all combined, can affect the issue of the present contest." In the African Church, a fortnight ago, he reiterated these extravagant propositions. Mr. BENJAMIN afterward took up the theme on the same rostrum, and spoke of evacuating this city with equal flippancy. Inconsiderate persons and newspapers, we observe with pain, repeat the same ideas; as if they positively desired the country to be taught that the abandonment of this vital position would not only be of no injury to the Confederacy, but of positive advantage.

Let not this fatal error be harbored till it takes root in the imagination. *The evacuation of Richmond would be the loss of all respect and authority toward the Confederate Government, the disintegration of the army, and the abandonment of the scheme of an independent Southern Confederation. The war would, after that, speedily degenerate into an irregular contest, in which passion would have more to do than purpose; which would have no other object than the mere defence or present safety of those immediately persisting in it. The hope of establishing a Confederacy and securing its recognition among nations, would be gone forever. The common sense of the country, the instinct of every man and woman in the land, contradicts the idea that any possibility of an independent South would remain after its capital was abandoned, its Government set adrift, and its army withdrawn into the solitudes of the interior.*

It is idle to pretend that Richmond is of no more importance than Savannah, Atlanta, Mobile or Norfolk, and that its fall would not be fatal to the Confederacy. If it had not been a vital point, why has so much effort been expended for its reduction and in its defence? It has been the great objective point of the enemy through four successive campaigns. The Confederacy has spared no pains or exertions, no cost of blood or treasure to make good its defence. It is the capital of the last of the border States, commanding the entire portion of Virginia east of the Alleghanies, and the most important division of North Carolina. It is situated 140 miles from the sea, yet large ships can unload from its wharves. The occupation of Richmond in strong force by the enemy would necessarily drive the Confederate armies out of Virginia, and render all Eastern North Carolina untenable; and, once gained by a power having command of the water, it could never, under any contingency, be recovered by the Confederacy.

Each contestant in the war has made Richmond the central object of all its plans and all its exertions. *It has become the symbol of the Confederacy. Its loss would be material ruin to the cause, and, in a moral point of view, absolutely destructive, crushing the heart and extinguishing the last hope of the country. Our armies would lose the incentive inspired by a great and worthy object of defence. Our military policy would be totally at sea; we should be without a hope or an object; without civil or military organization; without a treasury or a commissariat; without the means of keeping alive a wholesome and active public sentiment; without any of the appliances for supporting a cause depending upon the popular faith and enthusiasm; without the emblems of the semblance of nationality.*

The withdrawal of the army from Richmond into the interior would so narrow the area of conscription as greatly to reduce our military strength. As the army would dwindle in numbers, *it would move more and more rapidly westward, and before reaching the banks of the Mississippi would have degenerated into a mere body guard for a few officials.* From the hour of giving up the seat of government, our cause would sink into a mere rebellion in the estimation of foreign Powers; who would cease to accord to us the rights of belligerents; while the enemy would be free to treat our officers and soldiers as traitors and criminals; so that every "rebel" would fight thenceforward with a halter round his neck.

Virginia, though slow to come into the Confederacy, has been throughout the contest its main stay and support. It has borne the brunt of every campaign. It has suffered the ravages of war more severely than all the other States together. Every county in the State has felt the hand of the enemy. Its richest and best districts have been utterly desolated. Its sufferings have not only been severe beyond description, but continuous and unceasing. For four years it has been the common campaign and battle ground for the largest armies and bloodiest conflicts of modern times. No country in the world ever sustained as heavy losses or endured as hard a fate, with more heroism or fortitude. The evacuation of Richmond would be the abandonment of Richmond—forever—and without any rational hope of a return. Is it possible that such a desertion could be contemplated after the events of this war? Even if the act were not suicidal in policy, could the Confederacy now consent to cast away this worn and devastated but still powerful Commonwealth as an old shoe that could be put to no further use?

Aside from the disgrace that would attach to such ingratitude, the Confederacy could not afford to put Gen. GRANT into possession of Richmond, a depot and base a hundred and forty miles from the sea, and in the midst of Southern Virginia yet with water carriage to the door, and thus relinquish its last hold upon the last of the border States. It could not expect to continue the struggle with any hope of success, after abandoning States whence its most numerous recruits are obtained, a soil on which its arms have been uniformly victorious, and *withdrawing to States where defeat has constantly attended them.* The abandonment of Virginia would be equivalent to executing a quit claim deed to all the border States, together with Tennessee and North Carolina. Two lines of railways radiate from here into the most populous and influential districts of this latter State, subjecting its best portions to the control of any considerable military power having its base at Richmond. Is the Confederacy's wealth in population and territory now so great that it can afford to make a voluntary donation of all this territory; restricting its jurisdiction to the gulf States, and South Carolina, already overrun?

If Richmond be held but another six months, the fate of the Confederacy will have been favorably decided. The people will cling to the cause as long as the seat of Government is secure. Recent misfortunes will have awakened foreign Powers to the danger which would result to themselves from the restoration of the Union and pacification of this continent, now possessing a trained soldiery more numerous and formidable than any army in Europe. So long as Richmond and Virginia are ours, the very reverses which have been sustained will nerve our people to renewed exertion, and beguile the enemy into a false confidence. The war cannot be carried on much longer against us if we prove but true to ourselves; *and the single test of success will be our determination and ability to hold Richmond.* Other cities may fall, the rest of the Confederacy may succumb; but the cause still remains safe so long as Richmond and Virginia are held.

We have now before Richmond the best army which the Confederacy has ever possessed, impregnably posted, accustomed to victory and success. All its triumphs have been won in the defence of the Confederate capital. It has continued through every trial to make good that defence, and is honored throughout the Confederacy and the world for the prowess which it has exhibited in the successful effort. We have not the slightest belief or expectation that thoughtless friends or eager enemies will ever be gratified by the sight of such a national suicide as the evacuation of Richmond will be, while that noble army exists in any part; but with the hope of putting an end to the fall of the idle and short-sighted on this matter, we throw out these hints as to the consequences of the act of which they speak so lightly.

WILD SKEDADDLE OF THE REBEL CONGRESS.

From the Richmond Examiner, Feb. 27.

During the last four weeks *wild apprehensions of danger have disturbed the minds of the timid. The enemy has lately thrown his forces across lines of easy Congressional retreat to the West, and South, and, since that time, Senators and Representatives have one by one fled the Capitol, leaving the skeleton of the Legislature rapidly diminishing to a minimum number below a quorum.* It is true the President must stand firmer as national danger thickens; it is true the scared army must bare their breasts to the storm with more heroic courage, as the columns of the enemy converge on the liberty and existence of the country. *Should the President waver and imitate Congressional example there will be no difficulty in finding instances in history to illustrate his disgrace.*

THE RICHMOND AND PETERSBURGH LINES.

From the Richmond Dispatch, Feb. 27.

GRANT has again been massing his troops on Hatcher's Run, on our extreme right, ten miles southwest of Petersburgh, and it *is thought that another attempt by his columns to gain the Southside Railroad was prevented by the rain of Saturday. We think there can be little doubt that he will make this attempt so soon as the state of the roads will permit.* In their present miry condition, the movement of artillery is out of the question. GRANT has enough of the gambler in his character for the disastrous failure of his last advance toward the railroad to make him the more impatient to renew the attempt. At present, the extreme left, which may properly be considered the advance of the Yankee army, occupies a position on the left or north side of Hatcher's Run, between nine and ten miles southwest of Petersburgh, and about five miles in a direct line from the Southside Railroad.

SOUTH CAROLINA.

NOTHING TO TELL.

From the Richmond Examiner, Feb. 27.

In the absence of official information of military affairs in the Carolinas, we take nothing from other sources of intelligence, and omit the usual references to our file of Southern exchanges. We do so at the request of the authorities, and with the understanding that the other city journals have been put under obligations of reticence to the extent indicated above. The public will, no doubt, be properly patient in the interval of silence, and not take it as discouragement; for we are assured that there are good reasons for it, which look to an early official announcement of favorable results.

THE SHELLING OF COLUMBIA.

From the Richmond Examiner, Feb. 27.

One of the most atrocious crimes perpetrated since the beginning of this war, says the Charlotte *Bulletin*, was the shelling of Columbia, S. C., by the enemy, without a moment's warning. We are justified by truth in saying that two batteries were placed at commanding points on the west side of the river, and a bombardment opened upon the city whilst it was filled with women and children. Many of the houses were perforated by the missiles, and the flying of women and children from the terror thus created is said to have been a most heart-rending sight. No demand had been made for the surrender of the city. On the contrary, the enemy's approach was silently and steadily conducted. Some eight or ten persons were killed by the fragments thrown into the midst of helpless non-combatants. We are informed, *also, that after the surrender of the place, squads of the enemy marched about the city shooting down such citizens as they could find, urging as an excuse that they might be stragglers from* BEAUREGARD'S *army.*

From the same Paper, same date.

The news from Columbia corroborates the kind treatment of the inhabitants. The Ursuline Convent was protected by a guard. No public property was allowed to be burned in the city. SHERMAN'S *headquarters were at Nickerson's Hotel.*

From the best information received here, it appears probable that a considerable conflagration occurred in the western portion of Columbia, occasioned, it is supposed, by the cotton ignited in the streets. It is reported that the fire extended from Main-street to the Charlotte Depot—nearly three-fourths of a mile. The information is positive as to the occurrence of the fire, but doubt is entertained as to its magnitude.

Some of the refugees from Columbia are preparing to return.

The alarm in Charlotte has subsided.

The weather is bad, and the roads heavy, interfering with rapid military movements.

AN UNAUTHENTICATED RUMOR.

From the Richmond Dispatch, Feb. 27.

The usual number of Sunday rumors were in circulation yesterday, the most agreeable of which, though we regret to say not the most authentic, was that SHERMAN had been killed and his army routed and driven into the jungles of South Carolina.

GEN. JOHNSTON.

From the Richmond Dispatch, Feb. 27.

Gen. JOSEPH E. JOHNSTON, on Thursday evening last, assumed command of the army in SHERMAN'S front, lately commanded by Gen. BEAUREGARD.

NORTH CAROLINA.

UNION PRISONERS.

From the Richmond Examiner, Feb. 27.

The Raleigh *Confederate* of the 23d says:

"About twelve hundred Yankee prisoners—a dirty, ragged, and as hard-featured a set of men as ever were seen—were sent down from Salisbury, and stopped at the railroad depot, in this place awaiting orders to be sent to Wilmington for exchange. The Yankee authorities below Wilmington refused to receive a lot previously sent, but we understand that GRANT has sent instructions, through our exchange agent, to the officer in command there, ordering their reception at that point, and they were expected to leave last night.

It did not appear that a very strict guard was placed over them, or they were allowed unusual liberty by the officer in command. Many of them were seen straggling through the city during the morning unattended, and in perfect freedom.

A large Government warehouse was destroyed by fire in Fayetteville on Tuesday night last.

AFFAIRS AT CHARLOTTE.

From the Same.

The *Bulletin* of the 22d states that Col. HOKE, commanding post of Charlotte, is displaying the most commendable energy in the regulation of affairs connected with his immediate speciality. He has organized a military police force which occupy every public place, and the preservation of order, when everything is so favorable to confusion, is a task so difficult that its successful accomplishment is worthy al praise.

MISSISSIPPI.

A STATE CONVENTION TO BE CALLED.

From the Richmond Examiner, Feb. 27.

The Legislature of Mississippi is about to convene in extra session, for the purpose, it is said, of calling a State convention.

CHARLESTON.

Official Dispatch from General Gillmore.

The Extent and Importance of Our Captures.

Four Hundred and Fifty Guns Found in the Rebel Works.

Many Pieces of Foreign Manufacture Among Them.

DESTINATION OF HARDEE'S ARMY.

Rebel Apprehensions for Its Safety.

A Portion of Hood's Army Said to be in Front of Sherman.

SECRETARY STANTON TO GEN. DIX.

[OFFICIAL.]

WAR DEPARTMENT, WASHINGTON, March 1, 1865—8:10 P. M.

To Maj.-Gen. Dix, New-York:

The following telegram from Gen. GILLMORE has been transmitted to this department.

EDWIN M. STANTON, Secretary of War.

HEADQUARTERS DEPARTMENT OF THE SOUTH, CHARLESTON, S. C., Feb. 26, 1865.

Lieut.-Gen. U. S. Grant, and Maj.-Gen. H. W. Halleck, Chief of Staff, Washington:

An inspection of the rebel defences of Charleston shows that we have taken *over four hundred and fifty (450) pieces of ordnance*, being more than double what I first reported. The lot includes eight and ten inch Columbiads, a great many 32 and 42 pounder rifles, some seven-inch Brooks rifles, and many pieces of foreign make.

We also captured eight locomotives and a great number of passenger and platform cars, all in good condition.

Deserters report that the last of HARDEE'S army was to have crossed the Santee River yesterday, bound for Charlotte, N. C., and it was feared that SHERMAN had already intercepted their march.

It is reported, on similar authority, that the last of HOOD'S army, 12,000 strong, passed through Augusta last Sunday, the 19th, on the way to BEAUREGARD.

Georgetown has been evacuated by the enemy, and is now in our possession.

Deserters are coming in constantly. We have over 400 already.

(Signed,) Q. A. GILLMORE, Major-General Commanding.

ARRIVAL OF THE ARAGO.

The United States transport *Arago*, HENRY A. GADSDEN commanding, from Port Royal, &c., via Charleston Harbor the 26th inst., arrived at this city yesterday at 3:30 P. M.

When off Charleston Harbor (26th inst.) received the news of the burning of Columbia, South Carolina, on the 24th inst., by Gen. SHERMAN, and *also the report that Augusta had been taken possession of by the Union troops.*

OUR CHARLESTON CORRESPONDENCE.

Feeling Among the Citizens—Ruinous Appearance of the City—Fugitive Citizens Returning—A Union League in Charleston—The Quantity of Cotton Destroyed.

CHARLESTON, S. C., Tuesday, Feb. 21, 1865.

The confused state of affairs which prevailed for the first day or two after the evacuation of the city is rapidly assuming a more quiet and satisfactory condition. The citizens of the place are gradually becoming accustomed and reconciled to the new régime, and do not hesitate to appear on the streets or to visit their places of business. But a few complaints have been made to Provost-Marshal BENNETT, by citizens who have sustained some annoyance in the way of having their premises unceremoniously entered by the soldiers, and by other citizens who have had horses, vehicles, and other property suddenly confiscated. In a few days, however, a guard will be organized throughout the city, and the people will be assured of the safety of themselves and their effects.

The appearance of the city is desolate in the extreme. While on Morris Island I often heard the report that grass was growing in the streets at the lower end of Charleston, and now I am a witness to the truth of the statement. All along the water-front, and, in fact, for a long distance up the city, the buildings are either partially or wholly demolished. The walls of some present great, jagged holes, through which a horse and cart could easily pass, and that is the case not only in one but several streets. No wonder the rebels were solicitous to get beyond the reach of our shells! Such a punishment was never before inflicted upon any city. All of the hotels are closed, the furniture and appointments having been removed by the proprietors to the interior of the State some months ago. The Mills House was struck seventeen times, and at last the guests announced that they would not risk their lives by remaining longer in the building. The Charleston Hotel was also struck several times, so that it became necessary to close it.

While walking through the upper wards this morning, I was astonished to find that shells had even reached as far as the Georgia Railroad depot, thus showing that they had traveled a distance of five and six miles.

The first day of our entry into the city I noticed but few citizens made their appearance. I am told that the more prominent secessionists, and a great many of the Union sympathizers have gone into the country. But within the past few days a number of the latter have returned here, bringing their furniture with them. Unmistakably there is a strong Union feeling in Charleston. There is also a secesh element remaining which in course of time will die a natural death. As to the matter of subsistence the supply is limited, consisting mostly of meal and rice. The entire quantity was seized by our authorities on Saturday, and at noon to-day will be turned over to a committee of the citizens, of which committee Dr. A. G. MACKAY, one of the staunchest Union men in the place, is a member, to be distributed among the poor of the inhabitants. It seems to be inevitable that to prevent suffering, similar measures to those taken by the North in the case of Savannah must be adopted in behalf of the people of Charleston. It is contemplated by the citizens to hold a public meeting for the purpose of choosing delegates to repair to the North and lay before its people, an account of the destitute condition to which the rebellion has reduced them. I have taken special pains to inquire of a number of the inhabitants what general view was entertained in the South as to the results thus far of the war, and in every instance I was informed that the South would do well if it held out two months longer. Gen. HARDEE and other rebel military officers said before they left the city that their armies must concentrate in Virginia, or all would certainly be lost. Perhaps it will surprise many to learn that there was really a Union League established in Charleston. Such was the case, and it received the support of hundreds of the citizens, and many of the members were of such prominent standing that the military authorities dare not make open arrests.

According to the description given, the most inhuman and outrageous acts of cruelty were committed by the rebels when they evacuated. Women and children who had snatched from the flames a few bags of meal or corn, or an apronful of rice, were pursued by the cavalry and cut down with sabres. The rebels were exasperated to the nature of fiends when they approached a man who showed the least desire to share the fate of the city. Had they been allowed to exercise their own will, not a house would have been left standing. The firing of the Northeastern Railroad station together with its contents of rice, meal and flour was a proof of what they designed to do, with all the buildings. The rebels did their work too, regardless of human life and limb. In that railroad station were stored one hundred kegs of powder, which were purposely ignited while a large crowd of half-starved people were within gathering up a little quantity of meal to keep soul and body together. A most terrific explosion followed, the appalling result of which was the killing and mangling of 350 human beings.

The total quantity of cotton destroyed by fire was about 4,000 bales. It is thought that about 10,000 bales are still in the city. It is scattered around in small lots, some of the owners not having over two or three bales. Treasury Agent BROWNE and the Custom-House authorities were here yesterday, and will probably make an early disposition of this property.

In all, eight locomotives and twelve cars were captured. Two of the former are in running order to day. The remaining six will require more or less repairing before they can be of service. A large force of laborers has been put to work on the railroad leading to Wilmington, thus indicating that we are about to do something in that direction.

The city arsenal contains a considerable quantity of ammunition. Had our troops been five minutes later in reaching the city, the arsenal would have been fired by a party of rebels who were detailed for the purpose. In the open space opposite the citadel are piles of shells suited for the 600-pounder guns which Gen. HARDEE bursted on the morning he took his leave.

Every attention is paid to the wants of the citizens, who flock to the headquarters in vast numbers. Squads of cavalry have been sent out some distance into the interior, and a hundred or more prisoners have been captured.

Maj.-Gen. GILLMORE, Brig.-Gen. WEBSTER, and a large number of staff officers and civilians, including ladies, came up from Hilton Head yesterday morning, on the flag-steamer *W. W. Coit*, Capt. CROWELL.

In a short time measures will be instituted to rid the harbor and rivers of torpedoes. No explosions have yet occurred from that cause, although it is asserted by citizens that a large number of those machines have been sunk between here and Sumter. The monitors are lying off Sumter. Admiral DAHLGREN'S flagship lies a short distance from Vanderhorst Wharf. WHIT.

FROM BEAUFORT, N. C.

Beaufort to be Made a Depot of Supplies for our Armies in North Carolina.

FORTRESS MONROE Tuesday, Feb. 28.

The steamer *Ariel*, Capt. JONES, arrived this afternoon from Beaufort, N. C., bringing no news of importance.

Extensive preparations were making at Beaufort, N. C., for the purpose of making that place the general depot of supplies for our armies operating in the State of North Carolina; and also with a view to the rapid movement of Major-Gen. SHERMAN'S army northward, when Charleston and Savannah shall be no longer of any value as a basis of supplies of his forces.

The bad weather still continues, with the wind from the northeast, and occasional showers of rain.

NEWS FROM WASHINGTON.

Special Dispatches to the New-York Times.

WASHINGTON, Wednesday, March 1.

ADMIRAL PORTER.

The Committee on the Conduct of the War, having failed to get Admiral PORTER before them, have asked for an extension of twenty days, in order to complete the evidence in the Red River and Fort Fisher expeditions. Their request will be granted.

THE ENLISTMENT OF REBEL PRISONERS.

The Secretary of War sent to the House to-day, in compliance with a resolution of inquiry passed on Saturday, a statement from Provost-Marshal-Gen. FRY relative to the enlistment of rebel prisoners, from which it appears that the total number of such enlistments is 3,800. Nearly 1,500 were enlisted at Point Lookout, and sent to the Department of the Northwest. Four hundred and fifty were enlisted at Fort Delaware into the Third Maryland Cavalry, and sent to the Department of the Gulf. Seventeen hundred and fifty were enlisted at Rock Island and credited to localities in Pennsylvania, which paid them bounty, and sent to the Plains for service on the Overland route. All enlistments were stopped by order of the Secretary of War in September last, and no United States bounty has been paid to such recruits.

THE LOUISIANA QUESTION.

The question of admitting the Senators and Representatives from the State of Louisiana will not be acted on before the adjournment. They had a meeting to-day in regard to the matter, and after a free conference with the friends of the Senate resolution, it was decided that it was useless to press the matter any further.

THE PERMITS TO TRADE IN COTTON.

Mr. WASHBURNE, from the Committee on Commerce, submitted a report to the House, to-day, setting forth that the joint investigating committee had found much corruption and bribery existing under the operations of the act for the purchase of the products of insurrectionary districts, and submitting a bill for the repeal of the eighth section of the act which authorizes the trade. A joint resolution also passed the House, authorizing the continuance of the investigations of the committee after the adjournment of Congress.

MILITARY NOMINATIONS.

The Senate Military Committee at their meeting to-day reported upon all the military nominations recently sent to the Senate. There are now upward of twelve hundred names on the calendar unacted on. They will not be taken up before Monday next for want of time to consider them during the regular session.

THE ARMY APPROPRIATION BILL.

The report of the Conference Committee on the Army Appropriation Bill was presented to the House to-night. The committee having agreed to strike out the appropriation to the Illinois Central Railroad for Government transportation. The proposition was opposed by JAS. C. ALLEN, of Illinois, and warmly advocated by Messrs. WASHBURNE and STEVENS. The report was agreed to. The terms of the land grant to this company, it will be recollected, provide that it shall transport Government stores and troops free of cost.

THE MISSOURI CLAIMS.

The bill to reimburse the State of Missouri for moneys expended in the raising and equipment of troops was taken up in the House, and after a warm contest was finally laid on the table.

THE EXTRA PAY SETTLED.

The Conference Committee on the Executive and Judicial Appropriation Bill made a report to-day, in which the extra compensation of twenty per cent to the House employes, and the appropriation of $160,000 for the extension of the library was adopted.

AT WORK ON THE TAX BILL.

The Senate sat till after midnight last night on the Tax Bill, and have spent the entire day upon it, and will probably finish it to-night. The new section taxing State bank circulation ten per cent. was agreed to in Committee of the Whole. A motion to strike it out was lost by ayes 20, noes 22.

Dispatches to the Associated Press.

WASHINGTON, Wednesday, March 1.

GREAT SUCCESS OF RECRUITING.

The following important and encouraging information has been obtained from an authentic source:

On the 27th day of February, 1865, 6,685 men were enlisted into the service. The average number of men mustered daily for the last three days of February is 3,296. The average number of men mustered for the last ten days of that month was 3,216. (?) If recruiting be kept up, the army will be speedily reinforced to the extent necessary to put an end to the war.

THE PRESIDENT APPRISED OF HIS REELECTION.

Senator TRUMBULL and Representatives WILSON and DAWSON, as the Select Committee of the two houses of Congress, to-day waited upon President LINCOLN, and informed him of his reëlection. To this he responded:

"Having served four years in the depths of a great and yet unended national peril, I can view this call to a second term in no wise more flattering to myself than as an expression of the public judgment that I may better finish a difficult work, in which I have labored from the first, than could any one less severely schooled to the task. In this view, and with increased reliance on that Almighty Ruler who has so graciously sustained us thus far, and with increased gratitude to the generous people for their continued confidence, I accept the renewed trust, with its yet onerous and perplexing duties and responsibilities."

No response has yet been received from the Vice-President elect, who did not arrive here until to-night.

REPORT ON THE PETERSBURGH MINE.

The President sent to the Senate, to-day, a message inclosing the opinion and findings of the Court of Inquiry instituted by him in the Petersburgh mine. The opinion is signed by Maj.-Gen. W. S. HANCOCK, President of the court. After narrating the circumstances of the assault, the failure is ascribed to the following-named officers:

First—Gen. BURNSIDE, in not obeying the orders of the Commanding General in the formation of the assaulting column, in not preparing his parapet and abatis for the passage of his troops, and in not employing engineer officers to lead the columns with the working parties. Yet the court is satisfied that Gen. BURNSIDE believed the measures taken by him would insure success.

Second—Brig.-Gen. LEDLIE, in failing to push forward his troops promptly, and in blocking up the avenue designed for the passage of troops ordered to follow, he being most of the time in a bombproof ten rods in the rear of the main line, where the movement could not be witnessed.

Third—Brig.-Gen. FERRERO, for want of readiness for the assault, not going with his troops, but remaining in a bomb-proof.

Fourth—Col. Z. R. BLISS, of the Seventh Rhode Island, commanding a brigade, in remaining behind with one regiment, in a position where he could not see what was going on.

Fifth—Brig.-Gen. WILCOX, in lack of energy in carrying out Gen. BURNSIDE'S order, to push his troops forward to Cemetery Hill.

The Court concludes the opinion as follows: "Without intending to convey the impression that there was any disinclination on the part of the commander of the support to heartily coöperate in the attack on the 30th of July, the Court express their opinion that explicit orders should have been given assigning one officer to the command of all the troops intended to engage in the assault, when the Commanding General was not present in person to witness the operations."

THE SEARCH FOR FRAUDS IN THE NAVY.

The Secretary of the Navy, in response to a Senate resolution, submitted by Mr. HALE, says the department has been steadily assailed for abuses which it could not wholly prevent, and that implicated parties have been frequently the most boisterous in complaint. He states that investigations have eventuated in the detection of extensive frauds perpetrated by certain contractors, and that in some instances officers and employes of the Government have been implicated. There being no law officer attached to the department, special counsel was employed. Col. L. C. BAKER and subsequently Col. H. S. OLCUTT conducted these investigations, which embraced inquiries into abuses and malpractices connected with purchases for the Brooklyn, Charlestown, Portsmouth, Philadelphia and Washington Navy-yards. Provost-Marshals, police officers and other agents have been employed.

Mr. FRANKLIN SMITH and his brother, BENJAMIN G. SMITH, both contractors, were summoned before a Committee of Inquiry as witnesses, and were afterward arrested for fraudulent practices, arraigned before a Court-martial in September last, found guilty in January, and sentenced to fine and imprisonment. The testimony in the case covered 2,500 pages of manuscript, which was printed and largely circulated; and 500 copies were ordered by the Department that the Government might not be prejudiced by ex parte statements maliciously and ignorantly made, believing that the publication of the argument on one side justified and rendered necessary the publication of the argument on the other. These copies were distributed to members of Congress and others who were furnished with the argument for the defence. The expense was $500. The Secretary denies that he has given instructions to employes to inquire into the business transactions of any member of either House of Congress. The expenses of these examinations at the navy-yards were $14,894. Restitution to the amount of $47,661 has been made by persons arrested in consequence of these inquiries who have confessed their guilt. Parties have also been fined to the amount of $75,000.

A communication from Assistant Secretary FOX to Secretary WELLES is also presented, which embodies a personal defence against sundry charges and allegations, and gives the history of his attempt to garrison and provision Fort Sumter in 1861, with the official orders in the case.

THE LOAN BILL PASSED.

The Senate having passed the Six Hundred Million Loan Bill precisely as it went from the House, and as published in the New-York morning papers, it requires only President LINCOLN'S signature to become a law.

THE FORTIFICATION BILL.

The President has approved the Fortification Bill, the appropriations in which were cut down just one-half the amount which was originally reported. He has also approved the bill providing that no part of any ship or vessel shall be admeasured or registered for tonnage that is used for cabins or state-rooms, and constructed entirely above the first deck, which is not a deck to the hull.

POSTMASTER AT PORT ROYAL.

The Senate has confirmed Mr. S. L. BROTTON to be Postmaster at Port Royal, S. C., and Mr. JOHN M. ECKFIELDT to be master and refiner of the branch mint in California.

Atlantic Telegraph Company.

At the annual meeting of the shareholders of the Atlantic Telegraph Company, held in London on the 9th of February, the following gentlemen were elected Directors:

Mr. SAMUEL CUNARD, Bart., of London.
Mr. EDWARD CROPPER, of London.
Mr. GEORGE P. BIDDER, C. E., of London.
Mr. E. M. ARCHIBALD, of New-York.
Mr. PETER COOPER, of New-York.
Mr. WILSON G. HUNT, of New-York.
Mr. HUGH ALLEN, of Montreal.

Up to Friday evening, Feb. 17, 1,289 nautical miles of cable had been completed, and about 100 miles were being manufactured per week, and the *Great Eastern* will be all ready for sea with the entire cable on board by the 1st of June.

ARMY OF THE POTOMAC.

More Rebel Deserters—How they Manage to Escape—Their Stories About Depression in the South.

RIGHT WING ARMY OF THE POTOMAC, Monday, Feb. 27, 1865.

We are beginning to realize the fruits of the policy adopted by Lieut.-Gen. GRANT toward rebel deserters, in the rapid depletion of the army now cooped up in the defences of Richmond. During the week ending on Saturday night last, there were received at Headquarters of the Army of the Potomac, four hundred and ninety-seven deserters from the rebel army; and in the same time there were three hundred and fourteen received in the Army of the James—making an aggregate loss to Gen. LEE'S army on this account, of eight hundred and eight! These deserters arrive in squads of five, ten, or even as many, sometimes, as twenty. On Friday last one hundred and forty-six were received during the day, of whom forty-nine came together, and were members of the same regiment! I am informed that the rebel officers use every means at their command to stop this wholesale depletion of their army. Among other expedients, they send cavalry scouts along between the picket lines to hunt for deserters and bring them back, and within the last week six or eight of these scouts are reported as having come over with horses and equipments. Instead of taking back the others, they preferred to come over themselves.

It is no unusual thing for deserters to notify the pickets, when they reach our lines, that another squad will be over on the succeeding night, and it rarely happens that these predictions are not verified. They seem to have systematized the practice so perfectly that they can escape without difficulty, thus palpably indicating that many of those they leave behind do not regard desertion as a very heinous offence, nor endeavor to prevent it.

As for the stories the deserters tell, as far as they refer to public matters, there is very little dissimilarity, not enough to invalidate any of the statements, nor to make it interesting to publish them. *They all concur in representing that the gloom which pervades the public mind at the South is deepening constantly, and that all hopes of achieving their independence are abandoned* by the great mass of the citizens and soldiers. The only persons who even profess to hope for success now are the leaders. They are compelled to exert themselves to the utmost to continue the war, and are represented tobe in imminent danger of being arrested by the citizens and delivered over to our authorities. These statements must be received, however, with considerable allowance. If all they tell were true, the wonder would be that, instead of deserting by tens and twenties, they do not leave by brigades and divisions.

The intelligence of a rumor prevailing at the North that this army had been worsted in an engagement with Gen. LEE'S forces reached here yesterday, and excited considerable merriment. The idea seemed so preposterous, that the originator of it was universally held to be a genius to be able to induce anybody to credit his statement.

HARRY H. YOUNG.

FROM SHERIDAN'S ARMY.

The Late Ashby's Gap Disaster—Names of Killed and Wounded—The Weather.

From Our Own Correspondent.

WINCHESTER, Va., Thursday, Feb. 23, 1865.

Eight men, wounded in the unfortunate affair in the Gap last Sunday, were brought here late last night, and placed in the Taylor Hospital, in care of Surgeon WAGNER. Their names are as follows:

Capt. D. K. Duff, Co. K, 14th Penn. Cavalry, wounded in right arm, head and fingers.

Sergt. James R. Johnson, Co. C., 14th Penn. Cav., wounded in left hip.

Johnson Matthews, Co. G, 14th Penn. Cavalry, wounded in right shoulder.

Elisha Myers, Co. G, 14th Penn. Cavalry, wounded in right arm.

Hugh Townson, Co. B, 14th Penn. Cavalry, wounded in breast.

Samuel Bryson, Co. M., 14th Penn. Cavalry, wounded in left eye.

J. M. Kenner, Co. K, 14th Penn. Cavalry, wounded in left side.

Peter Ingis, Co. F, 14th Penn. Cavalry, wounded in neck and back.

Wounded men left in Ashby's Gap, but who will probably be brought in to-morrow, all belonging to the Fourteenth:

Privates Samuel McCarty, John Morris, Wm. M. Haney and Daniel Towdson.

A number of the slightly wounded are in the regimental camp.

Capt. DUFF knows of seven men who were killed, five of whom were buried by citizens near the church in the Gap, and two at the base of the mountain, near the Shenandoah. He could ascertain the names of only two of the seven:

First Sergt. PHILLIP R. PAUL, Co. D, 14th Penn. Cavalry—killed.

Private WILLIAM COOK, Co. B, 14th Penn. Cavalry—killed.

JAS. MARTIN, of Co. D, was among those captured.

This reduces the number of missing to fifty; most of these are doubtless prisoners, and some of them are slightly wounded. All of the returned wounded were paroled by Major RICHARDS, of MOSBY'S command.

Capt. DUFF commanded the rear guard when the attack was made, and five of the men known to have been killed belonged to his detachment. Had he been properly supported, it is now apparent the result would have been far different. The enemy, eighty strong, charged upon this litt band; they emptied their carbines without checking the attacking force, and having neither pistols or sabres, and no support to speak of from the balance of the command, the enemy had everything pretty much their own way.

The capture of GILMOR seems to have aroused the ire of the enemy, and for several days past small forces have been hovering about our lines, without doing any particular harm, however.

The warm rain storm continues, and the snow has nearly disappeared.

E. A. PAUL.

NEW-JERSEY LEGISLATURE.

Rejection of the Constitutional Amendment—Election of Senator Postponed.

TRENTON, N. J., March 1.

The discussion of the Constitutional Amendment continued during the principal part of the day. The vote was taken about five o'clock, and the amendment was defeated by a vote of 30 yeas against 30 nays. The result received cheers and hisses in the lobbies. It was a strict party vote.

The joint meeting of both branches was held. The election of United States Senator was postponed to March 15. JOSEPH B. WALKER was elected prison-keeper.

The Seven-Thirty Loan.

PHILADELPHIA, Wednesday, March 1.

JAY COOKE reports sales of seven-thirties to-day to the amount of $3,127,000, including one subscription from New-York of over $500,000, and another from Chicago of $92,000, and a large number of individual subscriptions.

Gov. Curtin's Visit South.

HARRISBURGH, Penn., Wednesday, March 1.

Gov. CURTIN leaves next Sunday for Charleston and Savannah, to see the Pennsylvania regiments and benefit his health. He will probably be absent two weeks.

Fire in Newburgh.

NEWBURGH, Wednesday, March 1.

The boiler shop of the Washington Iron Works in this city, was destroyed by fire this morning. Most of the machinery was removed to an adjacent building, and the business of the works will not be seriously interrupted.

DAILY DISPATCH.

VOLUME XXVIII. RICHMOND, VA., WEDNESDAY MORNING, FEBRUARY 15, 1865. NUMBER 89.

OFFICIAL.

HEADQ'RS ARMIES OF THE CONFEDERATE STATES, }
February 11, 1865. }

GENERAL ORDERS, NO. 2.—In entering upon the campaign about to open, the General-in-Chief feels assured that the soldiers who have so long and so nobly borne the hardships and dangers of the war, require no exhortation to respond to the calls of honor and duty.

With the liberty transmitted by their forefathers they have inherited the spirit to defend it.

The choice between war and abject submission is before them.

To such a proposal brave men, with arms in their hands, can have but one answer.

They cannot barter manhood for peace, nor the right of self-government for life or property.

But justice to them requires a sterner admonition to those who have abandoned their comrades in the hour of peril.

A last opportunity is offered them to wipe out the disgrace and escape the punishment of their crimes.

By authority of the President of the Confederate States, a pardon is announced to such deserters and men improperly absent as shall return to the commands to which they belong within the shortest possible time, not exceeding twenty days from the publication of this order, at the headquarters of the department in which they may be.

Those who may be prevented by interruption of communications, may report within the time specified to the nearest enrolling officer, or other officer on duty, to be forwarded as soon as practicable; and upon presenting a certificate from such officer, showing compliance with this requirement, will receive the pardon hereby offered.

Those who have deserted to the service of the enemy, or who have deserted after having been once pardoned for the same offence, and those who shall desert, or absent themselves without authority, after the publication of this order, are excluded from its benefits. Nor does the offer of pardon extend to other offences than desertion and absence without permission.

By the same authority, it is also declared that no general amnesty will again be granted, and those who refuse to accept the pardon now offered, or who shall hereafter desert or absent themselves without leave, shall suffer such punishment as the courts may impose, and no application for clemency will be entertained.

Taking new resolution from the fate which our enemies intend for us, let every man devote all his energies to the common defence.

Our resources, wisely and vigorously employed, are ample, and with a brave army, sustained by a determined and united people, success, with God's assistance, cannot be doubtful.

The advantages of the enemy will have but little value if we do not permit them to impair our resolution. Let us, then, oppose constancy to adversity, fortitude to suffering, and courage to danger, with the firm assurance that He who gave freedom to our fathers will bless the efforts of their children to preserve it. [fe 13—6t] R. E. LEE, General.

HEADQ'RS ARMIES OF THE CONFEDERATE STATES, }
February 11, 1865. }

GENERAL ORDERS, NO. 3.—The discipline and efficiency of the army have been greatly impaired by men leaving their proper commands to join others, in which they find service more agreeable.

This practice, almost as injurious in its consequences as the crime of desertion, by the Articles of War exposes the offender to a similar punishment, and subjects the officer receiving him to dismissal from the army.

It is therefore declared that the provisions of General Order No. 2, of this date, from army headquarters, apply to such men as have left their proper commands and joined others without being regularly transferred. They will receive the pardon promised in that order upon complying with its conditions, or suffer the consequences attached to neglecting it.

The names of such absentees will be forthwith reported to these headquarters by the officers with whom they are serving, and immediate measures taken to return them to their proper commands.

As soon as practicable, an inspection will be made, and charges will be preferred against those who neglect to enforce this order.

fe 13—6t R. E. LEE, General.

HEADQUARTERS ARMY OF NORTHERN VIRGINIA, }
January 25, 1865. }

TO ARM AND EQUIP AN ADDITIONAL force of cavalry, there is need of CARBINES, REVOLVERS, PISTOLS, SADDLES and other accoutrements of mounted men. Arms and equipments of the kind desired are believed to be held by citizens in sufficient numbers to supply our wants. Many keep them as trophies, and some with the expectation of using them in their own defence. But it should be remembered that arms are now required for use, and that they cannot be made so effectual for the defence of the country in any way as in the hands of organized troops. They are needed to enable our cavalry to cope with the well-armed and equipped cavalry of the enemy, not only in the general service, but in resisting those predatory expeditions which have inflicted so much loss upon the people of the interior.

To the patriotic I need make no other appeal than the wants of the service, but I beg to remind those who are reluctant to part with the arms and equipments in their possession, that by keeping them they diminish the ability of the army to defend their property, without themselves deriving any benefit from them. I therefore urge all persons not in the service to deliver promptly, to some of the officers designated below, such arms and equipments (especially those suitable for cavalry) as they may have, and to report to these officers the names of such persons as neglect to surrender those in their possession.

Every citizen who prevents a carbine or pistol from remaining unused will render a service to his country. Those who think to retain arms for their own defence should remember that if the army cannot protect them the arms will be of little use.—While no valid title can be acquired to public arms and equipments, except from the Government, it is reported that many persons have ignorantly purchased them from private parties. A fair compensation will, therefore, be made to all who deliver such arms and equipments to any ordnance officer, officer commanding at a post, officers and agents of the Quartermaster and Commissary Departments at any station, or officers in the enrolling service, or connected with the Nitre and Mining Bureau. All these officers are requested, and those connected with this army are directed, to receive and receipt for all arms and equipments, whatever their condition, and forward the same, with a duplicate receipt, to the Ordnance Department at Richmond, and report their proceedings to these headquarters. The person holding the receipt will be compensated upon presenting it to the Ordnance Bureau.

While it is hoped that no one will disregard this appeal, all officers connected with this army are required, and all others are requested, to take possession of any public arms and equipments they may find in the hands of persons unwilling to surrender them to the service of the country, and to give receipts therefor. A reasonable allowance for their expenses and trouble will be made to such patriotic citizens as will collect and deliver to any of the officers above designated such arms and equipments as they may find in the hands of persons not in service, or who will report the same to those officers. A prompt compliance with the call will greatly promote the efficiency and strength of the army, particularly of the cavalry, and render it better able to protect the homes and property of the people from outrage.

R. E. LEE, General.

The officers receiving arms or accoutrements under this appeal are requested to state upon the face of the duplicate receipts given by them the condition of the articles, whether in good order or otherwise, and if not in good order, the per centage which should be deducted on that account.

The receipts may be presented for payment to any one of the following-named ordnance officers:

Captain J. M. STEVENS,
Richmond Arsenal, Richmond, Va.
Major R. RANDOLPH,
Staunton, Va.
Major E. S. HUTTER,
Danville, Va.
Captain G. T. GETTY,
Lynchburg, Va.
Captain CHARLES SEMPLE,
Wytheville, Va.
Captain A. Q. BREVIZER,
Salisbury, N. C.

By order of J. GORGAS,
Brigadier-General, Chief of Ordnance.
Official: E. B. SMITH, Major.

fe 1—eod 1w

Richmond Dispatch.

BY J. A. COWARDIN & CO.

TERMS OF SUBSCRIPTION.

Daily Paper.—For one year, ONE HUNDRED DOLLARS; six months, FIFTY DOLLARS; three months, TWENTY-FIVE DOLLARS; one month, TEN DOLLARS.

Agents and News Dealers will be furnished at THIRTY DOLLARS per hundred copies.

All orders must be accompanied with the money, to insure attention; and all remittances by mail will be at the risk of those who make them.

Advertising.—Advertisements will be inserted at the rate of THREE DOLLARS per square for each insertion. Eight lines (or less) constitute a square.

Larger advertisements in exact proportion.

Advertisements published till forbid will be charged THREE DOLLARS per square for every insertion.

WEDNESDAY MORNING..FEBRUARY 15, 1865.

GENERAL LEE'S LAST APPEAL.

We invoke all good citizens, wherever it is in their power, to place before deserters and absentees from the army the last appeal that General Lee will ever make to them, to return to their duty and resume their place under the flag.—It will be seen that a full and free pardon is now offered to all who will come back within the specified time, but that thenceforth no pardons will be granted either to those who refuse the present offer or to those who are hereafter guilty of desertion. We are sure that General Lee must deeply deplore the necessity of such a determination. No man has a kinder and more benevolent heart; no official, civil or military, has a more honest and profound sympathy with the private soldier. He feels their suffering as his own; and they are well aware of the fact. Indeed, his tenderness to those under his command has been regarded by some as the only defect in his military character. For our part, we honor him for it, but when such a man feels the necessity of proclaiming that, if the present offer of Executive clemency is not regarded, there will be no more pardons hereafter, we feel assured that he means all that he says, and that he will be as inflexible in the execution of his duty as he is humane and merciful in seeking to avoid the terrible necessity.

We therefore earnestly entreat all the class whom he addresses to avail themselves of this last offer of pardon, and to return to the standards which they once illustrated by their valor, and to the comrades who are ready to welcome them once more to their side. The most discontented must now see that Lincoln is only aiming at the complete subjugation and ruin of their native land; at the elevation of the negro to an equality with themselves, and compelling them to fight longer and more dreadful wars against France and England than they will ever be called upon to fight under the Confederate flag. No one pretends to deny or to doubt; no Yankee hesitates to avow that, as soon as the United States succeeds in putting down "the rebellion," it will drive France from Mexico and England from Canada. The troops for that purpose will be drawn from the conquered South; and unless the deserters expect to pass their lives in a successful escape from military duty, they will be forced into the front of this battle. Their only hope as individuals is that of their country; in a triumphant resistance to Northern despotism. There is no safety for any man except in the path of duty.—We invoke the deserters and absentees to listen to their beloved commander, and hasten to retrieve their own honor and the flag of their country. Let them come back at once, and, with the blessing of God, our independence is secured.

"AFTER THAT THE DELUGE."

Perhaps no idea has had more influence in keeping the Conservatives of the North up to the war than the notion that the interests of the North are vitally involved in the suppression of the rebellion, and that internal peace and stability will follow the re-establishment of the old Government.

If there ever was a time when the first of these propositions was true, that time has gone by forever. Have not these Conservative classes always contended that slave labor was essential to the cultivation of those Southern staples upon which Northern commerce and manufactures depended? Have they not over and over again referred to the examples of Jamaica, St. Domingo and other West India islands, as evidences of the ruin which slave emancipation brings upon the agricultural and industrial interests of a country? Slavery is now abolished by their own Government throughout the United States, and we would like the Northern Conservatives to tell us why the results of such a measure, if it could be carried out, would be different in the Southern States from the West India islands? They must now perceive, if they are not willfully blind, that whilst, before the late abolition legislation of Congress, the re-establishment of the old Government was of vital importance to Northern commercial interests, its re-establishment now could only have the effect upon those interests that the abolition of negro slavery has produced in all other parts of the world. Cotton, rice and sugar cannot be cultivated except by negro labor, and negro labor, especially the labor of suddenly-emancipated slaves, set free in a paroxysm of national philanthropy, and unaccustomed to habits of self-reliance and self-government, is a phenomenon which the world has not yet witnessed. The commercial interests of the North have now more to expect from the success than the defeat of the Confederate cause. With our independence, slavery will still exist to produce the great staples of commerce, and the North, with the restoration of peace and commercial relations, could reap advantages from it which no other nation is in a position to obtain. With our overthrow, the cornerstone of their own industrial interests goes down, never to be restored. We submit that the late legislation of the Federal Congress has withdrawn from the so called Conservative classes of the North the principal reason for their support of the war, and furnished them a powerful motive in behalf of peace.

Equally illusory, it seems to us, is the conceit that internal stability and quiet will follow the overthrow of Southern Independence. There is no reliable foundation for concord and security in any country except liberty and justice. Where a people are, or conceive themselves to be, deprived of both, they will never give up the hope of reclaiming them till they cease to exist. Here the extermination theory comes in as an infallible panacea for the recovery of quiet and order. But even if it were practicable, it could not reach the causes of sectional agitation, which must be looked for, not in the South, but in the class and sectional legislation of the North. If the South should prove worth having under the new order of things, New England must cease to be New England if it does not seek to burthen the new proprietors with tariff and tribute, just as it did the old, and the new population will resent the infliction, and resist it, first by argument, and then by the sword, just as the South has done. But there are causes of disorganization in the very constitution of a democracy which always have, and always will, render it the most unstable of governments. To universal suffrage we may trace, in a considerable degree, the evils we are now suffering, and what must be its power for mischief when it is extended not only to the ignorant foreign mercenaries of the United States army, but to the millions of suddenly-emancipated African slaves? If these last are emancipated, without the rights of citizenship, will they be likely to remain quiet and content? It ought to be remembered that they will then be accustomed to the use of arms, and their numbers be no longer contemptible from ignorance of military affairs. If they are endowed with the right of suffrage, what a boundless field for demagogism of the lowest and vilest type! It will be putting firebrands in the hands of madmen. We address these reflections only to that class of Northern men which has really believed the interests of American society involved in Northern success. The truth is, when the Federal Government drew the sword at the beginning of this war it introduced an era of internal convulsions which have now no hope even of alleviation except in Southern Independence.

It appears that the Yankees work the negroes they have freed very hard.—Some ladies of Clinton were, a few days ago, down near Baton Rouge, and saw some Yankee negroes in the forest cutting wood. "Why are you not taking Christmas?" they asked. "We can't," answered the negroes. "Dey charges us fur every day we misses, and if we don't work we'll starve." "How much wood do you have to cut a day?" the ladies asked. "Three cords," was the reply.

The sons of Africa labor under a very agreeable delusion when they understand by liberty freedom from work. The Yankee, of all others, is the very instructor to free them from this pleasant error. What an ingenious way he has of leading his sable disciples along the flowery path to Freedom! No more bondage; no more right of one human being in another. Art thou not a man and a brother? take that axe and cut me three cords a day, and at the end of the week call up and reap the rewards of your labor. Only every day you devote to freedom, or doing nothing, is deducted—a word of three syllables, the meaning of which is explained at the end of the week, when Cuffee begins to understand that the Genius of Universal Emancipation has but one boon to bestow upon mankind—"Root, pig, or die."

Under the Southern master, two cords of wood a day would be the work of a very smart hand indeed, and Easter and Christmas holidays are the universal perquisites of the race. Christmas has always come in their latitudes to rich and poor, to white and black alike, and if any have suffered during that time-honored festival it has been the master, whose servants insist upon their periodical junketings, no matter who suffers.—But Christmas holds no high place on the Yankee calendar. The Fourth of July, when he calls upon the nations to acknowledge and admire the superior virtue and intelligence of his character; the Day of Thanksgiving, when he gorges to repletion with turkeys and pumpkin pie, and the Landing of the Pilgrims, who came to America to be at perfect liberty to deprive everybody else of their liberties, are his great festival days. But neither on festival nor fast is there to be any holiday for the new-born African sons of Freedom. "Dey charges us every day we misses, and if we don't work we'll starve."

This universal law of nature, "work or starve," is now, for the first time, made plain to African comprehension.—It is the decree of Providence; and those who do not heed it must disappear from the face of the earth. Under the beneficent system of Southern slavery, the negro was made to bear his part in the productive industry of the world; but his labor was moderate; it was alleviated by sympathies unknown to any peasantry in Europe, and by provisions for infancy and old age which cannot be expected, and are not even promised, under any other system. Freedom will not dandle upon its august lap his little ebonies, nor give him medicine when he is sick, nor feed and clothe and shelter him when he becomes old. Freedom requires him to pay for these luxuries out of his own pocket; to work as he never worked before, and "charges him every day when he misses," an operation by which, we are informed, Freedom generally manages, when pay-day comes, to bring the astonished Son of Africa in debt, or leaves him scarcely cash enough to drink her health in a glass of New England rum.

We are constrained to believe that, of all the sufferers by this war, the case of the emancipated negroes will be the most miserable and the most hopeless. The Yankees, if successful, are not going to lose the profits of this war by permitting the African to indulge his constitutional love of ease and pleasure. He will realize for the first time what work is when the Yankee runs the machine; and the practical knowledge of that fact will send his whole race, before the century is ended, to their only resting-place—the grave.

Admiral Goldsborough is said to be at Washington, perfecting the organization of a fine fleet for European waters.—Some of the largest and finest vessels of the United States service are to be included in this fleet. As the United States are not at war with any European Power, the object of the expedition is probably to give the benighted Europeans an insight into the latest improvements in naval construction and armaments, and to impress upon their incredulous minds a becoming appreciation and awe of the irresistible naval supremacy of the United States. England and France will be interested spectators of this magnificent display. If Napoleon wants the conceit taken out of him about the iron-clads in his squadrons he has only to make a trip to the seashore; and if England has any Nelsons in embryo, now is the time to hurry up their delivery. The United States, at present, claims to be mistress of the ocean, and is going to give the world a view of her credentials.

After the 4th of March next, the Federal as well as the Confederate Government will both be entirely in Southern hands. Having found a Southern-born man work so well as President, they took another in the person of Andy Johnson for Vice. Poor old Hannibal Hamlin had to return to New England. It seems the destiny of the North always to be governed by Southern men. Few men of Northern origin would have had the firmness to "put the foot down firmly" like Lincoln and take a "big job" like this war on their shoulders. The operation has nearly ruined the United States, and now that a double team of the same breed is about to be put on the machine, we look for a total wreck in the next four years. We take a natural pride in the fact that the South is equally great in creation and destruction. She can produce a Washington to build up the greatest of Republics in the shortest time, and a Lincoln, who can knock it down in a good deal less time than it took to build it up.

CALL OF THE GOVERNOR OF SOUTH CAROLINA.

Governor Magrath, of South Carolina, has issued an address to the people of that State, calling upon them to rise and resist the progress of Sherman through the State. We give some extracts from it:

PERSONS NOT WILLING TO FIGHT MUST LEAVE.

I call upon every man to lay aside selfish considerations, and prepare to do his duty to his State. Let the suggestions of ease and comfort become inglorious and unworthy; let those ends only be honorable which conduce to the defeat of the foe; let all who falter, now, or hesitate, be henceforth marked. All who have lived under the protection of the State, who have flourished under its laws, and shared its prosperity, will gladly arm to protect it from subjection. If any seek escape from duty and danger at this time, let them depart. The hour approaches when all who are true to the State will be found in the ranks of those who arm in its defence. There is no room in the State but for one class of men; they are the men who will fight in her cause.

PROPERTY TO BE REMOVED.

Remove your property from the reach of the enemy, carry what you can to a place of safety; then quickly rally and return to the field. What you cannot carry, destroy. Whatever you leave that will be of use to your foe, what he will not need, that will he destroy. Indulge no sickly hope that you will be spared by submission; terror will but whet his revenge. Think not that your property will be respected, and afterward recovered. No such feeling prompts him. You leave it but to support and sustain him; you save it but to help him on his course. Destroy what you cannot remove. He will make your return to your homes over a charred and blackened road; prepare you the same way for him as he advances. Let him read everywhere and in everything that in this State, from one portion of it to the other, there is but one purpose and fixed resolve—that purpose is to meet him at every point; fight him at every road; that resolve is to undergo all suffering, submit to every sacrifice, welcome any fate, sooner than subjection by his army, or submission to his terms.

FOREIGNERS TO GO IN THE RANKS OR LEAVE.

It is said there are some who think they are not bound to fight with us; who affect a desire not to forfeit what they call their allegiance to some foreign Power. It may be that there are some who hitherto have been misled. I will not believe that there lives in South Carolina now any man who, having been under the protection of the State, and treated as that State treats its own citizens, will, at this time, attempt to find in this affected zeal for an allegiance he has practically abjured an excuse for the succor he is bound to render. If there are such, let them depart. They shall not remain here and be the cold witnesses of the sufferings which others endure, while they are secure from danger. If they remain, they will do so with the full knowledge that the State expects and intends that every man shall do his duty.

THE INTENTIONS OF THE ENEMY.

You have not invaded their soil, nor sacked their cities, nor wasted their fields, nor murdered their relatives, nor violated their wives and daughters. They pretend not to the plea of visiting upon you the terrible punishment of retaliation. They claim a right to reduce you to subjection—to hold you in bondage—to strip you of more than life, when they deprive you of the privileges dearer than existence. Rise, then, with the truth before you, that the cause in which you are to arm is the cause of Justice and of Right! Strike with the belief strong in your hearts that the cause of Justice and of Right is the cause which a Power superior to the hosts seeking to oppress you will not suffer to be overthrown.—And even upon the soil of the State in which this monstrous tyranny was first defied shall it meet the fate it deserves, while imperishable honor will be awarded those who contributed to that great consummation, in which humanity will rejoice.

FROM SOUTH CAROLINA.—The Charleston *Courier* of the 6th instant has the following intelligence about the movements of the enemy in the interior of South Carolina:

"On Friday afternoon the enemy crossed the Salkehatchie between Broxton's and River's bridges, also above the river bridge, completely outflanking our forces, and compelling them to retire on Branchville. A sharp fight, lasting several hours, took place at River's bridge. General Wheeler kept the enemy in check, and made considerable havoc among them in the fight. We have no details or particulars as to the respective losses on either side, but that of the enemy is known to have been heavy.

"Our troops fell back to the second line of defences. The enemy, at latest accounts (Sunday evening), had not crossed River's bridge. The report that the Seventeenth army corps were at Barnwell Courthouse on Sunday, with a large force of cavalry, was discredited in military circles last evening. The general impression, however, was that they would make an effort to gain the road some time during the night. Up to a late hour the wires were working through to Augusta, and communication remained unbroken.

"Heavy cannonading was reported by passengers to have been heard all day in the direction of Bamberg. A number of prisoners were brought in Saturday and Sunday. They report that Sherman would make an attempt to cut the road at Midway. Passengers to Augusta report that Sherman was advancing on Branchville in two columns, with about forty thousand men.

"One transport and four of the enemy's barges landed a number of troops on Little Britain, and about two hundred men at Secret Post. About half-past two o'clock P. M. they advanced to King's creek, and, after skirmishing a short time, retired. Our picket line was re-established."

THE NEW YORK HERALD.

WHOLE NO. 10,401. NEW YORK, SUNDAY, FEBRUARY 19, 1865. PRICE FIVE CENTS.

SHERMAN IN THE HEART OF SOUTH CAROLINA.

Occupation of Columbia, the State Capital----Probable Evacuation of Charleston.

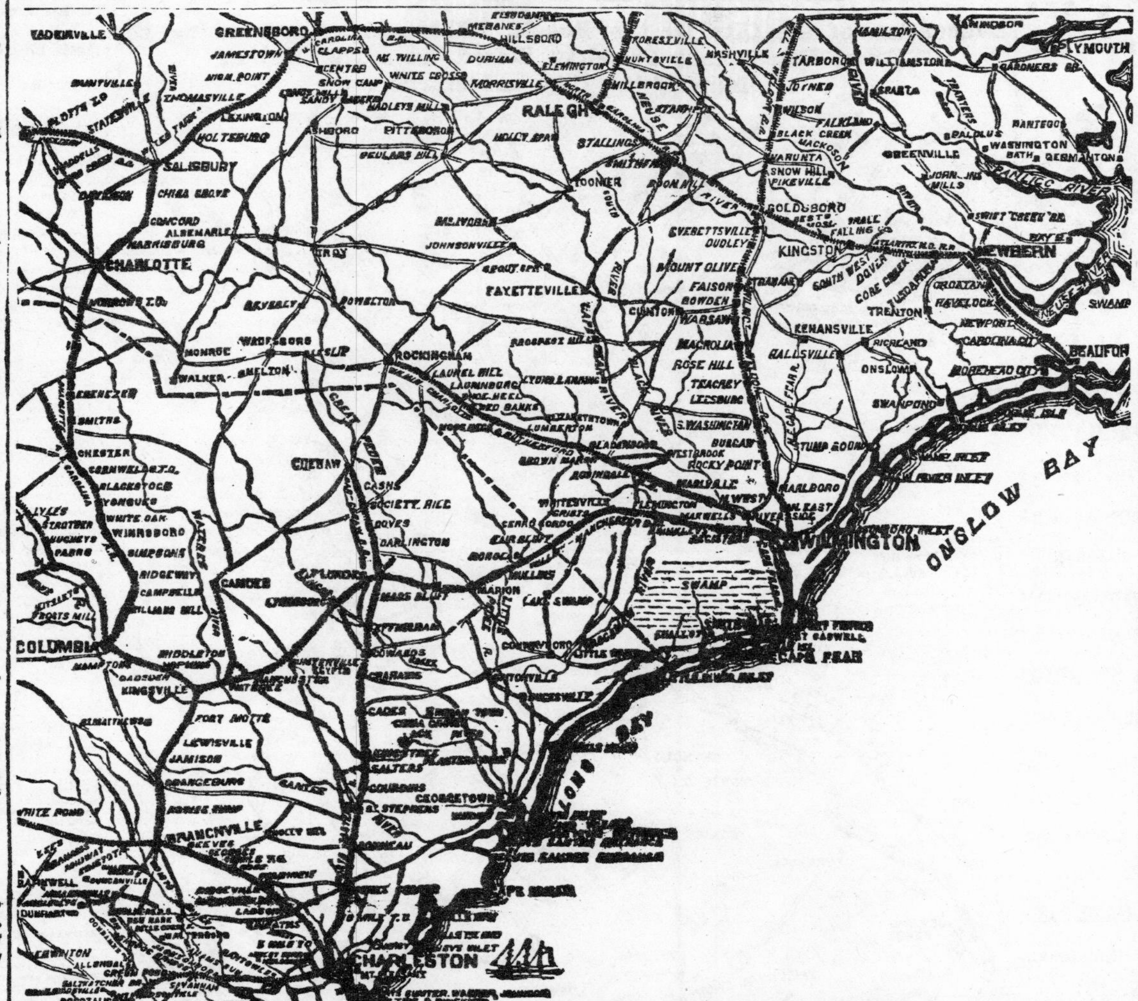

SHERMAN.

COLUMBIA OURS!

Occupation of the Capital of South Carolina.

Beauregard Officially Announces that Sherman Reached the City on February 17.

CHARLESTON IS BEING EVACUATED.

The Rebels Admit that the Occupation of Columbia Necessitates the Fall of Charleston.

It is Presumed that Sherman Will Make Charleston His Base.

Rumored Capture of Augusta, Georgia.

No General Engagement Has Occurred.

REBEL ACCOUNTS OF SHERMAN'S PROGRESS, &c., &c., &c.

THE OFFICIAL ANNOUNCEMENT.

Secretary Stanton to Major General Dix.

WAR DEPARTMENT, WASHINGTON, Feb. 18, 1865.

Major General DIX, New York—

The announcement of the occupation of Columbia, S. C., by General Sherman, and the probable evacuation of Charleston, has been communicated to the department in the following telegrams just received from Lieutenant General Grant.

EDWIN M. STANTON, Secretary of War.

General Grant to Secretary Stanton.

CITY POINT, Feb, 18—4:45 P. M.

Hon. E. M. STANTON, War Department:—

The Richmond Dispatch of this morning says *Sherman entered Columbia yesterday morning, and its fall necessitates, it presumes, the fall of Charleston*, which it thinks is *already being evacuated*.

U. S. GRANT, Lieutenant General.

SECOND DESPATCH.

CITY POINT, Va., Feb. 18, 1865.

Hon. E. M. STANTON, War Department:—

The following is taken from to-day's Richmond *Dispatch*:—

Columbia has fallen! Sherman marched into and took possession of the city yesterday morning. The intelligence was communicated *yesterday* by General Beauregard in an official despatch.

Columbia is situated on the north bank of the Congaree river, just below the confluence of the Saluda and Broad rivers.

From General Beauregard's despatch it appears that on Thursday evening the enemy approached the south bank of the Congaree and threw a number of shells into the city. During the night they moved up the river, and yesterday morning forded the Saluda and Broad rivers. While they were crossing these rivers our troops, under General Beauregard, evacuated Columbia. The enemy soon after took possession.

Through private sources we learn that two days ago, when it was decided not to attempt the defence of Columbia, a large quantity of medical stores, which it was thought it was impossible to remove, were destroyed. The female employes of the Treasury Department had been previously sent off to Charlotte, N. C., a hundred miles north of Columbia. We presume the Treasury lithographic establishment was also removed, although as to this we have no positive information.

The fall of Columbia *necessitates, we presume, the evacuation of Charleston*, which we think likely is already in process of evacuation.

It is impossible to say where Sherman will next direct his columns. The general opinion is that *he will go to Charleston and establish a base there;* but we confess we do not see what need he has of a base. It is to be presumed he is subsisting on the country, and he has had no battle to exhaust his ammunition. Before leaving Savannah he declared his intention to march to Columbia, thence to Augusta, and thence to Charleston. This was uttered as a boast and to hide his designs. We are disposed to believe that *he will next strike at Charlotte*, which is a hundred miles north of Columbia, on the Charlotte and Columbia Railroad, *or at Florence, S. C.*, the junction of the Columbia and Wilmington and the Charleston and Wilmington railroads, some ninety miles east of Columbia.

There was a report yesterday that *Augusta had also been taken by the enemy*. This we do not believe.

We have reason to feel assured that nearly the whole of Sherman's army is at Columbia, and that the report that Schofield was advancing on Augusta was untrue.

The Richmond *Whig* says:—

The Charleston *Mercury* of Saturday announces a brief suspension of that paper, with a view *to its temporary removal to another point*. This is rendered necessary by the progress of military events, cutting it off from the mail facilities for distributing its paper to a large portion of its subscribers, while the lack of transportation renders its supply of paper precarious.

Semmes has been made a rear admiral, and will take command of the James river squadron.

U. S. GRANT, Lieutenant General.

REBEL ACCOUNTS.

The Movement on Columbia.

SKIRMISHING IN FRONT OF THE CITY ON FEB. 14.

[From the Richmond Examiner, Feb. 16.]

Sherman's movements in South Carolina still draw attention. Parties who left Columbia on Friday last report a general belief that Sherman had cut loose from Branchville and was moving towards Kingsville or Columbia. The Congaree has to be crossed before reaching either place. At Kingsville Sherman would be able to destroy the Columbia and Charlotte and Wilmington and Manchester Railroads at one and the same time. But this is looking very far into the distance and over the head of a great many uncertainties.

We have but little that is substantial in these speculations beyond the general fact that Sherman's main force has turned Branchville, and has probably got as far as Orangeburg, on the Columbia road. The bridge across the Edisto, which was reported to have been burned by our troops in the face of Sherman's advance, is four miles on the east of Midway, and directly on the route to Orangeburg, fifteen miles distant.

It is probable that the movements on the road between Branchville and Augusta are merely those of detachments of cavalry and raiding parties. The main portion of the enemy's army is, undoubtedly, that which has demonstrated upon Branchville. Sherman, adventurous as he is, will hardly attempt the simultaneous capture of Charleston, Augusta and Columbia. But it may be, if he is permitted to hold Branchville, *he will determine at his leisure whether to move his main force upon Columbia or Augusta, or to take the third course, and go down to Charleston for a new base of operations*.

A Columbia paper of Sunday last says that General Beauregard and staff, consisting of Colonel Otey, Colonel Rice, Captain Beauregard, Captain Ferry and Dr. Brodie, had arrived in that city, and were stopping at Nickerson's Hotel there.

The same paper states that a portion of the enemy's forces have crossed the South Edisto at Bennaker's ferry, and are slowly pushing forward towards the north branch of that river; and it thinks that the probabilities are that this movement is made for the double purpose of cutting the Columbia and Charleston road and Wilmington and Manchester road at or near Kingsville. This, however, is speculation; and the facts are only those which were stated, in another and official form, some days ago.

LATER.

We learned at a late hour last night that a despatch had been received here in one of the offices of the government stating that the local force in Columbia had been ordered out, and that *skirmishing was going on with the enemy in the vicinity of that city*. The despatch is dated the 14th inst.

The Cavalry Movement Against Augusta.

FURTHER PARTICULARS OF THE CAVALRY BATTLE AT AIKEN.

[From the Augusta Chronicle, Feb. 10.]

The federals on Thursday morning were at Windsor, about fifteen miles from Aiken. It is not known in what force. No movements were made by them on Thursday. Cause of this not ascertained.

The troops in the vicinity of Windsor are Kilpatrick's corps.

It is reported that Generals Hampton and Wheeler engaged the enemy on the 7th and 8th, repulsing them at all points. Our loss about seventy killed, wounded and missing; that of the enemy much greater.

The enemy are reported to be moving towards the Congaree river.

A gentleman from Columbia states that Slocum's corps is moving on that city on this side of the Edisto. His main line, when last heard from, was on the railroad.

It is stated in Columbia that Kilpatrick's corps is protecting Slocum's left.

It is ascertained that Porter is again moving on Charleston. When last heard from he was at Green Pond.

It is not known where General Sherman himself is.

Barnwell court house was burned on Monday night.

The roads are teeming with vehicles, stock and all kinds of movable property, fleeing for Georgia and upper Carolina.

Anticipations Which Were Doomed to Disappointment.

[From the Columbia (S. C.) Carolinian, Feb. 12.]

The facts, briefly, are that a portion of the enemy's forces have crossed the South Edisto at Bennaker's ferry, and are slowly pushing forward towards the north branch of that river. The probabilities, briefly, are that this movement is made for the double purpose of cutting the Columbia and Charleston road and Wilmington and Manchester road at or near Kingsville. This done Sherman will have achieved what he may deem an important object preliminary to the capture of Charleston—namely, the bisection of three important branches of supply. That he will succeed in doing this we have doubts—very grave doubts; for we know something of the dangerous operations of an army in the hands of Beauregard; but admitting Sherman's success to the extent named, what reason is there to anticipate an immediate advance on Columbia? We can recall none. True, Columbia is the capital of the State, the abode of wealth, the theatre of much enterprise, but beyond these attractive features it is nothing compared to the grander game of Charleston, on the capture of which the energies of the whole Yankee army below us are now bent. They cannot operate on Charleston from Columbia, and they will not leave Columbia on a northward march while Charleston stands. To believe it is contrary to common sense, contrary to a knowledge of Sherman's character and matured determination, and contrary to all military strategy. Possibly a raid may be made here for the purpose of creating a diversion. *It will not find us unprepared.*

Long before Columbia falls *we look for a battle and a victory* commensurate in its consequences with the great interests now at stake—one which will prove that "God is fighting by our side, although with visor down," and that he *has vouchsafed to South Carolina the proud privilege of closing as she began this war—in triumph.*

The Valiant South Carolinians Propose to Let Sherman Alone if He Will Only Retire.

[From the Columbia Carolinian, Feb. 11.]

Whether Sherman's objective point is Augusta, Charleston, Columbia or Richmond, or all four, does not, to unskilled eyes, yet appear. One thing, however, is certain, that every mile of ground the federal army leaves behind it—provided the latter is promptly met and attacked at the proper time—*is so much gained to us.* We have troops, our generals are watchful, and we firmly believe that within twenty days *there will be such a concentration of strength and assault as will make the Yankee commander tremble for his safety.* He may be permitted to move on our railroads and to penetrate our interior, but these triumphs must be short. The condition of the country will compel him to go forward or back, and that right quickly. If he comes forward, a reception awaits him unlike that which he encountered in his career through Georgia; if he goes to Charleston, he may find himself afflicted in front and rear; if he returns the way he came that will be *just what we all desire him to do, and we shall be content to let him alone.* On the whole, though some hearts are perturbed with expectations of a sudden appearance of the enemy, we think the aspect not discouraging, especially if our people will but do their duty. By all means, wherever Sherman advances, let him find nothing on which to feed man or beast.

The Rebel Reports of the Behavior of Sherman's Troops.

[From the Columbia Guardian, Feb. 11.]

We have conversed with planters from Barnwell district, who have made their way through the lines of the enemy's advance, and who represent their conduct as still thoroughly characteristic of the most brutal vandalism. The village at Buford's Bridge has been burned to the ground; the residences of the planters on the route which were left unoccupied were invariably destroyed. And where the families still remained in their dwellings, they were subjected not only robbery, but to various kinds of insult. Pistols were clapped to the bosoms of women, mothers and wives; the robbers refused to wait until doors and drawers could be unlocked, broke open ruthlessly the finest cabinets and apartments, destroyed or carried off at pleasure, and, to enforce their demands, threatened the house with fire over the heads of the inhabitants. They traversed the precinct, it appears, in scattered bands of fifteen or twenty, sometimes with and sometimes without any officer. the officer in general command of these predatory parties being understood to be a Colonel Robbins, who evidently and eminently deserves that the letter G should be restored to his name, as of natural right belonging to it. He was probably chosen [illegible]

THE SOUTH.

Rumored Evacuation of Wilmington.

Heavy Concentration of Union Troops in North Carolina.

The Exchange of Prisoners Practically Resumed.

Lee Calls for a Large Force of Negroes.

They Are to be Placed at His Disposal to be Used as He Likes,

&c., &c., &c.

Reported Evacuation of Wilmington.

MOVEMENTS OF THE UNION TROOPS IN NORTH CAROLINA.

[From the Richmond Dispatch, Feb. 16.]

It was reported yesterday morning that *our troops were evacuating Wilmington*. The report is not confirmed by official despatches received yesterday. The Yankee papers state that General Terry is still in the vicinity of Fort Fisher, and waiting for General Hoke to attack him. Hitherto the Yankee press have represented Terry as about to march towards Wilmington with the confident expectation of taking the place. Fort Anderson proves a more effectual obstruction than they had anticipated.

General Baker, in command of our forces at Goldsboro, reports to the War Department that he has reason to believe *the enemy are concentrating at Newbern*, and that they have with them materials for repairing the railroad from Newbern to Kinston.

Scouts who came into Kinston on the night of the 11th report that Foster is in command at Newbern, and that two thousand of the Eighteenth army corps have arrived there, making the number of troops at the post about five thousand. It is reported, and believed, in Kinston that the enemy have landed two locomotives and two transport loads of railroad iron at Morehead City. It is not apprehended in Kinston that the enemy design an early movement in that direction.

The Exchange of Prisoners.

[From the Richmond Examiner, Feb. 16.]

More than two thousand Confederate prisoners have already been returned to Richmond since the reinstitution of the exchange. The truce boat went down yesterday, expecting to bring up from Boulware's landing about one thousand more. In addition to these we learn that Colonel Mulford expected there would arrive yesterday at Fortress Monroe, *en route* for exchange, two thousand of our prisoners. So far most of these men have been drawn from the prison at Point Lookout, and the most distant prisons will probably have their turn served last. Point Lookout is probably the most populous of the Yankee prisons, and contained some time ago seven thousand Confederate prisoners. The number of Confederates in the hands of the enemy, if reduced to privates, will, we learn, exceed forty thousand men. The return of our prisoners at this time is most beneficial in a military point of view.

PRISONERS SENT TO OUR LINES FROM RICHMOND.

[From the Richmond Examiner, Feb. 16.]

One thousand five hundred and eighteen Yankee prisoners of war, including one commissioned officer—Lieutenant Murray, Thirteenth New Hampshire regiment, a hostage who has been held in confinement for several months—were sent down the river yesterday. The Allison carried down four hundred and the Schultz four hundred and seventeen.

In view of the prospective exchange, seventeen hundred are expected down from Danville to-day, with a number of officers.

Operations on the Petersburg Lines.

[From the Richmond Dispatch, Feb. 16.]

There was a cannonade of several hours duration on our left, near the Appomattox, on Wednesday evening. With this exception nothing of moment occurred. On the Petersburg lines picket firing has, by the tacit consent of both parties, very much slackened within the past few days. The enemy are quiet in their intrenchments on Hatcher's run. Throughout Monday night the rumbling of wagons and artillery was heard on Grant's lines in the neighborhood of Dose Bottom. It was supposed that [illegible] transferring a heavy body of troops to the north [illegible] may be simply the return of the troops [illegible] to Petersburg to participate in the Hatcher's run [illegible] Monday.

Rebel Negro Soldiers.

LEE CALLS FOR A LARGE FORCE OF NEGROES.

[From the Richmond Examiner, Feb. 15.]

The idea of employing negroes to help in the defence of their homes has greatly ripened in the public mind; and especially since the atrocious ultimatum of the enemy at Hampton Roads has fully brought home to us all the imperative necessity of bringing out and using all the elements of force which we can possibly command. It is also very well known that General Lee, who has accepted the powers and responsibilities of General-in-Chief, *urgently calls for a large force of negroes* to be placed at his disposal, to be used according to his best judgment. *The country will not venture to deny to General Lee*, in the present position of affairs, *anything* he may ask for.

In the President's message at the opening of the present session the subject was most injudiciously presented for the first time to public attention, coupled as it was with a suggestion that emancipation might be held out to negro soldiers as a reward for faithful service. This suggestion was said, and justly said, to contain and to affirm the whole doctrine of abolition; because, if emancipation be a "reward" to negroes, then freedom is a better state for negroes than slavery. But in reply to this it was urged they think it a boon and a blessing; they will deem it a reward, and will give more zealous and faithful service in the hope of it. This implies that we, the white race, are no longer to judge for negroes, but leave them to judge for themselves; that we are not only to withdraw our care and guidance from them, but also to cheat them, by holding out to them as a blessing that which we know would prove a curse. This, therefore, is also abolition; and the worse sort of abolition, because it would be abandonment of the negro race in this country to misery and eventual extirpation: it is abolition, not of negro slavery only, but of negroes also.

Such were the obvious reflections which occurred to thoughtful minds on seeing the suggestion in the President's message; and up to this time the judgments of men upon the whole measure, as a practical measure, have been disturbed by the introduction of topics which raised a question of morals and right. So far as right and morality are concerned, the position of the Southern people is and has been impregnable. They feel that the relation of master and slave has been a blessing to the slave; that they have profited the negro race much more than that race has ever profited them; and what is more, they know that they, the *planters of the South, are the only defence of the negroes against that sanguinary Northern "philanthropy (?)* which would deprive them of the protection of owners, in order that they may disappear from the face of the earth and leave their place open *to miserable white laborers working for the minimum of daily bread.* Upon every ground of justice and humanity, this Southern people feels itself entitled, and indeed bound, to hold its existing relation with the black race, so long as possible. If compelled by the strong necessity of self preservation to abandon or to modify that relation, it will be under strong protest, and taking heaven and earth to witness that the blood of those simple creatures does not stain our hands.

It is also very certain that negroes are not intended for soldiers, and *will never fight when they can avoid it;* and that if we could but collect and bring back the absentees without leave, now on the rolls of our armies, we should never have to consider the project of alloying with this base material the pure metal of our Confederate ranks.

Yet, when all this has been said, still comes back the urgent question, how to meet the formidable and multitudinous hosts of a vindictive invader this very spring? and also the not less urgent demand of the great soldier on whom we all depend to command our armies, for power to use negroes in defence of the country. Who will take the responsibility of refusing that appeal?

Congress has now several bills before it, intended to authorize this description of force. But Congress is somewhat slow and timid this session: its legislation aims at too much exactitude in providing for every contingency and prescribing forms and restrictions; and the consequence is that time passes, and the needful thing still remains to be done. As we have a commander-in-chief—as this species of force is to be created at his express request, and as he will have the care of organizing and disposing it—something should be trusted to his discretion. And with this view we should greatly approve the simple amendment proposed on Tuesday, enacting "that the General-in-Chief be and is hereby invested with the full power to call into the service of the Confederate States, to perform any duty to which he may assign them, so many of the able-bodied slaves within the Confederate States, as, in his judgment, the exigencies of the public service may require." This makes no allusion to the future status of the slaves so to be employed. Congress cannot change that status, nor empower the General to change it. Therefore it leaves all that for future consideration in State Legislatures. It also avoids all special provisos as to the proportion of those taken from a particular plantation to those who are left, trusting that to the practical sagacity and justice of General Lee. It clothes him with great power, and loads him with heavy responsibility. If he is willing to wield that power, and shoulder that responsibility, in the name of God let him have them.

It has been too generally assumed in discussing this matter that you cannot fairly expect negroes to fight for the [illegible] without promising them freedom. Why? Would they have more stake in the country as freemen than as slaves? Would they have a better cause to fight for as freemen than as slaves? If so then they would be elevated and made happier by being made freemen. If so, here is abolitionism again—abolitionism pure and simple. Those who thus affirm either are abolitionists in their hearts, or else they can give so good reason why they are not. We desire to see this most urgent, practical question cleared and disembarrassed of theories and arguments. The thing to be done is to take the slaves and to get their service. It would not be the first time that slaves have fought for their country; and certainly negro slaves have a far stronger interest in defending a country where they have a master and protector and an assured home than one in which they would be left exposed, without defence, to the cruel benevolence of Yankee abolitionists. If we must use negroes in defence of our homes, *let us do so;* but, for their sake as well as for our own, let us beware of giving any consent or adhesion to the doctrine that people of that race gain by being turned wild—or "made free," if we are to use that improper Yankee cant.

General Lee's Idea of the Situation.

HE FEELS NO APPREHENSION ABOUT THE ISSUE OF THE WAR.

[From the Richmond Whig, Feb. 16.]

We copy from the Petersburg *Express* of yesterday, the following interesting correspondence, which "speaks for itself." The declaration to which General Wise refers is a declaration in favor of the prosecution of the war until our independence is achieved:—

HEADQUARTERS, WISE'S BRIGADE,
TRENCHES NEAR PETERSBURG, Va., Feb. 1, 1865.

To General ROBERT E. LEE, Commanding, &c:—

GENERAL—The foregoing declaration of sentiments was yesterday, the 31st day of January, ult., adopted in general meeting of the officers and men of this brigade, with but very few (some two or three) dissenting voices, and those differing but little, and more as to forms of expression than as to the matter.

I, in person, submitted the subject to the brigade, and took the vote, which was nearly unanimous in favor of the declaration as now presented. They have requested me to forward them to you as an expression of their confidence in you as a patriot and their commander-in-chief, and as an assurance of their devotion to the cause of their country. This I take great pleasure in doing, and I am, most respectfully, your obedient servant,

HENRY A. WISE, Brigadier General.

HEADQUARTERS, ARMY NORTHERN VIRGINIA,
Feb. 4, 1865.

Brigadier General HENRY A. WISE, Commanding, &c.:—

GENERAL:—I have received the declaration of principles and rights made by your brigade, and return my thanks to yourself, your officers and men. The spirit evinced in this document is the true one. If our people will sustain the noble soldiers of the confederacy and evince the same resolution and fortitude under their trials which have characterized the army, *I feel no apprehension about the issue of this contest.* I do not see how we can, by any compromise or negotiation, abate aught of the rights claimed in this admirable declaration without a surrender of the liberties we derived from our ancestors.

As long as our soldiers are animated by such sentiments and supported by the country, I believe that our overthrow is beyond the power of the enemy. Very respectfully, your obedient servant.

R. E. LEE, General.

SHENANDOAH.

Cavalry Expedition Up the Valley.

THE CAROLINA IRON WORKS DESTROYED.

Hot Skirmishing with the Rebel Cavalry,

&c., &c., &c.

Mr. Charles H. Farrell's Despatches.

WINCHESTER, Va., Feb. 17, 1865.

General Sheridan recently obtained information that the rebel military authorities were industriously working an iron furnace in the upper valley, conveying the iron after it was worked to Staunton, from thence per railroad to Richmond, where the iron was fabricated into shot and shell for the rebel army. The iron was conveyed in sleighs from the furnace to Staunton. General Sheridan placed the matter in the hands of Major General Merritt, temporary commander of the cavalry corps, who at once devised an expedition to destroy the rebel iron works.

For this duty a detachment of three hundred picked men of the First and Sixth regiments of Michigan cavalry, under the command of Lieutenant Colonel Maxwell, of the first named regiment, were detailed. The command left camp near this town at dusk on the evening of the 15th inst., proceeding up the main valley pike, over roads covered with snow, so that it was with difficulty the correct route could be pursued. The command passed through Kernstown, over Hog run, through Newtown and Middletown, passing the battle field of the 19th of October, crossed Cedar creek, passed through Strasburg, Fisher's Hill and Round Top, over Tom's Bank, Pew's creek and through Woodstock, all without molestation, until they reached a point within three miles of Edinburg.

The troops marched all night. Flankers, and advance and rear guards were thrown out, and everything kept well in hand to prevent surprise or sudden attack. The point above named was reached at three o'clock, A. M., when the advance guard came to the Shenandoah river, and were fired upon by a rebel picket stationed on the opposite side, near the bridge. Our troops soon discovered that the planks had been taken up from the bridge. The river was high, and not fordable, so that planks were speedily procured, the bridge repaired, and our troops crossed, the enemy's pickets, which had gathered in considerable numbers, disputing the passage by a constant fusilade.

On reaching the south side of the river a new obstacle presented itself, in the shape of a strong iron wire fence thrown across the road, and so obscure that it was not discovered until our troopers' horses ran against it. The removal of these obstacles occupied but a short time, as the troops moved with alacrity and good will. The command then pushed on, hoping to surprise the reserve or main body of the rebels, which were supposed to be within a half mile of the river. Our troops pushed on at a rapid trot, proceeded three miles beyond the river, but the main body of the rebels did not discover themselves. Three of our men were wounded, one of them mortally, while repairing the bridge.

Our troops remained at Edinburg until eleven A. M. on the 16th, gathering such information as might conduce to the success of the expedition.

The command was then divided, one-half returning down the Valley pike, and the other half proceeding through Fort Gap, between Three Top Mountain and Peaked Ridge, to a point on Water Lick creek, to the Caroline Iron Furnace—the objective point of the expedition. The furnace was in full blast, and hundreds of tons of iron ore and smelted iron were found on the ground. The hands at work at the furnace fled at the approach of our troops. The buildings and machinery for carrying on the works were destroyed. This accomplished, our second party of troops returned home by the way of Big Fort valley. On the route rebel guerillas and detachments of regular troops were seen and engaged by our troops. A number of the rebels were unsaddled and several captured. The command made a junction with the other detachment that evening, near Cedar creek, on the valley road.

The detachment that returned by the valley pike, accompanying which was Captain Martindale, of General Torbert's staff, and Lieutenant Baker, of General Merritt's staff, were not so fortunate. After they left Edinburg they were pursued by a squadron of one hundred rebel cavalry soldiers. At times they attacked our rear guard vigorously; when our men would stand to repel the attack the rebels would hesitate at our fire. At one time they charged between our main body and our rear guard of fourteen men, among whom was Captain Martindale. Our men, seeing their safety was in their determination, charged the rebels and rejoined the main force.

Passing through Woodstock—which was done after dark—our troops captured quite a number of horses. Our troops reached their camp after dark last night.

The result of the expedition may be summed up as follows:—The destruction of a valuable iron furnace, from which the rebels were getting out from sixty to one hundred tons of iron per day for military purposes, capturing fifteen rebel soldiers, killing and wounding several others.

Our loss was trifling. Captain Martindale's orderly was captured. Our wounded were brought into camp.

Our troops behaved with gallantry, and it was owing to this fact that the expedition was successful. The time occupied in accomplishing the work was a little over twenty-four hours, and the distance travelled nearly seventy miles.

Some of the rebel prisoners report that the main body of the rebel troops in the valley are at Staunton. Many of the rebels are absent on furlough, with orders to report to their commands by March 1.

Nine guerillas were captured last night near the Winchester and Martinsburg pike, north of Stevenson's depot. Their horses and equipments were also captured. The credit of this affair belongs to the regular cavalry brigade.

It is snowing in this section of the valley.

WINCHESTER, Va., Feb. 18—9:30 A. M.

A party of our scouts has just returned from an expedition up the valley bringing with them quite a number of prisoners, among whom is Colonel Thos. Magee, of the Twelfth Virginia rebel cavalry.

The Philadelphia Inquirer.

PRICE TWO CENTS. | PHILADELPHIA, TUESDAY, FEBRUARY 21, 1865. | PRICE TWO CENTS.

VICTORY!!!

OUR [FLAG] IS THERE!!

GLORIOUS NEWS!

CHARLESTON EVACUATED!

Stars and Stripes Wave Over the City!

THE GOOD OLD FLAG AVENGED!

South Carolina Chevaliers on the Run!

HARDEE PUSHING FOR NORTH CAROLINA!

Beauregard on the Double-Quick!

SHERMAN CLOSE IN HIS REAR!

His Army Moving Rapidly Northward!

PANIC AMONG THE SOUTHERN PEOPLE

Hampton's Rebel Cavalry Pillaging Towns.

A GRAND SERIES OF RAIDS

Union Thunder All Around!

OFFICIAL WAR GAZETTE.

Despatches from Lieut.-Gen. Grant.

CHARLESTON!!

Evacuation of the City by the Rebels. Sherman "Repossessing the Forts, Places and Property Seized from the Union."

Map of the City and Harbor.

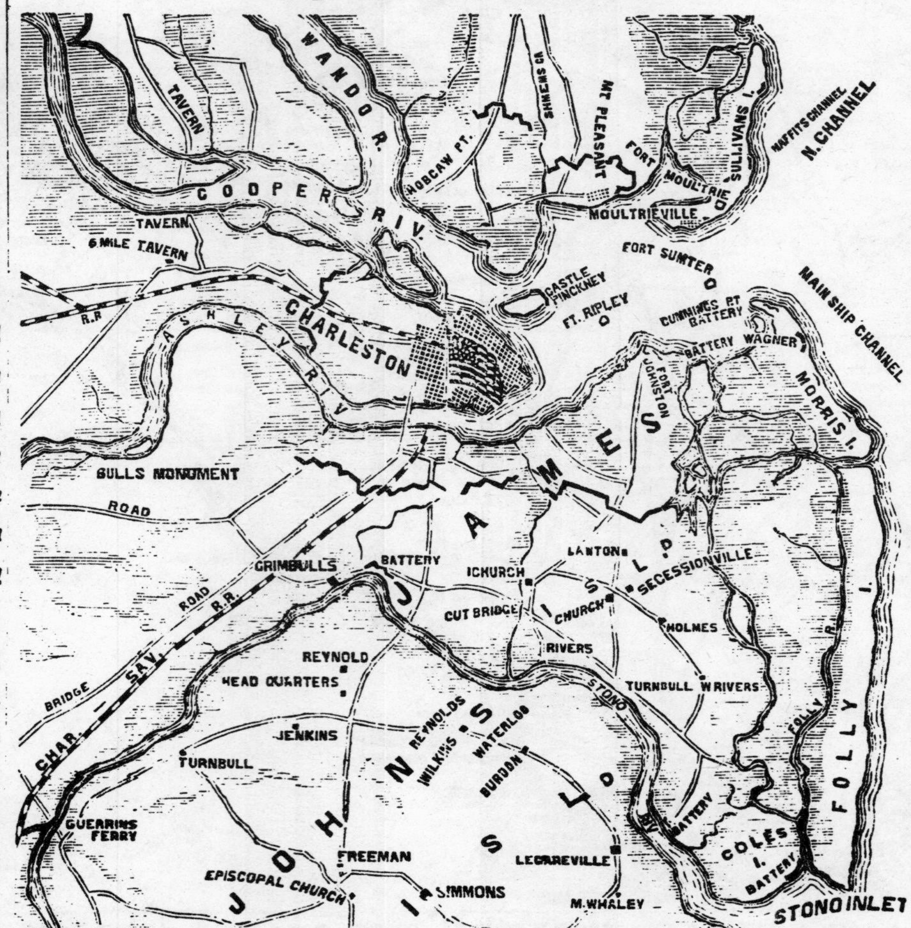

FIRST BULLETIN.

Important News from South Carolina—Evacuation of Charleston—The Fact Announced in Richmond Papers.

OFFICIAL GAZETTE.

WASHINGTON, Feb. 20, 12:40 P. M.—Major-General Dix, New York:—The evacuation of Charleston by the Rebels is announced in the following despatch, just received from General Grant.

E. M. STANTON, Secretary of War.

CITY POINT, Feb. 20.—Hon. E. M. Stanton:—The following despatch is just received.

U. S. GRANT, Lieutenant-General.

The Richmond *Examiner* of to-day, just received, says Charleston was evacuated on Tuesday last.

(Signed) G. WEITZEL Major-General.

SECOND BULLETIN.

Despatch from Secretary Stanton.

WASHINGTON, Feb. 20, 8 o'clock P. M.—Major-General Dix, New York:—The following details of military operations and the condition of affairs in the Rebel States, taken from the Richmond papers of to-day, have been forwarded by General Grant.

This Department has received no other intelligence in relation to the operations of our forces against Fort Anderson and Wilmington.

Admiral Dahlgren in Charleston.

A despatch from Admiral Dahlgren to the Secretary of the Navy, dated at Charleston harbor, on the 18th, states that the Rebels were abandoning Charleston that morning, and he was on his way to the city. EDWIN M. STANTON, Secretary of War.

Despatches from General Grant.

CITY POINT, Va., Feb. 20, 1865.—Hon. Edward M. Stanton, Secretary of War:—The following paragraphs are extracted from the Richmond papers of to-day:—

Beauregard Moving to Charlotte.

"We now know that Charleston was evacuated on Tuesday last, and that on Friday the enemy took possession of Columbia. It is reported that our forces under General Beauregard are moving in the direction of Charlotte."

Sherman Moving North.

Official information was received at the War Office last night that Sherman was advancing towards and was near Winnesboro', a point on the railroad leading to Charlotte, and thirty miles north of Columbia.

Charlotte is thronged with refugees from Columbia, who report that some of Wheeler's Cavalry plundered the city before the evacuation.

Valuables Removed from Columbia.

"Up to Tuesday last it was uncertain whether Columbia would come within the immediate range of Sherman's pursuers, and consequently the public mind was not prepared for such an early solution of the question. The Government had, however, just two weeks ago, taken the precaution to remove its special deposits there, amounting to several millions of dollars, and within the past few days all the dies and plates belonging to the Treasury Department, together with the supplies of Treasury notes on hand, were safely conveyed away.

Sherman's Strategy.

The enemy being in possession of Branchville, Orangeburg and Kingsville, precluded movements on the roads leading to Charleston, and an unfortunate accident upon the Charlotte road cutting off nearly all the rolling stock of the road from Columbia, prevented the authorities from making use of that avenue to save other valuable materials in the city.

Destruction of Property.

A large quantity of medical stores belonging to the Government were there, one-half of which were saved, and the rest, for want of time and transport, destroyed.

Rebel Treasury Note Establishment.

The presses and fixtures for printing Treasury Notes, in the establishments of Evans & Coggswell, and Keating & Ball, were necessarily abandoned, together with the other extensive machinery of those well-known firms. The first named establishment had one hundred and two printing presses, and is the best equipped publishing house in the South.

The Evacuation of Columbia.

The enemy's forces operating west of Columbia reached the banks of the Congaree, opposite the city, on Thursday evening, and threw in a number of shells, to which our batteries responded. A portion of this column moved up the river during the night, and crossed the Saluda and Broad Rivers, the main tributaries of the Congaree, which meet near Columbia, a few miles below the city.

During the movement General Beauregard evacuated the city, and on Friday morning the enemy entered and took possession without opposition. Our troops were withdrawn to a position some twenty miles from Columbia, where they remained on yesterday.

The Forces Entering Columbia.

The enemy's force entering Columbia consisted of Sherman's main army, a large portion of which immediately moved by the Charlotte road, while another portion has moved down in the direction of Charleston. The latter city has doubtless ere this been evacuated.

From Charleston.

CHARLESTON, Feb. 14.—The enemy's gunboats and one monitor have been shelling our picket lines on James Island all day. All is quiet in our immediate front. Nothing definite from above. The enemy keeps up a steady shelling of the city.

CHARLESTON, Feb. 15.—All is quiet along our lines. The enemy this morning are reported to be moving in force near Columbia, on the Lexington road. It is reported that they crossed the Congaree to-day.

From Wilmington—Furious Cannonading of Fort Anderson.

WILMINGTON, N. C., Feb. 18.—The enemy shelled Fort Anderson furiously yesterday afternoon, nearly all night and this morning. It is reported that a land force attacked our forces at Anderson, but were repulsed.

The cannonading is still going on at one o'clock P. M., but we have no particulars.

Another Raid on the Virginia and Tennessee Railroad.

A despatch has been received here stating that a force of the enemy 4000 strong, 200 of it being cavalry, are advancing from Knoxville, and had reached Greenville, which is fifty-four miles from Bristol. This expedition is supposed to be another raid on the Virginia and Tennessee Railroad.

Movements in North Carolina.

The telegraph operator at Weldon reported, on yesterday, that a raid from Washington or Newbern, North Carolina, was in progress, the supposed destination of the raiders being the Rocky Mount Station, on the Wilmington road in Edgecomb county. The wires continued to work, during yesterday evening, through to Wilmington, however, from which it would appear that they had not then struck the road.

A movement of the enemy was reported yesterday, in heavy force, upon Kinston, North Carolina, and it was supposed in official quarters that Foster's force had been moved up to Newbern.

A cavalry raid was also reported in the direction of Tarboro. The force moving from Newbern has fifty or sixty pieces of artillery. We shall hear more of these movements in a few days. We are quite convinced that they are in progress as we write.

Exchange of Prisoners.

Colonel Hatch, one of our Commissioners of Exchange, has gone to Wilmington, at which place he will during the week exchange ten thousand prisoners. We may remark here that the exchange of prisoners on the James River will at the same time go on uninterruptedly.

Desperate Fight of Deserters.

A desperate affair occurred last Tuesday in Lunenburg county, Virginia, between some deserters from the Confederate army and some of the Ninth Virginia Cavalry, aided by citizens. Several on both sides were wounded. The deserters were finally captured.

Robbery of Returned Prisoners.

General Ewell commanding the Department of Henrico, reports a wholesale robbery of one hundred paroled prisoners, on Saturday night, between Camp Lee and this city. Other robberies of returned prisoners are reported as occurring in the streets of Richmond.

U. S. GRANT, Lieutenant-General.

Despatch from Admiral Dahlgren—On the Way to Charleston.

WASHINGTON, Feb. 20.—The following despatch has been received at the Navy Department:—

FLAG-SHIP "HARVEST MOON," REBELLION ROADS, CHARLESTON HARBOR, Feb. 20.—Hon. Gideon Welles, Secretary of the Navy.—Sir:—Charleston was abandoned this morning by the Rebels. I am now on my way to the city, and have the honor to be, very respectfully, your obedient servant, JOHN A. DAHLGREN, Rear Admiral.

REBEL ACCOUNTS.

The Fall of Columbia.

From the Richmond Examiner, Feb. 18.

The State capital of South Carolina has fallen. Columbia is in the hands of Sherman. If the mere overrunning of a country were conquering it, the Yankee enemy might begin to boast of the subjugation of South Carolina. For so far they have advanced and penetrated the very heart of the State without serious opposition. But the only value of that advance, for the general purposes of the campaign, consists in its being a step towards co-operating with Grant in the investment of Richmond. Thus Sherman's enterprise is only beginning.

The future plans or present dispositions of Beauregard are unknown here. The little Confederate army, however, is safe, and may yet lead Sherman such a dance as Greene led Cornwallis over those same rivers and swamps. If the Federal army cannot reach the Danville railroad, then it had better have staid in Atlanta all this while. But "it is a far cry to Lochow."

It is true, the Federals can gratify their fine sense of "poetical justice" (or, as we should say, their petty malice), by laying waste the unprotected homesteads of that noble State, and wreaking upon the women and children of South Carolinians their noble revenge for the heroic resistance they have encountered on every field at the hands of the men. Yet that is not conquering a country. On the contrary, it is making it unconquerable where the breed of men is of the right kind. There is reason to believe that General Beauregard is carrying out a deliberate design; and that Sherman is near the end of his triumphs.

We may regard this [illegible]dacious march of the enemy through the h[illegible] of South Carolina as one of the consequen[illegible] removing Johnston from command of [illegible] of Tennessee.

Table of Distances.

The following table of distances, which we have compiled from reliable sources, will be found valuable to our readers for reference in tracing the various movements now taking place in the Carolinas:—

From Charleston to	Miles.	From Kingsville to	Miles.
Savannah	104	Columbia	25
Ashepoo Bridge	[illegible]	Florence	64
Pocotaligo	[illegible]	Wilmington	171
Kingstree	[illegible]	*From Columbia to*	
Florence	102	Florence	89
Augusta	137	Wilmington	196
Branchville	62	Charlotte	108
Orangeburg	79	Salisbury (inner line)	149
Kingsville	105	Raleigh (inner line)	[illegible]
Columbia	[illegible]	Goldsboro'	[illegible]
Aiken	[illegible]	Goldsboro' (by Wilm'n)	270
Augusta	137	Raleigh (by Wilm'n)	318
Wilmington (by rail)	[illegible]	*From Wilmington to*	
Richmond	[illegible]	Marion	86
Washington	[illegible]	Florence	107
From Branchville to		Goldsboro'	84
Charleston	62	Weldon	162
Orangeburg	17	Raleigh	132
Kingville	45	Hillsboro	172
Columbia	68	Greensboro'	214
Florence	108	Salisbury	[illegible]
Augusta	75	Charlotte	[illegible]
Wilmington	216	Petersburg	226
Charlotte	174	Richmond	248
From Newbern to		Washington	378
Beaufort	[illegible]		
Goldsboro'	[illegible]		

RECEPTION OF THE NEWS.

The News in Baltimore.

Special Despatch to the Inquirer.

BALTIMORE, Feb. 20.—Flags have been flying from the newspaper offices and other public buildings, in honor of the evacuation of Charleston, of Columbia, and Fort Sumter. There is much rejoicing here over the glorious achievements of Sherman. A grand salute is to be fired soon, and Washington's Birthday is to be observed as a general patriotic holiday.

The News in New York.

NEW YORK, Feb. 20.—There was a general display of bunting throughout the city to-day, on the announcement of the Rebel evacuation of Charleston.

INTERESTING FROM NORTH CAROLINA.

Effects of the Recent Union Victories.

NEWBERN, N. C., Feb. 20.—The fall of Fort Fisher is working a revolution in the minds of the people of this State, which, if there is any meaning in half of the threats emanating from the State Capital, must result in a separation of North Carolina from the Confederacy soon after Raleigh is garrisoned by the Union forces, which is a necessary protection required by the conservative party, a majority of whom, says a Rebel newspaper, favor a return to the Union, even with emancipation.

The enemy are removing their supplies from Wilmington, with a view, it is thought, of evacuating the city.

It is estimated that there is over one hundred and sixty millions of dollars' worth of cotton stored from Wilmington along the line of the railroads reaching into South Carolina and the southern part of North Carolina, which the enemy will order to be burned as soon as our forces approach.

Sherman's movements are regarded with much alarm by the Rebel papers of this State, which predict that he will attempt to hold Goldsborough and Raleigh.

The Raleigh (N. C.) *Standard* and the Raleigh *Progress*, and the other conservative papers in this State, are paying high tributes to the military genius of General Sherman whose approach they welcome with open manifestations of joy.

The experiment adopted here last year, by the Treasury Department, of leasing abandoned plantations to both white and black persons, who were placed on an equal footing in this respect, has brought forth results highly favorable to the blacks.

In the important report just published by Colonel Heaton, the Supervising Treasury Agent, he says:— "The sanguine expectation too often indulged in that legislation may now be exclusively depended upon as the sovereign antidote for all the temporal ills the freedman is heir to, is fallacious and visionary."

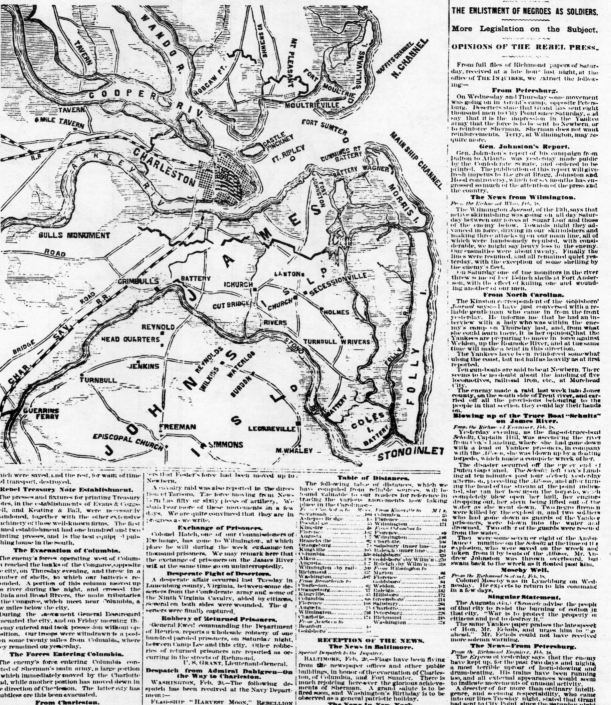

THE SOUTH.

The War News Around the Doomed Cities.

YANKEE OPERATIONS IN NORTH CAROLINA.

Destruction of the Truce-boat "Schultz."

THE ENLISTMENT OF NEGROES AS SOLDIERS.

More Legislation on the Subject.

OPINIONS OF THE REBEL PRESS.

From full files of Richmond papers of Saturday, received at a late hour last night, at the office of THE INQUIRER, we extract the following:—

From Petersburg.

On Wednesday and Thursday some movement was going on in Grant's camp, opposite Petersburg. Deserters state that Grant has sent eight thousand men to City Point since Saturday, and say that it is the impression in the Yankee army that the force is to be sent to Newbern, or to reinforce Sherman. Sherman does not want reinforcements. Terry, at Wilmington, may require more.

Gen. Johnston's Report.

Gen. Johnston's report of his campaign from Dalton to Atlanta was yesterday made public by the Confederate Senate, and ordered to be printed. The publication of this report will give fresh impetus to the great Bragg, Johnston and Hood controversy, which for six months has engrossed so much of the attention of the press and the country.

The News from Wilmington.

From the Richmond Whig, Feb. 18.

The Wilmington *Journal*, of the 15th, says that active skirmishing was going on all day Saturday between our forces at Sugar Loaf and those of the enemy below. Towards night they advanced in force, driving in our skirmishers and making three attacks upon our main line, all of which were handsomely repulsed, with considerable, we might say heavy loss to the enemy. Our casualties were about twenty. Finally the lines were resumed, and all remained quiet yesterday, with the exception of some shelling by the enemy's fleet.

On Saturday one of the monitors in the river threw some of her 15-inch shells at Fort Anderson, with the effect of killing one and wounding another of our men.

From North Carolina.

The Kinston correspondent of the Goldsboro' *Journal* says:—I have just conversed with a reliable gentleman who came in from the front yesterday. He informs me that he had an interview with a lady who was within the enemy's camp on Thursday last, and, from what she could learn there, it is her opinion that the Yankees are preparing to move in force against Weldon, up the Roanoke River, and at the same time will make a feint in this direction.

The Yankees have been reinforced somewhat along the coast, but not half as heavily as at first reported.

Ten gun-boats are said to be at Newbern. There seems to be no doubt about the landing of five locomotives, railroad iron, etc., at Morehead City.

The enemy made a raid last week into Jones county, on the south side of Trent river, and carried off all the provisions belonging to the people in that section they could lay their hands on.

Blowing up of the Truce Boat "Schultz" on James River.

From the Richmond Examiner, Feb. 18.

Yesterday evening, as the flag-of-truce-boat *Schultz*, Captain Hill, was ascending the river from Cox's Landing, where she had gone down with a load of Yankee prisoners, in company with the *Allison*, she was blown up by a floating torpedo, which made a complete wreck of her.

The disaster occurred off the upper end of Dutch Gap Canal. The *Schultz* left Cox's Landing at ten minutes past four o'clock yesterday afternoon, preceding the *Allison*, and after turning the head of the stream at the point indicated, she ran her bow upon the torpedo, which completely blew open her hull, her engines dropping out, her stern being lifted out of the water as she went down. Two negro firemen were killed by the explosion, and two soldiers who had gone down as guards of the Yankee prisoners, were blown into the water and drowned. Two other of the guards were rescued from the water.

There were some seven or eight of the Ambulance Committee on the *Schultz* at the time of the explosion, who were saved on the wreck and taken from it by boats of the *Allison*. Mr. Andrew Johnston was thrown overboard, but swam back to the wreck as it floated past him.

Mosby Well.

From the Richmond Sentinel, Feb. 18.

Colonel Mosby was in Lynchburg on Wednesday. He expects to return to his command in a few days.

Singular Statement.

The Augusta (Ga.) *Chronicle* advise the people of that city to resist the burning of cotton in that city. "War is to protect the property of citizens and not to destroy it."

The same Yankee paper praises the late speech of Hon. Mr. Echols, and urges him to "go ahead." Mr. Echols could not have received more solemn warning.

The News—From Petersburg.

From the Richmond Enquirer, Feb. 18.

The *Express* of yesterday says that the enemy have kept up, for the past two days and nights, a most terrible uproar of horn-blowing and drum-beating. His trains have been running too, and all external appearances would seem to indicate movements of unusual activity.

A deserter of far more than ordinary intelligence, and seeming respectability, who came into our lines Tuesday night, stated that Grant had sent to City Point since the Saturday night previous, from the left, not less than eight thousand men. This deserter states that the impression in the army was, these men were going South, either to Newbern or to Sherman. As Grant vainly endeavored to reach the Boydton plank and the South Side Railroad in his last movement, we think it probable that he will now reinforce at some point further South, and endeavor to make that part of his programme a success beyond peradventure.

Slaves for the Rebel Armies.

In the Rebel Senate, on Friday, Mr. Wigfall, from the Committee on Military Affairs, reported the following bill, which was read a third time and passed:—

The Congress of the Confederate States of America do enact, That it shall be competent for the Secretary of War to negotiate with the Governors or other authorities of the different States of the Confederacy, when he deems the same to be expedient, for any number of slaves to serve with the armies in the field, or for service in any of the bureaus of supply, or at posts, or hospitals, or for fortifications and mining, under any of the laws of the Confederate States, or to engage their assistance to execute the laws of the Confederacy relative to the impressment of slaves, and to make such contracts or engagements as may be necessary for forwarding an adequate supply of slave labor for all such purposes.

From the Trans-Mississippi Department.

Captain F. Mohl, who arrived in this city on yesterday, has kindly furnished us with files of Texas papers from December 24th to January 2d, from which we will extract hereafter. Among the items of interest in the budget before us we find that the forces under General Magruder are reported to be in excellent condition. Important events in his department are looked for in the coming spring.

General John A. Wharton, of the Confederate Army, we find, has arrived at his home in Brazoria county, Texas, after an absence of nearly three years and a half. He left Texas the Captain of a Company in the Terry Rangers, he returned a Major-General in the Confederate States army. He has won his rank, says the Houston *Telegraph*, by arduous service, and by the display of military ability. The State cherishes him with pride, and looks to him with confidence for still more signal service.

The New-York Times.

VOL. XIV......NO. 4194. NEW-YORK, SUNDAY, MARCH 5, 1865. PRICE FOUR CENTS.

THE INAUGURATION.

A Stormy Morning but a Clear Afternoon.

THE PROCESSION TO THE CAPITOL.

Imposing Display—Enthusiasm Among the People.

THE INAUGURATION CEREMONIES.

Vice-President Johnson Sworn in by Mr. Hamlin.

President Lincoln takes the Oath for the Second Term.

HIS INAUGURAL ADDRESS.

The Changes of Four Years—Both Sides Disappointed at the Length of the War.

THE SITUATION VERY HOPEFUL.

Our Object a Just and Lasting Peace Among Ourselves and with Others.

The Inauguration of President Lincoln.
Dispatches to the Associated Press.
WASHINGTON, Saturday, March 4.

The procession is now forming, though a heavy rain is falling, and the streets are almost impassable with mud.

The avenue is filled with a dense mass of people.

The ceremonies will take place in the Senate Chamber.

SECOND DISPATCH.

The procession reached the Capitol at about quarter to twelve o'clock, escorting the President elect.

At a subsequent period, the President and Vice-President, together with the Justices of the Supreme Court, Members and Ex-Members of Congress, Foreign Ministers, and other persons of distinction, assembled in the Senate Chamber.

There the Vice-President elect took the oath of office, preceding it by an address.

Chief Justice CHASE administered the oath of office on the eastern portico, when the President delivered his Inaugural Address.

There was a very large attendance, and the scene was one of marked interest.

THIRD DISPATCH.

The rain has ceased, and the procession is now passing down the avenue. This display is exceedingly grand. The sidewalks are jammed with people, and every window and house-top was filled with ladies and gentlemen, who are waving handkerchiefs and hats with great enthusiasm.

The visiting Philadelphia Fire Department and ours, attract great attention by their beautifully adorned apparatus.

Many bands of music are interspersed throughout the whole procession, and the line is one continual ring of music.

The *Chronicle* is represented in the procession by a large truck with a press upon it printing a *Chronicle Junior*, and scattering them to the dense mass of humanity.

The procession was one hour passing a given point, and the length of it is probably over a mile.

The Navy-yard delegation has a monitor in line, with the turret turning.

The streets are almost in an impassable condition, which makes the display not as magnificent as it would have been, though it is exceedingly beautiful.

One feature in the procession is the colored troops and the Odd-Fellows, with their band of music.

FOURTH DISPATCH.

The weather has cleared off bright and beautiful.

The President and others reached the platform. The band played "Hail to the Chief." Salutes were fired, and the President was cheered by an immense throng, composed of civilians and the military.

After delivering the Inaugural Address he was again cheered, salutes were fired, and the band played.

THE INAUGURAL ADDRESS.

Fellow-Countrymen:

At this second appearing to take the oath of the Presidential office, there is less occasion for an extended address than there was at the first. Then a statement somewhat in detail of a course to be pursued seemed very fitting and proper. Now, at the expiration of four years, during which public declarations have been constantly called forth on every point and phase of the great contest which still absorbs the attention and engrosses the energies of the nation, little that is new could be presented.

The progress of our arms, upon which all else chiefly depends, is as well known to the public as to myself, and it is, I trust, reasonably satisfactory and encouraging to all. With high hope for the future, no prediction in regard to it is ventured.

On the occasion corresponding to this four years ago, all thoughts were anxiously directed to an impending civil war. All dreaded it; all sought to avoid it. While the inaugural address was being delivered from this place, devoted altogether to saving the Union without war, insurgent agents were in the city seeking to destroy it without war—seeking to dissolve the Union and divide the effects by negotiation. Both parties deprecated war, but one of them would make war rather than let the nation survive, and the other would accept war rather than let it perish, and the war came.

One-eighth of the whole population were colored slaves, not distributed generally over the Union, but localized in the Southern part of it. These slaves constituted a peculiar and powerful interest. All knew that this interest was somehow the cause of the war. To strengthen, perpetuate and extend this interest, was the object for which the insurgents would rend the Union by war, while the Government claimed no right to do more than to restrict the territorial enlargement of it.

Neither party expected for the war the magnitude or the duration which it has already attained. Neither anticipated that the cause of the conflict might cease, or even before the conflict itself should cease. Each looked for an easier triumph, and a result less fundamental and astounding.

Both read the same Bible and pray to the same God, and each invokes His aid against the other. It may seem strange that any men should dare to ask a just God's assistance in wringing their bread from the sweat of other men's faces, but let us judge not, that we be not judged. The prayers of both should not be answered. That of neither has been answered fully. The Almighty has his own purposes. Woe unto the world because of offences, for it must needs be that offences come, but woe to that man by whom the offence cometh. If we shall suppose that American slavery is one of these offences, which in the Providence of God must needs come, but which having continued through His appointed time, He now wills to remove, and that He gives to both North and South this terrible war as the woe due to those by whom the offence came. Shall we discern there is any departure from those Divine attributes which the believers in a living God always ascribe to him? Fondly do we hope, fervently do we pray, that this mighty scourge of war may speedily pass away. Yet, if God wills that it continue until all the wealth piled by the bondman's two hundred and fifty years of unrequited toil shall be sunk, and until every drop of blood drawn with the lash shall be paid by another drawn with the sword, as was said three thousand years ago; so, still it must be said, that the judgments of the Lord are true and righteous altogether.

With malice toward none, with charity for all, with firmness in the right, as God gives us to see right, let us finish the work we are in, to bind up the nation's wounds, to care for him who shall have borne the battle and for his widow and his orphans, to do all which may achieve and cherish a just and a lasting peace among ourselves and with all nations.

ANOTHER ACCOUNT.

WASHINGTON, Saturday, March 4.

President LINCOLN was inaugurated for another term of four years at twelve o'clock, noon, to-day.

Overhead the weather was clear and beautiful, and on account of the recent rains the streets were filled with mud. Despite this fact the crowd that assembled was exceedingly large, and thousands proceeded to the capital to witness the inauguration ceremonies.

The procession moved from Sixteenth-street and Pennsylvania-avenue at about 11 o'clock.

President LINCOLN had been at the capital all day, and consequently did not accompany the procession to the scene of the interesting ceremonies.

Several bands of music, two regiments of the Invalid Corps, a squadron of cavalry, a battery of artillery, and four companies of colored troops, formed the military escort.

The Mayor and Councilmen of Washington, visiting Councilmen from Baltimore, the firemen of this city and the visiting firemen from Philadelphia, the Good Will, Franklin and Perseverance companies, each company drawing its engine along, were also in the procession.

Among the benevolent societies present were Lodges of Odd Fellows and Masons, including a colored Lodge of the latter fraternity.

The public and principal private buildings along Pennsylvania-avenue were gaily decorated with flags, and every window was thronged with faces to catch a glimpse of the President elect.

The oath to protect and maintain the Constitution of the United States, was administered to Mr. LINCOLN by Chief-Justice CHASE, in the presence of thousands, who witnessed the interesting ceremony while standing in mud almost knee-deep.

The Inaugural was then read, after which a national salute was fired by a battery stationed east of the Capitol.

The procession then again moved up Pennsylvania-avenue, the President being conveyed in an open barouche. Seated with him was his son and Senator FOSTER, of the Committee of Arrangements.

The President was escorted to the White House; after which, the procession separated.

Everything passed off in a most quiet and orderly manner, and although thousands participated in the ceremonies, not an accident occurred to mar the pleasures of the day.

FROM MISSISSIPPI.

Gen. Forrest Recounts his Exploits—He Warns his Soldiers to Prepare for Renewed Action.

CAIRO, Friday, March 3.

The Jackson, Miss., papers of the 18th ult. contain an address of the rebel Gen. FORREST to his troops, recounting the result of his operations during the past year. He says they have fought fifty battles, killed and captured sixteen thousand of the enemy, captured two thousand horses and mules, sixty-seven pieces of artillery, fourteen transports, twenty barges, three hundred wagons, fifty ambulances, one hundred and five stands of arms, forty blockhouses, destroyed thirty-six railroad bridges, two thousand miles of railroad, six locomotives, and one hundred cars, amounting to fifteen millions of property.

In accomplishing this he admits they were occasionally sustained by other troops, but says their regular number never exceeded five thousand. Two thousand had been killed or wounded and two thousand taken prisoners.

He tells them to prepare for renewed actions and warns them against being allured by syren songs of peace, for there can be no peace save upon their seperate independent nationality.

The river is still rapidly rising here. Much of the low land between Cairo, Mound City, and portions of the latter place are submerged, interfering with operations on ships and Navy-yard.

Hon. F. C. COLLIERY, Assistant Special Agent of the Transportation Department at Memphis, has been appointed Supervisor and Special Agent for the first special agency, comprising that part of the Mississippi Valley lying west of the Alleghany Mountains, east of the mouth of the Tennessee, and extending south to such parts of Alabama, Georgia, North Carolina and Virginia as is, or shall be occupied by the national forces operating from the North.

Gen. RHODES is in command of all the rebel military prisoners in Georgia, Alabama and Mississippi.

Great scarcity of breadstuffs is said to exist. RODES's division has been breaking up distilleries so that grain may be procured by suffering families and soldiers. Whisky is regarded as a worse enemy than the Yankees.

Gen. WIRT ADAMS has ordered all gins and cotton on the Big Black River to be removed.

Contemplated Rebel Raid on Oswego and Rochester.

OSWEGO, Saturday, March 4.

Maj. GRANT has received a dispatch from Gov. FENTON stating that the War Department at Washington had received information from Halifax that the rebels in the provinces are contemplating a raid on Oswego and Rochester. A public meeting is to be held in this city this afternoon to take such action in the matter as may be necessary.

Dry Goods Sale.

PHILADELPHIA, Saturday, March 4.

An immense sale of dry goods will take place here on March 9, when MYERS & Co. will dispose of 2,000 entire cases of domestic and foreign dry goods for cash.

Salute Fired in Boston.

BOSTON, Saturday, March 4.

A salute was fired at noon to-day and bells rung in honor of the late victories, and the inauguration of President LINCOLN. A heavy rain-storm prevails.

ADJOURNMENT OF CONGRESS.

Both Houses in Session All Night.

The Army Appropriation Bill Finally Passed.

Pay to the Illinois Central Railroad Refused.

The Bankrupt Bill Passed Over Without Notice.

Disagreement on the Civil Appropriation Bill.

THE BILL DEFEATED FOR WANT OF TIME.

CLOSING SCENES IN BOTH HOUSES.

Reorganization and Extra Session of the Senate.

Special Dispatches to the New-York Times.
WASHINGTON, Saturday, March 4.

CLOSING SCENES IN CONGRESS.

[The following is the continuation of the dispatch published in Saturday morning's TIMES.—ED.]

At 6 o'clock and five minutes A. M., another motion for a recess is made, but the House still refuse and grumble audibly at the Senate for its delay.

Gen. SCHENCK, from the Military Committee, then made a report upon the subject of the order which requires colored men to have passes before they can leave the District of Columbia. It was accompanied by a joint resolution declaring the order an improper practice, and requesting its abrogation. Discussion followed, but the Democrats are mostly asleep, and the resolution is adopted.

At 6:35 A. M., it is announced that the Senate has finished the "omnibus," having loaded it down with new amendments, rendering the labors of the Conference Committee herculean. Three of the most energetic members of the House are appointed to meet the elephant. HENRY WINTER DAVIS, D. C., LITTLEJOHN, and JAMES S. ROLLINS; and they go at it.

A few more unimportant matters come up; are speedily disposed of, and at 7:15 A. M., the House takes a recess until 9 A. M.

The scene in the Senate during the small hours of the night was interesting, and many times amusing. Eight patriotic ladies in the gallery bravely kept their bright eyes beaming upon the Senators until daydawn, while fifty or sixty male spectators listened, slept and yawned in the gentlemens' gallery.

SECOND DISPATCH.

9 A. M.—My dispatch for this morning's edition of the TIMES left off as the clock, which is my *vis-a-vis*, pointed the hour of 4 A. M. But the proceedings of the two Houses did not leave off there, by any means. The House had cleared the Speaker's desk of all important bills and amused itself by acting on unfinished business going over to the next session, while the members impatiently awaited the issue between the Senate and the House on the Miscellaneous Appropriation Bill.

At 5:35 A. M., the Committee of Conference reported another disagreement on the clause of the Army Appropriation Bill relating to the Illinois Central Railroad. The Senate would hear to nothing but striking out the clause which singles out this road as an exception to the general rule of payment. Mr. MORRILL moved that the House recede, as a last resort, pending which, several fiery speeches were made, but the motion prevailed, 62 to 47.

The time, thence to 3:45 A. M., was spent on various small bills coming up from the Speaker's tables, or reports of Conference Committee coming in.

Mr. STEVENS then moved a recess until 9 A. M., but it was voted down, because it gave no time for the appointment and meeting of the committee, which was the only hope of saving the important bill which the Senate had been laboring on all night.

The business on the Speaker's desk was proceeded with. Mr. SUMNER's bill, providing that color shall not be a disqualification for carrying the mails, when last before the House, was dropped from want of a quorum vote with the previous question pending. It came up now under the operation of the previous question, and was finally passed with few or no dissenting votes.

8 A. M.—The Appropriation Bill was most severely handled in the Senate, much to the disgust of the most earnest member there. Mr. SHERMAN, who finally gave up all hope of saving anything of the bill, save the light-house appropriations, and a few other commercial matters. Millions of dollars were added in various appropriations, but the great sticking point was the Winter Davis military arrest amendment. The Senate, after rejecting a substitute, rather milder in its form, offered by Mr. TRUMBULL, finally resolved to strike it out entirely. Among other things adopted in Committee of the Whole was a proposition which was soon recognized as an old customer, to wit: To purchase for each member of Congress one set of certain volumes of Congressional debates of sessions twenty or thirty years ago. This is known as the "Seaton Job," and would involve an expense of many thousands of dollars, and was rejected last Winter. It went through the Committee of the Whole, but when amendments came up for final adoption, Mr. CLARK demanded a separate vote on this, and it was rejected. The proposition to pay $4,000,000 to Missouri for expenses incurred in arming her militia, and $700,000 to Pennsylvania to reimburse her for moneys expended in repelling EARLY's last invasion, were also tacked on. Indeed, the majority of the Senate seemed to think no demand too enormous, and at least $7,000,000 or $8,000,000 were thus arranged for when it was positively certain that there was not a moment's time for a proper scrutiny of these items. To the credit of Senator SHERMAN be it said, that he protested earnestly against this style of legislation, but it was of no avail. At length the Senate consented to forego any further patchwork, and the Committee of Conference was soon at work on it. The Senate, at 7:15, then took a recess until 10 o'clock.

10 A. M.—The House did not meet very promptly, an hour and a half being too little time for members to get breakfast, and to refresh themselves for the duties of the day. It must be said that they bore the trying ordeal of the night with a far greater degree of equanimity, good feeling, and dignity than is usual on such occasions. It was reserved for the closing hour of the session to give birth to a series of disgraceful proceedings, and to perpetrate, at the very last moment of the constitutionally limited term, a scene of partisan filibustering that should cause shame and humiliation in the hearts of every one who promoted it.

At 10:20 A. M., Mr. HENRY WINTER DAVIS made a report from the Committee on Conference on the Miscellaneous Appropriation Bill, and reported that the committee had compromised everything but the section known as the Winter Davis Amendment; that could not be surmounted. The Senate insisted that it should not pass as a part of that bill, as that was no place for it; that body would be willing to receive it as a separate proposition, though the committee doubted if, in the present temper of the Senate on the subject, it could pass.

The House Committee are willing to make it a separate matter, but as they have no hope of effecting its passage in that way, Mr. DAVIS moves that the House insist, and on that motion makes a speech, which brings applause from the Democratic side. Mr. LITTLEJOHN, also a member of the Committee of Conference, speaks to the same effect, and the ball opens.

It is twenty minutes to eleven. The Democrats, headed mainly by Mr. ELDRIDGE, of Wisconsin, distinguished for nothing except the guerrilla warfare he has carried on against all Government measures, show signs of mischief.

Mr. ELDRIDGE rises in his seat and moves to adjourn.

The motion is declared out of order by Mr. GARFIELD, who is in the chair.

A motion is made to recede from the amendment, and the previous question demanded, and seconded, so the Chair states, when a message from the President (who is in his room in the Capitol, and where he seldom comes except on such an occasion as this,) is announced, and he communicates the fact that he has signed certain important bills.

Now comes confusion. Mr. ELDRIDGE says the previous question, which was pending, was not seconded.

Mr. COLFAX, (resuming the chair,) settles the matter, when Mr. PENDLETON moves to adjourn, on which Mr. ELDRIDGE demands the ayes and noes, and the demand being sustained, the clerk calls the roll.

It is eleven o'clock; the clerk proceeds rapidly, and at twenty minutes past eleven it is announced that the House will not adjourn.

Mr. ELDRIDGE moves to reconsider the vote by which the House refused to adjourn, and on that motion demands the ayes and noes; the demand is again sustained, and the clerk again calls the roll.

At eleven forty it is announced that the House refuses to reconsider.

Mr. KASSON, of Iowa, with characteristic good sense and a sincere desire to bring this matter to a conclusion, begs that unanimous consent may be given to strike out everything in the bill but the appropriations for the deaf and dumb and for the light-houses, for if these fail there will be suffering, shipwreck and loss of life.

This meets with a sentiment of apparent favor; but Mr. WINTER DAVIS rises in his seat, and says: "Mr. Speaker, I am in earnest, and not a single item of this bill shall pass if this amendment does not."

Mr. LITTLEJOHN says: "I agree with my colleague; the whole of the bill shall pass, or none."

It is now 11:45. The Conference Committee on the paper duty question make a report, fixing the duty at ten cents; and on a motion to recede from the House proposition to fix it at three cents, the yeas and nays are demanded, and the clerk once more calls the roll.

It is ten minutes of twelve. The call proceeds the clear sharp voice of the clerk ringing out above the confusion in the hall. And as the dial indicates the hour of twelve, the speaker orders the call suspended, and the term of the Thirty-eighth Congress expires, by constitutional limitation, in the midst of a call of the ayes and noes.

The Appropriation Bill is thus lost. Missouri and Pennsylvania get no reimbursements for militia expenses; the deaf and dumb starve; the light-houses are no beacon to the mariner; a hundred useful and necessary, and a few very suspicious and unworthy objects, are thus thrown overboard.

But perhaps it is best this Congress neglected its duty early in the session, or else this bill would have had ample consideration.

Speaker COLFAX rises from his chair, and the hall and galleries are breathless. In a brief but most felicitous speech, he returns thanks for the compliment paid him in the resolution of last evening, to the members for their courtesy, and with an eloquent allusion to the ceremony of the inauguration, which they are about to witness, he declares the House of Representatives of the Thirty-eighth Congress adjourned *sine die*.

THIRTY-EIGHTH CONGRESS.

SECOND SESSION.

SENATE.

WASHINGTON, Saturday, March 4.

The following is a continuation of the Senate proceedings from the point where they broke off at an early hour this morning:

CIVIL APPROPRIATION BILL.

The debate being long-continued on the Civil Appropriation Bill,

Mr. GRIMES, of Iowa, (Union,) interrupted Mr. COWAN, who was speaking, and intimated that Mr. COWAN, as a member of the Committee on Finance, charged with the management of this bill, was endangering its passage.

Mr. CLARK, of New-Hampshire, (Union) warned the Senate that lengthened discussion would soon prove fatal to the bill, and begged that the question might be taken on its passage. It was now nearly three o'clock, and the bill was to be engrossed, and much business had yet to be concluded. He hoped the Senate would come to a vote at once.

The Civil Appropriation Bill was then informally laid aside.

ENROLLMENT BILL PASSED.

Mr. WILSON, of Massachusetts, (Union,) made a report from the Committee of Conference on the Amendatory Enrollment Bill, which was concurred in.

TRIALS BY COURT-MARTIAL.

Mr. TRUMBULL, of Illinois, (Union,) then took the floor upon the amendment of Mr. LANE, of Indiana, to the Civil Appropriation bill, and offered a further amendment to include persons "employed" as well as "drafted or enlisted" who should be subject to trial by court-martial.

This was adopted.

The amendment as thus amended was then agreed to by yeas 22, nays 13, as follows:

YEAS—Messrs. Anthony, Brown, Chandler, Clark, Conness, Doolittle, Farwell, Foster, Grimes, Harlan, Harris, Howard, Lane of Indiana, Morgan, Morrill, Nye, Ramsey, Sherman, Stewart, Sumner, Wilkinson and Wilson—22.

NAYS—Messrs. Buckalew, Cowan, Hale, Hendricks, Johnson, McDougall, Nesmith, Powell, Riddle, Sprague, Trumbull, Van Winkle and Wade—13.

So the section was stricken out.

ARMY APPROPRIATION BILL.

Mr. HARRIS, of New-York, (Union,) here obtained leave to make a report of the Committee of Conference on the Army Appropriation Bill, saying the Senate Committee could not agree with the House Committee.

The Senate insisted on its action.

PENNSYLVANIA CLAIMS.

Mr. COWAN offered an amendment to the pending bill, the Civil or "Omnibus" Appropriation Bill, providing for the claim of Pennsylvania for money paid to the troops of that State, called out in 1863 to oppose the advance of Gen. LEE.

The amendment was adopted, by yeas 18, nays 16.

REPAIRS TO THE NAVAL ACADEMY.

An amendment was offered by Mr. GRIMES, providing for repairs at the Naval Academy at Annapolis, which was adopted.

NAVIGATION OF LAKE MICHIGAN.

Mr. CHANDLER, of Michigan, (Union,) offered an amendment appropriating $84,000 for improving the navigation of Lake Michigan, which was lost.

CIVIL APPROPRIATION BILL PASSED.

After acting upon several minor amendments, the bill was passed at 6 o'clock A. M.

EXECUTIVE SESSION.

After the passage of several private bills, at 6:45 A. M. the Senate went into Executive Session.

WASHINGTON, Saturday, March 4.

The Senate reassembled at 10 o'clock.

THREE-CENT PIECES

Mr. CLARK called up a bill to authorize the coinage of three-cent pieces and for other purposes, which was passed.

THE ARKANSAS SENATORS.

Mr. LANE, of Kansas, at 11 o'clock moved to take up a resolution for the admission of Senators from Arkansas.

Mr. SUMNER objected, and the resolution was not taken up.

EXTENDING COMMITTEES.

Mr. SPRAGUE, called up the joint resolution from the House authorizing the Committee on Commerce of both Houses, to sit after the 4th of March to investigate the subject of trade with the rebel States.

Mr. POWELL said the present Congress had no right to provide for the sitting of a committee after 12 o'clock to-day, and moved that the resolution be laid upon the table, which motion prevailed.

COLORED PEOPLE AS TRAVELERS.

Mr. CONNESS called up the bill to regulate commerce between the several States.

The pending question was on Mr. WILSON's amendment forbidding the exclusion of any citizen of the United States from any railroad-car, steamboat, or other conveyance, on account of any State law.

Mr. HALE moved, as an amendment to the amendment, to add that no citizen of the United States shall be excluded from any meeting-house, church or hotel, on account of any State law, or any regulation of any corporation. [Laughter.]

Mr. HALE's amendment was adopted.

The vote was then taken on Mr. WILSON's amendment as amended, and was decided in the affirmative, as follows:

YEAS—Messrs Brown, Clark, Collamer, Cowan, Dixon, Doolittle, Farwell, Foster, Grimes, Henderson, Lane of Kansas, Morrill, Nesmith, Pomeroy, Sumner, Ten Eyck, Wade, Willey, Wilson, and Wright—21.

NAYS—Messrs Chandler, Davis, Howard, Howe, Lane, of Indiana, McDougall, Morgan, Nye, Powell, Ramsey, Sherman, Sprague, Stewart, and Trumbull—14.

Mr. NESMITH moved to refer the bill to the Committee on the Conduct of the War, which was decided in the negative.

YEAS—Messrs Clark, Collamer, Cowan, Davis, Dixon, Hale, Lane, of Indiana, McDougall, Morrill, Nesmith, Powell, Ten Eyck, Trumbull, and Wright—14.

NAYS—Messrs Brown, Chandler, Howard, Lane of Kansas, Morgan, Nye, Pomeroy, Ramsey, Sherman, Sprague, Stewart, Sumner, Wade, Wilkinson, and Wilson—15.

Mr. MORRILL moved the indefinite postponement of the bill, which was disagreed to—YEAS 14, NAYS 21.

WAITING UPON THE PRESIDENT.

Mr. SHERMAN moved that a committee of three be appointed to wait upon the President and inquire if he had any further communication to make to the Senate. Carried.

Messrs. SHERMAN, COLLAMER and POWELL were appointed said committee.

INSTALLING THE NEW VICE-PRESIDENT.

At 11:45 Vice-President HAMLIN escorted the Vice-President elect into the Senate Chamber, and a few moments afterward Messrs. SEWARD, STANTON and SPEED entered, and seated themselves to the left of the chair. The judges of the Supreme Court entered immediately afterward, and seated themselves to the right of the chair.

At 12 o'clock Mr. HAMLIN briefly addressed the Senate, thanking the members for the kindness and consideration that had been shown to him on all occasions.

It was impossible to hear the speech of Mr. HAMLIN distinctly, owing to the confusion and conversation continually kept up between the women in the galleries.

Mr. JOHNSON, before taking the oath of office, made a short speech, which, as in the case of Mr. HAMLIN, was nearly inaudible, owing to the want of order which prevailed among the women in the galleries. By the choice of the people, he said, he had been made presiding officer of this body, and, in presenting himself here in obedience to the behests of the Constitution of the United States, it would, perhaps, not be out of place to remark just here what a striking thing the Constitution was. It was the Constitution of the people of the country, and under it, here to-day, before the American Senate, he felt that he was a man and an American citizen. He had a proud illustration of the fact that, under the Constitution, a man could rise from the ranks to occupy the second place in the gift of the American people and of the American Government. Those of us who have labored our whole lives for the establishment of a free Government knew how to cherish its great blessings. He would say to Senators and others before him—to the Supreme Court which sat before him, that they all got their power from the people of this country. Turning toward Mr. CHASE, Mr. JOHNSON said, And your exaltation and position depend upon the people. Then turning toward the Cabinet, he said, And I I will say to you, Mr. Secretary SEWARD, and to you, Mr. Secretary STANTON, and to you, Mr. Secretary—(to a gentleman near by, sotto voice, Who is Secretary of the Navy? the person addressed replied in a whisper, Mr. WELLS)—and to you, Mr. Secretary WELLS, I would say, you all derive your power from the people. Mr. JOHNSON then remarked that the great element of vitality in this Government was its nearness and proximity to the people. He wanted to say to all who heard him, in the face of the American people, that all power was derived from the people. He would say, in the hearing of the Foreign Ministers, for he was going to tell the truth here to-day, that he was a plebeian—he thanked God for it. It was the popular heart of this nation that was beating to sustain Cabinet officials and the President of the United States. It was a strange occasion that called forth a plebeian like him to tell such things as these. Mr. JOHNSON next adverted to affairs in Tennessee, and the abolition of slavery there. He thanked God Tennessee was a State in the Union, and had never been out. The State Government had been discontinued for a time—there had been an interregnum, a hiatus—but she had never been out of the Union. He stood here to-day as her representative. On this day she would elect a Governor and a Legislature, and she would very soon send Senators and members to Congress.

Mr. JOHNSON then took the oath of office, and Mr. HAMLIN declared the Senate adjourned *sine die*.

U. S. SENATE—EXTRA SESSION.

WASHINGTON, Saturday, March 4.

After the above proceedings, the proclamation convening the Senate in extra session was read by the Secretary, Mr. FORNEY.

The President's inaugural address was then read.

The Senators elect were next sworn in, after which the procession was formed, and proceeded to the east front of the Capitol building.

HOUSE OF REPRESENTATIVES.

WASHINGTON, Saturday, March 4.

CONCLUSION.

The following is the conclusion of the House proceedings from where our report broke off this morning:

MILITARY BUSINESS.

The report of Mr. GARFIELD on the disagreeing votes to the bill relating to various military subjects, was adopted by a vote of 71 to 57.

Much miscellaneous business was transacted.

STRUGGLE FOR PRECEDENCE.

[It is now 3 o'clock A. M. Almost every member has some little bill to be passed, and there were continuous struggles for the floor to offer their several measures. The galleries were nearly deserted. The ladies admitted to the floor had retired.]

COAL LOTS ON THE PUBLIC LANDS.

The House passed a bill to dispose of the coal lots on the public domain.

Some of the members exhausted by the long session had retired to sleep on the sofas.

DEPRIVING DESERTERS OF HOMESTEAD PRIVILEGES.

Mr. ALLISON, from the Committee on Public Lands, asked, but was refused permission, to report a bill to prevent deserters and others who may shirk military service from acquiring public lands under the Homestead law.

SUBSISTENCE DEPARTMENT.

Mr. SCHENCK, of Ohio, (Union,) made a report from the Committee of Conference, on the bill reorganizing the Subsistence Department, and it was adopted.

THANKS TO GEN. THOMAS.

Mr. SCHENCK reported back the joint resolution of thanks to Major-Gen. THOMAS, with the Senate's amendment thereto, which was disagreed to.

PRINTING CERTAIN REPORTS.

Mr. AMBROSE W. CLARK, from the Committee on Printing, reported in favor of printing 35,000 copies of the report of the commission on flax and hemp, 20,000 copies of the amended Internal Revenue Act, and 35,000 copies of the Agricultural Report for 1864, and it was agreed to.

EXTENSION OF TIME.

The House passed a bill extending the time for locating the Virginia military land warrants.

A RECESS REFUSED.

Mr. DAVIS, of Maryland, at 4 o'clock, moved to take a recess until 4 o'clock.

The Speaker deemed it his duty to say that if the House did so, two of the general Appropriation Bills would probably be lost.

The House refused to take a recess.

The business on the Speaker's table was taken up.

THE REBEL DEBT.

The House concurred in the Senate's joint resolution that this Government will never recognize the rebel debt on any conditions.

DUTY ON PRINTING PAPER.

The House then, by a vote of 53 against 67 non-concurred in the Senate's amendment to the joint resolution changing from three to fifteen per centum ad valorem the duty on printing paper used for books and newspapers exclusively. The House then, by a vote of 47 against 62, refused to lay the resolution on the table, and asked a committee of conference of the Senate.

THE ILLINOIS RAILROAD CLAIM.

Mr. THAYER, of Massachusetts, (Union,) made a report from the Conference Committee on the Army Appropriation Bill. He said the Senate struck out the proviso inserted by the House prohibiting any part of the money being paid to the Illinois Central Railroad Company. The difference seemed to rise on a point of law. Hence he proposed an amendment in order that the question may be settled by the Supreme Court of the United States as to whether that company is, by the Land Grant Law of 1850, bound to transport, free of charge, the troops, munitions, and other property of the United States.

Mr. KERNAN, of New-York, (Dem.,) did not think a further conference would adjust the difficulty between the two Houses.

Mr. MORRILL, of Vermont, (Union,) said it was now 5 o'clock in the morning. He thought the contest had continued as long as it was proper. When the land was granted, no one thought that such an extensive use would be made of the road. No man would inforce such a contract against his neighbor. It is the letter that killeth, but the spirit which maketh alive.

Mr. WASHBURNE, of Illinois, (Union,) thought that the amendment of Mr. THAYER would be received in a spirit of compromise. He was surprised that his friend from Vermont should make such arguments in favor of the company. That company had made twenty-five per cent. more by the war than if the war had not gone on. The war had been a blessing to the road. The company was interested in this bill to the extent of a million and a half of dollars.

Mr. WOODBRIDGE, of Vermont, (Union,) opposed Mr. THAYER's amendment, and in reply to Mr. WASHBURNE, said if it had not been for foreign capital, the Western railroads never would have been built. He maintained that in equity the company should be paid.

Mr. THAYER expressed his surprise that Mr. WOODBRIDGE should characterize his proposition as absurd, and that the gentleman, so swift to make the assertion, should sustain it by so weak an argument.

Mr. MORRILL moved that the House recede from its amendment concerning the Illinois Central Railroad, and this was agreed to by a vote of 62 against 47.

ARMY APPROPRIATION BILL PASSED.

The difficulty between the two Houses was thus removed, and the bill was passed.

RECESS AGAIN DENIED.

Mr. STEVENS, of Pennsylvania, (Union,) moved, at half-past five, that the House take a recess till nine o'clock.

This was disagreed to.

COLOR QUALIFICATION REPEALED.

The House took up the Senate bill removing all disqualification of color in carrying the mails.

Mr. ELDRIDGE moved that the bill be laid on the table, which was disagreed to by a vote of 30 against 65.

The bill was then passed.

NO PASSPORTS FOR COLORED PERSONS.

Mr. SCHENCK, from the Committee on Military Affairs, to whom was referred the letter of the Secretary of War on the subject, reported a resolution that in the judgment of the House, the order of Maj.-Gen. AUGUR, issued on 12th Jan., 1864, directing that no colored man be allowed to leave Washington, going north, without a pass, is a regulation which makes an odious discrimination, for a law of the United States has declared free alike all citizens and residents of the District of Columbia, and the President be requested to direct that the order be at once abrogated.

The resolution was agreed to by Ayes, 75; Nays, 24.

A STORM EXCITEMENT.

About 6:30 o'clock a heavy rain and wind storm broke over the Capitol, rattling on the glass and ceiling and causing a fierce whistling noise throughout the building.

This storm came up so suddenly and created so much noise that it alarmed many of the members of the House, who, affrighted, fled toward the doors.

The excitement and confusion, however, was soon quieted by the calm announcement of the Speaker that it was merely "a storm."

PENSION FOR A WIDOW.

A bill giving a pension to a widow being under consideration,

Mr. INGERSOLL earnestly spoke of the military services of the deceased husband, and sent up to be read some patriotic verses as illustrative of his argument.

At the conclusion of the reading members loudly and laughingly applauded them.

A RECESS AT LAST.

The House then, at 7:15 A. M., took a recess until 9 o'clock.

SATURDAY MORNING, 9 o'clock.

GOVERNMENT FOR THE INDIAN TERRITORY.

The House, on re-assembling, took up the Senate bill to establish a Civil Government for the Indian Territory.

It provides for the appointment of a Governor, Secretary of State, Judges, and all the other necessary machinery. Indians are to be elected to the Legislative Council. Involuntary servitude is forever prohibited, except as a punishment for crime. It also provides for the election of an Indian Delegate to Congress.

Mr. HOLMAN, of Indiana, (Dem.,) objected to the consideration of the bill.

MISCELLANEOUS WORK.

Much routine and miscellaneous business was then transacted, and questions were taken by yeas and nays on a number of private bills.

It was now 10 o'clock.

LANDS IN UTAH.

Mr. KINNEY, of Utah, unsuccessfully moved to suspend the rules in order to consider a bill confirming the citizens of Great Salt Lake in the possession of their lands.

CIVIL APPROPRIATION BILL DEFEATED.

The Committee of Conference on the Miscellaneous or Civil Appropriation Bill made a report.

Mr. DAVIS, of Maryland, (Union,) explained what had been done by the committee. They had struck out some of the provisions of the bill, including that to pay the Pennsylvania Volunteers, but retaining the section to pay the Missouri Volunteers.

The question left unsettled was that heretofore introduced by Mr. DAVIS, of Maryland, exempting civilians from trial by court-martial and military commissions.

Mr. LITTLEJOHN, of New-York, (Union,) owing to the few remaining minutes left to the House, moved that the report of the committee be concurred in, with the above exception.

Mr. ELDRIDGE moved to reconsider the vote by which the previous question was ordered.

Mr. PENDLETON, of Ohio, (Dem.,) moved that the House adjourn.

Thereupon Mr. HARDING called for the yeas and nays, which were ordered, and, being taken, the question was determined in the negative.

It was now 11 o'clock.

Mr. MALLORY, of Kentucky, (Dem.,) moved to lay the whole subject upon the table.

Mr. ELDRIDGE demanded the yeas and nays upon the motion, which were ordered.

It was now ten minutes to twelve o'clock.

The Clerk here commenced calling the roll, and when he had reached that of Mr. KNAPP, the hour of twelve had arrived.

THE PRESIDENT HAS NO MORE TO SAY.

The committee appointed to wait on President LINCOLN reported that they had performed that duty, and he had informed them that he had no further communication to make.

THE SPEAKER'S FAREWELL—CLOSE OF THE THIRTY-EIGHTH CONGRESS.

Mr. COLFAX, in taking leave of the members of the House, said:

GENTLEMEN OF THE HOUSE OF REPRESENTATIVES: The parting hour has come, and yonder clock, which takes note of time, will soon announce that the Congress of which we are members has passed into history. Honored by your vote with this responsible position, I have faithfully strive to perform its always complex and often perplexing duties without partizan bias, and with the sincerest impartiality. Whether I have realized the true ideal of a just presiding officer, aiding on the one hand the advance of the public business, with the responsibility of which the majority is charged, and on the other hand allowing no trespass on the parliamentary rights of the minority, must be left for others to decide. But looking back now over the entire Congress, I cannot remember a single word addressed to you which, "dying, I would wish to blot." On this day, which, by spontaneous consent, is being observed wherever our flag floats, as a day of national rejoicing, with a roar of cannons greeting the rising sun on the rock-bound coast of Maine, reëchoed and reëchoed by answering volleys from city to city, and from mountain peak to mountain peak, till from the golden gate they die away

Continued on Eighth Page.

THE NEW YORK HERALD.

WHOLE NO. 10,416. NEW YORK, MONDAY, MARCH 6, 1865. PRICE FOUR CENTS.

CAPTURE OF THE REBEL GENERAL EARLY.

Sheridan's New Movement Up the Shenandoah—Its Success—The Race for Lynchburg—Tightening of the Lines Around Richmond.

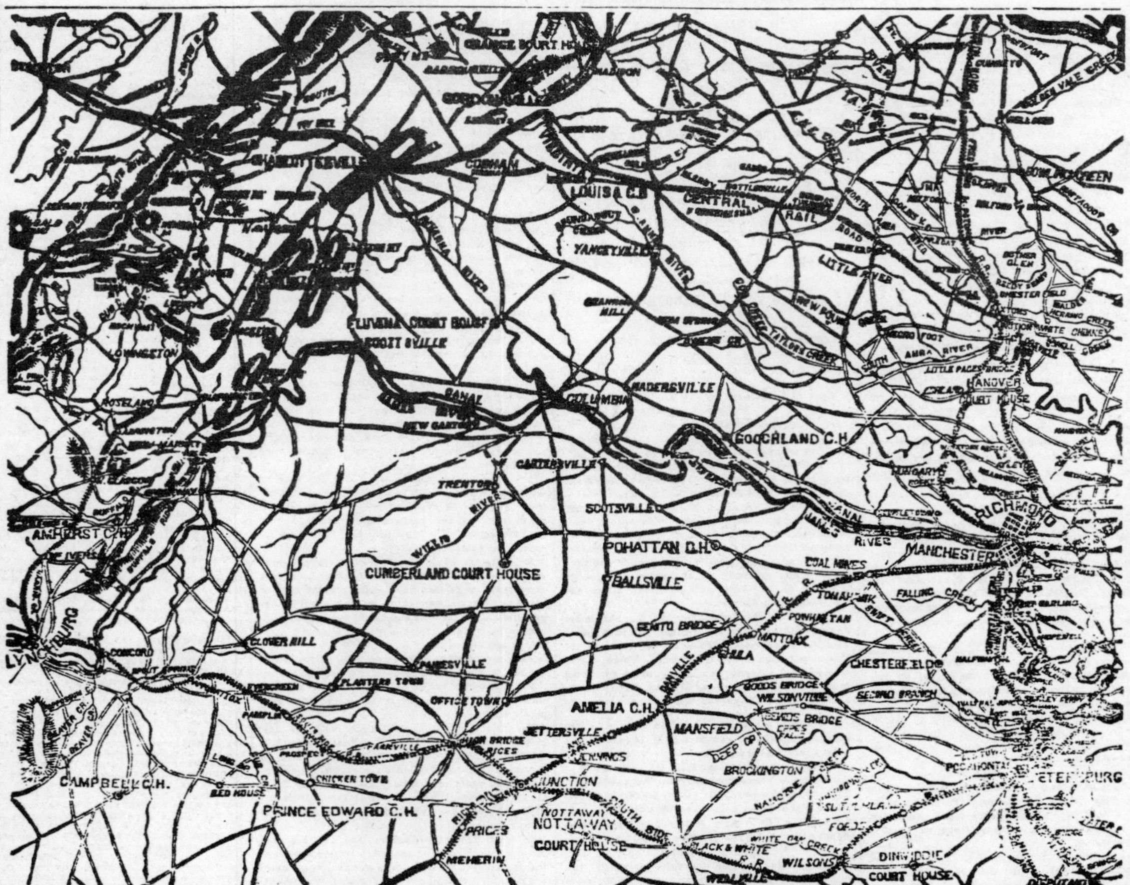

SHERIDAN.

Highly Important Despatches from General Grant.

Capture of the Rebel General Early and His Force.

One of the Results of Sheridan's New Movement Up the Shenandoah.

THE ALARM OF THE REBELS.

THE RACE FOR LYNCHBURG,

&c., &c., &c.

Secretary Stanton to General Dix.

WAR DEPARTMENT, WASHINGTON, March 5, 1865.

To Major General DIX, New York:—

The following despatches in relation to the reported defeat and capture of General Early by General Sheridan and the capture of Charlottesville have been received by this department.

General Sheridan and his force commenced their movement last Monday, and were at Staunton when last heard from. Major General Hancock was placed in charge of the Middle Military Division during the absence of General Sheridan, headquarters at Winchester.

E. M. STANTON, Secretary of War.

General Grant to Secretary Stanton.

CITY POINT, Va., March 5—11 A. M.

Hon. E. M. STANTON, Secretary of War:—

Deserters in this morning report that Sheridan had routed Early and captured Charlottesville. They report four regiments having gone from here (Richmond) to reinforce Early.

U. S. GRANT, Lieutenant General.

GENERAL GRANT'S SECOND DESPATCH.

CITY POINT, Va., March 5—2 P. M.

Hon. E. M. STANTON, Secretary of War:—

Deserters from every point of the enemy's lines confirm the capture of Charlottesville by General Sheridan. They say he captured General Early and nearly his entire force, consisting of eighteen hundred men. Four brigades were reported as being sent to Lynchburg, to get there before General Sheridan, if possible.

U. S. GRANT, Lieutenant General.

GENERAL GRANT'S THIRD DESPATCH.

CITY POINT, Va., March 5—4 P. M.

Hon. E. M. STANTON, Secretary of War:—

Refugees confirm the statement of deserters as to the capture of General Early and nearly his entire force. They say it took place on Thursday last, between Staunton and Charlottesville, and that the defeat was total.

U. S. GRANT, Lieutenant General.

Our Special Washington Despatch.

WASHINGTON, March 5—11 P. M.

It is reported that General Sheridan came upon Early and his forces near Charlottesville, on Thursday last, and, after a sharp engagement, whipped his forces and captured General Early. When the courier left Sheridan was pursuing the remnants of Early's army.

Mr. Charles H. Farrell's Despatch.

WINCHESTER, Va., March 3, 1865.

GENERAL SHERIDAN ON A RIDE UP THE VALLEY.

I am authorized to announce the fact that on Monday, the 27th ult., a large cavalry force left this department on an expedition up the valley. The expedition was well equipped, commanded in person by General Sheridan and his subordinates, Generals Merrit, Custer, Devins, Forsyth and Gibbs. No information has been received from this army since it left here.

AN ALLEGED CONSPIRACY TO CAPTURE GENERAL SHERIDAN.

A few days ago three Winchester families, by the names of Sherrard, Lee and Bunell, were sent without our lines, on the charge of disloyalty. It is alleged they conspired together to get up a sociable ball, to which General Sheridan was to be an invited guest, and that during its progress a detachment of Mosby's guerillas was to seize the General, take him captive and convey him to Richmond, à la Kelley and Crook. The plan was frustrated, and the ladies (!) who concocted it are now in full communion with those for whom they have exhibited such a warm sympathy.

A few days ago a scouting party, under the command of Sergeant Mulligan, went up the valley on special duty. On their return they were met by a body of guerillas, who attacked them, killing a scout by the name of Hall, and severely wounding private Goff, of the Seventeenth Pennsylvania cavalry. The affair took place near Middletown, thirteen miles south of this town.

An order has been issued discontinuing furloughs to officers and enlisted men. This looks like an early resumption of active military operations.

Williamsburg City News.

BIRTH IN A VAULT—ATTEMPTED INFANTICIDE.—About half past four o'clock yesterday afternoon a well dressed young woman was seen coming out of a house in Union avenue, near Huron street, Greenpoint, and shortly afterwards the cries of a new-born child were heard emanating from the vault in the yard. Mr. and Mrs. A. M. Rase and Mr. J. W. Coles were passing at the time, and these gentlemen, with others, entered the premises, and overturning the house over the vault, succeeded in rescuing from death a fine healthy male child. It is supposed that the girl had been visiting in the neighborhood, and the pains of labor coming on suddenly, she sought this place to hide her shame. The infant was taken home by Mrs. A. M. Rase, who will await the order of the Superintendent of the Poor. Captain Davis, of the Forty-seventh precinct, sent Sergeant Boch and officer Phelps to investigate the case, and the girl was traced to Franklin street, where, it is presumed, she took the cars for the Western District.

GRAND LARCENY.—A young girl, named Delia Mullin, was arrested on Saturday, by officer Videtto, of the Forty-fifth precinct, charged with stealing wearing apparel, &c., to the value of $191, from Mrs. Walsh, of 19 Nassau street, W. D. The girl had been living in the family of Mr. Swift, in Walton street, E. D., but was visiting at the residence of Mrs. Walsh at the time of the theft.

SUDDEN DEATH.—Last evening Coroner Barrett held an inquest upon the body of Harry Dobson, who died suddenly, of congestion of the brain on Saturday night in North Second street, near Fourth, Eastern District.

DESPERATE BURGLARS.—Early on Saturday morning the residence of Mr. Richard Williams, 296 Fourth street, Eastern District, was entered and robbed of various articles, to the value of $160, besides Mr. Williams' will. One of the burglars fired a pistol shot at the proprietor of the house, who had got up in consequence of the noise, the ball lodging in the wall near where he was standing.

Sailing of the Nova Scotian.

[illegible]

THE SOUTH.

The South Suffering from Wind on the Stomach.

THE REBEL CONGRESS REQUESTED TO QUIT TALKING AND GO TO WORK OR ADJOURN.

[From the Richmond Dispatch, March 2.]

We trust that when peace shall return to this belligerent land, and our universities and colleges are again in operation, there will be established in each of them a new department—the school of silence. In its professor's chair should be installed, grave and reflective, a Socrates, if such can now be found, not destitute himself of the capacity of eloquence, but chastened in oratorical fervor by the domestic declamation of Xantippe. At the feet of this professor should be laid the golden statue of Georgias, inventor of extemporaneous eloquence and founder of the school described by Plato as "wood-weavers." With his foot on this prostrate statue should our professor sit and bid his pupils look and shudder at the ruin which gales of speech, let loose by a rhetorical Æolus, have brought upon an afflicted land. Then, in due course of time, another generation will arise, which will appreciate at the proper value those representative bodies which, in times like these, discourse for months upon wind instruments, while that man of action, General Lee, in vain points out the only means and hope of their salvation. One of the greatest charms of spring is that it puts an end to deliberative bodies, as it is one of the consolations of fall that it puts an end to the kindred bore and annoyance of mosquitoes. The land is wearied and disgusted with debates, addresses and high-sounding resolutions. The passage and enactment four months ago of any law putting into the field all able bodied men, the Representatives included, would have done for the physical and moral strength of the confederacy more than four months of continuous eloquence. It is vain now to deplore the past; but we may at least invoke the representatives of the people to spare the world any further infliction of speeches which do not answer the arguments of Grant and Sherman, and of appeals which are not distinguished by the Demosthenean attribute of action. We do not observe that Sherman was anywhere stopped in his march by the one thousand rounds of oratorical Parrott guns which Governors and other public speakers let off at his advancing columns. Unless the representatives of the people take the field themselves and secure a position so close to the enemy that he can hear what they say, we have no hopes that he will put his fingers in his ears and run for his life.

News from Panama.

SPECULATIONS AS TO GEN. SICKLES' MISSION, ETC.

The Panama *Mercantile Chronicle* of February 13, received by the bark Idaho, contains the following:—

Our native friends are so greatly exercised in their conjectures relative to the mission of General Sickles to this government that we are induced to refer to it again without having any positive data on the subject. It is said that the General's object is to procure from the Colombian government a concession of lands on which the United States government will form a settlement of thirty thousand of the negroes emancipated by the great secession war. It is stated that one million of dollars will be given for this privilege, and it is feared that the settlement of thirty thousand emancipated slaves will lead to a repetition of Texan history.

We would first state that the American government will never pay $1,000,000 for this privilege, and in the second place our native friends do not understand the character of the American slaves or the relationship which would exist between them as emigrants and the United States government.

The object of the Americans, as disclosed in several of President Lincoln's speeches and despatches, is to remove these poor people from a country which has been thrown into a state bordering on destruction through their presence there in the condition of slaves. To leave these people as freed men in the Southern States after the war may have been concluded, would be a constant cause of irritation to the former masters, inducing disaffection and turmoil, as successors to a restoration of the Union. It is their wish, therefore, to settle them in one of the neighboring and friendly States, where the laws of the country will guarantee them safety, and where it will be easy for the United States government to extend a protecting hand to them in any hour of extremity. With such laudable motives we cannot but applaud the object of the United States government.

The Navy.

The United States steamer Florida, nine guns, having [illegible]

GRANT.

The Troops on the James Watching for the Rebel Fleet.

THE ARMIES MUD BOUND.

Rebel Indications of a Battle Before Richmond,

&c., &c., &c.

THE ARMY OF THE POTOMAC.

Mr. S. Cadwallader's Despatch.

CITY POINT, March 4, 1865.

BAD WEATHER AND BAD ROADS.

For three days past the weather has been rainy almost beyond precedent. This, added to what had fallen before, has rendered the roads as nearly impassable as mud can make them. The depth of the latter is fabulous. Nothing like it has been experienced this winter. As I write the rain continues to fall in torrents. Everything animate and inanimate has a dreary, sombre cast altogether depressing.

EXCHANGE OF MR. DENT.

Mr. John Dent, of St. Louis, Mo., and brother-in-law to Gen. Grant, has just been exchanged and arrived at headquarters yesterday on his way home. He was captured by the rebels at Skipworth's Landing, on the Mississippi river, more than a year ago, was taken to Canton, Miss., and thence to Demoplis. After a short stay at the latter place he was conveyed to Mobile for confinement until sent to Governor Bonham, of South Carolina. By the latter he was ordered into the hands of the Sheriff in Columbia, the capital of the State, for safe-keeping, and was ten months confined in the long corridor, five feet wide, which runs around the prison cells in the centre of the jail. During all this time he was never once outside of his prison walls, or touched his foot to the earth.

With one or two exceptions his treatment was courteous, and all was done for his comfort that his jailers could afford on the insufficient supplies permitted by the rebel government. At the time of his capture he had about two thousand dollars in greenbacks on his person, besides a good suit of clothes. The former was unceremoniously appropriated, and the latter so fancied by a rebel officer that Mr. Dent was induced to trade during his imprisonment. He was allowed to communicate with persons outside by letter, and had no difficulty in finding friends to relieve his necessities by advancing any sums of money that were necessary. A pair of very coarse linsey pantaloons cost him one hundred and eighty two dollars, and a pair of low-quartered, coarse Oxford ties eighty-five dollars; the latter were considered especially cheap, and his friends congratulated him on securing a bargain. Mr. Dent thinks the South very nearly past fighting. A general gloom and despondency prevails, and he thinks General Sherman will sweep everything before him, almost to Richmond, without opposition. Mr. Dent will leave here on to-morrow's mailboat for his home and family in St. Louis from whom he has been so long and painfully separated.

THE ARMY OF THE JAMES.

Mr. Wm. H. Merriam's Despatch.

DEPARTMENT HEADQUARTERS, March 4—A. M.

The enemy are just now indulging nightly in a heavy fire upon the extreme right of our lines, picked by the [illegible]

Mr. John A. Brady's Despatch.

[illegible]

... siderable excitement throughout the corps. For a long time we have expected the advent of Semmes, the Alabama pirate, and the rapid discharge from heavy guns led all to believe that at last the rebel fleet had determined to repeat the attempt which before proved a failure, and were dropping down the stream to carry out their programme of sinking our vessels and destroying our supplies at Jones' Neck, City Point and Bermuda. Couriers were sent in the proper direction to obtain information, and in a short time it was known that the fire was occasioned by a picket boat of the enemy. It seems that this boat has been in the habit of dropping down every night past our pickets and establishing itself almost within stone throw of Fort Brady. To prevent a further exhibition of this audacity on the part of the enemy, our pickets were thrown out to Graveyard Bend, with orders to fire on the boat if she again attempted to drop down the river. As soon, therefore, as she made her appearance behind the bend last evening she received a heavy musketry fire from the picket, which must have proved fatal to some of the crew. A bombardment immediately commenced, which was, however, confined entirely to the enemy, who opened from one of their land batteries and from their gunboat.

The Press Despatch.

HEADQUARTERS, ARMY OF THE POTOMAC, March 5, 1865.

Nothing of importance is transpiring in this department.

Deserters continue to come into our lines in large numbers, fifty-six having arrived to-day, nearly all bringing their arms and equipments with them, for which they are to be paid. The number of muskets received from deserters since February 22 is two hundred and forty, all of them in good order. In addition to the usual stories told by these men, they say that two companies from each regiment of several brigades have been detailed from the army defending Petersburg and sent to hunt up deserters, thousands of whom are said to be scattered through the country, endeavoring to reach their homes. This is particularly the case with the North and South Carolina troops, who are sick and tired of the contest, and anxious to join their families, now within our lines. These men are principally veterans of three and four years service, and many of them are those lately exchanged. All of them being refused furloughs, and not paid for a long time, nor any prospect of getting any soon, they took "French leave."

Anthony Raymond, of Company B, and Newell J. Engle, of Company H, of the Sixty-fourth New York Volunteers, were shot to-day for attempting to desert to the enemy. Five regiments of the First division of the Second corps, to which the criminals belonged, were assembled to witness the execution, the details of which were in charge of the Provost Marshal of the division.

The Ninety first New York Volunteers, a veteran regiment, arrived at the front to-day, and were assigned to the Third division of the Fifth corps. They numbered about six hundred men, and presented a splendid appearance.

REBEL ACCOUNTS.

Indications of a Battle Before Richmond.

[From the Richmond Sentinel, March 2.]

There is nothing of importance from the Army of Northern Virginia. Deserters in great numbers are coming into our lines from Grant's army, which is an *indication that they are in expectation of a battle*.

No Doubt Entertained of Grant's Intention to Move on the Rebel Right.

[From the Richmond Dispatch, March 3.]

Everything remains quiet on these lines, and is likely so to continue while the rain and mud lasts, and of these there seems to be no end. There is *no doubt that Grant will make another heavy movement on our right* so soon as the condition of the roads will permit.

Affairs in Lee's Army.

[From the Richmond Sentinel, March 3.]

The rain and the mud have put a stop to military operations in the vicinity of Richmond and Petersburg.

Deserters from Grant's army are coming in daily, and are sent on their way home rejoicing.

Deserters and absentees from the Confederate armies are returning to their commands in large numbers from all sections of the country, and are availing themselves of General Lee's amnesty proclamation. A deserter under sentence of death in the Army of Northern Virginia was released on the day appointed for his execution, the proclamation having been received about two hours previous to the time fixed for his being shot. He remarked, [illegible]

Marine Disasters.

[illegible]

City Sewerage.

TO THE EDITOR OF THE HERALD.

You have had occasion from time to time, as a matter of duty from the public journalist to the public itself, to remonstrate against the imperfections of our departments of sanitary regulation, and especially against the odious features of our ill-advised and unhealthy system of sewer construction.

Any one whom business may call into the Croton Aqueduct rotunda will find at all hours of the day groups of contractors, who are managing jobs on hand and jobs that are to be, and from all that appears on the outside or gleams from the inside these persons, rather than competent and educated officials, regulate the details of our public works and the special forms and methods of our underground city. Consequently we hear of the annual repetition of contracts for great lengths of oval brick receptacles and depositaries of filth, always forty-eight inches by thirty-two, which the Chief Engineer of the Board has recently declared to be elongated cess pools, detrimental to the public health and pertaining to a defective system of arrangement.

The philosophy of correct sewerage, as laid down by competent authorities, in the columns of the Journal of the Franklin Institute and other standard publications, may be thus stated:—

The results of experience in sewerage, ancient and modern, go to show that satisfactory operation depends to a great extent on the scouring action of the sewerage water, and that sewers without adequate flow are apt to clog up. It follows that, except for trunk mains, which receive aggregate discharges of house sewerage and rain fall, the intermediate lines should be so devised in grade, caliber, tightness and interior form as to pass most readily their ordinary contents and make most effective their ordinary water supply. Now, as tubes, with circular form, or with rounded basis, combine the greatest power of delivery with the least frictional surface, and may be very carefully made and put together, and as small tubes, by proper grades, have capacities for great discharges, there is a prudential limit quickly attained to their caliber, and they are to be preferred to all other forms and combinations for efficiency of operation, durability and limited cost, the first benefit involving all the sanitary considerations which make imperfect sewerage so serious an evil to public welfare. Under this theory it will be observed that all drains should be so devised as to concentrate the volume of the ordinary flow of sewerage water on the solid contents they receive [illegible]

Trunk Mains.	Feet.
72 inch	2,472
60 inch	6,099
54 inch	1,426
48 inch	15,405
42 inch	662
36 inch	21,282
Total	47,345
Tubular Pipe System.	Feet.
24 inch	34,123
18 inch	59,102
15 inch	112,049
12 inch	310,104
Total	515,378

[illegible]

Sales of Seven-Thirties.

[illegible]

SHERMAN.

The Army Somewhere in North Carolina.

Governor Vance Organizing to Oppose It.

The Rear Guard "Driven Out" of Columbia.

Grant and Sherman to be Beaten in Detail.

The Prospects of the Confederacy Unusually Brilliant.

Capture of the Rebel General Haygood's Brigade.

The Co-operative Columns Well Advanced Into North Carolina,

&c., &c., &c.

Reported Capture of General Haygood's Brigade, of Hoke's Division.

[From the Raleigh (N. C.) State Journal, March 2.]

As the train left Wilmington our Whitworth battery, planted at the head of the market, was firing upon the enemy, who had appeared upon the causeway on the western side of the Cape Fear river. Their main advance was then checked at Alligator creek; some few skirmishers pushed forward, but were driven off.

It is believed *that Haygood's brigade, with the exception of the Seventh battalion, has been captured.* Some accidental cases may have escaped. They probably have. They were on the west side of the Cape Fear. The other troops on that side escaped.

Hopes Entertained of the Capture of Sherman's Army.

[From the Richmond Whig, March 3.]

The Raleigh *Conservative* alludes to Sherman's operations, and indulges the hope, if our plans are not thwarted, that our able generals and brave troops in that quarter will be able to "bag" him or send him howling to the rear. If the report brought us by telegraph that the small force left by him at Columbia has been expelled be true, then the repulse in front, should he suffer much, would probably render his affairs desperate in the extreme. But we will not speculate further in regard to matters which must cease to be matters for mere speculation soon.

The Coming Battle to be Decisive.

SHERMAN AND GRANT TO BE BEATEN IN DETAIL.

[From the Richmond Enquirer, March 2.]

The wet season is at its height, and until the 1st of May the mud has no bottom in all the regions in the State of Virginia. Yankee deserters tell us that the enemy is massing on his left, and Confederate deserters inform the enemy that A. P. Hill's corps has been under marching orders for several days. The mud effectually blockades both. "It would mire a kitten," said a soldier, "between the city and camp;" and we can readily believe him, from the condition of the upper streets of this city.

Sherman had, in South Carolina, perhaps a better soil than the State of Virginia presents; but he must find a new base about Wilmington before he can prosecute further his great raid. His capture of Columbia, how has it benefited or advanced the prospect of our subjugation? He held the city not one week, burned a portion of it, and left without having conquered or subdued its people. He marches on towards Wilmington, which is already in his hands. His circuitous march around Charleston resulted in the capture of that city; but as it relieved an army from garrison duty to active service, the evacuation cannot be considered as having done any very great injury to our cause. When he enters North Carolina and leaves the sand country he enters the red mud of the Old North State, as sticky as its famous tar. There he encounters new enemies—tar, mud and tar people—and together they will hang upon him and stick to him. He will not be able to shake off either. Neither is noisy nor demonstrative. The people of that State are as firmly fixed in the purpose of independence as are the lofty pines in the soil of their State. The noisy few that induced the enemy to believe that treason would welcome them in that State served but to make their insignificance conspicuous, and demonstrated the unswerving fidelity of the people of that State. *Governor Vance is now actively at work rallying the people and organizing resistance.*

The military condition of these Confederate States, after four years of war, is by no means discouraging. The enemy has but two armies of all the hosts he once had in the field. Grant has literally stripped every section of the country, and concentrated all into two armies. In Western Virginia he has not left men enough to protect his major generals in their beds. No rest for the wicked out there. In Tennessee and Kentucky there are no troops. Mississippi, Alabama, Georgia, Florida and South Carolina have only small detachments, strongly fortified, dominating no country and holding only their camping grounds. In Trans-Mississippi the Confederates have no enemy. The army around Richmond and Sherman's movable columns only remain of all the hosts that once threatened these States. *These two armies disposed of, victory and independence are ours; the whole country returns to Confederate authority, and we confront again the frontiers of the enemy's country.* Never before has the prospect of final and sure victory presented itself to these people. Now, for the first time, is *the issue narrowed down to the ordeal of battle.* The enemy has apparently had many successes; but really he has been narrowing the issue, and *putting it within the reach of our resources and arms.* While scattered over half a continent it was impossible to win a decisive victory, but concentration has, after four years of effort, brought victory and independence within our reach, without hazarding our liberty upon the issue of battle. Grant has been driven to this, despite his successes. He has been compelled to denude his conquests and give up the fruits of his victories and concentrate all his armies into two. Defeat destroys first one army and then the other, and leaves the confederacy free of the foe. When the people look calmly at the real aspect of affairs they must [illegible]

Arrival of the Canada at Boston.

[illegible]

DAILY DISPATCH.

VOLUME XXIX — RICHMOND, VA., TUESDAY MORNING, MARCH 21, 1865. — NUMBER 66.

OFFICIAL.

Confederate States of America,
War Department,
Adjutant and Inspector General's Office,
Richmond, Va., March 15, 1865.

Sirs,—You are hereby authorized to raise a Company or Companies of Negro Soldiers, under the provisions of the act of Congress, approved March 13, 1865.

When the requisite number shall have been recruited, they will be mustered into the service for the war, and muster rolls forwarded to this office.

The Companies, when organized, will be subject to the rules and regulations governing the Provisional Army of the Confederate States.

By command of the Secretary of War.
Signed,
JOHN W. REILY, A. A. G.

To Maj. J. W. Pegram, and Maj. Thomas P. Turner, through Gen. Ewell.

COLORED TROOPS.

An Appeal to the People of Virginia.

It will be seen by the Order of the Secretary of War, published above, that the undersigned have been authorized to proceed at once with the organization of Companies composed of persons of Color, free and slave, who are willing to volunteer under the recent acts of Congress and the Legislature of Virginia. It is well known to the country that Gen. Lee has evinced the deepest interest on this subject, and that he regards prompt action in this matter, as vitally important to the country. In a letter addressed by him to Lt. Gen. Ewell, dated March 10th, he says, "I hope it will be found practicable to raise a considerable force in Richmond. * * * *. I attach great importance to the result of the first experiment, and nothing should be left undone to make it successful. The sooner this can be accomplished the better."

The undersigned have established a rendezvous on 21st, between Main and Cary streets, at the building known as "Smith's Factory;" and every arrangement has been made to secure the comfort of the new recruits, and to prepare them for service. It is recommended that each recruit be furnished, when practicable, with a grey jacket and pants, cap and blanket, and a good serviceable pair of shoes, but no delay should take place in forwarding the recruits in order to obtain these articles.

The governments, Confederate and State, having settled the policy of employing this element of strength, and this class of our population having given repeated evidence of their willingness to take up arms in the defence of their homes, it is believed that it is only necessary to put the matter before them in a proper light to cause them to rally with enthusiasm for the preservation of the homes in which they have been born and raised, and in which they have found contentment and happiness; and to save themselves and their race from the barbarous cruelty invariably practised upon them by a perfidious enemy claiming to be their friends.

Will not the people of Virginia, in this hour of peril and danger, promptly respond to the call of our loved General-in-Chief, and the demands of the Confederate and State governments?

Will those who have freely given their sons and brothers, their money and their property, to the achievment of the liberties of their country, now hold back from the cause their servants, who can well be spared, and who will gladly aid in bringing this fearful war to a speedy and glorious termination!

Let every man in the State consider himself a recruiting officer, and enter at once upon the duty of aiding in the organization of this force, by sending forward recruits to this rendezvous.

Every consideration of patriotism, the independence of our country, the safety of our homes, the happiness of our families, and the sanctity of our firesides, all prompt to immediate and energetic action for the defence of the country. Let the people but be true to themselves, and to the claims of duty, and our independence will be speedily secured, and peace be restored within our borders.

J. W. PEGRAM,
Maj. P. A. C. S.
TH. P. TURNER,
Maj. P. A. C. S

mh 16—6t

Richmond Dispatch.

BY J. A. COWARDIN & CO.

TERMS OF SUBSCRIPTION:

Daily Paper.—For one year, ONE HUNDRED DOLLARS; six months, FIFTY DOLLARS; three months, TWENTY-FIVE DOLLARS; one month, TEN DOLLARS.

Agents and News Dealers will be furnished at THIRTY DOLLARS per hundred copies.

All orders must be accompanied with the money, to insure attention; and all remittances by mail will be at the risk of those who make them.

Advertising.—Advertisements will be inserted at the rate of THREE DOLLARS per square for each insertion. Eight lines (or less) constitute a square.

Larger advertisements in exact proportion.

Advertisements published till forbid, will be charged THREE DOLLARS per square for every insertion.

TUESDAY MORNING..............MARCH 21, 1865.

Horace Walpole, in a letter to Sir Horace Mann, written during the Seven Years' War, expresses himself wearied with the slow process of military events. He says that no doubt the occurrences of Cæsar's day seemed to drag themselves along quite as tediously, although the conquests of Cæsar are proverbial for their rapidity. We read the commentaries, or the campaigns of Frederick, all in the bulk. We do not go through the tedious details of military operations in the newspapers, catching the news of a moment one day, and resting upon our information thus picked up for several others to come. The newspapers, and the dispatches and bulletins of the generals, only let us see a little at a time. A six months' campaign gathered this way, in detail, is wearisome enough. We must wait for the historian if we wish to read operations in the mass.

In addition to other causes of uneasiness, the great anxiety necessarily felt by contemporaries—especially by that portion of them whose countrymen and friends are engaged in the conflict—renders delay still more painful. Every moment is protracted into an hour—every hour apparently grows into a week—weeks become years, and years seem expanded to ages. Every man who looks back to the beginning of a war in which he is immediately interested, and which has already lasted four or five years, without looking at the intermediate events, will feel that he is contemplating the events of yesterday. It is like looking across a tremendous precipice, directly to the other side. He sees what is on the opposite cliff, but he sees nothing of the obstacles that lie between him and it. Let him look down, however, and he will find his brain reel and his eye sink. Even so is it with the man who looks, not merely at the starting point of a bloody war, but at the incidents which lie between him and it.—When he breaks the great whole into separate parts, for analysis and contemplation, he becomes overwhelmed and stupefied with the scene.

The events of this war have, no doubt, succeeded each other with sufficient rapidity, yet they are tedious to us, whatever they may be to the future historian. It seems to us like an age since Major Anderson was upturned at Fort Sumter; and when we read, the other day, that Mr. Dudley Field proposed to carry him back, and make him hoist his flag there again, we involuntarily asked whether he was still alive, or had not died of old age.

Xerxes is reported, by Herodotus, to have wept when he beheld his mighty comprehending five millions of the human race drawn out in the vast plain of Abydos, because the thought suddenly struck him that in one hundred years not a man of them would be left alive. In much less time than that the combatants in the present war will all have disappeared from the face of the earth, and then we may repeat Montaigne's standing question—*Au bono?* What is it all for? Oppressed and oppressors, so far as the vile integuments of humanity are concerned, will all have shared a common fate. Yet the glory of the patriot will last forever.

We write the above by way of experiment. We wish to see whether the public will tolerate anything not appertaining directly to the war.

ADDRESS OF CONGRESS TO THE PEOPLE OF THE CONFEDERATE STATES.

Fellow-Citizens,—The result of the "Peace Commission" is known to the country. The hopes of those who have hitherto believed that an honorable termination might be put to the war by negotiation have been rudely disappointed. The enemy, after drawing us into a conference, abruptly terminated it by insisting upon terms which they well knew we could never accept. Our absolute surrender and submission to the will of the conquerer are the only conditions vouchsafed by our arrogant foe. We are told that if we will lay down our arms, and place our lives, liberty, property and domestic institutions at the feet of President Lincoln, that he will be merciful to us! Upon his clemency we must rely to save us from universal confiscation and extermination! Yes! these are the conditions upon which the people of the sovereign States composing the Confederacy may be allowed to do—what? To return into "the Union" from which they solemnly and deliberately withdrew themselves because their interest and their honor required it, and their repugnance to which four years of remorseless and cruel war have served but to intensify! Thanks be to God, who controls and overrules the counsels of men, the haughty insolence of our enemies, which they hoped would intimidate and break the spirit of our people, is producing the very contrary effect! From every part of the country there comes up in response a shout of mingled indignation and defiance!

A noble enthusiasm re-animates our gallant army, who have been battling so long for freedom and independence! Let us all be united now. Let there be no parties or factions among us. Let us rise to the height of the great occasion. Let us all be willing to spend and be spent in the cause of our country. Let us contribute freely all that we have, if need be, to carry on the war until our final triumph is secured. Let us take fraternal counsel together, and calmly consider our condition and prospects. Such a survey, we believe, must tend to re-assure and encourage even the least sanguine. We have, it is true, recently met with serious disasters. Our fortitude is being severely tried. We have suffered much, and must be prepared to suffer more, in the cause for which we are struggling. Is the cause worth the sacrifice? To answer correctly we must constantly keep in mind the end for which we are contending. What is our object in this war? The establishment of our independence, through which alone are to be secured the sovereignty of the States and the right of self-government. What is the alternative? Our subjugation as a people! Is it possible to over-estimate the horrors of this terrible alternative? Can the imagination over-color the picture which would be presented in the event of our failure? If we fail, not only political degradation, but social humiliation must be our wretched lot. We would not only be political vassals, but social serfs. An enemy that has shown himself destitute of the ordinary sensibilities of human nature, and whose worst passions are embittered and enflamed against us, would assume the absolute control of our political and social destinies. In vain would a proud, though vanquished, people look even for that mercy which the conquered receive from a generous foe. Those "State Rights" which we have been taught to prize so dearly as the greatest bulwarks of Constitutional Liberty, and which, from the earliest period of our history, we have so jealously guarded, would be annihilated. The Confederate States would be held as conquered provinces by the despotic Government at Washington. They would be kept in subjugation by the stern hand of military power, as Venetia and Lombardy have been held by Austria—as Poland is held by the Russian Czar. Not only would we be deprived of every political franchise dear to freemen, but socially we would be degraded to the level of slaves; if, indeed, the refinement of malice in our enemies did not induce them to elevate the negro slave above his former master. Not only would the property and estates of vanquished "rebels" be confiscated, but they would be divided and distributed among our African bondsmen. But why pursue the hideous picture further?—Southern manhood revolts at the bare idea of the spectacle presented. Can you think of it unmoved? Can property—can life itself—be so dear to you as to allow you to weigh them for one moment against degradation so abject—against misery so profound? We do not, and cannot, believe it. If the proud memories and traditions of our first great revolution do not nerve you to eternal resistance to such a consummation—nor the example of our forefathers, who wrestled for the independence they bequeathed us during seven long years of suffering greater than we have endured—let not the precious blood that has been already shed by our bravest and best in the present struggle cry out to us from our yet reeking soil in vain! Fruitlessly, indeed, have these sons and brothers—martyrs of liberty—bled and died, if we falter now in the path which they have illumined before us!

In the Revolution of '76 our armies and our people suffered far more than we have done. Our cities then were almost all in the hands of the British, and we were entirely cut off from all supplies from abroad, while our facilities for producing them were infinitely less than they now are. Greene tells us that the battle of Eutaw was won by men who had scarcely shoes to their feet or shirts to their backs. They protected their shoulders from being galled by the bands of their cross-belts, by bunches of moss or tufts of grass. A detachment marching to Greene's assistance passed through a region so swept by both armies that they were compelled to subsist on green peaches as their only diet. There was scarcely any salt for fifteen months, and when obtained, it had to be used sparingly, mixed with hickory ashes. We need but allude to the terrible winter which Washington passed at Valley Forge, with an army unpaid, half starved and half naked, and shoeless, to convince us that much as our own brave soldiers are now enduring, their fathers, for a like cause, endured far more. Washington did not then despair. Lee does not now despair of the final triumph of a righteous cause. Why should we be doubtful—much less despondent—of our ultimate success?

The extent of our territory—the food-producing capacity of our soil—the amount and character of our population—are elements of strength which, carefully husbanded and wisely employed, are amply sufficient to insure our final triumph. The passage of hostile armies through our country, though productive of cruel suffering to our people and great pecuniary loss, gives the enemy no permanent advantage or foothold.

To subjugate a country, its civil government must be suppressed by a continuing military force, or supplanted by another, to which the inhabitants yield a voluntary or enforced obedience. The passage of hostile armies through our territory cannot produce this result.—Permanent garrisons would have to be stationed at a sufficient number of points to strangle all civil government before it could be pretended, even by the United States Government itself, that its authority was extended over these States. How many garrisons would it require? How many hundred thousand soldiers would suffice to suppress the civil governments of all the States of this Confederacy, and to establish over them, even in name and form, the authority of the United States? In a geographical point of view, therefore, it may be asserted that the conquest of these Confederate States is impracticable.

If we consider the food-producing capacity of our soil we need feel no apprehensions as to our ability to feed the people and any army we may put into the field. It is needless to go into detail or adduce statistics in proof of this. It is obvious to every well-informed mind. Although the occupation by the enemy, and his ruthless policy of destroying the harvests, granaries and agricultural implements of our people, wherever he moves, has undoubtedly diminished the amount of our cereals; still, in view of the fact that in every State, without exception, its agricultural labor has been devoted almost exclusively to the raising of breadstuffs, while before the war it was mainly devoted to the production of cotton, tobacco and other exports, it is impossible to doubt that there is an ample supply of food in the country.—It is true that the deportation of our slaves by the enemy, and the barbarous policy of arming them against us,—a policy reprobated by all authorities on ethics or international law,—has considerably diminished our agricultural labor. But when we reflect that, in 1860, our exports—almost entirely the products of slave labor—amounted to ($250,000,000) two hundred and fifty millions of dollars, it may be safely assumed that our slaves, though reduced in numbers, are fully equal to the task of feeding both the population at home and the army in the field. Our transportation, it is true, is defective and inadequate, but this may be infinitely improved by more energetic efforts and more thorough and systematic organization. We cannot believe, therefore, that on our bountiful soil, so richly blessed by nature, there is any danger of our failing in this great contest for want of food—of our being STARVED into submission to the hateful yoke of the conqueror!

But if we look to the amount and character of our population, we see especial reason why we should be encouraged to hope for—nay, to be assured of—our ultimate success. No people of our numbers can be subjugated, unless, false and recreant to themselves, their courage, faith and fortitude fail them.

We have upon our rolls a very large army of veteran soldiers. It is true—and it is a sad truth to confess—that the number present for duty is terribly disproportioned to the entire aggregate. This is too notorious for concealment—and we have no desire to conceal anything. We wish to speak frankly and truthfully to you of the actual condition of things. The number of absentees from your armies has been a fruitful cause of disaster. On many a hard-fought field the tide of success would have turned overwhelmingly in our favor had all been present whom duty required to participate in the strife. We will not stop to inquire into the causes of an evil which we have so much reason to deplore. The remedy is partly in the hands of Congress, and it is our province to apply it. But it is partly, also, in yours; and we appeal to you to use it. Let every good citizen frown down upon, and indignantly discountenance, all evasion of military duty—whether temporary or permanent—no matter how plausible the pretext or palliating the reason.

No duty, in this crisis of our affairs, can be more imperative than to fight for one's country, family and home. Let no skulker, deserter, or absentee without leave, from the army, be tolerated in any community. Let the reproachful glance of our women, between whose honor and the brutal foe our noble army stands as a flaming sword, drive him back to the field. With proper officers, strict discipline, and an elevated tone of public opinion throughout the country, desertion and absenteeism in the army can be arrested, and all men liable to military duty put into, and kept in, the ranks of our armies. If this be effected, we can maintain in the field a force sufficient to defy subjugation.

But it is in the character of our population, especially, that we find those elements of strength which impress us with the conviction that we never can be conquered. Our people are peculiarly military in their characteristics. Better soldiers than those in our army history has never shown. They have endured extreme hardships and suffering with a fortitude, and fought against constant odds with a gallantry, that has earned the gratitude of their country and extorted the admiration of the world. But, in addition to their military attributes, our people are pre-eminently of a proud and haughty spirit, and deeply imbued with the love of constitutional freedom. It belongs to their race and lineage; and, as Burke long ago remarked, their relation to the servile race in contact with them has intensified the feeling and invested this love of liberty with a sentiment of personal privilege. To suppose that a people with such military, political and social characteristics will ever voluntarily submit to be ruled by any other government than one of their own choice, is too insulting to their pride to be entertained for a moment. And to doubt their capacity to achieve independence and maintain themselves as a separate Power among the nations of the earth, is to close our eyes to all the teachings of history—to ignore the proof which our own forefathere have stamped upon its pages—to believe that human nature has changed, or that we are a degenerate race, unworthy descendants of our revolutionary sires!

The appointment by the President of General Lee as "General-in-Chief" has done much to restore confidence to the country and to reinspire the army. All feel that we may safely repose this weighty trust and responsibility in that great soldier and devoted patriot. All feel that we may lean upon him as our tower of strength. All feel that his calm courage and steadfast purpose, his military skill and wise judgment, will enable him to wield our armies with the maximum efficiency and strength. May God strengthen for the great task to which a confiding people have called him!

To provide means for carrying on the war, Congress has been compelled to impose upon the country a heavy burthen of taxation. But, heavy as it is, it is not too heavy for the country to bear, and not heavier than our wants imperatively demand. It is impossible to maintain the mighty contest in which we are engaged without vast expenditures of money. Money can only be raised by loans or by taxation. Our condition does not enable us to effect the former. We must of necessity, therefore, resort to the latter. We appeal to you with confidence to submit cheerfully to the burthens which the defence of your country, your homes and your liberties renders necessary. To contribute according to his means to that defence is as much an obligation upon the citizen as it is to peril his life upon the battle-field.

Let us, then, fellow-countrymen, tread the plain path of duty. No nation that has trod it faithfully and fearlessly ever, in the world's history, has stumbled and fallen. "Nations," says Burke, "never are murdered—they commit suicide."—Let us not be guilty of the folly and the crime of self-destruction. Let us show the fortitude, endurance and courage that belong to our race, and neither the brute force of our enemy's arms, nor the subtle poison of his lips, can extinguish the life of this Confederacy, breathed into it by the sovereign States which created it.

The people of the United States are becoming weary of this war. The foreign material for their armies is beginning to fail them. The mutterings of discontent at the prospect of a further draft upon their home population are beginning to be heard in their great cities.—The prospect of war, indefinitely prolonged, is alarming their capitalists.—Public credit must, sooner or later, collapse under the burthen of expenditures, the magnitude of which the most skillful financier cannot venture to predict. The debt of the United States is already equal to the national debt of England, which has been accumulating since the revolution of 1688. The interest on this debt is six per cent., while the interest on the English debt is only three per cent. It has been computed that the interest on the debt of the United States, together with the amount necessary to carry on its Government (even were the war at an end), would not fall much short of *five hundred millions per annum!*—a sum affirmed to be greater than the entire annual wealth of the Northern States. While a people, in self-defence, may submit cheerfully to any privations and sufferings—to any sacrifices of treasure and of blood—there is a limit beyond which a country, waging a war of aggression and conquest, will not go. We cannot stop this war without degradation, ruin, dishonor. Our enemies can have peace at any time by abandoning their wicked attempt at our subjugation, and allowing us to govern ourselves in accordance with those great principles for which their fathers and ours fought side by side.

Considered, therefore, in every point of view, it is impossible to believe that the people of the Confederate States will ever incur subjugation, or accept submission as the result of the great struggle in which we are engaged. Neither is it possible to believe that these States, compelled by long years of unjust and unconstitutional action towards them by the Northern States to withdraw from political union with them, can ever be tempted by any promises, or so-called "guaranties," to again unite themselves with them under a common government. Forced into this revolution by their faithless disregard of the obligations of the constitutional compact, and by the selfish and sectional legislation which they fastened upon us, what, in the course of this war, has occurred to change our opinion as to their character and purposes? The barbarity and unrelenting ferocity which has characterized their conduct of it has excited the indignant wonder of the world. Falsehood, duplicity and mean cunning marked their course in its inauguration—and, in its progress, every artifice of low diplomacy and persistent misrepresentation has been resorted to by them to lessen us in the estimation of mankind. Our struggle for the right of self-government—which they themselves have always declared to be inalienable—has been held up to the world as a contest for the maintenance of African slavery—a purely State institution, over which neither the Confederate States Government nor the United States Government has any constitutional control. To prevent foreign nations from according to us that recognition to which we were entitled by public law, and even the very language of existing treaties—a recognition which they have themselves accorded to other countries on far more slender grounds—they have deliberately falsified accounts of military operations and our capacity and resources for continuing the contest. A war which has been carried on for four years with ever varying fortunes, their Minister of State has again and again assured foreign Powers could not possibly be waged by us for more than two or three months. And, after all their insolent boasts of their power to crush us, they have been compelled to resort to foreign enlistments and the arming of our captured slaves in order to fill up the ranks of their armies. In spite of these practices—winked at, if not countenanced, by European Powers—they have practically confessed their inability to vanquish us in regular warfare by the inhuman policy of destroying the dwellings, the food and the agricultural implements of our non-combatant population; thus endeavoring, by the starvation of their wives and children, to break the indomitable spirit of our soldiers.

In the invasion of our soil neither private property, nor age, nor sex, has been spared from the rapacity and brutal passions of their mercenary legions.

Wherever they have passed over the surface of our fair land, the blackness of desolation has marked their path; and such barbarous devastation has been their devilish boast. Public records have been destroyed—institutions of learning—public and private libraries—pillaged or burnt, and the temples of God sacrilegiously defiled.

Fellow-countrymen, will you, can you, ever submit to be ruled by such a people? Can you ever join hands with them in fraternal union? Can you, with all these things freshly before you,—daily occurring on your native soil—ever return to a political union with these despoilers of your homes—these violators of your wives and daughters? Never! A dark crimson stream divides you, which all the skill of legislation can never bridge over. The Southern people have determined to be free and independent, and if their fortitude and courage do not fail them, it is impossible to doubt the issue. But there must be no halting—no hesitation—in the only path that leads to the goal. We must prove to our enemy, and prove to the world, that we cannot be conquered. We must convince them that, though our soil may be overrun, the faith of our people in the great cause for which they are contending is unbroken—their determination unchanged—their will invincible. Let us emulate the example of the Russian people when invaded by the grand army of Napoleon. Let us be willing to make any and every sacrifice, and

Evening Star.

VOL. XXV. WASHINGTON, D. C., MONDAY, APRIL 3, 1865. No. 3,772.

WASHINGTON EVENING STAR.
PUBLISHED DAILY, (EXCEPT SUNDAY,)
AT THE STAR BUILDINGS,
[illegible]
BY W. D. WALLACH.

The STAR is served by the carriers to their subscribers in the City and District for TWELVE AND A HALF CENTS PER WEEK.
PRICE FOR MAILING.—Single copy, three cents; one month, seventy five cents; three months, one dollar and fifty cents; six months, three dollars; one year, six dollars. No papers are sent from the office longer than paid for.
THE WEEKLY STAR one dollar and a half a year.

OFFICIAL.

The First Corps—Notice to Veterans.

HEADQUARTERS FIRST CORPS, WASHINGTON, D. C., Dec. 27, 1864.

Veterans desiring to enlist in the 1st Army Corps, should report in person at the office of Col. C. F. Johnson, Soldiers' Rest, Baltimore and Ohio Railroad Depot, Washington, D. C.

Any Veteran who has served two years, has been honorably discharged, and is physically qualified, may enlist in the Corps for one, two or three years.

Those enlisting will receive from the Government a bounty of $300 as soon as they are mustered in, and, in addition, the regular instalments from the Government, in proportion to the period of enlistment, as follows: $100 for one year's service, one-third paid on enlistment; $200 for two years' service, one-third on enlistment; $300 for three years' service, one-third on enlistment.

They will be credited to the quota of the district in which they or their families may be domiciled and will, therefore, be entitled to local bounties.

Free transportation will be furnished them to Washington by any Provost Marshal.

The best arms in the possession of the Government will be furnished these troops, and they will be allowed to retain their arms when honorably discharged.

Headquarters Major General Hancock:—158 F street, between 19th and 20th streets.

Office of the Board for the Examination of Officers—Brigadier General John R. Brooke, president, 183 G street, between 19th and 20th streets.

By order of Major General Hancock.

FINLEY ANDERSON, Assistant Adjutant General.
dec 27-tf

AMUSEMENTS.

CANTERBURY HALL,

MUSIC HALL AND THEATER — CANTERBURY HALL, CANTERBURY HALL, CANTERBURY HALL, CANTERBURY HALL — MUSIC HALL AND THEATER

LOUISIANA AVENUE, NEAR SIXTH STREET,
Rear of National and Metropolitan Hotels.

GEORGE LEA .... Proprietor
Also of the Varieties, New York, and Canterbury Alexandria, Va.
JOSH HART .... Stage Manager

By particular request, and
POSITIVELY FOR SIX NIGHTS ONLY.
POSITIVELY FOR SIX NIGHTS ONLY.
POSITIVELY FOR SIX NIGHTS ONLY.

commencing Monday, April 3, and terminating Saturday, April 9, the Star of the World, the Child Artiste, the Remarkable Juvenile,

EL NINO EDDIE.
EL NINO EDDIE.
EL NINO EDDIE.
EL NINO EDDIE.
EL NINO EDDIE.
EL NINO EDDIE.

in his perilous
ASCENSION FROM THE STAGE TO THE GALLERY,
ASCENSION FROM THE STAGE TO THE GALLERY,
on a Single Wire, over the heads of the audience.

TERROR! TERROR!! TERROR!!!
TERROR! TERROR!! TERROR!!!

may seize the human frame while witnessing this Mere Infant in so dangerous a task, yet it is safely accomplished nightly, and the Proprietor of the Canterbury, in behalf of the boy, assures the public there is no danger of the boy being dashed to pieces from falling off the wire, and this wonderful boy possesses remarkable strength of nerve and astonishing presence of mind, and has performed this dangerous undertaking so frequently that, by his cool, calm, and collected manner in the performance of the act, it dispels all unpleasant and trembling feelings from the audience for the safety of the little fellow, and for an act in which, at any moment, a person may fall and break their neck, yet, as Nino Eddie himself remarks, he never thinks of falling. The papers are all loud in his praise. He will remain for Six Nights Only, receiving for his several performances over

ONE THOUSAND DOLLARS.
ONE THOUSAND DOLLARS.
ONE THOUSAND DOLLARS.

First week of the Celebrated Banjoist and Ethiopian Delineator,
MR. DAN HOLT.
MR. DAN HOLT.
MR. DAN HOLT.

First week of a new Military Drama, entitled the
TRIALS OF A SOLDIER'S LIFE.
TRIALS OF A SOLDIER'S LIFE.
Characters by the Dramatic Company.

MULLIGAN. HART.
MULLIGAN. HART.
MULLIGAN. HART.
CLARE. REDDEN.
CLARE. REDDEN.
CLARE. REDDEN.
in Funny Ethiopian Eccentricities.

LAURA LE CLAIRE AND TILLY FORBES
LAURA LE CLAIRE AND TILLY FORBES
LAURA LE CLAIRE AND TILLY FORBES
in a New Comic Duet.

THE
BOQUET OF BEAUTY.
BOQUET OF BEAUTY.
consisting of the
GARDNER SISTERS,
LIZZIE SMITH,
KATE ULLMAN,
JENNIE JOHNSON,
MAGGIE CHAPMAN,
MARIE ROSE,
in their Charming Ballet Divertissements, under the direction of
MONS. LOUIS SZOLLOSY.

First time of the Roaring Irish Farce, entitled
O'FLANNIGAN AT THE FAIR.
O'FLANNIGAN AT THE FAIR;
OR,
THE PEEP O'DAY BOYS.
THE PEEP O'DAY BOYS.

Phelim O'Flannigan, a Peep O'Day Boy, ... John Mulligan
Biddy Muldoody, a Peep O'Day Woman, ... Josh Hart
Tearing Duffy .... John Redden
Billy Goleary .... J. S. Clark
Shorn, the Pedlar .... Dan Holt
Jack, the Showman .... W. White
Sporting Molly .... Miss Laura Le Claire
Peggy O'Flannigan .... Miss Tilly Forbes
Miss Finnegan .... Mary Gardner
Miss Muldoody .... Kate Ullman
Miss Patsey Marley .... Carrie Gardner

INCIDENTS.

Coggan Fair—Sporting Molly, from the county town—The history of Moses in the bulrushes—O'Flannigan kicking the fair before him like a football—"Tread on the tail of my coat"—Fire away, Flannigan—Song "Flaming O'Flannigan"—Double Irish jig—Song, "McEvoy"—Hurrah for the Shamrock Green—Country dance by all the characters—"That's the way we do it at home"—Who kissed Biddy—Terrific shellalah fight between O'Flannigan and Tearing Duffy—Tableau and death of O'Flannigan.

SATURDAY AFTERNOON AND NIGHT APRIL 8, 1865.
BENEFIT OF EL NINO EDDIE.
BENEFIT OF EL NINO EDDIE.
BENEFIT OF EL NINO EDDIE.
BENEFIT OF EL NINO EDDIE.

In the afternoon at 2 o'clock he will make an
ASCENSION OUTSIDE THE BUILDING.
ASCENSION OUTSIDE THE BUILDING.
ASCENSION OUTSIDE THE BUILDING,
from the roof of the Canterbury to the opposite side of the street.

In the evening, a
MAMMOTH ENTERTAINMENT.
MAMMOTH ENTERTAINMENT.
MAMMOTH ENTERTAINMENT.
MAMMOTH ENTERTAINMENT.

NOTICE.
In active preparation, a
NEW AND SPLENDID PANTOMIME.
NEW AND SPLENDID PANTOMIME.
NEW AND SPLENDID PANTOMIME.

AMUSEMENTS.

FORD'S NEW THEATER.
TENTH STREET, above Pennsylvania Avenue.

Mr. Ford takes great pleasure in announcing an engagement with the celebrated and popular comedienne,
MISS LAURA KEENE,
who will appear on
MONDAY EVENING, April 3,
when will be produced the great Moral Drama, by Miss Keene, entitled
THE WORKMEN OF WASHINGTON.

Martha Savage .... Miss Laura Keene
John Savage .... Mr J C McCollum
Mr Belcour, a millionaire .... Mr John Dyott
Mitty Dogan .... Harry Hawk
Lazy Lewis .... Mr C Warwick
Will Jones .... Mr T C Gourlay
Dr Mitchell .... Mr J Matthews
Sam .... Mr J H Evans
Josephine, (her first appearance) .... Miss M Hart
Rose Savage .... Miss J Gourlay
Mrs Vanderben .... Mrs Muzzy
Fanny .... Miss M Gourlay

GROVER'S NEW THEATER.
Pennsylvania Avenue, near Willard's.
MONDAY EVENING, April 3, 1865,
and every evening during the week, Grand Initial Performances of the Magnificent Oriental Spectacle,
ALADDIN;
OR, THE WONDERFUL LAMP,
presented after three months active preparation at a cost of
SIX THOUSAND THREE HUNDRED DOLLARS
New and magnificent Scenery, wonderful Mechanical Effects, new and elegant Properties, superb Costumes, entirely new Music for the Grand Choruses, all the original Dramatic Music, grand Ballets, Chinese Dances, Fairy Tableaux, &c.

OXFORD! OXFORD! OXFORD!
MUSIC HALL AND THEATRE.
Ninth street, fronting on Pennsylvania avenue
FOX, CURRAN & NORRIS .... Proprietors
THE CLIMAX ARRIVED AT.
HOUSES FULL TO REPLETION.

Hail, rain or shine makes no difference to the steady flow of Greenbacks into the Treasury of the now famous Oxford, famous for the unparalleled number of its stars, the immense size of its auditorium, the splendor of its decoration and the general management of the Institution. Sam Cowell, Adah Isaacs Menkin, Sam Sharpley, Charley White, J. H. Ogden, Agnes Sutherland, Miranda, Montani and Lady Herr Greff, Mme. Scombergh, Charley Fox, Mme. Valentini, Marietta Ravel, Sig. Paravilla, the unrivalled Marietta Zanfretta, James Melville and Sons, and, above all, by the astounding engagement with the incomparable Blondin, the hero of Niagara. And the predictions made of the impracticability of carrying out such ideas, and yet, when the success of the experiment was assured, how crazy those self-same fortune-tellers became to hire the same parties at still more fabulous prices.

Ladies' Matinee Saturday Afternoon.

FOR ONE WEEK ONLY.

UNPARALLELD COMBINATION OF ZOOLOGICAL AND EQUESTRIAN ATTRACTIONS.

VAN AMBURGH & CO.'S
MAMMOTH MENAGERIE,
from 539 and 541 Broadway, New York, combine with
THAYER & NOYES'
GREAT UNITED STATES CIRCUS,
will exhibit one week only,
AT THE FOOT OF SIXTH STREET,
NEAR PENNSYLVANIA AVENUE.
NEAR PENNSYLVANIA AVENUE.
AFTERNOON AND NIGHT.
AFTERNOON AND NIGHT.
BOTH COMPANIES
EXHIBITING IN ONE TENT
FOR ONE ADMISSION FEE.
Doors open at 2 and 7 o'clock.

LADIES AND FAMILY PARTIES
will find the
AFTERNOON EXHIBITIONS
less crowded than those given at night, while the performances will be equally attractive in every respect.

THAYER & NOYES'
UNITED STATES CIRCUS
includes
THE GREATEST FORCE OF TALENTED RIDERS, GYMNASTS, CLOWNS, ACROBATS, EQUILIBRISTS, VOLTIGEURS, &c.,
in the country, with
A STUD OF PERFORMING HORSES, PONIES AND MULES,
INCOMPARABLY SUPERIOR
to any other that can be produced upon this side of the Atlantic.

Prominent among the gifted performers attached to this
SUPERB CIRCUS TROUPE
will be found the names of
DR. J. L. THAYER, MR. G. W. NOYES,
MRS. T. KING, MR. T. KING,
MR. CHAS. REED, MR. JAS. REYNOLDS,
MR. O. KELLEY, MR. BURROWS,
MONS. MORESTE, MR. J. HAZELETT,
MR. SAUNDERS, MR. KINCAIDE,
MASTER COOK,
and a full corps of
GYMNASTS TUMBLERS AND ATHLETES.

VAN AMBURGH & CO.'S MENAGERIE,
comprises the
MOST SPLENDID COLLECTION OF LIVING WILD BEASTS, AND RARE AND CURIOUS BIRDS,
from every quarter of the globe, that has visited this city for many years, including among other prominent features the world-renowned
WAR ELEPHANT HANNIBAL,
A TWO-HUMPED BACTRIAN CAMEL,
the first one that has been seen in America for forty years; the first and only
HIMALAYA WHITE BEAR
ever brought to this country; a pair of
POONAH SLOTH BEARS,
the first ever exhibited here;
TWO WHITE ZEBUS,
together with
LIONS, TIGERS, LEOPARDS, HYENAS, BEARS, LLAMAS,
and an infinite variety of other rare specimens of the animal kingdom, forming the grandest exposition of
ANIMATED NATURE
ever presented to the Washington public.

THE PERFORMANCES
will include every imaginable variety of
DASHING HORSEMANSHIP AND CLASSIC OLYMPIC GAMES,
introducing
NEW AND STARTLING ACTS
never before given in this city. At each entertainment Mr. G. W. Noyes will introduce his famous
TRICK HORSE, GREY EAGLE, JR.,
the finest specimen of equine beauty in America; also his celebrated
PERFORMING MONKEY, SIGNOR VICTOR
the feats of which are comical beyond description.
A pupil of the great VAN AMBURGH will enter the dens of
LIONS, TIGERS AND LEOPARDS.

Each entertainment will commence with a
GRAND ORIENTAL CAVALCADE,
and conclude with the laughable performances of Dr. Thayer's
COMIC MULES, UNCLE SAM AND DICK,
MESSRS. THAYER & REYNOLDS, CLOWNS.

TO PREVENT DISAPPOINTMENT,
the public are requested to observe that the mammoth pavilion is located
AT THE FOOT OF SIXTH STREET, SOUTH OF PENNSYLVANIA AVENUE,
immediately in the rear of the Clarendon and Central Hotel.
Admission to the entire Mammoth Combination, 50 cents, Children under twelve, 25 cents.
mar 31-tf

SPECIAL NOTICES.

AMUSEMENTS.

THE STONE & ROSSTON
Circus Combination!

Organized on a scale of Unprecedented Magnificence, respectfully announce to the citizens of Washington and vicinity a short series of their SUPERB ENTERTAINMENTS, commencing on
THURSDAY EVENING, March 30,
and continue until further notice,
EVERY AFTERNOON AND EVENING.
Doors open at 2 and 7 p. m.
The spacious Pavilion will be erected on
NEW YORK AVENUE AND 6TH STREET.

The PROFUSION OF ATTRACTIONS will be presented with all the fascinating adjuncts essential to render them inimitable in superiority and marvelous in splendor.

Among the pre-eminent EQUESTRIANS, GYMNASTS, ACROBATS, PANCRATISTS, POSTURERS, EQUILIBRISTS, PANTOMIMISTS, HUMORISTS, DANSEUSES, and other Classic Artistes, are:

LE JEUNE BURTE, the Premier Horseman,
Messrs. MURRAY & HUTCHINSON, the Excelsior Gymnasts.
The DENZER BROTHERS, VALENTINE, RUDOLPH and CHARLES, the famous Acrobats.
The SAGRINEE FAMILY, consisting of Sigs. FERDINAND and PERELLE, M'lle SOPHIE and Master HENRI, Equestrians, Pancratists, Equilibrists, &c.,
Mr. DEN STONE, the accomplished Humorist,
Mr. CHARLES MONROE, the popular Clown and Vocalist.
Mr FRANK ROSSTON, the unequalled Equestrian Director,
Messrs. DREXEL, ANDROS, PICTON, GRAFF, BATTY, REMSEN, EBERLETTE, ECKBERG, MAGEE, TABOR, LIZARRO, WALDEN, ZARTIER and PILLOT, Masters LEON, AUTON, CLAUDE and CLARENCE, General Performers, constituting a

CONGRESS OF TALENT
ABSOLUTELY PEERLESS.

Prof. G. P. Hutchinson's WONDERFUL DOGS, trained to a point of perfection almost incredible, are attached to this Grand Combination.

The STUD OF HORSES and PONIES are unsurpassable as regards beauty and [illegible], and are splendid representatives of admired breeds.

The PAVILION, WARDROBE, TRAPPINGS, PROPERTIES, PARAPHERNALIA and GENERAL OUTFIT are entirely new, and were manufactured and imported expressly for Messrs. STONE & ROSSTON, at a cost of $50,000.

Admission, 50 cents. Reserved Seats, 75 cents. Children, to Reserved Seats, 50 cents.

For full details see Showmen's Pictorials, Illustrated Descriptive Bills and Programmes, Display Bills, Lithographs, &c. mh 30-tw

TELEGRAPHIC NEWS.

[FROM THE EXTRA STAR OF YESTERDAY.]

VICTORY!!!
LEE OVERWHELMED.
HIS LINES BROKEN!!
GRANT CRUSHING HIM ON THE EAST!!
SHERIDAN ON THE WEST!!!
SOUTHSIDE RAILROAD OURS!!!
Dispatches from the President.
Official War Bulletins.

WAR DEPARTMENT, WASHINGTON, D. C., 6 a. m., April 2, 1865.
Major General J. A. Dix, New York:

A dispatch just received from Gen. Grant at City Point, announces the triumphant success of our arms after three days of hard fighting, during which the forces on both sides exhibited unsurpassed valor.

EDWIN M. STANTON, Secretary of War.

"CITY POINT, VA., 5.30 a. m., April 2, 1865.—A dispatch from Gen. Grant states that Gen. Sheridan, commanding cavalry and infantry, has carried everything before him. He captured three brigades of infantry, a wagon train, and several batteries of artillery. The prisoners captured will amount to several thousand. Respectfully,

"T. S. BOWERS, A. A. G."

WAR DEPARTMENT, WASHINGTON, April 2, 1865, 11 a. m.
Major General Dix, New York:

The following dispatch from the President, dated at City Point, eight this morning, gives the latest intelligence from the front, where a furious battle was raging with continued success to the Union arms.

E. M. STANTON, Secretary of War.

"CITY POINT, VA., 8.30 a. m. April 2, 1865.—*Hon. E. M. Stanton, Secretary of War:* Last night Gen. Grant telegraphed that Gen. Sheridan, with his cavalry and 5th corps, had captured three brigades of infantry, a train of wagons, and several batteries, prisoners amounting to several thousand. This morning, Gen. Grant having ordered an attack along the whole line, telegraphs as follows:

"Both Wright and Parke got through the enemy's lines.

"The battle now rages furiously. General Sheridan, with his cavalry, the 5th corps, and Miles' division of the 2d corps, which was sent to him since one o'clock this morning, is now sweeping down from the west. All now looks highly favorable. General Ord is engaged, but I have not yet heard the result in his front.

A. LINCOLN."

WAR DEPARTMENT, WASHINGTON, April 2—12.30 P. M.
Major General John A. Dix, New York:

The President in the subjoined telegram gives the latest news from the front.

EDWIN M. STANTON, Secretary of War.

CITY POINT, 11 a. m. April 2, 1865.—*Hon. Edwin M. Stanton, Secretary of War:* Dispatches frequently coming in. All going finely. Parke, Wright and Ord, extending from the Appomattox to Hatcher's Run, have all broken through the enemy's entrenched lines, taking some guns, forts and prisoners. Sheridan with his own cavalry, 5th corps and part of the 2d, is coming in from the west on the enemy's flank, and Wright is already tearing up the Southside Railroad.

A. LINCOLN.

IMPORTANT FROM TEXAS.

That State to Secede from the Confederacy—General Lew. Wallace Meets the Rebel General Slaughter.

[Correspondence of the New York Herald.]

NEW ORLEANS, March 20.—I learn from a reliable gentleman, who has just returned from the Rio Grande, the following important facts:

The steamship Clinton carried out to Brazos Santiago Major General Lew. Wallace, who was sent to the Rio Grande on a special mission, supposed to concern the expulsion of our consul at Matamoras by Maximilian, and the return of rebel deserters by General Mejia.

The result of the consul affair is not known. It is not even known that any explanation whatever was demanded; but the conference with Mejia was entirely satisfactory. That officer had simply entered into an arrangement with the rebel General Slaughter for the delivery of murderers and thieves escaping from their respective States.

General Slaughter sent a note to General Wallace requesting an interview, which was granted, and the meeting took place at Point Isabel, Texas. The best feeling existed between the Union and rebel parties, and a good social time was enjoyed.

The result was that the Clinton, bearing a colonel of Wallace's staff, with despatches for General Canby, was sent back to New Orleans, *with orders to land at the wharf of Galveston on her return.*

General Wallace remained in Texas. He is probably now at Galveston, awaiting the arrival of the Clinton. She sails for that port to-night.

The Trans-Mississippi Rebel Army to Establish the Independent Republic of Texas.

The same informant states that the leaders of the trans-Mississippi army, fully convinced of the utter hopelessness of the rebel cause, have resolved to secede therefrom and proclaim the independence of Texas as a sovereign State, preparatory, probably, to seeking for readmission into the old Union.

The Brownsville Ranchero bitterly denounces this scheme, which proves that there must be some foundation for it.

APPALLING CALAMITY.

Burning of the Steamer Gen. Lyon—400 to 500 Troops and Refugees on Board—A Few Known to have been saved.

NEW YORK, April 2—The steamer General Sedgwick, from Wilmington on the 30th, has arrived here.

She reports that on the 31st inst., at 10.30 a. m., off Hatteras, she saw a steamer in shore on fire. She proved to be the General Lyon, from Wilmington for Fortress Monroe, with four or five hundred troops and refugees on board. The wind was blowing a gale, and the General Sedgwick could not launch boats, spars, wood work, &c. Seven were taken from the hospitals of Wilmington.

The list given of the saved by the General Sedgwick comprises only twenty-eight names, including most of the officers of General Lyon, a few few refugees and soldiers of the 99th, 89th and 6th New York, the 22d and the 5th Ohio regiments.

A schooner was seen picking up men, but it is not known how many she saved.

When the General Sedgwick left, the Lyon had burnt to a shell, and was fast drifting on to the breakers.

FROM HILTON HEAD, S. C.

Rebel Conscription in Georgia Resisted—Present Commerce of Savannah.

NEW YORK, April 2.—The steamer Arago from Hilton Head, brings files of the Savannah Herald to the 30th of March, inclusive. Hundreds are returning to their home and business.

Mr. Kilbourn, the Treasury agent, was in Savannah, en route for Fernandina, to establish an agency.

Since Sherman's capture of Savannah, two hundred and sixty steamships and steamers, fifteen ships, eight brigs, and sixty-six schooners have entered the port.

The village of [illegible], S. C., by its loyal leaders, is to [illegible] for its government a recorder, marshal, and [illegible]. Only freemen are to vote, and the [illegible] nominated are of the same class.

This is one of the reforms in South Carolina.

FROM MOBILE BAY.

Heavy Firing Heard in the Direction of the City—Operations of Our Land Forces.

CAIRO, March 31.—A despatch from Fish River Point, near Alabama city, of the 20th, says that the fleet went up the bay to-day and shelled Newport, Bells Row, and Howard landing, doing considerable damage. No response was made by the rebels.

NEW YORK, April 2.—The Herald's correspondence from the front of Mobile, dated March 23, says:

"Smith's 16th corps, accompanied by General Canby and staff, that day arrived at Derby's Mills, on Fish river, on the east side of Mobile Bay, ten miles distant from the bay and twenty-six miles from Mobile city. The entire 13th corps, under Generals Gordon and Granger was expected to join the 16th during the evening of the 23. The corps moved by land from Navy Cove, at the lower end of the bay, a distance of forty miles, and in the march not more than fifty rebel soldiers altogether were encountered.

"No opposition worthy of name was made to the advance of either corps, and no rebel works were encountered. The movement was a complete surprise. The reason for not expecting an advance was probably owing to the almost impassable nature of the country roads, which had to be corduroyed.

"General Canby's movement on the west side of the bay was probably a feint. Heavy firing in the direction of Mobile had been heard for twenty-four hours previous to the 22d, and it was supposed to proceed from an engagement between the monitors and rebel shore batteries."

A Fort Gaines letter of the 25th states that transports and gunboats were busily landing troops on the opposite side of Mobile Bay.

General Granger left for his command on the 19th. General Thomas had been heard from; he is all right.

A Barrancas letter states that Steele's army commenced their march in the advance on the 18th, taking the road to Perdido river, eight miles from Pensacola. He reported that his army would move through Baldwin county, Alabama, striking for Blakely Landing, forty-five miles above Mobile, where they expect to form a junction with the column from Mobile bay.

The rebel cavalry had made some skirmishing with the advance. Piers and wharves had been rebuilt at Pensacola. Several reconnoissances had been made in Mobile bay, and an attack was soon expected to be made.

FROM MONTREAL.

Secession Sympathizers Excited—Desperate Attempts to Influence Public Opinion.

MONTREAL, April 1.—Southern refugees and their sympathizers are having a lively time here to-day. Their leading organ has issued an extra, and they are circulating it throughout the city. It is headed "Infamous Conspiracy of the Provincial Executive for the Extradition of the St. Albans Raiders," and attempts to show that the accused after being re-arrested will be secretly removed to St. Catherine, and the charge of a breach of neutrality there will be prepared to fail, but they will be carried for examination and committal before the Toronto judges, who will obey the orders of the Government.

TORONTO, April 1.—A despatch from Montreal says that the money voted by Parliament has been paid to the St. Albans banks.

FROM NORTH CAROLINA.

Good News from Stoneman's Advance—Capture of the Town of Boone.

HEADQUARTERS EAST TENNESSEE, BOONE, N. C., March 27, via KNOXVILLE, April 1.—The advance of General Stoneman's force, commanded by Major Keagh, A. D. C., entered and captured the town of Boone, North Carolina, at 12 o'clock to-day.

The rebel force was routed with a loss of ten men killed, and sixty wounded and prisoners.

Major Barnes' battalion, 12th Kentucky cavalry, lost a few men wounded.

General Stoneman's command is now well into North Carolina, and will be heard from soon in the heart of the rebellion.

[Boone is the capital of the Watauga county, two hundred miles by north of Raleigh.]

FROM MEMPHIS.

Petition to Restore Civil Law in Tennessee—Action of Gen. Washburne.

MEMPHIS, March 30, via CAIRO, April 1.—Petitions have been signed by many merchants here praying the President to declare Tennessee no longer an insurrectionary State, and the Secretary of the Treasury will remit the present tax on goods from Northern States.

The Memphis and Charleston railroad is running to Collierville and will soon be further extended. The telegraph is working to Lafayette.

As another evidence of Gen. Washburne's desire to restore civil law, he has ordered the United States military police to confine their attention entirely to military offenders.

THE BATTLE ON FRIDAY.

Further Details of the Fight—Losses in the Fifth Corps—The Rebels Driven from the Field with Heavy Loss.

A letter from headquarters Army of the Potomac, dated Friday evening, says:

To-day there has been severe fighting on some part of the line, from morning till night, the result of which has been the extension of our line still further westward, although at considerable loss in killed and wounded.

The 2d division of the 5th corps, supported by the 3d, was thrown out by the White Oak road, west of the Boydton plank road, and ordered to reach and take position there. After crossing a small branch of Gravelly Run, and while about forming in line, our troops were fired upon by a heavy force of the enemy who were concealed in the woods, and also by the rebel artillery posted in favorable positions. Our men stood their ground for a while, but the enemy appearing to be moving to the left, as if to turn their flank, the line was forced back to their first position, where they were rallied and soon checked the enemy's advance.

About the same time another attack was made on the right flank of the 5th corps, but General Miles's division of the 2d, being posted here, made a brilliant charge and doubled up the enemy, driving them a long distance, leaving hundreds of their dead and wounded on the field.

This was a very handsome affair, and the division receives the highest praise for the manner in which it was done.

The loss on our side was about four hundred, as nearly as can be ascertained, nearly all in the first division.

The 5th corps, about noon, again took up the advance and drove the enemy back about a mile and a half, and long before dark had reached the White Oak road, which they had started for in the morning, and established their line across the same, driving the rebels into their strong works at Hatcher's Run. Their loss in the day's work will not be far from twelve hundred.

Among the casualties reported are Major Mills, A. A. G., on Gen. Humphrey's staff, killed by a shell; Col. Sergeant, 110th Pennsylvania, severely wounded; Gen. Dennison, commanding brigade in 2d division, 5th corps, slightly wounded.

An attack was also made in front of the 6th corps, but it was not successful.

After the rebels were driven back in front of the 5th corps an attack was made, with both infantry and cavalry, on Sheridan's force, about three miles from the Southside road, near Sutherland station, driving them back toward Dinwiddie, but he subsequently gained much more than he had lost.

The roads are in a terrible condition, it being almost impossible to move trains over them. The heavy rains have swollen the streams, and the engineers are busy day and night laying bridges and corduroys.

The loss of the enemy is not known, but, judging from the number of dead lying in the woods and ravines where the fighting occurred, it must be at least as heavy as our own. We took about one hundred and fifty prisoners during the day.

Financial.

[From N. Y. Sunday Herald.]

The gold market has been almost paralyzed since the recent panic, speculation having rested under the shock. The assault of the bears was so heavy and sudden that the bulls were driven from the field, and they have not yet had time to recover. The stormy days of the three weeks of intermittent panic have given place to quiet and stagnation. The gold room has been transformed from a howling and overcrowded pandemonium into a sparsely attended chamber of individuals waiting for something to turn up. The fluctuations in the price from day to day have hardly been worth their watching, while the prospect of decisive military events, and the prevailing belief in the possibility of an immediate peace, have deterred operators for a rise from venturing upon the market.

Yesterday, however, the latter showed increasing firmness, and but for the extreme depression under which it has been laboring, and the corresponding difficulty of influencing quotations, it would have probably shown considerable buoyancy, as the war news fell short of the general expectation in the street. Cash gold is still scarce, and ¼ per cent. is offered for it over the regular rate.

The money market is easy at 7 per cent. with exceptional transactions in governments at 6. Commercial paper is entirely out of favor, owing to the distrust of [illegible]. The best grade of commercial paper is quoted at [illegible] per cent.

Foreign exchange is dull at 109 a ¼ for bankers' sterling at sixty days, and 110¼ at three days.

On a Lee shore—the Confederacy.

The Clichy prison, in Paris, is to be abolished.

New Haven is divorcing at the rate of five couples per week.

The Philadelphia Inquirer.

PRICE TWO CENTS. | PHILADELPHIA, TUESDAY, APRIL 4, 1865. | PRICE TWO CENTS.

RICHMOND!

Babylon Is Fallen!!

GENERAL WEITZEL OCCUPIES THE CITY!

Philadelphia Colored Troops the First to Enter!

THE FLEEING REBELS FIRE THEIR CAPITAL.

Weitzel's Negroes Extinguish the Flames.

THE "INDOMITABLE ULYSSES" MARCHING ON.

Lee's Army In Full Retreat!

OUR FORCES CLOSE ON THEIR HEELS.

Enormous Losses of the Rebels!

OFFICIAL DESPATCHES FROM PRESIDENT LINCOLN.

The Whole Country in a Blaze of Enthusiasm!

JUBILEE AT THE NATIONAL CAPITAL.

Speeches by Stanton and Seward.

SPECIAL CORRESPONDENCE FROM THE FRONT.

OFFICIAL WAR GAZETTE.

FIRST BULLETIN.

WASHINGTON, April 3.—To Major-General Dix, New York:—The following telegram from the President, announcing the evacuation of Petersburg, and probably of Richmond, has just been received by the War Department.

E. M. STANTON, Secretary of War.

CITY POINT, Va., April 3.—Hon. E. M. Stanton, Secretary of War:—This morning General Grant reports Petersburg evacuated, and is confident Richmond also is. He is pushing forward to cut off, if possible, the retreating army.

A. LINCOLN.

SECOND BULLETIN.

Richmond is Ours.

WASHINGTON, April 3, 10·15 A. M.—Major-General Dix:—It appears from a despatch of General Weitzel, just received by this Department, that our forces under his command are in Richmond, having taken it at 8·15 this morning.

E. M. STANTON, Secretary of War.

THIRD BULLETIN.

Confirmation of the Capture of Richmond.

WASHINGTON, April 3, 12 M.—To Major-General Dix, New York:—The following official confirmation of the capture of Richmond, and announcing that the city is on fire, has just been received by this Department.

CITY POINT, Va., April 3, 11 A. M.—General Weitzel telegraphs as follows:—

"We took Richmond at 8.15 this morning. I captured many guns. The enemy left in great haste.

"The city is on fire in one place. We are making every effort to put it out.

"The people received us with enthusiastic expressions of joy.

"General Grant started early this morning, with the army, towards the Danville road, to cut off Lee's retreating army, if possible.

President Lincoln has gone to the front.

(Signed) T. S. BOWERS, Asst. Adjt.-Gen.

E. M. STANTON, Secretary of War.

FROM GRANT'S VICTORIOUS ARMY.

Special Correspondence of the Inquirer.

HEAD QUARTERS ARMY OF THE POTOMAC, Saturday, April 1, 1865—Midnight.

From out of the "wilderness" of scrub oaks, dwarf pines, swamps, ravines and knolls, through and over which our lines stretch, some intelligible idea of our operations yesterday begin to be apparent. This State of Virginia is worth fighting for as embodying a political principle; but as so many acres of ground, it is not worth one single human life. We thought at the Wilderness that we had reached the acme of all that was horrible and miserable and perplexing in the aspect of nature, but then we had not seen the country southwest of Petersburg. A tangled mass of ravines and hillocks, of small streamlets running in all possible directions, of little by-roads shooting off to every point of the compass, seeming to come from nowhere, and to be leading nowhere, intersecting each other at every conceivable angle of dense forests of the meanest and most detestable kind of scrub oak and pine; picture this, and throw in here and there a worn-out open field, with an old dilapidated farm-house in the centre, and you have a faint picture of the difficulties of the country in which we are operating. Out of this knotted mass the "special" must pluck the salient points for the information of the public; must ride miles on miles even to see the front of one Corps, and visit its various head-quarters, and tired, at night must write out what he has seen, what heard, what opines from both; is it any wonder that under circumstances like these his accounts are sometimes vague, sometimes unsatisfactory. Give him a fight like Fort Steadman, where he knows the ground, and where the ground is open, he does well enough. Put him in the kind of country we are in now and he does as well as he can.

Premising that the day has been comparatively quiet on the right of our offensive line, composed of the Second and Twenty-fourth Corps, it is the intention first to give the public some idea of

The Relative Position of the Two Armies.

A battle, fierce, sanguinary and decisive, may come off any day on this very ground, and the people will take a natural interest in a section that has already become historic, and may become sacred in the nation's calendar.

First, it must be premised that our old line in front of Petersburg, from the Appomattox to the left of the Weldon Road, remains intact and held precisely as they were before our present movement was initiated, running, until yesterday, to Hatcher's Run, but changed from Fort Sampson to the left, by the advance of the Twenty-fourth Corps, consequent upon the capture of the enemy's intrenched picket line.

From Petersburg to Hatcher's Run, by the Vaughn Road is seven and a half miles, and by the Boydton Road seven miles. The Fifth Corps front is a prolongation of our line beyond the Boydton Road, with the cavalry beyond them again, the line facing generally northeast, the flank being towards the South Side Road, from the bend of the road to the southwest.

Thus much by way of necessary preface. It remains to sketch events to the present moment, and beginning on the right with

The Twenty-fourth Corps,

Two divisions of which, those of Turner and Foster, with one of the Twenty-fifth Corps (Birney's), all under the command of Major-General Gibbons, are operating here. Birney's Division has been held as a reserve thus far. Foster is on the right of the Twenty-fourth, then Turner, forming connection with Hayes, holding the right of the Second Corps. Along General Gibbons' front the day has been quiet. This morning just before daybreak the Rebels essayed an attack upon Turner's pickets, coming in the old yelling style, but they quickly came to grief. Turner's line did not budge an inch, except to gather in sixty of the adventurous Rebels as prisoners and to kill and maim some few more. The prisoners sent to the rear, Turner's line quietly composed itself again, and during the remainder of the day the Rebels behaving themselves well, and we not yet being ready to disturb the apparent peacefulness of the neighborhood, it has been quiet until about 9·30 P. M., when a brisk cannonading begun and yet continues (10·20 P. M.). What it means it is impossible to-night to say. It seems by the sound to be general, on the Sixth Corps front as well as the Twenty-fourth, and an occasional distant rumble from the right indicates that the Ninth Corps is also adding to the uproar.

Passing still to the left, and

The Second Corps,

The day has been as peaceful as on the right. Occasional picket skirmishing has been going on, but nothing more serious in the way of fighting. The men of the Corps have been busy, however, building roads to the rear, cutting timber to the front for the artillery to get range, and other work preliminary to action. While mentioning roads it is but justice to notice the labors of the Chiefs of pioneers of the several divisions; Captain G. W. Cook, Sixty-first New York, of the First, Captain H. Y. Russell, of the Second, and Captain Charles Bowers, Eighth New Jersey, of the Third, whose tasks, although herculean and apparently impossible, have been successfully accomplished. Energy will accomplish wonders, and the energy of these officers has already made passable the impassable country around Dabney's Mills and beyond, substantial corduroy roads now cutting the country in every direction, and rendering access to the various parts of the line easy and sure.

Just beyond night the Second Division line was advanced somewhat, being pushed close up to the Rebel fort at Hatcher Run, General Smythe covering it with his musketry so entirely that the Rebels cannot use its guns. Were it not for the very extensive slashing in front of this line, both before the Second and Twenty-fourth Corps, we could easily carry it by assault, but this slashing is so intricate that men can hardly crawl through it singly, and it would be impossible to maintain a line of battle through it under anything like a respectable fire.

General Mott still holds his position on the left of General Hayes, and presses as close upon the Rebel line as his confrere, but his line, like that of Hayes, has been quiet.

General Miles still stretches across the Boydton Road in the position occupied yesterday. His fight yesterday was a brilliant one, and answered fully the purpose for which it was begun, being a diversion in favor of the Fifth Corps. His onslaught upon their line near Burgess Mill induced the Rebels to hurry men to the threatened point, and thus gave Warren and Sheridan less to contend against.

General Humphries was heard of to-day, only on his skirmish line. He is determined to know exactly the position of the enemy on the front of his corps, and so he goes where he can see it.

Proceeding still to the left with the story of to-day, I take up

The Fifth Corps.

The operations of Gen. Warren yesterday have already reached you. This morning early the Corps moved off on the Boydton Road. Griffin in advance, [illegible]

about two miles, and taking a road running nearly west, came in contact with the enemy near what the Rebels call Five Points, which, so near as it can be located with the assistance of imperfect maps, is from three to four miles northwest of Dinwiddie Court House.

In the afternoon General Warren got into line, with Griffin on the right, Ayres on the centre and Crawford on the left. It should be remembered here that this movement cut Sheridan and Warren off from all connection with the remainder of our army, and their fighting this afternoon has been an entirely independent affair. The distance at which the corps has been engaged, the difficulties of communication have been such that it is impossible to more than outline the affair, if even that can be done. Artillery was but little used, but the musketry was terrific along the whole line. The battle began at five in the afternoon, and by dark, when it ceased, the firing had receded far beyond the point of beginning, showing that our forces had driven the enemy from the field. The extent of our success, the relative losses of the contending forces, and other details necessary to a full knowledge of the history enacted to-day, it is impossible to send. The country in that section of Virginia corresponds to what surrounds us here, except that it is level. There are the same swamps, the same horrible pine forests, the same treacherous soil. Is this whole State of Virginia nothing but a wilderness of worn-out farms, swamps and pineries?

General Sheridan,

Moving this morning upon the left flank of Warren with the three cavalry divisions, has been, to-day at his old business of driving the Rebels before him. Custer, Devins and Davis have again proved themselves soldiers of mettle, but here, as with the Fifth Corps, we are without details. We know that Sheridan drove the enemy before him up the Boydton Road, and over the country to the neighborhood of Five Points; that he fought his infantry as well as cavalry in connection with the Fifth Corps, the battery attached to Custer's Division doing the most of the artillery work, and we are certain that the day has been a triumph for Sheridan and the Fifth Corps, but we know no more. The fighting has been an open field fight, and has occurred so near the South Side Railroad that a [illegible]

of the road, and although no news of the event has reached us here, the probabilities are that the cavalry and the Fifth Corps are already engaged in the work of tearing it to flinders. The distance from Five Points to the South Side Road is only about a mile and a half, and a defeat there is fatal to the railroad.

General Grant

Still has his head-quarters at Dabney Mills. That impertubable face of his tells no tales whatever; things may be all right or all wrong, but not a line of his countenance betrays the knowledge to the observer, hence we get no news from looking at him.

General Meade

Was, this afternoon, at a point above a mile to the right of the Vaughn road, and the same distance to the left of Hatcher Run. This meeting of Generals Grant and Meade at so near the angle made by the Rebels at Hatcher Run indicates stirring work in its neighborhood to-morrow.

General Ord

Has established his head-quarters at Humphries' Station, and is in charge of our whole old line, from Hatcher Run to the Appomattox, as well as his own line on the Bermuda Hundred front and on the north of the James.

What of

The Enemy

During all these movements of ours? Longstreet's Corps, composed of the divisions of Pickett, Constant and Kershaw, have been transferred from the north of the James to our extreme left, and, together with Fitzhugh Lee's cavalry, seven thousand strong, has been fighting Sheridan and Warren to-day. Hill's Corps and Bushrod Johnson's division of Anderson's Corps are opposite the Second and Twenty-fourth Corps, and Gordon's Corps opposite the Sixth and Ninth. What they have got opposite Weitzel, north of the James, it is hard to say, as their whole army is already accounted for, except one division of Anderson's Corps.

The heavy cannonading spoken of in the early part of this letter still (midnight) continues unabated along the whole front of the Sixth and Ninth Corps, and news has just reached me that is preliminary to an assault in front of Petersburg, ordered to be made by the Sixth and Ninth Corps at daylight in the morning. I may possibly yet close this letter by the announcement of the capture of the long beleaguered city.

Later.

April 2, 6 A. M.—The news from Sheridan and Warren this morning is that the victory is overwhelming. The South Side Road in our possession, Longstreet's Corps utterly broken to pieces. We having more prisoners than we can take care of.

The tremendous cannonading, which began last night at 10½ o'clock, yet continues. No assault has yet been made. [illegible]

R. [illegible]

RICHMOND!

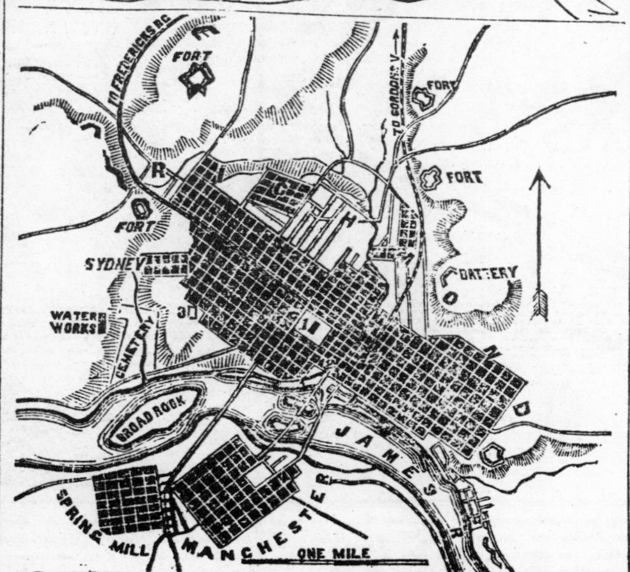

RICHMOND.

The Different Campaigns Against the Rebel Capital.

How Ulysses S. Grant (Unconditional Surrender Grant) Took the Rebel Stronghold.

Richmond, the great hot-bed of Secession and Rebellion, has fallen. After the long and weary months of anxious expectation through which we have passed, it is difficult to realize that the skillful plans and manoeuvrings of "the indomitable Ulysses," have at length been crowned with success. And at this important stage of the war, with the capital of the enemy in our hands, and his main army broken and scattered, it may not be unprofitable to cast a cursory glance at the campaigns heretofore conducted against the Rebel capital.

At the first outbreak of the Rebellion, flushed with the cowardly firing on the national standard at Fort Sumter, and over-confident of success, the popular cry of "On to Richmond" was raised, and our legions were hurried into the disastrous battle of Bull Run, in July, 1861. With its dearly bought experience ended the first campaign against the beleaguered city which now lies at the mercy of our colored troops.

Then it was that MCCLELLAN was placed in charge of our panic-stricken forces, and, after organizing and disciplining them, once more they were led "on to Richmond." The "Seven Days' Battles," the famous series of engagements presenting the strange military anomaly of seven distinct victories, combining to constitute a defeat, followed, ending in a second disastrous retreat in July, 1862. The enemy then assumed the offensive, and so continued a forward movement northward until his check at Antietam in September of that year. The campaign which was ended by that battle showed MCCLELLAN to be so entirely outgeneraled by LEE that he was removed by the Government, and succeeded by General BURNSIDE.

On the 15th of December 1863, the new commander commenced the third movement against the Rebel capital. Defeated in the memorable battle of Fredericksburg on the 13th of December, BURNSIDE was replaced by HOOKER, who, after the terrible battle of Chancellorsville, May 2 and 3, 1863, was in turn superseded by General MEADE. When the latter, under the orders of the President, took command, on the 28th of June 1863, his army was mainly concentrated at Frederick, Md. The enemy were supposed to be advancing on Harrisburg, Pa., then garrisoned by raw militia. Of course he was obliged to assume the defensive, until by his brilliant victory at Gettysburg, the first of July, the enemy were sent "whirling" back from whence they came. It was not, however, until the 1st of December, that MEADE crossed the Rapidan and inaugurated the fifth campaign against Richmond.

Little was done, however, until early in March, 1864, when "Unconditional Surrender GRANT," who had just been commissioned as Lieutenant-General of the Army of the United States, assumed command of the Army of the Potomac. Activity at once became the order of the day, and on the 4th of May he moved against the enemy. Then it was that the great series of movements was inaugurated that have just culminated in a success whose magnitude has almost frenzied with joy the loyal people of the land. It is unnecessary to recapitulate the great events that have transpired in the working out of the Lieutenant-General's plan of advance. The great battles of the Wilderness, in May, satisfied the Federal Commander that it was by slow and gradual advances that his end was to be gained, and not by hasty or precipitate movements. His strategic operations were commenced, and now, after four long and weary years of conflict for the nation, he has the satisfaction of announcing to his Government the capture of the hitherto impregnable Rebel stronghold, Richmond. All honor to him and to his gallant band of heroes. Long will their deeds of patriotism and daring be remembered, and imperishable will be the record they have inscribed on the pages of the book of fame and national glory.

THE GREAT STRUGGLE

Army of the Potomac

SHERIDAN'S TERRIBLE FIGHT.

Fifth Corps Goes to His Aid!

LEE'S FORCES FALL RAPIDLY BACK!

His Dead and Wounded Left In Our Hands.

Sheridan Takes 4000 Prisoners

A NUMBER OF CANNON CAPTURED!

The Rebels on the Full Retreat!

SOUTH SIDE RAILROAD SEVERED

Lee Hemmed In On All Points!

Details of Saturday's Movements.

HEAD-QUARTERS OF THE ARMY OF THE POTOMAC, April 1.—The greater portion of this army has not been engaged with the enemy to-day, the time being occupied in erecting works on the new line, and repairing the roads connecting the different corps.

The late rains rendered it impossible to move the wagon trains as fast as the troops advanced, one train taking forty-eight hours to move five miles, one thousand men assisting. But through the untiring energy and perseverance of the officers in charge of the Quartermaster and Commissary Departments the army has been almost as well supplied as while in their old quarters.

When the news of Sheridan's repulse reached here last evening, a part of the Fifth Corps was at once despatched to his aid, and it is expected that to-night or in the morning we shall receive good news from that quarter.

It appears that Sheridan was moving on the road leading to a place called the Five Forks, which is about three miles from the South Side Railroad, when two brigades of Pickett's Division, which had been ordered in a great hurry, came down on a road which runs from Sutherland Station to the one on which we were.

Sheridan's cavalry having, for the most part, passed the junction, this movement of the enemy threatened to cut him off. He, however, discovered his danger in time to get to his command with only a slight loss, at the same time taking about one hundred prisoners.

Both of the Lees were present, but one of them at a respectful distance. On being reinforced this morning by the Fifth Corps, the enemy fell back so rapidly that their dead and many of the wounded fell into our hands, as well as those of our own unavoidably left behind yesterday afternoon.

The attack made on the enemy's line in front of the Twenty fourth Corps was by Foster's Division, and about 200 prisoners were brought in, the One-hundred-and-forty-eighth New York taking the most of them.

Some three hundred or four hundred yards of ground was taken from them, and our picket line so much further advanced. At 4 A. M. this position was assaulted, and a few of our men captured, but in a very short time it was retaken with about sixty prisoners and a stand of colors.

Our loss up to the present time will not exceed 200, while that of the enemy on some parts of the line at least was greater than our own, but of course the total cannot be given. Major Dickinson, of the Fifteenth New York Heavy Artillery, is wounded and a prisoner.

The sharp-shooters brought into the Fifth Corps head-quarters this morning sixteen cavalrymen, belonging to William Henry Lee's command. They had been on picket, and were cut off by the force which went to the assistance of Sheridan.

[SECOND DESPATCH.]

HEAD-QUARTERS ARMY OF THE POTOMAC, April 1, Midnight.—A courier from Sheridan has just arrived with the most cheering news. The combined forces of cavalry and Warren's infantry advanced against the enemy this afternoon, driving them several miles, and capturing about four thousand prisoners and a number of guns.

They retreated to Five Forks, where they were flanked by a part of the Fifth Corps, which had moved down the White Oak road. It was here the large number of prisoners were taken. The Rebels then retreated south, along the White Oak Road, and were vigorously pursued by General Sheridan, while McKensil's cavalry, from the Army of the James, advanced west on the Ford Road, toward the South Side Road, and after the messenger left was only about three miles from it, and would undoubtedly reach it before morning.

Thus the last great line of railroad the Rebels have to supply their capital and Lee's army is about to be severed, and it is firmly believed they will immediately leave their present positions at Petersburg and Richmond.

Sharp cannonading is now going on near the centre of the line held by the left of the Sixth Corps.

Ice Freshet on the St. Lawrence.

MONTREAL, April 3.—The river rose several feet on Saturday and was piled with ice to a great height. One of the shoves came near striking a tube of the Victoria Bridge. Yesterday morning the river rose much higher, flooding Williams, Wellington, and other streets. Between five and six o'clock in the evening the ice shoved again, and the water rushed over the revetment wall, flooding Commission street. At about 11 o'clock it again rose as high as St. Paul and St. Giles streets.

The Grand Trunk Railroad between Bonaventure and the Tanneries is inundated.

This morning the inundated points of the city are covered with rafts formed with scows and boats.

At present by far the greater part of the Western portion of the city is inaccessible, except by boats. The flood is causing the greatest suffering and distress.

LATER.—Four o'clock P. M.—The water is slowly falling.

St. Domingo.

NEW YORK, April 3.—Advices received to-day from San Domingo deny the rumors of a counter revolution there. The Republic is free from any tumult, and the new Government is quietly organizing.

General F. de Rojas has been elected President, and nine eminent Dominicans, seven of them Generals in the army, have been appointed as his Cabinet or advisers. Among them are Antonio Polanco, brother of the President. A sovereign Constitutional Congress, consisting of nine representatives from each [illegible] has been called, and was to have been [illegible]

The New-York Times.

VOL. XIV......NO. 4220. NEW-YORK, TUESDAY, APRIL 4, 1865. PRICE FOUR CENTS

GRANT.

RICHMOND

AND

VICTORY!

The Union Army in the Rebel Capital.

Rout and Flight of the Great Rebel Army from Richmond.

Jeff. Davis and His Crew Driven Out.

Grant in Close Pursuit of Lee's Routed Forces.

Richmond and Petersburgh in Full Possession of Our Forces.

ENTHUSIASM IN THE REBEL CAPITAL.

The Citizens Welcome Our Army with Demonstrations of Joy.

RICHMOND FIRED BY THE ENEMY

Our Troops Save the City from Destruction.

THE EVACUATION OF PETERSBURGH.

FIRST DISPATCH.

[OFFICIAL.]

WAR DEPARTMENT, WASHINGTON, April 3—10 A. M.

To Major-Gen. Dix:

The following telegram from the President, announcing the EVACUATION OF PETERSBURGH and probably of Richmond, has just been received by this department:

EDWIN M. STANTON, Secretary of War.

CITY POINT, Va., April 3—8:30 A. M.

To Hon. Edwin M. Stanton, Secretary of War:

This morning Lieut.-Gen. GRANT reports Petersburgh evacuated, and he is confident that Richmond also is.

He is pushing forward to cut off, if possible, the retreating rebel army. A. LINCOLN.

THE CAPTURE OF RICHMOND.

SECOND DISPATCH.

WAR DEPARTMENT, WASHINGTON, D. C., April 3—10 A. M.

To Maj.-Gen. Dix:

It appears from a dispatch of Gen. WEITZEL just received by this Department, that our forces under his command ARE IN RICHMOND, having taken it at 8:15 this morning.

EDWIN M. STANTON, Secretary of War.

THIRD DISPATCH.

WAR DEPARTMENT, WASHINGTON, Monday, April 3—12 o'clock noon.

Maj.-Gen. Dix:

The following official confirmation of the capture of Richmond, and the announcement that the city is on fire has been received.

E. M. STANTON, Secretary of War.

CITY POINT, Monday, April 3—11 A. M.

To Edwin M. Stanton, Secretary of War:

Gen. WEITZEL telegraphs as follows:

"We took Richmond at 8:15 this morning. I captured many guns. The enemy left in great haste. The city is on fire in one place. Am making every effort to put it out. The people receive us with enthusiastic expressions of joy."

Gen. GRANT started early this morning with the army toward the Danville road, to cut off LEE's retreating army, if possible.

President LINCOLN has gone to the front.

T. S. BOWERS, A. A. G.

E. M. STANTON.

OUR SPECIAL ACCOUNTS.

Movements by Gen. Sheridan—His Call for Reinforcements—Four Thousand Prisoners Captured—Operations on the Petersburgh Front—The Gunboat Fleet Doing its Part.

From Our Own Correspondent.

HEADQUARTERS ARMY OF THE POTOMAC, Sunday, April 2—6 A. M.

After we quitted the field on Friday evening the left of the Fifth Corps swung about half a mile further round, and drove the enemy before them. But intelligence being received from Gen. SHERIDAN that the condition of the ground on his front was such that he could not operate with cavalry, and his advance had, therefore, been compelled to fall back. The Fifth Corps was ordered to go to his assistance, in order to relieve it and prevent its withdrawal. Being perceived and taken advantage of by the enemy, Gen. MILES' division of the Second Corps was advanced by the left flank in its front, and it was then withdrawn to the Boydtown road.

Gen. MILES' division of the Second then fell back to a position on the plankroad behind a temporary embankment that had been thrown up on Wednesday, leaving in the line he recently occupied nothing more than skirmishers, who were directed to fall back if attacked. The Second Division of the Fifth Corps, Gen. AYRES, set out early this morning to support Gen. SHERIDAN, and the divisions of Gen. GRIFFIN and Gen. CRAWFORD followed it about noon. They all formed a junction with Gen. SHERIDAN's Corps at a distance of some five miles from the Mrs. Butler house, and a general engagement commenced there about 3 o'clock.

I was not able to go out, as the distance is too great for me to accomplish anything in time for the mail. I understand, however, that the combined forces of Gens. SHERIDAN and WARREN succeeded, after a hotly contested fight, in putting the enemy to flight. They captured four thousand prisoners, four batteries of artillery, a large train of loaded wagons and a number of cattle. The rebel loss in killed and wounded, as well as our own was very heavy, but I am unable to give any estimate of the number.

On our lines during the day there was no fighting except on the Twenty-fourth Corps front. The rebels assaulted the pickets of that corps, and attempted to retake the picket line, from which they were driven yesterday. They were speedily repulsed with a loss of about twenty-five killed and wounded and sixty-four prisoners. Our loss was fifteen in the aggregate.

In the afternoon our troops were massed at three places in the Ninth Corps front, at two in the Sixth, and one in the Twenty-fourth, one in the Twenty-fifth, and two in the Second, with a view of making several demonstrations on the enemy's works and going through them, if necessary, for the complete development of the plan of attack. In pursuance with this design our artillery opened a furious cannonading along the entire front at about 11 P. M., which was continued with little intermission until 6 o'clock this morning. At 3 this morning, such of our troops as it was deemed proper to send in were got into position in front of our works and held ready to make the assault.

I have not yet had time to ascertain which troops were led to the assault, nor the results at different points, and am only able to speak of the Second Division, Gen. POTTER's, of the Ninth Corps. This division was posted on that part of the line between forts Sedgwick and Davis, and some time before the hour of attack arrived the Brigade Commanders Gens. GRIFFIN and CURTIN, perceiving the opportunity to do so without endangering their own men made a sortie and captured one hundred and thirty-three men and four officers of the rebel pickets.

His picket-line was completely surprised, and only knew of the attack when called upon to surrender. At this hour, 6 A. M., there is exceedingly heavy firing along the entire line from Deep Bottom to the Boydtown plank-road, and the fleet of gunboats on the James River are participating in it.

The assault on the enemy's works commenced at 4 o'clock in several places, and is still progressing, but with what success is not yet known. In the front of the Second Division of the Ninth Corps there seems to be more artillery engaged than elsewhere on the line, except at the point where the gunboats are engaged. But Gen. POTTER and his two able Brigade Generals, GRIFFIN and CURTIN, are holding their men well up the work, and the determination is universal throughout the division to go through if required. Gen. POTTER and his staff are in the hottest part of the field, overseeing the assault in person. The General feels, no doubt, that his front is one of the most important positions on the whole line, and from its proximity to the rebel works, most liable to be broken through, except that opposite Fort Steadman, and he is consequently extremely solicitous respecting it. The front at Fort Steadman is ably defended by Gen. WILCOX.

LATER.

Part of the line on the left is said to have made a successful demonstration and captured a number of prisoners. If possible to get it through in time, I will send you particulars, dispatching it to City Point by express before the boat leaves.

Among the prisoners captured by the Ninth Corps are eight officers, one of them a Major. Col. GOWAN, of the Forty-eighth Pennsylvania, was badly wounded, as also Col. WINSLOW and Major STEINBERGE, of the One Hundred and Sixth New-York; Col. GREGG, One Hundred and Seventy-ninth New-York, badly wounded and reported dead. The fighting was so severe that the loss on both sides must necessarily be very heavy. The rebels fought our men hand to hand when we were about climbing the parapet of the fort, although lying down at the time to avoid the fire of our advancing line. Gen. GRIFFIN, of the Second Brigade of the Division, led the way into their works, and when Gen. POTTER sent to ask if he could hold the works, and if not to fall back, his reply was, "Tell Gen. POTTER I can hold the works. Send me more men if you can; but I will hold the works." He took command of the division on Gen. POTTER being wounded. Gen. CURTIN, of the First Brigade, also behaved with great gallantry, holding his men up to the works till an entrance was effected, and then dashing forward at their head driving the enemy before him. This fight, even if not ultimately successful, proves the old Ninth Corps to be equal to any emergency. The task set for it is the worst this army ever had to do, and so far it has accomplished the object unaided. Everybody here thinks those who are left of us will quarter in Petersburgh to-night, and that the old stars and stripes will wave over the cockade city ere the setting of the sun. In taking Petersburgh we draw the cord that will soon strangle the rebellion in Richmond.

Gen. WILCOX is also in the field with his staff. The lines here are also very close together, and if our forces should be repulsed and disordered, the enemy would have an excellent opportunity to inflict serious damage, and make us pay dearly for the temerity we have evinced in attempting to assault such almost impregnable works as those he occupies along this line.

Gen. HARTRANFT's Division is engaged in the assault, but I am not able to say at what particular point or with what success. It is composed wholly of new troops who have never been in any engagement but that of the 25th ult., but they behaved so nobly on that occasion that great things are expected of them. And they have such regard for their brave and noble Division Commander that they will no doubt strive hard for the sake of his reputation and their own. Gen. PARKE, the Corps Commander, is also near the scene of action with his staff and within range of the enemy's guns directing the operations. From the present aspect of affairs he will have cause to be proud of his corps ere the day closes as we are no doubt already partially within the enemy's lines, strong as they are, whether we can hold them will soon be known. It is thought here that we can both take and hold them.

1 *o'clock. A. M.*—The demonstration in front of the Second division of the Ninth Corps promises to be a success. We have captured two of their forts, guns and all, and the line of works between and on either flank, and have taken two hundred more prisoners. The fight is still raging furiously. Our loss must be heavy, but at this hour it is impossible to give any estimate. We have succeeded in compelling them to bring their forces from the left and thus opened the way there for SHERIDAN and WARREN to operate successfully. Their force in this front, and which we are now fighting, is Gen. GORDON's corps, principally Southern troops from Alabama, Ga., and South Carolina. They have fought hard since the attack commenced, and still continue to dispute the ground inch by inch.

I regret to say that Gen. POTTER is severely wounded, being shot through the stomach. It is not classed as a mortal wound, but is highly dangerous.

I have not yet been able to learn how matters stand elsewhere, but we have now a strong force within their line of works and will hold them. By to-night, I hope to write you from Petersburgh.

H. H. YOUNG.

Skirmishing on March 30 Near Supporty Cross-Roads.

From Our Own Correspondent.

DINWIDDIE COURT-HOUSE, Va., Thursday, March 30. Via WASHINGTON, Monday, April 3—8:45 P. M.

The advance of Gen. SHERIDAN's command crossed Hatcher's Run yesterday, meeting only slight opposition and annoyance at that place from the enemy's cavalry.

W. H. F. LEE's cavalry, three brigades, was in front, but did not see fit to make a stand.

To-day, in an attempt to reach Supporty cross-roads, some of PICKETT's command and LEE's cavalry formed a line of battle and held the ground. In the skirmish that took place the following named persons were wounded:

KILLED AND WOUNDED.

John Leonard, Company F, Sixth United States Cavalry, left thigh, flesh; James N. Glosswax, Company A, Sixth United States Cavalry, hip; John Thompson, Company M, Sixth United States Cavalry; Henry M. Feelan, First United States Cavalry; Patrick Germon, Company F, Sixth United States Cavalry; John Mooney, Company M, Seventh Michigan; Sergt. Marsh, First Michigan, killed; Sergt. J. L. Cullek, Seventh Michigan, foot; Sergt. R. Harris, Fifth United States Cavalry; J. B. Morril, Company M, Fifth United States Cavalry; Sergt. Thomas M. Welles, Company F, Sixth United States Cavalry; Sergt. James Homer; Corp. E. Leabe, Fifth United States Cavalry, arm, severe; Sergt. J. Miller, Sixth United States; J. Davidson, First Michigan; Maj. Duggin, First Michigan; William Sherburne, Twentieth Pennsylvania; D. Duggin, First Michigan; George Nash; Corp. George Derrick; Sergt. Robert Rordan, Sixth New-York; Corp. George B. Lott, Twentieth Pennsylvania.

E. A. PAUL.

Details of the Victory.

Dispatches to the Associated Press.

HEADQUARTERS ARMY OF THE POTOMAC, Saturday, April 1.

The greater portion of the army has not been engaged with the enemy to-day. The time has been occupied in erecting works on the new line, and repairing the roads connecting the different corps. The late rains had rendered it impossible to move the wagon trains as fast as the troops advanced. One train took forty-eight hours to move five miles with the assistance of one thousand men. But through the untiring industry and perseverance of the officers in charge of the Quartermaster's and Commissary Departments, the army has been almost as well supplied as while in their old quarters.

When the news of SHERIDAN's repulse reached here last night, a part of the Fifth Corps was at once despatched to his aid, and it is expected that to-night or in the morning we shall receive good news from that quarter.

It appears that SHERIDAN was moving on the road leading to a place called the Three Forks, about three miles from the Southside Railroad, when two cavalry brigades of PICKETT's division, which had been moved out in a great hurry, came down on a road running from Sutherland Station. As SHERIDAN's cavalry had most of them passed the junction, this movement of the enemy threatened to cut him off. He, however, discovered his danger in time to get his command back with only a slight loss, at the same time taking about 100 prisoners. Both the LEES were present, but one of them was at a respectful distance.

On being reinforced this morning by the Fifth Corps, the enemy fell back so rapidly that their dead and many of their wounded fell into our hands, as well as those of our own that were unavoidably left behind yesterday afternoon.

The attack made on the enemy's line in front of the Twenty-fourth Corps was led by FOSTER's division, and about two hundred prisoners were brought in, the One Hundred and Forty-eighth New-York taking most of them. Some three hundred or four hundred yards of ground was taken from them, and our picket line so much further advanced.

At 4 o'clock this morning this position was assaulted, and a few of our men captured; but in a very short time it was retaken, with about sixty prisoners and a stand of colors.

Our losses up to the present time will not exceed twenty-five hundred; while those of the enemy, on some parts of the line, at least, were greater than our own; but, of course, the total cannot be given.

Major DYKEMAN, of the Fifteenth New-York Heavy Artillery, is reported wounded and a prisoner.

Three sharpshooters were brought into the Fifth Corps headquarters this morning, sixteen cavalrymen belonging to WM. HENRY LEE's command.

They had been on picket duty and were cut off by the force which went to the assistance of SHERIDAN.

SECOND DISPATCH.

HEADQUARTERS OF THE ARMY OF THE POTOMAC, April 1—Midnight.

A courier from Major-Gen. SHERIDAN has just arrived with the most cheering news.

The combined forces of cavalry and Major-Gen. WARREN's infantry advanced against the enemy this afternoon, driving them several miles, and capturing about 4,000 prisoners and a number of pieces of artillery.

They retreated to Five Forks, where they were flanked by a part of the Fifth Corps, which had moved down the White Oak road. It was here the large number of prisoners were taken.

The rebels then retreated south along the White Oak road, and were vigorously pursued by Gen. SHERIDAN, while MCKENZIE's cavalry from the Army of the James, advanced west on the Ford road toward the Southside road, and when the messenger left was only about three miles from it, and would undoubtedly reach it before morning.

Thus the last great line of railroad the rebels have to supply their capital and LEE's army by is about to be severed, and it is firmly believed that they will immediately leave their present position in Petersburgh and Richmond.

Sharp cannonading is now going on near the centre of the line, held by the left of the Sixth Corps.

REPORTS VIA BALTIMORE.

Capture of Forts Hell and Damnation—Heavy Losses.

Special Dispatch to the Evening Telegraph.

BALTIMORE, Monday, April 3.

The latest news here this morning is, that our forces had captured Fort Damnation last night, with all its armament and many prisoners. This fort is near Fort Hell, and one of the strongest and most important rebel forts.

It is also reported that Petersburgh has been captured.

The fighting has been terrible, and the losses heavy on both sides; but the rebel loss thus far is three times more than ours.

It is believed that SHERIDAN by this time has cut the Danville Railroad.

The Flood in the St. Lawrence—Submersion at Montreal—The Victoria Bridge in Danger.

MONTREAL, Monday, April 3.

The river rose several feet on Saturday and was piled with ice to a great heighth. One of the shoves came near striking a tube of the Victoria Bridge.

Yesterday morning, the river rose much higher, flooding William, Wellington and other streets. Between 5 and 6 o'clock in the evening, the ice shoved again and the water rushed over the revetment wall, flooding Commission-street. At about 11 o'clock, it again rose as high as St. Paul and St. Gill streets.

The Grand Trunk Railway track between Bonaventure and the tanneries is inundated.

The river rose a foot higher this morning.

The inundated parts of the city are covered with rafts formed with scows and boats.

At present, by far the greater part of the western end of the city is inaccessible except by boats.

The flood is causing the greatest suffering and distress.

Later—4 O'clock P. M.—The water is now slowly falling.

Fire at Louisville, Ky.

LOUISVILLE, Ky., Monday, April 3.

NUMONT's dry goods store, on Market-street, was burned this morning. EVERMAN's bakery and HILBURNS & Co.'s dry goods store, adjoining, were also injured by falling walls and water. The aggregate loss is $80,000, upon which there is very little insurance.

THE GLORIOUS NEWS.

Rejoicings in City and Country

Enthusiasm, Solemnity and Thanksgiving.

Business Suspended and Flags Displayed.

The Praise of the Army on Every Tongue.

Great Mass Meetings in Wall Street and at Union Square.

Patriotic Speeches and Patriotic Songs.

The Whole City Aglow with Excitement.

ILLUMINATIONS AND FIREWORKS.

At no time since the Fall of Sumter has the City of New-York been so thoroughly excited as it was yesterday upon the announcement of the occupation of Richmond. The news in the morning journals was sufficient to arouse the most latent patriotism, and cause the hardest heart to beat with gratitude. Scarcely, however, had the people settled themselves at their various avocations when a strange whisper filled the air, penetrating to the counting-room, the workshop and the school, as if by magic, and long before the newspaper extras stamped the joyful news upon the public mind, it was everywhere known that great news had come to hand, and that victory was ours. An interested crowd gathered about the TIMES Bulletin, and as the cheering words were read again and again, great hearty cheers went up from the multitude, and joy beamed from every eye. Soon the nimble feet of the newsboys had sped with the official dispatch throughout the town, and what had been but an intuitive surmise became a patent truth. The manifestations of exhilaration were boundless; flags were flung to the breeze from innumerable stores and dwellings, making Broadway to shine with the Stars and Stripes, and casting a stream of glory upon the harbor. At the ferries, as soon as the announcement was formally made, an order was issued to deck the boats with bunting, and at once the several fleets of double-enders steamed across the river gay with the flutter of our flag. The down-town shipping houses, most of which are provided with staffs, ran up their colors, so that South-street and West-street, Broad-street and Beaver-street, with the neighboring marts of traffic, vied in patriotic display with the hotels of Broadway and the mansions of the upper end. The magnetism of delight was upon every man. Not a dismal face, not an averted eye, not a pursed-up mouth was seen, nor a croaking tongue heard. No one suggested an "if" or a "but," but every one accepted the glad tidings as truth from the pen of an "honest man." Hand grasped hand in places where "how much" and "how low," are the ordinary salutation; "glorious news" and "thank God" sprang from lips more accustomed to "buyer sixty" and "seller ten;" hard pebbled spectacles that have weathered the beatings of the world and the buffetings of care for sixty years without a moisture, were wet with tears of gratitude, and men estranged for months grasped each others willing palm, while their hearts beat in harmonious thanksgiving. In the public and private schools as much and as genuine enthusiasm was displayed as in the harsher schools of Wall and William streets. Appropriate addresses were made in several of them by the Principals, and the national hymns were sung with a gusto which only school boys and girls can give. One theme was upon every lip—the boats, the cars, the restaurants, the stages, the streets were full of cheerful, happy, exulting, forgiving people, who waived all ceremony, all points of etiquette, and chatted busily each with his neighbor upon the one great occurrence of the day.

It would be idle to disguise the fact that our people rejoiced particularly over the fact that Richmond, the rebel capital, the home of the Confederate President, the seat of their government, the hub and centre of the contest, was at length occupied by our troops. Atlanta, Savannah, Wilmington and Charleston especially were each in turn the object of public attention and anxiety, but after all Richmond was the point after which the popular heart yearned. There it was that JEFF. and his satellites had reared their temple, there the skill of rebel engineers and the energies of their Gen. LEE had been spent in lines of defence and fortifications of strength. It has been the boast of any Southern man that come what might Richmond was forever theirs; that no power this side of Heaven could take it. For years this kind of talk has been made by the Southern people, and for years the sympathizing newspapers of this city and elsewhere have indorsed it, so that our people have felt within them an irrepressible longing for its possession. They wanted its lines of defence broken and its fortifications captured—they wanted JEFF. DAVIS driven out or hanged at his door post, and Gen. LEE swept from his intrenchments by besom of the Union. At length it came, and came, too, so suddenly, that the people were quite unprepared for it. It took the city several hours to accept the startling fact, to recognize its magnitude; and it is very doubtful if even yet the vast extent of the victory is duly appreciated. As each successive dispatch was placed upon the bulletins of the newspapers, the crowds increased in numbers, but the cup of enthusiasm was too full for further addition. Hardly would the paper be placed upon its board, before its contents would be thundered out to the people by some quick-sighted person, and after cheers were given for the news, he would be called upon for a repetition, and no let up was vouchsafed him until hoarse with shouting and perspiring with exertion, he gave way to a successor, who, in turn, read and reread the stirring dispatches.

Many were the jokes made at the expense of JEFF. and his gray coats; many were the queer suggestions and odd ideas thrown out as to Mr. LINCOLN's probable course. One man, who kept the crowd near our bulletin in a constant uproar, suggested that it would be a good idea if Old ABE would take rooms at the Spottswood House, and issue from thence a proclamation of amnesty to every mother's son in rebeldom, always excepting old JEFF., MASON, and SLI-

[Continued on Eighth Page.]

The Philadelphia Inquirer.

PRICE TWO CENTS. | PHILADELPHIA, MONDAY, APRIL 10, 1865. | PRICE TWO CENTS.

VICTORY!! VICTORY!!

GEN. GRANT'S SUN OF AUSTERLITZ!

LEE FINDS HIS WATERLOO.

SURRENDER OF THE REBEL ARMY!!

GEN. GRANT'S TERMS ACCEPTED BY LEE.

THE REBELS WANT PEACE.

A GREAT AMOUNT OF WAR MATERIAL GIVEN UP!

REBEL ARMY PAROLED!!

THE NATION'S THANKS TO ITS GLORIOUS HEROES.

OFFICIAL WAR GAZETTE.

FIRST BULLETIN.

WAR DEPARTMENT, WASHINGTON, D. C., April 9, 1865—9 P.M.—Maj.-Gen. John A. Dix, New York:—This Department has just received an official report of the surrender, this day, of Gen. Lee and his army, to Lieutenant-General Grant, on the terms proposed by General Grant. The details will be given as speedily as possible.

EDWIN M. STANTON,
Secretary of War.

HEAD-QUARTERS ARMIES OF UNITED STATES, April 9th—4·30 P. M.—Hon. Edwin M. Stanton, Secretary of War:—General Lee surrendered the Army of Northern Virginia, this afternoon, upon terms proposed by myself. The accompanying additional correspondence will show the conditions fully.

(Signed) U. S. GRANT,
Lieutenant-General.

April 9, 1865.—General:—I received your note of this morning on the picket line, whither I had come to meet you and ascertain definitely what terms were embraced in your proposition of yesterday with reference to the surrender of this army.

I now request an interview in accordance with the offer contained in your letter of yesterday, for that purpose.

Very respectfully your obed't ser't,
R. E. LEE, General.

To Lieutenant-General U. S. Grant, Commanding United States Armies.

April 9th, 1865.—General R. E. Lee, Commanding Confederate States Armies:—Your note of this date is but this moment (11·50) eleven fifty A. M., received.

In consequence of my having passed from the Richmond and Lynchburg road to the Farmville and Lynchburg road, I am at this writing about four miles west of Waller's Church, and will push forward to the front for the purpose of meeting you. Notice sent to me on this road where you wish the interview to take place will meet me.

Very respectfully, your obd't serv't,
U. S. GRANT,
Lieutenant-General.

APPOMATTOX COURT HOUSE, April 9, 1865.—General R. E. Lee, commanding C. S. A.:—In accordance with the substance of my letter to you of the 8th inst., I propose to receive the surrender of the Army of Northern Virginia on the following terms, to wit:—

Rolls of all the officers and men to be made in duplicate. One copy to be given to an officer designated by me, the other to be retained by such officer or officers as you may designate. The officers to give their individual paroles not to take arms against the Government of the United States until properly exchanged, and each company or regimental commander sign a like parole for the men of their commands.

The arms, artillery and public property to be parked and stacked, and turned over to the officers appointed by me to receive them. This will not embrace the side-arms of the officers, nor their private horses or baggage.

This done, each officer and man will be allowed to return to their homes, not to be disturbed by United States authority so long as they observe their parole and the laws in force where they may reside.

Very respectfully,
U. S. GRANT, Lieutenant-General.

HEAD-QUARTERS, ARMY NORTHERN VIRGINIA, 9th April, 1865.—Lieut.-Gen. U. S. Grant, Commanding United States Army.—General:—I have received your letter of this date containing the terms of surrender of the Army of Northern Virginia as proposed by you. As they are substantially the same as expressed in your letter of the 8th inst., they are accepted.

I will proceed to designate the proper officers to carry the stipulations into effect.

Very respectfully your obedient servant,
R. E. LEE, General.

The following is the previous correspondence between Lieutenant-General Grant and General Lee, referred to in the foregoing telegram to the Secretary of War:—

CLIFTON HOUSE, Va., April 9th, 1865.
Hon. Edwin M. Stanton, Secretary of War:—

The following correspondence has taken place between General Lee and myself. There has been no relaxation in the pursuit during its pendency:—

(Signed) U. S. GRANT, Lieut.-Gen.

April 7, 1865.—General R. E. LEE, Commanding C. S. A. General:—The result of the last week must convince you of the hopelessness of further resistance on the part of the Army of Northern Virginia in this struggle. I feel that it is so, and regard it as my duty to shift from myself the responsibility of any further effusion of blood by asking of you the surrender of that portion of the Confederate States Army known as the Army of Northern Virginia.

Very respectfully, your obedient servant,
U. S. GRANT,
Lieutenant-General Commanding Armies of the United States.

April 7th, 1865.—General:—I have received your note of this date. Though not entirely of the opinion you express of the hopelessness of further resistance on the part of the Army of Northern Virginia, I reciprocate your desire to avoid useless effusion of blood, and therefore, before considering your proposition, ask the terms you will offer on condition of its surrender.

(Signed) R. E. LEE, General.

To Lt.-Gen. Grant, Commanding Armies of the United States.

April 8th, 1865.—General R. E. Lee, Commanding C. S. A.:—General:—Your note of last evening, in reply to mine of same date, asking conditions on which I will accept the surrender of the Army of Northern Virginia is just received.

In reply, I would say, that peace being my first desire, there is but one condition I insist upon, viz: That the men surrendered shall be disqualified for taking up arms again against the Government of the United States until properly exchanged.

I will meet you, or designate officers to meet any officers you may name, for the same purpose, at any point agreeable to you, for the arranging definitely the terms upon which the surrender of the Army of Northern Virginia will be received.

Very respectfully, your obed't ser't,
U. S. GRANT, Lieut.-General,
Armies United States.

April 8th, 1865.—General:—I received at a late hour your note of to-day in answer to mine of yesterday. I did not intend to propose the surrender of the Army of Northern Virginia, but to ask the terms of your propositions.

To be frank with you, I do not think the emergency has arisen to call for the surrender of this army, but as the restoration of peace should be the sole object of all, I desire to know whether your proposals would tend to that end. I cannot, therefore, meet you with a view to surrender the Army of Northern Virginia, but as far as your proposition may affect the Confederate States forces under my command, and tend to the restoration of peace, I should be pleased to meet you at ten A. M. to-morrow, on the Old Stage road to Richmond, between the picket lines of the two armies.

Very respectfully, your obedient servant,
(Signed) R. E. LEE, General C. S. A.

April 9, 1865.—General R. E. Lee, Commanding C. S. A., General:—Your note of yesterday is received. As I have no authority to treat on the subject of peace the meeting proposed for ten A. M. to-day could have no good effect.

I will state, however, General, that I am equally anxious for peace with yourself, and the whole North entertain the same feeling. The terms upon which peace can be had are well understood.

By the South laying down their arms, they will hasten that most desirable event, save thousands of human lives and hundreds of millions of dollars' worth of property not yet destroyed. Sincerely hoping that all our difficulties may be settled without the loss of another life, I subscribe myself,

Very respectfully, your obd't serv't,
(Signed) U. S. GRANT,
Lieutenant-General U. S. A.

SECOND OFFICIAL BULLETIN.

WAR DEPARTMENT, WASHINGTON, D. C., April 9th, 1865, 9·30 P. M.—Lieutenant-General Grant:—Thanks be to Almighty God for the great victory with which he has this day crowned you and the gallant army under your command. The thanks of this Department, and of the Government, and of the people of the United States, their reverence and honor, have been deserved and will be rendered to you and the brave and gallant officers and soldiers of your army, for all time.

(Signed) EDWIN M. STANTON,
Secretary of War.

THIRD BULLETIN.

WAR DEPARTMENT, WASHINGTON, D. C., April 9th, 10, P. M., 1865.—Ordered that a salute of two hundred (200) guns be fired at the Head-quarters of every Army and Department, and at every Post and Arsenal in the United States, and at the Military Academy at West Point, on the day of the receipt of this order, in commemoration of the surrender of General R. E. Lee and the Army of Northern Virginia to Lieutenant-General Grant and the army under his command. Report of the receipt and execution of this order to be made to the Adjutant-General, Washington.

EDWIN M. STANTON,
Secretary of War.

The above message was received at the American Telegraph Office by operators Heber C. Robisson and Joseph Bradley, who feel that this is the last opportunity they or any other operator in Philadelphia will ever have of receiving news [illegible] enthusiasm.

OUR RICHMOND LETTER.

Special Correspondence of the Inquirer.

RICHMOND, Va., Thursday, April 5.

Full accounts of the occupation of the city having already been sent by other of your specials, there is, comparatively, little new for me to say. Still, Richmond as it is to-day, and its surroundings, will furnish materials for letters for a long while to come.

The Libby Prison.

The first object of attraction to the soldiers and civilians is Libby Prison. Old Libby still stands, though all around it is a scene of ruins. A photographer is making a picture, and what a picture! If it was a heaven-ordained thing that colored troops should save the residences of the city from destruction, while the business part had been swept away by their own hands, it was but a poetic sequel that Libby should be filled with Rebels, and the glorious old blue mount guard at the doorways!

And how it looked! Rebels peering through the grated windows and swarming over the roof; longing eyes turned towards their homes, over which waved the old flag (what must have been their thoughts, if *they dare to think*)! in the distance the legions of loved ones murdered in that hell-hole. What can they expect at our hands? "*Ye who enter here leave all hope behind!*" That has been the fearful inscription stamped upon the minds of tens of thousands of patriots whom accidents of war threw into the hands of men whose malignant hate knew no bounds, and whose depraved hearts caused them to commit deeds for which there should be no forgiveness here, if hereafter—men like Davis and Lee, Stephens and Benjamin, men who attended church upon the Sabbath, who knew of the torture our men were undergoing but a few steps from their gilded mansions, whose word would have changed the treatment in an hour.

It has been stated and reiterated over and over again, by Secession sympathizers in the North, that they were treated as well as they had the means to do. The condition of things I have found here I can prove to have existed for the last four years, which show this to be false. Lumber and machine shops are but a few yards distant; labor could have been had from the men themselves. The James River, but a few yards distant, and water at all times could have been had to keep the den clean. They had provision plenty stored in their immense warehouses close by; have always had plenty, and if their own army ever suffered it was because of the inefficiency of transportation from the canal and railroad here. At the base there should have been no want.

To pass through Libby and think of the sufferings that our men have been compelled to undergo, to see the loathsome corners where the sinks and water basins have emitted their foul vapors through the dark rooms, and to recall the names of the sick and faint murdered at the windows, where they had gone to get a few gasps of fresh air; to see samples of the food that was doled out, the wonder is that any men sustained life there for thirty days, summer or winter. That some epidemic never visited them, and swept all before it, is a marvel; and to-day I heard Rebel officers and privates whine, and even grow impudent, because they were put in such a place, and this too, when the privileges of sunning themselves on the roof and at the windows, and of receiving visits and food from their friends, were accorded them, which they denied to us. If there exists a man with the slightest desire to see the Rebel leaders and officers escape a single iota of the punishment they have earned, let him pay a visit to Libby, and if it does not vanish, then he is no friend of the soldier or of his country.

Captain Stewart

Who was selected to see to the forwarding and delivery of packages to our prisoners, is still here. For eight months he has stood by our boys, and like a ministering angel attended to their wants as best he could. He has still about five tons of boxes, &c., in his warehouse, which he has been unable to deliver for various causes. Last week there arrived about fifteen hundred of our prisoners from the South, taken from Sherman's army, in the most destitute condition. On Sunday last he was engaged clothing and shoeing them from 8 A. M. to 1 P. M., when an order came to put them on a boat at once, to go down and be exchanged. It was good news for the men, and he soon saw Libby empty, and its doors swing wide open. He suspected there was an intention of abandoning the city, but could not say or do anything. About midnight Major Turner came to him, and said, "Well, Captain, I am going to leave you Libby; we have concluded to evacuate the city." The Captain accepted it in the name of the United States.

At his request the warehouse adjoining Libby, in which our stores were, was not to be fired. Libby, adjoining, was spared for the same reason, and Pemberton, another jail the same as Libby, directly opposite, was also spared. On the opposite side from Pemberton was a tobacco warehouse filled with two million dollars' worth of French tobacco, which was fired in the morning. Captain Stewart and his clerk and two negroes got an axe, broke open Pemberton and tried to save it but failed; just as he would get the fire put out in one place it would catch in another, and his warehouse taking fire he was finally compelled to use his whole efforts to protect it, which he did.

Now, in the centre of two miles of charred ruins stands Libby, a monument to certify to the future the inhuman barbarity and degradation to which human slavery has sank the chivalry of Virginia. Let it remain, a satire upon the boasted civilization of the leaders of this Rebellion.

Among some letters that have fallen into our hands is one from the Rebel Adjutant-General, S. Cooper, addressed to his wife at Boydton, Mecklenburg county, Virginia. It is important as showing the utter despair of the Rebel cause. It shows that one week ago Jeff. Davis considered the capital lost and sent away his family. Mrs. Lee intended to have gone and Mrs. Mason could see no asylum nearer than Halifax:—

[No. 37.]

APRIL 1, 1865.

MY DEAR MARIA:—I received to-day your letter of March 24th, (No. 27). I find by it that you have received all my letters previous to the 21st of March. I have written you three since; that is, the 21st, 25th and 29th of March, and the one I am now writing is the 1st of April, so that there are but three letters from me besides this one, that are yet due you. I was pained on reading your letter that your mind is made up on coming to this city. You know not what you would have to encounter here, nor is it possible for you to know (unless you were here) of the privations which you would encounter here if you come. You say there is no place safer than where you are, except in Richmond, and that you expect to leave Clifton for this place in three weeks, by which time the roads will be passable.

Let me beg and urge you not to come here, and do not let your fancy picture comfort and safety to you here. Think of the distresses in Savannah and Columbia when Sherman's army took possession of those cities, and do not suppose that the same scenes may not be enacted here under like circumstances.

I met Mary Lee yesterday, and she told me her mother and sisters would not remain here, and also said the ladies in Savannah were selling their own clothing to buy themselves food. In all places the enemy have captured the Confederate money is considered by them as trash, and is not taken for the sale of any commodities. So will it be here. You know I have nothing but Confed. money, and how can you live upon that here under these circumstances? You will be reduced to starvation. That is lingering death to be sure, but it is not the less certain. You could not live upon your relations and friends here, as you seem to think, for a time, for they could no more live on the same means than yourself, and you would all be reduced to the same necessities and despair.

Call your mind to these facts, and do not let your apprehensions as to your present situation sway your judgment, and as you place *faith* in the protection of the Almighty, do not let that faith be shaken by the fear that He will fail you in the hour of need, which would only prove a *doubt* of His powers, or purpose to *save*.

Mrs. Davis and her children left here yesterday for the South, and other families are preparing to leave. Your sister Nannie, I understand, is much disturbed as to what to do, and inclines to leave the city. Grant is making every effort not to *fight* battles, but to starve the city and Lee's army by cutting off communications for supplies, and in that way gain an easy victory. His great purpose is to get possession of the Southside Railroad from Petersburg to Lynchburg, and if he accomplishes that, which he may possibly do, you will be prevented from reaching this city if you should start for it, and then you would be in a most helpless condition.

I give you these facts and suggestions for your consideration, and beg again that you will forgo your purpose to come here.

You tell me that Mr. Alexander seems most unwilling for you all to leave him; may God bless him for that; you could not be in better hands than in his. There is no necessity for you to leave him, and you could not be in better hands. Give my love to him and Miss Betty, and to his father. I must hurry Sam off to prevent you from coming; he has only been waiting the arrival of Cawood, who arrived two days since. He has brought all the things. * * * *

Fondest love to Jennie and Sally.

Ever affectionately yours,
S. C.

Mr. Ambler says your sister Eliza, Mrs. J. M. Mason, is going to Halifax for safety.

Castle Thunder Stands

On the upper side of the street, not very far from Libby. It is being cleaned out, and the lower part, formerly used for prisoners of State, will be taken for a guard-house for ordinary misdemeanors, while all Rebels will be consigned to Libby. Last Sunday the Rebels took out small numbers of prisoners, and started them under guards for Danville. Castle Thunder has its horrors, its untold tales of hope gone, stout hearts quailed, and maniacs come out, or the undertaker, a negro with a rude cart ended the case of "arbitrary arrests." About a dozen escaped from the guards, among whom are Captain S. Groonor, Lieutenant Church, and J. Hancock, of our army, charged with being spies.

The county jail was visited by Major Stevens, of the Fourth Massachusetts, and finding no provisions, and none having been had for twenty-four hours, he examined the books, and found from fifty to sixty men, women and children there, in the most squalid wretchedness. A little girl of about eight years of age attracted his attention, and he asked what she was in for. She replied, "she stole some bread to take home to her mother." The records proved her statements true, and as nearly all were in with the same charge—petty larcenies—the Major ordered the doors to be thrown wide open, and bid them "go and sin no more." A more grateful set could not have been found. Many thought they were there to die.

The "Examiner," "Dispatch," and "Enquirer"

Printing offices were burned. The *Whig* and *Sentinel* remain. The *Whig*, anxious to keep on the paying side, has come out for the Union and has accordingly been furnished with considerable United States advertising, among which we find the advertisement for the new Seven-thirty loan of Jay Cooke. Its editors and reporters remain, but have not all taken the oath of allegiance. The *Sentinel*, Jeff.'s organ, refuses to turn around, and is accordingly silent. The *Whig* comes out in the afternoon in a little sheet about the size of a sheet of foolscap. There is an excellent field for a loyal paper here.

President Lincoln and Lady in Richmond.

Mrs. Lincoln, accompanied by Senators Sumner and Harlan, and a dozen friends, arrived this morning, and spent the day in looking around the city, and will leave to-night on the *River Queen*.

Mr. Lincoln was here yesterday, and left last night, going down to City Point; he sent his own boat ahead, and got into the small yawl of Commodore Porter, and with a half dozen sailors he rode in it, in tow of a tug; part of the time he steered and seemed to enjoy the trip. He was very enthusiastically received wherever he went.

Major-General Devens

Has located himself in Governor Letcher's house. General Weitzel had his head-quarters in Jeff Davis' mansion, but has given it up for General Grant, Mrs. Grant having come up from City Point to-day. Assistant Secretary of War Dana and Mrs. Dana left to-night for City Point; he has been here two days looking after the interests of the Government.

Union Prisoners in the South.

Generals Hoffman and Mulford are here. There are no more prisoners of ours now in the enemy's lines, except such as are in Southern Georgia and in the Southwest. Those in the region of the Mississippi are to be exchanged at Vicksburg. No definite arrangements have been made yet for those in Georgia, but there will be soon.

The Markets were Very Thin

To-day. Shad at fifty cents (nothing but greenbacks and specie now recognized here); eggs, 60; butter, 75; beef, 25; some asparagus, I believe, was also offered. Ample facilities will be given to get in produce.

Mail Boats to Washington.

To-morrow we are to have a regular line of mail boats, leaving here at six A. M., arriving about half-past six P. M., and about twenty-eight hours from Washington.

The railroad to Petersburg will probably be completed to-morrow. It will take some time to rebuild the railroad bridge at this point, and in the meantime two pontoon bridges have been laid down.

Rebel Bonds "on the Street."

Among the papers and documents thrown to the winds on the exit of the Confederacy was about a million or two of Rebel bonds, some of them coupons. They are very cheap now, but as there is no designated place at which said coupons are to be paid they are not in very great demand.

Begging Papers and Food.

The people are nearly all out to-day on the streets, and are all either begging passes or food. White and black are all now on an equality; or the colored are rather the surest of favors, as no one questions their loyalty, and but few white folks have very comfortable records to dwell upon. No food or passes, without first taking the oath, is a bitter pill for some, but it is generally taken, with a gentle squirm. Nearly every one has an idea that Uncle Sam is an immense cornucopia, who has only to be squeezed and out comes an unlimited quantity of stores of all kinds, and as they are not to be expected to starve, *sequitur*, they are to be dealt out regular rations.

Richmond a Second New Orleans.

We have here a second New Orleans; perhaps not quite so bad, but bad enough, anyhow. The poorer classes of whites wont work if they can get along without by any make-shift. The seedy bankrupt F. F. V.'s don't expect to work. Their families want their servants to dress, feed and clothe them, but have no money to hire them, and the colored population have an idea that they must be paid in "Yankee money," "No Confeds." There is an absolute necessity for a social revolution, Confederate money is worthless; the State banks are no better, and the people have little else.

Richmond has great natural facilities for being a great commercial city, but unless she is *regenerated*, she *must die out*. No one looks for much of a change in the old Secesh here; they are ignorant, prejudiced and stupid; they will never learn, and cannot and do not want to forget their Secesh; they cling to the delusion with a strange fanaticism. They seem to admit that their cause is hopeless, and that it has not paid, but they go on and prate about being let alone, and being independent, won't reason, and cannot argue, and *never think*.

The merchants who have not been burned out, and whose hands are stained with treason—men who have aided and abetted, and many of whom have participated, have quit only because it *did not pay*.

Advent of the Sutlers.

The sutlers have come in the last three days like an avalanche! They are seizing the best stores and opening out their stocks marked at prices that sound like Confederate currency, but mean greenbacks. The popular dodge seems to be for a sutler to go to a Secesher and get him to take him in in order to throw around his house the mask of loyalty, and divert from his attention the Provost Marshal and the officers of the law. Some of these bargains should be looked into.

The Northern Papers in Richmond.

THE PHILADELPHIA INQUIRER and the New York papers made their appearance this morning, and were eagerly bought up at ten cents a piece. But few, if any of the citizens buy them. This afternoon the

Sequel to "the Great Mass Meeting

To fire the Southern heart," was held in the African Church. At an early hour the building was crowded to excess by the colored population and the services in honor of the *entree* of the Union army were held in the presence of about two thousand five hundred persons. The exercises were purely religious, but conducted in their own way. They are Baptists, but sing with with a native fervor that one seldom hears. They sang a hymn commencing with—

"Jesus, mine all, to Heaven is gone,
He whom I fix my hopes upon;"

And after each two lines the whole congregation would sing a chorus, repeating the same line four to six times.

"I am going to join this army of the Lord."

Half a dozen of the Christian Commission delegates being present, one of their number made a prayer. During his appeals for divine strength and guidance, the audience continued to exclaim, at intervals:—"Glory to God!" "Amen," "Bress God," "Bress de Lord," "Thank God," "Lord Jesus."

Rev. Prof. Burrows, of Andover, Massachusetts preached a sermon for them, and a more attentive and sincere congregation never were assembled before. Two front rows of seats were reserved for the colored soldiers, who, in their neat blue uniforms and shining buttons, made quite a display. Three or four of them were formerly slaves, and were recognised by some of their old acquaintances, who greeted them as though they had entered the city as conquerors.

They look upon our army as having been sent to avenge their many wrongs. They are wild with enthusiasm, and over fifty joined one of our regiments here doing guard duty. With a little exertion ten thousand can be had here in three weeks. A thorough investigation satisfies me that the Rebels did not get fifty men the whole month they tried to "fire the colored heart" to fasten tighter their own chains, but *Sambo* and *Cuffee* said they did not see it! The assurance that the Yanks would work them to death, and perpetrate all enormities that could be conceived of upon them did not answer. Major Turner had charge of the service; he drilled his men in a warehouse near Libby; he had about forty-five boys and idiots, who had no uniforms and no vim. He told Capt. Stewart that "nigger is gone up." The battalion we read of were the servants at the hospital, who refused to enlist into the regular service; and thus their frantic appeals of "help me or I sink," to a race they have robbed and degraded for over two centuries.

Davis' Next Base of Operations.

Opinion differs as to the next base of Davis; some say Danville, others Lynchburg. One thing is certain, a month ago he commenced his preparations to move to the latter place; at the time the canal was destroyed by Sheridan, he had commenced, and five boat loads were in transit and were returned and finally burned. The loss of their canal, which really was the main feeder of the city and army, was a very severe blow to him, his appeals to the farmers were mocked at; they were appalled at the magnitude of the destruction and merely said it was "no use to try;" he lost the South Side road; he had left but one railroad, it worthless, and despair seized him.

Lee's Confessions.

It is well known from official documents that were found that Lee, over two months ago, notified the Rebel Senate that he could not hold Richmond with his present army, but Davis insisted that it must be done. When the time came to retreat he had but the one road practicable, and that was to Danville. He set out for that point, and we now have a rumor that he subsequently turned toward Richmond. His private property was all got away, or sold, except his carriage, built in New Orleans. It has been a very fine affair, and was on the cars to go, but the train did not get off in time, and our cavalry coming in the train was fired, but some,

Continued on the Eighth Page.

The New-York Times.

VOL. XIV......NO. 4225. | NEW-YORK, MONDAY, APRIL 10, 1865. | PRICE FOUR CENTS

HANG OUT YOUR BANNERS

UNION

VICTORY!

PEACE!

Surrender of General Lee and His Whole Army.

THE WORK OF PALM SUNDAY.

Final Triumph of the Army of the Potomac.

The Strategy and Diplomacy of Lieut.-Gen. Grant.

Terms and Conditions of the Surrender.

The Rebel Arms, Artillery, and Public Property Surrendered.

Rebel Officers Retain Their Side Arms and Private Property.

Officers and Men Paroled and Allowed to Return to Their Homes.

The Correspondence Between Grant and Lee.

OFFICIAL.

WAR DEPARTMENT, WASHINGTON, April 9, 1865—9 o'clock P. M.

To Maj.-Gen. Dix:

This department has received the official report of the SURRENDER, THIS DAY, OF GEN. LEE AND HIS ARMY TO LIEUT.-GEN. GRANT, on the terms proposed by Gen. GRANT.

Details will be given as speedily as possible.

EDWIN M. STANTON, Secretary of War.

HEADQUARTERS ARMIES OF THE UNITED STATES, 4:30 P. M., April 9.

Hon. Edwin M. Stanton, Secretary of War:

GEN. LEE SURRENDERED THE ARMY OF NORTHERN VIRGINIA THIS AFTERNOON, upon the terms proposed by myself. The accompanying additional correspondence will show the conditions fully.

(Signed) U. S. GRANT, Lieut.-Gen'l.

SUNDAY, April 9, 1865.

GENERAL—I received your note of this morning, on the picket line, whither I had come to meet you and ascertain definitely what terms were embraced in your proposition of yesterday with reference to the surrender of this army.

I now request an interview in accordance with the offer contained in your letter of yesterday for that purpose.

Very respectfully, your obedient servant,

R. E. LEE, General.

To Lieut.-Gen. GRANT, Commanding United States Armies.

Sunday, April 9, 1865.

Gen. R. E. Lee, Commanding Confederate States Armies.

Your note of this date is but this moment, 11:50 A. M., received.

In consequence of my having passed from the Richmond and Lynchburgh road to the Farmville and Lynchburgh road, I am at this writing about four miles West of Walter's church, and will push forward to the front for the purpose of meeting you.

Notice sent to me, on this road, where you wish the interview to take place, will meet me.

Very respectfully, your ob'd't servant,

U. S. GRANT, Lieutenant-General.

APPOMATTOX COURT-HOUSE, April 9, 1865.

General R. E. Lee, Commanding C. S. A.:

In accordance with the substance of my letters to you of the 8th inst., I propose to receive the surrender of the Army of Northern Virginia on the following terms, to wit:

Rolls of all the officers and men to be made in duplicate, one copy to be given to an officer designated by me, the other to be retained by such officers as you may designate.

The officers to give their individual paroles not to take arms against the Government of the United States until properly exchanged, and each company or regimental commander sign a like parole for the men of their commands.

The arms, artillery and public property to be packed and stacked and turned over to the officers appointed by me to receive them.

This will not embrace the side-arms of the officers, nor their private horses or baggage.

This done, EACH OFFICER AND MAN WILL BE ALLOWED TO RETURN TO THEIR HOMES, not to be disturbed by United States authority so long as they observe their parole and the laws in force where they reside.

Very respectfully,

U. S. GRANT, Lieutenant-General.

HEADQUARTERS ARMY OF NORTHERN VIRGINIA, April 9, 1865.

Lieut.-Gen. U. S. Grant, Commanding U. S. A.:

GENERAL: I have received your letter of this date, CONTAINING THE TERMS OF SURRENDER OF THE ARMY OF NORTHERN VIRGINIA, as proposed by you. As they are substantially the same as those expressed in your letter of the 8th inst., THEY ARE ACCEPTED. I will proceed to designate the proper officers to carry the stipulations into effect.

Very respectfully,

Your obedient servant,

R. E. LEE, General.

THE PRELIMINARY CORRESPONDENCE.

The following is the previous correspondence between Lieut.-Gen. GRANT and Gen. LEE, referred to in the foregoing telegram to the Secretary of War:

CLIFTON HOUSE, VA., April 9, 1865.

Hon. Edwin M. Stanton, Secretary of War:

The following correspondence has taken place between Gen. LEE and myself. *There has been no relaxation in the pursuit during its pendency.*

U. S. GRANT, Lieutenant-General.

APRIL 7, 1865.

Gen. R. E. Lee, Commanding C. S. A.:

GENERAL: The result of the last week must convince you of the hopelessness of further resistance on the part of the Army of Northern Virginia in this struggle. I feel that it is so and regard it as my duty to shift from myself the responsibility of any further effusion of blood, by asking of you the surrender of that portion of the Confederate States Army, known as the Army of Northern Virginia.

Very Respectfully,

Your obedient servant,

U. S. GRANT,

Lieutenant-General,

Commanding Armies of the United States.

APRIL 7, 1865.

General: I have received your note of this date.

Though not entirely of the opinion you express of the hopelessness of further resistence on the part of the army of Northern Virginia, I reciprocate your desire to avoid useless effusion of blood, and therefore, before considering your proposition, *ask the terms you will offer, on condition of its surrender.*

R. E. LEE, General.

To Lieut.-Gen. U. S. GRANT, Commanding Armies of the United States.

APRIL 8, 1865.

To Gen. R. E. Lee, Commanding C. S. A.:

GENERAL: Your note of last evening in reply to mine of same date, asking the conditions on which I will accept the surrender of the Army of Northern Virginia, is just received.

In reply, I would say that *peace being my first desire, there is but one condition that I insist upon*, viz.:

That the men surrendered shall be disqualified for taking up arms again against the Government of the United States until properly exchanged.

I will meet you, or designate officers to meet any officers you may name, for the same purpose, at any point agreeable to you, for the purpose of arranging definitely the terms upon which the surrender of the Army of Northern Virginia will be received.

Very respectfully, your obedient servant,

U. S. GRANT, Lieut.-General,

Commanding armies of the United States.

April 8, 1865.

GENERAL: I received, at a late hour, your note of to-day, in answer to mine of yesterday.

I did not intend to propose the surrender of the Army of Northern Virginia, but *to ask the terms* of your proposition. To be frank, I do not think the emergency has arisen to call for the surrender.

But as *the restoration of peace should be the sole object of all*, I desire to know whether your proposals would tend to that end.

I cannot, therefore, meet you with a view to surrender the Army of Northern Virginia, but *as far as your proposition may affect the Confederate States forces under my command, and tend to the restoration of peace*, I should be pleased to meet you at 10 A. M., to-morrow, on the old stage road to Richmond, between the picket lines of the two armies.

Very respectfully, your obedient servant,

R. E. LEE,

General, C. S. A.

To Lieut.-Gen. GRANT, Commanding Armies of the United States.

APRIL 9, 1865.

General R. E. Lee, commanding C. S. A.:

GENERAL: Your note of yesterday is received. As I have no authority to treat on the subject of peace, the meeting proposed for 10 A. M. to-day could lead to no good. I will state, however, General, that *I am equally anxious for peace with yourself*; and the whole North entertain the same feeling. *The terms upon which peace can be had are well understood. By the South laying down their arms, they will hasten that most desirable event, save thousands of human lives, and hundreds of millions of property not yet destroyed.*

Sincerely hoping that all our difficulties may be settled *without the loss of another life*, I subscribe myself,

Very respectfully,

Your obedient servant,

U. S. GRANT,

Lieutenant-General United States Army.

REJOICINGS.

WILMINGTON, Del., Sunday, April 9.

Wilmington is in an uproar and blaze of glory, rejoicing over the greatest of victories yet achieved by our arms. Guns are firing, bells are ringing, and a large procession is proceeding through the streets. Such an excitement was never before witnessed in this city,

ALBANY, Monday, April 10—1 A. M.

There is great rejoicing here over the news of the surrender of Gen. LEE and his army.

The news was received at about 10 P. M., and about midnight State and Pearl streets were filled with people anxiously awaiting the particulars.

The bells are ringing, cannon firing, while the multitude are indulging in fireworks.

The Governor was called up and briefly addressed the throng around his residence.

The State House and many private residences are illuminated.

PHILADELPHIA, April 9.

The glorious announcement of LEE's surrender was received here about nine o'clock. It was telegraphed to all sections of the city, and was announced in the several churches. The *Ledger* office was illuminated in five minutes. The bell of Independence Hall was rung by the order of the Mayor. The firemen immediately assembled and blocked up the streets. Salutes were fired, and the whistles of the steam-engines and the cheers of the assembled multitudes made the whole city ring.

WORCESTER, Mass., Monday, April 9.

The news of the surrender of LEE and his army created an intense excitement here to-night. The bells were rung, guns were fired, bonfires kindled, the fire companies turned out, and many stores and buildings were illuminated.

PITTSBURGH, Pa., Sunday, April 9.

The news to-night brought nearly the entire population into the streets. The recruiting booths were turned into bonfires, salutes were fired, speeches were made, and bands played.

TRENTON, N. J., Sunday, April 9.

The glorious news was received here with cheering and ringing of bells. The people are turning out *en masse* to receive and rejoice over the glad tidings.

PROVIDENCE, R. I., Sunday, April 9—Midnight.

Bells are ringing, cannon are firing, and the citizens are out rejoicing over the news of LEE's surrender. A large bonfire is burning on Weybosset bridge.

FROM THE PACIFIC COAST.

Juarez said to be Coming to Washington by way of San Francisco—French Forces in Sinaloa—French War Steamers in California Ports—The Overland Mails.

SAN FRANCISCO, Friday, April 7.

The steamer *John L. Stephens*, from Mazatlan, brings $93,000 in treasure and a thousand bags of silver ore.

The Mazatlan *Times*, the Imperialist organ, give the report that JUAREZ was en route for Cape St. Lucas, whence he would sail for San Francisco on his way to Washington.

A French naval expedition had sailed, it was supposed, for Guaymas.

An Imperial force has moved to Sinaloa.

A correspondent of the San Francisco *Bulletin*, writing from Mazatlan, March 4, says that JUAREZ is still at Chihuahua with his ministers raising troops, though money, arms, and ammunition are scarce.

The French war steamer *Victoria* and transport *Du Rhine* was at Santa Barbara, on the coast of California. They hope to obtain supplies of coal at San Francisco.

The daily Overland Mail, hence to Salt Lake, resumed its trips yesterday. The first mail this way since the interruption arrived last night.

The recent meeting in behalf of the Christian Sanitary Commission, resulted in remittances, by telegraph, within the past few days, of $20,000 in gold.

The scarcity of flour and wheat continues. Extreme prices are obtained, and consequently trade does not improve much.

The Union Convention of Washington Territory have nominated A. A. DENY as Congressional Delegate.

Military celebrations for the national victories were held throughout the State to-day.

A mass meeting in aid of the Soldiers' Relief Association was held here to-night.

THE VICTORY.

Thanks to God, the Giver of Victory.

Honors to Gen. Grant and His Gallant Army.

A NATIONAL SALUTE ORDERED.

Two Hundred Guns to be Fired at the Headquarters of Every Army, Department, Post and Arsenal.

[OFFICIAL.]

WAR DEPARTMENT, WASHINGTON, D. C., April 9, 1865—9:30 P. M.

Lieut.-Gen. Grant:

Thanks be to Almighty God for the great victory with which he has this day crowned you and the gallant armies under your command.

The thanks of this Department and of the Government, and of the People of the United States—their reverence and honor have been deserved—will be rendered to you and the brave and gallant officers and soldiers of your army for all time.

EDWIN M. STANTON, Secretary of War.

WAR DEPARTMENT, WASHINGTON, D. C., April 9, 1865—10 o'clock P. M.

Ordered: That a salute of two hundred guns be fired at the headquarters of every army and department, and at every post and arsenal in the United States, and at the Military Academy at West Point on the day of the receipt of this order, in commemoration of the surrender of Gen. ROBERT E. LEE and the Army of Northern Virginia to Lieut.-Gen. GRANT and the army under his command. Report of the receipt and execution of this order to be made to the Adjutant-General at Washington.

EDWIN M. STANTON, Secretary of War.

FROM RICHMOND.

Perils and Excitements of a Voyage Up the James—Scenes and Incidents Along the River.

From Our Own Correspondent.

RICHMOND, Va., Wednesday, April 5.

The inspiration of the scene and the scope of the theme before us are far beyond the feeble descriptive powers of of the pen of your correspondent. No brilliant rhetoric, no vivid word-painting, no oratorical eloquence can portray the sublimity and immensity of the great victory. It is almost beyond the power of the human mind to comprehend its extent, and when you begin to descend to detail, the task is simply appalling in its magnitude. Think of a line of operations, held defensively and operated from offensively with such success, *thirty-nine miles long from flank to flank, thoroughly fortified throughout its entire length!* Think of the cities captured, of the fortifications stormed and taken, with their hundreds of guns, great and small, of the material of war now in our hands, yet beyond the possibility of computation of the terrible battles, and the overwhelming defeat, and rout of the chief army of the rebellion of the prisoners captured. Counted by the tens of thousands; of the terrified flight of the arch-traitor and his few desperate minions; of the triumphant entry of ABRAHAM LINCOLN into treason's fallen capital. Let every lover of his country depict the vast scene in his own imagination for words to fitly discribe it fails altogether.

Through the courtesy of Provost-Marshal Gen. PATRICK, I enjoyed an exceedingly pleasant sail from City Point to the Richmond wharves this morning, on his fleet flag ship, the *Mattino*. Accompanying the General were Hon. C. H. DANA, Assistant Secretary of War, his wife and son, and Hon. ROSCOE CONKLING, member of Congress from New-York. The snake-like bends of the James between City Point and Varina Landing, were quickly passed, and at the latter place assurance was given that the river was clear for our vessel to the very docks of Richmond; but I can assure you that the navigation of the tortuous channel of the James thence to Richmond, thickly sown with obstructions and supposed torpedoes, was an exceedingly delicate task, and full of excitement. Our pilot knew the channel of old, but he knew not the warlike devices of the enemy.

We were, however, very fortunate, and the approach to the city, especially during the last eight miles from Drewry's Bluff, was full of the intensest interest, for over these waters the Union flag had never before floated during the war. When we leave Dutch Gap and that famous canal, which looks as though it might have been washed out by a billow, we at once enter upon the lines held by the enemy. Howlett House Battery, famous for its determined resistance to our engineering operations on the north side of the river, stands abandoned and gloomy, with its twelve large guns still in the embrasures, but all silent as we steamed rapidly by. Another long and large earthwork appears on the left bank, mounting eight or ten guns, and bearing directly upon the mouth of the canal. This, too, like the rest, is abandoned, with its armament unimpaired. We next pass the wreck of the rebel gunboat, blown up by our batteries during the effort made to run through our fleet some months ago.

The next point of interest is Fort Brady, on the north bank of the river, and the left of the position of our Army of the James. What strikes one as very remarkable here is the fact that owing to the intricate windings of the James there are two rebel batteries, Howlett House and another, absolutely in the rear of this former position of our army. Fort Brady is the point where Gen. GIBBON opened on the retreating rebel rams. Had there been larger guns at his disposal, the range is so good that they would have stood a poor chance of escape.

We are now fairly in that part of the river held solely by the rebels, and a knowledge of the channel and obstructions is absolutely necessary to a safe voyage. The gunboat *Monticello* is therefore hailed, and on asking for information, a pilot who has been up and down is tendered with much politeness. The obstructions sunk by our own fleet are soon passed, likewise the fleet of monitors, and the next object which greets the vision is a gaily dressed tug, with a guard of marines, having in tow Admiral PORTER's barge with the President, on his return from Richmond, complacently seated in the stern sheets. It looks very much like a pic-nic. Following a short distance after is the President's handsome flag-ship, the *River Queen*. Not far behind is the beautiful steel gunboat *Bat*, ex-blockade runner, now general convoy to distinguished guests, and one of the fastest vessels in the navy. The *River Queen*, which took the President up the river, proceeded no farther than the obstructions at Drewry's Bluff. We are soon abreast of this historic fortification, and eager eyes scan closely its formidable walls and positions.

Here is the chief line of obstructions sunk by the rebels early in the war, and located as they are, directly under the guns of Fort Darling, subjecting every approaching thing to a terrible plunging fire, it is readily admitted that this was the impassable barrier to the naval advance on Richmond. The river here is very narrow, and the movement of large vessels attended with much danger. The obstructions were placed directly across the river, and filled it completely with the exception of a gap of fifty or sixty feet, left for the passage of the rebel fleet and flag-of-truce boats. They consist of the hulls of two or three old steamships, that formerly plyed between Richmond and New York. The wheel-houses, fast crumbling to decay, still rise above the water, and present the appearance of a melancholy ruin.

We pass so hurriedly under the guns of Fort Darling, that we have no good opportunity to observe its construction. We know it looks very strong, and on the north side it has one or two small outlying works on its flank. Our naval companions tell us that it is a casemated fortification, and with its surrounding field works, all parts of the fort itself, mounts not less than forty guns. All these, like hundreds more, are our trophies without blemish or injury.

Not far above Fort Darling lies the wreck of one of the famous rebel fleet in the James, the iron-clad *Virginia*. Whether she has been blown up or simply scuttled and sunk, cannot be ascertained from looking at her as she lies. She sank in deep water, and is careened over on her side, leaving a portion of her overhang visible above the water-line. Of the other iron-clad, the *Richmond*, we find no trace.

In the immediate vicinity of Fort Darling we pass through a very substantial bridge with a draw, used by LEE for the speedy transfer of troops from the north to the south side of the James. Ere reaching Richmond we pass two more of the same kind, though hardly so well built as the first; but all demonstrating that LEE had no pontoon bridges across the James anywhere—probably, because the rapid current rendered them unsafe, and probably, too, because he had not any pontoons to spare, when something else would answer just as well.

We have now steamed safely by all obstructions and chances of torpedoes, and the very pardonable trepidation which we felt in view of our possible danger, gives way to a feeling that just now is a moment in our lives, the significance, importance and sublimity of which cannot be justly appreciated. The City of Richmond is in view. The spires pointing heavenward; the smoke still rising from the conflagration's awful ruin, and the Stars and Stripes floating from a hundred house-tops and mastheads, all form a picture so sublimely grand and inspiring, that the human mind is simply lost in mute contemplation.

In a few moments we land at the Rockets, and a brisk walk of a mile and a half brings us to the Spotswood House, where we find dinner and a very comfortable room, amid hundreds of loyal guests.

L. L. CROUNSE.

First Impressions of Richmond—The Great Conflagration in the City—Who Was Responsible for it?—The Libby and Castle Thunder—Suffering for Food—Distribution of Supplies—Lee's Family.

From Our Own Correspondent.

RICHMOND, Thursday, April 6, 1865.

So many thousand facts are presented to the mind of the visitor here in such a very short space of time, that to record them systematically is almost impossible. The great features of the evacuation, the entrance of our troops, the conflagration, the President's visit and reception, have already been forwarded to you in detail by your correspondents who came in with the troops, and I will, therefore, allude to them only in a general way.

Let me say, though, at the outset, that the best part of the city is a ruin. That the awful fire kindled by the enemy, and which at first promised to consume but a few buildings, was so fanned by the rising wind, that before it could be got under subjection, *thirty squares, comprising not less than eight hundred buildings in the very best and most valuable business part of Richmond were in ashes.* What the pecuniary loss is no one can estimate. Nearly all the principal mills factories, warehouses, stores, banks and insurance offices were destroyed, and the losses being so heavy, the insurance companies, perhaps insolvent already from their countenance of the rebel currency, are now more than bankrupted, and thousands of property owners, computed wealthy in their actual possessions three days ago, are now reduced to beggary. It is among the things easily discernable, that this ruin, wrought by their own friends, to whom they have given all, and to whose tyranny they have submitted, with even cheerfulness, is the cause of far deeper gloom among many than that produced by the loss of the city or the defeat of their army. It is apparent indeed that the transfer of the city to the Union flag was not only *not distasteful to a very large portion of the people, many of them among the best classes, but even highly gratifying.* No captured city, not even Savannah nor Columbia, can present the ruin apparent here in Richmond. It will carry its painful evidences for half a score of years, and the only thing which will speedily alleviate the dire distress that must prevail, and give the city a chance for a speedy recovery from its present stagnation, is immediate peace. It is Richmond's only salvation. The origin of the fire and the incendiaries are so well and positively known that no extended investigation on these points is required. It seems that *Gen. Lee was not responsible for it, but that Jeff. Davis and his Secretary of War, Breckenridge, were.* The destruction of the supplies and the arsenal involved the destruction of the city, and it was so decided by the leading citizens. Gen. EWELL and Maj. CARRINGTON both protested against it in the most earnest manner, as did also a committee of citizens, but BRECKINRIDGE, in reply, exclaimed *that he didn't care a d—n if every house in Richmond was consumed, the warehouse must be burned.* Thus this wretched rebel, foisted into a powerful position with no constituents, is responsible for the dreadful ruin, and his master DAVIS is likewise responsible, because he silently countenanced it.

The fire was started in two places, among the supply warehouses near the wharves, and at the Danville Depot, where there were 1,500 hogsheads of tobacco belonging to the Confederate Government. This consumed the Danville Depot, also the Petersburgh Depot, and the bridge over the James to Manchester. The famous Libby Prison, and Castle Thunder, as I have already informed you, were not burned. They were reserved for a far more appropriate fate. I visited them yesterday, and found Castle Thunder used as a guard-house for factious and thieving negroes, caught in acts of plunder, while the Libby contained 700 rebel prisoners, officers and privates, temporarily shut up together. They looked through the iron gratings with gloomy countenances, while the Union guard outside seemed to richly enjoy the transition that the famous building had undergone, evidently having been there himself. The whirligig of time makes all things even, and the thousands of loyal officers and soldiers who have suffered the tortures and horrors of these dungeons may now contemplate their present uses with serene satisfaction, and yet without resentment.

A close inspection of Castle Thunder reveals one of the most hideous dungeons that can be conceived. We failed to see it, however, in all its filth and nastyness, for a strong force of men had been engaged two days in carrying out the accumulation of the past three years. The corporal of the guard who conducted us through, pointed out a spot on the floor on one of the main halls, not yet cleaned, where the dirt was three inches thick, and alive with vermin, *and yet on this floor, in this condition, prisoners were obliged to sleep either upon the dirt itself or upon palets of decaying straw.*

But I will not descant further upon this vile relic of the rebellion. Its career is too well known. The prisoners confined here, it will be recollected, were those against whom special vengeance was directed, prisoners of State, persons charged with harboring Union prisoners, Union officers charged with being spies, blockade-runners, &c. Well has it been said that a confinement in Castle Thunder is a foretaste of the tortures of the damned.

This building, together with the Libby belongs to the estate of JOHN ENDERS, and was leased by the rebel Government. They were originally built for stores, but subsequently turned into tobacco manufactories. But their base uses are now at an end.

This is the fourth day of the Union occupation, and the confusion in the city necessarily attendant upon such an evacuation, and such an occupation, is gradually subsiding. Could the ruins of the fire be removed from sight, Richmond would present an attractive appearance, for it is really a handsome city; but, after all, the saddest scenes are at the headquarters of the Provost-Martial, the Commissioners of Subsistence, and the office of Sanitary Commission, the latter being already established here. Gen. WEITZEL had no sooner established his headquarters here than thousands of citizens besieged him for rations. And as the city is now shut out from all supplies from the country, the crowd of applicants for subsistence is rapidly increasing. This morning there was nothing in the markets but a few small fish caught by negroes. The Capitol, the City Hall and the Capitol-square are filled with a great throng of all classes, condition, sexes and ages, with basket in hand and an appealing expression of face. What the regulations yet are in regard to the issue of rations to the citizens, I do not know, but a limited quantity is being supplied them at present.

In order to study this peculiar social feature of the rebellion, I mingled with these crowds this morning for a short time, to observe their temper, desires and condition. They were, of course, largely made up of what appeared to be the poorer classes, and many negroes were among them, some for subsistence for themselves and some as servants of families. I found many whose intelligent expression of countenance, fair features and attempted gentility of dress, indicated that they were of the higher classes, on whom the demands of want and hunger were as insatiable as upon those of less position. I noticed several ladies approach the officer in charge at the City Hall, genteelly attired, and with their faces so closely veiled as to defy the gaze of the keenest eye. They spoke in such tremulous tones when giving their names as to cause us to suspect their names were as foreign to them as the hunger they now sought to appease had been in days gone by. Many of the wealthiest families, however, who had the means, have far larger supplies of provisions on hand than was consistent with the repeated appeals of Confederate officials for such to spare from their bounty to feed the army.

The exodus of prominent citizens was confined mainly to those connected with the rebel government, and a few who had made themselves very conspicuous in rebel politics—all the rebel Cabinet and their chief assistants, though not much of their clerical force, got away. The preparations for the evacuation began very quietly among the officials. At noon of Sunday the important records of the departments were boxed up and carted to the depot; but very little suspicion was excited among the citizens as to the real state of the case. A strong guard was stationed at the Danville depot, and four trains were got ready, the first of which left, with DAVIS on board, at seven o'clock in the evening, and the last at midnight. DAVIS' family had gone into the country on the Friday preceeding, but not because of any apprehension that the city was to be given up. Very few families left the city, and there are very few vacant houses, the mansions of JEFF. DAVIS and GOV. BILLY SMITH being among those now in want of tenants. The family of Gen. LEE, consisting of his wife, who is an invalid, and three daughters, are among those who remain. They occupy a stylish house on Franklin-street, and for their protection a well disciplined guard is placed at the dwelling, and the family are scrupulously protected from annoyance of any character, the staring gaze of the passer-by hardly being allowed. This is the second time that Mrs. Gen. LEE has been in our hands. She was once captured by our cavalry near White House, in 1862, and sent through our lines to Richmond under flag of truce, by order of Gen. MCCLELLAN.

L. L. CROUNSE.

Union Sentiment in Richmond—Projects of Reconstruction—Distinguished Visitors—Recruiting Negro Troops—The Truth about Rebel Enlistment of Negroes.

From Our Own Correspondent.

RICHMOND, Friday, April 7, 1865.

I can give you news, to-day, which will gratify the heart of every loyal American. Virginia will return to the Union, and that right speedily. Desiring to ascertain the exact truth with reference to the alleged existence of a strong Union sentiment in the city, I availed myself of an opportunity to call upon certain gentlemen here whom I had heard alluded to by Secessionists as Union men, and I must say, that I spent two of the happiest hours of my life in full and free conversation with some of the most thorough and radical Union men in the country; men of wealth and position, whose faith has never wavered for an instant, and who, slaveholders, as they are, *demand that Virginia shall be taken back into the Union "under the Emancipation Proclamation;" that no vestige of the rebellion shall be tolerated; that the usurpation State, and Confederate, which has wrecked Virginia, shall not be recognized in a single respect*; that the State Government must be organized anew, by a convention of the people, as soon as that can be properly effected, and the State and its inhabitants thoroughly purged of treason in every shape.

Union sentiments, in this strong form exist here to a far greater extent than has yet been conceived; not alone among the poorer classes,—mechanics and laborers,—*but in wealthy and influential circles, where may be found men who have never lost faith in the Union*; who have confidently anticipated its triumph, and who greeted the old flag with tears of joy. They are men of the John Minor Botts school, and they are the leaven which shall leaven the whole lump here in this venerable old commonwealth of Virginia. They will delight to see the mass of the people treated with magnanimity, but they have felt too deeply the

Continued on Eighth Page.

The Philadelphia Inquirer.

PRICE TWO CENTS. PHILADELPHIA, WEDNESDAY, APRIL 12, 1865. PRICE TWO CENTS.

THE REBELLION AS IT WAS AND AS IT IS.

APRIL, 1861, AND APRIL, 1865.

THE LATEST NEWS

Important Presidential Proclamation

THE AMERICAN FLAG TO BE RESPECTED ABROAD.

SEVERE REBUKE TO "NEUTRAL" POWERS.

Latest Advices from Richmond!

SUNDAY IN THE REBEL CAPITAL.

An Arrogant Display of Secession

THE REBEL CLERGYMEN WON'T PRAY FOR PRESIDENT LINCOLN.

Weitzel Advises Coercion

RICHMOND IS TO HAVE A NATIONAL BANK.

Lee's Downfall Celebrated at His Late Residence.

PIERPOINT GOVERNMENT RECOGNIZED BY THE PRESIDENT.

The American Citizens of African Descent.

OUR SPECIAL RICHMOND CORRESPONDENCE.

Special Correspondence of the Inquirer.

RICHMOND, Monday, April 10—A. M.

Lee's Surrender in Richmond.

Last evening we had quite a sensation for Richmond. About eight P. M. General Weitzel received a despatch announcing the surrender of Lee and his entire army. A salute of one hundred guns was ordered to be fired, and Secesh at once started the story that a heavy battle was going on, and that Lee was to retake Richmond; but their joy was short-lived, for the contrabands soon got the true version, and, frantic with joy, ran in every direction, shouting "Lee has surrendered!" which sank like lead into the already almost broken hearts of the citizens.

The New Rebel Resting-Place.

Among the papers being brought to light is an order from Jeff Davis, dated on Sunday, the 2d inst., upon a Rebel Quartermaster, to ship his baggage and stores to Charlotte, N. C., where it is hoped he will fall into the hands of General Sherman.

Mrs. General Lee and Family.

Mrs. General Lee and her family continue to keep close in their house, and the shutters are all closed. No one disturbs them, and a sentry parades up and down the square, but does not interfere with the visits of their Secesh friends, to condole with them in their depths of despair.

Note from the Late Rebel Chieftain.

General Lee sent Mrs. Lee a note last Sunday, telling her that she must leave Richmond at once. He did not say where she should go and gave no further explanation. But she was then too sick to leave, and postponed it until Monday, when, in the panic, she was abandoned by Davis and Breckinridge, and the burning of a church in her front and the buildings in her rear, with the terrible explosions of the arsenals, and the general rushing to and fro, led her to make preparations to be carried out, but although all the houses around her on three sides were burned, the Lee mansion was not injured.

Bragg Unlucky as Usual.

General Bragg's house was consumed, with nearly all his furniture. But little was carried out, and that was appropriated by the poor whites.

Church Services.

The Episcopal church where Jeff. Davis was accustomed to attend was very well attended yesterday, but most of the audience were ladies, nine-tenths of whom were dressed in deep mourning.

Secesh Impudence.

One had two rows Confederate buttons upon a black silk sack, and another wore upon her sleeves the gold braid, indicating the rank of a Colonel. About a dozen Rebel officers attended in full uniform, and two or three minus one arm or leg were wearing *Confederate grey*. The pastor, Rev. C. Minnegrode, a German, and a very bitter Rebel, went through the regular Episcopal service, only *omitting the prayer for the President*. He read several chapters from the Bible containing the account of the persecutions of our Saviour by the Jews, his betrayal, his crucifixion and his resurrection. He seemed to dwell upon the passage, "Forgive them, Lord, they know not what they do." But the passage "*They who take up the sword shall perish by the sword*," was rather hastily run over. The citizens seemed very melancholy, and in following the pastor in the services responded very faintly. The choir consisted of a dozen ladies, towards the close a lame officer joined them. The organ was a very fine one but poorly played, and had it not been for it the choir would have broken down completely.

Jeff's Pew Vacant.

Jeff. Davis' pew, near the centre, was vacant, all around it were filled. Lee's pew was filled by some of our officers, it being well back to the rear. None of Lee's family or relatives attended, although he has about twenty here, a portion of whom attend the customary prayer meetings, where no Yankees are allowed to intrude. The other churches are about the same as this.

The fact is, Richmond is heart-broken. They are subjugated, and know it and feel it. They have lost their all, but hug their pride closer and closer as their troubles thicken and their relatives and friends are swept away.

A Rebel Commission.

The ex-Rebels had another meeting on Saturday, and appointed Judge Campbell, General J. R. Anderson (he of the Tredegar Works), N. P. Tyler (of the *Enquirer*), D. Burr (of the City Council), and H. W. Thornley, to visit Extra Billy Smith and endeavor to get him to make terms with Mr. Lincoln, and come back to Richmond. These represent the men who have tried to destroy the Union for four years; men who led the people and instigated the many damnable deeds that it makes one sick to recall to memory! They clung to the idea until all hope was gone, and they found themselves in our possession, and now they want to preserve the money they have made off the Rebellion, and secure further political power. They are still our enemies; still deem slavery a Christian institution; still look upon us as their hated conquerors, and upon themselves as innocent victims; but the love of wealth comes in, and they perjure themselves by taking the oath of allegiance. Talk to one of them five minutes, and he will betray himself every other sentence.

Another Class of Citizens.

Then there is another set of Union men, who have been marked and persecuted for four years. They are not so forward to make a display, but are none the less earnest and loyal. They have held several meetings, and to-morrow will hold another. Ex-Solicitor Whiting, of the War Department, is here counseling with them, and will meet them to-morrow morning.

URIAH H. PAINTER.

FROM ANOTHER CORRESPONDENT.

RICHMOND, VA., April 9th, 1865.

Special Correspondence of the Philadelphia Inquirer.

The First Sunday in Richmond,

Under the Union regime, has been a memorable one in many respects. The day has been a lovely one, the air mild and balmy, the sky cloudless, being one field of unsullied azure, and the entire city has presented a scene of quiet repose, unmarred by the slightest noise or disturbance, all of which is strictly in keeping with the sacred character of the day. The only sounds that have been wafted over the city by the soft spring breeze, consist of the peals of the various church bells, and the majestic strains of church organs, and the only signs of life and animation visible in the streets were throngs of people treading their way quietly and reverently to church.

Perhaps more from a sense of curiosity than proper devotion, I found myself moving in column with the church goers, and after crossing Capitol Square, directed my steps to the Monumental Protestant Episcopal Church, on Broad street. The church is a large one, octagonal in shape, capable of holding a numerous congregation, and contains a very fine organ. Entering, I found but a very small number of worshippers present, consisting of ladies, children, elderly gentlemen, and a very limited number of young men. The pastor, Rev. Mr. Woodbridge, took for his text the 28th verse of the 11th chapter of St. Matthew—"Come unto me all ye that labor and are heavy laden, and I will give you rest."

There was a peculiar fitness in the text, as the drift of the discourse was evidently intended to be a sort of balm to the Rebel sympathizers present for the anguish of mind and intense sorrow experienced by them in finding their fair city under control of and occupied by what they consider their deadliest enemies. The speaker proceeded to state that all those who had indulged in fair dreams of happiness and prosperity, and whose dreams had vanished like the morning mist, leaving the dreamer sad and dejected, and without rest, should remember the consoling words of Him who had so beautifully spoken in the words of the text. He spoke of the disappointment and soreness which ambitious minds experience at the success of those with whom they have placed themselves in rivalry, and to all such (evidently alluding to the defeat of the Rebel Generals) he would say, "Come unto me all ye who labor and are heavy laden, and I will give you rest." He alluded to the circumstance that man often leans upon the world, and the treacherous reed breaks, and he is without help or hope, and man's ever restless heart is buffeted about until it finds its rest in God.

The reverend gentleman touched upon the theme that those who perpetrate wrong, and whose restlessness leads them to the commission of acts of injustice, must render an account for their actions. He stated pointedly that the text of his sermon was intended for all who required consolation, no matter from what cause of grief. If any one present had no cause of sadness or grief, and felt contented within himself, his text and remarks did not apply to him. But to all afflicted ones he would say, if you are cast down with distress, sorrow or pain, go to Him, for He in his kindness will never cast out from His presence those who come unto him.

I noticed that the portion of the Episcopal ritual calling on the Heavenly Father to "bless the President of the United States and all others in authority," was omitted, and the words—"Bless all Christian rulers and magistrates," substituted.

The choir opened the services with an anthem entitled "Peace, troubled soul," and the soprano and alto seemed so affected at portions of the words, which probably reminded them of circumstances connected with the war, of a disagreeable character to them, that their voices trembled, and they could scarcely sing, and they were otherwise visibly affected.

The greater portion of the ladies present were in deep mourning, and a peculiar appearance of sadness seemed to pervade the entire congregation. A number of Union officers were present, who seemed to attract some attention. In the afternoon I visited St. Peter's Catholic Cathedral, and listened to vespers. Bishop Magill officiated, and the services were impressive. The cathedral is very large, the music extremely fine, and the interior is highly ornamented with paintings representing scenes in the life of our Saviour. The altar is composed of white marble, and an immense painting of the Crucifixion, a beautiful work of art, is erected in the rear of it. The attendance was slim, many of those present were Union soldiers, and I heard a member of the congregation say there were fewer persons present than he had ever known.

The four principal churches of Richmond, Episcopal, Methodist, Presbyterian and Catholic, are all very near each other and close by Capitol Square. Some of them are surmounted by tall and graceful spires, and they are all very handsome structures.

While penning the above in my room I heard an unusual commotion in the hotel, and some noise in the street, followed soon after by the thunder of artillery. I dropped my pen and proceeded to ascertain the cause, when I learned that a despatch had just been received at head-quarters that

Lee's Entire Army Had Surrendered.

The citizens had mostly retired for the night, but soon windows were thrown up and people poked their heads out to ascertain what was the matter. Others were running through the streets, and many, who had not heard of the contents of the official despatch regarding the surrender, spread a report that the Rebels were making an attack on the city.

Presently, a number of contrabands who had heard the news commenced jumping about in all directions, shouting "Lee's army has surrendered!" "Lee's army has surrendered," and it was not long before the delighted blacks made every person in town acquainted with the joyful or disagreeable intelligence, as the case might be.

The Secesh inhabitants on hearing the news quickly pulled down their windows or retired to their homes, not being inclined to believe the report. But not so the negroes, for they were entirely willing to believe what they wanted to believe and their joy and excitement knew no bounds. We know nothing as yet beyond the circumstance that an official despatch is said to be received worded, "General Lee and his whole army have surrendered," but a report prevails which I have not traced to any reliable authority, that

Jeff. Davis Has Been Captured

Near Charlotte, and also his wife and children with him. We are on the tip-toe of expectation for fresh developments of the glorious news, and I doubt not that Richmond will see many early risers to-morrow morning, bent on hearing all that can be learned regarding the downfall of Rebellion and the triumph of the Union.

For a number of days past a number of Rebel officers have been loafing about the streets of Richmond, holding high heads, and exhibiting a very much at home appearance. Provost Marshal Stevens issued an order that all such should at once report to him and take the oath of allegiance. Many of them declined to do so, when they were informed that unless they immediately obeyed orders a colored guard would be sent after them. This was too much for the chivalry, and many of them came forward at once.

The following is a list of Rebel officers who refused to take the oath, and were committed to Libby Prison:—

F. Gregory, General Rosser's staff.
Henry Taylor, General Loring's staff.
S. G. Short, Major and A. A. G. to General Martin.
D. P. Ramseur, Surgeon C. S. A.
S. B. Reardon, Assistant Paymaster C. S. A.
John J. McPherson, Assist. Paymaster C. S. A.
Captain C. O. Bigger, Invalid Corps.
Captain J. Thomas Buzzy, Second Maryland.
C. H. West, Jr., Flag Officer's Secretary.

Yesterday 298 Rebel prisoners took the oath, and 106 to-day. Lieutenant John Bishop is in charge of Libby Prison.

WM. H. CUNNINGTON.

NEAR PETERSBURG, Va., April 10, 1865.

"It never rains but it pours." Hardly had we done rejoicing over that great triumph of the Union arms, the taking of Richmond, than we are again called upon to strain our lungs with cheering, and to expend our gunpowder in celebrating the virtual end of this Rebellion, the

Surrender of General Lee and His Entire Army.

This great event occurred yesterday afternoon, but the exact nature of the ceremonies attending it have not yet transpired. You have, however, been already officially informed of the general terms of capitulation. The surrender took place about twelve miles from Burkesville, and constitutes an event in the history of the country, and even in the world's annals, of great and mighty import.

The Army of Northern Virginia has been no body of men to be despised; it died hard, and doubtless our own men, while contemplating it during the surrender, experienced—

"The stern joy which warriors feel
In foemen worthy of their steel."

It is universally conceded hereabouts that the surrender of General Lee ends the war. It lops off at one blow the head of the Rebellion, and the trunk is rotten and worthless.

It is anticipated by many that the Rebels yet in arms will now inaugurate a sort of guerrilla warfare, which may last for some time, but after a few of them have stretched hemp they will tire of that game, and peace will again bless the land, and the great American nation be greater and grander for having passed through the terrible ordeal of the past four years.

Last night the entire lines of the army, stretching around Petersburg, were illuminated with

Brilliant Bonfires.

Wild tumultuous cheers rent the air from the throats of thousands of sturdy warriors, and the greatest joy and enthusiasm pervaded every heart.

Artillery in all directions belched forth

Grand Salutes

Of one hundred guns, and bunting was displayed from every imaginable spot.

At daylight this morning,

The Gun-boats

In the James River, all the way from City Point to Richmond, made the welkin ring with the thunder of their guns of heavy calibre. The sailors manned the rigging and cheered most lustily, and I doubt not large quantities of apple-jack and old rye contributed their peculiar effect to the general rejoicing.

Four years ago Jeff. Davis gave utterance to some words at Stevenson, Alabama, which he has been compelled most reluctantly to eat. They have a peculiar fitness just now, as exhibiting the wide difference between his anticipations then and his realizations now. In February, 1861, he said to a number of his dupes, "Your Border States will gladly come into the Southern Confederacy within sixty days, as we will be your only friends. England will recognise us, and a glorious future is before us. The grass will grow in the Northern cities where the pavements have been worn by the tread of commerce.

"We will carry war where it is easy to advance, where food for the sword and torch await the armies, in the densely populated cities."

Mrs. General Grant

Is at City Point, and last evening was called upon by a great number of officers and influential citizens visiting here, who congratulated her on the great achievement of her illustrious husband.

The Head-quarters Band, belonging to the One-hundred-and-fourteenth Pennsylvania, was brought into requisition, and serenaded the lady and her guests.

Speculations

Are already on foot as to what course will be taken as far as reconstruction is concerned, and everybody has a theory of his own. Everybody is anxious to know what will be done with General Lee, and everybody also desires to be present at the final disposition of Jeff. Davis when he is captured, as he probably will be, if that event has not already transpired.

WM. H. CUNNINGTON.

PRESIDENT'S PROCLAMATION OF APRIL 11TH.

WASHINGTON, April 11th.—The Proclamation in reference to closing Southern ports is in accordance with a law passed as early as 1861. It was then understood, however, that while foreign powers would respect the effective blockade of those ports by naval force, a claim to exercise legal authority over them as over other ports of the United States, would not be respected. It is believed that the time has now come, however, when the United States Government can claim to exercise that legal authority over all its ports, whether blockaded or not, which belongs to every independent sovereign power. A sufficient number of Southern ports are left open for legitimate trade, and those now proclaimed closed will, it is presumed, be reopened after a time. Meanwhile blockade running is likely to be effectively ended. The issuing of this Proclamation is understood to be the business upon which Secretary Seward was about to visit City Point to confer with the President last week.

Another Presidential Proclamation.

Another important proclamation is issued to-day, claiming that our vessels of war in foreign ports shall no longer be subjected to restrictions as at present, but shall have the same rights and hospitalities which are extended to foreign men-of-war in ports of the United States, declaring that hereafter the cruisers of every nation will receive the treatment which in their ports they accord to ours.

By the President of the United States,

A PROCLAMATION.

Whereas for some time past vessels of war of the United States have been refused in certain foreign ports privileges and immunities to which they were entitled by treaty, public law, or the comity of nations, at the same time that vessels of war of the country wherein the said privileges and immunities have been withheld, have enjoyed them fully and uninterruptedly in ports of the United States, which condition of things has not always been forcibly resisted by the United States, although on the other hand they have not at any time failed to protest against, and declare their dissatisfaction with the same; In the view of the United States no condition any longer exists which can be claimed to justify the denial to them by any one of said nations of customary naval rights, such as has heretofore been so unnecessarily persisted in, and

Now, therefore, I, Abraham Lincoln, President of the United States, do hereby make known, that if after a reasonable time shall have elapsed for intelligence of this proclamation to have reached any foreign country in whose ports the said privileges and immunities shall have been refused as aforesaid, they shall continue to be so refused, then and thenceforth the same privileges and immunities shall be refused to the vessels of war of that country in like ports of the United States; and this refusal shall continue until war vessels of the United States shall have been placed upon an entire equality in the foreign ports aforesaid with similar vessels of other countries. *The United States, whatever claim or pretense may have existed heretofore, are now at least entitled to claim and concede an entire and friendly equality of rights and hospitalities with all maritime nations.*

In witness whereof I have hereunto set my hand and caused the seal of the United States to be affixed.

Done at the city of Washington this 11th day of April, in the year of our Lord 1865, and of the independence of the United States the 89th.

By the President, ABRAHAM LINCOLN.
W. H. SEWARD, Secretary of State.

The Fort Sumter Celebration.

FORTRESS MONROE, Va., April 10.—The steamship *Arago* arrived here at half-past three o'clock yesterday afternoon, with Henry Ward Beecher and party, from New York, bound to Fort Sumter. Owing to the southeasterly wind, the *Arago* was somewhat later in reaching here than was expected. Judge Holt, Provost Marshal General Fry, and others, were here yesterday, awaiting the arrival of the *Arago*, and [illegible] barked the steamer [illegible] and proceeded [illegible]. The weather at the time looked very unpromising, and indicated the approach of a storm. To-day the storm [illegible], rain having fallen all day, with a heavy [illegible] [illegible]

The New-York Times.

VOL. XIV......NO. 4229. | NEW-YORK, FRIDAY, APRIL 14, 1865. | PRICE FOUR CENTS

THE ERA OF PEACE.

Highly Important Order from the War Department.

THE CLOSING UP OF THE WAR.

All Drafting and Recruiting to be Stopped.

The Military Establishment to be Reduced.

Military Restrictions upon Trade and Commerce Removed.

[OFFICIAL.]

WAR DEPARTMENT, WASHINGTON, April 13, 1865—6 P. M.

To Maj.-Gen. Dix, New-York:

This department, after mature consideration, and consultation with the Lieutenant-General upon the results of the recent campaigns, has come to the following determinations, which will be carried into effect by appropriate orders, to be immediately issued:

First.—To stop all drafting and recruiting in the loyal States.

Second.—To curtail purchases for arms, ammunition, Quartermaster and Commissary supplies, and reduce the expenses of the military establishment in its several branches.

Third.—To reduce the number of general and staff-officers to the actual necessities of the service.

Fourth.—To remove all military restrictions upon trade and commerce, so far as may be consistent with public safety.

As soon as these measures can be put in operation, it will be made known by public orders.

EDWIN M. STANTON, Secretary of War.

IMPORTANT ORDER FROM GEN. GRANT.

The Order Suspending Trade Operations in Certain States Revoked.

HEADQUARTERS ARMIES OF THE UNITED STATES IN THE FIELD, VIRGINIA, April 11, 1865.

SPECIAL ORDER, No. 74.—Second paragraph of Special Orders, No. 48, of the date of March 10, 1865, from these headquarters suspending trade operations within the State of Virginia, except that portion known as the eastern shore, and the States of North Carolina and South Carolina, and that portion of the State of Georgia immediately bordering on the Atlantic, including the City of Savannah, until further orders, is hereby revoked.

By command of Lieut.-Gen. GRANT.

T. S. BOWERS, Assistant Adjutant-General.

IMPORTANT MOVEMENT.

The Legislature of Virginia Called to Richmond.

They Have Safe Conduct and Protection.

The Object a Return of the State to the Union.

From the Richmond Whig, April 12.

To the People of Virginia:

The undersigned members of the Legislature of the State of Virginia in connection with a number of citizens of the State, whose names are attached to this paper, in view of the evacuation of the City of Richmond by the Confederate Government, and its occupation by the military authorities of the United States, the surrender of the Army of Northern Virginia, and the suspension of the jurisdiction of the civil power of the State, are of the opinion that an immediate meeting of the General Assembly of the State is called for by the exigencies of the situation. The consent of the military authorities of the United States to a session of the Legislature in Richmond, in connection with the Governor and Lieutenant-Governor, to their free deliberation upon public affairs, and to the ingress and departure of all its members under safe conduct, has been obtained.

The United States authorities will afford transportation from any point under their control to any of the persons before mentioned.

The matters to be submitted to the Legislature are the restoration of peace to the State of Virginia, and the adjustment of questions involving life, liberty and property that have arisen in the State as a consequence of war.

We therefore earnestly request the Governor, Lieutenant-Governor, and members of the Legislature, to repair to this city by the 25th of April, instant.

We understand that full protection to persons and property will be afforded in the State, and we recommend to peaceful citizens to remain at their homes and pursue their usual avocations, with confidence that they will not be interrupted.

We earnestly solicit the attendance in Richmond, on or before the 25th of April instant, of the following persons, citizens of Virginia, to confer with us as to the best means of restoring peace to the State of Virginia. We have procured safe conduct from the military authorities of the United States for them to enter the city and depart without molestation. Hons. R. M. T. Hunter, A. T. Caperton, Wm. C. Rives, John Letcher, A. H. H. Stuart, R. L. Montague, Fayette McMullen, J. P. Holcombe, Alexander Rives, B. Johnson Barbour, James Barbour, Wm. L. Goggin, J. B. Baldwin, Thomas S. Gholson, Walter Staples, S. D. Miller, Thomas J. Randolph, Wm. T. Early, R. A. Claybrooke, John Critcher, Wm. Gallie, T. H. Eppes, and those other persons for whom passports have been procured, and especially others whom we consider it unnecessary to mention.

(Signed.)

A. J. MARSHALL, Senator from Fauquier.
JOHN NESSON, Senator from Marion.
JAMES VENABLE, Senator from Petersburgh.
DAVID I. BURR, of the House of Delegates, from Richmond.
DAVID J. SAUNDERS, of the House of Delegates, Richmond City.
L. S. HALL, the House of Delegates, Wetzel County.
J. J. ENGLISH, of the House of Delegates, Henrico County.
WM. AMBERS, of the House of Delegates, Chesterfield County.
A. M. KEILY, House of Delegates, Petersburgh.
H. W. THOMAS, Second Auditor, Virginia.
ST. L. L. MONCURE, Chief Clerk Second Auditor's Office.
JOSEPH MAYO, Mayor City of Richmond.
R. HOWARD, Clerk Hustings Court, Richmond City.
THOS. M. DUDLEY, Sergeant, Richmond City.
LYTTLETON TAZEWELL, Commonwealth's Attorney, Richmond City.
WM. T. JOYNES, Judge of the Circuit Court, Petersburgh.
JOHN A. MEREDITH, Judge Circuit Court, Richmond.
WM. H. LYONS, Judge Hustings Court, Richmond.
WM. C. WICKHAM, Member of Congress, Richmond District.
BENJ. S. EWELL, President William and Mary College.
NAT. TYLER, Editor Richmond *Enquirer*.
R. F. WALKER, Publisher *Examiner*.
J. R. ANDERSON, Richmond.
R. R. HOWISON, Richmond.
W. GODDIN, Richmond.
P. G. BAYLY, Richmond.
F. J. SMITH, Richmond.
FRANKLIN STERNS, Henrico.
JOHN LYON, Petersburgh.
THOMAS B. FISHER, Fauquier.
WM. M. HARRISON, Charles City.
CYRUS HALL, Ritchie.
THOS. W. GARNETT, King and Queen.
JAMES A. SCOTT, Richmond.

I concur in the preceding recommendation.

J. A. CAMPBELL.

Approved for publication in the *Whig* and in hand-bill form.

G. WEITZEL, Major-General Commanding Richmond, Va., April 11, 1865.

THE GEN. LYON DISASTER.

Complete List of the Passengers and Crew.

From Our Own Correspondent.

WILMINGTON, N. C., Thursday, April 6, 1865.

Below will be found as complete a list as the transportation records here furnish of the passengers on board the steamer *Gen. Lyon*, which burned off Hatteras last Thursday. She sailed from Smithville on Wednesday, and took a larger number of passengers than any other vessel that has left this port since our occupation of it. Her boats, properly manned, could save one hundred, and there were several sail in sight at the time of the accident, so that quite a number may have been saved:

Lieut. J. P. Alexander, Lieut. C. K. Johnson, Lieut. George Johnson, Sergt. Blake and 15 men Third Pennsylvania Artillery; E. C. Bray, Twenty-fourth Massachusetts. Refugees—M. A. Chauncey, Theo. Bletzen, A. Buchanan, Mrs. Brazil and family of seven, August Crummel, wife and two children; A. Paison, A. Scholz, Wm. Harrington, A. Leary, F. Schuan, Z. H. Amaniz, John Snyder, wife and three children; James Gilmore, wife and five children; James Hayes, wife and two children; Wm. Shamahan, Michael McNelty, John Bradbury, Wm. Dawsey, wife, seven children and servant; Henry Hurt, wife and three children; Henry Bawes and wife; Mary Ferrell and colored boy; H. Hurtz, Solomon Benjamin, Julia Brown, D. Windhom, wife and child, H. Windhom, J. C. Windhom, J. T. Hammond, lady and two children, C. B. Moss, Philip Burkhart, S. E. Russell, J. Burkhart, wife and child, Miss J. A. Banks, L. W. Snell, H. Snell and colored boy, H. A. Brooks, Thos. Carney, Clarence Dunn, T. S. Mansfield, Wm. Atkinson, D. McLardy, H. James, J. H. Brodshort, wife and three children, Mr. Shaller, Adrian Durenead, Edward W. Scholober, Chas. A. Letaie, Lewis Mognors, Alex Lee, W. Shaber, A. Cameron, Mrs. D. M. E. Williams, Jacob Doran, W. Duncan, wife and child, J. B. Bannister, George Stattler and wife, John A. Smith, J. McGuire, P. O'Hara, J. Rogan, Charles E. Bradley, colored; R. H. Warner, Frank Cowen, David Denvan, wife and child; Frank Curran, rebel deserter; Capt. Bullock, 1 officer and 22 recruits.

Isaac C. Cobby, 5th O V C	Rufus F. Wilson, 5th Tenn V.
Peter Wade, 5th O Vol Cal.	Wm E. Merritt, Bat [illegible] 1st Ill.
Tho W. Smith, 5th O V Cav	Peter Holt, Bat H 1st Ill.
Jas W. Zieur, 5th O V Cav.	P Munson, Bat H 1st Ill
Sergt Jno Wilfer, 1st O V C.	C Beckman, Bat H 1st Ill.
Lenard Dyer, 1st O V Cav	Jno Johnson, Bat H 1st Ill.
Wm J Smith, 82d Ohio.	Richard Clarey, 1st Sergt. 2d Ill
James Martin, 82d N. Y.	George Hewer, 17th Wis.
Henry Hoppe [illegible] N Y.	Over Beard, 123d Ohio.
E B Knig, 4th N Y.	John Emmerson
Wm Cullen, 5th Va Cav.	Charles Mott, 91st N Y.
Sephia [illegible], [illegible] N. Y.	W C Hailes, 5th Michigan
[illegible]	Robt Deede, 5th Virginia
Sam W [illegible] N Y.	P Lensey, 5th Virginia.
Jas Brown, 11th N Y.	Phillip Smith, 9th Illinois.
J Levy, 56th N Y	John Mully, 8th Illinois.
Henry Martin, 42d N Y	Geo Baker, 4th Pennsylvania.
Thos Sullivan, 2d N Y.	Jacob Stuarts, 148th Penn.
J Smith, 6th Michigan.	J Riley, 28th Ohio
Wm C Andrews, 14th N Y	Corp J W Ratliff, 2d Ohio
B W [illegible], 5th Tenn Cav.	J Lewis, 5th New York.
Wm H Call, 1st Penn.	C Corte[illegible], 15th N Y Cav.
Jas Arnett, 14th Iowa.	F. J. Longly, 122d Ohio.
Geo [illegible] Sanders, P V C	
Corp J M Braddy, 5th Pa Cav.	

Total number, 36.

PAROLED UNION PRISONERS.

M Robbins, 11th Penn.	J Wenbress, 2d Penn Cav.
W Roeb, 11th Pennsylvania.	A Gregg, 5th N Y Cav.
H O'hen, 21st Illinois.	H DePant, 85th New-York.
J B Wilber, 21st Illinois	C McDowell, 8th Iowa Cav.
J Pense, 21st Illinois.	J Welton, 5th Mich Cav.
W William, 142d Penn.	H Eby, 7th Penn Reserves.
A D Pearson, 14th Ill Cav.	A Deveraux, 8th N Y Art.
J Thompson, 4th Kentucky.	Flynn, 72d Ohio.
D Bayley, 137 New-York	W Milton, 4th Penn Cav.
A F Cook, 8th Indiana Cav	A Sacket, 8th Iowa Cav.
C Cox, 101st Pennsylvania.	A Spencer, 85th New-York.
C Horner, 101st New York.	S Horton, 103d Ohio.
C Cowdrey, 12th Mass	J F Burbridge, [illegible] Ohio.
D Reynolds, 15th Illinois Cavalry.	J C Downing, 24th Iowa.
B Gunway, 25th Iowa.	J Smith, 1st Virginia Cav.
J W Kirk, 13th Penn.	G Galusky, 106th N Y
H Knight, 122d New-York.	J C Thompson, 12th O Cav.
John Lawrence, 37th Mass.	A Northam, 2d Penn.
John Aveckson, 18th Wis	Thomas G Edwards, 6th Mass.
J McKrown, 3d N Y Cav.	Corp B F Fulkerson, 55th Ohio.
A Lennee, 35th N J Res.	F M Crabtree, 73d Ohio.
Joseph McDougall, 3d Ohio.	M D Donaldson, 39th Ohio.
J H Phillipp, 84th Ohio.	Peter Garrison, 47th Ohio.
Charles Henry, 32d Wis.	J McCarthy, 19th Mass.
J Johnson, 19th Penn Cav.	M Dietrick, 43d New-York.
J Purt, 24th Michigan.	H Warner, 9th Mich Cav.
T G Johnson, 20th Illinois.	A J Lookingbill, 6th Ind.
H S Smith, 104th Ohio.	J M Kendall, 8th New-York Cavalry
J Ward, 4th Kentucky.	S Smith, 1st N Y Cavalry.
J O Rouke, 92d Illinois.	E Martin, 8th Michigan.
J Yates, 101st Penn.	W Finney, 4th Mass Cav.
R Davis, 11th Iowa.	J Dyer, 1st Minnesota.
J Davidson, 27th Michigan.	A Cockran, 196th Penn.
L Beanshaw, 8th Ill Cav.	W J Conn, 10th Ohio Cav.
D H Hattelt, 11th Ohio.	G Simpson, 64th Ohio Cav.
A Miles, 69th New-York.	P Simpson, 54th Ohio Cav.
W Drake, 8th New-York Heavy Artillery.	E Goohort, 8th Ill Cav.
F Christian, 101st Penn.	W Burgen, 2d Bat. 16th U S.
H Isham, 6th Vermont.	J Smith, 63d Indiana.
D McDowell, 10th Penn.	J Base, 101st Ohio.
J Calvory, 3d Iowa Cav.	J Kilpatrick, 73d Illinois.
W Hennen, 1st Va Cav.	C A Russell, 1st Virginia Cavalry.
J Rhodes, 3d Iowa Cav.	B Berry, 25th Indiana.
T Heimick, 8th Ind Cav.	W Smith, 1st Mich. Engin.
E Carter, 8th Tenn.	Corp J. McDonald, 31st Ohio.
T Belknap, 17th Iowa.	R M Myers, 1st Ohio Cav.
E P Morris, 17th Iowa.	E Bowman, 53d Ind.
T O'Neil, 4th Ky Cav.	J Wilson, 1st N H Cav.
E Sutliff, 16th Conn.	J Cambell, 48th N Y.
C Denton, 20th Mass.	N Shanahan, 101st Ind.
M Desmond, 20th Mass.	Sgt E Mettetal, 24th Mich C.
J Harris, 66th N Y.	H Kisor, 7th Ohio.
H Wetty, 4th Ky.	G White, 60th Ill.
J Young, 11th Vt.	C Draper, 82 Ind.
J Rikey, 51st N Y.	
G Armstrong, 85th N Y.	

The names of the officers and crew I could not obtain. There was also about two hundred men of the Fifty-sixth Illinois, who had been mustered out of service and were on their way home, whose names I failed to get. Eleven discharged officers of the same organization are given as follows:

Maj Jas Files.	Capt Urber.
Capt Dungeory.	Lieut H S Dunlop.
Lieut Gowdie.	Lieut Rankins.
Lieut Haulbeck.	Lieut Joiner.
Lieut McKenzie.	Lieut Jas Griver.

The first officer of the *Gen. Lyon*, JNO. HAYDON, and several of the crew are in hospital here sick.

The Seven-Thirty Loan.

PHILADELPHIA, Thursday, April 13.

JAY COOKE reports the subscription to the Seven-thirty Loan, to-day, at $3,264,500, including $1,000,000 from the First National Bank of New-York, $138,000 from Pittsburgh, $50,000 from Nashville, and 2,291 individual subscriptions for amounts of $50 and $100.

THE SURRENDER.

Full Details of the Great Event from an Eye-Witness.

The Interview Between Grant and Lee.

The Dignified and Amiable Character of the Scene.

Signing of the Articles of Capitulation by Lee.

He Expresses Thanks for the Generous Conditions.

The Surrender Received by the Rebel Army with Cheers.

Social Meeting of Prominent Officers of the Two Armies.

A Second Interview Between Grant and Lee on Horseback.

General Lee Announces that He will Exert Himself for a Complete Cessation of Hostilities.

The Number of Men Surrendered 18,000 to 20,000.

From Our Own Correspondent.

ON BOARD STEAMER "CITY POINT," JAMES RIVER, VA., Wednesday, April 12, via WASHINGTON, D. C., April 13—12:20 P. M.

Lieut.-Gen. GRANT and staff arrived at City Point this morning at half-past four o'clock, having left Appomattox Court-house—the scene of the surrender of Gen. LEE and his army—on Tuesday morning at daylight. They came on horseback to Burkesville Station, on the Southside Railroad, and thence by rail to City Point. Appomattox Court-house is one hundred and three miles west of Petersburgh, and only twenty-two miles east of Lynchburgh. Gen. LEE did not arrive with them, but when the details of the surrender are complete, will proceed direct to Richmond.

I am able to lay before you the highly interesting and important details of the surrender, through the courtesy of Col. TAL. P. SHAFFNER, the eminent telegraph engineer, who was an eye-witness to the whole scene.

But in order to give a clear idea of the position where the event took place, and how the respective armies stood at the time, it is necessary to go back and very briefly follow the course of the armies from the time they left Petersburgh. When LEE began his retreat he crossed the Appomattox and moved westwardly with rapidity, while GRANT followed with part of his force directly in LEE's rear, and with the remainder of his infantry and SHERIDAN's cavalry, he struck out parallel with and on both sides of the Southside Railroad, for Burkesville, fifty-three miles west of Petersburgh, where the Danville road crosses the Southside road. By the most herculean efforts, the troops being cheered by the prospect of cutting off the rebel retreat, our forces reached Burkesville first, and the Danville Railroad was no longer available to LEE. In the meantime SHERIDAN had most sorely harrassed LEE's several retreating columns, and at Harpers Farm, on Thursday afternoon last, with the assistance of the Fifth and Sixth Corps, completely cut off and captured EWELL's entire column of nine thousand men, seven general officers, fifteen field pieces of artillery, twenty-nine battle flags, and six miles of wagon trains.

The details of this engagement are forwarded by your correspondent, Capt. PAUL, who witnessed it. As you may see by the map, the Appomattox west of Petersburgh is a very crooked stream, and has many tributaries, the country being rough and hilly. LEE was compelled to keep mainly north of the stream, on the line of the old stage road from Lynchburgh to Richmond.

After reaching Burkesville, Gen. MEADE, with the greater portion of the Army of the Potomac, took up the pursuit on the north side of the railroad, while SHERIDAN's cavalry and ORD's Twenty-fourth Corps moved rapidly along the south side of the road, SHERIDAN being constantly on LEE's flanks, frequently compelling him to halt and form line of battle, and as often engaging him, cutting off detachments, picking up stragglers, capturing cannon without number, and demoralizing the enemy at every stand. On Friday, at Farmville, 16 miles west of Burkesville, a considerable engagement occurred, in which the Second Corps participated largely and suffered some loss. Here Gen. THOS. A. SMYTH, commanding a brigade in the Second Division of the Second Corps, was killed while on the skirmish line, and in a charge subsequently Gen. MOTT, commanding the Third Division of the same corps, was wounded. Other troops were brought up, but before the enemy could be reengaged, they were on the retreat again. At High Bridge, over the Appomattox, LEE again crossed to the north side of the river, and two of our regiments, the Fifty-fourth Pennsylvania and One Hundred and Twenty-third Ohio, which were sent there to hold the bridge, were captured by a strong rebel cavalry force. The railroad bridge at this point a very high and long structure, was burned by the enemy. LEE now headed directly for Lynchburgh, in the hope of reaching a point where he could move around the front of our left wing, and escape toward Danville by a road which runs directly south from a point about twenty miles east of Lynchburgh. But GRANT was too vigorous—the pursuit was too hot. LEE's rear and flanks were so sorely pressed that he was compelled to skirmish nearly every step, and to destroy or abandon an immense amount of property, while SHERIDAN was rapidly shooting ahead of him. The position, therefore, on Sunday morning, was one from which LEE could not possibly extricate himself. His army lay massed a short distance west of Appomattox Court-house; his last avenue of escape toward Danville on the southwest was gone; he was completely hemmed in. MEADE was in his rear on the east and on his right flank north of Appomattox Court-house; SHERIDAN had headed him off completely, by getting between him and Lynchburgh; Gen. ORD was on the south of the court-house, near the railroad; the troops were in the most enthusiastic spirits, and the rebel army was doomed. LEE's last effort to escape was made on Sunday morning, by attempting to cut his way through SHERIDAN's lines, but it totally failed.

It will be recollected that Gen. GRANT's first letter to LEE was dated on the 7th, Friday, the day of the battle of Farmville, and the correspondence was kept up during the following day and up to 11 o'clock on Sunday, as already published. In response to Gen. GRANT's last letter, Gen. LEE appeared on the picket line of the Second Corps, MILES' division, with a letter addressed to Gen. MEADE, requesting a cessation of hostilities while he considered Gen. GRANT's terms of surrender. Gen. MEADE replied that he had no authority to accede to the request, but that he would wait two hours before making an attack. In the meantime Gen. GRANT sent word to Gen. MEADE that he would be up in half an hour, and the matter was turned over to him. A flag of truce proceeded to Appomattox Court-house shortly after noon, and at about 2 o'clock P. M. the two Generals met at the house of Mr. WILMER McLEAN. Gen. LEE was attended by Gen. MARSHAL, his Adjutant-General; Gen. GRANT, by Col. PARKER, one of his chief Aides-de Camp. The two Generals met and greeted each other with dignified courtesy, and proceeded at once to the business before them. Gen. LEE immediately alluded to the conditions of the surrender, characterized them as exceedingly lenient, and said he would gladly leave all the details to Gen. GRANT's own discretion. Gen. GRANT stated the terms of the parole that the arms should be stacked, the artillery parked, and the supplies and munitions turned over to him, the officers retaining their side arms, horses and personal effects. Gen. LEE promptly assented to the conditions, and the agreement of surrender was engrossed and signed by Gen. LEE at 3:30 o'clock.

Gen. LEE asked Gen. GRANT for an interpretation of the phrase, "personal effects," and said that many of his cavalrymen owned their own horses. Gen. GRANT said he construed it to mean that the horses must be turned over to the United States Government. *Gen. Lee admitted the correctness and justice of the interpretation*, when Gen. GRANT said he would instruct his officers to allow those men who owned their horses to retain them, as they would need them *for the purpose of tilling their farms.* Gen. LEE expressed a great sense of gratification for such a generous consideration, and said it would have a very good effect. He subsequently expressed a hope that each soldier might be furnished with a certificate of his parole, as evidence to prevent him from being forced into the army until regularly exchanged. Gen. GRANT assented to the suggestion, and the printing presses were soon put to work to print the documents required.

In regard to the strength of his army, Gen. LEE said he had no idea of the number of men that he should be able to deliver up. There had been so many engagements, and such heavy losses from desertion and other causes within the past few days, and the retreat so rapid, that no regular morning reports had been made since leaving Petersburgh; but it is generally believed by the best informed officers that LEE surrenders eighteen to twenty thousand men. Of the army horses, wagons, &c., there is yet no official account. Gen. LEE informed Gen. GRANT that his men were short of provisions, whereupon Gen. GRANT ordered twenty-five thousand rations to be distributed to them. Thus substantially ended the interview. Both Generals were the very impersonation of dignity and courtesy in their bearing. LEE is fine health, and though apparently impressed with the vital effect and importance of the act he was performing, he was cheerful and pleasant in his demeanor. The house where the stipulations were signed was a fair brick structure, with neat grounds, and quite neatly furnished. The room in which the interview took place was a comfortable parlor, about eighteen by twenty feet, and adorned by the usual furnishing common to the average of Virginia houses.

Both Generals were attired in full uniform. LEE wore a very fine sword. GRANT had no side-arms, having left camp the day previous, with the intention of being gone but a few hours, but, on the contrary, being gone all night. When the two Generals first met they were attended only by the staff officers already mentioned; but, during the interview, several of our officers entered and were introduced to Gen. LEE, who received them cordially and made no objections to their presence. They were Maj.-Gens. Ord and Sheridan, Brevet Maj.-Gen. Ingalls, Brig.-Gens. Williams, Rawlins and Barnard, Lieut.-Cols. Parker, Dent, Badeau, Bowers, A. A. G., Porter, Babcock, and Capt. Lincoln. Tal. P. Shaffner, Esq., was the only civilian present.

It should be said that Gen. GRANT had anticipated the surrender for several days, and had resolved beforehand not to require the same formalities which are required in a surrender between the forces of two foreign nations or belligerent powers; that they were our own people, and to exact no conditions for the mere purpose of humiliation.

After the interview, Gen. LEE returned to his own camp, about half a mile distant, where his leading officers were assembled awaiting his return.

He announced the result and the terms, whereupon they expressed great satisfaction at the leniency of the conditions. They then approached him in order of rank, shook hands, expressing satisfaction at his course and their regret at parting, all shedding tears on the occasion.

The fact of surrender and the liberal terms were then announced to the troops, and when Gen. LEE appeared among them he was loudly cheered. On Monday, between 9 and 10 o'clock A. M., Gen. GRANT and Staff rode out in the direction of the rebel lines, and on a hill just beyond the court-house, where a full view of the rebel army could be obtained, Gen. LEE was met, attended by but one staff officer and orderlies. The Generals halted, and, seated on their horses, conversed for nearly an hour upon the prospects of the future, each seeming to realize the mighty influence which the events of the present were to have upon it. Gen. LEE signified very emphatically his desire for a total cessation of hostilities, and indicated his intention to do all in his power to effect that end. The best of good feeling prevailed, and this was the last interview between the two Commanders. Gen. GRANT returned to McLEAN's house, and soon after Gens. LONGSTREET, GORDON, PICKETT and HETH, with a number of staff officers, arrived, and after recognitions and introductions, an hour of very friendly intercourse took place, during which many scenes and incidents of bye-gone college days and days of service together in the regular army, were revived and retold with much good nature.

Gen. GRANT gave Gen. LEE and his principal officers passes to proceed whither they wished. The parties then separated, and early on Tuesday morning Gen. GRANT and staff left the scene of the great event for their headquarters at City Point, arriving at 4:30 A. M. to-day. Gen. MEADE was left in command to superintend the details of the surrender, which would occupy several days, the work of providing each man and officer with an individual parole being a slow and tedious one; part of them are written and part printed by the little printing presses which accompany the headquarters.

Thus in exactly two weeks, to almost an hour, from the time Gen. GRANT and staff broke up their headquarters at City Point for the Spring campaign, they return with the Spring campaign not only complete, but the entire opposing army destroyed and the war substantially closed. The complete character of the destruction of LEE's army thus accomplished, forcibly appears from these facts, viz.: That when the operations began two weeks ago, his army numbered not less than 65,000 men; that we have captured from him 25,000 prisoners; that his killed and wounded are not less than 14,000; and that the balance of the army deserted on the retreat, or fell into our hands at the surrender.

The congratulations at headquarters this morning were very hearty.

As the various gentlemen of the staff appeared at their old homes, and as commemorative of their triumphant return, BRADY, the eminent photographer of New-York, preserved the group, Generals and all, for the admiration of all their friends in this and future generations.

L. L. CROUNSE.

The Peace Question as Affected by Lee's Surrender—The Capture of Lynchburgh—Sheridan Moving on Danville—Sherman Moving on Goldsboro—Incidents of the Late Campaign—Return of the Army to its Base.

From Our Own Correspondent.

CITY POINT, Va., Wednesday, April 12, 1865.

A point that attracts great attention in the correspondence which preceded the surrender of LEE and his army, is the direct and emphatic manner in which LEE alludes to his desire and intention to do all in his *power* to procure a speedy peace; that he, in fact, *surrenders for that purpose.* Gen. LEE, therefore, next to Gen. GRANT, becomes the most efficient peace-maker in the country. And as the entire Southern people have put their faith in him most implicitly, and declared that they would trust their cause in his hands, his action must wield an immense influence throughout the Southern States. As soon as the details of the surrender were executed, it was Gen. LEE's intention to return to Richmond, where his family are living. Mrs. Gen. LEE is represented as being much affected by the disaster to the rebel cause, but the reports about her serious illness have no foundation. She is an invalid, and for years has only been able to move from her bed to her chair. The entire family are now in our hands; Gen. ROBERT E. LEE, and his son, WILLIAM HENRY FITZHUGH LEE, who was *not* killed at Petersburgh, as has been reported, are prisoners on parole; his eldest son, G. W. CUSTIS LEE, is a prisoner of war in our custody, captured on Thursday last by SHERIDAN; his nephew, FITZHUGH LEE, whose wife is the owner of the White House estate on the Pamunkey, is also a prisoner on parole.

Though the surrender of the Army of Northern Virginia is an accomplished fact, our army is not idle, but whatever force is necessary to complete the entire work is even now in rapid motion. The Twenty-fourth Army Corps, a body of men that can outmarch any other body in the world, moved on Sunday for Lynchburgh, and just as Gen. GRANT left Burkesville for City Point on Tuesday afternoon, he received a dispatch announcing the occupation of that city by our troops without opposition.

As soon as SHERIDAN had rested his men and horses he moved directly for Danville, and has ere this occupied the place, as it was but seventy-five miles distant. This places his force directly in JOHNSTON's rear, and cuts off his hope of escape. Gen. SHERMAN moved from Goldsboro on Monday last for Raleigh and between SHERMAN and SHERIDAN the public may judge of JOHNSTON's chances of success. Important news from these columns is hourly expected.

The number of prisoners captured from the beginning of the campaign up to the present time, is over twenty-five thousand, aside from those surrendered and paroled. The nine thousand prisoners captured by Gens. SHERIDAN and WRIGHT on Thursday last, were yesterday between Wilson's Station and Petersburgh, on their way in from the front. Gens. EWELL, CUSTIS LEE, KERSHAW, BARTON, DUBOIS and two others were among them. The officers, six hundred in number, are expected here to-night.

Following the train on which came Gen. GRANT this morning, were two others, bringing two thousand of our wounded, among whom is Brevet Major Gen. MOTT, of the Second Corps, wounded on Friday last in the engagement at Farmsville.

One of the most singular and lamentable events of the war, carrying one back to the days of the chivalric Knights, when each foeman challenged his adversary to hand to hand conflict with the attendant hosts as spectators, occurred on Friday last, on the left of the line, during a skirmish between a portion of the Twenty-fourth Corps and a brigade of rebel cavalry. Gen. REED, Chief of Staff to Gen. ORD, being up at the front, suddenly recognized an old acquaintance in the person of Gen. ST. CLAIR DEARING, commanding a brigade of South Carolina Cavalry. Whether they had been in former times friends or foes I cannot say, but they met now as foes, and, in full view of the opposing forces present, they held a tournament of death, fighting with pistols, until, almost simultaneously, REED fell dead, and DEARING mortally wounded.

It is worthy of remark that in the late pursuit Gen. GRANT commanded in person, directing the movement of each army corps. Gen. MEADE had the Army of the Potomac proper, but his movements were mainly directly in the track of LEE, or on the right flank, while Gen. ORD, with the detachment of the Army of the James, pursued on the left flank, and SHERIDAN, supported by the Fifth Corps, finally accomplished the work of heading LEE off. The Ninth Corps has guarded the railroad from Petersburgh to Burkesville. Gen. GRANT leaves to-day for Richmond, and will, I learn, visit Washington in a day or two. Mrs. GRANT has awaited his return here on the flagship *Mary Martin.*

The greater portion of the Army of the Potomac will speedily return to the vicinity of Richmond and Petersburgh, to await further developments. The soldiers are all happy, and anticipate an early discharge and retirement to their homes.

L. L. CROUNSE.

ANOTHER ACCOUNT.

WASHINGTON, Thursday, April 13.

Correspondence from the Army of the Potomac says that very little fighting took place on the 7th inst., at Farmville. There was some skirmishing between the enemy's rear-guard and the Second Corps, with the Second Division of Cavalry, the result being unimportant. LEE had intended to fall back to Danville, but being cut off by our forces getting to Burkesville, he changed his course, and started toward Lynchburgh. Part of his army passed through Farmville on the morning of the 7th. After crossing the Appomattox the bridges were burned, and before our troops could get over the enemy had taken a position a mile from the river, where they erected works and made a stand in order to allow their wagons to get out of the way. On this side of the river, just outside of the town, a division of cavalry had taken up a position, determined to annoy our advance while reconstructing the bridge. The Second Division, under Gen. CROOK, attacked them vigorously, driving them back some distance. But they had a force dismounted lying in ambush, which poured a severe fire into our men as they advanced to the second attack, and they were compelled to fall back on their supports. The rebels soon after retired, being indisposed to await another charge. The loss on both sides was very light. The Second Corps soon after crossed the river, and pushing on after the enemy, drove them behind their newly built breastworks. Gen. SMYTH was severely, and it is believed, mortally wounded, in leading the charge. This was a sad loss to the command. Every man in it feels the loss as a personal one. A more gallant soldier never served his country, and he not only ranked high for bravery on the field, but as a gentleman and a friend he was beloved by all who knew him. The loss in the Second Corps will be about one hundred and fifty, mostly of SMYTH's brigade.

In the morning, before the enemy crossed the river, twelve guns were taken from them, and afterward six more, making eighteen during the day, and about two thousand prisoners.

The number of prisoners taken on the 6th is put down at seven thousand seven hundred, almost entirely of KERSHAW's and CUSTIS LEE's divisions.

The correspondent, after giving further details of events, but which have mainly been published through official sources, says the field where the surrender took place was almost covered with the enemy's dead—all of them, nearly, being shot in the head and upper part of the body. The position was a very favorable one for them, but our artillery had good range on an adjoining hill, and our men charged up the ascent with such impetuosity that some were bayoneted before they left their light breastworks. The road, for miles, was strewn with broken down wagons, caissons and baggage of all kinds, presenting a scene seldom witnessed on the part of LEE's army.

The loss on the 6th will sum up about one thousand in killed and wounded—the Sixth Corps suffering the heaviest.

Another letter, dated on the evening of the 8th, says: "Stragglers are found scattered all along the line of march, and, as the troops pass, they come in and surrender themselves, expressing their determination to fight no longer, as they consider the rebellion as good as over."

Four guns were brought in this morning, besides a long train of ambulances, many containing wounded, who were placed in hospitals and cared for.

Gen. GORDON sent four Surgeons through the line this afternoon, asking that they be allowed to minister to the wants of those left behind on the road. But, as we have plenty of such help, they will be returned to their army in the morning.

Gen. HAYS was relieved from the command of the Second Division of the Second Corps yesterday, for tardiness in moving the command in obedience to orders.

Another letter, dated the 9th of April, says: "Notwithstanding the correspondence between Gens. GRANT and LEE, yesterday, which led all to expect a formal surrender this morning, the latter exerted all his energies to escape the net laid for him. He marched rapidly all yesterday afternoon and evening, until he ran against SHERIDAN at the Appomattox Court-house.

A sharp fight ensued, resulting in the capture of a number of prisoners, and the checking of their retreat.

The Twenty-fourth and Fifth Corps were close up in support of the cavalry, and during the night took up a strong position across the main road, and on the south side, the Appomattox River on the north side, cutting them off from retreat in that direction.

Early this morning SHERIDAN attacked vigorously, and for some time a brisk engagement was carried on.

About 9 A. M. a flag of truce appeared in front of his line, and he was informed that hostilities had been suspended in order to arrange terms of surrender.

This was caused by agreement made by Gen. ORD, consenting to a cessation of firing so as to communicate with Gen. GRANT, and was done, it is said, without proper authority.

Gen. SHERIDAN's Adjutant General was allowed to come through the rebel column to communicate with Gen. MEADE, who stated that he knew of no such arrangement, and that he was about to move forward in accordance with his previous intentions.

Gen. LEE, however, sent another message, desiring to have an interview with Gen. GRANT, to arrange the terms of surrender, and Gen. MEADE was thus obliged to grant a two hours' armistice, in order to communicate with Gen. GRANT, who had moved around to the left during the night. Gen. GRANT consenting to see Gen. LEE and discuss the matter, about 4:30 o'clock Lieut.-Col. WHITTIER, of Gen. WRIGHT's Staff, came in and reported the terms arranged and the papers signed, when the greatest excitement prevailed throughout our lines, cheer upon cheer rending the air.

Soon after Gen. MEADE and Staff, with other officers, rode along the lines of the Second and Sixth Corps, and they were greeted with the most enthusiastic shouts, the men throwing their hats in the air, and fairly dancing with joy and delight.

No such scene has ever been witnessed in this army, and the thanks of the whole country are due to the brave men and their heroic commanders for such a great and glorious result.

It is understood that the men of Gen. LEE's army are to be paroled and allowed to return home. They gave up everything in their hands, but last night they destroyed large amounts of property in the shape of wagons, gun-carriages, baggage, papers, etc.

The number of Gen. LEE's force is put down at twenty thousand men. Very few guns were in their possession, as they abandoned nearly all they did not lose in action.

Thirty-eight guns were brought in yesterday, and several this morning.

The rank and file of LEE's army are said to be well satisfied to give up the struggle, believing that they have no hope of success, but say that if Gen. LEE had refused to surrender, they would have stuck to him to the last.

The officers are somewhat surly and discontented, but this feeling will soon wear off when they [illegible] how liberally and kindly our people are disposed to treat them.

Another letter from the Army of the Potomac, dated April 12, says:

"The final arrangements for the surrender of LEE's army were completed yesterday, and to-day they are at liberty to proceed to their homes or elsewhere, as they choose. The terms granted were certainly of a very liberal character.

A large number of officers, together with thousands of the men of this army, express their dissatisfaction not only at the unprecedented liberality granted to the Army of Northern Virginia, but at the manner in which they were paroled and allowed to go their way, without our men being permitted to enjoy the

Continued on Eighth Page

The Daily Picayune.

VOLUME XXIX. NEW ORLEANS, SATURDAY MORNING, APRIL 15, 1865. NUMBER 70.

The Daily Picayune.

DOUBLE SHEET

BATON ROUGE AND THE COAST.

Large Overflow from the Crevasse at Lobdell's—Apprehended Outbreak of the Water Opposite Baton Rouge—Precautions to Check It—Condition of the Levee and Probability of Crevasses along the Coast above New Orleans—The Planting Interest and Small Prospect of a Crop this Season—Sugar, Cotton, etc., etc.

Special Correspondence of the Picayune.]

BATON ROUGE, April 13, 1865.

I have just arrived here from New Orleans on board the steamer Ben Franklin. I send some notes on my observations along the coast, as I had a good opportunity of making them from the steamer's touching at very many points.

The vast amount of water flowing out of the Mississippi at Lobdell's store has covered the entire country this side of Bayou Grosse Tete, very nearly to the vicinity of Plaquemine. In many places, opposite Baton Rouge and below, the overflow can be seen from the river bank, and covers the surface to an undefined line, not more than half a mile back of it. This stream is from sixteen to twenty miles in width at many points, and is of considerable depth throughout its extent. Of course all cultivation and surface work have been suspended wherever this flood reaches. The intention of restoring the telegraph poles and wire through the crevasse, so as to have communication with Port Hudson and Morganza once more, will probably have to be abandoned for the present. It is also reported here that another impediment exists to the immediate restoration of telegraphic facilities between Baton Rouge and Port Hudson: for at the latter place the magnetic cable crossing the river is said to be carried away. If this is the case, another will have to be obtained and laid down before the line can be completed and worked satisfactorily.

Yesterday the water commenced running over the levee at the railroad depot in West Baton Rouge opposite here. As soon as the fact was known, a company of soldiers, from the 115th New York Volunteers, was sent over there with spades and shovels to assist in preventing a serious overflow. All the negroes and laborers in the vicinity were also pressed in to do a part of the work necessary to raise the levee and stop the small stream of water that was running over it. The batture of the depot grounds, back of the levee, was strong and firm. Sufficient earth was easily and readily obtained from this in a short time to fill up the place where the overflow had commenced, and relieve all the apprehensions that had existed at the first appearance of the danger.

The levees in many places between New Orleans and Baton Rouge are very poor and uncertain barriers against the flood in the Mississippi, which is still rising. In coming up here, I saw places in them, and sometimes long in extent, where the water was within a foot of their top, and the pressure very great against them. This is their condition for some distance above Bonnet Carré camp on the left bank of the river, where the levees are very high and not very strong. They are at this point from ten to sixteen feet in height, and have no battures back of them. They are, consequently, quite weak, and with the great force of the water now pressing against them should be under constant and strict espionage. By this precaution and readiness to stop an outbreak of the waters whenever it occurs, it is barely possible to prevent a crevasse in that locality. I regard the dangers there greater than at any other point.

I have conversed with many planters within a day or two, and they generally agree that the prospect for a crop of any kind along the coast the present season is a very gloomy and doubtful one. Considerable corn has been planted; but less cotton and sugar. An old planter told me he did not believe the entire product of the sugar crop in the parish of St. Charles this year could more than supply the wants of the people of the parish. There must, therefore, be a great falling off in the cultivation of the sugar cane this year over the last, which itself supplied only a very scanty crop. The cotton plant is coming up and looks very well, in a few places, but the heavy and frequent rains for weeks past, without much sunshine to dry the surface, have kept the soil compact, damp and cold. There must be a change in the weather, of a more favorable nature, before much can be said of the promise or success of this crop.

Rather Disagreeable.—The Paris correspondent of the London Morning Star, writing about criminal matters, says:

At the Toulon *bagne* those under sentence for murder are allowed an inclined plane as a bed, and one basket. To this board they are chained; and as these sleeping places are arranged in a line along a gallery, an iron rod is run through the chains attached to the legs of each prisoner. In case of the slightest disturbance at night this iron rod is raised by machinery, so as to suspend all the prisoners by their feet. A cannon, pointed towards the dormitories, is always ready loaded during the night in case of mutiny.

The *Opinion Nationale*, in a curious article on the bad marksmanship of the French Infantry, mentions that 15,000,000 cartridges were used at Solferino to shoot down 10,000 Austrians at the outside, which shows that it took 1,500 to kill or wound one man, and represents a weight of 200 pounds.

It is mentioned in a letter from Paris that there is a rumor in Madrid that the pecuniary difficulties felt at the palace are daily becoming more painful, and that an addition to the civil list is likely to be made to enable the Queen to discharge some of her debts, which, it is alleged, amount to nearly £300,000 sterling.

TELEGRAPHIC.

SURRENDER OF LEE.

EVACUATION OF RALEIGH.

GENERAL BANKS NOT AT CAIRO.

Gold in New York, 145.

[From our Extra of Yesterday.]

BATON ROUGE, April 14—10 A. M.—By the arrival of the W. R. Arthur we have received New York and Washington dates of the 9th.

WAR DEPARTMENT, Washington, April 9, 9 P. M.—*Major Gen. Dix*: This Department has received the official report of the surrender, this day, of Gen. Lee and his army to Lieut. Gen. Grant, on terms proposed by the latter.

E. M. STANTON,
Secretary of War.

HEADQUARTERS ARMIES OF THE UNITED STATES, April 9, 4:30 P. M.—*Hon. E. M Stanton, Secretary of War*: Gen. Lee surrendered the Army of Northern Virginia this afternoon, upon the terms proposed by myself. The accompanying additional correspondence will show the conditions more fully.

U. S. GRANT, Lieut. Gen.

APRIL 9.—*General*: I received your note of this morning on the picket line, whither I had come to meet you and ascertain definitely what terms were embraced in your proposition of yesterday with reference to the surrender of this army. I now request an interview in accordance with the offer contained in yours of yesterday for that purpose.

Very respectfully, your obe't servant,
R. E. LEE, Gen.

To Gen. Grant.

CAMP UNITED STATES ARMIES, April 9.—*Gen. R. E. Lee, Commanding Confederate States Armies*: Your note of this date is but this moment, 11:15 A. M., received. In consequence of my having passed from the Richmond and Lynchburg Railroad to the Danville and Lynchburg Railroad, I am at this writing about four miles west of Walter's Church, and will push forward to the front for the purpose of meeting you. Notice sent to me on this road where you wish the interview to take place will meet me.

Very respectfully, your obedient servant,
U. S. GRANT, Lieut. Gen.

APPOMATTOX COURT-HOUSE, April 9.—*Gen. R. E. Lee*: In accordance with the substance of my letter to you, of the 8th inst., I propose to receive the surrender of the Army of Northern Virginia on the following terms, to-wit: Rolls of all the officers and men to be made on duplicate; one copy to be given to any officer designated by me, the other to be retained by such officers as you may designate.

The officers do give their undivided paroles not to take up arms against the Government of the United States until properly exchanged, and each company or regiment commander sign a like parole for the men of their commands, the arms, artillery and public property to be packed, stacked and turned over to the officers appointed by me to receive them. This will not embrace the side arms of the officers, nor their private horses or baggage. This done each officer and man will be allowed to return to their homes, not to be disturbed by the United States authorities so long as they observe their parole and the laws in force where they may reside. Yours, respectfully,

U. S. GRANT, Lieut. Gen.

HEADQUARTERS ARMY NORTHERN VIRGINIA, April 9.—*Lieut. Gen. Grant*: I have received your letter of this date, containing terms of surrender of the Army of Northern Virginia, as proposed by you, and as they are the same expressed in your letter of the 8th inst., they are accepted. I will proceed to designate the proper officers to carry the stipulations into effect. Very respectfully,

R. E. LEE, General.

BUFFALO, April 10—There are great rejoicings here and at other cities over the glorious news.

CINCINNATI, April 10.—By an order from the War Department 200 guns were fired at noon to day. The city is lively with excitement and very little business doing.

The following is the previous correspondence between Grant and Lee, referred to in the foregoing telegram:

CLIFTON HOUSE, Va., April 9—*Hon. E. M. Stanton*: The following correspondence has taken place between Gen. Lee and myself. There has been no relaxation in pursuit during its pendency.

U. S. GRANT, Lieut. Gen.

APRIL 7, 1865.—*Gen. R. E Lee*: Results of the last week must convince you of the hopelessness of further resistance on the part of the Army of Northern Virginia in this struggle. I feel that it is so, and regard it as my duty to shift from myself the responsibility of any further effusion of blood by asking of you the surrender of that portion of the Confederate States Army known as the Army of Northern Virginia. Very respectfully,

U. S. GRANT, Lieut. Gen.

APRIL 7.—*General*: I have received your note of this date. Though not entirely of the opinion you express of the hopelessness of further resistance on the part of the Army of Northern Virginia, I respect your desire to evade the useless effusion of blood, and, therefore, before considering your proposition, ask the terms you will offer of conditions of surrender. R. E. LEE, Gen

APRIL 8.—Your note of last evening, in reply to mine of same date, asking on what conditions I will accept the surrender of the Army of Northern Virginia, is received. In reply, I would say that peace being my first desire there is but one condition that I insist on, that the men surrendered shall be disqualified for taking up arms against the Government of the United States until properly exchanged.

I will meet you or designate officers to meet any officers you may name for the same purpose, at any point agreeable to you, for the purpose of arranging definitely the terms on which the surrender of the Army of Northern Virginia will be received. Very respectfully,

U. S. GRANT, Lieut. Gen.

HEADQUARTERS ARMIES OF THE CONFEDERATE STATES, 1865.—*General*: I received at a late hour your note, in answer to mine yesterday. I did not intend to propose the surrender of the Army of Northern Virginia, but to ask the terms of your proposition be frank.

I do not think the emergency has arrived to call for a surrender, but as a restoration of peace should be the sole object of all, I desire to know whether your proposals would tend to that end. I cannot, therefore, meet you with a view to surrender the Army of Northern Virginia, but as far as your proposition may affect the Confederate States army forces under my command and tend to the restoration of peace, should be pleased to meet you at 10 A. M. tomorrow, at the old stage road to Richmond, between picket lines of the two armies.

Very respectfully, R. E LEE.

To Gen. Grant, U. S. A.

APRIL 9.—Your note of yesterday is received. As I have no authority to treat on the subject of peace, the meeting proposed for 10 A. M. to day could lead to no good. I will state, however, General, that I am equally anxious for peace with yourself, and the whole North entertains the same feeling. Terms upon which peace can be had are well understood by the South. By laying down their arms they will hasten that most desirable event, save thousands of human lives, and hundreds of millions of property not yet destroyed.

Sincerely hoping that all our difficulties may be settled without the loss of another life, I subscribe myself, very respectfully,

U. S. GRANT, Lieut. Gen.

WASHINGTON, April 9.—*To Lieut. Gen. Grant*: Thanks to Almighty God for the great victory with which He has this day crowned you and the gallant army under your command.

The thanks of this Department of the Government and of the people of the United States, their reverence and honor have been deserved, and will be rendered to you and the brave soldiers and gallant officers of your army for all time to come.

E. M. STANTON, Secretary of War.

WAR DEPARTMENT, WASHINGTON, April 9, 10 P. M.—Ordered that a salute of 200 guns be fired at the headquarters of every army and navy department and every arsenal in the United States, and at the Military Academy at West Point, on the day of the receipt of this order, in commemoration of the surrender of Gen. R. E. Lee and his army to Lieut. Gen. Grant. E. M. STANTON.

GOLDSBORO, N. C., April 6.—Deserters and refugees report the evacuation of Raleigh, and that the enemy were throwing up works on the Tar River at Rocky Mount, 40 miles from here, on the Weldon and Wilmington Railroad. The enemy are burning the bridges and ties on the railroad, and conveying off the rails. It is thought that Johnston will go to the relief of Lee. His army is much demoralized.

PADUCAH, April 10.—*To War Eagle*: A steamer just in from Eastport brings the gratifying intelligence of the complete route of Forrest's army in a recent battle with our forces. Particulars will be sent as soon as received.

SECOND DISPATCH.

PADUCAH, April 10.—The fight took place near Tuscaloosa, Ala. Forrest was first attempting to head off Gen. Wilson's cavalry force, moving towards the Gulf.

The enemy were badly beaten and many prisoners taken. Gen. Hatch commands at Eastport. Buford, with a small force, is near Corinth. The garrison at Eastport is more than sufficient to take care of him.

NEW YORK, April 10.—Gold opened at 144, rose to 145¾ and closed at 145. Noon Board—Cotton quiet, no quotations.

BATON ROUGE, April 14.—When the Arthur left Cairo, Gen. Banks had not arrived. The New Ruth is expected here within 24 hours, as she was to leave Cairo on the evening of the 10th.

EXAMINATIONS IN DIVINITY AT CAMBRIDGE (ENGLAND) UNIVERSITY.—Numerous stories are always afloat of wonderful blunders in divinity at Cambridge; some, of course, are inventions, and others facts, or founded on facts. Here are a couple of amusing specimens, which we credit with some foundation:

Examiner—"What can you tell me about St. Paul?"

Under-graduate—"He was also Saul, and was brought up at the feet of Gamaliel."

Examiner—"Yes, quite right. What do you know about Gamaliel?"

Under-graduate—"It is a mountain in Galilee."

The next, we believe, may be credited to Cambridge:

Examiner—"Why did Moses leave Egypt?"

Under-graduate, (with hesitation)—"Why, sir—hem—hem—"

Examiner—"Come, come, answer if you know."

Under-graduate—"Well, sir, I suppose that little affair with Potiphar's wife!"

For the following we do not attempt in any way to vouch, although we have heard its authenticity strenuously asserted:

Examiner—"Why was John the Baptist beheaded?"

Under-graduate, (falteringly)—"Because he would dance with Herodias's daughter."

[Cornhill Magazine.

☞ Strawberries have appeared in the New York market, and are marked at $5 per basket, or about twenty dollars per quart. They are of course ripened in conservatories.

LATEST NORTHERN NEWS.

ARRIVAL OF THE STEAMER W. R. ARTHUR.

PRESIDENT LINCOLN'S INTERVIEW WITH PROMINENT REBELS.

GUERRILLAS AT WORK.

CAPTURE OF SELMA, ALABAMA.

SERIOUS RAILROAD ACCIDENT.

The Markets.

By the arrival of the steamer W. R. Arthur, last night, we received St. Louis and Cairo papers of the 10th, and a Memphis Bulletin of the 11th. On examination, we find that the most important features of the intelligence contained in them were dispatched by telegraph, and will be found in our columns this morning. We have left, therefore, but a meagre supply whence to draw matter of interest.

The President and the Rebel Gentlemen.

NEW YORK, April 9.—The Herald's Richmond correspondent says Mr. Lincoln was on the 4th informed by Gens. Weitzel and Shepley, that prominent rebels desired an interview with him. He replied that he was willing to grant interviews, but in the presence of a friend. After the reception of the officers of the army and navy, it was announced to the President that Judge Campbell, the Assistant Secretary of War, and Mr. Meyers, of the late rebel Congress, were awaiting an audience with the President in another room.

The President, accompanied by Gen. Weitzel, immediately retired to the room and held a conference, which lasted but a short time and was adjourned to the flag ship Malvern. The result of these conferences cannot be made known, but auspicious results are known to occur from them.

The Guerrillas.

[Special Dispatch to the Missouri Democrat.]

CAIRO, April 8.—A General who arrived from Duvall's Bluff, states that on Sunday last a party of thirty-five guerrillas tore up some rails on the railroad between Little Rock and Duvall's Bluff, at the first station west of the Bluff, and thus threw off the train from Little Rock. Fortunately no one was hurt, but several persons who tried to escape by running from the train into the woods, were caught, robbed of their money and clothing, and sent back to the train, with the demand that all the passengers on board should surrender, and that the bearer of the message should return with an answer. This, however, was not done, and the guerrillas continuing to make an attack, were handsomely repulsed by colored troops, who chanced to be on board the train. Several horses of the guerrillas were killed. The scoundrels then beat a retreat. No one on the train was hurt by the shots. After some delay the track was repaired, and the train was able to proceed to Duvall's Bluff.

Capture of Selma.

CAIRO, April 9—The steamer Belle St. Louis, Capt Ziegler and Clerk Moody, furnishes Memphis dates up to the evening of the 8th. The Bulletin says there are well authenticated reports in circulation in the city that Selma, Ala., was captured and burned several days ago by a force of our cavalry from Gen. Thomas's command.

One report emanates from a merchant on Front Row. He was some distance out in the country a day or two since, and met and held conversation with a rebel soldier, who remarked, in the course of conversation: "I suppose you damned Memphis Yankees haven't heard yet that Selma was captured and burned the other day." The merchant replied that he had not. "Well, its so," said the soldier, and the interview ended.

Confirmatory of this is a report received from Senatobia, Miss., that Mr. Hunt, superintendent of Confederate foundries at Selma, had reached the former place, having narrowly escaped capture by the raiders, who, he stated, had sacked and burned Selma. He left his family at Selma, being unable to bring them away.

Railroad Accident.

On Thursday a serious accident occurred on the Memphis and Charleston Railroad at a place between Lafayette and Collierville, known as Turin Bridge, about eight miles from Memphis. The freshet had carried away a span of the bridge, and the train coming along at a pretty rapid rate, the locomotive, tender and platform cars were precipitated into the stream. An Irishman was killed and a colored man drowned. Other colored men were badly hurt. The locomotive has since been drawn out, and lies on dry land.

Capt. Wiley and his Band.

CAIRO, April 8.—On the morning of the 31st ult., Sergeant Louder, of Battery C, 2d Illinois Light Artillery, with fifteen men, attacked the thieving and marauding Capt. H. Wiley and his band, on White Oak Creek, 22 miles north of Fort Donelson. Wiley and two of his men were killed at the first fire, and the other guerrillas scattered in every direction, and two of them taking refuge in a mill, were notified to leave, but with curses refused. The mill was set on fire and they were burned with it. The mill belonged to the heirs of one Alsop, a notorious guerrilla, who had met his well merited fate at the hands of the same brave soldiers some three months ago.

New York Market.

NEW YORK April 8.—Cotton steady, at 35c. for Middling.

Flour heavy and 5@15c. lower, at $8@8 15 for extra State, $8 60@8 70 for extra round hoop Ohio, and $8 90@9 75 for trade brands, the market closing heavy.

Whisky more active and lower; Western, part last evening, at $2 15@2 16.

Wheat without decided change; amber at $1 50; winter red Western at $1 75; No. 1 spring at $1 62. Corn dull and heavy; red, yellow and white at $1 40. Oats selling retail at 80c. for Western.

Petroleum dull at 34c. for crude; 52@53c. for refined in bond, and 72@73c. for do free.

Pork dull and heavy at $28 50@28 87½ for new mess, closing at $28 75 for cash; $24@24 50 for 1863-4 do. cash and regular way, closing at $24 25 for cash; $24@24 50 for prime, and $26@26 50 for prime mess.

Beef quiet. Cut meats steady at 14½@15c. for shoulders, and 15@16c. for hams. Bacon steady at 14½@15½c. for Cumberland cut, and 15½c. for long ribbed. Lard rather firmer at 15½@16½c.

Money easy at 6@7 per cent., with a large supply. Sterling Exchange quiet at 108½@109½ for specie, first class bills. Gold without decided change, offering at 150, advancing to 150½, declining to 148½, and closing at 148¾. Total export of specie to-day, $328,460.

Evening Stock Exchange—Gold 148½; Erie 65½; Hudson 103¾; Reading 103; M. C. 92½; I. C. 100½; Pittsburg 62½; R. I. 91¾; N. W. 27¾; do. preferred 97½; Ft. Wayne 80½; O. & M. certificates 25; Canton 32½; Cumberland 41½; M. S. 60; Mariposa 15¼.

Market not very active.

Cincinnati Market.

CINCINNATI, April 8—P. M.—Flour unchanged and quiet, with but little done. Superfine at $7.

Wheat in fair demand. $1 50@1 55 for red. Corn dull. Rye held at 95c. Oats at 64c.

Whiskey dull, with small sales at $2 10.

Potatoes in large supply, and unsaleable to any extent; the best would not bring over $2 a barrel. Clover Seed $15, with the demand moderate. Butter unchanged; prime to choice at 25@30c. Eggs 20c.

Gold 147@149.

THE CITY.

GOOD FRIDAY—Yesterday was Good Friday, and despite the dull continuous rain, all of the Catholic, and most of the Episcopal Churches were frequented. It is one of the most beautiful and affecting ideas of the Ritual of both the Catholic and Episcopal Churches, that the life of Christ is to some extent lived over again, and almost reënacted in mourning by those who attend to the ordinances in the right way. It is expected that the minds and thoughts of all go with Him in the latter days of His life, and partake to some extent of his Passion. On Good Friday his sufferings culminated, and he was nailed to the Cross. He lay in the grave all day Saturday, and on Easter Sunday arose from the dead. The life of the good and true Catholic illustrates and relives that of the Savior, and the feasts and fasts of the Church are but commemorative institutions of different epochs in His history. We could not but be struck with the solemn scene we witnessed in the St. Louis Cathedral, where, in the vacant space near the doors, we saw so many kneelers, clad in black—principally ladies of the Creole part of our city—offering up their donations kneeling on the hard stone floor, and thinking of "those things wherewith the Atonement was made," and of Him who 1800 years ago was nailed to the Cross.

☞ Yesterday being a *dies non* in law, and State holiday, all the courts—the Provost Court, United States Court, Criminal and District Courts—were all closed. With the reorganization of the courts, we observe the rearrangement of some of the old court rooms. Much of the furniture carpeting, matting, etc. of which had become old. Abundant facilities will be offered next week for all the suits that "flesh is heir to," as next week all the courts will be in operation, and they are nearly all contiguous. Should a man receive any injury, he can be tried before the Recorder there, or be committed for final trial to the First District Court; or should his civil rights suffer, there are several courts of concurrent jurisdiction, or he can appeal to the Supreme Court, or finally, should he be killed, the Coroner will attend to the inquest, and we might be there to debate on the whole matter—all in the same building.

RECORDER VENNARD'S COURT.—The case of Mrs. Riley, Mrs. Kellahan, Mrs. Kenaugh, and Isabella Cassard, received a profane ventilation yesterday. Michael H. Samuels is a peaceful, well disposed citizen, who resides at 161 Robin street, which neighborhood he avers is respectable and he desires to keep it so, which motive does credit to his head and heart; but the parties above named are sad obstacles in the way. He says they are continually quarreling and fighting and creating a general disturbance of the otherwise Paridisical spot; that they use vulgar language toward his family; and, to his own knowledge, they have kept up such a course of conduct for six months; that the place seems to be a rendezvous for colored people, soldiers, etc.; wherefore, he prays that they be dealt with, for he will have no dealings with such people. The Recorder dealt with them to the extent of a $5 fine on each.

John Riley, a boy, accused of malicious mischief to the Boy's House of Refuge, was sent home to his anxious parents.

Peter Williams retired into the realms of the Workhouse as a contraband, accompanied, however, and indelibly attached to his name was the charge of stealing corn on the Levee. Alas poor Peter.

John Gardner, by dint of drinking, has made himself a habitual drunkard. John, when you were forming habits, when life was young and spread its inviting avenues before you, why did you not form good habits? Then the Recorder would not have been obliged to say to you, fined $5.

Also, you, John Coulise, drunk and before his Honor the second time, and noisy about that stable on Union street—was fined $5. John Henry, too, colored, and Henry Senaina, not colored, have $5 fine and five days' imprisonment awarded them.

Mary Sanders, imprisoned for thirty days; her conduct being somewhat like Potiphar's wife.

W. White and Lewis Jackson, John Dix and J. A. Harmon, regarded as contrabands, were similarly disposed of.

Mary Plott, for thirty days also, on a charge of seriously affecting her moral character.

Hugh McCann was dismissed, having been arrested for making a false accusation.

Mrs. Hardin was charged by Mrs. Campion with assault, insult and abuse. She was eloquent, and asked the Recorder to let her go home on account of Good Friday. She had a a very black eye. The Recorder said he would send her to the Workhouse for ten days, that her eye might get well.

RECORDER WOOLFLEY'S COURT.—Emma Reel, colored, and Josephine Brown were fined $5 each for violating city ordinance 1095.

Two knives, marked "St. James Hotel," and identified by George Moore as his property, were found by Policeman Hays, by virtue of a search warrant, in a house on Customhouse street.

Wm. Hainer was fined $5 for very improper conduct in the beef market.

☞ The record of the Coroner exhibits the following facts, though as yet there has been no jury of inquest:

On the steamer Gov. Morton, lying at the the foot of the Pontchartrain Railroad, there was the body of a colored man named Abraham Hollingsworth. He was 58 years old, and had died from the effects of a wound received by the fall of a limb of a tree.

Lucien Dubois was drowned in a well, at No. 325 Ursuline street. He was a colored man, 46 years old.

Arrest of a Female Spy.—The Louisville Journal states:

A highly important arrest has recently been made in St. Louis. A woman of prepossessing appearance, about thirty-four years of age, calling herself Mrs. John Smith, recently went to the Galt House. The landlord becoming suspicious that she was a rebel emissary, called the attention of the police to her. Detectives were put on the track, and she was discovered to be quite intimate with several secessionists. Some of the latter were arrested, and confessed that Mrs. Smith had furnished them with money to buy contraband goods. One of them also said that Mrs. Smith had visited the city six times during the last year, as a bearer of dispatches to and from Kirby Smith and Gen. Price. The woman was therefore taken into custody, and a pass from Gen. Price, dated February 26, 1865, found in her possession. This pass shows that the rebel General, in spite of reports to the contrary, still lives.

THE NEW YORK HERALD.

WHOLE NO. 10,456. NEW YORK, SATURDAY, APRIL 15, 1865. PRICE FOUR CENTS.

IMPORTANT.

ASSASSINATION OF PRESIDENT LINCOLN.

The President Shot at the Theatre Last Evening.

SECRETARY SEWARD DAGGERED IN HIS BED, BUT NOT MORTALLY WOUNDED.

Clarence and Frederick Seward Badly Hurt.

ESCAPE OF THE ASSASSINS.

Intense Excitement in Washington.

Scene at the Deathbed of Mr. Lincoln.

J. Wilkes Booth, the Actor, the Alleged [illegible] of the President, [illegible] &c.

THE OFFICIAL DESPATCH.

War Department, Washington, April 15—1:30 A. M.

Major General Dix, New York:—

This evening at about 9:30 P. M., at Ford's Theatre, the President, while sitting in his private box with Mrs. Lincoln, Mrs. Harris and Major Rathburn, was shot by an assassin, who suddenly entered the box and approached behind the President.

The assassin then leaped upon the stage, brandishing a large dagger or knife, and made his escape in the rear of the theatre.

The pistol ball entered the back of the President's head and penetrated nearly through the head. The wound is mortal.

The President has been insensible ever since it was inflicted, and is now dying.

About the same hour an assassin, whether the same or not, entered Mr. Seward's apartments, and under pretence of having a prescription was shown to the Secretary's sick chamber. The assassin immediately rushed to the bed and inflicted two or three stabs on the throat and two on the face.

It is hoped the wounds may no the mortal. My apprehension is that they will prove fatal.

The nurse alarmed Mr. Frederick Seward, who was in an adjoining room, and he hastened to the door of his father's room, when he met the assassin, who inflicted upon him one or more dangerous wounds. The recovery of Frederick Seward is doubtful.

It is not probable that the President will live through the night.

General Grant and wife were advertised to be at the theatre this evening, but he started to Burlington at six o'clock this evening.

At a Cabinet meeting, at which General Grant was present, the subject of the state of the country and the prospect of a speedy peace were discussed. The President was very cheerful and hopeful, and spoke very kindly of General Lee and others of the confederacy, and of the establishment of government in Virginia.

All the members of the Cabinet except Mr. Seward, are now in attendance upon the President.

I have seen Mr. Seward, but he and Frederick were both unconscious.

EDWIN M. STANTON, Secretary of War.

THE HERALD DESPATCHES.

Washington, April 14, 1865.

Assassination has been inaugurated in Washington. The bowie knife and pistol have been applied to President Lincoln and Secretary Seward. The former was shot in the throat, while at Ford's theatre to-night. Mr. Seward was badly cut about the neck, while in his bed at his residence.

SECOND DESPATCH.

Washington, April 14, 1865.

An attempt was made about ten o'clock this evening to assassinate the President and Secretary Seward. The President was shot at Ford's Theatre. Result not yet known. Mr. Seward's throat was cut, and his son badly wounded.

There is intense excitement here.

Details of the Assassination.

Washington, April 14, 1865.

Washington was thrown into an intense excitement a few minutes before eleven o'clock this evening, by the announcement that the President and Secretary Seward had been assassinated and were dead.

The wildest excitement prevailed in all parts of the city. Men, women and children, old and young, rushed [illegible] nearly every member of the Cabinet killed. Some time elapsed before authentic data could be ascertained in regard to the affair.

The President and Mrs. Lincoln were at Ford's theatre, listening to the performance of the American Cousin, occupying a box in the second tier. At the close of the third act a person entered the box occupied by the President, and shot Mr. Lincoln in the head. The shot entered the back of his head, and came out above the temple.

The assassin then jumped from the box upon the stage and ran across to the other side, exhibiting a dagger in his hand, flourishing it in a tragical manner, shouting the same words repeated by the desperado at Mr. Seward's house, adding to it, "The South is avenged," and then escaped from the back entrance to the stage, but in his passage dropped his pistol and his hat.

Mr. Lincoln fell forward from his seat, and Mrs. Lincoln fainted.

The moment the astonished audience could realize what had happened, the President was taken and carried to Mr. Petersen's house, in Tenth street, opposite to the theatre. Medical aid was immediately sent for, and the wound was at first supposed to be fatal, and it was announced that he could not live; but at half-past twelve he is still alive, though in a precarious condition.

As the assassin ran across the stage, Colonel J. B. Stewart, of this city, who was occupying one of the front seats in the orchestra, on the same side of the house as the box occupied by Mr. Lincoln, sprang to the stage and followed him; but he was obstructed in his passage across the stage by the fright of the actors, and reached the back door about three seconds after the assassin had passed out. Colonel Stewart got to the street just in time to see him mount his horse and ride away.

This operation shows that the whole thing was a preconcerted plan. The person who fired the pistol was a man about thirty years of age, about five feet nine, spare built, fair skin, dark hair, apparently bushy, with a large mustache. Laura Keene and the leader of the orchestra declare that they recognized him as J. Wilkes Booth the actor, and a rabid secessionist. Whoever he was, it is plainly evident that he thoroughly understood the theatre and all the approaches and modes of escape to the stage. A person not familiar with the theatre could not have possibly made his escape so well and quickly.

The alarm was sounded in every quarter. Mr. Stanton was notified, and immediately left his house.

All the other members of the Cabinet escaped attack.

Cavalrymen were sent out in all directions, and despatches sent to all the fortifications, and it is thought they will be captured.

About half-past ten o'clock this evening a tall, well dressed man made his appearance at Secretary Seward's residence, and applied for admission. He was refused admission by the servant, when the desperado stated that he had a prescription from the Surgeon General, and that he was ordered to deliver it in person. He was still refused, except upon the written order of the physician. This he pretended to show, and pushed by the servant and rushed up stairs to Mr. Seward's room. He was met at the door by Mr. Fred Seward, who notified him that he was master of the house, and would take charge of the medicine. After a few words had passed between them he dodged by Fred Seward and rushed to the Secretary's bed, and struck him in the neck with a dagger, and also in the breast.

It was supposed at first that Mr. Seward was killed instantly, but it was found afterwards that the wound was not mortal.

Major Wm. H. Seward, Jr., paymaster, was in the room, and rushed to the defence of his father, and was badly cut in the *mele* with the assassin, but not fatally.

The desperado managed to escape from the house, and was prepared for escape by having a horse at the door. He immediately mounted his horse, and sung out the motto of the State of Virginia, "*Sic Semper Tyrannis!*" and rode off.

Surgeon General Barnes was immediately sent for, and he *examined Mr. Seward and pronounced him safe*. His wounds were not fatal. The jugular vein was not cut, nor the wound in the breast deep enough to be fatal.

Washington, April 15—1 A. M.

The streets in the vicinity of Ford's Theatre are densely crowded by an anxious and excited crowd. A guard has been placed across Tenth street and F and E streets, and only official persons and particular friends of the President are allowed to pass.

The popular heart is deeply stirred, and the deepest indignation against leading rebels is freely expressed.

The scene at the house where the President lies *in extremis* is very affecting. Even Secretary Stanton is affected to tears.

When the news spread through the city that the President had been shot, the people, with pale faces and compressed lips, crowded every place where there was the slightest chance of obtaining information in regard to the affair.

After the President was shot, Lieutenant Rathbun, caught the assassin by the arm, who immediately struck him with a knife, and jumped from the box, as before stated.

The popular affection for Mr. Lincoln has been shown by this diabolical assassination, which will bring eternal infamy, not only upon its authors, but upon the hellish cause which they desire to avenge.

Vice President Johnson arrived at the White House, where the President lies, about one o'clock, and will remain with him to the last.

The President's family are in attendance upon him also.

As soon as intelligence could be got to the War Department, the electric telegraph and the Signal corps were put in requisition to endeavor to prevent the escape of the assassins, and all the troops around Washington are under arms.

Popular report points to a somewhat celebrated actor of known secession proclivities as the assassin; but it would be unjust to name him until some further evidence of his guilt is obtained. It is rumored that the person alluded to is in custody.

The latest advices from Secretary Seward reveals more desperate work there than at first supposed. Seward's wounds are not in themselves fatal; but, in connection with his recent injuries, and the great loss of blood he has sustained, his recovery is questionable.

It was Clarence A. Seward, instead of Wm. H. Seward, Jr., who was wounded. Fred. Seward was also badly cut, as were also three nurses, who were in attendance upon the Secretary, showing that a desperate struggle took place there. The wounds of the whole party were dressed.

One o'Clock A. M.

The President is perfectly senseless, and there is not the slightest hope of his surviving. Physicians believe that he will die before morning. All of his Cabinet, except Secretary Seward, are with him. Speaker Colfax, Senator Farwell, of Maine, and many other gentlemen, are also at the house awaiting the termination.

The scene at the President's bedside is described by one who witnessed it as most affecting. It was surrounded by his Cabinet ministers, all of whom were bathed in tears, not even excepting Mr. Stanton, who, when informed by Surgeon General Barnes, that the President could not live until morning, exclaimed, "Oh, no, General; no—no;" and with an impulse, natural as it was unaffected, immediately sat down on a chair near his bedside and wept like a child.

Senator Sumner was seated on the right of the President's couch, near the head, holding the right hand of the President in his own. He was sobbing like a woman, with his head bowed down almost on the pillow of the bed on which the President was lying.

Two o'Clock A. M.

The President is still alive, but there is no improvement in his condition.

THE PRESS DESPATCHES.

Washington, April 15—12:30 A. M.

The President was shot in a theatre to-night, and is perhaps mortally wounded.

SECOND DESPATCH.

Washington, April 15—1 A. M.

The President is not expected to live through the night. He was shot at a theatre.

Secretary Seward was also assassinated. No arteries were cut.

Additional Details of the Assassination.

Washington, April 15—1:30 A. M.

President Lincoln and wife, with other friends, this evening visited Ford's theatre, for the purpose of witnessing the performance of the American Cousin.

It was announced in the papers that General Grant would also be present; but that gentleman took the late train of cars for New Jersey.

The theatre was densely crowded, and all seemed delighted with the scene before them. During the third act, and while there was a temporary pause for one of the actors to enter, a sharp report of a pistol was heard, which merely attracted attention, but suggested nothing serious, until a man rushed to the front of the President's box, waving a long dagger in his right hand, and exclaiming "*Sic semper tyrannis!*" and immediately leaped from the box, which was in the second tier, to the stage beneath, and ran across to the opposite side, making his escape, amid the bewilderment of the audience, from the rear of the theatre, and, mounting a horse, fled.

The screams of Mrs. Lincoln first disclosed the fact to the audience that the President had been shot, when all present rose to their feet, rushing towards the stage, many exclaiming "Hang him! Hang him!"

The excitement was of the wildest possible description, and of course there was an abrupt termination of the theatrical performance.

There was a rush toward the President's box, when cries were heard:—"Stand back and give him air." "Has any one stimulants?"

On a hasty examination it was found that the President had been shot through the head, above and back of the temporal bone, and that some of the brain was oozing out.

He was removed to a private house [illegible] the theatre, and the Surgeon General [illegible] surgeons sent for to attend to his condition.

On an examination of the private box blood was discovered on the back of the cushioned rocking chair on which the President had been sitting, also on the partition and on the floor. A common single barreled pocket pistol was found on the carpet.

A military guard was placed in front of the private residence to which the President had been conveyed. An immense crowd was in front of it, all deeply anxious to learn the condition of the President. It had been previously announced that the wound was mortal, but all hoped otherwise. The shock to the community was terrible.

At midnight the Cabinet, with Messrs. Sumner, Colfax and Farnsworth, Judge Curtis, Governor Oglesby, General Meigs, Colonel Hay, and a few personal friends, with Surgeon General Barnes and his immediate assistants, were around his bedside.

The President was in a state of syncope, totally insensible, and breathing slowly. The blood oozed from the wound at the back of his head.

The surgeons exhausted every possible effort of medicinal skill; but all hope was gone.

The parting of his family with the dying President is too sad for description.

The President and Mrs. Lincoln did not start for the theatre until fifteen minutes after eight o'clock. Speaker Colfax was at the White House at the time, and the President stated to him that he was going. Mrs. Lincoln had not been well, because the papers had announced that General Grant and they were to be present, and, as General Grant had gone North, he did not wish the audience to be disappointed.

He went with apparent reluctance, and urged Mr. Colfax to go with him; but that gentleman had made other engagements, and, with Mr. Ashmun, of Massachusetts, bid him goodby.

When the excitement at the theatre was at its wildest height reports were circulated that Secretary Seward had also been assassinated.

On reaching this gentleman's residence a crowd and a military guard were found at the door, and on entering it was ascertained that the reports were based on truth.

Everybody there was so excited that scarcely an intelligible word could be gathered. But the facts are substantially as follows:—

About ten o'clock a man rang the bell, and the call having been answered by a colored servant, he said he had come from Dr. Verdi, Secretary Seward's family physician, with a prescription, at the same time holding in his hand a small piece of folded paper, and saying, in answer to a refusal, that he must see the Secretary, as he was entrusted with particular directions concerning the medicine.

He still insisted on going up, although repeatedly informed that no one could enter the chamber. The man pushed the servant aside, and walked hastily towards the Secretary's room, and was then met by Mr. Frederick Seward, of whom he demanded to see the Secretary, making the same representation which he did to the servant.

What further passed in the way of colloquy is not known; but the man struck him on the head with a billy, severely injuring the skull and felling him almost senseless.

The assassin then rushed into the chamber and attacked Major Seward, Paymaster United States Army, and Mr. Hansell, a messenger of the State Department, and two male nurses, disabling them all.

He then rushed upon the Secretary, who was lying in bed in the same room, and inflicted three stabs in the neck, but severing, it is thought and hoped, no arteries, though he bled profusely.

The assassin then rushed down stairs, mounted his horse at the door, and rode off before an alarm could be sounded, and in the same manner as the assassin of the President.

It is believed that the injuries of the Secretary are not fatal, nor those of either of the others, although both the Secretary and the Assistant Secretary are very seriously injured.

Secretaries Stanton and Welles, and other prominent officers of the Government, called at Secretary Seward's house to inquire into his condition, and there heard of the assassination of the President.

They then proceeded to the house where he was lying, exhibiting of course intense anxiety and solicitude.

An immense crowd was gathered in front of the President's house, and a strong guard was also stationed there. Many persons evidently supposing he would be brought to his home.

The entire city to-night presents a scene of wild excitement, accompanied by violent expression of indignation and the profoundest sorrow; many shed tears.

The military authorities have despatched mounted patrols in every direction, in order, if possible, to arrest the assassins. The whole metropolitan police are likewise vigilant for the same purpose.

The attacks, both at the theatre and at Secretary Seward's house, took place at about the same hour—ten o'clock—thus showing a preconcerted plan to assassinate those gentlemen. Some evidences of the guilt of the party who attacked the President are in the possession of the police.

Vice President Johnson is in the city, and his headquarters are guarded by troops.

THE STATE CAPITAL.

Rejection of the New York Fire Commissioners—Passage of the Central Railroad Fare Bill—Great Excitement Over the Health Bill, &c.

Albany, April 14—11:40 P. M.

Legislation each day is now so rapid here that a detail or analysis of its progress is out of the question. To-day the long pending Central Railroad bill passed the Senate, and is virtually a law if the Governor does not veto it. But the result may be foreshadowed in the veto sent in to day of the Dry Dock and Battery Railroad.

The Health bill, which two days since was bound by caucus rules to have a sure passage, was to-night defeated by republican votes. The Collector of the port of New York, who has had an elaborate organization up for his retention in the office of Commissioner of Charities, was thrown overboard and the power of all his patronage disregarded in the strife to secure this position, which has been his pet desire and speciality for many years. All these occurrences have a political significancy which it would take too much time and space to develop. The excitement of the day has been the Health bill, and that excitement has been so incoherent as to be indescribable. The attempt made last night to kill off the bill was renewed to-day at an early hour. It has been lost for want of a sufficient vote, and laid on the table for reconsideration. A motion was made to call it up for a final vote, a short time after the reading of the journal, by its opponents. The tactics against the measure were led by Weed, of Clinton, in which friends of the democrats have gained their [illegible] in this Legislature. He moved to take from the table, and upon that the previous question. The vote of sixty-seven to sixty-one disclosed the fact that the friends of the bill were in the minority, and a panic at once was created among them. An adroit suggestion [illegible] to be from [illegible] to rule the [illegible] Weed and others insisting that such action was out of order.

While the vote was being taken a few more republicans were drummed up, and the motion carried by one or two votes. Hereupon the wildest scenes of confusion took place, all the members gathered in a crowd before the Speaker's desk in the most excited condition, shouting, disputing and threatening each other and the Speaker. One member from New York got upon a desk, and in the midst of a clamor for bets, offered at a thousand dollars, shouted and taunted the republicans, daring any man to bet. He shook his two fists with handsfull of greenbacks. Others clamored in like manner, and the scene resembled the most exciting days at the gold room in New York. In the midst of all this were heard the clapping of hands and the triumphant imitations of the mock chanticleer of the republicans, while the democrats uttered the most violent denunciations of the Speaker to his face for his rulings.

This scene was disposed of only to be reproduced for the evening session. Mr. Weed renewed his assaults upon the bill to bring it to a final vote, while its diminished friends sought to postpone this action. Messrs. Van Buren, Stuart, Reed, Brandreth, Wood and Parker sought alternately to postpone or to kill time by filibustering, after prolonged, excited and most disorderly proceedings.

A final vote was forced upon the friends of the bill at a late hour. Sixty-one voted for the bill and fifty-one against it. Sixty five votes being necessary to its passage, it was lost. Mr. Salmon, of New York, who had made himself obnoxious by the vehemency of his opposition to the bill, was sought to be involved in proceedings before the bar of the House; but the Speaker was evidently discouraged from any such attempts. The management for the bill on the floor of the House was understood to be in the hands of the radicals, under the lead of Fields. Boole was in the lobby in person. Mayor Gunther, Carr and others of his opponents were here yesterday to urge on the passage of the bill. It is alleged that the republican interest was sold out by the radicals.

The Fire Commissioners encountered a decided capsize in executive session. The defeat of the Health bill was pending on their consideration, and the Assembly had adjourned in the extraordinary manner of the morning. The names were at first confirmed, Senator Laimbier, who had made the chief opposition, moving the confirmation. This action was, however, reconsidered on motion of Senator Andrews, on the ground of the promises made in the Assembly to the democrats, who passed it, that the board would comprise two democrats. The names were accordingly sent back to the Governor.

The continuation of Boole in office by the defeat of the Health bill is accompanied by the passage of a resolution continuing the Senate investigating committee, to sit during the summer and examine the other departments. The feeling here is that Boole was treated as an invidious exception, and the thing will be made even all round.

The action determined on in caucus yesterday in regard to Draper and the Board of Charities, was decked by resolution to-day, and is coupled with the defeat of Rufus F. Andrews as candidate for United States District Attorney at New York, as a satisfactory manifestation of Thurlow Weed's power.

The passage of the Central Railroad Fare bill was conducted through the form of third reading with no excitement, and with the limit of seven per cent dividends. The increase of half a cent per mile for three years is thought only reasonable.

IMPORTANT FROM SOUTH AMERICA.

Surrender of Montevideo to Gen. Flores—Brazil in Possession of the City, &c.

The Brazilian mail arrived at Lisbon April 2, bringing the following advices:—

Montevideo has surrendered to General Flores.

The Brazilians low (March 11) occupy the city.

Rio Janeiro, March 11, 1865.

Exchange 25¾ a 26¼.

Coffee—Sales of good firsts at 65.66. Shipments, 100,000 bags. Stock, 100,000 bags. Freights, 50.62½.

Bahia, March 11, 1865.

Exchange 26¼. Cotton nominal.

Pernambuco, March 11, 1865.

Exchange 26½ a 27.

News from San Francisco.

San Francisco, April 12, 1865.

The exports of treasure for the quarter just ended show a falling off of about six and a half millions as compared with the same period last year.

San Francisco, April 14, 1865.

The Pacific mail steamship Sacramento sailed to-day, with a large number of passengers, for New York, and $3,153,000 in treasure, of which nearly $700,000 go to New York.

The steamship Moses Taylor sailed for San Juan del Sur, with numerous passengers.

The market continues variable and unsettled, and traders pursue a continued policy. Prices of Eastern goods are slowly falling.

Sailed, ship Flying Eagle, for Boston.

New Orleans Markets.

New Orleans, April 5, Via Cairo, April 14, 1865.

The New Orleans markets are at a stand still. Low middling cotton is quoted at 42c per pound and good superfine flour at $9 per barrel.

THE REBELS.

JEFF. DAVIS AT DANVILLE.

His Latest Appeal to His Deluded Followers.

He Thinks the Fall of Richmond a Blessing in Disguise, as it Leaves the Rebel Armies Free to Move from Point to Point.

He Vainly Promises to Hold Virginia at All Hazards.

Lee and His Army Supposed to be Safe.

Breckinridge and the Rest of Davis' Cabinet Reach Danville Safely.

The Organ of Governor Vance, of North Carolina, Advises the Submission of the Rebels to President Lincoln's Terms, &c., &c., &c.

Jeff. Davis' Last Proclamation.

VIRGINIA TO BE HELD BY THE REBELS AT ALL HAZARDS.

Danville, Va., April 5, 1865.

The General-in-Chief found it necessary to make such movements of his troops as to uncover the capital. It would be unwise to conceal the *moral and material injury to our cause resulting from the occupation of our capital* by the enemy. It is equally unwise and unworthy of us to allow our own energies to falter and our efforts to become relaxed under adverses, however calamitous they may be. For many months *the largest and finest army* of the confederacy, under command of a leader whose presence inspires equal confidence in the troops and the people, has been greatly trammelled by the necessity of keeping constant watch over the approaches to the capital, and has thus been forced to forego more than one opportunity for promising enterprise. It is for us, my countrymen, to show by our bearing under reverses how wretched has been the self-deception of those who have believed us less able to endure misfortune with fortitude than to encounter dangers with courage.

We have now entered upon a new phase of the struggle. Relieved from the necessity of guarding particular points, *our army will be free to move from point to point* to strike the enemy in detail far from his base. *Let us but will it and we are free.*

Animated by that confidence in spirit and fortitude which never yet failed me, I announce to you, fellow countrymen, that it is my purpose to maintain your cause with my whole heart and soul; that I will never consent to abandon to the enemy one foot of the soil of any one of the States of the confederacy. That Virginia—noble State—whose ancient renown has been eclipsed by her still more glorious recent history; whose bosom has been bared to receive the main shock of this war; whose sons and daughters have exhibited heroism so sublime as to render her illustrious in all time to come—that Virginia, with the help of the people and by the blessing of Providence, *shall be held and defended*, and no peace ever be be made with the infamous invaders of her territory.

If by the stress of numbers we should ever be compelled to a temporary withdrawal from her limits, or those of any other border State, again and again will we return, until the baffled and exhausted enemy shall abandon in despair his endless and impossible task of making slaves of a people resolved to be free.

Let us, then, not despond, my countrymen; but, relying on God, meet the foe with fresh defiance and with unconquered and unconquerable hearts.

JEFFERSON DAVIS.

The Evacuation of the Rebel Capital.

THE FIRST REBEL ACCOUNT OF HOW THE CITY WAS ABANDONED.

[From the Danville (Va.) Register, April 5.]

Persons who left the capital Sunday night and Monday morning represent that the scene which followed the evacuation of the city by our troops beggars description. To preserve order and protect the property of the citizens who unavoidably remained there, as far as could be done, the Nineteenth Virginia militia, under Colonel Evans, was placed on police duty in the city, to await the coming of the enemy; but accounts state that they failed to render any aid or protection to the people whatever. On Sunday night a mob of the lower classes of the city, composed, it is said, mostly of the foreign element, visited a number of the largest storehouses of the city and robbed them of their contents. It is affirmed that Main street was pillaged, and then burned, and that some of the milling establishments were also committed to the flames. We have no doubt that a considerable portion of that brave city has been laid in ashes, and a number of its people insulted, outraged, robbed and massacred. How painful the thought that the place should be given over to rapine and plunder, even before the public enemy entered its limits. But the fact only proves that the people of Richmond have had secret enemies in their own midst scarcely less savage and even more treacherous and vindictive than the open foe.

We are told that the people banded together during the violent proceeding of the mob and resisted them with force, a street fight ensuing in which several persons were killed.

No intelligence has reached us of the enemy's troops occupying the city. The last trains on the Danville railroad which came out of the place left Monday morning, and passengers upon them had heard nothing from the enemy. The greater portion of Grant's army was transferred to the south side of James river some days ago, only the command of General Ord, which is composed mostly, if not entirely, of negro troops, being left on the north side. This command will enter and occupy the city. Some of our people who are acquainted with the character of General Ord think they have reason to hope that his treatment of the unfortunate people of Richmond will not be so hard, and cruel and inhuman as that which has fallen upon the heads of our fellow citizens in some other captured cities.

The newspapers of Richmond, we suppose, all fell into the hands of the enemy. The evacuation of the city was so sudden and unexpected—scarcely any one being prepared for it—that no time was left for the removal of so cumbrous an establishment as a city newspaper office. In a few days we may expect to hear that the *Enquirer* or the *Whig* or the *Examiner* is issued as a Yankee paper.

All the rolling stock of the Richmond and Danville Railroad in running order was saved on the retreat from Richmond. A few old cars, not in a movable condition, were left at Manchester. No train was captured by the enemy near the junction, as was at one time reported; and, indeed, we do not believe that any body of Yankees had struck the road at any point up to yesterday evening.

The Secretary of War, the Quartermaster General, Commissary General and a number of other officers of the government, left Richmond on horseback, and will probably arrive at this place to-morrow.

Should General Lee establish his lines east of the junction, we suppose the State Legislature will be convened at Lynchburg.

All the specie and other valuables belonging to the banks in Richmond were removed from the city on Sunday, and have been carried to places of safety.

A considerable amount of specie purchased by the State for distribution to the people, we regret to learn, had to be left behind. Also the State archives remained in the city; but we perceive no motive the enemy can have in destroying them, as they will, no doubt, endeavor to occupy the city permanently, and establish a State government at Richmond under the federal Union.

Lee's Army Supposed to be in a Safe Position.

[From the Raleigh Confederate, April 7.]

This is the time for rumor manufacturers who are engaged in a wholesale business. Sometimes they have it that whole brigades deserted in the last great battle; among others, Cook's brigade is selected as the bearer of this stigma. We are assured that such a statement has no foundation whatever; that no treachery induced the disaster at Petersburg; that our forces fought splendidly, and the enemy only succeeded by overwhelming numbers. We are convinced, too, from facts which we cannot mention, that *Lee's army is in a safe position*, and that *his future movements will be directed with the skill and energy which distinguish this great captain.*

Having anticipated the probable loss of Richmond, and fully recognizing the importance of the disaster, we are, nevertheless, not of the number of those who give up the cause. In the Southern confederacy this day there is military strength of men, material and supplies to make independence certain. It is with the *people themselves* whether they secure or lose their liberties.

Rebel Particulars of the Battle at Petersburg.

[From the Raleigh Confederate, April 7.]

An officer who left Richmond at nine o'clock on Monday morning last informs us that at the time he left the city was in flames from Cary to Canal streets. The Shockoe warehouse and other entrepots of supplies were burning. The bridges also had been fired.

No mob or violence of any kind had occurred up to the period when he left, so that the reports of a destructive mob on Sunday night are untrue. The enemy's cavalry entered the city as the train moved off that he came out in. The story of the mob, therefore, we hope, is entirely erroneous.

This officer describes the fighting on Saturday as terrific beyond description. The enemy forced column after column on our works, lapping our lines on the extreme right. They came nine columns deep. Eight lines faltered and were broken by the obstinacy of our defences; but the ninth broke over our forces like a whirlwind. He says the destruction of the enemy was immense. Our loss, we think, consisted mainly in the prisoners taken by the enemy. All the prisoners whom we captured were drunk, having been prepared according to Yankee tactics for this dreadful ordeal. Lieutenant General A. P. Hill was certainly killed. General Fitz. Lee was not killed, as reported, nor General W. H. F. Lee. No general officer from North Carolina was killed, as far as he heard. On Monday Sheridan attacked Fitz. Lee and was handsomely repulsed.

The Organ of Governor Vance, of North Carolina, Advising General Lee to Submit on Mr. Lincoln's Terms.

[From the Raleigh Confederate, April 7.]

The *Conservative* occasionally seems to fall into very mysterious hands, and to come under the control of an incomprehensible influence. On the day before yesterday that paper availed itself of a period of extreme reverse and disaster to renew the attempt to cast odium on a portion of our own citizens, which has been a favorite policy with its political leaders ever since the reverses began, and after it was no longer politic to claim that they "made the revolution." Yesterday it sends to the public a leader of still more extraordinary import. From what we comprehend of it, it seems to be *a distinct proposition to submit and surrender upon the terms proposed by Lincoln.* This has never yet, that we recollect of, been more distinctly proposed, even by journals whose loyalty has been called in question. The *Conservative* [illegible] to propose to treat with the [illegible] the concession that the confederacy is a government," and hence, says the *Conservative*, "if our authorities are determined to force this condition upon the North, as a basis of negotiation, then the North will never negotiate." What is this but surrender? Not only surrender, but an assertion to the world that the defence of the last four years has been of a position which is one of sheer nonsense—one which the North "never could admit!" We have not seen in this controversy so bold and unconditional a justification of the Northern invasion; for, if we sought to force a claim inconsistent with reason, and to demand an "admission" which "is an absurdity in anything like government," and the North only resisted such claim and refused such admission, then we are in the wrong and the Yankee government is right, and the writer of the article to which we are replying does well when he *advises General Lee not to "block up his way, at the threshold, by presenting a basis to which he knows the enemy will not yield,"* but "to meet him on his own ground," as "the only way to open the negotiation." When we remember what "his own ground" is, upon which the *Conservative* proposes to meet the enemy, we may readily understand how much it is prepared to concede. "His own ground" measured the length of three propositions; submission to the laws and constitution of the United States, the laying down of our arms, and acquiescence in Lincoln's proclamations. This is the ground on which the author of the editorial desires General Lee to meet Lincoln and "secure a talk about peace." We have no idea that Governor Vance will support this idea; but it is very unfortunate that now, at the very moment when everything should be said to uphold the hopes and confidence of the army and people, such sentiments should obtain publication in the organ of the Governor.

High Prices in an Overstocked Market.

[From the Raleigh Confederate, April 7.]

Our market, on the arrival of the Weldon train, on yesterday, *became overstocked* with shad; *they went off slowly at $50 per pair.*

Exchange of the Rebel General Vance.

[From the Ashville (N. C.) News.]

The exchange of prisoners seems to go steadily on. We have seen a large number of our mountain boys, who have reached home after a protracted imprisonment. Among others we were gratified to meet Brigadier General R. B. Vance, who reached home some days since. He looks rather worsted by his long confinement, but, as usual with him, is full of life, cheerful and buoyant. The General is a great favorite of the people of this section, and everybody was glad to see him.

City Intelligence.

Easter Sunday at St. Ann's Church.—The admirers of sacred music, made truly effective by a well trained choir, have an opportunity of indulging their taste by repairing to St. Ann's church on Easter Sunday evening, the doors opening at seven, the concert beginning at eight. Three of the pieces are from Gordigiani, three from Rossini and one from each of the composers Verdi, Donizetti, Verrimst, Dachauer and Gounod. We need only mention the names of Signor Remi and Messrs. Schmitz, Schubert and Dachauer to insure confidence in the vocal results. The ladies are quite distinguished for contralto and soprano execution, and no exertion will be spared to make the musical feast worthy of the day.

A New Church.—An advertisement among our religious notices announces the opening of the new Church of the Holy Trinity, Madison avenue, corner of Forty-second street, on Sunday. Sermons will be preached at the three sessions by Rev. Dr. Tyng, of St. George's; Rev. Dr. Dyer, and the Rev. Stephen H. Tyng, Jr., the pastor of the church. It promises to be an occasion of great interest to residents on Murray Hill.

Croton Aqueduct Contracts.—The following contracts have been issued by this department:—Laying crosswalks from southeast corner of Fifty-ninth street and Broadway to the junction of Broadway and Eighth avenue, Matthew Murray, $625. Cobble stone pavement in Hammond street, west of Thirteenth avenue, Christy Dowd, $1,896 50. Sewer in Forty-third street, from Lexington avenue to Fourth avenue, John Duffy, Jr., $1,913 50. Sewer in Forty-sixth street, from Eleventh avenue to seventy-five feet west of Tenth avenue, John Rourke, $5,223 50. Fifty-second street, sewer from Sixth to Seventh avenues, Joseph Moore, $4,880. Sewer in 125th street, from Fifth avenue through Manhattan street to Tenth avenue, James Cunningham, $22,941 25.

Miss Emma Hardinge delivers her able lecture on "Politics in the Pulpit" this evening, at Dodworth Hall. To test the lady's ability, any questions the audience desire to ask will be answered.

Man Drowned.—On the morning of the 13th instant a journeyman housepainter, whose name is believed to be Barnard Burns, was accidentally drowned at Guntherville, Long Island. His body has not yet been claimed by his friends. Mr. J. B. Acker, of No. 9 Macdougal street, will give facilities to any one who can identify the corpse.

The Philadelphia Inquirer.

PRICE TWO CENTS. PHILADELPHIA, SATURDAY, APRIL 15, 1865. PRICE TWO CENTS.

MURDER

OF

PRESIDENT LINCOLN!

His Assassination Last Night, While at Ford's Theatre, in Washington!

PISTOL BALL PENETRATES HIS BRAIN!

Mr. Linclon Dying at Midnight

Farewell of President's Family.

SAD AND SOLEMN SCENES

THE ASSASSIN IN HIS PRIVATE BOX.

The Murderer Leaps Upon the Stage and Escapes.

A HORSE IS WAITING FOR HIM.

ATTEMPT TO KILL SEC'Y SEWARD!

His Bedchamber Entered by the Villain.

Fred. W. and Major Seward Knocked Senseless.

SECRETARY SEWARD STABBED THREE TIMES IN THE NECK.

TERRIBLE EXCITEMENT IN WASHINGTON

WASHINGTON, April 14.—The President of the United States was shot while attending at Ford's Theatre to-night. It is feared that the wounds are mortal.

THE PARTICULARS.

WASHINGTON, April 14.—President Lincoln and his wife, together with other friends, this evening, visited Ford's Theatre for the purpose of witnessing the performance of the American Cousin.

It was announced in the papers that General Grant would also be present, but that gentleman instead took the late train of cars for New Jersey.

The theatre was densely crowded, and everybody seemed delighted with the scene before them.

During the third act, and while there was a temporary pause for one of the actors to enter, the sharp report of a pistol was heard, which merely attracted attention, but suggested nothing serious, until a man rushed to the front of the President's box, waving a long dagger in his right hand, and exclaiming "*Sic semper tyrannis!*" and immediately leaped from the box, which was of the second tier, to the stage beneath, and ran across to the opposite side, thus making his escape, amid the bewilderment of the audience, from the rear of the theatre, and, mounting a horse, fled.

The screams of Mrs. Lincoln first disclosed the fact to the audience that the President had been shot, when all present rose to their feet rushing toward the stage, many exclaiming "Hang him! hang him!"

The excitement was of the wildest possible description, and, of course, there was an abrupt termination of the theatrical performance.

There was a rush towards the Presidential box, when cries were heard, "Stand back! Give him air! Has any one stimulants?"

On a hasty examination it was found that the President had been shot through the head, above and back of the temporal bone, and that some of the brain was oozing out.

He was removed to a private house opposite to the theatre, and the Surgeon-General of the Army and other surgeons were sent for to attend to his condition.

On an examination of the private box blood was discovered on the back of the cushioned rocking-chair on which the President had been sitting, also on the partition and on the floor. A common single-barreled pocket pistol was found on the carpet.

A military guard was placed in front of the private residence to which the President had been conveyed. An immense crowd gathered in front of it, all deeply anxious to learn the condition of the President. It had been previously announced that the wound was mortal, but all hoped otherwise.

The shock to the community was terrible.

At midnight the Cabinet, with Messrs. Sumner, Colfax, and Farnsworth, Judge Carter, Governor Oglesby, General Meigs, Colonel Hay, and a few personal friends, with Surgeon-General Barnes, and his medical associates, were around his bed-side.

THE PRESIDENT IN A DYING CONDITION AT MIDNIGHT.

The President was in a state of *syncope*, totally insensible, and breathing slowly, the blood oozing from the wound at the back of his head. The surgeons were exhausting every possible effort of medical skill, but all hope was gone.

The parting of his family with the dying President is too sad for description.

The President and Mrs. Lincoln did not start to the theatre till fifteen minutes after eight o'clock. Speaker Colfax was at the White House at the time, and the President stated to him that he was going, although Mrs. Lincoln had not been well, because the papers had advertised that General Grant and they were to be present, and as General Grant had gone North, he did not wish the audience to be disappointed.

He went with apparent reluctance, and urged Mr. Colfax to go with him, but that gentleman had made other engagements, and with Mr. Ashman, of Massachusetts, bid him good-bye.

ATTEMPTED ASSASSINATION OF SECRETARY SEWARD.

When the excitement at the theatre was at its wildest height, reports were circulated that Secretary Seward had also been assassinated.

On reaching this gentleman's residence, a crowd and a military guard were found at the door, and on entering it was ascertained that the reports were based upon truth. Everybody there was so excited that scarcely an intelligible account could be gathered, but the facts are substantially as follows:—

About ten o'clock a man rang the bell, and the call having been answered by a colored servant, he said he had come from Dr. Verdi, Secretary Seward's family physician, with a prescription, at the same time holding in his hand a small piece of folded paper and saying, in answer to a refusal, that he must see the Secretary, as he was intrusted with a particular direction concerning the medicine.

He still insisted on going up, although repeatedly informed that no one could enter the chamber. The man pushed the servant aside and walked quickly to the Secretary's room, and was there met by Mr. Frederick W. Seward of whom he demanded to see the Secretary, making the same representation which he did to the servant.

What further passed in the way of colloquy is not known, but the man struck him on the head with a billy, severely injuring the skull, and felling him almost senseless. The assassin then rushed into the chamber and attacked Major Seward, Paymaster in the United States Army, and Mr. Hansell, a messenger of the State Department, and two male nurses, disabling them all. He then rushed upon the Secretary, who was lying in bed in the same room, and inflicted three stabs in the neck, but severing, it is thought, and hoped, no arteries.

The assassin then rushed down stairs, mounted his horse at the door and rode off before an alarm could be sounded, and in the same manner of the assassin of the President. It is believed the injuries of the Secretary are not fatal, nor those of the others, although both the Secretary and the Assistant Secretary are very seriously injured.

Secretaries Stanton and Welles, and other prominent officers of the Government, called at Secretary Seward's house to inquire into his condition, and there heard of the assassination of the President. They proceeded to the house where he was lying, exhibiting, of course, intense anxiety and solicitude.

An immense crowd was gathered in front of the President's House, and a strong guard also stationed there, many persons evidently supposing that he would be brought to his home.

The entire city to-night presents a scene of wild excitement, accompanied by violent expressions of indignation, and the profoundest sorrow. Many shed tears.

The military authorities have despatched mounted patrols in every direction, in order, if possible to arrest the assassin, while the Metropolitan police are alike vigilant for the same purpose.

The attack, both at the theatre and at Secretary Seward's house, took place at about the same hour (ten o'clock), thus showing a preconcerted plan to assassinate these gentlemen. Some evidences of the guilt of the party who attacked the President are in possession of the police.

Vice President Johnson is in the city, and his hotel quarters are guarded by troops.

General Grant Receives the News.

We learn that General Grant received intelligence of this sad calamity soon after midnight, when at Walnut street wharf, on his way to Burlington, New Jersey.

THE LATEST NEWS

Latest Advices from Richmond!

WEITZEL RELIEVED FROM COMMAND.

Gen. E. O. C. Ord His Successor.

A BUNCOMBE PROCLAMATION FROM JEFF. DAVIS.

He Hasn't Heard of Lee's Surrender.

HE THINKS EVERYTHING LOOKS WELL!

"Gen. Lee Will Never Give Up."

REBEL PROSPECTS PROMISING!

Usual Lying Braggadocia

GEN. LEE IN RICHMOND.

He Advises Johnston to Surrender!

GRANT ORDERS SHERMAN TO GIVE HIM A CHANCE.

Portuguese Insult to Our Flag.

PROMPT DEMAND OF OUR MINISTER.

Our Flag to be Everywhere Respected.

LATE ADVICES FROM [illegible]L QUARTERS.

OUR RICHMOND CORRESPONDENCE.

Special Correspondence of the I[illegible]r.

RICHMOND, Va., Wednesday Night, April 12, 1865.

The Great Event

Of the day has been the arrival of Major-General E. O. C. Ord, the commander of the Department of Virginia. General Ord through his whole career, has shown remarkable administrative qualifications, and brings to the discharge of the duties of his enlarged command a perfect acquaintance with its requirements, and a large experience in its details. Probably no officer could have been selected by General Grant who would better fill the difficult *role* General Ord will be called upon to perform. Nor is his capacity in council his only claim on the regard of his country. His services in the field have been arduous and brilliant, showing him one of our first soldiers. Twice wounded since the war began, his scars are honorable witnesses of his service and his bravery.

That the conflicting interests, the jealousies, the perplexities already arising around him will be fairly and fearlessly dealt with, none who know the man can doubt.

A Grand Salute

Of two hundred guns was fired to-day in honor of the surrender of Lee. The same salvos of joy were doubtless indulged in all over the Union, as the salute was in accordance with a General Order of the War Department.

The City

Is quiet and orderly, and fast becoming as respectable in appearance as circumstances will permit. Large gangs of negroes are kept constantly at work clearing the streets of the *debris* of the evacuation, but their progress in the burned district is very slow. There the ghastly monuments of Rebel barbarism will remain for weeks and months, silent but effective witnesses to the vindictive malignity of the despotism that attempted to destroy a city it could no longer hold. Outside of the burned district, however, Richmond is fast becoming again the beautiful city it was in its better days, and but for the ruin wrought by Breckinridge and Ewell the tourist would find little to remind him of its recent terrible history. One important adjunct of a city, viz., gas, was wanting during the first days of our occupation, but that has been remedied, and to-night all the houses are lighted with a very superior article.

Everybody's impression of Richmond, so long beleagured, so long defended, so long the centre of all that was false in American politics, will be interesting after the nation has recovered from the wild delirium of joy under which it is now laboring, and when that time comes mine shall be forthcoming.

A Trip to Burkesville

Was attempted yesterday, but resulted in a miserable failure. Leaving City Point at three A. M., the train which was going out specially to bring in General Grant, pounded and twisted and tortured along that miserable apology of a railroad called the South Side, until four miles beyond Wilson's Station, when a capsized locomotive barred further progress, and after hours of waiting a return train to City Point was taken. This episode of personal experience is mentioned only to anathematize that Southside Railroad. A more wretched affair it is impossible to conceive of, and it is hardly stretching truth to say that there is not a decent rail or sound tie in its whole length. How the Rebels managed to get the amount of work out of it they did it is hard to say. Want of repairs is its ailment. For four years it has not been ditched; rails have only been replaced when utterly worn out; new ties put down when the old absolutely refused to longer hold a spike. The force working the road was meagre in numbers; those employed in repairing it were more so. To a section of nine miles and a half east from Wilson's, five men were the allowance, and railroad men can easily imagine in what repair they would keep a road originally none of the best, and constantly worked beyond its capacity.

The road can hardly be called serviceable, and if the military situation shall demand its use for any time, we shall be obliged practically to rebuild it.

The Richmond and Petersburg Road

Is said to be in far better condition, and to be in reality a railroad. Our great interest, however, is centring in the Richmond, Fredericksburg and Potomac Road, and from it we have as yet no reliable advices. This whole community is anxious for speedier communication with the North than by the present out of the way route, via Fortress Monroe, and is waiting impatiently for the opening of the road to Aquia Creek. That it will soon be done everybody believes, but exactly when, nobody appears to know.

General Grant

Will in a few days proceed to Washington, and it is not now generally expected that he will visit the city he has captured. He announced to his staff to-day that he should give them immediately fifteen days leave of absence, and the military family that has been together so long will for that time be broken up. No staff in the army has been worked harder than that of the Lieutenant-General, and they have nobly earned a short respite from labor.

General Grant himself was to-day at City Point, giving no outward sign of the glorious history he created during the few days he was absent. He is the same imperturbable Grant. Looming to-day far above all compeers, or more correctly, having no compeer in all history, he seems himself to be the only man who is unconscious of the fact, and is the same man outwardly that he was during the earliest days of the war, when newspapers called him "the blunderer of the Mississippi." There is no exultation in his manner; not a change in his demeanor. This man who issues no congratulatory orders, who refuses to visit the city he has conquered, only because he has no business there, is great even in his unconsciousness of his greatness.

Exactly where General Grant will go next it is not proper to state, even were it definitely known; but there are faint remains of organized Rebellion in distant parts of the land, and his tireless energy will soon be at work on some of them.

An Incident

Of the late surrender exhibits Fitz Hugh Lee and Rosser in no enviable light. After General Lee had formally surrendered his army, these two men stole away, and were not to be found to give their parole. Neither of them were ever possessed of either talents or influence, and their defection is of no consequence to anybody but themselves. There is every probability that sooner or later they will fall into our hands, and then even their impudence can claim no immunity.

Impudence,

By the way, seems to be the great staple of nearly every man wearing the Rebel uniform. No organized force of the Rebellion remaining in Virginia, the officers on parole in Richmond still flaunt their grey before our eyes on the street, as if it were the badge of honorable service instead of what it is, the livery of a defeated, crushed, wiped-out Rebellion. Some of them seem to act as though they expected to wear it during their natural lives, and to glory in it forever. But even Southern chivalry may on this point be taught a lesson in good manners before long.

EDWARD CRAPSEY.

SHERMAN.

Reorganization of Sherman's Army—General Items of Interest.

Special Correspondence of the Inquirer.

GOLDSBORO, N. C., April 8, 1865.

A Reconstruction.

A nominal reorganization of General Sherman's army has been ordered, and the additional troops, under Schofield and Terry, have been formed into an integral part of the grand army now under his leadership.

The Army of Georgia.

The Fourteenth and Twentieth Corps, hitherto known as the left wing, will in future be designated "the Army of Georgia," and will be commanded by Major-General Slocum.

The Army of the Tennessee.

The Fifteenth and Seventeenth Corps, heretofore known as the right wing, will now be distinguished by the title of "The Army of the Tennessee," under the command of Major-General Oliver O. Howard. The "Army of the Ohio," consisting of the Twenty-third and Tenth Corps, will constitute the centre, under Major-General John M. Schofield.

Major-General Joseph A. Mower, lately commanding the First Division of the Seventeenth Corps, assumed the command of the Twentieth Corps, vice Williams.

Refugees

Are becoming fewer. All that arrive or have arrived are being sent to Newbern, except those in Government employ. Two thousand three hundred and seventy of these people have been supplied with Government rations since the occupation of Goldsboro'. These rations have been issued only to females, children, and aged and infirm men, far the greater number being women and children. These women are all without their natural male providers. In most cases they are wives whose husbands are or have been in the Rebel army. These recipients of the Government charity are all white. No rations whatever have been gratuitously issued to colored people. A camp of colored men has been formed beyond and in rear of the camp of the white soldiers. This camp of colored civilians had a population of 10,000.

A Change.

Captain Thomas B. Wilson, A. Q. M., who has been the Division Quartermaster of the Fourth Division of the Seventeenth Corps since Sherman commenced his movement from Atlanta, has been relieved from division duty, and assumes the important and onerous post of depot quartermaster to General Sherman's army.

Prisoners.

Two prisoners were taken on picket line yesterday, members of the Fiftieth North Carolina infantry. They are sullen and morose dogs, not at all communicative. From their admissions and assertions we gather that Johnston is working like a beaver in the vicinity of Smithfield. Whether concentrating an army there, hurrying an evacuating one, or supplying one at a distance with Smithfield for an important intermediate post, we are at a loss to determine.

A Fire

Broke out in a private residence on the main street, on the evening of the 6th. It originated among some cotton stowed in the loft. The soldiers busied themselves in removing the furniture from the building, and extinguishing the fire. Not one article was destroyed or stolen. Provost Marshal Hufty was on the ground superintending the removal of the furniture, and the suppression of the flames. When the fire was first discovered, many feared another Savannah conflagration.

A Review

Of the Twentieth Corps took place yesterday by its new commander, General Mower. The First and Third Divisions were reviewed in the forenoon, and the Second Division in the afternoon. The cleanliness and soldierly appearance of the Twentieth were favorably commented on by the throng of bystanders.

WILLIAM ANDERSON.

The Alleged Charges Against General Carrington.

CINCINNATI, April 14.—General Carrington publishes a card, saying the charges against him are all infamous attempts to obliterate the credit of his services in Indiana. His friends say the matter grows out of a misunderstanding with the paymasters, and all money for which he is responsible is deposited in bank ready to be turned over.

The Funeral of General Smyth.

WILMINGTON, Del., April 14.—The remains of Brigadier-General Thomas A. Smyth arrived here to-day at 1 o'clock, and will be interred on Monday afternoon at 2 o'clock with appropriate ceremonies.

WASHINGTON

DAVIS ISSUES A PROCLAMATION.

The Arrival of 440 Rebel Officers at the Capital.

THE GUERRILLAS BETWEEN RICHMOND AND WASHINGTON.

Steps Taken to Exterminate the Rascals.

RETRENCHMENT IN GOVERNMENT EXPENSES.

[SPECIAL DESPATCHES TO THE INQUIRER.]

WASHINGTON, April 14.

Jeff. Davis, on his Arrival

At Danville, issued a proclamation to the people of the South. He had not heard of the surrender of Lee. It contains nothing new. The same old story. Full of "sound and fury, signifying nothing."

Arrival of Rebel Officers.

A batch of four hundred and forty Rebel officers arrived here this afternoon from City Point. They comprise the officers captured by General Sheridan in the battle at Amelia Court House. Among them was Lieutenant-General Ewell, Major-General's Kershaw, Defose, Barton, Corse, Hunter, and Simms, also Commodores Hunter and Tucker of the Rebel navy. They were taken before Colonel Ingraham, Provost Marshal. It is understood that the latter officers are to be sent to Fort Warren, the others will be distributed among the other forts. They attracted considerable attention marching down Pennsylvania Avenue.

Guerrillas to be Exterminated.

Now that the largest part of Virginia is within the lines of our army, it is the intention of the Government to clear the country between Washington and Richmond of the scoundrelly set of robbers and thieves, in the shape of guerrillas infesting this region.

Retrenchment of Expenses.

It is estimated that the retrenchment of Government expenses to take place immediately will amount to upwards of one million dollars per day. Both the Secretary of War and the Secretary of the Navy have gone vigorously at work in this direction. The pruning hook will lop off all the diseased and rotten material in both branches of service.

[DESPATCHES TO THE ASSOCIATED PRESS.]

Sherman's Movements—Johnston Retreating South.

Intelligence has been received that General Sherman's army moved from Goldsboro on Monday.

General Johnston is reported to have retreated southward toward South Carolina, on learning of the surrender of General Lee's army.

It is supposed that the Rebels intend to make a stand in Georgia and the trans-Mississippi States, more with a view of obtaining favorable terms, than from any hope of establishing any independent Government.

If Johnston intends to fight or prolong the war, Sherman has the means and ability to crush him.

Secretary Seward's health does not yet cease to inspire some alarm, but it is believed that he will recover.

The political excitement on the great questions opening upon the nation is intense, and is apparently increasing.

Our Mexican Relations.

Some of the foreign journals have reported that it is the intention of our Government to acknowledge the Mexican empire. A recent act of the President does not, however, support that assertion, for he has recognized Jose A. Godey as Consul of the Mexican republic at San Francisco.

General Ord at Richmond.

General E. O. C. Ord, who is the ranking officer in the absence of General Grant, has taken command at Richmond. The colored troops under General Weitzel, will occupy Petersburg. Gen. Weitzel's administration of affairs at Richmond has given entire satisfaction both to the citizens and to our own authorities.

Harrisburg.

Special Despatch to the Inquirer.

HARRISBURG, April 14.—There is great rejoicing here over the order stopping the draft, as it indicates the end of the war. General Hinks, Provost Marshal-General of Pennsylvania, has ordered the Provost Marshals of the several districts to make their returns and close the business of their offices with as much facility as possible, announcing that recruiting and drafting in all the districts is suspended, and that accordingly telegraphic reports of musters will be discontinued.

Drafted men reporting are furloughed.

Immense preparations are making for a grand procession to-morrow, and a general illumination and torchlight parade in the evening. Flags are flying from every house. Bands of music are arriving.

The Governor is expected here to-morrow.

From Baltimore.

Special Despatch to the Inquirer.

BALTIMORE, April 14, 1865.—A large number of persons from Richmond and elsewhere south, and officers and soldiers of Lee's army, are arriving here. All seem glad to be enjoying such luxuries. I have it on reliable authority that Gen. Lee has gone to Johnston's army, by permission, to cause him to surrender.

Our City Council have deferred their approbation of celebrating the nineteenth of April. They prefer passing over so disgraceful an epoch of treason and rebellion as unworthy of observance.

The Seven-thirty loan is selling here very rapidly.

From Richmond.

THE CITIZENS RETURNING TO THEIR ALLEGIANCE—ARRIVAL OF GENERAL LEE.

BALTIMORE, April 14.—The Richmond *Whig*, of yesterday, contains little news of importance. It announces the arrival of General Lee on the night previously.

The *Whig* publishes the oath of allegiance, to which it says citizens will be required to swear and subscribe. The Provost Marshal's office is crowded with people anxious to take it, and the only question among the citizens seems to be who shall be the first to renew their citizenship.

Fire in Rochester.

ROCHESTER, N. Y., April 14.—The cabinet warehouse of James E. Haydon, of this city, was partially destroyed by fire this morning. The stock of Humphrey, Reedy & Co., stove dealers; Hastings & McVeagh, paper dealers; S. B. Roby, saddlery and hardware dealers, and the Agency of the American Tract Society were damaged. The total loss is thirty thousand dollars, with an insurance of twenty thousand dollars. The origin of the fire is unknown.

From Nassau and Galveston.

NEW YORK, April 14.—The steamer *Corsica*, from Nassau on the 10th, arrived here to-day.

The blockade runner *Banshee*, with 1000 bales of cotton, had arrived at Nassau from Galveston. She reports that Galveston was garrisoned by 1200 troops.

Twelve Federal ships were off the bar.

Six steamers had sailed recently from Havana for Galveston.

The New-York Times.

VOL. XIV......NO. 4230. NEW-YORK, SATURDAY, APRIL 15, 1865. PRICE FOUR CENTS

AWFUL EVENT.

President Lincoln Shot by an Assassin.

The Deed Done at Ford's Theatre Last Night.

THE ACT OF A DESPERATE REBEL

The President Still Alive at Last Accounts.

No Hopes Entertained of His Recovery.

Attempted Assassination of Secretary Seward.

DETAILS OF THE DREADFUL TRAGEDY.

[OFFICIAL.]

WAR DEPARTMENT,
WASHINGTON, April 15—1:30 A. M.

Maj.-Gen. Dix :

This evening at about 9:30 P. M., at Ford's Theatre, the President, while sitting in his private box with Mrs. LINCOLN, Mrs. HARRIS, and Major RATHBURN, was shot by an assassin, who suddenly entered the box and approached behind the President.

The assassin then leaped upon the stage, brandishing a large dagger or knife, and made his escape in the rear of the theatre.

The pistol ball entered the back of the President's head and penetrated nearly through the head. The wound is mortal. The President has been insensible ever since it was inflicted, and is now dying.

About the same hour an assassin, whether the same or not, entered Mr. SEWARD's apartments, and under the pretence of having a prescription, was shown to the Secretary's sick chamber. The assassin immediately rushed to the bed, and inflicted two or three stabs on the throat and two on the face. It is hoped the wounds may not be mortal. My apprehension is that they will prove fatal.

The nurse alarmed Mr. FREDERICK SEWARD, who was in an adjoining room, and hastened to the door of his father's room, when he met the assassin, who inflicted upon him one or more dangerous wounds. The recovery of FREDERICK SEWARD is doubtful.

It is not probable that the President will live throughout the night.

Gen. GRANT and wife were advertised to be at the theatre this evening, but he started to Burlington at 6 o'clock this evening.

At a Cabinet meeting at which Gen. GRANT was present, the subject of the state of the country and the prospect of a speedy peace was discussed. The President was very cheerful and hopeful, and spoke very kindly of Gen. LEE and others of the Confederacy, and of the establishment of government in Virginia.

All the members of the Cabinet except Mr. SEWARD, are now in attendance upon the President.

I have seen Mr. SEWARD, but he and FREDERICK were both unconscious.

EDWIN M. STANTON,
Secretary of War.

DETAIL OF THE OCCURRENCE.

WASHINGTON, Friday, April 14—12:30 A. M.

The President was shot in a theatre tonight, and is, perhaps, mortally wounded.

Secretary SEWARD was also assassinated.

SECOND DISPATCH.

WASHINGTON, Friday, April 14.

President LINCOLN and wife, with other friends, this evening visited Ford's Theatre for the purpose of witnessing the performance of the "American Cousin."

It was announced in the papers that Gen. GRANT would also be present, but he took the late train of cars for New-Jersey.

The theatre was densely crowded, and everybody seemed delighted with the scene before them. During the third act, and while there was a temporary pause for one of the actors to enter, a sharp report of a pistol was heard, which merely attracted attention, but suggesting nothing serious, until a man rushed to the front of the President's box, waving a long dagger in his right hand, and exclaiming "*Sic semper tyrannis*," and immediately leaped from the box, which was in the second tier, to the stage beneath, and ran across to the opposite side, making his escape amid the bewilderment of the audience from the rear of the theatre, and, mounting a horse, fled.

The screams of Mrs. LINCOLN first disclosed the fact to the audience that the President had been shot, when all present rose to their feet, rushing toward the stage, many exclaiming "Hang him! hang him!"

The excitement was of the wildest possible description, and of course there was an abrupt termination of the theatrical performance.

There was a rush toward the President's box, when cries were heard: "Stand back and give him air." "Has any one stimulants." On a hasty examination, it was found that the President had been shot through the head, above and back of the temporal bone, and that some of the brain was oozing out. He was removed to a private house opposite to the theatre, and the Surgeon-General of the army, and other surgeons sent for to attend to his condition.

On an examination of the private box blood was discovered on the back of the cushioned rocking chair on which the President had been sitting, also on the partition and on the floor. A common single-barreled pocket pistol was found on the carpet.

A military guard was placed in front of the private residence to which the President had been conveyed. An immense crowd was in front of it, all deeply anxious to learn the condition of the President. It had been previously announced that the wound was mortal; but all hoped otherwise. The shock to the community was terrible.

The President was in a state of syncope, totally insensible, and breathing slowly. The blood oozed from the wound at the back of his head. The surgeons exhausted every effort of medical skill, but all hope was gone. The parting of his family with the dying President is too sad for description.

At midnight, the Cabinet, with Messrs. SUMNER, COLFAX and FARNSWORTH, Judge CURTIS, Gov. OGLESBY, Gen. MEIGS, Col. HAY, and a few personal friends, with Surgeon-General BARNES and his immediate assistants, were around his bedside.

The President and Mrs. LINCOLN did not start for the theatre until fifteen minutes after eight o'clock. Speaker COLFAX was at the White House at the time, and the President stated to him that he was going, although Mrs. LINCOLN had not been well, because the papers had announced that Gen. GRANT and they were to be present, and, as Gen. GRANT had gone North, he did not wish the audience to be disappointed.

He went with apparent reluctance and urged Mr. COLFAX to go with him; but that gentleman had made other engagements, and with Mr. ASHMAN, of Massachusetts, bid him good bye.

When the excitement at the theatre was at its wildest height, reports were circulated that Secretary SEWARD had also been assassinated.

On reaching this gentleman's residence a crowd and a military guard were found at the door, and on entering it was ascertained that the reports were based on truth.

Everybody there was so excited that scarcely an intelligible word could be gathered, but the facts are substantially as follows:

About 10 o'clock a man rang the bell, and the call having been answered by a colored servant, he said he had come from Dr. VERDI, Secretary SEWARD's family physician, with a prescription, at the same time holding in his hand a small piece of folded paper, and saying in answer to a refusal that he must see the Secretary, as he was entrusted with particular directions concerning the medicine.

He still insisted on going up, although repeatedly informed that no one could enter the chamber. The man pushed the servant aside, and walked heavily toward the Secretary's room, and was then met by Mr. FREDERICK SEWARD, of whom he demanded to see the Secretary, making the same representation which he did to the servant. What further passed in the way of colloquy is not known, but the man struck him on the head with a "billy," severely injuring the skull and felling him almost senseless. The assassin then rushed into the chamber and attacked Major SEWARD, Paymaster of the United States army and Mr. HANSELL, a messenger of the State Department and two male nurses, disabling them all, he then rushed upon the Secretary, who was lying in bed in the same room, and inflicted three stabs in the neck, but severing, it is thought and hoped, no arteries, though he bled profusely.

The assassin then rushed down stairs, mounted his horse at the door, and rode off before an alarm could be sounded, and in the same manner as the assassin of the President.

It is believed that the injuries of the Secretary are not fatal, nor those of either of the others, although both the Secretary and the Assistant Secretary are very seriously injured.

Secretaries STANTON and WELLES, and other prominent officers of the government, called at Secretary SEWARD's house to inquire into his condition, and there heard of the assassination of the President.

They then proceeded to the house where he was lying, exhibiting of course intense anxiety and solicitude. An immense crowd was gathered in front of the President's house, and a strong guard was also stationed there, many persons evidently supposing he would be brought to his home.

The entire city to-night presents a scene of wild excitement, accompanied by violent expressions of indignation, and the profoundest sorrow—many shed tears. The military authorities have dispatched mounted patrols in every direction, in order, if possible, to arrest the assassins. The whole metropolitan police are likewise vigilant for the same purpose.

The attacks, both at the theatre and at Secretary SEWARD's house, took place at about the same hour—10 o'clock—thus showing a preconcerted plan to assassinate those gentlemen. Some evidence of the guilt of the party who attacked the President are in the possession of the police.

Vice-President JOHNSON is in the city, and his headquarters are guarded by troops.

ANOTHER ACCOUNT.

Special Dispatch to the New-York Times.

WASHINGTON, Friday, April 14.
11.15 P. M.

A stroke from Heaven laying the whole of the city in instant ruins could not have startled us as did the word that broke from Ford's Theatre a half hour ago that the President had been shot. It flew everywhere in five minutes, and set five thousand people in swift and excited motion on the instant.

It is impossible to get at the full facts of the case, but it appears that a young man entered the President's box from the theatre, during the last act of the play of "Our American Cousin," with pistol in hand. He shot the President in the head and instantly jumped from the box upon the stage, and immediately disappeared through the side scenes and rear of the theatre, brandishing a dirk knife and dropping a kid glove on the stage.

The audience heard the shot, but supposing it fired in the regular course of the play, did not heed it till Mrs. LINCOLN's screams drew their attention. The whole affair occupied scarcely half a minute, and then the assassin was gone. As yet he has not been found.

The President's wound is reported mortal. He was at once taken into the house opposite the theatre.

As if this horror was not enough, almost the same moment the story ran through the city that Mr. SEWARD had been murdered in his bed.

Inquiry showed this to be so far true also. It appears a man wearing a light coat, dark pants, slouch hat, called and asked to see Mr. SEWARD, and was shown to his room. He delivered to Major SEWARD, who sat near his father, what purported to be a physician's prescription, turned, and with one stroke cut Mr. SEWARD's throat as he lay on his bed, inflicting a horrible wound, but not severing the jugular vein, and not producing a mortal wound.

In the struggle that followed, Major SEWARD was also badly, but not seriously, wounded in several places. The assassin rushed down stairs, mounted the fleet horse on which he came, drove his spurs into him, and dashed away before any one could stop him.

Reports have prevailed that an attempt was also made on the life of Mr. STANTON.

MIDNIGHT.

The President is reported dead. Cavalry and infantry are scouring the city in every direction for the murderous assassins, and the city is overwhelmed with excitement. Who the assassins were no one knows, though every body supposes them to have been rebels.

SATURDAY MORNING—1 O'CLOCK.

The person who shot the President is represented as about 30 years of age, five feet nine inches in height, sparely built, of light complexion, dressed in dark clothing, and having a genteel appearance. He entered the box, which is known as the State box, being the upper box on the right hand side from the dress-circle in the regular manner, and shot the President from behind, the ball entering the skull about in the middle, behind, and going in the direction of the left eye; it did not pass through, but apparently broke the frontal bone and forced out the brain to some extent. The President is not yet dead, but is wholly insensible, and the Surgeon-General says he cannot live till day-break. The assassin was followed across the stage by a gentleman, who sprang out from an orchestra chair. He rushed through the side door into an alley, thence to the avenue and mounted a dark bay horse, which he apparently received from the hand of an accomplice, dashed up F, toward the back part of the city. The escape was so sudden that he effectually eluded pursuit. The assassin cried "*sic sempre*" in a sharp, clear voice, as he jumped to the stage, and dropped his hat and a glove.

Two or three officers were in the box with the President and Mrs. LINCOLN, who made efforts to stop the assassin, but were unsuccessful, and received some bruises. The whole affair, from his entrance into the box to his escape from the theatre, occupied scarcely a minute, and the strongest of the action found everybody wholly unprepared. The assault upon Mr. SEWARD appeared to have been made almost at the same moment as that upon the President. Mr. SEWARD's wound is not dangerous in itself, but may prove so in connection with his recent injuries. The two assassins have both endeavored to leave the city to the northwest, apparently not expecting to strike the river. Even so low down as Chain Bridge, cavalry have been sent in every direction to intercept them.

SATURDAY, 1.30 o'clock A. M.

The President still lies insensible. Messrs. STANTON, WELLS, McCULLOCH, SPEED and USHER are with him, as also the Vice-President, the Surgeon-General, and other Surgeons.

There is a great throng about the house, even at this hour.

2 o'clock A. M.

The President still lives, but lies insensible, as he has since the first moment, and no hopes are entertained that he can survive.

The most extravagant stories prevail, among which one is to effect, that Gen. GRANT was shot while on his was to Philaphia, of course this is not true.

Another is, that every member of Mr. SEWARD's family was wounded in the struggle with the assassin there. This also is untrue. Mr. FRED. SEWARD, the Assistant Secretary, and Major CLARENCE SEWARD, of the army, were wounded, neither of them dangerously.

THE CONDITION OF THE PRESIDENT.

WASHINGTON, April 15—2:12 A. M.

The President is still alive; but he is growing weaker. The ball is lodged in his brain, three inches from where it entered the skull. He remains insensible, and his condition is utterly hopeless.

The Vice-President has been to see him; but all company, except the members of the Cabinet and of the family, is rigidly excluded.

Large crowds still continue in the street, as near to the house as the line of guards allows.

THE SIEGE OF MOBILE.

Fierce Bombardment of the Spanish Fort—Mobile Papers Announce the Capture of Selma.

NEW-ORLEANS, Saturday, April 8, }
via CAIRO, Friday, April 14. }

A special dispatch to the New-Orleans *Times*, from the Spanish Fort, dated April 5, says:

"A furious fire was opened on the rebel forts last night from our entire line. During the bombardment a small magazine in the Spanish Fort exploded. The damage is unknown. Quiet prevailed on the 5th. Deserters report from 18,000 to 20,000 troops in and about Mobile, including all the State Reserves, and about 2,000 in the Spanish Fort. The loss outside the Spanish Fort up to the 4th instant amounted to about 500 killed and wounded. The rebel loss exceeds ours."

Adjt.-Gen. THOMAS arrived at New-Orleans on the morning of the 7th.

Mobile papers of the 4th inst. announce the capture of Selma, Alabama, with 23 pieces of artillery, and a large amount of Government property.

Fort Sumter Celebration in Bangor.

BANGOR, Me., Friday, April 14.

The restoration of the Old Flag to Fort Sumter was celebrated here to-day by a national salute at noon, by a display of all the flags on public and private buildings, and by the raising of the Stars and Stripes one thousand feet above the city by means of a monster kite bearing the name of U. S. GRANT.

The Madrid *Bolsa* says if the Pope should leave Rome, Spain would confer upon him the Balearic Isles.

The *Politica* says the Pope would rather inhabit the Montpensier Palace at Seville.

EUROPEAN NEWS.

TWO DAYS LATER BY THE EUROPA.

The Insult to Our Cruisers by Portugal.

The American Minister at Lisbon Demands Satisfaction.

Dismissal of the Commander of Fort Belan Requested.

Further Advance in Five-Twenties.

FINANCIAL AND COMMERCIAL.

HALIFAX, Friday, April 14.

The steamship *Europa*, from Liverpool on the 1st, via Queenstown on the 2d inst., arrived here at 2 o'clock this morning. She has 43 passengers for this port, and 30 for Boston. Her dates are two days later than those already received.

The steamship *Cuba*, from New-York, arrived at Liverpool at noon on the 1st inst.

THE STONEWALL AFFAIR.

A Lisbon dispatch, of the 31st of March, says that the American Minister at Lisbon has demanded satisfaction of the Portuguese Government for the firing upon the *Niagara* and *Sacramento* by the Portuguese forts. He also requests the dismissal of the Commander of Fort Belan, and a salute of twenty-one guns to the American flag.

Nothing as yet has been decided in regard to the matter.

A PROPHECY FROM RICHMOND.

The correspondent of the London *Times*, writing from Richmond on the 4th of March, says:

"I am daily more convinced that if Richmond falls and LEE and JOHNSTON are driven from the field, it is but the first stage of this colossal revolution which will then be completed. There will ensue a time when every important town of the South will require to be held by a Yankee garrison, when exultation in New-York will be exchanged for soberness and right reason, and when it will be realized that the closing scenes of this mightiest revolutionary drama will not be played out, save in the times of our children's children."

GREAT BRITAIN.

Parliamentary proceedings on the 30th ult. were unimportant.

In the House of Commons, on the 31st, Lord C. PAGET said that the Admiralty had received no proposal for sanctioning or supporting any fresh attempt to reach the North Pole. He was, therefore, unable to say what course the government would take if such a proposal were made.

Mr. NEWDEGATE put some questions as to the idea of the Pope taking up his residence in England, as indicated in some foreign journals.

Lord PALMERSTON replied that the government respected the Pope personally very much, but for him to come to England would be both an anachronism and a solecism.

The revenue returns for the financial year, ending March 31, show a net increase of over £104,000 on the year. Notwithstanding the great reductions in taxation, the revenue exceeds by nearly half a million sterling the estimates of Mr. GLADSTONE.

Messrs. BARING's circular says that large business has been done in 5-20 bonds, and that prices advanced early in the week to 57¾@58, but have since relapsed to 56⅜@57—the demand being chiefly from the continent.

On Friday, the telegrams per the steamship *Cuba* were received, and 5-20s again advanced to 57¼@58¼. Erie and Illinois Central Shares have also attracted attention, and have again advanced.

The Bank of England on the 30th ult. reduced its rate of discount to 4 per cent., at which there is a fair demand for money. This movement strengthened the English funds, and Consols are buoyant and advancing.

KELSON, TRITTON & Co., East India and general merchants, have suspended payment. Their liabilities are estimated at £900,000 sterling.

Another provincial bank has suspended, the Portsmouth and South Hants Banking Company. Their liabilities are about £170,000 sterling.

The Birmingham and Joint Stock Banking Company had agreed to take up the business of Atwood & Spooner's Bank, which lately suspended at Birmingham, and to pay the creditors 11s. 3d. on the pound.

The West India Mail steamer had arrived, with over two and a quarter millions of dollars in specie. She also brought several Captains of blockade-runners, whose occupations were gone.

THE ATLANTIC TELEGRAPH.

The French Government will probably send one or two steamers to accompany the two that are sent by the English Government with the *Great Eastern* across the Atlantic, at the time of laying the Atlantic cable, and it is hoped that the United States Government will do the same.

FRANCE.

Weekly returns from the Bank of France show an increase of cash on hand of over ten and a half millions francs.

In the French Chambers of the 30th, M. JULES FAVRE spoke upon the necessity for political liberty, but was interrupted by the President and declined to finish his speech. The amendment was rejected.

The amendment in favor of the liberty of the press was debated, but rejected by a large majority.

It is stated that NAPOLEON will leave Paris early in May, not returning until November. His physicians have recommended seven months' absence in the country air.

The Bourse is firm, 67.45.

SPAIN.

The *Epoca* states that the Minister of War tendered his resignation, and that Gen. LEORSUNDI refused to place him.

A later dispatch says the Minister of War resigned from ill health.

Gen. RIVERA succeeded to the office.

DENMARK.

The King relieved M. HELLSEN, Minister of Justice, of his functions. HELLSEN represented the alliance between the Reactionary and extreme Democratic parties. It is supposed that all members of the late Cabinet will return to their posts.

ITALY.

In the allocutions delivered at the last consistory the Pope expressed surprise and sorrow at the sad events which have recently taken place in Mexico. His Holiness hoped MAXIMILIAN would abandon the course upon which he had entered, and satisfy the just desires of the Holy See. The Pope further thanked the Bishops of the Catholic world, especially those of Italy, for defending the religion and liberties of the Church, despite the decrees of the secular authorities.

PRUSSIA.

In the Military Committee of Chambers, the Deputies amendment was introduced with the object of effecting a reconciliation between the government and chamber, and proposing a maximum strength of the army at 180,000 men, which was rejected by 11 to 8. The committee also rejected the general military estimates and navy estimates and amendments, thus refusing the whole military and naval proposals of the government.

AUSTRIA.

Count MENSDORFF had made some ministerial explanation in the Lower House Reichsrath. He said the views of the government on the question of the Duchies would be communicated in the Federal Diet on the 6th of April.

As regards relations with Italy, he said the government desired to promote the material interests of the two countries, but that Italy maintained a hostile attitude to the government. He desired to economize, but must maintain the position of Austria as a great Power.

INDIA.

A private Calcutta telegram of March 27 reports commercial affairs in much the same state as on the 25th, when slight improvement had taken place.

BRAZIL.

LONDON, Sunday, April 2.

The Brazilian mail has reached Lisbon, bringing the following dates:

RIO DE JANEIRO, Saturday, March 11.

Exchange 25⅞@26¼.

COFFEE.—Sales of good firsts at 65s.06. Shipments 100,000 bags. Stock, 100,000 bags. Freights 50@62¾.

BAHIA, Saturday, March 11.

Exchange 26¼.

Cotton nominal.

PERNAMBUCO, Saturday, March 11.

Exchange 26⅜@27.

Montivedeo has surrendered to Gen. FLORES. The Brazilians now occupy the city.

LATEST VIA LIVERPOOL.

LIVERPOOL, Saturday Evening, April 1, 1865.

The *Times* to-day has an editorial on the amended tariff law of the United States. It says: "It is impossible to find an excuse for it. Tried by the light of reason or by the results of experience it is alike condemned."

It ironically credits the framers of the scheme with peculiar wisdom in selecting the 1st of April for its inauguration.

The *Army & Navy Gazette* says: "The work of the United States Navy has now been accomplished, and it must be confessed that in the hands of FARRAGUT and PORTER the high reputation which the officers and seamen of that Power established soon after the national existence of itself, has been greatly enhanced."

LATEST VIA QUEENSTOWN.

LONDON, Saturday, April 1.

There is no news of importance this morning.

PARIS, Friday, March 31—P. M.

The Bourse is steady. The Rentes closed at 67f. 30c.

COMMERCIAL.

LIVERPOOL MARKET.

LIVERPOOL, April 31.—Evening.

The Market report was received per *Moravian*.

COTTON—The stock of Cotton in port is 680,000 bales by actual count, being 13,000 bales below the estimates, of which amount 49,000 bales are American.

TRADE REPORT.

The Manchester market was firmer with an upward tendency.

BREADSTUFFS—The market is easier. Messrs. RICHARDSON, SPENCE & Co., and others, report: Flour dull and easier. Wheat quiet and quotations are barely maintained; red Western 8s.@8s. 8d. Corn inactive; mixed 27s. 6d.

PROVISIONS—The market is downward, WAKEFIELD, NASH & Co., and others, report: Beef has a downward tendency. Pork heavy and declined 2s. 6d. Bacon firmer and holders demand an advance. Lard dull and easier at 58s.@61s. Butter flat and declining. Tallow downward.

PRODUCE.—Ashes easier at 29s. 6d. for Pots, and 30s. for Pearls. Sugar, flat. Coffee, quiet and steady. Rice, quiet and steady. Clover Seed, firmer. Jute, 10s.@30s. lower. Cod Oil, quiet at 57s. Sperm Oil, no sales. Linseed Oil, steady. Resin, very dull. Spirits Turpentine, quiet at 65s.@66s.

PETROLEUM—BOULT, ENGLISH & BRANDON report: Petroleum firm, at 1s. 11d.@2s. for refined; no crude in market.

LONDON MARKETS.

FLOUR firm; WHEAT steady. IRON advancing; bars and rails, £6 10s.@£6 15s; Scotch pig, 52s. 3d. SUGAR inactive. COFFEE active at a decline of 1s.@2s. TEA steady at 10½d. for common Congou. RICE steady. SPIRITS TURPENTINE firm at 67s. PETROLEUM steady at £18 for crude, 2s. for refined. SPERM OIL nominal at £82. TALLOW downward, at 40s.@43s. LINSEED OIL flat.

LATEST COMMERCIAL.

LIVERPOOL, Saturday, April 1—Evening.

COTTON—Sales to-day 6,000 bales, including 2,000 bales to speculators and exporters. The market is less firm but quiet and unchanged.

BREADSTUFFS—The market is quiet and steady.

PROVISIONS—The market is dull.

PRODUCE—The market is quiet and steady. Petroleum firm at 2s. @2s. 0½d. for refined.

LONDON, Saturday, April 1—Evening.

CONSOLS closed at 89⅞@90 for money.

AMERICAN STOCKS—Illinois Central Railroad 61⅜@62¼; Erie Railroad 36⅛@36¾; United States Five-twenties 57⅜@58⅜.

Gen. Lee in Richmond—The Oath of Allegiance.

BALTIMORE, Friday, April 14.

The Richmond *Whig* of yesterday contains little of importance. It announces the arrival of Gen. LEE on the night previous.

The *Whig* publishes the oath of allegiance, which it says citizens will be required to swear and subscribe to. The Provost-Marshal's office is crowded with people anxious to take it, and the only question among citizens seems to be who shall be first to renew their citizenship.

Rejoicings at Cincinnati.

CINCINNATI, Friday, April 14.

Business was entirely suspended to-day. The city was universally decorated with flags, and great enthusiasm prevailed. The procession was an immense affair, comprising the entire police force, Gens. HOOKER and WALLICH, with their staffs, four regiments of National Guards, discharged veterans, ward organizations, the Fenian Brotherhood, the Fire Department, and a large number of colored citizens. All the bells in the city were rung, and salutes were fired at 6 o,clock this evening. To-night the city is brilliantly illuminated, and there is generally a display of fireworks.

Fire.

ROCHESTER, N. Y., Friday, April 14.

The cabinet warehouse of JAMES E. HAYDON, of this city, was partially destroyed by fire this morning. The stocks of HUMPHREY REEDY & Co., stove dealers, HASTINGS & McVEAN, paper dealers, S. B. ROBY, saddlery and hardware dealers, and the agency of the American Tract Society, were damaged. Total loss, $30,000; insurance, $20,000. The origin of the fire is unknown.

The Funeral of Gen. T. A. Smyth.

WILMINGTON, Del., Friday, April 14.

The remains of Brig.-Gen. T. A. SMYTH arrived here to-day at 1 o'clock, and will be interred on Monday afternoon with appropriate ceremonies.

An Unseaworthy War Steamer.

To the Editor of the New-York Times:

UNITED STATES STEAMER MUSCOOTA. }
HAMPTON ROADS, Va., Wednesday, April 12, 1865. }

This vessel has returned to this port, having made her fourth attempt to make a cruise to the Pacific. On each occasion she has proved herself to be an unsafe sea boat. On her last trial she narrowly escaped being lost in the Gulf Stream. Inclosed you will find a list of her officers; please publish.

Respectfully, &c.,

ARTHUR BURTIS, Jr., Paymaster.

List of officers attached to the U. S. steamer *Muscoota*, one thousand tons, 10 guns:

Commander GEO. M. RANSOM, Lieut. Thos. S. Spencer, Ass't Paymaster Arthur Burtis, Jr., Ass't Surgeon Danl. McMurtrie, Act'g Master Geo. R. Durand, Act'g Ensigns Robt. M. Clark, Jas. Courtney, John D. Thomas, Chas. A. Stewart, Second Ass't Engineers Robert H. Gunnell, Jas. H. Grasmer, Henry Snyder, Act'g Third Ass't Engineers Robt. L. Case, Geo. Taylor, Geo. Westinghouse, Jr., Masters Fred'k. A. Beatie, A. I. Spinney, Wm. Merrill, Captain's Clerk Geo. S. Dana, Paymasters Clerk P. B. Hathaway.

Arrivals in the City.

Gov. Jos. A. Gilmore, Concord, N. H., is stopping at the Fifth-avenue Hotel.

Hon. O. N. Shannon, Cincinnati; Gen. B. F. Stringfellow, Atchison; Dr. N. Greene, Louisville, and Wm. D. Griswold, Terre Haute, are stopping at the Metropolitan Hotel.

COLLISION.—The steamship *La Favorite*, while returning from a trial trip and passing up the East River, collided with the Catharine Ferry-boat *Manhassett*, as she was entering her slip on the Brooklyn side, doing considerable damage to the *Manhassett*, by tearing away a portion of the gentlemen's cabin, and somewhat injuring the hull. Fortunately nobody was hurt.

WASHINGTON EVENING STAR.
PUBLISHED DAILY, (EXCEPT SUNDAY,)
AT THE STAR BUILDINGS,
Southwest corner of Pennsylvania av. and 11th street,
BY W. D. WALLACH.

The STAR is served by the carriers to their subscribers in the City and District for TWELVE AND A HALF CENTS PER WEEK.

PRICE FOR MAILING.—Single copy, three cents; one month, seventy five cents; three months, one dollar and fifty cents; six months, three dollars; one year, six dollars. No papers are sent from the office longer than paid for.

THE WEEKLY STAR one dollar and a half a year.

Evening Star.

Vol. XXV. WASHINGTON, D. C., SATURDAY, APRIL 15, 1865. No. 3,783.

ASSASSINATION OF THE PRESIDENT.

ATTEMPTED MURDER OF SECRETARY SEWARD AND SONS.

Despatches from Secretary Stanton.

WAR DEPARTMENT,
WASHINGTON, D. C., April 15—1.30 P. M.

Major General John A. Dix, New York:

Last evening, at 10.30 p. m., at Ford's Theater, the President, while sitting in his private box with Mrs. Lincoln, Miss Harris, and Maj. Rathbun, was shot by an assassin who suddenly entered the box. He approached behind the President. The assassin then leaped upon the stage, brandishing a large dagger or knife, and made his escape by the rear of the theater. The pistol ball entered the back of the President's head. The wound is mortal. The President has been insensible ever since it was inflicted, and is now dying.

About the same hour an assassin, either the same or another, entered Mr. Seward's house, and, under pretence of having a prescription, was shown to the Secretary's sick chamber. The Secretary was in bed, a nurse and Miss Seward with him. The assassin immediately rushed to the bed, inflicting two or three stabs on the throat, and two in the face. It is hoped the wounds may not be mortal. My apprehension is that they will prove fatal. The nurse alarmed Mr. Frederick Seward, who was in an adjoining room, and hastened to the door of his father's room, where he met the assassin, who inflicted upon him one or more dangerous wounds. The recovery of Frederick Seward is doubtful.

It is not probable that the President will live through the night.

Gen. Grant and wife were advertised to be at the theater this evening, but the latter started to Burlington at six o'clock last evening.

At a Cabinet meeting, at which Gen. Grant was present to-day, the subject of the state of the country, and the prospects of speedy peace was discussed. The President was very cheerful and hopeful, spoke very kindly of Gen. Lee and others of the Confederacy, and the establishment of Government in Virginia. All the members of the Cabinet, except Mr. Seward, are now in attendance upon the President. I have seen Mr. Seward, but he and Frederick were both unconscious.

E. M. STANTON, Secretary of War.

WAR DEPARTMENT,
WASHINGTON, D. C., 3 A. M., April 15, 1865.

Lieutenant General Grant:

The President still breathes, but is quite insensible, as he has been ever since he was shot. He evidently did not see the person who shot him, but was looking on the stage, as he was approached behind.

Mr. Seward has rallied, and it is hoped he may live. Frederick Seward's condition is very critical. The attendant who was present was stabbed through the lungs, and is not expected to live. The wounds of Major Seward are not serious.

Investigations strongly indicates J. Wilkes Booth as the assassin of the President. Whether it was the same, or a different person that attempted to murder Mr. Seward, remains in doubt.

Chief Justice Cartter is engaged in taking the evidence. Every exertion has been made to present the escape of the murderer. His horse has been found on the road near Washington.

EDWIN M. STANTON, Secretary of War.

WAR DEPARTMENT,
WASHINGTON, D. C., April 15,—4.10 A. M.

Major General Dix, New York:

The President continues insensible, and is sinking. Secretary Seward remains without change. Frederick Seward's skull is fractured in two places, besides a severe cut upon the head. The attendant is still alive, but hopeless.

Major Seward's wounds are not dangerous. It is now ascertained with reasonable certainty, that two assassins were engaged in the horrible crime—Wilkes Booth being the one that shot the President; the other, a companion of his, whose name is not known, but whose description is so clear that he can hardly escape.

It appears, from a letter found in Booth's trunk, that the murder was planned before the fourth of March, but fell through then because the accomplice backed out until Richmond could be heard from. Booth and his accomplice were at the livery stable at six o'clock last evening, and left there with their horses about ten o'clock, or shortly before that hour.

It would seem that they had for several days been seeking their chance, but for some unknown reason, it was not carried into effect until last night. One of them has evidently made his way to Baltimore, the other has not yet been traced.

EDWIN M. STANTON, Secretary of War.

TEN THOUSAND DOLLARS REWARD.

HEADQUARTERS DEP'T OF WASHINGTON,
April 15, 1865.

A REWARD OF TEN THOUSAND DOLLARS will be paid to the party or parties arresting the murderer of the President, Mr. Lincoln, and the assassin of the Secretary of State, Mr. Seward, and his son.

C. C. AUGUR,
Major General, Com'd'g Department.

GENERAL GRANT ADVISED OF PRESIDENT LINCOLN'S ASSASSINATION.

PHILADELPHIA, April 14.—General Grant received the news of the attempted assassination of the President when at Walnut street wharf, when about taking the cars for Burlington.

ASSOCIATED PRESS ACCOUNT.

President Lincoln and wife, together with other friends, last evening visited Ford's Theater for the purpose of witnessing the performance of the American Cousin. It was announced in the newspapers that Gen. Grant would also be present, but that gentleman, instead, took the late train of cars for New Jersey. The theater was densely crowded, and everybody seemed delighted with the scene before them.

During the third act, and while there was a temporary pause for one of the actors to enter, a sharp report of a pistol was heard, which merely attracted attention, but suggesting nothing serious, until a man rushed to the front of the President's box, waiving a long dagger in his right hand, and exclaiming "*Sic Semper Tyrannis*," and immediately leaped from the box, which was of the second tier, to the stage beneath, and ran across to the opposite side, thus making his escape, amid the bewilderment of the audience, from the rear of the theater, and, mounting a horse, fled.

The screams of Mrs. Lincoln first disclosed the fact to the audience that the President had been shot, when all present rose to their feet, rushing toward the stage, exclaiming, "Hang him!" "Hang him!"

The excitement was of the wildest possible character; and, of course, there was an abrupt termination of the theatrical performance.

There was a rush towards the President's box, when cries were heard, "Stand back!" "Give him air!" "Has any one stimulants!" &c.

On a hasty examination it was found that the President had been shot through the head, above and back of the temporal bone, and that some of the brain was oozing out. He was removed to the private residence of Mr. Peterson, opposite to the theater, and the Surgeon General of the Army and other surgeons sent for to attend to his condition.

On examination of the private box blood was discovered on the back of the cushioned rocking chair in which the President had been sitting, also on the partition and on the floor.

A common single barrelled pocket pistol was found on the carpet.

A military guard was placed in front of the private residence to which the President had been conveyed.

An immense crowd was in front of it, all deeply anxious to learn the condition of the President. It had been previously announced that the wound was mortal, but all hoped otherwise.

The shock to the community was terrible.

At midnight the Cabinet, with Messrs. Sumner, Colfax, Farnsworth, Judge Cartter, Gov. Oglesby, General Meigs, Major Hay, and a few personal friends, with Surgeon General Barnes and his medical associates, were around his bedside. The President was in a state of syncope, totally insensible, and breathing slowly, the blood oozing from the wound at the back of his head. The surgeons were exhausting every possible effort of medical skill, but all hope was gone. The parting of his family with the dying President is too sad for description.

The President and Mrs. Lincoln did not start to the theatre, till fifteen minutes past eight o'clock. Speaker Colfax was at the White House at the time, and the President stated to him that he was going, although Mrs. Lincoln had not been well, because the papers had advertised that General Grant and themselves were to be present, and, as General Grant had gone North, he did not wish the audience to be disappointed. He went with apparent reluctance, and urged Mr. Colfax to go with him; but that gentleman had made other engagements, and with Mr. Ashmun, of Massachusetts, bade him good-bye.

When the excitement at the theatre was at its wildest height, reports were circulated that Secretary Seward had also been assassinated.

On reaching this gentleman's residence a crowd and a military guard were found at the door, and, on entering, it was ascertained that reports were based upon truth.

Everybody was so much excited that scarcely an intelligible account could be gathered. But the facts are substantially as follows: About ten o'clock, a man rang the bell, and the call having been answered by a colored servant, he said he had come from Dr. Verdi, Secretary Seward's family physician, with a prescription, at the same time holding in his hand a small piece of folded paper, and saying, in answer to a refusal that he must see the Secretary, as he was intrusted with particular directions concerning the medicine. He still insisted on going up, although repeatedly informed that no one could enter the chamber.

The man pushed the servant aside and walked heavily toward the Secretary's room, and was there met by Mr. Frederick W. Seward of whom he demanded to see the Secretary, making the same representation which he did to the servant. What further passed in the way of colloquy is not known, but the man struck him on the head with a billy, severely injuring the skull, and felling him almost senseless.

The assassin then rushed into the chamber and attacked Major Seward (paymaster United States army) and Mr. Hansell, a messenger of the State Department, and two male nurses, disabling them all. He then rushed upon the Secretary, who was lying in bed in the same room, and inflicted three stabs in his neck, but severing, it is thought and hoped, no arteries, though he bled profusely.

The assassin then rushed down stairs, mounted his horse at the door and rode off before an alarm could be given; and in the same manner of the assassin of the President.

It is believed the injuries of the Secretary are not mortal, nor those of either of the others, although both the Secretary and the Assistant Secretary are very seriously injured.

Secretaries Stanton and Welles, and other prominent officers of the Government, called at Secretary Seward's house to inquire into his condition, and hearing there of the assassination of the President, proceeded to the house where he was lying, exhibiting, of course, intense anxiety and solicitude.

An immense crowd was gathered in front of the President's house, and a strong guard was also stationed there, many persons evidently supposing that he would be brought to his home.

The entire city last night presented a scene of wild excitement, accompanied by violent expressions of indignation, and the profoundest sorrow. Many persons shed tears.

The military authorities have despatched mounted patrols in every direction, in order, if possible, to arrest the assassins, while the Metropolitan police are alike vigilant for the same purpose. The attacks, both at the theater and at Secretary Seward's, took place at about the same hour—ten o'clock—thus showing a precented plan to assassinate these gentlemen.

Some evidence of the guilt of the party who attacked the President is in possession of the police.

Vice President Johnson is in the city, and his hotel quarters are guarded by troops.

2½ A. M.—The President is still alive, but is growing weaker. The ball is lodged in his brain, three inches from where it entered the skull. He remains insensible, and his condition utterly hopeless.

The Vice President has been to see him, but all company except the Cabinet, his family, and a few friends, are rigidly excluded.

Large crowds still continue in the street, as near to the house as the line of guards allow.

IMPORTANT ORDER BY A. C. RICHARDS, SUPERINTENDENT OF THE METROPOLITAN POLICE.

The following was issued by Superintendent Richards at 3 o'clock this morning:

In view of the melancholy events of last evening, I am directed to close all places where liquor is sold to be closed during this day and night.

The sergeants of the several precincts will see that this order is enforced.

A. C. RICHARDS, Superintendent.

FURTHER PARTICULARS OF THE ASSASSINATION.

[From the Chronicle.]

"At half-past ten o'clock last night, in the front upper left hand private box in Ford's Theater, while the scond scene of the third act of 'Our American Cousin' was being played, a pistol was fired, and Abraham Lincoln shot through the neck and lower part of the head. A second after the shot was fired, a man vaulted over the baluster of the box, saying, '*Sic Semper tyrannis!*' and, adding another sentence, which closed with the words, 'revenge for the South,' ran across the stage with a gleaming knife, double-edged and straight, in his right hand. The man was of middle stature, well-built, white faced and beardless, save that he wore a black moustache. His hair and eyes were black.

"The crowd ascended the stage; the actresses, pale beneath their rouge, ran wildly about. Miss Keene, whose benefit night it was, came forward, endeavoring to quiet the audience. Several gentlemen climbed to the box, and finally the audience were ordered out by some gentlemen.

"Mrs. Lincoln, Miss Harris and Maj. Rathburn were in the box with the President."

The assassin left behind him his hat and spur, which have been identified as belonging to the suspected man, (J. W. Booth.)

The ball entered three inches below the left ear and behind it a little, just beneath the base of the brain, taking an upward direction and lodging in the brain, where it could be felt by the surgeons, but not dislodged.

"Police Headquarters.

"No sooner had the dreadful event been announced in the street, than Superintendent Richards and his assistants were at work to discover the assassins. In a few moments the telegraph had aroused the whole police force of the city. Mayor Wallach, and several members of the city government, were soon on the spot. Every measure of precaution was taken to preserve order in the city, and every street was patrolled. At the request of Mr. Richards General Augur sent horses to mount the police. Every road out of Washington was picketed, and every possible avenue of escape thoroughly guarded. Steamboats about to depart down the Potomac were stopped.

"As it is suspected that this conspiracy originated in Maryland, the telegraph flashed the mournful news to Baltimore, and all the cavalry was immediately put upon active duty. Every road was picketed, and every precaution taken to prevent the escape of the assassins.

"As everything that tends to throw light upon this matter is of interest, we think it well to add, that last evening, a dark roan horse was hired at Thompson's stable, on the corner of E and 13th streets, at about ten minutes after ten o'clock. The horse had a black English saddle and ordinary stirrups. The man who hired him was dressed in black, and was some five feet six inches in height. When asked when he would return, he said, 'Probably in two hours, perhaps never.'—He wore a black mostache and goatee. One of the stable boys followed him, but lost sight of him on 10th street.

"After hearing of the assassinations, the same stable boy rushed to the Navy Yard, thinking to head the man and horse off, should he prove the criminal, but learned that the man and horse he described had passed over the bridge some time before; and being told that if he followed he would not be allowed back over the bridge, he followed no farther, but returned."

The *National Intelligencer* says:

"The President was seen to turn in his seat, and persons leaped upon the stage and clambered up to the box. His clothes were stripped from his shoulders, but no wound was at first found. He was entirely insensible. Further search revealed the fact that he had been shot in the head, as is described elsewhere. Major Potter, paymaster in the army, and Major Rathburn, (the latter having been in the box,) assisted by others, carried the President from the theater, the blood from the death wound falling upon the floor, stairway, and sidewalk as he was borne to the nearest house opposite, which was that of Mr. Ulke. Mrs. Lincoln was assisted in crossing the street with the President in a frantic condition, at the same time uttering heart-rending shrieks. She was attended by Miss Laura Keene and others. At the house, an army surgeon being at hand, called for a small quantity of brandy, which was administered, and it was thereupon announced to the pressing and excited crowd that he was alive, and not dead, as Mrs Lincoln, in her agony, insisted. It was then found that Major Rathburn had received a wound in the arm, which he had intentionally concealed to prevent excitement. He then fainted. The Surgeon General was sent for, and Drs. Hall and Stone also arrived.

An immense crowd had now assembled, but a strong military force arrived and guarded the entire locality.

Attack on Mr. Seward.

"Just as the man in charge of Lafayette Square called out that the gates were closed, a man made his way into Secretary Seward's house, representing that he was the bearer of a medicine prescribed by Surgeon General Barnes, and which he was ordered to deliver to Secretary Seward in person.

"Pushing into the Secretary's room, he seized the old, suffering statesman with one hand and cut him with a dagger-knife on both jaws, then turned and forced his way into the hall, where, meeting with Frederick Seward, the Secretary's son, he attacked him, and inflicted three wounds with a dagger-knife (probably the same) on the young man's head, breast, and hand. He also attacked Maj. Clarence Seward, another son of the Secretary of State, and inflicted upon him several serious wounds.

"The assassin then rushed out, mounted a bay horse, with light mane, and rode off, not at a gallop, but at what is called a 'pace.'

"The person who assassinated Secretary Seward left behind him a slouched hat and an old rusty navy revolver. The chambers were broken loose from the barrel; as if done by striking. The loads were drawn from the chambers, one being but a rough piece of lead, and the other balls smaller than the chambers, wrapped in paper, as if to keep them from falling out."

Crowds now gathered in all parts of the city. Nothing was talked of but the murder of the President, of Mr. Seward, and of the members of Mr. Seward's family. Intense excitement was added to the already nearly wild masses by a rumor that General Grant had been assassinated in the cars, en route for Philadelphia, and that Mr. Stanton had barely escaped with his life by being warned in time to exclude the conspirators from his house. (This is discredited.) It may be added that a person who was passing Mr. Seward's house saw the murderer mount his horse, pass up Fifteen-and-a-half street, where Mr. Seward resides, and thence rapidly to H street, where he disappeared.

FROM MOBILE.

Capture of Selma, Alabama, Confirmed—Twenty-three Guns Taken—A large Amount of Government Property Secured.

NEW ORLEANS, 8th, VIA CAIRO, 14th.—The Times' Spanish Fort special, dated 5th instant, says: A furious fire opened on the rebel forts last night from our entire line. During the bombardment a small magazine exploded in the Spanish fort. The damage loss outside of the Spanish fort, to 4th inst., amounted to five hundred killed and wounded. Rebel loss exceeds ours.

Adjutant General Thomas arrive on the morning of the 7th.

Mobile papers of the 4th, announces the capture of Selma, with twenty-three pieces of artillery and a large amount of Government property.

THE SURRENDER OF LEE.—General Lee was accompanied only by Colonel Marshall formerly of Baltimore, at present aid-de-camp on his staff, and Orderly Johns who served him in that capacity for fourteen months. Lee looked very much jaded and worn, but nevertheless, presented the same magnificent *physique* for which he has always been noted. He was neatly dressed in gray cloth, without embroidery or any insignia of rank, except three stars worn on the turned portion of his coat collar. His cheeks were very much bronzed by exposure, but still shone ruddy underneath it all. He is growing quite bald, and wears one of the side locks of his hair thrown across the upper portion of his forehead, which is as white and fair as a woman's. He stands fully six feet one inch in height, and weighs something over two hundred pounds, without being burdened with a pound of superfluous flesh. During the whole interview he was retired and dignified to a degree bordering on taciturnity, but was free from all exhibition of temper or mortification. His demeanor was that of a thoroughly possessed gentleman who had a a very disagreeable duty to perform, but was determined to get through it as well and as soon as he could.

He rode an ordinary gray horse, with plain equipments similar to those of our cavalry officers, and his orderly stated that it was the only animal he had here.

He bivouacked last night near a place known as the "Stone Chimney," in a grove, and made his breakfast this morning on a "corn dodger." His troops are even worse off.—*Correspondence N. Y. Herald, 9th.*

☞ The records of Libby Prison, from its commencement to its close, have been secured by Gen. Weitzel, and will be preserved for future reference. They show the date and homes of every man who entered there, and the date of his death or removal. The letter-books of the rebel treasury department have also been secured and will be sent to Washington.

GEN. LEE DESIROUS OF PEACE.—The Herald says that General Grant represents General Lee as zealous in his efforts to stop further effusion of blood, and instead of coming North, is now engaged in urging all other commanders of Southern armies to surrender without further resistance.

☞ Sherman's men have had green peas in Goldsboro'.

☞ Since Sherman's capture of Savannah, 360 steamships and steamers, 15 ships, 8 brigs and 66 schooners have entered the port.

☞ The duke de Galliera, a fast young blood in Paris, pays a house rent of $360,000 per annum.

LEGAL NOTICES.

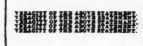

IN THE SUPREME COURT OF THE DISTRICT OF COLUMBIA.—MARY MYERS vs. PETER MYERS. In Equity, No. [illegible]. Bill for Divorce. The subpœna issued to compel the defendant's appearance having been returned into the Clerk's office by the Marshal, on the 31st day of December, 1864, endorsed "non est," and the defendant having failed to enter his appearance on the first rule day, occurring twenty days afterwards, and the complainant having filed an affidavit of a disinterested witness that the defendant has been absent from this District for over six months so that the process cannot be served on him, [illegible]

A true copy. R. J. MEIGS, Clerk.

IN THE SUPREME COURT OF THE DISTRICT OF COLUMBIA, [illegible]

OFFICIAL.

The First Corps—Notice to Veterans.

HEADQUARTERS FIRST CORPS,
WASHINGTON, D. C., Dec. 27, 1864.

Veterans desiring to enlist in the 1st Army Corps, should report in person at the office of Col. C. F. Johnson, Soldiers' Rest, Baltimore and Ohio Railroad Depot, Washington, D. C.

Any Veteran who has served two years, has been honorably discharged, and is physically qualified, may enlist in the Corps for one, two or three years.

Those enlisting will receive from the Government a bounty of $300 as soon as they are mustered in, and, in addition, the regular installments from the Government, in proportion to the period of enlistment, as follows: $100 for one year's service, one-third paid on enlistment; $200 for two years' service, one-third on enlistment; $300 for three years' service, one-third on enlistment.

They will be credited to the quota of the district in which they or their families may be domiciled and will, therefore, be entitled to local bounties.

Free transportation will be furnished them to Washington by any Provost Marshal.

The best arms in the possession of the Government will be furnished these troops, and they will be allowed to retain their arms when honorably discharged.

Headquarters Major General Hancock:—158 street, between 19th and 20th streets.

Office of the Board for the Examination of Officers:—Brigadier General John R. Brooke, President, 183 G street, between 19th and 20th streets.

By order of Major General Hancock.

FINLEY ANDERSON,
Assistant Adjutant General.

dec 27-tf

DENTISTRY.

TOOTH-ACHE CURED INSTANTLY BY THE external application of DR. SIGESMOND'S ESSENCE OF PALMETTO. It acts at once upon the nerves connected with the tooth aching, and relieves instantly. [illegible]

GREAT DISCOVERY IN DENTISTRY. TEETH EXTRACTED WITHOUT PAIN. [illegible]

S. B. LEWIS, M. D., Dentist.

JAMES S. TOPHAM & CO.'S PREMIUM TRUNK, SADDLERY, AND MILITARY EQUIPMENT MANUFACTORY, WHOLESALE AND RETAIL, 500 SEVENTH STREET, One Door North of Odd Fellows' Hall, [illegible] TRUNKS, VALISES, TRAVELING BAGS, SADDLES, HARNESS, HORSE COVERS, MILITARY HORSE EQUIPMENTS, SWORD BELTS, HAVERSACKS, WHIPS, BITS, SPURS, &c., &c., &c., AT LOW PRICES.

REPAIRING. Trunks, &c., repaired promptly and thoroughly.

THREE SILVER MEDALS [illegible]

SOLE AGENTS for District of Columbia and Alexandria, Va., for FRANK MILLER'S CELEBRATED PREPARED HARNESS OIL, supplied at the lowest FACTORY PRICES.

G. B. SMITH'S WILD CHERRY TONIC BITTERS. THIS PROPHYLATIC is sold by all Druggists and Grocers. This great PANACEA has been established 20 years. Its medicinal properties are TONIC, ASTRINGENT AND AROMATIC. It will eradicate all derangement of the STOMACH and BOWELS. It gives STRENGTH and BEAUTY to the YOUNG. REJUVENATES THE OLD. Cures DYSPEPSIA, LOSS OF APPETITE, INDIGESTION, LASSITUDE OF SYSTEM, CHRONIC DIARRHŒA, DYSENTERY, JAUNDICE, AGUE AND FEVER. [illegible]

NOTICE TO OFFICERS AND SOLDIERS. [illegible] JAMES M. MOORE, Capt. Ass't Qr. U. S. Army.

WATCHES, JEWELRY, &c. [illegible]

CONFIDENTIAL. YOUNG MEN [illegible] DR. CHAS. A. STEWART & CO. [illegible]

JEROME'S HAIR COLOR RESTORER [illegible]

REDFORD'S MEDICATED GINGER BREAD NUTS, for worms [illegible]

I AM ACQUAINTED WITH MR. H. T. HELMBOLD [illegible] POWERS & WEIGHTMAN [illegible]

FRENCH JUVENILE [illegible]

AMUSEMENTS.

CANTERBURY HALL,
MUSIC HALL AND THEATER. CANTERBURY HALL. CANTERBURY HALL. CANTERBURY HALL. CANTERBURY HALL. MUSIC HALL AND THEATER.
LOUISIANA AVENUE, NEAR SIXTH STREET,
Rear of National and Metropolitan Hotels.
GEORGE LEA .... Proprietor
Also of the Varieties, New York, and Canterbury Alexandria, Va.
JOSH HART .... Stage Manager

LAST WEEK OF THE WINTER SEASON.
LAST WEEK OF THE WINTER SEASON.
LAST WEEK OF THE WINTER SEASON.
LAST WEEK OF THE WINTER SEASON.
LAST WEEK OF THE WINTER SEASON.

CLOSING SCENES OF TRIUMPH

OVER ALL OPPOSITION!
OVER ALL OPPOSITION!
OVER ALL OPPOSITION!
OVER ALL OPPOSITION!
OVER ALL OPPOSITION!

The Manager is happy to announce an engagement with Mr.

CHARLES B. COLLINS,
CHARLES B. COLLINS,
CHARLES B. COLLINS,
CHARLES B. COLLINS,
CHARLES B. COLLINS,
CHARLES B. COLLINS,
CHARLES B. COLLINS.

THE ORIGINAL "CURE."
THE ORIGINAL "CURE."
THE ORIGINAL "CURE."
THE ORIGINAL "CURE."
THE ORIGINAL "CURE."

Whose various performances have been imitated by nearly all the half-fledged performers of the day. Patrons of this establishment are respectfully requested to be on hand to witness the

VERACITY OF THE ABOVE STATEMENT.
VERACITY OF THE ABOVE STATEMENT.
VERACITY OF THE ABOVE STATEMENT.
VERACITY OF THE ABOVE STATEMENT.
VERACITY OF THE ABOVE STATEMENT.

Mr. Collins will appear in two of his peculiar acts to-night, viz:

"THE CURE" AND THE "LIVELY YOUTH."
"THE CURE" AND THE "LIVELY YOUTH."
"THE CURE" AND THE "LIVELY YOUTH."
"THE CURE" AND THE "LIVELY YOUTH."
"THE CURE" AND THE "LIVELY YOUTH."

First night of the laughable Comic Pantomime, entitled

FLOURCOURED CLOWN.

Clown .... Josh Hart
Pantaloon .... Mons. Szolloay
Columbine .... Miss Laura Le Claire
Julia .... Miss Tilly Forbes

JOHN MULLIGAN
JOHN MULLIGAN
JOHN MULLIGAN

AND

DAN HOLT.
DAN HOLT.
DAN HOLT.

In a new Ethiopian Oddity, called

REDDEN AND CLARK

Will appear in a new act,

QUINTESSENCE OF AFRICA.

New Ballet Divertisement of the

SICILIAN VESPERS.

Arranged by Mons. Szolloay for the

BOUQUET OF BEAUTY.

Entire Change of Programme Every Night.

SPECIAL NOTICES.

A HINT TO BOTH SEXES.—HOW TO GAIN AND RETAIN AFFECTION.—It has been frequently suggested that PLANTATION BITTERS are, in another form, the "Elixir of Love" of the Ancients. That they do much to quiet "family jars," and reconcile fretful wives to cross husbands, we verily believe. When domestic quiet is restored and connubial felicity reigns supreme,

"How great the charm, how sweet the bliss
That finds expression in a kiss."

A free and proper use of PLANTATION BITTERS will inspire the souls of both sexes with pure and high-toned sentiments of affection, and a capacity for rare and exquisite enjoyment in each other's society. Remember there is no place like home, and no passion like love—and nothing to link the two together and you, to both like the great Family Blessing, PLANTATION BITTERS. ap 7-1w

PUBLIC HEALTH. THE PRESS

Advertising has been pronounced "undignified" by the medical faculty. A physician who advertises a valuable remedy to fifty people in his private practice would receive the cold shoulder from his professional brethren, should he make his merits known to millions through the business columns of a newspaper press. This may be "dignified,"—but is it benevolent, humane, or just? Whoever is fortunate enough to discover or invent anything that will prevent, or cure, or alleviate human suffering is bound to make it known through every channel of communication within his reach, to the general public. For many years the merits of HOSTETTER'S CELEBRATED STOMACH BITTERS have thus been proclaimed to the world, and multitudes have been restored to health or saved from fatal maladies in consequence. As new facts have been developed in relation to the operation of this most pure and potent of all Stomachics and Alteratives, they have been stated in simple language to the people of many lands; and if the proprietors of the medicine have derived profit from their dissemination, thousands upon thousands of individuals have been benefitted thereby to an extent beyond all estimate. In the West Indies, Canada, Australia and South America, HOSTETTER'S BITTERS are now recognised as the sole specific for Dyspepsia, the best possible safeguard against epidemics, and the finest invigorant in cases of General Debility, and the only diffusive stimulant, entirely free from noxious ingredients. ap 5-2w

IF PEOPLE WHO SUFFER from the dull stupidity that meets us everywhere in spring, and too often in all seasons of the year, knew how quick it could be cured by taking AYER'S SARSAPARILLA to purge the bile from their systems, we should have better neighbors as well as clearer heads to deal with. ap 7-1w

SPRING AND SUMMER CLOTHING. New styles Superb Stock of Dress, Sack, and Walking Coats, Pantaloons, Vests, and Boys' Clothing, Furnishing Goods, &c., &c. We are now prepared to exhibit our stock of Men's and Boys' Ready-made Clothing, which, for elegance of style, variety and excellence of fabric and faithfulness of manufacture, has not been surpassed by any stock heretofore offered in this [illegible]

STOP THAT SCRATCHING. [illegible]

THE BRIDAL CHAMBER, an Essay of Warning and Instruction for Young Men. [illegible]

COLGATE'S HONEY SOAP. [illegible]

SECRET DISEASES. [illegible]

DON'T FRET. [illegible]

AMUSEMENTS.

FORD'S NEW THEATER. TENTH STREET, above Pennsylvania Avenue.

THERE WILL BE NO PERFORMANCE AT THE THEATER TO-NIGHT.

WASHINGTON THEATER, corner of 11th and C sts. [illegible]

OXFORD! OXFORD! OXFORD! MUSIC HALL AND THEATER, Ninth street, fronting on Pennsylvania avenue. [illegible]

LADIES MATINEE SATURDAY AFTERNOON.

JOHN Q. WILLSON. [illegible] CABINET FURNITURE [illegible]

THE NATION MOURNS ITS LOSS.

The Philadelphia Inquirer.

PRICE TWO CENTS. | PHILADELPHIA, MONDAY, APRIL 17, 1865. | PRICE TWO CENTS.

THE GREAT TRAGEDY!

A Nation Mourns Its Honored President!

JOY CHANGED TO MOURNING!

The Great Martyr to Liberty!

MURDER OF THE PRESIDENT.

Full Details of the Assassination.

ACCOUNT OF A DISTINGUISHED EYE-WITNESS.

Mr. Lincoln's Death-bed Scenes

A NOBLE PATRIOT GONE TO REST!

Escape of the Dastard Assassin.

MR. SEWARD STILL ALIVE.

His Condition Is Favorable.

Andrew Johnson Inaugurated as President!

HIS INAUGURAL ADDRESS.

Views of the New President.

HE RETAINS THE OLD CABINET!

Official Gazette from Sec'y Stanton.

OUR SPECIAL DESPATCHES

THE GREAT NATIONAL TRAGEDY.

Special Despatch to the Inquirer.

WASHINGTON, April 16.

The monstrous crime of Friday night shocked this city with an agony unutterable. Yesterday morning men walked the streets, and looked into each other's eyes, and found no words willing to leave their lips. Their hearts were surcharged with grief and a wrath inexpressible.

That any Rebel ever could be so base as to assassinate the man who within the past ten days has held out the olive branch of peace, and exhibited so great a desire to forgive, was a crime for which Washington, as well as the nation, was unprepared. But the deed was consummated, and Washington, lowering her flags of joy, clothed them in habiliments of mourning. The transition from jubilance to grief and woe was a shock more sudden than ever before befel a community or people. The glorious banner which went up in the morning in honor of its restoration to Fort Sumter, in the short space of twenty-four hours came down to half-mast.

The rejoicing of Friday was turned to mourning, and the light of joy which illumed all faces but a few hours previous, gave way to tears and gloom. When the news of President Lincoln's death was announced, universal silence and grief pervaded the city. Everybody was impressed with the solemn and awful event. Funeral weeds were hung from every window, and the sables of mourning were draped on fronts and about the marble columns of all the public buildings.

THE ASSASSINATION.

From a distinguished officer of the army, who was sitting near the President's box at the time of the assassination, we have received the following interesting statement:—

Account of a Distinguished Eye-witness.

On the night of Friday, April 14th, 1865, in company with a friend, I went to Ford's Theatre, arriving there just after the entrance of President Lincoln and the party accompanying him. My friend and I, after viewing the Presidential party from the opposite side of the dress circle, went to the right side and took seats in the passage above the seats of the dress circle and about five feet from the door of the box. During the performance the attendant of the President came out and took the chair nearest the door.

I sat, and had been so sitting, about four feet to his left and rear for some time. A man, whose face I do not distinctly remember, passed me, and inquired of one sitting near me where the President's messenger was, and learning his identity, exhibited to him an envelope, apparently official, having a printed heading, and superscribed in a bold hand. I could not read the address, and did not try. I think now it was meant for Lieutenant-General Grant. The man went away. Some time after I was disturbed in my seat by the approach of a man, who desired to pass upon the aisle in which I was sitting.

Giving him room by bending my chair forward, he passed me, and stepped one step down upon the level below me. Standing there he was almost in the line of sight, and I saw him while watching the play. He stood, as I remember, one level above the messenger, and remained there perhaps one minute, apparently looking at the stage, and the orchestra below. Then he drew a number of visiting cards from his pocket, from which, with some attention, he [illegible] or selected one. These things I saw distinctly. I saw him stoop, and I think descend upon the level with the messenger, and by his right side. He showed the card to the messenger.

My attention was then more closely fixed upon the scene, and I do not know whether the card was carried in by the messenger, or his assent given to the entrance of the man who presented it. I saw, a few moments after, the man entering the door of the lobby leading to the box, and the door closing behind him. This was seen because I could not avoid observing it, the door side of the proscenium box and the stage being all within the direct and right oblique lines of sight. How long I watched the play after this entering, I do not know. It was, perhaps, two or three minutes, possibly four.

The house was still, the large audience listening to the dialogue between "Florence Trenchard" and "May Meredith," when the sharp report of a pistol rang through the house. It was apparently fired behind the scenes upon the right of the stage and behind the President's box. While it startled every one, yet it was evidently accepted by every one as an introduction to some new passage, several of which had been introduced in the early part of the play. A moment after a man leaped from off the box directly down, nine feet, on the stage, and ran rapidly across, bareheaded, and holding an unsheathed dagger in his right hand, the blade of which flashed brightly as he came within ten feet of the opposite exit.

In the gaslight I did not see his face as he leaped or ran, but I am confident that he was the man I saw enter. As he leaped he cried distinctly and aloud the motto of the State of Virginia—"*Sic semper tyrannis.*" The hearing of this and the sight of the dagger explained fully to me the nature of the deed he had committed. In a second more he had disappeared behind the side scene; consternation seemed for a moment or two to rivet every one to the seat. The next moment confusion reigned supreme. I saw the features of the man distinctly before he entered the box, having surveyed him contemptuously before he entered, supposing he was an ill-bred fellow who was pressing a selfish matter upon the President in his hours of leisure.

The Appearance of the Assassin.

The assassin of the President is about five feet nine-and-a-half inches in height, black hair, and I suppose, black eyes. He did not turn his face more than quarter front, as artists term it. His face was smooth, as I remember, with the exception of a moustache of moderate size. Of this I am not positive. He was clad in a black coat, approximating to a dress frock coat, dark pantaloons and wore a stiff-rimmed, flat-topped, round-cornered black hat of felt. He was a gentlemanly looking person, having no decided or obtrusive marks. He seemed for a moment or two to survey the house with the deliberation of a habitue of the theatre.

PARTICULARS OF THE DEATH OF MR. LINCOLN.

WASHINGTON, April 16.—Through the kindness of Hon. Maunsell B. Field, Assistant Secretary of the Treasury, who was present during the last hours of President Lincoln, we are furnished with the following interesting details:—

Account of Secretary Field,

Last Friday evening, at about half-past ten o'clock, I was sitting in the reading room at Willard's Hotel, engaged with a newspaper, when a person hurriedly entered the hotel and passed up the hall, announcing in a loud tone of voice that the President had just been shot at Ford's Theatre. I started to my feet and had hardly reached the office when two other persons came in and confirmed the report, which at first I was hardly able to credit. I had parted about fifteen minutes previously with Mr. Mellen, of the Treasury Department, who had retired to his room for the night, and I at once went to him and communicated what had occurred, and we started together for the scene of the tragedy.

We found the streets already crowded with excited masses of people, and when we reached the theatre there was a very large assemblage in front of it, as well as of the opposite house, belonging to Mr. Peterson, into which the President had been conveyed. The people around the theatre related to us substantially the general facts connected with the assassination, which have since been communicated to the public. The impression was prevalent, however, at that time, that the President had been shot in the breast, about the region of the heart, and that the wound might not prove fatal. After a few minutes we crossed the street, and endeavored to gain admission into the house where Mr. Lincoln lay. This I effected with some little difficulty.

The first person whom I met in the hall was Miss Harris, daughter of United States Senator Ira Harris, of New York, who had been at the theatre with the Presidential party. She informed me that the President was dying, but desired me not to communicate the fact to Mrs. Lincoln, who was in the front parlor. Several other persons who were there confirmed the statement as to Mr. Lincoln's condition. I then entered the front parlor, where I found Mrs. Lincoln in a state of indescribable agitation. She repeated over and over again, "Why didn't he kill me? why didn't he kill me?"

I asked her if there was any service I could render her, and she requested me to go for Dr. Stone or some other eminent physician. Both Dr. Stone and Surgeon-General Barnes had been already sent for, but neither had yet arrived. On my way out, I met Major T. T. Eckert, of the War Department, who told me that he was himself going for Dr. Stone. I then went for Dr. Hall one of the most distinguished surgeons in the district. I found him at home and he at once accompanied me. When we again reached the neighborhood of the house, access had become very difficult, guards having been stationed on every side.

After much effort I was enabled to obtain admission for Dr. Hall, but was not at that time permitted to enter myself; accordingly, I returned to Willard's. The whole population of the city was by this time out, and all kinds of conflicting stories were being circulated. At three or four o'clock I again started for Peterson's house. This time I was admitted without difficulty. I proceeded at once to the room in which the President was dying. It was a small chamber, in an extension or back building, on the level with the first or parlor floor. The President was lying on his back, diagonally across a low double bedstead, his head supported by two pillows on the outer side of the bed.

The persons in the room were the Secretaries McCulloch, Stanton, Welles and Harlan; Postmaster-General Dennison, the Attorney-General, the Assistant Secretary of the Interior, Senator Sumner, Massachusetts; General Halleck, General Augur, General Meigs, General J. F. Farnsworth, of Illinois; General Todd, of Dacotah; the President's Assistant Private Secretary, Major Hay, the medical gentlemen, and perhaps two or three others. Dr. Stone was sitting on the foot of the bed. An army surgeon was sitting opposite the President's

See Last Column.

J. WILKES BOOTH, THE ASSASSIN.

THE SCENE OF THE GREAT TRAGEDY.

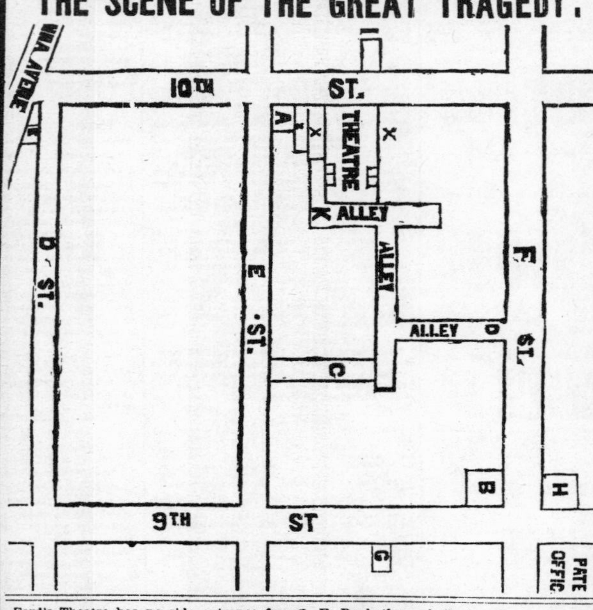

Ford's Theatre has no side entrance from the front.

A—Public School.

B—Herndon House (Hotel).

C—The only vacant lot communicating with the alley.

D—The only alley outlet to F street.

E—Bank (formerly Savings Bank).

I—Restaurants.

G—Newspaper Office.

H—Model House.

Most of the lots go back to the alleys.

I—House taken to after the act.

K—The alley by which the murderer escaped.

FORD'S THEATRE.

The Locality and Description of the Edifice.

Ford's Theatre, the scene of the late terrible disaster, is situated on Tenth street, just above E street, in Washington. It is a large edifice, constructed of brick, and of plain appearance. Its internal arrangements are somewhat novel, differing from those in our own city. There are eight private boxes instead of six, as is the case in the Philadelphia theatres. The four lower boxes, two on each side of the stage, are scarcely more than loopholes, and are very excellent points from which those who wish to see and remain unseen may take inspection. The apertures which appear above the stage are about three feet square. Consequently the boxes immediately above them are elevated but a short distance above the stage, a distance which any one could easily leap, even were his nerves not freshly braced from the commission of a murder.

The four upper boxes are *the* boxes of the theatre, and are very elegant and spacious. They give a tone of elegance to the auditorium, and are sumptuously appointed. It is in them that the most magnificent displays of toilette are made upon nights of opera, and that at once command the whole house, and are central points of inspection from it. Each accommodates quite a party, and the *locale* is so arranged that the greater portion of the occupants, except those in the back of the box, are in full view of the audience.

The box which the President occupied, and which was known as THE PRESIDENT'S BOX, consisted of the two upper boxes on the right hand side of the house as you face the stage, thrown into one. Mr. Lincoln was always accompanied by a party, which, although limited to personal friends and foreign officials, to whom courtesy required the extension of an invitation, was always sufficiently large to render more than one box necessary for comfort.

The proprietor of the theatre had, therefore, at the commencement of the present season, made arrangements by which these two boxes could at any time be thrown into one. They are fitted up with great elegance and taste. The curtains are of fine lace and buff satin, the paper dark and figured, the carpet Turkey, the seats velvet, and the exterior ornamentations are lit up with a chaste chandelier suspended from the outside. A winding staircase leads up to the lobbies which conduct to the box, and unless the arrangements are more stringent than they used to be, no decently dressed person would find much difficulty, probably, in entering one of those boxes after they had once been opened for the ingress of the party using them.

The Rest of the House.

The parquet consists of cane-seat chairs, rising in very gradual elevation, so that even the most distant observers obtain a fair view of the stage, and the entire parquette on an opera night, viewed from the stage or private boxes, resembles an exquisitely variegated parterre. The first tier or balcony is very commodious, and opens into a retiring-saloon elegantly illuminated and appointed. A second tier, corresponding to the family circle, completed the portion of the house dedicated to the accommodation of the audience. The house would hold probably between two and three thousand people.

The Murderer's Way of Exit.

There are two alleys at Ford's Theatre. One leads from the stage, along the east side of the theatre, between the theatre and a refreshment saloon, and so out to Tenth street. The alley is neatly paved, and is boarded and papered on both sides. The entry to it from the stage is through a glass door, and the exit from it on to Tenth street through a wooden one.

The other passage-way leads from the back of the theatre to a small alley which communicates with Ninth and other streets, and conducts to a livery stable locality. It was in this alley that the horse of the murderer was kept waiting.

The Tenth street door would have been too public, and escape, even temporary, a matter of impossibility. But the escape by the alley leading from the back of the stage was comparatively safe.

There are two doors there, one used for the egress and ingress of the actors, and the other devoted to the accommodation of scenery and machinery. It was through the smaller one that the assassin made his exit.

Circumstances have by this time settled the crime upon J. Wilkes Booth, who, from his engagements at this theatre, was perfectly familiar with all its minutiæ. He also kept a horse at the livery stable at the back of the theatre.

head, occasionally feeling his pulse, and applying his fingers to the arteries of the neck and the heart.

Mr. Lincoln seemed to be divested of all clothing except the bed coverings. His eyes were closed, and the lids and surrounding parts so injected with blood as to present the appearance of having been bruised. He was evidently totally unconscious, and was breathing regularly but heavily, and with an occasional sigh escaping with the breath; there was scarcely a dry eye in the room, and the scene was the most solemn and impressive one I ever witnessed. After a while Captain Robert Lincoln, of General Grant's staff, and eldest son of the President, entered the chamber and stood at the headboard, leaning over his father.

For a time his grief completely overpowered him, but he soon recovered himself and behaved in the most manly manner until the closing of the scene. As the morning wore on the condition of the President remained unchanged until about seven o'clock. In the meantime, it came on to rain heavily, and the scene from the windows was in dreary sympathy with that which was going on within. Just before this Mrs. Lincoln had been supported into the chamber and had thrown herself moaning upon her husband's body. She was permitted to remain but a few minutes, when she was carried out in an almost insensible condition.

At about seven o'clock the President's breathing changed in a manner to indicate that death was rapidly approaching. It became low and fitful, with frequent interruptions. Several times I thought that all was over, until the feeble respiration was resumed. At last, at just twenty-two minutes past seven o'clock, without a struggle, without a convulsive movement, without a tremor, he ceased breathing, and was no more. Thus died this great, pure, kind-hearted man, who never willingly injured a human being; the greatest martyr to liberty the world has ever seen.

Shortly after his death, finding that his eyes were not entirely closed, I placed my hands upon them. One of the attendant surgeons first put nickel cents upon them, and then substituted silver half dollars. It was twenty minutes or half an hour before the body commenced to grow cold. The lower jaw began to fall slightly, and the lower teeth were exposed. One of the medical gentlemen bound up the jaw with a pocket handkerchief. Mr. Stanton threw down the window shades, and I left the chamber of death. Immediately after the decease the Rev. Dr. Gurley had offered up a fervent and affecting prayer in the room, interrupted only by the sobs of those present.

When I left the room he was again praying in the front parlor. Poor Mrs. Lincoln's moans were distressing to listen to. After the prayer was over I entered the parlor and found Mrs. Lincoln supported in the arms of her son Robert. She was soon taken to her carriage. As she reached the front door she glanced at the theatre, opposite, and exclaimed several times, "Oh! that dreadful house!" "That dreadful house!" Immediately thereafter guards were stationed at the door of the room in which the President's body lay. In a few minutes I left myself. It is hoped that some historical painter will be found capable of portraying that momentous death scene.

Autopsy of the Late President.

The ball entered the skull midway between the left ear and the centre of the back of the head, and passed nearly to the right eye. The ball and two loose fragments of lead were found in the brain. Singularly enough, both orbital roofs were fractured inwardly, properly from contre coup. The tenacity of life was specially noticed by every surgeon in attendance. The brain was taken out, and will probably be weighed, although it may be difficult to arrive at its true weight, as a considerable portion escaped from the wound.

The autopsy of the President was made in the presence of Surgeon-General Barnes, Dr. Crane and Dr. Stone, of this city, by Drs. Woodward, Notson and Curtis, of the regular army.

The Corpse of Mr. Lincoln.

The corpse of the late President has been laid out in the room known as the guests' room, in the northwest wing of the White House. He is dressed in the suit of black clothes worn by him at his last inauguration.

A placid smile rests upon the features, and the deceased seems to be in a calm sleep, while flowers have been placed upon the pillow and over the breast above the kindest heart that ever throbbed. The corpse of the late President will be laid out in state, in the East Room, on Tuesday, in order to give the public an opportunity to see once more the features of him they loved so well. The preparations are being made to that end under the supervision of Mr. John Alexander, upholsterer. The catafalque upon which the body will rest is to be placed in the south part of the East Room, and is somewhat similar in style to that used on the occasion of the death of President Harrison.

Steps will be placed at the side to enable the public to mount to a position to get a perfect view of the face. The catafalque will be lined with fluted white satin, and on the outside it will be covered with black cloth and black velvet. Rev. Dr. Gurley, of the New York Avenue Presbyterian Church, where the President and family have been accustomed to worship, will doubtless be the officiating clergyman. The remains will be temporarily deposited in the vault of the Congressional Cemetery, and hereafter taken to Mr. Lincoln's home, at Springfield, Illinois. The remains of little Willie Lincoln are deposited in a vault at Oak Hill Cemetery, we believe.

The Funeral of President Lincoln.

Wednesday, it is understood, was determined upon to-day as the day for the funeral of our late President, Abraham Lincoln.

The Funeral Car.

The funeral car, which is being prepared for the occasion, is to be a magnificent affair. It is to be built on a hearse body, the extreme length fourteen feet. The body of the car will be covered with black cloth, from which will hang large festoons of cloth on the side and end, gathered and fastened by large rosettes of white and black satin over bows of white and black velvet. The bed of the car, on which the coffin will rest, will be eight feet from the ground, in order to give a full view of the coffin; and over this will rise the canopy, the supports of which will be draped with black cloth and velvet.

The top of the car will be decorated with plumes. The car will be drawn by six or eight horses, probably white, with black trappings, each led by a groom.

Voice of the Clergy.

The American Methodist Episcopal Conference also reported resolutions, which were unanimously adopted, lamenting the premature death of President Lincoln, as being irreparable to the nation. Rev. Doctors Gurley, Gillette, Hall, Regan, Butler and Channing, representing six Christian denominations,

Continued on the Eighth Page.

The Daily Picayune.

VOLUME XXIX | NEW ORLEANS, THURSDAY MORNING, APRIL 20, 1865. | NUMBER 74.

THE CITY OF NEW ORLEANS.

OFFICIAL.

[No. 6277.]

MAYORALTY OF NEW ORLEANS,
City Hall, March 31, 1865.

AN ORDINANCE to make certain local improvements, and authorize the city to levy a tax upon the property specially benefited thereby.

Whereas, no adequate means exist for the extinguishing of fires in the district bounded by Calliope, Tchoupitoulas and Canal streets and the river, in the First District of this city; and,

Whereas, the city possesses a quantity of iron pipe, thirty inches of diameter, with the necessary connections, purchased for the object above mentioned; therefore,

RESOLVED, That the Comptroller be and is hereby authorized to sell at public auction, after ten days' notice in the official journal, a contract for the work of laying the pipes, as hereinafter described—

Commencing at the intersection of Calliope and New Levee streets, there connecting with the pipes of the Commercial Water Works Company, and thence running up Calliope street to Front street, and thence down Front street to Canal street, and down Canal street to a junction with the main pipe of the said Water Works Company on Fulton street.

RESOLVED, That the aforesaid work shall be done in accordance with the specifications on file in the office of the City Surveyor.

RESOLVED, That in order to defray the cost of said work, exclusive of the main pipe, a tax of not more than thirty thousand dollars shall be levied upon all the taxable real estate below Gaiennié street, above Canal street, and in front and inclusive of all property fronting upon Tchoupitoulas street.

RESOLVED, That the pro-rata of the several properties hereinbefore made chargeable, shall be ascertained and determined from and in accordance with the city assessment rolls of the year 1864; and it is hereby made the duty of the Board of Assessors to prepare, from said rolls, a tableau containing a description of the said properties, the names of the owners thereof, the valuation thereof, and the pro-rata amount of said tax; and upon the approval of said tableau by the Mayor of the city, the amount so ascertained and determined shall be deemed a lien upon the property; said tableau shall thereupon be delivered to the City Comptroller, who shall cause tax receipts to be prepared, and, when completed, they shall be handed over to the City Treasurer, who shall collect the same in accordance with existing laws and ordinances.

(Signed) D. S. DEWEES,
Chairman Bureau Streets and Landings.
W. M. ABBATT,
Chairman Bureau of Finance.

Approved March 31, 1865.
(Signed) HU. KENNEDY, Mayor.
A true copy. Attest:
ap15—2dp D. L. GIBBENS, Sec'y.

[No. 6285.]

MAYORALTY OF NEW ORLEANS,
City Hall, April 13, 1865.

RESOLVED, That City Ordinance No. 6277, entitled "An Ordinance to make certain local improvements, and authorize the city to levy a tax upon the property specially benefited thereby," be so amended that the description shall read as follows:

Commencing at the intersection of Calliope and New Levee streets, there connecting with the pipes of the Commercial Water Works Company, and thence running up Calliope street to Front street, down Front street to Market street, up Market street to Delta street, and thence down Delta street to Canal street, and down Canal street to a junction with the main pipe of the said Water Works Company on Fulton street.

RESOLVED, That the time for adjudicating the contract for the above work be extended to the 20th inst.

(Signed) D. S. DEWEES,
Chairman Bureau Streets and Landings.
(Signed) G. BURKE,
Chairman Bureau of Finance.

Approved April 13, 1865.
(Signed) HU. KENNEDY, Mayor.
A true copy. Attest:
D. L. GIBBENS, Sec'y

COMPTROLLER'S OFFICE, CITY HALL,
New Orleans, April 5, 1865.

Notice is hereby given that I will sell at public auction, at this office, on THURSDAY, 20th inst., at 12 M., the contract for the above, in accordance with specification on file in Surveyor's office.

S. HOWELL,
ap14—td City Comptroller.

STREET COMMISSIONER'S OFFICE,
No. 7 City Hall, New Orleans, April 15, 1865.

Was brought to the First and Fourth District Pounds, on Market street, between Annunciation and Pacanier streets as estray—

One Bay HORSE, about twelve hands high, left hind fetlock white; no other mark.

Which, if not claimed within ten days and expenses thereon paid, will be sold at public auction at said Pound on THURSDAY, April 27, 1865, at 12 o'clock M.

JOHN PURCELL,
Street Commissioner.

For Comptroller:
ALEXANDER LEVY. ap16—5tin10d

NOTICE.

LOUISIANA STATE BANK,
New Orleans, March 27, 1865.

All parties indebted to this Institution are hereby required to make payment within thirty days. Such notes as shall remain unpaid after the above mentioned delay will be sued upon.

By order of Liquidating Commissioners.

mh28—3dp 3taw3d L. BERNARD, Sec'y.

PROPOSALS.

OFFICE ASSISTANT QUARTERMASTER,
27 Poydras street,
New Orleans, March 21, 1865.

Proposals will be received at this office until the 22d inst., for the building of a large Shed, Platforms and Fences at Hickok's Landing, at the terminus of the St. Joseph Street Railroad. Specifications furnished at this office.

For the Board: E. A. MORSE,
mh22—3dp Captain and A. Q. M.

The Daily Picayune.

DOUBLE SHEET

TELEGRAPHIC.

THE NATIONAL CALAMITY.

INTERESTING PARTICULARS OF THE AWFUL TRAGEDY.

THE PRESIDENT'S MURDERER.

JOHN WILKES BOOTH.

SECRETARY SEWARD LIVING AT LAST ACCOUNTS.

HIS SON'S CASE CRITICAL.

ONE OF HIS ATTENDANTS DEAD.

THE PLOT PARTIALLY FOILED.

THE VICE PRESIDENT AND SECRETARY OF WAR ESCAPED.

JOHNSON INAUGURATED.

ORGANIZES HIS CABINET.

IMPORTANT OFFICIAL DISPATCHES.

GEN. BANKS SPEAKS AT CAIRO.

War News from North Carolina.

A MOB SACKS AND BURNS RALEIGH.

JEFFERSON DAVIS ISSUES A PROCLAMATION.

North Carolina to Repeal Secession.

The steamer Pauline Carroll, arriving yesterday noon at Baton Rouge, the following dispatches were telegraphed to us from that place. They contain later and deeply interesting details of the mournful news already received by telegraph, and published in our columns:

WASHINGTON, April 15.—At an early hour this forenoon Hon. E. M. Stanton sent an official communication to Hon. A. Johnson, Vice President of the United States, stating that in consequence of the sudden and unexpected death of the Chief Magistrate, his inauguration should take place as soon as possible, and requesting him to state the place and hour at which the ceremonies should be performed. Mr. Johnson at once replied that it would be agreeable to him to have the proceedings take place at his rooms in Kirkwood House, as soon as arrangements could be perfected. Chief Justice Chase was informed of the fact, and repaired to the appointed place, in company with Secretary McCulloch, of the Treasury Department, Attorney General Speed, Hon. F. P. Blair, Hon. Montgomery Blair, Senators Foot, of Vermont, Ramsey, of Minnesota, Yates, of Illinois, Stuart, of Nevada, Hale, of New Hampshire, and Representative Farnsworth, of Illinois. At 11 o'clock the oath of office was administered by the Chief Justice of the United States, in the usual solemn and impressive manner. Mr. Johnson received the kind expressions of the gentlemen in a manner which showed his earnest sense of the great responsibility so suddenly devolved upon him, and made a brief speech in which he said "the duties of the office are mine. I will perform them. The consequences are with God. Gentlemen, I will lean upon you. I feel that I shall need your support. I am deeply impressed with the solemnity of the occasion, and the responsibility of the duties of the office I am assuming."

Mr. Johnson appeared to be in remarkably good health, and has a high and realizing sense of the hopes that are centred upon him. His manner was solemn and dignified, and his whole bearing produced a most gratifying impression upon those who participated in the ceremonies. It is probable that during the day President Johnson will issue his first proclamation to the American people.

It is expected, though nothing is definitely determined upon, that the funeral of the late President Lincoln will take place on or about Thursday next. It is supposed that his remains will be temporarily deposited in the Congressional Cemetery.

NEW YORK, April 15, 12:30 P. M.—A dispatch from Washington says Frederick Seward is not dead, but in a critical condition.

BURLINGTON, N. J., April 15.—Lieut. Gen. Grant left here for Washington at 6 o'clock this morning.

Mrs. U. S. GRANT.

WASHINGTON, April 15, 11 A. M.—The Star extra says, at 7:20 A. M. the President breathed his last, closing his eyes as if falling to sleep in perfect serenity. There was no indication of pain, and it was known that he was unconscious until the gradually decreasing respiration had ceased altogether.

The Rev. Dr. Gurley, of the New York Avenue Presbyterian Church, immediately on its being ascertained that life was extinct, knelt at the bedside and offered an impressive prayer, which was responded to by all present. Dr. Gurley then proceeded to the front parlor, where Mrs. Lincoln, Capt. Robt. Lincoln, Mr. J. Hay, private secretary, and others were waiting, when he again offered a prayer for the consolation of the family. Immediately after the President's death, a Cabinet meeting was held in the room in which the corpse lay. Secretary Stanton, Welles, and Asher, Postmaster General Dennison and Attorney General Speed were present.

CIRCULAR.

WAR DEPARTMENT, Provost Marshal General's Bureau, Washington, April 15, 9:40 A. M.—It is believed that the assassins of the President and Secretary Seward are attempting to cross from the United States into Canada. You will make a thorough and careful examination of all persons attempting to cross into Canada, and will arrest all suspicious persons. The most vigilant scrutiny on your part and the force at your disposal is demanded. A description of the parties supposed to be implicated in the murder will be telegraphed to you to-day; but in the meantime be active in preventing the crossing of any suspicious person. By order of the Secretary of War:

N. L. JEFFER, Brevet Brig. Gen.
Acting Prov't Marshal General.

Government offices are closed by order and will be draped with emblems of mourning. The roads leading to and from the city are guarded by the military, and the utmost circumspection is observed as to attempting to enter or leave the city.

BUFFALO, April 15.—The Governor of New York has issued a proclamation revoking the proposed thanksgiving for recent victories on April 20th, and changing it to one of prayer and humiliation for our great affliction.

NEW YORK, April 15.—The Post's Washington special says Mr. Hansall, messenger of the State Department, who was in attendance upon Mr. Seward, is dead. Secretary Seward is in a very precarious condition. It is reported that Booth was captured this morning. The story is that his horse threw him and injured him so that he was obliged to seek relief in a house on the Seventh street road. The Post also publishes a dispatch to Clarence A. Seward, which says Mr. Seward's wounds are bad but not mortal. He is composed. He has lost much blood, but no arteries are cut. Fred Seward's skull is fractured badly in two places above the temple. He is insensible, and, I fear, will die. His brother's wound is slight. The Governor's throat would have been cut if he had not rolled out of bed. The doctor says that Frederick's condition is highly critical, but not hopeless.

WASHINGTON, April 15.—There is no confirmation of the report that the murderer of the President has been arrested. Among circumstances tending to participation in the crime on Booth, were letters found in his trunk, one of which, apparently from a lady, supplicated him to desist from the perilous undertaking in which he was about to embark, as the time was inauspicious, and the mine not yet being ready to be sprung.

The extra Intelligencer says: From the evidence obtained it is rendered highly probable that the man who stabbed Mr. Seward and his sons, is John Survatt, of Prince George's county, Maryland. The horse he rode was hired at Taylor's stable on 14th street. Survatt is a young man with light hair and goatee. His father is said to have been Postmaster of Prince George's county. About 12 o'clock last night two men crossed the Anacostia Bridge, one of whom gave his name as Booth, and the other as Smith. Latter believed to be John Survatt. Last night a riderless horse was found, which has been identified by the proprietor of one of the stables previously mentioned as having been hired from his establishment. The accounts are conflicting as to whether Booth crossed the bridge on horseback or on foot, but as it is believed that he rode across it is presumed that he had exchanged his horse. From information in possession of the authorities, it is evident that the scope of the plot was intended to be much more comprehensive. The Vice President and other prominent members of the Administration were particularly inquired for by the suspected parties, and their precise locality accurately obtained, but providentially in their cases the scheme was miscarried. A boat was at once sent down the Potomac to notify the gunboats on the river of the awful crime, in order that all possible means should be taken for the arrest of the perpetrators. The most ample precautions have been taken, and it is not believed that the culprits will long succeed in evading the overtaking arm of justice.

OFFICIAL.

WAR DEPARTMENT, March 15.—*To Major Gen. Dix:* Official notice of the death of the late President, Abraham Lincoln, was given by the head of the Departments this A. M., and to Andrew Johnson, Vice President, upon whom the constitution devolved the office of President. Mr. Johnson, upon receiving the notice, appeared before Hon. Salmon P. Chase, Chief Justice of the United States, took the oath of office as President of the United States, and assumed the duties and functions at 12 o'clock. The President met the Heads of Departments in Cabinet meeting at the Treasury building. Among other business the following was transacted:

First. The arrangements for the funeral of the late President were assigned to the several Secretaries as far as related to the respective Departments.

Second. Wm. Hunter, Esq., was appointed Acting Secretary of State during the disability of Mr. Seward and his son Frederick Seward, the Assistant Secretary.

Third. The President formally announced that he desired to retain the present Secretaries of the Departments of his Cabinet, and they would go onward in the same manner as before the deplorable event that had changed the head of the Government.

All business in the Departments was suspended during the day. The surgeons report that the condition of Mr. Seward remains unchanged. He is doing well. No improvement in Mr. Frederick Seward. The murderers have not yet been apprehended.

E. M. STANTON.

The Herald's Goldsboro correspondent has a report from Raleigh, saying that Gov Vance will call the North Carolina Legislature together to repeal the secession ordinance. The World's Goldsboro dispatch, of the 10th, says the Raleigh Confederate, of the 9th, says the city was sacked and fired by a mob of the lower classes. The 16th Virginia reserve were left to protect the people, but were unable to do so. The mob took possession of some of the large warehouses and stores, and robbed them.

WASHINGTON, April 15.—The assassin of President Lincoln left behind him his hat and a spur. The hat was picked up in the President's box, and has been identified by parties to whom it has been shown as the one belonging to the suspected man, and accurately described by other parties—those who are not allowed to see it before describing it. The spur was dropped upon the stage, and that also has been identified as the one procured at a stable, where the same man hired a horse for the evening. Two gentlemen, who went to the Secretary of War to apprise him of the attack on Mr. Lincoln, met at the residence of the former a man muffled in a cloak, who, when accosted by them, hastened away. It had been Mr. Stanton's intention to accompany President Lincoln to the theatre, and occupy the same box, but the press of business prevented his going. It therefore seems evident that the aim of the plotter was to paralyze the country by at once striking down the head, the heart, and arm of the country. As soon as the dreadful events were announced in the streets, Superintendent Richards and his assistants were at work to discover the assassin. In a few moments the telegraph had aroused the whole police force of the city. Mayor Wallach and several members of the city government were soon on the spot, and every precaution was taken to preserve order and quiet in the city. Every street in the city was patrolled at the request of Mr. Richards. Gen. Augur sent horses to mount the police. Every road leading out of the city was strongly picketed, and every avenue of escape strongly guarded. Steam boats about to depart down the Potomac were stopped. The Daily Chronicle says it is suspected that this conspiracy originated in Maryland. The telegraph flashed the mournful news to Baltimore, and all the cavalry was immediately put upon active duty. Every road was picketed. A preliminary examination was made by Mr. Richards and his assistants. Several persons were called to testify, and the evidence as elicited before an informal tribunal and not under oath was conclusive and to the point. The murderer of President Lincoln was John Wilkes Booth. His hat was found in the private box, and identified by several persons who had seen him within the last two days, and the spur which he dropped by accident after he jumped to the stage was identified as one of those which he had obtained from the stable where he hired his horse. This man Booth has played more than once at Ford's Theatre, and is of course acquainted with its exit and entrances. The facility with which he escaped is easily understood. The person who attacked Secretary Seward left behind him a slouched hat and an old rusty navy revolver. The chambers were broken loose from the barrel as if done by striking. The loads were drawn from the chamber, one being but a rough piece of lead, and the other balls smaller than the chambers wrapped in paper, as if to keep them from falling out.

WASHINGTON, April 15.—The President's body was removed from the private residence opposite Ford's Theatre to the Executive Mansion this A. M. at 9:30, in a hearse, and wrapped in the American flag. It was escorted by a small guard of cavalry. Gen Augur and other military officers moved in front. A dense crowd accompanied the remains to the White House, where a guard excluded the crowd, allowing no one but the persons of the household and personal friends of the deceased to enter the premises. Stanton, Yates, and Representative Farnsworth were among the number. The body is being embalmed, with a view to its removal to Illinois.

NEW YORK, April 15.—The Herald's Goldsboro correspondent says Sherman's army commenced the advances on the 9th in three columns, under Howard, Slocum and Schofield. During the rejoicing over the news of the fall of Richmond, Sherman was called out by his troops and he addressed a few words to them, saying he was informed that Richmond had been captured, and Lee way flying in dismay. He said Grant wrote him he was pursuing Lee, and he hoped he (Sherman) would press Johnston, which, said Sherman, I think we will. The soldiers responded we will, we will. Sherman told his men that he did not mean to let Johnston have any rest.

Johnston has evacuated Raleigh, moving west and leaving the town in the possession of Hampton's Cavalry. On the evening of the 10th a small force of Howard's men was attacked by some rebel cavalry, who, however, were soon dispersed with the loss of 100 men and two pieces of cannon.

NEW YORK, April 15.—The following is the substance of Jeff. Davis's late proclamation, dated Danville, April [illegible]: His General-in-chief found it necessary to make such movements of his troops as to uncover the capital. It would be unwise to conceal the moral and material injury to our cause, resulting from the occupation of the capital by the enemy. It is equally unwise and unworthy of us to allow our efforts to become relaxed under reverses, however calamitous they may be for many months. The largest and finest army of the Confederacy, under command of a leader whose presence inspired equal confidence in the troops and the people, has been greatly trammeled by the necessity of keeping constant watch over the enemy's approach to our capital, and has been forced to forego more than one opportunity for promising enterprises.

CAIRO, April 15, 6 P. M.—The awful intelligence of the assassination of President Lincoln and the other victims of the desperado has made this a nation of mourning to-day. I gave the sad intelligence of the terrible event in my dispatches by the Sultana this A. M. Every house in the city is draped in mourning. Steamboats, churches and other bells are ringing a mournful knell for the loss of the nation's guide and hope.

Gen. Banks arrived here about noon, and shortly after addressed an immense audience in front of the Post Headquarters, deeply lamenting the loss of the illustrious man thus untimely slain. The General endeavored to convince his hearers by the assurances that his principles will live in the hearts of his countrymen, and would be fully consummated ere the memory of the glorious dead should be forgotten. The brave and gallant Gen. Banks, as he addressed the thronging crowd, could not refrain from tears, and as he went away the falling drops of every heart in the assembly deeply commiserated the loss that both he and the country has sustained. It was a sad but opportune moment for Gen. Banks to be amongst us. He was the friend and confidant of the head and counsel of the nation just ruthlessly slain, and his burning words and heart-wrung tears may lead a Christian feature to the bloody deed that has thrown a pall over our already deeply stricken land.

At the conclusion of the pronouncing of the benediction by Chaplain Johnson, Gen. Banks offered the following resolution, which was adopted by one unanimous and heartfelt aye:

Resolved, That we mourn deeply and beyond expression the death of the public servants who have fallen by the hand of the assassin; that we will show our devotion to their principles by renewed labors for their success, and that we will, with more energy and fervor and confidence than ever, maintain the Government they represented.

The fatigues of travel and the melancholy offices imposed upon him rendered it imperative upon Gen. Banks to seek the quietness of his state apartments on board the Pauline Carroll, upon which boat he leaves this evening for New Orleans, accompanied by his amiable lady and other cherished members of his devoted family, together with Brevet Lieut. Col. J. S. Crosby, and our old and familiar friend, William Palmer, long connected with the United States Military Telegraph in New Orleans.

Gen. Banks, I have authority for stating, returns to New Orleans to assume command of the Department of the Gulf. It was in contemplation to have given Gen. Banks a reception worthy of his exalted position upon the occasion of his passing through Cairo, but the melancholy news has made our city the home of sorrow and dismay instead of rejoicing and welcome.

BATON ROUGE, April 19.—All public offices and places of business are closed and draped in mourning.

THE VERY LATEST.

BATON ROUGE, April 19, 11 P. M.—By the arrival of the steamer Lady Gay we glean the following additional particulars of the event which has shrouded the nation in gloom and sorrow:

WASHINGTON, April 15.—An inquest was held this evening on the body of President Lincoln by Surgeon General Bardee and Dr. Stone, assisted by other medical men. The coffin is of mahogany, covered with black cloth and lined with lead—the latter being covered with white satin. A silver plate on the coffin over the breast bears the following inscription:

ABRAHAM LINCOLN,
Sixteenth President of the United States;
Born July 12, 1809;
Died April 15, 1865.

The remains have been embalmed. A few locks of hair were removed from the President's head for the family previous to the remains being placed in the coffin. The same special states that Secretary Seward has given a detailed description of the assassin. It is evident that he was a different person from the President's murderer. Frederick Seward is in a most critical condition, and surgeons are removing the broken fragments of his skull. A private dispatch to Mr. Seward's nephew now in this city, from a member of the family, says: "I have just left Mr. Seward's house. His wounds are not mortal. His wounds are not mortal. He lost much blood, but no arteries cut. Frederick's skull is fractured badly in two places above the temple. He is insensible and it is feared he will die. Secretary Seward has been informed of Mr. Lincoln's death."

NEW YORK, April 15.—The Commercial states: We have ascertained from a source perfectly reliable, that during a conversation yesterday, among members of a Spanish firm in this city, it was stated that on to-day the greatest news would be received that had yet been made known to the Republic. The fact of the statement was communicated to Gen. Peck by the clerk of the establishment.

A special to the Tribune says that J. Wilkes Booth was arrested about 9 o'clock this A. M., near Fort Hasting, on the Bladensburg Road. He boldly approached our pickets, and was arrested and brought to the city. This is not confirmed by any official dispatches from Washington up to this (Saturday) evening.

Another private dispatch states that Frederick Seward is out of danger.

Several street meetings have been held to-day and addressed by prominent gentlemen. The unanimous expression seems to be to hold the rebel leaders to a just account for their crime.

Two men expressing respect for Jeff. Davis were driven out of a newspaper counting-room and hunted by the crowd, they seeking safety by flight.

The steamship Atlanta sailed at 5:30 this evening with dispatches to our Ministers at foreign ports from Washington.

TORONTO, C. W., April 15.—The news of the assassination at Washington caused a profound sensation here. The flags on the Custom-House, American Consulate, the shipping in the harbor and in the city were displayed at half mast. Stores and places of business owned by Americans are closed. The feeling of grief by the Canadian people is intense, and it is contemplated giving some public expression.

WASHINGTON, April 15.—When the excitement at the theatre was at its wildest height reports were circulated that Secretary Seward was also assassinated. On reaching this gentleman's residence, a crowd and a military guard were round its doors, and on entering it was ascertained that the reports were based on truth. The facts are substantially as follows:

About 10 o'clock a man rang a bell, and the call having been answered by a colored servant, he said he had come from Dr. Viede, Secretary Seward's family physician, with a prescription, at the same time holding in his hand a small piece of folded paper, and saying, in answer to a refusal, that he must see the Secretary, as he was instructed with particular directions concerning the medicine. He insisted on going up, and although repeatedly informed that no one could enter the chambers he pushed the servant one side and walked hastily towards the Secretary's room. He was then met by Mr. Fred. Seward, of whom he demanded to see the Secretary, making the same representations which he did to the servant. What further passed in the way of colloquy is not known, but the man struck him on the head with a billet severely, injuring the skull and felling him almost senseless. The assassin then rushed into the chamber and attacked Mr. Seward, Paymaster of the United States Army, and Mr. Hansell, a messenger of the State Department, and two small nurses disabling them. He then rushed upon the Secretary, who was lying in the bed in the same room, and inflicted three stabs in the neck, but severing, it is thought and hoped, no arteries, though he bled profusely. The assassin rushed down stairs, mounted his horse at the door, and rode off before an alarm could be sounded, and in the same manner as the assassinator of the President. It is believed that the injuries of the Secretary are not fatal, nor those of the others; although both the Secretary and the Assistant Secretary are very severely injured.

Secretaries Stanton and Welles, and other prominent officers of the Government, called at Secretary Seward's house to inquire into his condition, and then heard of the assassination of the President. They then proceeded to the house where he was lying, exhibiting, of course, intense anxiety. Some evidences of the guilt of the party who attacked the President are in possession of the Board of Police.

THE POPE AND THE FINIAN BROTHERHOOD.—The following is the reply of the Sacred College to an application made by Archbishop Cullen, of Dublin, for a decree of condemnation of the Finian Brotherhood:

Most Illustrious and Most Reverend Sir—Many things have been reported to the Holy See concerning the so-called Society of Finian Brothers, as also concerning another named after St. Patrick, all of which have been submitted to the Supreme Council of the General Inquisition, to have a decision delivered thereupon.

Our Most Holy Sovereign Pope Pius IX, having therefore heard the opinions of the most Eminent Inquisition, has directed your Grace's attention to be drawn to the decree of Wednesday, August 5th, 1846, which is as follows: "The secret societies spoken of in the Pontifical constitutions understood to be all such as mediate anything against the Church or the State, whether an oath of secrecy be required or not." His Holiness desires it to be moreover intimated to you that recourse must be had to the Holy See, and all the circumstances carefully set forth, in case any difficulty should be experienced in applying said decree to either of the above mentioned societies.

Praying the Lord to keep you long in health and safety, I am, of your Grace, the most devoted.

AL. C. BARNABO, Pref.
P. CAPALTI, Secretary.

To the Most Reverend Paul Cullen, Archbishop of Dublin.

Grinning over the Greenbacks.—It was quite interesting this forenoon to see the dilapidated soldiers who have deserted from Lee's army receiving greenbacks, at the National Bank of the Metropolis, in Fifteenth street, in payment for the guns they brought away from secesh. Our Government pays eleven dollars and a half for each musket brought away; and as the ragged "butternuts" came into the bank and got their paymaster's checks cashed, they grinned over the welcome greenbacks with almost apparent delight.

[illegible] Persons in New York who were invited by the Secretary of War to the flag raising celebration at Fort Sumter have offered as much as one hundred dollars for a ticket.

The Philadelphia Inquirer.

PRICE TWO CENTS. PHILADELPHIA, TUESDAY, APRIL 25, 1865. PRICE TWO CENTS.

PRESIDENT LINCOLN'S REMAINS IN INDEPENDENCE HALL.

OUR DEAD PRESIDENT

Departure of the Remains from Philadelphia.

PASSAGE OF THE CORTEGE THRO' NEW JERSEY.

Thousands of Mourners Along the Route.

ARRIVAL AT NEW YORK.

The Corpse Lying in State at the City Hall.

METROPOLIS DRAPED IN MOURNING.

New York's Tribute to the Martyr.

THE SOLEMNITIES IN THE CITY.

AN INTERIOR VIEW OF THE RAILROAD CAR CONVEYING THE REMAINS OF PRESIDENT LINCOLN.

PROGRESS OF THE FUNERAL TRAIN.

NEW YORK, April 24, 10 A. M.—The funeral party started from the Continental Hotel, at Philadelphia, at two o'clock this morning, and halted before the State House until the coffin was conveyed to the funeral car. The transparency which adorned the front of the building, the portrait of the President, with a dark border representing a coffin, afforded a relief to the surrounding gloom of the morning, the words "Rest in Peace" still blazing from the gas jets above it. The Invincibles, and other city organizations, with torches, composed a part of the procession and the City Troop acted as the escort. A band of music played dirges on the march.

The procession reached the Kensington Depot at four o'clock. Thousands of men, women and children were still in the streets, and not a few half-dressed residents in that neighborhood, who apparently had just risen from their beds, ran forward to join the large crowd in waiting at the depot.

The funeral party with difficulty pressed their way to the cars. Mr. W. H. Gatzmer, General Agent, and Messrs. A. W. Markley, Joseph P. Bradley and John L. McKnight, Directors of the Camden and Amboy Railroad Company, and F. Walcott Jackson, General Superintendent, were among the civilians.

The running of the road was under the direction of Mr. R. S. Van Rensselaer.

At a few minutes after four o'clock the train started. A locomotive preceded it by ten minutes. The engine is trimmed with the national flag, draped with mourning, and there is a telegrapher and two signal men accompanying it to guard against accidents.

The train consisted of nine elegant cars, provided by the Camden and Amboy Railroad, all tastefully trimmed. The funeral car last night was additionally decorated; heavy silver fringe being placed at the end of the black covering of the several panels, and the festoons being fastened with stars and tassels of similar material.

First Lieutenant J. A. Durkee and Lieutenant Murphy spent the entire of last night in thus improving the exterior of the car and clothing the interior with additional drapery. The materials were contributed by Philadelphians.

There was on board the cars a committee from Newark, consisting of the Mayor of that city, Joseph P. Bradley, Esq., and the President and other members of Councils, together with eight additional citizens. These and the Mayor of Washington and other civilians occupied seats in the front car.

Next in order were the Senators and members of the House of Representatives, with their respective officers. Then followed the Iowa and Illinois delegations and representatives of the several States and Territories. The guard of honor occupied the next car, and after this was that containing the remains of the late President and his little son Willie. The last car was occupied by Rear-Admiral Davis, Major-Generals Dix and Hunter, Brigadier-General Townsend, Assistant Adjutant-General of the United States Army (Adjutant-General Thomas is detained at home by sickness), Brevet Brigadier-General Barnard, Generals Caldwell, Eaton, Ramsey, Major Field, of the Marine Corps, Captain Taylor and Captain Penrose, and other army and navy officers.

At a few minutes past four o'clock the train left the Kensington station and soon reached Bristol, where several hundred persons had assembled. The sun was now rising in its full glory, beautifully illuminating the rural scene.

Governor Parker came on board at the State line at Morrisville with his staff, consisting of Adjutant-General R. F. Stockton, Quartermaster-General Perrin, and others of his staff. They were accompanied by U. S. Senator John P. Stockton, Rev. Henry Miller, and Colonel Murphy, and were received by Governor Curtin, of Pennsylvania, who had joined the funeral party at Harrisburg.

The Delaware River was crossed at 5½ o'clock. As the train passed through Trenton the bells were tolled. Immense throngs of spectators had gathered on every hill-top, and the line of road, and other advantageous points were occupied. The train proceeded onward until it reached the station, where it stopped for thirty minutes.

The population were assembled in much larger numbers, for this was a much more attractive point. The station was elaborately festooned, and the national banner deeply draped.

A detachment of the Veteran Corps was drawn up in line on the platform, showing that the people of Trenton, like all other true patriots, were not unmindful of the great loss which has befallen the nation in the violent death of a beloved and honored President.

Through New Jersey.

TRENTON, April 24.—The funeral train reached here at 5·30 this morning. Governor Parker and staff, of New Jersey, were taken on board at the

Continued on the Eighth Page.

The Philadelphia Inquirer.

PRICE TWO CENTS. PHILADELPHIA, FRIDAY, APRIL 28, 1865. PRICE TWO CENTS.

BOOTH THE ASSASSIN

He is Traced to his Hiding Place

HE REFUSES TO SURRENDER HIMSELF

The Capture of Harold.

BOOTH SHOWS FIGHT

THE BARN SET ON FIRE.

Death of the Murderer of Lincoln!

HOW BOOTH WAS DISCOVERED.

Loyal Negroes Guide His Pursuers.

HIS BODY AT WASHINGTON.

Full Particulars of the Pursuit and Capture.

OFFICIAL GAZETTE.

WASHINGTON, April 27, 9·30 A. M.—Major-General Dix, New York:—J. Wilkes Booth and Harold were chased from the swamp in St. Mary's county, Maryland, to Garrett's farm, near Port Royal, on the Rappahannock, by Colonel Baker's force.

The rear of the barn in which they took refuge was fired. Booth, in making his escape, was shot through the head and killed, lingering about three hours, and Harold was captured.

Booth's body and Harold are now here.

(Signed) EDWIN M. STANTON,
Secretary of War.

[Port Royal, Va., near which Booth and Harold were taken, is on the south side of the Rappahannock, about twenty miles below Fredericksburg. The belief heretofore entertained that Booth, after committing his crime, took refuge in the southern counties of Maryland, with a view to crossing the Potomac into Virginia, is confirmed.]

THE PURSUIT AND DEATH OF BOOTH.

[SPECIAL DESPATCHES TO THE INQUIRER.]

WASHINGTON, April 27.

Booth, after assassinating President Lincoln and making a tragic exit from the stage of the theatre, mounted his horse and rode off, accompanied by an accomplice, named Harold, a young Marylander. To avoid suspicion, they separated, meeting at a place called Marlboro.

Booth in jumping from the box, had fractured one of the small bones of his left leg, just above the ankle, and the limb had swollen during the ride, causing much pain. Harold took him to the house of a Dr. Mudge, where the boot was cut off and the limb bandaged.

The two fugitives remained some days in Maryland, and Harold states that he saw the cavalry and detectives very near their place of concealment several times.

They were harbored by sympathizers with the Rebel cause, and the only persons who have given any information about them are those loyal Southerners who are easily distinguished by their dark skins.

Col. Baker on the Track of the Assassins.

Meanwhile, Colonel L. C. Baker, Provost Marshal of the War Department, had taken no part in the search made in Maryland for Booth by a large military force, aided by Colonel Olcott and the New York detectives, as he was waiting for some definite information of his whereabouts.

On Monday afternoon he received intelligence that Booth and Harold had probably crossed the Potomac at Swan's Point. Those engaged in searching for them did not know that they had crossed. Having consulted maps of Virginia, which he obtained from the office of the Coast Survey, Colonel Baker made up his mind that Booth and Harold must have gone to the vicinity of Port Royal, a quiet village below Fredericksburg, on the Rappahannock.

He accordingly wrote to General Hancock, requesting him to detail a commissioned officer and twenty-five cavalrymen to report to any one he might designate. He then gave instructions to two of his detective force, Lieutenant Luther B. Baker and E. J. Conger, formerly Lieutenant-Colonel of the cavalry regiment which Colonel Baker commanded.

The Escort,

Which subsequently reported and started off under the orders of Detectives Casker and Conger, belonged to the Sixteenth New York Cavalry, which has for some months been looking after Moseby's guerrillas over in Virginia.

The Commander of the Escort.

Lieutenant Edward P. Dougherty, who commanded the escort, was at one time a resident in Boston. When the Rebellion broke out he came here as a private in the New York Seventy-first, in which regiment he fought at the first Bull Run. He afterwards enlisted in the Berdan Sharp-shooters, and was then transferred into the Sixteenth New York cavalry, where he has so distinguished himself as to secure promotion.

He was especially commended last fall when, on making a reconnoissance near Culpeper Court House with a small force, he encountered Kershaw's Rebel cavalry Division, but gallantly cut his way out.

Booth's Executioner.

Sergeant Boston Corbett, who shot Booth, is a religious enthusiast, who has made the character of Cromwell his study. He was born in England, is about thirty-three years old, and is by trade a hat finisher.

About seven years since, while in Boston, he experienced religion, and when baptised, assumed the name of the city where he became converted, and since then he has always prayed for Divine instruction before taking any step in life, and he says that he has always been prompted what to do.

He was at one time a prisoner at Andersonville, Georgia, and was one of a party of sixteen who escaped. They were hunted down with bloodhounds, and only himself and one of his companions were brought back alive.

On the Sunday after President Lincoln was assassinated Sergeant Corbett obtained leave to attend services at McKendree Chapel here, and there prayed fervently that the assassins might be punished.

How the Assassins were Discovered.

The detectives and their escort went down on a steamboat to Belleplain, where they landed before day on Monday morning, and struck across for the Rappahannock.

There is a ferry above Port Royal and the ferryman denies having ferried over any men answering to the descriptions of Booth and Harrold. But a colored man looking over Lieutenant Baker's shoulder at a photograph of Booth, which he was showing the ferryman, exclaimed:—"I saw that man across the river—he was in a wagon with three other men." The loyal although sable Virginian was right. It appears that Booth and Harold had crossed the Potomac in a canoe, for which they paid three hundred dollars, and were met on the Virginia shore by two Confederate officers with a two-horse wagon. Booth wore a grey suit without any military insignia of rank.

At Port Royal the detectives learned that one of the Confederate officers had a sweetheart at Bowling Green, and had probably gone there. So the party started in pursuit, passing on their way a farm where resided two brothers, named William and John Garrett, who have been in the Rebel army, their house being about a quarter of a mile from the road.

After having gone about three miles from the Garretts' house the party met a loyal Virginian, of dark skin, of course, and from him learned that Booth and Harold were at the Garretts'. "Right about!" was the word, and about three o'clock in the morning the pursuers arrived there.

Statement of the Garretts.

Here let us state what the Garretts say about their visitors who came to their house on Friday or Saturday of last week.

The fugitives were brought in a wagon by two Confederate officers, who spoke of Booth as a wounded Marylander on his way home, and that they wished to leave him there a short time, and would take him away by the 26th.

Booth limped somewhat, and walked on crutches about the place, complaining of his ankle. He and Harold regularly took their meals at the house, and Booth kept up appearances well.

One day, at the dinner table, the conversation turned on the assassination of the President, when Booth denounced the assassination in the severest terms, saying that there was no punishment severe enough for the perpetrator. At another time some one said, in Booth's presence, that rewards, amounting to $200,000, had been offered for Booth, and that he would like to catch him, when Booth replied, "Yes, it would be a good haul, but the amount would doubtless soon be increased to $500,000.

After our cavalry passed towards Bowling Green, Booth and Harold applied to one of the Garretts for two horses, that they might ride to Louisa Court House, but he fearing that the horses would not be returned refused to let them go. Some words of recrimination passed between Booth and Harold, and the Garretts becoming suspicious that all was not right urged them to leave. This they refused to do unless they could be supplied with horses; and the Garretts then said that if they remained they must sleep in the barn. One of the Garretts went to sleep in the corn crib, fearing, as he says, that the strangers would steal their horses.

Preparations for the Capture.

On returning to the Garrett's House, Lieutenant Baker halted his force and going in obtained a reluctant confession from the brother there where the criminals were. Going out again, Lieutenant Baker aroused his escort, who had nearly all gone to sleep, and took them to the barn, around which he stationed then. He then advanced to the door and knocking with the butt of his revolver said, "Booth we want you." "Here I am," replied the assassin, "who are you, Confederate or Yankee?" Lieutenant Baker informed him who he was and summoned him to surrender, but met with a defiant refusal.

Quite a parley ensued, Harold at one time expressing a desire to surrender, which Booth rebuked, denouncing him as a coward. Booth could see the party outside through the cracks of the barn, but they could not see him. He swore that he would never be taken alive, and declared that he could kill at least five men and then kill himself, should they attempt to break into the barn.

The Barn Fired.

At last, Lieutenant Baker, fearing that the guerrillas and the paroled Rebel soldiers, with whom the country swarmed, would come to the rescue, posted the calvarymen around the barn, and going to one end of it, which was filled with hay, pulled some through a crack and lighted it. The flames ran up the crack to the top of the hay-mow, over which they spread. The inside of the barn was now lighted up.

When Booth first saw the fire he clambered up on the mow, and vainly attempted to extinguish it. He then returned to his position on the floor between the two doors, with his back against the hay-mow, a revolver in each hand, and a Spencer carbine between his legs.

Harold Surrenders.

Meanwhile, the soldiers had approached the barn, and Harold, dropping his pistol, gave himself up, receiving Booth's malediction as he left the burning barn.

Death of Booth.

Just afterwards the roof over the hay-mow began to crack as if it was falling in, and Booth made a movement. Some of those who were watching him say that he was about to kill himself, while others declare that he was intending to break out and escape. Be this as it may, Sergeant Corbett had a sight at him through a wide crack with his cavalry six-shooter, and pulled trigger. The ball entered about where the President was shot, but passed entirely through Booth's head. The murder has been avenged. "It's all up now," shrieked Booth, "I'm gone," and he staggered towards the door of the barn. Lieutenant Baker received him, and taking him from the blazing barn, laid him on the ground, then sat down and took his head in his lap.

Booth did not deny his crime, and showed no signs of repentance or of humanity, except to ask Lieutenant Doherty to give a message to his mother. His death was not easy, but at three minutes after seven his spirit passed away into the presence of an avenging God.

Return of the Escort.

Nothing remained for the party to do but to regain their steamboat at Belle Plain.

How Harold Was Taught to Walk.

They had to bring Booth's body in a cart, and at first Harold had to walk, to which he, as a Maryland gentleman, objected; but after a rope was placed around his neck with a slip noose, and the other end of it was fastened to a cavalryman's saddle he started off, taking good care that the rope should not tighten.

The Remains of Booth.

From Belle Plain Lieutenant-Colonel Conger rode overland to Alexandria, and reported to Colonel Baker yesterday afternoon, at half-past five.

When he left there were some hopes that Booth's wound was not mortal.

Colonel Baker went to Alexandria to meet the steamer, and since then the body of Booth, by direction of the Secretary of War, has remained in his custody.

Surgeon-General Barnes, with an assistant, made an autopsy on the remains this afternoon. Their final disposition is unknown to the public as yet.

Such are the leading events of the escape, pursuit and arrest of the assassin of President Lincoln, obtained from unquestionable sources.

Of course, every member of the expedition, civil or military, regards himself as the principal agent, and some wonderful stories are told; but what I have stated may be relied upon as correct.

This is, however, but the second act in the great conspiracy, the first act of which cost us our President. Other arrests have been made.

Other arrests are to be made, and in due time the public will learn the extent and the deliberate wickedness of the whole crime. They will also see that much of what has been published about arrests of the party who attacked Secretary Seward and other matters are bosh. Colonel Baker has detected the criminal, and the Secretary of War, who knows the facts better than any one else, gives him the credit.

Appearance of the Body.

Booth's moustache had been cut off apparently with scissors, and his beard allowed to grow, changing his appearance considerably. His hair had been cut somewhat shorter than he usually wore it.

Booth's body, which we have before described, was at once laid out on a bench and a guard placed over it. The lips of the corpse are tightly compressed, and the blood has settled in the lower part of the face and neck. Otherwise the face is pale and wears a wild, haggard look, indicating exposure to the elements and a rough time generally in his skulking flight. His hair is disarranged and dirty, and apparently had not been combed since he took his flight. The head and breast is alone exposed to view, the lower portion of his body, including the hands and feet, being covered with a tarpaulin thrown over it. The shot which terminated his accursed life entered on the left side at the back of the neck, a point, curiously enough, not far distant from that in which his victim, our lamented President, was shot.

A Spencer carbine, which Booth had with him in the barn at the time he was shot by Sergeant Corbett, and a large knife, with blood on it, supposed to be the one which Booth cut Major Rathbone with in the theatre box on the night of the murder of President Lincoln, and which was found on Booth's body, have been brought to the city. The carbine and knife are now in the possession of Colonel Baker, at his office.

Booth had upon his person some bills of exchange, but only about $175 in Treasury notes.

The bills of exchange, which are for a considerable amount, found on Booth's person, were drawn on banks in Canada in October last. About that time Booth was known to have been in Canada.

It is now thought that Booth's leg was fractured in jumping from the box in Ford's Theatre upon the stage, and not by the falling of his horse while endeavoring to make his escape, as was at first supposed.

The Captured Assassins.

The greatest curiosity is manifested to view the body of the murderer Booth, which yet remains on the gun-boat in the stream off the Navy Yard. Thousands of persons visited the yard to-day in hopes of getting a glimpse at the murderer's remains, but none were allowed to enter who were not connected with the yard. The wildest excitement has existed here all day, and regrets are expressed that Booth was not taken alive.

Sergeant Corbett.

It is said that in pulling the trigger upon Booth, he sent up an audible petition for the soul of the criminal.

The pistol used by Corbett was the regular large-sized cavalry pistol. He was offered a thousand dollars this morning for the weapon with its five undischarged loads.

An Autopsy.

This afternoon, Surgeon-General Barnes, with an assistant, held an autopsy on the body of Booth.

Booth not in Rebel Uniform.

It now appears that Booth an Harold had on clothing which was originally of some other color than the Confederate grey, but being faded and dusty, presented that appearance.

Booth's Mistress.

The news of Booth's death reached the ears of his mistress while she was in a street car, which caused her to weep bitterly, and drawing a photograph likeness of the murderer from her pocket, kissed it fondly several times.

The Demeanor of Harold.

Harold, thus far, has evaded every effort to be drawn into conversation by those who have necessarily come in contact with him since his capture, but his outward appearance indicates that he begins to realize the position in which he is placed, and that there is no hope for his escape from the awful doom that certainly awaits him. His relations and friends, in this city, are in the greatest distress over the disgrace that he has brought upon himself.

Bowling Green.

Bowling Green, near which place Booth was killed, is a post village, the capital of Caroline county, Virginia, on the road from Richmond to Fredericksburg, forty-five miles north of the former, and is situated in a fertile and healthy region. It contains two churches, three stores, two mills and about three hundred inhabitants.

DEATH SCENE OF THE ASSASSIN.

Map Showing the Place where Booth was Killed and Harold Captured.

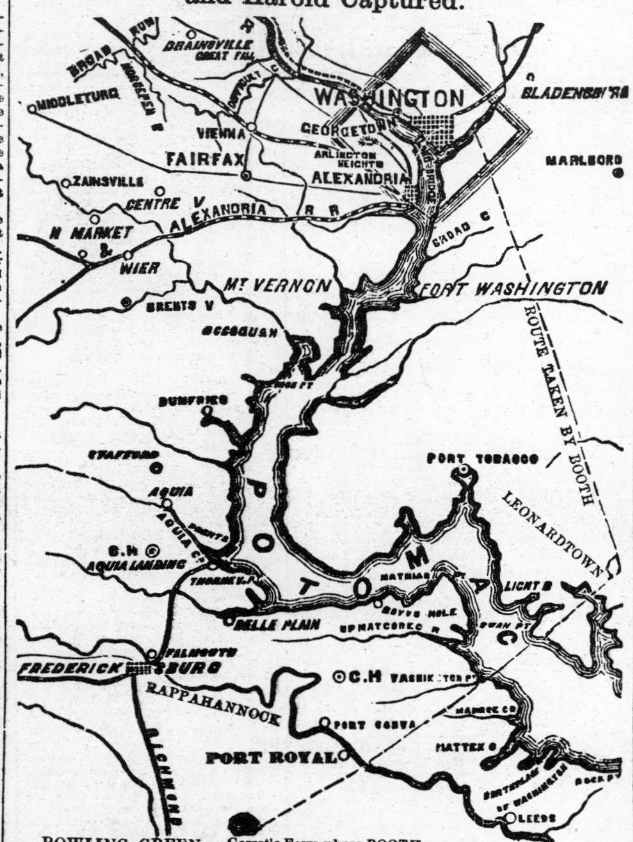

Garret's Farm where BOOTH was shot and HAROLD captured.

STONEMAN'S MOVEMENTS IN NORTH CAROLINA

KNOXVILLE, April 27.—Since the last intelligence from General Stoneman's command, the following is a summary of what it has accomplished:—

One portion of the command, under Colonel Palmer, moved down the Catawba River, dispersing parties going southwest from Johnston's army. He captured upwards of two thousand prisoners, and two pieces of artillery, and amongst other things destroyed, was the immense railroad bridge over the Catawba River, eleven hundred and twenty-five feet long, and sixty feet high. Then learning that a general armistice had been entered into between Sherman and Johnston, Colonel Palmer ceased operations.

The other portion of the command, under General Gillem, attacked and routed a Rebel force under Major-General McCowan, at Morgantown, taking one piece of artillery, and afterwards forcing the pass through the Blue Ridge held by the Rebel forces under General Martin, taking six guns, and could have captured or destroyed the whole force, had General Gillem not been met by General Martin, with a flag-of-truce, and bearing a letter from General Sherman, countersigned by General Johnston, and directed to General Stoneman, ordering a general suspension of hostilities, and a withdrawal of the forces under General Stoneman.

THE PRESIDENTIAL OBSEQUIES.

The Remains at Buffalo.

BUFFALO, N. Y., April 17.—The train was met at the depot in this city by a large concourse of people, and the funeral party were entertained at Bloomer's dining rooms by the city authorities.

The procession formed between seven and eight o'clock, and marched to St. James Hall, the coffin being prominently in view on the funeral car. The body was taken from the car and deposited on a dais in the hall.

In the gallery, outside the canopy, was the St. Cecilia Society, an amateur musical association, who, as the remains were brought in, sang with deep pathos, "Rest, spirit, rest."

The society then placed a heart composed of white flowers at the head of the coffin, and the public were then admitted.

BUFFALO, April 27.—As erroneous statements have been made in the press, it is necessary to say, on the authority of the embalmer and undertaker, that no perceptible change has taken place in the body of the late President since we left Washington. In that city the physicians removed a part of the brain only for the autopsy, but this was replaced so that no part of the body whatever is now deficient.

The remains were visited throughout the day, from 9·30 A. M. until 8 P. M., by an immense number of persons. The arrangements generally are pronounced better than elsewhere on the route. During the morning an anchor, made of camelias, was presented by a party of ladies from the Unitarian Church of Buffalo, and was laid on the coffin.

A cross of white flowers was also laid upon his coffin at the request of Major-General Dix. The procession, with the remains, left St. James' Hall at 8·45 P. M., escorted to the depot by military, followed by a large crowd. The depot was surrounded by persons anxious to get a last view of the coffin as the train left about 11 P. M. for Cleveland.

Treatment of a Traitor at Harrisburg.

Special Despatch to the Inquirer.

HARRISBURG, April 27.—On last Saturday week, when the news reached here of the assassination of the President, a man on the street gloried in the fact, and made a most obscene remark in regard to the corpse. The people desired to treat the man in a summary manner, but a guard of soldiers took possession of him. This afternoon he was marched through the principal streets to the tune of the Rogue's March, holding in his hand a board, with this inscription:—"William Young, a traitor too cowardly to fight for the Rebels, ejects his vulgar venom by insulting the remains of our dead President."

The soldiers desired to ride him on a rail, but the officers would not allow it.

On being released he was followed by a large crowd yelling and hooting at him, treating him rather roughly.

NORTH CAROLINA.

Sherman-Johnston Conference.

DETAILS OF THE INTERVIEW.

A Stormy Scene Between Kilpatrick and Wade Hampton.

THE REBEL STAFF COLD AND SUPERCILIOUS.

Torpedo Left on the Railroad by the Rebs.

GRAND REVIEWS OF THE TROOPS

OLD TECUMSEH AS A REVIEWING OFFICER.

A Description of Some of His Bright Particular Stars.

SHERMAN DESTROYING REBEL POWDER MILLS

Railway Travel Under the Rebel Rule.

Special Correspondence of the Inquirer.

RALEIGH, April 22.

The Conference

Between Sherman and Johnston, with its attendant incidents, was kept private. Now that the main features of the conditions agreed upon have been promulgated to the army, and the results of the carefully guarded interviews made known to the entire community, a brief *resume* of the circumstances and preliminaries incident to the meeting of the two great chieftains may be made public. A historic interest will ever surround this meeting of Sherman and Johnston.

Preparatory

To treating for terms our forces explored the railroad as far as within our lines. This act was performed under the direction of Colonel E. K. Kirby. On Saturday night, the 15th inst, the locomotive Walter Raleigh was slowly backing up the track of the North Carolina Railroad. The engine was manipulated by an engineer who, two days before, was in the service of the Rebels.

To prevent him rushing his engine into ambuscades or into unpleasant proximity to Rebel pickets, Colonel Kirby kept his revolver, loaded, capped and cocked, close to the head of the engineer. Ten miles from Morrisville Station, the tender of the engine, which was in advance, as the locomotive was backing, struck a torpedo, which exploded with a report loud as a six-pounder. The force of the explosion threw the tender from the track, and caused the occupants of the tender to throw impromptu somersaults through the air. No one, fortunately, was severely injured. A negro fireman, who sat on the front edge of the tender, was most severely injured of the party, sustaining the fracture of a leg. The tender was bent out of straight into curved lines. It was, however, replaced upon the track; and the engine run back to Gage's Station.

During Sunday, the 16th, the track was more successfully explored. The telegraph was repaired and put in working order to Durham Station.

The Interview.

Early on Monday morning, the 17th instant, General Sherman, attended by his staff and Colonel Kirby, of General Blair's staff, proceeded up the road to Durham Station. On reaching our cavalry line, they were joined by General Kilpatrick and his staff. The engine then proceeded to Durham. At this point General Kilpatrick had saddle-horses in waiting for the party. They rode five miles from Durham, and pulled up at an unpretending one-story frame house. The only attraction about this diminutive cot was, that it was embowered in umbrageous trees.

Generals Joseph E. Johnston and Wade Hampton, accompanied by a bevy of staff officers, were already on the ground. Generals Sherman and Johnston, alone and unattended, at once entered the cottage. They remained in conference for two hours. What passed between the Generals they alone can make known.

Outside the Cottage

Remained Generals Kilpatrick, Wade Hampton, and the staff officers. General Kilpatrick approached General Hampton and greeted him cordially. General Hampton replied coldly and superciliously. He told General Kilpatrick, "that for himself he was not disposed to give up the war, that he would never fraternize with us, but would retaliate with torch and sword, for the war that we had waged. He found a great deal of fault with our method of carrying on war. For a time General Kilpatrick was disposed to be conciliatory. But the supercilious taunts of Hampton, at last roused "Kill," and he retorted in more fitting terms to the groundless reproaches of the persistent Rebel. Hampton boasted of the surprise he carried out against General Kilpatrick's camp near Fayetteville. Though he did not allude to the champion captured in Georgia. The cavalry chiefs parted in no very amicable mood.

The Staff Officers

Of Wade Hampton imitated the boorish and senseless conduct of their sulky leader. General Sherman's officers were disposed to be sociable and friendly, but all their overtures were haughtily refused. They answered in monosyllables to direct questions, kept themselves together, and repelled all courteous intercourse. The Adjutant-General of Hampton, Captain McClellan, said to be a relative of George B. McClellan, delivered himself of some bitter remarks against the Union and its defenders. Two officers of General Johnston's *suite* proved an honorable exception in this ungentlemanly conduct of the Rebel staff officers. These two gentlemen, whose names we suppress from motives of delicacy, conducted themselves as officers and gentlemen, which is far more than can be said for their companions. The parting between the officers of the respective staffs was consequently very cool and distant.

Wade Hampton

Is a man of fine physique. He stands full six feet in height, and is symmetrically proportioned for strength and manly grace. He is of a decided dark complexion, has regular features, wears a full beard and moustache of glossy black. His black hair is, contrary to the prevailing Southern custom, cropped short. His dark eyes have a deep penetrating glance. From his appearance we would judge him to be forty.

Continued on the Eighth Page.

The Daily Picayune.

VOLUME XXIX. NEW ORLEANS, SATURDAY MORNING, APRIL 29, 1865. NUMBER 82.

Citizens' Mutual Insurance Company,

Office—No. 3 Carondelet street.

Amount of Premiums for the year ending 30th November, 1864 .... $158,148 39

Amount of Assets on the 30th November, 1864 303,890 06

Interests on Scrip payable on and after the second Monday in February, 1864.

OMER GAILLARD, President.

Hy. CASTAREDE, Secretary.

—TRUSTEES—

J. Lorber, Jas. A. White,
A. H. D. Méza, Ar. Miltenberger,
J. Lemore, Jno. Gauche,
Dque. Bouligny, J. A. Stouse,
A. Bidault, A. Verlotn DeGruy
A. Marquez, Avendano,
O. Gaillard Ja19, '65—1

Office of the Crescent Mutual Insurance Company.

NEW ORLEANS, January 6, 1865.

In conformity to ACT No. 176 approved March 17th, 1860, and with the Charter of this Company, public notice is hereby given that uncalled for Certificates of Scrip Dividends and Interest due for over three years are standing in the names of the following persons, and if not demanded by the legal owner or owners within thirty days of this notice from its first publication, will be cancelled and annulled:

NAMES.	Scrip Uncalled for.	Dividends and Interest.
Cammack & Converse		18 00
Cunningham C L	170	13 30
Gardiner & Lea	30	2 10
Harnden's Express	80	1 60
Jacobs F. Dussumier & Co	20	3 60
Keiner & McTeyre	90	1 80
Koch Bernard		81 70
Morgan J. C.		40 50
Morgan & Co., J. C.	30	60
Morrisett James D	30	3 30
Norris, Maul & Co.	60	9 00
Pennywit, Scott & Co		26 00
Pennywit & Co., P		663 90
Rapp John	70	6 90
Saliba J. & Radovitch	50	2 50
Schneider J. C.	[illegible]	1 00
Simmons Henry	[illegible]	2 70
Smith Ralph J	[illegible]	16 80
Titus Augustus	8	2 50
Todd John	60	3 00
Urquhart W & D	60	3 00

The above statement is a just, true and correct transcript from the Books of this Company.

THOS. A. ADAMS, President.

WM. H. RICE, Secretary, pro. tem.

Sworn to and subscribed before me, this the 31st day of December, 1864.

SAMUEL MYERS,

Second Justice of the Peace in and for the Parish of Orleans.

THE CITY OF NEW ORLEANS.

OFFICIAL.

[No. 6286.]

MAYORALTY OF NEW ORLEANS,
City Hall, April 24, 1865.

RESOLVED, That the adjudications for the sale of the contracts for "the cleaning of the paved and unpaved streets, and the repairing of the unpaved streets, and for the repairing and keeping in repair the paved streets," authorized to be sold by City Ordinance No. 6281, as reported by the City Controller, be and the same are hereby accepted.

RESOLVED, That the Mayor be and he is hereby authorized and empowered to enter into contract, by notarial act, with the following parties, to-wit:

For cleaning the paved and unpaved and repairing the unpaved streets of the

First Ward—Geo. Cronan $7,000
Security—John Coleman.
Second Ward—F. F. Trinchard 6,475
Security—W. R. Fish.
Third Ward—W. H. Waters 12,700
Security—W. R. Fish.
Fourth Ward—John Rooney 5,850
Security—S. W. Moore.
Fifth Ward—James McKeon 6,900
Security—M. Woods.
Sixth Ward—John Bietry 6,000
Security—John Wolff.
Seventh Ward—Samuel Plume 5,500
Security—W. Wakefield.
Eighth Ward—Tim. O'Connell 4,600
Security—E. D. White.
Ninth Ward—E. D. White 4,800
Security—Thomas Quilters.
Tenth Ward—Daniel Wilson 4,575
Security—James Stafford.
Eleventh Ward—Daniel Wilson 3,850
Security—James Stafford.

For repairing and keeping in repair the paved streets of the

First Ward—George Cronan 4,700
Security—John Coleman.
Second Ward—P. H. Cummins 5,975
Security—John McRoberts.
Third Ward—John Rooney 3,900
Security—S. W. Moore.
Fourth Ward—James McKeon 2,000
Security—M. Woods.
Fifth Ward—Dennis Cronan 3,000
Security—Mike Gernon.
Sixth Ward—Pat. Lane 2,550
Security—Philip Guelbeck.
Seventh Ward—Daniel Crowley 1,700
Security—E. D. White.
Eighth Ward—Tim. O'Connell 1,600
Security—E. D. White.
Ninth Ward—E. D. White 1,000
Security—Thomas Kavanaugh.
Tenth Ward—John Cronan 900
Security—George Cronan.
Eleventh Ward—Wm. Henry 975
Security—Daniel Wilson.

(Signed) G. BURKE,
Chairman Bureau of Finance.
(Signed) D. S. DEWEES,
Chairman Bureau Streets and Landings.
Approved April 24, 1865.
(Signed) HU. KENNEDY, Mayor.
A true copy. Attest:
ap25—3t D. L. GIBBENS, Sec'y.

STREET COMMISSIONER'S OFFICE,
No. City Hall, New Orleans, April 25, 1865.

Were brought to the Second and Third Districts Pound, corner Orleans and Claiborne streets, as estrays—

One dark brown mare mule, 12 hands high, branded U. C. on the right shoulder and U. on the left hip.

One dark brown mule, 13 hands high, branded U. C. on the left shoulder and C. over it.

One dark brown mule, 13 hands high, branded F. M. on the left shoulder, and

One cart.

Which if not claimed within ten days, and expenses thereon paid, will be sold at public auction at said pound, on Monday, May 18, 1865, at 12 o'clock M.

JOHN PURCELL,
Street Commissioner.

For Comptroller:
ALEXANDER LEVY. ap27—3tin10d

STREET COMMISSIONER'S OFFICE,
No. 7 City Hall, New Orleans, April 21, 1865.

Was brought to the First and Fourth District Pounds, in Market street, between Annunciation and Paccanier streets, as estray—

One Mare Pony about 11 hands high, branded U S on left shoulder and I C on left hip.

Which, if not claimed within ten days, and expenses thereon paid, will be sold at public auction at said Pound on WEDNESDAY, May 3, 1865, at 12 o'clock M. JOHN PURCELL,
Street Commissioner.

For Comptroller:
ALEXANDER LEVY. ap22—3tin10d

STREET COMMISSIONER'S OFFICE,
No. 7 City Hall, New Orleans April 20, 1865.

Was brought to the First and Fourth District Pounds on Market street, between Annunciation and Paccanier streets, as estray—

One dark bay Mare Pony, about 12 hands high, hind fetlocks white, and a white spot on the nose.

Which if not claimed within ten days and expenses thereon paid, will be sold at public auction at said Pound on MONDAY, May 1, 1865, at 12 o'clock M.

JOHN PURCELL,
Street Commissioner.

For Comptroller:
PAUL AUGRAND. ap22—3tin10d

STREET COMMISSIONER'S OFFICE,
No. 7 City Hall, New Orleans, April 15, 1865.

Was brought to the First and Fourth District Pounds, on Market street, between Annunciation and Paccanier streets as estray—

One Stud HORSE, about twelve hands high, left hind fetlock white; no other mark.

Which, if not claimed within ten days and expenses thereon paid, will be sold at public auction at said Pound on THURSDAY, April 27, 1865, at 12 o'clock M

JOHN PURCELL,
Street Commissioner.

For Comptroller:
ALEXANDER LEVY. ap16—3tin10d

The Daily Picayune.

DOUBLE SHEET

ADDITIONAL BY THE MOLLIE ABLE.

FROM SAVANNAH AND HILTON HEAD

PAROLED PRISONERS IN WASHINGTON.

Jeff. Davis and his Plunder.

GEN. GRANT TO GO TO NORTH CAROLINA.

Official Dispatch from Secretary Stanton.

SOUTHERN REFUGEES IN WASHINGTON.

Mr. Lincoln's Remains at Philadelphia.

TROPHIES OF SHERMAN'S EXPEDITION.

DESTRUCTIVE FIRE AT DAYTON.

JAY COOKE'S REPORT.

We give below additional telegraphic intelligence to that issued in our extra of yesterday afternoon, gleaned from the Western papers received by the Mollie Able. We copy principally from the Cairo Evening Times, of the 24th. A great portion of the St. Louis papers' telegrams have heretofore appeared in our columns from other sources:

Savannah and Hilton Head.

NEW YORK, April 24.—The steamer Blackstone, from Hilton Head, 20th, brings Savannah papers of the 19th.

The Savannah Herald, of the 18th, says intelligence was received there on the 15th confirming the news of the fall of Montgomery. The place was evacuated by the rebels and occupied by Federal troops on the 11th. The rebels retreated in the direction of Columbus. Government stores were being removed from Columbus, the fall of which place was expected by next news from Augusta.

A Savannah letter, of the 19th, says the receipt of the intelligence of the sad calamity that had befallen the nation cast the profoundest gloom over the city. Flags are suspended at half-mast, and other emblems of mourning are seen everywhere.

A meeting was held at Hilton Head, at which resolutions condoling with the nation and the family of the deceased, and calling for a most vigorous prosecution of the war, were adopted.

On the 20th seven arrests were made at Hilton Head.

On the receipt of the sad intelligence in Savannah, Gen. Grover requested the papers to withhold it until the next morning, and doubled the guards throughout the city.

Paroled Prisoners, etc.

NEW YORK, April 24.—The Tribune's Washington special says: So many paroled prisoners have arrived there—their former place of residence—that Government will have to take some action to rid the city of their presence. It has been deemed proper to place a guard around the residence of Chief Justice Chase.

About twelve per cent. of the clerks in the Bureau of Desertions have been dismissed as unnecessary.

The name of the dismissed hospital steward, who committed suicide, and was suspected of complicity in the assassination, is George B. Love.

Jeff. Davis and His Plunder—He is Probably Making for Mexico.

WASHINGTON, April 23.—The orders of Gen. Sherman for Gen. Stoneman to withdraw from Salisbury and join him, will probably open the way for Davis to escape to Mexico or Europe with his plunder, which is reported to be very large, including not only the plunder of the Richmond banks, but previous accumulations.

A dispatch received by this department from Richmond says: It is stated here by respectable parties that the amount of specie taken South by Jeff. Davis and his partisans is very large, including not only the plunders of Richmond banks, but previous accumulations. They hope, it is said, to make terms with Gen. Sherman or some other commander by which they will be permitted with their effects, including this gold plunder, to go to Mexico or Europe.

After the Cabinet meeting last night, Gen. Grant started for North Carolina to direct operations against Johnston's army.

Secretary Stanton's Dispatch.

WAR DEPARTMENT, Washington, April 22.—*To Major Gen. Dix:* In a dispatch dated Mobile, April 14, Gen. Canby reports as follows:

We find in Mobile and its defences on the west side of the bay over 1500 guns, a large amount of ammunition, supplies of all kinds, and about 1000 prisoners. Inventories are now being taken and a detailed report will be forwarded as soon as they are completed. The quantity of cotton captured will probably reach 3000 bales.

Gen. Hancock reports that nearly all of Mosby's men have surrendered, including nearly all of his officers, except Mosby himself.

The counties of Prince Charles and St. Mary have been noted for hostilities toward the Government, and its protection of rebel spies and every species of public enemy, and it is now supposed that Booth fled in that direction. If he escapes it will be owing to rebel accomplices.

E. M. STANTON.

Southern Refugees—Military Commands Female Employees.

WASHINGTON, April 23.—All the Southern refugees in Washington will call upon President Johnson on Monday morning.

Publication has been made of certain changes of several officers, including Gen. Halleck to command at Richmond. This is not correct. Gen. Ord remains in command of Virginia as heretofore. Gen. Halleck commands Virginia and North Carolina. Gen. Gilmore remains in command of the Department of the South.

"The female employés of the Treasury Department also called on the President, and some time was spent in hand shaking. Several bouquets were presented to him, one of which had a card accompanying it with the inscription: "May the angels of the Lord encamp around thee."

Mr. Lincoln's Remains at Philadelphia.

PHILADELPHIA, April 24.—The body of President Lincoln remained in state till 1 o'clock this morning. At 3 o'clock the line of march was taken to the Trenton railroad depot. The line consisted of nine elegant cars, provided by the Camden and Amboy Railroad, all tastefully draped. The funeral car last night was additionally decorated, heavy silver fringes being placed at the end of the black coverings of the several pannels, and the festoons being fastened with stars and tassels of similar material. The materials were contributed by the citizens of Philadelphia.

Gov. Parker came on board at Morrisville, with Adjt. Gen. Stockton, Quartermaster Perine, and others of his staff. They were accompanied by United States Senator J. P. Stockton, and were received by Gov. Curtin, of Pennsylvania, who was at Philadelphia.

Gen. Sherman's Trophies.

KNOXVILLE, TENN., April 23.—Among the tropies of Sherman's expedition are twelve battle flags and banners, one old New York flag found in the house of a loyal citizen. Salisbury, the famous pen where many unfortunate Union prisoners pined their lives away, was burned to the ground. A few New York prisoners, skeletons of their former selves. Almost all of them died on their way to Knoxville. They preferred to die under the shade of the stars and stripes than to be left in the loathsome hospitals of Salisbury.

Fire at Dayton, Ohio.

CINCINNATI, April 24.—Houston Hall, at Dayton, Ohio, was destroyed by fire this morning. Loss about $70,000. Insured for $25,000.

Jay Cooke's Report.

PHILADELPHIA, April 23.—Jay Cooke reports the sale of the 7-30 loan yesterday at $110,800. The largest Western subscription was $106,000, from Chicago; the largest Eastern $500,000, from New York. Total for five days this week, $15,209,700.

The Future Business of the Federal Armies.—The New York Times thus refers to the probable future use of the Federal armies:

We suppose that the Army of the Potomac will be divided up by the lieutenant general into bodies of some magnitude, and sent to occupy and garrison, for a time, the various important positions in Virginia, the Carolinas and Georgia; and the army of Sherman will, for a period, find like employment.

Sherman's great marches from November to April proved to us that the rebels have no army, and no material for an army, in the State of Georgia; that they have no army, and no material for an army in South Carolina; that, excluding Johnston, they have no army and no material for an army in North Carolina; and we know that they have no army, and, since Lee's men are all under parole, no material for an army, in Virginia. We know that, besides the garrison at Mobile, the rebels have no troops or military material in Alabama; that they have none in Mississippi; they have none anywhere in Tennessee. Kirby Smith has a good many men west of the Mississippi, but we should like to know if, under present circumstances, they propose to fight for the defunct Southern Confederacy.

Thus it is almost impossible that we should have any more fighting of any consequence on this side of the Mississippi River. Lee's men will all go home, in accordance with the terms of Gen. Grant; but even if they were not under parole, we may be very sure that they will fight no more.

Thus, in the future, the Army of the Potomac and the army of Sherman will be employed mainly as conservators of peace in the South. The term of service of a good number will expire before the close of this year; and of a very large number before the close of the next year. If Government finds it has absolutely no use for the men, it can disband at its pleasure.

A Cause for Rejoicing.—The New York Journal of Commerce, of the 15th inst., says the indefinite postponement of the draft was the great topic of rejoicing and congratulation yesterday. It was a practical manifestation of the coming of peace which all could appreciate. Drafted men were in a state of high delight; while substitute brokers and bounty jumpers lamented that their occupation was gone. The Recruiting Committee felt so good that they ordered a salute of one hundred guns in the Park. The barracks will be torn down and the materials sold for old lumber. Major Dodge, the Provost Marshal, came down gracefully in a special circular stating that the "business of recruiting and drafting will be discontinued in this district until further orders." He was at Washington at the time, and telegraphed the above announcement. All operations, of every description, under the draft, came to an end yesterday.

APPOINTMENTS FOR NEW ORLEANS.—We have seen a part of this announcement (that relating to the Collectorship) going the rounds of the Western papers, for a day or two past, but could not find it stated on any known authority. In this shape it appears in a special telegraph dispatch to the Boston Journal, from "Perley," the usually accurate Washington correspondent of that paper:

Hon. Wm. Pitt Kellogg, late Chief Justice of Nebraska, has been appointed Collector of Customs at New Orleans, vice Dennison, removed. Judge Daley, late delegate from Nebraska, and Judge Cutler of New Orleans, have been appointed Deputy Collectors of Customs of that city. A. T. Stone has been appointed Surveyor of the port of New Orleans.

☞ The Keans were to open at the Broadway Theatre, in New York, an engagement of eleven nights, on Easter Monday. Mr. Wood, the manager, announced this as their "first appearance in America!" Considering that each of them has played some four engagements all over the United States, years ago, this may be considered as a lively draft upon the credulity of the present generation.

TWO DAYS LATER FROM THE NORTH.

SURRENDER OF GEN. JOHNSTON.

TERMS BETWEEN SHERMAN AND JOHNSTON.

DISAPPROVAL OF PROCEEDINGS.

SURRENDER OF MOSBY.

GENERAL LEE'S PAROLED MEN.

BOOTH, THE ASSASSIN.

JEFF. DAVIS.

SENTENCE OF CHICAGO CONSPIRATORS.

ANOTHER PIRATE FITTING OUT.

[From Our Extra of Yesterday.]

The arrival of the Mollie Able this afternoon brings us the Cairo Times of the 24th. We subjoin the following:

WASHINGTON, April 22.—As reports have been in circulation for some time of a correspondence of Gens. Sherman and Johnston, as to the understanding or base of what was agreed upon between those two generals, and the results of which are as follows: The basis of agreement made this 18th day of April, 1865, near Duncharm's Station, in the State of North Carolina, by and between Gen. Jo. Johnston, commanding the Confederate forces, and Gen. Wm. T. Sherman, commanding the army of the United States in North Carolina; both present:

1. The Confederate armies now in the field to maintain their State guards until notice is given by the commanding general of either one to its opponents, reasonable time, say four hours, allowed.

2. The Confederate armies in existence to be disbanded and consolidated in their several State capitals, there to deposit their arms and public property in the State arsenals, and each officer and man to execute an agreement to cease all acts of war, and abide by the action of both State and Federal authority. The number of arms and munitions of war to be reported to the chief of ordnance at Washington City, subject to the further action of the Congress of the United States, and in the meantime to be used solely to maintain peace and order within the borders of the States respectively.

3. The recognition of the Executive of the United States of the several State Governments, in their officers and legislators, in taking the oath prescribed by the constitution of the United States. And where conflicting State Governments have resulted from the war, the legitimacy of all shall be submitted to the Superior Court of the United States.

4. The reestablishment of all Federal courts in all the States, with powers as defined by the constitution and laws of Congress.

5. The people and inhabitants of all the States to be guaranteed, so far as the Executive can, their political rights and franchise, as well as their rights of persons and property, as defined by the constitution of the United States and of the States respectively.

6. The Executive authority of the Government of the United States not to disturb any of the people by reason of the late war, so long as they remain in peace and quiet, and abstain from all acts of armed hostilities, and obey the laws in existence at the place of their residence.

7. In general terms, war to cease, general amnesty, so far as the Executive power of the United States can command, or on condition of the disbandment of the Confederate armies, and the distribution of arms and the resumption of peaceful pursuits by officers of and heretofore composing the said armies, and not being empowered by our respective principles to fulfill other terms, we individually and officially pledge ourselves to obtain the necessary authority to carry out the above programme.

W. T. SHERMAN,
Major Gen. Com'g U S. A. in N. Carolina.
JOE JOHNSTON,
Gen. Com'g C. S. A in North Carolina.

This proceeding of Gen. Sherman's was disapproved for the following, among other reasons:

1. It was an exercise of authority not vested in Gen. Sherman, and he (Johnston) knew that he (Sherman) had no authority to enter into any such arrangement.

2. It was a practical acknowledgement of the rebel Government.

3. It undertook to establish the rebel State Government, that had been over thrown at the sacrifice of many thousand loyal lives, and an immense treasury expended.

3. By the restoration of the rebel authorities in the respective States they would be enabled to re-establish slavery.

5. It might furnish a ground of responsibility by the Federal Government to pay the rebel debt.

6. It would put in dispute the existence of loyal State Government, and the new State of Western Virginia, which has been recognized by every department of the United States Government.

7. It practically abolishes the confiscation laws, and relieves rebels of every degree who have slaughtered our people.

8. It gave terms that had been repeatedly and solemnly rejected by President Lincoln.

9. It formed no basis of true and lasting peace, but relieved the rebels from the pressure of our victories and left them in a condition to renew their efforts to overthrow the United States Government, and subdue the loyal States whenever their strength was recruited.

All the Southern refugees in Washington will call upon President Johnson on Monday.

Surrender of Mosby.

NEW YORK, April 24.—The Times's Washington special says that Mosby secured a basis of agreement similar to that obtained by Johnston.

A person who was present at the consultation, informs the correspondent that the memorandum or basis of agreement was drawn up by Gen. Chapman, in the presence of twenty-two Federal and twenty rebel officers, and provided that Mosby should surrender upon the same terms as Johnston. If the latter should surrender, that two days armistice would be allowed to submit the agreement to Gen. Hancock for his approval; that if Gen. Hancock approved the terms, then ten days were to be allowed Mosby to get a reply from Johnston, and in the meantime no skirmishing should take place in Fauquier and Loudon counties; that if Johnston failed to surrender or get whipped, Mosby would surrender upon the terms upon which Lee surrendered.

Depredations of Gen. Lee's Men.

The World's Washington special says:

A letter from Burkeville, Va., states that some of the paroled men from Lee's army have been detected in tearing up the railroad between that place and Richmond. The parties were not caught, but if arrested they are liable to be tried and immediately shot for a violation of their parole.

The same special says that the last remnants of Lee's army, composed of some dozen regiments and one old ambulance, had, the day before, taken their melancholy departure home.

A good many of Lee's old officers declare that they can never live in the South or in the North, and that they would either go to Europe or to Mexico, though they prefer to join the North and enforce the Monroe doctrine on the latter.

Booth, the Assassin.

NEW YORK, April 23.—Circumstances which have come to the knowledge of the Government, render it nearly certain that Booth's horse fell with him, on Friday night, the 14th inst., and it is believed caused a fracture of his leg. It is also reported that he has divested himself of his moustache. The likeness of Booth published in Harper's Weekly is said to be correct. If Booth is lying wounded, the rewards offered and the detestation of his crime by all loyal citizens will soon bring him to light.

Jeff. Davis.

NEW YORK, April 23.—The Suffolk, Va., correspondent of the Herald states that rebel officers who have arrived there report that the news of Lee's surrender reached Jeff. Davis at Danville three days after his proclamation. Jeff. Davis stated that if he was hard pushed he should go to Texas, where he was sure he could raise an army around him and make another stand, and that he should never leave the limits of the Confederacy.

Chicago Conspirators.

CINCINNATI, April 23.—Considerable snow fell here yesterday and last night.

The Military Commission have passed the following sentences in the case of the Chicago conspirators:

Buckner, Senorris, Vincent and Marmaduke are acquitted, and will be discharged after taking the oath of allegiance. Charles and R. T. Semmes are found guilty of all specifications and charges, and are sentenced, the former to five and the latter to three years hard labor in the Ohio Penitentiary. The sentence against Greenfield and Daniels is not yet promulgated.

Mr. Seward.

SURGEON GENERAL'S OFFICE, WASHINGTON, April 24, 9 A. M.—*Hon. E. M. Stanton:* I have the honor to report that the Secretary of State is free from pain and stronger this morning. Mr. F. Seward passed a quiet night. Very respectfully, your obedient servant,

J. K. BARNES, Surg. Gen.

A Pirate Fitting Out.

NEW YORK, April 23.—Toronto papers contain an affidavit stating that the notorious McDonald, of that city, together with a member of the Toronto Council, named Dennison, had been discovered preparing a pirate at Collegwood, for plunder upon the lakes.

Gold and Stocks.

NEW YORK, April 23.—Money easier; 5 and 6 per cent. Sterling exchange quiet at 109 1-4 and 109 1-2 for gold and first class bills. Gold a little firmer and quiet, opening at 149 1-4 and closing at 148 3-4. Total exports of specie to-day, $34,646. Government stocks dull and quiet.

Address of the Ohio Delegation to President Johnson.

WASHINGTON, April 21.—This morning a delegation of over one hundred citizens of Ohio called upon President Johnson at the rooms of the Secretary of the Navy, to tender him expressions of their confidence and support upon his assuming the duties of the Executive chair, made vacant by the decease of Mr. Lincoln, our lamented President. These gentlemen, headed by Gov. Brough, proceeded to the rooms of the Secretary.

Gov. Brough said:

Mr. President—I have been requested by a small body of my constituents to present them to you this morning, in order that they may tender to you the assurance of their support and confidence in this hour of trial and labor. I am aware, sir, that the pressure of this presentation is severe upon you, yet I could not forego the request. We come to you with the assurance, as I have before said, of entire confidence in your guidance of the cause committed to your hands. We say to you frankly, that we sincerely and earnestly mourn the loss that has fallen on the country, by which you have been elevated to the position you occupy, but we beg to assure you that in our tears there is no bitterness or unkindness towards yourself.

In our sorrow there is no shadow of fear or apprehension that the banner of our country will fail to be borne in your hands with the same courage, the same fearlessness, the same integrity and honesty of purpose, that distinguished our leader so lately fallen. We do not come to ask of you any pledges or guarantees for the future. We do not come to ask any manifestations of the line of policy which it would probably be futile for you to attempt at this time to carry out, and which altered circumstances may entirely change or remodel. We simply come to say that we have an abiding faith that the sacred purpose of government will be carried out by you.

We come to congratulate you upon your assumption of the power of the country, not because we have forgotten the melancholy event that produced it, but because we feel that the vital principle of our Government is illustrated in the change so quietly and harmoniously made under the workings of our constitution. We come to say to you that we only seek that this rebellion shall be entirely crushed—that with rebellion its seeds and patent cause shall be annihilated—that the constitution and the laws shall be once more made to resume their places over the people of the country, and to suggest to you that the struggle has been as bloody and so terrible, so mournful in its consequences, so severe on the people of this land, that we shall not feel satisfied with the truth of our constitution and our laws, unless in its record we have some guarantee that such a rebellion shall not occur again, unless that history which records the rise and fall of this rebellion, shall, in its closing pages, present to the people of the land such an example and such a record that no man in future time, while that record lives, shall dare to raise his hand against the life of our nation, for the destruction of the best Government that God ever gave to man.

We do not ask this in any spirit of revenge—we do not ask that any monuments shall be raised to our dead leader, bearing inscriptions of the annihilation of those who inaugurated this great contest—but we simply ask it in the name of the Government which God has given us for our protection, and which has shed nothing but blessings upon the people from the date of its formation to the present day.

The State of Ohio, therefore, greets you and assures you that the same confidence, energy and vigilance with which she came to your support last fall for the second office of the Government will be extended to you throughout all your exertions while you occupy the position conferred upon you.

Reply of President Johnson.

President Johnson replied at length. The following are the leading points of his speech:

Respected Sirs—I might have adopted all that you have said on this occasion and present it as mine. I respond most cordially and endorse every sentiment you have uttered, and might thus conclude what I have to say in a much better manner than I could otherwise express it. This sad calamity, the affecting occurrence of the assassination of the President of the United States, is not more deeply felt by any one than myself, especially so while I occupy the position I do—being thrown into it by this sad event.

In entering upon the discharge of the duties that are imposed upon me in the office thus conferred, I feel and know the responsibility, and have on various occasions felt, as it were, overwhelmed, and I stand before you to-day embarrassed exceedingly as to how the responsibility shall be fulfilled. Hence the importance and value of the encouragement and support that you give here to-day.

The lack of that support may paralyze the most courageous, but the encouragement and countenance of an intelligent people is calculated to make even a coward courageous and to win merit in the discharge of his duties.

* * * * *

I cannot but say—and the saying it is a mere repetition of what has been expressed before—that the time has come with this Government when crime shall be understood. We are taught in all the States, and even in the courts of the United States, that the commission of various offences are crimes. Arson is a crime, burglary is a crime, murder is a crime. The time has come when the people should be educated and taught to understand that treason is a crime; [applause,] and not only a crime, but the highest of all crimes.

We look upon the assassination of the President, this diabolical and fiendish act which has been recently committed, as the highest crime, and the mind cannot conceive the penalty commensurate with it. It is a deed for which the human mind cannot invent a penalty severe enough. [Applause.] The assassins, in the garb and shape of treason, have lifted their impious arms against the Government under which they live. I will say, in this connection, in reference, as you have just remarked, to my future policy, that if my past course upon various public questions that have come up, and especially since this rebellion commenced, is any indication or evidence to you of what my future will be, any professions now made must be unnecessary. So far as regards my action in the disposition or winding up of the great drama, my past life must be taken as some indication of my future. In the progress of this question, in bringing it to a close, when justice is meted out and it becomes necessary to exercise mercy and clemency, we shall be sure to discriminate and ascertain which is mercy, because mercy is sometime misconceived and exercised improperly. If it is right and proper to take away the life of one individual for destroying that of another, what shall be done with those who destroy the life of the nation? Treason must be punished as the highest crime known to law. Some have committed treason, technically. Thousands and thousands have been taken from their homes for one cause and another; sometimes by conscription, sometimes by force of public opinion, sometimes misled by leaders. I would say, in the exercise of mercy, try to make the proper discrimination, visiting the penalties of treason on the conscious, intelligent, misleading traitors, and extending leniency to the great mass of the deceived. [Applause.]

Gen. Sherman to the North Carolina Farmers.—An application from certain North Carolina farmers to Gen. Sherman, for horses or mules for farming purposes, elicited the subjoined reply:

HEADQ'S MIL. DIV. OF MISSISSIPPI,
In the Field, April 4, 1865.

Messrs. Sutton and others, Mosely Hall, North Carolina:

Gentlemen—I cannot undertake to supply horses, or to encourage peaceful industry in North Carolina, until the State shall perform some public act, showing that, as to her, war is over.

I sympathize with the distress of families, but can not undertake to extend relief to individuals.

Very respectfully, your ob't serv't,
W. T. SHERMAN,
Major Gen. Commanding.

☞ The United States Mint has commenced the coinage of the recently authorized three cent piece. It is about the size of an English sixpence, the color of lead, and much of that dull appearance. It is a mixture of copper and nickel.

[New York Journal of Commerce.

The New-York Times.

VOL. XIV......NO. 4242. NEW-YORK, SATURDAY, APRIL 29, 1865. PRICE FOUR CENTS

JOHNSTON SURRENDERS

Gen. Grant Puts an End to the Sherman Truce.

The Rebels Give Up the Cause of Jeff. Davis.

They Surrender on the Same Terms Granted to Lee.

All the Rebel Troops East of Alabama Disbanded.

Substantial Close of the War East of the Mississippi.

WAR DEPARTMENT, WASHINGTON, D. C., April 28—3 P. M.

Maj.-Gen. Dix:

A dispatch from Gen. GRANT, dated at Raleigh, 10 P. M., April 26, just received by this department, states that "JOHNSTON surrendered the forces in his command, embracing all from here to the Chattahoochee, to Gen. SHERMAN, on the basis agreed upon between LEE and myself for the Army of Northern Virginia."

EDWIN M. STANTON, Secretary of War.

DISPATCH TO THE ASSOCIATED PRESS.

FORTRESS MONROE, Thursday, April 27, via BALTIMORE, Friday, April 28.

A steamer arrived here this morning, from Morehead City, bringing advices from Newbern, that Gen. GRANT has effectually put an end to the armistice agreed upon between Gen. SHERMAN and Gen. JOHNSTON.

Gen. GRANT had given Gen. JOHNSTON up to 6 o'clock yesterday (Wednesday) morning to surrender his army. The conditions are unknown.

Gen. GRANT announced that after that hour hostilities would at once be resumed.

To this Gen. JOHNSTON is said to have replied that if JEFFERSON DAVIS and the leading general officers of the Confederacy were pardoned, and permission given them to leave the country, he would be authorized to accept the terms proposed.

The Terms of Johnston's Surrender.

As the terms of surrender accorded to the rebel Gen. JOHNSTON are the same as those dictated to Gen. LEE, we refresh the reader's recollection by a republication of Gen. GRANT's note of the 9th inst.:

APPOMATTOX COURT-HOUSE, April 9.

Gen. R. E. Lee:

In accordance with the substance of my letter to you, of the 8th inst., I propose to receive the surrender of the Army of Northern Virginia on the following terms, to wit: Rolls of all the officers and men to be made in duplicate; one copy to be given to any officer designated by me, the other to be retained by such officers as you may designate. The officers to give their undivided paroles not to take up arms against the Government of the United States until properly exchanged, and each company or regiment commander sign a like parole for the men of their commands; the arms, artillery and public property to be packed, stacked and turned over to the officers appointed by me to receive them. This will not embrace the side arms of the officers, nor their private horses or baggage. This done, each officer and man will be allowed to return to their homes, not to be disturbed by the United States authorities so long as they observe their parole and the laws in force where they may reside. Yours, respectfully,

U. S. GRANT, Lieutenant-General.

BOOTH'S FATE.

PARTICULARS OF HIS CAPTURE AND DEATH.

Account of his Last Moments—His Sufferings and His Last Words.

Special Dispatch to the New-York Times.

WASHINGTON, Friday, April 28.

An unusual interest is manifested in hearing the details of the scenes and incidents in the capture and death of BOOTH, and especially in the circumstances from the time Col. BAKER's assistants approached the house of GARRETT, until the closing scene which ended with the death of the assassin. As yet these details have not been published in connected order, but after considerable trouble and labor, I have obtained from Lieut. L. B. BAKER a minute and exact statement of all the circumstances, from the time he and Col. CONGER, with a detachment of cavalry under command of Lieut. DOHERTY, approached the dwelling of GARRETT until they left the same with the dead body of BOOTH in charge. The other parties agree with Lieut. BAKER in the facts here stated, but inasmuch as the latter was present and with BOOTH continuously from the time he was shot until he died, and saw and heard everything that was done or said during that period, his statement is deemed the best authority. Besides this, it should be known that Lieut. BAKER is a gentleman of intelligence and a very close observer.

The party having arrived in the vicinity of GARRETT's house, moved cautiously up and surrounded it. The old man, GARRETT, came out of the kitchen door and asked, "What's this?" He was directed to light a candle, and he would be told; he went in to obey the order, and, in the meantime, Col. CONGER stationed a small guard near the barn. BAKER went into the house, and the old man soon joined him with a candle. BAKER caught him by the shoulder, holding a pistol near his head, saying, "I want to know where these two men are that were here this afternoon." The old man said he didn't know. BAKER said, "They are here, and if you don't bring them, I'll blow your brains out." The old man said they had gone to the woods in the afternoon when the cavalry passed (meaning BAKER's party.) BAKER again threatened to take GARRETT's life. At this moment CONGER returned. At the same instant GARRETT's son, who appeared to have been listening outside, entered the room, dressed in Confederate uniform. The son said, "Father, we had better tell them all." CONGER presented a pistol to young GARRETT's head and threatened to shoot him if he did not speak the truth. Young GARRETT then offered to conduct the parties to the barn where he said they were concealed. As they approached the barn they met another son of GARRETT, also dressed in Confederate uniform. The whole cavalry force had now surrounded the barn. BAKER told young GARRETT he must go in and bring out the arms of those men, and deliver them over. He hesitated, but finally said he would do it. He took the keys and unlocked the door. The barn was an old-fashioned building, thirty by forty feet, nearly empty; had in it some straw, hay, and farming utensils. GARRETT went in and soon returned, saying they refused to give up their arms, and had threatened to shoot him, and he had therefore come out. He locked the door and gave the keys to BAKER. CONGER, BAKER and DOHERTY held conference, and concluded to make BOOTH and HARROLD do one of two things, either put their arms in the hands of GARRETT (in whose custody they were found) and surrender, or they would fire the barn and the thing would end in bonfire and shooting match.

BAKER was to make these propositions. BAKER went up and addressed the parties in the barn, stating what he had concluded to do, telling them we had come to take them prisoners, and would treat them as prisoners, and would give them five minutes to consider. A voice from the inside, which afterward was found to be BOOTH, "Who are you, and what do you want of me?"

BAKER—We want you, and intend to take you.

BOOTH—This is a hard case. It may be that I am to be taken by my friends.

After some further conversation, he seemed to be convinced that he was surrounded, and said:

"Give me a chance for my life. I am a cripple, with but one leg. Withdraw your men one hundred yards, and I'll come out and fight you."

BAKER—We did not come to fight you, but to take you prisoner. You must give up your arms and surrender.

BOOTH asked time to consider, which was granted. A low conversation was heard going on between BOOTH and his companion. We could distinguish BOOTH's voice saying, "Go away from me, you d—d coward; leave me now, will you, you d—d coward."

While this was going on, the cavalry were dismounted and the horses taken out of reach of the contemplated firing.

BOOTH then called out, "Captain, who are you? I could have picked off half a dozen of your men while we were talking, and could have had a half dozen good shots at you."

BAKER—Then give up your arms and surrender. We have come here to take you, not to fight you.

BOOTH—I will never surrender. I shall never be taken alive.

BAKER—If you don't immediately surrender we will immediately set fire to the barn.

BOOTH—Well, my brave boys, prepare a stretcher for me.

A short pause ensued and further low-toned conversation was had inside of the barn. BOOTH directly said: "There is a man here that wants to surrender."

BAKER "Then let him hand out his arms and come out.

Another conversation took place inside, in which HARROLD seemed to be trying to get his arms from BOOTH, who was heard to say: "Go away from me; I don't want anything to do with you."

HARROLD then came to the door and asked to be let out.

BAKER went to the door and told him "No; hand out your arms."

HARROLD replied, "I have no arms."

BAKER said, "You have. You brought a carbine in the ferry-boat. Hand out the carbine and one pistol and you can come out."

BOOTH.—He has no arms. They are all mine. Upon my word as a gentleman he has no arms. They all belong to me.

BAKER opened the door a short distance, and HARROLD put out both hands. BAKER took hold of them, brought HARROLD out, and handed him over to DOHERTY, and immediately shut the door and locked it.

Col. CONGER went to the side of the barn, and drawing a small wisp of hay from the crack, set it on fire and thrust it back, and immediately the hay and straw inside caught and lighted up the barn as light as day.

The first seen of BOOTH he was standing near the middle of the barn, leaning on his crutch, with carbine in hand. On seeing the fire he immediately made toward it, dropping his crutch, with the apparent intention of extinguishing the fire or shooting the person who lighted it. When he came near the fire, he hesitated, turned partly around, and his face was seen distinctly by Col. CONGER, who says BOOTH's face was then the picture of despair. He then made toward the main door of the barn with his carbine in one hand and his pistol in the other, and when about the centre of the barn a pistol shot was heard from near the corner of the building.

During this time BAKER was holding the door partially open. Hearing the shot, he opened the door and went in just in time to see BOOTH fall. CONGER, who immediately entered the barn, said, "He has shot himself." BAKER reached the body and clasped BOOTH by the arms, thinking he was probably only wounded, but finding him powerless, with the aid of CONGER, DOHERTY, and two soldiers, he was carried out of the barn and laid upon the grass a short distance from the door. He appeared to be insensible, but by applications of water, and bathing his face and head, he revived, opened his eyes, and made an effort to speak. Col. CONGER placed his ear to BOOTH's mouth, and heard him say, "Tell mother I die for my country."

The heat became so intense that BOOTH was taken to the porch of GARRETT's house. Col. CONGER immediately sent to Port Royal for a surgeon. An hour elapsed before the surgeon arrived, during which time Lieut. BAKER constantly bathed BOOTH's head in ice-water, and placed in his mouth a wet cloth, BOOTH being unable to get his lips to a tumbler, owing to the fact that he could not be raised up.

In the meantime it was discovered that the wound was inflicted by a shot from a pistol in the hands of Sergeant CORBETT, of the Sixteenth New-York Cavalry, the ball passing entirely through his neck, perforating both sides of his shirt collar.

Shortly after BOOTH was laid upon the porch he made an effort to speak. He said, "Tell my mother I died for my country. I did what I thought was for the best." This was said with great difficulty and apparently in the greatest pain. He said two or three times at intervals, "Kill me; kill me;" and by signs indicated that he wanted to cough, and that he wanted CONGER to put his hand on his throat. CONGER did so, but BOOTH did not succeed in coughing.

He seemed now to be failing rapidly, but revived again and said, "My hands." His hands were lying motionless by his side. BAKER raised one of his hands so that BOOTH could see it, and bathed it in ice-water. BOOTH, with great effort, his eyes glaring at the hand, said, "Useless, useless." BAKER let go his hand, which fell powerless by the dying man's side. Again BOOTH sank away, and was fast failing when the surgeon arrived. He examined the wound for some minutes and said BOOTH might live for twenty-four hours; but BOOTH's countenance soon changed, his eyes assuming a glassy appearance. The surgeon then said he thought he was dying.

About this time Col. CONGER left for Washington, with orders to bring the body, when death ensued, to the boat at Belle Plain. BOOTH seemed now to be in the agonies of death; his face was terribly distorted, his chin drawn down and to one side, his countenance turned bluish, and he seemed to be in the greatest agony. It was soon over, and the surgeon pronounced him dead. He received the death-wound at 3:15, and died at 7:20 o'clock Wednesday morning.

Besides Lieuts. BAKER and DOHERTY, and the soldiers, there were present at the death-scene four or five ladies of the GARRETT family, and old GARRETT and his two sons.

After the Surgeon had pronounced BOOTH dead, Lieut. BAKER took his blanket from his saddle, and in it rolled the body, sewing the blanket up about the feet and head. Previous to this, the Surgeon had tied up the dead man's chin and hands, and closed his eyes. The body was placed on a rickety one-horse buggy wagon, belonging to a free negro near by, and taken thirty miles over the country, to Belle Plain, where the boat *Ida* was in readiness to bring the party to this city.

SECOND DISPATCH.

There is scarcely any abatement to-day in the excitement about the BOOTH capture, and the greatest curiosity exists as to the disposition of the body, all sorts of rumors are afloat, by some it is stated, as upon the best authority, that the family of BOOTH have made a request to be permitted to take the body and deliver it to BOOTH's mother, and that the authorities have consented.

The presence in this city of EDWIN BOOTH and Mr. CLARKE, brother-in law of BOOTH, gives plausibility to this story.

On the other hand it is said that in no event will the government permit the remains to pass into the hands of anybody, but that it will be disposed so that no traces of it can be hereafter found; and again, in corroboration of this, we have statements of persons who claim to have witnessed what they relate, and who say they saw the Surgeon-General take the autopsy that the body was afterward dissected and, in separate pieces, sewed in cloth, with heavy weights, and placed in a small vessel, which made a short, circuitous trip upon the Potomac, and, without landing, returned to the navy-yard, minus the body, again.

Another still inconfirmation of this says he watched his opportunity and secured a part of the body which he now has in his possession.

These are some of the dozens of rumors prevailing here and nearly of them received by the public with credence. Whether there be truth in any of these reports, I am unable to say.

And again it is said a great plot has been discovered, that there have been to-day more than a hundred arrests of well known citizens of this place in consequence of discoveries made since HARROLD was brought here.

Col. BAKER's immense body of detective aids and scouts are coming in by dozens, covered with dust, fatigued and disappointed.

Another report is that as Senator SUMNER was returning to his rooms last night he was shot at by some person who fled and was not recognized. How near the ball of the would-be assassin failed of its object is not known. This morning Mr. SUMNER received an anonymous letter, saying, "It is fortunate for you that my aim was not good."

DISPATCH TO THE ASSOCIATED PRESS.

WASHINGTON, Friday, April 28.

The excitement which prevailed in this city yesterday has considerably subsided. While all regret that the assassin, owing to the rashness of the soldiers engaged in the capture, was not taken alive, they at the same time felt grateful that the murderer had paid the penalty of his crime. Had he been brought to the Washington Navy-yard alive nothing could have withstood the fury of the excited congregated thousands.

What disposition was made of BOOTH's body after the autopsy upon it, it is impossible to ascertain, but that a fitting disposal, in keeping with his ignominious career, was made is certain.

The public breathe more freely, as the great burden which has been on their minds for the past two weeks has been removed.

HARROLD, who has been exhibiting great stoicism since his capture, now appears to seem to realize the awful position in which he is placed, and through the day has given way to frequent fits of weeping. He is quite young, and his appearance would indicate him to be not over twenty. Some time ago he was an applicant for the position of Surgeon's Steward on the Potomac flotilla, but was unsuccessful.

WASHINGTON, Friday, April 28.

Very great curiosity prevails as to the disposition to be made of the remains of BOOTH; but it seems the authorities are not willing to give the wretched carcase the honor of meeting the public gaze, and it will probably be deposited in whatever place promises the most obscurity for them. Yesterday a photographic view of the body was taken before it was taken from the monitor. It was then placed in an ordinary gray army blanket, in which it was sewed up. A plain casket-shaped box, measuring six feet by two, had been previously made in the joiner's shop for the remains, but it was not used.

THE BURIAL OF BOOTH.

CINCINNATI, Friday, April 28.

At a public meeting at Dayton yesterday, it was resolved that the body of BOOTH be taken to mid-ocean and there buried.

THE CASE OF THE "GEORGIAN."

The Examination of "Larry" McDonald—He is Committed for Trial.

From the Toronto Globe, April 27.

WILLIAM LAWRENCE MCDONALD, arrested on suspicion of violating the neutrality laws, was brought up yesterday morning, at the Police Court, before Alderman J. VANCE. The court-room was well filled with Southern sympathizers, among whom was the St. Albans raider Bennett H. Young, and the public generally. The court was delayed for some time, through Godfrey J. Hyams being before the Grand Jury in the case of Bennett H. Young. Mr. Patterson, of the firm of Harrison & Patterson, appeared for the Crown, and Mr. McMichael for the prisoner. The first witness placed in the box was Godfrey J. Hyams, who, after he had been sworn in the usual form on a copy of the New Testament, was asked by Mr. McMichael of what religion he was, to which Hyams replied, "none in particular," and as to his belief said: "I believe in God." Hyams said that he was once a Jew, that he had never abandoned his religion; that he was of whatever religion suited him. He believed in the Jewish and Christian religions alike. There were some things in the Bible that he did not believe, and also some things in the New Testament. Hyams was then sworn on a copy of the Bible, and, being examined by Mr. Patterson, said: I live in York-street in this city, and know the prisoner, McDonald; I have known him for upward of twelve months; he resided, when I first knew him, with his sister on Adelaide-street; his occupation within the past Winter and Fall has been making and preparing munitions of war as agent, under Col. Thompson, of the Confederate States of America; have seen him, during that time, making torpedoes, hand-shells, Greek fire, and other explosive missiles; in the process he used powder, shot, fine coal, and pitch; he had a small furnace and iron boiler in a house on Agnes-street, where those things were made and into which he moved in October last; there were several young men frequented his place; McDonald told me that these munitions and preparations were made to be used upon the steamer *Georgian*, which was to proceed from Collingwood upon raiding expeditions against the United States of America; I have been at McDonald's place on Agnes-street since the 6th day of February last; since that time I have seen in his place hand-shells and implements of war which he told me he was finishing and preparing to take to Collingwood for the steamer *Georgian*; I have been at Collingwood within the last three weeks; I saw McDonald there on the *Georgian*, together with another man named Bates, and others whose names I do not know; munitions of war have been concealed in the house on Agnes-street, deposited under the ground floor, through a small trap-door made for the purpose in the floor of the house.

Cross-examined by Mr. McMichael.—I am a shoemaker by trade; I have been engaged in some of the raids and occupations above mentioned, and by these means became informed of and intimate with the action of McDonald and others; I came from St. Catharines to Toronto in December last; I never saw McDonald in St. Catharines; when I said he left the munitions there for me, I knew it from a letter received from him; I know Mr. John Nasmith, of Toronto; I did not tell him that I received those munitions from Capt. Beall; I was not agent for the Confederate Government; I have seen McDonald's signature to a paper as agent of the Confederate Government; I did not know when I received the letter from McDonald that it was his handwriting; I have since had opportunity of knowing his handwriting, and knew that it was his; I burned the letter; I have seen documents in the hands of Dr. Bates, signed by McDonald as "agent of the Confederate Government;" McDonald told me in Collingwood that to divert suspicion they intended making some trips carrying wheat freight, &c., and then start upon a raid; I was sent to Collingwood by Capt. Prince, who paid my fare; at that time I had given information of the above matters; I have received money from Col. Thompson ($100;) I had volunteered information to Mr Thurston, American Consul here, before going to Collingwood, as mentioned; I asked McDonald for permission to go upon the expedition on board the *Georgian*; I told the facts to Mr. Thurston and Capt. Prince about three or four weeks ago; about two weeks since munitions of war were taken from my house at my instance by Detective McGarry; they were the same brought from St. Catharines; Mr. McDonald told me they were intended for the steamer *Georgian*; when the munitions and implements were taken from the house on Agnes-street; there was no person lying there; when I saw McDonald in this house in February last (since the 6th,) he was occupied in packing up various articles of war, munitions, &c., in small boxes, to take to Collingwood; I saw McDonald in Preston's tobacco factory, York-street, count out in Canadian bills and gold, and give to Dr. Bates, the sum of $18,000; Dr. Bates gave to McDonald a bond for 18,000 acres of land to which I was witness; I asked what was in the bond, and was told this was the substance, and that the land lay in Western Virginia and Mississippi; I believe in the Bible, the existence of God, and a future state of heaven and hell.

By Mr. Patterson.—McDonald frequently told me about the use of the *Georgian*; McDonald told me it was a mistake to have the *Georgian* in the name of a foreigner; he told me that Dr. Bates was making over-charges for the incidental expenses of the *Georgian*, and that the boat had been taken from him; I saw the papers by which the boat was turned over to McDonald.

By Mr. McMichael.—The raids were to be made upon the lakes, and against Detroit and other cities; the *Georgian* was to be confined for the present to the lakes, and afterwards to go farther; I heard McDonald say she would be "a mighty fine thing" for blockade-running.

Robert Spence sworn, said—I am Collector of Customs at Toronto; Collingwood is within my jurisdiction; upon instructions I proceeded thither on the morning of the 4th April last, to investigate matters of suspicious character reported to the government relative to the steamer *Georgian*; I there saw McDonald, who appeared to be in charge; after making precautionary arrangements to prevent the vessel leaving port, I returned to Toronto; I again went out to Collingwood on the 7th April, and found Mr. McDonald, who still appeared to be in charge; from instructions and information, I then took the vessel in charge, and placed my officer at Collingwood in custody, having unfitted her machinery for work, and consenting to another man named by Mr. Denison—the registered owner—being allowed to remain on board; the steamer *Georgian* appears by register to be owned by G. T. Denison, since 24th January last.

Cross-examined by Mr. McMichael—At that date she was under seizure for an action of our revenue laws; the government before this had been applied to, and consented to the transfer of the vessel from John Bates to G. T. Denison, and the registry was made the 24th of January; upon my first visit to Collingwood I did not search the vessel; I left another to do so, and by report from him was informed there was nothing of suspicious character in the form of munitions, &c., aboard; McDonald introduced himself to me by name; I saw no act of his beyond his general bearing that indicated him to be in charge of the *Georgian*; has told me the vessel was to be used in towing, also, that she was to run between Collingwood and Bedford; he told me that his business was that of a mechanic—a joiner I think; the expression that "McDonald appeared to be in charge," I intend to mean that from what I saw on board, the impression on my mind was that he was chief of those on board.

Sergt.-Maj. Hastings, City Police, sworn, said:—I know the house on Agnes-street in which McDonald lived; I went there on the 26th of March last; there was no person living in it then; I found a lot of bullet moulds, cartridges, potash kettle, with tar in it, a furnace, &c.; I reported to the Chief of Police afterwards, on the 31st of March; I went again and found in the cellar below the floor a torpedo, which I brought down to the Chief of Police; that night I went again, in company with Detective Mick and the witness Hyam, the latter of whom went into the cellar and handed up to me twenty-six torpedoes out of the water in the cellar.

J. A. Posey sworn, said—I have been living in Toronto for twelve months; I know McDonald and the house in which he lived on Agnes-street; I have been there several times; upon one occasion about Christmas I was there and helped to "stow away" some shells and a large kettle; McDonald was there and told me he expected that the house would be searched; there was a trap-door in the hall, and I helped to put the shells down this door; I carried them to a Mr. Heming's, and he put them down the hole; there might have been about fifty shells; I did not count them; I saw some powder canisters and some cartridges; saw a Southerner named Holt, and another named Norval; in November last McDonald asked me to meet him on York-street; I did not see him there, but met a man named Price, who took me to McDonald's house; McDonald there took down my name and the names of others, for the purpose, as he said, of going on an expedition upon the steamer *Georgian*; I afterward, on the 16th November, I think) went to Collingwood and took with me some cartridges; there were two others went with me; McDonald went with us as far as York-street, on our way to the cars, and gave one of us money to pay our fare; in Collingwood we met Holt, who told me not to go aboard the boat, as it would excite suspicion; Norval followed us from Toronto to Collingwood and told us that the expedition was not to take place, and we returned to Toronto; I afterwards was in McDonald's, in January; have not been there since; McDonald knew that Price paid me $10 the day I first went to his house.

Cross-examined by Mr. McMichael—The $10 were given me to help to pay off my board; I was to go on raids on board the *Georgian*; I was employed for such by Mr. McDonald; the raids were to be against the United States; I did not know where; in June last McDonald gave me money ($35) to go to the Confederate army.

At this stage the counsel for the Crown stated that a true bill had been found by the grand jury against McDonald in this matter, and proceedings would be stayed, and said the case for the prosecution was closed. He asked that the prisoner be committed for trial.

Mr. McMichael argued that there was not sufficient evidence to warrant a committal for trial. By the witnesses' statements it had been shown that the occurrences referred to took place before the 6th of February, and there was no evidence that munitions and material had been provided after the 6th of February, the date of the passing of the act.

Alderman Vance said that although before the 6th of February there was evidence of providing and preparing the means for an expedition, raid or enterprise against a foreign State, in all portions of the evidence referring to a date subsequent to that there was no evidence of an intention to do so. It simply closed by stating that the "munitions were being prepared and furnished to be taken to Collingwood by the steamer *Georgian*," without stating the objection, except by inference from former portions of the evidence, relating to dates prior to the 6th February, the date of the passing of the act. Under the circumstances he would leave it for a jury to decide, and commit the prisoner for trial at the next court of competent jurisdiction.

FROM CANADA.

Contemplated Rebel Raid into Vermont.

BURLINGTON, Vt., Friday, April 28.

Information was received here this morning that the rebel sympathizers in Canada were preparing for another raid on the frontier towns of this State.

The Federal and State militia authorities are on the alert, and are fully prepared to repel any invasion.

Guards have been placed on the steamers on Lake Champlain, and troops have been ordered to the more exposed frontier towns.

The militia of this city have been notified to be in readiness for any emergency.

The rebels will receive a warm reception if they should come along.

Suicide in Baltimore.

BALTIMORE, Friday, April 28.

A well-known citizen of Baltimore committed suicide last Monday, a short distance from this city, by shooting himself with a pistol. No cause could be assigned for the rash act, except that he had recently seemed depressed and melancholy.

Subsequent events have induced the suspicion that he was in some way implicated in the conspiracy, and last night the body was exhumed, embalmed, and sent to Washington, by orders of the government.

The affair causes much speculation, and there are many reports in connection with it, as well as some facts, which it is deemed imprudent to publish at present.

THE OBSEQUIES.

Westward Progress of the Funeral Cortege.

From New-York, Across Pennsylvania, into Ohio.

Official Reception of the Remains by Gen. Hooker and Gov. Brough.

Impressive Demonstrations Along the Route.

President Lincoln Drawing near to His Old Home.

WESTFIELD, N. Y., Friday, April 28.

The remains of ABRAHAM LINCOLN arrived here at 1 o'clock this morning. The bells were tolled and minute guns fired.

CLEVELAND, Friday, April 28.

All along the route from Buffalo to this city, which was reached this morning, the usual demonstrations of sorrow were witnessed. The remains were escorted by a large military and civic procession to a beautifully constructed temple prepared to receive them, and soon thereafter the face of the honored dead was open to the thousands of spectators, who in admirable order entered and retired from the inclosure.

The entire population of this city are abroad, all seemingly impressed with the solemnity of the occasion.

CLEVELAND, Ohio, Friday, April 28.

On the way to Cleveland, leaving Buffalo at 10:10 P. M., Thursday night, we successively passed Hamburgh, North Evans, Angola, Farnham, Irving and Silver Creek. At all the stations the immediate residents had assembled, some bearing lanterns and mourning flags in their hands, while on their houses were plainly discernable the usual drapery and mottoes expressive of the prevailing grief.

DUNKIRK, Friday, April 28—12:10.

Here, as at the preceding stations, the platform is elaborately decorated. Festoons of evergreens extend all along the eaves of the structure, while from the ceiling gracefully droop white and black folds. The background, covered with flags interlaced with crape, completes the artificial arrangement. But the chief feature is the group of thirty-six young ladies, representing the States of the Union. They are dressed in white, each with a broad, black scarf resting on the shoulder, and holding in the hand a national flag. We have a fine view of the tableaux by the glare of more than a hundred lamps and torches. The crowd here is dense. The tolling of bells, the solemn music by an instrumental band, and the firing of minute guns, contribute to the interest of the scene.

BROCTON, 12:30.

Many spectators are congregated here, and the place is illuminated.

WESTFIELD, 1 A. M.

We stop here for wood and water. A party of five ladies, namely: Mrs. DRAKE, wife of Col. DRAKE, killed at Cold Harbor; Mrs. BREWER, Mrs. SKINNER and the Misses TUCKER, brought in a cross and a wreath of flowers. On the cross were the words:

"Ours the Cross; Thine the Crown."

All of them were affected to tears, and considered it a sacred privilege to kiss the coffin.

Ripley has been passed and now (1:32) we are at the line which separates New-York from Pennsylvania. Maj.-Gen. DIX and staff took leave of us, and F. F. Farrar, Mayor of Erie, George W. Starr, F. B. Vincent, E. P. Bennett, J. T. Walsher and Capt. F. A. Roe, U. S. N., came on board.

Here Miss LEONORA CRAWFORD, aged 12 years, presented a cross and wreath with the words "Rest in Peace," attached. The scene was illuminated by a large bonfire and Chinese lanterns.

We pass Moreheads, Harbor Creek and Westerville, at all of which places crowds had assembled, manifesting unabated interest.

ERIE, 2:50.

There was no particular demonstration at this place.

The employes running this train are the same who were on the train that brought the late President to this point while on his way to Washington, just previous to his first inauguration.

Swanville, Fairview, Girard and Springfield are passed.

CONNEAUT, 3:48.

We are now in Ohio, and hurry on through Kingsville, Ashtabula, Saybrook, Geneva, Unionville, Madison, Perry, Paineville, Menter and Willoughby. The depot buildings are draped and large numbers of people are at these places assembled. Minute guns are fired and bells tolling.

WICKLIFFE—6:20.

The following gentlemen here came on board: Gov. BROUGH and staff, consisting of the following named officers: Gen. Cowen, Adjutant-General; Gen. Barlow, Quartermaster-General; Surgeon-General Barr and Col. Maxwell. Also, Maj.-Gen. Hooker, commanding the Department of the Ohio, with his staff, as follows: Col. Swords, Lieut.-Col. Simpson, Lieut.-Col. Lathrop, Major McFeely, Major Bannister, and Capt. Taylor. Also, United States Senator Sherman, Hon. S. Galloway, Hon. O. Waters and Maj. Montgmery. Also, the following-named gentlemen, to meet the remains: Hon. R. P. Spaulding, Ex-Gov. David Tod, Thomas Jones, Jr., Col. Anson Stager, Amasa Stone, Jr., Hon. H. B. Payne, Hon. John A. Foot, Hon. H. V. Wilson, Stillman Witt, Ansel Roberts, William Bingham, Hon. W. B. Castle, Charles Heckox, John Martin, Hon. W. Collins, H. N. Johnson, Dr. G. C. E. Webor, Dr. Proctor Thayer, H. B. Hurlbut, Jacob Hovey and James Warsick.

CLEVELAND—7 A. M.

As we pass the lake side of the city thousands of persons are gathered on the sloping green hillsides, all having a good view of the train. High up we see an arch, with the inscription, "ABRAHAM LINCOLN." It is draped in mourning, and the supports are covered with alternate stripes of black and white. Immediately under the arch is a lady, dressed in horizontal bars of the national colors, to represent the Genius of Liberty. She holds in her hand a flag, and this, together with her cap, is bandaged with mourning. It is a beautiful and expressive figure.

All places of business are closed. Colors are displayed at half-mast. A national salute of 36 guns is fired, and half-hour guns will be fired till sunset. We proceed to Euclid-street station in the cars. This is the point where Mr. LINCOLN embarked for Washington just previous to his first inauguration; and here the procession was formed.

The coffin was placed in a hearse, the roofing of which was covered with a national flag, with black plumes, and otherwise tastefully and appropriately adorned. The military escort embraced Maj.-Gen. HOOKER and Staff, and Gov. BROUGH, of Ohio, and Staff, and the civic escort of civic guard of honor was followed by the United States civil officers, veteran soldiers, members of the City Council, and City Officers of Cleaveland and other cities, members of the bar, the Board of Trade, Knights Templars, the Orders of Masons and Odd Fellows, Temperance Societies, Fenian Brotherhood, St. Vincent's Society, the German Benevolent Society, the Equal Rights League, &c., and all the Benevolent and other Associations and citizens on foot—a multitude of them.

The procession embraced all conditions of the people, without distinction of party or religion, and it presented a decidedly fine appearance, as it moved through the streets of this truly beautiful city from Euclid-street to Erie; down Erie to Superior and thence to the Park.

The sidewalks were densely crowded with mournful looking spectators, while thousands of persons beheld the cortège from the steps and windows of the beautiful residences which line the entire route. Emblems of mourning were everywhere prominent, together with expressive mottoes.

Every stranger is loud in his expressions of admiration of the splendid order of the arrangements.

In the park has been erected a building especially for the reception of the remains to which they have now been conveyed. The building is 24 by 36 feet in dimensions, and 14 feet high from the ground to the plate. The roof is of pagoda style, and the rafters are covered with white cloth over the centre of the main roof, and directly over the catafalque a second roof is raised about four feet, and covered in like manner. The catafalque consists of a raised dais four by twelve feet on the ground. The coffin rests on the dais about two feet above the floor. On the four corners stand columns supporting a canopy. The columns have been draped and wreathed with evergreens and white flowers in the most beautiful manner. Black cloth, falling as curtains, and fringed with silver, are caught and looped back to these columns. From the centre of the canopy, the floor and sides of the dais are covered with black cloth drooping from the four corners, bordered with silver fringe; and the borders of the cornice are brilliantly ornamented with white rosettes and stars of silver. The inside of the canopy is lined with black cloth, gathered in folds, and white and black crape serves as plumage to the posts. At the corners of the catafalque, in the centre, is a large star of black velvet, with thirty-six stars, one for each State in the Union. The floor of the dais is covered with flowers, and a figure of the Goddess of Liberty is placed at the head of the coffin. The ceiling of the building is hung with beautiful festoons of evergreen and flowers and white. The four posts which sustain on either side the pagoda roof are hung with large rosettes of mingled evergreen and magnolias of two varieties. Appropriate drapery hangs from the cornice of the building and swings from pillar to pillar of the fairy structure. Glass lamps have been attached to the pillars of the catafalque and to other points of the building so that the remains can be easily seen at night and to good advantage.

The religious services, after the remains had been placed upon the dais, were performed by Right Reverend Bishop MCILVAINE, who, in the course of his prayer, asked the blessing of heaven on the immediate family of the deceased, and a sanctification of the event which had called the nation to mourn to the good of him who had succeeded to the Chief Magistracy. He then read a part of the funeral service of the Episcopal Church, slightly altering their text to suit the occasion. These services were intensely solemn, and moved many of the listners to tears.

The remains were then exposed to public view. The arrangements are so perfect that every one who desires to see them will have no difficulty in being gratified. It is raining here to-day, but this is no impediment to the throngs passing to the park.

Cleveland has made a demonstration worthy of her citizens. Their sad countenances attest stronger than words the heavy grief which affects all hearts.

CLEVELAND—9 P. M.

The number who witnessed the remains of the President during the day was 150 a minute. Two rows of spectators were constantly passing, one on each side of the coffin. The lid was freshly covered with flowers in the form of harps, crosses and bouquets gathered in the hothouses of Cleveland and laid upon the coffin by ladies representing the Soldiers' Relief Association.

The funeral party were the guests of the corporate authorities. They were quartered at the Weddell House. A more liberal and friendly greeting could not have been extended.

CHARLES L. WILSON, of Chicago, on behalf of a Committee of One Hundred, was here to-day to extend the hospitalities of that city. This committee is to proceed to Michigan city to meet the remains, and will escort them to Springfield. The display at Chicago will be the largest ever known in that city. Forty-one organizations and societies, numbering 25,000 men, have already reported to the Chief Marshal.

At midnight we leave Cleveland, and will arrive at Columbus to-morrow morning. Everywhere deep sorrow has been manifested, and the feeling seems, if possible, to deepen, as we move Westward with the remains to their final resting place.

Gov. BROUGH to-night extended the hospitalities of his residence to the funeral party.

Change of Time of the Presidential Funeral.

SPRINGFIELD, Ill., Friday, April 28—1:50 P. M.

The time fixed for the funeral of the late President is changed from Saturday the 6th to Thursday the 4th of May.

A Case of Illegal Arrest and Imprisonment.

BOSTON, Friday, April 28.

A suit brought by Mr. LEONARD STURTEVANT against A. H. ALLEN for illegal arrest and imprisonment, which has been on trial here for some days in the Supreme Court, was closed this morning, the jury rendering a verdict in favor of Mr. STURTEVANT for $32,500.

At the breaking out of the war Mr. STURTEVANT was doing business in New-Orleans, and upon his coming North was arrested and lodged in jail upon charges of disloyalty preferred against him by Mr. ALLEN.

Missouri Threatened with Invasion.

ST. LOUIS, Friday, April 28.

Reports prevail that a force of from six to twelve thousand rebels, comprising remnants of JEFF. THOMPSON's and JOE SHELBY's brigades, are at Pocahontas, Arkansas, preparing to invade Missouri. A large number of people are leaving the southwest part of the State in consequence. Three regiments have been sent down the river. The reports are undoubtedly exaggerated.

Gen. Wilson's Late Raid

CINCINNATI, Friday, April 28.

Late Georgia papers give full accounts of Gen. WILSON's late raid, after defeating FORREST at Selma, Ala. After destroying the arsenals and manufactories there, WILSON moved eastward, capturing Montgomery, West Point, Columbus and Macon, scattering the militia on all sides, ruining the only remaining railroad, breaking up machine-shops, destroying stores, and rendering the manufacture of material for future campaigns impossible.

The Seven-Thirties.

PHILADELPHIA, Friday, April 28.

JAY COOKE reports the subscriptions to the seven-thirty loan to-day at $1,152,500. The largest single subscriptions were $100,000 from Cincinnati, $100,000 from Baltimore, $300,000 from New-York, $200,000 from Boston, and $200,000 from Syracuse. The number of individual subscriptions for amounts of $50 and $100, was 2,901.

The Daily Picayune.

VOLUME XXIX. NEW ORLEANS, FRIDAY MORNING, MAY 5, 1865. NUMBER 87.

THE CITY OF NEW ORLEANS.

OFFICIAL.

[No. 6266.]

MAYORALTY OF NEW ORLEANS, City Hall, April 24, 1865.

RESOLVED, That the adjudications for the sale of the contracts for "the cleaning of the paved and unpaved streets, and the repairing of the unpaved streets, and for the repairing and keeping in repair the paved streets," authorized to be sold by City Ordinance No. 6251, as reported by the City Controller, be and the same are hereby accepted.

RESOLVED, That the Mayor be and he is hereby authorized and empowered to enter into contract, by notarial act, with the following parties, to-wit

For cleaning the paved and unpaved and repairing the unpaved streets of the

First Ward—Geo. Cronan..........	$7,000
Security—John Coleman.	
Second Ward—F. F. Trinchard..........	6,375
Security—W. R. Fish.	
Third Ward—W. H. Waters..........	12,000
Security—W. R. Fish.	
Fourth Ward—John Rooney..........	5,250
Security—S. W. Moore.	
Fifth Ward—James McKeon..........	6,000
Security—M. Woods.	
Sixth Ward—John Bietry..........	6,000
Security—John Wolf.	
Seventh Ward—Samuel Flamm..........	5,503
Security—W. Wakefield.	
Eighth Ward—Tim. O'Connell..........	4,800
Security—E. D. White.	
Ninth Ward—E. D. White..........	4,000
Security—Thomas Gullison.	
Tenth Ward—Daniel Wilson..........	4,375
Security—James Stafford.	
Eleventh Ward—Daniel Wilson..........	3,250
Security—James Stafford.	

For repairing and keeping in repair the paved streets of the

First Ward—George Cronan..........	4,300
Security—John Coleman.	
Second Ward—F. H. Cummins..........	5,975
Security—John McRoberts.	
Third Ward—John Rooney..........	2,200
Security—S. W. Moore.	
Fourth Ward—James McKeon..........	2,000
Security—M. Woods.	
Fifth Ward—Dennis Cronan..........	3,000
Security—Mike Gernon.	
Sixth Ward—Pat. Lane..........	2,550
Security—Philip Guelbeck.	
Seventh Ward—Daniel Crowley..........	1,700
Security—E. D. White.	
Eighth Ward—Tim. O'Connell..........	1,000
Security—E. D. White.	
Ninth Ward—E. D. White..........	1,000
Security—Thomas Kavanaugh.	
Tenth Ward—John Crouse..........	900
Security—George Cronan.	
Eleventh Ward—Wm. Henry..........	975
Security—Daniel Wilson.	

(Signed) G. BURKE, Chairman Bureau of Finance.
(Signed) D. S. DEWEES, Chairman Bureau Streets and Landings.
Approved April 24, 1865.
(Signed) HU. KENNEDY, Mayor.
A true copy. Attest:
ap25—5t D. L. GIBBENS, Sec'y.

The City Park.

COMPTROLLER'S OFFICE, CITY HALL, New Orleans, May 4, 1865.

Sealed Proposals will be received at this office until SATURDAY, the 13th inst., at 12 M., for the pasturage, for one year, of the City Park, on Metairie Ridge.

Purchasers will not have the privilege of putting more than two hundred and fifty head of cattle at one time within the enclosure; and that portion of the Park between the Bayou and the Metairie Road, now used by visitors to the Park, is not included in the contract, and cattle will not be allowed there.

The timber on the premises must in no manner be disturbed, and the purchaser will be required to keep the fences in good order during the continuance of the lease, and shall be subject to such police regulations as are now and may hereafter be established.

Payments to be made monthly, in advance, and the time to commence from the acceptance of the proposal.

Proposals must be endorsed, "Proposals for the Pasturage of the City Park."

my1—td S. HOWELL, Comptroller.

STREET COMMISSIONER'S OFFICE, No. 7 City Hall, New Orleans, May 4, 1865.

Were brought to the Second and Third Districts Pound, corner Orleans and Claiborne streets, as estrays—

One bay mare and colt. The mare is 12½ hands high, hind feet white, Mexican brand on the left hip. The colt is black and about ten days old.

Which, if not claimed within ten days, and expenses thereon paid, will be sold at public auction at said pound, on TUESDAY, May 16, 1865, at 12 M.

GEO. W. McCERREN, Street Commissioner.

For Comptroller:
PAUL AUGRAIN. my5—3tin10d

STREET COMMISSIONER'S OFFICE, No. 7 City Hall, New Orleans May 2, 1865.

Was brought to the Second and Third Districts Pound one Bay Mare, 13 hands high, branded D. C. on the left hip, white face, black mane and tail, hind feet white, and heavy with foal.

Which if not claimed within ten days and expenses thereon paid, will be sold at public auction at said Pound on SATURDAY, May 13, 1865, at 12 o'clock M.

GEO. W. McCERREN, Street Commissioner.

For Comptroller:
ALEXANDER LEVY. my3—3tin10d

STREET COMMISSIONER'S OFFICE, No. City Hall, New Orleans, April 26, 1865.

Were brought to the Second and Third Districts Pound, corner Orleans and Claiborne streets, as estrays—

One dark brown mare mule, 12 hands high, branded U. C. on the right shoulder and U. on the left hip.

One dark brown mule, 13 hands high, branded U. C. on the left shoulder and C. over it.

One dark brown mule, 13 hands high, branded F. M. on the left shoulder, and

One cart.

Which if not claimed within ten days, and expenses thereon paid, will be sold at public auction at said pound, on Monday, May 8, 1865, at 12 o'clock M.

JOHN PURCELL, Street Commissioner.

For Comptroller:
ALEXANDER LEVY. ap27—3tin10d

STREET COMMISSIONER'S OFFICE, No. 7 City Hall, New Orleans, May 1, 1865.

Were brought to the Second and Third Districts Pound, corner of Orleans and Claiborne streets, as estrays—

One bay mare COLT, 12¼ hands high;

One gray HORSE, 13 hands high, branded with an inverse heart and a Z on right hip;

Which, if not claimed within ten days and expenses thereon paid, will be sold at public auction at said Pound on THURSDAY, May 11, 1865, at 12 o'clock M.

JOHN PURCELL, Street Commissioner.

For Comptroller:
PAUL AUGRAIN. my1—3tin10d

STREET COMMISSIONER'S OFFICE, No. 7, City Hall, New Orleans, April 24, 1865.

Were brought to the Second and Third District Pound, corner of Orleans and Claiborne streets, as estrays—

One red Cow, with bell, both ears split, white spots on right and left hip, and only three teats.

One dark brown Pony, 13 hands high, white star on forehead, both hind feet white, branded 1Ω on the right hip.

Which, if not claimed within ten days, and expenses thereon paid, will be sold at public auction at said Pound on FRIDAY, May 5th, at 12 o'clock M.

JOHN PURCELL, Street Commissioner.

For Comptroller:
ALEXANDER LEVY. ap25—3tin10d

The Daily Picayune.

DOUBLE SHEET

THE RUSSIAN PESTILENCE.

Afflicting and startling tidings come from Eastern Europe. Pestilence rages in St. Petersburg, the capital, and in several provinces of Russia. Like the Asiatic cholera, and all the great epidemics known to history, it is sweeping Westward, bearing ruthless death in its fearful train. Its appearance has excited intense alarm throughout thickly populated Europe. It may cross the broad Atlantic and commit great ravages in this fair country. We must prepare for its coming and, if possible, strip it of its terrors. Its progress, of course, will cause uneasiness and anxiety. If this only leads, as it should do, to the adoption of increased sanitary precautions on the part of the authorities, and a more rigorous attention to the laws of health on the part of individuals, the apprehension of coming evil may be productive of positive good; we may have cause to regard the threatening calamity as a blessing in disguise.

As a faithful journalist, whose duty it is to sound the alarm when anything occurs threatening danger to the community, we have carefully gathered all the information respecting the Russian pestilence within our reach, with a view of communicating it to our readers for their information. We have already given important details relative to the malady raging in the Russian capital, which was the first cause of alarm in Europe, furnished by Dr. Tillner, physician to the Grand Duchess Maria of Russia, and published in a Florence journal. In the English papers we find an account, dated April 5, received from the British Ambassador at St. Petersburg, which says:

The fever is contagious, and is called in French *fievre rechute*, in German *das recurrirende Fieber*, and "the relapsing or famine fever" in English. It is also styled "remittent fever," or "typhus recurrens," or "bilious typhoid fever," or "synocha," or "military fever," or "typhinia." It was unknown in Russia until eight months ago, when Prof. Botkin called attention to it as a fever he had never seen, though foreign physicians had described it. There is much ordinary typhus in St. Petersburg. The official journal states that the typhus and the typhoid fever and the "febris recurrens" prevailing in St. Petersburg have now slightly diminished. Lord Napier reports from Berlin, April 5, that an unknown disorder has appeared along the valley of the Vistula, and especially at Elbing. The Prussian Government is not aware that it came from St. Petersburg.

The Medical Gazette, of St. Petersburg, in an account of this epidemic, says:

It was during the last autumn that the disease broke out simultaneously in the north-east and south-west of the Russian empire. M. Gworling, the Government Doctor at Perm, announced that he had seen forty cases of the disease, which commences with cold and shivering, followed by heat without perspiration, accompanied by colic, headache, delirium, general debility, and sometimes with a flow of blood from the nose. The disease lasts from five to six days, after which the invalid recovers his appetite, falls into a sound sleep, and the fever quits him. The fever returns after a short interval, but again ceases, and the doctor has observed this to have happened three or four times. Quinine taken in large doses cures the fever, and removes delirium, but does not produce decisive effects, nor is it sufficient to arrest the progress of the disease. The doctor adds that he has seen more than 300 persons attacked with the disease in the course of the years 1857 and 1858 in America, where it raged with such violence that it was mistaken for the yellow fever.

Subsequent to the publications above noted, the London Times had the following telegram, dated Berlin, April 7. It gives the state of things in St. Petersburg a more alarming aspect:

Authentic intelligence states that three several maladies exist at St. Petersburg. The first is manifested by spasmodic affection of the brain and spinal cord, and the second typhus, gradually developed into febris recurrens. Quite recently the Siberian plague has broken out also. Of this seventy per cent. die within a few hours. A strong disposition to vomit, which cannot be satisfied, a swelling of the belly, pestilential carbuncles, and dark color of the skin, are its unmistakable symptoms. It is the black death. Dr. Erichson, surgeon to the Emperor Nicholas, aged 75, died while attending hospital.

The Times, of April 8, says:

St. Petersburg papers deny the existence of the plague in the capital, but the description of the disease shows its present stage greatly to resemble the plague. In many cases, indeed, it is difficult to distinguish plague from febris recurrens, at a time when typhoid epidemics are abroad. The disease is apparently on the decrease. In Poland also, and Eastern Prussia, an epidemic has broken out. It is manifested by severe inflammation of the membranes of the brain and spine; it is infectious, and as fatal as the worst form of cholera.

A letter in the Times from a Dr. Althaus attributes the prevalence of the epidemics at St. Petersburg to the extremely imperfect sanitary condition of that city, and the habits of the lower classes. Throughout Europe precautions against the spread of the pestilence are being promptly taken. In the British House of Lords on April 4th, and in the House of Commons on April 6th, the attention of the Government was called to the subject. In the Commons—

In reply to Sir John Pakington, Sir G. Grey, (the Home Secretary) said that the attention of the Government had been directed to the epidemic raging at St. Petersburg, and they had immediately sent instructions to Sir A. Buchanan at St. Petersburg, and Her Majesty's representatives at Berlin, Vienna, Stockholm, and Copenhagen, as well as to the Consuls at the ports of the Baltic, to procure without delay and report all the information which they could collect with respect to the origin and the nature of the disease and the modes of treatment. A medical officer had also been sent to St. Petersburg to investigate and report upon the character of the complaint; and instructions had also been given to the Custom-House officials to examine closely all vessels coming from the suspected ports. He had been informed by telegram from St. Petersburg that it was a fever not unknown in other parts of Europe, and it was now on the decline in that city. The information which he had received from Berlin and other places led him to believe that the apprehensions had been exaggerated.

The French Government has ordered all vessels arriving from Russian ports to be put in quarantine, the Austrian Government has sent a medical commission to St. Petersburg to examine into the nature of the raging pestilence and the best means of treating it, and the Prussian and all other European Governments appear to have taken preventive measures. Inasmuch as the telegraphic accounts of the news brought by the steamship Africa, which left Queenstown on April 15th, are silent as to the pestilence, we indulge the hope that it has abated. Meanwhile, it is satisfactory to know that the Collector at New York has promptly issued instructions that the arrival of any vessels infected with the plague or suspected of such infection, and also the arrival of any passenger who may at any time have been in the vicinity of the contagion, shall be immediately reported. We presume that similar action has been taken at other Northern ports.

In view of all the information received, we may yet hope that this continent will not be cursed by the presence of this pestilence. At all events, the experience afforded by past epidemic disorders shows us that, though we may not prevent their approach to our shores, we can do very much to mitigate their severity and circumscribe their area. Crowded dwellings, unwholesome food, filth, drink and dissolute living, are the great promoters of these disorders. Wide-spread reform in these respects would be a blessing both to individuals and the public. Let it not be forgotten that although contagious disorders cannot be entirely banished, even with the most perfect sanitary arrangements, that is no reason why we should neglect the simplest precautions which may be of service in the saving of human life. We renew the expression of our hope that all the measures that wisdom may suggest will be promptly adopted to preserve the health of our fair city. Then, if this latest form of the "plague" should visit us, we may not be without confidence that its ravages will be greatly circumscribed.

Internal Revenue Law in Regard to House Rent.

TREASURY DEPARTMENT, Office of Internal Revenue, Washington, April 14, 1864.

Sir—I reply to yours of the 6th inst., that the clause of section 117, of the act of June 30, 1864, relating to deduction of rent, is understood to mean:

1. That where rent is paid it shall be deducted; and

2. That the rental value of a homestead shall neither be included as income nor deducted therefrom; in other words, shall be made of no account.

Suppose A, who pays a rent of $700, to have a gross income of $3000; then A, having included all his items of income in the $3000, the law says his $700 rent shall not be included, but if he pay tax on $3000 it is included. The only way not to include is to deduct it.

Suppose B, who owns a house, the rental value of which is $700, has a gross income of $3000, the law says the rental value of his house shall not be included. If it were to be included, B would be assessed on $3700. The rental value thereof must neither be included nor deducted.

Very respectfully,
E. A. ROLLINS, Dep'y Com'r.
JAS. J. PULLAN, Cincinnati, Ohio.

President Johnson and the Figure Seven.—There is something remarkable in the frequent recurrence of the figure seven, in connection with the history of President Johnson, and I have taken the trouble to note the circumstance, which may be of interest to the public. His name, Johnson, it will be perceived has seven letters in it; he commenced to learn a trade at fourteen years of age, which is twice seven. He served seven years at his trade; finished his trade at twenty-one years of age, which is three times seven. He was elected an Alderman of the town of Greenville, N. C., in 1828, making a multiple of four times seven. He was elected to the Legislature of Tennessee in 1835, which is a multiple of five times seven, and was then aged twenty-seven. He was elected to Congress in 1843, aged thirty-five, which is five times seven. He was appointed the Military Governor of Tennessee on the seventh of March, 1862, and was nominated for the Vice Presidency in 1864, aged fifty-six, which is eight times seven. To say the least, this is a somewhat remarkable recurrence of a single figure, in one man's public life. He will no doubt be successful in bringing back the original seven secession States, and make the Union seven times as strong as it ever was before the rebellion. May God's blessing rest upon him, and may he live to aged seventy times seven!

The President's Secretaries.—Mr. Browning, of Nashville, and Col. R. D. Mussey, of the regular army, are acting as private Secretaries to President Johnson, in place of Messrs. Hay and Nicolay, who acted in similar capacities for Mr. Lincoln. Major Knox, of the War Department, has also been assigned to duty with the President.

TELEGRAPHIC.

LATER FROM THE NORTH.

GRANT AND JOHNSTON.

LEE'S OPINION ON THE SITUATION.

A BATTLE IN THE WEST.

GENERAL FORREST WOUNDED.

THE ASSASSINS.

DAVIS NOT CAPTURED.

PURSUIT OF THE RAM STONEWALL.

[From Our Extras of Yesterday.]

BATON ROUGE, May 4, 9:10 A. M.—By the arrival of the Joseph Pierce, from Vicksburg, we have New York dates to the 29th ult.

CAIRO, April 29, 6 P. M.—The following embraces all of importance in the dispatches received:

GRANT AND JOHNSTON.

NEW YORK, April 29.—Newbern advices state that Johnston attempted to higgle with Grant for terms which would provide for the pardon of Jeff. Davis and the other leading insurrectionary conspirators, but the Lieutenant General would listen to nothing of this kind, and Johnston was compelled to be satisfied with the conditions granted to Lee.

JEFF. DAVIS.

Intelligence of the arrival of Jeff Davis and his accompanying fugitives, as far south as South Carolina, has been received in Washington. It is thought he will be intercepted before reaching the Mississippi River.

GEN. LEE'S OPINIONS.

The Herald's Richmond correspondent recounts an interview he had with Gen. Lee. He called on him to obtain his political views in order to lay them before the public. On informing Gen. Lee of his object, the latter said: "I am a paroled prisoner, and I have never been a politician, and I know but little of political trade. I am a soldier." He further said he was ready to make any sacrifice or perform any honorable act that would tend to a restoration of peace and equality to the country. He said he was a believer in States rights. He had considered allegiance due primarily to his native State. He had opposed secession, but when his State went out he considered it his duty to go with it.

When he accepted a command under the rebel Government he considered he was serving his State. He regarded his surrender of the military as of no political significance; that it was not a surrender of the doctrine of States rights. When the South was wholly subdued only would the doctrine of States rights be surrendered. The surrender of a single army was only a military necessity.

When the South surrendered all its forces and returned to the Union, then only will she surrender her favorite doctrine of secession. That her principles will then be settled by military power. On the question of State sovereignty he concludes there exists a legitimate casus belli. The question was left unsettled in the conventions forming the organic law, and the war is destined to settle it; therefore the war raised on this issue cannot be called treason. If the South is forced to submit, it, of course, can only be looked upon as the triumph of Federal power over State rights and the forced annihilation of the latter.

The South have not been and are not yet prepared to beg for terms, but are ready to accept fair and honorable terms, their own political views being considered. As to slavery, they consider it dead, and the best men have long been anxious to do away with it.

He expressed the opinion that should arbitrary or vindictive or revengeful policies be attempted, the end was not yet. He remarked that the assassination of the President was a crime beyond execration. It would not be approved by any good man, from any conceivable motive.

As to terms of peace, to the suggestion that the political leaders only should be held to a strict accountability, he asked, would that be just? What has Mr. Davis done more than other Southerners that he should be punished? It is true, he occupied a prominent position as the agent of the whole people, but that has made him no more or less a rebel than the rest. His acts were the acts of the whole people, and the acts of the whole people were his acts. He is not accountable for the commencement of the war. On the contrary, he was one of the last to give in his adhesion to the secession movement, but strenuously opposed it from the outset, and portrayed its ruinous consequences by speeches and writing.

THE ASSASSINS.

NEW YORK, April 29.—The Herald's Washington special says the search after the assassin of President Lincoln and the would-be murderer of Seward, has developed a well laid and deliberately matured plan of assassination and nefarious rascality, murder and arson, unparalleled in the annals of crime.

The investigations have not yet reached the point where it is proper to disclose the intent and various ramifications of this murderous plot. Many unsuspected parties are involved, and the evidence is complete to show that it was not the freak of a madman or the act of an individual, but conducted by traitors of the rebellion, and held up by them in the hour of their most desperate need as a means of success in their great treasonable enterprise. The Times's special says that old officers and soldiers are among the inhabitants in the vicinity of Fredericksburg.

The officers, members of wealthy families, who never did a day's work, declare that they will not earn their living.

The Tribune's Washington special says Edwin Booth is here for the purpose, it is said, of procuring the body of his brother. His desire cannot be granted, as the grave of the assassin will never be known.

The New York Herald's Washington special says the post mortem examination of Booth's body showed the ball did not touch the brain, but striking the spinal column produced immediate paralysis. The opinion of the surgeon is that he must have died a horrible death, the brain being active, and consciousness complete up to the very moment of dissolution.

Nearly all the parties directly implicated are now in custody. Paine, the Seward assassin, is a brother of one of the St. Albans raiders. There are six brothers, all reckless and daring. Two were with Wagner, in North Carolina. Mr. Edwin Booth arrived in this city to-day, to ask for his brother's body. The request will not be granted.

FORREST.

The Herald's Selma, Ala., dispatch says among the prisoners captured here are 150 officers. Lieut Gen. Dick Taylor made his escape on a steamer. Forrest, Adams, Roddy, Armstrong and McCausland, under cover of the darkness, reached a swamp east of this city and evaded capture.

Officers comprising their staffs were taken. Forrest's ordnance officer, Capt. Bond, reports Forrest as wounded in two places in the arm. Croxton and McCook attacked Johnston's front and rear at Fryon.

The destruction of Centreville bridge over the Cahawba, and Croxton's movements towards Tuscaloosa, rendered it utterly impossible for Forrest to carry out his plans. Cahawba capitulated yesterday, and about 700 of our prisoners confined there for a long time were released. They had been well treated.

THE RAM STONEWALL.

The Herald's Washington special says information has reached Washington that the rebel steam ram Olinda, alias Stonewall, arrived at Teneriffe, in the Canary Islands, on the 1st of March, in thirty days from Lisbon. She was allowed to coal and provision. She was ordered to leave the port within twenty-four hours.

She left on the 1st inst., steaming southward, but her destination was not made public. The Navy Department, in anticipation of the appearance of the Stonewall in some of our harbors, is making a proper distribution of suitable vessels along the Atlantic seaboard.

THE FUNERAL CORTEGE.

The funeral cortege of the lamented President Lincoln had reached Carlington at 5:20 this A. M.

LOUISVILLE, April 30.—Nine hundred rebels surrendered at Cumberland Gap, yesterday, and were paroled.

NEW YORK, April 29.—Cotton quiet and lower. No gold quotations.

The Rebel Prisoners Disown Assassins.—A Washington dispatch (20th) to the New York World says:

On Tuesday the rebel prisoners at Point Lookout, through their sergeants of divisions, passed resolutions representing the voice of twenty-two thousand rebel prisoners, expressing their abhorrence of the assassination of the late President and their warm sympathy with the distressed family. The resolutions were to be sent to the War Department through Gen. Barnes, commandant at Point Lookout.

The French Government and the Stonewall (Olinda).—Says a Paris correspondent:

The French Government has not yet, I believe, given any document in writing as to who is responsible for the escape of the Olinda from out of the French hands into those of the Confederates, and the Government perhaps thinks that this is one of the cases in which haste is not good diplomacy. It is not a little singular that the *Moniteur*, in face of the fact that the French Government is probably liable for the escape of the Stonewall, should barefacedly publish from day to day a detailed account of the movements of this vessel.

SURRENDER OF JOHNSTON.

THE WAR IS VIRTUALLY CLOSED.

THE ARMY TO BE GREATLY REDUCED.

FUNERAL CORTEGE AT COLUMBUS.

THE AMNESTY PROCLAMATION MAY BE REPEALED.

NUMBER OF GOVERNMENT EMPLOYEES TO BE DISMISSED.

Gold on the 29th, 146 1-4.

BATON ROUGE, May 4—4 P. M.

By the arrival of the steamer Ben. Stickney we have New York dates to the 29th.

NAVAL.

NEW YORK, April 29.—The Herald's dispatch says Rear Admiral Porter has been detached from the command of the North Atlantic Squadron. Commodore Radford succeeds him.

THE WAR CLOSED.

The Commercial's Washington special says the surrender of Gen. Johnston to Gen. Sherman will soon work the termination of the war. It is not apprehended that any great difficulty will be encountered in determining the fate of the insurgents.

Gen. Grant having virtually concluded the war, will return to Washington and apply himself to the reduction of the military forces. The initiatory measures have already been taken for a large curtailment of expenses. The policy to be adopted towards the rebels in civil life who have not availed themselves of President Lincoln's amnesty, begins to excite attention. It is probable that they may soon find it too late to avail themselves of its provisions.

THE GOLD MARKET.

NEW YORK, April 29.—Transactions in gold are very limited and the price weak. The ruling figures this morning have been 146¼. Now that the military events have ceased to effect the standing of the public credit, the fluctuations in gold are chiefly the result of the changing aspect of foreign exchange, and other movements affecting the supply of gold.

THE FUNERAL.

COLUMBUS, April 29.—Notwithstanding the inclement weather, crowds of citizens gathered at the Cleveland depot to take their last look at the coffin. Left on time, and at 7 o'clock the rain ceased. Gov. Brown, Gen. Hooker, Senator Sherman and others from Columbus are on the train.

At 7:30 we reached Columbus. An immense assemblage received us. The committee of arrangements took charge of affairs. The coffin was slowly carried to the hearse, which was similar to those used in other cities. The flowers contributed at former places along the line still lie on the coffin. The procession then formed, the 88th Ohio Volunteers acting as escort and the veteran Reserve Corps as guard following.

COLUMBUS, April 29.—The rotunda of the Capitol was draped in mourning. The coffin was approached by steps. It rested on a mound of moss, on which were dotted the choicest flowers.

REDUCTION OF THE ARMY.

NEW YORK, April 29.—The Post's Washington correspondent says it is estimated that Secretary Stanton's order will dismiss from the military service at least 50,000 persons.

JEFF. DAVIS.

The latest advices show that there is a good prospect of capturing Jeff. Davis's specie and baggage train, if not himself and Cabinet.

MISCELLANEOUS MILITARY MATTERS.

Gen. Ingalls, Chief Quartermaster of the Army of the Potomac, and Gen. Gibbons, of the 2d Corps, arrived here from City Point on a special boat to-day. The latter brought up seventy-six rebel battle flags which will be presented to the War Department.

The Government is establishing military posts in St. Mary's, Prince George's and Charles counties, Md.

This is done in order to protect the loyal people in that vicinity, and to prevent any treasonable demonstrations by the disloyal. The protection which was given the murderer Booth plainly exhibited the extent of the latter. The troops are to forage on the country, and to give receipts for everything they take, which will be paid for to all persons proving their loyalty.

The Government has begun the work of retrenching its expenses, and on the 1st of May a large number of employés of the various departments will be dismissed. Since the restrictions on travel between this city and Richmond have been removed, hundreds of persons from the North have passed through here for the latter place on a visit of curiosity or pleasure.

THE NEW YORK HERALD.

WHOLE NO. 10,486. NEW YORK, MONDAY, MAY 15, 1865. PRICE FOUR CENTS.

JEFF. DAVIS.

DETAILS OF HIS CAPTURE.

His Camp Surprised at Daylight on the 10th Instant.

He Disguises Himself in His Wife's Clothing, and, Like His Accomplice Booth, Takes to the Woods.

He is Pursued and Forced to a Stand.

He Shows Fight and Flourishes a Dagger in the Style of the Assassin of the President.

His Wife Warns the Soldiers Not to "Provoke the President or He Might Hurt 'Em."

He Fails to Imitate Booth and Die in the Last Ditch.

HIS IGNOMINIOUS SURRENDER.

SKETCHES OF THE CAPTORS AND CAPTIVES,

&c., &c., &c.

DETAILS OF THE CAPTURE.

Secretary Stanton to Major General Dix.

WAR DEPARTMENT, WASHINGTON, May 14, 1865.

Major General JOHN A. DIX, New York:—

The following details of the capture of Jefferson Davis while attempting to make his escape in his wife's clothes have been received from Major General Wilson.

EDWIN M. STANTON.

General Wilson to Secretary Stanton.

MACON, Ga., May 12—11 A. M.

To Hon. E. M. STANTON, Secretary of War:—

The following despatch announcing the capture of Jeff. Davis has just been handed me by Colonel Minty, commanding Second division.

HEADQUARTERS, FOURTH MICHIGAN CAVALRY, CUMBERLANDVILLE, Ga., May 11, 1865.

To Capt. T. W. SCOTT, A. G., Second division:—

SIR—I have the honor to report that at daylight yesterday, at Irwinsville, I surprised and captured Jeff. Davis and family, together with his wife, sisters, and brother; his Postmaster General, Reagan; his private secretary, Colonel Harrison; Colonel Johnson, Aid-de-Camp on Davis' staff; Colonels Morris and Lubbick and Lieutenant Hathaway; also several important names and a train of five wagons and three ambulances, making a most perfect success.

Had not a most painful mistake occurred, by which the Fourth Michigan and First Wisconsin came in conflict, we should have done better. This mistake cost us two killed and Lieutenant Boutle wounded through the arm, in the Fourth Michigan, and four men wounded in the First Wisconsin. This occurred just at daylight after we had captured the camp. By the advance of the First Wisconsin they were mistaken for the enemy.

I returned to this point last night, and shall move right on to Macon, without waiting orders from you as directed, feeling that the whole object of the expedition is accomplished.

It will take me at least three days to reach Macon, as we are seventy-five miles out, and our stock much exhausted. I hope to reach Hawkinsville to-night.

I have the honor, &c.,

B. D. PRITCHARD,
Lieutenant Colonel Fourth Michigan cavalry.

The First Wisconsin belongs to Lagrange's brigade, of McCook's division, and had been sent due east by General Croxton via Dublin.

Colonel Minty had distributed his command all along the south bank of the Ocmulgee and Altamaha.

This accounts for the collision between parts of the First and Second divisions, and shows the zeal of the command in the pursuit.

I have directed increased vigilance on the part of the command, in the hope of catching the other assassins.

Our dispositions of men are good, and so far none of the rebel chiefs have been able to get through.

Breckinridge's son was captured the night before last eleven miles south of here.

Will send further details as soon as received.

J. H. WILSON, Brevet Major General.

GENERAL WILSON'S SECOND DESPATCH.

MACON, Ga., May 13—9:30 A. M.

Hon. E. M. STANTON, Secretary of War:—

Lieutenant Colonel Harden, commanding the First Wisconsin, has just arrived from Irwinsville. He struck the trail of Davis at Dublin, Lawrence county, on the evening of the 7th, and followed him closely night and day through the pine wilderness of Alligator creek and Green swamp, via Cumberlandsville, to Irwinsville.

At Cumberlandsville Colonel Harden met Colonel Pritchard, with one hundred and fifty picked men and horses, of the Fourth Michigan.

Harden followed the trail directly south, while Pritchard, having fresh horses, pushed down the Ocmulgee towards Hopewell, and thence by House creek to Irwinsville, arriving there at midnight of the 9th. Jeff. Davis had not arrived.

From a citizen Pritchard learned that his party were encamped two miles out of the town. He made dispositions of his men and surrounded the camp before day.

Harden had camped at nine P. M. within two miles, as he afterwards learned from Davis. The trail being too indistinct to follow, he pushed on at three A. M., and had gone but little more than a mile when his advance was fired upon by men of the Fourth Michigan.

A fight ensued, both parties exhibiting the greatest determination. Fifteen minutes elapsed before the mistake was discovered.

The firing in this skirmish was the first warning that Davis received.

The captors report that he hastily put on one of his wife's dresses and started for the woods, closely followed by our men, who at first thought him a woman, but, seeing his boots while he was running, they suspected his sex at once.

The race was a short one, and the rebel President was soon brought to bay. He brandished a bowie knife and showed signs of battle, but yielded promptly to the persuasions of Colt's revolvers, without compelling the men to fire. He expressed great indignation at the energy with which he was pursued, saying that he had believed our government more magnanimous than to hunt down women and children.

Mrs. Davis remarked to Colonel Harden, after the excitement was over, that the men had better not provoke the President or "he might hurt some of 'em."

Reagan behaved himself with dignity and resignation. The party evidently were making for the coast.

J. H. WILSON, Brevet Major General.

Our Special Washington Despatch.

WASHINGTON, May 14, 1865.

The news of the capture of Jeff. Davis spread rapidly through the city last evening, and was the occasion of much enthusiasm and rejoicing. It was announced in the various places of amusement and called forth the most tumultuous applause.

The details of his capture, published this afternoon in extras, has turned into ridicule what at first was supposed to have been invested with some element of dignity worthy of the occasion. It is regarded as a fitting termination to such a career as that of the leading actor in the tragedy that he should have been captured while trying to make his escape in his wife's petticoats, and should have surrendered without an effort at resistance, which might have dignified in a glorious death his exit from the scene on which he lagged too long. He will now come here to be tried for complicity in the assassination of President Lincoln, and will probably die not as a political martyr, but as a felon and murderer.

From the well known characteristics of General Wilson and his pertinacity in attention to minute details no doubt is entertained that the arch-traitor Jeff. will be safely delivered to the authorities here for trial and punishment.

DETAILS OF THE FLIGHT.

That Jeff. Davis would eventually be captured has been for some time a foregone conclusion, in which the public have so thoroughly acquiesced that the official announcement that he is in the hands of General J. H. Wilson will be received with few demonstrations of joy. The event has been so long anticipated that it falls as stillborn as an anti-climax to the greater acts of the assassination, the surrenders and the peace. "The capture of Jeff. Davis" is an announcement which, two years ago, would have been considered startling indeed, but when the people saw that Lee and Johnston and Dick Taylor had been unable to escape the combinations of General Grant, they felt that there was little fear that Davis would succeed. The combinations by which the rebellion has been destroyed east of the Mississippi find gratifying completeness in the capture of the arch-traitor himself.

Davis began his flight from Richmond on the night of April 2, and by the morning of the 3d had succeeded in doing by rail what Lee could not with his army—in fact, reach Danville and get beyond Grant's lines. He was at Danville on the 6th of April, anxiously awaiting the appearance of Lee, and employing himself in inditing a wild, wordy and windy proclamation, in which he vainly promised what he could never hope to perform. He declared there was no reason to be discouraged, and that he had no intention of abandoning the cause. He got the news of the surrender of Lee at nine o'clock at night on April 8, and at daylight the next morning he left in a private conveyance for Greensboro, N. C. Here he remained for several days. He was prominent, through his Secretary of War, Breckinridge, in arranging the terms of the Sherman-Johnston armistice, in which that admirable strategist, Sherman, failed so signally as a diplomatist. He remained at or near Greensboro during the time that elapsed in which the agreement of Sherman and Johnston was submitted to the authorities at Washington, and, as if confident the terms would not be accepted, he employed himself in organizing a detachment of cavalry, under Generals Wade Hampton and S. G. Dibbrell, as an escort for himself, his family staff and treasure to the coast of Florida or the Trans-Mississippi Department. On the receipt of the intelligence that the administration was not to be duped into the acceptance of the terms of the Sherman-Johnston armistice, he promptly decamped from Greensboro and continued "his flight."

His route from Greensboro to Irwinsville, Georgia, is not distinctly known. On April the 25th he left Charlotte, escorted by about three thousand cavalry. The men were mostly Kentuckians and Texans. Davis made a speech in Charlotte before leaving, in which, in his usual style, he promised to have a larger army in the field than ever very soon. He had with him a train of about twenty wagons. His escort were more desperadoes and adventurers, many of whom were formerly under John Morgan. He crossed the Savannah river a short distance above Augusta on May 2, and at Powellton, Hancock county, on May 5. In the meantime vengeance, on the wings of lightning, was pursuing him. By means of the rebel telegraph wires the President telegraphed his proclamation, accusing Davis of being in league with the assassins of President Lincoln, to General Wilson at Macon, Ga. General Wilson at once scattered handbills describing Davis throughout the country, and started his cavalry in search of the culprit. The result of the search is thus modestly announced by General Wilson:—

MACON, Ga., May 12—11 A. M.

Lieutenant General U. S. GRANT and Hon. SECRETARY OF WAR, Washington, D. C.—

I have the honor to report that at daylight of the 10th instant, Colonel Pritchard, commanding Fourth Michigan cavalry, captured Jeff. Davis and family, with Reagan, Postmaster General; Colonel Harrison, Private Secretary; Colonel Johnson, Aid-de-Camp; Colonel Morris, Colonel Lubbick, Lieutenant Hathaway, and others. Colonel Pritchard surprised their camp at Irwinsville, in Irwin county, Ga., seventy-five miles southeast of this place. They will be here to-morrow night, and will be forwarded under strong guard without delay.

I will send further particulars at once.

J. H. WILSON, Brevet Major General.

The despatches from General Wilson, which we publish elsewhere, give in detail the rest of the story.

THE NEWS IN THE CITY.

The capture of Jeff. Davis did not create in this city that degree of excitement which such an event might be expected to occasion. People took the matter quite coolly and calmly. Nobody, in fact, seemed much astonished or exercised in consequence, and things went on pretty much the same as usual to all outward appearances. The cause of this lack of excitement is doubtless the declining interest in everything concerning the rebellion. The community feel that the fighting is over and the Union restored, and therefore, care little for what may follow. Had the capture occurred a few months, or even weeks, sooner there would have been a very different condition of things to report; but occurring at this late day, and when people daily expected some such winding up of the arch-traitor's career, it only awakens the customary interest that any ordinary event might give rise to. It shows how very insignificant the rebel ex-President must have become, too, when people do not even think it worth their while to glory over his misfortune.

The probable disposition of Jeff. was much discussed yesterday. Some hoped he would be hanged without a moment's delay for his treason, while others expressed the views lately enunciated by Wendell Phillips, and were in favor of leaving him to the sting of his own conscience. All, however, agreed that if he is implicated in the assassination scheme hanging would be too good for him.

SKETCHES OF THE CAPTORS.

Sketch of Brevet Major General James H. Wilson.

No less great than the wonderful revelations of the material resources of the country has been the development of all grades of men equal to every emergency. Less than five years ago the subject of this sketch was a cadet at the government academy; to-day he leads an army, and his name is associated at the head of the finishing and one of the most brilliant raids of the war.

James H. Wilson, Brevet Major General of Volunteers, and Captain of Engineers United States Army, was born in Lower Illinois about the year 1840. He entered West Point as a cadet in 1856, and graduated fifth in his class, June 30, 1860. On the following day he was promoted to brevet second lieutenant Topographical Engineers. Upon the outbreak of the rebellion he was made full second lieutenant, to date from June 10, 1861. On the 9th of September following he became first lieutenant in his corps. Upon the organization, at Annapolis, Maryland, of the Sherman (T. W.) expedition to Hilton Head, South Carolina, Lieutenant Wilson was ordered to duty as chief of Topographical Engineers of that army. After the forces had secured a foothold in South Carolina Lieutenant Wilson conducted a number of reconnoissances through the rivers and other water courses in the vicinity of Fort Pulaski, on the Savannah river, with a view to future operations in that direction. On December [illegible] he left on a more extended and distant reconnoissance to discover whether a navigable passage existed between Callibogue Sound and the Savannah river. At this time the extreme advance of our forces rested on Dawfuskie Island. Leaving Callibogue Sound in two rowboats, with a detachment of seventy men of a Rhode Island regiment, Lieutenant Wilson proceeded by night through a number of intricate channels. At various points along the route the party spied the picket fires of the enemy, but passed them with muffled oars and without eliciting discovery. After a night of fruitless search the party drew up with the dawn of day and secreted themselves in the grass. When night returned they again took to their boats. Pushing on their way they soon entered Wright river, and, rounding the point of Jones' Island, entered the Savannah. The rest of the night was passed in making soundings, approaching under the very guns of Pulaski, and so near that the sentinels could be heard at their beat. Lieutenant Wilson now pushed up the Savannah beyond Venus Point, to the mouth of Mud river, whence he returned to the Wright, and thence to the headquarters of the army. The result of this reconnoissance was the discovery of a passage for gunboats drawing ten feet and clear of the guns of the fort. In the subsequent operations against Pulaski the troops followed Lieutenant Wilson's route, and a battery was established at Venus Point. Lieutenant Wilson remained in the Department of the South, conspicuously engaged on engineer duty until the summer of 1862, when he served for a short time as aid to General McClellan. On November 8, 1862, he was appointed assistant inspector general, with the rank of lieutenant colonel of volunteers, and assigned to General Grant, by whom he was for several months assigned to duty on the staff of Major General James B. McPherson. During the operations in Mississippi and against Vicksburg Colonel Wilson was again conspicuous for his engineering skill, and in the brilliant victories of General Grant, in the vicinity of Chattanooga, won the official commendation of Gen. W. F. Smith, with whom he was then acting. On December 31, 1863, he was nominated brigadier general of volunteers, to date from October 30, 1863, and was confirmed May 12, 1864, upon the recommendation of Lieutenant General Grant. In January, 1864, General Wilson was appointed chief of the Cavalry Bureau in Washington. In April following he was assigned to the command of the Third division, cavalry corps, Major General Sheridan, Army of the Potomac. During General Grant's Virginia campaign he acted independently, to the right and rear of the army, to destroy railroads. He also covered the rear from Coal Harbor to the south side of the James river. In June and the beginning of July he conducted a raid south of Richmond, destroying the railroads and throwing the enemy in a great state of alarm. After the necessity of cavalry operations in the vicinity of Richmond and Petersburg had passed General Wilson was transferred to the Shenandoah valley, where he added to his reputation as an efficient officer. For distinguished services he was breveted major general of volunteers, to date from Oct. 5, 1864. During the winter he was transferred to the Department of the Cumberland, and by General Thomas was placed in command of the cavalry corps of the Army of the Cumberland. On March 25, 1865, General Wilson started from Chickasaw, Alabama, with his troops well mounted and equipped. After routing Roddy at Monticello he moved on and annihilated the combined forces of Forrest, Lyon and Chalmers, under Forrest, and occupied Selma, Ala., on April 2. Thence he moved on to Montgomery, thence swept across Georgia, reaching Savannah on April 28, having marched six hundred and fifty miles.

As will be perceived by the telegraphic announcement, it was a portion of General Wilson's gallant corps which has the honor of putting a climax to the downfall of the rebellion by capturing its prime mover and leader.

General Wilson is not over twenty-five years of age, very young looking, about five feet eight inches in height, light hair and eyes, and rather boyish in manner. This latter peculiarity, however, does not detract from his merits as a soldier. He has the reputation of good judgment in the disposition of troops and the management of isolated expeditions. General Wilson's present rank in the regular army is captain in the corps of engineers, dating from May 7, 1863.

Sketch of Lieutenant Colonel Benjamin D. Pritchard, Fourth Michigan Cavalry.

By the official announcement of the capture of Jeff. Davis, the Fourth Michigan cavalry, commanded by Lieutenant Colonel Benjamin D Pritchard, has the glory of this crowning act. Col. Pritchard entered the service as captain in the Fourth Michigan cavalry, his commission dating August 13, 1862. His regiment rendezvoused at Detroit, was mustered into the United States service on August 29, and left for Kentucky in September following. Colonel Pritchard, during his captaincy, took part in the advance during the attack on Morgan's guerillas at Samford, and joined in the pursuit as far as Crab Orchard, Kentucky. On November 8, 1862, he took part in the chase after Morgan, in which the rebel chief was driven seven miles, and putting him completely to rout. Subsequently he participated in the operations against Murfreesboro and in pursuit of Forrest and Wheeler towards Fort Donelson. During the campaigns of 1863 and 1864, in Tennessee and Georgia, the Fourth Michigan took again a conspicuous part. For gallantry in the various actions of his regiment Captain Pritchard was promoted to the rank which he now holds.

It is unnecessary to repeat here the series of skilful and quickly executed movements, under the immediate command of Colonel Pritchard, which have resulted in Davis' capture. It is hoped this satisfactory success is but the forerunner of a more definite termination of the ex-Presidential rebel's career

SKETCHES OF THE CAPTIVES.

The Rebel Leader, Jeff. Davis.

Jeff. Davis was born in Kentucky, June 3, 1806. He was the son of James Davis, a noted horse trader, of Hopkinsville, Kentucky. The father fell under suspicion as a horse thief, and was forced to fly from Kentucky, and settled, when Jeff. was very young, near Vicksburg, Miss. He was able a few years after his removal to send his son Jeff. to Kentucky to complete his education at the Transylvania University, Lexington, and subsequently, through the influence of his money, secured for him an appointment to West Point, which young Jeff. entered at sixteen, forming part of the graduating class of 1828. He graduated near the foot of the class, and was commissioned in the First infantry as brevet second lieutenant, the lowest rank that could be given him. He was sent to Florida and served very creditably with Zach. Taylor, in the Black Hawk war, for which he got a commission as first lieutenant in the First dragoons. In 1832 he offended General Taylor by running away with and marrying his daughter, and the old General never recognized Davis until they happened to meet on the battle field of Buena Vista, Mexico. In 1835 Davis, having resigned his commission, settled near Vicksburg, and entered upon the arena of politics, in which he was so far successful as to be elected to the lower house of Congress.

When the Mexican war broke out Davis raised and commanded the First regiment of Mississippi rifles. The only significant feature in his career was the fact that he declined a United States commission as brigadier general of volunteers, on the ground that such an appointment by the federal Executive was a violation of State rights.

He re-entered political life in 1847, having been appointed by the Governor of Mississippi to fill the vacancy in the United States Senate caused by the death of Mr. Speight. At the ensuing election, in 1848, he was elected to fill the term expiring in 1851. On his return to Mississippi he became the State rights candidate for Governor, but was defeated by "Little Fidget" Foote, his lifetime enemy, who is now lying in Ludlow street jail in this city. About the same time he stumped the State for the purpose of advocating the repudiation of the State debt, and was subsequently honored as the originator and prime mover of that great swindle. In 1853 he was called by Pierce to a seat in his Cabinet, as Secretary of War. In 1857 he was re-elected United States Senator from Mississippi, which he held until his resignation (January, 1861), on the secession of his State. During the Congressional vacation of 1860, Davis made a visit to the North, and examined into the feeling which prevailed here at the time. He became satisfied that a strong party at the North were willing to entrust the control of the government again into the hands of a Southern President, and being ambitious for that position he made several speeches here announcing his intention to go home to Mississippi and labor for the preservation of the Union. On his return he found that other leaders had drawn the people into the meshes of secession, and with the selfishness which has always characterized him, he gave in his adherence to secession and became the leader in the rebellion. He was chosen Provisional President of the rebel confederation of States February 4, 1861; was inaugurated February 22, 1861, and re-elected in 1862 for the term of six years, for only half of which time he will be permitted to act. His administration of the affairs of the rebellious States has been marked by no great brilliancy or judgment. He has been the Marplot of almost every one of the rebel campaigns, and has done more by his obstinacy, envy, jealousy and malice to destroy the unity and effectiveness of his government and its armies than any other of its leaders. If the confederacy had possessed a leader less obstinate in the pursuit of bad plans, less envious of the fame of his subordinates, and less quarrelsome generally, it might have existed a few months longer.

There will be no difficulty whatever in conveying Davis and his party to Washington. No armed bands of the enemy remain in force to aid him, and there exists among his own people no such love for the obstinate and selfish old despot as will induce them to rise en masse to his rescue. He will be forwarded in hot haste to Washington, and be entered with the other criminals now before the military court to be tried for the murder of President Lincoln.

Mrs. Jefferson Davis.

The present wife of the arch-traitor, who has been captured with him, is his second wife, the daughter of General Taylor having died many years since. Mrs. Davis' maiden name was Varina Howell. She is said to be a granddaughter of General Howell, of New Jersey. She is still a young woman, with a family, we believe, of four children.

John H. Reagan, of Texas.

John H. Reagan, the rebel Postmaster General, is a native of Sevier county, Tennessee, where he was born on the 8th of October, 1818. He is, consequently, in his forty-seventh year. He is a lawyer by profession, and has occupied many civic and military positions in Texas, to which State he emigrated many years since. In 1852 he was appointed Judge of the District Court of Texas, and in 1857 he was elected a member of the Thirty-fifth Congress, and was chosen to sit on several committees. He has filled since 1861 the position of postmaster.

Colonel Burton N. Harrison, of Mississippi,

has been the private secretary of Davis ever since his inauguration as rebel President. Of his history previous to the war we know nothing. His career has been confined to the duties of a private secretary.

Colonel W. P. Johnston, of Kentucky.

William Preston Johnston, of Kentucky, is a native of Louisville, the son of a well known physician of that city and nephew of General William Preston, of the same city, formerly Minister to Spain. He is familiarly known in Louisville as "Boots" Johnston. He was known there as a young man of wild, loose habits, very fond of indulging in amateur theatrical performances. He was very fond of playing Sir Charles Coldstream, in Used Up, and played it with much taste. He affected the character in real life and tried to be an indolent blasé individual; but he has, doubtless, been thrown off his equanimity by late events as thoroughly as Sir Charles was by his supposed murder of the old blacksmith. Johnston married some years since the sister of Matt. Ward, who became notorious as the murderer of the Kentucky schoolmaster, Butler.

Colonel Lubbick, of Texas.

Francis R. Lubbick, an aide to the rebel President, reported by General Wilson as captured with him, is a native of Harris county, Texas. He was formerly Lieutenant Governor of that State, having been elected in 1857 with H. R. Runnels as Governor. His term expired in 1859. When the war began he went on the staff of General Longstreet, and served in that capacity at the first battle of Manassas or Bull run. He remained with Longstreet until 1864, when he was given the vacancy on the staff of Jeff. Davis, caused by the promotion of Colonel James Chestnut, of South Carolina, to be a brigadier general. He has since been serving in that capacity.

WILSON.

Occupation of Alabama by the National Armies.

The Sixteenth Army Corps in Montgomery.

GEN. ADAMS OPPOSED TO SURRENDERS.

He Burns Ninety-seven Thousand Bales of Cotton.

UNION SENTIMENT OF THE PEOPLE.

Political Complexion of Parties in Alabama.

MONTGOMERY UNDER THE OLD FLAG.

Civil Movement in Favor of the Union,

&c., &c., &c.

Mr. Wm. H. Wells' Despatch.

MONTGOMERY, Ala., April 27, 1865.

Accounts of the capture of Selma and Montgomery by General Wilson have doubtless reached you. A few days after the fall of Selma General Wilson took up the line of march for Montgomery. Very little resistance was encountered, and only a few unimportant skirmishes occurred with the demoralized rebel "buttermilks" under Adams and Buford, who abandoned the proud little capital of Alabama in somewhat indecent haste. The scenes which characterized their sudden departure are described by loyal eyewitnesses as thoroughly disgraceful and cowardly.

The city was evacuated by the troops under Adams and Buford on Wednesday, the 12th of April. A committee appointed from the City Council, with a deputation of citizens, went out about three o'clock A. M., under flag of truce, to surrender the place to the United States authorities, and to ask of the General commanding the Union forces protection for the non-combatant citizens and private property.

The committee appointed by the Council, together with the Mayor, repaired to the headquarters of General Adams, and stated that they came as the representatives of the city to inquire of him what were his intentions with regard to the city—whether he would attempt its defence or would retreat.

Adams replied that their query was based upon the most idle curiosity, which he would not gratify. He did not know whether he would "make a fight" or not.

The committee then desired to know his design with regard to the cotton in the city warehouses. They asked him if he intended to burn it, and if he did, could its destruction not be managed so as not to involve the safety of private property and the lives of women and children. His response to this reasonable and humane request was that he was determined at all hazards to burn the cotton, and if private property was destroyed he could not help it.

General Adams in turn asked the committee why they came to him with these interrogatories.

The Mayor stated that if the city was to be left without protection, it was the determination of the Council to go out to meet the Union General, and to ask at his hands, in the event of occupation by his troops, such protection for the citizens and private property as the circumstances might admit.

General Adams retorted that he *did not approve of surrenders of any end*, and that he would arrest any person attempting to leave the corporate limits with a flag of truce.

THE CONFLAGRATION.

At about five o'clock orders were issued for the destruction of the cotton, and the smoke from Johnson's wareware was to be the signal. The large cotton warehouses of Lehman, Durr & Co., Gilmer and others were fired simultaneously. The scene which followed beggars description. Dense columns of smoke piled high above the city, and almost shut out the light of the sun. Women, with affrighted countenances, were seen running hither and thither, crying and wringing their hands, and hundreds of excited persons were endeavoring to secure their furniture from the adjacent houses. The distress of the innocent persons endangered by the fury of the devastating element would have excited the pity even of the destroyers, if they had remained long enough to witness the execution of their desperate order. The flames enveloped the buildings and burned with great rapidity, and before night all these large warehouses, with their contents, lay in heaps of smouldering ruins. It was a miracle that the city was not utterly destroyed. The wind was setting in from the east, and carried the flames away from it. Still the escape seemed almost providential.

Ninety-seven thousand bales of cotton were burned.

INCIDENTS OF THE FIRE.

The city fire companies deserve the highest commendation. They worked with great energy and courage, and to their efforts, perhaps, the city is indebted for its salvation. The members of the negro fire company especially merit great praise. The brave fellows, reckless of life and limb, met the furious flame at every advance, and kept the conflagration in check.

An indiscriminate plunder of the warehouses and stores adjacent to the burned district was participated in by persons of every age, sex and color. The people crowded the roofs of the houses to prevent them catching fire.

THE CITY SURRENDERED.

All the stragglers having passed through, and the picket lines having been removed, the Mayor, with a deputation of Councilmen and citizens went out in the direction of Catoma creek, to meet the advance of the United States forces. They were received with great courtesy by General McCook, who was the commanding officer of the advance, and who assured the Mayor that all private property in the city should be respected so far as consistent with the military occupation. He said it might be necessary to press horses, only, for military purposes, but aside from that the citizens of Montgomery might rest assured of his protection. The Mayor then issued the following proclamation:—

TO THE PEOPLE OF MONTGOMERY:—

The city of Montgomery having been surrendered into the protection of the United States authorities, I am assured by Major General McCook, commanding United States forces in Montgomery, that all private property will be respected, so far as consistent with military operations, and that a military guard will be established for the better protection of the city and its inhabitants.

The General commanding requests, on the part of the people, that no citizen will attempt to leave the corporate limits.

W. L. COLEMAN, Mayor.

MONTGOMERY, April 12, 1865.

THE OCCUPATION.

On Wednesday morning, the 12th, a squad of about fifty mounted men dashed into Main street, and rode up to the Capitol, where they formed in line. In about half an hour General McCook, at the head of his columns, accompanied by the Mayor and committee of the Council, rode into Court House square, and from thence to the Capitol. Very soon thereafter the United States flag was floating from the Capitol dome, the Court House, the telegraph office, and from the Exchange Hotel, where General McCook established his headquarters. The flag of truce and the battle flag of the advance were placed one on each side of the Capitol stairs.

General Wilson, commanding the mounted army, arrived in the course of the day, and established his headquarters at the residence of Colonel Powell.

The troops poured into the city all through the day, and kept arriving all the next day. They were passed rapidly and in the strictest order through the city to encampments several miles beyond town. One division moved right on to Columbus, not even stopping to rest in this vicinity. The force was variously estimated at from ten to sixteen thousand, all well equipped and mounted.

THE CITY AGAIN EVACUATED.

General Wilson on Thursday gave notice to the municipal authorities that he was going to evacuate the place, and the people must take care of themselves. The troops commenced to move out on Thursday, and by Friday afternoon the last of the rear guard had departed.

ANOTHER CONFLAGRATION.

Before leaving General Wilson set fire to the railroad buildings, cars and locomotives, the government machine shops, nitre works and arsenal, and in a few hours all were a mass of ruins. In the destruction of public and private property by fire Montgomery has suffered fearfully.

ADVANCE OF THE SIXTEENTH ARMY CORPS.

After a weary and dusty march from the Gulf, we arrived in the vicinity of Dixie's first capital. The Second Maine cavalry, with the gallant and dashing Spurling at their head, constituted the advance of this corps, and entered Montgomery on the morning of the 24th of April. The citizens crowded the doorways and street corners, and observed the novel cavalcade with interest and curiosity. One of the local papers, announcing the event, remarks that:—"The forces of the United States have already entered the proud little city of Montgomery, the first capital of the confederacy. To some this may appear an unhappy event. Such persons must look upon the fact, however, as one of the fortunes of war, and make up their minds to bear it as good citizens and as gentlemen, and to afford such assistance and give such attentions as may facilitate the establishment of good order and good government."

THE GRAND ENTREE.

The main body of General Smith's army—McArthur's, Garrard's and Carr's divisions of the Sixteenth corps—entered the city about noon on the 25th, and passed through the streets with colors gaily flying and bands playing alternately "Dixie" and "Yankee Doodle." The troops and the long wagon trains were passing through all day. The white citizens crowded the sidewalks to get a glimpse of the "serried ranks of blue," while vast numbers of delighted little niggers followed closely after the bands. To many they came as deliverers, and frequent demonstrations of welcome greeted the sturdy column. To others, no doubt, they appeared "dreadful as an army with banners," and this class, though silent, gave unmistakable evidences of dissatisfaction in their looks.

THE FIRST REBEL CAPITAL.

A brief description of this little city of Montgomery may not prove uninteresting. It is situated in a pleasant valley, in a bend of the Alabama river, and its surroundings would be decidedly picturesque with a few hills, or even an approach to one, to relieve the monotony of the landscape. The only elevations of note are in the city itself, from the summits of which the eye extends over as fair and beautiful an area of table land as was ever desecrated by the devastating march of war.

Montgomery is a very pretty town, and many of the residences and gardens of the better class of inhabitants evince a degree of cultivated taste and refinement. The dwelling houses—chiefly frame ones, painted white—present a pretty contrast amid the green foilage in which they seem embowered. The Capitol, *where the first rebel Congress assembled, and from which was issued the memorable telegraphic despatch from the rebel Secretary, Pope Walker, inaugurating the war by directing the fire to open upon Fort Sumter*, is an imposing edifice of stone, situated upon the loftiest and most commanding eminence in the city. It has Corinthian columns, like the Capitol building at Nashville, and is not unlike that handsome structure.

One of the handsomest residences in the city is a large frame building, which was occupied by Jeff. Davis while presiding over the destinies of Rebeldom when this was the seat of rebel government. The grounds and gardens adjacent to this place are in the finest state of preservation.

SENTIMENT OF ALABAMA.

I am convinced that a majority of the people of this State, including the farmers and the working masses, with a large proportion of the leading influential and substantial men, do now and have ever desired the restoration of their State to its old position with her sisters of the Union, from which it was dragooned and precipitated into rebellion by the vilest system of political chicanery and intrigue. Among the faithful of Rebeldom Alabama was always considered unsound. Many of her people to-day are as true to the Union as ever. Here, in Montgomery, the conservatives have been scarcely permitted to open their mouths. Their friends and relatives have been torn from them by conscripting agents and forced to take part in the rebellion. Only for the past few months have they dared to speak out in bold and manly tones against the encroachments of the grinding despotism which manacled their limbs and bridled their tongues. In the State Legislature, though not in a majority, the conservatives managed to defeat the machinations of the Watts party of fire-eaters, and to bravely hold their own in the face of the reign of terror, and the most intolerant and fanatic spirit of proscription.

THE MONTGOMERY PRESS.

That notorious peripatetic concern, the Memphis-Grenada-Jackson-Atlanta-Montgomery *Appeal*, was printed here, but plumed its wings for a more congenial clime upon the first approach of Wilson's dashing dragoons. I understand it has gone to Macon, Ga., where, no doubt, it breathed its last sigh of desperation over the fallen fortunes of "Jeff.," as General Wilson now occupies that city. Its proprietors fondly hoped to make it the chief "thunderer" of the magnificent empire the rebels expected to establish.

The organ of the fire-eaters here, and the special toady of the boasting and vulgar Watts, who ruled the State pretty much as "Uncle Jeff." directed, was the Montgomery *Advertiser*, edited by the Simon-pure secesh in general, and nobody in particular. I understand it fled with the decamping Governor and his precious archives to Eufaula.

The only journal here, and indeed throughout the whole State, that seems to have evinced the least independence and spirit in defence of the people and in condemning and denouncing the Richmond despotism, is the Montgomery *Mail*, which is still in successful existence under the old Star Spangled Banner which floated over its cradle and birth. The *Mail* in better days was the *protégé* of Jonce Hooper, well known to the readers of the old New York *Spirit of the Times* as the author of "Simon Suggs." Its present editor is the Southern humorist, "John Happy" (Albert Roberts), late of the Nashville press. The *Mail* has done much good in directing the tone of Southern sentiments, and in combatting the absurd prejudices created by designing politicians of the Yancey and Davis school.

UNDER THE OLD FLAG.

Now that the citizens are once more under the shadow of the old flag of the Union, they begin pretty freely to express their devotion to the Union and their long repressed maledictions against the tyrants who had dragged them into a wicked rebellion against it.

I understand the people are soon to hold a mass meeting to consider the resumption of their allegiance thereto, and resolve themselves back into the Union, with their State, which many of them consider has never been out of the Union. Leading secessionists, at length convinced of the hopelessness of the Davis dynasty, are now prepared to effect a compromise with their more conservative neighbors, who have always been loyal, to return Alabama to her old position in the galaxy of loyal States.

THE MILITARY SITUATION

is just beginning to be correctly understood here. The capture of Columbus and Macon, Ga., by General Wilson, the entire and complete possession of their State, with the capture of every seaport and important inland town, and the surrender of the Army of Northern Virginia to General Grant, has satisfied even the most sanguine rebel that Dixie has pretty effectually "played out." As a general thing, the people, if not all disposed to rejoice at these important conclusions, seem at least highly satisfied with the immediate prospect of peace and the return of friends and relatives to their homes. The loss of the "divine institution" of slavery does not even excite a sigh of regret; and every sensible, reflecting Southern man I have met here rejoices that the war has at least relieved them of this incubus upon their agricultural and mechanical resources, upon their literature and general prosperity.

Fatal Accident in West Broadway.

About half-past nine o'clock last evening, as a Sixth avenue car was passing through West Broadway, on its return trip, one of a party of women essayed to cross the street before the car should have passed. In the attempt one of the horses struck her, knocking her down, she striking the pole in her fall. The driver did all in his power to stop the car, but owing to the fright the horses plunged, and before he could succeed the fore wheel of the car had passed completely over her, leaving her a mangled and bleeding corpse.

THE SEVEN-THIRTIES.

Immense Offerings of Money to the Government.

Over Thirty Millions Subscribed on Saturday.

The Balance of the Loan to be Put on the Market.

$230,000,000 MORE TO BE ISSUED.

POSTING THE NATIONAL BOOKS,

&c., &c., &c.

PHILADELPHIA, May 13, 1865.

The subscriptions to-day to the seven-thirty loan amounted to *thirty millions four hundred and fifty-one thousand nine hundred and fifty dollars*. The largest single Western subscription was one million and thirty five thousand dollars, from the Second National Bank, Chicago. The First National Bank of Cincinnati took one million dollars. The largest single Eastern subscription was five millions five hundred and fifty-four thousand dollars, from the Ninth National Bank, New York. The Bank of Commerce, New York, took one million. Fisk & Hatch, New York, $1,082,500. There were 21,307 individual subscriptions. Henry Clews & Co., New York, $1,000.000; National Metropolis, Washington, $400,000; National Exchange, Hartford, $200,000; Second National, Providence, $200,000; Second National, Boston, $500,000. The total sales for the week amounted to $98,384,650.

At the close of to-day's sales of the seven-thirties but little, if any, of the second series of the three hundred millions remained. All telegraphic orders received this day (Saturday) will be filled. If any of the loan remains over it will be given to the first applicants by telegraph on Monday morning.

Two weeks ago the amount of the second series sold and reported, inclusive of voucher conversions, was about one hundred and forty-five millions of dollars. The cash sales last week were about forty millions. This week they were ninety-eight millions.

The balance of the conversion of quartermasters' vouchers during the last two weeks, and which were not included in the daily published sales of the seven-thirties, together with the sales in California, and at the various sub-treasuries, also not included in the daily sales, will make about fifteen millions. Altogether the total sales are two hundred and ninety-eight millions of dollars.

The Secretary of the Treasury has decided to issue the balance of the loan that was authorized by the act of March, 1865, and which amounts to two hundred and thirty millions in seven and three-tenths notes, precisely similar in tenor, form and privileges to the seven-thirties already sold, payable three years from the 15th of next July, except that the government will reserve to itself the option of paying interest in gold coin at the rate of six per cent instead of seven and three-tenths in currency. Subscribers will deduct the interest in currency up to July 15 when they subscribe. The delivery of the notes of this third series of the seven-thirties will commence on the 1st of June, and will be made promptly and continuously after that date. Subscriptions, however, will be received at once, and interest at seven and three-tenths per cent allowed to subscribers up to the 15th of July, in the same manner as it was allowed for interval between the second series and the first series. Any excess of subscriptions to the present series will be filled with the new issue as speedily as the notes can be prepared at the Treasury. The slight change made in the conditions of this third series affect only the matter of interest. The payment in gold, if made, will be equivalent to the currency interest of the higher rate. The important privilege of converting the notes into the long and popular five-twenty gold bearing bonds, or of demanding payment of them at maturity, at the holder's option, is not interfered with. The takers of the seven-thirty loan will rejoice if the Secretary sooner or later avails himself of the option to pay them six per cent in gold in lieu of the larger rate of interest in currency. The return to specie payments, in the event of which only will this option be availed of, would so reduce and equalize prices that purchases made with six per cent in gold would be fully equal to those made with seven and three-tenths per cent in currency. The machinery used in popularizing the first two series of the seven-thirties will be occupied by the Secretary of the Treasury in the sale of this third series. It will be under the supervision of Jay Cooke, the government loan subscription agent, who will employ the sub-agencies heretofore employed, and with which the people are familiar. It is confidently expected that the whole amount will be sold in the next sixty or ninety days. When this two hundred and thirty millions is disposed of the last opportunity for those profitable investments in United States government securities will be gone.

The Navy.

ARRIVAL OF THE GUNBOATS GETTYSBURG AND DAYLIGHT.

The United States steamer Gettysburg arrived here yesterday, thirty-six hours from Fortress Monroe, with United States steamer Daylight in tow. The following is a list of her officers:—

Acting Volunteer Lieutenant Commanding—Samuel B. Washburne

Acting Assistant Paymaster—James S. Giraud.

Ensigns—Wm. J. Eldridge, M. C. Keith, S. S. La Dien and Charles Miller.

Mate—T. H. P. Gross.

Engineers—Acting First Assistant, G. S. Perkins; Second Assistants, J. M. Case, A. J. Pixley, E. B. Carter; Third Assistants, Jno. W. Homas, J. D. Wilbur, A. J. Donegan.

The United States steamer Daylight, eighteen guns, Acting Master Jos. A. Bullard commanding, forty-eight hours from Hampton Roads, was towed here by United States steamer Gettysburg. The following is a list of her officers:—

Acting Master Commanding—Jos. A. Bullard.
Acting Ensign and Executive Officer—J. Arnold Cross.
Acting Assistant Surgeon—Jas. R. May.
Acting Assistant Paymaster—Frederick C. Imlay.
Engineers—Acting First Assistant, in charge, Daniel B. Overton; Second Assistant, Robert Pallett; Third Assistant, Henry R. Allen.
Ensign—C. Lindemann.
Mates—Wm. H. Bolton, J. E. Merriman.

DEPARTURE OF THE SUPPLY STEAMER FOR THE SOUTH ATLANTIC BLOCKADING SQUADRON.

The supply steamer Massachusetts, Acting Volunteer Lieutenant commanding William West, was detained on Saturday last, her regular day of sailing, by order of the Navy Department. She will sail at noon to-morrow from Philadelphia. Letters for the South Atlantic blockading squadron, if forwarded to-day, will reach her in time.

Williamsburg City News.

FIGHT BETWEEN FIREMEN AND POLICEMEN—TWO OF THE FORMER SHOT.—About three o'clock A. M., yesterday, some firemen belonging to Hose Company No. 10, were congregated in North Second street, near Seventh, E. D., and acting in a disorderly manner. Officers Lee and Welsh, of the Forty-fifth precinct, went into the crowd and advised them to disperse and preserve order. This they did for a short time, but soon after attacked the officers with stones, and used them very roughly, officer Welsh having one of his hands badly mashed with a stone. The officers then grappled with two of them named Felix Doyle and Michael Farrell. The friends of these men then attempted a rescue, and succeeded in taking Doyle from officer Welsh, whose hand was so badly injured that it was useless for the time. Having succeeded in rescuing Doyle, the crowd became bolder, and poured volley after volley of stones at the officers. The latter then concluded to use their revolvers in self-defence, and after firing a few shots into the crowd surrounding them, they managed to get back to the station house with the prisoner Farrell. Two of the firemen are reported to be shot, one of them dangerously in the groin, but their names or whereabouts could not be ascertained.

The Philadelphia Inquirer.

PRICE TWO CENTS. PHILADELPHIA, THURSDAY, MAY 25, 1865. PRICE TWO CENTS.

THE ARMIES OF THE REPUBLIC.

THEIR TRIUMPHANT RETURN TO THE NATIONAL CAPITAL.

GEORGE G. MEADE.—WM. TECUMSEH SHERMAN.

WELCOME!

Second Day of the Grand Review

ARMIES OF GEORGIA AND THE TENNESSEE!

GEN. SHERMAN LEADS THE WARRIORS

Howard, Slocum, Logan, Blair, Geary, Jeff. C. Davis.

80,000 HEROES IN THE LINE!

Magnificent Appearance and Bearing of the Veterans!

SHERMAN'S "FORAGERS" AND "BUMMERS."

Spoils of the March from Atlanta to Richmond!

IMMENSE CROWD OF SPECTATORS!

Brilliant Spectacle on the Avenue.

SPLENDID SCENE AT THE REVIEWING STAND.

Assembled Wisdom and Heroism of the Nation!

GRANT AND HIS CHIEFS REVIEW THE MIGHTY HOST!

President Johnson, the Cabinet, Members of Congress and Diplomatic Corps Witness the Scene.

GREAT ENTHUSIASM OF THE PEOPLE

Scenes and Incidents on the Route.

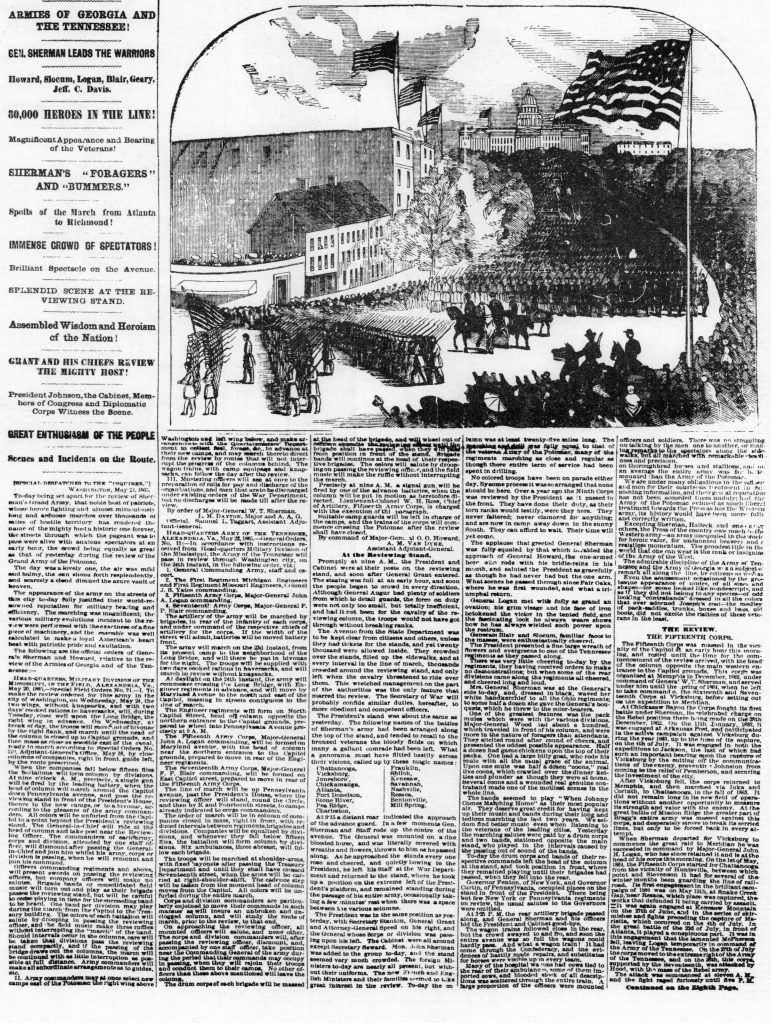

[SPECIAL DESPATCHES TO THE "INQUIRER."]

WASHINGTON, May 24, 1865.

To-day being set apart for the review of Sherman's Grand Army, that noble host of patriots, whose heroic fighting and almost miraculously long and arduous marches over thousands of miles of hostile territory has rendered the name of the mighty host a historic one forever, the streets through which the pageant was to pass were alive with anxious spectators at an early hour, the crowd being equally as great as that of yesterday during the review of the Grand Army of the Potomac.

The day was a lovely one, the air was mild and balmy, the sun shone forth resplendently, and scarcely a cloud dimmed the azure vault of heaven.

The appearance of the army on the streets of this city to-day fully justified their world-renowned reputation for military bearing and efficiency. The marching was magnificent; the various military evolutions incident to the review were performed with the exactness of a fine piece of machinery, and the *ensemble* was well calculated to make a loyal American's heart beat with patriotic pride and exultation.

The following are the official orders of Generals Sherman and Howard, relative to the review of the Armies of Georgia and of the Tennessee:—

HEAD-QUARTERS, MILITARY DIVISION OF THE MISSISSIPPI, IN THE FIELD, ALEXANDRIA, Va., May 20, 1865.—Special Field Orders No. 71.—I. To make the review ordered for this army in the city of Washington, on Wednesday, May 24, the two wings, without knapsacks, and with two days' cooked rations in haversacks, will, during Tuesday, close well upon the Long Bridge, the right wing in advance. On Wednesday, at break of day, the troops will move out of bivouac by the right flank, and march until the head of the column is closed up to Capitol grounds, and then mass as close as possible east of the canal, ready to march according to Special Orders No. 239, Adjutant-General's Office, May 18, by close columns of companies, right in front, guide left, by the route prescribed.

When the companies fall below fifteen files the battalions will form column by divisions. At nine o'clock A. M., precisely, a single gun will be fired by the leading battery, when the head of column will march around the Capitol down Pennsylvania avenue, and pass the reviewing stand in front of the President's House, thence to the new camps, or to a bivouac, according to the pleasure of the army commanders. All colors will be unfurled from the Capitol to a point beyond the President's reviewing stand. The General-in-Chief will ride at the head of column and take post near the Reviewing Officer. The commanders of each army, corps and division, attended by one staff officer, will dismount after passing the General-in-Chief and join him whilst his army, corps or division is passing, when he will remount and join his command.

Officers commanding regiments and above, will present swords on passing the reviewing officers, but company officers will make no salutes. Brigade bands or consolidated field music will turn out and play as their brigade passes the reviewing stand, but will be careful to cease playing in time for the succeeding band to be heard. One band per division may play during the march from the Capitol to the Treasury building. The colors of each battalion will salute by drooping in passing the reviewing officer, and the field music make three ruffles without interrupting the "march" of the band. Should intervals occur in the columns, care will be taken that divisions pass the reviewing stand compactly, and if the passing of the bridge draws out the columns, the march will be continued with as little interruption as possible at full distance. Army commanders will make all subordinate arrangements as to guides, etc.

II. Army commanders may at once select new camps east of the Potomac: the right wing above Washington and left wing below, and make arrangements with the Quartermasters' Department to collect fuel, forage, &c., in advance at their new camps, and may march thereto direct from the review by routes that will not interrupt the progress of the columns behind. The wagon trains, with camp equipage and knapsacks, can follow the day after the review.

III. Mustering officers will see at once to the preparation of rolls for pay and discharge of the organizations, and men that are to be discharged under existing orders of the War Department, but no discharges will be made till after the review.

By order of Major-General W. T. Sherman.

L. M. DAYTON, Major and A. A. G.

Official. Samuel L. Taggart, Assistant Adjutant-General.

HEAD-QUARTERS ARMY OF THE TENNESSEE, ALEXANDRIA, Va., May 22, 1865.—General Orders, No. 11:—In accordance with instructions received from Head-quarters Military Division of the Mississippi, the Army of the Tennessee will pass in review through Washington city, on the 24th instant, in the following order, viz.:

1. General Commanding Army, staff and escort.
2. The First Regiment Michigan Engineers and First Regiment Missouri Engineers, Colonel J. B. Yates commanding.
3. Fifteenth Army Corps, Major-General John A. Logan commanding.
4. Seventeenth Army Corps, Major-General F. P. Blair commanding.

The artillery of the army will be marched by brigades, in rear of the infantry of each corps, and under command of the respective chiefs of artillery for the corps. If the width of the street will admit, batteries will be moved battery front.

The army will march on the 23d instant, from its present camp to the neighborhood of the Long Bridge, and will there be put in bivouac for the night. The troops will be supplied with two days cooked rations in haversacks, and will march in review without knapsacks.

At daylight on the 24th instant, the army will commence crossing the Long Bridge, with Engineer regiments in advance, and will move by Maryland Avenue to the north and east of the Capitol, massing in streets contiguous to the line of march.

The Engineer regiments will form on North Capitol Street, head of column opposite the northern entrance to the Capitol grounds, prepared to wheel into Pennsylvania Avenue precisely at 9 A. M.

The Fifteenth Army Corps, Major-General John A. Logan commanding, will be formed on Maryland avenue, with the head of column near the northern entrance to the Capitol grounds, prepared to move in rear of the Engineer regiments.

The Seventeenth Army Corps, Major-General F. P. Blair commanding, will be formed on East Capitol street, prepared to move in rear of the Fifteenth Army Corps.

The line of march will be up Pennsylvania avenue, past the President's House, where the reviewing officer will stand, round the Circle, and then by K and Fourteenth streets, to camps already indicated to corps commanders.

The order of march will be in column of companies closed in mass, right in front, with reduced intervals between regiments, brigades and divisions. Companies will be equalized by divisions, and whenever they fall below fifteen files, the battalion will form column by divisions. Six ambulances, three abreast, will follow each brigade.

The troops will be marched at shoulder-arms, with fixed bayonets after passing the Treasury Department and until they shall have crossed Seventeenth street, when the arms will be carried at right-shoulder-shift. The cadence step will be taken from the moment head of column moves from the Capitol. All colors will be unfurled during the entire march.

Corps and division commanders are particularly enjoined to move their commands in such manner as will insure an unbroken and unclogged column, and will study the route of march, prior to the review, to that end.

On approaching the reviewing officer, all mounted officers will salute, and none other. The corps and division commanders will, after passing the reviewing officer, dismount, and, accompanied by one staff officer, take position near the Commanding General of the army during the period that their commands may occupy in passing, when they will rejoin their troops and conduct them to their camps. No other officers than those above mentioned will leave the column.

The drum corps of each brigade will be massed at the head of the brigade, and will wheel out of column opposite the reviewing officer until the brigade shall have passed, when they will pass from position in front of the stand. Brigade bands will continue at the head of their respective brigades. The colors will salute by drooping on passing the reviewing officer, and the field music will make the ruffle without interrupting the march.

Precisely at nine A. M. a signal gun will be fired by one of the advance batteries, when the column will be put in motion as heretofore directed. Lieutenant-Colonel W. H. Ross, Chief of Artillery, Fifteenth Army Corps, is charged with the execution of this paragraph.

Suitable camp guards will be left in charge of the camps, and the trains of the corps will commence crossing the Potomac after the review shall have closed.

By command of Major-General O. O. Howard,

A. M. VAN DYKE,
Assistant Adjutant-General.

At the Reviewing Stand.

Promptly at nine A. M., the President and Cabinet were at their posts on the reviewing stand, and soon after General Grant entered. The staging was full at an early hour, and soon the people began to crowd in every direction. Although General Augur had plenty of soldiers from which to detail guards, the force on duty were not only too small, but totally inefficient, and had it not been for the cavalry of the reviewing column, the troops would not have got through without breaking ranks.

The Avenue from the State Department was to be kept clear from citizens and others, unless they had tickets for the stands, and yet twenty thousand were allowed inside. They crowded over the stands, filled up the sidewalks, and at every interval in the line of march, thousands crowded around the reviewing stand, and only left when the cavalry threatened to ride over them. This wretched management on the part of the authorities was the only feature that marred the review. The Secretary of War will probably confide similar duties, hereafter, to more obedient and competent officers.

The President's stand was about the same as yesterday. The following names of the battles of Sherman's army had been arranged along the top of the stand, and tended to recall to the bronzed veterans the bloody fields on which many a gallant comrade had been left. What a panorama must have flitted hastily across their visions, called up by these magic names:

Chattanooga,	Franklin,
Vicksburg,	Shiloh,
Jonesboro',	Kenesaw,
Chickamauga,	Savannah,
Atlanta,	Nashville,
Fort Donelson,	Resaca,
Stone River,	Bentonville,
Pea Ridge,	Mill Spring.
Charleston,	

At 9·15 a distant roar indicated the approach of the advance guard. In a few moments Gen. Sherman and Staff rode up the centre of the avenue. The General was mounted on a fine blooded horse, and was literally covered with wreaths and flowers, thrown to him as he passed along. As he approached the stands every one rose and cheered, and quietly bowing to the President, he left his Staff at the War Department and returned to the stand, where he took up a position on the extreme left of the President's platform, and remained standing during the passage of his entire army, occasionally taking a few minutes' rest when there was a space between the various columns.

The President was in the same position as yesterday, with Secretary Stanton, General Grant and Attorney-General Speed on his right, and the General whose corps or division was passing upon his left. The Cabinet were all around except Secretary Seward. Hon. John Sherman was added to the group to-day, and the stand seemed very much crowded. The foreign Ministers to-day are nearly all present, but without their uniforms. The new French and English Ministers and their families seemed to take great interest in the review. To-day the column was at least twenty-five miles long. The marching and drill was fully equal to that of the veteran Army of the Potomac, many of the regiments marching as close and regular as though there entire term of service had been spent in drilling.

No colored troops have been on parade either day. By some process it was so arranged that none should be here. Over a year ago the Ninth Corps was reviewed by the President as it passed to the front. They have done their duty, as their torn ranks would testify, were they here. They never faltered; never clamored for anything; and are now in camp away down in the sunny South. They can afford to wait. Their time will yet come.

The applause that greeted General Sherman was fully equaled by that which heralded the approach of General Howard, the one-armed hero who rode with his bridle-reins in his mouth, and saluted the President as gracefully as though he had never had but the one arm. What scenes he passed through since Fair Oaks, where he was first wounded, and what a triumphal return.

General Logan met with fully as grand an ovation; his grim visage and his face of iron betokened the victor in the tented field, and the fascinating look he always wears shows how he has always wielded such power upon the rostrum.

Generals Blair and Slocum, familiar faces to the masses, were enthusiastically cheered.

The President presented a fine large wreath of flowers and evergreens to one of the Tennessee regiments as they passed along.

There was very little cheering to-day by the regiments, they having received orders to make no demonstrations; but when some of the rear divisions came along the regiments all cheered, and cheered long and loud.

Mrs. General Sherman was at the General's side to-day, and, dressed in black, waved her white handkerchief to all the Ohio regiments; to some half a dozen she gave the General's bouquets, which he threw to the color-bearers.

One of the greatest features was the pack mules which were with the various divisions. Major-General Wood had about a hundred, which traveled in front of his column, and were more in the nature of foragers than attendants. They elicited round after round of cheers, and presented the oddest possible appearance. Half a dozen had game chickens upon the top of their packs. One had a large billy goat, who rode his mule with all the usual grace of the animal. Upon one mule was half a dozen "coons," real live coons, which crawled over the dinner kettles and plunder as though they were at home. Several coons and a wounded real genuine contraband made one of the motliest scenes in the whole line.

The bands seemed to play "When Johnny Comes Marching Home" as their most popular air. They deserve great credit for having kept up their music and bands during their long and tedious marching the last two years. We seldom find better music even when listening to the veterans of the leading cities. Yesterday the marching salutes were paid by a drum corps and two bands, stationed opposite the main stand, who played in the intervals caused by the passing out of sound of the bands.

To-day the drum corps and bands of their respective commands left the head of the column at the stand, and took position in front, where they remained playing until their brigades had passed, when they fell into the rear.

Governor Fenton, of New York, and Governor Curtin, of Pennsylvania, occupied places on the stand in front of the President. There being but few New York or Pennsylvania regiments on review, the usual salutes to the Governors were omitted.

At 3·25 P. M. the rear artillery brigade passed along, and General Sherman and his officers bid the President and Cabinet good-bye.

The wagon trains followed close in the rear, but the crowd swayed to and fro, and soon the entire avenue was so full the wagons could hardly pass. And what a wagon train! It had come through the Confederacy, and the evidences of hastily made repairs, and substitutes for horses were visible upon every team.

Many of the hospital wagons had cows tied to the rear of their ambulances, some of them imported cows, and blooded stock of all descriptions was scattered through the entire train. A large proportion of the officers were mounted officers and soldiers. There was no straggling no talking by the men one to another, or making remarks to the spectators along the sidewalks, but all marched with remarkable steadiness and precision.

on thoroughbred horses and stallions, and on an average the entire army was far better mounted than the Army of the Potomac.

We are under many obligations to the officers and men for their courteous treatment in furnishing information, and their genial reputation has not been accorded them unduly; had the Army of the Potomac evinced as much liberal treatment towards the Press as has the Western army, its history would have been more fully and correctly written.

Excepting Sherman, Halleck and one or two others, the Press of the country owe much to the Western army—an army unequaled in the world for heroic valor, for undaunted bravery and a resistless momentum. The proudest title in the world that one can wear is the rank or insignias of the Army of the West.

The admirable discipline of the Army of Tennessee and the Army of Georgia was a subject of remark all along the line, by citizens as well as

Even the amusement occasioned by the grotesque appearance of mules, of all sizes and shapes—for some looked like nondescripts, and as if they did not belong to any species—of odd looking "contrabands" dressed in all the colors that ever adorned Joseph's coat—the medley of pack-saddles, trunks, boxes and bags, old boots, did not excite the risibles of these veterans in the least.

THE REVIEW.

THE FIFTEENTH CORPS.

The Fifteenth Corps was massed in the vicinity of the Capitol at an early hour this morning, and rested until the time for the commencement of the review arrived, with the head of the column opposite the main western entrance to the Capitol grounds. This corps was organized at Memphis in December, 1862, under command of General W. T. Sherman, and served under him until the spring of 1864, when he left to take command of the Sixteenth and Seventeenth Corps at Vicksburg, before setting out on the expedition to Meridian.

At Chickasaw Bayou the Corps fought its first battle under Sherman, its celebrated charge on the Rebel position there being made on the 28th December, 1862. On the 11th January, 1863, it was engaged at Arkansas Post, and participated in the active campaign against Vicksburg during the year 1863, up to the time of its capture, on the 4th of July. It was engaged in both the expeditions to Jackson, the last of which had such an important bearing upon the capture of Vicksburg by the cutting off the communications of the enemy, preventing Johnston from coming to the relief of Pemberton, and securing the investment of the city.

After Vicksburg fell, the corps returned to Memphis, and then marched via Iuka and Corinth, to Chattanooga, in the fall of 1863. It did not remain long in its new field of operations without another opportunity to measure its strength and valor with the enemy. At the great battle of Mission Ridge the greater part of Bragg's entire army was massed against this corps, and desperately strove to break its serried lines, but only to be forced back in every attempt.

When Sherman departed for Vicksburg to commence the great raid to Meridian he was succeeded in command by Major-General John H. Logan, who has since retained it and is at the head of his corps this morning. On the 1st of May, 1864, the Fifteenth Corps started for Chattanooga from the vicinity of Huntsville, between which point and Stevenson it had for several of the winter months been guarding the line of railroad. Its first engagement in the brilliant campaign of 1864 was on May 15th, at Snake Creek Gap, near Resaca, which place was captured, the works that defended it being carried by assault. It was again engaged at Kenesaw Mountain on the 27th of June, and in the series of skirmishes and fights preceding the capture of Marietta, which occurred on the 4th of July. In the great battle of the 22d of July, in front of Atlanta, it played a conspicuous part. It was in this engagement that the lamented McPherson fell, leaving Logan temporarily in command of the Army of the Tennessee. On the 27th of July the corps moved to the extreme right of the Army of the Tennessee, and on the 28th, this corps, supported by the Seventeenth, was attacked by Hood, with the mass of the Rebel army.

The attack was commenced at eleven A. M., and the fight raged furiously until five P. M.

Continued on the Eighth Page.

The New-York Times.

VOL. XIV......NO. 4266. | NEW-YORK, SUNDAY, MAY 28, 1865. | PRICE FOUR CENTS.

PEACE AT LAST.

Surrender of Gen. Kirby Smith's Entire Force.

Final Official Act of Insurgent Authority.

The Great Rebellion Has Passed Away.

Their Land and Naval Forces Declared Disbanded.

The Stars and Stripes Again Dominant Over All the Country.

All Military Prisoners During the War Set Free.

Re-Union, Peace, Freedom and Prosperity.

E PLURIBUS UNUM!

[OFFICIAL.]

FROM SECRETARY STANTON TO GEN. DIX.

WAR DEPARTMENT, WASHINGTON, May 27, 1865.

Maj.-Gen. Dix:

A dispatch from Gen. CANBY, dated at New-Orleans, yesterday, the 26th inst., states that arrangements for the surrender of the Confederate forces in the Trans-Mississippi Department have been concluded. They include the men and material of the army and navy.

EDWIN M. STANTON, Secretary of War.

MILITARY TRIBUNALS.

An Order from President Johnson.

WASHINGTON, Saturday, May 27.

The following order has just been issued from the War Department:

That in all cases of sentences by military tribunals of imprisonment during the war, the sentence be remitted, and that the prisoners be discharged.

The Adjutant-General will issue immediately the necessary instructions to carry this order into effect.

By order of the President.

(Signed) EDWIN M. STANTON, Secretary of War.

THE SOUTHWEST.

Disorganization Among the Rebels—Our Prisoners in Texas Purposely Allowed to Escape—Small Parties of Rebels Surrendering—Affairs in the Red River Region.

FORT SMITH, Saturday, May 27.

Rebel deserters and escaped prisoners of the Thirty-second Iowa Regiment, just arrived from Texas, report that the Federal prisoners confined at Tyler, Texas, are allowed to escape in large numbers, the guards saying that, when they are all gone, they will have nothing to do, and then can go home.

The enlisted men in the rebel army are unwilling to fight any longer, and do not respond to KIRBY SMITH's proclamation. They acknowledge themselves whipped and anxious for peace.

The surrender of the rebels east of the Mississippi was not credited at first, but it is now generally believed.

Gen. RUSSEY is now negotiating with the rebel officers of Western Arkansas for the surrender of their commands. Quite a number have already come in, and others will doubtless do so.

Guerrillas have ceased molesting boats and telegraph wires.

ST. LOUIS, Saturday, May 27.

The New-Orleans *Picayune*, of the 21st inst., learns, from rebel sources, that the Trans-Mississippi rebel army will soon surrender or disband in the absence of a large Federal force pressing them. The latter course will probably be pursued.

CAIRO, Saturday, May 27.

The New-Orleans *Times*, of the 22d inst., says that the gunboat *Little Rebel* arrived here yesterday from the mouth of the Red River, with dispatches from Lieut.-Commander FOSTER and Gen. KIRBY SMITH for Gen. CANBY.

The rebel flag-of-truce boat *Champion* that brought the Federal officers, Col. SPRAGUE and Maj. BUNDY, from Shreveport is still lying at the mouth of the Red River.

An exchange of prisoners was agreed upon at the mouth of the Red River on the 25th inst.

Two hundred and forty rebel exchanged prisoners arrived at Shreveport on the 16th inst.

Col. JULIAN E. BRYANT, nephew of WM. C. BRYANT, was drowned recently while bathing in the Gulf of Mexico.

The interior of Texas is in a terribly disorganized condition.

A telegraph line is to be constructed from San Antonio and Austin to Matamoras.

The French and English war vessels off the Rio Grande joined the United States sloop of war in firing half hour guns as a mark of respect to the memory of the late President LINCOLN.

Six hundred and forty bales of cotton passed here (Cairo) for St. Louis to-day, and upward of one thousand for Cincinnati.

Probable Surrender of Kirby Smith's Army.

BATON ROUGE, Tuesday, May 23, via CAIRO, Saturday, May 27.

Brig.-Gen. BRENT and Cols. DEBLAU, C. BURKE and SEIP, arrived here, to-day, as commissioners from KIRBY SMITH. Gen. HERRON and Lieut.-Commander FOSTER came down from Red River with them. Gen. HERRON has gone to Gen. CANBY, and it is believed here terms are arranged for the surrender of KIRBY SMITH's whole army.

Death of Dr. Henry McMurtrie.

PHILADELPHIA, Saturday, May 27.

Dr. HENRY MCMURTRIE, late Professor of Anatomy and Physiology in the general High School of this city, died yesterday afternoon, aged 73 years. Dr. MCMURTRIE was highly esteemed both by the profession and public.

FROM FLORIDA.

Capture of a Party of Rebels Attempting to Escape—Suspicious Statements—Who are the Men?

The following is from J. J. HOLLES, Lieutenant, commanding detachment Second Florida Cavalry, and is dated Cape Sable, Fla., May 18:

In obedience to orders received May 9, I proceeded to Cape Sable, with a detachment of the Second Florida Cavalry, to intercept any parties who might be making their escape from the Confederacy. On the morning of the 17th, at 2:30 A. M., a boat with sail was seen near shore; the picket boat immediately pulled for it, and upon challenging them and asking who they were, was answered, a fishing boat. The Corporal in charge of boat ordered them to surrender, which they did without resistance, their revolvers having been wet by the surf and consequently useless. On being brought to camp I examined every trunk, valise, &c., finding considerable Confederate money, some gold, and a few papers, which I still hold possession of. They appear to be an intelligent party of men, and undoubtedly have been holding important positions in the Confederacy. They all acknowledge to have recently been in Richmond. The party consisted of seven white men and a colored servant. The servant makes the following statement: I was hired at ten dollars per day, and my freedom after reaching Havana. We left Tallahassee on the 24th of April, went to Gainesville by railroad, from there to Chrystal River with three teams, one of six horses, the other of four. We brought the boat from Gainesville and launched it in Chrystal River on the 2d of May, and then went to Bay Port. Up to this time there had been but six white men in the party. Here we were joined by a man from Tallahassee, who came down in a buggy. We left Bay Port the 6th inst., at 9 A. M., running every night when we could, and sometimes during the day.

The men give their names as follows;

Frank P. Anderson, Richard S. McCullock, Fredk. Mohl, Henry W. McCormick, Julius C. Pratt, Thomas A. Harris, Isaac A. Homer.

The troops making the above arrest belong to the command of Gen. JOHN NEWTON, and have been in pursuit of this party of men since they first made their appearance at Crystal River. It is supposed that the men gave fictitious names to the officer making the arrest. As they have not yet been received at Key West, it is not known who they are, but their conduct looks very suspicious, and leads to the supposition that they are men of some importance.

FROM RICHMOND.

The Sixth Army Corps en Route to Washington—The Richmond Press and the Washington Chronicle—Arrest of Ex-Gov. Letcher and Hon. James Seddon.

From Our Own Correspondent.

RICHMOND, Tuesday, May 23, 1865.

The Sixth Army Corps marched through Richmond this morning, on its way to Washington.

They crossed the James at 7:30, marching up Seventeenth-street to Broad, thence to Brook's-avenue, and will encamp for to-night about seven miles on the road leading to Hanover Junction.

Maj.-Gen. WRIGHT and staff headed the advance column, which was formed of the Third Division. Maj.-Gen. RICKETTS, Maj.-Gen. HALLECK, and Maj.-Gen. ORD, with their respective staffs, reviewed the gallant corps as they filed past the City Hall.

It was a brilliant pageant, and drew out a large concourse of spectators.

In a recent editorial article of the Washington *Chronicle*, appeared a violent article upon the whole of the newspaper press of Richmond; many individuals now connected with it being singled out by name as fast enemies of the government, and, consequently, presumable to be so still.

From what I have been able to learn since coming here, I am bound to say that very grave errors are constantly made in the North respecting the aims and character of people here, and in this individual case I am able to assert that two parties, at least, are most unjustly treated, for they are both personally well known to me. Messrs. R. L. WALKER and J. W. LEWELLEN, of the Richmond *Republic*, are spoken of as men who, both before and during the war, have been in the habit of writing against the authority of the United States. This is not so. Neither of these gentlemen are, or ever have been, in any way connected with writing for the press.

Mr. LEWELLEN was connected with the Richmond *Dispatch* simply as book-keeper, and has always been openly and avowedly opposed to the rebel government, and who was probably saved by nothing but his age from falling into their clutches. As to Mr. WALKER, he, too, was never engaged in writing for any paper. He was a practical printer in the *Examiner* office, earning his livelihood like any other man in a newspaper office, without having anything to do with its opinions.

Both of these gentlemen were noted for the vehement support they gave JOHN MINOR BOTTS in the convention of 1860–61—merely because of his intense opposition to the doctrine of secession. If these two gentlemen were not honestly and sincerely desirous of restoring the authority of the United States, they would not have selected as editor of their paper such a man as Mr. R. J. HAMILTON, the well-known correspondent of the New-York TIMES for the past three years. One remarkable incident connected with this article in the *Chronicle* is worthy of mention During the first few days of the Federal occupation of Richmond, a gentleman named MCCARTNEY (professing to be one of the editors of the Washington *Chronicle*) met Mr. WALKER, and pressed him very urgently to join with him in starting a newspaper here. Now the question very naturally arises: If, in the opinion of the Washington *Chronicle*, Mr. WALKER's antecedents are such that he is not a proper man to be the proprietor of a journal in Richmond, was he exactly the kind of a person to be approached, in precisely the same capacity, by an editor of the Washington *Chronicle*?

The arrest of Ex-Gov. LETCHER and Hon. JAMES SEDDON, rebel Secretary of War, is announced, and excites no surprise.

R. D. FRANCIS.

NORTHERN MEXICO.

The Liberals at Monterey—Operations of Gen. Negrete—Alleged Attempt to Kidnap the Empress at Mexico.

CAIRO, Saturday, May 27.

The New Orleans *Times'* Brazos correspondent under date of the 12th inst., says:—The Liberal force which captured Monterey was 7,000 strong.

Gen. NEGRETE, after occupying the place, levied a forced loan of one hundred thousand dollars in specie.

At the fight at Saltillo the Imperialist Gens. VICTORIANO, LEPEDO and FIERRO were wounded, but escaped. In this fight CORTINA captured fifty thousand dollars in specie and nine hundred prisoners. While Gen. NEGRETE was attacking Matamoras on the 29th ult., the rebel Gen. SLAUGHTER fortified the left bank of the Rio Grande, and opened an artillery fire to prevent NEGRETE's troops from reaching the river for water.

A party of guerrillas recently attempted to kidnap the Empress from the City of Mexico, but was unsuccessful.

The unpopularity of MAXIMILIAN is still further confirmed.

The Boston Musical Festival.

BOSTON, Saturday, May 27.

The great Handel and Hayden musical festival, which has been in progress during the week, has proved a complete success, attracting very large and delighted audiences. All the seats in Music Hall have been taken for "Elijah" to-night, and also for "The Messiah," which will close the festival on Sunday night. The proceeds will show a handsome net income, one-half of which goes to the Christian and Sanitary Commission.

THE TRIAL OF THE ASSASSINS.

Report of the Testimony Taken on Saturday.

More Evidence of the Doings of Sanders and Thompson.

Their Connection with the St. Albans Robbery.

How Atzeroth Undertook to Make Sure of Vice-President Johnson.

Singular Weakness of the Testimony for the Defence.

They Will Probably Attempt to Justify the Murder as an Act of War.

Special Dispatch to the New-York Times.

WASHINGTON, Saturday, May 27.

Further evidence, on the part of the government, was offered to-day, in the trial of the assassins, to prove that THOMPSON, SANDERS and CLEARY, while in Canada, were acting by authority of the rebel government, and that Lieut. YOUNG was sent there on detached service to report to them, and to gather a party of twenty for such service as they might be required to perform.

The theory of the prosecution is understood to be that under this authority BOOTH and his accomplices acted in the assassination of the President, and the attempt upon the life of Mr. SEWARD.

It was also proven that ATZEROTH had called at the Kirkwood two days before the assassination and inquired for the Vice-President, and that the latter, while sitting at the dinner table, was pointed out to ATZEROTH. This proof is introduced to show that the prisoner was endeavoring to identify Mr. JOHNSON, and get the locality of his room, that he might make sure of his intended victim when the hour for the assassination should arrive.

Several witnesses were afterwards introduced by the defendants, but no important evidence was adduced in their favor. One witness, called to the stand by the counsel for Mrs. SURRATT, for the purpose of breaking down or in part discrediting the testimony of WEICHMAN, a witness for the government, was so skilfully interrogated by Judge-Advocate BURNETT that his testimony was turned to account for the prosecution.

This witness, who had been in the rebel army and recently a blockade-runner, in conclusion, admitted that he had never taken the oath of allegiance.

By analogy from the ruling of the Judge-Advocate-General on a former occasion, the testimony of this witness uncoroborated, so far as it affects the standing of the witness WEICHMAN, cannot be received.

The court-room was again crowded to its utmost capacity; about one-half the audience was composed of ladies.

Synopsis of Evidence Taken by the Court on Saturday.

WASHINGTON, Saturday, May 27.

The prosecution called GEORGE F. EDMONDS, of Burlington, Vt., who testified that he is an attorney and had charge, for the United States, of the St. Albans' Raid Case. JACOB THOMPSON, CLEMENT C. CLAY and SANDERS were in attendance on the court, and assumed to be the defenders of these raiders for the Confederate States.

The witness was shown a printed paper, which he believed was substantially if not an exact copy of the original which he had seen. This letter was dated Richmond, June 10, 1864, signed by JAMES A. SEDDON, rebel Secretary of War, and addressed to Lieut. YOUNG. It informed the latter that he was appointed for *special service*, and directed him to report to THOMPSON and CLAY for his instructions; and also to select twenty escaped Confederate soldiers for the execution of such enterprises as might be intrusted to him. The original paper was produced by the rebels on the trial of the St. Albans raiders.

Col. NEVINS, of Genesee, N. Y., testified to having seen ATZEROTH at the Kirkwood House on the 12th of April. This was between four and five in the afternoon. The prisoner inquired of and was informed by the witness where the Vice-President's room was, and pointed it out to the former. The witness did not know who ATZEROTH was nor his name, but immediately recognized the man on coming into this court.

The defence called several witnesses to impeach the veracity of some of those who have testified against Dr. MUDD, and to establish the fact that the Doctor had given no aid and comfort to the rebels. He had, however, provided food and shelter for some of the citizens in 1861, who had taken alarm lest they should be arrested at the time that Gen. SICKLES came into the county.

Full Report of the Evidence on Saturday.

WASHINGTON, Saturday, May 27.

After the evidence taken yesterday had been read, the following witnesses were to-day called for the prosecution:

Testimony of George F. Edmonds.

By Judge-Advocate Holt.—Q.—What is your profession. A.—Counsellor-at-law.

Q.—State whether not, on the trial which recently occurred in Canada of certain offenders known as the St. Albans raiders, you appeared as counsel for the Government of the United States? A.—I had charge of the matter for the Government of the United States.

Q.—State whether, in the performance of your professional duties there you made the acquaintance of Jacob Thompson, W. C. Cleary, C. C. Clay, George N. Sanders, and others of that clique? A.—In the sense in which the term is generally understood, I did not; I know those persons by their being pointed out to me daily; I did not have the honor, if it may be called such, of their acquaintance.

Q.—Were the defendants in court? A.—They were.

Q.—Were they engaged as officers of the Confederate government in defending these raiders? A.—They assumed to exercise those functions, and recognized each other accordingly.

Q.—Mention the persons whom you met there, and who were so recognized? A.—I do not think I saw Mr. Thompson more than once; I saw Mr. C. C. Clay during the early part of the proceedings almost daily, and Mr. Sanders during the whole of the period; Mr. Cleary, whom you mentioned, I saw to know at a later period, when he was examined as a witness on part of the defendants.

Q.—Did he represent in his testimony in that trial that these persons were engaged in the Confederate service, and that this raid was made under the authority of the Confederate government? A.—He so represented, as did all these persons, and they stood upon that defence.

Q.—Will you look at this paper and state whether or not you have seen the original of the document? A.—I have seen the original.

Q.—Was it or was it not given in evidence on the trial to which you refer? A.—It was given in evidence on the trial on the part of the defendants.

Q.—Given in evidence by them as a general document? A.—It was.

Q.—Is that a correct copy? A.—I cannot swear that it is an exact copy, but I examined the original very carefully, and I am able to swear that it is a substantial copy, and I have no doubt it is a literal copy.

The paper was then given in evidence, and was read, as follows:

CONFEDERATE STATES OF AMERICA, WAR DEPARTMENT, RICHMOND, Va., June 16, 1864.

To Lieut. Bennet H. Young:

LIEUTENANT: You have been appointed temporarily, First Lieutenant in the provisional army for special service. You will proceed without delay to the British provinces, where you will report to Messrs. Thompson and Clay for instructions. You will, under their directions, take such Confederate soldiers who have escaped from the enemy, not exceeding twenty in number, as you may deem suitable for the purpose, and will execute such enterprises as may be intrusted to you You will take care to commit no violation of the local law, and to obey implicitly their instructions. You and your men will receive from these gentlemen transportation and the customary rations and the commutation therefor.

JAMES A. SEDDON, Secretary of War.

Q.—Was the Young referred to in that connection one of the St. Albans' raiders? A.—I don't know that I can answer that question literally; he produced that document and professed to be the person.

Q.—He was on trial as such? A.—He was on trial as such and produced that document as authority for the acts he had committed.

The testimony of the witness having been concluded, Judge-Advocate Holt stated that since closing the case on the part of the government, so far as it concerned the individual prisoner, he had discovered an important witness, before unknown to him, whose examination he desired should now be made.

Mr. Ewing inquired as to which of the prisoners the proposed testimony was likely to affect.

Judge Holt replied that it referred directly to the case of Atzeroth.

Mr. Doester said that he had not opened the defence for Atzeroth, and therefore would not object to the reception of the testimony.

The witness was then called and testified as follows:—

Testimony of Col. Wm. R. Nevins.

By Judge-Advocate Holt—Q.—Where do you reside? A.—In New-York.

Q.—State whether or not you were in this city in the month of April last, and if so on what day? A.—I was here on the 12th of April; I think I recollect the day from the fact that a pass which I received from the War Department bears that date.

Q.—Where did you stop in this city? A.—At the Kirkwood House.

Q.—Look at the prisoners at the bar and see whether you recognize either of them as a person whom you met in the house on that day? A.—That one there (pointing to Atzeroth); I think he is the man.

Q.—State under what circumstances you met him, and what he said to you. A.—He had on a coat darker than that; as I was coming out he asked me if I knew where the Vice-President's room was; I told him that the Vice-President was then at dinner; there was no one there then except him and me.

Q.—Did he ask where the room of Vice-President Johnson was? A.—Yes, Sir; that was his first question; I did not know the number of the Vice-President's room, but I knew it was on the right-hand side, next the parlor; however, I said to him the Vice-President is eating his dinner.

Q.—Did you then part with him, or where did you go? A.—I passed on.

Q.—Did you leave him standing there or did he go away? A.—Well, he looked in the dining-room; I do not know whether he went in or not.

Q.—You say you pointed out the room to him? A.—Yes, Sir.

Q.—Was the room in view from where you pointed it out? A.—Yes, Sir. It was on the passage as you go into the dining-room; and between that and the steps as you go down to the dining-room is where the man met me.

Cross-examined by Mr. Doester—Q.—What time of day was this? A.—I think it was between 4 and 5 o'clock. There was no other person at dinner but the Vice-President himself. I was going away at the time, and was in a great hurry.

Q.—Whereabouts in the house did this conversation take place? A.—In the passage leading into the dining-room.

Q.—Did the prisoner look into the dining-room? A.—From the passage you cannot look into it, but by going down a few steps you can see it.

Q.—I understood you to say that he looked into the dining-room? A.—I pointed to the Vice-President, Mr. Johnson, who was sitting at the far end, with a yellow-looking man standing behind him.

Q.—What length of time was occupied in this conversation? A.—I do not suppose over three minutes.

Q.—Have you seen the prisoner since that time until you saw him to-day? A.—No, Sir.

Q.—Describe the dress and appearance of the prisoner? A.—I was in a hurry when I met the prisoner, and am therefore unable to give a very minute description; his dress was dark; he had on a low-crowned black hat; but it is his countenance by which I recognize him.

Q.—State to the court your age? A.—I was born Feb. 22, 1803.

By Judge-Advocate Holt—Q.—State whether or not, in coming into the presence of the prisoner Atzeroth, this morning, you recognized him at once, without his being pointed out to you? A.—I recognized him without his being pointed out to me.

Q.—No indication as to the person was made to you? A.—No, Sir.

Testimony of Bettie Washington, Colored.

By Mr. Stone—Q.—State where you reside? A.—I live at Dr. Samuel Mudd's, and have been living there since the Monday after Christmas.

Q.—Were you a slave before the emancipation proclamation was issued? A.—Yes, Sir.

In reply to a series of questions propounded to her, the witness then testified in substance that she had not been absent from the house of the prisoner, Dr. Samuel Mudd, for a single night since she first took up her abode with him until she came to Washington; that during that time the prisoner had been absent from home on three separate occasions—first at Mr. George Henry Gardiner's party, where he stayed late in the evening; second, at Giesboro, where he went to buy some horses; third, to Washington, from which place he returned on the day after his leaving home.

Q.—Did you not see the man called Herrold and Booth? A.—I saw only one of them—the small one; I was standing at the kitchen window, and just got a glimpse of him as he was going in the direction of the swamp.

Q.—How long after you saw him did you see Dr. Mudd? A.—I did not see Dr. Mudd with the man; I saw Dr. Mudd about two or three minutes afterward at the front door.

A photograph of Booth was here exhibited to the witness, but she failed to identify the likeness as that of any one she had ever seen.

During a brief cross-examination conducted by Assistant Judge-Advocate Bingham, the witness testified that an interval of about a week or two took place between the prisoner's departures from home, and that his brother accompanied him on these occasions.

Re-examination of Jeremiah T. Mudd.

By Mr. Ewing—Q.—Are you acquainted with the handwriting of the accused, Samuel A. Mudd. A.—Yes, Sir.

Q.—State whether you see his handwriting on that page, [exhibiting to the witness the register of the Pennsylvania Hotel, Washington, on page headed Friday, Dec. 23, 1864.] A.—I do.

Q.—Do you know at what hotel in Washington the prisoner was in the habit of stopping? A.—I do not.

Q.—Are you acquainted with Daniel G. Thomas, who has been a witness for the prosecution? A.—I am.

Q.—Do you know his reputation in the neighborhood in which he lives for truth and veracity? A.—I do; it is bad.

Q.—From your knowledge of his reputation for truth would you believe him under oath? A.—I do not think I could; it has been my impression that——

Judge Bingham—You need not state your impressions.

Mr. Ewing—Proceed with your answer.

A.—I have just stated that I did not think I could.

Cross-examined by Assistant Judge-Advocate Bingham—Q.—Do you base his general reputation upon your personal knowledge and acquaintance with him? A.—Yes, Sir; and upon what I generally heard spoken by others.

Q.—What do you say that you generally heard spoken by others in regard to his reputation for truth? A.—That it was pretty bad.

Q.—How many people did you ever hear speak of his general reputation for truth, before the taking of this testimony the other day? A.—I heard several speak of it.

Q.—How many—ten? A.—I think so; I will not say positively; I am speaking now from what I have heard generally.

Q.—Can you name the ten? A.—I really do not know.

Q.—Can you name half the ten? A.—I think I can; I might name a dozen.

Q.—Well, who are they? A.—I might name Dr. George Mudd for one.

Q.—When did you hear Dr. George Mudd speak on the subject? A.—I heard him speak of it as late as two years ago.

Q.—What did he say of the general character of the witness for truth? A.—That it was bad; that he did not believe his general character for truth was good.

Q.—How did he come to say that? A.—It was in connection with some matters that occurred about the time of stationing Col. Birney down there.

Q.—You did not understand that Thomas was opposed to Col. Birney? A.—Not at all; I simply mentioned that as being about the time.

Q.—State all the circumstances in that connection. A.—It was about the fact of Thomas' having a man named Payne arrested there; for what I don't know; the man who was arrested had a brother in the rebel army and some of his brother's friends came to his house.

Q.—Then the arrest was made on a charge of entertaining rebel soldiers? Yes, Sir; I presume it was.

Q.—Was that the only man whom you ever heard assail this man's character for truth? A.—I believe there were others.

Q.—Who were the others? A.—I do not know that I can name them.

Q.—If you cannot name two men who ever assailed his character for truth, how can you come to the conclusion that his general reputation for truth is bad? A.—Well, I heard a number so state.

By the Court—Q.—What relation are you to prisoner? A.—My father and his father were first cousins.

Q.—Have you been intimate with him? A.—Moderately so; we met frequently, as I live in his neighborhood.

By Mr. Stone—Q.—Have you been in the habit of serving on the juries in the county where you live? A.—I have frequently.

Q.—State whether Thomas has not frequently been a witness in court when you were present? A.—I do not recollect of his having been a witness in court.

By Judge Bingham—Q.—Have you ever heard any one assert that Mr. Thomas ever swore falsely in court? A.—No, Sir.

Q.—Are you aware of the fact that he has been a supporter of the government, and has acted as an official for the government since the rebellion broke out? A.—Yes, Sir.

Q.—Are you aware of another fact, that a very considerable portion of the people in Charles County are reputed somewhat disloyal and a good deal favorable to this rebellion? A.—I am aware that several young men from our section have gone into the rebel army.

Q.—Yes; and many of those left behind have been making a good deal of clamor, have they not, against the government and in favor of the rebellion? A.—Not to any great extent.

Q.—That is the general report, is it not? A.—Well, yes, Sir.

Q.—Are not the men who have spoken against this man (Thomas) of that class who bear the general reputation of being against the government? A.—I really do not know.

Q.—Have you any knowledge of rebels being fed and concealed in that neighborhood by residents there? A.—I have not; I have seen men in Bryantown passing and repassing, who, I was told, were rebels; as to their being fed or concealed in my immediate neighborhood I have no knowledge.

By Mr. Ewing—Q.—You have spoken of Dr. George Mudd as one of the men who said that he regarded the reputation of Thomas for veracity as bad; state whether Dr. George Mudd is a rebel sympathizer or not? A.—I regard him as having been throughout this war as strong a Union man as any in the United States; I never heard him express the slightest sympathy with the rebellion.

Q.—What is his reputation for loyalty? A.—I think there would be very little difficulty in establishing the fact of its being very good; he is so regarded universally.

By Judge Bingham—Q.—Did you ever hear Dr. George Mudd say anything against the rebellion? A.—Very often.

By Mr. Stone—Q.—Did Mr. Daniel Thomas hold any position under the government? A.—He said that he was a detective.

Q.—Do you know such to be a fact from any other source than himself? A.—I do not.

Q.—Under whose orders did he claim to have been acting? A.—I think under Col. Holland, the Provost-Marshal of our district.

Testimony of Benjamin P. Gwyn.

By Mr. Ewing.—Q.—State whether last Summer, in company with Capt. White, from Tennessee, Capt. Perry, Lieut. Perry, Andrew Gwyn and George Gwyn, or either of them, were about Dr. Samuel A. Mudd's house for a number of days. A.—I never saw any of these parties except Andrew Gwyn and George Gwyn, and have not been in Dr. Mudd's house since about the 1st of November, 1861, nor nearer to it than the church since the 6th of November, 1861.

Q.—State what occurred in 1861, when you were in the neighborhood of Dr. Mudd's house? A.—I was with my brother, Andrew J. Gwyn and Jerry Dyer; about that time Gen. Sickles came over into Maryland, arresting everybody; I was threatened with arrest, and left the neighborhood to avoid it; I went down to Charles County and stayed with my friends there, as everybody else was doing; there was a good deal of running around about that time.

Mr. Ewing—Go on and tell all about it.

Assistant Judge-Advocate Bingham objected to the witness being allowed to state anything further on this point, as it was not in issue what was done in 1861.

Mr. Ewing said that the prosecution had shown by four or five witnesses that a party, of whom the witness on the stand was one, had been concealed in the pines in the neighborhood of Dr. Mudd's house, having their meals brought to them by his servants; and had also attempted to show that those persons were in the Confederate service, and that Dr. Mudd was guilty of treason in attempting to secrete them. If the defence showed that this was not done last year, it would not be a complete refutation of the testimony, because it may be alleged to have been done previously. The defence wished to show that this concealment was the concealment of a much smaller party than was stated, and of men who were not in the Confederate service; and also that it occurred at another time than that stated. To deny the accused this opportunity would be to withhold a most legitimate line of defence; and to refuse to allow him to refute the whole mass of loose testimony of ignorant servants—ignorant as to dates—would be most unjust.

Judge Bingham contended that there was no color of excuse for the attempt to introduce testimony in regard to the year 1861. The reason why the objection was not made sooner was because the prosecution had been unable to perceive the purpose of the counsel for the defence in following such a course. It was proper for them to swear this witness as to his whereabouts, so as to contradict the testimony of Mary Simms, who had sworn to having seen him last Summer. To go further than that was not legitimate. If this course was persisted in and every witness called in regard to 1861, was to swear deliberately and maliciously false, there would be no power in the court to punish them for perjury, for the simple reason that no issue was before the Court, either in the evidence adduced or in the charges and specifications, which would authorize any inquiry about it.

The objection was sustained.

The commission then took a recess till two o'clock, at which time the body reassembled.

Re-examination of Benjamin F. Gwyn.

By Mr. Ewing—Q.—State where the party of whom you have spoken as being in the pines got their meals and slept. A.—They slept in the barn, near the spring, on bedding furnished from Dr. Mudd's, and were furnished with meals by Dr. Mudd; we remained there about four or five days.

Q.—State the circumstances of your being there, and what occurred. A.—As I said before, I went down there and stayed around the neighborhood, part of the time at Dr. Mudd's house and part of the time elsewhere; he gave us something to eat and some bed-clothing.

Q.—Were you and the party with you in his house during the time you were there? A.—Yes, Sir; almost every day, I think.

Q.—Where were your horses? A.—At the stable, I think; I do not know who attended to them.

Q.—Do you know where John H. Surratt was at that time? A.—I think he was at college.

Q.—Do you know whether there were any charges against you and the party that were there? A.—I came up to Washington about the first of November; and gave myself up, having got tired of staying away; they administered to me the oath and I then went home; I think they said there had not been any charges against me.

Q.—What induced the party to go to the pines to sleep? A.—To avoid arrest, I did.

Q.—What reason had you for supposing you would be arrested? A.—Almost everybody in our neighborhood was being arrested, and I understood I would be too, so I went down there.

Q.—Have you seen Surratt in Charles County since? A.—I have not; I wish to state here that it was not in November I slept in the pines; it was in August.

Q.—You spoke of Andrew J. Gwyn being there with you; will you state where he has been since? A.—He has been South.

Q.—What relation do you bear to him? A.—He is my brother; he lives in Prince George's County, some eight miles from my home.

Q.—Did you hear of Andrew J. Gwyn being in that section since 1861? A.—I heard he was there some time during last Winter, I think.

Q.—What time in 1861 did he go South? A.—In August.

Cross-examined by Judge-Advocate Holt—Q.—You spoke of the universality of arrests in 1861. Did you understand that they were confined to persons suspected of disloyalty and disloyal practices? A.—They were generally; there were several volunteer companies down there whose members were arrested.

Q.—Were those companies organized for the defence of the United States? A.—They were commissioned by Gov. Hicks.

Q.—On what grounds did you suppose you would be arrested? A.—I was Captain of a company down there.

Q.—Organized for what purpose? A.—It was called a home guard, and was for the purpose of protecting the neighbors; at that time there was a good deal of disaffection among the blacks; it was thought to be a proper time for raising companies through the county; I therefore petitioned Gov. Hicks, and he gave me a commission.

Q.—Was it not understood they were organized to stand by the State in any disloyal position she might take against the government of the United States? A.—Yes, Sir; I so understood it; they arrested several members of my company; and as I understood there was a warrant for my arrest, I left.

Q.—You slept in the pines for the sole purpose of escaping this arrest? A.—Yes, Sir.

Q.—Dr. Mudd, I suppose, concurred fully in your sentiments and the sentiments which pervaded these local organizations? A.—I do not know what his sentiments were at the time.

By Mr. Ewing—Q.—When was the company of which you were Captain organized? A.—I think in the Fall of 1859 or Winter of 1860.

Q.—Before or after the election of Mr. Lincoln? A.—I do not know; I think we commenced to organize our company before that, but were not fully organized until after that time.

Q.—How far was the locality of this organization from Dr. Mudd's place? A.—About ten miles.

Q.—Do you know whether Dr. Mudd was a member of any of those volunteer companies? A.—I think he was a member of a company gotten up in Bryantown.

Q.—Are you sure of that? A.—I do not know positively; I think so.

Testimony of Jerry Dyer.

Examined by Mr. Ewing—Q.—State where you live? A.—I live in Baltimore.

Q.—State where you lived prior to that? A.—In Charles County.

Q.—Do you know the prisoner, Dr. Samuel A. Mudd? A.—Yes, Sir.

Q.—How far do you live from the house of Dr. Mudd? A.—About a mile and a half in a direct line.

Q.—When did you leave your residence in Charles County? A.—In May, two years ago.

Q.—State how long before you went to Baltimore you had lived in Charles County? A.—I was raised there.

Q.—State whether you know Sylvester Elgan who has been on the witness stand? A.—I do not know him by that name; he was called "El;" he is a little boy—a servant of the father of Dr. Mudd.

Q.—Did you know his brother Frank? A.—Yes.

Q.—Do you know Dick Gardner, or Luke Gardner? A.—Not by that name; I know Dick and Luke Washington, who I presume are the ones you mean.

Q.—State whether in August, 1863, at the house of the accused, Dr. Mudd, under an oak tree, when you were in conversation with Walter Bowie and the accused, the accused said he would send Sylvester Elgan and his brother Frank, and others of his servants to Richmond? A.—Never had any such conversation with him in my life, and in August I was not in the county; I went to Baltimore the first day of August, and remained until October, when, hearing that some of my hands had left the farm, I went down to see about carrying on the farm; About thirty or forty hands left the neighborhood about that time.

Q.—And you never at that or any other time heard him threaten to send any of his servants to Richmond? A.—Never. I heard when I got down in the county that such a report had been started there by a certain man in the neighborhood. I never heard Dr. Mudd say any such thing.

Q.—Did you ever meet Dr. Mudd in company with Walter Bowie? A.—Not that I know of.

Q.—Can you say that you never met Dr. Mudd in company with Walter Bowie at the house of Dr. Mudd's father. A.—I am satisfied I never did; I recollect about two years ago, in the Fall of 1862 or Spring of 1863, when some one rode into the lane, I turned and asked who that was coming; he said "that is Walt. Bowie, I wonder what he wants here," and turned and went into the house; he stayed about for some two hours, got some whisky and went away; I don't recollect whether Dr. Mudd was there or not; my impression is he was not.

Q.—Do you know Andrew Gwyn? A.—Very well.

Q.—Do you know where has has been since 1861? A.—He has been in the rebel army.

Q.—Have you ever seen him since 1861? A.—I have not.

Q.—Did you meet him with Surratt and Dr. Blanford at the house of Dr. Mudd? A.—Never; I never saw Surratt there in my life; the only time I ever saw him at all was coming into Bryantown some two or three years ago.

Q.—Do you know whether or not any of Surratt's family were in Bryantown then? A.—He had a sister there at school.

Q.—Did you last year see Surratt drive up to the house of Dr. Mudd's father and take his horse out of the buggy? A.—I did not.

Q.—Are you acquainted with the witness, Milo Simms? A.—Yes; I know him, he used to live with Dr. Mudd.

Q.—Do you know Rachel Spencer, Elvina Washington, Elsie Elgan and Mary Simms? A.—Yes.

Q.—State whether any of them were servants of Dr. Mudd in 1861? A.—I think they all were; I know I bought the woman Elvina about 1860 or 1861.

Q.—State whether you were at Dr. Mudd's house, or in the neighborhood, with Benjamin Gwyn, in the Summer of 1861? A.—I was, in September, 1861.

Q.—How long were you at the house? A.—We were in the neighborhood about a week.

Q.—What were you doing? A.—We were knocking about in the bushes and pines; there was a report that everybody was to be arrested; they were arresting a good many men in that neighborhood; Mr. Gwyn came down and said that they had been to the house to arrest us; I also received notice that I was to be arrested; I came to Dr. Mudd's house and stayed about there, sleeping in the pines between his house and mine several nights; we were two nights very near his spring.

Q.—Where did you get your bed clothing? A.—At Dr. Mudd's house.

Q.—Where did you get your meals? A.—When we were near his house Dr. Mudd brought the meals in; a part of the time we were on the opposite side of the swamp; while we were on this side, about two hundred yards from this (Dr. Mudd's) house, he would sometimes bring down a basket with bread, meat, whisky, &c., and the girl, Mary Simms, sometimes brought coffee.

Q.—Who took care of the horses of the party? A.—I believe the horses were left at Dr. Mudd's stable; I suppose the boy Milo took care of them; he was about there.

Q.—State how the parties were dressed. A.—They had on citizens' clothes.

Q.—Who composed the party? A.—Benjamin Gwyn, Andrew Gwyn and myself.

Q.—Were apples and peaches ripe about that time? A.—It was about peach season.

Q.—Do you know whether a watch was left at Dr. Mudd's house when you were there? A.—I recollect telling the children to keep a lookout and let me know.

Q.—Do you know whether Albion Brooke was about the house at that time? A.—I think he was not living there, but he often came across there.

Q.—Do you know whether there was any warrant for your arrest or any charges against you? A.—I do not; there was a general stampede of people, and a great excitement in that whole community.

Q.—Do you know Daniel J. Thomas, one of the witnesses for the prosecution? A.—I have known him quite intimately since he was a boy. I have seen much of him for the last two or three years.

Q.—Are you acquainted with the reputation he held in the community in which he lives for veracity? A.—I only know from public rumor. There are very few who have any confidence in him.

Q.—From your knowledge of his reputation for veracity would you believe him under oath? A.—I would not.

Q.—Are you acquainted with the accused, Dr. Mudd? A.—Yes, I have known him from a boy.

Q.—What is his general reputation for peace, order and good citizenship? A.—I have never heard the slightest thing against him. He has always been regarded as a good citizen; as a man of peace. I have never known him to have any difficulty, but have always regarded him as a peaceable, quiet citizen.

Q.—What is his reputation as a master over his servants? A.—I have always considered him a very kind, humane master; I have not known anything to the contrary, with the single exception of his shooting that boy.

Cross-examined by Judge Holt—Q.—You say you would not believe Mr. Thomas under oath; have you ever heard him charged with having sworn falsely on any occasion? A.—I do not know as I have.

Q.—He is a rather talky, noisy man in the neighborhood, is he? A.—Yes.

Q.—He talks a good deal about the Union; a great deal against rebellion, don't he? A.—I believe he does.

Q.—He has a reputation of being intensely loyal to the government, has he? A.—I think he has; I believe he is considered loyal.

Q.—Have you been loyal yourself during the rebellion? A.—I do not know that I have been guilty of any act against the government.

Q.—I speak of your sentiments. Have you, during this rebellion, desired the government to succeed in putting it down? A.—I never wanted two governments.

Q.—The question is a direct and plain one; I desire you to answer it. A.—I can only answer that by saying I never wanted this government broken up; I would rather see one government.

Q.—Will you please answer the question directly, yes or no? A.—I hardly understand your question; I think I have desired the government to succeed.

Q.—You say you have committed no overt act of disloyalty? A.—Not that I am aware of.

Q.—Have you ever spoken kindly of the government and encouragingly to your loyal neighbors and friends? A.—I certainly have; I have endeavored to dissuade young men from going into the Southern army.

Q.—Were you not a member of a local organization, the object of which was to stand by the State of Maryland in the event of her taking ground against the Government of the United States? A.—I belonged to a military organization.

Q.—You stated you were at Dr. Mudd's in 1861; did not you suppose at that time that this organization of which you were a member was regarded as disloyal to the government? A.—I hardly know how to answer the question, circumstances have changed so since then; at that time everything was confusion and excitement, and I can hardly answer the question.

Q.—Have you any knowledge of the existence of a treasonable organization in this country known as the Knights of the Golden Circle or Sons of Liberty? A. I have not, except what I have seen in the papers.

Q.—At the time when you were a member of this organization, in the Summer or Fall of 1861, was not the subject of the Legislature of Maryland passing an ordinance of secession discussed among you? A.—Not to my knowledge; I may have heard such a thing spoken of, but I do not know that it was discussed to any extent.

Q.—Can you mention the names of the persons who have been most decided in expressing the opinion you have stated in regard to Mr. Thomas' character for truth? A.—It has been the talk of almost every man in the whole county.

Q.—Have you ever heard of a man of known loyalty, an ardent supporter of the government, speak of Mr. Thomas as a man not to be believed under oath? A.—I do not know as I have.

By the Court—Q.—Did not you rejoice at the success of the rebels at the first battle of Bull Run? A.—I do not know as I did particularly.

Q.—Did you generally? A.—I do not know as I did.

Q.—On which side were your sympathies at that time? A.—I suppose with the rebels at that time; I judge so; I do not know.

Q.—When Richmond was taken on which side were your sympathies? A.—With the United States Government; I wanted them to take Richmond, and the war to stop.

Q.—What time did your sympathies undergo a change, and what produced that change? A.—I do not know; the only thing that I objected to was the emancipation of the slaves; that I thought was wrong.

By Judge Burnett—Q.—How about the draft? A.—I joined a club.

Q.—To save yourself from being drafted? A.—Yes.

Q.—What did you say about the draft being enforced? A.—Not a word that I know of.

By Mr. Ewing—Q.—Was the understanding of which you have spoken as to the character of the witness, Thomas, for truth in his neighborhood during the war

Continued on Eighth Page.